against England in last summer's series were elegantly made. Graeme Hick and Courtney Walsh, with 2,004 runs and 118 wickets respectively, chose themselves, while the manner in which James Whitaker scored his runs, and the way he came back after having both hands broken to win a tour place to Australia, gave him the nod over several promising young England batsmen. John Childs's triumph over adversity of a different kind not only revived his career; it also helped Essex win the Britannic Assurance Championship, and he completes the Five.

Much of the pleasure of working on *Wisden* has been, and remains, the enthusiasm and the friendship of those who contribute to it. To all who help, journalists in England and abroad, the county secretaries and their staffs, members of the secretariats of MCC, TCCB and NCA, schoolmasters, all friends of *Wisden*, I am indeed grateful.

John Woodcock's decision to retire as editor filled me with sadness, but happily his connection did not end with that decision. As associate editor, he has been a great help to me in my first year as editor. I was, too, pleased that John Arlott was happy to continue with the Books, for his kind appraisal is enjoyed by many. These two Hampshiremen have provided much encouragement.

Finally, my special thanks to three people who know more than anyone what is involved in putting *Wisden* together: Mike Smith and Peter Bather, of the typesetters, SB Datagraphics, and Christine Forrest, who has worked with me on *Wisden* since 1979. We are a small team: one that has been together for some years now. That our various tasks never seem a chore, that we approach each edition with a new enthusiasm, says everything for the magic of *Wisden* and of cricket.

GRAEME WRIGHT

Eastcote,
Middlesex.

© John Wisden & Co Ltd 1987

ISBN

Cased edition 0 947766 07 3

Soft cover edition 0 947766 08 1

John Wisden & Co Ltd
6 Warwick Court
London WC1R 5DJ

Computer typeset by SB Datagraphics, Colchester

Printed in Great Britain by Spottiswoode Ballantyne Printers Ltd

LIST OF CONTRIBUTORS

The editor acknowledges with gratitude the assistance afforded in the preparation of the Almanack by the following:

Jack Arlidge (Sussex)
John Arlott (Books)
R. L. Arrowsmith (Obituaries)
Chris Aspin (Lancashire Leagues)
Diane Back
Jack Bannister (Warwickshire)
Brian Bearshaw (Lancashire)
Michael Berry
Scyld Berry
John Billot (Glamorgan)
J. Watson Blair (Scotland)
R. T. Brittenden
Robert Brooke (Births and Deaths)
Kenneth R. Bullock (Canada)
C. R. Buttery (New Zealand)
John Callaghan (Yorkshire)
Don Cameron
Terry Cooper (Middlesex)
Geoffrey Copinger
Tony Cozier (West Indies)
Patrick Eagar
Matthew Engel
Essex Chronicle
Paton Fenton (Oxford University)
David Field (Surrey)
Bill Frindall (Records)
David Frith
Nigel Fuller (Essex)
M. E. Gear
David Green
David Hallett (Cambridge University)
Les Hatton
Brian Hayward (Hampshire)
Eric Hill (Somerset)
Derek Hodgson
Grenville Holland (UAU)
Brian Hunt
Ken Ingman (ESCA)

Vic Isaacs
Martin Johnson (Leicestershire)
Abid Ali Kazi (Pakistan)
Ken Kelly
Brian Langley
Stephanie Lawrence
John Lawson (Nottinghamshire)
Edward Liddle
Peter Lush
John Mackinnon (Australia)
Vic Marks
Robin Marlar
Joanna Martin
John Minshull-Fogg
R. Mohan
Chris Moore (Worcestershire)
Dudley Moore (Kent)
Gerald Mortimer (Derbyshire)
David Munden
A. L. A. Pichanick (Zimbabwe)
Qamar Ahmed
Andrew Radd (Northamptonshire)
Netta Rheinberg
Dicky Rutnagur
Geoffrey Saulez
Derek Scott (Ireland)
Mike Selvey
Peter Sichel (South Africa)
Bill Smith
P. N. Sundaresan (India)
E. W. Swanton
John Thicknesse
Gerry Vaidyasekera (Sri Lanka)
Mary Vaux
D. R. Walsh (HMC Schools)
J. J. Warr
Geoffrey Wheeler (Gloucestershire)
A. S. R. Winlaw

CONTENTS

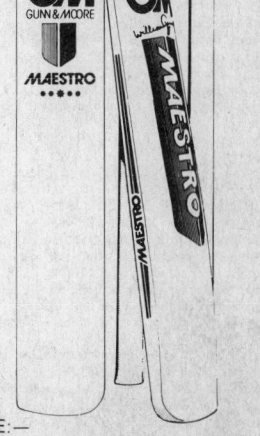

INDEX

Note: For reasons of space, certain entries which appear in alphabetical order in sections of the Almanack are not included in this index. These include names that appear in Test Cricketers, Births and Deaths of Cricketers, Individual batting and bowling performances in the 1986 first-class season, and Oxford and Cambridge Blues.

c. = catches; d. = dismissals; p'ship = partnership; r. = runs; w. = wickets.

* Signifies not out or an unbroken partnership

A

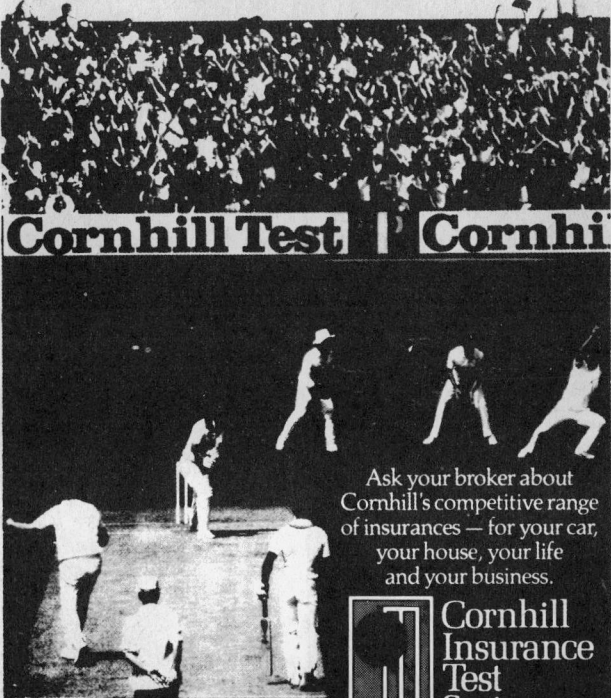

Bradman, Sir D. G. (Aust.):– *contd*
136; 29 Test hundreds, *176, 197, 221, 224, 229*; 13 hundreds in season, *136*; 6 hundreds in succession, *135*; 4 hundreds in succession, *135*; 2 hundreds in same Test, *171, 229*; 2 hundreds in match, *134*; Hundred and double-hundred, *135*; 10 successive fifties, *136*; Average of 115.66 in English season, *139*; 50 boundaries in innings, *146*; 30 r. in over, *145*; 451 for 2nd wkt, *146, 148, 179, 200*; 405 for 5th wkt, *149, 179, 200*; 346 for 6th wkt, *179, 200*; Test p'ship records, *200, 222, 229*.

Bradburn, W. P. (NZ):– Test p'ship record, *234*.

Bradley, W. M. (Eng.):– Wkt with 1st ball on Test début, *183*.

Brain, W. H. (Glos.):– w-k hat-trick, *156, 162*.

Braund, L. C. (Eng.):– All-round, *161*; 3 Test hundreds, *195, 204*; 8 w. in Test innings, *180*.

Brayshaw, I. J. (W. Aust.):– 10 w. in innings, *153*.

Brearley, J. M. (Eng.):– Test captain, *194, 211, 214, 217*; 25,185 r., *141*; 312* v North Zone in day, *132, 143*; 45 hundreds, *137*.

Brearley, W. (Eng.):– 17 w. in match, *154*; 4 w. with consecutive balls, *155*.

Briasco, P. S. (C. Dist.):– 317 for 2nd wkt, *148*.

Briggs, J. (Eng.):– 1 Test hundred, *195*; Test hat-trick, *184*; 2,221 w., *159*; 118 w. in Tests, *181*; 100 w. (12), *158*; 15 w. in Test, *180, 206*; 10 w. or more in Test (4), *200, 206*; 10 w. in innings, *152*; 8 w. for 11 r. in Test innings, *179*.

Bright, R. J. (Aust.):– 10 w. or more in Test (1), *232*.

Britannic Assurance Championship, *see* County Championship.

Broad, B. C. (Eng.):– 10,000 r., *265*.

Brockwell, W. (Eng.):– 379 for 1st wkt, *147*.

Bromfield, H. D. (SA):– Test p'ship record, *234*.

Bromley-Davenport, H. R. (Eng.):– Test p'ship record, *205*.

Brookes, D. (Eng.):– 30,874 r., *140*; 1,000 r. (17), *138*; 71 hundreds, *136*.

Brown, A. S. (Glos.):– 7 c. in innings, *164*.

Brown, D. J. (Eng.):– 79 w. in Tests, *182*.

Brown, F. R. (Eng.):– Test captain, *194, 203, 207, 211*.

Brown, G. (Eng.):– 37 hundreds, *137*.

Brown, J. T. (Eng.):– 1 Test hundred, *195*; 311 v Sussex, *132*; 300 v Derbyshire, *132*; 554 and 378 for 1st wkt, *146-7*.

Brown, J. (Scotland):– 7 d. in innings, *162*.

M

N

O

Index

Sutcliffe, H. (Eng.):– *contd*
  hundreds in same Test (2), *171, 197, 204;*
  2 hundreds in match (4), *134;* 313 v
  Essex, *132;* Avge of 96.96 in English
  season, *139;* 1st wkt hundreds, *147-8;*
  555 for 1st wkt, *146, 147, 148.*
Suttle, K. G. (Sussex):– 30,225 r., *140;*
  1,000 r. (17), *138;* 49 hundreds, *137;* 423
  consecutive Championship appearances,
  261.

T

Taber, H. B. (Aust.):– 20 d. in series, *187;*
  12 d. in match, *163;* 8 d. in Test, *186;* 7 d.
  in innings, *162.*
Taberer, H. M. (SA):– Test captain, *220.*
Tahir Naqqash (Pak.):– Test p'ship
  records, *248, 251.*
Talat Ali (Pak.):– Hundred and double-
  hundred, *135.*
Tallon, D. (Aust.):– 20 d. in series, *187;* 12
  d. in match, *163;* 7 d. in innings, *162.*
Tancred, A. B. (SA):– Carrying bat in Test,
  176.
Tancred, L. J. (SA):– Test captain, *203,
  220;* Test p'ship record, *222.*
Tarilton, P. H. (B'dos):– 304* v Trinidad,
  132.
Tariq Bashir (HBFC):– 355 for 5th wkt,
  149.
Tarrant, F. A. (Vic. and Middx):– All-
  round, *161;* 182* and 10 w., *160;* 100 w.
  (8), *158;* 10 w. in innings, *153;* 5 hat-
  tricks, *156;* 4 w. with consecutive balls,
  155.
Taslim Arif (Pak.):– 1 Test hundred, *231;*
  10 d. in match, *163;* 7 d. in innings, *162;*
  Test p'ship record, *232.*
Tate, M. W. (Eng.):– All-round, *161, 162;*
  All-round in Tests, *185;* 1 Test hundred,
  204; 2,784 w., *159;* 200 w. (3), *157;* 155
  w. in Tests, *181;* 116 w. in overseas
  season, *158;* 100 w. (14), *158;* 38 w. in
  series, *201;* 10 w. or more in Test (1), *201;*
  3 hat-tricks, *156;* Wkt with 1st ball on
  Test début, *183.*
Tattersall, R. (Eng.):– 100 w. (8), *158;* 10 w.
  or more in Test (1), *206.*
Tauseef Ahmed (Pak.):– Test p'ship record,
  251.
Tavaré, C. J. (Eng.):– 2 Test hundreds, *212,
  215;* Slow scoring in Test, *178;* 49 c. in
  season, *165;* Test p'ship record, *213.*
Tayfield, H. J. (SA):– 170 w. in Tests, *182;*
  37 w. in series, *181, 207;* 26 w. in series,
  207; 13 w. in Test (2), *180, 206, 222;* 9 w.
  in Test innings, *179;* 8 w. in Test innings,
  180; Test p'ship record, *234.*
Taylor, B. (Essex):– 1,294 d., *164;* 301
  consecutive Championship appearances,
  261.

Taylor, B. R. (NZ):– 2 Test hundreds, *236,
  242;* Hundred on Test début, *170, 242;*
  111 w. in Tests, *183;* All-round in Test,
  185; Test p'ship record, *242.*
Taylor, D. D. (NZ):– 1st wkt hundreds,
  147.
Taylor, H. W. (SA):– Test captain, *126, 203,
  220;* 2,936 r. in Tests, *174;* 582 r. in
  series, *206;* 7 Test hundreds, *205;* Test
  p'ship record, *206.*
Taylor, J. M. (Aust.):– 1 Test hundred, *199;*
  Test p'ship record, *200.*
Taylor, N. R. (Kent):– Hundred on début,
  133.
Taylor, R. W. (Eng.):– 1,648 d., *164;* 236 d.
  in JPL, *714;* 174 d. in Tests, *187;* 20 d. in
  series, *187;* 10 d. in Test, *186;* 10 d. in
  match (2), *163;* 7 d. in Test innings, *186;*
  7 d. in innings (3), *162;* Test p'ship
  records, *216, 218.*
Tennyson, Hon. L. H. (Lord Tennyson)
  (Eng.):– Test captain, *194.*
Terry, V. P. (Eng.):– 250 for 1st wkt, *263.*
Test and County Cricket Board:– Meet-
  ings, *1262, 1263-4;* Officers, *279;* XI v
  New Zealanders, *324-5.*
Test match grounds, *251-2.*
Test matches, duration of and qualification
  for, *1253-4.*
Test selectors, *1262.*
Texaco Trophy matches:– in 1986, *290-1,
  316-8;* in 1987, *1289.*
Thompson, G. J. (Eng.):– 1,591 w., *159;*
  100 w. (8), *158.*
Thomson, J. R. (Aust.):– 200 w. in Tests,
  182; 100 w. v England, *202.*
Thomson, K. (NZ):– Test p'ship record,
  242.
Thomson, N. I. (Eng.):– 1,597 w., *159;* 100
  w. (12), *158;* 10 w. in innings, *153.*
Thousand runs in May, *144.*
Throwing records, *260.*
Tied matches, *168-9, 257, 1252.*
Tilcon Trophy:– *657;* Fixtures, 1987, *1285.*
Titmus, F. J. (Eng.):– All-round, *161, 162;*
  All-round in Tests, *185;* 2,830 w., *159;*
  153 w. in Tests, *181;* 100 w. (16), *158.*
Todd, L. J. (Kent):– 38 hundreds, *137.*
Tolchard, R. W. (Eng.):– 1,037 d., *164.*
Toogood, G. J. (OUCC):– 149 and 10 w. v
  Cambridge, *343.*
Toohey, P. M. (Aust.):– 1 Test hundred,
  224.
Toshack, E. R. H. (Aust.):– 10 w. or more in
  Test (1), *230.*
Tours, Future, *926.*
Townsend, L. F. (Eng.):– All-round, *161.*
Trans-Tasman Trophy, *226.*
Tribe, G. E. (Aust.):– All-round, *161;* 100
  w. (8), *158.*
Troup, G. B. (NZ):– 10 w. or more in Test
  (1), *236.*

INDEX OF ADVERTISERS

INDEX OF FILLERS

NOTES BY THE EDITOR

"Just heard that India won the Lord's Test", wrote a correspondent from overseas last summer. "I have been an ardent supporter of England for over fifty years, and am both grieved and surprised at this defeat. I am still at a loss to understand – a) The poor standard of cricket in the two premier Universities – Cambridge and Oxford. In the past they have always produced clever Test captains and cricketers of Test standard. b) The lack of a firm, resolute captain of the calibre of Douglas Jardine and Len Hutton, both of whom rescued England when in the doldrums. c) The loss of English grit and determination in their batting. I wonder whether one-day cricket is killing Test cricket in England."

The influence of one-day, or limited-overs, cricket was also very much in the minds of those who prepared the Report of the TCCB Enquiry into the Standards of Play of English Cricket in Test and First-Class County Cricket: the Palmer Report, so named after the Enquiry's chairman, C. H. Palmer. Reading that report, full of valid points, I was nevertheless left wondering to what extent it, like the letter above, was out of tune with what England and English cricket have become and are becoming.

We live today in the age of the instant, be it the microwave oven, the fast-food outlet or the cricket match. So it seems inevitable that, if the public wants action and a winner to cheer, a match it can watch from beginning to end, the counties will supply it; not only because there is public interest but also because where there is public interest there will be sponsors. For the Test and County Cricket Board, on one hand trying to improve playing standards for Test matches while on the other planning the economic welfare of the county game, the dichotomy is that what is good for the game is not always good for the business.

In the same year that the Palmer Report considered limited-overs cricket to be the main cause of the decline in standards of batting and bowling in English cricket (and before the Indians and New Zealanders had shown the extent of that decline), the TCCB introduced a second limited-overs competition for the county Second XIs; and this summer the number of games in that competition has been virtually doubled by the playing of home and away ties in the three zonal rounds. Yet the Palmer Report advised: "The young cricketer now entering the first-class county game as presently organised has greater difficulty in acquiring the skills for success *in all types of cricket* [my italics] because of insufficient opportunity to serve a good apprenticeship in three-day cricket."

I am reminded of the television programme, *Yes Minister*, in which the Civil Service's answer to any call for action was to set up an enquiry. By the time it had reached its conclusion, everyone would have forgotten why it had been commissioned. The Palmer Report deserves better than to be shelved and forgotten, and it was appropriate that 1986 provided a timely reminder of its origins: widespread disappointment and genuine concern about the standards of play at Test and county level following the series of failures in Australia in 1982-83, in New Zealand and Pakistan in 1983-84, and against West Indies in England in 1984. Yet how quickly fortunes change.

England retain the Ashes

When they departed for Australia in October last year, England had gone
eleven Test matches without a win, having lost all five in the West Indies,
two to India and one to New Zealand. Before the year was out, however, they
had beaten Australia twice: at Brisbane in the first Test by seven wickets,
having made Australia follow on, and at Melbourne by an innings and 14
runs in three days. The second and third Tests, at Perth and Adelaide
respectively, were drawn, and so the Ashes, regained by Gower in 1985, were
retained by his successor as England's captain, Gatting.

After a year in the wilderness, these victories were a great morale boost for
the England players and their supporters. Viewed from a distance, they
appear to be the product of a happy, unified team, and much credit for this
must be given to the manager, P. M. Lush, and the assistant manager, M. J.
Stewart. Between them, they have restored pride to England's players.
Following the TCCB's decision to draw up terms of reference for the roles of
the management on tour, the choice of Mr Lush as manager was significantly
successful. The Public Relations and Marketing Manager of the TCCB, he
has experience of coping with the media and the marketing men and so was
able to absorb those external pressures which in the past have upset touring
teams. The assistant manager and the players, meanwhile, were able to
concentrate on their preparations and their cricket. It was a professional
approach and it paid dividends.

Gatting, on his first tour as England's captain, said that he did not enjoy all
aspects of the job, in which case success must have tasted all the sweeter.
There were times last year when he appeared to be waiting for something to
happen, rather than trying to make it happen, and it is hoped that his success
in Australia will have given him confidence. Leadership is a matter of
initiative as well as command; it is a quality Gatting has always shown in his
batting and should, now that he has some wins under his belt, be seen in his
captaincy. Gower's brief reign, in which series victories over India in India
and Australia in England in 1985 were offset by 5-0 defeats by West Indies at
home and away, ended when he was relieved of the England captaincy
following England's defeat by India at Lord's: the first Test of last summer.
The cry for a change was widespread. Had it been less strident, who is to say
that he would not have been just as successful as Gatting in Australia,
especially given Stewart's influence?

The parlous state of Australian cricket

Writing of the Australian side that toured England in 1985, my predecessor
said he was "not among those who maintain there is no such thing as a weak
Australian side". Has there ever been one as weak as that beaten by England
this past winter? Yet there are players with the potential to be good. What is
missing, it seems, is the tempering of that potential before it is exposed to
international cricket. The place for that is not in the succession of airport
terminals and one-day internationals through which the leading Australian
cricketers pass each season. It is in a healthy domestic first-class competition. In 1985-86 the Australian selectors called 24 players to the colours. It is
worth a glance at the Sheffield Shield matches which appear later in the

Almanack. State sides once proud with great names are frequently bare of current Australian players caught up in the commercial whirlpool of international cricket, simply to satisfy the television mogul and his marketing minions.

"Generally speaking", said the Palmer Report, "only players of genuine Test match standard will be competent to succeed consistently in limited-overs international matches." It was understandable that New Zealand, rather than compete for the prizemoney at the junket in Perth, chose instead to keep their Test men at home, strengthening their domestic competition so that younger players might profit from the experience of playing with and against them.

The loss of experienced players to South Africa did not help Australia's cause either. In improving the earning power of its top players, Mr Packer, the poacher turned gamekeeper, failed to take into account that while many may be called, usually only eleven are chosen: and that in a land where the dollar and success are the goalposts, those not chosen would become all too easy prey to the hand with the rand. Yet if the Australians continue to flounder, interest will fall away, not only at the grounds but also in the viewing figures. Even interest in one-day cricket will fall off if Australia are beaten regularly by the likes of New Zealand or India or Sri Lanka. The Australian Cricket Board already is concerned at the standard of the game there, but those who market it might do well to look also at their investment if they see cricket as a continuing commodity. There are those, of course, who would like to see the marketing men run even before they cut their losses.

Cause for English concern

It is not only for Australia's sake that it should be a power in world cricket. English cricket, dependent to quite some extent on Test match receipts for its financial well-being, needs the draw of a strong Australian side. Rarely last summer was there a full house on any day, even a Saturday, of a Test match, despite the fact that India and New Zealand were good sides with world-class players. At Lord's, for example, an overall attendance of 57,509 watched the Indians and 69,184 the New Zealanders; yet there were 93,329 to see the Australians the previous year, and 25,539 had earlier filled the ground for the third Texaco Trophy match, even though Australia had already won the series. At Birmingham, 42,750 watched the Indians, 51,550 the Australians. While it may be good for England to beat Australia, it is not good for either country if Australian cricket is so weak that it ceases to be regarded as a major sport by its success-oriented citizens.

India and New Zealand win their series

Following England's second successive whitewash by West Indies, the circumstances of which are told fully later in this *Wisden*, the Test victories of India and New Zealand last summer exposed serious flaws in England's technique and attitude. By India, England were outplayed in all departments, except wicket-keeping, although the bowling of Dilley was encouraging. More telling, though, was the accurate swing, seam and spin purveyed by the

Indians who, having perceived England's weaknesses, exploited them skilfully. "We want you to beat New Zealand", an Indian friend told *Wisden's* correspondent after the Headingley Test. "We don't want the world to think this series has been a pushover."

But that, too, was beyond England. I felt that by this time England had reached their nadir. New Zealand were a solid side, with two outstanding players in Hadlee and Martin Crowe, but I do not think that any England team, possessing pride and spirit, would have allowed themselves to be beaten by them. Noticeable in England's approach against India was a fear of failure; it was almost as if they had forgotten how to go about winning. At Trent Bridge, where they lost to New Zealand, once England had failed to gain an initiative, they looked resigned to defeat. What was needed was someone whose concern was not for his place in the team or his family: someone who was not conditioned by a fear of failure: who could take the game by the scruff and give it a shake. What was needed was Botham.

A guerrilla fighter impatient of discipline

Botham, it might be argued, is irresponsible; some wouldn't even bother to argue. But his lack of responsibility is more to himself that to his fellow-man. He bats and bowls not with concern for averages or place but for the joy of playing and the stimulus of competition. He, too, is a "guerrilla fighter impatient of discipline. A devotee of action who thrives on challenge and crisis." Those are words used to describe Winston Churchill in the 1930s: a man at times as much loved or loathed as Botham has been in recent years. Botham may not be everyone's ideal hero, but as Carlyle said, the hero can be poet, prophet, king, priest or whatever you will, according to the kind of world he finds himself born into. To a society that cries out for any extravagant gesture to alleviate the mediocrity, Botham by his deeds has indeed become a hero. In August, he presented the Leukaemia Research Fund with a cheque for £888,000 as a result of his great walk from John O'Groats to Land's End in 1985. The following week the Comptroller and Auditor General reported that the Ministry of Defence had overspent by £938 million on its major defence contracts and paid out more than £200 million on a further seven projects which were later cancelled. I suppose it's not quite cricket.

Botham's absence from the England side for all but the last Test match of the summer was due to his suspension by the TCCB from all first-class cricket from May 29 until July 31. His misdemeanour was bringing the game into disrepute by admitting to using cannabis (in a newspaper article on May 18), denying in the past that he had used cannabis, and making public pronouncements without the clearance of his county.

The suspension was not severe; a week later four auxiliary nurses at a Nottingham hospital were dismissed for allegedly smoking cannabis when they were off-duty and not on hospital premises. Botham erred. In 1985 the TCCB had taken no action against him following his conviction for possession of the drug, and it was felt then that it had been lenient. Moreover, the Board had agreed to support the Sports Council in its campaign against drug-taking, so it had not only to be responsible but be seen to be responsible.

With a similar sense of responsibility, it might also reflect on the condition of some of its customers after a day's imbibing. Cricket watching should be a pleasurable activity: the behaviour and language of certain spectators, from the hospitality boxes to the bleachers, were enough to make some people I spoke to think twice about attending major cricket matches, let alone taking children to them.

An unanswered question

Botham's suspension did, however, leave at least one question unanswered. The Board's action followed his admission in *The Mail on Sunday* that he did "take pot", albeit at a time predating the TCCB's anti-drugs resolution. The article was part of a settlement, between Botham and the newspaper, of a libel action instigated by Botham after allegations in that paper in March 1984 that he had smoked "pot" during England's tour of New Zealand. Commenting on the settlement, the editor of the newspaper, which had prepared its defence of the action, said that the view on both sides was that "it would be disastrous" for Ian Botham and English cricket if the case went to court. Yet in a carefully worded statement, following that England tour, the TCCB had said that "investigations have not substantiated any of the serious allegations made". The question raises itself. How deeply did that investigation dig?

The manager of that tour, A. C. Smith, has since become the Chief Executive of the TCCB: he will know the pitfalls that await the modern administrator. None the less, he and all with a responsibility for the game would do well to heed the words of Lord Harris in this bicentennial year of MCC.

"You do well to love it [cricket], for it is more free from anything sordid, anything dishonourable, than any game in the world. To play it keenly, honourably, self-sacrificingly is a moral lesson in itself ... protect it from anything that would sully it so that it may grow in favour with all men."

MCC's bicentenary

Whether, in this day of insider dealing, such a noble sentiment remains compatible with the business that cricket has become at first-class county level is debatable. But for those who care for the game, who cherish its lessons and its traditions, it is essential that the sentiment takes priority even over the business. Written more that half a century ago, those words seem no less appropriate in 1987 as MCC, of which Lord Harris was so much a part, celebrates its 200th anniversary, appositely under the presidency of M. C. Cowdrey. An imaginative programme has been arranged, with the highlight, for all cricket lovers at least, a five-day match at Lord's in August between MCC (a side chosen from all cricketers playing in the United Kingdom in 1987) and the Rest of the World. MCC's place in cricket is unique. If in recent years its role has been diminished, it still has a voice in the game's affairs which one trusts will be raised authoritatively should the ethic of cricket ever be threatened. *Wisden*, a mere 123 years old, congratulates the Club on its bicentenary and wishes it well.

A need for action

Given MCC's continuing involvement in cricket's affairs worldwide, by providing the International Cricket Conference with its Chairman and secretariat, what more welcome birthday gift could the members of the ICC give MCC than an agreement to curb short-pitched bowling and improve over-rates in Test cricket? I link the two intentionally, because action on the latter could have an effect on the former, as well as giving the spectator a fair return for his day's admission fee.

The great problem facing the game, certainly at Test match level, is short-pitched bowling, and unless cricket is to become a game which is administered by gentlemen and practised by thugs, action must be taken against those bowlers who practise intimidation as a means of containment and dismissal. For any bowler to defend his use of the bouncer against a tailender on the grounds that he is helmeted, protected and obstructive, is about on a par with the mugger who defends his right to rob old ladies because they live in an area of high crime and violence.

To see a batsman hit, even felled, by a ball is not an edifying sight. Or is it for some? We live in times when violence and ugliness are pronounced and promulgated, not least by the visual media. Those in public life are seen to be less concerned with truth and concern for people than with scoring political points and remaining in power. Our young people are not set a very good example by those who should be setting standards. Sport has become an outlet for patriotic aggression, and there are those for whom victory, however it is achieved, is more important than the way the game is played. Along with such a society, cricket has fallen from grace.

The answer to the problem of short-pitched bowling appears simple: a strict application of the Law. On a number of occasions last summer I saw bowlers threaten the batsman's person with no appearance of caution from the umpires. Umpires are not appointed simply to count the number of balls in an over any more than policemen are there to direct traffic. Their job is to uphold all the Laws: by no means a simple task and one full of responsibility. It requires, also, the full backing of the authorities, which applies both in this country and overseas.

That is why I would prefer independent umpires for Test matches, by which I do not mean "neutral" umpires; rather, umpires who are not appointed by the home country's board of control. I would advocate an international panel of leading umpires, appointed by and responsible to the ICC, which in turn would have to show a more positive attitude. It would cost money, but Test matches are cricket's money-spinner. They are also the world's window on the sport. Such a panel will stand later this year for World Cup matches; just as all countries have agreed to maintain a required over-rate or incur heavy fines. I feel that an international team of umpires, paid in accordance with their responsibilities, would feel less the servants of the national authorities who appoint them at present and, as a body, would have the confidence to enforce the Laws. With regard to the Law on short-pitched bowling, the TCCB will propose at this year's ICC annual meeting that bouncers be restricted to one per over, with bowlers receiving only one warning. Acceptance by the Test-playing countries would show they are more concerned for cricket than they are for national success.

Umpiring standards

English cricket has taken pride in the high standard of its umpires, and rightly so. But every now and then that standard slips. In the Test match at Headingley last summer, Shastri was given out off what should have been called a no ball; at the time Lever delivered it, there were three men behind the popping crease on the leg side: an infringement of Law 41.2. Similarly, in that Test, India had twelve players on the field during an over. Such an occurrence is understandable, given the umpires' attention to other matters, except that the player should not have returned to the field "without the consent of the umpire at the bowler's end" (Law 2.8) who should, at the same time, have made sure of the substitute's departure. I will return to the comings and goings of players, but first I wish to comment on the scores in New Zealand's fourth innings at Trent Bridge.

A matter of interpretation

The confusion arose from the action of Gower, who, with New Zealand 73 for two and requiring 1 run to win the second Test, was called upon by Gatting to bowl the last over and thoughtlessly "threw" his first delivery. Umpire Palmer called "no-ball", which effectively gave New Zealand the run they needed, but Martin Crowe, then 44, hit the ball for 4 runs. Were these to be added to his and New Zealand's scores? It was the interpretation of one of the umpires, when questioned by the editor of *Wisden Cricket Monthly* very soon afterwards, that they should not be. However, it does not appear that the umpires, at the end of the match, agreed with the official scorers on the correctness of the scores in accordance with Law 3.14. Subsequently, the Secretaries of MCC and the TCCB were of the opinion that the 4 runs should count towards the scores and this is how they appear in *Wisden*. The Secretary of MCC, which is responsible for the Laws, considered that the ball had not become dead on the call of "no-ball", there apparently having been no call of "time" immediately after the call of "no ball". Consequently, in accordance with Law 24.9, Crowe was entitled to hit the no-ball and have the resulting runs added to his score. There would have been no confusion had the umpires issued a statement immediately after the match, for they were not unaware that there was uncertainty.

Comings and goings

I am intrigued by the number of itinerant spear-bearers who have joined the play in recent years, bringing on or taking off helmets, glasses of water, dry batting gloves, salt tablets. Sometimes they are mentioned by name over the public address system: perhaps it's in the spear-bearers' union agreement. But thinking about it, the spectator has a right to know the extra's name, having paid to see this interruption to his day's cricket.

More serious are other comings and goings. One first-class umpire told me last year of an international fast bowler who, at the end of his spell, took his sweater and kept walking until he was back in the pavilion, without even telling his acting-captain that he was going, let alone requesting the umpire's consent. This consent is not just a courtesy (the day seems long past when courtesy is considered commonplace); it is a requirement of the Laws. One might ask why the umpires do not enforce it, but one can sympathise with them. In many walks of life, enforcement of the lesser laws produces counter-charges of "petty" or "nit-picking", so that it would seem to be the enforcer rather than the transgressor who is at fault. There is room here for captains, and the county clubs, to make sure that both the letter and the spirit of the Laws are adhered to.

Time to get on with the game

In this respect, counties and their captains could stand a reminder from the 1944 MCC Select Committee's report: "The Intervals and Hours of Play as provided for in the Laws of Cricket or in Match Regulations must be strictly adhered to. In particular, the two minutes allowed for the incoming batsman to take his place is a generous allowance *which should rarely be utilised to the full* [my italics] and never exceeded.

And then there is field-placing. It is not as if, by late in the summer, a captain does not know where his bowlers want their fieldsmen. The prevarication practised last summer by the England and Middlesex captain and the England and Middlesex spin bowlers when it came to setting a field may not have been deliberate time-wasting, but more often than not it was a waste of time. There are times, I regret to say, when it smacks of the shop floor and working to rule.

"War was gradually improved into an art and degraded into a trade", wrote Gibbon while describing the decline and fall of an earlier empire. It is hard, at times, watching some cricketers go about their daily business, not to reflect similarly on what had been improved into an art in the heyday of a more recent empire.

A more attacking approach

For all that modern society prefers action to aesthetic pleasures, style and personality continue to attract attention, and cricket must encourage those who breathe life into the game. Not only batsmen but also bowlers who by pace or wiles make cricket a contest rather than an exercise. When batsmen bat with a fear of being dismissed and bowlers bowl with a fear of being hit, stalemate and boredom set in. English cricket has, in batsmen like Botham, Gatting, Lamb, Whitaker, Bailey, and Gower – and Hick – players to break any stalemate, but there is a desperate need for attacking bowlers.

The time has come to encourage wicket-taking, and that is why I would like to see the TCCB, when it decides on bonus points for the County Championship in 1988, award them for bowling only. If pitches are to remain covered, and I suspect they will in the meantime, the batsmen already have sufficient in their favour. I would prefer to see cricket played on pitches which are more responsive to the vagaries of the English climate. It is said that to produce mature, exciting wines in some regions, the vines must suffer; the same could be said of young batsmen. But if pitches remain covered for Test cricket, bowlers must learn to take wickets on them.

Of late, some groundsmen have shown themselves able to prepare sporting pitches which give both batsmen and bowlers a chance, and others should be encouraged to do so. The Palmer Report stressed the need for pitches that are hard, fast and true to start with and then give spin bowlers some help later in the match. However, the practice of some counties of producing pitches which favour their own strengths is deprecable. As the rewards for winning increase, so the practices need more careful watching.

Changes for 1988

Looking at ways to improve the standard of first-class cricketers, the Palmer Report recommended a Championship of sixteen three-day matches and eight four-day matches per county; a knockout competition involving twenty teams in place of the current Benson and Hedges format; and a Sunday League of two divisions with each county playing only eight matches and then the top two in each division going into semi-finals and a final.

The response of the counties was, not surprisingly, less radical. However, from 1988, there will be four-day matches in the County Championship. Each county will play six four-day matches in addition to sixteen three-day matches. The zonal leagues format will be retained for the Benson and Hedges Cup, although there will not be quarter-finals; instead the top team from each group will go into the semi-final round. And the Sunday League, which from this year becomes the Refuge Assurance League, will be increased rather than cut back. Each county will continue to play the others once, and at the end of the season the top four counties will contest semi-finals, followed by a final.

I welcome the introduction of the four-day game if it is going to give young batsmen the opportunity to develop an innings properly instead of being forced into "one-day-style cricket" in pursuit of bonus points. Perhaps, too, it will reduce the number of contrived finishes, although the weather will always provide instances of final-day forfeitures. There is no excuse, though, when forfeitures become no more than a means to obtaining a result after two days of stalemate. I can understand the players' point of view. There is nothing worse than passing through an afternoon towards an inevitable draw in any kind of cricket. But when collusions, primed declarations and forfeitures make a nonsense of all that has gone before, it is not cricket. There were some marvellous Championship matches last year, played to an exciting finish, which resulted purely and simply from positive cricket, positive attitudes and skilful captaincy.

Valete?

Not retained under contract by Yorkshire, Boycott said late last year that he had retired from first-class cricket. It is not easy to imagine a season without him, especially with four-day Championship matches just around the corner. I have a feeling he will be back, for Yorkshire even. Last year also saw the retirement of the Australian fast bowler, Jeff Thomson. Devotees of the unquotable one-liner will be sad to see him go, but no batsman. In 51 Tests he took 200 wickets at 28.00; only five Australians have taken more; and in 21 Tests against England he took exactly 100 wickets. In all first-class cricket he took 675 wickets at 26.46.

A new man at the TCCB

Off the field, but never far away from it, D. B. Carr retired as Secretary of the TCCB after a life devoted to cricket. He made his first-class début at eighteen, playing for England against Australia in the Victory "Test" of 1945 at Lord's, and in 1951-52 he played in two Tests against India, captaining England at Madras. After being assistant secretary and secretary of Derbyshire, he became an Assistant Secretary of MCC in 1962 and then in 1974 was appointed Secretary of the newly formed Test and County Cricket Board. He is succeeded by A. C. Smith, who carries the designation of Chief Executive rather than Secretary, an indication perhaps that he is responsible for a business organisation, not a club. Previously secretary of Warwickshire, since 1976, and a Test selector, "A.C." played six times for England as wicket-keeper on E. R. Dexter's MCC tour of Australia and New Zealand in 1962-63.

If these Notes seem a catalogue of concerns, they are so because I am concerned about cricket: for the quality of cricket as I am for the quality of life. I do not see the game in isolation but in relation to what is happening in our society. That is, for me, a great part of cricket's attraction. Therefore it does concern me when, for example, I perceive a drift towards more limited-overs cricket, not just in England but internationally; because if cricket does indeed reflect stages of social history, our lives too must become more and more restricted to a set number of permutations. When the American short-story and baseball writer, Ring Lardner, died, Scott Fitzgerald wrote that "Ring moved in the company of a few dozen illiterates playing a boy's game. A boy's game with no more possibilities than a boy could master. A game bounded by walls which kept out danger, change or adventure."

Cricket must always be more than that. So must life.

FIVE CRICKETERS OF THE YEAR

JOHN CHILDS

Even in a game as notoriously fickle as cricket, there cannot be many instances of a player as well advanced in his career as JOHN HENRY CHILDS remodelling his method so successfully that, having been on the verge of disappearing from sight at the end of one season, he was knocking on the door of an England team to tour Australia twelve months later. In 1985, Childs, signed by Essex on a one-year contract at the age of 33 after a mixed decade with Gloucestershire, took five wickets at an average of 105.60. In 1986, despite being omitted from four Championship games and not bowling in another, he took 89 at 16.29 and his attacking left-arm spin was a crucial component in Essex's winning of the title. Had the Test selectors found room for a third spinner in the party to defend the Ashes, the place would have gone to Childs, who in four matches from mid-August took more wickets than Edmonds and Emburey all season. Instead, pencilled in as first reserve, he had the consolations of an Essex cap and a two-year contract that gave him the security to move his wife and two young sons from their Bristol home to one within easy reach of the county ground at Chelmsford.

In an era when the proposition that "nice guys never win" is a fashionable parrot-cry, it is gratifying that it was this very quality in Childs, allied to the club's continued faith in him, that persuaded Essex to keep him on after his dismal season in 1985. Analysing his failure that September, Doug Insole, the chairman, and Keith Fletcher, the outgoing captain, concluded that with the right guidance, his main fault – a too-slow flight – could be corrected. After discussing it with Childs, they decided that Fred Titmus, the former Middlesex and England off-spinner, was the man to send him to. In the Christmas holidays Childs spent four sessions in the Indoor School at Lord's with Titmus and the MCC head coach, Don Wilson, himself a former England slow left-armer, and was fitted with the method that within months transformed him into the most successful spinner in the country.

Childs's gratitude to Titmus and Wilson was mingled with astonishment that the change in his fortunes stemmed from nothing more complicated than a straighter, faster, longer run-up to the stumps. "Pitches have got slower in the ten years since I started, and my basic problem in 1985 was that, without the confidence of taking wickets, I had been running up and just 'putting' the ball there", he said. "The result was that even when the ball was turning, it had so little pace batsmen could generally adjust and play it off the pitch." Titmus described the flaw in a way which will strike a chord in all spin bowlers lacking confidence. "He was bowling as though he half expected the ball to come back like a bullet!"

Discarding their first notion of making Childs bowl with a slightly lower arm, Titmus and Wilson hit upon the straighter, nine-pace, run-up. "Until then, I had been running between the umpire and the stumps", said Childs. "But what might have been a problem in my new approach – getting side-on at the crease – turned out to be a help: to get into position, you have to lean back in the final stride, which gives your action greater snap." Childs, who had been filling in time in Bristol as a freelance sign-writer, the trade he learned on leaving school, then spent much of the remainder of the winter honing his new method in Gloucestershire's indoor nets. "I spent a lot of time bowling to Jack Russell, their wicket-keeper, who was working on his batting. He pulled my leg to start with, telling me I'd become a medium-pacer, but the experience was beneficial to us both."

Essex's reliance on their seamers on green early-season pitches kept Childs waiting till the second half of May to put his hours of practice to the test – in their third Championship game, on a slow turner at Northampton. A washed-out third day gave neither side a chance to win: but for Childs, with five for 97 in 43.3 overs, the contest was a watershed, in effect the making of his season. "I felt I'd started to come back to how I used to bowl, and I struck up a good rapport with David East. As our wicket-keeper he had seen both sides of me, the 1985 version and the new one, and he knew better than anyone what pace I should be bowling in any particular conditions. And having taken wickets, I now had the confidence to give the ball more air on a pitch that called for it."

Nothing gave Childs more pleasure than the nineteen stumpings off his bowling. "Catches at the wicket or at slip are the slow left-hander's traditional way of taking wickets. But when you have a batsman stumped, it usually means you've not only beaten him in the air but by hurrying the ball through you've given him no time to recover." Childs's bounce, product of a good high arm from his height of 6ft 2in, combined with his knack of giving the ball a form of over-spin by rotating it on an axis in line with second slip, made him a rewarding bowler to keep wicket to. Last season East had more than double the stumpings of any other 'keeper in the Championship.

A bronzed Devonian of sunny disposition, born in Plymouth on August 15, 1951, Childs paid tribute to Tom Woodward, a teacher at Audley Park Secondary School, Torquay, for his early coaching, which saw him progress from school and village cricket to the Devon Under-15 and Under-19 teams. "He wasn't a great cricketer himself, but he was one of those old-fashioned schoolteachers, happy to give all the help he could in his free time. Compared to now, I consider myself very lucky to have been at school in the 1960s." At twelve he had begun playing for his village, Kingskerswell, where in Bert Mitchell he was blessed with a fellow slow left-armer as captain who "knew when to put me on and take me off"; and at sixteen he moved up a class to the South Devon club in Newton Abbott.

Consistent success took him into Devon's minor county team where, with his apprenticeship as a sign-writer completed, his progress might easily have rested but for providential intervention. "Graham Wiltshire, the Gloucester-shire coach, came down to watch someone in the Cornwall side when we were playing them in 1974, saw me bowl, and instead offered me a trial. I'd never thought of playing professionally till then, but when Gloucestershire offered me a two-year contract I took it." Mike Procter awarded him his county cap in 1977 and in 1981, David Graveney's first year as captain, he took 75 wickets, until last season his best return. But with the attack losing balance through the retirement of Procter and Brian Brain, there was increasingly little work for two slow left-armers and Childs was released after playing only seven games in 1984. When his first year with Essex brought him only three wickets in the Championship, he was reconciled to being told "Thank you, but no thank you" when Insole asked to see him that September. Now he is resolved to show that 1986 was not just an Indian summer. Having rediscovered the pleasure of making batsmen hurry, the notion of dodging their straight drives holds no appeal whatever. – J.D.T.

GRAEME HICK

At any one time there are perhaps half-a-dozen cricketers in England who inspire people to say: "Ah, I think I'll go to that match tomorrow just to watch him play." Usually, such a compelling player is a batsman, such as David Gower or Viv Richards or Martin Crowe. In 1986, the name of Graeme Hick was added to that élite list of cricketers who actively excite followers of the game.

Nineteen years of age at the season's start, Hick was the first to make 1,000 first-class runs. A tall, broad, white-hatted wielder of a Duncan Fearnley blade, like Crowe, he went on to become one of two to score 2,000 runs, and thereby claimed another title: that of being, at twenty, the youngest batsman to reach this figure in an English season. Len Hutton was 21 when he did so in 1937. It is hard to think there have been many better players at his age than GRAEME ASHLEY HICK.

From the start he has been a prodigy. Born on May 23, 1966 in Harare, Zimbabwe, or Salisbury, Rhodesia, as the capital then was, Hick was six years and eight months old when he made his first century, with his own bat and without a box as he remembers. His 105 not out was scored against Mangula Junior School, and it contained 24 4s, the ball travelling quickly over a hard "bush" ground short of grass. His father, John Hick, had twice represented the district of Mashonaland as a middle-order batsman; he had already taken his son into Salisbury to watch Graeme Pollock bat in Currie Cup matches. But the schoolboy Hick, able at tennis, athletics and hockey (he came to play for the national schools team), did not give particular attention to cricket at first. He simply bowled his high, turning off-breaks for Banket Junior School in 1975 – and took 115 wickets for 347 runs, at an average of 3.02 each! As an opening batsman he had made no more than half-a-dozen hundreds by 1979, when he dropped to number three in the Prince Edward High School Under-14 team and served notice of his exceptional talent. That year he acquired the habit of making large, undefeated centuries, and averaged 185 for his school.

The following year, 1980, when living at the family home on the Trelawney tobacco-farming estate, he was found to have meningitis in its milder form. The delay was considerable, but the path already established. For the rest of his schooldays Hick ascended through the various grades: from the national Junior Schools team (of which he was captain), to the Fawns, to the Senior Schools side. So rapid was the progress that at seventeen, while still at school, Hick was selected as a member of the Zimbabwe World Cup party of 1983 – the youngest player to have been selected for that country, or for a World Cup tournament.

In 1984 he went to Worcestershire on a Zimbabwe Cricket Union scholarship: at the season's end he was allowed a Championship début against Surrey and had made 82 when time expired. In 1985, for Worcestershire and the touring Zimbabweans, he scored 1,265 runs at 52.70. His county, needless to say, were happy to preside over the growth of an extraordinary skill. They were especially impressed by the hungry way in which Hick approached his batting, often reaching the crease before the dismissed batsman had dragged himself from the field; by the orthodoxy and straightness of his style, tainted only by the steer through gully that has been forced upon so many by one-day cricket; by his strength, which he has developed through weight-lifting and is the strength of an amiable giant; by his pursuit of excellence, which somehow seems more attainable for a "colonial" than for someone bred in England; and by his method against short-pitched bowling. Hick pulls along the ground in front of square leg if he plays a shot – no top-edged hooking down to fine leg.

He began last season in fine form, having rewritten a few records at home during the winter. Ireland, touring Zimbabwe, had complained that they were not meeting good enough cricketers, and Hick was called in from his coaching duties around the schools. In a one-day game against Ireland he hit 155 not out (nine 6s, thirteen 4s) in 116 minutes. The next day, a three-day match began against them and Hick was 112 not out overnight. The following day he went on to 309 in less than seven hours (the next highest score was 58). His was the highest ever innings for Zimbabwe, or Rhodesia, or against Ireland.

Back with Worcestershire, centuries flowed like the Severn: two came in the Benson and Hedges Cup, bringing Gold Awards, and six in the Championship. He considered the double-century at Neath was "the most enjoyable", the best being the one against Gloucestershire on an uneven wicket at Worcester, when he took some bruises from Courtney Walsh and David Lawrence. Essex were the only other county to choose a batsman regularly as their one overseas player. Neither should Hick's capacious-handed slip-catching be forgotten, nor the potential of those off-breaks.

By the end of the season the question centred not on whether Hick was a great batsman in the making but on which country he would represent. Not Zimbabwe: reluctantly, yet understandably, Hick decided to sever the link with his native land in order to prove himself in Test cricket. New Zealand have sounded him out, offering a four-year qualification period. He was told that he could play for England only in 1991, after ten years' residence. By then many more runs will surely have flowed beneath the bridge beside New Road. – S.B.

DILIP VENGSARKAR

The view has always been held overseas that the true test of batsmanship is making runs in England, where conditions can alter with the passing overhead of a cloud and where pitches can vary so much in character. Even in contemporary times of covered pitches, the touring batsman still takes added glory from success in England.

One who has triumphed on every tour of England is DILIP BALVANT VENGSARKAR, born in Bombay on April 6, 1956, who holds the unique record of scoring a century on every one of his three Test appearances at Lord's. And this tall, elegant batsman reached his zenith in the summer of 1986 when his two hundreds, one at Lord's and another at Headingley, on one of the poorest Test pitches seen in England for some years, went so far towards India's achieving their 2-0 win in the three-match series. He finished it with an average of 90, by some margin the highest of any Indian batsman in England. Any suspicions that these hundreds were scored against a weak England team can be discounted. In each instance, Vengsarkar, having come in at the fall of the second wicket, was still short of his century when joined by the number eleven batsman. They were innings of the highest quality.

India's selectors have seldom been regarded as over-adventurous, but they could scarcely resist picking Vengsarkar in his first season of first-class cricket after seeing him make 110 in less than even time on a turning pitch against Prasanna, Bedi and Minna, a leg-spinner who was then regarded as a Test prospect. This classic innings was played in the annual fixture between the Ranji Trophy champions and the Rest of India, and when Vengsarkar went in, Bombay, the champions, were 100 for three and needing to score 211 to obtain a lead on first innings.

At that time, in 1975, the middle order of the Indian batting was fairly settled and the only vacant place was as Sunil Gavaskar's opening partner. Playing very straight as he did, Vengsarkar seemed to fit the role, but blooded against Sri Lanka, he was not an immediate success. He was out for 0 and 17 and was dropped for the remaining representative games. However, he held the selectors' attention by making a dour century against the touring team for the Indian Universities, and before he was quite twenty, he earned himself a place in the tour party to New Zealand and the West Indies in the spring of 1976.

Vengsarkar does not hail from a cricketing family, but his interest in the game was kindled when he was little more than a toddler as his home overlooked a large patch of green which is one of the main nurseries of Bombay cricket. Part of it was the home ground of Dadar Union, a club of high repute and tradition. Young Vengsarkar watched from his bedroom window, and when he was a little older he joined other boys in the neighbourhood in impromptu mid-week games. Nor was it just that he lived and grew up in the right environment. He was sent to the right school, King George, which produced many cricketers who played for Bombay and not a few who went on to play for India, including such greats of Indian cricket as Manjrekar and Gupte. By eleven, he was in King George's junior team as well as in the First XI, playing in the highly competitive Harris Shield competition (named after Lord Harris).

A year later, Vengsarkar was captain of both teams, and in the light of such early development it was surprising that he did not make a hundred in schools cricket before he was thirteen. Once he broke the barrier, however, several followed. One that opened new horizons was his 166 for Bombay Schools against Delhi Schools in 1970, for it led to his being picked for the West Zone Schools.

No sooner was he out of school than Vengsarkar was recruited by Dadar Union. Playing for the club alongside Gavaskar provided a close study in the building of a major innings, and this experience was quickly applied to his cricket at university, where he studied, and later graduated in, commerce. In 1974, Vengsarkar amassed 240 in the semi-finals of the collegiate competition and 170 against Delhi in the final of the Inter-University tournament. It was his passport into Bombay's Ranji Trophy squad, although he spent his first season in the reserves before getting his call in 1975, when Eknath Solkar was injured. He lost no time in establishing himself, and after only one season of first-class cricket climbed to the next level – a Test cap.

On the first leg of his maiden tour, in New Zealand, Vengsarkar played in all three Tests, opening the innings with Gavaskar each time, but without scoring over 30. There were no major scores either in the two Tests he played in the West Indies, but in the second of them he gave a clear hint of his promise and class. That was the contentious final Test match at Kingston, which was played on a newly laid pitch of very uneven bounce. The West

Indies pace bowlers, Holding, Daniel, Holder and Julien, were not averse to pitching short and three Indian batsmen took no further part in the match after being injured in the first innings. Indeed, Bedi declared as a protest against West Indies' intimidatory bowling. However, Vengsarkar, using his height to cope with the steep bounce, came out of the struggle with distinction, considering his lack of experience against pace bowling, scoring 39 and then 21 in the second innings, when five Indian batsmen were "absent injured". Notwithstanding this display of skill, he was not a fixture in the Test side until the tour of Australia in 1977-78, but from then until the series against England last summer he had missed only three Tests. By the time he returned to India for the series against Australia, he had 85 appearances to his name and an aggregate, including eleven centuries, of 4,985: only Gavaskar and Viswanath have scored more runs for India.

Although he frequently passed 50, Vengsarkar had to wait until his seventeenth Test match before achieving his maiden hundred: an occasion when he shared a record second-wicket stand of 344 with Gavaskar against West Indies, in Calcutta, in 1978-79. He has made runs everywhere, but all his overseas Test hundreds have been scored in England, where his reach and his technique of playing the ball late stand him in such good stead, as he demonstrated so amply last summer. – D.R.

COURTNEY WALSH

The revival of Gloucestershire – bottom of the County Championship table in 1984, third in 1985 and second last season – has been achieved through a team effort. Nevertheless, if one had to nominate a member of the side whose performances have been particularly influential, that man would surely be the West Indian fast bowler, Courtney Walsh, who in 1985 and 1986 took 203 wickets for the county at less than 19 runs apiece.

Walsh's bowling in 1986, when he was the country's leading wicket-taker with 118, was truly remarkable. His new-ball partner, David Lawrence, was less effective than in 1985, in addition to which Gloucestershire's penetrative third seamer, Kevin Curran, was prevented from bowling by a shoulder injury. These two factors imposed a burden on Walsh which he carried in heroic fashion as, showing great physical and mental stamina, he bowled with relentless hostility and reeled off match-winning performances week after week.

Of Gloucestershire's nine Championship victories last year, only one, at Leicester, came about through a contrived finish. The other eight were the result of natural cricket, and it is enlightening to list them with Walsh's match figures alongside.

Hampshire were beaten at Bournemouth by 146 runs; Walsh eleven for 94.

Kent, at Gloucester, by four wickets; Walsh seven for 107.

Surrey, at Bristol, by 96 runs; Walsh eleven for 113.

Glamorgan, at Cardiff, by five wickets; Walsh seven for 72.

Sussex, at Bristol, by one wicket; Walsh six for 129.

Somerset, at Bristol, by an innings and 7 runs; Walsh ten for 114.
    (His nine for 72 in Somerset's first innings was a career best.)

Worcestershire, at Worcester, by 78 runs; Walsh six for 97.

Hampshire, at Cheltenham, by 17 runs; Walsh twelve for 124.

His county captain, David Graveney, cannot praise Walsh highly enough. "He bowled 790 overs last season and *wanted* to bowl every one of them. He virtually carried our attack and did so without a murmur; he is a marvellous team man. When sides are chasing Championships, things can sometimes get a little tense in the dressing-room. Courtney has the knack of defusing awkward situations with a humorous remark or some genial clowning."

COURTNEY ANDREW WALSH was born in Kingston, Jamaica on October 30, 1962, and his early cricket was played there with the Melbourne club, which Michael Holding also represented. He made his first-class début in 1981-82 as a teenager, taking fifteen Shell Shield wickets at 25.20 runs apiece. Less successful in 1982-83, he really came to the fore in 1983-84 when he took 30 wickets at an average of 20.06, figures good enough to earn him a tour of England in 1984. However, faced with competition from Marshall, Garner, Holding, Baptiste, Davis and Small, he did not gain a Test place until the following winter when he played in all five Tests in Australia and one at home against New Zealand, taking sixteen wickets in all.

When England visited the West Indies in 1985-86, the emergence of Patrick Patterson restricted Walsh's opportunities, and so for all his talent he had yet to break through fully at Test level. There have been times when he felt he may never do so. "They want high pace all the time", he said, "and that isn't my way. As a young bowler my idols were Michael Holding and Andy Roberts, who were both slowing up a bit when I started to play. They could bowl the odd quick ball still, but they varied it a lot. I admired the way they out-thought batsmen with change of pace and length, and that's how I like to bowl."

Walsh's start with Gloucestershire was not unduly impressive. Tom Graveney, on a trip to the West Indies in 1983-84, had spotted something Holding-like in Walsh's rhythm and had recommended him to Gloucestershire, who signed him for the 1984 season. However, his selection for the West Indian party meant that he played only six matches for the county after the tour, and in those he took eighteen rather expensive wickets. His run seemed overlong and, perhaps because he had been told that the ball would automatically do odd things on English pitches, he tended to plop the ball on a length instead of hitting the deck with it.

He learned quickly, though, and in 1985 he showed himself a bowler of high quality, his 85 wickets costing only 20.07 runs each. He is tall – 6ft 5½in – lean, and loose-limbed with a high arm. His action is more chest-on than the purist would like, which means that movement in the air tends to be into the right-handed batsman, but his ability to hit the seam means that the in-swinger will often leave the bat off the pitch.

Walsh's pace, though considerable, is not of the very highest; but the steep bounce he commands has made him consistently hostile. His run-up has been reduced, as much to avoid fines for slow over-rates as to conserve energy, yet he remained distinctly sharp off thirteen or fourteen strides. Even his team-mates could not anticipate the speed at which the ball would emerge from his hand, so adept had he become at disguising his intentions. Informed opinion in the Gloucestershire dressing-room is that he has three distinct speeds, all delivered with the same action. There are also minute variations within these, so it is not surprising that Walsh hit batsmen's stumps at some times when they had completed their stroke and at others when they had scarcely started it. He has made sparing use of the bouncer, his shorter deliveries generally threatening the batsman's rib-cage, a tactic which, allied to change of pace, produced many catches in the short-leg area off splice or glove.

As a batsman, Walsh wields a useful long handle. In the field, he usually patrols the third man and fine leg areas, where he is subject to fits of abstraction; frantic bellows from his team-mates are sometimes necessary to alert him to an approaching ball. When concentrating he is an excellent ground fielder, swift, athletic and possessing a powerful arm. Certainly his rich talent and admirable temperament make him a marked asset to any side he plays in. At only 24 he has already made a great impact on county cricket and, his own over-modest doubts notwithstanding, must surely soon do the same in the international arena. – D.M.G.

JAMES WHITAKER

The fact that John Whitaker, who owns a flourishing chocolate manufacturing business in Yorkshire, is in a position to add "& Son" to the company name, but not "& Sons", is something for which Leicestershire are deeply grateful; and in the years ahead, England may well come to share that sentiment. John's elder son, William, did indeed join the family firm, but young James decided on a career in cricket. As the former is now the company's chief executive, and the latter also moved off the shop floor, so to speak, by way of selection for England's tour to Australia last winter, both have proved impeccable judges of a career.

When Brian Davison left Leicestershire at the end of the 1983 season, withdrawal symptoms were acute in the Grace Road members' enclosure. With the exception of David Gower, Davison was the one batsman who prompted spectators to raise the deckchairs an extra couple of notches as he emerged from the pavilion. Davison did not so much punish a cricket ball as inflict grievous bodily harm upon it. But already in that 1983 season there had been signs that an embryonic Davison was ready to emerge from the Second XI, a precocious, aggressive, 21-year-old with precisely the same uncomplicated approach. A bad ball was a bad ball whether delivered by Malcolm Marshall or Arthur Marshall.

JOHN JAMES WHITAKER was born in Skipton, on May 5, 1962, yet cannot be said to have slipped through Yorkshire's net. He learned his cricket at Uppingham School in Leicestershire under the guidance of their coach, Maurice Hallam, the former county opener, who quickly alerted the Grace Road management of the boy's talent. "It always seemed the most natural thing in the world for me to go on and play for Leicestershire", said Whitaker. "The fact that I was born in Yorkshire did not really come into it." Whitaker, as can be seen, does not get bogged down in theory, and his approach to batting after leaving Uppingham was further conditioned by watching, and batting with, Davison.

There are a number of similarities between the two. Whitaker, like Davison, does not consider a coaching manual to be required bedside reading: to him, marks for content are more valuable in this game than for artistic impression. He may lack a classical style, but his technique is sound and his eye razor sharp. Even the best county bowlers quickly discovered that there was little margin of error against Whitaker's facility to produce punishing strokes off both front and back foot. Again like Davison, he has immensely strong forearms, and one of his most distinctive strokes is a kind of speared drive; with minimal backlift and follow-through, more of a speared forearm jab, really, which brings him 6s anywhere in the arc between "cow corner" and extra cover.

His maiden century, against Somerset in 1984, was an innings that will linger long in the memory of those who witnessed it. He came in, with Leicestershire 30 for four, to face Ian Botham's hat-trick delivery, drove it through the covers for 4, and less than two hours later was in three figures. Whitaker, unlike Davison this time, is not one who goes in for conversation in the middle, and Botham's verbal joust with him was rather one-sided. As ball after ball came bouncing back from the boundary fence, Whitaker recalled, "He said one or two things, like 'hang about, it's Saturday not Sunday you know'; and when I was out, 'I knew the lucky so and so would nick one eventually'." As the "eventually" consisted of 160 runs, he did consider a parting comment but settled for a wry smile instead.

Whitaker appears to enjoy going in on a hat-trick. The next time it happened, at Old Trafford early last season, he scored another hundred. This time the bowler was Lancashire's Steve O'Shaughnessy, which provided a touch of irony as Whitaker had hitherto been best remembered at Old Trafford for his bowling (8-1-87-0), a motley assortment of right-arm rubbish which, in the last match of 1983, helped O'Shaughnessy to equal P. G. H. Fender's record for the fastest first-class century. Soon after his Old Trafford hundred, Whitaker was awarded his county cap, which was the major goal he had set himself for 1986; a place on the England tour was never in his mind until August, when he found himself being widely tipped in the press. "I'd decided, obviously, that I wanted to play for England, but didn't consider myself ready", he said. However, as tour selection drew closer, it became something he set his heart on and was ultimately thoroughly deserved.

Despite giving the impression that his approach to batting is instinctive, rather than meticulous, Whitaker is none the less a "planner", and his approach to the 1986 season began as early as the previous October. "I decided to take the winter off instead of going abroad, trained more or less every day, and thought about what I wanted to do in the summer. I set myself a target of at least 1,500 runs, and wanted to be fresh and eager come April." The plan worked so well that he won the first two Leicestershire Player of the Month awards, and a magnificent 200 not out, his highest first-class score, against Nottinghamshire at Grace Road at the end of June put him well on course to becoming the first of the season to 1,000 runs. His third 6 took him to 200, and his respective fifties came off 98, 53, 89 and 38 deliveries. "You sometimes get a feeling when it's going to be your day, and I had it that lunchtime when I was 30 odd not out."

He did not, one assumes, have that feeling for the next game, against Hampshire. Late on the first day he was struck on the right index finger by Marshall, and an almost identical blow followed next morning. Then Marshall hit him on the other hand, forcing him to retire. X-rays revealed two fractures, and he was grounded for almost five weeks on 911 runs while Worcestershire's Graeme Hick went on to be the first to four figures. However, Whitaker's comeback game, against his native Yorkshire, could scarcely have been more emphatic. In the first innings, after understandably struggling in the early stages, he scored an unbeaten century, emphasising in doing so that he is not one to play for intervals. He hit the last ball of the morning session for 6 and dealt similarly with the third ball after lunch. Then, in the second innings, he led a successful run-chase with an unbeaten 88. His overall performance prompted the comment from the beaten captain, David Bairstow, "The boy is a 'must' for Australia".

Whitaker did indeed go, albeit by a narrow vote over Northamptonshire's Robert Bailey, and despite his absence he also achieved his target of 1,500 runs. His selection provided much satisfaction for the Leicestershire vice-captain, Peter Willey, who had earlier made himself unavailable for Australia because of long-standing knee trouble. "The big thing about James", said Willey, "is that he is a batsman who can win you matches because of the rate at which he scores." Leicestershire might be well advised to bear that in mind when planning their future strategy for one-day matches: invariably Whitaker has batted too low down the order. His two John Player League centuries came first when he was promoted to open and then, batting at number three, when Ian Butcher was out to the first ball of the game. He is too good a player to have at number five, where so often there is no time to build an innings. – M.J.

i

BOTHAM'S WORLD RECORD

[*Patrick Eagar*

Ian Botham became the leading wicket-taker in Test cricket when umpire David Shepherd upheld his appeal for lbw against Jeff Crowe of New Zealand in the third Test at The Oval. Playing in his only Test of the summer, Botham had in the previous over equalled D. K. Lillee's record of 355 wickets by dismissing Bruce Edgar with his first ball.

THE ART OF PITCH PREPARATION

[*Patrick Eagar*

Two significant problems confronted England's batsmen at Sabina Park, Kingston, in the first Test against West Indies in 1986. One was Patrick Patterson, bowling here to Botham: the other was the pitch. Though the point is better illustrated in colour, this photo nevertheless reveals how the pitch was left bare at either end but sufficiently grassed in the middle to make even more menacing the short-pitching West Indian fast bowlers.

ENGLAND'S TEAM FOR THE OVAL TEST

[*Patrick Eagar*

The team which played New Zealand in the third Test at The Oval was the strongest and best-balanced England team of the summer. *Back row*: C. W. J. Athey, G. C. Small, J. E. Emburey, P. H. Edmonds, G. R. Dilley, P. Willey, B. N. French. *Front row*: A. J. Lamb, I. T. Botham, M. W. Gatting (*captain*), G. A. Gooch, D. I. Gower.

AN ENGLISH SETTING FOR AN INTERNATIONAL TOURNAMENT

[Ken Kelly

On the picturesque Cadbury's Ground, Bournville, with its century-old pavilion, Bermuda bat against Canada for a place in the semi-finals of the 1986 ICC Trophy tournament. Sixteen countries visited England for this gathering of Associate Members, playing 60 games on the grounds of Midlands clubs.

ZIMBABWE – 1986 ICC TROPHY WINNERS

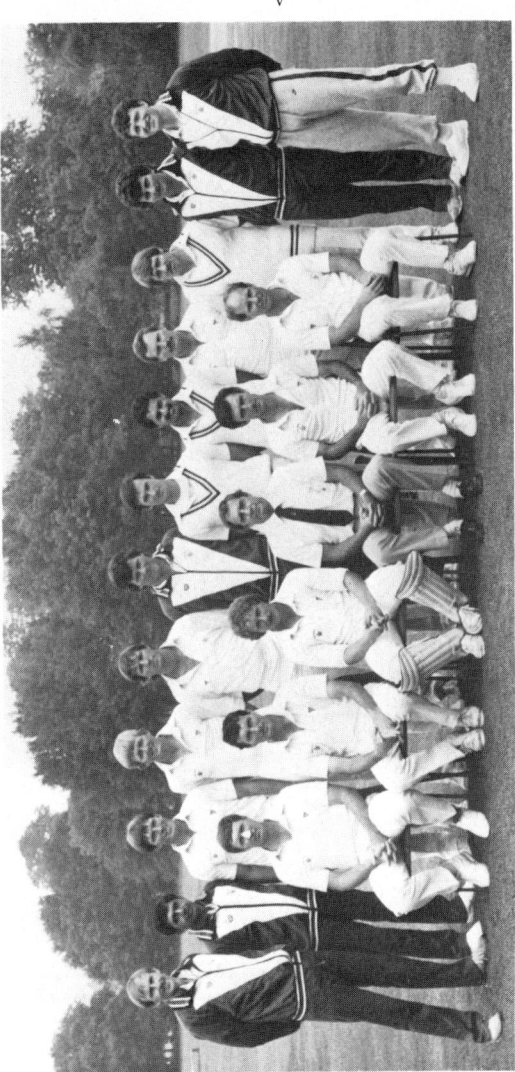

[*Ken Kelly*]

Zimbabwe retained the ICC Trophy, which they won in 1982, by beating Holland by 25 runs in the final at Lord's. Their squad was: *Back row*: C. J. Cox, B. Meman, A. C. Waller, D. H. Brain, G. A. Paterson, E. A. Brandes, I. P. Butchart, A. H. Shah, G. C. Wallace, M. P. Jarvis, C. Robertson, D. Roberts (*physiotherapist*). *Front row*: P. W. E. Rawson, R. D. Brown, D. L. Houghton (*captain*), D. A. Arnott (*manager*), A. J. Traicos, A. J. Pycroft.

HADLEE – NEW ZEALAND'S MATCH-WINNER

[Patrick Eagar

New Zealand's first series victory in England was the climax of a successful ten months for New Zealand and their remarkable all-rounder, Richard Hadlee, who in nine Test matches in that period took 68 wickets to become, with 334, the third-highest wicket-taker in Test cricket.

FIVE CRICKETERS OF THE YEAR

[Essex Chronicle Series

J. H. Childs (Essex)

FIVE CRICKETERS OF THE YEAR

[*Patrick Eagar*

G. A. Hick (Worcestershire)

FIVE CRICKETERS OF THE YEAR

[*Patrick Eagar*

D. B. Vengsarkar (India)

FIVE CRICKETERS OF THE YEAR

[*David Munden*

C. A. Walsh (Gloucestershire)

FIVE CRICKETERS OF THE YEAR

[*David Munden*

J. J. Whitaker (Leicestershire)

Sir George Allen, who in the Queen's Birthday Honours in 1986 was awarded a knighthood
for his services to cricket.

SIR GEORGE ALLEN

A SPECIAL PORTRAIT

By J. J. WARR

Sir George Oswald Browning Allen was born in Sydney, Australia, on July 31, 1902, being very much in the tradition of England captains who were not born in England. To name only some, Sir Pelham Warner was born in Trinidad, F. R. Brown in Peru, D. B. Carr in Germany, E. R. Dexter in Italy, and M. C. Cowdrey in India. D. R. Jardine in India. "Gubby", aged six, was brought to England with his brother and sister to be educated, and the family remained here ever after. His contribution to the national game of cricket has been immense, of which the award of the CBE followed in 1986 by a knighthood in the Queen's Birthday Honours is a clear recognition. Most people thought his knighthood was long overdue, but it did make him the last man in a hat-trick, following his grandfather and father.

However, there are other aspects of his life to demonstrate that cricket has not been his sole preoccupation. A highly successful stockbroker in peacetime, he also rose to the rank of Lieutenant-Colonel in military intelligence in the War Office in the Second World War, specialising in all aspects of German ground-to-air defences and particularly their siting; not unlike deciding on the field placing in a Test match. He saved many casualties among bomber pilots by his skill and knowledge and was awarded the Legion of Merit by the Americans.

One of the more colourful incidents of his military career occurred before he was posted to the War Office: when he was serving in the control room at Hawkinge during the Dunkirk evacuation. On hearing that his brother had been seriously wounded, he obtained permission to fly to break the news to their mother, who was living near Eton, at Datchet, and the aircraft, carrying Belgian markings, landed on the playing-fields of Eton as the nearest and most convenient place. Although they had the consent of Fighter Command to return to Hawkinge, before that happened, as Gubby found on his return from Datchet, the plane was surrounded by the Eton Home Guard under the command of Corporal Lord Porchester, now the Queen's racing manager. And even though Gubby went to Eton and was in the XI for three years, the intrepid patrol arrested him as a German spy, making him the only England cricket captain to suffer such a fate.

The incident did nothing to diminish Gubby's interest in racing, which was nurtured by all the great Newmarket trainers who regularly went to Fenner's to see the cricket. He has also known many of the leading politicians, both domestically and internationally. The foreword to the book, *Gubby Allen: Man of Cricket*, was written by a former Prime Minister and close friend in Lord Home of the Hirsel, and pride of place in Gubby's St John's Wood home is a suitably inscribed photograph of another personal friend, Sir Robert Menzies of Australia.

The game of cricket has been a linchpin in his life, however, and it was his own sister, Lady Dickson, who remarked that as a perpetual bachelor Gubby was "married to cricket". Whilst Gubby does not deny this, he is adamant that when Sir Pelham Warner proposed him first for the Middlesex committee and then the MCC cricket committee, he was very reluctant to accept. That notwithstanding, his first-class playing career stretched to more than 30 years, and it was only by liberal use of elastoplast and embrocation that he was still playing in the 1950s. Indeed, in those days, when he took the field he resembled the mummified figures of the great Pharoahs of Egypt. He is an authority on every muscle in the human body, having pulled most of them in his time. He has had five operations on his hips and it is said that he got so expert that he did the last two himself. Jim Swanton, his Boswell in *Gubby Allen: Man of Cricket*, once jokingly described him as a hypochondriacal megalomaniac and Gubby did not dissent.

Returning to his first-class career, there were four great highlights. In 1929 he took all ten wickets against Lancashire for Middlesex at Lord's, which has remained a unique feat in county cricket at Lord's to this day. It was only a late fitness test on the Friday that enabled him to play, and as he was delayed in the office on the Saturday, working for Debenham's, he did not take the new ball. His final figures were ten for 40 and eight of them were clean-bowled. Next would be his partnership with Les Ames of 246 in two and threequarter hours against New Zealand at Lord's in 1931: it remains a world record for the eighth wicket in a Test match and is the oldest such record to remain unbroken. Going in when England were 190 for seven, Gubby drove with power and, without making a mistake, finished with 122, his first and only Test century and still the highest innings by someone batting at number nine for England.

Then came his two tours of Australia, in 1932-33 and, as captain, in 1936-37. On the bodyline tour he emerged as a white knight, which was the image presented in the recent Australian television serial. There is a considerable grain of truth in that assessment, but it was spoilt by the totally inaccurate characterisation of people like P. G. H. Fender, who was depicted as a banjo-playing buffoon, and Sir Pelham Warner, as a whisky-swilling nonentity: two images as far from the truth as it is possible to imagine. Gubby is also shown as disagreeing with Douglas Jardine on the field, which is something he never did nor would ever have contemplated. He refused to bowl bodyline – a decision which was made in the dressing-room – but Gubby remained a firm friend of Jardine for the whole of Jardine's life.

The 1936-37 tour with Gubby as captain saw Bradman as something of an ogre. He had had marvellous tours of England in 1930 and 1934, and the memory of him in 1930 must have been one of the reasons why in 1932-33 Jardine was prepared to stretch the spirit and ethics of the game to breaking-point in order to snuff him out. As it turned out, with England bowling in an orthodox manner, the 1936-37 tour was one of the most exciting in the history of the Ashes. It also produced one of the most famous remarks in cricket. Gubby intended to console R. W. V. Robins when, in the second innings of the third Test, he dropped Bradman at 24 off Gubby's bowling: "Oh forget it, old boy, it will probably cost us the rubber but what the hell." Robbie recalled that remark endlessly, but always with amusement and not rancour.

The lifelong friendship between Gubby and Robbie is an interesting study in contrasts. R.W.V. was ebullient, volatile, totally unpredictable and much given to instant opinions followed by instant decisions, many of which carried a diplomatic backlash. G.O.A., on the other hand, prefers to weigh things up with great care and achieve his objectives by logical argument and with just a dash of lobbying. They had a close relationship as players, and I recall with particular pleasure the time when Gubby was a regular visitor as a batsman to the perfect wicket at Fenner's to play for the Free Foresters in the early 1950s. He was usually a scorer of a century in one innings or the other, and R.W.V. used to mock him, saying how easy it was to flog undergraduates round Fenner's. He added that if he played himself he would score 50 batting with a walking-stick. Gubby challenged him to turn out and try his luck using a proper bat. He did, and was bowled first ball in each innings: an Imperial pair! The late O. J. Wait bowled him in the first innings and I was the bowler in the second. The joke was enjoyed by all parties except for the same batsman who was on a hat-trick in both innings.

Distinguished as his playing career has been, it is in the administration and think-tanks of the game that Gubby has had his greatest influence. Despite his initial reluctance, he was elected to the MCC committee in 1935 and was at the time ten years younger than any other member of that committee. Subsequently he has been the Club's President, Treasurer and one of its Trustees, serving in one form or another for 51 years. He has been a distinguished chairman of selectors but does emphasise that silk purses cannot be made out of sows' ears: good selectors and good captains are only as good as the material they can choose and the players who play under them. He has held more offices in cricket than anyone in living memory, including being President of the Umpires' Association for more than 25 years. To him, though, his contribution to coaching the young has given him as much satisfaction as anything else. With H. S. Altham he wrote *The MCC Cricket Coaching Book* in 1952. It has remained the "bible" of coaching and has sold 100,000 copies.

Golf, in his spare time, has always been an abiding passion, and even in his eighties he is still making adjustments to his swing in search of perfection. His early tutor was Leonard Crawley, who had possibly one of the finest golf swings of all time. His lowest golf handicap has been four and, even now, one of his bad shots can produce a stream of verbal criticism of himself which would cause even Freddie Trueman to blush. Over the years he has derived immense pleasure from head to head confrontations with his friends, rather than seeking to put his name on trophies or golf club walls, while among his friends in the County Cricketers' Golf Society there is a term for the world's worst golfer: it is "Gubby's foursome partner". He can be seen at his beloved Berkshire or Sandwich outdoing Nigel Mansell at the wheel of his golf buggy, still hitting the ball straight but sacrificing length for accuracy, which is a polite way of saying that he doesn't hit it as far as he used to.

Jim Swanton has pointed out in "the book" how many cricket crises Sir George has lived through, and they were summed up by Prince Philip in his telegram to the President of MCC on the occasion of Gubby's 80th birthday celebration at Lord's: "No man has done more for MCC and for cricket over a long period when things have been far from easy. He deserves all the tributes he is bound to get. Philip."

Gubby spoke at the 150th MCC Anniversary Dinner in 1937 and it is hoped that he will do the same at the 200th in 1987. Like all great sportsmen, he identifies the one key moment of luck or fate which launched him on his career. In his case it was in 1922. Having had no success in the Freshmen's match at Cambridge, he was invited to play for Middlesex against the University and took six for 13 which, needless to say, got him into the University side. One of his victims was Hubert Ashton, the Cambridge captain, bowled by a trimmer, which might have helped his cause. For some reason he has never been one of *Wisden*'s Cricketers of the Year, but I suppose that is because he has been more sparing with his activities on the field than off.

MCC – 200 YEARS

A CELEBRATION

By E. W. SWANTON

There is no phrase more neatly expressive of the role of MCC in the evolution of the game than Sir Pelham Warner's well-worn description: a private club with a public function. It may well have been "Plum", too, who coined the aphorism that "MCC reigns but does not rule". In common parlance, while it has been accepted as the final seat of authority, it has not thrown its weight about. Pray notice the change of tense. We must write now in the past tense to the extent that, although Marylebone Cricket Club remains the maker and custodian of the Laws, just as it has been since its formation just two hundred years ago, and although it still provides the ICC, according to custom, with its venue, its Chairman and its secretariat, the Club has had since 1968 no more than a guiding voice in the governance of the English game in its various aspects, both amateur and professional.

When at that time Mr Harold Wilson's Labour administration agreed at last to make Government grants available to sports and games, they could scarcely treat with a private institution, however venerable and respected. Hence, in consultation with Mr Denis Howell, the Minister with special responsibility for sport, MCC made a voluntary devolution of its tacitly accepted though never explicit powers. The Test and County Cricket Board, formerly "The Advisory", would in future manage and control the first-class game, and a new body, the National Cricket Association, would be answerable for all aspects of the amateur game, with special emphasis on the coaching of the young. Both these bodies, along with MCC, would contribute equal representation, a third each, to a court of appeal known as The Cricket Council. The gist of all this is no doubt apprehended more or less by the average devotee of *Wisden*; but it is an outline perhaps worth defining afresh in this celebratory bicentennial year.

The future of MCC will be what its successive committees make of a wonderful heritage. Theirs is the ground, unique historically, perfectly placed geographically to remain, as it has always been, the natural headquarters of the game. When the spotlight turns on to Lord's this coming summer, it will show an arena better equipped to accommodate members and public than ever before. The handsome new Mound Stand complements and follows the contours of the recently built Tavern Stand, right up to the open decks of "free seats" at the Nursery End. As the eye moves anti-clockwise, the Grand and Warner Stands continue the line of the boundary round to the centre-piece of the Pavilion, that four-square monument to Victorian self-assurance which seems likewise to be the very emblem of cricket's permanence as a national institution.

Behind the Pavilion (which itself has been greatly modernised within and to which a library of fitting size and dignity has been appended), and contiguous with the tennis and squash courts and the Memorial Gallery, opened in 1950, the TCCB and NCA now comfortably and independently housed. So, alongside the Harris garden and in a separate building, is the Middlesex CCC. Away on the Nursery ground stands the MCC Indoor School, through which many thousand cricketers of all ages have passed since its opening ten years ago. Add to the picture the modern Tavern alongside the Grace Gates, and it strikes one afresh how greatly over the last two decades the face of Lord's has changed. What we must be truly thankful for is that the transitions have been wrought without loss of character. One cannot visualise further significant building in the immediate future, and so in 1987 Lord's can face the years ahead confidently as it is. Thank heaven it will always be a cricket ground – surely *the* cricket ground; never a stadium.

So much for "the plant", but what of the men who have made MCC and Lord's what they are today? The gallery is a remarkable one, starting with Thomas Lord himself whom that small band of noblemen commissioned to procure a ground for the club they were about to form. All that is known about Lord marks him as a man of quality. He had, say Lord Harris and F. S. Ashley-Cooper in *Lord's and the MCC*, a "handsome presence and possessed a *bonhomie* that was almost irresistible". Three grounds he had to find as London extended to the north, finally, in 1814, putting down his roots only just in time on the present site.

In those first days, two men of a very different temper held the stage: the Rev. Lord Frederick Beauclerk, reputedly the best cricketer in England around the turn of the nineteenth century, and the first Secretary of MCC, Benjamin Aislabie, who doted on the game though much too fat to be any good at it. Thomas Hughes portrayed him affectionately on the occasion in *Tom Brown's Schooldays* when he brought the MCC team to Rugby. In the earliest pavilions (the first was burned down in 1825), Aislabie cast on the scene a benevolence which held the club together, a necessary antidote no doubt to Beauclerk (descended from the union of Charles II and Nell Gwynne), who as a dictator of affairs on the field and off, and a sharp betting man to boot, comes across almost as a villain of old-style melodrama.

Following Aislabie's death in office in 1842, the affairs of MCC declined to a point which brought press agitation for a cricket parliament to depose the club from its position of authority. It was rescued from the hands of reactionaries such as Robert Grimston – who greeted with disgust the advent of the mowing machine – by a character ideally suited to the situation in R. A. Fitzgerald.

Bob Fitzgerald was clearly a popular personality and withal a lively one. "Whether it was the magnificence of his swagger, the luxuriance of his beard, the fun that rolled out of him so easily, or the power of his swiping, I do not know, but as regards each he could not escape notice", wrote Lord Harris, who as to the fun tells of Fitzgerald's favourite trick when a wicket fell of pretending to catch a mouse in the grass.

Fitzgerald reigned as Secretary of MCC from 1863 to 1876, having become in that time the first salaried occupant. As an undergraduate, Harris was a member of the team which Fitzgerald in 1872 took on a successful pioneering tour of Canada and the United States, the first ever undertaken by amateurs. He also took sides to Paris and Dublin, and flew the flags of MCC and I Zingari in many unfrequented places. (The MCC colours of red and yellow date from his time.) Fitzgerald was both reformer and innovator. Alas, he perhaps drove himself too hard, for his health completely failed and he died young. A tangible memorial to him in the MCC library is a collection of illustrated scrapbooks, donated by a grandson, T. G. Fitzgerald.

If young George Harris was on the threshold of a leading role in the rapid evolution of cricket, an even greater figure was another of Fitzgerald's North American party, W. G. Grace himself, already a rising star. The 1870s saw the dawn of county cricket, wherein the Graces of Gloucestershire led the way, and the game expanded mightily around the ample frame of W.G., who was, let it be said, ever a loyal MCC man. Middlesex began to play at Lord's in 1877, thus providing Londoners with a regular programme of first-class cricket. The following year came the event that popularised the game more than anything else; the first visit of the colonials from Australia and their defeat of MCC in a single day.

Although for some years yet the financial prosperity of MCC continued to depend greatly on the three classic fixtures, Eton v Harrow, begun in 1805, Gentlemen v Players, from 1806, and the University Match, from 1827, the frequent Australian visits, along with the appeal of Middlesex, brought an even wider public to Lord's.

No essay aiming to sketch the MCC story in its bicentenary year should omit mention of the longest-serving of all its officers, Sir Spencer Ponsonby-Fane, whose life was bound up with Lord's almost from his days as a Harrow boy in the mid-1830s until his death in 1915, aged 91. For 36 years he served the club as Treasurer, which was in his time and ever after the key post. Finding only two pictures in the place (admittedly Francis Haymans), he started the now incomparable art collection. Diplomat – he was secretary to Palmerston – and courtier, Ponsonby-Fane personified that close aristocratic involvement with MCC which was continuous from the foundation until after the Second World War.

On this point, a word here in parenthesis. Although its beginnings and the close connections with Eton, Harrow, Winchester, the other major schools and the Universities determined the style and pattern of its membership, MCC has not been, at least in living memory – and contrary to popular belief – a socially exclusive club. Granted a civilised standard of behaviour, good cricketers have always been welcome.

Next, chronologically, comes a very major figure in the story, Francis Lacey, a barrister by training, who took on the secretaryship at the age of 38 in 1898 and held it until 1926, when he was honoured with the first knighthood for services to cricket. Ignoring the advice of his predecessor, Henry Perkins, to "take no notice of the damned committee", Lacey put the club on a sound administrative footing. Where MCC had been loath to involve itself with the international and county scene, Lacey had a keener eye for the game's welfare and the Club's responsibilities. The Board of Control for Test Matches and "The Advisory" were formed early in his time, while in 1903 MCC (as the Melbourne CC had been urging it) undertook to choose and manage the tours to Australia.

Plum Warner led the first side out that winter and brought home the Ashes, and MCC has been a household name in cricket ever since. In due course, and over a span of 70-odd years, the MCC colours were flown in South Africa, the West Indies, New Zealand, India, Ceylon (now Sri Lanka) and Pakistan, as well as in many other countries not on the Test match circuit.

The post-Great War years saw the formidable Treasurer-Secretary partnership of Harris and Lacey, and it is fascinating if profitless to speculate whether, if old Lord Harris had lived another year or so, he might have scented the coming bodyline trouble in the late summer of 1932 and either scotched it at birth or at least apprehended the situation more swiftly when the first warning signals from Australia came wafting back. The bodyline message for cricket's rulers, so far as Test cricket was concerned, was to beware the sudden onset of unruly passions. There were storms to come, all right, but not yet. MCC was soon marking its 150th anniversary with three very successful matches and a celebratory dinner of many courses and toasts of which the writer, recently elected, retains only a blurred memory.

Through the Second World War – as distinct from the complete 1914-18 shut-down – MCC kept the flag flying admirably with a regular programme of cricket each summer, culminating in the "Victory Tests" between England and the Dominions. More people (413,856) watched cricket at Lord's in 1945 than in 1939 – an augury fulfilled by the vast crowds, in the first post-war years, of people anxious to dull the thought of past horrors and present shortages and discomforts.

MCC was more active than ever before in the period between the war's end and the transitions of 1968, presiding over ever more frequent Test exchanges, setting up enquiries at the behest of the counties – five of these, achieving much less than their labours deserved, sat within 30 years – and, especially, turning its attention to encouraging the young. The present comprehensive structure of School Associations' coaching and competitive cricket must be traced back to the foresight and energy in 1948 of G. O. (now Sir George) Allen and his subsequent partnership with H. S. Altham. Their *MCC Cricket Coaching Book*, regularly updated, has sold 100,000 copies.

Altham and Allen, successive Treasurers, apart from a single year, from 1950 to 1974, both steeped in all aspects of the game, served MCC in the Harris tradition, if using a softer touch, in harness with three Secretaries of contrasting personality but equal dedication, Colonel R. S. Rait Kerr, R. Aird and S. C. Griffith.

An extension of the hierarchy must be mentioned here. The modern President is expected – indeed obliged – to play a far more active role than ever before. What until the late 1940s was almost a sinecure has become a highly demanding post involving many hours a week, dealing with the complexities of both MCC itself and the ICC (of which the President of the day is the automatic Chairman), and the evolving relationship with the new bodies.

Whereas in the 40 years prior to the 1939-45 war only eight Presidents had been first-class cricketers, over the last 40 years the figure is 28. Most of these have brought to the job wide experience in cricket administration. When, however, a President has named as his successor a man of distinction outside the game – Lord Caccia, the late A. H. A. Dibbs, and the present Chairman of Finance, Sir Anthony Tuke, are recent examples – the Club has been invariably well served. It is easy to be too close to the game's problems and even to be insensitive to public opinion.

The most unfortunate instance of this was "the D'Oliveira Affair" when the Committee had to withstand, in the fateful year of 1968, a vote of no confidence – albeit fairly comfortably defeated – at a Special General Meeting. The Club, in the persons of the Chairman of ICC and its representatives, had come much more favourably from the "throwing crisis" of 1960. Harry Altham and Gubby Allen were chiefly involved here, ultimately with the decisive backing of Sir Donald Bradman.

When Kerry Packer's intrusion threatened to tear cricket apart in 1977, the ICC were lucky to find as their Chairmen two patient negotiators prepared to travel the world in search of a settlement in D. G. Clark and C. H. Palmer. Who shall say that the business might not have been brought to a less damaging conclusion by them on behalf of ICC than the subservient long-term accommodation suddenly accepted by the Australian Board?

These are waters under the bridge, and the concluding question to be asked is how well equipped is the MCC of 1987 to fulfil its more limited but still crucial stewardship of the game in the future? Writing on the eve of the bicentenary, I take the mood to be of competence and self-confidence. The Club today is a unique sporting institution with a value and annual turnover measured in many millions, run by a President and committee wherein cricket and business expertise are combined in a fairer mix of the generations than in some earlier days. It has 18,000 members and a waiting-list of embarrassing length. We are at the outset of a year marked by an ambitious series of large-scale events: a ball, dinners at Lord's and the Guildhall, a luncheon on the site of the original ground at Dorset Square, and more besides. Much imagination has gone into the programme, and the news is that everything is over-subscribed.

There remains the culmination of the festivities: the match between MCC, its team drawn from current county players regardless of nationality, and the Rest of the World. On this may Providence look kindly: fair weather, a good match worthy of the occasion, and – dare one hope? – something distinguished in the way of English participation.

TIME PRESENT AND TIME PAST

By VIC MARKS

Comparisons may well be odious but they are also irresistible. Who's the greater: Laver or Borg, Joe Davis or Steve, Steel or Owen, Bradman or Richards? Such debates are often endless and always fruitless, yet cricket enthusiasts, as well as slightly desperate biographers, can rarely shun picking their All-Time World XI. Usually the selectors plump for the heroes of their own era, and with an ageing population the lament that "Things ain't what they used to be" grows gradually louder. However, I do not intend here to deliver a polemic in defence of the modern cricketer; rather to examine some of the changes of the last few decades, as well as to observe some surprising similarities between cricketers past and present.

In the 1960s, cricket was compelled to react to the force of economic necessity. County clubs' coffers were like colanders, and the authorities' response was the introduction of instant cricket: the Gillette Cup knockout in 1963, the John Player Sunday League in 1969 and the Benson and Hedges competition in 1972. In addition, they permitted the influx of non-qualified overseas players in 1968. In retrospect, the authorities, so easily maligned, should be congratulated for ensuring the survival of all the first-class counties. Now the treasurer of a county cricket club is less susceptible to (stress induced) ulcers than his counterpart in the Football League.

Cricket has survived, but not without sacrifices. Instant cricket has created a demand for instant success; with four competitions each year there is less excuse if your club does not win one of them. Newcomers are now expected to match the contributions of their more experienced colleagues immediately. In 1964, Dennis Amiss could be assured of a slow and gentle baptism to first-class cricket, a luxury no longer afforded James Whitaker in 1984.

The advent of these new competitions had far-reaching consequences, such as the installation of a computer in the Pavilion at Lord's and a complete transformation of the fixture list. The county cricket season has become one prolonged, frenetic dash around the highways and byways of the country. County cricketers no longer check train schedules but instead tune into motoring flashes as they lurch from a JPL game at Canterbury back to a Championship match at Northampton. Our car insurance premiums have, unsurprisingly, rocketed.

These domestic changes have been mirrored at international level. In 1975 the first World Cup was a spectacular success and one-day internationals became a financial necessity. As a result, the commercial wizards planning a tour of Australia now insist that the intervals between Test matches are spent, not with missionary visits to the outback but in a series of lucrative one-day games. A modern international cricketer, when asked his impression of Australia, is scarcely able to give anything more than a vivid description of the airport lounges of Sydney, Melbourne and Perth. Many enthusiasts will have been astounded by Graham Gooch's decision not to tour last winter, but a regular tourist with a young family will understand his position much more easily. So, while our predecessors may envy the increased financial rewards available at the highest level, the modern player might yearn for the more leisurely existence of the 1950s – 32 Championship games and nothing else, and the chance to play golf on Sundays.

As the governing bodies, amidst general approval, have become more commercially minded, it is not surprising that some players have reacted in the same way, often to general condemnation. Modern players sometimes employ agents to maximise their earning capacity through endorsements and the newspapers during their short lifespan as a cricketer. This august Almanack has noted this trend: "Too many Australian and England cricketers appeared to be governed by commercial interests and cricket suffered accordingly." That was written by the editor of *Wisden* in 1964. Surely, then, it is a misconception to believe that it is only the cricketers of the last decade who have been rather keen to make some money from their prowess? Indeed, the established county player is unimpressed by the theory occasionally expressed in the columns of the *Daily Telegraph* that cricketers are overpaid. He earns approximately £8,500, a figure he is unlikely to match in the winter months and one which does not compare that favourably with the £10 a week that leading professionals received in 1933. And they didn't have to dive in the field.

Before England's tour to Australia in 1986, the TCCB in their tour contracts imposed restrictions on the players regarding their contributing to national newspapers. Those concerned, notably Phil Edmonds and Ian Botham, acquiesced and signed the contracts, presumably at some financial loss to themselves. However, this was no new problem. No doubt in Adelaide Sir Donald Bradman allowed himself a wry chuckle, recalling that he was in a similar position in 1932 when his newspaper released him from his contract, with full pay, to allow him to play against Jardine's tourists. Who can blame Bradman or Botham or the lesser mortals for trying to exploit their brief stay at the top? Cricket is a precarious profession; you might be dropped next week.

Today's cricketers have an uneasy relationship with the press. They enjoy praise and being offered writing contracts; they usually tolerate criticism of their performances on the field; but they detest the constant intrusions into their private lives. Of late, cricket tours have been covered by a gaggle of 50 or so pressmen, not just cricket reporters but newsmen as well, hunting for some saucy snippets for the tabloids.

"Dullness is feared and avoided. So unfortunately is fact. The News Room has invaded Sport and on the occasion of Test Matches, the cricket correspondent is often reinforced by a columnist or newshawk, who with furrowed brow, scours hotels and pavilions on his dark and dubious assignments. The technique of the game now ranks far below the 'story' and you will often hear reporters at the end of a full day's cricket lamenting that 'nothing has happened'. No one has fallen dead while taking guard or been arrested while placing the field".

To my surprise, that analysis of the press was written by Robertson-Glasgow in 1949, so bang goes the theory that such attention is a new phenomenon. However, the problem still remains, and it is sometimes exacerbated by the TV cameras. Every smile, every grimace, every expression of disappointment is relayed unerringly into our sitting-rooms so that a cricketer's behaviour is under the microscope as never before.

Finally, let me turn to what actually happens on the field. Have standards dropped to the extent that some of our commentators would have us believe? I can begin with confidence by making two assertions. Firstly, the overall level of fielding has improved as a result of one-day cricket; even Fred Trueman would agree with that. Secondly, the standard of wrist-spin has declined dramatically; no quarrels there even from Kim Barnett, one of the few left. Thereafter the picture becomes more blurred.

In an attempt to gain some perspective about the changes in the game, I examined the 1964 season; Simpson's Australians retained the Ashes 1–0, Worcestershire, led by Don Kenyon, won the County Championship, Sussex, under Dexter, retained the Gillette Cup in its second year, and Geoffrey Boycott was one of *Wisden's* Five Cricketers of the Year. Like any gnarled old pro I turned to the averages. Although I recognise that averages can be very misleading, especially when they refer to my own performances, certain trends were clearly established when placing them alongside those of 1986; namely that batsmen today dominate the game to a far greater extent and that spin bowlers in particular have become less effective over the last two decades. Here are some statistics: in 1964, 13 batsmen averaged over 40; in 1986, 48 batsmen averaged over 40 with Geoff Boycott, inevitably, being the common denominator.

Unsurprisingly the converse applies when examining the bowling averages. In 1964, 39 bowlers averaged under 22; in 1986, 9 bowlers averaged under 22 (common denominator – N. Gifford). Out of the top 30 bowlers in each year, twelve were spinners in 1964, only four in 1986.

One obvious explanation for the change is that the full covering of wickets, introduced in 1980, made batting a less precarious occupation and deprived spinners of twenty wickets per annum. However, I think that this trend has been exaggerated by the advent of one-day cricket, which has damaged our bowlers far more than our batsmen.

In the fifties and sixties, the great English bowlers such as Bedser, Laker, Titmus and Shackleton presumably rediscovered their optimum length and line in a net every April and they persevered with it until the Scarborough Festival. Minor adjustments might be made for individual players, but basically there was just one place to bowl – a good length at off stump – and they became superb bowling machines programmed solely for Championship and Test cricket. Now, every Sunday evening captains around the country are beseeching their bowlers to bowl anything but a good-length ball at off stump because such deliveries give the batsman too much room to swing his bat as he searches for that match-winning swat over mid-wicket at the end of the innings. Good-length bowling becomes a liability. Spinners are asked to attack leg stump as quickly as possible, in complete contrast to the requirements of Saturday and Monday. Even Norman Gifford admits that it's hard to make the adjustment, so what chance has Richard Illingworth? While one-day cricket has demanded greater aggression from the batsmen, often causing them to discover new, uncharted talents, as in the cases of Glenn Turner and Ravi Shastri, it has nurtured a negative, containing approach in many of our bowlers. Maidens rather than wickets become the goal. It may be no coincidence that the two leading wicket-takers in Test history, Ian Botham and Dennis Lillee, have seldom been fêted for their prowess as limited-overs bowlers.

Today's cricketers have had to become more adaptable as they turn their attentions to the differing demands of the various competitions, and unfortunately there is less scope for the out-and-out specialist. I'm afraid they have had to become fitter as well. They also need a comprehensive road atlas, a reliable car, an understanding wife and a thick skin. Whether they are any better or worse than their predecessors, I don't know. All I can say is that Hobbs and Hammond, May and Trueman, Botham and Gower would have triumphed in any era.

[*Ken Kelly*]

Dennis Amiss, happiest of men, celebrates his 100th hundred, having only minutes before
become the 21st batsman to achieve this feat with 101 not out against Lancashire at
Birmingham.

HOW AMISS WON HIS ENTRY CARD

By JACK BANNISTER

The crisis-ridden career of Dennis Leslie Amiss is an object lesson to those lesser cricketers who, when faced with their first major hurdle in professional cricket, show a deficiency in technique and temperament which precludes further progress. But because Amiss's make-up is generously threaded with toughened steel, in his 44th year – 29 of which have been spent on the Warwickshire staff – he was able to step into the "100 hundreds" club, as well as moving past Andrew Sandham into twelfth place in the list of the game's most prolific run-scorers. He continued to parade a technique and level of concentration which, far from showing the first understandable signs of decline, were as impressively solid as ever.

Because he has always been a batsman whose approach has been governed by an unflagging self-discipline, it might have been expected that the passing years would dull Amiss's appetite for runs. Instead, it is a measure of the man that he still relishes a batting challenge so voraciously that in 45 innings in 1986, his stumps were hit only four times – and one of those rare dismissals was a fast leg-break from the New Zealand seamer, Watson.

For Amiss, the Holy Grail became the 21st entry card into batting's most exclusive club. It shone brightly enough at the beginning of the summer to draw in, in seventeen innings, three of the four hundreds needed for glory, but then there was a tantalising wait as the hundredth century eluded him for sixteen more innings, in three of which he topped 50. And although it finally came in slightly anticlimactic fashion – the extra half-hour of a "dead" game against Lancashire being taken to enable the last 36 runs to be scored – the innings marked the personal high-point of a magnificent career which survived at least four major crises.

A brief entry into Test cricket ended with a shattering "pair" against Australia at Old Trafford in 1968, and a decline at county level precipitated the first crisis when, because of the signing of Kallicharran in 1972, and the short comeback of M. J. K. Smith, the only way Amiss could return to the county side, after being dropped, was to open the innings with Jameson. In the middle of June, in only his fifth Championship innings of the season, he scored an unbeaten 151 against Middlesex and followed it with four more hundreds in the next fifteen innings – against Worcestershire, Lancashire, Kent and Nottinghamshire. Hurdle number one was thus cleared with plenty to spare, but the special problems posed by the highest class of slow and fast bowling were soon to ask further searching questions.

The MCC tour of India in 1972-73, under the captaincy of Lewis, highlighted unexpected shortcomings against spin bowling as purveyed by that country's talented quartet of Bedi, Chandrasekhar, Prasanna and Venkataraghavan. But having failed to beat them, which resulted in his omission from the last two Tests, Amiss decided to join them by taking advantage of first-class cricket's magnanimous freemasonry.

"I was watching the fifth Test match in Bombay", Amiss recollected, "and I asked some of their bowlers what I could do to try to work my problems out. Bishan Bedi said he would come and bowl to me, and the others agreed to set up a net after the end of play out in the middle. The groundsman obliged with a pitch not far away from the actual Test strip, and away we went. I asked them where their imaginary fielders were, and I set out to survive against the world's best slow bowlers."

As they spun their web, so they drew Amiss in to extend his public torment into a private one, only for the Birmingham-forged steel to withstand, and then overcome, the pressure of such an examination.

"The result was a much-needed boost to my confidence, and when we went on to Pakistan, the whole tour turned round, thanks to that net."

In the first Test, at Lahore, he scored 112, the first of his eleven Test hundreds, and followed it with 158 at Hyderabad and 99 in the third Test, in Karachi. The second hurdle in his career had been surmounted and his Test place secured. However, as the 1970s unfolded, so did the insidious shift of emphasis at Test level from spin to pace. Amiss was mentally, as well as physically, affected by the bowling of Lillee and Thomson in Australia in 1974-75, and so he set out to rebuild his technique against sheer pace.

For once, unorthodoxy took over his thinking. He developed an extraordinary early back-foot shuffle before the ball was bowled, yet it was a method which led to a magnificent 203 against West Indies at The Oval in 1976. Whether his long innings was in spite of, and not because of, the ugly-looking change is arguable; but the result was undeniable: a triumphant fourth hundred in Tests against West Indies – a surprising statistic in view of his failure to reach three figures against Australia.

The innings was a psychological victory against odds which have defeated many better-looking players. No less a stern judge than Boycott is full of admiration for the way Amiss came to terms with fast bowling in spite of his predilection for a front-foot-based technique. He could not overcome Test fast bowling by hooking and pulling, therefore he had to endure it. Q.E.D. To settle for such a recurring war of attrition calls for special qualities, especially from a man aged 33, but the third hurdle was finally tackled successfully.

The following year, with a benefit safely gathered in and now out of the England side to make way for the return of Boycott, Amiss was a prime target for the Packer raid on the world bank of top-class cricketers. But unknown to him at the time of his slightly later acceptance date than that of England colleagues such as Greig, Snow, Underwood and Knott, the biggest hurdle of all was being built. Within twelve months, his signing for World Series Cricket would split the Warwickshire dressing-room one way and the county's membership the other.

The Warwickshire county committee, adhering to a verbal agreement with at least three other counties – all of whom subsequently reneged – publicly stated at the beginning of the 1978 season that Amiss would not be offered a contract thereafter until the Packer issue was resolved. For its part, the Packer organisation announced that no discussions could take place until Amiss was given a further contract. The battle lines were drawn; and far from his 2,030 runs in 1978, including seven Championship hundreds, causing the committee to have a change of heart, his magnificent season served only to emphasise the principle of employing cricketers who would always be available to play for their country.

The Warwickshire players supported the establishment line, but the club members did not, and a Special Members' Meeting was called to usurp the committee and reinstate Amiss. Even as the central figure in the furore, he had difficulty in persuading the conveners to defer the meeting for several months so that a mediatorial role by the Cricketers' Association could be explored. However, at the eleventh hour, in September 1978, his plea was acted upon.

Six months later, Amiss became the catalyst whose contractual position in March 1979 with Warwickshire drew the warring factions together after two acrimonious years. The last few steps to the peace table were faltering ones. For three weeks, Warwickshire refused to shift ground until an agreement was reached, and Packer's representatives refused to negotiate until they were satisfied that Amiss was not being victimised. Finally, over the Easter weekend, with his colleagues having already reported back for pre-season practice and training without him, Amiss's county accepted in good faith the assurances they had previously rebutted, and Test cricket resumed normal service. Amiss, at 36, was successfully over the fourth and most difficult hurdle in his distinguished career.

Yet despite an unsurpassed record in county cricket since those traumatic days of the late seventies, and despite the batting problems which have beset the England side, and the number of ordinary players to whom the selectors have turned in vain efforts to solve those problems, Amiss has never again played for his country. Instead, he has marched inexorably onwards, with natural skill, technique and experience fusing into a consistency of run-scoring.

The Packer revolution drew a significant dividing line across the career of the twelfth most prolific run accumulator in history. At the end of the 1977 season, his aggregate of 26,336 from 705 innings included 61 hundreds: one every 11.56 visits to the crease. But since then, at an age and stage of career when most batsmen wind down their output, Amiss has, in nine years, amassed 15,787 runs from 388 innings, including 39 hundreds: a century strike-rate of one in 9.94. Indeed, taking into account the various crisis points which have occurred in Amiss's 26-season career, he has shown a remarkable resilience to sustain a degree of excellence in both three-day and limited-overs cricket which is without parallel among the senior players in the game.

D. L. AMISS'S 100 HUNDREDS

1.	114	Warwickshire v Oxford University at Birmingham, 1964
2.	150*	Warwickshire v Scotland at Birmingham, 1966
3.	160*	Warwickshire v West Indians at Birmingham, 1966
4.	102	MCC Under-25 v President's XI at Rawalpindi, 1966-67
5.	131	MCC Under-25 v Pakistan Under-25 at Dacca, 1966-67
6.	138*	Warwickshire v Oxford University at Oxford, 1967
7.	151*	Warwickshire v Leicestershire at Birmingham, 1967
8.	176*	Warwickshire v Nottinghamshire at Coventry, 1967
9.	161*	Warwickshire v Northamptonshire at Northampton, 1967
10.	146	Warwickshire v Scotland at Birmingham, 1967
11.	109	International XI v Indian XI at Bombay, 1967-68
12.	126	Warwickshire v Worcestershire at Birmingham, 1968
13.	128	Warwickshire v Kent at Birmingham, 1968
14.	120	Warwickshire v Somerset at Birmingham, 1969
15.	110	Warwickshire v Gloucestershire at Gloucester, 1970
16.	105	MCC v Yorkshire at Scarborough, 1970
17.	112	Warwickshire v Yorkshire at Middlesbrough, 1971
18.	124	Warwickshire v Hampshire at Bournemouth, 1971

19.	151*	Warwickshire v Middlesex at Birmingham, 1972
20.	156*	Warwickshire v Worcestershire at Birmingham, 1972
21.	192	Warwickshire v Lancashire at Birmingham, 1972
22.	121*	Warwickshire v Kent at Dartford, 1972
23.	120	Warwickshire v Nottinghamshire at Coventry, 1972
24.	112	England v Pakistan at Lahore, 1972-73
25.	158	England v Pakistan at Hyderabad, 1972-73
26.	146*	England v MCC at Lord's, 1973
27.	106	MCC Tour XI v The Rest at Hove, 1973
28.	138*	England v New Zealand at Nottingham, 1973
29.	109	MCC v President's XI at Bridgetown, 1973-74
30.	174	England v West Indies at Port-of-Spain, 1973-74
31.	262*	England v West Indies at Kingston, 1973-74
32.	108	MCC v Guyana at Georgetown, 1973-74
33.	118	England v West Indies at Georgetown, 1973-74
34.	152	D. H. Robins' XI v Indians at Eastbourne, 1974
35.	195	Warwickshire v Middlesex at Birmingham, 1974
36.	188	England v India at Lord's, 1974
37.	112*	Warwickshire v Worcestershire at Worcester, 1974
38.	183	England v Pakistan at The Oval, 1974
39.	152	MCC v Victoria at Melbourne, 1974-75
40.	124	MCC v New South Wales at Sydney, 1974-75
41.	164*	England v New Zealand at Christchurch, 1974-75
42.	123	Warwickshire v Cambridge University at Cambridge, 1975
43.	143*	Warwickshire v Sussex at Hastings, 1975
44.	143	Warwickshire v Kent at Birmingham, 1975
45.	158*	Warwickshire v Northamptonshire at Birmingham, 1975
46.	164	MCC v Leicestershire at Lord's, 1976
47.	167	Warwickshire v Worcestershire at Worcester, 1976
48.	124*	England v The Rest at Bristol, 1976
49.	107*	Warwickshire v Kent at Tunbridge Wells, 1976
50.	101	Warwickshire v Derbyshire at Coventry, 1976
51.	178*	Warwickshire v Northamptonshire at Birmingham, 1976
52.	203	England v West Indies at The Oval, 1976
53.	135*	Warwickshire v Surrey at Birmingham, 1976
54.	179	England v India at Delhi, 1976-77
55.	138	MCC v South Zone at Hyderabad, 1976-77
56.	120	Warwickshire v Northamptonshire at Birmingham, 1977
57.	162*	Warwickshire v Surrey at The Oval, 1977
58.	100	Warwickshire v Essex at Birmingham, 1977
59.	144*	Warwickshire v Glamorgan at Nuneaton, 1977
60.	112	Warwickshire v Middlesex at Lord's, 1977
61.	160*	Warwickshire v Worcestershire at Birmingham, 1977
62.	127	Warwickshire v Yorkshire at Birmingham, 1978
63.	109	Warwickshire v Gloucestershire at Birmingham, 1978
64.	122*	Warwickshire v Essex at Colchester, 1978
65.	104	Warwickshire v Lancashire at Birmingham, 1978
66.	155*	⎫ Warwickshire v Worcestershire at Birmingham, 1978
67.	112	⎭
68.	162	Warwickshire v Glamorgan at Cardiff, 1978
69.	162	Warwickshire v Glamorgan at Swansea, 1979
70.	133	Warwickshire v Sussex at Hove, 1979
71.	119	Warwickshire v Yorkshire at Birmingham, 1979
72.	184	Warwickshire v Lancashire at Manchester, 1979

73.	130	Warwickshire v Nottinghamshire at Birmingham, 1979
74.	232*	Warwickshire v Gloucestershire at Bristol, 1979
75.	117*	Warwickshire v Lancashire at Liverpool, 1980
76.	109	} Warwickshire v Derbyshire at Derby, 1981
77.	127	
78.	103	Warwickshire v Glamorgan at Cardiff, 1981
79.	110	Warwickshire v Surrey at The Oval, 1981
80.	132	Warwickshire v Glamorgan at Birmingham, 1981
81.	145	Warwickshire v Worcestershire at Worcester, 1981
82.	156	Warwickshire v Somerset at Birmingham, 1982
83.	142	Warwickshire v Gloucestershire at Birmingham, 1983
84.	111	Warwickshire v Essex at Nuneaton, 1983
85.	164	Warwickshire v Kent at Folkestone, 1983
86.	100*	Warwickshire v Nottinghamshire at Birmingham, 1984
87.	121	Warwickshire v Northamptonshire at Northampton, 1984
88.	101*	Warwickshire v Worcestershire at Worcester, 1984
89.	118	Warwickshire v Lancashire at Manchester, 1984
90.	115*	Warwickshire v Glamorgan at Cardiff, 1984
91.	122	Warwickshire v Leicestershire at Birmingham, 1984
92.	100*	Warwickshire v Worcestershire at Worcester, 1985
93.	140	Warwickshire v Northamptonshire at Northampton, 1985
94.	125	Warwickshire v Oxford University at Oxford, 1985
95.	117	Warwickshire v Nottinghamshire at Nuneaton, 1985
96.	103*	Warwickshire v Yorkshire at Birmingham, 1985
97.	108*	Warwickshire v Essex at Birmingham, 1986
98.	104	Warwickshire v Gloucestershire at Bristol, 1986
99.	110	Warwickshire v Glamorgan at Swansea, 1986
100.	101*	Warwickshire v Lancashire at Birmingham, 1986

Of Amiss's 100 hundreds, 85 were scored in England (76 for Warwickshire), 2 in Australia, 3 in India, 1 in New Zealand, 4 in Pakistan and 5 in the West Indies.

* *Signifies not out.*

JIM LAKER – A TRIBUTE

By ROBIN MARLAR

In the early 1950s Everest had not yet been tamed. It stood alone among the high places of the world. Now, more than thirty years later, its climbs are still the test for real mountaineers, but even as they prove the efficacy of their thermal underwear, Everest seems to have shrunk. Hillary and Tensing have been followed to the top.

Down below, in kinder, greener conditions, the underwear is not for keeping out the cold but for mopping up the sweat. Even so, on the cricket field, conditions of wind and wear, of dust and damp still must be watched and taken into account. There, however, Jim Laker's achievement, nineteen wickets in a Test match, has not attracted followers. Nor may it ever be beaten. Twenty wickets in a match is still Everest, far more significant in a cricket context than any record for batting or even for all-round excellence.

Laker's nineteen looks less and less repeatable as the seasons pass. Even if some Caribbean or Oriental tyro emerges, as Sobers did to topple Hutton or Gavaskar to overtake Bradman, there is still that extra air of wondrous disbelief that Laker should have, could have, taken nineteen Australian wickets for England in a Test at Old Trafford. And with Lock, most avaricious of bowlers, bowling 69 overs at the other end for Burke's first-innings wicket; the one that got away from Laker. Nor should it pass notice that Statham and Bailey, both unquestioned occupants of the hall of fame, sent down 46 overs between them without a strike. Even if you accept that the 1956 Australians were not one of the best sides from that country, there were great cricketers in that team; Harvey, Miller, Lindwall, Benaud. In truth, even though it happened, we can describe Laker's feat only as incredible.

At 34, Laker was at the peak of his powers in 1956. As a slow off-break bowler in the classical tradition, he was the unchallenged master of his craft. His confidence soared. Surrey were in their run of seven successive Championships, then the only pudding for proof at county level. Stuart Surridge, the captain who made Laker, allowing his bowler the luxury of being able to live without ever needing to doubt his own ability, had an unshakeable belief in the destiny of Surrey and its players. Furthermore, Laker had something of a score to settle with the Australians. In 1948, during the last chapter in the Bradman saga which had earlier featured bodyline and all that, England were desperate for a victory; but at Leeds, where Australia were set to score 404 to win in 344 minutes, he had failed to bowl them out in the fourth innings. Afterwards he would talk gently about dropped catches and the lack of spin support, there being only Compton's occasional chinamen available. At Lord's, though, where this particular England defeat hurt more than most, there was a suspicion that when the crunch came, Laker was chicken.

After Laker's failure at Leeds, off-spinning was relegated to third place in the spinning hierarchy behind the left-arm spinners and leg-spinners. Not that it would have mattered who had bowled in the next Test in 1948, because at The Oval England were bowled out for 52. Laker won caps in the years that followed, but first Tattersall and then Appleyard kept him out of the

England XI. Both were fine bowlers, but neither was orthodox like Laker. Tattersall held his forefinger, a long one, alongside the seam and pushed his off-spinner in a manner that helped him disguise the away-swinger. Appleyard exploded on the scene as a fast-medium bowler with a deadly off-cutter. Later he slowed down and learned to spin while never losing his quick bowler's action. We have seen the same development since in Greig's bowling. Both Tattersall and Appleyard were deadly on wet wickets. Because of their actions, preceded by a longer run than that of Laker and his followers, they had the potential for an increase of pace and therefore penetration. But Laker, too, was a fearsome opponent on a wet wicket. His action, so grooved in its approach, so upright in delivery, was an instrument on which he could play the pace variations that he wanted, although never reaching medium pace.

Laker's principal asset, and the one he looked for first among spin bowlers in his later coaching and commentary career, was power of spin. His action, a slow bowler's action, enabled him to deliver the ball spun by the fingers and snapped forward with the wrist. He charged the ball with more menace than his rivals and, I suspect, almost all his followers. Not that Laker lacked an away-swinger or the ability to use the breeze from long leg. He was always reluctant to switch his slip to lock up the leg-trap, recognising that no matter how responsive the pitch, even the finger-spun ball might hustle on without deviation, taking the outside edge as a batsman played for the turn.

In another important aspect Laker was pre-eminent, certainly among his contemporaries. Not only did he have equal ability over and round the wicket, but he combined this with the shrewdest understanding of which batsman could be better discomforted by a change of angle. On good pitches, on-side players would be attacked from round the wicket on the basis that they would, if they played across the line of that angle, be candidates for a catch at the wicket or slip. Similarly, by using the full crease from over the wicket, he had a chance of getting through the off-side driver, or at least of taking his inside edge. When the ball was turning, the geometry spoke not only for itself but also to umpires, who would give leg-before decisions on the front foot only if the bowler was going round the wicket.

Laker's ability in this respect – and one not given to the leading Test wicket-taker of this type, Gibbs, who could not bowl round the wicket – depended on the position of his body. Operating round the wicket, he clung to the leg stump with his backside, his final stride short enough to give him perfect balance, enabling him to make maximum use of his six-foot frame. Because of this perfect action, he was able to maintain not only his tight control over direction and length but also those subtle variations in trajectory, in the "loop", which differentiated Laker from one breed of lesser performer. Only his splendid control gave Surridge, his captain, crowding helmetless in the danger zone, the courage to walk forward from short leg. Indeed, Laker was sure that some catches were missed because his close men were too keen.

Generations overlap, but the second overlap will inevitably take the players and their game into new territory, thus rendering comparisons deceptively, dangerously, impossible. In Laker's time pitches were un-covered, albeit progressively less so. Outfields were less like carpets. There was less grass on the squares and what there was, was cut shorter. The science of pitch preparation was in its infancy. Groundsmanship is not so unlike farming that we can fail to notice that in Laker's time there was no embarrassing food mountain. No batsman then wielded heavier willow than

2lb 7oz, and most bats were 2lb 4oz. Pads were less padded, and technique against the off-break was not so well developed that batsmen could avoid opening the "gate"; with the result that an off-break, when properly spun, could go through to bowl a highly rated player.

Match balls were hand-, not machine-stitched and less well dyed, although they did keep their shape better. If you gripped these balls tight with the fingers across the seam and ripped them across it, the skin on the fingers was eventually torn. Laker soaked his right forefinger in surgical spirit at the start of the season to harden the skin, but even so it tore, the split eventually deepening until it bled. Each spinner had a different solution to the problem, some even stopping giving the ball such a tweak. Not Laker. Never. He would use a concoction called Friar's Balsam, which seemed to give him antiseptic protection until a corn developed, although later in the season that corn would itself split and bleed.

It should not pass notice that in the second innings of that famous Old Trafford Test, Laker bowled 51 overs and two balls with hardly a break. Yet in all of the 1956 season he bowled only 959 overs: *only* because it was not uncommon for spin bowlers to break 1,000 or even 1,250 overs a season. Laker's spinning finger thickened with arthritis, noticeably so when compared with the same digit on the left hand, and from time to time, when confronted by these problems, he was, perhaps inevitably, not keen to fill the stock-bowling role as a Surrey match eased gently towards a draw. Like the voice of a Callas, a spin bowler's finger demanded judicious use.

No cricketer could have made an impression on the game as vividly as Laker without having the personality to deploy his talent. He might have gone to Surrey from Catford, but Jim Laker was the archetypal dry Yorkshireman. If his tongue could cut, his eye was keen. His humour depended on the detached observance of the passing scene, never better illustrated than in his story of the journey home after that Test, when he sat in a Lichfield pub alone and unrecognised whilst others celebrated what he had done. Nor were his years in banking wasted, for he invested shrewdly when he finally settled in Putney. After his brief flirtation with industry, commentating for television, together with his articles and books, kept him financially afloat. Cricket apart, he was not looking for the big one.

Not all cricketers travel contentedly through the rest of their lives. To all appearances Laker was one of the lucky ones. Perhaps an inner awareness of his stupendous achievement as a player, the bestest with the mostest, gave him lasting satisfaction. When he came back from his next winter tour in South Africa to pick up yet more awards, he found that the legislators had begun to interfere with the right of captains and bowlers to place their fielders at will. "They have made it harder for anyone to repeat my success", he told one audience, and as so often in his cricketing judgement, Laker is likely to be right. When shall we look upon his like again?

TEST CRICKETERS

FULL LIST FROM 1877 TO AUGUST 26, 1986

These lists have been compiled on a home and abroad basis, appearances abroad being printed in *italics*.

Abbreviations. E: England. A: Australia. SA: South Africa. WI: West Indies. NZ: New Zealand. In: India. P: Pakistan. SL: Sri Lanka.

All appearances are placed in this order of seniority. Hence, any England cricketer playing against Australia in England has that achievement recorded first and the remainder of his appearances at home (if any) set down before passing to matches abroad. Although the distinction between amateur and professional was abolished in 1963, initials of English professionals before that date are still given in brackets. The figures immediately following each name represent the total number of appearances in *all* Tests.

Where the season embraces two different years, the first year is given; i.e. 1876 indicates 1876-77.

When South Africa left the British Commonwealth in 1961 they ceased membership of the Imperial Cricket Conference, which in 1965 was renamed the International Cricket Conference. The rules of membership were changed then so that, although Pakistan have left the Commonwealth, they remain members of ICC.

ENGLAND

Number of Test cricketers: 521

Abel (R.) 13: v A 1888 (3) 1896 (3) 1902 (2); *v A 1891 (3)*; *v SA 1888 (2)*

Absolom, C. A. 1: *v A 1878*

Agnew, J. P. 3: v A 1985 (1); v WI 1984 (1); v SL 1984 (1)

Allen (D. A.) 39: v A 1961 (4) 1964 (1); v SA 1960 (2); v WI 1963 (2) 1966 (1); v P 1962 (4); *v A 1962 (1) 1965 (4)*; *v SA 1964 (4)*; *v WI 1959 (5)*; *v NZ 1965 (3)*; *v In 1961 (5)*; *v P 1961 (3)*

Allen, G. O. 25: v A 1930 (1) 1934 (2); v WI 1933 (1); v NZ 1931 (3); v In 1936 (3); *v A 1932 (5) 1936 (5)*; *v WI 1947 (3)*; *v NZ 1932 (2)*

Allom, M. J. C. 5: *v SA 1930 (1)*; *v NZ 1929 (4)*

Allott, P. J. W. 13: v A 1981 (1) 1985 (4); v WI 1984 (3); v In 1982 (2); v SL 1984 (1); *v In 1981 (1)*; *v SL 1981 (1)*

Ames (L. E. G.) 47: v A 1934 (5) 1938 (2); v SA 1929 (1) 1935 (4); v WI 1933 (3); v NZ 1931 (3) 1937 (3); v In 1932 (1); *v A 1932 (5) 1936 (5)*; *v SA 1938 (5)*; *v WI 1929 (4) 1934 (4)*; *v NZ 1932 (2)*

Amiss, D. L. 50: v A 1968 (1) 1975 (2) 1977 (2); v WI 1966 (1) 1973 (3) 1976 (1); v NZ 1973 (3); v In 1967 (2) 1971 (1) 1974 (3); v P 1967 (1) 1971 (3) 1974 (3); *v A 1974 (5) 1976 (1)*; *v WI 1973 (5) v NZ 1974 (2)*; *v In 1972 (3) 1976 (5)*; *v P 1972 (3)*

Andrew (K. V.) 2: v WI 1963 (1); *v A 1954 (1)*

Appleyard (R.) 9: v A 1956 (1); v SA 1955 (1); v P 1954 (1); *v A 1954 (4)*; *v NZ 1954 (2)*

Archer, A. G. 1: *v SA 1898*

Armitage (T.) 2: *v A 1876 (2)*

Arnold (E. G.) 10: v A 1905 (4); v SA 1907 (2); *v A 1903 (4)*

Arnold, G. G. 34: v A 1972 (3) 1975 (1); v WI 1973 (3); v NZ 1969 (1) 1973 (3); v In 1974 (2); v P 1967 (2) 1974 (3); *v A 1974 (4)*; *v WI 1973 (3)*; *v NZ 1974 (2)*; *v In 1972 (4)*; *v P 1972 (3)*

Arnold (J.) 1: v NZ 1931

Astill (W. E.) 9: *v SA 1927 (5)*; *v WI 1929 (4)*

Athey, C. W. J. 8: v A 1980 (1); v NZ 1986 (3); v In 1986 (2); *v WI 1980 (2)*

Attewell (W.) 10: v A 1890 (1); *v A 1884 (5) 1887 (1) 1891 (3)*

Bailey, T. E. 61: v A 1953 (5) 1956 (4); v SA 1951 (2) 1955 (5); v WI 1950 (2) 1957 (4); v NZ 1949 (4) 1958 (4); v P 1954 (3); *v A 1950 (4) 1954 (5) 1958 (5); v SA 1956 (5); v WI 1953 (5); v NZ 1950 (2) 1954 (2)*

Bairstow, D. L. 4: v A 1980 (1); v WI 1980 (1); v In 1979 (1); *v WI 1980 (1)*

Bakewell (A. H.) 6: v SA 1935 (2); v WI 1933 (1); v NZ 1931 (2); *v In 1933 (1)*

Balderstone J. C. 2: v WI 1976 (2)

Barber, R. W. 28: v A 1964 (1) 1968 (1); v SA 1960 (1) 1965 (3); v WI 1966 (2); v NZ 1965 (3); *v A 1965 (5); v SA 1964 (4); v In 1961 (5); v P 1961 (3)*

Barber (W.) 2: v SA 1935 (2)

Barlow, G. D. 3: v A 1977 (1); *v In 1976 (2)*

Barlow (R. G.) 17: v A 1882 (1) 1884 (3) 1886 (3); *v A 1881 (4) 1882 (4) 1886 (2)*

Barnes (S. F.) 27: v A 1902 (1) 1909 (3) 1912 (3); v SA 1912 (3); *v A 1901 (3) 1907 (5) 1911 (5); v SA 1913 (4)*

Barnes (W.) 21: v A 1880 (1) 1882 (1) 1884 (2) 1886 (2) 1888 (3) 1890 (2); *v A 1882 (4) 1884 (5) 1886 (1)*

Barnett (C. J.) 20: v A 1938 (3) 1948 (1); v SA 1947 (3); v WI 1933 (1); v NZ 1937 (3); v In 1936 (1); *v A 1936 (5); v In 1933 (3)*

Barratt (F.) 5: v SA 1929 (1); *v NZ 1929 (4)*

Barrington (K. F.) 82: v A 1961 (5) 1964 (5) 1968 (3); v SA 1955 (2) 1960 (4) 1965 (3); v WI 1963 (5) 1966 (2); v NZ 1965 (2); v In 1959 (5) 1967 (3); v P 1962 (4) 1967 (3); *v A 1962 (5) 1965 (5); v SA 1964 (5); v WI 1959 (5) 1967 (5); v NZ 1962 (3); v In 1961 (5) 1963 (1); v P 1961 (2)*

Barton (V. A.) 1: *v SA 1891*

Bates (W.) 15: *v A 1881 (4) 1882 (4) 1884 (5) 1886 (2)*

Bean (G.) 3: *v A 1891 (3)*

Bedser (A. V.) 51: v A 1948 (5) 1953 (5); v SA 1947 (2) 1951 (5) 1955 (1); v WI 1950 (3); v NZ 1949 (2); v In 1946 (3) 1952 (4); v P 1954 (2); *v A 1946 (5) 1950 (5) 1954 (1); v SA 1948 (5); v NZ 1946 (1) 1950 (2)*

Benson, M. R. 1: v In 1986

Berry (R.) 2: v WI 1950 (2)

Binks, J. G. 2: *v In 1963 (2)*

Bird M. C. 10: *v SA 1909 (5) 1913 (5)*

Birkenshaw J. 5: *v WI 1973 (2); v In 1972 (2); v P 1972 (1)*

Bligh, Hon. I. F. W. 4: *v A 1882 (4)*

Blythe (C.) 19: v A 1905 (1) 1909 (2); v SA 1907 (3); *v A 1901 (5) 1907 (1); v SA 1905 (5) 1909 (2)*

Board (J. H.) 6: *v SA 1898 (2) 1905 (4)*

Bolus, J. B. 7: v WI 1963 (2); *v In 1963 (5)*

Booth (M. W.) 2: *v SA 1913 (2)*

Bosanquet, B. J. T. 7: v A 1905 (3); *v A 1903 (4)*

Botham, I. T. 85: v A 1977 (2) 1980 (1) 1981 (6) 1985 (6); v WI 1980 (5) 1984 (5); v NZ 1978 (3) 1983 (4) 1986 (1); v In 1979 (4) 1982 (3); v P 1978 (3) 1982 (3); v SL 1984 (1); *v A 1978 (6) 1979 (3) 1982 (5); v WI 1980 (4) 1985 (5); v NZ 1977 (3) 1983 (3); v In 1979 (1) 1981 (6); v P 1983 (1); v SL 1981 (1)*

Bowden, M. P. 2: *v SA 1888 (2)*

Bowes (W. E.) 15: v A 1934 (3) 1938 (2); v SA 1935 (4); v WI 1939 (2); v In 1932 (1) 1946 (1); *v A 1932 (1); v NZ 1932 (1)*

Bowley (E. H.) 5: v SA 1929 (2); *v NZ 1929 (3)*

Boycott, G. 108: v A 1964 (4) 1968 (3) 1972 (2) 1977 (3) 1980 (1) 1981 (6); v WI 1966 (4) 1969 (3) 1973 (3) 1980 (5); v NZ 1965 (2) 1969 (3) 1973 (3) 1978 (2); v In 1967 (2) 1971 (1) 1974 (1) 1979 (4); v P 1967 (1) 1971 (2); *v A 1965 (5) 1970 (5) 1978 (6) 1979 (3); v SA 1964 (5); v WI 1967 (5) 1973 (5) 1980 (4); v NZ 1965 (2) 1977 (3); v In 1979 (1) 1981 (4); v P 1977 (3)*

Bradley, W. M. 2: v A 1899 (2)

Braund (L. C.) 23: v A 1902 (5); v SA 1907 (3); *v A 1901 (5) 1903 (5) 1907 (5)*

Brearley, J. M. 39: v A 1977 (5) 1981 (4); v WI 1976 (2); v NZ 1978 (3); v In 1979 (4); v P 1978 (3); *v A 1976 (1) 1978 (6) 1979 (3); v In 1976 (5) 1979 (1); v P 1977 (3)*

Brearley, W. 4: v A 1905 (1) 1909 (1); v SA 1912 (1)

Brennan, D. V. 2: v SA 1951 (2)

Briggs (John) 33: v A 1886 (3) 1888 (3) 1893 (2) 1896 (1) 1899 (1); *v A 1884 (5) 1886 (2) 1887 (1) 1891 (3) 1894 (5) 1897 (5); v SA 1888 (2)*

Broad, B. C. 5: v WI 1984 (4); v SL 1984 (1)

Brockwell (W.) 7: v A 1893 (1) 1899 (1); *v A 1894 (5)*

Bromley-Davenport, H. R. 4: *v SA 1895 (3) 1898 (1)*

Brookes (D.) 1: *v WI 1947*

Brown (A.) 2: *v In 1961 (1)*; *v P 1961 (1)*
Brown, D. J. 26: v A 1968 (4); v SA 1965 (2); v WI 1966 (1) 1969 (3); v NZ 1969 (1); v In 1967 (2): *v A 1965 (4)*; *v WI 1967 (4)*; *v NZ 1965 (2)*; *v P 1968 (3)*
Brown, F. R. 22: v A 1953 (1); v SA 1951 (5); v WI 1950 (1); v NZ 1931 (2) 1937 (1) 1949 (2); v In 1932 (1); *v A 1950 (5)*; *v NZ 1932 (2) 1950 (2)*
Brown (G.) 7: v A 1921 (3); *v SA 1922 (4)*
Brown (J. T.) 8: v A 1896 (2) 1899 (1); *v A 1894 (5)*
Buckenham (C. P.) 4: *v SA 1909 (4)*
Butcher, A. R. 1: *v In 1979*
Butcher, R. O. 3: *v WI 1980 (3)*
Butler (H. J.) 2: v SA 1947 (1); *v WI 1947 (1)*
Butt (H. R.) 3: *v SA 1895 (3)*

Calthorpe, Hon. F. S. G. 4: *v WI 1929 (4)*
Carr, A. W. 11: v A 1926 (4); v SA 1929 (2); *v SA 1922 (5)*
Carr, D. B. 2: *v In 1951 (2)*
Carr, D. W. 1: v A 1909
Cartwright, T. W. 5: v A 1964 (2); v SA 1965 (1); v NZ 1965 (1); *v SA 1964 (1)*
Chapman, A. P. F. 26: v A 1926 (4) 1930 (4); v SA 1924 (2); v WI 1928 (3); *v A 1924 (4) 1928 (4)*; *v SA 1930 (5)*
Charlwood (H. R. J.) 2: *v A 1876 (2)*
Chatterton (W.) 1: *v SA 1891*
Christopherson, S. 1: v A 1884
Clark (E. W.) 8: v A 1934 (2); v SA 1929 (2); v WI 1933 (2); *v In 1933 (3)*
Clay, J. C. 1: v SA 1935
Close (D. B.) 22: v A 1961 (1); v SA 1955 (1); v WI 1957 (2) 1963 (5) 1966 (1) 1976 (3); v NZ 1949 (1); v In 1959 (1) 1967 (3); v P 1967 (3); *v A 1950 (1)*
Coldwell (L. J.) 7: v A 1964 (2); v P 1962 (2); *v A 1962 (2)*; *v NZ 1962 (1)*
Compton (D. C. S.) 78: v A 1938 (4) 1948 (5) 1953 (5) 1956 (1); v SA 1947 (5) 1951 (5) 1955 (5); v WI 1939 (1) 1950 (1); v NZ 1937 (1) 1949 (4); v In 1946 (3) 1952 (2); v P 1954 (4); *v A 1946 (5) 1950 (4) 1954 (4)*; *v SA 1948 (5) 1956 (5)*; *v WI 1953 (5)*; *v NZ 1946 (1) 1950 (2)*
Cook (C.) 1: v SA 1947
Cook, G. 7: v In 1982 (3); *v A 1982 (3)*; *v SL 1981 (1)*
Cook, N. G. B. 9: v WI 1984 (3); v NZ 1983 (2); *v NZ 1983 (1)*; *v P 1983 (3)*
Cope, G. A. 3: *v P 1977 (3)*
Copson (W. H.) 3: v SA 1947 (1); v WI 1939 (2)
Cornford (W. L.) 4: *v NZ 1929 (4)*
Cottam, R. M. H. 4: *v In 1972 (2)*; *v P 1968 (2)*
Coventry, Hon. C. J. 2: *v SA 1888 (2)*
Cowans, N. G. 19: v A 1985 (1); v WI 1984 (1); v NZ 1983 (4); *v A 1982 (4)*; *v NZ 1983 (2)*; *v In 1984 (5)*; *v P 1983 (2)*
Cowdrey, C. S. 5: *v In 1984 (5)*
Cowdrey, M. C. 114: v A 1956 (5) 1961 (4) 1964 (3) 1968 (4); v SA 1955 (1) 1960 (5) 1965 (3); v WI 1957 (5) 1963 (2) 1966 (4); v NZ 1958 (4) 1965 (3); v In 1959 (5); v P 1962 (4) 1967 (2) 1971 (1); *v A 1954 (5) 1958 (5) 1962 (5) 1965 (4) 1970 (3) 1974 (5)*; *v SA 1956 (5)*; *v WI 1959 (5) 1967 (5)*; *v NZ 1954 (2) 1958 (2) 1962 (3) 1965 (3) 1970 (1)*; *v In 1963 (3)*; *v P 1968 (3)*
Coxon (A.) 1: v A 1948
Cranston, J. 1: v A 1890
Cranston, K. 8: v A 1948 (1); v SA 1947 (3); *v WI 1947 (4)*
Crapp (J. F.) 7: v A 1948 (3); *v SA 1948 (4)*
Crawford, J. N. 12: v SA 1907 (2); *v A 1907 (5)*; *v SA 1905 (5)*
Cuttell (W. R.) 2: *v SA 1898 (2)*

Dawson, E. W. 5: *v SA 1927 (1)*; *v NZ 1929 (4)*
Dean (H.) 3: v A 1912 (2); v SA 1912 (1)
Denness, M. H. 28: v A 1975 (1); v NZ 1969 (1); v In 1974 (3); v P 1974 (3); *v A 1974 (5)*; *v WI 1973 (5)*; *v NZ 1974 (2)*; *v In 1972 (5)*; *v P 1972 (3)*
Denton (D.) 11: v A 1905 (1); v SA 1905 (5) 1909 (5)
Dewes, J. G. 5: v A 1948 (1); v WI 1950 (2); *v A 1950 (2)*
Dexter, E. R. 62: v A 1961 (5) 1964 (5) 1968 (2); v SA 1960 (5); v WI 1963 (5); v NZ 1958 (1) 1965 (2); v In 1959 (2); v P 1962 (5); *v A 1958 (2) 1962 (5)*; *v SA 1964 (5)*; *v WI 1959 (5)*; *v NZ 1958 (2) 1962 (3)*; *v In 1961 (5)*; *v P 1961 (3)*

Dilley, G. R. 22: v A 1981 (3); v WI 1980 (3); v NZ 1983 (1) 1986 (2); v In 1986 (2); *v A 1979 (2); v WI 1980 (4); v In 1981 (4); v P 1983 (1)*

Dipper (A. E.) 1: v A 1921

Doggart, G. H. G. 2: v WI 1950 (2)

D'Oliveira, B. L. 44: v A 1968 (2) 1972 (5); v WI 1966 (4) 1969 (3); v NZ 1969 (3); v In 1967 (2) 1971 (3); v P 1967 (3) 1971 (3); *v A 1970 (6); v WI 1967 (5); v NZ 1970 (2); v P 1968 (3)*

Dollery (H. E.) 4: v A 1948 (2); v SA 1947 (1); v WI 1950 (1)

Dolphin (A.) 1: *v A 1920*

Douglas, J. W. H. T. 23: v A 1912 (1) 1921 (5); v SA 1924 (1); *v A 1911 (5) 1920 (5) 1924 (1); v SA 1913 (5)*

Downton, P. R. 27: v A 1981 (1) 1985 (6); v WI 1984 (5); v In 1986 (1); v SL 1984 (1); *v WI 1980 (3) 1985 (5); v In 1984 (5)*

Druce, N. F. 5: *v A 1897 (5)*

Ducat (A.) 1: v A 1921

Duckworth (G.) 24: v A 1930 (5); v SA 1924 (1) 1929 (4) 1935 (1); v WI 1928 (1); v In 1936 (3); *v A 1928 (5); v SA 1930 (3); v NZ 1932 (1)*

Duleepsinhji, K. S. 12: v A 1930 (4); v SA 1929 (1); v NZ 1931 (3); *v NZ 1929 (4)*

Durston (F. J.) 1: v A 1921

Edmonds, P. H. 41: v A 1975 (2) 1985 (5); v NZ 1978 (3) 1983 (2) 1986 (3); v In 1979 (4) 1982 (3) 1986 (2); v P 1978 (3); *v A 1978 (1); v WI 1985 (3); v NZ 1977 (3); v In 1984 (5); v P 1977 (2)*

Edrich, J. H. 77: v A 1964 (3) 1968 (5) 1972 (5) 1975 (4); v SA 1965 (1); v WI 1963 (3) 1966 (1) 1969 (3) 1976 (2); v NZ 1965 (1) 1969 (3); v In 1967 (2) 1971 (3) 1974 (3); v P 1971 (3) 1974 (3); *v A 1965 (5) 1970 (6) 1974 (4); v WI 1967 (5); v NZ 1965 (3) 1970 (2) 1974 (2); v In 1963 (2); v P 1968 (3)*

Edrich, W. J. 39: v A 1938 (4) 1948 (5) 1953 (3); v SA 1947 (4); v WI 1950 (2); v NZ 1949 (4); v In 1946 (1); v P 1954 (1); *v A 1946 (5) 1954 (4); v SA 1938 (5); v NZ 1946 (1)*

Elliott (H.) 4: v WI 1928 (1); *v SA 1927 (1); v In 1933 (2)*

Ellison, R. M. 11: v A 1985 (2); v WI 1984 (1); v In 1986 (1); v SL 1984 (1); *v WI 1985 (3); v In 1984 (3)*

Emburey, J. E. 37: v A 1980 (1) 1981 (4) 1985 (6); v WI 1980 (3); v NZ 1978 (1) 1986 (2); v In 1986 (3); *v A 1978 (4); v WI 1980 (4) 1985 (4); v In 1979 (1) 1981 (3); v SL 1981 (1)*

Emmett (G. M.) 1: v A 1948

Emmett (T.) 7: *v A 1876 (2) 1878 (1) 1881 (4)*

Evans, A. J. 1: v A 1921

Evans (T. G.) 91: v A 1948 (5) 1953 (5) 1956 (5); v SA 1947 (5) 1951 (3) 1955 (3); v WI 1950 (3) 1957 (5); v NZ 1949 (4) 1958 (5); v In 1946 (1) 1952 (4) 1959 (2); v P 1954 (4); *v A 1946 (5) 1950 (5) 1954 (4) 1958 (3); v SA 1948 (3) 1956 (5); v WI 1947 (4) 1953 (4); v NZ 1946 (1) 1950 (2) 1954 (2)*

Fagg (A. E.) 5: v WI 1939 (1); v In 1936 (2); *v A 1936 (2)*

Fane, F. L. 14: *v A 1907 (4); v SA 1905 (5) 1909 (5)*

Farnes, K. 15: v A 1934 (2) 1938 (4); *v A 1936 (2); v SA 1938 (5); v WI 1934 (2)*

Farrimond (W.) 4: v SA 1935 (1); *v SA 1930 (2); v WI 1934 (1)*

Fender, P. G. H. 13: v A 1921 (2); v SA 1924 (2) 1929 (1); *v A 1920 (3); v SA 1922 (5)*

Ferris, J. J. 1: *v SA 1891*

Fielder (A.) 6: *v A 1903 (2) 1907 (4)*

Fishlock (L. B.) 4: v In 1936 (2) 1946 (1); *v A 1946 (1)*

Flavell (J. A.) 4: v A 1961 (2) 1964 (2)

Fletcher, K. W. R. 59: v A 1968 (1) 1972 (1) 1975 (2); v WI 1973 (3); v NZ 1969 (2) 1973 (3); v In 1971 (2) 1974 (3); v P 1974 (3); *v A 1970 (5) 1974 (5) 1976 (1); v WI 1973 (4); v NZ 1970 (1) 1974 (2); v In 1972 (5) 1976 (3) 1981 (6); v P 1968 (3) 1972 (3); v SL 1981 (1)*

Flowers (W.) 8: v A 1893 (1); *v A 1884 (5) 1886 (2)*

Ford, F. G. J. 5: *v A 1894 (5)*

Foster, F. R. 11: v A 1912 (3); v SA 1912 (3); *v A 1911 (5)*

Foster, N. A. 14: v A 1985 (1); v WI 1984 (1); v NZ 1983 (1) 1986 (1); v In 1986 (1); *v WI 1985 (3); v NZ 1983 (2); v In 1984 (2); v P 1983 (2)*

Foster, R. E. 8: v SA 1907 (3); *v A 1903 (5)*

Fothergill (A. J.) 2: *v SA 1888 (2)*

Fowler, G. 21: v WI 1984 (5); v NZ 1983 (2); v P 1982 (1); v SL 1984 (1); *v A 1982 (3); v NZ 1983 (2); v In 1984 (5); v P 1983 (2)*

Freeman (A. P.) 12: v SA 1929 (3); v WI 1928 (3); *v A 1924 (2); v SA 1927 (4)*

French, B. N. 5: v NZ 1986 (3); v In 1986 (2)

Fry, C. B. 26: v A 1899 (5) 1902 (3) 1905 (4) 1909 (3) 1912 (3); v SA 1907 (3) 1912 (3); *v SA 1895 (2)*

Gatting, M. W. 48: v A 1980 (1) 1981 (6) 1985 (6); v WI 1980 (4) 1984 (1); v NZ 1983 (2) 1986 (3); v In 1986 (3); v P 1982 (3); *v WI 1980 (1) 1985 (1); v NZ 1977 (1) 1983 (2); v In 1981 (5) 1984 (5); v P 1977 (1) 1983 (3)*

Gay, L. H. 1: *v A 1894*

Geary (G.) 14: v A 1926 (2) 1930 (1) 1934 (2); v SA 1924 (1) 1929 (2); *v A 1928 (4); v SA 1927 (2)*

Gibb, P. A. 8: v In 1946 (2); *v A 1946 (1); v SA 1938 (5)*

Gifford, N. 15: v A 1964 (2) 1972 (3); v NZ 1973 (2); v In 1971 (2); v P 1971 (2); *v In 1972 (2); v P 1972 (2)*

Gilligan, A. E. R. 11: v SA 1924 (4); *v A 1924 (5); v SA 1922 (2)*

Gilligan, A. H. H. 4: *v NZ 1929 (4)*

Gimblett (H.) 3: v WI 1939 (1); v In 1936 (2)

Gladwin (C.) 8: v SA 1947 (2); v NZ 1949 (1); *v SA 1948 (5)*

Goddard (T. W.) 8: v A 1930 (1); v WI 1939 (2); v NZ 1937 (2); *v SA 1938 (3)*

Gooch, G. A. 59: v A 1975 (2) 1980 (1) 1981 (5) 1985 (6); v WI 1980 (5); v NZ 1978 (3) 1986 (3); v In 1979 (4) 1986 (3); v P 1978 (2); *v A 1978 (6) 1979 (2); v WI 1980 (4) 1985 (5); v In 1979 (1) 1981 (6); v SL 1981 (1)*

Gover (A. R.) 4: v NZ 1937 (2); v In 1936 (1) 1946 (1)

Gower, D. I. 86: v A 1980 (1) 1981 (5) 1985 (6); v WI 1980 (1) 1984 (5); v NZ 1978 (3) 1983 (4) 1986 (3); v In 1979 (4) 1982 (3) 1986 (2); v P 1978 (3) 1982 (3); v SL 1984 (1); *v A 1978 (6) 1979 (3) 1982 (5); v WI 1980 (4) 1985 (5); v NZ 1983 (3); v In 1979 (1) 1981 (6) 1984 (5); v P 1983 (3); v SL 1981 (1)*

Grace, E. M. 1: v A 1880

Grace, G. F. 1: v A 1880

Grace, W. G. 22: v A 1880 (1) 1882 (1) 1884 (3) 1886 (3) 1888 (3) 1890 (2) 1893 (2) 1896 (3) 1899 (1); *v A 1891 (3)*

Graveney (T. W.) 79: v A 1953 (5) 1956 (2) 1968 (5); v SA 1951 (1) 1955 (5); v WI 1957 (4) 1966 (4) 1969 (1); v NZ 1958 (4); v In 1952 (4) 1967 (3); v P 1954 (3) 1962 (4) 1967 (3); *v A 1954 (2) 1958 (5) 1962 (3); v WI 1953 (5) 1967 (5); v NZ 1954 (2) 1958 (2); v In 1951 (4); v P 1968 (3)*

Greenhough (T.) 4: v SA 1960 (1); v In 1959 (3)

Greenwood (A.) 2: *v A 1876 (2)*

Greig, A. W. 58: v A 1972 (5) 1975 (4) 1977 (5); v WI 1973 (3) 1976 (5); v NZ 1973 (3); v In 1974 (3); v P 1974 (3); *v A 1974 (6) 1976 (1); v WI 1973 (5); v NZ 1974 (2); v In 1972 (5) 1976 (5); v P 1972 (3)*

Greig, I. A. 2: v P 1982 (2)

Grieve, B. A. F. 2: *v SA 1888 (2)*

Griffith, S. C. 3: *v SA 1948 (2); v WI 1947 (1)*

Gunn (G.) 15: v A 1909 (1); *v A 1907 (5) 1911 (5); v WI 1929 (4)*

Gunn (J.) 6: v A 1905 (1); *v A 1901 (5)*

Gunn (W.) 11: v A 1888 (2) 1890 (2) 1893 (2) 1896 (1) 1899 (1); *v A 1886 (2)*

Haig, N. E. 5: v A 1921 (1); *v WI 1929 (4)*

Haigh (S.) 11: v A 1905 (2) 1909 (1) 1912 (1); *v SA 1898 (2) 1905 (5)*

Hallows (C.) 2: v A 1921 (1); v WI 1928 (1)

Hammond, W. R. 85: v A 1930 (5) 1934 (5) 1938 (4); v SA 1929 (4) 1935 (5); v WI 1928 (3) 1933 (3) 1939 (3); v NZ 1931 (3) 1937 (3); v In 1932 (1) 1936 (2) 1946 (3); *v A 1928 (5) 1932 (5) 1936 (5) 1946 (4); v SA 1927 (5) 1930 (5) 1938 (5); v WI 1934 (4); v NZ 1932 (2) 1946 (1)*

Hampshire, J. H. 8: v A 1972 (1) 1975 (1); v WI 1969 (1); *v A 1970 (2); v NZ 1970 (2)*

Hardinge (H. T. W.) 1: v A 1921

Hardstaff (J.) 5: *v A 1907 (5)*

Hardstaff (J. jun.) 23: v A 1938 (2) 1948 (1); v SA 1935 (1); v WI 1939 (3); v NZ 1937 (3); v In 1936 (2) 1946 (2); *v A 1936 (5) 1946 (1); v WI 1947 (3)*

Harris, Lord 4: v A 1880 (1) 1884 (2); *v A 1878 (1)*

Hartley, J. C. 2: *v SA 1905 (2)*

Hawke, Lord 5: *v SA 1895 (3) 1898 (2)*

Hayes (E. G.) 5: v A 1909 (1); v SA 1912 (1); *v SA 1905 (3)*

Hayes, F. C. 9: v WI 1973 (3) 1976 (2); *v WI 1973 (4)*

Hayward (T. W.) 35: v A 1896 (2) 1899 (2) 1902 (1) 1905 (5) 1909 (1); v SA 1907 (3); *v A 1897 (5) 1901 (5) 1903 (5); v SA 1895 (3)*

Hearne (A.) 1: *v SA 1891*

Hearne (F.) 2: *v SA 1888 (2)*

Hearne (G. G.) 1: *v SA 1891*

Hearne (J. T.) 12: v A 1896 (3) 1899 (3); *v A 1897 (5); v SA 1891 (1)*

Hearne (J. W.) 24: v A 1912 (3) 1921 (1) 1926 (1); v SA 1912 (2) 1924 (3); *v A 1911 (5) 1920 (2) 1924 (4); v SA 1913 (3)*

Hemmings, E. E. 5: v P 1982 (2); *v A 1982 (3)*

Hendren (E. H.) 51: v A 1921 (2) 1926 (5) 1930 (2) 1934 (4); v SA 1924 (5) 1929 (4); v WI 1928 (1); *v A 1920 (5) 1924 (5) 1928 (5); v SA 1930 (5); v WI 1929 (4) 1934 (4)*

Hendrick, M. 30: v A 1977 (3) 1980 (1) 1981 (2); v WI 1976 (2) 1980 (2); v NZ 1978 (2); v In 1974 (3) 1979 (4); *v A 1974 (2) 1978 (5); v NZ 1974 (1) 1977 (1)*

Heseltine, C. 2: v SA 1895 (2)

Higgs, K. 15: v A 1968 (1); v WI 1966 (5); v SA 1965 (1); v In 1967 (1); v P 1967 (3); *v A 1965 (1); v NZ 1965 (3)*

Hill (A.) 2: *v A 1876 (2)*

Hill, A. J. L. 3: *v SA 1895 (3)*

Hilton (M. J.) 4: v SA 1951 (1); v WI 1950 (1); *v In 1951 (2)*

Hirst (G. H.) 24: v A 1899 (1) 1902 (4) 1905 (3) 1909 (4); v SA 1907 (3); *v A 1897 (4) 1903 (5)*

Hitch (J. W.) 7: v A 1912 (1) 1921 (1); v SA 1912 (1); *v A 1911 (3) 1920 (1)*

Hobbs (J. B.) 61: v A 1909 (3) 1912 (3) 1921 (3) 1926 (5) 1930 (5); v SA 1912 (3) 1924 (4) 1929 (1); v WI 1928 (2); *v A 1907 (4) 1911 (5) 1920 (5) 1924 (5) 1928 (5); v SA 1909 (5) 1913 (5)*

Hobbs, R. N. S. 7: v In 1967 (3); v P 1967 (1) 1971 (1); *v WI 1967 (1); v P 1968 (1)*

Hollies (W. E.) 13: v A 1948 (1); v SA 1947 (3); v WI 1950 (2); v NZ 1949 (4); *v WI 1934 (3)*

Holmes, E. R. T. 5: v SA 1935 (1); *v WI 1934 (4)*

Holmes (P.) 7: v A 1921 (1); v In 1932 (1); *v SA 1927 (5)*

Hone, L. 1: *v A 1878*

Hopwood (J. L.) 2: v A 1934 (2)

Hornby, A. N. 3: v A 1882 (1) 1884 (1); *v A 1878 (1)*

Horton (M. J.) 2: v In 1959 (2)

Howard, N. D. 4: *v In 1951 (4)*

Howell (H.) 5: v A 1921 (1); v SA 1924 (1); *v A 1920 (3)*

Howorth (R.) 5: v WI 1947 (1); *v WI 1947 (4)*

Humphries (J.) 3: *v A 1907 (3)*

Hunter (J.) 5: *v A 1884 (5)*

Hutchings, K. L. 7: v A 1909 (2); *v A 1907 (5)*

Hutton (L.) 79: v A 1938 (3) 1948 (4) 1953 (5); v SA 1947 (5) 1951 (5); v WI 1939 (3) 1950 (3); v NZ 1937 (3) 1949 (4); v In 1946 (3) 1952 (4); v P 1954 (2); *v A 1946 (5) 1950 (5) 1954 (5); v SA 1938 (4) 1948 (5); v WI 1947 (2) 1953 (5); v NZ 1950 (2) 1954 (2)*

Hutton, R. A. 5: v In 1971 (3); v P 1971 (2)

Iddon (J.) 5: v SA 1935 (1); *v WI 1934 (4)*

Ikin (J. T.) 18: v SA 1951 (3) 1955 (1); v In 1946 (2) 1952 (2); *v A 1946 (5); v NZ 1946 (1); v WI 1947 (4)*

Illingworth (R.) 61: v A 1961 (2) 1968 (3) 1972 (5); v SA 1960 (4); v WI 1966 (2) 1969 (3) 1973 (3); v NZ 1958 (1) 1965 (1) 1969 (3) 1973 (3); v In 1959 (2) 1967 (3) 1971 (3); v P 1962 (1) 1967 (1) 1971 (3); *v A 1962 (2) 1970 (6); v WI 1959 (5); v NZ 1962 (3) 1970 (2)*

Insole, D. J. 9: v A 1956 (1); v SA 1955 (1); v WI 1950 (1) 1957 (1); *v SA 1956 (5)*

Jackman, R. D. 4: v P 1982 (2); *v WI 1980 (2)*

Jackson, F. S. 20: v A 1893 (2) 1896 (3) 1899 (5) 1902 (5) 1905 (5)

Jackson (H. L.) 2: v A 1961 (1); v NZ 1949 (1)

Jameson, J. A. 4: v In 1971 (2); *v WI 1973 (2)*

Jardine, D. R. 22: v WI 1928 (2) 1933 (2); v NZ 1931 (3); v In 1932 (1); *v A 1928 (5) 1932 (5); v NZ 1932 (1); v In 1933 (3)*

Jenkins (R. O.) 9: v WI 1950 (2); v In 1952 (2); *v SA 1948 (5)*

Jessop, G. L. 18: v A 1899 (1) 1902 (4) 1905 (1) 1909 (2); v SA 1907 (3) 1912 (2); *v A 1901 (5)*

Jones, A. O. 12: v A 1899 (1) 1905 (2) 1909 (2); *v A 1901 (5) 1907 (2)*

Jones, I. J. 15: v WI 1966 (2); *v A 1965 (4); v WI 1967 (5); v NZ 1965 (3); v In 1963 (1)*

Jupp (H.) 2: *v A 1876 (2)*

Jupp, V. W. C. 8: v A 1921 (2); v WI 1928 (2); *v SA 1922 (4)*

Keeton (W. W.) 2: v A 1934 (1); v WI 1939 (1)

Kennedy (A. S.) 5: *v SA 1922 (5)*
Kenyon (D.) 8: v A 1953 (2); v SA 1955 (3); *v In 1951 (3)*
Killick, E. T. 2: v SA 1929 (2)
Kilner (R.) 9: v A 1926 (4); v SA 1924 (2); *v A 1924 (3)*
King (J. H.) 1: v A 1909
Kinneir (S. P.) 1: *v A 1911*
Knight (A. E.) 3: *v A 1903 (3)*
Knight (B. R.) 29: v A 1968 (2); v WI 1966 (1) 1969 (3); v NZ 1969 (2); v P 1962 (2); *v A 1962 (1) 1965 (2); v NZ 1962 (3) 1965 (2); v In 1961 (4) 1963 (5); v P 1961 (2)*
Knight, D. J. 2: v A 1921 (2)
Knott, A. P. E. 95: v A 1968 (5) 1972 (5) 1975 (4) 1977 (5) 1981 (2); v WI 1969 (3) 1973 (3) 1976 (5) 1980 (4); v NZ 1969 (3) 1973 (3); v In 1971 (3) 1974 (3); v P 1967 (2) 1971 (3) 1974 (3); *v A 1970 (6) 1974 (6) 1976 (1); v WI 1967 (2) 1973 (5); v NZ 1970 (1) 1974 (2); v In 1972 (5) 1974 (5); v P 1968 (3) 1972 (3)*
Knox, N. A. 2: v SA 1907 (2)

Laker (J. C.) 46: v A 1948 (3) 1953 (3) 1956 (5); v SA 1951 (2) 1955 (1); v WI 1950 (1) 1957 (4); v NZ 1949 (1) 1958 (4); v In 1952 (4); v P 1954 (1); *v A 1958 (4); v SA 1956 (5); v WI 1947 (4) 1953 (4)*
Lamb, A. J. 46: v A 1985 (6); v WI 1984 (5); v NZ 1983 (4) 1986 (1); v In 1982 (3) 1986 (2); v P 1982 (3); v SL 1984 (1); *v A 1982 (5); v WI 1985 (5); v NZ 1983 (3); v In 1984 (5); v P 1983 (3)*
Langridge (James) 8: v SA 1935 (1); v WI 1933 (2); v In 1936 (1) 1946 (1); *v In 1933 (3)*
Larkins, W. 6: v A 1981 (1); v WI 1980 (3); *v A 1979 (1); v In 1979 (1)*
Larter (J. D. F.) 10: v SA 1965 (2); v NZ 1965 (1); v P 1962 (1); *v NZ 1962 (3); v In 1963 (3)*
Larwood (H.) 21: v A 1926 (2) 1930 (3); v SA 1929 (3); v WI 1928 (2); v NZ 1931 (1); *v A 1928 (5) 1932 (5)*
Leadbeater (E.) 2: *v In 1951 (2)*
Lee (H. W.) 1: *v SA 1930*
Lees (W. S.) 5: *v SA 1905 (5)*
Legge G. B. 5: *v SA 1927 (1); v NZ 1929 (4)*
Leslie, C. F. H. 4: *v A 1882 (4)*
Lever, J. K. 21: v A 1977 (3); v WI 1980 (1); v In 1979 (1) 1986 (1); *v A 1976 (1) 1978 (1) 1979 (1); v NZ 1977 (1); v In 1976 (5) 1979 (1) 1981 (2); v P 1977 (3)*
Lever, P. 17: v A 1972 (1) 1975 (1); v In 1971 (1); v P 1971 (3); *v A 1970 (5) 1974 (2); v NZ 1970 (2) 1974 (2)*
Leveson Gower, H. D. G. 3: *v SA 1909 (3)*
Levett, W. H. V. 1: *v In 1933*
Lewis, A. R. 9: v NZ 1973 (1); *v In 1972 (5); v P 1972 (3)*
Leyland (M.) 41: v A 1930 (3) 1934 (5) 1938 (1); v SA 1929 (5) 1935 (4); v WI 1928 (1) 1933 (1); v In 1936 (2); *v A 1928 (1) 1932 (5) 1936 (5); v SA 1930 (5); v WI 1934 (3)*
Lilley (A. A.) 35: v A 1896 (3) 1899 (4) 1902 (5) 1905 (5) 1909 (5); v SA 1907 (3); *v A 1901 (5) 1903 (5)*
Lillywhite (James jun.) 2: *v A 1876 (2)*
Lloyd, D. 9: v In 1974 (2); v P 1974 (3); *v A 1974 (4)*
Lloyd, T. A. 1: v WI 1984
Loader (P. J.) 13: v SA 1955 (1); v WI 1957 (2); v NZ 1958 (3); v P 1954 (1); *v A 1958 (2); v SA 1956 (4)*
Lock (G. A. R.) 49: v A 1953 (2) 1956 (4) 1961 (3); v SA 1955 (3); v WI 1957 (3) 1963 (3); v NZ 1958 (5); v In 1952 (2); v P 1962 (3); *v A 1958 (4); v SA 1956 (1); v WI 1953 (5) 1967 (2); v NZ 1958 (2); v In 1961 (5); v P 1961 (2)*
Lockwood (W. H.) 12: v A 1893 (2) 1899 (1) 1902 (4); *v A 1894 (5)*
Lohmann (G. A.) 18: v A 1886 (3) 1888 (3) 1890 (2) 1896 (1); *v A 1886 (2) 1887 (1) 1891 (3); v SA 1895 (3)*
Lowson (F. A.) 7: v SA 1951 (2) 1955 (1); *v In 1951 (4)*
Lucas, A. P. 5: v A 1880 (1) 1882 (1) 1884 (2); *v A 1878 (1)*
Luckhurst, B. W. 21: v A 1972 (4); v WI 1973 (2); v In 1971 (2); v P 1971 (3); *v A 1970 (5); 1974 (2); v NZ 1970 (2)*
Lyttelton, Hon. A. 4: v A 1880 (1) 1882 (1) 1884 (2)

Macaulay (G. G.) 8: v A 1926 (1); v SA 1924 (1); v WI 1933 (2); *v SA 1922 (4)*
MacBryan, J. C. W. 1: v SA 1924
McConnon (J. E.) 2: v P 1954 (2)

McGahey, C. P. 2: *v A 1901 (2)*
MacGregor, G. 8: v A 1890 (2) 1893 (3); *v A 1891 (3)*
McIntyre (A. J. W.) 3: v SA 1955 (1); v WI 1950 (1); *v A 1950 (10*
MacKinnon, F. A. 1: *v A 1878*
MacLaren, A. C. 35: v A 1896 (2) 1899 (4) 1902 (5) 1905 (4) 1909 (5); *v A 1894 (5) 1897 (5) 1901 (5)*
McMaster, J. E. P. 1: *v SA 1888*
Makepeace (H.) 4: *v A 1920 (4)*
Mann, F. G. 7: v NZ 1949 (2); *v SA 1948 (5)*
Mann, F. T. 5: *v SA 1922 (5)*
Marks, V. J. 6: v NZ 1983 (1); v P 1982 (1); *v NZ 1983 (1); v P 1983 (3)*
Marriott, C. S. 1: v WI 1933
Martin (F.) 2: v A 1890 (1); *v SA 1891 (1)*
Martin, J. W. 1: v SA 1947
Mason, J. R. 5: *v A 1897 (5)*
Matthews (A. D. G.) 1: v NZ 1937
May, P. B. H. 66: v A 1953 (2) 1956 (5) 1961 (4); v SA 1951 (2) 1955 (5); v WI 1957 (5); v NZ 1958 (5); v In 1952 (4) 1959 (3); v P 1954 (4); *v A 1954 (5) 1958 (5); v SA 1956 (5); v WI 1953 (5) 1959 (3); v NZ 1954 (2) 1958 (2)*
Mead (C. P.) 17: v A 1921 (2); *v A 1911 (4) 1928 (1); v SA 1913 (5) 1922 (5)*
Mead (W.) 1: v A 1899
Midwinter (W. E.) 4: *v A 1881 (4)*
Milburn, C. 9: v A 1968 (2); v WI 1966 (4); v In 1967 (1); v P 1967 (1); *v P 1968 (1)*
Miller, A. M. 1: v SA 1895
Miller, G. 34: v A 1977 (2); v WI 1976 (1) 1984 (2); v NZ 1978 (2); v In 1979 (3) 1982 (1); v P 1978 (3) 1982 (1); *v A 1978 (6) 1979 (1) 1982 (5); v WI 1980 (1); v NZ 1977 (3); v P 1977 (3)*
Milligan, F. W. 2: *v SA 1898 (2)*
Millman (G.) 6: v P 1962 (2); *v In 1961 (2); v P 1961 (2)*
Milton (C. A.) 6: v NZ 1958 (2); v In 1959 (2); *v A 1958 (2)*
Mitchell (A.) 6: v SA 1935 (2); v In 1936 (1); *v In 1933 (3)*
Mitchell, F. 2: *v SA 1898 (2)*
Mitchell (T. B.) 5: v A 1934 (2); v SA 1935 (1); *v A 1932 (1); v NZ 1932 (1)*
Mitchell-Innes, N. S. 1: v SA 1935
Mold (A. W.) 3: v A 1893 (3)
Moon, L. J. 4: *v SA 1905 (4)*
Morley (F.) 4: v A 1880 (1); *v A 1882 (3)*
Mortimore (J. B.) 9: v A 1964 (1); v In 1959 (2); *v A 1958 (1); v NZ 1958 (2); v In 1963 (3)*
Moss (A. E.) 9: v A 1956 (1); v SA 1960 (2); v In 1959 (3); *v WI 1953 (1) 1959 (2)*
Moxon, M. D. 2: v NZ 1986 (2)
Murdoch, W. L. 1: *v SA 1891*
Murray, J. T. 21: v A 1961 (5); v WI 1966 (1); v In 1967 (3); v P 1962 (3) 1967 (1); *v A 1962 (1); v SA 1964 (1); v NZ 1962 (1) 1965 (1); v In 1961 (3); v P 1961 (1)*

Newham (W.) 1: *v A 1887*
Nichols (M. S.) 14: v A 1930 (1); v SA 1935 (4); v WI 1933 (1) 1939 (1); *v NZ 1929 (4); v In 1933 (3)*

Oakman (A. S. M.) 2: v A 1956 (2)
O'Brien, T. C. 5: v A 1884 (1) 1888 (1); *v SA 1895 (3)*
O'Connor (J.) 4: v SA 1929 (1); *v WI 1929 (3)*
Old, C. M. 46: v A 1975 (3) 1977 (2) 1980 (1) 1981 (2); v WI 1973 (1) 1976 (2) 1980 (1); v NZ 1973 (2) 1978 (1); v In 1974 (3); v P 1974 (3) 1978 (3); *v A 1974 (2) 1976 (1) 1978 (1); v WI 1973 (4) 1980 (1); v NZ 1974 (1) 1977 (2); v In 1972 (4) 1976 (4); v P 1972 (1) 1977 (1)*
Oldfield (N.) 1: v WI 1939

Padgett (D. E. V.) 2: v SA 1960 (2)
Paine (G. A. E.) 4: *v WI 1934 (4)*
Palairet, L. C. H. 2: v A 1902 (2)
Palmer, C. H. 1: *v WI 1953*
Palmer, K. E. 1: *v SA 1964*
Parfitt (P. H.) 37: v A 1964 (4) 1972 (3); v SA 1965 (2); v WI 1969 (1); v NZ 1965 (2); v P 1962 (5); *v A 1962 (2); v SA 1964 (5); v NZ 1962 (3) 1965 (3); v In 1961 (2) 1963 (3); v P 1961 (2)*

Parker (C. W. L.) 1: v A 1921

Parker, P. W. G. 1: v A 1981

Parkhouse (W. G. A.) 7: v WI 1950 (2); v In 1959 (2); *v A 1950 (2); v NZ 1950 (1)*

Parkin (C. H.) 10: v A 1921 (4); v SA 1924 (1); *v A 1920 (5)*

Parks (J. H.) 1: v NZ 1937

Parks (J. M.) 46: v A 1964 (5); v SA 1960 (5) 1965 (3); v WI 1963 (4) 1966 (4); v NZ 1965 (3); v P 1954 (1); *v A 1965 (5); v SA 1964 (5); v WI 1959 (1) 1967 (3); v NZ 1965 (2); v In 1963 (5)*

Pataudi, Nawab of, 3: v A 1934 (1); *v A 1932 (2)*

Paynter (E.) 20: v A 1938 (4); v WI 1939 (2); v NZ 1931 (1) 1937 (2); v In 1932 (1); *v A 1932 (3); v SA 1938 (5); v NZ 1932 (2)*

Peate (E.) 9: v A 1882 (1) 1884 (3) 1886 (1); *v A 1881 (4)*

Peebles, I. A. R. 13: v A 1930 (2); v NZ 1931 (3); *v SA 1927 (4) 1930 (4)*

Peel (R.) 20: v A 1888 (3) 1890 (1) 1893 (1) 1896 (1); *v A 1884 (5) 1887 (1) 1891 (3) 1894 (5)*

Penn, F. 1: v A 1880

Perks (R. T. D.) 2: v WI 1939 (1); *v SA 1938 (1)*

Philipson, (H.) 5: *v A 1891 (1) 1894 (4)*

Pigott, A. C. S. 1: *v NZ 1983*

Pilling (R.) 8: v A 1884 (1) 1886 (1) 1888 (1); *v A 1881 (4) 1887 (1)*

Place (W.) 3: *v WI 1947 (3)*

Pocock, P. I. 25: v A 1968 (1); v WI 1976 (2) 1984 (2); v SL 1984 (1); *v WI 1967 (2) 1973 (4); v In 1972 (4) 1984 (5); v P 1968 (1) 1972 (3)*

Pollard (R.) 4: v A 1948 (2); v In 1946 (1); *v NZ 1946 (1)*

Poole (C. J.) 3: *v In 1951 (3)*

Pope (G. H.) 1: v SA 1947

Pougher (A. D.) 1: *v SA 1891*

Price, J. S. E. 15: v A 1964 (2) 1972 (1); v In 1971 (3); v P 1971 (1); *v SA 1964 (4); v In 1963 (4)*

Price (W. F. F.) 1: v A 1938

Prideaux, R. M. 3: v A 1968 (1); *v P 1968 (2)*

Pringle, D. R. 14: v WI 1984 (3); v NZ 1986 (1); v In 1982 (3) 1986 (3); v P 1982 (1); *v A 1982 (2)*

Pullar (G.) 28: v A 1961 (5); v SA 1960 (3); v In 1959 (3); v P 1962 (2); *v A 1962 (4); v WI 1959 (5); v In 1961 (3); v P 1961 (3)*

Quaife (Wm) 7: v A 1899 (2); *v A 1901 (5)*

Radford, N. V. 2: v NZ 1986 (1); v In 1986 (1)

Radley, C. T. 8: v NZ 1978 (3); v P 1978 (3); *v NZ 1977 (2)*

Randall, D. W. 47: v A 1977 (5); v WI 1984 (1); v NZ 1983 (3); v In 1979 (3) 1982 (3); v P 1982 (3); *v A 1976 (1) 1978 (6) 1979 (2) 1982 (4); v NZ 1977 (3) 1983 (3); v In 1976 (4); v P 1977 (3) 1983 (3)*

Ranjitsinhji, K. S. 15: v A 1896 (2) 1899 (5) 1902 (3); *v A 1897 (5)*

Read, H. D. 1: v SA 1935

Read (J. M.) 17: v A 1882 (1) 1890 (2) 1893 (1); *v A 1884 (5) 1886 (2) 1887 (1) 1891 (3); v SA 1888 (2)*

Read, W. W. 18: v A 1884 (2) 1886 (3) 1888 (3) 1890 (2) 1893 (2); *v A 1882 (4) 1887 (1); v SA 1891 (1)*

Relf (A. E.) 13: v A 1909 (1); *v A 1903 (2); v SA 1905 (5) 1913 (5)*

Rhodes (H. J.) 2: v In 1959 (2)

Rhodes (W.) 58: v A 1899 (3) 1902 (5) 1905 (4) 1909 (4) 1912 (3) 1921 (1) 1926 (1); v SA 1912 (3); *v A 1903 (5) 1907 (5) 1911 (5) 1920 (5); v SA 1909 (5) 1913 (5); v WI 1929 (4)*

Richardson (D. W.) 1: v WI 1957

Richardson (P. E.) 34: v A 1956 (5); v WI 1957 (5) 1963 (1); v NZ 1958 (4); *v A 1958 (4); v SA 1956 (5); v NZ 1958 (2); v In 1961 (5); v P 1961 (3)*

Richardson (T.) 14: v A 1893 (1) 1896 (3); *v A 1894 (5) 1897 (5)*

Richmond (T. L.) 1: v A 1921

Ridgway (F.) 5: *v In 1951 (5)*

Robertson (J. D.) 11: v SA 1947 (1); v NZ 1949 (1); *v WI 1947 (4); v In 1951 (5)*

Robins, R. W. V. 19: v A 1930 (2); v SA 1929 (1) 1935 (3); v WI 1933 (2); v NZ 1931 (1) 1937 (3); v In 1932 (1) 1936 (2); *v A 1936 (4)*

Robinson, R. T. 16: v A 1985 (6); v In 1986 (1); *v WI 1985 (4); v In 1984 (5)*

Roope, G. R. J. 21: v A 1975 (1) 1977 (2); v WI 1973 (1); v NZ 1973 (3) 1978 (1); v P 1978 (3); *v NZ 1977 (3); v In 1972 (2) 1977 (3)*

Root (C. F.) 3: v A 1926 (3)

Rose, B. C. 9: v WI 1980 (3); *v WI 1980 (1); v NZ 1977 (2); v P 1977 (3)*
Royle, V. P. F. A. 1: *v A 1878*
Rumsey, F. E. 5: v A 1964 (1); v SA 1965 (1); v NZ 1965 (3)
Russell (A. C.) 10: v A 1921 (2); *v A 1920 (4); v SA 1922 (4)*
Russell, W. E. 10: v SA 1965 (1); v WI 1966 (2); v P 1967 (1); *v A 1965 (1); v NZ 1965 (3); v In 1961 (1); v P 1961 (1)*

Sandham (A.) 14: v A 1921 (1); v SA 1924 (2); *v A 1924 (2); v SA 1922 (5); v WI 1929 (4)*
Schultz, S. S. 1: *v A 1878*
Scotton (W. H.) 15: v A 1884 (1) 1886 (3); *v A 1881 (4) 1884 (5) 1886 (2)*
Selby (J.) 6: *v A 1876 (2) 1881 (4)*
Selvey, M. W. W. 3: v WI 1976 (2); *v In 1976 (1)*
Shackleton (D.) 7: v SA 1951 (1); v WI 1950 (1) 1963 (4); *v In 1951 (1)*
Sharp (J.) 3: v A 1909 (3)
Sharpe (J. W.) 3: v A 1890 (1); *v A 1891 (2)*
Sharpe, P. J. 12: v A 1964 (2); v WI 1963 (3) 1969 (3); v NZ 1969 (3); *v In 1963 (1)*
Shaw (A.) 7: v A 1880 (1); *v A 1876 (2) 1881 (4)*
Sheppard, Rev. D. S. 22: v A 1956 (2); v WI 1950 (1) 1957 (2); v In 1952 (2); v P 1954 (2) 1962 (2); *v A 1950 (2) 1962 (5); v NZ 1950 (1) 1963 (3)*
Sherwin (M.) 3: v A 1888 (1); *v A 1886 (2)*
Shrewsbury (A.) 23: v A 1884 (2) 1886 (3) 1890 (2) 1893 (3); *v A 1881 (4) 1884 (5) 1886 (2) 1887 (1)*
Shuter, J. 1: v A 1888
Shuttleworth, K. 5: v P 1971 (1); *v A 1970 (2); v NZ 1970 (2)*
Sidebottom, A. 1: v A 1985
Simpson, R. T. 27: v A 1953 (3); v SA 1951 (3); v WI 1950 (3); v NZ 1949 (3); v In 1952 (2); v P 1954 (3); *v A 1950 (5) 1954 (1); v SA 1948 (1); v NZ 1950 (2) 1954 (2)*
Simpson-Hayward, G. H. 5: *v SA 1909 (5)*
Sims (J. M.) 4: v SA 1935 (1); v In 1936 (1); *v A 1936 (2)*
Sinfield (R. A.) 1: v A 1938
Slack, W. N. 3: v In 1986 (1); *v WI 1985 (2)*
Smailes (T. F.) 1: v In 1946
Small, G. C. 2: v NZ 1986 (2)
Smith, A. C. 6: *v A 1962 (4); v NZ 1962 (2)*
Smith, C. A. 1: *v SA 1888*
Smith (C. I. J.) 5: v NZ 1937 (1); *v WI 1934 (4)*
Smith, C. L. 8: v NZ 1983 (2); v In 1986 (1); *v NZ 1983 (2); v P 1983 (3)*
Smith (D.) 2: v SA 1935 (2)
Smith (D. R.) 5: *v In 1961 (5)*
Smith (D. V.) 3: v WI 1957 (3)
Smith (E. J.) 11: v A 1912 (3); v SA 1912 (3); *v A 1911 (4); v SA 1913 (1)*
Smith (H.) 1: v WI 1928
Smith, M. J. K. 50: v A 1961 (1) 1972 (3); v SA 1960 (4) 1965 (3); v WI 1966 (1); v NZ 1958 (3) 1965 (3); v In 1959 (2); *v A 1965 (5); v SA 1964 (5); v WI 1959 (5); v NZ 1965 (3); v In 1961 (4) 1963 (5); v P 1961 (3)*
Smith (T. P. B.) 4: v In 1946 (1); *v A 1946 (2); v NZ 1946 (1)*
Smithson (G. A.) 2: *v WI 1947 (2)*
Snow, J. A. 49: v A 1968 (5) 1972 (5) 1975 (4); v SA 1965 (1); v WI 1966 (3) 1969 (3) 1973 (1) 1976 (3); v NZ 1965 (1) 1969 (2) 1973 (3); v In 1967 (3) 1971 (2); v P 1967 (1); *v A 1970 (6); v WI 1967 (4); v P 1968 (2)*
Southerton (J.) 2: *v A 1876 (2)*
Spooner, R. H. 10: v A 1905 (2) 1909 (2) 1912 (3); v SA 1912 (3)
Spooner (R. T.) 7: v SA 1955 (1); *v In 1951 (5); v WI 1953 (1)*
Stanyforth, R. T. 4: *v SA 1927 (4)*
Staples (S. J.) 3: *v SA 1927 (3)*
Statham (J. B.) 70: v A 1953 (1) 1956 (3) 1961 (4); v SA 1951 (2) 1955 (4) 1960 (5) 1965 (1); v WI 1957 (3) 1963 (2); v NZ 1958 (2); v In 1959 (3); v P 1954 (4) 1962 (3); *v A 1954 (5) 1958 (4) 1962 (5); v SA 1956 (4); v WI 1953 (4) 1959 (3); v NZ 1950 (1) 1954 (2); v In 1951 (5)*
Steel, A. G. 13: v A 1880 (1) 1882 (1) 1884 (3) 1886 (3) 1888 (3); *v A 1882 (4)*
Steele, D. S. 8: v A 1975 (3); v WI 1976 (5)
Stevens, G. T. S. 10: v A 1926 (2); *v SA 1922 (1) 1927 (5); v WI 1929 (4)*
Stevenson, G. B. 2: *v WI 1980 (1); v In 1979 (1)*

Stewart (M. J.) 8: v WI 1963 (4); v P 1962 (2); *v In 1963* (2)
Stoddart, A. E. 16: v A 1893 (3) 1896 (2); *v A 1887 (1) 1891 (3) 1894 (5) 1897* (2)
Storer (W.) 6: v A 1899 (1); *v A 1897* (5)
Street (G. B.) 1: *v SA 1922*
Strudwick (H.) 28: v A 1921 (2) 1926 (5); v SA 1924 (1); *v A 1911 (1) 1920 (4) 1924 (5); v SA 1909 (5) 1913* (5)
Studd, C. T. 5: v A 1882 (1); *v A 1882* (4)
Studd, G. B. 4: *v A 1882* (4)
Subba Row, R. 13: v A 1961 (5); v SA 1960 (4); v NZ 1958 (1); v In 1959 (1); *v WI 1959* (2)
Sugg (F. H.) 2: v A 1888 (2)
Sutcliffe (H.) 54: v A 1926 (5) 1930 (4) 1934 (4); v SA 1924 (5) 1929 (5) 1935 (2); v WI 1928 (3) 1933 (2); v NZ 1931 (2); v In 1932 (1); *v A 1924 (5) 1928 (4) 1932 (5); v SA 1927 (5); v NZ 1932* (2)
Swetman (R.) 11: v In 1959 (3); *v A 1958 (2); v WI 1959 (4); v NZ 1958* (2)

Tate (F. W.) 1: v A 1902
Tate (M. W.) 39: v A 1926 (5) 1930 (5); v SA 1924 (5) 1929 (3) 1935 (1); v WI 1928 (3); v NZ 1931 (1); *v A 1924 (5) 1928 (5); v SA 1930 (5); v NZ 1932 (1)*
Tattersall (R.) 16: v A 1953 (1); v SA 1951 (5); v P 1954 (1); *v A 1950 (2); v NZ 1950 (2); v In 1951* (5)
Tavaré, C. J. 30: v A 1981 (2); v WI 1980 (2) 1984 (1); v NZ 1983 (4); v In 1982 (3); v P 1982 (3); v SL 1984 (1); *v A 1982 (5); v NZ 1983 (2); v In 1981 (6); v SL 1981 (1)*
Taylor (K.) 3: v A 1964 (1); v In 1959 (2)
Taylor, L. B. 2: v A 1985 (2)
Taylor, R. W. 57: v A 1981 (3); v NZ 1978 (3) 1983 (4); v In 1979 (3) 1982 (3); v P 1978 (3) 1982 (3); *v A 1978 (6) 1979 (3) 1982 (5); v NZ 1970 (1) 1977 (3) 1983 (3); v In 1979 (1) 1981 (6); v P 1977 (3) 1983 (3); v SL 1981 (1)*
Tennyson, Hon. L. H. 9: v A 1921 (4); *v SA 1913* (5)
Terry, V. P. 2: v WI 1984 (2)
Thomas, J. G. 5: v NZ 1986 (1); *v WI 1985* (4)
Thompson (G. J.) 6: v A 1909 (1); *v SA 1909* (5)
Thomson, N. I. 5: *v SA 1964* (5)
Titmus (F. J.) 53: v A 1964 (5); v SA 1955 (2) 1965 (3); v WI 1963 (4) 1966 (3); v NZ 1965 (3); v P 1962 (2) 1967 (2); *v A 1962 (5) 1965 (5) 1974 (4); v SA 1964 (5); v WI 1967 (2); v NZ 1962 (3); v In 1963* (5)
Tolchard, R. W. 4: *v In 1976* (4)
Townsend, C. L. 2: v A 1899 (2)
Townsend, D. C. H. 3: *v WI 1934* (3)
Townsend (L. F.) 4: *v WI 1929 (1); v In 1933* (3)
Tremlett (M. F.) 3: *v WI 1947* (3)
Trott (A. E.) 2: *v SA 1898* (2)
Trueman (F. S.) 67: v A 1953 (1) 1956 (2) 1961 (4) 1964 (4); v SA 1955 (1) 1960 (5); v WI 1957 (5) 1963 (5); v NZ 1958 (5) 1965 (2); v In 1952 (4) 1959 (5); v P 1962 (4); *v A 1958 (3) 1962 (5); v WI 1953 (3) 1959 (5); v NZ 1958 (2) 1962 (2)*
Tufnell, N. C. 1: *v SA 1909*
Turnbull, M. J. 9: v WI 1933 (2); v In 1936 (1); *v SA 1930 (5); v NZ 1929 (1)*
Tyldesley (E.) 14: v A 1921 (3) 1926 (1); v SA 1924 (1); v WI 1928 (3); *v A 1928 (1); v SA 1927* (5)
Tyldesley (J. T.) 31: v A 1899 (2) 1902 (5) 1905 (5) 1909 (4); v SA 1907 (3); *v A 1901 (5) 1903 (5); v SA 1898* (2)
Tyldesley (R. K.) 7: v A 1930 (2); v SA 1924 (4); *v A 1924 (1)*
Tylecote, E. F. S. 6: v A 1886 (2); *v A 1882* (4)
Tyler (E. J.) 1: *v SA 1895*
Tyson (F. H.) 17: v A 1956 (1); v SA 1955 (2); v P 1954 (1); *v A 1954 (5) 1958 (2); v SA 1956 (2); v NZ 1954 (2) 1958* (2)

Ulyett (G.) 25: v A 1882 (1) 1884 (3) 1886 (3) 1888 (2) 1890 (1); *v A 1876 (2) 1878 (1) 1881 (4) 1884 (5) 1887 (1); v SA 1888* (2)
Underwood, D. L. 86: v A 1968 (4) 1972 (2) 1975 (4) 1977 (5); v WI 1966 (2) 1969 (2) 1973 (3) 1976 (5) 1980 (1); v NZ 1969 (3) 1973 (1); v In 1971 (1) 1974 (3); v P 1967 (2) 1971 (1) 1974 (3); *v A 1970 (5) 1974 (5) 1976 (1) 1979 (3); v WI 1973 (4); v NZ 1970 (2) 1974 (2); v In 1972 (4) 1976 (5) 1979 (1) 1981 (6); v P 1968 (3) 1972 (2); v SL 1981 (1)*

Valentine, B. H. 7: *v SA 1938 (5); v In 1933* (2)
Verity (H.) 40: v A 1934 (5) 1938 (4); v SA 1935 (4); v WI 1933 (2) 1939 (1); v NZ 1931 (2) 1937 (1); v In 1936 (3); *v A 1932 (4) 1936 (5); v SA 1938 (5); v NZ 1932 (1); v In 1933* (3)
Vernon, G. F. 1: *v A 1882*
Vine (J.) 2: *v A 1911* (2)
Voce (W.) 27: v NZ 1931 (1) 1937 (1); v In 1932 (1) 1936 (1) 1946 (1); *v A 1932 (4) 1936 (5) 1946 (2); v SA 1930 (5); v WI 1929 (4); v NZ 1932* (2)

Waddington (A.) 2: *v A 1920* (2)
Wainwright (E.) 5: v A 1893 (1); *v A 1897* (4)
Walker (P. M.) 3: v SA 1960 (3)
Walters, C. F. 11: v A 1934 (5); v WI 1933 (3); *v In 1933* (3)
Ward (A.) 7: v A 1893 (2); *v A 1894* (5)
Wardle (J. H.) 28: v A 1953 (3) 1956 (1); v SA 1951 (2) 1955 (3); v WI 1950 (1) 1957 (1); v P 1954 (4); *v A 1954 (4); v SA 1956 (4); v WI 1947 (1) 1953 (2); v NZ 1954* (2)
Warner, P. F. 15: v A 1909 (1) 1912 (1); v SA 1912 (1); *v A 1903 (5); v SA 1898 (2) 1905* (5)
Warr, J. J. 2: *v A 1950* (2)
Warren (A. R.) 1: v A 1905
Washbrook (C.) 37: v A 1948 (4) 1956 (3); v SA 1947 (5); v WI 1950 (2); v NZ 1937 (1) 1949 (2); v In 1946 (3); *v A 1946 (5) 1950 (5); v SA 1948 (5); v NZ 1946 (1) 1950* (1)
Watkins (A. J.) 15: v A 1948 (1); v NZ 1949 (1); v In 1952 (3); *v SA 1948 (5); v In 1951* (5)
Watson (W.) 23: v A 1953 (3) 1956 (2); v SA 1951 (2) 1955 (1); v NZ 1958 (2); v In 1952 (1); *v A 1958 (2); v WI 1953 (5); v NZ 1958* (2)
Webbe, A. J. 1: *v A 1878*
Wellard (A. W.) 2: v A 1938 (1); v NZ 1937 (1)
Wharton (A.) 1: v NZ 1949
White (D. W.) 2: *v P 1961* (2)
White, J. C. 15: v A 1921 (1) 1930 (1); v SA 1929 (3); v WI 1928 (1); *v A 1928 (5); v SA 1930* (4)
Whysall (W. W.) 4: *v A 1930* (1); *v A 1924* (3)
Wilkinson (L. L.) 3: *v SA 1938* (3)
Willey, P. 26: v A 1980 (1) 1981 (4) 1985 (1); v WI 1976 (2) 1980 (5); v NZ 1986 (1); v In 1979 (1); *v A 1979 (3); v WI 1980 (4) 1985* (4)
Willis, R. G. D. 90: v A 1977 (5) 1981 (6); v WI 1973 (1) 1976 (2) 1980 (4) 1984 (3); v NZ 1978 (3) 1983 (4); v In 1974 (1) 1979 (3) 1982 (3); v P 1974 (1) 1978 (3) 1982 (2); *v A 1970 (4) 1974 (5) 1976 (1) 1978 (6) 1979 (3) 1982 (5); v WI 1973 (3); v NZ 1970 (1) 1977 (3) 1983 (3); v In 1976 (5) 1981 (5); v P 1977 (3) 1983 (1); v SL 1981* (1)
Wilson, C. E. M. 2: *v SA 1898* (2)
Wilson, D. 6: *v NZ 1970 (1); v In 1963* (5)
Wilson, E. R. 1: *v A 1920*
Wood (A.) 4: v A 1938 (1); v WI 1939 (3)
Wood, B. 12: v A 1972 (1) 1975 (3); v WI 1976 (1); v P 1978 (1); *v NZ 1974 (2); v In 1972 (3); v P 1972* (1)
Wood, G. E. C. 3: v SA 1924 (3)
Wood (H.) 4: v A 1888 (1); *v SA 1888 (2) 1891* (1)
Wood (R.) 1: *v A 1886*
Woods S. M. J. 3: *v SA 1895* (3)
Woolley (F. E.) 64: v A 1909 (1) 1912 (3) 1921 (5) 1926 (5) 1930 (2) 1934 (1); v SA 1912 (3) 1924 (5) 1929 (3); v NZ 1931 (1); v In 1932 (1); *v A 1911 (5) 1920 (5) 1924 (5); v SA 1909 (5) 1913 (5) 1922 (5); v NZ 1929* (4)
Woolmer, R. A. 19: v A 1975 (2) 1977 (5) 1981 (2); v WI 1976 (5) 1980 (2); *v A 1976 (1); v In 1976* (2)
Worthington (T. S.) 9: v In 1936 (2); *v A 1936 (3); v NZ 1929* (4)
Wright, C. W. 3: *v SA 1895* (3)
Wright (D. V. P.) 34: v A 1938 (3) 1948 (1); v SA 1947 (4); v WI 1939 (3) 1950 (1); v NZ 1949 (1); v In 1946 (2); *v A 1946 (5) 1950 (5); v SA 1938 (3) 1948 (3); v NZ 1946* (1)
Wyatt, R. E. S. 40: v A 1930 (1) 1934 (4); v SA 1929 (2) 1935 (5); v WI 1933 (2); v In 1936 (1); *v A 1932 (5) 1936 (2); v SA 1927 (5) 1930 (5); v WI 1929 (2) 1934 (4); v NZ 1932* (2)
Wynyard, E. G. 3: v A 1896 (1); *v SA 1905* (2)

Yardley, N. W. D. 20: v A 1948 (5); v SA 1947 (5); v WI 1950 (3); *v A 1946 (5); v SA 1938 (1); v NZ 1946* (1)

Young (H. I.) 2: v A 1899 (2)
Young (J. A.) 8: v A 1948 (3); v SA 1947 (1); v NZ 1949 (2); *v SA 1948 (2)*
Young, R. A. 2: *v A 1907 (2)*

AUSTRALIA

Number of Test cricketers: 337

A'Beckett, E. L. 4: v E 1928 (2); v SA 1931 (1); *v E 1930 (1)*
Alderman, T. M. 22: v E 1982 (1); v WI 1981 (2) 1984 (3); v P 1981 (3); *v E 1981 (6); v WI 1983 (3); v NZ 1981 (3); v P 1982 (1)*
Alexander, G. 2: v E 1884 (1); *v E 1880 (1)*
Alexander, H. H. 1 : v E 1932
Allan, F. E. 1: v E 1878
Allan, P. J. 1: v E 1965
Allen, R. C. 1: v E 1886
Andrews, T. J. E. 16: v E 1924 (3); *v E 1921 (5) 1926 (5); v SA 1921 (3)*
Archer, K. A. 5: v E 1950 (3); v WI 1951 (2)
Archer, R. G. 19: v E 1954 (4); v SA 1952 (1); *v E 1953 (3) 1956 (5); v WI 1954 (5); v P 1956 (1)*
Armstrong, W. W. 50: v E 1901 (4) 1903 (5) 1907 (5) 1911 (5) 1920 (5); v SA 1910 (5); *v E 1902 (5) 1905 (5) 1909 (5) 1921 (5); v SA 1902 (3)*

Badcock, C. L. 7: v E 1936 (3); *v E 1938 (4)*
Bannerman, A. C. 28: v E 1878 (1) 1881 (3) 1882 (4) 1884 (4) 1886 (1) 1887 (1) 1891 (3); *v E 1880 (1) 1882 (1) 1884 (3) 1888 (3) 1893 (3)*
Bannerman, C. 3: v E 1876 (2) 1878 (1)
Bardsley, W. 41: v E 1911 (4) 1920 (5) 1924 (3); v SA 1910 (5); *v E 1909 (5) 1912 (3) 1921 (5) 1926 (5); v SA 1912 (3) 1921 (3)*
Barnes, S. G. 13: v E 1946 (4); v In 1947 (3); *v E 1938 (1) 1948 (4); v NZ 1945 (1)*
Barnett, B. A. 4: *v E 1938 (4)*
Barrett, J. E. 2: *v E 1890 (2)*
Beard, G. R. 3: *v P 1979 (3)*
Benaud, J. 3: v P 1972 (2); *v WI 1972 (1)*
Benaud, R. 63: v E 1954 (5) 1958 (5) 1962 (5); v SA 1952 (1) 1963 (4); v WI 1951 (1) 1960 (5); *v E 1953 (3) 1956 (5) 1961 (4); v SA 1957 (5); v WI 1954 (5); v In 1956 (3) 1959 (5); v P 1956 (1) 1959 (3)*
Bennett, M. J. 3: v WI 1984 (2); *v E 1985 (1)*
Blackham, J. McC. 35: v E 1876 (2) 1878 (1) 1881 (4) 1882 (4) 1884 (2) 1886 (1) 1887 (1) 1891 (3) 1894 (1); *v E 1880 (1) 1882 (1) 1884 (3) 1886 (3) 1888 (3) 1890 (2) 1893 (3)*
Blackie, D. D. 3: v E 1928 (3)
Bonnor, G. J. 17: v E 1882 (4) 1884 (3); *v E 1880 (1) 1882 (1) 1884 (3) 1886 (2) 1888 (3)*
Boon, D. C. 16: v WI 1984 (3); v NZ 1985 (3); v In 1985 (3); *v E 1985 (4); v NZ 1985 (3)*
Booth, B. C. 29: v E 1962 (5) 1965 (3); v SA 1963 (4); v P 1964 (1); *v E 1961 (2) 1964 (5); v WI 1964 (5); v In 1964 (3); v P 1964 (1)*
Border, A. R. 81: v E 1978 (3) 1979 (3) 1982 (5); v WI 1979 (3) 1981 (3) 1984 (5); v NZ 1980 (3) 1985 (3); v In 1980 (3) 1985 (3); v P 1978 (2) 1981 (3) 1983 (5); *v E 1980 (1) 1981 (6) 1985 (6); v WI 1983 (3); v NZ 1981 (3) 1985 (3); v In 1979 (6); v P 1979 (3) 1982 (3); v SL 1982 (1)*
Boyle, H. F. 12: v E 1878 (1) 1881 (4) 1882 (1) 1884 (1); *v E 1880 (1) 1882 (1) 1884 (3)*
Bradman, D. G. 52: v E 1928 (4) 1932 (4) 1936 (5) 1946 (5); v SA 1931 (5); v WI 1930 (5); v In 1947 (5); *v E 1930 (5) 1934 (5) 1938 (4) 1948 (5)*
Bright, R. J. 22: v E 1979 (1); v WI 1979 (1); v NZ 1985 (1); v In 1985 (3); *v E 1977 (3) 1980 (1) 1981 (5); v NZ 1985 (2); v P 1979 (3) 1982 (2)*
Bromley, E. H. 2: v E 1932 (1); *v E 1934 (1)*
Brown, W. A. 22: v E 1936 (2); v In 1947 (3); *v E 1934 (5) 1938 (4) 1948 (2); v SA 1935 (5); v NZ 1945 (1)*
Bruce, W. 14: v E 1884 (2) 1891 (3) 1894 (4); *v E 1886 (2) 1893 (3)*
Burge, P. J. 42: v E 1954 (1) 1958 (1) 1962 (3) 1965 (4); v WI 1960 (2); *v E 1956 (3) 1961 (5) 1964 (5); v SA 1957 (1); v WI 1954 (1); v In 1956 (3) 1959 (2) 1964 (3); v P 1959 (2) 1964 (1)*
Burke, J. W. 24: v E 1950 (2) 1954 (2) 1958 (5); v WI 1951 (1); *v E 1956 (5); v SA 1957 (5); v In 1956 (3); v P 1956 (1)*

Burn, K. E. 2: *v E 1890 (2)*
Burton, F. J. 2: v E 1886 (1) 1887 (1)

Callaway, S. T. 3: v E 1891 (2) 1894 (1)
Callen, I. W. 1: v In 1977
Carkeek, W. 6: *v E 1912 (3); v SA 1912 (3)*
Carlson, P. H. 2: v E 1978 (2)
Carter, H. 28: v E 1907 (5) 1911 (5) 1920 (2); v SA 1910 (5); *v E 1909 (5) 1921 (4); v SA 1921 (2)*
Chappell, G. S. 87: v E 1970 (5) 1974 (6) 1976 (1) 1979 (3) 1982 (5); v WI 1975 (6) 1979 (3) 1981 (3); v NZ 1973 (3) 1980 (3); v In 1980 (3); v P 1972 (3) 1976 (3) 1981 (3) 1983 (5); *v E 1972 (5) 1975 (4) 1977 (5) 1980 (1); v WI 1972 (5); v NZ 1973 (3) 1976 (2) 1981 (3); v P 1979 (3); v SL 1982 (1)*
Chappell, I. M. 75: v E 1965 (2) 1970 (6) 1974 (6) 1979 (2); v WI 1968 (5) 1975 (6) 1979 (1); v NZ 1973 (3); v In 1967 (4); v P 1964 (1) 1972 (3); *v E 1968 (5) 1972 (5) 1975 (4); v SA 1966 (5) 1969 (4); v WI 1972 (5); v NZ 1973 (3); v In 1969 (5)*
Chappell, T. M. 3: *v E 1981 (3)*
Charlton, P. C. 2: *v E 1890 (2)*
Chipperfield, A. G. 14: v E 1936 (3); *v E 1934 (5) 1938 (1); v SA 1935 (5)*
Clark, W. M. 10: v In 1977 (5); v P 1978 (1); *v WI 1977 (4)*
Colley, D. J. 3: *v E 1972 (3)*
Collins, H. L. 19: v E 1920 (5) 1924 (5); *v E 1921 (3) 1926 (3); v SA 1921 (3)*
Coningham, A. 1: v E 1894
Connolly, A. N. 29: v E 1965 (1) 1970 (1); v SA 1963 (3); v WI 1968 (5); v In 1967 (3); *v E 1968 (5); v SA 1969 (4); v In 1964 (2); 1969 (5)*
Cooper, B. B. 1: v E 1876
Cooper, W. H. 2: v E 1881 (1) 1884 (1)
Corling, G. E. 5: *v E 1964 (5)*
Cosier, G. J. 18: v E 1976 (1) 1978 (2); v WI 1975 (3); v In 1977 (4); v P 1976 (3); *v WI 1977 (3); v NZ 1976 (2)*
Cottam, W. J. 1: v E 1886
Cotter, A. 21: v E 1903 (2) 1907 (2) 1911 (4); v SA 1910 (5); *v E 1905 (3) 1909 (5)*
Coultard, G. 1: v E 1881
Cowper, R. M. 27: v E 1965 (4); v In 1967 (4); v P 1964 (1); *v E 1964 (1) 1968 (4); v SA 1966 (5); v WI 1964 (5); v In 1964 (2); v P 1964 (1)*
Craig, I. D. 11: v SA 1952 (1); *v E 1956 (2); v SA 1957 (5); v In 1956 (2); v P 1956 (1)*
Crawford, W. P. A. 4: *v E 1956 (1); v In 1956 (3)*

Darling, J. 34: v E 1894 (5) 1897 (5) 1901 (3); *v E 1896 (3) 1899 (5) 1902 (5) 1905 (5); v SA 1902 (3)*
Darling, L. S. 12: v E 1932 (2) 1936 (1); *v E 1934 (4); v SA 1935 (5)*
Darling, W. M. 14: v E 1978 (4); v In 1977 (1); v P 1978 (1); *v WI 1977 (3); v In 1979 (5)*
Davidson, A. K. 44: v E 1954 (3) 1958 (5) 1962 (5); v WI 1960 (4); *v E 1953 (5) 1956 (2) 1961 (5); v SA 1957 (5); v In 1956 (1) 1959 (5); v P 1956 (1) 1959 (3)*
Davis, I. C. 15: v E 1976 (1); v NZ 1973 (3); v P 1976 (3); *v E 1977 (3); v NZ 1973 (3) 1976 (2)*
Davis, S. P. 1: *v NZ 1985*
De Courcy, J. H. 3: *v E 1953 (3)*
Dell, A. R. 2: v E 1970 (1); v NZ 1973 (1)
Donnan, H. 5: v E 1891 (2); *v E 1896 (3)*
Dooland, B. 3: v E 1946 (2); v In 1947 (1)
Duff, R. A. 22: v E 1901 (4) 1903 (5); *v E 1902 (5) 1905 (5); v SA 1902 (3)*
Duncan, J. R. F. 1: v E 1970
Dymock, G. 21: v E 1974 (1) 1978 (3) 1979 (3); v WI 1979 (2); v NZ 1973 (1); v P 1978 (1); *v NZ 1973 (2); v In 1979 (5); v P 1979 (3)*
Dyson, J. 30: v E 1982 (5); v WI 1981 (2) 1984 (3); v NZ 1980 (3); v In 1977 (3) 1980 (3); *v E 1981 (5); v NZ 1981 (3); v P 1982 (3)*

Eady, C. J. 2: v E 1901 (1); *v E 1896 (1)*
Eastwood, K. H. 1: v E 1970
Ebeling, H. I. 1: *v E 1934*
Edwards, J. D. 3: *v E 1888 (3)*
Edwards, R. 20: v E 1974 (5); v P 1972 (2); *v E 1972 (4) 1975 (4); v WI 1972 (5)*
Edwards, W. J. 3: v E 1974 (3)
Emery, S. H. 4: *v E 1912 (2); v SA 1912 (2)*

Evans, E. 6: v E 1881 (2) 1882 (1) 1884 (1); *v E 1886 (2)*

Fairfax, A. G. 10: v E 1928 (1); v WI 1930 (5); *v E 1930 (4)*
Favell, L. E. 19: v E 1954 (4) 1958 (2); v WI 1960 (4); *v WI 1954 (2); v In 1959 (4); v P 1959 (3)*
Ferris, J. J. 8: v E 1886 (2) 1887 (1); *v E 1888 (3) 1890 (2)*
Fingleton, J. H. 18: v E 1932 (3) 1936 (5); v SA 1931 (1); *v E 1938 (4); v SA 1935 (5)*
Fleetwood-Smith, L. O'B. 10: v E 1936 (3); *v E 1938 (4); v SA 1935 (3)*
Francis, B. C. 3: *v E 1972 (3)*
Freeman, E. W. 11: v WI 1968 (4); v In 1967 (2); *v E 1968 (2); v SA 1969 (2); v In 1969 (1)*
Freer, F. W. 1: v E 1946

Gannon, J. B. 3: v In 1977 (3)
Garrett, T. W. 19: v E 1876 (2) 1878 (1) 1881 (3) 1882 (3) 1884 (3) 1886 (2) 1887 (1); *v E 1882 (1) 1886 (3)*
Gaunt, R. A. 3: v SA 1963 (1); *v E 1961 (1); v SA 1957 (1)*
Gehrs, D. R. A. 6: v E 1903 (1); v SA 1910 (4); *v E 1905 (1)*
Giffen, G. 31: v E 1881 (3) 1882 (4) 1884 (3) 1891 (3) 1894 (5); *v E 1882 (1) 1884 (3) 1886 (3) 1893 (3) 1896 (3)*
Giffen, W. F. 3: v E 1886 (1) 1891 (2)
Gilbert, D. R. 7: v NZ 1985 (3); v In 1985 (2); *v E 1985 (1); v NZ 1985 (1)*
Gilmour, G. J. 15: v E 1976 (1); v WI 1975 (5); v NZ 1973 (2); v P 1976 (3); *v E 1975 (1); v NZ 1973 (1) 1976 (2)*
Gleeson, J. W. 29: v E 1970 (5); v WI 1968 (5); v In 1967 (4); *v E 1968 (5) 1972 (3); v SA 1969 (4); v In 1969 (3)*
Graham, H. 6: v E 1894 (2); *v E 1893 (3) 1896 (1)*
Gregory, D. W. 3: v E 1876 (2) 1878 (1)
Gregory, E. J. 1: v E 1876
Gregory, J. M. 24: v E 1920 (5) 1924 (5) 1928 (1); *v E 1921 (5) 1926 (5); v SA 1921 (3)*
Gregory, R. G. 2: v E 1936 (2)
Gregory, S. E. 58: v E 1891 (1) 1894 (5) 1897 (5) 1901 (5) 1903 (4) 1907 (2) 1911 (1); *v E 1890 (2) 1893 (3) 1896 (3) 1899 (5) 1902 (5) 1905 (3) 1909 (5) 1912 (3); v SA 1902 (3) 1912 (3)*
Grimmett, C. V. 37: v E 1924 (1) 1928 (5) 1932 (3); v SA 1931 (5); v WI 1930 (5); *v E 1926 (3) 1930 (5) 1934 (5); v SA 1935 (5)*
Groube, T. U. 1: *v E 1880*
Grout, A. T. W. 51: v E 1958 (5) 1962 (2) 1965 (5); v SA 1963 (5); v WI 1960 (5); *v E 1961 (5) 1964 (5); v SA 1957 (5); v WI 1964 (5); v In 1959 (4) 1964 (1); v P 1959 (3) 1964 (1)*
Guest, C. E. J. 1: v E 1962

Hamence, R. A. 3: v E 1946 (1); v In 1947 (2)
Hammond, J. R. 5: *v WI 1972 (5)*
Harry, J. 1: v E 1894
Hartigan, R. J. 2: v E 1907 (2)
Hartkopf, A. E. V. 1: v E 1924
Harvey, M. R. 1: v E 1946
Harvey, R. N. 79: v E 1950 (5) 1954 (5) 1958 (5) 1962 (5); v SA 1952 (5); v WI 1951 (5) 1960 (4); v In 1947 (2); *v E 1948 (2) 1953 (5) 1956 (5) 1961 (5); v SA 1949 (5) 1957 (4); v WI 1954 (5); v In 1956 (3) 1959 (5); v P 1956 (1) 1959 (3)*
Hassett, A. L. 43: v E 1946 (5) 1950 (5); v SA 1952 (5); v WI 1951 (4); v In 1947 (4); *v E 1938 (4) 1948 (5) 1953 (5); v SA 1949 (5); v NZ 1945 (1)*
Hawke, N. J. N. 27: v E 1962 (1) 1965 (4); v SA 1963 (4); v In 1967 (1); v P 1964 (1); *v E 1964 (5) 1968 (2); v SA 1966 (2); v WI 1964 (5); v In 1964 (1); v P 1964 (1)*
Hazlitt, G. R. 9: v E 1907 (2) 1911 (1); *v E 1912 (3); v SA 1912 (3)*
Hendry, H. L. 11: v E 1924 (1) 1928 (4); *v E 1921 (4); v SA 1921 (2)*
Hibbert, P. A. 1: v In 1977
Higgs, J. D. 22: v E 1978 (5) 1979 (1); v WI 1979 (1); v NZ 1980 (3); v In 1980 (2); *v WI 1977 (4); v In 1979 (6)*
Hilditch, A. M. J. 18: v E 1978 (1); v WI 1984 (2); v NZ 1985 (1); v P 1978 (2); *v E 1985 (6); v In 1979 (6)*
Hill, C. 49: v E 1897 (5) 1901 (5) 1903 (5) 1907 (5) 1911 (5); v SA 1910 (5); *v E 1896 (3) 1899 (3) 1902 (5) 1905 (5); v SA 1902 (3)*
Hill, J. C. 3: *v E 1953 (2); v WI 1954 (1)*
Hoare, D. E. 1: v WI 1960

Hodges, J. H. 2: v E 1876 (2)
Hogan, T. G. 7: v P 1983 (1); *v WI 1983 (5); v SL 1982 (1)*
Hogg, R. M. 38: v E 1978 (6) 1982 (3); v WI 1979 (2) 1984 (4); v NZ 1980 (2); v In 1980 (2); v P 1978 (2) 1983 (4); *v E 1981 (2); v WI 1983 (4); v In 1979 (6); v SL 1982 (1)*
Hole, G. B. 18: v E 1950 (1) 1954 (3); v SA 1952 (4); v WI 1951 (5); *v E 1953 (5)*
Holland, R. G. 11: v WI 1984 (3); v NZ 1985 (3); v In 1985 (1); *v E 1985 (4)*
Hookes, D. W. 23: v E 1976 (1) 1982 (5); v WI 1979 (1); v NZ 1985 (2); v In 1985 (2); *v E 1977 (5); v WI 1983 (5); v P 1979 (1); v SL 1982 (1)*
Hopkins, A. J. Y. 20: v E 1901 (2) 1903 (5); *v E 1902 (5) 1905 (3) 1909 (2); v SA 1902 (3)*
Horan, T. P. 15: v E 1876 (1) 1878 (1) 1881 (4) 1882 (4) 1884 (4); *v E 1882 (1)*
Hordern, H. V. 7: v E 1911 (5): v SA 1910 (2)
Hornibrook, P. M. 6: v E 1928 (1); *v E 1930 (5)*
Howell, W. P. 18: v E 1897 (3) 1901 (4) 1903 (3); *v E 1899 (5) 1902 (1); v SA 1902 (2)*
Hughes, K. J. 70: v E 1978 (6) 1979 (3) 1982 (5); v WI 1979 (3) 1981 (3) 1984 (4); v NZ 1980 (3); v In 1977 (2) 1980 (3); v P 1978 (2) 1981 (3) 1983 (5); *v E 1977 (1) 1980 (1) 1981 (6); v WI 1983 (5); v NZ 1981 (3); v In 1979 (6); v P 1979 (3) 1982 (3)*
Hughes, M. G. 1: v In 1985
Hunt, W. A. 1: v SA 1931
Hurst, A. G. 12: v E 1978 (6); v NZ 1973 (1); v In 1977 (1); v P 1978 (2); *v In 1979 (2)*
Hurwood, A. 2: v WI 1930 (2)

Inverarity, R. J. 6: v WI 1968 (1); *v E 1968 (2) 1972 (3)*
Iredale, F. A. 14: v E 1894 (5) 1897 (4); *v E 1896 (2) 1899 (3)*
Ironmonger, H. 14: v E 1928 (2) 1932 (4); v SA 1931 (4); v WI 1930 (4)
Iverson, J. B. 5: v E 1950 (5)

Jackson, A. 8: v E 1928 (2); v WI 1930 (4); *v E 1930 (2)*
Jarman, B. N. 19: v E 1962 (3); v WI 1968 (4); v In 1967 (4); v P 1964 (1); *v E 1968 (4); v In 1959 (1); 1964 (2)*
Jarvis, A. H. 11: v E 1884 (3) 1894 (4); *v E 1886 (2) 1888 (2)*
Jenner, T. J. 9: v E 1970 (2) 1974 (2); v WI 1975 (1); *v WI 1972 (4)*
Jennings, C. B. 6: *v E 1912 (3); v SA 1912 (3)*
Johnson I. W. 45: v E 1946 (4) 1950 (5) 1954 (4); v SA 1952 (1); v WI 1951 (4); v In 1947 (4); *v E 1948 (4) 1956 (5); v SA 1949 (5); v WI 1954 (5); v NZ 1945 (1); v In 1956 (2); v P 1956 (1)*
Johnson, L. J. 1: v In 1947
Johnston W. A. 40: v E 1950 (5) 1954 (4); v SA 1952 (5); v WI 1951 (4); v In 1947 (4); *v E 1948 (5) 1953 (3); v SA 1949 (5); v WI 1954 (4)*
Jones, D. M. 2: *v WI 1983 (2)*
Jones, E. 19: v E 1894 (1) 1897 (5) 1901 (2); *v E 1896 (3) 1899 (5) 1902 (2); v SA 1902 (1)*
Jones, S. P. 12: v E 1881 (2) 1884 (4) 1886 (1) 1887 (1); *v E 1882 (1) 1886 (3)*
Joslin, L. R. 1: v In 1967

Kelleway, C. 26: v E 1911 (4) 1920 (5) 1924 (5) 1928 (1); v SA 1910 (5); *v E 1912 (3); v SA 1912 (3)*
Kelly, J. J. 36: v E 1897 (5) 1901 (5) 1903 (5); *v E 1896 (3) 1899 (5) 1902 (5) 1905 (5); v SA 1902 (3)*
Kelly, T. J. D. 2: v E 1876 (1) 1878 (1)
Kendall, T. 2: v E 1876 (2)
Kent, M. F. 3: *v E 1981 (3)*
Kerr, R. B. 2: v NZ 1985 (2)
Kippax, A. F. 22: v E 1924 (1) 1928 (5) 1932 (1); v SA 1931 (4); v WI 1930 (5); *v E 1930 (5) 1934 (1)*
Kline L. F. 13: v E 1958 (2); v WI 1960 (2); *v SA 1957 (5); v In 1959 (3); v P 1959 (1)*

Laird, B. M. 21: v E 1979 (2); v WI 1979 (3) 1981 (3); v P 1981 (3); *v E 1980 (1); v NZ 1981 (3); v P 1979 (3) 1982 (3)*
Langley, G. R. A. 26: v E 1954 (2); v SA 1952 (5); v WI 1951 (5); *v E 1953 (4) 1956 (3); v WI 1954 (4); v In 1956 (2); v P 1956 (1)*
Laughlin, T. J. 3: v E 1978 (1); *v WI 1977 (2)*
Laver, F. 15: v E 1901 (1) 1903 (1); *v E 1899 (4) 1905 (5) 1909 (4)*
Lawry, W. M. 67: v E 1962 (5) 1965 (5) 1970 (5); v SA 1963 (5); v WI 1968 (5); v In 1967 (4); v P 1964 (1); *v E 1961 (5) 1964 (5) 1968 (4); v SA 1966 (5) 1969 (4); v WI 1964 (5); v In 1964 (3) 1969 (5); v P 1964 (1)*

Lawson, G. F. 36: v E 1982 (5); v WI 1981 (1) 1984 (5); v NZ 1980 (1) 1985 (2); v P 1983 (5); *v E 1981 (3) 1985 (6); v WI 1983 (5); v P 1982 (3)*

Lee, P. K. 2: v E 1932 (1); v SA 1931 (1)

Lillee, D. K. 70: v E 1970 (2) 1974 (6) 1976 (1) 1979 (3) 1982 (1); v WI 1975 (5) 1979 (3) 1981 (3); v NZ 1980 (3); v In 1980 (3); v P 1972 (3) 1976 (3) 1981 (3) 1983 (5); *v E 1972 (5) 1975 (4) 1980 (1) 1981 (6); v WI 1972 (1); v NZ 1976 (2) 1981 (3); v P 1979 (3); v SL 1982 (1)*

Lindwall, R. R. 61: v E 1946 (4) 1950 (5) 1954 (4) 1958 (2); v SA 1952 (4); v WI 1951 (5); v In 1947 (5); *v E 1948 (5) 1953 (5) 1956 (4); v SA 1949 (4); v WI 1954 (5); v NZ 1945 (1); v In 1956 (3) 1959 (2); v P 1956 (1) 1959 (2)*

Love, H. S. B. 1: v E 1932

Loxton, S. J. E. 12: v E 1950 (3); v In 1947 (1); *v E 1948 (3); v SA 1949 (5)*

Lyons, J. J. 14: v E 1886 (1) 1891 (3) 1894 (3) 1897 (1); *v E 1888 (1) 1890 (2) 1893 (3)*

McAlister, P. A. 8: v E 1903 (2) 1907 (4); *v E 1909 (2)*

Macartney, C. G. 35: v E 1907 (5) 1911 (1) 1920 (2); v SA 1910 (4); *v E 1909 (5) 1912 (3) 1921 (5) 1926 (5); v SA 1912 (3) 1921 (2)*

McCabe, S. J. 39: v E 1932 (5) 1936 (5); v SA 1931 (5); v WI 1930 (5); *v E 1930 (5) 1934 (5) 1938 (4); v SA 1935 (5)*

McCool, C. L. 14: v E 1946 (5); v In 1947 (3); *v SA 1949 (5) v NZ 1945 (1)*

McCormick, E. L. 12: v E 1936 (4); *v E 1938 (3); v SA 1935 (5)*

McCosker, R. B. 25: v E 1974 (3) 1976 (1) 1979 (2); v WI 1975 (4) 1979 (1); v P 1976 (3); *v E 1975 (4) 1977 (5); v NZ 1976 (2)*

McDermott, C. J. 14: v WI 1984 (2); v NZ 1985 (2); v In 1985 (2); *v E 1985 (6); v NZ 1985 (2)*

McDonald, C. C. 47: v E 1954 (2) 1958 (5); v SA 1952 (5); v WI 1951 (1) 1960 (5); *v E 1956 (5) 1961 (3); v SA 1957 (5); v WI 1954 (5); v In 1956 (2) 1959 (5); v P 1956 (1) 1959 (3)*

McDonald, E. A. 11: v E 1920 (3); *v E 1921 (5); v SA 1921 (3)*

McDonnell, P. S. 19: v E 1881 (4) 1882 (3) 1884 (2) 1886 (2) 1887 (1); *v E 1880 (1) 1884 (3) 1888 (3)*

McIlwraith, J. 1: *v E 1886*

Mackay K. D. 37: v E 1958 (5) 1962 (3); v WI 1960 (5); *v E 1956 (3) 1961 (5); v SA 1957 (5); v In 1956 (3) 1959 (5); v P 1959 (3)*

McKenzie, G. D. 60: v E 1962 (5) 1965 (4) 1970 (3); v SA 1963 (5); v WI 1968 (5); v In 1967 (2); v P 1964 (1); *v E 1961 (3) 1964 (5) 1968 (5); v SA 1966 (5) 1969 (3); v WI 1964 (5); v In 1964 (3) 1969 (5); v P 1964 (1)*

McKibbin, T. R. 5: v E 1894 (1) 1897 (2); *v E 1896 (2)*

McLaren, J. W. 1: v E 1911

Maclean, J. A. 4: v E 1978 (4)

McLeod, C. E. 17: v E 1894 (1) 1897 (5) 1901 (2) 1903 (3); *v E 1899 (1) 1905 (5)*

McLeod, R. W. 6: v E 1891 (3); *v E 1893 (3)*

McShane, P. G. 3: v E 1884 (1) 1886 (1) 1887 (1)

Maddocks, L. V. 7: v E 1954 (3); *v E 1956 (2); v WI 1954 (1); v In 1956 (1)*

Maguire, J. N. 3: v P 1983 (1); *v WI 1983 (2)*

Mailey, A. A. 21: v E 1920 (5) 1924 (5); *v E 1921 (3) 1926 (5); v SA 1921 (3)*

Mallett, A. A. 38: v E 1970 (2) 1974 (5) 1979 (1); v WI 1968 (1) 1975 (6) 1979 (1); v NZ 1973 (3); v P 1972 (2); *v E 1968 (1) 1972 (2) 1975 (4) 1980 (1); v SA 1969 (1); v NZ 1973 (3); v In 1969 (5)*

Malone, M. F. 1: *v E 1977*

Mann, A. L. 4: v In 1977 (4)

Marr, A. P. 1: v E 1884

Marsh, G. R. 6: v In 1985 (3); *v NZ 1985 (3)*

Marsh, R. W. 96: v E 1970 (6) 1974 (6) 1976 (1) 1979 (3) 1982 (5); v WI 1975 (6) 1979 (3) 1981 (3); v NZ 1973 (3) 1980 (3); v In 1980 (3); v P 1972 (3) 1976 (3) 1981 (3) 1983 (5); *v E 1972 (5) 1975 (4) 1977 (5) 1980 (1) 1981 (6); v WI 1972 (3); v NZ 1973 (3) 1976 (2) 1981 (3); v P 1979 (3) 1982 (3)*

Martin, J. W. 8: v SA 1963 (1); v WI 1960 (3); *v SA 1966 (1); v In 1964 (3); v P 1964 (1)*

Massie, H. H. 9: v E 1881 (4) 1882 (3) 1884 (1); *v E 1882 (1)*

Massie, R. A. L. 6: v P 1972 (2); *v E 1972 (4)*

Matthews, G. R. J. 14: v WI 1984 (1); v NZ 1985 (3); v In 1985 (3); v P 1983 (2); *v E 1985 (1); v WI 1983 (1); v NZ 1985 (3)*

Matthews, T. J. 8: v E 1911 (2); *v E 1912 (3); v SA 1912 (3)*

Mayne, E. R. 4: *v E 1912 (1); v SA 1912 (1) 1921 (2)*

Mayne, L. C. 6: *v SA 1969 (2); v WI 1964 (3); v In 1969 (1)*

Meckiff, I. 18: v E 1958 (4); v SA 1963 (1); v WI 1960 (2); *v SA 1957 (4); v In 1959 (5); v P 1959 (2)*
Meuleman, K. D. 1: *v NZ 1945*
Midwinter, W. E. 8: v E 1876 (2) 1882 (1) 1886 (2); *v E 1884 (3)*
Miller, K. R. 55: v E 1946 (5) 1950 (5) 1954 (4); v SA 1952 (4); v WI 1951 (5); v In 1947 (5); *v E 1948 (5) 1953 (5) 1956 (5); v SA 1949 (5); v WI 1954 (5); v NZ 1945 (1); v P 1956 (1)*
Minnett, R. B. 9: v E 1911 (5); *v E 1912 (1); v SA 1912 (3)*
Misson, F. M. 5: v WI 1960 (3); *v E 1961 (2)*
Moroney, J. R. 7: v E 1950 (1); v WI 1951 (1); *v SA 1949 (5)*
Morris, A. R. 46: v E 1946 (5) 1950 (5) 1954 (4); v SA 1952 (5); v WI 1951 (4); v In 1947 (4); *v E 1948 (5) 1953 (5); v SA 1949 (5); v WI 1954 (4)*
Morris, S. 1: v E 1884
Moses, H. 6: v E 1886 (2) 1887 (1) 1891 (2) 1894 (1)
Moss, J. K. 1: v P 1978
Moule, W. H. 1: *v E 1880*
Murdoch, W. L. 18: v E 1876 (1) 1878 (1) 1881 (4) 1882 (4) 1884 (1); *v E 1880 (1) 1882 (1) 1884 (3) 1890 (2)*
Musgrove, H. 1: v E 1884

Nagel, L. E. 1: v E 1932
Nash, L. J. 2: v E 1936 (1); v SA 1931 (1)
Nitschke, H. C. 2: v SA 1931 (2)
Noble, M. A. 42: v E 1897 (4) 1901 (5) 1903 (5) 1907 (5); *v E 1899 (5) 1902 (5) 1905 (5) 1909 (5); v SA 1902 (3)*
Noblet, G. 3: v SA 1952 (1); v WI 1951 (1); *v SA 1949 (1)*
Nothling, O. E. 1: v E 1928

O'Brien, L. P. J. 5: v E 1932 (2) 1936 (1); *v SA 1935 (2)*
O'Connor, J. D. A. 4: v E 1907 (3); *v E 1909 (1)*
O'Donnell, S. P. 6: v NZ 1985 (1); *v E 1985 (5)*
Ogilvie, A. D. 5: v In 1977 (3); *v WI 1977 (2)*
O'Keeffe, K. J. 24: v E 1970 (2) 1976 (1); v NZ 1973 (3); v P 1972 (2) 1976 (3); *v E 1977 (3); v WI 1972 (5); v NZ 1973 (3) 1976 (2)*
Oldfield, W. A. 54: v E 1920 (3) 1924 (5) 1928 (5) 1932 (4) 1936 (5); v SA 1931 (5); v WI 1930 (5); *v E 1921 (1) 1926 (5) 1930 (5) 1934 (5); v SA 1921 (1) 1935 (5)*
O'Neill, N. C. 42: v E 1958 (5) 1962 (5); v SA 1963 (4); v WI 1960 (5); *v E 1961 (5) 1964 (4); v WI 1964 (4); v In 1959 (5) 1964 (2); v P 1959 (3)*
O'Reilly, W. J. 27: v E 1932 (5) 1936 (5); v SA 1931 (2); *v E 1934 (5) 1938 (4); v SA 1935 (5); v WI 1945 (1)*
Oxenham, R. K. 7: v E 1928 (3); v SA 1931 (1); v WI 1930 (3)

Palmer, G. E. 17: v E 1881 (4) 1882 (4) 1884 (2); *v E 1880 (1) 1884 (3) 1886 (3)*
Park, R. L. 1: v E 1920
Pascoe, L. S. 14: v E 1979 (2); v WI 1979 (1) 1981 (1); v NZ 1980 (3); v In 1980 (3); *v E 1977 (3) 1980 (1)*
Pellew, C. E. 10: v E 1920 (4); *v E 1921 (5); v SA 1921 (1)*
Phillips, W. B. 27: v WI 1984 (2); v NZ 1985 (3); v In 1985 (3); v P 1983 (5); *v E 1985 (6); v WI 1983 (5); v NZ 1985 (3)*
Philpott, P. I. 8: v E 1965 (3); *v WI 1964 (5)*
Ponsford, W. H. 29: v E 1924 (5) 1928 (2) 1932 (3); v WI 1930 (5); *v E 1926 (2) 1930 (4) 1934 (4)*
Pope, R. J. 1: v E 1884

Rackemann, C. G. 5: v E 1982 (1); v WI 1984 (1); v P 1983 (2); *v WI 1983 (1)*
Ransford, V. S. 20: v E 1907 (5) 1911 (5); v SA 1910 (5); *v E 1909 (5)*
Redpath, I. R. 66: v E 1965 (1) 1970 (6) 1974 (6); v SA 1963 (1); v WI 1968 (5) 1975 (6); v In 1967 (3); v P 1972 (3); *v E 1964 (5) 1968 (5); v SA 1966 (5) 1969 (4); v WI 1972 (5); v NZ 1973 (3); v In 1964 (2) 1969 (5); v P 1964 (1)*
Reedman, J. C. 1: v E 1894
Reid, B. A. 6: v In 1985 (1); *v NZ 1985 (3)*
Renneberg, D. A. 8: v In 1967 (3); *v SA 1966 (5)*
Richardson, A. J. 9: v E 1924 (4); *v E 1926 (5)*

Richardson, V. Y. 19: v E 1924 (3) 1928 (2) 1932 (5); *v E 1930 (4); v SA 1935 (5)*
Rigg, K. E. 8: v E 1936 (3); v SA 1931 (4); v WI 1930 (1)
Ring, D. T. 13: v SA 1952 (5); v WI 1951 (5); v In 1947 (1); *v E 1948 (1) 1953 (1)*
Ritchie, G. M. 23: v WI 1984 (1); v NZ 1985 (3); v In 1985 (2); *v E 1985 (6); v WI 1983 (5); v NZ 1985 (3); v P 1982 (3)*
Rixon, S. J. 13: v WI 1984 (3); v In 1977 (5); *v WI 1977 (5)*
Robertson, W. R. 1: v E 1884
Robinson, R. D. 3: *v E 1977 (3)*
Robinson, R. H. 1: v E 1936
Rorke, G. F. 4: v E 1958 (2); *v In 1959 (2)*
Rutherford, J. W. 1: *v In 1956*
Ryder, J. 20: v E 1920 (5) 1924 (3) 1928 (5); *v E 1926 (4); v SA 1921 (3)*

Saggers, R. A. 6: *v E 1948 (1); v SA 1949 (5)*
Saunders, J. V. 14: v E 1901 (1) 1903 (2) 1907 (5); *v E 1902 (4); v SA 1902 (2)*
Scott, H. J. H. 8: v E 1884 (2); *v E 1884 (3) 1886 (3)*
Sellers, R. H. D. 1: *v In 1964*
Serjeant, C. S. 12: v In 1977 (4); *v E 1977 (3); v WI 1977 (5)*
Sheahan, A. P. 31: v E 1970 (2); v WI 1968 (5); v NZ 1973 (2); v In 1967 (4); v P 1972 (2); *v E 1968 (5) 1972 (2); v SA 1969 (4); v In 1969 (5)*
Shepherd, B. K. 9: v E 1962 (2); v SA 1963 (4); v P 1964 (1); *v WI 1964 (2)*
Sievers, M. W. 3: v E 1936 (3)
Simpson, R. B. 62: v E 1958 (1) 1962 (5) 1965 (3); v SA 1963 (5); v WI 1960 (5); v In 1967 (3) 1977 (5); v P 1964 (1); *v E 1961 (5) 1964 (5); v SA 1957 (5) 1966 (5); v WI 1964 (5) 1977 (5); v In 1964 (3); v P 1964 (1)*
Sincock, D. J. 3: v E 1965 (1); v P 1964 (1); *v WI 1964 (1)*
Slater, K. N. 1: v E 1958
Sleep, P. R. 4: v P 1978 (1); *v In 1979 (2); v P 1982 (1)*
Slight, J. 1: *v E 1880*
Smith, D. B. M. 2: *v E 1912 (2)*
Smith, S. B. 3: *v WI 1983 (3)*
Spofforth, F. R. 18: v E 1876 (1) 1878 (1) 1881 (1) 1882 (4) 1884 (3) 1886 (1); *v E 1882 (1) 1884 (3) 1886 (3)*
Stackpole, K. R. 43: v E 1965 (2) 1970 (6); v WI 1968 (5); v NZ 1973 (3); v P 1972 (1); *v E 1972 (5); v SA 1966 (5) 1969 (4); v WI 1972 (4); v NZ 1973 (3); v In 1969 (5)*
Stevens, G. B. 4: *v In 1959 (2); v P 1959 (2)*

Taber, H. B. 16: v WI 1968 (1); *v E 1968 (1); v SA 1966 (5) 1969 (4); v In 1969 (5)*
Tallon, D. 21: v E 1946 (5) 1950 (5); v In 1947 (5); *v E 1948 (4) 1953 (1); v NZ 1945 (1)*
Taylor, J. M. 20: v E 1920 (5) 1924 (5); *v E 1921 (5) 1926 (3); v SA 1921 (2)*
Thomas, G. 8: v E 1965 (3); *v WI 1964 (5)*
Thompson, N. 2: v E 1876 (2)
Thoms, G. R. 1: v WI 1951
Thomson, A. L. 4: v E 1970 (4)
Thomson, J. R. 51: v E 1974 (5) 1979 (1) 1982 (4); v WI 1975 (6) 1979 (1) 1981 (2); v In 1977 (5); v P 1972 (1) 1976 (1) 1981 (3); *v E 1975 (4) 1977 (5) 1985 (2); v WI 1977 (5); v NZ 1981 (3); v P 1982 (3)*
Thurlow, H. M. 1: v SA 1931
Toohey, P. M. 15: v E 1978 (5) 1979 (1); v WI 1979 (1); v In 1977 (5); *v WI 1977 (3)*
Toshack, E. R. H. 12: v E 1946 (5); v In 1947 (2); *v E 1948 (4); v NZ 1945 (1)*
Travers, J. P. F. 1: v E 1901
Tribe, G. E. 3: v E 1946 (3)
Trott, A. E. 3: v E 1894 (3)
Trott, G. H. S. 24: v E 1891 (3) 1894 (5) 1897 (5); *v E 1888 (3) 1890 (2) 1893 (3) 1896 (3)*
Trumble, H. 32: v E 1894 (1) 1897 (5) 1901 (5) 1903 (5); *v E 1890 (2) 1893 (3) 1896 (3) 1899 (5) 1902 (3); v SA 1902 (1)*
Trumble, J. W. 7: v E 1884 (4); *v E 1886 (3)*
Trumper, V. T. 48: v E 1901 (5) 1903 (5) 1907 (5) 1911 (5); v SA 1910 (5); *v E 1899 (5) 1902 (5) 1905 (5) 1909 (5); v SA 1902 (3)*
Turner, A. 14: v WI 1975 (6); v P 1976 (3); *v E 1975 (3); v NZ 1976 (2)*
Turner, C. T. B. 17: v E 1886 (2) 1887 (1) 1891 (3) 1894 (3); *v E 1888 (3) 1890 (2) 1893 (3)*

Veivers, T. R. 21: v E 1965 (4); v SA 1963 (3); v P 1964 (1); *v E 1964 (5); v SA 1966 (4); v In 1964 (3); v P 1964 (1)*

Waite, M. G. 2: *v E 1938 (2)*
Walker, M. H. N. 34: v E 1974 (6); 1976 (1); v WI 1975 (3); v NZ 1973 (1); v P 1972 (2) 1976 (2); *v E 1975 (4); 1977 (5); v WI 1972 (5); v NZ 1973 (3) 1976 (2)*
Wall, T. W. 18: v E 1928 (1) 1932 (4); v SA 1931 (3); v WI 1930 (1); *v E 1930 (5) 1934 (4)*
Walters, F. H. 1: v E 1884
Walters, K. D. 74: v E 1965 (5) 1970 (6) 1974 (6) 1976 (1); v WI 1968 (4); v NZ 1973 (3) 1980 (3); v In 1967 (2) 1980 (3); v P 1972 (1) 1976 (3); *v E 1968 (5) 1972 (4) 1975 (4) 1977 (5); v SA 1969 (4); v WI 1972 (5); v NZ 1973 (3) 1976 (2); v In 1969 (5)*
Ward, F. A. 4: v E 1936 (3); *v E 1938 (1)*
Watkins, J. R. 1: v P 1972
Watson, G. D. 5: *v E 1972 (2); v SA 1966 (3)*
Watson, W. 4: v E 1954 (1); *v WI 1954 (3)*
Waugh, S. R. 5: v In 1985 (2); *v NZ 1985 (3)*
Wellham, D. M. 5: v WI 1981 (1); v P 1981 (2); *v E 1981 (1) 1985 (1)*
Wessels, K. C. 24: v E 1982 (4); v WI 1984 (5); v NZ 1985 (1); v P 1983 (5); *v E 1985 (6); v WI 1983 (2); v SL 1982 (1)*
Whatmore, D. F. 7: v P 1978 (2); *v In 1979 (5)*
Whitney, M. R. 2: *v E 1981 (2)*
Whitty, W. J. 14: v E 1911 (2); v SA 1910 (5); *v E 1909 (1) 1912 (3); v SA 1912 (3)*
Wiener, J. M. 6: v E 1979 (2); v WI 1979 (2); *v P 1979 (2)*
Wilson, J. W. 1: *v In 1956*
Wood, G. M. 53: v E 1978 (6) 1982 (1); v WI 1981 (3) 1984 (5); v NZ 1980 (3); v In 1977 (1) 1980 (3); v P 1978 (1) 1981 (3); *v E 1980 (1) 1981 (6) 1985 (5); v WI 1977 (5) 1983 (1); v NZ 1981 (3); v In 1979 (2); v P 1982 (3); v SL 1982 (1)*
Woodcock, A. J. 1: v NZ 1973
Woodfull, W. M. 35: v E 1928 (5) 1932 (5); v SA 1931 (5); v WI 1930 (5); *v E 1926 (5) 1930 (5) 1934 (5)*
Woods, S. M. J. 3: *v E 1888 (3)*
Woolley, R. D. 2: *v WI 1983 (1); v SL 1982 (1)*
Worrall, J. 11: v E 1884 (1) 1887 (1) 1894 (1) 1897 (1); *v E 1888 (3) 1899 (4)*
Wright, K. J. 10: v E 1978 (2); v P 1978 (2); *v In 1979 (6)*

Yallop, G. N. 39: v E 1978 (6); v WI 1975 (3) 1984 (1); v In 1977 (1); v P 1978 (1) 1981 (1) 1983 (5); *v E 1980 (1) 1981 (6); v WI 1977 (4); v In 1979 (6); v P 1979 (3); v SL 1982 (1)*
Yardley, B. 33: v E 1978 (4) 1982 (5); v WI 1981 (3); v In 1977 (1) 1980 (2); v P 1978 (1) 1981 (3); *v WI 1977 (5); v NZ 1981 (3); v In 1979 (3); v P 1982 (2); v SL 1982 (1)*

Zoehrer, T. J. 3: *v NZ 1985 (3)*

SOUTH AFRICA

Number of Test cricketers: 235

Adcock, N. A. T. 26: v E 1956 (5); v A 1957 (5); v NZ 1953 (5) 1961 (2); *v E 1955 (4) 1960 (5)*
Anderson, J. H. 1: v A 1902
Ashley, W. H. 1: v E 1888

Bacher, A. 12: v A 1966 (5) 1969 (4); *v E 1965 (3)*
Balaskas, X. C. 9: v E 1930 (2) 1938 (1); v A 1935 (3); *v E 1935 (1); v NZ 1931 (2)*
Barlow, E. J. 30: v E 1964 (5); v A 1966 (5) 1969 (4); v NZ 1961 (5); *v E 1965 (3); v A 1963 (5); v NZ 1963 (3)*
Baumgartner, H. V. 1: v E 1913
Beaumont, R. 5: v E 1913 (2); *v E 1912 (1); v A 1912 (2)*
Begbie, D. W. 5: v E 1948 (2); v A 1949 (2)
Bell, A. J. 16: v E 1930 (3); *v E 1929 (3) 1935 (3); v A 1931 (5); v NZ 1931 (2)*
Bisset, M. 3: v E 1898 (2) 1909 (1)
Bissett, G. F. 4: v E 1927 (4)
Blanckenberg, J. M. 18: v E 1913 (5) 1922 (5); v A 1921 (3); *v E 1924 (5)*

Bland, K. C. 21: v E 1964 (5); v A 1966 (1); v NZ 1961 (5); *v E 1965 (3)*; *v A 1963 (4)*; *v NZ 1963 (3)*

Bock, E. G. 1: v A 1935

Bond, G. E. 1: v E 1938

Botten, J. T. 3: *v E 1965 (3)*

Brann, W. H. 3: v E 1922 (3)

Briscoe, A. W. 2: v E 1938 (1); v A 1935 (1)

Bromfield, H. D. 9: v E 1964 (3); v NZ 1961 (5); *v E 1965 (1)*

Brown, L. S. 2: *v A 1931 (1); v NZ 1931 (1)*

Burger, C. G. de V. 2: v A 1957 (2)

Burke, S. F. 2: v E 1964 (1); v NZ 1961 (1)

Buys, I. D. 1: v E 1922

Cameron, H. B. 26: v E 1927 (5) 1930 (5); *v E 1929 (4) 1935 (5)*; *v A 1931 (5)*; *v NZ 1931 (2)*

Campbell, T. 5: v E 1909 (4); *v E 1912 (1)*

Carlstein, P. R. 8: v A 1957 (1); *v E 1960 (5)*; *v A 1963 (2)*

Carter, C. P. 10: v E 1913 (2); v A 1921 (3); *v E 1912 (2) 1924 (3)*

Catterall, R. H. 24: v E 1922 (5) 1927 (5) 1930 (4); *v E 1924 (5) 1929 (5)*

Chapman, H. W. 2: v E 1913 (1); v A 1921 (1)

Cheetham, J. E. 24: v E 1948 (1); v A 1949 (3); v NZ 1953 (5); *v E 1951 (5) 1955 (3); v A 1952 (5); v NZ 1952 (2)*

Chevalier, G. A. 1: v A 1969

Christy, J. A. J. 10: v E 1930 (1); *v E 1929 (2); v A 1931 (5); v NZ 1931 (2)*

Chubb, G. W. A. 5: *v E 1951 (5)*

Cochran, J. A. K. 1: v E 1930

Coen, S. K. 2: v E 1927 (2)

Commaille, J. M. M. 12: v E 1909 (5) 1927 (2); *v E 1924 (5)*

Conyngham, D. P. 1: v E 1922

Cook, F. J. 1: v E 1895

Cooper, A. H. C. 1: v E 1913

Cox, J. L. 3: v E 1913 (3)

Cripps, G. 1: v E 1891

Crisp, R. J. 9: v A 1935 (4); *v E 1935 (5)*

Curnow, S. H. 7: v E 1930 (3); *v A 1931 (4)*

Dalton, E. L. 15: v E 1930 (1) 1938 (4); v A 1935 (1); *v E 1929 (1) 1935 (4); v A 1931 (2); v NZ 1931 (2)*

Davies, E. Q. 5: v E 1938 (3); v A 1935 (2)

Dawson, O. C. 9: v E 1948 (4); *v E 1947 (5)*

Deane, H. G. 17: v E 1927 (5) 1930 (2); *v E 1924 (5) 1929 (5)*

Dixon, C. D. 1: v E 1913

Dower, R. R. 1: v E 1898

Draper, R. G. 2: v A 1949 (2)

Duckworth, C. A. R. 2: v E 1956 (2)

Dumbrill, R. 5: v A 1966 (2); *v E 1965 (3)*

Duminy, J. P. 3: v E 1927 (2); *v E 1929 (1)*

Dunell, O. R. 2: v E 1888 (2)

Du Preez, J. H. 2: v A 1966 (2)

Du Toit, J. F. 1: v E 1891

Dyer, D. V. 3: *v E 1947 (3)*

Elgie, M. K. 3: v NZ 1961 (3)

Endean, W. R. 28: v E 1956 (5); v A 1957 (5); v NZ 1953 (5); *v E 1951 (1) 1955 (5); v A 1952 (5); v NZ 1952 (2)*

Farrer, W. S. 6: v NZ 1961 (3); *v NZ 1963 (3)*

Faulkner, G. A. 25: v E 1905 (5) 1909 (5); *v E 1907 (3) 1912 (3) 1924 (1); v A 1910 (5) 1912 (3)*

Fellows-Smith, J. P. 4: *v E 1960 (4)*

Fichardt, C. G. 2: v E 1891 (1) 1895 (1)

Finlason, C. E. 1: v E 1888

Floquet, C. E. 1: v E 1909

Francis, H. H. 2: v E 1898 (2)

Francois, C. M. 5: v E 1922 (5)
Frank, C. N. 3: v A 1921 (3)
Frank, W. H. B. 1: v E 1895
Fuller, E. R. H. 7: v A 1957 (1); *v E 1955 (2); v A 1952 (2); v NZ 1952 (2)*
Fullerton, G. M. 7: v A 1949 (2); *v E 1947 (2) 1951 (3)*
Funston, K. J. 18: v E 1956 (3); v A 1957 (5); v NZ 1953 (3); *v A 1952 (5); v NZ 1952 (2)*

Gamsy, D. 2: v A 1969 (2)
Gleeson, R. A. 1: v E 1895
Glover, G. K. 1: v E 1895
Goddard, T. L. 41: v E 1956 (5) 1964 (5); v A 1957 (5) 1966 (5) 1969 (3); *v E 1955 (5) 1960 (5); v A 1963 (5); v NZ 1963 (3)*
Gordon, N. 5: v E 1938 (5)
Graham, R. 2: v E 1898 (2)
Grieveson, R. E. 2: v E 1938 (2)
Griffin, G. M. 2: *v E 1960 (2)*

Hall, A. E. 7: v E 1922 (4) 1927 (2) 1930 (1)
Hall, G. G. 1: v E 1964
Halliwell, E. A. 8: v E 1891 (1) 1895 (3) 1898 (1); v A 1902 (3)
Halse, C. G. 3: *v A 1963 (3)*
Hands, P. A. M. 7: v E 1913 (5); v A 1921 (1); *v E 1924 (1)*
Hands, R. H. M. 1: v E 1913
Hanley, M. A. 1: v E 1948
Harris, T. A. 3: v E 1948 (1); *v E 1947 (2)*
Hartigan, G. P. D. 5: v E 1913 (3); *v E 1912 (1); v A 1912 (1)*
Harvey, R. L. 2: v A 1935 (2)
Hathorn, C. M. H. 12: v E 1905 (5); v A 1902 (3); *v E 1907 (3); v A 1910 (1)*
Hearne, F. 4: v E 1891 (1) 1895 (3)
Hearne, G. A. L. 3: v E 1922 (2); *v E 1924 (1)*
Heine, P. S. 14: v E 1956 (5); v A 1957 (4); v NZ 1961 (1); *v E 1955 (4)*
Hime, C. F. W. 1: v E 1895
Hutchinson, P. 2: v E 1888 (2)

Ironside, D. E. J. 3: v NZ 1953 (3)
Irvine, B. L. 4: v A 1969 (4)

Johnson, C. L. 1: v E 1895

Keith, H. J. 8: v E 1956 (3); *v E 1955 (4); v A 1952 (1)*
Kempis, G. A. 1: v E 1888
Kotze, J. J. 3: v A 1902 (2); *v E 1907 (1)*
Kuys, F. 1: v E 1898

Lance, H. R. 13: v A 1966 (5) 1969 (3); v NZ 1961 (2); *v E 1965 (3)*
Langton, A. B. C. 15: v E 1938 (5); v A 1935 (5); *v E 1935 (5)*
Lawrence, G. B. 5: v NZ 1961 (5)
Le Roux, F. le S. 1: v E 1913
Lewis, P. T. 1: v E 1913
Lindsay, D. T. 19: v E 1964 (3); v A 1966 (5) 1969 (2); *v E 1965 (3); v A 1963 (3); v NZ 1963 (3)*
Lindsay, J. D. 3: *v E 1947 (3)*
Lindsay, N. V. 1: v A 1921
Ling, W. V. S. 6: v E 1922 (3); v A 1921 (3)
Llewellyn, C. B. 15: v E 1895 (1) 1898 (1); v A 1902 (3); *v E 1912 (3); v A 1910 (5) 1912 (2)*
Lundie, E. B. 1: v E 1913

Macaulay, M. J. 1: v E 1964
McCarthy, C. N. 15: v E 1948 (5); v A 1949 (5); *v E 1951 (5)*
McGlew, D. J. 34: v E 1956 (1); v A 1957 (5); v NZ 1953 (5) 1961 (5); *v E 1951 (2) 1955 (5) 1960 (5); v A 1952 (4); v NZ 1952 (2)*
McKinnon, A. H. 8: v E 1964 (2); v A 1966 (2); v NZ 1961 (1); *v E 1960 (1) 1965 (2)*

McLean, R. A. 40: v E 1956 (5) 1964 (2); v A 1957 (4); v NZ 1953 (4) 1961 (5); *v E 1951 (3) 1955 (5) 1960 (5); v A 1952 (5); v NZ 1952 (2)*
McMillan, Q. 13: v E 1930 (5); *v E 1929 (2); v A 1931 (4); v NZ 1931 (2)*
Mann, N. B. F. 19: v E 1948 (5); v A 1949 (5); *v E 1947 (5) 1951 (4)*
Mansell, P. N. F. 13: *v E 1951 (2) 1955 (4); v A 1952 (5); v NZ 1952 (2)*
Markham, L. A. 1: v E 1948
Marx, W. F. E. 3: v A 1921 (3)
Meintjes, D. J. 2: v E 1922 (2)
Melle, M. G. 7: v A 1949 (2); *v E 1951 (1); v A 1952 (4)*
Melville, A. 11: v E 1938 (5) 1948 (1); *v E 1947 (5)*
Middleton, J. 6: v E 1895 (2) 1898 (2); v A 1902 (2)
Mills, C. 1: v E 1891
Milton, W. H. 3: v E 1888 (2) 1891 (1)
Mitchell, B. 42: v E 1930 (5) 1938 (5) 1948 (5); v A 1935 (5); *v E 1929 (5) 1935 (5) 1947 (5); v A 1931 (5); v NZ 1931 (2)*
Mitchell, F. 3: *v E 1912 (1); v A 1912 (2)*
Morkel, D. P. B. 16: v E 1927 (5); *v E 1929 (5); v A 1931 (5); v NZ 1931 (1)*
Murray, A. R. A. 10: v NZ 1953 (4); *v A 1952 (4); v NZ 1952 (2)*

Nel, J. D. 6: v A 1949 (5) 1957 (1)
Newberry, C. 4: v E 1913 (4)
Newson, E. S. 3: v E 1930 (1) 1938 (2)
Nicholson, F. 4: v A 1935 (4)
Nicolson, J. F. W. 3: v E 1927 (3)
Norton, N. O. 1: v E 1909
Nourse, A. D. 34: v E 1938 (5) 1948 (5); v A 1935 (5) 1949 (5); *v E 1935 (4) 1947 (5) 1951 (5)*
Nourse, A. W. 45: v E 1905 (5) 1909 (5) 1913 (5) 1922 (5); v A 1902 (3) 1921 (3); *v E 1907 (3) 1912 (3) 1924 (5); v A 1910 (5) 1912 (3)*
Nupen, E. P. 17: v E 1922 (4) 1927 (5) 1930 (3); v A 1921 (2) 1935 (1); *v E 1924 (2)*

Ochse, A. E. 2: v E 1888 (2)
Ochse, A. L. 3: v E 1927 (1); *v E 1929 (2)*
O'Linn, S. 7: v NZ 1961 (2); *v E 1960 (5)*
Owen-Smith, H. G. 5: *v E 1929 (5)*

Palm, A. W. 1: v E 1927
Parker, G. M. 2: *v E 1924 (2)*
Parkin, D. C. 1: v E 1891
Partridge, J. T. 11: v E 1964 (3); *v A 1963 (5); v NZ 1963 (3)*
Pearse, O. C. 3: *v A 1910 (3)*
Pegler, S. J. 16: v E 1909 (1); *v E 1912 (3) 1924 (5); v A 1910 (4) 1912 (3)*
Pithey, A. J. 17: v E 1956 (3) 1964 (5); *v E 1960 (2); v A 1963 (4); v NZ 1963 (3)*
Pithey, D. B. 8: v A 1966 (2); *v A 1963 (3); v NZ 1963 (3)*
Plimsoll, J. B. 1: *v E 1947*
Pollock, P. M. 28: v E 1964 (5); v A 1966 (5) 1969 (4); v NZ 1961 (3); *v E 1965 (3); v A 1963 (5); v NZ 1963 (3)*
Pollock, R. G. 23: v E 1964 (5); v A 1966 (5) 1969 (4); *v E 1965 (3); v A 1963 (5); v NZ 1963 (1)*
Poore, R. M. 3: v E 1895 (3)
Pothecary, J. E. 3: *v E 1960 (3)*
Powell, A. W. 1: v E 1898
Prince, C. F. H. 1: v E 1898
Procter, M. J. 7: v A 1966 (3) 1969 (4)
Promnitz, H. L. E. 2: v E 1927 (2)

Quinn, N. A. 12: v E 1930 (1); *v E 1929 (4); v A 1931 (5); v NZ 1931 (2)*

Reid, N. 1: v A 1921
Richards, A. R. 1: v E 1895
Richards, B. A. 4: v A 1969 (4)
Richards, W. H. 1: v E 1888
Robertson, J. B. 3: v A 1935 (3)
Rose-Innes, A. 2: v E 1888 (2)

Routledge, T. W. 4: v E 1891 (1) 1895 (3)
Rowan, A. M. B. 15: v E 1948 (5); *v E 1947 (5) 1951 (5)*
Rowan, E. A. B. 26: v E 1938 (4) 1948 (4); v A 1935 (3); 1949 (5); *v E 1935 (5) 1951 (5)*
Rowe, G. A. 5: v E 1895 (2) 1898 (2); v A 1902 (1)

Samuelson, S. V. 1: v E 1909
Schwarz, R. O. 20: v E 1905 (5) 1909 (4); *v E 1907 (3) 1912 (1); v A 1910 (5) 1912 (2)*
Seccull, A. W. 1: v E 1895
Seymour, M. A. 7: v E 1964 (2); v A 1969 (1); *v A 1963 (4)*
Shalders, W. A. 12: v E 1898 (1) 1905 (5); v A 1902 (3); *v E 1907 (3)*
Shepstone, G. H. 2: v E 1895 (1) 1898 (1)
Sherwell, P. W. 13: v E 1905 (5); *v E 1907 (3); v A 1910 (5)*
Siedle, I. J. 18: v E 1927 (1) 1930 (5); v A 1935 (5); *v E 1929 (3) 1935 (4)*
Sinclair, J. H. 25: v E 1895 (3) 1898 (2) 1905 (5) 1909 (4); v A 1902 (3); *v E 1907 (3); v A 1910 (5)*
Smith, C. J. E. 3: v A 1902 (3)
Smith, F. W. 3: v E 1888 (2) 1895 (1)
Smith, V. I. 9: v A 1949 (3) 1957 (1); *v E 1947 (4) 1955 (1)*
Snooke, S. D. 1: *v E 1907*
Snooke, S. J. 26: v E 1905 (5) 1909 (5) 1922 (3); *v E 1907 (3) 1912 (3); v A 1910 (5) 1912 (2)*
Solomon, W. R. 1: v E 1898
Stewart, R. B. 1: v E 1888
Stricker, L. A. 13: v E 1909 (4); *v E 1912 (2); v A 1910 (5) 1912 (2)*
Susskind, M. J. 5: *v E 1924 (5)*

Taberer, H. M. 1: v A 1902
Tancred, A. B. 2: v E 1888 (2)
Tancred, L. J. 14: v E 1905 (5) 1913 (1); v A 1902 (3); *v E 1907 (1) 1912 (2); v A 1912 (2)*
Tancred, V. M. 1: v E 1898
Tapscott, G. L. 1: v E 1913
Tapscott, L. E. 2: v E 1922 (2)
Tayfield, H. J. 37: v E 1956 (5); v A 1949 (5) 1957 (5); v NZ 1953 (5); *v E 1955 (5) 1960 (5); v A 1952 (5); v NZ 1952 (2)*
Taylor, A. I. 1: v E 1956
Taylor, D. 2: v E 1913 (2)
Taylor, H. W. 42: v E 1913 (5) 1922 (5) 1927 (5) 1930 (4); v A 1921 (3); *v E 1912 (3) 1924 (5) 1929 (3); v A 1912 (3) 1931 (5); v NZ 1931 (1)*
Theunissen, N. H. G. de J. 1: v E 1888
Thornton, P. G. 1: v A 1902
Tomlinson, D. S. 1: *v E 1935*
Traicos, A. J. 3: v A 1969 (3)
Trimborn, P. H. J. 4: v A 1966 (3) 1969 (1)
Tuckett, L. 9: v E 1948 (4); *v E 1947 (5)*
Tuckett, L. R. 1: v E 1913
Twentyman-Jones, P. S. 1: v A 1902

van der Bijl, P. G. V. 5: v E 1938 (5)
Van der Merwe, E. A. 2: v A 1935 (1); *v E 1929 (1)*
Van der Merwe, P. L. 15: v E 1964 (2); v A 1966 (5); *v E 1965 (3); v A 1963 (3); v NZ 1963 (2)*
Van Ryneveld, C. B. 19: v E 1956 (5); v A 1957 (4); v NZ 1953 (5); *v E 1951 (5)*
Varnals, G. D. 3: v E 1964 (3)
Viljoen, K. G. 27: v E 1930 (3) 1938 (4) 1948 (2); v A 1935 (4); *v E 1935 (4) 1947 (5); v A 1931 (4); v NZ 1931 (1)*
Vincent, C. L. 25: v E 1927 (5) 1930 (5); *v E 1929 (4) 1935 (4); v A 1931 (5); v NZ 1931 (2)*
Vintcent, C. H. 3: v E 1888 (2) 1891 (1)
Vogler, A. E. E. 15: v E 1905 (5) 1909 (5); *v E 1907 (3); v A 1910 (2)*

Wade, H. F. 10: v A 1935 (5); *v E 1935 (5)*
Wade, W. W. 11: v E 1938 (3) 1948 (5); v A 1949 (3)
Waite, J. H. B. 50: v E 1956 (5); 1964 (2); v A 1957 (5); v NZ 1953 (5) 1961 (5); *v E 1951 (4) 1955 (5) 1960 (5); v A 1952 (5) 1963 (4); v NZ 1952 (2) 1963 (3)*
Walter, K. A. 2: v NZ 1961 (2)
Ward, T. A. 23: v E 1913 (5) 1922 (5); v A 1921 (3); *v E 1912 (2) 1924 (5); v A 1912 (3)*

Watkins, J. C. 15: v E 1956 (2); v A 1949 (3); v NZ 1953 (3); *v A 1952 (5)*; *v NZ 1952 (2)*
Wesley, C. 3: *v E 1960 (3)*
Westcott, R. J. 5: v A 1957 (2); v NZ 1953 (3)
White, G. C. 17: v E 1905 (5) 1909 (4); *v E 1907 (3) 1912 (2)*; *v A 1912 (3)*
Willoughby, J. T. I. 2: v E 1895 (2)
Wimble, C. S. 1: v E 1891
Winslow, P. L. 5: v A 1949 (2); *v E 1955 (3)*
Wynne, O. E. 6: v E 1948 (3); v A 1949 (3)

Zulch, J. W. 16: v E 1909 (5) 1913 (3); v A 1921 (3); *v A 1910 (5)*

WEST INDIES

Number of Test cricketers: 187

Achong, E. 6: v E 1929 (1) 1934 (2); *v E 1933 (3)*
Alexander, F. C. M. 25: v E 1959 (5); v P 1957 (5); *v E 1957 (2)*; *v A 1960 (5)*; *v In 1958 (5)*; *v P 1958 (3)*
Ali, Imtiaz 1: v In 1975
Ali, Inshan 12: v E 1973 (2); v A 1972 (3); v In 1970 (1); v P 1976 (1); v NZ 1971 (3); *v E 1973 (1)*; *v A 1975 (1)*
Allan, D. W. 5: v A 1964 (1); v In 1961 (2); *v E 1966 (2)*
Asgarali, N. 2: *v E 1957 (2)*
Atkinson, D. St E. 22: v E 1953 (4); v A 1954 (4); v P 1957 (1); *v E 1957 (2)*; *v A 1951 (2)*; *v NZ 1951 (1) 1955 (4)*; *v In 1948 (4)*
Atkinson, E. St E. 8: v P 1957 (3); *v In 1958 (3)*; *v P 1958 (2)*
Austin, R. A. 2: v A 1977 (2)

Bacchus, S. F. A. F. 19: v A 1977 (2); *v E 1980 (5)*; *v A 1981 (2)*; *v In 1978 (6)*; *v P 1980 (4)*
Baichan, L. 3: *v A 1975 (1)*; *v P 1974 (2)*
Baptiste, E. A. E. 9: v A 1983 (3); *v E 1984 (5)*; *v In 1983 (1)*
Barrow, I. 11: v E 1929 (1) 1934 (1); *v E 1933 (3) 1939 (1)*; *v A 1930 (5)*
Barrett, A. G. 6: v E 1973 (2); v In 1970 (2); *v In 1974 (2)*
Bartlett, E. L. 5: *v E 1928 (1)*; *v A 1930 (4)*
Best, C. A. 3: v E 1985 (3)
Betancourt, N. 1: v E 1929
Binns, A. P. 5: v A 1954 (1); v In 1952 (1); *v NZ 1955 (3)*
Birkett, L. S. 4 *v A 1930 (4)*
Boyce, K. D. 21: v E 1973 (4); v A 1972 (4); v In 1970 (1); *v E 1973 (3)*; *v A 1975 (4)*; *v In 1974 (3)*; *v P 1974 (2)*
Browne, C. R. 4: v E 1929 (2); *v E 1928 (2)*
Butcher, B. F. 44: v E 1959 (2) 1967 (5); v A 1964 (5); *v E 1963 (5) 1966 (5) 1969 (3)*; *v A 1968 (5)*; *v NZ 1968 (3)*; *v In 1958 (5) 1966 (3)*; *v P 1958 (3)*
Butler, L. 1: v A 1954
Butts, C. G. 1: v NZ 1984
Bynoe, M. R. 4: *v In 1966 (3)*; *v P 1958 (1)*

Camacho, G. S. 11: v E 1967 (5); v In 1970 (2); *v E 1969 (2)*; *v A 1968 (2)*
Cameron, F. J. 5: *v In 1948 (5)*
Cameron, J. H. 2: *v E 1939 (2)*
Carew, G. M. 4: v E 1934 (1) 1947 (2); *v In 1948 (1)*
Carew, M. C. 19: v E 1967 (1); v NZ 1971 (3); v In 1970 (3); *v E 1963 (2) 1966 (1) 1969 (1)*; *v A 1968 (5)*; *v NZ 1968 (3)*
Challenor, G. 3: *v E 1928 (3)*
Chang, H. S. 1: *v In 1978*
Christiani, C. M. 4: v E 1934 (4)
Christiani, R. J. 22: v E 1947 (4) 1953 (1); v In 1952 (2); *v E 1950 (4)*; *v A 1951 (5)*; *v NZ 1951 (1)*; *v In 1948 (5)*
Clarke, C. B. 3: *v E 1939 (3)*
Clarke, S. T. 11: v A 1977 (1); *v A 1981 (1)*; *v In 1978 (5)*; *v P 1980 (4)*

Constantine, L. N. 18: v E 1929 (3) 1934 (3); *v E 1928 (3) 1933 (1) 1939 (3); v A 1930 (5)*
Croft, C. E. H. 27: v E 1980 (4); v A 1977 (2); v P 1976 (5); *v E 1980 (3); v A 1979 (3) 1981 (3); v NZ 1979 (3); v P 1980 (4)*

Da Costa, O. C. 5: v E 1929 (1) 1934 (1); *v E 1933 (3)*
Daniel, W. W. 10: v A 1983 (2); v In 1975 (1); *v E 1976 (4) v In 1983 (3)*
Davis, B. A. 4: v A 1964 (4)
Davis, C. A. 15: v A 1972 (2); v NZ 1971 (5); v In 1970 (4); *v E 1969 (3); v A 1968 (1)*
Davis, W. W. 11: v A 1983 (1); v NZ 1984 (2); v In 1982 (1); *v E 1984 (1); v In 1983 (6)*
De Caires, F. I. 3: v E 1929 (3)
Depeiza, C. C. 5: v A 1954 (3); *v NZ 1955 (2)*
Dewdney, T. 9: v A 1954 (2); v P 1957 (3); *v E 1957 (1); v NZ 1955 (3)*
Dowe, U. G. 4: v A 1972 (1); v NZ 1971 (1); v In 1970 (2)
Dujon, P. J. L. 37: v E 1985 (4); v A 1983 (5); v NZ 1984 (4); v In 1982 (5); *v E 1984 (5); v A 1981 (3) 1984 (5); v In 1983 (6)*

Edwards, R. M. 5: *v A 1968 (2); v NZ 1968 (3)*

Ferguson, W. 8: v E 1947 (4) 1953 (1); *v In 1948 (3)*
Fernandes, M. P. 2: v E 1929 (1); *v E 1928 (1)*
Findlay, T. M. 10: v A 1972 (1); v NZ 1971 (5); v In 1970 (2); *v E 1969 (2)*
Foster, M. L. C. 14: v E 1973 (1); v A 1972 (4) 1977 (1); v NZ 1971 (3); v In 1970 (2); v P 1976 (1); *v E 1969 (1) 1973 (1)*
Francis, G. N. 10: v E 1929 (1); *v E 1928 (3) 1933 (1); v A 1930 (5)*
Frederick, M. C. 1: v E 1953
Fredericks, R. C. 59: v E 1973 (5); v A 1972 (5); v NZ 1971 (5); v In 1970 (4) 1975 (4); v P 1976 (5); *v E 1969 (3) 1973 (3) 1976 (5); v A 1968 (4) 1975 (6); v NZ 1968 (3); v In 1974 (5); v P 1974 (2)*
Fuller, R. L. 1: v E 1934
Furlonge, H. A. 3: v A 1954 (1); *v NZ 1955 (2)*

Ganteaume, A. G. 1: v E 1947
Garner, J. 56: v E 1980 (4) 1985 (5); v A 1977 (2) 1983 (5); v NZ 1984 (4); v In 1982 (4); v P 1976 (5); *v E 1980 (5) 1984 (5); v A 1979 (3) 1981 (3) 1984 (5); v NZ 1979 (3); v P 1980 (3)*
Gaskin, B. B. M. 2: v E 1947 (2)
Gibbs, G. L. R. 1: v A 1954
Gibbs, L. R. 79: v E 1967 (5) 1973 (5); v A 1964 (5) 1972 (5); v NZ 1971 (2); v In 1961 (5) 1970 (1); v P 1957 (4); *v E 1963 (5) 1966 (5) 1969 (3) 1973 (3); v A 1960 (3) 1968 (5) 1975 (6); v NZ 1968 (3); v In 1958 (1) 1966 (3) 1974 (5); v P 1958 (3) 1974 (2)*
Gilchrist, R. 13: v P 1957 (4); *v In 1958 (4)*
Gladstone, G. 1: v E 1929
Goddard, J. D. C. 27: v E 1947 (4); *v E 1950 (4) 1957 (5); v A 1951 (4); v NZ 1951 (2) 1955 (3); v In 1948 (5)*
Gomes, H. A. 54: v E 1980 (4) 1985 (5); v A 1977 (3) 1983 (2); v NZ 1984 (4); v In 1982 (5); *v E 1976 (2) 1984 (5); v A 1981 (3) 1984 (5); v In 1978 (6) 1983 (6); v P 1980 (4)*
Gomez, G. E. 29: v E 1947 (4) 1953 (4); v In 1952 (4); *v E 1939 (2) 1950 (4); v A 1951 (5); v NZ 1951 (1); v In 1948 (5)*
Grant, G. C. 12: v E 1934 (4); *v E 1933 (3); v A 1930 (5)*
Grant, R. S. 7: v E 1934 (4); *v E 1939 (3)*
Greenidge, A. E. 6: v A 1977 (2); *v In 1978 (4)*
Greenidge, C. G. 71: v E 1980 (4) 1985 (5); v A 1977 (3) 1983 (5); v NZ 1984 (4); v In 1982 (5); v P 1976 (5); *v E 1976 (5) 1980 (5) 1984 (5); v A 1975 (2) 1979 (3) 1981 (2) 1984 (5); v NZ 1979 (3); v In 1974 (5) 1983 (6)*
Greenidge, G. A. 5: v A 1972 (3); v NZ 1971 (2)
Grell, M. G. 1: v E 1929
Griffith, C. C. 28: v E 1959 (1) 1967 (4); v A 1964 (5); *v E 1963 (5) 1966 (5); v A 1968 (3); v NZ 1968 (2); v In 1966 (3)*
Griffith, H. C. 13: v E 1929 (3); *v E 1928 (3) 1933 (2); v A 1930 (5)*
Guillen, S. C. 5: *v A 1951 (3); v NZ 1951 (2)*

Hall, W. W. 48: v E 1959 (5) 1967 (4); v A 1964 (5); v In 1961 (5); *v E 1963 (5) 1966 (5); v A 1960 (5) 1968 (2); v NZ 1968 (1); v In 1958 (5) 1966 (3); v P 1958 (3)*

Harper, R. A. 16: v E 1985 (2); v A 1983 (4); v NZ 1984 (1); *v E 1984 (5); v A 1984 (2); v In 1983 (2)*

Haynes, D. L. 59: v E 1980 (4) 1985 (5); v A 1977 (2) 1983 (5); v NZ 1984 (4); v In 1982 (5); *v E 1980 (5) 1984 (5); v A 1979 (3) 1981 (3) 1984 (5); v NZ 1979 (3); v In 1983 (6); v P 1980 (4)*

Headley, G. A. 22: v E 1929 (4) 1934 (4) 1947 (1) 1953 (1); *v E 1933 (3) 1939 (3); v A 1930 (5); v In 1948 (1)*

Headley, R. G. A. 2: *v E 1973 (2)*

Hendriks, J. L. 20: v A 1964 (4); v In 1961 (1); *v E 1966 (3) 1969 (1); v A 1968 (5); v NZ 1968 (3); v In 1966 (3)*

Hoad, E. L. G. 4: v E 1929 (1); *v E 1928 (1) 1933 (2)*

Holder, V. A. 40: v E 1973 (1); v A 1972 (3) 1977 (3); v NZ 1971 (4); v In 1970 (3) 1975 (1); v P 1976 (1); *v E 1969 (3) 1973 (2) 1976 (4); v A 1975 (3); v In 1974 (4) 1978 (6); v P 1974 (2)*

Holding, M. A. 59: v E 1980 (4) 1985 (4); v A 1983 (3); v NZ 1984 (3); v In 1975 (4) 1982 (5); *v E 1976 (4) 1980 (5) 1984 (4); v A 1975 (5) 1979 (5) 1981 (3) 1984 (3); v NZ 1979 (3); v In 1983 (6)*

Holford, D. A. J. 24: v E 1967 (4); v NZ 1971 (5); v In 1970 (1) 1975 (2); v P 1976 (1); *v E 1966 (5); v A 1968 (2); v NZ 1968 (3); v In 1966 (1)*

Holt, J. K. 17: v E 1953 (5); v A 1954 (5); *v In 1958 (5); v P 1958 (2)*

Howard, A. B. 1: v NZ 1971

Hunte, C. C. 44: v E 1959 (5); v A 1964 (5); v In 1961 (5); v P 1957 (5); *v E 1963 (5) 1966 (5); v A 1960 (5); v In 1958 (5) 1966 (3); v P 1958 (1)*

Hunte, E. A. C. 3: v E 1929 (3)

Hylton, L. G. 6: v E 1934 (4); *v E 1939 (2)*

Johnson, H. H. H. 3: v E 1947 (1); *v E 1950 (2)*

Johnson, T. F. 1: *v E 1939*

Jones, C. M. 4: v E 1929 (1) 1934 (3)

Jones, P. E. 9: v E 1947 (1); *v E 1950 (2); v A 1951 (1); v In 1948 (5)*

Julien, B. D. 24: v E 1973 (5); v In 1975 (4); v P 1976 (1); *v E 1973 (3) 1976 (2); v A 1975 (3); v In 1974 (4); v P 1974 (2)*

Jumadeen, R. R. 12: v A 1972 (1) 1977 (2); v NZ 1971 (1); v In 1975 (4); v P 1976 (1); *v E 1976 (1); v In 1978 (2)*

Kallicharran, A. I. 66: v E 1973 (5); v A 1972 (5) 1977 (5); v NZ 1971 (2); v In 1975 (4); v P 1976 (5); *v E 1973 (3) 1976 (3) 1980 (5); v A 1975 (5) 1979 (3); v NZ 1979 (3); v In 1974 (5) 1978 (6); v P 1974 (2) 1980 (4)*

Kanhai, R. B. 79: v E 1959 (5) 1967 (5) 1973 (5); v A 1964 (5) 1972 (5); v In 1961 (5) 1970 (5); v P 1957 (5); *v E 1957 (5) 1963 (5) 1966 (5) 1973 (3); v A 1960 (5) 1968 (5); v In 1958 (5) 1966 (3); v P 1958 (3)*

Kentish, E. S. M. 2: v E 1947 (1) 1953 (1)

King, C. L. 9: v P 1976 (1); *v E 1976 (3) 1980 (1); v A 1979 (1); v NZ 1979 (3)*

King, F. M. 14: v E 1953 (3); v A 1954 (4); v In 1952 (5); *v NZ 1955 (2)*

King, L. A. 2: v E 1967 (1); v In 1961 (1)

Lashley, P. D. 4: *v E 1966 (2); v A 1960 (2)*

Legall, R. 4: v In 1952 (4)

Lewis, D. M. 3: v In 1970 (3)

Lloyd, C. H. 110: v E 1967 (5) 1973 (5) 1980 (4); v A 1972 (3) 1977 (2) 1983 (4); v NZ 1971 (2); v In 1970 (5) 1975 (4) 1982 (5); v P 1976 (5); *v E 1969 (3) 1973 (3) 1976 (5) 1980 (4) 1984 (5); v A 1968 (4) 1975 (6) 1979 (2) 1981 (3) 1984 (5); v NZ 1968 (3) 1979 (3); v In 1966 (3) 1974 (5) 1983 (6); v P 1974 (2) 1980 (4)*

Logie, A. L. 13: v A 1983 (1); v NZ 1984 (4); v In 1982 (5); *v In 1983 (3)*

McMorris, E. D. A. 13: v E 1959 (4); v In 1961 (4); v P 1957 (1); *v E 1963 (2) 1966 (2)*

McWatt, C. A. 6: v E 1953 (5); v A 1954 (1)

Madray, I. S. 2: v P 1957 (2)

Marshall, M. D. 45: v E 1980 (1) 1985 (5); v A 1983 (4); v NZ 1984 (4); v In 1982 (5); *v E 1980 (4) 1984 (4); v A 1984 (5); v In 1978 (3) 1983 (6); v P 1980 (4)*

Marshall, N. E. 1: v A 1954

Marshall, R. E. 4: *v A 1951 (2); v NZ 1951 (2)*

Martin, F. R. 9: v E 1929 (1); *v E 1928 (3); v A 1930 (5)*

Martindale, E. A. 10: v E 1934 (4); *v E 1933 (3) 1939 (3)*

Mattis, E. H. 4: v E 1980 (4)
Mendonca, I. L. 2: v In 1961 (2)
Merry, C. A. 2: *v E 1933 (2)*
Miller, R. 1: v In 1952
Moodie, G. H. 1: v E 1934
Murray, D. A. 19: v E 1980 (4); v A 1977 (3); *v A 1981 (2)*; v In 1978 (6); *v P 1980* (4)
Murray, D. L. 62: v E 1967 (5) 1973 (5); v A 1972 (4) 1977 (2); v In 1975 (4); v P 1976 (5); *v E 1963 (5) 1973 (3) 1976 (5) 1980 (5); v A 1975 (6) 1979 (3); v NZ 1979 (3); v In 1974 (5); v P 1974 (2)*

Nanan, R. 1: *v P 1980*
Neblett, J. M. 1: v E 1934
Noreiga, J. M. 4: v In 1970 (4)
Nunes, R. K. 4: v E 1929 (1); *v E 1928 (3)*
Nurse, S. M. 29: v E 1959 (1) 1967 (5); v A 1964 (4); v In 1961 (1); *v E 1966 (5); v A 1960 (3) 1968 (5); v NZ 1968 (3); v In 1966 (2)*

Padmore, A. L. 2: v In 1975 (1); *v E 1976 (1)*
Pairaudeau, B. H. 13: v E 1953 (2); v In 1952 (5): *v E 1957 (2); v NZ 1955 (4)*
Parry, D. R. 12: v A 1977 (5); *v NZ 1979 (1); v In 1978 (6)*
Passailaigue, C. C. 1: v E 1929
Patterson, B. P. 5: v E 1985 (5)
Payne, T. R. O. 1: v E 1985
Phillip, N. 9: v A 1977 (3); *v In 1978 (6)*
Pierre, L. R. 1: v E 1947

Rae, A. F. 15: v In 1952 (2); *v E 1950 (4); v A 1951 (3); v NZ 1951 (1); v In 1948 (5)*
Ramadhin, S. 43: v E 1953 (5) 1959 (4); v A 1954 (4); v In 1952 (4); *v E 1950 (4) 1957 (5); v A 1951 (5) 1960 (2); v NZ 1951 (2) 1955 (4); v In 1958 (2); v P 1958 (2)*
Richards, I. V. A. 82: v E 1980 (4) 1985 (5); v A 1977 (2) 1983 (5); v NZ 1984 (4); v In 1975 (4) 1982 (5); v P 1976 (5); *v E 1976 (4) 1980 (5) 1984 (5); v A 1975 (6) 1979 (3) 1981 (3) 1984 (5); v In 1974 (5) 1983 (6); v P 1974 (2) 1980 (4)*
Richardson, R. B. 20: v E 1985 (5); v A 1983 (5); v NZ 1984 (4); *v A 1984 (5); v In 1983 (1)*
Rickards, K. R. 2: v E 1947 (1); *v A 1951 (1)*
Roach, C. A. 16: v E 1929 (4) 1934 (1); *v E 1928 (3) 1933 (3); v A 1930 (5)*
Roberts, A. M. E. 47: v E 1973 (1) 1980 (3); v A 1977 (2); v In 1975 (2) 1982 (5); v P 1976 (5); *v E 1976 (5) 1980 (3); v A 1975 (5) 1979 (3) 1981 (2); v NZ 1979 (2); v In 1974 (5) 1983 (2); v P 1974 (2)*
Roberts, A. T. 1: *v NZ 1955*
Rodriguez, W. V. 5: v E 1967 (1); v A 1964 (1); v In 1961 (2); *v E 1963 (1)*
Rowe, L. G. 30: v E 1973 (5); v A 1972 (3); v NZ 1971 (4); v In 1975 (4); *v E 1976 (2); v A 1975 (6) 1979 (3); v NZ 1979 (3)*

St Hill, E. L. 2: v E 1929 (2)
St Hill, W. H. 3: v E 1929 (1); *v E 1928 (2)*
Scarlett, R. O. 3: v E 1959 (3)
Scott, A. P. H. 1: v In 1952
Scott, O. C. 8: v E 1929 (1); *v E 1928 (2); v A 1930 (5)*
Sealey, B. J. 1: *v E 1933*
Sealy, J. E. D. 11: v E 1929 (2) 1934 (4); *v E 1939 (3); v A 1930 (2)*
Shepherd, J. N. 5: v In 1970 (2); *v E 1969 (3)*
Shillingford, G. C. 7: v NZ 1971 (2); v In 1970 (3); *v E 1969 (2)*
Shillingford, I. T. 4: v A 1977 (1); v P 1976 (3)
Shivnarine, S. 8: v A 1977 (3); *v In 1978 (5)*
Singh, C. K. 2: v E 1959 (2)
Small, J. A. 3: v E 1929 (1); *v E 1928 (2)*
Small, M. A. 2: v A 1983 (1); *v E 1984 (1)*
Smith, C. W. 5: v In 1961 (1); *v A 1960 (4)*
Smith, O. G. 26: v A 1954 (4); v P 1957 (5); *v E 1957 (5); v NZ 1955 (4); v In 1958 (5); v P 1958 (3)*
Sobers, G. S. 93: v E 1953 (1) 1959 (5) 1967 (5) 1973 (4); v A 1954 (4) 1964 (5); v NZ 1971 (5); v In 1961 (5); 1970 (5); v P 1957 (5); *v E 1957 (5) 1963 (5) 1966 (5) 1969 (3) 1973 (3); v A 1960 (5) 1968 (5); v NZ 1955 (4) 1968 (3); v In 1958 (5) 1966 (3); v P 1958 (3)*

Solomon, J. S. 27: v E 1959 (2); v A 1964 (4); v In 1961 (4); *v E 1963 (5); v A 1960 (5); v In 1958 (4); v P 1958 (3)*

Stayers, S. C. 4: v In 1961 (4)

Stollmeyer, J. B. 32: v E 1947 (2) 1953 (5); v A 1954 (2); v In 1952 (5); *v E 1939 (3) 1950 (4); v A 1951 (5); v NZ 1951 (2); v In 1948 (4)*

Stollmeyer, V. H. 1: *v E 1939*

Taylor, J. 3: v P 1957 (1); *v In 1958 (1); v P 1958 (1)*

Trim, J. 4: v E 1947 (1); *v A 1951 (1); v In 1948 (2)*

Valentine, A. L. 36: v E 1953 (3); v A 1954 (3); v In 1952 (5) 1961 (2); v P 1957 (1); *v E 1950 (4) 1957 (2); v A 1951 (5) 1960 (5); v NZ 1951 (2) 1955 (4)*

Valentine, V. A. 2: *v E 1933 (2)*

Walcott, C. L. 44: v E 1947 (4) 1953 (5) 1959 (2); v A 1954 (5); v In 1952 (5); v P 1957 (4); *v E 1950 (4) 1957 (5); v A 1951 (3); v NZ 1951 (2); v In 1948 (5)*

Walcott, L. A. 1: v E 1929

Walsh, C. A. 7: v E 1985 (1); v NZ 1984 (1); *v A 1984 (5)*

Watson, C. 7: v E 1959 (5); v In 1961 (1); *v A 1960 (1)*

Weekes, E. D. 48: v E 1947 (4) 1953 (5); v A 1954 (5); v In 1952 (5); v P 1957 (5); *v E 1950 (4) 1957 (5); v A 1951 (5); v NZ 1951 (2) 1955 (4); v In 1948 (5)*

Weekes, K. H. 2: *v E 1939 (2)*

White, W. A. 2: v A 1964 (2)

Wight, C. V. 2: v E 1929 (1); *v E 1928 (1)*

Wight, G. L. 1: v In 1952

Wiles, C. A. 1: *v E 1933*

Willett, E. T. 5: v A 1972 (4); *v In 1974 (2)*

Williams, A. B. 7: v A 1977 (3); *v In 1978 (4)*

Williams, E. A. V. 4: v E 1947 (3); *v E 1939 (1)*

Wishart, K. L. 1: v E 1934

Worrell, F. M. M. 51: v E 1947 (3) 1953 (4) 1959 (4); v A 1954 (4); v In 1952 (5) 1961 (5); *v E 1950 (4) 1957 (5) 1963 (5); v A 1951 (5) 1960 (5); v NZ 1951 (2)*

NEW ZEALAND

Number of Test cricketers: 160

Alabaster, J. C. 21: v E 1962 (2); v WI 1955 (1); v In 1967 (4); *v E 1958 (2); v SA 1961 (5); v WI 1971 (2); v In 1955 (4); v P 1955 (1)*

Allcott, C. F. W. 6: v E 1929 (2); v SA 1931 (1); *v E 1931 (3)*

Anderson, R. W. 9: v E 1977 (3); *v E 1978 (3); v P 1976 (3)*

Anderson, W. M. 1: v A 1945

Andrews, B. 2: *v A 1973 (2)*

Badcock, F. T. 7: v E 1929 (3) 1932 (2); v SA 1931 (2)

Barber, R. T. 1: v WI 1955

Bartlett, G. A. 10: v E 1965 (2); v In 1967 (2); v P 1964 (1); *v SA 1961 (5)*

Barton, P. T. 7: v E 1962 (3); *v SA 1961 (4)*

Beard, D. D. 4: v WI 1951 (2) 1955 (2)

Beck, J. E. F. 8: v WI 1955 (4); *v SA 1953 (4)*

Bell, W. 2: *v SA 1953 (2)*

Bilby, G. P. 2: v E 1965 (2)

Blain, T. E. 1: *v E 1986*

Blair, R. W. 19: v E 1954 (1) 1958 (2) 1962 (2); v SA 1952 (2) 1963 (3); v WI 1955 (2) *v E 1958 (3); v SA 1953 (4)*

Blunt, R. C. 9: v E 1929 (4); v SA 1931 (2); *v E 1931 (3)*

Bolton, B. A. 2: v E 1958 (2)

Boock, S. L. 26: v E 1977 (3) 1983 (2); v WI 1979 (3); v P 1978 (3) 1984 (2); *v E 1978 (3); v A 1985 (1); v WI 1984 (3); v P 1984 (3); v SL 1983 (3)*

Bracewell, B. P. 6: v P 1978 (1) 1984 (1); *v E 1978 (3); v A 1980 (1)*

Bracewell, J. G. 20: v A 1985 (2); v In 1980 (1); *v E 1983 (4) 1986 (3); v A 1980 (3) 1985 (2); v WI 1984 (1); v P 1984 (2); v SL 1983 (2)*
Bradburn, W. P. 2: v SA 1963 (2)
Brown, V. R. 2: *v A 1985 (2)*
Burgess, M. G. 50: v E 1970 (1) 1977 (3); v A 1973 (1) 1976 (2); v WI 1968 (2); v In 1967 (4) 1975 (3); v P 1972 (3) 1978 (3); *v E 1969 (2) 1973 (3) 1978 (3); v A 1980 (3); v WI 1971 (5); v In 1969 (3) 1976 (3); v P 1969 (3) 1976 (3)*
Burke, C. 1: v A 1945
Burtt, T. B. 10: v E 1946 (1) 1950 (2); v SA 1952 (1); v WI 1951 (2); *v E 1949 (4)*
Butterfield, L. A. 1: v A 1945

Cairns, B. L. 43: v E 1974 (1) 1977 (1) 1983 (3); v A 1976 (1) 1981 (3); v WI 1979 (3); v In 1975 (1) 1980 (3); v P 1978 (3) 1984 (3); v SL 1982 (2); *v E 1978 (2) 1983 (4); v A 1973 (1) 1980 (3) 1985 (1); v WI 1984 (2); v In 1976 (2); v P 1976 (2); v SL 1983 (2)*
Cameron, F. J. 19: v E 1962 (3); v SA 1963 (3); v P 1964 (3); *v E 1965 (2); v SA 1961 (5); v In 1964 (1); v P 1964 (2)*
Cave, H. B. 19: v E 1954 (2); v WI 1955 (3); *v E 1949 (4) 1958 (2); v In 1955 (5); v P 1955 (3)*
Chapple, M. E. 14: v E 1954 (1) 1965 (1); v SA 1952 (1) 1963 (3); v WI 1955 (1); *v SA 1953 (5) 1961 (2)*
Chatfield, E. J. 29: v E 1974 (1) 1977 (1) 1983 (3); v A 1976 (2) 1981 (1) 1985 (3); v P 1984 (3); v SL 1982 (2); *v E 1983 (3) 1986 (1); v A 1985 (2); v WI 1984 (4); v P 1984 (1); v SL 1983 (2)*
Cleverley, D. C. 2: v SA 1931 (1); v A 1945 (1)
Collinge, R. O. 35: v E 1970 (2) 1974 (2) 1977 (3); v A 1973 (3); v In 1967 (2) 1975 (3); v P 1964 (3) 1972 (2); *v E 1965 (3) 1969 (1) 1973 (3) 1978 (1); v In 1964 (2) 1976 (1); v P 1964 (2) 1976 (2)*
Colquhoun, I. A. 2: v E 1954 (2)
Coney, J. V. 49: v E 1983 (3); v A 1973 (2) 1981 (3) 1985 (3); v WI 1979 (3); v In 1980 (3); v P 1978 (3) 1984 (3); v SL 1982 (2); *v E 1983 (4) 1986 (3); v A 1973 (1) 1980 (2) 1985 (3); v WI 1984 (4); v P 1984 (3); v SL 1983 (3)*
Congdon, B. E. 61: v E 1965 (3) 1970 (2) 1974 (2) 1977 (3); v A 1973 (3) 1976 (2); v WI 1968 (3); v In 1967 (4) 1975 (3); v P 1964 (3) 1972 (3); *v E 1965 (3) 1969 (3) 1973 (3) 1978 (3); v A 1973 (3); v WI 1971 (5); v In 1964 (3) 1969 (3); v P 1964 (1) 1969 (3)*
Cowie, J. 9: v E 1946 (1); v A 1945 (1); *v E 1937 (3) 1949 (4)*
Cresswell G. F. 3: v E 1950 (2); *v E 1949 (1)*
Cromb, I. B. 5: v SA 1931 (2); *v E 1931 (3)*
Crowe, J. J. 26: v E 1983 (3); v SL 1982 (2); *v E 1983 (2) 1986 (3); v A 1985 (3); v WI 1984 (4); v P 1984 (3); v SL 1983 (3)*
Crowe, M. D. 32: v E 1983 (3); v A 1981 (3) 1985 (3); v P 1984 (3); *v E 1983 (4) 1986 (3); v A 1985 (3); v WI 1984 (4); v P 1984 (3); v SL 1983 (3)*
Cunis, R. S. 20: v E 1965 (3) 1970 (2); v SA 1963 (1); v WI 1968 (3); *v E 1969 (1); v WI 1971 (5); v In 1969 (3); v P 1969 (2)*

D'Arcy, J. W. 5: *v E 1958 (5)*
Dempster, C. S. 10: v E 1929 (4) 1932 (2); v SA 1931 (2); *v E 1931 (2)*
Dempster, E. W. 5: v SA 1952 (1); *v SA 1953 (4)*
Dick, A. E. 17: v E 1962 (3); v SA 1963 (2); v P 1964 (2); *v E 1965 (2); v SA 1961 (5); v P 1964 (3)*
Dickinson, G. R. 3: v E 1929 (2); v SA 1931 (1)
Donnelly, M. P. 7: *v E 1937 (3) 1949 (4)*
Dowling, G. T. 39: v E 1962 (3) 1970 (2); v In 1967 (4); v SA 1963 (1); v WI 1968 (3); v P 1964 (2); *v E 1965 (3) 1969 (3); v SA 1961 (4); v WI 1971 (2); v In 1964 (4) 1969 (3); v P 1964 (2) 1969 (3)*
Dunning, J. A. 4: v E 1932 (1); *v E 1937 (3)*

Edgar, B. A. 39: v E 1983 (3); v A 1981 (3) 1985 (3); v WI 1979 (3); v In 1980 (3); v P 1978 (3); v SL 1982 (2); *v E 1978 (3) 1983 (4) 1986 (3); v A 1980 (3) 1985 (3); v P 1984 (3)*
Edwards, G. N. 8: v E 1977 (1); v A 1976 (2); v In 1980 (3); *v E 1978 (2)*
Emery, R. W. G. 2: v WI 1951 (2)

Fisher, F. E. 1: v SA 1952
Foley, H. 1: v E 1929
Franklin, T. J. 2: v A 1985 (1); *v E 1983 (1)*
Freeman, D. L. 2: v E 1932 (2)

Gallichan, N. 1: *v E 1937*

Gedye, S. G. 4: v SA 1963 (3); v P 1964 (1)

Gillespie, S. R. 1: v A 1985

Gray, E. J. 7: *v E 1983 (2) 1986 (3); v P 1984 (2)*

Guillen, S. C. 3: v WI 1955 (3)

Guy, J. W. 12: v E 1958 (2); v WI 1955 (2); *v SA 1961 (2); v In 1955 (5); v P 1955 (1)*

Hadlee, D. R. 26: v E 1974 (2) 1977 (1); v A 1973 (3) 1976 (1); v In 1975 (3); v P 1972 (2); *v E 1969 (2) 1973 (3); v A 1973 (3); v In 1969 (3); v P 1969 (3)*

Hadlee, R. J. 66: v E 1977 (3) 1983 (3); v A 1973 (2) 1976 (2) 1981 (3) 1985 (3); v WI 1979 (3); v In 1975 (2) 1980 (3); v P 1972 (1) 1978 (3) 1984 (3); v SL 1982 (2); *v E 1973 (1) 1978 (3) 1983 (4) 1986 (3); v A 1973 (3) 1980 (3) 1985 (3); v WI 1984 (4); v In 1976 (3); v P 1976 (3); v SL 1983 (3)*

Hadlee, W. A. 11: v E 1946 (1) 1950 (2); v A 1945 (1); *v E 1937 (3) 1949 (4)*

Harford, N. S. 8: *v E 1958 (4); v In 1955 (2); v P 1955 (2)*

Harford, R. I. 3: v In 1967 (3)

Harris, P. G. Z. 9: v P 1964 (1); *v SA 1961 (5); v In 1955 (1); v P 1955 (2)*

Harris, R. M. 2: v E 1958 (2)

Hastings, B. F. 31: v E 1974 (2); v A 1973 (3); v WI 1968 (3); v In 1975 (1); v P 1972 (3); *v E 1969 (3) 1973 (3); v A 1973 (3); v WI 1971 (5); v In 1969 (2); v P 1969 (3)*

Hayes, J. A. 15: v E 1950 (2) 1954 (1); v WI 1951 (2); *v E 1958 (4); v In 1955 (5); v P 1955 (1)*

Henderson, M. 1: v E 1929

Hough, K. W. 2: v E 1958 (2)

Howarth, G. P. 47: v E 1974 (2) 1977 (3) 1983 (3); v A 1976 (2) 1981 (3); v WI 1979 (3); v In 1980 (3); v P 1978 (3) 1984 (3); v SL 1982 (2); *v E 1978 (3) 1983 (4); v A 1980 (2); v WI 1984 (4); v In 1976 (2); v P 1976 (2); v SL 1983 (3)*

Howarth, H. J. 30: v E 1970 (2) 1974 (2); v A 1973 (3) 1976 (2); v In 1975 (2); v P 1972 (3); *v E 1969 (3) 1973 (2); v WI 1971 (5); v In 1969 (3); v P 1969 (3)*

James, K. C. 11: v E 1929 (4) 1932 (2); v SA 1931 (3); *v E 1931 (3)*

Jarvis, T. W. 13: v E 1965 (1); v P 1972 (3); *v WI 1971 (4); v In 1964 (2); v P 1964 (3)*

Kerr, J. L. 7: v E 1932 (2); v SA 1931 (1); *v E 1931 (2) 1937 (2)*

Lees, W. K. 21: v E 1977 (2); v A 1976 (1); v WI 1979 (3); v P 1978 (3); v SL 1982 (2); *v E 1983 (2); v A 1980 (2); v In 1976 (3); v P 1976 (3)*

Leggat, I. B. 1: *v SA 1953*

Leggat, J. G. 9: v E 1954 (1); v WI 1951 (1) 1955 (1); *v In 1955 (3); v P 1955 (2)*

Lissette, A. F. 2: v WI 1955 (2)

Lowry, T. C. 7: v E 1929 (4); *v E 1931 (3)*

MacGibbon, A. R. 26: v E 1950 (2) 1954 (2); v SA 1952 (1); v WI 1955 (3); *v E 1958 (5); v SA 1953 (5); v In 1955 (5); v P 1955 (3)*

McEwan, P. E. 4: v WI 1979 (1); *v A 1980 (2); v P 1984 (1)*

McGirr, H. M. 2: v E 1929 (2)

McGregor, S. N. 25: v E 1954 (2) 1958 (2); v SA 1963 (3); v WI 1955 (4); v P 1964 (2); *v SA 1961 (5); v In 1955 (4); v P 1955 (3)*

McLeod E. G. 1: v E 1929

McMahon T. G. 5: v WI 1955 (1); *v In 1955 (3); v P 1955 (1)*

McRae, D. A. N. 1: v A 1945

Matheson, A. M. 2: v E 1929 (1); *v E 1931 (1)*

Meale, T. 2: *v E 1958 (2)*

Merritt, W. E. 6: v E 1929 (4); *v E 1931 (2)*

Meuli, E. M. 1: v SA 1952

Milburn, B. D. 3: v WI 1968 (3)

Miller, L. S. M. 13: v SA 1952 (2); v WI 1955 (3); *v E 1958 (4); v SA 1953 (4)*

Mills, J. E. 7: v E 1929 (3) 1932 (1); *v E 1931 (3)*

Moir, A. M. 17: v E 1950 (2) 1954 (2) 1958 (2); v SA 1952 (1); v WI 1951 (2) 1955 (1); *v E 1958 (2); v In 1955 (2); v P 1955 (3)*

Moloney D. A. R. 3: *v E 1937 (3)*

Mooney, F. L. H. 14: v E 1950 (2); v WI 1955 (3); *v E 1949 (3); v SA 1953 (5)*

Morgan, R. W. 20: v E 1965 (2) 1970 (2); v WI 1968 (1); v P 1964 (2); *v E 1965 (3); v WI 1971 (3); v In 1964 (4); v P 1964 (3)*

Morrison, B. D. 1: v E 1962
Morrison, J. F. M. 17: v E 1974 (2); v A 1973 (3) 1981 (3); v In 1975 (3); *v A 1973 (3); v In 1976 (1); v P 1976 (2)*
Motz, R. C. 32: v E 1962 (2) 1965 (3); v SA 1963 (2); v WI 1968 (3): v In 1967 (4); v P 1964 (3); *v E 1965 (3) 1969 (3); v SA 1961 (5); v In 1964 (3); v P 1964 (1)*
Murray, B. A. G. 13: v E 1970 (1); v In 1967 (4); *v E 1969 (2); v In 1969 (3); v P 1969 (3)*

Newman J. 3: v E 1932 (2); v SA 1931 (1)

O'Sullivan, D. R. 11: v In 1975 (1); v P 1972 (1); *v A 1973 (3); v In 1976 (3); v P 1976 (3)*
Overton, G. W. F. 3: *v SA 1953 (3)*

Page, M. L. 14: v E 1929 (4) 1932 (2); v SA 1931 (2); *v E 1931 (3) 1937 (3)*
Parker, J. M. 36: v E 1974 (2) 1977 (3); v A 1973 (3) 1976 (2); v WI 1979 (3); v In 1975 (3); v P 1972 (1) 1978 (2); *v E 1973 (3) 1978 (2); v A 1973 (3) 1980 (3); v In 1976 (3); v P 1976 (3)*
Parker, N. M. 3: *v In 1976 (2); v P 1976 (1)*
Petherick, P. J. 6: v A 1976 (1); v In 1976 (3); *v P 1976 (2)*
Petrie, E. C. 14: v E 1958 (2) 1965 (3); *v E 1958 (5); v In 1955 (2); v P 1955 (2)*
Playle, W. R. 8: v E 1962 (3); *v E 1958 (5)*
Pollard, V. 32: v E 1965 (3) 1970 (1); v WI 1968 (3); v In 1967 (4); v P 1972 (1); *v E 1965 (3) 1969 (3) 1973 (3); v In 1964 (4) 1969 (1); v P 1964 (3) 1969 (3)*
Poore, M. B. 14: v E 1954 (1); v SA 1952 (1); *v SA 1953 (5); v In 1955 (4); v P 1955 (3)*
Puna, N. 3: v E 1965 (3)

Rabone, G. O. 12: v E 1954 (2); v SA 1952 (1); v WI 1951 (2); *v E 1949 (4); v SA 1953 (3)*
Redmond, R. E. 1: v P 1972
Reid, J. F. 19: v A 1985 (3); v In 1980 (3); v P 1978 (1) 1984 (3); *v A 1985 (3); v P 1984 (3); v SL 1983 (3)*
Reid, J. R. 58: v E 1950 (2) 1954 (2) 1958 (2) 1962 (3); v SA 1952 (2) 1963 (3); v WI 1951 (2) 1955 (4); v P 1964 (3); *v E 1949 (2) 1958 (5) 1965 (3); v SA 1953 (5) 1961 (5); v In 1955 (5) 1964 (4); v P 1955 (3) 1964 (3)*
Roberts, A. D. G. 7: v In 1975 (2); *v In 1976 (3); v P 1976 (2)*
Roberts, A. W. 5: v E 1929 (1); v SA 1931 (2); *v E 1937 (2)*
Robertson, G. K. 1: v A 1985
Rowe, C. G. 1: v A 1945
Rutherford, K. R. 8: v A 1985 (3); *v E 1986 (1); v WI 1984 (4)*

Scott, R. H. 1: v E 1946
Scott, V. J. 10: v E 1946 (1) 1950 (2); v A 1945 (1); v WI 1951 (2); *v E 1949 (4)*
Shrimpton, M. J. F. 10: v E 1962 (2) 1965 (3) 1970 (2); v SA 1963 (1); *v A 1973 (2)*
Sinclair, B. W. 21: v E 1962 (3) 1965 (3); v SA 1963 (3); v In 1967 (2); v P 1964 (2); *v E 1965 (3); v In 1964 (2); v P 1964 (3)*
Sinclair, I. M. 2: v WI 1955 (2)
Smith, F. B. 4: v E 1946 (1); v WI 1951 (1); *v E 1949 (2)*
Smith, H. D. 1: v E 1932
Smith, I. D. S. 33: v E 1983 (3); v A 1981 (3) 1985 (3); v In 1980 (3); v P 1984 (3); *v E 1983 (2) 1986 (2); v A 1980 (1) 1985 (3); v WI 1984 (4); v P 1984 (3); v SL 1983 (3)*
Snedden, C. A. 1: v E 1946
Snedden, M. C. 11: v E 1983 (1); v A 1981 (3); v In 1980 (3); v SL 1982 (2); *v E 1983 (1); v A 1985 (1)*
Sparling, J. T. 11: v E 1958 (2) 1962 (1); v SA 1963 (2); *v E 1958 (3); v SA 1961 (3)*
Stirling, D. A. 6: *v E 1986 (2); v WI 1984 (1); v P 1984 (3)*
Sutcliffe, B. 42: v E 1946 (1) 1950 (2) 1954 (2) 1958 (2); v SA 1952 (2); v WI 1951 (2) 1955 (2); *v E 1949 (4) 1958 (4) 1965 (1); v SA 1953 (5); v In 1955 (5) 1964 (4); v P 1955 (3) 1964 (3)*

Taylor, B. R. 30: v E 1965 (1); v WI 1968 (3); v In 1967 (3); v P 1972 (3); *v E 1965 (2) 1969 (2) 1973 (3); v WI 1971 (4); v In 1964 (3) 1969 (2); v P 1964 (3) 1969 (1)*
Taylor, D. D. 3: v E 1946 (1); v WI 1955 (2)
Thomson, K. 2: v In 1967 (2)
Tindill, E. W. T. 5: v E 1946 (1); v A 1945 (1); *v E 1937 (3)*
Troup, G. B. 15: v A 1981 (2) 1985 (2); v WI 1979 (3); v In 1980 (3); v P 1978 (2); *v A 1980 (2); v WI 1984 (1); v In 1976 (1)*

Truscott, P. B. 1: v P 1964
Turner, G. M. 41: v E 1970 (2) 1974 (2); v A 1973 (3) 1976 (2); v WI 1968 (3); v In 1975 (3); v P 1972 (3); v SL 1982 (2); *v E 1969 (2) 1973 (3); v A 1973 (2); v WI 1971 (5); v In 1969 (3) 1976 (3); v P 1969 (1) 1976 (2)*

Vivian, G. E. 5: *v WI 1971 (4); v In 1964 (1)*
Vivian, H. G. 7: v E 1932 (1); v SA 1931 (1); *v E 1931 (2) 1937 (3)*

Wadsworth, K. J. 33: v E 1970 (2) 1974 (2); v A 1973 (3); v In 1975 (3); v P 1972 (3); *v E 1969 (3) 1973 (3); v A 1973 (3); v WI 1971 (5); v In 1969 (3); v P 1969 (3)*
Wallace, W. M. 13: v E 1946 (1) 1950 (2); v A 1945 (1); v SA 1952 (2); *v E 1937 (3) 1949 (4)*
Ward, J. T. 8: v SA 1963 (1); v In 1967 (1); v P 1964 (1); *v E 1965 (1); v In 1964 (4)*
Watson, W. 2: *v E 1986 (2)*
Watt, L. 1: v E 1954
Webb, M. G. 3: v E 1970 (1); v A 1973 (1); *v WI 1971 (1)*
Webb, P. N. 2: v WI 1979 (2)
Weir, G. L. 11: v E 1929 (3) 1932 (2); v SA 1931 (2); *v E 1931 (3) 1937 (1)*
Whitelaw, P. E. 2: v E 1932 (2)
Wright, J. G. 49: v E 1977 (3) 1983 (3); v A 1981 (3) 1985 (2); v WI 1979 (3); v In 1980 (3); v P 1978 (3) 1984 (3); v SL 1982 (2); *v E 1978 (2) 1983 (3) 1986 (3); v A 1980 (3) 1985 (3); v WI 1984 (4); v P 1984 (3); v SL 1983 (3)*

Yuile, B. W. 17: v E 1962 (2); v WI 1968 (3); v In 1967 (1); v P 1964 (3); *v E 1965 (1); v In 1964 (3) 1969 (1); v P 1964 (1) 1969 (2)*

INDIA

Number of Test cricketers: 174

Abid Ali, S. 29: v E 1972 (4); v A 1969 (1); v WI 1974 (2); v NZ 1969 (3); *v E 1971 (3) 1974 (3); v A 1967 (4); v WI 1970 (5); v NZ 1967 (4)*
Adhikari, H. R. 21: v E 1951 (3); v A 1956 (2); v WI 1948 (5) 1958 (1); v P 1952 (2); *v E 1952 (3); v A 1947 (5)*
Amarnath, L. 24: v E 1933 (3) 1951 (3); v WI 1948 (5); v P 1952 (5); *v E 1946 (3); v A 1947 (5)*
Amarnath, M. 56: v E 1976 (2) 1984 (5); v A 1969 (1) 1979 (1); v WI 1978 (2) 1983 (3); v NZ 1976 (3); v P 1983 (2); *v E 1979 (2)1986 (2); v A 1977 (5) 1985 (3); v WI 1975 (4) 1982 (5); v NZ 1975 (3); v P 1978 (3) 1982 (6) 1984 (2); v SL 1985 (2)*
Amarnath, S. 10: v E 1976 (2): *v WI 1975 (2); v NZ 1975 (3); v P 1978 (3)*
Amar Singh 7: v E 1933 (3); *v E 1932 (1) 1936 (3)*
Amir Elahi 1: *v A 1947*
Apte, A. L. 1: *v E 1959*
Apte, M. L. 7: v P 1952 (2); *v WI 1952 (5)*
Arun Lal 4: v SL 19821; *v P 1982 (3)*
Azad, K. 7: v E 1981 (2); v WI 1983 (2); v P 1983 (1); *v NZ 1980 (1)*
Azharuddin, M. 12: v E 1984 (3); *v E 1986 (3); v A 1985 (3); v SL 1985 (3)*

Baig, A. A. 10: v A 1959 (3); v WI 1966 (2); v P 1960 (3); *v E 1959 (2)*
Banerjee, S. A. 1: v WI 1948
Banerjee, S. N. 1: v WI 1948
Baqa Jilani, M. 1: *v E 1936*
Bedi, B. S. 67: v E 1972 (5) 1976 (5); v A 1969 (5); v WI 1966 (2) 1974 (4) 1978 (3); v NZ 1969 (3) 1976 (3); *v E 1967 (3) 1971 (3) 1974 (3) 1979 (3); v A 1967 (2) 1977 (5); v WI 1970 (5) 1975 (4); v NZ 1967 (4) 1975 (2); v P 1978 (3)*
Bhandari, P. 3: v A 1956 (1); v NZ 1955 (1); *v P 1954 (1)*
Bhat, A. R. 2: v WI 1983 (1); v P 1983 (1)
Binny, R. M. H. 24: v E 1979 (1); v WI 1983 (6); v P 1979 (6) 1983 (2); *v E 1986 (3); v A 1980 (1) 1985 (2); v NZ 1980 (1); v P 1984 (1); v SL 1985 (1)*
Borde, C. G. 55: v E 1961 (5) 1963 (5); v A 1959 (5) 1964 (3) 1969 (1); v WI 1958 (4) 1966 (3); v NZ 1964 (4); v P 1960 (5); *v E 1959 (4) 1967 (3); v A 1967 (4); v WI 1961 (5); v NZ 1967 (4)*

Chandrasekhar, B. S. 58: v E 1963 (4) 1972 (5) 1976 (5); v A 1964 (2); v WI 1966 (3) 1974 (4) 1978 (4); v NZ 1964 (2) 1976 (3); *v E 1967 (3) 1971 (3) 1974 (2) 1979 (1); v A 1967 (2) 1977 (5); v WI 1975 (4); v NZ 1975 (3); v P 1978 (3)*

Chauhan, C. P. S. 40: v E 1972 (2); v A 1969 (1) 1979 (6); v WI 1978 (6); v NZ 1969 (2); v P 1979 (6); *v E 1979 (4); v A 1977 (4) 1980 (3); v NZ 1980 (3); v P 1978 (3)*

Chowdhury, N. R. 2: v E 1951 (1); v WI 1948 (1)

Colah, S. H. M. 2: v E 1933 (1); *v E 1932 (1)*

Contractor, N. J. 31: v E 1961 (5); v A 1956 (1) 1959 (5); v WI 1958 (5); v NZ 1955 (4); v P 1960 (5); *v E 1959 (4); v WI 1961 (2)*

Dani, H. T. 1: v P 1952

Desai, R. B. 28: v E 1961 (4) 1963 (2); v A 1959 (3); v WI 1958 (1); v NZ 1964 (3); v P 1960 (5); *v E 1959 (5); v A 1967 (1); v WI 1961 (3); v NZ 1967 (1)*

Dilawar Hussain 3: v E 1933 (2); *v E 1936 (1)*

Divecha, R. V. 5: v E 1951 (2); v P 1952 (1); *v E 1952 (2)*

Doshi, D. R. 33: v E 1979 (1) 1981 (6); v A 1979 (6); v P 1979 (6) 1983 (1); v SL 1982 (1); *v E 1982 (3); v A 1980 (2); v NZ 1980 (2); v P 1982 (4)*

Durani, S. A. 29: v E 1961 (5) 1963 (5) 1972 (3); v A 1959 (1) 1964 (3); v WI 1966 (1); v NZ 1964 (3); *v WI 1961 (5) 1970 (3)*

Engineer, F. M. 46: v E 1961 (4) 1972 (5); v A 1969 (5); v WI 1966 (1) 1974 (5); v NZ 1964 (4) 1969 (2); *v E 1967 (3) 1971 (3) 1974 (3); v A 1967 (4); v WI 1961 (3); v NZ 1967 (4)*

Gadkari, C. V. 6: *v WI 1952 (3); v P 1954 (3)*

Gaekwad, A. D. 40: v E 1976 (4) 1984 (3); v WI 1974 (3) 1978 (5) 1983 (6); v NZ 1976 (3); v P 1983 (3); *v E 1979 (2); v A 1977 (1); v WI 1975 (3) 1982 (5); v P 1984 (2)*

Gaekwad, D. K. 11: v WI 1958 (1); v P 1952 (2) 1960 (1); *v E 1952 (1) 1959 (4); v WI 1952 (2)*

Gaekwad, H. G. 1: v P 1952

Gandotra, A. 2: v A 1969 (1); v NZ 1969 (1)

Gavaskar, S. M. 115: v E 1972 (5) 1976 (5) 1979 (1) 1981 (6) 1984 (5); v A 1979 (6); v WI 1974 (2) 1978 (6) 1983 (6); v NZ 1976 (3); v P 1979 (6) 1983 (3); v SL 1982 (1); *v E 1971 (3) 1974 (3) 1979 (4) 1982 (3) 1986 (3); v A 1977 (5) 1980 (3) 1985 (3); v WI 1970 (4) 1975 (4) 1982 (5); v NZ 1975 (3) 1980 (3); v P 1978 (3) 1982 (6) 1984 (2); v SL 1985 (3)*

Ghavri, K. D. 39: v E 1976 (3) 1979 (1); v A 1979 (6); v WI 1974 (3) 1978 (6); v NZ 1976 (2); v P 1979 (6); *v E 1979 (4); v A 1977 (3) 1980 (3); v NZ 1980 (1); v P 1978 (1)*

Ghorpade, J. M. 8: v A 1956 (1); v WI 1958 (1); v NZ 1955 (1); *v E 1959 (3); v WI 1952 (2)*

Ghulam Ahmed 22: v E 1951 (2); v A 1956 (2); v WI 1948 (3) 1958 (2); v NZ 1955 (1); v P 1952 (4); *v E 1952 (4); v P 1954 (4)*

Gopalan, M. J. 1: v E 1933

Gopinath, C. D. 8: v E 1951 (3); v A 1959 (1); v P 1952 (1); *v E 1952 (1); v P 1954 (2)*

Guard, G. M. 2: v A 1959 (1); v WI 1958 (1)

Guha, S. 4: v A 1969 (3); *v E 1967 (1)*

Gul Mahomed 8: v P 1952 (2); *v E 1946 (1); v A 1947 (5)*

Gupte, B. P. 3: v E 1963 (1); v NZ 1964 (1); v P 1960 (1)

Gupte, S. P. 36: v E 1951 (1) 1961 (2); v A 1956 (3); v WI 1958 (5); v NZ 1955 (5); v P 1952 (2) 1960 (3); *v E 1959 (5); v WI 1952 (5); v P 1954 (5)*

Hafeez, A. 3: *v E 1946 (3)*

Hanumant Singh 14: v E 1963 (2); v A 1964 (3); v WI 1966 (2); v NZ 1964 (4) 1969 (1); *v E 1967 (2)*

Hardikar, M. S. 2: v WI 1958 (2)

Hazare, V. S. 30: v E 1951 (5); v WI 1948 (5); v P 1952 (5); *v E 1946 (3) 1952 (4); v A 1947 (5); v WI 1952 (5)*

Hindlekar, D. D. 4: *v E 1936 (1) 1946 (3)*

Ibrahim, K. C. 4: v WI 1948 (4)

Indrajitsinhji, K. S. 4: v A 1964 (3); v NZ 1969 (1)

Irani, J. K. 2: *v A 1947 (2)*

Jahangir Khan, M. 4: *v E 1932 (1) 1936 (3)*

Jai, L. P. 1: v E 1933

Jaisimha, M. L. 39: v E 1961 (5) 1963 (5); v A 1959 (1) 1964 (3); v WI 1966 (2); v NZ 1964 (4) 1969 (1); v P 1960 (4); *v E 1959 (1); v A 1967 (2); v WI 1961 (4) 1970 (3); v NZ 1967 (4)*

Jamshedji, R. J. 1: v E 1933

Jayantilal, K. 1: *v WI 1970*

Joshi, P. G. 12: v E 1951 (2); v A 1959 (1); v WI 1958 (1); v P 1952 (1) 1960 (1); *v E 1959 (3); v WI 1952 (3)*

Kanitkar, H. S. 2: v WI 1974 (2)

Kapil Dev 77: v E 1979 (1) 1981 (6) 1984 (4); v A 1979 (6); v WI 1978 (6) 1983 (6); v P 1979 (6) 1983 (3); v SL 1982 (1); *v E 1979 (4) 1982 (3) 1986 (3); v A 1980 (3) 1985 (3); v WI 1982 (5); v NZ 1980 (3); v P 1978 (3) 1982 (6) 1984 (2); v SL 1985 (3)*

Kardar, A. H. (*see* Hafeez)

Kenny, R. B. 5: v A 1959 (4); v WI 1958 (1)

Kirmani, S. M. H. 88: v E 1976 (5) 1979 (1) 1981 (6) 1984 (5); v A 1979 (6); v WI 1978 (6) 1983 (6); v NZ 1976 (3); v P 1979 (6) 1983 (3); v SL 1982 (1); *v E 1982 (3); v A 1977 (5) 1980 (3) 1985 (3); v WI 1975 (4) 1982 (5); v NZ 1975 (3) 1980 (3); v P 1978 (3) 1982 (6) 1984 (2)*

Kischenchand, G. 5: v P 1952 (1); *v A 1947 (4)*

Kripal Singh, A. G. 14: v E 1961 (3) 1963 (2); v A 1956 (2) 1964 (1); v WI 1958 (1); v NZ 1955 (4); *v E 1959 (1)*

Krishnamurthy, P. 5: *v WI 1970 (5)*

Kulkarni, U. N. 4: *v A 1967 (3); v NZ 1967 (1)*

Kumar, V. V. 2: v E 1961 (1); v P 1960 (1)

Kunderan, B. K. 18: v E 1961 (1) 1963 (5); v A 1959 (3); v WI 1966 (2); v NZ 1964 (1); v P 1960 (2); *v E 1967 (2); v WI 1961 (2)*

Lall Singh 1: *v E 1932*

Madan Lal 39: v E 1976 (2) 1981 (6); v WI 1974 (2) 1983 (3); v NZ 1976 (1); v P 1983 (3); v SL 1982 (1); *v E 1974 (2) 1982 (3) 1986 (1); v A 1977 (2); v WI 1975 (4) 1982 (2); v NZ 1975 (3); v P 1982 (3) 1984 (1)*

Maka, E. S. 2: v P 1952 (1); *v WI 1952 (1)*

Malhotra, A. 7: v E 1981 (2) 1984 (1); v WI 1983 (3); *v E 1982 (1)*

Maninder Singh 18: v WI 1983 (4); v E 1986 (3); *v WI 1982 (3); v P 1982 (5) 1984 (1); v SL 1985 (2)*

Manjrekar, V. L. 55: v E 1951 (2) 1961 (5) 1963 (4); v A 1956 (3) 1964 (3); v WI 1958 (4); v NZ 1955 (5) 1964 (1); v P 1952 (3) 1960 (5); *v E 1952 (4) 1959 (2); v WI 1952 (4) 1961 (5); v P 1954 (5)*

Mankad, A. V. 22: v E 1976 (1); v A 1969 (5); v WI 1974 (1); v NZ 1969 (2) 1976 (3); *v E 1971 (3) 1974 (1); v A 1977 (3); v WI 1970 (3)*

Mankad, V. 44: v E 1951 (5); v A 1956 (3); v WI 1948 (5) 1958 (2); v NZ 1955 (4); v P 1952 (4); *v E 1946 (3) 1952 (3); v A 1947 (5); v WI 1952 (5); v P 1954 (5)*

Mansur Ali Khan (*see* Pataudi)

Mantri, M. K. 4: v E 1951 (1); *v E 1952 (2); v P 1954 (1)*

Meherhomji, K. R. 1: *v E 1936*

Mehra, V. L. 8: v E 1961 (1) 1963 (2); v NZ 1955 (2); *v WI 1961 (3)*

Merchant, V. M. 10: v E 1933 (3) 1951 (1); *v E 1936 (3) 1946 (3)*

Milkha Singh, A. G. 4: v E 1961 (1); v A 1959 (1); v P 1960 (2)

Modi, R. S. 10: v E 1951 (1); v WI 1948 (5); v P 1952 (1); *v E 1946 (3)*

More, K. S. 3: *v E 1986 (3)*

Muddiah, V. M. 2: v A 1959 (1); v P 1960 (1)

Mushtaq Ali, S. 11: v E 1933 (2) 1951 (1); v WI 1948 (3); *v E 1936 (3) 1946 (2)*

Nadkarni, R. G. 41: v E 1961 (1) 1963 (5); v A 1959 (5) 1964 (3); v WI 1958 (1) 1966 (1); v NZ 1955 (1) 1964 (4); v P 1960 (4); *v E 1959 (4); v A 1967 (3); v WI 1961 (5); v NZ 1967 (4)*

Naik, S. S. 3: v WI 1974 (2); *v E 1974 (1)*

Naoomal Jeoomal 3: v E 1933 (2); *v E 1932 (1)*

Narasimha Rao, M. V. 4: v A 1979 (2); v WI 1978 (2)

Navle, J. G. 2: v E 1933 (1); *v E 1932 (1)*

Nayak, S. V. 2: *v E 1982 (2)*

Nayudu, C. K. 7: v E 1933 (3); *v E 1932 (1) 1936 (3)*

Nayudu, C. S. 11: v E 1933 (2) 1951 (1); *v E 1936 (2) 1946 (2); v A 1947 (4)*

Nazir Ali, S. 2: v E 1933 (1); *v E 1932 (1)*

Nissar, Mahomed 6: v E 1933 (2); *v E 1932 (1) 1936 (3)*
Nyalchand, S. 1: v P 1952

Pai, A. M. 1: v NZ 1969
Palia, P. E. 2: *v E 1932 (1) 1936 (1)*
Pandit, C. S. 1: *v E 1986*
Parkar, G. A. 1: *v E 1982*
Parkar, R. D. 2: v E 1972 (2)
Parsana, D. D. 2: v WI 1978 (2)
Patankar, C. T. 1: v NZ 1955
Pataudi sen., Nawab of, 3: *v E 1946 (3)*
Pataudi jun., Nawab of (now Mansur Ali Khan) 46: v E 1961 (3) 1963 (5) 1972 (3); v A 1964 (3) 1969 (5); v WI 1966 (3) 1974 (4); v NZ 1964 (4) 1969 (3); *v E 1967 (3); v A 1967 (3); v WI 1961 (3); v NZ 1967 (4)*
Patel, B. P. 21: v E 1976 (5); v WI 1974 (3); v NZ 1976 (3); *v E 1974 (2); v A 1977 (2); v WI 1975 (3); v NZ 1975 (3)*
Patel, J. M. 7: v A 1956 (2) 1959 (3); v NZ 1955 (1); *v P 1954 (1)*
Patiala, Yuvraj of, 1: v E 1933
Patil, S. M. 29: v E 1979 (1) 1981 (4) 1984 (2); v WI 1983 (2); v P 1979 (2) 1983 (3); v SL 1982 (1); *v E 1982 (2); v A 1980 (3); v NZ 1980 (3); v P 1982 (4) 1984 (2)*
Patil, S. R. 1: v NZ 1955
Phadkar, D. G. 31: v E 1951 (4); v A 1956 (1); v WI 1948 (4) 1958 (1); v NZ 1955 (4); v P 1952 (2); *v E 1952 (4); v A 1947 (4); v WI 1952 (4); v P 1954 (3)*
Prabhakar, M. 2: v E 1984 (2)
Prasanna, E. A. S. 49: v E 1961 (1) 1972 (3) 1976 (4); v A 1969 (5); v WI 1966 (1) 1974 (5); v NZ 1969 (3); *v E 1967 (3) 1974 (2); v A 1967 (4) 1977 (4); v WI 1961 (1) 1970 (3) 1975 (1); v NZ 1967 (4) 1975 (3); v P 1978 (2)*
Punjabi, P. H. 5: *v P 1954 (5)*

Rai Singh, K. 1: *v A 1947*
Rajinder Pal 1: v E 1963
Rajindernath, V. 1: v P 1952
Rajput, L. S. 2: *v SL 1985 (2)*
Ramaswami, C. 2: *v E 1936 (2)*
Ramchand, G. S. 33: v A 1956 (3) 1959 (5); v WI 1958 (3); v NZ 1955 (5); v P 1952 (3); *v E 1952 (4); v WI 1952 (5); v P 1954 (5)*
Ramji, L. 1: v E 1933
Rangachary, C. R. 4: v WI 1948 (2); *v A 1947 (2)*
Rangnekar, K. M. 3: *v A 1947 (3)*
Ranjane, V. B. 7: v E 1961 (3) 1963 (1); v A 1964 (1); v WI 1958 (1); *v WI 1961 (1)*
Reddy, B. 4: *v E 1979 (4)*
Rege, M. R. 1: v WI 1948
Roy, A. 4: v A 1969 (2); v NZ 1969 (2)
Roy, Pankaj 43: v E 1951 (5); v A 1956 (3) 1959 (5); v WI 1958 (5); v NZ 1955 (3); v P 1952 (3) 1960 (1); *v E 1952 (4) 1959 (5); v WI 1952 (4); v P 1954 (5)*
Roy, Pranab 2: v E 1981 (2)

Sandhu, B. S. 8: v WI 1983 (1); *v WI 1982 (4); v P 1982 (3)*
Sardesai, D. N. 30: v E 1961 (1) 1963 (5) 1972 (1); v A 1964 (3) 1969 (1); v WI 1966 (2); v NZ 1964 (3); *v E 1967 (1) 1971 (3); v A 1967 (2); v WI 1961 (3) 1970 (5)*
Sarwate, C. T. 9: v E 1951 (1); v WI 1948 (1); *v E 1946 (1); v A 1947 (1)*
Saxena, R. C. 1: *v E 1967*
Sekar, T. A. P. 2: *v P 1982 (2)*
Sen, P. 14: v E 1951 (2); v WI 1948 (5); v P 1952 (2); *v E 1952 (2); v A 1947 (3)*
Sengupta, A. K. 1: v WI 1958
Sharma, Chetan 12: v E 1984 (3); *v E 1986 (2); v A 1985 (2); v P 1984 2; v SL 1985 (2)*
Sharma, Gopal 2: v E 1984 (1); *v SL 1985 (1)*
Sharma, P. 5: v E 1976 (2); v WI 1974 (2); *v WI 1975 (1)*
Shastri, R. J. 43: v E 1981 (6) 1984 (5); v WI 1983 (6); v P 1983 (2); *v E 1982 (3) 1986 (3); v A 1985 (3); v WI 1982 (5); v NZ 1980 (3); v P 1982 (2) 1984 (2); v SL 1985 (3)*
Shinde, S. G. 7: v E 1951 (3); v WI 1948 (1); *v E 1946 (1) 1952 (2)*
Shodhan, R. H. 3: v P 1952 (1); *v WI 1952 (2)*

Shukla, R. C. 1: v SL 1982
Sidhu, N. S. 2: v WI 1983 (2)
Sivaramakrishnan, L. 9: v E 1984 (5); *v A 1985 (2); v WI 1982 (1); v SL 1985 (1)*
Sohoni, S. W. 4: v E 1951 (1); *v E 1946 (2); v A 1947 (1)*
Solkar, E. D. 27: v E 1972 (5) 1976 (1); v A 1969 (4); v WI 1974 (4); v NZ 1969 (1); *v E 1971 (3) 1974 (3); v WI 1970 (5) 1975 (1)*
Sood, M. M. 1: v A 1959
Srikkanth, K. 17: v E 1981 (4) 1984 (2); *v E 1986 (3); v A 1985 (3); v P 1982 (2); v SL 1985 (3)*
Srinivasan, T. E. 1: *v NZ 1980*
Subramanya, V. 9: v WI 1966 (2); v NZ 1964 (1); *v E 1967 (2); v A 1967 (2); v NZ 1967 (2)*
Sunderram, G. 2: v NZ 1955 (2)
Surendranath, R. 11: v A 1959 (2); v WI 1958 (2); v P 1960 (2); *v E 1959 (5)*
Surti, R. F. 26: v E 1963 (1); v A 1964 (2) 1969 (1); v WI 1966 (2); v NZ 1964 (1) 1969 (2); v P 1960 (2); *v E 1967 (2); v A 1967 (4); v WI 1961 (5); v NZ 1967 (4)*
Swamy, V. N. 1: v NZ 1955

Tamhane, N. S. 21: v A 1956 (3) 1959 (1); v WI 1958 (4); v NZ 1955 (4); v P 1960 (2); *v E 1959 (2); v P 1954 (5)*
Tarapore, K. K. 1: v WI 1948

Umrigar, P. R. 59: v E 1951 (5) 1961 (4); v A 1956 (3) 1959 (3); v WI 1948 (1) 1958 (5); v NZ 1955 (5); v P 1952 (5) 1960 (5); *v E 1952 (4) 1959 (4); v WI 1952 (5) 1961 (5); v P 1954 (5)*

Vengsarkar, D. B. 85: v E 1976 (1) 1979 (1) 1981 (6) 1984 (5); v A 1979 (6); v WI 1978 (6) 1983 (5); v P 1979 (5) 1983 (1); v SL 1982 (1); *v E 1979 (4) 1982 (3) 1986 (3); v A 1977 (5) 1980 (3) 1985 (3); v WI 1975 (2) 1982 (5); v NZ 1975 (3) 1980 (3); v P 1978 (3) 1982 (6) 1984 (2); v SL 1985 (3)*
Venkataraghavan, S. 57: v E 1972 (2) 1976 (1); v A 1969 (5) 1979 (3); v WI 1966 (2) 1974 (2) 1978 (6); v NZ 1964 (4) 1969 (2) 1976 (3); v P 1983 (2); *v E 1967 (1) 1971 (3) 1974 (2) 1979 (4); v A 1977 (1); v WI 1970 (5) 1975 (3) 1982 (5); v NZ 1975 (1)*
Viswanath, G. R. 91: v E 1972 (5) 1976 (5) 1979 (1) 1981 (6); v A 1969 (4) 1979 (6); v WI 1974 (5) 1978 (6); v NZ 1976 (3); v SL 1982 (1); v P 1979 (6); *v E 1971 (3) 1974 (3) 1979 (4) 1982 (3); v A 1977 (5) 1980 (3); v WI 1970 (3) 1975 (4); v NZ 1975 (3) 1980 (3); v P 1978 (3) 1982 (6)*
Viswanath, S. 3: *v SL 1985 (3)*
Vizianagram, Maharaj Sir Vijaya 3: *v E 1936 (3)*

Wadekar, A. L. 37: v E 1972 (5); v A 1969 (5); v WI 1966 (2); v NZ 1969 (3); *v E 1967 (3) 1971 (3) 1974 (3); v A 1967 (4); v WI 1970 (5); v NZ 1967 (4)*
Wazir Ali, S. 7: v E 1933 (3); *v E 1932 (1) 1936 (3)*

Yadav, N. S. 26: v E 1979 (1) 1981 (1) 1984 (4); v A 1979 (5); v WI 1983 (3); v P 1979 (5); *v A 1980 (2) 1985 (3); v NZ 1980 (1); v P 1984 (1)*
Yajurvindra Singh 4: v E 1976 (2); v A 1979 (1); *v E 1979 (1)*
Yashpal Sharma 37: v E 1979 (1) 1981 (2); v A 1979 (6); v WI 1983 (1); v P 1979 (6) 1983 (3); v SL 1982 (1); *v E 1979 (3) 1982 (3); v A 1980 (3); v WI 1982 (5); v NZ 1980 (1); v P 1982 (2)*
Yograj Singh 1: *v NZ 1980*

Note: Hafeez, on going later to Oxford University, took his correct name, Kardar.

PAKISTAN

Number of Test cricketers: 104

Abdul Kadir 4: v A 1964 (1); *v A 1964 (1); v NZ 1964 (2)*
Abdul Qadir 38: v E 1977 (3) 1983 (3); v A 1982 (3); v WI 1980 (2); v NZ 1984 (3); v In 1982 (5) 1984 (1); v SL 1985 (3); *v E 1982 (3); v A 1983 (5); v NZ 1984 (2); v In 1979 (3); v SL 1985 (2)*
Afaq Hussain 2: v E 1961 (1); *v A 1964 (1)*
Aftab Baloch 2: v WI 1974 (1); v NZ 1969 (1)
Aftab Gul 6: v E 1968 (2); v NZ 1969 (1); *v E 1971 (3)*
Agha Saadat Ali 1: v NZ 1955

Agha Zahid 1: v WI 1974
Alim-ud-Din 25: v E 1961 (2); v A 1956 (1) 1959 (1); v WI 1958 (1); v NZ 1955 (3); v In 1954 (5); *v E 1954 (3) 1962 (3); v WI 1957 (5); v In 1960 (1)*
Amir Elahi 5: *v In 1952 (5)*
Anil Dalpat 9: v E 1983 (3); v NZ 1984 (3); *v NZ 1984 (3)*
Anwar Hussain 4: *v In 1952 (4)*
Anwar Khan 1: *v NZ 1978*
Arif Butt 3: *v A 1964 (1); v NZ 1964 (2)*
Ashraf Ali 5: v In 1984 (2); v SL 1981 (2) 1985 (1)
Asif Iqbal 58: v E 1968 (3) 1972 (3); v A 1964 (1); v WI 1974 (2); v NZ 1964 (3) 1969 (3) 1976 (3); v In 1978 (3); *n E 1967 (3) 1971 (3) 1974 (3); v A 1964 (1) 1972 (3) 1976 (3) 1978 (2); v WI 1976 (5); v NZ 1964 (3) 1972 (3) 1978 (2); v In 1979 (6)*
Asif Masood 16: v E 1968 (2) 1972 (1); v WI 1974 (2); v NZ 1969 (1); *v E 1971 (3) 1974 (3); v A 1972 (3) 1976 (1)*
Azeem Hafeez 18: v E 1983 (2); v NZ 1984 (3); v In 1984 (2); *v A 1983 (5); v NZ 1984 (3); v In 1983 (3)*
Azhar Khan 1: v A 1979
Azmat Rana 1: v A 1979

Burki, J. 25: v E 1961 (3); v A 1964 (1); v NZ 1964 (3) 1969 (1); *v E 1962 (5) 1967 (3); v A 1964 (1); v NZ 1964 (3); v In 1960 (5)*

D'Souza, A. 6: v E 1961 (2); v WI 1958 (1); *v E 1962 (3)*

Ehtesham-ud-Din 5: v A 1979 (1); *v E 1982 (1); v In 1979 (3)*

Farooq Hamid 1: *v A 1964*
Farrukh Zaman 1: v NZ 1976
Fazal Mahmood 34: v E 1961 (1); v A 1956 (1) 1959 (2); v WI 1958 (3); v NZ 1955 (2); v In 1954 (4); *v E 1954 (4) 1962 (2); v WI 1957 (5); v In 1952 (5) 1960 (5)*

Ghazali, M. E. Z. 2: *v E 1954 (2)*
Ghulam Abbas 1: *v E 1967*
Gul Mahomed 1: v A 1956

Hanif Mohammad 55: v E 1961 (3) 1968 (3); v A 1956 (1) 1959 (3) 1964 (1); v WI 1958 (1); v NZ 1955 (3) 1964 (3) 1969 (1); v In 1954 (5); *v E 1954 (4) 1962 (5) 1967 (3); v A 1964 (1); v WI 1957 (5); v NZ 1964 (3); v In 1952 (5) 1960 (5)*
Haroon Rashid 23: v E 1977 (3); v A 1979 (2) 1982 (3); v In 1982 (1); v SL 1981 (2); *v E 1978 (3) 1982 (1); v A 1976 (1) 1978 (1); v WI 1976 (5); v NZ 1978 (1)*
Haseeb Ahsan 12: v E 1961 (2); v A 1959 (1); v WI 1958 (1); *v WI 1957 (3); v In 1960 (5)*

Ibadulla, K. 4: v A 1964 (1); *v E 1967 (2); v NZ 1964 (1)*
Ijaz Butt 8: v A 1959 (2); v WI 1958 (3); *v E 1962 (3)*
Ijaz Faqih 2: v WI 1980 (1); *v A 1981 (1)*
Imran Khan 57: v A 1979 (2) 1982 (3); v WI 1980 (4); v NZ 1976 (3); v In 1978 (3) 1982 (6); v SL 1981 (1) 1985 (3); *v E 1971 (1) 1974 (3) 1982 (3); v A 1976 (3) 1978 (2) 1981 (3) 1983 (2); v WI 1976 (5); v NZ 1978 (2); v In 1979 (5); v SL 1985 (3)*
Imtiaz Ahmed 41: v E 1961 (3); v A 1956 (1) 1959 (3); v WI 1958 (3); v NZ 1955 (3); v In 1954 (5); *v E 1954 (4) 1962 (4); v WI 1957 (5); v In 1952 (5) 1960 (5)*
Intikhab Alam 47: v E 1961 (2) 1968 (3) 1972 (3); v A 1959 (1) 1964 (1); v WI 1974 (2); v NZ 1964 (3) 1969 (3) 1976 (3); *v E 1962 (3) 1967 (3) 1971 (3) 1974 (3); v A 1964 (1) 1972 (3); v WI 1976 (1); v NZ 1964 (3) 1972 (3); v In 1960 (3)*
Iqbal Qasim 41: v E 1977 (3); v A 1979 (3) 1982 (2); v WI 1980 (4); v NZ 1984 (5); v In 1978 (3) 1982 (2); v SL 1981 (3); *v E 1978 (3); v A 1976 (3) 1981 (2); v WI 1976 (2); v NZ 1984 (1); v In 1979 (6) 1983 (1)*
Israr Ali 4: v A 1959 (2); *v In 1952 (2)*

Jalal-ud-Din 6: v A 1982 (1); v In 1982 (2) 1984 (2); v SL 1985 (1)
Javed Akhtar 1: *v E 1962*
Javed Miandad 74: v E 1977 (3); v A 1979 (3) 1982 (3); v WI 1980 (4); v NZ 1976 (3) 1984 (3); v In 1978 (3) 1982 (6) 1984 (2); v SL 1981 (3) 1985 (3); *v E 1978 (3) 1982 (3); v A 1976 (3) 1978 (2) 1981 (3) 1983 (5); v WI 1976 (1); v NZ 1978 (3) 1984 (3); v In 1979 (6) 1983 (3); v SL 1985 (3)*

Kardar, A. H. 23: v A 1956 (1); v NZ 1955 (3); v In 1954 (5); *v E 1954 (4); v WI 1957 (5); v In 1952 (5)*

Khalid Hassan 1: *v E 1954*

Khalid Wazir 2: *v E 1954 (2)*

Khan Mohammad 13: v A 1956 (1); v NZ 1955 (3); v In 1954 (4); *v E 1954 (2); v WI 1957 (2); v In 1952 (1)*

Liaqat Ali 5: v E 1977 (2); v WI 1974 (1); *v E 1978 (2)*

Mahmood Hussain 27: v E 1961 (1); v WI 1958 (3); v NZ 1955 (1); v In 1954 (5); *v E 1954 (2) 1962 (3); v WI 1957 (3); v In 1952 (4) 1960 (5)*

Majid Khan 63: v E 1968 (3) 1972 (3); v A 1964 (1) 1979 (3); v WI 1974 (2) 1980 (4); v NZ 1964 (3) 1976 (3); v In 1978 (3) 1982 (1); v SL 1981 (1); *v E 1967 (3) 1971 (2) 1974 (3) 1982 (1); v A 1972 (3) 1976 (3) 1978 (2) 1981 (3); v WI 1976 (5); v NZ 1972 (3) 1978 (2); v In 1979 (6)*

Mansoor Akhtar 13: v A 1982 (3); v WI 1980 (2); v In 1982 (3); v SL 1981 (1); *v E 1982 (3); v A 1981 (1)*

Manzoor Elahi 2: v NZ 1984 (1); v In 1984 (1)

Maqsood Ahmed 16: v NZ 1955 (2); v In 1954 (5); *v E 1954 (4); v In 1952 (5)*

Mathias, Wallis 21: v E 1961 (1); v A 1956 (1) 1959 (2); v WI 1958 (3); v NZ 1955 (1); *v E 1962 (3); v WI 1957 (5); v In 1960 (5)*

Miran Bux 2: v In 1954 (2)

Mohammad Aslam 1: *v E 1954*

Mohammad Farooq 7: v NZ 1964 (3); *v E 1962 (2); v In 1960 (2)*

Mohammad Ilyas 10: v E 1968 (2); v NZ 1964 (3); *v E 1967 (1); v A 1964 (1); v NZ 1964 (3)*

Mohammad Munaf 4: v E 1961 (2); v A 1959 (2)

Mohammad Nazir 14: v E 1972 (1); v WI 1980 (4); v NZ 1969 (3); *v A 1983 (3); v In 1983 (3)*

Mohsin Kamal 3: v E 1983 (1); v SL 1985 (1); *v SL 1985 (1)*

Mohsin Khan 45: v E 1977 (1) 1983 (3); v A 1982 (3); v NZ 1984 (2); v In 1982 (6) 1984 (2); v SL 1981 (2) 1985 (2); *v E 1978 (3) 1982 (3); v A 1978 (1) 1981 (2) 1983 (5); v NZ 1978 (1) 1984 (3); v In 1983 (3); v SL 1985 (3)*

Mudassar Nazar 58: v E 1977 (3) 1983 (1); v A 1979 (3) 1982 (3); v NZ 1984 (3); v In 1978 (2) 1982 (6) 1984 (2); v SL 1981 (1) 1985 (3); *v E 1978 (3) 1982 (3); v A 1978 (1) 1978 (1) 1981 (3) 1983 (5); v NZ 1978 (1) 1984 (3); v In 1979 (5) 1983 (3); v SL 1985 (3)*

Mufasir-ul-Haq 1: *v NZ 1964*

Munir Malik 3: v A 1959 (1); *v E 1962 (2)*

Mushtaq Mohammad 57: v E 1961 (3) 1968 (3) 1972 (3); v WI 1958 (1) 1974 (2); v NZ 1969 (2) 1976 (3); v In 1978 (3); *v E 1962 (5) 1967 (3) 1971 (3) 1974 (3); v A 1972 (3) 1976 (3) 1978 (2); v WI 1976 (5); v NZ 1972 (2) 1978 (3); v In 1960 (5)*

Nasim-ul-Ghani 29: v E 1961 (2); v A 1959 (2) 1964 (1); v WI 1958 (3); *v E 1962 (5) 1967 (2); v A 1964 (1) 1972 (1); v WI 1957 (5); v NZ 1964 (3); v In 1960 (4)*

Naushad Ali 6: v NZ 1964 (3); *v NZ 1964 (3)*

Nazar Mohammad 5: *v In 1952 (5)*

Nazir Junior (*see* Mohammad Nazir)

Niaz Ahmed 2: v E 1968 (1); *v E 1967 (1)*

Pervez Sajjad 19: v E 1968 (1) 1972 (2); v A 1964 (1); v NZ 1964 (3) 1969 (3); *v E 1971 (3); v NZ 1964 (3) 1972 (3)*

Qasim Omar 23: v E 1983 (3); v NZ 1984 (3); v In 1984 (2); v SL 1985 (3); *v A 1983 (5); v NZ 1984 (3); v In 1983 (1); v SL 1985 (3)*

Ramiz Raja 6: v E 1983 (2); v SL 1985 (1); *v SL 1985 (3)*

Rashid Khan 4: v SL 1981 (2); *v A 1983 (1); v NZ 1984 (1)*

Rehman, S. F. 1: *v WI 1957*

Rizwan-uz-Zaman 3: v SL 1981 (2); *v A 1981 (1)*

Sadiq Mohammad 41: v E 1972 (3) 1977 (2); v WI 1974 (1) 1980 (3); v NZ 1969 (3) 1976 (3); v In 1978 (1); *v E 1971 (3) 1974 (3) 1978 (3); v A 1972 (3) 1976 (2); v WI 1976 (5); v NZ 1972 (3); v In 1979 (3)*

Saeed Ahmed 41: v E 1961 (3) 1968 (3); v A 1959 (3) 1964 (1); v WI 1958 (3); v NZ 1964 (3); *v E 1962 (5) 1967 (3) 1971 (1); v A 1964 (1) 1972 (2); v WI 1957 (5); v NZ 1964 (3); v In 1960 (5)*

Salah-ud-Din 5: v E 1968 (1); v NZ 1964 (3) 1969 (1)
Salim Altaf 21: v E 1972 (3); v NZ 1969 (2); v In 1978 (1); *v E 1967 (2) 1971 (2); v A 1972 (3) 1976 (2); v WI 1976 (3); v NZ 1972 (3)*
Salim Malik 30: v E 1983 (3); v NZ 1984 (3); v In 1982 (6) 1984 (2); v SL 1981 (2) 1985 (3); *v A 1983 (3); v NZ 1984 (3); v In 1983 (2); v SL 1985 (3)*
Salim Yousuf 3: v SL 1981 (1) 1985 (2)
Sarfraz Nawaz 55: v E 1968 (1) 1972 (2) 1977 (2) 1983 (3); v A 1979 (3); v WI 1974 (2) 1980 (2); v NZ 1976 (3); v In 1978 (3) 1982 (6); *v E 1974 (3) 1978 (2) 1982 (1); v A 1972 (2) 1976 (2) 1978 (2) 1981 (3) 1983 (3); v WI 1976 (4); v NZ 1972 (3) 1978 (3)*
Shafiq Ahmad 6: v E 1977 (3); v WI 1980 (2); *v E 1974 (1)*
Shafqat Rana 5: v E 1968 (2); v A 1964 (1); v NZ 1969 (2)
Shahid Israr 1: v NZ 1976
Shahid Mahmood 1: *v E 1962*
Sharpe, D. 3: v A 1959 (3)
Shoaib Mohammad 6: v E 1983 (1); v NZ 1984 (1); v SL 1985 (1); *v NZ 1984 (1); v In 1983 (2)*
Shuja-ud-Din 19: v E 1961 (2); v A 1959 (3); v WI 1958 (3); v NZ 1955 (3); v In 1954 (5); *v E 1954 (3)*
Sikander Bakht 26: v E 1977 (2); v WI 1980 (1); v NZ 1976 (1); v In 1978 (2) 1982 (1); *v E 1978 (3) 1982 (2); v A 1978 (2) 1981 (3); v WI 1976 (1); v NZ 1978 (3); v In 1979 (5)*

Tahir Naqqash 15: v A 1982 (3); v In 1982 (2); v SL 1981 (3); *v E 1982 (2); v A 1983 (1); v NZ 1984 (1); v In 1983 (3)*
Talat Ali 10: v E 1972 (3); *v E 1978 (2); v A 1972 (1); v NZ 1972 (1) 1978 (3)*
Taslim Arif 6: v A 1979 (3); v WI 1980 (2); *v In 1979 (1)*
Tauseef Ahmed 13: v E 1983 (2); v A 1979 (3); v NZ 1984 (1); v In 1984 (1); v SL 1981 (3) 1985 (1); *v SL 1985 (2)*

Waqar Hassan 21: v A 1956 (1) 1959 (1); v WI 1958 (1); v NZ 1955 (3); v In 1954 (5); *v E 1954 (4); v WI 1957 (1); v In 1952 (5)*
Wasim Akram 8: v SL 1985 (3); *v NZ 1984 (2); v SL 1985 (3)*
Wasim Bari 81: v E 1968 (3) 1972 (3) 1977 (3); v A 1982 (3); v WI 1974 (2) 1980 (2); v NZ 1969 (3) 1976 (2); v In 1978 (3) 1982 (6); *v E 1967 (3) 1971 (3) 1974 (3) 1978 (3) 1982 (3); v A 1972 (3) 1976 (3) 1978 (2) 1981 (3) 1983 (5); v WI 1976 (5); v NZ 1972 (3) 1978 (3); v In 1979 (6); 1983 (3)*
Wasim Raja 57: v E 1972 (1) 1977 (3) 1983 (3); v A 1979 (3); v WI 1974 (2) 1980 (4); v NZ 1976 (1) 1984 (1); v In 1982 (1) 1984 (1); v SL 1981 (3); *v E 1974 (2) 1978 (3) 1982 (1); v A 1978 (1) 1981 (3) 1983 (2); v WI 1976 (5); v NZ 1972 (3) 1978 (3) 1984 (2); v In 1979 (6) 1983 (3)*
Wazir Mohammad 20: v A 1956 (1) 1959 (1); v WI 1958 (3); v NZ 1955 (2); v In 1954 (5); *v E 1954 (2); v WI 1957 (5); v In 1952 (1)*

Younis Ahmed 2: v NZ 1969 (2)

Zaheer Abbas 78: v E 1972 (2) 1983 (3); v A 1979 (2) 1982 (3); v WI 1974 (2) 1980 (3); v NZ 1969 (1) 1976 (3) 1984 (3); v In 1978 (3) 1982 (6) 1984 (2); v SL 1981 (1) 1985 (2); *v E 1971 (3) 1974 (3) 1982 (3); v A 1972 (3) 1976 (3) 1978 (2) 1981 (2) 1983 (5); v WI 1976 (3); v NZ 1972 (3) 1978 (2) 1984 (2); v In 1979 (5) 1983 (3)*
Zakir Khan 1: *v SL 1985*
Zulfiqar Ahmed 9: v A 1956 (1); v NZ 1955 (3); *v E 1954 (2); v In 1952 (3)*
Zulqarnain 3: *v SL 1985 (3)*

SRI LANKA

Number of Test cricketers: 37

Ahangama, F. S. 3: v In 1985 (3)
Amalean, K. N. 1: v P 1985
Amerasinghe, A. M. J. G. 2: v NZ 1983 (2)
Anurasiri, S. D. 2: v P 1985 (2)

de Alwis, R. G. 7: v A 1982 (1); v NZ 1983 (3); v P 1985 (2); *v NZ 1982 (1)*

de Mel, A. L. F. 16: v E 1981 (1); v A 1982 (1); v In 1985 (3); v P 1985 (3); *v E 1984 (1); v In 1982 (1); v P 1981 (3) 1985 (3)*
de Silva, D. S. 12: v E 1981 (1); v A 1982 (1); v NZ 1983 (3); *v E 1984 (1); v NZ 1982 (2); v In 1982 (1); v P 1981 (3)*
de Silva, E. A. R. 3: v In 1985 (2); v P 1985 (1)
de Silva, G. R. A. 4: v E 1981 (1); *v In 1982 (1); v P 1981 (2)*
de Silva, P. A. 9: v In 1985 (2); v P 1985 (3); *v E 1984 (1); v P 1985 (3)*
Dias, R. L. 16: v E 1981 (1); v A 1982 (1); v NZ 1983 (2); v In 1985 (3); v P 1985 (1); *v E 1984 (1); v In 1982 (1); v P 1981 (3) 1985 (3)*

Fernando, E. R. N. S. 5: v A 1982 (1); v NZ 1983 (2); *v NZ 1982 (2)*

Goonatillake, H. M. 5: v E 1981 (1); *v In 1982 (1); v P 1981 (3)*
Gunasekera, Y. 2: *v NZ 1982 (2)*
Guneratne, R. P. W. 1: v A 1982
Gurusinha, A. P. 3: v P 1985 (2); *v P 1985 (1)*

Jayasekera, R. S. A. 1: *v P 1981*
Jeganathan, S. 2: *v NZ 1982 (2)*
John, V. B. 6: v NZ 1983 (3); *v E 1984 (1); v NZ 1982 (2)*
Jurangpathy, B. R. 1: v In 1985

Kaluperuma, L. W. 2: v E 1981 (1); *v P 1981 (1)*
Kaluperuma, S. M. S. 3: v NZ 1983 (3)
Kuruppuarachchi, A. K. 1: v P 1985

Madugalle, R. S. 18: v E 1981 (1); v A 1982 (1); v NZ 1983 (3); v In 1985 (3); *v E 1984 (1); v NZ 1982 (2); v In 1982 (1); v P 1981 (3) 1985 (3)*
Mahanama, R. S. 2: v P 1985 (2)
Mendis, L. R. D. 19: v E 1981 (1); v A 1982 (1); v NZ 1983 (3); v In 1985 (3); v P 1985 (3); *v E 1984 (1); v In 1982 (1); v P 1981 (3) 1985 (3)*

Ranasinghe, A. N. 2: *v In 1982 (1); v P 1981 (1)*
Ranatunga, A. 18: v E 1981 (1); v A 1982 (1); v NZ 1983 (3); v In 1985 (3); v P 1985 (3); *v E 1984 (1); v In 1982 (1); v P 1981 (2) 1985 (3)*
Ratnayake, R. J. 11: v A 1982 (1); v NZ 1983 (1); v In 1985 (3); v P 1985 (1); *v NZ 1982 (2); v P 1985 (3)*
Ratnayeke, J. R. 14: v NZ 1983 (2); v P 1985 (3); *v E 1984 (1); v NZ 1982 (2); v In 1982 (1); v P 1981 (2) 1985 (3)*

Silva, S. A. R. 8: v In 1985 (3); v P 1985 (1); *v E 1984 (1); v NZ 1982 (1); v P 1985 (2)*

Warnapura, B. 4: v E 1981 (1); *v In 1982 (1); v P 1981 (2)*
Warnaweera, K. P. J. 1: v P 1985
Weerasinghe, C. D. U. S. 1: v In 1985
Wettimuny, M. D. 2: *v NZ 1982 (2)*
Wettimuny, S. 20: v E 1981 (1); v A 1982 (1); v NZ 1983 (3); v In 1985 (3); v P 1985 (3); *v E 1984 (1); v NZ 1982 (2); v P 1981 (3) 1985 (3)*
Wijesuriya, R. G. C. E. 4: *v P 1981 (1) 1985 (3)*

TWO COUNTRIES

Twelve cricketers have appeared for two countries in Test matches, namely:

Amir Elahi, *India and Pakistan.*
J. J. Ferris, *Australia and England.*
S. C. Guillen, *West Indies and NZ.*
Gul Mahomed, *India and Pakistan.*
F. Hearne, *England and South Africa.*
A. H. Kardar, *India and Pakistan.*

W. E. Midwinter, *England and Australia.*
F. Mitchell, *England and South Africa.*
W. L. Murdoch, *Australia and England.*
Nawab of Pataudi, sen., *England and India.*
A. E. Trott, *Australia and England.*
S. M. J. Woods, *Australia and England.*

MOST TEST APPEARANCES FOR EACH COUNTRY

England: M. C. Cowdrey 114.
Australia: R. W. Marsh 96.
South Africa: J. H. B. Waite 50.
West Indies: C. H. Lloyd 110.

New Zealand: R. J. Hadlee 66.
India: S. M. Gavaskar 115.
Pakistan: Wasim Bari 81.
Sri Lanka: S. Wettimuny 20.

MOST TEST APPEARANCES AS CAPTAIN FOR EACH COUNTRY

England: P. B. H. May 41.
Australia: G. S. Chappell 48.
South Africa: H. W. Taylor 18.
West Indies: C. H. Lloyd 74.

New Zealand: J. R. Reid 34.
India: S. M. Gavaskar 46.
Pakistan: A. H. Kardar 23.
Sri Lanka: L. R. D. Mendis 15.

ENGLAND v REST OF THE WORLD

The following were awarded England caps for playing against the Rest of the World in England in 1970, although the five matches played are now generally considered not to have rated as full Tests: D. L. Amiss (1), G. Boycott (2), D. J. Brown (2), M. C. Cowdrey (4), M. H. Denness (1), B. L. D'Oliveira (4), J. H. Edrich (2), K. W. R. Fletcher (4), A. W. Greig (3), R. Illingworth (5), A. Jones (1), A. P. E. Knott (5), P. Lever (1), B. W. Luckhurst (5), C. M. Old (2), P. J. Sharpe (1), K. Shuttleworth (1), J. A. Snow (5), D. L. Underwood (3), A. Ward (1), D. Wilson (2).

HONOURS' LIST

In 1986, the following were decorated for their services to cricket:
New Year's Honours: J. G. Overy (England) OBE.
Queen's Birthday Honours: Sir George Allen (England) Kt; H. D. Bird (England) MBE, J. V. Coney (New Zealand) MBE, E. W. Dempster (New Zealand) MBE.
Sir Jack Hayward, who contributed to the cost of building the MCC Indoor School at Lord's and who has been a leading sponsor of women's cricket, received a knighthood in the New Year's Honours for charitable services, and J. Paul Getty II, who has made a number of gifts to cricket, was awarded an honorary knighthood in the Queen's Birthday Honours.

CRICKET RECORDS

Amended by BILL FRINDALL to end of the 1986 season in England

Unless stated to be of a minor character, all records apply only to first-class cricket including some performances in the distant past which have always been recognised as of exceptional merit.

* Denotes not out or an unbroken partnership.

(A), (SA), (WI), (NZ), (I), (P) or (SL) indicates either the nationality of the player, or the country in which the record was made.

FIRST-CLASS RECORDS

BATTING RECORDS

BOWLING RECORDS

ALL-ROUND RECORDS

WICKET-KEEPING RECORDS

FIELDING RECORDS

TEAM RECORDS

TEST MATCH RECORDS

BATTING RECORDS

TEST SERIES

LIMITED-OVERS INTERNATIONAL RECORDS

MISCELLANEOUS

FIRST-CLASS RECORDS

BATTING RECORDS

HIGHEST INDIVIDUAL SCORES

499	Hanif Mohammad	Karachi v Bahawalpur at Karachi	1958-59
452*	D. G. Bradman	NSW v Queensland at Sydney	1929-30
443*	B. B. Nimbalkar	Maharashtra v Kathiawar at Poona	1948-49
437	W. H. Ponsford	Victoria v Queensland at Melbourne	1927-28
429	W. H. Ponsford	Victoria v Tasmania at Melbourne	1922-23
428	Aftab Baloch	Sind v Baluchistan at Karachi	1973-74
424	A. C. MacLaren	Lancashire v Somerset at Taunton	1895
385	B. Sutcliffe	Otago v Canterbury at Christchurch	1952-53
383	C. W. Gregory	NSW v Queensland at Brisbane	1906-07
369	D. G. Bradman	South Australia v Tasmania at Adelaide	1935-36
365*	C. Hill	South Australia v NSW at Adelaide	1900-01
365*	G. S. Sobers	West Indies v Pakistan at Kingston	1957-58
364	L. Hutton	England v Australia at The Oval	1938
359*	V. M. Merchant	Bombay v Maharashtra at Bombay	1943-44
359	R. B. Simpson	NSW v Queensland at Brisbane	1963-64
357*	R. Abel	Surrey v Somerset at The Oval	1899
357	D. G. Bradman	South Australia v Victoria at Melbourne	1935-36
356	B. A. Richards	South Australia v W. Australia at Perth	1970-71
355	B. Sutcliffe	Otago v Auckland at Dunedin	1949-50
352	W. H. Ponsford	Victoria v NSW at Melbourne	1926-27
350	Rashid Israr	Habib Bank v National Bank at Lahore	1976-77
345	C. G. Macartney	Australians v Nottinghamshire at Nottingham	1921
344*	G. A. Headley	Jamaica v Lord Tennyson's XI at Kingston	1931-32
344	W. G. Grace	MCC v Kent at Canterbury	1876
343*	P. A. Perrin	Essex v Derbyshire at Chesterfield	1904
341	G. H. Hirst	Yorkshire v Leicestershire at Leicester	1905
340*	D. G. Bradman	NSW v Victoria at Sydney	1928-29
340	S. M. Gavaskar	Bombay v Bengal at Bombay	1981-82
338*	R. C. Blunt	Otago v Canterbury at Christchurch	1931-32
338	W. W. Read	Surrey v Oxford University at The Oval	1888
337*	Pervez Akhtar	Railways v Dera Ismail Khan at Lahore	1964-65
337†	Hanif Mohammad	Pakistan v West Indies at Bridgetown	1957-58
336*	W. R. Hammond	England v New Zealand at Auckland	1932-33
336	W. H. Ponsford	Victoria v South Australia at Melbourne	1927-28
334	D. G. Bradman	Australia v England at Leeds	1930
333	K. S. Duleepsinhji	Sussex v Northamptonshire at Hove	1930
332	W. H. Ashdown	Kent v Essex at Brentwood	1934
331*	J. D. Robertson	Middlesex v Worcestershire at Worcester	1949
325*	H. L. Hendry	Victoria v New Zealanders at Melbourne	1925-26
325	A. Sandham	England v West Indies at Kingston	1929-30
325	C. L. Badcock	South Australia v Victoria at Adelaide	1935-36
324	J. B. Stollmeyer	Trinidad v British Guiana at Port-of-Spain	1946-47
324	Waheed Mirza	Karachi Whites v Quetta at Karachi	1976-77
323	A. L. Wadekar	Bombay v Mysore at Bombay	1966-67
322	E. Paynter	Lancashire v Sussex at Hove	1937
322	I. V. A. Richards	Somerset v Warwickshire at Taunton	1985
321	W. L. Murdoch	NSW v Victoria at Sydney	1881-82
319	Gul Mahomed	Baroda v Holkar at Baroda	1946-47
318*	W. G. Grace	Gloucestershire v Yorkshire at Cheltenham	1876
317	W. R. Hammond	Gloucestershire v Nottinghamshire at Gloucester	1936
317	K. R. Rutherford	New Zealanders v D. B. Close's XI at Scarborough	1986
316*	J. B. Hobbs	Surrey v Middlesex at Lord's	1926
316*	V. S. Hazare	Maharashtra v Baroda at Poona	1939-40
316	R. H. Moore	Hampshire v Warwickshire at Bournemouth	1937

315*	T. W. Hayward	Surrey v Lancashire at The Oval	1898
315*	P. Holmes	Yorkshire v Middlesex at Lord's	1925
315*	A. F. Kippax	NSW v Queensland at Sydney	1927-28
314*	C. L. Walcott	Barbados v Trinidad at Port-of-Spain	1945-46
313	H. Sutcliffe	Yorkshire v Essex at Leyton	1932
312*	W. W. Keeton	Nottinghamshire v Middlesex at The Oval‡	1939
312*	J. M. Brearley	MCC Under 25 v North Zone at Peshawar	1966-67
311*	G. M. Turner	Worcestershire v Warwickshire at Worcester	1982
311	J. T. Brown	Yorkshire v Sussex at Sheffield	1897
311	R. B. Simpson	Australia v England at Manchester	1964
311	Javed Miandad	Karachi Whites v National Bank at Karachi	1974-75
310*	J. H. Edrich	England v New Zealand at Leeds	1965
310	H. Gimblett	Somerset v Sussex at Eastbourne	1948
309	V. S. Hazare	The Rest v Hindus at Bombay	1943-44
308*	F. M. M. Worrell	Barbados v Trinidad at Bridgetown	1943-44
307	M. C. Cowdrey	MCC v South Australia at Adelaide	1962-63
307	R. M. Cowper	Australia v England at Melbourne	1965-66
306*	A. Ducat	Surrey v Oxford University at The Oval	1919
306*	E. A. B. Rowan	Transvaal v Natal at Johannesburg	1939-40
305*	F. E. Woolley	MCC v Tasmania at Hobart	1911-12
305*	F. R. Foster	Warwickshire v Worcestershire at Dudley	1914
305*	W. H. Ashdown	Kent v Derbyshire at Dover	1935
304*	A. W. Nourse	Natal v Transvaal at Johannesburg	1919-20
304*	P. H. Tarilton	Barbados v Trinidad at Bridgetown	1919-20
304*	E. D. Weekes	West Indians v Cambridge University at Cambridge	1950
304	R. M. Poore	Hampshire v Somerset at Taunton	1899
304	D. G. Bradman	Australia v England at Leeds	1934
303*	W. W. Armstrong	Australians v Somerset at Bath	1905
303	Mushtaq Mohammad	Karachi Blues v Karachi University at Karachi	1967-68
302*	P. Holmes	Yorkshire v Hampshire at Portsmouth	1920
302*	W. R. Hammond	Gloucestershire v Glamorgan at Bristol	1934
302	W. R. Hammond	Gloucestershire v Glamorgan at Newport	1939
302	L. G. Rowe	West Indies v England at Bridgetown	1973-74
301*	E. H. Hendren	Middlesex v Worcestershire at Dudley	1933
301	W. G. Grace	Gloucestershire v Sussex at Bristol	1896
300*	V. T. Trumper	Australians v Sussex at Hove	1899
300*	F. B. Watson	Lancashire v Surrey at Manchester	1928
300*	Imtiaz Ahmed	PM's XI v Commonwealth XI at Bombay	1950-51
300	J. T. Brown	Yorkshire v Derbyshire at Chesterfield	1898
300	D. C. S. Compton	MCC v N. E. Transvaal at Benoni	1948-49
300	R. Subba Row	Northamptonshire v Surrey at The Oval	1958

† *Hanif Mohammad batted for 16 hours 10 minutes – the longest innings in first-class cricket.*
‡ *Played at The Oval because Lord's was required for Eton v Harrow.*

HIGHEST FOR TEAMS

For English Teams in Australia

307	M. C. Cowdrey	MCC v South Australia at Adelaide	1962-63
287	R. E. Foster	England v Australia at Sydney	1903-04

Against Australians in England

364	L. Hutton	England v Australia at The Oval	1938
219	A. Sandham	Surrey at The Oval (record for any county)	1934

For Australian Teams in England

345	C. G. Macartney	v Nottinghamshire at Nottingham	1921
334	D. G. Bradman	Australia v England at Leeds	1930

Against English Teams in Australia

307	R. M. Cowper	Australia v England at Melbourne	1965-66
280	A. J. Richardson	South Australia v MCC at Adelaide	1922-23

For Each First-Class County

Derbyshire	274	G. Davidson v Lancashire at Manchester		1896
Essex	343*	P. A. Perrin v Derbyshire at Chesterfield		1904
Glamorgan	287*	D. E. Davies v Gloucestershire at Newport		1939
Gloucestershire	318*	W. G. Grace v Yorkshire at Cheltenham		1876
Hampshire	316	R. H. Moore v Warwickshire at Bournemouth		1937
Kent	332	W. H. Ashdown v Essex at Brentwood		1934
Lancashire	424	A. C. MacLaren v Somerset at Taunton		1895
Leicestershire	252*	S. Coe v Northamptonshire at Leicester		1914
Middlesex	331*	J. D. Robertson v Worcestershire at Worcester		1949
Northamptonshire	300	R. Subba Row v Surrey at The Oval		1958
Nottinghamshire	312*	W. W. Keeton v Middlesex at The Oval†		1939
Somerset	322	I. V. A. Richards v Warwickshire at Taunton		1985
Surrey	357*	R. Abel v Somerset at The Oval		1899
Sussex	333	K. S. Duleepsinhji v Northamptonshire at Hove		1930
Warwickshire	305*	F. R. Foster v Worcestershire at Dudley		1914
Worcestershire	311*	G. M. Turner v Warwickshire at Worcester		1982
Yorkshire	341	G. H. Hirst v Leicestershire at Leicester		1905

† *Played at The Oval because Lord's was required for Eton v Harrow.*

HUNDRED ON DEBUT IN BRITISH ISLES

(The following list does not include instances of players who have previously appeared in first-class cricket outside the British Isles or who performed the feat before 1946. Particulars of the latter are in *Wisdens* prior to 1984.)

114	F. W. Stocks	Nottinghamshire v Kent at Nottingham	1946
108	A. Fairbairn	Middlesex v Somerset at Taunton	†‡1947
124	P. Hearn	Kent v Warwickshire at Gillingham	1947
215*	G. H. G. Doggart	Cambridge University v Lancashire at Cambridge	1948
106	J. R. Gill	Ireland v MCC at Dublin	1948
107*	G. Barker	Essex v Canadians at Clacton	†1954
135	J. K. E. Slack	Cambridge University v Middlesex at Cambridge	1954
100*	E. A. Clark	Middlesex v Cambridge University at Cambridge	1959
113	G. J. Chidgey	Free Foresters v Cambridge U. at Cambridge	1962
108	D. R. Shepherd	Gloucestershire v Oxford University at Oxford	1965
110*	A. J. Harvey-Walker	Derbyshire v Oxford University at Burton upon Trent	†1971
173	J. Whitehouse	Warwickshire v Oxford University at Oxford	1971
106	J. B. Turner	Minor Counties v Pakistanis at Jesmond	1974
112	J. A. Claughton	Oxford University v Gloucestershire at Oxford	†1976
100*	A. W. Lilley	Essex v Nottinghamshire at Nottingham	1978
146*	J. S. Johnson	Minor Counties v Indians at Wellington	1979
110	N. R. Taylor	Kent v Sri Lankans at Canterbury	1979
146*	D. G. Aslett	Kent v Hampshire at Bournemouth	1981
116	M. D. Moxon	Yorkshire v Essex at Leeds	†1981
100	D. A. Banks	Worcestershire v Oxford University at Oxford	1983
122	A. A. Metcalfe	Yorkshire v Nottinghamshire at Bradford	1983
117*	K. T. Medlycott	Surrey v Cambridge University at Banstead	§1984
101*	N. J. Falkner		
106	A. C. Storie	Northamptonshire v Hampshire at Northampton	†1985
102	M. P. Maynard	Glamorgan v Yorkshire at Swansea	1985
117*	R. J. Bartlett	Somerset v Oxford University at Oxford	1986
100*	P. D. Bowler	Leicestershire v Hampshire at Leicester	1986
145	I. L. Philip	Scotland v Ireland at Glasgow	1986

† *In his second innings.*

‡ *A. Fairbairn (Middlesex) in 1947 scored hundreds in the second innings of his first two matches in first-class cricket: 108 as above, 110* Middlesex v Nottinghamshire at Nottingham.*

§ *The only instance in England of two players performing the feat in the same match.*

Notes: A number of players abroad have also made a hundred on a first appearance.

The highest innings on début was hit by W. F. E. Marx when he made 240 for Transvaal against Griqualand West at Johannesburg in 1920-21.

There are three instances of a cricketer making two separate hundreds on début: A. R. Morris, New South Wales, 148 and 111 against Queensland in 1940-41, N. J. Contractor, Gujarat, 152 and 102* against Baroda in 1952-53, and Aamer Malik, Lahore "A", 132* and 110* against Railways in 1979-80.

J. S. Solomon, British Guiana, scored a hundred in each of his first three innings in first-class cricket: 114* v Jamaica; 108 v Barbados in 1956-57; 121 v Pakistanis in 1957-58.

R. Watson-Smith, Border, scored 310 runs before he was dismissed in first-class cricket, including not-out centuries in his first two innings: 183* v Orange Free State and 125* v Griqualand West in 1969-70.

G. R. Viswanath and D. M. Wellham alone have scored a hundred on both their début in first-class cricket and in Test cricket. Viswanath scored 230 for Mysore v Andhra in 1967-68 and 137 for India v Australia in 1969-70. Wellham scored 100 for New South Wales v Victoria in 1980-81 and 103 for Australia v England in 1981.

TWO SEPARATE HUNDREDS IN A MATCH

Eight times: Zaheer Abbas.
Seven times: W. R. Hammond.
Six times: J. B. Hobbs, G. M. Turner.
Five times: C. B. Fry.
Four times: D. G. Bradman, G. S. Chappell, J. H. Edrich, L. B. Fishlock, T. W. Graveney, C. G. Greenidge, H. T. W. Hardinge, E. H. Hendren, Javed Miandad, G. L. Jessop, P. A. Perrin, B. Sutcliffe, H. Sutcliffe.
Three times: L. E. G. Ames, G. Boycott, I. M. Chappell, D. C. S. Compton, M. C. Cowdrey, D. Denton, K. S. Duleepsinhji, R. E. Foster, R. C. Frederichs, S. M. Gavaskar, W. G. Grace, G. Gunn, M. R. Hallam, Hanif Mohammad, M. J. Harris, T. W. Hayward, V. S. Hazare, D. W. Hookes, L. Hutton, A. Jones, R. B. McCosker, P. B. H. May, C. P. Mead, A. C. Russell, Sadiq Mohammad, J. T. Tyldesley.
Twice: Agha Zahid, D. L. Amiss, L. Baichan, A. R. Border, B. J. T. Bosanquet, R. J. Boyd-Moss, C. C. Dacre, G. M. Emmett, A. E. Fagg, L. E. Favell, H. Gimblett, C. Hallows, R. A. Hamence, A. L. Hassett, G. A. Headley, A. I. Kallicharran, J. H. King, A. F. Kippax, P. N. Kirsten, J. G. Langridge, H. W. Lee, E. Lester, C. B. Llewellyn, C. G. Macartney, C. A. Milton, A. R. Morris, P. H. Parfitt, Nawab of Pataudi jun., E. Paynter, C. Pinch, R. G. Pollock, R. M. Prideaux, Qasim Omar, J. W. Rhodes, B. A. Richards, Rizwan-uz-Zaman, Pankaj Roy, James Seymour, R. B. Simpson, G. S. Sobers, E. Tyldesley, C. L. Walcott, W. W. Whysall, G. N. Yallop.

Notes: W. Lambert scored 107 and 157 for Sussex v Epsom at Lord's in 1817 and it was not until W. G. Grace made 130 and 102* for South of the Thames v North of the Thames at Canterbury in 1868 that the feat was repeated.

T. W. Hayward (Surrey) set up a unique record in 1906 when in one week – six days – he hit four successive hundreds, 144 and 100 v Nottinghamshire at Nottingham and 143 and 125 v Leicestershire at Leicester.

D. W. Hookes (South Australia) scored four successive hundreds in eleven days at Adelaide in 1976-77: 185 and 105 v Queensland (tied match) and 135 and 156 v New South Wales.

A. E. Fagg is alone in scoring two double-hundreds in the same match: 244 and 202* for Kent v Essex at Colchester, 1938.

L. G. Rowe is alone in scoring hundreds in each innings on his first appearance in Test cricket: 214 and 100* for West Indies v New Zealand at Kingston in 1971-72.

Zaheer Abbas (Gloucestershire) set a unique record in 1976 by twice scoring a double hundred and a hundred in the same match without being dismissed: 216* and 156* v Surrey at The Oval and 230* and 104* v Kent at Canterbury. In 1977 he achieved this feat for a third time, scoring 205* and 108* v Sussex at Cheltenham, and in 1981 for a fourth time, scoring 215* and 150* v Somerset at Bath.

M. R. Hallam (Leicestershire), opening the batting each time, achieved the following treble: 210* and 157 v Glamorgan at Leicester, 1959; 203* and 143* v Sussex at Worthing, 1961; 107* and 149* v Worcestershire at Leicester, 1965. In the last two matches he was on the field the whole time.

C. J. B. Wood, 107* and 117* for Leicestershire against Yorkshire at Bradford, 1911, is alone in carrying his bat and scoring hundreds in each innings.

W. L. Foster, 140 and 172*, and R. E. Foster, 134 and 101*, for Worcestershire v Hampshire at Worcester in July 1899, were the first brothers each to score two separate hundreds in the same first-class match.

The brothers I. M. Chappell, 145 and 121, and G. S. Chappell, 247* and 133, for Australia v New Zealand at Wellington in 1973-74, became the first players on the same side each to score a hundred in each innings of a Test match.

G. Gunn, 183, and G. V. Gunn, 100*, for Nottinghamshire v Warwickshire at Birmingham in 1931, provide the only instance of father and son each hitting a century in the same innings of a first-class match.

Most recent instances

In 1985-86

Rizwan-uz-Zaman	113* 175	Karachi Blues v Lahore City Blues at Lahore.
A. R. Border	140 114*	Australia v New Zealand at Christchurch.

In 1986: See Features of 1986.

HUNDRED AND DOUBLE-HUNDRED IN A MATCH

C. B. Fry	125 and 229	Sussex v Surrey at Hove	1900
W. W. Armstrong	157* and 245	Victoria v South Australia at Melbourne.	1920-21
H. T. W. Hardinge	207 and 102*	Kent v Surrey at Blackheath	1921
C. P. Mead	113 and 224	Hampshire v Sussex at Horsham	1921
K. S. Duleepsinhji	115 and 246	Sussex v Kent at Hastings	1929
D. G. Bradman	124 and 225	Woodfull's XI v Ryder's XI at Sydney	1929-30
B. Sutcliffe	243 and 100*	New Zealanders v Essex at Southend	1949
M. R. Hallam	210* and 157	Leicestershire v Glamorgan at Leicester	1959
M. R. Hallam	203* and 143*	Leicestershire v Sussex at Worthing	1961
Hanumant Singh	109 and 213*	Rajasthan v Bombay at Bombay	1966-67
Salah-ud-Din	256 and 102*	Karachi v East Pakistan at Karachi	1968-69
K. D. Walters	242 and 103	Australia v West Indies at Sydney	1968-69
S. M. Gavaskar	124 and 220	India v West Indies at Port-of-Spain	1970-71
L. G. Rowe	214 and 100*	West Indies v New Zealand at Kingston	1971-72
G. S. Chappell	247* and 133	Australia v New Zealand at Wellington	1973-74
L. Baichan	216* and 102	Berbice v Demerara at Georgetown	1973-74
Zaheer Abbas	216* and 156*	Gloucestershire v Surrey at Bristol	1976
Zaheer Abbas	230* and 104*	Gloucestershire v Kent at Canterbury	1976
Zaheer Abbas	205* and 108*	Gloucestershire v Sussex at Cheltenham	1977
Saadat Ali	141 and 222	Income Tax v Multan at Multan	1977-78
Talat Ali	214* and 104	PIA v Punjab at Lahore	1978-79
Shafiq Ahmed	129 and 217*	National Bank v MCB at Karachi	1978-79
D. W. Randall	209 and 146	Nottinghamshire v Middlesex at Nottingham	1979
Zaheer Abbas	215* and 150*	Gloucestershire v Somerset at Bath	1981
Qasim Omar	210* and 110	MCB v Lahore at Lahore	1982-83
A. I. Kallicharran	200* and 117*	Warwickshire v Northamptonshire at Birmingham	1984

FOUR HUNDREDS OR MORE IN SUCCESSION

Six in succession: C. B. Fry 1901; D. G. Bradman 1938-39; M. J. Procter 1970-71.

Five in succession: E. D. Weekes 1955-56.

Four in succession: A. R. Border 1985; D. G. Bradman 1931-32, 1948-49; D. C. S. Compton 1946-47; N. J. Contractor 1957-58; K. S. Duleepsinhji 1931; C. B. Fry 1911; C. G. Greenidge 1986; W. R. Hammond 1936-37, 1945-46; H. T. W. Hardinge 1913; T. W. Hayward 1906; J. B. Hobbs 1920, 1925; D. W. Hookes 1976-77; P. N. Kirsten 1976-77; J. G. Langridge 1949; C. G.

Macartney 1921; K. S. McEwan 1977; P. B. H. May 1956-57; V. M. Merchant 1941-42; A. Mitchell 1933; Nawab of Pataudi sen. 1931; L. G. Rowe 1971-72; Pankaj Roy 1962-63; Sadiq Mohammad 1976; Saeed Ahmed 1961-62; H. Sutcliffe 1931, 1939; E. Tyldesley 1926; W. W. Whysall 1930; F. E. Woolley 1929; Zaheer Abbas 1970-71, 1982-83.

Note: The most fifties in consecutive innings is ten – by E. Tyldesley in 1926 and by D. G. Bradman in the 1947-48 and 1948 seasons.

MOST HUNDREDS IN A SEASON

Eighteen: D. C. S. Compton in 1947. These included six hundreds against the South Africans in which matches his average was 84.78. His aggregate for the season was 3,816, also a record.

Sixteen: J. B. Hobbs in 1925, when aged 42, played 16 three-figure innings in first-class matches. It was during this season that he exceeded the number of hundreds obtained in first-class cricket by W. G. Grace.

Fifteen: W. R. Hammond in 1938.

Fourteen: H. Sutcliffe in 1932.

Thirteen: G. Boycott in 1971, D. G. Bradman in 1938, C. B. Fry in 1901, W. R. Hammond in 1933 and 1937, T. W. Hayward in 1906, E. H. Hendren in 1923, 1927 and 1928, C. P. Mead in 1928, and H. Sutcliffe in 1928 and 1931.

MOST HUNDREDS IN A CAREER

(35 or More)

	Hundreds Total	Abroad	100th 100		Hundreds Total	Abroad	100th 100
J. B. Hobbs	197	22	1923	D. G. Bradman	117	41†	1947-48
E. H. Hendren	170	19	1928-29	M. C. Cowdrey	107	27	1973
W. R. Hammond	167	33	1935	A. Sandham	107	20	1935
C. P. Mead	153	8	1927	Zaheer Abbas	107	70†	1982-83
G. Boycott	151	27	1977	T. W. Hayward	104	4	1913
H. Sutcliffe	149	14	1932	J. H. Edrich	103	13	1977
F. E. Woolley	145	10	1929	G. M. Turner	103	85†	1982
L. Hutton	129	24	1951	L. E. G. Ames	102	13	1950
W. G. Grace	126	1	1895	E. Tyldesley	102	8	1934
D. C. S. Compton	123	31	1952	D. L. Amiss	100	15	1986
T. W. Graveney	122	31	1964				

† *"Abroad" for D. G. Bradman is outside Australia; for Zaheer Abbas, outside Pakistan; for G. M. Turner, outside New Zealand.*

E. H. Hendren and D. G. Bradman scored their 100th hundreds in Australia, Zaheer Abbas scored his in Pakistan. Zaheer Abbas and G. Boycott did so in Test matches.

J. W. Hearne	96	S. M. Gavaskar	78	D. Brookes	71
C. B. Fry	94	K. F. Barrington	76	A. C. Russell	71
I. V. A. Richards	92	J. G. Langridge	76	D. Denton	69
W. J. Edrich	86	C. Washbrook	76	M. J. K. Smith	69
G. S. Sobers	86	H. T. W. Hardinge	75	R. E. Marshall	68
J. T. Tyldesley	86	R. Abel	74	R. N. Harvey	67
P. B. H. May	85	G. S. Chappell	74	P. Holmes	67
R. E. S. Wyatt	85	D. Kenyon	74	J. D. Robertson	67
J. Hardstaff, jun.	83	C. G. Greenidge	73	P. A. Perrin	66
A. I. Kallicharran	83	Majid Khan	73	Javed Miandad	65
R. B. Kanhai	83	Mushtaq Mohammad	72	R. T. Simpson	64
M. Leyland	80	J. O'Connor	72	K. S. McEwan	63
B. A. Richards	80	W. G. Quaife	72	K. W. R. Fletcher	62
C. H. Lloyd	79	K. S. Ranjitsinhji	72	G. Gunn	62

R. G. Pollock 62	M. J. Procter 48	M. W. Gatting 40
V. S. Hazare 60	A. C. MacLaren 47	J. Gunn 40
G. H. Hirst 60	W. H. Ponsford 47	M. J. Smith 40
R. B. Simpson 60	J. Iddon 46	C. L. Walcott 40
P. F. Warner 60	A. R. Morris 46	D. M. Young 40
I. M. Chappell 59	C. T. Radley 46	W. H. Ashdown 39
A. L. Hassett 59	W. W. Armstrong 45	J. B. Bolus 39
A. Shrewsbury 59	Asif Iqbal 45	W. A. Brown 39
A. E. Fagg 58	L. G. Berry 45	R. J. Gregory 39
P. H. Parfitt 58	A. R. Border 45	W. R. D. Payton 39
W. Rhodes 58	J. M. Brearley 45	J. R. Reid 39
G. A. Gooch 57	A. W. Carr 45	F. M. M. Worrell 39
L. B. Fishlock 56	C. Hill 45	F. L. Bowley 38
A. Jones 56	A. J. Lamb 45	P. J. Burge 38
C. A. Milton 56	N. C. O'Neill 45	J. F. Crapp 38
C. Hallows 55	E. Paynter 45	D. Lloyd 38
Hanif Mohammad 55	Shafiq Ahmed 45	V. L. Manjrekar 38
W. Watson 55	Rev. D. S. Sheppard . 45	Mudassar Nazar 38
D. J. Insole 54	K. D. Walters 45	A. W. Nourse 38
W. W. Keeton 54	H. H. I. Gibbons 44	N. Oldfield 38
W. Bardsley 53	V. M. Merchant 44	Rev. J. H. Parsons ... 38
B. F. Davison 53	A. Mitchell 44	D. W. Randall 38
A. E. Dipper 53	P. E. Richardson 44	W. W. Read 38
G. L. Jessop 53	B. Sutcliffe 44	J. Sharp 38
James Seymour 53	G. R. Viswanath 44	L. J. Todd 38
E. H. Bowley 52	Younis Ahmed 44	P. Willey 38
D. B. Close 52	E. J. Barlow 43	J. Arnold 37
A. Ducat 52	B. L. D'Oliveira 43	G. Brown 37
E. R. Dexter 51	J. H. Hampshire 43	G. M. Emmett 37
J. M. Parks 51	A. F. Kippax 43	W. Larkins 37
W. W. Whysall 51	H. Makepeace 43	H. W. Lee 37
G. Cox jun. 50	James Langridge 42	M. A. Noble 37
H. E. Dollery 50	H. W. Parks 42	H. S. Squires 37
K. S. Duleepsinhji ... 50	C. E. B. Rice 42	R. T. Virgin 37
H. Gimblett 50	T. F. Shepherd 42	C. J. B. Wood 37
W. M. Lawry 50	V. T. Trumper 42	N. F. Armstrong 36
Sadiq Mohammad 50	M. J. Harris 41	E. Oldroyd 36
F. B. Watson 50	P. N. Kirsten 41	W. Place 36
C. G. Macartney 49	K. R. Miller 41	D. B. Vengsarkar 36
M. J. Stewart 49	A. D. Nourse 41	A. L. Wadekar 36
K. G. Suttle 49	J. H. Parks 41	E. D. Weekes 36
P. M. Umrigar 49	R. M. Prideaux 41	K. C. Wessels 36
W. M. Woodfull 49	G. Pullar 41	C. S. Dempster 35
C. J. Barnett 48	W. E. Russell 41	D. I. Gower 35
W. Gunn 48	J. G. Wright 41	D. R. Jardine 35
E. G. Hayes 48	R. C. Fredericks 40	B. H. Valentine 35
B. W. Luckhurst 48		

3,000 RUNS IN A SEASON

	Season	I	NO	R	HI	100s	Avge
D. C. S. Compton	1947	50	8	3,816	246	18	90.85
W. J. Edrich	1947	52	8	3,539	267*	12	80.43
T. W. Hayward	1906	61	8	3,518	219	13	66.37
L. Hutton	1949	56	6	3,429	269*	12	68.58
F. E. Woolley	1928	59	4	3,352	198	12	60.94
H. Sutcliffe	1932	52	7	3,336	313	14	74.13
W. R. Hammond	1933	54	5	3,323	264	13	67.81
E. H. Hendren	1928	54	7	3,311	209*	13	70.44
R. Abel	1901	68	8	3,309	247	7	55.15

	Season	I	NO	R	HI	100s	Avge
W. R. Hammond	1937	55	5	3,252	217	13	65.04
M. J. K. Smith	1959	67	11	3,245	200*	8	57.94
E. H. Hendren	1933	65	9	3,186	301*	11	56.89
C. P. Mead	1921	52	6	3,179	280*	10	69.10
T. W. Hayward	1904	63	5	3,170	203	11	54.65
K. S. Ranjitsinhji	1899	58	8	3,159	197	8	63.18
C. B. Fry	1901	43	3	3,147	244	13	78.67
K. S. Ranjitsinhji	1900	40	5	3,065	275	11	87.57
L. E. G. Ames	1933	57	5	3,058	295	9	58.80
J. T. Tyldesley	1901	60	5	3,041	221	9	55.29
C. P. Mead	1928	50	10	3,027	180	13	75.67
J. B. Hobbs	1925	48	5	3,024	266*	16	70.32
E. Tyldesley	1928	48	10	3,024	242	10	79.57
W. E. Alley	1961	64	11	3,019	221*	11	56.96
W. R. Hammond	1938	42	2	3,011	271	15	75.27
E. H. Hendren	1923	51	12	3,010	200*	13	77.17
H. Sutcliffe	1931	42	11	3,006	230	13	96.96
J. H. Parks	1937	63	4	3,003	168	11	50.89
H. Sutcliffe	1928	44	5	3,002	228	13	76.97

Notes: W. G. Grace scored 2,739 runs in 1871 – the first batsman to reach 2,000 runs in a season. He made ten hundreds and twice exceeded 200, with an average of 78.25 in all first-class matches. At the time, the over consisted of four balls.

The highest aggregate in a season since the reduction of County Championship matches in 1969 is 2,559 by G. A. Gooch (45 innings) in 1984.

1,000 RUNS IN A SEASON MOST TIMES

(Includes Overseas Tours and Seasons)

28 times: W. G. Grace 2,000 (6); F. E. Woolley 3,000 (1), 2,000 (12).

27 times: M. C. Cowdrey 2,000 (2); C. P. Mead 3,000 (2), 2,000 (9).

26 times: G. Boycott 2,000 (3); J. B. Hobbs 3,000 (1), 2,000 (16).

25 times: E. H. Hendren 3,000 (3), 2,000 (12).

24 times: Wm. Quaife 2,000 (1); H. Sutcliffe 3,000 (3), 2,000 (12).

23 times: D. L. Amiss 2,000 (3); A. Jones.

22 times: T. W. Graveney 2,000 (7); W. R. Hammond 3,000 (3), 2,000 (9).

21 times: D. Denton 2,000 (5); J. H. Edrich 2,000 (6); W. Rhodes 2,000 (2).

20 times: D. B. Close; K. W. R. Fletcher; G. Gunn; T. W. Hayward 3,000 (2), 2,000 (8); James Langridge 2,000 (1); J. M. Parks 2,000 (3); A. Sandham 2,000 (8); M. J. K. Smith 3,000 (1), 2,000 (5); C. Washbrook 2,000 (2).

19 times: J. W. Hearne 2,000 (4); G. H. Hirst 2,000 (3); D. Kenyon 2,000 (7); E. Tyldesley 3,000 (1), 2,000 (5); J. T. Tyldesley 3,000 (1), 2,000 (4).

18 times: L. G. Berry 2,000 (1); H. T. W. Hardinge 2,000 (5); R. E. Marshall 2,000 (6); P. A. Perrin; G. M. Turner 2,000 (3); R. E. S. Wyatt 2,000 (5).

17 times: L. E. G. Ames 3,000 (1), 2,000 (5); T. E. Bailey 2,000 (1); D. Brookes 2,000 (6); D. C. S. Compton 3,000 (1), 2,000 (5); L. Hutton 3,000 (1), 2,000 (8); J. G. Langridge 2,000 (11); M. Leyland 2,000 (3); K. G. Suttle 2,000 (1), Zaheer Abbas 2,000 (2).

16 times: D. G. Bradman 2,000 (4); D. E. Davies 2,000 (1); C. G. Greenidge 2,000 (1); E. G. Hayes 2,000 (2); C. A. Milton 2,000 (1); J. O'Connor 2,000 (4); C. T. Radley; James Seymour 2,000 (1).

15 times: G. Barker; K. F. Barrington 2,000 (3); E. H. Bowley 2,000 (4); M. H. Denness; A. E. Dipper 2,000 (5); H. E. Dollery 2,000 (2); W. J. Edrich 3,000 (1), 2,000 (8); J. H. Hampshire; P. Holmes 2,000 (7); Mushtaq Mohammad; R. B. Nicholls 2,000 (1); P. H. Parfitt 2,000 (3); W. G. A. Parkhouse 2,000 (1); B. A. Richards 2,000 (1); I. V. A. Richards 2,000 (1); J. D. Robertson 2,000 (9); G. S. Sobers; M. J. Stewart 2,000 (1).

Notes: F. E. Woolley reached 1,000 runs in 28 consecutive seasons (1907-1938). C. P. Mead did so 27 seasons in succession (1906-1936).

Outside England, 1,000 runs in a season has been reached most times by D. G. Bradman (in 12 seasons in Australia).

Three batsmen have scored 1,000 runs in a season in each of four different countries: G. S. Sobers in West Indies, England, India and Australia; M. C. Cowdrey and G. Boycott in England, South Africa, West Indies and Australia.

HIGHEST AGGREGATES OUTSIDE ENGLAND

	Season	I	NO	R	HI	100s	Avge
In Australia D. G. Bradman	1928-29	24	6	1,690	340*	7	93.88
In South Africa J. R. Reid ....}	1961-62	30	2	1,915	203	7	68.39
In West Indies E. H. Hendren	1929-30	18	5	1,765	254*	6	135.76
In New Zealand G. M. Turner	1975-76	20	4	1,244	177*	5	77.75
In India C. G. Borde	1964-65	28	3	1,604	168	6	64.16
In Pakistan Saadat Ali	1983-84	27	1	1,649	208	4	63.42

Note: In more than one country, the following aggregates of over 2,000 runs have been recorded.

M. Amarnath (P/I/WI)	1982-83	34	6	2,234	207	9	79.78
J. R. Reid (SA/A/NZ)	1961-62	40	2	2,188	203	7	57.57
S. M. Gavaskar (I/P) .	1978-79	30	6	2,121	205	10	88.37
R. B. Simpson (I/P/A/WI)	1964-65	34	4	2,063	201	8	68.76

HIGHEST AVERAGES IN AN ENGLISH SEASON

(Qualification: 12 innings)

	Season	I	NO	R	HI	100s	Avge
D. G. Bradman	1938	26	5	2,429	278	13	115.66
G. Boycott	1979	20	5	1,538	175*	6	102.53
W. A. Johnston	1953	17	16	102	28*	0	102.00
G. Boycott	1971	30	5	2,503	233	13	100.12
D. G. Bradman	1930	36	6	2,960	334	10	98.66
H. Sutcliffe	1931	42	11	3,006	230	13	96.96
R. M. Poore	1899	21	4	1,551	304	7	91.23
D. R. Jardine	1927	14	3	1,002	147	5	91.09
D. C. S. Compton	1947	50	8	3,816	246	18	90.85
G. M. Turner	1982	16	3	1,171	311*	5	90.07
D. G. Bradman	1948	31	4	2,428	187	11	89.92
Zaheer Abbas	1981	36	10	2,306	215*	10	88.69
K. S. Ranjitsinhji	1900	40	5	3,065	275	11	87.57
D. R. Jardine	1928	17	4	1,133	193	3	87.15
W. R. Hammond	1946	26	5	1,783	214	7	84.90
D. G. Bradman	1934	27	3	2,020	304	10	84.16
R. B. Kanhai	1975	22	9	1,073	178*	3	82.53
Mudassar Nazar	1982	16	6	825	211*	4	82.50
C. G. Greenidge	1984	16	3	1,069	223	4	82.23
J. B. Hobbs	1928	38	7	2,542	200*	12	82.00
C. B. Fry	1903	40	7	2,683	234	9	81.30
W. J. Edrich	1947	52	8	3,539	267*	12	80.43

25,000 RUNS IN A CAREER

Dates in italics denote the first half of an overseas season; i.e. *1945* denotes the 1945-46 season.

	Career	R	I	NO	HI	100s	Avge
J. B. Hobbs	1905-34	61,237	1,315	106	316*	197	50.65
F. E. Woolley	1906-38	58,969	1,532	85	305*	145	40.75
E. H. Hendren	1907-38	57,611	1,300	166	301*	170	50.80
C. P. Mead	1905-36	55,061	1,340	185	280*	153	47.67
†W. G. Grace	1865-1908	54,896	1,493	105	344	126	39.55
W. R. Hammond	1920-51	50,551	1,005	104	336*	167	56.10
H. Sutcliffe	1919-45	50,138	1,088	123	313	149	51.95
G. Boycott	1962-86	48,426	1,014	162	261*	151	56.83
T. W. Graveney	1948-*71*	47,793	1,223	159	258	122	44.91
T. W. Hayward	1893-1914	43,551	1,138	96	315*	104	41.79
M. C. Cowdrey	1950-76	42,719	1,130	134	307	107	42.89
D. L. Amiss	1960-86	42,123	1,093	123	262*	100	43.42
A. Sandham	1911-*37*	41,284	1,000	79	325	107	44.82
L. Hutton	1934-60	40,140	814	91	364	129	55.51
M. J. K. Smith	1951-75	39,832	1,091	139	204	66	41.84
W. Rhodes	1898-1930	39,802	1,528	237	267*	58	30.83
J. H. Edrich	1956-78	39,790	979	104	310*	103	45.47
R. E. S. Wyatt	1923-57	39,405	1,141	157	232	85	40.04
D. C. S. Compton	1936-64	38,942	839	88	300	123	51.85
E. Tyldesley	1909-36	38,874	961	106	256*	102	45.46
J. T. Tyldesley	1895-1923	37,897	994	62	295*	86	40.60
J. W. Hearne	1909-36	37,252	1,025	116	285*	96	40.98
L. E. G. Ames	1926-51	37,248	951	95	295	102	43.51
D. Kenyon	1946-67	37,002	1,159	59	259	74	33.63
W. J. Edrich	1934-58	36,965	964	92	267*	86	42.39
J. M. Parks	1949-76	36,673	1,227	172	205*	51	34.76
D. Denton	1894-1920	36,479	1,163	70	221	69	33.37
K. W. R. Fletcher	1962-86	36,437	1,118	164	228*	62	38.19
G. H. Hirst	1891-1929	36,323	1,215	151	341	60	34.13
A. Jones	1957-83	36,049	1,168	72	204*	56	32.89
W. G. Quaife	1894-1928	36,012	1,203	185	255*	72	35.37
R. E. Marshall	*1945*-72	35,725	1,053	59	228*	68	35.94
G. Gunn	1902-32	35,208	1,061	82	220	62	35.96
D. B. Close	1949-86	34,994	1,225	173	198	52	33.26
J. G. Langridge	1928-55	34,380	984	66	250*	76	37.45
G. M. Turner	*1964*-82	34,346	792	101	311*	103	49.70
Zaheer Abbas	1965-85	34,289	747	89	274	107	52.11
C. Washbrook	1933-64	34,101	906	107	251*	76	42.67
M. Leyland	1920-48	33,659	932	101	263	80	40.50
H. T. W. Hardinge	1902-33	33,519	1,021	103	263*	75	36.51
R. Abel	1881-1904	33,124	1,007	73	357*	74	35.46
C. A. Milton	1948-74	32,150	1,078	125	170	56	33.73
J. D. Robertson	1937-59	31,914	897	46	331*	67	37.50
J. Hardstaff, jun.	1930-55	31,847	812	94	266	83	44.35
James Langridge	1924-53	31,716	1,058	157	167	42	35.20
K. F. Barrington	1953-68	31,714	831	136	256	76	45.63
C. H. Lloyd	*1963*-86	31,232	730	96	242*	79	49.26
Mushtaq Mohammad	*1956*-85	31,091	843	104	303*	72	42.07
C. G. Greenidge	1970-86	31,074	743	84	273*	73	47.15
C. B. Fry	1892-*1921*	30,886	658	43	258*	94	50.22
D. Brookes	1934-59	30,874	925	70	257	71	36.10
A. I. Kallicharran	*1966*-86	30,775	762	82	243*	83	45.25
P. Holmes	1913-35	30,574	810	84	315*	67	42.11
R. T. Simpson	*1944*-63	30,546	852	55	259	64	38.32
L. G. Berry	1924-51	30,225	1,056	57	232	45	30.25
K. G. Suttle	1949-71	30,225	1,064	92	204*	49	31.09

	Career	R	I	NO	HI	100s	Avge
P. A. Perrin	1896-1928	29,709	918	91	343*	66	35.92
P. F. Warner	1894-1929	29,028	875	75	244	60	36.28
R. B. Kanhai	*1954-81*	28,774	669	82	256	83	49.01
J. O'Connor	1921-39	28,764	903	79	248	72	34.90
T. E. Bailey	1945-67	28,642	1,072	215	205	28	33.42
I. V. A. Richards	*1971-86*	28,533	611	40	322	92	49.97
E. H. Bowley	1912-34	28,378	859	47	283	52	34.94
B. A. Richards	*1964-82*	28,358	576	58	356	80	54.74
G. S. Sobers	*1952-74*	28,315	609	93	365*	86	54.87
A. E. Dipper	1908-32	28,075	865	69	252*	53	35.27
D. G. Bradman	*1927-48*	28,067	338	43	452*	117	95.14
J. H. Hampshire	1961-84	28,059	924	112	183*	43	34.55
P. B. H. May	1948-63	27,592	618	77	285*	85	51.00
Majid Khan	*1961-84*	27,444	700	62	241	73	43.01
A. C. Russell	1908-30	27,358	717	59	273	71	41.57
E. G. Hayes	1896-1926	27,318	896	48	276	48	32.21
A. E. Fagg	1932-57	27,291	803	46	269*	58	36.05
James Seymour	1900-26	27,238	911	62	218*	53	32.08
P. H. Parfitt	1956-*73*	26,924	845	104	200*	58	36.33
B. F. Davison	*1967-85*	26,923	745	78	189	53	40.36
G. L. Jessop	1894-1914	26,698	855	37	286	53	32.63
D. E. Davies	1924-54	26,566	1,033	79	287*	32	27.84
A. Shrewsbury	1875-1902	26,505	813	90	267	59	36.65
M. J. Stewart	1954-72	26,492	898	93	227*	49	32.90
C. T. Radley	1964-86	26,068	867	131	200	46	35.41
P. E. Richardson	1949-65	26,055	794	41	185	44	34.60
M. H. Denness	1959-80	25,886	838	65	195	33	33.48
H. Makepeace	1906-30	25,799	778	66	203	43	36.23
W. Gunn	1880-1904	25,791	850	72	273	48	33.15
W. Watson	1939-64	25,670	753	109	257	55	39.86
G. Brown	1908-33	25,649	1,012	52	232*	37	26.71
G. M. Emmett	1936-59	25,602	865	50	188	37	31.41
J. B. Bolus	1956-75	25,598	833	81	202*	39	34.03
W. E. Russell	1956-72	25,525	796	64	193	41	34.87
C. J. Barnett	1927-*53*	25,389	821	45	259	48	32.71
Younis Ahmed	*1961-86*	25,388	746	114	221*	44	40.17
L. B. Fishlock	1931-52	25,376	699	54	253	56	39.34
D. J. Insole	1947-63	25,237	743	72	219*	54	37.61
J. M. Brearley	1961-83	25,185	768	102	312*	45	37.81
J. Vine	1896-1922	25,171	920	79	202	34	29.92
R. M. Prideaux	1958-*74*	25,136	808	75	202*	41	34.29
J. H. King	1895-1926	25,122	988	69	227*	34	27.33

† *In recent years some statisticians have removed from W. G. Grace's record a number of matches which they consider not to have been first-class. The above figures are those which became universally accepted upon appearance in W. G. Grace's obituary in the* Wisden *of 1916. Some works of reference give his career record as being 54,211–1,478–104–344–124–39.45. These figures also appeared in the 1981 edition of* Wisden.

CAREER AVERAGE OVER 50

(Qualification: 10,000 runs)

Avge		Career	I	NO	R	HI	100s
95.14	D. G. Bradman	*1927-48*	338	43	28,067	452*	117
71.22	V. M. Merchant	*1929-51*	229	43	13,248	359*	44
65.18	W. H. Ponsford	*1920-34*	235	23	13,819	437	47
64.99	W. M. Woodfull	*1921-34*	245	39	13,388	284	49
58.24	A. L. Hassett	*1932-53*	322	32	16,890	232	59

Avge		Career	I	NO	R	HI	100s
57.87	V. S. Hazare	1934-66	367	45	18,635	316*	60
57.22	A. F. Kippax	1918-35	256	33	12,762	315*	43
56.83	G. Boycott	1962-86	1,014	162	48,426	261*	151
56.55	C. L. Walcott	1941-63	238	29	11,820	314*	40
56.37	K. S. Ranjitsinhji	1893-1920	500	62	24,692	285*	72
56.22	R. B. Simpson	1952-77	436	62	21,029	359	60
56.10	W. R. Hammond	1920-51	1,005	104	50,551	336*	167
55.51	L. Hutton	1934-60	814	91	40,140	364	129
55.34	E. D. Weekes	1944-64	241	24	12,010	304*	36
54.87	G. S. Sobers	1952-74	609	93	28,315	365*	86
54.74	B. A. Richards	1964-82	576	58	28,358	356	80
54.47	R. G. Pollock	1961-85	429	53	20,484	274	62
54.24	F. M. M. Worrell	1941-64	326	49	15,025	308*	39
53.78	R. M. Cowper	1959-69	228	31	10,595	307	26
53.69	A. R. Border	1976-86	324	48	14,820	200	45
53.67	A. R. Morris	1940-63	250	15	12,614	290	46
53.30	Javed Miandad	1973-86	518	84	23,133	311	65
52.32	Hanif Mohammad	1951-75	371	45	17,059	499	55
52.27	P. R. Umrigar	1944-67	350	41	16,154	252*	49
52.20	G. S. Chappell	1966-83	542	72	24,535	247*	74
52.11	Zaheer Abbas	1965-85	747	89	34,289	274	107
51.95	H. Sutcliffe	1919-45	1,088	123	50,138	313	149
51.85	D. C. S. Compton	1936-64	839	88	38,942	300	123
51.53	A. D. Nourse	1931-52	269	27	12,472	260*	41
51.44	W. A. Brown	1932-49	284	15	13,840	265*	39
51.24	S. M. Gavaskar	1966-86	544	61	24,749	340	78
51.00	P. B. H. May	1948-63	618	77	27,592	285*	85
50.95	N. C. O'Neill	1955-67	306	34	13,859	284	45
50.93	R. N. Harvey	1946-62	461	35	21,699	231*	67
50.90	W. M. Lawry	1955-71	417	49	18,734	266	50
50.90	A. V. Mankad	1963-82	326	71	12,980	265	31
50.80	E. H. Hendren	1907-38	1,300	166	57,611	301*	170
50.65	J. B. Hobbs	1905-34	1,315	106	61,237	316*	197
50.36	Shafiq Ahmed	1967-85	349	42	15,461	217*	45
50.22	C. B. Fry	1892-1921	658	43	30,886	258*	94

FAST FIFTIES

Minutes

8†	C. C. Inman (57)	Leicestershire v Nottinghamshire at Nottingham ...	1965
11	C. I. J. Smith (66)	Middlesex v Gloucestershire at Bristol	1938
14	S. J. Pegler (50)	South Africans v Tasmania at Launceston	1910-11
14	F. T. Mann (53)	Middlesex v Nottinghamshire at Lord's	1921
14	H. B. Cameron (56)	Transvaal v Orange Free State at Johannesburg ...	1934-35
14	C. I. J. Smith (52)	Middlesex v Kent at Maidstone	1935

† *Full tosses were bowled to expedite a declaration.*

FASTEST HUNDREDS

Minutes

35	P. G. H. Fender (113*)	Surrey v Northamptonshire at Northampton ..	1920
35	S. J. O'Shaughnessy (105)	Lancashire v Leicestershire at Manchester	1983
37	C. M. Old (107)	Yorkshire v Warwickshire at Birmingham	1977
40	G. L. Jessop (101)	Gloucestershire v Yorkshire at Harrogate	1897
41	N. F. M. Popplewell (143)	Somerset v Gloucestershire at Bath	1983
42	G. L. Jessop (191)	Gentlemen of South v Players of South at Hastings	1907

Minutes

43	A. H. Hornby (106)	Lancashire v Somerset at Manchester	1905
43	D. W. Hookes (107)	South Australia v Victoria at Adelaide	1982-83
44	R. N. S. Hobbs (100)	Essex v Australians at Chelmsford	1975

Notes: The fastest recorded hundred in terms of balls received was scored off 34 balls by D. W. Hookes (above).

Research of the scorebook has shown that P. G. H. Fender scored his hundred from between 40 and 46 balls. He contributed 113 to an unfinished sixth-wicket partnership of 171 in 42 minutes with H. A. Peach.

S. J. O'Shaughnessy scored his hundred on the final afternoon of the season and against a succession of long-hops and full-tosses offered by occasional bowlers to expedite a declaration.

E. B. Alletson (Nottinghamshire) scored 189 out of 227 runs in 90 minutes against Sussex at Hove in 1911. It has been estimated that his last 139 runs took 37 minutes.

FASTEST DOUBLE-HUNDREDS

Minutes

113	R. J. Shastri (200*)	Bombay v Baroda at Bombay	1984-85
120	G. L. Jessop (286)	Gloucestershire v Sussex at Hove	1903
120	C. H. Lloyd (201*)	West Indians v Glamorgan at Swansea	1976
130	G. L. Jessop (234)	Gloucestershire v Somerset at Bristol	1905
131	V. T. Trumper (293)	Australians v Canterbury at Christchurch	1913-14

FASTEST TRIPLE-HUNDREDS

Minutes

181	D. C. S. Compton (300)	MCC v N. E. Transvaal at Benoni	1948-49
205	F. E. Woolley (305*)	MCC v Tasmania at Hobart	1911-12
205	C. G. Macartney (345)	Australians v Nottinghamshire at Nottingham .	1921
213	D. G. Bradman (369)	South Australia v Tasmania at Adelaide	1935-36

300 RUNS IN ONE DAY

345	C. G. Macartney	Australians v Nottinghamshire at Nottingham	1921
334	W. H. Ponsford	Victoria v New South Wales at Melbourne	1926-27
333	K. S. Duleepsinhji	Sussex v Northamptonshire at Hove	1930
331*	J. D. Robertson	Middlesex v Worcestershire at Worcester	1949
325*	B. A. Richards	S. Australia v W. Australia at Perth	1970-71
322†	E. Paynter	Lancashire v Sussex at Hove	1937
322	I. V. A. Richards	Somerset v Warwickshire at Taunton	1985
318	C. W. Gregory	New South Wales v Queensland at Brisbane	1906-07
317	K. R. Rutherford	New Zealanders v D. B. Close's XI at Scarborough ...	1986
316†	R. H. Moore	Hampshire v Warwickshire at Bournemouth	1937
315*	R. C. Blunt	Otago v Canterbury at Christchurch	1931-32
312*	J. M. Brearley	MCC Under 25 v North Zone at Peshawar	1966-67
311*	G. M. Turner	Worcestershire v Warwickshire at Worcester	1982
309*	D. G. Bradman	Australia v England at Leeds	1930
307*	W. H. Ashdown	Kent v Essex at Brentwood	1934
306*	A. Ducat	Surrey v Oxford University at The Oval	1919
305*	F. R. Foster	Warwickshire v Worcestershire at Dudley	1914

† *E. Paynter's 322 and R. H. Moore's 316 were scored on the same day: July 28, 1937.*

1,000 RUNS IN MAY

	Runs	Avge
W. G. Grace, May 9 to May 30, 1895 (22 days):		
13, 103, 18, 25, 288, 52, 257, 73*, 18, 169	1,016	112.88
"W.G." was within two months of completing his 47th year.		
W. R. Hammond, May 7 to May 31, 1927 (25 days):		
27, 135, 108, 128, 17, 11, 99, 187, 4, 30, 83, 7, 192, 14	1,042	74.42
Hammond scored his 1,000th run on May 28, thus equalling		
"W.G.'s" record of 22 days.		
C. Hallows, May 5 to May 31, 1928 (27 days):		
100, 101, 51*, 123, 101*, 22, 74, 104, 58, 34*, 232	1,000	125.00

1,000 RUNS IN APRIL AND MAY

	Runs	Avge
T. W. Hayward, April 16 to May 31, 1900:		
120*, 55, 108, 131*, 55, 193, 120, 5, 6, 3, 40, 146, 92	1,074	97.63
D. G. Bradman, April 30 to May 31, 1930:		
236, 185*, 78, 9, 48*, 66, 4, 44, 252*, 32, 47*	1,001	143.00
On April 30 Bradman scored 75 not out.		
D. G. Bradman, April 30 to May 31, 1938:		
258, 58, 137, 278, 2, 143, 145*, 5, 30*	1,056	150.85
Bradman scored 258 on April 30, and his 1,000th run on May 27.		
W. J. Edrich, April 30 to May 31, 1938:		
104, 37, 115, 63, 20*, 182, 71, 31, 53*, 45, 15, 245, 0, 9, 20*	1,010	84.16
Edrich scored 21 not out on April 30. All his runs were scored at		
Lord's.		
G. M. Turner, April 24 to May 31, 1973:		
41, 151*, 143, 85, 7, 8, 17*, 81, 13, 53, 44, 153*, 3, 2, 66*, 30, 10*,		
111	1,018	78.30

1,000 RUNS IN TWO SEPARATE MONTHS

Only four batsmen, C. B. Fry, K. S. Ranjitsinhji, H. Sutcliffe and L. Hutton, have scored over 1,000 runs in each of two months in the same season. L. Hutton, by scoring 1,294 in June 1949, made more runs in a single month than anyone else. He also made 1,050 in August 1949.

MOST RUNS SCORED OFF ONE OVER

(All instances refer to six-ball overs)

36	G. S. Sobers	off M. A. Nash, Nottinghamshire v Glamorgan at Swansea (six 6s)	1968
36	R. J. Shastri	off Tilak Raj, Bombay v Baroda at Bombay (six 6s)	1984-85
34	E. B. Alletson	off E. H. Killick, Nottinghamshire v Sussex at Hove (46604446; including two no-balls)	1911
34	F. C. Hayes	off M. A. Nash, Lancashire v Glamorgan at Swansea (646666)	1977
32	I. T. Botham	off I. R. Snook, England XI v Central Districts at Palmerston North (466466)	1983-84
32	C. C. Inman	off N. W. Hill, Leicestershire v Nottinghamshire at Nottingham (466664; full tosses were provided for him to hit)	1965
32	T. E. Jesty	off R. J. Boyd-Moss, Hampshire v Northamptonshire at Southampton (466662)	1984
32	P. W. G. Parker	off A. I. Kallicharran, Sussex v Warwickshire at Birmingham (466664)	1982

32	I. R. Redpath	off N. Rosendorff, Australians v Orange Free State at Bloemfontein (666644)	1969-70
32	C. C. Smart	off G. Hill, Glamorgan v Hampshire at Cardiff (664664)	1935
31	M. H. Bowditch (1) and M. J. Procter (30)	off A. A. Mallett, Western Province v Australians at Cape Town (Procter hit five 6s)	1969-70
31	A. W. Wellard	off F. E. Woolley, Somerset v Kent at Wells (666661)	1938
30	I. T. Botham	off P. A. Smith, Somerset v Warwickshire at Taunton (4466460 including one no-ball)	1982
30	D. G. Bradman	off A. P. Freeman, Australians v England XI at Folkestone (466464)	1934
30	H. B. Cameron	off H. Verity, South Africans v Yorkshire at Sheffield (444666)	1935
30	G. A. Gooch	off S. R. Gorman, Essex v Cambridge U. at Cambridge (662664)	1985
30	A. J. Lamb	off A. I. Kallicharran, Northamptonshire v Warwickshire at Birmingham (644664)	1982
30	D. T. Lindsay	off W. T. Greensmith, South African Fezela XI v Essex at Chelmsford (066666 to win the match)	1961
30	Majid Khan	off R. C. Davis, Pakistanis v Glamorgan at Swansea (606666)	1967
30	A. W. Wellard	off T. R. Armstrong, Somerset v Derbyshire at Wells (066666)	1936
30	D. Wilson	off R. N. S. Hobbs, Yorkshire v MCC at Scarborough (466266)	1966
30	P. L. Winslow	off J. T. Ikin, South Africans v Lancashire at Manchester (446646)	1955
30	Zaheer Abbas	off D. Breakwell, Gloucestershire v Somerset at Taunton (466626)	1979

Note: The greatest number of runs scored off an eight-ball over is 34 (40446664) by R. M. Edwards off M. C. Carew, Governor-General's XI v West Indians at Auckland, 1968-69.

MOST SIXES IN AN INNINGS

15	J. R. Reid (296)	Wellington v N. Districts at Wellington	1962-63
13	Majid Khan (147*)	Pakistanis v Glamorgan at Swansea	1967
13	C. G. Greenidge (273*)	D. H. Robins' XI v Pakistanis at Eastbourne	1974
13	C. G. Greenidge (259)	Hampshire v Sussex at Southampton	1975
13	G. W. Humpage (254)	Warwickshire v Lancashire at Southport	1982
13	R. J. Shastri (200*)	Bombay v Baroda at Bombay	1984-85
12	Gulfraz Khan (207)	Railways v Universities at Lahore	1976-77
12	I. T. Botham (138*)	Somerset v Warwickshire at Birmingham	1985
12	R. A. Harper (234)	Northamptonshire v Gloucestershire at Northampton	1986
11	C. K. Nayudu (153)	Hindus v MCC at Bombay	1926-27
11	C. J. Barnett (194)	Gloucestershire v Somerset at Bath	1934
11	R. Benaud (135)	Australians v T. N. Pearce's XI at Scarborough	1953

Note: W. J. Stewart (Warwickshire) hit seventeen 6s in the match v Lancashire, at Blackpool, 1959; ten in his first innings of 155 and seven in his second innings of 125.

MOST SIXES IN A SEASON

| 80 | I. T. Botham | 1985 | 66 | A. W. Wellard | 1935 |

Note: A. W. Wellard hit 50 or more sixes in a season four times. His number of 6s in 1935 has in the past been given as 72, but recent research has caused this to be adjusted.

MOST BOUNDARIES IN AN INNINGS

68	P. A. Perrin (343*)	Essex v Derbyshire at Chesterfield	1904
65	A. C. MacLaren (424)	Lancashire v Somerset at Taunton	1895
64	Hanif Mohammad (499)	Karachi v Bahawalpur at Karachi	1958-59
57	J. H. Edrich (310*)	England v New Zealand at Leeds	1965
55	C. W. Gregory (383)	NSW v Queensland at Brisbane	1906-07
54	G. H. Hirst (341)	Yorkshire v Leicestershire at Leicester	1905
53	A. W. Nourse (304*)	Natal v Transvaal at Johannesburg	1919-20
53	K. R. Rutherford (317)	New Zealanders v D. B. Close's XI at Scarborough.	1986
51	C. G. Macartney (345)	Australians v Nottinghamshire at Nottingham	1921
50	D. G. Bradman (369)	South Australia v Tasmania at Adelaide	1935-36
50	A. Ducat (306*)	Surrey v Oxford University at The Oval	1919
50	B. B. Nimbalkar (443*)	Maharashtra v Kathiawar at Poona	1948-49
50	J. R. Reid (296)	Wellington v N. Districts at Wellington	1962-63
50	I. V. A. Richards (322)	Somerset v Warwickshire at Taunton	1985

Note: Boundaries include sixes.

HIGHEST PARTNERSHIPS

577	V. S. Hazare (288) and Gul Mahomed (319), fourth wicket, Baroda v Holkar at Baroda	1946-47
574*	F. M. M. Worrell (255*) and C. L. Walcott (314*), fourth wicket, Barbados v Trinidad at Port-of-Spain	1945-46
561	Waheed Mirza (324) and Mansoor Akhtar (224*), first wicket, Karachi Whites v Quetta at Karachi	1976-77
555	P. Holmes (224*) and H. Sutcliffe (313), first wicket, Yorkshire v Essex at Leyton	1932
554	J. T. Brown (300) and J. Tunnicliffe (243), first wicket, Yorkshire v Derbyshire at Chesterfield	1898
502*	F. M. M. Worrell (308*) and J. D. C. Goddard (218*), fourth wicket, Barbados v Trinidad at Bridgetown	1943-44
490	E. H. Bowley (283) and J. G. Langridge (195), first wicket, Sussex v Middlesex at Hove	1933
487*	G. A. Headley (344*) and C. C. Passailaigue (261*), sixth wicket, Jamaica v Lord Tennyson's XI at Kingston	1931-32
470	A. I. Kallicharran (230*) and G. W. Humpage (254), fourth wicket, Warwickshire v Lancashire at Southport	1982
465*	J. A. Jameson (240*) and R. B. Kanhai (213*), second wicket, Warwickshire v Gloucestershire at Birmingham	1974
456	W. H. Ponsford (248) and E. R. Mayne (209), first wicket, Victoria v Queensland at Melbourne	1923-24
456	Khalid Irtiza (290) and Aslam Ali (236), third wicket, United Bank v Multan at Karachi	1975-76
455	K. V. Bhandarkar (205) and B. B. Nimbalkar (443*), second wicket, Maharashtra v Kathiawar at Poona	1948-49
451	D. G. Bradman (244) and W. H. Ponsford (266), second wicket, Australia v England, Fifth Test, at The Oval	1934
451*	S. Desai (218*) and R. M. H. Binny (211*), first wicket, Karnataka v Kerala at Chikmagalur	1977-78
451	Mudassar Nazar (231) and Javed Miandad (280*), third wicket, Pakistan v India, Fourth Test, at Hyderabad	1982-83

PARTNERSHIPS FOR FIRST WICKET

561	Waheed Mirza and Mansoor Akhtar, Karachi Whites v Quetta at Karachi	1976-77
555	P. Holmes and H. Sutcliffe, Yorkshire v Essex at Leyton	1932
554	J. T. Brown and J. Tunnicliffe, Yorkshire v Derbyshire at Chesterfield	1898
490	E. H. Bowley and J. G. Langridge, Sussex v Middlesex at Hove	1933
456	E. R. Mayne and W. H. Ponsford, Victoria v Queensland at Melbourne ...	1923-24
451*	S. Desai and R. M. H. Binny, Karnataka v Kerala at Chikmagalur	1977-78
428	J. B Hobbs and A. Sandham, Surrey v Oxford University at The Oval	1926
424	J. F. W. Nicholson and I. J. Siedle, Natal v Orange Free State at Bloemfontein	1926-27
421	S. M. Gavaskar and G. A. Parkar, Bombay v Bengal at Bombay	1981-82
418	Kamal Najamuddin and Khalid Alvi, Karachi v Railways at Karachi	1980-81
413	V. Mankad and Pankaj Roy, India v New Zealand at Madras (world Test record)	1955-56
405	C. P. S. Chauhan and M. S. Gupte, Maharashtra v Vidarbha at Poona ..	1972-73
395	D. M. Young and R. B. Nicholls, Gloucestershire v Oxford University at Oxford	1962
391	A. O. Jones and A. Shrewsbury, Nottinghamshire v Gloucestershire at Bristol	1899
390	G. L. Wight and G. L. R. Gibbs, B. Guiana v Barbados at Georgetown ..	1951-52
390	B. Dudleston and J. F. Steele, Leicestershire v Derbyshire at Leicester	1979
389	Majid Khan and Shafiq Ahmed, Punjab A v Sind A at Karachi	1974-75
389	Mudassar Nazar and Mansoor Akhtar, United Bank v Rawalpindi at Lahore	1981-82
388	K. C. Wessels and R. B. Kerr, Queensland v Victoria at St Kilda, Melbourne	1982-83
387	G. M. Turner and T. W. Jarvis, New Zealand v West Indies at Georgetown	1971-72
382	R. B. Simpson and W. M. Lawry, Australia v West Indies at Bridgetown .	1964-65
380	H. Whitehead and C. J. B. Wood, Leicestershire v Worcestershire at Worcester	1906
379	R. Abel and W. Brockwell, Surrey v Hampshire at The Oval	1897
378	J. T. Brown and J. Tunnicliffe, Yorkshire v Sussex at Sheffield	1897
377*	N. F. Horner and Khalid Ibadulla, Warwickshire v Surrey at The Oval ...	1960
375	W. H. Ponsford and W. M. Woodfull, Victoria v New South Wales at Melbourne	1926-27

FIRST-WICKET HUNDREDS IN BOTH INNINGS

B. Sutcliffe and D. D. Taylor, for Auckland v Canterbury in 1948-49, scored for the first wicket 220 in the first innings and 286 in the second innings. This is the only instance of two double-century opening stands in the same match.

T. W. Hayward and J. B. Hobbs in 1907 accomplished a performance without parallel by scoring over 100 together for Surrey's first wicket four times in one week: 106 and 125 v Cambridge University at The Oval, and 147 and 105 v Middlesex at Lord's.

L. Hutton and C. Washbrook, in three consecutive Test match innings which they opened together for England v Australia in 1946-47, made 138 in the second innings at Melbourne, and 137 and 100 at Adelaide. They also opened with 168 and 129 at Leeds in 1948.

J. B. Hobbs and H. Sutcliffe, in three consecutive Test match innings which they opened together for England v Australia in 1924-25, made 157 and 110 at Sydney and 283 at Melbourne. On 26 occasions – 15 times in Test matches – Hobbs and Sutcliffe took part in a three-figure first-wicket partnership. Seven of these stands exceeded 200.

G. Boycott and J. H. Edrich, in three consecutive Test match innings which they opened together for England v Australia in 1970-71, made 161* in the second innings at Melbourne, and 107 and 103 at Adelaide.

In 1971 R. G. A. Headley and P. J. Stimpson of Worcestershire shared in first-wicket hundred partnerships on each of the first four occasions they opened the innings together: 125 and 147 v Northamptonshire at Worcester, 102 and 128* v Warwickshire at Birmingham.

J. B. Hobbs during his career, which extended from 1905 to 1934, helped to make 100 or more for the first wicket in first-class cricket 166 times – 15 of them in 1926, when in consecutive innings he helped to make 428, 182, 106 and 123 before a wicket fell. As many as 117 of the 166 stands were made for Surrey. In all first-class matches Hobbs and A. Sandham shared 66 first-wicket partnerships of 100 or more runs.

P. Holmes and H. Sutcliffe made 100 or more runs for the first wicket of Yorkshire on 69 occasions; J. B. Hobbs and A. Sandham for Surrey on 63 occasions; W. W. Keeton and C. B. Harris of Nottinghamshire on 46; T. W. Hayward and J. B. Hobbs of Surrey on 40; G. Gunn and W. W. Whysall of Nottinghamshire on 40; J. D. Robertson and S. M. Brown of Middlesex on 34; C. B. Fry and J. Vine of Sussex on 33; R. E. Marshall and J. R. Gray of Hampshire on 33; D. E. Davies and A. H. Dyson of Glamorgan on 32; and G. Boycott and R. G. Lumb of Yorkshire on 27.

J. Douglas and A. E. Stoddart in 1896 scored over 150 runs for the Middlesex first wicket three times within a fortnight. In 1901, J. Iremonger and A. O. Jones obtained over 100 for the Nottinghamshire first wicket four times within eight days, scoring 134 and 144* v Surrey at The Oval, 238 v Essex at Leyton, and 119 v Derbyshire at Welbeck.

J. W. Lee and F. S. Lee, brothers, for Somerset in 1934, scored over 100 runs thrice in succession in the County Championship.

W. G. Grace and A. E. Stoddart, in three consecutive innings against the Australians in 1893, made over 100 runs for each opening partnership.

C. Hallows and F. B. Watson, in consecutive innings for Lancashire in 1928, opened with 200, 202, 107, 118; reached three figures twelve times, 200 four times.

H. Sutcliffe, in the period 1919-1939 inclusive, shared in 145 first-wicket partnerships of 100 runs or more.

There were four first-wicket hundred partnerships in the match between Somerset and Cambridge University at Taunton in 1960. G. Atkinson and R. T. Virgin scored 172 and 112 for Somerset and R. M. Prideaux and A. R. Lewis 198 and 137 for Cambridge University.

PARTNERSHIP RECORDS FOR ALL COUNTRIES

Best First-Wicket Stands

Pakistan	561	Waheed Mirza (324) and Mansoor Akhtar (224*), Karachi Whites v Quetta at Karachi	1976-77
English	555	P. Holmes (224*) and H. Sutcliffe (313), Yorkshire v Essex at Leyton	1932
Australian	456	W. H. Ponsford (248) and E. R. Mayne (209), Victoria v Queensland at Melbourne	1923-24
Indian	451*	S. Desai (218*) and R. M. H. Binny (211*), Karnataka v Kerala at Chikmagalur	1977-78
South African	424	J. F. W. Nicolson (252*) and I. J. Siedle (174), Natal v Orange Free State at Bloemfontein	1926-27
West Indian	390	G. L. Wight (262*) and G. L. R. Gibbs (216), British Guiana v Barbados at Georgetown	1951-52
New Zealand	387	G. M. Turner (259) and T. W. Jarvis (182), New Zealand v West Indies at Georgetown	1971-72

Best Second-Wicket Stands

English	465*	J. A. Jameson (240*) and R. B. Kanhai (213*), Warwickshire v Gloucestershire at Birmingham	1974
Indian	455	K. V. Bhandarkar (205) and B. B. Nimbalkar (443*), Maharashtra v Kathiawar at Poona	1948-49
Australian	451	W. H. Ponsford (266) and D. G. Bradman (244), Australia v England at The Oval	1934
West Indian	446	C. C. Hunte (260) and G. S. Sobers (365*), West Indies v Pakistan at Kingston	1957-58
Pakistan	426	Arshad Pervez (220) and Mohsin Khan (220), Habib Bank v Income Tax Dept at Lahore	1977-78
New Zealand	317	R. T. Hart (167*) and P. S. Briasco (157), Central Districts v Canterbury at New Plymouth	1983-84
South African	305	S. K. Coen (165) and J. M. M Commaille (186), Orange Free State v Natal at Bloemfontein	1926-27

Best Third-Wicket Stands

Pakistan	456	Khalid Irtiza (290) and Aslam Ali (236), United Bank v Multan at Karachi	1975-76
New Zealand	445	P. E. Whitelaw (195) and W. N. Carson (290), Auckland v Otago at Dunedin (in 268 minutes)	1936-37
West Indian	434	J. B. Stollmeyer (324) and G. E. Gomez (190), Trinidad v British Guiana at Port-of-Spain	1946-47
English	424*	W. J. Edrich (168*) and D. C. S. Compton (252*), Middlesex v Somerset at Lord's	1948
Indian	410	L. Amarnath (262) and R. S. Modi (156), India in England v The Rest at Calcutta	1946-47
Australian	390*	J. M. Wiener (221*) and J. K. Moss (200*), Victoria v Western Australia at St Kilda, Melbourne	1981-82
South African	341	E. J. Barlow (201) and R. G. Pollock (175), South Africa v Australia at Adelaide	1963-64

Best Fourth-Wicket Stands

Indian	577	V. S. Hazare (288) and Gul Mahomed (319), Baroda v Holkar at Baroda	1946-47
West Indian	574*	C. L. Walcott (314*) and F. M. M. Worrell (255*), Barbados v Trinidad at Port-of-Spain	1945-46
English	470	A. I. Kallicharran (230*) and G. W. Humpage (254), Warwickshire v Lancashire at Southport	1982
Australian	424	I. S. Lee (258) and S. O. Quin (210), Victoria v Tasmania at Melbourne	1933-34
Pakistan	350	Mushtaq Mohammad (201) and Asif Iqbal (175), Pakistan v New Zealand at Dunedin	1972-73
South African	342	E. A. B. Rowan (196) and P. J. M. Gibb (203), Transvaal v N. E. Transvaal at Johannesburg	1952-53
New Zealand	324	J. R. Reid (188*) and W. M. Wallace (197), New Zealanders v Cambridge University at Cambridge	1949

Best Fifth-Wicket Stands

Australian	405	S. G. Barnes (234) and D. G. Bradman (234), Australia v England at Sydney	1946-47
English	393	E. G. Arnold (200*) and W. B. Burns (196), Worcestershire v Warwickshire at Birmingham	1909
Indian	360	Uday Merchant (217) and M. N. Raiji (170), Bombay v Hyderabad at Bombay	1947-48
Pakistan	355	Altaf Shah (276) and Tariq Bashir (196), House Building Finance Corporation v Multan at Multan	1976-77
South African	338	R. G. Pollock (194) and A. L. Wilmot (152), Eastern Province v Natal at Port Elizabeth	1975-76
West Indian	335	B. F. Butcher (151) and C. H. Lloyd (201*), West Indians v Glamorgan at Swansea	1969
New Zealand	319	K. R. Rutherford (317) and E. J. Gray (88), New Zealanders v D. B. Close's XI at Scarborough	1986

Best Sixth-Wicket Stands

West Indian	487*	G. A. Headley (344*) and C. C. Passailaigue (261*), Jamaica v Lord Tennyson's XI at Kingston	1931-32
Australian	428	M. A. Noble (284) and W. W. Armstrong (172*), Australians v Sussex at Hove	1902

English	411	R. M. Poore (304) and E. G. Wynyard (225), Hampshire v Somerset at Taunton	1899
Indian	371	V. M. Merchant (359*) and R. S. Modi (168), Bombay v Maharashtra at Bombay	1943-44
Pakistan	353	Salah-ud-Din (256) and Zaheer Abbas (197), Karachi v East Pakistan at Karachi	1968-69
South African	244*	J. M. M. Commaille (132*) and A. W. Palm (106*), Western Province v Griqualand West at Johannesburg	1923-24
New Zealand	226	E. J. Gray (126) and R. W. Ormiston (93), Wellington v Central Districts at Wellington	1981-82

Best Seventh-Wicket Stands

West Indian	347	D. St E. Atkinson (219) and C. C. Depeiza (122), West Indies v Australia at Bridgetown	1954-55
English	344	K. S. Ranjitsinhji (230) and W. Newham (153), Sussex v Essex at Leyton	1902
Australian	335	C. W. Andrews (253) and E. C. Bensted (155), Queensland v New South Wales at Sydney	1934-35
Pakistan	308	Waqar Hassan (189) and Imtiaz Ahmed (209), Pakistan v New Zealand at Lahore	1955-56
South African	299	B. Mitchell (159) and A. Melville (153), Transvaal v Griqualand West at Kimberley	1946-47
Indian	274	K. C. Ibrahim (250) and K. M. Rangnekar (138), Bijapur XI v Bengal XI at Bombay	1942-43
New Zealand	265	J. L. Powell (164) and N. Dorreen (105*), Canterbury v Otago at Christchurch	1929-30

Best Eighth-Wicket Stands

Australian	433	A. Sims (184*) and V. T. Trumper (293), An Australian XI v Canterbury at Christchurch	1913-14
English	292	R. Peel (210*) and Lord Hawke (166), Yorkshire v Warwickshire at Birmingham	1896
West Indian	255	E. A. V. Williams (131*) and E. A. Martindale (134), Barbados v Trinidad at Bridgetown	1935-36
Pakistan	240	Gulfraz Khan (207) and Raja Sarfraz (102), Railways v Universities at Lahore	1976-77
Indian	236	C. T. Sarwate (235) and R. P. Singh (88), Holkar v Delhi and District at Delhi	1949-50
South African	222	D. P. B. Morkel (114) and S. S. L. Steyn (261*), Western Province v Border at Cape Town	1929-30
New Zealand	190*	J. E. Mills (104*) and C. F. W. Allcott (102*), New Zealanders v Civil Service at Chiswick	1927

Best Ninth-Wicket Stands

English	283	J. Chapman (165) and A. Warren (123), Derbyshire v Warwickshire at Blackwell	1910
Indian	245	V. S. Hazare (316*) and N. D. Nagarwalla (98), Maharashtra v Baroda at Poona	1939-40
New Zealand	239	H. B. Cave (118) and I. B. Leggat (142*), Central Districts v Otago at Dunedin	1952-53
Australian	232	C. Hill (365*) and E. Walkley (53), South Australia v New South Wales at Adelaide	1900-01
South African	221	N. V. Lindsay (160*) and G. R. McCubbin (97), Transvaal v Rhodesia at Bulawayo	1922-23
Pakistan	190	Asif Iqbal (146) and Intikhab Alam (51), Pakistan v England at The Oval	1967
West Indian	161	C. H. Lloyd (161*) and A. M. E. Roberts (68), West Indies v India at Calcutta	1983-84

Best Tenth-Wicket Stands

Australian	 307	A. F. Kippax (260*), and J. E. H. Hooker (62), New South Wales v Victoria at Melbourne	1928-29
Indian	 249	C. T. Sarwate (124*) and S. N. Banerjee (121), Indians v Surrey at The Oval	1946
English	 235	F. E. Woolley (185) and A. Fielder (112*), Kent v Worcestershire at Stourbridge	1909
Pakistan	..... 196*	Nadim Yousuf (202*) and Maqsood Kundi (109*) Muslim Commercial Bank v National Bank at Lahore	1981-82
New Zealand	.. 184	R. C. Blunt (338*) and W. Hawkesworth (21), Otago v Canterbury at Christchurch	1931-32
South African	.. 174	H. R. Lance (168) and D. Mackay-Coghill (57*), Transvaal v Natal at Johannesburg	1965-66
West Indian	... 138	E. L. G. Hoad (149*) and H. C. Griffith (84), West Indians v Sussex at Hove	1933

Note: All the English record wicket partnerships were made in the County Championship.

OUT HANDLED THE BALL

J. Grundy	MCC v Kent at Lord's	1857
G. Bennett	Kent v Sussex at Hove	1872
W. H. Scotton	Smokers v Non-Smokers at East Melbourne	1886-87
C. W. Wright	Nottinghamshire v Gloucestershire at Bristol	1893
E. Jones	South Australia v Victoria at Melbourne	1894-95
A. W. Nourse	South Africans v Sussex at Hove	1907
E. T. Benson	MCC v Auckland at Auckland	1929-30
A. W. Gilbertson	Otago v Auckland at Auckland	1952-53
W. R. Endean	South Africa v England at Cape Town	1956-57
P. J. Burge	Queensland v New South Wales at Sydney	1958-59
Dildar Awan	Services v Lahore at Lahore	1959-60
Mahmood-ul-Hasan	Karachi University v Railways-Quetta at Karachi	1960-61
Ali Raza	Karachi Greens v Hyderabad at Karachi	1961-62
Mohammad Yusuf	Rawalpindi v Peshawar at Peshawar	1962-63
A. Rees	Glamorgan v Middlesex at Lord's	1965
Pervez Akhtar	Multan v Karachi Greens at Sahiwal	1971-72
Javed Mirza	Railways v Punjab at Lahore	1972-73
R. G. Pollock	Eastern Province v Western Province at Cape Town	1973-74
C. I. Dey	Northern Transvaal v Orange Free State at Bloemfontein	1973-74
Nasir Valika	Karachi Whites v National Bank at Karachi	1974-75
Haji Yousuf	National Bank v Railways at Lahore	1974-75
Masood-ul-Hasan	PIA v National Bank 'B' at Lyallpur	1975-76
D. K. Pearse	Natal v Western Province at Cape Town	1978-79
A. M. J. Hilditch	Australia v Pakistan at Perth	1978-79
Musleh-ud-Din	Railways v Lahore at Lahore	1979-80
Jalal-ud-Din	IDBP v Habib Bank at Bahawalpur	1981-82
Mohsin Khan	Pakistan v Australia at Karachi	1982-83
D. L. Haynes	West Indies v India at Bombay	1983-84
K. Azad	Delhi v Punjab at Amritsar	1983-84
Athar A. Khan	Allied Bank v HBFC at Sialkot	1983-84
A. Pandya	Saurashtra v Baroda at Baroda	1984-85
G. N. Linton	Barbados v Windward Islands at Bridgetown	1985-86

OUT OBSTRUCTING THE FIELD

C. A. Absolom	Cambridge University v Surrey at The Oval	1868
T. Straw	Worcestershire v Warwickshire at Worcester	1899
T. Straw	Worcestershire v Warwickshire at Birmingham	1901
J. P. Whiteside	Leicestershire v Lancashire at Leicester	1901

L. Hutton	England v South Africa at The Oval	1951
J. A. Hayes	Canterbury v Central Districts at Christchurch	1954-55
D. D. Deshpande	Madhya Pradesh v Uttar Pradesh at Benares	1956-57
M. Mehra	Railways v Delhi at Delhi	1959-60
K. Ibadulla	Warwickshire v Hampshire at Coventry	1963
Qaiser Khan	Dera Ismail Khan v Railways at Lahore	1964-65
Ijaz Ahmed	Lahore Greens v Lahore Blues at Lahore	1973-74
Qasim Feroze	Bahawalpur v Universities at Lahore	1974-75
T. Quirk	Northern Transvaal v Border at East London	1978-79
Mahmood Rashid	United Bank v Muslim Commercial Bank at Bahawalpur	1981-82
Arshad Ali	Sukkur v Quetta at Quetta	1983-84
H. Wasu	Vidarbha v Rajasthan at Akola	1984-85
Khalid Javed	Railways v Lahore at Lahore	1985-86

OUT HIT THE BALL TWICE

H. E. Bull	MCC v Oxford University at Lord's	1864
H. R. J. Charlwood	Sussex v Surrey at Hove	1872
R. G. Barlow	North v South at Lord's	1878
P. S. Wimble	Transvaal v Griqualand West at Kimberley	1892-93
G. B. Nicholls	Somerset v Gloucestershire at Bristol	1896
A. A. Lilley	Warwickshire v Yorkshire at Birmingham	1897
J. H. King	Leicestershire v Surrey at The Oval	1906
A. P. Binns	Jamaica v British Guiana at Georgetown	1956-57
K. Bavanna	Andhra v Mysore at Guntur	1963-64
Zaheer Abbas	PIA 'A' v Karachi Blues at Karachi	1969-70
Anwar Miandad	IDBP v United Bank at Lahore	1979-80
Anwar Iqbal	Hyderabad v Sukkur at Hyderabad	1983-84
Iqtidar Ali	Allied Bank v Muslim Commercial Bank at Lahore	1983-84
Aziz Malik	Lahore Division v Faisalabad at Sialkot	1984-85

BOWLING RECORDS

TEN WICKETS IN ONE INNINGS

	O	M	R		
E. Hinkly (Kent)				v England at Lord's	1848
*J. Wisden (North)				v South at Lord's	1850
V. E. Walker (England)	43	17	74	v Surrey at The Oval	1859
E. M. Grace (MCC)	32.2	7	69	v Gents of Kent at Canterbury	1862
V. E. Walker (Middlesex)	44.2	5	104	v Lancashire at Manchester	1865
G. Wootton (All England)	31.3	9	54	v Yorkshire at Sheffield	1865
W. Hickton (Lancashire)	36.2	19	46	v Hampshire at Manchester	1870
S. E. Butler (Oxford)	24.1	11	38	v Cambridge at Lord's	1871
James Lillywhite (South)	60.2	22	129	v North at Canterbury	1872
W. G. Grace (MCC)	46.1	15	92	v Kent at Canterbury	1873
A. Shaw (MCC)	36.2	8	73	v North at Lord's	1874
E. Barratt (Players)	29	11	43	v Australians at The Oval	1878
G. Giffen (Australian XI)	26	10	66	v The Rest at Sydney	1883-84
W. G. Grace (MCC)	36.2	17	49	v Oxford University at Oxford	1886
G. Burton (Middlesex)	52.3	25	59	v Surrey at The Oval	1888
†A. E. Moss (Canterbury)	21.3	10	28	v Wellington at Christchurch	1889-90
S. M. J. Woods (Cambridge U.)	31	6	69	v Thornton's XI at Cambridge	1890
T. Richardson (Surrey)	15.3	3	45	v Essex at The Oval	1894
H. Pickett (Essex)	27	11	32	v Leicestershire at Leyton	1895
E. J. Tyler (Somerset)	34.3	15	49	v Surrey at Taunton	1895
W. P. Howell (Australians)	23.2	14	28	v Surrey at The Oval	1899
C. H. G. Bland (Sussex)	25.2	10	48	v Kent at Tonbridge	1899
J. Briggs (Lancashire)	28.5	7	55	v Worcestershire at Manchester	1900

	O	M	R		
A. E. Trott (Middlesex)	14.2	5	42	v Somerset at Taunton	1900
F. Hinds (A. B. St Hill's XI)	19.1	6	36	v Trinidad at Port-of-Spain	1900-01
A. Fielder (Players)	24.5	1	90	v Gentlemen at Lord's	1906
E. G. Dennett (Gloucestershire)	19.4	7	40	v Essex at Bristol	1906
A. E. E. Vogler (E. Province)	12	2	26	v Griqualand West at Johannesburg	1906-07
C. Blythe (Kent)	16	7	30	v Northamptonshire at Northampton	1907
A. Drake (Yorkshire)	8.5	0	35	v Somerset at Weston-super-Mare	1914
F. A. Tarrant (Maharaja of Cooch Behar's XI)	35.4	4	90	v Lord Willingdon's XI at Poona	1918-19
W. Bestwick (Derbyshire)	19	2	40	v Glamorgan at Cardiff	1921
A. A. Mailey (Australians)	28.4	5	66	v Gloucestershire at Cheltenham	1921
C. W. L. Parker (Glos.)	40.3	13	79	v Somerset at Bristol	1921
T. Rushby (Surrey)	17.5	4	43	v Somerset at Taunton	1921
J. C. White (Somerset)	42.2	11	76	v Worcestershire at Worcester	1921
G. C. Collins (Kent)	19.3	4	65	v Nottinghamshire at Dover	1922
H. Howell (Warwickshire)	25.1	5	51	v Yorkshire at Birmingham	1923
A. S. Kennedy (Players)	22.4	10	37	v Gentlemen at The Oval	1927
G. O. Allen (Middlesex)	25.3	10	40	v Lancashire at Lord's	1929
A. P. Freeman (Kent)	42	9	131	v Lancashire at Maidstone	1929
G. Geary (Leicestershire)	16.2	8	18	v Glamorgan at Pontypridd	1929
C. V. Grimmett (Australians)	22.3	8	37	v Yorkshire at Sheffield	1930
A. P. Freeman (Kent)	30.4	8	53	v Essex at Southend	1930
H. Verity (Yorkshire)	18.4	6	36	v Warwickshire at Leeds	1931
A. P. Freeman (Kent)	36.1	9	79	v Lancashire at Manchester	1931
V. W. C. Jupp (Northants)	39	6	127	v Kent at Tunbridge Wells	1932
H. Verity (Yorkshire)	19.4	16	10	v Nottinghamshire at Leeds	1932
T. W. Wall (South Australia)	12.4	2	36	v New South Wales at Sydney	1932-33
T. B. Mitchell (Derbyshire)	19.1	4	64	v Leicestershire at Leicester	1935
J. Mercer (Glamorgan)	26	10	51	v Worcestershire at Worcester	1936
T. W. Goddard (Glos.)	28.4	4	113	v Worcestershire at Cheltenham	1937
T. F. Smailes (Yorkshire)	17.1	5	47	v Derbyshire at Sheffield	1939
E. A. Watts (Surrey)	24.1	8	67	v Warwickshire at Birmingham	1939
*W. E. Hollies (Warwickshire)	20.4	4	49	v Nottinghamshire at Birmingham	1946
J. M. Sims (East)	18.4	2	90	v West at Kingston	1948
T. E. Bailey (Essex)	39.4	9	90	v Lancashire at Clacton	1949
J. K. Graveney (Glos.)	18.4	2	66	v Derbyshire at Chesterfield	1949
R. Berry (Lancashire)	36.2	9	102	v Worcestershire at Blackpool	1953
S. P. Gupte (Bombay)	24.2	7	78	v Combined XI at Bombay	1954-55
J. C. Laker (Surrey)	46	18	88	v Australians at The Oval	1956
J. C. Laker (England)	51.2	23	53	v Australia at Manchester	1956
G. A. R. Lock (Surrey)	29.1	18	54	v Kent at Blackheath	1956
K. Smales (Nottinghamshire)	41.3	20	66	v Gloucestershire at Stroud	1956
P. Chatterjee (Bengal)	19	11	20	v Assam at Jorhat	1956-57
J. D. Bannister (Warwickshire)	23.3	11	41	v Comb. Services at Birmingham	1959
A. J. G. Pearson (Cambridge University)	30.3	8	78	v Leicestershire at Loughborough	1961
N. I. Thomson (Sussex)	34.2	19	49	v Warwickshire at Worthing	1964
P. J. Allan (Queensland)	15.6	3	61	v Victoria at Melbourne	1965-66
I. J. Brayshaw (W. Australia)	17.6	4	44	v Victoria at Perth	1967-68
Shahid Mahmood (Karachi Whites)	25	5	58	v Khairpur at Karachi	1969-70
E. E. Hemmings (International XI)	49.3	14	175	v West Indies XI at Kingston	1982-83
P. Sunderam (Rajasthan)	22	5	78	v Vidarbha at Jodhpur	1985-86

* *J. Wisden and W. E. Hollies achieved the feat without the direct assistance of a fielder. Wisden's ten were all bowled; Hollies bowled seven and had three leg-before-wicket.*

† *On debut in first-class cricket.*

OUTSTANDING ANALYSES

	O	M	R	W		
H. Verity (Yorkshire)	19.4	16	10	10	v Nottinghamshire at Leeds	1932
G. Elliott (Victoria)	19	17	2	9	v Tasmania at Launceston	1857-58
Ahad Khan (Railways)	6.3	4	7	9	v Dera Ismail Khan at Lahore	1964-65
J. C. Laker (England)	14	12	2	8	v The Rest at Bradford	1950
D. Shackleton (Hampshire)	11.1	7	4	8	v Somerset at Weston-super-Mare	1955
E. Peate (Yorkshire)	16	11	5	8	v Surrey at Holbeck	1883
F. R. Spofforth (Australians)	8.3	6	3	7	v England XI at Birmingham	1884
W. A. Henderson (N.E. Transvaal)	9.3	7	4	7	v Orange Free State at Bloemfontein	1937-38
Rajinder Goel (Haryana)	7	4	4	7	v Jammu and Kashmir at Chandigarh	1977-78
V. I. Smith (South Africans)	4.5	3	1	6	v Derbyshire at Derby	1947
S. Cosstick (Victoria)	21.1	20	1	6	v Tasmania at Melbourne	1868-69
Israr Ali (Bahawalpur)	11	10	1	6	v Dacca U. at Bahawalpur	1957-58
A. D. Pougher (MCC)	3	3	0	5	v Australians at Lord's	1896
G. R. Cox (Sussex)	6	6	0	5	v Somerset at Weston-super-Mare	1921
R. K. Tyldesley (Lancashire)	5	5	0	5	v Leicestershire at Manchester	1924
P. T. Mills (Gloucestershire)	6.4	6	0	5	v Somerset at Bristol	1928

MOST WICKETS IN A MATCH

19-90	J. C. Laker	England v Australia at Manchester	1956
17-48	C. Blythe	Kent v Northamptonshire at Northampton	1907
17-50	C. T. B. Turner	Australians v England XI at Hastings	1888
17-54	W. P. Howell	Australians v Western Province at Cape Town	1902-03
17-56	C. W. L. Parker	Gloucestershire v Essex at Gloucester	1925
17-67	A. P. Freeman	Kent v Sussex at Hove	1922
17-89	W. G. Grace	Gloucestershire v Nottinghamshire at Cheltenham	1877
17-89	F. C. L. Matthews	Nottinghamshire v Northants at Nottingham	1923
17-91	H. Dean	Lancashire v Yorkshire at Liverpool	1913
17-91	H. Verity	Yorkshire v Essex at Leyton	1933
17-92	A. P. Freeman	Kent v Warwickshire at Folkestone	1932
17-103	W. Mycroft	Derbyshire v Hampshire at Southampton	1876
17-106	G. R. Cox	Sussex v Warwickshire at Horsham	1926
17-106	T. W. Goddard	Gloucestershire v Kent at Bristol	1939
17-119	W. Mead	Essex v Hampshire at Southampton	1895
17-137	W. Brearley	Lancashire v Somerset at Manchester	1905
17-159	S. F. Barnes	England v South Africa at Johannesburg	1913-14
17-201	G. Giffen	South Australia v Victoria at Adelaide	1885-86
17-212	J. C. Clay	Glamorgan v Worcestershire at Swansea	1937

Notes: H. A. Arkwright took eighteen wickets for 96 runs in a 12-a-side match for Gentlemen of MCC v Gentlemen of Kent at Canterbury in 1861.

W. Mead took seventeen wickets for 205 runs for Essex v Australians at Leyton in 1893, the year before Essex were raised to first-class status.

F. P. Fenner took seventeen wickets for Cambridge Town Club v University of Cambridge at Cambridge in 1844.

SIXTEEN OR MORE WICKETS IN A DAY

17-48	C. Blythe	Kent v Northamptonshire at Northampton	1907
17-91	H. Verity	Yorkshire v Essex at Leyton	1933
17-106	T. W. Goddard	Gloucestershire v Kent at Bristol	1939
16-38	T. Emmett	Yorkshire v Cambridgeshire at Hunslet	1869
16-52	J. Southerton	South v North at Lord's	1875
16-69	T. G. Wass	Nottinghamshire v Lancashire at Liverpool	1906
16-38	A. E. E. Vogler	E. Province v Griqualand West at Johannesburg .	1906-07
16-103	T. G. Wass	Nottinghamshire v Essex at Nottingham	1908
16-83	J. C. White	Somerset v Worcestershire at Bath	1919

FOUR WICKETS WITH CONSECUTIVE BALLS

J. Wells	Kent v Sussex at Brighton	1862
G. Ulyett	Lord Harris's XI v New South Wales at Sydney	1878-79
G. Nash	Lancashire v Somerset at Manchester	1882
J. B. Hide	Sussex v MCC and Ground at Lord's	1890
F. J. Shacklock	Nottinghamshire v Somerset at Nottingham	1893
A. D. Downes	Otago v Auckland at Dunedin	1893-94
F. Martin	MCC and Ground v Derbyshire at Lord's	1895
A. W. Mold	Lancashire v Nottinghamshire at Nottingham	1895
W. Brearley†	Lancashire v Somerset at Manchester	1905
S. Haigh	MCC v Army XI at Pretoria	1905-06
A. E. Trott‡	Middlesex v Somerset at Lord's	1907
F. A. Tarrant	Middlesex v Gloucestershire at Bristol	1907
A. Drake	Yorkshire v Derbyshire at Chesterfield	1914
S. G. Smith	Northamptonshire v Warwickshire at Birmingham	1914
H. A. Peach	Surrey v Sussex at The Oval	1924
A. F. Borland	Natal v Griqualand West at Kimberley	1926-27
J. E. H. Hooker†	New South Wales v Victoria at Sydney	1928-29
R. K. Tyldesley†	Lancashire v Derbyshire at Derby	1929
R. J. Crisp	Western Province v Griqualand West at Johannesburg ..	1931-32
R. J. Crisp	Western Province v Natal at Durban	1933-34
A. R. Gover	Surrey v Worcestershire at Worcester	1935
W. H. Copson	Derbyshire v Warwickshire at Derby	1937
W. A. Henderson	N.E. Transvaal v Orange Free State at Bloemfontein ...	1937-38
F. Ridgway	Kent v Derbyshire at Folkestone	1951
A. K. Walker§	Nottinghamshire v Leicestershire at Leicester	1956
S. N. Mohol	Board of Control President's XI v Minister for Small	
	Savings' XI at Poona	1965-66
P. I. Pocock	Surrey v Sussex at Eastbourne	1972

† *Not all in the same innings.*
‡ *Trott achieved another hat-trick in the same innings of this, his benefit match.*
§ *Walker dismissed Firth with the last ball of the first innings and Lester, Tompkin and Smithson with the first three balls of the second innings, a feat without parallel.*

Notes: In their match with England at The Oval in 1863, Surrey lost four wickets in the course of a four-ball over from G. Bennett.

Sussex lost five wickets in the course of the final (six-ball) over of their match with Surrey at Eastbourne in 1972. P. I. Pocock, who had taken three wickets in his previous over, captured four more, taking in all seven wickets with eleven balls, a feat unique in first-class matches. (The eighth wicket fell to a run-out.)

P. G. H. Fender (Surrey) took six Middlesex wickets with eleven balls (including five with seven) at Lord's in 1927.

HAT-TRICKS

Double Hat-Trick

Besides Trott's performance, which is given in the preceding section, the following instances are recorded of players having performed the hat-trick twice in the same match, Rao doing so in the same innings.

A. Shaw	Nottinghamshire v Gloucestershire at Nottingham	1884
T. J. Matthews	Australia v South Africa at Manchester	1912
C. W. L. Parker	Gloucestershire v Middlesex at Bristol	1924
R. O. Jenkins	Worcestershire v Surrey at Worcester	1949
J. S. Rao	Services v Northern Punjab at Amritsar	1963-64
Amin Lakhani	Combined XI v Indians at Multan	1978-79

Five Wickets with Six Consecutive Balls

W. H. Copson	Derbyshire v Warwickshire at Derby	1937
W. A. Henderson	NE Transvaal v Orange Free State at Bloemfontein	1937-38
P. I. Pocock	Surrey v Sussex at Eastbourne	1972

Most Hat-Tricks

Seven times: D. V. P. Wright.
Six times: T. W. Goddard, C. W. L. Parker.
Five times: S. Haigh, V. W. C. Jupp, A. E. G. Rhodes, F. A. Tarrant.
Four times: R. G. Barlow, J. T. Hearne, J. C. Laker, G. A. R. Lock, G. G. Macaulay, T. J. Matthews, M. J. Procter, T. Richardson, F. R. Spofforth, F. S. Trueman.
Three times: W. M. Bradley, H. J. Butler, W. H. Copson, R. J. Crisp, J. W. H. T. Douglas, J. A. Flavell, A. P. Freeman, G. Giffen, K. Higgs, A. Hill, W. A. Humphries, R. D. Jackman, R. O. Jenkins, A. S. Kennedy, W. H. Lockwood, E. A. McDonald, T. L. Pritchard, J. S. Rao, A. Shaw, J. B. Statham, M. W. Tate, H. Trumble, D. Wilson, G. A. Wilson.

Unusual Hat-Tricks

All "Stumped":	by W. H. Brain off C. L. Townsend, Gloucestershire v Somerset at Cheltenham	1893
All "Caught":	by G. J. Thompson off S. G. Smith, Northamptonshire v Warwickshire at Birmingham	1914
	by Cyril White off R. Beesly, Border v Griqualand West at Queenstown	1946-47
	by G. O. Dawkes (wicket-keeper) off H. L. Jackson, Derbyshire v Worcestershire at Kidderminster	1958
All "LBW":	H. Fisher, Yorkshire v Somerset at Sheffield	1932
	J. A. Flavell, Worcestershire v Lancashire at Manchester	1963
	M. J. Procter, Gloucestershire v Essex at Westcliff	1972
	B. J. Ikin, Griqualand West v OFS at Kimberley	1973-74
	M. J. Procter, Gloucestershire v Yorkshire at Cheltenham ...	1979
	Aamer Wasim, Zone C v Lahore at Lahore	1985-86

Most recent instances

Aamer Wasim	Zone C v Lahore at Lahore	1985-86
Aamer Wasim	Zone C v Railways at Faisalabad	1985-86
Habib Baloch	Zone A v HBFC at Bahawalpur	1985-86

In 1986: See Features of 1986.

200 WICKETS IN A SEASON

	Season	O	M	R	W	Avge
A. P. Freeman	1928	1,976.1	423	5,489	304	18.05
A. P. Freeman	1933	2,039	651	4,549	298	15.26
T. Richardson	1895‡	1,690.1	463	4,170	290	14.37
C. T. B. Turner**	1888†	2,427.2	1,127	3,307	283	11.68
A. P. Freeman	1931	1,618	360	4,307	276	15.60
A. P. Freeman	1930	1,914.3	472	4,632	275	16.84
T. Richardson	1897‡	1,603.4	495	3,945	273	14.45
A. P. Freeman	1929	1,670.5	381	4,879	267	18.27
W. Rhodes	1900	1,553	455	3,606	261	13.81
J. T. Hearne	1896	2,003.1	818	3,670	257	14.28
A. P. Freeman	1932	1,565.5	404	4,149	253	16.39
W. Rhodes	1901	1,565	505	3,797	251	15.12
T. W. Goddard	1937	1,478.1	359	4,158	248	16.76
W. C. Smith	1910	1,423.3	420	3,225	247	13.05
T. Richardson	1896‡	1,656.2	526	4,015	246	16.32
A. E. Trott	1899‡	1,772.4	587	4,086	239	17.09
T. W. Goddard	1947	1,451.2	344	4,119	238	17.30
M. W. Tate	1925	1,694.3	472	3,415	228	14.97
J. T. Hearne	1898‡	1,802.2	781	3,120	222	14.05
C. W. L. Parker	1925	1,512.3	478	3,311	222	14.91
G. A. Lohmann	1890‡	1,759.1	737	2,998	220	13.62
M. W. Tate	1923	1,608.5	331	3,061	219	13.97
C. F. Root	1925	1,493.2	416	3,770	219	17.21
C. W. L. Parker	1931	1,320.4	386	3,125	219	14.26
H. Verity	1936	1,289.3	463	2,847	216	13.18
G. A. R. Lock	1955	1,408.4	497	3,109	216	14.39
C. Blythe	1909	1,273.5	343	3,128	215	14.54
E. Peate	1882†	1,853.1	868	2,466	214	11.52
A. W. Mold	1895‡	1,629	598	3,400	213	15.96
W. Rhodes	1902	1,306.3	405	2,801	213	13.15
C. W. L. Parker	1926	1,739.5	556	3,920	213	18.40
J. T. Hearne	1893‡	1,741.4	667	3,492	212	16.47
A. P. Freeman	1935	1,503.2	320	4,562	212	21.51
G. A. R. Lock	1957	1,194.1	449	2,550	212	12.02
A. E. Trott	1900	1,547.1	363	4,923	211	23.33
G. G. Macaulay	1925	1,338.2	307	3,268	211	15.48
H. Verity	1935	1,279.2	453	3,032	211	14.36
J. Southerton	1870†	1,876.5	709	3,074	210	14.63
G. A. Lohmann	1888†	1,649.1	783	2,280	209	10.90
C. H. Parkin	1923	1,356.2	356	3,543	209	16.94
G. H. Hirst	1906	1,306.1	271	3,434	208	16.50
F. R. Spofforth	1884†	1,577	653	2,654	207	12.82
A. W. Mold	1894‡	1,288.3	456	2,548	207	12.30
C. W. L. Parker	1922	1,294.5	445	2,712	206	13.16
A. S. Kennedy	1922	1,346.4	366	3,444	205	16.80
M. W. Tate	1924	1,469.5	465	2,818	205	13.74
E. A. McDonald	1925	1,249.4	282	3,828	205	18.67
A. P. Freeman	1934	1,744.4	440	4,753	205	23.18
C. W. L. Parker	1924	1,303.5	411	2,913	204	14.27
G. A. Lohmann	1889‡	1,614.1	646	2,714	202	13.43
H. Verity	1937	1,386.2	487	3,168	202	15.68
A. Shaw	1878†	2,630	1,586	2,201	201	10.89
E. G. Dennett	1907	1,216.2	305	3,227	201	16.05
A. R. Gover	1937	1,219.4	191	3,816	201	18.98
C. H. Parkin	1924	1,162.5	357	2,735	200	13.67
T. W. Goddard	1935	1,553	384	4,073	200	20.36
A. R. Gover	1936	1,159.2	185	3,547	200	17.73
T. W. Goddard	1939§	819	139	2,973	200	14.86
R. Appleyard	1951	1,313.2	391	2,829	200	14.14

† *Indicates 4-ball overs; ‡ 5-ball overs. All others were 6-ball overs except § 8-ball overs.*
** *Exclusive of matches not reckoned as first-class.*

Notes: In four consecutive seasons (1928-31), A. P. Freeman took 1,122 wickets, and in eight consecutive seasons (1928-35), 2,090 wickets. In each of these eight seasons he took over 200 wickets.

T. Richardson took 1,005 wickets in four consecutive seasons (1894-97).

In 1896, J. T. Hearne took his 100th wicket as early as June 12. In 1931, C. W. L. Parker did the same and A. P. Freeman obtained his 100th wicket a day later.

The most wickets in a season since the reduction of Championship matches in 1969 is 134 by M. D. Marshall (822 overs) in 1982.

100 WICKETS IN AN ENGLISH SEASON MOST TIMES

23 times: W. Rhodes 200 wkts (3).

20 times: D. Shackleton (In successive seasons – 1949 to 1968 inclusive).

17 times: A. P. Freeman 300 wkts (1), 200 wkts (7).

16 times: T. W. Goddard 200 wkts (4), C. W. L. Parker 200 wkts (5), R. T. D. Perks, F. J. Titmus.

15 times: J. T. Hearne 200 wkts (3), G. H. Hirst 200 wkts (1), A. S. Kennedy 200 wkts (1).

14 times: C. Blythe 200 wkts (1), W. E. Hollies, G. A. R. Lock 200 wkts (2), M. W. Tate 200 wkts (3), J. C White.

13 times: J. B. Statham.

12 times: J. Briggs, E. G. Dennett 200 wkts (1), C. Gladwin, D. J. Shepherd, N. I. Thomson, F. S. Trueman.

11 times: A. V. Bedser, G. Geary, S. Haigh, J. C. Laker, M. S. Nichols, A. E. Relf.

10 times: W. Attewell, W. G. Grace, R. Illingworth, H. L. Jackson, V. W. C. Jupp, G. G. Macaulay 200 wkts (1), W. Mead, T. B. Mitchell, T. Richardson 200 wkts (3), J. Southerton 200 wkts (1), R. K. Tyldesley, D. L. Underwood, J. H. Wardle, T. G. Wass, D. V. P. Wright.

9 times: W. E. Astill, T. E. Bailey, W. E. Bowes, C. Cook, R. Howorth, J. Mercer, A. W. Mold 200 wkts (2), J. Newman, C. F. Root 200 wkts (1), A. Shaw 200 wkts (1), H. Verity 200 wkts (3).

8 times: T. W. Cartwright, H. Dean, J. A. Flavell, A. R. Gover 200 wkts (2), H. Larwood, G. A. Lohmann 200 wkts (3), R. Peel, J. M. Sims, F. A. Tarrant, R. Tattersall, G. J. Thompson, G. E. Tribe, A. W. Wellard, F. E. Woolley, J. A. Young.

100 WICKETS IN A SEASON OUTSIDE ENGLAND

W		Season	Country	R	Avge
116	M. W. Tate	1926-27	India/Ceylon	1,599	13.78
107	Ijaz Faqih	1985-86	Pakistan	1,719	16.06
106	C. T. B. Turner ...	1887-88	Australia	1,441	13.59
106	R. Benaud	1957-58	South Africa	2,056	19.39
104	S. F. Barnes	1913-14	South Africa	1,117	10.74
103	Abdul Qadir	1982-83	Pakistan	2,367	22.98

1,500 WICKETS IN A CAREER

Dates in italics denote the first half of an overseas season; i.e. *1970* denotes the 1970-71 season.

	Career	W	R	Avge
W. Rhodes	1898-1930	4,187	69,993	16.71
A. P. Freeman	1914-36	3,776	69,577	18.42
C. W. L. Parker	1903-35	3,278	63,817	19.46
J. T. Hearne	1888-1923	3,061	54,361	17.75
T. W. Goddard	1922-52	2,979	59,116	19.84
†W. G. Grace	1865-1908	2,876	51,545	17.92
A. S. Kennedy	1907-36	2,874	61,034	21.23
D. Shackleton	1948-69	2,857	53,303	18.65

	Career	W	R	Avge
G. A. R. Lock	1946-70	2,844	54,710	19.23
F. J. Titmus	1949-82	2,830	63,313	22.37
M. W. Tate	1912-37	2,784	50,567	18.16
G. H. Hirst	1891-1929	2,739	51,300	18.72
C. Blythe	1899-1914	2,506	42,136	16.81
W. E. Astill	1906-39	2,431	57,783	23.76
D. L. Underwood	1963-86	2,420	48,698	20.12
J. C. White	1909-37	2,356	43,759	18.57
W. E. Hollies	1932-57	2,323	48,656	20.94
F. S. Trueman	1949-69	2,304	42,154	18.29
J. B. Statham	1950-68	2,260	36,995	16.36
R. T. D. Perks	1930-55	2,233	53,770	24.07
J. Briggs	1879-1900	2,221	35,432	15.95
D. J. Shepherd	1950-72	2,218	47,298	21.32
E. G. Dennett	1903-26	2,147	42,568	19.82
T. Richardson	1892-1905	2,105	38,794	18.42
T. E. Bailey	1945-67	2,082	48,170	23.13
R. Illingworth	1951-83	2,072	42,023	20.28
F. E. Woolley	1906-38	2,068	41,066	19.85
G. Geary	1912-38	2,063	41,339	20.03
D. V. P. Wright	1932-57	2,056	49,305	23.98
J. Newman	1906-30	2,032	51,211	25.20
‡A. Shaw	1864-97	2,027	24,579	12.12
S. Haigh	1895-1913	2,012	32,091	15.94
N. Gifford	1960-86	2,001	46,634	23.30
H. Verity	1930-39	1,956	29,146	14.90
W. Attewell	1881-1900	1,950	29,896	15.33
J. C. Laker	1946-64	1,944	35,791	18.41
A. V. Bedser	1939-60	1,924	39,281	20.41
W. Mead	1892-1913	1,916	36,388	18.99
A. E. Relf	1900-21	1,897	39,724	20.94
P. G. H. Fender	1910-36	1,894	47,440	25.04
J. W. H. T. Douglas	1901-30	1,893	44,159	23.32
J. H. Wardle	1946-67	1,846	35,027	18.97
G. R. Cox	1895-1928	1,843	42,138	22.86
G. A. Lohmann	1884-97	1,841	25,298	13.74
J. W. Hearne	1909-36	1,839	44,944	24.43
G. G. Macaulay	1920-35	1,837	32,440	17.65
M. S. Nichols	1924-39	1,833	39,666	21.63
J. B. Mortimore	1950-75	1,807	41,904	23.18
C. Cook	1946-64	1,782	36,578	20.52
R. Peel	1882-99	1,776	28,758	16.19
H. L. Jackson	1947-63	1,733	30,101	17.36
T. P. B. Smith	1929-52	1,697	45,059	26.55
J. Southerton	1854-79	1,681	24,291	14.45
A. E. Trott	1892-1911	1,674	35,316	21.09
A. W. Mold	1889-1901	1,673	26,012	15.54
T. G. Wass	1896-1920	1,666	34,092	20.46
V. W. C. Jupp	1909-38	1,658	38,166	23.01
C. Gladwin	1939-58	1,653	30,265	18.30
W. E. Bowes	1928-47	1,639	27,470	16.76
J. K. Lever	1967-86	1,619	38,817	23.97
A. W. Wellard	1927-50	1,614	39,302	24.35
P. I. Pocock	1964-86	1,607	42,648	26.53
N. I. Thomson	1952-72	1,597	32,866	20.57
J. Mercer	1919-47	1,591	37,210	23.38
G. J. Thompson	1897-1922	1,591	30,060	18.89
J. M. Sims	1929-53	1,581	39,401	24.92
T. Emmett	1866-88	1,571	21,314	13.56
Intikhab Alam	1957-82	1,571	43,472	27.67
B. S. Bedi	1961-80	1,560	33,843	21.69

	Career	W	R	Avge
W. Voce	1927-52	1,558	35,961	23.08
A. R. Gover	1928-48	1,555	36,753	23.63
T. W. Cartwright	1952-77	1,536	29,357	19.11
K. Higgs	1958-86	1,536	36,267	23.61
James Langridge	1924-53	1,530	34,524	22.56
J. A. Flavell	1949-67	1,529	32,847	21.48
C. F. Root	1910-33	1,512	31,933	21.11
R. K. Tyldesley	1919-35	1,509	25,980	17.21

† *In recent years some statisticians have removed from W. G. Grace's record a number of matches which they consider not to have been first-class. The above figures are those which became universally accepted upon appearance in W. G. Grace's obituary in the* Wisden *of 1916. Some works of reference give his career record as being 2,809–50,999–18.15. These figures also appeared in the 1981 edition of* Wisden.

‡ *The figures for A. Shaw exclude one wicket for which no analysis is available.*

ALL-ROUND RECORDS

HUNDRED AND TEN WICKETS IN ONE INNINGS

V. E. Walker, England v Surrey at The Oval; ten for 74, four for 17, 20* and 108.   1859
W. G. Grace, MCC v Oxford University at Oxford; two for 60, ten for 49, and 104.   1886
F. A. Tarrant, Maharaja of Cooch Behar's XI v Lord Willingdon's XI at Poona; ten for 90, one for 22, 182* and 8*   1918-19

Note: E. M. Grace, for MCC v Gentlemen of Kent in a 12-a-side match at Canterbury in 1862, scored 192* and took five for 77 and ten for 69.

HUNDRED IN EACH INNINGS AND FIVE WICKETS TWICE

G. H. Hirst, Yorkshire v Somerset at Bath; six for 70, five for 45, 111 and 117* .   1906

HUNDRED AND HAT-TRICK

G. Giffen, Australians v Lancashire at Manchester; 13, 113, and six for 55 including hat-trick.   1884
W. E. Roller, Surrey v Sussex at The Oval; 204, four for 28 including hat-trick, and two for 16. (Unique instance of 200 and hat-trick.)   1885
W. B. Burns, Worcestershire v Gloucestershire at Worcester; 102*, three for 56, including hat-trick, and two for 21   1913
V. W. C. Jupp, Sussex v Essex at Colchester; 102, six for 61, including hat-trick, and six for 78   1921
R. E. S. Wyatt, MCC v Ceylon at Colombo; 124 and five for 39 including hat-trick.   1926-27
L. N. Constantine, West Indians v Northamptonshire at Northampton; seven for 45, including hat-trick, 107 (five 6s), and six for 67   1928
D. E. Davies, Glamorgan v Leicestershire at Leicester; 139, four for 27, and three for 31 including hat-trick   1937
V. M. Merchant, Dr C. R. Pereira's XI v Sir Homi Mehta's XI at Bombay; 1, 142, three for 31 including hat-trick, and no wicket for 17   1946-47
M. J. Procter, Gloucestershire v Essex at Westcliff-on-Sea; 51, 102, three for 43, and five for 30 including hat-trick (all lbw)........................   1972
M. J. Procter, Gloucestershire v Leicestershire at Bristol; 122, no wkt for 32, and seven for 26 including hat-trick   1979

Note: W. G. Grace, for MCC v Kent in a 12-a-side match at Canterbury in 1874, scored 123 and took five for 82 and six for 47 including a hat-trick.

SEASON DOUBLES

2,000 RUNS AND 200 WICKETS

1906   G. H. Hirst   2,385 runs and 208 wickets

3,000 RUNS AND 100 WICKETS

1937   J. H. Parks   3,003 runs and 101 wickets

2,000 RUNS AND 100 WICKETS

	Season	R	W		Season	R	W
W. G. Grace	1873	2,139	106	F. E. Woolley	1914	2,272	125
W. G. Grace	1876	2,622	129	J. W. Hearne	1920	2,148	142
C. L. Townsend ...	1899	2,440	101	V. W. C. Jupp	1921	2,169	121
G. L. Jessop	1900	2,210	104	F. E. Woolley	1921	2,101	167
G. H. Hirst	1904	2,501	132	F. E. Woolley	1922	2,022	163
G. H. Hirst	1905	2,266	110	F. E. Woolley	1923	2,091	101
W. Rhodes	1909	2,094	141	L. F. Townsend ...	1933	2,268	100
W. Rhodes	1911	2,261	117	D. E. Davies	1937	2,012	103
F. A. Tarrant	1911	2,030	111	James Langridge ..	1937	2,082	101
J. W. Hearne	1913	2,036	124	T. E Bailey	1959	2,011	100
J. W. Hearne	1914	2,116	123				

1,000 RUNS AND 200 WICKETS

	Season	R	W		Season	R	W
A. E. Trott	1899	1,175	239	M. W. Tate	1923	1,168	219
A. E. Trott	1900	1,337	211	M. W. Tate	1924	1,419	205
A. S. Kennedy	1922	1,129	205	M. W. Tate	1925	1,290	228

1,000 RUNS AND 100 WICKETS

Sixteen times: W. Rhodes.   **Fourteen times:** G. H. Hirst.
Ten times: V. W. C. Jupp.   **Nine times:** W. E. Astill.
Eight times: T. E. Bailey, W. G. Grace, M. S. Nichols, A. E. Relf, F. A. Tarrant, M. W. Tate, F. J. Titmus, F. E. Woolley.
Seven times: G. E. Tribe.
Six times: P. G. H. Fender, R. Illingworth, James Langridge.
Five times: J. W. H. T. Douglas, J. W. Hearne, A. S. Kennedy, J. Newman.
Four times: E. G. Arnold, J. Gunn, R. Kilner, B. R. Knight.
Three times: W. W. Armstrong (Australians), L. C. Braund, G. Giffen (Australians), N. E. Haig, R. Howorth, C. B. Llewellyn, J. B. Mortimore, Ray Smith, S. G. Smith, L. F. Townsend, A. W. Wellard.

Note: R. J. Hadlee in 1984 was the first player to perform the feat since the reduction of County Championship matches. A complete list of those performing the feat before then will be found on p. 202 of the 1982 *Wisden*.

WICKET-KEEPERS' DOUBLE

	Season	R	D
L. E. G. Ames	1928	1,919	122
L. E. G. Ames	1929	1,795	128
L. E. G. Ames	1932	2,482	104
J. T. Murray	1957	1,025	104

20,000 RUNS AND 2,000 WICKETS IN A CAREER

	Career	R	Avge	W	Avge	'Doubles'
W. E. Astill	1906-39	22,731	22.55	2,431	23.76	9
T. E. Bailey	1945-67	28,642	33.42	2,082	23.13	8
W. G. Grace	1865-1908	54,896	39.55	2,876	17.92	8
G. H. Hirst	1891-1929	36,323	34.13	2,739	18.72	14
R. Illingworth	1951-83	24,134	28.06	2,072	20.28	6
W. Rhodes	1898-1930	39,802	30.83	4,187	16.71	16
M. W. Tate	1912-37	21,717	25.01	2,784	18.16	8
F. J. Titmus	1949-82	21,588	23.11	2,830	22.37	8
F. E. Woolley	1906-38	58,969	40.75	2,068	19.85	8

WICKET-KEEPING RECORDS

MOST DISMISSALS IN AN INNINGS

8 (all ct)	A. T. W. Grout	Queensland v Western Australia at Brisbane	1959-60
8 (all ct)	D. E. East	Essex v Somerset at Taunton	†1985
7 (4ct, 3st)	E. J. Smith	Warwickshire v Derbyshire at Birmingham	1926
7 (6ct, 1st)	W. Farrimond	Lancashire v Kent at Manchester	1930
7 (all ct)	W. F. F. Price	Middlesex v Yorkshire at Lord's	1937
7 (3ct, 4st)	D. Tallon	Queensland v Victoria at Brisbane	1938-39
7 (all ct)	R. A. Saggers	New South Wales v Combined XI at Brisbane	1940-41
7 (1ct, 6st)	H. Yarnold	Worcestershire v Scotland at Dundee	1951
7 (4ct, 3st)	J. Brown	Scotland v Ireland at Dublin	1957
7 (all ct)	N. Kirsten	Border v Rhodesia at East London	1959-60
7 (all ct)	M. S. Smith	Natal v Border at East London	1959-60
7 (all ct)	K. V. Andrew	Northamptonshire v Lancashire at Manchester	1962
7 (all ct)	A. Long	Surrey v Sussex at Hove	1964
7 (all ct)	R. M. Schofield	Central Districts v Wellington at Wellington	1964-65
7 (all ct)	R. W. Taylor	Derbyshire v Glamorgan at Derby	1966
7 (6ct, 1st)	H. B. Taber	New South Wales v South Australia at Adelaide	1968-69
7 (6ct, 1st)	E. W. Jones	Glamorgan v Cambridge University at Cambridge.	1970
7 (6ct, 1st)	S. Benjamin	Central Zone v North Zone at Bombay	1973-74
7 (all ct)	R. W. Taylor	Derbyshire v Yorkshire at Chesterfield	1975
7 (6ct, 1st)	Shahid Israr	Karachi Whites v Quetta at Karachi	1976-77
7 (4ct, 3st)	Wasim Bari	PIA v Sind at Lahore	1977-78
7 (all ct)	J. A. Maclean	Queensland v Victoria at Melbourne	1977-78
7 (5ct, 2st)	Taslim Arif	National Bank v Punjab at Lahore	1978-79
7 (all ct)	Wasim Bari	Pakistan v New Zealand at Auckland	1978-79
7 (all ct)	R. W. Taylor	England v India at Bombay	1979-80
7 (all ct)	D. L. Bairstow	Yorkshire v Derbyshire at Scarborough	1982
7 (6ct, 1st)	R. B. Phillips	Queensland v New Zealanders at Bundaberg	1982-83
7 (3ct, 4st)	Masood Iqbal	Habib Bank v Lahore at Lahore	1982-83
7 (3ct, 4st)	Arif-ud-Din	United Bank v PACO at Sahiwal	1983-84
7 (6ct, 1st)	R. J. East	Orange Free State v Western Province 'B' at Cape Town	1984-85

† *The first eight wickets to fall.*

WICKET-KEEPERS' HAT-TRICKS

W. H. Brain, Gloucestershire v Somerset at Cheltenham, 1893 – three stumpings off successive balls from C. L. Townsend.

G. O. Dawkes, Derbyshire v Worcestershire at Kidderminster, 1958 – three catches off successive balls from H. L. Jackson.

R. C. Russell, Gloucestershire v Surrey at The Oval, 1986 – three catches off successive balls from C. A. Walsh and D. V. Lawrence (2).

MOST DISMISSALS IN A MATCH

12 (8ct, 4st)	E. Pooley	Surrey v Sussex at The Oval	1868
12 (9ct, 3st)	D. Tallon	Queensland v New South Wales at Sydney	1938-39
12 (9ct, 3st)	H. B. Taber	New South Wales v South Australia at Adelaide .	1968-69
11 (all ct)	A. Long	Surrey v Sussex at Hove	1964
11 (all ct)	R. W. Marsh	Western Australia v Victoria at Perth	1975-76
11 (all ct)	D. L. Bairstow	Yorkshire v Derbyshire at Scarborough	1982
10 (5ct, 5st)	H. Phillips	Sussex v Surrey at The Oval	1872
10 (2ct, 8st)	E. Pooley	Surrey v Kent at The Oval	1878
10 (9ct, 1st)	T. W. Oates	Nottinghamshire v Middlesex at Nottingham ...	1906
10 (1ct, 9st)	F. H. Huish	Kent v Surrey at The Oval	1911
10 (9ct, 1st)	J. C. Hubble	Kent v Gloucestershire at Cheltenham	1923
10 (8ct, 2st)	H. Elliott	Derbyshire v Lancashire at Manchester	1935
10 (7ct, 3st)	P. Corrall	Leicestershire v Sussex at Hove	1936
10 (9ct, 1st)	R. A. Saggers	New South Wales v Combined XI at Brisbane ..	1940-41
10 (all ct)	A. E. Wilson	Gloucestershire v Hampshire at Portsmouth	1953
10 (7ct, 3st)	B. N. Jarman	South Australia v New South Wales at Adelaide .	1961-62
10 (all ct)	L. A. Johnson	Northamptonshire v Sussex at Worthing	1963
10 (all ct)	R. W. Taylor	Derbyshire v Hampshire at Chesterfield	1963
10 (8ct, 2st)	L. A. Johnson	Northamptonshire v Warwickshire at Birmingham	1965
10 (9ct, 1st)	R. C. Jordon	Victoria v South Australia at Melbourne	1970-71
10 (all ct)	R. W. Marsh†	Western Australia v South Australia at Perth ...	1976-77
10 (6ct, 4st)	Taslim Arif	National Bank v Punjab at Lahore	1978-79
10 (9ct, 1st)	Arif-ud-Din	United Bank v Karachi 'B' at Karachi	1978-79
10 (all ct)	R. W. Taylor	England v India at Bombay	1979-80
10 (all ct)	R. J. Parks	Hampshire v Derbyshire at Portsmouth	1981
10 (9ct, 1st)	A. Ghosh	Bihar v Assam at Bhagalpur	1981-82
10 (8ct, 2st)	Z. Parkar	Bombay v Maharashtra at Bombay	1981-82
10 (all ct)	R. V. Jennings	Transvaal v Arosa Sri Lankans at Johannesburg .	1982-83
10 (9ct, 1st)	Kamal Najamuddin	Karachi v Lahore at Multan	1982-83
10 (all ct)	D. A. Murray	West Indies XI v South Africa at Port Elizabeth .	1983-84
10 (7ct, 3st)	Azhar Abbas	Bahawalpur v Lahore City Greens at Bahawalpur	1983-84
10 (7ct, 3st)	B. N. French	Nottinghamshire v Oxford University at Oxford .	1984
10 (8ct, 2st)	R. J. Ryall	Western Province v Transvaal at Cape Town ...	1984-85
10 (all ct)	S. J. Rixon	Australian XI v South Africa at Johannesburg ..	1985-86
10 (8ct, 2st)	Anil Dalpat	Karachi v United Bank at Lahore	1985-86

† Marsh also scored a hundred (104), a unique "double".

MOST DISMISSALS IN A SEASON

128 (79ct, 49st)	L. E. G. Ames	Kent	1929
122 (70ct, 52st)	L. E. G. Ames	Kent	1928
110 (63ct, 47st)	H. Yarnold	Worcestershire	1949
107 (77ct, 30st)	G. Duckworth	Lancashire	1928
107 (96ct, 11st)	J. G. Binks	Yorkshire	1960
104 (40ct, 64st)	L. E. G. Ames	Kent	1932
104 (82ct, 22st)	J. T. Murray	Middlesex	1957
102 (69ct, 33st)	F. H. Huish	Kent	1913
102 (95ct, 7st)	J. T. Murray	Middlesex	1960
101 (62ct, 39st)	F. H. Huish	Kent	1911
101 (85ct, 16st)	R. Booth	Worcestershire	1960
100 (91ct, 9st)	R. Booth	Worcestershire	1964

MOST DISMISSALS IN A CAREER

Dates in italics denote the first half of an overseas season; i.e. *1914* denotes the 1914-15 season.

	Career	Ct	St	Total
R. W. Taylor	1960-86	1,473	175	1,648
J. T. Murray	1952-75	1,270	257	1,527
H. Strudwick	1902-27	1,242	254	1,496
A. P. E. Knott	1965-85	1,211	133	1,344
F. H. Huish	1895-1914	933	377	1,310
B. Taylor	1949-73	1,082	212	1,294
D. Hunter	1889-1909	914	351	1,265
H. R. Butt	1890-1912	953	275	1,228
J. H. Board	1891-*1914*	852	355	1,207
H. Elliott	1920-47	904	302	1,206
J. M. Parks	1949-76	1,088	93	1,181
R. Booth	1951-70	949	177	1,126
L. E. G. Ames	1926-51	703	418	1,121
G. Duckworth	1923-47	751	339	1,090
H. W. Stephenson	1948-64	748	334	1,082
J. G. Binks	1955-75	895	176	1,071
T. G. Evans	1939-69	816	250	1,066
A. Long	1960-80	922	124	1,046
G. O. Dawkes	1937-61	895	148	1,043
R. W. Tolchard	1965-83	912	125	1,037
W. L. Cornford	1921-47	673	344	1,017

FIELDING RECORDS

(Excluding wicket-keepers)

Most Catches in an Innings

| 7 | M. J. Stewart | Surrey v Northamptonshire at Northampton | 1957 |
| 7 | A. S. Brown | Gloucestershire v Nottinghamshire at Nottingham | 1966 |

Most Catches in a Match

10	W. R. Hammond	Gloucestershire v Surrey at Cheltenham	†1928
8	W. B. Burns	Worcestershire v Yorkshire at Bradford	1907
8	A. H. Bakewell	Northamptonshire v Essex at Leyton	1928
8	W. R. Hammond	Gloucestershire v Worcestershire at Cheltenham	1932
8	K. J. Grieves	Lancashire v Sussex at Manchester	1951
8	C. A. Milton	Gloucestershire v Sussex at Hove	1952
8	G. A. R. Lock	Surrey v Warwickshire at The Oval	1957
8	J. M. Prodger	Kent v Gloucestershire at Cheltenham	1961
8	P. M. Walker	Glamorgan v Derbyshire at Swansea	1970
8	Javed Miandad	Habib Bank v Universities at Lahore	1977-78
8	Masood Anwar	Rawalpindi v Lahore Division at Rawalpindi	1983-84

† *Hammond also scored a hundred in each innings.*

Most Catches in a Season

78	W. R. Hammond	1928	65	D. W. Richardson	1961
77	M. J. Stewart	1957	64	K. F. Barrington	1957
73	P. M. Walker	1961	64	G. A. R. Lock	1957
71	P. J. Sharpe	1962	63	J. Tunnicliffe	1896
70	J. Tunnicliffe	1901	63	J. Tunnicliffe	1904
69	J. G. Langridge	1955	63	K. J. Grieves	1950
69	P. M. Walker	1960	63	C. A. Milton	1956
66	J. Tunnicliffe	1895	61	J. V. Wilson	1955
65	W. R. Hammond	1925	61	M. J. Stewart	1958
65	P. M. Walker	1959			

Note: The most catches by a fielder since the reduction of County Championship matches in 1969 is 49 by C. J. Tavaré in 1979.

Most Catches in a Career

Dates in italics denote the first half of an overseas season; i.e. *1970* denotes the 1970-71 season.

1,018	F. E. Woolley (1906-38)	786	J. G. Langridge (1928-55)
874	W. G. Grace (1865-1908)	764	W. Rhodes (1898-1930)
831	G. A. R. Lock (1946-*70*)	758	C. A. Milton (1948-74)
819	W. R. Hammond (1920-51)	754	E. H. Hendren (1907-38)
813	D. B. Close (1949-86)		

TEAM RECORDS

HIGHEST TOTALS

1,107	Victoria v New South Wales at Melbourne	1926-27
1,059	Victoria v Tasmania at Melbourne	1922-23
951-7 dec.	Sind v Baluchistan at Karachi	1973-74
918	New South Wales v South Australia at Sydney	1900-01
912-8 dec.	Holkar v Mysore at Indore	1945-46
910-6 dec.	Railways v Dera Ismail Khan at Lahore	1964-65
903-7 dec.	England v Australia at The Oval	1938
887	Yorkshire v Warwickshire at Birmingham	1896
849	England v West Indies at Kingston	1929-30
843	Australians v Oxford and Cambridge Universities Past and Present at Portsmouth	1893

HIGHEST FOR EACH FIRST-CLASS COUNTY

Derbyshire	645	v Hampshire at Derby	1898
Essex	692	v Somerset at Taunton	1895
Glamorgan	587-8	v Derbyshire at Cardiff	1951
Gloucestershire	653-6	v Glamorgan at Bristol	1928
Hampshire	672-7	v Somerset at Taunton	1899
Kent	803-4	v Essex at Brentwood	1934
Lancashire	801	v Somerset at Taunton	1895
Leicestershire	701-4	v Worcestershire at Worcester	1906
Middlesex	642-3	v Hampshire at Southampton	1923
Northamptonshire	557-6	v Sussex at Hove	1914
Nottinghamshire	739-7	v Leicestershire at Nottingham	1903
Somerset	675-9	v Hampshire at Bath	1924
Surrey	811	v Somerset at The Oval	1899
Sussex	705-8	v Surrey at Hastings	1902
Warwickshire	657-6	v Hampshire at Birmingham	1899
Worcestershire	633	v Warwickshire at Worcester	1906
Yorkshire	887	v Warwickshire at Birmingham	1896

LOWEST TOTALS

12	Oxford University v MCC and Ground at Oxford	†1877
12	Northamptonshire v Gloucestershire at Gloucester	1907
13	Auckland v Canterbury at Auckland	1877-78
13	Nottinghamshire v Yorkshire at Nottingham	1901
14	Surrey v Essex at Chelmsford	1983
15	MCC v Surrey at Lord's	1839
15	Victoria v MCC at Melbourne	†1903-04
15	Northamptonshire v Yorkshire at Northampton	†1908
15	Hampshire v Warwickshire at Birmingham	1922
	(Following on, Hampshire scored 521 and won by 155 runs.)	
16	MCC and Ground v Surrey at Lord's	1872
16	Derbyshire v Nottinghamshire at Nottingham	1879
16	Surrey v Nottinghamshire at The Oval	1880
16	Warwickshire v Kent at Tonbridge	1913
16	Trinidad v Barbados at Bridgetown	1942-43
16	Border v Natal at East London (first innings)	1959-60
17	Gentlemen of Kent v Gentlemen of England at Lord's	1850
17	Gloucestershire v Australians at Cheltenham	1896
18	The 'B's v England at Lord's	1831
18	Kent v Sussex at Gravesend	†1867
18	Tasmania v Victoria at Melbourne	1868-69
18	Australians v MCC and Ground at Lord's	†1896
18	Border v Natal at East London (second innings)	1959-60
19	Sussex v Surrey at Godalming	1830
19	Sussex v Nottinghamshire at Hove	†1873
19	MCC and Ground v Australians at Lord's	1878
19	Wellington v Nelson at Nelson	1885-86

† *Signifies that one man was absent.*

Note: At Lord's in 1810, The 'B's, with one man absent, were dismissed by England for 6.

LOWEST TOTAL IN A MATCH

34	(16 and 18) Border v Natal at East London	1959-60
42	(27 and 15) Northamptonshire v Yorkshire at Northampton	1908

Note: Northamptonshire batted one man short in each innings.

LOWEST FOR EACH FIRST-CLASS COUNTY

Derbyshire	16	v Nottinghamshire at Nottingham	1879
Essex	30	v Yorkshire at Leyton	1901
Glamorgan	22	v Lancashire at Liverpool	1924
Gloucestershire	17	v Australians at Cheltenham	1896
Hampshire	15	v Warwickshire at Birmingham	1922
Kent	18	v Sussex at Gravesend	1867
Lancashire	25	v Derbyshire at Manchester	1871
Leicestershire	25	v Kent at Leicester	1912
Middlesex	20	v MCC at Lord's	1864
Northamptonshire	12	v Gloucestershire at Gloucester	1907
Nottinghamshire	13	v Yorkshire at Nottingham	1901
Somerset	25	v Gloucestershire at Bristol	1947
Surrey	14	v Essex at Chelmsford	1983
Sussex	19	v Nottinghamshire at Hove	1873
Warwickshire	16	v Kent at Tonbridge	1913
Worcestershire	24	v Yorkshire at Huddersfield	1903
Yorkshire	23	v Hampshire at Middlesbrough	1965

HIGHEST MATCH AGGREGATES

2,376 for 38 wickets	Maharashtra v Bombay at Poona	1948-49
2,078 for 40 wickets	Bombay v Holkar at Bombay	1944-45
1,981 for 35 wickets	England v South Africa at Durban	1938-39
1,929 for 39 wickets	New South Wales v South Australia at Sydney	1925-26
1,911 for 34 wickets	New South Wales v Victoria at Sydney	1908-09
1,905 for 40 wickets	Otago v Wellington at Dunedin	1923-24

In England

1,723 for 31 wickets	England v Australia at Leeds	1948
1,601 for 29 wickets	England v Australia at Lord's	1930
1,507 for 28 wickets	England v West Indies at The Oval	1976
1,502 for 28 wickets	MCC v New Zealanders at Lord's	1927
1,499 for 31 wickets	T. N. Pearce's XI v Australians at Scarborough	1961
1,496 for 24 wickets	England v Australia at Nottingham	1938
1,494 for 37 wickets	England v Australia at The Oval	1934

LOWEST MATCH AGGREGATE

105 for 31 wickets	MCC v Australians at Lord's	1878

Note: The lowest aggregate since 1900 is 158 for 22 wickets, Surrey v Worcestershire at The Oval, 1954.

HIGHEST FOURTH INNINGS TOTALS

(Unless otherwise stated, the side making the runs won the match.)

654-5	England v South Africa at Durban	1938-39
	(After being set 696 to win. The match was left drawn on the tenth day.)	
604	Maharashtra v Bombay at Poona	1948-49
	(After being set 959 to win.)	
576-8	Trinidad v Barbados at Port-of-Spain	1945-46
	(After being set 672 to win. Match drawn on fifth day.)	
572	New South Wales v South Australia at Sydney	1907-08
	(After being set 593 to win.)	
529-9	Combined XI v South Africans at Perth	1963-64
	(After being set 579 to win. Match drawn on fourth day.)	
518	Victoria v Queensland at Brisbane	1926-27
	(After being set 753 to win.)	
507-7	Cambridge University v MCC and Ground at Lord's	1896
502-6	Middlesex v Nottinghamshire at Nottingham	1925
	(Game won by an unfinished stand of 271; a county record.)	
502-8	Players v Gentlemen at Lord's	1900
500-7	South African Universities v Western Province at Stellenbosch	1978-79

LARGEST VICTORIES

Largest Innings Victories

Inns and 851 runs:	Railways (910-6 dec.) v Dera Ismail Khan (Lahore)	1964-65
Inns and 666 runs:	Victoria (1,059) v Tasmania (Melbourne)	1922-23
Inns and 656 runs:	Victoria (1,107) v New South Wales (Melbourne)	1926-27
Inns and 605 runs:	New South Wales (918) v South Australia (Sydney)	1900-01
Inns and 579 runs:	England (903-7 dec.) v Australia (The Oval)	1938
Inns and 575 runs:	Sind (951-7 dec.) v Baluchistan (Karachi)	1973-74
Inns and 527 runs:	New South Wales (713) v South Australia (Adelaide)	1908-09
Inns and 517 runs:	Australians (675) v Nottinghamshire (Nottingham)	1921

Largest Victories by Runs Margin

685 runs: New South Wales (235 and 761-8 dec.) v Queensland (Sydney) 1929-30
675 runs: England (521 and 342-8 dec.) v Australia (Brisbane) 1928-29
638 runs: New South Wales (304 and 770) v South Australia (Adelaide) 1920-21
625 runs: Sargodha (376 and 416) v Lahore Municipal Corporation (Faisalabad) 1978-79
609 runs: Muslim Commercial Bank (575 and 282-0 dec.) v WAPDA (Lahore) 1977-78
571 runs: Victoria (304 and 649) v South Australia (Adelaide) 1926-27
562 runs: Australia (701 and 327) v England (The Oval) 1934

Victory Without Losing a Wicket

Lancashire (166-0 dec. and 66-0) beat Leicestershire by ten wickets (Manchester)   1956
Karachi 'A' (277-0 dec.) beat Sind 'A' by an innings and 77 runs (Karachi) 1957-58
Railways (236-0 dec. and 16-0) beat Jammu and Kashmir by ten wickets (Srinagar) 1960-61
Karnataka (451-0 dec.) beat Kerala by an innings and 186 runs (Chikmagalur) . 1977-78

TIED MATCHES IN FIRST-CLASS CRICKET

There have been 32 tied matches since the First World War.

Somerset v Sussex at Taunton 1919
(The last Sussex batsman not allowed to bat under Law 45 [subsequently Law
17 and now Law 31])
Orange Free State v Eastern Province at Bloemfontein 1925-26
(Eastern Province had two wickets to fall.)
Essex v Somerset at Chelmsford 1926
(Although Essex had one man to go in, MCC ruled that the game should rank
as a tie. The ninth wicket fell half a minute before time.)
Gloucestershire v Australians at Bristol 1930
Victoria v MCC at Melbourne 1932-33
(Victoria's third wicket fell to the last ball of the match when one run was
needed to win.)
Worcestershire v Somerset at Kidderminster 1939
Southern Punjab v Baroda at Patiala 1945-46
Essex v Northamptonshire at Ilford 1947
Hampshire v Lancashire at Bournemouth 1947
D. G. Bradman's XI v A. L. Hassett's XI at Melbourne 1948-49
Hampshire v Kent at Southampton 1950
Sussex v Warwickshire at Hove 1952
Essex v Lancashire at Brentwood 1952
Northamptonshire v Middlesex at Peterborough 1953
Yorkshire v Leicestershire at Huddersfield 1954
Sussex v Hampshire at Eastbourne 1955
Victoria v New South Wales at Melbourne 1956-57
T. N. Pearce's XI v New Zealanders at Scarborough 1958
Essex v Gloucestershire at Leyton 1959
Australia v West Indies (First Test) at Brisbane 1960-61
Bahawalpur v Lahore 'B' at Bahawalpur 1961-62
Hampshire v Middlesex at Portsmouth 1967
England XI v England Under-25 XI at Scarborough 1968
Yorkshire v Middlesex at Bradford 1973
Sussex v Essex at Hove 1974
South Australia v Queensland at Adelaide 1976-77
Central Districts v England XI at New Plymouth 1977-78
Victoria v New Zealanders at Melbourne 1982-83
Muslim Commercial Bank v Railways at Sialkot 1983-84
Sussex v Kent at Hastings 1984
Northamptonshire v Kent at Northampton 1984
Eastern Province 'B' v Boland at Albany SC, Port Elizabeth 1985-86
Natal 'B' v Eastern Province 'B' at Pietermaritzburg 1985-86

Note: Since 1948 a tie has been recognised only when the scores are level with all the wickets down in the fourth innings. This ruling applies to all grades of cricket, and in the case of a one-day match to the second innings, provided that the match has not been brought to a further conclusion.

MATCHES BEGUN AND FINISHED ON FIRST DAY.

Since 1900. A fuller list may be found in the Wisden of 1981 and preceding editions.

Yorkshire v Worcestershire at Bradford, May 7	1900
MCC and Ground v London County at Lord's, May 20	1903
Transvaal v Orange Free State at Johannesburg, December 30	1906
Middlesex v Gentlemen of Philadelphia at Lord's, July 20	1908
Gloucestershire v Middlesex at Bristol, August 26	1909
Eastern Province v Orange Free State at Port Elizabeth, December 26	1912
Kent v Sussex at Tonbridge, June 21	1919
Lancashire v Somerset at Manchester, May 21	1925
Madras v Mysore at Madras, November 4	1934
Ireland v New Zealanders at Dublin, September 11	1937
Derbyshire v Somerset at Chesterfield, June 11	1947
Lancashire v Sussex at Manchester, July 12	1950
Surrey v Warwickshire at The Oval, May 16	1953
Somerset v Lancashire at Bath, June 6 (H. T. F. Buse's benefit)	1953
Kent v Worcestershire at Tunbridge Wells, June 15	1960

TEST MATCH RECORDS

BATTING RECORDS

HIGHEST INDIVIDUAL INNINGS

365*	G. S. Sobers, West Indies v Pakistan at Kingston	1957-58
364	L. Hutton, England v Australia at The Oval	1938
337	Hanif Mohammad, Pakistan v West Indies at Bridgetown	1957-58
336*	W. R. Hammond, England v New Zealand at Auckland	1932-33
334	D. G. Bradman, Australia v England at Leeds	1930
325	A. Sandham, England v West Indies at Kingston	1929-30
311	R. B. Simpson, Australia v England at Manchester	1964
310*	J. H. Edrich, England v New Zealand at Leeds	1965
307	R. M. Cowper, Australia v England at Melbourne	1965-66
304	D. G. Bradman, Australia v England at Leeds	1934
302	L. G. Rowe, West Indies v England at Bridgetown	1973-74
299*	D. G. Bradman, Australia v South Africa at Adelaide	1931-32
291	I. V. A. Richards, West Indies v England at The Oval	1976
287	R. E. Foster, England v Australia at Sydney	1903-04
285*	P. B. H. May, England v West Indies at Birmingham	1957
280*	Javed Miandad, Pakistan v India at Hyderabad	1982-83
278	D. C. S. Compton, England v Pakistan at Nottingham	1954
274	R. G. Pollock, South Africa v Australia at Durban	1969-70
274	Zaheer Abbas, Pakistan v England at Birmingham	1971
270*	G. A. Headley, West Indies v England at Kingston	1934-35
270	D. G. Bradman, Australia v England at Melbourne	1936-37
268	G. N. Yallop, Australia v Pakistan at Melbourne	1983-84
266	W. H. Ponsford, Australia v England at The Oval	1934
262*	D. L. Amiss, England v West Indies at Kingston	1973-74
261	F. M. M. Worrell, West Indies v England at Nottingham	1950
260	C. C. Hunte, West Indies v Pakistan at Kingston	1957-58

259	G. M. Turner, New Zealand v West Indies at Georgetown	1971-72
258	T. W. Graveney, England v West Indies at Nottingham	1957
258	S. M. Nurse, West Indies v New Zealand at Christchurch	1968-69
256	R. B. Kanhai, West Indies v India at Calcutta	1958-59
256	K. F. Barrington, England v Australia at Manchester	1964
255*	D. J. McGlew, South Africa v New Zealand at Wellington	1952-53
254	D. G. Bradman, Australia v England at Lord's	1930
251	W. R. Hammond, England v Australia at Sydney	1928-29
250	K. D. Walters, Australia v New Zealand at Christchurch	1976-77
250	S. F. A. F. Bacchus, West Indies v India at Kanpur	1978-79

The highest individual innings for other countries are:

| 236* | S. M. Gavaskar, India v West Indies at Madras | 1983-84 |
| 190 | S. Wettimuny, Sri Lanka v England at Lord's | 1984 |

HUNDRED ON TEST DEBUT

C. Bannerman (165*)	Australia v England at Melbourne	1876-77
W. G. Grace (152)	England v Australia at The Oval	1880
H. Graham (107)	Australia v England at Lord's	1893
†K. S. Ranjitsinhji (154*)	England v Australia at Manchester	1896
†P. F. Warner (132*)	England v South Africa at Johannesburg	1898-99
†R. A. Duff (104)	Australia v England at Melbourne	1901-02
R. E. Foster (287)	England v Australia at Sydney	1903-04
G. Gunn (119)	England v Australia at Sydney	1907-08
†R. J. Hartigan (116)	Australia v England at Adelaide	1907-08
†H. L. Collins (104)	Australia v England at Sydney	1920-21
W. H. Ponsford (110)	Australia v England at Sydney	1924-25
A. A. Jackson (164)	Australia v England at Adelaide	1928-29
†G. A. Headley (176)	West Indies v England at Bridgetown	1929-30
J. E. Mills (117)	New Zealand v England at Wellington	1929-30
Nawab of Pataudi (102)	England v Australia at Sydney	1932-33
B. H. Valentine (136)	England v India at Bombay	1933-34
†L. Amarnath (118)	India v England at Bombay	1933-34
†P. A. Gibb (106)	England v South Africa at Johannesburg	1938-39
S. C. Griffith (140)	England v West Indies at Port-of-Spain	1947-48
A. G. Ganteaume (112)	West Indies v England at Port-of-Spain	1947-48
†J. W. Burke (101*)	Australia v England at Adelaide	1950-51
P. B. H. May (138)	England v South Africa at Leeds	1951
R. H. Shodhan (110)	India v Pakistan at Calcutta	1952-53
B. H. Pairaudeau (115)	West Indies v India at Port-of-Spain	1952-53
†O. G. Smith (104)	West Indies v Australia at Kingston	1954-55
A. G. Kripal Singh (100*)	India v New Zealand at Hyderabad	1955-56
C. C. Hunte (142)	West Indies v Pakistan at Bridgetown	1957-58
C. A. Milton (104*)	England v New Zealand at Leeds	1958
†A. A. Baig (112)	India v England at Manchester	1959
Hanumant Singh (105)	India v England at Delhi	1963-64
Khalid Ibadulla (166)	Pakistan v Australia at Karachi	1964-65
B. R. Taylor (105)	New Zealand v India at Calcutta	1964-65
K. D. Walters (155)	Australia v England at Brisbane	1965-66
J. H. Hampshire (107)	England v West Indies at Lord's	1969
†G. R. Viswanath (137)	India v Australia at Kanpur	1969-70
G. S. Chappell (108)	Australia v England at Perth	1970-71
‡L. G. Rowe (214, 100*)	West Indies v New Zealand at Kingston	1971-72
A. I. Kallicharran (100*)	West Indies v New Zealand at Georgetown	1971-72
R. E. Redmond (107)	New Zealand v Pakistan at Auckland	1972-73
†F. C. Hayes (106*)	England v West Indies at The Oval	1973
†C. G. Greenidge (107)	West Indies v India at Bangalore	1974-75
†L. Baichan (105*)	West Indies v Pakistan at Lahore	1974-75
G. J. Cosier (109)	Australia v West Indies at Melbourne	1975-76

S. Amarnath (124)	India v New Zealand at Auckland	1975-76
Javed Miandad (163)	Pakistan v New Zealand at Lahore	1976-77
†A. B. Williams (100)	West Indies v Australia at Georgetown	1977-78
†D. M. Wellham (103)	Australia v England at The Oval	1981
†Salim Malik (100*)	Pakistan v Sri Lanka at Karachi	1981-82
K. C. Wessels (162)	Australia v England at Brisbane	1982-83
W. B. Phillips (159)	Australia v Pakistan at Perth	1983-84
§M. Azharuddin (110)	India v England at Calcutta	1984-85

† *In his second innings of the match.*
‡ *L. G. Rowe is the only batsman to score a hundred in each innings on début.*
§ *M. Azharuddin is the only batsman to score hundreds in each of his first three Tests.*

300 RUNS IN FIRST TEST

314	L. G. Rowe (214, 100*)	West Indies v New Zealand at Kingston	1971-72
306	R. E. Foster (287, 19)	England v Australia at Sydney	1903-04

TWO SEPARATE HUNDREDS IN A TEST

Three times: S. M. Gavaskar v West Indies (1970-71), v Pakistan (1978-79), v West Indies (1978-79).

Twice in one series: C. L. Walcott v Australia (1954-55).

Twice: H. Sutcliffe v Australia (1924-25), v South Africa (1929); G. A. Headley v England (1929-30 and 1939); G. S. Chappell v New Zealand (1973-74), v West Indies (1975-76); ‡A. R. Border v Pakistan (1979-80), v New Zealand (1985-86).

Once: W. Bardsley v England (1909); A. C. Russell v South Africa (1922-23); W. R. Hammond v Australia (1928-29); E. Paynter v South Africa (1938-39); D. C. S. Compton v Australia (1946-47); A. R. Morris v England (1946-47); A. Melville v England (1947); B. Mitchell v England (1947); D. G. Bradman v India (1947-48); V. S. Hazare v Australia (1947-48); E. D. Weekes v India (1948-49); J. Moroney v South Africa (1949-50); G. S. Sobers v Pakistan (1957-58); R. B. Kanhai v Australia (1960-61); Hanif Mohammad v England (1961-62); R. B. Simpson v Pakistan (1964-65); K. D. Walters v West Indies (1968-69); †L. G. Rowe v New Zealand (1971-72); I. M. Chappell v New Zealand (1973-74); G. M. Turner v Australia (1973-74); C. G. Greenidge v England (1976); G. P. Howarth v England (1977-78); L. R. D. Mendis v India (1982-83); Javed Miandad v New Zealand (1984-85).

† *L. G. Rowe's two hundreds were on his Test début.*
‡ *A. R. Border scored 150* and 153 against Pakistan to become the first batsman to score 150 in each innings of a Test match.*

HUNDRED AND DOUBLE-HUNDRED IN SAME TEST

K. D. Walters (Australia)	242 and 103 v West Indies at Sydney	1968-69
S. M. Gavaskar (India)	124 and 220 v West Indies at Port-of-Spain	1970-71
†L. G. Rowe (West Indies)	214 and 100* v New Zealand at Kingston	1971-72
G. S. Chappell (Australia)	247* and 133 v New Zealand at Wellington	1973-74

† *On Test début.*

MOST RUNS IN A SERIES

	T	I	NO	R	HI	100s	Avge		
D. G. Bradman ...	5	7	0	974	334	4	139.14	A v E	1930
W. R. Hammond .	5	9	1	905	251	4	113.12	E v A	1928-29
R. N. Harvey	5	9	0	834	205	4	92.66	A v SA	1952-53
I. V. A. Richards .	4	7	0	829	291	3	118.42	WI v E	1976
C. L. Walcott	5	10	0	827	155	5	82.70	WI v A	1954-55
G. S. Sobers	5	8	2	824	365*	3	137.33	WI v P	1957-58
D. G. Bradman ...	5	9	0	810	270	3	90.00	A v E	1936-37
D. G. Bradman ...	5	5	1	806	299*	4	201.50	A v SA	1931-32
E. D. Weekes ...	5	7	0	779	194	4	111.28	WI v I	1948-49
†S. M. Gavaskar ..	4	8	3	774	220	4	154.80	I v WI	1970-71
Mudassar Nazar ..	6	8	2	761	231	4	126.83	P v I	1982-83
D. G. Bradman ...	5	8	0	758	304	2	94.75	A v E	1934
D. C. S. Compton ..	5	8	0	753	208	4	94.12	E v SA	1947

† *Gavaskar's aggregate was achieved in his first Test series.*

1,000 TEST RUNS IN A CALENDAR YEAR

	T	I	NO	R	HI	100s	Avge	Year
I. V. A. Richards (*West Indies*) .	11	19	0	1,710	291	7	90.00	1976
S. M. Gavaskar (*India*)	18	27	1	1,555	221	5	59.80	1979
G. R. Viswanath (*India*)	17	26	3	1,388	179	5	60.34	1979
R. B. Simpson (*Australia*)	14	26	3	1,381	311	3	60.04	1964
D. L. Amiss (*England*)	13	22	2	1,379	262*	5	68.95	1974
S. M. Gavaskar (*India*)	18	32	4	1,310	236*	5	46.78	1983
G. S. Sobers (*West Indies*) ..	7	12	3	1,193	365*	5	132.55	1958
D. B. Vengsarkar (*India*)	18	27	4	1,174	146*	5	51.04	1979
K. J. Hughes (*Australia*)	15	28	4	1,163	130*	2	48.45	1979
D. C. S. Compton (*England*) ..	9	15	1	1,159	208	6	82.78	1947
C. G. Greenidge (*West Indies*) .	14	22	4	1,149	223	4	63.83	1984
I. T. Botham (*England*)	14	22	0	1,095	208	3	49.77	1982
K. W. R. Fletcher (*England*) ...	13	22	4	1,090	178	2	60.55	1973
M. Amarnath (*India*)	14	24	1	1,077	120	4	46.82	1983
A. R. Border (*Australia*)	14	27	3	1,073	162	3	44.70	1979
C. Hill (*Australia*)	12	21	2	1,061	142	2	55.78	1902
D. I. Gower (*England*)	14	25	2	1,061	114	1	46.13	1982
W. M. Lawry (*Australia*)	14	27	2	1,056	157	2	42.24	1964
S. M. Gavaskar (*India*)	9	15	2	1,044	205	4	80.30	1978
K. F. Barrington (*England*) ...	12	22	2	1,039	132*	3	51.95	1963
E. R. Dexter (*England*)	11	15	1	1,038	205	2	74.14	1962
K. F. Barrington (*England*)	10	17	4	1,032	172	4	79.38	1961
Mohsin Khan (*Pakistan*)	10	17	3	1,029	200	4	73.50	1982
D. G. Bradman (*Australia*)	8	13	4	1,025	201	5	113.88	1948
S. M. Gavaskar (*India*)	11	20	1	1,024	156	4	53.89	1976

Note: The earliest date for completing 1,000 runs is May 3 by M. Amarnath in 1983.

MOST RUNS IN A CAREER

(Qualification: 2,000 runs)

ENGLAND

	T	I	NO	R	HI	100s	Avge
G. Boycott	108	193	23	8,114	246*	22	47.72
M. C. Cowdrey	114	188	15	7,624	182	22	44.06
W. R. Hammond	85	140	16	7,249	336*	22	58.45
L. Hutton	79	138	15	6,971	364	19	56.67
K. F. Barrington	82	131	15	6,806	256	20	58.67
D. I. Gower	86	148	11	6,149	215	13	44.88
D. C. S. Compton ...	78	131	15	5,807	278	17	50.06
J. B. Hobbs	61	102	7	5,410	211	15	56.94
J. H. Edrich	77	127	9	5,138	310*	12	43.54
T. W. Graveney	79	123	13	4,882	258	11	44.38
I. T. Botham	85	136	4	4,636	208	13	35.12
H. Sutcliffe	54	84	9	4,555	194	16	60.73
P. B. H. May	66	106	9	4,537	285*	13	46.77
E. R. Dexter	62	102	8	4,502	205	9	47.89
A. P. E. Knott	95	149	15	4,389	135	5	32.75
G. A. Gooch	59	105	4	3,746	196	7	37.08
D. L. Amiss	50	88	10	3,612	262*	11	46.30
A. W. Greig	58	93	4	3,599	148	8	40.43
E. H. Hendren	51	83	9	3,525	205*	7	47.63
F. E. Woolley	64	98	7	3,283	154	5	36.07
K. W. R. Fletcher	59	96	14	3,272	216	7	39.90
M. Leyland	41	65	5	2,764	187	9	46.06
M. W. Gatting	48	83	12	2,725	207	6	38.38
C. Washbrook	37	66	6	2,569	195	6	42.81
A. J. Lamb	46	79	6	2,500	137*	7	34.24
B. L. D'Oliveira	44	70	8	2,484	158	5	40.06
D. W. Randall	47	79	5	2,470	174	7	33.37
W. J. Edrich	39	63	2	2,440	219	6	40.00
T. G. Evans	91	133	14	2,439	104	2	20.49
L. E. G. Ames	47	72	12	2,434	149	8	40.56
W. Rhodes	58	98	21	2,325	179	2	30.19
T. E. Bailey	61	91	14	2,290	134*	1	29.74
M. J. K. Smith	50	78	6	2,278	121	3	31.63
P. E. Richardson	34	56	1	2,061	126	5	37.47

AUSTRALIA

	T	I	NO	R	HI	100s	Avge
G. S. Chappell	87	151	19	7,110	247*	24	53.86
D. G. Bradman	52	80	10	6,996	334	29	99.94
A. R. Border	81	143	24	6,199	196	18	52.09
R. N. Harvey	79	137	10	6,149	205	21	48.41
K. D. Walters	74	125	14	5,357	250	15	48.26
I. M. Chappell	75	136	10	5,345	196	14	42.42
W. M. Lawry	67	123	12	5,234	210	13	47.15
R. B. Simpson	62	111	7	4,869	311	10	46.81
I. R. Redpath	66	120	11	4,737	171	8	43.45
K. J. Hughes	70	124	6	4,415	213	9	37.41
R. W. Marsh	96	150	13	3,633	132	3	26.51
A. R. Morris	46	79	3	3,533	206	12	46.48
C. Hill	49	89	2	3,412	191	7	39.21
V. T. Trumper	48	89	8	3,163	214*	8	39.04

	T	I	NO	R	HI	100s	Avge
G. M. Wood	53	101	5	3,109	172	8	32.38
C. C. McDonald	47	83	4	3,107	170	5	39.32
A. L. Hassett	43	69	3	3,073	198*	10	46.56
K. R. Miller	55	87	7	2,958	147	7	36.97
W. W. Armstrong	50	84	10	2,863	159*	6	38.68
K. R. Stackpole	43	80	5	2,807	207	7	37.42
N. C. O'Neill	42	69	8	2,779	181	6	45.55
G. N. Yallop	39	70	3	2,756	268	8	41.13
S. J. McCabe	39	62	5	2,748	232	6	48.21
W. Bardsley	41	66	5	2,469	193*	6	40.47
W. M. Woodfull	35	54	4	2,300	161	7	46.00
P. J. Burge	42	68	8	2,290	181	4	38.16
S. E. Gregory	58	100	7	2,282	201	4	24.53
R. Benaud	63	97	7	2,201	122	3	24.45
C. G. Macartney	35	55	4	2,131	170	7	41.78
W. H. Ponsford	29	48	4	2,122	266	7	48.22
R. M. Cowper	27	46	2	2,061	307	5	46.84

SOUTH AFRICA

	T	I	NO	R	HI	100s	Avge
B. Mitchell	42	80	9	3,471	189*	8	48.88
A. D. Nourse	34	62	7	2,960	231	9	53.81
H. W. Taylor	42	76	4	2,936	176	7	40.77
E. J. Barlow	30	57	2	2,516	201	6	45.74
T. L. Goddard	41	78	5	2,516	112	1	34.46
D. J. McGlew	34	64	6	2,440	255*	7	42.06
J. H. B. Waite	50	86	7	2,405	134	4	30.44
R. G. Pollock	23	41	4	2,256	274	7	60.97
A. W. Nourse	45	83	8	2,234	111	1	29.78
R. A. McLean	40	73	3	2,120	142	5	30.28

WEST INDIES

	T	I	NO	R	HI	100s	Avge
G. S. Sobers	93	160	21	8,032	365*	26	57.78
C. H. Lloyd	110	175	14	7,515	242*	19	46.67
R. B. Kanhai	79	137	6	6,227	256	15	47.53
I. V. A. Richards	82	122	8	6,220	291	20	54.56
C. G. Greenidge	71	117	13	5,033	223	12	48.39
E. D. Weekes	48	81	5	4,455	207	15	58.61
A. I. Kallicharran	66	109	10	4,399	187	12	44.43
R. C. Fredericks	59	109	7	4,334	169	8	42.49
F. M. M. Worrell	51	87	9	3,860	261	9	49.48
C. L. Walcott	44	74	7	3,798	220	15	56.68
D. L. Haynes	59	97	10	3,703	184	8	42.56
C. C. Hunte	44	78	6	3,245	260	8	45.06
B. F. Butcher	44	78	6	3,104	209*	7	43.11
H. A. Gomes	54	81	10	3,032	143	9	42.70
S. M. Nurse	29	54	1	2,523	258	6	47.60
G. A. Headley	22	40	4	2,190	270*	10	60.83
J. B. Stollmeyer	32	56	5	2,159	160	4	42.33
L. G. Rowe	30	49	2	2,047	302	7	43.55

NEW ZEALAND

	T	I	NO	R	HI	100s	Avge
B. E. Congdon	61	114	7	3,448	176	7	32.22
J. R. Reid	58	108	5	3,428	142	6	33.28
G. M. Turner	41	73	6	2,991	259	7	44.64
B. Sutcliffe	42	76	8	2,727	230*	5	40.10
M. G. Burgess	50	92	6	2,684	119*	5	31.20
J. G. Wright	49	86	4	2,635	141	5	32.13
J. V. Coney	49	79	14	2,591	174*	3	39.86
G. P. Howarth	47	83	5	2,531	147	6	32.44
R. J. Hadlee	66	106	13	2,397	103	1	25.77
G. T. Dowling	39	77	3	2,306	239	3	31.16

INDIA

	T	I	NO	R	HI	100s	Avge
S. M. Gavaskar	115	201	16	9,367	236*	32	50.63
G. R. Viswanath	91	155	10	6,080	222	14	41.93
D. B. Vengsarkar	85	140	16	4,985	159	11	40.20
M. Amarnath	56	95	9	3,852	138	10	44.79
P. R. Umrigar	59	94	8	3,631	223	12	42.22
V. L. Manjrekar	55	92	10	3,208	189*	7	39.12
Kapil Dev	77	115	10	3,132	126*	3	29.82
C. G. Borde	55	97	11	3,061	177*	5	35.59
Nawab of Pataudi jun.	46	83	3	2,793	203*	6	34.91
S. M. H. Kirmani	88	124	22	2,759	102	2	27.04
F. M. Engineer	46	87	3	2,611	121	2	31.08
Pankaj Roy	43	79	4	2,442	173	5	32.56
V. S. Hazare	30	52	6	2,192	164*	7	47.65
A. L. Wadekar	37	71	3	2,113	143	1	31.07
V. Mankad	44	72	5	2,109	231	5	31.47
C. P. S. Chauhan	40	68	2	2,084	97	0	31.57
M. L. Jaisimha	39	71	4	2,056	129	3	30.68
D. N. Sardesai	30	55	4	2,001	212	5	39.23

PAKISTAN

	T	I	NO	R	HI	100s	Avge
Javed Miandad	74	115	17	5,413	280*	14	55.23
Zaheer Abbas	78	124	11	5,062	274	12	44.79
Majid Khan	63	106	5	3,931	167	8	38.92
Hanif Mohammad	55	97	8	3,915	337	12	43.98
Mushtaq Mohammad	57	100	7	3,643	201	10	39.17
Asif Iqbal	58	99	7	3,575	175	11	38.85
Mudassar Nazar	58	90	7	3,445	231	8	41.50
Saeed Ahmed	41	78	4	2,991	172	5	40.41
Wasim Raja	57	92	14	2,821	125	4	36.16
Mohsin Khan	45	73	6	2,661	200	7	39.71
Sadiq Mohammad	41	74	2	2,579	166	5	35.81
Imran Khan	57	83	12	2,140	123	2	30.14
Imtiaz Ahmed	41	72	1	2,079	209	3	29.28

SRI LANKA: The highest aggregate is 1,191, average 38.41, by A. Ranatunga.

HIGHEST AVERAGES

(Qualification: 20 innings)

Avge		*T*	*I*	*NO*	*R*	*HI*	*100s*
99.94	D. G. Bradman (*A*)	52	80	10	6,996	334	29
60.97	R. G. Pollock (*SA*)	23	41	4	2,256	274	7
60.83	G. A. Headley (*WI*)	22	40	4	2,190	270*	10
60.73	H. Sutcliffe (*E*)	54	84	9	4,555	194	16
59.23	E. Paynter (*E*)	20	31	5	1,540	243	4
58.67	K. F. Barrington (*E*)	82	131	15	6,806	256	20
58.61	E. D. Weekes (*WI*)	48	81	5	4,455	207	15
58.45	W. R. Hammond (*E*)	85	140	16	7,249	336*	22
57.78	G. S. Sobers (*WI*)	93	160	21	8,032	365*	26
56.94	J. B. Hobbs (*E*)	61	102	7	5,410	211	15
56.68	C. L. Walcott (*WI*)	44	74	7	3,798	220	15
56.67	L. Hutton (*E*)	79	138	15	6,971	364	19
55.23	Javed Miandad (*P*)	74	115	17	5,413	280*	14
55.00	E. Tyldesley (*E*)	14	20	2	990	122	3
54.56	I. V. A. Richards (*WI*)	82	122	8	6,220	291	20
54.20	C. A. Davis (*WI*)	15	29	5	1,301	183	4
53.86	G. S. Chappell (*A*)	87	151	19	7,110	247*	24
53.85	J. F. Reid (*NZ*)	13	22	2	1,077	180	5
53.81	A. D. Nourse (*SA*)	34	62	7	2,960	231	9
52.09	A. R. Border (*A*)	81	143	24	6,199	196	18
51.62	J. Ryder (*A*)	20	32	5	1,394	201*	3
50.63	S. M. Gavaskar (*I*)	115	201	16	9,367	236*	32
50.06	D. C. S. Compton (*E*)	78	131	15	5,807	278	17

MOST HUNDREDS

Total		*E*	*A*	*SA*	*WI*	*NZ*	*I*	*P*	*SL*
32	S. M. Gavaskar (*India*)	4	7	—	13	2	—	5	1
29	D. G. Bradman (*Australia*)	19	4	2	0	4	—	—	
26	G. S. Sobers (*West Indies*)	10	4	0	—	1	8	3	—
24	G. S. Chappell (*Australia*)	9	—	0	5	3	1	6	0
22	W. R. Hammond (*England*)	—	9	6	1	4	2	—	
22	M. C. Cowdrey (*England*)	—	5	3	6	2	3	3	—
22	G. Boycott (*England*)	—	7	1	5	2	4	3	0
21	R. N. Harvey (*Australia*)	6	—	8	3	0	4	0	—
20	K. F. Barrington (*England*)	—	5	2	3	3	3	4	—
20	I. V. A. Richards (*West Indies*)	8	4	—	—	1	6	1	—

CARRYING BAT THROUGH TEST INNINGS

(Figures in brackets show side's total)

A. B. Tancred	26* (47)	South Africa v England at Cape Town . .	1888-89
J. E. Barrett	67* (176)	Australia v England at Lord's	1890
R. Abel	132* (307)	England v Australia at Sydney	1891-92
P. F. Warner	132* (237)	England v South Africa at Johannesburg .	1898-99
W. W. Armstrong	159* (309)	Australia v South Africa at Johannesburg	1902-03
J. W. Zulch	43* (103)	South Africa v England at Cape Town . .	1909-10
W. Bardsley	193* (383)	Australia v England at Lord's	1926
W. M. Woodfull	30* (66)‡	Australia v England at Brisbane	1928-29
W. M. Woodfull	73* (193)†	Australia v England at Adelaide	1932-33
W. A. Brown	206* (422)	Australia v England at Lord's	1938
L. Hutton	202* (344)	England v West Indies at The Oval	1950

L. Hutton	156* (272)	England v Australia at Adelaide	1950-51
Nazar Mohammad ..	124* (331)	Pakistan v India at Lucknow	1952-53
F. M. M. Worrell ..	191* (372)	West Indies v England at Nottingham ...	1957
T. L. Goddard	56* (99)	South Africa v Australia at Cape Town ..	1957-58
D. J. McGlew	127* (292)	South Africa v New Zealand at Durban ..	1961-62
C. C. Hunte	60* (131)	West Indies v Australia at Port-of-Spain .	1964-65
G. M. Turner	43* (131)	New Zealand v England at Lord's	1969
W. M. Lawry	49* (107)	Australia v India at Delhi	1969-70
W. M. Lawry	60* (116)†	Australia v England at Sydney	1970-71
G. M. Turner	223* (386)	New Zealand v West Indies at Kingston .	1971-72
I. R. Redpath	159* (346)	Australia v New Zealand at Auckland ...	1973-74
G. Boycott	99* (215)	England v Australia at Perth	1979-80
S. M. Gavaskar ...	127* (286)	India v Pakistan at Faisalabad	1982-83
Mudassar Nazar ...	152* (323)	Pakistan v India at Lahore	1982-83
S. Wettimuny	63* (144)	Sri Lanka v New Zealand at Christchurch	1982-83
D. C. Boon	58* (103)	Australia v New Zealand at Auckland ...	1985-86

† *One man absent.*   ‡ *Two men absent.*

Notes: G. M. Turner (223*) holds the record for the highest score by a player carrying his bat through a Test innings. He is also the youngest player to do so, being 22 years 63 days old when he first achieved the feat (1969).

Nazar Mohammad and Mudassar Nazar are the only instance of father and son carrying their bat through a Test innings.

D. L. Haynes (55 and 105) opened the batting and was last man out in each innings for West Indies v New Zealand at Dunedin, 1979-80.

FASTEST FIFTIES

Minutes

28	J. T. Brown	England v Australia at Melbourne	1894-95
29	S. A. Durani	India v England at Kanpur	1963-64
30	E. A. V. Williams .	West Indies v England at Bridgetown	1947-48
30	B. R. Taylor	New Zealand v West Indies at Auckland	1968-69
33	C. A. Roach	West Indies v England at The Oval	1933
34	C. R. R. Browne ..	West Indies v England at Georgetown	1929-30

The fastest fifties in terms of balls received (where recorded) are:

Balls

32	I. T. Botham	England v New Zealand at The Oval	1986
33	R. C. Fredericks ...	West Indies v Australia at Perth	1975-76
33	Kapil Dev	India v England at Manchester	1982
33	I. V. A. Richards ..	West Indies v England at St John's	1985-86

FASTEST HUNDREDS

Minutes

70	J. M. Gregory	Australia v South Africa at Johannesburg	1921-22
75	G. L. Jessop	England v Australia at The Oval	1902
78	R. Benaud	Australia v West Indies at Kingston	1954-55
80	J. H. Sinclair	South Africa v Australia at Cape Town	1902-03
81	I. V. A. Richards	West Indies v England at St John's	1985-86
86	B. R. Taylor	New Zealand v West Indies at Auckland	1968-69

The fastest hundreds in terms of balls received (where recorded) are:

Balls

56	I. V. A. Richards ..	West Indies v England at St John's	1985-86
67	J. M. Gregory	Australia v South Africa at Johannesburg	1921-22
71	R. C. Fredericks ...	West Indies v Australia at Perth	1975-76
74	Majid Khan	Pakistan v New Zealand at Karachi	1976-77
75	G. L. Jessop	England v Australia at The Oval	1902

FASTEST DOUBLE-HUNDREDS

Minutes

214	D. G. Bradman ...	Australia v England at Leeds	1930
223	S. J. McCabe	Australia v England at Nottingham	1938
226	V. T. Trumper ..	Australia v South Africa at Adelaide	1910-11
234	D. G. Bradman ...	Australia v England at Lord's	1930
240	W. R. Hammond ..	England v New Zealand at Auckland	1932-33
241	S. E. Gregory ...	Australia v England at Sydney	1894-95
245	D. C. S. Compton .	England v Pakistan at Nottingham	1954

FASTEST TRIPLE-HUNDREDS

Minutes

288	W. R. Hammond ..	England v New Zealand at Auckland	1932-33
336	D. G. Bradman ...	Australia v England at Leeds	1930

MOST RUNS IN A DAY BY A BATSMAN

309	D. G. Bradman	Australia v England at Leeds	1930
295	W. R. Hammond	England v New Zealand at Auckland	1932-33
273	D. C. S. Compton ...	England v Pakistan at Nottingham	1954
271	D. G. Bradman	Australia v England at Leeds	1934

SLOWEST INDIVIDUAL BATTING

2* in 80 minutes	C. E. H. Croft, West Indies v Australia at Brisbane	1979-80
3* in 100 minutes	J. T. Murray, England v Australia at Sydney	1962-63
5 in 102 minutes	Nawab of Pataudi jun, India v England at Bombay	1972-73
7 in 123 minutes	G. Miller, England v Australia at Melbourne	1978-79
9 in 125 minutes	T. W. Jarvis, New Zealand v India at Madras	1964-65
10* in 133 minutes	T. G. Evans, England v Australia at Adelaide	1946-47
16 in 188 minutes	G. M. Ritchie, Australia v New Zealand at Sydney	1985-86
18 in 194 minutes	W. R. Playle, New Zealand v England at Leeds	1958
19 in 217 minutes	M. D. Crowe, New Zealand v Sri Lanka at Colombo (SSC)	1983-84
28* in 250 minutes	J. W. Burke, Australia v England at Brisbane	1958-59
31 in 264 minutes	K. D. Mackay, Australia v England at Lord's	1956
35 in 332 minutes	C. J. Tavaré, England v India at Madras	1981-82
55 in 336 minutes	B. A. Edgar, New Zealand v Australia at Wellington ...	1981-82
57 in 346 minutes	G. S. Camacho, West Indies v England at Bridgetown ..	1967-68
58 in 367 minutes	Ijaz Butt, Pakistan v Australia at Karachi	1959-60
60 in 390 minutes	D. N. Sardesai, India v West Indies at Bridgetown	1961-62
68 in 458 minutes	T. E. Bailey, England v Australia at Brisbane	1958-59
99 in 505 minutes	M. L. Jaisimha, India v Pakistan at Kanpur	1960-61
105 in 575 minutes	D. J. McGlew, South Africa v Australia at Durban	1957-58
114 in 591 minutes	Mudassar Nazar, Pakistan v England at Lahore	1977-78
158 in 648 minutes	C. T. Radley, England v New Zealand at Auckland	1977-78
172 in 708 minutes	S. M. Gavaskar, India v England at Bangalore	1981-82
337 in 970 minutes	Hanif Mohammad, Pakistan v West Indies at Bridgetown	1957-58

SLOWEST HUNDREDS

557 minutes	Mudassar Nazar, Pakistan v England at Lahore	1977-78
545 minutes	D. J. McGlew, South Africa v Australia at Durban	1957-58
488 minutes	P. E. Richardson, England v South Africa at Johannesburg	1956-57

Notes: The slowest hundred for any Test in England is 458 minutes (329 balls) by K. W. R. Fletcher, England v Pakistan, The Oval, 1974.

The slowest double-hundred in a Test took 652 minutes (426 balls): A. D. Gaekwad, India v Pakistan at Jullundur, 1983-84. It is also the slowest-ever first-class double-hundred.

HIGHEST WICKET PARTNERSHIPS

413 for 1st	V. Mankad (231) and Pankaj Roy (173) for India v New Zealand at Madras	1955-56
451 for 2nd	W. H. Ponsford (266) and D. G. Bradman (244) for Australia v England at The Oval	1934
451 for 3rd	Mudassar Nazar (231) and Javed Miandad (280*) for Pakistan v India at Hyderabad	1982-83
411 for 4th	P. B. H. May (285*) and M. C. Cowdrey (154) for England v West Indies at Birmingham	1957
405 for 5th	S. G. Barnes (234) and D. G. Bradman (234) for Australia v England at Sydney	1946-47
346 for 6th	J. H. W. Fingleton (136) and D. G. Bradman (270) for Australia v England at Melbourne	1936-37
347 for 7th	D. St E. Atkinson (219) and C. C. Depeiza (122) for West Indies v Australia at Bridgetown	1954-55
246 for 8th	L. E. G. Ames (137) and G. O. Allen (122) for England v New Zealand at Lord's	1931
190 for 9th	Asif Iqbal (146) and Intikhab Alam (51) for Pakistan v England at The Oval	1967
151 for 10th	B. F. Hastings (110) and R. O. Collinge (68*) for New Zealand v Pakistan at Auckland	1972-73

BOWLING RECORDS

MOST WICKETS IN AN INNINGS

10-53	J. C. Laker	England v Australia at Manchester	1956
9-28	G. A. Lohmann ...	England v South Africa at Johannesburg	1895-96
9-37	J. C. Laker	England v Australia at Manchester	1956
9-52	R. J. Hadlee	New Zealand v Australia at Brisbane	1985-86
9-69	J. M. Patel	India v Australia at Kanpur	1959-60
9-83	Kapil Dev	India v West Indies at Ahmedabad	1983-84
9-86	Sarfraz Nawaz	Pakistan v Australia at Melbourne	1978-79
9-95	J. M. Noreiga	West Indies v India at Port-of-Spain	1970-71
9-102	S. P. Gupte	India v West Indies at Kanpur	1958-59
9-103	S. F. Barnes	England v South Africa at Johannesburg	1913-14
9-113	H. J. Tayfield	South Africa v England at Johannesburg	1956-57
9-121	A. A. Mailey	Australia v England at Melbourne	1920-21
8-7	G. A. Lohmann ...	England v South Africa at Port Elizabeth	1895-96
8-11	J. Briggs	England v South Africa at Cape Town	1888-89
8-29	S. F. Barnes	England v South Africa at The Oval	1912
8-29	C. E. H. Croft	West Indies v Pakistan at Port-of-Spain	1976-77
8-31	F. Laver	Australia v England at Manchester	1909
8-31	F. S. Trueman	England v India at Manchester	1952
8-34	I. T. Botham	England v Pakistan at Lord's	1978
8-35	G. A. Lohmann ...	England v Australia at Sydney	1886-87
8-38	L. R. Gibbs	West Indies v India at Bridgetown	1961-62
8-43†	A. E. Trott	Australia v England at Adelaide	1894-95
8-43	H. Verity	England v Australia at Lord's	1934
8-43	R. G. D. Willis ...	England v Australia at Leeds	1981
8-51	D. L. Underwood ..	England v Pakistan at Lord's	1974

8-52	V. Mankad	India v Pakistan at Delhi	1952-53
8-53	G. B. Lawrence . . .	South Africa v New Zealand at Johannesburg .	1961-62
8-53†	R. A. L. Massie . . .	Australia v England at Lord's	1972
8-55	V. Mankad	India v England at Madras	1951-52
8-56	S. F. Barnes	England v South Africa at Johannesburg	1913-14
8-58	G. A. Lohmann . . .	England v Australia at Sydney	1891-92
8-58	Imran Khan	Pakistan v Sri Lanka at Lahore	1981-82
8-59	C. Blythe	England v South Africa at Leeds	1907
8-59	A. A. Mallett	Australia v Pakistan at Adelaide	1972-73
8-60	Imran Khan	Pakistan v India at Karachi	1982-83
8-65	H. Trumble	Australia v England at The Oval	1902
8-68	W. Rhodes	England v Australia at Melbourne	1903-04
8-69	H. J. Tayfield	South Africa v England at Durban	1956-57
8-69	Sikander Bakht . . .	Pakistan v India at Delhi	1979-80
8-70	S. J. Snooke	South Africa v England at Johannesburg	1905-06
8-71	G. D. McKenzie . . .	Australia v West Indies at Melbourne	1968-69
8-72	S. Venkataraghavan	India v New Zealand at Delhi	1964-65
8-76	E. A. S. Prasanna .	India v New Zealand at Auckland	1975-76
8-79	B. S. Chandrasekhar	India v England at Delhi	1972-73
8-81	L. C. Braund	England v Australia at Melbourne	1903-04
8-83	J. R. Ratnayeke . . .	Sri Lanka v Pakistan at Sialkot	1985-86
8-84†	R. A. L. Massie . . .	Australia v England at Lord's	1972
8-85	Kapil Dev	India v Pakistan at Lahore	1982-83
8-86	A. W. Greig	England v West Indies at Port-of-Spain	1973-74
8-92	M. A. Holding	West Indies v England at The Oval	1976
8-94	T. Richardson	England v Australia at Sydney	1897-98
8-103	I. T. Botham	England v West Indies at Lord's	1984
8-104†	A. L. Valentine . . .	West Indies v England at Manchester	1950
8-106	Kapil Dev	India v Australia at Adelaide	1985-86
8-107	B. J. T. Bosanquet .	England v Australia at Nottingham	1905
8-112	G. F. Lawson	Australia v West Indies at Adelaide	1984-85
8-126	J. C. White	England v Australia at Adelaide	1928-29
8-141	C. J. McDermott . .	Australia v England at Manchester	1985
8-143	M. H. N. Walker . .	Australia v England at Melbourne	1974-75

† *On Test début.*

MOST WICKETS IN A MATCH

19-90	J. C. Laker	England v Australia at Manchester	1956
17-159	S. F. Barnes	England v South Africa at Johannesburg	1913-14
16-137†	R. A. L. Massie . . .	Australia v England at Lord's	1972
15-28	J. Briggs	England v South Africa at Cape Town	1888-89
15-45	G. A. Lohmann . . .	England v South Africa at Port Elizabeth	1895-96
15-99	C. Blythe	England v South Africa at Leeds	1907
15-104	H. Verity	England v Australia at Lord's	1934
15-123	R. J. Hadlee	New Zealand v Australia at Brisbane	1985-86
15-124	W. Rhodes	England v Australia at Melbourne	1903-04
14-90	F. R. Spofforth	Australia v England at The Oval	1882
14-99	A. V. Bedser	England v Australia at Nottingham	1953
14-102	W. Bates	England v Australia at Melbourne	1882-83
14-116	Imran Khan	Pakistan v Sri Lanka at Lahore	1981-82
14-124	J. M. Patel	India v Australia at Kanpur	1959-60
14-144	S. F. Barnes	England v South Africa at Durban	1913-14
14-149	M. A. Holding	West Indies v England at The Oval	1976
14-199	C. V. Grimmett . . .	Australia v South Africa at Adelaide	1931-32

† *On Test début.*

Notes: The best for South Africa is 13-165 by H. J. Tayfield against Australia at Melbourne, 1952-53.

The best for Sri Lanka is 9-125 by R. J. Ratnayake against India at Colombo (PSO), 1985-86.

MOST WICKETS IN A SERIES

	T	R	W	Avge		
S. F. Barnes	4	536	49	10.93	England v South Africa.	1913-14
J. C. Laker	5	442	46	9.60	England v Australia ...	1956
C. V. Grimmett	5	642	44	14.59	Australia v South Africa	1935-36
T. M. Alderman	6	893	42	21.26	Australia v England ...	1981
R. M. Hogg	6	527	41	12.85	Australia v England ...	1978-79
Imran Khan	6	558	40	13.95	Pakistan v India	1982-83
A. V. Bedser	5	682	39	17.48	England v Australia ...	1953
D. K. Lillee	6	870	39	22.30	Australia v England ...	1981
M. W. Tate	5	881	38	23.18	England v Australia ...	1924-25
W. J. Whitty	5	632	37	17.08	Australia v South Africa	1910-11
H. J. Tayfield	5	636	37	17.18	South Africa v England.	1956-57
A. E. E. Vogler	5	783	36	21.75	South Africa v England.	1909-10
A. A. Mailey	5	946	36	26.27	Australia v England ...	1920-21
G. A. Lohmann	3	203	35	5.80	England v South Africa.	1895-96
B. S. Chandrasekhar	5	662	35	18.91	India v England	1972-73

MOST WICKETS IN A CAREER

(Qualification: 75 wickets)

ENGLAND

	T	Balls	R	W	Avge	5 W/i	10 W/m
I. T. Botham	85	19,356	9,663	357	27.06	26	4
R. G. D. Willis	90	17,357	8,190	325	25.20	16	—
F. S. Trueman	67	15,178	6,625	307	21.57	17	3
D. L. Underwood	86	21,862	7,674	297	25.83	17	6
J. B. Statham	70	16,056	6,261	252	24.84	9	1
A. V. Bedser	51	15,918	5,876	236	24.89	15	5
J. A. Snow	49	12,021	5,387	202	26.66	8	1
J. C. Laker	46	12,027	4,101	193	21.24	9	3
S. F. Barnes	27	7,873	3,106	189	16.43	24	7
G. A. R. Lock	49	13,147	4,451	174	25.58	9	3
M. W. Tate	39	12,523	4,055	155	26.16	7	1
F. J. Titmus	53	15,118	4,931	153	32.22	7	—
H. Verity	40	11,173	3,510	144	24.37	5	2
C. M. Old	46	8,858	4,020	143	28.11	4	—
A. W. Greig	58	9,802	4,541	141	32.20	6	2
T. E. Bailey	61	9,712	3,856	132	29.21	5	1
W. Rhodes	58	8,231	3,425	127	26.96	6	1
D. A. Allen	39	11,297	3,779	122	30.97	4	—
R. Illingworth	61	11,934	3,807	122	31.20	3	—
J. Briggs	33	5,332	2,094	118	17.74	9	4
G. G. Arnold	34	7,650	3,254	115	28.29	6	—
G. A. Lohmann	18	3,821	1,205	112	10.75	9	5
D. V. P. Wright	34	8,135	4,224	108	39.11	6	1
P. H. Edmonds	41	9,903	3,516	106	33.16	2	—
R. Peel	20	5,216	1,715	102	16.81	6	2
J. H. Wardle	28	6,597	2,080	102	20.39	5	1
C. Blythe	19	4,546	1,863	100	18.63	9	4
W. Voce	27	6,360	2,733	98	27.88	3	2
J. E. Emburey	37	8,331	2,970	97	30.61	4	—
T. Richardson	14	4,497	2,220	88	25.22	11	4
M. Hendrick	30	6,208	2,248	87	25.83	—	—
W. R. Hammond	85	7,969	3,138	83	37.80	2	—
F. E. Woolley	64	6,495	2,815	83	33.91	4	1

	T	Balls	R	W	Avge	5 W/i	10 W/m
G. O. Allen	25	4,386	2,379	81	29.37	5	1
D. J. Brown	26	5,098	2,237	79	28.31	2	—
H. Larwood	21	4,969	2,212	78	28.35	4	1
F. H. Tyson	17	3,452	1,411	76	18.56	4	1

AUSTRALIA

	T	Balls	R	W	Avge	5 W/i	10 W/m
D. K. Lillee	70	18,467	8,493	355	23.92	23	7
R. Benaud	63	19,108	6,704	248	27.03	16	1
G. D. McKenzie	60	17,681	7,328	246	29.78	16	3
R. R. Lindwall	61	13,650	5,251	228	23.03	12	—
C. V. Grimmett	37	14,513	5,231	216	24.21	21	7
J. R. Thomson	51	10,535	5,601	200	28.00	8	—
A. K. Davidson	44	11,587	3,819	186	20.53	14	2
K. R. Miller	55	10,461	3,906	170	22.97	7	1
W. A. Johnston	40	11,048	3,826	160	23.91	7	—
G. F. Lawson	36	8,405	4,250	145	29.31	10	2
W. J. O'Reilly	27	10,024	3,254	144	22.59	11	3
H. Trumble	32	8,099	3,072	141	21.78	9	3
M. H. N. Walker	34	10,094	3,792	138	27.47	6	—
A. A. Mallett	38	9,990	3,940	132	29.84	6	1
B. Yardley	33	8,909	3,986	126	31.63	6	1
R. M. Hogg	38	7,633	3,503	123	28.47	6	2
M. A. Noble	42	7,159	3,025	121	25.00	9	2
I. W. Johnson	45	8,780	3,182	109	29.19	3	—
G. Giffen	31	6,391	2,791	103	27.09	7	1
A. N. Connolly	29	7,818	2,981	102	29.22	4	—
C. T. B. Turner	17	5,179	1,670	101	16.53	11	2
A. A. Mailey	21	6,117	3,358	99	33.91	6	2
F. R. Spofforth	18	4,185	1,731	94	18.41	7	4
J. W. Gleeson	29	8,857	3,367	93	36.20	3	—
N. J. N. Hawke	27	6,974	2,677	91	29.41	6	1
A. Cotter	21	4,633	2,549	89	28.64	7	—
W. W. Armstrong	50	8,022	2,923	87	33.59	3	—
J. M. Gregory	24	5,582	2,648	85	31.15	4	—
T. M. Alderman	22	5,373	2,597	79	32.87	5	—
J. V. Saunders	14	3,565	1,796	79	22.73	6	—
G. Dymock	21	5,545	2,116	78	27.12	5	1
G. E. Palmer	17	4,517	1,678	78	21.51	6	2

SOUTH AFRICA

	T	Balls	R	W	Avge	5 W/i	10 W/m
H. J. Tayfield	37	13,568	4,405	170	25.91	14	2
T. L. Goddard	41	11,736	3,226	123	26.22	5	—
P. M. Pollock	28	6,522	2,806	116	24.18	9	1
N. A. T. Adcock	26	6,391	2,195	104	21.10	5	—
C. L. Vincent	25	5,851	2,631	84	31.32	3	—
G. A. Faulkner	25	4,227	2,180	82	26.58	4	—

WEST INDIES

	T	Balls	R	W	Avge	5 W/i	10 W/m
L. R. Gibbs	79	27,115	8,989	309	29.09	18	2
M. A. Holding	59	12,458	5,799	249	23.28	13	2
J. Garner	56	12,707	5,228	247	21.16	6	—
G. S. Sobers	93	21,599	7,999	235	34.03	6	—
M. D. Marshall	45	9,880	4,639	215	21.57	13	2

	T	Balls	R	W	Avge	5 W/i	10 W/m
A. M. E. Roberts	47	11,136	5,174	202	25.61	11	2
W. W. Hall	48	10,421	5,066	192	26.38	9	1
S. Ramadhin	43	13,939	4,579	158	28.98	10	1
A. L. Valentine	36	12,953	4,215	139	30.32	8	2
C. E. H. Croft	27	6,165	2,913	125	23.30	3	—
V. A. Holder	40	9,095	3,627	109	33.27	3	—
C. C. Griffith	28	5,631	2,683	94	28.54	5	—

NEW ZEALAND

	T	Balls	R	W	Avge	5 W/i	10 W/m
R. J. Hadlee	66	17,179	7,520	334	22.51	27	7
B. L. Cairns	43	10,628	4,280	130	32.92	6	1
R. O. Collinge	35	7,689	3,392	116	29.24	3	—
B. R. Taylor	30	6,334	2,953	111	26.60	4	—
R. C. Motz	32	7,034	3,148	100	31.48	5	—
E. J. Chatfield	29	6,834	2,719	88	30.89	3	1
H. J. Howarth	30	8,833	3,178	86	36.95	2	—
J. R. Reid	58	7,725	2,835	85	33.35	1	—

INDIA

	T	Balls	R	W	Avge	5 W/i	10 W/m
Kapil Dev	77	16,778	8,360	291	28.72	19	2
B. S. Bedi	67	21,364	7,637	266	28.71	14	1
B. S. Chandrasekhar ..	58	15,963	7,199	242	29.74	16	2
E. A. S. Prasanna	49	14,353	5,742	189	30.38	10	2
V. Mankad	44	14,686	5,236	162	32.32	8	2
S. Venkataraghavan ..	57	14,877	5,634	156	36.11	3	1
S. P. Gupte	36	11,284	4,403	149	29.55	12	1
D. R. Doshi	33	9,322	3,502	114	30.71	6	—
K. D. Ghavri	39	7,042	3,656	109	33.54	4	—
R. J. Shastri	43	10,129	3,764	98	38.40	2	—
R. G. Nadkarni	41	9,165	2,559	88	29.07	4	1
S. A. Durani	29	6,446	2,657	75	35.42	3	1
N. S. Yadav	26	6,197	2,670	75	35.60	2	—

PAKISTAN

	T	Balls	R	W	Avge	5 W/i	10 W/m
Imran Khan	57	13,971	5,857	264	22.18	17	4
Sarfraz Nawaz	55	13,927	5,798	177	32.75	4	1
Fazal Mahmood	34	9,834	3,434	139	24.70	13	4
Iqbal Qasim	41	10,786	3,994	137	29.15	5	2
Abdul Qadir	38	9,785	4,455	128	34.80	9	2
Intikhab Alam	47	10,474	4,494	125	35.95	5	2
Mushtaq Mohammad .	57	5,260	2,309	79	29.22	3	—

SRI LANKA: The highest aggregate is 58 wickets, average 35.53, by A. L. F. de Mel.

WICKET WITH FIRST BALL IN TEST CRICKET

	Batsman dismissed			
A. Coningham	A. C. MacLaren	A v E	Melbourne	1894-95
W. M. Bradley	F. Laver	E v A	Manchester	1899
E. G. Arnold	V. T. Trumper	E v A	Sydney	1903-04
G. G. Macaulay	G. A. L. Hearne	E v SA	Cape Town	1922-23
M. W. Tate	M. J. Susskind	E v SA	Birmingham	1924

Batsman dismissed

M. Henderson	E. W. Dawson	NZ v E ..... Christchurch	1929-30
H. D. Smith	E. Paynter	NZ v E ..... Christchurch	1932-33
T. F. Johnson	W. W. Keeton	WI v E ..... The Oval	1939
R. Howorth	D. V. Dyer	E v SA ..... The Oval	1947
Intikhab Alam	C. C. McDonald	P v A ...... Karachi	1959-60

HAT-TRICKS

F. R. Spofforth	Australia v England at Melbourne	1878-79
W. Bates	England v Australia at Melbourne	1882-83
J. Briggs	England v Australia at Sydney	1891-92
G. A. Lohmann	England v South Africa at Port Elizabeth	1895-96
J. T. Hearne	England v Australia at Leeds	1899
H. Trumble	Australia v England at Melbourne	1901-02
H. Trumble	Australia v England at Melbourne	1903-04
T. J. Matthews† ...	⎫ Australia v South Africa at Manchester	1912
T. J. Matthews	⎭	
M. J. C. Allom‡ ...	England v New Zealand at Christchurch	1929-30
T. W. Goddard	England v South Africa at Johannesburg	1938-39
P. J. Loader	England v West Indies at Leeds	1957
L. F. Kline	Australia v South Africa at Cape Town	1957-58
W. W. Hall	West Indies v Pakistan at Lahore	1958-59
G. M. Griffin	South Africa v England at Lord's	1960
L. R. Gibbs	West Indies v Australia at Adelaide	1960-61
P. J. Petherick‡ ...	New Zealand v Pakistan at Lahore	1976-77

† T. J. Matthews did the hat-trick in each innings of the same match.
‡ On Test début.

MOST BALLS BOWLED IN A TEST

S. Ramadhin (West Indies) sent down 774 balls in 129 overs against England at Birmingham, 1957. It was the most delivered by any bowler in a Test, beating H. Verity's 766 for England against South Africa at Durban, 1938-39. In this match Ramadhin also bowled the most balls (588) in any single first-class innings, including Tests.

It should be noted that six balls were bowled to the over in the Australia v England Test series of 1928-29 and 1932-33, when the eight-ball over was otherwise in force in Australia.

ALL-ROUND RECORDS

100 RUNS AND FIVE WICKETS IN AN INNINGS

England

A. W. Greig	148	6-164	v West Indies	Bridgetown	1973-74
I. T. Botham	103	5-73	v New Zealand	Christchurch	1977-78
I. T. Botham	108	8-34	v Pakistan	Lord's	1978
I. T. Botham	114	6-58 ⎱ 7-48 ⎰	v India	Bombay	1979-80
I. T. Botham	149*	6-95	v Australia	Leeds	1981
I. T. Botham	138	5-59	v New Zealand	Wellington	1983-84

Australia

C. Kelleway	114	5-33	v South Africa	Manchester	1912
J. M. Gregory	100	7-69	v England	Melbourne	1920-21
K. R. Miller	109	6-107	v West Indies	Kingston	1954-55
R. Benaud	100	5-84	v South Africa	Johannesburg	1957-58

South Africa
J. H. Sinclair	106	6-26	v England	Cape Town	1898-99
G. A. Faulkner	123	5-120	v England	Johannesburg	1909-10

West Indies
D. St E. Atkinson	219	5-56	v Australia	Bridgetown	1954-55
O. G. Smith	100	5-90	v India	Delhi	1958-59
G. S. Sobers	104	5-63	v India	Kingston	1961-62
G. S. Sobers	174	5-41	v England	Leeds	1966

New Zealand
B. R. Taylor†	105	5-86	v India	Calcutta	1964-65

India
V. Mankad	184	5-196	v England	Lord's	1952
P. R. Umrigar	172*	5-107	v West Indies	Port-of-Spain	1961-62

Pakistan
Mushtaq Mohammad	201	5-49	v New Zealand	Dunedin	1972-73
Mushtaq Mohammad	121	5-28	v West Indies	Port-of-Spain	1976-77
Imran Khan	117	6-98 } 5-82 }	v India	Faisalabad	1982-83

† *On début.*

100 RUNS AND FIVE DISMISSALS IN AN INNINGS

D. T. Lindsay	182	6ct	SA v A	Johannesburg	1966-67
I. D. S. Smith	113*	4ct, 1st	NZ v E	Auckland	1983-84
S. A. R. Silva	111	5ct	SL v I	Colombo (PSO)....	1985-86

100 RUNS AND TEN WICKETS IN A TEST

A. K. Davidson	44 80	5-135 } 6-87 }	A v WI	Brisbane	1960-61
I. T. Botham	114	6-58 } 7-48 }	E v I	Bombay	1979-80
Imran Khan	117	6-98 } 5-82 }	P v I	Faisalabad	1982-83

1,000 RUNS AND 100 WICKETS IN A CAREER

	Tests	Runs	Wkts	Tests for Double
England				
T. E. Bailey	61	2,290	132	47
I. T. Botham	85	4,636	357	21
A. W. Greig	58	3,599	141	37
R. Illingworth	61	1,836	122	47
W. Rhodes	58	2,325	127	44
M. W. Tate	39	1,198	155	33
F. J. Titmus	53	1,449	153	40
Australia				
R. Benaud	63	2,201	248	32
A. K. Davidson	44	1,328	186	34
G. Giffen	31	1,238	103	30
I. W. Johnson	45	1,000	109	45
R. R. Lindwall	61	1,502	228	38
K. R. Miller	55	2,958	170	33
M. A. Noble	42	1,997	121	27

	Tests	Runs	Wkts	Tests for Double
South Africa				
T. L. Goddard	41	2,516	123	36
West Indies				
G. S. Sobers	93	8,032	235	48
New Zealand				
R. J. Hadlee	66	2,397	334	28
India				
Kapil Dev	77	3,132	291	25
V. Mankad	44	2,109	162	23
Pakistan				
Imran Khan	57	2,140	264	30
Intikhab Alam	47	1,493	125	41
Sarfraz Nawaz	55	1,045	177	55

1,000 RUNS, 100 WICKETS AND 100 CATCHES

	Tests	Runs	Wkts	Ct
G. S. Sobers	93	8,032	235	109

WICKET-KEEPING RECORDS

Most Dismissals in an Innings

7 (all ct)	Wasim Bari	Pakistan v New Zealand at Auckland ...	1978-79
7 (all ct)	R. W. Taylor	England v India at Bombay	1979-80
6 (all ct)	A. T. W. Grout ...	Australia v South Africa at Johannesburg	1957-58
6 (5ct, 1st)	S. M. H. Kirmani .	India v New Zealand at Christchurch ...	1975-76
6 (all ct)	D. T. Lindsay	South Africa v Australia at Johannesburg	1966-67
6 (all ct)	R. W. Marsh	Australia v England at Brisbane	1982-83
6 (all ct)	J. T. Murray	England v India at Lord's	1967
6 (all ct)	S. A. R. Silva	Sri Lanka v India at Colombo (SSC)	1985-86

Most Dismissals in One Test

10 (all ct)	R. W. Taylor	England v India at Bombay	1979-80
9 (8ct, 1st)	G. R. A. Langley ..	Australia v England at Lord's	1956
9 (all ct)	R. W. Marsh	Australia v England at Brisbane	1982-83
9 (all ct)	D. A. Murray	West Indies v Australia at Melbourne ...	1981-82
9 (all ct)	S. A. R. Silva	Sri Lanka v India at Colombo (SSC)	1985-86
9 (8ct, 1st)	S. A. R. Silva	Sri Lanka v India at Colombo (PSO)	1985-86
8 (6ct, 2st)	L. E. G. Ames	England v West Indies at The Oval	1933
8 (6ct, 2st)	A. T. W. Grout ...	Australia v Pakistan at Lahore	1959-60
8 (all ct)	A. T. W. Grout ...	Australia v England at Lord's	1961
8 (all ct)	J. J. Kelly	Australia v England at Sydney	1901-02
8 (all ct)	G. R. A. Langley ..	Australia v West Indies at Kingston	1954-55
8 (all ct)	W. K. Lees	New Zealand v Sri Lanka at Wellington .	1982-83
8 (all ct)	D. T. Lindsay	South Africa v Australia at Johannesburg	1966-67
8 (all ct)	R. W. Marsh	Australia v West Indies at Melbourne ...	1975-76
8 (all ct)	R. W. Marsh	Australia v New Zealand at Christchurch	1976-77
8 (7ct, 1st)	R. W. Marsh	Australia v India at Sydney	1980-81
8 (all ct)	R. W. Marsh	Australia v England at Adelaide	1982-83
8 (all ct)	J. M. Parks	England v New Zealand at Christchurch .	1965-66
8 (7ct, 1st)	H. B. Taber	Australia v South Africa at Johannesburg	1966-67
8 (all ct)	Wasim Bari	Pakistan v England at Leeds	1971

Note: S. A. R. Silva made 18 dismissals in two successive Tests.

Most Dismissals in a Series

(Played in 5 Tests unless otherwise stated)

28 (all ct)	R. W. Marsh	Australia v England	1982-83
26 (all ct)	R. W. Marsh	Australia v West Indies (6 Tests)	1975-76
26 (23ct, 3st)	J. H. B. Waite	South Africa v New Zealand	1961-62
24 (21ct, 3st)	A. P. E. Knott	England v Australia (6 Tests)	1970-71
24 (all ct)	D. T. Lindsay	South Africa v Australia	1966-67
24 (22ct, 2st)	D. L. Murray	West Indies v England	1963
23 (22ct, 1st)	F. C. M. Alexander .	West Indies v England	1959-60
23 (21ct, 2st)	A. E. Dick	New Zealand v South Africa	1961-62
23 (20ct, 3st)	A. T. W. Grout ...	Australia v West Indies	1960-61
23 (22ct, 1st)	A. P. E. Knott	England v Australia (6 Tests)	1974-75
23 (21ct, 2st)	R. W. Marsh	Australia v England	1972
23 (all ct)	R. W. Marsh	Australia v England (6 Tests)	1981
23 (16ct, 7st)	J. H. B. Waite	South Africa v New Zealand	1953-54
22 (all ct)	S. J. Rixon	Australia v India	1977-78
22 (21ct, 1st)	S. A. R. Silva	Sri Lanka v India (3 Tests)	1985-86
21 (20ct, 1st)	A. T. W. Grout ...	Australia v England	1961
21 (16ct, 5st)	G. R. A. Langley ..	Australia v West Indies	1951-52
21 (all ct)	R. W. Marsh	Australia v Pakistan	1983-84
21 (13ct, 8st)	A. A. Saggers	Australia v South Africa	1949-50
21 (15ct, 6st)	H. Strudwick	England v South Africa	1913-14
20 (19ct, 1st)	P. R. Downton	England v Australia (6 Tests)	1985
20 (19ct, 1st)	P. J. L. Dujon	West Indies v Australia	1983-84
20 (18ct, 2st)	T. G. Evans	England v South Africa	1956-57
20 (17ct, 3st)	A. T. W. Grout ...	Australia v England	1958-59
20 (16ct, 4st)	G. R. A. Langley ..	Australia v West Indies (4 Tests)	1954-55
20 (19ct, 1st)	H. B. Taber	Australia v South Africa	1966-67
20 (16ct, 4st)	D. Tallon	Australia v England	1946-47
20 (18ct, 2st)	R. W. Taylor	England v Australia (6 Tests)	1978-79

Most Dismissals in a Career

	T	*Ct*	*St*	*Total*
R. W. Marsh (Australia)	96	343	12	355
A. P. E. Knott (England)	95	250	19	269
Wasim Bari (Pakistan)	81	201	27	228
T. G. Evans (England)	91	173	46	219
S. M. H. Kirmani (India)	88	160	38	198
D. L. Murray (West Indies)	62	181	8	189
A. T. W. Grout (Australia)	51	163	24	187
R. W. Taylor (England)	57	167	7	174
J. H. B. Waite (South Africa)	50	124	17	141
W. A. Oldfield (Australia)	54	78	52	130
P. J. L. Dujon (West Indies)	37	124	2	126
J. M. Parks (England)	46	103	11	114

Notes: The records for P. J. L. Dujon and J. M. Parks each include two catches taken when not keeping wicket in two and three Tests respectively.

I. D. S. Smith (92ct, 6st) made most dismissals for New Zealand and S. A. R. Silva (30ct, 1st) holds the record for Sri Lanka.

FIELDING RECORDS

(Excluding wicket-keepers)

Most Catches in an Innings

5	V. Y. Richardson	Australia v South Africa at Durban	1935-36
5	Yajurvindra Singh	India v England at Bangalore	1976-77

Most Catches in One Test

7	G. S. Chappell	Australia v England at Perth	1974-75
7	Yajurvindra Singh	India v England at Bangalore	1976-77
6	A. Shrewsbury	England v Australia at Sydney	1887-88
6	A. E. E. Vogler	South Africa v England at Durban	1909-10
6	F. E. Woolley	England v Australia at Sydney	1911-12
6	J. M. Gregory	Australia v England at Sydney	1920-21
6	B. Mitchell	South Africa v Australia at Melbourne	1931-32
6	V. Y. Richardson	Australia v South Africa at Durban	1935-36
6	R. N. Harvey	Australia v England at Sydney	1962-63
6	M. C. Cowdrey	England v West Indies at Lord's	1963
6	E. D. Solkar	India v West Indies at Port-of-Spain	1970-71
6	G. S. Sobers	West Indies v England at Lord's	1973
6	I. M. Chappell	Australia v New Zealand at Adelaide	1973-74
6	A. W. Greig	England v Pakistan at Leeds..................	1974
6	D. F. Whatmore	Australia v India at Kanpur	1979-80
6	A. J. Lamb	England v New Zealand at Lord's	1983

Most Catches in a Series

15	J. M. Gregory	Australia v England	1920-21
14	G. S. Chappell	Australia v England (6 Tests)	1974-75
13	R. B. Simpson	Australia v South Africa	1957-58
13	R. B. Simpson	Australia v West Indies	1960-61

Most Catches in a Career

G. S. Chappell (Australia) ...	122 in	87 matches
M. C. Cowdrey (England) ...	120 in	114 matches
R. B. Simpson (Australia) ...	110 in	62 matches
W. R. Hammond (England) .	110 in	85 matches
G. S. Sobers (West Indies) ..	109 in	93 matches
I. M. Chappell (Australia) ...	105 in	75 matches
S. M. Gavaskar (India)	100 in	115 matches

TEAM RECORDS

HIGHEST INNINGS TOTALS

903-7 dec.	England v Australia at The Oval	1938
849	England v West Indies at Kingston	1929-30
790-3 dec.	West Indies v Pakistan at Kingston	1957-58
758-8 dec.	Australia v West Indies at Kingston	1954-55
729-6 dec.	Australia v England at Lord's	1930
701	Australia v England at The Oval	1934
695	Australia v England at The Oval	1930
687-8 dec.	West Indies v England at The Oval	1976
681-8 dec.	West Indies v England at Port-of-Spain	1953-54
674-6	Pakistan v India at Faisalabad	1984-85
674	Australia v India at Adelaide	1947-48
668	Australia v West Indies at Bridgetown	1954-55
659-8 dec.	Australia v England at Sydney	1946-47
658-8 dec.	England v Australia at Nottingham	1938
657-8 dec.	Pakistan v West Indies at Bridgetown	1957-58
656-8 dec.	Australia v England at Manchester	1964
654-5	England v South Africa at Durban	1938-39
652-7 dec.	England v India at Madras	1984-85
652-8 dec.	West Indies v England at Lord's	1973
652	Pakistan v India at Faisalabad	1982-83
650-6 dec.	Australia v West Indies at Bridgetown	1964-65

The highest innings for the countries not mentioned on previous page are:

644-7 dec.	India v West Indies at Kanpur	1978-79
622-9 dec.	South Africa v Australia at Durban	1969-70
553-7 dec.	New Zealand v Australia at Brisbane	1985-86
491-7 dec.	Sri Lanka v England at Lord's	1984

HIGHEST FOURTH INNINGS TOTALS

To win

406-4	India v West Indies at Port-of-Spain	1975-76
404-3	Australia v England at Leeds	1948
362-7	Australia v West Indies at Georgetown	1977-78
348-5	West Indies v New Zealand at Auckland	1968-69
344-1	West Indies v England at Lord's	1984

To draw

654-5	England (needing 696 to win) v South Africa at Durban	1938-39
429-8	India (needing 438 to win) v England at The Oval	1979
423-7	South Africa (needing 451 to win) v England at The Oval	1947
408-5	West Indies (needing 836 to win) v England at Kingston	1929-30

To lose

445	India (lost by 47 runs) v Australia at Adelaide	1977-78
440	New Zealand (lost by 38 runs) v England at Nottingham	1973
417	England (lost by 45 runs) v Australia at Melbourne	1976-77
411	England (lost by 193 runs) v Australia at Sydney	1924-25

MOST RUNS IN A DAY (BOTH SIDES)

588	England (398-6), India (190-0) at Manchester (2nd day)	1936
522	England (503-2), South Africa (19-0) at Lord's (2nd day)	1924
508	England (221-2), South Africa (287-6) at The Oval (3rd day)	1935

MOST RUNS IN A DAY (ONE SIDE)

503	England (503-2) v South Africa at Lord's (2nd day)	1924
494	Australia (494-6) v South Africa at Sydney (1st day)	1910-11
475	Australia (475-2) v England at The Oval (1st day)	1934
471	England (471-8) v India at The Oval (1st day)	1936
458	Australia (458-3) v England at Leeds (1st day)	1930
455	Australia (455-1) v England at Leeds (2nd day)	1934

MOST WICKETS IN ONE DAY

27	England (18-3 to 53 out and 62) v Australia (60) at Lord's (2nd day)	1888
25	Australia (112 and 48-5) v England (61) at Melbourne (1st day)	1901-02

HIGHEST MATCH AGGREGATES

Runs	Wkts			Days played
1,981	35	South Africa v England at Durban	1938-39	10†
1,815	34	West Indies v England at Kingston	1929-30	9‡
1,764	39	Australia v West Indies at Adelaide	1968-69	5
1,753	40	Australia v England at Adelaide	1920-21	6
1,723	31	England v Australia at Leeds	1948	5
1,661	36	West Indies v Australia at Bridgetown	1954-55	6

† *No play on one day.*   ‡ *No play on two days.*

LOWEST INNINGS TOTALS

26	New Zealand v England at Auckland	1954-55
30	South Africa v England at Port Elizabeth	1895-96
30	South Africa v England at Birmingham	1924
35	South Africa v England at Cape Town	1898-99
36	Australia v England at Birmingham	1902
36	South Africa v Australia at Melbourne	1931-32
42	Australia v England at Sydney	1887-88
42	New Zealand v Australia at Wellington	1945-46
42†	India v England at Lord's	1974
43	South Africa v England at Cape Town	1888-89
44	Australia v England at The Oval	1896
45	England v Australia at Sydney	1886-87
45	South Africa v Australia at Melbourne	1931-32
47	South Africa v England at Cape Town	1888-89
47	New Zealand v England at Lord's	1958

The lowest innings for the countries not mentioned above are:

62	Pakistan v Australia at Perth	1981-82
76	West Indies v Pakistan at Dacca	1958-59
93	Sri Lanka v New Zealand at Wellington	1982-83

† *Batted one man short.*

FEWEST RUNS IN A FULL DAY'S PLAY

95 At Karachi, October 11, 1956. Australia 80 all out; Pakistan 15 for two (first day, 5½ hours).

104 At Karachi, December 8, 1959. Pakistan 0 for no wicket to 104 for five v Australia (fourth day, 5½ hours).

106 At Brisbane, December 9, 1958. England 92 for two to 198 all out v Australia (fourth day, 5 hours). *England were dismissed five minutes before the close of play, leaving no time for Australia to start their second innings.*

112 At Karachi, October 15, 1956. Australia 138 for six to 187 all out; Pakistan 63 for one (fourth day, 5½ hours).

117 At Madras, October 19, 1956. India 117 for five v Australia (first day, 5½ hours).

117 At Colombo (SSC), March 21, 1984. New Zealand 6 for no wicket to 123 for four (fifth day, 5 hours, 47 minutes).

In England

151 At Lord's, August 26, 1978. England 175 for two to 289 all out; New Zealand 37 for seven (third day, 6 hours).

159 At Leeds, July 10, 1971. Pakistan 208 for four to 350 all out; England 17 for one (third day, 6 hours).

LOWEST MATCH AGGREGATES

(For a completed match)

Runs	Wkts			Days played
234	29	Australia v South Africa at Melbourne	1931-32	3†
291	40	England v Australia at Lord's	1888	2
295	28	New Zealand v Australia at Wellington	1945-46	2
309	29	West Indies v England at Bridgetown	1934-35	3
323	30	England v Australia at Manchester ....·.......	1888	2

† *No play on one day.*

YOUNGEST TEST PLAYERS

Years	Days			
15	124	Mushtaq Mohammad ...	Pakistan v West Indies at Lahore ...	1958-59
16	191	Aftab Baloch	Pakistan v New Zealand at Dacca ...	1969-70
16	248	Nasim-ul-Ghani	Pakistan v West Indies at Bridgetown	1957-58
16	352	Khalid Hassan	Pakistan v England at Nottingham ..	1954
17	118	L. Sivaramakrishnan ...	India v West Indies at St John's ...	1982-83
17	122	J. E. D. Sealy	West Indies v England at Bridgetown	1929-30
17	189	C. D. U. S. Weerasinghe	Sri Lanka v India at Colombo (PSO)	1985-86
17	193	Maninder Singh	India v Pakistan at Karachi	1982-83
17	239	I. D. Craig	Australia v South Africa at Melbourne	1952-53
17	245	G. S. Sobers	West Indies v England at Kingston ..	1953-54
17	265	V. L. Mehra	India v New Zealand at Bombay	1955-56
17	300	Hanif Mohammad	Pakistan v India at Delhi	1952-53
17	341	Intikhab Alam	Pakistan v Australia at Karachi	1959-60

Note: The youngest Test players for countries not mentioned above are: England – D. B. Close, 18 years 149 days, v New Zealand at Manchester, 1949; New Zealand – D. L. Freeman, 18 years 197 days, v England at Christchurch, 1932-33; South Africa – A. E. Ochse, 19 years 1 day, v England at Port Elizabeth, 1888-89.

OLDEST PLAYERS ON TEST DEBUT

Years	Days			
49	119	J. Southerton	England v Australia at Melbourne ...	1876-77
47	284	Miran Bux	Pakistan v India at Lahore	1954-55
46	253	D. D. Blackie	Australia v England at Sydney	1928-29
46	237	H. Ironmonger	Australia v England at Brisbane	1928-29
42	242	N. Betancourt	West Indies v England at Port-of-Spain	1929-30
41	337	E. R. Wilson	England v Australia at Sydney	1920-21
41	27	R. J. D. Jamshedji	India v England at Bombay	1933-34
40	345	C. A. Wiles	West Indies v England at Manchester	1933
40	216	S. P. Kinneir	England v Australia at Sydney	1911-12
40	110	H. W. Lee	England v South Africa at Johannesburg	1930-31
40	56	G. W. A. Chubb	South Africa v England at Nottingham.	1951
40	37	C. Ramaswami	India v England at Manchester	1936

Note: The oldest Test player on début for New Zealand was H. M. McGirr, 38 years 101 days, v England at Auckland, 1929-30; for Sri Lanka, D. S. de Silva, 39 years 251 days, v England at Colombo (PSO), 1981-82.

OLDEST TEST PLAYERS

(Age on final day of their last Test match)

Years	Days			
52	165	W. Rhodes	England v West Indies at Kingston	1929-30
50	327	H. Ironmonger	Australia v England at Sydney	1932-33
50	320	W. G. Grace	England v Australia at Nottingham	1899
50	303	G. Gunn	England v West Indies at Kingston	1929-30
49	139	J. Southerton	England v Australia at Melbourne	1876-77
47	302	Miran Bux	Pakistan v India at Peshawar	1954-55
47	249	J. B. Hobbs	England v Australia at The Oval	1930
47	87	F. E. Woolley	England v Australia at The Oval	1934
46	309	D. D. Blackie	Australia v England at Adelaide	1928-29
46	206	A. W. Nourse	South Africa v England at The Oval	1924
46	202	H. Strudwick	England v Australia at The Oval	1926
46	41	E. H. Hendren	England v West Indies at Kingston	1934-35
45	245	G. O. Allen	England v West Indies at Kingston	1947-48
45	215	P. Holmes	England v India at Lord's	1932
45	140	D. B. Close	England v West Indies at Manchester	1976

MOST TEST MATCH APPEARANCES

For	Total		E	A	SA	WI	NZ	I	P	SL
England	114	M. C. Cowdrey	—	43	14	21	18	8	10	—
Australia	96	R. W. Marsh	42	—	—	17	14	3	20	—
South Africa	50	J. H. B. Waite	21	14	—	—	15	—	—	—
West Indies	110	C. H. Lloyd	34	29	—	—	8	28	11	—
New Zealand	66	R. J. Hadlee	17	19	—	7	—	8	10	5
India	115	S. M. Gavaskar	38	17	—	27	9	—	20	4
Pakistan	78	Zaheer Abbas	14	20	—	8	14	19	—	3
Sri Lanka	20	S. Wettimuny	2	1	—	—	5	3	9	—

MOST CONSECUTIVE TEST APPEARANCES

99	S. M. Gavaskar, India	Bombay 1974-75 to Birmingham 1986
87	G. R. Viswanath, India	Georgetown 1970-71 to Karachi 1982-83
85	G. S. Sobers, West Indies	Port-of-Spain 1954-55 to Port-of-Spain 1971-72
78	A. R. Border, Australia	Melbourne 1978-79 to Auckland 1985-86
71	I. M. Chappell, Australia	Adelaide 1965-66 to Melbourne 1975-76
66	Kapil Dev, India	Faisalabad 1978-79 to Delhi 1984-85
65	I. T. Botham, England	Wellington 1977-78 to Karachi 1983-84
65	A. P. E. Knott, England	Auckland 1970-71 to The Oval 1977
61	R. B. Kanhai, West Indies	Birmingham 1957 to Sydney 1968-69
58†	A. W. Greig, England	Manchester 1972 to The Oval 1977
58†	J. R. Reid, New Zealand	Manchester 1949 to Leeds 1965
57	D. L. Haynes, West Indies	Brisbane 1979-80 to St John's 1985-86
56	S. M. H. Kirmani, India	Madras 1979-80 to Kanpur 1984-85
53	K. J. Hughes, Australia	Brisbane 1978-79 to Sydney 1982-83
53	Javed Miandad, Pakistan	Lahore 1977-78 to Sydney 1983-84
52	R. W. Marsh, Australia	Brisbane 1970-71 to The Oval 1977
52	P. B. H. May, England	The Oval 1953 to Leeds 1959
52	F. E. Woolley, England	The Oval 1909 to The Oval 1926
51	G. S. Chappell, Australia	Perth 1970-71 to The Oval 1977

† *Indicates complete Test career.*

SUMMARY OF ALL TEST MATCHES

To end of 1986 season in England

		Tests				Won by					Tied	Drawn
			E	A	SA	WI	NZ	I	P	SL		
England	v Australia	257	86	96	–	–	–	–	–	–	–	75
	v South Africa	102	46	–	18	–	–	–	–	–	–	38
	v West Indies	90	21	–	–	35	–	–	–	–	–	34
	v New Zealand	63	30	–	–	–	4	–	–	–	–	29
	v India	75	30	–	–	–	–	11	–	–	–	34
	v Pakistan	39	13	–	–	–	–	–	3	–	–	23
	v Sri Lanka	2	1	–	–	–	–	–	–	0	–	1
Australia	v South Africa	53	–	29	11	–	–	–	–	–	–	13
	v West Indies	62	–	27	–	19	–	–	–	–	1	15
	v New Zealand	21	–	9	–	–	5	–	–	–	–	7
	v India	42	–	20	–	–	–	8	–	–	–	14
	v Pakistan	28	–	11	–	–	–	–	8	–	–	9
	v Sri Lanka	1	–	1	–	–	–	–	–	0	–	0
South Africa	v New Zealand	17	–	–	9	–	2	–	–	–	–	6
West Indies	v New Zealand	21	–	–	–	7	3	–	–	–	–	11
	v India	54	–	–	–	22	–	5	–	–	–	27
	v Pakistan	19	–	–	–	7	–	–	4	–	–	8
New Zealand	v India	25	–	–	–	–	4	10	–	–	–	11
	v Pakistan	27	–	–	–	–	3	–	10	–	–	14
	v Sri Lanka	5	–	–	–	–	4	–	–	0	–	1
India	v Pakistan	35	–	–	–	–	–	4	6	–	–	25
	v Sri Lanka	4	–	–	–	–	–	–	0	1	–	3
Pakistan	v Sri Lanka	9	–	–	–	–	–	–	5	1	–	3
		1,051	227	193	38	90	25	38	36	2	1	401

	Tests	Won	Lost	Drawn	Tied	Toss Won
England	628	227	167	234	–	309
Australia	464	193	137	133	1	231
South Africa	172	38	77	57	–	80
West Indies	246	90	60	95	1	132
New Zealand	179	25	75	79	–	88
India	235	38	83	114	–	119
Pakistan	157	36	39	82	–	81
Sri Lanka	21	2	11	8	–	11

ENGLAND v AUSTRALIA

		Captains					
Season	*England*		*Australia*	*T*	*E*	*A*	*D*
1876-77	James Lillywhite		D. W. Gregory	2	1	1	0
1878-79	Lord Harris		D. W. Gregory	1	0	1	0
1880	Lord Harris		W. L. Murdoch	1	1	0	0
1881-82	A. Shaw		W. L. Murdoch	4	0	2	2
1882	A. N. Hornby		W. L. Murdoch	1	0	1	0

THE ASHES

		Captains						
Season	*England*		*Australia*	*T*	*E*	*A*	*D*	*Held by*
1882-83	Hon. Ivo Bligh		W. L. Murdoch	4*	2	2	0	E
1884	Lord Harris[1]		W. L. Murdoch	3	1	0	2	E
1884-85	A. Shrewsbury		T. Horan[2]	5	3	2	0	E

Captains

Season	England	Australia	T	E	A	D	Held by
1886	A. G. Steel	H. J. H. Scott	3	3	0	0	E
1886-87	A. Shrewsbury	P. S. McDonnell	2	2	0	0	E
1887-88	W. W. Read	P. S. McDonnell	1	1	0	0	E
1888	W. G. Grace[3]	P. S. McDonnell	3	2	1	0	E
1890†	W. G. Grace	W. L. Murdoch	2	2	0	0	E
1891-92	W. G. Grace	J. McC. Blackham	3	1	2	0	A
1893	W. G. Grace[4]	J. McC. Blackham	3	1	0	2	E
1894-95	A. E. Stoddart	G. Giffen[5]	5	3	2	0	E
1896	W. G. Grace	G. H. S. Trott	3	2	1	0	E
1897-98	A. E. Stoddart[6]	G. H. S. Trott	5	1	4	0	A
1899	A. C. MacLaren[7]	J. Darling	5	0	1	4	A
1901-02	A. C. MacLaren	J. Darling[8]	5	1	4	0	A
1902	A. C. MacLaren	J. Darling	5	1	2	2	A
1903-04	P. F. Warner	M. A. Noble	5	3	2	0	E
1905	Hon. F. S. Jackson	J. Darling	5	2	0	3	E
1907-08	A. O. Jones[9]	M. A. Noble	5	1	4	0	A
1909	A. C. MacLaren	M. A. Noble	5	1	2	2	A
1911-12	J. W. H. T. Douglas	C. Hill	5	4	1	0	E
1912	C. B. Fry	S. E. Gregory	3	1	0	2	E
1920-21	J. W. H. T. Douglas	W. W. Armstrong	5	0	5	0	A
1921	Hon. L. H. Tennyson[10]	W. W. Armstrong	5	0	3	2	A
1924-25	A. E. R. Gilligan	H. L. Collins	5	1	4	0	A
1926	A. W. Carr[11]	H. L. Collins[12]	5	1	0	4	E
1928-29	A. P. F. Chapman[13]	J. Ryder	5	4	1	0	E
1930	A. P. F. Chapman[14]	W. M. Woodfull	5	1	2	2	A
1932-33	D. R. Jardine	W. M. Woodfull	5	4	1	0	E
1934	R. E. S. Wyatt[15]	W. M. Woodfull	5	1	2	2	A
1936-37	G. O. Allen	D. G. Bradman	5	2	3	0	A
1938†	W. R. Hammond	D. G. Bradman	4	1	1	2	A
1946-47	W. R. Hammond[16]	D. G. Bradman	5	0	3	2	A
1948	N. W. D. Yardley	D. G. Bradman	5	0	4	1	A
1950-51	F. R. Brown	A. L. Hassett	5	1	4	0	A
1953	L. Hutton	A. L. Hassett	5	1	0	4	E
1954-55	L. Hutton	I. W. Johnson[17]	5	3	1	1	E
1956	P. B. H. May	I. W. Johnson	5	2	1	2	E
1958-59	P. B. H. May	R. Benaud	5	0	4	1	A
1961	P. B. H. May[18]	R. Benaud[19]	5	1	2	2	A
1962-63	E. R. Dexter	R. Benaud	5	1	1	3	A
1964	E. R. Dexter	R. B. Simpson	5	0	1	4	A
1965-66	M. J. K. Smith	R. B. Simpson[20]	5	1	1	3	A
1968	M. C. Cowdrey[21]	W. M. Lawry[22]	5	1	1	3	A
1970-71†	R. Illingworth	W. M. Lawry[23]	6	2	0	4	E
1972	R. Illingworth	I. M. Chappell	5	2	2	1	E
1974-75	M. H. Denness[24]	I. M. Chappell	6	1	4	1	A
1975	A. W. Greig[25]	I. M. Chappell	4	0	1	3	A
1976-77‡	A. W. Greig	G. S. Chappell	1	0	1	0	—
1977	J. M. Brearley	G. S. Chappell	5	3	0	2	E
1978-79	J. M. Brearley	G. N. Yallop	6	5	1	0	E
1979-80‡	J. M. Brearley	G. S. Chappell	3	0	3	0	—
1980‡	I. T. Botham	G. S. Chappell	1	0	0	1	—
1981	J. M. Brearley[26]	K. J. Hughes	6	3	1	2	E
1982-83	R. G. D. Willis	G. S. Chappell	5	1	2	2	A
1985	D. I. Gower	A. R. Border	6	3	1	2	E

In Australia	....		134	49	66	19	
In England	....		123	37	30	56	
Totals	....		257	86	96	75	

* *The Ashes were awarded in 1882-83 after a series of three matches which England won 2-1. A fourth unofficial match was played, each innings being played on a different pitch, and this was won by Australia.*

† *The matches at Manchester in 1890 and 1938 and at Melbourne (Third Test) in 1970-71 were abandoned without a ball being bowled and are excluded.*

‡ *The Ashes were not at stake in these series.*

Notes: The following deputised for the official touring captain or were appointed by the home authority for only a minor proportion of the series:

[1]A. N. Hornby (First). [2]W. L. Murdoch (First), H. H. Massie (Third), J. McC. Blackham (Fourth). [3]A. G. Steel (First). [4]A. E. Stoddart (First). [5]J. McC. Blackham (First). [6]A. C. MacLaren (First, Second and Fifth). [7]W. G. Grace (First). [8]H. Trumble (Fourth and Fifth). [9]F. L. Fane (First, Second and Third). [10]J. W. H. T. Douglas (First and Second). [11]A. P. F. Chapman (Fifth). [12]W. Bardsley (Third and Fourth). [13]J. C. White (Fifth). [14]R. E. S. Wyatt (Fifth). [15]C. F. Walters (First). [16]N. W. D. Yardley (Fifth). [17]A. R. Morris (Second). [18]M. C. Cowdrey (First and Second). [19]R. N. Harvey (Second). [20]B. C. Booth (First and Third). [21]T. W. Graveney (Fourth). [22]B. N. Jarman (Fourth). [23]I. M. Chappell (Seventh). [24]J. H. Edrich (Fourth). [25]M. H. Denness (First). [26]I. T. Botham (First and Second).

HIGHEST INNINGS TOTALS

For England in England: 903-7 dec. at The Oval	....	1938
in Australia: 636 at Sydney	....	1928-29
For Australia in England: 729-6 dec. at Lord's	....	1930
in Australia: 659-8 dec. at Sydney	....	1946-47

LOWEST INNINGS TOTALS

For England in England: 52 at The Oval	....	1948
in Australia: 45 at Sydney	....	1886-87
For Australia in England: 36 at Birmingham	....	1902
in Australia: 42 at Sydney	....	1887-88

INDIVIDUAL HUNDREDS

For England (179)

132*‡	R. Abel, Sydney	1891-92	128*	G. Boycott, Lord's	1980
120	L. E. G. Ames, Lord's	1934	137	G. Boycott, The Oval	1981
185	R. W. Barber, Sydney	1965-66	103*	L. C. Braund, Adelaide	1901-02
134	W. Barnes, Adelaide	1884-85	102	L. C. Braund, Sydney	1903-04
129	C. J. Barnett, Adelaide	1936-37	121	J. Briggs, Melbourne	1884-85
126	C. J. Barnett, Nottingham	1938	140	J. T. Brown, Melbourne	1894-95
132*	K. F. Barrington, Adelaide	1962-63	121	A. P. F. Chapman, Lord's	1930
101	K. F. Barrington, Sydney	1962-63	102†	D. C. S. Compton, Nottingham	1938
256	K. F. Barrington, Manchester	1964	147 ⎫	D. C. S. Compton, Adelaide	1946-47
102	K. F. Barrington, Adelaide	1965-66	103* ⎭		
115	K. F. Barrington, Melbourne	1965-66	184	D. C. S. Compton, Nottingham	1948
119*	I. T. Botham, Melbourne	1979-80	145*	D. C. S. Compton, Manchester	1948
149*	I. T. Botham, Leeds	1981	102	M. C. Cowdrey, Melbourne	1954-55
118	I. T. Botham, Manchester	1981	100*	M. C. Cowdrey, Sydney	1958-59
113	G. Boycott, The Oval	1964	113	M. C. Cowdrey, Melbourne	1962-63
142*	G. Boycott, Sydney	1970-71			
119*	G. Boycott, Adelaide	1970-71			
107	G. Boycott, Nottingham	1977	104	M. C. Cowdrey, Melbourne	1965-66
191	G. Boycott, Leeds	1977			

104	M. C. Cowdrey, Birmingham	1968
188	M. H. Denness, Melbourne	1974-75
180	E. R. Dexter, Birmingham	1961
174	E. R. Dexter, Manchester	1964
158	B. L. D'Oliveira, The Oval	1968
117	B. L. D'Oliveira, Melbourne	1970-71
173†	K. S. Duleepsinhji, Lord's	1930
120†	J. H. Edrich, Lord's	1964
109	J. H. Edrich, Melbourne	1965-66
103	J. H. Edrich, Sydney	1965-66
164	J. H. Edrich, The Oval	1968
115*	J. H. Edrich, Perth	1970-71
130	J. H. Edrich, Adelaide	1970-71
175	J. H. Edrich, Lord's	1975
119	W. J. Edrich, Sydney	1946-47
111	W. J. Edrich, Leeds	1948
146	K. W. R. Fletcher, Melbourne	1974-75
287†	R. E. Foster, Sydney	1903-04
144	C. B. Fry, The Oval	1905
160	M. W. Gatting, Manchester	1985
100*	M. W. Gatting, Birmingham	1985
196	G. A. Gooch, The Oval	1985
102	D. I. Gower, Perth	1978-79
114	D. I. Gower, Adelaide	1982-83
166	D. I. Gower, Nottingham	1985
215	D. I. Gower, Birmingham	1985
157	D. I. Gower, The Oval	1985
152†	W. G. Grace, The Oval	1880
170	W. G. Grace, The Oval	1886
111	T. W. Graveney, Sydney	1954-55
110	A. W. Greig, Brisbane	1974-75
119†	G. Gunn, Sydney	1907-08
122*	G. Gunn, Sydney	1907-08
102*	W. Gunn, Manchester	1893
251	W. R. Hammond, Sydney	1928-29
200	W. R. Hammond, Melbourne	1928-29
119* 177 }	W. R. Hammond, Adelaide	1928-29
113	W. R. Hammond, Leeds	1930
112	W. R. Hammond, Sydney	1932-33
101	W. R. Hammond, Sydney	1932-33
231*	W. R. Hammond, Sydney	1936-37
240	W. R. Hammond, Lord's	1938
169*	J. Hardstaff jun., The Oval	1938
130	T. W. Hayward, Manchester	1899
137	T. W. Hayward, The Oval	1899
114	J. W. Hearne, Melbourne	1911-12
127*	E. H. Hendren, Lord's	1926
169	E. H. Hendren, Brisbane	1928-29
132	E. H. Hendren, Manchester	1934
126*	J. B. Hobbs, Melbourne	1911-12
187	J. B. Hobbs, Adelaide	1911-12
178	J. B. Hobbs, Melbourne	1911-12
107	J. B. Hobbs, Lord's	1912
122	J. B. Hobbs, Melbourne	1920-21
123	J. B. Hobbs, Adelaide	1920-21
115	J. B. Hobbs, Sydney	1924-25
154	J. B. Hobbs, Melbourne	1924-25
119	J. B. Hobbs, Adelaide	1924-25
119	J. B. Hobbs, Lord's	1926
100	J. B. Hobbs, The Oval	1926
142	J. B. Hobbs, Melbourne	1928-29
126	K. L. Hutchings, Melbourne	1907-08
100†	L. Hutton, Nottingham	1938
364	L. Hutton, The Oval	1938
122*	L. Hutton, Sydney	1946-47
156*‡	L. Hutton, Adelaide	1950-51
145	L. Hutton, Lord's	1953
103	Hon. F. S. Jackson, The Oval	1893
118	Hon. F. S. Jackson, The Oval	1899
128	Hon. F. S. Jackson, Manchester	1902
144*	Hon. F. S. Jackson, Leeds	1905
113	Hon. F. S. Jackson, Manchester	1905
104	G. L. Jessop, The Oval	1902
106*	A. P. E. Knott, Adelaide	1974-75
135	A. P. E. Knott, Nottingham	1977
137†	M. Leyland, Melbourne	1928-29
109	M. Leyland, Lord's	1934
153	M. Leyland, Manchester	1934
110	M. Leyland, The Oval	1934
126	M. Leyland, Brisbane	1936-37
111*	M. Leyland, Melbourne	1936-37
187	M. Leyland, The Oval	1938
131	B. W. Luckhurst, Perth	1970-71
109	B. W. Luckhurst, Melbourne	1970-71
120	A. C. MacLaren, Melbourne	1894-95
109	A. C. MacLaren, Sydney	1897-98
124	A. C. MacLaren, Adelaide	1897-98
116	A. C. MacLaren, Sydney	1901-02
140	A. C. MacLaren, Nottingham	1905
117	H. Makepeace, Melbourne	1920-21
104	P. B. H. May, Sydney	1954-55
101	P. B. H. May, Leeds	1956
113	P. B. H. May, Melbourne	1958-59
182*	C. P. Mead, The Oval	1921
102†	Nawab of Pataudi, Sydney	1932-33
216*	E. Paynter, Nottingham	1938
174†	D. W. Randall, Melbourne	1976-77
150	D. W. Randall, Sydney	1978-79
115	D. W. Randall, Perth	1982-83
154*†	K. S. Ranjitsinhji, Manchester	1896
175	K. S. Ranjitsinhji, Sydney	1897-98
117	W. W. Read, The Oval	1884
179	W. Rhodes, Melbourne	1911-12
104	P. E. Richardson, Manchester	1956
175†	R. T. Robinson, Leeds	1985
148	R. T. Robinson, Birmingham	1985
135*	A. C. Russell, Adelaide	1920-21

101	A. C. Russell, Manchester .	1921	143	H. Sutcliffe, Melbourne ...	1924-25
102*	A. C. Russell, The Oval	1921	161	H. Sutcliffe, The Oval	1926
105	J. Sharp, The Oval	1909	135	H. Sutcliffe, Melbourne ...	1928-29
113	Rev. D. S. Sheppard, Manchester	1956	161	H. Sutcliffe, The Oval	1930
			194	H. Sutcliffe, Sydney	1932-33
113	Rev. D. S. Sheppard, Melbourne	1962-63	138	J. T. Tyldesley, Birmingham	1902
105*	A. Shrewsbury, Melbourne .	1884-85	100	J. T. Tyldesley, Leeds	1905
164	A. Shrewsbury, Lord's	1886	112*	J. T. Tyldesley, The Oval ..	1905
106	A. Shrewsbury, Lord's	1893	149	G. Ulyett, Melbourne	1881-82
156*	R. T. Simpson, Melbourne .	1950-51	117	A. Ward, Sydney	1894-95
135*	A. G. Steel, Sydney	1882-83	112	C. Washbrook, Melbourne .	1946-47
148	A. G. Steel, Lord's	1884	143	C. Washbrook, Leeds	1948
134	A. E. Stoddart, Adelaide ..	1891-92	109†	W. Watson, Lord's	1953
173	A. E. Stoddart, Melbourne .	1894-95	133*	F. E. Woolley, Sydney	1911-12
112†	R. Subba Row, Birmingham	1961	123	F. E. Woolley, Sydney	1924-25
			149	R. A. Woolmer, The Oval .	1975
137	R. Subba Row, The Oval ..	1961	120	R. A. Woolmer, Lord's ...	1977
115†	H. Sutcliffe, Sydney	1924-25	137	R. A. Woolmer, Manchester	1977
176 127	} H. Sutcliffe, Melbourne ...	1924-25			

† *Signifies hundred on first appearance in England–Australia Tests.*
‡ *Carried his bat.*

Note: In consecutive innings in 1928-29, W. R. Hammond scored 251 at Sydney, 200 and 32 at Melbourne, and 119* and 177 at Adelaide.

For Australia (198)

133*	W. W. Armstrong, Melbourne	1907-08	103*	D. G. Bradman, Melbourne	1932-33
158	W. W. Armstrong, Sydney .	1920-21	304	D. G. Bradman, Leeds	1934
121	W. W. Armstrong, Adelaide	1920-21	244	D. G. Bradman, The Oval .	1934
123*	W. W. Armstrong, Melbourne	1920-21	270	D. G. Bradman, Melbourne	1936-37
118	C. L. Badcock, Melbourne .	1936-37	212	D. G. Bradman, Adelaide .	1936-37
165*‡	C. Bannerman, Melbourne .	1876-77	169	D. G. Bradman, Melbourne	1936-37
136 130	} W. Bardsley, The Oval	1909	144*	D. G. Bradman, Nottingham	1938
193*‡	W. Bardsley, Lord's	1926	102*	D. G. Bradman, Lord's ...	1938
234	S. G. Barnes, Sydney	1946-47	103	D. G. Bradman, Leeds	1938
141	S. G. Barnes, Lord's	1948	187	D. G. Bradman, Brisbane .	1946-47
128	G. J. Bonnor, Sydney	1884-85	234	D. G. Bradman, Sydney ...	1946-47
112	B. C. Booth, Brisbane	1962-63	138	D. G. Bradman, Nottingham	1948
103	B. C. Booth, Melbourne ...	1962-63	173*	D. G. Bradman, Leeds	1948
115	A. R. Border, Perth	1979-80	105	W. A. Brown, Lord's	1934
123*	A. R. Border, Manchester .	1981	133	W. A. Brown, Nottingham	1938
106*	A. R. Border, The Oval ...	1981			
196	A. R. Border, Lord's	1985	206*‡	W. A. Brown, Lord's	1938
146*	A. R. Border, Manchester .	1985	181	P. J. Burge, The Oval	1961
112	D. G. Bradman, Melbourne	1928-29	103	P. J. Burge, Sydney	1962-63
			160	P. J. Burge, Leeds	1964
123	D. G. Bradman, Melbourne	1928-29	120	P. J. Burge, Melbourne ...	1965-66
131	D. G. Bradman, Nottingham	1930	101*†	J. W. Burke, Adelaide	1950-51
254	D. G. Bradman, Lord's	1930	108†	G. S. Chappell, Perth	1970-71
334	D. G. Bradman, Leeds	1930	131	G. S. Chappell, Lord's ...	1972
232	D. G. Bradman, The Oval .	1930	113	G. S. Chappell, The Oval .	1972
			144	G. S. Chappell, Sydney ...	1974-75

102	G. S. Chappell, Melbourne	1974-75
112	G. S. Chappell, Manchester	1977
114	G. S. Chappell, Melbourne	1979-80
117	G. S. Chappell, Perth	1982-83
115	G. S. Chappell, Adelaide	1982-83
111	I. M. Chappell, Melbourne	1970-71
104	I. M. Chappell, Adelaide	1970-71
118	I. M. Chappell, The Oval	1972
192	I. M. Chappell, The Oval	1975
104†	H. L. Collins, Sydney	1920-21
162	H. L. Collins, Adelaide	1920-21
114	H. L. Collins, Sydney	1924-25
307	R. M. Cowper, Melbourne	1965-66
101	J. Darling, Sydney	1897-98
178	J. Darling, Adelaide	1897-98
160	J. Darling, Sydney	1897-98
104†	R. A. Duff, Melbourne	1901-02
146	R. A. Duff, The Oval	1905
102	J. Dyson, Leeds	1981
170*	R. Edwards, Nottingham	1972
115	R. Edwards, Perth	1974-75
100	J. H. Fingleton, Brisbane	1936-37
136	J. H. Fingleton, Melbourne	1936-37
161	G. Giffen, Sydney	1894-95
107†	H. Graham, Lord's	1893
105	H. Graham, Sydney	1894-95
100	J. M. Gregory, Melbourne	1920-21
201	S. E. Gregory, Sydney	1894-95
103	S. E. Gregory, Lord's	1896
117	S. E. Gregory, The Oval	1899
112	S. E. Gregory, Adelaide	1903-04
116†	R. J. Hartigan, Adelaide	1907-08
112†	R. N. Harvey, Leeds	1948
122	R. N. Harvey, Manchester	1953
162	R. N. Harvey, Brisbane	1954-55
167	R. N. Harvey, Melbourne	1958-59
114	R. N. Harvey, Birmingham	1961
154	R. N. Harvey, Adelaide	1962-63
128	A. L. Hassett, Brisbane	1946-47
137	A. L. Hassett, Nottingham	1948
115	A. L. Hassett, Nottingham	1953
104	A. L. Hassett, Lord's	1953
112	H. L. Hendry, Sydney	1928-29
119	A. M. J. Hilditch, Leeds	1985
188	C. Hill, Melbourne	1897-98
135	C. Hill, Lord's	1899
119	C. Hill, Sheffield	1902
160	C. Hill, Adelaide	1907-08
124	T. P. Horan, Melbourne	1881-82
129	K. J. Hughes, Brisbane	1978-79
117	K. J. Hughes, Lord's	1980
137	K. J. Hughes, Sydney	1982-83
140	F. A. Iredale, Adelaide	1894-95
108	F. A. Iredale, Manchester	1896
164†	A. A. Jackson, Adelaide	1928-29
147	C. Kelleway, Adelaide	1920-21
100	A. F. Kippax, Melbourne	1928-29
130	W. M. Lawry, Lord's	1961

102	W. M. Lawry, Manchester	1961
106	W. M. Lawry, Manchester	1964
166	W. M. Lawry, Brisbane	1965-66
119	W. M. Lawry, Adelaide	1965-66
108	W. M. Lawry, Melbourne	1965-66
135	W. M. Lawry, The Oval	1968
100	R. R. Lindwall, Melbourne	1946-47
134	J. J. Lyons, Sydney	1891-92
170	C. G. Macartney, Sydney	1920-21
115	C. G. Macartney, Leeds	1921
133*	C. G. Macartney, Lord's	1926
151	C. G. Macartney, Leeds	1926
109	C. G. Macartney, Manchester	1926
187*	S. J. McCabe, Sydney	1932-33
137	S. J. McCabe, Manchester	1934
112	S. J. McCabe, Melbourne	1936-37
232	S. J. McCabe, Nottingham	1938
104*	C. L. McCool, Melbourne	1946-47
127	R. B. McCosker, The Oval	1975
107	R. B. McCosker, Nottingham	1977
170	C. C. McDonald, Adelaide	1958-59
133	C. C. McDonald, Melbourne	1958-59
147	P. S. McDonnell, Sydney	1881-82
103	P. S. McDonnell, The Oval	1884
124	P. S. McDonnell, Adelaide	1884-85
112	C. E. McLeod, Melbourne	1897-98
110*	R. W. Marsh, Melbourne	1976-77
141*	K. R. Miller, Adelaide	1946-47
145*	K. R. Miller, Sydney	1950-51
109	K. R. Miller, Lord's	1953
155	A. R. Morris, Melbourne	1946-47
122 }	A. R. Morris, Adelaide	1946-47
124* }		
105	A. R. Morris, Lord's	1948
182	A. R. Morris, Leeds	1948
196	A. R. Morris, The Oval	1948
206	A. R. Morris, Adelaide	1950-51
153	A. R. Morris, Brisbane	1954-55
153*	W. L. Murdoch, The Oval	1880
211	W. L. Murdoch, The Oval	1884
133	M. A. Noble, Sydney	1903-04
117	N. C. O'Neill, The Oval	1961
100	N. C. O'Neill, Adelaide	1962-63
116	C. E. Pellew, Melbourne	1920-21
104	C. E. Pellew, Adelaide	1920-21
110†	W. H. Ponsford, Sydney	1924-25
128	W. H. Ponsford, Melbourne	1924-25
110	W. H. Ponsford, The Oval	1930
181	W. H. Ponsford, Leeds	1934
266	W. H. Ponsford, The Oval	1934
143*	V. S. Ransford, Lord's	1909
171	I. R. Redpath, Perth	1970-71
105	I. R. Redpath, Sydney	1974-75
100	A. J. Richardson, Leeds	1926
138	V. Y. Richardson, Melbourne	1924-25

146	G. M. Ritchie, Nottingham	1985	112	K. D. Walters, Brisbane ...	1970-71
201*	J. Ryder, Adelaide	1924-25	103	K. D. Walters, Perth	1974-75
112	J. Ryder, Melbourne	1928-29	103†	D. M. Wellham, The Oval .	1981
102	H. J. H. Scott, The Oval ...	1884	162†	K. C. Wessels, Brisbane ...	1982-83
311	R. B. Simpson, Manchester	1964	100	G. M. Wood, Melbourne ...	1978-79
225	R. B. Simpson, Adelaide ..	1965-66	112	G. M. Wood, Lord's	1980
207	K. R. Stackpole, Brisbane .	1970-71	172	G. M. Wood, Nottingham .	1985
136	K. R. Stackpole, Adelaide .	1970-71	141	W. M. Woodfull, Leeds ...	1926
114	K. R. Stackpole, Nottingham	1972	117	W. M. Woodfull, Manchester	1926
108	J. M. Taylor, Sydney	1924-25	111	W. M. Woodfull, Sydney ..	1928-29
143	G. H. S. Trott, Lord's	1896	107	W. M. Woodfull, Melbourne	1928-29
135*	V. T. Trumper, Lord's	1899			
104	V. T. Trumper, Manchester	1902	102	W. M. Woodfull, Melbourne	1928-29
185*	V. T. Trumper, Sydney ...	1903-04			
113	V. T. Trumper, Adelaide ..	1903-04	155	W. M. Woodfull, Lord's ..	1930
166	V. T. Trumper, Sydney ...	1907-08	102†	G. N. Yallop, Brisbane ...	1978-79
113	V. T. Trumper, Sydney ...	1911-12	121	G. N. Yallop, Sydney	1978-79
155†	K. D. Walters, Brisbane ...	1965-66	114	G. N. Yallop, Manchester .	1981
115	K. D. Walters, Melbourne .	1965-66			

† *Signifies hundred on first appearance in England–Australia Tests.*
‡ *Carried his bat.*

Notes: D. G. Bradman's scores in 1930 were 8 and 131 at Nottingham, 254 and 1 at Lord's, 334 at Leeds, 14 at Manchester, and 232 at The Oval.

D. G. Bradman scored a hundred in eight successive Tests against England in which he batted – three in 1936-37, three in 1938 and two in 1946-47. He was injured and unable to bat at The Oval in 1938.

W. H. Ponsford and K. D. Walters each hit hundreds in their first two Tests.

C. Bannerman and H. Graham each scored their maiden hundred in first-class cricket in their first Test.

No right-handed batsman has obtained two hundreds for Australia in a Test match against England, and no left-handed batsman for England against Australia.

H. Sutcliffe, in his first two games for England, scored 59 and 115 at Sydney and 176 and 127 at Melbourne in 1924-25. In the latter match, which lasted into the seventh day, he was on the field throughout except for 86 minutes, namely 27 hours and 52 minutes.

C. Hill made 98 and 97 at Adelaide in 1901-02, and F. E. Woolley 95 and 93 at Lord's in 1921.

H. Sutcliffe in 1924-25, C. G. Macartney in 1926 and A. R. Morris in 1946-47 made three hundreds in consecutive innings.

J. B. Hobbs and H. Sutcliffe shared eleven first-wicket three-figure partnerships.

L. Hutton and C. Washbrook twice made three-figure stands in each innings, at Adelaide in 1946-47 and at Leeds in 1948.

H. Sutcliffe, during his highest score of 194, v Australia in 1932-33, took part in three stands each exceeding 100, viz. 112 with R. E. S. Wyatt for the first wicket, 188 with W. R. Hammond for the second wicket, and 123 with the Nawab of Pataudi for the third wicket. In 1903-04 R. E. Foster, in his historic innings of 287, added 192 for the fifth wicket with L. C. Braund, 115 for the ninth with A. E. Relf, and 130 for the tenth with W. Rhodes.

When L. Hutton scored 364 at The Oval in 1938 he added 382 for the second wicket with M. Leyland, 135 for the third wicket with W. R. Hammond and 215 for the sixth wicket with J. Hardstaff jun.

D. C. S. Compton and A. R. Morris at Adelaide in 1946-47 provide the only instance of a player on each side hitting two separate hundreds in a Test match.

G. S. and I. M. Chappell at The Oval in 1972 provide the first instance in Test matches of brothers each scoring hundreds in the same innings.

RECORD PARTNERSHIPS FOR EACH WICKET

For England

323 for 1st	J. B. Hobbs and W. Rhodes at Melbourne	1911-12
382 for 2nd†	L. Hutton and M. Leyland at The Oval	1938
262 for 3rd	W. R. Hammond and D. R. Jardine at Adelaide	1928-29
222 for 4th	W. R. Hammond and E. Paynter at Lord's	1938

206 for 5th	E. Paynter and D. C. S. Compton at Nottingham	1938
215 for 6th	{ L. Hutton and J. Hardstaff jun. at The Oval	1938
	{ G. Boycott and A. P. E. Knott at Nottingham	1977
143 for 7th	F. E. Woolley and J. Vine at Sydney	1911-12
124 for 8th	E. H. Hendren and H. Larwood at Brisbane	1928-29
151 for 9th	W. H. Scotton and W. W. Read at The Oval	1884
130 for 10th†	R. E. Foster and W. Rhodes at Sydney	1903-04

For Australia

244 for 1st	R. B. Simpson and W. M. Lawry at Adelaide	1965-66
451 for 2nd†	W. H. Ponsford and D. G. Bradman at The Oval	1934
276 for 3rd	D. G. Bradman and A. L. Hassett at Brisbane	1946-47
388 for 4th†	W. H. Ponsford and D. G. Bradman at Leeds	1934
405 for 5th†‡	S. G. Barnes and D. G. Bradman at Sydney	1946-47
346 for 6th†	J. H. Fingleton and D. G. Bradman at Melbourne	1936-37
165 for 7th	C. Hill and H. Trumble at Melbourne	1897-98
243 for 8th†	R. J. Hartigan and C. Hill at Adelaide	1907-08
154 for 9th†	S. E. Gregory and J. McC. Blackham at Sydney	1894-95
127 for 10th†	J. M. Taylor and A. A. Mailey at Sydney	1924-25

† *Denotes record partnership against all countries.*
‡ *Record fifth-wicket partnership in first-class cricket.*

MOST RUNS IN A SERIES

England in England	732 (average 81.33)	D. I. Gower	1985
England in Australia	905 (average 113.12)	W. R. Hammond	1928-29
Australia in England	974 (average 139.14)	D. G. Bradman	1930
Australia in Australia	810 (average 90.00)	D. G. Bradman	1936-37

TEN WICKETS OR MORE IN A MATCH

For England (37)

13-163 (6-42, 7-121)	S. F. Barnes, Melbourne	1901-02
14-102 (7-28, 7-74)	W. Bates, Melbourne	1882-83
10-105 (5-46, 5-59)	A. V. Bedser, Melbourne	1950-51
14-99 (7-55, 7-44)	A. V. Bedser, Nottingham	1953
11-102 (6-44, 5-58)	C. Blythe, Birmingham	1909
11-176 (6-78, 5-98)	I. T. Botham, Perth	1979-80
10-253 (6-125, 4-128)	I. T. Botham, The Oval	1981
11-74 (5-29, 6-45)	J. Briggs, Lord's	1886
12-136 (6-49, 6-87)	J. Briggs, Adelaide	1891-92
10-148 (5-34, 5-114)	J. Briggs, The Oval	1893
10-104 (6-77, 4-27)†	R. M. Ellison, Birmingham	1985
10-179 (5-102, 5-77)†	K. Farnes, Nottingham	1934
10-60 (6-41, 4-19)	J. T. Hearne, The Oval	1896
11-113 (5-58, 6-55)	J. C. Laker, Leeds	1956
19-90 (9-37, 10-53)	J. C. Laker, Manchester	1956
10-124 (5-96, 5-28)	H. Larwood, Sydney	1932-33
11-76 (6-48, 5-28)	W. H. Lockwood, Manchester	1902
12-104 (7-36, 5-68)	G. A. Lohmann, The Oval	1886
10-87 (8-35, 2-52)	G. A. Lohmann, Sydney	1886-87
10-142 (8-58, 2-84)	G. A. Lohmann, Sydney	1891-92
12-102 (6-50, 6-52)†	F. Martin, The Oval	1890
10-58 (5-18, 5-40)	R. Peel, Sydney	1887-88
11-68 (7-31, 4-37)	R. Peel, Manchester	1888
15-124 (7-56, 8-68)	W. Rhodes, Melbourne	1903-04
10-156 (5-49, 5-107)†	T. Richardson, Manchester	1893
11-173 (6-39, 5-134)	T. Richardson, Lord's	1896

13-244 (7-168, 6-76)	T. Richardson, Manchester	1896
10-204 (8-94, 2-110)	T. Richardson, Sydney	1897-98
11-228 (6-130, 5-98)†	M. W. Tate, Sydney	1924-25
11-88 (5-58, 6-30)	F. S. Trueman, Leeds	1961
10-130 (4-45, 6-85)	F. H. Tyson, Sydney	1954-55
10-82 (4-37, 6-45)	D. L. Underwood, Leeds	1972
11-215 (7-113, 4-102)	D. L. Underwood, Adelaide	1974-75
15-104 (7-61, 8-43)	H. Verity, Lord's	1934
10-57 (6-41, 4-16)	W. Voce, Brisbane	1936-37
13-256 (5-130, 8-126)	J. C. White, Adelaide	1928-29
10-49 (5-29, 5-20)	F. E. Woolley, The Oval	1912

For Australia (35)

10-239 (4-129, 6-110)	L. O'B. Fleetwood-Smith, Adelaide	1936-37
10-160 (4-88, 6-72)	G. Giffen, Sydney	1891-92
11-82 (5-45, 6-37)†	C. V. Grimmett, Sydney	1924-25
10-201 (5-107, 5-94)	C. V. Grimmett, Nottingham	1930
10-122 (5-65, 5-57)	R. M. Hogg, Perth	1978-79
10-66 (5-30, 5-36)	R. M. Hogg, Melbourne	1978-79
12-175 (5-85, 7-90)†	H. V. Hordern, Sydney	1911-12
10-161 (5-95, 5-66)	H. V. Hordern, Sydney	1911-12
10-164 (7-88, 3-76)	E. Jones, Lord's	1899
11-134 (6-47, 5-87)	G. F. Lawson, Brisbane	1982-83
10-181 (5-58, 5-123)	D. K. Lillee, The Oval	1972
11-165 (6-26, 5-139)	D. K. Lillee, Melbourne	1976-77
11-138 (6-60, 5-78)	D. K. Lillee, Melbourne	1979-80
11-159 (7-89, 4-70)	D. K. Lillee, The Oval	1981
11-85 (7-58, 4-27)	C. G. Macartney, Leeds	1909
10-302 (5-160, 5-142)	A. A. Mailey, Adelaide	1920-21
13-236 (4-115, 9-121)	A. A. Mailey, Melbourne	1920-21
16-137 (8-84, 8-53)†	R. A. L. Massie, Lord's	1972
10-152 (5-72, 5-80)	K. R. Miller, Lord's	1956
13-77 (7-17, 6-60)	M. A. Noble, Melbourne	1901-02
11-103 (5-51, 6-52)	M. A. Noble, Sheffield	1902
10-129 (5-63, 5-66)	W. J. O'Reilly, Melbourne	1932-33
11-129 (4-75, 7-54)	W. J. O'Reilly, Nottingham	1934
10-122 (5-66, 5-56)	W. J. O'Reilly, Leeds	1938
11-165 (7-68, 4-97)	G. E. Palmer, Sydney	1881-82
10-126 (7-65, 3-61)	G. E. Palmer, Melbourne	1882-83
13-110 (6-48, 7-62)	F. R. Spofforth, Melbourne	1878-79
14-90 (7-46, 7-44)	F. R. Spofforth, The Oval	1882
11-117 (4-73, 7-44)	F. R. Spofforth, Sydney	1882-83
10-144 (4-54, 6-90)	F. R. Spofforth, Sydney	1884-85
12-89 (6-59, 6-30)	H. Trumble, The Oval	1896
10-128 (4-75, 6-53)	H. Trumble, Manchester	1902
12-173 (8-65, 4-108)	H. Trumble, The Oval	1902
12-87 (5-44, 7-43)	C. T. B. Turner, Sydney	1887-88
10-63 (5-27, 5-36)	C. T. B. Turner, Lord's	1888

† *Signifies ten wickets or more on first appearance in England–Australia Tests.*

Note: J. Briggs, J. C. Laker, T. Richardson in 1896, R. M. Hogg, A. A. Mailey, H. Trumble and C. T. B. Turner took ten wickets or more in successive Tests. J. Briggs was omitted, however, from the England team for the first Test match in 1893.

MOST WICKETS IN A SERIES

England in England	46 (average 9.60)	J. C. Laker	1956
England in Australia	38 (average 23.18)	M. W. Tate	1924-25
Australia in England	42 (average 21.26)	T. M. Alderman (6 Tests)	1981
Australia in Australia	41 (average 12.85)	R. M. Hogg (6 Tests)	1978-79

WICKET-KEEPING – MOST DISMISSALS

	M	Ct	St	Total
†R. W. Marsh (Australia)	42	141	7	148
A. P. E. Knott (England)	34	97	8	105
†W. A. Oldfield (Australia)	38	59	31	90
A. A. Lilley (England)	32	65	19	84
A. T. W. Grout (Australia)	22	69	7	76
T. G. Evans (England)	31	63	12	75

† *The number of catches by R. W. Marsh (141) and stumpings by W. A. Oldfield (31) are respective records in England–Australia Tests.*

SCORERS OF OVER 2,000 RUNS

	T	I	NO	R	HI	Avge
D. G. Bradman	37	63	7	5,028	334	89.78
J. B. Hobbs	41	71	4	3,636	187	54.26
G. Boycott	38	71	9	2,945	191	47.50
W. R. Hammond	31	58	3	2,852	251	51.85
H. Sutcliffe	27	46	5	2,741	194	66.85
C. Hill	41	76	1	2,660	188	35.46
J. H. Edrich	32	57	3	2,644	175	48.96
G. S. Chappell	35	65	8	2,619	144	45.94
M. C. Cowdrey	43	75	4	2,433	113	34.26
L. Hutton	27	49	6	2,428	364	56.46
R. N. Harvey	37	68	5	2,416	167	38.34
V. T. Trumper	40	74	5	2,263	185*	32.79
W. M. Lawry	29	51	5	2,233	166	48.54
S. E. Gregory	52	92	7	2,193	201	25.80
W. W. Armstrong	42	71	9	2,172	158	35.03
I. M. Chappell	30	56	4	2,138	192	41.11
K. F. Barrington	23	39	6	2,111	256	63.96
A. R. Morris	24	43	2	2,080	206	50.73
D. I. Gower	26	48	2	2,075	215	45.10

BOWLERS WITH 100 WICKETS

	T	Balls	R	W	5 W/i	Avge
D. K. Lillee	29	8,516	3,507	167	11	21.00
H. Trumble	31	7,895	2,945	141	9	20.88
I. T. Botham	29	7,361	3,556	136	8	26.14
R. G. D. Willis	35	7,294	3,346	128	7	26.14
M. A. Noble	39	6,845	2,860	115	9	24.86
R. R. Lindwall	29	6,728	2,559	114	6	22.44
W. Rhodes	41	5,791	2,616	109	6	24.00
S. F. Barnes	20	5,749	2,288	106	12	21.58
C. V. Grimmett	22	9,224	3,439	106	11	32.44
D. L. Underwood	29	8,000	2,770	105	4	26.38
A. V. Bedser	21	7,065	2,859	104	7	27.49
G. Giffen	31	6,325	2,791	103	7	27.09
W. J. O'Reilly	19	7,864	2,587	102	8	25.36
R. Peel	20	5,216	1,715	102	6	16.81
C. T. B. Turner	17	5,195	1,670	101	11	16.53
J. R. Thomson	21	4,951	2,418	100	5	24.18

ENGLAND v SOUTH AFRICA

	Captains					
Season	*England*	*South Africa*	*T*	*E*	*SA*	*D*
1888-89	C. A. Smith[1]	O. R. Dunell[2]	2	2	0	0
1891-92	W. W. Read	W. H. Milton	1	1	0	0
1895-96	Lord Hawke[3]	E. A. Halliwell[4]	3	3	0	0
1898-99	Lord Hawke	M. Bisset	2	2	0	0
1905-06	P. F. Warner	P. W. Sherwell	5	1	4	0
1907	R. E. Foster	P. W. Sherwell	3	1	0	2
1909-10	H. D. G. Leveson Gower[5]	S. J. Snooke	5	2	3	0
1912	C. B. Fry	F. Mitchell[6]	3	3	0	0
1913-14	J. W. H. T. Douglas	H. W. Taylor	5	4	0	1
1922-23	F. T. Mann	H. W. Taylor	5	2	1	2
1924	A. E. R. Gilligan[7]	H. W. Taylor	5	3	0	2
1927-28	R. T. Stanyforth[8]	H. G. Deane	5	2	2	1
1929	J. C. White[9]	H. G. Deane	5	2	0	3
1930-31	A. P. F. Chapman	H. G. Deane[10]	5	0	1	4
1935	R. E. S. Wyatt	H. F. Wade	5	0	1	4
1938-39	W. R. Hammond	A. Melville	5	1	0	4
1947	N. W. D. Yardley	A. Melville	5	3	0	2
1948-49	F. G. Mann	A. D. Nourse	5	2	0	3
1951	F. R. Brown	A. D. Nourse	5	3	1	1
1955	P. B. H. May	J. E. Cheetham[11]	5	3	2	0
1956-57	P. B. H. May	C. B. van Ryneveld[12]	5	2	2	1
1960	M. C. Cowdrey	D. J. McGlew	5	3	0	2
1964-65	M. J. K. Smith	T. L. Goddard	5	1	0	4
1965	M. J. K. Smith	P. L. van der Merwe	3	0	1	2
	In South Africa		58	25	13	20
	In England		44	21	5	18
	Totals		102	46	18	38

Notes: The following deputised for the official touring captain or were appointed by the home authority for only a minor proportion of the series:

[1]M. P. Bowden (Second). [2]W. H. Milton (Second). [3]Sir T. C. O'Brien (First). [4]A. R. Richards (Third). [5]F. L. Fane (Fourth and Fifth). [6]L. J. Tancred (Second and Third). [7]J. W. H. T. Douglas (Fourth). [8]G. T. S. Stevens (Fifth). [9]A. W. Carr (Fourth and Fifth). [10]E. P. Nupen (First), H. B. Cameron (Fourth and Fifth). [11]D. J. McGlew (Third and Fourth). [12]D. J. McGlew (Second).

HIGHEST INNINGS TOTALS

For England in England: 554-8 dec. at Lord's	1947
in South Africa: 654-5 at Durban	1938-39
For South Africa in England: 538 at Leeds	1951
in South Africa: 530 at Durban	1938-39

LOWEST INNINGS TOTALS

For England in England: 76 at Leeds	1907
in South Africa: 92 at Cape Town	1898-99
For South Africa in England: 30 at Birmingham	1924
in South Africa: 30 at Port Elizabeth	1895-96

INDIVIDUAL HUNDREDS

For England (87)

120	R. Abel, Cape Town	1888-89
148*	L. E. G. Ames, The Oval .	1935
115	L. E. G. Ames, Cape Town	1938-39
148*	K. F. Barrington, Durban	1964-65
121	K. F. Barrington, Johannesburg	1964-65
117	G. Boycott, Port Elizabeth	1964-65
104†	L. C. Braund, Lord's	1907
208	D. C. S. Compton, Lord's .	1947
163†	D. C. S. Compton, Nottingham	1947
115	D. C. S. Compton, Manchester	1947
113	D. C. S. Compton, The Oval	1947
114	D. C. S. Compton, Johannesburg	1948-49
112	D. C. S. Compton, Nottingham	1951
158	D. C. S. Compton, Manchester	1955
101	M. C. Cowdrey, Cape Town	1956-57
155	M. C. Cowdrey, The Oval .	1960
105	M. C. Cowdrey, Nottingham	1965
104	D. Denton, Johannesburg .	1909-10
172	E. R. Dexter, Johannesburg	1964-65
119†	J. W. H. T. Douglas, Durban	1913-14
219	W. J. Edrich, Durban	1938-39
191	W. J. Edrich, Manchester .	1947
189	W. J. Edrich, Lord's	1947
143	F. L. Fane, Johannesburg .	1905-06
129	C. B. Fry, The Oval	1907
106†	P. A. Gibb, Johannesburg .	1938-39
120	P. A. Gibb, Durban	1938-39
138*	W. R. Hammond, Birmingham	1929
101*	W. R. Hammond, The Oval	1929
136*	W. R. Hammond, Durban .	1930-31
181	W. R. Hammond, Cape Town	1938-39
120	W. R. Hammond, Durban .	1938-39
140	W. R. Hammond, Durban .	1938-39
122	T. W. Hayward, Johannesburg	1895-96
132	E. H. Hendren, Leeds	1924
142	E. H. Hendren, The Oval .	1924
124	A. J. L. Hill, Cape Town . .	1895-96
187	J. B. Hobbs, Cape Town . .	1909-10
211	J. B. Hobbs, Lord's	1924
100	L. Hutton, Leeds	1947
158	L. Hutton, Johannesburg .	1948-49
123	L. Hutton, Johannesburg .	1948-49

100	L. Hutton, Leeds	1951
110*	D. J. Insole, Durban	1956-57
102	M. Leyland, Lord's	1929
161	M. Leyland, The Oval	1935
136*	F. G. Mann, Port Elizabeth	1948-49
138†	P. B. H. May, Leeds	1951
112	P. B. H. May, Lord's	1955
117	P. B. H. May, Manchester .	1955
102	C. P. Mead, Johannesburg .	1913-14
117	C. P. Mead, Port Elizabeth	1913-14
181	C. P. Mead, Durban	1922-23
122*	P. H. Parfitt, Johannesburg	1964-65
108*	J. M. Parks, Durban	1964-65
117† 100 }	E. Paynter, Johannesburg .	1938-39
243	E. Paynter, Durban	1938-39
175	G. Pullar, The Oval	1960
152	W. Rhodes, Johannesburg .	1913-14
117†	P. E. Richardson, Johannesburg	1956-57
108	R. W. V. Robins, Manchester	1935
140 111 }	A. C. Russell, Durban	1922-23
137	R. T. Simpson, Nottingham	1951
121	M. J. K. Smith, Cape Town	1964-65
119†	R. H. Spooner, Lord's	1912
122	H. Sutcliffe, Lord's	1924
102	H. Sutcliffe, Johannesburg .	1927-28
114	H. Sutcliffe, Birmingham .	1929
100	H. Sutcliffe, Lord's	1929
104 109* }	H. Sutcliffe, The Oval	1929
100*	M. W. Tate, Lord's	1929
122†	E. Tyldesley, Johannesburg	1927-28
100	E. Tyldesley, Durban	1927-28
112	J. T. Tyldesley, Cape Town	1898-99
112	B. H. Valentine, Cape Town	1938-39
132*†‡	P. F. Warner, Johannesburg	1898-99
195	C. Washbrook, Johannesburg	1948-49
111	A. J. Watkins, Johannesburg	1948-49
134*	H. Wood, Cape Town	1891-92
115*	F. E. Woolley, Johannesburg	1922-23
134*	F. E. Woolley, Lord's	1924
154	F. E. Woolley, Manchester .	1929
113	R. E. S. Wyatt, Manchester	1929
149	R. E. S. Wyatt, Nottingham	1935

For South Africa (58)

138	E. J. Barlow, Cape Town . .	1964-65
144*	K. C. Bland, Johannesburg	1964-65

127	K. C. Bland, The Oval	1965
120	R. H. Catterall, Birmingham	1924

120	R. H. Catterall, Lord's ...	1924	112	A. D. Nourse, Cape Town .	1948-49
119	R. H. Catterall, Durban ..	1927-28	208	A. D. Nourse, Nottingham	1951
117	E. L. Dalton, The Oval ...	1935	129	H. G. Owen-Smith, Leeds .	1929
102	E. L. Dalton, Johannesburg	1938-39	154	A. J. Pithey, Cape Town ..	1964-65
116*	W. R. Endean, Leeds	1955	137	R. G. Pollock, Port Elizabeth	1964-65
123	G. A. Faulkner, Johannesburg	1909-10	125	R. G. Pollock, Nottingham	1965
112	T. L. Goddard, Johannesburg	1964-65	156*	E. A. B. Rowan, Johannesburg	1948-49
102	C. M. H. Hathorn, Johannesburg	1905-06	236	E. A. B. Rowan, Leeds ...	1951
			115	P. W. Sherwell, Lord's	1907
104*	D. J. McGlew, Manchester	1955	141	I. J. Siedle, Cape Town ..	1930-31
133	D. J. McGlew, Leeds	1955	106	J. H. Sinclair, Cape Town .	1898-99
142	R. A. McLean, Lord's ...	1955	109	H. W. Taylor, Durban	1913-14
100	R. A. McLean, Durban ..	1956-57	176	H. W. Taylor, Johannesburg	1922-23
109	R. A. McLean, Manchester	1960			
103	A. Melville, Durban	1938-39	101	H. W. Taylor, Johannesburg	1922-23
189 } 104*	A. Melville, Nottingham ..	1947	102	H. W. Taylor, Durban	1922-23
117	A. Melville, Lord's	1947	101	H. W. Taylor, Johannesburg	1927-28
123	B. Mitchell, Cape Town ..	1930-31			
164*	B. Mitchell, Lord's	1935	121	H. W. Taylor, The Oval ..	1929
128	B. Mitchell, The Oval	1935	117	H. W. Taylor, Cape Town .	1930-31
109	B. Mitchell, Durban	1938-39	125	P. G. V. van der Bijl, Durban	1938-39
120 } 189*	B. Mitchell, The Oval	1947	124	K. G. Viljoen, Manchester .	1935
120	B. Mitchell, Cape Town ...	1948-49	125	W. W. Wade, Port Elizabeth	1948-49
120	A. D. Nourse, Cape Town .	1938-39			
103	A. D. Nourse, Durban ...	1938-39	113	J. H. B. Waite, Manchester	1955
149	A. D. Nourse, Nottingham	1947			
115	A. D. Nourse, Manchester .	1947	147	G. C. White, Johannesburg	1905-06
129*	A. D. Nourse, Johannesburg	1948-49	118	G. C. White, Durban	1909-10
			108	P. L. Winslow, Manchester	1955

† *Signifies hundred on first appearance in England–South Africa Tests.*
‡ *P. F. Warner carried his bat through the second innings.*
Notes: The highest score by a South African batsman on début is 93* by A. W. Nourse at Johannesburg in 1905-06.
P. N. F. Mansell made 90 at Leeds in 1951, the best on début in England.
A. Melville's four hundreds were made in successive Test innings.
H. Wood scored the only hundred of his career in a Test match.

RECORD PARTNERSHIP FOR EACH WICKET

For England

359 for 1st†	L. Hutton and C. Washbrook at Johannesburg	1948-49
280 for 2nd	P. A. Gibb and W. J. Edrich at Durban	1938-39
370 for 3rd†	W. J. Edrich and D. C. S. Compton at Lord's	1947
197 for 4th	W. R. Hammond and L. E. G. Ames at Cape Town	1938-39
237 for 5th	D. C. S. Compton and N. W. D. Yardley at Nottingham	1947
206* for 6th	K. F. Barrington and J. M. Parks at Durban	1964-65
115 for 7th	M. C. Bird and J. W. H. T. Douglas at Durban	1913-14
154 for 8th	C. W. Wright and H. R. Bromley-Davenport at Johannesburg ..	1895-96
71 for 9th	H. Wood and J. T. Hearne at Cape Town	1891-92
92 for 10th	A. C. Russell and A. E. R. Gilligan at Durban	1922-23

For South Africa

260 for 1st†	I. J. Siedle and B. Mitchell at Cape Town	1930-31
198 for 2nd†	E. A. B. Rowan and C. B. van Ryneveld at Leeds	1951
319 for 3rd	A. Melville and A. D. Nourse at Nottingham	1947

214 for 4th†	H. W. Taylor and H. G. Deane at The Oval	1929
157 for 5th†	A. J. Pithey and J. H. B. Waite at Johannesburg	1964-65
171 for 6th	J. H. B. Waite and P. L. Winslow at Manchester	1955
123 for 7th	H. G. Deane and E. P. Nupen at Durban	1927-28
109* for 8th	B. Mitchell and L. Tuckett at The Oval	1947
137 for 9th†	E. L. Dalton and A. B. C. Langton at The Oval	1935
103 for 10th†	H. G. Owen-Smith and A. J. Bell at Leeds	1929

† *Denotes record partnership against all countries.*

MOST RUNS IN A SERIES

England in England	753 (average 94.12)	D. C. S. Compton .	1947
England in South Africa	653 (average 81.62)	E. Paynter	1938-39
South Africa in England	621 (average 69.00)	A. D. Nourse	1947
South Africa in South Africa .	582 (average 64.66)	H. W. Taylor	1922-23

TEN WICKETS OR MORE IN A MATCH

For England (23)

11-110 (5-25, 6-85)†	S. F. Barnes, Lord's	1912
10-115 (6-52, 4-63)	S. F. Barnes, Leeds	1912
13-57 (5-28, 8-29)	S. F. Barnes, The Oval	1912
10-105 (5-57, 5-48)	S. F. Barnes, Durban	1913-14
17-159 (8-56, 9-103)	S. F. Barnes, Johannesburg	1913-14
14-144 (7-56, 7-88)	S. F. Barnes, Johannesburg	1913-14
12-112 (7-58, 5-54)	A. V. Bedser, Manchester	1951
11-118 (6-68, 5-50)	C. Blythe, Cape Town	1905-06
15-99 (8-59, 7-40)	C. Blythe, Leeds	1907
10-104 (7-46, 3-58)	C. Blythe, Cape Town	1909-10
15-28 (7-17, 8-11)	J. Briggs, Cape Town	1888-89
13-91 (6-54, 7-37)†	J. J. Ferris, Cape Town	1891-92
10-207 (7-115, 3-92)	A. P. Freeman, Leeds	1929
12-171 (7-71, 5-100)	A. P. Freeman, Manchester	1929
12-130 (7-70, 5-60)	G. Geary, Johannesburg	1927-28
11-90 (6-7, 5-83)	A. E. R. Gilligan, Birmingham	1924
10-119 (4-64, 6-55)	J. C. Laker, The Oval	1951
15-45 (7-38, 8-7)†	G. A. Lohmann, Port Elizabeth	1895-96
12-71 (9-28, 3-43)	G. A. Lohmann, Johannesburg	1895-96
11-97 (6-63, 5-34)	J. B. Statham, Lord's	1960
12-101 (7-52, 5-49)	R. Tattersall, Lord's	1951
12-89 (5-53, 7-36)	J. H. Wardle, Cape Town	1956-57
10-175 (5-95, 5-80)	D. V. P. Wright, Lord's	1947

For South Africa (6)

11-112 (4-49, 7-63)†	A. E. Hall, Cape Town	1922-23
11-150 (5-63, 6-87)	E. P. Nupen, Johannesburg	1930-31
10-87 (5-53, 5-34)	P. M. Pollock, Nottingham	1965
12-127 (4-57, 8-70)	S. J. Snooke, Johannesburg	1905-06
13-192 (4-79, 9-113)	H. J. Tayfield, Johannesburg	1956-57
12-181 (5-87, 7-94)	A. E. E. Vogler, Johannesburg	1909-10

† *Signifies ten wickets or more on first appearance in England–South Africa Tests.*

Note: S. F. Barnes took ten wickets or more in his first five Tests v South Africa and in six of his seven Tests v South Africa. A. P. Freeman and G. A. Lohmann took ten wickets or more in successive matches.

MOST WICKETS IN A SERIES

England in England	34 (average 8.29)	S. F. Barnes	1912
England in South Africa	49 (average 10.93)	S. F. Barnes	1913-14
South Africa in England	26 (average 21.84)	H. J. Tayfield	1955
South Africa in England	26 (average 22.57)	N. A. T. Adcock ..	1960
South Africa in South Africa .	37 (average 17.18)	H. J. Tayfield	1956-57

ENGLAND v WEST INDIES

	Captains					
Season	*England*	*West Indies*	*T*	*E*	*WI*	*D*
1928	A. P. F. Chapman	R. K. Nunes	3	3	0	0
1929-30	Hon. F. S. G. Calthorpe	E. L. G. Hoad[1]	4	1	1	2
1933	D. R. Jardine[2]	G. C. Grant	3	2	0	1
1934-35	R. E. S. Wyatt	G. C. Grant	4	1	2	1
1939	W. R. Hammond	R. S. Grant	3	1	0	2
1947-48	G. O. Allen[3]	J. D. C. Goddard[4]	4	0	2	2
1950	N. W. D. Yardley[5]	J. D. C. Goddard	4	1	3	0
1953-54	L. Hutton	J. B. Stollmeyer	5	2	2	1
1957	P. B. H. May	J. D. C. Goddard	5	3	0	2
1959-60	P. B. H. May[6]	F. C. M. Alexander	5	1	0	4

THE WISDEN TROPHY

	Captains						
Season	*England*	*West Indies*	*T*	*E*	*WI*	*D*	*Held by*
1963	E. R. Dexter	F. M. M. Worrell	5	1	3	1	WI
1966	M. C. Cowdrey[7]	G. S. Sobers	5	1	3	1	WI
1967-68	M. C. Cowdrey	G. S. Sobers	5	1	0	4	E
1969	R. Illingworth	G. S. Sobers	3	2	0	1	E
1973	R. Illingworth	R. B. Kanhai	3	0	2	1	WI
1973-74	M. H. Denness	R. B. Kanhai	5	1	1	3	WI
1976	A. W. Greig	C. H. Lloyd	5	0	3	2	WI
1980	I. T. Botham	C. H. Lloyd[8]	5	0	1	4	WI
1980-81†	I. T. Botham	C. H. Lloyd	4	0	2	2	WI
1984	D. I. Gower	C. H. Lloyd	5	0	5	0	WI
1985-86	D. I. Gower	I. V. A. Richards	5	0	5	0	WI
	In England		49	14	20	15	
	In West Indies		41	7	15	19	
	Totals		90	21	35	34	

† *The Test match at Georgetown, scheduled as the second of the series, was cancelled owing to political pressure.*

Notes: The following deputised for the official touring captain or were appointed by the home authority for only a minor proportion of the series:

[1]N. Betancourt (Second), M. P. Fernandes (Third), R. K. Nunes (Fourth). [2]R. E. S. Wyatt (Third). [3]K. Cranston (First). [4]G. A. Headley (First), G. E. Gomez (Second). [5]F. R. Brown (Fourth). [6]M. C. Cowdrey (Fourth and Fifth). [7]M. J. K. Smith (First), D. B. Close (Fifth). [8]I. V. A. Richards (Fifth).

HIGHEST INNINGS TOTALS

For England in England: 619-6 dec. at Nottingham 1957
           in West Indies: 849 at Kingston 1929-30
For West Indies in England: 687-8 dec. at The Oval 1976
            in West Indies: 681-8 dec. at Port-of-Spain 1953-54

LOWEST INNINGS TOTALS

For England in England: 71 at Manchester 1976
           in West Indies: 103 at Kingston 1934-35
For West Indies in England: 86 at The Oval 1957
            in West Indies: 102 at Bridgetown 1934-35

INDIVIDUAL HUNDREDS

For England (81)

105	L. E. G. Ames, Port-of-Spain	1929-30
149	L. E. G. Ames, Kingston	1929-30
126	L. E. G. Ames, Kingston	1934-35
174	D. L. Amiss, Port-of-Spain	1973-74
262*	D. L. Amiss, Kingston	1973-74
118	D. L. Amiss, Georgetown	1973-74
203	D. L. Amiss, The Oval	1976
107†	A. H. Bakewell, The Oval	1933
128†	K. F. Barrington, Bridgetown	1959-60
121	K. F. Barrington, Port-of-Spain	1959-60
143	K. F. Barrington, Port-of-Spain	1967-68
116	G. Boycott, Georgetown	1967-68
128	G. Boycott, Manchester	1969
106	G. Boycott, Lord's	1969
112	G. Boycott, Port-of-Spain	1973-74
104*	G. Boycott, St John's	1980-81
120†	D. C. S. Compton, Lord's	1939
133	D. C. S. Compton, Port-of-Spain	1953-54
154†	M. C. Cowdrey, Birmingham	1957
152	M. C. Cowdrey, Lord's	1957
114	M. C. Cowdrey, Kingston	1959-60
119	M. C. Cowdrey, Port-of-Spain	1959-60
101	M. C. Cowdrey, Kingston	1967-68
148	M. C. Cowdrey, Port-of-Spain	1967-68
136*†	E. R. Dexter, Bridgetown	1959-60
110	E. R. Dexter, Georgetown	1959-60
146	J. H. Edrich, Bridgetown	1967-68
104	T. G. Evans, Manchester	1950
129*	K. W. R. Fletcher, Bridgetown	1973-74
106	G. Fowler, Lord's	1984
123	G. A. Gooch, Lord's	1980
116	G. A. Gooch, Bridgetown	1980-81
153	G. A. Gooch, Kingston	1980-81
154*	D. I. Gower, Kingston	1980-81
258	T. W. Graveney, Nottingham	1957
164	T. W. Graveney, The Oval	1957
109	T. W. Graveney, Nottingham	1966
165	T. W. Graveney, The Oval	1966
118	T. W. Graveney, Port-of-Spain	1967-68
148	A. W. Greig, Bridgetown	1973-74
121	A. W. Greig, Georgetown	1973-74
116	A. W. Greig, Leeds	1976
140†	S. C. Griffith, Port-of-Spain	1947-48
138	W. R. Hammond, The Oval	1939
107†	J. H. Hampshire, Lord's	1969
106*†	F. C. Hayes, The Oval	1973
205*	E. H. Hendren, Port-of-Spain	1929-30
123	E. H. Hendren, Georgetown	1929-30
159	J. B. Hobbs, The Oval	1928
196†	L. Hutton, Lord's	1939
165*	L. Hutton, The Oval	1939
202*‡	L. Hutton, The Oval	1950
169	L. Hutton, Georgetown	1953-54
205	L. Hutton, Kingston	1953-54
113	R. Illingworth, Lord's	1969
127	D. R. Jardine, Manchester	1933
116	A. P. E. Knott, Leeds	1976
110	A. J. Lamb, Lord's	1984
100	A. J. Lamb, Leeds	1984
100*	A. J. Lamb, Manchester	1984
135	P. B. H. May, Port-of-Spain	1953-54
285*	P. B. H. May, Birmingham	1957
104	P. B. H. May, Nottingham	1957
126*	C. Milburn, Lord's	1966
112†	J. T. Murray, The Oval	1966
101*†	J. M. Parks, Port-of-Spain	1959-60
107	W. Place, Kingston	1947-48

126	P. E. Richardson, Nottingham	1957
107	P. E. Richardson, The Oval	1957
133	J. D. Robertson, Port-of-Spain	1947-48
152†	A. Sandham, Bridgetown	1929-30
325	A. Sandham, Kingston	1929-30
108	M. J. K. Smith, Port-of-Spain	1959-60
106†	D. S. Steele, Nottingham	1976

100†	R. Subba Row, Georgetown	1959-60
122†	E. Tyldesley, Lord's	1928
114†	C. Washbrook, Lord's	1950
102	C. Washbrook, Nottingham	1950
116†	W. Watson, Kingston	1953-54
100*	P. Willey, The Oval	1980
102*	P. Willey, St John's	1980-81

For West Indies (91)

105	I. Barrow, Manchester	1933
133	B. F. Butcher, Lord's	1963
209*	B. F. Butcher, Nottingham	1966
107	G. M. Carew, Port-of-Spain	1947-48
103	C. A. Davis, Lord's	1969
101	P. J. Dujon, Manchester	1984
150	R. C. Fredericks, Birmingham	1973
138	R. C. Fredericks, Lord's	1976
109	R. C. Fredericks, Leeds	1976
112†	A. G. Ganteaume, Port-of-Spain	1947-48
143	H. A. Gomes, Birmingham	1984
104*	H. A. Gomes, Leeds	1984
134 }	C. G. Greenidge, Manchester	1976
101 }		
115	C. G. Greenidge, Leeds	1976
214*	C. G. Greenidge, Lord's	1984
223	C. G. Greenidge, Manchester	1984
184	D. L. Haynes, Lord's	1980
125	D. L. Haynes, The Oval	1984
131	D. L. Haynes, St John's	1985-86
176†	G. A. Headley, Bridgetown	1929-30
114 }	G. A. Headley, Georgetown	1929-30
112 }		
223	G. A. Headley, Kingston	1929-30
169*	G. A. Headley, Manchester	1933
270*	G. A. Headley, Kingston	1934-35
106 }	G. A. Headley, Lord's	1939
107 }		
105*	D. A. J. Holford, Lord's	1966
166	J. K. Holt, Bridgetown	1953-54
182	C. C. Hunte, Manchester	1963
108*	C. C. Hunte, The Oval	1963
135	C. C. Hunte, Manchester	1966
121	B. D. Julien, Lord's	1973
158	A. I. Kallicharran, Port-of-Spain	1973-74
119	A. I. Kallicharran, Bridgetown	1973-74
110	R. B. Kanhai, Port-of-Spain	1959-60
104	R. B. Kanhai, The Oval	1966
153	R. B. Kanhai, Port-of-Spain	1967-68
150	R. B. Kanhai, Georgetown	1967-68
157	R. B. Kanhai, Lord's	1973
118†	C. H. Lloyd, Port-of-Spain	1967-68
113*	C. H. Lloyd, Bridgetown	1967-68
132	C. H. Lloyd, The Oval	1973

101	C. H. Lloyd, Manchester	1980
100	C. H. Lloyd, Bridgetown	1980-81
137	S. M. Nurse, Leeds	1966
136	S. M. Nurse, Port-of-Spain	1967-68
106	A. F. Rae, Lord's	1950
109	A. F. Rae, The Oval	1950
232†	I. V. A. Richards, Nottingham	1976
135	I. V. A. Richards, Manchester	1976
291	I. V. A. Richards, The Oval	1976
145	I. V. A. Richards, Lord's	1980
182*	I. V. A. Richards, Bridgetown	1980-81
114	I. V. A. Richards, St John's	1980-81
117	I. V. A. Richards, Birmingham	1984
110*	I. V. A. Richards, St John's	1985-86
102	R. B. Richardson, Port-of-Spain	1985-86
160	R. B. Richardson, Bridgetown	1985-86
122	C. A. Roach, Bridgetown	1929-30
209	C. A. Roach, Georgetown	1929-30
120	L. G. Rowe, Kingston	1973-74
302	L. G. Rowe, Bridgetown	1973-74
123	L. G. Rowe, Port-of-Spain	1973-74
161†	O. G. Smith, Birmingham	1957
168	O. G. Smith, Nottingham	1957
226	G. S. Sobers, Bridgetown	1959-60
147	G. S. Sobers, Kingston	1959-60
145	G. S. Sobers, Georgetown	1959-60
102	G. S. Sobers, Leeds	1963
161	G. S. Sobers, Manchester	1966
163*	G. S. Sobers, Lord's	1966
174	G. S. Sobers, Leeds	1966
113*	G. S. Sobers, Kingston	1967-68
152	G. S. Sobers, Georgetown	1967-68
150*	G. S. Sobers, Lord's	1973
168*	C. L. Walcott, Lord's	1950
220	C. L. Walcott, Bridgetown	1953-54
124	C. L. Walcott, Port-of-Spain	1953-54
116	C. L. Walcott, Kingston	1953-54
141	E. D. Weekes, Kingston	1947-48
129	E. D. Weekes, Nottingham	1950
206	E. D. Weekes, Port-of-Spain	1953-54

137	K. H. Weekes, The Oval ..	1939	167	F. M. M. Worrell, Port-of-Spain	1953-54
131*	F. M. M. Worrell, Georgetown	1947-48	191*‡	F. M. M. Worrell, Nottingham	1957
261	F. M. M. Worrell, Nottingham	1950	197*	F. M. M. Worrell, Bridgetown	1959-60
138	F. M. M. Worrell, The Oval	1950			

† Signifies hundred on first appearance in England–West Indies Tests. S. C. Griffith provides the only instance for England of a player hitting his maiden century in first-class cricket in his first Test.
‡ Carried his bat.

RECORD PARTNERSHIPS FOR EACH WICKET

For England

212 for 1st	C. Washbrook and R. T. Simpson at Nottingham	1950
266 for 2nd	P. E. Richardson and T. W. Graveney at Nottingham	1957
264 for 3rd	L. Hutton and W. R. Hammond at The Oval	1939
411 for 4th†	P. B. H. May and M. C. Cowdrey at Birmingham	1957
130* for 5th	C. Milburn and T. W. Graveney at Lord's	1966
163 for 6th	A. W. Greig and A. P. E. Knott at Bridgetown	1973-74
197 for 7th†	M. J. K. Smith and J. M. Parks at Port-of-Spain	1959-60
217 for 8th	W. Graveney and J. T. Murray at The Oval	1966
109 for 9th	G. A. R. Lock and P. I. Pocock at Georgetown	1967-68
128 for 10th	K. Higgs and J. A. Snow at The Oval	1966

For West Indies

206 for 1st	R. C. Fredericks and L. G. Rowe at Kingston	1973-74
287* for 2nd	C. G. Greenidge and H. A. Gomes at Lord's	1984
338 for 3rd†	E. D. Weekes and F. M. M. Worrell at Port-of-Spain	1953-54
399 for 4th	G. S. Sobers and F. M. M. Worrell at Bridgetown	1959-60
265 for 5th	S. M. Nurse and G. S. Sobers at Leeds	1966
274* for 6th	G. S. Sobers and D. A. J. Holford at Lord's	1966
155* for 7th‡	G. S. Sobers and B. D. Julien at Lord's	1973
99 for 8th	C. A. McWatt and J. K. Holt at Georgetown	1953-54
150 for 9th	E. A. E. Baptiste and M. A. Holding at Birmingham	1984
67* for 10th	M. A. Holding and C. E. H. Croft at St John's	1980-81

† Denotes record partnership against all countries.
‡ 231 runs were added for this wicket in two separate partnerships: G. S. Sobers retired ill and was replaced by K. D. Boyce when 155 had been added.

TEN WICKETS OR MORE IN A MATCH

For England (10)

11-98 (7-44, 4-54)	T. E. Bailey, Lord's	1957
10-93 (5-54, 5-39)	A. P. Freeman, Manchester	1928
13-156 (8-86, 5-70)	A. W. Greig, Port-of-Spain	1973-74
11-48 (5-28, 6-20)	G. A. R. Lock, The Oval	1957
11-96 (5-37, 6-59)†	C. S. Marriott, The Oval	1933
10-142 (4-82, 6-60)	J. A. Snow, Georgetown	1967-68
10-195 (5-105, 5-90)†	G. T. S. Stevens, Bridgetown	1929-30
11-152 (6-100, 5-52)	F. S. Trueman, Lord's	1963
12-119 (5-75, 7-44)	F. S. Trueman, Birmingham	1963
11-149 (4-79, 7-70)	W. Voce, Port-of-Spain	1929-30

For West Indies (10)

11-147 (5-70, 6-77)†	K. D. Boyce, The Oval	1973
11-229 (5-137, 6-92)	W. Ferguson, Port-of-Spain	1947-48
11-157 (5-59, 6-98)†	L. R. Gibbs, Manchester	1963

10-106 (5-37, 5-69)	L. R. Gibbs, Manchester	1966
14-149 (8-92, 6-57)	M. A. Holding, The Oval	1976
10-96 (5-41, 5-55)†	H. H. H. Johnson, Kingston	1947-48
11-152 (5-66, 6-86)	S. Ramadhin, Lord's	1950
10-123 (5-60, 5-63)	A. M. E. Roberts, Lord's	1976
11-204 (8-104, 3-100)†	A. L. Valentine, Manchester	1950
10-160 (4-121, 6-39)	A. L. Valentine, The Oval	1950

† *Signifies ten wickets or more on first appearance in England–West Indies Tests.*

Note: F. S. Trueman took ten wickets or more in successive matches.

ENGLAND v NEW ZEALAND

		Captains				
Season	*England*	*New Zealand*	*T*	*E*	*NZ*	*D*
1929-30	A. H. H. Gilligan	T. C. Lowry	4	1	0	3
1931	D. R. Jardine	T. C. Lowry	3	1	0	2
1932-33	D. R. Jardine[1]	M. L. Page	2	0	0	2
1937	R. W. V. Robins	M. L. Page	3	1	0	2
1946-47	W. R. Hammond	W. A. Hadlee	1	0	0	1
1949	F. G. Mann[2]	W. A. Hadlee	4	0	0	4
1950-51	F. R. Brown	W. A. Hadlee	2	1	0	1
1954-55	L. Hutton	G. O. Rabone	2	2	0	0
1958	P. B. H. May	J. R. Reid	5	4	0	1
1958-59	P. B. H. May	J. R. Reid	2	1	0	1
1962-63	E. R. Dexter	J. R. Reid	3	3	0	0
1965	M. J. K. Smith	J. R. Reid	3	3	0	0
1965-66	M. J. K. Smith	B. W. Sinclair[3]	3	0	0	3
1969	R. Illingworth	G. T. Dowling	3	2	0	1
1970-71	R. Illingworth	G. T. Dowling	2	1	0	1
1973	R. Illingworth	B. E. Congdon	3	2	0	1
1974-75	M. H. Denness	B. E. Congdon	2	1	0	1
1977-78	G. Boycott	M. G. Burgess	3	1	1	1
1978	J. M. Brearley	M. G. Burgess	3	3	0	0
1983	R. G. D. Willis	G. P. Howarth	4	3	1	0
1983-84	R. G. D. Willis	G. P. Howarth	3	0	1	2
1986	M. W. Gatting	J. V. Coney	3	0	1	2
	In New Zealand		29	11	2	16
	In England		34	19	2	13
	Totals		63	30	4	29

Notes: The following deputised for the official touring captain or were appointed by the home authority for only a minor proportion of the series:
[1]R. E. S. Wyatt (Second). [2]F. R. Brown (Third and Fourth). [3]M. E. Chapple (First).

HIGHEST INNINGS TOTALS

For England in England: 546-4 dec. at Leeds	1965
in New Zealand: 593-6 dec. at Auckland	1974-75
For New Zealand in England: 551-9 dec. at Lord's	1973
in New Zealand: 537 at Wellington	1983-84

LOWEST INNINGS TOTALS

For England in England: 187 at Manchester	1937
in New Zealand: 64 at Wellington	1977-78
For New Zealand in England: 47 at Lord's	1958
in New Zealand: 26 at Auckland	1954-55

INDIVIDUAL HUNDREDS

For England (68)

122†	G. O. Allen, Lord's	1931
137†	L. E. G. Ames, Lord's	1931
103	L. E. G. Ames, Christchurch	1932-33
138*†	D. L. Amiss, Nottingham .	1973
164*	D. L. Amiss, Christchurch	1974-75
134*	T. E. Bailey, Christchurch .	1950-51
126†	K. F. Barrington, Auckland	1962-63
163	K. F. Barrington, Leeds ...	1965
137	K. F. Barrington, Birmingham	1965
103	I. T. Botham, Christchurch	1977-78
103	I. T. Botham, Nottingham .	1983
138	I. T. Botham, Wellington .	1983-84
109	E. H. Bowley, Auckland .	1929-30
115	G. Boycott, Leeds	1973
131	G. Boycott, Nottingham ...	1978
114	D. C. S. Compton, Leeds ..	1949
116	D. C. S. Compton, Lord's .	1949
128*	M. C. Cowdrey, Wellington	1962-63
119	M. C. Cowdrey, Lord's....	1965
181	M. H. Denness, Auckland .	1974-75
141	E. R. Dexter, Christchurch	1958-59
100	B. L. D'Oliveira, Christchurch	1970-71
117	K. S. Duleepsinhji, Auckland	1929-30
109	K. S. Duleepsinhji, The Oval	1931
310*†	J. H. Edrich, Leeds	1965
155	J. H. Edrich, Lord's	1969
115	J. H. Edrich, Nottingham .	1969
100	W. J. Edrich, The Oval	1949
178	K. W. R. Fletcher, Lord's .	1973
216	K. W. R. Fletcher, Auckland	1974-75
105†	G. Fowler, The Oval	1983
121	M. W. Gatting, The Oval .	1986
183	G. A. Gooch, Lord's	1986
111†	D. I. Gower, The Oval	1978
112*	D. I. Gower, Leeds	1983
108	D. I. Gower, Lord's	1983
131	D. I. Gower, The Oval	1986
139†	A. W. Greig, Nottingham .	1973
100*	W. R. Hammond, The Oval	1931
227	W. R. Hammond, Christchurch	1932-33
336*	W. R. Hammond, Auckland	1932-33
140	W. R. Hammond, Lord's .	1937
114†	J. Hardstaff jun., Lord's .	1937
103	J. Hardstaff jun., The Oval	1937
100	L. Hutton, Manchester	1937
101	L. Hutton, Leeds	1949
206	L. Hutton, The Oval	1949
125†	B. R. Knight, Auckland ...	1962-63
101	A. P. E. Knott, Auckland .	1970-71
102*†	A. J. Lamb, The Oval	1983
137*	A. J. Lamb, Nottingham ..	1983
196	G. B. Legge, Auckland	1929-30
113*	P. B. H. May, Leeds	1958
101	P. B. H. May, Manchester .	1958
124*	P. B. H. May, Auckland .	1958-59
104*†	C. A. Milton, Leeds	1958
131*†	P. H. Parfitt, Auckland ...	1962-63
158	C. T. Radley, Auckland ..	1977-78
164	D. W. Randall, Wellington	1983-84
104	D. W. Randall, Auckland .	1983-84
100†	P. E. Richardson, Birmingham	1958
121†	J. D. Robertson, Lord's ...	1949
111	P. J. Sharpe, Nottingham .	1969
103†	R. T. Simpson, Manchester	1949
117†	H. Sutcliffe, The Oval	1931
109*	H. Sutcliffe, Manchester ...	1931
109†	C. J. Tavaré, The Oval ...	1983
103*	C. Washbrook, Leeds	1949

For New Zealand (29)

110	J. G. Bracewell, Nottingham	1986
104	M. G. Burgess, Auckland ..	1970-71
105	M. G. Burgess, Lord's	1973
174*	J. V. Coney, Wellington .	1983-84
104	B. E. Congdon, Christchurch	1965-66
176	B. E. Congdon, Nottingham	1973
175	B. E. Congdon, Lord's ...	1973
128	J. J. Crowe, Auckland	1983-84
100	M. D. Crowe, Wellington .	1983-84
106	M. D. Crowe, Lord's	1986
136	C. S. Dempster, Wellington	1929-30
120	C. S. Dempster, Lord's	1931
206	M. P. Donnelly, Lord's	1949
116	W. A. Hadlee, Christchurch	1946-47
122 } 102 }	G. P. Howarth, Auckland .	1977-78
123	G. P. Howarth, Lord's	1978
117†	J. E. Mills, Wellington ...	1929-30
104	M. L. Page, Lord's	1931
121	J. M. Parker, Auckland ...	1974-75
116	V. Pollard, Nottingham ...	1973
105*	V. Pollard, Lord's	1973
100	J. R. Reid, Christchurch ..	1962-63
114	B. W. Sinclair, Auckland ..	1965-66

113*	I. D. S. Smith, Auckland	1983-84	130	J. G. Wright, Auckland	1983-84
101	B. Sutcliffe, Manchester	1949	119	J. G. Wright, The Oval	1986
116	B. Sutcliffe, Christchurch	1950-51			

† *Signifies hundred on first appearance in England–New Zealand Tests.*

RECORD PARTNERSHIPS FOR EACH WICKET

For England

223 for 1st	G. Fowler and C. J. Tavaré at The Oval	1983
369 for 2nd	J. H. Edrich and K. F. Barrington at Leeds	1965
245 for 3rd	W. R. Hammond and J. Hardstaff jun. at Lord's	1937
266 for 4th	M. H. Denness and K. W. R. Fletcher at Auckland	1974-75
242 for 5th	W. R. Hammond and L. E. G. Ames at Christchurch	1932-33
240 for 6th†	P. H. Parfitt and B. R. Knight at Auckland	1962-63
149 for 7th	A. P. E. Knott and P. Lever at Auckland	1970-71
246 for 8th†	L. E. G. Ames and G. O. Allen at Lord's	1931
163* for 9th†	M. C. Cowdrey and A. C. Smith at Wellington	1962-63
59 for 10th	A. P. E. Knott and N. Gifford at Nottingham	1973

For New Zealand

276 for 1st	C. S. Dempster and J. E. Mills at Wellington	1929-30
131 for 2nd	B. Sutcliffe and J. R. Reid at Christchurch	1950-51
210 for 3rd	B. A. Edgar and M. D. Crowe at Lord's	1986
154 for 4th	J. G. Wright and J. J. Crowe at Auckland	1983-84
177 for 5th	B. E. Congdon and V. Pollard at Nottingham	1973
117 for 6th	M. G. Burgess and V. Pollard at Lord's	1973
104 for 7th	B. Sutcliffe and V. Pollard at Birmingham	1965
104 for 8th	A. W. Roberts and D. A. R. Moloney at Lord's	1937
118 for 9th†	J. V. Coney and B. L. Cairns at Wellington	1983-84
57 for 10th	F. L. H. Mooney and J. Cowie at Leeds	1949

† *Denotes record partnership against all countries.*

TEN WICKETS OR MORE IN A MATCH

For England (7)

11-140 (6-101, 5-39)	I. T. Botham, Lord's	1978
10-149 (5-98, 5-51)	A. W. Greig, Auckland	1974-75
11-65 (4-14, 7-51)	G. A. R. Lock, Leeds	1958
11-84 (5-31, 6-53)	G. A. R. Lock, Christchurch	1958-59
11-70 (4-38, 7-32)†	D. L. Underwood, Lord's	1969
12-101 (6-41, 6-60)	D. L. Underwood, The Oval	1969
12-97 (6-12, 6-85)	D. L. Underwood, Christchurch	1970-71

For New Zealand (4)

10-144 (7-74, 3-70)	B. L. Cairns, Leeds	1983
10-140 (4-73, 6-67)	J. Cowie, Manchester	1937
10-100 (4-74, 6-26)	R. J. Hadlee, Wellington	1977-78
10-140 (6-80, 4-60)	R. J. Hadlee, Nottingham	1986

† *Signifies ten wickets or more on first appearance in England–New Zealand Tests.*

Note: D. L. Underwood took twelve wickets in successive matches against New Zealand in 1969 and 1970-71.

HAT-TRICK AND FOUR WICKETS IN FIVE BALLS

M. J. C. Allom, in his first Test match, v New Zealand at Christchurch in 1929-30, dismissed C. S. Dempster, T. C. Lowry, K. C. James, and F. T. Badcock to take four wickets in five balls (w-www).

ENGLAND v INDIA

Captains

Season	England	India	T	E	I	D
1932	D. R. Jardine	C. K. Nayudu	1	1	0	0
1933-34	D. R. Jardine	C. K. Nayudu	3	2	0	1
1936	G. O. Allen	Maharaj of Vizianagram	3	2	0	1
1946	W. R. Hammond	Nawab of Pataudi sen.	3	1	0	2
1951-52	N. D. Howard[1]	V. S. Hazare	5	1	1	3
1952	L. Hutton	V. S. Hazare	4	3	0	1
1959	P. B. H. May[2]	D. K. Gaekwad[3]	5	5	0	0
1961-62	E. R. Dexter	N. J. Contractor	5	0	2	3
1963-64	M. J. K. Smith	Nawab of Pataudi jun.	5	0	0	5
1967	D. B. Close	Nawab of Pataudi jun.	3	3	0	0
1971	R. Illingworth	A. L. Wadekar	3	0	1	2
1972-73	A. R. Lewis	A. L. Wadekar	5	1	2	2
1974	M. H. Denness	A. L. Wadekar	3	3	0	0
1976-77	A. W. Greig	B. S. Bedi	5	3	1	1
1979	J. M. Brearley	S. Venkataraghavan	4	1	0	3
1979-80	J. M. Brearley	G. R. Viswanath	1	1	0	0
1981-82	K. W. R. Fletcher	S. M. Gavaskar	6	0	1	5
1982	R. G. D. Willis	S. M. Gavaskar	3	1	0	2
1984-85	D. I. Gower	S. M. Gavaskar	5	2	1	2
1986	M. W. Gatting[4]	Kapil Dev	3	0	2	1

In England		35	20	3	12
In India		40	10	8	22
Totals		75	30	11	34

Notes: The 1932 Indian touring team was captained by the Maharaj of Porbandar but he did not play in the Test match.

The following deputised for the official touring captain or were appointed by the home authority for only a minor proportion of the series:

[1]D. B. Carr (Fifth). [2]M. C. Cowdrey (Fourth and Fifth). [3]Pankaj Roy (Second). [4]D. I. Gower (First).

HIGHEST INNINGS TOTALS

For England in England: 633-5 dec. at Birmingham 1979
            in India: 652-7 dec. at Madras 1984-85

For India in England: 510 at Leeds 1967
            in India: 553-8 dec. at Kanpur 1984-85

LOWEST INNINGS TOTALS

For England in England: 101 at The Oval 1971
            in India: 102 at Bombay 1981-82

For India in England: 42 at Lord's 1974
            in India: 83 at Madras 1976-77

INDIVIDUAL HUNDREDS

For England (61)

188	D. L. Amiss, Lord's	1974	200*†	D. I. Gower, Birmingham .	1979
179	D. L. Amiss, Delhi	1976-77	175†	T. W. Graveney, Bombay .	1951-52
151*	K. F. Barrington, Bombay .	1961-62	151	T. W. Graveney, Lord's ...	1967
172	K. F. Barrington, Kanpur .	1961-62	148	A. W. Greig, Bombay	1972-73
113*	K. F. Barrington, Delhi ...	1961-62	106	A. W. Greig, Lord's	1974
137	I. T. Botham, Leeds	1979	103	A. W. Greig, Calcutta	1976-77
114	I. T. Botham, Bombay	1979-80	167	W. R. Hammond, Man-	
142	I. T. Botham, Kanpur	1981-82		chester	1936
128	I. T. Botham, Manchester .	1982	217	W. R. Hammond, The Oval	1936
208	I. T. Botham, The Oval ...	1982	205*	J. Hardstaff jun., Lord's ...	1946
246*†	G. Boycott, Leeds	1967	150	L. Hutton, Lord's	1952
155	G. Boycott, Birmingham .	1979	104	L. Hutton, Manchester	1952
125	G. Boycott, The Oval	1979	107	R. Illingworth, Manchester	1971
105	G. Boycott, Delhi	1981-82	127	B. R. Knight, Kanpur	1963-64
160	M. C. Cowdrey, Leeds	1959	107	A. J. Lamb, The Oval	1982
107	M. C. Cowdrey, Calcutta ..	1963-64	125	A. R. Lewis, Kanpur	1972-73
151	M. C. Cowdrey, Delhi	1963-64	214*	D. Lloyd, Birmingham ...	1974
118	M. H. Denness, Lord's	1974	101	B. W. Luckhurst, Man-	
100	M. H. Denness, Birming-			chester	1971
	ham	1974	106	P. B. H. May, Nottingham .	1959
126*	E. R. Dexter, Kanpur	1961-62	121	P. H. Parfitt, Kanpur	1963-64
109†	B. L. D'Oliveira, Leeds ...	1967	131	G. Pullar, Manchester	1959
100*	J. H. Edrich, Manchester .	1974	119	G. Pullar, Kanpur	1961-62
104	T. G. Evans, Lord's	1952	126	D. W. Randall, Lord's	1982
113	K. W. R. Fletcher, Bombay	1972-73	160	R. T. Robinson, Delhi	1984-85
123*	K. W. R. Fletcher, Man-		119	D. S. Sheppard, The Oval .	1952
	chester	1974	100†	M. J. K. Smith, Manchester	1959
201	G. Fowler, Madras	1984-85	149	C. J. Tavaré, Delhi	1981-82
136	M. W. Gatting, Bombay ..	1984-85	136†	B. H. Valentine, Bombay .	1933-34
207	M. W. Gatting, Madras ...	1984-85	102	C. F. Walters, Madras ...	1933-34
183*	M. W. Gatting, Birmingham	1986	137*†	A. J. Watkins, Delhi	1951-52
129	G. A. Gooch, Madras	1981-82	128	T. S. Worthington, The	
114	G. A. Gooch, Lord's	1986		Oval	1936

For India (50)

118†	L. Amarnath, Bombay	1933-34	108	V. L. Manjrekar, Madras ..	1963-64
110†	M. Azharuddin, Calcutta .	1984-85	184	V. Mankad, Lord's	1952
105	M. Azharuddin, Madras ...	1984-85	114	V. M. Merchant, Man-	
122	M. Azharuddin, Kanpur ..	1984-85		chester	1936
112†	A. A. Baig, Manchester ...	1959	128	V. M. Merchant, The Oval	1946
121	F. M. Engineer, Bombay ..	1972-73	154	V. M. Merchant, Delhi ...	1951-52
101	S. M. Gavaskar, Man-		112	Mushtaq Ali, Manchester ..	1936
	chester	1974	122*	R. G. Nadkarni, Kanpur ..	1963-64
108	S. M. Gavaskar, Bombay ..	1976-77	103	Nawab of Pataudi jun.,	
221	S. M. Gavaskar, The Oval .	1979		Madras	1961-62
172	S. M. Gavaskar, Bangalore	1981-82	203*	Nawab of Pataudi jun.,	
105†	Hanumant Singh, Delhi ...	1963-64		Delhi	1963-64
164*	V. S. Hazare, Delhi	1951-52	148	Nawab of Pataudi jun.,	
155	V. S. Hazare, Bombay	1951-52		Leeds	1967
127	M. L. Jaisimha, Delhi	1961-62	129*	S. M. Patil, Manchester ...	1982
129	M. L. Jaisimha, Calcutta ..	1963-64	115	D. G. Phadkar, Calcutta ..	1951-52
116	Kapil Dev, Kanpur	1981-82	140	Pankaj Roy, Bombay	1951-52
102	S. M. H. Kirmani, Bombay	1984-85	111	Pankaj Roy, Madras	1951-52
192	B. K. Kunderan, Madras ..	1963-64	142	R. J. Shastri, Bombay	1984-85
100	B. K. Kunderan, Delhi	1963-64	111	R. J. Shastri, Calcutta	1984-85
133	V. L. Manjrekar, Leeds ...	1952	130*	P. R. Umrigar, Madras ...	1951-52
189*	V. L. Manjrekar, Delhi ...	1961-62	118	P. R. Umrigar, Manchester	1959

147*	P. R. Umrigar, Kanpur ... 1961-62	113	G. R. Viswanath, Bombay . 1972-73
103	D. B. Vengsarkar, Lord's .. 1979	113	G. R. Viswanath, Lord's . 1979
157	D. B. Vengsarkar, Lord's .. 1982	107	G. R. Viswanath, Delhi ... 1981-82
137	D. B. Vengsarkar, Kanpur . 1984-85	222	G. R. Viswanath, Madras . 1981-82
126*	D. B. Vengsarkar, Lord's .. 1986	140	Yashpal Sharma, Madras .. 1981-82
102*	D. B. Vengsarkar, Leeds .. 1986		

† *Signifies hundred on first appearance in England–India Tests.*

Note: M. Azharuddin scored hundreds in each of his first three Tests.

RECORD PARTNERSHIPS FOR EACH WICKET

For England

178 for 1st	G. Fowler and R. T. Robinson at Madras	1984-85
241 for 2nd	G. Fowler and M. W. Gatting at Madras	1984-85
169 for 3rd	R. Subba Row and M. J. K. Smith at The Oval	1959
266 for 4th	W. R. Hammond and T. S. Worthington at The Oval	1936
254 for 5th†	K. W. R. Fletcher and A. W. Greig at Bombay	1972-73
171 for 6th	I. T. Botham and R. W. Taylor at Bombay	1979-80
125 for 7th	D. W. Randall and P. H. Edmonds at Lord's	1982
168 for 8th	R. Illingworth and P. Lever at Manchester	1971
83 for 9th	K. W. R. Fletcher and N. Gifford at Madras	1972-73
70 for 10th	P. J. W. Allott and R. G. D. Willis at Lord's	1982

For India

213 for 1st	S. M. Gavaskar and C. P. S. Chauhan at The Oval	1979
192 for 2nd	F. M. Engineer and A. L. Wadekar at Bombay	1972-73
316 for 3rd†‡	G. R. Viswanath and Yashpal Sharma at Madras	1981-82
222 for 4th†	V. S. Hazare and V. L. Manjrekar at Leeds	1952
214 for 5th†	M. Azharuddin and R. J. Shastri at Calcutta	1984-85
130 for 6th	S. M. H. Kirmani and Kapil Dev at The Oval	1982
235 for 7th†	R. J. Shastri and S. M. H. Kirmani at Bombay	1984-85
128 for 8th	R. J. Shastri and S. M. H. Kirmani at Delhi	1981-82
104 for 9th	R. J. Shastri and Madan Lal at Delhi	1981-82
51 for 10th	⎰ R. G. Nadkarni and B. S. Chandrasekhar at Calcutta ...	1963-64
	⎱ S. M. H. Kirmani and C. Sharma at Madras	1984-85

† *Denotes record partnership against all countries.*

‡ *415 runs were added between the fall of the 2nd and 3rd wickets: D. B. Vengsarkar retired hurt when he and Viswanath had added 99 runs.*

TEN WICKETS OR MORE IN A MATCH

For England (7)

10-78 (5-35, 5-43)†	G. O. Allen, Lord's	1936
11-145 (7-49, 4-96)†	A. V. Bedser, Lord's	1946
11-93 (4-41, 7-52)	A. V. Bedser, Manchester	1946
13-106 (6-58, 7-48)	I. T. Botham, Bombay	1979-80
11-163 (6-104, 5-59)†	N. A. Foster, Madras	1984-85
10-70 (7-46, 3-24)†	J. K. Lever, Delhi	1976-77
11-153 (7-49, 4-104)	H. Verity, Madras	1933-34

For India (4)

10-177 (6-105, 4-72)	S. A. Durani, Madras	1961-62
12-108 (8-55, 4-53)	V. Mankad, Madras	1951-52
10-188 (4-130, 6-58)	Chetan Sharma, Birmingham	1986
12-181 (6-64, 6-117)†	L. Sivaramakrishnan, Bombay	1984-85

† *Signifies ten wickets or more on first appearance in England–India Tests.*

Note: A. V. Bedser took eleven wickets in a match in the first two Tests of his career.

ENGLAND v PAKISTAN

Season	England		Pakistan	T	E	P	D
		Captains					
1954	L. Hutton[1]		A. H. Kardar	4	1	1	2
1961-62	E. R. Dexter		Imtiaz Ahmed	3	1	0	2
1962	E. R. Dexter[2]		Javed Burki	5	4	0	1
1967	D. B. Close		Hanif Mohammad	3	2	0	1
1968-69	M. C. Cowdrey		Saeed Ahmed	3	0	0	3
1971	R. Illingworth		Intikhab Alam	3	1	0	2
1972-73	A. R. Lewis		Majid Khan	3	0	0	3
1974	M. H. Denness		Intikhab Alam	3	0	0	3
1977-78	J. M. Brearley[3]		Wasim Bari	3	0	0	3
1978	J. M. Brearley		Wasim Bari	3	2	0	1
1982	R. G. D. Willis[4]		Imran Khan	3	2	1	0
1983-84	R. G. D. Willis[5]		Zaheer Abbas	3	0	1	2
	In England			24	12	2	10
	In Pakistan			15	1	1	13
	Totals			39	13	3	23

Notes: [1]D. S. Sheppard captained in Second and Third Tests. [2]M. C. Cowdrey captained in Third Test. [3]G. Boycott captained in Third Test. [4]D. I. Gower captained in Second Test. [5]D. I. Gower captained in Second and Third Tests.

HIGHEST INNINGS TOTALS

For England in England: 558-6 dec. at Nottingham 1954
in Pakistan: 546-8 dec. at Faisalabad 1983-84
For Pakistan in England: 608-7 dec. at Birmingham 1971
in Pakistan: 569-9 dec. at Hyderabad 1972-73

LOWEST INNINGS TOTALS

For England in England: 130 at The Oval 1954
in Pakistan: 159 at Karachi 1983-84
For Pakistan in England: 87 at Lord's 1954
in Pakistan: 199 at Karachi 1972-73

INDIVIDUAL HUNDREDS

For England (36)

112	D. L. Amiss, Lahore	1972-73
158	D. L. Amiss, Hyderabad ..	1972-73
183	D. L. Amiss, The Oval	1974
139†	K. F. Barrington, Lahore ..	1961-62
148	K. F. Barrington, Lord's ..	1967
109*	K. F. Barrington, Nottingham	1967
142	K. F. Barrington, The Oval	1967
100†	I. T. Botham, Birmingham .	1978
108	I. T. Botham, Lord's	1978
121*	G. Boycott, Lord's	1971
112	G. Boycott, Leeds	1971
100*	G. Boycott, Hyderabad	1977-78
278	D. C. S. Compton, Nottingham	1954
159†	M. C. Cowdrey, Birmingham	1962
182	M. C. Cowdrey, The Oval .	1962
100	M. C. Cowdrey, Lahore ...	1968-69
205	E. R. Dexter, Karachi	1961-62

172	E. R. Dexter, The Oval	1962
114*	B. L. D'Oliveira, Dacca	1968-69
122	K. W. R. Fletcher, The Oval	1974
152	D. I. Gower, Faisalabad	1983-84
173*	D. I. Gower, Faisalabad	1983-84
153	T. W. Graveney, Lord's	1962
114	T. W. Graveney, Nottingham	1962
105	T. W. Graveney, Karachi	1968-69
116	A. P. E. Knott, Birmingham	1971
108*†	B. W. Luckhurst, Birmingham	1971
139	C. Milburn, Karachi	1968-69
111	P. H. Parfitt, Karachi	1961-62
101*	P. H. Parfitt, Birmingham	1962
119	P. H. Parfitt, Leeds	1962
101*	P. H. Parfitt, Nottingham	1962
165	G. Pullar, Dacca	1961-62
106†	C. T. Radley, Birmingham	1978
105	D. W. Randall, Birmingham	1982
101	R. T. Simpson, Nottingham	1954

For Pakistan (25)

109	Alim-ud-Din, Karachi	1961-62
146	Asif Iqbal, The Oval	1967
104*	Asif Iqbal, Birmingham	1971
102	Asif Iqbal, Lahore	1972-73
138†	Javed Burki, Lahore	1961-62
140	Javed Burki, Dacca	1961-62
101	Javed Burki, Lord's	1962
111 / 104	Hanif Mohammad, Dacca	1961-62
187*	Hanif Mohammad, Lord's	1967
122†	Haroon Rashid, Lahore	1977-78
108	Haroon Rashid, Hyderabad	1977-78
138	Intikhab Alam, Hyderabad	1972-73
200	Mohsin Khan, Lord's	1982
104	Mohsin Khan, Lahore	1983-84
114†	Mudassar Nazar, Lahore	1977-78
100*	Mushtaq Mohammad, Nottingham	1962
100	Mushtaq Mohammad, Birmingham	1971
157	Mushtaq Mohammad, Hyderabad	1972-73
101	Nasim-ul-Ghani, Lord's	1962
119	Sadiq Mohammad, Lahore	1972-73
116	Salim Malik, Faisalabad	1983-84
112	Wasim Raja, Faisalabad	1983-84
274†	Zaheer Abbas, Birmingham	1971
240	Zaheer Abbas, The Oval	1974

† *Signifies hundred on first appearance in England–Pakistan Tests.*

Note: Three batsmen – Majid Khan, Mushtaq Mohammad and D. L. Amiss – were dismissed for 99 at Karachi, 1972-73: the only instance in Test matches.

RECORD PARTNERSHIPS FOR EACH WICKET

For England

198 for 1st	G. Pullar and R. W. Barber at Dacca	1961-62
248 for 2nd	M. C. Cowdrey and E. R. Dexter at The Oval	1962
201 for 3rd	K. F. Barrington and T. W. Graveney at Lord's	1967
188 for 4th	E. R. Dexter and P. H. Parfitt at Karachi	1961-62
192 for 5th	D. C. S. Compton and T. E. Bailey at Nottingham	1954
153* for 6th	P. H. Parfitt and D. A. Allen at Birmingham	1962
167 for 7th	D. I. Gower and V. J. Marks at Faisalabad	1983-84
99 for 8th	P. H. Parfitt and D. A. Allen at Leeds	1962
76 for 9th	T. W. Graveney and F. S. Trueman at Lord's	1962
79 for 10th	R. W. Taylor and R. G. D. Willis at Birmingham	1982

For Pakistan

173 for 1st	Mohsin Khan and Shoaib Mohammad at Lahore	1983-84
291 for 2nd†	Zaheer Abbas and Mushtaq Mohammad at Birmingham	1971
180 for 3rd	Mudassar Nazar and Haroon Rashid at Lahore	1977-78
153 for 4th	Javed Burki and Mushtaq Mohammad at Lahore	1961-62
	Mohsin Khan and Zaheer Abbas at Lord's	1982
197 for 5th	Javed Burki and Nasim-ul-Ghani at Lord's	1962
145 for 6th	Mushtaq Mohammad and Intikhab Alam at Hyderabad	1972-73
75 for 7th	Salim Malik and Abdul Qadir at Karachi	1983-84
130 for 8th†	Hanif Mohammad and Asif Iqbal at Lord's	1967
190 for 9th†	Asif Iqbal and Intikhab Alam at The Oval	1967
62 for 10th	Sarfraz Nawaz and Asif Masood at Leeds	1974

† *Denotes record partnership against all countries.*

TEN WICKETS OR MORE IN A MATCH

For England (2)

11-83 (6-65, 5-18)†	N. G. B. Cook, Karachi	1983-84
13-71 (5-20, 8-51)	D. L. Underwood, Lord's	1974

For Pakistan (2)

10-194 (5-84, 5-110)	Abdul Qadir, Lahore	1983-84
12-99 (6-53, 6-46)	Fazal Mahmood, The Oval	1954

† *Signifies ten wickets or more on first appearance in England–Pakistan Tests.*

FOUR WICKETS IN FIVE BALLS

C. M. Old, v Pakistan at Birmingham in 1978, dismissed Wasim Raja, Wasim Bari, Iqbal Qasim and Sikander Bakht to take four wickets in five balls (ww-ww).

ENGLAND v SRI LANKA

		Captains				
Season	*England*	*Sri Lanka*	*T*	*E*	*SL*	*D*
1981-82	K. W. R. Fletcher	B. Warnapura	1	1	0	0
1984	D. I. Gower	L. R. D. Mendis	1	0	0	1
	Totals		2	1	0	1

Highest innings total for England: 370 at Lord's	1984
for Sri Lanka: 491-7 dec. at Lord's	1984
Lowest innings total for England: 223 at Colombo (PSO)	1981-82
for Sri Lanka: 175 at Colombo (PSO)	1981-82

INDIVIDUAL HUNDREDS

For England (1)

107†	A. J. Lamb, Lord's	1984

For Sri Lanka (3)

111	L. R. D. Mendis, Lord's	1984
102*†	S. A. R. Silva, Lord's	1984
190	S. Wettimuny, Lord's	1984

† *Signifies hundred on first appearance in England–Sri Lanka Tests.*

Best bowling in an innings for England: 6-33 by J. E. Emburey at Colombo (PSO)	1981-82
for Sri Lanka: 4-70 by A. L. F. de Mel at Colombo (PSO)	1981-82
Best wicket partnerships for England: 87 for 6th by A. J. Lamb and R. M. Ellison at Lord's	1984
for Sri Lanka: 150 for 5th by S. Wettimuny and L. R. D. Mendis at Lord's	1984

ENGLAND v REST OF THE WORLD

In 1970, owing to the cancellation of the South African tour to England, a series of matches was arranged, with the trappings of a full Test series, between England and the Rest of the World. It was played for the Guinness Trophy.

The following players represented the Rest of the World: E. J. Barlow (5), F. M. Engineer (2), L. R. Gibbs (4), Intikhab Alam (5), R. B. Kanhai (5), C. H. Lloyd (5), G. D. McKenzie (3), D. L. Murray (3), Mushtaq Mohammad (2), P. M. Pollock (1), R. G. Pollock (5), M. J. Procter (5), B. A. Richards (5), G. S. Sobers (5).

A list of players who appeared for England in these matches may be found on page 126.

AUSTRALIA v SOUTH AFRICA

Season	Australia	*Captains* South Africa	T	A	SA	D
1902-03*S*	J. Darling	H. M. Taberer[1]	3	2	0	1
1910-11*A*	C. Hill	P. W. Sherwell	5	4	1	0
1912*E*	S. E. Gregory	F. Mitchell[2]	3	2	0	1
1921-22*S*	H. L. Collins	H. W. Taylor	3	1	0	2
1931-32*A*	W. M. Woodfull	H. B. Cameron	5	5	0	0
1935-36*S*	V. Y. Richardson	H. F. Wade	5	4	0	1
1949-50*S*	A. L. Hassett	A. D. Nourse	5	4	0	1
1952-53*A*	A. L. Hassett	J. E. Cheetham	5	2	2	1
1957-58*S*	I. D. Craig	C. B. van Ryneveld[3]	5	3	0	2
1963-64*A*	R. B. Simpson[4]	T. L. Goddard	5	1	1	3
1966-67*S*	R. B. Simpson	P. L. van der Merwe	5	1	3	1
1969-70*S*	W. M. Lawry	A. Bacher	4	0	4	0
	In South Africa		30	15	7	8
	In Australia		20	12	4	4
	In England		3	2	0	1
	Totals		53	29	11	13

S Played in South Africa.   A Played in Australia.   E Played in England.

Notes: The following deputised for the official touring captain or were appointed by the home authority for only a minor proportion of the series:
[1]J. H. Anderson (Second), E. A. Halliwell (Third). [2]L. J. Tancred (Third). [3]D. J. McGlew (First). [4]R. Benaud (First).

HIGHEST INNINGS TOTALS

For Australia in Australia: 578 at Melbourne	1910-11
in South Africa: 549-7 dec. at Port Elizabeth	1949-50
For South Africa in Australia: 595 at Adelaide	1963-64
in South Africa: 622-9 dec. at Durban	1969-70

LOWEST INNINGS TOTALS

For Australia in Australia: 153 at Melbourne	1931-32
in South Africa: 75 at Durban	1949-50
For South Africa in Australia: 36† at Melbourne	1931-32
in South Africa: 85 at Johannesburg	1902-03

† *Scored 45 in the second innings giving the smallest aggregate of 81 (12 extras) in Test cricket.*

INDIVIDUAL HUNDREDS

For Australia (55)

159*‡	W. W. Armstrong, Johannesburg	1902-03
132	W. W. Armstrong, Melbourne	1910-11
132†	W. Bardsley, Sydney	1910-11
121	W. Bardsley, Manchester ..	1912
164	W. Bardsley, Lord's	1912
122	R. Benaud, Johannesburg ..	1957-58
100	R. Benaud, Johannesburg ..	1957-58
169†	B. C. Booth, Brisbane	1963-64
102*	B. C. Booth, Sydney	1963-64
226†	D. G. Bradman, Brisbane .	1931-32
112	D. G. Bradman, Sydney ...	1931-32
167	D. G. Bradman, Melbourne	1931-32
299*	D. G. Bradman, Adelaide .	1931-32
121	W. A. Brown, Cape Town .	1935-36
189	J. W. Burke, Cape Town ..	1957-58
109†	A. G. Chipperfield, Durban	1935-36
203	H. L. Collins, Johannesburg	1921-22
112	J. H. Fingleton, Cape Town	1935-36
108	J. H. Fingleton, Johannesburg	1935-36
118	J. H. Fingleton, Durban ...	1935-36
119	J. M. Gregory, Johannesburg	1921-22
178	R. N. Harvey, Cape Town .	1949-50
151*	R. N. Harvey, Durban ...	1949-50
116	R. N. Harvey, Port Elizabeth	1949-50
100	R. N. Harvey, Johannesburg	1949-50
109	R. N. Harvey, Brisbane ...	1952-53
190	R. N. Harvey, Sydney	1952-53
116	R. N. Harvey, Adelaide ...	1952-53
205	R. N. Harvey, Melbourne .	1952-53
112†	A. L. Hassett, Johannesburg	1949-50
167	A. L. Hassett, Port Elizabeth	1949-50
163	A. L. Hassett, Adelaide ..	1952-53
142†	C. Hill, Johannesburg	1902-03
191	C. Hill, Sydney	1910-11
100	C. Hill, Melbourne	1910-11
114	C. Kelleway, Manchester ..	1912
102	C. Kelleway, Lord's	1912
157	W. M. Lawry, Melbourne .	1963-64
101†	S. J. E. Loxton, Johannesburg	1949-50
137	C. G. Macartney, Sydney ..	1910-11
116	C. G. Macartney, Durban .	1921-22
149	S. J. McCabe, Durban	1935-36
189*	S. J. McCabe, Johannesburg	1935-36
154	C. C. McDonald, Adelaide	1952-53
118 101*	J. Moroney, Johannesburg .	1949-50
111	A. R. Morris, Johannesburg	1949-50
157	A. R. Morris, Port Elizabeth	1949-50
127†	K. E. Rigg, Sydney	1931-32
142	J. Ryder, Cape Town	1921-22
153	R. B. Simpson, Cape Town	1966-67
134	K. R. Stackpole, Cape Town	1966-67
159	V. T. Trumper, Melbourne	1910-11
214*	V. T. Trumper, Adelaide ..	1910-11
161	W. M. Woodfull, Melbourne	1931-32

For South Africa (36)

114†	E. J. Barlow, Brisbane	1963-64
109	E. J. Barlow, Melbourne ..	1963-64
201	E. J. Barlow, Adelaide	1963-64
127	E. J. Barlow, Cape Town .	1969-70
110	E. J. Barlow, Johannesburg	1969-70
126	K. C. Bland, Sydney	1963-64
162*	W. R. Endean, Melbourne .	1952-53
204	G. A. Faulkner, Melbourne	1910-11
115	G. A. Faulkner, Adelaide ..	1910-11
122*	G. A. Faulkner, Manchester	1912
152	C. N. Frank, Johannesburg	1921-22
102	B. L. Irvine, Port Elizabeth	1969-70
182	D. T. Lindsay, Johannesburg	1966-67
137	D. T. Lindsay, Durban ...	1966-67
131	D. T. Lindsay, Johannesburg	1966-67
108	D. J. McGlew, Johannesburg	1957-58
105	D. J. McGlew, Durban ...	1957-58
231	A. D. Nourse, Johannesburg	1935-36
114	A. D. Nourse, Cape Town .	1949-50
111	A. W. Nourse, Johannesburg	1921-22
122	R. G. Pollock, Sydney	1963-64
175	R. G. Pollock, Adelaide ...	1963-64
209	R. G. Pollock, Cape Town .	1966-67
105	R. G. Pollock, Port Elizabeth	1966-67
274	R. G. Pollock, Durban ...	1969-70
140	B. A. Richards, Durban ...	1969-70
126	B. A. Richards, Port Elizabeth	1969-70
143	E. A. B. Rowan, Durban ..	1949-50

101	J. H. Sinclair, Johannes-		115	J. H. B. Waite, Johannes-	
	burg	1902-03		burg	1957-58
104	J. H. Sinclair, Cape Town .	1902-03	134	J. H. B. Waite, Durban . . .	1957-58
103	S. J. Snooke, Adelaide	1910-11	105	J. W. Zulch, Adelaide	1910-11
111	K. G. Viljoen, Melbourne .	1931-32	150	J. W. Zulch, Sydney	1910-11

† *Signifies hundred on first appearance in Australia–South Africa Tests.*
‡ *Carried his bat.*

RECORD PARTNERSHIPS FOR EACH WICKET

For Australia

233 for 1st	J. H. Fingleton and W. A. Brown at Cape Town	1935-36
275 for 2nd	C. C. McDonald and A. L. Hassett at Adelaide	1952-53
242 for 3rd	C. Kelleway and W. Bardsley at Lord's	1912
168 for 4th	R. N. Harvey and K. R. Miller at Sydney	1952-53
143 for 5th	W. W. Armstrong and V. T. Trumper at Melbourne	1910-11
107 for 6th	C. Kelleway and V. S. Ransford at Melbourne	1910-11
160 for 7th	R. Benaud and G. D. McKenzie at Sydney	1963-64
83 for 8th	A. G. Chipperfield and C. V. Grimmett at Durban	1935-36
78 for 9th	{ D. G. Bradman and W. J. O'Reilly at Adelaide	1931-32
	{ K. D. Mackay and I. Meckiff at Johannesburg	1957-58
82 for 10th	V. S. Ransford and W. J. Whitty at Melbourne	1910-11

For South Africa

176 for 1st	D. J. McGlew and T. L. Goddard at Johannesburg	1957-58
173 for 2nd	L. J. Tancred and C. B. Llewellyn at Johannesburg	1902-03
341 for 3rd†	E. J. Barlow and R. G. Pollock at Adelaide	1963-64
206 for 4th	C. N. Frank and A. W. Nourse at Johannesburg	1921-22
129 for 5th	J. H. B. Waite and W. R. Endean at Johannesburg	1957-58
200 for 6th†	R. G. Pollock and H. R. Lance at Durban	1969-70
221 for 7th	D. T. Lindsay and P. L. van der Merwe at Johannesburg	1966-67
124 for 8th†	A. W. Nourse and E. A. Halliwell at Johannesburg	1902-03
85 for 9th	R. G. Pollock and P. M. Pollock at Cape Town	1966-67
53 for 10th	L. A. Stricker and S. J. Pegler at Adelaide	1910-11

† *Denotes record partnership against all countries.*

TEN WICKETS OR MORE IN A MATCH

For Australia (5)

14-199 (7-116, 7-83)	C. V. Grimmett, Adelaide	1931-32
10-88 (5-32, 5-56)	C. V. Grimmett, Cape Town	1935-36
10-110 (3-70, 7-40)	C. V. Grimmett, Johannesburg	1935-36
13-173 (7-100, 6-73)	C. V. Grimmett, Durban	1935-36
11-24 (5-6, 6-18)	H. Ironmonger, Melbourne	1931-32

For South Africa (2)

10-116 (5-43, 5-73)	C. B. Llewellyn, Johannesburg	1902-03
13-165 (6-84, 7-81)	H. J. Tayfield, Melbourne	1952-53

Note: C. V. Grimmett took ten wickets or more in three consecutive matches in 1935-36.

AUSTRALIA v WEST INDIES

Captains

Season	Australia	West Indies	T	A	WI	T	D
1930-31A	W. M. Woodfull	G. C. Grant	5	4	1	0	0
1951-52A	A. L. Hassett[1]	J. D. C. Goddard[2]	5	4	1	0	0
1954-55W	I. W. Johnson	D. S. Atkinson[3]	5	3	0	0	2
1960-61A	R. Benaud	F. M. M. Worrell	5†	2	1	1	1

THE FRANK WORRELL TROPHY

Captains

Season	Australia	West Indies	T	A	WI	T	D	Held by
1964-65W	R. B. Simpson	G. S. Sobers	5	1	2	0	2	WI
1968-69A	W. M. Lawry	G. S. Sobers	5	3	1	0	1	A
1972-73W	I. M. Chappell	R. B. Kanhai	5	2	0	0	3	A
1975-76A	G. S. Chappell	C. H. Lloyd	6	5	1	0	0	A
1977-78W	R. B. Simpson	A. I. Kallicharran[4]	5	1	3	0	1	WI
1979-80A	G. S. Chappell	C. H. Lloyd[5]	3	0	2	0	1	WI
1981-82A	G. S. Chappell	C. H. Lloyd	3	1	1	0	1	WI
1983-84W	K. J. Hughes	C. H. Lloyd[6]	5	0	3	0	2	WI
1984-85A	A. R. Border[7]	C. H. Lloyd	5	1	3	0	1	WI

		T	A	WI	T	D
In Australia		37	20	11	1	5
In West Indies		25	7	8	0	10
Totals		62	27	19	1	15

† *The First Test at Brisbane resulted in a tie. This is the only instance of a Test match resulting in a tie.*

A Played in Australia.   W Played in West Indies.

Notes: The following deputised for the official touring captain or were appointed by the home authority for only a minor proportion of the series:
[1] A. R. Morris (Third). [2] J. B. Stollmeyer (Fifth). [3] J. B. Stollmeyer (Second and Third). [4] C. H. Lloyd (First and Second). [5] D. L. Murray (First). [6] I. V. A. Richards (Second). [7] K. J. Hughes (First and Second).

HIGHEST INNINGS TOTALS

For Australia in Australia: 619 at Sydney	....	1968-69
in West Indies: 758-8 dec. at Kingston	....	1954-55
For West Indies in Australia: 616 at Adelaide	....	1968-69
in West Indies: 573 at Bridgetown	....	1964-65

LOWEST INNINGS TOTALS

For Australia in Australia: 76 at Perth	....	1984-85
in West Indies: 90 at Port-of-Spain	....	1977-78
For West Indies in Australia: 78 at Sydney	....	1951-52
in West Indies: 109 at Georgetown	....	1972-73

INDIVIDUAL HUNDREDS

For Australia (64)

128	R. G. Archer, Kingston ...	1954-55
121	R. Benaud, Kingston	1954-55
117	B. C. Booth, Port-of-Spain	1964-65
126	A. R. Border, Adelaide ...	1981-82
100*	A. R. Border, Port-of-Spain	1983-84
223	D. G. Bradman, Brisbane .	1930-31
152	D. G. Bradman, Melbourne	1930-31
106	G. S. Chappell, Bridgetown	1972-73
123 109*	‡G. S. Chappell, Brisbane .	1975-76
182*	G. S. Chappell, Sydney ...	1975-76
124	G. S. Chappell, Brisbane .	1979-80
117†	I. M. Chappell, Brisbane ..	1968-69
165	I. M. Chappell, Melbourne	1968-69
106*	I. M. Chappell, Bridgetown	1972-73
109	I. M. Chappell, Georgetown	1972-73
156	I. M. Chappell, Perth	1975-76
109†	G. J. Cosier, Melbourne ...	1975-76
143	R. M. Cowper, Port-of-Spain	1964-65
102	R. M. Cowper, Bridgetown	1964-65
127*†	J. Dyson, Sydney	1981-82
133	R. N. Harvey, Kingston ...	1954-55
133	R. N. Harvey, Port-of-Spain	1954-55
204	R. N. Harvey, Kingston ...	1954-55
132	A. L. Hassett, Sydney	1951-52
102	A. L. Hassett, Melbourne ..	1951-52
113†	A. M. J. Hilditch, Melbourne	1984-85
130*†	R. J. Hughes, Brisbane ...	1979-80
100*	R. J. Hughes, Melbourne ..	1981-82
146†	A. F. Kippax, Adelaide ...	1930-31
210	W. M. Lawry, Bridgetown .	1964-65
105	W. M. Lawry, Brisbane ...	1968-69
205	W. M. Lawry, Melbourne ..	1968-69
151	W. M. Lawry, Sydney	1968-69
118	R. R. Lindwall, Bridgetown	1954-55
109*	R. B. McCosker, Melbourne	1975-76
110	C. C. McDonald, Port-of-Spain	1954-55
127	C. C. McDonald, Kingston	1954-55
129	K. R. Miller, Sydney	1951-52
147	K. R. Miller, Kingston ...	1954-55
137	K. R. Miller, Bridgetown ..	1954-55
109	K. R. Miller, Kingston ...	1954-55
111	A. R. Morris, Port-of-Spain	1954-55
181†	N. C. O'Neill, Brisbane ...	1960-61
120	W. B. Phillips, Bridgetown .	1983-84
183	W. H. Ponsford, Sydney ..	1930-31
109	W. H. Ponsford, Brisbane .	1930-31
132	I. R. Redpath, Sydney	1968-69
102	I. R. Redpath, Melbourne .	1975-76
103	I. R. Redpath, Adelaide ..	1975-76
101	I. R. Redpath, Melbourne .	1975-76
124	C. S. Serjeant, Georgetown	1977-78
201	R. B. Simpson, Bridgetown	1964-65
142	K. R. Stackpole, Kingston .	1972-73
122	P. M. Toohey, Kingston ...	1977-78
136	A. Turner, Adelaide	1975-76
118	K. D. Walters, Sydney ...	1968-69
110	K. D. Walters, Adelaide ..	1968-69
242 103	K. D. Walters, Sydney ...	1968-69
102*	K. D. Walters, Bridgetown .	1972-73
112	K. D. Walters, Port-of-Spain	1972-73
173	K. C. Wessels, Sydney	1984-85
126	G. M. Wood, Georgetown .	1977-78

‡ *G. S. Chappell is the only player to score hundreds in both innings of his first Test as captain.*

For West Indies (63)

108	F. C. M. Alexander, Sydney	1960-61
219	D. St E. Atkinson, Bridgetown	1954-55
117	B. F. Butcher, Port-of-Spain	1964-65
101	B. F. Butcher, Sydney	1968-69
118	B. F. Butcher, Adelaide ..	1968-69
122	C. C. Depeiza, Bridgetown .	1954-55
130	P. J. L. Dujon, Port-of-Spain	1983-84
139	P. J. L. Dujon, Perth	1984-85
125†	M. L. C. Foster, Kingston .	1972-73
169	R. C. Fredericks, Perth ...	1975-76
101†	H. A. Gomes, Georgetown .	1977-78
115	H. A. Gomes, Kingston ...	1977-78
126	H. A. Gomes, Sydney	1981-82
124*	H. A. Gomes, Adelaide	1981-82
127	H. A. Gomes, Perth	1984-85
120*	H. A. Gomes, Adelaide	1984-85
120*	C. G. Greenidge, Georgetown	1983-84
127	C. G. Greenidge, Kingston .	1983-84
103*	D. L. Haynes, Georgetown .	1983-84
145	D. L. Haynes, Bridgetown .	1983-84
102*	G. A. Headley, Brisbane ..	1930-31
105	G. A. Headley, Sydney	1930-31
110	C. C. Hunte, Melbourne ...	1960-61
101	A. I. Kallicharran, Brisbane	1975-76
127	A. I. Kallicharran, Port-of-Spain	1977-78
126	A. I. Kallicharran, Kingston	1977-78
106	A. I. Kallicharran, Adelaide	1979-80
117 115	R. B. Kanhai, Adelaide ...	1960-61

129	R. B. Kanhai, Bridgetown .	1964-65	154	R. B. Richardson, St John's	1983-84
121	R. B. Kanhai, Port-of-Spain	1964-65	138	R. B. Richardson, Brisbane.	1984-85
			107	L. G. Rowe, Brisbane	1975-76
105	R. B. Kanhai, Bridgetown .	1972-73	104†	O. G. Smith, Kingston	1954-55
129†	C. H. Lloyd, Brisbane	1968-69	132	G. S. Sobers, Brisbane	1960-61
178	C. H. Lloyd, Georgetown .	1972-73	168	G. S. Sobers, Sydney	1960-61
149	C. H. Lloyd, Perth	1975-76	110	G. S. Sobers, Adelaide	1968-69
102	C. H. Lloyd, Melbourne . .	1975-76	113	G. S. Sobers, Sydney	1968-69
121	C. H. Lloyd, Adelaide	1979-80	104	J. B. Stollmeyer, Sydney . . .	1951-52
114	C. H. Lloyd, Brisbane	1984-85	108	C. L. Walcott, Kingston . . .	1954-55
123*	F. R. Martin, Sydney	1930-31	126	C. L. Walcott, Port-of-Spain	1954-55
201	S. M. Nurse, Bridgetown . .	1964-65	110		
137	S. M. Nurse, Sydney	1968-69	155	C. L. Walcott, Kingston . . .	1954-55
101	I. V. A. Richards, Adelaide	1975-76	110		
140	I. V. A. Richards, Brisbane	1979-80	139	E. D. Weekes, Port-of-Spain	1954-55
178	I. V. A. Richards, St John's	1983-84			
208	I. V. A. Richards, Melbourne	1984-85	100†	A. B. Williams, Georgetown	1977-78
131*	R. B. Richardson, Bridgetown	1983-84	108	F. M. M. Worrell, Melbourne	1951-52

† *Signifies hundred on first appearance in Australia–West Indies Tests.*

Note: F. C. M. Alexander and C. C. Depeiza scored the only hundreds of their careers in a Test match.

RECORD PARTNERSHIPS FOR EACH WICKET

For Australia

382 for 1st†	W. M. Lawry and R. B. Simpson at Bridgetown	1964-65
298 for 2nd	W. M. Lawry and I. M. Chappell at Melbourne	1968-69
295 for 3rd†	C. C. McDonald and R. N. Harvey at Kingston	1954-55
336 for 4th	W. M. Lawry and K. D. Walters at Sydney	1968-69
220 for 5th	K. R. Miller and R. G. Archer at Kingston	1954-55
206 for 6th	K. R. Miller and R. G. Archer at Bridgetown	1954-55
134 for 7th	A. K. Davidson and R. Benaud at Brisbane	1960-61
137 for 8th	R. Benaud and I. W. Johnson at Kingston	1954-55
97 for 9th	K. D. Mackay and J. W. Martin at Melbourne	1960-61
97 for 10th	T. G. Hogan and R. M. Hogg at Georgetown	1983-84

For West Indies

250* for 1st	C. G. Greenidge and D. L. Haynes at Georgetown	1983-84
165 for 2nd	M. C. Carew and R. B. Kanhai at Brisbane	1968-69
308 for 3rd	R. B. Richardson and I. V. A. Richards at St John's	1983-84
198 for 4th	L. G. Rowe and A. I. Kallicharran at Brisbane	1975-76
210 for 5th	R. B. Kanhai and M. L. C. Foster at Kingston	1972-73
165 for 6th	R. B. Kanhai and D. L. Murray at Bridgetown	1972-73
347 for 7th†‡	D. St E. Atkinson and C. C. Depeiza at Bridgetown	1954-55
82 for 8th	H. A. Gomes and A. M. E. Roberts at Adelaide	1981-82
122 for 9th	D. A. J. Holford and J. L. Hendriks at Adelaide	1968-69
56 for 10th	J. Garner and C. E. H. Croft at Brisbane	1979-80

† *Denotes record partnership against all countries.*
‡ *Record seventh-wicket partnership in first-class cricket.*

TEN WICKETS OR MORE IN A MATCH

For Australia (9)

11-222 (5-135, 6-87)†	A. K. Davidson, Brisbane	1960-61
11-183 (7-87, 4-96)†	C. V. Grimmett, Adelaide	1930-31
10-115 (6-72, 4-43)	N. J. N. Hawke, Georgetown	1964-65
10-144 (6-54, 4-90)	R. G. Holland, Sydney	1984-85
11-79 (7-23, 4-56)	H. Ironmonger, Melbourne	1930-31
11-181 (8-112, 3-69)	G. F. Lawson, Adelaide	1984-85
10-127 (7-83, 3-44)	D. K. Lillee, Melbourne	1981-82
10-159 (8-71, 2-88)	G. D. McKenzie, Melbourne	1968-69
10-185 (3-87, 7-98)	B. Yardley, Sydney	1981-82

For West Indies (3)

10-113 (7-55, 3-58)	G. E. Gomez, Sydney	1951-52
11-107 (5-45, 6-62)	M. A. Holding, Melbourne	1981-82
10-107 (5-69, 5-38)	M. D. Marshall, Adelaide	1984-85

† *Signifies ten wickets or more on first appearance in Australia–West Indies Tests.*

AUSTRALIA v NEW ZEALAND

Season	Australia	New Zealand	T	A	NZ	D
		Captains				
1945-46N	W. A. Brown	W. A. Hadlee	1	1	0	0
1973-74A	I. M. Chappell	B. E. Congdon	3	2	0	1
1973-74N	I. M. Chappell	B. E. Congdon	3	1	1	1
1976-77N	G. S. Chappell	G. M. Turner	2	1	0	1
1980-81A	G. S. Chappell	G. P. Howarth[1]	3	2	0	1
1981-82N	G. S. Chappell	G. P. Howarth	3	1	1	1

TRANS-TASMAN TROPHY

Season	Australia	New Zealand	T	A	NZ	D	Held by
		Captains					
1985-86A	A. R. Border	J. V. Coney	3	1	2	0	NZ
1985-86N	A. R. Border	J. V. Coney	3	0	1	2	NZ

	T	A	NZ	D
In Australia	9	5	2	2
In New Zealand	12	4	3	5
Totals	21	9	5	7

A Played in Australia. N Played in New Zealand.

Note: The following deputised for the official touring captain: [1]M. G. Burgess (Second).

HIGHEST INNINGS TOTALS

For Australia in Australia: 477 at Adelaide		1973-74
in New Zealand: 552 at Christchurch		1976-77
For New Zealand in Australia: 553-7 dec. at Brisbane		1985-86
in New Zealand: 484 at Wellington		1973-74

LOWEST INNINGS TOTALS

For Australia in Australia: 162 at Sydney		1973-74
in New Zealand: 103 at Auckland		1985-86
For New Zealand in Australia: 121 at Perth		1980-81
in New Zealand: 42 at Wellington		1945-46

INDIVIDUAL HUNDREDS

For Australia (20)

152*	A. R. Border, Brisbane	1985-86
140		
114*	A. R. Border, Christchurch	1985-86
247*		
133	G. S. Chappell, Wellington.	1973-74
176	G. S. Chappell, Christchurch	1981-82
145		
121	I. M. Chappell, Wellington	1973-74
101	G. J. Gilmour, Christchurch	1976-77
118	G. R. Marsh, Auckland ...	1985-86
132	R. W. Marsh, Adelaide ...	1973-74
115†	G. R. J. Matthews, Brisbane	1985-86
130	G. R. J. Matthews, Wellington	1985-86
159*‡	I. R. Redpath, Auckland ..	1973-74
122†	K. R. Stackpole, Melbourne	1973-74
104*	K. D. Walters, Auckland ..	1973-74
250	K. D. Walters, Christchurch	1976-77
107	K. D. Walters, Melbourne .	1980-81
111†	G. M. Wood, Brisbane	1980-81
100	G. M. Wood, Auckland ...	1981-82

For New Zealand (13)

101*	J. V. Coney, Wellington ...	1985-86
132	B. E. Congdon, Wellington .	1973-74
107*	B. E. Congdon, Christchurch	1976-77
188	M. D. Crowe, Brisbane ...	1985-86
137	M. D. Crowe, Christchurch	1985-86
161	B. A. Edgar, Auckland	1981-82
101	B. F. Hastings, Wellington .	1973-74
117	J. F. M. Morrison, Sydney .	1973-74
108	J. M. Parker, Sydney	1973-74
108†	J. F. Reid, Brisbane	1985-86
101		
110*	G. M. Turner, Christchurch	1973-74
141	J. G. Wright, Christchurch .	1981-82

† *Signifies hundred on first appearance in Australia–New Zealand Tests.*
‡ *Carried his bat.*

Notes: G. S. and I. M. Chappell at Wellington in 1973-74 provide the only instance in Test matches of brothers both scoring a hundred in each innings and in the same Test.

G. S. Chappell's match aggregate of 380 (247* and 133) for Australia at Wellington in 1973-74 is the record in Test matches.

RECORD PARTNERSHIPS FOR EACH WICKET

For Australia

106 for 1st	B. M. Laird and G. M. Wood at Auckland		1981-82
168 for 2nd	G. R. Marsh and W. B. Phillips at Auckland		1985-86
264 for 3rd	I. M. Chappell and G. S. Chappell at Wellington		1973-74
106 for 4th	I. R. Redpath and I. C. Davis at Christchurch		1973-74
213 for 5th	G. M. Ritchie and G. R. J. Matthews at Wellington		1985-86
197 for 6th	A. R. Border and G. R. J. Matthews at Brisbane		1985-86
217 for 7th†	K. D. Walters and G. J. Gilmour at Christchurch		1976-77
93 for 8th	G. J. Gilmour and K. J. O'Keeffe at Auckland		1976-77
57 for 9th	R. W. Marsh and L. S. Pascoe at Perth		1980-81
60 for 10th	K. D. Walters and J. D. Higgs at Melbourne		1980-81

For New Zealand

107 for 1st	G. M. Turner and J. M. Parker at Auckland		1973-74
108 for 2nd	G. M. Turner and J. F. M. Morrison at Wellington		1973-74
224 for 3rd†	J. F. Reid and M. D. Crowe at Brisbane		1985-86
229 for 4th†	B. E. Congdon and B. F. Hastings at Wellington		1973-74
88 for 5th	J. V. Coney and M. G. Burgess at Perth		1980-81
109 for 6th	K. R. Rutherford and J. V. Coney at Wellington		1985-86
132* for 7th	J. V. Coney and R. J. Hadlee at Wellington		1985-86
53 for 8th	B. A. Edgar and R. J. Hadlee at Brisbane		1980-81
73 for 9th	H. J. Howarth and D. R. Hadlee at Christchurch		1976-77
124 for 10th	J. G. Bracewell and S. L. Boock at Sydney		1985-86

† *Denotes record partnership against all countries.*

TEN WICKETS OR MORE IN A MATCH

For Australia (2)

10-174 (6-106, 4-68)   R. G. Holland, Sydney 1985-86
11-123 (5-51, 6-72)   D. K. Lillee, Auckland 1976-77

For New Zealand (3)

10-106 (4-74, 6-32)   J. G. Bracewell, Auckland 1985-86
15-123 (9-52, 6-71)   R. J. Hadlee, Brisbane 1985-86
11-155 (5-65, 6-90)   R. J. Hadlee, Perth 1985-86

AUSTRALIA v INDIA

Season	Australia	*Captains* India	T	A	I	D
1947-48*A*	D. G. Bradman	L. Amarnath	5	4	0	1
1956-57*I*	I. W. Johnson[1]	P. R. Umrigar	3	2	0	1
1959-60*I*	R. Benaud	G. S. Ramchand	5	2	1	2
1964-65*I*	R. B. Simpson	Nawab of Pataudi jun.	3	1	1	1
1967-68*A*	R. B. Simpson[2]	Nawab of Pataudi jun.[3]	4	4	0	0
1969-70*I*	W. M. Lawry	Nawab of Pataudi jun.	5	3	1	1
1977-78*A*	R. B. Simpson	B. S. Bedi	5	3	2	0
1979-80*I*	K. J. Hughes	S. M. Gavaskar	6	0	2	4
1980-81*A*	G. S. Chappell	S. M. Gavaskar	3	1	1	1
1985-86*A*	A. R. Border	Kapil Dev	3	0	0	3
	In Australia		20	12	3	5
	In India		22	8	5	9
	Totals		42	20	8	14

A Played in Australia. I Played in India.

Notes: The following deputised for the official touring captain or were appointed by the home authority for only a minor proportion of the series:
[1]R. R. Lindwall (Second). [2]W. M. Lawry (Third and Fourth). [3]C. G. Borde (First).

HIGHEST INNINGS TOTALS

For Australia in Australia: 674 at Adelaide 1947-48
             in India: 523-7 dec. at Bombay 1956-57

For India in Australia: 600-4 dec. at Sydney 1985-86
         in India: 510-7 dec. at Delhi 1979-80

LOWEST INNINGS TOTALS

For Australia in Australia: 83 at Melbourne 1980-81
             in India: 105 at Kanpur 1959-60

For India in Australia: 58 at Brisbane 1947-48
         in India: 135 at Delhi 1959-60

INDIVIDUAL HUNDREDS

For Australia (41)

112	S. G. Barnes, Adelaide	1947-48	198*	A. L. Hassett, Adelaide	1947-48
123†	D. C. Boon, Adelaide	1985-86	100	K. J. Hughes, Madras	1979-80
131	D. C. Boon, Sydney	1985-86	213	K. J. Hughes, Adelaide	1980-81
162†	A. R. Border, Madras	1979-80	100	W. M. Lawry, Melbourne	1967-68
124	A. R. Border, Melbourne	1980-81	105	A. L. Mann, Perth	1977-78
163	A. R. Border, Melbourne	1985-86	100*	G. R. J. Matthews, Melbourne	1985-86
185†	D. G. Bradman, Brisbane	1947-48			
132 127*	D. G. Bradman, Melbourne	1947-48	100*	A. R. Morris, Melbourne	1947-48
			163	N. C. O'Neill, Bombay	1959-60
201	D. G. Bradman, Adelaide	1947-48	113	N. C. O'Neill, Calcutta	1959-60
161	J. W. Burke, Bombay	1956-57	128†	G. M. Ritchie, Adelaide	1985-86
204†	G. S. Chappell, Sydney	1980-81	114	A. P. Sheahan, Kanpur	1969-70
151	I. M. Chappell, Melbourne	1967-68	103	R. B. Simpson, Adelaide	1967-68
138	I. M. Chappell, Delhi	1969-70	109	R. B. Simpson, Melbourne	1967-68
108	R. M. Cowper, Adelaide	1967-68	176	R. B. Simpson, Perth	1977-78
165	R. M. Cowper, Sydney	1967-68	100	R. B. Simpson, Adelaide	1977-78
101	L. E. Favell, Madras	1959-60	103†	K. R. Stackpole, Bombay	1969-70
153	R. N. Harvey, Melbourne	1947-48	102	K. D. Walters, Madras	1969-70
140	R. N. Harvey, Bombay	1956-57	125	G. M. Wood, Adelaide	1980-81
114	R. N. Harvey, Delhi	1959-60	121†	G. N. Yallop, Adelaide	1977-78
102	R. N. Harvey, Bombay	1959-60	167	G. N. Yallop, Calcutta	1979-80

For India (27)

100	M. Amarnath, Perth	1977-78	111	V. Mankad, Melbourne	1947-48
138	M. Amarnath, Sydney	1985-86	128*†	Nawab of Pataudi, Madras	1964-65
108	N. J. Contractor, Bombay	1959-60	174	S. M. Patil, Adelaide	1980-81
113†	S. M. Gavaskar, Brisbane	1977-78	123	D. G. Phadkar, Adelaide	1947-48
127	S. M. Gavaskar, Perth	1977-78	109	G. S. Ramchand, Bombay	1956-57
118	S. M. Gavaskar, Melbourne	1977-78	116	K. Srikkanth, Sydney	1985-86
115	S. M. Gavaskar, Delhi	1979-80	112	D. B. Vengsarkar, Bangalore	1979-80
123	S. M. Gavaskar, Bombay	1979-80			
166*	S. M. Gavaskar, Adelaide	1985-86	137†	G. R. Viswanath, Kanpur	1969-70
172	S. M. Gavaskar, Sydney	1985-86	161*	G. R. Viswanath, Bangalore	1979-80
116 145	V. S. Hazare, Adelaide	1947-48	131	G. R. Viswanath, Delhi	1979-80
101	M. L. Jaisimha, Brisbane	1967-68	114	G. R. Viswanath, Melbourne	1980-81
101*	S. M. H. Kirmani, Bombay	1979-80			
116	V. Mankad, Melbourne	1947-48	100*	Yashpal Sharma, Delhi	1979-80

† *Signifies hundred on first appearance in Australia–India Tests.*

RECORD PARTNERSHIPS FOR EACH WICKET

For Australia

217 for 1st	D. C. Boon and G. R. Marsh at Sydney	1985-86
236 for 2nd	S. G. Barnes and D. G. Bradman at Adelaide	1947-48
222 for 3rd	A. R. Border and K. J. Hughes at Madras	1979-80
159 for 4th	R. N. Harvey and S. J. E. Loxton at Melbourne	1947-48
223* for 5th	A. R. Morris and D. G. Bradman at Melbourne	1947-48
151 for 6th	T. R. Veivers and B. N. Jarman at Bombay	1964-65
64 for 7th	T. R. Veivers and J. W. Martin at Madras	1964-65
73 for 8th	T. R. Veivers and G. D. McKenzie at Madras	1964-65
87 for 9th	I. W. Johnson and W. P. A. Crawford at Madras	1956-57
77 for 10th	A. R. Border and D. R. Gilbert at Melbourne	1985-86

For India

192 for 1st	S. M. Gavaskar and C. P. S. Chauhan at Bombay	1979-80
224 for 2nd	S. M. Gavaskar and M. Amarnath at Sydney	1985-86
159 for 3rd	S. M. Gavaskar and G. R. Viswanath at Delhi	1979-80
159 for 4th	D. B. Vengsarkar and G. R. Viswanath at Bangalore	1979-80
109 for 5th	A. A. Baig and R. B. Kenny at Bombay	1959-60
188 for 6th	V. S. Hazare and D. G. Phadkar at Adelaide	1947-48
132 for 7th	V. S. Hazare and H. R. Adhikari at Adelaide	1947-48
127 for 8th	S. M. H. Kirmani and K. D. Ghavri at Bombay	1979-80
57 for 9th	S. M. H. Kirmani and K. D. Ghavri at Sydney	1980-81
94 for 10th	S. M. Gavaskar and N. S. Yadav at Adelaide	1985-86

TEN WICKETS OR MORE IN A MATCH

For Australia (7)

11-105 (6-52, 5-53)	R. Benaud, Calcutta	1956-57
12-124 (5-31, 7-93)	A. K. Davidson, Kanpur	1959-60
12-166 (5-99, 7-67)	G. Dymock, Kanpur	1979-80
10-91 (6-58, 4-33)†	G. D. McKenzie, Madras	1964-65
10-151 (7-66, 3-85)	G. D. McKenzie, Melbourne	1967-68
10-144 (5-91, 5-53)	A. A. Mallett, Madras	1969-70
11-31 (5-2, 6-29)†	E. R. H. Toshack, Brisbane	1947-48

For India (6)

10-194 (5-89, 5-105)	B. S. Bedi, Perth	1977-78
12-104 (6-52, 6-52)	B. S. Chandrasekhar, Melbourne	1977-78
10-130 (7-49, 3-81)	Ghulam Ahmed, Calcutta	1956-57
11-122 (5-31, 6-91)	R. G. Nadkarni, Madras	1964-65
14-124 (9-69, 5-55)	J. M. Patel, Kanpur	1959-60
10-174 (4-100, 6-74)	E. A. S. Prasanna, Madras	1969-70

† *Signifies ten wickets or more on first appearance in Australia–India Tests.*

AUSTRALIA v PAKISTAN

Season	Australia	Captains Pakistan	T	A	P	D
1956-57 P	I. W. Johnson	A. H. Kardar	1	0	1	0
1959-60 P	R. Benaud	Fazal Mahmood[1]	3	2	0	1
1964-65 P	R. B. Simpson	Hanif Mohammad	1	0	0	1
1964-65 A	R. B. Simpson	Hanif Mohammad	1	0	0	1
1972-73 A	I. M. Chappell	Intikhab Alam	3	3	0	0
1976-77 A	G. S. Chappell	Mushtaq Mohammad	3	1	1	1
1978-79 A	G. N. Yallop[2]	Mushtaq Mohammad	2	1	1	0
1979-80 P	G. S. Chappell	Javed Miandad	3	0	1	2
1981-82 A	G. S. Chappell	Javed Miandad	3	2	1	0
1982-83 P	K. J. Hughes	Imran Khan	3	0	3	0
1983-84 A	K. J. Hughes	Imran Khan[3]	5	2	0	3
	In Pakistan		11	2	5	4
	In Australia		17	9	3	5
	Totals		28	11	8	9

A Played in Australia. P Played in Pakistan.

Notes: [1]Imtiaz Ahmed captained in Second Test. [2]K. J. Hughes captained in Second Test.
[3]Zaheer Abbas captained in First, Second and Third Tests.

HIGHEST INNINGS TOTALS

For Australia in Australia: 585 at Adelaide 1972-73
              in Pakistan: 617 at Faisalabad 1979-80
For Pakistan in Australia: 624 at Adelaide 1983-84
              in Pakistan: 501-6 dec. at Faisalabad 1982-83

LOWEST INNINGS TOTALS

For Australia in Australia: 125 at Melbourne 1981-82
              in Pakistan: 80 at Karachi 1956-57
For Pakistan in Australia: 62 at Perth 1981-82
              in Pakistan: 134 at Dacca 1959-60

INDIVIDUAL HUNDREDS

For Australia (32)

142	J. Benaud, Melbourne	1972-73	105	R. B. McCosker, Melbourne	1976-77
105†	A. R. Border, Melbourne	1978-79	118†	R. W. Marsh, Adelaide	1972-73
150*	A. R. Border, Lahore	1979-80	134	N. C. O'Neill, Lahore	1959-60
153			159†	W. B. Phillips, Perth	1983-84
118	A. R. Border, Brisbane	1983-84	135	I. R. Redpath, Melbourne	1972-73
117*	A. R. Border, Adelaide	1983-84	106*	G. M. Ritchie, Faisalabad	1982-83
116*	G. S. Chappell, Melbourne	1972-73	127	A. P. Sheahan, Melbourne	1972-73
121	G. S. Chappell, Melbourne	1976-77	153†	R. B. Simpson, Karachi	1964-65
235	G. S. Chappell, Faisalabad	1979-80	115		
201	G. S. Chappell, Brisbane	1981-82	107	K. D. Walters, Adelaide	1976-77
150*	G. S. Chappell, Brisbane	1983-84	179	K. C. Wessels, Adelaide	1983-84
182	G. S. Chappell, Sydney	1983-84	100	G. M. Wood, Melbourne	1981-82
196	I. M. Chappell, Adelaide	1972-73	172	G. N. Yallop, Faisalabad	1979-80
168	G. J. Cosier, Melbourne	1976-77	141	G. N. Yallop, Perth	1983-84
105†	I. C. Davis, Adelaide	1976-77	268	G. N. Yallop, Melbourne	1983-84
106	K. J. Hughes, Perth	1981-82			
106	K. J. Hughes, Adelaide	1983-84			

For Pakistan (25)

152*	Asif Iqbal, Adelaide	1976-77	135	Mohsin Khan, Lahore	1982-83
120	Asif Iqbal, Sydney	1976-77	149	Mohsin Khan, Adelaide	1983-84
134*	Asif Iqbal, Perth	1978-79	152	Mohsin Khan, Melbourne	1983-84
101*	Hanif Mohammad, Karachi	1959-60	121	Mushtaq Mohammad, Sydney	1972-73
104	Hanif Mohammad, Melbourne	1964-65	113	Qasim Omar, Adelaide	1983-84
129*	Javed Miandad, Perth	1978-79	137	Sadiq Mohammad, Melbourne	1972-73
106*	Javed Miandad, Faisalabad	1979-80	105	Sadiq Mohammad, Melbourne	1976-77
138	Javed Miandad, Lahore	1982-83			
131	Javed Miandad, Adelaide	1983-84	166	Saeed Ahmed, Lahore	1959-60
166†	Khalid Ibadulla, Karachi	1964-65	210*	Taslim Arif, Faisalabad	1979-80
158	Majid Khan, Melbourne	1972-73	101	Zaheer Abbas, Adelaide	1976-77
108	Majid Khan, Melbourne	1978-79	126	Zaheer Abbas, Faisalabad	1982-83
110*	Majid Khan, Lahore	1979-80			
111	Mansoor Akhtar, Faisalabad	1982-83			

† *Signifies hundred on first appearance in Australia-Pakistan Tests.*

RECORD PARTNERSHIPS FOR EACH WICKET

For Australia

134 for 1st	I. C. Davis and A. Turner at Melbourne	1976-77
259 for 2nd	W. B. Phillips and G. N. Yallop at Perth	1983-84
203 for 3rd	G. N. Yallop and K. J. Hughes at Melbourne	1983-84
217 for 4th	G. S. Chappell and G. N. Yallop at Faisalabad	1979-80
171 for 5th	G. S. Chappell and G. J. Cosier at Melbourne	1976-77
	A. R. Border and G. S. Chappell at Brisbane	1983-84
139 for 6th	R. M. Cowper and T. R. Veivers at Melbourne	1964-65
185 for 7th	G. N. Yallop and G. R. J. Matthews at Melbourne	1983-84
117 for 8th	G. J. Cosier and K. J. O'Keeffe at Melbourne	1976-77
83 for 9th	J. R. Watkins and R. A. L. Massie at Sydney	1972-73
52 for 10th	D. K. Lillee and M. H. N. Walker at Sydney	1976-77
	G. F. Lawson and T. M. Alderman at Lahore	1982-83

For Pakistan

249 for 1st†	Khalid Ibadulla and Abdul Kadir at Karachi	1964-65
233 for 2nd	Mohsin Khan and Qasim Omar at Adelaide	1983-84
223* for 3rd	Taslim Arif and Javed Miandad at Faisalabad	1979-80
155 for 4th	Mansoor Akhtar and Zaheer Abbas at Faisalabad	1982-83
186 for 5th	Javed Miandad and Salim Malik at Adelaide	1983-84
115 for 6th	Asif Iqbal and Javed Miandad at Sydney	1976-77
104 for 7th	Intikhab Alam and Wasim Bari at Adelaide	1972-73
111 for 8th	Majid Khan and Imran Khan at Lahore	1979-80
56 for 9th	Intikhab Alam and Afaq Hussain at Melbourne	1964-65
87 for 10th	Asif Iqbal and Iqbal Qasim at Adelaide	1976-77

† *Denotes record partnership against all countries.*

TEN WICKETS OR MORE IN A MATCH

For Australia (2)

10-111 (7-87, 3-24)†	R. J. Bright, Karachi	1979-80
10-135 (6-82, 4-53)	D. K. Lillee, Melbourne	1976-77
11-118 (5-32, 6-86)†	C. G. Rackemann, Perth	1983-84

For Pakistan (5)

11-218 (4-76, 7-142)	Abdul Qadir, Faisalabad	1982-83
13-114 (6-34, 7-80)†	Fazal Mahmood, Karachi	1956-57
12-165 (6-102, 6-63)	Imran Khan, Sydney	1976-77
11-118 (4-69, 7-49)	Iqbal Qasim, Karachi	1979-80
11-125 (2-39, 9-86)	Sarfraz Nawaz, Melbourne	1978-79

† *Signifies ten wickets or more on first appearance in Australia–Pakistan Tests.*

AUSTRALIA v SRI LANKA

		Captains				
Season	Australia	Sri Lanka	T	A	SL	D
1982-83SL	G. S. Chappell	L. R. D. Mendis	1	1	0	0

SL Played in Sri Lanka.

The only match played was at Kandy.

INDIVIDUAL HUNDREDS

For Australia (2)

143*† D. W. Hookes, Kandy ... 1982-83 │ 141† K. C. Wessels, Kandy ... 1982-83

† Signifies hundred on first appearance in Australia–Sri Lanka Tests.

Highest score for Sri Lanka: 96 by S. Wettimuny.

Best bowling in an innings for Australia: 5-66 by T. G. Hogan.
for Sri Lanka: 2-113 by A. L. F. de Mel.

Best wicket partnerships for Australia: 170 for the 2nd by K. C. Wessels and G. N. Yallop.
155* for the 5th by D. W. Hookes and A. R. Border.
for Sri Lanka: 96 for the 5th by L. R. D. Mendis and
A. Ranatunga.

Highest innings total for Australia: 514-4 dec.
for Sri Lanka: 271.

SOUTH AFRICA v NEW ZEALAND

		Captains				
Season	South Africa	New Zealand	T	SA	NZ	D
1931-32N	H. B. Cameron	M. L. Page	2	2	0	0
1952-53N	J. E. Cheetham	W. M. Wallace	2	1	0	1
1953-54S	J. E. Cheetham	G. O. Rabone[1]	5	4	0	1
1961-62S	D. J. McGlew	J. R. Reid	5	2	2	1
1963-64N	T. L. Goddard	J. R. Reid	3	0	0	3
	In New Zealand		7	3	0	4
	In South Africa		10	6	2	2
	Totals		17	9	2	6

N Played in New Zealand. S Played in South Africa.

Note: [1]B. Sutcliffe captained in Fourth and Fifth Tests.

HIGHEST INNINGS TOTALS

For South Africa in South Africa: 464 at Johannesburg 1961-62
in New Zealand: 524-8 at Wellington 1952-53

For New Zealand in South Africa: 505 at Cape Town 1953-54
in New Zealand: 364 at Wellington 1931-32

LOWEST INNINGS TOTALS

For South Africa in South Africa: 148 at Johannesburg 1953-54
in New Zealand: 223 at Dunedin 1963-64

For New Zealand in South Africa: 79 at Johannesburg 1953-54
in New Zealand: 138 at Dunedin 1963-64

INDIVIDUAL HUNDREDS

For South Africa (11)

122*	X. C. Balaskas, Wellington	1931-32	101	R. A. McLean, Durban ...	1953-54	
103†	J. A. J. Christy, Christ-church	1931-32	113	R. A. McLean, Cape Town	1961-62	
116	W. R. Endean, Auckland ..	1952-53	113†	B. Mitchell, Christchurch ..	1931-32	
255*†	D. J. McGlew, Wellington .	1952-53	109†	A. R. A. Murray, Welling-ton	1952-53	
127*‡	D. J. McGlew, Durban ...	1961-62				
120	D. J. McGlew, Johannes-burg	1961-62	101	J. H. B. Waite, Johannes-burg	1961-62	

For New Zealand (7)

109	P. T. Barton, Port Eliza-beth	1961-62	135	J. R. Reid, Cape Town	1953-54
101	P. G. Z. Harris, Cape Town	1961-62	142	J. R. Reid, Johannes-burg	1961-62
107	G. O. Rabone, Durban	1953-54	138	B. W. Sinclair, Auckland ..	1963-64
			100†	H. G. Vivian, Wellington .	1931-32

† *Signifies hundred on first appearance in South Africa–New Zealand Tests.*
‡ *Carried his bat.*

RECORD PARTNERSHIPS FOR EACH WICKET

For South Africa

196 for 1st	J. A. J. Christy and B. Mitchell at Christchurch	1931-32
76 for 2nd	J. A. J. Christy and H. B. Cameron at Wellington	1931-32
112 for 3rd	D. J. McGlew and R. A. McLean at Johannesburg	1961-62
135 for 4th	K. J. Funston and R. A. McLean at Durban	1953-54
130 for 5th	W. R. Endean and J. E. Cheetham at Auckland	1952-53
83 for 6th	K. C. Bland and D. T. Lindsay at Auckland	1963-64
246 for 7th†	D. J. McGlew and A. R. A. Murray at Wellington	1952-53
95 for 8th	J. E. Cheetham and H. J. Tayfield at Cape Town	1953-54
60 for 9th	P. M. Pollock and N. A. T. Adcock at Port Elizabeth	1961-62
47 for 10th	D. J. McGlew and H. D. Bromfield at Port Elizabeth	1961-62

For New Zealand

126 for 1st	G. O. Rabone and M. E. Chapple at Cape Town	1953-54
51 for 2nd	W. P. Bradburn and B. W. Sinclair at Dunedin	1963-64
94 for 3rd	M. B. Poore and B. Sutcliffe at Cape Town	1953-54
171 for 4th	B. W. Sinclair and S. N. McGregor at Auckland	1963-64
174 for 5th	J. R. Reid and J. E. F. Beck at Cape Town	1953-54
100 for 6th	H. G. Vivian and F. T. Badcock at Wellington	1931-32
84 for 7th	J. R. Reid and G. A. Bartlett at Johannesburg	1961-62
73 for 8th	P. G. Z. Harris and G. A. Bartlett at Durban	1961-62
69 for 9th	C. F. W. Allcott and I. B. Cromb at Wellington	1931-32
49* for 10th	A. E. Dick and F. J. Cameron at Cape Town	1961-62

† *Denotes record partnership against all countries.*

TEN WICKETS OR MORE IN A MATCH

For South Africa (1)

11-196 (6-128, 5-68)†   S. F. Burke, Cape Town 1961-62

† *Signifies ten wickets or more on first appearance in South Africa–New Zealand Tests.*

Note: The best match figures by a New Zealand bowler are 8-180 (4-61, 4-119), J. C. Alabaster at Cape Town, 1961-62.

WEST INDIES v NEW ZEALAND

		Captains				
Season	*West Indies*	*New Zealand*	*T*	*WI*	*NZ*	*D*
1951-52N	J. D. C. Goddard	B. Sutcliffe	2	1	0	1
1955-56N	D. St E. Atkinson	J. R. Reid[1]	4	3	1	0
1968-69N	G. S. Sobers	G. T. Dowling	3	1	1	1
1971-72W	G. S. Sobers	G. T. Dowling[2]	5	0	0	5
1979-80N	C. H. Lloyd	G. P. Howarth	3	0	1	2
1984-85W	I. V. A. Richards	G. P. Howarth	4	2	0	2
	In New Zealand		12	5	3	4
	In West Indies		9	2	0	7
	Totals		21	7	3	11

N Played in New Zealand.   W Played in West Indies.

Notes: The following deputised for the official touring captain or were appointed by the home authority for only a minor proportion of the series:
[1]H. B. Cave (First). [2]B. E. Congdon (Third, Fourth and Fifth).

HIGHEST INNINGS TOTALS

For West Indies in West Indies: 564-8 at Bridgetown 1971-72
in New Zealand: 546-6 dec. at Auckland 1951-52

For New Zealand in West Indies: 543-3 dec. at Georgetown 1971-72
in New Zealand: 460 at Christchurch 1979-80

LOWEST INNINGS TOTALS

For West Indies in West Indies: 133 at Bridgetown 1971-72
in New Zealand: 77 at Auckland 1955-56

For New Zealand in West Indies: 94 at Bridgetown 1984-85
in New Zealand: 74 at Dunedin 1955-56

INDIVIDUAL HUNDREDS

By West Indies (23)

109†	M. C. Carew, Auckland ...	1968-69
183	C. A. Davis, Bridgetown ..	1971-72
163	R. C. Fredericks, Kingston	1971-72
100	C. G. Greenidge, Port-of-Spain	1984-85
105†	D. L. Haynes, Dunedin ...	1979-80
122	D. L. Haynes, Christchurch	1979-80
100*†	A. I. Kallicharran, Georgetown	1971-72
101	A. I. Kallicharran, Port-of-Spain	1971-72
100*	C. L. King, Christchurch ..	1979-80
168†	S. M. Nurse, Auckland ...	1968-69
258	S. M. Nurse, Christchurch .	1968-69

105	I. V. A. Richards, Bridgetown	1984-85
185	R. B. Richardson, Georgetown	1984-85
214† 100*	L. G. Rowe, Kingston	1971-72
100	L. G. Rowe, Christchurch .	1979-80
142	G. S. Sobers, Bridgetown ..	1971-72
152	J. B. Stollmeyer, Auckland .	1951-52
115	C. L. Walcott, Auckland ..	1951-52
123	E. D. Weekes, Dunedin ...	1955-56
103	E. D. Weekes, Christchurch	1955-56
156	E. D. Weekes, Wellington .	1955-56
100	F. M. M. Worrell, Auckland	1951-52

By New Zealand (14)

101	M. G. Burgess, Kingston ..	1971-72
166*	B. E. Congdon, Port-of-Spain	1971-72
126	B. E. Congdon, Bridgetown	1971-72
112	J. J. Crowe, Kingston	1984-85
188	M. D. Crowe, Georgetown	1984-85
127	B. A. Edgar, Auckland	1979-80
103	R. J. Hadlee, Christchurch .	1979-80
117*	B. F. Hastings, Christchurch	1968-69
105	B. F. Hastings, Bridgetown	1971-72
147	G. P. Howarth, Christchurch	1979-80
182	T. W. Jarvis, Georgetown .	1971-72
188†	B. R. Taylor, Auckland ...	1968-69
223*‡	G. M. Turner, Kingston ...	1971-72
259	G. M. Turner, Georgetown .	1971-72

† *Signifies hundred on first appearance in West Indies–New Zealand Tests.*
‡ *Carried his bat.*

Notes: E. D. Weekes in 1955-56 made three hundreds in consecutive innings.
   L. G. Rowe and A. I. Kallicharran each scored hundreds in their first two innings in Test cricket, Rowe being the only batsman to do so in his first match.

RECORD PARTNERSHIPS FOR EACH WICKET

For West Indies

225 for 1st	C. G. Greenidge and D. L. Haynes at Christchurch	1979-80
269 for 2nd	R. C. Fredericks and L. G. Rowe at Kingston	1971-72
185 for 3rd	C. G. Greenidge and R. B. Richardson at Port-of-Spain	1984-85
162 for 4th	{ E. D. Weekes and O. G. Smith at Dunedin	1955-56
	{ C. G. Greenidge and A. I. Kallicharran at Christchurch	1979-80
189 for 5th	F. M. M. Worrell and C. L. Walcott at Auckland	1951-52
254 for 6th	C. A. Davis and G. S. Sobers at Bridgetown	1971-72
143 for 7th	D. St E. Atkinson and J. D. C. Goddard at Christchurch	1955-56
83 for 8th	I. V. A. Richards and M. D. Marshall at Bridgetown	1984-85
70 for 9th	M. D. Marshall and J. Garner at Bridgetown	1984-85
31 for 10th	T. M. Findlay and G. C. Shillingford at Bridgetown	1971-72

For New Zealand

387 for 1st†	G. M. Turner and T. W. Jarvis at Georgetown	1971-72
210 for 2nd†	G. P. Howarth and J. J. Crowe at Kingston	1984-85
75 for 3rd	B. E. Congdon and B. F. Hastings at Christchurch	1968-69
175 for 4th	B. E. Congdon and B. F. Hastings at Bridgetown	1971-72
142 for 5th	M. D. Crowe and J. V. Coney at Georgetown	1984-85
220 for 6th†	G. M. Turner and K. J. Wadsworth at Kingston	1971-72
143 for 7th	M. D. Crowe and I. D. S. Smith at Georgetown	1984-85
136 for 8th†	B. E. Congdon and R. S. Cunis at Port-of-Spain	1971-72
62* for 9th	V. Pollard and R. S. Cunis at Auckland	1968-69
41 for 10th	B. E. Congdon and J. C. Alabaster at Port-of-Spain	1971-72

† *Denotes record partnership against all countries.*

TEN WICKETS OR MORE IN A MATCH

For West Indies (1)

11-120 (4-40, 7-80)	M. D. Marshall, Bridgetown	1984-85

For New Zealand (3)

10-124 (4-51, 6-73)†	E. J. Chatfield, Port-of-Spain	1984-85
11-102 (5-34, 6-68)†	R. J. Hadlee, Dunedin	1979-80
10-166 (4-71, 6-95)	G. B. Troup, Auckland	1979-80

† *Signifies ten wickets or more on first appearance in West Indies–New Zealand Tests.*

WEST INDIES v INDIA

Captains

Season	West Indies	India	T	WI	I	D
1948-49*I*	J. D. C. Goddard	L. Amarnath	5	1	0	4
1952-53*W*	J. B. Stollmeyer	V. S. Hazare	5	1	0	4
1958-59*I*	F. C. M. Alexander	Ghulam Ahmed[1]	5	3	0	2
1961-62*W*	F. M. M. Worrell	N. J. Contractor[2]	5	5	0	0
1966-67*I*	G. S. Sobers	Nawab of Pataudi jun.	3	2	0	1
1970-71*W*	G. S. Sobers	A. L. Wadekar	5	0	1	4
1974-75*I*	C. H. Lloyd	Nawab of Pataudi jun.[3]	5	3	2	0
1975-76*W*	C. H. Lloyd	B. S. Bedi	4	2	1	1
1978-79*I*	A. I. Kallicharran	S. M. Gavaskar	6	0	1	5
1982-83*W*	C. H. Lloyd	Kapil Dev	5	2	0	3
1983-84*I*	C. H. Lloyd	Kapil Dev	6	3	0	3
	In India		30	12	3	15
	In West Indies		24	10	2	12
	Totals		54	22	5	27

I Played in India.   W Played in West Indies.

Notes: The following deputised for the official touring captain or were appointed by the home authority for only a minor proportion of the series:
[1]P. R. Umrigar (First), V. Mankad (Fourth), H. R. Adhikari (Fifth). [2]Nawab of Pataudi jun. (Third, Fourth and Fifth). [3]S. Venkataraghavan (Second).

HIGHEST INNINGS TOTALS

For West Indies in West Indies: 631-8 dec. at Kingston		1961-62
in India: 644-8 dec. at Delhi		1958-59
For India in West Indies: 469-7 at Port-of-Spain		1982-83
in India: 644-7 dec. at Kanpur.................................		1978-79

LOWEST INNINGS TOTALS

For West Indies in West Indies: 214 at Port-of-Spain		1970-71
in India: 151 at Madras		1978-79
For India in West Indies: 97† at Kingston		1975-76
in India: 90 at Calcutta		1983-84

† *Five men absent hurt.*

INDIVIDUAL HUNDREDS

For West Indies (67)

250	S. F. A. F. Bacchus, Kanpur	1978-79	107†	C. G. Greenidge, Bangalore	1974-75
103	B. F. Butcher, Calcutta ...	1958-59	154*	C. G. Greenidge, St John's	1982-83
142	B. F. Butcher, Madras	1958-59	194	C. G. Greenidge, Kanpur .	1983-84
107†	R. J. Christiani, Delhi	1948-49	136	D. L. Haynes, St John's ...	1982-83
125*	C. A. Davis, Georgetown ..	1970-71	123	J. K. Holt, Delhi	1958-59
105	C. A. Davis, Port-of-Spain	1970-71	101	C. C. Hunte, Bombay	1966-67
110	P. J. L. Dujon, St John's ..	1982-83	124†	A. I. Kallicharran, Bangalore	1974-75
100	R. C. Fredericks, Calcutta .	1974-75	103*	A. I. Kallicharran, Port-of-Spain	1975-76
104	R. C. Fredericks, Bombay ..	1974-75			
123	H. A. Gomes, Port-of-Spain	1982-83	187	A. I. Kallicharran, Bombay	1978-79
101†	G. E. Gomez, Delhi	1948-49	256	R. B. Kanhai, Calcutta ...	1958-59

138	R. B. Kanhai, Kingston ...	1961-62
139	R. B. Kanhai, Port-of-Spain	1961-62
158*	R. B. Kanhai, Kingston ...	1970-71
163	C. H. Lloyd, Bangalore ...	1974-75
242*	C. H. Lloyd, Bombay	1974-75
102	C. H. Lloyd, Bridgetown ...	1975-76
143	C. H. Lloyd, Port-of-Spain .	1982-83
106	C. H. Lloyd, St John's ...	1982-83
103	C. H. Lloyd, Delhi ...	1983-84
161*	C. H. Lloyd, Calcutta ...	1983-84
130	A. L. Logie, Bridgetown ...	1982-83
125†	E. D. A. McMorris, Kingston	1961-62
115†	B. H. Pairaudeau, Port-of-Spain	1952-53
104	A. F. Rae, Bombay	1948-49
109	A. F. Rae, Madras	1948-49
192*	I. V. A. Richards, Delhi	1974-75
142	I. V. A. Richards, Bridgetown	1975-76
130	I. V. A. Richards, Port-of-Spain	1975-76
177	I. V. A. Richards, Port-of-Spain	1975-76
109	I. V. A. Richards, Georgetown	1982-83
120	I. V. A. Richards, Bombay	1983-84
100	O. G. Smith, Delhi	1958-59
142*†	G. S. Sobers, Bombay	1958-59
198	G. S. Sobers, Kanpur	1958-59
106*	G. S. Sobers, Calcutta	1958-59
153	G. S. Sobers, Kingston	1961-62
104	G. S. Sobers, Kingston	1961-62
108*	G. S. Sobers, Georgetown .	1970-71
178*	G. S. Sobers, Bridgetown .	1970-71
132	G. S. Sobers, Port-of-Spain	1970-71
100*	J. S. Solomon, Delhi	1958-59
160	J. B. Stollmeyer, Madras ..	1948-49
104*	J. B. Stollmeyer, Port-of-Spain	1952-53
152†	C. L. Walcott, Delhi	1948-49
108	C. L. Walcott, Calcutta	1948-49
125	C. L. Walcott, Georgetown	1952-53
118	C. L. Walcott, Kingston ...	1952-53
128†	E. D. Weekes, Delhi	1948-49
194	E. D. Weekes, Bombay	1948-49
162 / 101	E. D. Weekes, Calcutta ...	1948-49
207	E. D. Weekes, Port-of-Spain	1952-53
161	E. D. Weekes, Port-of-Spain	1952-53
109	E. D. Weekes, Kingston ...	1952-53
111	A. B. Williams, Calcutta ..	1978-79
237	F. M. M. Worrell, Kingston	1952-53

For India (49)

114*†	H. R. Adhikari, Delhi	1948-49
101*	M. Amarnath, Kanpur ...	1978-79
117	M. Amarnath, Port-of-Spain	1982-83
116	M. Amarnath, St John's ...	1982-83
163*	M. L. Apte, Port-of-Spain	1952-53
109	C. G. Borde, Delhi ...	1958-59
121	C. G. Borde, Bombay ...	1966-67
125	C. G. Borde, Madras ...	1966-67
104	S. A. Durani, Port-of-Spain	1961-62
109	F. M. Engineer, Madras ...	1966-67
102	A. D. Gaekwad, Kanpur ...	1978-79
116	S. M. Gavaskar, Georgetown	1970-71
117*	S. M. Gavaskar, Bridgetown	1970-71
124 / 220	S. M. Gavaskar, Port-of-Spain	1970-71
156	S. M. Gavaskar, Port-of-Spain	1975-76
102	S. M. Gavaskar, Port-of-Spain	1975-76
205	S. M. Gavaskar, Bombay ..	1978-79
107 / 182*	S. M. Gavaskar, Calcutta .	1978-79
120	S. M. Gavaskar, Delhi	1978-79
147*	S. M. Gavaskar, Georgetown	1982-83
121	S. M. Gavaskar, Delhi ...	1983-84
236*	S. M. Gavaskar, Madras ..	1983-84
134*	V. S. Hazare, Bombay	1948-49
122	V. S. Hazare, Bombay	1948-49
126*	Kapil Dev, Delhi ...	1978-79
100*	Kapil Dev, Port-of-Spain ..	1982-83
118	V. L. Manjrekar, Kingston	1952-53
102	R. S. Modi, Bombay ...	1948-49
106†	Mushtaq Ali, Calcutta ...	1948-49
115*	B. P. Patel, Port-of-Spain	1975-76
150	P. Roy, Kingston ...	1952-53
212	D. N. Sardesai, Kingston ..	1970-71
112	D. N. Sardesai, Port-of-Spain	1970-71
150	D. N. Sardesai, Bridgetown	1970-71
102	R. J. Shastri, St John's ...	1982-83
102	E. D. Solkar, Bombay ...	1974-75
130	P. R. Umrigar, Port-of-Spain	1952-53
117	P. R. Umrigar, Kingston ..	1952-53
172*	P. R. Umrigar, Port-of-Spain	1961-62
157*	D. B. Vengsarkar, Calcutta	1978-79
109	D. B. Vengsarkar, Delhi ...	1978-79
159	D. B. Vengsarkar, Delhi ..	1983-84
100	D. B. Vengsarkar, Bombay	1983-84
139	G. R. Viswanath, Calcutta .	1974-75
112	G. R. Viswanath, Port-of-Spain	1975-76
124	G. R. Viswanath, Madras .	1978-79
179	G. R. Viswanath, Kanpur .	1978-79

† *Signifies hundred on first appearance in West Indies–India Tests.*

RECORD PARTNERSHIPS FOR EACH WICKET

For West Indies

296 for 1st†	C. G. Greenidge and D. L. Haynes at St John's	....	1982-83
255 for 2nd	E. D. A. McMorris and R. B. Kanhai at Kingston	....	1961-62
220 for 3rd	I. V. A. Richards and A. I. Kallicharran at Bridgetown	....	1975-76
267 for 4th	C. L. Walcott and G. E. Gomez at Delhi	....	1948-49
219 for 5th	E. D. Weekes and B. H. Pairaudeau at Port-of-Spain	....	1952-53
250 for 6th	C. H. Lloyd and D. L. Murray at Bombay	....	1974-75
130 for 7th	C. G. Greenidge and M. D. Marshall at Kanpur	....	1983-84
124 for 8th†	I. V. A. Richards and K. D. Boyce at Delhi	....	1974-75
161 for 9th†	C. H. Lloyd and A. M. E. Roberts at Calcutta	............,.....	1983-84
98* for 10th†	F. M. M. Worrell and W. W. Hall at Port-of-Spain	....	1961-62

For India

153 for 1st	S. M. Gavaskar and C. P. S. Chauhan at Bombay	....	1978-79
344* for 2nd†	S. M. Gavaskar and D. B. Vengsarkar at Calcutta	....	1978-79
159 for 3rd	M. Amarnath and G. R. Viswanath at Port-of-Spain	....	1975-76
172 for 4th	G. R. Viswanath and A. D. Gaekwad at Kanpur	....	1978-79
204 for 5th	S. M. Gavaskar and B. P. Patel at Port-of-Spain	....	1975-76
170 for 6th	S. M. Gavaskar and R. J. Shastri at Madras	....	1983-84
186 for 7th	D. N. Sardesai and E. D. Solkar at Bridgetown	....	1970-71
107 for 8th	Yashpal Sharma and B. S. Sandhu at Kingston	....	1982-83
143* for 9th	S. M. Gavaskar and S. M. H. Kirmani at Madras	....	1983-84
62 for 10th	D. N. Sardesai and B. S. Bedi at Bridgetown	....	1970-71

† *Denotes record partnership against all countries.*

TEN WICKETS OR MORE IN A MATCH

For West Indies (2)

11-126 (6-50, 5-76)	W. W. Hall, Kanpur		1958-59
12-121 (7-64, 5-57)	A. M. E. Roberts, Madras	....	1974-75

For India (3)

11-235 (7-157, 4-78)†	B. S. Chandrasekhar, Bombay	....	1966-67
10-223 (9-102, 1-121)	S. P. Gupte, Kanpur	....	1958-59
10-135 (1-52, 9-83)	Kapil Dev, Ahmedabad	....	1983-84

† *Signifies ten wickets or more on first appearance in West Indies–India Tests.*

WEST INDIES v PAKISTAN

	Captains					
Season	West Indies	Pakistan	T	WI	P	D
1957-58*W*	F. C. M. Alexander	A. H. Kardar	5	3	1	1
1958-59*P*	F. C. M. Alexander	Fazal Mahmood	3	1	2	0
1974-75*P*	C. H. Lloyd	Intikhab Alam	2	0	0	2
1976-77*W*	C. H. Lloyd	Mushtaq Mohammad	5	2	1	2
1980-81*P*	C. H. Lloyd	Javed Miandad	4	1	0	3
	In West Indies	....	10	5	2	3
	In Pakistan	....	9	2	2	5
	Totals	....	19	7	4	8

P Played in Pakistan.   W Played in West Indies.

HIGHEST INNINGS TOTALS

For West Indies in West Indies: 790-3 dec. at Kingston 1957-58
　　　　　　　　　　in Pakistan: 493 at Karachi 1974-75
For Pakistan in West Indies: 657-8 dec. at Bridgetown 1957-58
　　　　　　　　　　in Pakistan: 406-8 dec. at Karachi 1974-75

LOWEST INNINGS TOTALS

For West Indies in West Indies: 154 at Port-of-Spain 1976-77
　　　　　　　　　　in Pakistan: 76 at Dacca 1958-59
For Pakistan in West Indies: 106 at Bridgetown 1957-58
　　　　　　　　　　in Pakistan: 104 at Lahore 1958-59

INDIVIDUAL HUNDREDS

For West Indies (17)

105*† L. Baichan, Lahore	1974-75	157　C. H. Lloyd, Bridgetown ..	1976-77
120　R. C. Fredericks, Port-of-Spain	1976-77	120*　I. V. A. Richards, Multan .	1980-81
100　C. G. Greenidge, Kingston	1976-77	120　I. T. Shillingford, Georgetown	1976-77
142†　C. C. Hunte, Bridgetown .	1957-58	365*　G. S. Sobers, Kingston	1957-58
260　C. C. Hunte, Kingston	1957-58	125 ⎫ G. S. Sobers, Georgetown .	1957-58
114　C. C. Hunte, Georgetown .	1957-58	109* ⎭	
101　B. D. Julien, Karachi	1974-75	145　C. L. Walcott, Georgetown	1957-58
115　A. I. Kallicharran, Karachi	1974-75	197†　E. D. Weekes, Bridgetown .	1957-58
217　R. B. Kanhai, Lahore	1958-59		

Pakistan (14)

135　Asif Iqbal, Kingston	1976-77	121　Mushtaq Mohammad, Port-of-Spain	1976-77
337†　Hanif Mohammad, Bridgetown	1957-58	150　Saeed Ahmed, Georgetown	1957-58
103　Hanif Mohammad, Karachi	1958-59	107*　Wasim Raja, Karachi	1974-75
122　Imtiaz Ahmed, Kingston ...	1957-58	117*　Wasim Raja, Bridgetown ..	1976-77
123　Imran Khan, Lahore	1980-81	106　Wazir Mohammad, Kingston	1957-58
100　Majid Khan, Karachi	1974-75		
167　Majid Khan, Georgetown .	1976-77	189　Wazir Mohammad, Port-of-Spain	1957-58
123　Mushtaq Mohammad, Lahore	1974-75		

† *Signifies hundred on first appearance in West Indies–Pakistan Tests.*

RECORD PARTNERSHIPS FOR EACH WICKET

For West Indies

182 for 1st	R. C. Fredericks and C. G. Greenidge at Kingston	1976-77
446 for 2nd†	C. C. Hunte and G. S. Sobers at Kingston	1957-58
162 for 3rd	R. B. Kanhai and G. S. Sobers at Lahore	1958-59
188* for 4th	G. S. Sobers and C. L. Walcott at Kingston	1957-58
185 for 5th	E. D. Weekes and O. G. Smith at Bridgetown	1957-58
151 for 6th	C. H. Lloyd and D. L. Murray at Bridgetown	1976-77
70 for 7th	C. H. Lloyd and J. Garner at Bridgetown	1976-77
50 for 8th	B. D. Julien and V. A. Holder at Karachi	1974-75
46 for 9th	J. Garner and C. E. H. Croft at Port-of-Spain	1976-77
44 for 10th	R. Nanan and S. T. Clarke at Faisalabad	1980-81

For Pakistan

159 for 1st‡	Majid Khan and Zaheer Abbas at Georgetown	1976-77
178 for 2nd	Hanif Mohammad and Saeed Ahmed at Karachi	1958-59
169 for 3rd	Saeed Ahmed and Wazir Mohammad at Port-of-Spain	1957-58
154 for 4th	Wazir Mohammad and Hanif Mohammad at Port-of-Spain	1957-58
87 for 5th	Mushtaq Mohammad and Asif Iqbal at Kingston	1976-77
166 for 6th	Wazir Mohammad and A. H. Kardar at Kingston	1957-58
128 for 7th	Wasim Raja and Wasim Bari at Karachi	1974-75
73 for 8th	Imran Khan and Sarfraz Nawaz at Port-of-Spain	1976-77
73 for 9th	Wasim Raja and Sarfraz Nawaz at Bridgetown	1976-77
133 for 10th†	Wasim Raja and Wasim Bari at Bridgetown	1976-77

† *Denotes record partnership against all countries.*

‡ *219 runs were added for this wicket in two separate partnerships: Sadiq Mohammad retired hurt and was replaced by Zaheer Abbas when 60 had been added. The highest partnership by two opening batsmen is 152 by Hanif Mohammad and Imtiaz Ahmed at Bridgetown, 1957-58.*

TEN WICKETS OR MORE IN A MATCH

For Pakistan (1)

12-100 (6-34, 6-66) Fazal Mahmood, Dacca 1958-59

Note: The best match figures by a West Indian bowler are 9-187 (5-66, 4-121), A. M. E. Roberts at Lahore, 1974-75, and 9-95 (8-29, 1-66), C. E. H. Croft at Port-of-Spain, 1976-77.

NEW ZEALAND v INDIA

Season	New Zealand	*Captains* India	T	NZ	I	D
1955-56 *I*	H. B. Cave	P. R. Umrigar[1]	5	0	2	3
1964-65 *I*	J. R. Reid	Nawab of Pataudi jun.	4	0	1	3
1967-68 *N*	G. T. Dowling[2]	Nawab of Pataudi jun.	4	1	3	0
1969-70 *I*	G. T. Dowling	Nawab of Pataudi jun.	3	1	1	1
1975-76 *N*	G. M. Turner	B. S. Bedi[3]	3	1	1	1
1976-77 *I*	G. M. Turner	B. S. Bedi	3	0	2	1
1980-81 *N*	G. P. Howarth	S. M. Gavaskar	3	1	0	2
	In India		15	1	6	8
	In New Zealand		10	3	4	3
	Totals		25	4	10	11

I Played in India.   N Played in New Zealand.

Notes: [1]Ghulam Ahmed captained in First Test. [2]B. W. Sinclair captained in First Test. [3]S. M. Gavaskar captained in First Test.

HIGHEST INNINGS TOTALS

For New Zealand in New Zealand: 502 at Christchurch	1967-68
in India: 462-9 dec. at Calcutta	1964-65
450-2 dec. at Delhi	1955-56
For India in New Zealand: 414 at Auckland	1975-76
in India: 537-3 dec. at Madras	1955-56

LOWEST INNINGS TOTALS

For New Zealand in New Zealand: 100 at Wellington 1980-81
              in India: 127 at Bombay 1969-70

For India in New Zealand: 81 at Wellington 1975-76
         in India: 88 at Bombay 1964-65

INDIVIDUAL HUNDREDS

For New Zealand (16)

120	G. T. Dowling, Bombay ...	1964-65	120	J. R. Reid, Calcutta	1955-56
143	G. T. Dowling, Dunedin ..	1967-68	137*†	B. Sutcliffe, Hyderabad ...	1955-56
239	G. T. Dowling, Christchurch	1967-68	230*	B. Sutcliffe, Delhi	1955-56
			151*	B. Sutcliffe, Calcutta	1964-65
102†	J. W. Guy, Hyderabad	1955-56	105†	B. R. Taylor, Calcutta	1964-65
137*	G. P. Howarth, Wellington	1980-81	117	G. M. Turner, Christchurch	1975-76
104	J. M. Parker, Bombay	1976-77			
123*	J. F. Reid, Christchurch .	1980-81	113	G. M. Turner, Kanpur	1976-77
119*	J. R. Reid, Delhi	1955-56	110	J. G. Wright, Auckland ...	1980-81

For India (20)

124†	S. Amarnath, Auckland ..	1975-76	153	Nawab of Pataudi jun., Calcutta	1964-65
109	C. G. Borde, Bombay	1964-65			
116†	S. M. Gavaskar, Auckland	1975-76	113	Nawab of Pataudi jun., Delhi	1964-65
119	S. M. Gavaskar, Bombay ..	1976-77			
100*†	A. G. Kripal Singh, Hyderabad	1955-56	106*	G. S. Ramchand, Calcutta .	1955-56
			100	Pankaj Roy, Calcutta	1955-56
118†	V. L. Manjrekar, Hyderabad	1955-56	173	Pankaj Roy, Madras	1955-56
			200*	D. N. Sardesai, Bombay ..	1964-65
177	V. L. Manjrekar, Delhi ...	1955-56	106	D. N. Sardesai, Delhi	1964-65
102*	V. L. Manjrekar, Madras .	1964-65	223†	P. R. Umrigar, Hyderabad	1955-56
223	V. Mankad, Bombay	1955-56	103*	G. R. Viswanath, Kanpur .	1976-77
231	V. Mankad, Madras	1955-56	143	A. L. Wadekar, Wellington	1967-68

† *Signifies hundred on first appearance in New Zealand–India Tests. B. R. Taylor provides the only instance for New Zealand of a player scoring his maiden hundred in first-class cricket in his first Test.*

RECORD PARTNERSHIPS FOR EACH WICKET

For New Zealand

126 for 1st	B. A. G. Murray and G. T. Dowling at Christchurch	1967-68
155 for 2nd	G. T. Dowling and B. E. Congdon at Dunedin	1967-68
222* for 3rd†	B. Sutcliffe and J. R. Reid at Delhi	1955-56
103 for 4th	G. T. Dowling and M. G. Burgess at Christchurch	1967-68
119 for 5th	G. T. Dowling and K. Thomson at Christchurch	1967-68
87 for 6th	J. W. Guy and A. R. MacGibbon at Hyderabad	1955-56
163 for 7th	B. Sutcliffe and B. R. Taylor at Calcutta	1964-65
81 for 8th	V. Pollard and G. E. Vivian at Calcutta	1964-65
69 for 9th	M. G. Burgess and J. C. Alabaster at Dunedin	1967-68
61 for 10th	J. T. Ward and R. O. Collinge at Madras	1964-65

For India

413 for 1st†	V. Mankad and Pankaj Roy at Madras	1955-56
204 for 2nd	S. M. Gavaskar and S. Amarnath at Auckland	1975-76
238 for 3rd	P. R. Umrigar and V. L. Manjrekar at Hyderabad	1955-56
171 for 4th	P. R. Umrigar and A. G. Kripal Singh at Hyderabad	1955-56
127 for 5th	V. L. Manjrekar and G. S. Ramchand at Delhi	1955-56
193* for 6th†	D. N. Sardesai and Hanumant Singh at Bombay	1964-65
116 for 7th	B. P. Patel and S. M. H. Kirmani at Wellington	1975-76
143 for 8th†	R. G. Nadkarni and F. M. Engineer at Madras	1964-65
105 for 9th	⎰ S. M. H. Kirmani and B. S. Bedi at Bombay	1976-77
	⎱ S. M. H. Kirmani and N. S. Yadav at Auckland	1980-81
57 for 10th	R. B. Desai and B. S. Bedi at Dunedin	1967-68

† *Denotes record partnership against all countries.*

TEN WICKETS OR MORE IN A MATCH

For New Zealand (1)

11-58 (4-35, 7-23)	R. J. Hadlee, Wellington	1975-76

For India (2)

11-140 (3-64, 8-76)	E. A. S. Prasanna, Auckland	1975-76
12-152 (8-72, 4-80)	S. Venkataraghavan, Delhi	1964-65

NEW ZEALAND v PAKISTAN

Season	New Zealand	*Captains* Pakistan	T	NZ	P	D
1955-56*P*	H. B. Cave	A. H. Kardar	3	0	2	1
1964-65*N*	J. R. Reid	Hanif Mohammad	3	0	0	3
1964-65*P*	J. R. Reid	Hanif Mohammad	3	0	2	1
1969-70*P*	G. T. Dowling	Intikhab Alam	3	1	0	2
1972-73*P*	B. E. Congdon	Intikhab Alam	3	0	1	2
1976-77*P*	G. M. Turner[1]	Mushtaq Mohammad	3	0	2	1
1978-79*N*	M. G. Burgess	Mushtaq Mohammad	3	0	1	2
1984-85*P*	J. V. Coney	Zaheer Abbas	3	0	2	1
1984-85*N*	G. P. Howarth	Javed Miandad	3	2	0	1
In Pakistan			15	1	8	6
In New Zealand			12	2	2	8
Totals			27	3	10	14

N Played in New Zealand.   P Played in Pakistan.
Note: [1] J. M. Parker captained in Third Test.

HIGHEST INNINGS TOTALS

For New Zealand in New Zealand 492 at Wellington	1984-85
in Pakistan: 482-6 dec. at Lahore	1964-65
For Pakistan in New Zealand: 507-6 dec. at Dunedin	1972-73
in Pakistan: 565-9 dec. at Karachi	1976-77
561 at Lahore	1955-56

LOWEST INNINGS TOTALS

For New Zealand in New Zealand: 156 at Dunedin	1972-73
in Pakistan: 70 at Dacca	1955-56
For Pakistan in New Zealand: 169 at Auckland	1984-85
in Pakistan: 114 at Lahore	1969-70

INDIVIDUAL HUNDREDS

For New Zealand (16)

119*	M. G. Burgess, Dacca	1969-70	107†	R. E. Redmond, Auckland	1972-73
111	M. G. Burgess, Lahore	1976-77	106	J. F. Reid, Hyderabad	1984-85
111*	J. V. Coney, Dunedin	1984-85	148	J. F. Reid, Wellington	1984-85
129†	B. A. Edgar, Christchurch	1978-79	158*	J. F. Reid, Auckland	1984-85
110	B. F. Hastings, Auckland	1972-73	128	J. R. Reid, Karachi	1964-65
114	G. P. Howarth, Napier	1978-79	130	B. W. Sinclair, Lahore	1964-65
152	W. K. Lees, Karachi	1976-77	110†	G. M. Turner, Dacca	1969-70
111	S. N. McGregor, Lahore	1955-56	107	J. G. Wright, Karachi	1984-85

For Pakistan (26)

175	Asif Iqbal, Dunedin	1972-73	126	Mohammad Ilyas, Karachi	1964-65
166	Asif Iqbal, Lahore	1976-77	106	Mudassar Nazar, Hyderabad	1984-85
104	Asif Iqbal, Napier	1978-79	201	Mushtaq Mohammad, Dunedin	1972-73
103	Hanif Mohammad, Dacca	1955-56			
100*	Hanif Mohammad, Christchurch	1964-65	101	Mushtaq Mohammad, Hyderabad	1976-77
203*	Hanif Mohammad, Lahore	1964-65	107	Mushtaq Mohammad, Karachi	1976-77
209	Imtiaz Ahmed, Lahore	1955-56			
163†	Javed Miandad, Lahore	1976-77	166	Sadiq Mohammad, Wellington	1972-73
206	Javed Miandad, Karachi	1976-77			
160*	Javed Miandad, Christchurch	1978-79	103*	Sadiq Mohammad, Hyderabad	1976-77
104 / 103*	Javed Miandad, Hyderabad	1984-85	172	Saeed Ahmed, Karachi	1964-65
110	Majid Khan, Auckland	1972-73	119*	Salim Malik, Karachi	1984-85
112	Majid Khan, Karachi	1976-77	189	Waqar Hassan, Lahore	1955-56
119*	Majid Khan, Napier	1978-79	135	Zaheer Abbas, Auckland	1978-79

† *Signifies hundred on first appearance in New Zealand–Pakistan Tests.*

Note: Mushtaq and Sadiq Mohammad, at Hyderabad in 1976-77, provide the fourth instance in Test matches, after the Chappells (thrice), of brothers each scoring hundreds in the same innings.

RECORD PARTNERSHIPS FOR EACH WICKET

For New Zealand

159 for 1st	R. E. Redmond and G. M. Turner at Auckland	1972-73
195 for 2nd	J. G. Wright and G. P. Howarth at Napier	1978-79
178 for 3rd	B. W. Sinclair and J. R. Reid at Lahore	1964-65
128 for 4th	B. F. Hastings and M. G. Burgess at Wellington	1972-73
183 for 5th†	M. G. Burgess and R. W. Anderson at Lahore	1976-77
145 for 6th	J. F. Reid and R. J. Hadlee at Wellington	1984-85
186 for 7th†	W. K. Lees and R. J. Hadlee at Karachi	1976-77
100 for 8th	B. W. Yuile and D. R. Hadlee at Karachi	1969-70
96 for 9th	M. G. Burgess and R. S. Cunis at Dacca	1969-70
151 for 10th†	B. F. Hastings and R. O. Collinge at Auckland	1972-73

For Pakistan

147 for 1st‡	Sadiq Mohammad and Majid Khan at Karachi	1976-77
114 for 2nd	Mohammad Ilyas and Saeed Ahmed at Rawalpindi	1964-65
212 for 3rd	Mudassar Nazar and Javed Miandad at Hyderabad	1984-85
350 for 4th†	Mushtaq Mohammad and Asif Iqbal at Dunedin	1972-73
281 for 5th†	Javed Miandad and Asif Iqbal at Lahore	1976-77
217 for 6th†	Hanif Mohammad and Majid Khan at Lahore	1964-65
308 for 7th†	Waqar Hassan and Imtiaz Ahmed at Lahore	1955-56
89 for 8th	Anil Dalpat and Iqbal Qasim at Karachi	1984-85
52 for 9th	Intikhab Alam and Arif Butt at Auckland	1964-65
65 for 10th	Salah-ud-Din and Mohammad Farooq at Rawalpindi	1964-65

† *Denotes record partnership against all countries.*
‡ *In the preceding Test of this series, at Hyderabad, 164 runs were added for this wicket by Sadiq Mohammad, Majid Khan and Zaheer Abbas. Sadiq Mohammad retired hurt after 136 had been scored.*

TEN WICKETS OR MORE IN A MATCH

For Pakistan (4)

10-182 (5-91, 5-91)	Intikhab Alam, Dacca	1969-70
11-130 (7-52, 4-78)	Intikhab Alam, Dunedin	1972-73
10-128 (5-56, 5-72)	Wasim Akram, Dunedin	1984-85
11-79 (5-37, 6-42)†	Zulfiqar Ahmed, Karachi	1955-56

† *Signifies ten wickets or more on first appearance in New Zealand–Pakistan Tests.*
Note: The best match figures by a New Zealand bowler are 9-70 (4-36, 5-34), F. J. Cameron at Auckland, 1964-65.

NEW ZEALAND v SRI LANKA

	Captains					
Season	New Zealand	Sri Lanka	T	NZ	SL	D
1982-83N	G. P. Howarth	D. S. de Silva	2	2	0	0
1983-84S	G. P. Howarth	L. R. D. Mendis	3	2	0	1
	Totals		5	4	0	1

N Played in New Zealand. S Played in Sri Lanka.

HIGHEST INNINGS TOTALS

For New Zealand in New Zealand: 344 at Christchurch	1982-83
in Sri Lanka: 459 at Colombo (CCC)	1983-84
For Sri Lanka in New Zealand: 240 at Wellington	1982-83
in Sri Lanka: 289-9 dec. at Colombo (SSC)	1983-84

LOWEST INNINGS TOTALS

For New Zealand in New Zealand: 201 at Wellington	1982-83
in Sri Lanka: 198 at Colombo (SSC)	1983-84
For Sri Lanka in New Zealand: 93 at Wellington	1982-83
in Sri Lanka: 97 at Kandy	1983-84

INDIVIDUAL HUNDREDS

For New Zealand (1)	**For Sri Lanka** (1)
180 J. F. Reid, Colombo (CCC) 1983-84	108† R. L. Dias, Colombo (SSC) 1983-84

† *Signifies hundred on first appearance in New Zealand–Sri Lanka Tests.*

Best wicket partnership for New Zealand: 133 for the 6th by J. F. Reid and J. V.
Coney at Colombo (CCC)   1983-84
for Sri Lanka: ‡159* for the 3rd by S. Wettimuny and
R. L. Dias at Colombo (SSC)   1983-84
‡ *163 runs were added for this wicket in two separate partnerships: S. Wettimuny retired hurt and was replaced by L. R. D. Mendis when 159 had been added.*

TEN WICKETS OR MORE IN A MATCH

For New Zealand (1)

10-102 (5-73, 5-29)   R. J. Hadlee, Colombo (CCC)   1983-84
Note: The best match figures by a Sri Lankan bowler are 8-159 (5-86, 3-73), V. B. John at
Colombo (SSC), 1983-84.

INDIA v PAKISTAN

			Captains				
Season	India		Pakistan	T	I	P	D
1952-53*I*	L. Amarnath		A. H. Kardar	5	2	1	2
1954-55*P*	V. Mankad		A. H. Kardar	5	0	0	5
1960-61*I*	N. J. Contractor		Fazal Mahmood	5	0	0	5
1978-79*P*	B. S. Bedi		Mushtaq Mohammad	3	0	2	1
1979-80*I*	S. M. Gavaskar[1]		Asif Iqbal	6	2	0	4
1982-83*P*	S. M. Gavaskar		Imran Khan	6	0	3	3
1983-84*I*	Kapil Dev		Zaheer Abbas	3	0	0	3
1984-85*P*	S. M. Gavaskar		Zaheer Abbas	2	0	0	2
	In India			19	4	1	14
	In Pakistan			16	0	5	11
	Totals			35	4	6	25

I Played in India.   P Played in Pakistan.
Note: [1]G. R. Viswanath captained in Sixth Test.

HIGHEST INNINGS TOTALS

For India in India: 539-9 dec. at Madras   1960-61
in Pakistan: 500 at Faisalabad   1984-85
For Pakistan in India: 448-8 dec. at Madras   1960-61
in Pakistan: 674-6 at Faisalabad   1984-85

LOWEST INNINGS TOTALS

For India in India: 106 at Lucknow   1952-53
in Pakistan: 145 at Karachi   1954-55
For Pakistan in India: 150 at Delhi   1952-53
in Pakistan: 158 at Dacca   1954-55

INDIVIDUAL HUNDREDS

For India (23)

109*	M. Amarnath, Lahore	1982-83
120	M. Amarnath, Lahore	1982-83
103*	M. Amarnath, Karachi....	1982-83
101*	M. Amarnath, Lahore	1984-85
177*	C. G. Borde, Madras	1960-61
201	A. D. Gaekwad, Jullundur .	1983-84
111 137	} S. M. Gavaskar, Karachi ..	1978-79
166	S. M. Gavaskar, Madras ..	1979-80
127*‡	S. M. Gavaskar, Faisalabad	1982-83
103*	S. M. Gavaskar, Bangalore	1983-84
146*	V. S. Hazare, Bombay	1952-53

127	S. M. Patil, Faisalabad	1984-85
128	R. J. Shastri, Karachi.....	1982-83
139	R. J. Shastri, Faisalabad ..	1984-85
110†	R. H. Shodhan, Calcutta ..	1952-53
102	P. R. Umrigar, Bombay ..	1952-53
108	P. R. Umrigar, Peshawar ..	1954-55
115	P. R. Umrigar, Kanpur ..	1960-61
117	P. R. Umrigar, Madras ..	1960-61
112	P. R. Umrigar, Delhi	1960-61
146*	D. B. Vengsarkar, Delhi ..	1979-80
145†	G. R. Viswanath, Faisalabad	1978-79

For Pakistan (31)

103*	Alim-ud-Din, Karachi	1954-55
104†	Asif Iqbal, Faisalabad	1978-79
142	Hanif Mohammad, Bahawalpur	1954-55
160	Hanif Mohammad, Bombay	1960-61
135	Imtiaz Ahmed, Madras ..	1960-61
117	Imran Khan, Faisalabad ..	1982-83
154*†	Javed Miandad, Faisalabad	1978-79
100	Javed Miandad, Karachi ..	1978-79
126	Javed Miandad, Faisalabad	1982-83
280*	Javed Miandad, Hyderabad	1982-83
101*†	Mohsin Khan, Lahore	1982-83
126	Mudassar Nazar, Bangalore	1979-80
119	Mudassar Nazar, Karachi ..	1982-83
231	Mudassar Nazar, Hyderabad	1982-83

152*†	Mudassar Nazar, Lahore ..	1982-83
152	Mudassar Nazar, Karachi .	1982-83
199	Mudassar Nazar, Faisalabad	1984-85
101	Mushtaq Mohammad, Delhi	1960-61
124*‡	Nazar Mohammad, Lucknow	1952-53
210	Qasim Omar, Faisalabad ..	1984-85
121†	Saeed Ahmed, Bombay	1960-61
103	Saeed Ahmed, Madras	1960-61
107	Salim Malik, Faisalabad ..	1982-83
102*	Salim Malik, Faisalabad ..	1984-85
125	Wasim Raja, Jullundur	1983-84
176†	Zaheer Abbas, Faisalabad ..	1978-79
235*	Zaheer Abbas, Lahore	1978-79
215	Zaheer Abbas, Lahore	1982-83
186	Zaheer Abbas, Karachi ..	1982-83
168	Zaheer Abbas, Faisalabad ..	1982-83
168*	Zaheer Abbas, Lahore	1984-85

† *Signifies hundred on first appearance in India–Pakistan Tests.*
‡ *Carried his bat.*

RECORD PARTNERSHIPS FOR EACH WICKET

For India

192 for 1st	S. M. Gavaskar and C. P. S. Chauhan at Lahore	1978-79
125 for 2nd	S. M. Gavaskar and M. Amarnath at Hyderabad	1982-83
190 for 3rd	M. Amarnath and Yashpal Sharma at Lahore	1982-83
183 for 4th	V. S. Hazare and P. R. Umrigar at Bombay	1952-53
200 for 5th	S. M. Patil and R. J. Shastri at Faisalabad	1984-85
121 for 6th	A. D. Gaekwad and R. M. H. Binny at Jullundur	1983-84
155 for 7th	R. M. H. Binny and Madan Lal at Bangalore	1983-84
122 for 8th	S. M. H. Kirmani and Madan Lal at Faisalabad	1982-83
149 for 9th†	P. G. Joshi and R. B. Desai at Bombay	1960-61
109 for 10th†	H. R. Adhikari and Ghulam Ahmed at Delhi	1952-53

For Pakistan

162 for 1st	Hanif Mohammad and Imtiaz Ahmed at Madras.............	1960-61
250 for 2nd	Mudassar Nazar and Qasim Omar at Faisalabad	1984-85
451 for 3rd†	Mudassar Nazar and Javed Miandad at Hyderabad	1982-83
287 for 4th	Javed Miandad and Zaheer Abbas at Faisalabad.............	1982-83
213 for 5th	Zaheer Abbas and Mudassar Nazar at Karachi	1982-83
207 for 6th	Salim Malik and Imran Khan at Faisalabad	1982-83
142 for 7th	Zaheer Abbas and Ashraf Ali at Lahore	1984-85
95 for 8th	Wasim Raja and Tahir Naqqash at Jullundur	1983-84
60 for 9th	Wasim Bari and Iqbal Qasim at Bangalore	1979-80
104 for 10th	Zulfiqar Ahmed and Amir Elahi at Madras	1952-53

† *Denotes record partnership against all countries.*

TEN WICKETS OR MORE IN A MATCH

For India (2)

11-146 (4-90, 7-56)	Kapil Dev, Madras	1979-80
13-131 (8-52, 5-79)†	V. Mankad, Delhi	1952-53

For Pakistan (5)

12-94 (5-52, 7-42)	Fazal Mahmood, Lucknow	1952-53
11-79 (3-19, 8-60)	Imran Khan, Karachi	1982-83
11-180 (6-98, 5-82)	Imran Khan, Faisalabad	1982-83
10-175 (4-135, 6-40)	Iqbal Qasim, Bombay	1979-80
11-190 (8-69, 3-121)	Sikander Bakht, Delhi	1979-80

† *Signifies ten wickets or more on first appearance in India–Pakistan Tests.*

INDIA v SRI LANKA

Season	India	Captains Sri Lanka	T	I	SL	D
1982-83*I*	S. M. Gavaskar	B. Warnapura	1	0	0	1
1985-86*S*	Kapil Dev	L. R. D. Mendis	3	0	1	2
	In India		1	0	0	1
	In Sri Lanka		3	0	1	2
	Totals		4	0	1	3

I Played in India.   S Played in Sri Lanka.

HIGHEST INNINGS TOTALS

For India in India: 566-6 dec. at Madras................................	1982-83
in Sri Lanka: 325-5 dec. at Kandy................................	1985-86
For Sri Lanka in India: 394 at Madras	1982-83
in Sri Lanka: 385 at Colombo (PSO)	1985-86

LOWEST INNINGS TOTALS

For India in India: 566-6 dec. at Madras 1982-83
         in Sri Lanka: 198 at Colombo (PSO) 1985-86
For Sri Lanka in India: 346 at Madras 1982-83
           in Sri Lanka: 198 at Kandy 1985-86

INDIVIDUAL HUNDREDS

For India (3)

116*	M. Amarnath, Kandy	1985-86	114*†	S. M. Patil, Madras	1982-83
155†	S. M. Gavaskar, Madras ..	1982-83			

For Sri Lanka (7)

106	R. L. Dias, Kandy	1985-86	124	L. R. D. Mendis, Kandy ..	1985-86
103	R. S. Madugalle, Colombo (SSC)	1985-86	111	A. Ranatunga, Colombo (SSC)	1985-86
105 } 105	†L. R. D. Mendis, Madras.	1982-83	111	S. A. R. Silva, Colombo (PSO)	1985-86

† Signifies hundred on first appearance in India–Sri Lanka Tests.

RECORD PARTNERSHIPS FOR EACH WICKET

For India

156 for 1st	S. M. Gavaskar and Arun Lal at Madras	1982-83
173 for 2nd	S. M. Gavaskar and D. B. Vengsarkar at Madras	1982-83
76 for 3rd	L. S. Rajput and D. B. Vengsarkar at Colombo (SSC)	1985-86
76 for 4th	K. Srikkanth and L. Sivaramakrishnan at Colombo (PSO)	1985-86
78 for 5th	M. Amarnath and M. Azharuddin at Kandy	1985-86
90 for 6th	S. M. Gavaskar and M. Amarnath at Colombo (PSO)	1985-86
78* for 7th	S. M. Patil and Madan Lal at Madras	1982-83
70 for 8th	Kapil Dev and L. Sivaramakrishnan at Colombo (PSO)	1985-86
16 for 9th	S. M. Gavaskar and Gopal Sharma at Colombo (SSC)	1985-86
29 for 10th	Kapil Dev and Chetan Sharma at Colombo (PSO)	1985-86

For Sri Lanka

74 for 1st	S. Wettimuny and S. A. R. Silva at Colombo (PSO)	1985-86
95 for 2nd	S. A. R. Silva and R. S. Madugalle at Colombo (PSO)	1985-86
153 for 3rd	R. L. Dias and L. R. D. Mendis at Madras	1982-83
216 for 4th	R. L. Dias and L. R. D. Mendis at Kandy	1985-86
144 for 5th	R. S. Madugalle and A. Ranatunga at Colombo (SSC)	1985-86
89 for 6th	L. R. D. Mendis and A. N. Ranasinghe at Madras	1982-83
77 for 7th†	R. S. Madugalle and D. S. de Silva at Madras	1982-83
40* for 8th	P. A. de Silva and A. L. F. de Mel at Kandy	1985-86
42 for 9th	J. R. Ratnayeke and A. L. F. de Mel at Madras	1982-83
32 for 10th	D. S. de Silva and G. R. A. de Silva at Madras .....,......	1982-83

† Denotes record partnership against all countries.

Best bowling in an innings

For India: 5-85 D. R. Doshi, Madras 1982-83
For Sri Lanka: 6-85 R. J. Ratnayake, Colombo (SSC) 1985-86

PAKISTAN v SRI LANKA

		Captains				
Season	*Pakistan*	*Sri Lanka*	*T*	*P*	*SL*	*D*
1981-82*P*	Javed Miandad	B. Warnapura[1]	3	2	0	1
1985-86*P*	Javed Miandad	L. R. D. Mendis	3	2	0	1
1985-86*S*	Imran Khan	L. R. D. Mendis	3	1	1	1
	In Pakistan		6	4	0	2
	In Sri Lanka		3	1	1	1
	Totals		9	5	1	3

P Played in Pakistan. S Played in Sri Lanka.

Note: [1]L. R. D. Mendis captained in the Second Test.

HIGHEST INNINGS TOTALS

For Pakistan in Pakistan: 555-3 at Faisalabad	1985-86
in Sri Lanka: 318 at Colombo (PSO)	1985-86
For Sri Lanka in Pakistan: 479 at Faisalabad	1985-86
in Sri Lanka: 323-3 at Colombo (PSO)	1985-86

LOWEST INNINGS TOTALS

For Pakistan in Pakistan: 259 at Sialkot	1985-86
in Sri Lanka: 132 at Colombo (CCC)	1985-86
For Sri Lanka in Pakistan: 149 at Karachi	1981-82
in Sri Lanka: 101 at Kandy	1985-86

INDIVIDUAL HUNDREDS

For Pakistan (7)

153†	Haroon Rashid, Karachi .	1981-82	122	Ramiz Raja, Colombo	
203*	Javed Miandad, Faisalabad	1985-86		(PSO)	1985-86
129	Mohsin Khan, Lahore ...	1981-82	100*†	Salim Malik, Karachi	1981-82
206†	Qasim Omar, Faisalabad .	1985-86	134†	Zaheer Abbas, Lahore ...	1981-82

For Sri Lanka (6)

122†	P. A. de Silva, Faisalabad	1985-86	135*	A. Ranatunga, Colombo	
105	P. A. de Silva, Karachi ..	1985-86		(PSO)	1985-86
109	R. L. Dias, Lahore	1981-82	157	S. Wettimuny, Faisalabad	1981-82
116*	A. P. Gurusinha, Colombo				
	(PSO)	1985-86			

† *Signifies hundred on first appearance in Pakistan-Sri Lanka Tests.*

RECORD PARTNERSHIPS FOR EACH WICKET

For Pakistan

98* for 1st	Mudassar Nazar and Mohsin Khan at Karachi	1985-86
151 for 2nd	Mohsin Khan and Majid Khan at Lahore	1981-82
397 for 3rd	Qasim Omar and Javed Miandad at Faisalabad	1985-86
162 for 4th	Salim Malik and Javed Miandad at Karachi	1981-82
102 for 5th	Mudassar Nazar and Salim Malik at Kandy	1985-86
100 for 6th	Zaheer Abbas and Imran Khan at Lahore	1981-82
104 for 7th	Haroon Rashid and Tahir Naqqash at Karachi	1981-82
29 for 8th	Ashraf Ali and Iqbal Qasim at Faisalabad	1981-82
	Salim Yousuf and Abdul Qadir at Sialkot	1985-86
	Salim Yousuf and Abdul Qadir at Karachi	1985-86
127 for 9th	Haroon Rashid and Rashid Khan at Karachi	1981-82
48 for 10th	Rashid Khan and Tauseef Ahmed at Faisalabad	1981-82

For Sri Lanka

77 for 1st†	S. Wettimuny and H. M. Goonatillake at Faisalabad	1981-82
217 for 2nd†	S. Wettimuny and R. L. Dias at Faisalabad	1981-82
85 for 3rd	S. Wettimuny and R. L. Dias at Faisalabad	1985-86
240* for 4th†	A. P. Gurusinha and A. Ranatunga at Colombo (PSO)	1985-86
58 for 5th	R. L. Dias and L. R. D. Mendis at Lahore	1981-82
121 for 6th	A. Ranatunga and P. A. de Silva at Faisalabad	1985-86
66 for 7th	P. A. de Silva and J. R. Ratnayeke at Faisalabad	1985-86
61 for 8th†	R. S. Madugalle and D. S. de Silva at Faisalabad	1981-82
52 for 9th†	P. A. de Silva and R. J. Ratnayeke at Faisalabad	1985-86
36 for 10th	R. J. Ratnayake and R. G. C. E. Wijesuriya at Faisalabad	1985-86

† *Denotes record partnership against all countries.*

TEN WICKETS OR MORE IN A MATCH

For Pakistan (1)

14-116 (8-58, 6-58)   Imran Khan, Lahore 1981-82

Note: The best match figures by a Sri Lankan bowler are 9-162 (4-103, 5-59), D. S. de Silva at
Faisalabad, 1981-82.

TEST MATCH GROUNDS

In Chronological Sequence

City and Ground	Date of First Test	Match
1. Melbourne, Melbourne Cricket Ground	March 15, 1877	Australia v England
2. London, Kennington Oval	September 6, 1880	England v Australia
3. Sydney, Sydney Cricket Ground (No. 1)	February 17, 1882	Australia v England
4. Manchester, Old Trafford	July 11, 1884	England v Australia

This match was due to have started on July 10, but rain prevented any play.

5. London, Lord's	July 21, 1884	England v Australia
6. Adelaide, Adelaide Oval	December 12, 1884	Australia v England

City and Ground	Date of First Test	Match
7. Port Elizabeth, St George's Park	March 12, 1889	South Africa v England
8. Cape Town, Newlands	March 25, 1889	South Africa v England
9. Johannesburg, Old Wanderers*	March 2, 1896	South Africa v England
10. Nottingham, Trent Bridge	June 1, 1899	England v Australia
11. Leeds, Headingley	June 29, 1899	England v Australia
12. Birmingham, Edgbaston	May 29, 1902	England v Australia
13. Sheffield, Bramall Lane*	July 3, 1902	England v Australia
14. Durban, Lord's*	January 21, 1910	South Africa v England
15. Durban, Kingsmead	January 18, 1923	South Africa v England
16. Brisbane, Exhibition Ground*	November 30, 1928	Australia v England
17. Christchurch, Lancaster Park	January 10, 1930	New Zealand v England
18. Bridgetown, Kensington Oval	January 11, 1930	West Indies v England
19. Wellington, Basin Reserve	January 24, 1930	New Zealand v England
20. Port-of-Spain, Queen's Park Oval	February 1, 1930	West Indies v England
21. Auckland, Eden Park	February 17, 1930	New Zealand v England

This match was due to have started on February 14, but rain prevented any play on the first two days. February 16 was a Sunday.

22. Georgetown, Bourda	February 21, 1930	West Indies v England
23. Kingston, Sabina Park	April 3, 1930	West Indies v England
24. Brisbane, Woolloongabba	November 27, 1931	Australia v South Africa
25. Bombay, Gymkhana Ground*	December 15, 1933	India v England
26. Calcutta, Eden Gardens	January 5, 1934	India v England
27. Madras, Chepauk	February 10, 1934	India v England
28. Delhi, Feroz Shah Kotla	November 10, 1948	India v West Indies
29. Bombay, Brabourne Stadium*	December 9, 1948	India v West Indies
30. Johannesburg, Ellis Park*	December 27, 1948	South Africa v England
31. Kanpur, Green Park	January 12, 1952	India v England
32. Lucknow, University Ground*	October 25, 1952	India v Pakistan
33. Dacca, Dacca Stadium*	January 1, 1955	Pakistan v India
34. Bahawalpur, Dring Stadium	January 15, 1955	Pakistan v India
35. Lahore, Lawrence Gardens (Bagh-i-Jinnah)*	January 29, 1955	Pakistan v India
36. Peshawar, Peshawar Club Ground	February 13, 1955	Pakistan v India
37. Karachi, National Stadium	February 26, 1955	Pakistan v India
38. Dunedin, Carisbrook	March 11, 1955	New Zealand v England
39. Hyderabad, Fateh Maidan (Lal Bahadur Stadium)	November 19, 1955	India v New Zealand
40. Madras Corporation Stadium*	January 6, 1956	India v New Zealand
41. Johannesburg, New Wanderers	December 24, 1956	South Africa v England
42. Lahore, Gaddafi Stadium	November 21, 1959	Pakistan v Australia
43. Rawalpindi, Rawalpindi Club Ground	March 27, 1965	Pakistan v New Zealand
44. Nagpur, Vidarbha Cricket Association Ground	October 3, 1969	India v New Zealand
45. Perth, Western Australian Cricket Association Ground	December 11, 1970	Australia v England
46. Hyderabad, Niaz Stadium	March 16, 1973	Pakistan v England
47. Bangalore, Karnataka State Cricket Association Ground	November 22, 1974	India v West Indies
48. Bombay, Wankhede Stadium	January 23, 1975	India v West Indies
49. Faisalabad, Iqbal Park	October 16, 1978	Pakistan v India
50. Napier, McLean Park	February 16, 1979	New Zealand v Pakistan
51. Multan, Ibn-e-Qasim Bagh Stadium	December 30, 1980	Pakistan v West Indies
52. St John's (Antigua), Recreation Ground	March 27, 1981	West Indies v England
53. Colombo, P. Saravanamuttu Oval	February 17, 1982	Sri Lanka v England
54. Kandy, Asgiriya Stadium	April 22, 1983	Sri Lanka v Australia
55. Jullundur, Burlton Park	September 24, 1983	India v Pakistan
56. Ahmedabad, Gujarat Stadium	November 12, 1983	India v West Indies
57. Colombo, Sinhalese Sports Club Ground	March 16, 1984	Sri Lanka v New Zealand
58. Colombo, Colombo Cricket Club Ground	March 24, 1984	Sri Lanka v New Zealand
59. Sialkot, Jinnah Park	October 27, 1985	Pakistan v Sri Lanka

* *Denotes no longer used for Test matches. In some instances the ground is no longer in existence.*

FAMILIES IN TEST CRICKET

FATHERS AND SONS

England
M. C. Cowdrey (114 Tests, 1954-55–1974-75) and C. S. Cowdrey (5 Tests, 1984-85).
J. Hardstaff (5 Tests, 1907-08) and J. Hardstaff jun. (23 Tests, 1935–1948).
L. Hutton (79 Tests, 1937–1954-55) and R. A. Hutton (5 Tests, 1971).
F. T. Mann (5 Tests, 1922-23) and F. G. Mann (7 Tests, 1948-49–1949).
J. H. Parks (1 Test, 1937) and J. M. Parks (46 Tests, 1954–1967-68).
F. W. Tate (1 Test, 1902) and M. W. Tate (39 Tests, 1924–1935).
C. L. Townsend (2 Tests, 1899) and D. C. H. Townsend (3 Tests, 1934-35).

Australia
E. J. Gregory (1 Test, 1876-77) and S. E. Gregory (58 Tests, 1890–1912).

South Africa
F. Hearne (4 Tests, 1891-92–1895-96) and G. A. L. Hearne (3 Tests, 1922-23–1924).
  F. Hearne also played 2 Tests for England in 1888-89.
J. D. Lindsay (3 Tests, 1947) and D. T. Lindsay (19 Tests, 1963-64–1969-70).
A. W. Nourse (45 Tests, 1902-03–1924) and A. D. Nourse (34 Tests, 1935–1951).
L. R. Tuckett (1 Test, 1913-14) and L. Tuckett (9 Tests, 1947–1948-49).

West Indies
G. A. Headley (22 Tests, 1929-30–1953-54) and R. G. A. Headley (2 Tests, 1973).
O. C. Scott (8 Tests, 1928–1930-31) and A. P. H. Scott (1 Test, 1952-53).

New Zealand
W. M. Anderson (1 Test, 1945-46) and R. W. Anderson (9 Tests, 1976-77–1978).
W. A. Hadlee (11 Tests, 1937–1950-51) and D. R. Hadlee (26 Tests, 1969–1977-78); R. J. Hadlee (66 Tests, 1972-73–1986).
H. G. Vivian (7 Tests, 1931–1937) and G. E. Vivian (5 Tests, 1964-65–1971-72).

India
L. Amarnath (24 Tests, 1933-34–1952-53) and M. Amarnath (56 Tests, 1969-70–1986); S. Amarnath (10 Tests, 1975-76–1978-79).
D. K. Gaekwad (11 Tests, 1952–1960-61) and A. D. Gaekwad (40 Tests, 1974-75–1984-85).
Nawab of Pataudi (Iftikhar Ali Khan) (3 Tests, 1946) and Nawab of Pataudi (Mansur Ali Khan) (46 Tests, 1961-62–1974-75).
  Nawab of Pataudi sen. also played 3 Tests for England, 1932-33–1934.
V. Mankad (44 Tests, 1946–1958-59) and A. V. Mankad (22 Tests, 1969-70–1977-78).
Pankaj Roy (43 Tests, 1951-52–1960-61) and Pranab Roy (2 Tests, 1981-82).

India and Pakistan
M. Jahangir Khan (4 Tests, 1932–1936) and Majid Khan (63 Tests, 1964-65–1982-83).
S. Wazir Ali (7 Tests, 1932–1936) and Khalid Wazir (2 Tests, 1954).

Pakistan
Hanif Mohammad (55 Tests, 1954–1969-70) and Shoaib Mohammad (6 Tests, 1983-84–1985-86).
Nazar Mohammad (5 Tests, 1952-53) and Mudassar Nazar (58 Tests, 1976-77–1985-86).

GRANDFATHERS AND GRANDSONS

Australia
V. Y. Richardson (19 Tests, 1924-25–1935-36) and G. S. Chappell (87 Tests, 1970-71–1983-84); I. M. Chappell (75 Tests, 1964-65–1979-80); T. M. Chappell (3 Tests, 1981).

GREAT-GRANDFATHER AND GREAT-GRANDSON

Australia

W. H. Cooper (2 Tests, 1881-82 and 1884-85) and A. P. Sheahan (31 Tests, 1967-68–1973-74).

BROTHERS IN SAME TEST TEAM

England

E. M., G. F. and W. G. Grace: 1 Test, 1880.
C. T. and G. B. Studd: 4 Tests, 1882-83.
A. and G. G. Hearne: 1 Test, 1891-92.
    F. Hearne, their brother, played in this match for South Africa.
D. W. and P. E. Richardson: 1 Test, 1957.

Australia

E. J. and D. W. Gregory: 1 Test, 1876-77.
C. and A. C. Bannerman: 1 Test, 1878-79.
G. and W. F. Giffen: 2 Tests, 1891-92.
G. H. S. and A. E. Trott: 3 Tests, 1894-95.
I. M. and G. S. Chappell: 43 Tests, 1970-71–1979-80.

South Africa

S. J. and S. D. Snooke: 1 Test, 1907.
D. and H. W. Taylor: 2 Tests, 1913-14.
R. H. M. and P. A. M. Hands: 1 Test, 1913-14.
E. A. B. and A. M. B. Rowan: 9 Tests, 1948-49–1951.
P. M. and R. G. Pollock: 23 Tests, 1963-64–1969-70.
A. J. and D. B. Pithey: 5 Tests, 1963-64.

West Indies

G. C. and R. S. Grant: 4 Tests, 1934-35.
J. B. and V. H. Stollmeyer: 1 Test, 1939.
D. St E. and E. St E. Atkinson: 1 Test, 1957-58.

New Zealand

J. J. and M. D. Crowe: 24 Tests, 1983–1986.
D. R. and R. J. Hadlee: 10 Tests, 1973-1977-78.
H. J. and G. P. Howarth: 4 Tests, 1974-75–1976-77.
J. M. and N. M. Parker: 3 Tests, 1976-77.
B. P. and J. G. Bracewell: 1 Test, 1980-81.

India

S. Wazir Ali and S. Nazir Ali: 2 Tests, 1932–1933-34.
L. Ramji and Amar Singh: 1 Test, 1933-34.
C. K. and C. S. Nayudu: 4 Tests, 1933-34–1936.
A. G. Kripal Singh and A. G. Milkha Singh: 1 Test, 1961-62.
S. and M. Amarnath: 8 Tests, 1975-76–1978-79.

Pakistan

Wazir and Hanif Mohammad: 18 Tests, 1952-53–1959-60.
Wazir and Mushtaq Mohammad: 1 Test, 1958-59.
Hanif and Mushtaq Mohammad: 19 Tests, 1960-61–1969-70.
Hanif, Mushtaq and Sadiq Mohammad: 1 Test, 1969-70.
Mushtaq and Sadiq Mohammad: 26 Tests, 1969-70–1978–79.
Wasim and Ramiz Raja: 2 Tests, 1983-84.

Sri Lanka

M. D. and S. Wettimuny: 2 Tests, 1982-83.

LIMITED-OVERS INTERNATIONAL RECORDS

Note: Limited-overs international matches do not have first-class status.

3,000 OR MORE RUNS

	M	I	NO	R	HI	100s	Avge
I. V. A. Richards (*West Indies*)	109	99	19	4,600	189*	8	57.50
D. L. Haynes (*West Indies*)	104	103	14	3,801	148	8	42.70
A. R. Border (*Australia*)	130	121	17	3,254	127*	3	31.28

HIGHEST INDIVIDUAL SCORE FOR EACH COUNTRY

189*	I. V. A. Richards	**West Indies** v England at Manchester	1984
175*	Kapil Dev	**India** v Zimbabwe at Tunbridge Wells	1983
171*	G. M. Turner	**New Zealand** v East Africa at Birmingham	1975
158	D. I. Gower	**England** v New Zealand at Brisbane	1982-83
138*	G. S. Chappell	**Australia** v New Zealand at Sydney	1980-81
123	Zaheer Abbas	**Pakistan** v Sri Lanka at Lahore	1981-82
121	R. L. Dias	**Sri Lanka** v India at Bangalore	1982-83

FIVE OR MORE HUNDREDS

Total		E	A	WI	NZ	I	P	SL	Others
8	D. L. Haynes (*West Indies*)	0	6	–	2	0	0	0	0
8	I. V. A. Richards (*West Indies*) ..	3	3	–	0	2	0	0	0
7	D. I. Gower (*England*)	–	2	0	3	0	1	1	0
7	Zaheer Abbas (*Pakistan*)	0	2	0	1	3	–	1	0
6	C. G. Greenidge (*West Indies*) ..	0	0	–	1	2	1	1	1

HIGHEST PARTNERSHIP FOR EACH WICKET

193 for 1st	G. A. Gooch (91) and C. W. J. Athey (142*), England v New Zealand at Manchester	1986
221 for 2nd	C. G. Greenidge (115) and I. V. A. Richards (149), West Indies v India at Jamshedpur	1983-84
224* for 3rd	D. M. Jones (99*) and A. R. Border (118*), Australia v Sri Lanka at Adelaide	1984-85
157* for 4th	R. B. Kerr (87*) and D. M. Jones (78*), Australia v England at Melbourne	1984-85
152 for 5th	I. V. A. Richards (98) and C. H. Lloyd (89*), West Indies v Sri Lanka at Brisbane	1984-85
144 for 6th	Imran Khan (102*) and Shahid Mahboob (77), Pakistan v Sri Lanka at Leeds	1983
108 for 7th	Ramiz Raja (75) and Anil Dalpat (37), Pakistan v New Zealand at Christchurch	1984-85
68 for 8th	B. E. Congdon (52*) and B. L. Cairns (23), New Zealand v England at Scarborough	1978
126* for 9th	Kapil Dev (175*) and S. M. H. Kirmani (24*), India v Zimbabwe at Tunbridge Wells	1983
106* for 10th	I. V. A. Richards (189*) and M. A. Holding (12*), West Indies v England at Manchester	1984

100 OR MORE WICKETS

	M	Balls	R	W	BB	4Wi	Avge
M. A. Holding (*West Indies*) ...	96	5,146	2,872	135	5-26	6	21.27
J. Garner (*West Indies*)	85	4,628	2,359	129	5-31	4	18.28
R. J. Hadlee (*New Zealand*) ...	91	4,856	2,606	126	5-25	5	20.68
E. J. Chatfield (*New Zealand*)..	81	4,341	2,504	105	5-34	2	23.84
Kapil Dev (*India*)	83	4,364	2,632	105	5-43	2	25.06
I. T. Botham (*England*)	78	4,068	2,761	103	4-56	1	26.80
D. K. Lillee (*Australia*)	63	3,593	2,145	103	5-34	6	20.82

BEST BOWLING FOR EACH COUNTRY

7-51	W. W. Davis	**West Indies** v Australia at Leeds	1983
6-14	G. J. Gilmour	**Australia** v England at Leeds	1975
6-14	Imran Khan	**Pakistan** v India at Sharjah	1984-85
5-20	V. J. Marks	**England** v New Zealand at Wellington	1983-84
5-23	R. O. Collinge	**New Zealand** v India at Christchurch	1975-76
5-26	U. S. H. Karnain	**Sri Lanka** v New Zealand at Moratuwa	1983-84
5-43	Kapil Dev	**India** v Australia at Nottingham	1983

HAT-TRICKS

Jalal-ud-Din	Pakistan v Australia at Hyderabad	1982-83
B. A. Reid	Australia v New Zealand at Sydney	1985-86

CAREER DISMISSALS

	M	Ct	St	Total
R. W. Marsh (*Australia*)	91	119	4	123
P. J. L. Dujon (*West Indies*)	79	91	8	99
Wasim Bari (*Pakistan*)	51	52	10	62

ALL-ROUND

1,000 Runs and 50 Wickets

	M	R	W
I. T. Botham (*England*)	78	1,299	103
J. V. Coney (*New Zealand*)	84	1,767	52
G. S. Chappell (*Australia*)	73	2,329	71
R. J. Hadlee (*New Zealand*)	91	1,259	126
Imran Khan (*Pakistan*)	72	1,212	69
Kapil Dev (*India*)	83	1,679	105
Mudassar Nazar (*Pakistan*)	89	2,063	85
I. V. A. Richards (*West Indies*)	109	4,600	63
R. J. Shastri (*India*)	61	1,300	55

1,000 Runs and 100 Dismissals

	M	R	D
R. W. Marsh	91	1,220	123

HIGHEST INNINGS TOTALS

338-5	(60 overs)	**Pakistan** v Sri Lanka at Swansea	1983
334-4	(60 overs)	**England** v India at Lord's	1975
333-8	(45 overs)	**West Indies** v India at Jamshedpur	1983-84
333-9	(60 overs)	England v Sri Lanka at Taunton	1983
330-6	(60 overs)	Pakistan v Sri Lanka at Nottingham	1975
328-5	(60 overs)	**Australia** v Sri Lanka at The Oval	1975
323-2	(50 overs)	Australia v Sri Lanka at Adelaide	1984-85
322-6	(60 overs)	England v New Zealand at The Oval	1983
320-8	(55 overs)	England v Australia at Birmingham	1980
320-9	(60 overs)	Australia v India at Nottingham	1983
313-9	(50 overs)	West Indies v Australia at St John's	1977-78
309-6	(50 overs)	West Indies v Sri Lanka at Perth	1984-85
309-5	(60 overs)	**New Zealand** v East Africa at Birmingham	1975
304-5	(50 overs)	New Zealand v Sri Lanka at Auckland	1982-83
302-8	(50 overs)	Australia v New Zealand at Melbourne	1982-83

Note: The highest score by **India** is 282-5 (47 overs) v West Indies at Berbice, Guyana, 1982-83, and the highest by **Sri Lanka** is 288-9 (60 overs) v Pakistan at Swansea, 1983.

HIGHEST TOTALS BATTING SECOND

Winning

297-6	(48.5 overs)	New Zealand v England at Adelaide	1982-83

Losing

288-9	(60 overs)	Sri Lanka v Pakistan at Swansea	1983

HIGHEST MATCH AGGREGATES

626-14	(120 overs)	Pakistan v Sri Lanka at Swansea	1983
619-19	(118 overs)	England v Sri Lanka at Taunton	1983
604-9	(120 overs)	Australia v Sri Lanka at The Oval	1975

LOWEST INNINGS TOTALS

45	(40.3 overs)	Canada v England at Manchester	1979
63	(25.5 overs)	**India** v Australia at Sydney	1980-81
64	(35.5 overs)	**New Zealand** v Pakistan at Sharjah	1985-86
70	(25.2 overs)	**Australia** v England at Birmingham	1977
70	(26.3 overs)	Australia v New Zealand at Adelaide	1985-86
74	(29 overs)	New Zealand v Australia at Wellington	1981-82
79	(34.2 overs)	India v Pakistan at Sialkot	1978-79
85	(47 overs)	**Pakistan** v England at Manchester	1978
86	(37.2 overs)	**Sri Lanka** v West Indies at Manchester	1975
87	(32.5 overs)	Pakistan v India at Sharjah	1984-85
91	(35.5 overs)	Sri Lanka v Australia at Adelaide	1984-85
93	(36.2 overs)	**England** v Australia at Leeds	1975
94	(31.7 overs)	England v Australia at Melbourne	1978-79
94	(52.3 overs)	East Africa v England at Birmingham	1975
96	(41 overs)	Sri Lanka v India at Sharjah	1983-84

Note: This section does not take into account those matches in which the number of overs was reduced.

The lowest innings total by **West Indies** is 111 (41.4 overs) v Pakistan at Melbourne, 1983-84.

TIED MATCH

West Indies 222-5 (50 overs), Australia 222-9 (50 overs) at Melbourne   1983-84

WORLD CUP FINALS

1975   West Indies (291-8) beat Australia (274) by 17 runs at Lord's.
1979   West Indies (286-9) beat England (194) by 92 runs at Lord's.
1983   India (183) beat West Indies (140) by 43 runs at Lord's.

MISCELLANEOUS

LARGE ATTENDANCES

Test Series

943,000	Australia v England (5 Tests)	1936-37

In England

549,650	England v Australia (5 Tests)	1953

Test Match

†350,534	Australia v England, Melbourne (Third Test)	1936-37
325,000+	India v England, Calcutta (Second Test)	1972-73

In England

158,000+	England v Australia, Leeds (Fourth Test)	1948
137,915	England v Australia, Lord's (Second Test)	1953

Test Match Day

90,800	Australia v West Indies, Melbourne (Fifth Test, 2nd day)	1960-61

Other First-Class Matches in England

80,000+	Surrey v Yorkshire, The Oval (3 days)	1906
78,792	Yorkshire v Lancashire, Leeds (3 days)	1904
76,617	Lancashire v Yorkshire, Manchester (3 days)	1926

One-day International

86,133	Australia v West Indies, Melbourne	1983-84

† *Although no official figures are available, the attendance at the Fourth Test between India and England at Calcutta, 1981-82, was thought to have exceeded this figure.*

LORD'S CRICKET GROUND

Lord's and the MCC were founded in 1787. The Club has enjoyed an uninterrupted career since that date, but there have been three grounds known as Lord's. The first (1787-1810) was situated where Dorset Square now is; the second (1809-13), at North Bank, had to be abandoned owing to the cutting of the Regent's Canal; and the third, opened in 1814, is the present one at St John's Wood. It was not until 1866 that the freehold of Lord's was secured by the MCC. The present pavilion was erected in 1890 at a cost of £21,000.

HIGHEST INDIVIDUAL SCORES MADE AT LORD'S

316*	J. B. Hobbs	Surrey v Middlesex	1926
315*	P. Holmes	Yorkshire v Middlesex	1925
281*	W. H. Ponsford	Australians v MCC	1934
278	W. Ward	MCC v Norfolk (with E. H. Budd, T. Vigne and F. Ladbroke)	1820

| 278 | D. G. Bradman | .... | Australians v MCC | .... | 1938 |
| 277* | E. H. Hendren | .... | Middlesex v Kent | .... | 1922 |

Note: The longest innings in a Test match at Lord's was played by S. Wettimuny (642 minutes, 190 runs) for Sri Lanka v England, 1984.

HIGHEST TOTALS OBTAINED AT LORD'S

First-Class Matches

729-6	Australia v England	....	1930
665	West Indians v Middlesex	....	1939
652-8	West Indies v England	....	1973
629	England v India	....	1974
612-8	Middlesex v Nottinghamshire	....	1921
610-5	Australians v Gentlemen	....	1948
609-8	Cambridge University v MCC and Ground	....	1913
608-7	Middlesex v Hampshire	....	1919
607	MCC and Ground v Cambridge University	....	1902

Minor Match

| 735-9 | MCC and Ground v Wiltshire | .... | 1888 |

BIGGEST HIT AT LORD'S

The only known instance of a batsman hitting a ball over the present pavilion at Lord's occurred when A. E. Trott, appearing for MCC against Australians on July 31, August 1, 2, 1899, drove M. A. Noble so far and high that the ball struck a chimney pot and fell behind the building.

HIGHEST IN A MINOR COUNTY MATCH

| 323* | F. E. Lacey | Hampshire v Norfolk at Southampton | .... | 1887 |

HIGHEST IN MINOR COUNTIES CHAMPIONSHIP

282	E. Garnett	Berkshire v Wiltshire at Reading	....	1908
254	H. E. Morgan	Glamorgan v Monmouthshire at Cardiff	....	1901
253*	G. J. Whittaker	Surrey II v Gloucestershire II at The Oval	....	1950
253	A. Booth	Lancashire II v Lincolnshire at Grimsby	....	1950
252	J. A. Deed	Kent II v Surrey II at The Oval (on début)	....	1924

HIGHEST FOR ENGLISH PUBLIC SCHOOL

| 278 | J. L. Guise | Winchester v Eton at Eton | .... | 1921 |

HIGHEST IN OTHER MATCHES

628*	A. E. J. Collins, Clark's House v North Town at Clifton College. (A Junior House match. His innings of 6 hours 50 minutes was spread over four afternoons.)	....	1899
566	C. J. Eady, Break-o'-Day v Wellington at Hobart	....	1901-02
515	D. R. Havewalla, B.B. and C.I. Rly v St Xavier's at Bombay	....	1933-34
506*	J. C. Sharp, Melbourne GS v Geelong College at Melbourne	....	1914-15
502*	Chaman Lal, Mehandra Coll., Patiala v Government Coll., Rupar at Patiala		1956-57
485	A. E. Stoddart, Hampstead v Stoics at Hampstead	....	1886
475*	Mohammad Iqbal, Muslim Model HS v Islamia HS, Sialkot at Lahore	....	1958-59
466*	G. T. S. Stevens, Beta v Lambda (University College School House match) at Neasden	....	1919
459	J. A. Prout, Wesley College v Geelong College at Geelong	....	1908-09

RECORD HIT

The Rev. W. Fellows, while at practice on the Christ Church ground at Oxford in 1856, drove a ball bowled by Charles Rogers 175 yards from hit to pitch.

THROWING THE CRICKET BALL

140 yards 2 feet, Robert Percival, on the Durham Sands, Co. Durham Racecourse   c 1882
140 yards 9 inches, Ross Mackenzie, at Toronto   1872

Notes: W. F. Forbes, on March 16, 1876, threw 132 yards at the Eton College Sports. He was then 18 years of age.

William Yardley, while a boy at Rugby, threw 100 yards with his right hand and 78 yards with his left .

Charles Arnold, of Cambridge, once threw 112 yards with the wind and 108 against.

W. H. Game, at The Oval in 1875, threw the ball 111 yards and then back the same distance. W. G. Grace threw 109 yards one way and back 105, and George Millyard 108 with the wind and 103 against. At The Oval in 1868, W. G. Grace made three successive throws of 116, 117 and 118 yards, and then threw back over 100 yards. D. G. Foster (Warwickshire) threw 133 yards, and in 1930 he made a Danish record with 120.1 metres – about 130 yards.

DATES OF FORMATION OF COUNTY CLUBS NOW FIRST-CLASS

County	First known county organisation	Original date	Present Club Reorganisation, if substantial
Derbyshire	November 4, 1870	November 4, 1870	—
Essex	By May, 1790	January 14, 1876	—
Glamorgan	1863	July 6, 1888	—
Gloucestershire	November 3, 1863	1871	—
Hampshire	April 3, 1849	August 12, 1863	July, 1879
Kent	August 6, 1842	March 1, 1859	December 6, 1870
Lancashire	January 12, 1864	January 12, 1864	—
Leicestershire	By August, 1820	March 25, 1879	—
Middlesex	December 15, 1863	February 2, 1864	—
Northamptonshire . .	1820	1820	July 31, 1878
Nottinghamshire	March/April, 1841	March/April, 1841	December 11, 1866
Somerset	October 15, 1864	August 18, 1875	—
Surrey	August 22, 1845	August 22, 1845	—
Sussex	June 16, 1836	March 1, 1839	August, 1857
Warwickshire	May, 1826	1882	—
Worcestershire	1844	March 5, 1865	—
Yorkshire	March 7, 1861	January 8, 1863	December 10, 1891

DATES OF FORMATION OF CLUBS IN THE CURRENT MINOR COUNTIES CHAMPIONSHIP

County	First known county organisation	Present Club
Bedfordshire	May, 1847	November 3, 1899
Berkshire	By May, 1841	March 17, 1895
Buckinghamshire . . .	November, 1864	January 15, 1891
Cambridgeshire	March 13, 1844	June 6, 1891
Cheshire	1819	September 29, 1908
Cornwall	1813	November 12, 1894
Cumberland	January 2, 1884	April 10, 1948

County	First known county organisation	Present Club
Devon	1824	November 26, 1899
Dorset	1862 *or* 1871	February 5, 1896
Durham	January 24, 1874	May 10, 1882
Hertfordshire	1838	March 8, 1876
Lincolnshire	1853	September 28, 1906
Norfolk	January 11, 1827	October 14, 1876
Northumberland	1834	December, 1895
Oxfordshire	1787	December 14, 1921
Shropshire	1819 or 1829	June 28, 1956
Staffordshire	November 24, 1871	November 24, 1871
Suffolk	July 27, 1864	August, 1932
Wiltshire	February 24, 1881	January, 1893

CONSTITUTION OF COUNTY CHAMPIONSHIP

There are references in the sporting press to a champion county as early as 1825, but the list is not continuous and in some years only two counties contested the title. The earliest reference in any cricket publication is from 1864, and at this time there were eight leading counties who have come to be regarded as first-class from that date – Cambridgeshire, Hampshire, Kent, Middlesex, Nottinghamshire, Surrey, Sussex and Yorkshire. The newly formed Lancashire club began playing inter-county matches in 1865, Gloucestershire in 1870 and Derbyshire in 1871, and they are therefore regarded as first-class from these respective dates. Cambridgeshire dropped out after 1871, Hampshire, who had not played inter-county matches in certain seasons, after 1885, and Derbyshire after 1887. Somerset, who had played matches against the first-class counties since 1879, were regarded as first-class from 1882 to 1885, and were admitted formally to the Championship in 1891. In 1894, Derbyshire, Essex, Leicestershire and Warwickshire were granted first-class status, but did not compete in the Championship until 1895 when Hampshire returned. Worcestershire, Northamptonshire and Glamorgan were admitted to the Championship in 1899, 1905 and 1921 respectively and are regarded as first-class from these dates. An invitation in 1921 to Buckinghamshire to enter the Championship was declined, owing to the lack of necessary playing facilities, and an application by Devon in 1948 was unsuccessful.

MOST COUNTY CHAMPIONSHIP APPEARANCES

763	W. Rhodes	....	Yorkshire	1898-1930
707	F. E. Woolley	......	Kent	1906-38
665	C. P. Mead	....	Hampshire	1906-36

MOST CONSECUTIVE COUNTY CHAMPIONSHIP APPEARANCES

423	K. G. Suttle	Sussex	1954-69
412	J. G. Binks	Yorkshire	1955-69
399	J. Vine	Sussex	1899-1914
344	E. H. Killick	Sussex	1898-1912
326	C. N. Woolley	Northamptonshire	1913-31
305	A. H. Dyson	Glamorgan	1930-47
301	B. Taylor	Essex	1961-72

Notes: J. Vine made 417 consecutive appearances for Sussex in all first-class matches between July 1900 and September 1914.

J. G. Binks did not miss a Championship match for Yorkshire between making his début in June 1955 and retiring at the end of the 1969 season.

FEATURES OF 1986

Triple-Hundred and 300 Runs in a Day

K. R. Rutherford ... 317   New Zealanders v D. B. Close's XI at Scarborough.

Double-Hundreds

R. J. Bailey (2)	200*	Northamptonshire v Yorkshire at Luton.
	224*	Northamptonshire v Glamorgan at Swansea.
C. G. Greenidge	222	Hampshire v Northamptonshire at Northampton.
R. A. Harper	234	Northamptonshire v Gloucestershire at Northampton.
G. A. Hick (2)	227*	Worcestershire v Nottinghamshire at Worcester.
	219*	Worcestershire v Glamorgan at Neath.
		(In successive innings)
T. E. Jesty	221	Surrey v Essex at The Oval.
P. M. Roebuck	221*	Somerset v Nottinghamshire at Nottingham.
J. J. Whitaker	200*	Leicestershire v Nottinghamshire at Leicester.

Four Hundreds in Successive Innings

C. G. Greenidge (Hampshire) – 222, 103, 180* and 126.

Hundred in Each Innings of a Match

C. G. Greenidge	103	180*	Hampshire v Derbyshire at Derby.
M. D. Moxon	123	112*	Yorkshire v Indians at Scarborough.

Fastest Hundred

(For the Walter Lawrence Trophy)

I. V. A. Richards ... 48 balls Somerset v Glamorgan at Taunton.
In 57 minutes and including six 6s and twelve 4s.

Hundred Before Lunch

M. Amarnath	101*	Indians v Northamptonshire at Northampton (2nd day).
C. G. Greenidge	125*	Hampshire v Sussex at Hove (1st day).
I. V. A. Richards ...	102	Somerset v Glamorgan at Taunton (2nd day).
K. R. Rutherford ...	101*	New Zealanders v D. B. Close's XI at Scarborough (2nd day).
		Rutherford then scored 199* between lunch and tea.

Hundred on First-Class Début

R. J. Bartlett	117*	Somerset v Oxford University at Oxford.
P. D. Bowler	100*	Leicestershire v Hampshire at Leicester.
I. L. Philip	145	Scotland v Ireland at Titwood, Glasgow.

First to 1,000 Runs

G. A. Hick (Worcestershire) on July 17.

First to 2,000 Runs

C. G. Greenidge (Hampshire) on September 10.

Youngest to Score 2,000 Runs

G. A. Hick (Worcestershire) aged 20 years, 112 days.

Carrying Bat Through Completed Innings

G. S. Clinton ...... 84* (171)   Surrey v Yorkshire at Leeds.
W. N. Slack .... 105* (252)   Middlesex v Yorkshire at Leeds.

Innings totals shown in brackets.

Fifty Boundaries in an Innings

K. R. Rutherford (45 × 4, 8 × 6) New Zealanders v D. B. Close's XI at Scarborough.

Twelve Sixes in an Innings

R. A. Harper   Northamptonshire v Gloucestershire at Northampton.

Notable Partnerships

First Wicket
282   M. D. Moxon/A. A. Metcalfe, Yorkshire v Lancashire at Manchester.
273*   N. A. Felton/P. M. Roebuck, Somerset v Hampshire at Taunton.
250†   C. G. Greenidge/V. P. Terry, Hampshire v Northamptonshire at Northampton.

   A. J. Moles and P. A. Smith shared opening partnerships of 161 and 155 for Warwickshire v Somerset at Weston-super-Mare.

Second Wicket
344†   G. Cook/R. J. Boyd-Moss, Northamptonshire v Lancashire at Northampton.
287*†   T. S. Curtis/G. A. Hick, Worcestershire v Glamorgan at Neath.

Fourth Wicket
273*   P. Willey/P. D. Bowler, Leicestershire v Hampshire at Leicester.

Fifth Wicket
319‡   K. R. Rutherford/E. J. Gray, New Zealanders v D. B. Close's XI at Scarborough.

Seventh Wicket
193   R. A. Harper/D. Ripley, Northamptonshire v Gloucestershire at Northampton.

Tenth Wicket
132†   A. Hill/M. Jean-Jacques, Derbyshire v Yorkshire at Sheffield.

   † *County record.*   ‡ *New Zealand record.*

Fourteen Wickets in a Match

T. M. Alderman .... 14-144 Kent v Leicestershire at Canterbury.
V. J. Marks .... 14-212 Somerset v Glamorgan at Cardiff.

Eight or More Wickets in an Innings

N. V. Radford 9-70   Worcestershire v Somerset at Worcester.
C. A. Walsh 9-72   Gloucestershire v Somerset at Bristol.
T. M. Alderman (2) . 8-46   Kent v Derbyshire at Derby.
                    8-70   Kent v Leicestershire at Canterbury.
P. Bainbridge 8-53   Gloucestershire v Somerset at Bristol.
J. H. Childs (2) .... 8-61 Essex v Northamptonshire at Colchester.
                    8-58   Essex v Gloucestershire at Colchester.
                            (In successive innings)
Imran Khan 8-34   Sussex v Middlesex at Lord's.
M. Jean-Jacques 8-77   Derbyshire v Kent at Derby.
V. J. Marks 8-100   Somerset v Glamorgan at Cardiff.
R. C. Ontong 8-101   Glamorgan v Nottinghamshire at Cardiff.
A. Sidebottom 8-72   Yorkshire v Leicestershire at Middlesbrough.

Hat-tricks

A. M. Babington ... Sussex v Gloucestershire at Bristol.
G. R. Dilley .... Kent v Essex at Chelmsford.

Outstanding Analyses

D. L. Underwood ...... 35.5–29–11–7 Kent v Warwickshire at Folkestone.
D. J. Wild .... 6.3–4–4–4   Northamptonshire v Cambridge U. at Cambridge.
J. K. Lever 9–9–0–2   Essex v Cambridge U. at Cambridge.

First to 100 Wickets

C. A. Walsh (Gloucestershire) on August 11.

1,000 Runs and 50 Wickets

V. J. Marks (Somerset) – 1,057 runs and 59 wickets.

Six Wicket-Keeping Dismissals in an Innings

6 S. A. Marsh (5ct, 1st) .... Kent v Warwickshire at Folkestone.
6 R. J. Parks (5ct, 1st) .... Hampshire v Nottinghamshire at Southampton.

Five Catches in the Field

5   M. Azharuddin . . . .   Indians v Somerset at Taunton.
5   R. J. Bailey . . . .   Northamptonshire v Worcestershire at Northampton.
5   C. S. Cowdrey . . . .   Kent v Warwickshire at Folkestone.

Hat-Trick of Catches

R. C. Russell . . . .   Gloucestershire v Surrey at The Oval.

Highest Innings Totals

590-7 dec. . . . . . .   Kent v Oxford University at Oxford.
519-7 dec. . . . . . .   New Zealanders v D. B. Close's XI at Scarborough.
503 . . . .   Northamptonshire v Gloucestershire at Northampton.
500-9 dec. . . . . . .   Surrey v Worcestershire at The Oval.

Lowest Innings Totals

44 . . . .   Essex v Northamptonshire at Colchester.
58 . . . .   Nottinghamshire v Leicestershire at Leicester.
64 . . . .   Surrey v Hampshire at Basingstoke.
65 . . . .   Warwickshire v Kent at Folkestone.
70 . . . .   Middlesex v Sussex at Lord's.

Most Extras in an Innings

53 (B1, l-b 30, w 5, n-b 17) . . . .   Gloucestershire v Derbyshire at Chesterfield.

Career Aggregate Milestones†

100 hundreds   . . . . . .   D. L. Amiss.
30,000 runs . . . .   C. G. Greenidge, A. I. Kallicharran.
10,000 runs . . . .   B. C. Broad, T. A. Lloyd, D. N. Patel, R. T. Robinson, W. N. Slack,
                            C. L. Smith.
2,000 wickets   . . . . . .   N. Gifford.
1,000 wickets   . . . . .   E. E. Hemmings, M. D. Marshall.
500 dismissals . . . . .   P. R. Downton, I. J. Gould, C. J. Richards.
500 catches . . . .   C. T. Radley.

  † *Achieved since September 1985.*

FIRST-CLASS AVERAGES, 1986

BATTING

(Qualification: 8 innings, average 10.00)

* Signifies not out.   *† Denotes a left-handed batsman.*

	M	I	NO	R	HI	100s	Avge
C. G. Greenidge (*Hampshire*)	20	34	4	2,035	222	8	67.83
J. J. Whitaker (*Leicestershire*)	22	32	9	1,526	200*	5	66.34
G. A. Hick (*Worcestershire*)	24	37	6	2,004	227*	6	64.64
A. J. Lamb (*Northamptonshire*) ...	18	27	4	1,359	160*	4	59.08
B. M. McMillan (*Warwickshire*)	12	21	4	999	136	3	58.76
R. J. Bailey (*Northamptonshire*) ...	28	43	9	1,915	224*	4	56.32
†A. I. Kallicharran (*Warwickshire*) ...	14	23	5	1,005	163*	5	55.83
M. W. Gatting (*Middlesex*)	18	23	3	1,091	183*	4	54.55
G. Boycott (*Yorkshire*)	13	20	1	992	135*	2	52.21
†R. J. Hadlee (*Nottinghamshire and New Zealand*)	17	21	5	813	129*	2	50.81
T. S. Curtis (*Worcestershire*)	24	40	10	1,498	153	2	49.93
†C. H. Lloyd (*Lancashire*)	7	8	1	347	128	1	49.57
†A. R. Border (*Essex*)	20	32	4	1,385	150	4	49.46
A. J. Moles (*Warwickshire*)	11	18	3	738	102	2	49.20
†N. H. Fairbrother (*Lancashire*)	22	33	8	1,217	131	3	48.68
Imran Khan (*Sussex*)	11	18	1	730	135*	2	48.66
C. L. Smith (*Hampshire*)	20	30	8	1,061	114*	2	48.22
R. T. Robinson (*Nottinghamshire*) ...	21	34	5	1,398	159*	4	48.20
I. T. Botham (*Somerset*)	13	20	2	863	139	4	47.94
D. N. Patel (*Worcestershire*)	24	30	9	1,005	132*	3	47.85
P. M. Roebuck (*Somerset*)	22	35	8	1,288	221*	4	47.70
A. C. S. Pigott (*Sussex*)	19	18	6	572	104*	1	47.66
J. E. Morris (*Derbyshire*)	26	40	3	1,739	191	4	47.00
A. J. Stewart (*Surrey*)	25	39	3	1,665	166	3	46.25
A. M. Ferreira (*Warwickshire*)	12	15	6	413	69*	0	45.88
A. A. Metcalfe (*Yorkshire*)	26	41	1	1,803	151	4	45.07
C. E. B. Rice (*Nottinghamshire*) ...	22	31	6	1,118	156*	2	44.72
P. Willey (*Leicestershire*)	18	30	5	1,117	172*	4	44.68
P. W. G. Parker (*Sussex*)	25	43	7	1,595	125	6	44.30
V. J. Marks (*Somerset*)	25	36	12	1,057	110	1	44.04
C. W. Scott (*Nottinghamshire*)	10	8	3	220	69*	0	44.00
R. J. Bartlett (*Somerset*)	6	9	2	307	117*	1	43.85
K. M. Curran (*Gloucestershire*)	26	39	8	1,353	117*	4	43.64
†B. C. Rose (*Somerset*)	14	23	5	784	129	2	43.55
I. V. A. Richards (*Somerset*)	18	28	1	1,174	136	4	43.48
†D. M. Smith (*Worcestershire*)	20	28	4	1,041	165*	3	43.37
†J. W. Lloyds (*Gloucestershire*)	26	39	9	1,295	111	1	43.16
A. Hill (*Derbyshire*)	24	40	6	1,438	172*	3	42.29
G. Cook (*Northamptonshire*)	22	30	4	1,084	183	3	41.69
K. Saxelby (*Nottinghamshire*)	11	8	5	124	34	0	41.33
R. A. Smith (*Hampshire*)	25	38	8	1,237	128*	2	41.23
C. W. J. Athey (*Gloucestershire*) ...	19	31	4	1,233	171*	1	41.10
M. Newell (*Nottinghamshire*)	19	30	9	862	112*	1	41.04
W. K. M. Benjamin (*Leicestershire*) .	20	20	10	404	95*	0	40.40
†J. Abrahams (*Lancashire*)	24	38	7	1,251	189*	3	40.35
C. J. Richards (*Surrey*)	23	34	9	1,006	115	2	40.24
†Younis Ahmed (*Glamorgan*)	15	23	2	845	105*	1	40.23
G. D. Mendis (*Lancashire*)	23	37	3	1,363	108	2	40.08
†B. C. Broad (*Nottinghamshire*)	25	42	2	1,593	122	6	39.82
B. J. M. Maher (*Derbyshire*)	14	24	5	752	126	1	39.57

	M	I	NO	R	HI	100s	Avge
†D. I. Gower (*Leicestershire*)	14	23	2	830	131	1	39.52
†M. R. Benson (*Kent*)	23	39	2	1,461	128	2	39.48
P. Johnson (*Nottinghamshire*)	26	37	5	1,250	128	3	39.06
†G. Fowler (*Lancashire*)	20	32	2	1,163	180	3	38.76
T. J. Boon (*Leicestershire*)	23	36	10	1,003	117	1	38.57
G. W. Humpage (*Warwickshire*)	26	42	4	1,462	130	3	38.47
†K. Sharp (*Yorkshire*)	19	31	6	958	181	2	38.32
†W. N. Slack (*Middlesex*)	23	35	3	1,224	106	3	38.25
G. A. Gooch (*Essex*)	19	32	0	1,221	183	3	38.15
C. M. Wells (*Sussex*)	24	38	9	1,098	106	1	37.86
P. R. Downton (*Middlesex*)	24	29	5	906	126*	2	37.75
P. A. Smith (*Warwickshire*)	25	44	4	1,508	119	1	37.70
D. L. Amiss (*Warwickshire*)	26	45	6	1,450	110	4	37.17
K. J. Barnett (*Derbyshire*)	26	45	3	1,544	143	2	36.76
P. A. Neale (*Worcestershire*)	25	34	7	987	118*	1	36.55
†D. R. Turner (*Hampshire*)	10	14	1	472	96	0	36.30
†H. Morris (*Glamorgan*)	26	44	2	1,522	128*	2	36.23
R. A. Harper (*Northamptonshire*)	25	30	4	933	234	1	35.88
P. E. Robinson (*Yorkshire*)	8	13	2	392	104*	1	35.63
J. Derrick (*Glamorgan*)	18	24	8	569	78*	0	35.56
N. J. Falkner (*Surrey*)	11	18	2	567	102	1	35.43
R. I. Alikhan (*Sussex*)	18	28	4	843	72	0	35.12
J. D. Love (*Yorkshire*)	21	29	5	831	109	1	34.62
T. E. Jesty (*Surrey*)	20	30	1	998	221	2	34.41
M. A. Lynch (*Surrey*)	25	39	3	1,234	152	3	34.27
J. D. Birch (*Nottinghamshire*)	21	28	7	718	79*	0	34.19
E. A. E. Baptiste (*Kent*)	7	8	0	273	113	1	34.12
J. D. Carr (*Middlesex*)	17	26	3	782	84*	0	34.00
P. J. Hartley (*Yorkshire*)	15	17	4	441	87*	0	33.92
D. W. Varey (*Lancashire*)	6	10	2	271	83	0	33.87
M. D. Moxon (*Yorkshire*)	20	33	4	982	147	3	33.86
†D. J. Wild (*Northamptonshire*)	14	21	3	608	101	1	33.77
K. W. R. Fletcher (*Essex*)	20	28	6	736	91	0	33.45
M. P. Maynard (*Glamorgan*)	22	34	4	1,002	148	2	33.40
C. J. Tavaré (*Kent*)	26	42	4	1,267	123	2	33.34
R. J. Harden (*Somerset*)	22	36	3	1,093	108	2	33.12
†G. S. Clinton (*Surrey*)	23	35	4	1,027	117	1	33.12
A. P. Wells (*Sussex*)	23	34	7	891	150*	1	33.00
Asif Din (*Warwickshire*)	24	38	14	788	69*	0	32.83
P. J. Prichard (*Essex*)	26	44	3	1,342	147*	1	32.73
P. Whitticase (*Leicestershire*)	18	21	4	554	67*	0	32.58
†I. J. Gould (*Sussex*)	20	24	6	586	78*	0	32.55
†J. G. Wright (*Derbyshire and New Zealanders*)	14	22	1	682	119	1	32.47
C. Maynard (*Lancashire*)	19	26	5	662	132*	1	31.52
A. M. Green (*Sussex*)	25	46	3	1,343	179	3	31.23
N. R. Taylor (*Kent*)	26	42	5	1,151	106	1	31.10
†A. J. T. Miller (*Middlesex*)	23	35	4	963	111*	1	31.06
R. O. Butcher (*Middlesex*)	26	37	4	1,016	171	1	30.78
S. A. Marsh (*Kent*)	26	36	8	857	70	0	30.60
R. J. Boyd-Moss (*Northamptonshire*)	27	42	3	1,192	155	2	30.56
M. W. Alleyne (*Gloucestershire*)	10	16	5	336	116*	0	30.54
†N. A. Felton (*Somerset*)	23	37	3	1,030	156*	3	30.29
D. Ripley (*Northamptonshire*)	13	15	5	301	134*	1	30.10
S. J. Rhodes (*Worcestershire*)	25	27	10	509	77*	0	29.94
G. S. le Roux (*Sussex*)	14	16	6	298	72*	0	29.80
†J. J. E. Hardy (*Somerset*)	19	29	0	863	79	0	29.75
B. R. Hardie (*Essex*)	22	35	5	883	113*	2	29.43
D. J. Capel (*Northamptonshire*)	28	36	7	853	111	2	29.41
C. T. Radley (*Middlesex*)	25	33	6	792	113*	2	29.33
T. M. Tremlett (*Hampshire*)	21	23	12	322	59*	0	29.27

	M	I	NO	R	HI	100s	Avge
R. Sharma (*Derbyshire*)	15	17	6	321	71	0	29.18
C. S. Cowdrey (*Kent*)	22	33	3	873	100	1	29.10
K. P. Tomlins (*Gloucestershire*)	16	29	5	696	75	0	29.00
R. J. Maru (*Hampshire*)	17	10	6	116	23	0	29.00
D. A. Thorne (*Warwickshire and Oxford U.*)	14	21	4	490	104*	1	28.82
A. W. Stovold (*Gloucestershire*)	26	43	4	1,123	118	1	28.79
D. B. D'Oliveira (*Worcestershire*)	25	41	3	1,094	146*	1	28.78
R. A. Cobb (*Leicestershire*)	25	41	3	1,092	91	0	28.73
T. C. Middleton (*Hampshire*)	8	14	3	316	68*	0	28.72
J. A. Hopkins (*Glamorgan*)	15	26	0	738	142	1	28.38
G. C. Holmes (*Glamorgan*)	26	44	5	1,106	107	1	28.35
†T. A. Lloyd (*Warwickshire*)	16	28	0	793	100	1	28.32
S. N. Hartley (*Yorkshire*)	21	30	2	785	87	0	28.03
V. P. Terry (*Hampshire*)	23	36	4	896	80	0	28.00
†D. J. Thomas (*Surrey*)	9	12	4	222	47*	0	27.75
D. J. Fell (*Cambridge U.*)	9	17	3	388	114	1	27.71
D. L. Bairstow (*Yorkshire*)	24	33	4	796	88	0	27.44
P. Bainbridge (*Gloucestershire*)	26	43	4	1,065	105	1	27.30
P. J. W. Allott (*Lancashire*)	17	19	5	382	65	0	27.28
J. P. Stephenson (*Essex*)	14	25	1	647	85	0	26.95
A. E. Warner (*Derbyshire*)	20	28	6	593	91	0	26.95
†R. C. Russell (*Gloucestershire*)	27	31	9	585	71	0	26.59
W. Larkins (*Northamptonshire*)	17	29	4	664	86	0	26.56
P. A. C. Bail (*Somerset and Cambridge U.*)	11	20	0	530	174	1	26.50
S. J. O'Shaughnessy (*Lancashire*)	10	14	3	291	74	0	26.45
M. A. Feltham (*Surrey*)	12	14	5	237	76	0	26.33
K. R. Brown (*Middlesex*)	10	16	2	367	65	0	26.21
†S. G. Hinks (*Kent*)	23	38	2	936	131	2	26.00
N. G. Cowley (*Hampshire*)	19	21	7	360	78*	0	25.71
D. A. Reeve (*Sussex*)	19	21	9	307	51	0	25.58
†A. R. Butcher (*Surrey*)	16	25	0	634	157	1	25.36
D. W. Browne (*Cambridge U.*)	7	13	4	228	61*	0	25.33
I. G. Swallow (*Yorkshire*)	9	11	5	152	43*	0	25.33
†A. L. Jones (*Glamorgan*)	13	21	4	429	50	0	25.23
A. W. Lilley (*Essex*)	15	26	2	604	87	0	25.16
J. Simmons (*Lancashire*)	13	17	5	300	61	0	25.00
†K. D. James (*Hampshire*)	12	13	2	275	62	0	25.00
J. G. Thomas (*Glamorgan*)	22	27	6	523	70	0	24.90
P. D. Bowler (*Leicestershire*)	8	11	1	249	100*	1	24.90
M. A. Roseberry (*Middlesex*)	5	8	1	174	70*	0	24.85
P. B. Clift (*Leicestershire*)	15	16	1	370	49	0	24.66
C. D. M. Tooley (*Oxford U.*)	6	10	1	221	60	0	24.55
P. Carrick (*Yorkshire*)	25	33	7	637	51	0	24.50
D. A. Hagan (*Oxford U.*)	9	16	1	364	88	0	24.26
S. N. V. Waterton (*Northamptonshire*)	14	17	4	314	58*	0	24.15
†R. M. Ellison (*Kent*)	20	29	6	552	62*	0	24.00
M. R. Chadwick (*Lancashire*)	10	18	0	423	61	0	23.50
J. F. Steele (*Glamorgan*)	12	17	5	282	41*	0	23.50
A. K. Golding (*Cambridge U.*)	7	11	3	188	47	0	23.50
D. W. Randall (*Nottinghamshire*)	14	22	1	493	101*	1	23.47
R. J. Parks (*Hampshire*)	25	23	5	420	80	0	23.33
A. J. Wright (*Gloucestershire*)	15	26	0	603	87	0	23.19
M. Jean-Jacques (*Derbyshire*)	9	12	3	208	73	0	23.11
R. J. Finney (*Derbyshire*)	17	17	5	277	54	0	23.08
P. A. J. DeFreitas (*Leicestershire*)	27	30	2	645	106	1	23.03
R. J. Doughty (*Surrey*)	15	19	2	387	61	0	22.76
D. B. Pauline (*Glamorgan*)	12	20	0	455	97	0	22.75
B. Roberts (*Derbyshire*)	25	37	3	772	124*	1	22.70
R. C. Ontong (*Glamorgan*)	24	37	4	744	80*	0	22.54

	M	I	NO	R	HI	100s	Avge
D. G. Aslett (*Kent*)	17	23	0	517	63	0	22.47
C. Marples (*Derbyshire*)	15	24	3	466	57	0	22.19
P. J. Newport (*Worcestershire*)	23	17	4	285	68	0	21.92
D. R. Pringle (*Essex*)	20	32	4	611	97	0	21.82
N. J. Lenham (*Sussex*)	18	29	4	544	77	0	21.76
T. Davies (*Glamorgan*)	24	28	13	316	41	0	21.06
P. W. Romaines (*Gloucestershire*)	15	27	4	476	67*	0	20.69
G. Miller (*Derbyshire*)	20	27	2	512	65	0	20.48
I. S. Anderson (*Derbyshire*)	13	23	1	449	93	0	20.40
D. E. East (*Essex*)	25	40	4	730	100*	1	20.27
G. Monkhouse (*Surrey*)	10	12	4	162	51	0	20.25
L. Potter (*Leicestershire*)	20	30	3	545	81*	0	20.18
B. N. French (*Nottinghamshire*)	20	23	5	361	58	0	20.05
N. A. Foster (*Essex*)	23	30	7	458	53*	0	19.91
M. J. Kilborn (*Oxford U.*)	7	12	1	219	59	0	19.90
M. C. J. Nicholas (*Hampshire*)	24	32	2	564	55	0	18.80
J. C. Balderstone (*Leicestershire*)	14	23	1	410	115	1	18.63
J. E. Emburey (*Middlesex*)	18	22	3	354	75	0	18.63
M. Watkinson (*Lancashire*)	21	25	4	389	58*	0	18.52
P. W. Jarvis (*Yorkshire*)	15	17	7	183	47	0	18.30
M. S. Ahluwalia (*Cambridge U.*)	6	11	0	198	36	0	18.00
D. K. Standing (*Sussex*)	17	26	3	412	65	0	17.91
†A. Walker (*Northamptonshire*)	19	15	10	87	40*	0	17.40
E. E. Hemmings (*Nottinghamshire*)	21	23	4	330	54*	0	17.36
R. K. Illingworth (*Worcestershire*)	18	15	4	191	39	0	17.36
S. T. Clarke (*Surrey*)	14	13	4	156	32*	0	17.33
K. J. Kerr (*Warwickshire*)	14	12	5	120	45*	0	17.14
A. Needham (*Surrey*)	11	17	2	256	52	0	17.06
G. R. Cowdrey (*Kent*)	17	26	1	425	75	0	17.00
†G. J. Parsons (*Warwickshire*)	21	24	5	322	58*	0	16.94
M. J. Weston (*Worcestershire*)	8	12	2	167	49	0	16.70
J. Garner (*Somerset*)	18	15	4	182	47	0	16.54
M. A. Holding (*Derbyshire*)	14	20	2	295	36*	0	16.38
G. C. Small (*Warwickshire*)	25	26	7	304	45*	0	16.00
N. G. Cowans (*Middlesex*)	21	21	7	223	44*	0	15.92
†M. R. Davis (*Somerset*)	9	8	4	63	21*	0	15.75
A. C. Storie (*Northamptonshire*)	8	11	0	171	38	0	15.54
J. E. Davidson (*Cambridge U.*)	9	10	3	108	41*	0	15.42
I. P. Butcher (*Leicestershire*)	12	19	1	273	58	0	15.16
K. T. Medlycott (*Surrey*)	14	15	2	197	61	0	15.15
D. G. Price (*Cambridge U.*)	8	15	1	207	60	0	14.78
N. G. B. Cook (*Northamptonshire*)	27	27	3	351	45	0	14.62
P. H. Edmonds (*Middlesex*)	17	19	5	201	31	0	14.35
A. A. G. Mee (*Oxford U.*)	8	14	1	183	51	0	14.07
W. W. Daniel (*Middlesex*)	16	16	6	140	33	0	14.00
D. J. Makinson (*Lancashire*)	15	13	6	96	43	0	13.71
N. V. Radford (*Worcestershire*)	20	16	3	178	30	0	13.69
†J. H. Childs (*Essex*)	22	23	7	214	34	0	13.37
I. R. Payne (*Gloucestershire*)	11	12	4	106	30*	0	13.25
†K. E. Cooper (*Nottinghamshire*)	17	13	5	105	19	0	13.12
†C. Gladwin (*Essex*)	8	15	0	195	73	0	13.00
J. P. Agnew (*Leicestershire*)	19	20	6	181	35*	0	12.92
†R. A. Pick (*Nottinghamshire*)	19	17	1	206	55	0	12.87
S. R. Gorman (*Cambridge U.*)	6	9	3	76	37	0	12.66
†C. H. Dredge (*Somerset*)	17	21	3	227	40	0	12.61
T. D. Topley (*Essex*)	9	11	2	113	45	0	12.55
M. D. Marshall (*Hampshire*)	23	23	2	263	51*	0	12.52
S. P. Hughes (*Middlesex*)	23	26	2	296	47	0	12.33
C. A. Walsh (*Gloucestershire*)	23	24	6	221	52	0	12.27
†G. R. Dilley (*Kent*)	18	26	8	218	30	0	12.11
T. Gard (*Somerset*)	20	25	6	228	36	0	12.00

	M	I	NO	R	HI	100s	Avge
N. A. Mallender (*Northamptonshire*) .	22	20	10	119	37	0	11.90
K. R. Pont (*Essex*)	7	13	1	142	36	0	11.83
D. L. Underwood (*Kent*)	24	26	5	243	29	0	11.57
R. I. H. B. Dyer (*Warwickshire*)	5	10	2	91	28	0	11.37
A. N. Hayhurst (*Lancashire*)	10	14	0	156	31	0	11.14
D. A. Graveney (*Gloucestershire*) . . .	22	18	9	94	30*	0	10.44
S. J. Dennis (*Yorkshire*)	16	12	4	82	18*	0	10.25

BOWLING

(Qualification: 10 wickets in 10 innings)

† *Denotes left-arm bowler.*

	O	M	R	W	BB	Avge
M. D. Marshall (*Hampshire*)	656.3	171	1,508	100	6-51	15.08
R. J. Hadlee (*Nottinghamshire and New Zealand*)	547.3	150	1,215	76	6-31	15.98
†J. H. Childs (*Essex*)	640.1	212	1,449	89	8-58	16.28
S. T. Clarke (*Surrey*)	341.3	95	806	48	5-31	16.79
C. A. Walsh (*Gloucestershire*)	789.5	193	2,145	118	9-72	18.17
A. H. Gray (*Surrey*)	342.3	69	966	51	7-23	18.94
T. M. Alderman (*Kent*)	610	139	1,882	98	8-46	19.20
M. A. Holding (*Derbyshire*)	388.1	110	1,045	52	7-97	20.09
J. Simmons (*Lancashire*)	230.5	52	762	36	7-79	21.16
P. W. Jarvis (*Yorkshire*)	428.4	82	1,332	60	7-55	22.20
M. P. Bicknell (*Surrey*)	196	43	600	27	3-27	22.22
P. B. Clift (*Leicestershire*)	413.3	120	1,002	45	4-35	22.26
J. E. Emburey (*Middlesex*)	473.3	170	872	39	5-51	22.35
N. A. Foster (*Essex*)	806.2	179	2,349	105	6-57	22.37
W. W. Daniel (*Middlesex*)	402.1	52	1,387	62	4-27	22.37
P. A. J. DeFreitas (*Leicestershire*) . . .	743.3	139	2,171	94	7-44	23.09
G. C. Small (*Warwickshire*)	639.3	158	1,781	77	5-35	23.12
A. M. Babington (*Sussex*)	117.5	16	348	15	4-18	23.20
J. Garner (*Somerset*)	419	95	1,091	47	5-56	23.21
T. D. Topley (*Essex*)	249.4	60	744	32	5-52	23.25
Imran Khan (*Sussex*)	317.2	72	866	37	8-34	23.40
†A. R. Butcher (*Surrey*)	111	28	305	13	4-25	23.46
O. H. Mortensen (*Derbyshire*)	416.2	111	1,082	46	5-35	23.52
A. P. Pridgeon (*Worcestershire*)	535	134	1,396	59	6-52	23.66
N. G. Cowans (*Middlesex*)	435.2	94	1,380	58	5-61	23.79
K. E. Cooper (*Nottinghamshire*)	410.5	106	1,026	43	5-102	23.86
†N. Gifford (*Warwickshire*)	564.4	157	1,409	59	6-27	23.88
D. R. Pringle (*Essex*)	506.3	128	1,348	56	7-46	24.07
P. J. W. Allott (*Lancashire*)	405.1	106	1,053	43	5-32	24.48
P. J. Newport (*Worcestershire*)	632.3	90	2,146	85	6-48	25.24
C. E. B. Rice (*Nottinghamshire*)	413.3	115	1,111	44	4-54	25.25
P. M. Such (*Nottinghamshire*)	231.3	69	566	22	5-36	25.72
G. R. Dilley (*Kent*)	505.2	86	1,634	63	6-57	25.93
S. P. Hughes (*Middlesex*)	529.4	123	1,652	63	7-35	26.22
†D. L. Underwood (*Kent*)	638.1	259	1,371	52	7-11	26.36
N. G. Cowley (*Hampshire*)	385.2	78	1,060	40	5-17	26.50
P. J. Hartley (*Yorkshire*)	321.1	49	1,095	41	6-68	26.70
N. V. Radford (*Worcestershire*)	665.4	132	2,164	81	9-70	26.71
A. Sidebottom (*Yorkshire*)	226.1	37	671	25	8-72	26.84
D. A. Reeve (*Sussex*)	525.5	127	1,411	52	5-32	27.13
M. Jean-Jacques (*Derbyshire*)	159	16	599	22	8-77	27.22
B. P. Patterson (*Lancashire*)	391.4	69	1,309	48	6-31	27.27

	O	M	R	W	BB	Avge
D. E. Malcolm (*Derbyshire*)	216.2	38	765	28	5-42	27.32
C. Shaw (*Yorkshire*)	300.1	64	848	31	5-38	27.35
R. A. Harper (*Northamptonshire*)	825.2	275	1,700	62	5-84	27.41
P. Bainbridge (*Gloucestershire*)	414.1	89	1,185	43	8-53	27.55
D. L. Acfield (*Essex*)	401.1	107	912	33	5-38	27.63
R. C. Ontong (*Glamorgan*)	606.4	153	1,774	64	8-101	27.71
J. P. Agnew (*Leicestershire*)	522.5	118	1,528	55	5-27	27.78
A. C. S. Pigott (*Sussex*)	390	48	1,363	49	5-50	27.81
†R. J. Maru (*Hampshire*)	497.5	146	1,336	48	5-38	27.83
T. A. Munton (*Warwickshire*)	297.4	68	905	32	4-60	28.28
†J. K. Lever (*Essex*)	638.1	154	1,990	70	6-57	28.42
D. J. Wild (*Northamptonshire*)	132.3	17	429	15	4-4	28.60
†K. T. Medlycott (*Surrey*)	356.2	86	1,166	40	6-63	29.15
E. E. Hemmings (*Nottinghamshire*) ..	818.3	259	2,134	73	7-102	29.23
†P. H. Edmonds (*Middlesex*)	529	162	1,111	38	4-31	29.23
T. M. Tremlett (*Hampshire*)	453.4	110	1,263	43	5-46	29.37
A. N. Jones (*Sussex*)	171	26	620	21	3-36	29.52
†N. G. B. Cook (*Northamptonshire*) ..	870.2	290	1,890	64	6-72	29.53
S. J. W. Andrew (*Hampshire*)	141.2	32	419	14	3-25	29.92
L. B. Taylor (*Leicestershire*)	280.3	66	809	27	4-106	29.96
M. A. Feltham (*Surrey*)	224	48	781	26	4-47	30.03
†S. J. Dennis (*Yorkshire*)	407.3	79	1,318	43	5-71	30.65
R. A. Pick (*Nottinghamshire*)	469.1	88	1,570	50	6-68	31.40
†L. Potter (*Leicestershire*)	113	31	318	10	3-37	31.80
†J. A. Afford (*Nottinghamshire*)	492.4	131	1,455	45	6-81	32.33
D. J. Capel (*Northamptonshire*)	633.1	131	2,044	63	7-86	32.44
C. H. Dredge (*Somerset*)	389	83	1,151	35	3-10	32.88
†K. D. James (*Hampshire*)	228.4	55	692	21	5-34	32.95
C. A. Connor (*Hampshire*)	541.4	123	1,616	49	5-60	32.97
J. W. Lloyds (*Gloucestershire*)	369.2	71	1,221	37	5-111	33.00
J. E. Davidson (*Cambridge U.*)	326	54	998	30	5-35	33.26
†D. A. Graveney (*Gloucestershire*) ...	446	137	999	30	4-17	33.30
W. K. M. Benjamin (*Leicestershire*) .	465.3	89	1,541	46	6-33	33.50
C. S. Cowdrey (*Kent*)	266.2	45	905	27	5-69	33.51
K. Saxelby (*Nottinghamshire*)	284	54	905	27	4-47	33.51
R. J. Doughty (*Surrey*)	300	50	1,104	32	4-52	34.50
†D. J. Makinson (*Lancashire*)	322.1	66	1,044	30	4-69	34.80
B. J. Griffiths (*Northamptonshire*) ...	237.3	49	741	21	4-59	35.28
G. S. le Roux (*Sussex*)	303.2	60	928	26	3-27	35.69
V. J. Marks (*Somerset*)	744.5	198	2,121	59	8-100	35.94
N. A. Mallender (*Northamptonshire*) .	611	138	1,693	47	5-110	36.02
†I. Folley (*Lancashire*)	349	98	1,046	29	4-42	36.06
D. V. Lawrence (*Gloucestershire*)	588.1	85	2,299	63	5-84	36.49
P. I. Pocock (*Surrey*)	394.5	107	1,095	30	4-45	36.50
S. J. Base (*Glamorgan*)	222.5	40	774	21	4-74	36.85
R. Sharma (*Derbyshire*)	140.5	33	407	11	3-72	37.00
S. R. Barwick (*Glamorgan*)	292.4	61	964	26	3-25	37.07
C. M. Wells (*Sussex*)	458.2	103	1,373	37	4-23	37.10
†R. J. Finney (*Derbyshire*)	318.4	60	1,057	28	7-54	37.75
G. J. Parsons (*Warwickshire*)	371.1	72	1,179	31	5-24	38.03
I. R. Payne (*Gloucestershire*)	215.1	58	576	15	3-48	38.40
J. G. Thomas (*Glamorgan*)	478.5	70	1,746	45	4-56	38.80
K. J. Kerr (*Warwickshire*)	316	52	955	24	5-47	39.79
A. Walker (*Northamptonshire*)	422	76	1,314	33	6-50	39.81
S. M. McEwan (*Worcestershire*)	180.1	31	638	16	3-33	39.87
K. B. S. Jarvis (*Kent*)	155.2	42	487	12	2-15	40.58
J. Derrick (*Glamorgan*)	265.2	47	897	22	3-19	40.77
S. D. Fletcher (*Yorkshire*)	414	82	1,273	31	5-90	41.06
I. T. Botham (*Somerset*)	311.1	65	1,043	25	6-125	41.72
D. N. Patel (*Worcestershire*)	453.2	115	1,255	30	5-88	41.83
G. Monkhouse (*Surrey*)	233.1	69	589	14	4-37	42.07

	O	M	R	W	BB	Avge
N. S. Taylor (*Somerset*)	342.2	62	1,222	29	4-40	42.13
G. Miller (*Derbyshire*)	634.2	187	1,406	33	5-37	42.60
A. E. Warner (*Derbyshire*)	349.1	67	1,200	28	4-38	42.85
A. N. Hayhurst (*Lancashire*)	114.1	13	429	10	4-69	42.90
†P. Carrick (*Yorkshire*)	621.3	187	1,550	36	4-111	43.05
J. D. Inchmore (*Worcestershire*)	221.1	49	562	13	2-41	43.23
†A. M. G. Scott (*Sussex and Cambridge U.*)	283	71	814	18	4-100	45.22
G. C. Holmes (*Glamorgan*)	131	21	499	11	2-22	45.36
D. J. Hickey (*Glamorgan*)	281.5	39	1,102	24	5-57	45.91
B. M. McMillan (*Warwickshire*)	220	34	808	17	3-47	47.52
R. M. Ellison (*Kent*)	385.4	90	1,103	23	4-36	47.95
†R. K. Illingworth (*Worcestershire*)	564.2	189	1,361	28	5-64	48.60
†D. J. Thomas (*Surrey*)	166.3	29	588	12	2-44	49.00
T. A. J. Dawson (*Oxford U.*)	194	38	649	13	3-65	49.92
M. Watkinson (*Lancashire*)	504.4	86	1,753	35	5-90	50.08
†R. V. J. Coombs (*Somerset*)	256.5	58	844	16	3-60	52.75
A. M. Ferreira (*Warwickshire*)	178	47	532	10	2-61	53.20
†D. A. Thorne (*Warwickshire and Oxford U.*)	239.3	70	593	11	3-42	53.72
C. S. Mays (*Sussex*)	212.5	45	706	13	3-77	54.30
P. A. Smith (*Warwickshire*)	159	19	743	13	3-36	57.15
†M. R. Davis (*Somerset*)	167.3	21	631	11	2-43	57.36
A. K. Golding (*Cambridge U.*)	252	51	685	10	3-51	68.50

The following bowlers took ten wickets but bowled in fewer than ten innings:

	O	M	R	W	BB	Avge
C. C. Ellison (*Cambridge U.*)	127	41	325	14	5-82	23.21
N. F. Williams (*Middlesex*)	79.3	9	264	10	3-44	26.40
E. A. E. Baptiste (*Kent*)	146	40	351	13	4-53	27.00
G. J. F. Ferris (*Leicestershire*)	104	20	356	13	4-54	27.38
A. J. Murphy (*Lancashire*)	91	16	288	10	3-67	28.80
C. Penn (*Kent*)	117.3	24	407	14	5-65	29.07
A. P. Igglesden (*Kent*)	125	25	372	11	4-46	33.81
A. R. C. Fraser (*Middlesex*)	156	40	370	10	3-19	37.00
R. S. Rutnagur (*Oxford U.*)	164	34	528	14	3-50	37.71
C. D. Fraser-Darling (*Nottinghamshire*)	120	16	461	12	5-84	38.41
E. A. Moseley (*Glamorgan*)	124.3	14	447	11	4-70	40.63
†G. E. Sainsbury (*Gloucestershire*)	169.1	46	498	12	4-146	41.50

COUNTY BENEFITS AWARDED IN 1987

Derbyshire	J. G. Wright.	Northamptonshire	B. J. Griffiths (Testimonial).
Gloucestershire	A. W. Stovold.		
Hampshire	M. D. Marshall.	Nottinghamshire	E. E. Hemmings.
Kent	K. B. S. Jarvis.	Somerset	C. H. Dredge.
Leicestershire	D. I. Gower.	Surrey	S. T. Clarke.
Middlesex	C. T. Radley.	Sussex	Imran Khan.
		Warwickshire	G. W. Humpage.

No benefits have been awarded by Essex, Glamorgan, Lancashire, Worcestershire or Yorkshire.

INDIVIDUAL SCORES OF 100 AND OVER

There were 255 three-figure innings in first-class cricket in 1986, 54 fewer than in 1985. The list includes 202 hit in the County Championship, and 34 in other first-class games, but not the eight hit by the Indian touring team, nor the eleven hit by the New Zealand touring team, which can be found in their respective sections.

Signifies not out.

C. G. Greenidge (8)
222   Hants v Northants, Northampton
103 ⎱ Hants v Derbys., Derby
180* ⎰
148   Hants v Somerset, Bournemouth
144* Hants v Derbys., Portsmouth
127* Hants v Lancs., Manchester
126   Hants v Sussex, Hove
118   Hants v Notts., Nottingham

B. C. Broad (6)
122   Notts. v Yorks., Worksop
120   Notts. v Essex, Nottingham
116   Notts. v Warwicks., Nottingham
116   Notts. v Sussex, Hove
112   Notts. v Northants, Nottingham
105   Notts. v Glos., Cheltenham

G. A. Hick (6)
227* Worcs. v Notts., Worcester
219* Worcs. v Glam., Neath
134   Worcs. v Glos., Worcester
107   Worcs. v Glam., Worcester
103   Worcs. v Surrey, Worcester
100   Worcs. v Sussex, Hove

A. A. Metcalfe (6)
151   Yorks. v Northants, Luton
151   Yorks. v Lancs., Manchester
149   Yorks. v Glam., Leeds
123   Yorks. v Kent, Scarborough
108   Yorks. v Worcs., Worcester
108   Yorks. v Notts., Sheffield

P. W. G. Parker (6)
125   Sussex v Worcs., Worcester
120   Sussex v Glos., Bristol
111   Sussex v Notts., Hove
109   Sussex v Cambridge U., Hove
107   Sussex v Middx, Lord's
100* Sussex v Derbys., Eastbourne

A. I. Kallicharran (5)
163* Warwicks. v Glam., Birmingham
132* Warwicks. v Glos., Bristol
121   Warwicks. v Cambridge U., Cambridge
103* Warwicks. v Yorks., Birmingham
102* Warwicks. v Glam., Swansea

J. J. Whitaker (5)
200* Leics. v Notts., Leicester
175   Leics. v Derbys., Chesterfield
106* Leics. v Derbys., Leicester
102* Leics. v Lancs., Manchester
100* Leics. v Yorks., Leicester

D. L. Amiss (4)
110   Warwicks. v Glam., Swansea
108* Warwicks. v Essex, Birmingham
104   Warwicks. v Glos., Bristol
101* Warwicks. v Lancs., Birmingham

R. J. Bailey (4)
224* Northants v Glam., Swansea
200* Northants v Yorks., Luton
114   Northants v Derbys., Derby
106   Northants v Leics., Northampton

A. R. Border (4)
150   Essex v Glam., Swansea
138   Essex v Surrey, The Oval
110   Essex v Derbys., Derby
108* Essex v Sussex, Eastbourne

K. M. Curran (4)
117* Glos. v Notts., Cheltenham
116   Glos. v Glam., Cardiff
103* Glos. v Oxford U., Oxford
103* Glos. v Surrey, The Oval

M. W. Gatting (4)
183* England v New Zealand, Birmingham
158   Middx v Northants, Lord's
135   Middx v New Zealanders, Lord's
121   England v New Zealand, The Oval

A. J. Lamb (4)
160* Northants v Middx, Northampton
159   Northants v Derbys., Derby
157   Northants v Sussex, Hastings
117   Northants v Middx, Lord's

J. E. Morris (4)
191   Derbys. v Kent, Derby
153   Derbys. v Lancs., Liverpool
127   Derbys. v Northants, Derby
118   Derbys. v Leics., Leicester

I. V. A. Richards (4)
136 Somerset v Glam., Cardiff
128 Somerset v Kent, Bath
115 Somerset v Warwicks., Weston-super-
     Mare
102 Somerset v Glam., Taunton

R. T. Robinson (4)
159* Notts. v Kent, Nottingham
108 Notts. v Glos., Cheltenham
105 Notts. v Yorks., Worksop
104 Notts. v Leics., Nottingham

P. M. Roebuck (4)
221* Somerset v Notts., Nottingham
147* Somerset v Worcs., Weston-super-
     Mare
128* Somerset v Middx, Lord's
102* Somerset v Hants, Taunton

P. Willey (4)
172* Leics. v Hants, Leicester
168* Leics. v Derbys., Leicester
119 Leics. v Notts., Leicester
104 Leics. v Kent, Canterbury

J. Abrahams (3)
189* Lancs. v Glam., Swansea
117 Lancs. v Oxford U., Oxford
100* Lancs. v Worcs., Manchester

G. Cook (3)
183 Northants v Lancs., Northampton
120 Northants v Glam., Northampton
109* Northants v Kent, Canterbury

N. H. Fairbrother (3)
131 Lancs. v Worcs., Manchester
116* Lancs. v Yorks., Manchester
115* Lancs. v Somerset, Manchester

N. A. Felton (3)
156* Somerset v Hants, Taunton
110 Somerset v Leics., Leicester
104 Somerset v Indians, Taunton

G. A. Gooch (3)
183 England v New Zealand, Lord's
151 Essex v Worcs., Southend
114 England v India, Lord's

A. M. Green (3)
179 Sussex v Glam., Cardiff
132 Sussex v Cambridge U., Hove
114 Sussex v Hants, Hove

A. Hill (3)
172* Derbys. v Yorks., Sheffield
130* Derbys. v Sussex, Eastbourne
119* Derbys. v Hants, Derby

G. W. Humpage (3)
130 Warwicks. v Lancs., Manchester
125 Warwicks. v Cambridge U.,
     Cambridge
100* Warwicks. v New Zealanders,
     Birmingham

P. Johnson (3)
128 Notts. v Essex, Chelmsford
120* Notts. v Lancs., Nottingham
105* Notts. v Yorks., Worksop

M. A. Lynch (3)
152 Surrey v Notts., The Oval
128* Surrey v Warwicks., The Oval
119* Surrey v Kent, Dartford

B. M. McMillan (3)
136 Warwicks. v Notts., Nottingham
134 Warwicks. v Yorks., Leeds
106 Warwicks. v Kent, Birmingham

M. D. Moxon (3)
147 Yorks. v Lancs., Manchester
123 ⎫
112* ⎭ Yorks. v Indians, Scarborough

D. N. Patel (3)
132* Worcs. v Surrey, The Oval
128 Worcs. v Essex, Southend
108 Worcs. v Middx, Worcester

W. N. Slack (3)
106 Middx v Northants, Northampton
105* Middx v Yorks., Leeds
100 Middx v Derbys., Derby

D. M. Smith (3)
165* Worcs. v Somerset, Weston-super-
     Mare
102 Worcs. v Warwicks., Birmingham
100 Worcs. v Glam., Worcester

A. J. Stewart (3)
166 Surrey v Kent, The Oval
144 Surrey v Middx, Uxbridge
105 Surrey v Kent, Dartford

K. J. Barnett (2)
143 Derbys. v Northants, Derby
114 Derbys. v Glos., Chesterfield

M. R. Benson (2)
128 Kent v Indians, Canterbury
123 Kent v Surrey, Dartford

I. T. Botham (2)
139 Somerset v Lancs., Manchester
104* Somerset v Worcs., Weston-super-Mare

G. Boycott (2)
135* Yorks. v Surrey, Leeds
127 Yorks. v Leics., Middlesbrough

R. J. Boyd-Moss (2)
155 Northants v Lancs., Northampton
148* Northants v Glam., Northampton

D. J. Capel (2)
111 Northants v Leics., Northampton
103* Northants v Somerset, Bath

T. S. Curtis (2)
153 Worcs. v Somerset, Worcester
122* Worcs. v Yorks., Worcester

P. R. Downton (2)
126* Middx v Oxford U., Oxford
104 Middx v Warwicks., Uxbridge

R. J. Hadlee (2)
129* Notts. v Somerset, Nottingham
105* Notts. v Surrey, The Oval

R. J. Harden (2)
108 Somerset v Sussex, Taunton
102 Somerset v Kent, Maidstone

B. R. Hardie (2)
113* Essex v Somerset, Taunton
110 Essex v Yorks., Chelmsford

S. G. Hinks (2)
131 Kent v Hants, Canterbury
103 Kent v Somerset, Maidstone

Imran Khan (2)
135* Sussex v Warwicks., Birmingham
104 Sussex v Hants, Southampton

T. E. Jesty (2)
221 Surrey v Essex, The Oval
179 Surrey v Worcs., The Oval

M. P. Maynard (2)
148 Glam. v Oxford U., Oxford
129 Glam. v Warwicks., Birmingham

G. D. Mendis (2)
108 Lancs. v Notts., Nottingham
100 Lancs. v Glam., Swansea

A. J. Moles (2)
102 Warwicks. v Somerset, Weston-super-Mare
100 Warwicks. v Glos., Nuneaton

H. Morris (2)
128* Glam. v Kent, Maidstone
114 Glam. v Worcs., Worcester

C. T. Radley (2)
113* Middx v Somerset, Lord's
103* Middx v Derbys., Lord's

C. E. B. Rice (2)
156* Notts. v Middx, Nottingham
120 Notts. v Derbys., Derby

C. J. Richards (2)
115 Surrey v Glos., The Oval
100 Surrey v Middx, Uxbridge

B. C. Rose (2)
129 Somerset v Middx, Lord's
107* Somerset v Kent, Bath

K. Sharp (2)
181 Yorks. v Glos., Harrogate
114* Yorks. v Warwicks., Leeds

C. L. Smith (2)
114* Hants v Sussex, Hove
103* Hants v Somerset, Bournemouth

R. A. Smith (2)
128* Hants v Sussex, Southampton
101 Hants v Surrey, Basingstoke

C. J. Tavaré (2)
123 Kent v Oxford U., Oxford
105 Kent v Northants, Canterbury

The following each played one three-figure innings:

M. W. Alleyne, 116*, Glos. v Sussex, Bristol; C. W. J. Athey, 171*, Glos. v Northants, Northampton.
P. A. C. Bail, 174, Cambridge U. v Oxford U., Lord's; P. Bainbridge, 105, Glos. v Notts., Cheltenham; J. C. Balderstone, 115, Leics. v Sussex, Leicester; E. A. E. Baptiste, 113, Kent v Oxford U., Oxford; G. D. Barlow, 107, Middx v Sussex, Lord's; R. J. Bartlett, 117*, Somerset v Oxford U., Oxford; T. J. Boon, 117, Leics. v Yorks., Middlesbrough; P. D. Bowler, 100*, Leics. v Hants, Leicester; A. R. Butcher, 157, Surrey v Cambridge U., Cambridge; R. O. Butcher, 171, Middx v Surrey, Uxbridge.

G. S. Clinton, 117, Surrey v Somerset, Taunton; C. S. Cowdrey, 100, Kent v Warwicks., Folkestone.

P. A. J. DeFreitas, 106, Leics. v Kent, Canterbury; D. B. D'Oliveira, 146*, Worcs. v Glos., Bristol.

D. E. East, 100*, Essex v Glos., Colchester.

N. J. Falkner, 102, Surrey v Middx, Uxbridge; D. J. Fell, 114, Cambridge U. v Sussex, Hove; G. Fowler, 180, Lancs. v Sussex, Hove.

D. I. Gower, 131, England v New Zealand, The Oval.

R. A. Harper, 234, Northants v Glos., Northampton; G. C. Holmes, 107, Glam. v Worcs., Worcester; J. A. Hopkins, 142, Glam. v New Zealanders, Swansea.

Javed Miandad, 102*, D. B. Close's XI v New Zealanders, Scarborough.

C. H. Lloyd, 128, Lancs. v Warwicks., Birmingham; T. A. Lloyd, 100, Warwicks. v Yorks., Leeds; J. W. Lloyds, 111, Glos. v Derbys., Gloucester; J. D. Love, 109, Yorks. v Northants, Scarborough.

B. J. M. Maher, 126, Derbys. v New Zealanders, Derby; V. J. Marks, 110, Somerset v Sussex, Taunton; C. Maynard, 132*, Lancs. v Yorks., Leeds; A. J. T. Miller, 111*, Middx v Hants, Lord's.

P. A. Neale, 118*, Worcs. v Middx, Worcester; M. Newell, 112*, Notts. v Oxford U., Oxford.

I. L. Philip, 145, Scotland v Ireland, Glasgow; A. C. S. Pigott, 104*, Sussex v Warwicks., Birmingham; P. J. Prichard, 147*, Essex v Notts., Chelmsford.

D. W. Randall, 101*, Notts. v Oxford U., Oxford; D. Ripley, 134*, Northants v Yorks., Scarborough; B. Roberts, 124*, Derbys. v Somerset, Chesterfield; P. E. Robinson, 104*, Yorks. v Kent, Scarborough.

P. A. Smith, 119, Warwicks. v Worcs., Birmingham; A. W. Stovold, 118, Glos. v Derbys., Chesterfield.

N. R. Taylor, 106, Kent v Oxford U., Oxford; D. A. Thorne, 104*, Oxford U. v Cambridge U., Lord's.

A. P. Wells, 150*, Sussex v Notts., Hove; C. M. Wells, 106, Sussex v Essex, Eastbourne; D. J. Wild, 101, Northants v Cambridge U., Cambridge.

Younis Ahmed, 105*, Glam. v Sussex, Cardiff.

TEN WICKETS IN A MATCH

There were 34 instances of bowlers taking ten or more wickets in a match in first-class cricket in 1986, eighteen more than in 1985. The list includes 31 in the County Championship, two by the New Zealand touring team and one by the Indian touring team.

C. A. Walsh (4)
12-124 Glos. v Hants, Cheltenham
11-94   Glos. v Hants, Bournemouth
11-113 Glos. v Surrey, Bristol
10-114 Glos. v Somerset, Bristol

T. M. Alderman (3)
14-144 Kent v Leics., Canterbury
11-130 Kent v Derbys., Derby
10-135 Kent v Glos., Gloucester

J. H. Childs (3)
11-95   Essex v Glos., Colchester
10-98   Essex v Glam., Swansea
10-123 Essex v Kent, Folkestone

N. V. Radford (3)
11-129 Worcs. v Somerset, Worcester
10-129 Worcs. v Northants, Northampton
10-169 Worcs. v Sussex, Worcester

N. A. Foster (2)
11-157 Essex v Worcs., Southend
10-154 Essex v Notts., Chelmsford

R. J. Hadlee (2)
10-72   Notts. v Surrey, Nottingham
10-140 New Zealand v England, Nottingham

E. E. Hemmings (2)
10-164 Notts. v Essex, Chelmsford
10-175 Notts. v Lancs., Southport

P. W. Jarvis (2)
11-92   Yorks. v Middx, Lord's
10-108 Yorks. v Surrey, Leeds

The following each took ten wickets in a match on one occasion:

J. A. Afford, 10-103, Notts. v Kent, Nottingham.
J. G. Bracewell, 10-77, New Zealanders v Oxford & Cambridge U., Cambridge.
Chetan Sharma, 10-188, India v England, Birmingham.
P. A. J. DeFreitas, 13-86, Leics. v Essex, Southend; G. R. Dilley, 10-110, Kent v Lancs.,
   Canterbury.
A. H. Gray, 12-113, Surrey v Warwicks., The Oval.
M. Jean-Jacques, 10-125, Derbys. v Kent, Derby.
V. J. Marks, 14-212, Somerset v Glam., Cardiff; K. T. Medlycott, 10-155, Surrey v Middx,
   Uxbridge.
P. J. Newport, 11-100, Worcs. v Hants, Worcester.
R. C. Ontong, 13-127, Glam. v Notts., Cardiff.
B. P. Patterson, 10-89, Lancs. v Essex, Manchester.
J. Simmons, 10-145, Lancs. v Glam., Lytham.

SIX WICKETS IN AN INNINGS

There were 73 instances of bowlers taking six or more wickets in an innings in first-class cricket
in 1986, one fewer than in 1985. The list includes 66 in the County Championship, four by the
New Zealand touring team, two by the Indian touring team and one in another first-class match.

C. A. Walsh (7)
9-72 Glos. v Somerset, Bristol
7-62 Glos. v Derbys., Chesterfield
6-26 Glos. v Hants, Bournemouth
6-90 ⎫
6-34 ⎭ Glos. v Hants, Cheltenham
6-41 Glos. v Surrey, Bristol
6-83 Glos. v Essex, Colchester

T. M. Alderman (6)
8-46 Kent v Derbys., Derby
8-70 ⎫
6-74 ⎭ Kent v Leics., Canterbury
6-49 Kent v Glos., Gloucester
6-56 Kent v Hants, Southampton
6-70 Kent v Sussex, Tunbridge Wells

R. J. Hadlee (6)
6-31 Notts. v Derbys., Derby
6-33 Notts. v Surrey, Nottingham
6-42 Notts. v Warwicks., Nottingham
6-51 Notts. v Essex, Nottingham
6-80 New Zealand v England,
         Nottingham
6-80 New Zealand v England, Lord's

J. H. Childs (4)
8-58 Essex v Glos., Colchester
8-61 Essex v Northants, Colchester
7-58 Essex v Kent, Folkestone
7-51 Essex v Glam., Swansea

P. A. J. DeFreitas (3)
6-42 ⎫
7-44 ⎭ Leics. v Essex, Southend
6-21 Leics. v Kent, Canterbury

A. H. Gray (3)
7-23 Surrey v Kent, The Oval
6-83 ⎫
6-30 ⎭ Surrey v Warwicks., The Oval

P. W. Jarvis (3)
7-55 Yorks. v Surrey, Leeds
6-47 Yorks. v Middx, Lord's
6-78 Yorks. v Essex, Chelmsford

N. A. Foster (2)
6-57 Essex v Middx, Lord's
6-93 Essex v Worcs., Southend

E. E. Hemmings (2)
7-102 Notts. v Essex, Chelmsford
6-45 Notts. v Glam., Cardiff

V. J. Marks (2)
6-112 ⎫
8-100 ⎭ Somerset v Glam., Cardiff

P. J. Newport (2)
6-48 Worcs. v Hants, Worcester
6-49 Worcs. v Derbys., Derby

B. P. Patterson (2)
6-31 Lancs. v Oxford U., Oxford
6-46 Lancs. v Essex, Manchester

N. V. Radford (2)
9-70 Worcs. v Somerset, Worcester
7-94 Worcs. v Sussex, Worcester

The following each took six wickets in an innings on one occasion:

J. A. Afford, 6-81, Notts. v Kent, Nottingham.

P. Bainbridge, 8-53, Glos. v Somerset, Bristol; W. K. M. Benjamin, 6-33, Leics. v Notts., Leicester; J. G. Bracewell, 6-55, New Zealanders v Oxford & Cambridge U., Cambridge; I. T. Botham, 6-125, Somerset v Leics., Leicester.

D. J. Capel, 7-86, Northants v Derbys., Derby; Chetan Sharma, 6-58, India v England, Birmingham; N. G. B. Cook, 6-72, Northants v Worcs., Northampton.

G. R. Dilley, 6-57, Kent v Lancs., Canterbury.

R. J. Finney, 7-54, Derbys. v Leics., Chesterfield.

N. Gifford, 6-27, Warwicks. v Northants, Northampton; E. J. Gray, 7-61, New Zealanders v Essex, Chelmsford.

P. J. Hartley, 6-68, Yorks. v Notts., Sheffield; M. A. Holding, 7-97, Derbys v Worcs., Derby; S. P. Hughes, 7-35, Middx v Surrey, The Oval.

Imran Khan, 8-34, Sussex v Middx, Lord's.

M. Jean-Jacques, 8-77, Derbys. v Kent, Derby.

J. K. Lever, 6-57, Essex v Glam., Swansea.

M. D. Marshall, 6-51, Hants v Glos., Bournemouth; K. T. Medlycott, 6-63, Surrey v Kent, The Oval.

R. C. Ontong, 8-101, Glam. v Notts., Cardiff.

R. A. Pick, 6-68, Notts. v Yorks., Worksop; A. P. Pridgeon, 6-52, Worcs. v Middx, Worcester; D. R. Pringle, 7-46, Essex v Yorks., Chelmsford.

A. Sidebottom, 8-72, Yorks. v Leics., Middlesbrough; J. Simmons, 7-79, Lancs. v Glam., Lytham.

D. L. Underwood, 7-11, Kent v Warwicks., Folkestone.

A. Walker, 6-50, Northants v Lancs., Northampton.

N. S. Yadav, 6-30, Indians v Somerset, Taunton.

MCC SCHOOL OF MERIT

A School of Merit, organised by MCC at the Indoor School at Lord's and sponsored by Thorn Lighting, held its opening term last winter. Its aim is to provide regular coaching during the winter months for up to 30 young cricketers, aged between twelve and eighteen and chosen from all over the country, in the hope that they will graduate to county and, in time, national teams.

THE CRICKET COUNCIL

The Cricket Council, which was set up in 1968 and reconstituted in 1974 and 1983, acts as the governing body for cricket in the British Isles. It comprises the following, the officers listed being those for 1985-86.

Chairman: R. Subba Row.
Vice-Chairman: J. D. Robson.
8 Representatives of the Test and County Cricket Board: R. Subba Row, C. R. M. Atkinson, D. J. Insole, F. G. Mann, H. J. Pocock, A. C. Smith, A. D. Steven, F. M. Turner.
5 Representatives of the National Cricket Association: J. D. Robson, F. R. Brown, F. H. Elliott, E. K. Ingman, J. G. Overy.
3 Representatives of the Marylebone Cricket Club: D. G. Clark, G. H. G. Doggart, M. D. Mence.
1 Representative (non-voting) of the Minor Counties Cricket Association: G. L. B. August.
1 Representative (non-voting) of the Irish Cricket Union: D. Scott.
1 Representative (non-voting) of the Scottish Cricket Union: R. W. Barclay.

Secretary: D. B. Carr.

THE TEST AND COUNTY CRICKET BOARD

The TCCB was set up in 1968 to be responsible for Test matches, official tours, and first-class and minor county competitions. It is composed of representatives of the seventeen first-class counties; Marylebone Cricket Club; Minor Counties Cricket Association; Oxford University Cricket Club, Cambridge University Cricket Club, the Irish Cricket Union and the Scottish Cricket Union.

Officers 1985-86

Chairman: R. Subba Row.

Chairmen of Committees: R. Subba Row (Executive); F. G. Mann (Adjudication); M. C. Cowdrey (County Pitches); D. J. Insole (Cricket, Overseas Tours); C. R. M. Atkinson (Discipline); A. D. Steven (Finance); B. Coleman (PR and Marketing); D. R. W. Silk (Registration); P. B. H. May (Selection); D. B. Carr (Umpires); M. D. Vockins (Under-25 and Second XI Competitions).

Secretary: D. B. Carr. (Chief Executive from January 1987: A. C. Smith.) *Assistant Secretary (Administration):* B. Langley. *Assistant Secretary (Cricket):* M. E. Gear. *PR and Marketing Manager:* P. M. Lush. *Sales and Promotion Manager:* K. Deshayes.

THE NATIONAL CRICKET ASSOCIATION

With the setting up of the Cricket Council in 1968 it was necessary to form a separate organisation to represent the interests of all cricket below the first-class game, and it is the National Cricket Association that carries out this function. It comprises representatives from 51 county cricket associations and seventeen national cricketing organisations.

Officers 1985-86

President: F. R. Brown.
Chairman: J. D. Robson.
Vice-Chairman: F. H. Elliott.

Secretary: B. J. Aspital.
Director of Coaching: K. V. Andrew.
Hon. Treasurer: D. W. Carter.

THE INDIANS IN ENGLAND, 1986

[Patrick Eagar

The Indian team which toured England last year, winning the Test series 2-0 by defeating England at Lord's and at Headingley. *Back row*: S. M. Patil, Chetan Sharma, M. Prabhakar, R. Lamba, Maninder Singh, V. B. Prabhudesai (*assistant manager*), K. S. More, K. Srikkanth, M. Azharuddin, C. S. Pandit. *Front row*: R. M. H. Binny, D. B. Vengsarkar, M. Amarnath, Kapil Dev (*captain*), Raj Singh (*manager*), R. J. Shastri, S. M. Gavaskar, N. S. Yadav.

THE INDIANS IN ENGLAND, 1986

As the Indians began their tour in cold, rainy weather in the West Country, two questions came to mind. Why were they filling the first half of a twin-tour summer when, having toured first in 1982, they could have followed New Zealand in 1986? And could their bowlers, on the evidence presented, bowl England out twice to win a Test match?

The answer to the first question was that it was the choice of India's Board of Control. With two tours of India scheduled for 1986-87, they wanted their international players fresh at the start of the season rather than returning from a tour of England. While sensible, this none the less condemned Kapil Dev's team to the colder, more unsettled half of the English season. And the wisdom of it was called into question when India went into the first one-day international, having lost a third of their playing time to the weather. Furthermore, it meant there was no place in the touring team for the leg-spinner, Laxman Sivaramakrishnan, whose art would be nullified by wickets still not hard.

India won the first one-day international; they won the Texaco Trophy; and they beat England in the first Test, so winning their second Test in England and their first at headquarters. In doing so they answered, convincingly, the second question, and they did so again at Headingley, embarrassingly, dismissing England for 102 and 128.

The turning-point came at Northampton, where Kapil Dev, Roger Binny and Chetan Sharma bowled the county side out for 118. This success, and especially that of Kapil who, moving the ball from leg to off or cutting it back, took four wickets in eight balls, brought home to the Indians the vulnerability of English batsmen in English conditions. Subsequently, in the Test series, their seam bowlers adhered to the traditional virtues of line and length, while the selection of two left-arm spinners reinforced the strategy of attacking the England batsmen on and outside off stump. Consequently, players programmed by limited-overs cricket to working the ball to leg were forced to adjust their method. And when the conditions encouraged movement in the air or off the pitch, as they did for the Indian bowlers in all three Tests, the deficiencies in English batting techniques were exposed.

Chetan Sharma, a pocket battleship of a fast-medium bowler, took most wickets on tour and in the Tests, his six for 58 in England's second innings at Birmingham giving him ten wickets for the match. Aggressive and volatile, he none the less bowled with great control, and the ball that came back from outside off stump found more than one open gate. Binny, whose medium-pace bowling had been a leading factor in India's World Cup success in 1983, put his back into his work more as the tour progressed and gained an extra half yard of pace without any loss of accuracy. He saved his best for the Test matches, as indeed he seemed to save his best catches for his own bowling. Manoj Prabhakar offered little more than swing, obtaining little movement off the pitch, and when Chetan Sharma was ruled out of the second Test by injury, the Indians called up Madan Lal from the Central Lancashire League. It was a wise decision.

Maninder Singh, a veteran of fifteen Tests at the age of twenty, was not expected (by English commentators) to have a role in the Tests yet played in all three and topped India's averages. He turned 21 on tour, by which time his control of flight and spin, as well as his colourful *patkas*, had revived memories of Bishan Bedi *and* set India on the way to a historic win at Lord's. Shivlal Yadav bowled his off-spin well, and tactics rather than form kept him out of the Test team. By way of compensation he was rewarded with career-best figures of six for 30 at Taunton, where Mohammad Azharuddin held five catches close to the bat. The enthusiastic fielding and throwing of this Indian side contributed largely to its success.

While the technique of England's batsmen was found wanting, that of the Indians was not. Krishnamachari Srikkanth, by the impulsive nature of his game, always gave bowlers a chance, but if Sunil Gavaskar failed to make the same impact as on his four previous Test-match tours, that owed more to his own approach than to any lessening of technique. So often in the past the main course, Gavaskar preferred this time to be a lively *hors d'oeuvre*, whetting the appetite for the batting that followed.

In Dilip Vengsarkar, India had the batsman of the series. At Lord's and at Headingley, his hundreds were the platform from which India pushed for victory. In both innings of both Tests he top-scored for India, was rarely forced to play a false stroke, and made every movement elegant. His 126 not out in the first Test was his third in a Test match at Lord's, unique for an overseas player, and his achievements are recognised earlier in the Almanack.

On either side of him, India could bat the experienced Mohinder Amarnath and their exciting new talent, Azharuddin. At Lord's, the former threatened for a time to emulate his performance at Northampton the previous week by scoring a hundred before lunch, and although injury kept him from the second Test, he enjoyed a good tour and a good series. Azharuddin, on his first tour of England, scored most runs for the Indians and was one of three to average more than 50. Fluent and wristy, he looked happiest early on when flicking the ball off his legs or playing off the back foot, but by the tour's end he was revealing a more all-round game. His concentration, apt to oscillate, also improved.

Yet the real strength of India's batting was its depth. In the Test matches there was no tail to speak of. Kapil Dev, with the responsibility of the captaincy and of spearheading the bowling, played his most exciting innings away from the Test arenas. His confidence and his personality flowered after the win at Lord's. Ravi Shastri, his vice-captain, looked to own his reputation as a world-class all-rounder but gave little more than glimpses of it as either batsman or slow left-arm spinner. Mature and experienced for his 24 years, he led the side capably in Kapil's absence.

Both wicket-keepers served India well. Each averaged around 40 and kept to a high standard. Kiran More received the nod for the Tests after the ebullient Chandrakant Pandit had played in the one-day internationals. And when Amarnath was unfit for Headingley, Pandit played as a batsman ahead of Lamba and Patil. An opener in the Srikkanth mould, flashy but impermanent, Raman Lamba batted most attractively in the Indians' victory over Yorkshire at the end of the tour and stated firmly his potential. But Sandeep Patil, a star of the 1982 side, seemed to have lost the confidence that made him such an exciting batsman.

A happy team spirit prevailed throughout the tour, fostered by a genial but firm manager, Raj Singh. Mr Prabhudesai, from the Bombay Cricket Association, was assistant manager. A winning team is usually a happy one, but it was greatly to India's advantage, and to the credit of the players concerned, that during the Indians' tour of Australia, Kapil Dev and Gavaskar had formed a bond of friendship, the outcome of which was to be India's most successful tour of England. – G.W.

INDIAN TOUR RESULTS

Test matches – Played 3: Won 2, Drawn 1.
First-class matches – Played 11: Won 3, Drawn 8.
Wins – England (2), Yorkshire.
Draws – England, Worcestershire, Gloucestershire, Hampshire, Kent, Northamptonshire, Leicestershire, Somerset.
Non first-class matches – Played 10: Won 6, Lost 2, Drawn 1, No result 1. *Wins* – England, Surrey, Ireland, League Cricket Conference, Scotland (2). *Losses* – England, Lavinia Duchess of Norfolk's XI. *Draw* – Oxford & Cambridge Universities. *No result* – Ireland.

TEST MATCH AVERAGES

ENGLAND – BATTING

	T	I	NO	R	HI	100s	Avge
M. W. Gatting ...	3	6	2	293	183*	1	73.25
G. A. Gooch	3	6	0	175	114	1	29.16
D. I. Gower	2	4	0	101	49	0	25.25
D. R. Pringle	3	6	0	136	63	0	22.66
C. W. J. Athey ...	2	4	0	78	38	0	19.50
A. J. Lamb	2	4	0	65	39	0	16.25
J. E. Emburey	3	6	1	74	38	0	14.80
P. H. Edmonds ...	2	4	1	42	18	0	14.00
G. R. Dilley	2	4	1	18	10	0	6.00
B. N. French	2	4	0	22	8	0	5.50

Played in one Test: M. R. Benson 21, 30; P. R. Downton 5, 29; R. M. Ellison 12, 19; N. A. Foster 17, 0; J. K. Lever 0*, 0; N. V. Radford 0, 1; R. T. Robinson 35, 11; W. N. Slack 0, 19; C. L. Smith 6, 28.

* *Signifies not out.*

BOWLING

	O	M	R	W	BB	Avge
D. R. Pringle	126.3	31	302	13	4-73	23.23
P. H. Edmonds	85	27	178	7	4-31	25.42
J. K. Lever	53	9	166	6	4-64	27.66
G. R. Dilley	85.2	19	299	10	4-146	29.90
J. E. Emburey	76.5	28	141	4	2-40	35.25
N. A. Foster	63	18	141	4	3-93	35.25

Also bowled: R. M. Ellison 35-11-80-1; M. W. Gatting 2-0-10-0; G. A. Gooch 13-2-31-1; N. V. Radford 38-3-148-2.

FIELDING

9 – B. N. French; 5 – G. A. Gooch; 4 – J. E. Emburey, D. R. Pringle; 3 – M. W. Gatting; 2 – D. I. Gower, A. J. Lamb, W. N. Slack; 1 – G. R. Dilley, P. R. Downton, P. H. Edmonds.

INDIA – BATTING

	T	I	NO	R	HI	100s	Avge
D. B. Vengsarkar ...	3	6	2	360	126*	2	90.00
K. S. More	3	5	2	156	48	0	52.00
M. Amarnath	2	4	0	172	79	0	43.00
M. Azharuddin	3	6	1	157	64	0	31.40
S. M. Gavaskar	3	6	0	175	54	0	29.16
R. M. H. Binny	3	4	0	81	40	0	20.25
Kapil Dev	3	5	1	81	31	0	20.25
K. Srikkanth	3	6	0	105	31	0	17.50
R. J. Shastri	3	6	1	74	32	0	14.80
Chetan Sharma	2	2	0	11	9	0	5.50
Maninder Singh	3	4	1	10	6	0	3.33

Played in one Test: Madan Lal 20, 22; C. S. Pandit 23, 17.

* Signifies not out.

BOWLING

	O	M	R	W	BB	Avge
Maninder Singh	114.1	41	187	12	4-26	15.58
Chetan Sharma	102.3	·20	300	16	6-58	18.75
R. M. H. Binny	87.2	11	251	12	5-40	20.91
Kapil Dev	128.2	36	306	10	4-52	30.60
R. J. Shastri	80	24	161	5	1-5	32.20

Also bowled: M. Amarnath 11–4–20–0; Madan Lal 20.5–5–48–3.

FIELDING

16 – K. S. More; 3 – M. Amarnath, M. Azharuddin, R. M. H. Binny, S. M. Gavaskar, K. Srikkanth; 2 – Kapil Dev, R. J. Shastri; 1 – Maninder Singh, C. S. Pandit, D. B. Vengsarkar.

INDIAN AVERAGES – FIRST-CLASS MATCHES

BATTING

	M	I	NO	R	HI	100s	Avge
D. B. Vengsarkar ...	8	11	3	536	126*	2	67.00
Kapil Dev	6	9	4	273	115*	1	54.60
M. Azharuddin	10	14	3	596	142	2	54.18
M. Amarnath	9	13	3	473	101	1	47.30
R. Lamba	5	7	0	301	116	1	43.00
C. S. Pandit	6	8	2	252	91	0	42.00
K. S. More	7	8	2	228	52	0	38.00
S. M. Gavaskar	8	12	1	372	136*	1	33.81
R. J. Shastri	8	10	2	220	70*	0	27.50
Chetan Sharma	9	5	2	79	39	0	26.33
K. Srikkanth	9	14	0	344	90	0	24.57
S. M. Patil	6	8	0	188	57	0	23.50
R. M. H. Binny	8	9	1	182	64	0	22.75
N. S. Yadav	7	2	2	22	13*	0	—
M. Prabhakar	6	6	1	77	33	0	15.40
Maninder Singh	8	5	2	16	6*	0	5.33

Played in one match: Madan Lal 20, 22.

* Signifies not out.

BOWLING

	O	M	R	W	BB	Avge
Kapil Dev	186.2	50	461	20	5-35	23.05
Chetan Sharma	221.3	34	736	31	6-58	23.74
Maninder Singh	257.1	71	612	21	4-26	29.14
N. S. Yadav	188.4	39	534	15	6-30	35.60
M. Prabhakar	119	25	353	9	3-42	39.22
R. M. H. Binny	182.2	29	637	16	5-40	39.81
R. J. Shastri	217	57	494	12	3-44	41.16

Also bowled: M. Amarnath 43.2-12-68-4; M. Azharuddin 20-1-68-0; R. Lamba 16-4-49-1; Madan Lal 20.5-5-48-3; C. S. Pandit 2.1-0-14-0; S. M. Patil 38-6-122-2; K. Srikkanth 20-0-91-3.

FIELDING

23 – K. S. More (22 ct, 1 st); 12 – M. Azharuddin; 10 – C. S. Pandit; 7 – M. Amarnath; 6 – R. M. H. Binny; 5 – S. M. Gavaskar, Kapil Dev, K. Srikkanth; 4 – S. M. Patil, R. J. Shastri; 3 – Maninder Singh, D. B. Vengsarkar, N. S. Yadav; 2 – Chetan Sharma; 1 – R. Lamba, M. Prabhakar.

HUNDREDS FOR INDIANS

The following nine three-figure innings were played for the Indians, eight in first-class matches and one in a non first-class match.

M. Azharuddin (2)
142 v Leics., Leicester
100* v Northants, Northampton

D. B. Vengsarkar (2)
126* v England, Lord's (First Test)
102* v England, Leeds (Second Test)

M. Amarnath (1)
101 v Northants, Northampton

S. M. Gavaskar (1)
136* v Somerset, Taunton

Kapil Dev (1)
115* v Hants, Southampton

R. Lamba (1)
116 v Yorks., Scarborough

K. Srikkanth (1)
†113 v Oxford & Cambridge U., Oxford

* *Signifies not out.* † *Not first-class.*

Note: Those matches which follow which were not first-class are signified by the use of a dagger.

†LAVINIA, DUCHESS OF NORFOLK'S XI v INDIANS

At Arundel, May 4. Lavinia, Duchess of Norfolk's XI won by five wickets, rain having reduced their target to 178 off 41 overs. Toss: Lavinia, Duchess of Norfolk's XI.

Indians

K. Srikkanth b Monkhouse	37	Chetan Sharma not out	49
R. Lamba b Monkhouse	14	N. S. Yadav b Igglesden	11
M. Azharuddin lbw b Igglesden	1	Maninder Singh not out	1
M. Amarnath b Monkhouse	6	B 4, l-b 10, w 3	17
S. M. Patil lbw b Knight	31		—
*Kapil Dev b Jesty	16	1/36 2/49 3/62 (9 wkts, 50 overs)	217
†C. S. Pandit st Taylor b Butcher	34	4/63 5/101 6/151	
R. M. H. Binny st Taylor b Knight	0	7/153 8/153 9/201	

Bowling: Igglesden 10-0-39-2; Jesty 10-4-37-1; Monkhouse 10-2-57-3; Knight 10-3-26-2; Butcher 8-1-22-1; Sykes 2-0-22-0.

Lavinia, Duchess of Norfolk's XI

A. R. Butcher c Azharuddin b Maninder	25	G. Monkhouse not out	0
M. A. Lynch b Azharuddin	24		
M. A. Roseberry c Srikkanth b Maninder	3	L-b 6	6
T. E. Jesty b Binny	74		—
D. G. Aslett c Pandit b Kapil Dev	45	1/45 2/51 3/56 (5 wkts, 39 overs)	181
R. D. V. Knight not out	4	4/173 5/177	

J. F. Sykes, D. Wilson, *†R. W. Taylor and A. P. Igglesden did not bat.

Bowling: Kapil Dev 10-1-44-1; Binny 10-1-46-1; Azharuddin 9-1-36-1; Maninder 6-1-21-2; Chetan 4-0-28-0.

Umpires: D. J. Dennis and J. G. Langridge.

WORCESTERSHIRE v INDIANS

At Worcester, May 6, 7, 8. Drawn. Toss: Indians. Rain ruined the prospects of an interesting finish to the touring team's opening first-class fixture by washing out the final day's play. Contrasting half-centuries from Azharuddin, who took 222 minutes over his 76, and Kapil Dev, with 51 off 47 balls against his former county colleagues, pulled the Indians round after D'Oliveira had held three sharp slip catches as they slipped to 106 for five. Srikkanth had made a characteristically lively start, including four boundaries in an over by Ellcock as he and Gavaskar put on 75 in fourteen overs. The highlight of the match, however, was another polished innings from Hick, whose 70 on the opening morning included ten 4s and one 6.

Worcestershire

T. S. Curtis b Shastri	24	– not out	23
D. B. D'Oliveira c Gavaskar b Kapil Dev	12	– not out	27
G. A. Hick c Azharuddin b Maninder	70		
D. N. Patel c Patil b Chetan	14		
*P. A. Neale c More b Chetan	8		
M. J. Weston c More b Prabhakar	49		
†S. J. Rhodes lbw b Chetan	3		
P. J. Newport c Maninder b Prabhakar	4		
N. V. Radford c Patil b Prabhakar	21		
R. K. Illingworth not out	6		
R. M. Ellcock not out	0		
B 4, l-b 2, n-b 13	19	B 2, l-b 2, n-b 2	6
	—		—
1/19 2/92 3/131 4/137 (9 wkts dec.)	230	(no wkt)	56
5/152 6/166 7/193			
8/208 9/229			

Bowling: *First Innings*—Kapil Dev 16-4-34-1; Prabhakar 18-8-42-3; Azharuddin 6-1-19-0; Chetan 19-1-70-3; Shastri 16-7-38-1; Maninder 13-4-21-1. *Second Innings*—Prabhakar 5-2-19-0; Chetan 4-2-13-0; Kapil Dev 4-1-15-0; Maninder 5-3-5-0; Shastri 1-1-0-0.

Indians

S. M. Gavaskar c Patel b Radford 28	M. Prabhakar c Weston b Radford 16
K. Srikkanth c Illingworth b Newport . 43	Chetan Sharma c Rhodes b Ellcock ... 39
R. J. Shastri c D'Oliveira b Ellcock 11	†K. S. More b Patel 1
D. B. Vengsarkar c D'Oliveira	Maninder Singh not out 6
b Newport . 1	L-b 15, n-b 7 22
M. Azharuddin c D'Oliveira b Patel ... 76	
S. M. Patil c D'Oliveira b Ellcock 3	1/75 2/76 3/79 4/98 5/106 297
*Kapil Dev b Illingworth 51	6/193 7/227 8/270 9/275

Bowling: Ellcock 17–1–77–3; Radford 18–3–63–2; Newport 15–2–65–2; Weston 9–1–22–0; Illingworth 13–1–51–1; Patel 2.2–0–4–2.

Umpires: J. Birkenshaw and D. R. Shepherd.

GLOUCESTERSHIRE v INDIANS

At Victoria Cricket Ground, Cheltenham, May 10, 11, 12. Drawn. Toss: Gloucestershire. The return of first-class cricket to the Cheltenham Town ground, after a gap of 49 years, proved a commercial success, but the wretched May weather made playing and watching hard work. And although both captains showed a willingness to open up the game, rain on the third day ruled out all chances of a victory. The slow pitch provided little help for any bowler, and the Indians batted consistently after being put in, the highlight of their first innings being a partnership of 89 in 22 overs between Patil and Vengsarkar. Patil reached his fifty off 59 balls, hitting two 6s and six 4s, Shastri hit Graveney for a couple of 6s, and Pandit also batted brightly. Gloucestershire's reply, with Athey out of touch, was something of a struggle until Bainbridge took control. Curran, in good early-season form, struck some powerful blows, including a 6 and eight 4s, to set up the declaration late on Sunday afternoon. Rain delayed the start on the third day, and with a little over three hours' play possible, the Indians were content with batting practice against spin and medium-pace bowling while Lawrence rested a hip injury.

Indians

K. Srikkanth c Curran b Lawrence	22	– b Sainsbury	31
R. Lamba c Athey b Sainsbury	23	– c Russell b Bainbridge	23
M. Amarnath b Bainbridge	19	– not out	43
D. B. Vengsarkar c Russell b Graveney	74	– (5) not out	21
S. M. Patil b Lawrence	57		
*R. J. Shastri not out	70		
†C. S. Pandit not out	50		
R. M. H. Binny (did not bat)		– (4) c Bainbridge b Athey	0
L-b 1, n-b 6	7	B 4, l-b 10, w 1, n-b 2	17

1/27 2/60 3/88   (5 wkts dec.) 322   1/43 2/84 3/85   (3 wkts dec.) 135
4/177 5/230

Chetan Sharma, M. Prabhakar and N. S. Yadav did not bat.

Bowling: *First Innings*—Lawrence 16–2–59–2; Sainsbury 16–2–53–1; Payne 23–9–66–0; Lloyds 15–2–53–0; Bainbridge 14–1–54–1; Graveney 10–2–36–1. *Second Innings*—Lawrence 5–1–21–0; Sainsbury 15–7–26–1; Athey 11–4–14–1; Payne 12–6–15–0; Bainbridge 12–5–17–1; Lloyds 8–1–18–0; Graveney 8–4–10–0; Stovold 1–1–0–0.

Gloucestershire

A. W. Stovold c Pandit b Prabhakar .. 20	I. R. Payne not out 30
P. W. Romaines c Binny b Patil 23	
C. W. J. Athey c Pandit b Yadav 23	B 1, l-b 4, n-b 8 13
P. Bainbridge c Srikkanth b Yadav 58	
J. W. Lloyds c and b Binny 35	1/42 2/48 3/129 (5 wkts dec.) 271
K. M. Curran not out 69	4/140 5/215

*D. A. Graveney, †R. C. Russell, D. V. Lawrence and G. E. Sainsbury did not bat.

Bowling: Prabhakar 11–3–20–1; Binny 16–0–68–1; Patil 9–0–27–1; Chetan 13–1–45–0; Yadav 20–3–62–2; Shastri 18–3–44–0.

Umpires: H. D. Bird and A. G. T. Whitehead.

†SURREY v INDIANS

At The Oval, May 15. Indians won by five wickets. Toss: Indians. Butcher batted for 48 overs and hit four 6s and seven 4s in his 140.

Surrey

A. R. Butcher lbw b Kapil Dev	140	M. A. Feltham not out 0
N. J. Falkner c Srikkanth b Binny	6	G. Monkhouse c Srikkanth b Kapil Dev 8
A. J. Stewart b Maninder	9	B 1, l-b 1, w 1, n-b 5 8
T. E. Jesty b Chetan	30	
D. M. Ward c Pandit b Chetan	24	1/21 2/48 3/161 (8 wkts, 50 overs) 230
†C. J. Richards c Pandit b Kapil Dev	3	4/215 5/217 6/222
S. T. Clarke b Chetan	2	7/222 8/230

A. H. Gray and *P. I. Pocock did not bat.

Bowling: Kapil Dev 10–1–40–3; Binny 9–1–29–1; Chetan 10–0–30–3; Maninder 10–1–48–1; Shastri 8–0–47–0; Azharuddin 3–0–34–0.

Indians

K. Srikkanth run out	14	*Kapil Dev not out 12
S. M. Gavaskar lbw b Clarke	81	
M. Azharuddin run out	55	L-b 8, w 4, n-b 5 17
D. B. Vengsarkar not out	51	
S. M. Patil c and b Feltham	0	1/51 2/162 3/166 (5 wkts, 47.3 overs) 231
R. J. Shastri c Falkner b Feltham	1	4/166 5/172

†C. S. Pandit, Chetan Sharma, Maninder Singh and R. M. H. Binny did not bat.

Bowling: Gray 10–0–52–0; Clarke 9–0–33–1; Feltham 9.3–0–62–2; Monkhouse 9–0–46–0; Pocock 10–0–30–0.

Umpires: J. A. Jameson and R. A. White.

HAMPSHIRE v INDIANS

At Southampton, May 17, 18, 19. Drawn. Toss: Indians. After the opening day was lost to rain, the Indians chose to bat, but the man to celebrate early on was Bakker, a medium-pace bowler from the Netherlands, who dismissed Gavaskar with his third ball in first-class cricket. The tourists lost five wickets for 113 before Kapil Dev and Binny flourished in a sixth-wicket partnership of 158 in 30 overs. Kapil was the dominant partner, hitting four 6s and eleven 4s to reach the Indians' first century of the tour in 92 balls. After his declaration, Greenidge and Terry made a spirited reply, and Robin Smith also batted well before Nicholas declared 146 behind. This led to Hampshire's being set a target of 279 in 115 minutes plus twenty overs. Although given another good start by Greenidge and Terry, they slipped from 124 for one to 210 for five in their quest for runs and the initiative moved to the Indians.

Indians

S. M. Gavaskar c Maru b Bakker	6	– (6) c Greenidge b Cowley	15
R. Lamba run out	2	– c Parks b Bakker	12
M. Amarnath b Cowley	46	– c C. L. Smith b Nicholas	2
M. Azharuddin c Parks b Andrew	22	– not out	55
S. M. Patil lbw b Cowley	27	– c and b Maru	30
R. M. H. Binny c Parks b Tremlett	64		
*Kapil Dev not out	115	– not out	10
M. Prabhakar not out	6	– (1) c R. A. Smith b Andrew	0
B 3, l-b 3, n-b 3	9	L-b 3, n-b 5	8

1/7 2/9 3/60 4/95   (6 wkts dec.) 297   1/8 2/12 3/29   (5 wkts dec.) 132
5/113 6/271   4/60 5/96

N. S. Yadav, †K. S. More and Maninder Singh did not bat.

Bowling: *First Innings*—Andrew 17–5–50–1; Bakker 16–3–85–1; Tremlett 15–4–48–1; Maru 17–1–51–0; Cowley 14–3–57–2. *Second Innings*—Andrew 7–5–5–1; Bakker 8–3–27–1; Nicholas 7–2–27–1; Maru 9–1–48–1; Cowley 7–1–22–1.

Hampshire

C. G. Greenidge lbw b Prabhakar	33	– b Prabhakar	86
V. P. Terry not out	65	– c Kapil Dev b Prabhakar	57
R. A. Smith not out	44	– (4) c Azharuddin b Prabhakar	13
*M. C. J. Nicholas (did not bat)		– (3) st More b Maninder	30
C. L. Smith (did not bat)		– lbw b Kapil Dev	19
N. G. Cowley (did not bat)		– b Kapil Dev	9
T. M. Tremlett (did not bat)		– not out	4
†R. J. Parks (did not bat)		– not out	1
L-b 3, w 1, n-b 5	9	L-b 8	8

1/57   (1 wkt dec.) 151   1/124 2/171 3/179   (6 wkts) 227
                                       4/194 5/210 6/225

R. J. Maru, S. J. W. Andrew and P. J. Bakker did not bat.

Bowling: *First Innings*—Prabhakar 8–2–25–1; Kapil Dev 6–2–13–0; Binny 12–2–59–0; Maninder 12–2–30–0; Yadav 6–1–21–0. *Second Innings*—Kapil Dev 9–1–27–2; Binny 6–0–32–0; Maninder 18–1–95–1; Prabhakar 15–1–65–3.

Umpires: D. J. Constant and K. E. Palmer.

KENT v INDIANS

At Canterbury, May 21, 22, 23. Drawn. Toss: Kent. Only 80 minutes of play were possible on the first day and Kent, to the annoyance of the visitors, batted throughout the second day. Benson took the opportunity to register a century and batted for 320 minutes, hitting seventeen 4s, as all the Kent batsmen played useful innings. Unfortunately for India, rain prevented any play on the third day.

Kent

M. R. Benson c Amarnath b Yadav	128	†S. A. Marsh not out 21
S. G. Hinks b Chetan	21	G. R. Dilley not out 4
*C. J. Tavaré b Chetan	58	L-b 8, w 2, n-b 4 14
N. R. Taylor c Prabhakar b Maninder	64	
G. R. Cowdrey c Maninder b Chetan	42	1/59 2/180 3/243 4/309 (6 wkts) 378
E. A. E. Baptiste b Maninder	26	5/345 6/359

C. S. Dale, T. M. Alderman and K. B. S. Jarvis did not bat.

Bowling: Prabhakar 23–2–76–0; Chetan 24–5–70–3; Yadav 31–8–76–1; Amarnath 8–4–6–0; Shastri 31–10–81–0; Maninder 21–4–61–2.

Indians

K. Srikkanth, R. Lamba, M. Amarnath, D. B. Vengsarkar, M. Azharuddin, *R. J. Shastri, †C. S. Pandit, Chetan Sharma, M. Prabhakar, N. S. Yadav and Maninder Singh.

Umpires: J. H. Harris and D. O. Oslear.

†ENGLAND v INDIA

First Texaco Trophy Match

At The Oval, May 24. India won by nine wickets. The aptitude of this Indian team for limited-overs cricket was always in evidence from the moment Kapil Dev put England in to bat. Indeed, even before that, in choosing to play their two slow left-armers, Shastri and Maninder Singh, India stole a march on England, who favoured another seam bowler instead of Edmonds on a true pitch. The Indians bowled straight and to a length, while the field-placing and fielding were of the highest class. Binny brought off a breathtaking caught and bowled. England never controlled the game. Put under pressure by Fowler's uncertain start (22 overs for 20), they lost Gooch, Fowler (colliding with Gatting in mid-wicket), Gower to his first ball and Lamb before lunch. Gatting (58 balls) and Pringle (66 balls) were the mainstays, but only Emburey's final flourish took England past 150. India's innings began with a sensation: Srikkanth caught behind off the first ball. Had Dilley, soon after, held Gavaskar's return catch, England might have been in with a chance. Instead, Gavaskar and Azharuddin took charge, despatching the wayward Dilley and Taylor through the on side with wristy flicks and drives. After ten overs India were 50: England, in the field, looked tardy. Emburey bowled as the occasion demanded, but with wickets and overs in hand, the batsmen had no need for risks.

Man of the Match: M. Azharuddin.　　　*Attendance:* 14,811; *receipts* £142,608.

England

G. A. Gooch c Azharuddin b Chetan	30	J. E. Emburey run out		20
G. Fowler run out	20	G. R. Dilley c Pandit b Chetan		6
M. W. Gatting c Kapil Dev b Shastri	27	L. B. Taylor not out		1
*D. I. Gower c Kapil Dev b Shastri	0	B 1, l-b 10, w 3, n-b 2		16
A. J. Lamb c Kapil Dev b Maninder	0			
D. R. Pringle c Azharuddin b Chetan	28	1/54 2/67 3/67	(55 overs)	162
†P. R. Downton c Azharuddin b Binny	4	4/70 5/102 6/115		
R. M. Ellison c and b Binny	10	7/131 8/138 9/151		

Bowling: Kapil Dev 11–1–32–0; Binny 11–2–38–2; Chetan 11–2–25–3; Maninder 11–1–31–1; Shastri 11–0–25–2.

India

K. Srikkanth c Downton b Dilley	0	
S. M. Gavaskar not out	65	
M. Azharuddin not out	83	
L-b 9, w 4, n-b 2	15	

1/0　　　　　　　(1 wkt, 47.2 overs) 163

D. B. Vengsarkar, S. M. Patil, R. J. Shastri, *Kapil Dev, †C. S. Pandit, Chetan Sharma, R. M. H. Binny and Maninder Singh did not bat.

Bowling: Dilley 11–0–53–1; Taylor 7–1–30–0; Pringle 8.2–4–20–0; Ellison 10–1–36–0; Emburey 11–2–15–0.

Umpires: D. R. Shepherd and A. G. T. Whitehead.

†ENGLAND v INDIA

Second Texaco Trophy Match

At Manchester, May 26. England won by five wickets. A marvellous match of fluctuating fortunes and mounting excitement was blessed by welcome sunshine and graced by good cricket throughout. Put in, India lost Gavaskar in Ellison's first over, but Srikkanth (93 balls) was in typically enterprising form. Emburey's two wickets before lunch, and Dilley's dismissal of Patil with the first ball of the afternoon session, swung the pendulum England's way (130 for five), only for Shastri (72 balls) and Kapil Dev (45 balls), helped by a missed stumping and some loose bowling, to steal the initiative with exhilarating and inventive batting, 90 coming off the last ten overs. Their running between the wickets (matched later by that of Gower and Lamb) turned ones into twos, twos into threes as the slow outfield restricted boundaries. Gower, with his lovely strokeplay, underpinned England's reply. There was a setback when Lamb (71 balls) was run out when Gower's straight drive was deflected by the boot of Chetan Sharma, the bowler; and Gower was bowled, pulling across the line, in the 39th over as he tried to improve the run-rate. Pringle, however, again looked untroubled, Gatting was all urgency, and with good running they hauled in a requirement of almost 7 runs an over. Pringle eased the pressure with a straight-driven 4 off Binny, and after two wides by Chetan Sharma in the penultimate over, he drove him through the covers for the winning boundary.

India, by virtue of their faster run-rate in the two matches, won the Texaco Trophy. England, to have taken it, would have had to score their 255 runs in 47.1 overs.

Man of the Match: D. I. Gower.   *Attendance:* 16,202; *receipts* £126,200.

Men of the Series: D. I. Gower (England) and R. J. Shastri (India).

India

K. Srikkanth c Fowler b Emburey	....	67	*Kapil Dev c Downton b Dilley	......	51
S. M. Gavaskar c Gooch b Ellison	....	4	Chetan Sharma not out	....	8
M. Azharuddin c Gower b Edmonds	..	7	B 5, l-b 4, w 2, n-b 3	....	14
D. B. Vengsarkar b Emburey	....	29			
S. M. Patil b Dilley	....	12	1/4 2/49 3/109 (6 wkts, 55 overs)		254
R. J. Shastri not out	....	62	4/117 5/130 6/234		

†C. S. Pandit, R. M. H. Binny and Maninder Singh did not bat.

Bowling: Dilley 11–2–46–2; Ellison 11–0–55–1; Pringle 11–0–49–0; Edmonds 11–1–49–1; Emburey 11–1–46–2.

England

G. A. Gooch lbw b Kapil Dev	....	10	†P. R. Downton not out	....	4
G. Fowler c and b Binny	....	10			
*D. I. Gower b Binny	....	81	L-b 13, w 5	....	18
A. J. Lamb run out	....	45			
M. W. Gatting run out	....	39	1/18 2/27 3/142 (5 wkts, 53.5 overs)		256
D. R. Pringle not out	....	49	4/157 5/242		

P. H. Edmonds, J. E. Emburey, R. M. Ellison and G. R. Dilley did not bat.

Bowling: Kapil Dev 10–0–41–1; Binny 10–1–47–2; Chetan 9.5–0–49–0; Shastri 11–0–37–0; Maninder 11–0–55–0; Azharuddin 2–0–14–0.

Umpires: H. D. Bird and D. J. Constant.

†IRELAND v INDIANS

At Belfast, May 28. No result. Toss: Ireland. The weather having delayed the start by 90 minutes, it brought play to an end when torrential rain fell at lunch.

Indians

K. Srikkanth c Prior b Corlett	0	S. M. Patil not out	15
R. Lamba not out	21	W 1, n-b 3	4
C. S. Pandit b Jones	8		
M. Azharuddin b Garth	9	1/0 2/17 3/30 (3 wkts, 18 overs) 57	

*R. J. Shastri, M. Prabhakar, †K. S. More, R. M. H. Binny, N. S. Yadav and Maninder Singh did not bat.

Bowling: Corlett 5–1–10–1; Jones 7–1–22–1; Garth 4–0–16–1; Halliday 2–0–9–0.

Ireland

S. J. S. Warke, M. A. Masood, D. G. Dennison, M. F. Cohen, J. A. Prior, J. D. Garth, S. C. Corlett, A. McBrine, †P. B. Jackson, *M. Halliday and E. Jones.

Umpires: H. J. Henderson and P. Lunney.

†IRELAND v INDIANS

At Downpatrick, May 29. Indians won by 9 runs. Toss: Ireland.

Indians

†C. S. Pandit st Jackson b McBrine	44	M. Prabhakar not out	7
R. Lamba c Jackson b Jones	3	N. S. Yadav not out	2
M. Azharuddin c Corlett b Garth	11	B 5, l-b 3, w 3	11
S. M. Patil st Jackson b Halliday	61		
D. B. Vengsarkar c Cohen b Garth	46	1/19 2/32 3/75 (7 wkts, 55 overs) 210	
*R. J. Shastri b Corlett	7	4/144 5/158	
Chetan Sharma b Corlett	18	6/182 7/206	

K. S. More and Maninder Singh did not bat.

Bowling: Corlett 11–1–38–2; Jones 11–1–26–1; Garth 9–2–35–2; McBrine 11–2–45–1; Halliday 11–1–34–1; Prior 2–0–24–0.

Ireland

M. A. Masood b Maninder	40	S. C. Corlett not out	10
S. J. S. Warke st More b Yadav	46	A. McBrine not out	3
D. G. Dennison c Vengsarkar b Shastri	12	L-b 9, w 3, n-b 3	15
M. F. Cohen c and b Chetan	25		
J. A. Prior b Shastri	9	1/75 2/97 3/106 (6 wkts, 55 overs) 201	
J. D. Garth c Maninder b Prabhakar	41	4/117 5/161 6/196	

†P. B. Jackson, *M. Halliday and E. Jones did not bat.

Bowling: Chetan 10–2–38–1; Prabhakar 6–1–22–1; Patil 7–0–35–0; Yadav 11–3–22–1; Maninder 11–2–43–1; Shastri 10–2–32–2.

Umpires: M. A. C. Moore and F. O'Brien.

NORTHAMPTONSHIRE v INDIANS

At Northampton, May 31, June 1, 2. Drawn. Toss: Indians. The touring team, desperately short of preparation for the first Test, made up for lost time after rain had allowed only eight deliveries to be bowled on the first day. But those eight did not pass without incident, the last of them accounting for Gavaskar to give Smith, a nineteen-year-old left-arm fast bowler from County Durham, a prize wicket with his second ball in first-class cricket. On Sunday, Amarnath cruised to a hundred before lunch with a 6 and seventeen 4s, while Azharuddin's stay lasted for 177 minutes, Kapil Dev declaring as soon as he reached three figures. The Indian captain then wrecked the county's innings with a spell of high-class new-ball bowling which included four wickets in eight balls without conceding a run. Bailey and Walker, with a career-best 40 not out, averted a total disaster, but Northamptonshire followed on 183 behind. Despite two early dismissals, they found the going easier as Kapil opted to give his other bowlers practice, and the match was comfortably saved thanks to Boyd-Moss, Capel and a stylish contribution from Wild late on the final afternoon.

Indians

S. M. Gavaskar c Waterton b Smith ...	5	*Kapil Dev not out	16
K. Srikkanth c Waterton b Capel	19		
M. Amarnath c Waterton b Walker ...	101	B 4, l-b 2, n-b 1	7
D. B. Vengsarkar st Waterton b Cook .	20		
M. Azharuddin not out	100	1/7 2/56 3/117	(5 wkts dec.) 301
R. M. H. Binny c Bailey b Wild	33	4/174 5/268	

Chetan Sharma, †K. S. More, N. S. Yadav and Maninder Singh did not bat.

Bowling: Walker 15–2–49–1; Smith 17–4–38–1; Capel 10–3–34–1; Cook 20–2–89–1; Wild 11–2–42–1; Kapur 10–2–30–0; Boyd-Moss 1.3–0–13–0.

Northamptonshire

A. C. Storie c More b Binny	1	– lbw b Kapil Dev	1
R. J. Bailey c More b Chetan	37	– c Chetan b Binny	14
R. J. Boyd-Moss c More b Kapil Dev	0	– c Kapil Dev b Maninder	79
A. J. Lamb c More b Kapil Dev	0	– b Kapil Dev	33
D. J. Capel lbw b Kapil Dev	0	– not out	67
D. J. Wild b Kapil Dev	0	– not out	41
*R. A. Harper lbw b Kapil Dev	12		
†S. N. V. Waterton c Kapil Dev b Chetan ...	0		
N. G. B. Cook c Vengsarkar b Chetan	5		
A. Walker not out	40		
G. Smith b Amarnath	4		
L-b 6, w 1, n-b 12	19	W 2, n-b 2	4

1/9 2/12 3/18 4/18 5/18	118	1/4 2/21 3/90 4/166 (4 wkts) 239
6/48 7/61 8/62 9/96		

Bowling: *First Innings*—Kapil Dev 13–4–35–5; Binny 11–4–44–1; Chetan 8–0–27–3; Amarnath 2.2–0–2–1; Yadav 1–0–4–0. *Second Innings*—Kapil Dev 10–2–31–2; Binny 11–2–52–1; Chetan 10–2–61–0; Maninder 19–6–48–1; Yadav 16–2–45–0; Amarnath 1–0–1–0; Srikkanth 1–0–1–0.

Umpires: C. Cook and B. J. Meyer.

ENGLAND v INDIA

First Cornhill Test

At Lord's, June 5, 6, 7, 9, 10. India won by five wickets, their first Test victory at Lord's and only their second in 33 Tests in England. It was, in addition, England's sixth successive defeat since regaining the Ashes so comprehensively the previous season, and at the end of the match Gower was informed by the chairman of selectors, Mr P. B. H. May, that he had been relieved of the captaincy. Gatting, the vice-captain, was promoted to lead England in the next two Tests.

Gower's tenure began to look insecure on the third afternoon when, with Vengsarkar suffering from cramp in his left arm, India's last two wickets put on 77 runs in 25 overs. So ebbed England's prospects of victory. And when India's bowlers, Kapil Dev and Maninder Singh especially, exposed all manner of deficiencies in England's batting on the fourth day, Gower's fate was sealed. England could not even rely on the weather: when they batted, the cloud came down to encourage movement through the air and off the seam; when India batted, the cloud was high and the sun shone in approval of their batsmen's technique.

Yet by the end of the first day, England at 245 for five had overcome the disadvantage of being asked to bat on an overcast morning and the loss after lunch of three leading batsmen in the space of eleven balls from Chetan Sharma: Gower edging a lazy pull, Gatting bowled through a slow-closing gate, and Lamb well held low down at short leg as he pushed forward. Gooch, however, always looked in control. His square- and on-drives boomed with authority, and while his sixth Test hundred (316 minutes, 255 balls) was not his most commanding, it suited the circumstances. So, too, did Pringle's first fifty in a Test match. The Essex pair had added 147 when, five minutes before the close, Gooch was bowled by Chetan Sharma's nip-backer. His 114, from 280 balls, contained a 6 and twelve 4s.

Friday produced just 132 runs from 83 overs, light rain having delayed the start and interrupted the afternoon. Yet it was not a dull day. India's fielding was sharp, their bowling was nagging to a degree on an off-stump line, and they took all the honours in the first session as the English batsmen progressed to 271 for eight at lunch. Forty minutes later England were all out, having scored 49 from their last 33 overs. India began purposefully and were 83 for the loss of Srikkanth by stumps, Dilley and Ellison both having passed the bat a number of times and Pringle having bowled tidily.

Gavaskar looked determined to score the Test hundred that had eluded him at Lord's, so it came as a surprise when, in the second over of Saturday morning, he played at a ball well wide of him and was caught at third slip. Vengsarkar settled in and Amarnath set pulses racing with 14 from one over by Dilley. However, Emburey, beginning with four successive maiden overs, put on a brake and Edmonds reaped the reward when Amarnath tried to break free of the spinners' hold, only to find the tall figure of Pringle at mid-on.

The new ball, taken early in the afternoon, brought a flurry of runs from Azharuddin before Dilley cut short his bravura with a smart return catch off a back-foot drive. The collapse that followed might have stranded Vengsarkar short of his hundred. He was 81 when Pringle knocked over Chetan Sharma's off stump. Instead, More announced himself as a batsman of higher ranking than ten, Maninder (coming in when Vengsarkar was 95) proved equal to the occasion, and Vengsarkar, with a push for a single, became the first overseas batsman to score three hundreds in Test matches at Lord's. G. Boycott, D. C. S. Compton, J. H. Edrich, J. B. Hobbs and L. Hutton had done so for England. Off 170 balls in 266 minutes, his tenth Test century was one of classical elegance, charm and responsibility. Of the sixteen 4s in his unbeaten 126 (213 balls, 326 minutes) many came from handsome drives.

England had four overs before the close in which they scored 8 without loss. At 5.54 on Monday evening they were all out for 180, leaving India needing 134 to win on the last day. Lamb and Gatting made the most of the attacking fields which Kapil Dev maintained throughout the day, but only Downton showed the technique and the judgement that was required if England were to avoid defeat. Ellison might have been better attacking Maninder than defending when runs were just as important as minutes to England, but India's young left-arm spinner was able to bowl to a length and with a maturity which belied his twenty years. His figures – three for 9 from 20.4 overs – tell their own story.

In truth, though, England had been fighting off their heels from the morning session when Kapil Dev removed Gooch, Robinson and Gower for 1 run in nineteen balls. The next afternoon the Indian captain set the seal on a momentous match for his country by hitting Edmonds for 18 in one over; three 4s and the 6 over mid-wicket with which the game was won. There were other candidates for the Man of the Match award but it was appropriate that it went to Kapil Dev, for whom it was his first victory in 21 Tests as captain of India. There was no way, given India's performance at Lord's, that it would be his last.

The attendance for the match was 57,509, with takings of £455,184. – G.W.

England

G. A. Gooch b Chetan	114	– lbw b Kapil Dev	8
R. T. Robinson c Azharuddin b Maninder	35	– c Amarnath b Kapil Dev	11
*D. I. Gower c More b Chetan	18	– lbw b Kapil Dev	8
M. W. Gatting b Chetan	0	– b Chetan	40
A. J. Lamb c Srikkanth b Chetan	6	– c More b Shastri	39
D. R. Pringle b Binny	63	– c More b Kapil Dev	6
J. E. Emburey c Amarnath b Kapil Dev	7	– (9) c and b Maninder	1
†P. R. Downton lbw b Chetan	5	– (7) c Shastri b Maninder	29
R. M. Ellison c Kapil Dev b Binny	12	– (8) c More b Binny	19
G. R. Dilley c More b Binny	4	– not out	2
P. H. Edmonds not out	7	– c Binny b Maninder	7
L-b 15, w 1, n-b 7	23	L-b 6, w 1, n-b 3	10

1/66 2/92 3/92 4/98 5/245	294	1/18 2/23 3/35 4/108 5/113	180
6/264 7/269 8/271 9/287		6/121 7/164 8/170 9/170

Bowling: *First Innings*—Kapil Dev 31–8–67–1; Binny 18.2–4–55–3; Chetan 32–10–64–5; Maninder 30–15–45–1; Amarnath 7–1–18–0; Shastri 10–3–30–0. *Second Innings*—Kapil Dev 22–7–52–4; Chetan 17–4–48–1; Binny 15–3–44–1; Shastri 20–8–21–1; Maninder 20.4–12–9–3; Amarnath 2–2–0–0.

India

S. M. Gavaskar c Emburey b Dilley	34	– c Downton b Dilley	22
K. Srikkanth c Gatting b Dilley	20	– c Gooch b Dilley	0
M. Amarnath c Pringle b Edmonds	69	– lbw b Pringle	8
D. B. Vengsarkar not out	126	– b Edmonds	33
M. Azharuddin c and b Dilley	33	– run out	14
R. J. Shastri c Edmonds b Dilley	1	– not out	20
R. M. H. Binny lbw b Pringle	9		
*Kapil Dev c Lamb b Ellison	1	– (7) not out	23
Chetan Sharma b Pringle	2		
†K. S. More lbw b Pringle	25		
Maninder Singh c Lamb b Emburey	6		
L-b 5, w 1, n-b 9	15	B 1, l-b 9, w 1, n-b 5	16

1/31 2/90 3/161 4/232 5/238   341   1/10 2/31 3/76 4/78   (5 wkts) 136
6/252 7/253 8/264 9/303   5/110

Bowling: *First Innings*—Dilley 34–7–146–4; Ellison 29–11–63–1; Emburey 27–13–28–1; Edmonds 22–7–41–1; Pringle 25–7–58–3. *Second Innings*—Dilley 10–3–28–2; Ellison 6–0–17–0; Pringle 15–5–30–1; Edmonds 11–2–51–1.

Umpires: K. E. Palmer and D. R. Shepherd.

†OXFORD & CAMBRIDGE UNIVERSITIES v INDIANS

At Oxford, June 12, 13. Drawn. Toss: Oxford & Cambridge Universities.

Indians

R. Lamba c Thorne b Rutnagur	77	– (5) lbw b Scott	2
K. Srikkanth b Davidson	113		
M. Azharuddin b Davidson	74		
S. M. Patil st Brown b Golding	60		
*Kapil Dev not out	6	– (3) c Tooley b Davidson	25
†C. S. Pandit not out	5	– (4) not out	51
R. M. H. Binny (did not bat)		– (1) c Rutnagur b Davidson	35
M. Prabhakar (did not bat)		– (2) b Davidson	10
K. S. More (did not bat)		– (6) not out	18
B 2, l-b 9, w 1, n-b 1	13	L-b 2, w 1	3

1/180 2/208 3/322 4/348   (4 wkts dec.) 348   1/34 2/59 3/80   (4 wkts dec.) 144
4/87

N. S. Yadav and Maninder Singh did not bat.

Bowling: *First Innings*—Davidson 22–1–81–2; Scott 12–1–71–0; Rutnagur 13–1–86–1; Golding 17–0–74–1; Thorne 7–1–25–0. *Second Innings*—Davidson 11–2–52–3; Thorne 7–1–41–0; Scott 6–1–34–1; Rutnagur 4–0–6–0; Golding 1.4–1–9–0.

Oxford & Cambridge Universities

D. A. Hagan c Lamba b Maninder	34	– c Kapil Dev b Prabhakar	2
P. A. C. Bail c and b Maninder	52	– c Kapil Dev b Prabhakar	16
D. J. Fell lbw b Maninder	0	– not out	25
C. D. M. Tooley c Srikkanth b Yadav	45	– c Kapil Dev b Prabhakar	1
*D. A. Thorne c Azharuddin b Yadav	52	– c Pandit b Maninder	3
D. G. Price not out	23	– retired hurt	5
R. S. Rutnagur run out	3	– b Yadav	3
A. K. Golding lbw b Yadav	1	– c More b Srikkanth	2
†A. D. Brown c Srikkanth b Maninder	5	– not out	0
L-b 2, n-b 6	8	B 1, l-b 3, n-b 3	7

1/80 2/82 3/98 4/171   (8 wkts dec.) 223   1/11 2/21 3/24   (6 wkts) 64
5/200 6/212 7/216 8/223   4/27 5/61 6/64

A. M. G. Scott and J. E. Davidson did not bat.

Bowling: *First Innings*—Prabhakar 10–2–36–0; Binny 9–0–53–0; Lamba 3–0–16–0; Yadav 21–2–55–3; Maninder 19–7–52–4; Kapil Dev 1–0–6–0; Srikkanth 1–0–3–0. *Second Innings*—Kapil Dev 9–7–3–0; Prabhakar 13–3–43–3; Maninder 8–5–10–1; Yadav 4–1–4–1; Srikkanth 1–1–0–1.

Umpires: H. J. Rhodes and R. A. White.

LEICESTERSHIRE v INDIANS

At Leicester, June 14, 15, 16. Drawn. Toss: Leicestershire. An entertaining two days were overshadowed by an incident involving the Indian seam bowler, Chetan Sharma, who became the subject of a police enquiry after an autograph-seeking spectator complained of being punched in the face as the players left the field following Shastri's declaration on Sunday afternoon. No action was subsequently taken. Leicestershire were sustained by Benjamin's 95 not out, his highest score, in two and a half hours: he hit one 6 and thirteen 4s. Azharuddin, having reached his hundred in almost four hours, batted for another hour and a half to put the Indians ahead, his fluent strokeplay bringing him one 6 and fourteen 4s. The declaration on his dismissal soon after tea opened the way for an exciting finish, but Leicestershire, 59 without loss at the close, batted much too slowly on the third morning. When Willey's token declaration set the touring side to score 242 in 68 minutes and twenty overs, only the effervescent Srikkanth, with thirteen boundaries including four 4s in one over off DeFreitas, kept the spectators' interest alive.

Leicestershire

L. Potter c Pandit b Chetan	12	– c Pandit b Shastri	65
R. A. Cobb c Vengsarkar b Prabhakar	0	– c Pandit b Srikkanth	80
I. P. Butcher c Shastri b Amarnath	26	– b Yadav	14
J. J. Whitaker c Gavaskar b Amarnath	18	– not out	47
T. J. Boon b Chetan	32	– not out	22
*P. Willey c Pandit b Chetan	12		
P. B. Clift c Yadav b Chetan	16		
P. A. J. DeFreitas c Patil b Amarnath	5		
W. K. M. Benjamin not out	95		
J. P. Agnew c Amarnath b Shastri	18		
†P. Gill c Azharuddin b Shastri	8		
B 5, l-b 4, n-b 18	27	B 4, l-b 3, n-b 9	16

1/5 2/19 3/46 4/78 5/111   269   1/113 2/156   (3 wkts dec.) 244
6/116 7/131 8/146 9/205   3/179

Bowling: *First Innings*—Chetan 22–1–89–4; Prabhakar 10–1–32–1; Amarnath 21–4–39–3; Yadav 7–2–18–0; Shastri 16.4–1–56–2; Patil 7–1–26–0. *Second Innings*—Prabhakar 15–2–36–0; Patil 14–3–50–0; Azharuddin 3–0–8–0; Yadav 34–8–68–1; Shastri 18–3–27–1; Srikkanth 8–0–35–1; Chetan 4–1–13–0.

Indians

S. M. Gavaskar c Benjamin b DeFreitas	7		
†C. S. Pandit b Agnew	0 – (3) run out		3
M. Azharuddin c Butcher b Clift	142		
D. B. Vengsarkar c Willey b Benjamin	60		
K. Srikkanth b Benjamin	0 – (1) c Whitaker b Willey		90
M. Amarnath retired hurt	10		
S. M. Patil b Clift	7 – (4) b Clift		6
*R. J. Shastri c Gill b Clift	1		
M. Prabhakar b Clift	8 – (2) b Clift		33
Chetan Sharma not out	22 – (5) not out		7
L-b 7, n-b 8	15	B 1, l-b 5	6

1/1 2/19 3/164 4/164   (8 wkts dec.) 272   1/108 2/120 3/135   (4 wkts) 145
5/228 6/232 7/243 8/272   4/145

N. S. Yadav did not bat.

Bowling: *First Innings*—Agnew 20-0-83-1; DeFreitas 19-4-52-1; Clift 15.1-3-54-4; Benjamin 14-4-35-2; Willey 10-1-41-0. *Second Innings*—Agnew 8-0-38-0; DeFreitas 5-1-30-0; Benjamin 5-1-26-0; Clift 8-1-40-2; Willey 0.3-0-5-1.

Umpires: D. G. L. Evans and P. B. Wight.

ENGLAND v INDIA

Second Cornhill Test

At Leeds, June 19, 20, 21, 23. India won by 279 runs. Hammonds Sauce Works Band, playing in front of the Football Stand, was the indisputable success for England during a match which India won by a resounding margin in under three and a half days. This victory, their first in England outside London, gave them a decisive 2-0 lead in the three-match series. Summing up England's performance, their chairman of selectors said: "We were outplayed in every department."

It could be argued that there were extenuating circumstances. For the first time since 1978, England took the field without either Botham, who was suspended, or Gower, who, after practising on the Wednesday, withdrew to nurse a shoulder injury. Furthermore, Gooch, England's third player with pretensions to world class, had an unlucky but poor match. Whatever the reason, England, a summer tapestry in 1985, was ragged around the edges and coming apart at the seams one year later. It was an unhappy start to Gatting's term as captain.

First use of a quickly deteriorating pitch was to prove vital, and India won the toss. Lever, recalled at the age of 37 as the swing and seam expert to take advantage of Headingley's known idiosyncracies, made a surprisingly nervous start, conceding 18 runs in his first two overs, and then 31 in seven. Pringle's steadying influence was needed somewhat sooner than his captain might have anticipated. By the time Srikkanth paid his usual tax on impetuosity, India were 64 off twenty overs. To dismiss Gavaskar, who entered the match with a Test average of 51, was a bonus. Shastri and Vengsarkar added 53 in nineteen overs, and the latter went on to demonstrate his dominance of this series. Fifth out at 203, for 61, he batted for seven minutes over three hours while each partner in turn struggled at the other end.

India, resuming at 235 for eight, batted for eleven overs and two balls on the second morning, the late-order batsmen frustrating England's bowlers while adding 37 more runs. England's batsmen were similarly inconvenienced, falling immediately into trouble. With Chetan Sharma injured, India had sent for Madan Lal, the professional for Ashton in the Central Lancashire League, and the veteran of 38 Tests quickly demonstrated his mastery and experience of English conditions, providing support for Kapil Dev and inspiration for Binny. Slack was bowled second ball, Gooch was caught at gully off a ball from Kapil that kicked and Smith groped ineffectively at one that came back considerably. Either side of lunch (41 for four), Gatting and Lamb were the first victims in a spell by Binny that brought him four wickets for 17 in 37 balls. When Athey, surprisingly low at number six, turned Binny for 2 runs the crowd cheered an England score of 74 for eight, relieved that the follow-on figure had been passed.

India's first-innings lead of 170 looked unbeatable until England's bowlers learned to enlist the unpredictable surface. India's first three wickets fell for 29 runs and they were 70 for five at the close as the seam attack revelled, Lever having figures of three for 9 in 28 balls. Already, however, Vengsarkar had demonstrated, on the ground that nurtured Sutcliffe, Hutton and Boycott, the art of batting on a bad pitch. He returned on the Saturday to progress from 33 to 102 not out and prompt his tailenders into a caning of a dispirited attack. As at Lord's, he reached his hundred in the company of Maninder Singh, the number eleven batsman. Gatting almost certainly must have wished that he could have exchanged one of his six batsmen for Edmonds, who had been omitted from England's squad along with Ellison.

Needing to score 408 to win, more than any side had achieved, England sought only survival. But with half the playing time remaining when the innings began, even that hope grew forlorn as six wickets fell for 90 runs in the 41.1 overs before the close on Saturday evening. The Indian spinners found that the pitch was adding turn to its erratic bounce, and on Monday morning, only another 75 minutes were required for England's humiliation to be completed, all out in 63.3 overs for a total of 128. In an innings of characteristic defiance, Gatting remained 31 not out.

The respective wicket-keepers, French, in his first Test, and More, in his second, made an excellent impression; as indeed did India's other wicket-keeper, Pandit, who was playing as a batsman in place of the injured Amarnath. The same, regretfully, can not be said of those spectators who tried to recreate the "human wave" effect by synchronised waving of the arms when Azharuddin was batting on Friday afternoon. Their mindless imitation of the football crowds at the World Cup in Mexico did not help the batsman's concentration and left Headingley's reputation as a ground for cricket lovers as much in tatters as the reputation of the England team.

The attendance on the first day was disappointingly small and for the match amounted to 33,850 with takings of £229,004. Vengsarkar was named Man of the Match. – D.H.

India

S. M. Gavaskar c French b Pringle	35	– c French b Lever	1
K. Srikkanth c Emburey b Pringle	31	– b Dilley	8
R. J. Shastri c Pringle b Dilley	32	– lbw b Lever	3
D. B. Vengsarkar c French b Lever	61	– not out	102
M. Azharuddin lbw b Gooch	15	– lbw b Lever	2
C. S. Pandit c Emburey b Pringle	23	– b Pringle	17
*Kapil Dev lbw b Lever	0	– (8) c Gatting b Lever	31
R. M. H. Binny c Slack b Emburey	6	– (10) lbw b Pringle	26
Madan Lal c Gooch b Dilley	20	– run out	22
†K. S. More not out	36	– (7) c Slack b Pringle	16
Maninder Singh c Gooch b Dilley	3	– c Gatting b Pringle	1
L-b 5, n-b 5	10	B 4, l-b 4	8

1/64 2/75 3/128 4/163 5/203   272   1/9 2/9 3/29 4/35 5/70   237
6/203 7/211 8/213 9/267   6/102 7/137 8/173 9/233

Bowling: *First Innings*—Dilley 24.2–7–54–3; Lever 30–4–102–2; Pringle 27–6–47–3; Emburey 17–4–45–1; Gooch 6–0–19–1. *Second Innings*—Dilley 17–2–71–1; Lever 23–5–64–4; Pringle 22.3–6–73–4; Emburey 7–3–9–0; Gooch 7–2–12–0.

England

G. A. Gooch c Binny b Kapil Dev	8	– c Srikkanth b Kapil Dev	5
W. N. Slack b Madan Lal	0	– c Gavaskar b Binny	19
C. L. Smith b Madan Lal	6	– c More b Shastri	28
A. J. Lamb c Pandit b Binny	10	– c More b Binny	10
*M. W. Gatting c More b Binny	13	– not out	31
C. W. J. Athey c More b Madan Lal	32	– c More b Maninder	8
D. R. Pringle c Srikkanth b Binny	8	– (8) lbw b Maninder	8
J. E. Emburey c Kapil Dev b Binny	0	– (9) c Azharuddin b Kapil Dev	1
†B. N. French b Binny	8	– (10) c Vengsarkar b Maninder	5
G. R. Dilley b Shastri	10	– (11) run out	2
J. K. Lever not out	0	– (7) c More b Maninder	0
B 1, l-b 2, n-b 4	7	L-b 9, n-b 2	11

1/4 2/14 3/14 4/38 5/41   102   1/12 2/46 3/63 4/77 5/90   128
6/63 7/63 8/71 9/100   6/90 7/101 8/104 9/109

Bowling: *First Innings*—Kapil Dev 18–7–36–1; Madan Lal 11.1–3–18–3; Binny 13–1–40–5; Shastri 3–1–5–1. *Second Innings*—Kapil Dev 19.2–7–24–2; Madan Lal 9.4–2–30–0; Maninder 16.3–6–26–4; Binny 8–1–18–2; Shastri 10–3–21–1.

Umpires: J. Birkenshaw and D. J. Constant.

†LEAGUE CRICKET CONFERENCE v INDIANS

At Chester-le-Street, June 26. Indians won by 72 runs. Toss: League Cricket Conference. Hooper, the Guyana and Young West Indies batsman, who was the professional for Werneth, hit 50 of his 75 in boundaries (three 6s, eight 4s). Yadav bowled one over more than the maximum eleven permitted by the rules for a 55-overs match.

Indians

K. Srikkanth c Hooper b Merrick 24	M. Prabhakar c Hooper b Davis 6
R. Lamba c Haynes b Davis 9	N. S. Yadav not out 2
M. Amarnath c Hooper b Johnson 13	
S. M. Patil c Haynes b Johnson 61	B 7, w 4, n-b 11 22
M. Azharuddin c Merrick b Haynes .. 45	
D. B. Vengsarkar b Haynes 71	1/38 2/38 3/71 (8 wkts, 55 overs) 321
*R. J. Shastri b Davis 40	4/144 5/236 6/242
†C. S. Pandit not out 28	7/289 8/308

Maninder Singh did not bat.

Bowling: Davis 11–0–58–3; Merrick 10–3–56–1; Johnson 11–0–55–2; Nevins 11–1–56–0; Haynes 10–0–67–2; Knowles 2–0–22–0.

League Cricket Conference

J. Foster c Maninder b Patil 61	W. W. Davis c Amarnath b Srikkanth . 20
M. Bowyer lbw b Azharuddin 6	D. L. Nevins not out 0
C. L. Hooper c Maninder b Azharuddin 75	B 4, l-b 10, w 5, n-b 8 27
R. C. Haynes c Amarnath b Patil 20	
*B. Knowles lbw b Patil 3	1/21 2/157 3/164 (7 wkts, 55 overs) 249
P. G. Wood not out 22	4/178 5/189
†D. Borthwick c Azharuddin b Shastri . 15	6/224 7/244

T. A. Merrick and G. Johnson did not bat.

Bowling: Prabhakar 6–1–35–0; Lamba 2–0–14–0; Azharuddin 8–1–29–2; Maninder 11–3–19–0; Yadav 12–2–42–0; Patil 11–1–50–3; Shastri 3–0–23–1; Srikkanth 2–0–23–1.

Umpires: T. Fiddes and J. H. Lowery.

SOMERSET v INDIANS

At Taunton, June 28, 29, 30. Drawn. Toss: Somerset. In great heat and on a pitch taking turn, Somerset collapsed against Yadav, whose off-spin brought him career-best figures, and Shastri. Both bowlers were supported by excellent close-catching, especially by Azharuddin at silly point. After Shastri and Lamba had provided a lively opening of 130 in 25 overs, Gavaskar, who played for Somerset in 1980, steadily built his hundred, ending with four 6s and fourteen 4s from 78 overs. Rain shortened the second day and took 65 minutes from the third, when Somerset were soon in trouble at 45 for two. However, Felton, who used up 50 overs for his first 31 and was joined by Harden in a vital third-wicket stand of 64 in 30 overs, steadied them. He then opened up enterprisingly to have two 6s and eleven 4s in his 104 from 204 balls. Although Somerset were still 48 behind, India declined to take the extra half hour.

Somerset

N. A. Felton c Pandit b Binny	28	– c and b Patil	104
*P. M. Roebuck c Azharuddin b Yadav	23	– c Pandit b Chetan	4
J. J. E. Hardy c Azharuddin b Shastri	11	– c Shastri b Yadav	34
R. J. Harden c Pandit b Yadav	4	– run out	36
R. J. Bartlett c Azharuddin b Yadav	0	– c Yadav b Chetan	19
V. J. Marks c Azharuddin b Yadav	19	– (7) not out	0
J. C. M. Atkinson c Azharuddin b Shastri	10	– (6) not out	12
†T. Gard c Lamba b Yadav	0		
G. V. Palmer c Binny b Yadav	2		
N. S. Taylor not out	17		
R. V. J. Coombs b Shastri	1		
B 1, l-b 8, w 1, n-b 3	13	B 1, n-b 3	4

1/52 2/67 3/71 4/72 5/92 128   1/4 2/45 3/109   (5 wkts) 213
6/107 7/107 8/109 9/111   4/182 5/212

Bowling: *First Innings*—Chetan 4–1–11–0; Prabhakar 6–2–15–0; Binny 8–3–19–1; Shastri 19.2–3–44–3; Yadav 14–4–30–6. *Second Innings*—Prabhakar 8–2–23–0; Chetan 10–0–31–2; Yadav 24–9–70–1; Shastri 17–5–43–0; Binny 5–2–14–0; Patil 8–2–19–1; Lamba 3–0–12–0.

Indians

*R. J. Shastri c Roebuck b Palmer	64	M. Prabhakar c Bartlett b Atkinson	14
R. Lamba c Gard b Atkinson	69	N. S. Yadav not out	13
M. Amarnath lbw b Taylor	33		
S. M. Patil st Gard b Harden	8	B 2, l-b 4, w 5, n-b 2	13
S. M. Gavaskar not out	136		
M. Azharuddin b Marks	27	1/130 2/142 3/161 (8 wkts dec.) 389
†C. S. Pandit c Roebuck b Harden	12	4/216 5/289 6/312
R. M. H. Binny b Marks	0	7/313 8/358

Chetan Sharma did not bat.

Bowling: Taylor 26–3–81–1; Atkinson 24–6–80–2; Coombs 9–2–37–0; Marks 21–5–71–2; Palmer 18–2–59–1; Harden 15–2–55–2.

Umpires: J. W. Holder and R. Palmer.

ENGLAND v INDIA

Third Cornhill Test

At Birmingham, July 3, 4, 5, 7, 8. Drawn. A stoppage of 48 minutes for bad light and rain after tea on the fifth day tantalisingly denied both sides the opportunity of winning a match which fluctuated throughout on a dry, brown pitch. Needing 236 to register a record third successive victory over England, who would then have equalled their worst losing streak of eight successive Tests, established in 1921, India ended 62 runs short with five wickets in hand.

In deciding to revert to five specialist batsmen, England made five changes, including one enforced by Dilley's reporting unfit on the morning of the game with a tooth abscess. Benson and Radford made their Test débuts, while Foster, Gower, and Edmonds returned. The changes brought the number of players used by England in the three-match series to nineteen, compared with thirteen by India, who reverted to the side which won at Lord's, Amarnath and Chetan Sharma having recovered after injury.

Gatting won the toss and batted, but superb swing bowling by Kapil Dev sent back Gooch and Athey in seven balls without a run on the board. Although Gower hit a brilliant 49 off 81 deliveries in 112 minutes, when he was out at 88, Gatting was the last front-line batsman left. Moreover, Gatting was dependent on a brittle-looking middle-lower order to extract maximum benefit from first use of a wearing pitch. Yet the next four partnerships added 96, 94, 49 and 40 with the captain playing an unbeaten innings of 183 in 387 minutes. Gatting faced 294 balls and hit two 6s and twenty 4s in a demonstration of technique and character which forced Kapil Dev into a less positive approach than he had shown in the previous two Tests.

England's total of 390 should have ensured a crucial first-innings lead on a pitch which was unreliable in bounce and, although slow in pace, became more helpful to seam and spin bowlers alike as the game progressed. Such a pitch was hardly satisfactory for a five-day game. But Foster alone, among a disappointing trio of faster bowlers, threatened consistently to take wickets. This, combined with a surprising under-use of Emburey, who did not bowl on the third day until the 62nd over, allowed India also to reach 390. It was the first time both innings had finished level in a Test match since New Zealand and Pakistan, 402 each at Auckland, and West Indies and Australia, 428 each at Kingston, accomplished the feat in February 1973. Amarnath and Azharuddin, with 79 and 64 respectively, came nearest to a major innings, but it was India's batting depth which denied England any advantage after three days, other than that of bowling last.

In England's second innings, their first five batsmen all established themselves, but none played a decisive innings. Hostile seam bowling by Chetan Sharma more than compensated for Kapil's absence with a back injury by inducing a mid-innings collapse which reduced the home side from 152 for two to 190 for seven in fifteen overs. His six wickets gave him ten for 188 in the match, making him only the fourth Indian to take ten wickets in a match against England, and India were left a minimum of 84 overs in which to win.

For the second time in the match, Gavaskar and Srikkanth punished Foster and Radford, each conceding 17 runs from their first three overs. They put on 58 in 39 minutes, but once Edmonds came on to bowl to the worn Pavilion end, India's confident progress was checked. He had Srikkanth caught, sweeping, and almost an hour later broke through with three of the four wickets to fall in 38 deliveries for 4 runs. A score of 126 for five off 55 overs at the tea interval promised an exciting last session, with England holding a slight advantage, but the weather's intervention snuffed out India's chance of victory.

Azharuddin held firm against Gatting's attacking fields in the eighteen overs after the final resumption, and his unbeaten 29 in 37 overs, together with More's 31 in 36, denied England a win they could have achieved had they bowled better in the first innings – and still might have achieved had Emburey been used more judiciously in both innings.

The Man of the Match was Gatting. The attendance for the five days was 42,750 with takings of £248,323. – J.B.

England

G. A. Gooch c More b Kapil Dev	0	– lbw b Chetan	40
M. R. Benson b Maninder	21	– b Shastri	30
C. W. J. Athey c More b Kapil Dev	0	– c More b Chetan	38
D. I. Gower lbw b Chetan	49	– c Gavaskar b Chetan	26
*M. W. Gatting not out	183	– lbw b Chetan	26
D. R. Pringle c Amarnath b Shastri	44	– c More b Maninder	7
J. E. Emburey c Shastri b Maninder	38	– not out	27
N. A. Foster b Binny	17	– run out	0
P. H. Edmonds b Chetan	18	– c Binny b Maninder	10
†B. N. French b Chetan	8	– c More b Chetan	1
N. V. Radford c Gavaskar b Chetan	0	– c Azharuddin b Chetan	1
L-b 7, n-b 5	12	B 10, l-b 6, w 2, n-b 11	29

1/0 2/0 3/61 4/88 5/184	390	1/49 2/102 3/152 4/163 5/190 235
6/278 7/327 8/367 9/384		6/190 7/190 8/217 9/229

Bowling: *First Innings*—Kapil Dev 31–6–89–2; Binny 17–1–53–1; Chetan 29.3–2–130–4; Maninder 25–3–66–2; Shastri 14–1–45–1. *Second Innings*—Kapil Dev 7–1–38–0; Binny 16–1–41–0; Chetan 24–4–58–6; Amarnath 2–1–2–0; Maninder 22–5–41–2; Shastri 23–8–39–1.

India

S. M. Gavaskar b Pringle	29	– c French b Foster	54
K. Srikkanth c Pringle b Radford	23	– c Pringle b Edmonds	23
M. Amarnath b Edmonds	79	– c French b Edmonds	16
D. B. Vengsarkar c Gooch b Radford	38	– c French b Edmonds	0
M. Azharuddin c French b Foster	64	– not out	29
R. J. Shastri c Gooch b Foster	18	– c Emburey b Edmonds	0
*Kapil Dev c French b Foster	26		
†K. S. More c French b Emburey	48	– (7) not out	31
R. M. H. Binny c Gower b Emburey	40		
Chetan Sharma c Gower b Pringle	9		
Maninder Singh not out	0		
B 1, l-b 9, w 1, n-b 5	16	B 1, l-b 15, w 1, n-b 4	21

1/53 2/58 3/139 4/228 5/266   390   1/58 2/101 3/101   (5 wkts) 174
6/275 7/302 8/370 9/385   4/104 5/105

Bowling: *First Innings*—Radford 35–3–131–2; Foster 41–9–93–3; Pringle 21–2–61–2; Edmonds 24–7–55–1; Emburey 18.5–7–40–2. *Second Innings*—Foster 22–9–48–1; Radford 3–0–17–0; Pringle 16–5–33–0; Edmonds 28–11–31–4; Emburey 7–1–19–0; Gatting 2–0–10–0.

Umpires: H. D. Bird and B. J. Meyer.

†SCOTLAND v INDIANS

At Dumfries, July 10. Indians won by three wickets. Toss: Scotland.

Scotland

I. L. Philip c Shastri b Yadav	7	†D. Fleming b Prabhakar	5
W. A. Donald b Shastri	41	J. E. Ker not out	8
*R. G. Swan b Shastri	12	A. W. J. Stevenson not out	4
O. Henry lbw b Maninder	19	B 1, l-b 7, w 8, n-b 2	18
A. B. Russell c Binny b Patil	8		
N. W. Burnett st Pandit b Maninder	42	1/23 2/56 3/73 (9 wkts, 55 overs) 192
A. Brown c Lamba b Patil	26	4/97 5/105 6/171
P. G. Duthie c Pandit b Prabhakar	2	7/171 8/178 9/179

Bowling: Prabhakar 7–2–19–2; Chetan 4–0–10–0; Yadav 11–2–31–1; Shastri 11–3–21–2; Maninder 11–1–50–2; Patil 11–0–53–2.

Indians

†C. S. Pandit run out	15	R. M. H. Binny not out	11
R. Lamba c and b Henry	8	*R. J. Shastri not out	6
M. Azharuddin c Henry b Ker	35	L-b 1, w 4, n-b 4	9
S. M. Patil c Russell b Stevenson	26		
Chetan Sharma c Fleming b Duthie	25	1/20 2/29 3/85 (7 wkts, 47.5 overs) 195
D. B. Vengsarkar b Ker	29	4/88 5/125
M. Prabhakar b Stevenson	31	6/164 7/188

Maninder Singh and N. S. Yadav did not bat.

Bowling: Duthie 11–1–39–1; Ker 11–1–40–2; Henry 6–0–30–1; Burnett 5–0–25–0; Stevenson 8–1–37–2; Donald 6.5–0–23–0.

Umpires: J. B. Connell and W. B. Smith.

†SCOTLAND v INDIANS

At Dumfries, July 11. Indians won by 52 runs. Toss: Scotland.

Indians

K. Srikkanth c Henry b Duthie	2	M. Prabhakar run out	19
R. Lamba st Fleming b Henry	53	N. S. Yadav not out	14
M. Azharuddin c Philip b Kirkwood	18	Maninder Singh not out	0
C. S. Pandit b Donald	0	B 1, l-b 3, w 6	10
*S. M. Patil c Kirkwood b Burnett	16		
S. M. Gavaskar c Fleming b Ker	1	1/2 2/39 3/41 (9 wkts, 50 overs)	211
†K. S. More run out	19	4/95 5/97 6/115	
Chetan Sharma c Philip b Henry	59	7/134 8/174 9/208	

Bowling: Duthie 10-0-41-1; Ker 8-0-26-1; Donald 10-2-39-1; Kirkwood 7-0-30-1; Burnett 5-0-30-1; Henry 10-0-41-2.

Scotland

I. L. Philip c More b Chetan	9	†D. Fleming st More b Azharuddin	9
W. A. Donald c More b Maninder	23	J. E. Ker not out	14
*R. G. Swan c More b Maninder	21		
O. Henry c Azharuddin b Patil	25	B 14, l-b 5, w 4, n-b 2	25
A. B. Russell c Prabhakar b Maninder	10		
N. W. Burnett st More b Srikkanth	3	1/19 2/46 3/85 (9 wkts, 50 overs)	159
A. Brown b Patil	14	4/91 5/110 6/127	
P. G. Duthie run out	1	7/128 8/134 9/159	

G. R. Kirkwood did not bat.

Bowling: Prabhakar 7-1-18-0; Chetan 7-2-11-1; Maninder 10-3-27-3; Yadav 10-0-28-0; Patil 10-2-28-2; Srikkanth 4-0-10-1; Azharuddin 2-0-18-1.

Umpires: J. B. Connell and W. B. Smith.

YORKSHIRE v INDIANS

At Scarborough, July 12, 13, 14. Indians won by five wickets. Toss: Yorkshire. Both sides were without key players because of injuries, but there was entertaining batting throughout on an easy-paced pitch. Moxon had the distinction of scoring a century in both innings, the first Yorkshire batsman to make two hundreds for the county in a match against a touring side. Lamba hit a stylish 116 in 230 minutes, a number of his eighteen boundaries coming from square cuts and powerful on-side strokes. With Amarnath's declaration, a stalemate appeared to have developed on the second day, and Carrick, Yorkshire's acting-captain, changed his batting order to give players practice. The plan misfired, however, when Maninder took three for 1 in eight balls. Moxon and Hartley brought about a recovery and the tourists were set a target of 255 in 53 overs. They began slowly, but Lamba and More struck 39 from the first ten balls after tea and as Yorkshire wilted, the run-chase became a formality. Patil hit five 4s and three 6s in his half-century, despite being troubled by a leg strain, and the Indians recorded their first win over Yorkshire.

Yorkshire

M. D. Moxon c Amarnath b Yadav	123	– (6) not out	112
†R. J. Blakey b Yadav	44	– b Lamba	0
A. A. Metcalfe c and b Srikkanth	92	– (5) c Chetan b Maninder	0
K. Sharp c and b Yadav	1	– (1) b Maninder	9
S. N. Hartley c Amarnath b Yadav	22	– (3) b Srikkanth	87
P. E. Robinson c Azharuddin b Maninder	15	– (4) b Maninder	4
*P. Carrick not out	24		
I. G. Swallow run out	3	– (7) not out	8
B 5, l-b 7, w 1, n-b 6	19	B 3, l-b 8, n-b 5	16

1/95 2/268 3/269 4/280	(7 wkts dec.) 343	1/0 2/34 3/38	(5 wkts dec.) 236
5/306 6/334 7/343		4/38 5/191	

C. Shaw, S. D. Fletcher and S. J. Dennis did not bat.

Bowling: *First Innings*—Chetan 1–0–6–0; Binny 12–2–59–0; Lamba 9–4–22–0; Maninder 29–4–106–1; Yadav 22.4–1–95–4; Azharuddin 6–0–27–0; Srikkanth 4–0–16–1. *Second Innings*—Binny 14–3–39–0; Lamba 4–0–15–1; Maninder 26–6–59–3; Yadav 13–1–45–0; Srikkanth 7–0–39–1; Azharuddin 5–0–14–0; Pandit 2.1–0–14–0.

Indians

K. Srikkanth c Fletcher b Swallow	29	– (2) c Fletcher b Dennis	5
R. Lamba c Dennis b Carrick	116	– (1) c and b Carrick	56
†K. S. More c Robinson b Shaw	19	– c Robinson b Carrick	52
M. Azharuddin lbw b Fletcher	0	– b Shaw	17
C. S. Pandit c Sharp b Carrick	91	– (6) not out	56
*M. Amarnath c and b Carrick	33	– (7) not out	14
R. M. H. Binny not out	4		
N. S. Yadav not out	9		
S. M. Patil (did not bat)		– (5) b Fletcher	50
B 6, l-b 10, n-b 8	24	L-b 6, n-b 1	7

1/57 2/107 3/108 4/216 (6 wkts dec.) 325   1/14 2/106 3/131 (5 wkts) 257
5/307 6/312   4/141 5/222

Maninder Singh and Chetan Sharma did not bat.

Bowling: *First Innings*—Dennis 11–2–37–0; Fletcher 15–2–52–1; Swallow 23–1–93–1; Carrick 20–2–68–3; Shaw 10–1–25–1; Moxon 8–1–23–0; Hartley 3–1–11–0. *Second Innings*—Dennis 12–2–51–1; Fletcher 10–1–49–1; Shaw 9–3–50–1; Swallow 7–0–31–0; Carrick 11–0–70–2.

Umpires: B. Leadbeater and D. Lloyd.

INDIA BEAT PAKISTAN IN HARROGATE

In the first match between the two countries in England, India beat Pakistan by one wicket off the first ball of the final over at Harrogate on July 15 last year. An estimated 10,000 spectators attended the fixture, which was played in aid of Help the Aged.

Pakistan 195 for five (40 overs) (Salim Malik 79 not out); India 196 for nine (39.1 overs) (K. Srikkanth 58, D. B. Vengsarkar 43).

THE NEW ZEALANDERS IN ENGLAND, 1986

To say that Richard Hadlee was the difference between England and New Zealand in the 1986 Test series between the two countries is not an exaggeration. And yet to say so does an injustice to the fifteen of his countrymen who comprised the tenth New Zealand side to visit England on a Test-match tour. The record partnership between Bruce Edgar and Martin Crowe at Lord's; Evan Gray's determined half-century and John Bracewell's hundred at Trent Bridge; John Wright's long innings at The Oval: all were essential to the touring party's prime aim. This was to win; for the first time, a series in England, and with victory by eight wickets at Trent Bridge, that aim was realised.

Hadlee's influence, however, cannot be overestimated. At 35 he was a master of the arts of fast-medium seam and swing bowling. Only at The Oval, late in a full season for him, did English batsmen play him with confidence. As New Zealand's only experienced fast bowler, once Ewen Chatfield's broken thumb ruled him out of the first two Tests, Hadlee maintained fitness, form and concentration so that Jeremy Coney, his captain, was able to bowl him in short, demanding spells. Few passed without a wicket falling. His nineteen wickets in the series took his total in Test cricket to 334, with only Botham and Lillee ahead of him.

With the consent of the Test and County Cricket Board, Hadlee played in the Test matches only. Otherwise he appeared for his county, Nottinghamshire, who had granted him a benefit in 1986. Regarded by some as a dubious precedent, it was none the less appreciated by the New Zealand Cricket Council, who wanted to use the tour to bring on young seam bowlers. With Chatfield 36 and Lance Cairns retired, replacements for them and Hadlee are New Zealand's greatest need.

Three possible candidates toured: Derek Stirling, a tall, heavily built man who had represented his country in Pakistan and West Indies, and two youngsters from Auckland, Willie Watson, twenty, and Brian Barrett, nineteen. None achieved as much as had been hoped of them. Stirling's most important contribution, perhaps, was with the bat, rather than the ball, in the second Test. Otherwise his approach looked long and laboured, his control variable. Watson, prone to an open-chested action, looked to have more potential as a stock bowler with ability to move the ball late, while Barrett, who played for Worcestershire in 1985 by virtue of qualification for Ireland, hoped mostly for movement off the seam, some bounce and a modicum of away-swing.

In the absence of an established seam attack, New Zealand were fortunate in their contrasting spin bowlers – Bracewell, an off-spinner, and Gray, a slow left-armer. Both had toured in 1983. Bracewell, having played a leading part in New Zealand's recent success over Australia, was thought to be the bowler around whom New Zealand's future attack would revolve. Tall, with good control and the confidence to give the ball air, he arrived with a striking-rate in Test cricket superior to that of Edmonds and Emburey and yet was not bowled as often as Gray in the series. Gray's accuracy allowed him to be Coney's stock bowler, but his success in this role owed something to the shortcomings of England's strokemakers. Both had batting averages of more than 50 on tour to emphasise their all-round value to a side which possessed a solid, consistent batting order.

THE NEW ZEALANDERS IN ENGLAND, 1986

[Patrick Eagar

The New Zealand party which toured England last year and won the Test series 1–0. R. J. Hadlee, who joined the team only for the Test matches, does not appear in this team group. *Back row*: M. R. Plummer (*physiotherapist*), K. R. Rutherford, E. J. Gray, W. Watson, T. J. Franklin, B. J. Barrett, D. A. Stirling, J. G. Bracewell, T. E. Blain, B. J. Curgenven (*scorer*). *Front row*: G. M. Turner (*cricket manager*), M. D. Crowe, E. J. Chatfield, R. A. Vance (*manager*), J. V. Coney (*captain*), J. G. Wright, J. J. Crowe, B. A. Edgar, I. D. S. Smith.

Martin Crowe's balance, his stillness at the crease, his selection of stroke, all bore the hallmark of a world-class batsman. His century at Lord's was his fifth in 30 Tests. Little he did was clumsy or inelegant. Back trouble, however, restricted his use as a seam bowler.

The New Zealand batting was not as dependent on Martin Crowe as the bowling was on Hadlee. The left-handed opening pair of Wright and Edgar scored heavily on tour and one or the other put down roots in the Test matches. But there was a problem at number three, the position so capably filled at home in recent years by John Reid, who had chosen not to tour. Jeff Crowe and Ken Rutherford were tried but neither gave an air of permanence. Rutherford, a pleasing strokemaker who opens for his province, may need no more than a long Test innings to give him the confidence to make the difficult transition to the highest level. His 317 at Scarborough, though not against an attack of county standard, showed he has an appetite for runs.

Crowe, on the other hand, remained an enigma. Attacking the bowling in the one-day internationals and on tour, he looked little less a player than his younger brother. But in the serious environment of Test cricket – and these New Zealanders did regard it as serious – some of the technical flaws which were apparent in 1983 were still in evidence. Trevor Franklin began his second tour of England with runs but broke a thumb at Nottingham before the first Test. Even more unluckily, he suffered multiple fractures when a luggage trolley hit his leg at Gatwick Airport on the day of the team's departure.

Ian Smith and Tony Blain were more wicket-keeper-batsmen than specialists, which meant that with Hadlee also in the lower-middle order, the New Zealand batting had the shortest tails. When Smith was unfit for the third Test, and returned home during it, Blain batted with assurance in a pleasing, old-fashioned manner and kept neatly to suggest a ready replacement should Smith's international career have ended.

For Coney, New Zealand's defeat of England was his third successful series in a year. If once or twice his tactics were open to question, he was firmly in charge and kept the morale of his younger players high when the distractions of Hadlee's benefit activities could easily have introduced an air of disenchantment. Moreover, his team lost only one game – the second one-day international, though they did take the Texaco Trophy. Since Coney's last visit to England, his batting, then built on solid defence, had become a means to counter-attack, while his slow-medium swing bowling appeared even slower but was no less lacking in guile.

The collective experience of the side was strengthened by the presence of Glenn Turner, the former Worcestershire and New Zealand opening batsman, as cricket manager. When Mr Bob Vance, the manager and Chairman of the New Zealand Cricket Council Board of Control, took ill early in the tour and returned to New Zealand, his duties were shared by Turner, Chatfield (while he was injured) and Edgar, who acted as treasurer. Such resourcefulness, however, was not surprising in a touring party whose great strength was that its players worked for themselves, their team and their country. – G.W.

NEW ZEALAND TOUR RESULTS

Test matches – Played 3: Won 1, Drawn 2.
First-class matches – Played 15: Won 4, Drawn 11.
Wins – England, Oxford & Cambridge Universities, Essex, Minor Counties.
Draws – England (2), Middlesex, Sussex, Warwickshire, Nottinghamshire, Northampton-shire, Derbyshire, TCCB XI, Glamorgan, D. B. Close's XI.
Non first-class matches – Played 3: Won 1, Lost 1, Drawn 1. *Win* – England. *Loss* – England, *Draw* – Lavinia, Duchess of Norfolk's XI.

TEST MATCH AVERAGES

ENGLAND – BATTING

	T	I	NO	R	HI	100s	Avge
D. I. Gower	3	5	0	293	131	1	58.60
G. A. Gooch	3	5	0	268	183	1	53.60
J. E. Emburey	2	3	1	92	75	0	46.00
M. W. Gatting ...	3	5	0	170	121	1	34.00
B. N. French	3	3	2	33	21	0	33.00
M. D. Moxon	2	4	0	111	74	0	27.75
C. W. J. Athey ...	3	5	0	138	55	0	27.60
G. C. Small	2	2	1	14	12	0	14.00
P. H. Edmonds ...	3	4	1	35	20	0	11.66

Played in two Tests: G. R. Dilley 17. Played in one Test: I. T. Botham 59*; N. A. Foster 8; A. J. Lamb 0; D. R. Pringle 21, 9; N. V. Radford 12*; J. G. Thomas 28, 10; P. Willey 44, 42.

* Signifies not out.

BOWLING

	O	M	R	W	BB	Avge
G. R. Dilley	69.3	16	179	9	4-82	19.88
P. H. Edmonds	101	32	212	8	4-97	26.50
G. C. Small	64	20	134	4	3-88	33.50
J. E. Emburey	79.5	33	141	4	2-87	35.25

Also bowled: I. T. Botham 26–4–82–3; N. A. Foster 28–7–69–1; G. A. Gooch 19-9–38–1; D. I. Gower 1–0–5–0; D. R. Pringle 22–1–74–0; N. V. Radford 25–4–71–1; J. G. Thomas 43–5–140–2.

FIELDING

6 – G. A. Gooch, 3 – C. W. J. Athey, P. H. Edmonds, B. N. French, D. I. Gower; 2 – M. W. Gatting; 1 – M. D. Moxon.

NEW ZEALAND – BATTING

	T	I	NO	R	HI	100s	Avge
M. D. Crowe	3	5	2	206	106	1	68.66
J. G. Bracewell ...	3	3	1	114	110	1	57.00
J. V. Coney	3	4	1	133	51	0	44.33
D. A. Stirling	2	2	1	44	26	0	44.00
J. G. Wright	3	6	1	191	119	1	38.20
R. J. Hadlee	3	3	0	93	68	0	31.00
E. J. Gray	3	3	0	91	50	0	30.33
B. A. Edgar	3	5	1	92	83	0	23.00
J. J. Crowe	3	4	0	51	23	0	12.75
I. D. S. Smith	2	2	0	20	18	0	10.00
W. Watson	2	2	1	9	8*	0	9.00

Played in one Test: T. E. Blain 37; E. J. Chatfield 5; K. R. Rutherford 0, 24*.

* Signifies not out.

BOWLING

	O	M	R	W	BB	Avge
R. J. Hadlee	153.5	42	390	19	6-80	20.52
J. G. Bracewell	75.4	22	213	6	3-29	35.50
W. Watson	72.5	18	196	4	2-51	49.00
E. J. Gray	117	40	271	5	3-83	54.20

Also bowled: E. J. Chatfield 21–7–73–3; J. V. Coney 16–1–48–0; M. D. Crowe 12–1–51–0; K. R. Rutherford 3–0–8–0; D. A. Stirling 44–8–181–3.

FIELDING

7 – I. D. S. Smith; 4 – M. D. Crowe; 2 – J. V. Coney, J. J. Crowe, E. J. Gray, W. Watson; 1 – D. A. Stirling.

NEW ZEALAND AVERAGES – FIRST-CLASS MATCHES

BATTING

	M	I	NO	R	HI	100s	Avge
J. G. Bracewell	12	11	6	386	110	2	77.20
M. D. Crowe	12	18	6	787	106	2	65.58
J. V. Coney	13	17	5	688	140*	1	57.33
K. R. Rutherford ...	12	19	3	848	317	2	53.00
E. J. Gray	13	13	4	467	108	1	51.88
B. A. Edgar	12	19	5	590	110*	1	42.14
J. G. Wright	12	19	1	668	119	1	37.11
J. J. Crowe	13	19	2	624	159	1	36.70
I. D. S. Smith	9	9	3	215	48	0	35.83
R. J. Hadlee	3	3	0	93	68	0	31.00
D. A. Stirling	11	7	3	116	26	0	29.00
T. E. Blain	9	9	2	172	37	0	24.57
T. J. Franklin	7	10	0	227	96	0	22.70
W. Watson	12	6	3	30	10	0	10.00
B. J. Barrett	8	4	3	8	5*	0	8.00
E. J. Chatfield	7	2	1	5	5	0	5.00

* Signifies not out.

BOWLING

	O	M	R	W	BB	Avge
R. J. Hadlee	153.5	42	390	19	6-80	20.52
J. V. Coney	75	23	194	7	2-14	27.71
J. G. Bracewell	411	122	1,042	37	6-55	28.16
E. J. Gray	438.2	144	1,087	37	7-61	29.37
E. J. Chatfield	191.4	47	457	13	3-73	35.15
D. A. Stirling	255	36	1,025	28	5-98	36.60
W. Watson	308.1	60	963	26	4-31	37.03
B. J. Barrett	157.5	18	610	15	3-32	40.66

Also bowled: M. D. Crowe 49.5–8–190–2; B. A. Edgar 1–0–2–0; T. J. Franklin 1–0–5–0; K. R. Rutherford 5–0–25–0; I. D. S. Smith 2–0–8–0; J. G. Wright 4–1–13–0.

FIELDING

22 – T. E. Blain (19 ct, 3 st); 19 – I. D. S. Smith (17 ct, 2 st); 11 – J. J. Crowe; 10 – M. D. Crowe; 9 – E. J. Gray; 7 – J. V. Coney, K. R. Rutherford; 5 – B. A. Edgar, T. J. Franklin; 4 – D. A. Stirling, J. G. Wright; 3 – E. J. Chatfield, W. Watson; 2 – J. G. Bracewell, substitute (T. E. Blain); 1 – B. J. Barrett.

HUNDREDS FOR NEW ZEALANDERS

The following eleven three-figure innings were played for the New Zealanders, all in first-class matches.

J. G. Bracewell (2)
   110 v England, Nottingham
        (Second Test)
   100* v Northants, Northampton

M. D. Crowe (2)
   106 v England, Lord's (First Test)
   100* v Essex, Chelmsford

K. R. Rutherford (2)
   317 v D. B. Close's XI, Scarborough
   104 v TCCB XI, Birmingham

   * Signifies not out.

J. V. Coney (1)
   140* v Glam., Swansea

J. J. Crowe (1)
   159 v Glam., Swansea

B. A. Edgar (1)
   110* v Derbys., Derby

E. J. Gray (1)
   108 v Minor Counties, Lakenham

J. G. Wright (1)
   119 v England, The Oval (Third Test)

Note: Those matches which follow which were not first-class are signified by the use of a dagger.

†LAVINIA, DUCHESS OF NORFOLK'S XI v NEW ZEALANDERS

At Arundel, June 22. Drawn. Toss: New Zealanders.

New Zealanders

T. J. Franklin b Kelleher	74	E. J. Gray not out		1
J. G. Wright b Kelleher	5	†I. D. S. Smith not out		10
K. R. Rutherford b Kelleher	3	B 1, l-b 10, n-b 2		13
M. D. Crowe c Goldsmith b Bracewell	70			
J. J. Crowe st Blain b Bracewell	35	1/19 2/36 3/141	(6 wkts dec.)	255
*J. V. Coney c Scott b Clarke	44	4/176 5/219 6/243		

D. A. Stirling, W. Watson and E. J. Chatfield did not bat.

Bowling: Clarke 14–2–45–1; Kelleher 16–3–44–3; Knight 7–0–27–0; Bracewell 17–3–64–2; Dale 12–0–64–0.

Lavinia, Duchess of Norfolk's XI

S. C. Goldsmith c Smith b Chatfield	28	J. G. Bracewell b Gray		15
B. A. Edgar c Rutherford b Watson	7	*R. D. V. Knight not out		19
A. J. Stewart c J. J. Crowe				
b M. D. Crowe	24	L-b 3, n-b 10		13
†T. E. Blain c M. D. Crowe b Chatfield	0			
T. E. Jesty not out	68	1/19 2/64 3/64	(6 wkts)	184
R. J. Scott b Coney	10	4/64 5/90 6/112		

S. T. Clarke, D. J. M. Kelleher and C. S. Dale did not bat.

Bowling: Stirling 9–1–36–0; Watson 8–0–51–1; Gray 7–1–37–1; M. D. Crowe 4–1–10–1; Chatfield 6–4–7–2; Coney 5–1–22–1; Rutherford 2–0–18–0.

Umpires: D. J. Dennis and J. G. Langridge.

OXFORD & CAMBRIDGE UNIVERSITIES v NEW ZEALANDERS

At Cambridge, June 25, 26, 27. New Zealanders won by 139 runs. Toss: Oxford & Cambridge Universities. The New Zealanders batted steadily throughout the opening day, but Coney's positive attitude, declaring at the overnight score, left Rutherford 9 short of his century. Contained by the off-spin of Bracewell and left-arm spin of Gray, the Universities' batsmen had every reason to be grateful for the early runs that came off Stirling by way of third man. Bail and Hagan put on the first 20 in even time: the follow-on was avoided by 19. In 105 minutes before the close, Gray and Franklin added 84 comfortably, and in the morning Coney delayed his declaration until Franklin's dismissal, caught on the boundary attempting to reach his hundred. He hit twelve 4s and a straight 6 through a pavilion window. The Universities' target of 294 in 280 minutes was more academic than attainable as Bracewell, bowling unchanged, again dictated the terms. Bail and Hagan set off with determination but the last seven wickets fell for 48 runs.

New Zealanders

B. A. Edgar c sub b Davidson	75			
J. G. Wright c Price b Thorne	40			
K. R. Rutherford not out	91			
J. J. Crowe c Tooley b Scott	13			
*J. V. Coney not out	56			
T. J. Franklin (did not bat)		– (1) c Scott b Davidson		96
E. J. Gray (did not bat)		– (2) not out		56
L-b 6, w 1, n-b 6	13	L-b 9, n-b 2		11
1/108 2/132 3/159	(3 wkts dec.) 288	1/163	(1 wkt dec.)	163

†T. E. Blain, J. G. Bracewell, D. A. Stirling and W. Watson did not bat.

Bowling: *First Innings*—Davidson 27–4–77–1; Thorne 17–4–48–1; Scott 23–6–52–1; Rutnagur 17–4–56–0; Golding 21–4–49–0. *Second Innings*—Davidson 11–3–44–1; Thorne 6–2–15–0; Scott 5–0–30–0; Rutnagur 11–2–33–0; Golding 11–1–32–0.

Oxford & Cambridge Universities

P. A. C. Bail lbw b Watson	22	– c Blain b Bracewell ... 27
D. A. Hagan c Franklin b Watson	11	– b Stirling ... 19
D. J. Fell c Franklin b Bracewell	9	– not out ... 0
C. D. M. Tooley c Edgar b Gray	5	– (5) b Gray ... 20
D. A. Thorne b Bracewell	18	– (6) b Bracewell ... 11
*D. G. Price c Blain b Stirling	12	– (7) c Coney b Gray ... 8
R. S. Rutnagur c Rutherford b Bracewell	26	– (8) c Gray b Bracewell ... 6
A. K. Golding b Watson	28	– (4) c Rutherford b Bracewell ... 26
†A. D. Brown c Crowe b Bracewell	0	– b Watson ... 8
A. M. G. Scott not out	4	– b Bracewell ... 8
J. E. Davidson b Watson	0	– b Bracewell ... 5
B 10, l-b 5, n-b 8	23	B 4, l-b 6, w 1, n-b 5 16

1/28 2/42 3/54 4/59 5/91   158   1/41 2/59 3/90 4/106 5/116   154
6/93 7/126 8/126 9/158   6/130 7/132 8/145 9/149

In the second innings, D. J. Fell retired hurt and resumed at 149.

Bowling: *First Innings*—Stirling 18-3-71-1; Watson 15.2-5-31-4; Gray 19-8-19-1; Bracewell 30-17-22-4. *Second Innings*—Stirling 10-2-29-1; Watson 5-1-24-1; Bracewell 35.2-18-55-6; Gray 25-12-36-2.

Umpires: H. D. Bird and K. E. Palmer.

MIDDLESEX v NEW ZEALANDERS

At Lord's, June 28, 29, 30. Drawn. Toss: New Zealanders. Middlesex, struggling in the Championship, made all the running in the touring side's first match against a county. Cowans put in a fiery opening spell and Gatting took the important wicket of Crowe, who disturbed the bails as he tried to deflect his falling helmet from the stumps. Coney symbolised his authority with a measured 93, receiving brisk help from Smith. Middlesex began their innings on the first evening and batted into the third morning. The sun was hot and the pitch near-perfect. Gatting made his first score above 43 of the summer and rehabilitated himself over 262 minutes, hitting fifteen 4s and two 6s. When the New Zealanders were 44 for two soon after lunch, Middlesex scented a possible victory, but Crowe, violent in brief bursts against Hughes and Fraser, put the loss of Wright, Franklin and Coney in a twenty-ball span by Fraser into perspective. Although at 176 for six, with 95 minutes left, the visitors again looked in trouble, Smith and Gray ensured the draw without difficulty.

New Zealanders

B. A. Edgar lbw b Hughes	27	– lbw b Cowans ... 0
J. G. Wright c Butcher b Cowans	13	– c Downton b Fraser ... 40
K. R. Rutherford c Downton b Cowans	4	– lbw b Hughes ... 23
M. D. Crowe hit wkt b Gatting	2	– c Downton b Gatting ... 78
T. J. Franklin c Emburey b Hughes	5	– lbw b Fraser ... 0
*J. V. Coney c Gatting b Edmonds	93	– c Miller b Fraser ... 10
E. J. Gray c Emburey b Cowans	6	– not out ... 53
†I. D. S. Smith b Edmonds	48	– not out ... 24
J. G. Bracewell b Miller b Edmonds	16	
D. A. Stirling b Gatting	6	
W. Watson not out	4	
B 2, l-b 3, n-b 3	8	B 6, l-b 2, n-b 3 11

1/25 2/31 3/47 4/54 5/55   232   1/0 2/44 3/111 4/111   (6 wkts) 239
6/78 7/166 8/194 9/221   5/131 6/176

Bowling: *First Innings*—Cowans 14-2-43-3; Fraser 11-2-37-0; Gatting 11-0-36-2; Hughes 8-3-27-2; Edmonds 20.2-5-31-3; Emburey 20-2-53-0. *Second Innings*—Cowans 9-2-35-1; Hughes 15-3-57-1; Edmonds 29-8-67-0; Fraser 9-1-46-3; Gatting 10-4-25-1; Miller 1-0-1-0.

Middlesex

A. J. T. Miller c Coney b Bracewell ...	56	S. P. Hughes c Crowe b Bracewell	20
W. N. Slack c Crowe b Stirling	10	N. G. Cowans b Stirling	0
*M. W. Gatting st Smith b Bracewell ..	135	A. G. J. Fraser c Edgar b Bracewell ...	2
C. T. Radley c Edgar b Stirling	42		
R. O. Butcher b Stirling	30	B 1, l-b 7, n-b 10	18
†P. R. Downton not out	77		
J. E. Emburey b Stirling	15	1/16 2/131 3/232 4/256 5/290	436
P. H. Edmonds c and b Gray	31	6/325 7/392 8/427 9/427	

Bowling: Stirling 31–6–98–5; Watson 25–3–76–0; Crowe 6–1–14–0; Bracewell 41.5–4–144–4; Gray 20–3–82–1; Coney 4–0–14–0.

Umpires: M. J. Kitchen and D. O. Oslear.

ESSEX v NEW ZEALANDERS

At Chelmsford, July 2, 3, 4. New Zealanders won by six wickets. Toss: Essex. The touring team, with 207 minutes in which to score 162, achieved victory with 5.2 overs of the final twenty remaining. With seven established Essex players missing, either through injury or Test duty, Stephenson came in for only his second first-class game and grasped his opportunity with a fluent 63 containing twelve 4s. Prichard also batted well before the New Zealanders scored freely against a depleted attack. Martin Crowe, with eighteen 4s in his 125-ball hundred, led the spree to enable Coney to declare 46 ahead. The flight and control of the left-arm spinner, Gray, proved too much for Essex in their second innings. They were 86 for four on the second evening, and only the ninth-wicket stand of 79 between Ian Pont and Childs made the New Zealanders' target in any way challenging.

Essex

C. Gladwin b Barrett	5	– c Coney b Barrett	12
J. P. Stephenson c Edgar b Bracewell	63	– b Gray	33
P. J. Prichard c J. J. Crowe b Barrett	65	– st Blain b Gray	14
A. R. Border c Gray b Bracewell	14	– c Blain b Gray	14
K. R. Pont c and b Stirling	36	– lbw b Bracewell	27
†D. E. East b Bracewell	13	– (7) c J. J. Crowe b Gray	1
S. Turner c Blain b Bracewell	10	– (8) c Blain b Gray	5
I. L. Pont b Bracewell	6	– (9) c Coney b Gray	43
T. D. Topley c Wright b Gray	45	– (6) st Blain b Gray	10
J. H. Childs not out	31	– c J. J. Crowe b Barrett	34
*D. L. Acfield b Barrett	11	– not out	0
B 2, l-b 12, n-b 4	18	B 6, l-b 6, n-b 2	14

1/21 2/113 4/162 5/181	307	1/47 2/47 3/66 4/83 5/109	207
6/207 7/210 8/217 9/278		6/118 7/119 8/128 9/207	

Bowling: *First Innings*—Stirling 11–0–50–1; Barrett 10.4–0–54–3; Bracewell 38–10–110–5; Coney 6–3–24–0; Gray 21–6–55–1. *Second Innings*—Stirling 4–0–27–0; Barrett 14.5–1–45–2; Gray 32–16–61–7; Bracewell 29–11–62–1.

New Zealanders

J. G. Wright b Childs	96		
B. A. Edgar c East b Turner	51	– c and b Acfield	41
K. R. Rutherford c Prichard b Topley	63		
M. D. Crowe not out	100		
J. J. Crowe not out	21	– (3) lbw b Acfield	6
†T. E. Blain (did not bat)		– (1) c Topley b Acfield	24
*J. V. Coney (did not bat)		– (4) not out	36
E. J. Gray (did not bat)		– (5) c I. L. Pont b Childs	14
J. G. Bracewell (did not bat)		– (6) not out	30
L-b 16, n-b 6	22	B 7, l-b 7	14

1/131 2/194 3/244	(3 wkts dec.) 353	1/62 2/69 3/74 4/113	(4 wkts) 165

D. A. Stirling and B. J. Barrett did not bat.

Bowling: *First Innings*—I. L. Pont 13–2–49–0; Topley 21–2–69–1; Turner 19–6–66–1; Acfield 26–10–54–0; Childs 24–6–74–1; Border 3–1–8–0; K. R. Pont 4–1–17–0. *Second Innings*—I. L. Pont 5–2–11–0; Topley 5–3–7–0; Childs 23.4–4–66–1; Acfield 21–5–55–3; Border 2–0–12–0.

Umpires: D. J. Constant and J. H. Hampshire.

SUSSEX v NEW ZEALANDERS

At Hove, July 5, 6, 7. Drawn. Toss: Sussex. Only nine overs could be bowled on the first day because of rain, and an undistinguished game petered out when, with Sussex asked to score 275 in 195 minutes, another stoppage put paid to any chance of a result. Mays, making his first appearance for Sussex at Hove, bowled his off-spin in long spells, while Crowe's 41 and 31 were workmanlike innings for the visitors.

New Zealanders

K. R. Rutherford lbw b Pigott	6	– (2) lbw b Imran	2
B. A. Edgar retired hurt	14	– (5) not out	56
T. J. Franklin b Imran	20	– (1) c Alikhan b Standing	23
J. J. Crowe c Green b C. M. Wells	41	– (3) c Gould b Standing	31
*J. V. Coney c Parker b Mays	30	– (4) st Gould b Mays	22
T. E. Blain c A. P. Wells b Imran	34	– not out	12
†I. D. S. Smith c Reeve b Mays	4		
J. G. Bracewell lbw b Mays	36		
B. J. Barrett b Reeve	0		
W. Watson b Imran	10		
E. J. Chatfield not out	0		
L-b 4, n-b 2	6	L-b 1, n-b 1	2

1/6 2/41 3/99 4/122 5/127   201   1/3 2/55 3/58   (4 wkts dec.) 148
6/177 7/179 8/196 9/201   4/114

Bowling: *First Innings*—Pigott 11–1–36–1; Imran 18.5–8–37–3; C. M. Wells 9–3–15–1; Reeve 9–0–32–1; Mays 22–3–77–3. *Second Innings*—Imran 4–2–4–1; Reeve 8–0–11–0; Mays 20–4–68–1; Standing 12–1–28–2; C. M. Wells 8–0–28–0; Green 3–0–8–0.

Sussex

D. K. Standing not out	29	– c Crowe b Chatfield	13
A. M. Green c Franklin b Chatfield	34	– c Rutherford b Chatfield	24
P. W. G. Parker not out	7	– not out	20
Imran Khan (did not bat)		– c Rutherford b Watson	1
C. M. Wells (did not bat)		– not out	35
W 1, n-b 4	5	N-b 2	2

1/63   (1 wkt dec.) 75   1/35 2/38 3/40   (3 wkts) 95

A. P. Wells, R. I. Alikhan, *†I. J. Gould, D. A. Reeve, C. S. Mays and A. C. S. Pigott did not bat.

Bowling: *First Innings*—Barrett 9–0–43–0; Chatfield 8–2–9–1; Watson 8–1–23–0. *Second Innings*—Barrett 6–1–35–0; Chatfield 13–3–27–2; Watson 9–2–24–1; Bracewell 4–2–9–0.

Umpires: N. T. Plews and R. A. White.

MINOR COUNTIES v NEW ZEALANDERS

At Lakenham, July 9, 10, 11. New Zealanders won by ten wickets. Toss: Minor Counties. Gray dominated the match with a fine century and a return of nine wickets for 106. A patient 69 from Plumb was the mainstay of the Minor Counties' first innings, which fell away after tea to the slow left-arm bowling of Gray. The New Zealanders, having disappointingly accepted an offer of bad light after only four overs in the evening, batted throughout the second day. Jeff Crowe hit twelve 4s in his 69 before falling to a superb leg-side stumping by Ashley, playing in his first representative match, and Gray went on to his hundred (one 6, eighteen 4s) in two and three-quarter hours. Minor Counties began their second innings well enough after Wright declared at the overnight score, but they collapsed, losing nine wickets for 59 runs, once Gray, who had been off the field for the first hour owing to a stomach upset, returned to the attack.

Minor Counties

P. A. Todd c and b Stirling	4	– c Smith b Chatfield	21
S. G. Plumb lbw b Gray	69	– c Franklin b Gray	29
S. Greensword c Blain b Gray	35	– b Barrett	34
G. R. J. Roope c Blain b Chatfield	15	– run out	3
*N. A. Riddell c Barrett b Stirling	20	– c Chatfield b Gray	7
A. S. Patel b Stirling	30	– c Wright b Barrett	7
R. Herbert c Gray b Watson	10	– b Watson	23
†D. J. Ashley c Blain b Gray	4	– c Stirling b Barrett	0
W. G. Merry c Franklin b Gray	3	– (10) st Blain b Gray	5
D. Surridge not out	0	– (11) not out	1
A. J. Murphy c Smith b Gray	0	– (9) c Smith b Gray	6
L-b 3, n-b 16	19	B 1, l-b 2, w 1, n-b 1	5

1/5 2/81 3/122 4/144 5/182   209   1/32 2/82 3/92 4/92 5/102   141
6/188 7/194 8/207 9/207   6/108 7/114 8/129 9/134

Bowling: *First Innings*—Stirling 15-1-82-3; Barrett 12-1-22-0; Watson 12-3-28-1; Chatfield 14-6-20-1; Gray 27-9-54-5. *Second Innings*—Chatfield 7-0-15-1; Stirling 6-0-32-0; Gray 15.4-2-52-4; Barrett 12-4-32-3; Watson 3-1-7-1.

New Zealanders

T. J. Franklin c Todd b Greensword	20		
*J. G. Wright c Patel b Murphy	65		
J. J. Crowe st Ashley b Plumb	69		
E. J. Gray b Surridge	108		
M. D. Crowe b Merry	26		
†T. E. Blain c Riddell b Murphy	0		
†I. D. S. Smith lbw b Murphy	7		
D. A. Stirling c Riddell b Surridge	18	– (1) not out	13
W. Watson not out	7		
B. J. Barrett not out	3	– (2) not out	5
B 2, l-b 8, n-b 1	11		

1/55 2/107 3/201 4/262   (8 wkts dec.) 334   (no wkt) 18
5/273 6/287 7/309 8/328

E. J. Chatfield did not bat.

Bowling: *First Innings*—Murphy 27-3-85-3; Merry 20-5-47-1; Surridge 19-5-61-2; Greensword 13-4-33-1; Herbert 8-3-24-0; Patel 11-3-41-0; Plumb 9-1-33-1. *Second Innings*—Roope 2-0-9-0; Riddell 1-0-5-0; Todd 1-0-4-0.

Umpires: D. J. Halfyard and T. G. Wilson.

WARWICKSHIRE v NEW ZEALANDERS

At Birmingham, July 12, 13, 14. Drawn. Toss: New Zealanders. Only twenty wickets fell in a match which produced three declarations but no result after the touring side had been set a target of 270 in 170 minutes. Humpage's hundred, the 28th of his career, was made in 150 minutes, and included ten 4s and three 6s. The New Zealanders all batted attractively on the second day, with Martin Crowe particularly impressive while scoring 86 in 121 minutes, many of his fourteen 4s the product of his powerful driving and cutting. Warwickshire struggled to 75 for four before the close and were 157 for nine at lunch on the third day – a lead of 216. However, an unbeaten stand of 53 in 65 minutes between Kerr and Munton, followed by two quick wickets for Small, swung the match away from the New Zealanders.

Warwickshire

D. A. Thorne b M. D. Crowe	18	– c Blain b Chatfield 2
P. A. Smith c Bracewell b Coney	77	– b Watson 0
B. M. McMillan b Bracewell	65	– (5) c J. J. Crowe b Bracewell .. 39
*D. L.-Amiss c Blain b Coney	0	– (3) b Watson 16
†G. W. Humpage not out	100	– (6) run out 21
Asif Din lbw b Bracewell	21	– (4) b M. D. Crowe 17
A. M. Ferreira not out	31	– c Chatfield b Gray 28
G. J. Parsons (did not bat)		– c Watson b Bracewell 13
G. C. Small (did not bat)		– lbw b Gray 10
K. J. Kerr (did not bat)		– not out 33
T. A. Munton (did not bat)		– not out 11
B 4, l-b 12, n-b 2	18	B 9, l-b 7, n-b 4 20

1/36 2/161 3/161   (5 wkts dec.) 330   1/2 2/18 3/20   (9 wkts dec.) 210
4/189 5/239   4/55 5/95 6/122
                                              7/132 8/153 9/157

Bowling: *First Innings*—Chatfield 24.4–6–64–0; Watson 14–4–59–0; M. D. Crowe
9–1–37–1; Bracewell 23–5–57–2; Coney 11–3–32–2; Gray 14–1–65–0. *Second Innings*—
Chatfield 12–2–21–1; Watson 7–1–30–2; M. D. Crowe 10–2–38–1; Bracewell 32–15–56–2;
Gray 26–12–49–2.

New Zealanders

B. A. Edgar c McMillan b Munton	43	– (2) lbw b Small 0
J. G. Wright c Thorne b Munton	66	– (1) lbw b Small 16
K. R. Rutherford b Munton	14	– not out 52
M. D. Crowe not out	86	
*J. V. Coney c Munton b Asif Din	56	
J. J. Crowe (did not bat)		– (4) not out 65
L-b 2, n-b 4	6	L-b 2, n-b 1 3

1/97 2/122 3/139 4/271   (4 wkts dec.) 271   1/5 2/18   (2 wkts) 136

E. J. Gray, †T. E. Blain, J. G. Bracewell, W. Watson and E. J. Chatfield did not bat.

Bowling: *First Innings*—Small 9–2–25–0; McMillan 9–0–45–0; Ferreira 14–4–55–0; Parsons
11–0–53–0; Kerr 20–6–42–0; Munton 14–4–35–3; Thorne 2–0–14–0; Asif Din 1.4–1–0–1.
Second Innings—Small 6–0–18–2; McMillan 4–0–11–0; Parsons 3–1–10–0; Asif Din
15–4–51–0; Munton 6–2–16–0; Thorne 5–2–10–0; Smith 3–1–18–0.

Umpires: J. Birkenshaw and A. G. T. Whitehead.

†ENGLAND v NEW ZEALAND

First Texaco Trophy Match

At Leeds, July 16. New Zealand won by 47 runs. England, requiring fewer than 4 runs an
over, should not have lost this match. They contrived to do so chiefly by three run-outs, each
one equally indefensible by players accustomed to the pressures of one-day cricket. New
Zealand's bowling was steady but no more on a pitch which had eased since the morning
when the New Zealanders, choosing to bat first, had indeed struggled. Ten overs passed
before the first boundary, and when it seemed they were over the worst, Ellison with
controlled away-swing took three wickets in twenty balls. Jeff Crowe worked hard for 28
overs, and with Gray batting sensibly, New Zealand mustered 79 from the last thirteen overs.
England began steadily, but in the 28th over Gower, driving loosely, was bowled by Coney.
There followed errors and no comedy. Lamb, in form, was run out after playing the ball to
short third man. Gatting, involved in that indiscretion, tried to repeat the straight 6 off Gray
with which he opened his scoring and was bowled by a flighted ball which turned and
bounced. Pringle, dropped twice when 1, survived again by turning down Richards's
invitation to a 22-yard dash – but Richards could not get back. And finally Ellison, who was
looking capable of rescuing England, found in Foster an unwilling run-stealer.

Man of the Match: J. J. Crowe.   *Attendance*: 14,000; receipts £116,325.

New Zealand

B. A. Edgar lbw b Foster	0	†I. D. S. Smith run out	4
J. G. Wright c Richards b Ellison	21	J. G. Bracewell not out	10
K. R. Rutherford b Ellison	11		
M. D. Crowe b Ellison	9	L-b 18, w 7, n-b 3	28
*J. V. Coney run out	27		
J. J. Crowe c and b Foster	66	1/9 2/36 3/48 (8 wkts, 55 overs) 217	
R. J. Hadlee lbw b Dilley	11	4/54 5/112 6/138	
E. J. Gray not out	30	7/165 8/187	

E. J. Chatfield did not bat.

Bowling: Dilley 11–1–37–1; Foster 9–1–27–2; Pringle 9–0–42–0; Ellison 11–1–43–3; Emburey 11–0–30–0; Gooch 4–0–20–0.

England

G. A. Gooch b Hadlee	18	R. M. Ellison run out	12
M. R. Benson c Chatfield b Bracewell	24	N. A. Foster b Hadlee	5
D. I. Gower b Coney	18	G. R. Dilley not out	2
A. J. Lamb run out	33	L-b 1, w 2	3
*M. W. Gatting b Gray	19		
D. R. Pringle c Rutherford b Gray	28	1/38 2/48 3/83 (48.2 overs) 170	
†C. J. Richards run out	4	4/103 5/131 6/143	
J. E. Emburey lbw b Bracewell	0	7/144 8/162 9/165	

Bowling: Hadlee 9.2–0–29–2; Chatfield 8–2–24–0; Bracewell 11–2–27–2; M. D. Crowe 4–0–15–0; Gray 11–1–55–2; Coney 5–0–19–1.

Umpires: J. Birkenshaw and B. J. Meyer.

†ENGLAND v NEW ZEALAND

Second Texaco Trophy Match

At Manchester, July 18. England won by six wickets, but New Zealand won the Texaco Trophy on their faster run-rate in the two matches. The batting of Gooch and especially Athey made amends for England's poor, at times slovenly, showing in the field after they had put New Zealand in. Rutherford played attractively, but the highlight of the innings was the strokeplay of Martin Crowe, whose power and placement made a nonsense of Gatting's field-setting. He hit two 6s and eleven 4s in 74 balls, his last 43 runs coming off thirteen balls. With his brother also timing the ball well, the last nine overs produced 126 runs; the last four 71 as England lost control. Foster's seventh over (the 53rd) cost 20 runs and the 55th, bowled by Gooch, cost 26 (including 5 wides) as Hadlee in six balls added to the mayhem. The crowd's displeasure, warranted but crudely expressed, turned to pleasure as Gooch and Athey compiled the highest first-wicket partnership in a one-day international, Gooch's 91 taking just 102 balls. Needing slightly more than 5 an over, they were on course with 128 after 25 overs and had improved the asking-rate when 92 were needed off the last twenty. Athey, opening in place of the unfit Benson, played his best innings for England, hitting fourteen 4s in 172 balls, driving and sweeping with assurance despite problems from a muscle spasm in his thigh. New Zealand missed the control of Chatfield, who had broken his left thumb catching Martin at Headingley.

Man of the Match: C. W. J. Athey.   *Attendance:* 19,000; *receipts* £150,000.

Men of the Series: C. W. J. Athey (England) and M. D. Crowe (New Zealand).

New Zealand

J. G. Wright c Pringle b Emburey 39	R. J. Hadlee not out 18
B. A. Edgar lbw b Dilley 5	
K. R. Rutherford b Edmonds 63	L-b 2, w 14, n-b 1 17
M. D. Crowe not out 93	
*J. V. Coney run out 1	1/16 2/89 3/133 (5 wkts, 55 overs) 284
J. J. Crowe b Pringle 48	4/136 5/249

E. J. Gray, †I. D. S. Smith, J. G. Bracewell and W. Watson did not bat.

Bowling: Dilley 9–0–55–1; Foster 7–0–40–0; Pringle 10–2–63–1; Gooch 7–0–48–0; Edmonds 11–1–42–1; Emburey 11–1–34–1.

England

G. A. Gooch c and b Coney 91	D. R. Pringle not out 0
C. W. J. Athey not out 142	L-b 5, w 3, n-b 1 9
D. I. Gower c Wright b Coney 9	
A. J. Lamb b Bracewell 28	1/193 2/219 3/265 (4 wkts, 53.4 overs) 286
*M. W. Gatting b M. D. Crowe 7	4/274

†C. J. Richards, J. E. Emburey, N. A. Foster, P. H. Edmonds and G. R. Dilley did not bat.

Bowling: Hadlee 11–1–34–0; Watson 11–1–46–0; M. D. Crowe 6–0–36–1; Bracewell 10.4–0–67–1; Gray 4–0–39–0; Coney 11–0–59–2.

Umpires: K. E. Palmer and N. T. Plews.

NOTTINGHAMSHIRE v NEW ZEALANDERS

At Nottingham, July 19, 20, 21. Drawn. Toss: Nottinghamshire. After the New Zealanders had lost both openers at 12, Martin Crowe inspired a revival with a sparkling 80 in 113 minutes. On the second day, when conditions favoured the seam bowlers, Nottinghamshire collapsed against the left-arm spin of Gray and might well have been in danger of following on had Newell not held the innings together for three hours, twenty minutes. With Martin Crowe hitting three 6s and six 4s in another rapid half-century, Coney was able to set Nottinghamshire to score 265 in 225 minutes. A superb 70 out of 111 by Broad put them on course, and when the last twenty overs began the requirement was 94 with six wickets in hand. However, the game was swinging the touring team's way until French produced a defiant innings to force a draw.

New Zealanders

B. A. Edgar c French b Cooper	5	– (2) not out 48
T. J. Franklin c Broad b Pick	7	
K. R. Rutherford c Birch b Cooper	33	– (1) b Pick 45
M. D. Crowe c Saxelby b Hemmings	80	– not out 56
*J. V. Coney c Robinson b Saxelby	45	
J. J. Crowe c Robinson b Saxelby	75	– (3) c Broad b Saxelby 6
E. J. Gray b Hemmings	10	
†I. D. S. Smith not out	46	
D. A. Stirling c French b Pick	20	
L-b 5	5	B 2, l-b 5, w 3 10

1/12 2/12 3/124 4/126   (8 wkts dec.) 326   1/72 2/87   (2 wkts dec.) 165
5/183 6/234 7/286 8/326

B. J. Barrett and W. Watson did not bat.

Bowling: *First Innings*—Pick 14.5–2–54–2; Cooper 21–5–49–2; Saxelby 17–2–75–2; Evans 11–2–53–0; Hemmings 27–11–90–2. *Second Innings*—Pick 10–1–22–1; Cooper 15–3–37–0; Hemmings 11–4–30–0; Evans 11–1–61–0; Saxelby 6–2–8–1.

Nottinghamshire

B. C. Broad c sub b Barrett	47	– c Gray b Watson	70
R. T. Robinson b Stirling	7	– b Gray	26
K. Saxelby not out	25		
P. Johnson c M. D. Crowe b Watson	3	– c Smith b Watson	0
M. Newell c Rutherford b Gray	53	– (3) b Watson	26
*J. D. Birch lbw b Stirling	31	– (5) c Rutherford b Stirling	25
K. P. Evans c J. J. Crowe b Watson	0	– (6) b Coney	14
†B. N. French c J. J. Crowe b Gray	5	– (7) not out	32
R. A. Pick c sub b Gray	26	– (8) c Smith b Coney	0
E. E. Hemmings c M. D. Crowe b Gray	20	– (9) not out	10
K. E. Cooper c M. D. Crowe b Gray	0		
B 4, l-b 3, w 1, n-b 2	10	B 8, l-b 6, n-b 2	16

1/33 2/100 3/105 4/173 5/174   227   1/48 2/111 3/111 4/148 (7 wkts) 219
6/181 7/187 8/223 9/227   5/171 6/189 7/189

Bowling: *First Innings*—Stirling 17–2–68–2; Barrett 24–4–63–1; Watson 23–6–38–2; Gray 19.4–5–51–5. *Second Innings*—Stirling 12–3–34–1; Watson 13–3–33–3; Gray 19–3–82–1; Barrett 8–2–25–0; M. D. Crowe 4–1–17–0; Coney 6–1–14–2.

Umpires: B. Dudleston and D. R. Shepherd.

ENGLAND v NEW ZEALAND

First Cornhill Test

At Lord's, July 24, 25, 26, 28, 29. Drawn. England may have been spared another Lord's defeat in the 1980s when the sort of weather that spoiled so many Test matches there in the 1970s robbed this match of almost half the fourth day. None the less, England needed a long and commanding innings from Gooch, his second Test hundred at Lord's in 1986, to save the game.

It would hardly be a drawn Lord's Test without rain and bad light plus a much-discussed, if short-lived, controversy. This came on the second day when French, England's injured wicket-keeper, was replaced by the former England wicket-keeper, R. W. Taylor. French had been struck on the back of the helmet when he turned away from a Hadlee bouncer, the resulting cut requiring three stitches and the blow leaving him groggy until after the weekend. Athey deputised for two overs at the start of New Zealand's innings until Taylor could hurry round the ground – from his duties as host for Cornhill, the match's sponsor – and equip himself with an assortment of borrowed kit, although he did, far-sightedly, have his own gloves in his car. Despite having retired from first-class cricket two years earlier, Taylor, at the age of 45, kept almost without blemish. He did his old job until the 76th over, near the lunch interval on Saturday, after which R. J. Parks of Hampshire, following his grandfather and father, appeared in a Test match. However, Parks, a more authentic substitute, should have been on stand-by at the start of play because recovery from such a head wound is seldom immediate. French finally assumed his appointed role for one ball on Monday morning. All these switches were made with the generous permission of New Zealand's captain, Coney. With substitutes also needed for Willey and Foster and for Coney and Jeff Crowe, 29 players took the field at various times.

Even before the match, injuries had given England anxieties. Willey was called in after Emburey broke his nose in a Sunday League match and Pringle was declared unfit just before the toss, which meant that England's XI was pre-determined for the second consecutive Test.

Dilley, the man who withdrew at Birmingham on the first morning of the third Test against India, was back. Moxon, who replaced Benson as Gooch's opening partner, underpinned England's steady development to 248 for five after Gatting had won the toss. However, it was soon evident that two different games were taking place – one when Hadlee was bowling and the other when he was out of the attack. He took a wicket in each of his first two spells and in his fourth disposed of Moxon and Gatting. On the second day he and Watson went through England's later batsmen, and with six for 80 Hadlee equalled I. T. Botham's record of five or more wickets in a Test innings 26 times.

Dilley's fast, accurate opening spell brought the wickets of Wright and Rutherford, but Edgar and Martin Crowe responded in their characteristic ways. Edgar existed at 1 run an over for most of his 298-ball innings while Crowe eased the situation with increasing aggression. Both were 52 not out at the end of a day in which 25 overs were lost, and gradually they transformed a recovery into a position from which their side could strike for victory. Crowe's range of strokes during an innings of 5 hours, 40 minutes (247 balls, eleven of which he hit for 4) showed the English cricket-watcher that he had entered the ranks of world-class batsmen. Their partnership of 210 was a record for New Zealand's third wicket against England, surpassing Hastings and Congdon's 190, also at Lord's, in 1973. When they were dismissed in successive overs, Coney made a brisk, consolidating half-century, and only Edmonds prevented the match from running entirely New Zealand's way. Their innings was ended by the first ball on Monday, their lead 35.

Hadlee made his customary initial breakthrough and Gray, turning the ball out of the footmarks, achieved a remarkable double by bowling a right-hander, Athey, and a left-hander, Gower, around their legs as they made technically inept attempts to combat him. From then on, pads were frequently favoured to counter the slow left-armer as he toiled for 46 overs.

Only 21 overs were bowled after lunch, and at 110 for three, only 75 ahead, England were looking to a long partnership between Gooch and Gatting. Instead, the latter's over-ambitious stroke on the final morning put an extra burden on the former. Gooch, however, coped in masterly fashion and had the ideal partner in the resolute Willey. The new ball, taken with England 146 in front with four hours left, was the last obstacle, and when it was surmounted Gooch played with great freedom in the afternoon sun. He had batted for 441 minutes, received 368 balls and hit 22 4s when his dismissal to a catch at long-off brought the declaration. This allowed England to dismiss two top-order New Zealand batsmen for 0 for the second time – Wright for a "pair" – both falling to slip catches by Gower that deserved a more meaningful setting.

For his innings which secured the draw for England, Gooch was named Man of the Match. The overall attendance was 69,184 and receipts £531,434. – T.C.

England

G. A. Gooch c Smith b Hadlee	18	– c Watson b Bracewell	183
M. D. Moxon lbw b Hadlee	74	– lbw b Hadlee	5
C. W. J. Athey c J. J. Crowe b Hadlee	44	– b Gray	16
D. I. Gower c M. D. Crowe b Bracewell	62	– b Gray	3
*M. W. Gatting b Hadlee	2	– c M. D. Crowe b Gray	26
P. Willey lbw b Watson	44	– b Bracewell	42
P. H. Edmonds c M. D. Crowe b Hadlee	6	– not out	9
†B. N. French retired hurt	0		
G. R. Dilley c Smith b Hadlee	17		
N. A. Foster b Watson	8		
N. V. Radford not out	12		
B 6, l-b 7, n-b 7	20	L-b 6, w 1, n-b 4	11

1/27 2/102 3/196 4/198 5/237   307   1/9 2/68 3/72   (6 wkts dec.) 295
6/258 7/271 8/285 9/307   4/136 5/262 6/295

B. N. French retired hurt at 259-6.

Bowling: *First Innings*—Hadlee 37.5–11–80–6; Watson 30–7–70–2; M. D. Crowe 8–1–38–0; Coney 4–0–12–0; Bracewell 26–8–65–1; Gray 13–9–29–0. *Second Innings*—Hadlee 27–3–78–1; Watson 17–2–50–0; Gray 46–14–83–3; M. D. Crowe 4–0–13–0; Bracewell 23.4–7–57–2; Rutherford 3–0–8–0.

New Zealand

J. G. Wright b Dilley	0	– (2) c Gower b Dilley	0
B. A. Edgar c Gatting b Gooch	83	– (1) c Gower b Foster	0
K. R. Rutherford c Gooch b Dilley	0	– not out	24
M. D. Crowe c and b Edmonds	106	– not out	11
J. J. Crowe c Gatting b Edmonds	18		
*J. V. Coney c Gooch b Radford	51		
E. J. Gray c Gower b Edmonds	11		
R. J. Hadlee b Edmonds	19		
†D. S. Smith c Edmonds b Dilley	18		
J. G. Bracewell not out	1		
W. Watson lbw b Dilley	1		
B 4, l-b 9, w 6, n-b 15	34	L-b 4, n-b 2	6

1/2 2/5 3/215 4/218 5/274   342   1/0 2/8   (2 wkts) 41
6/292 7/310 8/340 9/340

Bowling: *First Innings*—Dilley 35.1–9–82–4; Foster 25–6–56–0; Radford 25–4–71–1; Edmonds 42–10–97–4; Gooch 13–6–23–1. *Second Innings*—Foster 3–1–13–1; Dilley 6–3–5–1; Edmonds 5–0–18–0; Gower 1–0–1–0.

Umpires: H. D. Bird and A. G. T. Whitehead.

NORTHAMPTONSHIRE v NEW ZEALANDERS

At Northampton, July 30, 31, August 1. Drawn. Toss: Northamptonshire. Rain delayed the start until 1.30 p.m. on the second day and ruined the match as a contest. Bailey was again outstanding with a hard-hit 95 off 98 balls, including seventeen 4s, and he shared a fourth-wicket stand of 145 with Williams, who made the most of his first-team recall with a 6 and eighteen 4s. Gouldstone, a 23-year-old, played some pleasing strokes on his début against an attack in which none of the young New Zealand seam bowlers impressed. Given a welcome opportunity for batting practice, the visitors lost half their side for 111 after a sound start, but Bracewell, striking three 6s and fifteen 4s from a varied county attack, reached his second first-class century at a run a minute off 94 balls.

Northamptonshire

M. R. Gouldstone lbw b Barrett	35	D. J. Wild c Blain b Barrett	8
A. Fordham c Blain b Watson	4	†D. Ripley not out	1
R. J. Boyd-Moss b Stirling	1	L-b 3, w 1, n-b 11	15
R. G. Williams c Blain b Stirling	93		
R. J. Bailey c Blain b Gray	95	1/15 2/16 3/73 (6 wkts dec.) 300	
D. J. Capel not out	48	4/218 5/275 6/291	

*G. Cook, N. G. B. Cook and A. Walker did not bat.

Bowling: Stirling 17–1–76–2; Watson 18–4–66–1; Barrett 15–2–62–2; Gray 14–3–45–1; Bracewell 14–2–48–0.

New Zealanders

B. A. Edgar lbw b Wild	27	J. G. Bracewell not out	100
J. G. Wright c G. Cook b Capel	48	†T. E. Blain not out	17
K. R. Rutherford b Wild	5	L-b 6, w 1	7
J. J. Crowe run out	4		
*J. V. Coney c Williams b Wild	21	1/73 2/76 3/81 (5 wkts) 246	
E. J. Gray retired hurt	17	4/96 5/111	

D. A. Stirling, W. Watson and B. J. Barrett did not bat.

Bowling: Walker 13–2–41–0; Capel 11–2–25–1; Williams 21–6–57–0; Wild 24–4–50–3; N. G. B. Cook 10–2–25–0; Boyd-Moss 3.1–1–7–0; Bailey 3–0–35–0.

Umpires: J. H. Hampshire and R. A. White.

DERBYSHIRE v NEW ZEALANDERS

At Derby, August 2, 3, 4. Drawn. Toss: New Zealanders. Maher, Derbyshire's reserve wicket-keeper, who won a place as an opening batsman in July, scored an accomplished maiden century in the county's highest total against the New Zealanders. It also equalled their best for any tour match – against the Indians in 1946. When Maher was run out, he had been at the crease for almost six hours, faced 289 balls and hit nineteen 4s against an attack which showed how much New Zealand depended on Hadlee. Warner, with two 6s and seven 4s, raced to his fourth half-century of the season on the second day, which was curtailed by rain just as the New Zealanders were beginning their innings. Consequently, helped by dropped catches, they took batting practice on the third day with Edgar taking 241 balls to score his only century of the tour in preparation for the second Test.

Derbyshire

*K. J. Barnett c Smith b Barrett	18		R. J. Finney c M. D. Crowe b Stirling		2
B. J. M. Maher run out	126		D. E. Malcolm c Smith b Stirling		7
A. M. Brown c Smith b Stirling	23		J. P. Taylor not out		9
J. E. Morris c and b Gray	49				
B. Roberts lbw b Coney	1		B 1, l-b 4, n-b 1		6
G. Miller lbw b Barrett	51				
†C. Marples c Smith b Watson	24		1/24 2/94 3/199 4/200 5/230		366
A. E. Warner lbw b Stirling	50		6/269 7/339 8/341 9/353		

Bowling: Stirling 26–7–95–4; Watson 28–4–100–1; Barrett 16.2–2–71–2; M. D. Crowe 5–2–10–0; Coney 15–6–29–1; Gray 30–14–43–1; Wright 4–1–13–0.

New Zealanders

J. G. Wright b Malcolm	2		E. J. Gray not out		5
B. A. Edgar not out	110				
K. R. Rutherford c Roberts b Taylor	29		B 7, l-b 7, n-b 8		22
M. D. Crowe c Brown b Miller	51				
J. J. Crowe c Marples b Taylor	5		1/4 2/63 3/160	(5 wkts dec.)	266
*I. V. Coney st Marples b Barnett	42		4/177 5/248		

†I. D. S. Smith, B. J. Barrett, D. A. Stirling and W. Watson did not bat.

Bowling: Malcolm 13–3–30–1; Warner 8–1–14–0; Finney 17–2–71–0; Taylor 15–2–45–2; Miller 30–7–66–1; Barnett 9–3–26–1.

Umpires: R. Julian and D. Lloyd.

ENGLAND v NEW ZEALAND

Second Cornhill Test

At Nottingham, August 7, 8, 9, 11, 12. New Zealand won by eight wickets, their fourth Test victory over England since the 48-year drought broke in 1978. It was a thoroughly deserved and comprehensive win too, dominated by Hadlee, who reacted to the challenge of facing England on his adopted home ground in his customarily combative manner. He took ten wickets in a Test for the seventh time (a feat achieved before only by Barnes, Grimmett and Lillee) and played an important role in New Zealand's first-innings batting recovery, which in the end marked the difference between the teams. When New Zealand were 144 for five, chasing England's 256, the game was nicely balanced. But on the Saturday England's bowlers were outwitted by the capable set of batsmen masquerading as the New Zealand tail, and Bracewell went on to make 110 from 200 deliveries, only the third century of his life.

For New Zealand, this was further confirmation of their new high standing in world cricket; a triumph for Hadlee's exceptional qualities and the whole team's professionalism, resilience and adaptability. For England, it was yet another dismal game, the eighth defeat in ten Tests, and one that was heavily laden with off-the-field murmurings. Gooch was under pressure to announce his availability or otherwise for the tour of Australia (he said no three days after the game); Gower's inclusion became a matter for debate because his form and spirits had understandably declined after he had lost the England captaincy; and then, on the rest day, 50 miles away at Wellingborough, Botham broke the Sunday League 6-hitting record. It was like a distant thunderclap.

The game itself was played in murky, storm-laden weather, except on the Saturday when a large crowd had to share the sunshine with a plague of flying ants. And for the first time all summer Botham, released from his ban the previous week, might have played. Instead the selectors hardly considered him and decided to reconstruct their seam attack in a different way. Foster and Radford were dropped, Dilley again withdrew through injury, and Willey was made twelfth man. Pringle and Emburey were both fit again, and there was a fresh new-ball attack of Thomas, playing his first home Test, and Small, playing his first anywhere.

New Zealand weakened their batting, in theory, and strengthened their bowling by bringing in Stirling for Rutherford; and Coney put England in on a pitch which, though it had a little more life than the featherbed used in 1985, rolled out into a pleasant if still sluggish batting surface. However, demoralised England at once started tumbling to Hadlee, who found movement denied to everyone else and took six for 80 in the first innings; *en route* he rose to third in the list of all-time Test wicket-takers, ahead of Willis, behind Lillee and Botham.

Only Athey and Gower, the two batsmen whose places seemed most in jeopardy, held out for long. Gower brushed aside his problems with one of his most personalised and instinctive innings. There was some debate as to whether he was playing brilliantly or luckily, though he was dismissed only when a delivery from Gray cannoned low and freakishly out of the rough.

At first New Zealand's batsmen found things just as hard. England's attack never looked penetrative, but Small proved an economical and well-organised addition to the attack and the spinners at first proved almost unhittable. However, Hadlee swung the bat as effectively as he had the ball to start the recovery, Gray batted five hours for 50, and Bracewell hit ten 4s in a highly effective percentage innings while the England captain and bowlers went on to auto-pilot. Bracewell's two previous centuries were also against English bowling; at Auckland in a tour match and at Northampton the previous week. He also gave his team more encouragement by getting Gooch caught close in on the Saturday evening.

Monday was frustrating for New Zealand, with only 75 minutes' cricket possible. But even that was remarkable after ferocious storms over the weekend, and it was time enough for Moxon and Athey to be caught by Smith, who thus passed the national wicket-keeping record of 96 Test dismissals, held by the late K. J. Wadsworth.

Next day England caved in again. Their hopes of a draw effectively disappeared when Gower and Gatting both failed, and the nearest thing to counter-attack came from Emburey, who jerked and jabbed his way to 75 in just over two hours until Hadlee returned with the new ball and stopped the nonsense. New Zealand had almost an hour, plus the final twenty overs, to make the 74 they needed, and they got there with eight overs to spare. Hadlee's Man of the Match earned gave the Nottinghamshire crowd something to cheer; England's supporters further afield were beginning to turn distinctly restless. The match attendance was 34,495 with receipts totalling £221,660. – M.E.

England

G. A. Gooch lbw b Hadlee	18	– c Coney b Bracewell	17
M. D. Moxon b Hadlee	9	– c Smith b Hadlee	23
C. W. J. Athey lbw b Watson	55	– (4) c Smith b Bracewell	6
D. I. Gower lbw b Gray	71	– (5) c J. J. Crowe b Bracewell	26
*M. W. Gatting b Hadlee	17	– (6) c Smith b Gray	4
D. R. Pringle c Watson b Stirling	21	– (7) c Gray b Stirling	9
J. E. Emburey c Smith b Hadlee	8	– (8) c M. D. Crowe b Hadlee	75
P. H. Edmonds c Smith b Hadlee	0	– (3) lbw b Hadlee	20
J. G. Thomas b Hadlee	28	– c Gray b Stirling	10
†B. N. French c Coney b Watson	21	– not out	12
G. C. Small not out	2	– lbw b Hadlee	12
B 1, l-b 3, n-b 2	6	B 4, l-b 9, w 1, n-b 2	16

1/18 2/43 3/126 4/170 5/176   256   1/23 2/47 3/63 4/87 5/98   230
6/191 7/191 8/205 9/240   6/104 7/178 8/203 9/203

Bowling: *First Innings*—Hadlee 32–7–80–6; Stirling 17–3–62–1; Gray 13–4–30–1; Watson 16.5–6–51–2; Coney 7–1–18–0; Bracewell 4–1–11–0. *Second Innings*—Hadlee 33.1–15–60–4; Stirling 18–5–48–2; Bracewell 11–5–29–3; Watson 9–3–25–0; Gray 24–9–55–1.

New Zealand

J. G. Wright c Athey b Small	58	– b Emburey		7
B. A. Edgar lbw b Thomas	8			
J. J. Crowe c French b Small	23	– (2) lbw b Small		2
M. D. Crowe c Edmonds b Emburey	28	– (3) not out		48
*J. V. Coney run out	24	– (4) not out		20
E. J. Gray c Athey b Edmonds	50			
R. J. Hadlee c Gooch b Thomas	68			
J. G. Bracewell c Moxon b Emburey	110			
†I. D. S. Smith lbw b Edmonds	2			
D. A. Stirling b Small	26			
W. Watson not out	8			
L-b 4, w 2, n-b 2	8			

1/39 2/85 3/92 4/142 5/144   413   1/5 2/19   (2 wkts) 77
6/239 7/318 8/326 9/391

Bowling: *First Innings*—Small 38–12–88–3; Thomas 39–5–124–2; Pringle 20–1–58–0; Edmonds 28–11–52–2; Emburey 42.5–17–87–2; Gooch 2–2–0–0. *Second Innings*—Small 8–3–10–1; Thomas 4–0–16–0; Emburey 6–1–15–1; Edmonds 4–1–16–0; Pringle 2–0–16–0; Gower 0.0–0–4–0.

Note: D. I. Gower's only delivery was a no-ball that was hit for 4.

Umpires: D. J. Constant and K. E. Palmer.

TCCB XI v NEW ZEALANDERS

At Birmingham, August 13, 14, 15. Drawn. Toss: TCCB XI. The New Zealanders having already played Warwickshire, and Lancashire, the other county scheduled to play them on these days, being involved in a NatWest Bank Trophy semi-final, a TCCB XI was selected to fill the fixture. Batting first in poor light, the New Zealanders were 36 for three before Wright and Jeff Crowe steadied the innings, and Wright was able to declare three-quarters of an hour before the close. On the second day Metcalfe played positively and impressively, but Bailey, usually so free-hitting, began with unusual restraint, taking twenty overs to score 11. Morris and Whitaker, whose 22 included five 4s, gave the innings the impetus it needed. The touring side lost Wright and Franklin cheaply before the close, but on the third day Rutherford elegantly compiled his first hundred of the tour, putting on 167 for the third wicket with Martin Crowe. Although Such and Capel had impressed on the first day, DeFreitas was the only bowler to trouble the New Zealanders in their second innings. Barnett fielded superbly, being responsible for the run-out of Rutherford and the dismissal of Jeff Crowe. When the TCCB XI were given an improbable target of 242 in 75 minutes and twenty overs, Metcalfe again demonstrated his ability with twelve 4s in an unbeaten 71 off 81 balls.

New Zealanders

*J. G. Wright b Capel	59	– c Whitaker b Lawrence		2
T. J. Franklin lbw b DeFreitas	11	– b DeFreitas		0
K. R. Rutherford c Russell b Lawrence	2	– run out		104
M. D. Crowe c Whitaker b Capel	4	– c DeFreitas b Such		61
J. J. Crowe c Whitaker b Such	58	– c Barnett b Capel		18
T. E. Blain c Russell b DeFreitas	29	– c Russell b Capel		16
†I. D. S. Smith b Bailey b Such	31	– not out		35
J. G. Bracewell lbw b Capel	8	– not out		41
W. Watson lbw b Capel	0			
B. J. Barrett not out	0			
L-b 7, n-b 9	16	B 4, l-b 6, n-b 4		14

1/16 2/20 3/36 4/122 5/146   (9 wkts dec.) 218   1/2 2/6 3/173   (6 wkts dec.) 291
6/197 7/216 8/216 9/218   4/187 5/208 6/221

E. J. Chatfield did not bat.

Bowling: *First Innings*—Lawrence 15-2-47-1; DeFreitas 19.5-6-39-2; Capel 17-5-61-4; Such 28-11-37-2; Barnett 10-1-27-0. *Second Innings*—Lawrence 10-2-38-1; DeFreitas 19.1-4-59-1; Capel 23.3-6-76-2; Such 33-5-91-1; Barnett 3-0-17-0.

TCCB XI

K. J. Barnett c Blain b Watson	35	– c Wright b Barrett	7
A. A. Metcalfe b Chatfield	58	– not out	71
R. J. Bailey b Barrett	68	– not out	42
J. E. Morris c Wright b Watson	36		
J. J. Whitaker b Bracewell	22		
*M. C. J. Nicholas c Rutherford b Bracewell	20		
D. J. Capel not out	6		
L-b 10, w 1, n-b 12	23	L-b 1	1

1/73 2/109 3/187 4/218   (6 wkts dec.) 268   1/21   (1 wkt) 121
5/262 6/268

P. A. J. DeFreitas, †R. C. Russell, P. M. Such and D. V. Lawrence did not bat.

Bowling: *First Innings*—Chatfield 23-8-53-1; Barrett 16-1-85-1; Watson 17-1-58-2; Bracewell 23.4-4-57-2; Franklin 1-0-5-0. *Second Innings*—Chatfield 9-1-34-0; Barrett 6-0-37-1; Bracewell 7-2-13-0; Watson 4-0-20-0; Smith 2-0-8-0; Rutherford 1-0-8-0.

Umpires: A. A. Jones and K. J. Lyons.

GLAMORGAN v NEW ZEALANDERS

At Swansea, August 16, 17, 18. Drawn. Toss: Glamorgan. Rain washed out the final day with the contest finely poised and both captains prepared to embrace risks in order to bring about a result. Morris, awarded his county cap before play began, declared Glamorgan's first innings 75 runs behind and the touring side lost three wickets before play ended on Sunday evening. The opening day had produced superb batting by Jeff Crowe and Coney after the visitors had been asked to bat on a damp and greenish pitch. They put on 218 in stylish manner, Crowe's 159 including one 6 and 26 4s in 144 deliveries and Coney's unbeaten 140 one 6 and eighteen 4s in 153 balls. The Sunday saw a spectacular success for Hopkins, marking his benefit year with a timely sense of occasion. He struck five 6s (three in one over) and sixteen 4s in making 142 off 209 deliveries, and his partnership of 180 with Holmes was the highest for any wicket by Glamorgan against the New Zealanders. Previously the record had been established by A. H. Dyson and D. E. Davies with 157 for the first wicket at Swansea in 1937.

New Zealanders

J. G. Wright c Davies b Barwick	6	– c Jones b Derrick	24
K. R. Rutherford c Davies b Thomas	10	– c Hopkins b Barwick	24
J. J. Crowe c Hopkins b Barwick	159	– b Derrick	2
M. D. Crowe run out	28	– not out	8
*J. V. Coney not out	140	– not out	4
E. J. Gray lbw b Thomas	19		
J. G. Bracewell not out	9		
L-b 5, w 1, n-b 1	7	L-b 5, w 4	9

1/13 2/21 3/74   (5 wkts dec.) 378   1/57 2/57 3/66   (3 wkts) 71
4/292 5/367

†I. D. S. Smith, D. A. Stirling, B. J. Barrett and E. J. Chatfield did not bat.

Bowling: *First Innings*—Thomas 19-1-83-2; Barwick 25-3-92-2; North 17-2-57-0; Derrick 17-1-91-0; Holmes 10-1-50-0. *Second Innings*—Thomas 6-0-24-0; Barwick 11-2-34-1; Derrick 5-1-8-2.

Glamorgan

J. A. Hopkins c Smith b Bracewell	142	P. A. Cottey not out 9
*H. Morris c Gray b Stirling	 0	
A. L. Jones c J. J. Crowe b Chatfield	.. 16	L-b 7, n-b 13 20
G. C. Holmes st Smith b Gray	 74	
M. P. Maynard c Bracewell b Chatfield	16	1/7 2/51 3/231 (5 wkts. dec.) 303
J. Derrick not out	 26	4/258 5/274

J. G. Thomas, †T. Davies, P. D. North and S. R. Barwick did not bat.

Bowling: Stirling 11–0–51–1; Barrett 8–0–36–0; Chatfield 22–4–38–2; Gray 18–5–61–1; Bracewell 23–2–86–1; Coney 5–4–1–0; M. D. Crowe 3.5–0–23–0.

Umpires: B. Leadbeater and D. S. Thompsett.

ENGLAND v NEW ZEALAND

Third Cornhill Test

At The Oval, August 21, 22, 23, 25, 26. Drawn. England's attempts to square the series were frustrated first by Wright's grim resolve for seven hours, seven minutes and finally by rain and bad light, which accounted for 15 hours, 40 minutes. On the third day, the only one to pass without interruption, Gower and Gatting, in an unbroken partnership of 219 in 55 overs, had given England a platform from which to advance on the final two days. And on the fourth morning Botham, in his first match of the summer for England, had launched his own spectacular assault – 59 from 36 balls – to put England 101 runs ahead with almost eleven hours remaining. Instead, the weather allowed only six balls more.

From the side that lost at Trent Bridge, England omitted Thomas, Moxon and Pringle. Dilley was again fit: Lamb as well as Botham was recalled. It was England's best-balanced side of the summer. New Zealand, for whom Chatfield was again available, left out Watson and brought in Blain for Smith, who was not fit.

Gatting won the toss and, after a delay of 35 minutes, New Zealand batted on a pitch which looked firm, fast and full of runs. Yet only Coney, with 38 from 41 balls, batted in attacking vein, one lofted drive off Small clearing the mid-off boundary. Had Edmonds, at mid-off, held Gray off Emburey three overs later, New Zealand would have been 115 for five. However, when rain foreclosed after 58 overs, they were 142 for four: Wright 63 not out, Gray 15 not out, Botham three for 36 off eleven overs.

Botham's return to Test cricket was a dramatic one: a wicket with his first ball when Edgar dabbed a lifting delivery to Gooch at first slip. Thus he equalled D. K. Lillee's record of 355 Test wickets. The next ball Jeff Crowe edged low past the left hand of Emburey at third slip, but it was a short-lived reprieve. The last ball of Botham's second over cut back at Crowe and Botham had become the leading wicket-taker in Test cricket.

On the second morning, New Zealand lost three wickets while adding 67 off 31 overs. It was patient work. Wright, who edged a low chance to Botham off Emburey when 90, moved to his hundred soon after lunch, having batted for 374 minutes (291 balls) and hit seven 4s. His fifth in Tests, it was also the first hundred for New Zealand at The Oval. Rain cut two and a half hours from the afternoon, and in the 49 minutes' play that followed the resumption, New Zealand made five scoring strokes from 100 balls and lost Wright, bowled off stump by an Edmonds delivery which was drifting towards the left-hander's middle stump, pitched and turned outside his defence. Blain made a good impression, despite going for 67 minutes for just 1 run on Friday evening and Saturday morning.

England's innings began at mid-day and by lunch they had lost Athey, being tried as an opening batsman. At 62 for three, England were in a familiar position, but Gatting joined Gower for England's best batting of the summer. Gatting's firmly punched drives, cuts and sure footwork against the spin bowlers were complemented by Gower's elegant, powerful and persuasive strokes, which drew out the sun to watch. Even Hadlee was reduced to a sequence of bouncers at Gower which warranted more than simply a private word from umpire Bird. Gower's hundred, in 213 minutes (147 balls), was his fourth against New Zealand and his thirteenth for England.

There was little more than an hour's play on Monday, but in that time England advanced from 281 for three to 388 for five, achieving a first-innings lead for the first time in eleven Tests. Gatting set the pace, hitting 35 off 35 balls as he raced to 121, his sixth Test hundred coming in 288 minutes (175 balls) with his third 4 in an over by Gray. In all he hit thirteen 4s; Gower hit fourteen in his 131.

The remainder of the morning was Botham's as, with ferocious drives and hooks, he rose to the challenge of Hadlee and the new ball. When 20, mis-hooking Stirling, he sent up a steepling catch under which the hapless Blain circled for eight seconds. In his next over, Stirling went for 24 (4646·4) as Botham equalled A. M. E. Roberts's record for the most runs by one batsman off a six-ball over in a Test match (off Botham himself at Port-of-Spain in 1980-81). Hadlee went for 22 in his first two overs with the new ball, Botham hitting 17 of them. New Zealand's field placing resembled something set for the last overs of a Sunday League thrash. When heavy rain drove the players off, Botham had hit two 6s and eight 4s in 54 minutes at the crease, his fifty having come off 32 balls. There was no further play that day, and on the final day Botham bowled one over in separate three-ball spells either side of three o'clock.

Wright was named as Man of the Match, attendance for which was 47,434, with takings of £382,972. The Man of the Series for England was Gower, and for New Zealand, Hadlee. – G.W.

New Zealand

J. G. Wright b Edmonds	119 – not out				7
B. A. Edgar c Gooch b Botham	1 – not out				0
J. J. Crowe lbw b Botham	8				
M. D. Crowe lbw b Dilley	13				
*J. V. Coney c Gooch b Botham	38				
E. J. Gray b Dilley	30				
R. J. Hadlee c French b Edmonds	6				
J. G. Bracewell c Athey b Emburey	3				
†T. E. Blain c Gooch b Dilley	37				
D. A. Stirling not out	18				
E. J. Chatfield c French b Dilley	5				
B 1, w 1, n-b 7	9				

1/17 2/31 3/59 4/106 5/175   287   (no wkt) 7
6/192 7/197 8/251 9/280

Bowling: *First Innings*—Dilley 28.2-4-92-4; Small 18-5-36-0; Botham 25-4-75-3; Emburey 31-15-39-1; Edmonds 22-10-29-2; Gooch 4-1-15-0. *Second Innings*—Botham 1-0-7-0.

England

G. A. Gooch c Stirling b Hadlee	32	J. E. Emburey not out	9
C. W. J. Athey lbw b Hadlee	17		
D. I. Gower b Chatfield	131	L-b 9, w 5, n-b 5	19
A. J. Lamb b Chatfield	0		
*M. W. Gatting b Chatfield	121	1/38 2/62 3/62 (5 wkts dec.) 388	
I. T. Botham not out	59	4/285 5/326	

†B. N. French, P. H. Edmonds, G. R. Dilley and G. C. Small did not bat.

Bowling: Hadlee 23.5-6-92-2; Stirling 9-0-71-0; Chatfield 21-7-73-3; Gray 21-4-74-0; Bracewell 11-1-51-0; Coney 5-0-18-0.

Umpires: H. D. Bird and D. R. Shepherd.

D. B. CLOSE'S XI v NEW ZEALANDERS

At Scarborough, August 31, September 1, 2. Drawn. Toss: D. B. Close's XI. Rutherford re-wrote the record books on the second day when he amassed 317 runs in 230 minutes off 245 balls, his eight 6s and 45 4s being the most boundaries in an innings by a New Zealander. His 317 was the highest score by a New Zealander abroad; the most runs by a New Zealander in one day and the sixth-highest number in a day by any batsman in England; the highest by a player for a New Zealand side and the third-highest score by any New Zealander – the others being B. Sutcliffe with 355 in 1949-50 and R. C. Blunt with 338 not out in 1931-32. (Both were playing for Otago, Rutherford's province.) It was also the highest innings played at Scarborough, comfortably passing J. B. Hobbs's 266 in 1925. Rutherford made 101 before lunch and 199 between lunch and tea, during which session he hit Doshi for four successive 6s, reaching 200 in 186 minutes and scoring his third hundred off 33 balls in 35 minutes. At 219 minutes his was the fifth-fastest first-class triple-hundred and the second-fastest in England, behind C. G. Macartney's in 205 minutes in 1921. Rutherford's stand of 319 for the fifth wicket in 154 minutes with Gray was a new Zealand record for that wicket, surpassing B. Sutcliffe and W. S. Haig's 266 in 1949-50. Despite their big total, 417 runs of which were added when Rutherford was at the crease, the New Zealanders were prevented from forcing victory on the third day by the Pakistan Test players, Sadiq Mohammad and Javed Miandad. On the first day Boycott, who took an hour over his first 9 runs, had looked set to make his 152nd hundred on the placid pitch, but at 81 he lost his middle stump to Chatfield, a fate which befell him again on the third day when Stirling was the bowler.

D. B. Close's XI

G. Boycott b Chatfield	81	– b Stirling	21
Sadiq Mohammad c Chatfield b Bracewell	37	– b Coney	77
M. A. Harper lbw b Bracewell	0	– lbw b Coney	55
Javed Miandad c Edgar b Watson	41	– not out	102
C. L. King b Watson	1	– run out	48
*D. B. Close c Blain b Stirling	22	– c Blain b Watson	4
C. M. Old c Blain b Stirling	0		
F. D. Stephenson lbw b Bracewell	33	– (7) not out	22
†R. W. Taylor c Coney b Bracewell	21		
R. O. Estwick c Blain b Stirling	2		
D. R. Doshi not out	9		
L-b 5, n-b 5	10	B. 1, l-b 11, n-b 17	29
	257	**(5 wkts)**	**358**

1/68 2/68 3/155 4/160 5/177
6/178 7/222 8/224 9/239

1/70 2/144 3/183
4/260 5/306

Bowling: *First Innings*—Stirling 15-1-56-3; Chatfield 19-5-52-1; Watson 14-2-57-2; Bracewell 16.3-6-51-4; Gray 11-3-36-0. *Second Innings*—Stirling 18-2-75-1; Chatfield 19-3-51-0; Gray 10-2-25-0; Watson 20-1-93-1; Coney 12-5-32-2; Bracewell 18-2-59-0; Edgar 1-0-2-0; Rutherford 1-0-9-0.

New Zealanders

T. J. Franklin c Boycott b Doshi	45	J. G. Bracewell not out	32
B. A. Edgar c Sadiq b Estwick	1	D. A. Stirling not out	15
K. R. Rutherford c Taylor b Close	317	L-b 15, n-b 2	17
M. D. Crowe lbw b Estwick	1		
*J. V. Coney c Taylor b Estwick	0	1/15 2/99 3/113	**(7 wkts dec.)** 519
E. J. Gray c Harper b Stephenson	88	4/113 5/432	
†T. E. Blain c Harper b Sadiq	3	6/451 7/476	

W. Watson and E. J. Chatfield did not bat.

Bowling: Estwick 23-4-95-3; Stephenson 23-3-90-1; Old 8-0-46-0; Doshi 22-2-142-1; Close 10-1-71-1; King 4-0-39-0; Sadiq 4-0-21-1.

Umpires: R. Julian and B. Leadbeater.

THE ICC TROPHY, 1986

By MICHAEL BERRY

The third tournament for the ICC Trophy, contested by the Associate Members of the International Cricket Conference, was an unqualified success for all involved. The organisation and common sense of the administrators, co-ordinated with flair and unfaltering diplomacy by Mr Bob Evans, the chairman of the ICC Trophy committee, were refreshing. So too was the hospitality of the Midland clubs, who undertook to host more than 200 fixtures, including many friendly matches. And whereas the tournaments of 1979 and 1982, staged similarly in the Midlands, had been severely affected by poor weather, in 1986 the sun shone on the competition and the cricket achieved new heights.

What disappointments there were arose mainly from the failure of the full complement of eighteen Associate Members to take part. West Africa failed to respond to numerous requests to clarify their entry and were expelled. Singapore, having paid their deposit to the Metropole Hotel at the National Exhibition Centre in Birmingham, the headquarters of the competition for the month of its duration, and having registered their squad, unfortunately were forced to withdraw when some of their selected players could not make the trip.

The favourites were always Zimbabwe, the 1982 winners, who were making their third visit to the United Kingdom in five years. Even the loss of Graeme Hick, whose term of qualification for England would have been set back by his appearance for his native country, did not cause them undue concern. Their experience of first-class cricket at home and abroad, and particularly their knowledge of English conditions, gave them a great advantage. Their range of talents was vast. Andrew Pycroft, Peter Rawson and Grant Paterson all scored centuries, and the variety and craft of their bowling was reflected by the penetration of Eddo Brandes, Ian Butchart and Rawson and the spin of John Traicos, the 39-year-old former South African Test player, who was born in Egypt of Greek parentage. Only by Holland in the final, which for the first time was played at Lord's, was Zimbabwe's defence of the Trophy seriously challenged. Indeed, had it not been for injuries to two of their players, Holland and not Zimbabwe might have represented the Associate Members at this year's World Cup in India and Pakistan.

For those actively promoting cricket in The Netherlands, the performances of the Dutch were a source of satisfaction. Their batting was particularly strong, with Steve Atkinson, a Minor Counties player for Durham, scoring 503 runs and Rupert Gomes, from Trinidad, scoring 499. Both qualified to play for Holland under the four-year residential rule. Paul-Jan Bakker, who played for Hampshire in 1986, was their key bowler with 21 wickets, and they had two highly rated all-rounders in Ron Elferink and Roland Lefebvre.

Close behind Holland came their European rivals, Denmark, who beat Bermuda in the play-off between the losing semi-finalists to take third place. The Danes, whose average height was 6ft 2in, were strengthened by the presence of their two county seam bowlers, Derbyshire's Ole Mortensen, who took 22 wickets, and Søren Henriksen of Lancashire. Bermuda, losing finalists in 1982, selected a young, relatively inexperienced side and almost failed to qualify for the last four after a surprise defeat by the United States. In the end they squeezed through by virtue of their superior run-rate, only to be outclassed by Zimbabwe. Their traditional assets were flamboyant batting, hostile bowling which was spearheaded by Anthony Edwards (nineteen wickets), and spectacular fielding.

Of Bermuda's "local" rivals, the happy-go-lucky Americans fared better than the Canadians, their sustained and somewhat unexpected assault on the semi-finals being built on the example of the captain, Sew Shivnarine, the former Guyana and West Indies all-rounder. Canada, like the United States, also had a predominantly Caribbean complexion, and they found some consolation for their collective disappointment in the batting of Paul Prashad, a 22-year-old from Guyana who had played in Wales for Swansea. His aggregate of 533 runs at 88.33 included centuries against Papua New Guinea, Israel and Fiji.

Other outstanding batting feats came from Papua New Guinea and Hong Kong. On the opening day of the tournament, Hong Kong's Simon Myles, a Mansfield-born batsman who was to make 408 runs, established a new individual scoring record with 172 off 127 balls against Gibraltar. Babina Harry, aged nineteen, scored 338 runs in the unorthodox style that mirrored the Papuan philosophy, and his 127 against Gibraltar helped his side establish a record total of 455 for nine. Papua New Guinea's colourful participation was matched by the Fijians, whose round trip of 24,000 miles brought a string of defeats but no loss of enthusiasm in either their cricket or their melodic post-match pursuits.

Malaysia, who had never won an ICC Trophy match, made amends by reeling off three straight victories over East Africa, Argentina and Bangladesh. However, defeats followed against Kenya, Zimbabwe and Denmark. Kenya and East Africa were overshadowed by Malaysia's flying start, although Kenya almost pulled off an upset when they went close to toppling Denmark. The Danes' last-wicket pair, coming together at 96 for nine, had to add 26 runs to achieve victory. Kenya, led by Tom Tikolo, their first African-born captain, and East Africa both introduced some promising players, as did Bangladesh, although Bangladesh's performances were a shadow of their cricket in 1982, when they were semi-finalists.

Argentina, Gibraltar and Israel happily overcame sparse resources to play their part, although the gulf between these three and most of their opponents prompted a call from some quarters for a streamlining or seeding of the competition in future years. Yet even in defeat, often of massive proportions, they provided their share of personalities on a cosmopolitan stage that was a triumph for cricket and its unrivalled good fellowship.

Group One

	Played	Won	Lost	Points	Run-rate
Zimbabwe	6	6	0	24	4.92
Denmark	6	5	1	20	3.68
Malaysia	6	3	3	12	2.85
Kenya	6	3	3	12	2.73
East Africa	6	2	4	8	3.07
Bangladesh	6	2	4	8	2.82
Argentina	6	0	6	0	2.52

Group Two

	Played	Won	Lost	Points	Run-rate
Holland	8	7	1	28	5.03
Bermuda	8	7	1	28	4.62
USA	8	7	1	28	4.21
Canada	8	5	3	20	4.42
Papua New Guinea	8	4	4	16	5.08
Hong Kong	8	3	5	12	3.58
Fiji	8	2	6	8	3.23
Gibraltar	8	1	7	4	2.58
Israel	8	0	8	0	2.78

GROUP ONE

At Moseley, June 11. Zimbabwe won by 144 runs. Zimbabwe 315 for seven (60 overs) (A. J. Pycroft 135); Bangladesh 171 for eight (60 overs) (M. P. Jarvis four for 28).

At Kenilworth, June 11. Denmark won by 121 runs. Denmark 221 for seven (50 overs) (S. Henriksen 56); Argentina 100 (46.4 overs) (O. H. Mortensen four for 15).

At Burton, June 11. Malaysia won by two wickets. East Africa 140 (55.3 overs) (P. Desai 48; D. John four for 27); Malaysia 141 for eight (54.2 overs) (P. Banerji 56; D. Patel four for 19).

At Wednesbury, June 13. Bangladesh won by 9 runs. Bangladesh 143 (54.4 overs) (Minhazul Abedin 50); Kenya 134 (59 overs).

At Studley, June 13. Malaysia won by 138 runs. Malaysia 226 for nine (60 overs) (P. Budin 58; A. Gooding four for 37); Argentina 88 (54.1 overs) (D. Culley 41).

At Sutton Coldfield, June 16. Zimbabwe won by seven wickets. Kenya 82 (36 overs); Zimbabwe 85 for three (28.2 overs).

At Old Edwardians, June 16. Denmark won by 113 runs. Denmark 274 for seven (60 overs) (S. Mikkelsen 60, O. H. Mortensen 59 not out, S. Henriksen 50); East Africa 161 (46.4 overs).

At Fordhouses, June 18. Zimbabwe won by 207 runs. Zimbabwe 357 for seven (60 overs) (P. W. E. Rawson 125, G. C. Wallace 77); Argentina 150 (45 overs).

At Moseley Ashfield, June 18. Malaysia won by 57 runs. Malaysia 239 (56.5 overs) (A. Stevens 68, Y. Imran 64 not out; Jahangir Badsha four for 39); Bangladesh 182 (51.4 overs) (Rafiqul Alam 51, Gazi Ashraf 41, N. Hoshain 40; D. John five for 40).

At Kidderminster, June 20. Zimbabwe won by eight wickets. Denmark 146 (58.2 overs) (N. Bindslev 42; E. A. Brandes four for 21); Zimbabwe 148 for two (34.5 overs) (G. A. Paterson 86 not out).

At Coventry and North Warwickshire, June 20. East Africa won by six wickets. Bangladesh 162 (58.5 overs) (S. Lakha four for 31); East Africa 166 for four (57.4 overs) (B. Bouri 66 not out, F. Gool 53).

At Himley, June 20. Kenya won by five wickets. Malaysia 154 (54.3 overs) (A. Stevens 66); Kenya 158 for five (42.4 overs) (T. Tikolo 45 not out, T. Iqbal 42).

At Egerton Park, June 23. Zimbabwe won by eight wickets. Malaysia 89 (36.2 overs) (E. A. Brandes four for 13, P. W. E. Rawson four for 21); Zimbabwe 90 for two (21.2 overs).

At Stourbridge, June 23. East Africa won by 84 runs. East Africa 261 for eight (60 overs) (S. Walusimbi 48, G. R. Shariff 48, A. Kumar 44, V. Tarmohamed 41 not out); Argentina 177 (53.4 overs) (L. Alonso 43; A. Kumar six for 26).

At Nantwich, June 25. Zimbabwe won by ten wickets. East Africa 140 (35.2 overs) (G. R. Shariff 72; E. A. Brandes five for 37); Zimbabwe 143 for no wkt (27 overs) (D. L. Houghton 87 not out, G. A. Paterson 55 not out).

At Hereford, June 25. Bangladesh won by seven wickets. Argentina 122 (49.2 overs); Bangladesh 125 for three (39.1 overs) (Raquibul Hassan 47 not out).

At Kenilworth Wardens, June 25. Denmark won by one wicket. Kenya 121 (46.5 overs); Denmark 122 for nine (46 overs).

At Tamworth, June 27. Kenya won by 63 runs. Kenya 209 for nine (60 overs) (A. Patel 65); East Africa 146 (50.1 overs) (A. Kumar 45; Z. Sheikh four for 20).

At Bewdley, June 27. Denmark won by 87 runs. Denmark 265 for eight (60 overs) (O. H. Mortensen 55 not out; A. Stevens four for 48); Malaysia 178 (59.5 overs) (V. Vijayalingham 51).

At Colwall, June 30. Denmark won by four wickets. Bangladesh 147 (54.3 overs) (N. Hoshain 56; O. H. Mortensen four for 31); Denmark 148 for six (43.3 overs) (J. Jensen 49).

At Walmley, June 30. Kenya won by 87 runs. Kenya 228 (53.5 overs) (T. Iqbal 55, T. Tikolo 48); Argentina 141 (48.4 overs) (D. Culley 44 not out; Z. Sheikh four for 25).

GROUP TWO

At Hinckley, June 11. USA won by 72 runs. USA 151 (59.1 overs) (T. Foster 40; D. Abraham four for 27); Canada 79 (39.5 overs) (K. Khan four for 22).

At Wolverhampton, June 11. Holland won by 219 runs. Holland 271 for six (60 overs) (R. E. Lifmann 98, R. J. Elferink 64); Papua New Guinea 52 (20.5 overs) (P. J. Bakker five for 18).

At Wellington, June 11. Bermuda won by 235 runs. Bermuda 304 for nine (60 overs) (W. A. E. Manders 75, R. Hill 41, S. Lightbourne 41); Fiji 69 (20.1 overs) (A. Edwards six for 39, T. Burgess four for 29).

At Bridgnorth, June 11. Hong Kong won by 144 runs. Hong Kong 324 for three (60 overs) (S. D. Myles 172, N. Stearns 62); Gibraltar 180 for five (60 overs) (G. De'Ath 63).

At Market Harborough, June 13. USA won by 49 runs. USA 283 for seven (60 overs) (K. Khan 73, N. Lashkari 50); Papua New Guinea 234 (56 overs) (K. Au 62, T. Vai 41).

At Cheltenham CC, June 13. Holland won by six wickets. Canada 225 (59.5 overs) (D. Singh 50); Holland 226 for four (57 overs) (R. Gomes 82, S. W. Lubbers 51).

At Griff and Coton, Nuneaton, June 13. Bermuda won by 227 runs. Bermuda 407 for eight (60 overs) (A. N. Gibbons 125 not out, R. Hill 84, S. Lightbourne 50); Hong Kong 180 for six (60 overs) (M. Sabine 55).

At Birmingham Municipal, June 13. Fiji won by nine wickets. Israel 155 (60 overs) (D. Moss 108; A. Waqa four for 24); Fiji 157 for one (41 overs) (S. Campbell 68 not out; C. A. C. Browne 46 not out).

At Solihull, June 16. Holland won by ten wickets. USA 88 (34.2 overs) (P. J. Bakker five for 20); Holland 89 for no wkt (23.4 overs) (S. R. Atkinson 45 not out).

At Walsall, June 16. Canada won by 89 runs. Canada 356 for five (60 overs) (P. Prashad 164 not out, D. Singh 65); Papua New Guinea 267 for nine (60 overs) (K. Au 67, T. Vai 51; F. Waithe four for 37, D. Etwaroo four for 64).

At Aldridge, June 16. Bermuda won by nine wickets. Israel 86 (34 overs) (T. Burgess four for 10); Bermuda 87 for one (13.5 overs) (W. A. Reid 63 not out).

At Banbury, June 16. Fiji won by six wickets. Gibraltar 185 for eight (60 overs) (T. Buzaglo 88); Fiji 187 for four (34 overs) (E. Vakausausa 55, T. Batina 47, S. Campbell 44).

At Cannock and Rugeley, June 18. Papua New Guinea won by 369 runs. Papua New Guinea 455 for nine (60 overs) (B. Harry 127, C. Amini 97, A. Leka 69, R. Ila 60 not out; G. De'Ath five for 88); Gibraltar 86 (35 overs) (W. Maha five for 12, G. Ravu four for 16).

At Halesowen, June 18. Canada won by four wickets. Hong Kong 261 for seven (60 overs) (N. Stearns 86, S. D. Myles 82); Canada 265 for six (58.3 overs) (O. Dipchand 76, F. Kirmani 51).

At Old Silhillians, June 18. Holland won by 267 runs. Holland 425 for four (60 overs) (S. R. Atkinson 162, R. E. Lifmann 110, R. Gomes 64 not out, S. W. Lubbers 50); Israel 158 (59.1 overs) (D. Moss 62, S. Perlman 51; R. J. Elferink six for 22).

At Stratford-upon-Avon, June 18. USA won by three wickets. Bermuda 224 for nine (60 overs) (R. Hill 58, W. A. E. Manders 56); USA 225 for seven (56.2 overs) (T. Mills 46 not out).

At Blossomfield, June 20. USA won by five wickets. Fiji 251 (59.3 overs) (C. A. C. Browne 57); USA 255 for five (52.1 overs) (N. Lashkari 104 not out, K. Khan 74).

At Swindon, June 20. Canada won by ten wickets. Gibraltar 46 (25.4 overs) (D. Abraham five for 9); Canada 48 for no wkt (3.5 overs).

At Worcester, June 20. Papua New Guinea won by 277 runs. Papua New Guinea 377 for six (60 overs) (B. Harry 162, K. Au 56, W. Maha 52); Israel 100 (39.4 overs) (C. Amini five for 19).

At Wroxeter and Uppington, June 20. Holland won by 170 runs. Holland 327 for seven (60 overs) (S. R. Atkinson 107, R. Gomes 101); Hong Kong 157 for nine (60 overs) (N. Stearns 47, M. Sabine 45).

At Leamington, June 23. USA won by five wickets. Hong Kong 144 (54 overs) (C. Collins 53); USA 148 for five (24.4 overs).

At Shrewsbury, June 23. Canada won by 235 runs. Canada 329 for seven (60 overs) (P. Prashad 120, C. Neblett 63, F. Kirmani 57); Israel 94 (38.3 overs) (D. Singh four for 34).

At Old Hill, June 23. Papua New Guinea won by 195 runs. Papua New Guinea 381 for eight (60 overs) (W. Maha 113, C. Amini 43, K. Au 41); Fiji 186 (41.2 overs) (N. Tiana four for 50).

At Aston Unity, June 23. Bermuda won by seven wickets. Gibraltar 143 for seven (60 overs); Bermuda 147 for three (27.4 overs) (W. A. Reid 45).

At Aston Manor, June 25. USA won by eight wickets. Gibraltar 136 (44.3 overs) (G. De'Ath 47; U. Prabhudas five for 23); USA 137 for two (25 overs) (S. Shivnarine 70 not out, T. Foster 41 not out).

At Bournville, June 25. Bermuda won by eight wickets. Canada 119 (52 overs) (N. A. Gibbons four for 18); Bermuda 123 for two (35.4 overs) (S. Lightbourne 70 not out).

At Gloucester, June 25. Holland won by nine wickets. Fiji 103 (40.3 overs) (R. J. Elferink six for 14); Holland 106 for one (20.4 overs) (S. R. Atkinson 52 not out).

At Barnt Green, June 25. Hong Kong won by eight wickets. Israel 158 (56 overs) (S. Perlman 41); Hong Kong 159 for two (47 overs) (S. D. Myles 87 not out).

At Solihull Municipal, June 27. USA won by 247 runs. USA 396 for four (60 overs) (K. Khan 143 not out, H. Blackman 83, S. Shivnarine 66, K. Lorick 50 not out); Israel 149 (40.5 overs) (U. Prabhudas four for 34).

At Nuneaton, June 27. Bermuda won by six wickets. Papua New Guinea 184 (51.2 overs) (R. Ila 73, A. Leka 43; T. Burgess four for 47); Bermuda 188 for four (49.5 overs) (R. Hill 65, W. A. E. Manders 49).

At Wellesbourne, June 27. Holland won by eight wickets. Gibraltar 134 (48.5 overs); Holland 137 for two (11 overs) (S. R. Atkinson 70 not out).

At Knowle and Dorridge, June 27. Hong Kong won by seven wickets. Fiji 87 (35.5 overs) (B. Gohel six for 11); Hong Kong 88 for three (31.3 overs).

At Kings Heath, June 30. Canada won by 247 runs. Canada 356 for two (60 overs) (P. Prashad 129, O. Dipchand 105, R. S. A. Jayasekera 41); Fiji 109 (39.3 overs).

At Olton, June 30. Papua New Guinea won by two wickets. Hong Kong 257 for eight (60 overs) (B. Catton 63, R. Brewster 55); Papua New Guinea 259 for eight (58 overs) (T. Vai 55, W. Maha 50).

At Smethwick, June 30. Bermuda won by 30 runs. Bermuda 217 (56.4 overs) (N. A. Gibbons 51, W. A. Reid 46); Holland 187 (59.1 overs) (R. P. Lefebvre 41; S. Lightbourne four for 44).

At Warwick, June 30. Gibraltar won by three wickets. Israel 262 (57.5 overs) (S. Moshe 77, S. Perlman 69, S. Nemblett 63; P. White five for 48); Gibraltar 263 for seven (58.4 overs) (R. Buzaglo 49, C. Rocca 49, W. Scott 44, J. Buzaglo 42).

SEMI-FINALS

BERMUDA v ZIMBABWE

At West Bromwich Dartmouth, July 2. Zimbabwe won by ten wickets.

Bermuda

R. Hill c Houghton b Rawson	24	J. A. Tucker c Paterson b Rawson	15
W. A. Reid b Butchart	7	†A. C. Douglas not out	10
S. Lightbourne b Rawson	7	B 1, l-b 8, w 2	11
A. N. Gibbons c Traicos b Butchart	58		
*W. A. E. Manders c Pycroft b Traicos	33	1/26 2/40 3/41 (7 wkts, 60 overs) 201	
C. M. Marshall c Waller b Shah	1	4/113 5/114	
O. W. Jones not out	35	6/161 7/188	

A. Edwards and T. Burgess did not bat.

Bowling: Rawson 12-4-28-3; Butchart 12-2-58-2; Shah 12-2-30-1; Brandes 12-2-41-0; Traicos 12-1-35-1.

Zimbabwe

R. D. Brown not out	61
G. A. Paterson not out	123
B 1, l-b 3, w 12, n-b 5	21

(no wkt, 38.5 overs) 205

A. H. Shah, A. J. Pycroft, *†D. L. Houghton, A. C. Waller, G. C. Wallace, P. W. E. Rawson, I. P. Butchart, E. A. Brandes and A. J. Traicos did not bat.

Bowling: Edwards 7-1-30-0; Burgess 2-0-19-0; Lightbourne 1-0-11-0; Manders 8-1-40-0; Gibbons 12-0-54-0; Reid 8-0-43-0; Douglas 0.5-0-4-0.

Umpires: B. Morris and B. Turner.

DENMARK v HOLLAND

At Mitchells & Butlers, Edgbaston, July 2. Holland won by five wickets.

Denmark

†N. Bindslev lbw b Elferink	18	M. Seider b Lefebvre	1
J. Jensen c Entrop b Van Weelde	6	*T. Nielsen not out	4
S. Mikkelsen c Schoonheim b Elferink	5	B 4, l-b 25, w 7	36
A. From Hansen c Lefebvre b Visee	14		
S. Henriksen c Gomes b Elferink	42	1/19 2/32 3/54 (8 wkts, 60 overs)	224
J. Morild run out	86	4/62 5/161 6/208	
O. H. Mortensen b Bakker	12	7/211 8/224	

T. Skov Nielsen and S. Thomsen did not bat.

Bowling: Bakker 12–3–32–1; Van Weelde 8–2–44–1; Elferink 12–4–28–3; Lubbers 11–3–33–0; Visee 5–1–17–1; Lefebvre 12–0–41–1.

Holland

S. R. Atkinson lbw b Mortensen	5	P. C. Entrop not out	2
R. E. Lifmann st Bindslev b Skov Nielsen	26		
R. Gomes not out	127		
S. W. Lubbers lbw b Nielsen	0	B 2, l-b 9, w 3, n-b 2	16
R. J. Elferink c Bindslev b Nielsen	7		
R. P. Lefebvre c Mortensen b Skov Nielsen	42	1/13 2/85 3/86 (5 wkts, 54.2 overs)	225
		4/96 5/213	

A. D. Visee, †R. F. Schoonheim, P. J. Bakker and *R. A. H. Van Weelde did not bat.

Bowling: Mortensen 9–2–36–1; Thomsen 12–3–33–0; Henriksen 10–1–34–0; Skov Nielsen 11.2–0–50–2; Nielsen 8–0–42–2; Morild 4–0–19–0.

Umpires: F. Law and G. Wenman.

THIRD PLACE MATCH

At Halesowen, July 4. Denmark won by six wickets. Bermuda 155 (37.3 overs) (W. A. E. Manders 45; S. Henriksen four for 26); Denmark 158 for four (26 overs) (A. From Hansen 78).

FINAL

HOLLAND v ZIMBABWE

At Lord's, July 7, 8. Zimbabwe won by 25 runs. Toss: Holland. Rain caused delays on the first day, when Brown anchored Zimbabwe's innings for 51 overs on a greenish pitch helping the bowlers. In contrast, Waller hit his half-century off 51 balls and the last nine overs yielded 73 runs. Dropped catches marred the Dutch effort, and their misfortune at seeing Elferink injured when he slipped on the wet outfield was compounded on the second day when Lubbers damaged ankle ligaments at a crucial stage of their reply. Resuming at 11 without loss, Holland were 109 for one in the 36th over, and the loss of four wickets was countered by stylish driving from Elferink and Lubbers as they rallied to 182 for six in the 52nd over. Then came Lubbers's injury, and even though he returned at 216 for eight in the 58th over, Zimbabwe had made sure of retaining the ICC Trophy and qualifying for the 1987 World Cup.

Zimbabwe

R. D. Brown c Van Weelde b Lubbers	60	I. P. Butchart not out	13
G. A. Paterson c Visee b Van Weelde	11	E. A. Brandes b Bakker	6
A. H. Shah c Lifmann b Van Weelde	12	A. J. Traicos not out	0
A. J. Pycroft c Schoonheim b Lubbers	30	L-b 8, w 12, n-b 2	22
*†D. L. Houghton b Lubbers	3		
A. C. Waller run out	59	1/18 2/41 3/93 (9 wkts, 60 overs) 243	
G. C. Wallace c Schoonheim b Lefebvre	26	4/101 5/170 6/204	
P. W. E. Rawson run out	1	7/205 8/229 9/238	

Bowling: Bakker 12-0-58-1; Van Weelde 12-1-46-2; Elferink 9-2-31-0; Lefebvre 12-2-34-1; Lubbers 11-0-44-3; Visee 4-1-22-0.

Holland

S. R. Atkinson c Pycroft b Traicos	31	P. J. Bakker b Rawson	11
R. E. Lifmann lbw b Shah	41	†R. F. Schoonheim b Butchart	2
R. Gomes c Rawson b Butchart	27	*R. A. H. Van Weelde b Butchart	0
S. W. Lubbers not out	35	B 1, l-b 19, w 6, n-b 1	27
R. P. Lefebvre b Brandes	8		
P. C. Entrop b Shah	0	1/50 2/109 3/109 (58.4 overs) 218	
A. D. Visee b Brandes	5	4/129 5/130 6/139	
R. J. Elferink b Butchart	31	7/206 8/216 9/218	

Bowling: Rawson 11-3-27-1; Butchart 11.4-1-33-4; Traicos 12-2-31-1; Brandes 12-1-52-2; Shah 12-0-55-2.

Umpires: A. Inman and P. Ogden.

WORLD CUP, 1987

The fourth World Cup tournament, to be staged this year in India and Pakistan, and sponsored by Reliance Industries Limited, the Indian textile and industrial group, commences on October 8. The winners will receive the Reliance Cup and prizemoney of £30,000. The fixtures are:

Group A: Oct. 9-10, Australia v India (Madras); Oct. 10-11, New Zealand v Zimbabwe (Hyderabad, India); Oct. 13-14, Australia v Zimbabwe (Madras); Oct. 14-15, India v New Zealand (Bangalore); Oct. 17-18, India v Zimbabwe (Bombay); Oct. 18-19, Australia v New Zealand (Indore); Oct. 22-23, Australia v India (Delhi); Oct. 23-24, New Zealand v Zimbabwe (Calcutta); Oct. 26-27, India v Zimbabwe (Ahmedabad); Oct. 27-28, Australia v New Zealand (Chandigarh); Oct. 30-31, Australia v Zimbabwe (Cuttack); Oct. 31-Nov. 1, India v New Zealand (Nagpur).

Group B: Oct. 8-9, Pakistan v Sri Lanka (Hyderabad, Pakistan); Oct. 9-10, England v West Indies (Gujranwala); Oct. 12-13, England v Pakistan (Rawalpindi); Oct. 13-14, Sri Lanka v West Indies (Karachi); Oct. 16-17, Pakistan v West Indies (Lahore); Oct. 17-18, England v Sri Lanka (Peshawar); Oct. 20-21, England v Pakistan (Karachi); Oct. 21-22, Sri Lanka v West Indies (Kanpur); Oct. 25-26, Pakistan v Sri Lanka (Faisalabad); Oct. 26-27, England v West Indies (Jaipur); Oct. 30-31, England v Sri Lanka (Pune); Oct. 30-31, Pakistan v West Indies (Karachi).

Semi-finals: Nov. 4-5 at Lahore and Nov. 5-6 at Bombay.

Final: Nov. 8-10 at Calcutta.

The matches will be of 50 overs per team, and a graded system of fines has been devised by the ICC in an effort to ensure that teams bowl their 50 overs in the required time. The fines will become heavier in the semi-finals and final.

THE MARYLEBONE CRICKET CLUB, 1986

At the 199th Annual Meeting of MCC, held at Lord's on May 7, 1986, at which
the President took the chair, C. G. A. Paris's acceptance of the Committee's
invitation to become a Life Vice-President of the club and the appointment of
an Assistant Secretary (M. D. Mence) with special responsibility for ICC
affairs were announced.

As forecast in the previous year's accounts, work on refurbishing the Pavilion following the move of TCCB and NCA to their new premises, plus additional work on the indoor school, involved exceptional expenditure, amounting to over £300,000. Following the serious fire and loss of life at Bradford City's football ground in April, 1985, the club were obliged to undertake, at considerable cost, revised safety measures. The cost of work on the new Mound Stand was now expected to be nearer £4 million than £3 million, and the replacement of lighting in the indoor school as well as the discovery of dry rot in the Library added unforeseen expenditure. As a result of all this, the final surplus after tax was no more than £2,140.

The membership of the club on December 31, 1985, was 18,121, made up of 10,906 town members, 2,352 country members, 3,237 at the special over-65 rate, 278 at the under-25 rate, 273 at the special schoolmasters' rate, 754 on the abroad list, 72 life members, 22 60-year life members, 39 honorary cricket members and 188 honorary life members. In addition there were 30 out-match members, and the number of candidates on the waiting list was 11,503. In 1985, 577 vacancies occurred, owing to 226 deaths, 213 resignations and 148 lapsed memberships. The Committee decided, in view of the size of the waiting list, to limit members to proposing only two candidates a year.

M. C. Cowdrey, CBE, was nominated by J. G. W. Davies to succeed him as President of MCC on October 1, 1986. This assigned to the post for the club's bicentenary year one of the great names of post-war cricket, a former captain of England, winner of 114 Test caps, the maker of 7,624 Test runs and 107 first-class hundreds, and a diligent servant of both MCC and TCCB since his retirement from regular cricket in 1976.

Because there were more nominations than vacancies for the Committee of 1986-87, a postal ballot was held among members, as a result of which Field-Marshal Sir Edwin Bramall, M. C. Cowdrey, I. C. MacLaurin and M. E. L. Melluish were nominated to join the Committee on October 1, 1986. Those due for rotational retirement from the Committee on September 30, 1986, were C. A. Fry, F. G. Mann, Sir Anthony Tuke and J. A. F. Vallance. Following the approval at a Special General Meeting in 1985 of the reintroduction of Associate Members, with a limitation of 2,000 at any one time, all such vacancies were already filled. To avoid overcrowding, Full Membership is to be reduced to 15,000 over a period of years.

MCC v MIDDLESEX

At Lord's, April 23, 24, 25. Abandoned. For the second time in four years, on each occasion with Middlesex as the champion county, the weather prevented any play. By tradition the England captain is offered the captaincy of MCC, but Gower had earlier advised the club that he would not be able to accept. Nicholas, the appointed captain, had led England B on their winter tour of Sri Lanka. Before the match Thomas, the England and Glamorgan fast bowler, withdrew and was replaced by Radford.

MCC

C. L. Smith, M. D. Moxon, *M. C. J. Nicholas, C. W. J. Athey, R. J. Bailey, R. M. Ellison, †B. N. French, R. J. Maru, N. V. Radford, N. G. B. Cook and D. V. Lawrence.

Middlesex

G. D. Barlow, W. N. Slack, *M. W. Gatting, R. O. Butcher, C. T. Radley, †P. R. Downton, J. E. Emburey, P. H. Edmonds, N. F. Williams, N. G. Cowans and W. W. Daniel.

Umpires: J. W. Holder and A. G. T. Whitehead.

†At Cambridge, May 10, 11, 12. MCC drew with Cambridge University (See Cambridge University section).

†At Lord's, May 13. Drawn. MCC 199 for one dec. (R. T. Virgin 72, G. K. Brown 78 not out); MCC Young Cricketers 193 for five (P. Bent 50, I. J. F. Hutchinson 57).

†At Oxford, June 18, 19, 20. MCC beat Oxford University by 254 runs (See Oxford University section).

†At Dublin, July 19, 20, 21. MCC drew with Ireland (See Other Matches, 1986).

†At Lord's, August 21, 22. Drawn. Scotland 246 for six dec. (A. B. Russell 78, O. Henry 51) and 121 for six dec.; MCC 20 for one dec. and 180 for three (Sadiq Mohammad 81, R. J. Lanchbury 75).

†At Roehampton, August 27, 28. MCC won by 80 runs. MCC 156 for seven dec. (R. D. V. Knight 48) and 175 for four dec. (R. V. Lewis 69, J. A. Claughton 52); Wales 134 for four dec. (N. Gumbs 54) and 117 (C. Elward 61; D. Wilson five for 14).

†At Lensbury CC, August 29. Drawn. MCC 201 for six dec. (B. Hassan 96); NAYC 187 for nine (M. A. Atherton 44; R. Merryman four for 42).

MCC ENGLAND HONORARY CRICKET MEMBERS

C. J. Barnett	T. E. Bailey	M. C. Cowdrey, CBE
W. E. Bowes	M. J. K. Smith, OBE	J. T. Murray, MBE
H. Larwood	J. Hardstaff	J. M. Parks
L. E. G. Ames, CBE	J. B. Statham, CBE	D. B. Close, CBE
Sir Leonard Hutton	F. S. Trueman	B. L. D'Oliveira, OBE
D. C. S. Compton, CBE	T. W. Graveney, OBE	R. Illingworth, CBE
D. V. P. Wright	G. A. R. Lock	G. Pullar
T. G. Evans, CBE	C. Milburn	F. J. Titmus, MBE
C. Washbrook	D. A. Allen	D. J. Brown
A. V. Bedser, CBE	R. W. Barber	M. H. Denness
P. B. H. May, CBE	E. R. Dexter	J. M. Brearley, OBE
W. Watson	P. H. Parfitt	R. W. Taylor, MBE
P. E. Richardson	F. H. Tyson	R. G. D. Willis, MBE

OTHER MATCHES AT LORD'S, 1986

June 5, 6, 7, 9, 10. First Cornhill Test. ENGLAND lost to INDIA by five wickets (See Indian tour section).

OXFORD UNIVERSITY v CAMBRIDGE UNIVERSITY

July 2, 3, 4. Cambridge University won by five wickets to record their 54th victory in the 142-match history of the fixture. Few can have finished more dramatically, the winning run coming from a leg-bye off the final ball after Cambridge had chased 106 from sixteen overs – and then 30 from the last three. Getting them, with Thorne and Rutnagur bowling tightly, owed much to some brave hitting from their promoted tailender, Davidson: when he was run out off the fourth ball of the last over, only 4 were needed. Rutnagur's fifth delivery was adjudged a wide, Browne hit 2 off the next ball to bring the scores level, and then came the leg-bye. On the first day Davidson had taken four wickets for 13 in 25 balls as Oxford, put in, crashed from 163 for five to 167 all out after tea. Bail, a Freshman, then established Cambridge's superiority, hitting two 6s and twenty 4s and impressing with the quality of his cover drives as he compiled the seventh-highest score in a University match (174). Thorne, Oxford's captain, batted defiantly for 3 hours, 40 minutes on the last day and looked to be bowling his side to a draw until Davidson's charge brought Cambridge the victory they had been promising throughout.

Oxford University

D. A. Hagan (*Trinity, Leamington Spa and St Edmund Hall*) c Lea b Davidson	12	– c Lea b Ellison	31
A. A. G. Mee (*Merchant Taylors', Northwood and Oriel*) c Brown b Ellison	41	– c Bail b Davidson	0
M. J. Kilborn (*Univ. of NSW and St John's*) c Brown b Ellison	28	– c Brown b Scott	59
*D. A. Thorne (*Bablake and Keble*) b Davidson	61	– not out	104
C. D. M. Tooley (*St Dunstan's and Magdalen*) c Bail b Golding	2	– b Davidson	31
R. S. Rutnagur (*Westminster and New*) b Golding	5	– b Golding	5
N. V. Salvi (*Rossall and Christ Church*) run out	7	– c Browne b Davidson	10
R. A. Rydon (*Sherborne and Pembroke*) c Bail b Davidson	2	– c Browne b Golding	2
†J. E. B. Cope (*St John's, Leatherhead and Keble*) lbw b Davidson	1	– c Lea b Golding	0
T. A. J. Dawson (*Mill Hill and Linacre*) not out	1	– c Brown b Davidson	0
M. P. Lawrence (*Manchester GS and Merton*) b Davidson	0	– lbw b Scott	0
L-b 6, n-b 1	7	B 3, l-b 16, w 4, n-b 3	26
	167		**268**

1/26 2/72 3/97 4/117 5/123
6/163 7/165 8/166 9/167

1/2 2/84 3/121 4/199 5/218
6/229 7/245 8/267 9/267

Bowling: *First Innings*—Davidson 19.1–3–58–5; Scott 15–4–36–0; Ellison 10–5–19–2; Golding 22–8–39–2; Lea 3–0–9–0. *Second Innings*—Scott 17.5–6–43–2; Davidson 30–4–92–4; Golding 30–10–51–3; Ellison 11–5–21–1; Lea 10–0–42–0.

Cambridge University

P. A. C. Bail (*Millfield and Downing*) lbw b Rydon	174	– c Tooley b Thorne	7
M. S. Ahluwalia (*Latymer Upper and Emmanuel*) lbw b Thorne	9		
D. J. Fell (*John Lyon and Trinity*) lbw b Rutnagur	22	– c Lawrence b Rutnagur	20
D. W. Browne (*Stamford and St Catharine's*) c Cope b Rutnagur	2	– (6) not out	13
*D. G. Price (*Haberdashers' Aske's and Homerton*) lbw b Thorne	0	– c Kilborn b Rutnagur	7
A. E. Lea (*High Arcal GS and Churchill*) c Lawrence b Dawson	19	– (2) b Rutnagur	19
A. K. Golding (*Colchester GS and St Catharine's*) b Dawson	47	– not out	0
†A. D. Brown (*Clacton HS and Magdalene*) b Dawson	4		
J. E. Davidson (*Penglais and Trinity*) not out	41	– (4) run out	26
A. M. G. Scott (*Seaford Head and Queens'*) not out	1		
L-b 7, w 3, n-b 1	11	B 1, l-b 12, w 1	14

1/37 2/93 3/97 4/100   (8 wkts dec.) 330   1/12 2/52 3/55   (5 wkts) 106
5/171 6/269 7/280 8/289   4/68 5/102

C. C. Ellison (*Tonbridge and Homerton*) did not bat.

Bowling: *First Innings*—Thorne 32–11–42–2; Rydon 21–4–89–1; Rutnagur 26–3–69–2; Dawson 28–4–92–3; Lawrence 10–2–31–0. *Second Innings*—Thorne 8–0–43–1; Rutnagur 8–0–50–3.

Umpires: M. J. Kitchen and D. O. Oslear.

OXFORD v CAMBRIDGE, RESULTS AND HUNDREDS

The University match dates back to 1827. Altogether there have been 142 official matches, Cambridge winning 54 and Oxford 46, with 42 drawn. Results since 1950:

1950	Drawn	1969	Drawn
1951	Oxford won by 21 runs	1970	Drawn
1952	Drawn	1971	Drawn
1953	Cambridge won by two wickets	1972	Cambridge won by an innings and 25 runs
1954	Drawn		
1955	Drawn	1973	Drawn
1956	Drawn	1974	Drawn
1957	Cambridge won by an innings and 186 runs	1975	Drawn
		1976	Oxford won by ten wickets
1958	Cambridge won by 99 runs	1977	Drawn
1959	Oxford won by 85 runs	1978	Drawn
1960	Drawn	1979	Cambridge won by an innings and 52 runs
1961	Drawn		
1962	Drawn	1980	Drawn
1963	Drawn	1981	Drawn
1964	Drawn	1982	Cambridge won by seven wickets
1965	Drawn	1983	Drawn
1966	Oxford won by an innings and 9 runs	1984	Oxford won by five wickets
1967	Drawn	1985	Drawn
1968	Drawn	1986	Cambridge won by five wickets

Ninety-two three-figure innings have been played in the University matches. For those scored before 1919 see 1940 *Wisden*. Those subsequent to 1919 include the seven highest:

238*	Nawab of Pataudi	1931 Oxford		119	J. M. Brearley	1964 Cam.
211	G. Goonesena	1957 Cam.		118	H. Ashton	1921 Cam.
201*	M. J. K. Smith	1954 Oxford		118	D. R. W. Silk	1954 Cam.
201	A. Ratcliffe	1931 Cam.		117	M. J. K. Smith	1956 Oxford
200	Majid Khan	1970 Cam.		116*	D. R. W. Silk	1953 Cam.
193	D. C. H. Townsend	1934 Oxford		116	M. C. Cowdrey	1953 Oxford
174	P. A. C. Bail	1986 Cam.		115	A. W. Allen	1934 Cam.
170	M. Howell	1919 Oxford		114*	D. R. Owen-Thomas	1972 Cam.
167	B. W. Hone	1932 Oxford		114	J. F. Pretlove	1955 Cam.
158	P. M. Roebuck	1975 Cam.		113*	J. M. Brearley	1962 Cam.
157	D. R. Wilcox	1932 Cam.		113	E. R. T. Holmes	1927 Oxford
155	F. S. Goldstein	1968 Oxford		112*	E. D. Fursdon	1975 Oxford
149	J. T. Morgan	1929 Cam.		111*	G. W. Cook	1957 Cam.
149	G. J. Toogood	1985 Oxford		109	C. H. Taylor	1923 Cam.
146	R. O'Brien	1956 Cam.		109	G. J. Toogood	1984 Oxford
146	D. R. Owen-Thomas	1971 Cam.		108	F. G. H. Chalk	1934 Oxford
145*	H. E. Webb	1948 Oxford		106	Nawab of Pataudi	1929 Oxford
145	D. P. Toft	1967 Oxford		105	E. J. Craig	1961 Cam.
142	M. P. Donnelly	1946 Oxford		104*	D. A. Thorne	1986 Oxford
139	R. J. Boyd-Moss	1983 Cam.		104	H. J. Enthoven	1924 Cam.
136	E. T. Killick	1930 Cam.		104	M. J. K. Smith	1955 Oxford
135	H. A. Pawson	1947 Oxford		103*	A. R. Lewis	1962 Cam.
131	Nawab of Pataudi	1960 Oxford		103*	D. R. Pringle	1979 Cam.
129	H. J. Enthoven	1925 Cam.		102*	A. P. F. Chapman	1922 Cam.
128*	A. J. T. Miller	1984 Oxford		101*	R. W. V. Robins	1928 Cam.
127	D. S. Sheppard	1952 Cam.		101	N. W. D. Yardley	1937 Cam.
124	A. K. Judd	1927 Cam.		100*	M. Manasseh	1964 Oxford
124	A. Ratcliffe	1932 Cam.		100	P. J. Dickinson	1939 Cam.
124	R. J. Boyd-Moss	1983 Cam.		100	N. J. Cosh	1967 Cam.
122	P. A. Gibb	1938 Cam.		100	R. J. Boyd-Moss	1982 Cam.
121	J. N. Grover	1937 Oxford				

* Signifies not out.

Highest Totals

503	Oxford	1900		432-9	Cambridge	1936
457	Oxford	1947		431	Cambridge	1932
453-8	Oxford	1931		425	Cambridge	1938

Lowest Totals

32	Oxford	1878		42	Oxford	1890
39	Cambridge	1858		47	Cambridge	1838

Notes: A. P. F. Chapman and M. P. Donnelly enjoy the following distinction: Chapman scored a century at Lord's in the University match (102*, 1922); for Gentlemen v Players (160, 1922), (108, 1926); and for England v Australia (121, 1930). M. P. Donnelly scored a century at Lord's in the University match (142, 1946); for Gentlemen v Players (162*, 1947); and for New Zealand v England (206, 1949).

A. Ratcliffe's 201 for Cambridge remained a record for the match for only one day, being beaten by the Nawab of Pataudi's 238* for Oxford next day.

M. J. K. Smith (Oxford) and R. J. Boyd-Moss (Cambridge) are the only players who have scored three hundreds. Smith scored 201* in 1954, 104 in 1955, and 117 in 1956; Boyd-Moss scored 100 in 1982 and 139 and 124 in 1983. His aggregate of 489 surpassed Smith's previous record of 477.

The following players have scored two hundreds: W. Yardley (Cambridge) 100 in 1870 and 130 in 1872; H. J. Enthoven (Cambridge) 104 in 1924 and 129 in 1925; Nawab of Pataudi (Oxford) 106 in 1929 and 238* in 1931; A. Ratcliffe (Cambridge) 201 in 1931 and 124 in 1932; D. R. W. Silk (Cambridge) 116* in 1953 and 118 in 1954; J. M. Brearley (Cambridge) 113* in 1962 and 119 in 1964; D. R. Owen-Thomas (Cambridge) 146 in 1971 and 114* in 1972; G. J. Toogood (Oxford) 109 in 1984 and 149 in 1985.

F. C. Cobden, in the Oxford v Cambridge match in 1870, performed the hat-trick by taking the last three wickets and won an extraordinary game for Cambridge by 2 runs. The feat is without parallel in first-class cricket. Other hat-tricks, all for Cambridge, have been credited to A. G. Steel (1879), P. H. Morton (1880), J. F. Ireland (1911), and R. G. H. Lowe (1926).

S. E. Butler, in the 1871 match, took all the wickets in the Cambridge first innings. The feat is unique in University matches. He bowled 24.1 overs. In the follow-on he took five wickets for 57, giving him match figures of fifteen for 95 runs.

The best all-round performances in the history of the match have come from P. R. Le Couteur, who scored 160 and took eleven Cambridge wickets for 66 runs in 1910, and G. J. Toogood, who in 1985 scored 149 and took ten Cambridge wickets for 93.

D. W. Jarrett (Oxford 1975, Cambridge 1976), S. M. Wookey (Cambridge 1975-76), Oxford 1978) and G. Pathmanathan (Oxford 1975-78, Cambridge 1983) are alone in gaining cricket Blues for both Universities.

ETON v HARROW

July 5. Drawn. The overnight rain that delayed the start until three o'clock returned in the late afternoon after Eton, who won the toss, had dismissed Harrow for 37, their lowest total since 1827. Eton were unable to commence their innings and the match was abandoned, leaving members and others to recall another famous collapse by Harrow: "Fowler's Match" in 1910 when the Eton captain took eight for 23 in the second innings to bowl his side to victory by 9 runs. Harrow's score on that occasion was 45.

Harrow

*R. A. Pyman c MacLeay b Pettifer ...	4	A. C. W. Snow c Lunt b Pym	0	
D. I. H. Greenall c MacLeay b York ..	0	N. C. Morgan b Norman	0	
A. W. Sexton retired hurt	5	†A. K. C. Green not out	2	
M. D. S. Raper c Teeger b Pettifer	10			
J. J. Pethers c Winter b Pettifer	3	L-b 2	2	
B. W. M. Burgess b Pym	8			
D. C. Manasseh st Teeger b Norman ..	3	1/1 2/9 3/21 4/24 5/31		37
R. T. Brankin-Frisby lbw b Norman ..	0	6/35 7/35 8/35 9/37		

Bowling: York 9–5–6–1; Pettifer 9–2–22–3; Pym 6.1–3–6–2; Norman 6–5–1–3.

Eton

†J. A. Teeger, R. D. O. MacLeay, *A. D. A. Zagoritis, W. A. C. Pym, L. G. Fernandes, D. E. Pearson, C. E. C. Winter, A. R. G. Lunt, J. D. Norman, H. D. Pettifer and C. York.

Umpires: A. Powley and G. Powley.

ETON v HARROW, RESULTS AND HUNDREDS

Of the 151 matches played Eton have won 50, Harrow 44 and 57 have been drawn. This is the generally published record, but Harrow men object strongly to the first game in 1805 being treated as a regular contest between the two schools, contending that it is no more correct to count that one than the fixture of 1857 which has been rejected.

The matches played during the war years 1915-18 and 1940-45 are not reckoned as belonging to the regular series.

Results since 1950:

1950	Drawn	1969	Drawn
1951	Drawn	1970	Eton won by 97 runs
1952	Harrow won by seven wickets	1971	Drawn
1953	Eton won by ten wickets	1972	Drawn
1954	Harrow won by nine wickets	1973	Drawn
1955	Eton won by 38 runs	1974	Harrow won by eight wickets
1956	Drawn	1975	Harrow won by an innings and 151 runs
1957	Drawn		
1958	Drawn	1976	Drawn
1959	Drawn	1977	Eton won by six wickets
1960	Harrow won by 124 runs	1978	Drawn
1961	Harrow won by an innings and 12 runs	1979	Drawn
		1980	Drawn
1962	Drawn	1981	Drawn
1963	Drawn	1982	Drawn
1964	Eton won by eight wickets	1983	Drawn
1965	Harrow won by 48 runs	1984	Drawn
1966	Drawn	1985	Eton won by 3 runs
1967	Drawn	1986	Drawn
1968	Harrow won by seven wickets		

Forty-five three-figure innings have been played in matches between these two schools. Those since 1918:

161*	M. K. Fosh	1975 Harrow	106	D. M. Smith	1966 Eton
159	E. W. Dawson	1923 Eton	104	R. Pulbrook	1932 Harrow
158	I. S. Akers-Douglas	1928 Eton	103	L. G. Crawley	1921 Harrow
153	N. S. Hotchkin	1931 Eton	103	T. Hare	1947 Eton
151	R. M. Tindall	1976 Harrow	102*	P. H. Stewart-Brown	1923 Harrow
135	J. C. Atkinson-Clark	1930 Eton	102	R. V. C. Robins	1953 Eton
115	E. Crutchley	1939 Harrow	100	R. H. Cobbold	1923 Eton
112	A. W. Allen	1931 Eton	100*	P. V. F. Cazalet	1926 Eton
112*	T. M. H. James	1978 Harrow	100	A. N. A. Boyd	1934 Eton
111	R. A. A. Holt	1937 Harrow	100*	P. M. Studd	1935 Harrow
109	K. F. H. Hale	1929 Eton	100	S. D. D. Sainsbury	1947 Eton
109	N. S. Hotchkin	1932 Eton	100	M. J. J. Faber	1968 Eton
107	W. N. Coles	1946 Eton			

* Signifies not out.

In 1904, D. C. Boles of Eton, making 183, set a record for the match, beating the 152 obtained for Eton in 1841 by Emilius Bayley, afterwards the Rev. Sir John Robert Laurie Emilius Bayley Laurie. M. C. Bird, Harrow, in 1907, scored 100 not out and 131, the only batsman who has made two 100s in the match. N. S. Hotchkin, Eton, played the following innings: 1931, 153; 1932, 109 and 96; 1933, 88 and 12.

July 7, 8. ICC Trophy final. ZIMBABWE beat HOLLAND by 25 runs (See ICC Trophy section).

July 12. Benson and Hedges Cup final. MIDDLESEX beat KENT by 2 runs (See Benson and Hedges Cup section).

July 24, 25, 26, 28, 29. First Cornhill Test. ENGLAND drew with NEW ZEALAND (See New Zealand tour section).

MCC SCHOOLS v NATIONAL ASSOCIATION OF YOUNG CRICKETERS

August 6, 7. Drawn. Toss: NAYC. Instead of its usual dates immediately following the schools trials, now held at Oxford, the fixture was played later because of the Test match. The outstanding performance was that of the sixteen-year-old Middlesex schoolboy, Ramprakash, who on the opening day scored his second hundred of the week in representative cricket, having hit 117 for English Schools against Scotland at Dartford, and followed it with a half-century on the second day. At the close of the first day, during which some 95 minutes were lost because of rain, NAYC were 27 for two, with Lloyd, son of the former England and Lancashire left-hander, not out 16. He went on to a neat 59. With bad weather about, NAYC declared as soon as they were past the follow-on figure, and despite a stoppage of 45 minutes, MCC Schools were able to declare a second time, leaving NAYC to score 233 to win. Although the first four batsmen all scored runs, some initiative was lacking and little attempt was made to match a rate of almost 6 runs an over.

MCC Schools

M. R. Ramprakash (*Gayton HS*) not out	116	– c Taylor b Hutchings 61
S. P. Titchard (*Priestley College*) c Bailey b Taylor	0	– c Boiling b Speak 21
*M. A. Atherton (*Manchester GS*) c Hutchings b Kendrick	37	– not out 15
M. A. Crawley (*Manchester GS*) lbw b Boiling	26	– st Bailey b Hodgson 33
N. A. Stanley (*Bedford Modern*) b Boiling	41	
P. N. Gover (*Eastleigh College*) not out	1	
B 3, l-b 2, w 2, n-b 2	9	W 3, n-b 1 4

1/0 2/73 3/132 4/209   (4 wkts. dec.) 230   1/75 2/86 3/134   (3 wkts. dec.) 134

H. R. J. Trump (*Millfield*), †R. J. Turner (*Millfield*), P. J. Martin (*Danum School*), M. R. Newton (*Peter Symonds*) and I. J. Houseman (*Harrogate GS*) did not bat.

Bowling: *First Innings*—Taylor 9-4-13-1; Winterborne 7-1-28-0; Kendrick 26-8-76-1; Ealham 14-4-44-0; Boiling 21-2-64-2. *Second Innings*—Taylor 5-1-19-0; Winterborne 2-0-12-0; Kendrick 3-3-0-0; Ealham 3-0-14-0; Boiling 4-2-9-0; Speak 6-0-42-1; Hutchings 3-0-14-1; Hodgson 3-0-24-1.

National Association of Young Cricketers

N. Hutchings (*Hampshire*) c Turner b Houseman	0	– c Trump b Atherton 28
G. Lloyd (*Lancashire*) lbw b Newton	59	– c Ramprakash b Houseman 25
N. J. Speak (*Lancashire*) b Martin	5	– c Crawley b Newton 61
J. Boiling (*Surrey*) st Turner b Newton	18	
*G. D. Hodgson (*Lancashire*) not out	26	– b Martin 31
D. C. Percival (*Warwickshire*) not out	13	
M. Ealham (*Kent*) (did not bat)		– not out 10
B 1, l-b 2, w 2, n-b 6	11	B 4, l-b 1, w 2, n-b 3 10

1/0 2/24 3/81 4/100   (4 wkts. dec.) 132   1/44 2/69 3/140 4/165   (4 wkts) 165

†M. J. Bailey (*Staffordshire*), G. Winterborne (*Surrey*), N. M. Kendrick (*Surrey*) and M. Taylor (*Middlesex*) did not bat.

Bowling: *First Innings*—Houseman 11-2-35-1; Martin 8-2-25-1; Newton 10-0-43-2; Trump 7-1-26-0. *Second Innings*—Houseman 9-1-34-1; Martin 14-3-38-1; Newton 5-0-40-1; Trump 2-0-16-0; Atherton 10-3-32-1.

Umpires: D. F. Dean and F. S. Tillson.

The National Cricket Association after the match selected the following to play for NCA Young Cricketers against Combined Services: S. P. Titchard (Cheshire), M. R. Ramprakash (Middlesex), *M. A. Atherton (Lancashire), G. D. Hodgson (Lancashire), N. J. Speak (Lancashire), G. Lloyd (Lancashire), H. R. J. Trump (Somerset), †R. J. Turner (Somerset), P. J. Martin (Yorkshire), I. J. Houseman (Yorkshire) and M. Taylor (Middlesex).

August 8. Drawn. Combined Services 252 for five dec. (L. M. J. Willatt 53, E. C. Gordon-Lennox 123); NCA Young Cricketers 165 for seven (M. R. Ramprakash 47, M. A. Atherton 48).

August 11. SRI LANKA YOUNG CRICKETERS beat ENGLAND YOUNG CRICKETERS by four wickets (See Sri Lankan Young Cricketers tour section).

WILLIAM YOUNGER CUP FINAL

August 23. Stourbridge beat Weston-super-Mare by four wickets and so for the third year in succession a Birmingham League club won the National Club Championship. Put in, Weston were going nicely until Smith, aged 49, brought himself into the attack with off-spin and Brewer, also 49, bowled slow left-arm. From 73 without loss off twenty overs, they faltered to 84 for two in the next eleven. In the final over, Lampitt, who played once for Worcestershire during the season, hit the stumps three times, taking a wicket with his last two balls. When his turn came to bat, he and Patel, another with Worcestershire experience, set Stourbridge on the way to victory, which Tolley, a promising young all-rounder, made certain of after Cup final nerves had resulted in an unnecessary loss of wickets. Stourbridge, in addition to the trophy, received £1,000, the runners-up £600, while the Man of the Match award went to Hill, Weston's fast bowler.

Weston-super-Mare

C. Norton b Smith	39		*J. Scott not out	3
E. Langford lbw b Brewer	23		K. Farrow b Lampitt	0
†S. J. Turner run out	30		D. Hill b Lampitt	0
M. Dyer c Smith b Banks	26			
D. Sperring b Lampitt	2		L-b 4, w 7, n-b 5	16
N. Evans c sub b Lampitt	32			
R. J. Turner b Lampitt	4		1/73 2/75 3/127 4/132 5/160 (45 overs) 175
N. Brown lbw b Banks	0		6/169 7/169 8/175 9/175

Bowling: Lampitt 9–0–43–5; Tolley 9–3–28–0; Banks 9–0–43–2; Smith 9–1–37–1; Brewer 9–1–2–1.

Stourbridge

H. V. Patel c Scott b Hill	54		D. Collins c Norton b Scott	11
J. P. Wright c S. J. Turner b Hill	0		G. Haynes not out	2
D. A. Banks c Farrow b Evans	23		B 2, l-b 14, w 2	18
S. R. Lampitt lbw b Hill	42			
P. Fox run out	3		1/17 2/58 3/134 (6 wkts, 43.4 overs) 176
C. Tolley not out	23		4/135 5/145 6/174

†G. Saint, M. Brewer and *G. Smith did not bat.

Bowling: Hill 9–2–37–3; Evans 9–1–29–1; Scott 8.4–0–40–1; Farrow 9–0–20–0; Brown 8–0–34–0.

Umpires: A. Davies and G. Newport.

NATIONAL CLUB CHAMPIONSHIP WINNERS 1969-86

D. H. Robins Trophy

1969 HAMPSTEAD beat Pocklington Pixies by 14 runs.
1970 CHELTENHAM beat Stockport by three wickets.
1971 BLACKHEATH beat Ealing by eight wickets.
1972 SCARBOROUGH beat Brentham by six wickets.
1973 WOLVERHAMPTON beat The Mote by five wickets.
1974 SUNBURY beat Tunbridge Wells by seven wickets.
1975 YORK beat Blackpool by six wickets.

John Haig Trophy

1976   SCARBOROUGH beat Dulwich by five wickets.
1977   SOUTHGATE beat Bowdon by six wickets.
1978   CHELTENHAM beat Bishop's Stortford by 15 runs.
1979   SCARBOROUGH beat Reading by two wickets.
1980   MOSELEY beat Gosport Borough by nine wickets.
1981   SCARBOROUGH beat Blackheath by 57 runs.
1982   SCARBOROUGH beat Finchley by 4 runs.

William Younger Cup

1983   SHREWSBURY beat Hastings and St Leonards Priory by 2 runs.
1984   OLD HILL beat Bishop's Stortford by five wickets.
1985   OLD HILL beat Reading by nine wickets.
1986   STOURBRIDGE beat Weston-super-Mare by four wickets.

NORSK HYDRO VILLAGE CHAMPIONSHIP FINAL

August 24. Forge Valley beat Ynysygerwn by 5 runs. The Welsh village had lost once before to a Yorkshire village in a Lord's final – in 1979 – and the same fate awaited them. Electing to bat first, Forge Valley, from near Scarborough, started slowly, not reaching double figures until the tenth over, but Wall and Ridsdale gave the innings a solid foundation and Grayson sped up the scoring. For Ynysygerwn, Steve Williams, a junior rugby international, stood out in the field, saving many runs and taking three good catches, while Curtis, the only working collieryman in the Welsh side, took four wickets. As their innings developed, the Welshmen looked to be in control, but they too lost wickets at critical times, leaving Thomas, a survivor of the 1979 defeat, to carry the burden. This he did with great skill until the last ball of the 39th over when he was seventh out with the score 160, and not until the final ball could the Yorkshiremen be certain of victory. Mr J. G. W. Davies, President of MCC, presented the trophy and a cheque for £500 to the winners and the runners-up received £350.

Forge Valley

M. J. Wall lbw b Curtis	24	T. S. Glaves run out	15
C. J. Ridsdale run out	41	C. D. Northgraves not out	0
A. J. Grayson c Prowt b Curtis	29		
*M. C. Shepherdson b Curtis	10	L-b 13, w 6, n-b 3	22
D. E. Pettitt run out	12		
D. W. Hartley c S. Williams b Harris	3	1/60 2/106 3/119 (9 wkts, 40 overs) 170	
J. B. Sowden c S. Williams b Harris	1	4/138 5/139 6/142	
N. H. Pettitt c S. Williams b Curtis	13	7/142 8/164 9/170	

†E. Willmore did not bat.

Bowling: Evans 9-3-19-0; Jenkins 9-0-29-0; Curtis 9-0-38-4; R. Williams 4-0-24-0; Harris 9-0-47-2.

Ynysygerwn

J. W. Harris b Shepherdson	9	D. L. Evans not out	0
*R. Williams b Shepherdson	23	†C. J. Prowt run out	5
A. W. Jenkins c Sowden b N. H. Pettitt	15		
R. W. Hicks run out	22	L-b 9, w 6, n-b 1	16
D. W. Thomas b Glaves	55		
S. Williams b Glaves	13	1/20 2/46 3/49 (9 wkts, 40 overs) 165	
D. C. Owen b Glaves	6	4/104 5/139 6/159	
H. Jenkins b Sowden	1	7/160 8/160 9/165	

J. Curtis did not bat.

Bowling: Shepherdson 9-3-21-2; Northgraves 7-1-18-0; Hartley 7-0-31-0; N. H. Pettitt 3-0-13-1; Glaves 8-1-34-3; Sowden 6-0-39-1.

Umpires: M. C. Baylis and R. P. Wilby.

VILLAGE CHAMPIONSHIP WINNERS 1972-86

Sponsored by John Haig Ltd

1972 TROON (Cornwall) beat Astwood Bank (Worcestershire) by seven wickets.
1973 TROON (Cornwall) beat Gowerton (Glamorgan) by 12 runs.
1974 BOMARSUND (Northumberland) beat Collingham (Nottinghamshire) by three
      wickets.
      (Played at Edgbaston after being rained off at Lord's).
1975 GOWERTON (Glamorgan) beat Isleham (Cambridgeshire) by six wickets.
1976 TROON (Cornwall) beat Sessay (Yorkshire) by 18 runs.
1977 COOKLEY (Worcestershire) beat Lindal Moor (Cumbria) by 28 runs.

Sponsored by *The Cricketer*

1978 LINTON PARK (Kent) beat Toft (Cheshire) by four wickets.

Sponsored by Samuel Whitbread and Co. Ltd

1979 EAST BIERLEY (Yorkshire) beat Ynysygerwn (Glamorgan) by 92 runs.
1980 MARCHWIEL (Clwyd) beat Longparish (Hampshire) by 79 runs.
1981 ST FAGANS (Glamorgan) beat Broad Oak (Yorkshire) by 22 runs.
1982 ST FAGANS (Glamorgan) beat Collingham (Nottinghamshire) by six wickets.
1983 QUARNDON (Derbyshire) beat Troon (Cornwall) by eight wickets.
1984 MARCHWIEL (Clwyd) beat Hursley Park (Hampshire) by 8 runs.

No sponsor: organised by *The Cricketer*

1985 FREUCHIE (Fifeshire) beat Rowledge (Surrey) by virtue of fewer wickets lost with
      the scores level.

Sponsored by Norsk Hydro Fertilizers

1986 FORGE VALLEY (Yorkshire) beat Ynysygerwn (Glamorgan) by 5 runs.

September 6. NatWest Bank Trophy final. SUSSEX beat LANCASHIRE by seven wickets
(See NatWest Bank Trophy section).

GETTY'S GIFTS TO CRICKET

J. Paul Getty II, who in 1985 contributed £1.5 million towards the cost of the new Mound
Stand at Lord's, made further generous donations to cricket in 1986. These included £380,000
to help create the Arundel Castle Cricket Foundation, the aim of which is to provide cricket
and cricket coaching for young people who might otherwise have little or no opportunity to
play the game. The Foundation is to be administered by J. R. T. Barclay, until last season the
captain of Sussex. Other donations by Getty included £10,000 each to Kent, as a contribution
towards the cost of the new stand at Canterbury, to Gloucestershire, for help with the cost of a
new cricket school at the Phoenix County Ground in Bristol, and to Leicestershire, in support
of an indoor sports centre.

BRITANNIC ASSURANCE
COUNTY CHAMPIONSHIP, 1986

Three bowling points on the first day of their penultimate match, against Nottinghamshire at Trent Bridge, clinched for Essex their third title in four seasons. Only briefly out of the top three, in July, they led for much of the time, won more games than any other county and were worthy champions.

Gloucestershire, top of the table from early in July until the last week of August, encouraged their supporters as they had in 1985, but Essex had games in hand and once again Gloucestershire could not last the distance, failing to win any of their last seven games. By September, Nottinghamshire were Essex's most likely challenger, but they were unable to win at Hove or beat Essex. When Walker, the last Northamptonshire batsman, held out against them in the final match of the season, they had to settle for fourth place.

Surrey were third, an improvement of three places, although they never really threatened the front-runners and were a little fortunate to pip Nottinghamshire. Worcestershire retained fifth place, and having built their team methodically in recent years they must now look for a higher position. Hampshire, well placed for much of the season, finally had to settle for sixth, a disappointment after being runners-up in 1985. A more positive approach might have seen Leicestershire do better than seventh, and more enterprise at certain times would have placed Kent higher than eighth.

Continued over

BRITANNIC ASSURANCE CHAMPIONSHIP

Win = 16 points	Played	Won	Lost	Drawn	Bonus points Batting	Bowling	Points
1 – Essex (4)	24	10	6	8	51	76	287
2 – Gloucestershire (3)	24	9	3	12	50	65	259
3 – Surrey (6)	24	8	6	10	54	66	248
4 – Nottinghamshire (8)	24	7	2	15	55	80	247
5 – Worcestershire (5)	24	7	5	12	58	72	242
6 – Hampshire (2)	23	7	4	12	54	69	235
7 – Leicestershire (16)	24	5	7	12	55	67	202
8 – Kent (9)	24	5	7	12	42	75	197
9 – Northamptonshire (10) ...	24	5	3	16	53	60	193
10 – Yorkshire (11)	24	4	5	15	62	59	193
11 – Derbyshire (13)	24	5	5	14	42	70	188
12 { Middlesex (1)	24	4	9	11	47	65	176
{ Warwickshire (15)	24	4	5	15	61	51	176
14 – Sussex (7)	23	4	7	12	46	56	166
15 – Lancashire (14)	23	4	5	14	41	51	156
16 – Somerset (17)	23	3	7	13	52	52	152
17 – Glamorgan (12)	24	2	7	15	39	47	118

1985 positions are shown in brackets.
The total for Derbyshire includes 12 points for a win in a one-innings match and that for Yorkshire includes 8 points for levelling the scores in a drawn match.
Where sides are equal on points, the one with the most wins has priority.

The following two matches were abandoned and are not included in the above table: May 31, June 2, 3 – Sussex v Somerset at Horsham; September 13, 15, 16 – Hampshire v Lancashire at Southampton.

Northamptonshire were a difficult side to beat and advanced one place to ninth, while Yorkshire, after two early wins, settled into the middle order for a similar advance from eleventh to tenth. Few of their experienced players did themselves justice but observers sensed a pinprick of light at the tunnel's end. Derbyshire began slowly but as in 1985 they developed as the season progressed, their eleventh position being an improvement of two places.

Middlesex, the defending champions, suffered such a collapse that for a time in July they were on the bottom rung of the ladder. The return of their Test players and two late victories took them to twelfth equal alongside Warwickshire, but the time may have come for a reappraisal of the multi-talented Metropolitan county. Warwickshire's advance of three places hardly justified some of the optimism at Edgbaston, and a fall of seven places to fourteenth by Sussex was of concern to a club with such potential.

Lancashire were top of the table at the beginning of June with two wins and 28 bonus points, but after this false dawn began the slide to fifteenth. The dismissal of their manager and coach, and the replacement of Lloyd as captain, were sad sequels to a dismal season. At Somerset, so concerned were the committee over their sixteenth position, and other failures, that brave if not universally popular measures were taken. Glamorgan's committee deserved praise for their imaginative decision in mid-season to appoint the young Hugh Morris as their captain. It is hoped that their courage is rewarded in 1987 by a move away from seventeenth. – R.W.B.

REGULATIONS FOR BRITANNIC ASSURANCE CHAMPIONSHIP

(As applied in 1986)

1. Prizemoney

First (Essex)	£22,000
Second (Gloucestershire)	£10,500
Third (Surrey)	£5,250
Fourth (Nottinghamshire)	£2,750
Fifth (Worcestershire)	£1,375
Winner of each match	£210
Championship Player of the Year (P. A. J. DeFreitas)	£500
County of the Month	£750
Player of the Month	£250

2. Scoring of Points

(*a*) For a win, sixteen points, plus any points scored in the first innings.

(*b*) In a tie, each side to score eight points, plus any points scored in the first innings.

(*c*) If the scores are equal in a drawn match, the side batting in the fourth innings to score eight points, plus any points scored in the first innings.

(*d*) **First Innings Points** (awarded only for performances **in the first 100 overs** of each first innings and retained whatever the result of the match).

   (i) A maximum of four batting points to be available as under:
      150 to 199 runs – 1 point; 200 to 249 runs – 2 points; 250 to 299 runs – 3 points; 300 runs or over – 4 points.

(*e*) If play starts when fewer than eight hours' playing time remains and a one innings match is played, no first innings points shall be scored. The side winning on the one innings to score twelve points.

(*f*) The side which has the highest aggregate of points gained at the end of the season shall be the Champion County. Should any sides in the Championship table be equal on points the side with most wins will have priority.

3. Hours of Play

1st and 2nd days . . . . . 11.00 a.m. to 6.30 p.m. or after 110 overs, whichever is the later. (For Sunday play, the home county may decide to play from 12 noon to 7.30 p.m.)

3rd day . . . . 11.00 a.m. to 6.00 p.m. or after 102 overs, whichever is the later.

(*a*) If play is suspended (including any interval between innings) the minimum number of overs to be bowled in a day to be reduced by one over for each full $3\frac{1}{2}$ minutes of such suspension or suspensions in aggregate.

(*b*) If at 5.00 p.m. on the third day more than 82 overs have been bowled (or a proportionately reduced number in the event of any suspension), a minimum of 20 overs to be bowled in accordance with Law 17.6 and 17.7, except that all calculations in regard to suspensions or the start of a new innings to be based on $3\frac{1}{2}$ minutes per over. Play may cease on the third day at any time between 5.30 p.m. and 6.00 p.m. by mutual agreement of the captains.

(*c*) The captain's may agree or, in the event of disagreement, the umpires may decide to play 30 minutes (or minimum ten overs) extra time at the end of the first and/or second day's play if, in their opinion, it would bring about a definite result on that day. In the event of the possibility of a finish disappearing before the full period has expired, the whole period must be played out. Any time so claimed does not effect the timing for cessation of play on the third day.

(*d*) If an innings ends during the course of an over, that part shall count as a full over so far as the minimum number of overs per day is concerned.

Intervals

Lunch: 1.15 p.m. to 1.55 p.m. (1st and 2nd days), 2.15 p.m. to 2.55 p.m. on Sundays when play commences at 12 noon
1.00 p.m. to 1.40 p.m. (3rd day)

Tea: 4.10 p.m. to 4.30 p.m. (1st and 2nd days), 5.10 p.m. to 5.30 p.m. on Sundays when play commences at 12 noon, or when 40 overs remain to be bowled, whichever is the later.
3.40 p.m. to 4.00 p.m. (3rd day), or when 40 overs remain to be bowled, whichever is the later.

4. Substitutes

A substitute shall be allowed as of right in the event of a cricketer currently playing in a Championship match being required to join the England team for a Test match (or one-day international). Such substitutes may be permitted to bat or bowl in that match, subject to the approval of the TCCB. The player who is substituted may not take further part in the match, even though he might not be required by England. If batting at the time, the player substituted shall be retired "not out" and his substitute may be permitted to bat subject to the approval of the TCCB.

5. New ball

The captain of the fielding side shall have the choice of taking the new ball after 100 overs have been bowled with the old one.

6. Covering of Pitches

The whole pitch shall be covered:

(*a*) The night before a match and, if necessary, until the first ball is bowled.

(*b*) On each night of a match and, if necessary, throughout Sunday.

(*c*) In the event of play being suspended on account of bad light or rain during the specified hours of play.

7. Declarations

Law 14 will apply, but, in addition, a captain may also forfeit his first innings, subject to the provisions set out in Law 14.2. If, owing to weather conditions, the match has not started when fewer than eight hours of playing time remain, the first innings of each side shall automatically be forfeited and a one-innings match played.

CHAMPION COUNTY SINCE 1864

Note: The earliest county champions were decided usually by the fewest matches lost, but in 1888 an unofficial points system was introduced. In 1890, the Championship was constituted officially. From 1977 to 1983 it was sponsored by Schweppes, and since 1984 by Britannic Assurance.

1864	Surrey	1900	Yorkshire	1950	{ Lancashire / Surrey
1865	Nottinghamshire	1901	Yorkshire		
1866	Middlesex	1902	Yorkshire	1951	Warwickshire
1867	Yorkshire	1903	Middlesex	1952	Surrey
1868	Nottinghamshire	1904	Lancashire	1953	Surrey
1869	{ Nottinghamshire / Yorkshire	1905	Yorkshire	1954	Surrey
		1906	Kent	1955	Surrey
1870	Yorkshire	1907	Nottinghamshire	1956	Surrey
1871	Nottinghamshire	1908	Yorkshire	1957	Surrey
1872	Nottinghamshire	1909	Kent	1958	Surrey
1873	{ Gloucestershire / Nottinghamshire	1910	Kent	1959	Yorkshire
		1911	Warwickshire	1960	Yorkshire
1874	Gloucestershire	1912	Yorkshire	1961	Hampshire
1875	Nottinghamshire	1913	Kent	1962	Yorkshire
1876	Gloucestershire	1914	Surrey	1963	Yorkshire
1877	Gloucestershire	1919	Yorkshire	1964	Worcestershire
1878	Undecided	1920	Middlesex	1965	Worcestershire
1879	{ Nottinghamshire / Lancashire	1921	Middlesex	1966	Yorkshire
		1922	Yorkshire	1967	Yorkshire
1880	Nottinghamshire	1923	Yorkshire	1968	Yorkshire
1881	Lancashire	1924	Yorkshire	1969	Glamorgan
1882	{ Nottinghamshire / Lancashire	1925	Yorkshire	1970	Kent
		1926	Lancashire	1971	Surrey
1883	Nottinghamshire	1927	Lancashire	1972	Warwickshire
1884	Nottinghamshire	1928	Lancashire	1973	Hampshire
1885	Nottinghamshire	1929	Nottinghamshire	1974	Worcestershire
1886	Nottinghamshire	1930	Lancashire	1975	Leicestershire
1887	Surrey	1931	Yorkshire	1976	Middlesex
1888	Surrey	1932	Yorkshire	1977	{ Middlesex / Kent
1889	{ Surrey / Lancashire / Nottinghamshire	1933	Yorkshire		
		1934	Lancashire	1978	Kent
		1935	Yorkshire	1979	Essex
1890	Surrey	1936	Derbyshire	1980	Middlesex
1891	Surrey	1937	Yorkshire	1981	Nottinghamshire
1892	Surrey	1938	Yorkshire	1982	Middlesex
1893	Yorkshire	1939	Yorkshire	1983	Essex
1894	Surrey	1946	Yorkshire	1984	Essex
1895	Surrey	1947	Middlesex	1985	Middlesex
1896	Yorkshire	1948	Glamorgan	1986	Essex
1897	Lancashire	1949	{ Middlesex / Yorkshire		
1898	Yorkshire				
1899	Surrey				

Notes: The title has been won outright as follows: Yorkshire 31 times, Surrey 18, Nottinghamshire 13, Middlesex 8, Lancashire 8, Kent 6, Essex 4, Gloucestershire 3, Warwickshire 3, Worcestershire 3, Glamorgan 2, Hampshire 2, Derbyshire 1, Leicestershire 1.

Eight times the title has been shared as follows: Nottinghamshire 5, Lancashire 4, Middlesex 2, Surrey 2, Yorkshire 2, Gloucestershire 1, Kent 1.

The earliest date the Championship has been won in any season since it was expanded in 1895 was August 12, 1910, by Kent.

BRITANNIC ASSURANCE CHAMPIONSHIP
STATISTICS FOR 1986

County	For			Against		
	Runs	*Wickets*	*Avge*	*Runs*	*Wickets*	*Avge*
Derbyshire	9,846	317	31.05	9,279	281	33.02
Essex	8,827	329	26.82	8,777	365	24.04
Glamorgan	8,644	314	27.52	8,739	219	39.90
Gloucestershire	9,176	308	29.79	9,068	307	29.53
Hampshire	8,192	240	34.13	8,528	312	27.33
Kent	8,568	330	25.96	9,011	311	28.97
Lancashire	8,753	280	31.26	8,264	233	35.46
Leicestershire	8,940	290	30.82	8,606	300	28.68
Middlesex	8,042	280	28.72	7,661	268	28.58
Northamptonshire ..	9,504	270	35.20	9,891	300	32.97
Nottinghamshire	9,402	265	35.47	10,089	351	28.74
Somerset	9,657	290	33.30	9,549	241	39.62
Surrey	9,287	305	30.44	8,719	295	29.55
Sussex	9,226	287	32.14	9,558	262	36.48
Warwickshire	10,046	289	34.76	9,059	254	35.66
Worcestershire	9,417	240	39.23	10,256	330	31.07
Yorkshire	9,097	277	32.84	9,570	282	33.93
	154,624	4,911	31.48	154,624	4,911	31.48

COUNTY CHAMPIONSHIP – MATCH RESULTS, 1864-1986

County	*Years of Play*	*Played*	*Won*	*Lost*	*Tied*	*Drawn*
Derbyshire	1871-87; 1895-1986	2,022	495	748	0	779
Essex	1895-1986	1,985	553	583	5	844
Glamorgan	1921-1986	1,520	334	525	0	661
Gloucestershire ..	1870-1986	2,261	673	834	1	753
Hampshire	1864-85; 1895-1986	2,094	547	731	4	812
Kent	1864-1986	2,382	877	725	4	776
Lancashire	1865-1986	2,460	921	498	3	1,038
Leicestershire ...	1895-1986	1,952	417	740	1	794
Middlesex	1864-1986	2,163	814	556	5	788
Northamptonshire	1905-1986	1,719	406	615	3	695
Nottinghamshire .	1864-1986	2,292	696	601	0	995
Somerset	1882-85; 1891-1986	1,992	471	832	3	686
Surrey	1864-1986	2,539	1,020	555	4	960
Sussex	1864-1986	2,432	691	838	5	898
Warwickshire ...	1895-1986	1,966	515	577	1	873
Worcestershire ..	1899-1986	1,907	459	692	1	755
Yorkshire	1864-1986	2,561	1,175	414	2	970
Cambridgeshire .	1864-69; 1871	19	8	8	0	3
		18,133	11,072	11,072	21	7,040

Notes: Matches abandoned without a ball bowled are wholly excluded.

Counties participated in the years shown, except that there were no matches in the years 1915-18 and 1940-45; Hampshire did not play inter-county matches in 1868-69, 1871-74 and 1879; Worcestershire did not take part in the Championship in 1919.

COUNTY CHAMPIONSHIP – FINAL POSITIONS, 1890-1986

	Derbyshire	Essex	Glamorgan	Gloucestershire	Hampshire	Kent	Lancashire	Leicestershire	Middlesex	Northamptonshire	Nottinghamshire	Somerset	Surrey	Sussex	Warwickshire	Worcestershire	Yorkshire
1890	—	—	—	6	—	3	2	—	7	—	5	—	1	8	—	—	3
1891	—	—	—	9	—	5	2	—	3	—	4	5	1	7	—	—	8
1892	—	—	—	7	—	7	4	—	5	—	2	3	1	9	—	—	6
1893	—	—	—	9	—	4	2	—	3	—	6	8	5	7	—	—	1
1894	—	—	—	9	—	4	4	—	3	—	7	6	1	8	—	—	2
1895	5	9	—	4	10	14	2	12	6	—	12	8	1	11	6	—	3
1896	7	5	—	10	8	9	2	13	3	—	6	11	4	14	12	—	1
1897	14	3	—	5	9	12	1	13	8	—	10	11	2	6	7	—	4
1898	9	5	—	3	12	7	6	13	2	—	8	13	4	9	9	—	1
1899	15	6	—	9	10	8	4	13	2	—	10	13	1	5	7	12	3
1900	13	10	—	7	15	3	2	14	7	—	5	11	7	3	6	12	1
1901	15	10	—	14	7	7	3	12	2	—	9	12	6	4	5	11	1
1902	10	13	—	14	15	7	5	11	12	—	3	7	4	2	6	9	1
1903	12	8	—	13	14	8	4	14	1	—	5	10	11	2	7	6	3
1904	10	14	—	9	15	3	1	7	4	—	5	12	11	6	7	13	2
1905	14	12	—	8	16	6	2	5	11	13	10	15	4	3	7	8	1
1906	16	7	—	9	8	1	4	15	11	11	5	11	3	10	6	14	2
1907	16	7	—	10	12	8	6	11	5	15	1	14	4	13	9	2	2
1908	14	11	—	10	9	2	7	13	4	15	8	16	3	5	12	6	1
1909	15	14	—	16	8	1	2	13	6	7	10	11	5	4	12	8	3
1910	15	11	—	12	6	1	4	10	3	9	5	16	2	7	14	13	8
1911	14	6	—	12	11	2	4	15	3	10	8	16	5	13	1	9	7
1912	12	15	—	11	6	3	4	13	5	2	8	14	7	10	9	16	1
1913	13	15	—	9	10	1	8	14	6	4	5	16	3	7	11	12	2
1914	12	8	—	16	5	3	11	13	2	9	10	15	1	6	7	14	4
1919	9	14	—	8	7	2	5	9	13	12	3	5	4	11	15	—	1
1920	16	9	—	8	11	5	2	13	1	14	7	10	3	6	12	15	4
1921	12	15	17	7	6	4	5	11	1	13	8	10	2	9	16	14	3
1922	11	8	16	13	6	4	5	14	7	15	2	10	3	9	12	17	1
1923	10	13	16	11	7	5	3	14	8	17	2	9	4	6	12	15	1
1924	17	15	13	6	12	5	4	11	2	16	6	8	3	10	9	14	1
1925	14	7	17	10	9	5	3	12	6	11	4	15	2	13	8	16	1
1926	11	9	8	15	7	3	1	13	6	16	4	14	5	10	12	17	2
1927	5	8	15	12	13	4	1	7	9	16	2	14	6	10	11	17	3
1928	10	16	15	5	12	2	1	9	8	13	3	14	6	7	11	17	4
1929	7	12	17	4	11	8	2	9	6	13	1	15	10	4	14	16	2
1930	9	6	11	2	13	5	1	12	16	17	4	13	8	7	15	10	3
1931	7	10	15	2	12	3	6	16	11	17	5	13	8	4	9	14	1
1932	10	14	15	13	8	3	6	12	10	16	4	7	5	2	9	17	1
1933	6	4	16	10	14	3	5	17	12	13	8	11	9	2	7	15	1
1934	3	8	13	7	14	5	1	12	10	17	9	15	11	2	4	16	5
1935	2	9	13	15	16	10	4	6	3	17	5	14	11	7	8	12	1
1936	1	9	16	4	10	8	11	15	2	17	5	7	6	14	13	12	3
1937	3	6	7	4	14	12	9	16	2	17	10	13	8	5	11	15	1
1938	5	6	16	10	14	9	4	15	2	17	12	7	3	8	13	11	1
1939	9	4	13	3	15	5	6	17	2	16	12	14	8	10	11	7	1
1946	15	8	6	5	10	6	3	11	2	17	16	13	4	11	17	14	8
1947	5	11	9	2	16	4	3	14	1	17	11	11	6	9	15	7	7
1948	6	13	1	8	9	15	5	11	3	17	14	12	2	16	7	10	4
1949	15	9	8	7	16	13	11	17	1	6	11	9	5	13	4	3	1

	Derbyshire	Essex	Glamorgan	Gloucestershire	Hampshire	Kent	Lancashire	Leicestershire	Middlesex	Northamptonshire	Nottinghamshire	Somerset	Surrey	Sussex	Warwickshire	Worcestershire	Yorkshire
1950	5	17	11	7	12	9	1	16	14	10	15	7	1	13	4	6	3
1951	11	8	5	12	9	16	3	15	7	13	17	14	6	10	1	4	2
1952	4	10	7	9	12	15	3	6	5	8	16	17	1	13	10	14	2
1953	6	12	10	6	14	16	3	3	5	11	8	17	1	2	9	15	12
1954	3	15	4	13	14	11	10	16	7	7	5	17	1	9	6	11	2
1955	8	14	16	12	3	13	9	6	5	7	11	17	1	4	9	15	2
1956	12	11	13	3	6	16	2	17	5	4	8	15	1	9	14	9	7
1957	4	5	9	12	13	14	6	17	7	2	15	8	1	9	11	16	3
1958	5	6	15	14	2	8	7	12	10	4	17	3	1	13	16	9	11
1959	7	9	6	2	8	13	5	16	10	11	17	12	3	15	4	14	1
1960	5	6	11	8	12	10	2	17	3	9	16	14	7	4	15	13	1
1961	7	6	14	5	1	11	13	9	3	16	17	10	15	8	12	4	2
1962	7	9	14	4	10	11	16	17	13	8	15	6	5	12	3	2	1
1963	17	12	2	8	10	13	15	16	6	7	9	3	11	4	4	14	1
1964	12	10	11	17	12	7	14	16	6	3	15	8	4	9	2	1	5
1965	9	15	3	10	12	5	13	14	6	2	17	7	8	16	11	1	4
1966	9	16	14	15	11	4	12	8	12	5	17	3	7	10	6	2	1
1967	6	15	14	17	12	2	11	2	7	9	15	8	4	13	10	5	1
1968	8	14	3	16	5	2	6	9	10	13	4	12	15	17	11	7	1
1969	16	6	1	2	5	10	15	14	11	9	8	17	3	7	4	12	13
1970	7	12	2	17	10	1	3	15	16	14	11	13	5	9	7	6	4
1971	17	10	16	8	9	4	3	5	6	14	12	7	1	11	2	15	13
1972	17	5	13	3	9	2	15	6	8	4	14	11	12	16	1	7	10
1973	16	8	11	5	1	4	12	9	13	3	17	10	2	15	7	6	14
1974	17	12	16	14	2	10	8	4	6	3	15	5	7	13	9	1	11
1975	15	7	9	16	3	5	4	1	11	8	13	12	6	17	14	10	2
1976	15	6	17	3	12	14	16	4	1	2	13	7	9	10	5	11	8
1977	7	6	14	3	11	1	16	5	1	9	17	4	14	8	10	13	12
1978	14	2	13	10	8	1	12	6	3	17	7	5	16	9	11	15	4
1979	16	1	17	10	12	5	13	6	14	11	9	8	3	4	15	2	7
1980	9	8	13	7	17	16	15	10	1	12	3	5	2	4	14	11	6
1981	12	5	14	13	7	9	16	8	4	15	1	3	6	2	17	11	10
1982	11	7	16	15	3	13	12	2	1	9	4	6	5	8	17	14	10
1983	9	1	15	12	3	7	12	4	2	6	14	10	8	11	5	16	17
1984	12	1	13	17	15	5	16	4	3	11	2	7	8	6	9	10	14
1985	13	4	12	3	2	9	14	16	1	10	8	17	6	7	15	5	11
1986	11	1	17	2	6	8	15	7	12	9	4	16	3	14	12	5	10

Note: From 1969 onwards, positions have been given in accordance with the Championship regulations which state that "Should *any* sides in the table be equal on points the side with most wins will have priority".

DERBYSHIRE

President: The Duke of Devonshire
Chairman: C. N. Middleton
Chairman, Cricket Committee: G. L. Willatt
Secretary/Chief Executive: R. Pearman
   County Ground, Nottingham Road, Derby
   DE2 6DA (Telephone: 0332-383211)
Captain: K. J. Barnett
Coach: P. E. Russell

Derbyshire ended the 1986 season knowing, as they had a year earlier, that strengthening is required if they are to challenge for any of the four trophies. They had good days and have moved forward from the dismal era of the early 1970s, but they lacked the strength which produces consistency. Their scanning of the retained lists was given more urgency by Geoff Miller's decision to join Essex and the retirement, to take charge of the Second XI, of Alan Hill.

Miller, not seen at his best for two seasons, sought his release with a year to run on his contract. His request met with no opposition which, for a Derbyshire-born player in a cosmopolitan dressing-room, was sad. Only R. W. Taylor played more times for England while with the county, but there was a feeling that Miller's output did not reflect his ability. Derbyshire hope that the improving Rajeshwar Sharma will prove an adequate replacement. Hill's stance became more extraordinary with each season, but his determination remained undimmed and he ended, in his benefit year, with the highest aggregate of his career. His solid contribution will be missed by a county already short of batting.

John Morris had a fine season, especially in the Britannic Assurance Championship, in which Derbyshire showed modest gains by winning two more matches than in 1985 and rising two places in the table. Morris set out to occupy the crease on a more permanent basis and to exchange tantalisingly brief glimpses of quality for more sustained success. He was one of four players awarded county caps during the summer but, of the others, only Ole Mortensen had a prosperous season. He was absent for a month playing for Denmark in the ICC Trophy but rediscovered his nip and hostility. Bruce Roberts, uneasily cast as a wicket-keeper in the early weeks for the purpose of one-day competitions, later lost his batting touch and, after being capped, Paul Newman did not play again because of a back injury.

Kim Barnett, although never entirely fit after his early return from the England B tour of Sri Lanka with an undiagnosed infection, again passed 1,500 runs in his aggressive style and, despite receiving little support on Sundays, set a Derbyshire record with 700 runs in the John Player League. The only other batting of note in the top half of the order came from Bernard Maher. Iain Anderson's unconvincing form let in Maher, then reserve wicket-keeper, as an opening batsman in mid-July. He averaged almost 40 in the first-class list and won back his place behind the stumps from Chris Marples, who was released at the end of the season.

Fortunately, there were some entertaining assaults from the later batsmen, especially the fast bowler, Allan Warner, who came back with credit after savage treatment in the Benson and Hedges Cup quarter-final. Martin Jean-Jacques made a startling entry into first-class cricket after being spotted playing for Buckinghamshire and the London club, Shepherd's Bush. In his first match, against Yorkshire at Sheffield, he scored 73 batting at number eleven and shared a county record last-wicket stand of 132 with Hill. The 93 raised by J. Humphries and J. Horsley against Lancashire had survived since 1914 and Derbyshire became the last of the seventeen first-class counties to manage three figures for the tenth wicket. In his fourth match, Jean-Jacques took eight for 77 in Kent's first innings, and though he was unlikely to maintain those peaks, he showed obvious promise. Another record partnership came from Anderson and Hill, who added 286 against Cornwall in the NatWest Bank Trophy, the best for any wicket in all the limited-overs competitions.

After winning all four of their Benson and Hedges Cup zonal matches, Derbyshire disappointed in limited-overs games. Bowling let them down against Kent in the quarter-final and, just as surely, their batting betrayed them against Surrey in the second round of the NatWest Trophy. A modest John Player League season had its high point with victory over Yorkshire by ten wickets.

Michael Holding bowled extremely well when available under the terms of his contract and was appointed vice-captain for 1987. His deputy, Devon Malcolm, advanced significantly, which Derbyshire recognised by offering him a five-year contract. Genuinely fast, Malcolm was still classified as an overseas player, despite seven years' residence after coming to England to rejoin his parents and complete his education. Injuries to Newman and Roger Finney upset the balance of the attack and this, combined with uncertain weather, produced a number of contrived finishes. Barnett, whose inclination is to gamble, saw these as preferable to playing out inevitable draws, but a better answer came from the determined effort to produce fast, bouncy pitches at Derby, matching those at Chesterfield. These helped to produce magnificent Championship cricket against Kent and Middlesex in July.

There is no doubt that Derbyshire are bent on improvement in every area, especially now that their facilities are good. They are moving towards a more stable organisation, with Barnett settled as captain, and they hope to avoid the rapid turnover of staff which followed their 1981 NatWest Trophy success. Of that team, only Barnett, John Wright and Newman remain. – J.G.M.

DERBYSHIRE 1986

[*Bill Smith*

Back row: B. Roberts, O. H. Mortensen, R. Sharma, D. E. Malcolm, M. Jean-Jacques, A. E. Warner, B. J. M. Maher. *Front row*: C. Marples, A. Hill, K. J. Barnett (*captain*), G. Miller, J. E. Morris. *Insets*: R. J. Finney, I. S. Anderson, M. A. Holding, P. G. Newman.

DERBYSHIRE RESULTS

All first-class matches – Played 25 : Won 5, Lost 5, Drawn 15.

County Championship matches – Played 24 : Won 5, Lost 5, Drawn 14.

Bonus points – Batting 42, Bowling 70.

Competition placings – Britannic Assurance County Championship, 11th; NatWest Bank Trophy, 2nd round; Benson and Hedges Cup, q-f; John Player League, 9th equal.

BRITANNIC ASSURANCE CHAMPIONSHIP AVERAGES

BATTING

	Birthplace	M	I	NO	R	HI	Avge
‡J. E. Morris	Crewe	24	38	3	1,654	191	47.25
‡A. Hill	Buxworth	24	40	6	1,438	172*	42.29
‡K. J. Barnett ...	Stoke-on-Trent	24	42	3	1,484	143	38.05
B. J. M. Maher ...	Hillingdon	13	23	5	626	77*	34.77
‡P. G. Newman ...	Leicester	3	4	2	62	34	31.00
R. Sharma	Nairobi, Kenya	15	17	6	321	71	29.18
A. E. Warner	Birmingham	19	27	6	543	91	25.85
‡R. J. Finney	Darley Dale	16	16	5	275	54	25.00
‡B. Roberts	Lusaka, N. Rhodesia	24	36	3	771	124*	23.36
M. Jean-Jacques ...	Soufrière, Dominica	9	12	3	208	73	23.11
C. Marples	Chesterfield	14	23	3	442	57	22.10
‡I. S. Anderson ...	Derby	13	23	1	449	93	20.40
‡G. Miller	Chesterfield	19	26	2	461	65	19.20
‡M. A. Holding ...	Kingston, Jamaica	14	20	2	295	36*	16.38
D. E. Malcolm ...	Kingston, Jamaica	8	6	4	30	29*	15.00
‡O. H. Mortensen ..	Vejle, Denmark	16	17	9	69	31*	8.62
J. P. Taylor	Ashby-de-la-Zouch	3	4	1	9	6	3.00

Also batted: A. M. Brown (*Heanor*) (1 match) 21, 9*; C. F. B. P. Rudd (*Sutton Coldfield*) (1 match) 1; L. J. Wood (*Ruislip*) (2 matches) 5, 2; ‡J. G. Wright (*Darfield, NZ*) (2 matches) 3, 7, 4.

* *Signifies not out.*   ‡ *Denotes county cap.*

The following played a total of ten three-figure innings for Derbyshire in County Championship matches: J. E. Morris 4, A. Hill 3, K. J. Barnett 2, B. Roberts 1.

BOWLING

	O	M	R	W	BB	Avge
M. A. Holding	388.1	110	1,045	52	7-97	20.09
O. H. Mortensen ...	416.2	111	1,082	46	5-35	23.52
D. E. Malcolm	203.2	35	735	27	5-42	27.22
M. Jean-Jacques ...	159	16	599	22	8-77	27.22
R. J. Finney	301.4	58	986	28	7-54	35.21
R. Sharma	140.5	33	407	11	3-72	37.00
G. Miller	604.2	180	1,340	32	5-37	41.87
A. E. Warner	341.1	66	1,186	28	4-38	42.35

Also bowled: K. J. Barnett 95–25–333–5; A. Hill 9–3–22–1; B. J. M. Maher 33–2–151–3; C. Marples 4–0–48–0; J. E. Morris 44.4–5–245–1; P. G. Newman 73.1–16–198–9; B. Roberts 22–5–53–2; C. F. B. P. Rudd 28.3–7–90–0; J. P. Taylor 72–10–254–6; L. J. Wood 39–10–95–2.

Wicket-keepers: C. Marples 30 ct, 3 st; B. J. M. Maher 23 ct; B. Roberts 2 ct, 1 st.

Leading Fielders: K. J. Barnett 23; R. Sharma 14; G. Miller 13.

At Lord's, April 26, 28, 29. DERBYSHIRE drew with MIDDLESEX.

DERBYSHIRE v SOMERSET

At Chesterfield, April 30, May 1, 2. Drawn. Derbyshire 5 pts, Somerset 8 pts. Toss: Derbyshire. Derbyshire began their home season with an unbalanced team containing five seam bowlers and Roberts as wicket-keeper, this being their plan for limited-overs matches. Richards wrapped up Derbyshire's uneven first innings, and when Somerset batted Botham drove massively to score 61 off 50 balls. Newman returned his best figures for 22 months to restrict Somerset's lead to 86, but although Derbyshire began the third day 124 for two, neither side was capable of creating a position from which the match could be won. With Somerset's attack weakened by the withdrawal of Botham, with a strained side, Hill and Morris added 153 before Roberts beat his previous best score, hitting three 6s and thirteen 4s as he reached his hundred in 145 minutes.

Derbyshire

*K. J. Barnett c Garner b Dredge	64	– b Richards	51
I. S. Anderson b Botham	3	– c Botham b Garner	12
A. Hill b Garner	17	– lbw b Davis	93
J. E. Morris c Richards b Botham	53	– c Roebuck b Marks	81
†B. Roberts c Gard b Richards	40	– not out	124
R. Sharma c Roebuck b Richards	7	– c sub b Roebuck	24
P. G. Newman c Gard b Botham	3	– not out	25
R. J. Finney not out	25		
A. E. Warner c Garner b Richards	0		
M. A. Holding c Roebuck b Richards	5		
O. H. Mortensen c Roebuck b Garner	2		
L-b 1, n-b 3	4	B 6, l-b 14, w 2, n-b 6	28

1/30 2/74 3/94 4/166 5/186   223   1/41 2/85 3/238   (5 wkts dec.) 438
6/188 7/192 8/193 9/199   4/274 5/399

Bonus points – Derbyshire 2, Somerset 4.

Bowling: *First Innings*—Garner 14-1-34-2; Botham 18-1-61-3; Davis 9-0-44-0; Dredge 12-0-47-1; Richards 11-3-36-4. *Second Innings*—Garner 21-5-45-1; Botham 13-1-45-0; Davis 22-3-73-1; Dredge 21-6-49-0; Richards 18-5-56-1; Hardy 1-0-5-0; Marks 27-9-83-1; Roebuck 12-2-30-1; Rose 5-0-29-0; Felton 1-0-3-0.

Somerset

N. A. Felton c Newman b Warner	24	J. Garner b Newman	16
*P. M. Roebuck lbw b Newman	14	C. H. Dredge c Roberts b Newman	5
J. J. E. Hardy c Morris b Newman	73	†T. Gard not out	0
I. V. A. Richards c Barnett b Mortensen	22		
B. C. Rose c Anderson b Newman	28	B 4, l-b 16, w 3, n-b 13	36
I. T. Botham c Roberts b Holding	61		
V. J. Marks lbw b Finney	27	1/44 2/50 3/86 4/152 5/247	309
M. R. Davis run out	3	6/256 7/285 8/291 9/306	

Bonus points – Somerset 4, Derbyshire 3 (Score at 100 overs: 300-8).

Bowling: Holding 24-8-57-1; Mortensen 26-7-54-1; Newman 24.1-7-62-5; Warner 10-1-53-1; Finney 19-5-63-1.

Umpires: H. D. Bird and B. J. Meyer.

DERBYSHIRE v NOTTINGHAMSHIRE

At Derby, May 24, 25, 26. Drawn. Derbyshire 5 pts, Nottinghamshire 7 pts. Toss: Nottinghamshire. After struggling to find his touch, Rice hit fifteen 4s in his 120 and, although Nottinghamshire lost their last five wickets for 45 runs, Hadlee had Derbyshire 62 for five by the close. Finney's solid 54 enabled them to avoid the follow-on but, by the end of the second day, Nottinghamshire led by 337. Rice decided to bat on for seven overs, which became an important factor as Derbyshire recovered astonishingly from 26 for six. Morris batted well with good support from Finney. Surprisingly little use was made of Cooper as Marples frustrated Nottinghamshire with the first half-century of his career. Mortensen, awarded his county cap on the first day, saw out the last 21 overs with Marples to earn for Derbyshire a remarkable draw.

Nottinghamshire

R. T. Robinson lbw b Mortensen	5	– b Warner ... 31
B. C. Broad c Hill b Mortensen	9	– lbw b Finney ... 34
D. W. Randall b Mortensen	43	– lbw b Mortensen ... 31
*C. E. B. Rice c and b Miller	120	– (5) c Miller b Mortensen ... 1
P. Johnson c Anderson b Miller	9	– (4) lbw b Finney ... 71
M. Newell c Morris b Miller	28	– not out ... 26
R. J. Hadlee not out	30	– c and b Miller ... 20
†C. W. Scott b Warner	11	– not out ... 7
E. E. Hemmings b Miller	3	
K. E. Cooper c Miller b Warner	0	
J. A. Afford b Warner	0	
L-b 17, n-b 4	21	B 4, l-b 7, n-b 3 ... 14
	279	(6 wkts dec.) **235**

1/6 2/27 3/113 4/134 5/223
6/234 7/263 8/270 9/272

1/48 2/84 3/137
4/139 5/197 6/225

Bonus points – Nottinghamshire 3, Derbyshire 4.

Bowling: *First Innings*—Mortensen 16–3–42–3; Finney 16–5–49–0; Miller 41–13–88–4; Warner 18.4–2–51–3; Barnett 7–0–32–0. *Second Innings*—Mortensen 17–9–35–2; Finney 14–1–38–2; Miller 34–2–114–1; Warner 13–2–37–1.

Derbyshire

*K. J. Barnett c Scott b Afford	3	– c Johnson b Rice ... 1
I. S. Anderson b Hadlee	0	– c Scott b Hadlee ... 6
A. Hill lbw b Hadlee	7	– b Cooper ... 3
J. G. Wright c Scott b Hadlee	3	– c Scott b Afford ... 7
J. E. Morris c Rice b Hadlee	1	– st Scott b Afford ... 81
B. Roberts c Robinson b Hadlee	42	– b Afford ... 0
G. Miller c Scott b Cooper	21	– c Scott b Cooper ... 2
R. J. Finney c Scott b Hadlee	54	– c Randall b Afford ... 45
†C. Marples lbw b Cooper	0	– not out ... 50
A. E. Warner c Robinson b Afford	4	– b Afford ... 39
O. H. Mortensen not out	10	– not out ... 2
L-b 6	6	B 1, l-b 10, w 1 ... 12
	151	(9 wkts) **248**

1/1 2/11 3/11 4/12 5/31
6/64 7/97 8/103 9/110

1/12 2/12 3/22 4/22
5/23 6/26 7/147 8/154 9/218

Bonus points – Derbyshire 1, Nottinghamshire 4.

Bowling: *First Innings*—Hadlee 18.5–6–31–6; Cooper 13–4–32–2; Afford 23–5–63–2; Hemmings 18–9–19–0. *Second Innings*—Hadlee 17–3–43–1; Rice 10–3–16–1; Afford 38–15–71–5; Cooper 10–5–17–2; Hemmings 34–10–90–0.

Umpires: R. Palmer and R. A. White.

DERBYSHIRE v ESSEX

At Derby, May 31, June 2, 3. Essex won by 116 runs. Essex 20 pts, Derbyshire 3 pts. Toss: Essex. There was no play on the first day. On the second, after Mortensen had taken two wickets in his second over, Border scored his first Championship century, reaching 100 in 195 minutes. In all he batted for 207 minutes and hit fourteen 4s. When rain washed out the third morning, Barnett declared and Essex forfeited their second innings, leaving Derbyshire to score 257 in a minimum of 76 overs. Fletcher had taken over the captaincy of Essex because Gooch had returned to attend the birth of his twins. Lever bowled extremely well and Foster was unlucky to have three catches dropped, but Derbyshire's batting was poor. They neither chased nor defended effectively and only Finney showed much resistance. Childs bowled steadily, and Essex won with more than thirteen overs to spare.

Essex

*G. A. Gooch c Barnett b Mortensen ..	3	N. A. Foster not out 53
B. R. Hardie b Mortensen	48	J. K. Lever not out 9
P. J. Prichard lbw b Mortensen	0	
A. R. Border c sub b Finney 110		B 11, l-b 5, w 1, n-b 4 21
K. W. R. Fletcher st Roberts b Wood .	53	
D. R. Pringle lbw b Finney	0	1/15 2/15 3/132 (7 wkts dec.) 300
†D. E. East c Wright b Wood	3	4/200 5/204 6/211 7/288

J. H. Childs and D. L. Acfield did not bat.

Bonus points – Essex 4, Derbyshire 3.

Bowling: Mortensen 22–7–49–3; Finney 12.2–3–38–2; Rudd 28.3–7–90–0; Wood 30–4–82–2; Barnett 6.4–1–25–0.

Essex forfeited their second innings.

Derbyshire

*K. J. Barnett not out	26	– b Childs 20
I. S. Anderson not out	16	– c East b Lever 25
A. Hill (did not bat)		– c East b Lever 31
J. G. Wright (did not bat)		– c Fletcher b Lever 4
J. E. Morris (did not bat)		– c Hardie b Lever 0
†B. Roberts (did not bat)		– st East b Childs 17
R. Sharma (did not bat)		– c Border b Lever 1
R. J. Finney (did not bat)		– not out 29
C. F. B. P. Rudd (did not bat)		– c East b Childs 1
L. J. Wood (did not bat)		– c Fletcher b Childs 5
O. H. Mortensen (did not bat)		– lbw b Acfield 0
L-b 1, w 1	2	L-b 7 7

(no wkt dec.) 44	1/30 2/72 3/76 4/76 5/87	140
	6/105 7/105 8/114 9/134	

Bowling: *First Innings*—Lever 7–2–13–0; Foster 5–2–19–0; Childs 4–1–7–0; Acfield 3–1–4–0. *Second Innings*—Lever 17–9–32–5; Foster 17–6–41–0; Childs 22–10–36–4; Pringle 3–1–10–0; Acfield 9.2 3–14–1.

Umpires: D. J. Constant and J. A. Jameson.

At Sheffield, June 4, 5, 6. DERBYSHIRE beat YORKSHIRE by 99 runs.

At The Oval, June 7, 9, 10. DERBYSHIRE lost to SURREY by nine wickets.

At Gloucester, June 14, 16, 17. DERBYSHIRE drew with GLOUCESTERSHIRE.

DERBYSHIRE v GLOUCESTERSHIRE

At Chesterfield, June 21, 22, 23. Drawn. Derbyshire 5 pts, Gloucestershire 8 pts. Toss:
Derbyshire. Walsh was too much for Derbyshire on a lively pitch, taking seven wickets on the
first day and cracking Miller's spinning finger when he was 39 to interrupt the only worthwhile
stand – that with Hill. Poor bowling enabled Gloucestershire to reply briskly. They were 162 for
one overnight and, after a blank second morning, Stovold completed his fifth century against
Derbyshire in 173 minutes, with fifteen 4s. Taylor and Holding bowled Derbyshire back into the
game, but the loss of 52 overs to the weather on the second day reduced the options for either
side to force a victory. Barnett played gloriously to reach his first century of the season in 143
minutes, arriving with a straight 6 off Lloyds to add to his twelve 4s. Anderson shared an
opening stand of 189 with his captain, but Finney's good sense was needed before Derbyshire
were safe.

Derbyshire

*K. J. Barnett c Russell b Walsh	14	– c Alleyne b Lloyds	114
I. S. Anderson c Russell b Walsh	1	– c Russell b Lloyds	93
A. Hill b Walsh	71	– c Russell b Payne	13
J. E. Morris c Russell b Lawrence	0	– c Bainbridge b Lloyds	5
B. Roberts c Lawrence b Walsh	4	– c Stovold b Lawrence	2
G. Miller c and b Lloyds	40		
†C. Marples c Alleyne b Walsh	12	– (6) c Russell b Lawrence	14
R. J. Finney c Russell b Walsh	0	– (7) not out	41
M. A. Holding c Payne b Lloyds	9	– (8) c Bainbridge b Lawrence	1
A. E. Warner not out	10	– (9) c Walsh b Lawrence	0
J. P. Taylor c Lloyds b Walsh	6	– (10) not out	3
B 8, l-b 6, w 3, n-b 14	31	B 11, l-b 3, w 1, n-b 9	24

1/7 2/18 3/27 4/39 5/149   198   1/189 2/221 3/240   (8 wkts) 310
6/151 7/177 8/179 9/180   4/241 5/243 6/270
                                                     7/273 8/279

Bonus points – Derbyshire 1, Gloucestershire 4.

Bowling: *First Innings*—Lawrence 15–2–55–1; Walsh 26.5–10–62–7; Payne 13–2–27–0;
Bainbridge 6–0–21–0; Lloyds 9–3–19–2. *Second Innings*—Lawrence 15–1–84–4; Walsh
27–4–72–0; Payne 18–6–40–1; Bainbridge 10–2–32–0; Lloyds 26–5–63–3; Stovold 3–1–5–0.

Gloucestershire

A. J. Wright b Holding	15	I. R. Payne c Anderson b Taylor 12
A. W. Stovold c Hill b Taylor	118	D. V. Lawrence c Holding b Taylor ... 6
K. P. Tomlins c Marples b Finney	40	C. A. Walsh c Marples b Warner 0
*P. Bainbridge c Barnett b Holding	39	
K. M. Curran c Marples b Taylor	5	B 1, l-b 30, w 5, n-b 17 ... 53
J. W. Lloyds c Marples b Holding	24	
†R. C. Russell not out	22	1/42 2/177 3/219 4/225 5/279 334
M. W. Alleyne c Taylor b Holding	0	6/288 7/288 8/312 9/328

Bonus points – Gloucestershire 4, Derbyshire 4.

Bowling: Holding 26–6–76–4; Warner 21.4–2–69–1; Finney 24–4–77–1; Taylor 19–1–81–4.

Umpires: B. Leadbeater and D. O. Oslear.

At Liverpool, June 28, 30, July 1. DERBYSHIRE drew with LANCASHIRE.

DERBYSHIRE v WORCESTERSHIRE

At Derby, July 2, 3, 4. Drawn. Derbyshire 5 pts, Worcestershire 8 pts. Toss: Worcestershire. Newport's control and movement troubled Derbyshire on a lively but unreliable pitch until Miller played with assurance. Warner's unbeaten 57, containing two 6s and eight 4s, boosted the innings and Holding should have taken the first hat-trick of his career before the close of the opening day. Neale and Weston were dismissed with successive balls but Rhodes was dropped at first slip off the next and went on to add 88 with the impressive Hick. Curtis, who had retired hurt on the first day with a cut lip, after being hit on the helmet, shared a stand of 125 with Newport and, although Holding returned seven to 97, his best for the county to date, Worcestershire led by 89. Derbyshire had to work hard to achieve safety, but helped by a second explosive half-century from Warner, this one containing four 6s and three 4s, they took away Worcestershire's hopes of victory.

Derbyshire

*K. J. Barnett c Rhodes b Pridgeon	0	– b Illingworth	62
I. S. Anderson c Hick b Weston	25	– c Hick b Illingworth	20
A. Hill b Newport	14	– c Hick b Newport	59
J. E. Morris c Patel b Newport	36	– (5) c Curtis b Illingworth	·54
B. Roberts c Curtis b Newport	3	– (6) c Rhodes b Pridgeon	16
G. Miller c Hick b Newport	65	– (7) b Newport	10
†C. Marples b Pridgeon	21	– (4) c Curtis b Illingworth	0
M. Jean-Jacques c Rhodes b Newport	7	– not out	21
M. A. Holding c Patel b McEwan	18	– c Rhodes b Newport	5
A. E. Warner not out	57	– c McEwan b Illingworth	52
J. P. Taylor lbw b Newport	0		
L-b 11, w 1, n-b 2	14	B 8, l-b 5, w 2	15

1/0 2/47 3/47 4/61 5/90   260   1/66 2/96 3/98   (9 wkts dec.) 314
6/130 7/142 8/188 9/242   4/166 5/195 6/219
                                  7/232 8/245 9/314

Bonus points – Derbyshire 3, Worcestershire 4.

Bowling: *First Innings*—Pridgeon 19-6-74-2; McEwan 15-3-52-1; Weston 15-6-48-1; Newport 17.5-4-49-6; Illingworth 8-2-23-0; Patel 2-1-3-0. *Second Innings*—Pridgeon 24-5-61-1; McEwan 14-2-51-0; Weston 4-1-13-0; Newport 28-5-106-3; Illingworth 44-22-64-5; Patel 2-0-6-0.

Worcestershire

T. S. Curtis c Barnett b Holding	67	– not out	4
D. B. D'Oliveira b Warner	0	– not out	43
G. A. Hick c Miller b Jean-Jacques	94		
D. N. Patel c Marples b Holding	21		
*P. A. Neale c Marples b Holding	17		
M. J. Weston c Barnett b Holding	0		
†S. J. Rhodes c Hill b Warner	28		
P. J. Newport c Roberts b Holding	68		
R. K. Illingworth lbw b Holding	8		
S. M. McEwan not out	1		
A. P. Pridgeon b Holding	3		
B 17, l-b 10, w 11, n-b 4	42	B 4, w 2, n-b 2	8

1/0 2/59 3/86 4/86 5/174   349   (no wkt) 55
6/194 7/319 8/342 9/345

Bonus points – Worcestershire 4, Derbyshire 2 (Score at 100 overs: 319-6).

Bowling: *First Innings*—Holding 29.4-7-97-7; Warner 16-4-51-2; Jean-Jacques 18-4-71-1; Taylor 17-1-65-0; Miller 27-12-32-0; Barnett 3-2-6-0. *Second Innings*—Holding 6-4-4-0; Warner 7-0-40-0; Jean-Jacques 5-2-6-0; Taylor 4-3-1-0.

Umpires: B. Leadbeater and K. J. Lyons.

DERBYSHIRE v KENT

At Derby, July 5, 7, 8. Derbyshire won by 28 runs. Derbyshire 20 pts, Kent 6 pts. Toss: Kent. Alderman bowled magnificently in helpful conditions for the best figures of his career, eight for 46, but Kent's batsmen did not take full advantage on the first day, six wickets falling for 128 in 46 overs. Holding suffered a groin strain, but Jean-Jacques, in only his fourth Championship match, excelled with eight for 77. In Derbyshire's second innings, Morris scored a splendid 191 off 243 balls in 289 minutes (two 6s, 22 4s), equalling the county's highest against Kent, by G. M. Lee at Derby in 1926. Kent, requiring 260 for victory in what would have been 72 overs, were set back by Mortensen's early burst and Miller's fine control. Ellison and Marsh added 74 for the seventh wicket and Kent continued to chase the runs until Miller's fifth wicket gave Derbyshire victory with sixteen balls to spare. It was a fine match, with no need for contrivance as 988 runs were scored and 40 wickets fell.

Derbyshire

*K. J. Barnett b Alderman	4	– lbw b C. S. Cowdrey	40
I. S. Anderson c Taylor b Dilley	6	– lbw b Alderman	26
A. Hill c Hinks b Alderman	12	– c Marsh b Alderman	17
J. E. Morris c Marsh b C. S. Cowdrey	16	– c Marsh b Alderman	191
B. Roberts c Aslett b Alderman	0	– c Hinks b Underwood	6
G. Miller lbw b Alderman	0	– c C. S. Cowdrey b Dilley	8
†C. Marples b Alderman	13	– c Aslett b Dilley	19
M. Jean-Jacques c Taylor b Alderman	21	– b Dilley	0
M. A. Holding not out	36	– (10) c G. R. Cowdrey b Underwood	13
A. E. Warner c Hinks b Alderman	3	– (9) c Marsh b Dilley	53
O. H. Mortensen lbw b Alderman	1	– not out	0
W 1, n-b 4	5	B 4, l-b 4, w 1, n-b 9	18

1/5 2/22 3/42 4/42 5/42   117   1/67 2/69 3/147 4/165 5/231   391
6/42 7/74 8/77 9/85   6/231 7/323 8/339 9/388

Bonus points – Kent 4.

Bowling: First Innings—Dilley 8–2–21–1; Alderman 15–2–46–8; Ellison 11–3–33–0; C. S. Cowdrey 4–2–17–1. *Second Innings*—Dilley 29–2–112–4; Alderman 20–2–84–3; Ellison 18–0–86–0; C. S. Cowdrey 14–3–43–1; Underwood 18.4–5–58–2.

Kent

D. G. Aslett b Jean-Jacques	17	– c Roberts b Mortensen	39
S. G. Hinks c Roberts b Jean-Jacques	33	– b Mortensen	7
C. J. Tavaré c Marples b Warner	15	– b Mortensen	6
N. R. Taylor b Jean-Jacques	9	– c Marples b Miller	13
*C. S. Cowdrey c Barnett b Mortensen	23	– c Marples b Miller	15
G. R. Cowdrey c Marples b Jean-Jacques	11	– b Jean-Jacques	4
D. L. Underwood c Roberts b Jean-Jacques	19	– (10) lbw b Miller	3
R. M. Ellison c Morris b Jean-Jacques	57	– (7) c Marples b Jean-Jacques	42
†S. A. Marsh b Jean-Jacques	39	– (8) st Marples b Miller	60
G. R. Dilley c Hill b Jean-Jacques	1	– (9) st Marples b Miller	28
T. M. Alderman not out	1	– not out	2
L-b 9, w 11, n-b 4	24	B 1, l-b 3, w 4, n-b 4	12

1/33 2/66 3/76 4/106 5/117   249   1/46 2/55 3/56 4/79 5/84   231
6/123 7/193 8/222 9/240   6/106 7/180 8/216 9/226

Bonus points – Kent 2, Derbyshire 4.

Bowling: First Innings—Holding 13–3–35–0; Mortensen 20–3–50–1; Jean-Jacques 19–1–77–8; Warner 18–5–49–1; Miller 9–1–29–0. *Second Innings*—Mortensen 21–3–69–3; Warner 7–1–33–0; Miller 31.2–5–77–5; Jean-Jacques 11–2–48–2.

Umpires: B. Leadbeater and K. J. Lyons.

At Birmingham, July 16, 17, 18. DERBYSHIRE drew with WARWICKSHIRE.

DERBYSHIRE v MIDDLESEX

At Derby, July 19, 21, 22. Derbyshire won by one wicket. Derbyshire 21 pts, Middlesex 4 pts.
Toss: Middlesex. A hostile opening burst by Mortensen helped him to his best figures for three
years and Middlesex would have been in worse trouble had Butcher been caught at slip when 19.
Hill battled sternly and Morris completed his 1,000 runs for the season, but Derbyshire's lead
was only 35. With Gatting unfit, Emburey led Middlesex but withdrew after having his nose
broken in the Sunday game, Radley taking over. Slack's first century of the season, containing
eight 4s off 113 balls in 108 minutes, put Middlesex in a better position and Daniel's hard-hit 33
(eight 4s) made the Derbyshire target 289 in 91 overs. From the comfort of 210 for four, they lost
four wickets in seven overs before Holding and Warner hit cleanly to add 47 in six overs.
Warner clinched an exciting victory by hitting Daniel back over his head.

Middlesex

A. J. T. Miller c Maher b Holding	4	– c Miller b Holding	29
W. N. Slack lbw b Mortensen	8	– c Maher b Mortensen	100
J. D. Carr c Marples b Mortensen	0	– b Mortensen	22
R. O. Butcher c Warner b Miller	66	– c Barnett b Mortensen	58
C. T. Radley c Barnett b Holding	1	– lbw b Holding	25
†P. R. Downton c Roberts b Mortensen	21	– lbw b Holding	16
*J. E. Emburey c Marples b Roberts	0	– absent injured	
P. H. Edmonds b Holding	25	– (7) not out	23
S. P. Hughes b Mortensen	5	– (8) c Maher b Mortensen	0
N. G. Cowans b Maher b Mortensen	8	– (9) b Holding	0
W. W. Daniel not out	0	– (10) b Warner	33
B 2, l-b 2	4	B 2, l-b 14, w 1	17

1/12 2/12 3/16 4/22 5/102   142   1/76 2/121 3/208 4/225 5/259   323
6/102 7/116 8/127 9/139   6/272 7/273 8/276 9/323

Bonus points – Derbyshire 4.

Bowling: First Innings—Holding 17.3-4-61-3; Mortensen 15-4-35-5; Warner 5-0-24-0;
Roberts 6-1-18-1; Miller 3-3-0-1. *Second Innings*—Holding 26-6-86-4; Mortensen
28-7-85-4; Warner 19-3-48-1; Miller 34-11-66-0; Roberts 8-2-15-0; Barnett 1-0-7-0.

Derbyshire

*K. J. Barnett c Downton b Hughes	19	– c Butcher b Hughes	16
B. J. M. Maher lbw b Cowans	0	– c Radley b Daniel	12
A. Hill c Emburey b Cowans	45	– b Edmonds	45
J. E. Morris c Butcher b Hughes	28	– (7) c Cowans b Daniel	9
B. Roberts b Edmonds	22	– (4) lbw b Daniel	55
I. S. Anderson b Daniel	9	– (5) lbw b Cowans	42
G. Miller b Emburey	8	– (6) b Cowans	20
†C. Marples c Slack b Daniel	13	– st Downton b Edmonds	6
M. A. Holding b Cowans	19	– b Daniel	31
A. E. Warner not out	5	– not out	23
O. H. Mortensen c Carr b Daniel	0	– not out	0
B 1, l-b 6, w 1, n-b 1	9	B 1, l-b 16, w 1, n-b 13	31

1/3 2/34 3/67 4/118 5/120   177   1/21 2/32 3/110 4/167   (9 wkts) 290
6/135 7/141 8/171 9/177   5/210 6/213 7/230 8/231 9/278

Bonus points – Derbyshire 1, Middlesex 4.

Bowling: First Innings—Daniel 14.5-1-52-3; Cowans 16-2-40-3; Hughes 13-1-42-2;
Edmonds 13-5-19-1; Emburey 10-3-17-1. *Second Innings*—Daniel 20.3-4-89-4; Cowans
14-2-51-2; Hughes 17-4-42-1; Edmonds 33-10-91-2.

Umpires: J. Birkenshaw and R. Julian.

At Portsmouth, July 23, 24, 25. DERBYSHIRE lost to HAMPSHIRE by 5 runs.

At Abergavenny, July 26, 28, 29. DERBYSHIRE beat GLAMORGAN by three wickets.

At Derby, August 2, 3, 4. DERBYSHIRE drew with NEW ZEALANDERS (See New Zealand tour section).

At Eastbourne, August 6, 7, 8. DERBYSHIRE lost to SUSSEX by three wickets.

DERBYSHIRE v LANCASHIRE

At Buxton, August 9, 11, 12. Drawn. Derbyshire 4 pts, Lancashire 1 pt. Toss: Lancashire. The first Championship match to contain Danes, Mortensen and Henriksen, on each side was spoiled by traditional Buxton weather, rain washing out the second day. Lancashire struggled on a slow pitch against Holding and Warner, and Derbyshire were heading for a good position by the close. In the hope of achieving a positive result, they declared before the start of play on the third morning, fed runs to Lancashire, and set about chasing 280 in 65 overs. But after a sound start, Derbyshire lost six wickets in eleven overs from Simmons and Folley and had to play out the last sixteen overs with survival now the aim. Roberts and Finney batted through to deny Lancashire their first victory since early June. Fowler and then Varey kept wicket for Lancashire after Maynard injured his thumb.

Lancashire

G. D. Mendis b Holding	5	– c Finney b Roberts	65
G. Fowler c Barnett b Warner	41	– c Barnett b Hill	86
D. W. Varey c Maher b Warner	17	– not out	15
N. H. Fairbrother c Maher b Mortensen	45	– not out	4
J. Abrahams c Sharma b Warner	4		
*C. H. Lloyd lbw b Mortensen	11		
†C. Maynard c Warner b Sharma	11		
J. Simmons not out	18		
I. Folley c Maher b Holding	2		
D. J. Makinson c Barnett b Holding	2		
S. Henriksen b Warner	1		
B 1, l-b 5, n-b 10	16	B 2, l-b 1, w 2, n-b 3	8

1/9 2/61 3/90 4/94 5/129   173   1/147 2/166   (2 wkts dec.) 178
6/134 7/149 8/165 9/167

Bonus points – Lancashire 1, Derbyshire 4.

Bowling: *First Innings*—Holding 20-4-42-3; Mortensen 15-3-43-2; Finney 12-5-31-0; Sharma 6-3-13-1; Warner 14.1-4-38-4. *Second Innings*—Finney 8-3-15-0; Warner 8-2-35-0; Barnett 8-1-44-0; Marples 4-0-48-0; Hill 9-3-22-1; Roberts 5-1-11-1.

Derbyshire

*K. J. Barnett b Henriksen	11	– c Varey b Makinson	20
†B. J. M. Maher not out	31	– b Simmons	51
A. Hill not out	27	– c Simmons b Folley	51
J. E. Morris (did not bat)		– c and b Folley	15
B. Roberts (did not bat)		– not out	25
C. Marples (did not bat)		– st Varey b Simmons	3
A. E. Warner (did not bat)		– c sub b Simmons	0
M. A. Holding (did not bat)		– c Henriksen b Folley	0
R. J. Finney (did not bat)		– not out	1
L-b 3	3	B 3, l-b 1, w 2, n-b 7	13

1/25   (1 wkt dec.) 72   1/30 2/129 3/133   (7 wkts) 179
                                    4/157 5/162 6/170 7/171

O. H. Mortensen and R. Sharma did not bat.

Bowling: *First Innings*—Makinson 13–4–32–0; Henriksen 6–0–26–1; Simmons 7–1–11–0. *Second Innings*—Makinson 10.4–1–49–1; Henriksen 2–0–11–0; Fairbrother 8–3–13–0; Simmons 22–7–56–3; Folley 19–5–44–3; Abrahams 3–2–2–0.

Umpires: H. D. Bird and R. A. White.

DERBYSHIRE v YORKSHIRE

At Chesterfield, August 16, 18, 19. Drawn. Derbyshire 4 pts, Yorkshire 1 pt. Toss: Derbyshire. Holding bowled superbly in Yorkshire's first innings but, although Derbyshire dominated the early stages, progress was limited by bad light on the first day and heavy rain on the second. As so often, previous play counted for little as the captains reached agreement to attempt a result on the third day. Yorkshire, offered easy runs, declared to set Derbyshire 272 for victory in 70 overs. On a pitch still helping bowlers, they started slowly but Morris raised the tempo and Warner hit powerfully, seven 4s and four 6s contributing to his 64 off 53 balls. Requiring 141 from the last twenty overs, Derbyshire called off the chase when their seventh wicket fell.

Yorkshire

M. D. Moxon c Sharma b Holding	0	– c Maher b Barnett	33
A. A. Metcalfe c Roberts b Warner	20	– lbw b Finney	7
S. N. Hartley b Hill b Holding	8	– not out	41
P. E. Robinson c Maher b Holding	23	– not out	70
J. D. Love lbw b Finney	32		
*†D. L. Bairstow c Morris b Finney	17		
P. Carrick c Maher b Holding	9		
P. J. Hartley b Holding	10		
S. J. Dennis c Roberts b Mortensen	9		
C. Shaw not out	7		
S. D. Fletcher c Miller b Mortensen	24		
B 1, l-b 14, w 1, n-b 2	18	L-b 7, w 2, n-b 2	11

1/0 2/14 3/46 4/77 5/99   177   1/19 2/61   (2 wkts dec.) 162
6/114 7/129 8/145 9/147

Bonus points – Yorkshire 1, Derbyshire 4.

Bowling: *First Innings*—Holding 21–7–46–5; Mortensen 22–6–61–2; Finney 12–1–40–2; Warner 11–6–15–1. *Second Innings*—Finney 10–3–26–1; Warner 8–0–24–0; Barnett 6–0–43–1; Morris 8–0–62–0.

Derbyshire

*K. J. Barnett not out	34	– c Moxon b P. J. Hartley	3
†B. J. M. Maher not out	14	– c Bairstow b Shaw	19
A. Hill (did not bat)		– c Bairstow b P. J. Hartley	23
J. E. Morris (did not bat)		– c Bairstow b P. J. Hartley	42
B. Roberts (did not bat)		– lbw b P. J. Hartley	2
G. Miller (did not bat)		– not out	51
A. E. Warner (did not bat)		– c P. J. Hartley b Dennis	64
M. A. Holding (did not bat)		– c Moxon b Dennis	18
R. Sharma (did not bat)		– not out	7
B 4, l-b 7, n-b 9	20	B 5, l-b 5, n-b 5	15

(no wkt dec.) 68   1/4 2/45 3/55 4/75   (7 wkts) 244
5/93 6/200 7/221

R. J. Finney and O. H. Mortensen did not bat.

Bowling: *First Innings*—Dennis 6–1–19–0; P. J. Hartley 6–1–22–0; Shaw 3–1–12–0; Fletcher 2–0–4–0. *Second Innings*—Dennis 14–2–53–2; P. J. Hartley 17–2–57–4; Fletcher 14–2–48–0; Shaw 15–3–38–1; Carrick 9.4–4–38–0.

Umpires: A. A. Jones and B. J. Meyer.

DERBYSHIRE v LEICESTERSHIRE

At Chesterfield, August 20, 21, 22. Drawn. Derbyshire 8 pts, Leicestershire 6 pts. Toss: Leicestershire. Chesterfield week continued to suffer from poor weather, despite an exhilarating first day. On a lively pitch, the bat was often beaten but the bowlers' direction strayed and the catching was erratic. Warner hit his highest score, 91 off 90 balls including five 6s and nine 4s, but ran out of steam when the prospect of a century loomed. Not so Whitaker, who batted brilliantly on the second day despite four stoppages. His century came off 117 balls, with two 6s and nineteen 4s on a pitch which continued to help bowlers, and after the third morning was lost to the weather, he continued to dominate, ending with four 6s and 27 4s. Nobody else had much answer to Finney who, in a welcome return to rhythm following a back injury, took the last four Leicestershire wickets in eight balls and achieved the best figures of his career.

Derbyshire

*K. J. Barnett c Whitticase b Taylor	1	– c Whitticase b Agnew	15
†B. J. M. Maher c Whitticase b Agnew	22	– not out	6
A. Hill c Whitticase b Taylor	56	– not out	8
J. E. Morris c Boon b Taylor	62		
B. Roberts c DeFreitas b Agnew	15		
G. Miller run out	30		
A. E. Warner c Benjamin b DeFreitas	91		
R. J. Finney lbw b Agnew	0		
M. Jean-Jacques c Benjamin b DeFreitas	2		
M. A. Holding not out	34		
O. H. Mortensen not out	31		
L-b 14, w 5, n-b 15	34	B 2, l-b 1, w 1, n-b 6	10

1/4 2/65 3/142 4/165 5/195   (9 wkts dec.) 378   1/26   (1 wkt) 39
6/257 7/270 8/283 9/332

Bonus points – Derbyshire 4, Leicestershire 3 (Score at 100 overs: 326-8).

Bowling: *First Innings*—Taylor 24–7–57–3; DeFreitas 31–6–100–2; Benjamin 20–2–70–0; Agnew 34–8–133–3; Potter 1–0–4–0. *Second Innings*—Taylor 4–0–10–0; DeFreitas 5–1–11–0; Agnew 8–4–8–1; Benjamin 4–1–7–0; Balderstone 3–3–0–0.

Leicestershire

*J. C. Balderstone c Maher b Mortensen	29	W. K. M. Benjamin not out	5
R. A. Cobb c Barnett b Finney	24	J. P. Agnew b Finney	0
L. Potter lbw b Finney	1	L. B. Taylor b Finney	0
J. J. Whitaker b Warner	175		
T. J. Boon b Warner	6	B 2, l-b 5, w 1, n-b 11	19
P. D. Bowler lbw b Finney	21		
P. A. J. DeFreitas b Finney	11	1/39 2/51 3/121 4/162 5/264	293
†P. Whitticase lbw b Warner	2	6/286 7/286 8/293 9/293	

Bonus points – Leicestershire 3, Derbyshire 4.

Bowling: Holding 23–8–64–0; Mortensen 20–10–30–1; Finney 17.5–4–54–7; Warner 16–2–68–2; Jean-Jacques 18–1–70–0.

Umpires: J. Birkenshaw and A. A. Jones.

At Nottingham, August 23, 25, 26. DERBYSHIRE drew with NOTTINGHAMSHIRE.

At Leicester, August 27, 28, 29. DERBYSHIRE drew with LEICESTERSHIRE.

DERBYSHIRE v HAMPSHIRE

At Derby, August 30, September 1, 2. Hampshire won by nine wickets. Hampshire 21 pts, Derbyshire 2 pts. Toss: Hampshire. Greenidge scored two centuries of fearsome power, the second making a mockery of Barnett's declaration, which set Hampshire 256 to win in 130 minutes plus the final twenty overs. Barnett played well on the first day but, in poor light on the second morning, Marshall's pace was too much for Derbyshire. The umpires suspended play only when Sharma was hit on the head by a ball from Marshall and taken to hospital, where he was detained overnight. Nicholas declared when Greenidge reached his century in 183 minutes with his fourteenth 4 and was then out. Hill responded with an unbeaten 119 before the second declaration. Greenidge won the game with his third century in successive innings. He was completely in charge on a day which saw the end of Miller's Derbyshire career, scoring 180 not out in 175 minutes from 168 balls, including three 6s and twenty 4s.

Derbyshire

*K. J. Barnett c R. A. Smith b Cowley	98	– c R. A. Smith b Marshall	9
†B. J. M. Maher b Marshall	43	– lbw b Marshall	7
A. Hill c Parks b James	5	– not out	119
J. E. Morris c James b Cowley	15	– c Parks b R. A. Smith	26
B. Roberts c R. A. Smith b Marshall	3	– st Parks b R. A. Smith	11
G. Miller lbw b Marshall	0	– not out	39
A. E. Warner lbw b Marshall	8		
R. Sharma retired hurt	0		
R. J. Finney b Tremlett	19		
O. H. Mortensen b Marshall	4		
D. E. Malcolm not out	0		
B 7, l-b 1, n-b 6	14	L-b 10, n-b 1	11

1/128 2/147 3/161 4/174 5/174	209	1/16 2/31 3/77 (4 wkts dec.) 222
6/182 7/199 8/203 9/209		4/123

Bonus points – Derbyshire 2, Hampshire 4.

Bowling: *First Innings*—Marshall 21–5–49–5; James 13–4–28–1; Maru 17–8–36–0; Tremlett 12.4–3–34–1; Cowley 23–8–54–2. *Second Innings*—James 6–2–10–0; Maru 12–9–5–0; Tremlett 5–2–5–0; Cowley 8–4–10–0; Marshall 7–4–12–2; R. A. Smith 18.4–1–102–2; C. L. Smith 15–1–60–0; Nicholas 2–0–8–0.

Hampshire

C. G. Greenidge b Mortensen	103	– not out	180
V. P. Terry b Malcolm	12		
C. L. Smith not out	54	– not out	33
*M. C. J. Nicholas (did not bat)		– (2) run out	32
L-b 1, w 1, n-b 5	7	B 3, l-b 7, w 1, n-b 1	12

1/24 2/176   (2 wkts dec.) 176   1/105   (1 wkt) 257

R. A. Smith, T. M. Tremlett, K. D. James, M. D. Marshall, †R. J. Parks, R. J. Maru and N. G. Cowley did not bat.

Bonus point – Hampshire 1.

Bowling: *First Innings*—Malcolm 12–2–59–1; Mortensen 15.3–3–45–1; Finney 9–3–39–0; Warner 6–3–19–0; Miller 10–3–13–0. *Second Innings*—Malcolm 9.1–0–57–0; Miller 21–5–65–0; Finney 14–1–67–0; Sharma 8–1–58–0.

Umpires: A. A. Jones and P. B. Wight.

DERBYSHIRE v NORTHAMPTONSHIRE

At Derby, September 3, 4, 5. Drawn. Derbyshire 6 pts, Northamptonshire 7 pts. Toss: Derbyshire. After suffering from Greenidge on the previous day, the Derbyshire bowlers were flayed by Lamb and Bailey, who scored centuries and added 217 in only 38 overs. Lamb, in rich form since being dropped by England, needed only 102 balls for his century and broke £200-worth of glass patio door with a 6 to the pavilion balcony. He also hit 27 4s in his 160-ball innings while Bailey's 114 included a 6 and thirteen 4s. Derbyshire required 272 to avoid the follow-on and, despite a grim grind, failed by 5 runs as Capel, showing good control, took seven wickets. When he had scored 21, Hill achieved his highest aggregate in a season (1,359). After overnight consideration the follow-on was enforced, but Barnett and Morris scored centuries in a partnership of 221 in 57 overs to put victory out of Northamptonshire's reach.

Northamptonshire

*G. Cook c Maher b Jean-Jacques	31	N. G. B. Cook b Finney	4
W. Larkins b Holding	14	N. A. Mallender b Jean-Jacques	2
R. J. Boyd-Moss c Maher b Holding	0	G. Smith b Finney	3
A. J. Lamb c Maher b Jean-Jacques	159		
R. J. Bailey b Holding	114	B 5, l-b 11, w 1, n-b 11	28
D. J. Capel c Maher b Jean-Jacques	5		
R. A. Harper lbw b Finney	35	1/24 2/24 3/83 4/300 5/322	421
†D. Ripley not out	26	6/342 7/384 8/398 9/409	

Bonus points – Northamptonshire 4, Derbyshire 4.

Bowling: Holding 24–3–86–3; Warner 18–1–95–0; Jean-Jacques 23–2–99–4; Finney 20.3–1–76–3; Sharma 11–1–49–0.

Derbyshire

*K. J. Barnett lbw b Capel	13	– c G. Cook b Smith	143
†B. J. M. Maher c Ripley b Capel	50	– c G. Cook b Capel	0
A. Hill lbw b Capel	55	– c Ripley b Mallender	6
J. E. Morris c Smith b Capel	3	– c G. Cook b Boyd-Moss	127
B. Roberts lbw b N. G. B. Cook	40	– c and b Boyd-Moss	8
A. M. Brown c Lamb b Harper	21	– (7) not out	9
A. E. Warner c G. Cook b Harper	6	– (6) c Lamb b N. G. B. Cook	5
R. Sharma lbw b Capel	4	– not out	0
R. J. Finney c Harper b Capel	4		
M. Jean-Jacques not out	29		
M. A. Holding lbw b Capel	21		
L-b 6, w 10, n-b 5	21	B 5, l-b 8, w 1	14

1/19 2/112 3/130 4/131 5/179   267   1/8 2/32 3/253   (6 wkts dec.) 312
6/195 7/199 8/208 9/209   4/279 5/300 6/304

Bonus points – Derbyshire 2, Northamptonshire 3 (Score at 100 overs: 204-7).

Bowling: *First Innings*—Mallender 22–8–57–0; Capel 26–5–86–7; N. G. B. Cook 29–16–43–1; Smith 9–0–33–0; Harper 29–14–37–2; Boyd-Moss 2–0–5–0. *Second Innings*—Mallender 10–1–33–1; Capel 15–4–37–1; N. G. B. Cook 33–10–71–1; Smith 14–4–61–1; Harper 10–4–27–0; Boyd-Moss 19–4–70–2.

Umpires: D. Lloyd and P. B. Wight.

At Taunton, September 13, 15, 16. DERBYSHIRE beat SOMERSET by three wickets.

SPORT AID – WEST INDIES v REST OF THE WORLD

Although the efforts of the Edgbaston groundsman, Rob Franklin, and his staff, plus the willingness of the players to take the field in wet, slippery conditions, came to nothing when heavy rain returned to force the abandonment of the charity match between West Indies and a Rest of the World XI on May 20 last year, approximately £150,000 was raised through sponsorship and receipts for the Sport Aid appeal in aid of famine relief.

The teams were: *West Indies* – C. G. Greenidge, R. B. Richardson, C. H. Lloyd, A. L. Logie, I. V. A. Richards (captain), H. A. Gomes, T. R. O. Payne, E. A. E. Baptiste, M. A. Holding, J. Garner and A. H. Gray. *Rest of the World XI* – S. M. Gavaskar, J. G. Wright, D. I. Gower (captain), B. F. Davison, C. E. B. Rice, I. T. Botham, Imran Khan, Kapil Dev, R. J. Shastri, P. R. Downton and T. M. Alderman. In the 13.3 overs of play possible, West Indies scored 78 for one, with Richardson 39 not out.

ESSEX

President: T. N. Pearce
Chairman: D. J. Insole
Chairman, Cricket Committee: D. J. Insole
Secretary/General Manager: P. J. Edwards
County Ground, New Writtle Street,
Chelmsford CM2 0PG
(Telephone: 0245-354533)
Captain: G. A. Gooch

In winning their third County Championship title in four years, Essex overcame problems that would have left many counties struggling in the middle reaches. England selection frequently deprived them of two or three players, and Keith Fletcher and Brian Hardie missed several matches because of injuries. In such times, however, a lack of experience was compensated for by the performances of younger players, notably John Stephenson and Donald Topley. This depth of playing staff also stood Essex in good stead in the John Player League, which they just failed to take for a third successive year, having to settle for second place. In the Benson and Hedges Cup and NatWest Bank Trophy, they were knocked out in the quarter-finals and second round respectively.

Graham Gooch, in his first year as captain, led the county with great enthusiasm as well as a bold, positive approach. As a batsman, he did not impose himself as he had in previous seasons but he still finished with more than 1,200 runs, two of his three hundreds coming in Test matches. When he was away on international duty, Fletcher, the man he succeeded, underlined what was already known – that he is a master tactician and motivator.

The biggest bonus for Essex was the form of John Childs, the left-arm spinner. In 1985, he took only three Championship wickets at 125 apiece. Last summer he collected 85 at an average of 15.03, four times claiming seven or more wickets in an innings. More than half his wickets were taken in the last seven weeks of the season as Essex, 54 points adrift of the leaders in the first week of August, came through to win the title by 28 points.

Yet it was Neil Foster who finished the season as the county's leading wicket-taker, his 105 overall representing his most successful summer. He showed great stamina and ten times took five or more wickets in an innings. His selection for England's tour of Australia was deservedly won. John Lever's 70 first-class wickets were fewer than in previous seasons, but he remained a reliable and effective performer, as the England selectors acknowledged when they recalled him to Test cricket, at the age of 37, after an absence of more than four years. Essex's fourth England player, Derek Pringle, again proved his qualities as an all-rounder, his seven for 46 against Yorkshire at Chelmsford and 97 against Kent at Folkestone being important match-winning contributions. The former earned Essex their first Championship win and the latter virtually guaranteed the county's winning their ninth major title in eight years.

Allan Border, signed by Essex to replace Ken McEwan, who returned
to South Africa in 1985, scored 1,385 runs for a first-class average of
nearly 50 before setting off a month ahead of the end of the season to
captain Australia in India. Initially he struggled to find his touch, not
reaching 50 in the Championship until the end of May, but he
immediately went on to three figures and finished with four hundreds.
Perhaps his most significant innings, however, was an unbeaten 59 on a
difficult Lord's pitch to see his side to victory over Middlesex. Hardie
continued to give the county great service, whether as an opening
batsman or providing substance in the middle order, while Paul Prichard
offered further evidence of his talent by scoring 1,000 runs for the first
time. He was awarded his county cap, as were Alan Lilley and Childs,
but before he can aspire to greater heights, Prichard will have to build
bigger scores from his firm foundations. He passed 50 eleven times in
first-class games, yet only once went on to a hundred.

David East again performed most competently and was the country's
leading wicket-keeper with 83 dismissals, including nineteen stumpings.
No-one else had more than eight stumpings. However, his batting
remained frustrating. By the middle of August he had scored just 350
runs, but a late flourish, which included 82 and 100 not out against
Championship rivals Gloucestershire, when opening the innings, more
than doubled his aggregate in the final month. East was one of several
players used to open the innings, among them Stephenson who, after a
successful season captaining Durham University, filled the position
against the New Zealanders, responded with 63 and 33, and kept his
place for the rest of the season. His defence and temperament were sound
and, provided he opts for a career in the game, he looked likely to make a
bigger impact.

Topley, who bowled at medium pace, was another young player to
make his mark. Although he made only seven Championship appearances, in two of those he took seventeen wickets, against Sussex and
Middlesex, to point the way to unexpected victories at a time when
Essex's ranks were depleted. Certainly he should fill the gap left by
Stuart Turner, one of two stalwarts who announced their retirement – the
other being Keith Pont.

Between them, these two served Essex for almost 40 years. Pont always
gave the appearance of playing for fun and had a sense of humour which
will be missed in the dressing-room. Turner, on the other hand, snarled
his way from one match to another, treating every opposing player as an
enemy on the field of play. It can be argued that Pont never quite made
the most of his ability, but Turner did. His 9,411 first-class runs and
821 wickets were testimony to his talent, and he was the only player to
achieve the double of 3,000 runs and 300 wickets in the John Player
League.

Essex followers will be saddened by their departure, but they will
welcome the arrival of two new recruits. Hugh Page, a fast-medium
bowler from Transvaal, has become the county's overseas signing in
place of Border, while the former England off-spinner, Geoff Miller, has
moved to Chelmsford from Derbyshire. – N.F.

ESSEX 1986

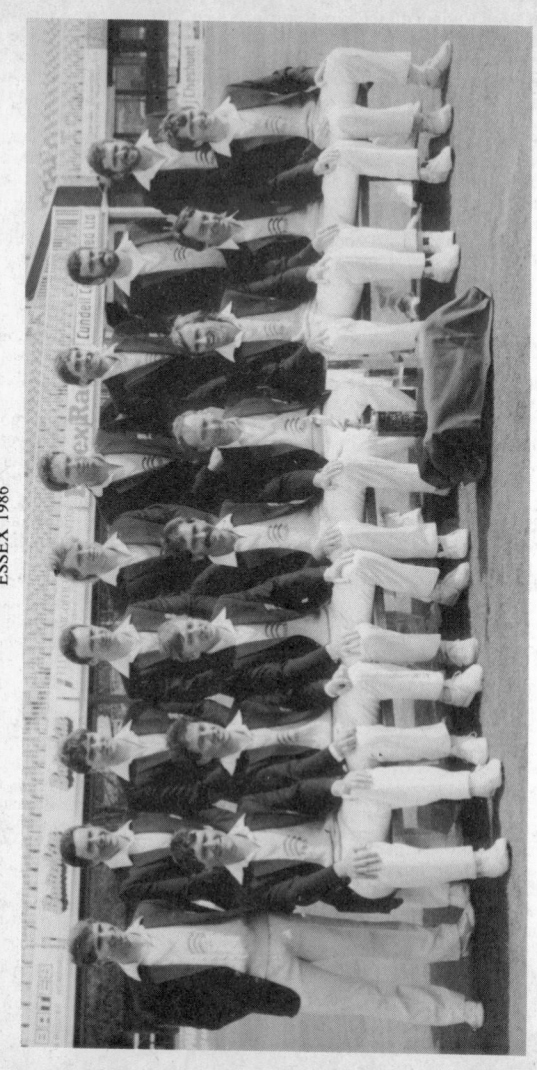

[Bill Smith]

Back row: P. J. Prichard, J. H. Childs, C. Gladwin, A. W. Lilley, I. L. Pont, D. R. Pringle, N. A. Foster, T. D. Topley, A. R. Border. Front row: D. E. East, B. R. Hardie, S. Turner, G. A. Gooch (captain), K. W. R. Fletcher, J. K. Lever, D. L. Acfield, K. R. Pont.

ESSEX RESULTS

All first-class matches – Played 26: Won 10, Lost 7, Drawn 9.

County Championship matches – Played 24: Won 10, Lost 6, Drawn 8.

Bonus points – Batting 51, Bowling 76.

Competition placings – Britannic Assurance County Championship, winners; NatWest Bank Trophy, 2nd round; Benson and Hedges Cup, q-f; John Player League, 2nd.

BRITANNIC ASSURANCE CHAMPIONSHIP AVERAGES

BATTING

	Birthplace	M	I	NO	R	HI	Avge
‡A. R. Border	Sydney, Australia	18	29	4	1,287	150	51.48
‡G. A. Gooch	Leytonstone	13	21	0	778	151	37.04
‡P. J. Prichard	Billericay	24	40	3	1,165	147*	31.48
‡K. W. R. Fletcher	Worcester	19	27	5	691	91	31.40
‡B. R. Hardie	Stenhousemuir	21	33	4	831	113*	28.65
‡A. W. Lilley	Ilford	14	24	2	557	87	25.31
J. P. Stephenson ..	Stebbing	13	23	1	551	85	25.04
I. L. Pont	Brentwood	2	4	3	24	14*	24.00
‡N. A. Foster	Colchester	21	27	7	433	53*	21.65
‡D. E. East	Clapton	23	37	4	712	100*	21.57
‡D. R. Pringle	Nairobi, Kenya	15	22	2	370	97	18.50
‡C. Gladwin	East Ham	7	13	0	178	73	13.69
‡J. K. Lever	Stepney	21	25	5	199	38	9.95
‡J. H. Childs	Plymouth	20	21	6	149	30	9.93
T. D. Topley	Canterbury	7	9	2	58	23	8.28
‡K. R. Pont	Wanstead	6	11	1	79	31	7.90
‡D. L. Acfield	Chelmsford	17	17	9	41	10	5.12

Also batted: N. D. Burns (*Chelmsford*) (2 matches) 18, 7, 29; ‡S. Turner (*Chester*) (1 match) 32, 25*.

* Signifies not out. ‡ Denotes county cap.

The following played a total of nine three-figure innings for Essex in County Championship matches: A. R. Border 4, B. R. Hardie 2, D. E. East 1, G. A. Gooch 1, P. J. Prichard 1.

BOWLING

	O	M	R	W	BB	Avge
J. H. Childs	566.3	186	1,278	85	8-58	15.03
T. D. Topley	207.1	46	651	31	5-52	21.00
N. A. Foster	715.2	154	2,139	100	6-57	21.39
D. R. Pringle	336.1	85	946	41	7-46	23.07
D. L. Acfield	327.1	78	765	25	4-50	30.60
J. K. Lever	564.1	130	1,812	58	6-57	31.24

Also bowled: A. R. Border 21–2–100–1; D. E. East 0.2–0–1–0; G. A. Gooch 127.4–34–329–7; B. R. Hardie 12–0–58–0; A. W. Lilley 18.3–1–104–2; I. L. Pont 32.2–2–130–3; K. R. Pont 31.5–7–85–4; J. P. Stephenson 2–0–5–0; S. Turner 21–5–72–1.

Wicket-keepers: D. E. East 61 ct, 19 st; N. D. Burns 2 ct, 2 st.

Leading Fielders: K. W. R. Fletcher 25; B. R. Hardie 19; P. J. Prichard 18; A. R. Border 14; N. A. Foster 12.

At Cambridge, April 23, 24, 25. ESSEX drew with CAMBRIDGE UNIVERSITY.

At Birmingham, April 26, 27, 28. ESSEX drew with WARWICKSHIRE.

ESSEX v KENT

At Chelmsford, May 7, 8, 9. Kent won by 25 runs. Kent 22 pts, Essex 4 pts. Toss: Essex. Dilley performed the second hat-trick of his career during the Essex first innings when he dismissed Fletcher with his last ball of the morning session and Lilley and East in the afternoon following a delay of 40 minutes after lunch because of rain. Dilley's pace and lift, combined with Alderman's movement and accuracy, gave Kent a lead of 98 on first innings. Kent, having been put in, had faltered on the first day after a century partnership between Benson and Hinks, and in the second innings it needed Chris Cowdrey's resolute, unbeaten 70 to hold them together. Later in the day, with Essex chasing 269 in 74 overs, the Kent captain stopped their progress with three wickets in four balls to make victory almost certain after Alderman, in his first game of the season, had claimed the first five Essex wickets.

Kent

M. R. Benson c Gooch b Foster	64	– c Border b Lever	30
S. G. Hinks lbw b Pringle	67	– b Lever	9
C. J. Tavaré b Lever	29	– c East b Lever	4
N. R. Taylor lbw b Lever	9	– lbw b Lever	14
*C. S. Cowdrey c East b Foster	9	– not out	70
G. R. Cowdrey run out	13	– b Pringle	10
R. M. Ellison c East b Foster	4	– lbw b Foster	15
†S. A. Marsh lbw b Lever	27	– lbw b Foster	0
G. R. Dilley not out	26	– c Border b Foster	0
D. L. Underwood c Fletcher b Lever	6	– b Pringle	16
T. M. Alderman not out	10		
B 2, l-b 4, w 1, n-b 1	8	L-b 1, w 1	2

1/121 2/145 3/171 4/172　　　(9 wkts dec.) 272　　1/37 2/44 3/57　　(9 wkts dec.) 170
5/190 6/196 7/200 8/240 9/252　　　　　　　　　　4/60 5/92 6/139 7/145
　　　　　　　　　　　　　　　　　　　　　　　　8/151 9/170

Bonus points – Kent 2, Essex 3 (Score at 100 overs: 234-7).

Bowling: *First Innings*—Lever 29-10-57-4; Foster 27-6-69-3; Pringle 24-8-76-1; Gooch 21-9-41-0; Acfield 14-5-23-0. *Second Innings*—Lever 26-6-69-4; Foster 27-7-81-3; Pringle 14.5-7-19-2.

Essex

*G. A. Gooch c Alderman b Dilley	60	– lbw b Alderman	21
B. R. Hardie c Hinks b Alderman	2	– c Underwood b Alderman	5
P. J. Prichard c Marsh b Alderman	31	– lbw b Alderman	25
A. R. Border lbw b Dilley	14	– c Tavaré b Alderman	38
K. W. R. Fletcher c C. S. Cowdrey b Dilley	16	– c Marsh b Underwood	51
D. R. Pringle run out	15	– c Marsh b Alderman	0
A. W. Lilley c Tavaré b Dilley	3	– lbw b C. S. Cowdrey	29
†D. E. East c Benson b Dilley	0	– c Dilley b C. S. Cowdrey	21
N. A. Foster c C. S. Cowdrey b Alderman	3	– c G. R. Cowdrey b Dilley	25
J. K. Lever b Alderman	2	– lbw b C. S. Cowdrey	0
D. L. Acfield not out	0	– not out	1
B 4, l-b 2, w 1, n-b 21	28	B 1, l-b 17, w 3, n-b 6	27

1/8 2/96 3/123 4/129 5/157　　　　　　174　　1/14 2/43 3/77 4/157 5/157　　243
6/165 7/165 8/172 9/174　　　　　　　　　　6/167 7/217 8/217 9/217

Bonus points – Essex 1, Kent 4.

Bowling: *First Innings*—Dilley 13.5–0–69–5; Alderman 13–1–59–4; Ellison 5–0–19–0; C. S. Cowdrey 7–1–21–0. *Second Innings*—Dilley 15.5–1–81–1; Alderman 17–3–46–5; Ellison 14–3–30–0; C. S. Cowdrey 8–2–31–3; Underwood 10–2–37–1.

Umpires: A. A. Jones and K. E. Palmer.

At Northampton, May 17, 19, 20. ESSEX drew with NORTHAMPTONSHIRE.

ESSEX v YORKSHIRE

At Chelmsford, May 21, 22, 23. Essex won by 26 runs. Essex 19 pts, Yorkshire 4 pts. Toss: Yorkshire. With the first day having been lost to the weather, declarations on the final day brought about a thrilling finish. Set a target of 279 in 70 overs, Yorkshire looked to have no chance when they lost their eighth wicket at 120. However, Peter Hartley and Jarvis added 124 in only twenty overs, during which both achieved career-best scores, before Pringle, who had been responsible for Yorkshire's earlier problems, returned to claim the final two wickets and end with figures of seven for 46. The previous day, the promising Jarvis had bowled well for his six wickets. For Essex, Hardie and Prichard, despite having retired at 14 with a badly bruised arm, batted confidently on a pitch which was not always trustworthy, each hitting thirteen 4s.

Essex

*G. A. Gooch b Sidebottom	11			
B. R. Hardie c Moxon b Jarvis	110			
P. J. Prichard b Jarvis	82			
A. R. Border b Jarvis	1			
K. W. R. Fletcher lbw b Jarvis	2			
D. R. Pringle b Fletcher	25			
A. W. Lilley lbw b Jarvis	0	– (1) not out	29
†D. E. East lbw b Sidebottom	4	– (2) not out	5
N. A. Foster b Carrick	25			
J. K. Lever not out	4			
D. L. Acfield c Bairstow b Jarvis	0			
B 3, l-b 17, n-b 11	31			

1/38 2/89 3/95 4/146 5/221   295   (no wkt dec.) 34
6/221 7/246 8/289 9/295

Bonus points – Essex 3, Yorkshire 4.

Bowling: *First Innings*—Sidebottom 16–4–38–2; Jarvis 21.5–2–78–6; P. J. Hartley 12–2–50–0; Fletcher 15–1–43–1; Carrick 24–6–66–1. *Second Innings*—Sharp 3–0–30–0; Love 2.2–0–4–0.

Yorkshire

K. Sharp not out	25	– c Gooch b Lever	6
M. D. Moxon not out	25	– b Foster	2
J. D. Love (did not bat)		– lbw b Lever	0
S. N. Hartley (did not bat)		– b Pringle	24
A. A. Metcalfe (did not bat)		– lbw b Pringle	57
*†D. L. Bairstow (did not bat)		– c Hardie b Pringle	0
P. Carrick (did not bat)		– lbw b Pringle	16
A. Sidebottom (did not bat)		– c Hardie b Pringle	2
P. J. Hartley (did not bat)		– not out	87
P. W. Jarvis (did not bat)		– b Pringle	47
S. D. Fletcher (did not bat)		– c Prichard b Pringle	3
B 1	1	B 4, l-b 4	8

(no wkt dec.) 51   1/6 2/8 3/10 4/71 5/71   252
6/101 7/109 8/120 9/244

Bowling: *First Innings*—Lever 6–2–16–0; Foster 6–2–19–0; Pringle 3–2–7–0; Acfield 3–1–8–0. *Second Innings*—Lever 20–4–74–2; Foster 17–4–60–1; Pringle 17.5–6–46–7; Gooch 3–2–4–0; Acfield 10–1–60–0.

Umpires: K. J. Lyons and N. T. Plews.

At Derby, May 31, June 2, 3. ESSEX beat DERBYSHIRE by 116 runs.

At Swansea, June 4, 5, 6. ESSEX beat GLAMORGAN by an innings and 73 runs.

ESSEX v NOTTINGHAMSHIRE

At Chelmsford, June 7, 9, 10. Drawn. Essex 6 pts, Nottinghamshire 7 pts. Toss: Nottinghamshire. Excellent hundreds from two 21-year-olds were the highlights of this game. Johnson, whose 128 from 132 deliveries included two 6s and twenty 4s, steered Nottinghamshire away from a precarious 67 for five on the opening day. Hadlee's 43 off 38 balls (nine 4s) helped to relieve the immediate pressure. For Essex, in similar straits, the rescue came from a career-best 147 not out by Prichard as Hemmings worked his way through the innings on a pitch offering encouragement to spin. Prichard, who hit twenty 4s in his four and a half hours at the wicket, gained most support from the stubborn Lever, the pair putting on 101 for the eighth wicket. Another five wickets by Foster in Nottinghamshire's second innings brought the Essex fast bowler a ten-wicket haul in a Championship match for the first time. Hemmings also finished with ten wickets as Essex, following another fine contribution from Prichard, fell 71 runs short of their target of 293 in 260 minutes.

Nottinghamshire

B. C. Broad c East b Foster	8	– lbw b Acfield	11
M. Newell lbw b Lever	0	– b Lever	43
D. W. Randall c East b Foster	25	– c East b Foster	60
*C. E. B. Rice c Gladwin b Foster	30	– (5) b Foster	27
P. Johnson c East b Childs	128	– (4) b Foster	20
J. D. Birch b Foster	0	– b Foster	17
R. J. Hadlee b Acfield	43	– c Foster b Childs	3
†B. N. French c East b Lever	30	– not out	17
E. E. Hemmings st East b Childs	10	– lbw b Childs	1
K. E. Cooper b Foster	5	– c Foster b Childs	17
J. A. Afford not out	9	– c East b Foster	0
B 8, l-b 3	11	B 7, l-b 8, w 2	17

1/3 2/19 3/58 4/65 5/67   299   1/16 2/109 3/133 4/148 5/183   233
6/129 7/228 8/280 9/285   6/192 7/196 8/201 9/225

Bonus points – Nottinghamshire 3, Essex 4.

Bowling: *First Innings*—Lever 21–1–107–2; Foster 23–3–85–5; Acfield 14–2–34–1; Childs 18–4–62–2. *Second Innings*—Lever 10–4–29–1; Foster 27.2–5–69–5; Acfield 8–1–27–1; Childs 29–8–93–3.

Essex

C. Gladwin c Rice b Hemmings	8	– c Cooper b Rice	5
B. R. Hardie c Rice b Hadlee	3		
P. J. Prichard not out	147	– lbw b Hadlee	78
A. R. Border lbw b Hemmings	13	– c Hadlee b Hemmings	50
*K. W. R. Fletcher b Hemmings	3	– c Randall b Hemmings	9
K. R. Pont c French b Hemmings	6	– not out	8
†D. E. East c Cooper b Hemmings	2	– (2) c sub b Hemmings	47
N. A. Foster b Hemmings	4	– (7) not out	9
J. K. Lever run out	25		
D. L. Acfield c Broad b Hemmings	3		
J. H. Childs c French b Hadlee	11		
B 3, l-b 10, n-b 2	15	B 4, l-b 12	16

1/11 2/17 3/44 4/50 5/70 240   1/26 2/92 3/173   (5 wkts) 222
6/84 7/94 8/195 9/214   4/193 5/213

Bonus points – Essex 2, Nottinghamshire 4.

Bowling: *First Innings*—Hadlee 21.2-6-36-2; Rice 12-5-17-0; Hemmings 42-15-102-7; Cooper 10-3-23-0; Afford 13-4-49-0. *Second Innings*—Hadlee 11-3-31-1; Hemmings 35-9-62-3; Rice 5-2-12-1; Afford 26-7-78-0; Cooper 6-0-23-0.

Umpires: J. W. Holder and B. Leadbeater.

ESSEX v HAMPSHIRE

At Ilford, June 14, 16, 17. Hampshire won by 12 runs. Hampshire 23 pts, Essex 5 pts. Toss: Hampshire. Although a hostile pitch always favoured the bowlers, there were nevertheless some good batting performances. Robin Smith and Parks – the latter's 68 was his Championship best – swung the balance Hampshire's way on the first day. Nineteen wickets fell on the second day for 323 runs. Border was the only Essex player to look at ease and Parks again had to come to the visitors' rescue as they struggled in their second innings. Left with a target of 198, and all of the final day in which to advance from 27 for two, Essex looked capable of getting the runs while Border remained, but when he was out soon after completing his second half-century of the match, Marshall and Maru bowled Hampshire to an exciting victory just before the tea interval.

Hampshire

C. G. Greenidge c Lilley b Pringle	26	– c sub b Foster	11
V. P. Terry c East b Foster	2	– c Border b Lever	6
C. L. Smith c East b Foster	15	– c Pringle b Foster	23
*M. C. J. Nicholas c sub b Pringle	0	– b Foster	10
R. A. Smith b Foster	87	– c Lilley b Acfield	3
D. R. Turner lbw b Pringle	22	– b Acfield	5
M. D. Marshall lbw b Pringle	9	– lbw b Foster	0
N. G. Cowley c East b Pringle	0	– c Acfield b Pringle	25
†R. J. Parks lbw b Foster	68	– b Pringle	37
R. J. Maru b Foster	23	– not out	7
C. A. Connor not out	0	– lbw b Childs	0
B 4, l-b 1, w 2, n-b 1	8	B 2, l-b 3, w 1, n-b 2	8

1/9 2/43 3/45 4/49 5/112 260   1/18 2/19 3/43 4/55 5/57 135
6/130 7/130 8/202 9/255   6/61 7/69 8/106 9/134

Bonus points – Hampshire 3, Essex 4.

Bowling: *First Innings*—Lever 20-4-66-0; Foster 26.2-8-64-5; Pringle 26-8-65-5; Childs 8-1-27-0; Acfield 11-1-25-0; Gooch 2-1-8-0. *Second Innings*—Lever 7-1-28-1; Foster 16-5-36-4; Pringle 8-2-27-2; Acfield 12-4-28-2; Childs 1.5-0-11-1.

Essex

*G. A. Gooch b Maru	19	– c Terry b Connor	1
†D. E. East c Parks b Connor	4	– run out	37
P. J. Prichard lbw b Connor	5	– b Maru	6
J. K. Lever b Marshall	11	– c Parks b Marshall	5
A. R. Border c C. L. Smith b Cowley	71	– c Parks b Marshall	54
D. R. Pringle c Parks b Maru	0	– c Nicholas b Cowley	22
A. W. Lilley lbw b Marshall	8	– c Maru b Marshall	21
C. Gladwin c Parks b Connor	17	– c Parks b Maru	0
N. A. Foster c Parks b Connor	9	– c R. A. Smith b Maru	17
J. H. Childs st Parks b Cowley	30	– c Nicholas b Marshall	5
D. L. Acfield not out	3	– not out	0
B 1, l-b 10, n-b 10	21	B 4, l-b 9, w 1, n-b 3	17

1/15 2/35 3/35 4/50 5/51   198   1/3 2/20 3/36 4/75 5/116   185
6/68 7/119 8/137 9/185   6/156 7/157 8/159 9/179

Bonus points – Essex 1, Hampshire 4.

Bowling: First Innings—Marshall 17-6-60-2; Connor 17-5-54-4; Maru 13-4-34-2; Cowley 14-3-39-2. *Second Innings*—Marshall 21-7-26-4; Connor 12-3-33-1; Maru 25.2-5-74-3; Cowley 12-1-36-1; C. L. Smith 1-0-3-0.

Umpires: B. J. Meyer and K. E. Palmer.

ESSEX v SUSSEX

At Ilford, June 18, 19, 20. Essex won by 69 runs. Essex 22 pts, Sussex 4 pts. Toss: Essex. Only sixteen balls remained of the match when Acfield claimed the final wicket to give Essex victory on a pitch which had been the subject of much discussion on the first day. Prichard and Fletcher provided the backbone of the home side's first innings before Sussex crashed to 16 for six by the close, Topley celebrating his first Championship appearance of the season with some accurate medium-pace seam bowling (four for 7 in seven overs). Imran and Alikhan, who was making his Championship début, made sure that Sussex would not have to follow on, but Border, with five 6s and nine 4s in his 110-minute 96, sped Essex to a declaration 359 runs ahead. Two wickets down for 11 overnight, Sussex restored their pride with stubborn resistance throughout the last day. Alikhan battled for more than three hours in making 27, and there was also great determination from Reeve, who had gone in as night-watchman, and Gould, who had taken over the county captaincy the previous week.

Essex

C. Gladwin c A. P. Wells b Imran	8	– c Reeve b Standing	12
B. R. Hardie c Standing b Imran	7	– retired hurt	5
P. J. Prichard c C. M. Wells b Pigott	68	– b Bredin	55
A. R. Border b Reeve	17	– (5) not out	96
*K. W. R. Fletcher c Gould b Pigott	52	– (8) not out	2
K. R. Pont c Gould b Reeve	5	– (4) b Reeve	31
†D. E. East c Pigott b Reeve	6	– (6) c C. M. Wells b Reeve	15
N. A. Foster not out	51	– (7) c Parker b Bredin	0
T. D. Topley c Parker b Pigott	4		
J. H. Childs c Green b Pigott	3		
D. L. Acfield b Pigott	2		
B 4, l-b 11, n-b 4	19	B 6, l-b 6, n-b 1	13

1/9 2/22 3/51 4/149 5/157   242   1/54 2/92 3/152 (5 wkts dec.) 229
6/167 7/208 8/224 9/238   4/205 5/212

Bonus points – Essex 2, Sussex 4.

Bowling: First Innings—Imran 23-2-71-2; Pigott 24.4-4-57-5; C. M. Wells 6-2-12-0; Reeve 18-5-40-3; Standing 17-5-35-0; Bredin 4-1-12-0. *Second Innings*—Imran 13-3-38-0; Pigott 7-0-32-0; Standing 11-1-43-1; Bredin 12-2-50-2; Reeve 15-2-39-2; C. M. Wells 2-0-15-0.

Sussex

D. K. Standing c East b Topley	7	– b Childs	3
A. M. Green c Gladwin b Foster	4	– lbw b Topley	6
P. W. G. Parker lbw b Topley	0	– (4) c Fletcher b Childs	7
D. A. Reeve run out	0	– (3) c Gladwin b Topley	51
C. M. Wells c Hardie b Topley	0	– (6) lbw b Topley	39
Imran Khan st East b Childs	49	– (5) c Prichard b Topley	28
A. P. Wells c Hardie b Topley	0	– c Childs b Foster	35
R. I. Alikhan st East b Childs	25	– not out	27
*†I. J. Gould lbw b Topley	3	– c Foster b Childs	68
A. C. S. Pigott not out	19	– c Fletcher b Childs	0
A. M. Bredin lbw b Acfield	3	– c East b Acfield	2
L-b 2	2	B 9, l-b 6, w 4, n-b 5	24

1/9 2/9 3/11 4/11 5/13   112   1/8 2/11 3/50 4/83 5/126   290
6/15 7/84 8/89 9/91   6/146 7/190 8/279 9/281

Bonus points – Essex 4.

Bowling: *First Innings*—Foster 19–2–44–1; Topley 21–4–52–5; Childs 13–6–13–2; Acfield 1.3–0–1–1. *Second Innings*—Foster 31–7–63–1; Topley 25–5–68–4; Childs 40–14–84–4; Acfield 23.2–4–60–1.

Umpires: B. J. Meyer and K. E. Palmer.

At Lord's, June 21, 23, 24. ESSEX beat MIDDLESEX by five wickets.

At Chelmsford, July 2, 3, 4. ESSEX lost to NEW ZEALANDERS by six wickets (See New Zealand tour section).

At Manchester, July 5, 7. ESSEX lost to LANCASHIRE by an innings and 22 runs.

ESSEX v LEICESTERSHIRE

At Southend, July 16, 17. Leicestershire won by ten wickets. Leicestershire 23 pts, Essex 5 pts. Toss: Essex. DeFreitas fully exploited a pitch of uneven bounce to send Essex tumbling to their second consecutive defeat within two days. His hostility and movement brought him career-best figures on the opening day, and he bettered them on the second to return a match analysis of thirteen for 86. Given the new ball in the second innings, he bowled with added pace to take his first four wickets for 8 runs in a twenty-ball spell. Only Border and Prichard offered any resistance in the home side's first innings and East and Topley in the second. Leicestershire's innings was built on solid batting right down the order.

Essex

*B. R. Hardie c Potter b Benjamin	2	– c Gill b DeFreitas	0
J. P. Stephenson c Potter b DeFreitas	19	– c Willey b DeFreitas	0
P. J. Prichard lbw b Benjamin	56	– c Gill b Agnew	9
A. R. Border b DeFreitas	45	– c Clift b DeFreitas	12
A. W. Lilley lbw b DeFreitas	0	– c Clift b DeFreitas	8
K. R. Pont c Clift b DeFreitas	0	– c Gill b DeFreitas	1
†D. E. East lbw b Agnew	2	– lbw b Agnew	33
T. D. Topley c Gill b DeFreitas	9	– c Willey b DeFreitas	23
J. K. Lever b Clift	1	– c Gill b Agnew	6
J. H. Childs c Clift b DeFreitas	6	– c Clift b DeFreitas	13
D. L. Acfield not out	3	– not out	2
B 1, l-b 4, w 2, n-b 3	10	W 1, n-b 3	4

1/3 2/49 3/115 4/128 5/128   153   1/0 2/9 3/9 4/23 5/25   111
6/131 7/133 8/140 9/146   6/48 7/74 8/87 9/104

Bonus points – Essex 1, Leicestershire 4.

Bowling: *First Innings*—Agnew 13–5–40–1; Benjamin 8.4–2–21–2; DeFreitas 17.5–2–42–6; Clift 14–4–45–1. *Second Innings*—DeFreitas 16.1–5–44–7; Agnew 13–2–37–3; Clift 15–4–30–0.

Leicestershire

J. C. Balderstone c Topley b Lever	7		
R. A. Cobb lbw b Lever	13		
*P. Willey c Stephenson b Topley	5		
L. Potter lbw b Acfield	25		
T. J. Boon c Border b Topley	46		
P. D. Bowler lbw b Acfield	14		
P. B. Clift lbw b Topley	46		
W. K. M. Benjamin c East b Topley	25		
P. A. J. DeFreitas lbw b Topley	19		
J. P. Agnew not out	35	– (1) not out	1
†P. Gill c Border b Childs	17	– (2) not out	0
L-b 7, n-b 5	12		

1/19 2/27 3/31 4/100 5/112   264   (no wkt) 1
6/128 7/170 8/195 9/219

Bonus points – Leicestershire 3, Essex 4.

Bowling: *First Innings*—Lever 33–8–86–2; Topley 32–7–120–5; Pont 3–0–13–0; Acfield 15–7–21–2; Childs 6–1–17–1. *Second Innings*—East 0.2–0–1–0.

Umpires: J. W. Holder and H. J. Rhodes.

ESSEX v WORCESTERSHIRE

At Southend, July 19, 21, 22. Essex won by 91 runs. Essex 24 pts, Worcestershire 6 pts. Toss: Worcestershire. Foster, with sustained spells of accurate fast-medium bowling, returned career-best match figures of eleven for 157 as Essex won with six of the final twenty overs remaining. The opening day brought Gooch's first Championship hundred of the summer – he hit 21 4s in all – and a highest score of 85 for Stephenson as the pair shared in an opening stand of 214 in 205 minutes. Gooch again excelled as Essex chased quick runs in their second innings, his 79 coming off 88 balls. Worcestershire, in danger on the second morning of being asked to follow on, recovered dramatically through the efforts of Patel, whose 128 in four hours included eighteen 4s and one 6 and came after he had been confined to bed 24 hours earlier with a virus infection.

Essex

*G. A. Gooch c Rhodes b Radford	151	– b Radford	79
J. P. Stephenson c Hick b Pridgeon	85	– c Hick b Pridgeon	9
P. J. Prichard c Rhodes b Radford	27	– c sub b Newport	15
A. R. Border b Pridgeon	56	– c D'Oliveira b Inchmore	13
B. R. Hardie not out	34	– c Hick b Radford	10
D. R. Pringle b Pridgeon	0	– b Newport	15
A. W. Lilley not out	6	– (9) b Newport	0
†D. E. East (did not bat)		– (7) c Smith b Pridgeon	29
N. A. Foster (did not bat)		– (8) c Rhodes b Pridgeon	11
J. K. Lever (did not bat)		– not out	3
J. H. Childs (did not bat)		– c Rhodes b Newport	5
L-b 10, n-b 1	11	B 4, l-b 6, n-b 3	13

1/214 2/262 3/281   (5 wkts dec.) 370   1/76 2/97 3/110 4/122 5/134   202
4/343 5/343   6/175 7/188 8/189 9/193

Bonus points – Essex 4, Worcestershire 2.

Bowling: *First Innings*—Radford 23–2–113–2; Pridgeon 22–5–58–3; Inchmore 19–3–58–0; Newport 20–4–83–0; Patel 13–2–48–0. *Second Innings*—Radford 17–2–74–2; Pridgeon 14–1–59–3; Newport 9.5–1–42–4; Inchmore 6–0–17–1.

Worcestershire

T. S. Curtis b Lever	4	– lbw b Foster	22
D. B. D'Oliveira c sub b Lever	35	– c Pringle b Lever	4
†S. J. Rhodes c Lilley b Foster	0	– (7) not out	33
G. A. Hick c Border b Lever	51	– (3) b Pringle	29
D. M. Smith c East b Foster	21	– (4) c sub b Foster	16
*P. A. Neale lbw b Foster	2	– (5) c Gooch b Foster	11
D. N. Patel c East b Foster	128	– (6) b Foster	0
P. J. Newport lbw b Pringle	34	– c Gooch b Foster	5
N. V. Radford c Gooch b Foster	21	– c Hardie b Lever	30
J. D. Inchmore not out	23	– b Lever	2
A. P. Pridgeon b Foster	3	– lbw b Lever	0
L-b 1	1	L-b 6	6

1/8 2/11 3/90 4/91 5/98   323   1/5 2/53 3/57 4/87 5/87   158
6/130 7/241 8/282 9/313   6/92 7/98 8/146 9/158

Bonus points – Worcestershire 4, Essex 4.

Bowling: *First Innings*—Lever 25–2–110–3; Foster 32.3–7–93–6; Pringle 12–2–49–1; Gooch 14–2–40–0; Childs 9–1–30–0. *Second Innings*—Lever 16–2–55–4; Foster 24–5–64–5; Pringle 14–4–31–1; Childs 3–1–2–0.

Umpires: J. W. Holder and H. J. Rhodes.

At The Oval, July 23, 24, 25. ESSEX drew with SURREY.

At Eastbourne, August 2, 4, 5. ESSEX drew with SUSSEX.

ESSEX v MIDDLESEX

At Chelmsford, August 6, 7, 8. Essex won by an innings and 92 runs. Essex 24 pts, Middlesex 3 pts. Toss: Essex. Middlesex lost their last five wickets for 32 runs in the first hour of the final day as Essex completed a Championship double over the defending champions. Foster, who had nine wickets in the match for 107, prompted the visitors' demise. Only Slack offered any resistance when Middlesex followed on early on the second afternoon, Foster and Lever having used the heavy cloud cover to full advantage in the morning. Not out 89 at the close, he batted in all for approximately three and three-quarter hours before being well caught, low down, at first slip. An enterprising partnership of 167 between Fletcher and Lilley was the feature of the Essex innings, in which Prichard reached 1,000 runs in a season for the first time. Burns, making his first appearance as wicket-keeper for Essex, gave an encouraging performance, the highlight of which was his stumping of Downton in the first innings.

Essex

B. R. Hardie c Radley b Cowans 21	J. K. Lever not out 3	
J. P. Stephenson c Brown b Sykes 54	J. H. Childs not out 3	
P. J. Prichard lbw b Hughes 18		
A. R. Border c Butcher b Sykes 45	B 8, l-b 9, n-b 11 28	
A. W. Lilley b Daniel 87		
*K. W. R. Fletcher st Downton b Sykes 91	1/34 2/62 3/141 (8 wkts dec.) 382	
†N. D. Burns b Sykes 29	4/156 5/323 6/367	
N. A. Foster b Hughes 3	7/376 8/378	

D. L. Acfield did not bat.

Bonus points – Essex 4, Middlesex 3.

Bowling: Daniel 21–1–73–1; Cowans 21–6–54–1; Hughes 24–2–93–2; Sykes 26–4–102–4; Slack 8–1–43–0.

Middlesex

A. J. T. Miller b Lever 0	– c Hardie b Lever 5	
W. N. Slack c Hardie b Lever 15	– c Prichard b Foster 92	
K. R. Brown lbw b Foster 32	– c Prichard b Childs 16	
R. O. Butcher c Burns b Foster 3	– lbw b Foster 3	
*C. T. Radley c Burns b Foster 14	– lbw b Childs 9	
J. D. Carr b Lever 11	– b Acfield 12	
†P. R. Downton st Burns b Childs 15	– lbw b Foster 2	
J. F. Sykes not out 12	– c Border b Foster 26	
S. P. Hughes b Childs 0	– b Childs 2	
W. W. Daniel b Foster 0	– st Burns b Childs 1	
N. G. Cowans b Foster 7	– not out 0	
B 5, l-b 1, n-b 1 7	B 1, l-b 4, w 1 6	

1/2 2/33 3/38 4/51 5/69	116 1/9 2/48 3/62 4/96 5/137	174
6/90 7/100 8/106 9/107	6/143 7/162 8/173 9/173	

Bonus points – Essex 4.

Bowling: *First Innings*—Lever 12–4–35–3; Foster 17.2–2–51–5; Childs 14–5–24–2. *Second Innings*—Lever 14–2–40–1; Foster 20–4–56–4; Childs 27.1–8–64–4; Acfield 9–2–9–1.

Umpires: D. Lloyd and R. A. White.

At Leicester, August 9, 11, 12. ESSEX beat LEICESTERSHIRE by 130 runs.

ESSEX v NORTHAMPTONSHIRE

At Colchester, August 16, 18, 19. Northamptonshire won by 102 runs. Northamptonshire 24 pts, Essex 8 pts. Toss: Northamptonshire. On a pitch which crumbled rapidly, Essex, needing 147 to win in a minimum of 56 overs, were dismissed for the lowest score of the season in 85 minutes, or 20.1 overs. Nick Cook and Mallender were the destroyers, with only Gooch managing to reach double figures. An aggressive innings from Lamb, his 81 in 91 minutes containing ten 4s and two 6s, and a more sedate one from Bailey, set Northamptonshire in hand for maximum batting points, but second time around, after resuming on the third morning at 36 for one, they collapsed to the left-arm spin of Childs as the pitch presented problems from the start. Gooch struck fifteen 4s and a 6 to help Essex to a narrow first-innings lead, and Prichard and Hardie also batted attractively. However, these efforts were in total contrast to the dramatic finale in which Northamptonshire claimed the last eight Essex wickets for 13 runs.

Northamptonshire

*G. Cook c East b Foster	8	– c Prichard b Childs	9
W. Larkins lbw b Pringle	29	– st East b Childs	34
R. J. Boyd-Moss c Childs b Foster	10	– lbw b Pringle	7
A. J. Lamb lbw b Pringle	81	– c Hardie b Childs	27
R. J. Bailey c Prichard b Foster	63	– c Fletcher b Childs	5
D. J. Capel b Childs	40	– c Fletcher b Childs	11
R. A. Harper c East b Foster	13	– st East b Childs	39
†S. N. V. Waterton c East b Foster	24	– c Gooch b Childs	11
N. G. B. Cook c Border b Gooch	17	– lbw b Pringle	23
N. A. Mallender lbw b Acfield	10	– not out	3
A. Walker not out	0	– c Fletcher b Childs	2
B 1, l-b 6	7	B 7, l-b 3	10

1/9 2/31 3/84 4/159 5/236   302   1/23 2/50 3/50 4/65 5/86   181
6/238 7/255 8/291 9/302   6/97 7/125 8/168 9/176

Bonus points – Northamptonshire 4, Essex 4.

Bowling: First Innings—Lever 14-2-53-0; Foster 23.1-7-83-5; Pringle 21-3-64-2; Childs 24-5-75-1; Acfield 3-2-4-1; Gooch 8-3-16-1. *Second Innings*—Lever 4-0-11-0; Foster 8-0-27-0; Childs 30.2-9-61-8; Acfield 9-0-36-0; Pringle 14-4-36-2.

Essex

*G. A. Gooch c Walker b Harper	87	– lbw b N. G. B. Cook	12
†D. E. East c Bailey b Mallender	9	– c Lamb b N. G. B. Cook	1
J. K. Lever c Waterton b Mallender	17	– (9) b Mallender	3
P. J. Prichard c Waterton b N. G. B. Cook	72	– (3) c Waterton b Mallender	9
A. R. Border b N. G. B. Cook	28	– (4) b N. G. B. Cook	6
B. R. Hardie c Lamb b Mallender	66	– (5) c Lamb b N. G. B. Cook	0
D. R. Pringle b Mallender	0	– c Harper b N. G. B. Cook	0
K. W. R. Fletcher c Harper b N. G. B. Cook	9	– (6) c Lamb b Mallender	1
N. A. Foster c Bailey b Mallender	0	– (8) lbw b Mallender	0
J. H. Childs not out	14	– run out	2
D. L. Acfield c and b N. G. B. Cook	8	– not out	0
L-b 8, n-b 19	27	B 2, l-b 1, n-b 7	10

1/38 2/96 3/150 4/223 5/256   337   1/13 2/14 3/31 4/31 5/32   44
6/291 7/296 8/298 9/323   6/35 7/35 8/36 9/44

Bonus points – Essex 4, Northamptonshire 4 (Score at 100 overs: 333-9).

Bowling: First Innings—Mallender 27-1-110-5; Capel 9-1-55-0; Harper 24-7-52-1; Walker 9-0-36-0; N. G. B. Cook 32-7-76-4. *Second Innings*—Mallender 9.1-0-22-4; N. G. B. Cook 10-4-14-5; Harper 1-0-5-0.

Umpires: D. Lloyd and N. T. Plews.

ESSEX v GLOUCESTERSHIRE

At Colchester, August 20, 21, 22. Drawn. Essex 8 pts, Gloucestershire 5 pts. Toss: Essex. Bainbridge, who had defended stubbornly for around four hours, and Lawrence survived the last nineteen deliveries to enable the Championship leaders to stave off defeat by their nearest rivals after they had been set to score 301 in 91 overs. Some 25 minutes were lost to rain late in the day. The pitch, although offering the bowlers encouragement, was not as troublesome as that used in the previous match, as East confirmed when he followed up his first-innings 82 with an unbeaten century from 167 balls. His only one of the season, it contained four 6s and nine 4s and was a robust exhibition of clean hitting. Walsh was the pick of the visiting bowlers, taking five wickets in an innings for the eleventh time in the season, while Childs again demonstrated his liking for the conditions at Colchester with eight wickets in an innings for the second time in the week to return his best figures for Essex.

Essex

J. P. Stephenson c Russell b Walsh	8	– c Lloyds b Graveney	29
†D. E. East lbw b Walsh	82	– not out	100
P. J. Prichard c Lloyds b Walsh	65	– c Russell b Graveney	5
B. R. Hardie c and b Walsh	26	– c Curran b Graveney	7
*K. W. R. Fletcher c Graveney b Bainbridge	35		
D. R. Pringle c Lloyds b Lawrence	6	– run out	11
A. W. Lilley c Lloyds b Bainbridge	37	– (5) c Curran b Graveney	16
N. A. Foster c Graveney b Lawrence	22		
J. K. Lever b Walsh	2		
J. H. Childs not out	8		
D. L. Acfield b Walsh	2		
B 4, l-b 3, n-b 11	18	L-b 2, n-b 2	4

1/53 2/131 3/194 4/196 5/207   311   1/73 2/78 3/98   (5 wkts dec.) 172
6/269 7/274 8/286 9/300   4/142 5/172

Bonus points – Essex 4, Gloucestershire 4.

Bowling: *First Innings*—Walsh 28–7–83–6; Lawrence 23–0–113–2; Bainbridge 15–3–42–2; Graveney 13–3–35–0; Lloyds 9–1–31–0. *Second Innings*—Walsh 13.4–3–40–0; Lawrence 6–0–27–0; Graveney 19–3–73–4; Lloyds 12–2–30–0.

Gloucestershire

P. W. Romaines c Prichard b Childs	22	– c Fletcher b Childs	0
K. P. Tomlins c East b Childs	43	– c Prichard b Pringle	23
†R. C. Russell c Prichard b Childs	9	– (8) c East b Acfield	2
P. Bainbridge st East b Childs	10	– (3) not out	53
A. W. Stovold c Acfield b Childs	9	– (4) lbw b Pringle	23
K. M. Curran c Stephenson b Childs	14	– (5) lbw b Pringle	0
J. W. Lloyds c Stephenson b Foster	52	– (6) c Prichard b Acfield	11
M. W. Alleyne b Childs	7	– (7) lbw b Pringle	8
*D. A. Graveney c Fletcher b Childs	0	– (10) c Hardie b Childs	2
C. A. Walsh not out	5	– (9) st East b Childs	4
D. V. Lawrence b Foster	0	– not out	1
B 2, l-b 10	12	B 4, l-b 3, n-b 5	12

1/41 2/61 3/78 4/95 5/100   183   1/23 2/23 3/63 4/63   (9 wkts) 139
6/137 7/159 8/159 9/183   5/82 6/112 7/122
                                    8/129 9/137

Bonus points – Gloucestershire 1, Essex 4.

Bowling: *First Innings*—Lever 6–2–19–0; Foster 12.3–3–53–2; Childs 22–6–58–8; Acfield 4–0–9–0; Pringle 12–2–32–0. *Second Innings*—Lever 5–2–14–0; Foster 1–1–0–0; Childs 41–21–37–3; Acfield 32–12–54–2; Pringle 12–4–27–4.

Umpires: D. Lloyd and N. T. Plews.

ESSEX v SURREY

At Chelmsford, August 23, 25, 26. Drawn. Essex 5 pts, Surrey 5 pts. Rain washed out the final day's play after only 25 overs had been possible on the second. The main talking-point of this match, which brought together the second- and third-placed counties in the Championship race, was the visit to the press box of the Surrey captain, Pocock, on the first day to describe the pitch as "absolutely disgraceful". Its top, he claimed, had disintegrated before lunch, and Essex's collapse from 111 for two gave some credence to these views. Clinton displayed greater resolution with 49 not out as Surrey replied with 97 for two before the close, but Childs was making inroads when the weather intervened.

Essex

†D. E. East lbw b Thomas	20	J. K. Lever c Jesty b Clarke	22
J. P. Stephenson c Medlycott b Feltham	12	J. H. Childs not out	10
P. J. Prichard c Stewart b Pocock	31	D. L. Acfield c Lynch b Clarke	10
B. R. Hardie c Jesty b Medlycott	38		
*K. W. R. Fletcher lbw b Pocock	2	L-b 9, n-b 4	13
D. R. Pringle run out	43		
A. W. Lilley b Medlycott	17	1/22 2/41 3/111 4/111 5/114	222
N. A. Foster c Lynch b Medlycott	4	6/149 7/155 8/199 9/207	

Bonus points – Essex 2, Surrey 4.

Bowling: Clarke 12.5–3–37–2; Feltham 8–3–22–1; Thomas 5–0–31–1; Pocock 21–4–65–2; Medlycott 17–3–58–3.

Surrey

A. R. Butcher c East b Acfield	23	M. A. Feltham c Foster b Childs	5
G. S. Clinton c Prichard b Childs	55	K. T. Medlycott not out	9
A. J. Stewart c East b Childs	4		
T. E. Jesty c East b Foster	23	B 7, l-b 2	9
M. A. Lynch c Fletcher b Childs	16		
†C. J. Richards run out	3	1/40 2/49 3/107 4/115	(7 wkts) 166
D. J. Thomas not out	19	5/123 6/142 7/148	

S. T. Clarke and *P. I. Pocock did not bat.

Bonus points – Surrey 1, Essex 3.

Bowling: Lever 10–4–19–0; Foster 12–3–27–1; Acfield 21–5–39–1; Pringle 4–1–10–0; Childs 26–9–62–4.

Umpires: D. J. Constant and D. O. Oslear.

At Taunton, August 27, 28, 29. ESSEX beat SOMERSET by 9 runs.

At Folkestone, August 30, September 1, 2. ESSEX beat KENT by 23 runs.

At Nottingham, September 10, 11, 12. ESSEX drew with NOTTINGHAMSHIRE.

ESSEX v GLAMORGAN

At Chelmsford, September 13, 15, 16. Glamorgan won by 112 runs. Glamorgan 16 pts, Essex 2 pts. Toss: Glamorgan. The Welsh county gained their second Championship win of the season following the decision of the captains, Gooch and Morris, to set up a finish after rain had seriously disrupted the first two days. Glamorgan were fed easy runs, and the declaration left Essex a target of 301 in a minimum of 69 overs for victory. Thomas, however, quickly had the new champions in disarray with three wickets in his first six overs, those of East and Prichard coming off successive balls, and only a forthright 62 off 73 balls from Lilley gave Essex's innings a semblance of respectability.

Glamorgan

J. A. Hopkins c East b Foster	25	– c East b Lilley	79
*H. Morris c Gooch b Foster	17	– c East b Lilley	62
A. L. Jones not out	31	– not out	27
G. C. Holmes c and b Topley	4	– not out	16
M. P. Maynard b Foster	2		
R. C. Ontong c Fletcher b Foster	0		
J. G. Thomas c East b Smith	3		
M. J. Cann not out	16		
L-b 4, w 3, n-b 2	9	B 1, l-b 6, w 2	9

1/44 2/46 3/53 4/58   (6 wkts dec.) 107   1/133 2/162   (2 wkts dec.) 193
5/58 6/63

I. Smith, †M. L. Roberts and S. R. Barwick did not bat.

Bonus points – Essex 2.

Bowling: *First Innings*—Foster 21–1–51–4; Pringle 14–4–24–0; Gooch 2–0–2–0; Topley 13–6–25–2; Childs 2–1–1–0. *Second Innings*—Hardie 12–0–58–0; Lilley 18.3–1–104–2; Gooch 7–1–24–0.

Essex

Essex forfeited their first innings.

†D. E. East c Maynard b Thomas	24	N. A. Foster st Roberts b Ontong	8
J. P. Stephenson c Cann b Thomas	6	T. D. Topley not out	5
P. J. Prichard c Roberts b Thomas	9	J. H. Childs c Jones b Barwick	4
*G. A. Gooch run out	10		
B. R. Hardie b Barwick	3	B 4, l-b 4, w 1, n-b 2	11
D. R. Pringle c and b Smith	13		
K. W. R. Fletcher b Thomas	33		188
A. W. Lilley b Barwick	62		

1/11 2/41 3/41 4/51 5/55
6/78 7/119 8/149 9/180

Bowling: Thomas 18–1–60–4; Barwick 14.4–1–43–3; Smith 7–2–18–1; Ontong 12–1–59–1; Cann 1–1–0–0.

Umpires: H. D. Bird and B. Dudleston.

GLAMORGAN

Patron: HRH The Prince of Wales
President: His Honour Judge Rowe Harding
Chairman: G. Craven
Chairman, Cricket Committee: D. W. Lewis
Secretary: P. G. Carling
   Sophia Gardens, Cardiff CF1 9XR
   (Telephone: 0222-43478)
Assistant Secretary (Cricket): J. F. Steele
Captains: 1986 – R. C. Ontong and H. Morris
         1987 – H. Morris
Coach: A. Jones

Those who looked for encouraging signs, rather than anticipating improved results, derived some small satisfaction from Glamorgan's dismal record in the Britannic Assurance Championship. Few imagined that bottom of the table was to be the county's final position, even when it became evident at an early stage in the season that Javed Miandad had burned his boats by failing to rejoin the team in time for the Benson and Hedges Cup qualifying rounds. Alas, the team failed to win a home Championship game, and the two victories, at Leicester and in the final game at Chelmsford after Essex had made certain of the title, involved declarations when rain had reduced the playing time.

The Miandad episode loomed large, with reverberations throughout the season because of the team's lack of success. A handful of members felt that a conciliation should have been effected when he unexpectedly arrived in Swansea and sought reinstatement during mid-season. However, his terms were unacceptable, and his former team-mates endorsed the club's decision that Miandad's severence was irrevocable. Glamorgan were deeply wounded that he had let them down by not reporting for the opening matches.

It was suggested that Javed Miandad resented Glamorgan's decision to re-sign Ezra Moseley, the West Indian fast bowler, for midweek games when he was available from his Central Lancashire League commitments. Ironically, Moseley never measured up to requirements with the new ball, his eleven wickets costing 40.63 runs each, and he did not play after the Worcestershire match in mid-July, when Hick devastated the Glamorgan bowling. Shortly after the end of the season it was announced that the Indian all-rounder, Ravi Shastri, had agreed a two-year contract. The 24-year-old left-arm spinner fills the gap left by the retirement of John Steele, who has become assistant secretary with a special brief as adviser to the captain. And in November, the county signed Alan Butcher from Surrey on a three-year contract.

The captaincy changed at the end of July when Rodney Ontong asked to be relieved of command. He intended originally to hand over at the end of the season, but decided that a new captain would benefit from experience gained during the remainder of the summer. Philip Carling, the county secretary, had visited South Africa during the winter to discuss matters of captaincy and policy with Ontong, and it had been hoped that all problems had been settled. Unfortunately, the lull was all too short. Ontong felt he needed to relax to give his talents, as one of the country's leading all-rounders, freedom of expression.

There was not a great deal of choice, but Glamorgan responded boldy by appointing Hugh Morris, at 22 the youngest captain to occupy the position in the county's history. The left-hander opened the innings with reassuring maturity and scored 1,522 runs at an average of 36.23. Only Younis Ahmed had a better average in scoring 845 runs, and he left the county before the season ended.

Morris enjoyed immediate success. His first match as captain saw his team win at Leicester, and his temperament indicates a long and notable career. Even so, his apprenticeship in the mysteries that surround captaincy may not be entirely painless; but with the worldly-wise Steele as his confidant, his progress need not be exposed to some of the less pleasant experiences. Already he has had to stand up to the fact that there is nothing lower than last place, and a captain feels the humiliation more than anyone.

Mr Carling warned that it would be wrong to suggest that a young side, which had more than its share of difficulties on the field in 1986, could be a major force in 1987. "Nor will a new overseas player transform the situation overnight", he said. "As long as not too much is expected too soon, this young side can develop and compete with the best."

Glamorgan signed Duncan Pauline, a batsman from Surrey, and Simon Base, a 26-year-old fast-medium bowler who had played in South Africa and in Yorkshire league cricket. And during the season, Denis Hickey, an Australian at Glamorgan on an Esso Scholarship, was allowed to play in the Championship on overseas registration. However, neither bowler took twenty wickets in the Championship and both were expensive. Once again, Ontong was the most successful bowler with his off-breaks, his 64 wickets at 27.71 including a match analysis of thirteen for 127 against Nottinghamshire on a Cardiff turner. His batting, though, was disappointing, his highest innings being an unbeaten 80 in his final game as captain against Northamptonshire at Swansea.

Ontong's lack of success was shared by Gregory Thomas, who returned from the West Indies as a Test bowler but, hampered by slow pitches on his home grounds, failed to do himself justice. Matthew Maynard, a natural strokemaker and outstanding in the field, passed 1,000 runs in his first full season; John Derrick enjoyed considerable progress as a useful all-rounder in the making; and Geoff Holmes again batted responsibly. John Hopkins, in his benefit season, and Alan Lewis Jones lost their places for a time before returning to bat reliably, Jones later undergoing a second shoulder operation in September after suffering a recurrence of a serious dislocation.

Although for a second consecutive year Glamorgan failed to produce a bowler to take twenty wickets in the John Player League, in which they enjoyed a rise of two places, Morris passed Javed Miandad's record of 573 runs in a season by scoring 587. Another significant feature was the establishment of the club's headquarters at Sophia Gardens, the first time the offices had been sited at a playing venue. The Wilfred Wooller Room was opened as part of the complex, and electrically operated scoreboards were installed at Cardiff and Swansea. Significant improvements are being made, and it is hoped that these will be reflected soon in improvements on the field. – J.B.

GLAMORGAN 1986

[Bill Smith]

Back row: P. D. North, M. P. Maynard, D. B. Pauline, J. Derrick, S. J. Base, T. Jones (*physiotherapist*), I. Smith, D. R. Williams, S. W. Maddock, H. Morris, P. A. Cottey, G. Lewis (*scorer*). *Front row*: Younis Ahmed, T. Davies, J. G. Thomas, J. F. Steele, P. G. Carling (*secretary*), R. C. Ontong, A. Jones (*coach*), J. A. Hopkins, A. L. Jones, G. C. Holmes, S. R. Barwick. *Note*: R. C. Ontong was captain until July 22 when H. Morris was appointed.

GLAMORGAN RESULTS

All first-class matches – Played 26: Won 3, Lost 7, Drawn 16.

County Championship matches – Played 24: Won 2, Lost 7, Drawn 15.

Bonus points – Batting 39, Bowling 47.

Competition placings – Britannic Assurance County Championship, 17th; NatWest Bank Trophy, 2nd round; Benson and Hedges Cup, 5th in Group C; John Player League, 12th equal.

BRITANNIC ASSURANCE CHAMPIONSHIP AVERAGES

BATTING

	Birthplace	M	I	NO	R	HI	Avge
‡Younis Ahmed	Jullundur, India	15	23	2	845	105*	40.23
‡H. Morris	Cardiff	24	42	2	1,512	128*	37.80
J. Derrick	Cwmaman	16	22	6	496	78*	31.00
M. P. Maynard ...	Oldham	20	32	4	838	129	29.92
‡A. L. Jones	Alltwen	12	20	4	413	50	25.81
‡J. G. Thomas	Trebanos	19	25	6	485	70	25.52
‡G. C. Holmes	Newcastle-upon-Tyne	24	42	5	939	107	25.37
‡J. A. Hopkins ...	Maesteg	14	25	0	596	93	23.84
D. B. Pauline	Aberdeen	11	19	0	435	97	22.89
‡R. C. Ontong	Johannesburg, SA	24	37	4	744	80*	22.54
‡T. Davies	St Albans	22	28	13	316	41	21.06
‡J. F. Steele	Stafford	11	16	4	251	41*	20.91
‡E. A. Moseley	Christchurch, Barbados	6	8	1	55	19	7.85
S. J. Base	Maidstone	11	11	4	53	13*	7.57
P. D. North	Newport	4	5	2	22	17*	7.33
S. R. Barwick	Neath	10	8	2	33	9	5.50
D. J. Hickey	Moorapana, Australia	12	9	5	19	9*	4.75

Also batted: M. J. Cann (*Cardiff*) (1 match) 16*; P. A. Cottey (*Swansea*) (2 matches) 2, 0, 7; M. L. Roberts (*Mullion*) (2 matches) 8; I. Smith (*Chopwell*) (3 matches) 0, 0. S. L. Watkin (*Maesteg*) (1 match) did not bat.

* *Signifies not out.*   ‡ *Denotes county cap.*

The following played a total of five three-figure innings for Glamorgan in County Championship matches: H. Morris 2, G. C. Holmes 1, M. P. Maynard 1, Younis Ahmed 1.

BOWLING

	O	M	R	W	BB	Avge
R. C. Ontong	606.4	153	1,774	64	8-101	27.71
S. R. Barwick	256.4	56	838	23	3-25	36.43
J. G. Thomas	397.5	60	1,478	39	4-56	37.89
S. J. Base	199.5	34	727	19	4-74	38.26
E. A. Moseley	124.3	14	447	11	4-70	40.63
J. Derrick	213.2	39	705	16	3-19	44.06
D. J. Hickey	243.5	29	996	17	3-87	58.58

Also bowled: M. J. Cann 1–1–0–0; G. C. Holmes 107–14–427–9; J. A. Hopkins 1.5–0–12–0; M. P. Maynard 4–0–13–0; H. Morris 11–4–44–0; P. D. North 43.4–11–92–4; D. B. Pauline 14–0–67–2; I. Smith 24–3–111–1; J. F. Steele 134–20–534–6; S. L. Watkin 16–1–82–2; Younis Ahmed 20–4–82–0.

Wicket-keepers: T. Davies 25 ct, 7 st; M. L. Roberts 2 ct, 1 st.

Leading Fielders: G. C. Holmes 17; M. P. Maynard 12.

At Bristol, April 26, 27, 28. GLAMORGAN drew with GLOUCESTERSHIRE.

At Southampton, April 30, May 1, 2. GLAMORGAN drew with HAMPSHIRE.

At Taunton, May 7, 8, 9. GLAMORGAN drew with SOMERSET.

At Lord's, May 21, 22, 23. GLAMORGAN drew with MIDDLESEX.

GLAMORGAN v SOMERSET

At Cardiff, May 24, 26, 27. Drawn. Glamorgan 6 pts, Somerset 6 pts. Toss: Glamorgan. An absorbing contest throughout, this match featured a magnificent century by Richards, his 90th in first-class cricket, and a match analysis of fourteen for 212 by Marks, a personal best and indeed the best figures at Sophia Gardens, exceeding the thirteen for 102 by Underwood for Kent in 1979. The pitch took spin progressively at the Cathedral Road end and made for an exciting final day. Glamorgan, 45 runs behind on first innings, must have held little hope of averting defeat at 144 for eight midway through the final day; but then Derrick and Davies added 99, the best ninth-wicket stand for Glamorgan against Somerset since Wooller and H. G. Davies put on 68 at Swansea in 1948. So Somerset were left to get 199 at just over 7 runs an over. Botham, opening with Richards, hit 47 off 29 balls, but superb catching and three wickets by Ontong in four deliveries completely changed the situation. However, the abiding memory was of Richards's 136, scored off 172 balls with two 6s and eighteen 4s. He even made being sent back and run out look regal.

Glamorgan

J. A. Hopkins st Gard b Marks	43	– c Gard b Dredge	12
A. L. Jones lbw b Botham	24	– c Dredge b Garner	11
H. Morris c Hardy b Marks	67	– c Botham b Marks	29
G. C. Holmes c Harden b Marks	15	– c Harden b Marks	5
Younis Ahmed c Hardy b Marks	20	– c Hardy b Marks	22
*R. C. Ontong c Dredge b Marks	78	– c Gard b Marks	14
M. P. Maynard st Gard b Marks	4	– b Marks	3
J. G. Thomas not out	50	– c Garner b Marks	32
J. Derrick not out	2	– not out	61
†T. Davies (did not bat)		– c and b Marks	41
S. J. Base (did not bat)		– lbw b Marks	0
B 3, l-b 5, w 2, n-b 1	11	L-b 1, w 4, n-b 8	13

1/50 2/78 3/111 4/147   (7 wkts dec.) 314   1/23 2/26 3/47 4/72 5/89   243
5/209 6/219 7/310   6/96 7/111 8/144 9/243

Bonus points – Glamorgan 2, Somerset 2 (Score at 100 overs: 226-6).

Bowling: *First Innings*—Garner 15–4–41–0; Taylor 12–2–35–0; Botham 12–3–29–1; Dredge 13–1–40–0; Marks 43–11–112–6; Palmer 8–0–15–0; Harden 1–0–3–0; Richards 10–1–31–0. *Second Innings*—Garner 18–6–36–1; Botham 13–4–28–0; Marks 31.3–7–100–8; Dredge 11–4–21–1; Taylor 3–0–20–0; Palmer 5–1–14–0; Richards 5–0–23–0.

Somerset

V. J. Marks b Thomas	0	– (4) c Davies b Derrick	16
*P. M. Roebuck c Morris b Base	40	– (8) not out	4
R. J. Harden b Ontong	42	– b Ontong	10
I. V. A. Richards run out	136	– (2) c Holmes b Base	15
I. T. Botham c Jones b Holmes	49	– (1) c Jones b Ontong	47
G. V. Palmer c Younis b Holmes	17	– (5) c Jones b Ontong	0
†T. Gard c and b Ontong	30	– not out	5
J. J. E. Hardy c Jones b Base	8		
C. H. Dredge b Base	4		
N. S. Taylor b Ontong	3		
J. Garner not out	5	– (6) b Ontong	1
B 1, l-b 10, w 1, n-b 13	25	B 4, l-b 6, w 1, n-b 2	13

1/0 2/68 3/121 4/211 5/260   359   1/42 2/78 3/79 4/79   (6 wkts) 111
6/314 7/343 8/347 9/351   5/82 6/103

Bonus points – Somerset 4, Glamorgan 4.

Bowling: *First Innings*—Thomas 20–4–64–1; Base 16–4–56–3; Holmes 16–3–66–2; Derrick 15–1–45–0; Ontong 21.2–5–82–3; Younis 7–0–35–0. *Second Innings*—Thomas 9–0–40–0; Base 4–0–45–1; Ontong 8.4–4–10–4; Derrick 4–1–6–1.

Umpires: J. Birkenshaw and J. H. Hampshire.

GLAMORGAN v ESSEX

At Swansea, June 4, 5, 6. Essex won by an innings and 73 runs. Essex 24 pts, Glamorgan 3 pts. Toss: Essex. Border's 150 on the first day, an innings of classical majesty in just under four and a half hours with one 6 and 22 4s, was the springboard from which Essex overwhelmed the home side on a turning pitch. But for interruptions through rain, the match could have been completed inside two days as the extra half hour was taken. Only five overs and four balls were needed on the final morning to capture the last two wickets. Glamorgan never came to grips with the hostile accuracy of Lever and then the left-arm spin of Childs. Childs finished with a match analysis of ten for 98; an admirable performance.

Essex

C. Gladwin c Davies b Derrick	73	J. K. Lever run out	0
B. R. Hardie b Moseley	18	J. H. Childs c Hopkins b Moseley	2
P. J. Prichard c Davies b Moseley	0	D. L. Acfield not out	1
A. R. Border b Steele	150		
*K. W. R. Fletcher c Base b Moseley	67	B 4, l-b 3, w 1, n-b 6	14
K. R. Pont b Steele	5		
†D. E. East c Ontong b Base	6	1/39 2/39 3/164 4/301 5/323	366
N. A. Foster c Younis b Derrick	30	6/323 7/340 8/341 9/361	

Bonus points – Essex 4, Glamorgan 2 (Score at 100 overs: 323-6).

Bowling: Moseley 20–3–70–4; Base 18–2–81–1; Holmes 6–1–11–0; Derrick 202–5–54–2; Ontong 27–4–98–0; Steele 16–4–45–2.

Glamorgan

J. A. Hopkins c East b Lever	0	– st East b Childs	6
A. L. Jones b Foster	24	– c Border b Acfield	13
H. Morris c Fletcher b Lever	30	– c Fletcher b Acfield	16
G. C. Holmes lbw b Lever	14	– lbw b Childs	9
Younis Ahmed c Fletcher b Lever	28	– c Hardie b Border	41
*R. C. Ontong c East b Childs	1	– st East b Childs	6
J. F. Steele c Prichard b Childs	4	– b Childs	9
J. Derrick st East b Childs	27	– c Prichard b Childs	17
†T. Davies b Lever	20	– b Childs	2
E. A. Moseley lbw b Lever	0	– c East b Childs	2
S. J. Base not out	3	– not out	3
L-b 8, n-b 1	9	B 4, l-b 5	9

1/0 2/40 3/70 4/104 5/105   **160**   1/19 2/19 3/44 4/48 5/60   **133**
6/109 7/109 8/157 9/157   6/102 7/123 8/125 9/126

Bonus points – Glamorgan 1, Essex 4.

Bowling: *First Innings*—Lever 28.5–10–57–6; Foster 12–3–19–1; Acfield 10–2–29–0; Childs 13–2–47–3. *Second Innings*—Lever 3–0–17–0; Foster 2–0–2–0; Childs 28.4–10–51–7; Acfield 25–8–46–2; Border 3–0–8–1.

Umpires: C. Cook and R. Julian.

At Birmingham, June 7, 9, 10. GLAMORGAN drew with WARWICKSHIRE.

At Oxford, June 14, 16, 17. GLAMORGAN beat OXFORD UNIVERSITY by an innings and 26 runs.

GLAMORGAN v WARWICKSHIRE

At Swansea, June 18, 19, 20. Warwickshire won by 284 runs. Warwickshire 24 pts, Glamorgan 5 pts. Toss: Glamorgan. Amiss's 99th hundred in first-class cricket, coming off 134 deliveries, set the scene for this overwhelming victory after Warwickshire had been asked to bat on a pitch which provided early lift and then reverted to type, wearing encouragingly for the spinners. Amiss struck nine 4s in his first fourteen scoring strokes and nineteen 4s in all, a number with pleasing late-cuts, and Humpage rendered lively assistance with his 55 in a third-wicket stand worth 127. Ontong's defiance helped to avert the follow-on; but after Kallicharran's unbeaten 102 (two 6s, ten 4s), his fourth hundred in ten innings, Glamorgan collapsed against the spin of Gifford and Kerr. Kerr's five for 47 were the best figures of his brief career.

Warwickshire

T. A. Lloyd c Davies b Moseley	39	– c Davies b Derrick	57
P. A. Smith c Derrick b Ontong	9		
A. I. Kallicharran lbw b Holmes	6	– not out	102
D. L. Amiss c Davies b Moseley	110	– c Holmes b Steele	48
†G. W. Humpage b Thomas	55		
Asif Din b Thomas	0	– (5) not out	22
A. M. Ferreira b Thomas	6		
G. J. Parsons not out	24	– (2) c Holmes b Ontong	47
K. J. Kerr c Holmes b Moseley	1		
G. C. Small b Thomas	13		
*N. Gifford c Holmes b Ontong	0		
B 5, l-b 8, w 7, n-b 18	38	L-b 6, w 1, n-b 7	14

1/59 2/70 3/197 4/198 5/209   **301**   1/89 2/137 3/232   (3 wkts dec.) **290**
6/266 7/271 8/272 9/294

Bonus points – Warwickshire 4, Glamorgan 4.

In the first innings P. A. Smith, when 8, retired hurt at 52 and resumed at 266.

Bowling: *First Innings*—Thomas 21–1–89–4; Moseley 20–3–67–3; Holmes 5–0–28–1; Derrick 4–0–20–0; Maynard 4–0–13–0; Ontong 10.1–5–19–2; Steele 17–1–52–0. *Second Innings*—Thomas 4–0–26–0; Moseley 10–1–30–0; Ontong 27–6–95–1; Derrick 14–1–44–1; Steele 10–0–70–1; Pauline 5–0–19–0.

Glamorgan

D. B. Pauline lbw b Small	4	– c Kallicharran b Small	31
H. Morris lbw b Parsons	0	– b Small	20
G. C. Holmes b Gifford	20	– b Kerr	2
Younis Ahmed c Humpage b Small	16	– st Humpage b Kerr	35
M. P. Maynard lbw b Gifford	20	– c Asif Din b Kerr	13
*R. C. Ontong c Humpage b Small	50	– c Asif Din b Kerr	3
J. F. Steele c Humpage b Gifford	38	– b Gifford	1
J. G. Thomas run out	11	– not out	9
J. Derrick c Humpage b Kerr	6	– c Ferreira b Gifford	0
†T. Davies c Kallicharran b Gifford	10	– c Lloyd b Gifford	0
E. A. Moseley not out	4	– c Ferreira b Kerr	0
W 1, n-b 6	7	B 4, l-b 1, n-b 2	7

1/4 2/6 3/27 4/56 5/64   186   1/39 2/50 3/60 4/95 5/103   121
6/139 7/166 8/166 9/174   6/112 7/114 8/118 9/118

Bonus points – Glamorgan 1, Warwickshire 4.

Bowling: *First Innings*—Small 21–5–60–3; Parsons 7–2–18–1; Gifford 18.1–8–42–4; Smith 2–0–12–0; Kerr 23–9–44–1; Ferreira 9–4–10–0. *Second Innings*—Small 13–3–40–2; Parsons 4–2–12–0; Kerr 13.5–2–47–5; Gifford 5–1–17–3.

Umpires: M. J. Kitchen and P. B. Wight.

GLAMORGAN v LANCASHIRE

At Swansea, June 21, 23, 24. Drawn. Glamorgan 4 pts, Lancashire 5 pts. Toss: Lancashire. The second match of the Swansea Festival Week was washed out with no play on the final day. Lancashire raised a massive 475 before declaring after batting on into Monday morning. Mendis's first hundred for Lancashire came off 135 balls (eighteen 4s) and Abrahams hit an excellent 189 not out from 330 deliveries with two 6s and 30 4s. There was a fierce burst to accelerate the rate by Chris Maynard, who struck one 6 and ten 4s in making 60 from 66 deliveries. Glamorgan, facing a long rearguard action, had as their first priority a target of 326 to avoid following on. Pauline set an example of stubborn endurance with 50 runs in 51 overs, but Glamorgan were fortunate that they did not have to contend with Simmons. The Lancashire off-spinner was unable to bowl because of extensive bruising when a ball landed on his instep during the Sunday League game.

Lancashire

G. D. Mendis c Davies b Ontong	100	J. Simmons c Holmes b Hickey	1
G. Fowler c Steele b Hickey	14	P. J. W. Allott c Pauline b Thomas	46
J. Abrahams not out	189	
N. H. Fairbrother c Younis b Ontong	1	L-b 8, w 7, n-b 7	22
*C. H. Lloyd lbw b Ontong	14	
†C. Maynard c Holmes b Steele	60	1/26 2/164 3/175 4/226 (8 wkts dec.) 475
M. Watkinson c Holmes b Hickey	28	5/325 6/374 7/376 8/475

D. J. Makinson and I. Folley did not bat.

Bonus points – Lancashire 4, Glamorgan 2 (Score at 100 overs: 371-5).

Bowling: Thomas 24.5–4–97–1; Hickey 22–2–102–3; Derrick 12–2–34–0; Holmes 4–0–14–0; Steele 20–4–118–1; Ontong 35–12–102–3.

Glamorgan

D. B. Pauline c Allott b Watkinson ...	53
H. Morris c Abrahams b Makinson ...	54
G. C. Holmes c Allott b Makinson	2
Younis Ahmed c Maynard b Watkinson	68
M. P. Maynard not out	36

*R. C. Ontong not out	7
B 2, l-b 2, w 1, n-b 5	10
1/82 2/90 3/163 4/191 (4 wkts)	230

J. F. Steele, J. G. Thomas, †T. Davies, J. Derrick and D. J. Hickey did not bat.

Bonus points – Glamorgan 2, Lancashire 1.

Bowling: Allott 12.2–5–22–0; Makinson 16–0–61–2; Watkinson 24–10–59–2; Folley 32–11–84–0.

Umpires: M. J. Kitchen and P. B. Wight.

At Maidstone, June 28, 30, July 1. GLAMORGAN drew with KENT.

GLAMORGAN v SUSSEX

At Cardiff, July 2, 3, 4. Drawn. Glamorgan 4 pts, Sussex 5 pts. Toss: Sussex. Run-making was always laboured on a pitch of low bounce. Green, whose maiden century had been against Glamorgan in 1985, batted for just over five hours, his 179 (fifteen 4s) being the highest innings by a Sussex batsman on a Welsh ground. The record had been established 55 years earlier by John Langridge (161) at Cardiff Arms Park. Reeve's three wickets in six balls without cost on the second day revived memories of his three Glamorgan wickets in four balls at Hove the previous year, but Glamorgan now had their own man of substance in Younis Ahmed. He scored an unbeaten 105 off 210 deliveries, driving powerfully although being curbed by the off-spin of Standing. Ontong declared 57 runs behind, only for rain to wash out the final day. Eight of the nine dismissals on the second day were for lbw and all were adjudged by Mr Julian.

Sussex

D. K. Standing lbw b Holmes	16	– lbw b Base	3
A. M. Green c Pauline b Base	179	– lbw b Base	15
P. W. G. Parker c Ontong b Steele	75	– (4) not out	1
A. P. Wells not out	43		
C. M. Wells not out	27		
D. A. Reeve (did not bat)		– (3) not out	7
L-b 3, w 1, n-b 7	11	L-b 1	1

1/80 2/269 3/281 (3 wkts dec.)	351	1/18 2/19 (2 wkts) 27

R. I. Alikhan, *†I. J. Gould, A. C. S. Pigott, C. S. Mays and A. M. Babington did not bat.

Bonus points – Sussex 3, Glamorgan 1 (Score at 100 overs: 281-3).

Bowling: *First Innings*—Hickey 19–1–71–0; Base 17–1–79–1; Ontong 19–4–62–0; Derrick 22–6–47–0; Holmes 8–2–32–1; Steele 27–6–57–1. *Second Innings*—Hickey 7–0–19–0; Base 7–4–7–2.

Glamorgan

D. B. Pauline c Gould b C. M. Wells ..	33
H. Morris lbw b C. M. Wells	37
G. C. Holmes lbw b Reeve	61
Younis Ahmed not out	105
M. P. Maynard lbw b Reeve	0
*R. C. Ontong lbw b Reeve	0
J. F. Steele lbw b C. M. Wells	15

†T. Davies lbw b Pigott	22
J. Derrick not out	1
B 9, l-b 6, w 1, n-b 4	20
1/75 2/80 3/189 (7 wkts dec.)	294
4/189 5/189 6/229 7/290	

D. J. Hickey and S. J. Base did not bat.

Bonus points – Glamorgan 3, Sussex 2 (Score at 100 overs: 259-6).

Bowling: Pigott 10–0–31–1; Reeve 21–9–30–3; Mays 25–4–84–0; Babington 13–0–46–0; C. M. Wells 19–7–30–3; Standing 19–3–50–0; Green 2–1–8–0.

Umpires: J. A. Jameson and R. Julian.

GLAMORGAN v GLOUCESTERSHIRE

At Cardiff, July 5, 7, 8. Gloucestershire won by five wickets. Gloucestershire 23 pts, Glamorgan 6 pts. Toss: Gloucestershire. The home county, after being 228 for three, lost their last seven wickets while adding 17 runs as Walsh set about them in the final session of Saturday's play. They were to collapse again at their second attempt, demoralised by the fearsome pace of Lawrence, who took three wickets for 11 runs in his first five overs on the final morning. Morris, who scored a staunch 98 in the first innings, again stood firm with a half-century; but Gloucestershire's target of 188 at fewer than 3 an over was not exacting. Curran distinguished their first innings with his maiden Championship century, scored off 100 deliveries, and in his career-best 116 he struck three 6s and fourteen 4s. In Gloucestershire's second innings, Lloyd's unbeaten half-century guided them to a success which carried them to the top of the Championship table.

Glamorgan

D. B. Pauline c Russell b Lawrence	16	– c Russell b Walsh	20
H. Morris c and b Lloyds	98	– c Graveney b Lawrence	55
G. C. Holmes c Russell b Walsh	1	– c and b Graveney	23
M. P. Maynard c Wright b Graveney	61	– c Walsh b Lloyds	43
*R. C. Ontong c Wright b Lloyds	42	– (6) c Wright b Lawrence	0
J. G. Thomas lbw b Walsh	0	– (9) b Lawrence	19
P. A. Cottey b Walsh	2	– c Wright b Lawrence	0
J. F. Steele c Wright b Walsh	0	– c Lloyds b Graveney	13
†T. Davies c Bainbridge b Lloyds	0	– (5) b Lloyds	22
S. J. Base lbw b Walsh	4	– not out	10
D. J. Hickey not out	2	– b Walsh	0
B 5, l-b 10, w 1, n-b 3	19	B 1, l-b 5, n-b 6	12

1/23 2/23 3/160 4/228 5/233   245   1/29 2/71 3/140 4/150 5/152   217
6/233 7/238 8/239 9/239   6/156 7/187 8/193 9/216

Bonus points – Glamorgan 2, Gloucestershire 4.

Bowling: First Innings—Lawrence 18–4–58–1; Walsh 19.2–7–34–5; Bainbridge 5–1–13–0; Lloyds 26–8–85–3; Graveney 25–7–40–1. *Second Innings*—Lawrence 17–4–45–4; Walsh 20.2–6–38–2; Lloyds 19–3–73–2; Graveney 17–2–55–2.

Gloucestershire

A. W. Stovold b Thomas	12	– c Davies b Thomas	9
A. J. Wright c Holmes b Steele	55	– c Maynard b Hickey	14
†R. C. Russell b Thomas	0		
K. P. Tomlins c Davies b Hickey	2	– (3) c Thomas b Ontong	18
P. Bainbridge b Base	24	– (4) lbw b Thomas	48
K. M. Curran c Maynard b Ontong	116	– (5) lbw b Ontong	23
J. W. Lloyds c Cottey b Thomas	35	– (6) not out	56
M. W. Alleyne not out	17	– (7) not out	6
C. A. Walsh c Base b Ontong	6		
*D. A. Graveney b Thomas	1		
D. V. Lawrence c and b Ontong	0		
L-b 6, n-b 1	7	B 4, l-b 6, n-b 4	14

1/23 2/23 3/28 4/71 5/165   275   1/12 2/46 3/63   (5 wkts) 188
6/247 7/251 8/266 9/274   4/99 5/152

Bonus points – Gloucestershire 3, Glamorgan 4.

Bowling: First Innings—Thomas 22–4–56–4; Hickey 13–1–58–1; Base 18–5–55–1; Steele 8–0–23–1; Ontong 24.1–4–77–3. *Second Innings*—Thomas 15.2–2–31–2; Hickey 10–2–35–1; Base 4–0–16–0; Ontong 17–3–72–2; Steele 6–0–24–0.

Umpires: J. A. Jameson and R. Julian.

GLAMORGAN v WORCESTERSHIRE

At Neath, July 16, 17, 18. Worcestershire won by seven wickets. Worcestershire 23 pts, Glamorgan 2 pts. Toss: Glamorgan. Hick dominated this match, playing one of the greatest innings seen on a Welsh ground. There was none of the artificiality of bowlers feeding runs for a declaration: Glamorgan were trying desperately to get him out in both innings. With explosive power he struck eight 6s and 25 4s, the majority of the one-bounce variety, in making the highest first-class score on the Gnoll ground: 219 not out off 146 deliveries in 172 minutes during which he and Curtis added 287 to pass their county's second-wicket record: 274, set 53 years earlier by H. H. I. Gibbons and the Nawab of Pataudi against Kent and equalled a year later by the same pair against Glamorgan. When 119, Hick became the first batsman to score 1,000 runs in the season. In the second innings, he launched Worcestershire towards a target of 225 at just under 7 runs an over with a display of mini-magic: 52 from 22 balls with three 6s and six 4s. Welsh cricket watchers had witnessed a reincarnation of Gilbert Jessop. It was a dramatic contrast to the intense defiance of Holmes on the first day – 85 in nearly four and a half hours – and Pauline on the last – 97 in five and a quarter hours. Curtis batted admirably without being dismissed and on Hick's departure Neale assumed the role of the big-hitter (three 6s, six 4s) to maintain Worcestershire's momentum and bring victory with nine balls to spare.

Glamorgan

H. Morris c D'Oliveira b Pridgeon	3	– lbw b Radford	1
D. B. Pauline c Rhodes b Radford	13	– b Radford	97
G. C. Holmes c Hick b Newport	85	– (10) c Hick b Pridgeon	1
Younis Ahmed c D'Oliveira b Illingworth	37	– (3) b Radford	3
M. P. Maynard c Smith b Patel	4	– (4) lbw b Pridgeon	1
*R. C. Ontong lbw b Radford	38	– (5) c Newport b Patel	51
J. Derrick run out	6	– (6) st Rhodes b Newport	38
J. G. Thomas b Radford	24	– (7) run out	6
J. F. Steele not out	24	– (8) c Rhodes b Radford	7
†T. Davies not out	19	– (9) not out	17
E. A. Moseley (did not bat)		– c Newport b Pridgeon	15
B 2, l-b 5, w 5, n-b 3	15	B 12, l-b 4, w 3	19

1/10 2/18 3/96 4/102 (8 wkts dec.) 268   1/8 2/12 3/13 4/114 5/179   256
5/173 6/194 7/195 8/228   6/195 7/217 8/235 9/240

Bonus points – Glamorgan 2, Worcestershire 3 (Score at 100 overs: 235-8).

Bowling: *First Innings*—Radford 26-5-57-3; Pridgeon 15-5-20-1; Newport 17-2-44-1; Illingworth 26-5-54-1; Patel 26-6-86-1. *Second Innings*—Pridgeon 19.4-9-25-3; Radford 29-4-72-4; Newport 14-4-20-1; Illingworth 35-12-84-0; Patel 13-3-32-1; Hick 3-1-6-0; D'Oliveira 1-0-1-0.

Worcestershire

T. S. Curtis not out	66	– not out	63
D. B. D'Oliveira lbw b Thomas	7	– c Davies b Moseley	7
G. A. Hick not out	219	– c Steele b Ontong	52
D. M. Smith (did not bat)		– b Thomas	9
*P. A. Neale (did not bat)		– not out	70
B 1, l-b 5, w 1, n-b 1	8	B 4, l-b 17, w 1, n-b 2	24

1/13 (1 wkt dec.) 300   1/27 2/95 3/110 (3 wkts) 225

D. N. Patel, †S. J. Rhodes, P. J. Newport, N. V. Radford, A. P. Pridgeon and R. K. Illingworth did not bat.

Bonus points – Worcestershire 4.

Bowling: *First Innings*—Thomas 13-1-72-1; Moseley 14-2-50-0; Derrick 8.5-0-49-0; Steele 12-2-65-0; Ontong 8-2-58-0. *Second Innings*—Thomas 13-1-74-1; Moseley 9.3-0-70-1; Ontong 6-0-39-1; Derrick 3-0-21-0.

Umpires: J. H. Hampshire and D. O. Oslear.

GLAMORGAN v NORTHAMPTONSHIRE

At Swansea, July 19, 21, 22. Drawn. Glamorgan 4 pts, Northamptonshire 5 pts. Toss: Northamptonshire. Glamorgan were saved from defeat by the three players involved in the changes in team management announced during the final day's play. Ontong, who resigned as captain, steered his team through the danger of the follow-on with an unbeaten 80. When, after some unusual high-altitude slow bowling by Morris to hasten the second Northamptonshire declaration, Glamorgan were set to score 264 off a minimum of 42 overs, Morris, appointed the youngest captain in his county's history at 22 years of age, led the way with a well-struck 88 to follow his first-innings 90. And finally Steele, named as assistant secretary with special responsibility for team management, blocked in characteristic manner for nearly 90 minutes after Harper, bounding in with a high, lissom action and bowling his off-breaks with well-disguised variation, had torn the middle out of the innings. On the first day, Bailey's double-century provided exceptional entertainment as he hit six 6s and 24 4s, receiving notable support from Harper and Boyd-Moss.

Northamptonshire

*G. Cook b Hickey	14		
W. Larkins retired hurt	5	– (1) not out	40
R. J. Boyd-Moss c Steele b Base	68	– (2) c Younis b Hickey	0
R. J. Bailey not out	224	– (3) not out	74
D. J. Capel b Ontong	48		
D. J. Wild b Base	5		
R. A. Harper lbw b Pauline	88		
†S. N. V. Waterton c and b Pauline	10		
N. G. B. Cook not out	8		
B 5, l-b 6, w 3, n-b 5	19		

1/17 2/144 3/276 4/285   (6 wkts dec.) 489   1/0   (1 wkt dec.) 114
5/433 6/457

N. A. Mallender and A. Walker did not bat.

Bonus points – Northamptonshire 4, Glamorgan 2 (Score at 100 overs: 444-5).

Bowling: First Innings—Thomas 14-2-64-0; Hickey 15-2-89-1; Base 22-4-84-2; Holmes 11-0-67-0; Ontong 27-5-79-1; Pauline 9-0-48-2; Steele 8-0-47-0. *Second Innings*—Thomas 4-2-4-0; Hickey 4-1-23-1; Younis 11-4-43-0; Morris 11-4-44-0.

Glamorgan

H. Morris c Waterton b Harper	90	– b Mallender	88
D. B. Pauline c and b Capel	38	– lbw b Mallender	0
G. C. Holmes c N. G. B. Cook b Harper	24	– c N. G. B. Cook b Mallender	2
Younis Ahmed c Waterton b Mallender	66	– c N. G. B. Cook b Walker	4
M. P. Maynard c N. G. B. Cook b Harper	0	– b Harper	17
*R. C. Ontong not out	80	– st Waterton b Harper	17
J. G. Thomas c Bailey b Mallender	11	– c N. G. B. Cook b Harper	0
J. F. Steele not out	10	– not out	41
†T. Davies (did not bat)		– c Walker b Harper	8
S. J. Base (did not bat)		– c Bailey b Mallender	2
D. J. Hickey (did not bat)		– not out	5
L-b 7, w 3, n-b 11	21	B 4, l-b 1, n-b 7	12

1/67 2/119 3/174 4/184   (6 wkts dec.) 340   1/0 2/7 3/22 4/56   (9 wkts) 196
5/266 6/313   5/92 6/101 7/146
                                                  8/173 9/187

Bonus points – Glamorgan 2, Northamptonshire 1 (Score at 100 overs: 227-4).

Bowling: First Innings—Mallender 29-8-67-2; Walker 19-1-71-0; Capel 24-5-63-1; N. G. B. Cook 24-9-37-0; Harper 41-16-71-3; Wild 7-0-24-0. *Second Innings*—Mallender 13-3-30-4; Walker 12-1-52-1; Capel 7-1-40-0; Harper 18-7-39-4; N. G. B. Cook 5-0-30-0.

Umpires: J. H. Hampshire and D. O. Oslear.

At Leicester, July 23, 24, 25. GLAMORGAN beat LEICESTERSHIRE by 13 runs.

GLAMORGAN v DERBYSHIRE

At Abergavenny, July 26, 28, 29. Derbyshire won by three wickets. Derbyshire 20 pts, Glamorgan 4 pts. Toss: Glamorgan. Positive captaincy revived this game after the second day had been washed out. Barnett closed his side's first innings 25 runs in arrears, fed Glamorgan's batsmen, and waited for his challenge to be accepted. It was, with the visitors being set to score 261 at just over 4 runs an over and pledged to keep up the attack regardless. Barnett, scorer of an unbeaten 84 on the first day, when seventeen wickets fell, now steered his side towards their target with 93 off 145 deliveries, and there was bold strokeplay by Roberts, Miller, Marples and Warner. During the interlude when Glamorgan were assembling their second innings against amiable bowling, Morris made the most of the offerings, while Derrick's 78 not out (thirteen 4s) was his highest first-class score.

Glamorgan

D. B. Pauline lbw b Malcolm	5	– c Warner b Barnett	22
*H. Morris c Miller b Malcolm	13	– not out	81
G. C. Holmes c Marples b Malcolm	21	– b Morris	17
Younis Ahmed lbw b Mortensen	46		
M. P. Maynard b Sharma	31	– (4) c Marples b Maher	0
R. C. Ontong c Morris b Sharma	4	– (5) c Malcolm b Maher	25
J. Derrick b Mortensen	10	– (6) not out	78
J. G. Thomas c Marples b Warner	17		
†T. Davies not out	9		
D. J. Hickey lbw b Mortensen	0		
S. R. Barwick b Warner	3		
B 5, l-b 2, n-b 2	9	B 11, w 1	12

1/10 2/33 3/48 4/95 5/123   168   1/49 2/70 3/73   (4 wkts dec.) 235
6/129 7/149 8/155 9/159   4/128

Bonus points – Glamorgan 1, Derbyshire 4.

Bowling: *First Innings*—Malcolm 10–3–31–3; Mortensen 22–7–45–3; Miller 10–2–17–0; Warner 9.3–0–23–2; Sharma 12–1–45–2. *Second Innings*—Barnett 12–3–36–1; Sharma 8–0–16–0; Morris 25.4–5–103–1; Maher 22–2–69–2.

Derbyshire

*K. J. Barnett not out	84	– lbw b Ontong	93
B. J. M. Maher c Davies b Hickey	8	– c Maynard b Ontong	29
A. Hill lbw b Hickey	1	– (8) run out	0
J. E. Morris b Thomas	23	– (3) c Ontong b Barwick	4
B. Roberts st Davies b Barwick	0	– (4) c Morris b Thomas	31
G. Miller lbw b Barwick	0	– (5) st Davies b Ontong	26
†C. Marples c Maynard b Ontong	12	– (6) not out	32
R. Sharma c Davies b Ontong	0	– (9) not out	3
A. E. Warner not out	8	– (7) c and b Thomas	27
L-b 5, n-b 2	7	B 5, l-b 10, n-b 2	17

1/44 2/50 3/93 4/100   (7 wkts dec.) 143   1/67 2/74 3/160 4/197   (7 wkts) 262
5/100 6/131 7/135   5/208 6/241 7/243

D. E. Malcolm and O. H. Mortensen did not bat.

Bonus points – Glamorgan 3.

Bowling: *First Innings*—Thomas 10–2–38–1; Hickey 9–1–51–2; Barwick 19–8–36–2; Ontong 7–4–13–2. *Second Innings*—Thomas 16.1–0–103–2; Hickey 4–0–27–0; Barwick 16–0–62–1; Ontong 23–3–55–3.

Umpires: K. E. Palmer and N. T. Plews.

At Northampton, August 6, 7, 8. GLAMORGAN drew with NORTHAMPTONSHIRE.

At Leeds, August 9, 11, 12. GLAMORGAN drew with YORKSHIRE.

At Swansea, August 16, 17, 18. GLAMORGAN drew with NEW ZEALANDERS (See New Zealand tour section).

At Lytham, August 20, 21, 22. GLAMORGAN drew with LANCASHIRE.

GLAMORGAN v KENT

At Cardiff, August 23, 25, 26. Drawn. Glamorgan 1 pt, Kent 3 pts. Toss: Glamorgan. The second and third days were washed out by rain, but the Saturday produced a tussle of absorbing intensity; a contest between the guile and faultless precision of Underwood and the batsmen he overawed. Glamorgan began badly, five wickets falling for 58 and only Morris showing the necessary resolution. With Underwood conceding just 24 runs from 24 overs while dismissing Maynard and Ontong, the partnership of 92 between Holmes and Derrick was essential in preventing the home team's innings from disintegrating.

Glamorgan

J. A. Hopkins lbw b Penn	11		J. G. Thomas not out		1
*H. Morris c Marsh b Alderman	33		†T. Davies not out		2
A. L. Jones c Cowdrey b Alderman	7				
G. C. Holmes lbw b Ellison	41		L-b 3, w 3, n-b 3		9
M. P. Maynard lbw b Underwood	1				
R. C. Ontong lbw b Underwood	0		1/27 2/53 3/57 4/58	(7 wkts)	157
J. Derrick b Alderman	52		5/58 6/150 7/154		

S. R. Barwick and D. J. Hickey did not bat.

Bonus points – Glamorgan 1, Kent 3.

Bowling: Alderman 30–12–41–3; Ellison 25.1–8–50–1; Penn 11–1–39–1; Underwood 24–14–24–2; Tavaré 1–1–0–0.

Kent

M. R. Benson, N. R. Taylor, C. J. Tavaré, S. G. Hinks, D. G. Aslett, *C. S. Cowdrey, R. M. Ellison, †S. A. Marsh, C. Penn, D. L. Underwood and T. M. Alderman.

Umpires: B. J. Meyer and R. Palmer.

GLAMORGAN v SURREY

At Swansea, August 27, 28, 29. Drawn. Toss: Glamorgan. Rain having washed out the first two days, a one-innings match was played with twelve points the prize for the winning side. As it transpired, Glamorgan lost both opening batsmen cheaply and decided that the challenge to score at around four and a half runs an over for 47 overs was too hazardous on a damp pitch. Butcher's 69 for the visitors included one 6 and seven 4s. Clinton helping him in a commanding opening partnership worth 122. However, after Feltham's initial breakthrough, Jones and Maynard ensured there would be no reward for Surrey.

Surrey

A. R. Butcher b Ontong	69	D. J. Thomas st Davies b Ontong	5
G. S. Clinton c Davies b Ontong	44	S. T. Clarke not out	16
A. J. Stewart lbw b Barwick	23	B 6, l-b 5	11
T. E. Jesty b Barwick	13		
M. A. Lynch b Barwick	11	1/122 2/133 3/152	(6 wkts dec.) 210
†C. J. Richards not out	18	4/161 5/182 6/189	

M. A. Feltham, K. T. Medlycott and *P. I. Pocock did not bat.

Bowling: Thomas 8–0–21–0; Barwick 23–5–90–3; Ontong 22–7–56–3; Derrick 6–0–32–0.

Glamorgan

J. A. Hopkins c Clinton b Feltham	3	R. C. Ontong not out	1
*H. Morris c Thomas b Feltham	5		
A. L. Jones c Stewart b Pocock	50	B 2, l-b 1, w 1	4
G. C. Holmes c Clinton b Medlycott	25		
M. P. Maynard not out	29	1/6 2/9 3/54 4/115	(4 wkts) 117

J. Derrick, J. G. Thomas, †T. Davies, P. D. North and S. R. Barwick did not bat.

Bowling: Clarke 12–4–29–0; Feltham 4–4–0–2; Pocock 17–5–41–1; Medlycott 9–1–40–1; Butcher 3–2–4–0.

Umpires: B. J. Meyer and R. Palmer.

GLAMORGAN v NOTTINGHAMSHIRE

At Cardiff, September 3, 4, 5. Nottinghamshire won by 24 runs. Nottinghamshire 20 pts, Glamorgan 6 pts. Toss: Nottinghamshire. Throughout this was a contest of fluctuating fortunes, dominated by spin bowling. Ontong's five wickets were a significant factor in the dismissal of Nottinghamshire before lunch on the first day, but Glamorgan's expectations of a commanding first-innings lead never materialised as Afford, slow left-arm, replied in kind for the visitors. Ontong and Thomas put on 126 for the sixth wicket, but their team led by only 98 and there was little doubt that batting last would be perilous. Had Glamorgan been able to remove French on the second afternoon the issue would have been resolved in their favour, but the Nottinghamshire wicket-keeper's rock-like determination as he faced 88 balls saved his side after the splendid start by Broad and Robinson. Ontong's second-innings figures of eight for 101 bettered the best performance by a Glamorgan bowler in a home match against Nottinghamshire – seven for 48 by D. J. Shepherd at the Arms Park 30 years earlier – while his match figures of thirteen for 127 were the best for the county at Sophia Gardens, surpassing M. A. Nash's twelve for 131 against Gloucestershire in 1975. With all of the final day in which to make 173, Glamorgan floundered against the spin and often wicked bounce obtained by Hemmings and Afford. Once the defiant Hopkins had gone for 49 in 51 overs, they were doomed to go through the season without a Championship victory in Wales.

Nottinghamshire

B. C. Broad lbw b Thomas	0	– c Morris b Ontong	56
R. T. Robinson c Hopkins b Barwick	45	– c Holmes b Ontong	47
M. Newell b Thomas	2	– c Holmes b Ontong	0
P. Johnson b Barwick	37	– c Maynard b Ontong	0
*C. E. B. Rice b Ontong	4	– lbw b Ontong	15
J. D. Birch c Barwick b Ontong	20	– (7) c sub b Ontong	24
R. J. Hadlee c Morris b Barwick	0	– (6) c sub b Ontong	15
†B. N. French lbw b Ontong	1	– lbw b Barwick	58
R. A. Pick c Hopkins b Ontong	6	– lbw b Barwick	9
E. E. Hemmings lbw b Ontong	0	– not out	19
J. A. Afford not out	0	– lbw b Ontong	4
B 2, w 1, n-b 3	6	B 13, l-b 7, w 1, n-b 2	23

1/0 2/10 3/70 4/75 5/107	121	1/114 2/120 3/120 4/131 5/138	270
6/108 7/111 8/121 9/121		6/156 7/202 8/234 9/255	

Bonus points – Glamorgan 4.

Bowling: *First Innings*—Thomas 6–1–42–2; Smith 5–1–26–0; Barwick 10–2–25–3; Ontong 9.1–1–26–5. *Second Innings*—Thomas 17–2–57–0; Smith 2–0–11–0; Barwick 31–5–81–2; Ontong 40.1–13–101–8.

Glamorgan

J. A. Hopkins b Afford	21	– c Johnson b Afford	49
*H. Morris c French b Hadlee	2	– c French b Hemmings	20
A. L. Jones c French b Afford	33	– c Broad b Hemmings	5
G. C. Holmes c Birch b Hadlee	13	– lbw b Hemmings	5
M. P. Maynard c French b Rice	0	– st French b Afford	20
R. C. Ontong c French b Afford	60	– c Pick b Afford	0
J. G. Thomas c and b Afford	70	– (8) c Rice b Afford	13
†T. Davies not out	4	– (7) not out	18
I. Smith c French b Afford	0	– c Newell b Hemmings	0
S. R. Barwick b Pick	1	– b Hemmings	9
P. D. North b Pick	0	– c Johnson b Hemmings	0
L-b 10, w 3, n-b 2	15	B 3, l-b 6	9

1/15 2/55 3/68 4/69 5/78   219   1/50 2/64 3/84 4/94 5/102   148
6/204 7/216 8/216 9/217   6/105 7/124 8/124 9/148

Bonus points – Glamorgan 2, Nottinghamshire 4.

Bowling: *First Innings*—Hadlee 15–5–19–2; Pick 15.3–3–27–2; Afford 30–7–80–5; Hemmings 19–4–51–0; Rice 14–5–32–1. *Second Innings*—Hadlee 10–5–5–0; Pick 3–0–8–0; Afford 29–7–71–4; Rice 6–1–10–0; Hemmings 25.5–10–45–6.

Umpires: D. J. Constant and J. A. Jameson.

At Worcester, September 10, 11, 12. GLAMORGAN lost to WORCESTERSHIRE by seven wickets.

At Chelmsford, September 13, 15, 16. GLAMORGAN beat ESSEX by 112 runs.

COUNTY CAPS AWARDED IN 1986

Derbyshire	J. E. Morris, O. H. Mortensen, P. G. Newman, B. Roberts.
Essex	A. R. Border, J. H. Childs, A. W. Lilley, P. J. Prichard.
Glamorgan	H. Morris, J. G. Thomas.
Hampshire	R. J. Maru.
Kent	S. A. Marsh.
Lancashire	C. Maynard, G. D. Mendis.
Leicestershire	T. J. Boon, R. A. Cobb, P. A. J. DeFreitas, J. J. Whitaker.
Northamptonshire	D. J. Capel, R. A. Harper, D. J. Wild.
Nottinghamshire	P. Johnson.
Somerset	N. A. Felton.
Sussex	A. N. Jones, D. A. Reeve, A. P. Wells.
Warwickshire	P. A. Smith.
Worcestershire	G. A. Hick, R. K. Illingworth, P. J. Newport, M. J. Weston.
Yorkshire	P. W. Jarvis, A. A. Metcalfe.

No caps were awarded by Gloucestershire, Middlesex or Surrey.

GLOUCESTERSHIRE

Patron: HRH The Princess of Wales
President: G. W. Parker
Chairman: D. N. Perry
Chairman, Cricket Committee: D. G. Stone
Secretary: P. G. M. August
   Phoenix County Ground, Nevil Road, Bristol
   BS7 9EJ (Telephone: 0272-45216)
Captain: D. A. Graveney
Senior Coach: J. N. Shepherd
Youth Coach: G. G. Wiltshire

Early in August, when David Graveney's side led the Britannic Assurance Championship by 54 points, it seemed that the elusive title would at last be won. But, as in 1985, Gloucestershire finished not in a blaze of glory but with a series of defeats and drawn matches. Not one of the last seven games was won and just 28 points were obtained. Yet it was not a case of Gloucestershire collapsing under pressure. The weather played a crucial part in their last four weeks, forcing stalemates or improbable run-chases in which they were often on the wrong side of the equation. The only time the rain proved an ally was at Colchester, where Phil Bainbridge's defensive innings prevented rivals Essex from gaining the match points.

Providing, as they did, only one bowler in the top 45 of the national averages and not one batsman in the top 30, Gloucestershire's players could be proud at having made such a valiant tilt at the Championship. However, the team did have, in Courtney Walsh, the most potent match-winner in the county game in 1986. The West Indian, in his second full season with the county, was so successful that he took his 100th wicket on August 11, the fastest to reach the target since L. R. Gibbs in 1971. He bowled the bouncer as well as any of his Caribbean colleagues, but it was the variety of his bowling which was responsible for the dismissal of so many batsmen. On twelve occasions Walsh took five wickets in an innings and four times ten wickets in a match, with Gloucestershire's close-catching often rising to the heights in support.

Walsh missed only one Championship game, while David Lawrence, his new-ball partner, was absent for only two matches – a wonderful record of fitness by the opening pair. For Lawrence, however, it was an in-different season compared with 1985. His total of 59 Championship wickets was twenty fewer than the previous year, and at 36 runs apiece they were 50 per cent more expensive. If anything, Lawrence tried too hard, and with the attacking fields employed by Gloucestershire, he paid the penalty in boundaries, conceding too many runs for a bowler with Test match ambitions. Nevertheless he has enthusiasm, skilled advisers and time on his side.

With Kevin Curran unfit to bowl, following a shoulder operation, Bainbridge was often employed as first change and had successful days, notably a career-best eight for 53 in the rout of Somerset at Bristol. However, he could not compare with Curran for pace and aggression, or for the ability to maintain pressure while the fast bowlers rested. He scored fewer runs than in his golden summer of 1985, too often getting out when well set, but he did valuable work as vice-captain. Graveney, often troubled by a back injury, was less successful than in some previous seasons but took a number of tremendous catches in the gully.

There were useful all-round performances from the off-spinner, Jeremy Lloyds, who was, after Walsh, the most valuable member of the team. Batting at number six or seven, he scored 1,295 runs and with Curran, who hit three of the eight Championship centuries, made a formidable middle-order pairing, able to repair early damage or attack with a will. If Curran can come again as a bowler he will be a fine all-rounder.

Bill Athey, when not playing for England, was a consistent run-getter, but the problem of finding a settled opening partnership was never solved satisfactorily. Andrew Stovold had a better season, scoring his 1,000 runs, but in August he dropped down the order to allow Keith Tomlins, the former Middlesex player, a run in the opening position. Paul Romaines, his season truncated by injury, passed 50 only twice, while Tony Wright, after a match-winning innings against Kent, was unable to maintain that standard and lost his place.

Although no-one was able to replace Brian Davison, whose contract was cancelled by mutual consent when the Home Office refused to grant him British citizenship, thus making him ineligible under the qualification regulations, Gloucestershire had in Mark Alleyne one of the batting discoveries of the summer. A product of the Haringey Cricket School in London, he hit the winning run in his first match and scored a hundred in his eighth first-class innings after being 99 overnight. Selection for England Young Cricketers restricted his appearances, but at eighteen he showed such good technique and composure that a bright future was forecast for him.

Jack Russell, the wicket-keeper, had another good season and narrowly missed a place in England's team to Australia. His batting average of 26 was an improvement on 1985, and he gained from his experience as an opener in the John Player League, one of the few good points to emerge from Gloucestershire's limited-overs season. They were bottom of the Sunday competition; interest in the Benson and Hedges Cup never went beyond the zonal stage; and they lost at Bristol to Leicestershire in the second round of the NatWest Bank Trophy. And to add to these injuries, a slow over-rate in the Championship again brought a hefty fine.

Yet if three-day cricket remains the true test of a side's mettle, Gloucestershire passed with honours. They advanced one place in the Championship, won two more matches, and obtained eighteen more points. Their three defeats came when chasing a target in rain-affected matches. Graveney has been asked to stay on as captain for the final two years of his contract and he must be hopeful of winning at least one competition, preferably the Championship, in that period. – G.J.W.

GLOUCESTERSHIRE 1986

[*Bill Smith*]

Back row: K. P. Tomlins, D. J. Taylor, J. W. Lloyds, I. R. Payne, C. W. J. Athey, R. C. Russell. *Middle row*: J. N. Shepherd (*coach*), R. G. P. Ellis, D. V. Lawrence, D. A. Burrows, G. E. Sainsbury, A. J. Wright, G. G. Wiltshire (*coach*). *Front row*: P. W. Romaines, P. Bainbridge, D. A. Graveney (*captain*), D. G. Collier (*secretary/manager*), A. W. Stovold, A. J. Brassington. *Insets*: M. W. Alleyne, K. M. Curran, C. A. Walsh.

GLOUCESTERSHIRE RESULTS

All first-class matches – Played 26: Won 9, Lost 3, Drawn 14.

County Championship matches – Played 24: Won 9, Lost 3, Drawn 12.

Bonus points – Batting 50, Bowling 65.

Competition placings – Britannic Assurance County Championship, 2nd; NatWest Bank Trophy, 2nd round; Benson and Hedges Cup, 3rd in Group C; John Player League, 17th.

BRITANNIC ASSURANCE CHAMPIONSHIP AVERAGES

BATTING

	Birthplace	M	I	NO	R	HI	Avge
‡C. W. J. Athey ...	Middlesbrough	13	21	1	994	171*	49.70
‡J. W. Lloyds	Penang, Malaya	24	36	9	1,232	111	45.62
‡K. M. Curran	Rusape, S. Rhodesia	24	37	6	1,181	117*	38.09
M. W. Alleyne ...	Tottenham	10	16	5	336	116*	30.54
‡A. W. Stovold ...	Bristol	24	40	4	1,072	118	29.77
K. P. Tomlins	Kingston-upon-Thames	15	27	4	676	75	29.39
‡R. C. Russell	Stroud	24	31	9	585	71	26.59
‡P. Bainbridge ...	Stoke-on-Trent	24	41	4	941	105	25.43
A. J. Wright	Stevenage	14	24	0	530	87	22.08
‡P. W. Romaines ..	Bishop Auckland	13	24	4	429	67*	21.45
‡C. A. Walsh	Kingston, Jamaica	23	24	6	221	52	12.27
‡D. A. Graveney ...	Bristol	20	17	8	93	30*	10.33
‡D. V. Lawrence ...	Gloucester	22	25	5	198	34*	9.90
I. R. Payne	Kennington	9	10	2	53	12	6.62

Also batted: G. E. Sainsbury (*Wanstead*) (4 matches) 1*, 14*, 13; P. H. Twizell (*Rothbury*) (1 match) 0.

* *Signifies not out.*   ‡ *Denotes county cap.*

The following played a total of eight three-figure innings for Gloucestershire in County Championship matches – K. M. Curran 3, M. W. Alleyne 1, C. W. J. Athey 1, P. Bainbridge 1, J. W. Lloyds 1, A. W. Stovold 1.

BOWLING

	O	M	R	W	BB	Avge
C. A. Walsh	789.5	193	2,145	118	9-72	18.17
P. Bainbridge	381.1	81	1,095	41	8-53	26.70
J. W. Lloyds	329.2	61	1,119	34	5-111	32.91
D. A. Graveney	418	125	942	27	4-17	34.88
I. R. Payne	160.3	35	459	13	3-48	35.30
D. V. Lawrence	542.1	78	2,134	59	5-84	36.16

Also bowled: C. W. J. Athey 7–1–46–0; K. M. Curran 18–3–50–0; P. W. Romaines 21.1–0–152–0; G. E. Sainsbury 109.1–25–376–8; A. W. Stovold 26–1–132–2; K. P. Tomlins 6–0–34–0; P. H. Twizell 11.1–3–38–0; A. J. Wright 1–0–10–0.

Wicket-keeper: R. C. Russell 51 ct, 4 st.

Leading Fielders: K. M. Curran 28; J. W. Lloyds 22; D. A. Graveney 19; C. W. J. Athey 17; A. J. Wright 14.

At Oxford, April 23, 24, 25. GLOUCESTERSHIRE drew with OXFORD UNIVERSITY.

GLOUCESTERSHIRE v GLAMORGAN

At Bristol, April 26, 27, 28. Drawn. Gloucestershire 3 pts, Glamorgan 4 pts. Toss: Gloucestershire. The loss of the first day, as well as much of the third afternoon, made it impossible for either team to force a result on a green, sluggish pitch. Lawrence extracted some life out of it to trouble Glamorgan early on, while Hopkins reached 10,000 runs for his county before he was caught at third slip. However, any hopes Gloucestershire had of a complete breakthrough were dashed by a typically wristy innings from Younis in which he hit a 6 and eleven 4s. On the third day, Gloucestershire's batsmen struggled to come to terms with Derrick's in-swing before the rain returned.

Glamorgan

J. A. Hopkins c Curran b Lawrence	33	– lbw b Lawrence		0
A. L. Jones c Graveney b Lawrence	13	– not out		20
H. Morris c Wright b Bainbridge	10	– c Curran b Lawrence		0
G. C. Holmes c Athey b Bainbridge	17	– not out		27
Younis Ahmed lbw b Bainbridge	94			
*R. C. Ontong c Russell b Walsh	0			
J. F. Steele c Lloyds b Lawrence	18			
J. G. Thomas not out	18			
†T. Davies c Wright b Bainbridge	10			
J. Derrick not out	1			
L-b 4, n-b 8	12	W 1		1

1/25 2/42 3/76 4/105   (8 wkts dec.) 226   1/4 2/9   (2 wkts) 48
5/110 6/173 7/207 8/221

S. J. Base did not bat.

Bonus points – Glamorgan 2, Gloucestershire 3.

Bowling: *First Innings*—Lawrence 22-3-70-3; Walsh 22-10-33-1; Curran 10-3-11-0; Bainbridge 28-4-85-4; Graveney 13-6-16-0; Lloyds 3-1-7-0. *Second Innings*—Lawrence 6-3-6-2; Walsh 2-0-6-0; Bainbridge 4-0-12-0; Graveney 4-0-11-0; Lloyds 4-0-11-0; Athey 1-0-2-0.

Gloucestershire

A. W. Stovold b Thomas	20	J. W. Lloyds not out		13
P. W. Romaines c Ontong b Derrick	10			
C. W. J. Athey lbw b Derrick	11	B 4, w 5, n-b 1		10
P. Bainbridge c Thomas b Holmes	11			
A. J. Wright b Derrick	4	1/35 2/49 3/56	(5 wkts dec.) 83
K. M. Curran not out	4	4/66 5/66	

*D. A. Graveney, †R. C. Russell, C. A. Walsh and D. V. Lawrence did not bat.

Bonus points – Glamorgan 2.

Bowling: Thomas 10-2-23-1; Base 8-1-19-0; Derrick 7-3-19-3; Holmes 6-2-18-1.

Umpires: D. R. Shepherd and P. B. Wight.

At Northampton, May 7, 8, 9. GLOUCESTERSHIRE drew with NORTHAMPTONSHIRE.

At Cheltenham Town CC, May 10, 11, 12. GLOUCESTERSHIRE drew with INDIANS (See Indian tour section).

At Taunton, May 21, 22, 23. GLOUCESTERSHIRE lost to SOMERSET by 118 runs.

At Bournemouth, May 24, 26, 27. GLOUCESTERSHIRE beat HAMPSHIRE by 146 runs.

At Leicester, May 31, June 2, 3. GLOUCESTERSHIRE beat LEICESTERSHIRE by six wickets.

GLOUCESTERSHIRE v WARWICKSHIRE

At Bristol, June 4, 5, 6. Drawn. Gloucestershire 5 pts, Warwickshire 8 pts. Toss: Warwickshire. The 80th and 98th first-class hundreds of Kallicharran and Amiss respectively were the main features of a high-scoring game. Gloucestershire found few perils in the pitch or the bowling, with Curran and Lloyds putting on 182 in 44 overs for the fifth wicket. Only Parsons, of the seam bowlers, found consistency of line and length and he bowled well for his five wickets. After Lloyd had launched Warwickshire's innings with a flurry of strokes, Kallicharran took his career aggregate beyond 30,000 runs before Gifford declared 52 behind. Warwickshire's target on the final afternoon was 315 in four hours, and while Kallicharran and Amiss were putting on 154 for the third wicket, they looked capable of achieving it. However, Graveney's dismissal of both and the ensuing collapse left Gloucestershire nearer victory.

Gloucestershire

A. J. Wright b Munton	43	– c Humpage b Small	6
A. W. Stovold c Kallicharran b Parsons	9	– lbw b Moles	64
C. W. J. Athey c Kallicharran b Smith	37	– c and b Asif Din	98
P. Bainbridge c Amiss b Parsons	30	– b Asif Din	37
K. M. Curran c Asif Din b Parsons	92	– not out	20
J. W. Lloyds c Lloyd b Munton	79	– not out	33
I. R. Payne c Kallicharran b Small	2		
*D. A. Graveney lbw b Munton	0		
D. V. Lawrence c Humpage b Parsons	9		
†R. C. Russell c Asif Din b Parsons	14		
C. A. Walsh not out	9		
B 5, l-b 16, w 2, n-b 5	28	L-b 4	4

1/12 2/78 3/132 4/132 5/314   352   1/22 2/131 3/206   (4 wkts dec.) 262
6/314 7/314 8/325 9/325   4/217

Bonus points – Gloucestershire 4, Warwickshire 4.

Bowling: *First Innings*—Small 21-1-90-1; Munton 23-4-76-3; Parsons 26.2-6-75-5; Smith 5-0-27-1; Moles 11-2-32-0; Gifford 9-0-31-0. *Second Innings*—Small 11-3-15-1; Parsons 4-1-16-0; Gifford 2-0-4-0; Asif Din 24-1-93-2; Moles 13-1-40-1; Lloyd 11-0-80-0; Munton 4-0-10-0.

Warwickshire

T. A. Lloyd b Bainbridge	56	– c Curran b Lawrence	15
P. A. Smith c Bainbridge b Lawrence	13	– b Lawrence	3
A. I. Kallicharran not out	132	– b Graveney	76
D. L. Amiss c Lloyds b Bainbridge	10	– c Lloyds b Graveney	104
†G. W. Humpage c Russell b Lloyds	75	– c Curran b Walsh	23
Asif Din not out	3	– c Russell b Stovold	2
G. J. Parsons (did not bat)		– c Payne b Graveney	0
A. J. Moles (did not bat)		– c Payne b Walsh	6
G. C. Small (did not bat)		– not out	5
T. A. Munton (did not bat)		– not out	0
L-b 6, w 4, n-b 1	11	L-b 10, w 2, n-b 3	15

1/38 2/94 3/126 4/295   (4 wkts dec.) 300   1/7 2/26 3/180 4/235   (8 wkts) 249
5/235 6/236 7/239 8/249

*N. Gifford did not bat.

Bonus points – Warwickshire 4, Gloucestershire 1.

Bowling: *First Innings*—Lawrence 11–1–57–1; Walsh 19–4–52–0; Lloyds 15–2–49–1; Bainbridge 27–8–62–2; Payne 14–2–34–0; Graveney 12–1–40–0. *Second Innings*—Lawrence 10.3–3–51–2; Walsh 27.3–2–96–2; Bainbridge 8–2–23–0; Lloyds 1–0–13–0; Payne 4–0–17–0; Graveney 13.5–4–36–3; Stovold 1–0–3–1.

Umpires: H. D. Bird and A. A. Jones.

At Harrogate, June 7, 9, 10. GLOUCESTERSHIRE drew with YORKSHIRE.

GLOUCESTERSHIRE v DERBYSHIRE

At Gloucester, June 14, 16, 17. Drawn. Gloucestershire 2 pts, Derbyshire 6 pts. Toss: Gloucestershire. Derbyshire, 127 without loss, looked to have control of the match at the end of the first day but timid batting, after a splendid opening partnership, allowed Gloucestershire a way out. On the Saturday, Malcolm seized his first opportunity of the season so effectively against some loose batting that Gloucestershire were all out before tea. The home side's bowling appeared equally out of sorts, but it tightened up on Monday to such an extent that Derbyshire gained only two batting points and their innings of 313 occupied 128.1 overs. Gloucestershire lost five wickets clearing the deficit of 131, Malcolm again bowling well, but Athey and Lloyds steadied them. Lloyds, whose second hundred for the county occupied three and a half hours and contained fourteen 4s, found another splendid partner in Russell, and their stand of 127 made the game safe.

Gloucestershire

A. J. Wright c Barnett b Malcolm	16	– b Miller	19
A. W. Stovold c Marples b Warner	41	– b Taylor	25
C. W. J. Athey c Sharma b Malcolm	0	– c Marples b Malcolm	46
P. Bainbridge b Malcolm	20	– c Marples b Malcolm	4
K. M. Curran c Marples b Malcolm	43	– c Sharma b Malcolm	12
K. P. Tomlins run out	9	– c Sharma b Miller	1
J. W. Lloyds b Malcolm	8	– b Sharma	111
†R. C. Russell c Sharma b Warner	20	– b Malcolm	63
*D. A. Graveney b Miller	5	– absent injured	
D. V. Lawrence c Marples b Taylor	12	– (9) b Miller	10
C. A. Walsh not out	0	– (10) not out	15
B 1, l-b 4, w 2, n-b 1	8	B 12, l-b 4, w 2, n-b 8	26

1/42 2/50 3/57 4/121 5/130   182   1/52 2/58 3/69 4/99 5/100   332
6/130 7/141 8/162 9/182   6/166 7/293 8/310 9/332

Bonus points – Gloucestershire 1, Derbyshire 4.

Bowling: *First Innings*—Malcolm 16–2–42–5; Warner 11–2–47–2; Taylor 13–2–49–1; Miller 21.4–5–39–1. *Second Innings*—Malcolm 27–5–91–4; Warner 15–1–52–0; Taylor 19–3–58–1; Miller 45–18–76–3; Sharma 6.5–0–25–1; Barnett 3–0–14–0.

Derbyshire

*K. J. Barnett b Walsh	95			
I. S. Anderson lbw b Bainbridge	62			
A. Hill c Russell b Graveney	26			
J. E. Morris c Lloyds b Walsh	56			
B. Roberts c and b Bainbridge	9			
G. Miller c Athey b Lawrence	2			
R. Sharma c Graveney b Walsh	14			
†C. Marples b Lawrence	24	– (1) not out	24	
A. E. Warner run out	4			
J. P. Taylor b Walsh	0			
D. E. Malcolm not out	0	– (2) not out	29	
B 11, l-b 6, n-b 4	21			

1/145 2/176 3/197 4/210 5/241　　　　313　(no wkt)　　　　53
6/271 7/290 8/313 9/313

Bonus points – Derbyshire 2, Gloucestershire 1 (Score at 100 overs: 228-4).

Bowling: *First Innings*—Lawrence 32.1–9–104–2; Walsh 35–11–84–4; Graveney 32–15–55–1; Bainbridge 25–10–39–2; Lloyds 4–0–14–0. *Second Innings*—Lawrence 2–0–17–0; Walsh 1–0–2–0; Wright 1–0–10–0; Athey 2–0–16–0; Tomlins 1–0–8–0.

Umpires: J. W. Holder and K. J. Lyons.

GLOUCESTERSHIRE v KENT

At Gloucester, June 18, 19, 20. Gloucestershire won by four wickets. Gloucestershire 20 pts, Kent 6 pts. Toss: Gloucestershire. At one time in serious danger of having to follow on, Gloucestershire came back strongly to win a match dominated by bowlers of medium pace and above. Bainbridge, leading Gloucestershire in the absence of Graveney, who was having an operation to his back, did the damage in Kent's first innings, ending a threatening partnership between the Cowdrey brothers in an over in which he took three wickets. Kent's 238 looked a winning total as Alderman played havoc with Gloucestershire's batting on the second day, but Kent's second-innings collapse was even more complete. A stomach complaint delayed Hinks's entrance until the end, and Christopher Cowdrey retired hurt after being hit on the left foot by Lawrence, not returning until the fall of the seventh wicket. Gloucestershire, requiring 227 on a pitch of uneven bounce, began the last day 83 for one. Wright battled on to 87, his best score for two years, in four and a quarter hours, and the winning hit came from Alleyne, an eighteen-year-old making his début.

Kent

M. R. Benson b Payne	13	– c Curran b Lloyds	42	
S. G. Hinks c Wright b Walsh	27	– (10) not out	19	
C. J. Tavaré c Russell b Walsh	0	– lbw b Lawrence	1	
N. R. Taylor c Stovold b Bainbridge	44	– (2) b Walsh	11	
*C. S. Cowdrey c Curran b Bainbridge	51	– (4) b Walsh	6	
G. R. Cowdrey c Russell b Bainbridge	61	– (5) b Bainbridge	4	
†S. A. Marsh lbw b Bainbridge	0	– (6) st Russell b Payne	12	
C. Penn b Bainbridge	0	– (7) c and b Lloyds	0	
D. L. Underwood b Lawrence	19	– (8) b Walsh	5	
T. M. Alderman b Walsh	9	– (9) b Payne	0	
K. B. S. Jarvis not out	0	– b Walsh	4	
B 3, l-b 10, n-b 1	14	B 3, l-b 2, n-b 4	9	

1/44 2/44 3/54 4/109 5/184　　　238　1/20 2/24 3/48 4/79 5/79　　　113
6/184 7/184 8/223 9/238　　　　　　　6/79 7/79 8/86 9/87

Bonus points – Kent 2, Gloucestershire 4.

Bowling: *First Innings*—Lawrence 17.4–3–46–1; Walsh 33–9–78–3; Payne 22–10–44–1; Bainbridge 22–10–49–5; Lloyds 5–1–8–0. *Second Innings*—Lawrence 14–2–42–1; Walsh 12.1–4–29–4; Bainbridge 7–1–19–1; Payne 8–2–15–2; Lloyds 2–1–3–2.

Gloucestershire

A. J. Wright c G. R. Cowdrey b Jarvis	21	– c Tavaré b Alderman	87
A. W. Stovold b Alderman	3	– c Alderman b Jarvis	40
†R. C. Russell lbw b Alderman	13	– c Taylor b Alderman	17
K. P. Tomlins c G. R. Cowdrey b Alderman	3	– b Alderman	14
*P. Bainbridge c Marsh b Alderman	15	– lbw b Alderman	6
K. M. Curran c Taylor b Jarvis	1	– b Penn	23
J. W. Lloyds not out	45	– not out	13
M. W. Alleyne lbw b Alderman	2	– not out	13
I. R. Payne lbw b Penn	1		
D. V. Lawrence c Alderman b Penn	10		
C. A. Walsh lbw b Alderman	10		
L-b 1	1	L-b 8, w 1, n-b 5	14

1/17 2/31 3/34 4/50 5/51   125   1/75 2/105 3/150   (6 wkts) 227
6/69 7/71 8/76 9/96   4/158 5/201 6/201

Bonus points – Kent 4.

Bowling: *First Innings*—Alderman 21.4–8–49–6; Jarvis 14–2–48–2; Penn 7–0–27–2. *Second Innings*—Alderman 26–4–86–4; Jarvis 20–8–39–1; Underwood 22–7–35–0; Penn 16.5–3–59–1.

Umpires: J. W. Holder and K. J. Lyons.

At Chesterfield, June 21, 22, 23. GLOUCESTERSHIRE drew with DERBYSHIRE.

GLOUCESTERSHIRE v SURREY

At Bristol, June 28, 30, July 1. Gloucestershire won by 96 runs. Gloucestershire 21 pts, Surrey 5 pts. Toss: Surrey. Another splendid performance by Walsh paved the way for Gloucestershire's first win in the Championship at Bristol since 1982 and eased them into second place. Seventeen dismissals and two batsmen retired hurt was the first day's tally on a pitch of uneven bounce. Surrey were kept in the game by Stewart, who bobbed and weaved bravely, took his knocks, and still played some high-class strokes. Gloucestershire's lead was kept to 27 almost solely by his efforts. Gloucestershire lost three second-innings wickets for 37 but took control through Lloyds and Curran, who added 132 in 45 overs. Lloyds completed a good all-round match by dismissing three of the leading batsmen when Surrey were making a bid to score 312 in 87 overs. Going in to tea at 156 for four, they were still well placed to save the match, but Walsh, off his shorter run, bowled to such a demanding line and length that he took five wickets in 61 balls without assistance from wicket-keeper or fieldsmen.

Gloucestershire

A. J. Wright c Clinton b Bicknell	56	– c and b Bicknell		4
A. W. Stovold c Clinton b Gray	16	– c Falkner b Doughty		5
C. W. J. Athey c Needham b Gray	2	– (7) lbw b Bicknell		47
P. Bainbridge c Richards b Bicknell	11	– (3) c Lynch b Gray		3
K. M. Curran b Doughty	12	– c sub b Doughty		67
J. W. Lloyds c Needham b Gray	27	– (4) lbw b Butcher		74
†R. C. Russell c Richards b Doughty	17	– (6) c Clinton b Bicknell		29
I. R. Payne retired hurt	4			
*D. A. Graveney c Needham b Pocock	3			
D. V. Lawrence not out	14	– (8) c sub b Gray		10
C. A. Walsh c Gray b Pocock	12	– (9) not out		2
L-b 1, w 1, n-b 9	11	B 12, l-b 24, w 1, n-b 6		43

1/25 2/28 3/74 4/89 5/115   185   1/6 2/12 3/37   (8 wkts dec.) 284
6/140 7/155 8/164 9/185   4/169 5/184 6/271
                                        7/278 8/284

Bonus points – Gloucestershire 1, Surrey 4.

Bowling: *First Innings*—Gray 15–4–36–3; Doughty 12–1–55–2; Butcher 5–0–25–0; Bicknell 11–0–41–2; Pocock 6.5–2–27–2. *Second Innings*—Gray 31.2–6–68–2; Doughty 14–3–50–2; Bicknell 19–5–48–3; Pocock 24–6–48–0; Needham 18–6–26–0; Butcher 4–1–8–1.

Surrey

A. R. Butcher c Graveney b Walsh	7	– c Lloyds b Graveney		26
G. S. Clinton retired hurt	5	– c Bainbridge b Lloyds		34
A. J. Stewart not out	65	– lbw b Lloyds		52
M. A. Lynch c Graveney b Walsh	13	– b Lloyds		23
N. J. Falkner run out	9	– not out		40
A. Needham c sub b Bainbridge	8	– lbw b Walsh		8
†C. J. Richards c Lloyds b Graveney	16	– b Walsh		0
R. J. Doughty c Russell b Walsh	17	– b Walsh		9
M. P. Bicknell c Russell b Walsh	0	– b Walsh		0
A. H. Gray lbw b Walsh	2	– b Walsh		4
*P. I. Pocock c Graveney b Walsh	9	– c Curran b Lloyds		0
L-b 5, n-b 2	7	B 1, l-b 6, n-b 12		19

1/10 2/33 3/74 4/91 5/113   158   1/45 2/105 3/128 4/152 5/172   215
6/138 7/138 8/146 9/158   6/172 7/186 8/199 9/213

Bonus points – Surrey 1, Gloucestershire 4.

Bowling: *First Innings*—Lawrence 20–3–67–0; Walsh 17.1–5–41–6; Graveney 9–4–20–1; Bainbridge 12–3–25–1. *Second Innings*—Lawrence 10–0–37–0; Walsh 30–8–72–5; Lloyds 17.4–5–60–4; Graveney 15–5–39–1.

Umpires: K. E. Palmer and D. R. Shepherd.

GLOUCESTERSHIRE v YORKSHIRE

At Bristol, July 2, 3, 4. Drawn. Gloucestershire 6 pts, Yorkshire 7 pts. Toss: Yorkshire. An exciting finish was in prospect when rain intervened, washing out the final day. Gloucestershire, close to a two-day defeat at one point, were back with a good chance with Yorkshire, needing 151 for victory, having lost two wickets for 20. Moreover, Boycott might not have batted because of a badly bruised hand. Some poor Yorkshire catching enabled Gloucestershire to reach a useful first-innings total on a green pitch, and then Lawrence, with his first five-wicket return of the season, played a leading role in restricting Yorkshire's lead to 23. This quickly assumed substantial proportions when the young Yorkshire seam bowlers removed Gloucestershire's first five batsmen for 38. But as they tired, Walsh swung his bat effectively to score a maiden half-century.

Gloucestershire

A. J. Wright c Love b Jarvis	0 – lbw b Jarvis	4
A. W. Stovold c Jarvis b Shaw	43 – b Fletcher	0
*P. Bainbridge c Bairstow b Moxon	24 – c Jarvis b Shaw	9
J. W. Lloyds c Jarvis b Fletcher	23 – c Love b Shaw	8
K. M. Curran c Bairstow b Shaw	61 – b Fletcher	36
M. W. Alleyne b Jarvis	8 – run out	0
†R. C. Russell c Bairstow b Shaw	26 – c Carrick b Fletcher	23
I. R. Payne c Sharp b Jarvis	8 – lbw b Shaw	9
D. V. Lawrence c Moxon b Jarvis	33 – c Boycott b Jarvis	13
C. A. Walsh b Fletcher	4 – st Bairstow b Carrick	52
G. E. Sainsbury not out	1 – not out	14
B 1, l-b 8, n-b 6	15	L-b 4, w 1	5

1/0 2/70 3/119 4/144 5/190   246   1/2 2/6 3/16 4/38 5/38   173
6/197 7/197 8/236 9/241   6/83 7/90 8/102 9/123

Bonus points – Gloucestershire 2, Yorkshire 4.

Bowling: *First Innings*—Jarvis 20.5–1–75–4; Fletcher 16–0–72–2; Shaw 14–1–47–3; Hartley 4–1–21–0; Carrick 1–0–4–0; Moxon 9–4–18–1. *Second Innings*—Jarvis 19–3–64–2; Fletcher 18–3–58–3; Shaw 19–3–39–3; Carrick 1.5–0–8–1.

Yorkshire

G. Boycott c Bainbridge b Lawrence	8	
M. D. Moxon b Bainbridge	55 – (1) c Lawrence b Walsh	0
A. A. Metcalfe lbw b Lawrence	0 – (2) b Lawrence	8
K. Sharp b Bainbridge	71 – not out	3
J. D. Love c Russell b Lawrence	9	
P. W. Jarvis c Curran b Lawrence	10	
S. N. Hartley c Wright b Lawrence	6	
*†D. L. Bairstow c Curran b Payne	43	
P. Carrick run out	19 – (3) not out	7
C. Shaw b Walsh	0	
S. D. Fletcher not out	2	
B 12, l-b 18, w 4, n-b 12	46	N-b 2	2

1/32 2/35 3/111 4/142 5/178   269   1/9 2/10   (2 wkts) 20
6/190 7/193 8/248 9/255

Bonus points – Yorkshire 3, Gloucestershire 4.

Bowling: *First Innings*—Walsh 25–7–51–1; Lawrence 24–2–84–5; Payne 6.3–0–28–1; Bainbridge 13–4–32–2; Sainsbury 14–4–44–0. *Second Innings*—Walsh 2.5–1–4–1; Lawrence 2–0–16–1.

Umpires: K. E. Palmer and D. R. Shepherd.

At Cardiff, July 5, 7, 8. GLOUCESTERSHIRE beat GLAMORGAN by five wickets.

GLOUCESTERSHIRE v SUSSEX

At Bristol, July 16, 17, 18. Gloucestershire won by one wicket. Gloucestershire 22 pts, Sussex 2 pts. Toss: Sussex. This was a splendid contest, packed with incident, and a fine advertisement for the three-day game. First to make an impact was Alleyne, who scored a maiden hundred in only his eighth first-class innings. The eighteen-year-old ended the first day 99 and next morning became Gloucestershire's youngest century-maker, reaching three figures in 229 minutes with twelve 4s. Lawrence's second-over broadside of three wickets in four balls sent Sussex tumbling to the follow-on, 248 in arrears, but they cleared the deficit for the loss of three wickets, Parker stroking fifteen 4s in a timely century from 172 balls. Lloyds broke through, however, and Gloucestershire required no more than 94 to win. It was almost too many as Imran and Babington, another youngster, reduced the Championship leaders to 31 for six, Babington dismissing Bainbridge, Curran and Lloyds with successive balls. Alleyne and Russell halted the procession, but when a hobbling Lawrence joined Russell, 12 runs were needed from the last wicket. Lawrence bravely hooked Imran for 6, and some scrambled singles ended the agonies of the players and spectators.

Gloucestershire

A. J. Wright b Imran	46	– b Imran 0
A. W. Stovold b Imran	62	– c Parker b Babington 6
K. P. Tomlins c Green b Mays	51	– b Imran 13
P. Bainbridge b Imran	1	– c A. P. Wells b Babington 5
K. M. Curran b Mays	0	– c Gould b Babington 0
J. W. Lloyds c Imran b Mays	17	– c Green b Babington 0
M. W. Alleyne not out	116	– lbw b Reeve 19
†R. C. Russell not out	45	– not out 23
C. A. Walsh (did not bat)		– lbw b Imran 0
*D. A. Graveney (did not bat)		– c Gould b Imran 10
D. V. Lawrence (did not bat)		– not out 7
B 1, l-b 7, w 1, n-b 3	12	B 2, l-b 3, w 4, n-b 2 11

1/110 2/112 3/112 4/112		(6 wkts dec.) 350	1/0 2/9 3/17 4/17		(9 wkts) 94
5/152 6/265							5/17 6/31 7/57 8/62 9/82

Bonus points – Gloucestershire 2, Sussex 2 (Score at 100 overs: 222-5).

Bowling: *First Innings*—Imran 28.4–10–59–3; Pigott 15–5–37–0; C. M. Wells 15–1–56–0; Babington 8–1–28–0; Reeve 17–0–58–0; Mays 31–10–78–3; Standing 16–2–26–0. *Second Innings*—Imran 18–7–42–4; Babington 8–1–18–4; Mays 6–0–17–0; Reeve 5–1–12–1.

Sussex

D. K. Standing b Lawrence	16	– b Walsh 9
A. M. Green c Russell b Lawrence	0	– b Walsh 35
P. W. G. Parker b Lawrence	0	– b Walsh 120
Imran Khan c Russell b Lawrence	0	– st Russell b Lloyds 47
C. M. Wells c Graveney b Walsh	13	– c Russell b Lloyds 50
A. P. Wells c Stovold b Graveney	19	– c Stovold b Lloyds 0
D. A. Reeve c Wright b Walsh	27	– b Lloyds 31
*†I. J. Gould c Wright b Graveney	2	– lbw b Lloyds 5
A. C. S. Pigott c Bainbridge b Graveney	3	– b Walsh 17
C. S. Mays not out	8	– b Graveney 4
A. M. Babington b Graveney	1	– not out 0
L-b 5, n-b 8	13	B 5, l-b 5, w 5, n-b 8 23

1/2 2/2 3/2 4/20 5/50				102	1/43 2/44 3/152 4/267 5/273		341
6/60 7/67 8/84 9/101					6/290 7/315 8/328 9/333

Bonus points – Gloucestershire 4.

Bowling: *First Innings*—Lawrence 11–1–34–4; Walsh 17–5–34–2; Bainbridge 5–1–12–0; Graveney 11.4–4–17–4; Lloyds 1–1–0–0. *Second Innings*—Walsh 28.1–5–95–4; Bainbridge 2–0–7–0; Graveney 25–7–61–1; Lawrence 10–0–57–0; Lloyds 30–2–111–5.

Umpires: M. J. Kitchen and R. A. White.

GLOUCESTERSHIRE v SOMERSET

At Bristol, July 19, 21. Gloucestershire won by an innings and 7 runs. Gloucestershire 24 pts, Somerset 4 pts. Toss: Gloucestershire. Somerset, below full strength, had no answer to career-best bowling performances by Walsh and Bainbridge and were beaten inside two days. Only Garner in the Somerset team could look back on the match with any satisfaction. He showed what the pitch had to offer for pace bowlers on the first day when Gloucestershire did well to achieve maximum batting points. Walsh took his cue so effectively that he had the first six Somerset batsmen back in the pavilion by Saturday's close, and he just failed to complete the full set on Monday when Sainsbury intervened to dismiss Garner. When Somerset followed on it was Bainbridge, at no more than brisk medium, who did the damage, virtually ensuring their fate with four wickets in seven balls at the cost of a single. Garner hit out fiercely, striking six 6s and denting Bainbridge's figures, but he could not make Gloucestershire bat a second time.

Gloucestershire

A. J. Wright lbw b Davis	13
A. W. Stovold c Richards b Garner	6
C. W. J. Athey c Gard b Garner	55
P. Bainbridge run out	51
K. M. Curran b Dredge	3
J. W. Lloyds c Richards b Garner	29
M. W. Alleyne c Marks b Garner	21
†R. C. Russell c Gard b Marks	49
C. A. Walsh c Gard b Davis	9
*D. A. Graveney not out	30
G. E. Sainsbury b Marks	13
B 16, l-b 8, w 1, n-b 4	29
	308

1/8 2/31 3/108 4/115 5/165 6/182 7/222 8/249 9/266

Bonus points – Gloucestershire 4, Somerset 4.

Bowling: Garner 20–6–59–4; Davis 16–1–66–2; Dredge 20–5–88–1; Richards 8–2–17–0; Coombs 10–2–36–0; Marks 6.3–3–18–2.

Somerset

J. G. Wyatt c Curran b Walsh	0	– (2) b Bainbridge	13
N. A. Felton c Curran b Walsh	4	– (1) st Russell b Bainbridge	19
J. J. E. Hardy c Russell b Walsh	11	– lbw b Bainbridge	0
*I. V. A. Richards c Alleyne b Walsh	35	– c Wright b Bainbridge	0
R. J. Harden c Bainbridge b Walsh	1	– c Athey b Bainbridge	28
V. J. Marks c Wright b Walsh	18	– c Alleyne b Bainbridge	26
†T. Gard lbw b Walsh	1	– c Athey b Graveney	0
M. R. Davis not out	14	– b Bainbridge	0
C. H. Dredge c Russell b Walsh	11	– b Walsh	8
J. Garner c Graveney b Sainsbury	14	– c Athey b Bainbridge	47
R. V. J. Coombs b Walsh	18	– not out	0
L-b 12, n-b 8	20	B 1, l-b 5, n-b 7	13
	147		154

1/2 2/7 3/14 4/38 5/65 6/73 7/87 8/100 9/119

1/35 2/35 3/37 4/38 5/93 6/98 7/98 8/98 9/154

Bonus points – Gloucestershire 4.

Bowling: *First Innings*—Walsh 21.3–6–72–9; Sainsbury 13–6–45–1; Bainbridge 4–1–12–0; Graveney 4–3–6–0. *Second Innings*—Walsh 14–3–42–1; Sainsbury 7–1–17–0; Bainbridge 16.2–2–53–8; Graveney 10–2–36–1.

Umpires: M. J. Kitchen and R. A. White.

At Worcester, July 26, 28, 29. GLOUCESTERSHIRE beat WORCESTERSHIRE by 78 runs.

GLOUCESTERSHIRE v HAMPSHIRE

At Cheltenham, August 2, 4, 5. Gloucestershire won by 17 runs. Gloucestershire 22 pts, Hampshire 7 pts. Toss: Hampshire. Gloucestershire's fifth successive victory, which extended their lead in the Championship to 54 points, was hard-gained on a pitch tailor-made for fast bowling. As Marshall, Walsh and Lawrence made the ball fly, batsmen needed to be brave as well as skilled and fortunate to survive. None was braver than Chris Smith who, batting virtually one-handed after the third finger of his right hand was broken by Lawrence, helped Tremlett add 112 for the ninth wicket to earn Hampshire a first-innings lead of 69. Gloucestershire did well to clear the deficit for the loss of only two wickets but then foundered against James, whose five for 34 were his best Championship figures. Hampshire were left needing 116 to win and Greenidge and Terry had made 39 of them before Walsh and Lawrence swept all before them, aided by close catching of a remarkable brilliance. Hampshire, unsure of what approach to adopt, were put out for 98 as Walsh completed his second six-wicket return of the match and took ten wickets for the fourth time in the season.

Gloucestershire

P. W. Romaines c Parks b Tremlett	10	– c Middleton b Marshall	0
K. P. Tomlins c C. L. Smith b Tremlett	10	– b James	30
C. W. J. Athey lbw b Tremlett	42	– c Parks b Connor	36
P. Bainbridge c Greenidge b Connor	22	– c R. A. Smith b Marshall	21
A. W. Stovold c Parks b Connor	17	– lbw b James	48
K. M. Curran c R. A. Smith b Marshall	25	– c R. A. Smith b James	14
J. W. Lloyds c C. L. Smith b Marshall	35	– b James	0
†R. C. Russell c Parks b James	16	– c Terry b James	9
*D. A. Graveney not out	7	– not out	2
C. A. Walsh lbw b Marshall	0	– b Marshall	3
D. V. Lawrence c Parks b James	0	– b Marshall	0
B 2, l-b 6, w 2, n-b 7	17	B 1, l-b 18, n-b 2	21

1/19 2/26 3/87 4/109 5/132   201   1/0 2/55 3/96 4/102 5/147   184
6/151 7/184 8/197 9/200   6/148 7/178 8/179 9/184

Bonus points – Gloucestershire 2, Hampshire 4.

Bowling: *First Innings*—Marshall 19–4–42–3; Connor 20–4–63–2; Tremlett 15–2–55–3; James 9.4–3–33–2. *Second Innings*—Marshall 22–6–44–4; Connor 12–0–44–1; Tremlett 15–4–43–0; James 16–4–34–5.

Hampshire

C. G. Greenidge lbw b Lawrence	38	– c Athey b Lawrence	26
V. P. Terry c Bainbridge b Walsh	0	– b Walsh	13
T. C. Middleton c Russell b Walsh	27	– c Athey b Lawrence	1
C. L. Smith not out	72	– (10) c Curran b Walsh	5
R. A. Smith c Lloyds b Walsh	25	– (4) b Walsh	23
†R. J. Parks c Lawrence b Walsh	0	– (9) c Curran b Lawrence	4
*M. C. J. Nicholas c Curran b Walsh	25	– (5) c Romaines b Walsh	7
K. D. James run out	1	– (6) c Graveney b Walsh	6
M. D. Marshall c Walsh b Lawrence	3	– (7) c Athey b Walsh	5
T. M. Tremlett c Athey b Bainbridge	52	– (8) c Russell b Lawrence	3
C. A. Connor c Russell b Walsh	0	– not out	0
B 8, l-b 9, n-b 10	27	N-b 5	5

1/1 2/71 3/75 4/124 5/124   270   1/39 2/39 3/63 4/69 5/74   98
6/134 7/148 8/157 9/269   6/83 7/88 8/92 9/97

Bonus points – Hampshire 3, Gloucestershire 4.

In the first innings C. L. Smith, when 15, retired hurt at 131 and resumed at 157.

Bowling: *First Innings*—Walsh 33–12–90–6; Lawrence 29–7–92–2; Bainbridge 20–3–42–1; Graveney 10–5–18–0; Lloyds 2–0–11–0. *Second Innings*—Walsh 16.5–5–34–6; Lawrence 16–2–64–4.

Umpires: A. A. Jones and R. Palmer.

GLOUCESTERSHIRE v NOTTINGHAMSHIRE

At Cheltenham, August 6, 7, 8. Drawn. Gloucestershire 5 pts, Nottinghamshire 7 pts. Toss: Nottinghamshire. Graveney left himself out of the Gloucestershire side in the belief that the pitch would again favour the fast bowlers, but this proved far from the case. Four batsmen made centuries, beginning with Bainbridge, whose only three-figure score of the season helped his side to maximum batting points after nearly half of the first day's play had been lost to rain. Nottinghamshire's response was an opening partnership of 221 in 54 overs between Robinson and Broad, the left-hander batting particularly well and handling Walsh with assurance. Less than five hours remained when Rice declared, but his probing new-ball spell helped reduce Gloucestershire to 58 for five with at least 64 overs left. However, Stovold thwarted Nottinghamshire's hopes of victory with a spirited counter-attack, and Curran enlivened the final stages with two 6s and eighteen 4s as he ended a run of low scores with his third century of the summer.

Gloucestershire

P. W. Romaines c Scott b Cooper	32	– b Rice	0
K. P. Tomlins c Newell b Saxelby	27	– c Rice b Cooper	37
*P. Bainbridge b Robinson b Saxelby	105	– c Broad b Rice	1
A. W. Stovold b Pick	81	– (7) not out	74
K. M. Curran c Birch b Fraser-Darling	17	– not out	117
J. W. Lloyds c Scott b Cooper	3	– c Birch b Fraser-Darling	1
M. W. Alleyne c Johnson b Saxelby	23	– (4) c Johnson b Cooper	15
†R. C. Russell c Robinson b Cooper	2		
C. A. Walsh c Pick b Cooper	2		
D. V. Lawrence not out	34		
P. H. Twizell c Birch b Cooper	0		
L-b 14, w 1, n-b 4	19	L-b 3, n-b 1	4

1/54 2/99 3/237 4/274 5/283   345   1/1 2/7 3/45   (5 wkts dec.) 249
6/283 7/291 8/295 9/336   4/57 5/58

Bonus points – Gloucestershire 4, Nottinghamshire 3 (Score at 100 overs: 300-8).

Bowling: *First Innings*—Pick 18–5–45–1; Rice 9–2–33–0; Cooper 39.4–8–102–5; Saxelby 25–8–81–3; Fraser-Darling 14–1–70–1. *Second Innings*—Saxelby 11–3–50–0; Rice 14–3–40–2; Cooper 12–2–37–2; Fraser-Darling 14–1–55–1; Broad 6–1–35–0; Birch 3–0–4–0; Johnson 3–0–25–0.

Nottinghamshire

B. C. Broad lbw b Bainbridge	105	*C. E. B. Rice not out	33
R. T. Robinson c and b Bainbridge	108		
C. D. Fraser-Darling c Russell			
b Lawrence	20	B 4, l-b 4, n-b 3	11
M. Newell not out	23	1/221 2/226 3/255 (3 wkts dec.) 300	

P. Johnson, J. D. Birch, †C. W. Scott, K. E. Cooper, R. A. Pick and K. Saxelby did not bat.

Bonus points – Nottinghamshire 4, Gloucestershire 1.

Bowling: Walsh 22–3–102–0; Lawrence 18–2–74–1; Bainbridge 18–4–47–2; Lloyds 6–0–31–0; Twizell 11.1–3–38–0.

Umpires: C. Cook and R. Palmer.

GLOUCESTERSHIRE v MIDDLESEX

At Cheltenham, August 9, 11, 12. Middlesex won by 104 runs. Middlesex 20 pts, Gloucestershire 2 pts. Toss: Gloucestershire. Another rain-affected match brought Gloucestershire's second Championship defeat of the season and Middlesex's second win. Graveney's decision to insert Middlesex on the first day might have borne fruit had Gloucestershire's catching been up to previous high standards, but with Brown a solid anchorman, Middlesex batted consistently to 302 for five and, following a weekend storm, continued their innings when play resumed on Monday afternoon. Walsh became the first bowler to take 100 wickets when he bowled Rose, the fastest to achieve the feat since L. R. Gibbs did so on August 5, 1971. Altogether 78 overs were lost on the second day, and Gloucestershire declared at their overnight score to encourage Downton, captaining Middlesex for the first time, to set a target. It was 357 in a minimum of 90 overs, but after Middlesex's fast bowlers had half the side out for 90, Lloyds's forceful innings of 94 in 105 minutes did little more than delay the inevitable.

Middlesex

W. N. Slack c Romaines b Lawrence	47	– c Russell b Stovold	17
A. J. T. Miller c Curran b Bainbridge	32	– not out	32
K. R. Brown c Russell b Walsh	66	– not out	17
R. O. Butcher c Romaines b Walsh	33		
C. T. Radley lbw b Walsh	15		
J. D. Carr c and b Walsh	66		
*†P. R. Downton c Curran b Lawrence	46		
G. D. Rose b Walsh	9		
S. P. Hughes c Curran b Lawrence	5		
W. W. Daniel b Lawrence	4		
N. G. Cowans not out	8		
L-b 13, w 2, n-b 7	22	W 2	2

1/63 2/104 3/161 4/206 5/223   349   1/39   (1 wkt dec.) 68
6/326 7/327 8/341 9/341

Bonus points – Middlesex 3, Gloucestershire 2 (Score at 100 overs: 272-5).

Bowling: *First Innings*—Walsh 35–9–95–5; Lawrence 25.1–2–112–4; Bainbridge 10–2–16–1; Graveney 32–10–62–0; Lloyds 17–3–51–0. *Second Innings*—Romaines 4.1–0–39–0; Stovold 4–0–29–1.

Gloucestershire

P. W. Romaines c Downton b Daniel	0	– c Miller b Hughes	27
K. P. Tomlins not out	35	– c Carr b Cowans	0
A. J. Wright b Daniel	13	– c Radley b Daniel	6
P. Bainbridge c Brown b Rose	9	– c Miller b Hughes	34
†R. C. Russell not out	0	– (8) c Daniel b Butcher	27
A. W. Stovold (did not bat)	–	(5) c Downton b Cowans	13
K. M. Curran (did not bat)	–	(6) c Slack b Cowans	11
J. W. Lloyds (did not bat)	–	(7) c Downton b Butcher	94
*D. A. Graveney (did not bat)	–	lbw b Hughes	7
C. A. Walsh (did not bat)	–	not out	17
D. V. Lawrence (did not bat)	–	c Miller b Hughes	0
N-b 4	4	B 6, l-b 7, n-b 3	16

1/0 2/19 3/48   (3 wkts dec.) 61   1/0 2/13 3/77 4/86 5/90   252
6/131 7/180 8/231 9/252

Bonus point – Middlesex 1.

Bowling: *First Innings*—Daniel 8–1–15–2; Cowans 7–1–19–0; Hughes 4–1–11–0; Rose 4–0–16–1. *Second Innings*—Daniel 6–1–17–1; Cowans 13–4–60–3; Rose 4–0–32–0; Carr 11–0–53–0; Hughes 11.4–4–40–4; Butcher 9–0–37–2.

Umpires: C. Cook and J. H. Hampshire.

At Nuneaton, August 16, 18, 19. GLOUCESTERSHIRE lost to WARWICKSHIRE by 163 runs.

At Colchester, August 20, 21, 22. GLOUCESTERSHIRE drew with ESSEX.

At Manchester, August 23, 25, 26. GLOUCESTERSHIRE drew with LANCASHIRE.

GLOUCESTERSHIRE v WORCESTERSHIRE

At Bristol, August 27, 28, 29. Drawn. Gloucestershire 3 pts, Worcestershire 8 pts. Toss: Worcestershire. Failure to win more than three points in this match cost Gloucestershire their position as Championship leaders, and although they could again point to the inclemency of the weather as a factor, they were outplayed in most departments by a Worcestershire side which adapted better to the slow, turning pitch. With Athey an admirable exception, they batted nervously to 209 for nine on the first day as Patel and Illingworth called the tune. Rain ended play at the tea interval and there were only 50 overs possible on the second day, used to splendid purpose by Worcestershire, who rattled up 191 for the loss of two wickets. The following morning Neale opted to bat on for full bonus points. D'Oliveira and Hick took their partnership to 157 from 26 overs, and D'Oliveira went on to a career-best 146 not out from 203 balls, not even Walsh causing him concern.

Gloucestershire

P. W. Romaines c and b Pridgeon	22	– c D'Oliveira b Radford	10
K. P. Tomlins c D'Oliveira b Radford	0	– not out	46
C. W. J. Athey b Illingworth	73	– b D'Oliveira	42
P. Bainbridge c Rhodes b Patel	2	– c Radford b D'Oliveira	1
A. W. Stovold b Patel	12		
K. M. Curran b Patel	12		
J. W. Lloyds c Rhodes b Illingworth	38		
†R. C. Russell lbw b Patel	23	– (5) not out	11
C. A. Walsh st Rhodes b Patel	3		
*D. A. Graveney not out	5		
D. V. Lawrence not out	9		
B 4, l-b 5, n-b 1	10		

1/1 2/63 3/73 4/93   (9 wkts dec.) 209   1/18 2/89 3/95   (3 wkts) 110
5/115 6/161 7/177
8/189 9/196

Bonus points – Gloucestershire 2, Worcestershire 4.

Bowling: *First Innings*—Radford 16-6-48-1; Pridgeon 9-6-12-1; Newport 6-1-13-0; Illingworth 24-7-39-2; Patel 25-7-88-5. *Second Innings*—Radford 6-1-21-1; Pridgeon 4-1-10-0; Patel 7-1-18-0; Illingworth 17-6-41-0; Newport 2-0-3-0; D'Oliveira 10-5-17-2.

Worcestershire

T. S. Curtis c sub b Lloyds	42	D. N. Patel not out	1
D. B. D'Oliveira not out	146	B 3, l-b 3, n-b 1	7
D. M. Smith c and b Graveney	5		
G. A. Hick c Athey b Walsh	85	1/69 2/76 3/233	(4 wkts dec.) 300
*P. A. Neale c Athey b Bainbridge	14	4/281	

†S. J. Rhodes, P. J. Newport, N. V. Radford, R. K. Illingworth and A. P. Pridgeon did not bat.

Bonus points – Worcestershire 4, Gloucestershire 1.

Bowling: Walsh 21-3-100-1; Lawrence 12-0-55-0; Lloyds 17-2-76-1; Graveney 18-1-42-1; Bainbridge 3.3-1-21-1.

Umpires: J. H. Hampshire and P. B. Wight.

At The Oval, September 3, 4, 5. GLOUCESTERSHIRE drew with SURREY.

HAMPSHIRE

President: C. G. A. Paris
Chairman: D. Rich
Chairman, Cricket Committee: C. J. Knott
Chief Executive: A. F. Baker
  Northlands Road, Southampton SO9 2TY
  (Telephone: 0703-333788)
Captain: M. C. J. Nicholas
Coach: P. J. Sainsbury

Hampshire's winning of the John Player League for the third time was a deserved success in a season which was tinged with the disappointment of the team's failure to play to full potential in the other major competitions. Having finished second in the Britannic Assurance Championship the previous season, the county had entertained high expectations of challenging for the season's premier title, but these were not always matched by performance. A final position of sixth had to be accepted.

However, the most bitter pill was again Hampshire's failure to qualify for a Lord's final, something which Mark Nicholas, their enterprising captain, continued to find particularly irritating. In the Benson and Hedges Cup they failed to advance to the quarter-finals, and they were beaten at Southampton by Worcestershire in the second round of the NatWest Bank Trophy. This left them with the stigma, the word used by Nicholas, of being the only county not to have played in a one-day final at Lord's.

Success in the John Player League was a proper advance from third place in 1985, although there were some anxious moments, such as losing to Sussex and Middlesex on successive Sundays in August after sharing first place in the table with Northamptonshire at the end of July. However, Hampshire came down the final straight like champions, winning their last four games and clinching the title in the penultimate fixture against Surrey at The Oval. There were a number of splendid contributions to the success, but especially consistent were Robin Smith and Tim Tremlett. Smith hit six half-centuries as he scored 629 runs to top the national Sunday League averages, while Tremlett took 26 wickets – the most by a Hampshire bowler since J. M. Rice's 25 in 1975 and two short of P. J. Sainsbury's record of 28.

In the County Championship, Hampshire were splendidly served by Gordon Greenidge and Malcolm Marshall, their established West Indies Test cricketers. Greenidge, whose aggregate of runs in the first-class game, 2,035, was the highest by a Hampshire player since B. A. Richards's 2,395 in 1968, topped the national batting averages, and Marshall, taking 100 wickets for the second time, led the bowling to give the county a first-time double.

However, Hampshire's pre-season confidence for Championship success was based on the potential of their first five batsmen, and as the season unfolded, this was not realised. Greenidge was outstanding and finished the summer in brilliant fashion by scoring four hundreds in successive Championship innings, the first Hampshire batsman to achieve the feat. But only two others, Chris and Robin Smith, also scored first-class hundreds, as opposed to eight players doing so in 1985. Paul Terry, the vice-captain, struggled throughout the season to rediscover his form, while Nicholas had an even worse time. Both failed to score 1,000 runs for the first time since establishing themselves as regular members of the team. The Smith brothers also scored fewer runs than in the previous season, although Chris Smith twice had the misfortune to break a finger.

Indeed, injuries contributed significantly to Hampshire's having to settle for sixth place. The absence of Chris Smith did weaken the batting, but perhaps an even more serious setback was the loss of Rajesh Maru, the slow left-arm spinner, who had made such a considerable advance in 1985. Maru broke the joint at the top of his spinning finger while fielding against Surrey at Basingstoke towards the end of June and he was forced to miss eight matches. The extent to which he was missed was underlined when he returned to take 26 wickets in seven games and was awarded his county cap. Cardigan Connor turned in some useful performances, especially in the John Player League, while Nigel Cowley improved his total of first-class wickets and played a leading part in Hampshire's winning the Asda Challenge at the Scarborough Festival.

With Tremlett unable to reproduce his 1985 form in the Championship, Marshall again provided the cutting edge to the Hampshire attack. He bowled more overs than any county team-mate, took his 100 wickets at an average of 15.08, and towards the end of the season reached 1,000 first-class wickets, 531 of them for Hampshire. Encouragingly, there were useful all-round performances from Kevan James, in his second season, and his unbeaten 54 at The Oval was a vital contribution to Hampshire's winning the John Player League title that afternoon.

But for the loss to the weather of the last five days of their home Championship programme, Hampshire might have finished higher than sixth place. Certainly, Bobby Parks, their consistently efficient wicket-keeper, had reason to regret the September rain. Without the loss of those days he would almost certainly have passed L. Harrison's record for the most dismissals in a season by a Hampshire wicket-keeper. Instead, he finished just two short of Harrison's 1959 total of 83. – B.H.

HAMPSHIRE 1986

[Bill Smith]

Back row: I. J. Chivers, T. C. Middleton, A. N. Aymes, C. A. Connor, R. J. Scott, M. E. O'Connor. Middle row: C. L. Smith, K. J. Shine, P. J. Bakker, J. R. Ayling, S. J. W. Andrew, K. D. James, R. A. Smith, P. J. Sainsbury (coach). Front row: C. F. E. Goldie, N. G. Cowley, D. R. Turner, M. C. J. Nicholas (captain), V. P. Terry, T. M. Tremlett, R. J. Parks, R. J. Maru. Insets: M. D. Marshall, C. G. Greenidge.

HAMPSHIRE RESULTS

All first-class matches – Played 25: Won 7, Lost 4, Drawn 14. Abandoned 1.

County Championship matches – Played 23: Won 7, Lost 4, Drawn 12. Abandoned 1.

Bonus points – Batting 54, Bowling 69.

*Competition placings – Britannic Assurance County Championship, 6th; NatWest Bank Trophy,
2nd round; Benson and Hedges Cup, 3rd in Group D; John Player League, winners.*

BRITANNIC ASSURANCE CHAMPIONSHIP AVERAGES

BATTING

	Birthplace	M	I	NO	R	HI	Avge
‡C. G. Greenidge ..	St Peter, Barbados	19	32	4	1,916	222	68.42
‡C. L. Smith	Durban, SA	17	25	8	964	114*	56.70
‡R. A. Smith	Durban, SA	23	34	6	1,100	128*	39.28
‡T. M. Tremlett ...	Wellington, Somerset	19	21	11	317	59*	31.70
‡D. R. Turner	Chippenham	9	13	0	403	96	31.00
T. C. Middleton ...	Winchester	8	14	3	316	68*	28.72
‡N. G. Cowley	Shaftesbury	17	18	6	329	78*	27.41
‡R. J. Maru	Nairobi, Kenya	15	9	5	108	23	27.00
K. D. James	Lambeth	12	13	2	275	62	25.00
‡R. J. Parks	Cuckfield	23	21	4	419	80	24.64
‡V. P. Terry	Osnabruck, WG	21	33	3	704	80	23.46
‡M. C. J. Nicholas .	London	21	28	2	489	55	18.80
‡M. D. Marshall ...	St Michael, Barbados	23	23	2	263	51*	12.52
C. A. Connor	The Valley, Anguilla	20	13	5	41	16	5.12
S. J. W. Andrew ..	London	5	5	2	15	7	5.00

Also batted: P. J. Bakker (*Vlaardingen, Netherlands*) (1 match) 3*, 3.

* *Signifies not out.*   ‡ *Denotes county cap.*

The following played a total of twelve three-figure innings for Hampshire in County
Championship matches: C. G. Greenidge 8, C. L. Smith 2, R. A. Smith 2.

BOWLING

	O	M	R	W	BB	Avge
M. D. Marshall	656.3	171	1,508	100	6-51	15.08
R. J. Maru	438.3	132	1,177	41	4-33	28.70
N. G. Cowley	345.2	69	949	33	5-17	28.75
T. M. Tremlett	424.4	103	1,175	40	5-46	29.37
K. D. James	228.4	55	692	21	5-34	32.95
C. A. Connor	541.4	123	1,616	49	5-60	32.97
S. J. W. Andrew ...	97.2	15	331	10	3-25	33.10

Also bowled: P. J. Bakker 24–5–73–1; T. C. Middleton 8–1–39–1; M. C. J. Nicholas
57–11–171–2; R. J. Parks 23–1–110–0; C. L. Smith 37–4–177–1; R. A. Smith 42.4–7–189–2;
V. P. Terry 1–1–0–0; D. R. Turner 3–1–6–0.

Wicket-keeper: R. J. Parks 68 ct, 6 st.

Leading Fielders: R. A. Smith 19; C. G. Greenidge 17; V. P. Terry 16; C. L. Smith 13;
M. C. J. Nicholas 12.

At Nottingham, April 26, 27, 28. HAMPSHIRE beat NOTTINGHAMSHIRE by nine wickets.

HAMPSHIRE v GLAMORGAN

At Southampton, April 30, May 1, 2. Drawn. Hampshire 8 pts, Glamorgan 5 pts. Toss: Hampshire. Two wickets fell for 19 before Glamorgan were rallied by a stand of 67 in 28 overs between Morris and Holmes. However, the dismissal of Morris triggered a collapse which saw five wickets fall for 48 runs. Hampshire made a positive reply with Chris Smith, in his 100th first-class game for the county, dominating a third-wicket partnership of 142 in 35 overs with Terry. Glamorgan's second innings was spirited and determined. They never looked like being dismissed on a pitch which became slower and slower, especially after Marshall left the field with a back injury.

Glamorgan

J. A. Hopkins c Greenidge b Connor	5	– lbw b Connor	22
A. L. Jones c Terry b Tremlett	6		
H. Morris c Parks b Marshall	34	– (2) b Cowley	58
G. C. Holmes c Greenidge b Tremlett	52	– (3) b Tremlett	29
Younis Ahmed b Tremlett	17	– (4) c R. A. Smith b Maru	85
*R. C. Ontong c Parks b Connor	4	– (5) c Maru b Tremlett	52
J. F. Steele run out	25	– (6) c Parks b Connor	10
J. Derrick run out	4	– (7) c C. L. Smith b Connor	15
J. G. Thomas lbw b Connor	20	– (8) not out	37
†T. Davies not out	13	– (9) not out	2
E. A. Moseley c C. L. Smith b Marshall	13		
L-b 4, w 3, n-b 1	8	B 4, l-b 24, w 3, n-b 1	32

1/5 2/19 3/86 4/118 5/125   201   1/35 2/98 3/158   (7 wkts dec.) 342
6/125 7/134 8/170 9/175   4/264 5/283 6/303 7/310

Bonus points – Glamorgan 2, Hampshire 4.

Bowling: *First Innings*—Marshall 20.5–5–46–2; Connor 29–9–57–3; Tremlett 27–11–40–3; Cowley 5–0–13–0; Nicholas 4–0–11–0; Maru 6–1–30–0. *Second Innings*—Marshall 15–5–42–0; Connor 27–13–45–3; Tremlett 27–9–78–2; Maru 35–19–67–1; Cowley 21–7–59–1; C. L. Smith 5–2–21–0; R. A. Smith 3–2–2–0.

Hampshire

C. G. Greenidge c Holmes b Thomas	0	†R. J. Parks c Holmes b Thomas	3
V. P. Terry c Ontong b Derrick	80	R. J. Maru not out	0
R. A. Smith b Derrick	19		
C. L. Smith b Thomas	79	B 5, l-b 5, w 1, n-b 16	27
*M. C. J. Nicholas c Derrick b Holmes	26		
M. D. Marshall b Holmes	45	1/2 2/54 3/196	(8 wkts dec.) 308
N. G. Cowley c sub b Derrick	21	4/196 5/262 6/273	
T. M. Tremlett not out	8	7/305 8/308	

C. A. Connor did not bat.

Bonus points – Hampshire 4, Glamorgan 3.

Bowling: Thomas 20–3–66–3; Moseley 24–4–60–0; Derrick 17–4–67–3; Holmes 18–3–71–2; Steele 4–0–25–0; Ontong 6–1–9–0.

Umpires: J. W. Holder and M. J. Kitchen.

At Manchester, May 7, 8, 9. HAMPSHIRE drew with LANCASHIRE.

At Southampton, May 17, 18, 19. HAMPSHIRE drew with INDIANS (See Indian tour section).

At Cambridge, May 21, 22, 23. HAMPSHIRE drew with CAMBRIDGE UNIVERSITY.

HAMPSHIRE v GLOUCESTERSHIRE

At Bournemouth, May 24, 26, 27. Gloucestershire won by 146 runs. Gloucestershire 22 pts, Hampshire 2 pts. Toss: Hampshire. Stovold and Romaines's opening partnership of 106 laid the foundation for a comfortable total after Gloucestershire had been put in on a green pitch under overcast skies. On the second day, Hampshire were unhinged by Walsh, who extracted life from the pitch and was well supported by Payne. Gloucestershire increased their lead to 129 by the close, and although Marshall took all six wickets to fall the following morning, they were able to set a target of 257 off a minimum of 62 overs. Terry and Chris Smith gave Hampshire a good start, but they collapsed in dismal fashion: from 57 for no wicket to 110 all out in 80 minutes. Walsh was the principal agent, enjoying a return of six for 26 and match figures of eleven for 94. It was the first time Hampshire had been dismissed twice in a match since late August 1984 – by Kent, also at Bournemouth, when Underwood was the chief destroyer.

Gloucestershire

P. W. Romaines b Tremlett	52	– c C. L. Smith b Marshall 29
A. W. Stovold c Andrew b Marshall	65	– c Parks b Marshall 14
A. J. Wright c Marshall b Maru	28	– b Marshall 13
P. Bainbridge c Parks b Maru	7	– b Marshall 22
J. W. Lloyds lbw b Andrew	48	– (6) lbw b Marshall 22
K. M. Curran c Maru b Andrew	62	– (5) not out 38
I. R. Payne not out	9	– c Maru b Marshall 6
D. V. Lawrence c Parks b Bakker	1	
†R. C. Russell not out	1	
B 1, l-b 9, w 2, n-b 11	23	L-b 1, w 1, n-b 4 6

1/106 2/140 3/166 4/177   (7 wkts dec.) 296   1/23 2/45 3/69   (6 wkts dec.) 150
5/278 6/285 7/287   4/111 5/139 6/150

*D. A. Graveney and C. A. Walsh did not bat.

Bonus points – Gloucestershire 2, Hampshire 1 (Score at 100 overs: 236-4).

Bowling: *First Innings*—Marshall 20-4-42-1; Bakker 18-3-51-1; Andrew 16-3-58-2; Tremlett 22-4-69-1; Maru 34-9-64-2; Nicholas 5-3-2-0. *Second Innings*—Marshall 23-5-51-6; Andrew 8-1-26-0; Tremlett 7-2-31-0; Maru 7-2-19-0; Bakker 6-2-22-0.

Hampshire

V. P. Terry c Russell b Walsh	17	– c Curran b Walsh 31
C. L. Smith lbw b Walsh	27	– c Curran b Payne 26
R. A. Smith c Russell b Payne	1	– c Russell b Walsh 0
*M. C. J. Nicholas c Russell b Walsh	11	– c Russell b Walsh 2
D. R. Turner c Payne b Lawrence	35	– c Curran b Lawrence 20
M. D. Marshall b Payne	23	– c Stovold b Payne 0
T. M. Tremlett c Stovold b Payne	5	– lbw b Walsh 5
†R. J. Parks b Walsh	36	– lbw b Lawrence 6
R. J. Maru c Wright b Walsh	17	– c Lawrence b Walsh 1
S. J. W. Andrew b Bainbridge	0	– not out 4
P. J. Bakker not out	3	– c Russell b Walsh 3
B 1, l-b 5, n-b 9	15	B 5, w 4, n-b 3 12

1/40 2/42 3/57 4/66 5/103   190   1/57 2/57 3/61 4/63 5/68   110
6/125 7/130 8/165 9/179   6/85 7/102 8/103 9/103

Bonus points – Hampshire 1, Gloucestershire 4.

Bowling: *First Innings*—Lawrence 12–1–52–1; Walsh 26.2–7–68–5; Payne 22–6–48–3; Bainbridge 5–0–16–1. *Second Innings*—Lawrence 8–0–43–2; Walsh 13.1–3–26–6; Payne 8–1–32–2; Graveney 1–0–4–0.

Umpires: C. Cook and A. A. Jones.

HAMPSHIRE v NOTTINGHAMSHIRE

At Southampton, May 31, June 2, 3. Drawn. Hampshire 4 pts, Nottinghamshire 3 pts. Toss: Hampshire. Rain prevented play on the first day, delayed the start for 90 minutes on the second, and returned to wash out the third. Nottinghamshire were put in on a pitch which provided plenty of life and Marshall, relishing the conditions, took the first four wickets on his way to figures of five for 38. Parks, the Hampshire wicket-keeper, claimed six victims in an innings for the third time in his career. Hadlee, who had batted belligerently in Nottinghamshire's innings, helped to ensure that Hampshire's batsmen struggled in turn.

Nottinghamshire

R. T. Robinson c Maru b Marshall	....	8	R. A. Pick c Parks b Cowley	5
B. C. Broad c Parks b Marshall	......	12	K. E. Cooper st Parks b Cowley	6
D. W. Randall c Parks b Marshall	....	17	J. A. Afford not out	0
*C. E. B. Rice c Parks b Marshall	....	11		
P. Johnson c C. L. Smith b Andrew	....	25	W 2, n-b 5	7
J. D. Birch c Parks b Andrew	....	11		
R. J. Hadlee b Connor	....	44	1/9 2/33 3/48 4/55 5/84	162
†B. N. French lbw b Marshall	....	16	6/101 7/146 8/156 9/162	

Bonus points – Nottinghamshire 1, Hampshire 4.

Bowling: Marshall 13–3–38–5; Connor 18–5–53–1; Nicholas 3–1–19–0; Andrew 9–0–47–2; Maru 2–2–0–0; Cowley 2.1–1–5–2.

Hampshire

C. G. Greenidge c Johnson b Hadlee	..	1	N. G. Cowley not out	8
V. P. Terry b Birch b Pick	....	19		
C. L. Smith c Birch b Rice	....	26	L-b 1, n-b 3	4
*M. C. J. Nicholas c French b Cooper	.	15		
R. A. Smith not out	....	6	1/2 2/32 3/53	(5 wkts dec.) 80
M. D. Marshall c Robinson b Rice	....	1	4/66 5/70	

R. J. Maru, †R. J. Parks, C. A. Connor and S. J. W. Andrew did not bat.

Bonus points – Nottinghamshire 2.

Bowling: Hadlee 11–7–14–1; Pick 8–1–37–1; Cooper 8–3–18–1; Rice 6–3–10–2.

Umpires: B. Dudleston and R. A. White.

HAMPSHIRE v SOMERSET

At Bournemouth, June 7, 8, 9. Drawn. Hampshire 6 pts, Somerset 7 pts. Toss: Somerset. Greenidge marked his 250th first-class game for Hampshire with a century containing four 6s and twenty 4s, many of them powerful strokes. When Hampshire's middle order collapsed, Greenidge subdued his aggressive instincts, but he began to express himself again when Cowley gave him good support. Connor made quick inroads into the Somerset reply with three wickets in thirteen balls on Saturday evening, but Hardy, once with Hampshire, and Marks led a recovery on the Sunday. Hampshire were 130 runs ahead with seven wickets in hand at the close, and an absorbing final day brought maximum effort from both sides to achieve a result. Chris Smith, whose first century of the season was made in 225 minutes (one 6, twelve 4s), and brother Robin put on 179 in 53 overs for the fourth wicket. Left to score 282 for victory in at least 59 overs, Somerset were 200 for eight when Hampshire settled for a draw with just one ball remaining.

Hampshire

C. G. Greenidge c Harden b Taylor	148	– c Dredge b Taylor 15
V. P. Terry c Richards b Dredge	35	– lbw b Dredge 23
C. L. Smith c Hardy b Dredge	4	– not out 103
*M. C. J. Nicholas c Blitz b Marks	18	– c Blitz b Taylor 1
R. A. Smith b Garner	0	– c Marks b Dredge 94
M. D. Marshall lbw b Garner	1	
N. G. Cowley b Dredge	28	– (6) not out 3
†R. J. Parks b Garner	18	
R. J. Maru c Blitz b Taylor	21	
C. A. Connor c Garner b Taylor	7	
S. J. W. Andrew not out	2	
L-b 11, n-b 5	16	L-b 4, n-b 2 6

1/84 2/96 3/150 4/151 5/153   298   1/24 2/50 3/51   (4 wkts dec.) 245
6/240 7/250 8/282 9/292   4/230

Bonus points – Hampshire 3, Somerset 4.

Bowling: *First Innings*—Garner 19-6-49-3; Taylor 17.4-2-78-3; Dredge 24-4-90-3; Richards 8-1-25-0; Marks 12-4-30-1; Harden 3-1-15-0. *Second Innings*—Garner 14-8-14-0; Taylor 24-7-84-2; Dredge 19.5-3-68-2; Marks 12-1-40-0; Harden 8-0-35-0.

Somerset

N. A. Felton c Parks b Connor	9	– c Parks b Connor 56
*P. M. Roebuck b Connor	6	– c Cowley b Andrew 10
J. J. E. Hardy c Parks b Connor	59	– c Greenidge b Connor 37
I. V. A. Richards c Terry b Connor	9	– c Greenidge b Maru 29
R. J. Harden lbw b Marshall	20	– c Parks b Maru 32
B. C. Rose c Parks b Connor	37	– c Parks b Cowley 14
V. J. Marks not out	83	– not out 14
†R. J. Blitz lbw b Cowley	18	– lbw b Marshall 0
C. H. Dredge not out	11	– b Marshall 4
J. Garner (did not bat)	–	– not out 1
L-b 5, w 3, n-b 2	10	L-b 1, w 2 3

1/13 2/16 3/26 4/67   (7 wkts dec.) 262   1/22 2/105 3/110 4/136   (8 wkts) 200
5/134 6/153 7/235   5/181 6/181 7/183 8/191

N. S. Taylor did not bat.

Bonus points – Somerset 3, Hampshire 3.

Bowling: *First Innings*—Marshall 19-4-49-1; Connor 20-3-60-5; Andrew 18-2-65-0; Maru 18-6-37-0; Cowley 11.2-2-43-1; Nicholas 2-0-3-0. *Second Innings*—Marshall 8.5-5-11-2; Connor 11-5-34-2; Andrew 8-3-15-1; Maru 21-5-88-2; Cowley 13-1-51-1.

Umpires: J. H. Hampshire and N. T. Plews.

At Ilford, June 14, 16, 17. HAMPSHIRE beat ESSEX by 12 runs.

HAMPSHIRE v SURREY

At Basingstoke, June 18, 19. Hampshire won by an innings and 193 runs. Hampshire 24 pts, Surrey 2 pts. Toss: Hampshire. Pocock, the Surrey captain, was critical of his team's performance after they had been beaten by an innings for the second time in a week. He said: "I have never before seen any side beaten by an innings on such a good cricket wicket. We batted very badly and Hampshire bowled very well." On the first day, Hampshire had also batted well, Greenidge just missing a century and Robin Smith reaching his off 162 balls, having hit one 6 and sixteen 4s. Hampshire's total surpassed their previous best at the ground – 389 against

Derbyshire in 1914. Surrey, 21 without loss overnight, were bundled out in 42 overs on the second day. Only Richards showed any resistance. Following on 257 behind, they showed even less resolution as they were dismissed for 64 in 20.1 overs and 87 minutes. On the third day, for which sponsorship marquees had been sold well in advance, the two teams played a match of 40 overs each for a stake of £2,000. Hampshire won by 10 runs (Hampshire 249 for seven; Surrey 239).

Hampshire

C. G. Greenidge b Doughty	97	N. G. Cowley not out	6
V. P. Terry lbw b Gray	44		
D. R. Turner c Pocock b Doughty	12	B 11, l-b 15, w 4, n-b 10	40
*M. C. J. Nicholas b Bicknell	50		—
R. A. Smith lbw b Pocock	101	1/142 2/178 3/188 (5 wkts dec.)	401
M. D. Marshall not out	51	4/291 5/375	

†R. J. Parks, T. M. Tremlett, R. J. Maru and C. A. Connor did not bat.

Bonus points – Hampshire 4, Surrey 2.

Bowling: Gray 19–3–59–1; Doughty 17–3–76–2; Bicknell 17–4–55–1; Butcher 14–2–52–0; Pocock 23–3–81–1; Needham 10–1–52–0.

Surrey

A. J. Stewart b Connor	8	c Turner b Marshall	4
G. S. Clinton c Nicholas b Marshall	22	b Connor	20
M. A. Lynch c Greenidge b Connor	0	c Nicholas b Marshall	0
T. E. Jesty c Greenidge b Marshall	0	c Parks b Marshall	0
A. Needham lbw b Tremlett	7	c Parks b Connor	0
†C. J. Richards not out	56	c Parks b Tremlett	13
A. R. Butcher b Tremlett	0	c Greenidge b Tremlett	7
R. J. Doughty c Greenidge b Maru	16	run out	17
M. P. Bicknell b Marshall	1	c Parks b Tremlett	0
A. H. Gray c Parks b Connor	11	c sub b Tremlett	0
*P. I. Pocock b Marshall	10	not out	0
L-b 5, w 3, n-b 5	13	L-b 1, w 1, n-b 1	3

1/36 2/37 3/37 4/41 5/55	144	1/13 2/21 3/21 4/25 5/38	64
6/59 7/88 8/98 9/123		6/40 7/59 8/59 9/64	

Bonus points – Hampshire 4.

Bowling: *First Innings*—Marshall 17–7–26–4; Connor 17–4–77–3; Tremlett 8–4–17–2; Maru 3–1–8–1; Cowley 4–1–11–0. *Second Innings*—Marshall 6–2–15–3; Connor 10–0–34–2; Tremlett 4.1–0–14–4.

Umpires: B. Dudleston and A. A. Jones.

HAMPSHIRE v KENT

At Southampton, June 21, 23, 24. Kent won by five wickets. Kent 21 pts, Hampshire 6 pts. Toss: Kent. Hampshire were given a good start by Greenidge and Terry with an opening partnership of 103, but Underwood removed both in the space of four balls to undermine the innings. Kent replied with 107 for two by the close, but on Monday Cowley, Hampshire's off-spinner, helped his county to a lead of 25 on first innings with five wickets for 17, including a spell of four wickets for 2 runs in 28 balls either side of lunch. Underwood again caused Hampshire problems by dismissing Greenidge, Smith and Marshall in eight balls, but Alderman, with six for 56, was the most successful bowler in conditions helping the swing bowler. Kent, needing 169 in 80 overs, got home thanks to another sound innings from Benson, who batted for 255 minutes for his unbeaten 97.

Hampshire

C. G. Greenidge b Underwood	53	– c Cowdrey b Underwood	49
V. P. Terry b Underwood	47	– c Marsh b Jarvis	1
D. R. Turner b Underwood	5	– b Alderman	12
*M. C. J. Nicholas c Marsh b Alderman	7	– lbw b Alderman	39
R. A. Smith c Marsh b Ellison	29	– c Aslett b Underwood	0
M. D. Marshall c and b Underwood	1	– b Underwood	0
N. G. Cowley c Marsh b Jarvis	18	– lbw b Alderman	1
†R. J. Parks c Marsh b Alderman	13	– lbw b Alderman	0
T. M. Tremlett	31	– not out	14
C. A. Connor lbw b Jarvis	0	– lbw b Alderman	16
S. J. W. Andrew b Alderman	7	– b Alderman	2
L-b 2, n-b 1	3	L-b 9	9
	214		143

1/103 2/104 3/113 4/127 5/129
6/157 7/175 8/183 9/183

1/6 2/36 3/84 4/84 5/88
6/103 7/103 8/114 9/137

Bonus points – Hampshire 2, Kent 4.

Bowling: *First Innings*—Alderman 23.1–4–71–3; Jarvis 16–5–57–2; Ellison 15.4–3–54–1; Underwood 22–13–30–4. *Second Innings*—Alderman 27.1–8–56–6; Jarvis 13–3–45–1; Underwood 17–10–21–3; Ellison 3–1–12–0.

Kent

M. R. Benson lbw b Cowley	90	– not out	97
T. R. Ward c Terry b Marshall	29	– b Cowley	12
*C. J. Tavaré c Greenidge b Marshall	0	– b Andrew	12
N. R. Taylor c Greenidge b Cowley	17	– c Parks b Andrew	6
G. R. Cowdrey c Parks b Connor	14	– c Parks b Andrew	4
D. G. Aslett b Andrew	8	– lbw b Marshall	6
R. M. Ellison c Andrew b Cowley	10	– not out	22
†S. A. Marsh c Nicholas b Cowley	0		
D. L. Underwood c Terry b Connor	4		
T. M. Alderman c and b Cowley	2		
K. B. S. Jarvis not out	0		
L-b 10, n-b 5	15	B 3, l-b 6, w 1, n-b 3	13
	189	(5 wkts)	172

1/62 2/62 3/143 4/149 5/167
6/181 7/181 8/186 9/189

1/34 2/69 3/82
4/94 5/104

Bonus points – Kent 1, Hampshire 4.

Bowling: *First Innings*—Marshall 17–4–38–2; Connor 20–4–58–2; Andrew 11–3–33–1; Tremlett 11–4–33–0; Cowley 17.4–7–17–5. *Second Innings*—Marshall 13–2–34–1; Connor 11–2–36–0; Cowley 20–4–38–1; Tremlett 12–3–26–0; Andrew 8–0–25–3; Smith 1–0–4–0.

Umpires: J. W. Holder and J. A. Jameson.

At Worcester, June 28, 30, July 1. HAMPSHIRE lost to WORCESTERSHIRE by six wickets.

At Leicester, July 2, 3, 4. HAMPSHIRE drew with LEICESTERSHIRE.

At Taunton, July 5, 7, 8. HAMPSHIRE drew with SOMERSET.

HAMPSHIRE v WARWICKSHIRE

At Portsmouth, July 19, 21. Hampshire won by an innings and 43 runs. Hampshire 24 pts, Warwickshire 2 pts. Toss: Warwickshire. Put in, Hampshire lost two wickets cheaply, but that was the only time in the match they had cause for concern. The Smith brothers established the innings with a partnership of 91 in 31 overs, during which Chris reached 10,000 runs in first-class cricket, and Turner and James, both left-handers, batted with enterprise as 148 runs were added in 35 overs. Lloyd, the Warwickshire opener, suffered a broken nose while fielding at slip when James edged a ball from Gifford into his face, and the visitors' problems increased as they were tumbled out for 110 by Marshall and Connor on the second morning. Following on, Warwickshire looked as if they might carry the game into the third day while McMillan was sharing stands with Amiss and Humpage, but when they went, James quickly accounted for the tailenders.

Hampshire

V. P. Terry c and b McMillan	12	N. G. Cowley not out		6
C. L. Smith b Small	58	T. M. Tremlett not out		11
*M. C. J. Nicholas lbw b McMillan	2	B 12, l-b 11, n-b 7		30
R. A. Smith c Humpage b Parsons	73			
D. R. Turner c Parsons b Gifford	96	1/17 2/31 3/122	(6 wkts dec.)	350
K. D. James c Smith b Gifford	62	4/183 5/331 6/336		

M. D. Marshall, †R. J. Parks and C. A. Connor did not bat.

Bonus points – Hampshire 4, Warwickshire 2.

Bowling: Small 23–3–71–1; McMillan 13–3–54–2; Parsons 15–4–43–1; Munton 16–2–52–0; Thorne 9–0–35–0; Gifford 18–5–54–2; Smith 3–0–18–0.

Warwickshire

D. A. Thorne b Connor	5	– b Connor	11
P. A. Smith lbw b Marshall	11	– c Parks b Tremlett	23
B. M. McMillan c R. A. Smith b Marshall	0	– c Parks b Marshall	61
G. J. Parsons c Parks b Marshall	14	– (7) c Terry b Marshall	0
D. L. Amiss c James b Marshall	2	– (4) c R. A. Smith b Tremlett	33
†G. W. Humpage b Connor	4	– (5) c R. A. Smith b James	30
Asif Din not out	50	– (6) not out	14
G. C. Small b Marshall	0	– c C. L. Smith b James	7
T. A. Munton b Connor	19	– lbw b James	0
*N. Gifford b Connor	0	– c Marshall b James	0
T. A. Lloyd absent injured		– absent injured	
B 1, l-b 1, w 1, n-b 2	5	B 8, l-b 8, n-b 2	18

1/5 2/8 3/23 4/31 5/37	110	1/29 2/61 3/115 4/167 5/175 197
6/39 7/41 8/110 9/110		6/176 7/193 8/193 9/197

Bonus points – Hampshire 4.

Bowling: *First Innings*—Marshall 15–6–22–5; Connor 15.4–4–34–4; James 5–1–25–0; Tremlett 6–1–27–0. *Second Innings*—Connor 16–8–60–1; Marshall 19–4–51–2; Tremlett 18–5–54–2; James 7.5–3–16–4.

Umpires: D. J. Constant and B. J. Meyer.

HAMPSHIRE v DERBYSHIRE

At Portsmouth, July 23, 24, 25. Hampshire won by 5 runs. Hampshire 21 pts, Derbyshire 6 pts. Toss: Derbyshire. The visitors benefited from winning the toss as Hampshire struggled to 166 for six on the rain-affected opening day and early on the second lost their four remaining wickets for 18 runs. Maher and Hill appeared to be putting Derbyshire in a strong position, but Tremlett took five wickets as Hampshire fought back to keep the first-innings deficit to 32 and wipe it out for the loss of one wicket by the close. When Hampshire reached

86 for one at lunch on the final day, Derbyshire turned to Maher and Morris to feed the batsmen runs before a declaration, allowing Greenidge and Parks to take their partnership to 197 in 38 overs. Greenidge was unbeaten with 144 (sixteen 4s) off 135 balls, having scored 30,000 runs in first-class cricket. Derbyshire's target was 223 in 52 overs, and while Morris was batting they were favourites to win. They needed 89 off the last twenty overs, 56 off ten and 6 off the final over, but Warner, going for a second run, was run out off the first ball.

Hampshire

C. G. Greenidge c Anderson b Holding	24	– not out 144
V. P. Terry c Hill b Holding	8	– lbw b Holding 2
T. C. Middleton c Maher b Miller	33	– (4) not out 8
C. L. Smith c Holding b Warner	19	
R. A. Smith b Warner	12	
*M. C. J. Nicholas c Marples b Mortensen	55	
K. D. James run out	16	
M. D. Marshall b Holding	8	
†R. J. Parks c Morris b Holding	2	– (3) c Barnett b Maher 80
T. M. Tremlett c Barnett b Holding	1	
C. A. Connor not out	2	
L-b 3, w 1	4	B 8, l-b 8, w 2, n-b 2 20

1/12 2/39 3/62 4/84 5/114   **184**   1/32 2/229   (2 wkts dec.) **254**
6/153 7/168 8/170 9/172

Bonus points – Hampshire 1, Derbyshire 4.

Bowling: *First Innings*—Holding 24–5–89–5; Mortensen 13.1–1–31–1; Warner 16–9–36–2; Miller 7–2–16–1; Roberts 3–1–9–0. *Second Innings*—Holding 12–3–37–1; Mortensen 9–4–11–0; Warner 10–3–28–0; Morris 11–0–80–0; Maher 11–0–82–1.

Derbyshire

*K. J. Barnett c Nicholas b Marshall	4	– lbw b Marshall 16
B. J. M. Maher b Tremlett	69	– b Marshall 3
A. Hill b James	43	– c Parks b Tremlett 24
J. E. Morris run out	25	– c Terry b Connor 78
B. Roberts c and b James	6	– c Middleton b Marshall ... 10
I. S. Anderson lbw b Connor	7	– c Greenidge b Marshall 4
G. Miller c Parks b Tremlett	0	– c Parks b Connor 22
†C. Marples b Tremlett	18	– c Connor b Tremlett 34
M. A. Holding b Tremlett	26	– c Nicholas b Tremlett 5
A. E. Warner c Nicholas b Tremlett	2	– run out 11
O. H. Mortensen not out	0	– not out 0
L-b 9, w 1, n-b 6	16	B 1, l-b 3, n-b 6 10

1/4 2/115 3/127 4/146 5/166   **216**   1/14 2/21 3/101 4/132 5/140   **217**
6/169 7/169 8/187 9/197   6/141 7/185 8/200 9/210

Bonus points – Derbyshire 2, Hampshire 4.

Bowling: *First Innings*—Marshall 19–4–46–1; Connor 25–8–71–1; James 16–5–44–2; Tremlett 22.4–8–46–5. *Second Innings*—Marshall 17–1–54–4; Connor 10–0–54–2; James 9–2–33–0; C. L. Smith 4–0–20–0; Tremlett 11.1–0–52–3.

Umpires: D. J. Constant and B. J. Meyer.

At Cheltenham, August 2, 4, 5. HAMPSHIRE lost to GLOUCESTERSHIRE by 17 runs.

At Canterbury, August 6, 7, 8. HAMPSHIRE drew with KENT.

HAMPSHIRE v SUSSEX

At Southampton, August 9, 11, 12. Drawn. Hampshire 5 pts, Sussex 6 pts. Toss: Hampshire. Consistent, attractive batting saw Hampshire prosper on a flat pitch, as did Sussex on the second day after Connor had removed Green and Alikhan in a good opening spell. Parker and Imran put on 167 in 50 overs with Imran hitting two 6s and nine 4s in his first century of the season. Both sides did their best on the final day to achieve a positive result. Greenidge was again in form and Robin Smith thrived on the occasional bowlers, hitting a 6 and fifteen 4s. Sussex, set 261 to win in a minimum of 46 overs, which Nicholas's use of his spin bowlers, Maru and Cowley, increased to 60, were saved from defeat by their ninth-wicket pair, who survived the last eight overs.

Hampshire

C. G. Greenidge c Gould b Reeve	78	– c Parker b A. P. Wells	79
T. C. Middleton lbw b Reeve	30	– b le Roux	6
D. R. Turner c Alikhan b Imran	79		
R. A. Smith b Babington	30	– (3) not out	128
*M. C. J. Nicholas b Reeve	6	– (4) not out	13
T. M. Tremlett retired hurt	59		
N. G. Cowley c Parker b Babington	22		
M. D. Marshall not out	11		
L-b 4, n-b 1	5	B 5, l-b 11	16

1/72 2/121 3/176 4/188   (6 wkts dec.) 320   1/20 2/205   (2 wkts dec.) 242
5/254 6/320

R. J. Maru, †R. J. Parks and C. A. Connor did not bat.

Bonus points – Hampshire 4, Sussex 2 (Score at 100 overs: 304-5).

Bowling: *First Innings*—Imran 24–6–74–1; le Roux 15–3–42–0; Reeve 24–7–64–3; Babington 13.5–3–38–2; C. M. Wells 9–1–34–0; Green 10–2–33–0; Lenham 7–1–31–0. *Second Innings*—Imran 6–3–9–0; le Roux 4–0–15–1; Reeve 12–6–20–0; Green 13–2–39–0; C. M. Wells 7–4–7–0; Babington 4–0–15–0; Lenham 13–0–45–0; A. P. Wells 9–0–42–1; Alikhan 5–0–34–0.

Sussex

R. I. Alikhan c Parks b Connor	14	– b Cowley	14
A. M. Green c Nicholas b Connor	17	– st Parks b Maru	40
P. W. G. Parker c Middleton b Nicholas	83	– c and b Maru	36
Imran Khan b Maru	104	– c Parks b Marshall	31
C. M. Wells not out	56	– run out	41
A. P. Wells not out	13	– not out	25
*†I. J. Gould (did not bat)		– c Connor b Cowley	13
G. S. le Roux (did not bat)		– b Cowley	0
N. J. Lenham (did not bat)		– c Parks b Maru	4
D. A. Reeve (did not bat)		– not out	3
B 4, l-b 6, w 5	15	L-b 2	2

1/30 2/51 3/198 4/265   (4 wkts dec.) 302   1/51 2/59 3/120 4/138   (8 wkts) 209
5/171 6/197 7/197 8/202

A. M. Babington did not bat.

Bonus points – Sussex 4, Hampshire 1.

Bowling: *First Innings*—Marshall 16–3–43–0; Connor 18–8–34–2; Maru 30.1–6–87–1; Cowley 18–1–74–0; Nicholas 15–1–54–1. *Second Innings*—Connor 9–1–30–0; Marshall 13.5–4–26–1; Cowley 16–3–59–3; Maru 21–3–92–3.

Umpires: H. J. Rhodes and D. R. Shepherd.

At Lord's, August 16, 18, 19. HAMPSHIRE drew with MIDDLESEX.

HAMPSHIRE v WORCESTERSHIRE

At Bournemouth, August 20, 21, 22. Drawn. Hampshire 6 pts, Worcestershire 4 pts. Toss: Worcestershire. Terry, leading Hampshire in the absence through injury of Nicholas, batted with great determination to emerge from a bad spell. It took him 48 minutes to score 2 and 80 minutes to reach double figures, but he found his touch in the afternoon. When eighth out he had batted for 222 minutes. On the second day play was possible only before lunch; time enough, though, for Hampshire to make rapid inroads by taking eight Worcestershire wickets for 104, and the innings was soon ended after a delayed start on the third day. Hampshire did their best to win the match by racing to 91 in fourteen overs and setting a target of 209 in 43 overs, which became a possible 51, so quickly did they get through their overs. Hick, with 60 of his 81 in boundaries, and D'Oliveira put on 108 in 26 overs for the third wicket, but after their dismissal and that of Neale, Worcestershire concentrated on a draw with 71 wanted from ten overs and five wickets in hand.

Hampshire

C. G. Greenidge b McEwan	16	– c Hick b Newport	42
T. C. Middleton c Rhodes b Newport	24		
R. A. Smith c Neale b Newport	7	– run out	5
C. L. Smith c Rhodes b Newport	36	– not out	6
*V. P. Terry c Smith b McEwan	74	– (2) b McEwan	23
T. M. Tremlett c Rhodes b Newport	2	– not out	1
K. D. James c Newport b Pridgeon	9		
M. D. Marshall c Neale b Newport	22	– (5) c Weston b Pridgeon	0
†R. J. Parks c and b Pridgeon	20		
R. J. Maru not out	9		
C. A. Connor c Rhodes b Pridgeon	1		
L-b 8, w 3, n-b 6	17	L-b 14	14

1/25 2/41 3/59 4/97 5/107   237   1/71 2/81 3/85   (4 wkts dec.) 91
6/131 7/183 8/219 9/233   4/88

Bonus points – Hampshire 2, Worcestershire 4.

Bowling: *First Innings*—Pridgeon 21.2-9-33-3; Newport 26-3-74-5; McEwan 19-2-45-2; Weston 20-9-46-0; Patel 12-3-31-0. *Second Innings*—Pridgeon 4-0-15-1; Newport 6-0-41-1; McEwan 4-0-21-1.

Worcestershire

L. K. Smith c Parks b Marshall	2	– c Terry b Maru	2
T. S. Curtis b James	33	– c Greenidge b Marshall	9
S. M. McEwan c Terry b Marshall	7		
G. A. Hick c Parks b Marshall	0	– (3) c Greenidge b Maru	81
D. B. D'Oliveira c James b Connor	8	– (4) b Marshall	26
*P. A. Neale c Terry b Maru	6	– lbw b Marshall	2
D. N. Patel c Parks b James	28	– (5) not out	10
M. J. Weston not out	16	– (7) not out	17
†S. J. Rhodes c Parks b Maru	5		
P. J. Newport c Greenidge b Maru	2		
A. P. Pridgeon c Tremlett b Maru	4		
L-b 4, n-b 5	9	L-b 11, n-b 2	13

1/4 2/16 3/16 4/29 5/45   120   1/9 2/20 3/128   (5 wkts) 160
6/85 7/92 8/103 9/111   4/130 5/134

Bonus points – Hampshire 4.

Bowling: *First Innings*—Marshall 22-11-30-3; Connor 10-3-23-1; Maru 14-4-33-4; Tremlett 6-1-13-0; James 12-4-17-2. *Second Innings*—Marshall 12-3-32-3; Connor 6-3-22-0; Maru 17-8-49-2; Tremlett 9-1-34-0; James 2-0-12-0; C. L. Smith 1-1-0-0.

Umpires: M. J. Kitchen and K. J. Lyons.

HAMPSHIRE v YORKSHIRE

At Bournemouth, August 23, 25, 26. Drawn. Hampshire 4 pts, Yorkshire 3 pts. Toss: Yorkshire. Play was possible only on the first day, when there was cause for a double celebration for Marshall. After learning he had been appointed vice-captain of West Indies on their tour to Pakistan, he took his 1,000th first-class wicket when he bowled Moxon for 1. Heavy rain washed out play on the second and third days.

Yorkshire

M. D. Moxon b Marshall	1	P. J. Hartley c and b Maru	0
A. A. Metcalfe lbw b James	47	S. J. Dennis run out	11
S. N. Hartley c Terry b Maru	12	S. D. Fletcher c Greenidge b Connor	10
J. D. Love c Parks b James	31		
K. Sharp c Middleton b Marshall	15	B 1, l-b 5, w 3, n-b 7	16
*†D. L. Bairstow c Middleton b Marshall	9		
P. Carrick c Marshall b Tremlett	17	1/17 2/44 3/83 4/111 5/117	212
I. G. Swallow not out	43	6/127 7/159 8/164 9/187	

Bonus points – Yorkshire 2, Hampshire 4.

Bowling: Marshall 19–6–52–3; Connor 10.3–3–14–1; Tremlett 11–2–37–1; James 19–7–45–2; Maru 15–2–58–2.

Hampshire

C. G. Greenidge lbw b Dennis	0	T. M. Tremlett not out	10
T. C. Middleton run out	13		
C. L. Smith lbw b Dennis	7	L-b 1, n-b 1	2
R. A. Smith b Dennis	5		
*V. P. Terry not out	21	1/0 2/18 3/24 4/34 (4 wkts)	58

K. D. James, M. D. Marshall, †R. J. Parks, R. J. Maru and C. A. Connor did not bat.

Bonus point – Yorkshire 1.

Bowling: Dennis 8.4–5–19–3; P. J. Hartley 8–1–27–0; Fletcher 6–3–10–0; Carrick 2–1–1–0.

Umpires: M. J. Kitchen and K. J. Lyons.

At Northampton, August 27, 28, 29. HAMPSHIRE beat NORTHAMPTONSHIRE by 169 runs.

At Derby, August 30, September 1, 2. HAMPSHIRE beat DERBYSHIRE by nine wickets.

At Hove, September 10, 11, 12. HAMPSHIRE drew with SUSSEX.

HAMPSHIRE v LANCASHIRE

At Southampton, September 13, 15, 16. Abandoned.

KENT

Patron: HRH The Duke of Kent
President: F. S. Bird
Chairman: M. A. O'B. ffrench Blake
Secretary: D. B. Dalby
St Lawrence Ground, Old Dover Road,
Canterbury CT1 3NZ
(Telephone: 0227-456886)
Captain: C. S. Cowdrey
Director of Coaching: J. C. T. Page
Cricket Administrator: B. W. Luckhurst

At full strength, Kent could include seven Test men in their side, irrespective of which overseas player featured. Moreover, two of those Test players, Terry Alderman, operating exclusively in the Championship, and Graham Dilley, in a campaign restricted by England appearances, took 142 Championship wickets between them, Alderman falling two short of 100 wickets because of an arm injury which caused him to miss the last two matches. It was a cruel end to a season in which he had performed superbly. And yet despite their reservoir of talent and Alderman's success, Kent flattered only to deceive in the Britannic Assurance Championship. The nearest they came to winning their first trophy since 1978 was in the Benson and Hedges Cup, in which they suffered their third defeat in a final at Lord's in four seasons, albeit a defeat as narrow as in 1984 in the NatWest Bank Trophy final.

Once again Kent made an encouraging start. Essex were beaten early in the Championship; the John Player League season began with three successive victories; and Kent qualified for the quarter-finals of the Benson and Hedges Cup. As in 1985, however, lack of consistency told against them. Championship and Sunday League form was variable, and once the final at Lord's had been lost, all the hopes for the summer were destined to remain unfulfilled.

The evidence would point to inconsistent batting, and rightly so. Only Lancashire and Glamorgan registered fewer batting points than Kent, who had to wait until the first week in August before they gained the maximum four for the first time. Fittingly, it was the game during which the Duke of Kent, the club's Patron, opened the new £600,000 stand at the St Lawrence Ground at Canterbury. The match itself, against Leicestershire, will be remembered, not because it was the only time Kent gained 24 points in the season, but because it provided Championship cricket that was full of fine individual performances, was not contrived, and developed over three entertaining days to a marvellous climax. But only two players – Mark Benson, who shrugged off his knee problems so effectively that he played for England, and Chris Tavaré – scored 1,000 runs in Championship cricket. And while Neil Taylor and Simon Hinks went close, the captain, Christopher Cowdrey, did not reach 900. Nor did the combined runs of Graham Cowdrey and Derek Aslett, who shared the other main batting place. Indeed, no-one from Kent appeared in the top 50 in the national averages.

A glance at the leading 30 names in the bowling figures would reveal that Alderman was Kent's only representative, from which it may be deduced that all was not well in that department either. Once Dilley had shown that he was back to his best form, Test and international calls limited his availability; and without him, the support accorded to Alderman was frequently disappointing. Kevin Jarvis, who takes a well-deserved benefit in 1987, was first injured and then unwell, while Richard Ellison had the sort of bowling season, particularly in first-class cricket, that he will want to put behind him. Derek Underwood, who had a second benefit in 1986, also had, by his own high standards, a lean season. Eldine Baptiste, the other overseas player, played in all the limited-overs games, with particular success in the John Player League.

There appeared to be some consolation midway through the season when Alan Igglesden, a twenty-year-old fast bowler, was called into the side and took his chance eagerly. He was fast and he took wickets, but a badly pulled muscle in his side cut short his season just when he was beginning to attract attention. Igglesden could yet prove to be a bonus. The new wicket-keeper-batsman, Steven Marsh, already has. He refused to allow himself to be burdened by the pressure of following in the footsteps of Alan Knott. Wicket-keepers take time to settle into the first-class game and Marsh, appreciating that, turned in some impressive batting displays. He had spent the winter in South Africa, playing in Cape Town for the Avendale club, with which the former Kent and England cricketer, Bob Woolmer, is associated, and Woolmer's influence was not wasted on young Marsh. He scored nearly 900 runs in the Championship and in his first full season enjoyed the distinction of six dismissals in an innings to equal a Kent wicket-keeping record.

Since Kent last won an honour in 1978, there has been much talk of transition. Suddenly, it seems, the side has gone through several such periods since then and nothing has yet emerged to provide the success that is so keenly awaited. With such a strong playing staff the wait should not be long, but to bring the barren days of the 1980s to an end, the team must play more often to its full potential. – D.M.

KENT 1986

[*Bill Smith*]

Back row: C. S. Dale, D. J. M. Kelleher, R. P. Davis, T. R. Ward, S. C. Goldsmith, P. Farbrace. *Middle row*: B. W. Luckhurst (*cricket manager*), G. Popplewell (*physiotherapist*), S. G. Hinks, G. R. Cowdrey, S. A. Marsh, C. Penn, A. P. Igglesden, E. A. E. Baptiste, J. C. T. Page (*director of coaching*), C. Lewis (*scorer*). *Front row*: M. R. Benson, C. J. Tavaré, D. G. Aslett, D. L. Underwood, C. S. Cowdrey (*captain*), K. B. S. Jarvis, N. R. Taylor, G. R. Dilley, R. M. Ellison. *Inset*: T. M. Alderman.

KENT RESULTS

All first-class matches – Played 26: Won 5, Lost 7, Drawn 14.

County Championship matches – Played 24: Won 5, Lost 7, Drawn 12.

Bonus points – Batting 42, Bowling 75.

Competition placings – Britannic Assurance County Championship, 8th; NatWest Bank Trophy, 2nd round; Benson and Hedges Cup, finalists; John Player League, 6th equal.

BRITANNIC ASSURANCE CHAMPIONSHIP AVERAGES

BATTING

	Birthplace	M	I	NO	R	HI	Avge
‡M. R. Benson	Shoreham	20	34	1	1,229	123	37.24
‡C. J. Tavaré	Orpington	24	40	4	1,086	105	30.16
‡S. A. Marsh	Westminster	24	34	6	829	70	29.60
‡C. S. Cowdrey	Farnborough, Kent	21	32	3	820	100	28.27
‡N. R. Taylor	Orpington	24	40	5	981	88	28.02
‡S. G. Hinks	Northfleet	21	35	1	893	131	26.26
‡R. M. Ellison	Ashford, Kent	19	27	6	521	62*	24.80
‡D. G. Aslett	Dover	17	23	0	517	63	22.47
‡E. A. E. Baptiste ..	Liberta, Antigua	5	6	0	134	80	22.33
G. R. Cowdrey	Farnborough, Kent	15	24	1	353	75	15.34
‡G. R. Dilley	Dartford	13	20	6	179	30	12.78
‡D. L. Underwood ..	Bromley	23	26	5	243	29	11.57
‡T. M. Alderman ..	Perth, Australia	19	21	8	102	25	7.84
A. P. Igglesden ...	Farnborough, Kent	5	5	2	22	8*	7.33
‡K. B. S. Jarvis	Dartford	5	6	4	9	4*	4.50
C. Penn	Dover	5	6	1	11	9	2.20

Also batted: C. S. Dale (*Canterbury*) (2 matches) 0*, 2, 16; R. P. Davis (*Westbrook*) (1 match) 0*; T. R. Ward (*Farningham*) (1 match) 29, 12.

* *Signifies not out.* ‡ *Denotes county cap.*

The following played a total of five three-figure innings for Kent in County Championship matches: S. G. Hinks 2, M. R. Benson 1, C. S. Cowdrey 1, C. J. Tavaré 1.

BOWLING

	O	M	R	W	BB	Avge
T. M. Alderman ...	610	139	1,882	98	8-46	19.20
E. A. E. Baptiste ...	137	38	327	13	4-53	25.15
G. R. Dilley	350.3	51	1,156	44	6-57	26.27
C. Penn	100.5	18	369	14	5-65	26.35
D. L. Underwood ..	627.1	251	1,368	51	7-11	26.82
A. P. Igglesden	125	25	372	11	4-46	33.81
C. S. Cowdrey	258.2	43	886	26	5-69	34.07
R. M. Ellison	350.4	79	1,023	22	4-36	46.50
K. B. S. Jarvis	139.2	33	472	10	2-48	47.20

Also bowled: D. G. Aslett 35–3–187–4; M. R. Benson 7–0–55–2; G. R. Cowdrey 7–1–26–1; C. S. Dale 34–5–142–0; R. P. Davis 59.5–22–121–6; C. J. Tavaré 27–6–107–2; N. R. Taylor 76.3–8–252–3.

Wicket-keeper: S. A. Marsh 48 ct, 3 st.

Leading Fielders: C. S. Cowdrey 31; C. J. Tavaré 21; D. G. Aslett 17; S. G. Hinks 15.

At Leicester, April 26, 27, 28. KENT drew with LEICESTERSHIRE.

KENT v NORTHAMPTONSHIRE

At Canterbury, April 30, May 1, 2. Drawn. Kent 3 pts, Northamptonshire 6 pts. Toss: Kent. Kent had to struggle for runs on a soft pitch, and when Christopher Cowdrey was seventh out at 175 they looked in serious trouble. Then Ellison, who batted for 165 minutes for his half-century, and Marsh added 97 off 35 overs. Northamptonshire's reply was built upon a third-wicket partnership of 110 in 34 overs between Cook and Lamb, who made 72 in 123 minutes with one 6 and ten 4s. Cook reached his hundred in 306 minutes, with ten 4s, and when he declared 22 behind, his bowlers had Kent 19 for two at the close. Tavaré came to the rescue, reaching 100 out of 141 in 205 minutes with two 6s and ten 4s, and Graham Cowdrey – to 50 in 200 minutes – helped in a stand of 110 off 43 overs.

Kent

M. R. Benson c G. Cook b Mallender	10	– c and b Capel	15
S. G. Hinks c and b Harper	43	– b Mallender	8
C. J. Tavaré lbw b Capel	14	– (4) b N. G. B. Cook	105
N. R. Taylor b Griffiths	41	– (5) c Lamb b Harper	3
*C. S. Cowdrey c Storie b Harper	48	– (6) c Storie b Harper	10
G. R. Cowdrey lbw b N. G. B. Cook	0	– (7) c Mallender b Bailey	75
E. A. E. Baptiste lbw b N. G. B. Cook	3	– (8) b N. G. B. Cook	2
R. M. Ellison not out	62	– (9) not out	22
†S. A. Marsh not out	46	– (3) lbw b Griffiths	1
G. R. Dilley (did not bat)	–	not out	1
L-b 3, w 2	5	B 1, l-b 5, w 1, n-b 1	8

1/27 2/56 3/86 4/138   (7 wkts dec.) 272   1/18 2/19 3/36   (8 wkts dec.) 250
5/139 6/143 7/175   4/45 5/69 6/179
     7/183 8/249

D. L. Underwood did not bat.

Bonus points – Kent 2, Northamptonshire 3 (Score at 100 overs: 227-7).

Bowling: *First Innings*—Mallender 25–5–69–1; Griffiths 17–3–58–1; Capel 19–7–42–1; Harper 28–7–70–2; N. G. B. Cook 24–11–30–2. *Second Innings*—Mallender 17–3–38–1; Griffiths 18–5–45–1; N. G. B. Cook 24–8–51–2; Harper 27–13–39–2; Capel 13–2–43–1; Boyd-Moss 5–0–20–0; Bailey 3–1–8–1; Lamb 2–2–0–0.

Northamptonshire

*G. Cook not out	109	R. J. Bailey not out 30
A. C. Storie c Dilley b C. S. Cowdrey	26	L-b 1, w 3, n-b 5 9
R. J. Boyd-Moss c Tavaré b Dilley	4	
A. J. Lamb c G. R. Cowdrey b Dilley	72	1/83 2/89 3/199 (3 wkts dec.) 250

D. J. Capel, R. A. Harper, †D. Ripley, N. G. B. Cook, N. A. Mallender and B. J. Griffiths did not bat.

Bonus points – Northamptonshire 3, Kent 1.

Bowling: Dilley 14–2–38–2; Ellison 16–5–43–0; Baptiste 24–7–67–0; Underwood 21–6–56–0; C. S. Cowdrey 12–3–29–1; Taylor 7–0–16–0.

Umpires: C. Cook and K. E. Palmer.

At Chelmsford, May 7, 8, 9. KENT beat ESSEX by 25 runs.

At Canterbury, May 21, 22, 23. KENT drew with INDIANS (See Indian tour section).

KENT v WORCESTERSHIRE

At Tunbridge Wells, May 31, June 2, 3. Drawn. Kent 2 pts. Toss: Worcestershire. The weather, which was to wreak havoc with the Festival Week, delayed a start until 12.15 on the second day, whereupon Kent quickly lost Benson. Hinks, however, played superbly as he and Tavaré added 120 off 39 overs, but with his dismissal the tempo slowed. Tavaré batted for four and a half hours for his unbeaten 75. No play was possible on the third day.

Kent

M. R. Benson b Radford	....	1
S. G. Hinks c Curtis b Pridgeon	......	86
*C. J. Tavaré not out	....	75
N. R. Taylor not out	....	37
L-b 3, w 2, n-b 4	....	9

1/3 2/123   (2 wkts) 208

G. R. Cowdrey, D. G. Aslett, R. M. Ellison, †S. A. Marsh, G. R. Dilley, T. M. Alderman and D. L. Underwood did not bat.

Bonus points – Kent 2.

Bowling: Radford 24–6–75–1; Pridgeon 17–7–20–1; Newport 12–1–42–0; Patel 11–3–28–0; Illingworth 21–7–40–0.

Worcestershire

T. S. Curtis, D. B. D'Oliveira, D. M. Smith, G. A. Hick, *P. A. Neale, D. N. Patel, †S. J. Rhodes, P. J. Newport, N. V. Radford, R. K. Illingworth and A. P. Pridgeon.

Umpires: J. H. Hampshire and N. T. Plews.

KENT v SUSSEX

At Tunbridge Wells, June 4, 5, 6. Drawn. Kent 5 pts, Sussex 4 pts. Toss: Kent. Parker, with 66 not out in 117, held Sussex together in the 2 hours 40 minutes' play on the opening day. A full day's play on the Thursday began with Alderman continuing to cause problems for the batsman, and when Kent batted, a bright half-century in 48 balls by Marsh (two 6s, seven 4s) led to Cowdrey's declaration 68 in arrears. On the final day, the start of which was delayed by rain and bad light, Sussex set Kent a target of 242 in 160 minutes, but another stoppage for bad light upset those calculations. During the Week rain and bad light accounted for nearly half the playing time.

Sussex

N. J. Lenham c Marsh b Alderman	....	4	– b Underwood	 33
A. M. Green c Hinks b Alderman	....	0	– b Underwood	 10
P. W. G. Parker c Taylor b Alderman	....	79	– c Alderman b Underwood	 36
A. P. Wells c Marsh b Jarvis	....	35	– c Tavaré b Underwood	 0
D. A. Reeve c C. S. Cowdrey b Jarvis	....	5		
C. M. Wells c Hinks b Alderman	....	29	– (5) not out	 43
D. K. Standing c Marsh b Alderman	....	2		
*†J. J. Gould not out	....	60	– (6) c C. S. Cowdrey b Taylor	... 36
G. S. le Roux retired hurt	....	5		
A. C. S. Pigott c C. S. Cowdrey b Alderman	...	16		
A. M. Bredin c Tavaré b Underwood	....	2		
L-b 2, w 2, n-b 5	....	9	B 8, l-b 2, w 3, n-b 2	 15

1/4 2/7 3/106 4/117 5/145   246   1/24 2/75 3/75   (5 wkts dec.) 173
6/148 7/169 8/243 9/246   4/104 5/173

Bonus points – Sussex 2, Kent 4.

Bowling: *First Innings*—Jarvis 22–7–61–2; Alderman 20–2–70–6; Penn 12–1–55–0; Underwood 29.3–9–58–1; Taylor 1–1–0–0. *Second Innings*—Alderman 7–0–18–0; Jarvis 2–1–2–0; Underwood 21–5–59–4; Taylor 18.3–1–73–1; C. S. Cowdrey 2–0–11–0.

Kent

M. R. Benson c Standing b Reeve	31	– lbw b Reeve	20
S. G. Hinks b Pigott	15	– c Standing b Pigott	8
C. J. Tavaré b Reeve	6	– not out	40
N. R. Taylor c Green b Reeve	3	– not out	6
*C. S. Cowdrey c Parker b Bredin	23		
G. R. Cowdrey not out	33		
C. Penn c sub b Bredin	9		
†S. A. Marsh not out	52		
L-b 5, n-b 1	6	B 1, w 1, n-b 1	3

1/21 2/42 3/57 4/68   (6 wkts dec.) 178   1/14 2/50   (2 wkts) 77
5/90 6/104

T. M. Alderman, D. L. Underwood and K. B. S. Jarvis did not bat.

Bonus points – Kent 1, Sussex 2.

Bowling: *First Innings*—Pigott 13–2–38–1; Reeve 22–9–34–3; C. M. Wells 8.2–3–11–0; Bredin 18–4–88–2; Lenham 1–0–2–0. *Second Innings*—Pigott 5–0–23–1; Reeve 9–2–18–1; Standing 12–6–17–0; Bredin 7–3–17–0; A. P. Wells 1–0–1–0; Green 1–1–0–0; Parker 1–1–0–0.

Umpires: J. H. Hampshire and N. T. Plews.

At Oxford, June 7, 9, 10. KENT drew with OXFORD UNIVERSITY.

At Bath, June 14, 16, 17. KENT lost to SOMERSET by an innings and 24 runs.

At Gloucester, June 18, 19, 20. KENT lost to GLOUCESTERSHIRE by four wickets.

At Southampton, June 21, 23, 24. KENT beat HAMPSHIRE by five wickets.

KENT v GLAMORGAN

At Maidstone, June 28, 30, July 1. Drawn. Kent 7 pts, Glamorgan 7 pts. Toss: Kent. Glamorgan were given a fine start by Pauline and Morris, whose opening stand occupied 42 overs; and later Morris, who hit twelve 4s in 269 minutes, was given encouraging support by Maynard, who stroked nine 4s in a 94-minute half-century. However, Alderman struck back with five wickets for 30 in 10.1 overs as seven Glamorgan batsmen went for 41 runs. Only a splendid 93 by Tavaré, who hit two 6s and eleven 4s in 182 minutes, enabled Kent to go ahead by 5 runs on the second afternoon. Morris, with a century in 256 minutes, including thirteen 4s, dominated Glamorgan's batting on the final day, when Kent were set 260 to win in 150 minutes. Without Thomas, and with Barwick handicapped by injury, Glamorgan fought hard for victory after Ontong had taken three for 11 in twenty balls, but Taylor, who had raced to 50 in 55 minutes, adopted a defensive role to deny them.

Glamorgan

D. B. Pauline lbw b Dilley	55	– lbw b Alderman	7
H. Morris c Marsh b Alderman	92	– not out	128
G. C. Holmes c Tavaré b Dilley	0	– c Hinks b Underwood	42
Younis Ahmed c Dilley b C. S. Cowdrey	15	– c Marsh b Jarvis	20
M. P. Maynard b Underwood	52	– c C. S. Cowdrey b Taylor	12
*R. C. Ontong c C. S. Cowdrey b Alderman	0	– c Taylor b Underwood	26
J. G. Thomas c and b Dilley	17		
†T. Davies c Tavaré b Alderman	0	– (7) lbw b G. R. Cowdrey	12
J. Derrick c Hinks b Alderman	8	– (8) not out	3
S. R. Barwick c Marsh b Alderman	4		
D. J. Hickey not out	9		
B 8, l-b 4, w 6, n-b 7	25	B 1, l-b 5, n-b 8	14
	277	(6 wkts dec.)	264

1/104 2/104 3/143 4/236 5/236
6/244 7/244 8/263 9/263

1/9 2/99 3/151
4/168 5/217 6/256

Bonus points – Glamorgan 3, Kent 4.

Bowling: *First Innings*—Dilley 21-2-66-3; Alderman 26.1-9-57-5; Jarvis 19-3-71-0; C. S. Cowdrey 15-5-35-1; Underwood 14-6-23-1; Taylor 3-0-13-0. *Second Innings*—Dilley 6-2-16-0; Alderman 12-3-31-1; Underwood 24-11-36-2; Jarvis 10.2-1-31-1; Taylor 30-6-84-1; C. S. Cowdrey 11-0-43-0; G. R. Cowdrey 4-1-17-1.

Kent

M. R. Benson c Thomas b Holmes	46	– c Barwick b Ontong	37
S. G. Hinks c Davies b Thomas	22	– c Holmes b Hickey	0
†S. A. Marsh c Davies b Hickey	55	– (7) lbw b Holmes	0
C. J. Tavaré c Maynard b Hickey	93	– (3) b Hickey	2
N. R. Taylor c Maynard b Ontong	19	– (4) not out	82
*C. S. Cowdrey c Davies b Hickey	2	– (5) b Ontong	5
G. R. Cowdrey b Ontong	2	– (6) st Davies b Ontong	7
G. R. Dilley c Davies b Ontong	0	– not out	4
D. L. Underwood c Davies b Thomas	1		
T. M. Alderman b Thomas	13		
K. B. S. Jarvis not out	1		
B 4, l-b 7, w 5, n-b 12	28	L-b 2, n-b 4	6
	282	(6 wkts)	143

1/34 2/122 3/146 4/184 5/187
6/200 7/200 8/207 9/247

1/1 2/15 3/87 4/93
5/111 6/114

Bonus points – Kent 3, Glamorgan 4.

Bowling: *First Innings*—Thomas 25-8-63-3; Hickey 19.5-1-87-3; Ontong 26-9-66-3; Barwick 11-2-26-0; Holmes 10-0-27-1; Derrick 2-1-2-0. *Second Innings*—Hickey 9-1-39-2; Barwick 10-1-46-0; Ontong 16-7-27-3; Holmes 8-0-29-1.

Umpires: J. Birkenshaw and D. G. L. Evans.

KENT v SOMERSET

At Maidstone, July 2, 3, 4. Drawn. Kent 5 pts, Somerset 6 pts. Toss: Somerset. Somerset's tailenders, led by Dredge, lifted them from 154 for seven after Igglesden, summoned on the morning of the match to make his début when Jarvis was declared unfit, took two for 5 in fifteen balls. Kent, 58 for three overnight, were all out soon after lunch on the second day. Harden retrieved a poor start by Somerset and went on to his first Championship century in 174 minutes with one 6 and fourteen 4s, he and Marks adding 123 in 30 overs. Penn had career-best bowling figures of five for 65. Roebuck's declaration left Kent all of the final day to score 367 to win, and they were on target as Hinks and Tavaré put on 165 in 54 overs. Hinks's hundred, in 238 minutes, contained one 6 and fourteen 4s. Kent needed 103 off the last twenty overs, but when they lost three wickets for 10 runs in four overs the chase was abandoned.

Somerset

N. A. Felton c Alderman b Igglesden	30	– c Tavaré b Alderman	6
*P. M. Roebuck c Marsh b Penn	5	– c sub b Alderman	5
R. J. Harden c G. R. Cowdrey b C. S. Cowdrey	20	– c Aslett b Penn	102
I. V. A. Richards c C. S. Cowdrey b Underwood	29	– c Aslett b Penn	31
B. C. Rose b Igglesden	5	– c and b Penn	5
V. J. Marks c Marsh b Penn	24	– c Aslett b Penn	61
J. C. M. Atkinson c Penn b C. S. Cowdrey	13	– c Tavaré b Underwood	16
†T. Gard c Alderman b C. S. Cowdrey	23	– (9) b Penn	10
C. H. Dredge c C. S. Cowdrey b Alderman	40	– (8) c Hinks b Underwood	1
J. Garner not out	20	– not out	26
N. S. Taylor c Hinks b Underwood	13	– not out	0
B 4, l-b 15, w 7, n-b 1	27	L-b 4, w 1, n-b 4	9

1/10 2/61 3/96 4/104 5/113   249   1/10 2/22 3/72   (9 wkts dec.) 272
6/132 7/154 8/210 9/218   4/82 5/205 6/229
                                      7/230 8/235 9/254

Bonus points – Somerset 2, Kent 4.

Bowling: First Innings—Alderman 29–10–76–1; Penn 17–7–30–2; Igglesden 20–3–59–2; C. S. Cowdrey 21–5–55–3; Underwood 5.3–2–10–2. *Second Innings*—Alderman 14–3–58–2; Igglesden 14–4–31–0; Penn 14–1–65–5; C. S. Cowdrey 8–0–34–0; Underwood 17–4–80–2.

Kent

D. G. Aslett b Taylor	21	– lbw b Garner	13
S. G. Hinks c Dredge b Garner	21	– c Gard b Taylor	103
C. J. Tavaré c Gard b Garner	0	– c Gard b Dredge	80
N. R. Taylor c Richards b Taylor	50	– c Gard b Dredge	60
†S. A. Marsh c Harden b Dredge	11	– (7) c Marks b Dredge	1
*C. S. Cowdrey c Richards b Garner	1	– (5) not out	49
G. R. Cowdrey lbw b Garner	0	– (6) run out	2
C. Penn c Richards b Dredge	0	– not out	2
D. L. Underwood c Harden b Marks	25		
T. M. Alderman c Rose b Marks	8		
A. P. Igglesden not out	5		
L-b 4, n-b 9	13	B 5, l-b 8, n-b 1	14

1/31 2/32 3/55 4/91 5/92   155   1/18 2/183 3/225   (6 wkts) 324
6/98 7/100 8/131 9/148   4/302 5/304 6/312

Bonus points – Kent 1, Somerset 4.

Bowling: First Innings—Garner 17–2–56–4; Taylor 10–2–38–2; Dredge 14–4–35–2; Marks 10.1–4–15–2; Richards 2–0–7–0. *Second Innings*—Garner 20–4–52–1; Taylor 22–3–88–1; Atkinson 4–0–18–0; Dredge 20–1–51–3; Richards 7–4–7–0; Marks 25.5–3–87–0; Harden 4–0–8–0.

Umpires: J. Birkenshaw and D. G. L. Evans.

At Derby, July 5, 7, 8. KENT lost to DERBYSHIRE by 28 runs.

At The Oval, July 16, 17, 18. KENT lost to SURREY by 234 runs.

KENT v LANCASHIRE

At Canterbury, July 19, 21, 22. Kent won by eight wickets. Kent 21 pts, Lancashire 5 pts. Toss: Kent. Bowlers were always on top until the final morning, when Lancashire could bowl the injured Patterson for only five overs and Tavaré took control. Dilley, who had a tremendous match, always had Lancashire struggling on the opening day and Kent fared little better against the pace of Patterson and Allott, reaching 123 for seven by the close. Ellison linked up with Dilley to dismiss Lancashire cheaply again with both O'Shaughnessy and Fairbrother batting lower in the order, and with runners, because of injury. Stoppages for bad light cut 32 overs from the second day, which ended with Kent, needing 171 to win, 42 for the loss of Hinks. Within an over of lunch on the final day they were comfortable winners, Tavaré having dominated an unbroken stand of 123 in 34 overs with Taylor, his 159-minute innings including fourteen 4s.

Lancashire

G. D. Mendis c Marsh b Igglesden	47	– c Marsh b Ellison	44
*G. Fowler c Marsh b Alderman	3	– b Ellison	21
M. R. Chadwick b Dilley	1	– c Hinks b Igglesden	12
N. H. Fairbrother b Dilley	36	– (8) c Ellison b Alderman	7
J. Abrahams b Dilley	4	– (4) lbw b Ellison	4
S. J. O'Shaughnessy lbw b Dilley	0	– (7) lbw b Dilley	5
†C. Maynard c Marsh b Alderman	6	– (5) c Marsh b Ellison	3
M. Watkinson b Dilley	6	– (6) lbw b Dilley	25
P. J. W. Allott not out	35	– c Igglesden b Dilley	5
I. Folley c Igglesden b Dilley	9	– c Cowdrey b Dilley	13
B. P. Patterson b Ellison	4	– not out	12
B 1, l-b 11, n-b 5	17	L-b 8, w 1, n-b 5	14

1/8 2/27 3/82 4/95 5/98   162   1/69 2/70 3/85 4/95 5/95   165
6/110 7/110 8/112 9/141   6/125 7/132 8/139 9/141

Bonus points – Lancashire 1, Kent 4.

Bowling: *First Innings*—Dilley 22–4–57–6; Alderman 24–7–59–2; Igglesden 10–1–27–1; Ellison 7.4–4–7–1. *Second Innings*—Dilley 17.4–3–53–4; Alderman 14–5–36–1; Ellison 14–4–36–4; Igglesden 11–2–32–1.

Kent

M. R. Benson c Allott b Patterson	16	– b Allott	37
S. G. Hinks c Maynard b Allott	4	– c Watkinson b Patterson	0
C. J. Tavaré c Maynard b O'Shaughnessy	37	– not out	90
N. R. Taylor c Maynard b O'Shaughnessy	16	– not out	36
D. G. Aslett c Watkinson b Allott	11		
*C. S. Cowdrey c Watkinson b Allott	19		
R. M. Ellison lbw b Patterson	3		
†S. A. Marsh lbw b Allott	6		
G. R. Dilley c Chadwick b Patterson	7		
T. M. Alderman not out	15		
A. P. Igglesden b Patterson	2		
L-b 9, w 1, n-b 11	21	N-b 8	8

1/12 2/27 3/78 4/85 5/114   157   1/8 2/48   (2 wkts) 171
6/121 7/123 8/135 9/139

Bonus points – Kent 1, Lancashire 4.

Bowling: *First Innings*—Patterson 17.4–3–43–4; Allott 18–5–42–4; Watkinson 10–2–35–0; O'Shaughnessy 9–2–28–2. *Second Innings*—Patterson 12–1–41–1; Allott 17–4–50–1; Watkinson 6–1–32–0; Folley 8–3–19–0; Abrahams 5–1–29–0.

Umpires: C. Cook and D. G. L. Evans.

At Scarborough, July 23, 24, 25. KENT drew with YORKSHIRE.

KENT v LEICESTERSHIRE

At Canterbury, August 2, 4, 5. Kent won by 5 runs. Kent 24 pts, Leicestershire 4 pts. Toss: Kent. One of the best Championship finishes rounded off a thoroughly absorbing three days of cricket. Consistent batting, with Cowdrey, the captain, returning to form and reaching 50 in 78 minutes, enabled Kent to declare on the Saturday evening and benefit immediately by having Leicestershire 21 for three at the close. Leicestershire's problems continued on the second day as Alderman took four for 13 in his first six overs, but DeFreitas brought them back into the game. First he rescued the innings with a maiden first-class century, scoring 100 out of 141 in 106 minutes with seventeen 4s and adding 149 off 34 overs with Whitticase. Then, following the example of Alderman as regards line and length, he took six wickets as Kent were shot out for 87. Before the day was over, Alderman had Leicestershire in trouble again with a spell of three for 5 in fifteen balls. Leicestershire began the final day needing 179 to win with seven wickets in hand, and although Underwood upset their middle-order batting, Willey stood firm. His century, in 234 minutes with thirteen 4s, kept his side in the hunt, but Alderman dismissed him and wrapped up the innings to give himself fourteen wickets for the match and Kent a narrow and exciting victory.

Kent

M. R. Benson b DeFreitas	29	– c Whitticase b Agnew	0
S. G. Hinks b DeFreitas	34	– c sub b DeFreitas	8
C. J. Tavaré c Butcher b DeFreitas	35	– b DeFreitas	27
N. R. Taylor c and b Taylor	40	– c Whitticase b DeFreitas	4
D. G. Aslett b Agnew	4	– b Agnew	16
*C. S. Cowdrey c Gower b Ferris	60	– lbw b Ferris	7
R. M. Ellison c and b Ferris	26	– lbw b DeFreitas	17
†S. A. Marsh not out	52	– b Ferris	2
G. R. Dilley b Ferris	0	– not out	3
D. L. Underwood not out	26	– b DeFreitas	0
T. M. Alderman (did not bat)		– b DeFreitas	0
L-b 14, w 1, n-b 8	23	L-b 1, n-b 2	3

1/62 2/75 3/125 4/141　　　(8 wkts dec.) 329　　1/0 2/24 3/32 4/44 5/64　　87
5/185 6/250 7/251 8/253　　　　　　　　　　　　　6/66 7/74 8/87 9/87

Bonus points – Kent 4, Leicestershire 3.

Bowling: First Innings—Agnew 27–6–79–1; Taylor 15–2–55–1; DeFreitas 21–4–87–3; Ferris 20–4–58–3; Willey 17–5–36–0. *Second Innings*—Agnew 13–2–46–2; DeFreitas 10.4–0–21–6; Willey 1–1–0–0; Ferris 6–2–19–2.

Leicestershire

I. P. Butcher b Dilley	0	– (2) lbw b Alderman	1
J. C. Balderstone c Cowdrey b Alderman	14	– (1) lbw b Alderman	11
R. A. Cobb b Dilley	0	– lbw b Alderman	1
J. P. Agnew b Alderman	9	– (9) not out	27
*D. I. Gower b Alderman	6	– (4) c Marsh b Alderman	29
P. Willey c Aslett b Alderman	10	– (5) c Cowdrey b Alderman	104
T. J. Boon lbw b Alderman	0	– (6) c Cowdrey b Underwood	1
†P. Whitticase not out	41	– (7) b Underwood	1
P. A. J. DeFreitas c Aslett b Alderman	106	– (8) b Underwood	16
L. B. Taylor lbw b Alderman	0	– c Alderman b Dilley	10
G. J. F. Ferris b Alderman	6	– lbw b Alderman	1
L-b 2, w 1, n-b 4	7	B 1, l-b 5, n-b 4	10

1/1 2/1 3/10 4/21 5/40　　　　199　　1/6 2/12 3/19 4/63 5/96　　212
6/40 7/43 8/192 9/192　　　　　　　　6/106 7/136 8/193 9/209

Bonus points – Leicestershire 1, Kent 4.

Bowling: *First Innings*—Dilley 18-4-54-2; Alderman 21-5-70-8; Underwood 9-4-12-0; Ellison 8-1-56-0; Cowdrey 2-0-5-0. *Second Innings*—Alderman 32-8-74-6; Dilley 21-2-59-1; Ellison 13-3-46-0; Underwood 19-9-27-3.

Umpires: J. A. Jameson and D. R. Shepherd.

KENT v HAMPSHIRE

At Canterbury, August 6, 7, 8. Drawn. Kent 8 pts, Hampshire 4 pts. Toss: Hampshire. Cowdrey, with a spell of three for 0 in ten balls in a career-best bowling performance, set back Hampshire. They were rescued by Cowley, who batted for 187 minutes and hit eight 4s. Kent, with three of their fast bowlers out with injuries, lost a fourth when Igglesden tore a muscle in his side after half an hour, and were further handicapped when Underwood could not take the field after tea because of a muscle spasm in his neck. Consequently, the final session of the day saw Kent's cricket administrator, 47-year-old Brian Luckhurst, and his twenty-year-old son, Tim, fielding as substitutes. Benson and Hinks gave Kent a wonderful start by putting on 191 off 54 overs, the best first-wicket stand for the county in the Championship for thirteen seasons. Hinks's career-best 131 was made in 257 minutes with one 6 and eighteen 4s, and when Cowdrey declared on the final morning Hampshire had to score 197 to avoid an innings defeat. Underwood, his neck encased in a special collar, toiled for 23 overs in a bid to open the way for victory but Smith made sure of a draw, scoring 50 out of 75 in 110 minutes with eight 4s.

Hampshire

C. G. Greenidge b Baptiste	26	– c Marsh b Baptiste 17
T. C. Middleton b Baptiste	23	– b Underwood 49
D. R. Turner c Marsh b Baptiste	12	– b Taylor 33
R. A. Smith b Underwood	39	– not out 55
*M. C. J. Nicholas b Cowdrey	4	– c Cowdrey b Aslett 15
K. D. James b Cowdrey	0	– c and b Tavaré 0
M. D. Marshall c Marsh b Cowdrey	0	
N. G. Cowley not out	78	
T. M. Tremlett b Cowdrey	20	– (7) not out 5
†R. J. Parks lbw b Cowdrey	13	
C. A. Connor c Cowdrey b Ellison	0	
L-b 5, w 5, n-b 9	19	B 4, w 1, n-b 2 7

1/48 2/72 3/73 4/84 5/84	234	1/27 2/98 3/116 (5 wkts) 181
6/84 7/141 8/211 9/233		4/155 5/156

Bonus points – Hampshire 2, Kent 4.

Bowling: *First Innings*—Igglesden 5-0-20-0; Ellison 23-5-58-1; Cowdrey 29-8-69-5; Baptiste 25-5-70-3; Underwood 8-5-9-1; Taylor 1-0-3-0. *Second Innings*—Baptiste 16-2-41-1; Cowdrey 12-3-48-0; Ellison 4-0-12-0; Underwood 23-13-32-1; Taylor 3-0-14-1; Aslett 9-1-27-1; Tavaré 5-2-3-1.

Kent

M. R. Benson b Cowley	94	R. M. Ellison not out 44
S. G. Hinks b Marshall	131	†S. A. Marsh c Smith b James 30
C. J. Tavaré c Parks b Cowley	14	L-b 14, n-b 6 20
N. R. Taylor c Marshall b Tremlett	42	
D. G. Aslett lbw b Marshall	0	1/191 2/224 3/248 (8 wkts dec.) 431
*C. S. Cowdrey c and b Tremlett	38	4/248 5/324 6/339
E. A. E. Baptiste b Connor	18	7/368 8/431

D. L. Underwood and A. P. Igglesden did not bat.

Bonus points – Kent 4, Hampshire 2 (Score at 100 overs: 340-6).

Bowling: Marshall 26-8-34-2; Connor 28.5-1-138-1; James 19.5-2-78-1; Tremlett 22-1-88-2; Cowley 25.1-3-70-2; Nicholas 2-1-9-0.

Umpires: J. A. Jameson and D. R. Shepherd.

At Birmingham, August 9, 11, 12. KENT drew with WARWICKSHIRE.

At Hove, August 16, 18, 19. KENT lost to SUSSEX by six wickets.

KENT v SURREY

At Dartford, August 20, 21, 22. Drawn. Kent 6 pts, Surrey 6 pts. Toss: Kent. An opening stand of 212 off 64 overs gave Kent early control as Benson hit twenty 4s in an innings of 246 minutes, but Feltham temporarily put the brakes on their progress with a spell of three for 10 in seventeen balls. When Kent declared seven overs into the second morning, Surrey made a dismal start as Alderman took three wickets for 31 in 5.5 overs. They recovered through Stewart and Lynch, who added 96 off 24 overs, Lynch going on to 100 in 210 minutes with a 6 and fourteen 4s. Surrey declared that evening, and Kent, taking the chance of quick runs on the final morning, left them to score 294 in a minimum of 57 overs. Although rain intervened after lunch, reducing the overs available to a minimum of 28, Surrey responded to an opening attack of Tavaré and Benson by thrashing 132 from thirteen overs, Lynch and Stewart scoring 115 off ten. Stewart reached 100 out of 150 in 70 minutes with seven 6s and six 4s, but at the same time Kent were picking up valuable wickets and ultimately both sides had to be content with a draw.

Kent

M. R. Benson b Feltham	123	– c Clinton b Feltham	22
N. R. Taylor lbw b Feltham	88	– c Clinton b Lynch	65
C. J. Tavaré b Pocock	32	– c Jesty b Thomas	5
S. G. Hinks c Clarke b Feltham	2	– b Medlycott	0
D. G. Aslett b Thomas	17	– c Jesty b Richards	57
*C. S. Cowdrey st Richards b Pocock	10	– not out	24
R. M. Ellison c Lynch b Clarke	32	– not out	26
†S. A. Marsh b Clarke	47		
C. S. Dale not out	0		
B 15, l-b 2, n-b 11	28	B 8, l-b 4, w 1, n-b 2	15

1/212 2/232 3/234 4/269   (8 wkts dec.) 379   1/34 2/54 3/57   (5 wkts dec.) 214
5/291 6/303 7/372 8/379   4/146 5/176

D. L. Underwood and T. M. Alderman did not bat.

Bonus points – Kent 4, Surrey 2 (Score at 100 overs: 311-6).

Bowling: *First Innings*—Clarke 28.1–16–37–2; Feltham 24–3–110–3; Pocock 26–7–61–2; Thomas 17–4–65–1; Butcher 8–2–27–0; Medlycott 14–3–62–0. *Second Innings*—Clarke 6–0–14–0; Feltham 5–0–36–1; Thomas 8–1–15–1; Medlycott 8–1–35–1; Pocock 4–0–20–0; Lynch 5–0–48–1; Richards 5–0–34–1.

Surrey

A. R. Butcher c Marsh b Alderman	8	– c Ellison b Benson	12
G. S. Clinton lbw b Alderman	23	– st Marsh b Tavaré	1
A. J. Stewart b Ellison	61	– (4) c Aslett b Benson	105
T. E. Jesty c Tavaré b Alderman	11	– (5) st Marsh b Underwood	5
M. A. Lynch not out	119	– (3) b Alderman	47
†C. J. Richards c Ellison b Underwood	21	– c Tavaré b Underwood	4
D. J. Thomas not out	47	– run out	0
M. A. Feltham (did not bat)		– not out	25
K. T. Medlycott (did not bat)		– lbw b Alderman	9
S. T. Clarke (did not bat)		– not out	32
L-b 5, n-b 5	10	B 2, l-b 1, n-b 2	5

1/22 2/41 3/53 4/149   (5 wkts dec.) 300   1/9 2/33 3/148 4/158   (8 wkts) 245
5/204   5/164 6/164 7/189 8/201

*P. I. Pocock did not bat.

Bonus points – Surrey 4, Kent 2.

Bowling: *First Innings*—Alderman 17–1–89–3; Ellison 15–1–61–1; Underwood 22.4–6–70–1; Dale 13–2–59–0; Cowdrey 4–0–16–0. *Second Innings*—Tavaré 6–0–64–1; Benson 7–0–55–2; Dale 3–0–21–0; Underwood 8–1–37–2; Alderman 10–0–63–2; Ellison 1–0–2–0.

Umpires: B. Dudleston and D. O. Oslear.

At Cardiff, August 23, 25, 26. KENT drew with GLAMORGAN.

At Nottingham, August 27, 28, 29. KENT lost to NOTTINGHAMSHIRE by 132 runs.

KENT v ESSEX

At Folkestone, August 30, September 1, 2. Essex won by 23 runs. Essex 22 pts, Kent 6 pts. Toss: Essex. A masterly innings by Gooch, with fine support from Fletcher, kept Essex going against the spin of Underwood, and after Christopher Cowdrey had broken through with a spell of four for 4 in eighteen balls, Pringle steered them to respectability, batting in all for 238 minutes and hitting four 6s and two 4s. Kent struggled initially against the pace of Foster and then the spin of Acfield and Childs on a cold second day, but the Kent captain's unbeaten 45 and the loss of 65 minutes for bad light arrested Essex's progress. On the third day, having gathered in the last three Kent wickets, Essex gathered quick runs to set Kent 184 to win in a minimum of 47 overs. They started well and were 47 without loss at tea, but in the final session they had no answer to the left-arm spin of Childs, who had a staunch ally in Acfield on a pitch with little sympathy for batsmen.

Essex

*G. A. Gooch lbw b Underwood	74	– b Ellison	8
J. P. Stephenson c Dilley b Underwood	8	– not out	71
P. J. Prichard c C. S. Cowdrey b Underwood	6	– lbw b Dilley	3
B. R. Hardie b Underwood	0	– c Dilley b Aslett	36
K. W. R. Fletcher c Tavaré c C. S. Cowdrey	47	– not out	5
D. R. Pringle c C. S. Cowdrey b Dilley	97		
†D. E. East c Aslett b C. S. Cowdrey	8		
N. A. Foster c and b C. S. Cowdrey	0		
J. K. Lever c Taylor b C. S. Cowdrey	1		
J. H. Childs run out	15		
D. L. Acfield not out	6		
L-b 9, w 1, n-b 8	18	L-b 2, n-b 2	4

1/46 2/54 3/54 4/114 5/176   280   1/9 2/14 3/97   (3 wkts dec.) 127
6/185 7/186 8/190 9/247

Bonus points – Essex 2, Kent 4 (Score at 100 overs: 248-9).

Bowling: *First Innings*—Dilley 20.2–4–57–1; Alderman 9–2–15–0; Underwood 40–13–96–4; C. S. Cowdrey 12–3–24–4; Ellison 23–6–63–0; Tavaré 3–0–7–0; G. R. Cowdrey 3–0–9–0. *Second Innings*—Dilley 6–1–21–1; Ellison 8–0–24–1; Aslett 6–0–46–1; Underwood 8–2–30–0; C. S. Cowdrey 0.2–0–4–0.

Kent

M. R. Benson c East b Foster	12	– b Childs	25
N. R. Taylor c and b Foster	27	– c Fletcher b Lever	20
C. J. Tavaré c Fletcher b Acfield	17	– c Prichard b Acfield	1
D. G. Aslett b Foster	24	– st East b Childs	37
G. R. Cowdrey c Prichard b Childs	16	– c East b Childs	9
*C. S. Cowdrey st East b Childs	60	– b Childs	7
R. M. Ellison st East b Acfield	4	– lbw b Childs	1
†S. A. Marsh c East b Childs	7	– st East b Acfield	38
G. R. Dilley st East b Acfield	30	– c Gooch b Childs	12
D. L. Underwood not out	7	– c Acfield b Childs	2
T. M. Alderman b Acfield	1	– not out	0
B 9, l-b 9, w 1	19	B 1, l-b 6, n-b 1	8

1/42 2/49 3/73 4/93 5/125   224   1/47 2/48 3/52 4/72 5/86   160
6/140 7/157 8/206 9/214   6/92 7/117 8/150 9/160

Bonus points – Kent 2, Essex 4 (Score at 100 overs: 217-9).

Bowling: *First Innings*—Lever 8–0–21–0; Foster 24–10–59–3; Childs 39–15–65–3; Pringle 9–5–11–0; Acfield 25.2–5–50–4. *Second Innings*—Lever 5–0–12–1; Foster 4–1–13–0; Childs 21–9–58–7; Acfield 21.4–3–70–2.

Umpires: K. J. Lyons and A. G. T. Whitehead.

KENT v WARWICKSHIRE

At Folkestone, September 3, 4, 5. Kent won by an innings and 30 runs. Kent 22 pts, Warwickshire 4 pts. Toss: Warwickshire. Bad light and rain brought five interruptions on the first day of a match in which bowlers generally had the better of the conditions. Moles and Amiss retrieved Warwickshire's fortunes with a stand of 114 off 34 overs, and on a more pleasant second day Kent fared better as their captain, Cowdrey, moved towards his only hundred of the season. Not out 82 overnight, he went on to reach three figures in 167 minutes with two 6s and five 4s, and Marsh, who had equalled the Kent wicket-keeping record of six dismissals in Warwickshire's innings, hit a career-best 70. Gifford's marathon spell – on the second day he had taken his 2,000th first-class wicket – forecast trouble for Warwickshire in their second innings and so it proved when Underwood returned one of his most remarkable analyses. He was backed by some fine close catching, Christopher Cowdrey holding five catches in an innings for the second time in his career, and was well supported by another left-arm spinner, Davis, who was making his county début.

Warwickshire

A. J. Moles b Baptiste	82	– b Davis	8
P. A. Smith c Marsh b C. S. Cowdrey	11	– c C. S. Cowdrey b Underwood	14
A. I. Kallicharran c Marsh b Baptiste	2	– c C. S. Cowdrey b Underwood	2
D. L. Amiss b Davis	73	– c C. S. Cowdrey b Underwood	5
†G. W. Humpage c Marsh b Baptiste	19	– c Tavaré b Underwood	23
Asif Din c Davis b Underwood	11	– c C. S. Cowdrey b Underwood	5
A. M. Ferreira st Marsh b Davis	26	– c C. S. Cowdrey b Underwood	0
K. J. Kerr c Marsh b Baptiste	1	– c G. R. Cowdrey b Davis	0
G. C. Small b Davis	28	– (10) c Aslett b Underwood	2
T. A. Munton c Marsh b Underwood	0	– (11) not out	0
*N. Gifford not out	2	– (9) b Davis	2
B 3, l-b 5, w 2, n-b 2	12	N-b 1	1

1/21 2/32 3/146 4/195 5/196   267   1/11 2/18 3/26 4/29 5/56   65
6/219 7/221 8/246 9/247   6/56 7/59 8/62 9/65

Bonus points – Warwickshire 2, Kent 3 (Score at 100 overs 234-7).

Bowling: *First Innings*—Ellison 12–1–26–0; Baptiste 26–9–53–4; C. S. Cowdrey 12–1–49–1; Davis 28.5–4–83–3; Underwood 32–18–48–2. *Second Innings*—Baptiste 8–3–12–0; Underwood 35.5–29–11–7; Davis 31–18–38–3; Tavaré 2–1–4–0.

Kent

M. R. Benson c Ferreira b Small	2	R. M. Ellison b Kerr	8
N. R. Taylor c Moles b Small	10	D. L. Underwood b Kerr	1
C. J. Tavaré c Humpage b Gifford	43	R. P. Davis not out	0
D. G. Aslett b Gifford	63		
G. R. Cowdrey c Humpage b Gifford	7	B 12, l-b 21, n-b 3	36
*C. S. Cowdrey lbw b Small	100		
E. A. E. Baptiste lbw b Gifford	22	1/2 2/23 3/114 4/131 5/150	362
†S. A. Marsh b Gifford	70	6/224 7/328 8/348 9/356	

Bonus points – Kent 3, Warwickshire 2 (Score at 100 overs: 295-6).

Bowling: Small 21–4–64–3; Smith 2–0–13–0; Ferreira 9–2–32–0; Gifford 49.5–15–96–5; Kerr 46–2–120–2; Munton 2–0–4–0.

Umpires: K. J. Lyons and A. G. T. Whitehead.

KENT v MIDDLESEX

At Canterbury, September 13, 15, 16. Drawn. Toss: Middlesex. Rain, coming just before lunch, washed out the first day and no play was possible on the remaining two days. It was a disappointing end to the season.

Middlesex

W. N. Slack c Marsh b Baptiste	11
A. J. T. Miller not out	30
J. D. Carr not out	44
B 4, w 5, n-b 7	16
1/22	(1 wkt) 101

*M. W. Gatting, C. T. Radley, R. O. Butcher, †P. R. Downton, J. E. Emburey, P. H. Edmonds, S. P. Hughes and N. G. Cowans did not bat.

Bowling: Dilley 10–2–22–0; Baptiste 9–2–26–1; C. S. Cowdrey 6–0–33–0; Ellison 3–0–10–0; Underwood 2–0–6–0.

Kent

N. R. Taylor, S. G. Hinks, C. J. Tavaré, D. G. Aslett, *C. S. Cowdrey, G. R. Cowdrey, E. A. E. Baptiste, †S. A. Marsh, R. M. Ellison, G. R. Dilley and D. L. Underwood.

Umpires: A. A. Jones and D. O. Oslear.

ESSO SCHOLARSHIPS

The four young Australian cricketers who received Esso Scholarships to play in England in 1986 were: K. Bradshaw (Tasmania) for Sussex, D. J. Hickey (Victoria) for Glamorgan, G. S. Trimble (Queensland) for Essex and M. E. Waugh (New South Wales) for MCC.

LANCASHIRE

Patron: HM The Queen
President: 1986 – C. D. Peaker
1987 – B. J. Howard
Chairman: C. S. Rhoades
Secretary: C. D. Hassell
County Cricket Ground, Old Trafford,
Manchester M16 0PX
(Telephone: 061-848 7021)
Cricket Manager: 1986 – J. D. Bond
Captain: 1986 – C. H. Lloyd
1987 – D. P. Hughes
Coaches: 1986 – J. S. Savage and P. Lever
1987 – J. A. Ormrod and J. S. Savage

Yet another miserable season for Lancashire ended with the manager, Jack Bond, and the coach, Peter Lever, being dismissed, but with the entire playing staff being retained. Lancashire finished in the bottom five of both the Britannic Assurance Championship and the John Player League and failed to qualify for the knockout stages of the Benson and Hedges Cup, losing three of their zonal matches including that against Scotland. They played well in the NatWest Bank Trophy but faltered in the final against Sussex, who were comfortable winners. Two days later the news was announced that Bond and Lever would not be retained, and in November Clive Lloyd was replaced as captain by David Hughes, at 39 the club's longest-serving player.

There was nothing simple or straightforward about Lancashire's summer. They started by winning two of the first four Championship matches and for a few days they basked in the glorious sunshine at the head of the table. But like most English summers, there was plenty of rain to go with the sun and Lancashire felt the full force as they lost six of their first seven limited-overs matches. They started the John Player League with three defeats and hit rock-bottom at Perth when they batted through 55 overs in the Benson and Hedges Cup and still could not overtake Scotland's 156 for nine.

So by the beginning of June they were out of one competition, almost certainly out of another, and yet were top of the Championship. That was soon to change. Before the end of the month they were in the bottom half of the table, and after slipping to sixteenth after the 22nd game, they managed to hoist themselves into fifteenth while extending to eleven years their unhappy run of finishing in the bottom six places.

The NatWest Bank Trophy kept interest bubbling in the second half of the season and Lancashire played some spirited cricket to win at Taunton, Leicester and The Oval. Their semi-final victory over Surrey, by 4 runs, came close to rivalling the famous 1971 Gloucestershire match for excitement. A modest bowling attack was magnificently supported by outstanding fielding and Lancashire deserved their place in a 60-overs final for the first time for ten years. Unfortunately, the bubble burst at Lord's and Lloyd, clearly crestfallen, sat unhappily in the dressing-room for a long time after the game was finished.

Lloyd captained Lancashire again last season, but he played in only six Championship matches because of the qualification regulations. Lancashire understandably preferred to play Patrick Patterson, the West Indian fast bowler, in an attempt to rise to a more respectable position in the table. He played in seventeen Championship games but, upset by niggling injuries, took only 40 wickets at just over 30 runs each. The Old Trafford pitches were consistently good, as England discovered when they won two Texaco Trophy matches by chasing totals in excess of 250, and Patterson was given only one to his liking – a green one for the match against Essex. The eventual champions, weakened by injuries and Test calls, lost by an innings in two days, with Patterson taking ten wickets in the match, his best return of the season and a repeat of his display at Ilford the previous season.

The bowling lacked real authority throughout the summer, and for only the third time in the club's history – all have come in the last five years – none of the bowlers took 50 wickets. Patterson took eight against Oxford University to finish with 48, and Paul Allott had 43, all in the Championship, but it was 45-year-old Jack Simmons who headed the averages with 36 wickets at 21 runs each, including a match return of ten for 145 against Glamorgan. Of England-qualified bowlers, only John Childs of Essex finished ahead of him in the national averages.

The batting, which had been woefully weak in 1985, recovered last year and four players reached 1,000 runs. Graeme Fowler happily returned to form right from the start with 180 in his first innings, against Sussex at Hove. John Abrahams, too, recovered his ability, Gehan Mendis proved a worthwhile signing from Sussex and was leading run-scorer, and Neil Fairbrother, 22, continued his advance from 1984 (average 31.60) and 1985 (39.85) by averaging nearly 49 and finishing eighth among the England-qualified batsmen. Wicket-keeper Chris Maynard also had his best season as a batsman, scoring a magnificent maiden century against Yorkshire at Headingley and topping 600 runs.

The county's batting was often at its best in difficult situations. Lancashire were left with six rearguard actions after conceding large first-innings leads and recovered so well in one, against Somerset at Old Trafford in the penultimate Championship match, that they turned a 237-run deficit into a 26-run win. They batted through the final day three times to deny Derbyshire, Nottinghamshire and Yorkshire, they took Northamptonshire to the final hour after following on 256 behind, and failed totally only when they went down by an innings to Middlesex at Lord's.

The appointment of Lloyd as captain and Simmons as vice-captain provided Lancashire with one or two headaches, and with Fowler and Abrahams also stepping in, the Championship team had four different captains. The county looked particularly ridiculous in the opening game at Hove when Lloyd stood down in favour of Patterson, Simmons was simply not selected, and Fowler had to lead them for the first time. Yet all was not chaos. The second team, under the guidance of Hughes and Alan Ormrod, won the Second Eleven Championship for the first time since 1964, giving rise to hope for the future. – B.B.

LANCASHIRE 1986

[*Bill Smith*

Back row: I. Folley, M. R. Chadwick, D. J. Makinson, B. P. Patterson, M. Watkinson, C. Maynard, G. D. Mendis. *Front row*: S. J. O'Shaughnessy,
G. Fowler, C. H. Lloyd (*captain*), J. Abrahams, N. H. Fairbrother. *Insets*: J. Simmons, P. J. W. Allott, A. J. Murphy, A. N. Hayhurst, J. Stanworth.

LANCASHIRE RESULTS

All first-class matches – Played 24: Won 5, Lost 5, Drawn 14. Abandoned 1.

County Championship matches – Played 23: Won 4, Lost 5, Drawn 14. Abandoned 1.

Bonus points – Batting 41, Bowling 51.

Competition placings – Britannic Assurance County Championship, 15th; NatWest Bank Trophy, finalists; Benson and Hedges Cup, 4th in Group B; John Player League, 12th equal.

BRITANNIC ASSURANCE CHAMPIONSHIP AVERAGES

BATTING

	Birthplace	M	I	NO	R	HI	Avge
‡C. H. Lloyd	Georgetown, BG	6	7	0	328	128	46.85
‡N. H. Fairbrother .	Warrington	21	32	7	1,158	131	46.32
‡G. D. Mendis	Colombo, Ceylon	22	36	3	1,265	108	38.33
‡G. Fowler	Accrington	19	30	1	1,110	180	38.27
‡J. Abrahams	Cape Town, SA	23	37	7	1,134	189*	37.80
D. W. Varey	Darlington	6	10	2	271	83	33.87
‡C. Maynard	Haslemere, Surrey	19	26	5	662	132*	31.52
‡P. J. W. Allott ..	Altrincham	17	19	5	382	65	27.28
‡S. J. O'Shaughnessy	Bury	10	14	3	291	74	26.45
‡J. Simmons	Clayton-le-Moors	13	17	5	300	61	25.00
M. R. Chadwick ..	Rochdale	10	18	0	423	61	23.50
M. Watkinson ...	Westhoughton	20	24	3	377	58*	17.95
D. J. Makinson ...	Eccleston	14	13	6	96	43	13.71
A. N. Hayhurst ...	Manchester	9	12	0	146	31	12.16
I. Folley	Burnley	16	19	2	159	20*	9.35
B. P. Patterson ..	Portland, Jamaica	17	15	5	54	12*	5.40

Also batted: K. A. Hayes (*Thurnscoe*) (1 match) 17; W. K. Hegg (*Whitefield*) (2 matches) 0, 4; S. Henriksen (*Rodoure, Denmark*) (2 matches) 6*, 1; A. J. Murphy (*Manchester*) (4 matches) 1*, 0*, 1*; J. Stanworth (*Oldham*) (2 matches) 2, 11*.

* *Signifies not out.*   ‡ *Denotes county cap.*

The following played a total of ten three-figure innings for Lancashire in County Championship matches: N. H. Fairbrother 3, J. Abrahams 2, G. D. Mendis 2, G. Fowler 1, C. H. Lloyd 1, C. Maynard 1.

BOWLING

	O	M	R	W	BB	Avge
J. Simmons	230.5	52	762	36	7-79	21.16
P. J. W. Allott	405.1	106	1,053	43	5-32	24.48
B. P. Patterson	356	61	1,222	40	6-46	30.55
D. J. Makinson	285.1	55	963	30	4-69	32.10
I. Folley	327	90	1,009	26	4-42	38.80
M. Watkinson	454.4	69	1,632	30	5-90	54.40

Also bowled: J. Abrahams 37.5–4–161–1; M. R. Chadwick 5–0–51–0; N. H. Fairbrother 22–8–48–0; G. Fowler 4–0–34–2; A. N. Hayhurst 106.1–8–418–8; S. Henriksen 17–2–61–1; A. J. Murphy 64–13–203–7; S. J. O'Shaughnessy 97–18–363–5.

Wicket-keepers: C. Maynard 29 ct, 3 st; W. K. Hegg 2 ct, 2 st; J. Stanworth 4; D. W. Varey 1 ct, 1 st.

Leading Fielders: M. Watkinson 14; J. Abrahams 12.

At Hove, April 26, 27, 28. LANCASHIRE beat SUSSEX by nine wickets.

LANCASHIRE v LEICESTERSHIRE

At Manchester, April 30, May 1, 2. Drawn. Lancashire 6 pts, Leicestershire 8 pts. Toss: Lancashire. Lancashire's middle order collapsed after a second-wicket partnership of 134 between Fowler and Varey and it needed a stand of 65 between Maynard and Allott to help Lancashire get full batting points. Leicestershire's night-watchman, Whitticase, batted until after lunch for a career-best 60, Whitaker scored a century after going in on a hat-trick, and with Lancashire, 89 for one overnight, having to recover from the loss of five wickets in an hour and a half on the third morning, there was no time for Leicestershire to chase victory.

Lancashire

G. D. Mendis c Whitticase b Agnew	0	– b Clift	28
*G. Fowler b Benjamin	72	– c Whitaker b Agnew	56
D. W. Varey c Boon b Agnew	72	– (4) c Gower b Benjamin	15
N. H. Fairbrother c DeFreitas b Clift	1	– (5) not out	64
S. J. O'Shaughnessy lbw b Benjamin	4	– (6) c Potter b Clift	14
J. Abrahams c Butcher b Agnew	3	– (7) c Gower b DeFreitas	0
†C. Maynard c Boon b Clift	59	– (8) run out	37
M. Watkinson st Whitticase b Clift	13	– (9) not out	39
P. J. W. Allott c Cobb b Clift	42	– (3) c Cobb b Agnew	16
D. J. Makinson not out	11		
B. P. Patterson not out	1		
B 5, l-b 12, n-b 6	23	B 2, l-b 4, w 2, n-b 7	15

1/0 2/134 3/141 4/154   (9 wkts dec.) 301   1/70 2/101 3/116   (7 wkts dec.) 284
5/160 6/161 7/205   4/118 5/135 6/152
8/270 9/290   7/226

Bonus points – Lancashire 4, Leicestershire 4.

Bowling: *First Innings*—Agnew 19–7–38–3; Benjamin 28–4–93–2; DeFreitas 19–3–66–0; Clift 34–9–87–4. *Second Innings*—Agnew 16–3–58–2; Benjamin 23–4–92–1; DeFreitas 27–6–74–1; Clift 29–10–49–2; Potter 2–1–1–0; Butcher 2–0–4–0.

Leicestershire

I. P. Butcher c Maynard b Patterson	39	– c Fowler b Makinson	10
R. A. Cobb c Abrahams b Patterson	4	– lbw b Allott	5
†P. Whitticase c Fairbrother b O'Shaughnessy	60		
*D. I. Gower b Allott	76		
L. Potter lbw b O'Shaughnessy	0	– (3) not out	17
J. J. Whitaker not out	102		
W. K. M. Benjamin not out	5		
T. J. Boon (did not bat)		– (4) not out	6
B 4, l-b 2, w 4, n-b 7	17	N-b 2	2

1/8 2/109 3/109   (5 wkts dec.) 303   1/7 2/19   (2 wkts) 40
4/109 5/289

P. B. Clift, P. A. J. DeFreitas and J. P. Agnew did not bat.

Bonus points – Leicestershire 4, Lancashire 2.

Bowling: *First Innings*—Patterson 17–6–43–2; Allott 23.2–5–74–1; Watkinson 16–3–62–0; Makinson 9–2–51–0; O'Shaughnessy 12–3–45–2; Abrahams 7–0–22–0. *Second Innings*—Allott 6–4–5–1; Makinson 9–5–14–1; Watkinson 7–3–9–0; O'Shaughnessy 4–0–12–0.

Umpires: D. J. Constant and R. A. White.

LANCASHIRE v HAMPSHIRE

At Manchester, May 7, 8, 9. Drawn. Lancashire 1 pt, Hampshire 3 pts. Toss: Hampshire. Greenidge took his total of runs in the county in four years, whether for Hampshire or the West Indians, to more than 1,000 for an average of 335 with his seventh three-figure score. He reached his hundred off 154 balls with two 6s and thirteen 4s, and hit another six boundaries before the end of play. The start of the game was delayed by 90 minutes and the last two days were washed out.

Hampshire

C. G. Greenidge not out	127	*M. C. J. Nicholas not out	14
V. P. Terry c Maynard b Allott	2	L-b 10, n-b 7	17
R. A. Smith c Maynard b Patterson	21		
C. L. Smith b Allott	70	1/6 2/65 3/232 (3 wkts) 251	

M. D. Marshall, N. G. Cowley, R. J. Maru, T. M. Tremlett, †R. J. Parks and C. A. Connor did not bat.

Bonus points – Hampshire 3, Lancashire 1.

Bowling: Patterson 12.2–2–38–1; Allott 19–4–65–2; Folley 17–3–72–0; O'Shaughnessy 6–2–20–0; Watkinson 14–0–46–0.

Lancashire

*G. Fowler, G. D. Mendis, D. W. Varey, N. H. Fairbrother, J. Abrahams, S. J. O'Shaughnessy, †C. Maynard, M. Watkinson, I. Folley, P. J. W. Allott and B. P. Patterson.

Umpires: B. Leadbeater and J. H. Hampshire.

At Worcester, May 21, 22, 23. LANCASHIRE beat WORCESTERSHIRE by 3 runs.

At Leeds, May 24, 26, 27. LANCASHIRE drew with YORKSHIRE.

LANCASHIRE v WARWICKSHIRE

At Manchester, May 31, June 2, 3. Drawn. Lancashire 3 pts, Warwickshire 5 pts. Toss: Lancashire. After Humpage had scored his second century of the season, hitting sixteen 4s and two 6s, Lancashire tried to make up for time lost on Saturday by declaring 149 behind. Play could not start until two o'clock on the final day when Fowler took his first wickets in England – with successive balls – and Lancashire were left to score 270 to win in 53 overs. A seventh-wicket partnership of 92 between Maynard and Simmons took them close but Allott and Makinson could manage only 10 of the 15 needed from the last over.

Warwickshire

T. A. Lloyd b Makinson	17	– c Maynard b Allott	0
P. A. Smith lbw b Makinson	20	– c Maynard b Allott	9
A. I. Kallicharran b Makinson	14	– c Maynard b Fowler	28
D. L. Amiss c Watkinson b Allott	30	– not out	37
†G. W. Humpage b Makinson	130	– b Fowler	0
Asif Din not out	69	– not out	40
A. J. Moles not out	1		
B 1, l-b 14, n-b 5	20	L-b 4, w 1, n-b 1	6

1/38 2/47 3/76 4/110	(5 wkts dec.) 301	1/0 2/11 3/60 (4 wkts dec.) 120	
5/293		4/60	

G. J. Parsons, G. C. Small, T. A. Munton and *N. Gifford did not bat.

Bonus points – Warwickshire 4, Lancashire 2.

Bowling: *First Innings*—Patterson 21–2–85–0; Allott 23–6–44–1; Makinson 24–3–69–4; Watkinson 16–3–41–0; Simmons 10–0–47–0. *Second Innings*—Allott 5–1–13–2; Makinson 5–1–14–0; Fairbrother 2–1–2–0; Simmons 2–1–2–0; Chadwick 5–0–51–0; Fowler 4–0–34–2.

Lancashire

G. D. Mendis c Kallicharran b Small	44	– c Smith b Small	25
G. Fowler lbw b Small	4	– b Parsons	8
M. R. Chadwick c Humpage b Small	61	– c Humpage b Smith	47
N. H. Fairbrother not out	25	– c Amiss b Smith	36
J. Abrahams c Amiss b Smith	6	– c Humpage b Smith	0
†C. Maynard not out	7	– b Small	64
M. Watkinson (did not bat)		– b Gifford	0
*J. Simmons (did not bat)		– c Smith b Small	44
P. J. W. Allott (did not bat)		– not out	22
D. J. Makinson (did not bat)		– not out	2
L-b 3, n-b 2	5	B 4, l-b 11, n-b 2	17

1/7 2/104 3/123 4/141   (4 wkts dec.) 152   1/20 2/52 3/116 4/116   (8 wkts) 265
                                          5/134 6/135 7/227 8/248

B. P. Patterson did not bat.

Bonus points – Lancashire 1, Warwickshire 1.

Bowling: *First Innings*—Small 15–4–41–3; Parsons 12–4–18–0; Munton 8–2–22–0; Moles 7–0–30–0; Gifford 12–3–25–0; Smith 2.4–0–13–1. *Second Innings*—Small 14–1–60–3; Parsons 5–0–28–1; Gifford 16–1–74–1; Munton 7–2–32–0; Smith 8–0–36–3; Asif Din 3–0–20–0.

Umpires: J. H. Harris and R. Palmer.

At Oxford, June 4, 5, 6. LANCASHIRE beat OXFORD UNIVERSITY by nine wickets.

LANCASHIRE v MIDDLESEX

At Manchester, June 7, 9, 10. Drawn. Lancashire 4 pts, Middlesex 4 pts. Toss: Lancashire. Mendis hit his highest score since joining Lancashire, who needed a partnership of 135 between Lloyd and Simmons to help them achieve full batting points. Twenty-eight overs were lost on the first day, 68 on the second, and the third was totally washed out. Middlesex were without seven first-team players with Edmonds, Emburey, Gatting and Downton playing for England, and Cowans, Williams and Barlow unfit.

Lancashire

G. D. Mendis c Miller b Daniel	66	P. J. W. Allott not out	9
G. Fowler c Slack b Hughes	0	D. J. Makinson c Slack b Hughes	4
J. Abrahams run out	28	A. J. Murphy not out	1
N. H. Fairbrother b Daniel	42	B 2, l-b 12, n-b 9	23
*C. H. Lloyd c Tufnell b Hughes	79		
†C. Maynard c Hughes b Daniel	0	1/8 2/82 3/138 (9 wkts dec.) 313
M. Watkinson b Daniel	0	4/149 5/149 6/153
J. Simmons c Miller b Hughes	61	7/288 8/303 9/308

Bonus points – Lancashire 4, Middlesex 4.

Bowling: Daniel 25–2–98–4; Hughes 27–6–77–4; Fraser 29–5–60–0; Tufnell 18–3–64–0.

Middlesex

A. J. T. Miller not out	....	16
W. N. Slack b Makinson	....	11
K. R. Brown not out	....	25
B 4, l-b 2	....	6

1/16   (1 wkt) 58

*C. T. Radley, R. O. Butcher, J. D. Carr, †C. P. Metson, S. P. Hughes, A. R. C. Fraser, P. C. R. Tufnell and W. W. Daniel did not bat.

Bowling: Allott 10–3–19–0; Makinson 6–1–23–1; Simmons 4–2–6–0; Watkinson 2–0–4–0.

Umpires: J. Birkenshaw and A. G. T. Whitehead.

LANCASHIRE v WORCESTERSHIRE

At Manchester, June 14, 16, 17. Drawn. Lancashire 7 pts, Worcestershire 4 pts. Toss: Lancashire. Fairbrother and Abrahams both scored their first Championship hundreds of the season and shared in a fourth-wicket partnership of 243. Patel saw off the threat of the follow-on for Worcestershire on the second day, and after Abrahams had taken his total of runs in the match to 173 without getting out, Worcestershire were left 57 overs in which to score 285 to win. After the fall of early wickets, they settled for a draw.

Lancashire

G. D. Mendis c Illingworth b Patel	66	– st Rhodes b Illingworth 27
G. Fowler c Newport b Patel	22	
M. R. Chadwick c and b Illingworth	28	– (2) c Hick b Patel 48
N. H. Fairbrother c Rhodes b Inchmore	131	– not out 10
J. Abrahams not out	100	– (3) not out 73
†C. Maynard not out	0	
B 5, l-b 5, w 5, n-b 5	20	B 2, l-b 6, w 2, n-b 2 12

1/67 2/120 3/120 4/363   (4 wkts dec.) 367   1/57 2/128   (2 wkts dec.) 170

A. N. Hayhurst, M. Watkinson, *J. Simmons, P. J. W. Allott and B. P. Patterson did not bat.

Bonus points – Lancashire 3, Worcestershire 1 (Score at 100 overs: 257-3).

Bowling: *First Innings*—Radford 9.2–2–40–0; Inchmore 27–6–55–1; Newport 25.2–3–98–0; Patel 35–9–82–2; Illingworth 29.4–9–82–1. *Second Innings*—Newport 5–0–30–0; Illingworth 17–2–68–1; Inchmore 6–0–17–0; Patel 13–2–42–1; Hick 2–0–5–0.

Worcestershire

T. S. Curtis c Allott b Simmons	29	– not out 55
D. B. D'Oliveira c Maynard b Allott	6	– c sub b Allott 24
D. M. Smith c Simmons b Allott	13	– c Maynard b Allott 0
G. A. Hick st Maynard b Watkinson	13	– run out 9
*P. A. Neale c Allott b Hayhurst	23	– lbw b Watkinson 13
D. N. Patel c and b Simmons	94	– not out 35
†S. J. Rhodes c Allott b Watkinson	5	
P. J. Newport c sub b Patterson	9	
R. K. Illingworth not out	18	
N. V. Radford b Watkinson	24	
J. D. Inchmore c Fairbrother b Simmons	1	
B 4, l-b 2, n-b 7	13	B 1, l-b 4, w 1, n-b 4 10

1/20 2/40 3/61 4/89 5/126   253   1/30 2/32 3/50 4/88   (4 wkts) 146
6/140 7/176 8/219 9/252

Bonus points – Worcestershire 3, Lancashire 4.

Bowling: *First Innings*—Patterson 16–5–27–1; Allott 20–7–41–2; Hayhurst 8–1–28–1; Watkinson 24–5–92–3; Simmons 20.3–5–53–3; Abrahams 2–0–6–0. *Second Innings*—Patterson 11–5–23–0; Allott 11–1–45–2; Watkinson 16–3–51–1; Simmons 8–3–16–0; Fairbrother 3–1–6–0.

Umpires: H. D. Bird and J. A. Jameson.

At Swansea, June 21, 23, 24. LANCASHIRE drew with GLAMORGAN.

LANCASHIRE v DERBYSHIRE

At Liverpool, June 28, 30, July 1. Drawn. Lancashire 2 pts, Derbyshire 8 pts. Toss: Lancashire. Lancashire faced an uphill struggle from the opening day, which ended with Derbyshire 78 ahead with seven wickets in hand. Morris, Newman and Roberts were capped by Derbyshire on the second day and Morris responded with a career-best 153 (25 4s) and a partnership of 155 with Roberts before the declaration. Lancashire, needing 371 to avoid an innings defeat, batted with resolution through the final day to save the match, Fowler dropping down the order to have his best innings since the opening day of the season.

Lancashire

G. D. Mendis c Finney b Newman	35	– b Malcolm	20
*G. Fowler c Morris b Finney	8	– (5) not out	88
M. R. Chadwick lbw b Finney	6	– (2) c Barnett b Malcolm	48
N. H. Fairbrother b Newman	0	– c and b Sharma	52
J. Abrahams b Malcolm	0	– (3) b Miller	29
†C. Maynard c Marples b Newman	0	– not out	4
M. Watkinson c Anderson b Miller	7		
P. J. W. Allott c and b Malcolm	5		
D. J. Makinson lbw b Malcolm	5		
I. Folley not out	13		
B. P. Patterson st Marples b Miller	5		
L-b 1, w 1, n-b 8	10	B 14, l-b 3, w 5, n-b 7	29

1/26 2/49 3/54 4/56 5/56   94   1/33 2/86 3/120 4/231   (4 wkts) 270
6/61 7/67 8/74 9/74

Bonus points – Derbyshire 4.

Bowling: *First Innings*—Malcolm 15–5–43–3; Finney 12–4–21–2; Newman 12–5–16–3; Miller 15.3–9–13–2. *Second Innings*—Finney 6–0–20–0; Malcolm 21–4–81–2; Newman 15–1–51–0; Miller 41–20–44–1; Sharma 19–8–22–1; Barnett 11–2–35–0.

Derbyshire

*K. J. Barnett c Fowler b Folley	49	R. J. Finney c Abrahams b Folley	0
I. S. Anderson c Maynard b Makinson	6	P. G. Newman not out	0
A. Hill c Maynard b Makinson	11		
J. E. Morris c Abrahams b Patterson	153	B 9, l-b 8, w 1, n-b 22	40
B. Roberts c Watkinson b Makinson	87		
G. Miller c Maynard b Makinson	22	1/37 2/54 3/83	(9 wkts dec.) 465
R. Sharma c Maynard b Patterson	40	4/238 5/308 6/379	
†C. Marples c Chadwick b Folley	57	7/459 8/464 9/465	

D. E. Malcolm did not bat.

Bonus points – Derbyshire 4, Lancashire 2 (Score at 100 overs: 335-5).

Bowling: Patterson 20.1–1–77–2; Allott 30–8–91–0; Makinson 25–3–105–4; Folley 28–11–69–3; Watkinson 23–2–86–0; Abrahams 2–0–14–0; Fairbrother 1–0–6–0.

Umpires: J. A. Jameson and N. T. Plews.

LANCASHIRE v ESSEX

At Manchester, July 5, 7. Lancashire won by an innings and 22 runs. Lancashire 22 pts, Essex 3 pts. Toss: Lancashire. This win, achieved in two days, was Lancashire's first over Essex in thirteen years. Patterson took advantage of a grassy pitch to record his best Championship figures of the season against an Essex team severely weakened by injuries and Test calls. Mendis batted superbly to pass 50 for the fifth time in six matches as Lancashire took a first-innings lead of 169. Border fought hard to try to avoid the innings defeat, but Essex lost their last seven wickets for 23 runs.

Essex

C. Gladwin b Patterson	11	– lbw b Allott	6
J. P. Stephenson c Watkinson b Patterson	7	– c Maynard b Allott	20
P. J. Prichard b Patterson	0	– b Allott	0
A. R. Border c Maynard b Allott	6	– c Fowler b Watkinson	51
A. W. Lilley c Maynard b Makinson	10	– b Patterson	32
K. R. Pont c Chadwick b Patterson	4	– c Fairbrother b Patterson	5
†D. E. East c Fairbrother b Patterson	0	– lbw b Watkinson	0
I. L. Pont c Allott b Makinson	4	– not out	5
T. D. Topley not out	15	– c Maynard b Patterson	0
*J. K. Lever c Fairbrother b Patterson	3	– b Patterson	0
J. H. Childs b Patterson	1	– c Makinson b Watkinson	3
L-b 4, w 1, n-b 5	10	B 4, l-b 10, w 5, n-b 6	25

1/12 2/16 3/30 4/30 5/35   71   1/12 2/12 3/61 4/124 5/128   147
6/35 7/43 8/54 9/69   6/128 7/143 8/143 9/143

Bonus points – Lancashire 4.

Bowling: *First Innings*—Allott 12–7–10–2; Patterson 12.4–2–46–6; Makinson 8–2–11–2. *Second Innings*—Patterson 13–1–43–4; Allott 11–3–31–3; Makinson 8–2–23–0; Watkinson 9.4–2–36–3.

Lancashire

G. D. Mendis c East b Lever	86	P. J. W. Allott c K. R. Pont b I. L. Pont	3
*G. Fowler b Childs	21	D. J. Makinson not out	1
M. R. Chadwick c Border b Lever	20	B. P. Patterson c East b I. L. Pont	1
N. H. Fairbrother b Childs	3		
J. Abrahams c East b Lever	30	B 4, l-b 4, n-b 3	11
†C. Maynard c Border b Topley	9		
I. Folley c Stephenson b Childs	20	1/70 2/128 3/137 4/137 5/175	240
M. Watkinson lbw b I. L. Pont	35	6/177 7/231 8/237 9/239	

Bonus points – Lancashire 2, Essex 3 (Score at 100 overs: 237-8).

Bowling: Lever 26.1–9–41–3; I. L. Pont 18.2–2–68–3; Topley 29–8–67–1; K. R. Pont 5.5–1–9–0; Childs 25–9–47–3.

Umpires: D. R. Shepherd and A. G. T. Whitehead.

At Northampton, July 16, 17, 18. LANCASHIRE lost to NORTHAMPTONSHIRE by ten wickets.

At Canterbury, July 19, 21, 22. LANCASHIRE lost to KENT by eight wickets.

LANCASHIRE v NOTTINGHAMSHIRE

At Southport, July 23, 24, 25. Drawn. Lancashire 4 pts, Nottinghamshire 8 pts. Toss: Nottinghamshire. Nottinghamshire batted consistently throughout the opening day, and when they made Lancashire follow on 168 behind, on a wicket taking spin, Lancashire were facing their third successive defeat. Rain came to their help, 37 overs being lost on the second day, and beginning the third day 6 without loss, they batted with more resolution in another successful rearguard action. Hemmings finished with ten wickets in the match, and there was a remarkable catch in Lancashire's first innings by Robinson, who held the ball one-handed as he lay on his back, after slipping in the outfield, to dismiss Watkinson.

Nottinghamshire

B. C. Broad lbw b Murphy	51	E. E. Hemmings not out 26
R. T. Robinson c Abrahams b Hayhurst	97	K. E. Cooper not out 5
M. Newell c Fowler b Folley	33	
*C. E. B. Rice b Allott	43	B 5, l-b 9, w 1, n-b 2 17
P. Johnson b Murphy	23	
J. D. Birch lbw b Murphy	0	1/82 2/169 3/191 (8 wkts dec.) 350
†C. W. Scott c Murphy b Folley	41	4/239 5/239 6/263
R. A. Pick lbw b Folley	14	7/304 8/316

P. M. Such did not bat.

Bonus points – Nottinghamshire 4, Lancashire 3 (Score at 100 overs: 308-7).

Bowling: Allott 24–8–63–1; Murphy 21–5–67–3; Watkinson 23–0–88–0; Folley 30–8–73–3; Hayhurst 12–1–45–1.

Lancashire

G. D. Mendis b Pick	13	c Newell b Hemmings 69
G. Fowler c Johnson b Hemmings	30	c Newell b Hemmings 37
M. R. Chadwick c Newell b Such	3	lbw b Such 0
J. Abrahams b Hemmings	20	b Hemmings 16
*C. H. Lloyd b Hemmings	19	c Birch b Hemmings 75
A. N. Hayhurst c Robinson b Hemmings	22	c Newell b Such 3
†C. Maynard c Such b Pick	59	c Broad b Hemmings 13
M. Watkinson c Robinson b Such	3	not out 58
P. J. W. Allott c Rice b Pick	6	not out 17
I. Folley b Hemmings	3	
A. J. Murphy not out	0	
L-b 3, w 1	4	B 4, l-b 4, n-b 5 13

1/33 2/47 3/51 4/81 5/98   182   1/61 2/70 3/121 4/138 (7 wkts) 301
6/113 7/132 8/149 9/182   5/153 6/190 7/252

Bonus points – Lancashire 1, Nottinghamshire 4.

Bowling: *First Innings*—Pick 15.3–4–48–3; Cooper 7–5–4–0; Such 20–6–57–2; Hemmings 28–12–70–5. *Second Innings*—Pick 12–0–48–0; Cooper 11–2–38–0; Hemmings 43–14–105–5; Such 26–3–90–2; Rice 10–4–12–0.

Umpires: J. Birkenshaw and P. B. Wight.

At Birmingham, July 26, 28, 29. LANCASHIRE drew with WARWICKSHIRE.

LANCASHIRE v YORKSHIRE

At Manchester, August 2, 4, 5. Drawn. Lancashire 1 pt, Yorkshire 8 pts. Toss: Yorkshire. A run of nine successive draws in Roses matches looked likely to end when the second day ended with Lancashire, 229 behind on the first innings, standing at 14 for two in their second. But Fairbrother scored his third Roses century from 213 balls, Abrahams resisted for four hours, and Lancashire batted through the final day to deny Yorkshire. The feature of the first innings had been the partnership of 282 between Metcalfe and Moxon, the highest Yorkshire opening stand in a Roses match and the third best by a county first-wicket pair at Old Trafford.

Lancashire

G. D. Mendis c Bairstow b P. J. Hartley	54	– lbw b Carrick	25
G. Fowler b Jarvis	35	– c Bairstow b Jarvis	0
J. Abrahams c Bairstow b Jarvis	4	– (4) c Metcalfe b Carrick	80
N. H. Fairbrother b Jarvis	1	– (5) not out	116
A. N. Hayhurst lbw b P. J. Hartley	8	– (6) c Bairstow b P. J. Hartley	14
M. Watkinson c Moxon b P. J. Hartley	0	– (7) lbw b P. J. Hartley	1
*J. Simmons b Fletcher	7	– (8) not out	8
P. J. W. Allott c S. N. Hartley b Dennis	36		
I. Folley c Bairstow b Jarvis	1	– (3) lbw b Dennis	1
†J. Stanworth c Moxon b Dennis	2		
B. P. Patterson not out	6		
B 8, l-b 7, n-b 1	16	L-b 3, w 1, n-b 2	6

1/79 2/84 3/92 4/113 5/115   170   1/1 2/2 3/74 4/156   (6 wkts) 251
6/118 7/151 8/161 9/163   5/220 6/227

Bonus points – Lancashire 1, Yorkshire 4.

Bowling: *First Innings*—Jarvis 18–6–36–4; Dennis 17.3–2–38–2; Fletcher 19–8–29–1; P. J. Hartley 11–1–31–3; Carrick 10–4–21–0. *Second Innings*—Jarvis 18–4–37–1; Dennis 19–2–47–1; P. J. Hartley 21–8–42–2; Carrick 33–16–67–2; Fletcher 19–5–39–0; Love 4–0–16–0.

Yorkshire

M. D. Moxon run out	147	P. J. Hartley c Hayhurst b Patterson	5
A. A. Metcalfe c Stanworth b Hayhurst	151	P. W. Jarvis not out	3
S. N. Hartley c Stanworth b Hayhurst	11	B 1, l-b 6, w 2, n-b 1	11
P. E. Robinson b Hayhurst	1		
J. D. Love not out	53	1/282 2/317 3/318 (7 wkts dec.) 399	
*†D. L. Bairstow lbw b Allott	3	4/327 5/336	
P. Carrick c Folley b Hayhurst	14	6/363 7/377	

S. D. Fletcher and S. J. Dennis did not bat.

Bonus points – Yorkshire 4 (Score at 100 overs: 318-2).

Bowling: Patterson 18–2–76–1; Allott 29–6–84–1; Watkinson 22–2–77–0; Hayhurst 26–3–69–4; Folley 8–0–35–0; Simmons 15–2–43–0; Fairbrother 3–1–7–0.

Umpires: M. J. Kitchen and B. Leadbeater.

At The Oval, August 6, 7, 8. LANCASHIRE lost to SURREY by two wickets.

At Buxton, August 9, 11, 12. LANCASHIRE drew with DERBYSHIRE.

At Nottingham, August 16, 18, 19. LANCASHIRE lost to NOTTINGHAMSHIRE by seven wickets.

LANCASHIRE v GLAMORGAN

At Lytham, August 20, 21, 22. Drawn. Lancashire 4 pts, Glamorgan 5 pts. Toss: Lancashire. Lytham, staging its second Championship match since taking over as a venue from Blackpool, was blessed with sunshine on the opening day when Abrahams, watchful and patient, held the innings together before the last six wickets fell for 7 runs. Rain reduced the second day to 55 overs, and on a wicket taking spin, seventeen wickets fell on the last day, sixteen to spinners. Simmons opened the bowling after setting Glamorgan 178 to win in 45 overs and almost brought victory with one of the best returns of his career. Hegg, an eighteen year old who played for English Schools in 1985, made his début as Lancashire's wicket-keeper.

Lancashire

K. A. Hayes c Maynard b Barwick	17		
M. R. Chadwick run out	2	– (1) c Derrick b North	50
J. Abrahams c Davies b Derrick	99	– b Ontong	17
N. H. Fairbrother c Hopkins b Barwick	8	– b Ontong	2
S. J. O'Shaughnessy c Hopkins b Hickey	27	– not out	27
A. N. Hayhurst b Ontong	19	– (2) b Ontong	16
*J. Simmons c Hopkins b Ontong	0	– (6) b Ontong	1
†W. K. Hegg c Davies b Derrick	0	– st Davies b North	4
I. Folley c Hopkins b Ontong	2	– run out	1
D. J. Makinson not out	0	– (7) c Morris b North	6
B. P. Patterson b Derrick	0	– (10) c Hickey b North	4
B 2, l-b 8, w 2, n-b 6	18	B 10, l-b 10, n-b 1	21

1/12 2/27 3/47 4/105 5/185	192	1/35 2/93 3/95 (9 wkts dec.) 149
6/189 7/190 8/192 9/192		4/99 5/102 6/117
		7/136 8/143 9/149

Bonus points – Lancashire 1, Glamorgan 4.

Bowling: *First Innings*—Hickey 23–5–48–1; Barwick 26–6–60–2; Derrick 24.1–10–37–3; Ontong 23–14–30–3; North 2–0–7–0. *Second Innings*—Hickey 5–1–11–0; Barwick 12–7–25–0; Ontong 31–12–44–4; North 24.4–6–49–4.

Glamorgan

*H. Morris c Chadwick b Makinson	0	– c Abrahams b Simmons	49
J. A. Hopkins c Simmons b Folley	36	– c Hegg b Folley	7
A. L. Jones lbw b Simmons	35	– b Simmons	8
G. C. Holmes c Chadwick b Simmons	19	– c Makinson b Simmons	16
M. P. Maynard b Folley	4	– b Simmons	25
R. C. Ontong c and b Simmons	28	– st Hegg b Simmons	32
J. Derrick c sub b Folley	0	– b Simmons	0
†T. Davies lbw b Folley	14	– c Folley b Simmons	8
P. D. North not out	17	– not out	5
S. R. Barwick not out	3	– not out	4
B 1, l-b 6, w 1	8	L-b 2	2

1/0 2/70 3/94 4/94	(8 wkts dec.) 164	1/10 2/39 3/67 4/98 (8 wkts) 156
5/114 6/114 7/144 8/144		5/115 6/117
		7/127 8/152

D. J. Hickey did not bat.

Bonus points – Glamorgan 1, Lancashire 3.

Bowling: *First Innings*—Patterson 10–3–15–0; Makinson 12–3–22–1; Hayhurst 2–0–12–0; Simmons 21–4–66–3; Folley 22–8–42–4. *Second Innings*—Patterson 1–0–2–0; Simmons 22–5–79–7; Folley 19–3–65–1; Abrahams 3–1–8–0.

Umpires: B. J. Meyer and R. Palmer.

LANCASHIRE v GLOUCESTERSHIRE

At Manchester, August 23, 25, 26. Drawn. Lancashire 2 pts, Gloucestershire 4 pts. Toss: Gloucestershire. Gloucestershire's fading hopes of winning the Championship received another setback when rain brought the game to an end ten minutes before lunch on the second day. They had batted positively on the opening day with a second-wicket partnership of 155 between Tomlins and Bainbridge.

Gloucestershire

K. P. Tomlins lbw b Makinson	59	M. W. Alleyne b Makinson		8
P. W. Romaines c Fairbrother		C. A. Walsh st Hegg b Folley		16
b Patterson .	0	D. V. Lawrence c and b Folley		0
P. Bainbridge c Hegg b Makinson	98	†R. C. Russell not out		16
K. M. Curran b O'Shaughnessy	38	B 5, l-b 10, n-b 2		17
A. W. Stovold c O'Shaughnessy				
b Patterson .	26	1/4 2/159 3/184 4/232 (8 wkts dec.) 354		
J. W. Lloyds not out	76	5/244 6/279 7/320 8/320		

*D. A. Graveney did not bat.

Bonus points – Gloucestershire 4, Lancashire 2 (Score at 100 overs: 318-6).

Bowling: Patterson 16–2–33–2; Makinson 28–6–85–3; Hayhurst 11–1–36–0; O'Shaughnessy 12–2–42–1; Folley 20–7–50–2; Watkinson 22–3–89–0; Abrahams 2–0–4–0.

Lancashire

G. D. Mendis not out	61
M. R. Chadwick lbw b Graveney	15
*J. Abrahams not out	13
B 1, l-b 1, n-b 2	4
1/38 (1 wkt) 93	

N. H. Fairbrother, S. J. O'Shaughnessy, A. N. Hayhurst, M. Watkinson, †W. K. Hegg, I. Folley, D. J. Makinson and B. P. Patterson did not bat.

Bowling: Walsh 10–4–25–0; Lawrence 11–0–47–0; Graveney 11–4–19–1.

Umpires: J. H. Hampshire and J. A. Jameson.

At Lord's, August 27, 28, 29. LANCASHIRE lost to MIDDLESEX by an innings and 157 runs.

LANCASHIRE v SOMERSET

At Manchester, September 10, 11, 12. Lancashire won by 26 runs. Lancashire 21 pts, Somerset 8 pts. Toss: Lancashire. In a remarkable finish to the season at Old Trafford, Botham hit a hundred in 60 balls and Lancashire snatched victory after trailing on the first innings by 237 runs. Somerset, without Richards, Roebuck and Garner, bowled out Lancashire before tea on the opening day and were 163 for five when Botham walked out to bat the following morning. He stayed only 82 minutes and hit seventeen 4s and nine 6s off 79 balls in front of Old Trafford's largest crowd of the season for a Championship match. Fairbrother, with his third century of the season, led Lancashire's recovery and Somerset, set a target of 209 in 30 overs, willingly chased victory until the ninth wicket fell in the 29th over.

Lancashire

G. D. Mendis c Bartlett b Botham	9	– lbw b Botham	21
D. W. Varey c Bartlett b Botham	25	– c Harden b Taylor	83
J. Abrahams b Taylor	9	– c Gard b Dredge	92
N. H. Fairbrother c Hardy b Marks	65	– (5) not out	115
A. N. Hayhurst c Felton b Botham	1	– (6) lbw b Botham	31
†C. Maynard run out	36	– (7) c and b Marks	66
M. Watkinson c Taylor b Marks	2	– (8) not out	2
*J. Simmons c and b Marks	2		
I. Folley lbw b Marks	5	– (4) c Gard b Taylor	18
B. P. Patterson b Taylor	12		
A. J. Murphy not out	1		
L-b 1, n-b 3	4	L-b 14, w 2, n-b 1	17

1/21 2/34 3/54 4/58 5/133   171   1/40 2/157 3/196   (6 wkts dec.) 445
6/145 7/153 8/156 9/169   4/263 5/330 6/441

Bonus points – Lancashire 1, Somerset 4.

Bowling: *First Innings*—Botham 21–8–43–3; Taylor 21.4–3–66–2; Dredge 8–3–20–0; Marks 12–4–41–4. *Second Innings*—Botham 25–5–98–2; Taylor 26–3–102–2; Harman 21–1–61–0; Marks 38–10–103–1; Dredge 20–2–67–1.

Somerset

P. A. C. Bail c Simmons b Hayhurst	55	– c Maynard b Simmons	47
N. A. Felton c Varey b Simmons	40	– c Watkinson b Murphy	6
J. J. E. Hardy c Varey b Watkinson	24	– c Watkinson b Hayhurst	5
R. J. Harden c Murphy b Folley	22	– b Simmons	13
†T. Gard c Maynard b Folley	6	– (8) c Abrahams b Simmons	0
R. J. Bartlett c Watkinson b Murphy	35	– (7) c Maynard b Folley	43
I. T. Botham c Patterson b Simmons	139	– (5) c Varey b Folley	1
*V. J. Marks not out	43	– (6) st Maynard b Watkinson	33
M. D. Harman c Folley b Watkinson	15	– (11) lbw b Simmons	0
C. H. Dredge b Watkinson	0	– (9) b Simmons	25
N. S. Taylor c Folley b Watkinson	13	– (10) not out	1
B 2, l-b 11, n-b 3	16	B 1, l-b 5, n-b 2	8

1/80 2/117 3/143 4/154 5/163   408   1/17 2/38 3/59 4/62 5/80   182
6/314 7/349 8/386 9/388   6/147 7/148 8/174 9/182

Bonus points – Somerset 4, Lancashire 4 (Score at 100 overs: 395-9).

Bowling: *First Innings*—Patterson 17–3–44–0; Murphy 19–3–69–1; Simmons 17–2–108–2; Hayhurst 5–0–25–1; Watkinson 20.5–5–59–4; Folley 23–10–90–2. *Second Innings*—Hayhurst 6–0–28–1; Murphy 5–1–21–1; Folley 7–0–55–2; Simmons 8.5–1–53–5; Watkinson 2–0–19–1.

Umpires: R. Julian and B. J. Meyer.

At Southampton, September 13, 15, 16. HAMPSHIRE v LANCASHIRE. Abandoned.

LEICESTERSHIRE

Chairman: C. H. Palmer
Chairman, Cricket Committee: J. J. Palmer
Secretary/Cricket Manager: F. M. Turner
  County Cricket Ground, Grace Road,
  Leicester LE2 8AD
  (Telephone: 0533-831880/832128)
Captain: 1986 – D. I. Gower
      1987 – P. Willey
Coach: K. Higgs

Injuries, and a lack of balance in the bowling, produced a somewhat disappointing season for Leicestershire; one which culminated in the removal of David Gower as captain less than three months after his being replaced as England's captain. Gower had just announced that he was to miss the county's last three matches because of "mental and physical exhaustion" when Mr Mike Turner, the secretary-manager, recommended to the committee that he be given a "rest" from the position to which he was appointed at the end of the 1983 season. Gower's absences because of his England commitments had become increasingly detrimental, Turner felt, and there was evidence that he found it difficult to motivate himself adequately on his return to county cricket. In addition, Gower has a benefit in 1987, which could have proved a further distraction to his captaincy. Gower described the decision as "disappointing but understandable".

With Gower playing for England, the vice-captain, Peter Willey, out of domestic cricket until June following surgery on a continuing knee injury, and Nigel Briers suffering a fractured wrist at Hove in the same month, Leicestershire called on Paddy Clift as their fourth captain in July. And when Clift missed the later stages of the season through injury, Chris Balderstone became the fifth player to lead the county. At various stages, the attack was also without Les Taylor, Winston Benjamin and Jonathan Agnew, and all things considered, Leicestershire's recovery to seventh in the Britannic Assurance Championship, from sixteenth in 1985, was satisfactory.

Solace was also found in the form of James Whitaker and Phillip DeFreitas, who headed the batting and bowling averages and were selected for England's tour of Australia. Whitaker, one of *Wisden*'s Five Cricketers of the Year, was, furthermore, second in the national averages, having scored 1,526 runs in his aggressive style despite losing five weeks in mid-season. He had bones in both hands fractured while batting against Marshall of Hampshire, but showed his class with an unbeaten hundred and a spectacular 82 not out in a successful run-chase against Yorkshire in his comeback game.

It is a measure of the progress made by DeFreitas, in his first full season, that he deprived Whitaker of Leicestershire's "Player of the Season" award. He made attractive runs at number eight or nine, including a maiden century against Kent at Canterbury, but more important he was an aggressive, penetrating bowler, narrowly failing to take 100 wickets. DeFreitas, Dominican born, troubled even the best batsmen, both with his ability to move the ball either way and with the extra bounce generated by his high, whippy action.

What Leicestershire lacked was a spinner to provide variation. Willey is essentially a limited-overs specialist, and the signing of Laurie Potter from Kent failed to offset the departure of Nick Cook to Northamptonshire. Leicestershire had described Potter as an all-rounder, but his left-arm spin fell a long way short of the quality needed in first-class cricket. His batting, too, was a disappointment, although there were flashes of brilliance to raise hopes for the future.

Tim Boon completed 1,000 runs in first-class matches for the second time, a splendid achievement given that he missed the whole of 1985 following a car accident in South Africa and played throughout 1986 with a foot-long metal pin in his thigh. Russell Cobb, with the opportunity to open regularly, scored 1,000 runs for the first time, even though his maiden century remained an elusive goal. He passed 50 eight times in the season – making it seventeen times in his career – without reaching three figures, but by adding extra aggression to a splendid technique, he made an important contribution, particularly with Ian Butcher losing form dramatically.

Nevertheless, it was strange that Cobb was preferred to Chris Balderstone in the early rounds of the Benson and Hedges Cup, which Leicestershire were defending. Balderstone, who had done as much as anyone to secure Leicestershire the trophy in 1985, was adjudged surplus to requirements, yet with Willey unavailable, it was lack of experience in the top-order batting which had a decisive influence on Leicestershire's being out of contention after three of their four zonal matches. Balderstone was recalled later in the season, and at 45 he did well enough to earn another one-year contract. In 1987, he undertakes more duties on the coaching side, working alongside Ken Higgs, who at the age of 49 made a dramatic return to first-class cricket to relieve the problem of injuries.

In the John Player League, Leicestershire's selection at times appeared to be made with an eye to the future at the expense of what constituted the best side. And in a competition that makes heavy demands on fielding, theirs was rarely ever more than adequate. The best chance of honours appeared to be in the NatWest Bank Trophy, despite Leicestershire's poor record in the 60-overs competition. They moved comfortably into the second round with victory over Ireland and recorded a fine win over Gloucestershire at Bristol, only to be knocked out in the quarterfinals by the eventual finalists, Lancashire. Leicestershire lost an important toss to bat first on a damp pitch at Grace Road, but after recovering to set a challenging total they performed too poorly in the field to defend it. – M.J.

LEICESTERSHIRE 1986

[*Bill Smith*]

Back row: P. Whitticase, R. A. Cobb, T. J. Boon, P. A. J. DeFreitas, W. K. M. Benjamin, G. J. F. Ferris, L. Potter, I. P. Butcher. *Front row*: J. C. Balderstone, P. Willey, D. I. Gower (*captain*), L. B. Taylor, J. P. Agnew. *Insets*: N. E. Briers, P. Gill, P. B. Clift, J. J. Whitaker, P. D. Bowler.

LEICESTERSHIRE RESULTS

All first-class matches – Played 26: Won 5, Lost 7, Drawn 14.

County Championship matches – Played 24: Won 5, Lost 7, Drawn 12.

Bonus points – Batting 55, Bowling 67.

Competition placings – Britannic Assurance County Championship, 7th; NatWest Bank Trophy, q-f; Benson and Hedges Cup, 4th in Group A; John Player League, 15th.

BRITANNIC ASSURANCE CHAMPIONSHIP AVERAGES

BATTING

	Birthplace	M	I	NO	R	HI	Avge
‡J. J. Whitaker	Skipton	19	28	8	1,382	200*	69.10
‡P. Willey	Sedgefield	16	27	5	1,019	172*	46.31
‡N. E. Briers	Leicester	5	6	1	220	83	44.00
‡T. J. Boon	Doncaster	21	33	9	933	117	38.87
‡D. I. Gower	Tunbridge Wells	9	14	2	436	83	36.33
P. Whitticase	Solihull	17	20	4	554	67*	34.62
W. K. M. Benjamin	St John's, Antigua	18	18	9	309	57*	34.33
‡R. A. Cobb	Leicester	23	38	3	982	91	28.05
P. D. Bowler	Plymouth	8	11	1	249	100*	24.90
‡P. A. J. DeFreitas	Scotts Head, Dominica	24	28	2	630	106	24.23
‡P. B. Clift	Salisbury, S. Rhodesia	13	14	0	311	49	22.21
‡J. C. Balderstone ..	Huddersfield	14	23	1	410	115	18.63
L. Potter	Bexleyheath	18	27	3	444	81*	18.50
G. J. F. Ferris ...	Urlings Village, Antigua	5	6	1	67	17*	13.40
‡J. P. Agnew	Macclesfield	17	18	5	158	35*	12.15
‡I. P. Butcher	Farnborough, Kent	10	16	1	175	39	11.66
P. Gill	Manchester	7	10	4	60	17	10.00
‡L. B. Taylor	Earl Shilton	15	15	6	48	13	5.33

Also batted: G. A. R. Harris (*Tottenham*) (1 match) 6, 0*; ‡K. Higgs (*Sandyford*) (2 matches) 3*, 8; L. Tennant (*Walsall*) (2 matches) 12*, 1.

* *Signifies not out.*   ‡ *Denotes county cap.*

The following played a total of thirteen three-figure innings for Leicestershire in County Championship matches: J. J. Whitaker 5, P. Willey 4, J. C. Balderstone 1, T. J. Boon 1, P. D. Bowler 1, P. A. J. DeFreitas 1.

BOWLING

	O	M	R	W	BB	Avge
P. A. J. DeFreitas ..	675.1	123	1,977	89	7-44	22.21
P. B. Clift	384.2	113	901	39	4-35	23.10
J. P. Agnew	486.5	114	1,397	53	5-27	26.35
G. J. F. Ferris	104	20	356	13	4-54	27.38
L. B. Taylor	280.3	66	809	27	4-106	29.96
L. Potter	112	30	318	10	3-37	31.80
W. K. M. Benjamin	438.3	83	1,449	42	6-33	34.50

Also bowled: J. C. Balderstone 45–9–143–2; T. J. Boon 30.3–2–170–5; P. D. Bowler 25.4–10–57–0; N. E. Briers 13–0–60–2; I. P. Butcher 2–0–4–0; R. A. Cobb 10–3–41–0; G. A. R. Harris 8–1–34–0; K. Higgs 36–10–71–5; L. Tennant 8–1–35–0; J. J. Whitaker 5.2–0–47–1; P. Willey 165.5–48–372–6.

Wicket-keepers: P. Whitticase 23 ct, 1 st; P. Gill 23; D. I. Gower 1 st.

Leading Fielders: L. Potter 17; J. J. Whitaker 14; T. J. Boon 12; P. B. Clift 12.

At Cambridge, April 19, 21, 22. LEICESTERSHIRE drew with CAMBRIDGE UNIVERSITY.

LEICESTERSHIRE v KENT

At Leicester, April 26, 27, 28. Drawn. Leicestershire 6 pts, Kent 3 pts. Toss: Leicestershire. Kent were bowled out for 85 soon after lunch on the opening day, the result of a combination of poor shots and accurate bowling on a slow, seamers' pitch. Cobb's patient application and Whitaker's aggression helped Leicestershire take a lead of 157, and, in retrospect, the home county's decision to begin Sunday play at noon instead of eleven o'clock proved unwise. Kent were in trouble at 73 for three in their second innings against the moving ball before bad light halted play an hour early. Although bitterly cold, conditions were easier on the third day, and with Baptiste and Graham Cowdrey putting on 123 for the sixth wicket, Leicestershire could not bowl Kent out quickly enough to force a victory.

Kent

M. R. Benson lbw b Agnew	14	– lbw b DeFreitas	39
S. G. Hinks c Potter b Benjamin	6	– c Potter b DeFreitas	14
C. J. Tavaré b Clift	3	– b Benjamin	33
N. R. Taylor c Gill b Clift	4	– b Clift	4
G. R. Cowdrey c Gill b DeFreitas	6	– (6) b DeFreitas	59
E. A. E. Baptiste c Whitaker b Agnew	9	– (7) c Gill b DeFreitas	80
R. M. Ellison c Gill b DeFreitas	6	– (8) c Gill b Agnew	0
*C. S. Cowdrey lbw b Agnew	1	– (5) c Gill b Potter	24
†S. A. Marsh not out	12	– not out	21
G. R. Dilley c and b Agnew	12	– c Gill b Agnew	4
D. L. Underwood c Gower b Agnew	1	– b Agnew	0
L-b 9, w 1, n-b 1	11	B 1, l-b 6, n-b 14	21
	—		—
	85		299

1/15 2/24 3/29 4/38 5/46   85
6/52 7/58 8/59 9/81

1/53 2/59 3/73 4/126 5/143   299
6/266 7/270 8/280 9/299

Bonus points – Leicestershire 4.

Bowling: *First Innings*—Agnew 17–6–27–5; Benjamin 15–8–21–1; Clift 8–3–11–2; DeFreitas 9–3–17–2. *Second Innings*—Agnew 34.4–12–74–3; Benjamin 23–7–64–1; DeFreitas 29–6–61–4; Clift 16–3–52–1; Potter 9–2–41–1.

Leicestershire

I. P. Butcher lbw b Baptiste	6		
R. A. Cobb b Baptiste	74		
*D. I. Gower c C. S. Cowdrey b Baptiste	3	– (1) not out	3
L. Potter b Ellison	4	– (3) not out	0
J. J. Whitaker c Hinks b Dilley	57	– (2) b Ellison	0
T. J. Boon c Hinks b Underwood	11		
P. B. Clift c Ellison b Underwood	11		
P. A. J. DeFreitas c Taylor b Dilley	4		
W. K. M. Benjamin not out	29		
J. P. Agnew c Benson b Dilley	1		
†P. Gill c and b Baptiste	13		
B 5, l-b 10, w 1, n-b 13	29	L-b 2	2
	—		—
	242		(1 wkt) 5

1/34 2/44 3/49 4/145 5/168   242   1/4   (1 wkt) 5
6/186 7/193 8/208 9/211

Bonus points – Leicestershire 2, Kent 3 (Score at 100 overs: 208-8).

Bowling: *First Innings*—Dilley 31–9–74–3; Ellison 23–11–37–1; Baptiste 29–10–58–4; Underwood 24–12–33–2; C. S. Cowdrey 7–1–25–0. *Second Innings*—Dilley 2–0–3–0; Ellison 1–1–0–1.

Umpires: H. D. Bird and B. Leadbeater.

At Manchester, April 30, May 1, 2. LEICESTERSHIRE drew with LANCASHIRE.

At Lord's, May 7, 8, 9. LEICESTERSHIRE drew with MIDDLESEX.

At Nottingham, May 21, 22, 23. LEICESTERSHIRE lost to NOTTINGHAMSHIRE by five wickets.

At Northampton, May 24, 26, 27. LEICESTERSHIRE drew with NORTHAMPTONSHIRE.

LEICESTERSHIRE v GLOUCESTERSHIRE

At Leicester, May 31, June 2, 3. Gloucestershire won by six wickets. Gloucestershire 20 pts, Leicestershire 4 pts. Toss: Gloucestershire. Rain on the first day and third morning meant that the captains had to conspire to set up a finish. Graveney appointed Stovold and Romaines, with a total of five first-class wickets between them, to lob up a variety of tempting deliveries for Potter and Cobb to hit, and Gower then asked Gloucestershire to make 236 in 46 overs. Stovold got them going with an aggressive 61, but 146 off the final twenty overs appeared too demanding. However, Leicestershire's bowling and fielding inexplicably fell apart and Gloucestershire achieved their win with nine balls to spare. Whitticase sustained a shoulder injury making a frantic dive to prevent 4 byes, which led to Gower putting on the gloves and coming up with a collectors-item stumping. The TCCB later ruled that Gloucestershire were entitled to three rather than four bowling points because only eight Leicestershire batsmen were dismissed, Whitaker and Benjamin having been laid low by a virus.

Leicestershire

R. A. Cobb lbw b Payne	66	– (2) not out	68
L. Potter c Graveney b Lawrence	2	– (1) not out	81
P. Willey b Walsh	12		
*D. I. Gower b Walsh	4		
J. J. Whitaker retired ill	4		
N. E. Briers c Lloyds b Lawrence	81		
P. B. Clift c Russell b Graveney	23		
†P. Whitticase c Athey b Lawrence	30		
P. A. J. DeFreitas c Payne b Graveney	5		
J. P. Agnew not out	1		
W. K. M. Benjamin absent ill			
B 2, l-b 3, w 1, n-b 5	11		

1/2 2/43 3/53 4/99 5/170   239   (no wkt dec.) 149
6/216 7/227 8/239

Bonus points – Leicestershire 2, Gloucestershire 3.

Bowling: *First Innings*—Lawrence 23.4–6–72–3; Walsh 20–4–50–2; Payne 8–1–27–1; Bainbridge 5–1–23–0; Lloyds 12–2–43–0; Graveney 18–8–19–2. *Second Innings*—Stovold 11–0–68–0; Romaines 10–0–81–0.

Gloucestershire

P. W. Romaines c Willey b DeFreitas	4	– retired hurt	4
A. W. Stovold b Agnew	24	– b DeFreitas	61
C. W. J. Athey lbw b Clift	35	– st Gower b Potter	61
P. Bainbridge c Clift b DeFreitas	23	– (6) not out	2
K. M. Curran c Briers b Agnew	40	– c Whitaker b Clift	52
J. W. Lloyds not out	11	– (7) not out	4
I. R. Payne lbw b Clift	0		
†R. C. Russell not out	4		
D. V. Lawrence (did not bat)		– (4) b Benjamin	26
L-b 3, w 1, n-b 8	12	B 8, l-b 11, n-b 7	26

1/26 2/40 3/83 4/119   (6 wkts. dec.) 153   1/104 2/141 3/224   (4 wkts) 236
5/140 6/142   4/232

*D. A. Graveney and C. A. Walsh did not bat.

Bonus points – Gloucestershire 1, Leicestershire 2.

Bowling: *First Innings*—Agnew 15–5–45–2; DeFreitas 16–3–66–2; Clift 12–4–24–2; Willey 5–1–15–0. *Second Innings*—Agnew 13–1–63–0; Benjamin 10–2–50–1; Potter 4–0–17–1; Clift 9.3–1–37–1; DeFreitas 8–0–50–1.

Umpires: J. W. Holder and A. G. T. Whitehead.

LEICESTERSHIRE v SURREY

At Hinckley, June 4, 5, 6. Leicestershire won by six wickets. Lebcestershire 23 pts, Surrey 7 pts. Toss: Leicestershire. Neither side found batting straightforward on a slow, uneven pitch. After Clift had precipitated a Surrey decline from 185 for three to 215 for nine, Gray and Doughty responded in turn for the visitors on the second morning, but a stand of 95 in seventeen overs between DeFreitas and Benjamin gave the home side a useful lead. Fast bowling of a high class from Agnew and Benjamin left Leicestershire to score 131 in 42 overs for victory, which, with the pitch at its trickiest, was not as clear-cut as those figures might suggest. However, from a shaky platform of 34 for three, Whitaker, hitting thirteen 4s, saw Leicestershire home with four overs to spare.

Surrey

N. J. Falkner lbw b DeFreitas	20	– lbw b Benjamin	28
G. S. Clinton c Whitaker b DeFreitas	73	– b DeFreitas	31
A. J. Stewart c Potter b Benjamin	56	– c Whitaker b Agnew	20
M. A. Lynch c Gill b DeFreitas	1	– c Potter b Benjamin	8
D. M. Ward lbw b Clift	9	– b Benjamin	0
A. Needham not out	44	– c Boon b Agnew	27
†C. J. Richards b Benjamin	1	– c Clift b Agnew	7
R. J. Doughty b Clift	8	– c Potter b Benjamin	18
G. Monkhouse b Clift	0	– not out	1
A. H. Gray b Clift	0	– (11) lbw b Benjamin	7
*P. I. Pocock c Boon b DeFreitas	11	– (10) c Gill b Agnew	7
B 1, l-b 17, w 5, n-b 8	31	B 2, l-b 5, n-b 3	10

1/57 2/148 3/150 4/185 5/195   254   1/61 2/63 3/79 4/79 5/91   164
6/198 7/215 8/215 9/215   6/107 7/145 8/145 9/155

Bonus points – Surrey 3, Leicestershire 4.

Bowling: *First Innings*—Agnew 18–7–41–0; Benjamin 19–3–50–2; Clift 30–10–70–4; DeFreitas 28–5–67–4; Willey 3–1–5–0; Potter 2–0–3–0. *Second Innings*—Agnew 21–5–61–4; Benjamin 19.2–6–41–5; DeFreitas 15–5–30–1; Clift 8–2–19–0; Potter 1–0–6–0.

Leicestershire

L. Potter lbw b Gray	14	– c Lynch b Doughty	5
R. A. Cobb b Doughty	16	– c Gray b Monkhouse	2
*P. Willey c Lynch b Gray	21	– lbw b Doughty	0
J. J. Whitaker c Pocock b Doughty	6	– not out	88
N. E. Briers b Gray	15	– b Gray	23
T. J. Boon c Richards b Monkhouse	41	– not out	5
P. B. Clift lbw b Pocock	43		
P. A. J. DeFreitas lbw b Doughty	63		
W. K. M. Benjamin not out	52		
†P. Gill lbw b Gray	2		
J. P. Agnew c Pocock b Doughty	2		
B 1, l-b 4, n-b 8	13	B 4, l-b 1, n-b 3	8

1/33 2/41 3/49 4/79 5/82　　　　288　　　1/6 2/6 3/34 4/105　　(4 wkts) 131
6/157 7/173 8/268 9/275

Bonus points – Leicestershire 3, Surrey 4.

Bowling: *First Innings*—Gray 29–6–92–4; Monkhouse 31–10–87–1; Doughty 21.3–5–52–4; Pocock 15–7–48–1; Needham 2–0–4–0. *Second Innings*—Gray 15–4–58–1; Doughty 10–1–43–2; Monkhouse 13–4–25–1.

Umpires: J. W. Holder and A. G. T. Whitehead.

At Hove, June 7, 9, 10. LEICESTERSHIRE beat SUSSEX by 21 runs.

At Leicester, JUNE 14, 15, 16. LEICESTERSHIRE drew with INDIANS (See Indian tour section).

At Birmingham, June 21, 23, 24. LEICESTERSHIRE drew with WARWICKSHIRE.

LEICESTERSHIRE v NOTTINGHAMSHIRE

At Leicester, June 28, 30, July 1. Leicestershire won by 275 runs. Leicestershire 24 pts, Nottinghamshire 3 pts. Toss: Leicestershire. Whitaker scored a magnificent, career-best 200 not out, hitting thirty 4s and three 6s and dominating a partnership of 244 in 69 overs with his vice-captain, Willey. Whitaker's respective 50s were scored off 98, 53, 89 and finally 38 balls. Nottinghamshire's reply was held together by Johnson after Pick, the night-watchman, had frustrated Leicestershire's early breakthrough, but it required the return of Robinson, who had broken a finger while fielding in the Sunday League match, to prevent the follow-on. Gower's fluent 80 enabled him to set a target of 334 in a minimum of 82 overs, but this was never within Nottinghamshire's capabilities as they collapsed in under two hours to the pace of Benjamin, who returned career-best figures of six for 33.

Leicestershire

L. Potter c French b Rice	4	– c Randall b Pick	47
I. P. Butcher lbw b Rice	0	– c Hemmings b Saxelby	4
P. Willey c and b Such	119	– b Saxelby	5
*D. I. Gower b Saxelby	23	– not out	80
J. J. Whitaker not out	200	– c Rice b Pick	11
T. J. Boon not out	20	– c French b Pick	9
P. A. J. DeFreitas (did not bat)	–	not out	36
L-b 8, n-b 2	10	L-b 6, w 1, n-b 5	12

1/4 2/5 3/58 4/302   (4 wkts dec.) 376   1/16 2/36 3/81   (5 wkts dec.) 204
                                                      4/107 5/135

†P. Whitticase, W. K. M. Benjamin, J. P. Agnew and L. B. Taylor did not bat.

Bonus points – Leicestershire 4, Nottinghamshire 1 (Score at 100 overs: 359-4).

Bowling: *First Innings*—Pick 16.5-3-96-0; Rice 16-5-43-2; Saxelby 18-4-69-1; Hemmings 24-6-72-0; Such 27-4-82-1; Broad 1-0-6-0. *Second Innings*—Pick 17-2-58-3; Rice 9-3-23-0; Saxelby 7-1-23-2; Such 14-4-47-0; Hemmings 18-4-47-0.

Nottinghamshire

R. T. Robinson c Whitaker b DeFreitas	12	– absent injured	
B. C. Broad c Whitaker b Agnew	0	– (1) c Whitaker b Benjamin	0
R. A. Pick c Butcher b DeFreitas	55	– (7) b Benjamin	0
D. W. Randall b Benjamin	9	– (3) c Gower b Benjamin	11
*C. E. B. Rice b DeFreitas	10	– (4) c sub b Benjamin	2
P. Johnson c and b Benjamin	80	– (5) lbw b Agnew	5
D. J. R. Martindale c Agnew b DeFreitas	9	– (6) lbw b Agnew	4
†B. N. French b DeFreitas	11	– (2) b Benjamin	11
E. E. Hemmings c Butcher b Benjamin	3	– (8) hit wkt b Agnew	17
K. Saxelby not out	32	– (9) not out	0
P. M. Such run out	6	– (10) c DeFreitas b Benjamin	1
B 5, l-b 10, w 1, n-b 4	20	L-b 6, n-b 1	7

1/1 2/38 3/55 4/138 5/180   247   1/11 2/21 3/23 4/30 5/40   58
6/185 7/194 8/212 9/228   6/40 7/52 8/57 9/58

Bonus points – Nottinghamshire 2, Leicestershire 4.

Bowling: *First Innings*—Agnew 19-2-62-1; Benjamin 20-2-66-3; DeFreitas 21-2-73-5; Willey 6-1-31-0. *Second Innings*—Benjamin 11.5-2-33-6; Agnew 11-4-19-3.

Umpires: D. J. Constant and J. H. Harris.

LEICESTERSHIRE v HAMPSHIRE

At Leicester, July 2, 3, 4. Drawn. Leicestershire 7 pts, Hampshire 4 pts. Toss: Leicestershire. Bowler, 22, from Tasmania but English born, became the first batsman to score a hundred for Leicestershire on his first-class début, and he was within 38 runs of becoming the first player in English cricket to score a century in both innings of his maiden first-class match. He figured in an unbroken fourth-wicket partnership of 273 with Willey, whose 172 not out from 320 deliveries (24 4s) was his highest score for the county. Marshall, on a slow pitch, bowled with little effect in the first innings, but he swung the game Hampshire's way with a spell of three for 13 on the second evening. The visitors were left to rue dropping Clift three times in the slips on the final day after Leicestershire were 41 for four – leading by only 59 and in effect with only five wickets remaining because Whitaker had suffered fractures to both hands after being hit twice by Marshall. Leicestershire recovered through Bowler and DeFreitas, and Willey declined to make a challenging declaration.

Leicestershire

L. Potter b Connor	2	– c Parks b Marshall 0
R. A. Cobb c Terry b James	12	– c Parks b Connor 13
*P. Willey not out	172	– lbw b Marshall 6
J. J. Whitaker c Parks b Tremlett	6	– (5) retired hurt 13
P. D. Bowler not out	100	– (6) lbw b Cowley 62
J. P. Agnew (did not bat)	–	(4) c Parks b Marshall 0
P. B. Clift (did not bat)	–	c R. A. Smith b Connor 49
P. A. J. DeFreitas (did not bat)	–	c Turner b Tremlett 66
W. K. M. Benjamin (did not bat)	–	c Cowley b Nicholas 12
†P. Gill (did not bat)	–	not out 4
L. B. Taylor (did not bat)	–	not out 0
B 3, l-b 1, w 3, n-b 14 21		B 6, l-b 7, w 1, n-b 12 ... 26

1/6 2/33 3/40   (3 wkts dec.) 313   1/4 2/16 3/16   (8 wkts dec.) 251
4/41 5/124 6/223
7/246 8/250

Bonus points – Leicestershire 4, Hampshire 1.

Bowling: *First Innings*—Marshall 15–5–32–0; Connor 21–3–63–1; Tremlett 24–4–77–1; James 22.4–5–74–1; Cowley 15–2–57–0; C. L. Smith 1–0–6–0. *Second Innings*—Connor 18–2–45–2; Marshall 21–4–53–3; James 4–1–17–0; Cowley 13–3–35–1; Tremlett 20–4–61–1; Nicholas 8–2–27–1; Terry 1–1–0–0.

Hampshire

V. P. Terry lbw b Agnew	0	– not out 11
C. L. Smith retired hurt	58	
*M. C. J. Nicholas c Gill b Benjamin	30	
R. A. Smith b Taylor	14	
D. R. Turner b Clift	49	
K. D. James b Taylor	47	
M. D. Marshall b Taylor	6	
N. G. Cowley c Gill b Willey	37	
†R. J. Parks not out	12	– (2) not out 14
T. M. Tremlett not out	6	
B 8, l-b 12, n-b 16 36		B 4, l-b 1 5

1/0 2/70 3/115 4/200   (7 wkts dec.) 295   (no wkt) 30
5/211 6/263 7/275

C. A. Connor did not bat.

Bonus points – Hampshire 3, Leicestershire 3 (Score at 100 overs: 279-7).

Bowling: *First Innings*—Agnew 22–4–57–1; Benjamin 18–6–53–1; Taylor 19–7–34–3; DeFreitas 5–0–32–0; Willey 16–2–50–1; Potter 6–2–13–0; Clift 15–5–36–1; Bowler 1–1–0–0. *Second Innings*—Potter 14–9–9–0; Bowler 9–7–5–0; Benjamin 10–7–3–0; Cobb 4–3–8–0.

Umpires: C. Cook and J. H. Harris.

At Middlesbrough, July 5, 7, 8. LEICESTERSHIRE drew with YORKSHIRE.

At Southend, July 16, 17. LEICESTERSHIRE beat ESSEX by ten wickets.

LEICESTERSHIRE v SUSSEX

At Leicester, July 19, 21, 22. Drawn. Leicestershire 5 pts, Sussex 5 pts. Toss: Leicestershire. Despite the fact that Sussex were without four front-line pace bowlers, and Leicestershire three, the respective attacks were still able to gain assistance from a dry pitch of uncertain pace and bounce. Twenty wickets had fallen before 12.30 p.m. on the second day. However, Sussex were further handicapped by injuries to Babington and Reeve, and Balderstone's 32nd first-class hundred ultimately enabled Gower to set a target of 282 in five hours. This was beyond Sussex, particularly with Parker unable to bat because of a knee injury, but Leicestershire's bowling was poor on a pitch which now offered every encouragement to the spin bowlers. Sussex also benefited from three dropped catches by the slips.

Leicestershire

J. C. Balderstone lbw b Babington	7	– b Mays	115
R. A. Cobb b Mays	10	– b Reeve	15
P. Willey lbw b Reeve	41	– c sub b Lenham	57
*D. I. Gower b Mays	39	– c Gould b Lenham	6
L. Potter lbw b Reeve	0	– c A. P. Wells b Lenham	10
T. J. Boon c Reeve b Babington	3	– not out	29
P. B. Clift lbw b Babington	0	– c sub b C. M. Wells	22
P. A. J. DeFreitas c Standing b C. M. Wells	15	– b Lenham	17
†P. Gill c Gould b C. M. Wells	6	– not out	6
L. Tennant not out	12		
G. J. F. Ferris b C. M. Wells	17		
L-b 7, w 1, n-b 4	12	B 5, l-b 11, w 2, n-b 6	24

1/12 2/41 3/93 4/97 5/101   162   1/59 2/151 3/159   (7 wkts dec.) 301
6/104 7/105 8/120 9/135   4/183 5/239 6/271 7/292

Bonus points – Leicestershire 1, Sussex 4.

Bowling: *First Innings*—Babington 13–3–32–3; Reeve 22–9–29–2; C. M. Wells 18.4–6–49–3; Mays 12–2–45–2. *Second Innings*—Babington 9–1–26–0; Reeve 20–7–40–1; Mays 15–4–38–1; C. M. Wells 30–7–81–1; Standing 6–1–15–0; Lenham 30–7–85–4.

Sussex

N. J. Lenham lbw b Ferris	0	– c Cobb b Willey	35
A. M. Green c Gill b DeFreitas	9	– b DeFreitas	23
P. W. G. Parker lbw b Ferris	48		
A. P. Wells b Ferris	1	– c sub b Clift	14
C. M. Wells c Gill b Ferris	52	– not out	39
R. I. Alikhan lbw b DeFreitas	16	– (3) not out	64
D. K. Standing not out	18		
D. A. Reeve b DeFreitas	2		
*†I. J. Gould b Clift	9		
C. S. Mays b Clift	2		
A. M. Babington lbw b Clift	0		
B 9, l-b 10, w 3, n-b 3	25	B 4, l-b 2, w 3, n-b 2	11

1/1 2/13 3/16 4/120 5/127   182   1/40 2/75 3/125   (3 wkts) 186
6/166 7/168 8/180 9/182

Bonus points – Sussex 1, Leicestershire 4.

Bowling: *First Innings*—DeFreitas 24–5–64–3; Ferris 14–3–54–4; Clift 23.2–9–45–3. *Second Innings*—DeFreitas 20–4–49–1; Tennant 4–1–11–0; Ferris 7–2–18–0; Willey 24–9–40–1; Clift 19–4–52–1; Potter 3–0–10–0.

Umpires: B. Leadbeater and K. E. Palmer.

LEICESTERSHIRE v GLAMORGAN

At Leicester, July 23, 24, 25. Glamorgan won by 13 runs. Glamorgan 17 pts, Leicestershire 4 pts. Toss: Glamorgan. Morris, aged 22, led Glamorgan to their first Championship win of the season, and away from the bottom of the table, in his first match as captain. It was enterprising captaincy from Clift, however, in charge of Leicestershire for the first time with

Gower and Willey on Test duty, and Briers injured, that brought about an exciting finish after bad weather had allowed fewer than eighteen overs' play on the first day. Morris responded to Clift's first-innings declaration by setting a target of 287 in a minimum of 81 overs (ultimately 87), and on an unpredictable pitch a stand of 143 in 38 overs between Boon and Cobb looked to have made the game Leicestershire's. However, Ontong dismissed both in quick succession and, despite a brave 49 from Clift, who batted with torn knee ligaments, a hostile spell from Thomas brought Glamorgan victory with thirteen balls to spare.

Glamorgan

D. B. Pauline c Gill b Agnew	4	– c Taylor b Clift	33
*H. Morris c Butcher b Clift	8	– c sub b Potter	15
G. C. Holmes lbw b DeFreitas	37	– c Gill b Potter	9
Younis Ahmed c Potter b Clift	15	– not out	48
M. P. Maynard c Gill b Taylor	50	– b DeFreitas	11
R. C. Ontong c Butcher b Clift	1	– c Butcher b Potter	4
J. G. Thomas b DeFreitas	0	– not out	23
J. F. Steele not out	32		
†T. Davies c Gill b Taylor	2		
S. J. Base b DeFreitas	8		
D. J. Hickey c Gill b DeFreitas	1		
B 2, l-b 7, w 2, n-b 14	25	B 1, n-b 6	7

1/6 2/41 3/70 4/72 5/73   183 1/47 2/63 3/64 (5 wkts dec.) 150
6/77 7/158 8/160 9/177   4/81 5/112

Bonus points – Glamorgan 1, Leicestershire 4.

Bowling: *First Innings*—DeFreitas 23.5–4–44–4; Agnew 8–0–28–1; Taylor 19–1–65–2; Clift 13–3–22–3; Potter 3–0–15–0. *Second Innings*—DeFreitas 10–2–26–1; Taylor 11–4–24–0; Clift 12–2–24–1; Potter 14–4–37–3; Bowler 7.4–0–38–0.

Leicestershire

J. C. Balderstone b Thomas	13	– lbw b Hickey	4
I. P. Butcher not out	23	– lbw b Thomas	1
R. A. Cobb not out	3	– c Steele b Ontong	77
L. Potter (did not bat)		– c Steele b Base	15
T. J. Boon (did not bat)		– b Ontong	80
P. D. Bowler (did not bat)		– c Holmes b Ontong	0
*P. B. Clift (did not bat)		– c Davies b Thomas	49
P. A. J. DeFreitas (did not bat)		– lbw b Thomas	14
J. P. Agnew (did not bat)		– c Base b Ontong	4
†P. Gill (did not bat)		– c Hickey b Thomas	8
L. B. Taylor (did not bat)		– not out	5
B 4, l-b 2, n-b 2	8	B 2, l-b 7, w 1, n-b 6	16

1/33   (1 wkt dec.) 47 1/5 2/5 3/34 4/177 5/177   273
                6/204 7/241 8/260 9/260

Bowling: *First Innings*—Thomas 9–2–22–1; Hickey 4–2–8–0; Base 1–0–8–0; Ontong 5–2–3–0; Steele 1–1–0–0. *Second Innings*—Thomas 25.5–2–83–4; Hickey 12–3–30–1; Ontong 27–3–88–4; Base 10–3–22–1; Holmes 5–0–30–0; Steele 5–2–8–0.

Umpires: B. Leadbeater and K. E. Palmer.

At Canterbury, August 2, 4, 5. LEICESTERSHIRE lost to KENT by 5 runs.

LEICESTERSHIRE v YORKSHIRE

At Leicester, August 6, 7, 8. Leicestershire won by seven wickets. Leicestershire 22 pts, Yorkshire 6 pts. Toss: Yorkshire. Higgs, the former England fast bowler, 49 years of age and Leicestershire's coach, made a romantic return to first-class cricket after a four-year absence, taking five wickets in an innings for the 50th time with model line-and-length bowling on an uneven pitch. Called up because of injuries in the county's ranks, he undermined Yorkshire's first innings with a spell of three for 1 in 28 balls. On the second day the spotlight shifted to Whitaker, who came back after a month's absence because of his hand injuries to score his first century against his native county, needing only 129 deliveries and hitting three 6s and nine 4s. He was dropped twice, as indeed he was in Leicestershire's second innings, when his 84-ball 82 not out (two 6s, nine 4s), along with important contributions from two other Yorkshire "exiles", Boon and Balderstone, sustained the home side's chase for 238 in 57 overs. Carrick came in for particularly heavy punishment and Leicestershire coasted to victory with fourteen balls to spare. During the match DeFreitas was awarded his Leicestershire cap.

Yorkshire

R. J. Blakey c Potter b Higgs	32	– lbw b Taylor	8
A. A. Metcalfe lbw b Higgs	60	– c Cobb b Taylor	35
S. N. Hartley c and b Ferris	23	– lbw b DeFreitas	22
P. E. Robinson c Potter b Higgs	2	– c Butcher b Boon	71
J. D. Love c Whitticase b DeFreitas	8	– b Ferris	10
*†D. L. Bairstow c Whitticase b DeFreitas	15	– not out	52
P. Carrick lbw b DeFreitas	25	– c and b Boon	27
P. J. Hartley lbw b Higgs	30	– c Higgs b Boon	15
S. J. Dennis not out	5		
C. Shaw lbw b Higgs	0		
S. D. Fletcher c Balderstone b DeFreitas	2		
L-b 6, n-b 8	14	B 1, l-b 7, w 1, n-b 7	16

1/96 2/103 3/113 4/132 5/136   216   1/19 2/69 3/73   (7 wkts dec.) 256
6/175 7/187 8/213 9/213   4/86 5/185 6/232 7/256

Bonus points – Yorkshire 2, Leicestershire 4.

Bowling: *First Innings*—DeFreitas 22.4-3-94-4; Ferris 21-6-62-1; Taylor 10-2-32-0; Higgs 11-4-22-5. *Second Innings*—DeFreitas 17-4-63-1; Taylor 14-7-18-2; Potter 17-1-81-0; Ferris 8-1-31-1; Balderstone 3-0-23-0; Boon 8.3-0-40-3.

Leicestershire

I. P. Butcher lbw b Dennis	19	– c and b P. J. Hartley	7
*J. C. Balderstone b Dennis	14	– c Carrick b Fletcher	48
R. A. Cobb c Carrick b Shaw	47	– lbw b Dennis	5
T. J. Boon lbw b Fletcher	9	– not out	78
J. J. Whitaker not out	100	– not out	82
L. Potter c Bairstow b Dennis	7		
P. A. J. DeFreitas c Bairstow b P. J. Hartley	5		
†P. Whitticase c Robinson b P. J. Hartley	0		
L. B. Taylor c Bairstow b P. J. Hartley	1		
G. J. F. Ferris c and b Shaw	16		
K. Higgs not out	3		
B 1, l-b 9, n-b 4	14	B 7, l-b 9, w 1, n-b 2	19

1/22 2/63 3/84 4/106   (9 wkts dec.) 235   1/7 2/29 3/102   (3 wkts) 239
5/136 6/159 7/163
8/171 9/219

Bonus points – Leicestershire 2, Yorkshire 4.

Bowling: *First Innings*—P. J. Hartley 21-5-61-3; Dennis 25.4-6-85-3; Carrick 2-1-2-0; Fletcher 19-5-47-1; Shaw 15-6-30-2. *Second Innings*—Dennis 14.4-3-58-1; P. J. Hartley 6-0-46-1; Carrick 17-2-56-0; Shaw 4-1-15-0; Fletcher 12-1-40-1; Love 1-0-8-0.

Umpires: A. A. Jones and R. Julian.

LEICESTERSHIRE v ESSEX

At Leicester, August 9, 11, 12. Essex won by 130 runs. Essex 18 pts, Leicestershire 4 pts. Toss: Essex. Essex managed two batting points on a green pitch on the opening day, thanks largely to excellent innings from Hardie and Foster. And on the third day Foster took five wickets in an innings for the ninth time in the season to confound Leicestershire's quest for 321 in 80 overs and set Essex up for the match points. That target was manufactured after play had not been possible on the second day, Essex scoring 159 runs in 52 minutes against "feed" bowling following Leicestershire's declaration at their weekend score. Leicestershire were already struggling at 69 for three, and when Whitaker, Potter and Boon fell at that total in the space of four deliveries, Essex could be the only winners. Whitticase held them up with a valiant half-century but they eventually won with plenty in hand to make further ground on the Championship leaders, Gloucestershire.

Essex

†D. E. East c Boon b Agnew	20	– c DeFreitas b Boon	20
J. P. Stephenson c Willey b Ferris	5	– c Ferris b Boon	30
P. J. Prichard b Ferris	23	– not out	40
A. R. Border lbw b Agnew	0		
*K. W. R. Fletcher c Whitticase b Agnew	16		
B. R. Hardie c Balderstone b DeFreitas	53	– (5) not out	1
A. W. Lilley lbw b Taylor	32	– (4) c Ferris b Whitaker	63
N. A. Foster not out	48		
T. D. Topley lbw b Willey	0		
J. K. Lever run out	6		
J. H. Childs c Whitticase b Taylor	0		
B 5, l-b 3, n-b 5	13	B 2, l-b 2, w 1	5

1/19 2/43 3/45 4/74 5/86   216   1/55 2/55 3/142   (3 wkts dec.) 159
6/151 7/188 8/189 9/216

Bonus points – Essex 2, Leicestershire 4.

Bowling: *First Innings*—Taylor 17.2–3–36–2; Ferris 15–1–58–2; Agnew 22–6–55–3; DeFreitas 20–6–50–1; Willey 9–4–9–1. *Second Innings*—Cobb 6–0–33–0; Boon 8–1–81–2; Whitaker 4.2–0–41–1.

Leicestershire

J. C. Balderstone b Foster	7	– c Topley b Foster	18
R. A. Cobb not out	29	– c East b Foster	0
*P. Willey c and b Topley	3	– c East b Foster	31
T. J. Boon not out	12	– c Prichard b Topley	7
J. J. Whitaker (did not bat)		– c Topley b Foster	5
L. Potter (did not bat)		– c East b Foster	0
P. A. J. DeFreitas (did not bat)		– c Hardie b Topley	22
†P. Whitticase (did not bat)		– not out	55
J. P. Agnew (did not bat)		– c Lilley b Topley	21
G. J. F. Ferris (did not bat)		– lbw b Childs	10
L. B. Taylor (did not bat)		– lbw b Childs	7
N-b 4	4	L-b 1, w 3, n-b 10	14

1/11 2/27   (2 wkts dec.) 55   1/3 2/48 3/59 4/69 5/69   190
                                         6/69 7/119 8/146 9/176

Bowling: *First Innings*—Lever 7–1–20–0; Foster 10–6–21–1; Topley 5–1–10–1; Childs 1–0–4–0. *Second Innings*—Foster 22–3–84–5; Topley 18–3–69–3; Childs 13.5–6–36–2.

Umpires: A. A. Jones and P. B. Wight.

At Worcester, August 16, 18, 19. LEICESTERSHIRE lost to WORCESTERSHIRE by four wickets.

At Chesterfield, August 20, 21, 22. LEICESTERSHIRE drew with DERBYSHIRE.

LEICESTERSHIRE v NORTHAMPTONSHIRE

At Leicester, August 23, 25, 26. Drawn. Leicestershire 3 pts, Northamptonshire 2 pts. Toss:
Leicestershire. The weather ruined this traditional Bank Holiday fixture, with only 21.2 overs
bowled on the second day and none at all on the third. This was a big disappointment for the
club and for spectators, just as Saturday had brought disappointment for Cobb, who once
again missed out when within sight of an elusive maiden century. His 91, containing twelve
4s and spanning four and a half hours, was a career best, but his concentration faltered
immediately after the tea interval and he was caught at slip off his former Leicestershire
colleague, Nick Cook. The innings' entertainment came from Benjamin, whose 24-ball half-
century contained five 4s and four 6s, two each off Cook and Harper.

Leicestershire

J. C. Balderstone lbw b Capel	37	W. K. M. Benjamin not out	57
R. A. Cobb c Harper b N. G. B. Cook	91	J. P. Agnew st Ripley b N. G. B. Cook	0
*P. Willey c G. Cook b Walker	40	L. B. Taylor not out	4
J. J. Whitaker c G. Cook b Harper	51		
T. J. Boon b N. G. B. Cook	37	B 5, l-b 8, w 1, n-b 7	21
P. D. Bowler lbw b Harper	2		
P. A. J. DeFreitas c Walker		1/78 2/147 3/227 (9 wkts dec.) 367	
b N. G. B. Cook	19	4/233 5/238 6/293	
†P. Whitticase c Larkins b Harper	8	7/304 8/306 9/308	

Bonus points – Leicestershire 3, Northamptonshire 2 (Score at 100 overs: 257-5).

Bowling: Mallender 23–4–64–0; Capel 22–4–72–1; Walker 19–3–72–1; N. G. B. Cook
31.2–10–69–4; Harper 29–11–77–3.

Northamptonshire

*G. Cook, W. Larkins, R. J. Boyd-Moss, R. J. Bailey, D. J. Capel, R. A. Harper,
†D. Ripley, N. G. B. Cook, N. A. Mallender, A. Walker and R. G. Williams.

Umpires: J. Birkenshaw and R. A. White.

LEICESTERSHIRE v DERBYSHIRE

At Leicester, August 27, 28, 29. Drawn. Leicestershire 7 pts, Derbyshire 8 pts. Toss: Leicestershire. Off-the-field announcements held more interest than a match which never rose above
the mundane. Gower announced that he was resting until the end of the season, giving as his
reason "mental and physical exhaustion", and passing on the captaincy to Willey, who struck
21 4s in his fourth hundred of the season before announcing that he would not be available to
tour Australia because of concern about his knee. Barnett, Morris and Whitaker then pressed
their claims for inclusion in the England party, the last-mentioned two scoring chanceless
hundreds, but with little in the way of enterprise from the captains, the match petered out into
a draw.

Leicestershire

J. C. Balderstone c Maher b Mortensen	8	– c Sharma b Malcolm	12
R. A. Cobb c Sharma b Finney	17	– c Sharma b Miller	45
*P. Willey not out	168	– (8) not out	0
J. J. Whitaker b Finney	0	– not out	106
T. J. Boon c Hill b Malcolm	25	– (3) c Sharma b Miller	42
P. D. Bowler c Maher b Mortensen	22	– (5) c Miller b Sharma	6
P. A. J. DeFreitas lbw b Finney	17	– c Roberts b Miller	0
†P. Whitticase c Jean-Jacques b Malcolm	4	– (6) c Mortensen b Miller	45
W. K. M. Benjamin b Malcolm	8		
J. P. Agnew c Sharma b Mortensen	16		
L. B. Taylor c Maher b Mortensen	0		
B 3, w 1, n-b 3	7	L-b 2, w 4	6

1/11 2/36 3/44 4/88 5/154   292   1/14 2/75 3/150 4/167   (6 wkts) 262
6/195 7/210 8/224 9/280   5/252 6/262

Bonus points – Leicestershire 3, Derbyshire 4.

Bowling: *First Innings*—Malcolm 22–2–61–3; Mortensen 15.4–3–61–4; Finney 22–4–74–3; Miller 19–7–45–0; Jean-Jacques 11–1–48–0. *Second Innings*—Malcolm 8–0–48–1; Mortensen 2–1–2–0; Miller 39–9–114–4; Finney 2–0–5–0; Barnett 6–2–29–0; Sharma 25–7–62–1.

Derbyshire

*K. J. Barnett b DeFreitas	96	M. Jean-Jacques c Whitticase b Taylor	8
†B. J. M. Maher c Cobb b Taylor	14	O. H. Mortensen lbw b Willey	3
A. Hill c Whitticase b Benjamin	12	D. E. Malcolm not out	0
J. E. Morris c Whitaker b Willey	118		
B. Roberts lbw b DeFreitas	23	L-b 2, n-b 9	11
G. Miller b DeFreitas	0		
R. Sharma c Benjamin b DeFreitas	38	1/66 2/122 3/133 4/191 5/191 336
R. J. Finney c Whitticase b DeFreitas	13	6/244 7/288 8/300 9/331

Bonus points – Derbyshire 4, Leicestershire 4.

Bowling: Taylor 18–4–76–2; Benjamin 24–1–104–1; Willey 14.5–3–25–2; DeFreitas 27–4–92–5; Agnew 9–2–33–0; Bowler 2–0–4–0.

Umpires: J. Birkenshaw and B. Dudleston.

LEICESTERSHIRE v SOMERSET

At Leicester, August 30, September 1, 2. Drawn. Leicestershire 7 pts, Somerset 4 pts. Toss: Somerset. An eventful match was eventually overshadowed by events off the field, with the announcement on the final morning that Leicestershire's secretary-manager, Mr F. M. Turner, was to recommend to the full committee the replacement of Gower as county captain. Leicestershire were disappointed at failing to record a victory in their final home match after bowling Somerset out for 113 and asking them to follow on 180 runs behind. Roebuck and Felton, the latter scoring his third century of the season, figured in an opening partnership of 198, and when four wickets fell on the final morning to raise the home side's hopes, the fifth-wicket stand of 136 between Botham and Harden dashed them most effectively.

Leicestershire

J. C. Balderstone c Gard b Botham	16	– not out	18
R. A. Cobb lbw b Botham	29	– b Taylor	7
*P. Willey c Gard b Botham	7		
J. J. Whitaker b Botham	31		
T. J. Boon c Botham b Davis	83	– (3) not out	41
P. D. Bowler lbw b Botham	18		
P. A. J. DeFreitas b Marks	9		
†P. Whitticase not out	67		
W. K. M. Benjamin lbw b Dredge	10		
K. Higgs c Gard b Botham	8		
L. B. Taylor c Gard b Davis	0		
B 1, l-b 12, n-b 2	15	L-b 1, w 1, n-b 2	4

1/44 2/45 3/78 4/91 5/146　　　　　　293　　1/11　　　　　　(1 wkt) 70
6/165 7/243 8/264 9/291

Bonus points – Leicestershire 3, Somerset 4.

Bowling: *First Innings*—Botham 43–12–125–6; Taylor 11–2–39–0; Dredge 14–3–36–1; Davis 13.4–2–43–2; Marks 12–2–37–1. *Second Innings*—Taylor 7–0–38–1; Dredge 6–1–26–0; Botham 2–2–0–0; Harden 2–0–5–0.

Somerset

N. A. Felton lbw b Taylor	4	– c Willey b Taylor	110
*P. M. Roebuck b Taylor	2	– c Whitticase b DeFreitas	72
J. J. E. Hardy c Boon b Benjamin	19	– b DeFreitas	8
R. J. Harden b Benjamin	8	– c Taylor b Benjamin	63
B. C. Rose b Benjamin	16	– b Taylor	8
I. T. Botham c Whitticase b DeFreitas	10	– b Taylor	74
V. J. Marks c Boon b DeFreitas	2	– not out	23
†T. Gard lbw b Benjamin	3	– b Taylor	3
C. H. Dredge b Benjamin	23	– c Boon b Willey	7
N. S. Taylor not out	0	– b DeFreitas	7
M. R. Davis absent injured		– not out	0
B 1, l-b 10, w 1, n-b 14	26	B 2, l-b 16, w 6, n-b 17	41

1/11 2/12 3/46 4/54 5/70　　　　　113　　1/198 2/207 3/216　　(9 wkts dec.) 416
6/76 7/85 8/93 9/113　　　　　　　　　4/233 5/369 6/375
　　　　　　　　　　　　　　　　　　7/383 8/404 9/416

Bonus points – Leicestershire 4.

Bowling: *First Innings*—Taylor 12–2–28–2; Higgs 7–3–6–0; Benjamin 11.5–1–45–5; DeFreitas 7–0–23–2. *Second Innings*—Benjamin 24–2–92–1; Taylor 25–5–106–4; DeFreitas 40.3–8–96–3; Higgs 18–3–43–0; Willey 22–9–51–1; Bowler 6–2–10–0.

Umpires: B. Dudleston and B. J. Meyer.

At The Oval, September 13, 15, 16. LEICESTERSHIRE lost to SURREY by 90 runs.

MIDDLESEX

Patron: HRH The Duke of Edinburgh
President: F. G. Mann
Chairman: M. P. Murray
Chairman, Cricket Committee: R. V. C. Robins
Secretary: T. M. Lamb
Lord's Cricket Ground, St John's Wood,
London NW8 8QN (Telephone: 01-289 1300)
Captain: M. W. Gatting
Coach: D. Bennett

There was universal surprise and local disappointment at Middlesex's non-existent defence of their Britannic Assurance Championship pennant. It had been expected that they would again overcome the loss of key players to England duties, but neither the full-strength side nor the second-string team performed to the level achieved in 1985. The midsummer weeks near, or at, the foot of the table brought grumblings from impatient supporters.

The reality was that, having been denied a winning start *with* Mike Gatting, John Emburey and Phil Edmonds, Middlesex had little prospect of winning without them. A further reality was that the 1985 Championship was a near-miracle in the similar circumstances of a constantly changing team.

"Supporters quickly forget", ruminated Middlesex's coach, Don Bennett, referring specifically to criticism even after the Benson and Hedges Cup had been won. Gatting said: "Our Benson displays included the best cricket in my Middlesex career." Certainly, wins by six, seven and eight wickets and 134 runs in the zonal matches set the mood for the knockout stages, in which home ties in the quarter- and semi-finals enabled their supporters to relish more commanding cricket as Sussex and Nottinghamshire were eliminated by 84 runs and five wickets respectively.

The final against Kent was more testing, but victory from the twilight, rain-drenched, last-ball finish meant that Gatting had received a trophy in all four summers of his captaincy. In eleven seasons Middlesex have won five Championships (one of them shared) and five Lord's finals. The continuing disappointment has been the Sunday League. Middlesex were equal ninth, compared with twelfth in 1985, one reason plausibly advanced being that they play attacking bowlers in a competition which rewards unambitious, defensive seamers. The NatWest Bank Trophy saw Middlesex drawn in the toughest first round; the only tie involving first-class counties. They won at Northampton, but, away again, lost to Yorkshire.

The Championship defence was already going wrong when two important men reported distressing effects from back injuries. Graham Barlow hit a hundred against Sussex late in May, but played only two more innings before being compelled to retire. His eighteen seasons left a memory of 12,387 runs, at 35.90, and breathtaking fielding. Neil Williams also ended his season after four games, and these setbacks meant that almost half the expected full-strength team was unavailable during Tests. Yet even with all their stars in action, Middlesex had not flourished. The first three games brought sixteen points. Later, Clive Radley's ever-changing second-string squad endured a run of defeats by Sussex, Worcestershire, Nottinghamshire, Essex and Surrey. It was a grim contrast to 1985 when Radley organised bonus points so productively that the title campaign never sagged.

The Nottinghamshire defeat made Middlesex sixteenth for more than a month, and when Glamorgan beat Leicestershire, Middlesex were last on July 25. However, Gatting was certain that the capacity to win was merely dormant. Northamptonshire were disposed of in true champions' style for a belated first win on August 5. Radley, Emburey's stand-in as vice-captain, handed the leadership to Paul Downton, who immediately led his men to victory over Gloucestershire. Lancashire and Warwickshire were overwhelmed and there were no defeats in the last month, although nine losses were the most since 1959 – a 28-match Championship. The final placing was twelfth equal.

As a result of the increased fixture clashes with Test matches and an extra Texaco Trophy series, Gatting was away for fourteen matches, Edmonds and Emburey for thirteen. Even when they played, their contribution was less than hoped for. Gatting attacked the bowling in customary fashion, but he played only ten innings; and spin was frequently subsidiary to pace in a damp summer. Only at Edgbaston did Edmonds and Emburey manage a wicket-taking alliance.

Wilf Slack experienced a lop-sided year. Lacking his old partner, Barlow, shell-shocked after the West Indies series, and encountering personal problems, he was unsettled and his technique faltered critically. He lost the ability to play well forward and straight, qualities that were the foundation of his game. He rediscovered his reliable technique in a six-week burst which brought two centuries, two 92s and five other scores over 40, but he was none the less a surprise in England's tour party to Australia.

Radley and Roland Butcher were included in the general decline. Victories will be rare when numbers four and five average around 30. Radley, though, was the cornerstone of the Benson and Hedges Cup wins, and his worth was confirmed with a three-year contract at the age of 42. Butcher experienced some dreadful sequences, one such reading 3, 3, 33, 3, 4 and 4.

It was as well that Andrew Miller and John Carr continued their development, Miller just missing 1,000 runs in his first full season and Carr finishing with some solid scores. "On this form Carr will be a very good player", was Gatting's view, but the demanding Bennett wanted a noticeable improvement from both. However, Carr's promising off-spin has vanished and his seamers were inadequate.

Simon Hughes was the pick of the quick bowlers, swinging the ball away and often making it seam towards the slips – as he demonstrated on one remarkable morning at The Oval. Alastair and Angus Fraser, especially Alastair, hinted that the pace bowling future is bright, but if Emburey and Edmonds stay in international cricket, there might be a problem with spinners. Philip Tufnell and Jamie Sykes did not look the part. Their toils must be set in the context of playing in a struggling side; of spin bowlers needing years to learn their art; and of Middlesex requiring the highest standards. – T.C.

MIDDLESEX 1986

[Bill Smith

Back row: R. O. Butcher, A. J. T. Miller, W. W. Daniel, N. G. Cowans, W. N. Slack, S. P. Hughes, H. P. H. Sharp (*scorer*). *Front row:* P. R. Downton, J. E. Emburey, M. W. Gatting (*captain*), C. T. Radley, P. H. Edmonds. *Insets:* J. D. Carr, N. F. Williams.

MIDDLESEX RESULTS

All first-class matches – Played 26: Won 5, Lost 9, Drawn 12. Abandoned 1.

County Championship matches – Played 24: Won 4, Lost 9, Drawn 11.

Bonus points – Batting 47, Bowling 65.

Competition placings – Britannic Assurance County Championship, 12th equal; NatWest Bank Trophy, 2nd round; Benson and Hedges Cup, winners; John Player League, 9th equal.

BRITANNIC ASSURANCE CHAMPIONSHIP AVERAGES

BATTING

	Birthplace	M	I	NO	R	HI	Avge
‡M. W. Gatting	Kingsbury	10	10	1	452	158	50.22
‡G. D. Barlow	Folkestone	4	5	1	190	107	47.50
‡W. N. Slack	Troumaca, St Vincent	20	30	2	1,136	106	40.57
J. D. Carr	St John's Wood	17	26	3	782	84*	34.00
‡P. R. Downton	Farnborough, Kent	21	25	3	669	104	30.40
A. J. T. Miller	Chesham	22	34	4	907	111*	30.23
‡R. O. Butcher	St Philip, Barbados	24	34	3	933	171	30.09
‡C. T. Radley	Hertford	23	31	6	738	113*	29.52
K. R. Brown	Edmonton	10	16	2	367	66	26.21
M. A. Roseberry ...	Houghton-le-Spring	5	8	1	174	70*	24.85
J. F. Sykes	Shoreditch	3	4	1	63	26	21.00
‡J. E. Emburey	Peckham	11	10	1	163	49	18.11
‡N. G. Cowans	Enfield St Mary, Jamaica	19	19	7	195	44*	16.25
G. D. Rose	Tottenham	5	6	1	74	52	14.80
‡W. W. Daniel	St Philip, Barbados	16	16	6	140	33	14.00
‡P. H. Edmonds ...	Lusaka, N. Rhodesia	11	10	3	93	25	13.28
‡S. P. Hughes	Kingston-upon-Thames	21	24	2	255	47	11.59
A. R. C. Fraser ...	Billinge	5	6	1	39	13	7.80
C. P. Metson	Cuffley	3	4	0	29	15	7.25
P. C. R. Tufnell ...	Barnet	6	7	1	32	9	5.33

Also batted: G. K. Brown (*Welling*) (1 match) 14, 3; A. G. J. Fraser (*Edgware*) (3 matches) 19*, 11*; ‡N. F. Williams (*Hope Well, St Vincent*) (4 matches) 1, 11.

* *Signifies not out.*   ‡ *Denotes county cap.*

The following played a total of ten three-figure innings for Middlesex in County Championship matches: W. N. Slack 3, C. T. Radley 2, G. D. Barlow 1, R. O. Butcher 1, P. R. Downton 1, M. W. Gatting 1, A. J. T. Miller 1.

BOWLING

	O	M	R	W	BB	Avge
J. E. Emburey	251	79	505	24	5-51	21.04
W. W. Daniel	402.1	52	1,387	62	4-27	22.37
N. G. Cowans	396.2	85	1,265	52	5-61	24.32
S. P. Hughes	478.3	109	1,522	54	7-35	28.18
P. H. Edmonds	293.4	90	623	20	4-67	31.15

Also bowled: K. R. Brown 0.4-0-10-0; R. O. Butcher 13.4-2-49-2; J. D. Carr 93.2-17-284-1; A. G. J. Fraser 36.4-12-82-5; A. R. C. Fraser 131-32-327-8; M. W. Gatting 42-18-99-5; A. J. T. Miller 1-0-5-0; G. D. Rose 64-10-277-7; W. N. Slack 17-3-75-1; J. F. Sykes 43.3-5-161-5; P. C. R. Tufnell 148-32-479-5; N. F. Williams 59.3-7-214-8.

Wicket-keepers: P. R. Downton 35 ct, 5 st; C. P. Metson 3 ct.

Leading Fielders: R. O. Butcher 14; C. T. Radley 14; P. H. Edmonds 13; W. N. Slack 13.

At Lord's, April 23, 24, 25. MCC v MIDDLESEX. Abandoned.

MIDDLESEX v DERBYSHIRE

At Lord's, April 26, 28, 29. Drawn. Middlesex 7 pts, Derbyshire 3 pts. Toss: Derbyshire. Fewer than two hours' play was possible on the first day, when Gatting hit Miller for a 6 and five 4s to enliven the brief ration. Holding dismissed him on the second morning with a ball that came back, and both Holding and Finney bowled so accurately that Slack and Radley had to work hard for runs. Slack batted for five hours, while Radley's unbeaten hundred – his 45th – came off 188 balls. Middlesex appeared to have a chance when Derbyshire were 59 for three when bad light brought the day to an early close, but Morris, Roberts and Newman battled soundly on the last day to prevent the follow-on.

Middlesex

G. D. Barlow b Miller	16	– not out	52
W. N. Slack b Newman	96	– lbw b Holding	9
*M. W. Gatting lbw b Holding	43		
C. T. Radley not out	103		
R. O. Butcher c Anderson b Mortensen	34	– (3) b Barnett	60
B 1, l-b 5, n-b 8	14	B 5, l-b 3, n-b 2	10

1/29 2/90 3/217 4/306   (4 wkts dec.) 306   1/23 2/131   (2 wkts dec.) 131

†P. R. Downton, J. E. Emburey, P. H. Edmonds, N. F. Williams, N. G. Cowans and W. W. Daniel did not bat.

Bonus points – Middlesex 3, Derbyshire 1 (Score at 100 overs: 289-3).

Bowling: *First Innings*—Holding 22-6-37-1; Mortensen 25.4-6-63-1; Miller 9-3-34-1; Newman 15-2-49-1; Finney 15-3-45-0; Warner 17-1-72-0. *Second Innings*—Holding 6-1-18-1; Mortensen 7-3-14-0; Newman 7-1-20-0; Finney 7-0-31-0; Warner 5-2-26-0; Barnett 6.3-2-14-1.

Derbyshire

*K. J. Barnett lbw b Cowans	23	M. A. Holding c Downton b Williams . 17
I. S. Anderson lbw b Cowans	4	O. H. Mortensen not out	2
A. Hill c Downton b Edmonds	19	G. Miller absent ill
J. E. Morris b Daniel	44	
R. J. Finney b Cowans	13	L-b 3, w 1, n-b 9 13
†B. Roberts c Edmonds b Williams	28	
P. G. Newman c Emburey b Williams . 34		1/13 2/41 3/50 4/92 5/119 202
A. E. Warner b Cowans	5	6/177 7/182 8/184 9/202

Bonus points – Derbyshire 2, Middlesex 4.

Bowling: Daniel 9-1-43-1; Cowans 18-4-64-4; Emburey 21-10-20-0; Edmonds 18-7-28-1; Williams 12.3-1-44-3; Gatting 2-2-0-0.

Umpires: J. W. Holder and A. G. T. Whitehead.

At Oxford, April 30, May 1, 2. MIDDLESEX beat OXFORD UNIVERSITY by 177 runs.

MIDDLESEX v LEICESTERSHIRE

At Lord's, May 7, 8, 9. Drawn. Middlesex 3 pts, Leicestershire 3 pts. Toss: Middlesex. Entering in unpromising circumstances, Gower none the less played with his usual nonchalance, making 83 from 120 balls with two 6s and nine 4s. One pulled 6 off Daniel went many yards over the square-leg boundary. Whitaker, impressively belligerent, hurried to his 50 off 51 balls, cracking ten 4s. The shortened first day ended with Leicestershire 234 for six, but rain allowed only 41 minutes on the second morning and none on the last day.

Leicestershire

R. A. Cobb c Gatting b Cowans	34	†P. Whitticase not out		5
I. P. Butcher c Downton b Daniel	4	P. A. J. DeFreitas c Slack b Williams	.	9
L. Potter run out	1	W. K. M. Benjamin not out		11
*D. I. Gower b Williams	83	B 2, l-b 4, n-b 7		13
J. J. Whitaker b Cowans	60			
T. J. Boon lbw b Williams	22	1/9 2/11 3/115 4/169 5/191	(8 wkts)	259
P. B. Clift c Butcher b Daniel	17	6/221 7/236 8/246		

L. B. Taylor did not bat.

Bonus points – Leicestershire 3, Middlesex 3.

Bowling: Cowans 20–8–47–2; Daniel 20–3–79–2; Williams 20–1–86–3; Gatting 11–5–20–0; Emburey 2–0–10–0; Edmonds 7–2–11–0.

Middlesex

G. D. Barlow, W. N. Slack, *M. W. Gatting, R. O. Butcher, C. T. Radley, †P. R. Downton, J. E. Emburey, P. H. Edmonds, N. F. Williams, N. G. Cowans and W. W. Daniel.

Umpires: J. A. Jameson and R. Palmer.

MIDDLESEX v GLAMORGAN

At Lord's, May 21, 22, 23. Drawn. Middlesex 4 pts, Glamorgan 2 pts. Toss: Middlesex. On a pitch which had pace and gave movement to the fast bowlers, an intriguing struggle looked in prospect despite the loss of the first day. Daniel was the main architect of Glamorgan's early collapse, benefiting from the safe hands of Brown, who held three catches in seven balls off him – two low at fourth slip and the third off the face of the bat at short leg. Maynard organised the recovery, attacking the faster bowlers confidently and playing the spinners from down the pitch. Thomas and Moseley wrecked Middlesex's start, and the home county finished in disarray when Gatting, after a burst of strokes, was bowled without offering one. The return of the rain to wash out the third day made it all of little consequence.

Glamorgan

J. A. Hopkins lbw b Williams	3	E. A. Moseley c Downton b Gatting	...	19
A. L. Jones c Brown b Daniel	7	†T. Davies not out		5
H. Morris c Brown b Daniel	0	S. J. Base c Radley b Emburey		4
G. C. Holmes c Brown b Daniel	6			
Younis Ahmed c Downton b Williams	1	L-b 9, w 4, n-b 6		19
*R. C. Ontong c Brown b Emburey	19			
M. P. Maynard hit wkt b Gatting	57	1/11 2/13 3/14 4/19 5/25		159
J. G. Thomas b Daniel	19	6/79 7/121 8/134 9/152		

Bonus points – Glamorgan 1, Middlesex 4.

Bowling: Williams 16–4–43–2; Daniel 16–4–34–4; Cowans 10–3–18–0; Edmonds 14–3–26–0; Emburey 7–3–11–2; Gatting 9–4–18–2.

Middlesex

A. J. T. Miller b Thomas	3	R. O. Butcher not out		18
K. R. Brown lbw b Moseley	9			
*M. W. Gatting b Moseley	35	L-b 3, w 2, n-b 6		11
J. E. Emburey c Thomas b Moseley	0			
C. T. Radley not out	18	1/6 2/44 3/49 4/56	(4 wkts)	81

†P. R. Downton, P. H. Edmonds, N. F. Williams, N. G. Cowans and W. W. Daniel did not bat.

Bonus point – Glamorgan 1.

Bowling: Thomas 6–2–13–1; Moseley 9–1–39–3; Base 4–0–12–0; Holmes 3–1–14–0.

Umpires: B. J. Meyer and P. B. Wight.

MIDDLESEX v SUSSEX

At Lord's, May 24, 26, 27. Sussex won by seven wickets. Sussex 22 pts, Middlesex 6 pts. Toss: Sussex. Imran gave the merest hint of what was to come by beating both Middlesex openers repeatedly, but after this early phase Barlow and Miller were in command. Butcher consolidated Middlesex's position with a half-century off 38 balls. On the second day Parker toiled for almost five hours, but his major partners, Green and Imran, were more assertive. Indeed, Imran was out in the same over as Parker. Sussex declared on achieving full batting points and the match was tilting their way when Imran removed Barlow and Hughes before the close. Next day he produced a *tour de force*: his speed and movement on a lively pitch were too much for Middlesex. Imran recorded his career-best bowling figures, surpassing his eight for 58 for Pakistan against Sri Lanka in 1981-82, and he rounded off his day with six 4s and the winning 6 as Sussex reached their target with 38 overs to spare.

Middlesex

G. D. Barlow b Jones	107	– c Gould b Imran	3
A. J. T. Miller c Parker b Jones	73	– c Green b Imran	10
K. R. Brown b Reeve	31	– (4) lbw b le Roux	1
*C. T. Radley lbw b Pigott	4	– (5) c Gould b Imran	2
R. O. Butcher b Reeve	50	– (6) c Jones b Imran	23
J. D. Carr lbw b Pigott	23	– (7) lbw b Imran	1
G. D. Rose lbw b le Roux	7	– (8) lbw b Imran	0
†C. P. Metson b Pigott	15	– (9) c Gould b Jones	5
N. F. Williams c Parker b Reeve	11	– (10) lbw b Imran	11
S. P. Hughes not out	3	– (3) lbw b Imran	4
N. G. Cowans not out	5	– not out	0
L-b 11, w 8, n-b 4	23	B 4, l-b 3, w 2, n-b 1	10

1/194 2/199 3/212 4/277   (9 wkts dec.) 342   1/9 2/18 3/19 4/22 5/43   70
5/283 6/297 7/328 8/331 9/334   6/45 7/45 8/52 9/70

Bonus points – Middlesex 4, Sussex 2 (Score at 100 overs: 308-6).

Bowling: *First Innings*—Imran 21-4-57-0; le Roux 19-5-37-1; Pigott 17-1-71-3; Reeve 29-5-86-3; Jones 10-1-36-2; C. M. Wells 6-1-19-0; Lenham 8-1-25-0. *Second Innings*—Imran 14.3-4-34-8; le Roux 9-3-15-1; Reeve 3-1-9-0; Jones 2-1-5-1.

Sussex

N. J. Lenham c Carr b Hughes	1	– c Metson b Hughes	5
A. M. Green c Barlow b Hughes	88	– b Rose	24
P. W. G. Parker c Metson b Rose	107	– c Metson b Rose	13
Imran Khan run out	60	– (5) not out	43
C. M. Wells lbw b Carr	3	– (4) not out	25
A. P. Wells not out	22		
*†I. J. Gould not out	7		
L-b 8, w 1, n-b 3	12	L-b 2, w 1	3

1/1 2/160 3/267   (5 wkts dec.) 300   1/10 2/43 3/44   (3 wkts) 113
4/267 5/275

G. S. le Roux, D. A. Reeve, A. N. Jones and A. C. S. Pigott did not bat.

Bonus points – Sussex 4, Middlesex 2.

Bowling: *First Innings*—Cowans 24-5-58-0; Hughes 24-4-81-2; Rose 19-5-66-1; Williams 11-1-41-0; Carr 21.2-4-46-1. *Second Innings*—Hughes 11-2-34-1; Cowans 5-1-11-0; Rose 8-1-40-2; Carr 2-0-11-0; Miller 1-0-5-0; Brown 0.4-0-10-0.

Umpires: B. J. Meyer and P. B. Wight.

At The Oval, May 31, June 2, 3. MIDDLESEX drew with SURREY.

At Worcester, June 4, 5, 6. MIDDLESEX lost to WORCESTERSHIRE by an innings and 1 run.

At Manchester, June 7, 9, 10. MIDDLESEX drew with LANCASHIRE.

MIDDLESEX v YORKSHIRE

At Lord's, June 14, 16, 17. Yorkshire won by 69 runs. Yorkshire 22 pts, Middlesex 3 pts. Toss: Yorkshire. Boycott seemed determined to score his 150th century on the occasion of his 600th first-class match, his first innings occupying 4 hours, 40 minutes, during which he received 228 balls in 83 overs. When Radley caught him, very close in, Bairstow immediately helped to double the run-rate. Boycott later failed to mark his 1,000th innings with a big score, but events around it vindicated his first effort. Jarvis bowled superbly, moving the ball off the helpful pitch at high speed, yet attacking the stumps accurately enough to earn four second-innings lbws. Having been in danger of following on, Middlesex in their second innings looked as if they might make 257 in 90 overs only when Gatting was progressing freely.

Yorkshire

G. Boycott c Radley b Emburey	69	– b Fraser		31
M. D. Moxon c Downton b Fraser	20	– c Edmonds b Hughes		13
A. A. Metcalfe c Gatting b Emburey	7	– lbw b Fraser		29
K. Sharp c Miller b Edmonds	11	– b Fraser		2
J. D. Love c and b Cowans	8	– c Downton b Cowans		16
S. N. Hartley c sub b Emburey	56	– c Downton b Cowans		10
*†D. L. Bairstow c Emburey b Edmonds	46	– (9) c and b Edmonds		25
P. Carrick lbw b Gatting	11	– (10) not out		8
A. Sidebottom c Slack b Edmonds	9	– (11) c Edmonds b Cowans		0
P. W. Jarvis not out	9	– (7) c Miller b Emburey		0
S. J. Dennis st Downton b Edmonds	8	– (8) b Cowans		15
B 4, l-b 16, n-b 2	22	B 1, l-b 2, n-b 1		4

1/44 2/56 3/83 4/101 5/143	276	1/14 2/74 3/78 4/79 5/101 153
6/224 7/235 8/245 9/255		6/104 7/104 8/129 9/153

Bonus points – Yorkshire 2, Middlesex 2 (Score at 100 overs: 203-5).

Bowling: *First Innings*—Cowans 13–5–26–1; Hughes 13–7–30–0; Fraser 23–5–48–1; Edmonds 40.4–10–71–4; Emburey 33–6–74–3; Gatting 4–2–7–1. *Second Innings*—Cowans 13–3–49–4; Hughes 6–2–18–1; Edmonds 12–3–35–1; Emburey 8–0–29–1; Fraser 9–2–19–3.

Middlesex

A. J. T. Miller run out	5	– b Carrick		17
W. N. Slack c Bairstow b Jarvis	12	– c Dennis b Jarvis		30
*M. W. Gatting b Sidebottom	29	– lbw b Jarvis		37
R. O. Butcher lbw b Jarvis	0	– c Sharp b Carrick		23
C. T. Radley st Bairstow b Carrick	14	– lbw b Jarvis		16
†P. R. Downton c Love b Sidebottom	2	– lbw b Jarvis		22
J. E. Emburey c Boycott b Jarvis	49	– b Sidebottom		11
P. H. Edmonds c Jarvis b Dennis	5	– c Bairstow b Sidebottom		3
S. P. Hughes lbw b Jarvis	18	– lbw b Jarvis		11
A. R. C. Fraser b Jarvis	12	– not out		7
N. G. Cowans not out	7	– b Jarvis		0
B 4, l-b 12, n-b 4	20	B 3, l-b 6, n-b 1		10

1/14 2/49 3/50 4/66 5/70	173	1/38 2/69 3/108 4/122 5/133 187
6/77 7/84 8/139 9/160		6/149 7/165 8/172 9/185

Bonus points – Middlesex 1, Yorkshire 4.

Bowling: *First Innings*—Sidebottom 18–5–39–2; Jarvis 17–2–45–5; Dennis 8–2–35–1; Carrick 14–4–38–1. *Second Innings*—Sidebottom 16–2–43–2; Jarvis 18.2–7–47–6; Dennis 9–1–30–0; Carrick 29–6–58–2.

Umpires: R. Julian and N. T. Plews.

At Nottingham, June 18, 19, 20. MIDDLESEX lost to NOTTINGHAMSHIRE by 126 runs.

MIDDLESEX v ESSEX

At Lord's, June 21, 23, 24. Essex won by five wickets. Essex 20 pts, Middlesex 6 pts. Toss: Essex. Essex may have thought they had the worst of the first day, in which 17 wickets fell, the last seven being their own for 109. Butcher had defied all the restrictions imposed on most others by the testing conditions, hitting one 6 and thirteen 4s, and Cowans, in a hostile opening spell, had taken four Essex wickets for 2 runs in his first 21 balls. Gladwin and Foster kept Essex afloat, and their deficit of 78 did not look such a handicap when Middlesex submitted in their second innings. Topley again thrived, but Foster was even more devastating on a pitch of erratic bounce which gave considerable movement off the seam. With eleven wickets falling on the second morning, it seemed unlikely that the third day would be necessary, but rain dictated otherwise. Essex, 29 for one at the start of the last day, required 147 more, and Border needed all his skill to see Essex home.

Middlesex

A. J. T. Miller b Topley	12	– c East b Foster 13
K. R. Brown c Fletcher b Topley	6	– c East b Topley 0
†P. R. Downton c Fletcher b Foster	7	– b Topley 36
R. O. Butcher c Prichard b Topley	86	– lbw b Foster 0
*C. T. Radley c East b Pont	1	– c Topley b Foster 9
J. D. Carr lbw b Topley	1	– c Gladwin b Foster 3
M. A. Roseberry c Topley b Pont	36	– c Foster b Topley 0
P. H. Edmonds lbw b Pont	1	– (9) c Border b Topley 11
S. P. Hughes c East b Foster	14	– (8) lbw b Foster 2
N. G. Cowans b Pont	17	– b Foster 3
W. W. Daniel not out	17	– not out 13
L-b 6, w 2, n-b 2	10	B 3, l-b 4 7

1/18 2/20 3/38 4/59 5/66   208   1/2 2/26 3/26 4/52 5/64   97
6/148 7/160 8/160 9/186   6/64 7/66 8/67 9/77

Bonus points – Middlesex 2, Essex 4.

Bowling: *First Innings*—Foster 19.3–5–66–2; Topley 24–4–67–4; Pont 23–6–63–4; Acfield 2–0–6–0. *Second Innings*—Foster 15–2–57–6; Topley 14.1–5–33–4.

Essex

C. Gladwin lbw b Hughes	26	– c Roseberry b Daniel 7
A. W. Lilley c Carr b Cowans	0	– (7) c Edmonds b Hughes 36
P. J. Prichard c Edmonds b Cowans	0	– c Edmonds b Cowans 35
A. R. Border b Cowans	4	– not out 59
*K. W. R. Fletcher c Downton b Cowans	5	– retired hurt 8
K. R. Pont b Daniel	14	– c Hughes b Daniel 0
†D. E. East c Cowans b Daniel	4	– (2) lbw b Cowans 5
N. A. Foster c Downton b Daniel	47	– not out 17
T. D. Topley lbw b Cowans	2	
J. H. Childs not out	5	
D. L. Acfield b Daniel	0	
B 5, l-b 11, n-b 7	23	B 4, l-b 3, w 1, n-b 4 ... 12

1/1 2/7 3/11 4/18 5/50   130   1/10 2/44 3/48   (5 wkts) 179
6/63 7/76 8/112 9/128   4/69 5/137

Bonus points – Middlesex 4.

Bowling: *First Innings*—Cowans 16–2–61–5; Daniel 14.2–2–27–4; Hughes 4–1–21–1; Edmonds 11–7–5–0. *Second Innings*—Cowans 18–4–65–2; Daniel 18–2–60–2; Hughes 17–7–35–1; Edmonds 2–0–7–0; Butcher 0.4–0–5–0.

Umpires: C. Cook and B. Dudleston.

At Lord's, June 28, 29, 30. MIDDLESEX drew with NEW ZEALANDERS (See New Zealand tour section).

MIDDLESEX v SURREY

At Uxbridge, July 2, 3, 4. Surrey won by 197 runs. Surrey 23 pts, Middlesex 7 pts. Toss: Surrey. Middlesex dominated the first morning's play, but Falkner and Medlycott, beginning their sixth-wicket partnership before lunch, were not separated until after tea. Falkner's first Championship century came in under four hours, and before the day was over another Surrey novice, Bicknell, took two wickets as Middlesex slipped to 47 for three. By lunch next day, Butcher had made 125 of Middlesex's 165 runs, his 100 arriving off 95 balls, and in all he hit a century in 4s as well as striking three 6s – a dazzling exhibition on a pitch on which the ball kept low for the quicker bowlers and helped the spinners. The match turned on two hard-earned centuries from Stewart and Richards which left Middlesex to score 357 in 66 overs. With 30 overs left and nine wickets to fall, a draw looked certain, but when Miller and Roseberry were parted, Pocock and Medlycott, helped by the close catching of Butcher, worked their way through the innings.

Surrey

A. R. Butcher c Butcher b Hughes	34	– c Butcher b Cowans	2
G. S. Clinton c Carr b Daniel	7	– (7) not out	16
A. J. Stewart run out	8	– c Downton b Daniel	144
M. A. Lynch b Daniel	8	– lbw b Cowans	48
N. J. Falkner c sub b Hughes	102	– (2) c Downton b Daniel	4
†C. J. Richards c Butcher b Tufnell	20	– (5) b Tufnell	100
K. T. Medlycott c Daniel b Hughes	61	– (6) c Miller b Tufnell	7
M. A. Feltham run out	20	– not out	8
S. T. Clarke not out	14		
M. P. Bicknell b Daniel	0		
*P. I. Pocock b Daniel	0		
L-b 6, w 1, n-b 7	14	B 2, l-b 11, n-b 11	24
	288	(6 wkts dec.)	**353**

1/36 2/45 3/60 4/64 5/97 6/224 7/259 8/288 9/288

1/8 2/8 3/131 4/259 5/279 6/337

Bonus points – Surrey 3, Middlesex 4.

Bowling: *First Innings*—Daniel 22–4–65–4; Cowans 9–3–35–0; Hughes 25–7–71–3; Tufnell 30–10–83–1; Carr 10–5–24–0; Butcher 1–0–4–0. *Second Innings*—Daniel 20–0–84–2; Cowans 16–3–64–2; Hughes 15–1–81–0; Tufnell 25–5–81–2; Carr 11–2–30–0.

Middlesex

A. J. T. Miller c Pocock b Bicknell	7	– b Medlycott	34
W. N. Slack c Richards b Bicknell	4	– c Lynch b Bicknell	0
†P. R. Downton lbw b Clarke	0	– (7) c Lynch b Medlycott	0
R. O. Butcher st Richards b Medlycott	171	– b Pocock	0
*C. T. Radley lbw b Bicknell	12	– c Butcher b Pocock	22
J. D. Carr st Richards b Pocock	34	– c Butcher b Medlycott	3
M. A. Roseberry c Lynch b Medlycott	3	– (3) st Richards b Pocock	59
S. P. Hughes c Bicknell b Medlycott	4	– b Medlycott	6
P. C. R. Tufnell c Falkner b Medlycott	2	– (10) c Butcher b Pocock	1
W. W. Daniel c and b Medlycott	11	– (11) not out	0
N. G. Cowans not out	17	– (9) c Richards b Medlycott	24
B 1, l-b 11, w 2, n-b 6	20	L-b 4, w 5, n-b 1	10

1/14 2/15 3/23 4/56 5/169   285   1/8 2/91 3/96 4/103 5/114   159
6/215 7/247 8/256 9/257   6/114 7/134 8/134 9/159

Bonus points – Middlesex 3, Surrey 4.

Bowling: *First Innings*—Clarke 10–2–45–1; Bicknell 22–4–88–3; Pocock 9–1–35–1; Feltham 6–1–34–0; Medlycott 19.3–3–71–5. *Second Innings*—Bicknell 7–3–9–1; Feltham 7–3–17–0; Medlycott 27–9–84–5; Pocock 23.1–11–45–4.

Umpires: B. Dudleston and A. A. Jones.

MIDDLESEX v WARWICKSHIRE

At Uxbridge, July 5, 7, 8. Drawn. Middlesex 4 pts, Warwickshire 4 pts. Toss: Middlesex. The first day and much of the second morning were lost to rain. Small and McMillan, moving the ball about sharply, undermined Middlesex's start, Small's first ten overs bringing him three for 10. Downton, however, settled in, first with Carr and then Rose, who assisted in a forthright manner during a stand of 124. When Middlesex batted into the third day, Warwickshire forfeited their first innings and were soon set a target of 331 in 70 overs. Warwickshire opened with two tailenders to counter the new ball on an awkward pitch, but they were swept aside in four overs. When Lloyd went first ball, leaving Warwickshire 11 for three at lunch, their chance of winning had gone. Middlesex in turn were foiled by Smith (43 overs), McMillan, brief showers and finally the ninth-wicket pair, who held on for the last two and a half overs.

Middlesex

A. J. T. Miller c McMillan b Small	4		
W. N. Slack c McMillan b Small	3		
M. A. Roseberry lbw b McMillan	4		
R. O. Butcher b McMillan	13		
*C. T. Radley lbw b Small	2		
J. D. Carr lbw b Parsons	17		
†P. R. Downton st Humpage b Gifford	104		
G. D. Rose c Amiss b Thorne	52		
S. P. Hughes b Gifford	47		
A. G. J. Fraser not out	19	– (1) not out	11
P. C. R. Tufnell b Parsons	6	– (2) not out	6
B 8, l-b 19, w 1, n-b 13	41	L-b 1	1

1/5 2/13 3/19 4/21 5/33   312   (no wkt dec.) 18
6/89 7/213 8/262 9/289

Bonus points – Middlesex 4, Warwickshire 4 (Score at 100 overs: 312-9).

Bowling: *First Innings*—Small 24–5–41–3; McMillan 16–2–68–2; Gifford 29–5–76–2; Parsons 10.2–3–23–2; Smith 4–2–7–0; Kerr 5–1–26–0; Thorne 12–2–44–1. *Second Innings*—Gifford 2–0–8–0; Thorne 2–0–5–0; Asif Din 1–0–4–0.

Warwickshire

Warwickshire forfeited their first innings.

K. J. Kerr c Radley b Hughes	4	Asif Din c Downton b Fraser	16
G. J. Parsons c Carr b Rose	4	D. A. Thorne not out	0
T. A. Lloyd b Hughes	0	G. C. Small not out	12
P. A. Smith st Downton b Tufnell	44	L-b 14, w 1, n-b 5	20
D. L. Amiss c Downton b Rose	14		
†G. W. Humpage c Downton b Fraser	21	1/4 2/4 3/11 4/33	(8 wkts) 198
B. M. McMillan c Radley b Tufnell	63	5/57 6/142 7/186 8/186	

*N. Gifford did not bat.

Bowling: Hughes 20–4–61–2; Rose 11–2–39–2; Fraser 14.5–6–37–2; Tufnell 18–4–47–2; Carr 3–3–0–0.

Umpires: B. Dudleston and A. A. Jones.

MIDDLESEX v SOMERSET

At Lord's, July 16, 17, 18. Drawn. Middlesex 4 pts, Somerset 6 pts. Toss: Middlesex. Slack, emerging cautiously from a poor patch, batted for almost five hours. Only at the start of Carr's innings did Middlesex score freely, and the third batting point was not earned until the 95th over. Radley, 68 overnight, engineered 76 quick runs on the second morning, when he achieved the distinction of a century against all the other counties, and two more hundreds followed as Rose and Roebuck compiled their second consecutive double-century opening partnership. Rose played with great dash and audacity, hitting twenty boundaries, while Roebuck was typically patient, needing 277 minutes to reach three figures. Having declared at their overnight score, Somerset were set 257 in 195 minutes, but with the injured Rose not permitted to bat above No. 7 and the makeshift opening pair being swept aside by the new ball, the target was not attacked.

Middlesex

W. N. Slack c Gard b Coombs	92	– (2) c Gard b Coombs 57
A. J. T. Miller b Garner	14	– (1) b Marks 78
J. D. Carr c Marks b Coombs	75	– st Gard b Coombs 14
R. O. Butcher c Rose b Dredge	9	– not out 10
*C. T. Radley not out	113	– not out 8
M. A. Roseberry run out	0	
†P. R. Downton c Coombs b Marks	56	
L-b 4, n-b 13	17	B 5, l-b 11, n-b 1 17

1/21 2/138 3/176 (6 wkts dec.) 376   1/108 2/144 3/174 (3 wkts dec.) 184
4/217 5/219 6/376

S. P. Hughes, N. G. Cowans, P. C. R. Tufnell and W. W. Daniel did not bat.

Bonus points – Middlesex 3, Somerset 2 (Score at 100 overs: 261-5).

Bowling: *First Innings*—Garner 23–7–57–1; Davis 21–3–76–0; Dredge 17–2–55–1; Marks 32.1–10–73–1; Coombs 29–8–101–2; Harden 3–0–10–0. *Second Innings*—Garner 5–2–7–0; Davis 6–0–23–0; Dredge 6–1–16–0; Marks 17–2–76–1; Coombs 12–0–46–2.

Somerset

B. C. Rose c Downton b Daniel	129	
*P. M. Roebuck not out	128	– b Daniel 3
J. J. E. Hardy b Hughes	2	– (1) b Cowans 5
R. J. Harden run out	23	– (3) lbw b Cowans 54
N. A. Felton lbw b Cowans	5	– (4) not out 53
V. J. Marks not out	2	– (5) not out 7
B 5, l-b 4, w 1, n-b 5	15	B 3, l-b 1 4

1/225 2/234 3/275 4/293 (4 wkts dec.) 304   1/5 2/17 3/115 (3 wkts) 126

†T. Gard, M. R. Davis, C. H. Dredge, J. Garner and R. V. J. Coombs did not bat.

Bonus points – Somerset 4, Middlesex 1.

Bowling: *First Innings*—Daniel 12–0–36–1; Cowans 19–3–82–1; Hughes 24–7–50–1; Tufnell 23–3–73–0; Carr 11–1–36–0; Slack 6–2–18–0. *Second Innings*—Daniel 9–3–20–1; Cowans 11–3–19–2; Hughes 9–0–33–0; Tufnell 13–3–28–0; Carr 6–1–22–0; Butcher 1–1–0–0.

Umpires: A. A. Jones and K. J. Lyons.

At Derby, July 19, 21, 22. MIDDLESEX lost to DERBYSHIRE by one wicket.

At Northampton, July 26, 28, 29. MIDDLESEX lost to NORTHAMPTONSHIRE by four wickets.

MIDDLESEX v NORTHAMPTONSHIRE

At Lord's, August 2, 4, 5. Middlesex won by an innings and 43 runs. Middlesex 24 pts, Northamptonshire 2 pts. Toss: Middlesex. The defending champions had spent the previous week at the foot of the County Championship table, but they removed themselves from this ignominious position by recording their first win of the summer. Gatting, in his most powerful, disdainful mood, collected the big score he had been seeking all season, hitting a 6 and 24 4s off his 195 balls. Radley, without a boundary, and Downton completed half-centuries before the end of the first day, and on Monday morning the tail was permitted to add 94 to begin another day of unbroken command for Middlesex. Northamptonshire's openers were out of the action by lunch, Cook having been struck on the arm by Daniel, but the key wicket was Lamb's, caught hooking first ball. Northamptonshire's first five wickets fell in sixteen overs, but the second half lasted for 41. Middlesex needed eight wickets on the last day and took two of them swiftly, but Lamb played a sparkling knock. Even when he was caught down the pitch by the diving Downton, Middlesex were taken into the final twenty overs.

Middlesex

A. J. T. Miller b N. G. B. Cook	.....	39
W. N. Slack c Waterton b Walker	.....	0
*M. W. Gatting b Mallender	....	158
R. O. Butcher c Boyd-Moss b Walker	..	42
C. T. Radley c Waterton b Capel	.....	50
†P. R. Downton c and b Harper	.....	50
P. H. Edmonds retired hurt	....	8
J. E. Emburey c Harper b Capel	......	15

S. P. Hughes c Lamb b N. G. B. Cook	.	23
W. W. Daniel b Mallender	....	3
N. G. Cowans not out	....	44
B 7, l-b 4, n-b 4	....	15
		—
1/1 2/145 3/231 4/244 5/334		447
6/353 7/371 8/382 9/447		

Bonus points – Middlesex 4, Northamptonshire 1 (Score at 100 overs: 321–4).

Bowling: Mallender 30–4–96–2; Walker 19–3–85–2; N. G. B. Cook 26–6–74–2; Harper 26–6–71–1; Capel 25–4–110–2.

Northamptonshire

*G. Cook retired hurt	....	2	26 – (5) b Cowans 2
W. Larkins c Edmonds b Daniel	....	16	– lbw b Emburey 43
R. J. Boyd-Moss c Edmonds b Daniel	....	6	– (4) c Edmonds b Daniel 3
A. J. Lamb c Slack b Hughes	....	0	– (6) c Downton b Emburey 117
R. J. Bailey c Downton b Hughes	....	5	– (7) b Daniel 13
D. J. Capel c Downton b Hughes	....	0	– (8) c Radley b Edmonds 27
R. A. Harper b Emburey	....	27	– (9) not out 20
†S. N. V. Waterton b Daniel	....	16	– (1) c Downton b Daniel 4
N. G. B. Cook c Miller b Emburey	....	37	– (3) c Butcher b Daniel 2
N. A. Mallender not out	....	10	– c and b Emburey 0
A. Walker c Downton b Daniel	....	12	– run out 0
B 1, l-b 2, w 1	......	4	B 5, l-b 3, n-b 6 14
		—	—
1/44 2/50 3/50 4/50 5/55		159	1/4 2/6 3/16 4/31 5/127 245
6/95 7/112 8/142 9/159			6/162 7/206 8/234 9/237

Bonus points – Northamptonshire 1, Middlesex 4.

Bowling: *First Innings*—Daniel 16.3–3–50–4; Cowans 10–0–52–0; Hughes 11–5–20–3; Edmonds 9–3–15–0; Emburey 8–3–10–2; Gatting 2–0–9–0. *Second Innings*—Daniel 18–4–55–4; Hughes 7–3–27–0; Emburey 33–12–75–3; Cowans 6–2–20–1; Edmonds 34–14–57–1; Butcher 1–0–3–0; Gatting 1–1–0–0.

Umpires: J. H. Harris and K. J. Lyons.

At Chelmsford, August 6, 7, 8. MIDDLESEX lost to ESSEX by an innings and 92 runs.

At Cheltenham, August 9, 11, 12. MIDDLESEX beat GLOUCESTERSHIRE by 104 runs.

MIDDLESEX v HAMPSHIRE

At Lord's, August 16, 18, 19. Drawn. Middlesex 4 pts, Hampshire 5 pts. Toss: Middlesex. Carr, Radley and Downton found themselves in a familiar role, restructuring the innings, after Marshall and an unevenly bouncing pitch had brought Middlesex early trouble. Gatting's dismissal by Connor, though, was almost self-inflicted. The Middlesex bowlers pegged back Hampshire, Edmonds taking three wickets on the first evening, and declarations became necessary after the weather allowed only 23 overs on the second day. Miller made his first Championship century on the third day, but Greenidge showed little enthusiasm for the chase when Hampshire were set 224 in 54 overs. He faced 147 balls for his unbeaten 70, and marched off when the umpires offered to call a halt with eleven overs left and 95 required. In contrast, when Hampshire had wanted 140 from the last twenty overs, Tremlett had prompted 35 runs from the first five overs to show what was possible. Greenidge's action was taken while his captain was attending to a personal matter and Nicholas was not pleased with the abandonment of the challenge.

Middlesex

W. N. Slack c Parks b Marshall	1	– b Cowley	49
A. J. T. Miller b Marshall	9	– not out	111
*M. W. Gatting b Connor	5		
R. O. Butcher lbw b Marshall	3	– (3) lbw b Maru	4
J. D. Carr lbw b Cowley	37	– (4) c Terry b Middleton	56
C. T. Radley c Middleton b Tremlett	14	– (5) not out	5
†P. R. Downton not out	33		
J. E. Emburey b Tremlett	21		
P. H. Edmonds c Middleton b Maru	5		
S. P. Hughes b Maru	10		
N. G. Cowans c Cowley b Maru	0		
L-b 8, w 1, n-b 8	17	W 1	1

1/4 2/17 3/20 4/28 5/82   155   1/79 2/84 3/200   (3 wkts dec.) 226
6/83 7/130 8/135 9/149

Bonus points – Middlesex 1, Hampshire 4.

Bowling: *First Innings*—Marshall 16–2–38–3; Connor 10–2–35–1; Tremlett 19–5–31–2; Maru 11.1–3–27–3; Cowley 6–2–16–1. *Second Innings*—Marshall 4.2–1–4–0; Connor 6–1–19–0; Maru 12–3–34–1; Tremlett 3–0–16–0; Cowley 9–1–36–1; Smith 10–0–48–0; Parks 10–1–56–0; Middleton 2–0–13–1.

Hampshire

C. G. Greenidge c Downton b Edmonds	17	– not out	70
T. C. Middleton lbw b Hughes	10	– c Radley b Emburey	22
R. A. Smith c Gatting b Edmonds	39	– c and b Edmonds	2
*M. C. J. Nicholas c Radley b Edmonds	6		
V. P. Terry lbw b Hughes	18	– (4) c Butcher b Emburey	2
T. M. Tremlett not out	42	– (5) not out	28
N. G. Cowley b Cowans	2		
M. D. Marshall lbw b Hughes	13		
†R. J. Parks not out	0		
B 5, l-b 3, w 3	11	L-b 5	5

1/13 2/67 3/68 4/77   (7 wkts dec.) 158   1/40 2/51 3/78   (3 wkts) 129
5/105 6/121 7/147

R. J. Maru and C. A. Connor did not bat.

Bonus points – Hampshire 1, Middlesex 3.

Bowling: *First Innings*—Hughes 17–6–37–3; Cowans 18–3–63–1; Edmonds 21–9–24–3; Emburey 14–3–26–0; Butcher 1–1–0–0. *Second Innings*—Hughes 6–3–13–0; Cowans 6–0–19–0; Edmonds 16–3–54–1; Emburey 15–5–38–2.

Umpires: R. A. White and P. B. Wight.

At Leeds, August 20, 21, 22. MIDDLESEX drew with YORKSHIRE.

At Hove, August 23, 25, 26. MIDDLESEX drew with SUSSEX.

MIDDLESEX v LANCASHIRE

At Lord's, August 27, 28, 29. Middlesex won by an innings and 157 runs. Middlesex 24 pts, Lancashire 2 pts. Toss: Middlesex. On a first day shortened by 21 overs, a century opening stand gave Middlesex an excellent start to a performance of the sort that was common currency in recent seasons. Resuming at 245 for five, they made rapid progress on the second day, Radley and Downton batting expertly in collecting the fourth batting point with two balls to spare, declaring at lunchtime, and bowling Lancashire out cheaply. Hughes made the breach, Cowans widened it, and Lancashire could not counter Gatting or Fraser. Following on, Mendis and Fowler survived until the close, and Lancashire looked settled at 134 for one at lunch. However, Cowans took three for 6 in 21 balls and came back later to end the prolonged resistance for the ninth wicket of Simmons and Folley.

Middlesex

A. J. T. Miller c Maynard b Patterson	44	J. E. Emburey not out	32
W. N. Slack lbw b Folley	83	S. P. Hughes lbw b Simmons	4
J. D. Carr run out	34	B 2, l-b 14, n-b 3	19
R. O. Butcher lbw b Watkinson	53		
*M. W. Gatting c Fowler b Simmons	8	1/114 2/150 3/169 (8 wkts dec.) 432	
C. T. Radley st Maynard b Simmons	71	4/180 5/237 6/381	
†P. R. Downton b Watkinson	84	7/399 8/432	

N. G. Cowans and A. G. J. Fraser did not bat.

Bonus points – Middlesex 4, Lancashire 2 (Score at 100 overs: 301-5).

Bowling: Patterson 17–4–56–1; Allott 9–1–10–0; Hayhurst 19–2–77–0; Watkinson 22–1–95–2; Simmons 21.4–5–56–3; O'Shaughnessy 14–2–48–0; Folley 22–4–74–1.

Lancashire

G. D. Mendis c Carr b Hughes	7	– c Emburey b Hughes	28
G. Fowler lbw b Hughes	5	– lbw b Cowans	70
J. Abrahams c Slack b Cowans	0	– c Butcher b Emburey	45
S. J. O'Shaughnessy lbw b Gatting	17	– c Slack b Cowans	4
A. N. Hayhurst lbw b Cowans	0	– c Carr b Cowans	3
†C. Maynard b Hughes	0	– b Hughes	6
*J. Simmons c Downton b Fraser	5	– not out	13
M. Watkinson c Downton b Fraser	18	– c Radley b Emburey	3
P. J. W. Allott c Cowans b Gatting	4	– b Emburey	2
I. Folley c Slack b Emburey	10	– lbw b Cowans	17
B. P. Patterson not out	0	– c Downton b Fraser	9
L-b 4, n-b 1	5	B 1, l-b 2, n-b 1	4

1/9 2/12 3/16 4/20 5/21   71   1/60 2/137 3/145 4/149 5/153   204
6/33 7/40 8/44 9/67   6/161 7/164 8/166 9/195

Bonus points – Middlesex 4.

Bowling: *First Innings*—Cowans 9–3–12–2; Hughes 9–2–19–3; Fraser 9.5–4–12–2; Emburey 13–9–16–1; Gatting 4–2–8–2. *Second Innings*—Hughes 21–4–80–2; Fraser 12–2–33–1; Cowans 15–4–36–4; Emburey 23–11–26–3; Gatting 6–1–26–0.

Umpires: D. J. Constant and B. Leadbeater.

At Birmingham, August 30, September 1, 2. MIDDLESEX beat WARWICKSHIRE by 100 runs.

At Canterbury, September 13, 15, 16. MIDDLESEX drew with KENT.

FIELDING IN 1986

(Qualification: 20 dismissals)

83	D. E. East (64 ct, 19 st)	29	K. M. Curran
81	R. J. Parks (73 ct, 8 st)	29	G. A. Hick
66	S. J. Rhodes (58 ct, 8 st)	28	C. E. B. Rice
60	R. C. Russell (56 ct, 4 st)	26	K. W. R. Fletcher
51	S. A. Marsh (48 ct, 3 st)	24	K. J. Barnett
49	G. W. Humpage (41 ct, 8 st)	24	J. D. Birch
48	P. R. Downton (43 ct, 5 st)	24	P. Gill
48	B. N. French (44 ct, 4 st)	24	P. Johnson
44	D. L. Bairstow (41 ct, 3 st)	24	P. Whitticase (23 ct, 1 st)
44	C. J. Richards (39 ct, 5 st)	23	R. J. Bailey
40	T. Davies (32 ct, 8 st)	23	B. J. M. Maher
39	M. A. Lynch	23	C. W. Scott (22 ct, 1 st)
37	I. J. Gould (36 ct, 1 st)	22	G. A. Gooch
37	S. N. V. Waterton (32 ct, 5 st)	22	J. W. Lloyds
36	T. Gard (30 ct, 6 st)	21	C. W. J. Athey
35	C. Marples (31 ct, 4 st)	21	R. A. Smith
32	C. S. Cowdrey	21	C. J. Tavaré
32	R. A. Harper	20	D. A. Graveney
32	C. Maynard (29 ct, 3 st)	20	P. J. Prichard

NORTHAMPTONSHIRE

Patron: The Earl of Dalkeith
President: D. C. Lucas
Chairman: W. R. F. Chamberlain
Chairman, Cricket Committee: A. P. Arnold
Secretary/Manager: S. P. Coverdale
   County Ground, Wantage Road,
   Northampton NN1 4TJ
   (Telephone: 0604-32917)
Captain: G. Cook
Coach: R. M. Carter
Cricket Development Officer: B. L. Reynolds

That a season which featured many outstanding individual performances – mostly with the bat – should produce so little improvement in the team's final placings was a source of disappointment for Northamptonshire in 1986. The belief of the secretary-manager, Mr Stephen Coverdale, in the county's capacity to beat any side in the country "on our day" looked justifiable in view of the blend of youth and experience available. But the only progress was a rise of one place to ninth in the Britannic Assurance Championship with the same number of wins, five, as in 1985.

As in the past, the least convincing performances came in the vital "run-in" period. From potential John Player League champions in August, Northamptonshire slipped to fifth place – just out of the money for the second year running. In the Benson and Hedges Cup and NatWest Bank Trophy, defeats by Worcestershire in the quarter-finals and Middlesex in the first round came after promising positions had been allowed to drift when concentration wavered.

In the three-day game, the problem was another familiar one: that of bowling sides out in the absence of a consistently effective pace spearhead. David Capel, who matured considerably as an all-rounder in 1986, showed promise as a strike bowler, but Neil Mallender, although suffering more that most from poor close catching, failed to find his rhythm for much of the season and his potential remained unfulfilled. Neither Jim Griffiths, who was not offered a new contract for 1987, nor Alan Walker, who replaced him at the end of June, was able to provide penetration either, and it was not surprising that the club felt it necessary to announce plans for improving the pace and bounce of Northampton pitches. Such action, it was hoped, would encourage the fast bowlers currently on the staff, as well as making Northamptonshire a more attractive proposition for pacemen from elsewhere.

Much was expected of the spinners, Nick Cook and Roger Harper. They finished as the county's leading wicket-takers in first-class matches, sending down nearly 1,700 overs between them, and they also furnished strong evidence to support the view that slow bowling has a place in the limited-overs game. Cook's approach, in his first season with the county, was splendidly competitive, while Harper, like the quicker bowlers, would benefit from some extra bounce at the County Ground. However, they rarely looked sufficiently threatening when operating in tandem in

Championship matches, and this greatly reduced Northamptonshire's chances of success. The dismissal of Essex for only 44 at Colchester in August rewrote some records, but in the context of the season it was more a curiosity than an accurate gauge of bowling strength.

Two of the four Championship wins in July, over Sussex and Middlesex, came as the result of outstanding innings from Allan Lamb, whose omission from the England side proved a blessing for his county. The value of Lamb when he devotes his full energies to the county game is enormous, and during his match-winning 157 against Sussex, at Hastings, he passed 10,000 runs for Northamptonshire in nine, often incomplete, seasons.

Despite Lamb's brilliance, though, both the club's and the supporters' choice as player of the year was Robert Bailey. He enjoyed a memorable summer, tainted only by the absence of a Test call to play against India or New Zealand, or of a place in the touring party for Australia. Hitting the ball with obvious power but little apparent effort, the 22-year-old Bailey registered two double-hundreds in four weeks and narrowly missed reaching 2,000 runs in only his third full season.

In addition to Lamb and Bailey, Geoff Cook and Robin Boyd-Moss also passed 1,000 runs. Although hampered by a variety of injuries, Cook, Northamptonshire's longest-serving captain, still has a lot of cricket in him. But Boyd-Moss was in many ways a frustrating batsman. Fine centuries against Lancashire and Glamorgan left one in no doubt as to his talent, but lack of confidence sometimes held him back and he ended the season with only 106 runs in his final eleven innings. Wayne Larkins was out of action for the first month with a football injury, and subsequently missed out on a Test recall – which would have given his benefit season a much-needed filip – because of a broken finger. The leading run-scorer for the previous four seasons, he never settled down to play a long innings.

Harper and Capel both struggled with the bat in the closing weeks, although in Harper's case a sense of anticlimax was almost inevitable after his leading off with a magnificent 234 against Gloucestershire. Capel should make a significant contribution to Northamptonshire cricket for many years to come, but for Duncan Wild, whose career for so long ran roughly parallel with his fellow Northamptonian's, it was a case of filling the "standby" role again. He played some impressive innings when given the chance, but he has yet to enjoy a full season in which to prove himself as an early-order batsman.

The most contentious selection was that of the wicket-keepers, David Ripley and Stuart Waterton. Ripley started and finished the season in possession, while the newcomer from Kent performed creditably in between until troubled by illness. However, with so much potential at Northamptonshire, an extension in 1987 of the county's six-year spell without a title must surely prompt some searching questions about approach and ability to play good cricket under pressure. – A.R.

NORTHAMPTONSHIRE 1986

[Bill Smith]

Back row: S. N. V. Waterton, D. J. Capel, N. G. B. Cook, R. J. Bailey, D. J. Wild, A. Walker. *Front row:* N. A. Mallender, A. J. Lamb, G. Cook (*captain*), R. A. Harper, R. J. Boyd-Moss. *Insets:* A. C. Storie, W. Larkins, R. G. Williams, D. Ripley, A. Fordham.

NORTHAMPTONSHIRE RESULTS

All first-class matches – Played 27: Won 5, Lost 3, Drawn 19.

County Championship matches – Played 24: Won 5, Lost 3, Drawn 16.

Bonus points – Batting 53, Bowling 60.

Competition placings – Britannic Assurance County Championship, 9th; NatWest Bank Trophy, 1st round; Benson and Hedges Cup, q-f; John Player League, 5th.

BRITANNIC ASSURANCE CHAMPIONSHIP AVERAGES

BATTING

	Birthplace	*M*	*I*	*NO*	*R*	*HI*	*Avge*
‡A. J. Lamb	*Langebaanweg, SA*	14	20	4	1,261	160*	78.81
‡R. J. Bailey	*Stoke-on-Trent*	24	36	7	1,562	224*	53.86
‡G. Cook	*Middlesbrough*	20	29	4	1,057	183	42.28
‡R. A. Harper	*Georgetown, BG*	24	29	4	921	234	36.84
D. Ripley	*Leeds*	11	12	3	286	134*	31.77
‡R. J. Boyd-Moss	*Hatton, Ceylon*	24	37	3	1,033	155	30.38
‡D. J. Wild	*Northampton*	11	16	1	448	85	29.86
‡W. Larkins	*Roxton*	17	29	4	664	86	26.56
‡D. J. Capel	*Northampton*	24	30	4	685	111	26.34
S. N. V. Waterton	*Dartford*	13	16	4	314	58*	26.16
A. C. Storie	*Bishopbriggs, Glasgow*	6	7	0	152	38	21.71
N. G. B. Cook	*Leicester*	24	25	3	343	45	15.59
‡N. A. Mallender	*Kirk Sandall*	21	19	9	116	37	11.60
A. Walker	*Emley*	17	14	9	47	13*	9.40
‡R. G. Williams	*Bangor*	3	4	0	35	18	8.75
‡B. J. Griffiths	*Wellingborough*	9	6	3	18	7	6.00

Also batted: A. Fordham (*Bedford*) (1 match) 5, 17; G. Smith (*Jarrow*) (1 match) 3.

** Signifies not out.		‡ Denotes county cap.*

The following played a total of seventeen three-figure innings for Northamptonshire in County Championship matches: R. J. Bailey 4, A. J. Lamb 4, G. Cook 3, R. J. Boyd-Moss 2, D. J. Capel 2, R. A. Harper 1, D. Ripley 1.

BOWLING

	O	*M*	*R*	*W*	*BB*	*Avge*
R. A. Harper	815.2	273	1,670	62	5-84	26.93
N. G. B. Cook	807.2	264	1,746	61	6-72	28.62
D. J. Capel	549.4	109	1,774	52	7-86	34.11
B. J. Griffiths	208.3	40	666	19	4-59	35.05
N. A. Mallender	585	128	1,636	45	5-110	36.35
A. Walker	394	72	1,224	32	6-50	38.25

Also bowled: R. J. Bailey 11.5-6-12-2; R. J. Boyd-Moss 75.3-18-212-7; G. Cook 17-4-38-1; A. J. Lamb 2-2-0-0; G. Smith 23-4-94-1; D. J. Wild 87-5-329-7; R. G. Williams 36-7-111-3.

Wicket-keepers: S. N. V. Waterton 29 ct, 4 st; D. Ripley 11 ct, 4 st.

Leading Fielders: R. A. Harper 32; R. J. Bailey 20; N. G. B. Cook 18; G. Cook 16; W. Larkins 13; A. J. Lamb 12.

At Cambridge, April 26, 28, 29. NORTHAMPTONSHIRE drew with CAMBRIDGE
UNIVERSITY.

At Canterbury, April 30, May 1, 2. NORTHAMPTONSHIRE drew with KENT.

NORTHAMPTONSHIRE v GLOUCESTERSHIRE

At Northampton, May 7, 8, 9. Drawn. Northamptonshire 5 pts, Gloucestershire 5 pts. Toss:
Gloucestershire. A memorable innings by Harper dominated a match in which the batsmen
were always in control. The Guyanan all-rounder, 23 not out on the second evening, raced to a
maiden double-hundred with clean, controlled hitting which produced twelve 6s and 25 4s. His
234 came at exactly a run a minute, off 213 balls; the third 50 off only 27; and his seventh-wicket
partnership of 193 in 48 overs with Ripley was only 36 runs short of the county's 60-year-old
record. Harper's innings overshadowed Athey's unbeaten 171, his highest score in England,
which occupied just over six hours. On such an easy-paced pitch a result – even a contrived one –
always looked unlikely, but few could complain at the entertainment on the final day.

Gloucestershire

A. W. Stovold b Griffiths		2 – not out	12
P. W. Romaines lbw b Mallender		17 – not out	18
C. W. J. Athey not out	171		
P. Bainbridge c Griffiths b Harper	55		
J. W. Lloyds c and b Harper	6		
K. M. Curran not out	39		
L-b 10, n-b 1	11		

1/7 2/47 3/173 4/191   (4 wkts dec.) 301   (no wkt) 30

I. R. Payne, *D. A. Graveney, †R. C. Russell, D. V. Lawrence and G. E. Sainsbury did not bat.

Bonus points – Gloucestershire 3, Northamptonshire 1 (Score at 100 overs: 265-4).

Bowling: *First Innings*—Mallender 25–9–61–1; Griffiths 22.3–3–72–1; Capel 23–7–61–0;
N. G. B. Cook 15–3–48–0; Harper 24–7–49–2. *Second Innings*—Capel 4–1–9–0; Griffiths
4–1–5–0; Boyd-Moss 5–0–14–0; Bailey 4–3–2–0.

Northamptonshire

A. C. Storie c Curran b Sainsbury	0	N. G. B. Cook not out	17
*G. Cook c Payne b Sainsbury	82	N. A. Mallender c Athey b Lloyds	2
R. J. Boyd-Moss c Lloyds b Sainsbury	4	B. J. Griffiths st Russell b Lloyds	6
A. J. Lamb c Lawrence b Sainsbury	50		
R. J. Bailey c Russell b Graveney	25	B 5, l-b 6, n-b 7	18
D. J. Capel c Athey b Payne	22		
R. A. Harper c and b Lloyds	234	1/2 2/16 3/95 4/123 5/177	503
†D. Ripley b Lloyds	43	6/231 7/424 8/487 9/497	

Bonus points – Northamptonshire 4, Gloucestershire 2 (Score at 100 overs: 395-6).

Bowling: Lawrence 19–3–100–0; Sainsbury 43–9–146–4; Payne 18–2–96–1; Graveney
20–7–51–1; Bainbridge 12–1–60–0; Lloyds 12.4–3–39–4.

Umpires: R. Julian and R. A. White.

NORTHAMPTONSHIRE v ESSEX

At Northampton, May 17, 19, 20. Drawn. Northamptonshire 2 pts, Essex 4 pts. Toss:
Northamptonshire. Play was possible only on the second day, when Geoff Cook held his side's
innings together. The other batsmen struggled against the contrasting spin of Acfield and
Childs, who bowled with excellent control to return his best figures since joining Essex. The
Northamptonshire captain was seventh out after 3 hours, 40 minutes of concentration.

Northamptonshire

*G. Cook b Acfield	81	N. G. B. Cook c and b Childs	16
A. C. Storie c Hardie b Pringle	9	A. Walker not out	1
R. J. Boyd-Moss c and b Childs	29	B. J. Griffiths b Childs	7
A. J. Lamb c Hardie b Pringle	1		
R. J. Bailey c Border b Acfield	26	B 7, l-b 5	12
D. J. Capel c Fletcher b Childs	8		
R. A. Harper st East b Childs	40	1/44 2/89 3/92 4/136 5/157	244
†D. Ripley c Hardie b Acfield	14	6/161 7/197 8/233 9/236	

Bonus points – Northamptonshire 2, Essex 4 (Score at 100 overs: 238-9).

Bowling: Lever 8-3-10-0; Foster 10-3-32-0; Childs 43.3-15-97-5; Pringle 19-4-39-2;
Acfield 22-4-54-3.

Essex

*G. A. Gooch lbw b Griffiths	4	A. R. Border not out	14
B. R. Hardie b Griffiths	1		
P. J. Prichard not out	4	1/4 2/5	(2 wkts) 23

K. W. R. Fletcher, D. R. Pringle, †D. E. East, N. A. Foster, D. L. Acfield, J. H. Childs
and J. K. Lever did not bat.

Bowling: Griffiths 7-3-18-2; Walker 3-1-3-0; Harper 4-2-2-0.

Umpires: D. O. Oslear and D. R. Shepherd.

At Birmingham, May 21, 22, 23. NORTHAMPTONSHIRE drew with WARWICKSHIRE.

NORTHAMPTONSHIRE v LEICESTERSHIRE

At Northampton, May 24, 26, 27. Drawn. Northamptonshire 5 pts, Leicestershire 5 pts. Toss:
Northamptonshire. Leicestershire's plan to build a sizeable first-innings lead and catch
Northamptonshire on a pitch offering increasing help to the spin bowlers provided a sluggish
second day on which only 291 runs were scored off 126 overs. The tactic ultimately failed when
Clift, bowling off-spin, and Balderstone were unable to exploit the conditions adequately. With
Agnew and DeFreitas always threatening on the first day, the home side owed much to
contrasting innings from Bailey (two 6s, ten 4s in 135 minutes) and Capel, whose first hundred
for three years lasted four and a quarter hours and included fourteen boundaries. Briers, the
acting-captain, set the tone of the Leicestershire reply, his 83 taking him 68 overs to compile,
although Whitticase later batted with flair and enterprise. Northamptonshire never looked in
danger on the final afternoon and Bailey again shone with a two-hour century against some
variable slow bowling, hitting two 6s and eleven 4s.

Northamptonshire

*G. Cook c Clift b Agnew	3			
W. Larkins b Agnew	8	– b Clift	10	
R. J. Boyd-Moss c Clift b DeFreitas	16	– c Whitaker b Briers	53	
R. J. Bailey c Clift b Agnew	88	– (1) c Whitaker b Briers	106	
R. G. Williams c Whitticase b DeFreitas	0	– (4) b Balderstone	17	
D. J. Capel c Whitticase b Benjamin	111	– (5) not out	60	
R. A. Harper c Balderstone b DeFreitas	10	– (6) b Balderstone	49	
†D. Ripley b DeFreitas	2	– (7) not out	16	
N. G. B. Cook c Cobb b DeFreitas	19			
A. Walker c Whitaker b Agnew	10			
B. J. Griffiths not out	0			
L-b 4, n-b 2	6	B 2, l-b 5	7	
	273		**(5 wkts) 318**	

1/11 2/16 3/72 4/72 5/135   273   1/42 2/168 3/179   (5 wkts) 318
6/158 7/166 8/240 9/273   4/200 5/292

Bonus points – Northamptonshire 3, Leicestershire 4 (Score at 100 overs: 273-9).

Bowling: *First Innings*—Agnew 25.1–4–81–4; Benjamin 20–3–74–1; DeFreitas 26–5–54–5; Clift 29–11–60–0. *Second Innings*—Agnew 4–0–12–0; Benjamin 3–0–18–0; Clift 19.2–2–58–1; DeFreitas 2–0–15–0; Balderstone 39–6–120–2; Briers 11–0–54–2; Boon 11–1–28–0; Whitaker 1–0–6–0.

Leicestershire

I. P. Butcher c sub b Harper	32	P. A. J. DeFreitas b N. G. B. Cook	4	
R. A. Cobb c and b Harper	41	W. K. M. Benjamin not out	43	
J. C. Balderstone c Ripley b Harper	2	J. P. Agnew c N. G. B. Cook b Boyd-Moss	16	
J. J. Whitaker c Walker b Williams	27			
T. J. Boon c Bailey b Harper	38	B 4, l-b 10, n-b 2	16	
*N. E. Briers b N. G. B. Cook	83			
P. B. Clift c sub b Griffiths	12	1/62 2/79 3/88 4/116 5/179	371	
†P. Whitticase c Bailey b Harper	57	6/213 7/289 8/311 9/314		

Bonus points – Leicestershire 1, Northamptonshire 2 (Score at 100 overs: 187-5).

Bowling: Walker 17–1–46–0; Griffiths 17–1–56–1; N. G. B. Cook 46–13–83–2; Harper 44–17–84–5; Capel 13–4–36–0; Williams 21–5–52–1; Boyd-Moss 0.3–0–0–1.

Umpires: B. Leadbeater and N. T. Plews.

At Northampton, May 31, June 1, 2. NORTHAMPTONSHIRE drew with INDIANS (See Indian tour section).

†At Northampton, June 6. Northamptonshire won by seven wickets. Zimbabweans 249 for six (60 overs) (A. J. Pycroft 46, A. C. Waller 60); Northamptonshire 255 for three (51.4 overs) (R. J. Bailey 57, D. J. Capel 73 not out, R. A. Harper 69 not out).

NORTHAMPTONSHIRE v WORCESTERSHIRE

At Northampton, June 7, 9, 10. Drawn. Northamptonshire 5 pts, Worcestershire 7 pts. Toss: Worcestershire. An interesting match ended with Northamptonshire, having been set 250 to win in 62 overs, struggling to avoid defeat after losing six wickets in 21 balls to Radford and Pridgeon. They salvaged a draw thanks to Wild and Waterton, who added 113 in 31 overs and, despite the state of the game, always looked to punish the loose ball. Radford bowled with aggression in each innings, extracting rare pace and bounce from a slow Northampton pitch to achieve a match return of ten for 129. In contrast, Northamptonshire's left-arm spinner, Nick Cook, took the honours on the first day with his best performance for his new county. Neale's responsible innings paved the way for a respectable Worcestershire total, the bowling of Radford and Illingworth secured a lead of 81 on the second day, and the visitors then moved positively towards a declaration through Rhodes, who ran superbly between the wickets in an unbroken stand of 56 with Illingworth.

Worcestershire

T. S. Curtis c Bailey b N. G. B. Cook	39	– c Waterton b N. G. B. Cook	27
D. B. D'Oliveira c Waterton b N. G. B. Cook	47	– b N. G. B. Cook	29
D. M. Smith c Bailey b N. G. B. Cook	1		
G. A. Hick c Waterton b N. G. B. Cook	39	– (3) c Harper b Griffiths	1
*P. A. Neale not out	76	– c Harper b Griffiths	27
D. N. Patel c Bailey b Williams	1	– (4) c Waterton b Griffiths	18
†S. J. Rhodes c Bailey b Williams	0	– (6) not out	40
N. V. Radford c and b N. G. B. Cook	10	– (7) c Waterton b Griffiths	0
R. K. Illingworth st Waterton b N. G. B. Cook	22	– (8) not out	17
J. D. Inchmore c Bailey b Harper	12		
A. P. Pridgeon c Capel b Griffiths	3		
B 6, l-b 14, n-b 2	22	B 4, l-b 3, w 1, n-b 1	9

1/72 2/83 3/126 4/165 5/166   272   1/54 2/59 3/61   (6 wkts dec.) 168
6/166 7/187 8/241 9/256   4/99 5/112 6/112

Bonus points – Worcestershire 3, Northamptonshire 4 (Score at 100 overs: 260-9).

Bowling: *First Innings*—Mallender 8–6–5–0; Griffiths 10.2–3–19–1; Wild 6–1–27–0; N. G. B. Cook 39–18–72–6; Capel 4–1–12–0; Harper 25–5–58–1; Williams 15–2–59–2. *Second Innings*—Mallender 10–0–40–0; Griffiths 18–4–59–4; N. G. B. Cook 26–10–50–2; Harper 3–0–12–0.

Northamptonshire

*G. Cook b Illingworth	38	– lbw b Radford	2
R. J. Bailey lbw b Radford	4	– lbw b Radford	9
N. G. B. Cook c Curtis b Radford	10	– (9) c Rhodes b Radford	7
R. J. Boyd-Moss c Rhodes b Inchmore	2	– (3) c D'Oliveira b Pridgeon	0
D. J. Wild c Rhodes b Illingworth	0	– (4) b Radford	68
R. G. Williams c Inchmore b Radford	18	– (5) c Illingworth b Pridgeon	0
D. J. Capel b Illingworth	28	– (6) b Radford	0
R. A. Harper c Radford b Patel	47	– (7) lbw b Pridgeon	4
†S. N. V. Waterton c and b Radford	36	– (8) not out	58
N. A. Mallender not out	4	– not out	1
B. J. Griffiths b Radford	0		
B 2, l-b 2	4	L-b 6, n-b 5	11

1/9 2/23 3/38 4/39 5/64   191   1/11 2/13 3/13 4/13   (8 wkts) 160
6/93 7/110 8/177 9/191   5/16 6/23 7/136 8/156

Bonus points – Northamptonshire 1, Worcestershire 4.

Bowling: *First Innings*—Radford 25.3–6–66–5; Pridgeon 3–1–9–0; Illingworth 27–10–72–3; Inchmore 14–7–18–1; Patel 10–3–22–1. *Second Innings*—Radford 17–3–63–5; Pridgeon 7.5–2–10–3; Illingworth 12–3–32–0; Inchmore 3–1–13–0; Patel 10–3–24–0; D'Oliveira 2–0–12–0.

Umpires: D. J. Constant and M. J. Kitchen.

NORTHAMPTONSHIRE v WARWICKSHIRE

At Northampton, June 14, 16, 17. Warwickshire won by 117 runs. Warwickshire 17 pts, Northamptonshire 5 pts. Toss: Warwickshire. Gifford, jeered by the home spectators for prolonging Warwickshire's laboured first innings into the 140th over before declaring on the second morning, bowled his side to their first Championship win of the season with a display of flight and variation. Northamptonshire opened up the game on the second evening with a declaration, 64 runs behind, which halted a third-wicket partnership of 137 in 36 overs between Boyd-Moss and Lamb. Warwickshire responded positively, putting on 163 in the first session of the final day. Smith (one 6, ten 4s) batted attractively, supported by Amiss. Facing a target of 295 to win in three and a half hours, Northamptonshire lost two wickets to Small before Gifford went to work; and although Storie batted gamely for 35 overs and Waterton showed solid technique, Warwickshire won with ten overs to spare.

Warwickshire

T. A. Lloyd c Waterton b Mallender	2	– c Capel b Mallender	2
P. A. Smith run out	39	– b Cook	83
A. I. Kallicharran lbw b Mallender	0	– lbw b Capel	16
D. L. Amiss c Waterton b Griffiths	12	– c Cook b Wild	62
†G. W. Humpage c Boyd-Moss b Harper	26	– run out	10
Asif Din b Harper	30	– st Waterton b Cook	25
A. M. Ferreira c Harper b Capel	19	– not out	11
G. J. Parsons not out	58	– not out	11
G. C. Small b Wild	25		
A. R. K. Pierson not out	42		
B 2, l-b 7, n-b 4	13	B 4, l-b 5, w 1	10

1/5 2/5 3/37 4/83   (8 wkts dec.) 266   1/2 2/49 3/141   (6 wkts dec.) 230
5/89 6/125 7/149 8/188   4/161 5/202 6/208

*N. Gifford did not bat.

Bonus points – Warwickshire 1, Northamptonshire 3 (Score at 100 overs: 187-7).

Bowling: *First Innings*—Mallender 21–4–41–2; Griffiths 20–4–46–1; Capel 18–2–49–1; Cook 36–16–48–0; Harper 34–10–52–2; Wild 6–0–15–1; Boyd-Moss 5–1–6–0. *Second Innings*—Mallender 7–1–14–1; Griffiths 8–2–34–0; Harper 12–1–38–0; Cook 14–3–48–2; Capel 7–1–29–1; Wild 10–0–58–1.

Northamptonshire

A. C. Storie c Amiss b Gifford	32	– c Lloyd b Gifford	38
R. J. Bailey lbw b Small	9	– b Small	6
R. J. Boyd-Moss not out	66	– lbw b Small	11
A. J. Lamb not out	79	– b Gifford	8
D. J. Capel (did not bat)		– b Gifford	13
D. J. Wild (did not bat)		– c Asif Din b Gifford	0
*R. A. Harper (did not bat)		– lbw b Asif Din	39
†S. N. V. Waterton (did not bat)		– st Humpage b Gifford	41
N. G. B. Cook (did not bat)		– c Kallicharran b Gifford	3
N. A. Mallender (did not bat)		– lbw b Small	4
B. J. Griffiths (did not bat)		– not out	5
B 6, l-b 4, w 1, n-b 5	16	L-b 7, n-b 2	9

1/19 2/65   (2 wkts dec.) 202   1/9 2/33 3/42 4/75 5/79   177
                                    6/88 7/128 8/138 9/149

Bonus points – Northamptonshire 2.

Bowling: *First Innings*—Small 10–4–26–1; Parsons 10–2–22–0; Smith 4–0–26–0; Ferreira 9–3–32–0; Gifford 14–6–25–1; Pierson 10–2–35–0; Asif Din 6–0–26–0. *Second Innings*—Small 17–6–42–3; Parsons 5–1–24–0; Gifford 21.5–11–27–6; Ferreira 3–0–16–0; Asif Din 12–2–48–1; Smith 1–0–13–0.

Umpires: J. H. Hampshire and A. A. Jones.

At Bath, June 18, 19, 20. NORTHAMPTONSHIRE drew with SOMERSET.

NORTHAMPTONSHIRE v YORKSHIRE

At Luton, June 21, 23, 24. Drawn. Northamptonshire 6 pts, Yorkshire 5 pts. Toss: Northamptonshire. Wardown Park's first first-class match, played on a pitch which drew praise from both sides, was marked by outstanding batting from Bailey and Metcalfe. Bailey transformed the game with a magnificent display, hitting a 6 and 25 4s and reaching his maiden double-century in 292 minutes with a single off the last ball of the day. Yorkshire, as Northamptonshire had been, were in early trouble before Metcalfe's second century in successive Championship matches retrieved the position. His five-hour innings included 22 boundaries, and he shared in a stand of 164 with Bairstow, who made light of a painful back injury. Northamptonshire set Yorkshire 265 to win in 48 overs, and despite losing four wickets in three overs, they kept up the chase until the end.

Northamptonshire

A. C. Storie lbw b Sidebottom	29	– c Sharp b P. J. Hartley	18
W. Larkins c Metcalfe b P. J. Hartley	11	– b Dennis	2
R. J. Boyd-Moss c and b P. J. Hartley	67	– c Sharp b Carrick	58
R. J. Bailey not out	200	– c Sharp b P. J. Hartley	19
D. J. Wild c Dennis b Carrick	36	– (9) not out	16
D. J. Capel not out	18	– (5) lbw b Dennis	2
*R. A. Harper (did not bat)	–	(6) not out	41
†S. N. V. Waterton (did not bat)	–	(7) c Sharp b Carrick	4
N. G. B. Cook (did not bat)	–	(8) c Love b Jarvis	13
B 4, l-b 7, w 2, n-b 11	24	B 8, l-b 10, n-b 2	20

1/15 2/64 3/225 4/318   (4 wkts dec.) 385   1/5 2/44 3/65   (7 wkts dec.) 193
4/106 5/110 6/136
7/151

N. A. Mallender and B. J. Griffiths did not bat.

    Bonus points – Northamptonshire 4, Yorkshire 1 (Score at 100 overs: 336-4).

    Bowling: *First Innings*—Sidebottom 20–4–58–1; Jarvis 20–3–72–0; P. J. Hartley 22–6–92–2; Dennis 16–5–50–0; Carrick 23–5–61–1; Love 9–1–41–0. *Second Innings*—Dennis 12–2–38–2; Jarvis 15–4–49–1; P. J. Hartley 11–0–61–2; Carrick 13–3–27–2.

Yorkshire

G. Boycott c Bailey b Mallender	3	– c Waterton b Capel	68
A. A. Metcalfe c Harper b Griffiths	151	– c Capel b Mallender	35
K. Sharp c Harper b Mallender	0	– c Storie b Harper	26
S. N. Hartley c Harper b Capel	11	– c Larkins b Harper	19
J. D. Love c Larkins b Mallender	46	– not out	28
*†D. L. Bairstow b Cook	88	– (7) lbw b Capel	1
P. Carrick not out	0	– (6) run out	1
P. J. Hartley (did not bat)	–	c Larkins b Harper	54
P. W. Jarvis (did not bat)	–	c Mallender b Cook	0
S. J. Dennis (did not bat)	–	not out	4
L-b 12, w 2, n-b 1	15	L-b 4	4

1/6 2/6 3/34 4/146   (6 wkts dec.) 314   1/51 2/118 3/152   (8 wkts) 240
5/310 6/314   4/156 5/158 6/161
7/230 8/236

A. Sidebottom did not bat.

    Bonus points – Yorkshire 4, Northamptonshire 2.

    Bowling: *First Innings*—Mallender 19–6–58–3; Griffiths 14–1–67–1; Capel 11–1–57–1; Harper 20–7–52–0; Cook 7.5–1–33–1; Wild 10–0–35–0. *Second Innings*—Mallender 13–0–57–1; Griffiths 4–0–21–0; Capel 12–0–73–2; Cook 6–1–25–1; Harper 12.5–0–60–3.

    Umpires: D. G. L. Evans and K. J. Lyons.

At Hastings, June 28, 30, July 1. NORTHAMPTONSHIRE beat SUSSEX by one wicket.

At The Oval, July 5, 7, 8. NORTHAMPTONSHIRE beat SURREY by 100 runs.

NORTHAMPTONSHIRE v LANCASHIRE

At Northampton, July 16, 17, 18. Northamptonshire won by ten wickets. Northamptonshire 24 pts, Lancashire 1 pt. Toss: Northamptonshire. Career-best performances from Geoff Cook, Boyd-Moss and Walker were the highlights of a convincing display which gave Northamptonshire their third successive Championship victory, and their first over Lancashire at Northampton for thirteen years. Cook and Boyd-Moss dominated the Lancashire attack with their assertive strokeplay, exceeding by 2 runs the previous county second-wicket record partnership, set by Larkins and Willey, also against Lancashire, in 1983, as they added 344 in 90 overs. Cook hit a 6 and 25 4s in his 338-minute stay while Boyd-Moss found the boundary 22 times in 321 minutes. Walker's spell of six for 12 in eight overs after lunch on the second day forced the visitors to follow on, when they made a better fight of it on a good batting pitch. O'Shaughnessy and Makinson provided stubborn resistance on the last afternoon to ensure that Northamptonshire would have to bat again, but once Nick Cook broke through, the home side won comfortably.

Northamptonshire

*G. Cook c Makinson b Abrahams	183	– not out 7
W. Larkins lbw b Makinson	17	– not out 19
R. J. Boyd-Moss c and b Watkinson	155	
R. J. Bailey not out	17	
D. J. Capel not out	8	
B 4, l-b 1, w 1, n-b 14	20	W 1, n-b 7 8

1/30 2/374 3/374   (3 wkts dec.) 400   (no wkt) 34

D. J. Wild, R. A. Harper, †S. N. V. Waterton, N. G. B. Cook, N. A. Mallender and A. Walker did not bat.

Bonus points – Northamptonshire 4, Lancashire 1.

Bowling: *First Innings*—Patterson 18-4-69-0; Makinson 15-2-69-1; Watkinson 31-6-106-1; O'Shaughnessy 11-3-58-0; Folley 15-5-42-0; Abrahams 9.3-0-51-1. *Second Innings*—Patterson 2-0-19-0; Makinson 1.3-0-15-0.

Lancashire

G. D. Mendis c G. Cook b Mallender	9	– c Waterton b Walker 69
*G. Fowler b Capel	50	– c Waterton b Capel 14
I. Folley lbw b Mallender	0	– (10) c Larkins b Walker 6
M. R. Chadwick c N. G. B. Cook b Walker	38	– (3) c N. G. B. Cook b Capel ... 5
N. H. Fairbrother c Harper b Walker	20	– (4) c Larkins b Harper 20
J. Abrahams c Waterton b Walker	0	– (5) c Harper b Capel 10
S. J. O'Shaughnessy b Walker	10	– (6) c G. Cook b N. G. B. Cook . 74
†C. Maynard retired hurt	1	– c Boyd-Moss b Harper 19
M. Watkinson c Waterton b Walker	2	– (7) c Bailey b Harper 1
D. J. Makinson not out	1	– (9) c Larkins b N. G. B. Cook . 43
B. P. Patterson b Walker	0	– not out 0
B 1, l-b 5, n-b 7	13	B 4, l-b 6, n-b 17 27

1/12 2/12 3/89 4/120 5/120   144   1/44 2/56 3/120 4/133 5/135   288
6/131 7/131 8/143 9/144   6/139 7/171 8/227 9/288

Bonus points – Northamptonshire 4.

Bowling: *First Innings*—Mallender 11–3–39–2; Walker 23–6–50–6; Harper 18–8–33–0; N. G. B. Cook 13–10–6–0; Capel 6–2–10–1. *Second Innings*—Mallender 24–5–49–0; Walker 22–4–59–2; N. G. B. Cook 30.1–9–56–2; Capel 23–4–62–3; Harper 34–18–41–3; Wild 2–0–11–0.

Umpires: J. A. Jameson and P. B. Wight.

At Swansea, July 19, 21, 22. NORTHAMPTONSHIRE drew with GLAMORGAN.

NORTHAMPTONSHIRE v MIDDLESEX

At Northampton, July 26, 28, 29. Northamptonshire won by four wickets. Northamptonshire 20 pts, Middlesex 6 pts Toss: Middlesex. Lamb's highest score for Northamptonshire since 1981, off 183 deliveries, secured victory after a generous declaration from Radley, seeking Middlesex's first Championship win of the season, left the home side needing 318 in five hours. There were still three overs remaining when Lamb drove Sykes for his third 6 to reach the target, his fine innings having also included eighteen 4s. On the first day Middlesex were indebted to Miller's watchful innings (258 minutes, fourteen 4s), the value of which was shown clearly when hostile pace bowling from Daniel, Cowans and Hughes secured a first-innings lead of 91. Enterprising batting from Slack (207 minutes, ten 4s) and especially Roseberry (101 balls) set up an interesting finish, but as long as Lamb remained, Northamptonshire looked on course, despite the loss of three wickets in as many overs near the end.

Middlesex

W. N. Slack lbw b Mallender	0	– c Bailey b Mallender	106
A. J. T. Miller c Harper b N. G. B. Cook	92		
M. A. Roseberry lbw b Mallender	2	– not out	70
R. O. Butcher c G. Cook b Capel	12	– not out	25
*C. T. Radley c Larkins b Harper	24		
†P. R. Downton c and b N. G. B. Cook	7	– (2) c Bailey b Capel	18
J. F. Sykes c Harper b Walker	10		
S. P. Hughes not out	12		
N. G. Cowans b Walker	14		
W. W. Daniel b Walker	18		
P. C. R. Tufnell lbw b N. G. B. Cook	0		
B 6, l-b 6, n-b 12	24	B 3, l-b 4	7

1/0 2/9 3/37 4/115 5/132   216   1/71 2/186   (2 wkts dec.) 226
6/164 7/174 8/191 9/211

Bonus points – Middlesex 2, Northamptonshire 4.

Bowling: *First Innings*—Mallender 16–3–37–2; Walker 21–6–50–3; Capel 9–1–28–1; Harper 21–4–51–1; N. G. B. Cook 23–11–38–3. *Second Innings*—Mallender 17–3–54–1; Walker 15–2–63–0; N. G. B. Cook 21–5–42–0; Capel 11–0–35–1; Harper 13–3–25–0.

Northamptonshire

*G. Cook b Daniel	6	– lbw b Daniel	21
W. Larkins c Butcher b Cowans	26	– b Cowans	28
R. J. Boyd-Moss b Cowans	2	– lbw b Cowans	34
A. J. Lamb b Cowans	12	– not out	160
R. J. Bailey b Daniel	1	– c Butcher b Daniel	38
D. J. Capel run out	18	– c Radley b Sykes	0
R. A. Harper c Slack b Daniel	30	– lbw b Daniel	3
†S. N. V. Waterton b Hughes	13	– not out	13
N. G. B. Cook b Hughes	1		
N. A. Mallender b Daniel	1		
A. Walker not out	0		
B 1, l-b 6, w 4, n-b 4	15	B 8, l-b 3, n-b 13	24

1/12 2/36 3/57 4/61 5/65   125   1/54 2/58 3/191 4/294   (6 wkts) 321
6/106 7/112 8/116 9/119   5/295 6/298

Bonus points – Middlesex 4.

Bowling: *First Innings*—Daniel 16–0–76–4; Cowans 14–2–35–3; Tufnell 1–1–0–0; Hughes 2.3–1–7–2. *Second Innings*—Daniel 21–2–81–3; Cowans 15–1–65–2; Hughes 17–2–78–0; Tufnell 7–0–27–0; Sykes 17.3–1–59–1.

Umpires: J. W. Holder and R. A. White.

At Northampton, July 30, 31, August 1. NORTHAMPTONSHIRE drew with NEW ZEALANDERS (See New Zealand tour section).

At Lord's, August 2, 4, 5. NORTHAMPTONSHIRE lost to MIDDLESEX by an innings and 43 runs.

NORTHAMPTONSHIRE v GLAMORGAN

At Northampton, August 6, 7, 8. Drawn. Northamptonshire 6 pts, Glamorgan 2 pts. Toss: Northamptonshire. Three consecutive century partnerships ensured a commanding total for Northamptonshire, but they failed to press home their advantage on the final day when solid batting from Morris and Hopkins saw Glamorgan to safety. Geoff Cook and Larkins took charge on the first day with an opening stand of 151 in 146 minutes, and as the onslaught continued only Glamorgan's young left-arm spinner, North, posed the batsmen any problems. Cook (276 minutes, eleven 4s) again settled for the supporting role as he and Boyd-Moss, playing at the top of his form, put on 130 in even time, and finally Boyd-Moss, who hit 21 4s in a stay of less than three hours, and Lamb added 139 in nineteen hectic overs. Struggling at 120 for five soon after tea on the second afternoon, Glamorgan rallied through Maynard and Derrick, but after a tense struggle they finished 10 runs short of avoiding the follow-on. Cook chose to enforce it rather than offer the visitors an incentive of victory, but on a pitch which became slower as the match progressed, Glamorgan never looked in danger.

Northamptonshire

*G. Cook c Hopkins b Barwick	120	R. J. Bailey not out	9
W. Larkins c Roberts b Hickey	86	B 2, l-b 7, w 1, n-b 12	22
R. J. Boyd-Moss not out	148		
A. J. Lamb c Maynard b Barwick	56	1/151 2/281 3/420 (3 wkts dec.)	441

D. J. Capel, R. A. Harper, †S. N. V. Waterton, N. G. B. Cook, N. A. Mallender and A. Walker did not bat.

Bonus points – Northamptonshire 4 (Score at 100 overs: 347-2).

Bowling: Hickey 30–2–122–1; Barwick 24–5–120–2; Derrick 15–0–72–0; Ontong 35–10–82–0; North 17–5–36–0.

Glamorgan

J. A. Hopkins c and b N. G. B. Cook	34	– c Waterton b Boyd-Moss	54
*H. Morris c Waterton b Mallender	18	– b Bailey	52
D. B. Pauline b Capel	3	– hit wkt b Walker	0
G. C. Holmes b Harper	21	– not out	20
M. P. Maynard b Mallender	77		
R. C. Ontong c G. Cook b Harper	14		
J. Derrick b N. G. B. Cook	76		
P. D. North c Bailey b Harper	0		
†M. L. Roberts c Harper b N. G. B. Cook	8		
S. R. Barwick b Harper	0		
D. J. Hickey not out	0		
B 4, l-b 11, w 1, n-b 15	31	B 4, l-b 5, n-b 3	12

1/30 2/48 3/86 4/95 5/120   282   1/96 2/97 3/138   (3 wkts) 138
6/257 7/259 8/279 9/282

Bonus points – Glamorgan 2, Northamptonshire 2 (Score at 100 overs: 223-5).

Bowling: *First Innings*—Mallender 21–5–63–2; Capel 15–2–33–1; Harper 43.3–15–83–4; N. G. B. Cook 39–12–77–3; G. Cook 1–1–0–0; Walker 6–2–11–0. *Second Innings*—Mallender 7–1–13–0; Capel 3–3–0–0; Harper 14–7–20–0; N. G. B. Cook 16–5–27–0; G. Cook 6–2–10–0; Walker 10–2–34–1; Boyd-Moss 14–8–23–1; Bailey 4.5–2–2–1.

Umpires: B. Leadbeater and A. G. T. Whitehead.

NORTHAMPTONSHIRE v SOMERSET

At Wellingborough School, August 9, 11, 12. Drawn. Northamptonshire 5 pts, Somerset 4 pts. Toss: Somerset. Roebuck's decision to bat first looked suspect as Somerset struggled at the start, and with better direction the Northamptonshire attack could have made greater inroads. Instead, Marks produced a determined innings of 2 hours, 40 minutes before running out of partners. In the final session of the first day Larkins gave a dazzling display, 48 of his 59 runs, scored off 66 balls, coming in boundaries. He was particularly severe on Botham, whose opening nine overs cost 66 runs. No play was possible on the second day, but Lamb soon made up for lost time, almost upstaging Larkins with two 6s and fifteen 4s in 83 from 79 deliveries. Somerset hesitated over a second-innings declaration after Capel sent back Felton, Richards and Botham in twelve balls; yet set an unlikely 221 to win in 90 minutes, the home side briefly flirted with the idea as Larkins again savaged the bowling with four 6s and four 4s. His dismissal ended their optimistic chase.

Somerset

B. C. Rose c G. Cook b Capel	....	1	– c and b Capel	17
*P. M. Roebuck b Walker	....	14	– c Waterton b Capel	5
N. A. Felton c Larkins b Harper	....	28	– b Capel	14
I. V. A. Richards c Lamb b Walker	....	0	– c Lamb b Capel	43
R. J. Harden lbw b Mallender	....	33	– not out	53
I. T. Botham b Harper	....	16	– b Capel	0
V. J. Marks not out	....	76	– c Boyd-Moss b N. G. B. Cook	33
†T. Gard c Harper b Walker	....	13	– not out	19
M. R. Davis b Capel	....	3		
J. Garner c Harper b Capel	....	11		
R. V. J. Coombs b Harper	....	8		
B 3, l-b 3, n-b 1	....	7	B 1, l-b 5, n-b 5	11

1/3 2/30 3/30 4/71 5/79	210	1/10 2/34 3/69 (6 wkts dec.) 195
6/101 7/127 8/164 9/182		4/86 5/86 6/148

Bonus points – Somerset 2, Northamptonshire 4.

Bowling: *First Innings*—Mallender 17–6–35–1; Capel 24–8–42–3; Walker 18–3–60–3; Harper 18.4–5–50–3; N. G. B. Cook 8–3–17–0. *Second Innings*—Mallender 11–3–40–0; Capel 19–3–61–5; Harper 12–4–32–0; N. G. B. Cook 11–2–25–1; Walker 6–0–31–0.

Northamptonshire

*G. Cook c Marks b Garner	....	12	– st Gard b Coombs	10
W. Larkins c Gard b Coombs	....	59	– c Davis b Marks	47
R. J. Boyd-Moss c Richards b Garner	....	0	– not out	11
A. J. Lamb c Gard b Marks	....	83		
N. G. B. Cook c Botham b Garner	....	4		
R. J. Bailey not out	....	11		
R. A. Harper (did not bat)	....	–	– (4) not out	12
L-b 5, n-b 11	....	16		

1/54 2/54 3/99 4/123	(5 wkts dec.) 185	1/29 2/67 (2 wkts) 80
5/185		

D. J. Capel, †S. N. V. Waterton, N. A. Mallender and A. Walker did not bat.

Bonus points – Northamptonshire 1, Somerset 2.

Bowling: *First Innings*—Garner 17–3–73–3; Botham 12–1–73–0; Coombs 5–1–31–1; Marks 1.5–1–3–1. *Second Innings*—Garner 3–2–1–0; Botham 3–1–7–0; Marks 7–1–47–1; Coombs 7–0–25–1.

Umpires: B. Leadbeater and A. G. T. Whitehead.

At Colchester, August 16, 18, 19. NORTHAMPTONSHIRE beat ESSEX by 102 runs.

NORTHAMPTONSHIRE v NOTTINGHAMSHIRE

At Northampton, August 20, 21, 22. Drawn. Northamptonshire 4 pts, Nottinghamshire 5 pts. Toss: Northamptonshire. Rain on the final afternoon washed out further play with Northamptonshire chasing a victory target of 268 in 50 overs. Put in to bat, Nottinghamshire progressed carefully, Broad providing the backbone with a valuable innings which lasted four hours, twenty minutes, featured fourteen boundaries and ended when he offered no shot to a ball from Nick Cook. Fraser-Darling, a strongly built all-rounder, cashed in on two missed chances to reach a maiden half-century on the first evening and had the home side in trouble with a career-best bowling performance on a rain-affected second day, although Bailey counter-attacked magnificently, hitting thirteen 4s. Northamptonshire declared upon avoiding the follow-on, but despite the efforts of the captains to produce an interesting finish, the weather had the decisive say.

Nottinghamshire

B. C. Broad lbw b N. G. B. Cook	92	– c Mallender b N. G. B. Cook	43
M. Newell b Harper	29	– not out	53
P. Johnson c G. Cook b Harper	24	– b N. G. B. Cook	1
*J. D. Birch c Wild b Harper	3	– not out	16
D. W. Randall c Ripley b Walker	5		
†C. W. Scott lbw b Harper	40		
C. D. Fraser-Darling b Walker	61		
K. P. Evans c Bailey b Mallender	1		
E. E. Hemmings lbw b Capel	31		
K. Saxelby not out	16		
J. A. Afford lbw b Capel	4		
B 4, l-b 7, w 1, n-b 10	22	L-b 4, n-b 1	5

1/77 2/106 3/126 4/137 5/178   328   1/67 2/72   (2 wkts. dec.) 118
6/231 7/232 8/284 9/320

Bonus points – Nottinghamshire 2, Northamptonshire 3 (Score at 100 overs: 248-7).

Bowling: *First Innings*—Mallender 25–4–81–1; Capel 31.5–9–84–2; Walker 22–6–55–2; Wild 4–0–21–0; Harper 29–12–50–4; N. G. B. Cook 13–5–26–1. *Second Innings*—Walker 7–1–19–0; Capel 7–1–28–0; N. G. B. Cook 10–2–33–2; Wild 9–1–34–0.

Northamptonshire

*G. Cook c Birch b Fraser-Darling	3	– not out	27
W. Larkins c Evans b Fraser-Darling	2	– not out	20
R. J. Boyd-Moss lbw b Fraser-Darling	9		
R. J. Bailey c Afford b Saxelby	98		
D. J. Capel b Saxelby	17		
D. J. Wild c and b Fraser-Darling	12		
R. A. Harper c Birch b Saxelby	4		
†D. Ripley c Scott b Fraser-Darling	1		
N. G. B. Cook not out	17		
N. A. Mallender not out	1		
B 4, l-b 6, w 1, n-b 4	15	B 1, l-b 1	2

1/4 2/8 3/31 4/66   (8 wkts. dec.) 179   (no wkt) 49
5/93 6/98 7/112 8/176

A. Walker did not bat.

Bonus points – Northamptonshire 1, Nottinghamshire 3.

Bowling: *First Innings*—Saxelby 25–5–49–3; Fraser-Darling 25.4–6–84–5; Evans 9–1–35–0; Afford 1–0–1–0; Hemmings 2–2–0–0. *Second Innings*—Saxelby 6–1–13–0; Fraser-Darling 7–0–28–0; Hemmings 1–0–6–0.

Umpires: J. H. Hampshire and R. A. White.

At Leicester, August 23, 25, 26. NORTHAMPTONSHIRE drew with LEICESTERSHIRE.

NORTHAMPTONSHIRE v HAMPSHIRE

At Northampton, August 27, 28, 29. Hampshire won by 169 runs. Hampshire 20 pts. Toss: Northamptonshire. A spineless batting display by Northamptonshire handed the visitors victory after each side had forfeited an innings to counteract the effect of a blank first day. Hampshire were given a superb start by Greenidge and Terry, whose opening partnership of 250 beat the 26-year-old county record by 1 run. Greenidge's memorable and masterly innings included three 6s and 28 4s, and he demonstrated every stroke during his 281 minutes at the crease. In sharp contrast, Terry's 55 runs took him 78 overs to compile. Northamptonshire were given a full day to score 339 but struggled against Maru before Marshall returned to run through the tail. Nick Cook was last out, after a defiant effort, with an hour and a half remaining.

Hampshire

C. G. Greenidge c Harper b Mallender 222
V. P. Terry c Ripley b Walker 55
C. L. Smith not out 23
R. A. Smith not out 16
B 2, l-b 15, n-b 5 22
—
1/250 2/309   (2 wkts dec.) 338

*M. C. J. Nicholas, N. G. Cowley, K. D. James, T. M. Tremlett, †R. J. Parks, M. D. Marshall and R. J. Maru did not bat.

Bonus points – Hampshire 4 (Score at 100 overs: 335-2).

Bowling: Mallender 13–1–33–1; Walker 18–0–87–1; N. G. B. Cook 25–6–81–0; Harper 25–5–66–0; Boyd-Moss 8–1–21–0; Capel 12–4–33–0.

Hampshire forfeited their second innings.

Northamptonshire

Northamptonshire forfeited their first innings.

*G. Cook c Terry b Maru 34	N. G. B. Cook c R. A. Smith b Marshall 30	
W. Larkins lbw b Marshall 0	N. A. Mallender b Marshall 0	
R. J. Boyd-Moss st Parks b Maru 25	A. Walker not out 0	
A. J. Lamb c Greenidge b Maru 32		
R. J. Bailey c Parks b Tremlett 10	B 2, l-b 6 8	
D. J. Capel c and b Maru 2		
R. A. Harper lbw b Marshall 24	1/5 2/59 3/62 4/93 5/102 169	
†D. Ripley lbw b Tremlett 4	6/113 7/120 8/166 9/166	

Bowling: Marshall 17.4–3–41–4; James 11–5–21–0; Maru 24–8–47–4; Tremlett 16–2–39–2; Cowley 9–5–6–0; C. L. Smith 1–0–7–0.

Umpires: J. A. Jameson and A. A. Jones.

At Derby, September 3, 4, 5. NORTHAMPTONSHIRE drew with DERBYSHIRE.

At Scarborough, September 10, 11, 12. NORTHAMPTONSHIRE drew with YORKSHIRE.

At Nottingham, September 13, 15, 16. NORTHAMPTONSHIRE drew with NOTTING-HAMSHIRE.

NOTTINGHAMSHIRE

President: J. W. Baddiley
Chairman: C. F. Ward
Chairman, Cricket Committee: R. T. Simpson
Secretary: B. Robson
County Cricket Ground, Trent Bridge,
Nottingham NG2 6AG
(Telephone: 0602-821525)
Cricket Manager: K. A. Taylor
Captain: C. E. B. Rice

Not for the first time in recent years, Nottinghamshire promised much in terms of winning trophies but had to be content with the lesser prize-money. They finished fourth in the Britannic Assurance Championship, third in the John Player League, reached the semi-finals of the Benson and Hedges Cup and faltered in the quarter-finals of the NatWest Bank Trophy. And with the possibility of the Clive Rice–Richard Hadlee era coming to a close, they were left to reflect on the fact that, despite such outstanding all-round talents, only in the Championship year of 1981 had a major honour found its way to Trent Bridge.

Nottinghamshire's followers were always guaranteed entertaining fare. Few sides could match the county's run-scoring rate and there was never anything dour about the way they tackled each challenge. They were also consistent. After the defeat by Hampshire in the opening match of the season, they suffered only one further setback in the Championship, losing at Leicester late in June when they were hurried out for 58 in their second innings.

With that in mind, it may seem surprising that Nottinghamshire did not put more pressure on Essex, the eventual champions, even though the Championship was not settled until the penultimate match. Their shortcoming, however, was their inability to finish off the opposition on occasions numerous enough to leave a feeling of frustration long after the season had finished. The most obvious example was in May, when Nottinghamshire had Derbyshire on the point of defeat at 26 for six in their second innings, yet even with the match-winning penetration of Hadlee could not press home their advantage. Derbyshire recovered to 248 for nine, with the last pair batting for more than an hour to save the game.

Nor was this an isolated case. The trait stayed with Nottinghamshire until the last ball of the season when they were striving for the victory over Northamptonshire which would have given them the runners-up position behind Essex. On that September day, there was not the long drawn-out frustration at being unable to bowl out the opposition, but there was none the less an air of disappointment when Northamptonshire clung on for a draw with their last pair at the wicket.

The level of disappointment, however, is curbed when consideration is given to the fact that not so many years have passed since the county trundled from one season to the next on the lower rungs of the County Championship ladder. But soon Nottinghamshire must face the prospect

of a team without Hadlee and Rice, around whom so much of the
county's recent ascendency has revolved. Hadlee, when he was not
tormenting English batsmen in the Test matches last summer, again
illustrated his immense value to the side, heading both the batting and
bowling averages in his benefit season. Rice, for his part, completed
1,000 runs in first-class cricket for the twelfth successive season, and in
the John Player League he equalled the record number of wickets in a
season, 34, taken by Somerset's R. J. Clapp in 1974.

Nottinghamshire have, under the experienced and astute eye of the
cricket manager, Ken Taylor, been planning for the future, and it is to
the increasing band of talented youngsters that the county will look for
fresh inspiration in coming seasons. Paul Johnson, a prodigious
strokemaker, typified the exuberance in evidence at Trent Bridge when,
at the age of 21 years and three months, he became last season the
youngest player in the club's history to score 1,000 runs. Mick Newell,
another promising young batsman, had to work harder and longer for his
opportunity in the first team, but his dedication and perseverance were
rewarded during a summer in which he edged Derek Randall out of the
side on merit. Randall suffered one of those seasons when form was
elusive. He looked to be recapturing it towards the end of the season in
the one-day games and it was hoped that he would return in 1987
refreshed and full of enthusiasm.

With the experience and scoring power of two England openers, Chris
Broad and Tim Robinson, Nottinghamshire's batting continued to be as
productive as any in the country, although it was still prone to most
unlikely collapses. Its run-scoring potential should be boosted if John
Birch can produce in 1987 the form he showed in the first half of last
season before injuries received in a motor accident curtailed his
involvement.

As a bowling side, backed to the highest standard by the wicket-
keeping skills of Bruce French, at last capped by England, Nottinghamshire relied heavily on Hadlee's special talents, but two young contenders
did enough in 1986 to suggest that they would be around the county scene
for years to come. Andy Pick took 50 wickets to underline his mounting
value as a medium-fast bowler, and Andy Afford, a left-arm spinner,
showed at 22 remarkable control and a mature approach. It says much
for Afford's contribution that the highly rated Peter Such found his
opportunities restricted. If these youngsters do come of age soon,
Nottinghamshire may yet lose the tag of county cricket's "nearly"
men. – J.L.

NOTTINGHAMSHIRE 1986

[*Bill Smith*]

Back row: R. J. Evans, P. M. Such, C. D. Fraser-Darling, K. P. Evans, J. A. Afford, M. Newell. *Middle row:* C. W. Scott, D. J. R. Martindale, R. A. Pick, K. E. Cooper, B. C. Broad, K. Saxelby, D. J. Millns, P. Johnson. *Front row:* R. T. Robinson, E. E. Hemmings, D. W. Randall, R. J. Hadlee, K. A. Taylor (*manager*), C. E. B. Rice (*captain*), J. D. Birch, B. N. French, M. K. Bore.

NOTTINGHAMSHIRE RESULTS

All first-class matches – Played 26: Won 8, Lost 2, Drawn 16.

County Championship matches – Played 24: Won 7, Lost 2, Drawn 15.

Bonus points – Batting 55, Bowling 80.

Competition placings – Britannic Assurance County Championship, 4th; NatWest Bank Trophy, q-f; Benson and Hedges Cup, s-f; John Player League, 3rd.

BRITANNIC ASSURANCE CHAMPIONSHIP AVERAGES

BATTING

	Birthplace	M	I	NO	R	HI	Avge
‡R. J. Hadlee	Christchurch, NZ	14	18	5	720	129*	55.38
‡R. T. Robinson	Sutton-in-Ashfield	19	30	5	1,319	159*	52.76
‡C. E. B. Rice	Johannesburg, SA	22	31	6	1,118	146*	44.72
C. W. Scott	Thorpe-on-the-Hill	9	8	3	220	69*	44.00
‡P. Johnson	Newark	24	34	5	1,156	128	39.86
‡B. C. Broad	Bristol	24	40	2	1,476	122	38.84
C. D. Fraser-Darling	Sheffield	5	4	0	142	61	35.50
M. Newell	Blackburn	17	27	8	671	80	35.31
‡J. D. Birch	Nottingham	19	25	6	636	79*	33.47
‡K. Saxelby	Worksop	9	7	4	99	34	33.00
‡B. N. French	Warsop	14	14	2	269	58	22.41
‡D. W. Randall	Retford	13	21	0	392	60	18.66
‡E. E. Hemmings	Leamington Spa	20	21	3	300	54*	16.66
‡K. E. Cooper	Hucknall	16	12	5	105	19	15.00
R. A. Pick	Nottingham	17	15	1	180	55	12.85
J. A. Afford	Crowland	14	12	7	19	9*	3.80
P. M. Such	Helensburgh	4	4	0	9	6	2.25

Also batted: K. P. Evans (*Calverton*) (2 matches) 1; D. J. R. Martindale (*Harrogate*) (2 matches) 9, 4, 14.

* Signifies not out.   ‡ Denotes county cap.

The following played a total of seventeen three-figure innings for Nottinghamshire in County Championship matches: B. C. Broad 6, R. T. Robinson 4, P. Johnson 3, R. J. Hadlee 2, C. E. B. Rice 2.

BOWLING

	O	M	R	W	BB	Avge
R. J. Hadlee	393.4	108	825	57	6-31	14.47
K. E. Cooper	374.5	98	940	41	5-102	22.93
C. E. B. Rice	413.2	115	1,111	44	4-54	25.25
E. E. Hemmings	780.3	244	2,014	71	7-102	28.36
K. Saxelby	240	45	763	24	4-47	31.79
R. A. Pick	419.2	75	1,455	42	6-68	34.64
J. A. Afford	466.4	119	1,426	41	6-81	34.78
P. M. Such	132	33	382	10	3-39	38.20
C. D. Fraser-Darling	120	16	461	12	5-84	38.41

Also bowled: J. D. Birch 11-1-24-1; B. C. Broad 7-1-41-0; K. P. Evans 15-2-73-0; P. Johnson 19-2-113-0; M. Newell 2-0-19-0; D. W. Randall 3-0-17-0; R. T. Robinson 2-0-18-0.

Wicket-keepers: B. N. French 30 ct, 4 st; C. W. Scott 22 ct, 1 st; M. Newell 1 st.

Leading Fielders: C. E. B. Rice 28; P. Johnson 24; J. D. Birch 21; B. C. Broad 17; M. Newell 14; D. W. Randall 13; R. T. Robinson 13.

NOTTINGHAMSHIRE v HAMPSHIRE

At Nottingham, April 26, 27, 28. Hampshire won by nine wickets. Hampshire 21 pts, Nottinghamshire 5 pts. Toss: Hampshire. Hampshire raced to an emphatic victory thanks to Rice's generous declaration and the uninhibited strokeplay of Greenidge. Greenidge made light of the target of 206, in 42 overs, with 118 (four 6s, ten 4s) in 105 minutes off 99 balls. His hundred came in 89 minutes off 88 balls. Terry played a fine supporting role. On the Saturday Nottinghamshire had made 265 on a slow pitch, but half-centuries by Robin Smith and Parks, in conditions favouring the bowlers, denied them a substantial lead. Broad and Robinson saw Nottinghamshire move comfortably towards a declaration which, with the benefit of hindsight, could have been delayed.

Nottinghamshire

R. T. Robinson c Nicholas b Tremlett	65	– c Parks b Connor	48
B. C. Broad c Parks b Maru	18	– not out	68
D. W. Randall b Marshall	18	– c R. A. Smith b Cowley	7
*C. E. B. Rice c c C. L. Smith b Cowley	76	– c Maru b Cowley	31
P. Johnson b Maru	11	– not out	17
J. D. Birch b Marshall	24		
R. J. Hadlee run out	1		
†B. N. French lbw b Maru	12		
E. E. Hemmings b Maru	23		
K. E. Cooper not out	10		
J. A. Afford c Parks b Cowley	0		
L-b 7	7	L-b 10	10

1/42 2/89 3/115 4/159 5/210   265   1/76 2/97 3/156   (3 wkts dec.) 181
6/211 7/217 8/249 9/262

Bonus points – Nottinghamshire 2, Hampshire 3 (Score at 100 overs: 232-7).

Bowling: *First Innings*—Marshall 24-7-48-2; Connor 16-3-54-0; Maru 31-8-71-4; Tremlett 24-8-48-1; Cowley 19.4-4-37-2. *Second Innings*—Marshall 7-2-26-0; Connor 19-4-41-1; Tremlett 8-2-19-0; Maru 17-3-50-0; Cowley 10-1-29-2; C. L. Smith 1-0-6-0.

Hampshire

C. G. Greenidge b Rice	21	– c French b Hemmings	118
V. P. Terry c Broad b Rice	14	– not out	74
R. A. Smith c Randall b Cooper	50	– not out	13
C. L. Smith c Rice b Cooper	9		
*M. C. J. Nicholas c Johnson b Cooper	23		
M. D. Marshall c and b Rice	35		
N. G. Cowley lbw b Rice	4		
T. M. Tremlett c Johnson b Hadlee	5		
†R. J. Parks not out	51		
R. J. Maru not out	17		
B 3, l-b 5, w 1, n-b 3	12	B 2, l-b 2	4

1/37 2/42 3/90 4/100   (8 wkts dec.) 241   1/170   (1 wkt) 209
5/155 6/159 7/168 8/174

C. A. Connor did not bat.

Bonus points – Hampshire 2, Nottinghamshire 3 (Score at 100 overs: 209-8).

Bowling: *First Innings*—Hadlee 18-4-54-1; Cooper 24-13-30-3; Hemmings 21-9-24-0; Rice 17-4-54-4; Afford 28-9-71-0. *Second Innings*—Hadlee 5-0-19-0; Cooper 5-0-33-0; Hemmings 15.1-2-67-1; Afford 10-0-54-0; Rice 5-0-32-0.

Umpires: R. Julian and D. O. Oslear.

At The Oval, April 30, May 1, 2. NOTTINGHAMSHIRE drew with SURREY.

At Oxford, May 7, 8, 9. NOTTINGHAMSHIRE beat OXFORD UNIVERSITY by 210 runs.

NOTTINGHAMSHIRE v LEICESTERSHIRE

At Nottingham, May 21, 22, 23. Nottinghamshire won by five wickets. Nottinghamshire 20 pts, Leicestershire 4 pts. Toss: Nottinghamshire. Nottinghamshire captured their first Championship victory of the season with five wickets and seven balls to spare. After the loss of more than a day to wet conditions, Gower and Whitaker eased Leicestershire away from their early problems with a stand of 137. Both sides forfeited an innings after Leicestershire's declaration on the final morning, and Nottinghamshire, with 92 overs to reach their target, paced themselves perfectly. Robinson made 104, his first hundred of the season, in 263 minutes, and was run out when DeFreitas, following through after bowling, kicked the ball into the stumps. Rice then assumed control and Nottinghamshire were just 27 runs short of victory when he was dismissed.

Leicestershire

I. P. Butcher b Hadlee	9	P. A. J. DeFreitas b Rice	55
R. A. Cobb b Hadlee	4	W. K. M. Benjamin not out	34
L. Potter lbw b Pick	3	L. B. Taylor not out	1
*D. I. Gower c Birch b Hadlee	82	B 4, l-b 1, n-b 2	7
J. J. Whitaker c Rice b Cooper	76		
N. E. Briers c Randall b Hadlee	1	1/5 2/10 3/34	(9 wkts. dec.) 312
P. B. Clift c Rice b Hadlee	4	4/171 5/172 6/181	
†P. Whitticase run out	36	7/188 8/261 9/278	

Bonus points – Leicestershire 4, Nottinghamshire 4.

Bowling: Hadlee 17-5-41-5; Pick 15-2-84-1; Cooper 19-3-42-1; Afford 14-1-47-0; Rice 14-2-60-1; Randall 3-0-17-0; Johnson 2-1-16-0.

Leicestershire forfeited their second innings.

Nottinghamshire

Nottinghamshire forfeited their first innings.

R. T. Robinson run out	104	R. J. Hadlee not out	9
B. C. Broad c Clift b Benjamin	4		
D. W. Randall b Clift	26	L-b 12, w 9, n-b 7	28
*C. E. B. Rice c Whitticase b Clift	86		
P. Johnson c Whitticase b DeFreitas	22	1/14 2/73 3/220	(5 wkts) 315
J. D. Birch not out	36	4/256 5/286	

†B. N. French, R. A. Pick, K. E. Cooper and J. A. Afford did not bat.

Bowling: Taylor 21-5-57-0; Benjamin 22.5-4-101-1; DeFreitas 25-4-68-1; Clift 20-3-71-2; Briers 2-0-6-0.

Umpires: H. D. Bird and J. A. Jameson.

At Derby, May 24, 25, 26. NOTTINGHAMSHIRE drew with DERBYSHIRE.

At Southampton, May 31, June 2, 3. NOTTINGHAMSHIRE drew with HAMPSHIRE.

NOTTINGHAMSHIRE v SOMERSET

At Nottingham, June 4, 5, 6. Drawn. Nottinghamshire 5 pts, Somerset 6 pts. Toss: Nottinghamshire. Although put in to bat, Somerset restricted Nottinghamshire to one bowling point as Roebuck painstakingly made his way to a career-best 221 not out, which included 22 4s, in more than eight hours. Hadlee's century in Nottinghamshire's reply – he batted for 98 minutes and hit nineteen 4s – was in stark contrast as he shared an unbroken stand of 206 with Birch. Cooper took three wickets in successive overs when Somerset batted again, but a typical innings from Richards enabled them to declare, leaving Nottinghamshire to score 295 in three hours. Rice briefly took up the challenge, hitting three 6s and ten 4s, but a draw always seemed the most likely result.

Somerset

N. A. Felton c Rice b Cooper	51	– lbw b Cooper	37
*P. M. Roebuck not out	221		
J. J. E. Hardy c Broad b Pick	46	– lbw b Cooper	0
I. V. A. Richards b Cooper	6	– c Hadlee b Afford	65
R. J. Harden b Pick	77	– not out	35
B. C. Rose not out	43	– (2) c French b Cooper	24
V. J. Marks (did not bat)	–	(6) not out	15
B 1, l-b 11, n-b 3	15	B 5, l-b 3, n-b 1	9

1/86 2/195 3/213   (4 wkts dec.) 459   1/59 2/66 3/69   (4 wkts dec.) 185
4/357   4/145

†R. J. Blitz, J. Garner, C. H. Dredge and N. S. Taylor did not bat.

Bonus points – Somerset 4, Nottinghamshire 1 (Score at 100 overs: 312-3).

Bowling: *First Innings*—Hadlee 27-8-38-0; Cooper 28-0-96-2; Pick 33-1-110-2; Rice 17-1-63-0; Afford 31-3-140-0. *Second Innings*—Hadlee 4-2-3-0; Pick 3-0-15-0; Afford 17-0-98-1; Cooper 9-2-26-3; Johnson 7-0-35-0.

Nottinghamshire

B. C. Broad c Garner b Dredge	52	– b Garner	2
M. Newell b Garner	4	– not out	51
D. W. Randall c Hardy b Marks	21	– lbw b Dredge	10
*C. E. B. Rice c Felton b Garner	8	– not out	87
P. Johnson b Dredge	51		
J. D. Birch not out	79		
R. J. Hadlee not out	129		
L-b 2, w 1, n-b 3	6	B 2, l-b 2, n-b 3	7

1/28 2/56 3/66   (5 wkts dec.) 350   1/2 2/33   (2 wkts) 157
4/139 5/144

†B. N. French, R. A. Pick, K. E. Cooper and J. A. Afford did not bat.

Bonus points – Nottinghamshire 4, Somerset 2.

Bowling: *First Innings*—Garner 20-4-85-2; Taylor 13-4-57-0; Marks 33-8-108-1; Dredge 11-2-58-2; Richards 9-0-40-0. *Second Innings*—Garner 6-0-16-1; Taylor 10-2-39-0; Marks 18-1-65-0; Dredge 7-3-30-1; Richards 3-1-3-0.

Umpires: D. J. Constant and D. G. L. Evans.

At Chelmsford, June 7, 9, 10. NOTTINGHAMSHIRE drew with ESSEX.

NOTTINGHAMSHIRE v SURREY

At Nottingham, June 14, 16. Nottinghamshire won by an innings and 7 runs. Nottinghamshire 23 pts, Surrey 4 pts. Toss: Nottinghamshire. On a lively pitch, Nottinghamshire raced to a two-day victory over Surrey as Hadlee returned match figures of ten for 72. Nottinghamshire built the foundations for their win on the opening day when they compiled a steady 294. Gray, who bowled with aggression for his four wickets, lacked the support to bowl the home side out cheaply. Robinson and Randall shared a useful partnership of 90 in seventeen overs and Birch, who batted for 202 minutes for his unbeaten 67, held the middle order together. Surrey lost three wickets for 38 before the close and, in humid conditions with the ball moving extravagantly, were all out in 45 minutes on Monday morning. Jesty and Needham resisted to greater effect in the second innings, but the return of Hadlee to the attack brought an end to Surrey's resistance.

Nottinghamshire

R. T. Robinson c Doughty b Gray	 52	E. E. Hemmings c Doughty b Bicknell	.	1
B. C. Broad c and b Gray	 2	K. E. Cooper c and b Bicknell	....	9
D. W. Randall c Stewart b Jesty	 46	P. M. Such b Bicknell	....	2
*C. E. B. Rice c Richards b Pocock	... 3			
P. Johnson lbw b Gray	 11	L-b 20, w 3, n-b 10	....	33
J. D. Birch not out	 67			
R. J. Hadlee b Doughty	 32	1/9 2/99 3/113 4/134 5/135		294
†B. N. French c Stewart b Gray	 36	6/194 7/252 8/266 9/278		

Bonus points – Nottinghamshire 3, Surrey 4.

Bowling: Gray 23–3–59–4; Doughty 15–1–54–1; Bicknell 18–0–72–3; Jesty 3–0–18–1; Pocock 20–7–44–1; Needham 7–2–15–0; Butcher 5–1–12–0.

Surrey

A. R. Butcher lbw b Hadlee	....	1 – c French b Hadlee	 21
G. S. Clinton lbw b Hadlee	....	5 – c Randall b Hadlee	 18
A. J. Stewart c French b Cooper	....	18 – b Such	 15
M. A. Lynch c Johnson b Rice	....	1 – c Robinson b Such	 1
†C. J. Richards c Randall b Cooper	..	25 – (7) b Hadlee	 2
T. E. Jesty c French b Hadlee	....	5 – (5) lbw b Rice	 55
A. Needham lbw b Rice	....	5 – (6) c Rice b Such	 48
R. J. Doughty c Birch b Cooper	.....	1 – b Hadlee	 5
M. P. Bicknell c Johnson b Hadlee	...	1 – not out	 9
A. H. Gray c Cooper b Hemmings	....	18 – b Hadlee	 0
*P. I. Pocock not out	....	0 – c Rice b Hadlee	 4
L-b 3, n-b 3	....	6	B 4, l-b 7, w 1, n-b 2 ... 14

1/2 2/11 3/24 4/63 5/69	95	1/33 2/50 3/51 4/66 5/142	192
6/69 7/70 8/71 9/95		6/160 7/166 8/182 9/184	

Bonus points – Nottinghamshire 4.

Bowling: *First Innings*—Hadlee 17–4–39–4; Rice 9–2–23–2; Cooper 8–1–22–3; Hemmings 1.2–0–8–1. *Second Innings*—Rice 15–3–40–1; Cooper 10–2–22–0; Such 16–7–39–3; Hadlee 15.3–6–33–6; Hemmings 16–3–47–0.

Umpires: C. Cook and D. O. Oslear.

NOTTINGHAMSHIRE v MIDDLESEX

At Nottingham, June 18, 19, 20. Nottinghamshire won by 126 runs. Nottinghamshire 21 pts, Middlesex 4 pts. Toss: Nottinghamshire. From the end of the first day, Nottinghamshire always appeared to be heading for victory, but they were made to wait until the last hour of the match. Another resourceful innings by Birch enabled them to make 192 on a pitch with uneven bounce and sufficient movement to encourage the faster bowlers. Carr provided the backbone of Middlesex's reply, but he could not prevent Hemmings from disposing quickly of the late order before the close to give Nottinghamshire a lead of 57. As the wicket eased on the second day, Rice punished the bowling for an unbeaten 156, which took him 305 minutes and included eighteen 4s. Middlesex, set 404 in a day plus eighteen overs, were soon in trouble and 26 for two overnight. However, Radley, for 204 minutes, Downton, for 163 minutes, and Hughes, for 27 overs, questioned Nottinghamshire's ability to force home their advantage.

Nottinghamshire

R. T. Robinson b Hughes	17	– b Daniel	67
B. C. Broad c G. K. Brown b Hughes	22	– lbw b Cowans	4
D. W. Randall b Daniel	0	– c Butcher b Daniel	8
*C. E. B. Rice b Fraser	17	– not out	156
P. Johnson c K. R. Brown b Fraser	29	– lbw b Fraser	26
J. D. Birch b Cowans	46	– not out	54
†C. W. Scott b Daniel	10		
R. A. Pick c G. K. Brown b Cowans	7		
E. E. Hemmings c Downton b Cowans	16		
K. E. Cooper not out	14		
P. M. Such c K. R. Brown b Cowans	0		
B 4, l-b 3, w 3, n-b 4	14	B 8, l-b 11, w 3, n-b 9	31

1/43 2/45 3/47 4/70 5/111   192   1/16 2/42 3/156   (4 wkts dec.) 346
6/130 7/158 8/167 9/192   4/221

Bonus points – Nottinghamshire 1, Middlesex 4.

Bowling: *First Innings*—Daniel 15-0-58-2; Cowans 10.2-4-22-4; Hughes 13-1-71-2; Fraser 13-4-34-2. *Second Innings*—Daniel 19-0-88-2; Cowans 18-2-72-1; Fraser 17-3-60-1; Hughes 18-3-56-0; Carr 17-1-51-0.

Middlesex

K. R. Brown c Randall b Cooper	32	– lbw b Pick	4
A. J. T. Miller c Johnson b Cooper	5	– lbw b Cooper	6
†P. R. Downton c Scott b Pick	1	– (8) b Cooper	53
R. O. Butcher c Scott b Pick	1	– (3) c Johnson b Pick	17
*C. T. Radley b Rice	9	– (6) c Birch b Pick	58
J. D. Carr c Birch b Cooper	57	– (7) b Hemmings	31
G. K. Brown lbw b Hemmings	14	– (4) c Randall b Such	3
S. P. Hughes b Hemmings	1	– (5) c Randall b Such	26
A. R. C. Fraser c Birch b Hemmings	0	– c Broad b Cooper	4
N. G. Cowans c Randall b Hemmings	6	– b Rice	26
W. W. Daniel not out	0	– not out	8
B 1, l-b 4, w 1, n-b 3	9	B 10, l-b 20, w 5, n-b 6	41

1/28 2/42 3/44 4/44 5/81   135   1/10 2/21 3/48 4/90 5/158   277
6/121 7/122 8/122 9/128   6/194 7/202 8/224 9/260

Bonus points – Nottinghamshire 4.

Bowling: *First Innings*—Pick 13-4-39-2; Rice 10-0-32-1; Such 9-2-21-0; Cooper 14-5-26-3; Hemmings 6.3-4-12-4. *Second Innings*—Pick 27-4-85-3; Cooper 25.1-11-43-3; Such 20-7-46-2; Hemmings 32-10-57-1; Rice 8-3-16-1.

Umpires: C. Cook and D. O. Oslear.

At Leicester, June 28, 30, July 1. NOTTINGHAMSHIRE lost to LEICESTERSHIRE by 275 runs.

NOTTINGHAMSHIRE v WARWICKSHIRE

At Nottingham, July 2, 3, 4. Drawn. Nottinghamshire 8 pts, Warwickshire 3 pts. Toss: Nottinghamshire. Although they were in charge of the match from the moment Rice won the toss, Nottinghamshire had to settle for a draw. On a lively pitch, Warwickshire struggled against the pace, bounce and movement of Hadlee, who was well supported by his fieldsmen. Asif Din and Small lent token respectability as all ten Warwickshire batsmen fell to catches. The vagaries of the pitch did not seem evident as Nottinghamshire moved resolutely to 451. Before the end of the first day Broad had scored his first hundred of the season, batting in all for 197 minutes (139 balls) and hitting seventeen 4s. With a lead of 322, Nottinghamshire had a day and a half in which to force victory but Warwickshire, 111 for three overnight, resisted stubbornly, and an hour and a half was lost to bad light on the final day. McMillan's 136, which included twenty 4s, occupied 304 minutes and was his highest score; and at the end, Small and Munton batted for 27 overs to frustrate Nottinghamshire's ambitions.

Warwickshire

T. A. Lloyd c and b Hadlee	3	– b Hadlee	40
P. A. Smith c Broad b Hadlee	3	– c Broad b Hadlee	5
B. M. McMillan c Rice b Hadlee	0	– lbw b Saxelby	136
D. L. Amiss c Newell b Pick	5	– (5) c Johnson b Hemmings	46
†G. W. Humpage c Randall b Hadlee	14	– (6) c Pick b Saxelby	6
Asif Din c Rice b Hadlee	53	– (7) lbw b Hemmings	1
G. J. Lord c Johnson b Hemmings	17	– (8) c Rice b Saxelby	0
G. J. Parsons c Johnson b Hemmings	0	– (4) b Hadlee	3
G. C. Small c Rice b Hadlee	30	– not out	45
T. A. Munton c Hadlee b Hemmings	1	– not out	11
*N. Gifford not out	0		
L-b 2, n-b 1	3	L-b 8, w 2	10

1/5 2/5 3/8 4/27 5/27   129   1/17 2/104 3/110   (8 wkts) 303
6/74 7/74 8/122 9/129   4/202 5/236 6/241
                                     7/243 8/244

Bonus points – Nottinghamshire 4.

Bowling: *First Innings*—Hadlee 18–6–42–6; Rice 9–3–16–0; Pick 10–3–35–1; Saxelby 6–1–15–0; Hemmings 8.3–4–19–3. *Second Innings*—Hadlee 25–7–44–3; Pick 18–3–73–0; Saxelby 24–3–72–3; Rice 14–3–45–0; Hemmings 39–18–61–2.

Nottinghamshire

B. C. Broad c Amiss b Gifford	116	†C. W. Scott not out	69
M. Newell c McMillan b Munton	17	E. E. Hemmings c and b Smith	1
D. W. Randall c McMillan b Small	8	K. Saxelby b Munton	34
*C. E. B. Rice c Lord b McMillan	70		
R. A. Pick c Humpage b Small	10		
P. Johnson b Gifford	44	B 8, l-b 5, w 4, n-b 10	27
D. J. R. Martindale lbw b Munton	14		
R. J. Hadlee b Parsons	41		451

1/83 2/122 3/171 4/198 5/261
6/292 7/294 8/375 9/378

Bonus points – Nottinghamshire 4, Warwickshire 3 (Score at 100 overs: 365-7).

Bowling: Small 22–7–65–2; McMillan 17–3–71–1; Parsons 26–3–104–1; Gifford 25–9–59–2; Smith 11–0–61–1; Munton 20.5–3–78–3.

Umpires: A. G. T. Whitehead and P. B. Wight.

At Worcester, July 5, 7, 8. NOTTINGHAMSHIRE drew with WORCESTERSHIRE.

NOTTINGHAMSHIRE v YORKSHIRE

At Worksop, July 16, 17, 18. Nottinghamshire won by an innings and 8 runs. Nottinghamshire 24 pts, Yorkshire 3 pts. Toss: Nottinghamshire. Having elected to bat, Nottinghamshire set themselves up for a conclusive victory with a remarkable scoring spree on the opening day. Broad and Robinson, each hitting sixteen 4s in their hundreds, gave the innings its momentum with an opening stand of 226 in 64 overs, and Johnson maintained it with an unbeaten 105 in 140 minutes, also hitting sixteen 4s. Despite typical resistance from Boycott for three and a half hours, Pick's best bowling to date enabled Nottinghamshire to enforce the follow-on on the second day, by the close of which Yorkshire were 70 for four and facing an innings defeat. With Pick quickly accounting for Hartley and Jarvis, the overnight pair, such a fate had become a certainty by lunch.

Nottinghamshire

B. C. Broad c Bairstow b Shaw	122	M. Newell not out	3
R. T. Robinson c Moxon b Jarvis	105	B 4, l-b 11, w 2, n-b 3	20
P. Johnson not out	105		
*C. E. B. Rice b Fletcher	49	1/226 2/242 3/389 (3 wkts dec.)	404

K. P. Evans, †B. N. French, R. A. Pick, E. E. Hemmings, K. Saxelby and K. E. Cooper did not bat.

Bonus points – Nottinghamshire 4, Yorkshire 1 (Score at 100 overs: 393-3).

Bowling: Jarvis 22–3–92–1; Fletcher 22–1–97–1; Shaw 20–1–78–1; Carrick 22–3–62–0; Hartley 4–0–28–0; Swallow 12–2–32–0.

Yorkshire

G. Boycott c Newell b Hemmings	56	– c French b Cooper	6
M. D. Moxon lbw b Pick	14	– lbw b Rice	1
A. A. Metcalfe lbw b Pick	12	– c French b Saxelby	6
K. Sharp c French b Pick	56	– c Newell b Pick	37
S. N. Hartley c Newell b Pick	7	– c Hemmings b Pick	28
*†D. L. Bairstow c Newell b Hemmings	20	– (7) c French b Cooper	25
P. Carrick b Pick	0	– (8) b Saxelby	21
I. G. Swallow c Rice b Hemmings	26	– (9) c Hemmings b Saxelby	13
P. W. Jarvis b Cooper	28	– (6) c French b Pick	2
C. Shaw not out	5	– not out	8
S. D. Fletcher b Pick	16	– b Hemmings	1
L-b 3	3	L-b 2, n-b 3	5
1/21 2/41 3/121 4/131 5/160	243	1/3 2/10 3/14 4/63 5/83	153
6/165 7/169 8/222 9/222		6/110 7/110 8/133 9/148	

Bonus points – Yorkshire 2, Nottinghamshire 4.

Bowling: *First Innings*—Pick 21.1–4–68–6; Saxelby 14–2–48–0; Cooper 14–4–30–1; Rice 9–4–28–0; Hemmings 27–15–50–3; Evans 3–0–16–0. *Second Innings*—Pick 17–6–41–3; Rice 10–5–21–1; Saxelby 11–2–35–3; Cooper 12–2–19–2; Evans 3–1–22–0; Hemmings 8.5–3–13–1.

Umpires: B. Dudleston and D. R. Shepherd.

At Nottingham, July 19, 20, 21. NOTTINGHAMSHIRE drew with NEW ZEALANDERS (See New Zealand tour section).

At Southport, July 23, 24, 25. NOTTINGHAMSHIRE drew with LANCASHIRE.

At Sheffield, July 26, 28, 29. NOTTINGHAMSHIRE drew with YORKSHIRE.

At Cheltenham, August 6, 7, 8. NOTTINGHAMSHIRE drew with GLOUCESTERSHIRE.

NOTTINGHAMSHIRE v LANCASHIRE

At Nottingham, August 16, 18, 19. Nottinghamshire won by seven wickets. Nottinghamshire 17 pts, Lancashire 3 pts. Toss: Nottinghamshire. Injury-hit Lancashire were on the receiving end of a history-making effort by Johnson which brought Nottinghamshire victory after two declarations had left the home team a generous target of 295 in a minimum of 89 overs. The 21-year-old batsman became the youngest Nottinghamshire player to score 1,000 runs in a season during the course of his unbeaten 120, which came in 137 minutes and included twenty 4s. Broad and Robinson had laid the foundations with a stand of 113 in 123 minutes. On the opening day Mendis hit thirteen 4s in an innings of 108, and Fairbrother, 89 at the close, struck one 6 and fifteen 4s in his 97, but the loss of the second afternoon to rain changed the path along which the match was proceeding.

Lancashire

G. D. Mendis c Rice b Fraser-Darling	108			
G. Fowler c Johnson b Rice	57			
J. Abrahams c Broad b Rice	3	– (2) c French b Birch	2
N. H. Fairbrother run out	97	– (1) not out	28
S. J. O'Shaughnessy c Robinson b Hemmings	4	– (3) not out	12
A. N. Hayhurst c Broad b Saxelby	29		
†C. Maynard c Newell b Saxelby	6		
*J. Simmons lbw b Fraser-Darling	1		
D. J. Makinson not out	2		
B 6, l-b 9, n-b 2	17		

1/116 2/132 3/189 4/203   (8 wkts dec.) 324   1/13   (1 wkt dec.) 42
5/311 6/321 7/321 8/324

B. P. Patterson and I. Folley did not bat.

Bonus points – Lancashire 3, Nottinghamshire 1 (Score at 100 overs: 290-4).

Bowling: *First Innings*—Saxelby 26–5–89–2; Rice 17–6–31–2; Fraser-Darling 24.2–4–87–2; Cooper 11–3–12–0; Hemmings 32–9–90–1. *Second Innings*—Birch 3–1–4–1; Johnson 5–1–19–0; Newell 2–0–19–0.

Nottinghamshire

R. T. Robinson c Makinson b Patterson	0	– (5) not out	23
B. C. Broad lbw b Patterson	12	– (1) c Hayhurst b Simmons	66
M. Newell not out	19	– (2) c sub b Patterson	61
P. Johnson not out	36	– (3) not out	120
J. D. Birch (did not bat)	–	– (4) c Folley b Makinson	15
L-b 2, w 2, n-b 1	5	L-b 2, w 1, n-b 7	10

1/5 2/18   (2 wkts dec.) 72   1/113 2/173 3/208   (3 wkts) 295

*C. E. B. Rice, C. D. Fraser-Darling, †B. N. French, E. E. Hemmings, K. E. Cooper and K. Saxelby did not bat.

Bowling: *First Innings*—Patterson 8–1–20–2; Makinson 9–3–20–0; Hayhurst 5–0–26–0; Folley 1–0–4–0. *Second Innings*—Patterson 17–4–59–1; Makinson 15–2–57–1; O'Shaughnessy 12–1–68–0; Folley 14–1–39–0; Simmons 8–2–20–1; Hayhurst 6.1–0–50–0.

Umpires: B. Dudleston and K. E. Palmer.

Nottinghamshire in 1986   531

At Northampton, August 20, 21, 22. NOTTINGHAMSHIRE drew with NORTHAMP-
TONSHIRE.

NOTTINGHAMSHIRE v DERBYSHIRE

At Nottingham, August 23, 25, 26. Drawn. Nottinghamshire 3 pts, Derbyshire 3 pts. Toss:
Derbyshire. Rain soon after lunch stopped play on the second day and none was possible on
the third. With sixteen overs also lost on the first day, Derbyshire batted on into the second,
resuming at 243 for seven, and Nottinghamshire's reply lasted 89 minutes before the weather
intervened.

Derbyshire

*K. J. Barnett c Scott b Rice	77	R. J. Finney not out	23
†B. J. M. Maher b Afford	31	L. J. Wood b Hemmings	2
A. Hill b Hemmings	15	D. E. Malcolm b Hemmings	0
J. E. Morris c Robinson b Hemmings	15		
B. Roberts c and b Rice	37	B 9, l-b 19	28
G. Miller c Scott b Cooper	6		
A. E. Warner c Scott b Pick	12	1/112 2/125 3/152 4/161 5/172	275
R. Sharma lbw b Hemmings	29	6/201 7/237 8/255 9/267	

Bonus points – Derbyshire 3, Nottinghamshire 3 (Score at 100 overs: 255-7).

Bowling: Pick 12–4–19–1; Cooper 18–4–45–1; Hemmings 42–10–107–5; Afford 18–4–44–1;
Rice 17–5–32–2.

Nottinghamshire

B. C. Broad c Barnett b Malcolm	0
R. T. Robinson not out	47
M. Newell not out	26
B 1, l-b 2, n-b 2	5

1/2   (1 wkt) 78

*C. E. B. Rice, P. Johnson, J. D. Birch, †C. W. Scott, R. A. Pick, E. E. Hemmings,
K. E. Cooper and J. A. Afford did not bat.

Bowling: Malcolm 7–1–20–1; Finney 3–0–8–0; Warner 2–0–17–0; Wood 9–6–13–0; Miller
8–2–17–0.

Umpires: R. Julian and D. Lloyd.

NOTTINGHAMSHIRE v KENT

At Nottingham, August 27, 28, 29. Nottinghamshire won by 132 runs. Nottinghamshire
22 pts, Kent 4 pts. Toss: Nottinghamshire. A sound all-round performance took Nottinghamshire to victory with their left-arm spinner, Afford, returning career-best match figures of ten
for 103. Nottinghamshire were in trouble at 31 for four on the first day after Alderman's three
wickets in five balls but Hadlee effected a recovery with 88 in 136 minutes. The New Zealand
all-rounder then joined forces with Afford to dismiss Kent for 140, only Marsh's brave 61, his
highest for the county, saving them from having to follow on. A sparkling 159, which included
four 6s and eleven 4s, by Robinson in 208 minutes saw Nottinghamshire race to a declaration
before the end of the second day. Kent, with all of the last day to score 324, could not hold
out against the spin of Afford, whose six for 81 was his best innings return, and Hemmings,
who finished with four for 59.

Nottinghamshire

B. C. Broad lbw b Alderman	8	– c Tavaré b Alderman	47
R. T. Robinson c Aslett b Alderman	52	– not out	159
M. Newell b Alderman	0	– not out	34
*C. E. B. Rice lbw b Alderman	0		
P. Johnson c Aslett b Alderman	4		
J. D. Birch c Aslett b Dilley	24		
R. J. Hadlee c Tavaré b Ellison	88		
†B. N. French c sub b Dilley	17		
R. A. Pick c Aslett b Ellison	16		
E. E. Hemmings lbw b Ellison	0		
J. A. Afford not out	0		
B 1, l-b 10	11	L-b 1	1

1/19 2/19 3/19 4/31 5/86   240   1/116   (1 wkt dec.) 241
6/168 7/202 8/239 9/239

Bonus points – Nottinghamshire 2, Kent 4.

Bowling: *First Innings*—Dilley 26–2–81–2; Alderman 21–6–84–5; Underwood 18–6–39–0; Ellison 9.2–3–18–3; Dale 6–1–7–0. *Second Innings*—Dilley 13–1–41–0; Alderman 18–3–47–1; Underwood 20–5–73–0; Ellison 6–1–24–0; Dale 12–2–55–0.

Kent

M. R. Benson lbw b Hadlee	7	– b Afford	20
N. R. Taylor lbw b Hadlee	7	– lbw b Afford	6
*C. J. Tavaré b Pick	4	– b Hemmings	21
D. G. Aslett b Hadlee	7	– c Hadlee b Afford	40
R. M. Ellison c Johnson b Hemmings	23	– (6) st French b Hemmings	26
†S. A. Marsh c Broad b Hemmings	61	– (7) b Hemmings	32
S. G. Hinks b Afford	15	– (5) c Johnson b Afford	10
G. R. Dilley c Pick b Afford	0	– c Newell b Afford	7
D. L. Underwood b Afford	5	– (10) lbw b Afford	15
C. S. Dale c Johnson b Afford	2	– (9) b Hemmings	16
T. M. Alderman not out	7	– not out	2
L-b 2	2	B 7, l-b 6, w 1	14

1/14 2/15 3/19 4/33 5/59   140   1/27 2/30 3/90 4/95 5/122   209
6/108 7/120 8/126 9/131   6/165 7/174 8/174 9/207

Bonus points – Nottinghamshire 4.

Bowling: *First Innings*—Hadlee 11–2–16–3; Pick 10–3–33–1; Hemmings 18–4–51–2; Rice 4–0–16–0; Afford 10–2–22–4. *Second Innings*—Hadlee 11–3–20–0; Pick 7–2–28–0; Hemmings 26–8–59–4; Rice 2–1–8–0; Afford 33.2–11–81–6.

Umpires: R. Julian and N. T. Plews.

At Hove, August 30, 31, September 1. NOTTINGHAMSHIRE drew with SUSSEX.

At Cardiff, September 3, 4, 5. NOTTINGHAMSHIRE beat GLAMORGAN by 24 runs.

NOTTINGHAMSHIRE v ESSEX

At Nottingham, September 10, 11, 12. Drawn. Nottinghamshire 7 pts, Essex 4 pts. Toss: Essex. Essex picked up the three bonus points they needed to win the County Championship and went on to deny Nottinghamshire the victory that would have given them second-place prizemoney. Nottinghamshire, having been put in on a green pitch, reached 267 thanks largely to Broad's 120, which took 285 minutes and included twelve 4s. Seam bowling of the highest class by Hadlee and Rice in helpful conditions earned Nottinghamshire a lead of 128, and with bad light ending play at tea on the second afternoon, it required enterprising batting by Robinson and Hadlee to enable Rice to set a target of 313 in a minimum of 84 overs. When Essex were 97 for five, Nottinghamshire's victory looked likely, but Fletcher occupied the crease for 167 minutes to deny them.

Nottinghamshire

B. C. Broad c East b Foster	120	– c East b Lever	20
R. T. Robinson c East b Lever	10	– c East b Foster	64
M. Newell b Foster	14	– c East b Foster	6
P. Johnson c Pringle b Lever	23	– c Lilley b Foster	7
*C. E. B. Rice c East b Lever	5	– b Pringle	4
J. D. Birch lbw b Lever	0	– lbw b Pringle	5
R. J. Hadlee c Pringle b Lever	21	– not out	55
†B. N. French c East b Gooch	18	– b Pringle	0
E. E. Hemmings c Fletcher b Foster	25	– c and b Pringle	19
K. E. Cooper c Gooch b Foster	19		
J. A. Afford not out	2		
B 2, l-b 6, w 2	10	L-b 2, n-b 2	4

1/31 2/91 3/133 4/141 5/141   267   1/63 2/92 3/99   (8 wkts dec.) 184
6/177 7/207 8/234 9/259   4/104 5/106 6/111
                                  7/111 8/184

Bonus points – Nottinghamshire 3, Essex 4.

Bowling: *First Innings*—Lever 23–5–87–5; Foster 25.1–4–77–4; Pringle 16–1–64–0; Childs 6–0–15–0; Gooch 12–3–16–1. *Second Innings*—Lever 9–1–37–1; Foster 18.2–0–74–3; Gooch 6.4–0–24–0; Pringle 9.3–1–47–4.

Essex

*G. A. Gooch c French b Hadlee	36	– b Hemmings	41
J. P. Stephenson c Birch b Hadlee	38	– b Afford	32
P. J. Prichard b Afford	22	– lbw b Rice	14
†D. E. East b Hadlee	3	– (8) not out	44
B. R. Hardie c French b Rice	1	– (4) c Johnson b Rice	1
K. W. R. Fletcher c Afford b Rice	6	– (5) not out	44
D. R. Pringle c French b Hadlee	0	– (6) c Rice b Hemmings	0
A. W. Lilley b Rice	17	– (7) b Cooper	41
N. A. Foster c French b Hadlee	8		
J. K. Lever b Hadlee	4		
J. H. Childs not out	2		
L-b 1, n-b 1	2	B 1, l-b 9, w 4, n-b 1	15

1/50 2/90 3/96 4/101 5/103   139   1/71 2/79 3/95 4/96   (6 wkts) 232
6/104 7/112 8/124 9/128   5/97 6/179

Bonus points – Nottinghamshire 4.

Bowling: *First Innings*—Hadlee 16–3–51–6; Cooper 5–0–39–0; Hemmings 7–4–20–0; Afford 6–2–10–1; Rice 9.2–3–18–3. *Second Innings*—Hadlee 16–1–46–0; Rice 20–9–34–2; Cooper 12–5–28–1; Hemmings 25–7–42–2; Afford 14–2–72–1.

Umpires: A. A. Jones and B. Leadbeater.

NOTTINGHAMSHIRE v NORTHAMPTONSHIRE

At Nottingham, September 13, 15, 16. Drawn. Nottinghamshire 4 pts, Northamptonshire 6 pts. Toss: Nottinghamshire. Needing to win to finish second in the Championship, Nottinghamshire batted badly in testing conditions and Northamptonshire, resuming on Monday morning at 86 for four, earned a lead of 71 through the application of their lower-order batsmen. Nottinghamshire were without Hadlee, pleading exhaustion as the reason for his absence. Broad's 112, which occupied 231 minutes, included fifteen 4s, and was his sixth hundred of the season, plus Hemmings's season's best of 54 not out, brought the home side back into contention and Northamptonshire were set a target of 243 in a minimum of 43 overs. Larkins and Bailey put them in with a chance, but an excellent spell by Afford swung the match Nottinghamshire's way. They needed two wickets in the last over, and although Rice removed Cook with the first ball, Walker held on to give the visitors a draw and demote Nottinghamshire to fourth place.

Nottinghamshire

B. C. Broad c Ripley b Walker	27	– c Capel b Harper	112
R. T. Robinson c Larkins b Capel	1	– c Ripley b Walker	43
†M. Newell b Capel	0	– c Ripley b Walker	11
P. Johnson c Capel b Walker	15	– c Harper b Walker	0
*C. E. B. Rice c Ripley b Mallender	20	– b Harper	17
J. D. Birch run out	6	– c Larkins b Harper	11
C. D. Fraser-Darling c Larkins b Cook	40	– c Ripley b Harper	21
R. A. Pick c and b Harper	0	– (9) run out	1
E. E. Hemmings b Harper	23	– (8) not out	54
K. E. Cooper lbw b Harper	3	– not out	17
J. A. Afford not out	0		
B 2, l-b 7, w 1	10	B 11, l-b 14, n-b 1	26

1/2 2/6 3/36 4/58 5/70   **145**   1/87 2/127 3/127   (8 wkts dec.) **313**
6/90 7/96 8/140 9/144   4/162 5/205 6/206
                                           7/267 8/269

Bonus points – Northamptonshire 4.

Bowling: *First Innings*—Mallender 11–3–33–1; Capel 16–6–49–2; Walker 17–6–40–2; Harper 7.5–4–10–3; Cook 6–3–4–1. *Second Innings*—Mallender 6–0–30–0; Capel 8–0–35–0; Walker 28–3–78–3; Cook 21–3–74–0; Harper 44–13–71–4.

Northamptonshire

R. J. Boyd-Moss c Broad b Pick	25	– c Hemmings b Afford	5
W. Larkins c Broad b Cooper	20	– lbw b Cooper	27
R. J. Bailey b Rice	16	– b Cooper	39
D. J. Wild c Broad b Afford	19	– st Newell b Hemmings	13
D. J. Capel c Birch b Rice	3	– c Fraser-Darling b Afford	7
A. Fordham b Afford	5	– (7) lbw b Afford	17
*R. A. Harper c Rice b Afford	19	– (6) b Afford	24
†D. Ripley b Afford	20	– c Fraser-Darling b Rice	25
N. G. B. Cook c Johnson b Rice	22	– c Robinson b Rice	6
N. A. Mallender b Pick	37	– not out	0
A. Walker not out	7	– not out	0
B 6, l-b 6, w 1, n-b 10	23	B 12, l-b 10, n-b 1	23

1/43 2/47 3/82 4/86 5/87   **216**   1/37 2/55 3/88 4/96   (9 wkts) **186**
6/113 7/138 8/193 9/200   5/121 6/128 7/169
                                          8/179 9/182

Bonus points – Northamptonshire 2, Nottinghamshire 4.

Bowling: *First Innings*—Pick 19–1–67–2; Cooper 10–3–28–1; Fraser-Darling 5–0–15–0; Afford 25.5–11–43–4; Rice 14–4–33–3; Hemmings 5–2–18–0. *Second Innings*—Pick 2–0–13–0; Rice 8–3–20–2; Afford 23–12–55–4; Cooper 10–2–33–2; Hemmings 15–6–43–1.

Umpires: M. J. Kitchen and P. B. Wight.

SOMERSET

President: C. R. M. Atkinson
Chairman: M. F. Hill
Chairman, Cricket Committee:
  1986 – B. A. Langford
  1987 – R. E. Marshall
Secretary: A. S. Brown
  The County Ground, St James's Street,
  Taunton TA1 1JT (Telephone: 0823-72946)
Captain: P. M. Roebuck
Coach: P. J. Robinson

After a start of some promise under the new captain, Peter Roebuck, Somerset again failed to live up to expectations and, worst of all, the season ended with the club in the grip of internal strife. The crux of this was the decision of the committee, in late August, not to renew the contracts of Vivian Richards and Joel Garner, who had played such a large part in the successful years from 1978 to 1983. The cricketing reasons for this bold move were sound, but they quickly became swamped by the sentimental response of a large number of members. Ian Botham, who had come back from nine weeks' suspension by the TCCB with some thunderous performances, even by his standards, threatened to leave the county if the two West Indian Test players were not reinstated.

In due course, a Special General Meeting was requisitioned, calling for the resignation of the committee – and by inference the re-engagement of Richards and Garner. However, at Shepton Mallet on November 8, a motion of no confidence in the committee was defeated by 1,828 votes to 798, and a motion for the committee to stand down was defeated by 1,863 to 743.

A review of the season reveals the on-field reasons for the committee's concern. Interest in the Benson and Hedges Cup did not extend beyond the group matches, while early ambitions in the John Player League, which saw Somerset top of the table in mid-June, were quenched by four heavy defeats that set the scene for a narrow defeat by Lancashire in the second round of the NatWest Bank Trophy. Botham missed this match because of his suspension, but otherwise his enforced absence made little difference to the county. England calls would have taken him away from ten Championship and six Sunday games: the suspension cost eight Championship and seven John Player games.

In the Britannic Assurance Championship, some good performances in games shortened by the weather helped Somerset to fourth by mid-June, but a poor July and four defeats in the final five matches reduced them to sixteenth – one place higher than in 1985 with two more victories to show. The context of these two very poor seasons was the expectation engendered in 1984 when, with Richards and Garner playing for the touring West Indians and with Martin Crowe excelling as player and clubman, a blend of experience and young promise took the county to seventh in the Championship and to two quarter-finals. Somerset had retained Crowe's registration, but with other counties interested in the New Zealander, the committee had to choose between playing him as

their overseas player or retaining Richards and Garner. Looking to the
future, they offered Crowe a three-year contract.

Although there were a number of fallible days, the batting was
generally sound. Roebuck, who played for several weeks early on with a
cracked finger, applied himself splendidly and was the leading scorer.
Richards, who hit a hundred at the beginning of May in 48 balls, the
fastest of the season, came back strongly after a long, quiet spell and
finished with four in all, while Brian Rose hit two in another summer
shortened by injury. Richard Harden had an excellent first full season,
making his first Championship hundreds, scoring 1,000 runs for the first
time, and improving his fielding. Nigel Felton also reached his first 1,000
runs, after an early injury.

Jonathan Hardy, who joined Somerset from Hampshire, showed much
pedigree with his cultured left-handed batting. He started splendidly,
played through a shoulder injury when the side was short of batsmen, had
a poor spell and then came back well in the final few matches. Botham
again produced several astonishing performances, notably in the John
Player League. With 12 needed from the last three balls to beat
Middlesex, and with Daniel bowling, he struck a 6, stopped a yorker, and
swung the final ball high over square leg – an amazing effort. Making
175 not out at Wellingborough School against Northamptonshire, he hit
a record thirteen 6s.

Ricky Bartlett, on his début, made 117 not out at Oxford, the first
hundred of the season; Paul Bail impressed with his 174 for Cambridge
at Lord's. Both made useful contributions late in the season and hold
promise. Julian Wyatt had his arm broken early on and thereafter had
few chances.

The bowling was less reassuring. Only Garner (47), Colin Dredge (35)
and Vic Marks (59) returned acceptable first-class figures, Marks again
demonstrating his value as an all-rounder and his quality as a team man.
Botham doubled his Championship return of 1985 and Nick Taylor, a
seam bowler formerly of Yorkshire and Surrey, had some good days,
especially in the limited-overs games.

But once again the younger bowlers disappointed. Robert Coombs, the
left-arm spinner who encouraged high hopes in 1985, began too early
perhaps while at university and split his spinning finger. He was released
at the end of the season. Trevor Gard, the wicket-keeper, recovered from
a severe neck injury in early June to end soundly, while Rayner Blitz,
from Essex, who deputised for Gard, put in some sturdy batting
performances but suffered, like most wicket-keepers, on the low pitches
at Bath.

In view of the 1985 results and the 1986 weather, gate receipts and
membership held up well, with Bath creating a record in the best week
of the season. The interest aroused by Botham's return from suspension
was remarkable, but how the public will react to the events which
followed last season remains to be seen. The members have shown
where their support lies and the future is now in the hands of a new
generation. – E.H.

537

SOMERSET 1986

[Bill Smith]

Back row: R. J. Blitz, N. A. Felton, R. J. Bartlett, S. C. Booth, R. J. Harden, J. J. E. Hardy, N. S. Taylor, R. V. J. Coombs, M. S. Turner, G. V. Palmer, M. R. Davis, J. G. Wyatt. *Front row*: C. H. Dredge, V. J. Marks, I. V. A. Richards, P. M. Roebuck (*captain*), B. C. Rose, I. T. Botham, P. J. Robinson (*coach*), T. Gard, D. Waight (*physiotherapist*). *Inset*: J. Garner.

SOMERSET RESULTS

All first-class matches – Played 25 : Won 3, Lost 7, Drawn 15. Abandoned 1.

County Championship matches – Played 23 : Won 3, Lost 7, Drawn 13. Abandoned 1.

Bonus points – Batting 52, Bowling 52.

*Competition placings – Britannic Assurance County Championship, 16th ; NatWest Bank Trophy,
2nd round ; Benson and Hedges Cup, 4th in Group C ; John Player League, 6th equal.*

BRITANNIC ASSURANCE CHAMPIONSHIP AVERAGES

BATTING

	Birthplace	M	I	NO	R	HI	Avge
‡P. M. Roebuck ...	Oxford	20	32	8	1,261	221*	52.54
‡V. J. Marks	Middle Chinnock	23	33	11	1,029	110	46.77
‡B. C. Rose	Dartford	13	22	5	784	129	46.11
‡I. T. Botham	Heswall	12	19	1	804	139	44.66
‡I. V. A. Richards ..	St John's, Antigua	18	28	1	1,174	136	43.48
R. J. Bartlett	Ash Priors	4	6	1	171	43	34.20
R. J. Harden	Bridgwater	21	34	3	1,053	108	33.96
J. J. E. Hardy ..	Nakaru, Kenya	17	26	0	779	79	29.96
‡N. A. Felton	Guildford	21	34	3	898	156*	28.96
M. R. Davis	Kilve	8	7	4	60	21*	20.00
‡J. Garner	Christ Church, Barbados	18	15	4	182	47	16.54
J. C. M. Atkinson .	Butleigh	3	4	1	49	16*	16.33
R. V. J. Coombs ..	Barnet	8	5	3	30	18	15.00
‡T. Gard	West Lambrook	19	24	6	228	36	12.66
‡C. H. Dredge	Frome	16	20	2	215	40	11.94
M. D. Harman ...	Aylesbury	3	5	2	27	15	9.00
R. J. Blitz	Watford	4	4	0	33	18	8.25
J. G. Wyatt	Paulton	3	5	0	41	20	8.20
N. S. Taylor	Holmfirth	14	16	5	87	24*	7.90
G. V. Palmer	Taunton	3	5	0	29	17	5.80

Also batted : P. A. C. Bail (*Burnham-on-Sea*) (2 matches) 55, 47, 0; D. J. Foster (*Tottenham*)
(1 match) 0; N. J. Pringle (*Weymouth*) (1 match) 10, 11. M. S. Turner (*Shaftesbury*) (1 match)
did not bat.

* *Signifies not out.*   ‡ *Denotes county cap.*

The following played a total of seventeen three-figure innings for Somerset in County
Championship matches : I. V. A. Richards 4, P. M. Roebuck 4, I. T. Botham 2, N. A. Felton
2, R. J. Harden 2, B. C. Rose 2, V. J. Marks 1.

BOWLING

	O	M	R	W	BB	Avge
J. Garner	419	95	1,091	47	5-56	23.21
C. H. Dredge	385	81	1,146	34	3-10	33.70
V. J. Marks	719.5	191	2,046	57	8-100	35.89
N. S. Taylor	314.2	57	1,141	28	4-40	40.75
I. T. Botham	285.1	61	961	22	6-125	43.68
R. V. J. Coombs ...	247.5	56	807	16	3-60	50.43
M. R. Davis	163.3	18	630	10	2-43	63.00

Also bowled : J. C. M. Atkinson 10–1–52–0; N. A. Felton 1–0–3–0; D. J. Foster 5–0–29–0;
R. J. Harden 39–3–153–2; J. J. E. Hardy 1–0–5–0; M. D. Harman 60.3–12–149–1; G. V.
Palmer 63–7–231–4; N. J. Pringle 10–0–48–0; I. V. A. Richards 161–32–500–9; P. M.
Roebuck 24–3–120–1; B. C. Rose 11–0–57–2; M. S. Turner 15–3–55–2.

Wicket-keepers: T. Gard 29 ct, 5 st; R. J. Blitz 8 ct.

Leading Fielders: I. V. A. Richards 19; R. J. Harden 12; J. J. E. Hardy 12.

At Oxford, April 19, 21, 22. SOMERSET drew with OXFORD UNIVERSITY.

SOMERSET v YORKSHIRE

At Taunton, April 26, 27, 28. Yorkshire won by 5 runs off the last ball of the match. Yorkshire 19 pts, Somerset 1 pt. Toss: Somerset. After the first eight hours had been lost to the weather, Yorkshire batted solidly in slow, damp conditions. Love, with 46 from 56 balls, provided the early impetus, while Sharp batted fluently for 169 balls. Two forfeitures of innings opened up the possibility of a result, with Somerset requiring 324 in a minimum of 76 overs. An effective start was accelerated by Hardy's fine 79 in 102 balls, and after Roebuck's solid, 150-ball innings ended, Somerset pursued their target to the end. Bad light cost them two overs, and off the last over, from Carrick, they needed 16. Dredge struck the second ball for 4, and when the field closed in, straight drove the fifth for 6. He was brilliantly caught at wide long-on attempting the 6 off the final ball which would have brought Somerset victory.

Yorkshire

M. D. Moxon c Roebuck b Marks	73	P. Carrick not out	0
A. A. Metcalfe run out	55		
K. Sharp b Marks	96	B 1, l-b 15, n-b 2	18
J. D. Love b Dredge	46		
S. N. Hartley b Dredge	31	1/129 2/151 3/218 (5 wkts dec.)	323
*†D. L. Bairstow not out	4	4/316 5/318	

A. Sidebottom, G. B. Stevenson, P. J. Hartley and I. G. Swallow did not bat.

Bonus points – Yorkshire 3, Somerset 1 (Score at 100 overs: 252-3).

Bowling: Garner 10-2-27-0; Botham 10-4-20-0; Coombs 31-8-95-0; Dredge 25-7-64-2; Marks 38-9-90-2; Richards 6-0-11-0.

Yorkshire forfeited their second innings.

Somerset

Somerset forfeited their first innings.

N. A. Felton b P. J. Hartley	29	C. H. Dredge c P. J. Hartley b Carrick	24
*P. M. Roebuck b P. J. Hartley	60	†T. Gard b P. J. Hartley	1
J. J. E. Hardy c Love b Carrick	79	R. V. J. Coombs not out	4
I. V. A. Richards run out	25		
I. T. Botham c Metcalfe b Sidebottom	30	B 5, l-b 8, n-b 18	31
B. C. Rose c Bairstow b Sidebottom	18		
V. J. Marks b Sidebottom	16	1/63 2/185 3/195 4/234 5/257	318
J. Garner run out	1	6/281 7/282 8/296 9/300	

Bowling: Sidebottom 24-5-71-3; P. J. Hartley 20-1-90-3; Carrick 11-0-65-2; Stevenson 13-2-48-0; Swallow 7-0-31-0.

Umpires: B. Dudleston and A. A. Jones.

At Chesterfield, April 30, May 1, 2. SOMERSET drew with DERBYSHIRE.

SOMERSET v GLAMORGAN

At Taunton, May 7, 8, 9. Drawn. Somerset 4 pts, Glamorgan 1 pt. Toss: Glamorgan. A century by Richards from 48 balls, including six 6s and twelve 4s, and an exciting finish brought a rain-spoiled game to life. Two declarations left Glamorgan needing 291 in 95 overs, but only Holmes, in 44 overs, and Thomas, in fourteen, suggested a Glamorgan victory. Rather, it seemed as if Somerset would take the sixteen points, but rain removed fourteen overs from the final 105 minutes, coming to the assistance of a splendidly defiant last-wicket stand of eighteen overs between Davies and Base, the latter playing his first Championship innings.

Somerset

N. A. Felton c Jones b Base	55		
*P. M. Roebuck not out	76		
J. J. E. Hardy c Steele b Thomas	24		
I. V. A. Richards st Davies b Ontong	102		
R. J. Harden c Steele b Base	8		
R. J. Bartlett not out	18		
V. J. Marks (did not bat)	–	(1) not out	12
†T. Gard (did not bat)	–	(2) not out	4
L-b 4, w 3, n-b 10	17		

1/72 2/130 3/245 4/256   (4 wkts dec.) 300   (no wkt dec.) 16

J. Garner, N. S. Taylor and M. S. Turner did not bat.

Bonus points – Somerset 4, Glamorgan 1.

Bowling: *First Innings*—Thomas 17.2–1–100–1; Moseley 18–0–61–0; Base 24–3–71–2; Ontong 13–2–64–1. *Second Innings*—Younis 2–0–4–0; Hopkins 1.5–0–12–0.

Glamorgan

J. A. Hopkins c Felton b Garner	0	– lbw b Garner	14
A. L. Jones not out	12	– c Felton b Garner	14
H. Morris c Richards b Garner	8	– c Richards b Taylor	20
G. C. Holmes not out	3	– c sub b Marks	68
Younis Ahmed (did not bat)	–	c sub b Richards	11
*R. C. Ontong (did not bat)	–	c Richards b Turner	11
J. F. Steele (did not bat)	–	c Garner b Turner	4
J. G. Thomas (did not bat)	–	c Richards b Garner	31
†T. Davies (did not bat)	–	not out	28
E. A. Moseley (did not bat)	–	b Marks	2
S. J. Base (did not bat)	–	not out	15
N-b 3	3	N-b 12	12

1/0 2/13   (2 wkts dec.) 26   1/21 2/36 3/67   (9 wkts) 230
                                            4/80 5/107 6/138
                                            7/164 8/192 9/195

Bowling: *First Innings*—Garner 7.5–0–18–2; Taylor 7–3–8–0. *Second Innings*—Garner 23–3–53–3; Taylor 19–4–59–1; Turner 15–3–55–2; Richards 15–4–25–1; Marks 12–1–38–2.

Umpires: C. Cook and D. Lloyd.

SOMERSET v GLOUCESTERSHIRE

At Taunton, May 21, 22, 23. Somerset won by 118 runs. Somerset 20 pts, Gloucestershire 3 pts. Toss: Gloucestershire. Following a blank first day, Marks gave Somerset a good start which was developed by Botham, in 84 balls, and Harden, whose highest score in the Championship came off 180 balls. An early declaration and a forfeiture left Gloucestershire a target of 330 in 90 overs, but a slightly grassy pitch and the combination of Garner, Taylor and Dredge proved too much for them. Only Athey, who hit eight 4s from 172 balls, and Romaines, with whom he added 59, made any realistic progress, and Gloucestershire's last six wickets fell in eight overs for 47 runs.

Somerset

V. J. Marks b Walsh 65	C. H. Dredge c Curran b Bainbridge .. 5
*P. M. Roebuck c Romaines b Walsh . 10	N. S. Taylor not out 24
J. J. E. Hardy c Curran b Bainbridge .. 28	J. Garner c Curran b Graveney 1
I. V. A. Richards lbw b Walsh 4	B 3, l-b 12, w 2, n-b 5 22
I. T. Botham b Lawrence 61	
R. J. Harden b Lawrence 81	1/51 2/106 3/120 348
G. V. Palmer c Stovold b Payne ... 11	4/126 5/217 6/230
†T. Gard c Russell b Walsh 36	7/301 8/322 9/331

Bonus points – Somerset 4, Gloucestershire 3 (Score at 100 overs: 330-8).

Bowling: Lawrence 21–4–73–2; Walsh 29–6–72–4; Payne 19–3–51–1; Bainbridge 17–0–78–2; Graveney 11.3–4–23–1; Lloyds 10–3–36–0.

Somerset forfeited their second innings.

Gloucestershire

A. W. Stovold not out 7	– c Richards b Garner 0
P. W. Romaines not out 10	– c Garner b Taylor 29
C. W. J. Athey (did not bat)	– c Dredge b Garner 75
P. Bainbridge (did not bat)	– c Richards b Taylor 13
J. W. Lloyds (did not bat)	– c Richards b Taylor 18
K. M. Curran (did not bat)	– b Dredge 18
I. R. Payne (did not bat)	– b Garner 2
*D. A. Graveney (did not bat)	– c Gard b Garner 0
†R. C. Russell (did not bat)	– not out 17
D. V. Lawrence (did not bat)	– b Dredge 0
C. A. Walsh (did not bat)	– c Hardy b Dredge 17
L-b 1, w 1 2	B 8, l-b 7, w 1, n-b 6 22

(no wkt dec.) 19   1/0 2/59 3/89 4/115 5/164   211
                    6/170 7/176 8/177 9/184

Bowling: *First Innings*—Taylor 3–1–4–0; Palmer 4–0–14–0; Harden 2–2–0–0. *Second Innings*—Garner 16–3–35–4; Botham 8–0–27–0; Dredge 12.4–3–36–3; Richards 3–1–7–0; Marks 10–2–28–0; Taylor 10–1–41–3; Palmer 4–0–22–0.

Umpires: A. A. Jones and D. J. Constant.

At Cardiff, May 24, 26, 27. SOMERSET drew with GLAMORGAN.

At Horsham, May 31, June 2, 3. SUSSEX v SOMERSET. Abandoned.

At Nottingham, June 4, 5, 6. SOMERSET drew with NOTTINGHAMSHIRE.

At Bournemouth, June 7, 8, 9. SOMERSET drew with HAMPSHIRE.

SOMERSET v KENT

At Bath, June 14, 16, 17. Somerset won by an innings and 24 runs. Somerset 24 pts, Kent 4 pts.
Toss: Somerset. A dry, slow pitch, which gave gradually increasing turn and on which the ball
tended to keep low, was well used by Garner – match figures of nine for 85 – and the spinners,
Marks and Coombs. Somerset's batsmen gave the home county a brisk start, especially
Richards, who hit three 6s and seventeen 4s from 144 balls. Despite the defiance in both innings
of Tavaré and Marsh, Kent, who received almost twice as many deliveries as Somerset, could
not stave off Garner and his colleagues, who won the match with a little more than two hours to
spare. Indeed, the Kent batsmen never really recovered from an amazing spell from Garner on
the second afternoon when, in 38 balls, he dismissed four of the top five batsmen without
conceding a run and precipitated the follow-on.

Somerset

N. A. Felton lbw b Alderman	26	V. J. Marks b Alderman	68
*P. M. Roebuck c Marsh b Alderman	2		
J. J. E. Hardy lbw b Ellison	33	B 1, l-b 10, w 1, n-b 6	18
I. V. A. Richards b Alderman	128		
R. J. Harden c Alderman b Dilley	51	1/8 2/60 3/70	(6 wkts dec.) 433
B. C. Rose not out	107	4/228 5/266 6/433	

C. H. Dredge, J. Garner, †R. J. Blitz and R. V. J. Coombs did not bat.

Bonus points – Somerset 4, Kent 2.

Bowling: Dilley 20–4–83–1; Alderman 23.5–3–122–4; Ellison 15–3–65–1; C. S. Cowdrey
13–1–63–0; Underwood 20–3–59–0; Taylor 7–0–30–0.

Kent

M. R. Benson c and b Coombs	55	– b Garner	8
S. G. Hinks b Garner	20	– c Blitz b Garner	25
C. J. Tavaré b Garner	38	– c Harden b Coombs	39
N. R. Taylor lbw b Garner	20	– b Garner	4
*C. S. Cowdrey c Blitz b Garner	6	– b Garner	43
G. R. Cowdrey b Coombs	0	– c Rose b Marks	3
R. M. Ellison b Marks	10	– lbw b Garner	6
†S. A. Marsh b Coombs	43	– b Coombs	35
G. R. Dilley c Harden b Dredge	8	– c Dredge b Marks	0
D. L. Underwood not out	6	– b Marks	5
T. M. Alderman b Marks	2	– not out	0
B 14, l-b 3, n-b 1	18	B 8, l-b 2, w 1, n-b 4	15

1/44 2/101 3/140 4/145 5/146   226   1/17 2/58 3/64 4/92 5/122   183
6/154 7/170 8/185 9/219   6/127 7/146 8/163 9/183

Bonus points – Kent 2, Somerset 4.

Bowling: *First Innings*—Garner 18–9–29–4; Dredge 18–6–42–1; Marks 30.3–12–65–2;
Coombs 28–7–60–3; Harden 2–0–13–0. *Second Innings*—Garner 22–7–56–5; Dredge
16–5–26–0; Coombs 22–11–48–2; Marks 32.1–20–43–3.

Umpires: J. H. Harris and D. R. Shepherd.

SOMERSET v NORTHAMPTONSHIRE

At Bath, June 18, 19, 20. Drawn. Somerset 4 pts, Northamptonshire 8 pts. Toss: Somerset.
On a grassy pitch, never totally reliable yet never playing as its appearance suggested,
Northamptonshire prospered after a poor start. Capel hit two 6s and sixteen 4s in his unbeaten
103 from 161 balls. Despite quick, adventurous half-centuries from Hardy (two 6s, six 4s) and

Richards (one 6, ten 4s), Somerset's ninth-wicket pair of Marks and Davis had to fight hard to avoid the follow-on. Their stoic defence was again needed in Somerset's second innings when a late collapse forced them to play out the final thirteen overs, Marks having batted through 27 overs. Only when Hardy (two 6s and five 4s in 43 balls) and Roebuck, and later Roebuck and Rose, who added 70 in twenty overs, were batting did Somerset challenge the target of 323 in 74 overs.

Northamptonshire

*G. Cook lbw b Garner	5 – b Marks	70
W. Larkins b Davis	12 – lbw b Davis	0
R. J. Boyd-Moss c Hardy b Marks	36 – c and b Palmer	37
R. J. Bailey b Davis	69 – c Blitz b Palmer	1
D. J. Wild c Roebuck b Richards	85 – b Davis	29
D. J. Capel not out	103 – c Blitz b Palmer	10
R. A. Harper c Harden b Richards	2 – c Hardy b Palmer	11
†S. N. V. Waterton not out	24 – c Blitz b Garner	11
N. G. B. Cook (did not bat)	– b Marks	2
N. A. Mallender (did not bat)	– c Felton b Marks	4
B. J. Griffiths (did not bat)	– not out	0
B 9, l-b 5, n-b 5	19	B 3, l-b 13, n-b 4 ... 20

1/12 2/34 3/116 4/169   (6 wkts dec.) 355   1/0 2/65 3/67 4/129 5/145   195
5/274 6/290   6/163 7/181 8/191 9/195

Bonus points – Northamptonshire 4, Somerset 2 (Score at 100 overs: 351-6).

Bowling: *First Innings*—Garner 15-1-57-1; Davis 18.1-2-67-2; Palmer 20-2-89-0; Richards 18-2-55-2; Marks 29-10-73-1. *Second Innings*—Garner 12-2-25-1; Davis 17-2-49-2; Palmer 22-4-77-4; Marks 13.2-5-28-3.

Somerset

N. A. Felton c Waterton b Griffiths	7 – c Waterton b Mallender	5
*P. M. Roebuck b Mallender	0 – c Bailey b N. G. B. Cook	62
†R. J. Blitz c N. G. B. Cook b Wild	15 – (9) lbw b Mallender	0
J. J. E. Hardy c Waterton b Wild	50 – (3) b Harper	50
I. V. A. Richards c Larkins b N. G. B. Cook	59 – (4) c N. G. B. Cook b Griffiths	0
R. J. Harden c Mallender b N. G. B. Cook	17 – (5) lbw b Wild	14
B. C. Rose c and b Capel	18 – (6) c Griffiths b N. G. B. Cook	34
V. J. Marks b Mallender	20 – (7) not out	35
G. V. Palmer c Waterton b Capel	1 – (8) c G. Cook b Griffiths	0
M. R. Davis not out	19 – not out	21
J. Garner c Waterton b Griffiths	6	
L-b 11, w 5	16	B 10, l-b 8, w 1, n-b 1 ... 20

1/5 2/7 3/77 4/103 5/150   228   1/8 2/75 3/76 4/99   (8 wkts) 241
6/181 7/183 8/192 9/217   5/169 6/182 7/183 8/200

Bonus points – Somerset 2, Northamptonshire 4.

Bowling: *First Innings*—Mallender 20-6-68-2; Griffiths 13.4-4-33-2; Wild 9-2-36-2; N. G. B. Cook 15-6-29-2; Harper 7-3-11-0; Capel 11-3-40-2. *Second Innings*—Mallender 15-5-44-2; Griffiths 15-3-62-2; Harper 21-6-45-1; Wild 4-0-13-1; Capel 11.5-0-50-0; N. G. B. Cook 7-4-9-2.

Umpires: D. R. Shepherd and J. H. Harris.

At Taunton, June 28, 29, 30. SOMERSET drew with INDIANS (See Indian tour section).

At Maidstone, July 2, 3, 4. SOMERSET drew with KENT.

SOMERSET v HAMPSHIRE

At Taunton, July 5, 7, 8. Drawn. Somerset 3 pts, Hampshire 6 pts. Toss: Hampshire. Three hours were lost on the first day and, more important, the first two hours of the final day, which made that day largely meaningless. Somerset batted well on a seaming pitch to reach 189 for four on Saturday, Hardy playing especially well. Marshall broke through on Monday morning, and then Middleton, in only his second first-class match, provided the basis of a firm reply in better conditions. Nicholas's declaration, 11 runs behind, gave Somerset 70 minutes' batting in the evening, and on the last day, largely against occasional bowlers, Roebuck and Felton put together Somerset's highest partnership against Hampshire before Roebuck's declaration gave Hampshire twenty minutes in which to bat.

Somerset

N. A. Felton b James	25	– not out	156
*P. M. Roebuck c Parks b Marshall	33	– not out	102
J. J. E. Hardy c Smith b Marshall	65		
I. V. A. Richards b Tremlett	12		
R. J. Harden c Parks b Andrew	30		
V. J. Marks b Marshall	19		
J. C. M. Atkinson lbw b Marshall	4		
†T. Gard not out	4		
C. H. Dredge b Marshall	5		
J. Garner b Tremlett	6		
N. S. Taylor b Tremlett	0		
B 1, l-b 4, w 5, n-b 18	28	B 5, l-b 2, w 2, n-b 6	15

1/50 2/85 3/105 4/174 5/191	231	(no wkt dec.) 273
6/210 7/212 8/223 9/231		

Bonus points – Somerset 2, Hampshire 4.

Bowling: *First Innings*—Marshall 21–7–40–5; Connor 14–2–51–0; Andrew 18–3–58–1; James 9–0–34–1; Tremlett 17–4–43–3. *Second Innings*—Marshall 11–0–29–0; Andrew 1.2–0–4–0; Connor 14.4–3–37–0; James 13–2–44–0; Smith 9–4–28–0; Nicholas 16–3–38–0; Middleton 6–1–26–0; Parks 13–0–54–0; Turner 3–1–6–0.

Hampshire

V. P. Terry lbw b Taylor	1		
T. C. Middleton not out	68	– (4) not out	2
*M. C. J. Nicholas lbw b Taylor	37		
R. A. Smith b Richards	53		
D. R. Turner b Dredge	23		
K. D. James not out	21	– (3) not out	22
†R. J. Parks (did not bat)		– (1) c Hardy b Harden	11
C. A. Connor (did not bat)		– (2) st Gard b Harden	4
B 4, l-b 9, w 2, n-b 2	17	L-b 2	2

1/7 2/63 3/137 4/180	(4 wkts dec.) 220	1/13 2/34	(2 wkts) 41

M. D. Marshall, T. M. Tremlett and S. J. W. Andrew did not bat.

Bonus points – Hampshire 2, Somerset 1.

Bowling: *First Innings*—Taylor 14–2–50–2; Dredge 18–3–48–1; Garner 6–3–5–0; Atkinson 6–1–34–0; Richards 14–6–30–1; Marks 11–2–40–0. *Second Innings*—Roebuck 5–1–15–0; Harden 4–0–24–2.

Umpires: D. O. Oslear and J. H. Harris.

At Lord's, July 16, 17, 18. SOMERSET drew with MIDDLESEX.

At Bristol, July 19, 21. SOMERSET lost to GLOUCESTERSHIRE by an innings and 7 runs.

SOMERSET v WORCESTERSHIRE

At Weston-super-Mare, August 2, 4, 5. Somerset won by five wickets. Somerset 20 pts, Worcestershire 5 pts. Toss: Worcestershire. In a match dominated by the bat, Smith dropped when 69, batted excellently for his unbeaten 165 off 286 balls, hitting 22 4s and two 6s. Somerset's poor start became a fading memory as Botham, making his first appearance since his suspension, held the stage. His astonishing innings comprised seven 6s and ten 4s from 66 balls in 64 minutes; his hundred came off 65 balls. Somerset declared 93 runs behind, but two hours of rain frustrated them, and on the final day they fed easy runs before being given a target of 341 in 200 minutes plus twenty overs. Roebuck's superbly controlled 147 not out from 228 balls (fourteen 4s) held the innings together as first Rose and Harden played well and then, after a mid-innings slump, Marks hit a 6 and eleven 4s in 77 balls as their decisive stand of 133 in 25 overs won the match for Somerset with four balls to spare.

Worcestershire

T. S. Curtis b Botham	64	– c Harden b Rose	74
D. B. D'Oliveira c and b Garner	30	– c Botham b Rose	91
D. M. Smith not out	165	– not out	38
G. A. Hick c Richards b Coombs	30	– not out	43
*P. A. Neale c Coombs b Davis	70		
D. N. Patel not out	1		
B 1, l-b 14, n-b 4	19	N-b 1	1

1/58 2/175 3/239 4/374   (4 wkts dec.) 379   1/143 2/182   (2 wkts dec.) 247

†S. J. Rhodes, R. K. Illingworth, P. J. Newport, A. P. Pridgeon and N. V. Radford did not bat.

Bonus points – Worcestershire 4, Somerset 1 (Score at 100 overs: 325-3).

Bowling: *First Innings*—Garner 13-3-37-1; Davis 11-3-55-1; Botham 20-3-70-1; Coombs 24-3-87-1; Marks 33-13-66-0; Richards 8-1-41-0; Harden 3-0-8-0. *Second Innings*—Botham 8-1-55-0; Davis 2.4-0-9-0; Richards 6-0-40-0; Roebuck 7-0-75-0; Rose 6-0-28-2; Marks 4-0-17-0; Coombs 4-1-19-0; Harden 1-0-4-0.

Somerset

B. C. Rose c Patel b Radford	6	– b Newport	56
*P. M. Roebuck c Illingworth b Patel	68	– not out	147
R. J. Harden c Rhodes b Radford	10	– c Curtis b Radford	28
I. V. A. Richards b Newport	36	– lbw b Radford	4
N. A. Felton not out	52	– (6) c Smith b Radford	0
I. T. Botham not out	104	– (5) b Newport	17
V. J. Marks (did not bat)		– not out	71
L-b 5, n-b 5	10	B 1, l-b 13, n-b 4	18

1/6 2/31 3/78 4/163   (4 wkts dec.) 286   1/99 2/160 3/173   (5 wkts) 341
4/207 5/208

†T. Gard, M. R. Davis, J. Garner and R. V. J. Coombs did not bat.

Bonus points – Somerset 3, Worcestershire 1.

Bowling: *First Innings*—Radford 22-3-77-2; Pridgeon 10-3-34-0; Newport 13.4-2-72-1; Illingworth 12-3-40-0; Patel 16-2-58-1. *Second Innings*—Radford 18-0-89-3; Pridgeon 21-3-93-0; Patel 13-1-43-0; Newport 13-0-50-2; Illingworth 12.2-2-52-0.

Umpires: H. D. Bird (R. Thorne and A. G. T. Whitehead on the second day, Whitehead on the third) and J. H. Hampshire.

SOMERSET v WARWICKSHIRE

At Weston-super-Mare, August 6, 7, 8. Drawn. Somerset 2 pts, Warwickshire 4 pts. Toss: Warwickshire. After the first morning was lost to rain, four batsmen dominated much of the match on a slow pitch. Smith and Moles, the latter reaching a maiden century from 242 balls, compiled opening stands of 161 and 155 for Warwickshire. Somerset declared 116 runs behind after Rose and Richards had put on 122 in 25 overs and the third declaration set a target of 356 in three hours plus twenty overs. Rose, who faced 163 balls in all, and Richards, five 6s and eleven 4s in 94 balls, put together 164 off 33 overs, but when Richards was out with 160 needed from a probable 25 overs, the match died without recourse to the final half-hour.

Warwickshire

A. J. Moles b Coombs	66	– c Felton b Marks	102
P. A. Smith c Gard b Garner	87	– c Davis b Marks	78
B. M. McMillan c Richards b Marks	36	– not out	48
D. L. Amiss lbw b Coombs	53	– not out	1
†G. W. Humpage not out	32		
D. A. Thorne not out	11		
B 2, l-b 6, w 2, n-b 7	17	B 6, l-b 1, w 1, n-b 2	10

1/161 2/165 3/240 4/268   (4 wkts dec.) 302   1/155 2/235   (2 wkts dec.) 239

Asif Din, K. J. Kerr, G. J. Parsons, T. A. Munton and *N. Gifford did not bat.

Bonus points – Warwickshire 4, Somerset 1.

Bowling: *First Innings*—Garner 16–1–40–1; Davis 18–2–62–0; Richards 4–0–10–0; Marks 29–6–79–1; Coombs 24.5–6–82–2; Harden 4–0–21–0. *Second Innings*—Garner 3–0–7–0; Davis 9–0–63–0; Coombs 30–6–82–0; Marks 31–9–74–2; Richards 3–1–6–0.

Somerset

B. C. Rose not out	76	– not out	96
*P. M. Roebuck retired hurt	4		
J. G. Wyatt b Parsons	20	– (2) b McMillan	5
I. V. A. Richards not out	74	– b McMillan	115
N. A. Felton (did not bat)		– (3) c Humpage b McMillan	1
R. J. Harden (did not bat)		– (5) not out	8
B 2, l-b 7, w 1, n-b 2	12	B 1, l-b 1, w 1, n-b 4	7

1/64   (1 wkt dec.) 186   1/30 2/32 3/196   (3 wkts) 232

V. J. Marks, †T. Gard, M. R. Davis, J. Garner and R. V. J. Coombs did not bat.

Bonus points – Somerset 1.

Bowling: *First Innings*—McMillan 6–2–14–0; Smith 9–3–24–0; Asif Din 1–0–8–0; Parsons 11–1–28–1; Kerr 15–2–42–0; Munton 8–0–61–0. *Second Innings*—McMillan 10–1–47–3; Smith 7–1–31–0; Parsons 9–0–34–0; Kerr 7–0–32–0; Munton 9–0–40–0; Gifford 13–0–46–0.

Umpires: J. H. Hampshire and M. J. Kitchen.

At Wellingborough School, August 9, 11, 12. SOMERSET drew with NORTHAMPTON-SHIRE.

SOMERSET v SURREY

At Taunton, August 16, 18, 19. Surrey won by 178 runs. Surrey 20 pts, Somerset 4 pts. Toss: Surrey. After early problems against Garner and Botham, Clinton provided the base for Surrey's large total on the opening day, facing 161 balls and hitting seventeen 4s. Stewart, missed before scoring, struck thirteen 4s in his confident 78 from 66 balls and Richards sustained the final 39 overs of Surrey's innings. Rain prevented any play on Monday, and when Somerset had added 49 to their score on the final morning, their target was 345 from a minimum 95 overs. After Clarke's early burst of three for 2 in eleven deliveries, only a belligerent Botham, with a 6 and six 4s in 26 balls, Marks, playing brightly for 35 balls, and Garner, who hit three 6s off Pocock, held Surrey up for long. They romped home with 205 minutes in hand.

Surrey

A. R. Butcher c Felton b Taylor	29	K. T. Medlycott c Felton b Coombs	...	3
G. S. Clinton c sub b Marks	117	S. T. Clarke b Garner		21
A. J. Stewart c Roebuck b Coombs	78			
M. A. Lynch c Harden b Taylor	14	B 8, l-b 4, w 3, n-b 5		20
N. J. Falkner c and b Marks	37			
†C. J. Richards not out	70	1/49 2/163 3/207	(9 wkts dec.)	427
D. J. Thomas c Gard b Botham	27	4/272 5/305 6/344		
M. A. Feltham lbw b Garner	11	7/385 8/398 9/427		

*P. I. Pocock did not bat.

Bonus points – Surrey 4, Somerset 4.

Bowling: Garner 19.1–0–62–2; Botham 14–2–58–1; Taylor 13–1–75–2; Marks 24–5–88–2; Richards 3–0–30–0; Coombs 21–3–95–2; Harden 2–0–7–0.

Surrey forfeited their second innings.

Somerset

B. C. Rose not out	43	– b Thomas	3
*P. M. Roebuck not out	31	– b Clarke	9
N. A. Felton (did not bat)		– c Lynch b Clarke	6
I. V. A. Richards (did not bat)		– b Clarke	7
R. J. Harden (did not bat)		– c Clarke b Pocock	16
I. T. Botham (did not bat)		– c Clinton b Feltham	34
V. J. Marks (did not bat)		– run out	37
†T. Gard (did not bat)		– c Lynch b Clarke	16
J. Garner (did not bat)		– c Falkner b Pocock	27
N. S. Taylor (did not bat)		– c Stewart b Clarke	2
R. V. J. Coombs (did not bat)		– not out	0
B 4, l-b 1, w 1, n-b 3	9	B 3, l-b 1, w 1, n-b 4	9
(no wkt dec.)	83	1/3 2/22 3/30 4/38 5/82	166
		6/82 7/133 8/158 9/166	

Bowling: *First Innings*—Clarke 5–1–11–0; Thomas 4–0–18–0; Pocock 1–1–0–0; Falkner 1–0–6–0; Stewart 2–0–34–0; Lynch 1–0–9–0. *Second Innings*—Clarke 12.3–1–31–5; Thomas 6–1–25–1; Butcher 2–0–14–0; Feltham 5–0–41–1; Pocock 9–1–51–2.

Umpires: C. Cook and J. W. Holder.

SOMERSET v SUSSEX

At Taunton, August 20, 21, 22. Drawn. Somerset 3 pts, Sussex 1 pt. Toss: Somerset. Set back first by Jones and then Colin Wells, Somerset recovered through a splendid fifth-wicket partnership between Harden, who reached his hundred in 207 balls, and Marks, whose three figures came up off 184 balls. They added 187 in 59 overs before Pigott's second new-ball spell brought him four wickets for 25 in 9.3 overs. Somerset batted on for twenty minutes on the second day, but after seventeen overs of the Sussex reply heavy rain fell, not only ending play for the day but for the rest of the contest.

Somerset

J. G. Wyatt lbw b Jones	3	M. D. Harman not out	8
*P. M. Roebuck c Speight b C. M. Wells	39	N. S. Taylor b Pigott	12
N. A. Felton b Jones	0	D. J. Foster lbw b Pigott	0
I. V. A. Richards lbw b C. M. Wells	41		
R. J. Harden b Pigott	108	B 1, l-b 2, n-b 4	7
V. J. Marks c Speight b C. M. Wells	110		
†T. Gard c sub b Pigott	5	1/9 2/9 3/61 4/108 5/295	333
J. Garner c Speight b Pigott	0	6/305 7/305 8/315 9/333	

Bonus points – Somerset 3, Sussex 1 (Score at 100 overs: 282-4).

Bowling: Jones 14–3–33–2; Pigott 27.3–4–81–5; C. M. Wells 31–4–77–3; Mays 28–5–78–0; Green 4–1–13–0; Lenham 2–0–13–0; Standing 12–1–35–0.

Sussex

R. I. Alikhan b Marks	15
A. M. Green not out	27
*P. W. G. Parker not out	19
N-b 5	5
1/45	(1 wkt) 66

N. J. Lenham, C. M. Wells, A. P. Wells, D. K. Standing, †M. P. Speight, A. C. S. Pigott, A. N. Jones and C. S. Mays did not bat.

Bowling: Garner 6–1–15–0; Foster 5–0–29–0; Taylor 3–0–6–0; Marks 3–1–16–1.

Umpires: C. Cook and J. W. Holder.

SOMERSET v ESSEX

At Taunton, August 27, 28, 29. Essex won by 9 runs. Essex 20 pts, Somerset 6 pts. Toss: Essex. Only East's half-century saved Essex from being routed after they had chosen to bat on a damp pitch. A typical 53 off 52 balls from Richards and Botham's unbeaten 36 took Somerset into the second day with a lead of 5 runs and four wickets in hand, from which another 66 runs were gathered. In easier conditions Hardie, well supported throughout, compiled a patient 113 not out from 356 balls and Gooch was able to set a target of 273 in 68 overs. Richards, 94 from 94 balls with three 6s and nine 4s, Marks, 56 off 86 balls, and Botham, who left his sick-bed to hit 41 in 29 balls, made achieving it look a probability. Immediately before Botham's dismissal, 20 runs were needed in eighteen overs from the last five wickets, but he disdained the opportunity to win the match in singles and was caught on the boundary, the first of five wickets to fall for 10 runs as Essex won the match with a possible 53 balls remaining.

Essex

*G. A. Gooch c Richards b Botham	0	– lbw b Taylor	38
J. P. Stephenson c Botham b Taylor	0	– c Gard b Taylor	11
P. J. Prichard c Richards b Taylor	1	– c Hardy b Marks	38
B. R. Hardie c Roebuck b Taylor	18	– not out	113
K. W. R. Fletcher c Roebuck b Botham	7	– c Harden b Marks	28
D. R. Pringle lbw b Botham	2	– run out	21
†D. E. East not out	58	– (8) c Roebuck b Harman	41
N. A. Foster c Gard b Taylor	14	– (9) not out	0
J. K. Lever c Harman b Dredge	18	– (7) b Dredge	38
J. H. Childs c Botham b Dredge	7		
D. L. Acfield c Gard b Dredge	0		
L-b 2, n-b 2	4	B 6, l-b 9	15
1/0 2/0 3/2 4/29 5/29	129	1/32 2/64 3/115 (7 wkts dec.) 343	
6/36 7/57 8/109 9/129		4/163 5/207	
		6/259 7/343	

Bonus points – Somerset 4.

Bowling: *First Innings*—Botham 21–5–77–3; Taylor 15–5–40–4; Dredge 5.3–1–10–3. *Second Innings*—Botham 7–2–32–0; Taylor 25–9–58–2; Dredge 21–6–51–1; Marks 39–10–99–2; Harman 39.3–11–88–1.

Somerset

N. A. Felton c Prichard b Childs	10	– lbw b Lever	6
*P. M. Roebuck b Childs	10	– lbw b Foster	24
J. J. E. Hardy run out	11	– c Pringle b Foster	19
I. V. A. Richards c Fletcher b Gooch	53	– c Hardie b Lever	94
R. J. Harden c Fletcher b Childs	14	– c Fletcher b Foster	4
I. T. Botham c Foster b Lever	67	– (7) c Stephenson b Childs	41
†T. Gard c Lever b Childs	0	– (8) lbw b Pringle	0
V. J. Marks run out	4	– (6) b Pringle	56
C. H. Dredge c East b Foster	24	– not out	4
M. D. Harman not out	4	– run out	0
N. S. Taylor b Foster	2	– lbw b Childs	2
L-b 1	1	B 5, l-b 7, n-b 1	13

1/16 2/21 3/72 4/96 5/133	200	1/30 2/38 3/100 4/110 5/198	263
6/133 7/150 8/194 9/196		6/253 7/254 8/259 9/261	

Bonus points – Somerset 2, Essex 4.

Bowling: *First Innings*—Lever 21–7–59–1; Foster 26.3–7–62–2; Childs 8–0–27–4; Pringle 4–0–23–0; Gooch 4–0–28–1. *Second Innings*—Lever 18–2–104–2; Foster 20–4–79–3; Pringle 12–1–45–2; Childs 9.1–2–23–2.

Umpires: K. J. Lyons and R. A. White.

At Leicester, August 30, September 1, 2. SOMERSET drew with LEICESTERSHIRE.

At Worcester, September 3, 4. SOMERSET lost to WORCESTERSHIRE by an innings and 9 runs.

At Manchester, September 10, 11, 12. SOMERSET lost to LANCASHIRE by 26 runs.

SOMERSET v DERBYSHIRE

At Taunton, September 13, 15, 16. Derbyshire won by three wickets. Derbyshire 12 pts. Toss: Derbyshire. Rain having prevented a start on the first two days, a one-innings match was played. On a seamers' pitch Somerset struggled to 182 all out, owing much to a responsible innings by Hardy, Bartlett's 41 in 63 balls, and a characteristic if somewhat untimely 36 in twelve balls by Botham. Maher and Hill seemed to make the match safe for Derbyshire, adding 89 in 22 overs, but only after a collapse, in which there was a fine catch by Botham, did Morris (34 from 35 balls) see his side home with seven balls to spare.

Somerset

N. A. Felton lbw b Holding	4	†T. Gard b Warner	17
P. A. C. Bail lbw b Mortensen	0	C. H. Dredge c Maher b Jean-Jacques	0
J. J. E. Hardy lbw b Mortensen	52	N. S. Taylor c Maher b Warner	1
R. J. Harden b Jean-Jacques	1		
R. J. Bartlett c Holding b Finney	41	L-b 8, n-b 2	10
I. T. Botham b Mortensen	36		
*V. J. Marks c Warner b Holding	4	1/2 2/16 3/27 4/93 5/139	182
J. C. M. Atkinson not out	16	6/140 7/144 8/176 9/177	

Bowling: Holding 21–8–46–2; Mortensen 13–4–33–3; Jean-Jacques 11–2–44–2; Finney 7–1–47–1; Warner 4.1–1–4–2.

Derbyshire

*K. J. Barnett b Taylor	14	M. A. Holding c Taylor b Marks	0
†B. J. M. Maher b Marks	49	R. Sharma not out	3
A. Hill c Gard b Dredge	45	B 1, l-b 6, n-b 3	10
J. E. Morris not out	34		
B. Roberts b Marks	10	1/24 2/113 3/117	(7 wkts) 184
A. E. Warner c Gard b Dredge	19	4/138 5/171	
M. Jean-Jacques c Botham b Dredge	0	6/171 7/172	

R. J. Finney and O. H. Mortensen did not bat.

Bowling: Botham 13–2–48–0; Taylor 9–0–31–1; Marks 12.5–1–58–3; Dredge 9–1–40–3.

Umpires: B. Leadbeater and K. J. Lyons.

STATUS OF MATCHES IN THE UK

(a) Automatic First-Class Matches

The following matches of three or more days' duration should automatically be considered first-class:

(i) County Championship matches.

(ii) Official representative tourist matches from Full Member Countries, unless specifically excluded.

(iii) MCC v any First-Class County.

(iv) Oxford v Cambridge and either University against First-Class Counties.

(v) Scotland v Ireland.

(b) Excluded from First-Class Status

The following matches of three or more days' duration should not normally be accorded first-class status:

(i) County "friendly" matches.

(ii) Matches played by Scotland or Ireland, other than their annual match against each other.

(iii) Unofficial tourist matches, unless circumstances are exceptional.

(iv) MCC v Oxford/Cambridge.

(v) Matches involving privately raised teams, unless included officially in a touring team's itinerary.

(c) Consideration of Doubtful Status

Matches played by unofficial touring teams of exceptional ability can be considered in advance and decisions taken accordingly.

Certain other matches comprising 22 recognised first-class cricketers might also be considered in advance.

SURREY

Patron: HM The Queen
President: 1986-87 – M. F. Turner
1987-88 – A. V. Bedser
Chairman: D. H. Newton
Secretary: I. F. B. Scott-Browne
Kennington Oval, London SE11 5SS
(Telephone: 01-582 6660)
Director of Cricket: M. J. Stewart
Captain: 1986 – P. I. Pocock
Coaches: G. G. Arnold and C. E. Waller

Surrey's mercurial season was unexpectedly gladdened by Northampton-shire's number eleven batsman, Alan Walker. For while Surrey were celebrating their win over Leicestershire at The Oval, 130 miles away at Trent Bridge Walker survived the last five balls of the Britannic Assurance Championship to deny Nottinghamshire the victory which would have put them second. Sixth at the start of the last round, Surrey thus found themselves filling third place in the table instead of fourth and winning £5,250 instead of £2,750. It was a satisfying reversal of the previous season's finish when Worcestershire had taken fifth place in the closing moments to exclude Surrey from the prizemoney.

Third in the Championship – Surrey's best since being second in 1980 – and failing by just 5 runs to reach the NatWest Bank Trophy final would, for many counties, represent a successful season. At The Oval, however, it was a familiar scenario of sighting an honour without making the final push to win one. Yet with their deep cupboard of talent and blossoming youth programme, Surrey should have figured more promi-nently in the list of winners in recent years.

Lack of new-ball support for the two West Indians, Sylvester Clarke and Tony Gray, who played virtually alternately because of the qualification regulations, weakened the attack's ability to dismiss sides quickly, and Surrey collected ten fewer bowling points than in 1985. The emergence of Martin Bicknell, a seventeen-year-old fast bowler who joined Clarke and Gray in the top ten of the national averages, gave the county a potentially match-winning pairing of strike bowlers, but while individual figures were often impressive, the performances were rarely in tandem. Bicknell's contribution, unfortunately, was restricted by bruised shoulder tendons resulting from a collision with an advertising board at The Oval.

The success of Bicknell, and of Nick Falkner, the opening batsman, was a reward for the quality and depth of the schoolboy scheme developed by Micky Stewart when he became team manager in 1979. But their progress was fostered amidst tales of dressing-room disharmony, which gave Pat Pocock a difficult introduction to captaincy in what was to be his last season with Surrey. Monte Lynch was suspended from the Sunday League match against Sussex at the end of July, and for the rest of the summer his discontent with the club was rumoured. Alan Butcher, the vice-captain, was released after fifteen seasons, as were Richard

Doughty and Graham Monkhouse, the latter to concentrate on the family farming business in Cumbria.

The county's performance in the John Player League continued to be a source of bewilderment and frustration. Twelfth equal, with five wins, was an improvement after finishing last in 1985, but a one-wicket victory over the previous year's winners, Essex, was the summit of their achievement. Nor did they give a worthwhile account of themselves in the Benson and Hedges Cup, failing to reach the quarter-finals for the second successive season.

In the NatWest Bank Trophy, Surrey overcame a wonderful all-round display by Nottinghamshire's Hadlee in the quarter-finals, and against Lancashire were taken splendidly to the verge of the final by a century from Trevor Jesty. This fighting innings came amid a rich vein of form in an otherwise disappointing season in which, despite a double-hundred against Essex and 179 against Worcestershire, Jesty failed to score 1,000 runs.

Lynch, who began with two hundreds, was another unable to reproduce his consistency of the previous season, and the regular scoring became the responsibility of Alec Stewart, who made 1,665 runs in a most stylish manner. A bonus was the batting of Jack Richards, the wicket-keeper, who passed 1,000 runs for the first time. His form with the bat won him selection for England's two Texaco Trophy matches against New Zealand and a place on the winter tour of Australia, for which Micky Stewart had been appointed assistant manager.

In mid-season, Surrey lost six of nine consecutive Championship matches ending in a result. Two of those defeats, against Nottinghamshire and Hampshire, came in two days within the same week. But in the middle of this period they defeated Middlesex at Uxbridge in a match which announced the arrival of Falkner and the left-arm spinner, Keith Medlycott. Falkner posted his maiden Championship century, and Medlycott captured ten wickets on a grassless pitch.

Three wins in four matches took Surrey into contention for the title, their position improving from ninth to third, but they suffered a setback with the wet weather in late August. They took only five points from the match against Essex at Chelmsford, and none at all when the first two days were washed out at Swansea and Pocock set Glamorgan perhaps too demanding a target in a one-innings match. It was undoubtedly the phase of the season which ended their serious challenge.

Pocock said his farewells to Surrey after more than half his life on the staff. His business commitments had become too demanding, and age also had its say. "P.P. does not stand for Peter Pan", he said poignantly on his departure. – D.W.F.

SURREY 1986

[Bill Smith

Back row: J. Robinson, K. T. Medlycott, D. M. Ward, N. J. Falkner, Zahid Sadiq. Middle row: G. G. Arnold (coach), T. Billson (scorer), G. E. Brown, A. Needham, J. Deary (physiotherapist), T. E. Jesty, A. J. Stewart, D. J. Thomas, C. K. Bullen, M. A. Feltham, M. P. Bicknell, R. J. Doughty, G. Monkhouse, C. E. Waller (coach). Front row: S. T. Clarke, A. R. Butcher, P. I. Pocock (captain), M. J. Stewart (manager), C. J. Richards, G. S. Clinton, M. A. Lynch. Inset: A. H. Gray.

SURREY RESULTS

All first-class matches – Played 25: Won 8, Lost 6, Drawn 11.

County Championship matches – Played 24: Won 8, Lost 6, Drawn 10.

Bonus points – Batting 54, Bowling 66.

Competition placings – Britannic Assurance County Championship, 3rd; NatWest Bank Trophy, s-f; Benson and Hedges Cup, 4th in Group D; John Player League, 12th equal.

BRITANNIC ASSURANCE CHAMPIONSHIP AVERAGES

BATTING

	Birthplace	M	I	NO	R	HI	Avge
‡A. J. Stewart	Merton	24	38	3	1,629	166	46.54
‡C. J. Richards	Penzance	23	34	9	1,006	115	40.24
N. J. Falkner	Redhill	11	18	2	567	102	35.43
‡M. A. Lynch	Georgetown, BG	24	38	3	1,201	152	34.31
‡T. E. Jesty	Gosport	19	29	1	955	221	34.10
‡G. S. Clinton	Sidcup	22	34	4	1,004	117	33.46
‡D. J. Thomas	Solihull	9	12	4	222	47*	27.75
M. A. Feltham	St John's Wood	11	13	4	217	76	24.11
R. J. Doughty	Bridlington	14	18	2	366	61	22.87
‡G. Monkhouse	Langwathby	10	12	4	162	51	20.25
D. M. Ward	Croydon	4	6	1	100	34	20.00
‡A. R. Butcher	Croydon	15	24	0	477	71	19.87
‡A. Needham	Calow	10	16	2	256	52	18.28
‡S. T. Clarke	Christ Church, Barbados	13	12	3	156	32*	17.33
K. T. Medlycott ..	Whitechapel	13	14	2	170	61	14.16
‡A. H. Gray	Port-of-Spain, Trinidad	11	14	2	108	28	9.00
‡P. I. Pocock	Bangor	21	20	9	93	16*	8.45
M. P. Bicknell	Guildford	9	10	2	21	9*	2.62

Also batted: G. E. Brown (*Balham*) (1 match) 0*, 2*.

* *Signifies not out.* ‡ *Denotes county cap.*

The following played a total of twelve three-figure innings for Surrey in County Championship matches: M. A. Lynch 3, A. J. Stewart 3, T. E. Jesty 2, C. J. Richards 2, G. S. Clinton 1, N. J. Falkner 1.

BOWLING

	O	M	R	W	BB	Avge
S. T. Clarke	341.3	95	806	48	5-31	16.79
A. H. Gray	342.3	69	966	51	7-23	18.94
M. P. Bicknell	196	43	600	27	3-27	22.22
K. T. Medlycott ..	309.4	71	1,077	36	6-63	29.91
M. A. Feltham	191	32	741	23	4-47	32.21
R. J. Doughty	279	46	1,056	31	4-52	34.06
P. I. Pocock	394.5	107	1,095	30	4-45	36.50
G. Monkhouse	233.1	69	589	14	4-37	42.07
D. J. Thomas	166.3	29	588	12	2-44	49.00

Also bowled: A. R. Butcher 68-12-249-6; G. S. Clinton 3-1-12-0; N. J. Falkner 4-1-9-1; T. E. Jesty 59-21-155-5; M. A. Lynch 23.2-2-119-2; A. Needham 67-21-163-0; C. J. Richards 5-0-34-1; A. J. Stewart 5-0-55-0.

Wicket-keepers: C. J. Richards 39 ct, 5 st; G. E. Brown 4 ct, 1 st.

Leading Fielders: M. A. Lynch 38; A. J. Stewart 15.

At Worcester, April 26, 27, 28. SURREY drew with WORCESTERSHIRE.

SURREY v NOTTINGHAMSHIRE

At The Oval, April 30, May 1, 2. Drawn. Surrey 6 pts, Nottinghamshire 7 pts. Toss: Nottinghamshire. The flags were flown at half-mast in memory of Jim Laker, who died a week earlier, and the players wore black armbands. The sombre mood was lightened by an outstanding innings from Lynch, who heralded the new season with a 6 and 24 4s in an audacious, career-best 152 after Nottinghamshire's acting-captain, Hadlee, had misread the pitch. Lynch received cultured support from Jesty in a stand of 224 which sped Surrey to a declaration that evening. Lynch's century came off 111 balls, and there was another of almost equal belligerence off 126 balls from Hadlee, whose partnership of 112 with Birch took Nottinghamshire from the threat of the follow-on to a declaration. Surrey's second declaration left them 215 minutes in which to bowl out Nottinghamshire. That they just failed to do so was the result of a dogged rearguard action in which Hadlee showed the determined side of his cricketing nature by batting 81 minutes for 8.

Surrey

A. R. Butcher c Hemmings b Saxelby	7	– c French b Pick	11
G. S. Clinton c Hemmings b Saxelby	6	– c Birch b Hemmings	61
A. J. Stewart b Pick	19	– lbw b Hemmings	76
M. A. Lynch c Saxelby b Hemmings	152	– c Robinson b Afford	27
T. E. Jesty c Johnson b Hemmings	99	– lbw b Hemmings	9
D. M. Ward st French b Afford	3	– st French b Hemmings	34
†C. J. Richards c Birch b Pick	14	– not out	50
M. A. Feltham not out	23	– not out	0
R. J. Doughty not out	25		
L-b 7, w 2, n-b 8	17	L-b 3, n-b 1	4

1/15 2/17 3/50 4/274 (7 wkts dec.) 365   1/24 2/137 3/168 (6 wkts dec.) 272
5/286 6/308 7/316   4/188 5/189 6/264

S. T. Clarke and *P. I. Pocock did not bat.

Bonus points – Surrey 4, Nottinghamshire 3 (Score at 100 overs: 355-7).

Bowling: *First Innings*—Hadlee 20-3-60-0; Saxelby 16-5-62-2; Pick 16-2-65-2; Hemmings 29-10-83-2; Afford 19.5-4-88-1. *Second Innings*—Saxelby 5-1-18-0; Pick 10-2-45-1; Hemmings 26-7-95-4; Afford 20.4-3-75-1; Johnson 2-0-18-0; Robinson 2-0-18-0.

Nottinghamshire

R. T. Robinson c Lynch b Clarke	7	– lbw b Clarke	4
B. C. Broad c Lynch b Feltham	37	– c Richards b Clarke	8
R. A. Pick c Lynch b Doughty	29	– (9) not out	8
D. W. Randall b Feltham	5	– (3) c sub b Doughty	4
P. Johnson b Feltham	33	– (4) b Pocock	46
J. D. Birch c Richards b Doughty	62	– (5) c Lynch b Clarke	37
*R. J. Hadlee not out	105	– (6) c Clarke b Butcher	8
†B. N. French not out	37	– (7) c Clarke b Pocock	5
E. E. Hemmings (did not bat)		– (8) c Butcher b Pocock	6
K. Saxelby (did not bat)		– c Doughty b Pocock	5
J. A. Afford (did not bat)		– not out	0
L-b 11, n-b 1	12	B 8, l-b 13	21

1/16 2/66 3/80 4/101 (6 wkts dec.) 327   1/14 2/27 3/31 (9 wkts) 152
5/132 6/244   4/103 5/119 6/129
                                           7/135 8/144 9/152

Bonus points – Nottinghamshire 4, Surrey 2.

Bowling: *First Innings*—Clarke 23–11–32–1; Doughty 24–6–101–2; Pocock 26.1–5–79–0; Feltham 18–1–77–3; Jesty 4–0–27–0. *Second Innings*—Clarke 18–4–38–3; Doughty 13–5–19–1; Pocock 23–5–45–4; Feltham 6–2–25–0; Butcher 2–1–4–1.

Umpires: J. H. Hampshire and A. G. T. Whitehead.

SURREY v WARWICKSHIRE

At The Oval, May 7, 8, 9. Surrey won by an innings and 73 runs. Surrey 24 pts, Warwickshire 3 pts. Toss: Surrey. Gray replaced his fellow West Indian, Clarke, in the home XI and responded with a match analysis of twelve for 113, figures which reflected his faultless line and frequent steep bounce and which took Surrey to their second successive innings victory at The Oval over the Midlands county. Gray's bowling was richly augmented by another spectacular innings from Lynch, who reached his hundred in 148 minutes. Interruptions because of bad light on the opening day kept Gray fresh, and apart from a resourceful 58 from McMillan, Warwickshire had little to offer. More delays on the second day, with a thunderstorm in the afternoon costing 32 overs, obliged Surrey's batsmen to score as quickly as possible, and on the final morning Lynch and Richards added 36 in twenty minutes before Pocock closed the innings. Warwickshire fell apart as Gray, supported by outstanding close-catching, claimed six for 30 to wrap up the match with an hour and 40 minutes to spare. It was Gray's eighth return of five wickets or more in an innings in twenty matches.

Warwickshire

T. A. Lloyd c Richards b Doughty	27	– c Stewart b Gray	0
R. I. H. B. Dyer c Doughty b Monkhouse	9	– c Stewart b Gray	14
Asif Din c Richards b Gray	14	– c Doughty b Gray	0
D. L. Amiss c Lynch b Gray	20	– c Richards b Doughty	26
†G. W. Humpage c Clinton b Jesty	20	– (7) lbw b Monkhouse	10
B. M. McMillan c Richards b Gray	58	– (5) c Lynch b Monkhouse	17
P. A. Smith c Lynch b Gray	3	– (6) c Doughty b Gray	4
G. J. Parsons not out	1	– c Lynch b Gray	2
G. C. Small c Jesty b Gray	8	– retired hurt	1
T. A. Munton c Richards b Gray	0	– b Gray	1
*N. Gifford b Doughty	1	– not out	5
L-b 3, w 1, n-b 9	13	B 2, l-b 3, n-b 4	9

1/35 2/50 3/68 4/76 5/142   174   1/0 2/12 3/17 4/63 5/63,   89
6/160 7/161 8/170 9/173   6/76 7/78 8/80 9/84

Bonus points – Warwickshire 1, Surrey 4.

Bowling: *First Innings*—Gray 17–2–83–6; Doughty 12.1–5–44–2; Monkhouse 13–2–41–1; Jesty 5–2–3–1. *Second Innings*—Gray 13.3–4–30–6; Doughty 11–5–39–1; Monkhouse 9–3–15–2; Pocock 1–1–0–0.

Surrey

A. R. Butcher c McMillan b Small	0	†C. J. Richards not out	31
G. S. Clinton lbw b Parsons	60		
A. J. Stewart c Humpage b Munton	76	B 4, l-b 22, n-b 4	30
M. A. Lynch not out	128		
T. E. Jesty c Humpage b Munton	9	1/6 2/110 3/224 (5 wkts dec.)	336
A. Needham lbw b Parsons	2	4/254 5/259	

G. Monkhouse, R. J. Doughty, A. H. Gray and *P. I. Pocock did not bat.

Bonus points – Surrey 4, Warwickshire 2.

Bowling: Small 23–4–75–1; McMillan 25–0–113–0; Munton 17–6–52–2; Parsons 18–2–70–2.

Umpires: K. J. Lyons and P. B. Wight.

†At The Oval, May 15. SURREY lost to INDIANS by five wickets (See Indian tour section).

At Hove, May 21, 22, 23. SURREY drew with SUSSEX.

SURREY v MIDDLESEX

At The Oval, May 31, June 2, 3. Drawn. Surrey 2 pts, Middlesex 5 pts. Toss: Middlesex. Hughes, the Middlesex seam bowler, sandwiched a career-best return of seven for 35 between the first and third days which were both fully lost to the rain. In trying, murky conditions, only Needham provided any real substance in the middle order before the last five wickets tumbled for 14 runs, Hughes capturing five for 7 in fourteen balls. Surrey's 109, occupying fewer than 35 overs, was their lowest total for two seasons. Middlesex, 55 for two, were making sound progress when bad light forced a stoppage, after which they declined to 162 for six and were indebted to Miller for his chanceless 62.

Surrey

N. J. Falkner c Downton b Daniel	....	6	G. Monkhouse c Emburey b Hughes	.. 0
G. S. Clinton c Emburey b Hughes	....	20	S. T. Clarke c Gatting b Hughes	 0
A. J. Stewart c Downton b Daniel	....	10	*P. I. Pocock c Gatting b Hughes	 1
M. A. Lynch c Downton b Hughes	....	7		
T. E. Jesty lbw b Fraser	....	15	L-b 4, w 1, n-b 2	 7
A. Needham not out	....	34		
†C. J. Richards c Emburey b Hughes	..	4	1/24 2/34 3/45 4/50 5/88	109
R. J. Doughty c Emburey b Hughes	..	5	6/95 7/101 8/105 9/105	

Bonus points – Middlesex 4.

Bowling: Daniel 9–0–31–2; Fraser 12–2–34–1; Hughes 11.2–2–35–7; Edmonds 2–0–5–0.

Middlesex

G. D. Barlow c Monkhouse b Clarke	..	12	J. E. Emburey lbw b Jesty	 4
W. N. Slack c Falkner b Monkhouse	..	27	P. H. Edmonds not out	 6
A. J. T. Miller c Falkner b Jesty	......	62	L-b 2, w 2, n-b 3	 7
*M. W. Gatting c Lynch b Clarke	....	31		
R. O. Butcher c Richards b Doughty	..	1	1/25 2/55 3/94 4/114	(6 wkts) 162
†P. R. Downton not out	....	12	5/147 6/152	

S. P. Hughes, A. R. C. Fraser and W. W. Daniel did not bat.

Bonus points – Middlesex 1, Surrey 2.

Bowling: Clarke 16–3–46–2; Doughty 13–0–37–1; Monkhouse 16–3–46–1; Jesty 7–1–14–2; Pocock 4–0–17–0.

Umpires: H. D. Bird and B. Leadbeater.

At Hinckley, June 4, 5, 6. SURREY lost to LEICESTERSHIRE by six wickets.

SURREY v DERBYSHIRE

At The Oval, June 7, 9, 10. Surrey won by nine wickets. Surrey 22 pts, Derbyshire 5 pts. Toss: Surrey. Clarke, recently troubled by muscle wastage around a knee, showed no ill effects as he made fairly short work of Derbyshire's first innings. Surrey, 86 for five at the close, were grateful to Monkhouse, 8 not out overnight, who defended stubbornly for 210 minutes for 51, his best score for two years, and to Doughty's aggressive 61 for their lead. Clarke again made early inroads when Derbyshire batted, and Morris, with 62, stood alone in sustaining their innings. Bicknell, aged seventeen and making his first-class début, swept Derbyshire aside on the final morning by taking three for 4 in eleven deliveries, and Surrey's task of making 95 to win their second Championship match of the season proved a formality.

Derbyshire

*K. J. Barnett c Richards b Clarke	0	– lbw b Clarke	4
I. S. Anderson c Lynch b Clarke	48	– c Pocock b Monkhouse	26
A. Hill c Richards b Doughty	4	– b Clarke	0
J. E. Morris b Doughty	0	– c sub b Doughty	62
B. Roberts c Doughty b Clarke	43	– c Richards b Clarke	10
G. Miller lbw b Clarke	5	– c Richards b Bicknell	16
R. J. Finney c Doughty b Clarke	4	– lbw b Pocock	4
†C. Marples c Richards b Bicknell	15	– c Falkner b Bicknell	7
M. Jean-Jacques b Bicknell	12	– (11) not out	1
M. A. Holding c Clinton b Doughty	21	– (9) c sub b Bicknell	5
O. H. Mortensen not out	5	– (10) run out	0
B 5, l-b 15, w 1, n-b 1	22	B 1, n-b 2	3

1/0 2/14 3/15 4/76 5/82   179   1/8 2/8 3/73 4/94 5/110   138
6/86 7/122 8/144 9/159   6/119 7/127 8/136 9/137

Bonus points – Derbyshire 1, Surrey 4.

Bowling: *First Innings*—Clarke 18–3–43–5; Doughty 9.2–2–17–3; Monkhouse 12–2–44–0; Bicknell 13–5–23–2; Jesty 4–3–3–0; Pocock 5–1–29–0. *Second Innings*—Clarke 13.4–5–30–3; Doughty 11–3–38–1; Bicknell 11–6–30–3; Monkhouse 9–3–31–1; Pocock 6–4–8–1.

Surrey

N. J. Falkner b Finney	14	– not out	46
G. S. Clinton run out	7		
A. J. Stewart c Miller b Holding	1	– not out	1
M. A. Lynch c Barnett b Holding	3	– (2) c sub b Barnett	45
T. E. Jesty c Barnett b Finney	3		
†C. J. Richards c Morris b Holding	49		
G. Monkhouse c Hill b Mortensen	51		
R. J. Doughty run out	61		
M. P. Bicknell b Mortensen	2		
S. T. Clarke c Miller b Mortensen	0		
*P. I. Pocock not out	5		
B 7, l-b 11, w 1, n-b 8	27	B 1, l-b 1, n-b 2	4

1/25 2/26 3/30 4/33 5/40   223   1/79   (1 wkt) 96
6/121 7/212 8/218 9/218

Bonus points – Surrey 2, Derbyshire 4.

Bowling: *First Innings*—Holding 25–11–49–3; Mortensen 21.2–5–46–3; Finney 15–2–50–2; Miller 15–3–43–0; Barnett 4–0–17–0. *Second Innings*—Holding 5–2–17–0; Mortensen 7–1–48–0; Finney 2–0–6–0; Barnett 4.5–1–22–1; Miller 4–3–1–0.

Umpires: J. H. Harris and R. A. White.

At Nottingham, June 14, 16. SURREY lost to NOTTINGHAMSHIRE by an innings and 7 runs.

At Basingstoke, June 18, 19. SURREY lost to HAMPSHIRE by an innings and 193 runs.

At Cambridge, June 21, 23, 24. SURREY drew with CAMBRIDGE UNIVERSITY.

At Bristol, June 28, 30, July 1. SURREY lost to GLOUCESTERSHIRE by 96 runs.

At Uxbridge, July 2, 3, 4. SURREY beat MIDDLESEX by 197 runs.

SURREY v NORTHAMPTONSHIRE

At The Oval, July 5, 7, 8. Northamptonshire won by 100 runs. Northamptonshire 20 pts, Surrey 2 pts. Toss: Surrey. Two forfeitures in a rain-bedevilled match ushered Surrey to their fourth Championship defeat in five matches. Put in, Northamptonshire had been restricted to 26 overs' batting by the adverse weather on the first day, but on the second Boyd-Moss and Wild, resuming at 91 for three, engineered the initial growth and Lamb added a flourish with thirteen boundaries in a bustling 83 off 96 balls. Cook declared first thing on the final day and a flexible attitude on the part of both captains left Surrey with a target of 331. Clinton and Falkner gave them a solid start, but despite brisk efforts from Lynch and Doughty, Surrey rarely threatened to take control and Northamptonshire won with seventeen overs to spare.

Northamptonshire

*G. Cook c Ward b Doughty	32	R. A. Harper b Feltham	10
D. J. Capel b Gray	5	†S. N. V. Waterton not out	37
R. J. Boyd-Moss b Feltham	77	B 6, l-b 6, n-b 2	14
R. J. Bailey b Doughty	5		
D. J. Wild b Feltham	67	1/13 2/57 3/79 (6 wkts. dec.)	330
A. J. Lamb not out	83	4/175 5/212 6/228	

N. G. B. Cook, N. A. Mallender and A. Walker did not bat.

Bonus points – Northamptonshire 4, Surrey 2.

Bowling: Gray 23-1-66-1; Bicknell 22-1-78-0; Doughty 20-1-100-2; Feltham 18-1-74-3.

Northamptonshire forfeited their second innings.

Surrey

Surrey forfeited their first innings.

N. J. Falkner c Lamb b Wild	45	M. A. Feltham lbw b N. G. B. Cook	0
G. S. Clinton c Wild b Capel	28	A. H. Gray st Waterton b Harper	10
A. J. Stewart b Walker	18	M. P. Bicknell c G. Cook b Capel	7
M. A. Lynch c Waterton b Mallender	36	*P. I. Pocock c Walker b Capel	6
D. M. Ward c G. Cook b Harper	28	L-b 8	8
†C. J. Richards c Boyd-Moss b N. G. B. Cook	3	1/53 2/95 3/95 4/146 5/163	230
R. J. Doughty not out	41	6/163 7/165 8/199 9/220	

Bowling: Mallender 16-6-34-1; Capel 20-4-70-3; Walker 14-5-14-1; Harper 16-8-32-2; Wild 11-1-28-1; N. G. B. Cook 12-2-44-2.

Umpires: D. J. Constant and R. Palmer.

SURREY v KENT

At The Oval, July 16, 17, 18. Surrey won by 234 runs. Surrey 22 pts, Kent 6 pts. Toss: Surrey. Outstanding individual performances by Stewart, Medlycott and Gray were the basis of Surrey's comprehensive victory over their neighbours. Stewart's strength on the drive brought him ten 4s and a half-century in 54 balls on the first day, and there were 26 4s in his second-innings 166 off 233 balls, which surpassed his previous highest: 158, also off Kent's bowling. However, Surrey's 201 in their first innings was disappointing on a fast pitch on which

Igglesden bowled effectively in only his second Championship match. Kent, with eight wickets in hand, were only 80 behind them at the close, but as the surface became conducive to spin on the second morning, Surrey asserted command. Their left-arm spinner, Medlycott, turned the ball sharply to return career-best figures of six for 63, including a spell of three for 0 in fourteen balls. On the last day, Kent had to bat for at least 79 overs to save the match – or win it if someone batted like Stewart. Instead, they were devastated by the giant Gray, who loped in menacingly from the Vauxhall End to claim seven wickets. Medlycott provided ideal, contrasting support to finish with match figures of nine for 100.

Surrey

N. J. Falkner c Marsh b Igglesden	0	– c Marsh b C. S. Cowdrey	48
G. S. Clinton b C. S. Cowdrey	34	– (7) c Tavaré b Jarvis	5
A. J. Stewart lbw b C. S. Cowdrey	55	– c Marsh b Igglesden	166
M. A. Lynch c Jarvis b Igglesden	23	– (2) c Marsh b Igglesden	10
*T. E. Jesty c G. R. Cowdrey b Underwood	0	– (4) b Alderman	39
A. Needham lbw b Igglesden	0	– (5) lbw b Alderman	0
K. T. Medlycott b Alderman	0	– (6) lbw b Alderman	0
G. Monkhouse c C. S. Cowdrey b Alderman	31	– c Hinks b Underwood	24
R. J. Doughty b Underwood	24	– run out	4
A. H. Gray b Igglesden	28	– not out	4
†G. E. Brown not out	0	– not out	2
B 1, l-b 1, w 4	6	B 1, l-b 14, w 1, n-b 4	20

1/2 2/88 3/93 4/102 5/113   201   1/28 2/123 3/239   (9 wkts dec.) 322
6/114 7/114 8/158 9/197   4/239 5/245 6/278
                                                              7/294 8/311 9/319

Bonus points – Surrey 2, Kent 4.

Bowling: *First Innings*—Igglesden 17–6–46–4; Alderman 17–5–40–2; Jarvis 7–1–46–0; C. S. Cowdrey 11–3–37–2; Underwood 15–6–30–2. *Second Innings*—Igglesden 23–8–46–2; Alderman 13–4–44–3; Jarvis 16–2–72–1; Underwood 23–8–63–1; C. S. Cowdrey 10–0–48–1; Taylor 6–0–19–0; Aslett 5–1–15–0.

Kent

D. G. Aslett st Brown b Medlycott	53	– c Brown b Gray	0
S. G. Hinks c Needham b Doughty	24	– c Brown b Gray	7
C. J. Tavaré b Gray	39	– c Monkhouse b Medlycott	23
D. L. Underwood run out	29	– (10) not out	10
N. R. Taylor hit wkt b Gray	12	– (4) lbw b Medlycott	3
G. R. Cowdrey c Brown b Medlycott	13	– (5) c Brown b Gray	0
*C. S. Cowdrey c Stewart b Medlycott	8	– (6) c sub b Medlycott	16
†S. A. Marsh c Lynch b Medlycott	0	– (7) c Lynch b Gray	1
T. M. Alderman c Needham b Medlycott	25	– (8) b Gray	0
A. P. Igglesden c Gray b Medlycott	7	– (9) b Gray	0
K. B. S. Jarvis not out	0	– c Doughty b Gray	4
B 4, l-b 2, n-b 1	7	B 5, n-b 3	8

1/54 2/115 3/121 4/143 5/171   217   1/0 2/36 3/37 4/40 5/41   72
6/182 7/182 8/187 9/213   6/42 7/46 8/54 9/62

Bonus points – Kent 2, Surrey 4.

Bowling: *First Innings*—Gray 24–3–61–2; Doughty 13–1–41–1; Monkhouse 7–3–11–0; Needham 9–3–28–0; Jesty 2–1–7–0; Medlycott 22–8–63–6. *Second Innings*—Gray 10.4–3–23–7; Doughty 3–1–7–0; Medlycott 7–1–37–3.

Umpires: D. G. L. Evans and R. Julian.

At Leeds, July 19, 20, 21. SURREY lost to YORKSHIRE by seven wickets.

SURREY v ESSEX

At The Oval, July 23, 24, 25. Drawn. Surrey 8 pts, Essex 5 pts. Toss: Surrey. Jesty returned to
his best form in the most magnificent manner after four cyphers in his previous seven visits to
the crease. But his first Championship double-hundred was countered on the last day by
Border's phlegmatic century, which steered Essex clear of defeat despite the constant threat of
Gray. Border's 52 stabilised Essex as they reached 243 for nine on a rain-curtailed first day,
but their 250 was unceremoniously swamped when Jesty cut loose on the second day. He hit
two 6s and 34 4s in 269 balls, and Stewart and Lynch also displayed their handsome strokes as
Surrey swept to maximum batting points in just 68 overs. They declared late in the day with a
lead of 198, and when they had Essex 92 for three with 67 overs remaining, victory beckoned.
Border, however, found a reliable ally in Hardie, who helped the Australian captain add 101
and, more important, use up 27 overs. Border batted in all for 62 overs and Surrey eventually
acknowledged the draw with ten overs still available.

Essex

C. Gladwin c Richards b Doughty	0	– lbw b Doughty	5
J. P. Stephenson c Monkhouse b Gray	23	– c Stewart b Thomas	35
P. J. Prichard c Hardie b Gray	34	– c Medlycott b Gray	13
A. R. Border c Richards b Thomas	52	– b Medlycott	138
*B. R. Hardie run out	12	– c Stewart b Gray	25
N. D. Burns c sub b Thomas	18	– c Stewart b Gray	7
†D. E. East c Monkhouse b Gray	38	– c Stewart b Thomas	4
S. Turner c Lynch b Monkhouse	32	– not out	25
I. L. Pont not out	14	– not out	1
T. D. Topley b Gray	0		
J. K. Lever run out	8		
L-b 6, w 1, n-b 12	19	L-b 4, w 1, n-b 18	23

1/12 2/41 3/95 4/120 5/143   250   1/18 2/41 3/92 4/193   (7 wkts) 276
6/155 7/210 8/233 9/234   5/209 6/228 7/262

Bonus points – Essex 3, Surrey 4.

Bowling: *First Innings*—Gray 28–9–50–4; Doughty 10–0–70–1; Thomas 12–2–44–2;
Monkhouse 27.2–8–57–1; Needham 15–8–16–0; Medlycott 3–0–7–0. *Second Innings*—Gray
24–2–73–3; Monkhouse 9–4–16–0; Doughty 11–1–40–1; Thomas 13–1–44–2; Needham
6–1–22–0; Medlycott 21–2–69–1; Lynch 3–0–8–0.

Surrey

A. Needham c Hardie b Lever	3	D. J. Thomas not out	0
N. J. Falkner c Hardie b Topley	5		
A. J. Stewart c Hardie b Topley	67	B 2, l-b 20, n-b 5	27
*T. E. Jesty run out	221		
M. A. Lynch c Stephenson b Turner	85	1/4 2/16 3/186 (5 wkts dec.) 448
†C. J. Richards not out	40	4/359 5/426	

G. Monkhouse, R. J. Doughty, K. T. Medlycott and A. H. Gray did not bat.

Bonus points – Surrey 4, Essex 2.

Bowling: Lever 25–1–124–1; Topley 26–3–140–2; Turner 21–5–72–1; Pont 14–0–62–0;
Border 9–1–28–0.

Umpires: D. G. L. Evans and N. T. Plews.

SURREY v SUSSEX

At Guildford, July 26, 28, 29. Surrey won by five wickets. Surrey 22 pts, Sussex 4 pts. Toss:
Sussex. Surrey's fifth Championship win lifted them four places to third in the table and was a
personal triumph for their talented opening batsman, Falkner. His 95 in 129 balls was the
basis of their first innings and a bristling 68 (two 6s, six 4s) from 83 deliveries set up the

victory after Surrey had been set to score 248 in two and three-quarter hours. Imran and Gould both scored half-centuries after Clarke's considerable pace had claimed the top three Sussex wickets, and following persistent drizzle on the second day, Surrey declared 94 runs behind on the third morning in expectation of a target. Gould, the Sussex captain, responded with imagination. At first le Roux gave Sussex the advantage, but the issue was put beyond doubt as Falkner and Lynch exploited the short boundaries to add 89 in 49 minutes.

Sussex

R. I. Alikhan b Clarke	7	– c and b Medlycott	40
A. M. Green c Jesty b Clarke	15	– c Clarke b Bicknell	28
P. W. G. Parker b Clarke	4	– c and b Medlycott	39
Imran Khan c and b Medlycott	55	– b Falkner	24
C. M. Wells c Lynch b Thomas	26	– b Medlycott	0
A. P. Wells b Medlycott	33	– c Bicknell b Lynch	17
N. J. Lenham c Falkner b Bicknell	41	– not out	0
*†I. J. Gould c Richards b Bicknell	54		
G. S. le Roux c Jesty b Bicknell	36		
D. A. Reeve lbw b Clarke	9		
C. S. Mays not out	0		
B 3, l-b 5, w 3, n-b 3	14	B 1, w 1, n-b 3	5

1/23 2/28 3/29 4/78 5/144   294   1/48 2/97 3/114   (6 wkts dec.) 153
6/151 7/240 8/247 9/294   4/114 5/147 6/153

Bonus points – Sussex 3, Surrey 4.

Bowling: *First Innings*—Clarke 22.3-7-60-4; Thomas 21-6-52-1; Bicknell 20-7-41-3; Pocock 18-2-66-0; Medlycott 16-2-67-2. *Second Innings*—Clarke 5-0-22-0; Thomas 7-1-29-0; Bicknell 5-1-18-1; Pocock 5-0-20-0; Medlycott 10-5-19-3; Lynch 4.2-1-18-1; Falkner 3-1-3-1; Jesty 11-4-23-0.

Surrey

N. J. Falkner c le Roux b Reeve	95	– c Lenham b Mays	68
G. S. Clinton b Reeve	31	– b le Roux	12
A. J. Stewart c Gould b le Roux	7	– lbw b le Roux	12
T. E. Jesty not out	27	– c Mays b le Roux	1
M. A. Lynch not out	28	– b Mays	63
†C. J. Richards (did not bat)	–	not out	35
D. J. Thomas (did not bat)	–	not out	45
B 1, l-b 8, n-b 3	12	B 3, l-b 8, n-b 2	13

1/119 2/140 3/140   (3 wkts dec.) 200   1/30 2/50 3/55   (5 wkts) 249
                                                      4/144 5/170

M. P. Bicknell, K. T. Medlycott, S. T. Clarke and *P. I. Pocock did not bat.

Bonus points – Surrey 2, Sussex 1.

Bowling: *First Innings*—Imran 15-1-55-0; le Roux 15-4-57-1; Mays 3-0-8-0; Reeve 14-1-53-2; C. M. Wells 3-1-12-0; Alikhan 1-0-4-0; A. P. Wells 1-1-0-0; Green 0.2-0-2-0. *Second Innings*—Imran 11-0-45-0; le Roux 9-1-27-3; Reeve 10-0-60-0; C. M. Wells 3-0-39-0; Mays 7.5-0-62-2; Green 2-0-5-0.

Umpires: D. J. Constant and A. A. Jones.

SURREY v LANCASHIRE

At The Oval, August 6, 7, 8. Surrey won by two wickets. Surrey 21 pts, Lancashire 5 pts. Toss: Lancashire. With Lancashire troubled by injuries, at one time requiring three substitute fielders on the last day, the demanding target of 295 in 52 overs set by Simmons was understandable in view of his limited bowling resources. However, a sustained spell of hitting won the match for Surrey with seven balls to spare and strengthened their hold on third place in the Championship. On the first day, Lancashire were inhibited by a pitch which allowed generous deviation, especially for the lively Feltham, who claimed three of the first five wickets. Abrahams batted for two and a half hours for his 28. That Lancashire took a first-innings lead of 2 runs was due largely to Simmons's three wickets in seventeen balls at the end of a Surrey innings which had been shored up by Lynch's 72 (one 6, twelve 4s). After Fowler and Mendis had given Lancashire a good start, the persevering Abrahams spent three and three-quarter hours making an unbeaten 81 to achieve what they estimated were sufficient runs. The calculations were upset by a sparkling stand of 138 in 23 overs between Stewart and Jesty, including 92 in their first twelve, which left Lancashire seeking their first victory at The Oval after a quarter-century of trying.

Lancashire

G. D. Mendis c Lynch b Thomas	2	– c Lynch b Feltham	25
G. Fowler c Richards b Feltham	20	– lbw b Pocock	68
J. Abrahams c Lynch b Clarke	28	– not out	81
N. H. Fairbrother b Feltham	0	– (5) c Richards b Pocock	55
S. J. O'Shaughnessy run out	43		
*J. Simmons c Stewart b Feltham	23	– not out	36
M. Watkinson c Medlycott b Clarke	29		
P. J. W. Allott b Clarke	5		
I. Folley lbw b Feltham	13	– (4) b Clarke	5
†J. Stanworth not out	11		
B. P. Patterson c Butcher b Clarke	0		
B 4, l-b 4, n-b 10	18	B 14, l-b 3, n-b 5	22

1/10 2/37 3/38 4/82 5/112   192   1/82 2/115 3/127   (4 wkts dec.) 292
6/140 7/158 8/165 9/191   4/212

Bonus points – Lancashire 1, Surrey 4.

Bowling: *First Innings*—Clarke 24.5–7–51–4; Feltham 17–4–47–4; Thomas 8–1–23–1; Monkhouse 23–9–52–0; Pocock 3–2–1–0; Medlycott 7–4–10–0. *Second Innings*—Clarke 17–5–36–1; Thomas 12–4–34–0; Feltham 14–2–52–1; Pocock 28–13–36–2; Medlycott 27–7–117–0.

Surrey

A. R. Butcher b Patterson	11	– c Fairbrother b Simmons	26
G. Monkhouse retired hurt	7		
A. J. Stewart lbw b Allott	13	– c Watkinson b Patterson	69
M. A. Lynch lbw b Simmons	72	– (5) b Folley	7
T. E. Jesty c sub b Folley	24	– (4) c Folley	71
†C. J. Richards c Stanworth b Patterson	33	– not out	46
D. J. Thomas c sub b Simmons	0	– (2) c and b Patterson	10
M. A. Feltham c Stanworth b Simmons	0	– (7) c sub b Watkinson	15
K. T. Medlycott c Simmons b Patterson	5	– c sub b Simmons	5
S. T. Clarke c sub b Simmons	13	– (8) c Abrahams b Simmons	29
*P. I. Pocock not out	0	– (10) not out	0
B 4, l-b 5, n-b 3	12	B 5, l-b 9, w 2, n-b 1	17

1/14 2/31 3/124 4/140 5/142   190   1/33 2/47 3/185 4/185   (8 wkts) 295
6/146 7/171 8/190 9/190   5/194 6/217 7/283 8/294

Bonus points – Surrey 1, Lancashire 4.

Bowling: *First Innings*—Patterson 15.1–0–80–3; Allott 8–4–20–1; O'Shaughnessy 8–1–22–0; Watkinson 3–1–7–0; Folley 9–3–31–1; Simmons 11–4–21–4. *Second Innings*—Patterson 16–1–99–2; Watkinson 11–0–64–1; Simmons 10.5–1–56–3; Folley 13–2–62–2.

Umpires: J. H. Harris and B. J. Meyer.

SURREY v WORCESTERSHIRE

At The Oval, August 9, 11, 12. Drawn. Surrey 6 pts, Worcestershire 6 pts. Toss: Surrey. A pitch devoid of malice, the unsettled weather, and high-class batting combined to leave this match with rarely a scent of a result. Curtis opened Worcestershire's account solidly and by the afternoon the platform was there for Patel to cut loose stylishly with an unbeaten 132, his second fifty needing only 28 balls as he and Rhodes took their sixth-wicket partnership to 191 from 37 overs before Neale's declaration on Saturday evening. Clinton was quickly dislodged, but on Monday Surrey's night-watchman, Feltham, stood them in good stead for sixteen overs. Any chance of the follow-on was comfortably averted as Jesty, in a rich vein of form, hit his second century of the summer and, assisted by Lynch's fourth fifty in six innings, saw Surrey to 286 for four before poor light and rain cut into the last session. Jesty went on to 179 on the final day, his boundaries made up of two 6s and 21 4s, and with the tenor of the match favouring a draw, Pocock extended Surrey's innings to 500 for nine, the highest total by any side during the summer. Thereafter, Curtis and Smith enjoyed some batting practice.

Worcestershire

T. S. Curtis c Lynch b Gray	51	– not out	64
D. B. D'Oliveira b Butcher	42		
D. M. Smith c Lynch b Butcher	34	– not out	42
G. A. Hick b Medlycott	31		
*P. A. Neale c Richards b Medlycott	5		
D. N. Patel not out	132		
†S. J. Rhodes not out	67	– (2) c Lynch b Feltham	2
B 2, l-b 9, w 1, n-b 7	19	B 2, l-b 8, n-b 5	15

1/80 2/119 3/172 4/172 5/190   (5 wkts dec.) 381   1/26   (1 wkt) 123

P. J. Newport, N. V. Radford, A. P. Pridgeon and S. M. McEwan did not bat.

Bonus points – Worcestershire 4, Surrey 2.

Bowling: *First Innings*—Gray 21-8-57-1; Thomas 11.3-0-71-0; Feltham 16-0-69-0; Butcher 13-2-40-2; Pocock 17-4-56-0; Medlycott 18-4-77-2. *Second Innings*—Gray 8-1-27-0; Thomas 9-1-33-0; Feltham 7-1-16-1; Medlycott 7-3-17-0; Pocock 2-1-6-0; Stewart 2-0-8-0; Lynch 2-1-6-0.

Surrey

A. R. Butcher c Pridgeon b Newport	45	K. T. Medlycott c Rhodes b Smith	0
G. S. Clinton b Pridgeon	2	A. H. Gray not out	12
M. A. Feltham c Hick b Newport	16	*P. I. Pocock not out	16
A. J. Stewart c Rhodes b Pridgeon	24	B 7, l-b 20, w 1, n-b 7	35
T. E. Jesty c Pridgeon b Newport	179		
M. A. Lynch c Rhodes b Newport	77	1/8 2/73 3/79	(9 wkts dec.) 500
†C. J. Richards c Hick b Smith	60	4/112 5/305 6/424	
D. J. Thomas c sub b Hick	34	7/464 8/464 9/474	

Bonus points – Surrey 4, Worcestershire 2 (Score at 100 overs: 334-5).

Bowling: Radford 10-2-27-0; Pridgeon 15-4-41-2; McEwan 19-4-89-0; Newport 36-0-136-4; Patel 24-7-71-0; Hick 20.4-4-74-1; Smith 10-2-35-2.

Umpires: J. H. Harris and B. J. Meyer.

At Taunton, August 16, 18, 19. SURREY beat SOMERSET by 178 runs.

At Dartford, August 20, 21, 22. SURREY drew with KENT.

At Chelmsford, August 23, 25, 26. SURREY drew with ESSEX.

At Swansea, August 27, 28, 29. SURREY drew with GLAMORGAN.

SURREY v GLOUCESTERSHIRE

At The Oval, September 3, 4, 5. Drawn. Surrey 7 pts, Gloucestershire 7 pts. Toss: Surrey. Essex's victory over Kent the previous day left Surrey and Gloucestershire without a chance of winning the Championship. Second place was the best prize available and Surrey gained an early chance of attaining that objective by putting Gloucestershire in on a well-grassed pitch. In such conditions, Clarke provided chilling opposition, although Athey, scoring profitably off his legs, and Lloyds made a positive response in Gloucestershire's 252 for eight in the 72 overs permitted by the weather on the first day. In a bizarre start to Surrey's first innings, only four overs were bowled in half an hour as Clinton retired with a damaged elbow, Jesty and two fielders were also injured, and Stewart, Butcher and Lynch were dismissed off successive balls, all caught by Russell – a feat performed only once before; by G. O. Dawkes for Derbyshire against Worcestershire in 1958. Russell having earlier scored 71, it was a memorable match for the Gloucestershire wicket-keeper. However, his counterpart, Richards, restored Surrey with a splendid century in 124 balls and Feltham hit a career-best 76. Curran took advantage of a varied attack to hit a robust hundred in 128 minutes on the last day and Graveney gave his bowlers at least 47 overs to win the match. Some outstanding catching precipitated a struggle for Surrey and it was left to Stewart to plot a course to safety. However, Surrey's chance of finishing runners-up had vanished.

Gloucestershire

P. W. Romaines b Clarke	0	– b Feltham	25
K. P. Tomlins lbw b Bicknell	16	– (6) not out	53
C. W. J. Athey c Lynch b Doughty	76	– c Richards b Clarke	2
P. Bainbridge b Clarke	5	– c Richards b Clarke	17
A. W. Stovold lbw b Feltham	20	– (2) c Richards b Clarke	55
K. M. Curran b Feltham	6	– (5) not out	103
J. W. Lloyds c Stewart b Butcher	66		
†R. C. Russell c Richards b Bicknell	71		
C. A. Walsh lbw b Clarke	0		
*D. A. Graveney not out	17		
D. V. Lawrence c and b Medlycott	0		
B 6, l-b 10, w 3, n-b 1	20	B 1, l-b 1, w 4, n-b 8	14

1/2 2/41 3/69 4/102 5/114   **297**   1/78 2/88 3/88   **(4 wkts dec.) 269**
6/136 7/221 8/232 9/296   4/127

Bonus points – Gloucestershire 3, Surrey 4.

Bowling: *First Innings*—Clarke 26–3–81–3; Bicknell 17–4–38–2; Feltham 22–4–75–2; Doughty 9–1–49–1; Medlycott 3.5–0–21–1; Butcher 6–0–17–1. *Second Innings*—Clarke 15–3–30–3; Feltham 10–1–36–1; Bicknell 7–0–32–0; Medlycott 22–5–62–0; Doughty 7–0–37–0; Jesty 2–1–1–0; Lynch 7–0–30–0; Butcher 3–0–32–0; Clinton 1–0–7–0.

Surrey

*A. R. Butcher c Russell b Lawrence	2	– c Tomlins b Walsh	0
G. S. Clinton retired hurt	0	– c Walsh b Lawrence	1
A. J. Stewart c Russell b Walsh	3	– not out	86
T. E. Jesty b Bainbridge	7	– c Lloyds b Walsh	38
M. A. Lynch c Russell b Lawrence	0	– c Graveney b Walsh	4
†C. J. Richards c Curran b Walsh	115	– c and b Walsh	0
M. A. Feltham c Athey b Lloyds	76	– c Athey b Lawrence	18
K. T. Medlycott c Russell b Walsh	0	– not out	23
R. J. Doughty b Walsh	25		
S. T. Clarke b Walsh	22		
M. P. Bicknell not out	1		
L-b 3, n-b 2	5	B 8, l-b 7, w 1, n-b 5	21

1/5 2/5 3/5 4/40 5/194   **256**   1/0 2/2 3/70 4/79   **(6 wkts) 191**
6/194 7/219 8/243 9/256   5/83 6/127

Bonus points – Surrey 3, Gloucestershire 4.

Bowling: *First Innings*—Walsh 20.3–4–61–5; Lawrence 17–0–79–2; Bainbridge 8–0–34–1; Curran 5–0–19–0; Lloyds 12–2–60–1. *Second Innings*—Walsh 17.3–1–67–4; Lawrence 9–3–44–2; Bainbridge 5–1–23–0; Graveney 10–6–12–0; Curran 3–0–20–0; Lloyds 2–0–10–0.

Umpires: R. Palmer and N. T. Plews.

SURREY v LEICESTERSHIRE

At The Oval, September 13, 15, 16. Surrey won by 90 runs. Surrey 19 pts, Leicestershire 1 pt. Toss: Surrey. In sixth position and in danger of being excluded from the Championship prize-money for the second successive summer, Surrey gained from two forfeitures in this rain-swept match. Their prospects were far from optimistic when the weather restricted their progress to 53 for two on the first day and to 104 for two on the second, which contained only 35 minutes' play. However, a full third day gave Surrey their chance. Stewart and Jesty added 80 from nineteen overs in the first hour, and after DeFreitas dismissed both of them in quick succession, Richards struck an unbeaten half-century, full of firm, confident strokes, to pass 1,000 runs in a season for the first time. Leicestershire forfeited their first innings and Surrey their second to leave the visitors requiring 271 in 64 overs. Three early wickets by Bicknell had Surrey sensing victory, spinners Pocock and Medlycott kept up the pressure, and they were held up only by a characteristically defiant 76 from Willey before Leicestershire were bowled out in the 59th over.

Surrey

G. S. Clinton c Whitticase b DeFreitas .	11	D. M. Ward not out		26
M. A. Lynch b Taylor	17	B 6, l-b 8, n-b 11		25
A. J. Stewart c Potter b DeFreitas	81			
T. E. Jesty c Whitaker b DeFreitas	56	1/31 2/53 3/178	(4 wkts dec.)	270
†C. J. Richards not out	54	4/187		

M. A. Feltham, K. T. Medlycott, A. H. Gray, M. P. Bicknell and *P. I. Pocock did not bat.

Bonus points – Surrey 3, Leicestershire 1.

Bowling: Taylor 12–4–36–1; DeFreitas 24–1–66–3; Ferris 13–1–64–0; Tennant 4–0–24–0; Willey 13–1–49–0; Boon 2–0–17–0.

Surrey forfeited their second innings.

Leicestershire

Leicestershire forfeited their first innings

J. C. Balderstone lbw b Gray	7	L. Tennant run out		1
R. A. Cobb c Richards b Bicknell	5	G. J. F. Ferris not out		17
*P. Willey c Feltham b Gray	76	L. B. Taylor c Lynch b Medlycott		13
J. J. Whitaker c Richards b Bicknell	11			
T. J. Boon c Stewart b Bicknell	3	B 7, l-b 2		9
L. Potter c Lynch b Pocock	8			
P. A. J. DeFreitas lbw b Pocock	6	1/12 2/24 3/39 4/45 5/73		180
†P. Whitticase st Richards b Pocock	24	6/99 7/143 8/147 9/157		

Bowling: Gray 16–6–32–2; Bicknell 7–3–27–3; Feltham 4–2–10–0; Medlycott 13.2–4–36–1; Pocock 18–0–66–3.

Umpires: J. H. Hampshire and J. A. Jameson.

SUSSEX

President: A. M. Caffyn
Chairman: R. M. Leadley
Chairman, Cricket & Ground Sub-Committee:
　　D. J. Church
Secretary: R. H. Renold
　　County Ground, Eaton Road,
　　Hove BN3 3AN
　　(Telephone: 0273-732161)
Captain: 1986 – J. R. T. Barclay
　　　　　1987 – I. J. Gould
Coach: S. J. Storey

Sussex finished the season with a flourish, beating Lancashire decisively and handsomely at Lord's to win the NatWest Bank Trophy for the first time and record their fourth victory in seven appearances in the final of the 60-overs competition. All very exciting, this grand finale none the less tended to cover over the cracks of a disappointing performance in the Britannic Assurance Championship, the county slumping from seventh in 1985 to a place dangerously near the bottom of the table. Fourth place in the John Player League, to accompany the NatWest success, gave a fair indication of where Sussex's talents lay.

It was not a lucky season for John Barclay, the captain, who took a benefit in 1986. A serious finger injury kept him out of action for almost all of the summer, and having handed over the captaincy of the team to Ian Gould, while remaining on hand to offer willing advice as club captain, he later announced his retirement. Barclay first played for Sussex as a talented sixteen-year-old whose batting for Eton was making a favourable impression, and he proved a knowledgeable and enthusiastic captain. He scored 1,000 runs in a season four times, with a highest score of 119 against Leicestershire at Hove in 1980, while his off-spin bowling brought him 324 wickets, including a best return of six for 61 against the Sri Lankans in 1979.

Imran Khan, who will be touring with the Pakistan team in 1987, as well as taking his Sussex benefit, proved yet again his class and all-round ability, heading both the batting and the bowling averages. He played many thrilling innings and produced some stirring bowling, especially going flat out down the Hove slope and notably at Lord's, where Sussex beat Middlesex by seven wickets. Imran took eight for 34 in the second innings, between scoring 60 and 43 not out.

The seam support for Imran was strong, comprising Garth le Roux, still a formidable competitor, the sharpish Adrian Jones, whose season was troubled by injury, Tony Pigott, Colin Wells and Dermot Reeve. But of spinners there were none. Chris Waller had returned to The Oval to coach, and although such youngsters as Andy Bredin, slow left-arm, and the former Lancing College off-spinner, Chris Mays, were tried, Sussex were essentially a pace-bowling outfit. A successful formula in limited-overs games, the all-seam attack proved expensive in fines for slow over-rates. But this should not be the sole reason for the county's search for a top-class spinner. Without one, Sussex lack the balance to challenge for the Championship.

Paul Parker was the leading run-scorer with 1,595 runs, hitting six hundreds and eight fifties, delighting all with his fine strokeplay. But the only other batsman to pass 1,000 runs in the Championship was the opening batsman, Allan Green, who played many neat and composed innings. He was particularly severe on the Glamorgan bowling with centuries in the Championship and second round of the NatWest Trophy. Rehan Alikhan, drafted into the side from club cricket, lent stability to the top-order batting. Green was again a smart and fearless fieldsman close to the bat, while Parker shone as always in the covers.

Gould handled the captaincy very ably, fully deserving the emotional moment of receiving a trophy on the balcony of the Pavilion at Lord's. In addition to his usual bag of dismissals, he held a respectable position in the batting averages and hit seven half-centuries in all competitions. To his obvious delight – evidenced by a lively cartwheel – he took two wickets against Derbyshire at Eastbourne when an injury kept him from keeping wicket. A week later, Gould split the muscle sheath over his hip bone, and while he was out of action, his place behind the stumps was filled with much aplomb by the Hurstpierpoint College captain, Martin Speight.

Pigott filled second place in the batting averages, following an unbeaten maiden century at Edgbaston, and was fourth in the bowling averages behind 23-year-old Andy Babington, whose nine wickets included a hat-trick at Bristol. Reeve, the Man of the Match at Lord's, was the leading wicket-taker, but worryingly was the only one to capture more than 50. Colin Wells, dependable as ever, maintained with his promising younger brother, Alan, Sussex's remarkable family record, as did Neil Lenham, son of the former opening batsman, Les. More than 40 pairs of brothers have played for Sussex, while the Lenhams follow, among others, the Tates, Langridges, Coxes and Parks.

The Championship fixture at Horsham against Somerset was abandoned without a ball bowled, the first time this has happened at the attractive rural ground. However, play, albeit abbreviated, was possible in the John Player game, thanks to the Horsham club's enthusiastic president, Dr John Dew, and his band of helpers, who pumped more than 1,000 gallons of water into the nearby river. It had been raining, Dr Dew reported, for eighteen hours.

It was learned that the Central Ground at Hastings is to become a shopping complex, and within a few years matches will be played at Summerfields, a new ground described as a "major step forward" by a Hastings councillor. Among those with fond memories of the Central Ground will be Kent's Derek Underwood, who scored his maiden century there in 1984, having twenty years earlier demoralised Sussex with a remarkable bowling performance of nine for 28.

The day after their NatWest triumph at Lord's, Sussex beat Yorkshire to maintain their interest in the John Player League prizemoney. It was disappointing, though, to see only a small crowd at Hove to celebrate their success. When Brighton and Hove Albion were beaten by Manchester United in the 1983 FA Cup final, they were cheered by thousands as they paraded around the town. Sussex followers are equally proud of their team, but in a less demonstrative fashion, it seems. – J.A.

569

SUSSEX 1986

[*Bill Smith*]

Back row: N. J. Lenham, A. M. Bredin, D. K. Standing, A. M. Green. *Middle row*: C. P. Cale (*assistant coach*), I. C. Waring, A. N. Jones, D. A. Reeve, P. Moores, A. P. Wells, S. J. Storey (*coach*). *Front row*: P. W. G. Parker, A. C. S. Pigott, C. M. Wells, J. R. T. Barclay (*captain*), I. J. Gould, C. P. Phillipson, G. S. le Roux. *Insets*: R. I. Alikhan, C. S. Mays, Imran Khan, A. M. Babington.

SUSSEX RESULTS

All first-class matches – Played 25: Won 4, Lost 7, Drawn 14. Abandoned 1.

County Championship matches – Played 23: Won 4, Lost 7, Drawn 12. Abandoned 1.

Bonus points – Batting 46, Bowling 56.

Competition placings – Britannic Assurance County Championship, 14th; NatWest Bank Trophy, winners; Benson and Hedges Cup, q-f; John Player League, 4th.

BRITANNIC ASSURANCE CHAMPIONSHIP AVERAGES

BATTING

	Birthplace	M	I	NO	R	HI	Avge
‡Imran Khan	Lahore, Pakistan	10	17	3	729	135*	52.07
‡A. C. S. Pigott	London	18	18	6	572	104*	47.66
‡P. W. G. Parker . .	Bulawayo, S. Rhodesia	23	40	5	1,459	125	41.68
‡C. M. Wells	Newhaven	22	36	8	994	106	35.50
R. I. Alikhan	London	16	26	3	808	72	35.13
‡A. P. Wells	Newhaven	21	32	6	842	150*	32.38
‡I. J. Gould	Slough	18	23	5	561	78*	31.16
‡G. S. le Roux	Cape Town, SA	14	16	6	298	72*	29.80
‡A. M. Green	Pulborough	23	42	3	1,106	179	28.35
‡D. A. Reeve	Kowloon, Hong Kong	18	21	9	307	51	25.58
N. J. Lenham	Worthing	17	28	3	544	77	21.76
D. K. Standing	Brighton	15	22	1	321	65	15.28
‡A. N. Jones	Woking	11	10	3	55	13	7.85
A. M. Bredin	Wimbledon	6	6	2	26	8*	6.50
C. S. Mays	Brighton	7	6	2	19	8*	4.75

Also batted: A. M. Babington (*London*) (5 matches) 1, 0*, 0; ‡J. R. T. Barclay (*Bonn, WG*) (2 matches) 4, 28, 4; C. P. Phillipson (*Brindaban, India*) (1 match) 6; A. M. G. Scott (*Guildford*) (1 match) 0; M. P. Speight (*Walsall*) (5 matches) 4, 17.

* *Signifies not out.* ‡ *Denotes county cap.*

The following played a total of twelve three-figure innings for Sussex in County Championship matches: P. W. G. Parker 5, A. M. Green 2, Imran Khan 2, A. C. S. Pigott 1, A. P. Wells 1, C. M. Wells 1.

BOWLING

	O	M	R	W	BB	Avge
Imran Khan	294.3	62	825	33	8-34	25.00
D. A. Reeve	508.5	127	1,368	51	5-32	26.82
A. C. S. Pigott	379	47	1,327	48	5-50	27.64
A. N. Jones	171	26	620	21	3-36	29.52
C. M. Wells	415.2	93	1,263	36	4-23	35.08
G. S. le Roux	303.2	66	928	26	3-27	35.69

Also bowled: R. I. Alikhan 10–0–65–0; A. M. Babington 83.5–11–242–9; J. R. T. Barclay 13–2–65–0; A. M. Bredin 84–20–316–6; I. J. Gould 18.3–0–96–2; A. M. Green 170.1–25–574–7; N. J. Lenham 131–25–409–9; C. S. Mays 170.5–38–561–9; P. W. G. Parker 2–1–4–0; A. M. G. Scott 17–3–70–1; D. K. Standing 156–37–451–2; A. P. Wells 11–1–43–1.

Hat-trick: A. M. Babington v Gloucestershire at Bristol.

Wicket-keepers: I. J. Gould 33 ct; M. P. Speight 6 ct.

Leading Fielders: P. W. G. Parker 18; substitutes 12.

SUSSEX v LANCASHIRE

At Hove, April 26, 27, 28. Lancashire won by nine wickets. Lancashire 24 pts, Sussex 2 pts.
Toss: Sussex. The pitch looked slightly green when Barclay put Lancashire in, but Fowler,
captaining Lancashire in the absence of Lloyd and Simmons, played soundly, hitting 28 4s in
his first Championship hundred since his double-hundred against Kent in July 1984. He and
Fairbrother put on 234 of Lancashire's 331 for four on the first day, and there was little
evidence of help for the bowlers when O'Shaughnessy and Abrahams added 100 in an hour
and a half before the declaration. Yet Sussex, against Patterson and especially Allott in lively
form, were 157 for nine when bad light brought an early close to the second day. Parker batted
attractively for three hours when Sussex followed on, striking confident square cuts and
sweetly timed cover drives, but Allott again bowled demandingly and Watkinson claimed five
wickets with his off-breaks to end Sussex's rearguard action. Needing only 23 to win,
Lancashire reached their target with four of the available nine overs in hand.

Lancashire

G. D. Mendis c Barclay b le Roux	0	– not out 11
*G. Fowler c le Roux b C. M. Wells	180	– c Green b Jones 0
D. W. Varey c Standing b Reeve	25	– not out 11
N. H. Fairbrother c C. M. Wells b Reeve	84	
S. J. O'Shaughnessy not out	50	
J. Abrahams not out	73	
L-b 12, n-b 7	19	L-b 1 1

1/6 2/60 3/294 4/298   (4 wkts dec.) 431   1/4   (1 wkt) 23

M. Watkinson, D. J. Makinson, †C. Maynard, P. J. W. Allott and B. P. Patterson did not bat.

Bonus points – Lancashire 4, Sussex 1 (Score at 100 overs: 311-4).

Bowling: *First Innings*—le Roux 20–7–37–1; Jones 22–5–80–0; Reeve 35–7–99–2; C. M.
Wells 30–8–88–1; Barclay 13–2–65–0; Standing 12–1–50–0. *Second Innings*—le Roux
3–0–19–0; Jones 2–0–3–1.

Sussex

N. J. Lenham b Patterson	1	– b Allott 22
A. M. Green c Maynard b Allott	35	– c Watkinson b Patterson 27
P. W. G. Parker b Patterson	8	– b Allott 78
C. M. Wells c Fowler b Patterson	7	– c O'Shaughnessy b Watkinson .. 17
A. P. Wells c Maynard b Makinson	5	– c Varey b Patterson 10
D. K. Standing lbw b Allott	15	– b Watkinson 14
*J. R. T. Barclay c O'Shaughnessy b Allott	4	– lbw b Makinson 28
†I. J. Gould c Abrahams b Makinson	32	– c O'Shaughnessy b Watkinson .. 42
G. S. le Roux b Allott	34	– c Abrahams b Watkinson 22
D. A. Reeve not out	7	– c O'Shaughnessy b Watkinson .. 1
A. N. Jones c Makinson b Allott	2	– not out 4
L-b 5, n-b 5	10	B 9, l-b 10, n-b 9 28

1/4 2/33 3/47 4/58 5/62   160   1/43 2/59 3/112 4/126 5/159   293
6/69 7/108 8/148 9/155   6/190 7/247 8/269 9/272

Bonus points – Sussex 1, Lancashire 4.

Bowling: *First Innings*—Patterson 13–2–55–3; Allott 17–4–32–5; Makinson 11–4–36–2;
Watkinson 13–6–32–0. *Second Innings*—Patterson 15–3–62–2; Allott 20–4–54–2; Makinson
13–1–48–1; Watkinson 26.1–5–90–5; O'Shaughnessy 9–2–20–0.

Umpires: D. J. Constant and R. Palmer.

At Leeds, May 7, 8, 9. SUSSEX lost to YORKSHIRE by one wicket.

SUSSEX v SURREY

At Hove, May 21, 22, 23. Drawn. Sussex 4 pts, Surrey 4 pts. Toss: Sussex. Play was possible only on the second day when Surrey, put in, built up a formidable total. Clinton played a sheet-anchor innings of 98, hitting fourteen 4s, while the more enterprising Lynch had ten 4s in his 59 from 63 balls. Babington, on his début for Sussex, made a good impression with his wholehearted pace bowling, conceding only 39 runs in fifteen overs. Sussex had already lost Lenham and Parker when umpires Hampshire and Shepherd made their final excursion to the damp square.

Surrey

A. R. Butcher lbw b Reeve	50	G. Monkhouse not out	34
G. S. Clinton c Babington b Bredin	98	S. T. Clarke c A. P. Wells b Pigott	4
A. J. Stewart lbw b Reeve	37	*P. I. Pocock c Reeve b Green	14
M. A. Lynch c Babington b C. M. Wells	59		
T. E. Jesty c A. P. Wells b C. M. Wells	6	L-b 9, n-b 4	13
A. Needham c Reeve b Bredin	18		
†C. J. Richards c Bredin b Pigott	18	1/81 2/141 3/221 4/240 5/275	365
R. J. Doughty c Gould b Reeve	14	6/280 7/297 8/316 9/320	

Bonus points – Surrey 4, Sussex 4 (Score at 100 overs: 357-9).

Bowling: Pigott 17-0-68-2; Babington 15-2-39-0; C. M. Wells 18-5-62-2; Reeve 22-4-83-3; Bredin 25-7-80-2; Standing 2-0-11-0; Green 2-0-13-1.

Sussex

N. J. Lenham c Doughty b Clarke 1
A. M. Green not out 23
P. W. G. Parker c Clarke b Doughty .. 3
C. M. Wells not out 10
    L-b 1 1

1/6 2/9   (2 wkts) 38

A. P. Wells, D. K. Standing, *†I. J. Gould, D. A. Reeve, A. C. S. Pigott, A. M. Babington and A. M. Bredin did not bat.

Bowling: Clarke 5-3-7-1; Doughty 3-0-12-1; Clinton 2-1-5-0; Stewart 1-0-13-0.

Umpires: J. H. Hampshire and D. R. Shepherd.

At Lord's, May 24, 26, 27. SUSSEX beat MIDDLESEX by seven wickets.

SUSSEX v SOMERSET

At Horsham, May 31, June 2, 3. Abandoned.

At Tunbridge Wells, June 4, 5, 6. SUSSEX drew with KENT.

SUSSEX v LEICESTERSHIRE

At Hove, June 7, 9, 10. Leicestershire won by 21 runs. Leicestershire 22 pts, Sussex 4 pts. Toss: Leicestershire. The lively seam bowling of Leicestershire's DeFreitas, who undid the Sussex cause with four wickets for 8 runs in fifteen balls, and the robust batting of the Wells brothers were the principal ingredients of an interesting last day. There were a dozen cracking 4s and a fiercely struck 6 in Alan Wells's 76, but when he became DeFreitas's fifth victim Sussex were still 42 runs short of their target of 278 with only the last-wicket pair remaining. With Gill injured, I. P. Butcher kept wicket for Leicestershire. During the match, Sussex announced that Barclay, their club captain, who was troubled by injuries, would stand down from the side, though it was hoped he would return "in due course".

Leicestershire

L. Potter c Parker b Imran	3	– lbw b Lenham	55
R. A. Cobb c Parker b Pigott	7	– c sub b Pigott	67
*P. Willey c Gould b Imran	59	– c Green b Imran	3
J. J. Whitaker c Lenham b Imran	18	– c Parker b Imran	26
N. E. Briers retired hurt	17	– absent injured	
T. J. Boon c sub b Jones	49	– (5) c sub b Imran	1
P. B. Clift c Gould b Jones	27	– (6) c sub b Imran	0
P. A. J. DeFreitas lbw b Pigott	25	– (7) not out	21
W. K. M. Benjamin lbw b C. M. Wells	7	– (8) lbw b C. M. Wells	1
†P. Gill retired hurt	4	– lbw b Imran	0
J. P. Agnew not out	5	– (9) c Lenham b Pigott	18
L-b 11, n-b 4	15	L-b 7	7
	236		**199**

1/10 2/10 3/35 4/136 5/188   236   1/84 2/101 3/145 4/148 5/148   199
6/211 7/225 8/227   6/168 7/169 8/198 9/199

Bonus points – Leicestershire 2, Sussex 3.

Bowling: *First Innings*—Imran 18.4-6-55-3; Pigott 20-5-54-2; Jones 9.3-1-29-2; Reeve 8-2-21-0; C. M. Wells 10-0-28-1; Lenham 2.3-0-13-0; Bredin 6-0-25-0. *Second Innings*—Imran 21.5-5-52-5; Pigott 16-1-63-2; Jones 10-1-34-0; C. M. Wells 7-1-16-1; Lenham 8-2-23-1; Bredin 1-0-4-0.

Sussex

N. J. Lenham b Clift	13	– c sub b DeFreitas	40
A. M. Green c Potter b Agnew	25	– c sub b Agnew	20
P. W. G. Parker b DeFreitas	13	– b Clift	1
A. P. Wells c Boon b Clift	34	– (6) c Potter b DeFreitas	76
A. C. S. Pigott c Gould b DeFreitas	31	– (9) b Clift	20
C. M. Wells lbw b Clift	0	– (5) c Benjamin b DeFreitas	46
Imran Khan lbw b Benjamin	1	– (4) lbw b Clift	0
*†I. J. Gould run out	5	– (7) c Boon b DeFreitas	8
D. A. Reeve c Potter b Benjamin	15	– (8) b DeFreitas	3
A. N. Jones not out	7	– c Benjamin b Agnew	13
A. M. Bredin b DeFreitas	4	– not out	8
B 2, l-b 2, n-b 6	10	B 13, l-b 7, n-b 1	21
	158		**256**

1/29 2/54 3/63 4/117 5/117   158   1/26 2/27 3/27 4/116 5/121   256
6/118 7/123 8/146 9/146   6/135 7/139 8/191 9/236

Bonus points – Sussex 1, Leicestershire 4.

Bowling: *First Innings*—Agnew 17-2-49-1; Benjamin 19-5-59-2; Clift 19-8-29-3; DeFreitas 11.4-3-17-3. *Second Innings*—Agnew 21-5-68-2; Benjamin 18-2-62-0; DeFreitas 19-3-61-5; Clift 18-8-45-3.

Umpires: R. Julian and K. J. Lyons.

SUSSEX v CAMBRIDGE UNIVERSITY

At Hove, June 14, 15, 16. Drawn. Toss: Cambridge University. Sussex, fielding seven uncapped players, lost one of them in the first over when Lenham's right hand index finger was broken in two places by a ball from Scott, who played for their Second XI in 1985. A feast of strokeplay followed this misfortune as Green and Parker put on 199 in 50 overs. On the second day, Fell took 269 minutes to compile his highest score, and when he declared Cambridge's innings at their overnight score, Sussex increased their lead to 249. Requiring approximately 5 runs an over, Cambridge never looked capable of winning, but the resolute defence of Browne and Gorman for fourteen overs had ensured a draw when the match was called off with eight overs unbowled.

Sussex

N. J. Lenham retired hurt	0		
A. M. Green b Lea	132	– c and b Scott	47
P. W. G. Parker c Gorman b Lea	109		
A. P. Wells st Brown b Lea	1	– (3) not out	48
C. M. Wells b Davidson	69		
D. K. Standing lbw b Scott	11	– (4) not out	38
R. I. Alikhan not out	22	– (1) c and b Golding	13
*†I. J. Gould not out	25		
B 4, l-b 3, w 3	10	B 1, l-b 2, w 2, n-b 2	7

1/199 2/213 3/287   (5 wkts dec.) 379   1/63 2/65   (2 wkts dec.) 153
4/311 5/344

I. C. Waring, A. M. Bredin and A. M. Babington did not bat.

Bowling: *First Innings*—Scott 26-6-59-1; Davidson 28-0-130-1; Browne 1-0-5-0; Golding 24-2-89-0; Gorman 4-0-28-0; Lea 18-1-61-3. *Second Innings*—Davidson 17-2-64-0; Scott 17-7-27-1; Golding 13-1-54-1; Lea 2-0-5-0.

Cambridge University

P. A. C. Bail c sub b Babington	13	– b Waring	26
M. S. Ahluwalia c and b Babington	36	– c Gould b Babington	0
*D. J. Fell c and b Babington	114	– (5) b Babington	8
D. W. Browne not out	61	– (6) not out	33
T. J. Head not out	40	– (4) c Waring b Bredin	10
A. E. Lea (did not bat)		– (3) c Gould b Babington	2
S. R. Gorman (did not bat)		– not out	12
B 1, l-b 9, w 1, n-b 8	19	L-b 1, n-b 5	6

1/19 2/117 3/214   (3 wkts dec.) 283   1/1 2/7 3/38 4/43   (5 wkts) 97
5/54

A. K. Golding, †A. D. Brown, A. M. G. Scott and J. E. Davidson did not bat.

Bowling: *First Innings*—Babington 20-3-61-3; C. M. Wells 25-7-66-0; Bredin 22-2-57-0; Standing 18-3-45-0; Waring 15-5-29-0; Green 1-0-1-0; Gould 4-0-14-0. *Second Innings*—Babington 14-2-45-3; Waring 7-1-16-1; C. M. Wells 1-0-1-0; Bredin 9-3-12-1; Standing 9-4-12-0; A. P. Wells 2-1-1-0; Parker 1-0-9-0.

Umpires: M. J. Kitchen and R. Palmer.

At Ilford, June 18, 19, 20. SUSSEX lost to ESSEX by 69 runs.

At Worcester, June 21, 23, 24. SUSSEX drew with WORCESTERSHIRE.

SUSSEX v NORTHAMPTONSHIRE

At Hastings, June 28, 30, July 1. Northamptonshire won by one wicket. Northamptonshire 19 pts, Sussex 7 pts. Toss: Sussex. The future of the Central Ground, on which there have been many famous matches and performances, may be in doubt, but no question mark could be raised over the entertainment provided by this match. It reflected credit on both teams and on the County Championship, with interest maintained until the end when Northamptonshire's number eleven batsman, Walker, drove the winning single off Imran Khan after he and Mallender had needed to score 20 runs. Earlier Lamb, omitted from the England team announced on the Sunday, scored a magnificent, fighting 157 off 153 balls on a pitch of dubious character, hitting 27 boundaries and leading his county towards victory in partnerships of 172 with Capel and 87 with Bailey, whose 57 came off 52 balls. Yet the previous day Northamptonshire had escaped following on by 2 runs, and Sussex, with Imran in marvellous all-round form, must have fancied their chances of bowling Northamptonshire out when they declared before the start of the third day. It was learnt later that Larkins had chipped a bone in his right hand when playing the lifting ball from Pigott which dismissed him and he withdrew from the England team for the third Test against India.

Sussex

D. K. Standing c Cook b Harper	22	– c Harper b Capel	16
A. M. Green b Harper	55	– lbw b Capel	28
P. W. G. Parker c and b Cook	26	– b Wild	54
Imran Khan c Waterton b Capel	59	– not out	62
C. M. Wells c Lamb b Harper	11	– not out	12
A. P. Wells lbw b Capel	44		
R. I. Alikhan not out	27		
*†I. J. Gould b Cook	1		
D. A. Reeve c Walker b Cook	10		
A. C. S. Pigott c Boyd-Moss b Mallender	10		
B 8, l-b 5, n-b 5	18	L-b 1	1

1/72 2/83 3/133 4/148 5/232   (9 wkts dec.) 283   1/43 2/52 3/146   (3 wkts dec.) 173
6/235 7/236 8/258 9/283

A. M. Bredin did not bat.

Bonus points – Sussex 3, Northamptonshire 3 (Score at 100 overs: 259-8).

Bowling: *First Innings*—Mallender 13.5–3–28–1; Walker 11–2–37–0; Capel 12–0–30–2; Harper 29–8–79–3; Cook 34–11–72–3; Boyd-Moss 4–1–14–0; Wild 3–0–10–0. *Second Innings*—Mallender 12–5–26–0; Walker 13–4–42–0; Cook 16–6–30–0; Capel 12–0–48–2; Harper 5–1–9–0; Wild 6–0–17–1.

Northamptonshire

D. J. Capel c Parker b Pigott	13	– b Imran	54
W. Larkins c Gould b Imran	9	– c C. M. Wells b Pigott	0
R. J. Boyd-Moss c Gould b C. M. Wells	17	– b Imran	0
A. J. Lamb c Standing b Imran	20	– c sub b Pigott	157
R. J. Bailey c Alikhan b Reeve	7	– c Gould b C. M. Wells	57
D. J. Wild lbw b Reeve	0	– c Reeve b C. M. Wells	18
*R. A. Harper lbw b C. M. Wells	22	– lbw b C. M. Wells	0
†S. N. V. Waterton lbw b C. M. Wells	9	– run out	3
N. G. B. Cook b Imran	18	– b C. M. Wells	1
N. A. Mallender not out	7	– not out	8
A. Walker c Standing b C. M. Wells	1	– not out	13
B 3, l-b 7, n-b 3	13	B 1, l-b 6, n-b 3	10

1/25 2/25 3/46 4/57 5/57   136   1/0 2/1 3/173 4/260   (9 wkts) 321
6/94 7/99 8/111 9/135   5/282 6/282 7/285
                                 8/288 9/301

Bonus points – Sussex 4.

Bowling: *First Innings*—Imran 16–2–44–3; Pigott 9–3–19–1; Reeve 11–5–26–2; Standing 6–1–14–0; C. M. Wells 7.2–2–23–4. *Second Innings*—Imran 18.5–1–66–2; Pigott 15–4–61–2; Reeve 10–3–46–0; Standing 8–1–35–0; C. M. Wells 17–2–72–4; Bredin 6–2–34–0.

Umpires: A. A. Jones and R. Julian.

At Cardiff, July 2, 3, 4. SUSSEX drew with GLAMORGAN.

At Hove, July 5, 6, 7. SUSSEX drew with NEW ZEALANDERS (See New Zealand tour section).

At Bristol, July 16, 17, 18. SUSSEX lost to GLOUCESTERSHIRE by one wicket.

At Leicester, July 19, 21, 22. SUSSEX drew with LEICESTERSHIRE.

SUSSEX v WORCESTERSHIRE

At Hove, July 23, 24, 25. Sussex won by five wickets. Sussex 20 pts, Worcestershire 7 pts. Toss: Sussex. Following an attractive century by the impressive Hick, who began belligerently after tea on the second afternoon and finished with a blitz on the final morning, Neale, the Worcestershire captain, set a challenging target of 291 in at least 75 overs. Sussex took it up, and with Parker in strokemaking form, completing his 1,000 runs for the season on the way, the mountain was scaled with fourteen balls to spare. The Worcestershire seam bowlers always made the batsmen work for their runs, and it needed Alan Wells and Gould to hit out boldly in their sixth-wicket stand of 77 for Sussex to enjoy only their second Championship success of the season.

Worcestershire

T. S. Curtis b le Roux	92	– b Lenham	36
D. B. D'Oliveira c and b le Roux	62	– c Lenham b Scott	19
G. A. Hick c Phillipson b le Roux	4	– c Parker b Lenham	100
D. M. Smith c Gould b Mays	63	– c Scott b C. M. Wells	21
*P. A. Neale c A. P. Wells b C. M. Wells	7	– b C. M. Wells	4
†S. J. Rhodes b Lenham	16	– not out	19
S. R. Lampitt not out	11		
P. J. Newport not out	15	– (7) not out	6
L-b 4, w 1, n-b 5	10	B 1, l-b 4, n-b 3	8

1/96 2/104 3/214 4/232	(6 wkts dec.) 280	1/34 2/102 3/175 (5 wkts dec.) 213
5/236 6/265		4/183 5/193

A. P. Pridgeon, J. D. Inchmore and R. K. Illingworth did not bat.

Bonus points – Worcestershire 3, Sussex 2 (Score at 100 overs: 264-5).

Bowling: *First Innings*—le Roux 19–4–48–3; Scott 12–2–47–0; C. M. Wells 23–6–63–1; Lenham 17.3–9–42–1; Mays 31–9–75–1; Green 1–0–1–0. *Second Innings*—le Roux 11–2–41–0; Scott 5–1–23–1; Lenham 16–1–64–2; C. M. Wells 14–1–58–2; Mays 7–3–22–0; Green 1–1–0–0.

Sussex

R. I. Alikhan c Rhodes b Inchmore	67	– c Neale b Pridgeon	56
A. M. Green c Newport b Illingworth	60	– c Rhodes b Pridgeon	9
P. W. G. Parker b Pridgeon	33	– c Neale b Newport	97
N. J. Lenham c Hick b Newport	4	– b Newport	24
C. M. Wells c Rhodes b Newport	0	– b Newport	18
A. P. Wells c Smith b Illingworth	15	– not out	42
C. P. Phillipson c Rhodes b Illingworth	6		
*†I. J. Gould b Pridgeon	4	– (7) not out	35
G. S. le Roux not out	7		
C. S. Mays c Hick b Pridgeon	0		
A. M. G. Scott c Smith b Illingworth	0		
L-b 2, n-b 5	7	L-b 6, n-b 5	11

1/120 2/133 3/151 4/151 5/180   203   1/15 2/115 3/170   (5 wkts) 292
6/188 7/193 8/194 9/194   4/206 5/215

Bonus points – Sussex 2, Worcestershire 4.

Bowling: *First Innings*—Pridgeon 16–5–43–3; Inchmore 14–6–26–1; Newport 15–3–57–2; Illingworth 30.5–12–54–4; Lampitt 7–1–21–0. *Second Innings*—Pridgeon 16–3–57–2; Inchmore 14–4–32–0; Newport 15–0–73–3; Illingworth 29–2–120–0; D'Oliveira 0.4–0–4–0.

Umpires: M. J. Kitchen and K. J. Lyons.

At Guildford, July 26, 28, 29. SUSSEX lost to SURREY by five wickets.

SUSSEX v ESSEX

At Eastbourne, August 2, 4, 5. Drawn. Sussex 6 pts, Essex 8 pts. Toss: Essex. An absorbing match ended in a tense finish as Essex, enthusiastically chasing a target of 319 in 49 overs, finished just 16 runs short with Border 108 not out, having thrilled a large ring of spectators as he hammered the Sussex bowling to all parts of the spacious Saffrons ground. In 86 balls, Border hit one 6 and eleven 4s. Colin Wells hit his only century of the summer off 130 balls in Sussex's first innings and followed this exciting, boundary-sprinkled display with eleven 4s in his second-innings 59 on a pitch which gave encouragement to bowlers as well as batsmen. There were spirited spells from Foster and Pringle for Essex, and for Sussex le Roux put a brake on Essex's victory drive by dismissing Fletcher and East in the same over. Having required 78 from the last ten overs, Essex needed 22 off the final over from le Roux and not even Border in his aggressive vein could manage that.

Sussex

R. I. Alikhan lbw b Foster	19	– lbw b Pringle	59
A. M. Green lbw b Lever	8	– c Gooch b Lever	5
P. W. G. Parker c East b Foster	7	– lbw b Foster	0
N. J. Lenham c Foster b Pringle	68	– b Foster	8
C. M. Wells b Gooch	106	– b Pringle	59
D. K. Standing c and b Foster	31	– c Foster b Pringle	21
*†I. J. Gould c and b Foster	1	– not out	43
G. S. le Roux not out	44	– not out	72
A. C. S. Pigott st East b Childs	35		
C. S. Mays st East b Childs	5		
A. N. Jones c East b Foster	7		
L-b 12, w 3	15	L-b 2, w 1, n-b 2	5

1/17 2/34 3/39 4/209 5/247   346   1/9 2/10 3/26   (6 wkts dec.) 272
6/253 7/258 8/323 9/337   4/110 5/148 6/161

Bonus points – Sussex 4, Essex 4.

Bowling: *First Innings*—Lever 23–2–116–1; Foster 27.4–3–84–5; Pringle 19–3–67–1; Gooch 13–6–33–1; Childs 11–4–34–2. *Second Innings*—Lever 16–4–47–1; Foster 27–5–99–2; Pringle 19–4–57–3; Childs 7–3–10–0; Stephenson 2–0–5–0; Border 5–1–52–0.

Essex

*G. A. Gooch lbw b Pigott	31	– c Lenham b Wells	78
J. P. Stephenson lbw b Wells	43	– b le Roux	6
†D. E. East lbw b le Roux	5	– (8) lbw b le Roux	0
P. J. Prichard c Gould b Jones	21	– (3) c Jones b Wells	60
A. R. Border lbw b Wells	2	– (4) not out	108
K. W. R. Fletcher not out	57	– (7) c Alikhan b le Roux	11
B. R. Hardie c Green b Pigott	80	– (6) c le Roux b Jones	4
D. R. Pringle not out	42	– (5) c Mays b Jones	12
N. A. Foster (did not bat)		– not out	11
B 2, l-b 9, w 3, n-b 5	19	B 3, l-b 8, w 1, n-b 1	13

1/36 2/62 3/109 4/111   (6 wkts dec.) 300   1/11 2/126 3/152 4/197   (7 wkts) 303
5/115 6/243   5/221 6/259 7/260

J. K. Lever and J. H. Childs did not bat.

Bonus points – Essex 4, Sussex 2.

Bowling: *First Innings*—le Roux 20–9–36–1; Jones 14–2–51–1; Pigott 22–4–77–2; Wells 21–8–45–2; Mays 1–0–14–0; Lenham 7–0–16–0; Green 12–1–50–0. *Second Innings*—le Roux 12.5–2–44–3; Jones 10–1–55–2; Mays 4–1–40–0; Pigott 12–0–72–0; Wells 11–1–81–2.

Umpires: B. Dudleston and P. B. Wight.

SUSSEX v DERBYSHIRE

At Eastbourne, August 6, 7, 8. Sussex won by three wickets. Sussex 21 pts, Derbyshire 3 pts. Toss: Sussex. On the final day Gould, the Sussex captain, was forced to hand over the wicket-keeping duties to Reeve because of an injury to his left hand, whereupon he went on to take his first first-class wickets while encouraging Derbyshire towards a declaration, and later he scored 78 not out in aggressive fashion as Sussex met their target with eleven balls to spare. Hill hit a stubborn first-innings 130 not out as Derbyshire batted into the second afternoon following the loss of 36 overs on the first day, but Parker's range of strokes and a close-of-play declaration put Sussex in a position to bid for victory.

Derbyshire

*K. J. Barnett c Pigott b Jones	39	– c le Roux b Wells	10
B. J. M. Maher b Reeve	8	– not out	77
A. Hill not out	130	– c Parker b Gould	35
J. E. Morris b le Roux	31	– c Standing b Gould	26
B. Roberts c and b Reeve	9	– not out	19
G. Miller lbw b le Roux	40		
†C. Marples c Gould b le Roux	11		
A. E. Warner c Gould b Reeve	7		
R. Sharma not out	64		
B 1, l-b 4, w 6, n-b 1	12	L-b 1, n-b 1	2

1/50 2/62 3/98 4/120   (7 wkts dec.) 351   1/20 2/77 3/129   (3 wkts dec.) 169
5/191 6/203 7/216

R. J. Finney and D. E. Malcolm did not bat.

Bonus points – Derbyshire 3, Sussex 3 (Score at 100 overs: 256-7).

Bowling: *First Innings*—le Roux 27–3–104–3; Pigott 18–1–48–0; Reeve 33–12–71–3; Jones 5–3–9–1; Wells 9–3–13–0; Standing 3–1–13–0; Lenham 4–0–16–0; Gould 5.3–0–29–0. *Second Innings*—Reeve 8–3–12–0; Wells 8–2–20–1; Green 10–0–39–0; Gould 13–0–67–2; Alikhan 3–0–26–0; Parker 1–0–4–0.

Sussex

R. I. Alikhan c Roberts b Miller	64	– c Hill b Finney	72
A. M. Green c Barnett b Malcolm	3	– c Marples b Warner	13
P. W. G. Parker not out	100	– c Miller b Malcolm	1
N. J. Lenham not out	25	– c Marples b Warner	77
C. M. Wells (did not bat)		– c Maher b Sharma	50
*†I. J. Gould (did not bat)		– not out	78
G. S. le Roux (did not bat)		– b Sharma	7
D. K. Standing (did not bat)		– b Malcolm	4
D. A. Reeve (did not bat)		– not out	6
L-b 7, n-b 6	13	B 6, l-b 3, n-b 2	11

1/19 2/129   (2 wkts dec.) 205   1/30 2/31 3/143 4/182   (7 wkts) 319
                                                    5/263 6/275 7/298

A. N. Jones and A. C. S. Pigott did not bat.

Bonus points – Sussex 2.

Bowling: First Innings—Malcolm 13-3-57-1; Warner 12-4-41-0; Finney 6-2-14-0; Miller 24.5-3-76-1; Sharma 8-2-10-0. *Second Innings*—Malcolm 14.1-1-91-2; Warner 11-0-52-2; Finney 16-4-52-1; Miller 19-1-92-0; Sharma 4-0-23-2.

Umpires: B. Dudleston and P. B. Wight.

At Southampton, August 9, 11, 12. SUSSEX drew with HAMPSHIRE.

SUSSEX v KENT

At Hove, August 16, 18, 19. Sussex won by six wickets. Sussex 23 pts, Kent 5 pts. Toss: Sussex. The wicket was greenish, the weather generally overcast, and the seam bowlers took full advantage of the conditions. Pigott had match figures of nine for 82, Dilley's were seven for 148, and the highest score was Colin Wells's 82, 46 of which came from typically robust boundaries. Sussex were only 22 runs behind Kent with five first-innings wickets in hand after the first day, and with Kent batting even more tentatively on the Monday, Sussex won shortly after lunch on the third day, Parker contributing an attractive, unbeaten half-century. Worryingly for Sussex, however, Gould aggravated a hip injury in the Sunday League match and was told he must rest for at least ten days. In his absence, Kent allowed M. P. Speight, an eighteen-year-old from Hurstpierpoint College, to keep wicket and he made a fine impression, taking two catches, on a pitch of uneven bounce.

Kent

M. R. Benson c Gould b le Roux	0	– c sub b Jones	31
S. G. Hinks c Reeve b le Roux	12	– c C. M. Wells b le Roux	12
C. J. Tavaré c Gould b Jones	1	– b Pigott	3
N. R. Taylor c Gould b Reeve	13	– c and b Pigott	0
D. G. Aslett lbw b Pigott	44	– c Alikhan b Pigott	1
*C. S. Cowdrey lbw b Reeve	31	– c Lenham b le Roux	34
R. M. Ellison c Green b Jones	6	– lbw b Jones	10
†S. A. Marsh c Gould b Pigott	32	– c Alikhan b Pigott	20
G. R. Dilley not out	23	– not out	13
D. L. Underwood c Reeve b Pigott	9	– c sub b Jones	16
T. M. Alderman c Gould b Pigott	5	– c A. P. Wells b Pigott	0
L-b 7, w 2, n-b 6	15	L-b 3, n-b 2	5

1/0 2/1 3/25 4/35 5/76   191   1/19 2/40 3/40 4/46 5/54   145
6/98 7/122 8/161 9/175   6/74 7/109 8/121 9/144

Bonus points – Kent 1, Sussex 4.

Bowling: *First Innings*—le Roux 13–5–35–2; Jones 12–5–47–2; Reeve 19–5–50–2; Pigott 12–1–32–4; C. M. Wells 3–0–12–0; Green 2–0–8–0. *Second Innings*—le Roux 15–3–37–2; Jones 13–1–36–3; Pigott 16.2–3–50–5; C. M. Wells 7–2–19–0.

Sussex

R. I. Alikhan c Benson b Dilley	18	– c Alderman b Dilley	0
A. M. Green c Taylor b Ellison	39	– c Cowdrey b Alderman	15
P. W. G. Parker c and b Ellison	0	– not out	51
A. P. Wells c Tavaré b Ellison	0	– c Aslett b Dilley	2
C. M. Wells lbw b Dilley	82	– c Marsh b Alderman	5
N. J. Lenham lbw b Dilley	22	– not out	11
D. A. Reeve not out	22		
G. S. le Roux c Cowdrey b Dilley	10		
A. C. S. Pigott c Benson b Ellison	35		
A. N. Jones b Dilley	3		
*†I. J. Gould absent injured			
B 4, l-b 8, n-b 9	21	N-b 1	1

1/50 2/53 3/54 4/81 5/168   252   1/0 2/52 3/55 4/63   (4 wkts) 85
6/170 7/189 8/226 9/252

Bonus points – Sussex 3, Kent 4.

Bowling: *First Innings*—Dilley 24–3–101–5; Alderman 22–6–56–0; Ellison 21.5–6–53–4; Cowdrey 4–0–23–0; Underwood 2–0–7–0. *Second Innings*—Dilley 11.5–1–47–2; Alderman 11–2–38–2.

Umpires: J. Birkenshaw and D. J. Constant.

At Taunton, August 20, 21, 22. SUSSEX drew with SOMERSET.

SUSSEX v MIDDLESEX

At Hove, August 23, 25, 26. Drawn. Sussex 2 pts, Middlesex 3 pts. Toss: Sussex. Play was possible only on the first day, relentless rain, accompanied by high winds, making it a dismal Bank Holiday for cricket lovers. Put in, Middlesex scored steadily on a good wicket with three heartily struck 6s featuring among some robust holiday-style strokes, but all prospects of an entertaining battle were dampened by cricket's ancient enemy.

Middlesex

A. J. T. Miller c Speight b Imran	44	†P. R. Downton c Speight b Pigott	0
W. N. Slack b Pigott	46	G. D. Rose not out	0
K. R. Brown c A. P. Wells b Pigott	60	L-b 7, w 1, n-b 10	18
J. D. Carr c Alikhan b Jones	32		
R. O. Butcher c Jones b Pigott	69	1/88 2/122 3/182	(6 wkts) 284
*C. T. Radley not out	15	4/208 5/284 6/284	

S. P. Hughes, N. G. Cowans and A. G. J. Fraser did not bat.

Bonus points – Middlesex 3, Sussex 2.

Bowling: Jones 12–0–27–1; le Roux 20–5–58–0; Imran 17–3–47–1; Pigott 21.3–0–91–4; C. M. Wells 20–4–45–0; Green 6–2–9–0.

Sussex

A. M. Green, R. I. Alikhan, *P. W. G. Parker, Imran Khan, C. M. Wells, N. J. Lenham, A. P. Wells, A. N. Jones, †M. P. Speight, G. S. le Roux and A. C. S. Pigott.

Umpires: N. T. Plews and A. G. T. Whitehead.

SUSSEX v NOTTINGHAMSHIRE

At Hove, August 30, 31, September 1. Drawn. Sussex 2 pts, Nottinghamshire 8 pts. Toss: Nottinghamshire. The visitors were in command until the final day when career-best innings by Alan Wells (two 6s, 27 4s) and Pigott (ten 4s), and Parker's sixth hundred of the summer, taking him past 1,500 runs for the season, checked Nottinghamshire's Championship bid. Broad's sound 116 (two 6s, thirteen 4s) and Johnson's attractive 65 off 72 balls had given them a first-innings lead of 130, but with Parker 82 not out, Sussex fought back to level terms at 135 for three on Sunday evening. When they were 191 for six on the last morning, with Colin Wells unable to bat because of a stomach upset, Nottinghamshire must have entertained hopes of victory, but Alan Wells and Pigott dashed them with their eighth-wicket stand of 149 in 105 minutes. Parker's declaration, 300 runs ahead, left 80 minutes' batting for Nottinghamshire, only for bad light to bring the game quickly to a close.

Sussex

R. I. Alikhan run out	33	– lbw b Rice	16
A. M. Green lbw b Hadlee	3	– lbw b Pick	11
*P. W. G. Parker c French b Hadlee	0	– c Birch b Hemmings	111
Imran Khan c Newell b Fraser-Darling	11	– c French b Pick	20
C. M. Wells c French b Rice	10		
N. J. Lenham c Broad b Rice	0	– lbw b Fraser-Darling	3
A. P. Wells lbw b Hadlee	63	– not out	150
G. S. le Roux b Rice	6	– lbw b Fraser-Darling	2
†M. P. Speight lbw b Hemmings	4	– b Hadlee	17
A. C. S. Pigott not out	40	– (5) lbw b Hemmings	80
A. N. Jones b Pick	7	– (10) not out	1
L-b 3, n-b 2	5	B 4, l-b 8, n-b 7	19

1/3 2/3 3/21 4/32 5/42   182   1/22 2/54 3/135   (8 wkts dec.) 430
6/90 7/99 8/123 9/151   4/185 5/189 6/191
                            7/227 8/376

Bonus points – Sussex 1, Nottinghamshire 4.

In the second innings A. C. S. Pigott, when 15, retired hurt at 183 and resumed at 227.

Bowling: *First Innings*—Hadlee 15-7-18-3; Pick 10.2-3-38-1; Fraser-Darling 7-1-36-1; Rice 12-4-35-3; Hemmings 15-4-52-1. *Second Innings*—Hadlee 26-4-60-1; Pick 19-1-76-2; Rice 16-2-84-1; Fraser-Darling 23-3-86-2; Hemmings 26.2-6-96-2; Birch 5-0-16-0.

Nottinghamshire

B. C. Broad lbw b Lenham	116	– not out	4
R. T. Robinson b Imran	4	– not out	0
M. Newell c sub b Green	46		
P. Johnson b Pigott	65		
*C. E. B. Rice not out	41		
J. D. Birch not out	23		
L-b 12, n-b 5	17		

1/18 2/138 3/243 4/247   (4 wkts dec.) 312   (no wkt) 4

R. J. Hadlee, †B. N. French, E. E. Hemmings, R. A. Pick and C. D. Fraser-Darling did not bat.

Bonus points – Nottinghamshire 4, Sussex 1.

Bowling: *First Innings*—Imran 19-2-57-1; Jones 2.3-0-16-0; Pigott 22-7-59-1; le Roux 11.3-1-61-0; Green 23-5-73-1; Lenham 15-4-34-1. *Second Innings*—Imran 1-0-4-0.

Umpires: J. W. Holder and R. A. White.

SUSSEX v HAMPSHIRE

At Hove, September 10, 11, 12. Drawn. Sussex 7 pts, Hampshire 6 pts. Toss: Hampshire.
Greenidge's fourth successive century and 125 before lunch, including two 6s and eighteen 4s,
was countered by Green's four-and-a-half-hour innings containing thirteen 4s. Parker's fifty
in 85 minutes was livelier. Hampshire, needing match points to improve their prospects
of Championship prizemoney, increased their lead to 87 on the second evening, and an
enterprising 180 off 44 overs by Chris and Robin Smith allowed Nicholas to give his bowlers
three and a half hours in which to provide a victory. Instead, Sussex, despite losing Green and
Parker as Marshall claimed his 100th wicket of the season, set their sights on the target of 281.
Alikhan took on the anchor role, and the balance of fortune swung as contributions came all
the way down the order.

Hampshire

C. G. Greenidge c le Roux b Green	126	– c and b Green	30
V. P. Terry c Parker b Pigott	48	– b Pigott	0
C. L. Smith c A. P. Wells b Reeve	31	– not out	114
R. A. Smith b Green	39	– not out	87
*M. C. J. Nicholas b Pigott	7		
K. D. James b Pigott	36		
N. G. Cowley not out	65		
M. D. Marshall b Reeve	1		
R. J. Maru not out	13		
B 1, l-b 10, w 4, n-b 4	19	B 3, l-b 6, n-b 5	14

1/143 2/190 3/255 4/257   (7 wkts dec.) 385   1/2 2/65   (2 wkts dec.) 245
5/265 6/350 7/351

†R. J. Parks and C. A. Connor did not bat.

Bonus points – Hampshire 4, Sussex 3 (Score at 100 overs: 380-7).

Bowling: *First Innings*—le Roux 16-4-52-0; Pigott 21-0-91-3; C. M. Wells 11-2-47-0;
Reeve 24-3-101-2; Green 21-5-58-2; Standing 8-1-25-0. *Second Innings*—le Roux
14-2-40-0; Pigott 10-1-49-1; Green 16-1-48-1; Reeve 12.2-1-47-0; Standing 10-1-52-0.

Sussex

R. I. Alikhan c C. L. Smith b Marshall	0	– c Connor b Cowley	48
A. M. Green c James b Maru	114	– c R. A. Smith b Marshall	0
*P. W. G. Parker b Marshall	51	– c R. A. Smith b Marshall	0
A. P. Wells c sub b Cowley	39	– b Maru	28
C. M. Wells lbw b Cowley	20	– c C. L. Smith b Maru	24
N. J. Lenham c sub b Cowley	3	– c and b Maru	17
D. K. Standing st Parks b Maru	23	– c Terry b Maru	5
A. C. S. Pigott not out	75	– c R. A. Smith b C. L. Smith	40
G. S. le Roux not out	12	– not out	37
D. A. Reeve (did not bat)		– not out	34
B 1, l-b 7, n-b 5	13	L-b 5, n-b 5	10

1/8 2/101 3/179 4/213   (7 wkts dec.) 350   1/1 2/2 3/75 4/105   (8 wkts) 243
5/233 6/239 7/328   5/107 6/121 7/148 8/181

†M. P. Speight did not bat.

Bonus points – Sussex 4, Hampshire 2 (Score at 100 overs: 311-6).

Bowling: *First Innings*—Marshall 14-3-41-2; James 18-3-67-0; Maru 28-4-96-2; Connor
20-4-56-0; Cowley 24.2-1-77-3; R. A. Smith 1-0-5-0. *Second Innings*—Marshall 9-1-42-2;
James 3-1-11-0; Maru 24.5-9-71-4; Cowley 16-2-49-1; Connor 3-0-11-0; C. L. Smith
8-0-54-1.

Umpires: H. D. Bird and K. J. Lyons.

At Birmingham, September 13, 15, 16. SUSSEX drew with WARWICKSHIRE.

WARWICKSHIRE

President: The Earl of Aylesford
Chairman: A. D. Steven
Chairman, Cricket Committee:
 1986 – D. M. W. Heath
Secretary: 1986 – A. C. Smith and
  D. M. W. Heath
 1987 – D. M. W. Heath
 County Ground, Edgbaston,
 Birmingham B5 7QU
 (Telephone: 021-440 4292)
Cricket Manager: D. J. Brown
Captain: N. Gifford
Coach: A. S. M. Oakman

A number of good individual performances could not prevent another disappointing season of transition for Warwickshire. Three of the four competitions were out of reach much too soon, and in the NatWest Bank Trophy, the quarter-final tie at Worcester was marked by an abject performance on a difficult pitch.

Only bottom-place Glamorgan obtained fewer bowling points in the Britannic Assurance Championship, although the advance of Tim Munton, together with the sustained form and fitness of Gladstone Small and Norman Gifford, meant fewer repetitions of the poor bowling performances of previous years, when an inability to contain resulted in high scores being conceded quickly. Munton paid welcome attention to the old-fashioned tenets of line and length, and any further development will turn him into a top-class seam bowler. His progress contributed to the Committee's decision to release four seam bowlers – Stephen Wall, Steven Monkhouse, Philip Threlfall and Dean Hoffman.

Another consistent season from the 46-year-old Gifford took him past the landmark of 2,000 first-class wickets. He became only the tenth post-war bowler to achieve this, and the 33rd in history. His form, fitness and enthusiasm showed no signs of waning. Small's single-handed strike-bowling efforts deservedly earned recognition from the England selectors with two games against New Zealand and a place in the England touring party to Australia. The signing of an Antiguan fast bowler, Anthony Merrick, should ensure a more equitable division of new-ball labour – when he plays. For Merrick's arrival complicates still further an already difficult situation with regard to overseas players. In 1986, Warwickshire had to make a choice of either Alvin Kallicharran and Anton Ferreira, or the young South African, Brian McMillan.

McMillan was signed as a fast bowler, but he made a greater impact as a batsman, hitting three hundreds and six other scores over 50 in 21 innings to finish fifth in the national averages. Consequently, Kallicharran's opportunities were limited to fourteen first-class matches. After a moderate 1985 season, in which he was affected by a shoulder injury, he repeated his heavy scoring of previous years, his 1,005 runs containing five hundreds.

Among the younger batsmen, the most progress was made by Paul Smith, whose 1,508 runs earned him his county cap, and Andy Moles, a newcomer who took full advantage of the opportunity afforded him by injuries to Andy Lloyd. Smith exceeded his previous best aggregate, in 1984, by 468, and the decision to promote him to open the innings was rewarded with a much more responsible approach. His bowling figures were again unimpressive, but they do not reflect a welcome sign of improvement towards the end of the season. There was a glimpse of sustained control, particularly when he clinched the home victory over Yorkshire, and improvement would enhance his all-round value. He struck up a remarkably productive opening partnership with Moles, the two youngsters sharing four century stands and four more over 50 in their first ten innings together. Possessing an unspectacular but solid technique, Moles scored 738 runs, including two hundreds and five fifties, at an average of just under 50.

At senior level, the form of Dennis Amiss showed no decline, and his 100th first-class hundred gave further proof, if needed, of his right to a place among the great batting names. His 1,450 runs took him past Andrew Sandham into twelfth place in the list of highest aggregates in the history of the game. Geoff Humpage outscored every other wicket-keeper in England by a considerable margin, which was still not wide enough to persuade the England selectors that he was worth taking to Australia. It is strange, but probably true, that had he not kept wicket during the last three years, he might have played for England as a specialist batsman. His consistent heavy scoring merited an opportunity.

A considerable amount of team building is under way at Edgbaston, as evidenced by the non-retention at the end of the season of more than a third of the full-time playing staff. Nevertheless the season was a steadier one, and the off-spin bowling of Kevin Kerr provided an unexpected bonus. He came to Edgbaston as part of a reciprocal scholarship arrangement between Warwickshire and the Transvaal Cricket Union, but only in June was it discovered that he was born in Glasgow, and therefore was qualified to play for England. He bowled consistently well and any decision by him not to return for the 1987 season, because of examinations and job prospects, would be a disappointment to Warwickshire's cricket management. Their long-standing slow bowling problem has been partly ameliorated by Gifford's four seasons with the club, but his pending retirement will leave the cupboard bare.

The county has enough talent on the staff to provide the basis of an effective side who should achieve higher final positions in the Championship and Sunday League than the twelfth and ninth of 1986. Much will depend on how they resolve the issue concerning overseas players. No other county has a more complicated situation to unravel. But if Small is given overdue support with the new ball, and if Gifford's burden in the spin department is shared, supporters can look forward to watching a team capable of challenging for honours.

Warwickshire's already strong administrative links with the Test and County Cricket Board were further strengthened by the appointment of Mr Alan Smith, the club's secretary, as the Board's new chief executive. He took up his duties on January 1, and his successor at Edgbaston was the chairman of cricket, Mr David Heath. – J.D.B.

WARWICKSHIRE 1986

[*Bill Smith*

Back row: P. W. Threlfall, S. Wall, P. A. Smith, B. M. McMillan, T. A. Munton, R. I. H. B. Dyer, A. R. K. Pierson, W. Morton, D. S. Hoffman, G. J. Parsons, Asif Din. *Middle row*: G. C. Small, T. A. Lloyd, A. I. Kallicharran, N. Gifford (*captain*), D. L. Amiss, G. W. Humpage, A. M. Ferreira. *Front row*: R. S. Weir, W. J. P. Matthews, G. J. Lord, G. A. Tedstone. *Insets*: A. J. Moles, D. A. Thorne.

WARWICKSHIRE RESULTS

All first-class matches – Played 26: Won 5, Lost 5, Drawn 16.

County Championship matches – Played 24: Won 4, Lost 5, Drawn 15.

Bonus points – Batting 61, Bowling 51.

Competition placings – Britannic Assurance County Championship, 12th equal; NatWest Bank Trophy, q-f; Benson and Hedges Cup, 3rd in Group A; John Player League, 9th equal.

BRITANNIC ASSURANCE CHAMPIONSHIP AVERAGES

BATTING

	Birthplace	M	I	NO	R	HI	Avge
B. M. McMillan ..	Welkom, SA	11	19	4	895	136	59.66
‡A. I. Kallicharran .	Paidama, BG	13	22	5	884	163*	52.00
A. J. Moles	Solihull	11	18	3	738	102	49.20
‡A. M. Ferreira ..	Pretoria, SA	10	13	5	354	69*	44.25
‡D. L. Amiss	Birmingham	24	42	5	1,418	110	38.32
‡P. A. Smith	Jesmond	24	42	4	1,431	119	37.65
Asif Din	Kampala, Uganda	23	36	14	750	69*	34.09
‡G. W. Humpage ..	Birmingham	24	39	3	1,216	130	33.77
‡T. A. Lloyd	Oswestry	15	26	0	791	100	30.42
D. A. Thorne	Coventry	6	8	3	107	58	21.40
G. J. Parsons	Slough	19	23	5	309	58*	17.16
‡G. C. Small	St George, Barbados	21	23	6	280	45*	16.47
K. J. Kerr	Airdrie	13	11	4	87	45*	12.42
R. I. H. B. Dyer .	Hertford	4	8	1	69	28	9.85
G. J. Lord	Birmingham	2	4	0	38	17	9.50
T. A. Munton	Melton Mowbray	17	13	5	44	19	5.50
‡N. G. Gifford	Ulverston	24	14	6	27	8	3.37

Also batted: S. Monkhouse (*Bury*) (1 match) 0; A. R. K. Pierson (*Enfield*) (2 matches) 42*, 0*.

* *Signifies not out.*　　‡ *Denotes county cap.*

The following played a total of sixteen three-figure innings for Warwickshire in County Championship matches: D. L. Amiss 4, A. I. Kallicharran 4, B. M. McMillan 3, A. J. Moles 2, G. W. Humpage 1, T. A. Lloyd 1, P. A. Smith 1.

BOWLING

	O	M	R	W	BB	Avge
G. C. Small	537.3	126	1,573	68	5-35	23.13
N. Gifford	542.3	148	1,377	58	6-27	23.74
T. A. Munton	246.4	51	803	25	4-60	32.12
K. J. Kerr	296	46	913	24	5-47	38.04
B. M. McMillan ...	207	34	752	17	3-47	44.23
G. J. Parsons	316.4	58	1,028	23	5-75	44.69
P. A. Smith	156	18	725	13	3-36	55.76

Also bowled: Asif Din 87-8-358-4; A. M. Ferreira 125-31-391-8; A. I. Kallicharran 9-0-65-2; T. A. Lloyd 15-0-109-0; A. J. Moles 64.3-10-198-5; S. Monkhouse 10-4-34-1; A. R. K. Pierson 36-5-133-2; D. A. Thorne 53-6-174-1.

Wicket-keeper: G. W. Humpage 37 ct, 8 st.

Leading Fielder: A. I. Kallicharran 12.

WARWICKSHIRE v ESSEX

At Birmingham, April 26, 27, 28. Drawn. Warwickshire 6 pts, Essex 7 pts. Toss: Essex. With an hour and three-quarters lost on the last morning because of rain, a draw was inevitable. Put in to bat, Warwickshire lost their first six wickets for 146 before a seventh-wicket stand of 105 between Smith and Parsons pulled the innings round. Hardie played the anchor role in the Essex reply with 81 in four and three-quarter hours, and on the last day, Amiss scored his 97th first-class hundred, hitting one 6 and fourteen 4s. McMillan, on an exchange scholarship from Transvaal, underlined his promise with a polished innings of 64 to add to his 33 in the first innings.

Warwickshire

T. A. Lloyd c East b Foster	5	– c East b Foster	22
R. I. H. B. Dyer lbw b Gooch	28	– retired hurt	17
G. J. Lord b Pringle	10	– c Pringle b Foster	11
D. L. Amiss lbw b Gooch	16	– not out	108
†G. W. Humpage c Gooch b Lever	22	– c Foster b Lever	22
B. M. McMillan c East b Pringle	33	– c East b Gooch	64
P. A. Smith c Fletcher b Lever	88	– not out	3
G. J. Parsons not out	42		
G. C. Small c Acfield b Lever	17		
L-b 6, w 3, n-b 1	10	L-b 3	3

1/11 2/36 3/54 4/71 5/95   (8 wkts dec.) 271   1/39 2/57 3/91 4/233   (4 wkts) 250
6/146 7/251 8/271

T. A. Munton and *N. Gifford did not bat.

Bonus points – Warwickshire 3, Essex 3 (Score at 100 overs: 255-7).

Bowling: *First Innings*—Lever 28.1–13–71–3; Foster 24–6–81–1; Pringle 20–8–40–2; Acfield 9–2–27–0; Gooch 22–6–46–2. *Second Innings*—Lever 13–1–56–1; Foster 15–2–75–2; Pringle 9–0–30–0; Gooch 13–1–47–1; Acfield 10–3–27–0; Border 4–0–12–0.

Essex

*G. A. Gooch lbw b McMillan	14	N. A. Foster b Small	14
B. R. Hardie lbw b Gifford	81	J. K. Lever not out	8
P. J. Prichard b McMillan	38		
A. R. Border b Munton	34	L-b 14, w 2, n-b 6	22
K. W. R. Fletcher b Smith	31		
D. R. Pringle not out	46	1/17 2/99 3/154 (8 wkts dec.) 303
A. W. Lilley st Humpage b Gifford	3	4/212 5/220 6/231	
†D. E. East c Lord b Small	12	7/244 8/279	

D. L. Acfield did not bat.

Bonus points – Essex 4, Warwickshire 3.

Bowling: Small 22–8–58–2; McMillan 23–5–64–2; Parsons 14–3–49–0; Munton 15–4–41–1; Gifford 17–5–33–2; Smith 8–0–44–1.

Umpires: K. J. Lyons and B. J. Meyer.

At Cambridge, April 30, May 1, 2. WARWICKSHIRE beat CAMBRIDGE UNIVERSITY by nine wickets.

At The Oval, May 7, 8, 9. WARWICKSHIRE lost to SURREY by an innings and 73 runs.

WARWICKSHIRE v NORTHAMPTONSHIRE

At Birmingham, May 21, 22, 23. Drawn. Warwickshire 2 pts, Northamptonshire 4 pts. Toss: Northamptonshire. Although the first day was lost to rain, and there were interruptions on the second, two declarations led to an interesting finish as Lamb, with a belligerent 52, helped Northamptonshire chase a target of 273. Shrewd spin bowling by Gifford checked their progress, with three wickets falling for 5 runs at a crucial stage, and Harper's flourishing 59 off 49 balls provided entertainment rather than any prospect of victory. The most impressive batting of the match came from Bailey, whose 83 in the first innings was studded with splendid drives and pulls.

Warwickshire

T. A. Lloyd c Harper b Walker	2	– run out	64
R. I. H. B. Dyer c Ripley b Griffiths	0	– lbw b Griffiths	0
P. A. Smith st Ripley b N. G. B. Cook	34	– b Walker	51
D. L. Amiss lbw b Capel	21	– c Harper b Boyd-Moss	7
†G. W. Humpage c and b Capel	41	– b G. Cook	32
B. M. McMillan c Harper b N. G. B. Cook	10	– not out	50
Asif Din lbw b Capel	4	– st Ripley b Boyd-Moss	9
G. J. Parsons c Harper b N. G. B. Cook	25	– st Ripley b Boyd-Moss	9
G. C. Small c and b Harper	13	– not out	0
T. A. Munton not out	4		
*N. Gifford c Capel b Harper	0		
B 3, l-b 5, w 3	11	B 3, l-b 6	9

1/2 2/10 3/41 4/85 5/110   165   1/0 2/119 3/122   (7 wkts dec.) 231
6/118 7/119 8/157 9/161   4/145 5/175
                                                     6/206 7/228

Bonus points – Warwickshire 1, Northamptonshire 4.

Bowling: *First Innings*—Walker 13–5–33–1; Griffiths 9–1–36–1; Capel 16–5–39–3; N. G. B. Cook 21–6–39–3; Harper 9.3–4–10–2. *Second Innings*—Walker 13–1–40–1; Griffiths 11–2–35–1; Harper 11–5–9–0; N. G. B. Cook 14–0–37–0; Capel 5–0–34–0; Boyd-Moss 13–3–39–3; G. Cook 10–1–28–1.

Northamptonshire

*G. Cook lbw b McMillan	6	– c Lloyd b Gifford	43
R. J. Bailey c Dyer b Munton	83	– c McMillan b Small	16
R. J. Boyd-Moss c and b McMillan	16	– c Small b McMillan	18
A. J. Lamb not out	12	– b Gifford	52
D. J. Capel (did not bat)	–	st Humpage b Gifford	18
R. A. Harper (did not bat)	–	not out	59
†D. Ripley (did not bat)	–	b Gifford	0
N. G. B. Cook (did not bat)	–	c Dyer b McMillan	16
A. Walker (did not bat)	–	not out	0
L-b 4, n-b 3	7	B 1, l-b 4, n-b 5	10

1/15 2/103 3/124   (3 wkts dec.) 124   1/38 2/65 3/119 4/153   (7 wkts) 232
                                                     5/158 6/158 7/224

A. C. Storie and B. J. Griffiths did not bat.

Bonus point – Warwickshire 1.

Bowling: *First Innings*—Small 6–0–36–0; McMillan 9–1–35–2; Parsons 4–0–31–0; Gifford 4–0–15–0; Munton 1.5–1–3–1. *Second Innings*—Small 12.5–0–73–1; McMillan 14–1–56–2; Gifford 17–0–78–4; Parsons 6–0–20–0; Asif Din 1–1–0–0.

Umpires: D. Lloyd and K. E. Palmer.

WARWICKSHIRE v WORCESTERSHIRE

At Birmingham, May 24, 26, 27. Worcestershire won by 71 runs. Worcestershire 22 pts, Warwickshire 7 pts. Toss: Worcestershire. A high-scoring first innings from each side was followed by two batting collapses on a pitch which offered help to spin and seam alike on the last day. David Smith for Worcestershire (five 6s, ten 4s) and Warwickshire's Paul Smith (fifteen 4s) both scored hundreds, it being the latter's maiden Championship century. A third-day collapse by the visitors, in which they lost their last eight wickets for 43, was brought about by Gifford and Small, who bowled with impressive hostility after deciding to operate off his shorter Sunday League run-up. Needing 206 to win, Warwickshire batted poorly against the spin bowling of Patel and Illingworth. They lost half their wickets for 26, and sound contributions from McMillan, Asif Din and Parsons could not avert defeat.

Worcestershire

M. J. Weston c and b Kerr	30	– b Smith	4
D. B. D'Oliveira c Humpage b Small	9	– b Gifford	35
D. M. Smith lbw b Parsons	102	– c Dyer b Small	8
G. A. Hick c Kerr b Parsons	62	– b Gifford	53
*P. A. Neale not out	84	– (7) c Humpage b Small	5
D. N. Patel c Humpage b Small	12	– (5) b Small	11
†S. J. Rhodes run out	42	– (6) c Dyer b Gifford	8
N. V. Radford lbw b Parsons	4	– b Small	0
R. K. Illingworth b Kerr	2	– c Humpage b Small	3
J. D. Inchmore (did not bat)		– b Gifford	0
A. P. Pridgeon (did not bat)		– not out	4
B 4, l-b 4, n-b 5	13	B 7, l-b 2, w 1, n-b 5	15

1/19 2/100 3/200 4/215   (8 wkts. dec.) 360   1/20 2/33 3/103 4/124 5/126   146
5/252 6/341 7/351 8/360   6/136 7/136 8/142 9/142

Bonus points – Worcestershire 4, Warwickshire 3.

Bowling: *First Innings*—Small 16–1–53–2; McMillan 14–3–44–0; Parsons 22–0–108–3; Kerr 22–3–97–2; Gifford 20–6–50–0. *Second Innings*—Small 17.3–4–35–5; Smith 5–0–29–1; Kerr 5–3–15–0; Gifford 24–9–34–4; Parsons 9–2–24–0.

Warwickshire

T. A. Lloyd c Rhodes b Pridgeon	70	– c Rhodes b Patel	11
R. I. H. B. Dyer run out	0	– c Smith b Patel	1
P. A. Smith st Rhodes b Illingworth	119	– c Inchmore b Radford	4
D. L. Amiss b Patel	46	– c Rhodes b Inchmore	1
†G. W. Humpage b Illingworth	31	– st Rhodes b Patel	1
B. M. McMillan not out	9	– run out	29
Asif Din not out	8	– st Rhodes b Illingworth	27
G. J. Parsons (did not bat)		– b Illingworth	24
K. J. Kerr (did not bat)		– c and b Illingworth	12
G. C. Small (did not bat)		– b Patel	7
*N. Gifford (did not bat)		– not out	0
L-b 8, w 3, n-b 7	18	B 5, l-b 5, w 2, n-b 5	17

1/11 2/121 3/210   (5 wkts. dec.) 301   1/8 2/18 3/21 4/21 5/26   134
4/282 5/285   6/79 7/97 8/113 9/128

Bonus points – Warwickshire 4, Worcestershire 2.

Bowling: First Innings—Radford 22–2–81–0; Inchmore 13–2–46–0; Pridgeon 15–2–37–1; Patel 21–6–64–1; Weston 5–1–13–0; Illingworth 23–6–52–2. *Second Innings*—Radford 6–2–9–1; Inchmore 10–5–10–1; Pridgeon 6–0–21–0; Patel 22–9–37–4; Illingworth 19.2–8–47–3.

Umpires: D. Lloyd and K. E. Palmer.

At Manchester, May 31, June 2, 3. WARWICKSHIRE drew with LANCASHIRE.

At Bristol, June 4, 5, 6. WARWICKSHIRE drew with GLOUCESTERSHIRE.

WARWICKSHIRE v GLAMORGAN

At Birmingham, June 7, 9, 10. Drawn. Warwickshire 8 pts, Glamorgan 5 pts. Toss: Glamorgan. Batsmen thrived on a blameless pitch in a match much interrupted by rain and bad light. Kallicharran, whose appearances had been limited because of Warwickshire's decision to play McMillan as their overseas player, marked his first Championship appearance of the season at Edgbaston with a magnificent unbeaten 163 in 263 minutes, hitting one 6 and 24 4s after an opening stand of 137 between Lloyd and the promoted Smith. For Glamorgan, Maynard, a player of promise, scored 129, his second first-class hundred, which came off only 158 balls and included a 6 and twenty 4s.

Warwickshire

T. A. Lloyd b Base	99		G. J. Parsons c Thomas b Ontong		22
P. A. Smith b Thomas	79				
A. I. Kallicharran not out	163		B 4, l-b 8, w 2, n-b 2		16
D. L. Amiss c Davies b Derrick	0				
Asif Din c Holmes b Derrick	21		1/137 2/253 3/258	(6 wkts dec.)	443
†G. W. Humpage c Morris b Thomas	43		4/300 5/365 6/443		

K. J. Kerr, G. C. Small, T. A. Munton and *N. Gifford did not bat.

Bonus points – Warwickshire 4, Glamorgan 1 (Score at 100 overs: 300-4).

Bowling: Thomas 23–9–56–2; Hickey 21–4–97–0; Derrick 25–4–86–2; Base 28–6–98–1; Ontong 30.3–3–86–1; Holmes 2–0–8–0.

Glamorgan

D. B. Pauline lbw b Small	1		†T. Davies not out		13
G. C. Holmes b Small	10		S. J. Base c Humpage b Parsons		4
Younis Ahmed c and b Small	48		D. J. Hickey not out		0
H. Morris b Smith	2				
M. P. Maynard hit wkt b Parsons	129		L-b 2, n-b 3		5
*R. C. Ontong b Munton	14				
J. G. Thomas c Asif Din b Kerr	32		1/2 2/29 3/45 4/78 5/120	(9 wkts dec.)	300
J. Derrick lbw b Parsons	42		6/172 7/275 8/285 9/297		

Bonus points – Glamorgan 4, Warwickshire 4.

Bowling: Small 23–6–71–3; Parsons 20–4–55–3; Kerr 9–1–43–1; Smith 10–2–57–1; Munton 7–1–47–1; Gifford 2–0–6–0; Asif Din 5–1–19–0.

Umpires: H. D. Bird and B. Dudleston.

At Northampton, June 14, 16, 17. WARWICKSHIRE beat NORTHAMPTONSHIRE by 117 runs.

At Swansea, June 18, 19, 20. WARWICKSHIRE beat GLAMORGAN by 284 runs.

WARWICKSHIRE v LEICESTERSHIRE

At Birmingham, June 21, 23, 24. Drawn. Warwickshire 7 pts, Leicestershire 3 pts. Toss: Warwickshire. Sound batting in both innings gave the home side an advantage on a slow pitch which they were unable to convert into a win. Following a third-wicket partnership of 135 between the obdurate Cobb and attacking Whitaker (one 6, fifteen 4s), Leicestershire collapsed in their first innings, losing their last eight wickets for 58. Gifford bowled steadily after his second declaration left the visitors a target of 247 at under 4 runs an over, but with the bounce uneven and the turn occasionally generous, Leicestershire preferred to play for a draw. Willey's unbeaten 34 occupied 38 overs.

Warwickshire

T. A. Lloyd b Potter	70	– b Taylor	23
P. A. Smith retired hurt	0		
A. I. Kallicharran lbw b Taylor	2	– retired hurt	0
D. L. Amiss c Whitticase b Benjamin	54	– c Cobb b Taylor	10
†G. W. Humpage b Potter	34	– b Potter	56
Asif Din c Benjamin b Agnew	61	– b Agnew	31
A. M. Ferreira b Potter	68	– not out	7
G. J. Parsons c Potter b Agnew	5	– (2) lbw b Agnew	1
K. J. Kerr not out	8	– (8) not out	3
G. C. Small lbw b Agnew	0		
B 4, l-b 9, w 1, n-b 6	20	L-b 6, w 5	11

1/12 2/117 3/170 4/177   (8 wkts dec.) 322   1/17 2/32 3/67   (5 wkts dec.) 142
5/283 6/306 7/322 8/322   4/132 5/132

*N. Gifford did not bat.

Bonus points – Warwickshire 3, Leicestershire 1 (Score at 100 overs: 273-4).

Bowling: *First Innings*—Agnew 20–1–55–3; Taylor 14–3–43–1; DeFreitas 16–3–49–0; Benjamin 21–2–74–1; Willey 20–6–43–0; Potter 26–9–45–3. *Second Innings*—Agnew 13–4–40–2; Taylor 12–3–28–2; DeFreitas 5–0–39–0; Benjamin 3–0–18–0; Potter 3–1–11–1.

Leicestershire

R. A. Cobb c Ferreira b Small	78	– c Amiss b Gifford	4
L. Potter c Humpage b Kerr	9	– c sub b Gifford	68
*P. Willey run out	0	– (4) not out	34
J. J. Whitaker c Humpage b Small	90	– (5) c Lloyd b Gifford	5
T. J. Boon lbw b Parsons	4	– (6) not out	12
†P. Whitticase lbw b Ferreira	0		
I. P. Butcher c and b Kerr	9	– (3) c Gifford b Kerr	11
W. K. M. Benjamin c Ferreira b Small	0		
P. A. J. DeFreitas c Kallicharran b Small	7		
J. P. Agnew c Ferreira b Kerr	1		
L. B. Taylor not out	0		
B 9, l-b 6, w 1, n-b 3	19	B 12, l-b 2, n-b 2	16

1/25 2/25 3/160 4/170 5/175   218   1/34 2/69 3/107 4/115   (4 wkts) 150
6/205 7/208 8/217 9/218

Bonus points – Leicestershire 2, Warwickshire 4.

Bowling: *First Innings*—Small 21.5–9–41–4; Parsons 12–4–29–1; Kerr 32–6–67–3; Gifford 6–0–30–0; Ferreira 10–2–32–1; Asif Din 1–0–4–0. *Second Innings*—Small 9.2–2–32–0; Parsons 3–2–8–0; Gifford 26–14–26–3; Kerr 18–4–46–1; Ferreira 6–0–20–0; Asif Din 1–0–4–0.

Umpires: D. R. Shepherd and R. A. White.

At Leeds, June 28, 29, 30. WARWICKSHIRE drew with YORKSHIRE.

At Nottingham, July 2, 3, 4. WARWICKSHIRE drew with NOTTINGHAMSHIRE.

At Uxbridge, July 5, 7, 8. WARWICKSHIRE drew with MIDDLESEX.

At Birmingham, July 12, 14, 15. WARWICKSHIRE drew with NEW ZEALANDERS (See New Zealand tour section).

WARWICKSHIRE v DERBYSHIRE

At Birmingham, July 16, 17, 18. Drawn. Warwickshire 4 pts, Derbyshire 4 pts. Toss: Derbyshire. Derbyshire's tactic of batting into the second day was frustrated by the slow pitch and dogged tail-end resistance from Warwickshire in their second innings after being set 275 to win in a minimum of 62 overs. The Derbyshire first innings lasted 467 minutes and represented a recovery from 188 for six, Sharma having led the fight-back with 71 in 131 minutes. Off-spinner Miller bowled 81 overs in the match, taking five of his six wickets on the last day, including that of Amiss who became the second player to pass 1,000 runs for the season.

Derbyshire

*K. J. Barnett b McMillan	77	– b Small	3
B. J. M. Maher lbw b Small	31	– not out	52
A. Hill c Lloyd b Gifford	30	– st Humpage b Pierson	18
J. E. Morris b Gifford	13	– not out	50
B. Roberts c Asif Din b Gifford	3		
G. Miller lbw b Small	9		
†C. Marples c Humpage b Gifford	45		
R. Sharma b Pierson	71		
M. Jean-Jacques lbw b Small	34		
A. E. Warner not out	28		
D. E. Malcolm b Smith	1		
B 1, l-b 16, n-b 15	32	B 2, l-b 10, n-b 5	17

1/99 2/124 3/142 4/152 5/168   374   1/8 2/53   (2 wkts dec.) 140
6/188 7/239 8/315 9/373

Bonus points – Derbyshire 2, Warwickshire 2 (Score at 100 overs: 214-6).

Bowling: *First Innings*—Small 24–7–67–3; McMillan 18–4–51–1; Parsons 17–5–44–0; Gifford 48–24–72–4; Thorne 8–2–35–0; Pierson 18–3–65–1; Smith 6.1–0–22–1; Asif Din 1–0–1–0. *Second Innings*—Small 3–2–1–1; McMillan 2–0–4–0; Pierson 8–0–33–1; Asif Din 12–0–54–0; Gifford 3–2–2–0; Thorne 3–0–5–0; Lloyd 4–0–29–0.

Warwickshire

T. A. Lloyd c Barnett b Jean-Jacques	46	– c Miller b Malcolm	6
P. A. Smith c Warner b Sharma	39	– b Warner	20
D. L. Amiss b Miller	66	– (4) c Maher b Miller	38
D. A. Thorne c and b Sharma	58	– (7) b Miller	8
†G. W. Humpage b Sharma	2	– c Barnett b Miller	9
B. M. McMillan not out	6	– (3) c Warner b Miller	35
Asif Din not out	0	– (6) not out	7
G. J. Parsons (did not bat)		– c Sharma b Miller	0
G. C. Small (did not bat)		– c Marples b Barnett	3
A. R. K. Pierson (did not bat)		– not out	0
B 8, l-b 7, w 2, n-b 6	23	L-b 10, w 5, n-b 3	18

1/64 2/117 3/193   (5 wkts dec.) 240   1/19 2/30 3/85 4/114   (8 wkts) 144
4/202 5/237   5/121 6/122 7/134 8/140

*N. Gifford did not bat.

Bonus points – Warwickshire 2, Derbyshire 2 (Score at 100 overs: 237-5).

Bowling: *First Innings*—Malcolm 15–5–25–0; Warner 5–3–9–0; Miller 46–10–93–1; Jean-Jacques 9–1–25–1; Barnett 1–0–1–0; Sharma 26–5–72–3. *Second Innings*—Malcolm 14–2–29–1; Warner 7–2–30–1; Miller 35–21–37–5; Jean-Jacques 6–0–18–0; Sharma 7–5–12–0; Barnett 15–11–8–1.

Umpires: C. Cook and A. G. T. Whitehead.

At Portsmouth, July 19, 21. WARWICKSHIRE lost to HAMPSHIRE by an innings and 43 runs.

WARWICKSHIRE v LANCASHIRE

At Birmingham, July 26, 28, 29. Drawn. Warwickshire 4 pts, Lancashire 7 pts. Toss: Warwickshire. The match was notable for the 100th hundred of Amiss's career. He became the 21st player to achieve this feat, thanks to the sportsmanship of Lloyd, the Lancashire captain, who agreed to play out the last twenty overs, even though the result was certain to be a draw following the rain which prevented any play the previous day. Amiss batted for 114 minutes and faced 127 deliveries, from which he hit one 6 and fourteen 4s. Fifteen wickets fell on the Saturday. In Warwickshire's first innings, Ferreira avoided a complete collapse by hitting eleven 4s in his unbeaten 69, while Lancashire were rescued by Lloyd after Small had continued his recent penetrative form with three early wickets. Not out 72 in their close-of-play 183 for five, he went on to his only hundred of the summer when the match resumed three days later.

Warwickshire

P. A. Smith b Allott	4	– (2) lbw b Allott 10
A. J. Moles lbw b Murphy	1	– (1) lbw b Folley 67
A. I. Kallicharran c Watkinson b Allott	2	– lbw b Folley 29
D. L. Amiss c Allott b Murphy	33	– not out 101
†G. W. Humpage c Abrahams b Allott	0	– not out 38
Asif Din c Maynard b Watkinson	3	
A. M. Ferreira not out	69	
G. J. Parsons c Folley b Watkinson	8	
G. C. Small c Maynard b Watkinson	6	
*N. Gifford c Fairbrother b Allott	4	
S. Monkhouse b Allott	0	
L-b 6, n-b 2	8	B 4, l-b 4, w 1, n-b 1 10

1/4 2/6 3/19 4/23 5/36 138   1/27 2/93 3/141   (3 wkts) 255
6/52 7/69 8/101 9/138

Bonus points – Lancashire 4.

Bowling: *First Innings*—Allott 21.3–5–55–5; Murphy 14–3–29–2; Watkinson 15–1–48–3. *Second Innings*—Allott 9–2–17–1; Murphy 5–1–17–0; Watkinson 22–1–96–0; Hayhurst 6–0–22–0; Folley 20–6–59–2; Abrahams 4.2–0–25–0; Fairbrother 2–0–11–0.

Lancashire

G. D. Mendis b Small	0	P. J. W. Allott c Humpage b Ferreira . 21
G. Fowler c Parsons b Ferreira	76	I. Folley not out 20
J. Abrahams lbw b Monkhouse	2	
N. H. Fairbrother c Humpage b Small	0	B 1, l-b 11, n-b 5 17
*C. H. Lloyd c Moles b Small	128	
A. N. Hayhurst c sub b Small	0	1/2 2/19 3/20 (9 wkts dec.) 293
†C. Maynard lbw b Small	26	4/122 5/123 6/188
M. Watkinson lbw b Parsons	3	7/193 8/235 9/293

A. J. Murphy did not bat.

Bonus points – Lancashire 3, Warwickshire 4.

Bowling: Small 27–5–85–5; Monkhouse 10–4–34–1; Parsons 19–2–76–1; Ferreira 20–5–61–2; Gifford 2–1–1–0; Smith 5–0–24–0.

Umpires: M. J. Kitchen and B. Leadbeater.

At Weston-super-Mare, August 6, 7, 8. WARWICKSHIRE drew with SOMERSET.

WARWICKSHIRE v KENT

At Birmingham, August 9, 11, 12. Drawn. Warwickshire 4 pts, Kent 2 pts. Toss: Warwickshire. No play was possible on the second day because of rain, but three declarations all but brought a rare home victory. After Kent had been set 361 to win in four and a half hours plus twenty overs, splendid seam bowling by the improving Munton gave the home side an advantage they narrowly failed to press home. On the first day McMillan batted for 245 minutes and hit a 6 and seventeen 4s to take his season's aggregate to 999.

Warwickshire

A. J. Moles c Marsh b Penn	44	– not out 37
P. A. Smith c Marsh b Penn	55	– not out 17
B. M. McMillan b Aslett	106	
D. L. Amiss lbw b Alderman	5	
†G. W. Humpage c Cowdrey b Penn	59	
Asif Din not out	40	
D. A. Thorne not out	4	
B 1, l-b 9, n-b 3	13	B 1, l-b 2 3

1/77 2/111 3/117   (5 wkts dec.) 326   (no wkt dec.) 57
4/206 5/318

G. J. Parsons, K. J. Kerr, T. A. Munton and *N. Gifford did not bat.

Bonus points – Warwickshire 4, Kent 2.

Bowling: *First Innings*—Alderman 24–5–89–1; Ellison 17–3–47–0; Underwood 24–9–49–0; Penn 23–5–94–3; Cowdrey 3–0–19–0; Tavaré 7–2–8–0; Aslett 2–0–10–1. *Second Innings*—Aslett 4–0–33–0; Tavaré 3–0–21–0.

Kent

M. R. Benson not out	13	– c Humpage b Munton 82
S. G. Hinks not out	8	– c Humpage b Kerr 38
C. J. Tavaré (did not bat)		– c Humpage b Munton 14
N. R. Taylor (did not bat)		– c McMillan b Gifford 81
*C. S. Cowdrey (did not bat)		– c Moles b Gifford 20
D. G. Aslett (did not bat)		– c Amiss b Moles 13
R. M. Ellison (did not bat)		– c Humpage b Munton 14
†S. A. Marsh (did not bat)		– not out 12
C. Penn (did not bat)		– c Humpage b Munton 0
D. L. Underwood (did not bat)		– not out 3
L-b 2	2	B 6, l-b 7, n-b 9 22

(no wkt dec.) 23   1/100 2/117 3/163   (8 wkts) 299
4/217 5/249 6/274
7/292 8/293

T. M. Alderman did not bat.

Bowling: *First Innings*—Parsons 4–2–9–0; Smith 3–0–12–0. *Second Innings*—McMillan 18–3–55–0; Smith 5–1–16–0; Munton 29–9–60–4; Parsons 12–1–34–0; Kerr 8–3–22–1; Gifford 15–1–81–2; Moles 5–0–18–1.

Umpires: B. Dudleston and R. Palmer.

WARWICKSHIRE v GLOUCESTERSHIRE

At Nuneaton, August 16, 18, 19. Warwickshire won by 163 runs. Warwickshire 20 pts, Gloucestershire 3 pts. Toss: Warwickshire. Much of the second day having been lost through rain, two declarations on the third morning left the Championship leaders with the stiff task of scoring 369 runs from a minimum of 75 overs to win. Hostile bowling by Small, who took three of the first five wickets to fall, settled the issue, and despite brave innings from Curran and Lloyds, Warwickshire won with 95 minutes to spare. On the first day, their new opener, Moles, had continued his good form with his second Championship hundred in three matches, while for Gloucestershire, Romaines twice batted well on the ground where, four years previously, he hit his highest score of 186.

Warwickshire

A. J. Moles c Russell b Lloyds	100	– not out		29
P. A. Smith b Graveney	32	– not out		70
A. I. Kallicharran c and b Lloyds	19			
D. L. Amiss c Graveney b Lloyds	8			
†G. W. Humpage c Lloyds b Bainbridge	44			
Asif Din b Lloyds	47			
A. M. Ferreira c Graveney b Lloyds	47			
K. J. Kerr not out	45			
G. C. Small b Walsh	13			
T. A. Munton b Walsh	0			
*N. Gifford not out	3			
B 4, l-b 16, n-b 3	23	L-b 2, w 1		3

1/60 2/113 3/123 4/209   (9 wkts dec.) 381   (no wkt dec.) 102
5/219 6/310 7/311
8/348 9/348

Bonus points – Warwickshire 4, Gloucestershire 3 (Score at 100 overs: 311-7).

Bowling: *First Innings*—Walsh 20-2-58-2; Lawrence 16-3-74-0; Lloyds 38-10-124-5; Graveney 36-9-81-1; Bainbridge 5-0-24-1. *Second Innings*—Bainbridge 5-0-15-0; Tomlins 5-0-26-0; Romaines 7-0-32-0; Stovold 7-0-27-0.

Gloucestershire

P. W. Romaines not out	67	– b Munton		41
K. P. Tomlins lbw b Munton	22	– c Humpage b Small		0
C. W. J. Athey c Humpage b Ferreira	20	– c Kallicharran b Small		36
P. Bainbridge not out	0	– c Kerr b Ferreira		1
A. W. Stovold (did not bat)		– lbw b Small		8
K. M. Curran (did not bat)		– c Ferreira b Gifford		57
J. W. Lloyds (did not bat)		– c Smith b Gifford		31
†R. C. Russell (did not bat)		– c Moles b Gifford		7
C. A. Walsh (did not bat)		– c Small b Kerr		19
D. V. Lawrence (did not bat)		– c and b Kerr		1
*D. A. Graveney (did not bat)		– not out		0
L-b 4, n-b 2	6	L-b 2, w 1, n-b 1		4

1/55 2/114   (2 wkts dec.) 115   1/3 2/71 3/72 4/87 5/98   205
                             6/145 7/175 8/200 9/205

Bowling: *First Innings*—Small 7-3-16-0; Smith 6-0-33-0; Munton 11-3-25-1; Ferreira 9-4-16-1; Kerr 7-1-15-0; Gifford 3-0-6-0. *Second Innings*—Small 13-2-49-3; Smith 6-0-17-0; Gifford 12-1-56-3; Ferreira 8-2-19-1; Munton 9-0-31-1; Kerr 6.1-0-31-2.

Umpires: J. H. Hampshire and R. Julian.

At Worcester, August 23, 25, 26. WARWICKSHIRE drew with WORCESTERSHIRE.

WARWICKSHIRE v YORKSHIRE

At Birmingham, August 27, 28, 29. Warwickshire won by 54 runs. Warwickshire 19 pts. Toss: Yorkshire. Only 21 overs were possible on the first two days, but two forfeited innings on the third day enabled Warwickshire to set Yorkshire 283 to win in 140 minutes plus twenty overs. In the home side's innings, Kallicharran hit the 83rd hundred of his career, the second 50 coming in 21 minutes, after Moles and Smith had shared their fourth century opening stand in ten innings. Good bowling by Small and Smith clinched the win, with Smith taking the last wicket with the first ball of the final over.

Warwickshire

A. J. Moles b Fletcher	....	91
P. A. Smith c Moxon b Shaw	....	55
A. I. Kallicharran not out	....	103
D. L. Amiss not out	....	8
B 2, l-b 10, w 4, n-b 9	....	25

1/109 2/272   (2 wkts dec.) 282

†G. W. Humpage, Asif Din, A. M. Ferreira, K. J. Kerr, G. C. Small, T. A. Munton and *N. Gifford did not bat.

Bonus points – Warwickshire 3.

Bowling: Dennis 19–3–63–0; P. J. Hartley 4–0–16–0; Fletcher 17–3–61–1; Shaw 11–3–45–1; S. N. Hartley 3.2–1–12–0; Moxon 6.4–2–35–0; Sharp 4–0–32–0; Love 3–2–6–0.

Warwickshire forfeited their second innings.

Yorkshire

Yorkshire forfeited their first innings.

M. D. Moxon b Smith	....	13	S. J. Dennis lbw b Gifford	 0
A. A. Metcalfe b Small	....	10	C. Shaw lbw b Smith	 3
S. N. Hartley lbw b Smith	....	10	S. D. Fletcher not out	 4
J. D. Love b Munton	....	24		
K. Sharp c Gifford b Munton	....	8	L-b 7, w 5, n-b 6	 18
*†D. L. Bairstow lbw b Small	....	57		
P. J. Hartley b Ferreira	....	80	1/21 2/25 3/42 4/68 5/115	228
P. Carrick lbw b Small	....	1	6/150 7/164 8/175 9/218	

Bowling: Small 17–6–56–3; Smith 9.1–2–46–3; Munton 10–2–34–2; Gifford 5–2–15–1; Ferreira 14–2–70–1.

Umpires: J. H. Harris and M. J. Kitchen.

WARWICKSHIRE v MIDDLESEX

At Birmingham, August 30, September 1, 2. Middlesex won by 100 runs. Middlesex 22 pts, Warwickshire 8 pts. Toss: Middlesex. A pitch which afforded an increasing amount of assistance to the spin bowlers brought about an astonishing second-innings collapse by the home side against Middlesex's England spin bowlers. Edmonds took four wickets in four overs for 4 runs to start Warwickshire's decline from 131 for three to 150 all out. On the first two days, batsmen on both sides were in command, but at one point on the third morning, when Middlesex were 138 for six, a home win seemed likely. However, Gatting and Slack batted attractively to set up a generous-looking target of 251 in a minimum of 67 overs. Warwickshire made steady progress, and when the final twenty overs began were 131 for three. Twelve overs later they had been crushed by Edmonds and Emburey, who took nine wickets between them, the other wicket to fall resulting from a run-out.

Middlesex

A. J. T. Miller b Munton	38	– c Amiss b Small ... 7
W. N. Slack c Humpage b Munton	51	– (8) not out ... 41
J. D. Carr lbw b Munton	33	– st Humpage b Gifford ... 14
R. O. Butcher c Small b Ferreira	15	– b Gifford ... 0
*M. W. Gatting b Gifford	56	– (7) not out ... 50
C. T. Radley c Ferreira b Kerr	28	– (5) b Gifford ... 23
†P. R. Downton not out	35	– (2) c Smith b Kerr ... 47
J. E. Emburey b Gifford	8	– (6) b Kerr ... 23
P. H. Edmonds lbw b Kerr	6	
S. P. Hughes c and b Kerr	24	
N. G. Cowans c Kallicharran b Gifford	9	
B 1, l-b 14, n-b 1	16	B 9, l-b 15, n-b 2 ... 26

1/91 2/96 3/143 4/147 5/228   319   1/14 2/70 3/70   (6 wkts dec.) 231
6/234 7/247 8/256 9/300   4/98 5/116 6/138

Bonus points – Middlesex 4, Warwickshire 4 (Score at 100 overs: 308-9).

Bowling: *First Innings*—Small 13–3–47–0; Smith 9–0–46–0; Munton 16–5–43–3; Ferreira 14–3–42–1; Kerr 19–4–55–3; Gifford 27.4–7–61–3; Moles 3–1–10–0. *Second Innings*—Small 11–6–8–1; Smith 7–3–13–0; Kerr 28–0–108–2; Gifford 25–3–78–3.

Warwickshire

A. J. Moles lbw b Cowans	11	– c Miller b Emburey ... 12
P. A. Smith b Edmonds	24	– c Edmonds b Emburey ... 79
A. I. Kallicharran c Gatting b Cowans	73	– run out ... 1
D. L. Amiss c Radley b Emburey	7	– c Butcher b Emburey ... 2
†G. W. Humpage st Downton b Edmonds	81	– b Edmonds ... 37
Asif Din not out	62	– c and b Edmonds ... 7
A. M. Ferreira not out	36	– c Slack b Emburey ... 0
K. J. Kerr (did not bat)		– lbw b Edmonds ... 0
G. C. Small (did not bat)		– c Downton b Edmonds ... 0
*N. Gifford (did not bat)		– not out ... 2
T. A. Munton (did not bat)		– c Radley b Emburey ... 0
L-b 3, n-b 3	6	B 5, l-b 5 ... 10

1/23 2/68 3/81   (5 wkts dec.) 300   1/50 2/62 3/65 4/131 5/138   150
4/141 5/231   6/148 7/148 8/148 9/148

Bonus points – Warwickshire 4, Middlesex 2.

Bowling: *First Innings*—Hughes 8–0–35–0; Cowans 10–2–41–2; Emburey 37–6–102–1; Edmonds 34–5–108–2; Gatting 3–1–11–0. *Second Innings*—Hughes 3–0–17–0; Cowans 2–0–5–0; Edmonds 27–9–67–4; Emburey 27–8–51–5.

Umpires: J. H. Harris and M. J. Kitchen.

At Folkestone, September 3, 4, 5. WARWICKSHIRE lost to KENT by an innings and 30 runs.

WARWICKSHIRE v SUSSEX

At Birmingham, September 13, 15, 16. Drawn. Warwickshire 6 pts, Sussex 7 pts. Toss: Sussex. The loss of two hours through rain on the first day and an hour to bad light on the second prevented Sussex from offering a more generous target than 280 in 51 overs. Imran Khan held his side's first innings together with a fine, unbeaten 135 (one 6, sixteen 4s) in 278 minutes, and Standing's 65 out of a sixth-wicket stand of 159 in 52 overs was a career best. By the end of the second day the home side had secured maximum batting points in 69.5 overs, and the third day of this high-scoring match was marked by a maiden hundred from Pigott in 85 minutes off 98 deliveries, with 90 of his runs coming from boundaries (21 4s and one 6).

Sussex

R. I. Alikhan b Small	5	– lbw b Moles	61
A. M. Green c Kallicharran b Munton	29	– lbw b Small	0
*P. W. G. Parker lbw b Munton	1		
Imran Khan not out	135		
C. M. Wells b Ferreira	2	– st Humpage b Kallicharran	34
A. P. Wells c Amiss b Moles	19	– (4) lbw b Asif Din	19
D. K. Standing c Kallicharran b Moles	65	– (3) b Munton	19
A. C. S. Pigott not out	18	– (6) not out	104
G. S. le Roux (did not bat)		– (7) c Smith b Kallicharran	4
D. A. Reeve (did not bat)		– (8) not out	30
B 4, l-b 13, w 1, n-b 11	29	L-b 7	7

1/30 2/40 3/57 4/68   (6 wkts dec.) 303   1/3 2/56 3/97   (6 wkts dec.) 278
5/115 6/274   4/107 5/178 6/186

†M. P. Speight did not bat.

Bonus points – Sussex 4, Warwickshire 2.

Bowling: *First Innings*—Small 22–6–42–1; Smith 6–0–31–0; Munton 17–2–48–2; Ferreira 14–4–41–1; Moles 20.3–5–57–2; Gifford 8–1–28–0; Thorne 12–1–39–0. *Second Innings*—Small 7–1–25–1; Smith 6–3–25–0; Munton 4–0–20–1; Thorne 7–1–11–0; Moles 5–1–11–1; Asif Din 17–2–74–1; Gifford 7–1–40–0; Kallicharran 9–0–65–2.

Warwickshire

A. J. Moles lbw b Pigott	55	– b le Roux	0
P. A. Smith lbw b Reeve	52	– b Reeve	10
A. I. Kallicharran c Speight b C. M. Wells	41	– c A. P. Wells b Green	42
D. L. Amiss lbw b le Roux	25	– lbw b Reeve	37
†G. W. Humpage b Green	32	– not out	57
Asif Din c Parker b Reeve	10	– not out	28
A. M. Ferreira not out	60		
D. A. Thorne b Standing	10		
G. C. Small not out	2		
B 6, l-b 9	15	B 2, l-b 3	5

1/93 2/115 3/149 4/208   (7 wkts dec.) 302   1/0 2/18 3/85 4/109   (4 wkts) 179
5/220 6/246 7/278

T. A. Munton and *N. Gifford did not bat.

Bonus points – Warwickshire 4, Sussex 3.

Bowling: *First Innings*—le Roux 11–2–52–1; Imran 8–3–16–0; Reeve 19–6–40–2; Pigott 12–0–69–1; Green 8.5–0–51–1; C. M. Wells 6–0–38–1; Standing 5–1–21–1. *Second Innings*—le Roux 5–0–14–1; Reeve 11–2–34–2; Green 15–0–81–1; C. M. Wells 6–0–37–0; Standing 5–1–7–0; Alikhan 1–0–1–0.

Umpires: C. Cook and R. Julian.

599

WORCESTERSHIRE

Patron: The Duke of Westminster
President: D. Kenyon
Chairman: C. D. Fearnley
Chairman, Cricket Committee: M. G. Jones
Secretary: M. D. Vockins
   County Ground, New Road, Worcester
   WR2 4QQ (Telephone: 0905-422694)
Captain: P. A. Neale
Coach: B. L. D'Oliveira

Not even the entertainment and enjoyment provided by Graeme Hick could over-ride the disappointment of Worcestershire's two defeats in the semi-finals of the knockout competitions, making it three falls in succession at the final fence on the run-in to Lord's. Worcestershire went out by 11 runs to Kent in the semi-finals of the Benson and Hedges Cup and for the second year running were beaten at the same stage of the NatWest Bank Trophy, Sussex winning by five wickets.

Yet surprisingly for a side so well equipped for the limited-overs game, Worcestershire made no headway in the John Player League. For the second successive season, they finished second from bottom. Coincidently, their fifth place in the Britannic Assurance Championship was also the same as in 1985, although their seven wins were the most by the county since they were runners-up in 1979. One of the most memorable and most satisfying was that over Middlesex by an innings and 1 run. It was Worcestershire's first win by an innings in the Championship for six years, and later in the summer they dealt Somerset a similar fate.

Hick, who withdrew from the Zimbabwean team for the ICC Trophy so as not to interrupt his period of qualification for England, allowed little argument that he is now the best batsman in the world for his age. Majestic in his strokemaking, the twenty-year-old became the youngest ever to score 2,000 runs in a first-class season, 914 of them coming during July. He needed 103 runs from his final innings, against Glamorgan at New Road, to reach the landmark in his first full season and achieved it with his sixth Championship hundred of the summer. Two of those were unbeaten double-hundreds: 227 against Nottinghamshire – including Hadlee – and 219 against Glamorgan, during which Hick became the first batsman in the country to reach 1,000 runs. Inevitably the Worcestershire Supporters' Association Player of the Year, Hick was also the county's leading run-scorer in the Benson and Hedges Cup and the John Player League, for good measure winning Gold Awards for two innings of 103 not out against Nottinghamshire and Northamptonshire in the Benson and Hedges competition.

Four other batsmen – Tim Curtis, Dipak Patel, David Smith and Damian D'Oliveira – passed 1,000 runs for the season, while the captain, Phil Neale, was just 13 runs short. A deserving and popular winner of the Dick Lygon Award for the Clubman of the Year, Curtis over the summer developed into one of the most consistent openers on the county circuit, and his career-highest aggregate of 1,498 runs at 49.93 included a career-best 153 against Somerset. D'Oliveira's unbeaten 146 against Gloucestershire was also his highest innings, and by taking his career aggregate in the John Player League past 1,000 runs he provided a unique instance of a father, Basil, and son achieving that landmark in the competition.

The only bowler in the country to take 100 wickets in 1985, Neal Radford graduated to the England team in the middle of the summer but failed to do himself full justice in two Test match appearances. Though playing six games fewer in 1986, he took 78 wickets for Worcestershire, including the season's best return of nine for 70 against Somerset at New Road. It was the best analysis by a Worcestershire bowler since J. A. Flavell's nine for 56 against Middlesex in 1964.

Worcestershire's leading wicket-taker, however, was not Radford but the up-and-coming Philip Newport, who almost doubled his previous best haul to finish with 85 wickets and was awarded his county cap. So too were Hick, Martin Weston and Richard Illingworth. Steven Rhodes, after proving the major success on the England B tour to Sri Lanka, missed out on further international recognition, but it must be only a matter of time before he keeps wicket for England.

Paul Pridgeon, who did not play one Championship match in 1985 following two shoulder operations, underlined his return to full fitness by heading the bowling averages, his 59 wickets including a career-best six for 52 against Middlesex. Before announcing his retirement at the end of the season, John Inchmore in his 38th year became the first bowler to complete 500 first-class wickets for the county since Basil D'Oliveira, now the county's coach, did so in 1976. Worcestershire have a ready-made replacement for Inchmore in Steve McEwan. With the exception of Inchmore, all the playing staff have been retained, confirming the committee's belief that there is sufficient maturing talent and potential to ensure that Worcestershire will provide an even sterner challenge in 1987. – C.M.

601

WORCESTERSHIRE 1986

[*Bill Smith*

Back row: J. W. Sewter (*scorer*), S. J. Rhodes, T. S. Curtis, P. J. Newport, G. A. Hick, S. M. McEwan, R. K. Illingworth, D. B. D'Oliveira. *Front row:* D. M. Smith, D. N. Patel, P. A. Neale (*captain*), A. P. Pridgeon, N. V. Radford. *Inserts:* R. M. Ellcock, J. D. Inchmore, S. R. Lampitt, M. J. Weston.

WORCESTERSHIRE RESULTS

All first-class matches – Played 25: Won 7, Lost 5, Drawn 13.

County Championship matches – Played 24: Won 7, Lost 5, Drawn 12.

Bonus points – Batting 58, Bowling 72.

Competition placings – Britannic Assurance County Championship, 5th; NatWest Bank Trophy, s-f; Benson and Hedges Cup, s-f; John Player League, 16th.

BRITANNIC ASSURANCE CHAMPIONSHIP AVERAGES

BATTING

	Birthplace	M	I	NO	R	HI	Avge
‡G. A. Hick	Salisbury, Rhodesia	23	36	6	1,934	227*	64.46
‡T. S. Curtis	Chislehurst	23	38	9	1,451	153	50.03
‡D. N. Patel	Nairobi, Kenya	23	29	9	991	132*	49.55
‡D. M. Smith	Balham	20	28	4	1,041	165*	43.37
‡P. A. Neale	Scunthorpe	24	33	7	979	118*	37.65
S. J. Rhodes	Bradford	24	26	10	506	77*	31.62
‡D. B. D'Oliveira . .	Cape Town, SA	24	39	2	1,055	146*	28.51
‡P. J. Newport	High Wycombe	22	16	4	281	68	23.41
‡R. K. Illingworth . .	Bradford	17	14	3	185	39	16.81
‡N. V. Radford	Luanshya, N. Rhodesia	17	12	2	144	30	14.40
‡M. J. Weston	Worcester	7	11	2	118	30	13.11
J. D. Inchmore	Ashington	9	8	2	55	23*	9.16
‡A. P. Pridgeon	Wall Heath	20	10	3	44	10*	6.28

Also batted: R. M. Ellcock (*Bridgetown, Barbados*) (1 match) 4*; S. R. Lampitt (*Wolverhampton*) (1 match) 11*; S. M. McEwan (*Worcester*) (8 matches) 5*, 1*, 7; L. K. Smith (*Mirfield*) (1 match) 2, 2.

* *Signifies not out.* ‡ *Denotes county cap.*

The following played a total of sixteen three-figure innings for Worcestershire in County Championship matches: G. A. Hick 6, D. N. Patel 3, D. M. Smith 3, T. S. Curtis 2, D. B. D'Oliveira 1, P. A. Neale 1.

BOWLING

	O	M	R	W	BB	Avge
A. P. Pridgeon	535	134	1,396	59	6-52	23.66
N. V. Radford	584.4	122	1,882	76	9-70	24.76
P. J. Newport	617.3	88	2,081	83	6-48	25.07
S. M. McEwan	180.1	31	638	16	3-33	39.87
J. D. Inchmore	221.1	49	562	13	2-41	43.23
D. N. Patel	451	115	1,251	28	5-88	44.67
R. K. Illingworth . . .	551.2	188	1,310	27	5-64	48.51

Also bowled: D. B. D'Oliveira 27.4–6–118–5; R. M. Ellcock 15–1–40–1; G. A. Hick 28.4–5–109–3; S. R. Lampitt 7–1–21–0; D. M. Smith 11–3–35–2; M. J. Weston 126–36–354–5.

Wicket-keeper: S. J. Rhodes 57 ct, 8 st.

Leading Fielders: G. A. Hick 29; D. B. D'Oliveira 12.

WORCESTERSHIRE v SURREY

At Worcester, April 26, 27, 28. Drawn. Worcestershire 6 pts, Surrey 6 pts. Toss: Surrey. A successful appeal against the light by the Surrey captain and number eleven, Pocock, immediately on reaching the wicket, denied Worcestershire the chance of forcing victory with seventeen balls remaining. Surrey, set to score 260 in 55 overs, had been 126 for three at the start of the final twenty overs, but Newport's four wickets swung the game Worcestershire's way. On the opening day Rhodes, equalling his highest score, repaired the damage after Worcestershire had been 64 for five, and half-centuries by Stewart and Needham kept Surrey close. Hick, with some majestic strokeplay, struck three 6s and fifteen 4s in reaching 103 off 142 balls to set up the declaration.

Worcestershire

T. S. Curtis c Lynch b Monkhouse	9	– c Lynch b Clarke	0
D. B. D'Oliveira c Richards b Clarke	22	– b Clarke	4
G. A. Hick b Clarke	5	– c Richards b Clarke	103
D. N. Patel c Lynch b Monkhouse	7	– lbw b Clarke	39
*P. A. Neale lbw b Butcher	32	– (6) c and b Jesty	3
M. J. Weston c Clarke b Monkhouse	4	– (7) c Pocock b Monkhouse	29
†S. J. Rhodes not out	77	– (8) not out	42
P. J. Newport lbw b Thomas	26	– (9) c Monkhouse b Pocock	9
N. V. Radford lbw b Thomas	0	– (10) not out	0
R. K. Illingworth c Richards b Clarke	3	– (5) c Richards b Clarke	10
A. P. Pridgeon c Richards b Monkhouse	8		
B 16, l-b 15, w 1, n-b 6	38	B 1, l-b 10, n-b 4	15

1/38 2/40 3/44 4/58 5/64   **231**   1/0 2/18 3/113   (8 wkts dec.) **254**
6/136 7/203 8/203 9/222   4/134 5/159 6/175
7/227 8/250

Bonus points – Worcestershire 2, Surrey 4.

Bowling: *First Innings*—Clarke 24–8–57–3; Thomas 24–7–64–2; Monkhouse 21.5–10–37–4; Pocock 11–2–25–0; Jesty 8–6–3–0; Butcher 3–1–14–1. *Second Innings*—Clarke 27–6–69–5; Thomas 9–0–40–0; Monkhouse 14–0–60–1; Jesty 13–3–56–1; Pocock 5.4–3–18–1.

Surrey

A. R. Butcher lbw b Radford	15	– c Illingworth b Weston	71
G. S. Clinton b Patel	19	– run out	28
A. J. Stewart lbw b Radford	53	– c Radford b Weston	4
M. A. Lynch c D'Oliveira b Weston	3	– lbw b Newport	22
T. E. Jesty lbw b Radford	17	– lbw b Radford	18
A. Needham c Patel b Radford	52	– (7) lbw b Radford	0
†C. J. Richards c and b Newport	27	– (6) b Newport	31
D. J. Thomas b Newport	0	– c Hick b Newport	35
G. Monkhouse c Hick b Illingworth	10	– not out	1
S. T. Clarke c sub b Illingworth	5	– lbw b Newport	0
*P. I. Pocock not out	0	– not out	0
B 6, l-b 10, w 3, n-b 6	25	B 2, l-b 14, n-b 2	18

1/32 2/80 3/83 4/124 5/129   **226**   1/88 2/107 3/108 4/148 (9 wkts) **228**
6/191 7/198 8/214 9/226   5/171 6/172 7/200 8/220 9/228

Bonus points – Surrey 2, Worcestershire 4.

Bowling: *First Innings*—Radford 24–9–66–4; Pridgeon 4–1–10–0; Newport 20–6–39–2; Weston 14–5–36–1; Patel 6–1–18–1; Illingworth 21.1–7–41–2; D'Oliveira 1–1–0–0. *Second Innings*—Radford 14–2–62–2; Newport 12.1–2–58–4; Patel 6–3–20–0; Pridgeon 13–1–43–0; Weston 7–0–29–2.

Umpires: J. A. Jameson and N. T. Plews.

At Worcester, May 6, 7, 8. WORCESTERSHIRE drew with INDIANS (See Indian tour section).

WORCESTERSHIRE v LANCASHIRE

At Worcester, May 21, 22, 23. Lancashire won by 3 runs. Lancashire 19 pts, Worcestershire 4 pts. Toss: Worcestershire. Worcestershire, who forfeited their first innings after rain had prevented any play on the opening day, failed by just 4 runs to reach a target of 323 in 87 overs. D'Oliveira (89 in 191 minutes) and Rhodes (61 off 91 balls) kept them on course, with Radford putting on 71 for the eighth wicket with Rhodes. Inchmore and Illingworth, coming together with 24 needed off five overs, reduced that to 5 from the final over from Allott. But off the second ball Illingworth slipped while backing up and was run out by a direct throw from Fairbrother.

Lancashire

G. D. Mendis c Rhodes b Radford	15	– not out 11
G. Fowler c Rhodes b Inchmore	3	– c Rhodes b Inchmore 21
J. Abrahams c Rhodes b Patel	43	– not out 3
N. H. Fairbrother b Radford	54	
*C. H. Lloyd b Inchmore	2	
†C. Maynard c Rhodes b Radford	26	
M. Watkinson b Illingworth	40	
J. Simmons b Radford	42	
P. J. W. Allott c Curtis b Newport	22	
D. J. Makinson lbw b Radford	5	
S. Henriksen not out	6	
B 4, l-b 5, w 4, n-b 8	21	L-b 6, w 1, n-b 1 8

1/9 2/40 3/87 4/100 5/156   279   1/34   (1 wkt dec.) 43
6/165 7/222 8/249 9/270

Bonus points – Lancashire 3, Worcestershire 4.

Bowling: *First Innings*—Radford 29.2–8–77–5; Inchmore 19–5–41–2; Newport 20–3–59–1; Illingworth 10–2–43–1; Patel 16–2–50–1. *Second Innings*—Radford 6–2–16–0; Inchmore 5–0–19–1; Illingworth 2–2–0–0; Patel 1–0–2–0.

Worcestershire

Worcestershire forfeited their first innings.

T. S. Curtis lbw b Allott 10	P. J. Newport c Fairbrother b Makinson 22
D. B. D'Oliveira c Fairbrother	N. V. Radford lbw b Makinson 26
b Watkinson . 89	J. D. Inchmore not out 13
D. M. Smith lbw b Allott 3	R. K. Illingworth run out 7
G. A. Hick lbw b Makinson 18	L-b 6, n-b 6 12
*P. A. Neale c Fowler b Simmons 35	
D. N. Patel b Watkinson 23	1/16 2/34 3/69 4/121 5/176 319
†S. J. Rhodes c Maynard b Makinson . 61	6/189 7/227 8/298 9/299

Bowling: Allott 22.2–4–88–2; Henriksen 9–2–24–0; Makinson 24–4–80–4; Watkinson 23–1–91–2; Simmons 8–2–30–1.

Umpires: B. Dudleston and J. W. Holder.

At Birmingham, May 24, 26, 27. WORCESTERSHIRE beat WARWICKSHIRE by 71 runs.

At Tunbridge Wells, May 31, June 2, 3. WORCESTERSHIRE drew with KENT.

WORCESTERSHIRE v MIDDLESEX

At Worcester, June 4, 5, 6. Worcestershire won by an innings and 1 run. Worcestershire 24 pts, Middlesex 3 pts. Toss: Worcestershire. The county champions, without six of their Test players, were bowled out in their second innings in under four hours as Worcestershire achieved their first win by an innings for six years. Neale celebrated his 32nd birthday with an unbeaten 118, hitting a 6 and fifteen 4s and putting on 195 in 52 overs with Patel after Hick had set Worcestershire alight in his 70. On the last morning Pridgeon took the first three Middlesex wickets for 5 runs in sixteen balls before going on to take six for 52, his best Championship return at New Road. Only Carr offered prolonged resistance, following his maiden half-century in the first innings with an unbeaten 40.

Middlesex

A. J. T. Miller b Newport	9	– c Rhodes b Pridgeon	21
W. N. Slack lbw b Radford	9	– c Rhodes b Pridgeon	14
K. R. Brown c Pridgeon b Radford	9	– lbw b Pridgeon	23
R. O. Butcher c Rhodes b Pridgeon	27	– c Radford b Pridgeon	0
*C. T. Radley b Radford	22	– c Hick b Newport	30
J. D. Carr not out	84	– not out	40
†C. P. Metson c Rhodes b Newport	8	– c Hick b Pridgeon	1
S. P. Hughes b Radford	30	– lbw b Radford	0
A. R. C. Fraser run out	3	– c Illingworth b Pridgeon	13
W. W. Daniel b Radford	0	– b Radford	16
P. C. R. Tufnell run out	8	– b Newport	9
L-b 25, w 5, n-b 5	35	B 8, w 1	9

1/13 2/31 3/32 4/75 5/99   244   1/36 2/41 3/41 4/74 5/92   176
6/121 7/194 8/201 9/205   6/104 7/105 8/143 9/167

Bonus points – Middlesex 2, Worcestershire 4.

Bowling: *First Innings*—Radford 27.1–5–80–5; Pridgeon 18–3–40–1; Newport 19–3–69–2; Illingworth 10–6–17–0; Patel 4–0–13–0. *Second Innings*—Radford 27–14–50–2; Pridgeon 25–8–52–6; Newport 19.4–4–66–2.

Worcestershire

T. S. Curtis b Daniel	45	†S. J. Rhodes c Slack b Daniel	8
D. B. D'Oliveira c Carr b Hughes	2	P. J. Newport not out	22
D. M. Smith lbw b Hughes	26	B 1, l-b 9, w 2, n-b 10	22
G. A. Hick c Miller b Hughes	70		
*P. A. Neale not out	118	1/8 2/47 3/139	(6 wkts dec.) 421
D. N. Patel c Hughes b Slack	108	4/163 5/358 6/378	

N. V. Radford, R. K. Illingworth and A. P. Pridgeon did not bat.

Bonus points – Worcestershire 4, Middlesex 1 (Score at 100 overs: 352-4).

Bowling: Daniel 35–5–123–2; Hughes 36–7–115–3; Fraser 28–11–72–0; Tufnell 13–3–76–0; Carr 1–0–11–0; Slack 3–0–14–1.

Umpires: D. O. Oslear and P. B. Wight.

At Northampton, June 7, 9, 10. WORCESTERSHIRE drew with NORTHAMPTONSHIRE.

At Manchester, June 14, 16, 17. WORCESTERSHIRE drew with LANCASHIRE.

WORCESTERSHIRE v YORKSHIRE

At Worcester, June 18, 19, 20. Drawn. Worcestershire 6 pts, Yorkshire 4 pts. Toss: Worcestershire. Having been given the platform of a second-wicket stand of 181 in 50 overs between Metcalfe and Boycott, Yorkshire batted on into the second day to reach their highest score at New Road for 33 years. Metcalfe's hundred, containing seventeen 4s, was his first since he made 122 on his début in 1983. Curtis and Smith steered Worcestershire comfortably past the follow-on mark, and Neale declared at the end of the day with a full hand of batting points. Worcestershire's target was 302 from 53 overs, which became 116 from the last twenty with Hick in apparent command. His dismissal, however, effectively ended the run-chase.

Yorkshire

G. Boycott c Hick b Inchmore	76	– lbw b D'Oliveira	36
M. D. Moxon b Pridgeon	1	– st Rhodes b Hick	82
A. A. Metcalfe b Pridgeon	108	– st Rhodes b Hick	17
K. Sharp b Newport	4	– (5) not out	12
J. D. Love run out	24	– (6) not out	43
S. N. Hartley c and b McEwan	48		
*†D. L. Bairstow b Patel	15	– (4) c Pridgeon b D'Oliveira	0
P. Carrick not out	50		
A. Sidebottom c Rhodes b Inchmore	12		
P. W. Jarvis c D'Oliveira b McEwan	29		
S. J. Dennis c Pridgeon b Newport	8		
B 8, l-b 16, w 2, n-b 4	30	L-b 5, n-b 1	6
	405	(4 wkts dec.)	**196**

1/3 2/184 3/197 4/207 5/246 6/274 7/321 8/342 9/393

1/91 2/126 3/133 4/143

Bonus points – Yorkshire 4, Worcestershire 2 (Score at 100 overs: 321-6).

Bowling: *First Innings*—Pridgeon 32-6-89-2; Inchmore 24-3-82-2; McEwan 29-3-96-2; Newport 27.5-5-87-2; Patel 18-6-27-1. *Second Innings*—Pridgeon 8-4-17-0; Inchmore 6-0-13-0; Newport 8-0-34-0; McEwan 7-2-23-0; Patel 6-0-20-0; D'Oliveira 8-0-60-2; Hick 3-0-24-2.

Worcestershire

T. S. Curtis not out	122	– b Hartley	37
D. B. D'Oliveira c Jarvis b Hartley	42	– lbw b Sidebottom	22
D. M. Smith b Sidebottom	82	– (4) c Metcalfe b Dennis	15
G. A. Hick not out	36	– (3) c Bairstow b Hartley	60
*P. A. Neale (did not bat)		– lbw b Hartley	30
D. N. Patel (did not bat)		– b Jarvis	26
†S. J. Rhodes (did not bat)		– b Jarvis	7
P. J. Newport (did not bat)		– not out	16
S. M. McEwan (did not bat)		– not out	5
B 2, l-b 4, w 1, n-b 11	18	L-b 24, w 1, n-b 3	28
	(2 wkts dec.) **300**	(7 wkts)	**246**

1/78 2/245

1/56 2/80 3/103 4/164 5/195 6/208 7/241

J. D. Inchmore and A. P. Pridgeon did not bat.

Bonus points – Worcestershire 4.

Bowling: *First Innings*—Sidebottom 15-1-54-1; Jarvis 13-2-49-0; Dennis 17-2-62-0; Hartley 14.2-2-63-1; Carrick 15-4-40-0; Love 8-2-26-0. *Second Innings*—Sidebottom 13-1-57-1; Jarvis 15.4-1-73-2; Dennis 6-0-31-1; Hartley 13-1-59-3; Carrick 5-4-2-0.

Umpires: R. Palmer and A. G. T. Whitehead.

WORCESTERSHIRE v SUSSEX

At Worcester, June 21, 23, 24. Drawn. Worcestershire 4 pts, Sussex 7 pts. Toss: Sussex.
Worcestershire, somewhat uncharacteristically, made not even a token attempt on a target of
261 in 51 overs; although in their defence it has to be added that Smith was nursing a bruised
finger after the Sunday League game and that Hick had been omitted so that Ellcock could
make his first Championship appearance of the season. For the fourth time in successive games,
Radford took five or more wickets in an innings as he claimed career-best figures of seven
for 94 on the opening day. Parker batted for 305 minutes for his 125 and hit nineteen 4s.
Worcestershire, beginning the second day 38 for one, were dismissed in three hours for 148 in
grey, gloomy conditions. Colin Wells made the early breakthrough and Reeve polished off the
later batting with four wickets for 11 in 39 balls. Sussex fared no better, being 83 for five when
bad light stopped play an hour early, but from being interestingly balanced, the game drifted
towards a draw after rain caused a 90-minute delay on the final morning.

Sussex

D. K. Standing lbw b Radford	2	– b Newport	8
A. M. Green b Ellcock	5	– b Weston	22
P. W. G. Parker c and b Radford	125	– b Radford	22
R. I. Alikhan lbw b Radford	39	– c Rhodes b Radford	2
C. M. Wells lbw b Radford	2	– (6) not out	36
A. P. Wells lbw b Radford	3	– (5) c sub b Radford	0
*†I. J. Gould lbw b Radford	30	– c Rhodes b Newport	25
D. A. Reeve run out	0	– not out	9
A. C. S. Pigott not out	19		
A. N. Jones b Radford	0		
A. M. Bredin not out	7		
L-b 12, w 1, n-b 5	18	B 8, l-b 17, n-b 9	34

1/7 2/12 3/102 4/116 5/127   (9 wkts dec.) 250   1/30 2/51 3/68   (6 wkts dec.) 158
6/223 7/224 8/225 9/227   4/69 5/74 6/140

Bonus points – Sussex 3, Worcestershire 4.

Bowling: *First Innings*—Ellcock 15-1-40-1; Radford 25.5-3-94-7; Newport 13-4-27-0;
Weston 7-3-11-0; Illingworth 22-10-36-0; Patel 15-4-30-0. *Second Innings*—Radford
24-5-75-3; Newport 12-3-22-2; Weston 14-6-35-1; Illingworth 1-0-1-0.

Worcestershire

T. S. Curtis c Parker b Jones	6	– not out	43
D. B. D'Oliveira c Gould b C. M. Wells	10	– c Parker b C. M. Wells	14
R. K. Illingworth b C. M. Wells	39		
D. N. Patel lbw b Reeve	15		
*P. A. Neale c Gould b C. M. Wells	37	– (3) not out	28
M. J. Weston c and b Jones	0		
†S. J. Rhodes b Reeve	0		
P. J. Newport c Jones b Reeve	3		
N. V. Radford b Reeve	6		
D. M. Smith c Gould b Reeve	6		
R. M. Ellcock not out	4		
L-b 8, w 1, n-b 13	22	L-b 8, w 1, n-b 8	17

1/6 2/50 3/70 4/89 5/90   148   1/34   (1 wkt) 102
6/95 7/108 8/120 9/142

Bonus points – Sussex 4.

Bowling: *First Innings*—Jones 14-2-60-2; Pigott 4-1-15-0; Reeve 22.2-5-32-5; C. M. Wells
20-7-33-3. *Second Innings*—Jones 8-0-33-0; Reeve 13-3-32-0; C. M. Wells 9-2-21-1;
Standing 4-2-2-0; Bredin 5-1-6-0.

Umpires: R. Palmer and A. G. T. Whitehead.

WORCESTERSHIRE v HAMPSHIRE

At Worcester, June 28, 30, July 1. Worcestershire won by six wickets. Worcestershire 22 pts, Hampshire 5 pts. Toss: Hampshire. Newport's six for 48, his best figures to date, gave him a match return of eleven for 100 and left Worcestershire with all of the final day in which to score the 111 needed for victory. No batsman had managed more than 44 in the two first innings, but on the second afternoon Chris Smith held out for almost four hours to give his bowlers a chance of thwarting Worcestershire. For a time it looked as if they might as Marshall made the most of an increasingly suspect pitch on the final morning, capturing three wickets quickly, including that of Hick, out without scoring for the first time in a Championship match. Marshall also forced Smith to retire hurt after a blow on the finger, but Curtis, with determination and technique, and Patel, with seven boundaries in his unbeaten 49, made sure that Worcestershire would achieve their third Championship win of the season.

Hampshire

C. G. Greenidge c Pridgeon b Radford	12	– (7) lbw b Newport	0
V. P. Terry c Curtis b Pridgeon	8	– (1) c Rhodes b Pridgeon	1
C. L. Smith b Pridgeon	0	– (2) b Pridgeon	66
*M. C. J. Nicholas lbw b Newport	24	– (3) b Newport	10
R. A. Smith b Illingworth	9	– (4) c and b Newport	15
K. D. James c Rhodes b Pridgeon	41	– (5) c Rhodes b Radford	14
M. D. Marshall b Newport	4	– (6) b Newport	24
N. G. Cowley b Newport	0	– b Pridgeon	5
†R. J. Parks c Radford b Newport	31	– c Radford b Newport	0
T. M. Tremlett b Newport	7	– b Newport	2
C. A. Connor not out	11	– not out	0
L-b 8, n-b 3	11	B 1, l-b 5	19

1/24 2/24 3/24 4/45 5/63   158   1/1 2/23 3/43 4/80 5/127   156
6/67 7/67 8/130 9/140   6/127 7/144 8/147 9/156

Bonus points – Hampshire 1, Worcestershire 4.

Bowling: *First Innings*—Radford 18-7-36-1; Pridgeon 16.1-3-46-3; Newport 18-3-52-5; Illingworth 16-12-16-1. *Second Innings*—Radford 15-3-44-1; Pridgeon 14.2-6-19-3; Newport 17-1-48-6; Illingworth 13-8-26-0; Patel 1-0-5-0.

Worcestershire

T. S. Curtis lbw b Tremlett	14	– c Parks b Marshall	21
D. B. D'Oliveira run out	33	– lbw b Marshall	6
G. A. Hick c Nicholas b Marshall	21	– b Marshall	0
D. M. Smith c and b Marshall	44	– retired hurt	6
*P. A. Neale c Nicholas b Marshall	0	– c C. L. Smith b Marshall	13
R. K. Illingworth run out	14		
D. N. Patel c C. L. Smith b Connor	0	– (6) not out	49
*S. J. Rhodes c Parks b Connor	0	– (7) not out	3
P. J. Newport lbw b Marshall	31		
N. V. Radford not out	23		
A. P. Pridgeon c Parks b Cowley	3		
B 1, l-b 9, w 1, n-b 10	21	B 3, l-b 6, w 4, n-b 1	14

1/35 2/73 3/73 4/73 5/100   204   1/9 2/13 3/43 4/87   (4 wkts) 112
6/100 7/100 8/170 9/190

Bonus points – Worcestershire 2, Hampshire 4.

Bowling: *First Innings*—Marshall 23-2-70-4; James 9-1-27-0; Connor 19-2-42-2; Tremlett 16-5-29-1; Cowley 11-2-26-1. *Second Innings*—Marshall 15-6-29-4; Connor 8-1-34-0; Cowley 2-0-2-0; Tremlett 6-2-16-0; James 3.4-0-22-0.

Umpires: C. Cook and J. H. Hampshire.

At Derby, July 2, 3, 4. WORCESTERSHIRE drew with DERBYSHIRE.

WORCESTERSHIRE v NOTTINGHAMSHIRE

At Worcester, July, 5, 7, 8. Drawn. Worcestershire 4 pts, Nottinghamshire 8 pts. Toss: Worcestershire. A magnificent 227 not out by Hick, his first double-century for Worcestershire, changed the pattern of the game after Nottinghamshire had threatened to win inside two days. Hadlee followed up his four wickets in Worcestershire's first innings with 76 runs off 101 balls on the second day before removing the home side's openers for 26. Worcestershire began the final day only 36 runs ahead with seven wickets in hand. But Hick, 76 not out overnight, added another 151 in spectacular style, smashing five 6s off Hemmings – three over the pavilion – and 31 4s. Altogether he batted for 288 minutes and received 307 balls. That, however, was the end of the entertainment. Nottinghamshire, left to score 263 in 57 overs, reduced by rain to 50 overs, declined the challenge and shut up shop.

Worcestershire

T. S. Curtis c Scott b Saxelby	18	– lbw b Hadlee	13
D. B. D'Oliveira b Pick	2	– b Hadlee	2
G. A. Hick c Scott b Hadlee	0	– not out	227
D. N. Patel b Hadlee	51	– c Hadlee b Afford	46
*P. A. Neale c Randall b Rice	42	– c Rice b Hemmings	57
M. J. Weston c Scott b Hadlee	1	– c and b Hemmings	8
†S. J. Rhodes c Rice b Saxelby	7	– not out	15
P. J. Newport c Scott b Saxelby	3		
R. K. Illingworth c Afford b Hadlee	29		
J. D. Inchmore b Saxelby	4		
A. P. Pridgeon not out	10		
B 1, l-b 20, w 1, n-b 3	25	B 2, l-b 7, w 1, n-b 2	12

1/7 2/8 3/67 4/115 5/121   192   1/9 2/26 3/111   (5 wkts dec.) 380
6/138 7/147 8/150 9/154   4/249 5/309

Bonus points – Worcestershire 1, Nottinghamshire 4.

Bowling: *First Innings*—Hadlee 16-7-24-4; Pick 12-4-36-1; Saxelby 21-3-47-4; Rice 19-5-54-1; Hemmings 1-0-10-0. *Second Innings*—Hadlee 12-1-38-2; Pick 10-1-28-0; Hemmings 33-4-154-2; Afford 36-10-113-1; Saxelby 8-0-38-0.

Nottinghamshire

B. C. Broad lbw b Newport	23	– b Newport	23
M. Newell b Pridgeon	80	– b Inchmore	15
D. W. Randall c Rhodes b Inchmore	34	– run out	4
*C. E. B. Rice c Neale b Pridgeon	3	– not out	37
P. Johnson c Weston b Illingworth	15	– not out	38
R. J. Hadlee c Neale b Newport	76		
†C. W. Scott not out	38		
R. A. Pick c Hick b Newport	1		
E. E. Hemmings c D'Oliveira b Pridgeon	13		
K. Saxelby not out	1		
L-b 16, n-b 10	26	B 6, l-b 1, n-b 4	11

1/32 2/108 3/115 4/133   (8 wkts dec.) 310   1/25 2/44 3/50   (3 wkts) 128
5/230 6/257 7/261 8/303

J. A. Afford did not bat.

Bonus points – Nottinghamshire 4, Worcestershire 3 (Score at 100 overs: 302-7).

Bowling: *First Innings*—Pridgeon 21-3-57-3; Inchmore 18-4-47-1; Newport 21-2-62-3; Patel 15-4-44-0; Weston 13-1-48-0; Illingworth 15-7-36-1. *Second Innings*—Pridgeon 11-2-38-0; Inchmore 6-1-17-1; Newport 8-0-22-1; Illingworth 8-4-23-0; Weston 5-0-21-0.

Umpires: M. J. Kitchen and K. E. Palmer.

At Neath, July 16, 17, 18. WORCESTERSHIRE beat GLAMORGAN by seven wickets.

At Southend, July 19, 21, 22. WORCESTERSHIRE lost to ESSEX by 91 runs.

At Hove, July 23, 24, 25. WORCESTERSHIRE lost to SUSSEX by five wickets.

WORCESTERSHIRE v GLOUCESTERSHIRE

At Worcester, July 26, 28, 29. Gloucestershire won by 78 runs. Gloucestershire 20 pts, Worcestershire 4 pts. Toss: Gloucestershire. While Hick was building on his fourth century in five Championship games, Worcestershire harboured hopes of achieving their target of 313 in 88 overs. But his departure for 134, which took his first-class aggregate in July to 914 runs, signalled the beginning of the end. The next four wickets tumbled for only 21 runs, three of them to Walsh in ten balls. Gloucestershire, having elected to bat first on an untrustworthy pitch, were indebted to a fifth-wicket stand of 146 between Lloyds and Tomlins after Pridgeon had reduced them to 23 for four. Rain washed out the second day's play, leaving Worcestershire with little alternative but to declare at their Saturday score and wait to be set a target.

Gloucestershire

A. J. Wright c Curtis b Pridgeon	3	– (2) c Hick b Pridgeon	5
A. W. Stovold c Illingworth b Pridgeon	4	– (1) run out	5
K. P. Tomlins c Rhodes b Patel	75	– not out	23
P. Bainbridge c Smith b Pridgeon	10	– not out	17
K. M. Curran lbw b Pridgeon	0		
J. W. Lloyds c Rhodes b Newport	82		
M. W. Alleyne not out	73		
†R. C. Russell c Hick b Newport	9		
C. A. Walsh b Inchmore	16		
D. V. Lawrence c Inchmore b Newport	2		
*D. A. Graveney not out	1		
B 2, l-b 15, w 1, n-b 7	25		

1/7 2/8 3/23 4/23 5/169   (9 wkts dec.) 300   1/8 2/8   (2 wkts dec.) 50
6/211 7/256 8/291 9/299

Bonus points – Gloucestershire 4, Worcestershire 4.

Bowling: *First Innings*—Pridgeon 20–2–60–4; Inchmore 17.1–2–51–1; Newport 22–5–66–3; Patel 23–6–75–1; Illingworth 13–3–31–0. *Second Innings*—Pridgeon 5.4–1–24–1; Newport 5–0–26–0.

Worcestershire

T. S. Curtis b Walsh	10	– c Graveney b Lawrence	0
D. B. D'Oliveira c Russell b Walsh	6	– c Russell b Lawrence	21
R. K. Illingworth not out	13	– (9) c Russell b Walsh	0
G. A. Hick not out	4	– (3) c Russell b Graveney	134
D. M. Smith (did not bat)		– (4) lbw b Walsh	6
*P. A. Neale (did not bat)		– (5) c Russell b Bainbridge	7
D. N. Patel (did not bat)		– (6) b Bainbridge	21
†S. J. Rhodes (did not bat)		– (7) lbw b Walsh	9
P. J. Newport (did not bat)		– (8) c Graveney b Bainbridge	10
J. D. Inchmore (did not bat)		– b Walsh	0
A. P. Pridgeon (did not bat)		– not out	6
L-b 1, n-b 4	5	B 8, l-b 5, w 1, n-b 6	20

1/17 2/24   (2 wkts dec.) 38   1/1 2/56 3/67 4/92 5/162   234
                                            6/213 7/215 8/215 9/219

Bowling: *First Innings*—Walsh 6–2–17–2; Lawrence 5–1–20–0. *Second Innings*—Walsh 25–6–80–4; Lawrence 14–3–63–2; Bainbridge 15.2–4–46–3; Lloyds 5–0–19–0; Graveney 10–5–13–1.

Umpires: J. A. Jameson and B. J. Meyer.

At Weston-super-Mare, August 2, 4, 5. WORCESTERSHIRE lost to SOMERSET by five wickets.

At The Oval, August 9, 11, 12. WORCESTERSHIRE drew with SURREY.

WORCESTERSHIRE v LEICESTERSHIRE

At Worcester, August 16, 18, 19. Worcestershire won by four wickets. Worcestershire 20 pts, Leicestershire 2 pts. Toss: Worcestershire. Despite having to concede an 81-run lead after play on the second day had been reduced by the weather to eleven overs, Worcestershire cruised to their fifth Championship win of the season. Making the most of a responsive wicket, Pridgeon, Newport and McEwan bowled Leicestershire out in their second innings for 114 in under three hours, Newport's nine wickets in the match consolidating his standing as the county's leading wicket-taker. This gave Worcestershire 53 overs to score 196 to win, and Smith steered them to within 22 runs of their target, hitting ten 4s and a 6 in his 76 off 99 balls. Patel's unbeaten 43 saw them home with three overs and four wickets to spare.

Leicestershire

J. C. Balderstone b McEwan	11	– b Pridgeon		2
R. A. Cobb b Pridgeon	13	– b McEwan		25
P. Willey c Pridgeon b Newport	19	– c Hick b Pridgeon		6
*D. I. Gower c Rhodes b McEwan	0	– b Newport		2
J. J. Whitaker c Rhodes b McEwan	18	– b McEwan		14
T. J. Boon c Hick b Newport	63	– lbw b McEwan		4
P. A. J. DeFreitas c Newport b Pridgeon	25	– b Newport		26
†P. Whitticase c Hick b Newport	26	– c Rhodes b Newport		26
W. K. M. Benjamin b Newport	6	– c Rhodes b Pridgeon		1
L. B. Taylor not out	5	– b Newport		2
G. A. R. Harris c Hick b Newport	6	– not out		0
L-b 4, n-b 1	17	L-b 4, n-b 2		6

1/25 2/25 3/25 4/53 5/69   209   1/6 2/22 3/25 4/43 5/52   114
6/135 7/181 8/192 9/203   6/57 7/110 8/111 9/113

Bonus points – Leicestershire 2, Worcestershire 4.

Bowling: *First Innings*—Pridgeon 18–6–36–2; Newport 20.4–3–76–5; McEwan 17–1–53–3; Weston 15–2–40–0; Patel 1–1–0–0; Smith 1–1–0–0. *Second Innings*—Pridgeon 16–6–33–3; Newport 12.5–3–30–4; McEwan 10–1–33–3; Weston 7–2–14–0.

Worcestershire

T. S. Curtis not out	48	– lbw b Benjamin		4
D. B. D'Oliveira c DeFreitas b Benjamin	14	– b Taylor		1
D. M. Smith c Whitaker b DeFreitas	15	– lbw b Benjamin		76
G. A. Hick not out	45	– c Whitticase b Taylor		34
*P. A. Neale (did not bat)		– c Gower b DeFreitas		16
D. N. Patel (did not bat)		– not out		43
M. J. Weston (did not bat)		– b Benjamin		9
†S. J. Rhodes (did not bat)		– not out		5
L-b 2, n-b 4	6	L-b 8, n-b 3		11

1/23 2/48   (2 wkts dec.) 128   1/5 2/29 3/65 4/96   (6 wkts) 199
                                                 5/174 6/188

P. J. Newport, S. M. McEwan and A. P. Pridgeon did not bat.

Bowling: *First Innings*—Benjamin 12–2–36–1; Taylor 16–6–41–0; DeFreitas 13–3–31–1; Harris 5–0–18–0; Willey 2–2–0–0. *Second Innings*—Taylor 17.1–1–63–2; DeFreitas 11.5–2–38–1; Benjamin 17–1–70–3; Harris 3–1–16–0; Boon 1–0–4–0.

Umpires: D. O. Oslear and R. Palmer.

At Bournemouth, August 20, 21, 22. WORCESTERSHIRE drew with HAMPSHIRE.

WORCESTERSHIRE v WARWICKSHIRE

At Worcester, August 23, 25, 26. Drawn. Worcestershire 3 pts, Warwickshire 2 pts. Toss: Warwickshire. Only 68 overs were possible on the opening day before rain came and washed out the remainder of the match.

Warwickshire

A. J. Moles lbw b Newport	26	G. J. Parsons c and b Radford		9
P. A. Smith c Rhodes b Pridgeon	45	K. J. Kerr not out		6
A. I. Kallicharran b Radford	31			
D. L. Amiss c Hick b Newport	33	B 8, l-b 4, w 2, n-b 6		20
†G. W. Humpage c Radford b Newport	28			
Asif Din not out	12	1/63 2/89 3/127 4/141	(7 wkts)	215
A. M. Ferreira b McEwan	5	5/175 6/181 7/206		

T. A. Munton and *N. Gifford did not bat.

Bonus points – Warwickshire 2, Worcestershire 3.

Bowling: Radford 22–1–80–2; Pridgeon 14–2–35–1; Newport 19–2–64–3; McEwan 13–5–24–1.

Worcestershire

T. S. Curtis, D. B. D'Oliveira, D. M. Smith, G. A. Hick, *P. A. Neale, D. N. Patel, †S. J. Rhodes, P. J. Newport, N. V. Radford, S. M. McEwan and A. P. Pridgeon.

Umpires: J. W. Holder and P. B. Wight.

At Bristol, August 27, 28, 29. WORCESTERSHIRE drew with GLOUCESTERSHIRE.

WORCESTERSHIRE v SOMERSET

At Worcester, September 3, 4. Worcestershire won by an innings and 9 runs. Worcestershire 24 pts, Somerset 2 pts. Toss: Worcestershire. Victory in two days brought Worcestershire their first innings win over Somerset since 1952. Radford was their destroyer-in-chief, returning a career-best nine for 70 to force the visitors to follow on 218 runs behind. Having taken the first eight wickets to fall, including a spell of four for 1 in twelve balls, Radford was in sight of becoming the first bowler for 22 years to take ten wickets in an innings in England when Newport broke the sequence. His return, in addition to being the best in the Championship in 1986, was the best by a Worcestershire bowler for 22 years. The previous day Curtis, hitting 22 4s, had laid the foundation of the home team's total with a career-best 153 in 313 minutes.

Worcestershire

T. S. Curtis c Hardy b Marks	153	D. N. Patel b Botham		40
D. B. D'Oliveira lbw b Botham	34	B 2, l-b 7, n-b 1		10
D. M. Smith c Dredge b Marks	52			
G. A. Hick b Dredge	13	1/61 2/194 3/217	(5 wkts dec.)	345
*P. A. Neale not out	43	4/296 5/345		

†S. J. Rhodes, P. J. Newport, N. V. Radford, S. M. McEwan and A. P. Pridgeon did not bat.

Bonus points – Worcestershire 4, Somerset 2.

Bowling: Botham 22.1–4–65–2; Taylor 19–1–85–0; Dredge 16–4–32–1; Pringle 10–0–48–0; Marks 29–4–106–2.

Somerset

N. A. Felton b Radford	16	– b McEwan	4
*P. M. Roebuck c Rhodes b Radford	22	– c D'Oliveira b Newport	33
†T. Gard b Radford	0	– (9) not out	32
J. J. E. Hardy lbw b Radford	4	– (3) c Patel b Newport	67
R. J. Harden c D'Oliveira b Radford	21	– (4) b Patel	6
R. J. Bartlett b Radford	23	– (5) b Radford	11
I. T. Botham b Radford	0	– (6) b Patel	17
V. J. Marks b Radford	2	– (7) lbw b Radford	7
N. J. Pringle c Smith b Newport	10	– (8) c McEwan b Patel	11
C. H. Dredge c McEwan b Radford	14	– c McEwan b Patel	0
N. S. Taylor not out	6	– c McEwan b Newport	1
L-b 2, n-b 7	9	B 3, l-b 2, w 2, n-b 13	20
1/18 2/18 3/34 4/47 5/85	127	1/6 2/102 3/124 4/124 5/141	209
6/85 7/90 8/91 9/116		6/159 7/162 8/204 9/204	

Bonus points – Worcestershire 4.

Bowling: *First Innings*—Radford 19.2–4–70–9; Pridgeon 12–3–31–0; Newport 7–0–24–1. *Second Innings*—Pridgeon 8–0–34–0; McEwan 9–2–33–1; Radford 14–1–59–2; Patel 23–9–56–4; Newport 10.4–4–22–3.

Umpires: B. Dudleston and R. Julian.

WORCESTERSHIRE v GLAMORGAN

At Worcester, September 10, 11, 12. Worcestershire won by seven wickets. Worcestershire 21 pts, Glamorgan 6 pts. Toss: Glamorgan. Hick became the youngest player in the history of the game to complete 2,000 runs in a season as Worcestershire achieved their target of 302 in 52 overs with three balls remaining. The twenty-year-old Zimbabwean needed 103 in his last innings to reach the landmark in his first full season and got there by hitting his sixth hundred of the summer. His 107, off 121 balls in 147 minutes, took his aggregate against the Welsh county to 699 from six innings, including an unbeaten 219 at Neath earlier in the season. Centuries from Morris, his first in the Championship as captain, and Holmes saw Glamorgan dominate the first day, and they batted on to compile their highest total of the season. With the batsmen continuing to reign supreme, it eventually fell to Morris to set a target, and allowing for the genius of Hick, his calculation was just right.

Glamorgan

J. A. Hopkins c McEwan b Radford	0	– c Illingworth b Newport	93
*H. Morris c Rhodes b Patel	114	– c Hick b Patel	35
A. L. Jones c D'Oliveira b McEwan	44	– c Neale b D'Oliveira	29
G. C. Holmes b Patel	107	– (5) not out	15
M. P. Maynard b Radford	24	– (4) not out	21
R. C. Ontong c Rhodes b Radford	47		
J. G. Thomas c Radford b McEwan	22		
†T. Davies not out	6		
B 5, l-b 7, w 4, n-b 19	35	B 2, l-b 9, w 1, n-b 1	13

1/0 2/115 3/283 4/292   (7 wkts dec.) 399   1/98 2/166 3/177   (3 wkts dec.) 206
5/342 6/382 7/399

I. Smith, S. R. Barwick and S. L. Watkin did not bat.

Bonus points – Glamorgan 4, Worcestershire 1 (Score at 100 overs: 334-4).

Bowling: *First Innings*—Radford 38.1–11–130–3; McEwan 15–2–89–2; Patel 31–10–83–2; Newport 12–0–41–0; Illingworth 22–8–44–0. *Second Innings*—Radford 10–1–31–0; McEwan 9.1–4–29–0; Illingworth 11–1–32–0; Newport 11–2–54–1; Patel 10–1–25–1; D'Oliveira 5–0–24–1.

Worcestershire

T. S. Curtis st Davies b Ontong	50	– retired hurt	7
D. B. D'Oliveira c and b Barwick	12	– b Barwick	49
D. M. Smith c Holmes b Ontong	100	– lbw b Ontong	67
G. A. Hick c Morris b Watkin	61	– c Maynard b Barwick	107
*P. A. Neale c Maynard b Watkin	22	– not out	60
D. N. Patel not out	29	– not out	2
†S. J. Rhodes not out	7		
B 7, l-b 13, w 1, n-b 2	23	B 3, l-b 3, n-b 4	10

1/17 2/164 3/197   (5 wkts dec.) 304   1/83 2/165 3/293   (3 wkts) 302
4/259 5/264

P. J. Newport, N. V. Radford, R. K. Illingworth and S. M. McEwan did not bat.

Bonus points – Worcestershire 4, Glamorgan 2.

Bowling: *First Innings*—Thomas 19.2–4–66–0; Barwick 18–4–47–1; Ontong 26–4–68–2; Watkin 15–1–74–2; Smith 7–0–29–0. *Second Innings*—Thomas 7–0–48–0; Smith 3–0–27–0; Barwick 22–2–125–2; Ontong 18.3–2–88–1; Watkin 1–0–8–0.

Umpires: D. O. Oslear and D. R. Shepherd.

YORKSHIRE

Patron: HRH The Duchess of Kent
President: The Viscount Mountgarret
Chairman: B. Walsh
Chairman, Cricket Committee: D. B. Close
Secretary: J. Lister
   Headingley Cricket Ground, Leeds LS6 3BU
   (Telephone: 0532-787394)
Captain: 1986 – D. L. Bairstow
        1987 – P. Carrick

After a disappointing season, Yorkshire, still with much promise unfulfilled, ended their association with Geoff Boycott, and in November David Bairstow was replaced as captain by Phil Carrick. The cricket committee voted 4-1 against offering Boycott another year's contract, and when this recommendation was put before the general committee, an amendment aimed at extending his career failed by 12-9. Also released was Graham Stevenson, whose appearances in the past two years had been limited by back and groin strains.

Boycott, whose final record with Yorkshire in the Championship was 29,485 runs at an average of 58.27, again headed the county's averages, despite missing nine Britannic Assurance Championship matches with a broken bone in his left wrist. County officials paid due tribute to the 45-year-old opener, while stressing that the committee wanted to give younger talent the chance to develop, particularly as several outstanding prospects had gone to other counties in the past.

Injuries set Yorkshire back seriously, for Arnie Sidebottom and Paul Jarvis were also long-term absentees. The county's main strike force, they appeared together in only eight Championship and nine John Player League games. Jarvis, who along with Ashley Metcalfe received his county cap, demonstrated an impressive ability to cut through an innings. He played the leading role in the Championship victories over Middlesex at Lord's and Surrey at Headingley, but at 21 rather too much was expected of him. The tendency to bowl him in long spells resulted, not surprisingly, in a nasty back strain. A broken toe caused Sidebottom to miss the last twelve Championship matches.

Thus in early August Yorkshire found themselves in the same position as the previous year, relying heavily on their less experienced seam bowlers. Peter Hartley, Stuart Fletcher, Simon Dennis and Chris Shaw all did well, but all the seam bowlers' figures could have been improved by better close-catching. Bairstow, plagued by a series of bumps, bruises and strains which would have disabled a less resolute man, battled bravely without having all that successful a time behind the stumps, while Carrick, at first slip, finished with a less than 50 per cent record. Such a situation inevitably took some of the heart out of the attack, and when Bairstow was relieved of the captaincy, one reason given was that his wicket-keeping had suffered as a result of his extra responsibilities.

Among the slower bowlers, only Carrick appeared regularly, but he had a lean time. Although he conceded no more than 2.39 runs an over,

the slow left-armer would have served the team's needs better had he
tossed up the ball and persuaded errors. His striking-rate of one wicket
per 114 deliveries pinpointed a serious weakness in Yorkshire's
approach. In theory, they were prepared to risk defeat in pursuit of
victory, but in practice Bairstow and Carrick, his appointed deputy,
lacked the courage of the club's conviction for positive cricket and set a
defensive tone. This was evident in the field as Yorkshire stood back and
waited to see what would happen, although they were ever ready to
negotiate when the weather intervened.

Yorkshire could not have hoped for a better start, with wins in their
first two Championship games and their best opening run in the Sunday
League with four successes. The batting proved reliable, too, with their
62 bonus points the most by any county. Yet the side never capitalised,
improving by only one place to tenth in the Championship.

Metcalfe stood out with six hundreds and more than 1,500 runs. Under
the guidance during the winter of the former Australian opener, Keith
Stackpole, he had adjusted his initial foot movement and so avoided
being caught behind the wicket, a flaw which had made him look
vulnerable against fast bowling. Last summer, the 22-year-old opener put
a miserable 1985 well behind him and scored freely, his runs coming
at a rate of 58.11 per 100 balls. His partnership with Martyn Moxon
promised much until Moxon, having gained selection for England, lost
his form and finally his place.

Kevin Sharp also made satisfactory progress and would have passed
1,000 runs had he not had a toe broken in late July. In contrast, Jim Love
experienced mixed fortunes and Neil Hartley, despite occupying the
crease for lengthy periods, rarely looked at ease. Neither can feel his
place is secure from the challenge of Richard Blakey and Phil Robinson,
whose limited appearances raised a question mark over the selection
policy. Blakey scored heavily with the Colts, represented Young England
and did enough to demand greater opportunity, while Robinson, less
stylish, could be effective in the middle order, where he hits the ball hard
and often.

Robinson was more in evidence in the John Player League, where
Yorkshire experimented by batting first when they won the toss. For
most of the season they stayed in touch with the leaders, nursing hopes of
prizemoney, but they lost three of the last four games and tied with
Warwickshire as they faded to eighth. It was much the same in the other
competitions. After a flourish in the opening group game of the Benson
and Hedges Cup, beating Lancashire, they failed to reach the quarter-
finals, and an impressive victory over Middlesex in the NatWest Bank
Trophy preceded a heavy defeat at the hands of Sussex. A poor pitch was
a contributory factor after Sussex had won the toss, but Yorkshire had
held a clear advantage at one stage.

Much in the future will depend on the guidance offered to the younger
players. Boycott's departure left a gap in the sense that he represented the
last playing link with the highly successful side of the 1960s and his
experience will be missed. In the circumstances, Close and other former
players on the committee will have to play an active role, if only in
making themselves readily available to those who want advice. If a
happy relationship can be established between the committee- and
dressing-rooms, Yorkshire might just cause one or two surprises. – J.C.

YORKSHIRE 1986

[Bill Smith]

Back row: P. E. Robinson, S. D. Fletcher, S. J. Dennis, C. Shaw, M. D. Moxon, A. A. Metcalfe. Front row: S. N. Hartley, K. Sharp, P. Carrick, D. L. Bairstow (captain), A. Sidebottom, J. D. Love. Insets: I. G. Swallow, P. A. Booth, G. Boycott, R. J. Blakey, P. W. Jarvis.

YORKSHIRE RESULTS

All first-class matches – Played 25: Won 4, Lost 6, Drawn 15.

County Championship matches – Played 24: Won 4, Lost 5, Drawn 15.

Bonus points – Batting 62, Bowling 59.

Competition placings – Britannic Assurance County Championship, 10th; NatWest Bank Trophy, q-f; Benson and Hedges Cup, 3rd in Group B; John Player League, 8th.

BRITANNIC ASSURANCE CHAMPIONSHIP AVERAGES

BATTING

	Birthplace	M	I	NO	R	HI	Avge
‡G. Boycott	Fitzwilliam	12	18	1	890	135*	52.35
‡A. A. Metcalfe	Horsforth	24	37	0	1,582	151	42.75
P. E. Robinson ...	Keighley	7	11	2	373	104*	41.44
‡K. Sharp	Leeds	18	29	6	948	181	41.21
‡J. D. Love	Leeds	21	29	5	831	109	34.62
P. J. Hartley	Keighley	15	17	4	441	87*	33.92
I. G. Swallow	Barnsley	8	9	4	141	43*	28.20
‡D. L. Bairstow ...	Bradford	24	33	4	796	88	27.44
‡M. D. Moxon	Barnsley	17	27	3	636	147	26.50
‡S. N. Hartley	Shipley	20	28	2	676	78	26.00
‡P. Carrick	Leeds	24	32	6	613	51	23.57
R. J. Blakey	Huddersfield	3	5	0	99	46	19.80
‡P. W. Jarvis	Redcar	15	17	7	183	47	18.30
‡S. J. Dennis	Scarborough	15	12	4	82	18*	10.25
S. D. Fletcher	Keighley	14	10	3	67	24	9.57
C. Shaw	Hemsworth	13	10	4	57	21	9.50
‡A. Sidebottom	Barnsley	10	9	2	65	18	9.28

Also batted: P. J. Berry (*Saltburn*) (1 match) 4*; D. Byas (*Kilham*) (1 match) 0; ‡G. B. Stevenson (*Ackworth*) (2 matches) 58*.

* *Signifies not out.* ‡ *Denotes county cap.*

The following played a total of thirteen three-figure innings for Yorkshire in County Championship matches: A. A. Metcalfe 6, G. Boycott 2, K. Sharp 2, J. D. Love 1, M. D. Moxon 1, P. E. Robinson 1.

BOWLING

	O	M	R	W	BB	Avge
P. W. Jarvis	428.4	82	1,332	60	7-55	22.20
C. Shaw	281.1	60	773	29	5-38	26.65
P. J. Hartley	321.1	49	1,095	41	6-68	26.70
A. Sidebottom	226.1	37	671	25	8-72	26.84
S. J. Dennis	384.3	75	1,230	42	5-71	29.28
S. D. Fletcher	389	79	1,172	29	5-90	40.41
P. Carrick	590.3	185	1,412	31	4-111	45.54

Also bowled: D. L. Bairstow 5–3–7–0; P. J. Berry 39–13–83–1; R. J. Blakey 10.3–1–68–1; D. Byas 2–0–15–0; S. N. Hartley 45.4–8–195–4; J. D. Love 39.2–7–146–0; A. A. Metcalfe 18.1–4–75–0; M. D. Moxon 27.4–9–90–2; P. E. Robinson 11–0–115–0; K. Sharp 29–4–192–3; G. B. Stevenson 29–8–75–2; I. G. Swallow 142–36–386–5.

Wicket-keepers: D. L. Bairstow 41 ct, 3 st; R. J. Blakey 4 ct; K. Sharp 4 ct; P. E. Robinson 1 ct.

Leading Fielder: M. D. Moxon 12.

At Taunton, April 26, 27, 28. YORKSHIRE beat SOMERSET by 5 runs.

YORKSHIRE v SUSSEX

At Leeds, May 7, 8, 9. Yorkshire won by one wicket. Yorkshire 20 pts, Sussex 1 pt. Toss: Sussex.
With the first day lost to rain, the teams had to contrive a finish. Yorkshire's seam bowlers were
difficult to force away on a slow pitch, and Sussex would have been in desperate trouble but for
Lenham's 198-minute innings. Further rain took 38 overs from the second day and on the third
Yorkshire forfeited their first innings. Sussex were given easy runs and their declaration set a
target of 251 in 58 overs. Yorkshire also struggled against accurate bowling, but their strength in
depth proved crucial when they needed 112 from the last twenty overs with only four wickets in
hand. Carrick, dropped when 24, led the way with 51 from 76 balls and Stevenson reached his
half-century from 36. Reeve bowled extremely well for Sussex and might have won the game,
for, off the first ball of the final over, Jarvis edged him for the final boundary through the gloves
of the diving wicket-keeper, Gould.

Sussex

N. J. Lenham c and b Hartley	75	– b Sharp	7
A. M. Green c Carrick b Jarvis	3	– not out	34
P. W. G. Parker b Sidebottom	0	– not out	10
A. P. Wells c Love b Jarvis	36		
*J. R. T. Barclay lbw b Sidebottom	4		
D. K. Standing c Jarvis b Hartley	2		
†I. J. Gould lbw b Stevenson	0		
G. S. le Roux c Hartley b Stevenson	0		
D. A. Reeve not out	35		
A. C. S. Pigott b Jarvis	10		
A. N. Jones b Hartley	11		
B 2, l-b 10, n-b 7	19	L-b 1, n-b 3	4

1/14 2/21 3/106 4/117 5/130   195   1/11   (1 wkt dec.) 55
6/131 7/132 8/132 9/162

Bonus points – Sussex 1, Yorkshire 4.

Bowling: *First Innings*—Sidebottom 19–3–47–2; Jarvis 20–6–44–3; Stevenson 16–6–27–2;
Hartley 17.1–2–46–3; Carrick 6–1–19–0. *Second Innings*—Sharp 5–1–36–1; Metcalfe
4.1–0–18–0.

Yorkshire

Yorkshire forfeited their first innings.

G. Boycott c Gould b le Roux	12	G. B. Stevenson not out	58
M. D. Moxon c Gould b Reeve	28	P. J. Hartley c and b Reeve	15
K. Sharp c Green b le Roux	7	P. W. Jarvis not out	16
J. D. Love c Standing b Pigott	12	L-b 7, n-b 18	25
A. A. Metcalfe c Pigott b Reeve	9		
*†D. L. Bairstow lbw b Reeve	0	1/26 2/53 3/73	(9 wkts) 251
P. Carrick b Pigott	51	4/74 5/75 6/100	
A. Sidebottom c Gould b Jones	18	7/140 8/195 9/219	

Bowling: le Roux 14–1–57–2; Jones 11–0–66–1; Reeve 20.1–2–82–4; Pigott 12–0–39–2.

Umpires: B. Dudleston and N. T. Plews.

At Chelmsford, May 21, 22, 23. YORKSHIRE lost to ESSEX by 26 runs.

YORKSHIRE v LANCASHIRE

At Leeds, May 24, 26, 27. Drawn. Yorkshire 8 pts, Lancashire 7 pts. Toss: Lancashire. Lancashire batted first because they suspected the pitch would offer help to the spinners on the last day, but they lost half their side for only 47 to hostile pace bowling. Sidebottom and Jarvis were kept on too long, however, and when they tired Yorkshire had little to offer. Maynard took full advantage of the situation with his first century in first-class cricket, making his runs in four and three-quarter hours with a 6 and fourteen 4s. Yorkshire made a solid reply on the second day, their runs coming almost in even time although the occasional delivery did enough to confound the most assured batsmen. For most of the last day Lancashire operated in the shadow of defeat under grey, stormy skies. The ball turned slowly, and at 168 for six Simmons was missed at slip first ball. He then shared in a stand worth 67 in twelve overs with Watkinson, who also gave a clear chance when 27. Yorkshire showed no interest in a target of 251 in 75 minutes plus twenty overs.

Lancashire

G. D. Mendis b Jarvis	8	– b Swallow	62
M. R. Chadwick c S. N. Hartley b Sidebottom	13	– lbw b Swallow	26
D. W. Varey lbw b Jarvis	0	– b Swallow	8
N. H. Fairbrother b Jarvis	20	– c S. N. Hartley b Carrick	16
J. Abrahams c Jarvis b Sidebottom	3	– c Sharp b Carrick	21
†C. Maynard not out	132	– lbw b Carrick	12
M. Watkinson c Bairstow b Jarvis	24	– c Moxon b Carrick	44
*J. Simmons lbw b Jarvis	0	– not out	38
P. J. W. Allott st Bairstow b Swallow	65	– not out	21
D. J. Makinson c Bairstow b P. J. Hartley	14		
B. P. Patterson c Bairstow b P. J. Hartley	0		
B 4, l-b 6, n-b 7	17	B 2, l-b 6, w 4, n-b 8	20

1/13 2/13 3/33 4/41 5/47   296   1/73 2/107 3/108   (7 wkts dec.) 268
6/131 7/131 8/265 9/289   4/137 5/152
                                  6/168 7/235

Bonus points – Lancashire 3, Yorkshire 4.

Bowling: *First Innings*—Sidebottom 26–4–70–2; Jarvis 28–5–86–5; P. J. Hartley 13.3–2–51–2; Carrick 13–4–42–0; Swallow 14–4–37–1. *Second Innings*—Sidebottom 5–1–19–0; P. J. Hartley 8–3–15–0; Carrick 47–13–111–4; Swallow 41–12–109–3; Love 2–0–6–0.

Yorkshire

K. Sharp c and b Patterson	1	– (3) not out	22
M. D. Moxon c Chadwick b Allott	1	– (1) not out	36
I. G. Swallow c Allott b Simmons	41		
A. A. Metcalfe c and b Watkinson	42	– (2) lbw b Makinson	27
J. D. Love lbw b Allott	41		
S. N. Hartley lbw b Patterson	34		
*†D. L. Bairstow c Makinson b Watkinson	41		
P. Carrick b Makinson	50		
A. Sidebottom c Abrahams b Allott	6		
P. J. Hartley lbw b Allott	31		
P. W. Jarvis not out	5		
B 6, l-b 9, w 1, n-b 5	21	L-b 5	5

1/2 2/11 3/78 4/111 5/146   314   1/41   (1 wkt) 90
6/208 7/221 8/238 9/302

Bonus points – Yorkshire 4, Lancashire 4.

Bowling: *First Innings*—Patterson 20–4–67–2; Allott 21.4–4–68–4; Makinson 13–2–56–1; Watkinson 19–2–69–2; Simmons 14–5–39–1. *Second Innings*—Allott 6–1–10–0; Watkinson 12–1–49–0; Makinson 10–4–23–1; Fairbrother 3–2–3–0.

Umpires: R. Julian and M. J. Kitchen.

YORKSHIRE v DERBYSHIRE

At Sheffield, June 4, 5, 6. Derbyshire won by 99 runs. Derbyshire 22 pts, Yorkshire 7 pts. Toss: Derbyshire. Derbyshire batted very slowly on an easy-paced pitch and carried their first innings into the second day. Hill used up 440 balls and 467 minutes to make a career-best 172, and with Jean-Jacques, a former Minor County player making his début, shared in a record stand for Derbyshire's tenth wicket. Their 132 was also the highest by a last pair against Yorkshire. Yorkshire, throwing the game open, declared 139 behind, offered easy runs, and were set a target of 280 in 81 overs. However, they quickly fell well behind the required rate. Boycott made only 6 in twenty overs, with Mortensen bowling well outside the off stump. Towards the end the bounce became unreliable and Holding exploited the conditions superbly, taking five for 9 in 23 balls to give Derbyshire their second win in 29 years against Yorkshire. Only a defiant innings by Bairstow, who hammered 41 from as many deliveries, prevented the margin being greater.

Derbyshire

*K. J. Barnett c Bairstow b Dennis	19	– b Dennis	0
I. S. Anderson c Bairstow b Dennis	3	– c Moxon b Sharp	5
A. Hill not out	172	– not out	76
J. E. Morris lbw b Sidebottom	24	– not out	53
B. Roberts c Love b Jarvis	11		
G. Miller b Hartley	19		
R. Sharma lbw b Jarvis	16		
†C. Marples b Jarvis	12		
M. A. Holding c Hartley b Dennis	11		
O. H. Mortensen c Jarvis b Carrick	9		
M. Jean-Jacques b Dennis	73		
L-b 9, n-b 20	29	L-b 4, n-b 2	6

1/8 2/31 3/81 4/97 5/130   **398**   1/0 2/21   (2 wkts dec.) **140**
6/163 7/185 8/206 9/266

Bonus points – Derbyshire 3, Yorkshire 4 (Score at 100 overs: 268-9).

Bowling: *First Innings*—Jarvis 32–6–82–3; Dennis 26.5–4–89–4; Sidebottom 27–3–103–1; Hartley 25–3–83–1; Carrick 19–9–21–1; Love 4–1–11–0. *Second Innings*—Dennis 3–1–4–1; Hartley 2–0–6–0; Sharp 10–1–74–1; Metcalfe 9–0–52–0.

Yorkshire

G. Boycott b Jean-Jacques	22	– c and b Holding	69
M. D. Moxon c Marples b Holding	10	– lbw b Mortensen	9
A. A. Metcalfe b Jean-Jacques	67	– c Marples b Jean-Jacques	10
K. Sharp b Mortensen	74	– c Marples b Jean-Jacques	2
J. D. Love b Holding	8	– c Holding b Miller	2
*†D. L. Bairstow c and b Holding	4	– c Barnett b Mortensen	41
P. Carrick b Holding	43	– c Roberts b Holding	25
A. Sidebottom not out	15	– b Holding	2
P. J. Hartley not out	1	– c Marples b Holding	7
P. W. Jarvis (did not bat)		– not out	1
S. J. Dennis (did not bat)		– lbw b Holding	0
B 4, l-b 4, w 4, n-b 3	15	B 5, l-b 6, w 1	12

1/28 2/52 3/148 4/160   (7 wkts dec.) **259**   1/17 2/50 3/52 4/61 5/131   **180**
5/164 6/234 7/244   6/159 7/163 8/179 9/180

Bonus points – Yorkshire 3, Derbyshire 3.

Bowling: *First Innings*—Holding 22–5–70–4; Mortensen 22–3–70–1; Jean-Jacques 16–0–55–2; Miller 24–7–56–0. *Second Innings*—Holding 21–9–28–5; Mortensen 21–8–60–2; Jean-Jacques 12–0–38–2; Miller 11–0–43–1.

Umpires: J. Birkenshaw and J. H. Harris.

YORKSHIRE v GLOUCESTERSHIRE

At Harrogate, June 7, 9, 10. Drawn. Yorkshire 6 pts, Gloucestershire 4 pts. Toss: Gloucestershire. Yorkshire were put in on a good batting pitch largely because Gloucestershire, with a weakened attack, did not want to set a fourth-innings target. Sharp took the opportunity to hit the highest score of his first-class career, his runs coming from 339 balls with 24 4s, but Yorkshire could not score quickly enough and continued their innings into the second day, reaching their highest score for sixteen years. When Gloucestershire batted, Yorkshire were without Sidebottom, who went home with flu, but Peter Hartley bowled particularly well into a strong wind. Wright, although mostly filling the anchor role, hit three 6s in a sudden burst, and Bainbridge also played well. Some late successes encouraged Yorkshire's hopes of enforcing the follow-on, but heavy rain washed out the whole of the third day.

Yorkshire

G. Boycott b Walsh	81	P. W. Jarvis b Walsh	0
A. A. Metcalfe lbw b Sainsbury	3	S. J. Dennis not out	0
K. Sharp b Bainbridge	181		
J. D. Love c Athey b Lloyds	14	B 1, l-b 5, n-b 2	8
S. N. Hartley b Sainsbury	78		
*†D. L. Bairstow c Curran b Sainsbury	40	1/13 2/156 3/185 (8 wkts dec.)	450
P. Carrick b Walsh	30	4/355 5/377 6/422	
P. J. Hartley not out	15	7/444 8/444	

A. Sidebottom did not bat.

Bonus points – Yorkshire 4, Gloucestershire 1 (Score at 100 overs: 303-3).

Bowling: Walsh 32–5–80–3; Sainsbury 32.1–5–124–3; Graveney 17–0–58–0; Bainbridge 43–12–112–1; Athey 4–1–28–0; Lloyds 12–1–42–1.

Gloucestershire

A. W. Stovold retired hurt	13	†R. C. Russell c Bairstow b Dennis	0
A. J. Wright b Carrick	59	*D. A. Graveney not out	3
C. W. J. Athey lbw b Carrick	29		
P. Bainbridge lbw b Dennis	75	L-b 8, w 1, n-b 4	13
K. P. Tomlins c Bairstow b P. J. Hartley	26		
K. M. Curran b P. J. Hartley	0	1/93 2/118 3/189 (6 wkts)	257
J. W. Lloyds not out	39	4/189 5/252 6/252	

G. E. Sainsbury and C. A. Walsh did not bat.

Bonus points – Gloucestershire 3, Yorkshire 2.

Bowling: Jarvis 18–5–82–0; P. J. Hartley 20–3–52–2; Dennis 14–2–44–2; S. N. Hartley 2–1–2–0; Carrick 28–11–51–2; Love 5–1–18–0.

Umpires: J. A. Jameson and D. O. Oslear.

At Lord's, June 14, 16, 17. YORKSHIRE beat MIDDLESEX by 69 runs.

At Worcester, June 18, 19, 20. YORKSHIRE drew with WORCESTERSHIRE.

At Luton, June 21, 23, 24. YORKSHIRE drew with NORTHAMPTONSHIRE.

YORKSHIRE v WARWICKSHIRE

At Leeds, June 28, 29, 30. Drawn. Yorkshire 5 pts, Warwickshire 5 pts. Toss: Warwickshire. Warwickshire batted slowly on an easy-paced pitch, McMillan's career-best 134 taking rather too long (320 balls) for his team's needs, and Gifford chose to bat on into the second day. Yorkshire's weakened attack performed creditably. Sharp held Yorkshire together after their early setback against Small, who moved the new ball, his hundred taking almost four and a half hours. Bairstow injected much-needed urgency into the proceedings, and then gave Warwickshire a lead of 85 by declaring at the overnight score. Lloyd, reaching his century from 145 balls, carried Warwickshire to a position of strength, but, with runs coming at better than 4 an over, Gifford delayed his declaration too long. He eventually set a target of 287 in 185 minutes or a minimum of 50 overs. Small took three for 14 in a 33-ball burst that forced Yorkshire on to the defensive, and some poor batting saw them decline to 56 for seven. However, Hartley showed more spirit and a better technique than most of his colleagues as he and Carrick, without taking any risks, put on 98 in the last 85 minutes to ensure a draw.

Warwickshire

T. A. Lloyd c Sharp b Shaw	15	– c and b Fletcher	100
P. A. Smith b Hartley	19	– b Fletcher	63
B. M. McMillan lbw b Fletcher	134		
D. L. Amiss c Metcalfe b Swallow	83	– (3) c Bairstow b Fletcher	18
†G. W. Humpage b Shaw	39	– (4) b Carrick	10
Asif Din c Bairstow b Fletcher	16	– (5) not out	2
G. J. Parsons lbw b Fletcher	4		
K. J. Kerr b Carrick	4		
G. C. Small b Hartley	43		
T. A. Munton not out	8		
*N. Gifford c Moxon b Hartley	8		
L-b 8, w 1, n-b 7	16	L-b 7, n-b 1	8

1/34 2/44 3/193 4/260 5/303   385   1/142 2/174 3/191 (4 wkts dec.) 201
6/304 7/321 8/339 9/369   4/201

Bonus points – Warwickshire 3, Yorkshire 1 (Score at 100 overs: 286-4).

Bowling: *First Innings*—Fletcher 26–5–74–3; Shaw 22–3–63–2; Hartley 20–1–69–3; Carrick 38–6–123–1; Swallow 19–4–48–1. *Second Innings*—Fletcher 13.1–1–64–3; Shaw 5–1–22–0; Carrick 21–2–50–1; Hartley 3–0–22–0; Swallow 6–0–36–0.

Yorkshire

G. Boycott c Asif Din b Small	4	– lbw b McMillan	26
M. D. Moxon c Humpage b Small	13	– c Humpage b Small	1
A. A. Metcalfe lbw b Small	30	– c Humpage b Small	0
K. Sharp not out	114	– b Small	6
J. D. Love c McMillan b Gifford	37	– c Asif Din b Gifford	0
*†D. L. Bairstow b Parsons	47	– c Parsons b McMillan	6
P. Carrick b Gifford	26	– not out	38
I. G. Swallow not out	14	– lbw b Kerr	1
P. J. Hartley (did not bat)		– not out	61
B 6, l-b 7, n-b 2	15	B 4, l-b 7, w 4	15

1/4 2/45 3/56 4/115   (6 wkts dec.) 300   1/5 2/5 3/27 4/28   (7 wkts) 154
5/203 6/269   5/41 6/49 7/56

C. Shaw and S. D. Fletcher did not bat.

Bonus points – Yorkshire 4, Warwickshire 2.

Bowling: *First Innings*—Small 15–3–50–3; McMillan 12–3–54–0; Gifford 22–3–60–2; Kerr 24–4–73–0; Munton 12–5–24–0; Parsons 12–2–26–1. *Second Innings*—Small 15–2–38–3; McMillan 10–3–22–2; Gifford 14–4–21–1; Kerr 8–1–30–1; Asif Din 2–1–3–0; Smith 6–1–29–0.

Umpires: B. Leadbeater and R. A. White.

At Bristol, July 2, 3, 4. YORKSHIRE drew with GLOUCESTERSHIRE.

YORKSHIRE v LEICESTERSHIRE

At Middlesbrough, July 5, 7, 8. Drawn. Yorkshire 5 pts, Leicestershire 5 pts. Toss: Leicestershire. With the pitch offering exceptional lift at one end, Leicestershire batted slowly to 291 for seven on the opening day and on into the second. Boon had the satisfaction of a century against his native county, but his innings took four and a quarter hours. Yorkshire were similarly subdued. Boycott dominated their reply, scoring his 150th century off 263 balls to become Yorkshire's leading century-maker, and moving on into third place in the list of runmakers for the county behind H. Sutcliffe and D. Denton. Altogether he occupied the crease for six and a half hours, receiving 337 balls and hitting fourteen boundaries. His historic innings overshadowed Sidebottom's career-best bowling of eight for 72, and the match had been killed as a contest before rain washed out the last morning and ensured a draw.

Leicestershire

J. C. Balderstone c Jarvis b Sidebottom	3	– run out	7
R. A. Cobb c Bairstow b Sidebottom	8	– lbw b Moxon	23
*P. Willey c Hartley b Jarvis	17	– (6) not out	4
L. Potter b Jarvis	63		
T. J. Boon c sub b Sidebottom	117	– (4) not out	29
P. D. Bowler lbw b Sidebottom	4	– (3) c Carrick b Shaw	0
P. B. Clift lbw b Sidebottom	8		
†P. Whitticase c and b Sidebottom	55	– (5) c Metcalfe b Carrick	11
J. P. Agnew c and b Sidebottom	1		
P. A. J. DeFreitas lbw b Sidebottom	8		
W. K. M. Benjamin not out	3		
B 1, l-b 15, n-b 11	27	B 3, l-b 2, w 2, n-b 1	8

1/12 2/13 3/42 4/161 5/168   314   1/15 2/19 3/40 4/61   (4 wkts) 82
6/196 7/285 8/297 9/304

Bonus points – Leicestershire 3, Yorkshire 2 (Score at 100 overs: 259-6).

Bowling: *First Innings*—Jarvis 19-4-48-2; Sidebottom 27.1-4-72-8; Fletcher 25-8-75-0; Shaw 18-6-33-0; Carrick 22-6-55-0; Moxon 4-1-15-0. *Second Innings*—Fletcher 5-2-13-0; Shaw 7-2-9-1; Carrick 20-12-21-1; Metcalfe 5-4-5-0; Moxon 8-2-22-1; Bairstow 5-3-7-0.

Yorkshire

G. Boycott lbw b DeFreitas	127	C. Shaw c Cobb b Clift	21
M. D. Moxon lbw b Benjamin	8	S. D. Fletcher c Benjamin b Clift	5
A. A. Metcalfe lbw b Clift	44	A. Sidebottom not out	1
K. Sharp c DeFreitas b Potter	31		
S. N. Hartley c Potter b Clift	14	L-b 14, n-b 11	25
*†D. L. Bairstow retired hurt	6		
P. Carrick c Bowler b Agnew	19	1/12 2/89 3/169 4/201 5/257	309
P. W. Jarvis c Bowler b Agnew	8	6/273 7/295 8/306 9/309	

Bonus points – Yorkshire 3, Leicestershire 2 (Score at 100 overs: 270-5).

Bowling: Agnew 34-7-88-2; Benjamin 13-4-32-1; DeFreitas 31-8-97-1; Potter 7-1-25-1; Willey 13-3-18-0; Clift 21.3-8-35-4.

Umpires: J. H. Hampshire and P. B. Wight.

At Scarborough, July 12, 13, 14. YORKSHIRE lost to INDIANS by five wickets (See Indian tour section).

At Worksop, July 16, 17, 18. YORKSHIRE lost to NOTTINGHAMSHIRE by an innings and 8 runs.

YORKSHIRE v SURREY

At Leeds, July 19, 20, 21. Yorkshire won by seven wickets. Yorkshire 23 pts, Surrey 5 pts. Toss: Surrey. On a pitch lacking pace but offering some turn, Surrey batted badly. Stewart battled through 69 overs for his 90 and his late-order colleagues ensured at least respectability. Boycott, overcoming the pain from what turned out to be a broken bone in his left wrist, dominated Yorkshire's reply over almost six hours. Metcalfe was more enterprising and Sharp displayed a wristy authority, but Boycott held everything together with his chanceless, unbeaten century. Surrey, losing three wickets almost at once in their second innings, were under pressure throughout the last day as Jarvis achieved career-best figures. Clinton, despite a muscle strain, carried his bat, and by concentrating on defence he survived where others lost their wickets to poor strokes. Yorkshire's second innings was little more than batting practice and they had six overs to spare when they completed a comfortable victory.

Surrey

N. J. Falkner lbw b Jarvis	0	– lbw b Jarvis		0
G. S. Clinton b Jarvis	26	– not out		84
A. J. Stewart c Dennis b Carrick	90	– (4) b Dennis		0
M. A. Lynch lbw b Shaw	0	– (5) b Jarvis		14
T. E. Jesty lbw b Dennis	4	– (6) lbw b Jarvis		0
†C. J. Richards c Bairstow b Carrick	24	– (7) b Carrick		16
G. Monkhouse c Moxon b Carrick	2	– (8) lbw b Jarvis		1
K. T. Medlycott c Bairstow b Dennis	47	– (3) lbw b Jarvis		1
R. J. Doughty b Jarvis	48	– b Jarvis		28
A. H. Gray lbw b Dennis	6	– b Jarvis		6
*P. I. Pocock not out	0	– lbw b Carrick		10
B 9, l-b 9, w 2, n-b 2	22	B 4, l-b 5, n-b 2		11

1/0 2/54 3/55 4/64 5/138   269   1/0 2/2 3/3 4/37 5/37   171
6/148 7/162 8/263 9/265   6/79 7/92 8/146 9/154

Bonus points – Surrey 3, Yorkshire 3 (Score at 100 overs: 262-7).

Bowling: *First Innings*—Jarvis 22–5–53–3; Dennis 23.5–7–57–3; Shaw 16–5–34–1; Carrick 26–8–66–3; Swallow 16–3–41–0. *Second Innings*—Jarvis 25–7–55–7; Dennis 13–2–34–1; Carrick 25–9–49–2; Shaw 2–1–7–0; Swallow 11–4–17–0.

Yorkshire

G. Boycott not out	135			
M. D. Moxon lbw b Gray	3	– (1) not out		42
A. A. Metcalfe c Lynch b Pocock	55	– (2) c Richards b Monkhouse		20
K. Sharp b Gray	76	– (3) c Richards b Gray		4
S. N. Hartley lbw b Gray	0	– (4) b Pocock		11
*†D. L. Bairstow lbw b Medlycott	0	– (5) not out		44
P. Carrick c Monkhouse b Medlycott	12			
I. G. Swallow not out	0			
B 9, l-b 5, n-b 12	26	B 6, l-b 5, w 2		13

1/4 2/118 3/277 4/277   (6 wkts dec.) 307   1/36 2/43 3/69   (3 wkts) 134
5/278 6/302

C. Shaw, P. W. Jarvis and S. J. Dennis did not bat.

Bonus points – Yorkshire 4, Surrey 2.

Bowling: *First Innings*—Gray 14–3–36–3; Doughty 15–0–57–0; Monkhouse 20–5–59–0; Medlycott 35–6–101–2; Pocock 16–6–40–1. *Second Innings*—Gray 11–1–56–1; Doughty 5–1–18–0; Monkhouse 8–3–8–1; Pocock 7–3–17–1; Medlycott 3–0–24–0.

Umpires: J. A. Jameson and P. B. Wight.

YORKSHIRE v KENT

At Scarborough, July 23, 24, 25. Drawn. Yorkshire 4 pts, Kent 6 pts. Toss: Yorkshire. After rain had delayed the start for more than two hours, Metcalfe became the first Yorkshire batsman to 1,000 runs as he took advantage of an easy-paced pitch to score freely, his runs coming in 212 minutes. Robinson, with twelve 4s in his overnight 66, punished some poor bowling as he went on to record his first century for the county, although he was kept in check in the later stages of his innings. His 104 not out contained eighteen 4s. Benson, with 94 in under two and a half hours, set the stage for an interesting finish as Kent declared late on the second day, giving Yorkshire a lead of 91. They then offered easy runs, Robinson accepting 91 from 76 balls, and were set a target of 298 in 60 overs. Peter Hartley, capped before the match, broke the back of their challenge with a spell of three wickets for 4 runs in fourteen deliveries, but Yorkshire were frustrated by the last pair, Ellison and Igglesden, who held out for ten overs to save the game.

Yorkshire

K. Sharp c Benson b Igglesden	0	– (2) retired hurt	25
A. A. Metcalfe c Hinks b Cowdrey	123	– (1) c Marsh b Alderman	26
S. N. Hartley c Tavaré b Underwood	40	– not out	51
P. E. Robinson not out	104	– c Taylor b Aslett	91
J. D. Love c Cowdrey b Ellison	9	– not out	1
P. J. Hartley c Aslett b Cowdrey	27		
*†D. L. Bairstow c Tavaré b Ellison	4		
P. Carrick c Marsh b Cowdrey	5		
P. W. Jarvis not out	17		
L-b 4, n-b 8	12	B 2, l-b 1, w 3, n-b 6	12

1/0 2/124 3/222 4/247   (7 wkts dec.) 341   1/50 2/199   (2 wkts dec.) 206
5/301 6/306 7/315

S. J. Dennis and C. Shaw did not bat.

Bonus points – Yorkshire 4, Kent 3.

Bowling: *First Innings*—Igglesden 18–1–86–1; Alderman 21–4–69–0; Ellison 18–3–51–2; Underwood 16–6–50–1; Cowdrey 24–2–81–3. *Second Innings*—Igglesden 7–0–25–0; Alderman 11–2–39–1; Cowdrey 7–0–23–0; Underwood 12–2–60–0; Aslett 9–1–56–1.

Kent

M. R. Benson b Jarvis	94	– b P. J. Hartley	23
S. G. Hinks b Jarvis	46	– c Metcalfe b Dennis	17
C. J. Tavaré not out	62	– lbw b Carrick	23
N. R. Taylor not out	21	– c Bairstow b P. J. Hartley	34
D. G. Aslett (did not bat)		– b P. J. Hartley	26
*C. S. Cowdrey (did not bat)		– c Carrick b P. J. Hartley	0
R. M. Ellison (did not bat)		– not out	25
†S. A. Marsh (did not bat)		– lbw b Jarvis	4
D. L. Underwood (did not bat)		– c Bairstow b Jarvis	10
T. M. Alderman (did not bat)		– lbw b Jarvis	0
A. P. Igglesden (did not bat)		– not out	8
B 5, l-b 10, w 1, n-b 11	27	B 2, l-b 16, n-b 4	22

1/138 2/179   (2 wkts dec.) 250   1/46 2/48 3/82 4/123   (9 wkts) 192
5/123 6/142 7/156
8/166 9/166

Bonus points – Kent 3.

Bowling: *First Innings*—Jarvis 17–3–58–2; Dennis 17–3–81–0; Shaw 11.1–0–45–0; P. J. Hartley 12–2–43–0; Carrick 10–7–8–0. *Second Innings*—Jarvis 15–0–72–3; P. J. Hartley 18–3–45–4; Dennis 8–3–23–1; Shaw 2–1–4–0; Carrick 16–11–20–1; Love 1–0–10–0.

Umpires: D. O. Oslear and R. Palmer.

YORKSHIRE v NOTTINGHAMSHIRE

At Sheffield, July 26, 28, 29. Drawn. Yorkshire 12 pts (including 8 pts as the batting side in the fourth innings with the scores equal), Nottinghamshire 5 pts. Toss: Nottinghamshire. The seam bowlers on both sides dominated the early exchanges on a pitch allowing extra bounce and giving them every encouragement to keep the ball up and let it move about. Sixteen wickets fell on the first day, but rain complicated the issue and altogether cut 124 overs from the game. In an attempt to make up the time lost, Yorkshire lobbed a series of full tosses and half-volleys from which Nottinghamshire scored 188 from only 23 overs. Yorkshire's target was 234 in 54 overs, and the emergency opening partnership of Metcalfe and Blakey gave them a good start, putting on 117 in 33 overs and appearing to have established control. However, Rice handled his attack well and came back himself near the end to upset Yorkshire with a hostile, accurate spell. They needed 6 runs from the last over but lost three wickets to good fielding and tight bowling, Shaw being run out from the final delivery with the scores level. In the hectic closing minutes, Bairstow hit two 6s off Hemmings, who bowled very tidily, and Peter Hartley was "called" by umpire Hampshire for running 1 run short.

Nottinghamshire

B. C. Broad c Robinson b P. J. Hartley	7	– run out	15
R. T. Robinson c Robinson b P. J. Hartley	4	– not out	90
M. Newell b P. J. Hartley	47		
*C. E. B. Rice c Bairstow b Shaw	47	– not out	65
P. Johnson b Carrick	15		
J. D. Birch c Jarvis b P. J. Hartley	18	– (3) b Blakey	18
†C. W. Scott lbw b P. J. Hartley	4		
R. A. Pick c Bairstow b Shaw	19		
E. E. Hemmings lbw b Fletcher	9		
K. Saxelby b P. J. Hartley	11		
K. E. Cooper not out	0		
B 4, l-b 4, n-b 2	10		

1/11 2/16 3/98 4/116 5/132   191   1/32 2/84   (2 wkts dec.) 188
6/144 7/153 8/167 9/191

Bonus points – Nottinghamshire 1, Yorkshire 4.

Bowling: *First Innings*—Jarvis 13–3–30–0; P. J. Hartley 22.3–2–68–6; Fletcher 14–0–43–1; Shaw 10–2–26–2; Carrick 9–2–16–1. *Second Innings*—Jarvis 1–0–5–0; P. J. Hartley 1–1–0–0; Robinson 11–0–115–0; Blakey 10.3–1–68–1.

Yorkshire

R. J. Blakey b Rice	1	– lbw b Hemmings	46
A. A. Metcalfe c Broad b Rice	0	– c Cooper b Hemmings	108
S. N. Hartley c Johnson b Cooper	33	– c Birch b Hemmings	7
P. E. Robinson c Scott b Pick	1	– run out	8
J. D. Love run out	59	– c Scott b Rice	8
*†D. L. Bairstow c Rice b Cooper	0	– run out	22
P. Carrick c Rice b Saxelby	31	– c Saxelby b Rice	5
P. J. Hartley c Rice b Pick	0	– c Robinson b Rice	3
P. W. Jarvis c Scott b Pick	6	– not out	2
C. Shaw c Birch b Cooper	5	– run out	1
S. D. Fletcher not out	0		
L-b 6, n-b 4	10	B 5, l-b 17, n-b 1	23

1/0 2/4 3/5 4/56 5/56   146   1/117 2/131 3/163   (9 wkts) 233
6/113 7/116 8/124 9/144   4/191 5/199 6/205
                             7/228 8/229 9/233

Bonus points – Nottinghamshire 4.

Bowling: *First Innings*—Pick 20–7–50–3; Rice 15–5–34–2; Cooper 14–4–34–3; Saxelby 9–1–22–1. *Second Innings*—Pick 9–0–40–0; Rice 12–2–34–3; Cooper 10–2–38–0; Hemmings 15–0–67–3; Saxelby 8–0–32–0.

Umpires: J. H. Hampshire and R. Palmer.

At Manchester, August 2, 4, 5. YORKSHIRE drew with LANCASHIRE.

At Leicester, August 6, 7, 8. YORKSHIRE lost to LEICESTERSHIRE by seven wickets.

YORKSHIRE v GLAMORGAN

At Leeds, August 9, 11, 12. Drawn. Yorkshire 8 pts, Glamorgan 3 pts. Toss: Glamorgan. A weakened Yorkshire attack cut through hesitant Glamorgan batting on a slow pitch which allowed a little movement off the seam. The match was ruined by the rain that washed out all but a few minutes of the second day, but Yorkshire tried hard to force a victory. Metcalfe enjoyed the unique distinction of becoming the first Yorkshireman to follow a hundred on his début with one in his first match as a capped player, having been recognised on the Saturday. He reached three figures from 118 balls. Glamorgan, however, had good reason to regret missing Love at slip before he had scored, at which point Yorkshire were 51 for four, for Love and Metcalfe went on to make 181 from 49 overs. Following Yorkshire's declaration, Glamorgan could do little but play out time, which they did without difficulty, Maynard mixing resolute defence with some beautifully timed drives.

Glamorgan

J. A. Hopkins c Metcalfe b Dennis	2	– c sub b Carrick	44
*H. Morris c Hartley b Shaw	20	– b Shaw	28
G. C. Holmes c Bairstow b Fletcher	16	– c Robinson b Shaw	19
M. P. Maynard c Bairstow b Shaw	6	– not out	85
R. C. Ontong c Robinson b Shaw	0	– not out	15
J. Derrick c Bairstow b Fletcher	49		
P. A. Cottey lbw b Dennis	7		
†T. Davies not out	9		
S. J. Base lbw b Dennis	0		
S. R. Barwick c Byas b Fletcher	9		
D. J. Hickey lbw b Dennis	2		
B 4, l-b 7, n-b 3	14	B 1, l-b 8, w 3, n-b 9	21

1/2 2/21 3/36 4/38 5/90   134   1/57 2/81 3/147   (3 wkts) 212
6/106 7/110 8/110 9/121

Bonus points – Yorkshire 4.

Bowling: *First Innings*—Dennis 18–7–26–4; Fletcher 21–6–51–3; Shaw 13–6–22–3; Hartley 5–2–10–0; Swallow 4–1–14–0. *Second Innings*—Dennis 15–2–39–0; Fletcher 19–2–64–0; Shaw 13–2–51–2; Carrick 11–4–32–1; Swallow 3–2–2–0; Byas 2–0–15–0.

Yorkshire

S. N. Hartley c Davies b Barwick	2	*†D. L. Bairstow c Hickey b Base	42
A. A. Metcalfe c Morris b Base	149	I. G. Swallow not out	3
P. Carrick c Davies b Base	1	L-b 10, w 7, n-b 6	23
D. Byas c Davies b Barwick	0		
P. E. Robinson c Ontong b Base	2	1/4 2/29 3/35 4/51 (7 wkts dec.) 310
J. D. Love c sub b Derrick	88	5/232 6/288 7/310

C. Shaw, S. J. Dennis and S. D. Fletcher did not bat.

Bonus points – Yorkshire 4, Glamorgan 3.

Bowling: Hickey 17–0–79–0; Barwick 20–8–52–2; Base 18.5–1–74–4; Ontong 6–1–16–0; Holmes 5–2–9–0; Derrick 14–1–70–1.

Umpires: J. W. Holder and N. T. Plews.

At Chesterfield, August 16, 18, 19. YORKSHIRE drew with DERBYSHIRE.

YORKSHIRE v MIDDLESEX

At Leeds, August 20, 21, 22. Drawn. Yorkshire 6 pts, Middlesex 6 pts. Toss: Middlesex. A series of unforced errors proved costly for Middlesex on another slow, low pitch. Slack, however, was an exception and carried his bat, having received 246 deliveries and resisted for 310 minutes. Prepared to wait for the bad ball but nonetheless hitting a 6 and fifteen 4s, the left-hander brought Middlesex unexpected batting bonus points in a last-wicket stand of 64 in sixteen overs with Daniel. Yorkshire in turn collapsed against Daniel and Hughes, the latter, aided by interruptions from the weather, keeping one end going throughout the innings. Yorkshire were in desperate trouble at 98 for six, but Love and Bairstow, who had dropped down the order because of an infected toe, effected a recovery with 95 in 24 overs. Bairstow made his runs from 64 balls and declared in arrears in an attempt to bring about a positive finish. Rain, though, washed out the whole of the last day.

Middlesex

W. N. Slack not out	105	J. F. Sykes lbw b Fletcher			15
A. J. T. Miller c Bairstow b Dennis	2	S. P. Hughes b Fletcher			4
K. R. Brown c Shaw b Fletcher	36	W. W. Daniel b Fletcher			20
R. O. Butcher c Bairstow b Fletcher	4				
J. D. Carr c Metcalfe b Dennis	38	L-b 4, n-b 3			7
*C. T. Radley lbw b Dennis	13				
†P. R. Downton lbw b Dennis	2	1/2 2/52 3/56 4/111 5/145			252
G. D. Rose lbw b Dennis	6	6/151 7/158 8/184 9/188			

Bonus points – Middlesex 3, Yorkshire 4.

Bowling: Dennis 25–5–71–5; Fletcher 28.5–6–90–5; Shaw 14–4–38–0; Carrick 7–1–30–0; Swallow 9–4–19–0.

Yorkshire

M. D. Moxon c Carr b Daniel	5	S. J. Dennis c Daniel b Rose			4
A. A. Metcalfe lbw b Hughes	39	C. Shaw not out			7
S. N. Hartley b Daniel	39				
P. E. Robinson c Carr b Hughes	0	B 2, l-b 5, n-b 3			10
J. D. Love not out	65				
P. Carrick lbw b Daniel	5	1/14 2/84 3/88	(8 wkts dec.)		216
I. G. Swallow c Downton b Hughes	0	4/92 5/97 6/98			
*†D. L. Bairstow lbw b Hughes	42	7/193 8/206			

S. D. Fletcher did not bat.

Bonus points – Yorkshire 2, Middlesex 3.

Bowling: Daniel 17–9–33–3; Hughes 34–10–92–4; Rose 18–2–84–1.

Umpires: J. A. Jameson and R. Julian.

At Bournemouth, August 23, 25, 26. YORKSHIRE drew with HAMPSHIRE.

At Birmingham, August 27, 28, 29. YORKSHIRE lost to WARWICKSHIRE by 54 runs.

YORKSHIRE v NORTHAMPTONSHIRE

At Scarborough, September 10, 11, 12. Drawn. Yorkshire 7 pts, Northamptonshire 3 pts.
Toss: Yorkshire. Yorkshire made slow progress on a pitch lacking pace and offering uneven
bounce. Boycott ignored some wide, short-pitched bowling, particularly by Mallender, but the
tempo increased under the influence of Love. He completed his first Championship century
for more than two years, reaching three figures from 172 balls as he punished some inaccurate
deliveries by the left-arm spinner, Cook. Northamptonshire raced along in reply, reaching 98
for two in an hour on the second morning. But they collapsed against the nagging accuracy of
Shaw, who achieved career-best figures of five for 38. Most of their batsmen were out to
careless strokes and the last six wickets fell for 27 runs in eleven overs. Yorkshire enforced the
follow-on, although they had their problems. Bairstow was off the field with a broken bone
in his left hand – Blakey kept wicket in both innings – and Dennis had a painful back strain.
By way of balance, Geoff Cook, Northamptonshire's captain, had broken the index finger on
his right hand in the first innings and Larkins suffered a stomach upset, which necessitated a
change in their batting order. Yorkshire made good progress towards victory, taking four
wickets for 158 before the close, but on the last day they were denied mainly by Northamptonshire's Leeds-born wicket-keeper, Ripley, who hit his maiden first-class hundred. He gave a
sharp chance to Carrick at slip as he reached 50, but showed determination and skill in
scoring an unbeaten 134 from 310 balls in almost five hours. Yorkshire displayed little
imagination under the leadership of Carrick on the last afternoon, when it was clear that the
weakened pace attack had lost its cutting edge.

Yorkshire

G. Boycott run out	61	S. J. Dennis not out	18
A. A. Metcalfe lbw b Capel	15	P. J. Berry not out	4
R. J. Blakey c Bailey b N. G. B. Cook	12		
K. Sharp c N. G. B. Cook b Harper	33	B 6, l-b 8, n-b 3	17
J. D. Love c Bailey b Walker	109		
*†D. L. Bairstow c Harper b Walker	37	1/25 2/59 3/117 (7 wkts dec.) 352	
P. Carrick b Capel	46	4/129 5/193 6/301 7/348	

S. D. Fletcher and C. Shaw did not bat.

Bonus points – Yorkshire 3, Northamptonshire 2 (Score at 100 overs: 285-5).

Bowling: Mallender 21-3-67-0; Capel 25-4-89-2; Walker 19-4-56-2; N. G. B. Cook
24-7-78-1; Harper 25-6-48-1.

Northamptonshire

*G. Cook lbw b Shaw	47	– (9) b Sharp	26
W. Larkins c Berry b Dennis	40	– (3) c Metcalfe b Carrick	40
R. J. Boyd-Moss b Fletcher	10	– (1) c Carrick b Fletcher	4
R. J. Bailey c Blakey b Shaw	47	– (2) c Berry b Dennis	18
D. J. Capel c Carrick b Berry	14	– (4) lbw b Fletcher	20
D. J. Wild c Boycott b Shaw	6	– (5) b Shaw	74
R. A. Harper c Blakey b Dennis	1	– (6) c Blakey b Dennis	14
†D. Ripley b Shaw	1	– (7) not out	134
N. G. B. Cook c Sharp b Shaw	5	– (8) c Carrick b Shaw	45
N. A. Mallender c Blakey b Dennis	11	– not out	11
A. Walker not out	1		
B 3, l-b 6, w 1, n-b 4	14	B 13, l-b 13, w 3, n-b 7	36

1/74 2/98 3/123 4/153 5/170	197	1/18 2/42 3/79 (8 wkts dec.) 422
6/173 7/176 8/182 9/195		4/138 5/186 6/213
		7/309 8/362

Bonus points – Northamptonshire 1, Yorkshire 4.

Bowling: *First Innings*—Dennis 16.2-3-71-3; Fletcher 12-2-45-1; Shaw 17-3-38-5;
Carrick 7-0-24-0; Berry 4-1-10-1. *Second Innings*—Fletcher 46-15-105-2; Shaw 30-5-77-2;
Dennis 12-0-63-2; Berry 35-12-73-0; Carrick 33-16-58-1; Sharp 7-2-20-1.

Umpires: B. Dudleston and J. A. Jameson.

THE UNIVERSITIES IN 1986

OXFORD

President: M. J. K. Smith (St Edmund Hall)
Hon. Treasurer: Dr S. R. Porter (St Cross)

Captain: D. A. Thorne (Coventry School – Bablake and Keble)
Secretary: M. P. Lawrence (Manchester Grammar School and Merton)

Captain for 1987: C. D. M. Tooley (St Dunstan's College and Magdalen)
Secretary: D. A. Hagan (Trinity School, Leamington Spa and
    St Edmund Hall)

Oxford University experienced another disastrous season and there is little that can be said in mitigation. Not a single first-class match was won in The Parks, and the University fared no better in non first-class matches. The departure of Andrew Miller and John Carr, both of whom joined Middlesex, left the new captain, David Thorne, short of experienced batsmen, while the absence of Thorne and Giles Toogood for the greater part of the season, owing to examinations, deprived the team of its two genuine all-rounders. The intake of Freshmen produced little talent.

In every phase, Oxford were no match for the counties, several of which lessened the margin of victory by preferring batting practice to enforcing the follow-on. But if the University teams of today can not be expected to be the equal of first-class sides in batting and bowling, they should be able to match them in fielding. Worryingly, there was a serious deterioration in Oxford's out-cricket in 1986, and at times discipline looked close to breaking point. There was even a world of difference in the seriousness and effort put into the pre-match warm-up by the University and their opponents, and it was reflected in the counties' superior fielding.

It all emphasised the need for a full-time coach, the services of which Oxford University dispensed with several years ago in the interests of economy. However, the University's cricket has fallen to such a low level that the appointment of a coach should be the top priority irrespective of the cost.

Oxford's batting lacked consistency and depth, and only five times was an individual score of 50 or more achieved against a county. The highest in The Parks was 88 by David Hagan, who shared noteworthy opening partnerships of 76 against Lancashire and 65 against Kent with Adrian Mee. The bowling was the weakest for many years. Without Thorne and Toogood, the opening attack was not even of medium pace, which was one of the reasons why The Parks was again a paradise for visiting batsmen. Ten centuries were scored from eleven innings by the counties, and a further six were hit in other matches. In the main, the slow bowling was undertaken by Tim Dawson, an off-spinner, and Mark Lawrence, slow left-arm, and both suffered from an excess of dropped catches and questionable field placings.

However, the Dark Blues did play their part in a memorable University Match. Thorne's unbeaten 104 in the second innings at Lord's was Oxford's only century in a first-class match, and Cambridge's exciting win off the seventh delivery of the last over helped compensate for a dearth of talent at both Universities.

OXFORD UNIVERSITY 1986

Back row: J. E. B. Cope, A. A. G. Mee, R. A. Rydon, M. J. Kilborn, T. A. J. Dawson, N. V. Salvi, R. E. Morris. *Front row*: D. A. Hagan, C. D. M. Tooley, D. A. Thorne (*captain*), M. P. Lawrence, R. S. Rutnagur.

[*Bill Smith*

A wet and depressing season was further saddened by the death, after a short illness, of Ron Grimshaw, who reported Oxford University cricket and rugby for the *Oxford Mail* for well over a decade. He will be sadly missed. – P.F.

OXFORD UNIVERSITY RESULTS

First-class matches – Played 8: Lost 5, Drawn 3.

FIRST-CLASS AVERAGES – BATTING

	M	I	NO	R	HI	Avge
D. A. Thorne	6	9	1	334	104*	41.75
C. D. M. Tooley	5	8	1	196	60	28.00
D. A. Hagan	8	14	1	334	88	25.69
N. V. Salvi	4	7	1	126	36	21.00
M. J. Kilborn	7	12	1	219	59	19.90
A. A. G. Mee	8	14	1	183	51	14.07
J. D. Quinlan	5	5	1	46	24*	11.50
R. A. Rydon	5	9	1	64	20	8.00
R. S. Rutnagur	5	7	0	56	24	8.00
T. A. J. Dawson	7	9	5	32	10*	8.00
T. Patel	6	8	0	63	18	7.87
D. P. Taylor	4	6	0	39	17	6.50
J. E. B. Cope	4	5	2	11	8*	3.66
P. C. MacLarnon	4	5	1	9	4	2.25
M. P. Lawrence	6	10	2	12	10*	1.50

Played in two matches: G. J. Toogood 1, 11. Played in one match: M. R. Sygrove 2, 6; S. D. Weale 12, 28.

* *Signifies not out.*

D. A. Thorne played the only three-figure innings for Oxford University.

BOWLING

	O	M	R	W	BB	Avge
R. S. Rutnagur	136	28	439	14	3-50	31.35
D. A. Thorne	156.3	56	330	9	3-42	36.66
T. A. J. Dawson	194	38	649	13	3-65	49.92
M. P. Lawrence	156	29	554	7	2-28	79.14
R. A. Rydon	119	21	471	5	3-106	94.20

Also bowled: D. A. Hagan 0.1–0–4–0; P. C. MacLarnon 26.5–5–89–2; T. Patel 2–0–12–0; J. D. Quinlan 103.3–14–369–4; M. R. Sygrove 17–0–85–2; G. J. Toogood 58–16–155–4.

FIELDING

6 – D. P. Taylor; 5 – J. E. B. Cope; 4 – M. J. Kilborn; 3 – A. A. G. Mee, D. A. Thorne, C. D. M. Tooley; 2 – T. A. J. Dawson, D. A. Hagan, M. P. Lawrence, J. D. Quinlan, R. S. Rutnagur; 1 – T. Patel, R. A. Rydon, N. V. Salvi.

OXFORD UNIVERSITY v SOMERSET

At Oxford, April 19, 21, 22. Drawn. Toss: Oxford University. The opening match in The Parks was restricted to five and a half hours because of rain. Bartlett, a nineteen-year-old from Taunton School, became the youngest Somerset player to score a hundred on début, his century taking 181 minutes and containing thirteen 4s. He added 53 with Dredge for the last wicket before the county declared, leaving Oxford 45 minutes in which to bat. No play was possible on the second and third days.

Somerset

J. G. Wyatt lbw b Rutnagur	40	M. R. Davis lbw b Toogood	3
*P. M. Roebuck b Toogood	0	N. S. Taylor c Mee b Dawson	3
J. J. E. Hardy c and b Dawson	39	C. H. Dredge not out	12
N. A. Felton b Rutnagur	0	B 3, l-b 3, w 1, n-b 6	13
R. J. Bartlett not out	117		
B. C. Rose c Patel b Rutnagur	0	1/3 2/64 3/64	(9 wkts dec.) 236
V. J. Marks run out	9	4/101 5/120 6/125	
†R. J. Blitz b Dawson	0	7/137 8/170 9/183	

Bowling: Toogood 22–4–56–2; Thorne 14.3–2–41–0; Rutnagur 19–4–62–3; Dawson 23–3–65–3; Quinlan 1–0–6–0.

Oxford University

D. A. Hagan lbw b Davis	0
A. A. G. Mee c Bartlett b Dredge	0
C. D. M. Tooley not out	6
P. C. MacLarnon not out	1
B 1, w 3	4

1/1 2/5   (2 wkts) 11

G. J. Toogood *D. A. Thorne, T. Patel, R. S. Rutnagur, †D. P. Taylor, J. D. Quinlan and T. A. J. Dawson did not bat.

Bowling: Davis 4–3–1–1; Taylor 2–2–0–0; Marks 4–2–4–0; Dredge 4–2–5–1.

Umpires: J. Birkenshaw and D. Lloyd.

OXFORD UNIVERSITY v GLOUCESTERSHIRE

At Oxford, April 23, 24, 25. Drawn. Toss: Oxford University. Gloucestershire's recovery was begun by Wright and Bainbridge after Thorne had dismissed their openers for 39. Curran took over after lunch, hitting six 6s and eight 4s in a punishing maiden century which took 127 minutes. Oxford also started badly, but Tooley and Thorne steadied the innings with a partnership of 62 before a thunderstorm ended play soon after lunch, and next day Thorne went on to complete the University's first half-century of the season. Oxford declared 130 behind the county, who set them to score 210 in two hours after closing their second innings at tea. However, only seven minutes' play was possible before the rain returned.

Gloucestershire

A. W. Stovold c Cope b Thorne	20	– c Rutnagur b Thorne	11
P. W. Romaines c Cope b Thorne	4	– b Dawson	20
A. J. Wright b Quinlan	39	– c Mee b Dawson	34
P. Bainbridge c and b Thorne	66		
K. P. Tomlins c Tooley b Rutnagur	9	– (4) not out	11
K. M. Curran not out	103		
J. W. Lloyds c Mee b Quinlan	28	– (5) c Cope b Rutnagur	0
I. R. Payne not out	23		
*D. A. Graveney (did not bat)		– (6) not out	1
B 2, l-b 5, w 4, n-b 6	17	B 1, n-b 1	2

1/4 2/39 3/104 4/147   (6 wkts dec.) 309   1/15 2/38 3/78   (4 wkts dec.) 79
5/155 6/232   4/78

†R. C. Russell and G. E. Sainsbury did not bat.

Bowling: *First Innings*—Quinlan 19–3–98–2; Thorne 20–10–42–3; Rutnagur 22–5–78–1; Dawson 19–3–70–0; MacLarnon 2.5–0–14–0. *Second Innings*—Quinlan 12–4–30–0; Thorne 8–5–12–1; Dawson 10–5–21–2; Rutnagur 6–1–15–1.

Oxford University

D. A. Hagan b Sainsbury	9	– not out	1
A. A. G. Mee b Payne	2	– not out	0
C. D. M. Tooley b Lloyds	44		
*D. A. Thorne c Payne b Lloyds	72		
T. Patel c Graveney b Lloyds	8		
M. J. Kilborn lbw b Sainsbury	0		
R. S. Rutnagur c Stovold b Graveney	8		
P. C. MacLarnon c Stovold b Payne	3		
†J. E. B. Cope not out	8		
J. D. Quinlan b Graveney	6		
T. A. J. Dawson not out	0		
B 7, l-b 1, w 1, n-b 10	19	L-b 1, n-b 1	2

1/6 2/42 3/104 4/136   (9 wkts dec.) 179   (no wkt) 3
5/139 6/160 7/163
8/163 9/175

Bowling: *First Innings*—Sainsbury 29–12–43–2; Curran 15–5–33–0; Payne 19–8–34–2; Graveney 10–6–11–2; Bainbridge 6–1–19–0; Lloyds 17–7–31–3. *Second Innings*—Bainbridge 1–1–0–0; Payne 0.4–0–2–0.

Umpires: J. Birkenshaw and D. Lloyd.

OXFORD UNIVERSITY v MIDDLESEX

At Oxford, April 30, May 1, 2. Middlesex won by 177 runs. Toss: Oxford University. The University did well to restrict the county champions to 83 for two at lunch on the first day but their four bowlers were severely punished afterwards. Downton led the spree with a career-best 126 in 205 minutes, his unbeaten innings containing two 6s and seventeen 4s. Oxford's batting was disappointing. Mee hit 51 in the first innings and Hagan, the other opener, made the same in the second, but there were two alarming collapses. In the first innings, the last six wickets fell for 21 runs, and on the last afternoon Emburey and Hughes again did the damage as the same number of wickets fell for 13 runs. Although leading by 187 on the first innings, Middlesex did not enforce the follow-on, and in a bid to score runs quickly lost six wickets for 109 before declaring on the second evening, leaving Oxford to score 297 or bat throughout the last day.

Middlesex

G. D. Barlow c Taylor b Thorne	4		
W. N. Slack b Rutnagur	59	– (8) not out	0
*M. W. Gatting c Kilborn b Lawrence	41		
†P. R. Downton not out	126		
N. F. Williams c Kilborn b Lawrence	16	– (6) not out	23
J. E. Emburey c and b Rutnagur	10	– (2) c Taylor b Thorne	0
R. O. Butcher not out	45	– lbw b Lawrence	8
C. T. Radley (did not bat)		– (1) c Thorne b MacLarnon	12
S. P. Hughes (did not bat)		– (3) c Thorne b Lawrence	21
A. R. C. Fraser (did not bat)		– (4) lbw b MacLarnon	2
N. G. Cowans (did not bat)		– (5) c Tooley b Dawson	28
B 1, l-b 5, n-b 2	8	B 11, l-b 3, w 1	15

1/13 2/80 3/136 4/221   (5 wkts dec.) 309   1/0 2/30 3/36   (6 wkts dec.) 109
5/245   4/40 5/83 6/109

Bowling: *First Innings*—Rutnagur 29–8–76–2; Thorne 23–6–51–1; Dawson 18–4–61–0; Lawrence 29–1–115–2. *Second Innings*—Rutnagur 6–4–17–0; Thorne 8–3–12–1; MacLarnon 10–2–25–2; Lawrence 13–4–28–2; Dawson 6–2–13–1.

Oxford University

D. A. Hagan c Slack b Emburey	6	– b Hughes		51
A. A. G. Mee c Radley b Emburey	51	– lbw b Cowans		3
P. C. MacLarnon c Barlow b Emburey	0	– (8) c Radley b Emburey		1
C. D. M. Tooley c Emburey b Fraser	19	– (3) c Downton b Williams		6
*D. A. Thorne c Gatting b Williams	15	– (4) c Downton b Hughes		21
T. Patel lbw b Fraser	12	– (5) c Downton b Hughes		9
M. J. Kilborn not out	9	– (6) run out		10
R. S. Rutnagur c Downton b Emburey	1	– (7) b Cowans		4
†D. P. Taylor b Hughes	3	– b Emburey		0
T. A. J. Dawson b Hughes	0	– not out		5
M. P. Lawrence b Hughes	0	– c Slack b Emburey		0
B 4, n-b 2	6	L-b 3, w 4, n-b 2		9

1/10 2/10 3/49 4/89 5/101   122   1/15 2/34 3/73 4/83 5/106   119
6/109 7/110 8/116 9/122   6/113 7/113 8/114 9/119

Bowling: *First Innings*—Fraser 17–5–25–2; Williams 13–2–30–1; Emburey 31–21–20–4; Hughes 12.1–4–18–3; Cowans 5–1–20–0; Gatting 2–0–5–0. *Second Innings*—Cowans 11–4–17–2; Hughes 16–4–28–3; Fraser 8–3–18–0; Williams 7–0–20–1; Emburey 14.5–7–12–3; Gatting 7–2–21–0.

Umpires: R. Julian and D. R. Shepherd.

OXFORD UNIVERSITY v NOTTINGHAMSHIRE

At Oxford, May 7, 8, 9. Nottinghamshire won by 210 runs. Toss: Oxford University. Oxford were outclassed by Nottinghamshire after putting them in. Newell's hundred, which took 241 minutes and contained fifteen 4s, was his first. Randall's, his 38th, took eight minutes longer. Oxford were spun out for 98 on the second afternoon, only Hagan and Thorne, who added 53 for the third wicket, batting with any confidence. Johnson and Martindale began Nottinghamshire's second assault, and when Martindale, 74 overnight, failed to reach his hundred, Birch declared. Oxford again collapsed after lunch with Pick and Such bringing back memories of their performance in The Parks in 1984.

Nottinghamshire

D. W. Randall not out	101			
M. Newell not out	112			
P. Johnson (did not bat)		– (1) c Rydon b Lawrence		91
D. J. R. Martindale (did not bat)		– (2) c Kilborn b Quinlan		88
*J. D. Birch (did not bat)		– (3) not out		26
L-b 13, w 1, n-b 1	15	B 1, l-b 4, w 1		6

(no wkt dec.) 228   1/129 2/211   (2 wkts dec.) 211

K. P. Evans, R. A. Pick, †C. W. Scott, K. Saxelby, J. A. Afford and P. M. Such did not bat.

Bowling: *First Innings*—Quinlan 10–2–21–0; Thorne 13–6–30–0; Rydon 21–4–62–0; Dawson 19–4–51–0; Lawrence 18–5–51–0. *Second Innings*—Quinlan 16.3–2–58–1; Rydon 14–5–76–0; Dawson 5–0–37–0; Lawrence 12–2–35–1.

Oxford University

D. A. Hagan c Birch b Such	39	– lbw b Afford	30
A. A. G. Mee run out	0	– b Pick	0
M. J. Kilborn lbw b Pick	0	– b Pick	17
*D. A. Thorne c Newell b Such	27	– c Saxelby b Pick	23
T. Patel c and b Such	4	– lbw b Pick	0
S. D. Weale b Such	12	– c Randall b Such	28
R. A. Rydon lbw b Afford	7	– b Such	11
†J. E. B. Cope c Pick b Afford	0	– not out	2
J. D. Quinlan b Afford	0	– b Such	1
T. A. J. Dawson not out	2	– b Such	5
M. P. Lawrence b Such	0	– c Birch b Evans	2
B 2, l-b 2, w 3	7	B 1, l-b 10, w 1	12

1/15 2/16 3/69 4/74 5/77   **98**   1/4 2/49 3/69 4/69 5/76   **131**
6/90 7/95 8/96 9/97   6/113 7/120 8/122 9/128

Bowling: *First Innings*—Saxelby 8–3–15–0; Pick 8–3–13–1; Evans 4–0–12–0; Such 19.3–10–36–5; Afford 16–9–18–3. *Second Innings*—Saxelby 13–2–44–0; Pick 17–7–26–4; Evans 10.2–3–19–1; Afford 10–3–11–1; Such 19–10–20–4.

Umpires: H. D. Bird and D. S. Thompsett.

OXFORD UNIVERSITY v LANCASHIRE

At Oxford, June 4, 5, 6. Lancashire won by nine wickets. Toss: Lancashire. Oxford, bowled out for 96 in the first innings, with Patterson taking six for 31, batted well second time round to avoid an innings defeat. Hagan and Mee opened with a partnership of 76, which was followed by a similar stand between Hagan and Kilborn. In Lancashire's first innings, Mendis and Abrahams put on 169 for the second wicket and Abrahams went on to his first century of the season.

Oxford University

D. A. Hagan b Watkinson	11	– c Fairbrother b Abrahams	88
A. A. G. Mee c Fowler b Patterson	2	– c Mendis b Watkinson	21
M. J. Kilborn b Patterson	3	– c Patterson b Abrahams	37
G. J. Toogood c Abrahams b Patterson	1	– b Patterson	11
T. Patel c Folley b Watkinson	18	– c Folley b Patterson	11
N. V. Salvi c Mendis b Watkinson	7	– (7) c Fowler b Folley	35
R. A. Rydon lbw b Patterson	20	– (8) c and b Folley	14
†D. P. Taylor b Patterson	6	– (6) b Watkinson	12
J. D. Quinlan c Makinson b Folley	15	– not out	24
M. R. Sygrove b Patterson	2	– b Hayhurst	6
*M. P. Lawrence not out	0	– lbw b Hayhurst	0
B 5, l-b 4, w 1, n-b 1	11	B 7, l-b 14, w 2, n-b 3	26

1/14 2/14 3/18 4/23 5/34   **96**   1/76 2/152 3/169 4/174 5/194   **285**
6/47 7/69 8/86 9/96   6/196 7/247 8/257 9/285

Bowling: *First Innings*—Patterson 17.4–6–31–6; Makinson 7–2–7–0; Watkinson 19–9–44–3; Folley 3–1–5–1. *Second Innings*—Patterson 18–2–56–2; Makinson 30–9–74–0; Hayhurst 8–5–11–2; Fairbrother 1–1–0–0; Watkinson 31–8–77–2; Folley 19–7–32–2; Abrahams 7–1–14–2.

Lancashire

G. D. Mendis c Quinlan b Sygrove	98		
G. Fowler c Salvi b Toogood	16	– not out	37
J. Abrahams c Quinlan b Toogood	117		
N. H. Fairbrother not out	59		
A. N. Hayhurst c Taylor b Quinlan	10	– (1) c Hagan b Sygrove	0
M. Watkinson not out	12		
*C. H. Lloyd (did not bat)		– (3) not out	19
L-b 3, w 5	8	B 4, l-b 1, w 1, n-b 1	7

1/36 2/205 3/255 4/285   (4 wkts dec.) 320   1/9   (1 wkt) 63

†J. Stanworth, I. Folley, D. J. Makinson and B. P. Patterson did not bat.

Bowling: *First Innings*—Quinlan 21–1–66–1; Toogood 29–10–77–2; Rydon 9–0–33–0; Lawrence 18–5–70–0; Sygrove 13–0–66–1; Patel 1–0–5–0. *Second Innings*—Toogood 7–2–22–0; Sygrove 4–0–19–1; Rydon 3–0–13–0; Hagan 0.1–0–4–0.

Umpires: M. Hendrick and D. S. Thompsett.

OXFORD UNIVERSITY v KENT

At Oxford, June 7, 9, 10. Drawn. Toss: Kent. Oxford's weak attack – they were without four bowlers, including Thorne – was put to the sword by Kent. Tavaré, Taylor and Baptiste scored hundreds and a declaration at lunch on the second day deprived Penn of one. Rain and poor light accounted for most of the afternoon's play, and on the final day Hagan and Mee resumed promisingly for the University in a partnership of 65. However, the customary slump was in evidence when more rain, twenty minutes after tea, brought the match to an early finish. Altogether six hours and ten minutes were lost on the last two days.

Kent

M. R. Benson b Rydon	40	C. Penn not out	84
S. G. Hinks c Cope b Rydon	14	†S. A. Marsh not out	7
C. J. Tavaré b Dawson	123	B 6, l-b 7, w 7	20
N. R. Taylor c Hagan b Lawrence	106		
*C. S. Cowdrey b Dawson	53	1/43 2/67 3/252 (7 wkts dec.) 590	
G. R. Cowdrey lbw b Rydon	30	4/342 5/349	
E. A. E. Baptiste b Dawson	113	6/459 7/548	

D. L. Underwood and K. B. S. Jarvis did not bat.

Bowling: Quinlan 24–2–90–0; Rydon 31–4–106–3; MacLarnon 14–3–50–0; Lawrence 35–5–163–1; Dawson 44–10–161–3; Patel 1–0–7–0.

Oxford University

D. A. Hagan c and b C. S. Cowdrey	38	R. A. Rydon not out	7
A. A. G. Mee lbw b Hinks	25		
M. J. Kilborn c and b Jarvis	9	B 5, l-b 5, w 1	11
P. C. MacLarnon lbw b Underwood	4		
T. Patel lbw b Jarvis	1	1/65 2/74 3/80 (5 wkts) 120	
N. V. Salvi not out	25	4/86 5/94	

†J. E. B. Cope, J. D. Quinlan, T. A. J. Dawson and *M. P. Lawrence did not bat.

Bowling: Jarvis 16–9–15–2; Penn 16.4–6–38–0; Baptiste 9–2–24–0; C. S. Cowdrey 8–2–19–1; Hinks 8–2–10–1; Taylor 1–1–0–0; Underwood 11–8–3–1; G. R. Cowdrey 3–2–1–0.

Umpires: M. Hendrick and D. S. Thompsett.

OXFORD UNIVERSITY v GLAMORGAN

At Oxford, June 14, 16, 17. Glamorgan won by an innings and 26 runs. Toss: Oxford University. Oxford finished their first-class fixtures in The Parks with another heavy defeat, despite fielding their strongest side. Batting first, they lost only one wicket before lunch, but when Mee was bowled by Thomas to end a partnership of 53 with Tooley, the usual collapse ensued. The last nine wickets fell for 86. Glamorgan made a poor start, losing their first three wickets for 53, but there followed the county's highest partnership against Oxford or Cambridge. Maynard, with a career-best 148 which included two 6s and seventeen 4s, and Holmes put on 234 in a little over three hours for the fourth wicket. Glamorgan's declaration gave Oxford 43 minutes' batting, in which they lost two wickets for 14 runs, and after Tooley and Kilborn had added another 62 for the third wicket on the final day, the only resistance came from Salvi, who hit 36.

Oxford University

D. A. Hagan c Pauline b Hickey	16	– c Davies b Hickey	2
A. A. G. Mee b Thomas	38	– c Steele b Base	0
C. D. M. Tooley c Maynard b Steele	60	– c Davies b Holmes	28
M. J. Kilborn lbw b Thomas	2	– c Steele b Derrick	45
*D. A. Thorne c Davies b Base	5	– b Derrick	6
N. V. Salvi b Hickey	6	– (7) lbw b Steele	36
R. S. Rutnagur c Holmes b Hickey	24	– (6) c Cottey b Derrick	9
R. A. Rydon c Thomas b Derrick	0	– c Davies b Holmes	1
†D. P. Taylor b Hickey	1	– c Morris b Hickey	17
T. A. J. Dawson not out	10	– st Davies b Steele	9
M. P. Lawrence c Davies b Hickey	0	– not out	10
L-b 5, w 1, n-b 3	9	L-b 2, w 2, n-b 7	11
	171		**174**

1/32 2/85 3/91 4/113 5/127
6/141 7/159 8/159 9/161

1/3 2/8 3/76 4/89 5/97
6/101 7/112 8/143 9/156

Bowling: First Innings—Thomas 13–4–21–2; Hickey 16.1–3–57–5; Derrick 14–5–39–1; Base 9–1–21–1; Steele 14–3–28–1. *Second Innings*—Hickey 21.5–7–49–2; Base 14–5–26–1; Derrick 16–1–54–3; Holmes 14–6–22–2; Steele 8–4–21–2.

Glamorgan

D. B. Pauline c Taylor b Rutnagur	20	*J. F. Steele not out	31
P. A. Cottey c Taylor b Rydon	6		
H. Morris c Taylor b Rutnagur	10	B 6, l-b 5, w 1, n-b 4	16
G. C. Holmes lbw b Lawrence	93		
M. P. Maynard c and b Dawson	148	1/8 2/44 3/53 (5 wkts dec.)	371
J. Derrick not out	47	4/287 5/293	

J. G. Thomas, †T. Davies, S. J. Base and D. J. Hickey did not bat.

Bowling: Thorne 30–13–57–0; Rydon 20–4–92–1; Rutnagur 20–3–72–2; Lawrence 21–5–61–1; Dawson 22–3–78–1.

Umpires: H. J. Rhodes and R. A. White.

†At Oxford, June 18, 19, 20. MCC won by 254 runs. MCC 377 for five dec. (R. J. Lanchbury 101, Sadiq Mohammad 56, D. P. Hughes 119, C. R. Trembath 83) and 148 for three dec. (M. E. Waugh 101 not out); Oxford University 102 (D. P. Hughes four for 20) and 169 (D. A. Hagan 47, R. A. Rydon 46).

At Lord's, July 2, 3, 4. OXFORD UNIVERSITY lost to CAMBRIDGE UNIVERSITY by five wickets (See Other Matches at Lord's, 1986).

CAMBRIDGE

President: Sir John Butterfield (Downing)

Captain: D. G. Price (Haberdashers' Aske's and Homerton)
Secretary: S. R. Gorman (St Peter's, York and Emmanuel)

Captain for 1987: D. G. Price
Secretary: A. M. G. Scott (Seaford Head and Queens')

Although some early problems suggested that it might be otherwise, Cambridge were stronger than for some time, particularly in their trio of seam bowlers, John Davidson, Alastair Scott and Charles Ellison. There was promise, too, in the batting, even if the lack of experience led to problems during the wet term at Fenner's which ruled out the possibility of hard, fast pitches.

Indeed, the slow and low pitches caused the groundsman, Tony Pocock, considerable anxiety, and the TCCB's Inspector of Pitches was called in. Any suggestion of digging up the square was ruled out, but the authorities were sufficiently concerned to order remedial work during the close season. Not that the pitches were as bad as some batsmen made them appear.

Given these problems, coupled with examinations, which always over-shadow a University season, Cambridge did well to keep their heads above water. Much credit for this was due to David Price, the captain, who led the side with great assurance on and off the field. In this, he was helped by the former Essex player, Graham Saville, who took over as Cambridge's coach and played an important part in developing the team spirit that carried Cambridge to victory in the University Match. The captaincy also encouraged Price to develop as the side's most accomplished player at Fenner's.

The most talented batsman was Paul Bail, a Freshman who played for Somerset in 1985, although until scoring a remarkable maiden hundred against Oxford at Lord's, he did not produce the major innings upon which the University's batting was relying. The only century against a county was David Fell's career-best 114 against Sussex at Hove, and he again went to Lord's as Cambridge's leading run-scorer. David Browne also scored more than 200 runs, but the brittleness of the batting line-up was reflected by the absence of a three-figure partnership.

Andrew Golding made useful runs in the lower order and, occasionally, showed glimpses of form as a left-arm spin bowler. He, more than most it seemed, suffered from dropped catches. Ellison, who started the season with five wickets against Leicestershire, topped the bowling averages, but Davidson was the leading wicket-taker with 28, worthy of distinction in such a truncated University season. Scott was dependable but lacked the pace necessary to bowl out sides.

Finally, mention has to be made of the wicket-keeping of Adrian Brown, whose skills when standing up to the seam bowlers made so much difference to the attack. He also tidied up the side's out-cricket, making Cambridge look an efficient unit in the field, and his fifteen catches and two stumpings were testimony to his ability. – D.H.

CAMBRIDGE UNIVERSITY 1986

[*Bill Smith*]

Back row: G. J. Saville (*coach*), M. S. Ahluwalia, A. K. Golding, C. C. Ellison, A. D. Brown, J. E. Davidson, S. R. Gorman, P. A. C. Bail, T. J. Head. *Front row*: D. J. Fell, D. W. Browne, D. G. Price (*captain*), A. M. G. Scott, A. E. Lea.

CAMBRIDGE UNIVERSITY RESULTS

First-class matches – Played 8: Won 1, Lost 1, Drawn 6.

FIRST-CLASS AVERAGES – BATTING

	M	I	NO	R	HI	Avge
D. J. Fell	8	15	2	379	114	29.15
C. C. Ellison	5	3	1	54	51*	27.00
D. W. Browne	7	13	4	228	61*	25.33
P. A. C. Bail	8	15	0	379	174	25.26
A. K. Golding	6	9	3	134	47	22.33
J. E. Davidson	8	8	3	103	41*	20.60
M. S. Ahluwalia	6	11	0	198	36	18.00
A. M. G. Scott	7	6	5	17	5	17.00
D. G. Price	7	13	1	187	60	15.58
T. J. Head	3	5	1	62	40*	15.50
S. R. Gorman	6	9	3	76	37	12.66
A. E. Lea	5	8	0	79	19	9.87
A. D. Brown	8	9	1	78	30	9.75
T. M. Lord	2	4	0	31	23	7.75

Played in one match: S. D. Heath 10, 6; J. M. Tremellen 3, 4*.

* Signifies not out.

The following played a total of two three-figure innings for Cambridge University – P. A. C. Bail 1, D. J. Fell 1.

BOWLING

	O	M	R	W	BB	Avge
C. C. Ellison	127	41	325	14	5-82	23.21
J. E. Davidson	288	47	877	28	5-35	31.32
A. E. Lea	54	6	191	6	3-61	31.83
A. M. G. Scott	238	62	662	16	4-100	41.37
A. K. Golding	220	46	604	10	3-51	60.40

Also bowled: P. A. C. Bail 4-0-28-0; D. W. Browne 23-5-76-1; S. R. Gorman 49-10-184-2; S. D. Heath 7-0-39-0; D. G. Price 1.2-0-11-0; J. M. Tremellen 7-0-32-0.

FIELDING

17 – A. D. Brown (15ct, 2st); 6 – A. E. Lea; 5 – P. A. C. Bail; 4 – D. W. Browne, S. R. Gorman; 3 – D. G. Price, A. M. G. Scott; 2 – J. E. Davidson, A. K. Golding, substitutes; 1 – C. C. Ellison, D. J. Fell, T. J. Head.

CAMBRIDGE UNIVERSITY v LEICESTERSHIRE

At Cambridge, April 19, 21, 22. Drawn. Toss: Leicestershire. After a full opening day's play, the weather intervened to rule out all but eighteen minutes on the second day and 84 on the third. There was an encouraging start by the Cambridge seam bowlers with Ellison taking five wickets and Scott three with economical returns.

Leicestershire

I. P. Butcher c Lea b Scott	58	†P. Whitticase lbw b Scott	0
R. A. Cobb c Browne b Scott	30	W. K. M. Benjamin c Head b Ellison	0
L. Potter c Fell b Ellison	24	J. P. Agnew not out	5
T. J. Boon run out	16	B 4, l-b 3, w 1	8
J. J. Whitaker c and b Ellison	57		
*N. E. Briers st Brown b Ellison	3	1/63 2/100 3/131	(9 wkts dec.) 254
P. B. Clift not out	43	4/132 5/136 6/203	
P. A. J. DeFreitas lbw b Ellison	10	7/236 8/241 9/242	

Bowling: Davidson 24–5–64–0; Scott 33–9–61–3; Ellison 34–11–82–5; Gorman 11–3–40–0.

Cambridge University

T. J. Head c Butcher b Agnew	1	D. W. Browne not out	7
A. E. Lea c Butcher b Benjamin	4		
D. J. Fell not out	32	L-b 2, n-b 3	5
P. A. C. Bail c Clift b Benjamin	9		
*D. G. Price c Cobb b DeFreitas	6	1/6 2/6 3/39 4/49	(4 wkts) 64

S. R. Gorman, †A. D. Brown, C. C. Ellison, J. E. Davidson and A. M. G. Scott did not bat.

Bowling: Agnew 8–4–10–1; Benjamin 8–1–31–2; Clift 6–3–7–0; DeFreitas 5.2–1–14–1; Potter 1–1–0–0.

Umpires: M. Hendrick and M. J. Kitchen.

CAMBRIDGE UNIVERSITY v ESSEX

At Cambridge, April 23, 24, 25. Drawn. Toss: Cambridge University. Essex batted with great caution and not a little suspicion of a pitch recovering from the rain of the previous days. Border, in his first game for the county, was made to work for his runs by Davidson and Ellison. His 50 took 87 balls with ten 4s, and he hit a 6 and three more 4s before being bowled by the persevering Davidson. After Lever had taken two wickets without conceding a run in his nine overs, Cambridge were kept on the rack by the off-spin of Acfield, and only some defiant batting by Cambridge's off-spinner, Gorman, enabled them to reach three figures. Fletcher did not enforce the follow-on, allowing the Essex batsmen time in the middle until lunch on the third day. It was a relief for Cambridge when bad light and then a thunderstorm washed out play soon after tea, following a session punctuated by showers.

Essex

A. W. Lilley c Lea b Gorman	44	– c Price b Scott	3
B. R. Hardie c Lea b Ellison	27	– retired hurt	25
P. J. Prichard c Brown b Davidson	21	– c sub b Gorman	77
A. R. Border b Davidson	80		
*K. W. R. Fletcher not out	45		
D. R. Pringle not out	12	– (4) not out	63
†D. E. East (did not bat)		– (5) c Browne b Davidson	4
B 16, l-b 12, w 1, n-b 8	37	B 6, l-b 8, w 2, n-b 3	19
1/59 2/98 3/135 4/229	(4 wkts dec.) 266	1/3 2/169 3/191	(3 wkts dec.) 191

J. H. Childs, J. K. Lever, T. D. Topley and D. L. Acfield did not bat.

Bowling: *First Innings*—Davidson 31–8–61–2; Scott 25–9–60–0; Ellison 26–5–66–1; Gorman 11–1–28–1; Browne 6–1–23–0. *Second Innings*—Davidson 16.5–2–62–1; Scott 19–5–64–1; Ellison 3–1–6–0; Gorman 11–2–45–1.

Cambridge University

T. J. Head c Border b Lever	10	– c Border b Lever	1
A. E. Lea c Pringle b Lever	6	– c Border b Lever	3
D. J. Fell c Pringle b Acfield	6	– not out	10
P. A. C. Bail c Fletcher b Acfield	3	– c East b Lever	1
*D. G. Price lbw b Acfield	26	– lbw b Lever	0
D. W. Browne b Childs	4	– c Prichard b Childs	6
S. R. Gorman c East b Pringle	37	– not out	0
†A. D. Brown lbw b Pringle	4		
C. C. Ellison c Lilley b Acfield	3		
J. E. Davidson b Acfield	0		
A. M. G. Scott not out	3		
B 3, l-b 4	7	L-b 3, w 1	4

1/13 2/23 3/23 4/28 5/39   109   1/2 2/5 3/13   (5 wkts) 25
6/67 7/74 8/95 9/95   4/13 5/25

Bowling: *First Innings*—Lever 9–9–0–2; Pringle 17.5–7–26–2; Topley 5–2–7–0; Acfield 27–14–38–5; Childs 23–13–31–1. *Second Innings*—Lever 12–6–12–4; Pringle 4–4–0–0; Topley 11.3–7–10–0; Childs 3–3–0–1.

Umpires: M. Hendrick and M. J. Kitchen.

CAMBRIDGE UNIVERSITY v NORTHAMPTONSHIRE

At Cambridge, April 26, 28, 29. Drawn. Toss: Cambridge University. The three Cambridge seam bowlers gave little away on another slow pitch, Boyd-Moss needing 138 minutes for his half-century before falling to a leg-side catch by Brown. Bailey played with a little more freedom. The county declared after the first day and Cambridge replied carefully. Price, hitting a 6 and seven 4s in a little over two hours, gave the innings substance, but Wild, in six overs, took four wickets as the last five wickets tumbled for 13. He then took up with the bat what he had begun with the ball, reaching 53 before the close and going on next morning to a hundred in 152 minutes off 124 balls. He hit a 6 and fourteen 4s. The declaration invited the University to score 304 or bat for four hours to save the game. They achieved the latter with determined resistance against seven bowlers.

Northamptonshire

*G. Cook c Price b Scott	27		
A. C. Storie c Bail b Ellison	13	– (1) lbw b Scott	4
R. J. Boyd-Moss c Brown b Scott	61	– (4) c Brown b Ellison	18
R. J. Bailey lbw b Ellison	55	– (5) not out	42
R. G. Williams run out	26	– (7) b Davidson	7
D. J. Capel c Scott b Ellison	45	– c Gorman b Golding	2
D. J. Wild not out	10	– (3) hit wkt b Davidson	101
†D. Ripley not out	0	– (2) c Brown b Ellison	14
N. G. B. Cook (did not bat)		– (8) c Brown b Golding	3
N. A. Mallender (did not bat)		– (9) not out	3
B 4, l-b 6, n-b 1	11	B 5, l-b 5, n-b 1	11

1/41 2/47 3/135 4/172   (6 wkts dec.) 248   1/11 2/62 3/134   (7 wkts dec.) 205
5/200 6/247   4/155 5/158 6/175
                                    7/186

B. J. Griffiths did not bat.

Bowling: *First Innings*—Davidson 19–3–48–0; Scott 28–7–75–2; Ellison 16–6–37–3; Golding 26–7–56–0; Gorman 3–0–22–0. *Second Innings*—Davidson 18–3–58–2; Scott 13–3–44–1; Ellison 16–7–50–2; Golding 17–3–43–2.

Cambridge University

M. S. Ahluwalia lbw b Capel	12	– (2) b Griffiths	13
D. W. Browne lbw b Mallender	0	– (3) c Ripley b Mallender	20
D. J. Fell run out	40	– (4) b N. G. B. Cook	22
P. A. C. Bail b Capel	0	– (1) b Capel	35
*D. G. Price c N. G. B. Cook b Wild	60	– not out	22
S. R. Gorman lbw b Griffiths	2	– not out	9
A. K. Golding lbw b N. G. B. Cook	11		
†A. D. Brown c Bailey b Wild	0		
C. C. Ellison b Wild	0		
A. M. G. Scott not out	2		
J. E. Davidson lbw b Wild	11		
L-b 8, w 2, n-b 2	12	B 4, l-b 1, n-b 3	8

1/7 2/38 3/38 4/82 5/84   150   1/47 2/57 3/84   (4 wkts) 129
6/137 7/137 8/137 9/137   4/110

Bowling: *First Innings*—Mallender 12–5–35–1; Griffiths 17–5–55–1; N. G. B. Cook 21–14–18–1; Capel 10–5–18–2; Williams 10–7–12–0; Wild 6.3–4–4–4. *Second Innings*—Mallender 14–5–22–1; Griffiths 12–4–20–1; Capel 12–1–56–1; N. G. B. Cook 12–8–12–1; Williams 7–2–10–0; Wild 4–2–4–0; Bailey 1–1–0–0.

Umpires: J. Birkenshaw and H. J. Rhodes.

CAMBRIDGE UNIVERSITY v WARWICKSHIRE

At Cambridge, April 30, May 1, 2. Warwickshire won by nine wickets. Toss: Cambridge University. Batting first for the first time, the University made slow progress until Ellison hit seven 4s in his 55-minute half-century, enabling Cambridge to enjoy the rare opportunity of a declaration. In the final twenty minutes Warwickshire lost two wickets, and two more in fifteen minutes on the second day. That, however, was the end of Cambridge's hold on the match. Kallicharran, who took four hours, twenty minutes to reach his hundred, hitting twelve 4s, and Humpage, with sixteen 4s in his 200-minute century, put on 224 for the fifth wicket. And then Parsons, with two wickets before the close and another two when play resumed on the third morning, sealed Cambridge's fate. At lunch they were 77 for seven, and Warwickshire won with two hours to spare.

Cambridge University

M. S. Ahluwalia b Ferreira	26	– lbw b Parsons	5
T. M. Lord b Munton	23	– c Humpage b Parsons	0
D. J. Fell lbw b Small	32	– b Parsons	26
P. A. C. Bail lbw b Munton	45	– c Humpage b Parsons	4
*D. G. Price lbw b Gifford	1	– c Dyer b Small	2
S. R. Gorman c Amiss b Small	5	– b Ferreira	9
A. K. Golding c Humpage b Parsons	10	– c Humpage b Munton	2
†A. D. Brown c Kallicharran b Parsons	8	– b Munton	14
C. C. Ellison not out	51	– absent injured	
J. E. Davidson b Parsons	0	– c Amiss b Parsons	20
A. M. G. Scott not out	3	– (9) not out	3
B 8, l-b 10, n-b 4	22	B 6, l-b 8, n-b 5	19

1/51 2/59 3/146 4/147   (9 wkts dec.) 226   1/7 2/8 3/32 4/45 5/45   104
5/152 6/159 7/166   6/51 7/71 8/78 9/104
8/213 9/213

Bowling: *First Innings*—Small 10–3–17–2; Parsons 23.3–7–64–3; Munton 20–4–42–2; Ferreira 25–6–65–1; Gifford 15–7–20–1. *Second Innings*—Small 13–7–14–1; Parsons 17–6–24–5; Gifford 7–2–12–0; Lloyd 1–0–4–0; Munton 11–7–9–2; Ferreira 14–6–21–1; Lord 1–0–6–0.

Warwickshire

T. A. Lloyd c Price b Scott	1	– c sub b Scott	1
R. I. H. B. Dyer c Gorman b Davidson	9	– not out	13
G. J. Lord c Brown b Davidson	1	– not out	24
T. A. Munton b Scott	3		
A. I. Kallicharran c Davidson b Scott	121		
†G. W. Humpage b Scott	125		
D. L. Amiss not out	16		
L-b 13, w 2	15	L-b 1, w 1	2

1/1 2/8 3/16 4/17   (6 wkts dec.) 291   1/3   (1 wkt) 40
5/241 6/291

A. M. Ferreira, G. J. Parsons, G. C. Small and *N. Gifford did not bat.

Bowling: *First Innings*—Davidson 15–5–26–2; Scott 24.1–3–100–4; Ellison 11–1–44–0; Golding 27–5–67–0; Gorman 9–4–21–0; Bail 3–0–20–0. *Second Innings*—Davidson 5–1–9–0; Scott 6–3–15–1; Golding 3–2–4–0; Price 1.2–0–11–0.

Umpires: J. Birkenshaw and H. J. Rhodes.

†At Cambridge, May 10, 11, 12. Drawn. MCC 226 for seven dec. (B. Dudleston 53, Sadiq Mohammad 65) and 259 for seven dec. (R. J. Lanchbury 54, N. R. C. MacLaurin 54, C. J. C. Rowe 55); Cambridge University 198 for four dec. (P. A. C. Bail 60, D. J. Fell 68, D. W. Browne 47) and 213 for eight (D. W. Browne 100 not out).

CAMBRIDGE UNIVERSITY v HAMPSHIRE

At Cambridge, May 21, 22, 23. Drawn. Toss: Cambridge University. No play was possible on the first day, but Cambridge still had a struggle to avoid defeat. Robin and Chris Smith shared an opening partnership of 88 at a run a minute before both were bowled by Davidson, who then bowled Nicholas in a profitable eight-ball spell. Turner and Terry's 134 picked up the impetus, and after Hampshire's mid-afternoon declaration, Maru was the principal agent as Cambridge were bowled out in three hours. Davidson, with career-best figures, prevented Hampshire from racing towards an advantageous declaration, although the University still had to bat for two and a half hours to save the match.

Hampshire

R. A. Smith b Davidson	58	– (3) not out	22
C. L. Smith b Davidson	32	– c Brown b Davidson	12
*M. C. J. Nicholas b Davidson	2	– (1) b Davidson	23
D. R. Turner not out	69		
V. P. Terry c Davidson b Golding	70		
N. G. Cowley not out	3	– (5) c Brown b Davidson	19
†R. J. Parks (did not bat)		– (4) c Brown b Davidson	0
T. M. Tremlett (did not bat)		– (6) b Davidson	1
R. J. Maru (did not bat)		– (7) not out	8
B 3, l-b 4, w 1, n-b 2	10	B 4, l-b 2	6

1/88 2/90 3/97 4/231   (4 wkts dec.) 244   1/39 2/50 3/50   (5 wkts dec.) 91
                                  4/76 5/78

S. J. W. Andrew and P. J. Bakker did not bat.

Bowling: *First Innings*—Davidson 22–3–75–3; Tremellen 7–0–32–0; Browne 7–1–22–0; Golding 15–2–69–1; Heath 7–0–39–0. *Second Innings*—Davidson 16–5–35–5; Browne 3–1–13–0; Golding 13–4–37–0.

Cambridge University

M. S. Ahluwalia c and b Cowley	33	– c Parks b Bakker	3
T. M. Lord c Parks b Andrew	1	– lbw b Cowley	7
D. J. Fell c and b Maru	15	– c Terry b Andrew	29
P. A. C. Bail lbw b Bakker	11	– c R. A. Smith b Cowley	10
D. W. Browne c Andrew b Tremlett	39	– c C. L. Smith b Cowley	4
S. D. Heath st Parks b Maru	10	– (7) c Nicholas b Maru	6
*D. G. Price c C. L. Smith b Maru	0	– (6) b R. A. Smith	3
A. K. Golding b Tremlett	0	– not out	11
†A. D. Brown st Parks b Maru	11	– b Bakker	1
J. M. Tremellen b Maru	3	– not out	4
J. E. Davidson not out	0		
L-b 4, n-b 2	6	B 6, l-b 9, n-b 5	20

1/9 2/37 3/50 4/69 5/101	129	1/5 2/23 3/41 4/53	(8 wkts) 98
6/115 7/115 8/115 9/122		5/61 6/65 7/75 8/78	

Bowling: *First Innings*—Andrew 10–4–17–1; Bakker 12–6–20–1; Maru 21.2–9–38–5; Tremlett 14–3–40–2; Cowley 6–1–10–1. *Second Innings*—Andrew 10–3–16–1; Bakker 6.5–3–15–2; Cowley 13–4–22–3; Maru 12–3–22–1; C. L. Smith 3–3–0–0; R. A. Smith 6–3–8–1.

Umpires: D. S. Thompsett and A. G. T. Whitehead.

†At Cambridge, June 9. Canada won by seven wickets. Cambridge University 253 for seven (55 overs) (M. S. Ahluwalia 50, D. J. Fell 73); Canada 257 for four (53.4 overs) (P. Prashad 73, R. Jayasekera 61 not out, F. Kirmani 59).

At Hove, June 14, 15, 16. CAMBRIDGE UNIVERSITY drew with SUSSEX.

†At Cambridge, June 18, 19, 20. Drawn. Combined Services 210 (M. Fleming 83) and 251 for three dec. (E. C. Gordon-Lennox 103 not out, B. W. P. Bennett 68 not out); Cambridge University 367 for seven dec. (M. S. Ahluwalia 79, D. W. Browne 128) and 217 for eight (P. A. C. Bail 67, D. W. Browne 59; N. J. Pringle five for 49).

CAMBRIDGE UNIVERSITY v SURREY

At Cambridge, June 21, 23, 24. Drawn. Toss: Surrey. Cambridge, having failed to avoid the follow-on by 3 runs, batted through the last day to save the game. Butcher, leading Surrey in the absence of Pocock, dominated the first day, batting for 216 minutes to score 157 from 199 balls, 23 of which were sent for 4. Without Ellison, who was injured, the Cambridge attack lacked penetration, and useful contributions all the way down the order allowed the county to declare in a strong position at the close on the first day. At 164 for eight Cambridge were in trouble, but the tail prolonged the innings by 90 minutes while adding another 59. Without Clarke, who did not bowl because of a back injury, Surrey looked unlikely to bowl out the University a second time, despite the acting-captain's four for 25 in 23 overs.

Surrey

*A. R. Butcher c Scott b Davidson	157	M. A. Feltham not out	20
G. S. Clinton lbw b Browne	23	S. T. Clarke not out	0
†A. J. Stewart c Golding b Davidson	36		
M. A. Lynch b Lea	33	B 8, l-b 4, w 1, n-b 2	15
T. E. Jesty c Gorman b Davidson	43		
A. Needham c Brown b Lea	0	1/52 2/196 3/237	(8 wkts dec.) 375
R. J. Doughty c Bail b Golding	21	4/267 5/267 6/308	
K. T. Medlycott c Brown b Lea	27	7/334 8/367	

G. Winterborne did not bat.

Bowling: Scott 14–0–78–0; Davidson 27–3–95–3; Browne 6–2–13–1; Golding 30–2–95–1; Lea 21–5–74–3; Bail 1–0–8–0.

Cambridge University

P. A. C. Bail c Clarke b Needham	27	– c and b Medlycott	14
M. S. Ahluwalia c Clarke b Medlycott	28	– c Needham b Butcher	33
D. J. Fell lbw b Butcher	0	– run out	3
D. W. Browne c Lynch b Butcher	0	– b Doughty	39
*D. G. Price b Butcher	47	– c Doughty b Butcher	13
A. E. Lea c Jesty b Medlycott	8	– c Doughty b Butcher	18
S. R. Gorman b Feltham	2	– b Butcher	0
A. K. Golding b Feltham	33	– not out	20
†A. D. Brown b Medlycott	30	– not out	6
A. M. G. Scott b Feltham	5		
J. E. Davidson not out	5		
B 13, l-b 13, w 4, n-b 8	38	B 10, l-b 3, w 1	14

1/55 2/57 3/60 4/74 5/84   223   1/22 2/27 3/89 4/97   (7 wkts) 160
6/87 7/143 8/164 9/204   5/126 6/130 7/135

Bowling: *First Innings*—Feltham 28–13–36–3; Winterborne 14–3–34–0; Butcher 20–6–31–3; Needham 30–13–47–1; Medlycott 24.4–10–43–3; Doughty 3–0–6–0. *Second Innings*—Doughty 18–4–42–1; Feltham 5–3–4–0; Medlycott 22–5–46–1; Butcher 23–10–25–4; Needham 12–5–17–0; Winterborne 6–2–13–0; Lynch 1–1–0–0.

Umpires: H. D. Bird and K. E. Palmer.

At Lord's, July 2, 3, 4. CAMBRIDGE UNIVERSITY beat OXFORD UNIVERSITY by five wickets (See Other Matches at Lord's, 1986).

YOUNG CRICKETER OF THE YEAR

(*Elected by the Cricket Writers Club*)

1950	R. Tattersall	1969	A. Ward
1951	P. B. H. May	1970	C. M. Old
1952	F. S. Trueman	1971	J. Whitehouse
1953	M. C. Cowdrey	1972	D. R. Owen-Thomas
1954	P. J. Loader	1973	M. Hendrick
1955	K. F. Barrington	1974	P. H. Edmonds
1956	B. Taylor	1975	A. Kennedy
1957	M. J. Stewart	1976	G. Miller
1958	A. C. D. Ingleby-Mackenzie	1977	I. T. Botham
1959	G. Pullar	1978	D. I. Gower
1960	D. A. Allen	1979	P. W. G. Parker
1961	P. H. Parfitt	1980	G. R. Dilley
1962	P. J. Sharpe	1981	M. W. Gatting
1963	G. Boycott	1982	N. G. Cowans
1964	J. M. Brearley	1983	N. A. Foster
1965	A. P. E. Knott	1984	R. J. Bailey
1966	D. L. Underwood	1985	D. V. Lawrence
1967	A. W. Greig	1986	{ A. A. Metcalfe
1968	R. M. H. Cottam		{ J. J. Whitaker

An additional award, in memory of Norman Preston, Editor of *Wisden* from 1952 to 1980, was made to C. W. J. Athey in 1980.

OXFORD AND CAMBRIDGE BLUES

From 1946 to 1986, and some others

A full list of Blues from 1837 may be found in all Wisdens published between 1923 and 1939. Between 1948 and 1972 the list was confined to all those who had won Blues after 1880, plus some of "special interest for personal or family reasons". Between 1972 and 1982 the list was restricted to those who had won Blues since 1919. Such adjustments have been necessary owing to the exigencies of space.

OXFORD

Aamer Hameed (Central Model HS and Punjab U.) 1979
Abell, G. E. B. (Marlborough) 1924, 1926-27
Allan, J. M. (Edinburgh Academy) 1953-56
Allerton, J. W. O. (Stowe) 1969
Allison, D. F. (Greenmore Coll.) 1970
Altham, H. S. (Repton) 1911-12
Arenhold, J. A. (Diocesan Coll., SA) 1954

Baig, A. A. (Aliya and Osmania U., India) 1959-62
Baig, M. A. (Osmania U., India) 1962-64
Bailey, J. A. (Christ's Hospital) (Capt. in 1958) 1956-58
Barber, A. T. (Shrewsbury) (Capt. in 1929) 1927-29
Barker, A. H. (Charterhouse) 1964-65, 1967
Bartlett, J. H. (Chichester) 1946, 1951
Bettington, R. H. B. (The King's School, Parramatta) (Capt. in 1923) 1920-23
Bird, W. S. (Malvern) (Capt. in 1906) 1904-06
Birrell, H. B. (St Andrews, SA) 1953-54
Blake, P. D. S. (Eton) (Capt. in 1952) 1950-52
Bloy, N. C. F. (Dover) 1946-47
Boobbyer, B. (Uppingham) 1949-52
Bosanquet, B. J. T. (Eton) 1898-1900
Botton, N. D. (King Edward's, Bath) 1974
Bowman, R. C. (Fettes) 1957
Brettell, D. N. (Cheltenham) 1977
Bristowe, W. R. (Charterhouse) 1984-85
Brooks, R. A. (Quintin and Bristol U.) 1967
Burchnall, R. L. (Winchester) 1970-71
Burki, J. (St Mary's, Rawalpindi and Punjab U.) 1958-60
Burton, M. St J. W. (Umtali HS, Rhodesia and Rhodes U.) (Capt. in 1970) 1969-71
Bury, T. E. O. (Charterhouse) 1980
Bush, J. E. (Magdalen Coll. Sch.) 1952

Campbell, A. N. (Berkhamsted) 1970
Campbell, I. P. (Canford) 1949-50
Campbell, I. P. F. (Repton) (Capt. in 1913) 1911-13
Cantlay, C. P. T. (Radley) 1975
Carr, D. B. (Repton) (Capt. in 1950) 1949-51
Carr, J. D. (Repton) 1983-85
Carroll, P. R. (Newington Coll. and Sydney U.) 1971

Chalk, F. G. H. (Uppingham) (Capt. in 1934) 1931-34
Chesterton, G. 'H. (Malvern) 1949
Claughton, J. A. (King Edward's, Birmingham) (Capt. in 1978) 1976-79
Clements, S. M. (Ipswich) (Capt. in 1979) 1976, 1979
Clube, S. V. M. (St John's, Leatherhead) 1956
Cope, J. E. B. (St John's, Leatherhead) 1986
Corlett, S. C. (Worksop) 1971-72
Corran, A. J. (Gresham's) 1958-60
Coutts, I. D. F. (Dulwich) 1952
Cowan, R. S. (Lewes Priory CS) 1980-82
Cowdrey, M. C. (Tonbridge) (Capt. in 1954) 1952-54
Coxon, A. J. (Harrow CS) 1952
Crawley, A. M. (Harrow) 1927-30
Crutchley, G. E. V. (Harrow) 1912
Cullinan, M. R. (Hilton Coll., SA) 1983-84
Curtis, I. J. (Whitgift) 1980, 1982
Cushing, V. G. B. (KCS Wimbledon) 1973
Cuthbertson, J. L. (Rugby) 1962-63

Davidson, W. W. (Brighton) 1947-48
Davis, F. J. (Blundell's) 1963
Dawson, T. A. J. (Mill Hill) 1986
Delisle, G. P. S. (Stonyhurst) 1955-56
de Saram, F. C. (Royal Coll., Colombo) 1934-35
Divecha, R. V. (Podar HS and Bombay U.) 1950-51
Dixon, E. J. H. (St Edward's, Oxford) (Capt. in 1939) 1937-39
Donnelly, M. P. (New Plymouth BHS and Canterbury U., NZ) (Capt. in 1947) 1946-47
Dowding, A. L. (St Peter's, Adelaide) (Capt. in 1953) 1952-53
Drybrough, C. D. (Highgate) (Capt. in 1961-62) 1960-62
Duff, A. R. (Radley) 1960-61
Dyer, A. W. (Mill Hill) 1965-66
Dyson, E. M. (QEGS, Wakefield) 1958

Eagar, M. A. (Rugby) 1956-59
Easter, J. N. C. (St Edward's, Oxford) 1967-68
Edbrooke, R. M. (Queen Elizabeth's Hospital) 1984

Ellis, R. G. P. (Haileybury) (Capt. in 1982) 1981-83

Elviss, R. W. (Leeds GS) 1966-67

Ezekowitz, R. A. B. (Westville BHS, Durban and Cape Town U., SA) 1980-81

Faber, M. J. J. (Eton) 1972

Fane, F. L. (Charterhouse) 1897-98

Fasken, D. K. (Wellington) 1953-55

Fellows-Smith, J. P. (Durban HS, SA) 1953-55

Fillary, E. W. J. (St Lawrence) 1963-65

Findlay, W. (Eton) (Capt. in 1903) 1901-03

Fisher, P. B. (St Ignatius, Enfield) 1975-78

Foster, G. N. (Malvern) 1905-08

Foster, H. K. (Malvern) 1894-96

Foster, R. E. (Malvern) (Capt. in 1900) 1897-1900

Franks, J. G. (Stamford) 1984-85

Fry, C. A. (Repton) 1959-61

Fry, C. B. (Repton) (Capt. in 1894) 1892-95

Fursdon, E. D. (Sherborne) 1974-75

Gamble, N. W. (Stockport GS) 1967

Garofall, A. R. (Latymer Upper) 1967-68

Gibbs, P. J. K. (Hanley GS) 1964-66

Gibson, I. (Manchester GS) 1955-58

Gilliat, R. M. C. (Charterhouse) (Capt. in 1966) 1964-67

Gilligan, F. W. (Dulwich) (Capt. in 1920) 1919-20

Glover, T. R. (Lancaster RGS) (Capt. in 1975) 1973-75

Goldstein, F. S. (Falcon Coll., Bulawayo) (Capt. in 1968-69) 1966-69

Green, D. M. (Manchester GS) 1959-61

Grover, J. N. (Winchester) (Capt. in 1938) 1936-38

Groves, M. G. M. (Diocesan Coll., SA) 1964-66

Guest, M. R. J. (Rugby) 1964-66

Guise, J. L. (Winchester) (Capt. in 1925) 1924-25

Gurr, D. R. (Aylesbury GS) 1976-77

Hagan, D. A. (Trinity, Leamington Spa) 1986

Halliday, S. J. (Downside) 1980

Hamblin, C. B. (King's, Canterbury) 1971-73

Hamilton, A. C. (Charterhouse) 1975

Harris, C. R. (Buckingham RLS) 1964

Harris, Hon. G. R. C. (Lord Harris) (Eton) 1871-72, 1874

Hayes, K. A. (QEGS, Blackburn) (Capt. in 1984) 1981-84

Heal, M. G. (St Brendan's, Bristol) 1970, 1972

Heard, H. (QE Hosp. Sch.) 1969-70

Henderson, D. (St Edward's, Oxford) 1950

Henley, D. F. (Harrow) 1947

Heseltine, P. G. (Holgate GS) 1983

Hiller, R. B. (Bec) 1966

Hobbs, J. A. D. (Liverpool Coll.) 1957

Hofmeyr, M. B. (Pretoria, SA) (Capt. in 1951) 1949-51

Holmes, E. R. T. (Malvern) (Capt. in 1927) 1925-27

Hone, B. W. (Adelaide U.) (Capt. in 1933) 1931-33

Howell, M. (Repton) (Capt. in 1919) 1914, 1919

Huxford, P. N. (Richard Hale) 1981

Imran Khan (Aitchison Coll., Lahore and Worcester RGS) (Capt. in 1974) 1973-75

Jakobson, T. R. (Charterhouse) 1961

Jardine, D. R. (Winchester) 1920-21, 1923

Jardine, M. R. (Fettes) (Capt. in 1891) 1889-92

Jarrett, D. W. (Wellington) 1975

Johns, R. L. (St Albans and Keele U.) 1970

Jones, A. K. C. (Solihull) (Capt. in 1973) 1971-73

Jones, P. C. H. (Milton HS, Rhodesia and Rhodes U.) (Capt. in 1972) 1971-72

Jose, A. D. (Adelaide U.) 1950-51

Jowett, D. C. P. R. (Sherborne) 1952-55

Jowett, R. L. (Bradford GS) 1957-59

Kamm, A. (Charterhouse) 1954

Kardar, A. H. (Islamia Coll. and Punjab U.) 1947-49

Kayum, D. A. (Selhurst GS and Chatham House GS) 1977-78

Keighley, W. G. (Eton) 1947-48

Kentish, E. S. M. (Cornwall Coll., Jamaica) 1956

Khan, A. J. (Aitchison Coll., Lahore and Punjab U.) 1968-69

Kilborn, M. J. (Farrer Agric. HS and Univ. of NSW) 1986

Kingsley, P. G. T. (Winchester) (Capt. in 1930) 1928-30

Kinkead-Weekes, R. C. (Eton) 1972

Knight, D. J. (Malvern) 1914, 1919

Knight, J. M. (Oundle) 1979

Knott, C. H. (Tonbridge) (Capt. in 1924) 1922-24

Knott, F. H. (Tonbridge) (Capt. in 1914) 1912-14

Knox, F. P. (Dulwich) (Capt. in 1901) 1899-1901

Lamb, Hon. T. M. (Shrewsbury) 1973-74

Lawrence, M. P. (Manchester GS) 1984-86

Lee, R. J. (Church of England GS and Sydney U.) 1972-74

Legge, G. B. (Malvern) (Capt. in 1926) 1925-26

L'Estrange, M. G. (St Aloysius Coll. and Sydney U.) 1977, 1979

Leveson Gower, H. D. G. (Winchester) (Capt. in 1896) 1893-96

Lewis, D. J. (Cape Town U.) 1951

Lloyd, M. F. D. (Magdalen Coll. Sch.) 1974
Luddington, R. S. (KCS, Wimbledon) 1982

McCanlis, M. A. (Cranleigh) (Capt. in 1928) 1926-28
Macindoe, D. H. (Eton) (Capt. in 1946) 1937-39, 1946
McKinna, G. H. (Manchester GS) 1953
MacLarnon, P. C. (Loughborough GS) 1985
Majendie, N. L. (Winchester) 1962-63
Mallett, A. W. H. (Dulwich) 1947-48
Mallett, N. V. H. (St Andrew's Coll. and Cape Town U.) 1981
Manasseh, M. (Epsom) 1964
Marie, G. V. (Western Australia U. and Reading U.) (Capt. in 1979, but injury prevented him playing v Cambridge) 1978
Marks, V. J. (Blundell's) (Capt. in 1976-77) 1975-78
Marsden, R. (Merchant Taylors', Northwood) 1982
Marshall, J. C. (Rugby) 1953
Marsham, C. D. B. (Private) (Capt. in 1857-58) 1854-58
Marsham, C. H. B. (Eton) (Capt. in 1902) 1900-02
Marsham, C. J. B. (Private) 1851
Marsham, R. H. B. (Private) 1856
Marsland, G. P. (Rossall) 1954
Martin, J. D. (Magdalen Coll. Sch.) (Capt. in 1965) 1962-63, 1965
Maudsley, R. H. (Malvern) 1946-47
May, B. (Prince Edward's, Salisbury and Cape Town U.) (Capt. in 1971) 1970-72
Mee, A. A. G. (Merchant Taylors', Northwood) 1986
Melville, A. (Michaelhouse, SA) (Capt. in 1931-32) 1930-33
Melville, C. D. M. (Michaelhouse, SA) 1957
Metcalfe, S. G. (Leeds GS) 1956
Millener, D. J. (Auckland GS and Auckland U.) 1969-70
Miller, A. J. T. (Haileybury) (Capt. in 1985) 1983-85
Minns, R. E. F. (King's, Canterbury) 1962-63
Mitchell, W. M. (Dulwich) 1951-52
Mitchell-Innes, N. S. (Sedbergh) (Capt. in 1936) 1934-37
Moore, D. N. (Shrewsbury) (Capt. in 1931, when he did not play v Cambridge owing to illness) 1930
Morgan, A. H. (Hastings GS) 1969
Morrill, N. D. (Sandown GS and Millfield) 1979
Moulding, R. P. (Haberdashers' Aske's) (Capt. in 1981) 1978-83
Mountford, P. N. G. (Bromsgrove) 1963

Neate, F. W. (St Paul's) 1961-62
Newton-Thompson, J. O. (Diocesan Coll., SA) 1946
Niven, R. A. (Berkhamsted) 1968-69, 1973

O'Brien, T. C. (St Charles' College, Notting-Hill) 1884-85
Orders, J. O. D. (Winchester) 1978-81
Owen-Smith, H. G. (Diocesan College, SA) 1931-33

Palairet, L. C. H. (Repton) (Capt. in 1892-93) 1890-93
Pataudi, Nawab of (Chief's College, Lahore) 1929-31
Pataudi, Nawab of (Winchester) (Capt. in 1961, when he did not play v Cambridge owing to a car accident and 1963) 1960, 1963
Pathmanathan, G. (Royal Coll., Colombo and Sri Lanka U.) 1975-78
Paver, R. G. L. (Fort Victoria HS and Rhodes U.) 1973-74
Pawson, A. C. (Winchester) 1903
Pawson, A. G. (Winchester) (Capt. in 1910) 1908-11
Pawson, H. A. (Winchester) (Capt. in 1948) 1947-48
Pearce, J. P. (Ampleforth) 1979
Peebles, I. A. R. (Glasgow Academy) 1930
Petchey, M. D. (Latymer Upper) 1983
Phillips, J. B. M. (King's, Canterbury) 1955
Piachaud, J. D. (St Thomas's, Colombo) 1958-61
Pithey, D. B. (Plumtree HS and Cape Town U.) 1961-62
Porter, S. R. (Peers School) 1973
Potter, I. C. (King's, Canterbury) 1961-62
Potts, H. J. (Stand GS) 1950
Price, V. R. (Bishop's Stortford) (Capt. in 1921) 1919-22
Pycroft, J. (Bath) 1836

Quinlan, J. D. (Sherborne) 1985

Rawlinson, H. T. (Eton) 1983-84
Raybould, J. G. (Leeds GS) 1959
Ridge, S. P. (Dr Challenor's GS) 1982
Ridley, G. N. S. (Milton HS, Rhodesia) (Capt. in 1967) 1965-68
Ridley, R. M. (Clifton) 1968-70
Robertson-Glasgow, R. C. (Charterhouse) 1920-23
Robinson, G. A. (Preston Cath. Coll.) 1971
Robinson, H. B. O. (North Shore Coll., Vancouver) 1947-48
Rogers, J. J. (Sedbergh) 1979-81
Ross, C. J. (Wanganui CS and Wellington U., NZ) (Capt. in 1980) 1978-80
Rudd, C. R. D. (Eton) 1949
Rumbold, J. S. (St Andrew's Coll., NZ) 1946
Rutnagur, R. S. (Westminster) 1985-86
Rydon, R. A. (Sherborne) 1986

Sabine, P. N. B. (Marlborough) 1963
Sale, R. (Repton) 1910
Sale, R. (Repton) 1939, 1946
Salvi, N. V. (Rossall) 1986

Sanderson, J. F. W. (Westminster) 1980

Saunders, C. J. (Lancing) 1964

Savage, R. Le Q. (Marlborough) 1976-78

Sayer, D. M. (Maidstone GS) 1958-60

Scott, M. D. (Winchester) 1957

Singleton, A. P. (Shrewsbury) (Capt. in 1937) 1934-37

Siviter, K. (Liverpool) 1976

Smith, A. C. (King Edward's, Birmingham) (Capt. in 1959-60) 1958-60

Smith, G. O. (Charterhouse) 1895-96

Smith, M. J. K. (Stamford) (Capt. in 1956) 1954-56

Stallibrass, M. J. D. (Lancing) 1974

Stevens, G. T. S. (UCS) (Capt. in 1922) 1920-23

Sutcliffe, S. P. (King George V GS, Southport) 1980-81

Sutton, M. A. (Ampleforth) 1946

Tavaré, C. J. (Sevenoaks) 1975-77

Taylor, C. H. (Westminster) 1923-26

Taylor, T. J. (Stockport GS) 1981-82

Thackeray, P. R. (St Edward's, Oxford and Exeter U.) 1974

Thomas, R. J. A. (Radley) 1965

Thorne, D. A. (Bablake) (Capt. in 1986) 1984-86

Toft, D. P. (Tonbridge) 1966-67

Toogood, G. J. (N. Bromsgrove HS) (Capt. in 1983) 1982-85

Tooley, C. D. M. (St Dunstan's) 1985-86

Topham, R. D. N. (Shrewsbury and Australian National U., Canberra) 1976

Travers, B. H. (Sydney U.) 1946, 1948

Twining, R. H. (Eton) (Capt. in 1912) 1910-13

van der Bijl, P. G. (Diocesan Coll., SA) 1932

Van Ryneveld, C. B. (Diocesan Coll., SA) (Capt. in 1949) 1948-50

Varey, J. G. (Birkenhead) 1982-83

Wagstaffe, M. C. (Rossall and Exeter U.) 1972

Walford, M. M. (Rugby) 1936, 1938

Walker, D. F. (Uppingham) (Capt. in 1935) 1933-35

Waller, G. de W. (Hurstpierpoint) 1974

Walsh, D. R. (Marlborough) 1967-69

Walshe, A. P. (Milton HS, Rhodesia) 1953, 1955-56

Walton, A. C. (Radley) (Capt. in 1957) 1955-57

Ward, J. M. (Newcastle-u-Lyme HS) 1971-73

Warner, P. F. (Rugby) 1895-96

Watson, A. G. M. (St Lawrence) 1965-66, 1968

Webb, H. E. (Winchester) 1948

Webbe, A. J. (Harrow) (Capt. in 1877-78) 1875-78

Wellings, E. M. (Cheltenham) 1929, 1931

Westley, S. A. (Lancaster RGS) 1968-69

Wheatley, G. A. (Uppingham) 1946

Whitcombe, P. A. (Winchester) 1947-49

Whitcombe, P. J. (Worcester RGS) 1967-69

Wiley, W. G. A. (Diocesan Coll., SA) 1952

Williams, C. C. P. (Westminster) (Capt. in 1955) 1953-55

Wilson, P. R. B. (Milton HS, Rhodesia and Cape Town U.) 1968, 1970

Wilson, R. W. (Warwick) 1957

Wingfield Digby, A. R. (Sherborne) 1971, 1975-77

Winn, C. E. (KCS, Wimbledon) 1948-51

Woodcock, R. G. (Worcester RGS) 1957-58

Wookey, S. M. (Malvern and Cambridge U.) 1978

Wordsworth, Chas. (Harrow) (Capt. both years, first Oxford Capt.) 1827, 1829

Worsley, D. R. (Bolton) (Capt. in 1964) 1961-64

Wrigley, M. H. (Harrow) 1949

CAMBRIDGE

Acfield, D. L. (Brentwood) 1967-68

Aers, D. R. (Tonbridge) 1967

Ahluwalia, M. S. (Latymer Upper) 1986

Aird, R. (Eton) 1923

Alexander, F. C. M. (Wolmer's Coll., Jamaica) 1952-53

Allbrook, M. E. (Tonbridge) 1975-78

Allen, G. O. (Eton) 1922-23

Allom, M. J. C. (Wellington) 1927-28

Andrew, C. R. (Barnard Castle) (Capt. in 1985) 1984-85

Ashton, C. T. (Winchester) (Capt. in 1923) 1921-23

Ashton, G. (Winchester) (Capt. in 1921) 1919-21

Ashton, H. (Winchester) (Capt. in 1922) 1920-22

Atkins, G. (Dr Challenor's GS) 1960

Aworth, C. J. (Tiffin) (Capt. in 1975) 1973-75

Bail, P. A. C. (Millfield) 1986

Bailey, T. E. (Dulwich) 1947-48

Baker, R. K. (Brentwood) 1973-74

Bannister, C. S. (Caterham) 1976

Barber, R. W. (Ruthin) 1956-57

Barford, M. T. (Eastbourne) 1970-71

Barrington, W. E. J. (Lancing) 1982

Bartlett, H. T. (Dulwich) (Capt. in 1936) 1934-36

Beaumont, D. J. (West Bridgford GS and Bramshill Coll.) 1978

Benke, A. F. (Cheltenham) 1962

Bennett, B. W. P. (Welbeck and RMA Sandhurst) 1979

Bennett, C. T. (Harrow) (Capt. in 1925) 1923, 1925

Bernard, J. R. (Clifton) 1958-60

Bhatia, A. N. (Doon School, India) 1969

Bligh, Hon. Ivo F. W. (Lord Darnley) (Eton) (Capt. in 1881) 1878-81

Blofeld, H. C. (Eton) 1959

Bodkin, P. E. (Bradfield) (Capt. in 1946) 1946

Boyd-Moss, R. J. (Bedford) 1980-83

Brearley, J. M. (City of London) (Capt. in 1963-64) 1961-64

Breddy, M. N. (Cheltenham GS) 1984

Brodie, J. B. (Union HS, SA) 1960

Brodrick, P. D. (Royal GS, Newcastle) 1961

Bromley, R. C. (Christ's Coll. and Canterbury U., NZ) 1970

Brooker, M. E. W. (Lancaster RGS and Burnley GS) 1976

Brown, A. D. (Clacton HS) 1986

Brown, F. R. (The Leys) 1930-31

Browne, D. W. (Stamford) 1986

Burnett, A. C. (Lancing) 1949

Burnley, I. D. (Queen Elizabeth, Darlington) 1984

Bushby, M. H. (Dulwich) (Capt. in 1954) 1952-54

Calthorpe, Hon. F. S. G. (Repton) 1912-14, 1919

Cameron, J. H. (Taunton) 1935-37

Cangley, B. G. M. (Felsted) 1947

Carling, P. G. (Kingston GS) 1968, 1970

Chambers, R. E. J. (Forest) 1966

Chapman, A. P. F. (Oakham and Uppingham) 1920-22

Close, P. A. (Haileybury) 1965

Cobden, F. C. (Harrow) 1870-72

Cockett, J. A. (Aldenham) 1951

Coghlan, T. B. L. (Rugby) 1960

Conradi, E. R. (Oundle) 1946

Cook, G. W. (Dulwich) 1957-58

Cooper, N. H. C. (St Brendan's, Bristol and East Anglia U.) 1979

Cosh, N. J. (Dulwich) 1966-68

Cotterell, T. A. (Downside) 1983-85

Cottrall, G. A. (Kingston GS) (Capt. in 1968) 1966-68

Cottrell, P. R. (Chislehurst and Sidcup GS) 1979

Coverdale, S. P. (St Peter's, York) 1974-77

Craig, E. J. (Charterhouse) 1961-63

Crawford, N. C. (Shrewsbury) 1979-80

Crawley, E. (Harrow) 1887-89

Crawley, L. G. (Harrow) 1923-25

Croft, P. D. (Gresham's) 1955

Crookes, D. V. (Michaelhouse, SA) 1953

Curtis, T. S. (Worcester RGS) 1983

Daniell, J. (Clifton) 1899-1901

Daniels, D. M. (Rutlish) 1964-65

Datta, P. B. (Asutosh Coll., Calcutta) 1947

Davies, A. G. (Birkenhead) 1984-85

Davies, J. G. W. (Tonbridge) 1933-34

Davidson, J. E. (Penglais) 1985-86

Dawson, E. W. (Eton) (Capt. in 1927) 1924-27

Day, S. H. (Malvern) (Capt. in 1901) 1899-1902

Dewes, A. R. (Dulwich) 1978

Dewes, J. G. (Aldenham) 1948-50

Dexter, E. R. (Radley) (Capt. in 1958) 1956-58

Dickinson, D. C. (Clifton) 1953

Doggart, A. G. (Bishop's Stortford) 1921-22

Doggart, G. H. G. (Winchester) (Capt. in 1950) 1948-50

Doggart, S. J. G. (Winchester) 1980-83

Douglas-Pennant, S. (Eton) 1959

Duleepsinhji, K. S. (Cheltenham) 1925-26, 1928

Edmonds, P. H. (Gilbert Rennie HS, Lusaka, Skinner's and Cranbrook) (Capt. in 1973) 1971-73

Edwards, T. D. W. (Sherborne) 1981

Elgood, B. C. (Bradfield) 1948

Ellison, C. C. (Tonbridge) 1982-83, 1985-86

Enthoven, H. J. (Harrow) (Capt. in 1926) 1923-26

Estcourt, N. S. D. (Plumtree, Southern Rhodesia) 1954

Falcon, M. (Harrow) (Capt. in 1910) 1908-11

Farnes, K. (Royal Liberty School, Romford) 1931-33

Fell, D. J. (John Lyon) 1985-86

Field, M. N. (Bablake) 1974

Fitzgerald, J. F. (St Brendan's, Bristol) 1968

Ford, A. F. J. (Repton) 1878-81

Ford, F. G. J. (Repton) (Capt. in 1889) 1887-90

Ford, W. J. (Repton) 1873

Fosh, M. K. (Harrow) 1977-78

Gardiner, S. J. (St Andrew's, Bloemfontein) 1978

Garlick, P. L. (Sherborne) 1984

Gibb, P. A. (St Edward's, Oxford) 1935-38

Gibson, C. H. (Eton) 1920-21

Gilligan, A. E. R. (Dulwich) 1919-20

Goldie, C. F. E. (St Paul's) 1981-82

Golding, A. K. (Colchester GS) 1986

Goodfellow, A. (Marlborough) 1961-62

Goonesena, G. (Royal Coll., Colombo) (Capt. in 1957) 1954-57

Gorman, S. R. (St Peter's, York) 1985

Grace, W. G., jun. (Clifton) 1895-96

Grant, G. C. (Trinidad) 1929-30

Grant, R. S. (Trinidad) 1933

Green, D. J. (Burton GS) (Capt. in 1959) 1957-59

Greig, I. A. (Queen's Coll., SA) (Capt. in 1979) 1977-79

Grierson, H. (Bedford GS) 1911

Grimes, A. D. H. (Tonbridge) 1984

Griffith, M. G. (Marlborough) 1963-65
Griffith, S. C. (Dulwich) 1935
Griffiths, W. H. (Charterhouse) 1946-48

Hadley, R. J. (Sanfields CS) 1971-73
Hall, J. E. (Ardingly) 1969
Hall, P. J. (Geelong) 1949
Harvey, J. R. W. (Marlborough) 1965
Hawke, Hon. M. B. (Eton) (Capt. in 1885) 1882-83, 1885
Hayes, P. J. (Brighton) 1974-75, 1977
Hays, D. L. (Highgate) 1966, 1968
Hayward, W. I. D. (St Peter's Coll., Adelaide) 1950-51, 1953
Haywood, D. C. (Nottingham HS) 1968
Hazelrigg, A. G. (Eton) (Capt. in 1932) 1930-32
Henderson, S. P. (Downside and Durham U.) (Capt. in 1983) 1982-83
Hewitt, S. G. P. (Bradford GS) 1983
Hignell, A. J. (Denstone) (Capt. in 1977-78) 1975-78
Hobson, B. S. (Taunton) 1946
Hodgson, K. I. (Oundle) 1981-83
Hodson, R. P. (QEGS, Wakefield) 1972-73
Holliday, D. C. (Oundle) 1979-81
Howat, M. G. (Abingdon) 1977, 1980
Howland, C. B. (Dulwich) (Capt. in 1960) 1958-60
Hughes, G. (Cardiff HS) 1965
Human, J. H. (Repton) (Capt. in 1934) 1932-34
Hurd, A. (Chigwell) 1958-60
Hutton, R. A. (Repton) 1962-64
Huxter, R. J. A. (Magdalen Coll. Sch.) 1981

Insole, D. J. (Monoux, Walthamstow) (Capt. in 1949) 1947-49

Jackson, E. J. W. (Winchester) 1974-76
Jackson, F. S. (Harrow) (Capt. in 1892-93) 1890-93
Jahangir Khan (Lahore), 1933-36
James, R. M. (St John's, Leatherhead) 1956-58
Jameson, T. E. N. (Taunton and Durham U.) 1970
Jarrett, D. W. (Wellington and Oxford U.) 1976
Jefferson, R. I. (Winchester) 1961
Jenner, Herbert (Eton) (Capt. in 1827, First Cambridge Capt.) 1827
Jessop, G. L. (Cheltenham GS) (Capt. in 1899) 1896-99
Johnson, P. D. (Nottingham HS) 1970-72
Jones, A. O. (Bedford Modern) 1893
Jorden, A. M. (Monmouth) (Capt. in 1969-70) 1968-70

Kelland, P. A. (Repton) 1950

Kemp-Welch, G. D. (Charterhouse) (Capt. in 1931) 1929-31
Kendall, M. P. (Gillingham GS) 1972
Kenny, C. J. M. (Ampleforth) 1952
Kerslake, R. C. (Kingswood) 1963-64
Killick, E. T. (St Paul's) 1928-30
Kirby, D. (St Peter's, York) (Capt. in 1961) 1959-61
Kirkman, M. C. (Dulwich) 1963
Knight, R. D. V. (Dulwich) 1967-70
Knightley-Smith, W. (Highgate) 1953

Lacey, F. E. (Sherborne) 1882
Lacy-Scott, D. G. (Marlborough) 1946
Lea, A. E. (High Arcal GS) 1984-86
Lewis, A. R. (Neath GS) (Capt. in 1962) 1960-62
Lewis, L. K. (Taunton) 1953
Littlewood, D. J. (Enfield GS) 1978
Lowry, T. C. (Christ's College, NZ) (Capt. in 1924) 1923-24
Lumsden, V. R. (Munro College, Jamaica) 1953-55
Lyttelton, 4th Lord (Eton) 1838
Lyttelton, Hon. Alfred (Eton) (Capt. in 1879) 1876-79
Lyttelton, Hon. C. F. (Eton) 1908-09
Lyttelton, Hon. C. G. (Lord Cobham) (Eton) 1861-64
Lyttelton, Hon. Edward (Eton) (Capt. in 1878) 1875-78
Lyttelton, Hon. G. W. S. (Eton) 1866-67

McAdam, K. P. W. J. (Prince of Wales, Nairobi and Millfield) 1965-66
MacBryan, J. C. W. (Exeter) 1920
McCarthy, C. N. (Maritzburg Coll., SA) 1952
McDowall, J. I. (Rugby) 1969
MacGregor, G. (Uppingham) (Capt. in 1891) 1888-91
McLachlan, A. A. (St Peter's, Adelaide) 1964-65
McLachlan, I. M. (St Peter's, Adelaide) 1957-58
Majid J. Khan (Aitchison Coll., Lahore and Punjab U.) (Capt. in 1971-72) 1970-72
Malalasekera, V. P. (Royal Coll., Colombo) 1966-67
Mann, E. W. (Harrow) (Capt. in 1905) 1903-05
Mann, F. G. (Eton) 1938-39
Mann, F. T. (Malvern) 1909-11
Marlar, R. G. (Harrow) (Capt. in 1953) 1951-53
Marriott, C. S. (St Columba's) 1920-21
Mathews, K. P. A. (Felsted) 1951
May, P. B. H. (Charterhouse) 1950-52
Melluish, M. E. L. (Rossall) (Capt. in 1956) 1954-56
Meyer, R. J. O. (Haileybury) 1924-26
Miller, M. E. (Prince Henry GS, Hohne, WG) 1963

Mills, J. M. (Oundle) (Capt. in 1948) 1946-48
Mills, J. P. C. (Oundle) (Capt. in 1982) 1979-82
Mischler, N. M. (St Paul's) 1946-47
Mitchell, F. (St Peter's, York) (Capt. in 1896) 1894-97
Morgan, J. T. (Charterhouse) (Capt. in 1930) 1928-30
Morgan, M. N. (Marlborough) 1954
Morris, R. J. (Blundell's) 1949
Morrison, J. S. F. (Charterhouse) (Capt. in 1919) 1912, 1914, 1919
Moses, G. H. (Ystalyfera GS) 1974
Moylan, A. C. D. (Clifton) 1977
Mubarak, A. M. (Royal Coll., Colombo and Sri Lanka U.) 1978-80
Murray, D. L. (Queen's RC, Trinidad) (Capt. in 1966) 1965-66
Murrills, T. J. (The Leys) (Capt. in 1976) 1973-74, 1976

Nevin, M. R. S. (Winchester) 1969
Norris, D. W. W. (Harrow) 1967-68

O'Brien, R. P. (Wellington) 1955-56
Odendaal, A. (Queen's Coll. and Stellenbosch U., SA) 1980
Owen-Thomas, D. R. (KCS, Wimbledon) 1969-72

Palfreman, A. B. (Nottingham HS) 1966
Palmer, R. W. M. (Bedford) 1982
Parker, G. W. (Crypt, Gloucester) (Capt. in 1935) 1934-35
Parker, P. W. G. (Collyer's GS) 1976-78
Parsons, A. B. D. (Brighton) 1954-55
Pathmanathan, G. (Royal Coll., Colombo, Sri Lanka U. and Oxford U.) 1983
Paull, R. K. (Millfield) 1967
Payne, M. W. (Wellington) (Capt. in 1907) 1904-07
Pearman, H. (King Alfred's and St Andrew's U.) 1969
Pearson, A. J. G. (Downside) 1961-63
Peck, I. G. (Bedford) (Capt. in 1980-81) 1980-81
Pepper, J. (The Leys) 1946-48
Pieris, P. I. (St Thomas's, Colombo) 1957-58
Pollock, A. J. (Shrewsbury) (Capt. in 1984) 1982-84
Ponniah, C. E. M. (St Thomas's, Colombo) 1967-69
Ponsonby, Hon. F. G. B. (Lord Bessborough) (Harrow) 1836
Popplewell, N. F. M. (Radley) 1977-79
Popplewell, O. B. (Charterhouse) 1949-51
Pretlove, J. F. (Alleyn's) 1954-56
Price, D. G. (Haberdashers' Aske's) (Capt. in 1986) 1984-86
Prideaux, R. M. (Tonbridge) 1958-60
Pringle, D. R. (Felsted) (Capt. in 1982, when he did not play v Oxford owing to Test selection) 1979-81

Pritchard, G. C. (King's, Canterbury) 1964
Pryer, B. J. K. (City of London) 1948
Pyemont, C. P. (Marlborough) 1967

Ranjitsinhji, K. S. (Rajkumar Coll., India) 1893
Ratcliffe, A. (Rydal) 1930-32
Reddy, N. S. K. (Doon School, India) 1959-61
Rimell, A. G. J. (Charterhouse) 1949-50
Robins, R. W. V. (Highgate) 1926-28
Roebuck, P. G. P. (Millfield) 1984-85
Roebuck, P. M. (Millfield) 1975-77
Roopnaraine, R. (Queen's RC, BG) 1965-66
Rose, M. H. (Pocklington) 1963-64
Ross, N. P. G. (Marlborough) 1969
Roundell, J. (Winchester) 1973
Russell, D. P. (West Park GS, St Helens) 1974-75
Russell, S. G. (Tiffin) (Capt. in 1967) 1965-67
Russom, N. (Huish's GS) 1980-81

Scott, A. M. G. (Seaford Head) 1985-86
Seabrook, F. J. (Haileybury) (Capt. in 1928) 1926-28
Seager, C. P. (Peterhouse, Rhodesia) 1971
Selvey, M. W. W. (Battersea GS and Manchester U.) 1971
Sheppard, D. S. (Sherborne) (Capt. in 1952) 1950-52
Short, R. L. (Denstone) 1969
Shuttleworth, G. M. (Blackburn GS) 1946-48
Silk, D. R. W. (Christ's Hospital) (Capt. in 1955) 1953-55
Singh, S. (Khalsa Coll. and Punjab U.) 1955-56
Sinker, N. D. (Winchester) 1966
Slack, J. K. E. (UCS) 1954
Smith, C. S. (William Hulme's GS) 1954-57
Smith, D. J. (Stockport GS) 1955-56
Smyth, R. I. (Sedbergh) 1973-75
Snowden, W. (Merchant Taylors', Crosby) (Capt. in 1974) 1972-75
Spencer, J. (Brighton and Hove GS) 1970-72
Steele, H. K. (King's Coll., NZ) 1971-72
Stevenson, M. H. (Rydal) 1949-52
Studd, C. T. (Eton) (Capt. in 1883) 1880-83
Studd, G. B. (Eton) (Capt. in 1882) 1879-82
Studd, J. E. K. (Eton) (Capt. in 1884) 1881-84
Studd, P. M. (Harrow) (Capt. in 1939) 1937-39
Studd, R. A. (Eton) 1895
Subba Row, R. (Whitgift) 1951-53
Surridge, D. (Richard Hale and Southampton U.) 1979
Swift, B. T. (St Peter's, Adelaide) 1957

Taylor, C. R. V. (Birkenhead) 1971-73
Thomson, R. H. (Bexhill) 1961-62
Thwaites, I. G. (Eastbourne) 1964
Tindall, M. (Harrow) (Capt. in 1937) 1935-37
Tordoff, G. G. (Normanton GS) 1952

Trapnell, B. M. W. (UCS) 1946
Turnbull, M. J. (Downside) (Capt. in 1929) 1926, 1928-29

Urquhart, J. R. (King Edward VI School, Chelmsford) 1948

Valentine, B. H. (Repton) 1929
Varey, D. W. (Birkenhead) 1982-83

Wait, O. J. (Dulwich) 1949, 1951
Warr, J. J. (Ealing County GS) (Capt. in 1951) 1949-52
Watts, H. E. (Downside) 1947
Webster, W. H. (Highgate) 1932
Weedon, M. J. H. (Harrow) 1962
Wells, T. U. (King's Coll., NZ) 1950
Wheatley, O. S. (King Edward's, Birmingham) 1957-58
Wheelhouse, A. (Nottingham HS) 1959

White, R. C. (Hilton Coll., SA) (Capt. in 1965) 1962-65
Wilcox, D. R. (Dulwich) (Capt. in 1933) 1931-33
Wilenkin, B. C. G. (Harrow) 1956
Wilkin, C. L. A. (St Kitts GS) 1970
Willard, M. J. L. (Judd) 1959-61
Willatt, G. L. (Repton) (Capt. in 1947) 1946-47
Windows, A. R. (Clifton) 1962-64
Wood, G. E. C. (Cheltenham) (Capt. in 1920) 1914, 1919-20
Wookey, S. M. (Malvern) 1975-76
Wooller, W. (Rydal) 1935-36
Wright, S. (Mill Hill) 1973

Yardley, N. W. D. (St Peter's, York) (Capt. in 1938) 1935-38
Young, R. A. (Repton) (Capt. in 1908) 1905-08

UMPIRES FOR 1987

TEST MATCH UMPIRES

Six umpires comprise the panel for the five Test matches and three one-day internationals between England and Pakistan in 1987. They are: H. D. Bird, D. J. Constant, B. J. Meyer, K. E. Palmer, D. R. Shepherd and A. G. T. Whitehead.

FIRST-CLASS UMPIRES

The first-class list shows one change for 1987, with D. Lloyd, the former Lancashire and England opening batsman, replacing C. Cook, who has retired. B. Hassan, the former Nottinghamshire player, and P. J. Eele, who was on the first-class list from 1981 to 1984, have gone on to the Reserve list. The full list is: H. D. Bird, J. Birkenshaw, D. J. Constant, B. Dudleston, D. G. L. Evans, J. H. Hampshire, J. H. Harris, J. W. Holder, J. A. Jameson, A. A. Jones, R. Julian, M. J. Kitchen, B. Leadbeater, D. Lloyd, K. J. Lyons, B. J. Meyer, D. O. Oslear, K. E. Palmer, R. Palmer, N. T. Plews, D. R. Shepherd, R. A. White, A. G. T. Whitehead and P. B. Wight. *Reserves:* P. J. Eele, B. Hassan, M. Hendrick, H. J. Rhodes and D. S. Thompsett.

MINOR COUNTIES UMPIRES

N. P. Atkins, K. Bray, C. J. Chapman, R. H. Duckett, P. J. Eele, Dr D. Fawkner-Corbett, W. H. Gillingham, D. J. Halfyard, D. B. Harrison, B. Knight, T. Lynan, G. I. McLean, T. G. A. Morley, D. Norton, M. K. Reed, K. S. Shenton, C. Smith, C. T. Spencer, G. A. Stickley, A. R. Tayler, R. C. Tolchard, J. van Geloven, T. V. Wilkins, R. T. Wilson and T. G. Wilson. *Reserves:* P. Adams, R. Bell, P. Brown, R. F. Elliott, R. G. Evans, P. Gray, M. A. Johnson, S. T. Lamb, R. Pattinson, J. B. Seward, T. P. Stevens, J. Stobart, J. H. Symons, J. Thornton, R. Walker and B. Wilson.

OTHER MATCHES, 1986

†At Coleraine, June 11, 12, 13. Ireland won by seven wickets. Wales 326 for seven dec. (C. Elward 123, G. Ellis 67; S. C. Corlett four for 70) and 139 for three dec. (N. Roberts 60); Ireland 225 for four dec. (M. A. Masood 69, M. F. Cohen 64) and 241 for three (S. J. S. Warke 100).

†At Dublin, July 19, 20, 21. Drawn. MCC 399 for seven dec. (M. E. Waugh 239 not out) and 205 for two dec. (B. Hassan 61, M. E. Waugh 101 not out); Ireland 326 for nine dec. (S. J. S. Warke 68, D. G. Dennison 85, M. Halliday 62 not out; C. R. Trembath six for 93) and 231 for eight (M. A. Masood 44, J. D. Garth 64, M. Halliday 45).

THE TILCON TROPHY

History was repeated on the first day of the Harrogate Festival when, after rain, the match between Warwickshire and Yorkshire was decided by each player bowling twice at a single stump. This followed the system devised for the final in 1985 by the umpires, D. O. Oslear, who was standing again on this occasion, and J. W. Holder, rather than the newly adopted rules for the Benson and Hedges Cup and NatWest Bank Trophy, in which five players from each team bowl twice at three stumps. For Warwickshire, the holders, Gifford and Smith hit the stump, while Bairstow achieved Yorkshire's only success.

Leicestershire's victory over Gloucestershire on the second day was decided in the orthodox manner, although conditions were such that the captains, Bainbridge and Willey, agreed that the seam bowlers should operate off shortened run-ups. Gloucestershire, fielding first after losing the toss, were without Walsh for two hours, owing to the breakdown of his car. Bainbridge's six for 38, including the stumping of DeFreitas by Russell off a wide, was the best return in the eleven years of the competition.

On the third day, Leicestershire went on to regain the trophy they had lost to Warwickshire in 1985 and win £1,500. Batting first after winning the toss, they were 117 for eight before Whitticase and Agnew put on 55 in nineteen overs. Agnew then reduced Warwickshire to 12 for three, from which they never recovered.

†June 11. Warwickshire beat Yorkshire 2-1 in a bowling competition.

†June 12. Leicestershire won by 73 runs. Leicestershire 197 (53.4 overs) (P. Bainbridge six for 38); Gloucestershire 124 (41.5 overs) (P. Willey four for 16). *Man of the Match*: P. Bainbridge.

†June 13. Leicestershire won by 68 runs. Leicestershire 172 for eight (55 overs) (J. J. Whitaker 41, P. Whitticase 45 not out); Warwickshire 104 (48.5 overs). *Man of the Match*: P. Whitticase.

SCOTLAND v IRELAND

At Glasgow, August 16, 17, 18. Drawn. Toss: Scotland. Had a wet outfield not delayed the start, Scotland might have forced victory, for when stumps were drawn on the final day, Ireland, having followed on, were still 5 runs in arrears with only three wickets in hand. The first day belonged to Philip, of Stenhousemuir, who hit a hundred in his first first-class match and at the close had scored an unbeaten 142 of Scotland's 216 for two. The Scots batted on until after lunch on the second day, and took a firm hold on the match after tea as seven Irish wickets fell for 85 runs. Beginning their second innings early on the final morning, and 210 runs behind, Ireland faced defeat at 62 for five, but an excellent stand of 118 between Harrison and Corlett thwarted Scotland. When Harrison was out, Corlett steered Ireland through the remaining 54 minutes.

Other Matches, 1986

Scotland

I. L. Philip c J. McBrine b A. McBrine	145	P. G. Duthie not out	54
W. A. Donald b A. McBrine	29	J. E. Ker not out	7
*R. G. Swan lbw b Corlett	30	B 3, l-b 14, w 7, n-b 1	25
A. B. Russell b Corlett	24		
A. Brown b A. McBrine	74	1/88 2/186 3/219 (7 wkts dec.)	396
N. W. Burnett lbw b Corlett	4	4/269 5/273	
D. G. Moir c Jackson b Corlett	4	6/285 7/376	

†D. Fleming and A. W. J. Stevenson did not bat.

Bowling: Corlett 40–3–113–4; J. McBrine 27–4–67–0; Garth 19–7–34–0; A. McBrine 23–5–64–3; Halliday 28–8–74–0; Harrison 12–2–27–0.

Ireland

S. J. S. Warke lbw b Donald	47	– b Duthie	10
M. A. Masood c Fleming b Duthie	0	– (3) run out	12
M. F. Cohen c Swan b Stevenson	29	– (2) c Russell b Moir	10
J. D. Garth b Donald	1	– c Fleming b Moir	6
J. A. Prior c Philip b Donald	1	– c Fleming b Stevenson	12
G. D. Harrison c Russell b Moir	13	– c Brown b Duthie	68
*M. Halliday c Donald b Moir	15	– (8) lbw b Moir	7
A. McBrine b Moir	0		
S. C. Corlett b Moir	23	– (7) not out	44
J. McBrine not out	27	– (9) not out	2
†P. B. Jackson b Ker	2		
B 12, l-b 7, w 4, n-b 5	28	B 10, l-b 13, w 1, n-b 10	34

1/3 2/80 3/81 4/82 5/89	186	1/23 2/35 3/46 4/53 (7 wkts)	205
6/116 7/116 8/130 9/182		5/62 6/180 7/190	

Bowling: *First Innings*—Duthie 18–5–34–1; Ker 9.4–2–15–1; Burnett 8–1–22–0; Donald 21–14–17–3; Moir 23–4–53–4; Stevenson 12–3–26–1. *Second Innings*—Duthie 12–4–29–2; Ker 11–5–10–0; Burnett 5–2–8–0; Donald 11–3–20–0; Moir 29–5–64–3; Stevenson 15–4–51–1.

Umpires: P. Brown and W. B. Smith.

THE ASDA CHALLENGE

Owing to a water-logged ground, no play was possible on the first day of the Asda Challenge at Scarborough. Essex beat Lancashire on the toss of a coin. On the second day, Yorkshire, electing to bat, compiled a solid total, and when the first four Hampshire batsmen were out for 98 in 22 overs, the home county looked likely winners. However, Robin Smith added 61 in the next fifteen overs to take his side towards a three-wicket win. Hampshire's success continued in the final when they comfortably beat Essex by 87 runs with almost eight overs to spare. Parks took four catches as well as contributing a bright 32 in Hampshire's total of 250 after they had been sent in to bat, but the Man of the Match award went to Cowley, who took three wickets for 25 runs.

†September 3. Essex beat Lancashire on the toss of a coin.

†September 4. Hampshire won by three wickets. Yorkshire 222 for five (50 overs) (A. A. Metcalfe 44, K. Sharp 52, P. E. Robinson 50 not out); Hampshire 225 for seven (48.3 overs) (C. G. Greenidge 41, R. A. Smith 57). *Man of the Match:* R. A. Smith.

†September 5. Hampshire won by 87 runs. Hampshire 250 for nine (50 overs) (V. P. Terry 61); Essex 163 (42.1 overs) (C. Gladwin 59). *Man of the Match:* N. G. Cowley.

NATWEST BANK TROPHY, 1986

Sussex, in winning the NatWest Bank Trophy for the first time, increased to four their victories in the final of the 60-overs competition, so equalling the record of Lancashire, their opponents at Lord's in the sixth final under the auspices of the National Westminster Bank and the 24th since the inception of the competition in 1963. Both counties were making their seventh appearance in the final since then, also a record. Winners by seven wickets, Sussex received £19,000 in addition to the trophy, while Lancashire received £9,500. The losing semi-finalists, Surrey and Worcestershire, each received £4,500, and Leicestershire, Nottinghamshire, Warwickshire and Yorkshire each received £2,250 as the losing quarter-finalists. Dermot Reeve, adjudged Man of the Match in the final by Sir Leonard Hutton, received £550. The Man of the Match in each semi-final received £275; in each quarter-final £200; in each second-round match £125; and in each first-round match £100. Total prizemoney for the competition was £51,000, £4,000 more than in 1985.

FIRST ROUND

BERKSHIRE v GLOUCESTERSHIRE

At Reading, June 25. Gloucestershire won by 120 runs. Toss: Gloucestershire.
Man of the Match: D. V. Lawrence.

Gloucestershire

A. W. Stovold st Stevens b Lewington	58	*D. A. Graveney not out	11
A. J. Wright c and b Roope	51	D. V. Lawrence b New	0
C. W. J. Athey c Stevens b Lewington	4	C. A. Walsh not out	25
P. Bainbridge c New b Lewington	14	B 4, l-b 7, w 9, n-b 1	21
K. M. Curran b New	38		
J. W. Lloyds c and b Jackson	1	1/120 2/122 3/132 (9 wkts, 60 overs) 249
I. R. Payne c Lickley b New	23	4/145 5/148 6/203	
†R. C. Russell c Simmons b Jones	3	7/211 8/217 9/219	

Bowling: Jones 12–0–95–1; Jackson 12–2–30–1; New 12–0–58–3; Roope 12–2–32–1; Lewington 12–5–23–3.

Berkshire

M. G. Lickley c Russell b Lawrence	18	†M. E. Stevens c and b Graveney	23
D. B. Gorman c Athey b Lawrence	1	J. H. Jones not out	12
G. R. J. Roope c and b Lawrence	12	P. J. Lewington b Lloyds	0
M. L. Simmons c Walsh b Lloyds	26	L-b 4, w 4, n-b 10	18
K. S. Murray c Lloyds b Walsh	1		
*J. F. Harvey b Walsh	0	1/8 2/38 3/39 (37.3 overs) 129
B. Jackson st Russell b Graveney	14	4/52 5/52 6/60	
P. M. New b Lawrence	4	7/104 8/105 9/128	

Bowling: Lawrence 8–0–36–4; Walsh 7–0–30–2; Lloyds 11.3–3–35–2; Graveney 11–2–24–2.

Umpires: D. J. Dennis and D. G. L. Evans.

CHESHIRE v SURREY

At Birkenhead, June 25. Surrey won by 39 runs. Toss: Surrey.
Man of the Match: A. R. Butcher.

FIELDING POSITIONS Nº5

SILLY MID-ON

Over the years, we've taken up some interesting positions ourselves.

In 328 years of banking, we've achieved quite a bit and after only seven years' major involvement in cricket, our record is already impressive.

In 1981 we introduced the NatWest Trophy; one of the country's most sought after limited overs trophies.

Each season the competition attracts over 100,000 spectators to cricket grounds.

And we're active off the field, too. Together with the National Cricket Association we've produced a first-class series of coaching films.

We lend our support to the Under 13's Ken Barrington Cup.

And the National Cricket Association Proficiency Award Scheme also gets our backing.

Right now our relationship with cricket couldn't be sunnier. Nor our position clearer.

Surrey

A. R. Butcher c J. S. Hitchmough			M. A. Feltham c and b J. S. Hitchmough	1
	b Crawley	38	M. P. Bicknell run out	2
G. S. Clinton c Crawley			A. H. Gray st Cummings b Wood	3
	b J. S. Hitchmough	49	*P. I. Pocock not out	2
A. J. Stewart c J. S. Hitchmough				
	b Mudassar	31	B 1, l-b 5, w 2	8
M. A. Lynch c Yates b Wood		29		
T. E. Jesty c O'Brien b Wood		8	1/55 2/109 3/149 (9 wkts, 60 overs) 198	
A. Needham st Cummings b Wood		4	4/162 5/163 6/166	
†C. J. Richards not out		23	7/168 8/172 9/180	

Bowling: J. S. Hitchmough 12–3–37–2; Mudassar 10–2–31–1; Crawley 10–1–23–1; Sutton 8–1–19–0; Wood 12–1–56–4; O'Brien 8–1–26–0.

Cheshire

B. Wood lbw b Gray		1	K. Teasdale c and b Bicknell	18
S. C. Yates c Needham b Butcher		20	*J. A. Sutton c and b Pocock	8
Mudassar Nazar lbw b Gray		0	†S. Cummings not out	1
I. Cockbain c and b Bicknell		15	B 1, l-b 9, w 3, n-b 2	15
N. T. O'Brien c Stewart b Gray		23		
J. J. Hitchmough c Jesty b Needham		20	1/2 2/2 3/31 (55.4 overs) 159	
J. S. Hitchmough b Feltham		22	4/42 5/84 6/93	
S. T. Crawley c Bicknell b Feltham		16	7/129 8/130 9/153	

Bowling: Gray 12–3–23–3; Feltham 10–3–27–2; Butcher 12–3–27–1; Bicknell 8–1–36–2; Pocock 9.4–3–24–1; Needham 4–1–12–1.

Umpires: B. J. Meyer and C. Smith.

DERBYSHIRE v CORNWALL

At Derby, June 25. Derbyshire won by 204 runs. Toss: Cornwall. Hill and Anderson added 286 for Derbyshire's second wicket, which was not only a record for the competition, but also the highest partnership for any wicket in the three domestic limited-overs competitions. Derbyshire's total was the third-highest in the 60-overs competition, while their margin of victory was the fifth-highest in runs.

Man of the Match: A. Hill.

Derbyshire

*K. J. Barnett b Lovell		26	†B. Roberts not out	2
I. S. Anderson b Toseland		134	L-b 5, w 30, n-b 3	38
A. Hill c Willcock b Toseland		153		
J. E. Morris not out		12	1/58 2/344 3/357 (3 wkts, 60 overs) 365	

R. J. Finney, R. Sharma, M. A. Holding, M. Jean-Jacques, P. G. Newman and P. E. Russell did not bat.

Bowling: Snowdon 12–1–97–0; Lovell 12–0–83–1; Hunt 12–0–87–0; Furse 12–1–52–0; Toseland 12–2–41–2.

Cornwall

*E. G. Willcock b Jean-Jacques		5	C. C. Lovell b Sharma	0
T. J. Angove b Finney		13	D. A. Toseland b Barnett	39
P. J. Stephen c Morris b Sharma		54	†S. P. Eva not out	0
M. S. T. Dunstan c Holding b Newman		11	B 1, l-b 4, w 9, n-b 3	17
J. M. Cradick c Barnett b Sharma		10		
A. E. Snowdon c Morris b Barnett		9	1/6 2/37 3/63 (58.1 overs) 161	
S. A. Hunt b Sharma		2	4/94 5/115 6/118	
R. G. Furse c Roberts b Barnett		1	7/120 8/120 9/121	

Bowling: Holding 6–2–8–0; Jean-Jacques 5–1–14–1; Finney 6–0–25–1; Newman 6–2–13–1; Russell 9–2–20–0; Sharma 12–3–29–4; Barnett 11.1–3–34–3; Hill 3–0–13–0.

Umpires: A. Jepson and M. J. Kitchen.

DEVON v NOTTINGHAMSHIRE

At Exmouth, June 25. Nottinghamshire won by 59 runs. Toss: Devon.
Man of the Match: N. R. Gaywood.

Nottinghamshire

B. C. Broad c and b Donohue	32	R. A. Pick not out	9
R. T. Robinson c Turpin b Yeabsley	9	E. E. Hemmings not out	4
D. W. Randall c N. A. Folland b Allin	53		
*C. E. B. Rice c Edwards b Donohue	15	L-b 6, w 2, n-b 2	10
P. Johnson c N. A. Folland b Donohue	4		
R. J. Hadlee c Gaywood b Allin	20	1/28 2/46 3/75 (8 wkts, 60 overs)	212
†B. N. French c Edwards b Brown	46	4/83 5/117 6/159	
K. P. Evans c Turpin b Brown	10	7/195 8/197	

K. Saxelby did not bat.

Bowling: Donohue 12–0–42–3; Yeabsley 12–2–32–1; Allin 12–2–45–2; Brown 12–1–49–2; Tierney 12–2–38–0.

Devon

K. G. Rice lbw b Hadlee	6	†R. C. Turpin lbw b Pick	14
N. A. Folland b Pick	4	A. W. Allin not out	1
N. G. Folland st French b Hemmings	30		
N. R. Gaywood b Saxelby	49	B 6, l-b 9, w 4, n-b 2	21
J. K. Tierney c Johnson b Saxelby	0		
*J. H. Edwards b Hadlee	5	1/10 2/10 3/98 (8 wkts, 60 overs)	153
K. Donohue c Randall b Hemmings	9	4/100 5/100 6/118	
P. A. Brown not out	14	7/120 8/152	

D. I. Yeabsley did not bat.

Bowling: Hadlee 9–3–10–2; Pick 11–1–23–2; Saxelby 12–2–36–2; Hemmings 12–2–27–2; Rice 10–2–19–0; Evans 6–0–23–0.

Umpires: J. H. Harris and D. R. Shepherd.

HAMPSHIRE v HERTFORDSHIRE

At Southampton, June 25. Hampshire won by four wickets. Toss: Hertfordshire.
Man of the Match: R. J. Hailey.

Hertfordshire

W. M. Osman c Nicholas b Tremlett	20	T. S. Smith c Greenidge b Connor	7
S. A. Dean b Connor	6	W. G. Merry c Parks b Marshall	0
D. G. Ottley b James	4	R. J. Hailey not out	7
E. P. Neal c C. L. Smith b James	0	B 4, l-b 9, w 12, n-b 2	25
M. C. G. Wright lbw b Tremlett	1		
*F. E. Collyer c and b Cowley	26	1/25 2/42 3/42 (58.3 overs)	122
†M. W. C. Olley st Parks b Cowley	20	4/44 5/47 6/93	
A. R. Garofall st Parks b Cowley	6	7/105 8/106 9/107	

Bowling: Connor 11.3–2–23–2; Marshall 12–4–12–1; Tremlett 12–1–29–2; James 7–1–19–2; Cowley 12–3–19–3; Nicholas 4–1–9–0.

Hampshire

C. G. Greenidge c Olley b Merry	18	N. G. Cowley b Hailey	4
V. P. Terry b Merry	1	M. D. Marshall not out	15
C. L. Smith c Osman b Hailey	25	B 1, l-b 3, w 5	9
*M. C. J. Nicholas c Ottley b Hailey	17		
R. A. Smith c Garofall b Hailey	18	1/8 2/39 3/65 (6 wkts, 41.2 overs)	124
K. D. James not out	17	4/87 5/96 6/100	

T. M. Tremlett, †R. J. Parks and C. A. Connor did not bat.

Bowling: Merry 12–3–27–2; Neal 8–1–29–0; Garofall 3–1–11–0; Hailey 12–3–32–4; Smith 6–3–17–0; Ottley 0.2–0–4–0.

Umpires: J. W. Holder and R. Julian.

LANCASHIRE v CUMBERLAND

At Manchester, June 25. Lancashire won by eight wickets. Toss: Lancashire.
Man of the Match: J. Abrahams.

Cumberland

M. D. Woods c Mendis b O'Shaughnessy	22	S. D. Philbrook not out	14
C. J. Stockdale b Allott	8		
G. D. Hodgson b Folley	35	L-b 7, w 8, n-b 2	17
B. W. Reidy c Watkinson b Abrahams	33		
S. Sharp not out	40	1/26 2/36 3/101 (5 wkts, 60 overs)	178
*J. R. Moyes lbw b Abrahams	9	4/117 5/142	

D. Halliwell, †W. N. Boustead, J. B. Elleray and E. K. Sample did not bat.

Bowling: Allott 12–2–32–1; Watkinson 11–0–29–0; Makinson 7–1–30–0; O'Shaughnessy 6–1–22–1; Folley 12–1–32–1; Abrahams 12–3–26–2.

Lancashire

G. D. Mendis b Reidy	25
G. Fowler c Elleray b Halliwell	8
J. Abrahams not out	67
*C. H. Lloyd not out	57
B 9, l-b 8, w 5	22

1/28 2/81 (2 wkts, 51.2 overs) 179

N. H. Fairbrother, †C. Maynard, S. J. O'Shaughnessy, M. Watkinson, I. Folley, P. J. W. Allott and D. J. Makinson did not bat.

Bowling: Halliwell 12–2–29–1; Sample 9.2–2–29–0; Reidy 12–2–34–1; Woods 10–0–44–0; Elleray 8–1–26–0.

Umpires: M. Hendrick and A. A. Jones.

LEICESTERSHIRE v IRELAND

At Leicester, June 25. Leicestershire won by 167 runs. Toss: Ireland. Willey and Gower put on 209 for Leicestershire's third wicket, surpassing by 30 the previous record for the competition.
Man of the Match: D. I. Gower.

Leicestershire

R. A. Cobb c Vincent b Milling	26	W. K. M. Benjamin b Milling	5
L. Potter c Garth b Corlett	11	B 1, l-b 4, w 10, n-b 1	16
P. Willey b Milling	101		
*D. I. Gower not out	121	1/36 2/48 3/257 (5 wkts, 60 overs) 305	
J. J. Whitaker c Cohen b Milling	25	4/289 5/305	

T. J. Boon, †P. Whitticase, P. A. J. DeFreitas, J. P. Agnew and L. B. Taylor did not bat.

Bowling: Corlett 12–0–53–1; Milling 12–0–63–4; Garth 12–1–43–0; Halliday 7–0–41–0; McBrine 12–1–65–0; Masood 5–0–35–0.

Ireland

S. J. S. Warke b DeFreitas	12	J. D. Garth not out	8
M. F. Cohen c Cobb b Potter	32	L-b 8, w 11, n-b 7	26
D. G. Dennison c and b Willey	12		
M. A. Masood c Boon b Taylor	26	1/48 2/77 3/88 (4 wkts, 60 overs) 138	
D. A. Vincent not out	22	4/121	

A. McBrine, S. C. Corlett, †P. B. Jackson, *M. Halliday and H. Milling did not bat.

Bowling: Agnew 6–2–12–0; Taylor 10–1–28–1; Benjamin 11–0–23–0; DeFreitas 7–2–18–1; Willey 12–3–19–1; Potter 12–2–28–1; Boon 1–0–2–0; Whitaker 1–1–0–0.

Umpires: R. H. Duckett and N. T. Plews.

NORTHAMPTONSHIRE v MIDDLESEX

At Northampton, June 25. Middlesex won by seven wickets. Toss: Middlesex.
Man of the Match: M. W. Gatting.

Northamptonshire

W. Larkins c Emburey b Hughes	40	N. G. B. Cook b Emburey	13
*G. Cook run out	57	N. A. Mallender b Emburey	0
A. J. Lamb c Emburey b Hughes	80	A. Walker not out	3
R. J. Bailey c Downton b Daniel	34	B 4, l-b 10, w 3	17
D. J. Capel c Miller b Hughes	13		
R. A. Harper lbw b Daniel	1	1/77 2/136 3/205 (60 overs) 259	
D. J. Wild b Daniel	0	4/228 5/229 6/229	
†S. N. V. Waterton b Daniel	1	7/235 8/250 9/254	

Bowling: Daniel 12–2–33–4; Cowans 8–0–35–0; Hughes 12–1–52–3; Edmonds 12–0–62–0; Emburey 12–0–43–2; Slack 2–0–14–0; Gatting 2–0–6–0.

Middlesex

A. J. T. Miller st Waterton b Harper	35	R. O. Butcher not out	10
W. N. Slack c Waterton b Capel	18	L-b 10, w 4	14
*M. W. Gatting not out	118		
C. T. Radley c and b Mallender	67	1/38 2/97 3/230 (3 wkts, 59 overs) 262	

†P. R. Downton, J. E. Emburey, P. H. Edmonds, S. P. Hughes, N. G. Cowans and W. W. Daniel did not bat.

Bowling: Mallender 12–0–44–1; Capel 12–1–29–1; Walker 11–1–53–0; Wild 7–0–32–0; N. G. B. Cook 6–0–38–0; Harper 11–0–56–1.

Umpires: K. J. Lyons and P. B. Wight.

NORTHUMBERLAND v ESSEX

At Jesmond, June 25. Essex won by 79 runs. Toss: Essex. Lilley, batting with a broken thumb and breaking a finger when 88, faced 90 balls and hit six 6s and nine 4s.
Man of the Match: A. W. Lilley.

Essex

*G. A. Gooch b Halliday	44	†D. E. East b Williams	28
C. Gladwin c Graham b Scott	10	J. K. Lever not out	1
P. J. Prichard c and b Graham	10		
A. R. Border c Corby b Graham	23	B 1, l-b 14, w 5, n-b 1	21
D. R. Pringle c Old b Williams	22		
A. W. Lilley b Old	113	1/32 2/60 3/82 (9 wkts, 60 overs) 298		
K. R. Pont b Scott	20	4/93 5/163 6/217	
N. A. Foster c Dreyer b Halliday	6	7/224 8/284 9/298	

D. L. Acfield did not bat.

Bowling: Old 12–2–73–1; Scott 12–3–55–2; Williams 12–3–52–2; Graham 12–3–28–2; Halliday 12–0–75–2.

Northumberland

G. D. Halliday b Pringle	57	†K. Corby not out	3
K. Pearson c East b Gooch	61		
R. Dreyer run out	26	L-b 11, w 4	15
K. C. Williams c Border b Foster	33		
P. G. Cormack b Foster	5	1/118 2/126 3/188 (5 wkts, 60 overs) 219		
*M. E. Younger not out	19	4/188 5/197	

G. R. Morris, C. M. Old, P. C. Graham and S. P. Scott did not bat.

Bowling: Lever 10–4–26–0; Foster 12–2–30–2; Gooch 12–3–43–1; Pringle 9–2–36–1; Acfield 7–1–27–0; Pont 8–1–35–0; Border 2–0–11–0.

Umpires: B. Leadbeater and D. Lloyd.

SCOTLAND v KENT

At Edinburgh, June 25. Kent won by eight wickets. Toss: Kent.
Man of the Match: G. R. Dilley.

Scotland

I. L. Philip c Baptiste b G. R. Cowdrey	27	P. G. Duthie lbw b Dilley	1
W. A. Donald c C. S. Cowdrey b Dilley	9	†J. D. Knight b Dilley	2
*R. G. Swan not out	64	A. W. J. Stevenson b Dilley	0
A. B. Russell run out	17	B 1, l-b 14, w 4, n-b 3	22
N. W. Burnett run out	21		
O. Henry run out	2	1/20 2/58 3/101 (58.5 overs) 165		
D. L. Snodgrass lbw b Jarvis	0	4/144 5/150 6/151	
D. G. Moir c Baptiste b Dilley	0	7/153 8/156 9/165	

Bowling: Dilley 9.5–0–29–5; Jarvis 9–1–27–1; G. R. Cowdrey 11–2–30–1; Baptiste 6–0–16–0; Underwood 12–5–17–0; Taylor 9–3–19–0; C. S. Cowdrey 2–0–12–0.

Kent

M. R. Benson c Henry b Stevenson	18	
N. R. Taylor st Knight b Henry	26	
C. J. Tavaré not out	48	
*C. S. Cowdrey not out	62	
L-b 2, w 10	12	
1/39 2/64 (2 wkts, 53.2 overs) 166		

G. R. Cowdrey, D. G. Aslett, E. A. E. Baptiste, K. B. S. Jarvis, †S. A. Marsh, G. R. Dilley and D. L. Underwood did not bat.

Bowling: Duthie 9–1–22–0; Burnett 9.2–1–28–0; Moir 11–4–32–0; Stevenson 9–2–31–1; Henry 10–2–34–1; Donald 5–0–17–0.

Umpires: J. H. Hampshire and T. G. Wilson.

SOMERSET v DORSET

At Taunton, June 25. Somerset won by eight wickets. Toss: Somerset.
Man of the Match: N. A. Felton.

Dorset

R. P. Merriman lbw b Dredge	11	I. E. W. Sanders c Felton b Richards	2
R. V. Lewis c Harden b Garner	0	†D. A. Ridley c Roebuck b Atkinson	5
S. J. Halliday lbw b Taylor	2	B. K. Shantry c Dredge b Taylor	6
*A. Kennedy b Garner	39		
V. B. Lewis b Garner	11	L-b 6, w 4, n-b 7	17
S. J. Turrill lbw b Garner	0		
C. Stone not out	32	1/2 2/19 3/25 (54.1 overs) 132	
A. R. Wingfield Digby st Gard		4/65 5/65 6/70	
b Richards	7	7/87 8/91 9/115	

Bowling: Garner 9–0–36–4; Taylor 9.1–2–21–2; Dredge 6–1–16–1; Marks 12–5–15–0; Richards 12–3–22–2; Atkinson 6–2–16–1.

Somerset

N. A. Felton not out	59	I. V. A. Richards not out	6
*P. M. Roebuck c Kennedy		B 2, l-b 3, w 1, n-b 4	10
b Wingfield Digby	41		
J. J. E. Hardy c Ridley b Kennedy	19	1/77 2/111 (2 wkts, 33.2 overs) 135	

R. J. Harden, V. J. Marks, J. C. M. Atkinson, †T. Gard, J. Garner, C. H. Dredge and N. S. Taylor did not bat.

Bowling: Shantry 10.2–2–48–0; Sanders 4–0–20–0; Wingfield Digby 9–2–30–1; Stone 6–0–26–0; Kennedy 4–1–6–1.

Umpires: C. Cook and D. J. Halfyard.

STAFFORDSHIRE v GLAMORGAN

At Stone, June 25. Glamorgan won by 61 runs. Toss: Staffordshire. The unbroken stand of 71 between Ontong and Davies for Glamorgan was an eighth-wicket record for the competition. Davies went on to take four catches and make two stumpings to equal R. W. Taylor's wicket-keeping record of six dismissals in an innings.
Man of the Match: R. C. Ontong.

Glamorgan

J. A. Hopkins lbw b Webster	5	E. A. Moseley b Flower	4
H. Morris st Griffiths b Cartledge	48	†T. Davies not out	30
G. C. Holmes b Benjamin	13	B 5, l-b 8, w 5, n-b 3	21
Younis Ahmed b Benjamin	2		
M. P. Maynard st Griffiths b Flower	9	1/17 2/54 3/63 (7 wkts, 60 overs) 205	
R. C. Ontong not out	54	4/76 5/104	
J. G. Thomas c Archer b Cartledge	19	6/129 7/134	

J. Derrick and J. F. Steele did not bat.

Bowling: Webster 12–1–43–1; Maguire 8–1–24–0; Blank 9–2–33–0; Benjamin 11–2–37–2; Flower 12–3–34–2; Cartledge 8–1–21–2.

Staffordshire

S. J. Dean lbw b Holmes	23	D. C. Blank c Thomas b Steele	7
D. Cartledge c Davies b Holmes	13	R. W. Flower c Moseley b Derrick	4
G. S. Warner c Davies b Holmes	19	K. R. Maguire not out	0
D. A. Banks c Thomas b Ontong	37	L-b 3, w 1, n-b 1	5
*N. J. Archer c Davies b Derrick	15		
†A. Griffiths st Davies b Ontong	2	1/34 2/43 3/87 (49.3 overs) 144
A. J. Webster c Davies b Ontong	0	4/103 5/108 6/108
J. E. Benjamin st Davies b Steele	19	7/129 8/135 9/141

Bowling: Thomas 9-2-29-0; Moseley 7-1-12-0; Holmes 12-3-21-3; Ontong 12-3-50-3; Derrick 5.3-0-21-2; Steele 4-1-8-2.

Umpires: J. A. Jameson and C. T. Spencer.

SUSSEX v SUFFOLK

At Hove, June 25. Sussex won by seven wickets. Toss: Sussex.
Man of the Match: D. A. Reeve.

Suffolk

M. S. A. McEvoy b Standing	19	R. C. Green b Imran	6
G. Morgan c and b Imran	7	R. A. Pybus b Babington	4
*S. M. Clements c Jones b Standing	13	†M. Sturgeon lbw b Babington	0
R. Herbert c sub b Reeve	2		
P. J. Caley b Reeve	12	B 2, l-b 3, w 9, n-b 1	15
K. G. Brooks not out	26		
P. J. Hayes run out	0	1/20 2/35 3/39 4/49 (49 overs) 108
M. D. Bailey b Imran	4	5/62 6/70 7/77 8/96 9/106

Bowling: Imran 12-1-27-3; Jones 7-0-25-0; Reeve 12-7-8-2; Wells 3-1-7-0; Standing 12-3-27-2; Babington 3-0-9-2.

Sussex

R. I. Alikhan lbw b Green	0	D. K. Standing not out	1
A. M. Green b Bailey	22	B 8, l-b 2, w 3, n-b 5	18
P. W. G. Parker not out	40		
Imran Khan c Green b Hayes	28	1/0 2/39 3/103 (3 wkts, 35.1 overs) 109

C. M. Wells, C. P. Phillipson, *†I. J. Gould, D. A. Reeve, A. M. Babington and A. N. Jones did not bat.

Bowling: Green 7-1-16-1; Pybus 4-0-27-0; Bailey 7.1-0-24-1; Hayes 9-4-8-1; Herbert 8-1-24-0.

Umpires: B. Dudleston and D. S. Thompsett.

WARWICKSHIRE v DURHAM

At Birmingham, June 25. Warwickshire won by 135 runs. Toss: Warwickshire. The substitute, A. R. Fothergill, kept wicket for Durham when Mercer went off with a back injury.
Man of the Match: A. I. Kallicharran.

Warwickshire

T. A. Lloyd b Malone	4	G. J. Parsons b Malone	2
P. A. Smith c sub b Greensword	79	K. J. Kerr run out	3
A. I. Kallicharran st sub b Kippax	99		
D. L. Amiss b Johnson	77	L-b 7	7
†G. W. Humpage c Wasim Raja b Kippax	7	1/4 2/141 3/243 (8 wkts, 60 overs) 317
Asif Din lbw b Kippax	7	4/251 5/261 6/298
A. M. Ferreira not out	32	7/305 8/317

G. C. Small and *N. Gifford did not bat.

Bowling: Malone 12–1–51–2; Johnson 10–1–50–1; Greensword 12–1–50–1; Conn 4–0–27–0; Wasim Raja 10–0–71–0; Kippax 12–0–61–3.

Durham

J. W. Lister b Parsons	19	I. E. Conn c Humpage b Ferreira	0
S. Greensword st Humpage b Kerr	9	S. J. Malone b Ferreira	6
*N. A. Riddell c Humpage b Smith	33	†R. A. D. Mercer not out	0
Wasim Raja c Humpage b Kerr	18	B 1, l-b 14, w 2, n-b 3	20
A. S. Patel c Amiss b Ferreira	59		
G. Hurst lbw b Smith	6	1/31 2/51 3/81 (55.1 overs) 182
P. J. Kippax c Amiss b Lloyd	6	4/97 5/138 6/159
G. Johnson b Asif Din	6	7/170 8/170 9/182

Bowling: Small 6–1–17–0; Parsons 8–2–14–1; Kerr 12–2–32–2; Ferreira 10–2–28–3; Smith 12–1–28–2; Lloyd 6–0–43–1; Asif Din 1.1–0–5–1.

Umpires: R. Palmer and A. G. T. Whitehead.

WORCESTERSHIRE v OXFORDSHIRE

At Worcester, June 25. Worcestershire won by 144 runs. Toss: Oxfordshire.
Man of the Match: D. B. D'Oliveira.

Worcestershire

T. S. Curtis c Crossley b Hobbins	14	M. J. Weston not out	44
D. B. D'Oliveira c and b Porter	99	†S. J. Rhodes not out	11
G. A. Hick c Wise b Curtis	27	B 4, l-b 6, w 8	18
D. M. Smith c Curtis b Evans	17		
*P. A. Neale b Porter	42	1/46 2/101 3/169 (6 wkts, 60 overs) 292
D. N. Patel c Busby b Porter	20	4/174 5/209 6/247

N. V. Radford, J. D. Inchmore and A. P. Pridgeon did not bat.

Bowling: Busby 12–3–40–0; Arnold 12–0–79–0; Hobbins 5–1–25–1; Curtis 8–1–47–1; Evans 12–1–33–1; Porter 11–1–58–3.

Oxfordshire

G. C. Ford c Curtis b Hick	50	G. R. Hobbins not out	15
M. D. Nurton c Radford b Patel	31	L-b 7, w 2, n-b 5	14
D. A. J. Wise c Patel b D'Oliveira	14		
*P. J. Garner not out	24	1/78 2/98 3/120 (3 wkts, 60 overs) 148

†A. Crossley, S. R. Porter, R. N. Busby, R. A. Evans, I. J. Curtis and K. A. Arnold did not bat.

Bowling: Radford 10–1–28–0; Pridgeon 8–1–15–0; Inchmore 9–1–19–0; Weston 9–1–20–0; Patel 7–4–8–1; D'Oliveira 8–1–24–1; Hick 7–1–21–1; Smith 1–0–5–0; Rhodes 1–0–1–0.

Umpires: P. J. Eele and R. A. White.

YORKSHIRE v CAMBRIDGESHIRE

At Leeds, June 25. Yorkshire won by seven wickets. Toss: Yorkshire.
Man of the Match: J. D. R. Benson.

Cambridgeshire

*G. V. Miller c Sharp b Fletcher	9	M. G. Stephenson not out	8
N. T. Gadsby b Carrick	25	D. C. Collard not out	4
†M. A. Garnham c Blakey b Fletcher	8		
D. R. Parry c Sharp b Fletcher	6	L-b 9, w 10, n-b 2	21
J. D. R. Benson c Blakey b Hartley	85		
C. Lethbridge b Carrick	0	1/18 2/29 3/39 (8 wkts, 60 overs)	176
D. R. Vincent lbw b Hartley	6	4/77 5/104 6/112	
I. S. Lawrence c Blakey b Hartley	4	7/144 8/167	

D. C. Wing did not bat.

Bowling: Dennis 12–3–39–0; Jarvis 12–4–19–0; Fletcher 12–1–53–3; Hartley 12–1–49–3; Carrick 12–8–7–2.

Yorkshire

G. Boycott run out	31	J. D. Love not out	8
M. D. Moxon run out	75	B 2, l-b 2, w 3	7
A. A. Metcalfe lbw b Stephenson	23		
K. Sharp not out	33	1/69 2/112 3/159 (3 wkts, 53.1 overs)	177

†R. J. Blakey, *P. Carrick, P. J. Hartley, P. W. Jarvis, S. J. Dennis and S. D. Fletcher did not bat.

Bowling: Lethbridge 9–0–20–0; Wing 9–0–25–0; Pollard 11–1–31–0; Parry 12–0–42–0; Stephenson 10–0–42–1; Benson 2.1–0–13–0.

Umpires: H. J. Rhodes and D. O. Oslear.

SECOND ROUND

DERBYSHIRE v SURREY

At Derby, July 9. Surrey won by 62 runs. Toss: Derbyshire.
Man of the Match: C. J. Richards.

Surrey

G. S. Clinton c Holding b Miller	18	G. Monkhouse b Mortensen	18
A. R. Butcher c Morris b Jean-Jacques	21	S. T. Clarke not out	13
A. J. Stewart b Jean-Jacques	16	B 7, l-b 6, w 7, n-b 1	21
M. A. Lynch c Roberts b Holding	20		
N. J. Falkner c and b Jean-Jacques	36	1/33 2/56 3/57 (7 wkts, 60 overs)	229
A. Needham c Sharma b Miller	13	4/92 5/115	
†C. J. Richards not out	53	6/168 7/202	

M. P. Bicknell and *P. I. Pocock did not bat.

Bowling: Mortensen 10–1–47–1; Warner 6–0–49–0; Jean-Jacques 12–0–43–3; Holding 12–2–24–1; Miller 12–2–30–2; Sharma 8–1–23–0.

Derbyshire

*K. J. Barnett run out	47	M. A. Holding c Clinton b Needham	0
I. S. Anderson c Richards b Bicknell	0	M. Jean-Jacques b Monkhouse	16
A. Hill c Butcher b Needham	16	O. H. Mortensen c Falkner b Monkhouse	11
J. E. Morris b Needham	0	B 4, l-b 8, w 4, n-b 2	18
†B. Roberts c sub b Pocock	12		
R. Sharma lbw b Pocock	9	1/9 2/59 3/59 (53.5 overs)	167
A. E. Warner b Needham	6	4/84 5/87 6/100	
G. Miller not out	32	7/100 8/100 9/129	

Bowling: Clarke 9–3–19–0; Bicknell 9–2–25–1; Monkhouse 11.5–1–55–2; Needham 12–2–32–4; Pocock 12–5–24–2.

Umpires: D. O. Oslear and R. A. White.

GLOUCESTERSHIRE v LEICESTERSHIRE

At Bristol, July 9, 10. Leicestershire won by six wickets. Toss: Leicestershire.
Man of the Match: J. C. Balderstone.

Gloucestershire

A. J. Wright run out	43	I. R. Payne b DeFreitas		12
A. W. Stovold c Willey b Benjamin	11	*D. A. Graveney not out		0
C. W. J. Athey b Taylor	2	D. V. Lawrence b DeFreitas		0
P. Bainbridge c Whitticase b Clift	24	L-b 15, w 1		16
K. M. Curran b Benjamin	21			
K. P. Tomlins c Potter b Taylor	8	1/16 2/21 3/84	(55.4 overs)	177
†R. C. Russell c Whitticase b Benjamin	39	4/114 5/122 6/131		
C. A. Walsh b Clift	1	7/134 8/175 9/177		

Bowling: Benjamin 10–2–28–3; Taylor 12–2–44–2; DeFreitas 9.4–3–24–2; Willey 12–1–27–0; Clift 12–1–39–2.

Leicestershire

J. C. Balderstone c Stovold b Walsh	66	T. J. Boon not out		10
R. A. Cobb st Russell b Graveney	23	B 4, l-b 8, w 4, n-b 2		18
*D. I. Gower c Stovold b Bainbridge	1			
P. Willey not out	37	1/98 2/101 3/107	(4 wkts, 56.1 overs)	179
L. Potter c Graveney b Bainbridge	24	4/162		

P. B. Clift, †P. Whitticase, P. A. J. DeFreitas, W. K. M. Benjamin and L. B. Taylor did not bat.

Bowling: Lawrence 8–0–27–0; Walsh 12–2–21–1; Bainbridge 11–2–45–2; Payne 12–3–35–0; Graveney 11–4–15–1; Tomlins 1–0–10–0; Athey 1.1–0–14–0.

Umpires: J. H. Harris and K. J. Lyons.

HAMPSHIRE v WORCESTERSHIRE

At Southampton, July 9. Worcestershire won by 66 runs. Toss: Hampshire.
Man of the Match: T. S. Curtis.

Worcestershire

T. S. Curtis b James	94	†S. J. Rhodes not out		32
D. B. D'Oliveira c Parks b Marshall	50			
G. A. Hick c Parks b Connor	9	L-b 14, w 3, n-b 8		25
D. M. Smith run out	1			
*P. A. Neale b Connor	36	1/88 2/102 3/107	(5 wkts, 60 overs)	278
D. N. Patel not out	31	4/205 5/212		

P. J. Newport, N. V. Radford, J. D. Inchmore and A. P. Pridgeon did not bat.

Bowling: Marshall 12–1–50–1; Connor 12–2–30–2; James 10–0–72–1; Tremlett 10–1–48–0; Cowley 12–0–36–0; Nicholas 4–0–28–0.

Hampshire

V. P. Terry b Radford	8	†R. J. Parks c Rhodes b Newport		6
C. L. Smith b Radford	1	T. M. Tremlett not out		28
*M. C. J. Nicholas lbw b Inchmore	29	C. A. Connor c Radford b Pridgeon		5
R. A. Smith c Neale b Newport	39	L-b 8, w 6, n-b 6		20
D. R. Turner c Rhodes b Pridgeon	17			
K. D. James b Inchmore	19	1/7 2/10 3/75	(53.1 overs)	212
M. D. Marshall run out	32	4/92 5/113 6/137		
N. G. Cowley c Neale b Newport	8	7/160 8/168 9/186		

Bowling: Radford 9–1–43–2; Pridgeon 11.1–1–28–2; Inchmore 9–1–40–2; Newport 12–0–62–3; Patel 12–4–31–0.

Umpires: J. Birkenshaw and A. A. Jones.

NOTTINGHAMSHIRE v KENT

At Nottingham, July 9. Nottinghamshire won by six wickets. Toss: Nottinghamshire.
Man of the Match: B. C. Broad.

Kent

M. R. Benson c Rice b Evans	32	†S. A. Marsh c French b Pick	1
S. G. Hinks b Hadlee	44	G. R. Dilley not out	14
C. J. Tavaré b Evans	0	D. L. Underwood not out	2
N. R. Taylor c Hadlee b Evans	21	B 5, l-b 5, w 1	11
*C. S. Cowdrey c Randall b Hadlee	1		
G. R. Cowdrey c French b Hadlee	22	1/72 2/72 3/89 (9 wkts, 60 overs)	161
E. A. E. Baptiste c Hadlee b Evans	4	4/91 5/119 6/129	
R. M. Ellison c French b Saxelby	9	7/136 8/137 9/147	

Bowling: Hadlee 9–2–17–3; Pick 12–5–15–1; Rice 11–0–35–0; Saxelby 7–0–29–1; Hemmings 9–2–25–0; Evans 12–2–30–4.

Nottinghamshire

R. T. Robinson c Marsh b Ellison	49	†B. N. French not out	2
B. C. Broad c Benson b Baptiste	73		
D. W. Randall retired hurt	5	L-b 5, w 2, n-b 5	12
P. Johnson c Tavaré b Ellison	0		
*C. E. B. Rice not out	15	1/120 2/138 3/139 (4 wkts, 41.4 overs)	162
R. J. Hadlee c Marsh b Baptiste	6	4/146	

R. A. Pick, E. E. Hemmings, K. Saxelby and K. P. Evans did not bat.

Bowling: Dilley 5–0–15–0; Baptiste 12–3–46–2; Ellison 10.4–2–46–2; C. S. Cowdrey 7–0–31–0; Underwood 7–1–19–0.

Umpires: J. A. Jameson and M. J. Kitchen.

SOMERSET v LANCASHIRE

At Taunton, July 9. Lancashire won by 3 runs. Toss: Somerset.
Man of the Match: G. D. Mendis.

Lancashire

G. D. Mendis c Roebuck b Marks	72	P. J. W. Allott c Richards b Taylor	4
G. Fowler b Richards	17	D. J. Makinson not out	8
J. Abrahams c Harden b Dredge	52	I. Folley b Dredge	1
*C. H. Lloyd run out	36	B 1, l-b 4, n-b 1	6
N. H. Fairbrother b Garner	7		
S. J. O'Shaughnessy c Gard b Garner	1	1/40 2/137 3/163 (60 overs)	221
†C. Maynard c Hardy b Taylor	5	4/173 5/175 6/180	
M. Watkinson c Harden b Taylor	12	7/205 8/208 9/213	

Bowling: Garner 12–3–23–2; Taylor 12–1–47–3; Richards 12–0–40–1; Dredge 12–1–46–2; Marks 12–0–60–1.

672   *NatWest Bank Trophy, 1986*

Somerset

N. A. Felton c Maynard b Watkinson . 14
*P. M. Roebuck lbw b Allott 0
J. J. E. Hardy c O'Shaughnessy b Folley 53
I. V. A. Richards c and b Folley 50
R. J. Harden c Lloyd b Makinson 17
B. C. Rose not out 43
V. J. Marks c and b Watkinson 8
†T. Gard c Maynard b O'Shaughnessy . 3

C. H. Dredge c sub b Watkinson 8
J. Garner b Makinson 8
N. S. Taylor not out 1
    L-b 4, w 4, n-b 5 13

1/1 2/30 3/109   (9 wkts, 60 overs) 218
4/139 5/139 6/158
7/166 8/179 9/197

Bowling: Allott 12–1–40–1; Watkinson 12–0–44–3; Makinson 12–2–49–2; O'Shaughnessy 12–2–47–1; Folley 12–1–34–2.

Umpires: D. G. L. Evans and R. Julian.

SUSSEX v GLAMORGAN

At Hove, July 9. Sussex won by 29 runs. Toss: Sussex. Green hit his first hundred in limited-overs cricket off 131 deliveries.
Man of the Match: Imran Khan.

Sussex

N. J. Lenham run out 6
A. M. Green c and b Base 102
P. W. G. Parker c Steele b Base 21
Imran Khan c and b Steele 54
C. M. Wells b Hickey 28
*†I. J. Gould run out 20
A. P. Wells run out 21
R. I. Alikhan not out 0

D. A. Reeve run out 1
D. K. Standing retired hurt 0
A. M. Babington not out 4
    B 4, w 3, n-b 5 12

1/21 2/59 3/194   (8 wkts, 60 overs) 269
4/196 5/227 6/251
7/263 8/264

Bowling: Thomas 12–1–45–0; Hickey 9–0–64–1; Base 12–0–49–2; Holmes 12–1–39–0; Ontong 8–0–44–0; Steele 7–0–24–1.

Glamorgan

J. A. Hopkins c A. P. Wells
           b C. M. Wells . 47
H. Morris c and b C. M. Wells 27
G. C. Holmes c Reeve b Lenham 45
Younis Ahmed c Gould b Babington . . 31
M. P. Maynard b Babington 7
*R. C. Ontong c Babington b Imran . . 32
J. G. Thomas c Imran b Reeve 1
†T. Davies run out 16

J. F. Steele b Imran 0
S. J. Base b Imran 2
D. J. Hickey not out 0

    B 1, l-b 15, w 8, n-b 8 32

1/65 2/107 3/167   (59.2 overs) 240
4/179 5/186 6/194
7/231 8/233 9/240

Bowling: Imran 11.2–3–16–3; Babington 10–0–45–2; C. M. Wells 12–0–35–2; Reeve 12–0–53–1; Standing 5–0–27–0; Lenham 9–0–48–1.

Umpires: B. Dudleston and R. Palmer.

WARWICKSHIRE v ESSEX

At Birmingham, July 9. Warwickshire won by 64 runs. Toss: Warwickshire.
Man of the Match: G. W. Humpage.

Warwickshire

T. A. Lloyd c East b Gooch	44	G. C. Small lbw b Pringle	0
P. A. Smith c Acfield b Gooch	26	K. J. Kerr b Pringle	13
D. L. Amiss c East b Gooch	10	*N. Gifford c Gooch b Pringle	0
†G. W. Humpage st East b Acfield	70	L-b 11, w 6	17
B. M. McMillan lbw b Foster	10		
Asif Din not out	38	1/69 2/82 3/94	(59.5 overs) 255
D. A. Thorne c Gooch b Foster	21	4/141 5/182 6/214	
G. J. Parsons b Foster	6	7/234 8/235 9/255	

Bowling: Foster 12-1-31-3; Lever 11-0-69-0; Pringle 10.5-0-47-3; Acfield 10-0-46-1; Gooch 12-2-31-3; Pont 4-0-20-0.

Essex

*G. A. Gooch lbw b Small	48	N. A. Foster b Small	20
J. P. Stephenson lbw b Parsons	55	J. K. Lever c Humpage b McMillan	7
P. J. Prichard c Lloyd b Gifford	2	D. L. Acfield not out	4
A. R. Border b McMillan	6	L-b 7, w 4	11
D. R. Pringle b Gifford	33		
A. W. Lilley c Humpage b Kerr	5	1/98 2/111 3/113	(51.4 overs) 191
K. R. Pont lbw b McMillan	0	4/127 5/140 6/143	
†D. E. East run out	0	7/144 8/174 9/183	

Bowling: Small 8-0-25-2; Parsons 12-4-34-1; McMillan 11.4-1-54-3; Kerr 12-1-42-1; Gifford 8-1-29-2.

Umpires: J. H. Hampshire and J. W. Holder.

YORKSHIRE v MIDDLESEX

At Leeds, July 9, 10. Yorkshire won by 20 runs. Toss: Yorkshire. Middlesex, from 177 for five, in the 54th over, lost their last five wickets for 8 runs in 26 balls.

Man of the Match: M. D. Moxon.

Yorkshire

M. D. Moxon lbw b Daniel	65	A. Sidebottom b Hughes	1
A. A. Metcalfe lbw b Cowans	0	C. Shaw c Downton b Hughes	2
K. Sharp b Cowans	2	S. D. Fletcher not out	1
S. N. Hartley c and b Emburey	24	B 2, l-b 20, w 4, n-b 1	27
P. E. Robinson c Butcher b Cowans	66		
*†D. L. Bairstow b Daniel	8	1/1 2/7 3/62	(9 wkts, 60 overs) 205
P. Carrick lbw b Cowans	0	4/141 5/184 6/185	
P. W. Jarvis not out	9	7/187 8/190 9/192	

Bowling: Cowans 10-4-24-4; Daniel 12-1-40-2; Hughes 11-0-39-2; Edmonds 12-1-36-0; Emburey 12-1-35-1; Gatting 3-1-9-0.

Middlesex

W. N. Slack b Shaw	27	S. P. Hughes c Moxon b Carrick	3
A. J. T. Miller b Fletcher	34	N. G. Cowans b Jarvis	1
*M. W. Gatting b Jarvis	8	W. W. Daniel not out	1
R. O. Butcher c Sidebottom b Jarvis	30	L-b 10, w 2, n-b 2	14
C. T. Radley b Sidebottom	29		
†P. R. Downton st Bairstow b Carrick	31	1/57 2/66 3/95	(57.3 overs) 185
J. E. Emburey b Shaw	7	4/121 5/158 6/177	
P. H. Edmonds c and b Carrick	0	7/177 8/183 9/183	

Bowling: Sidebottom 12-0-31-1; Jarvis 10.3-2-32-3; Shaw 12-2-34-2; Fletcher 11-0-38-1; Carrick 12-4-40-3.

Umpires: B. Leadbeater and P. B. Wight.

QUARTER-FINALS

LEICESTERSHIRE v LANCASHIRE

At Leicester, July 30, 31, August 1. Lancashire won by six wickets. Toss: Lancashire. Play did not begin until the second day, when more than two hours were lost during six stoppages for rain and bad light. Leicestershire struggled on a moist pitch until a dashing innings from DeFreitas (one 6, six 4s), with good support from Whitticase, revived their fortunes. Leicestershire slipped to 28 for three in the evening gloom, but on the third morning Fairbrother (thirteen 4s), first with Abrahams and then with O'Shaughnessy, relished an appetising diet of moderate bowling and Lancashire cruised to victory with 39 balls to spare.

Man of the Match: N. H. Fairbrother.

Leicestershire

J. C. Balderstone c Stanworth b Hayhurst	45	P. A. J. DeFreitas c Fairbrother b Allott	69
R. A. Cobb lbw b Allott	8	J. P. Agnew not out	5
P. Willey c Stanworth b Allott	1	L. B. Taylor not out	6
*D. I. Gower c O'Shaughnessy		B 1, l-b 5, w 13, n-b 5	24
b Hayhurst	13		
T. J. Boon b Hayhurst	19	1/28 2/32 3/72 (8 wkts, 60 overs) 223	
L. Potter c Stanworth b Hayhurst	1	4/91 5/93 6/107	
†P. Whitticase c Stanworth b Allott	32	7/204 8/212	

G. J. F. Ferris did not bat.

Bowling: Allott 12–3–28–4; Watkinson 10–0–49–0; O'Shaughnessy 10–0–59–0; Hayhurst 12–1–40–4; Simmons 12–6–18–0; Abrahams 4–0–23–0.

Lancashire

G. Fowler c Gower b Taylor	12	S. J. O'Shaughnessy not out	53
G. D. Mendis c Whitticase b Agnew	2	L-b 5, w 16, n-b 5	26
J. Abrahams c Potter b Willey	34		
*C. H. Lloyd c Gower b Taylor	6	1/4 2/20 3/28 (4 wkts, 53.3 overs) 226	
N. H. Fairbrother not out	93	4/133	

†J. Stanworth, M. Watkinson, J. Simmons, P. J. W. Allott and A. N. Hayhurst did not bat.

Bowling: Agnew 11–5–30–1; Taylor 9–1–35–2; DeFreitas 10–1–50–0; Potter 2–1–7–0; Willey 12–1–46–1; Ferris 9–0–49–0; Gower 0.3–0–4–0.

Umpires: D. O. Oslear and B. Leadbeater.

SURREY v NOTTINGHAMSHIRE

At The Oval. July 30. Surrey won by 46 runs. Toss: Nottinghamshire. Few sides would expect victory after encountering a spectacular individual performance with bat and ball from Hadlee. That Surrey managed it was due to a splendid attacking innings from Thomas and to Nottinghamshire's failure to support their all-rounder. Fresh from taxing England's batsmen as New Zealand's strike bowler in the Lord's Test the day before, Hadlee took four of Surrey's first five wickets to leave them limply placed at 72 with half their batting gone. However, Thomas, in his third game after a ten-week absence through injury, hit 65 from 107 balls to take Surrey past 200. Nottinghamshire were themselves in dire trouble at 70 for six, but Hadlee, although taking 23 balls to score, needed only 47 more to pass 50.

Man of the Match: R. J. Hadlee.

Surrey

N. J. Falkner b Hadlee	0	S. T. Clarke c Randall b Hadlee	23
G. S. Clinton c French b Evans	10	*P. I. Pocock not out	9
A. J. Stewart c Broad b Hadlee	5	M. P. Bicknell not out	2
T. E. Jesty b Hadlee	21	L-b 13, w 3	16
M. A. Lynch lbw b Cooper	26		
†C. J. Richards c French b Hadlee	10	1/2 2/12 3/37 (9 wkts, 60 overs)	204
D. J. Thomas c French b Rice	65	4/72 5/72 6/92	
G. Monkhouse c Hadlee b Pick	17	7/136 8/174 9/200	

Bowling: Hadlee 12–4–17–5; Cooper 12–3–48–1; Rice 9–2–29–1; Pick 10–0–58–1; Evans 5–2–11–1; Hemmings 12–4–28–0.

Nottinghamshire

B. C. Broad st Richards b Pocock	34	R. A. Pick c Stewart b Monkhouse	7
R. T. Robinson hit wkt b Clarke	0	E. E. Hemmings not out	3
D. W. Randall lbw b Thomas	5	K. E. Cooper b Monkhouse	0
P. Johnson c Jesty b Pocock	18		
*C. E. B. Rice c Clarke b Bicknell	1	B 4, l-b 10, w 1, n-b 7	22
R. J. Hadlee c Richards b Thomas	55		
K. P. Evans lbw b Clarke	1	1/1 2/9 3/62 4/63 5/69 (51.5 overs)	158
†B. N. French c Lynch b Monkhouse	12	6/70 7/115 8/151 9/157	

Bowling: Clarke 10–6–7–2; Thomas 10–0–57–2; Pocock 12–3–21–2; Bicknell 10–2–19–1; Monkhouse 8.5–0–34–3; Lynch 1–0–5–0.

Umpires: D. J. Constant and N. T. Plews.

WORCESTERSHIRE v WARWICKSHIRE

At Worcester, July 30, 31. Worcestershire won by eight wickets. Worcestershire, having put Warwickshire in, fashioned a comprehensive victory by establishing an early stranglehold that never looked like being broken. Play was a day and 75 minutes late starting after heavy rain, and Warwickshire's fears were quickly realised on a wicket that provided plenty of encouragement for seam bowlers. They laboured to 23 for one in seventeen overs before lunch, lost Amiss and Moles immediately afterwards, and had used up half their overs in reaching 48 before Kallicharran, who curbed his attacking instincts in making 39 from 118 balls, hit Patel for the first boundary of the innings. Half-centuries from Smith and Curtis, who put on 120 for the second wicket, saw Worcestershire home with eight wickets and 20.3 overs to spare.

Man of the Match: D. M. Smith.

Warwickshire

A. J. Moles b Patel	14	G. J. Parsons b Radford	7
P. A. Smith b Inchmore	4	G. C. Small not out	3
A. I. Kallicharran c Radford b Patel	39		
D. L. Amiss c Hick b Radford	0	L-b 3, w 5, n-b 1	9
†G. W. Humpage b Patel	2		
Asif Din c Rhodes b Newport	10	1/14 2/23 3/24 (8 wkts, 60 overs)	136
D. A. Thorne c Patel b Radford	21	4/38 5/58 6/85	
A. M. Ferreira not out	27	7/106 8/125	

*N. Gifford did not bat.

Bowling: Radford 12–1–23–3; Pridgeon 12–0–28–0; Newport 12–3–19–1; Inchmore 12–1–27–1; Patel 12–2–36–3.

Worcestershire

T. S. Curtis not out 51
D. B. D'Oliveira b Small 11
D. M. Smith c Humpage b Ferreira ... 62
G. A. Hick not out 0
      B 1, l-b 5, w 3, n-b 4 13

1/16 2/136   (2 wkts, 39.3 overs) 137

*P. A. Neale, D. N. Patel, †S. J. Rhodes, P. J. Newport, N. V. Radford, J. D. Inchmore and
A. P. Pridgeon did not bat.

Bowling: Small 10–4–26–1; Parsons 8–2–21–0; Ferreira 9.3–0–24–1; Smith 5–0–29–0;
Thorne 1–0–4–0; Moles 6–0–27–0.

Umpires: D. G. L. Evans and D. R. Shepherd.

YORKSHIRE v SUSSEX

At Leeds, July 30, 31. Sussex won by 88 runs. Toss: Sussex. Although the pitch, that used for
the second Test match against India, was subsequently reported to Lord's as unfit, Sussex
batted with great determination in an innings spread over two days because of rain. They
were 86 for six, but Gould, whose innings measured exactly the difference between the teams,
hit his 88 from 80 balls. It was his highest score in major limited-overs cricket. Yorkshire,
who, like their opponents, had felt that 180 was a winning score, collapsed against the hostile
bowling of Jones and le Roux, losing four wickets for 1 run in a spell which effectively ruined
their cause.

Man of the Match: I. J. Gould.

Sussex

R. I. Alikhan c Robinson b Fletcher ...	14	G. S. le Roux not out	39
A. M. Green b P. J. Hartley	5	D. A. Reeve not out	1
P. W. G. Parker c Carrick b P. J. Hartley	3		
Imran Khan lbw b P. J. Hartley	23	L-b 10, w 6	16
C. M. Wells c Bairstow b Shaw	20		
A. P. Wells c Carrick b Shaw	4	1/7 2/19 3/49 (7 wkts, 60 overs) 213	
*†I. J. Gould c Love b Fletcher	88	4/64 5/73 6/86 7/201	

A. C. S. Pigott and A. N. Jones did not bat.

Bowling: Jarvis 12–1–41–0; P. J. Hartley 12–3–47–3; Shaw 12–2–56–2; Fletcher
12–3–37–2; Carrick 12–5–22–0.

Yorkshire

M. D. Moxon c Gould b Jones	6	P. W. Jarvis run out	10
A. A. Metcalfe lbw b le Roux	6	S. D. Fletcher not out	2
S. N. Hartley c sub b le Roux	0	C. Shaw b le Roux	0
P. E. Robinson c Gould b Jones	0		
J. D. Love b le Roux	12	L-b 3, w 4, n-b 2	9
*†D. L. Bairstow b Jones	3		
P. Carrick c Gould b Jones	54	1/15 2/15 3/15 4/16 (38.3 overs) 125	
P. J. Hartley c Gould b Reeve	23	5/23 6/42 7/96 8/122 9/124	

Bowling: Imran 6–0–16–0; le Roux 10.3–2–17–4; Jones 8–2–26–4; Pigott 2–0–12–0; C. M.
Wells 8–0–27–0; Reeve 4–0–24–1.

Umpires: J. Birkenshaw and J. W. Holder.

SEMI-FINALS

SURREY v LANCASHIRE

At The Oval, August 13. Lancashire won by 4 runs. Toss: Surrey. Jesty's heroic 112 narrowly failed to put Surrey into the final. His single-handed effort, while his colleagues frittered away their wickets to a series of imprudent strokes, was hampered from the time he was 79 by a pulled hamstring, which required him to bat with a runner. Yet the confines imposed by this injury added a new dimension of quality to his strokeplay. Surrey's failure, however, made possible another romantic episode in the career of Lancashire's captain, Clive Lloyd, who was assured of his ninth and probably last Lord's final in the week after his 42nd birthday. Lloyd played a significant role in Lancashire's victory, coming in at 8 for two, scoring 65, and sharing a vital stand of 101 at almost 5 runs an over with O'Shaughnessy. Clarke had been in his element on a pitch that was fast and full of bounce. Lancashire defended their total with tight out-cricket but, Jesty apart, Surrey's batsmen appeared to think that the way to win was to hit the ball out of sight. As a result, none reached 20. Jesty, who hit a 6 and fourteen 4s, kept his head until the penultimate over, when he swung his 139th delivery to long-on, where Fowler made ground to take an outstanding catch.

Man of the Match: T. E. Jesty.

Lancashire

G. Fowler c Richards b Clarke	0	J. Simmons b Clarke	9
G. D. Mendis c Clarke b Bicknell	1	P. J. W. Allott c Stewart b Clarke	0
J. Abrahams b Feltham	15	M. Watkinson not out	2
*C. H. Lloyd c Richards b Pocock	65	B 1, l-b 18, w 9, n-b 4	32
N. H. Fairbrother lbw b Thomas	18		
S. J. O'Shaughnessy c Lynch b Clarke	62		229
A. N. Hayhurst c Richards b Butcher	3		
†C. Maynard c Stewart b Feltham	22		

1/1 2/8 3/28 (58.3 overs) 229
4/57 5/158 6/177
7/214 8/222 9/222

Bowling: Clarke 11.3–4–21–4; Bicknell 10–1–25–1; Thomas 9–2–40–1; Feltham 12–0–51–2; Pocock 9–0–43–1; Butcher 7–0–30–1.

Surrey

A. R. Butcher c Watkinson b Allott	6	S. T. Clarke c Fairbrother b Watkinson	19
G. S. Clinton c Simmons b Allott	11	*P. I. Pocock b Allott	2
A. J. Stewart lbw b Watkinson	7	M. P. Bicknell not out	1
T. E. Jesty c Fowler b Hayhurst	112		
M. A. Lynch run out	15		
†C. J. Richards c Maynard b O'Shaughnessy	9	L-b 9, w 6, n-b 4	19
D. J. Thomas c Abrahams b Simmons	12		225
M. A. Feltham c O'Shaughnessy b Simmons	12		

1/9 2/30 3/30 (58.5 overs) 225
4/75 5/109 6/141
7/173 8/201 9/206

Bowling: Allott 12–3–47–3; Watkinson 11–1–37–2; Hayhurst 11.5–0–52–1; O'Shaughnessy 12–0–48–1; Simmons 12–3–32–2.

Umpires: N. T. Plews and A. G. T. Whitehead.

WORCESTERSHIRE v SUSSEX

At Worcester, August 13, 14, 15. Sussex won by five wickets. Toss: Sussex. Worcestershire, who on the first day used a helicopter to help dry out their ground, under water earlier in the week, were undone by their former all-rounder, Imran Khan. Having struggled to 82 for two at the halfway stage, they lost their last eight wickets for 43 runs in twenty overs. The damage was done in the first ten overs after tea on the second day when six wickets tumbled for just

17. Imran took three for 6 in five overs, including the wicket of Hick, whom he bowled second ball. Sussex were 31 for two at the close, and on the third day, despite a splendid spell from Radford, they moved resolutely towards a place in the final. It was Worcestershire's third defeat in consecutive limited-overs semi-finals.

Man of the Match: Imran Khan.

Worcestershire

T. S. Curtis c Alikhan b C. M. Wells ..	22	N. V. Radford lbw b le Roux	0
D. B. D'Oliveira run out	21	R. K. Illingworth c Gould b Pigott	8
D. M. Smith b Jones	21	A. P. Pridgeon not out	4
G. A. Hick b Imran	1		
*P. A. Neale lbw b Imran	1	L-b 14, w 4, n-b 5	23
D. N. Patel c Gould b Imran	6		
†S. J. Rhodes c Gould b Jones	3	1/40 2/66 3/82 4/82 (51 overs) 125	
P. J. Newport run out	15	5/84 6/93 7/98 8/99 9/118	

Bowling: Imran 12–2–26–3; le Roux 12–1–31–1; C. M. Wells 12–3–24–1; Jones 8–1–23–2; Reeve 5–2–7–0; Pigott 2–2–0–1.

Sussex

A. M. Green c Hick b Radford	11	*†I. J. Gould not out	1
R. I. Alikhan c Rhodes b Pridgeon	41		
P. W. G. Parker lbw b Radford	2	B 3, l-b 7, w 2, n-b 7	19
Imran Khan c Hick b Radford	4		
C. M. Wells not out	45	1/17 2/23 3/31 (5 wkts, 49 overs) 126	
A. P. Wells c Radford b Smith	3	4/103 5/124	

G. S. le Roux, D. A. Reeve, A. C. S. Pigott and A. N. Jones did not bat.

Bowling: Radford 12–3–20–3; Pridgeon 12–4–23–1; Newport 12–2–33–0; Illingworth 4–1–12–0; Patel 5–0–24–0; Hick 3–0–4–0; Smith 1–1–0–1.

Umpires: D. O. Oslear and R. Palmer.

FINAL

LANCASHIRE v SUSSEX

At Lord's, September 6. Sussex won by seven wickets. No team batting second had previously scored 243 to win either of the two domestic one-day finals at Lord's, and yet so commonplace was Lancashire's bowling that Sussex never looked like falling short, achieving their target with ten balls to spare. Reeve, their medium-pace bowler, made their victory possible, taking four wickets for 12 runs in 25 balls after Fowler and Mendis had put on 50 in thirteen overs to question Gould's decision to insert Lancashire. The most important wicket was that of Lloyd, who was given a standing ovation, in which the Sussex players all joined, as he made his way to the wicket in what seemed likely to be his last appearance in a Lord's final. With the first ball of this over, his third, Reeve had trapped Mendis; with his fifth he dismissed Lloyd for 0. Throughout his twelve overs, Reeve bowled commendably to a full length on a slowish pitch, obtaining movement both ways off the seam. Gould backed him, as he also did Colin Wells, by maintaining an attacking field, keeping two slips and having only two men outside the fielding circle. After 40 overs Lancashire were 112 for five, but Hayhurst, with forthright blows, turned the innings. He also gave Fairbrother, after a shaky start, encouragement to trust his own strokeplay. They put on 100 together in twenty overs, Fairbrother going on to his fifty off 96 balls. It was good, positive cricket except for the failure of Sussex's all-seam attack to bowl their overs fast enough. Their last five were in "over-time".

After Alikhan's dismissal in the tenth over, Green and Parker set about their task with a sure confidence. Both drove fluently square and through the V, Parker's bat in particular having the sonority of a strokemaker in form. Both were adept at taking the weight off a shot and running to a fieldsman: both brought up their fifties with handsome off-side boundaries,

Green's off 106 balls with seven 4s and Parker's off 69 balls with an on-driven 6 in Simmons's first over and five 4s. In the 60s, Parker suffered cramp but preferred salt tablets to a runner, and not even the dismissal of Green in the 43rd over brought relief to Lancashire. Imran Khan batted with a casual elegance which denied any possibility of last-minute collapses, and although Colin Wells's thumping 6 into the Tavern off the penultimate ball was more the stuff of one-day encounters, there was so much to savour in the orthodoxy and classical strokeplay of Parker and Imran.

Man of the Match: D. A. Reeve.

Lancashire

G. D. Mendis lbw b Reeve 17	M. Watkinson not out 15
G. Fowler c Gould b C. M. Wells 24	J. Simmons not out 6
J. Abrahams c Pigott b Reeve 20	
*C. H. Lloyd lbw b Reeve 0	B 1, l-b 17, w 6, n-b 6 30
N. H. Fairbrother b Pigott 63	
S. J. O'Shaughnessy b Reeve 4	1/50 2/56 3/56 (8 wkts, 60 overs) 242
A. N. Hayhurst c Gould b Imran 49	4/85 5/100 6/203
†C. Maynard c Gould b Imran 14	7/205 8/217

P. J. W. Allott did not bat.

Bowling: Imran 12–2–43–2; le Roux 9–0–43–0; Jones 3–0–25–0; C. M. Wells 12–3–34–1; Reeve 12–4–20–4; Pigott 12–1–59–1.

Sussex

R. I. Alikhan b Allott 6	C. M. Wells not out 17
A. M. Green st Maynard b Simmons .. 62	L-b 17, w 6 23
P. W. G. Parker c Abrahams b Hayhurst 85	
Imran Khan not out 50	1/19 2/156 3/190 (3 wkts, 58.2 overs) 243

A. P. Wells, *†I. J. Gould, G. S. le Roux, D. A. Reeve, A. C. S. Pigott and A. N. Jones did not bat.

Bowling: Watkinson 11.2–0–40–0; Allott 11–3–34–1; O'Shaughnessy 6–0–52–0; Hayhurst 12–2–38–1; Simmons 12–2–31–1; Abrahams 3–0–15–0; Fairbrother 3–0–16–0.

Umpires: H. D. Bird and K. E. Palmer.

NATWEST BANK TROPHY RECORDS

(Including Gillette Cup, 1963-80)

Batting

Highest individual scores: 206, A. I. Kallicharran, Warwickshire v Oxfordshire, Birmingham, 1984; 177, C. G. Greenidge, Hampshire v Glamorgan, Southampton, 1975; 165 not out, V. P. Terry, Hampshire v Berkshire, Southampton, 1985; 158, G. D. Barlow, Middlesex v Lancashire, Lord's, 1984; 158, Zaheer Abbas, Gloucestershire v Leicestershire, Leicester, 1983; 156, D. I. Gower, Leicestershire v Derbyshire, Leicester, 1984; 155, J. J. Whitaker, Leicestershire v Wiltshire, Swindon, 1984; 153, A. Hill, Derbyshire v Cornwall, Derby, 1986. (93 hundreds were scored in the Gillette Cup; 52 hundreds have been scored in the NatWest Bank Trophy.)

Fastest hundred: R. E. Marshall in 77 minutes, Hampshire v Bedfordshire at Goldington, 1968.

Highest innings total: 392 for five off 60 overs, Warwickshire v Oxfordshire, Birmingham, 1984; 371 for four off 60 overs, Hampshire v Glamorgan, Southampton, 1975; 365 for three off 60 overs, Derbyshire v Cornwall, Derby, 1986; 354 for seven off 60 overs, Leicestershire v Wiltshire, Swindon, 1984; 349 for six off 60 overs, Lancashire v Gloucestershire, Bristol, 1984; 339 for four off 60 overs, Hampshire v Berkshire, Southampton, 1985; 330 for four off 60 overs, Somerset v Glamorgan, Cardiff, 1978; 327 for seven off 60 overs, Gloucestershire v Berkshire, Reading, 1966; 327 for six off 60 overs, Essex v Scotland, Chelmsford, 1984; 326 for six off 60 overs, Leicestershire v Worcestershire, Leicester, 1979; 321 for four off 60 overs, Hampshire v Bedfordshire, Goldington, 1968; 317 for four off 60 overs, Yorkshire v Surrey (in the final), Lord's, 1965; 317 for eight off 60 overs, Warwickshire v Durham, Birmingham, 1986; 312 for five off 60 overs, Worcestershire v Lancashire, Manchester, 1985; 305 for five off 60 overs, Leicestershire v Ireland, Leicester, 1986.

Highest innings total by a minor county: 256 off 58 overs, Oxfordshire v Warwickshire, Birmingham, 1983.

Highest totals by a side batting second: 306 for six off 59.3 overs, Gloucestershire v Leicestershire, Leicester, 1983; 298 off 59 overs, Lancashire v Worcestershire, Manchester, 1985; 297 for four off 57.1 overs, Somerset v Warwickshire, Taunton, 1978; 296 for four off 58 overs, Kent v Surrey, Canterbury, 1985; 290 for seven off 59.3 overs, Yorkshire v Worcestershire, Leeds, 1982; 287 for six off 59 overs, Warwickshire v Glamorgan, Birmingham, 1976; 287 off 60 overs, Essex v Somerset, Taunton, 1978; 282 for nine off 60 overs, Leicestershire v Gloucestershire, Leicester, 1975. Gloucestershire's 306 for six v Leicestershire, Leicester, 1983 was the highest by a side batting second and winning the match.

Highest innings by a side batting first and losing: 302 for five off 60 overs, Leicestershire v Gloucestershire, Leicester, 1983.

Lowest innings in the final at Lord's: 118 off 60 overs, Lancashire v Kent, 1974.

Lowest completed innings totals: 39 off 26.4 overs, Ireland v Sussex, Hove, 1985; 41 off 20 overs, Cambridgeshire v Buckinghamshire, Cambridge, 1972; 41 off 19.4 overs, Middlesex v Essex, Westcliff, 1972; 41 off 36.1 overs, Shropshire v Essex, Wellington, 1974.

Lowest total by a side batting first and winning: 98 off 56.2 overs, Worcestershire v Durham, Chester-le-Street, 1968.

Shortest innings: 10.1 overs (60 for one), Worcestershire v Lancashire, Worcester, 1963.

Matches re-arranged on a reduced number of overs are excluded from the above.

Record partnerships for each wicket

227 for 1st	R. E. Marshall and B. L. Reed, Hampshire v Bedfordshire at Goldington	1968
286 for 2nd	I. S. Anderson and A. Hill, Derbyshire v Cornwall, Derby	1986
209 for 3rd	P. Willey and D. I. Gower, Leicestershire v Ireland, Leicester	1986
234* for 4th	D. Lloyd and C. H. Lloyd, Lancashire v Gloucestershire at Manchester	1978
166 for 5th	M. A. Lynch and G. R. J. Roope, Surrey v Durham at The Oval	1982
105 for 6th	G. S. Sobers and R. A. White, Nottinghamshire v Worcestershire at Worcester	1974
160* for 7th	C. J. Richards and I. R. Payne, Surrey v Lincolnshire at Sleaford	1983
71* for 8th	R. C. Ontong and T. Davies, Glamorgan v Staffordshire at Stone	1986
87 for 9th	M. A. Nash and A. E. Cordle, Glamorgan v Lincolnshire at Swansea	1974
81 for 10th	S. Turner and R. E. East, Essex v Yorkshire at Leeds	1982

Bowling

Hat-tricks: J. D. F. Larter, Northamptonshire v Sussex, Northampton, 1963; D. A. D. Sydenham, Surrey v Cheshire, Hoylake, 1964; R. N. S. Hobbs, Essex v Middlesex, Lord's, 1968; N. M. McVicker, Warwickshire v Lincolnshire, Birmingham, 1971; G. S. le Roux, Sussex v Ireland, Hove, 1985.

Four wickets in five balls: D. A. D. Sydenham, Surrey v Cheshire, Hoylake, 1964.

Best analyses: seven for 15, A. L. Dixon, Kent v Surrey, The Oval, 1967; seven for 30, P. J. Sainsbury, Hampshire v Norfolk, Southampton, 1965; seven for 32, S. P. Davis, Durham v Lancashire, Chester-le-Street, 1983; seven for 33, R. D. Jackman, Surrey v Yorkshire, Harrogate, 1970; seven for 37, N. A. Mallender, Northamptonshire v Worcestershire, Northampton, 1984.

Results

Largest victories in runs: Sussex by 244 runs v Ireland, Hove, 1985; Warwickshire by 227 runs v Oxfordshire, Birmingham, 1984; Essex by 226 runs v Oxfordshire, Chelmsford, 1985; Leicestershire by 214 runs v Staffordshire, Longton, 1975; Derbyshire by 204 runs v Cornwall, Derby, 1986; Sussex by 200 runs v Durham, Hove, 1964; and in the final by 175 runs, Yorkshire v Surrey, Lord's 1965.

Quickest finishes: both at 2.20 p.m. Worcestershire beat Lancashire by nine wickets at Worcester, 1963; Essex beat Middlesex by eight wickets at Westcliff, 1972.

Scores level: Nottinghamshire 215, Somerset 215 for nine at Taunton, 1964; Surrey 196, Sussex 196 for eight at The Oval, 1970; Somerset 287 for six, Essex 287 at Taunton, 1978; Surrey 195 for seven, Essex 195 at Chelmsford, 1980; Essex 149, Derbyshire 149 for eight at Derby, 1981; Northamptonshire 235 for nine, Derbyshire 235 for six in the final at Lord's, 1981; Middlesex 222 for nine, Somerset 222 for eight at Lord's, 1983; Hampshire 224 for eight, Essex 224 for seven at Southampton, 1985. Under the rules the side which lost fewer wickets won.

Minor Counties: Durham became the first minor county to defeat a first-class county when they beat Yorkshire at Harrogate by five wickets in 1973, Lincolnshire became the second when they beat Glamorgan at Swansea by six wickets in 1974 and Shropshire the first in the NatWest Bank Trophy when they beat Yorkshire at Telford by 37 runs in 1984. Hertfordshire were the first minor county to reach the third round when they beat Essex at Hitchin by 33 runs in 1976. Durham became the first minor county to defeat first-class opposition on two occasions when they beat Derbyshire at Derby in 1985.

WINNERS

Gillette Cup

1963	SUSSEX beat Worcestershire by 14 runs.
1964	SUSSEX beat Warwickshire by eight wickets.
1965	YORKSHIRE beat Surrey by 175 runs.
1966	WARWICKSHIRE beat Worcestershire by five wickets.
1967	KENT beat Somerset by 32 runs.
1968	WARWICKSHIRE beat Sussex by four wickets.
1969	YORKSHIRE beat Derbyshire by 69 runs.
1970	LANCASHIRE beat Sussex by six wickets.
1971	LANCASHIRE beat Kent by 24 runs.
1972	LANCASHIRE beat Warwickshire by four wickets.
1973	GLOUCESTERSHIRE beat Sussex by 40 runs.
1974	KENT beat Lancashire by four wickets.
1975	LANCASHIRE beat Middlesex by seven wickets.
1976	NORTHAMPTONSHIRE beat Lancashire by four wickets.
1977	MIDDLESEX beat Glamorgan by five wickets.
1978	SUSSEX beat Somerset by five wickets.
1979	SOMERSET beat Northamptonshire by 45 runs.
1980	MIDDLESEX beat Surrey by seven wickets.

NatWest Bank Trophy

1981	DERBYSHIRE beat Northamptonshire by losing fewer wickets with the scores level.
1982	SURREY beat Warwickshire by nine wickets.
1983	SOMERSET beat Kent by 24 runs.
1984	MIDDLESEX beat Kent by four wickets.
1985	ESSEX beat Nottinghamshire by 1 run.
1986	SUSSEX beat Lancashire by seven wickets.

BENSON AND HEDGES CUP, 1986

Middlesex, whose previous success in the competition had come in 1983, won the Benson and Hedges Cup when they beat Kent by 2 runs in an exciting finish at Lord's. In addition to the trophy, which they hold for a year, Middlesex received £19,000 in prizemoney. Kent, as runners-up, took £9,500.

The losing semi-finalists, Nottinghamshire and Worcestershire, received £4,500 each, while Derbyshire, Essex, Northamptonshire and Sussex, the losing quarter-finalists, received £2,250 each.

John Emburey, nominated by David Gower for the Gold Award in the final for his useful batting, tight, economical bowling and a spectacular diving catch at slip, received £550, while the Gold Award winners in the semi-finals each received £275, in the quarter-finals £200, and in the group matches £125 each.

Total prizemoney for the competition was £82,400, an increase of £4,000 over the previous year. Benson and Hedges increased their total sponsorship to the TCCB for 1986 to £422,000.

FINAL GROUP TABLE

	Played	Won	Lost	Pts	Bowlers' Striking Rate
Group A					
DERBYSHIRE	4	4	0	8	31.82
NORTHAMPTONSHIRE	4	3	1	6	52.64
Warwickshire	4	2	2	4	44.58
Leicestershire	4	1	3	2	40.43
Minor Counties	4	0	4	0	49.30
Group B					
WORCESTERSHIRE	4	3	1	6	37.76
NOTTINGHAMSHIRE	4	3	1	6	54.29
Yorkshire	4	2	2	4	36.29
Lancashire	4	1	3	2	49.84
Scotland	4	1	3	2	51.12
Group C					
ESSEX	4	4	0	8	38.64
SUSSEX	4	3	1	6	29.48
Gloucestershire	4	2	2	4	38.06
Somerset	4	1	3	2	41.25
Glamorgan	4	0	4	0	51.60
Group D					
MIDDLESEX	4	4	0	8	32.53
KENT	4	2	2	4	36.69
Hampshire	4	2	2	4	41.24
Surrey	4	2	2	4	56.82
Oxford & Cambridge Univs	4	0	4	0	105.87

The top two teams in each section qualified for the quarter-finals.

Where two or more teams finished with the same number of points, the position in the group was determined by their bowlers' striking-rates.

GROUP A

DERBYSHIRE v LEICESTERSHIRE

At Chesterfield, May 3, 5. Derbyshire won on faster scoring-rate after rain ended play. Toss: Leicestershire.
Gold Award: M. A. Holding.

Derbyshire

*K. J. Barnett c Whitaker b Benjamin .	52	R. J. Finney not out	7
I. S. Anderson c Butcher b Benjamin ..	0	P. E. Russell not out	6
A. Hill c Butcher b DeFreitas	24		
J. E. Morris c Gower b Clift	13	B 1, l-b 10, n-b 10	21
†B. Roberts b Benjamin	5		
G. Miller c DeFreitas b Taylor	32	1/47 2/80 3/95 (8 wkts, 55 overs)	236
M. A. Holding b Agnew	69	4/101 5/109 6/193	
P. G. Newman b Agnew	7	7/215 8/222	

O. H. Mortensen did not bat.

Bowling: Agnew 11–1–54–2; Benjamin 11–1–45–3; Taylor 11–0–33–1; DeFreitas 11–3–34–1; Clift 11–0–59–1.

Leicestershire

†I. P. Butcher c Roberts b Holding	0	P. A. J. DeFreitas not out	8
R. A. Cobb c Anderson b Mortensen .	4	W. K. M. Benjamin not out	4
L. Potter c Miller b Mortensen	5	L-b 2, n-b 2	4
*D. I. Gower c Finney b Holding	11		
J. J. Whitaker c Anderson b Mortensen	2	1/0 2/9 3/11 (7 wkts, 20 overs)	53
N. E. Briers c Finney b Miller	8	4/26 5/26	
P. B. Clift c Anderson b Miller	7	6/38 7/45	

L. B. Taylor and J. P. Agnew did not bat.

Bowling: Holding 7–1–13–2; Mortensen 6–1–17–3; Miller 4–1–13–2; Russell 3–0–8–0.

Umpires: H. D. Bird and B. J. Meyer.

MINOR COUNTIES v NORTHAMPTONSHIRE

At Slough, May 3. Northamptonshire won by five wickets. Toss: Northamptonshire.
Gold Award: R. Herbert.

Minor Counties

S. R. Atkinson c Ripley b Mallender ..	4	R. Herbert not out	26
†N. Priestley run out	2		
P. A. Todd b Harper	32	B 1, l-b 14, w 2	17
G. R. J. Roope b Wild	17		
*N. A. Riddell c Boyd-Moss b Cook ...	0	1/8 2/14 3/56 (5 wkts, 55 overs)	135
S. G. Plumb not out	37	4/59 5/75	

K. A. Arnold, J. S. Hitchmough, W. G. Merry and D. Surridge did not bat.

Bowling: Mallender 7–2–10–1; Capel 11–2–20–0; Walker 8–0–32–0; Harper 11–5–17–1; Cook 11–7–18–1; Wild 7–0–23–1.

Northamptonshire

*G. Cook c Surridge b Arnold	14	D. J. Wild not out	17
R. J. Bailey c Plumb b Arnold	38		
R. J. Boyd-Moss not out	32	B 8, l-b 4, w 5, n-b 1	18
A. J. Lamb st Priestley b Herbert	0		
R. A. Harper run out	16	1/48 2/56 3/61 (5 wkts, 39.2 overs) 138	
D. J. Capel b Herbert	3	4/89 5/102	

†D. Ripley, N. A. Mallender, N. G. B. Cook and A. Walker did not bat.

Bowling: Merry 5–0–23–0; Surridge 5–1–25–0; Arnold 7–0–16–2; Herbert 11–3–30–2; Hitchmough 5–2–13–0; Plumb 6.2–4–19–0.

Umpires: J. H. Harris and J. W. Holder.

LEICESTERSHIRE v WARWICKSHIRE

At Leicester, May 10. Warwickshire won by one wicket. Toss: Warwickshire.
Gold Award: B. M. McMillan.

Leicestershire

L. Potter c McMillan b Small	6	†P. Whitticase b Small	13
R. A. Cobb c and b Parsons	22	P. A. J. DeFreitas not out	3
T. J. Boon run out	43	B 1, l-b 14, w 4, n-b 6	25
*D. I. Gower b Gifford	36		
J. J. Whitaker c Smith b Munton	12	1/22 2/45 3/106 (7 wkts, 55 overs) 192	
N. E. Briers run out	7	4/126 5/137	
P. B. Clift not out	25	6/143 7/186	

W. K. M. Benjamin and L. B. Taylor did not bat.

Bowling: Small 11–1–40–2; McMillan 11–1–43–0; Munton 11–1–20–1; Parsons 11–0–46–1; Gifford 11–2–28–1.

Warwickshire

T. A. Lloyd c Potter b DeFreitas	22	G. C. Small lbw b DeFreitas	2
R. I. H. B. Dyer b DeFreitas	13	*N. Gifford not out	1
B. M. McMillan b Benjamin	51	T. A. Munton not out	0
D. L. Amiss lbw b Briers	13	L-b 11, w 3, n-b 7	21
†G. W. Humpage c Gower b Taylor	21		
Asif Din b Benjamin	14	1/39 2/42 3/74 (9 wkts, 55 overs) 193	
P. A. Smith c Whitticase b Taylor	26	4/128 5/150 6/151	
G. J. Parsons c Whitticase b Taylor	9	7/185 8/190 9/192	

Bowling: Taylor 11–0–23–3; Benjamin 11–2–42–2; DeFreitas 11–2–28–3; Potter 8–0–32–0; Briers 7–0–26–1; Clift 7–0–31–0.

Umpires: D. O. Oslear and K. E. Palmer.

NORTHAMPTONSHIRE v DERBYSHIRE

At Northampton, May 10. Derbyshire won by 38 runs. Toss: Derbyshire.
Gold Award: B. Roberts.

Derbyshire

*K. J. Barnett b Capel	7	†B. Roberts not out	86
I. S. Anderson c Harper b Wild	25	B 4, l-b 8, w 4	16
A. Hill not out	90		
J. E. Morris st Ripley b Harper	1	1/13 2/68 3/70 (3 wkts, 55 overs) 225	

G. Miller, P. G. Newman, M. A. Holding, R. J. Finney, P. E. Russell and O. H. Mortensen did not bat.

Bowling: Capel 8–2–16–1; Mallender 9–1–26–0; Walker 11–1–53–0; Harper 11–3–33–1; N. G. B. Cook 11–0–47–0; Wild 5–0–38–1.

Northamptonshire

*G. Cook b Holding	1	N. G. B. Cook c Miller b Newman	...	19
R. J. Bailey lbw b Mortensen	17	N. A. Mallender run out		3
R. J. Boyd-Moss lbw b Holding	0	A. Walker not out		3
A. J. Lamb c Newman b Mortensen	4	B 8, l-b 15, w 5, n-b 3		31
R. A. Harper lbw b Miller	23			
D. J. Capel run out	22		(50.2 overs)	187
D. J. Wild st Roberts b Russell	38	1/8 2/8 3/23		
†D. Ripley run out	26	4/24 5/49 6/119		
		7/123 8/167 9/176		

Bowling: Mortensen 11–2–30–2; Holding 9–4–25–2; Finney 7–0–29–0; Miller 11–1–34–1; Newman 8.2–1–28–1; Russell 4–0–18–1.

Umpires: R. Julian and R. A. White.

MINOR COUNTIES v WARWICKSHIRE

At Walsall, May 13. Warwickshire won by 47 runs. Toss: Warwickshire.
Gold Award: D. L. Amiss.

Warwickshire

T. A. Lloyd b Webster	2	A. R. K. Pierson run out		11
R. I. H. B. Dyer run out	0	*N. Gifford b Webster		2
B. M. McMillan lbw b Malone	4	T. A. Munton not out		0
D. L. Amiss c Herbert b Plumb	73	L-b 16, w 3		19
†G. W. Humpage c Roope b Malone	9			
Asif Din b Hitchmough	9	1/2 2/2 3/12	(54.4 overs)	184
P. A. Smith c Priestley b Hitchmough	35	4/32 5/63 6/130		
G. J. Parsons b Malone	20	7/146 8/176 9/181		

Bowling: Malone 10.4–1–26–3; Webster 10–2–31–2; Hitchmough 11–3–41–2; Merry 8–1–25–0; Herbert 8–2–25–0; Plumb 7–1–20–1.

Minor Counties

P. A. Todd b Pierson	44	R. Herbert c Amiss b Parsons		6
†N. Priestley c Humpage b Munton	10	W. G. Merry c Humpage b McMillan		3
G. R. J. Roope c Humpage b Munton	8	S. J. Malone not out		1
*N. A. Riddell b Gifford	20	L-b 11, w 5		16
S. G. Plumb lbw b McMillan	9			
A. Patel run out	15	1/46 2/61 3/67	(50.4 overs)	137
J. S. Hitchmough c Humpage b Parsons	1	4/94 5/120 6/121		
A. J. Webster b Parsons	4	7/124 8/129 9/135		

Bowling: McMillan 9–1–12–2; Parsons 10.4–1–36–3; Pierson 11–3–25–1; Munton 11–0–25–2; Gifford 9–0–28–1.

Umpires: D. Lloyd and B. J. Meyer.

NORTHAMPTONSHIRE v LEICESTERSHIRE

At Northampton, May 13. Northamptonshire won by 23 runs. Toss: Northamptonshire.
Lamb and Capel established a new Benson and Hedges Cup record of 160 for the fifth wicket.
Gold Award: A. J. Lamb.

Northamptonshire

*G. Cook lbw b DeFreitas	19	D. J. Wild not out		1
R. J. Bailey c Butcher b Agnew	0			
R. J. Boyd-Moss lbw b Clift	24	L-b 16, w 12, n-b 1		29
A. J. Lamb c Briers b Benjamin	106			
R. A. Harper c Butcher b Clift	4	1/2 2/38 3/55	(5 wkts, 55 overs)	226
D. J. Capel not out	43	4/61 5/221		

†D. Ripley, N. A. Mallender, N. G. B. Cook and A. Walker did not bat.

Bowling: Agnew 11–2–42–1; Benjamin 10–3–23–1; DeFreitas 11–0–46–1; Clift 11–2–43–2; Potter 7–2–33–0; Briers 5–0–23–0.

Leicestershire

L. Potter c Harper b Mallender	28	P. A. J. DeFreitas c Capel b Mallender		11
I. P. Butcher lbw b Wild	12	W. K. M. Benjamin b Mallender		0
N. E. Briers c N. G. B. Cook b Harper	37	J. P. Agnew b Mallender		2
*D. I. Gower c Walker b Harper	42	L-b 8, w 4		12
J. J. Whitaker b Mallender	30			
T. J. Boon c Boyd-Moss b Wild	10	1/41 2/42 3/127	(54.2 overs)	203
P. B. Clift c N. G. B. Cook b Wild	0	4/129 5/146 6/146		
†P. Whitticase not out	19	7/179 8/197 9/197		

Bowling: Mallender 10.2–0–53–5; Capel 5–1–16–0; N. G. B. Cook 11–0–33–0; Wild 11–1–40–3; Harper 11–1–22–2; Walker 6–0–31–0.

Umpires: A. A. Jones and R. Palmer.

DERBYSHIRE v MINOR COUNTIES

At Derby, May 15, 16. Derbyshire won by seven wickets. Toss: Minor Counties.
Gold Award: K. J. Barnett.

Minor Counties

P. A. Todd c Holding b Mortensen	4	W. G. Merry not out		5
†N. Priestley b Newman	14	S. J. Malone not out		1
R. Herbert c Miller b Mortensen	4			
G. R. J. Roope c Morris b Miller	26	L-b 8, w 5		13
*N. A. Riddell lbw b Miller	12			
S. G. Plumb lbw b Newman	20	1/8 2/20 3/44	(8 wkts, 55 overs)	138
A. S. Patel b Warner	35	4/65 5/65 6/115		
A. J. Webster run out	4	7/131 8/133		

D. Surridge did not bat.

Bowling: Holding 11–1–25–0; Mortensen 11–3–16–2; Newman 11–0–27–2; Finney 8–4–19–0; Miller 11–2–39–2; Warner 3–1–4–1.

Derbyshire

*K. J. Barnett lbw b Herbert	62	†B. Roberts not out		22
I. S. Anderson c Roope b Herbert	26	L-b 3, w 5		8
A. Hill not out	16			
J. E. Morris b Herbert	6	1/76 2/95 3/107	(3 wkts, 40 overs)	140

G. Miller, P. G. Newman, M. A. Holding, R. J. Finney, A. E. Warner and O. H. Mortensen did not bat.

Bowling: Malone 6–0–21–0; Webster 8–0–43–0; Merry 7–2–17–0; Surridge 9–1–30–0; Herbert 10–1–26–3.

Umpires: B. Leadbeater and K. J. Lyons.

WARWICKSHIRE v NORTHAMPTONSHIRE

At Birmingham, May 15, 16. Northamptonshire won by 156 runs. Toss: Warwickshire. Northamptonshire's total was their highest in the competition.

Gold Award: R. J. Bailey.

Northamptonshire

*G. Cook lbw b Munton	37	D. J. Wild not out 1
R. J. Bailey b Parsons	86	
R. J. Boyd-Moss c Parsons b McMillan	58	B 1, l-b 18, w 13, n-b 3 35
A. J. Lamb c Munton b McMillan	39	
R. A. Harper c Asif Din b McMillan ..	19	1/96 2/194 3/211 (5 wkts, 55 overs) 283
D. J. Capel not out	8	4/250 5/273

†D. Ripley, N. A. Mallender, N. G. B. Cook and A. Walker did not bat.

Bowling: Small 11–0–61–0; McMillan 11-2-51-3; Munton 10-2-57-1; Parsons 10-0-41-1; Gifford 11–2–34–0; Lloyd 2-0-20-0.

Warwickshire

T. A. Lloyd b Capel	0	G. J. Parsons c Lamb b Walker 3
R. I. H. B. Dyer b Mallender	1	G. C. Small not out 5
D. L. Amiss c Ripley b Capel	6	L-b 6, w 3 9
P. A. Smith b Capel	4	
B. M. McMillan lbw b Capel	39	1/0 2/4 3/11 (7 wkts, 55 overs) 127
†G. W. Humpage c Bailey b Mallender	8	4/12 5/35
Asif Din not out	52	6/82 7/110

T. A. Munton and *N. Gifford did not bat.

Bowling: Capel 11-2-29-4; Mallender 8-2-19-2; N. G. B. Cook 4-0-10-0; Wild 11–2–16–0; Harper 10-5-18-0; Walker 8-1-29-1; Bailey 3-3-0-0.

Umpires: B. Dudleston and J. H. Harris.

LEICESTERSHIRE v MINOR COUNTIES

At Leicester, May 17, 19. Leicestershire won by 109 runs. Toss: Minor Counties.

Gold Award: L. Potter.

Leicestershire

L. Potter c Plumb b Merry	112	W. K. M. Benjamin not out 19
I. P. Butcher not out	103	L-b 12, w 11, n-b 3 26
*D. I. Gower b Merry	1	
J. J. Whitaker b Malone	17	1/196 2/201 3/249 (3 wkts, 55 overs) 278

N. E. Briers, T. J. Boon, P. B. Clift, †P. Whitticase, P. A. J. DeFreitas and L. B. Taylor did not bat.

Bowling: Malone 10-0-48-1; Merry 10-1-37-2; Hitchmough 3-0-22-0; Herbert 11–0–55–0; Webster 11-1-66-0; Plumb 10-0-38-0.

Minor Counties

†N. Priestley b Clift	37	A. J. Webster lbw b Taylor 5
M. A. Fell b Benjamin	12	S. J. Malone b Benjamin 0
P. A. Todd c Whitticase b Benjamin ..	0	W. G. Merry not out 1
G. R. J. Roope lbw b Clift	8	L-b 4, w 1 5
*N. A. Riddell c Whitticase b Benjamin	74	
S. G. Plumb c Benjamin b Potter	16	1/19 2/23 3/37 (50.4 overs) 169
J. S. Hitchmough b Benjamin	5	4/129 5/151 6/152
R. Herbert c Butcher b Potter	6	7/159 8/168 9/168

Bowling: Taylor 8–3–15–1; Benjamin 9.4–2–17–5; Clift 11–3–14–2; DeFreitas 7–1–15–0; Briers 5–0–34–0; Potter 10–0–70–2.

Umpires: C. Cook and K. J. Lyons.

WARWICKSHIRE v DERBYSHIRE

At Birmingham, May 17, 19. Derbyshire won by three wickets. Toss: Warwickshire. Amiss became the fifth player to score 2,000 runs in the competition.
Gold Award: B. M. McMillan.

Warwickshire

T. A. Lloyd lbw b Mortensen	1	G. C. Small b Holding	2
G. J. Lord c Holding b Mortensen	0	A. R. K. Pierson b Holding	0
B. M. McMillan run out	76		
D. L. Amiss c Barnett b Warner	59	B 3, l-b 6, w 12, n-b 5	26
†G. W. Humpage b Finney	16		
Asif Din c Miller b Warner	4	1/2 2/6 3/114 (9 wkts, 55 overs) 213	
P. A. Smith c Barnett b Warner	18	4/141 5/152 6/185	
G. J. Parsons not out	11	7/204 8/213 9/213	

*N. Gifford did not bat.

Bowling: Holding 11–1–40–2; Mortensen 11–1–34–2; Finney 11–1–34–1; Miller 11–4–29–0; Warner 11–0–67–3.

Derbyshire

*K. J. Barnett c McMillan b Small	12	R. Sharma c Humpage b Small	2
I. S. Anderson b Parsons	42	R. J. Finney not out	12
A. Hill run out	51	L-b 18, w 9, n-b 2	29
J. E. Morris c and b Pierson	5		
†B. Roberts c Small b Parsons	35	1/21 2/100 3/107 (7 wkts, 54.5 overs) 215	
G. Miller not out	25	4/151 5/170	
M. A. Holding b McMillan	2	6/174 7/183	

A. E. Warner and O. H. Mortensen did not bat.

Bowling: Small 10.5–1–36–2; McMillan 11–0–55–1; Pierson 11–1–33–1; Parsons 11–1–47–2; Gifford 11–3–26–0.

Umpires: H. D. Bird and A. G. T. Whitehead.

GROUP B

LANCASHIRE v YORKSHIRE

At Manchester, May 3, 5. Yorkshire won by eight wickets. Toss: Yorkshire.
Gold Award: M. D. Moxon.

Lancashire

G. Fowler c and b Sidebottom	7	P. J. W. Allott b Stevenson	2
G. D. Mendis lbw b Sidebottom	0	J. Simmons not out	10
S. J. O'Shaughnessy b Stevenson	8	M. Watkinson b Sidebottom	0
*C. H. Lloyd c P. J. Hartley		L-b 3, w 2, n-b 4	9
b Sidebottom	101		
N. H. Fairbrother b Carrick	23	1/0 2/9 3/36 (9 wkts, 55 overs) 208	
J. Abrahams c Sidebottom b Jarvis	39	4/87 5/181 6/195	
†C. Maynard b Stevenson	9	7/197 8/203 9/208	

D. J. Makinson did not bat.

Bowling: Sidebottom 11–6–24–4; Jarvis 11–1–32–1; Stevenson 11–0–58–3; P. J. Hartley 11–0–55–0; Carrick 11–1–36–1.

Yorkshire

M. D. Moxon not out 106
G. Boycott c Maynard b Allott 55
K. Sharp lbw b Simmons 0
J. D. Love not out 34
        L-b 15, w 1, n-b 1 17

1/123 2/130   (2 wkts, 51 overs) 212

S. N. Hartley, *†D. L. Bairstow, P. Carrick, A. Sidebottom, P. J. Hartley, G. B. Stevenson and P. W. Jarvis did not bat.

Bowling: Makinson 6–0–16–0; Allott 10–1–31–1; Watkinson 11–0–50–0; O'Shaughnessy 9–1–47–0; Simmons 11–0–38–1; Abrahams 4–1–15–0.

Umpires: D. J. Constant and R. A. White.

SCOTLAND v WORCESTERSHIRE

At Glasgow, May 3, 4. Worcestershire won by two wickets after being 57 for seven at the end of the first day. Toss: Worcestershire.
Gold Award: T. S. Curtis.

Scotland

I. L. Philip run out 1
W. A. Donald c Patel b Pridgeon 0
†A. Brown b Illingworth 26
N. W. Burnett c Illingworth b Patel . . . 15
*O. Henry st Rhodes b Hick 10
A. B. Russell c Rhodes b Patel 5
D. L. Snodgrass c Weston b D'Oliveira . 18
D. G. Moir lbw b D'Oliveira 2

J. E. Ker st Rhodes b D'Oliveira 8
P. G. Duthie not out 8
G. R. Kirkwood not out 1
    B 4, l-b 3, w 7, n-b 1 15

1/0 2/4 3/48   (9 wkts, 55 overs) 109
4/51 5/63 6/67
7/72 8/94 9/99

Bowling: Radford 7–1–16–0; Pridgeon 6–2–9–1; Newport 4–0–9–0; Illingworth 11–1–22–1; Patel 11–4–12–2; Hick 8–1–22–1; D'Oliveira 8–2–12–3.

Worcestershire

T. S. Curtis not out 40
D. B. D'Oliveira c Henry b Ker 8
G. A. Hick c Snodgrass b Duthie 0
D. N. Patel lbw b Duthie 2
*P. A. Neale c Russell b Moir 0
M. J. Weston b Donald 11
†S. J. Rhodes lbw b Henry 3
P. J. Newport run out 5

N. V. Radford b Henry 11
R. K. Illingworth not out 17
    B 1, l-b 4, w 7, n-b 1 13

1/14 2/14 3/23   (8 wkts, 49.5 overs) 110
4/24 5/41 6/46
7/53 8/71

A. P. Pridgeon did not bat.

Bowling: Duthie 11–2–18–2; Ker 5–0–16–1; Moir 10.5–2–22–1; Donald 11–4–20–1; Henry 11–4–17–2; Kirkwood 1–0–12–0.

Umpires: B. Dudleston and D. O. Oslear.

NOTTINGHAMSHIRE v YORKSHIRE

At Nottingham, May 10, 12. Nottinghamshire won by 8 runs. Toss: Nottinghamshire.
Gold Award: D. W. Randall.

Nottinghamshire

R. T. Robinson b Stevenson	19	J. D. Birch b Sidebottom	15
B. C. Broad c Bairstow b Carrick	70	†B. N. French not out	1
D. W. Randall not out	82	B 1, l-b 10, w 2	13
*C. E. B. Rice c Bairstow b P. J. Hartley	9		
P. Johnson c Bairstow b P. J. Hartley	2	1/37 2/136 3/159 (6 wkts, 55 overs) 227
R. J. Hadlee c P. J. Hartley b Sidebottom	16	4/167 5/191 6/224

R. A. Pick, K. E. Cooper and K. Saxelby did not bat.

Bowling: Sidebottom 11–1–48–2; Jarvis 11–4–30–0; P. J. Hartley 11–0–49–2; Stevenson 11–1–42–1; Carrick 11–0–47–1.

Yorkshire

G. Boycott retired hurt	27	A. Sidebottom b Rice	13
M. D. Moxon b Cooper	40	P. J. Hartley not out	29
K. Sharp c Johnson b Pick	14	P. W. Jarvis not out	6
J. D. Love b Rice	15	L-b 10, w 1	11
S. N. Hartley b Hadlee	13		
*†D. L. Bairstow b Saxelby	31	1/73 2/95 3/103 (8 wkts, 55 overs) 219
G. B. Stevenson run out	10	4/127 5/150 6/168
P. Carrick run out	10	7/172 8/197

Bowling: Hadlee 11–2–32–1; Cooper 11–2–28–1; Pick 11–0–43–1; Saxelby 11–0–61–1; Rice 11–0–45–2.

Umpires: J. W. Holder and P. B. Wight.

SCOTLAND v LANCASHIRE

At Perth, May 10, 11. Scotland won by 3 runs, so achieving in their 25th match their first win in the competition. Toss: Lancashire.
Gold Award: R. G. Swan.

Scotland

I. L. Philip c Fairbrother b Hughes	28	D. G. Moir b Allott	21
W. A. Donald c and b Patterson	4	P. G. Duthie b Allott	8
*R. G. Swan b Abrahams	31	†J. D. Knight not out	1
O. Henry c Hughes b Watkinson	9	B 8, l-b 7, w 2, n-b 2	19
N. W. Burnett lbw b Patterson	27		
A. B. Russell b Allott	8	1/10 2/62 3/80 (9 wkts, 55 overs) 156
D. L. Snodgrass c Fairbrother		4/97 5/125 6/125
b Patterson	0	7/125 8/146 9/156

A. W. J. Stevenson did not bat.

Bowling: Allott 10–2–24–3; Patterson 9–2–31–3; Watkinson 11–3–25–1; Simmons 7–2–17–0; Hughes 11–1–24–1; O'Shaughnessy 2–0–9–0; Abrahams 5–0–11–1.

Lancashire

G. D. Mendis b Stevenson	30	*J. Simmons not out	16
G. Fowler lbw b Duthie	1	P. J. W. Allott b Moir	13
J. Abrahams b Henry	31	B. P. Patterson not out	3
S. J. O'Shaughnessy b Duthie	9	B 3, l-b 3, w 5	11
M. Watkinson c Moir b Henry	16		
N. H. Fairbrother b Duthie	12	1/2 2/62 3/72 (9 wkts, 55 overs) 153
D. P. Hughes c Knight b Burnett	4	4/93 5/93 6/109
†C. Maynard st Knight b Donald	7	7/109 8/119 9/139

Bowling: Duthie 11–4–31–3; Donald 10–0–40–1; Moir 11–0–36–1; Stevenson 11–3–20–1; Henry 11–4–19–2; Burnett 1–0–1–1.

Umpires: J. H. Hampshire and B. Leadbeater.

NOTTINGHAMSHIRE v SCOTLAND

At Nottingham, May 13. Nottinghamshire won by eight wickets. Toss: Scotland.
Gold Award: I. L. Philip.

Scotland

W. A. Donald lbw b Cooper	5	D. L. Snodgrass not out		20
I. L. Philip c Hemmings b Hadlee	73	D. G. Moir not out		8
*R. G. Swan b Pick	24	L-b 20, w 3, n-b 1		24
A. B. Russell c Johnson b Pick	6			
O. Henry run out	3	1/13 2/91 3/115	(6 wkts, 55 overs)	166
N. W. Burnett c French b Pick	3	4/120 5/125 6/142		

P. G. Duthie, †J. D. Knight and A. W. J. Stevenson did not bat.

Bowling: Pick 11–1–41–3; Hemmings 11–3–24–0; Cooper 11–3–22–1; Rice 11–1–29–0; Hadlee 11–2–30–1.

Nottinghamshire

R. T. Robinson not out	76
B. C. Broad run out	10
D. W. Randall b Henry	44
*C. E. B. Rice not out	27
L-b 9, w 4	13
1/27 2/117 (2 wkts, 44.4 overs)	170

P. Johnson, J. D. Birch, R. J. Hadlee, †B. N. French, E. E. Hemmings, K. E. Cooper and R. A. Pick did not bat.

Bowling: Duthie 11–1–44–0; Donald 4–0–10–0; Stevenson 9.4–0–38–0; Henry 10–1–33–1; Burnett 3–0–9–0; Moir 7–0–27–0.

Umpires: R. Julian and K. J. Lyons.

WORCESTERSHIRE v LANCASHIRE

At Worcester, May 13. Lancashire won on their faster scoring-rate after the first 30 overs, the match having finished at 8.26 p.m. with the scores level and both sides having lost the same number of wickets. Toss: Lancashire. Although this was the seventh occasion on which a Benson and Hedges match had finished with the scores level, it was the first instance of a match ending as a tie.
Gold Award: P. J. W. Allott.

Worcestershire

T. S. Curtis lbw b Allott	3	N. V. Radford not out		3
D. B. D'Oliveira c Simmons b Allott	6	J. D. Inchmore not out		2
D. M. Smith lbw b Makinson	14			
G. A. Hick lbw b Makinson	32	B 1, l-b 18, n-b 9		28
*P. A. Neale run out	52			
D. N. Patel run out	76	1/11 2/23 3/65	(8 wkts, 55 overs)	231
†S. J. Rhodes c Fowler b Makinson	0	4/77 5/182 6/184		
P. J. Newport c Fairbrother b Allott	15	7/222 8/226		

A. P. Pridgeon did not bat.

Bowling: Patterson 11–1–43–0; Allott 11–3–30–3; Makinson 11–3–36–3; Watkinson 6–0–42–0; Simmons 10–2–31–0; Abrahams 6–0–30–0.

Lancashire

G. D. Mendis lbw b Inchmore	21	P. J. W. Allott not out	6
G. Fowler b Newport	76	D. J. Makinson not out	0
J. Abrahams b Radford	20		
N. H. Fairbrother c sub b Hick	47	B 4, l-b 19, w 4, n-b 5	32
D. P. Hughes b Inchmore	1		
†C. Maynard lbw b Patel	14	1/42 2/125 3/146	(8 wkts, 55 overs) 231
M. Watkinson b Pridgeon	7	4/149 5/188 6/208	
*J. Simmons c D'Oliveira b Hick	7	7/223 8/225	

B. P. Patterson did not bat.

Bowling: Radford 11–2–36–1; Pridgeon 10–3–38–1; Newport 11–0–39–1; Inchmore 11–0–40–2; Patel 8–0–30–1; Hick 4–0–25–2.

Umpires: C. Cook and A. G. T. Whitehead.

WORCESTERSHIRE v NOTTINGHAMSHIRE

At Worcester, May 15. Worcestershire won by eight wickets. Toss: Worcestershire.
Gold Award: G. A. Hick.

Nottinghamshire

R. T. Robinson c Hick b Illingworth	29	†B. N. French run out	7
B. C. Broad lbw b Inchmore	40	R. A. Pick not out	3
D. W. Randall c Rhodes b Weston	12	B 1, l-b 22, w 6, n-b 1	30
*C. E. B. Rice b Inchmore	44		
P. Johnson c Radford b Weston	18	1/53 2/81 3/87	(7 wkts, 55 overs) 218
R. J. Hadlee c Weston b Illingworth	16	4/145 5/173	
J. D. Birch not out	19	6/185 7/205	

K. E. Cooper and P. M. Such did not bat.

Bowling: Radford 11–2–35–0; Inchmore 11–2–33–2; Newport 11–0–43–0; Illingworth 11–1–49–2; Weston 11–1–35–2.

Worcestershire

M. J. Weston b Hadlee	3
D. B. D'Oliveira c Rice b Hadlee	22
D. M. Smith not out	81
G. A. Hick not out	103
B 8, n-b 2	10

1/18 2/29   (2 wkts, 52.1 overs) 219

*P. A. Neale, D. N. Patel, †S. J. Rhodes, P. J. Newport, N. V. Radford, J. D. Inchmore and R. K. Illingworth did not bat.

Bowling: Hadlee 9.1–5–22–2; Cooper 11–2–35–0; Pick 11–2–41–0; Such 11–0–58–0; Rice 10–0–55–0.

Umpires: J. H. Hampshire and B. J. Meyer.

YORKSHIRE v SCOTLAND

At Leeds, May 15. Yorkshire won by 167 runs. Toss: Scotland. Yorkshire's total, in which Sharp hit his 105 not out off 102 balls, was their highest in the competition.
Gold Award: P. J. Hartley.

Yorkshire

M. D. Moxon c Moir b Burnett 83	G. B. Stevenson not out 27
A. A. Metcalfe b Henry 31	
K. Sharp not out 105	L-b 14, w 7, n-b 3 24
J. D. Love b De Neef 25	
S. N. Hartley lbw b Duthie 0	1/61 2/167 3/219 (5 wkts, 55 overs) 317
*†D. L. Bairstow b Burnett 22	4/220 5/263

P. Carrick, A. Sidebottom, P. W. Jarvis and P. J. Hartley did not bat.

Bowling: Duthie 10-0-56-1; De Neef 11-0-68-1; Moir 8-0-51-0; Donald 6-0-26-0; Henry 11-0-42-1; Burnett 9-0-60-2.

Scotland

I. L. Philip lbw b Stevenson 11	P. G. Duthie b Carrick 33
W. A. Donald c Moxon b P. J. Hartley 52	D. De Neef c Sidebottom b Carrick . . . 5
*R. G. Swan lbw b Stevenson 0	†J. D. Knight not out 1
A. B. Russell c Sharp b P. J. Hartley . . 5	B 1, l-b 5, w 2, n-b 1 9
N. W. Burnett lbw b P. J. Hartley . . . 7	
O. Henry lbw b Jarvis 2	1/42 2/42 3/61 (40.4 overs) 150
A. Brown lbw b P. J. Hartley 12	4/77 5/80 6/96
D. G. Moir c and b P. J. Hartley 13	7/96 8/110 9/118

Bowling: Sidebottom 8-0-44-0; Stevenson 7-0-19-2; P. J. Hartley 11-0-43-5; Jarvis 11-1-24-1; Carrick 3.4-0-14-2.

Umpires: J. W. Holder and N. T. Plews.

LANCASHIRE v NOTTINGHAMSHIRE

At Liverpool, May 17, 19. Nottinghamshire won by 20 runs. Toss: Lancashire.
Gold Award: R. J. Hadlee.

Nottinghamshire

R. T. Robinson c Abrahams b Simmons 58	†B. N. French run out 2
B. C. Broad lbw b Allott 2	
D. W. Randall c Maynard b Allott 0	L-b 12, w 6, n-b 8 26
*C. E. B. Rice c Maynard b Allott 71	
P. Johnson c Makinson b Simmons 19	1/8 2/8 3/123 (7 wkts, 55 overs) 263
J. D. Birch not out 48	4/158 5/162
R. J. Hadlee b Makinson 37	6/260 7/263

R. A. Pick, K. E. Cooper and P. M. Such did not bat.

Bowling: Watkinson 10-0-50-0; Allott 11-2-53-3; Makinson 9-0-37-1; O'Shaughnessy 5-0-39-0; Simmons 11-3-33-2; Abrahams 9-1-39-0.

Lancashire

G. Fowler c Broad b Hadlee 2	J. Simmons not out 7
G. D. Mendis c French b Hadlee 35	P. J. W. Allott not out 23
J. Abrahams b Cooper 0	
S. J. O'Shaughnessy st French b Such . . 14	B 1, l-b 9, w 8, n-b 3 21
*C. H. Lloyd c Rice b Pick 67	
N. H. Fairbrother b Pick 33	1/7 2/9 3/43 (8 wkts, 55 overs) 243
†C. Maynard c and b Hadlee 22	4/80 5/166 6/174
M. Watkinson c Broad b Hadlee 19	7/200 8/218

D. J. Makinson did not bat.

Bowling: Hadlee 11-0-53-4; Cooper 11-2-25-1; Pick 11-0-60-2; Such 11-0-43-1; Rice 11-0-52-0.

Umpires: A. A. Jones and P. B. Wight.

YORKSHIRE v WORCESTERSHIRE

At Leeds, May 17, 19. Worcestershire won by 44 runs. Toss: Yorkshire.
Gold Award: D. B. D'Oliveira.

Worcestershire

M. J. Weston b S. N. Hartley	42	J. D. Inchmore b Sidebottom	11
D. B. D'Oliveira b P. J. Hartley	66	R. K. Illingworth not out	5
D. M. Smith b Carrick	1	A. P. Pridgeon not out	1
G. A. Hick b Carrick	35	B 1, l-b 7, w 1, n-b 4	13
*P. A. Neale b Sidebottom	28		
D. N. Patel st Bairstow b Stevenson	6	1/69 2/73 3/137 (9 wkts, 55 overs) 213	
†S. J. Rhodes lbw b Jarvis	3	4/158 5/175 6/178	
N. V. Radford b Sidebottom	2	7/185 8/206 9/207	

Bowling: Sidebottom 10–1–36–3; Jarvis 11–0–34–1; Carrick 11–1–38–2; Stevenson 7–1–29–1; P. J. Hartley 8–1–38–1; S. N. Hartley 8–0–30–1.

Yorkshire

M. D. Moxon run out	2	A. Sidebottom not out	18
A. A. Metcalfe lbw b Radford	11	P. J. Hartley run out	0
K. Sharp b Pridgeon	17	P. W. Jarvis run out	0
J. D. Love c Hick b Pridgeon	25	B 4, l-b 11, w 2, n-b 10	27
S. N. Hartley b Inchmore	28		
*†D. L. Bairstow lbw b Illingworth	6	1/13 2/14 3/66 (49 overs) 169	
P. Carrick run out	14	4/70 5/83 6/116	
G. B. Stevenson c Patel b Pridgeon	21	7/129 8/159 9/159	

Bowling: Radford 9–2–28–1; Inchmore 9–1–23–1; Illingworth 11–3–21–1; Pridgeon 11–0–57–3; Patel 8–1–24–0; Weston 1–0–1–0.

Umpires: B. Leadbeater and R. A. White.

GROUP C

GLOUCESTERSHIRE v SOMERSET

At Bristol, May 3, 5. Gloucestershire won by eight wickets. Toss: Gloucestershire.
Gold Award: D. V. Lawrence.

Somerset

N. A. Felton c Russell b Lawrence	0	J. Garner b Payne	0
*P. M. Roebuck c Russell b Lawrence	11	C. H. Dredge c Russell b Lawrence	6
J. J. E. Hardy run out	14	†T. Gard not out	4
I. V. A. Richards c Lawrence b Bainbridge	29	B 2, l-b 5, w 1, n-b 15	23
I. T. Botham c Athey b Lawrence	24		
B. C. Rose run out	49	1/1 2/21 3/56 (54.1 overs) 178	
V. J. Marks c Curran b Graveney	11	4/67 5/106 6/143	
M. R. Davis lbw b Payne	7	7/156 8/156 9/168	

Bowling: Lawrence 11–1–36–4; Walsh 11–0–38–0; Payne 11–2–38–2; Bainbridge 8.1–0–35–1; Graveney 11–1–18–1; Lloyds 2–0–6–0.

Gloucestershire

A. W. Stovold not out	72
P. W. Romaines c Richards b Davis ...	79
C. W. J. Athey b Dredge	8
P. Bainbridge not out	9
B 6, l-b 5, w 1, n-b 2	14

1/146 2/166   (2 wkts, 53.2 overs) 182

K. M. Curran, J. W. Lloyds, I. R. Payne, *D. A. Graveney, †R. C. Russell, D. V. Lawrence and C. A. Walsh did not bat.

Bowling: Garner 11–5–16–0; Davis 11–0–55–1; Richards 11–2–28–0; Dredge 10.2–2–35–1; Marks 10–1–37–0.

Umpires: R. Palmer and N. T. Plews.

SUSSEX v ESSEX

At Hove, May 3, 5. Essex won by 18 runs. Toss: Essex. Imran Khan, who reached his hundred off 84 balls, hit his second fifty off 30 balls. Sussex were fined £1,000 for failing by ten overs to achieve the required rate of 55 overs in 205 minutes.
Gold Award: Imran Khan.

Essex

*G. A. Gooch c Green b Jones	73	†D. E. East run out	1
B. R. Hardie not out	119		
A. R. Border b Jones	11	L-b 9, w 12, n-b 7	28
D. R. Pringle c le Roux b Imran	7		
K. W. R. Fletcher c Gould b Imran ...	8	1/139 2/180 3/187 (7 wkts, 55 overs) 277
P. J. Prichard c Barclay b Pigott	15	4/208 5/238
A. W. Lilley run out	15	6/269 7/277

S. Turner, N. A. Foster and J. K. Lever did not bat.

Bowling: le Roux 10–0–50–0; Imran 11–0–46–2; Reeve 10–0–54–0; C. M. Wells 2–0–15–0; Pigott 11–0–53–1; Jones 11–0–50–2.

Sussex

A. M. Green run out	50	A. P. Wells b Pringle	17
*J. R. T. Barclay c East b Lever	9	C. M. Wells not out	23
P. W. G. Parker b Pringle	20	L-b 8, n-b 1	9
Imran Khan not out	112		
†I. J. Gould c Border b Foster	16	1/27 2/82 3/93 (6 wkts, 55 overs) 259
G. S. le Roux b Lever	3	4/124 5/140 6/193

D. A. Reeve, A. C. S. Pigott and A. N. Jones did not bat.

Bowling: Lever 11–2–44–2; Foster 11–0–70–1; Gooch 11–1–48–0; Turner 11–2–42–0; Pringle 11–2–47–2.

Umpires: K. J. Lyons and A. G. T. Whitehead.

GLAMORGAN v SUSSEX

At Swansea, May 10, 12. Sussex won by 5 runs in a match restricted by rain to ten overs a side. Toss: Glamorgan.
Gold Award: G. S. le Roux.

Sussex

Imran Khan not out 48
P. W. G. Parker c Morris b Holmes ... 13
†I. J. Gould run out 25
      B 4, l-b 5, w 3 12

1/30 2/98   (2 wkts, 10 overs) 98

A. M. Green, *J. R. T. Barclay, A. P. Wells, C. P. Phillipson, G. S. le Roux, D. A. Reeve, A. C. S. Pigott and A. N. Jones did not bat.

Bowling: Derrick 2–0–21–0; Holmes 2–0–10–1; Pauline 1–0–18–0; Ontong 1–0–11–0; Thomas 2–0–11–0; Moseley 2–0–18–0.

Glamorgan

J. A. Hopkins c Barclay b le Roux 26	H. Morris not out 7
A. L. Jones c Phillipson b Jones 2	E. A. Moseley not out 9
G. C. Holmes lbw b Imran 29	B 3, l-b 6, w 1, n-b 1 11
M. P. Maynard c Gould b le Roux 0	
J. G. Thomas c Gould b le Roux 0	1/8 2/60 3/61 (6 wkts, 10 overs) 93
*R. C. Ontong run out 9	4/61 5/65 6/83

D. B. Pauline, †T. Davies and J. Derrick did not bat.

Bowling: Reeve 2–0–15–0; Jones 2–0–23–1; Pigott 2–0–23–0; Imran 2–0–10–1; le Roux 2–0–13–3.

Umpires: J. H. Harris and M. J. Kitchen.

SOMERSET v ESSEX

At Taunton, May 10, 12. Essex won by 12 runs. Toss: Somerset.
Gold Award: D. R. Pringle.

Essex

*G. A. Gooch lbw b Garner 16	S. Turner c Dredge b Botham 41
B. R. Hardie c Botham b Dredge 13	N. A. Foster run out 8
P. J. Prichard b Dredge 3	J. K. Lever not out 0
A. R. Border c Richards b Dredge 7	B 1, l-b 16, w 2, n-b 2 21
K. W. R. Fletcher lbw b Dredge 5	
D. R. Pringle c Marks b Botham 65	1/23 2/32 3/42 (55 overs) 206
A. W. Lilley c Richards b Marks 18	4/52 5/55 6/102
†D. E. East c Hardy b Botham 9	7/118 8/190 9/200

Bowling: Garner 11–0–48–1; Botham 11–0–53–3; Taylor 7–1–17–0; Dredge 11–0–30–4; Richards 6–2–19–0; Marks 9–2–22–1.

Somerset

*P. M. Roebuck c East b Turner 26	C. H. Dredge run out 25
N. A. Felton c Lilley b Lever 3	J. Garner not out 14
J. J. E. Hardy c Pringle b Turner 8	N. S. Taylor b Pringle 9
I. V. A. Richards c Lever b Pringle ... 22	L-b 10, w 8, n-b 1 19
I. T. Botham b Foster 41	
R. J. Bartlett lbw b Turner 0	1/8 2/23 3/59 (54 overs) 194
V. J. Marks c Border b Pringle 0	4/69 5/69 6/70
†T. Gard c East b Lever 27	7/119 8/169 9/170

Bowling: Lever 10–2–20–2; Foster 11–1–40–1; Turner 11–2–43–3; Pringle 11–0–42–3; Gooch 11–1–39–0.

Umpires: C. Cook and D. Lloyd.

ESSEX v GLOUCESTERSHIRE

At Chelmsford, May 13. Essex won by 17 runs. Toss: Gloucestershire.
Gold Award: N. A. Foster.

Essex

*G. A. Gooch b Walsh	51	S. Turner c Bainbridge b Lawrence	0
B. R. Hardie c Stovold b Lawrence	4	N. A. Foster not out	4
P. J. Prichard b Bainbridge	52	L-b 14, w 8, n-b 2	24
A. R. Border b Bainbridge	31		
K. W. R. Fletcher c Bainbridge b Walsh	42	1/40 2/79 3/142 (7 wkts, 55 overs) 271	
D. R. Pringle not out	56	4/158 5/245	
†D. E. East c Athey b Lawrence	7	6/260 7/261	

T. D. Topley and J. K. Lever did not bat.

Bowling: Lawrence 11-1-57-3; Walsh 11-0-65-2; Payne 11-2-57-0; Bainbridge 11-1-25-2; Athey 4-0-24-0; Graveney 7-0-29-0.

Gloucestershire

A. W. Stovold c East b Lever	0	D. V. Lawrence c Topley b Turner	5
P. W. Romaines c East b Foster	42	†R. C. Russell b Lever	11
C. W. J. Athey run out	78	C. A. Walsh not out	2
K. M. Curran c Prichard b Foster	47	L-b 10, w 10, n-b 4	24
P. Bainbridge lbw b Foster	9		
I. R. Payne b Turner	0	1/1 2/110 3/181 (9 wkts, 55 overs) 254	
K. P. Tomlins run out	1	4/192 5/193 6/195	
*D. A. Graveney not out	35	7/195 8/203 9/250	

Bowling: Lever 11-1-44-2; Foster 11-1-42-3; Topley 11-1-40-0; Turner 11-0-61-2; Pringle 11-0-57-0.

Umpires: D. O. Oslear and R. A. White.

SOMERSET v GLAMORGAN

At Taunton, May 13. Somerset won by 75 runs. Toss: Somerset. Botham's 126 not out, off 95 balls, included eight 6s and ten 4s.
Gold Award: I. T. Botham.

Somerset

V. J. Marks c Hopkins b Ontong	32	†T. Gard b Thomas	14
*P. M. Roebuck lbw b Thomas	1	C. H. Dredge not out	0
J. J. E. Hardy run out	25	B 3, l-b 2, w 7	12
I. V. A. Richards st Davies b Steele	20		
I. T. Botham not out	126	1/14 2/61 3/64 (7 wkts, 55 overs) 258	
R. J. Harden b Derrick	24	4/97 5/143	
R. J. Bartlett run out	4	6/149 7/244	

J. Garner and N. S. Taylor did not bat.

Bowling: Thomas 11-2-42-2; Base 8-1-70-0; Steele 11-2-41-1; Ontong 11-0-38-1; Holmes 8-0-45-0; Derrick 6-0-17-1.

Glamorgan

J. A. Hopkins c Harden b Botham	 5	†T. Davies b Garner	11
A. L. Jones c Gard b Botham	 0	J. F. Steele not out	6
H. Morris c Taylor b Dredge	 51	S. J. Base c Richards b Taylor	4
G. C. Holmes lbw b Taylor	 30	L-b 9, w 1, n-b 1	11
J. G. Thomas c and b Taylor	 0		
D. B. Pauline lbw b Taylor	 4	1/0 2/9 3/67	(49.5 overs) 183
*R. C. Ontong c Gard b Taylor	 56	4/67 5/77 6/130	
J. Derrick c Taylor b Dredge	 5	7/139 8/171 9/175	

Bowling: Garner 9–2–19–1; Botham 8–3–10–2; Dredge 11–2–56–2; Taylor 10.5–0–51–5; Marks 11–0–38–0.

Umpires: B. Dudleston and P. B. Wight.

ESSEX v GLAMORGAN

At Chelmsford, May 15. Essex won by six wickets. Toss: Glamorgan.
Gold Award: K. W. R. Fletcher.

Glamorgan

J. A. Hopkins lbw b Turner	 31	J. Derrick run out	8
A. L. Jones c Gooch b Topley	 16	†T. Davies lbw b Lever	2
H. Morris c and b Lever	 21	J. F. Steele not out	2
G. C. Holmes c East b Topley	 0	L-b 12, w 3, n-b 3	18
D. B. Pauline b Foster	 15		
*R. C. Ontong not out	 58	1/49 2/58 3/63	(9 wkts, 55 overs) 205
J. G. Thomas c Gooch b Lever	 9	4/88 5/108 6/121	
E. A. Moseley c Gooch b Foster	 25	7/174 8/185 9/190	

Bowling: Lever 11–2–38–3; Foster 11–1–33–2; Pringle 11–0–50–0; Topley 11–2–34–2; Turner 11–3–38–1.

Essex

*G. A. Gooch c Davies b Holmes	 30	D. R. Pringle not out	54
B. R. Hardie c Morris b Steele	 25	B 1, l-b 4, w 3, n-b 3	11
P. J. Prichard b Derrick b Steele	 18		
A. R. Border c Holmes b Steele	 17	1/39 2/78 3/79	(4 wkts, 52 overs) 206
K. W. R. Fletcher not out	 51	4/98	

T. D. Topley, †D. E. East, S. Turner, N. A. Foster and J. K. Lever did not bat.

Bowling: Thomas 9–1–36–0; Moseley 10–2–49–0; Holmes 6–0–24–1; Derrick 5–1–12–0; Ontong 11–1–43–0; Steele 11–2–37–3.

Umpires: R. Julian and M. J. Kitchen.

GLOUCESTERSHIRE v SUSSEX

At Bristol, May 15, 16. Sussex won by seven wickets. Toss: Sussex.
Gold Award: A. N. Jones.

Gloucestershire

A. W. Stovold b Jones	 3	D. V. Lawrence c C. M. Wells b Pigott	4
P. W. Romaines b C. M. Wells	 24	C. A. Walsh lbw b Jones	8
C. W. J. Athey c Gould b Jones	 2	G. E. Sainsbury b le Roux	4
*P. Bainbridge c Gould b Imran	 9	L-b 9, w 3, n-b 6	18
K. M. Curran c Barclay b Pigott	 37		
J. W. Lloyds c Lenham b C. M. Wells	6	1/3 2/7 3/36	(46.1 overs) 134
I. R. Payne not out	 19	4/67 5/92 6/92	
†R. C. Russell c and b Imran	 0	7/96 8/101 9/120	

Bowling: le Roux 6.1–0–14–1; Jones 7–3–14–3; C. M. Wells 11–2–36–2; Imran 11–0–37–2; Pigott 11–5–24–2.

Sussex

N. J. Lenham lbw b Sainsbury 33	C. M. Wells not out 27
A. M. Green c Bainbridge b Lloyds ... 32	B 3, l-b 1, w 3, n-b 8 15
P. W. G. Parker c Lloyds b Walsh 9	
Imran Khan not out 20	1/54 2/83 3/92 (3 wkts, 30.5 overs) 136

*J. R. T. Barclay, A. P. Wells, †I. J. Gould, G. S. le Roux, A. C. S. Pigott and A. N. Jones did not bat.

Bowling: Lawrence 9–0–41–0; Walsh 9–1–40–1; Sainsbury 3.2–1–14–1; Payne 2.3–0–15–0; Lloyds 7–1–22–1.

Umpires: C. Cook and A. A. Jones.

GLAMORGAN v GLOUCESTERSHIRE

At Swansea, May 17, 19. Gloucestershire won by 45 runs. Toss: Glamorgan.
Gold Award: I. R. Payne.

Gloucestershire

A. W. Stovold c Jones b Base 4	*D. A. Graveney not out 25
P. W. Romaines lbw b Thomas 36	D. V. Lawrence not out 4
C. W. J. Athey lbw b Derrick 35	B 4, l-b 6, w 9, n-b 4 23
P. Bainbridge b Derrick 10	
J. W. Lloyds run out 3	1/19 2/59 3/74 (7 wkts, 55 overs) 196
K. M. Curran c Jones b Holmes 16	4/81 5/104
I. R. Payne c Thomas b Base 40	6/138 7/188

†R. C. Russell and C. A. Walsh did not bat.

Bowling: Thomas 11–3–44–1; Base 11–0–34–2; Derrick 11–0–34–2; Ontong 11–5–20–0; Smith 7–0–32–0; Holmes 4–0–22–1.

Glamorgan

J. A. Hopkins b Payne 23	†T. Davies run out 9
A. L. Jones run out 32	I. Smith c Payne b Lloyds 6
H. Morris lbw b Payne 0	S. J. Base not out 4
G. C. Holmes b Payne 0	L-b 9, w 2, n-b 1 12
D. B. Pauline c Russell b Bainbridge . 31	
*R. C. Ontong c and b Lloyds 22	1/62 2/63 3/63 (50.2 overs) 151
J. G. Thomas c and b Lloyds 4	4/66 5/116 6/122
J. Derrick lbw b Walsh 8	7/122 8/139 9/140

Bowling: Walsh 9–4–19–1; Lawrence 4–0–20–0; Payne 11–2–22–3; Bainbridge 10–3–39–1; Graveney 6–1–21–0; Lloyds 10.2–1–21–3.

Umpires: D. Lloyd and R. Palmer.

SUSSEX v SOMERSET

At Hove, May 17, 19. Sussex won by 42 runs. Toss: Somerset.
Gold Award: N. J. Lenham.

Sussex

N. J. Lenham st Gard b Marks	82	D. A. Reeve not out	21
A. M. Green c Gard b Garner	13	A. C. S. Pigott lbw b Botham	21
P. W. G. Parker b Dredge	9	A. N. Jones not out	1
Imran Khan c Gard b Palmer	25	B 1, l-b 6, n-b 3	10
C. M. Wells b Marks	0		
A. P. Wells lbw b Botham	21	1/16 2/55 3/135 (9 wkts, 55 overs) 218	
G. S. le Roux c Gard b Palmer	7	4/135 5/137 6/152	
*†I. J. Gould c Gard b Garner	8	7/169 8/185 9/217	

Bowling: Garner 11–2–34–2; Botham 9–3–44–2; Dredge 10–1–34–1; Taylor 8–0–43–0; Marks 11–1–36–2; Palmer 6–1–20–2.

Somerset

V. J. Marks b Jones	24	C. H. Dredge c Pigott b Jones	3
*P. M. Roebuck hit wkt b Reeve	13	N. S. Taylor b Pigott	1
J. J. E. Hardy b Reeve	11	J. Garner not out	6
I. V. A. Richards c Green b Jones	14		
I. T. Botham c Gould b Pigott	6	B 5, l-b 2, w 1, n-b 3	11
R. J. Harden b Jones	0		
G. V. Palmer c and b le Roux	53	1/31 2/44 3/62 4/64 5/65 (51 overs) 176	
†T. Gard c Imran b Pigott	34	6/75 7/154 8/162 9/165	

Bowling: le Roux 11–1–34–1; Imran 11–2–36–0; Reeve 11–3–32–2; Jones 8–0–32–4; C. M. Wells 1–0–2–0; Pigott 9–2–33–3.

Umpires: J. A. Jameson and R. Julian.

GROUP D

MIDDLESEX v SURREY

At Lord's, May 3. Middlesex won by six wickets. Toss: Middlesex.
  Gold Award: M. W. Gatting.

Surrey

A. R. Butcher c Downton b Gatting	65	S. T. Clarke b Emburey	0
G. S. Clinton lbw b Cowans	47	M. A. Feltham not out	0
A. J. Stewart lbw b Gatting	5	B 1, l-b 11, w 3, n-b 5	20
M. A. Lynch c Radley b Cowans	5		
T. E. Jesty not out	42	1/120 2/130 3/136 (7 wkts, 55 overs) 207	
†C. J. Richards c Gatting b Williams	13	4/137 5/175	
R. J. Doughty b Emburey	10	6/191 7/191	

G. Monkhouse and *P. I. Pocock did not bat.

Bowling: Cowans 11–2–30–2; Daniel 11–0–36–0; Williams 11–2–46–1; Emburey 11–2–35–2; Edmonds 2–0–12–0; Gatting 9–2–36–2.

Middlesex

G. D. Barlow b Monkhouse	30	†P. R. Downton not out	13
W. N. Slack c Butcher b Monkhouse	28	B 1, l-b 4, w 3	8
*M. W. Gatting not out	90		
C. T. Radley c Butcher b Jesty	34	1/61 2/62 3/159 (4 wkts, 53.3 overs) 208	
R. O. Butcher c Butcher b Clarke	10	4/186	

J. E. Emburey, P. H. Edmonds, N. F. Williams, N. G. Cowans and W. W. Daniel did not bat.

Bowling: Clarke 11–2–15–1; Doughty 11–2–40–0; Feltham 10.3–0–54–0; Monkhouse 11–2–35–2; Pocock 4–0–29–0; Jesty 6–0–30–1.

Umpires: J. H. Hampshire and K. E. Palmer.

OXFORD & CAMBRIDGE UNIVS v HAMPSHIRE

At Oxford, May 3. Hampshire won by eight wickets. Toss: Hampshire.
 Gold Award: C. G. Greenidge.

Oxford & Cambridge Univs

P. A. C. Bail lbw b Cowley 59	†A. D. Brown b Connor 7
C. D. M. Tooley b Bakker 15	A. M. G. Scott not out 0
G. J. Toogood b Bakker 3	J. E. Davidson b Connor 0
D. J. Fell lbw b Nicholas 10	L-b 10, w 4 14
D. A. Thorne c Tremlett b Connor 2	
*D. G. Price b Connor 30	1/32 2/45 3/97 (52.5 overs) 146
R. S. Rutnagur b Tremlett 2	4/97 5/102 6/120
A. K. Golding c Greenidge b Nicholas 4	7/134 8/141 9/146

 Bowling: Connor 9.5–0–35–4; Bakker 11–5–19–2; Tremlett 11–0–35–1; Nicholas 10–2–20–2; Cowley 11–2–27–1.

Hampshire

C. G. Greenidge not out 83
V. P. Terry c Thorne b Toogood 20
R. A. Smith c Brown b Scott 0
D. R. Turner not out 40
L-b 4 4

1/45 2/58   (2 wkts, 30 overs) 147

C. L. Smith, *M. C. J. Nicholas, N. G. Cowley, T. M. Tremlett, †R. J. Parks, C. A. Connor and P. J. Bakker did not bat.

 Bowling: Davidson 4–0–12–0; Scott 11–1–44–1; Toogood 8–1–50–1; Golding 4–0–28–0; Thorne 3–0–9–0.

 Umpires: R. Julian and D. R. Shepherd.

HAMPSHIRE v MIDDLESEX

At Southampton, May 10, 12. Middlesex won by seven wickets. Toss: Middlesex. Gatting hit his unbeaten 60 off 30 balls. In a match begun on the first day but later abandoned owing to the weather, Hampshire were 27 for no wicket after six overs in reply to Middlesex's total of 230 for seven off 55 overs.
 Gold Award: M. W. Gatting.

Hampshire

C. G. Greenidge b Cowans 1	D. R. Turner not out 0
R. A. Smith c Gatting b Edmonds ... 37	B 1, l-b 1, w 1 3
V. P. Terry run out 31	
M. D. Marshall run out 2	1/2 2/61 3/73 (5 wkts, 10 overs) 77
*M. C. J. Nicholas run out 3	4/77 5/77

C. L. Smith, N. G. Cowley, T. M. Tremlett, †R. J. Parks and C. A. Connor did not bat.

 Bowling: Cowans 2–0–8–1; Williams 1–0–5–0; Daniel 2–0–18–0; Edmonds 2–0–24–1; Hughes 1–0–10–0; Emburey 2–0–10–0.

Middlesex

W. N. Slack b Connor	5	†P. R. Downton not out	6
C. T. Radley c Cowley b Connor	7	W 2	2
*M. W. Gatting not out	60		
R. O. Butcher run out	0	1/11 2/50 3/50 (3 wkts, 9 overs) 80

J. E. Emburey, P. H. Edmonds, N. F. Williams, S. P. Hughes, N. G. Cowans and W. W. Daniel did not bat.

Bowling: Tremlett 2–0–20–0; Connor 2–0–13–2; Nicholas 2–0–26–0; Cowley 1–0–13–0; Marshall 2–0–8–0.

Umpires: J. A. Jameson and R. Palmer.

KENT v SURREY

At Canterbury, May 10, 12. Surrey won by four wickets. Toss: Surrey.
Gold Award: T. E. Jesty.

Kent

M. R. Benson lbw b Monkhouse	28	E. A. E. Baptiste b Pocock	3
S. G. Hinks c Stewart b Feltham	9	R. M. Ellison not out	6
C. J. Tavaré run out	35	B 2, l-b 6, w 4	12
N. R. Taylor c Richards b Clarke	23		
*C. S. Cowdrey not out	89	1/18 2/60 3/95 (6 wkts, 55 overs) 270
G. R. Cowdrey b Clarke	65	4/107 5/234 6/239

†S. A. Marsh, G. R. Dilley and D. L. Underwood did not bat.

Bowling: Clarke 11–0–35–2; Doughty 8–1–62–0; Feltham 11–3–47–1; Monkhouse 11–2–37–1; Pocock 9–1–41–1; Jesty 5–0–40–0.

Surrey

A. R. Butcher c Marsh b Ellison	1	R. J. Doughty c Marsh b Dilley	30
G. S. Clinton b Baptiste	13	G. Monkhouse not out	2
†C. J. Richards c Tavaré b Hinks	45	L-b 8, w 4, n-b 4	16
M. A. Lynch b Dilley	58		
T. E. Jesty not out	94	1/1 2/49 3/72 (6 wkts, 53.5 overs) 274
A. J. Stewart c Tavaré b Dilley	15	4/180 5/198 6/268

M. A. Feltham, S. T. Clarke and *P. I. Pocock did not bat.

Bowling: Dilley 11–1–41–3; Ellison 10.5–1–48–1; Hinks 7–0–29–1; Baptiste 10–0–54–1; Underwood 8–0–50–0; C. S. Cowdrey 7–0–44–0.

Umpires: J. Birkenshaw and A. A. Jones.

OXFORD & CAMBRIDGE UNIVS v KENT

At Cambridge, May 13. Kent won by eight wickets. Toss: Oxford & Cambridge Univs.
Gold Award: R. M. Ellison.

Oxford & Cambridge Univs

P. A. C. Bail c Hinks b Ellison	3	C. C. Ellison c Marsh b Underwood	1
C. D. M. Tooley c Tavaré b Dilley	8	†A. D. Brown not out	5
D. J. Fell b Penn	3	A. M. G. Scott c Marsh b Ellison	2
G. J. Toogood c Tavaré b Dilley	5		
*D. A. Thorne c Marsh b Penn	1	B 1, l-b 3, w 3, n-b 1	8
D. G. Price c and b Baptiste	13		
R. S. Rutnagur b Ellison	32	1/11 2/14 3/21 4/24 5/25 (38 overs) 81
A. K. Golding c Tavaré b Underwood	0	6/54 7/60 8/66 9/78

Bowling: Dilley 6–1–16–2; Ellison 11–6–11–3; Baptiste 6–1–20–1; Penn 8–2–23–2; Underwood 7–5–7–2.

Kent

M. R. Benson st Brown b Golding 35
S. G. Hinks b Rutnagur 25
*C. J. Tavaré not out 18
N. R. Taylor not out 0
    L-b 5, w 1 6

1/66 2/66   (2 wkts, 29.3 overs) 84

C. Penn, G. R. Cowdrey, E. A. E. Baptiste, R. M. Ellison, †S. A. Marsh, G. R. Dilley and D. L. Underwood did not bat.

Bowling: Toogood 6–3–14–0; Thorne 6–1–13–0; Ellison 3–0–8–0; Scott 4–0–16–0; Golding 5.3–1–20–1; Rutnagur 5–2–8–1.

Umpires: J. A. Jameson and N. T. Plews.

SURREY v HAMPSHIRE

At The Oval, May 13. Hampshire won by three wickets. Toss: Hampshire.
Gold Award: T. M. Tremlett.

Surrey

A. R. Butcher c R. A. Smith b Tremlett 59
†C. J. Richards c Parks b Tremlett 10
A. J. Stewart c R. A. Smith b Tremlett. 25
M. A. Lynch run out 22
T. E. Jesty not out 71
A. Needham c Nicholas b Tremlett ... 8
R. J. Doughty st Parks b Cowley 13

S. T. Clarke b Marshall 4
M. A. Feltham not out 6
    L-b 8, w 12, n-b 1 21

1/26 2/99 3/103   (7 wkts, 55 overs) 239
4/132 5/151
6/191 7/204

G. Monkhouse and *P. I. Pocock did not bat.

Bowling: Marshall 11–1–34–1; Connor 11–1–43–0; Tremlett 11–1–30–4; Cowley 11–0–50–1; Nicholas 11–0–74–0.

Hampshire

C. G. Greenidge lbw b Doughty 58
V. P. Terry c Monkhouse b Doughty .. 32
R. A. Smith c Richards b Pocock 20
C. L. Smith run out 67
*M. C. J. Nicholas run out 1
D. R. Turner c Lynch b Monkhouse ... 21
M. D. Marshall b Pocock 2

N. G. Cowley not out 21
T. M. Tremlett not out 7
    B 2, l-b 5, w 3, n-b 1 11

1/91 2/92 3/128   (7 wkts, 54.2 overs) 240
4/135 5/188
6/195 7/213

†R. J. Parks and C. A. Connor did not bat.

Bowling: Clarke 11–1–36–0; Doughty 8–0–46–2; Feltham 10.2–0–59–0; Monkhouse 11–1–46–1; Pocock 11–2–37–2; Jesty 3–0–9–0.

Umpires: H. D. Bird and M. J. Kitchen.

HAMPSHIRE v KENT

At Southampton, May 15. Kent won by 63 runs. Toss: Hampshire.
Gold Award: G. R. Cowdrey.

Kent

M. R. Benson c Terry b Tremlett	65	E. A. E. Baptiste not out	25
S. G. Hinks c Parks b Connor	2		
C. J. Tavaré c Parks b Nicholas	11	L-b 11, w 2	13
N. R. Taylor c R. A. Smith b Cowley	67		
*C. S. Cowdrey c C. L. Smith b Marshall	7	1/4 2/38 3/148 (5 wkts, 55 overs) 250	
G. R. Cowdrey not out	60	4/154 5/162	

R. M. Ellison, †S. A. Marsh, G. R. Dilley and D. L. Underwood did not bat.

Bowling: Marshall 11–4–25–1; Connor 11–0–51–1; Nicholas 11–0–43–1; Tremlett 11–0–51–1; Cowley 11–0–69–1.

Hampshire

C. G. Greenidge lbw b Ellison	6	T. M. Tremlett not out	36
V. P. Terry b Baptiste	41	†R. J. Parks lbw b Ellison	16
R. A. Smith c and b Baptiste	4	C. A. Connor not out	4
C. L. Smith c Ellison b Underwood	21		
D. R. Turner c Benson b Underwood	1	B 1, l-b 8, w 4	13
*M. C. J. Nicholas c Tavaré b Underwood	7	1/11 2/37 3/77 (9 wkts, 55 overs) 187	
M. D. Marshall c Tavaré b Underwood	33	4/80 5/80 6/90	
N. G. Cowley c Marsh b Dilley	5	7/100 8/147 9/172	

Bowling: Dilley 11–0–40–1; Ellison 11–2–39–2; C. S. Cowdrey 11–1–54–0; Baptiste 11–2–19–2; Underwood 11–2–26–4.

Umpires: D. Lloyd and P. B. Wight.

MIDDLESEX v OXFORD & CAMBRIDGE UNIVS

At Lord's, May 15. Middlesex won by eight wickets. Toss: Middlesex.
Gold Award: C. D. M. Tooley.

Oxford & Cambridge Univs

P. A. C. Bail c and b Edmonds	30	†A. D. Brown b Emburey	2
D. A. Hagan c Emburey b Daniel	10	C. C. Ellison not out	1
D. J. Fell run out	44		
C. D. M. Tooley b Daniel	62	B 3, l-b 14, w 1, n-b 5	23
*D. A. Thorne not out	36		
D. G. Price c Edmonds b Emburey	0	1/25 2/59 3/149 (8 wkts, 55 overs) 209	
R. S. Rutnagur run out	1	4/186 5/187 6/197	
A. K. Golding c Radley b Williams	0	7/199 8/207	

A. M. G. Scott did not bat.

Bowling: Cowans 11–2–27–0; Daniel 11–0–43–2; Edmonds 11–4–32–1; Williams 10–1–37–1; Emburey 11–0–43–2; Gatting 1–0–10–0.

Middlesex

G. D. Barlow c Scott b Rutnagur	48
W. N. Slack b Rutnagur	52
*M. W. Gatting not out	39
C. T. Radley not out	62
L-b 6, w 2, n-b 1	9

1/97 2/117   (2 wkts, 43.3 overs) 210

R. O. Butcher, †P. R. Downton, J. E. Emburey, P. H. Edmonds, N. F. Williams, N. G. Cowans and W. W. Daniel did not bat.

Bowling: Scott 8–1–36–0; Ellison 8–1–30–0; Rutnagur 11–2–31–2; Golding 10–0–71–0; Thorne 6.3–0–36–0.

Umpires: J. Birkenshaw and R. Palmer.

KENT v MIDDLESEX

At Canterbury, May 17, 19. Middlesex won by 134 runs. Toss: Kent.
Gold Award: M. W. Gatting.

Middlesex

G. D. Barlow c C. S. Cowdrey b Jarvis	1	P. H. Edmonds c Baptiste b Jarvis	....	9
W. M. Slack c Tavaré b Baptiste	21	N. G. Cowans not out	....	0
*M. W. Gatting b Hinks	62			
C. T. Radley c Tavaré b Baptiste	48	B 1, l-b 17, w 7, n-b 1	....	26
R. O. Butcher c Ellison b Jarvis	22			
†P. R. Downton not out	53	1/10 2/49 3/138 (8 wkts, 55 overs)		258
J. E. Emburey run out	8	4/153 5/181 6/201		
N. F. Williams c Tavaré b Ellison	8	7/237 8/257		

W. W. Daniel did not bat.

Bowling: Jarvis 11–0–54–3; Ellison 11–2–27–1; C. S. Cowdrey 11–0–49–0; Baptiste 10–0–56–2; Underwood 7–0–39–0; Hinks 5–0–15–1.

Kent

M. R. Benson not out	57	†S. A. Marsh c Emburey b Cowans	...	15
S. G. Hinks b Williams	10	D. L. Underwood b Cowans	....	0
C. J. Tavaré b Cowans	0	K. B. S. Jarvis c Emburey b Edmonds	.	0
N. R. Taylor c sub b Emburey	5	B 2, l-b 3, w 8, n-b 1	....	14
*C. S. Cowdrey c and b Emburey	3			
G. R. Cowdrey b Daniel	13	1/26 2/34 3/49 (42.4 overs)		124
E. A. E. Baptiste c Williams b Daniel	4	4/58 5/83 6/87		
R. M. Ellison c Downton b Daniel	3	7/97 8/123 9/123		

Bowling: Williams 8–0–20–1; Cowans 11–2–26–3; Emburey 11–3–22–2; Daniel 10–1–38–3; Edmonds 2.4–0–13–1.

Umpires: J. H. Hampshire and M. J. Kitchen.

SURREY v OXFORD & CAMBRIDGE UNIVS

At The Oval, May 17, 19. Surrey won by eight wickets. Toss: Oxford & Cambridge Univs.
Gold Award: A. J. Stewart.

Oxford & Cambridge Univs

P. A. C. Bail c Clinton b Monkhouse	.. 40	A. K. Golding not out	....	31
D. A. Hagan lbw b Pocock	 11	†A. D. Brown not out	....	10
D. J. Fell c Richards b Doughty	4			
C. D. M. Tooley c Lynch b Butcher	... 1	B 4, l-b 5, w 3, n-b 7	....	19
*D. A. Thorne lbw b Butcher	 14			
D. G. Price c Butcher b Monkhouse	... 25	1/25 2/31 3/59 (6 wkts, 55 overs)		161
R. S. Rutnagur retired hurt	 6	4/72 5/82 6/136		

C. C. Ellison and A. M. G. Scott did not bat.

Bowling: Gray 11–1–33–0; Doughty 6–1–18–1; Butcher 7–2–23–2; Monkhouse 10–1–41–2; Pocock 11–5–16–1; Needham 10–3–21–0.

Surrey

A. R. Butcher c Golding b Scott 1
G. S. Clinton b Bail 22
A. J. Stewart not out 63
M. A. Lynch not out 68
     B 1, l-b 1, w 3, n-b 3 8

1/6 2/52   (2 wkts, 38.1 overs) 162

T. E. Jesty, †C. J. Richards, A. Needham, R. J. Doughty, G. Monkhouse, A. H. Gray and
*P. I. Pocock did not bat.

Bowling: Scott 9.1–3–26–1; Thorne 5–0–15–0; Golding 11–1–48–0; Bail 4–0–20–1; Ellison
8–0–45–0; Tooley 1–0–6–0.

Umpires: B. Dudleston and N. T. Plews.

QUARTER-FINALS

DERBYSHIRE v KENT

At Derby, May 28. Kent won by four wickets. Toss: Kent. Derbyshire were made to struggle,
especially by Dilley, on a lively pitch in the first session but, importantly, lost only three
wickets. This opened the way for an exciting stand of 91 between Morris and Roberts, Morris
scoring at a run a ball in a fine innings. Derbyshire's total should have been enough to win the
game but Kent also kept wickets in hand for a final assault. The Cowdrey brothers added 56
in seven overs and Warner was expensive at an important stage, being hit for 79 in 58 balls.
Chris Cowdrey, who had earlier taken two wickets, saw Kent to victory with strong support
from Ellison.

Gold Award: C. S. Cowdrey.

Derbyshire

*K. J. Barnett c Hinks b Ellison 8	M. A. Holding run out 4
I. S. Anderson b Baptiste 24	A. E. Warner not out 17
A. Hill c Tavaré b Baptiste 29	B 2, l-b 6, w 6, n-b 5 19
J. E. Morris b C. S. Cowdrey 65	
†B. Roberts b C. S. Cowdrey 43	1/11 2/64 3/79 (6 wkts, 55 overs) 238
G. Miller not out 29	4/170 5/191 6/203

P. G. Newman, R. J. Finney and O. H. Mortensen did not bat.

Bowling: Dilley 11–1–52–0; Ellison 11–1–44–1; Baptiste 11–0–38–2; C. S. Cowdrey
9–0–49–2; Hinks 2–0–10–0; Underwood 11–2–37–0.

Kent

M. R. Benson c Miller b Newman 12	E. A. E. Baptiste b Holding 1
S. G. Hinks c Morris b Finney 41	R. M. Ellison not out 34
C. J. Tavaré b Finney 1	L-b 10, w 2, n-b 3 15
N. R. Taylor c Barnett b Newman 41	
*C. S. Cowdrey not out 63	1/36 2/37 3/65 (6 wkts, 53.4 overs) 242
G. R. Cowdrey b Warner 34	4/136 5/192 6/193

†S. A. Marsh, G. R. Dilley and D. L. Underwood did not bat.

Bowling: Holding 10–2–33–1; Mortensen 11–2–36–0; Finney 11–2–26–2; Newman
9–0–41–2; Miller 3–0–17–0; Warner 9.4–0–79–1.

Umpires: J. Birkenshaw and J. W. Holder.

ESSEX v NOTTINGHAMSHIRE

At Chelmsford, May 28, 29. Nottinghamshire won by three wickets. Toss: Essex. Hadlee, whose unbeaten 61 off 57 deliveries contained three 6s and six 4s, took Nottinghamshire into the semi-finals with a straight 6 off Lever, having come to the crease after Rice had helped rescue the visitors from a precarious position of 39 for three. On the first day Rice had enjoyed most success when Essex batted, finding enough movement to trouble all the batsmen. Gooch produced an admirable spell for Essex before Hadlee decided the tie with a typical flourish.

Gold Award: C. E. B. Rice.

Essex

*G. A. Gooch b Pick	25	S. Turner b Rice	2
B. R. Hardie c Birch b Hadlee	2	N. A. Foster lbw b Rice	0
P. J. Prichard c Randall b Rice	16	J. K. Lever not out	2
A. R. Border b Rice	15	B 1, l-b 12, w 5, n-b 3	21
K. W. R. Fletcher b Hadlee	37		
D. R. Pringle b Rice	35	1/22 2/39 3/59 (9 wkts, 55 overs)	195
K. R. Pont b Rice	24	4/70 5/124 6/163	
†D. E. East not out	16	7/177 8/180 9/180	

Bowling: Hadlee 11–1–30–2; Cooper 11–2–34–0; Pick 11–0–27–2; Rice 11–0–48–5; Hemmings 11–4–43–0.

Nottinghamshire

B. C. Broad c East b Gooch	7	†B. N. French c East b Foster	7
R. T. Robinson c Gooch b Lever	2	E. E. Hemmings not out	2
D. W. Randall c Pringle b Foster	6	L-b 10, w 8, n-b 1	19
*C. E. B. Rice lbw b Gooch	50		
P. Johnson c Gooch b Pringle	22	1/14 2/14 3/39 (7 wkts, 51.1 overs)	196
J. D. Birch lbw b Gooch	20	4/70 5/112	
R. J. Hadlee not out	61	6/125 7/161	

R. A. Pick and K. E. Cooper did not bat.

Bowling: Lever 10.1–1–40–1; Foster 11–1–58–2; Gooch 11–3–26–3; Pringle 10–1–25–1; Turner 9–2–37–0.

Umpires: D. O. Oslear and K. E. Palmer.

MIDDLESEX v SUSSEX

At Lord's, May 28, 29. Middlesex won by 84 runs. Toss: Sussex. The Middlesex openers, having survived Imran's initial burst, were unseated by Reeve as soon as he began, but a foundation had been laid. Gatting and Butcher added 62 in the next eight overs, and Butcher and Radley 44 from nine more. Sussex again bowled their overs slower than required, so incurring a £600 fine, and then thunderstorms allowed them just ten balls on the first day. On the second morning, with the conditions favouring the bowlers, there was only occasional dominance by the batsmen. No sooner was Parker run out than Green and Gould were caught off consecutive balls from Cowans, who bowled his overs straight through, Wells ran himself out, and Imran was left without support.

Gold Award: R. O. Butcher.

Middlesex

G. D. Barlow c Wells b Reeve	14	J. E. Emburey not out	9
W. N. Slack b Reeve	24		
*M. W. Gatting c Barclay b Pigott	42	B 2, l-b 10, w 6, n-b 4	22
R. O. Butcher c and b Pigott	65		
C. T. Radley not out	48	1/46 2/49 3/133 (5 wkts, 55 overs)	256
†P. R. Downton run out	32	4/177 5/244	

P. H. Edmonds, S. P. Hughes, N. G. Cowans and W. W. Daniel did not bat.

Bowling: Imran 11–2–24–0; le Roux 11–2–55–0; Jones 11–0–52–0; Reeve 11–0–54–2; Pigott 11–0–59–2.

Sussex

N. J. Lenham c Downton b Cowans ...	6	*J. R. T. Barclay not out	3
A. M. Green c Edmonds b Cowans ...	33	A. C. S. Pigott c and b Edmonds	2
P. W. G. Parker run out	9	A. N. Jones b Hughes	20
Imran Khan lbw b Daniel	47	L-b 6, w 6, n-b 2	14
†I. J. Gould c Downton b Cowans	0		
C. M. Wells run out	26	1/19 2/51 3/53 (48 overs) 172	
G. S. le Roux b Edmonds	6	4/53 5/108 6/124	
D. A. Reeve b Edmonds	6	7/137 8/146 9/149	

Bowling: Daniel 9–0–41–1; Cowans 11–3–27–3; Hughes 8–1–15–1; Edmonds 11–0–52–3; Emburey 9–0–31–0.

Umpires: D. J. Constant and A. G. T. Whitehead.

WORCESTERSHIRE v NORTHAMPTONSHIRE

At Worcester, May 28, 29. Worcestershire won by eight wickets. Toss: Worcestershire. An unbroken third-wicket stand of 179 in 31 overs between Hick and Smith took Worcestershire to their first semi-final for six years. Hick reached his century off only 88 balls (two 6s, eight 4s) after Worcestershire had resumed at 52 for one on the second morning, needing 182 at 5.27 runs an over. The turning-point came when Hick, on 24, was caught on the boundary by Boyd-Moss off Harper, only for umpire Shepherd to call "no-ball" because Lamb had strayed outside the fielding circle. Northamptonshire's own innings was interrupted four times by the weather on the first day, and after a stand of 120 between Lamb and Harper they lost four wickets in eleven balls.

Gold Award: G. A. Hick.

Northamptonshire

*G. Cook c Hick b Weston	30	N. G. B. Cook not out	14
R. J. Bailey b Radford	6	N. A. Mallender not out	1
R. J. Boyd-Moss c Rhodes b Pridgeon .	31		
A. J. Lamb c D'Oliveira b Inchmore ..	71	B 1, l-b 13, n-b 2	16
R. A. Harper c Hick b Pridgeon	56		
D. J. Capel b Radford	8	1/17 2/66 3/86 (8 wkts, 55 overs) 233	
D. J. Wild run out	0	4/206 5/209 6/210	
†D. Ripley run out	0	7/211 8/231	

A. Walker did not bat.

Bowling: Radford 11–0–58–2; Inchmore 11–2–40–1; Pridgeon 11–0–43–2; Weston 11–3–23–1; Illingworth 6–0–33–0; Patel 5–0–22–0.

Worcestershire

M. J. Weston c Ripley b Walker	15	G. A. Hick not out 103	
D. B. D'Oliveira c Lamb		L-b 8, w 2, n-b 1	11
b N. G. B. Cook .	15		
D. M. Smith not out	90	1/18 2/55 (2 wkts, 52.2 overs) 234	

*P. A. Neale, D. N. Patel, †S. J. Rhodes, R. K. Illingworth, N. V. Radford, J. D. Inchmore and A. P. Pridgeon did not bat.

Bowling: Mallender 9.2–1–40–0; Capel 10–3–35–0; Walker 11–1–52–1; Harper 11–2–42–0; N. G. B. Cook 11–0–57–1.

Umpires: J. H. Harris and D. R. Shepherd.

SEMI-FINALS

MIDDLESEX v NOTTINGHAMSHIRE

At Lord's, June 11, 12. Middlesex won by five wickets. Toss: Middlesex. Play began at 3.00 p.m. on the first day, by which time Middlesex had sorted out several injuries. One who reported fit was Emburey, who had experienced back trouble in the Test match the day before, and he went on to return personal best bowling figures for the competition, including the wickets of Broad and Randall, who had played effectively in their contrasting styles. From 115 for one Nottinghamshire descended without distinction. Daniel's pace defeated Rice and Johnson with successive balls; Emburey held a stinging return catch to remove the danger of Hadlee. As in their quarter-final, Middlesex had to block out a world-class fast bowler and succeeded. However, three quick wickets, then Butcher's dismissal at 155, meant that Radley needed to organise 46 runs from ten overs. He did so in his usual capable fashion.

Gold Award: J. E. Emburey.

Nottinghamshire

B. C. Broad b Emburey	42	R. A. Pick c Miller b Emburey	0
R. T. Robinson b Hughes	2	E. E. Hemmings not out	26
D. W. Randall lbw b Emburey	65		
*C. E. B. Rice b Daniel	0	L-b 7, w 10, n-b 7	24
P. Johnson b Daniel	0		
J. D. Birch not out	28	1/4 2/115 3/118 (8 wkts, 55 overs) 189
R. J. Hadlee c and b Emburey	1	4/120 5/134 6/136
†B. N. French b Fraser	1	7/137 8/140

K. E. Cooper did not bat.

Bowling: Hughes 8–0–36–1; Daniel 11–1–36–2; Edmonds 11–2–30–0; Fraser 11–1–36–1; Emburey 11–2–22–4; Gatting 3–0–22–0.

Middlesex

A. J. T. Miller c Pick b Cooper	27	J. E. Emburey not out	15
W. N. Slack c Randall b Rice	65		
*M. W. Gatting run out	3	L-b 8	8
R. O. Butcher lbw b Hadlee	36		
C. T. Radley not out	36	1/89 2/92 3/119 (5 wkts, 53.2 overs) 193
†P. R. Downton run out	3	4/144 5/155

P. H. Edmonds, S. P. Hughes, A. R. C. Fraser and W. W. Daniel did not bat.

Bowling: Hadlee 11–3–27–1; Cooper 11–4–22–1; Pick 10–1–44–0; Hemmings 11–2–34–0; Rice 10.2–0–58–1.

Umpires: J. Birkenshaw and J. H. Harris.

WORCESTERSHIRE v KENT

At Worcester, June 11. Kent won by 11 runs. Toss: Worcestershire. Tavaré and Taylor put Kent on course with a third-wicket stand of 139 in 25 overs, Taylor scoring his 68 off 75 balls. Having chosen to chase a target, Worcestershire faced an uphill struggle after being restricted to 12 runs from the first eleven overs by Ellison and Jarvis. Hick and Neale kept the contest alive with a stand of 118 in 26 overs, but in successive overs Worcestershire's hopes were dashed. A direct throw from Chris Cowdrey ran out Neale, and then Ellison returned to trap Hick lbw.

Gold Award: N. R. Taylor.

Kent

M. R. Benson st Rhodes b Patel	22	†S. A. Marsh not out	3
S. G. Hinks lbw b Weston	41	D. L. Underwood not out	1
C. J. Tavaré c Rhodes b Radford	68		
N. R. Taylor run out	68	L-b 7, w 4, n-b 1	12
*C. S. Cowdrey b Radford	12		
G. R. Cowdrey b Inchmore	2	1/56 2/66 3/205 (8 wkts, 55 overs)	252
E. A. E. Baptiste run out	21	4/206 5/217 6/221	
R. M. Ellison c Smith b Inchmore	2	7/245 8/248	

K. B. S. Jarvis did not bat.

Bowling: Radford 11–0–62–2; Inchmore 11–1–49–2; Pridgeon 8–1–42–0; Patel 11–1–32–1; Weston 11–1–37–1; Illingworth 3–0–23–0.

Worcestershire

D. N. Patel c G. R. Cowdrey b Jarvis	1	N. V. Radford not out	29
D. B. D'Oliveira c Marsh b Baptiste	18	J. D. Inchmore not out	18
D. M. Smith lbw b Ellison	5	B 2, l-b 10, w 5, n-b 1	18
G. A. Hick lbw b Ellison	72		
*P. A. Neale run out	53	1/1 2/10 3/38 (7 wkts, 55 overs)	241
†S. J. Rhodes c Tavaré b Underwood	4	4/156 5/162	
M. J. Weston run out	23	6/171 7/205	

R. K. Illingworth and A. P. Pridgeon did not bat.

Bowling: Ellison 11–3–49–2; Jarvis 11–4–28–1; Underwood 11–1–56–1; Baptiste 11–1–56–1; C. S. Cowdrey 11–0–40–0.

Umpires: B. Leadbeater and B. J. Meyer.

FINAL

KENT v MIDDLESEX

At Lord's, July 12. Middlesex won by 2 runs. A dramatic finish, in murky light and heavy rain, was adequate compensation for a match which, though tightly fought, had been a somewhat dull affair until late in the day. Put in on a morning humid after heavy overnight rain, Middlesex had in fact the better of the conditions, though it was only Kent's tardy over-rate (four overs beyond the time allowed) which sentenced their batsmen to darkness visible. The ball swung extravagantly throughout, as the number of wides indicates.

The successive dismissals of Gatting and Butcher by Ellison in the fifteenth over arrested Middlesex just when they needed to accelerate, and with only 10 runs coming from the next seven overs, they were 89 for four at lunch after 35 overs. As so often, Radley's method and Downton's running, plus some vigorous hitting from Emburey and Edmonds, saw them set a challenging target. Daniel, in a hostile opening spell, made sure it remained so. When Taylor was without a run in the 25 minutes before tea, taken at 5.50 p.m., Kent at 71 for four were in need of something special. Graham Cowdrey and Baptiste provided it with a partnership full of courageous strokeplay and hard running. In the dark, damp evening, the game came alive. Daniel's return for the 46th over (116 for five) brought an offer from the umpires to go off: it was turned down. When Baptiste was bowled, Ellison took up the attack with bold, straight hitting. Kent needed 31 runs from the last three overs but the dismissal of Cowdrey in the first of them was the turning-point. Edmonds came back to bowl the penultimate over, dismissed Ellison and gave away just 5 runs, leaving 14 to be scored off the 55th over. Hughes, despite Marsh's 6, kept his head and his line.

Gold Award: J. E. Emburey.

Attendance: 19,316 (excluding members); *receipts*: £258,510.

Middlesex

W. N. Slack b Dilley	0	P. H. Edmonds not out	15
A. J. T. Miller c Marsh b C. S. Cowdrey	37	S. P. Hughes not out	4
*M. W. Gatting c Marsh b Ellison	25	L-b 8, w 11, n-b 4	23
R. O. Butcher c Marsh b Ellison	0		
C. T. Radley run out	54	1/6 2/66 3/66 (7 wkts, 55 overs)	199
†P. R. Downton lbw b Ellison	13	4/85 5/131	
J. E. Emburey b Baptiste	28	6/163 7/183	

N. G. Cowans and W. W. Daniel did not bat.

Bowling: Dilley 11–2–19–1; Baptiste 11–0–61–1; C. S. Cowdrey 11–0–48–1; Ellison 11–2–27–3; Underwood 11–4–36–0.

Kent

M. R. Benson c Downton b Cowans	1	†S. A. Marsh not out	14
S. G. Hinks lbw b Cowans	13	G. R. Dilley not out	4
C. J. Tavaré c Downton b Daniel	3		
N. R. Taylor c Miller b Edmonds	19	L-b 9, w 8	17
*C. S. Cowdrey c Emburey b Hughes	19		
G. R. Cowdrey c Radley b Hughes	58	1/17 2/20 3/20 (8 wkts, 55 overs)	197
E. A. E. Baptiste b Edmonds	20	4/62 5/72 6/141	
R. M. Ellison b Edmonds	29	7/178 8/182	

D. L. Underwood did not bat.

Bowling: Cowans 9–2–18–2; Daniel 11–1–43–1; Gatting 4–0–18–0; Hughes 9–2–35–2; Emburey 11–5–16–0; Edmonds 11–1–58–3.

Umpires: D. J. Constant and D. R. Shepherd.

BENSON AND HEDGES CUP RECORDS

Highest individual scores: 198 not out, G. A. Gooch, Essex v Sussex, Hove 1982; 173 not out, C. G. Greenidge, Hampshire v Minor Counties (South), Amersham, 1973; 158 not out, B. F. Davison, Leicestershire v Warwickshire, Coventry, 1972. (129 hundreds have been scored in the competition.)

Highest totals in 55 overs: 350 for three, Essex v Oxford & Cambridge Univs, Chelmsford, 1979; 327 for four, Leicestershire v Warwickshire, Coventry, 1972; 327 for two, Essex v Sussex, Hove, 1982; 321 for one, Hampshire v Minor Counties (South), Amersham, 1973.

Highest total by a side batting second: 291 for five (53.5 overs), Warwickshire v Lancashire, Manchester, 1981.

Highest match aggregate: 593 for fourteen wickets, Gloucestershire (282) v Hampshire (311-4), Bristol, 1974.

Lowest totals: 56 in 26.2 overs, Leicestershire v Minor Counties, Wellington, 1982; 59 in 34 overs, Oxford & Cambridge Univs v Glamorgan, Cambridge, 1983; 60 in 26 overs, Sussex v Middlesex, Hove, 1978; 62 in 26.5 overs, Gloucestershire v Hampshire, Bristol, 1975.

Best bowling: Seven for 12, W. W. Daniel, Middlesex v Minor Counties (East), Ipswich, 1978; seven for 22, J. R. Thomson, Middlesex v Hampshire, Lord's, 1981; seven for 32, R. G. D. Willis, Warwickshire v Yorkshire, Birmingham, 1981.

Hat-tricks: G. D. McKenzie, Leicestershire v Worcestershire, Worcester, 1972; K. Higgs, Leicestershire v Surrey in the final, Lord's, 1974; A. A. Jones, Middlesex v Essex, Lord's 1977; M. J. Procter, Gloucestershire v Hampshire, Southampton, 1977; W. Larkins, Northamptonshire v Oxford & Cambridge Univs, Northampton, 1980; E. A. Moseley, Glamorgan v Kent, Cardiff, 1981; G. C. Small, Warwickshire v Leicestershire, Leicester, 1984.

Record partnership for each wicket

241 for 1st	S. M. Gavaskar and B. C. Rose, Somerset v Kent at Canterbury ...	1980
285* for 2nd	C. G. Greenidge and D. R. Turner, Hampshire v Minor Counties (South) at Amersham	1973
268* for 3rd	G. A. Gooch and K. W. R. Fletcher, Essex v Sussex at Hove	1982
184* for 4th	D. Lloyd and B. W. Reidy, Lancashire v Derby at Chesterfield	1980
160 for 5th	A. J. Lamb and D. J. Capel, Northamptonshire v Leicestershire at Northampton	1986
114 for 6th	Majid Khan and G. P. Ellis, Glamorgan v Gloucestershire at Bristol	1975
149* for 7th	J. D. Love and C. M. Old, Yorkshire v Scotland at Bradford	1981
109 for 8th	R. E. East and N. Smith, Essex v Northamptonshire at Chelmsford.	1977
83 for 9th	P. G. Newman and M. A. Holding, Derbyshire v Nottinghamshire at Nottingham	1985
80* for 10th	D. L. Bairstow and M. Johnson, Yorkshire v Derbyshire at Derby ..	1981

WINNERS 1972-86

1972 LEICESTERSHIRE beat Yorkshire by five wickets.
1973 KENT beat Worcestershire by 39 runs.
1974 SURREY beat Leicestershire by 27 runs.
1975 LEICESTERSHIRE beat Middlesex by five wickets.
1976 KENT beat Worcestershire by 43 runs.
1977 GLOUCESTERSHIRE beat Kent by 64 runs.
1978 KENT beat Derbyshire by six wickets.
1979 ESSEX beat Surrey by 35 runs.
1980 NORTHAMPTONSHIRE beat Essex by 6 runs.
1981 SOMERSET beat Surrey by seven wickets.
1982 SOMERSET beat Nottinghamshire by nine wickets.
1983 MIDDLESEX beat Essex by 4 runs.
1984 LANCASHIRE beat Warwickshire by six wickets.
1985 LEICESTERSHIRE beat Essex by five wickets.
1986 MIDDLESEX beat Kent by 2 runs.

WINS BY OXFORD AND CAMBRIDGE UNIVERSITIES

1973 OXFORD beat Northamptonshire at Northampton by two wickets.
1975 OXFORD & CAMBRIDGE beat Worcestershire at Cambridge by 66 runs.
1975 OXFORD & CAMBRIDGE beat Northamptonshire at Oxford by three wickets.
1976 OXFORD & CAMBRIDGE beat Yorkshire at Barnsley by seven wickets.
1984 OXFORD & CAMBRIDGE beat Gloucestershire at Bristol by 27 runs.

WINS BY MINOR COUNTIES AND SCOTLAND

1980 MINOR COUNTIES beat Gloucestershire at Chippenham by 3 runs.
1981 MINOR COUNTIES beat Hampshire at Southampton by 3 runs.
1982 MINOR COUNTIES beat Leicestershire at Wellington by 131 runs.
1986 SCOTLAND beat Lancashire at Perth by 3 runs.

JOHN PLAYER LEAGUE, 1986

In its eighteenth and final season, the John Player League was won for a third time by Hampshire, champions previously in 1975 and 1978. From late in June they were always one of the front-runners – Essex, Nottinghamshire and Northamptonshire were the others – and had at least one game in hand until the penultimate Sunday, when they beat Surrey at The Oval to claim the John Player Trophy. They were then four points clear of Essex, and even if they had lost their last match and Essex won theirs at Chelmsford, Hampshire would still have been champions by virtue of one more away win. As it was, they beat Lancashire by eight wickets at Southampton to head the table with 50 points.

Essex fought hard to retain the title, taking up the running from Northamptonshire by beating them on August 17 as Hampshire were losing to Middlesex. But the following week Essex lost at home to lowly-placed Surrey and Hampshire began the sequence of victories that made them champions. Essex finished as runners-up, followed by Nottinghamshire, whose defeat of Northamptonshire on the final Sunday enabled Sussex to partake of the prizemoney for the fifth consecutive season. Northamptonshire had gone to the top of the table on August 10, having shared two points with Somerset at Wellingborough School where, before the rain fell, I. T. Botham struck thirteen 6s to beat C. G. Greenidge and G. B. Stevenson's record for the Sunday League. However, three defeats in Northamptonshire's last four games allowed Sussex, who won their last three, to edge them out of fourth place.

Seven counties failed to win the John Player League in its eighteen seasons: Derbyshire, Glamorgan, Gloucestershire, Middlesex, Northamptonshire, Nottinghamshire and Surrey. The John Player Trophy, which Hampshire

Continued over.

JOHN PLAYER LEAGUE

		P	W	L	T	NR	Pts	6s	4W	Away Wins
1	Hampshire (3)	15	12	3	0	1	50	37	5	6
2	Essex (1)	16	11	4	0	1	46	37	3	5
3	Nottinghamshire (12) ..	15	10	5	0	1	42	23	5	5
4	Sussex (2)	16	10	6	0	0	40	28	6	6
5	Northamptonshire (5) .	15	9	5	0	2	40	33	2	2
6	Somerset (10)	16	8	6	0	2	36	61	1	3
	Kent (10)	14	7	5	1	3	36	18	5	4
8	Yorkshire (6)	15	7	6	1	2	34	26	3	2
	Derbyshire (4)	16	7	9	0	0	28	35	0	3
9	Warwickshire (6)	15	5	7	2	2	28	13	1	3
	Middlesex (12)	14	5	7	1	3	28	10	1	2
	Lancashire (14)	16	6	9	0	1	26	29	0	1
12	Glamorgan (14)	15	6	9	0	1	26	19	4	1
	Surrey (17)	15	5	8	1	2	26	20	2	2
15	Leicestershire (6)	15	5	10	0	1	22	18	4	0
16	Worcestershire (16) ...	16	5	11	0	0	20	21	2	1
17	Gloucestershire (6)	14	3	11	0	2	16	8	0	1

1985 positions in brackets.

No play was possible in the following seven matches: August 3 – Gloucestershire v Hampshire, Kent v Leicestershire, Middlesex v Northamptonshire, Nottinghamshire v Glamorgan, Warwickshire v Surrey. August 10 – Gloucestershire v Middlesex. September 14 – Kent v Yorkshire.

hold until the end of the 1987 season, will be donated by the sponsors for permanent display in the Memorial Gallery at Lord's.

Third-placed Nottinghamshire provided the season's leading batsman, B. C. Broad (701 runs), and bowler, C. E. B. Rice, whose 34 wickets equalled the record for the most wickets in a season set by R. J. Clapp of Somerset in 1974. Rice's feat of taking four or more wickets in a match five times in 1986 was without parallel in the history of the League. A. N. Jones's seven for 41 for Sussex against Nottinghamshire was the season's best return, and the fourth best ever, while Botham's 175 not out against Northamptonshire was the highest score of 1986. He was just 1 run short of G. A. Gooch's John Player League record and his final total of 23 6s was only three short of the record 26 hit by I. V. A. Richards in 1977.

The last season of John Player's sponsorship saw several century landmarks reached. Greenidge, two weeks after losing his share of the 6-hitting record to Botham, scored his tenth hundred, leaving on nine the South Africans, K. E. McEwan and B. A. Richards. He also, in the course of 1986, played his 100th consecutive Sunday League innings without being dismissed without scoring, a unique achievement. K. W. R. Fletcher, deputising for Gooch as captain of Essex, became the first player to lead a county to 100 wins, while J. F. Steele, the League's leading catcher, took his total to 101.

Four batsmen scored more than 6,000 runs in the John Player League: D. L. Amiss of Warwickshire (6,861), C. T. Radley of Middlesex (6,536), G. M. Turner of Worcestershire (6,144) and Hampshire's Greenidge (6,049). There were three bowlers with 300 wickets: D. L. Underwood of Kent (344), J. K. Lever of Essex (344) and S. Turner of Essex (303). Turner, who also scored 3,165 runs and held 82 catches, was the League's leading all-rounder. Of the wicket-keepers, R. W. Taylor of Derbyshire made 236 dismissals (187 ct, 49 st), E. W. Jones of Glamorgan 223 (184 ct, 39 st), A. P. E. Knott of Kent 218 (183 ct, 35 st) and D. L. Bairstow of Yorkshire 215 (196 ct, 19 st). Radley (88) and R. E. East of Essex (85) came closest to Steele in the list of catches by a fieldsman. J. Simmons of Lancashire, with 261 appearances, played in the most John Player League games.

DISTRIBUTION OF PRIZEMONEY

The total prizemoney was £73,450.

£19,000 and John Player Trophy: HAMPSHIRE.
£9,500 to runners-up: ESSEX.
£4,250 for third place: NOTTINGHAMSHIRE.
£2,500 for fourth place: SUSSEX.
£275 each match to the winners – shared if tied or no result.

Batting award: £400 to I. T. Botham (Somerset) who hit 23 6s in the season.

Other leading 6-hitters:

15 – I. V. A. Richards (Somerset).
11 – C. G. Greenidge (Hampshire).
10 – C. H. Lloyd (Lancashire), C. E. B. Rice (Nottinghamshire), R. A. Smith (Hampshire).
 9 – G. A. Gooch (Essex), P. W. G. Parker (Sussex), B. Roberts (Derbyshire).
 8 – A. J. Lamb (Northamptonshire), A. E. Warner (Derbyshire).
 7 – A. R. Border (Essex), R. A. Harper (Northamptonshire), L. Potter (Leicestershire),
     P. E. Robinson (Yorkshire).

In all, 445 6s were hit in the League in 1986.

Fastest televised match fifty
49 balls – C. T. Radley, Middlesex v Somerset, Taunton, May 11, and A. P. Wells, Sussex v Glamorgan, Hove, July 13.

Bowling award: £400 to C. E. B. Rice (Nottinghamshire) who took four wickets or more in an innings on five occasions.

E. A. E. Baptiste (Kent) took four wickets in an innings four times and P. A. J. DeFreitas (Leicestershire), N. A. Foster (Essex), A. N. Jones (Sussex) and K. D. James (Hampshire) twice. 27 players each took four wickets in an innings once.

DERBYSHIRE

At Leicester, May 4. DERBYSHIRE lost to LEICESTERSHIRE by 19 runs.

DERBYSHIRE v SUSSEX

At Derby, May 11. Derbyshire won by eight wickets. Toss: Sussex. Barnett and Morris established a new Derbyshire record for the competition of 132 unbroken for the third wicket.

Sussex

A. M. Green b Finney 22	C. P. Phillipson not out 12
P. W. G. Parker b Finney 22	D. A. Reeve not out 2
Imran Khan b Holding 55	L-b 13, w 6, n-b 1 20
A. P. Wells c Newman b Mortensen ... 23	
†I. J. Gould c and b Holding 2	1/40 2/56 3/105 (6 wkts, 40 overs) 163
G. S. le Roux lbw b Holding 5	4/111 5/120 6/161

*J. R. T. Barclay, A. N. Jones and A. C. S. Pigott did not bat.

Bowling: Newman 4-0-14-0; Mortensen 8-0-37-1; Finney 8-1-20-2; Miller 8-1-16-0; Holding 8-1-37-3; Warner 4-0-26-0.

Derbyshire

*K. J. Barnett not out 74	
I. S. Anderson c Gould b le Roux 11	
A. Hill c Gould b Jones 4	
J. E. Morris not out 66	
L-b 7, w 2 9	

1/15 2/32   (2 wkts, 37.3 overs) 164

†B. Roberts, G. Miller, P. G. Newman, M. A. Holding, R. J. Finney, A. E. Warner and O. H. Mortensen did not bat.

Bowling: le Roux 7-0-27-1; Jones 8-1-28-1; Imran 8-1-16-0; Reeve 6-0-32-0; Pigott 6.3-0-34-0; Barclay 2-0-20-0.

Umpires: D. O. Oslear and K. E. Palmer.

DERBYSHIRE v WARWICKSHIRE

At Leek, May 18. Warwickshire won by five wickets. Toss: Warwickshire.

Derbyshire

*K. J. Barnett c McMillan b Munton . .	23	R. J. Finney b McMillan	16
I. S. Anderson run out	11	A. E. Warner not out	3
A. Hill b McMillan.	43	O. H. Mortensen b Gifford	1
J. E. Morris run out	13	B 1, l-b 7, w 4, n-b 2	14
†B. Roberts lbw b Munton	8		
G. Miller lbw b Gifford	0	1/24 2/54 3/76 　　　　　(38.4 overs) 132	
M. A. Holding b Parsons	0	4/92 5/103 6/104	
R. Sharma b McMillan	0	7/106 8/128 9/129	

Bowling: Small 7–1–20–0; McMillan 8–2–22–3; Parsons 8–0–33–1; Munton 8–0–34–2; Gifford 7.4–1–15–2.

Warwickshire

T. A. Lloyd run out	1	P. A. Smith not out	1
D. L. Amiss c Roberts b Mortensen . . .	4		
G. J. Lord lbw b Finney	6	B 6, l-b 9, w 9, n-b 2	26
B. M. McMillan not out	37		
†G. W. Humpage c Miller b Mortensen	25	1/1 2/15 3/15 　　　　(5 wkts, 39 overs) 133	
Asif Din lbw b Warner	33	4/70 5/131	

G. J. Parsons, G. C. Small, T. A. Munton and *N. Gifford did not bat.

Bowling: Holding 8–2–18–0; Finney 7–2–20–1; Mortensen 8–0–32–2; Miller 8–1–22–0; Warner 6–0–15–1; Sharma 2–0–11–0.

Umpires: A. A. Jones and P. B. Wight.

DERBYSHIRE v ESSEX

At Derby, June 1. Essex won by eight wickets. Toss: Essex. The match was reduced to 30 overs a side after rain had interrupted Derbyshire's innings at 55 for four.

Derbyshire

*K. J. Barnett c East b Foster	5	P. G. Newman lbw b Foster	1
I. S. Anderson b Foster	2	R. J. Finney not out	13
A. Hill c East b Foster	2		
J. E. Morris c Border b Gooch	13	L-b 1, w 3	4
†B. Roberts not out	53		
G. Miller b Foster	11	1/7 2/8 3/20 4/35 　　(7 wkts, 30 overs) 108	
M. A. Holding c Foster b Lever	4	5/60 6/65 7/69	

P. E. Russell and O. H. Mortensen did not bat.

Bowling: Foster 8–3–17–5; Lever 8–2–30–1; Pringle 6–0–30–0; Gooch 4–0–8–1; Acfield 4–0–22–0.

Essex

*G. A. Gooch not out	50
B. R. Hardie c and b Holding	5
A. R. Border c Roberts b Holding	10
D. R. Pringle not out	32
B 1, l-b 7, w 4, n-b 2	14

1/21 2/39 　　　　　(2 wkts, 26 overs) 111

K. W. R. Fletcher, P. J. Prichard, A. W. Lilley, D. L. Acfield, †D. E. East, N. A. Foster and J. K. Lever did not bat.

Bowling: Holding 8–2–29–2; Mortensen 8–1–29–0; Newman 5–1–20–0; Finney 5–0–25–0.

Umpires: D. J. Constant and J. A. Jameson.

At The Oval, June 8. DERBYSHIRE beat SURREY by three wickets.

At Gloucester, June 15. DERBYSHIRE beat GLOUCESTERSHIRE by five wickets.

DERBYSHIRE v KENT

At Derby, July 6. Kent won by 11 runs. Toss: Kent.

Kent

D. G. Aslett c Roberts b Mortensen ...	18	†S. A. Marsh b Warner	8
S. G. Hinks c Hill b Jean-Jacques	10	G. R. Dilley not out	1
C. J. Tavaré c Roberts b Mortensen ..	38		
N. R. Taylor retired hurt	75	B 5, l-b 3, w 4, n-b 5	17
*C. S. Cowdrey c Sharma b Warner ...	31		
G. R. Cowdrey c Malcolm b Warner ..	6	1/24 2/42 3/89 (7 wkts, 40 overs)	225
E. A. E. Baptiste b Malcolm	6	4/182 5/194	
R. M. Ellison not out	15	6/203 7/222	

D. L. Underwood did not bat.

Bowling: Jean-Jacques 8-0-42-1; Malcolm 8-0-47-1; Miller 8-0-39-0; Mortensen 8-2-26-2; Sharma 2-0-25-0; Warner 6-0-38-3.

Derbyshire

*K. J. Barnett lbw b C. S. Cowdrey ...	71	R. Sharma b Ellison	27
I. S. Anderson b Dilley	2	A. E. Warner not out	1
A. Hill b Underwood	5	B 2, l-b 8, w 3, n-b 3	16
J. E. Morris b C. S. Cowdrey	52		
†B. Roberts c Hinks b C. S. Cowdrey .	18	1/13 2/34 3/113 (6 wkts, 40 overs)	214
G. Miller not out	22	4/140 5/163 6/211	

O. H. Mortensen, M. Jean-Jacques and D. E. Malcolm did not bat.

Bowling: Dilley 8-0-35-1; Ellison 8-0-37-1; Baptiste 8-0-40-0; Underwood 8-0-49-1; C. S. Cowdrey 8-0-43-3.

Umpires: B. Leadbeater and K. J. Lyons.

At Finedon, July 13. DERBYSHIRE lost to NORTHAMPTONSHIRE by 97 runs.

DERBYSHIRE v MIDDLESEX

At Derby, July 20. Derbyshire won by seven wickets. Toss: Middlesex.

Middlesex

W. N. Slack c Barnett b Miller	24	P. H. Edmonds not out	14
A. J. T. Miller c Roberts b Miller	14	S. P. Hughes c Roberts b Warner	7
N. R. C. MacLaurin c Holding b Roberts	3	N. G. Cowans not out	4
C. T. Radley run out	30	B 1, l-b 8, w 2	11
J. D. Carr b Mortensen	12		
†P. R. Downton c Maher b Warner ...	40	1/39 2/43 3/54 (8 wkts, 40 overs)	161
*J. E. Emburey retired hurt	0	4/74 5/131 6/135	
G. D. Rose b Holding	2	7/141 8/154	

Bowling: Mortensen 8-0-33-1; Holding 8-1-22-1; Warner 8-0-36-2; Miller 8-1-22-2; Roberts 8-0-39-1.

Derbyshire

*K. J. Barnett not out	85	B. J. M. Maher not out	11
†C. Marples c Downton b Rose	1	L-b 3, w 6, n-b 1	10
A. Hill c Downton b Rose	2		
B. Roberts b Cowans	55	1/10 2/28 3/136 (3 wkts, 39 overs) 164	

J. E. Morris, G. Miller, M. A. Holding, A. E. Warner, I. S. Anderson and O. H. Mortensen did not bat.

Bowling: Rose 8-0-31-2; Cowans 8-0-28-1; Hughes 4-0-24-0; Slack 4-0-21-0; Edmonds 8-1-25-0; Carr 7-0-32-0.

Umpires: J. Birkenshaw and R. Julian.

At Ebbw Vale, July 27. DERBYSHIRE lost to GLAMORGAN by 4 runs.

DERBYSHIRE v LANCASHIRE

At Buxton, August 10. Derbyshire won by three wickets. Toss: Derbyshire.

Lancashire

G. D. Mendis b Holding	2	I. D. Austin c Sharma b Holding	4
G. Fowler c Barnett b Finney	17	†C. Maynard not out	13
J. Abrahams c Roberts b Finney	3	L-b 12, w 3, n-b 4	19
*C. H. Lloyd c Morris b Warner	22		
N. H. Fairbrother not out	52	1/9 2/23 3/31 (6 wkts, 40 overs) 149	
D. P. Hughes b Warner	17	4/66 5/104 6/121	

J. Simmons, D. J. Makinson and S. Henriksen did not bat.

Bowling: Mortensen 8-1-28-0; Holding 8-1-30-2; Finney 8-0-23-2; Sharma 8-1-24-0; Warner 8-0-32-2.

Derbyshire

*K. J. Barnett lbw b Simmons	12	A. E. Warner b Makinson	2
C. Marples c Maynard b Makinson	2	R. Sharma not out	7
A. Hill run out	6	B 1, l-b 6, w 4, n-b 2	13
J. E. Morris run out	5		
B. Roberts not out	60	1/3 2/26 3/33 (7 wkts, 39.4 overs) 155	
†B. J. M. Maher lbw b Abrahams	21	4/37 5/99	
M. A. Holding c Mendis b Simmons	27	6/137 7/141	

R. J. Finney and O. H. Mortensen did not bat.

Bowling: Henriksen 4-0-7-0; Makinson 8-2-22-2; Austin 8-1-25-0; Simmons 7.4-2-41-2; Abrahams 8-1-24-1; Hughes 4-0-29-0.

Umpires: H. D. Bird and R. A. White.

DERBYSHIRE v YORKSHIRE

At Chesterfield, August 17. Derbyshire won by ten wickets. Toss: Derbyshire.

Yorkshire

M. D. Moxon c Sharma b Holding	10	S. J. Dennis b Holding	1
A. A. Metcalfe lbw b Mortensen	1	C. Shaw not out	4
S. N. Hartley b Mortensen	13	S. D. Fletcher not out	2
P. E. Robinson c Miller b Mortensen	5	B 3, w 4, n-b 3	10
J. D. Love c Holding b Finney	10		
*†D. L. Bairstow c Roberts b Warner	4	1/11 2/11 3/20 (9 wkts, 40 overs) 132	
P. Carrick c Finney b Holding	36	4/33 5/44 6/61	
P. J. Hartley run out	35	7/109 8/116 9/129	

Bowling: Mortensen 8–4–18–3; Holding 8–1–16–3; Finney 8–1–40–1; Warner 8–0–37–1; Miller 8–1–18–0.

Derbyshire
*K. J. Barnett not out 72
A. Hill not out 47
　　　L-b 5, w 3, n-b 8 16

　　　　(no wkt, 28.1 overs) 135

†B. J. M. Mayer, J. E. Morris, B. Roberts, G. Miller, R. Sharma, M. A. Holding, A. E. Warner, R. J. Finney and O. H. Mortensen did not bat.

Bowling: Dennis 8–0–42–0; P. J. Hartley 8–0–24–0; Shaw 6.1–1–42–0; Fletcher 6–0–22–0.

Umpires: A. A. Jones and B. J. Meyer.

At Nottingham, August 24. DERBYSHIRE lost to NOTTINGHAMSHIRE by 23 runs.

DERBYSHIRE v HAMPSHIRE

At Heanor, August 31. Hampshire won by 73 runs. Toss: Derbyshire.

Hampshire
C. G. Greenidge b Roberts 51	N. G. Cowley not out 5
V. P. Terry lbw b Finney 1	T. M. Tremlett not out 4
R. A. Smith c Morris b Holding .. 95	L-b 11, w 4, n-b 2 17
*M. C. J. Nicholas b Warner 6	
C. L. Smith c Warner b Holding 73	1/5 2/75 3/104 (6 wkts, 40 overs) 257
M. D. Marshall c Warner b Holding .. 5	4/219 5/244 6/249

K. D. James, †R. J. Parks and C. A. Connor did not bat.

Bowling: Holding 8–2–29–3; Finney 8–0–51–1; Miller 2–0–26–0; Mortensen 8–0–53–0; Roberts 6–0–28–1; Warner 8–0–59–1.

Derbyshire
*K. J. Barnett c Terry b James 6	R. Sharma c James b Connor 37
A. Hill run out 17	R. J. Finney c and b Connor 2
J. E. Morris lbw b Connor 6	O. H. Mortensen not out 1
B. Roberts c Greenidge b Cowley 6	L-b 11, n-b 5 16
†B. J. M. Maher lbw b Cowley 21	
G. Miller c R. A. Smith b Cowley 1	1/12 2/29 3/30 (32.5 overs) 184
A. E. Warner c Terry b Connor 68	4/42 5/52 6/69
M. A. Holding b Marshall 3	7/104 8/179 9/183

Bowling: James 8–0–32–1; Connor 6.5–0–25–4; Cowley 8–1–48–3; Marshall 6–0–33–1; Tremlett 4–0–35–0.

Umpires: A. A. Jones and P. B. Wight.

At Worcester, September 7. DERBYSHIRE beat WORCESTERSHIRE by one wicket.

At Taunton, September 14. DERBYSHIRE lost to SOMERSET by three wickets.

ESSEX

ESSEX v WARWICKSHIRE

At Chelmsford, May 4. Essex won by 47 runs. Toss: Essex. The unbroken fifth-wicket stand of 185 in 25 overs between Asif Din and McMillan of Warwickshire was a new record for the competition.

Essex

*G. A. Gooch c Lord b Parsons	100	P. J. Prichard not out	6
B. R. Hardie c Lloyd b Parsons	95	L-b 16, w 4, n-b 3	23
A. R. Border b Small	40		
D. R. Pringle not out	16	1/184 2/240 3/261 (4 wkts, 40 overs) 284	
K. W. R. Fletcher b McMillan	4	4/270	

A. W. Lilley, S. Turner, †D. E. East, N. A. Foster and J. K. Lever did not bat.

Bowling: McMillan 8–0–56–1; Small 8–0–30–1; Munton 8–0–43–0; Parsons 8–0–67–2; Gifford 7–0–51–0; Smith 1–0–21–0.

Warwickshire

T. A. Lloyd run out	8	Asif Din not out	108
D. L. Amiss c Prichard b Foster	0	L-b 15, w 2	17
†G. W. Humpage b Gooch	23		
G. J. Lord b Gooch	3	1/4 2/12 3/20 (4 wkts, 40 overs) 237	
B. M. McMillan not out	78	4/52	

P. A. Smith, G. J. Parsons, *N. Gifford, T. A. Munton and G. C. Small did not bat.

Bowling: Lever 7–0–37–0; Foster 8–0–30–1; Gooch 8–0–47–2; Turner 8–0–52–0; Pringle 8–0–55–0; Lilley 1–0–1–0.

Umpires: J. Birkenshaw and B. Leadbeater.

At Swindon, May 18. ESSEX beat GLOUCESTERSHIRE by nine wickets.

At Sheffield, May 25. ESSEX lost to YORKSHIRE by two wickets.

At Derby, June 1. ESSEX beat DERBYSHIRE by eight wickets.

ESSEX v NOTTINGHAMSHIRE

At Chelmsford, June 8. Essex won by 11 runs. Toss: Nottinghamshire.

Essex

P. J. Prichard run out	23	J. K. Lever b Pick	0
B. R. Hardie c Pick b Cooper	29	T. D. Topley not out	0
A. R. Border c Birch b Hemmings	58		
*K. W. R. Fletcher b Hemmings	12	B 1, l-b 7, w 7, n-b 1	16
A. W. Lilley c Cooper b Hemmings	7		
K. R. Pont not out	26	1/46 2/91 3/121 (8 wkts, 40 overs) 190	
†D. E. East c Broad b Hadlee	10	4/135 5/145 6/165	
N. A. Foster b Pick	9	7/189 8/189	

D. L. Acfield did not bat.

Bowling: Hadlee 8–1–25–1; Cooper 8–0–40–1; Pick 6–0–43–2; Hemmings 8–1–26–3; Rice 5–0–22–0; Evans 5–0–26–0.

Nottinghamshire

B. C. Broad c East b Acfield	33	R. A. Pick run out	1
D. W. Randall lbw b Foster	33	E. E. Hemmings not out	1
*C. E. B. Rice b Pont	15	B 4, l-b 7, w 2	13
P. Johnson b Topley	34		
J. D. Birch b Topley	3	1/68 2/78 3/101 (8 wkts, 40 overs) 179	
R. J. Hadlee c Border b Foster	24	4/113 5/132 6/163	
†B. N. French c Fletcher b Foster	14	7/173 8/176	
K. P. Evans not out	8		

K. E. Cooper did not bat.

Bowling: Lever 8–0–40–0; Foster 8–1–43–3; Topley 8–0–26–2; Pont 8–0–25–1; Acfield 8–0–34–1.

Umpires: J. W. Holder and B. Leadbeater.

ESSEX v HAMPSHIRE

At Ilford, June 15. Hampshire won by six wickets. Toss: Essex.

Essex

*G. A. Gooch b Marshall	39	A. W. Lilley not out	5
P. J. Prichard c R. A. Smith b Nicholas	15		
A. R. Border c Nicholas b Tremlett	75	B 4, l-b 21, w 9, n-b 2	36
D. R. Pringle c Nicholas b Marshall	0		
K. W. R. Fletcher run out	62	1/49 2/126 3/126 (5 wkts, 39 overs) 256	
K. R. Pont not out	24	4/205 5/250	

†D. E. East, N. A. Foster, J. K. Lever and D. L. Acfield did not bat.

Bowling: Connor 8–0–51–0; Marshall 8–1–30–2; Tremlett 8–0–33–1; Nicholas 8–0–62–1; Cowley 7–2–55–0.

Hampshire

C. G. Greenidge lbw b Pringle	20	*M. C. J. Nicholas not out	53
V. P. Terry c East b Gooch	17	L-b 18, w 4, n-b 1	23
D. R. Turner b Pont	37		
R. A. Smith c Gooch b Foster	32	1/36 2/73 3/95 (4 wkts, 37.3 overs) 257	
C. L. Smith not out	75	4/153	

M. D. Marshall, N. G. Cowley, T. M. Tremlett, †R. J. Parks and C. A. Connor did not bat.

Bowling: Foster 8–1–49–1; Lever 7.3–0–57–0; Gooch 8–0–38–1; Pringle 7–0–51–1; Pont 7–0–44–1.

Umpires: B. J. Meyer and K. E. Palmer.

At Lord's, June 22. MIDDLESEX v ESSEX. No result.

At Manchester, July 6. ESSEX lost to LANCASHIRE by 2 runs.

ESSEX v SOMERSET

At Chelmsford, July 13. Essex won by 35 runs. Toss: Essex.

Essex

*G. A. Gooch b Taylor	52	A. W. Lilley not out	6
P. J. Prichard c Feltham b Taylor	69	B 1, l-b 14, w 4	19
A. R. Border c Harden b Garner	40		
D. R. Pringle not out	64	1/97 2/156 3/207 (4 wkts, 40 overs) 253	
B. R. Hardie b Davis	3	4/229	

K. R.Pont, †D. E. East, N. A. Foster, J. K. Lever and D. L. Acfield did not bat.

Bowling: Garner 8–0–43–1; Davis 8–0–41–1; Taylor 8–0–36–2; Dredge 8–0–49–0; Marks 3–0–20–0; Richards 5–0–49–0.

Somerset

B. C. Rose c East b Lever	9	C. H. Dredge c Lever b Pringle	3
*P. M. Roebuck c Hardie b Lever	1	†T. Gard b Lever	0
R. J. Harden c Lilley b Foster	1	N. S. Taylor not out	1
I. V. A. Richards c Pringle b Acfield	29	B 4, l-b 7, w 6	17
N. A. Felton c East b Foster	96		
V. J. Marks run out	32	1/5 2/9 3/13 (37.4 overs) 218	
J. Garner c Gooch b Lever	23	4/70 5/182 6/184	
M. R. Davis b Lever	6	7/214 8/214 9/214	

Bowling: Lever 7–0–21–5; Foster 8–1–33–2; Pringle 6.4–0–31–1; Gooch 8–0–35–0; Acfield 7–0–63–1; Pont 1–0–24–0.

Umpires: J. A. Jameson and P. B. Wight.

ESSEX v WORCESTERSHIRE

At Southend, July 20. Essex won by 43 runs. Toss: Worcestershire.

Essex

*G. A. Gooch b Radford	94	J. P. Stephenson not out	35
P. J. Prichard c Rhodes b Radford	0	†D. E. East not out	1
A. R. Border lbw b Illingworth	17	B 2, l-b 14, w 11, n-b 1	28
D. R. Pringle c Inchmore b Illingworth	5		
B. R. Hardie c Curtis b Weston	41	1/1 2/47 3/55 (6 wkts, 40 overs) 273	
A. W. Lilley c Newport b Inchmore	52	4/161 5/230 6/244	

T. D. Topley, N. A. Foster and J. K. Lever did not bat.

Bowling: Radford 8–0–38–2; Inchmore 8–0–40–1; Newport 8–0–64–0; Illingworth 8–1–49–2; Weston 8–0–66–1.

Worcestershire

T. S. Curtis c Gooch b Foster	82	R. K. Illingworth b Pringle	10
D. B. D'Oliveira c Lever b Pringle	21	N. V. Radford not out	5
G. A. Hick lbw b Foster	47	J. D. Inchmore b Lever	3
D. M. Smith b Gooch	19	B 1, l-b 21, w 2	24
*P. A. Neale c East b Gooch	0		
†S. J. Rhodes c Stephenson b Pringle	15	1/56 2/132 3/186 (39 overs) 230	
M. J. Weston c and b Foster	3	4/186 5/190 6/198	
P. J. Newport run out	1	7/202 8/214 9/222	

Bowling: Lever 8–0–47–1; Foster 8–0–41–3; Pringle 7–0–38–3; Gooch 8–0–36–2; Topley 8–0–46–0.

Umpires: J. W. Holder and H. J. Rhodes.

At Eastbourne, August 3. ESSEX beat SUSSEX by 39 runs.

At Leicester, August 10. ESSEX beat LEICESTERSHIRE by 24 runs.

ESSEX v NORTHAMPTONSHIRE

At Colchester, August 17. Essex won by 32 runs. Toss: Essex.

Essex

*G. A. Gooch c Lamb b N. G. B. Cook	45	K. W. R. Fletcher not out		7
B. R. Hardie run out	109			
A. R. Border c Larkins b Wild	25	B 2, l-b 11, w 5, n-b 1		19
D. R. Pringle c Walker b Mallender	20			
A. W. Lilley run out	2	1/104 2/149 3/213 (5 wkts, 40 overs)		234
P. J. Prichard not out	7	4/214 5/224		

†D. E. East, N. A. Foster, J. K. Lever and D. L. Acfield did not bat.

Bowling: Mallender 6–0–28–1; Capel 5–0–25–0; N. G. B. Cook 8–0–30–1; Harper 8–1–40–0; Walker 7–0–55–0; Wild 6–0–43–1.

Northamptonshire

R. J. Bailey c Border b Gooch	63	N. G. B. Cook not out		11
W. Larkins c Lever b Foster	7	N. A. Mallender st East b Border		1
A. J. Lamb b Gooch	18	A. Walker not out		0
D. J. Capel c Hardie b Pringle	33	L-b 5, w 4		9
R. A. Harper b Gooch	26			
*G. Cook c Gooch b Foster	5	1/10 2/51 3/117 (9 wkts, 40 overs)		202
D. J. Wild c East b Pringle	1	4/152 5/159 6/162		
†S. N. V. Waterton c Gooch b Pringle	28	7/166 8/197 9/202		

Bowling: Foster 8–0–52–2; Lever 7–0–35–0; Acfield 8–0–29–0; Gooch 8–0–40–3; Pringle 8–0–36–3; Border 1–0–5–1.

Umpires: D. Lloyd and N. T. Plews.

ESSEX v SURREY

At Chelmsford, August 24. Surrey won by one wicket. Toss: Essex. When Lever dismissed Feltham, he passed D. L. Underwood's record, to become the most successful bowler in John Player League matches, with 341 wickets.

Essex

C. Gladwin c Bullen b Gray	28	T. D. Topley not out		8
B. R. Hardie c Bullen b Gray	8	J. K. Lever not out		0
P. J. Prichard lbw b Bullen	19			
D. R. Pringle b Pocock	15	B 1, l-b 7, w 1, n-b 3		12
*K. W. R. Fletcher b Pocock	3			
A. W. Lilley b Bullen	9	1/35 2/47 3/68 (8 wkts, 40 overs)		163
†D. E. East b Gray	23	4/79 5/84 6/106		
N. A. Foster c Lynch b Feltham	38	7/117 8/159		

D. L. Acfield did not bat.

Bowling: Butcher 8–0–32–0; Feltham 8–0–51–1; Gray 8–0–24–3; Pocock 8–0–30–2; Bullen 8–1–18–2.

Surrey

A. R. Butcher c East b Foster	10	C. K. Bullen c East b Lever	0
G. S. Clinton b Topley	14	A. H. Gray not out	24
M. A. Lynch b Topley	8	*P. I. Pocock not out	2
A. J. Stewart b Lever	59	L-b 12, w 3	15
T. E. Jesty c Lever b Acfield	13		
†C. J. Richards run out	4	1/24 2/38 3/43 (9 wkts, 40 overs) 167	
D. J. Thomas run out	7	4/75 5/103 6/111	
M. A. Feltham b Lever	11	7/133 8/133 9/160	

Bowling: Foster 8-0-28-1; Lever 8-1-33-3; Topley 8-2-22-2; Pringle 8-1-33-0; Acfield 8-1-39-1.

Umpires: D. J. Constant and D. O. Oslear.

At Folkestone, August 31. ESSEX beat KENT by two wickets.

ESSEX v GLAMORGAN

At Chelmsford, September 14. Essex won by seven wickets. Toss: Essex.

Glamorgan

J. A. Hopkins c and b Pringle	20	†M. L. Roberts not out	6
*H. Morris c Stephenson b Gooch	31	S. R. Barwick b Foster	2
G. C. Holmes c East b Topley	8	S. L. Watkin run out	7
R. C. Ontong c East b Gooch	8	L-b 9, w 7, n-b 1	17
P. A. Cottey lbw b Topley	1		
M. P. Maynard c Fletcher b Lever	28	1/44 2/65 3/74 (40 overs) 136	
J. G. Thomas c Fletcher b Lever	8	4/77 5/85 6/102	
I. Smith b Gooch	0	7/110 8/122 9/125	

Bowling: Lever 8-2-21-2; Foster 8-0-28-1; Pringle 8-0-26-1; Topley 8-0-24-2; Gooch 8-0-28-3.

Essex

*G. A. Gooch c Roberts b Ontong	61	K. W. R. Fletcher not out	8
B. R. Hardie b Barwick	38	B 4, l-b 2, w 1, n-b 11	18
P. J. Prichard b Watkin	5		
D. R. Pringle not out	8	1/98 2/119 3/123 (3 wkts, 32.1 overs) 138	

J. P. Stephenson, A. W. Lilley, †D. E. East, N. A. Foster, J. K. Lever and T. D. Topley did not bat.

Bowling: Thomas 8-0-27-0; Barwick 6-0-22-1; Watkin 8-0-37-1; Ontong 8-1-33-1; Holmes 2.1-0-13-0.

Umpires: H. D. Bird and B. Dudleston.

GLAMORGAN

GLAMORGAN v HAMPSHIRE

At Cardiff, May 4. Hampshire won by 20 runs. Toss: Glamorgan. Ontong was stumped off a wide ball – the first instance of this happening in the John Player League.

Hampshire

C. G. Greenidge c Maynard b Steele ..	56	M. D. Marshall c Holmes b Thomas ...	14
V. P. Terry c Davies b Base	6	N. G. Cowley not out	4
R. A. Smith b Holmes	69	B 3, l-b 4, w 4, n-b 1	12
D. R. Turner b Ontong	5		
C. L. Smith b Holmes	24	1/12 2/113 3/123 (6 wkts, 40 overs)	242
*M. C. J. Nicholas not out	52	4/168 5/173 6/216	

T. M. Tremlett, †R. J. Parks and C. A. Connor did not bat.

Bowling: Base 4–0–33–1; Thomas 7–0–47–1; Ontong 8–0–36–1; Steele 8–0–35–1; Derrick 8–0–53–0; Holmes 5–0–31–2.

Glamorgan

J. A. Hopkins lbw b Marshall	8	†T. Davies not out	16
H. Morris lbw b Cowley	79	J. Derrick not out	17
Younis Ahmed st Parks b Cowley	16	B 8, l-b 7, w 2	17
G. C. Holmes st Parks b Nicholas	12		
*R. C. Ontong st Parks b Tremlett ...	19	1/21 2/60 3/85 (7 wkts, 40 overs)	222
M. P. Maynard b Tremlett	14	4/137 5/149	
J. G. Thomas c Nicholas b Tremlett ...	24	6/176 7/193	

S. J. Base and J. F. Steele did not bat.

Bowling: Marshall 8–0–35–1; Connor 8–0–31–0; Nicholas 8–0–56–1; Tremlett 8–0–53–3; Cowley 8–0–32–2.

Umpires: R. Palmer and N. T. Plews.

GLAMORGAN v LEICESTERSHIRE

At Swansea, May 11. Glamorgan won by six wickets. Toss: Leicestershire.

Leicestershire

N. E. Briers c Holmes b Steele	36	W. K. M. Benjamin not out	19
L. Potter lbw b Thomas	7	I. P. Butcher not out	8
*D. I. Gower c Davies b Derrick	15	B 4, l-b 2, w 6	12
J. J. Whitaker c Morris b Ontong	10		
T. J. Boon b Holmes	19	1/15 2/41 3/69 (6 wkts, 40 overs)	132
P. B. Clift c Steele b Holmes	6	4/80 5/99 6/100	

P. A. J. DeFreitas, †P. Whitticase and L. B. Taylor did not bat.

Bowling: Thomas 7–1–25–1; Base 5–0–19–0; Derrick 8–1–19–1; Ontong 8–1–26–1; Steele 5–0–17–1; Holmes 7–0–20–2.

Glamorgan

J. A. Hopkins c Taylor b Clift	26	*R. C. Ontong not out	3
H. Morris c Whitticase b Potter	38	L-b 10, w 5	15
D. B. Pauline c Gower b Benjamin	22		
G. C. Holmes not out	27	1/65 2/76 3/113 (4 wkts, 36.1 overs)	135
M. P. Maynard b Benjamin	4	4/128	

J. G. Thomas, †T. Davies, J. F. Steele, S. J. Base and J. Derrick did not bat.

Bowling: Taylor 6.1–0–18–0; Benjamin 7–0–33–2; DeFreitas 7–0–19–0; Clift 8–1–20–1; Potter 8–1–35–1.

Umpires: J. H. Harris and M. J. Kitchen.

At The Oval, May 18. GLAMORGAN lost to SURREY by 12 runs.

GLAMORGAN v SOMERSET

At Cardiff, May 25. Somerset won by three wickets. Toss: Somerset.

Glamorgan

J. A. Hopkins b Taylor	49	J. G. Thomas not out	6
H. Morris c Richards b Palmer	57	B 5, l-b 6, w 4	15
Younis Ahmed lbw b Taylor	16		
G. C. Holmes run out	55	1/117 2/118	(4 wkts, 40 overs) 216
*R. C. Ontong not out	18	3/153 4/207	

M. P. Maynard, †T. Davies, D. B. Pauline, S. J. Base and J. Derrick did not bat.

Bowling: Garner 8–1–47–0; Botham 6–0–26–0; Richards 2–0–13–0; Marks 6–0–32–0;
Dredge 5–0–27–0; Taylor 8–0–38–2; Palmer 5–0–22–1.

Somerset

*P. M. Roebuck run out	48	M. S. Turner not out	22
V. J. Marks b Base	13	C. H. Dredge not out	28
I. V. A. Richards c Thomas b Ontong	1	B 1, l-b 9, w 7	17
I. T. Botham c Davies b Younis	48		
R. J. Harden c Holmes b Derrick	37	1/24 2/81 3/82	(7 wkts, 39.1 overs) 217
G. V. Palmer b Holmes	1	4/154 5/161	
†T. Gard c Morris b Younis	2	6/166 7/170	

J. Garner and N. S. Taylor did not bat.

Bowling: Thomas 6–1–26–0; Base 4–0–15–1; Derrick 8–0–46–1; Ontong 8–0–52–1; Younis
6–0–28–2; Holmes 7.1–0–40–1.

Umpires: J. Birkenshaw and J. H. Hampshire.

At Birmingham, June 8. GLAMORGAN beat WARWICKSHIRE by 8 runs.

GLAMORGAN v LANCASHIRE

At Swansea, June 22. Glamorgan won by five wickets. Toss: Lancashire.

Lancashire

G. D. Mendis c Davies b Hickey	3	J. Simmons run out	0
G. Fowler c Hickey b Ontong	19	P. J. W. Allott c Morris b Hickey	15
J. Abrahams c Davies b Thomas	6	D. J. Makinson not out	0
*C. H. Lloyd c Hickey b Steele	27	L-b 8, w 4, n-b 2	14
N. H. Fairbrother c Steele b Ontong	14		
†C. Maynard run out	6	1/2 2/18 3/30	(37.4 overs) 147
S. J. O'Shaughnessy run out	34	4/54 5/74 6/92	
M. Watkinson run out	9	7/117 8/117 9/147	

Bowling: Thomas 7–1–28–1; Hickey 5.4–1–5–2; Derrick 8–0–42–0; Ontong 8–0–24–2;
Holmes 4–0–12–0; Steele 5–0–28–1.

Glamorgan

J. A. Hopkins c Maynard b Allott	65	*R. C. Ontong not out	1
H. Morris c and b Watkinson	5	J. G. Thomas not out	6
Younis Ahmed run out	50	L-b 11, w 1, n-b 4	16
G. C. Holmes c Maynard			
b O'Shaughnessy	0	1/15 2/115 3/122	(5 wkts, 38 overs) 152
M. P. Maynard c sub b Abrahams	9	4/142 5/145	

J. F. Steele, †T. Davies, J. Derrick and D. J. Hickey did not bat.

Bowling: Watkinson 6–1–12–1; Allott 8–1–26–1; O'Shaughnessy 6–1–28–1; Makinson 8–0–32–0; Simmons 8–0–37–0; Abrahams 2–1–6–1.

Umpires: M. J. Kitchen and P. B. Wight.

At Maidstone, June 29. GLAMORGAN lost to KENT by 94 runs.

GLAMORGAN v GLOUCESTERSHIRE

At Cardiff, July 6. Glamorgan won by 45 runs. Toss: Gloucestershire. Hopkins and Holmes's 123 for the second wicket was a Glamorgan record in the John Player League.

Glamorgan

J. A. Hopkins c Wright b Walsh	89	†T. Davies not out	1
H. Morris c Russell b Walsh	5		
G. C. Holmes c Tomlins b Graveney	54	B 1, l-b 13, w 1, n-b 2	17
M. P. Maynard run out	31		
*R. C. Ontong not out	23	1/18 2/141 3/191　(5 wkts, 40 overs)	222
J. G. Thomas run out	2	4/211 5/217	

P. A. Cottey, J. F. Steele, J. Derrick and D. J. Hickey did not bat.

Bowling: Sainsbury 8–0–40–0; Walsh 8–0–33–2; Payne 7–0–34–0; Bainbridge 6–0–35–0; Graveney 8–0–49–1; Lloyds 3–0–17–0.

Gloucestershire

A. W. Stovold c and b Steele	33	†R. C. Russell c Hickey b Derrick	9
A. J. Wright lbw b Thomas	0	C. A. Walsh c Davies b Hickey	35
K. P. Tomlins lbw b Ontong	38	G. E. Sainsbury not out	7
P. Bainbridge c Derrick b Ontong	2	L-b 6, w 1	7
K. M. Curran b Ontong	6		
J. W. Lloyds b Ontong	9	1/2 2/75 3/78　(39.5 overs)	177
I. R. Payne lbw b Steele	0	4/79 5/91 6/92	
*D. A. Graveney b Hickey	31	7/94 8/111 9/154	

Bowling: Thomas 8–0–32–1; Hickey 7.5–1–33–2; Steele 8–0–29–2; Ontong 8–0–28–4; Holmes 4–0–17–0; Derrick 4–0–32–1.

Umpires: J. A. Jameson and R. Julian.

At Hove, July 13. GLAMORGAN lost to SUSSEX by 28 runs.

GLAMORGAN v NORTHAMPTONSHIRE

At Neath, July 20. Glamorgan won by 50 runs. Toss: Glamorgan.

Glamorgan

J. A. Hopkins c Mallender b Capel	15	J. Derrick lbw b Wild	12
H. Morris c Harper b N. G. B. Cook	51	†T. Davies not out	3
G. C. Holmes not out	65	B 1, l-b 14, w 5, n-b 1	21
M. P. Maynard run out	0		
*R. C. Ontong run out	17	1/36 2/110 3/112　(6 wkts, 40 overs)	188
J. G. Thomas c Harper b Wild	4	4/141 5/161 6/182	

P. A. Cottey, D. J. Hickey and S. R. Barwick did not bat.

Bowling: Capel 8–0–17–1; Mallender 5–1–15–0; Walker 7–0–37–0; N. G. B. Cook 8–0–37–1; Harper 8–0–41–0; Wild 4–0–26–2.

Northamptonshire

R. J. Bailey c Ontong b Hickey	16	N. G. B. Cook c Davies b Derrick	5	
R. J. Boyd-Moss b Thomas	0	N. A. Mallender b Holmes	2	
A. J. Lamb b Holmes	66	A. Walker not out	9	
D. J. Capel run out	13	L-b 1, w 5, n-b 6	12	
R. A. Harper run out	3			
D. J. Wild b Ontong	8		(35.4 overs) 138	
*G. Cook c Derrick b Holmes	2	1/0 2/27 3/62		
†S. N. V. Waterton c Davies b Holmes	2	4/67 5/81 6/90		
		7/121 8/122 9/126		

Bowling: Thomas 6–2–14–1; Hickey 5–0–26–1; Ontong 8–1–16–1; Barwick 8–0–31–0; Derrick 4–0–23–1; Holmes 4.4–0–27–4.

Umpires: J. H. Hampshire and D. O. Oslear.

GLAMORGAN v DERBYSHIRE

At Ebbw Vale, July 27. Glamorgan won by 4 runs. Toss: Glamorgan.

Glamorgan

J. A. Hopkins run out	34	J. Derrick not out	14	
*H. Morris c Warner b Roberts	100	†T. Davies not out	3	
G. C. Holmes lbw b Holding	18	B 1, l-b 14, w 4	19	
M. P. Maynard b Warner	18			
R. C. Ontong c Roberts b Holding	17	1/73 2/139 3/175	(6 wkts, 40 overs) 223	
J. G. Thomas b Warner	0	4/198 5/198 6/214		

P. A. Cottey, S. R. Barwick and D. J. Hickey did not bat.

Bowling: Mortensen 8–0–35–0; Holding 8–1–34–2; Roberts 8–0–61–1; Warner 8–0–43–2; Sharma 8–1–35–0.

Derbyshire

*K. J. Barnett c Morris b Derrick	45	A. E. Warner c Ontong b Thomas	9	
†C. Marples b Hickey	10	R. Sharma c Morris b Derrick	5	
J. E. Morris c Cottey b Barwick	24	O. H. Mortensen not out	0	
B. Roberts b Barwick	12	L-b 14, w 6, n-b 3	23	
B. J. M. Maher run out	45			
M. A. Holding lbw b Derrick	1	1/29 2/63 3/91	(9 wkts, 40 overs) 219	
I. S. Anderson not out	19	4/127 5/136 6/161		
G. Miller c Morris b Derrick	26	7/192 8/207 9/215		

Bowling: Hickey 6–0–24–1; Thomas 8–0–40–1; Ontong 8–0–40–0; Barwick 8–0–37–2; Derrick 8–0–48–4; Holmes 2–0–16–0.

Umpires: K. E. Palmer and N. T. Plews.

At Nottingham, August 3. NOTTINGHAMSHIRE v GLAMORGAN. No result.

At Scarborough, August 10. GLAMORGAN lost to YORKSHIRE by 19 runs.

At Worcester, August 24. GLAMORGAN lost to WORCESTERSHIRE by 63 runs.

GLAMORGAN v MIDDLESEX

At Cardiff, September 7. Middlesex won by nine wickets. Toss: Middlesex.

Glamorgan

J. A. Hopkins c Miller b Hughes	 31	I. Smith not out	....	3
*H. Morris run out	 21	S. R. Barwick not out	....	1
G. C. Holmes c Cowans b Emburey	... 9			
R. C. Ontong c Gatting b Carr	 12	B 5, l-b 10, w 6, n-b 2	 23
M. P. Maynard b Emburey	 13			
J. G. Thomas b Carr	 7	1/45 2/79 3/82	(8 wkts, 40 overs) 132
†T. Davies run out	 10	4/103 5/113 6/116	
P. A. Cottey lbw b Emburey	 2	7/123 8/129	

S. L. Watkin did not bat.

Bowling: Gatting 8–0–18–0; Cowans 6–1–21–0; Sykes 8–1–25–0; Hughes 7–0–18–1; Emburey 8–1–25–3; Carr 3–0–10–2.

Middlesex

W. N. Slack run out	 7
C. T. Radley not out	 75
J. D. Carr not out	 45
L-b 3, w 1, n-b 2	 6
1/19	(1 wkt, 29.3 overs) 133

A. J. T. Miller, R. O. Butcher, *M. W. Gatting, †P. R. Downton, J. E. Emburey, J. F. Sykes, S. P. Hughes and N. G. Cowans did not bat.

Bowling: Thomas 5–0–23–0; Barwick 6.3–1–30–0; Ontong 8–0–23–0; Watkin 4–0–22–0; Holmes 6–0–32–0.

Umpires: J. W. Holder and D. R. Shepherd.

At Chelmsford, September 14. GLAMORGAN lost to ESSEX by seven wickets.

GLOUCESTERSHIRE

At Canterbury, May 4. GLOUCESTERSHIRE lost to KENT by 104 runs.

GLOUCESTERSHIRE v ESSEX

At Swindon, May 18. Essex won by nine wickets in a match restricted by rain and a damp pitch to 25 overs a side. Toss: Essex.

Gloucestershire

P. W. Romaines run out	 33	D. V. Lawrence not out	 16
C. W. J. Athey c Border b Acfield	 10		
P. Bainbridge c Lever b Foster	 37	B 2, l-b 5, n-b 2	 9
K. M. Curran c Gooch b Turner	 0		
J. W. Lloyds run out	 1	1/32 2/61 3/65	(7 wkts, 25 overs) 126
I. R. Payne c Turner b Pringle	 9	4/68 5/96	
*D. A. Graveney b Lever	 11	6/97 7/126	

†R. C. Russell, C. A. Walsh and G. E. Sainsbury did not bat.

Bowling: Lever 5–1–30–1; Foster 5–0–29–1; Acfield 5–1–18–1; Turner 5–0–19–1; Pringle 5–0–23–1.

Essex

*G. A. Gooch st Russell b Lloyds	43
B. R. Hardie not out	71
A. R. Border not out	12
L-b 2, w 2	4

1/80   (1 wkt, 23.4 overs) 130

D. R. Pringle, P. J. Prichard, A. W. Lilley, S. Turner, †D. E. East, N. A. Foster, J. K. Lever and D. L. Acfield did not bat.

Bowling: Lawrence 5–1–19–0; Walsh 4.4–0–19–0; Payne 2–0–13–0; Sainsbury 5–1–27–0; Graveney 2–0–15–0; Lloyds 3–0–19–1; Bainbridge 2–0–16–0.

Umpires: D. Lloyd and R. Palmer.

At Hove, May 25. GLOUCESTERSHIRE lost to SUSSEX by 114 runs.

At Leicester, June 1. GLOUCESTERSHIRE lost to LEICESTERSHIRE by nine wickets.

At Leeds, June 8. GLOUCESTERSHIRE beat YORKSHIRE by 68 runs.

GLOUCESTERSHIRE v DERBYSHIRE

At Gloucester, June 15. Derbyshire won by five wickets. Toss: Derbyshire.

Gloucestershire

A. J. Wright c Roberts b Taylor	2	C. A. Walsh run out	1
C. W. J. Athey lbw b Warner	56	†R. C. Russell not out	1
P. Bainbridge b Taylor	0	B 5, l-b 8, w 6	19
K. M. Curran c and b Taylor	38		
J. W. Lloyds c Anderson b Warner	4	1/2 2/2 3/101 (7 wkts, 40 overs) 163
K. P. Tomlins b Holding	30	4/111 5/111
I. R. Payne not out	12	6/138 7/160

*D. A. Graveney and G. E. Sainsbury did not bat.

Bowling: Taylor 5–0–14–3; Warner 8–1–27–2; Holding 8–2–38–1; Miller 8–0–31–0; Russell 8–0–25–0; Sharma 3–0–15–0.

Derbyshire

*K. J. Barnett c Curran b Walsh	8	M. A. Holding not out	2
I. S. Anderson b Lloyds	30		
A. Hill b Walsh	34	B 5, l-b 12, n-b 1	18
J. E. Morris b Walsh	38		
†B. Roberts c and b Sainsbury	29	1/11 2/77 3/115 (5 wkts, 39.2 overs) 166
G. Miller not out	7	4/142 5/160

R. Sharma, J. P. Taylor, A. E. Warner and P. E. Russell did not bat.

Bowling: Sainsbury 7–0–22–1; Walsh 7.2–1–29–3; Bainbridge 7–0–21–0; Payne 6–0–33–0; Graveney 5–0–18–0; Lloyds 7–0–26–1.

Umpires: J. W. Holder and K. J. Lyons.

GLOUCESTERSHIRE v SURREY

At Bristol, June 29. Surrey won by eight wickets in a match restricted by rain to 37 overs a side.
Toss: Surrey.

Gloucestershire

A. W. Stovold c Gray b Bicknell	26	C. A. Walsh c Ward b Feltham	0
C. W. J. Athey c Needham b Doughty	15	*D. A. Graveney not out	1
K. P. Tomlins c and b Needham	11	G. E. Sainsbury not out	0
K. M. Curran c Richards b Gray	52	L-b 10, w 3, n-b 2	15
J. W. Lloyds st Richards b Needham	1		
P. Bainbridge b Needham	12	1/20 2/58 3/66 (9 wkts, 37 overs)	157
†R. C. Russell c Richards b Feltham	21	4/70 5/86 6/135	
D. V. Lawrence c Bicknell b Gray	3	7/154 8/154 9/157	

Bowling: Doughty 5–1–13–1; Feltham 6–0–36–2; Needham 8–1–24–3; Bicknell 6–0–27–1;
Gray 8–1–24–2; Pocock 4–0–23–0.

Surrey

G. S. Clinton not out	67
M. A. Lynch c Russell b Sainsbury	14
A. J. Stewart b Lloyds	17
†C. J. Richards not out	55
L-b 4, w 4	8

1/41 2/79 (2 wkts, 33 overs) 161

D. M. Ward, A. Needham, M. A. Feltham, R. J. Doughty, M. P. Bicknell, A. H. Gray and
*P. I. Pocock did not bat.

Bowling: Sainsbury 8–0–28–1; Walsh 8–0–30–0; Lawrence 4–0–25–0; Lloyds 6–0–27–1;
Graveney 2–0–13–0; Bainbridge 5–0–34–0.

Umpires: K. E. Palmer and D. R. Shepherd.

At Cardiff, July 6. GLOUCESTERSHIRE lost to GLAMORGAN by 45 runs.

At Nottingham, July 13. GLOUCESTERSHIRE lost to NOTTINGHAMSHIRE by 12 runs.

GLOUCESTERSHIRE v SOMERSET

At Bristol, July 20. Gloucestershire won by eight wickets. Toss: Gloucestershire.

Somerset

N. A. Felton b Twizell	19	C. H. Dredge not out	7
J. G. Wyatt c Curran b Bainbridge	38	M. R. Davis not out	0
R. J. Harden c Alleyne b Bainbridge	26	B 1, l-b 7, w 2	10
*I. V. A. Richards c Curran b Walsh	52		
J. J. E. Hardy st Russell b Bainbridge	8	1/39 2/85 3/89 (7 wkts, 40 overs)	213
V. J. Marks run out	30	4/129 5/170	
J. Garner run out	23	6/183 7/211	

†T. Gard and N. S. Taylor did not bat.

Bowling: Sainsbury 7–0–41–0; Walsh 8–1–36–1; Twizell 5–0–20–1; Payne 8–0–48–0;
Bainbridge 8–1–38–3; Graveney 4–0–22–0.

Gloucestershire

†R. C. Russell c Hardy b Garner 6
C. W. J. Athey lbw b Dredge 26
P. Bainbridge not out 106
K. M. Curran not out 66
      B 1, l-b 10, w 2 13

1/10 2/59   (2 wkts, 37.5 overs) 217

M. W. Alleyne, K. P. Tomlins, I. R. Payne, *D. A. Graveney, P. H. Twizell, C. A. Walsh and
G. E. Sainsbury did not bat.

Bowling: Garner 8–0–30–1; Davis 5–0–21–0; Taylor 6.5–0–49–0; Dredge 8–0–37–1;
Richards 7–0–45–0; Marks 3–0–24–0.

Umpires: M. J. Kitchen and R. A. White.

At Hereford, July 27. GLOUCESTERSHIRE lost to WORCESTERSHIRE by 3 runs.

GLOUCESTERSHIRE v HAMPSHIRE

At Cheltenham, August 3. No result.

GLOUCESTERSHIRE v MIDDLESEX

At Cheltenham, August 10. No result.

At Birmingham, August 17. GLOUCESTERSHIRE lost to WARWICKSHIRE by 46 runs.

GLOUCESTERSHIRE v NORTHAMPTONSHIRE

At Moreton-in-Marsh, August 31. Northamptonshire won by 12 runs. Toss: Northamptonshire.

Northamptonshire

†R. J. Bailey b Bainbridge 36	R. J. Boyd-Moss not out 18	
W. Larkins c Athey b Curran 6	N. G. B. Cook not out 13	
A. J. Lamb c Graveney b Twizell 43		
D. J. Capel b Bainbridge 4	L-b 8, w 5 13	
R. A. Harper c Athey b Sainsbury 28		
*G. Cook retired hurt 14	1/20 2/66 3/76 (6 wkts, 40 overs) 182	
D. J. Wild b Sainsbury 7	4/108 5/141 6/159	

N. A. Mallender and A. Walker did not bat.

Bowling: Sainsbury 8–0–32–2; Curran 8–0–36–1; Walsh 8–2–31–0; Twizell 8–0–46–1;
Bainbridge 8–0–29–2.

Gloucestershire

C. W. J. Athey lbw b Mallender	0
†R. C. Russell c Bailey b Capel	0
P. Bainbridge c Boyd-Moss b Wild	71
K. M. Curran c Boyd-Moss	
b N. G. B. Cook .	24
P. W. Romaines c and b Harper	21
C. A. Walsh b Wild	1
J. W. Lloyds run out	25

K. P. Tomlins not out	11
*D. A. Graveney not out	6
B 4, l-b 5, w 2	11
1/2 2/4 3/83 (7 wkts, 40 overs)	170
4/114 5/117	
6/150 7/152	

G. E. Sainsbury and P. H. Twizell did not bat.

Bowling: Capel 6–0–23–1; Mallender 6–1–17–1; Walker 8–1–38–0; N. G. B. Cook 8–1–20–1; Harper 8–0–35–1; Wild 4–0–28–2.

Umpires: D. G. L. Evans and K. E. Palmer.

GLOUCESTERSHIRE v LANCASHIRE

At Bristol, September 7. Gloucestershire won by nine wickets. Toss: Gloucestershire.

Lancashire

G. D. Mendis c Sainsbury b Bainbridge	39
G. Fowler lbw b Walsh	17
J. Abrahams run out	49
M. Watkinson c Athey b Graveney ...	10
S. J. O'Shaughnessy run out	30
N. H. Fairbrother c Athey b Sainsbury .	19
†C. Maynard b Sainsbury	1
*C. H. Lloyd c Athey b Sainsbury	2

A. N. Hayhurst not out	1
D. J. Makinson not out	12
B 1, l-b 9, w 5, n-b 1	16
1/27 2/116 3/121 (8 wkts, 40 overs)	196
4/139 5/174 6/176	
7/181 8/182	

J. Simmons did not bat.

Bowling: Sainsbury 7–0–24–3; Walsh 8–0–60–1; Curran 4–0–23–0; Payne 8–0–31–0; Bainbridge 8–0–25–1; Graveney 5–0–23–1.

Gloucestershire

C. W. J. Athey c Lloyd b O'Shaughnessy	73
†R. C. Russell not out	94
P. Bainbridge not out	27
L-b 3, n-b 2	5

1/142   (1 wkt, 38 overs) 199

K. M. Curran, M. W. Alleyne, J. W. Lloyds, P. W. Romaines, I. R. Payne, G. E. Sainsbury, *D. A. Graveney and C. A. Walsh did not bat.

Bowling: Makinson 7–0–44–0; Watkinson 7–0–31–0; Simmons 8–0–30–0; Hayhurst 5–0–23–0; O'Shaughnessy 7–0–46–1; Abrahams 4–0–22–0.

Umpires: J. H. Harris and P. B. Wight.

HAMPSHIRE

At Cardiff, May 4. HAMPSHIRE beat GLAMORGAN by 20 runs.

HAMPSHIRE v NORTHAMPTONSHIRE

At Southampton, May 11. Hampshire won by 4 runs. Toss: Northamptonshire.

Hampshire

C. G. Greenidge c Bailey b Mallender	12	N. G. Cowley b Walker		18
V. P. Terry b N. G. B. Cook	32	T. M. Tremlett not out		4
R. A. Smith c Wild b Capel	0	†R. J. Parks not out		4
D. R. Turner run out	2	L-b 7, w 3		10
C. L. Smith c G. Cook b Mallender	31			—
*M. C. J. Nicholas b Walker	41	1/23 2/30 3/32	(8 wkts, 40 overs)	158
M. D. Marshall c Bailey b Mallender	4	4/59 5/124 6/126		
		7/130 8/154		

C. A. Connor did not bat.

Bowling: Mallender 8–0–42–3; Capel 8–0–24–1; N. G. B. Cook 8–1–20–1; Harper 8–1–21–0; Walker 8–0–44–2.

Northamptonshire

*G. Cook lbw b Nicholas	12	N. G. B. Cook run out		6
R. J. Bailey lbw b Nicholas	11	N. A. Mallender not out		1
A. J. Lamb c Parks b Nicholas	0			
R. J. Boyd-Moss c Parks b Tremlett	0	L-b 5, w 8		13
R. A. Harper run out	37			—
D. J. Capel c Turner b Nicholas	38	1/24 2/24 3/25	(8 wkts, 40 overs)	154
D. J. Wild c Parks b Tremlett	0	4/28 5/101 6/101		
†D. Ripley not out	36	7/127 8/145		

A. Walker did not bat.

Bowling: Marshall 8–2–27–0; Connor 8–1–29–0; Tremlett 8–0–24–2; Nicholas 8–0–41–4; Cowley 8–1–28–0.

Umpires: J. A. Jameson and R. Palmer.

HAMPSHIRE v NOTTINGHAMSHIRE

At Southampton, June 1. Nottinghamshire won by seven wickets. Toss: Hampshire.

Hampshire

C. G. Greenidge b Hadlee	16	N. G. Cowley not out		1
V. P. Terry c French b Pick	14			
D. R. Turner c Hadlee b Hemmings	40	L-b 2, w 12, n-b 2		16
R. A. Smith not out	82			—
C. L. Smith c French b Rice	0	1/26 2/38 3/97	(5 wkts, 40 overs)	197
*M. C. J. Nicholas c Johnson b Rice	28	4/102 5/191		

M. D. Marshall, T. M. Tremlett, †R. J. Parks and C. A. Connor did not bat.

Bowling: Hadlee 8–0–31–1; Cooper 8–0–19–0; Pick 8–0–44–1; Hemmings 8–0–46–1; Rice 8–0–55–2.

Nottinghamshire

R. T. Robinson c Terry b Cowley	67	R. J. Hadlee not out		4
B. C. Broad c Greenidge b Nicholas	94	L-b 2, w 6		8
*C. E. B. Rice not out	27			—
P. Johnson c Parks b Nicholas	0	1/159 2/189 3/189	(3 wkts, 39.3 overs)	200

D. W. Randall, J. D. Birch, †B. N. French, R. A. Pick, K. E. Cooper and E. E. Hemmings did not bat.

Bowling: Marshall 8–0–28–0; Connor 8–0–42–0; Tremlett 8–0–24–0; Nicholas 8–0–49–2; Cowley 7.3–0–55–1.

Umpires: B. Dudleston and R. A. White.

At Ilford, June 15. HAMPSHIRE beat ESSEX by six wickets.

HAMPSHIRE v KENT

At Basingstoke, June 22. Hampshire won by four wickets. Toss: Hampshire.

Kent

M. R. Benson b James	14	C. Penn c Terry b Tremlett	4
N. R. Taylor c Marshall b Cowley	28	D. L. Underwood not out	1
C. J. Tavaré lbw b James	1	K. B. S. Jarvis not out	0
G. R. Cowdrey c and b Tremlett	10	B 4, l-b 5, w 6, n-b 2	17
*C. S. Cowdrey b Tremlett	45		
E. A. E. Baptiste c Greenidge b Cowley	4	1/28 2/30 3/55 (9 wkts, 40 overs) 149	
D. G. Aslett b Connor	22	4/60 5/68 6/112	
†S. A. Marsh c Connor b Nicholas	3	7/127 8/139 9/148	

Bowling: Marshall 8-0-44-0; Connor 8-1-18-1; James 8-1-17-2; Tremlett 8-0-28-3; Nicholas 5-0-21-1; Cowley 3-0-12-2.

Hampshire

C. G. Greenidge run out	41	N. G. Cowley b Baptiste	16
V. P. Terry b Underwood	42	K. D. James not out	0
D. R. Turner c Penn b Underwood	12		
R. A. Smith not out	23	L-b 8, w 3	11
*M. C. J. Nicholas c Marsh			
b C. S. Cowdrey	1	1/89 2/93 3/104 (6 wkts, 37.3 overs) 150	
M. D. Marshall c and b Underwood	4	4/112 5/117 6/149	

T. M. Tremlett, †R. J. Parks and C. A. Connor did not bat.

Bowling: Jarvis 7-1-29-0; Baptiste 7.3-0-29-1; C. S. Cowdrey 7-0-42-1; Penn 8-0-37-0; Underwood 8-3-5-3.

Umpires: J. W. Holder and J. A. Jameson.

At Worcester, June 29. HAMPSHIRE beat WORCESTERSHIRE by nine wickets.

At Taunton, July 6. HAMPSHIRE beat SOMERSET by eight wickets.

HAMPSHIRE v WARWICKSHIRE

At Portsmouth, July 20. Hampshire won by six wickets. Toss: Hampshire.

Warwickshire

D. L. Amiss lbw b Marshall	30	G. C. Small c Parks b James	23
B. M. McMillan c Parks b Connor	8	*N. Gifford c Terry b Marshall	2
†G. W. Humpage c sub b James	7	T. A. Munton c Nicholas b Tremlett	3
P. A. Smith c Cowley b Tremlett	4	L-b 6, w 2	8
D. A. Thorne c Parks b Tremlett	24		
Asif Din lbw b Connor	16	1/26 2/39 3/52 (35.5 overs) 152	
A. J. Moles lbw b Nicholas	18	4/53 5/82 6/112	
G. J. Parsons not out	9	7/112 8/136 9/142	

Bowling: James 7-0-41-2; Connor 6-0-23-2; Tremlett 7.5-0-16-3; Marshall 8-0-29-2; Cowley 2-0-12-0; Nicholas 5-0-25-1.

Hampshire

V. P. Terry c McMillan b Small	8	M. D. Marshall not out		39
C. L. Smith run out	4	L-b 4, w 5, n-b 1		10
*M. C. J. Nicholas c Humpage b Small	1			
R. A. Smith not out	58	1/9 2/10	(4 wkts, 35.5 overs)	154
K. D. James c Humpage b Munton	34	3/15 4/94		

D. R. Turner, N. G. Cowley, †R. J. Parks, T. M. Tremlett and C. A. Connor did not bat.

Bowling: Small 6–1–16–2; McMillan 5.5–0–38–0; Parsons 8–0–22–0; Smith 2–0–10–0; Munton 6–0–24–1; Thorne 7–0–29–0; Moles 1–0–11–0.

Umpires: D. J. Constant and B. J. Meyer.

HAMPSHIRE v LEICESTERSHIRE

At Southampton, July 27. Hampshire won on faster scoring-rate. Toss: Leicestershire. After rain interrupted their innings, Leicestershire were set a revised target of 187 off 27 overs.

Hampshire

C. G. Greenidge hit wkt b Potter	73	M. D. Marshall not out		2
V. P. Terry c Balderstone b Taylor	142	L-b 8, w 2, n-b 5		15
R. A. Smith c Balderstone b DeFreitas	31			
*M. C. J. Nicholas not out	13	1/163 2/260 3/264	(3 wkts, 40 overs)	276

C. L. Smith, K. D. James, N. G. Cowley, †R. J. Parks, T. M. Tremlett and C. A. Connor did not bat.

Bowling: Taylor 8–0–64–1; Tennant 8–0–42–0; Ferris 8–0–38–0; Potter 8–0–56–1; DeFreitas 8–0–68–1.

Leicestershire

I. P. Butcher st Parks b Tremlett	31	L. B. Taylor run out		0
*J. C. Balderstone hit wkt b Marshall	14	G. J. F. Ferris not out		2
L. Potter c Terry b Tremlett	28	L-b 2, w 1, n-b 1		4
T. J. Boon c James b Tremlett	35			
P. D. Bowler b Marshall	34	1/31 2/68 3/80	(7 wkts, 27 overs)	184
P. A. J. DeFreitas b Connor	32	4/142 5/167		
†P. Whitticase not out	4	6/182 7/182		

R. A. Cobb and L. Tennant did not bat.

Bowling: James 2–0–26–0; Connor 8–0–76–1; Marshall 8–0–27–2; Tremlett 8–0–44–3; Cowley 1–0–9–0.

Umpires: B. Dudleston and D. G. L. Evans.

At Cheltenham, August 3. GLOUCESTERSHIRE v HAMPSHIRE. No result.

HAMPSHIRE v SUSSEX

At Bournemouth, August 10. Sussex won by seven wickets after rain had reduced their target to 199 off 36 overs. Toss: Sussex.

Hampshire

C. G. Greenidge c A. P. Wells b le Roux 43	K. D. James lbw b le Roux 0
V. P. Terry lbw b Reeve 15	
D. R. Turner c Phillipson b le Roux ... 23	B 2, l-b 11, w 7 20
R. A. Smith not out 57	
*M. C. J. Nicholas c C. M. Wells b Imran 34	1/40 2/89 3/90 (6 wkts, 40 overs) 221
N. G. Cowley b le Roux 29	4/156 5/221 6/221

M. D. Marshall, †R. J. Parks, P. J. Bakker and C. A. Connor did not bat.

Bowling: Imran 8–1–37–1; C. M. Wells 8–0–37–0; Reeve 8–0–54–1; le Roux 8–0–40–4; Lenham 8–0–40–0.

Sussex

P. W. G. Parker c James b Bakker 92	*†I. J. Gould not out 2
A. P. Wells b Cowley 63	B 4, l-b 5, w 3 12
Imran Khan c James b Bakker 19	
C. M. Wells not out 11	1/147 2/182 3/196 (3 wkts, 35.1 overs) 199

A. M. Green, G. S. le Roux, C. P. Phillipson, D. A. Reeve, N. J. Lenham and J. R. T. Barclay did not bat.

Bowling: Connor 8–0–32–0; James 4.1–0–20–0; Bakker 7–0–46–2; Marshall 8–0–34–0; Cowley 8–0–58–1.

Umpires: H. J. Rhodes and D. R. Shepherd.

At Lord's, August 17. HAMPSHIRE lost to MIDDLESEX by eight wickets.

HAMPSHIRE v YORKSHIRE

At Bournemouth, August 24. Hampshire won by seven wickets. Toss: Hampshire. Greenidge, who reached his hundred off 89 balls with three 6s and sixteen 4s, became the first player to score ten hundreds in John Player League matches.

Yorkshire

K. Sharp c Cowley b Tremlett 30	P. J. Hartley not out 14
A. A. Metcalfe run out 45	S. J. Dennis not out 3
S. N. Hartley c Greenidge b Marshall . 14	L-b 12, w 4, n-b 2 18
J. D. Love c Terry b Tremlett 55	
P. E. Robinson c Parks b Connor 8	1/74 2/86 3/127 (7 wkts, 40 overs) 196
*†D. L. Bairstow c Parks b Connor 4	4/138 5/156
P. Carrick c R. A. Smith b Cowley ... 2	6/167 7/180

C. Shaw and S. D. Fletcher did not bat.

Bowling: Connor 8–1–29–2; James 8–1–26–0; Marshall 8–0–28–1; Tremlett 8–0–44–2; Cowley 8–0–57–1.

Hampshire

C. G. Greenidge not out 125	C. L. Smith not out 1
V. P. Terry b Carrick 21	B 2, l-b 15, n-b 2 19
R. A. Smith run out 11	
*M. C. J. Nicholas run out 20	1/84 2/144 3/188 (3 wkts, 36.1 overs) 197

K. D. James, N. G. Cowley, T. M. Tremlett, M. D. Marshall, †R. J. Parks and C. A. Connor did not bat.

Bowling: Dennis 7.1–1–41–0; P. J. Hartley 8–0–44–0; Fletcher 8–0–52–0; Shaw 8–1–23–0; Carrick 5–0–20–1.

Umpires: M. J. Kitchen and K. J. Lyons.

At Heanor, August 31. HAMPSHIRE beat DERBYSHIRE by 73 runs.

At The Oval, September 7. HAMPSHIRE beat SURREY by 3 runs.

HAMPSHIRE v LANCASHIRE

At Southampton, September 14. Hampshire won by eight wickets. Toss: Hampshire. The match was reduced by rain to 30 overs a side.

Lancashire

G. D. Mendis c Connor b James	7
D. W. Varey c Tremlett b James	3
*J. Abrahams b Connor	11
N. H. Fairbrother b Cowley	15
S. J. O'Shaughnessy c Connor b Tremlett	51
†C. Maynard c and b Tremlett	5
M. Watkinson c Greenidge b Cowley	2
A. N. Hayhurst c c C. L. Smith b James	19
D. J. Makinson c R. A. Smith b James	9
J. Simmons not out	3
A. J. Murphy not out	2
B 3, l-b 10, w 4	17

1/12 2/16 3/24   (9 wkts, 30 overs) 144
4/62 5/72 6/78
7/120 8/129 9/139

Bowling: James 6–1–23–4; Bakker 6–0–20–0; Connor 6–0–20–1; Tremlett 6–1–38–2; Cowley 6–0–30–2.

Hampshire

C. G. Greenidge b Watkinson	27
V. P. Terry not out	63
R. A. Smith c Watkinson b Murphy	39
*M. C. J. Nicholas not out	5
L-b 10, w 3, n-b 1	14

1/44 2/132   (2 wkts, 25.4 overs) 148

C. L. Smith, K. D. James, N. G. Cowley, T. M. Tremlett, †R. J. Parks, P. J. Bakker and C. A. Connor did not bat.

Bowling: Makinson 3–0–10–0; Murphy 6–0–33–1; Watkinson 4.4–0–25–1; Hayhurst 6–0–30–0; Simmons 3–0–20–0; O'Shaughnessy 3–0–20–0.

Umpires: K. E. Palmer and R. A. White.

KENT

KENT v GLOUCESTERSHIRE

At Canterbury, May 4. Kent won by 104 runs. Toss: Kent.

Kent

M. R. Benson b Graveney	37
S. G. Hinks b Lawrence	26
C. J. Tavaré c Payne b Walsh	88
E. A. E. Baptiste c Lloyds b Graveney	5
*C. S. Cowdrey b Athey	9
G. R. Cowdrey b Walsh	48
R. M. Ellison not out	16
N. R. Taylor not out	3
B 3, l-b 7, w 5, n-b 2	17

1/40 2/97 3/124   (6 wkts, 40 overs) 249
4/168 5/187 6/234

†S. A. Marsh, G. R. Dilley and D. L. Underwood did not bat.

Bowling: Lawrence 8–0–55–1; Walsh 8–0–56–2; Payne 8–0–38–0; Graveney 8–0–42–2; Bainbridge 6–0–37–0; Athey 2–0–11–1.

Gloucestershire

P. W. Romaines lbw b Dilley	6	†R. C. Russell b Baptiste	4
C. W. J. Athey c Marsh b Ellison	2	D. V. Lawrence c Marsh b Ellison	0
P. Bainbridge lbw b C. S. Cowdrey	32	C. A. Walsh b Dilley	0
K. M. Curran c Hinks b Baptiste	14		
J. W. Lloyds not out	45	B 2, l-b 9, w 7, n-b 2	20
K. P. Tomlins b Baptiste	17		
I. R. Payne c Marsh b Baptiste	0	1/13 2/29 3/60	(36.5 overs) 145
*D. A. Graveney c G. R. Cowdrey		4/70 5/106 6/106	
b Underwood	5	7/119 8/133 9/142	

Bowling: Dilley 6.5–1–18–2; Ellison 6–2–16–2; C. S. Cowdrey 8–0–43–1; Baptiste 8–0–35–4; Underwood 8–1–22–1.

Umpires: K. J. Lyons and A. G. T. Whitehead.

At Worcester, May 11. KENT beat WORCESTERSHIRE by six wickets.

At Lord's, May 18. KENT beat MIDDLESEX by 7 runs.

KENT v SURREY

At Canterbury, May 25. Tied. Toss: Kent.

Kent

M. R. Benson c Richards b Feltham	11	†S. A. Marsh b Clarke	6
S. G. Hinks c Richards b Doughty	37	D. L. Underwood not out	6
C. J. Tavaré b Clarke	18	K. B. S. Jarvis not out	1
N. R. Taylor c Ward b Needham	16	B 4, l-b 3	7
*C. S. Cowdrey st Richards b Monkhouse	10		
G. R. Cowdrey c Stewart b Feltham	21	1/31 2/55 3/74	(9 wkts, 40 overs) 187
E. A. E. Baptiste b Clarke	52	4/87 5/93 6/135	
C. Penn run out	2	7/165 8/178 9/181	

Bowling: Doughty 8–0–29–1; Feltham 8–0–42–2; Needham 8–0–45–1; Monkhouse 8–0–23–1; Clarke 8–0–41–3.

Surrey

*A. R. Butcher c Marsh b Baptiste	64	G. Monkhouse run out	2
G. S. Clinton b Baptiste	9	M. A. Feltham run out	3
A. J. Stewart c Penn b C. S. Cowdrey	16		
T. E. Jesty lbw b C. S. Cowdrey	3	L-b 10, w 2, n-b 1	13
A. Needham b Penn	49		
D. M. Ward c C. S. Cowdrey b Baptiste	5	1/28 2/55 3/64	(9 wkts, 40 overs) 187
†C. J. Richards not out	23	4/134 5/154 6/155	
R. J. Doughty b Baptiste	0	7/157 8/171 9/187	

S. T. Clarke did not bat.

Bowling: Jarvis 8–1–39–0; Baptiste 8–1–22–4; Hinks 4–0–14–0; Penn 8–0–33–1; C. S. Cowdrey 8–0–42–2; Underwood 4–0–27–0.

Umpires: B. J. Meyer and P. B. Wight.

At Bath, June 15. KENT lost to SOMERSET by 103 runs.

At Basingstoke, June 22. KENT lost to HAMPSHIRE by four wickets.

KENT v GLAMORGAN

At Maidstone, June 29. Kent won by 94 runs. Toss: Glamorgan.

Kent

M. R. Benson c Ontong b Hickey	0	G. R. Dilley b Hickey	2
S. G. Hinks run out	99	D. L. Underwood not out	1
N. R. Taylor c and b Ontong	28	K. B. S. Jarvis not out	0
*C. S. Cowdrey b Thomas	59	B 1, l-b 15, w 6, n-b 3	25
E. A. E. Baptiste b Holmes	13		
G. R. Cowdrey c Thomas b Hickey	38	1/2 2/81 3/172 (9 wkts, 40 overs) 269	
D. G. Aslett c Davies b Thomas	0	4/197 5/243 6/243	
†S. A. Marsh c Holmes b Hickey	4	7/255 8/263 9/268	

Bowling: Thomas 8–0–51–2; Hickey 7–0–41–4; Derrick 8–0–53–0; Ontong 8–0–42–1; Steele 4–0–30–0; Holmes 5–0–36–1.

Glamorgan

J. A. Hopkins c Baptiste b Jarvis	31	†T. Davies b Underwood	5
H. Morris c Jarvis b Underwood	39	J. F. Steele not out	1
Younis Ahmed b C. S. Cowdrey	6	D. J. Hickey b Underwood	0
G. C. Holmes c Taylor b Jarvis	25	L-b 8, w 1, n-b 2	11
M. P. Maynard c Aslett b Jarvis	4		
*R. C. Ontong c Aslett b Underwood	25	1/64 2/71 3/100 (33.2 overs) 175	
J. G. Thomas c Aslett b Underwood	2	4/105 5/112 6/116	
J. Derrick c Underwood b Dilley	26	7/166 8/169 9/175	

Bowling: Dilley 6–0–23–1; Baptiste 8–0–44–0; Jarvis 8–0–39–3; C. S. Cowdrey 4–0–18–1; Underwood 7.2–0–43–5.

Umpires: J. Birkenshaw and D. G. L. Evans.

At Derby, July 6. KENT beat DERBYSHIRE by 11 runs.

KENT v LANCASHIRE

At Canterbury, July 20. Lancashire won by 37 runs. Toss: Kent.

Lancashire

G. D. Mendis c Marsh b Dilley	66	†C. Maynard not out	4
G. Fowler b Baptiste	112		
*C. H. Lloyd run out	35	L-b 10, w 7, n-b 1	18
N. H. Fairbrother c Marsh b Baptiste	2		
P. J. W. Allott run out	11	1/177 2/204 3/212 (5 wkts, 40 overs) 251	
M. Watkinson not out	3	4/230 5/245	

J. Abrahams, S. J. O'Shaughnessy, I. Folley and D. J. Makinson did not bat.

Bowling: Dilley 8–0–46–1; Ellison 8–0–34–0; Baptiste 8–0–55–2; C. S. Cowdrey 5–0–35–0; Underwood 8–0–47–0; Hinks 3–0–24–0.

Kent

M. R. Benson b O'Shaughnessy	63	†S. A. Marsh c Fairbrother b Makinson	8
S. G. Hinks c Fowler b Allott	45	G. R. Dilley c Lloyd b Allott	1
C. J. Tavaré c Fairbrother b Folley	10	D. L. Underwood not out	2
N. R. Taylor c Makinson b Folley	32	B 5, l-b 8, w 8, n-b 3	24
*C. S. Cowdrey b Abrahams	18		
G. R. Cowdrey c Allott b Makinson	4	1/75 2/99 3/140 (36.3 overs) 214	
E. A. E. Baptiste b O'Shaughnessy	2	4/186 5/189 6/191	
R. M. Ellison st Maynard b Abrahams	5	7/201 8/203 9/207	

Bowling: Watkinson 5–0–27–0; Makinson 6.3–0–44–2; Allott 7–1–19–2; Folley 8–0–57–2; O'Shaughnessy 8–0–43–2; Abrahams 2–0–11–2.

Umpires: C. Cook and D. G. L. Evans.

At Northampton, July 27. KENT lost to NORTHAMPTONSHIRE by 100 runs.

KENT v LEICESTERSHIRE

At Canterbury, August 3. No result.

At Birmingham, August 10. WARWICKSHIRE v KENT. No result.

At Hove, August 17. KENT beat SUSSEX by one wicket.

KENT v ESSEX

At Folkestone, August 31. Essex won by two wickets. Toss: Kent.

Kent

M. R. Benson run out	42	R. M. Ellison c Gladwin b Pringle	0
N. R. Taylor lbw b Acfield	26	†S. A. Marsh not out	0
C. J. Tavaré c Foster b Lever	50	B 2, l-b 6, w 3	11
G. R. Cowdrey c Acfield b Gooch	12		
E. A. E. Baptiste b Gooch	9	1/65 2/77 3/99 (7 wkts, 40 overs) 168	
*C. S. Cowdrey c Foster b Pringle	10	4/125 5/150	
D. G. Aslett not out	8	6/159 7/164	

G. R. Dilley and D. L. Underwood did not bat.

Bowling: Lever 8–0–42–1; Foster 8–2–22–0; Gooch 8–1–27–2; Acfield 8–0–39–1; Pringle 8–0–30–2.

Essex

*G. A. Gooch c Tavaré b Ellison	1	N. A. Foster not out	8
B. R. Hardie lbw b Ellison	72	J. K. Lever not out	1
P. J. Prichard c G. R. Cowdrey b Baptiste	22		
D. R. Pringle c Marsh b Baptiste	6	L-b 9, w 7, n-b 1	17
K. W. R. Fletcher c Marsh b Underwood	18		
C. Gladwin b Baptiste	5	1/1 2/48 3/70 (8 wkts, 40 overs) 169	
A. W. Lilley c Tavaré b Ellison	12	4/99 5/126 6/145	
†D. E. East c Marsh b Baptiste	7	7/160 8/160	

D. L. Acfield did not bat.

Bowling: Dilley 8–0–24–0; Ellison 8–0–39–3; Baptiste 8–0–43–4; C. S. Cowdrey 8–0–37–0; Underwood 8–0–17–1.

Umpires: K. J. Lyons and A. G. T. Whitehead.

KENT v NOTTINGHAMSHIRE

At Canterbury, September 7. Kent won by six wickets. Toss: Nottinghamshire.

Nottinghamshire

B. C. Broad b Underwood	30	R. A. Pick lbw b Ellison	7
R. T. Robinson c Marsh b Ellison	2	E. E. Hemmings lbw b Baptiste	2
P. Johnson c Marsh b Dilley	7	K. Saxelby not out	1
*C. E. B. Rice lbw b C. S. Cowdrey	10		
D. W. Randall b Underwood	12	B 1, l-b 8, w 4	13
R. J. Hadlee c and b Dilley	31		
C. D. Fraser-Darling c Underwood		1/4 2/20 3/36	(35.4 overs) 122
b C. S. Cowdrey	3	4/63 5/88 6/101	
†B. N. French c Marsh b Underwood	4	7/108 8/116 9/120	

Bowling: Dilley 8–1–20–2; Ellison 5.4–1–17–2; C. S. Cowdrey 8–0–37–2; Baptiste 6–0–21–1; Underwood 8–3–18–3.

Kent

M. R. Benson c French b Saxelby	3	G. R. Cowdrey not out	25
S. G. Hinks c Johnson b Saxelby	7		
C. J. Tavaré not out	63	L-b 6, w 8, n-b 2	16
D. G. Aslett c French b Rice	3		
*C. S. Cowdrey c French		1/5 2/16 3/26	(4 wkts, 35.1 overs) 123
b Fraser-Darling	6	4/45	

E. A. E. Baptiste, R. M. Ellison, †S. A. Marsh, G. R. Dilley and D. L. Underwood did not bat.

Bowling: Hadlee 8–2–31–0; Saxelby 8–1–25–2; Pick 7.1–0–29–0; Rice 6–1–14–1; Fraser-Darling 6–1–18–1.

Umpires: R. Palmer and N. T. Plews.

KENT v YORKSHIRE

At Canterbury, September 14. No result.

LANCASHIRE

LANCASHIRE v SUSSEX

At Manchester, May 4. Sussex won by five wickets. Toss: Sussex.

Lancashire

G. D. Mendis c Phillipson b le Roux	13	J. Simmons c and b Pigott	15
G. Fowler lbw b Jones	25	P. J. W. Allott c Parker b Pigott	20
*C. H. Lloyd c Gould b Pigott	53	D. J. Makinson not out	0
N. H. Fairbrother c le Roux b Pigott	17	L-b 6, w 2, n-b 3	11
S. J. O'Shaughnessy c Gould b Jones	9		
J. Abrahams c Gould b Pigott	2	1/30 2/67 3/101	(38.4 overs) 176
†C. Maynard run out	8	4/119 5/125 6/129	
M. Watkinson c Barclay b le Roux	3	7/138 8/146 9/176	

Bowling: C. M. Wells 8–1–30–0; le Roux 8–1–30–2; Imran 7–0–43–0; Jones 8–0–43–2; Pigott 7.4–0–24–5.

Sussex

A. M. Green c Fowler b Allott	15	C. M. Wells not out	18
P. W. G. Parker c Allott b Simmons	35		
Imran Khan b O'Shaughnessy	27	B 3, l-b 12, n-b 1	16
†I. J. Gould b Simmons	17		—
G. S. le Roux c Allott b Simmons	24	1/29 2/78 3/89 (5 wkts, 39.3 overs) 178	
A. P. Wells not out	26	4/128 5/129	

*J. R. T. Barclay, C. P. Phillipson, A. N. Jones and A. C. S. Pigott did not bat.

Bowling: Watkinson 8–1–31–0; Allott 7.3–1–27–1; O'Shaughnessy 8–1–33–1; Makinson 8–0–39–0; Simmons 8–1–33–3.

Umpires: D. J. Constant and R. A. White.

At Leicester, May 18. LANCASHIRE lost to LEICESTERSHIRE by nine wickets.

LANCASHIRE v WARWICKSHIRE

At Manchester, June 1. Warwickshire won by 11 runs. Toss: Lancashire. A match of ten overs a side was played after the original match, reduced to 22 overs a side, was abandoned when further rain interrupted play with Warwickshire 44 for two off twelve overs.

Warwickshire

A. I. Kallicharran st Maynard b Simmons	23	D. L. Amiss not out	11
†G. W. Humpage b Simmons	9	B 6, w 2	8
Asif Din c Lloyd b Hayhurst	8		—
P. A. Smith not out	28	1/35 2/44 3/55 (3 wkts, 10 overs) 87	

T. A. Lloyd, A. J. Moles, G. J. Parsons, G. C. Small, T. A. Munton and *N. Gifford did not bat.

Bowling: Allott 2–0–11–0; Watkinson 2–0–26–0; Hayhurst 2–0–17–1; Makinson 2–0–10–0; Simmons 2–0–17–2.

Lancashire

G. Fowler c and b Parsons	17	P. J. W. Allott b Gifford	4
*C. H. Lloyd not out	30	L-b 4, w 2, n-b 3	9
A. N. Hayhurst c Humpage b Munton	1		—
N. H. Fairbrother b Small	12	1/28 2/32 3/66 (5 wkts, 10 overs) 76	
†C. Maynard run out	3	4/70 5/76	

G. D. Mendis, J. Abrahams, M. Watkinson, J. Simmons and D. J. Makinson did not bat.

Bowling: Small 2–0–13–1; Parsons 2–0–12–1; Moles 2–0–14–0; Munton 2–0–20–1; Gifford 2–0–13–1.

Umpires: J. H. Harris and R. Palmer.

LANCASHIRE v MIDDLESEX

At Manchester, June 8. Lancashire won by six wickets. Toss: Lancashire.

Middlesex

A. J. T. Miller c Fowler b Allott	37	†C. P. Metson not out	4
W. N. Slack b Simmons	50	A. R. C. Fraser not out	2
R. O. Butcher lbw b Allott	11	B 2, l-b 18, w 3, n-b 1	24
*C. T. Radley c Watkinson b Simmons	14		—
G. K. Brown c Fowler b Simmons	4	1/68 2/90 3/119 (7 wkts, 40 overs) 170	
G. D. Rose c Lloyd b Watkinson	16	4/131 5/132	
S. P. Hughes b Watkinson	8	6/163 7/164	

A. G. J. Fraser and W. W. Daniel did not bat.

Bowling: Watkinson 8–0–19–2; Makinson 8–1–36–0; Allott 8–0–22–2; Hayhurst 8–0–39–0; Simmons 8–0–34–3.

Lancashire

G. D. Mendis c Metson b A. G. J. Fraser	23	†C. Maynard not out	49
G. Fowler run out	40	L-b 8, w 4	12
J. Abrahams b Hughes	8		—
*C. H. Lloyd c Metson b A. R. C. Fraser	4	1/56 2/79 3/81 (4 wkts, 39.5 overs)	174
N. H. Fairbrother not out	38	4/90	

A. N. Hayhurst, M. Watkinson, J. Simmons, P. J. W. Allott and D. J. Makinson did not bat.

Bowling: Daniel 7.5–2–34–0; Rose 8–1–31–0; A. G. J. Fraser 8–0–25–1; Hughes 8–0–33–1; A. R. C. Fraser 8–1–43–1.

Umpires: J. Birkenshaw and A. G. T. Whitehead.

LANCASHIRE v WORCESTERSHIRE

At Manchester, June 15. Lancashire won by 39 runs. Toss: Worcestershire.

Lancashire

G. D. Mendis b Newport	31	M. Watkinson not out	13
G. Fowler c Patel b Pridgeon	107	L-b 8, w 2, n-b 1	11
*C. H. Lloyd c Neale b Patel	64		
N. H. Fairbrother c and b Pridgeon	11	1/76 2/178 (4 wkts, 40 overs)	249
†C. Maynard not out	12	3/197 4/232	

J. Abrahams, J. Simmons, P. J. W. Allott, A. N. Hayhurst and D. J. Makinson did not bat.

Bowling: Pridgeon 8–0–60–2; Inchmore 8–0–43–0; Patel 8–0–48–1; Newport 8–0–32–1; Weston 4–0–30–0; Illingworth 4–0–28–0.

Worcestershire

M. J. Weston c Maynard b Watkinson	18	J. D. Inchmore not out	5
D. B. D'Oliveira b Simmons	44	R. K. Illingworth not out	14
D. M. Smith b Hayhurst	9		
G. A. Hick b Simmons	68	L-b 9, w 6, n-b 1	16
*P. A. Neale b Allott	14		
D. N. Patel c Fowler b Simmons	9	1/28 2/52 3/119 (8 wkts, 40 overs)	210
†S. J. Rhodes run out	4	4/141 5/167 6/175	
P. J. Newport hit wkt b Watkinson	9	7/179 8/191	

A. P. Pridgeon did not bat.

Bowling: Makinson 8–0–43–0; Watkinson 8–0–34–2; Hayhurst 8–0–42–1; Allott 8–0–44–1; Simmons 8–0–38–3.

Umpires: H. D. Bird and J. A. Jameson.

At Swansea, June 22. LANCASHIRE lost to GLAMORGAN by five wickets.

LANCASHIRE v ESSEX

At Manchester, July 6. Lancashire won by 2 runs. Toss: Essex.

Lancashire

G. D. Mendis b Pont 48
G. Fowler c Stephenson b Acfield 20
*C. H. Lloyd not out 91
N. H. Fairbrother not out 43
     B 1, l-b 6, w 3, n-b 2 12

1/58 2/100   (2 wkts, 40 overs) 214

J. Abrahams, S. J. O'Shaughnessy, †C. Maynard, M. Watkinson, I. Folley, P. J. W. Allott and D. J. Makinson did not bat.

Bowling: Topley 8–0–51–0; Lever 8–0–37–0; Turner 8–0–54–0; Acfield 8–1–29–1; Pont 8–1–36–1.

Essex

C. Gladwin c Maynard b Watkinson .. 2	†D. E. East not out 2
J. P. Stephenson b Abrahams 45	
A. R. Border run out 5	L-b 13, w 4, n-b 1 18
P. J. Prichard not out 103	
A. W. Lilley b O'Shaughnessy 23	1/2 2/21 3/127 (5 wkts, 40 overs) 212
K. R. Pont c Maynard b Makinson ... 14	4/168 5/210

T. D. Topley, S. Turner, *J. K. Lever and D. L. Acfield did not bat.

Bowling: Watkinson 8–1–34–1; Makinson 8–1–38–1; O'Shaughnessy 6–0–39–1; Allott 8–1–35–0; Folley 2–0–13–0; Abrahams 8–1–40–1.

Umpires: D. R. Shepherd and A. G. T. Whitehead.

At Canterbury, July 20. LANCASHIRE beat KENT by 37 runs.

At Taunton, July 27. LANCASHIRE lost to SOMERSET by eight wickets.

LANCASHIRE v YORKSHIRE

At Manchester, August 3. No result after rain ended play. Toss: Yorkshire.

Lancashire

G. D. Mendis c Metcalfe b Fletcher ... 18	M. Watkinson not out 3
G. Fowler c Metcalfe b P. J. Hartley .. 71	
*C. H. Lloyd c P. J. Hartley b Carrick . 2	L-b 18, w 3 21
N. H. Fairbrother run out 20	
J. Abrahams not out 41	1/51 2/57 3/105 (5 wkts, 40 overs) 184
P. J. W. Allott c Fletcher b P. J. Hartley 8	4/143 5/160

S. J. O'Shaughnessy, †J. Stanworth, J. Simmons and A. N. Hayhurst did not bat.

Bowling: Jarvis 8–1–38–0; P. J. Hartley 8–0–49–2; Fletcher 8–0–33–1; Shaw 8–0–27–0; Carrick 8–0–19–1.

Yorkshire

M. D. Moxon not out 17
A. A. Metcalfe lbw b Allott 4
S. N. Hartley not out 15
   L-b 5 5

1/8   (1 wkt, 12 overs) 41

P. E. Robinson, J. D. Love, *†D. L. Bairstow, P. Carrick, P. J. Hartley, S. D. Fletcher, P. W. Jarvis and C. Shaw did not bat.

Bowling: Watkinson 6–0–18–0; Allott 6–1–18–1.

Umpires: M. J. Kitchen and B. Leadbeater.

At Buxton, August 10. LANCASHIRE lost to DERBYSHIRE by three wickets.

At Nottingham, August 17. LANCASHIRE lost to NOTTINGHAMSHIRE by 26 runs.

LANCASHIRE v NORTHAMPTONSHIRE

At Manchester, August 24. Lancashire won by five wickets. Toss: Northamptonshire.

Northamptonshire

W. Larkins b Allott	0	D. J. Wild not out		35
*G. Cook run out	11			
R. J. Bailey run out	75	L-b 10, w 2		12
D. J. Capel lbw b Makinson	8			
R. J. Boyd-Moss b Allott	18	1/2 2/38 3/60	(5 wkts, 40 overs)	195
R. A. Harper not out	36	4/109 5/129		

†D. Ripley, N. G. B. Cook, N. A. Mallender and A. Walker did not bat.

Bowling: Watkinson 6–0–28–0; Allott 8–0–35–2; Makinson 8–0–54–1; O'Shaughnessy 2–0–17–0; Hayhurst 8–0–20–0; Simmons 8–1–31–0.

Lancashire

G. D. Mendis c Capel b N. G. B. Cook	22	P. J. W. Allott not out		0
G. Fowler b N. G. B. Cook	46			
*C. H. Lloyd c Wild b Mallender	85	B 1, l-b 3, w 1		5
J. Abrahams b Walker	11			
S. J. O'Shaughnessy b Mallender	22	1/62 2/78 3/126	(5 wkts, 38.5 overs)	196
†C. Maynard not out	5	4/191 5/192		

D. J. Makinson, A. N. Hayhurst, M. Watkinson and J. Simmons did not bat.

Bowling: Capel 8–1–17–0; Mallender 7.5–0–63–2; Harper 8–1–23–0; N. G. B. Cook 8–0–32–2; Walker 7–0–57–1.

Umpires: J. H. Hampshire and J. A. Jameson.

LANCASHIRE v SURREY

At Manchester, August 31. Lancashire won by four wickets. Toss: Lancashire.

Surrey

A. R. Butcher lbw b Hayhurst	25	D. J. Thomas b Simmons		1
G. S. Clinton lbw b Allott	0	R. J. Doughty not out		15
T. E. Jesty c Lloyd b Allott	26	A. H. Gray not out		20
†C. J. Richards c Fowler				
b O'Shaughnessy	52	L-b 14		14
A. J. Stewart c Hayhurst b Simmons	7			
M. A. Lynch b Watkinson	23	1/12 2/50 3/64	(8 wkts, 40 overs)	184
A. Needham c Hayhurst		4/89 5/139 6/142		
b O'Shaughnessy	1	7/147 8/149		

*P. I. Pocock did not bat.

Bowling: Watkinson 8–1–39–1; Allott 8–3–20–2; O'Shaughnessy 8–0–33–2; Hayhurst 8–0–40–1; Simmons 8–0–38–2.

Lancashire

G. D. Mendis c and b Thomas	4	†C. Maynard not out	24
G. Fowler c Lynch b Doughty	23	M. Watkinson not out	4
J. Abrahams c Richards b Gray	45	L-b 6, w 3, n-b 2	11
*C. H. Lloyd c Richards b Gray	26		
N. H. Fairbrother b Thomas	25	1/9 2/42 3/90 (6 wkts, 39.3 overs) 185	
S. J. O'Shaughnessy run out	23	4/127 5/134 6/181	

A. N. Hayhurst, J. Simmons and P. J. W. Allott did not bat.

Bowling: Doughty 8-0-29-1; Thomas 6-1-40-2; Needham 8-0-31-0; Gray 8-0-39-2; Pocock 5-1-30-0; Butcher 4.3-0-10-0.

Umpires: D. J. Constant and D. O. Oslear.

At Bristol, September 7. LANCASHIRE lost to GLOUCESTERSHIRE by nine wickets.

At Southampton, September 14. LANCASHIRE lost to HAMPSHIRE by eight wickets.

LEICESTERSHIRE

LEICESTERSHIRE v DERBYSHIRE

At Leicester, May 4. Leicestershire won by 19 runs. Toss: Derbyshire.

Leicestershire

N. E. Briers c Russell b Miller	26	W. K. M. Benjamin not out	7
L. Potter b Newman	105		
*D. I. Gower c Newman b Mortensen	28	L-b 18, w 2	20
J. J. Whitaker c Anderson b Newman	17		
T. J. Boon lbw b Newman	14	1/88 2/152 3/188 (5 wkts, 40 overs) 230	
P. B. Clift not out	13	4/201 5/212	

P. A. J. DeFreitas, I. P. Butcher, †P. Whitticase and L. B. Taylor did not bat.

Bowling: Mortensen 8-0-31-1; Holding 8-0-43-0; Newman 7-0-38-3; Miller 8-0-43-1; Russell 5-0-22-0; Finney 4-0-35-0.

Derbyshire

*K. J. Barnett c Whitticase b Benjamin	6	R. J. Finney b Taylor	1
I. S. Anderson c Butcher b Clift	63	P. E. Russell b DeFreitas	1
A. Hill lbw b Benjamin	6	O. H. Mortensen not out	1
J. E. Morris c Boon b Potter	11	B 2, l-b 9, w 2, n-b 1	14
†B. Roberts b Briers	11		
G. Miller not out	73	1/8 2/22 3/42 (9 wkts, 40 overs) 211	
M. A. Holding run out	1	4/62 5/157 6/160	
P. G. Newman b DeFreitas	23	7/191 8/194 9/207	

Bowling: Benjamin 8-1-28-2; Taylor 8-0-41-1; Briers 5-0-32-1; Potter 6-0-24-1; DeFreitas 7-0-41-2; Clift 6-0-34-1.

Umpires: R. Julian and D. R. Shepherd.

At Swansea, May 11. LEICESTERSHIRE lost to GLAMORGAN by six wickets.

LEICESTERSHIRE v LANCASHIRE

At Leicester, May 18. Leicestershire won by nine wickets. Toss: Leicestershire.

Lancashire

G. D. Mendis c Potter b Taylor	7	M. Watkinson not out	2
G. Fowler c Whitticase b Benjamin	2	D. J. Makinson run out	0
J. Abrahams c Butcher b Benjamin	55	P. J. W. Allott not out	10
*C. H. Lloyd c Whitaker b Clift	10	L-b 10, w 7, n-b 2	19
N. H. Fairbrother c Whitticase			
b DeFreitas	0	1/8 2/14 3/38	(8 wkts, 40 overs) 141
A. N. Hayhurst c Boon b Benjamin	34	4/39 5/121 6/129	
†C. Maynard b Benjamin	2	7/129 8/130	

J. Simmons did not bat.

Bowling: Benjamin 8–1–19–4; Taylor 8–0–35–1; Clift 8–2–18–1; DeFreitas 8–1–24–1; Potter 4–0–12–0; Briers 4–0–23–0.

Leicestershire

N. E. Briers c Lloyd b Watkinson	52
L. Potter not out	63
*D. I. Gower not out	16
B 2, l-b 7, n-b 2	11

1/124   (1 wkt, 34.5 overs) 142

J. J. Whitaker, T. J. Boon, P. B. Clift, W. K. M. Benjamin, I. P. Butcher, P. A. J. DeFreitas, †P. Whitticase and L. B. Taylor did not bat.

Bowling: Watkinson 7–0–25–1; Allott 5–0–9–0; Hayhurst 8–0–33–0; Makinson 6.5–0–41–0; Simmons 8–0–25–0.

Umpires: C. Cook and K. J. Lyons.

At Northampton, May 25. LEICESTERSHIRE lost to NORTHAMPTONSHIRE by 47 runs.

LEICESTERSHIRE v GLOUCESTERSHIRE

At Leicester, June 1. Leicestershire won by nine wickets, having been set a revised target of 148 in 36 overs after rain interrupted play. Toss: Gloucestershire.

Gloucestershire

P. W. Romaines lbw b Agnew	6	D. V. Lawrence not out	21
C. W. J. Athey st Whitticase b Potter	40	†R. C. Russell not out	7
K. M. Curran c Taylor b DeFreitas	29	B 1, l-b 4, w 3, n-b 5	13
P. Bainbridge c Whitticase b DeFreitas	0		
K. P. Tomlins b Clift	26	1/13 2/76 3/76	(7 wkts, 37 overs) 152
*D. A. Graveney c DeFreitas b Taylor	8	4/92 5/115	
I. R. Payne c Potter b Taylor	2	6/119 7/135	

G. E. Sainsbury and C. A. Walsh did not bat.

Bowling: Agnew 6–0–24–1; Taylor 8–0–35–2; DeFreitas 6–1–18–2; Clift 8–0–33–1; Potter 5–0–24–1; Briers 4–0–13–0.

Leicestershire

N. E. Briers not out	....	60
L. Potter lbw b Payne	....	24
*D. I. Gower not out	....	51
B 4, l-b 7, w 2, n-b 2	....	15

1/50   (1 wkt, 32 overs) 150

J. J. Whitaker, T. J. Boon, I. P. Butcher, P. B. Clift, P. A. J. DeFreitas, †P. Whitticase, J. P. Agnew and L. B. Taylor did not bat.

Bowling: Lawrence 8–0–41–0; Sainsbury 4–0–15–0; Walsh 8–1–29–0; Payne 3–0–18–1; Bainbridge 6–0–18–0; Graveney 3–0–18–0.

Umpires: J. W. Holder and A. G. T. Whitehead.

At Birmingham, June 22. LEICESTERSHIRE lost to WARWICKSHIRE on scoring-rate.

LEICESTERSHIRE v NOTTINGHAMSHIRE

At Leicester, June 29. Nottinghamshire won by seven wickets. Toss: Nottinghamshire.

Leicestershire

L. Potter b Saxelby	....	63	T. J. Boon not out	....	31
P. Willey b Hadlee	....	59	W. K. M. Benjamin not out	....	3
*D. I. Gower b Hemmings	....	2	L-b 12, w 1	....	13
J. J. Whitaker c sub b Rice	....	3			
P. D. Bowler c Rice b Evans	....	4	1/101 2/104 3/115	(6 wkts, 40 overs) 191	
P. A. J. DeFreitas b Hadlee	....	13	4/136 5/139 6/182		

†P. Whitticase, J. P. Agnew and L. B. Taylor did not bat.

Bowling: Hadlee 8–1–24–2; Rice 8–0–34–1; Pick 6–0–44–0; Hemmings 8–1–29–1; Evans 2–0–8–1; Saxelby 8–0–40–1.

Nottinghamshire

B. C. Broad run out	....	60	R. J. Hadlee not out	....	9
D. W. Randall c Willey b Benjamin	...	9	L-b 7, w 3, n-b 1	....	11
P. Johnson c Potter b Agnew	....	90			
*C. E. B. Rice not out	....	16	1/34 2/154 3/178	(3 wkts, 36.1 overs) 195	

R. T. Robinson, E. E. Hemmings, †B. N. French, K. P. Evans, R. A. Pick and K. Saxelby did not bat.

Bowling: Benjamin 8–1–38–1; Agnew 7.1–0–28–1; DeFreitas 6–0–28–0; Taylor 7–0–47–0; Willey 6–0–32–0; Potter 2–0–15–0.

Umpires: D. J. Constant and J. H. Harris.

At Middlesbrough, July 6. LEICESTERSHIRE lost to YORKSHIRE by five wickets.

LEICESTERSHIRE v MIDDLESEX

At Leicester, July 13. Leicestershire won by seven wickets. Toss: Middlesex.

Middlesex

A. J. T. Miller run out	20	G. D. Rose not out	11
C. T. Radley b Benjamin	8	S. P. Hughes b DeFreitas	1
N. R. C. MacLaurin lbw b DeFreitas	0	N. G. Cowans not out	0
R. O. Butcher b DeFreitas	14	B 1, l-b 8, w 4, n-b 2	15
J. D. Carr b DeFreitas	38		
†P. R. Downton c Whitticase b Agnew	20	1/21 2/28 3/46 (9 wkts, 40 overs) 137	
*J. E. Emburey c Willey b Clift	2	4/54 5/95 6/105	
P. H. Edmonds b Benjamin	8	7/122 8/128 9/137	

Bowling: Benjamin 8–1–22–2; Agnew 8–0–35–1; DeFreitas 7–1–20–4; Taylor 8–0–26–0; Clift 7–1–17–1; Willey 2–0–8–0.

Leicestershire

L. Potter c Butcher b Edmonds	52	P. D. Bowler not out	6
P. Willey lbw b Hughes	23	L-b 5, w 2	7
*D. I. Gower not out	43		
T. J. Boon lbw b Cowans	7	1/57 2/102 3/118 (3 wkts, 36.4 overs) 138	

†P. Whitticase, P. B. Clift, P. A. J. DeFreitas, W. K. M. Benjamin, J. P. Agnew and L. B. Taylor did not bat.

Bowling: Cowans 8–0–30–1; Rose 4–0–24–0; Emburey 8–2–11–0; Edmonds 8–0–37–1; Hughes 8–1–30–1; Butcher 0.4–0–1–0.

Umpires: R. Julian and D. O. Oslear.

LEICESTERSHIRE v SUSSEX

At Leicester, July 20. Sussex won by 46 runs. Toss: Sussex. Tennant, playing in his first John Player League game, bowled two wides and took two wickets in his first over.

Sussex

A. M. Green c Willey b Tennant	0	C. P. Phillipson not out	27
P. W. G. Parker b Clift	55	D. A. Reeve not out	3
Imran Khan c Willey b Tennant	0	L-b 9, w 5, n-b 1	15
C. M. Wells c Gower b Willey	68		
*†I. J. Gould c Gower b Clift	16	1/0 2/1 3/119 (6 wkts, 40 overs) 222	
A. P. Wells run out	38	4/136 5/178 6/204	

N. J. Lenham, D. K. Standing and A. M. Babington did not bat.

Bowling: Tennant 8–1–21–2; Benjamin 7.1–0–42–0; Willey 8–0–39–1; Clift 8–0–44–2; DeFreitas 8–0–54–0; Potter 0.5–0–13–0.

Leicestershire

L. Potter c Standing b C. M. Wells	17	†P. Gill b A. P. Wells	3
I. P. Butcher run out	0	L. Tennant not out	2
*D. I. Gower c and b C. M. Wells	0		
P. Willey c Gould b C. M. Wells	15	L-b 5, w 7	12
T. J. Boon not out	49		
P. D. Bowler c Gould b Reeve	7	1/0 2/1 3/31 (8 wkts, 40 overs) 176	
P. A. J. DeFreitas b Imran	13	4/34 5/132 6/148	
P. B. Clift c and b Standing	10	7/162 8/168	

W. K. M. Benjamin did not bat.

Bowling: C. M. Wells 8–1–22–3; Imran 7–2–13–1; Babington 8–2–38–0; Standing 8–0–40–1; Reeve 8–0–51–1; A. P. Wells 1–0–7–1.

Umpires: B. Leadbeater and K. E. Palmer.

At Southampton, July 27. LEICESTERSHIRE lost to HAMPSHIRE on scoring-rate.

At Canterbury, August 3. KENT v LEICESTERSHIRE. No result.

LEICESTERSHIRE v ESSEX

At Leicester, August 10. Essex won by 24 runs in a match reduced by rain to eighteen overs.
Toss: Leicestershire.

Essex

P. J. Prichard run out	27
B. R. Hardie run out	80
A. R. Border c Taylor b DeFreitas	13
*K. W. R. Fletcher not out	25
L-b 2, w 3, n-b 1	6

1/57 2/83 3/151   (3 wkts, 18 overs) 151

J. P. Stephenson, A. W. Lilley, †D. E. East, T. D. Topley, N. A. Foster, D. L. Acfield
and S. Turner did not bat.

Bowling: Tennant 3–0–25–0; Willey 3–0–31–0; DeFreitas 4–0–25–1; Benjamin 4–0–32–0;
Taylor 4–0–36–0.

Leicestershire

L. Potter b Acfield	36	†P. Whitticase c East b Foster	0
*P. Willey run out	33	L. B. Taylor not out	2
J. J. Whitaker c Turner b Border	1	R. A. Cobb not out	10
T. J. Boon b Foster	17	B 2, l-b 3, w 1	6
P. D. Bowler b Acfield	3		
P. A. J. DeFreitas st East b Border	1	1/53 2/54 3/74 (8 wkts, 18 overs) 127
W. K. M. Benjamin c Stephenson		4/78 5/88 6/108	
b Topley	18	7/108 8/116	

L. Tennant did not bat.

Bowling: Topley 3–0–23–1; Turner 4–0–32–0; Border 4–0–21–2; Acfield 3–0–25–2; Foster
4–0–21–2.

Umpires: A. A. Jones and P. B. Wight.

At Worcester, August 17. LEICESTERSHIRE lost to WORCESTERSHIRE by 12 runs.

LEICESTERSHIRE v SOMERSET

At Leicester, August 31. Leicestershire won by 56 runs. Toss: Somerset.

Leicestershire

L. Potter c and b Davis	30	P. A. J. DeFreitas not out	8
T. J. Boon b Garner	0	W. K. M. Benjamin not out	2
J. J. Whitaker c Botham b Taylor	73	B 4, l-b 8, w 1	13
*P. Willey c Gard b Taylor	51		
P. D. Bowler b Garner	19	1/1 2/59 3/151 (7 wkts, 40 overs) 217
†P. Whitticase c sub b Taylor	4	4/166 5/176	
M. Blackett b Botham	17	6/197 7/215	

L. Tennant and L. B. Taylor did not bat.

Bowling: Garner 8–2–30–2; Botham 8–0–44–1; Dredge 8–0–36–0; Davis 7.5–0–56–1; Harden 0.1–0–0–0; Taylor 8–0–39–3.

Somerset

B. C. Rose b Tennant	4	C. H. Dredge b Willey	8
*P. M. Roebuck c Potter b Willey	31	N. S. Taylor b DeFreitas	28
R. J. Harden c Whitticase b Tennant	0	M. R. Davis not out	1
I. T. Botham b Tennant	0	B 6, l-b 1, w 5, n-b 3	15
N. A. Felton c Potter b DeFreitas	59		
J. J. E. Hardy b Willey	1	1/12 2/14 3/20	(36.2 overs) 161
J. Garner b DeFreitas	11	4/64 5/66 6/78	
†T. Gard c Tennant b Willey	3	7/87 8/106 9/152	

Bowling: Tennant 8–1–25–3; Taylor 6–0–29–0; Willey 8–0–37–4; Benjamin 8–0–32–0; DeFreitas 6.2–0–31–3.

Umpires: B. Dudleston and B. J. Meyer.

At The Oval, September 14. LEICESTERSHIRE lost to SURREY by two wickets.

MIDDLESEX

MIDDLESEX v NOTTINGHAMSHIRE

At Lord's, May 4. Nottinghamshire won by 46 runs. Toss: Middlesex.

Nottinghamshire

B. C. Broad c Downton b Fraser	28
R. T. Robinson b Gatting	42
*C. E. B. Rice not out	94
P. Johnson not out	61
B 1, l-b 4, w 1, n-b 6	12

1/65 2/84   (2 wkts, 40 overs) 237

J. D. Birch, D. W. Randall, R. J. Hadlee, †B. N. French, E. E. Hemmings, R. A. Pick and K. E. Cooper did not bat.

Bowling: Williams 8–0–28–0; Daniel 8–0–37–0; Carr 3–0–21–0; Fraser 8–0–45–1; Gatting 5–0–43–1; Emburey 8–0–58–0.

Middlesex

G. D. Barlow b Hemmings	45	N. F. Williams c Rice b Hemmings	6
W. N. Slack b Cooper	2	A. R. C. Fraser not out	6
*M. W. Gatting c Randall b Cooper	0	W. W. Daniel b Rice	4
C. T. Radley b Pick	36	B 2, l-b 22, n-b 3	27
R. O. Butcher lbw b Pick	1		
†P. R. Downton c Robinson b Hemmings	11	1/16 2/16 3/81	(37.4 overs) 191
J. D. Carr lbw b Pick	4	4/84 5/105 6/108	
J. E. Emburey b Rice	49	7/116 8/133 9/187	

Bowling: Hadlee 7–0–30–0; Cooper 8–3–12–2; Rice 6.4–0–32–2; Pick 8–0–37–3; Hemmings 8–0–56–3.

Umpires: J. H. Hampshire and K. E. Palmer.

At Taunton, May 11. MIDDLESEX lost to SOMERSET by six wickets.

MIDDLESEX v KENT

At Lord's, May 18. Kent won by 7 runs. Toss: Middlesex.

Kent

M. R. Benson c Slack b Fraser	25	†S. A. Marsh b Emburey	6
S. G. Hinks b Hughes	46	D. L. Underwood b Daniel	2
C. J. Tavaré c and b Emburey	4	K. B. S. Jarvis not out	0
*C. S. Cowdrey b Daniel	45	B 1, l-b 8, w 1, n-b 3	13
G. R. Cowdrey b Hughes	10		
E. A. E. Baptiste c Radley b Fraser	16	1/63 2/75 3/89 (38.1 overs) 177	
N. R. Taylor c Downton b Daniel	9	4/106 5/135 6/157	
C. Penn c Carr b Emburey	1	7/158 8/173 9/177	

Bowling: Daniel 7.1–0–20–3; Cowans 8–0–39–0; Fraser 8–0–41–2; Hughes 8–0–39–2; Emburey 7–2–29–3.

Middlesex

W. N. Slack lbw b Jarvis	2	A. R. C. Fraser run out	2
C. T. Radley c Hinks b Baptiste	5	N. G. Cowans b Baptiste	0
*M. W. Gatting lbw b C. S. Cowdrey	43	W. W. Daniel not out	1
R. O. Butcher c Marsh b Penn	12	B 4, l-b 12, w 2, n-b 1	19
†P. R. Downton run out	39		
J. D. Carr lbw b Baptiste	41	1/10 2/12 3/51 (39.5 overs) 170	
J. E. Emburey c Taylor b Hinks	2	4/77 5/134 6/138	
S. P. Hughes b Baptiste	4	7/161 8/168 9/169	

Bowling: Jarvis 8–0–30–1; Baptiste 7.5–0–25–4; C. S. Cowdrey 8–0–26–1; Penn 8–0–33–1; Underwood 6–0–30–0; Hinks 2–0–10–1.

Umpires: B. Dudleston and M. J. Kitchen.

At The Oval, June 1. MIDDLESEX beat SURREY by four wickets.

At Manchester, June 8. MIDDLESEX lost to LANCASHIRE by six wickets.

MIDDLESEX v YORKSHIRE

At Lord's, June 15. Middlesex won by nine wickets. Toss: Middlesex. Emburey's four wickets were taken in the 40th over of Yorkshire's innings. Slack and Miller compiled a first-wicket record for Middlesex in the John Player League.

Yorkshire

K. Sharp run out	52	P. W. Jarvis b Emburey	0
M. D. Moxon c Radley b Edmonds	48	P. Carrick b Emburey	0
A. A. Metcalfe c Gatting b Edmonds	13	S. J. Dennis not out	1
S. N. Hartley c Radley b Hughes	15	L-b 12, w 3, n-b 2	17
P. E. Robinson b Fraser	29		
*†D. L. Bairstow b Hughes	34	1/103 2/119 3/128 (40 overs) 210	
A. Sidebottom b Emburey	1	4/144 5/199 6/209	
P. J. Hartley st Downton b Emburey	0	7/209 8/209 9/209	

Bowling: Rose 8–1–22–0; Fraser 8–0–30–1; Hughes 8–0–51–2; Edmonds 8–0–43–2; Emburey 8–0–52–4.

Middlesex

A. J. T. Miller c Dennis b S. N. Hartley 69
W. N. Slack not out 101
*M. W. Gatting not out 36
    L-b 8 8

1/148   (1 wkt, 37.3 overs) 214

J. D. Carr, C. T. Radley, †P. R. Downton, J. E. Emburey, P. H. Edmonds, S. P. Hughes, G. D. Rose and A. R. C. Fraser did not bat.

Bowling: Dennis 5–0–27–0; Sidebottom 5.3–0–29–0; Carrick 8–0–36–0; Jarvis 8–0–53–0; P. J. Hartley 4–0–24–0; S. N. Hartley 7–0–37–1.

Umpires: R. Julian and N. T. Plews.

MIDDLESEX v ESSEX

At Lord's, June 22. No result after bad light ended play. Toss: Middlesex. Rain delayed the start of Middlesex's innings and interrupted play again when Middlesex were 50 for one.

Essex

C. Gladwin c Rose b Edmonds 28	†D. E. East not out 8
P. J. Prichard lbw b Cowans 97	N. A. Foster not out 6
A. R. Border c Radley b Edmonds 29	B 1, l-b 19, w 3, n-b 1 24
A. W. Lilley c Cowans b Hughes 11	
*K. W. R. Fletcher b Daniel 11	1/66 2/133 3/159 (6 wkts, 40 overs) 217
K. R. Pont c Carr b Cowans 3	4/193 5/201 6/203

T. D. Topley, J. H. Childs and D. L. Acfield did not bat.

Bowling: Rose 8–1–35–0; Cowans 8–0–42–2; Daniel 8–1–28–1; Edmonds 8–0–36–2; Hughes 8–0–56–1.

Middlesex

A. J. T. Miller not out 30
M. A. Roseberry c Fletcher b Acfield . . 23
R. O. Butcher b Pont 11
*C. T. Radley not out 8
    L-b 9, w 8 17

1/46 2/80   (2 wkts, 17 overs) 89

G. D. Rose, †P. R. Downton, J. D. Carr, P. H. Edmonds, S. P. Hughes, N. G. Cowans and W. W. Daniel did not bat.

Bowling: Foster 3–0–13–0; Topley 5–0–24–0; Pont 5–0–21–1; Acfield 4–0–22–1.

Umpires: C. Cook and B. Dudleston.

MIDDLESEX v WARWICKSHIRE

At Lord's, July 6. Tied. Toss: Warwickshire.

Warwickshire

T. A. Lloyd c Roseberry b Carr	61	G. C. Small not out	7
D. L. Amiss c Rose b Hughes	6	K. J. Kerr not out	5
B. M. McMillan c Carr b Fraser	9		
†G. W. Humpage b Sykes	9	B 1, l-b 10, w 2	13
P. A. Smith c Downton b Slack	12		
Asif Din run out	11	1/22 2/43 3/75 (8 wkts, 40 overs) 168	
D. A. Thorne run out	12	4/102 5/117 6/125	
G. J. Parsons b Hughes	23	7/133 8/162	

*N. Gifford did not bat.

Bowling: Rose 6–0–22–0; Hughes 7–0–38–2; Fraser 5–0–19–1; Sykes 8–0–27–1; Slack 8–0–29–1; Carr 6–1–22–1.

Middlesex

A. J. T. Miller b Parsons	23	G. D. Rose c McMillan b Gifford	3
W. N. Slack b Parsons	9		
M. A. Roseberry run out	22	L-b 7, w 5, n-b 1	13
R. O. Butcher b Kerr	12		
*C. T. Radley c Parsons b Gifford	38	1/22 2/52 3/69 (7 wkts, 40 overs) 168	
†P. R. Downton c Gifford b Small	41	4/73 5/147	
J. D. Carr not out	7	6/163 7/168	

J. F. Sykes, S. P. Hughes and A. G. J. Fraser did not bat.

Bowling: Small 8–1–20–1; Parsons 8–1–29–2; Kerr 8–1–23–1; McMillan 8–0–38–0; Gifford 5–0–32–2; Thorne 3–0–19–0.

Umpires: B. Dudleston and A. A. Jones.

At Leicester, July 13. MIDDLESEX lost to LEICESTERSHIRE by seven wickets.

At Derby, July 20. MIDDLESEX lost to DERBYSHIRE by seven wickets.

MIDDLESEX v NORTHAMPTONSHIRE

At Lord's, August 3. No result.

At Cheltenham, August 10. GLOUCESTERSHIRE v MIDDLESEX. No result.

MIDDLESEX v HAMPSHIRE

At Lord's, August 17. Middlesex won by eight wickets. Toss: Middlesex.

Hampshire

C. G. Greenidge b Cowans	13	T. M. Tremlett not out	3
V. P. Terry c Gatting b Edmonds	26		
R. A. Smith c and b Emburey	65	L-b 8, w 5, n-b 3	16
*M. C. J. Nicholas c Miller b Emburey	41		
N. G. Cowley c Downton b Cowans	23	1/24 2/71 3/146 (5 wkts, 40 overs) 195	
R. J. Scott not out	8	4/154 5/186	

K. D. James, M. D. Marshall, †R. J. Parks and C. A. Connor did not bat.

Bowling: Hughes 8–0–40–0; Cowans 8–1–39–2; Edmonds 8–0–28–1; Emburey 8–1–23–2; Gatting 6–0–39–0; Carr 2–0–18–0.

Middlesex

C. T. Radley c Smith b James 47
W. N. Slack b Cowley 75
R. O. Butcher not out 42
J. D. Carr not out 26
L-b 4, w 6 10

1/115 2/147   (2 wkts, 39 overs) 200

A. J. T. Miller, *M. W. Gatting, †P. R. Downton, J. E. Emburey, P. H. Edmonds, S. P. Hughes and N. G. Cowans did not bat.

Bowling: Connor 7–0–38–0; James 8–0–30–1; Tremlett 8–0–46–0; Cowley 8–0–40–1; Marshall 8–0–42–0.

Umpires: R. A. White and P. B. Wight.

At Hove, August 24. MIDDLESEX lost to SUSSEX by 101 runs.

MIDDLESEX v WORCESTERSHIRE

At Lord's, August 31. Middlesex won by five wickets. Toss: Middlesex.

Worcestershire

T. S. Curtis run out 5		M. J. Weston run out 0
†S. J. Rhodes c Slack b Hughes 22		N. V. Radford not out 24
G. A. Hick c Cowans b Sykes 36		L-b 8, w 2 10
D. N. Patel not out 40		
D. B. D'Oliveira c Downton b Hughes . 0		1/19 2/69 3/69 (6 wkts, 40 overs) 183
*P. A. Neale c Butcher b Emburey 46		4/72 5/145 6/146

S. M. McEwan, R. K. Illingworth and A. P. Pridgeon did not bat.

Bowling: Rose 8–0–35–0; Cowans 8–1–22–0; Sykes 6–0–28–1; Hughes 8–0–25–2; Emburey 8–0–52–1; Gatting 2–0–13–0.

Middlesex

C. T. Radley c and b Weston 21		J. E. Emburey not out 44
W. N. Slack b Illingworth 52		
J. D. Carr b Radford 0		B 3, l-b 6, n-b 3 12
R. O. Butcher c Rhodes b Patel 12		
*M. W. Gatting b Radford 16		1/50 2/51 3/70 (5 wkts, 39.2 overs) 185
†P. R. Downton not out 28		4/93 5/125

G. D. Rose, J. F. Sykes, S. P. Hughes and N. G. Cowans did not bat.

Bowling: Pridgeon 7.2–0–45–0; Weston 8–0–29–1; Radford 8–1–24–2; Patel 8–0–36–1; McEwan 6–0–32–0; Illingworth 2–1–10–1.

Umpires: J. A. Jameson and R. Palmer.

At Cardiff, September 7. MIDDLESEX beat GLAMORGAN by nine wickets.

NORTHAMPTONSHIRE

At Southampton, May 11. NORTHAMPTONSHIRE lost to HAMPSHIRE by 4 runs.

NORTHAMPTONSHIRE v LEICESTERSHIRE

At Northampton, May 25. Northamptonshire won by 47 runs. Toss: Leicestershire.

Northamptonshire

R. J. Bailey lbw b Clift	89	†D. Ripley not out	7
M. R. Gouldstone b Benjamin	4	N. G. B. Cook not out	4
R. J. Boyd-Moss lbw b DeFreitas	12	L-b 7, w 5	12
D. J. Capel b Benjamin	54		
R. A. Harper b Benjamin	4	1/10 2/40 3/153 (7 wkts, 40 overs)	202
*G. Cook b Agnew	4	4/157 5/177	
R. G. Williams c Gill b Agnew	12	6/190 7/192	

N. A. Mallender and A. Walker did not bat.

Bowling: Agnew 8-0-22-2; Benjamin 8-1-39-3; Clift 8-0-55-1; DeFreitas 8-1-31-1; Briers 8-0-48-0.

Leicestershire

*N. E. Briers run out	32	M. Blackett not out	3
J. C. Balderstone st Ripley b Harper	47	†P. Gill not out	2
J. J. Whitaker c Harper b Walker	6		
T. J. Boon lbw b Williams	13	B 4, l-b 8, w 2	14
P. A. J. DeFreitas c and b Harper	1		
P. B. Clift st Ripley b Harper	7	1/63 2/78 3/103 (8 wkts, 40 overs)	155
I. P. Butcher run out	18	4/105 5/107 6/127	
W. K. M. Benjamin c Mallender b Walker	12	7/145 8/151	

J. P. Agnew did not bat.

Bowling: Mallender 5-1-13-0; Capel 4-0-21-0; N. G. B. Cook 8-1-34-0; Walker 7-0-29-2; Harper 8-0-18-3; Williams 8-0-28-1.

Umpires: B. Leadbeater and N. T. Plews.

NORTHAMPTONSHIRE v WORCESTERSHIRE

At Northampton, June 8. Northamptonshire won by 29 runs. Toss: Worcestershire.

Northamptonshire

*G. Cook c Rhodes b Inchmore	4	R. A. Harper not out	25
R. J. Bailey not out	118	L-b 5, w 1	6
R. J. Boyd-Moss c Radford b Weston	14		
D. J. Capel c Weston b Radford	61	1/13 2/51 3/174 (3 wkts, 40 overs)	228

D. J. Wild, R. G. Williams, †S. N. V. Waterton, N. G. B. Cook, N. A. Mallender and A. Walker did not bat.

Bowling: Radford 8-0-47-1; Inchmore 8-0-43-1; Pridgeon 8-1-34-0; Weston 8-0-34-1; Illingworth 6-0-38-0; Patel 2-0-27-0.

Worcestershire

D. N. Patel c Waterton b Capel	0	J. D. Inchmore c G. Cook b Walker	2
D. B. D'Oliveira c and b Harper	41	R. K. Illingworth b Walker	3
D. M. Smith b N. G. B. Cook	52	A. P. Pridgeon not out	0
G. A. Hick b N. G. B. Cook	14		
*P. A. Neale run out	1	L-b 9, w 2	11
M. J. Weston st Waterton			
b N. G. B. Cook	18	1/0 2/68 3/101	(39.3 overs) 199
†S. J. Rhodes c Harper b Mallender	46	4/103 5/125 6/143	
N. V. Radford c G. Cook b Walker	11	7/161 8/169 9/191	

Bowling: Capel 4-0-23-1; Mallender 6.3-1-31-1; Walker 8-1-38-3; Harper 8-0-42-1; N. G. B. Cook 8-0-32-3; Wild 5-0-24-0.

Umpires: D. J. Constant and M. J. Kitchen.

NORTHAMPTONSHIRE v WARWICKSHIRE

At Northampton, June 15. Northamptonshire won by seven wickets. Toss: Northamptonshire.

Warwickshire

T. A. Lloyd c Lamb b Capel	13	G. C. Small lbw b Walker	1
D. L. Amiss b Harper	44	A. R. K. Pierson not out	5
A. I. Kallicharran c Cook b Walker	5		
†G. W. Humpage c Capel b Wild	12	B 1, l-b 1, w 2	4
P. A. Smith lbw b Wild	13		
Asif Din not out	24	1/18 2/36 3/62	(8 wkts, 40 overs) 132
A. M. Ferreira run out	10	4/87 5/91 6/105	
G. J. Parsons c Waterton b Harper	1	7/108 8/111	

*N. Gifford did not bat.

Bowling: Capel 5-0-19-1; Mallender 6-0-25-0; Cook 8-0-26-0; Walker 7-1-21-2; Wild 6-0-21-2; Harper 8-1-18-2.

Northamptonshire

R. G. Williams c Kallicharran b Parsons	9	*R. A. Harper not out	26
R. J. Bailey c Kallicharran b Smith	31	B 4, l-b 3, n-b 1	8
R. J. Boyd-Moss not out	37		
A. J. Lamb b Asif Din	22	1/19 2/58 3/96	(3 wkts, 36 overs) 133

D. J. Capel, D. J. Wild, †S. N. V. Waterton, N. G. B. Cook, N. A. Mallender and A. Walker did not bat.

Bowling: Small 6-1-25-0; Parsons 6-2-13-1; Pierson 8-1-30-0; Smith 6-0-21-1; Gifford 8-0-26-0; Asif Din 2-0-11-1.

Umpires: J. H. Hampshire and A. A. Jones.

NORTHAMPTONSHIRE v YORKSHIRE

At Luton, June 22. Northamptonshire won by seven wickets. Toss: Northamptonshire. Rain interrupted play when Northamptonshire were 150 for three, resulting in their being set a revised target of 199 off 36 overs.

Yorkshire

K. Sharp run out 94	P. J. Hartley c G. Cook b Wild 4
A. A. Metcalfe c Waterton b Capel ... 9	P. W. Jarvis c Harper b Mallender 10
S. N. Hartley run out 46	S. J. Dennis not out 0
*†D. L. Bairstow c Walker	
b N. G. B. Cook . 7	B 12, w 2 14
P. E. Robinson lbw b Wild 0	
J. D. Love lbw b Harper 11	1/23 2/128 3/146 (38.3 overs) 220
P. Carrick run out 25	4/146 5/174 6/177
A. Sidebottom retired hurt 0	7/181 8/219 9/220

Bowling: Mallender 6.3–1–29–1; Capel 5–0–27–1; Walker 7–0–42–0; Harper 8–0–36–1; Wild 7–0–42–2; N. G. B. Cook 5–0–32–1.

Northamptonshire

R. J. Bailey c Bairstow b P. J. Hartley . 13	R. A. Harper not out 20
W. Larkins c sub b P. J. Hartley 92	L-b 8, w 5, n-b 1 14
R. J. Boyd-Moss lbw b P. J. Hartley .. 28	
D. J. Capel not out 32	1/37 2/139 3/150 (3 wkts, 33.4 overs) 199

*G. Cook, D. J. Wild, †S. N. V. Waterton, N. G. B. Cook, N. A. Mallender and A. Walker did not bat.

Bowling: Jarvis 6.4–0–45–0; P. J. Hartley 8–0–47–3; Dennis 7–0–29–0; S. N. Hartley 4–0–19–0; Love 5–0–31–0; Carrick 3–0–20–0.

Umpires: D. G. L. Evans and K. J. Lyons.

At Hastings, June 29. NORTHAMPTONSHIRE beat SUSSEX by 88 runs.

NORTHAMPTONSHIRE v SURREY

At Tring, July 6. Northamptonshire won by 69 runs. Toss: Surrey.

Northamptonshire

R. J. Boyd-Moss c and b Monkhouse .. 86	*G. Cook not out 4
R. J. Bailey c Ward b Needham 58	
A. J. Lamb c Lynch b Pocock 56	B 3, l-b 5, w 6 14
D. J. Capel c Bicknell b Monkhouse .. 16	
R. A. Harper not out 24	1/82 2/164 3/212 (5 wkts, 40 overs) 264
D. J. Wild c Needham b Monkhouse .. 6	4/226 5/255

†S. N. V. Waterton, N. G. B. Cook, N. A. Mallender and A. Walker did not bat.

Bowling: Doughty 6–0–30–0; Monkhouse 8–0–48–3; Needham 8–0–51–1; Clarke 8–1–44–0; Bicknell 6–0–44–0; Pocock 4–0–39–1.

Surrey

A. R. Butcher c Capel b Mallender 13	S. T. Clarke c Lamb b N. G. B. Cook . 15
M. A. Lynch b Mallender 4	M. P. Bicknell b Walker 13
A. J. Stewart b Harper 40	*P. I. Pocock not out 1
†C. J. Richards c Mallender b Walker . 14	
D. M. Ward b N. G. B. Cook 17	L-b 14, w 3 17
A. Needham b Harper 20	
R. J. Doughty st Waterton	1/9 2/40 3/83 (9 wkts, 40 overs) 195
b N. G. B. Cook . 22	4/83 5/116 6/126
G. Monkhouse not out 19	7/148 8/169 9/194

Bowling: Mallender 6–1–14–2; Capel 5–0–24–0; Walker 7–0–35–2; Harper 8–0–44–2; N. G. B. Cook 8–0–33–3; Wild 6–0–31–0.

Umpires: D. J. Constant and R. Palmer.

NORTHAMPTONSHIRE v DERBYSHIRE

At Finedon, July 13. Northamptonshire won by 97 runs. Toss: Derbyshire.

Northamptonshire

R. J. Boyd-Moss lbw b Miller	20	*G. Cook not out	8
R. J. Bailey b Warner	34		
A. J. Lamb run out	97	B 1, l-b 16, w 8, n-b 1	26
D. J. Capel b Malcolm	47		
R. A. Harper c Barnett b Warner	4	1/50 2/73 3/195 (6 wkts, 40 overs) 242	
D. J. Wild c Marples b Malcolm	6	4/217 5/224 6/242	

†S. N. V. Waterton, N. G. B. Cook, N. A. Mallender and A. Walker did not bat.

Bowling: Malcolm 8–0–40–2; Jean-Jacques 8–0–53–0; Mortensen 8–1–33–0; Miller 4–0–20–1; Warner 8–0–55–2; Sharma 4–0–24–0.

Derbyshire

*K. J. Barnett c Lamb b Wild	46	M. Jean-Jacques run out	1
†C. Marples c Mallender b Walker	42	O. H. Mortensen not out	3
A. Hill b N. G. B. Cook	1	D. E. Malcolm b Wild	16
J. E. Morris c Bailey b N. G. B. Cook	11	B 1, l-b 3, w 4	8
B. Roberts b Harper	0		
G. Miller b Wild	9	1/76 2/88 3/102 (36.1 overs) 145	
R. Sharma c Mallender b Wild	3	4/103 5/107 6/118	
A. E. Warner c Waterton b Wild	5	7/119 8/121 9/125	

Bowling: Capel 3–0–27–0; Mallender 4–0–21–0; N. G. B. Cook 8–0–32–2; Walker 5–0–18–1; Harper 8–1–25–1; Wild 7.1–2–7–5; Boyd-Moss 1–0–11–0.

Umpires: H. D. Bird and B. Dudleston.

At Neath, July 20. NORTHAMPTONSHIRE lost to GLAMORGAN by 50 runs.

NORTHAMPTONSHIRE v KENT

At Northampton, July 27. Northamptonshire won by 100 runs. Toss: Northamptonshire.

Northamptonshire

R. J. Bailey c Hinks b Baptiste	52	*G. Cook not out	15
W. Larkins c Hinks b C. S. Cowdrey	31	B 1, l-b 8, w 4, n-b 2	15
A. J. Lamb b C. S. Cowdrey	17		
D. J. Capel run out	41	1/65 2/99 3/111 (4 wkts, 40 overs) 228	
R. A. Harper not out	57	4/200	

D. J. Wild, †S. N. V. Waterton, N. G. B. Cook, N. A. Mallender and A. Walker did not bat.

Bowling: Jarvis 8–0–57–0; Ellison 8–0–36–0; Baptiste 8–0–49–1; C. S. Cowdrey 8–1–32–2; Underwood 8–0–45–0.

Kent

M. R. Benson b Capel	23	†S. A. Marsh c Capel b Walker	10
S. G. Hinks c Waterton b Mallender	5	D. L. Underwood c Harper b Walker	2
C. J. Tavaré c Wild b Capel	11	K. B. S. Jarvis not out	3
N. R. Taylor c and b N. G. B. Cook	45	L-b 3, w 1	4
*C. S. Cowdrey c Waterton b Capel	0		
G. R. Cowdrey c and b Walker	1	1/13 2/38 3/43 (35.1 overs) 128	
E. A. E. Baptiste lbw b Harper	9	4/43 5/52 6/74	
R. M. Ellison c Bailey b N. G. B. Cook	15	7/97 8/115 9/123	

Bowling: Mallender 5–0–13–1; Capel 8–0–28–3; Walker 6.1–0–15–3; N. G. B. Cook 8–0–40–2; Harper 4–0–15–1; Wild 4–0–14–0.

Umpires: J. W. Holder and R. A. White.

At Lord's, August 3. MIDDLESEX v NORTHAMPTONSHIRE. No result.

NORTHAMPTONSHIRE v SOMERSET

At Wellingborough School, August 10. No result after rain ended play. Botham hit a new John Player League record of thirteen 6s, as well as twelve 4s in his 27-over innings. His 175 not out was 1 run short of G. A. Gooch's record for the competition. Toss: Northamptonshire.

Somerset

B. C. Rose c G. Cook b Capel	7	J. Garner not out	3
*P. M. Roebuck lbw b Mallender	9		
I. V. A. Richards lbw b Capel	21	L-b 6, w 6, n-b 1	13
I. T. Botham not out	175		
N. A. Felton c Harper b N. G. B. Cook	35	1/16 2/18 3/51 (5 wkts, 39 overs) 272	
R. J. Harden c Harper b Walker	9	4/185 5/234	

V. J. Marks, †T. Gard, M. R. Davis and G. V. Palmer did not bat.

Bowling: Mallender 7–0–48–1; Capel 8–1–31–2; Wild 8–0–57–0; Walker 8–0–64–1; Harper 5–0–39–0; N. G. B. Cook 3–0–27–1.

Northamptonshire

R. J. Bailey c Roebuck b Richards	1
W. Larkins not out	38
A. J. Lamb not out	14
L-b 1	1
1/3 (1 wkt, 15 overs) 54	

*G. Cook, D. J. Capel, D. J. Wild, R. A. Harper, †S. N. V. Waterton, N. G. B. Cook, N. A. Mallender and A. Walker did not bat.

Bowling: Garner 5–1–8–0; Richards 7–1–21–1; Palmer 2–0–16–0; Davis 1–0–8–0.

Umpires: B. Leadbeater and A. G. T. Whitehead.

At Colchester, August 17. NORTHAMPTONSHIRE lost to Essex by 32 runs.

At Manchester, August 24. NORTHAMPTONSHIRE lost to LANCASHIRE by five wickets.

At Moreton-in-Marsh, August 31. NORTHAMPTONSHIRE beat GLOUCESTERSHIRE by 12 runs.

At Nottingham, September 14. NORTHAMPTONSHIRE lost to NOTTINGHAMSHIRE by seven wickets.

NOTTINGHAMSHIRE

At Lord's, May 4. NOTTINGHAMSHIRE beat MIDDLESEX by 46 runs.

NOTTINGHAMSHIRE v WARWICKSHIRE

At Nottingham, May 11. Warwickshire won by 48 runs. Toss: Nottinghamshire.

Warwickshire

T. A. Lloyd run out	58	G. J. Lord not out	1
D. L. Amiss b Rice	40	G. J. Parsons not out	6
†G. W. Humpage b Rice	86	L-b 13, w 3	16
Asif Din lbw b Pick	14		
P. A. Smith b Rice	14	1/73 2/148 3/199 (6 wkts, 40 overs) 236
B. M. McMillan lbw b Rice	1	4/219 5/225 6/230

A. R. K. Pierson, T. A. Munton and *N. Gifford did not bat.

Bowling: Hadlee 8-0-43-0; Cooper 8-1-21-0; Saxelby 8-0-55-0; Rice 8-1-49-4; Pick 8-0-55-1.

Nottinghamshire

R. T. Robinson c Lloyd b McMillan	7	R. A. Pick b Gifford	6
B. C. Broad b Pierson	17	K. Saxelby not out	4
*C. E. B. Rice c Gifford b Munton	11	K. E. Cooper c Humpage b McMillan	5
P. Johnson lbw b Parsons	1	B 5, l-b 9, w 3	17
D. W. Randall c Smith b Gifford	33		
J. D. Birch b McMillan	66	1/27 2/31 3/32 (37.3 overs) 188
R. J. Hadlee c Lord b Munton	9	4/51 5/96 6/113
†B. N. French c Lord b Pierson	12	7/158 8/172 9/180

Bowling: McMillan 6.3-1-23-3; Parsons 8-0-33-2; Munton 8-1-31-2; Pierson 7-0-48-1; Gifford 7-0-26-2; Smith 1-0-13-0.

Umpires: J. W. Holder and P. B. Wight.

NOTTINGHAMSHIRE v SUSSEX

At Nottingham, May 18. Sussex won by one wicket. Toss: Sussex. Jones scored 12 runs off the last over, having earlier taken seven wickets for 41 – the fourth-best return, and the best by a Sussex bowler, in the John Player League.

Nottinghamshire

R. T. Robinson c le Roux b Jones	 55	R. A. Pick b Jones	 5
B. C. Broad lbw b Reeve	 46	K. E. Cooper not out	 1
*C. E. B. Rice b Jones	 23		
P. Johnson c le Roux b Jones	 10	L-b 16, w 9, n-b 1	 26
D. W. Randall c and b Jones	 12		
R. J. Hadlee b Jones	 2	1/89 2/142 3/151	(8 wkts, 40 overs) 198
J. D. Birch c Pigott b Jones	 4	4/155 5/165 6/174	
†B. N. French not out	 14	7/181 8/197	

J. A. Afford did not bat.

Bowling: C. M. Wells 5-0-21-0; le Roux 7-0-20-0; Imran 5-0-24-0; Reeve 8-0-35-1; Jones 7-0-41-7; Pigott 8-0-41-0.

Sussex

A. M. Green b Pick	 36	*J. R. T. Barclay not out	 6
P. W. G. Parker c French b Cooper	... 22	A. C. S. Pigott run out	 0
Imran Khan c French b Pick	 15	A. N. Jones not out	 17
C. M. Wells c Rice b Pick	 11	L-b 13, w 4, n-b 5	 22
A. P. Wells st French b Afford	 2		
†I. J. Gould c Birch b Rice	 63	1/57 2/81 3/82	(9 wkts, 40 overs) 203
G. S. le Roux lbw b Rice	 1	4/88 5/113 6/133	
D. A. Reeve lbw b Rice	 8	7/164 8/180 9/181	

Bowling: Hadlee 8-0-40-0; Cooper 8-0-25-1; Afford 8-1-27-1; Pick 8-0-40-3; Rice 8-0-58-3.

Umpires: H. D. Bird and A. G. T. Whitehead.

At Southampton, June 1. NOTTINGHAMSHIRE beat HAMPSHIRE by seven wickets.

At Chelmsford, June 8. NOTTINGHAMSHIRE lost to ESSEX by 11 runs.

NOTTINGHAMSHIRE v SURREY

At Nottingham, June 15. Nottinghamshire won by three wickets. Toss: Nottinghamshire.

Surrey

G. S. Clinton c French b Pick	 21	G. Monkhouse not out	 24
M. A. Lynch c Randall b Hemmings	... 78	A. H. Gray b Hadlee	 6
A. R. Butcher c French b Pick	 2	*P. I. Pocock not out	 1
A. J. Stewart c Rice b Hemmings	 17	B 6, w 6	 12
T. E. Jesty lbw b Hemmings	 4		
A. Needham c Rice b Cooper	 5	1/45 2/53 3/80	(9 wkts, 40 overs) 193
†C. J. Richards c Robinson b Hadlee	... 22	4/102 5/123 6/143	
R. J. Doughty b Rice	 1	7/149 8/167 9/190	

Bowling: Hadlee 8-1-37-2; Cooper 8-1-34-1; Rice 8-0-34-1; Pick 8-0-41-2; Hemmings 8-0-41-3.

Nottinghamshire

R. T. Robinson b Gray	60	†B. N. French not out		1
B. C. Broad b Needham	44	R. A. Pick not out		1
P. Johnson st Richards b Pocock	1	B 1, l-b 6, w 3		13
*C. E. B. Rice c and b Monkhouse	35			—
D. W. Randall c and b Gray	26	1/98 2/106 3/122	(7 wkts, 39.5 overs)	194
J. D. Birch b Gray	5	4/176 5/177		
R. J. Hadlee b Butcher	8	6/191 7/193		

E. E. Hemmings and K. E. Cooper did not bat.

Bowling: Doughty 8–0–38–0; Monkhouse 8–0–31–1; Pocock 8–0–36–1; Gray 8–0–35–3; Needham 7–0–42–1; Butcher 0.5–0–2–1.

Umpires: C. Cook and D. O. Oslear.

At Bath, June 22. NOTTINGHAMSHIRE beat SOMERSET by 32 runs.

At Leicester, June 29. NOTTINGHAMSHIRE beat LEICESTERSHIRE by seven wickets.

At Worcester, July 6. NOTTINGHAMSHIRE beat WORCESTERSHIRE by seven wickets.

NOTTINGHAMSHIRE v GLOUCESTERSHIRE

At Nottingham, July 13. Nottinghamshire won by 12 runs. Toss: Gloucestershire.

Nottinghamshire

R. T. Robinson c and b Payne	24	†B. N. French not out		2
B. C. Broad b Bainbridge	38			
P. Johnson c Tomlins b Bainbridge	54	L-b 6, w 3		9
*C. E. B. Rice c Athey b Walsh	40			—
R. J. Evans c Athey b Sainsbury	11	1/49 2/93 3/136	(6 wkts, 40 overs)	181
K. P. Evans b Walsh	3	4/175 5/177 6/181		

K. E. Cooper, R. A. Pick, E. E. Hemmings and K. Saxelby did not bat.

Bowling: Sainsbury 8–0–26–1; Walsh 8–0–35–2; Bainbridge 8–0–40–2; Payne 8–1–20–1; Graveney 5–0–30–0; Athey 3–0–24–0.

Gloucestershire

C. W. J. Athey c Robinson b Rice	21	C. A. Walsh not out		0
A. W. Stovold c French b Saxelby	0			
P. Bainbridge c Broad b Pick	17	L-b 10, w 2, n-b 2		14
K. M. Curran not out	71			—
M. W. Alleyne c Hemmings b R. J. Evans	1	1/0 2/39 3/49	(5 wkts, 40 overs)	169
K. P. Tomlins run out	45	4/52 5/166		

I. R. Payne, *D. A. Graveney, †R. C. Russell and G. E. Sainsbury did not bat.

Bowling: Saxelby 8–1–36–1; Cooper 8–1–17–0; Pick 7–0–40–1; Rice 7–2–25–1; R. J. Evans 7–1–22–1; Hemmings 3–0–19–0.

Umpires: B. J. Meyer and N. T. Plews.

At Hull, July 27. NOTTINGHAMSHIRE lost to YORKSHIRE by 102 runs.

NOTTINGHAMSHIRE v GLAMORGAN

At Nottingham, August 3. No result.

NOTTINGHAMSHIRE v LANCASHIRE

At Nottingham, August 17. Nottinghamshire won by 26 runs. Toss: Lancashire.

Nottinghamshire

B. C. Broad c Lloyd b Makinson	15	C. D. Fraser-Darling not out		1
R. T. Robinson lbw b Watkinson	9			
P. Johnson run out	10	B 1, l-b 15, w 6, n-b 2		24
D. W. Randall run out	88			
*C. E. B. Rice lbw b Hayhurst	70	1/22 2/42 3/44	(5 wkts, 40 overs)	237
J. D. Birch not out	20	4/171 5/231		

†B. N. French, K. P. Evans, E. E. Hemmings and K. Saxelby did not bat.

Bowling: Watkinson 8–0–34–1; Makinson 8–0–41–1; Hayhurst 8–1–38–1; O'Shaughnessy 8–0–55–0; Simmons 8–1–53–0.

Lancashire

G. D. Mendis b Saxelby	1	J. Simmons b Rice		0
G. Fowler c Saxelby b Fraser-Darling	10	D. J. Makinson b Rice		2
J. Abrahams b Saxelby	0	A. N. Hayhurst b Rice		10
*C. H. Lloyd c Robinson b Fraser-Darling	43	B 1, l-b 14, w 4		19
N. H. Fairbrother c Rice b Saxelby	79			
S. J. O'Shaughnessy lbw b Rice	33	1/3 2/12 3/20	(39.3 overs)	211
†C. Maynard run out	10	4/104 5/181 6/183		
M. Watkinson not out	4	7/201 8/201 9/206		

Bowling: Saxelby 8–0–37–3; Fraser-Darling 8–1–32–2; Evans 8–0–48–0; Rice 7.3–1–25–4; Hemmings 8–0–54–0.

Umpires: B. Dudleston and K. E. Palmer.

NOTTINGHAMSHIRE v DERBYSHIRE

At Nottingham, August 24. Nottinghamshire won by 23 runs. Toss: Nottinghamshire.

Nottinghamshire

B. C. Broad not out	104
R. T. Robinson lbw b Finney	2
*C. E. B. Rice c Barnett b Finney	64
D. W. Randall not out	49
L-b 11, w 1, n-b 2	14
1/3 2/131 (2 wkts, 40 overs)	233

P. Johnson, J. D. Birch, †C. W. Scott, R. A. Pick, E. E. Hemmings, K. Saxelby and C. D. Fraser-Darling did not bat.

Bowling: Finney 8–0–42–2; Holding 8–0–49–0; Warner 8–0–42–0; Miller 8–0–46–0; Mortensen 8–0–43–0.

Derbyshire

*K. J. Barnett c Pick b Hemmings	37	R. Sharma not out		12
A. Hill st Scott b Hemmings	36	R. J. Finney c Saxelby b Rice		14
J. E. Morris c and b Fraser-Darling	41	O. H. Mortensen not out		0
B. Roberts b Fraser-Darling	15	L-b 9, w 1, n-b 1		11
A. E. Warner lbw b Pick	4			
†B. J. M. Maher lbw b Rice	4	1/65 2/87 3/135	(9 wkts, 40 overs)	210
G. Miller b Rice	21	4/140 5/140 6/152		
M. A. Holding c sub b Saxelby	15	7/181 8/186 9/204		

Bowling: Saxelby 8–0–49–1; Fraser-Darling 8–1–35–2; Pick 8–0–32–1; Hemmings 8–0–43–2; Rice 8–0–42–3.

Umpires: R. Julian and D. Lloyd.

At Canterbury, September 7. NOTTINGHAMSHIRE lost to KENT by six wickets.

NOTTINGHAMSHIRE v NORTHAMPTONSHIRE

At Nottingham, September 14. Nottinghamshire won by seven wickets. Toss: Nottinghamshire. Rice became the first bowler to take four wickets in an innings five times in a season in the John Player League as well as taking his season's haul to 34 wickets, equalling R. J. Clapp's record for the competition, set in 1974.

Northamptonshire

W. Larkins c Robinson b Hadlee	46	N. A. Mallender not out		1
R. J. Bailey c Cooper b Fraser-Darling	30	D. J. Wild b Rice		13
R. J. Boyd-Moss c Johnson b Rice	11			
D. J. Capel c Rice b Saxelby	27	B 6, l-b 10, w 9		25
R. A. Harper c Johnson b Rice	11			
*G. Cook b Saxelby	7	1/64 2/88 3/106	(9 wkts, 40 overs)	174
†D. Ripley run out	1	4/139 5/153 6/168		
N. G. B. Cook b Rice	2	7/170 8/172 9/174		

A. Walker did not bat.

Bowling: Cooper 8–4–16–0; Hadlee 8–0–24–1; Pick 5–0–24–0; Saxelby 8–0–34–2; Fraser-Darling 3–0–27–1; Rice 8–0–33–4.

Nottinghamshire

B. C. Broad c Harper b Mallender	25	D. W. Randall not out		10
R. T. Robinson c Larkins b Walker	20	B 1, l-b 4, w 1		6
†P. Johnson c N. G. B. Cook b Mallender	79			
*C. E. B. Rice not out	38	1/34 2/73 3/151	(3 wkts, 37.3 overs)	178

J. D. Birch, R. J. Hadlee, C. D. Fraser-Darling, R. A. Pick, K. E. Cooper and K. Saxelby did not bat.

Bowling: Mallender 8–0–28–2; Capel 8–0–44–0; N. G. B. Cook 5–0–24–0; Walker 7.3–0–36–1; Harper 8–0–35–0; Wild 1–0–6–0.

Umpires: M. J. Kitchen and P. B. Wight.

SOMERSET

At Leeds, May 4. SOMERSET lost to YORKSHIRE by five wickets.

SOMERSET v MIDDLESEX

At Taunton, May 11. Somerset won by six wickets. Toss: Somerset.

Middlesex

G. D. Barlow st Gard b Marks	18	S. P. Hughes c and b Turner	13
W. N. Slack b Botham	5	A. R. C. Fraser not out	9
*M. W. Gatting c Dredge b Marks	15	L-b 5, w 2, n-b 1	8
C. T. Radley not out	78		
R. O. Butcher c Dredge b Marks	0	1/11 2/40 3/40 (7 wkts, 40 overs)	196
†P. R. Downton c Richards b Turner	50	4/41 5/138	
J. E. Emburey b Botham	0	6/145 7/169	

N. G. Cowans and W. W. Daniel did not bat.

Bowling: Garner 8–1–17–0; Botham 8–0–39–2; Dredge 8–0–31–0; Marks 8–1–31–3; Turner 7–0–63–2; Richards 1–0–10–0.

Somerset

*P. M. Roebuck c Hughes b Emburey	68	R. J. Harden not out	5
J. G. Wyatt retired hurt	48		
J. J. E. Hardy lbw b Daniel	3	L-b 11, w 8, n-b 2	21
I. V. A. Richards b Fraser	19		
I. T. Botham not out	28	1/122 2/153 (4 wkts, 40 overs)	197
V. J. Marks b Daniel	5	3/168 4/178	

C. H. Dredge, M. S. Turner, J. Garner and †T Gard did not bat.

Bowling: Cowans 8–1–18–0; Daniel 8–0–56–2; Fraser 8–0–33–1; Hughes 8–0–30–0; Emburey 8–0–49–1.

Umpires: C. Cook and D. Lloyd.

At Cardiff, May 25. SOMERSET beat GLAMORGAN by three wickets.

At Horsham, June 1. SOMERSET beat SUSSEX by eight wickets.

SOMERSET v KENT

At Bath, June 15. Somerset won by 103 runs. Toss: Kent.

Somerset

V. J. Marks b Ellison	7	G. V. Palmer not out	7
*P. M. Roebuck c Taylor b C. S. Cowdrey	75	J. Garner not out	5
R. J. Harden c Benson b Underwood	17	L-b 14, w 10, n-b 1	25
I. V. A. Richards c Baptiste b Underwood	2		
B. C. Rose b Baptiste	66	1/28 2/85 3/96 (6 wkts, 40 overs)	244
J. J. E. Hardy b Ellison	40	4/140 5/231 6/231	

C. H. Dredge, †R. J. Blitz and N. S. Taylor did not bat.

Bowling: Jarvis 8–0–36–0; Ellison 8–0–51–2; Underwood 8–0–32–2; C. S. Cowdrey 8–0–41–1; Baptiste 8–0–70–1.

Kent

M. R. Benson run out	6	†S. A. Marsh not out	22
S. G. Hinks c Blitz b Garner	8	D. L. Underwood c Hardy b Palmer	2
C. J. Tavaré c sub b Palmer	30	K. B. S. Jarvis b Marks	0
N. R. Taylor run out	36	L-b 4, w 2, n-b 1	7
*C. S. Cowdrey c Harden b Palmer	14		
G. R. Cowdrey lbw b Taylor	14	1/9 2/16 3/68 (30.4 overs) 141	
E. A. E. Baptiste c Roebuck b Palmer	1	4/96 5/99 6/110	
R. M. Ellison c Harden b Taylor	1	7/113 8/121 9/128	

Bowling: Garner 4–1–7–1; Taylor 8–1–28–2; Dredge 5–0–14–0; Marks 5.4–0–46–1; Palmer 6–0–28–4; Richards 2–0–14–0.

Umpires: J. H. Harris and D. R. Shepherd.

SOMERSET v NOTTINGHAMSHIRE

At Bath, June 22. Nottinghamshire won by 32 runs. Toss: Somerset.

Nottinghamshire

R. T. Robinson b Garner	9	K. P. Evans b Taylor	1
B. C. Broad not out	100	R. A. Pick not out	12
*C. E. B. Rice c Dredge b Garner	68	B 1, l-b 10, w 2	13
R. J. Hadlee c Harden b Taylor	30		
†P. Johnson c Garner b Taylor	0	1/22 2/148 3/197 (7 wkts, 40 overs) 241	
D. W. Randall b Richards	4	4/197 5/201	
D. J. R. Martindale lbw b Richards	4	6/217 7/218	

E. E. Hemmings and M. K. Bore did not bat.

Bowling: Garner 8–1–33–2; Taylor 8–0–42–3; Marks 7–0–49–0; Dredge 8–0–41–0; Palmer 4–0–38–0; Richards 5–0–27–2.

Somerset

V. J. Marks c Johnson b Rice	18	J. Garner b Rice	0
*P. M. Roebuck lbw b Hadlee	0	†R. J. Blitz b Pick	1
R. J. Harden b Evans	71	N. S. Taylor b Pick	0
I. V. A. Richards b Hadlee	64	L-b 10, w 6, n-b 1	17
B. C. Rose b Rice	25		
J. J. E. Hardy b Hadlee	12	1/2 2/83 3/114 (36.3 overs) 209	
G. V. Palmer not out	1	4/183 5/197 6/207	
C. H. Dredge b Rice	0	7/208 8/208 9/209	

Bowling: Hadlee 8–0–38–3; Bore 6–0–30–0; Pick 6.3–0–28–2; Evans 8–0–56–1; Hemmings 1–0–14–0; Rice 7–0–33–4.

Umpires: A. A. Jones and R. Julian.

SOMERSET v HAMPSHIRE

At Taunton, July 6. Hampshire won by eight wickets. Toss: Hampshire.

Somerset

N. A. Felton b James	0	C. H. Dredge b Tremlett	17
*P. M. Roebuck lbw b Tremlett	25	J. Garner not out	2
R. J. Harden c Marshall b James	3	N. S. Taylor b Tremlett	2
I. V. A. Richards b James	0	B 4, l-b 6, w 3, n-b 1	14
B. C. Rose c Terry b Connor	21		
J. J. E. Hardy lbw b Tremlett	0	1/0 2/28 3/31	(34 overs) 103
V. J. Marks c Parks b James	0	4/33 5/37 6/40	
†T. Gard c Parks b Marshall	19	7/69 8/97 9/99	

Bowling: James 8–0–24–4; Connor 6–0–13–1; Tremlett 7–0–18–4; Marshall 7–1–20–1; Cowley 6–0–18–0.

Hampshire

V. P. Terry c Gard b Garner	5
D. R. Turner not out	40
*M. C. J. Nicholas c Felton b Garner	1
R. A. Smith not out	46
L-b 5, w 5, n-b 2	12
1/6 2/12 (2 wkts, 28.1 overs)	104

C. L. Smith, K. D. James, M. D. Marshall, N. G. Cowley, T. M. Tremlett, †R. J. Parks and C. A. Connor did not bat.

Bowling: Garner 8–2–21–2; Taylor 6–0–34–0; Dredge 4–0–13–0; Marks 4–0–12–0; Richards 6.1–0–19–0.

Umpires: J. H. Harris and D. O. Oslear.

At Chelmsford, July 13. SOMERSET lost to ESSEX by 35 runs.

At Bristol, July 20. SOMERSET lost to GLOUCESTERSHIRE by eight wickets.

SOMERSET v LANCASHIRE

At Taunton, July 27. Somerset won by eight wickets. Toss: Somerset.

Lancashire

G. D. Mendis b Davis	3	†C. Maynard b Taylor	8
G. Fowler c Gard b Turner	0	M. Watkinson not out	34
J. Abrahams not out	103	L-b 6, w 4, n-b 1	11
*C. H. Lloyd c Garner b Marks	7		
N. H. Fairbrother c Rose b Davis	39	1/6 2/20 3/59	(6 wkts, 40 overs) 211
S. J. O'Shaughnessy b Taylor	6	4/122 5/143 6/153	

J. Simmons, P. J. W. Allott and D. J. Makinson did not bat.

Bowling: Davis 8–0–35–2; Turner 7–0–45–1; Marks 6–0–30–1; Taylor 8–0–37–2; Garner 8–0–29–0; Richards 3–0–29–0.

Somerset

B. C. Rose c Maynard b Allott 30
*P. M. Roebuck not out 75
I. V. A. Richards b Simmons 62
R. J. Harden not out 28
        L-b 12, w 5 17
                       —

1/65 2/153   (2 wkts, 38.2 overs) 212

N. A. Felton, V. J. Marks, M. S. Turner, N. S. Taylor, M. R. Davis, J. Garner and †T. Gard did not bat.

Bowling: Watkinson 7.2-0-34-0; Makinson 7-0-39-0; Allott 8-0-25-1; O'Shaughnessy 8-0-43-0; Simmons 8-0-59-1.

Umpires: K. J. Lyons and D. R. Shepherd.

SOMERSET v WORCESTERSHIRE

At Weston-super-Mare, August 3. Somerset won by four wickets. Toss: Somerset. Rain, which had already reduced the match to 25 overs a side, reduced Somerset's target to 124 off twenty overs.

Worcestershire

T. S. Curtis c Richards b Palmer 39	R. K. Illingworth run out 1
D. M. Smith b Richards 1	S. M. McEwan not out 7
G. A. Hick b Richards 4	
D. N. Patel b Davis 31	L-b 7, w 5, n-b 1 13
*P. A. Neale c Marks b Taylor 15	
D. B. D'Oliveira c Harden b Botham .. 23	1/5 2/27 3/67 (8 wkts, 24 overs) 147
†S. J. Rhodes not out 12	4/84 5/114 6/131
N. V. Radford lbw b Botham 1	7/135 8/136

A. P. Pridgeon did not bat.

Bowling: Taylor 4-0-30-1; Richards 5-0-25-2; Marks 3-0-21-0; Palmer 3-0-20-1; Davis 5-0-26-1; Botham 4-0-18-2.

Somerset

I. T. Botham c and b Pridgeon 3	G. V. Palmer b Radford 33
B. C. Rose c and b Illingworth 15	M. R. Davis not out 0
I. V. A. Richards run out 10	L-b 4, w 3 7
R. J. Harden c Rhodes b McEwan 12	
N. A. Felton c Rhodes b McEwan 13	1/6 2/29 3/32 (6 wkts, 19.3 overs) 125
V. J. Marks not out 32	4/56 5/62 6/115

*P. M. Roebuck, †T. Gard and N. S. Taylor did not bat.

Bowling: Radford 5-0-36-1; Pridgeon 4.3-0-39-1; Illingworth 5-0-25-1; McEwan 5-1-21-2.

Umpires: H. D. Bird and J. H. Hampshire.

At Wellingborough School, August 10. NORTHAMPTONSHIRE v SOMERSET. No result.

SOMERSET v SURREY

At Taunton, August 17. No result after rain ended play. Toss: Somerset.

Surrey

A. R. Butcher c and b Marks	....	50
G. S. Clinton c Felton b Taylor	....	70
A. J. Stewart b Taylor	....	1
M. A. Lynch c Taylor b Botham	......	15
†C. J. Richards not out	....	47
D. M. Ward lbw b Garner	....	1

D. J. Thomas not out 5

L-b 3, w 6 9
————
1/110 2/113 3/133   (5 wkts, 36 overs) 198
4/162 5/168

R. J. Doughty, S. T. Clarke, *P. I. Pocock and A. Needham did not bat.

Bowling: Garner 6–1–23–1; Richards 5–0–21–0; Botham 6–0–48–1; Marks 8–0–33–1; Taylor 8–0–41–2; Palmer 3–0–29–0.

Somerset

*P. M. Roebuck, N. A. Felton, R. J. Harden, I. V. A. Richards, B. C. Rose, I. T. Botham, V. J. Marks, †T. Gard, G. V. Palmer, J. Garner and N. S. Taylor.

Umpires: C. Cook and J. W. Holder.

At Birmingham, August 24. SOMERSET beat WARWICKSHIRE by six wickets.

At Leicester, August 31. SOMERSET lost to LEICESTERSHIRE by 56 runs.

SOMERSET v DERBYSHIRE

At Taunton, September 14. Somerset won by three wickets. Toss: Somerset.

Derbyshire

*K. J. Barnett c Botham b Marks	.....	40
A. Hill b Richards	....	50
J. E. Morris b Dredge	....	10
B. Roberts not out	....	40
†B. J. M. Maher b Garner	....	14
M. A. Holding b Botham	....	14

A. E. Warner not out 27

B 1, l-b 8, w 2, n-b 1 12
————
1/63 2/92 3/128   (5 wkts, 40 overs) 207
4/158 5/177

R. Sharma, R. J. Finney, O. H. Mortensen and M. Jean-Jacques did not bat.

Bowling: Garner 8–1–27–1; Botham 8–0–60–1; Taylor 4–0–16–0; Marks 8–0–39–1; Dredge 8–1–35–1; Richards 4–0–21–1.

Somerset

N. A. Felton c Maher b Finney	.....	3
P. A. C. Bail b Finney	....	18
R. J. Harden run out	....	25
I. V. A. Richards b Jean-Jacques	.....	55
I. T. Botham c Sharma b Warner	.....	32
J. J. E. Hardy c Morris b Finney	.....	12
*V. J. Marks not out	....	23

J. Garner run out 13
C. H. Dredge not out 14
L-b 6, w 6, n-b 4 16
————
1/5 2/31 3/77   (7 wkts, 39 overs) 211
4/141 5/157
6/157 7/185

N. S. Taylor and †T.Gard did not bat.

Bowling: Mortensen 8–0–39–0; Finney 8–0–40–3; Jean-Jacques 8–0–39–1; Holding 7–0–36–0; Warner 8–0–51–1.

Umpires: K. J. Lyons and B. Leadbeater.

SURREY

SURREY v YORKSHIRE

At The Oval, May 11. Yorkshire won by six wickets. Toss: Yorkshire.

Surrey

A. R. Butcher c and b Sidebottom	1	G. Monkhouse c Love b Sidebottom	5
G. S. Clinton not out	92	M. A. Feltham not out	0
A. J. Stewart b P. J. Hartley	28	L-b 8, w 4, n-b 1	13
M. A. Lynch b Carrick	10		
T. E. Jesty c S. N. Hartley b Fletcher	11	1/2 2/64 3/87 (7 wkts, 40 overs) 206	
†C. J. Richards b P. J. Hartley	32	4/110 5/162	
R. J. Doughty c Love b Sidebottom	14	6/196 7/204	

S. T. Clarke and *P. I. Pocock did not bat.

Bowling: Fletcher 8–0–30–1; Sidebottom 8–0–47–3; Carrick 8–0–32–1; S. N. Hartley 2–0–20–0; P. J. Hartley 6–0–34–2; Jarvis 8–0–35–0.

Yorkshire

K. Sharp b Jesty	9	*†D. L. Bairstow not out	83
M. D. Moxon b Jesty	11	B 1, l-b 8, w 3, n-b 1	13
A. A. Metcalfe not out	74		
J. D. Love c and b Pocock	13	1/17 2/30 3/59 (4 wkts, 37 overs) 210	
S. N. Hartley c Richards b Clarke	7	4/80	

S. D. Fletcher, P. Carrick, P. J. Hartley, P. W. Jarvis and A. Sidebottom did not bat.

Bowling: Jesty 8–0–28–2; Doughty 8–0–25–0; Pocock 4–0–37–1; Clarke 6–0–13–1; Monkhouse 6–0–48–0; Feltham 5–0–50–0.

Umpires: J. Birkenshaw and A. A. Jones.

SURREY v GLAMORGAN

At The Oval, May 18. Surrey won by 12 runs. Toss: Glamorgan.

Surrey

*A. R. Butcher c Morris b Thomas	5	A. Needham not out	10
G. S. Clinton b Base	66	M. A. Feltham not out	4
A. J. Stewart st Davies b Ontong	31	B 3, l-b 2, w 5	10
M. A. Lynch c Davies b Ontong	0		
T. E. Jesty run out	26	1/11 2/67 3/75 (7 wkts, 40 overs) 161	
†C. J. Richards c Steele b Base	8	4/134 5/138	
R. J. Doughty b Base	1	6/143 7/153	

G. Monkhouse and S. T. Clarke did not bat.

Bowling: Thomas 7–1–24–1; Base 8–0–31–3; Ontong 8–0–28–2; Steele 8–0–26–0; Derrick 5–0–25–0; Holmes 4–0–22–0.

Glamorgan

J. A. Hopkins c Clarke b Doughty	 12	J. Derrick not out	6
H. Morris c Doughty b Butcher	 44	J. F. Steele b Monkhouse	11
D. B. Pauline c Butcher b Needham	.. 4	S. J. Base run out	1
G. C. Holmes b Needham	 4	B 1, l-b 7, w 5	13
*R. C. Ontong run out	 23		
M. P. Maynard c Richards b Clarke	.. 12	1/34 2/52 3/60	(39.1 overs) 149
J. G. Thomas run out	 16	4/80 5/102 6/127	
†T. Davies c and b Monkhouse	 3	7/128 8/132 9/146	

Bowling: Clarke 7.1-0-18-1; Feltham 6-1-32-0; Doughty 4-0-21-1; Needham 8-2-13-2; Monkhouse 8-1-21-2; Jesty 3-0-21-0; Butcher 3-0-15-1.

Umpires: J. H. Hampshire and N. T. Plews.

At Canterbury, May 25. SURREY tied with KENT.

SURREY v MIDDLESEX

At The Oval, June 1. Middlesex won by three wickets. Toss: Middlesex.

Surrey

*A. R. Butcher c Rose b Hughes	 47	†C. J. Richards not out	 15
G. S. Clinton c Edmonds b Fraser	 32		
A. J. Stewart c Emburey b Hughes	 0	B 1, l-b 14, w 1, n-b 4	 20
M. A. Lynch c Rose b Hughes	 12		
T. E. Jesty not out	 40	1/85 2/87 3/99	(5 wkts, 40 overs) 187
A. Needham b Emburey	 21	4/111 5/144	

R. J. Doughty, G. Monkhouse, M. A. Feltham and S. T. Clarke did not bat.

Bowling: Daniel 8-0-36-0; Fraser 8-0-32-1; Emburey 8-2-42-1; Hughes 8-0-33-3; Edmonds 8-1-29-0.

Middlesex

G. D. Barlow c and b Needham	 15	S. P. Hughes not out	 8
A. J. T. Miller b Needham	 37	P. H. Edmonds not out	 2
*M. W. Gatting b Doughty	 12	B 1, l-b 2, w 7	 10
R. O. Butcher c Doughty b Needham	.. 21		
†P. R. Downton b Feltham	 46	1/28 2/55 3/89	(7 wkts, 39.1 overs) 188
J. E. Emburey c Clarke b Feltham	 33	4/92 5/159	
G. D. Rose run out	 4	6/173 7/178	

A. R. C. Fraser and W. W. Daniel did not bat.

Bowling: Doughty 8-0-29-1; Feltham 8-1-37-2; Needham 8-0-46-3; Clarke 8-0-28-0; Monkhouse 7.1-0-45-0.

Umpires: H. D. Bird and B. Leadbeater.

SURREY v DERBYSHIRE

At The Oval, June 8. Derbyshire won by three wickets. Toss: Derbyshire.

Surrey

G. S. Clinton c Sharma b Mortensen .. 55	S. T. Clarke not out 7
M. A. Lynch c Holding b Mortensen .. 45	M. P. Bicknell not out 0
A. J. Stewart c Morris b Miller 18	
T. E. Jesty run out 5	L-b 5, w 7 12
D. M. Ward c Holding b Sharma 17	
†C. J. Richards c Anderson b Finney .. 35	1/83 2/111 3/120 (8 wkts, 40 overs) 198
G. Monkhouse c Mortensen b Holding . 3	4/137 5/159 6/171
M. A. Feltham c Mortensen b Holding 1	7/188 8/191

*P. I. Pocock did not bat.

Bowling: Holding 8-1-19-2; Finney 5-0-30-1; Taylor 4-0-30-0; Miller 8-0-33-1; Mortensen 8-0-42-2; Sharma 7-0-39-1.

Derbyshire

*K. J. Barnett c Lynch b Monkhouse .. 92	R. Sharma not out 0
I. S. Anderson c Stewart b Pocock 25	R. J. Finney not out 2
A. Hill c Lynch b Pocock 14	
J. E. Morris run out 1	L-b 7 7
†B. Roberts run out 44	
G. Miller lbw b Clarke 0	1/68 2/115 3/131 (7 wkts, 38 overs) 199
M. A. Holding st Richards b Monkhouse 14	4/153 5/163 6/191

O. H. Mortensen and J. P. Taylor did not bat.

Bowling: Bicknell 8-0-27-0; Feltham 7-0-39-0; Monkhouse 7-1-50-2; Clarke 7-1-32-1; Pocock 8-0-30-2; Jesty 1-0-14-0.

Umpires: J. H. Harris and R. A. White.

At Nottingham, June 15. SURREY lost to NOTTINGHAMSHIRE by three wickets.

At Bristol, June 29. SURREY beat GLOUCESTERSHIRE by eight wickets.

At Tring, July 6. SURREY lost to NORTHAMPTONSHIRE by 69 runs.

SURREY v SUSSEX

At Guildford, July 27. Sussex won by 11 runs. Toss: Surrey.

Sussex

A. M. Green c Clarke b Feltham 69	D. A. Reeve run out 2
P. W. G. Parker lbw b Doughty 8	A. C. S. Pigott not out 1
Imran Khan st Richards b Monkhouse 13	A. N. Jones not out 9
C. M. Wells c Lynch b Feltham 34	B 3, l-b 9, w 3, n-b 3 18
A. P. Wells c Stewart b Clarke 21	
*†I. J. Gould c Medlycott b Feltham .. 30	1/20 2/56 3/124 (9 wkts, 40 overs) 214
G. S. le Roux c Feltham b Clarke 4	4/145 5/176 6/195
C. P. Phillipson c Clarke b Feltham ... 5	7/197 8/202 9/202

Bowling: Doughty 8-1-38-1; Clarke 8-0-35-2; Monkhouse 8-0-31-1; Thomas 8-0-42-0; Feltham 6-0-35-4; Medlycott 2-0-21-0.

Surrey

A. J. Stewart lbw b C. M. Wells	0	M. A. Feltham c and b Imran	37
G. S. Clinton run out	56	S. T. Clarke not out	9
M. A. Lynch b Jones	34	G. Monkhouse not out	1
*T. E. Jesty b le Roux	9	L-b 7, n-b 1	8
†C. J. Richards c A. P. Wells b le Roux	13		
D. J. Thomas run out	0	1/0 2/60 3/73 (9 wkts, 40 overs) 203	
R. J. Doughty b Imran	36	4/93 5/94 6/136	
K. T. Medlycott b Reeve	0	7/139 8/181 9/198	

Bowling: C. M. Wells 8–0–24–1; Imran 7–0–31–2; le Roux 8–0–36–2; Jones 8–0–44–1; Pigott 4–0–22–0; Reeve 5–0–39–1.

Umpires: D. J. Constant and A. A. Jones.

At Birmingham, August 3. WARWICKSHIRE v SURREY. No result.

SURREY v WORCESTERSHIRE

At The Oval, August 10. Surrey won by four wickets. Toss: Surrey.

Worcestershire

D. M. Smith c and b Bullen	32	P. J. Newport c Feltham b Gray	3
†S. J. Rhodes c Richards b Thomas	45	N. V. Radford not out	4
G. A. Hick c Bullen b Thomas	27	L-b 7, w 1, n-b 3	11
D. N. Patel lbw b Feltham	31		
*P. A. Neale not out	25	1/77 2/99 3/143 (6 wkts, 40 overs) 189	
D. B. D'Oliveira c Lynch b Gray	11	4/150 5/171 6/182	

R. K. Illingworth, J. D. Inchmore and A. P. Pridgeon did not bat.

Bowling: Gray 8–0–31–2; Doughty 8–1–41–0; Feltham 8–0–39–1; Bullen 8–0–26–1; Thomas 8–0–45–2.

Surrey

*A. R. Butcher lbw b Inchmore	24	D. J. Thomas not out	37
G. S. Clinton c Neale b Pridgeon	59	R. J. Doughty not out	9
M. A. Lynch c Inchmore b Patel	4	L-b 7, w 5, n-b 1	13
A. J. Stewart lbw b Patel	1		
T. E. Jesty b Pridgeon	31	1/48 2/64 3/67 (6 wkts, 38.3 overs) 191	
†C. J. Richards c Neale b Pridgeon	13	4/127 5/132 6/159	

M. A. Feltham, C. K. Bullen and A. H. Gray did not bat.

Bowling: Radford 7.3–1–43–0; Pridgeon 8–0–36–3; Inchmore 5–0–25–1; Patel 8–1–28–2; Illingworth 8–0–34–0; Newport 2–0–18–0.

Umpires: J. H. Harris and B. J. Meyer.

At Taunton, August 17. SOMERSET v SURREY. No result.

At Chelmsford, August 24. SURREY beat ESSEX by one wicket.

At Manchester, August 31. SURREY lost to LANCASHIRE by four wickets.

SURREY v HAMPSHIRE

At The Oval, September 7. Hampshire won by 3 runs to become the John Player League champions. Toss: Surrey.

Hampshire

C. G. Greenidge c Richards b Gray	...	16	T. M. Tremlett run out	...	4
V. P. Terry hit wkt b Thomas	...	2	†R. J. Parks not out	...	10
R. A. Smith lbw b Bicknell	...	21			
*M. C. J. Nicholas c Bullen b Gray	...	0	B 6, l-b 5, w 11, n-b 3	...	25
C. L. Smith c Bullen b Butcher	...	16			
K. D. James not out	...	54	1/13 2/32 3/32 (8 wkts, 40 overs)		149
N. G. Cowley c Richards b Butcher	...	0	4/56 5/94 6/94		
M. D. Marshall c Richards b Bicknell	.	1	7/95 8/114		

C. A. Connor did not bat.

Bowling: Gray 8–1–37–2; Thomas 8–1–41–1; Bullen 8–1–13–0; Bicknell 8–1–19–2; Needham 4–0–16–0; Butcher 4–0–12–2.

Surrey

*A. R. Butcher c Terry b Tremlett	...	44	A. H. Gray not out	...	2
G. S. Clinton c R. A. Smith b Marshall		6	C. K. Bullen not out	...	0
M. A. Lynch c Parks b Connor	...	0			
†C. J. Richards lbw b Tremlett	...	10	L-b 4, n-b 7	...	11
D. M. Ward lbw b Marshall	...	3			
N. J. Falkner b Marshall	...	31	1/17 2/17 3/38 (8 wkts, 40 overs)		146
D. J. Thomas c James b Connor	...	34	4/45 5/96 6/117		
A. Needham run out	...	5	7/143 8/145		

M. P. Bicknell did not bat.

Bowling: Marshall 8–0–27–2; Connor 8–0–21–2; Tremlett 8–0–34–3; James 8–0–32–0; Cowley 8–1–28–0.

Umpires: D. G. L. Evans and A. G. T. Whitehead.

SURREY v LEICESTERSHIRE

At The Oval, September 14. Surrey won by two wickets in a match reduced by rain to 37 overs a side. Toss: Surrey.

Leicestershire

L. Potter c Stewart b Gray	...	4	W. K. M. Benjamin c Richards b Gray		4
T. J. Boon b Gray	...	39	R. A. Cobb not out	...	1
J. J. Whitaker c Lynch b Bicknell	...	16	L-b 3, n-b 4	...	7
*P. Willey c Bicknell b Bullen	...	0			
†P. Whitticase c Lynch b Thomas	...	19	1/10 2/37 3/37 (8 wkts, 37 overs)		123
P. D. Bowler c Lynch b Gray	...	18	4/71 5/100 6/105		
P. A. J. DeFreitas run out	...	15	7/121 8/123		

L. Tennant and L. B. Taylor did not bat.

Bowling: Gray 8–0–21–4; Thomas 7–1–22–1; Bicknell 7–0–21–1; Bullen 8–2–24–1; Feltham 6–0–30–0; Jesty 1–0–2–0.

Surrey

G. S. Clinton c Benjamin b Taylor	18	A. H. Gray c Potter b DeFreitas	5
M. A. Lynch run out	29	C. K. Bullen not out	1
T. E. Jesty c Whitticase b Benjamin	0		
*†C. J. Richards b DeFreitas	30	B 1, l-b 8, w 6	15
A. J. Stewart c Whitticase b DeFreitas	1		
D. M. Ward b Willey	10	1/43 2/43 3/84 (8 wkts, 35.3 overs) 124	
D. J. Thomas b Tennant	4	4/85 5/86 6/104	
M. A. Feltham not out	11	7/106 8/121	

M. P. Bicknell did not bat.

Bowling: Taylor 7–1–27–1; Tennant 6–0–32–1; DeFreitas 8–2–15–3; Benjamin 8–0–20–1; Willey 6.3–0–21–1.

Umpires: J. H. Hampshire and J. A. Jameson.

SUSSEX

At Manchester, May 4. SUSSEX beat LANCASHIRE by five wickets.

At Derby, May 11. SUSSEX lost to DERBYSHIRE by eight wickets.

At Nottingham, May 18. SUSSEX beat NOTTINGHAMSHIRE by one wicket.

SUSSEX v GLOUCESTERSHIRE

At Hove, May 25. Sussex won by 114 runs. Toss: Gloucestershire.

Sussex

A. M. Green b Graveney	58	C. M. Wells not out	11
P. W. G. Parker c Lawrence b Walsh	78		
Imran Khan lbw b Walsh	9	L-b 12, n-b 1	13
†I. J. Gould run out	11		
A. P. Wells c Graveney b Bainbridge	0	1/112 2/141 3/159 (5 wkts, 40 overs) 221	
G. S. le Roux not out	41	4/159 5/191	

D. A. Reeve, *J. R. T. Barclay, A. C. S. Pigott and A. N. Jones did not bat.

Bowling: Lawrence 6–0–36–0; Sainsbury 8–1–32–0; Payne 8–0–37–0; Graveney 6–1–30–1; Walsh 8–0–49–2; Bainbridge 4–0–25–1.

Gloucestershire

P. W. Romaines run out	19	D. V. Lawrence lbw b Reeve	4
A. W. Stovold b Jones	35	C. A. Walsh b Reeve	0
K. M. Curran b Jones	2	G. E. Sainsbury c Barclay b Reeve	1
P. Bainbridge c Reeve b Pigott	7	B 1, l-b 7, w 4, n-b 5	17
J. W. Lloyds c Gould b Pigott	0		
I. R. Payne c Parker b Pigott	1	1/32 2/41 3/63 (31.2 overs) 107	
*D. A. Graveney not out	20	4/65 5/69 6/88	
†R. C. Russell lbw b Reeve	1	7/95 8/103 9/103	

Bowling: Imran 4–1–13–0; le Roux 4–0–14–0; Reeve 7.2–1–22–4; Jones 8–1–30–2; Pigott 8–1–20–3.

Umpires: C. Cook and A. A. Jones.

SUSSEX v SOMERSET

At Horsham, June 1. Somerset won by eight wickets in a match reduced by rain to 25 overs a side. Toss: Somerset.

Sussex

A. M. Green c and b Palmer	11	D. A. Reeve run out	1
P. W. G. Parker b Garner	25	A. C. S. Pigott not out	18
Imran Khan c Dredge b Marks	2	A. N. Jones not out	1
C. M. Wells c sub b Dredge	4	L-b 12, w 2	14
A. P. Wells run out	0		
†I. J. Gould c Hardy b Dredge	16	1/26 2/30 3/56	(9 wkts, 25 overs) 108
G. S. le Roux c Richards b Dredge	1	4/63 5/63 6/68	
*J. R. T. Barclay c Hardy b Palmer	15	7/68 8/76 9/100	

Bowling: Taylor 5-0-14-0; Dredge 5-0-31-3; Marks 5-0-19-1; Palmer 5-0-24-2; Garner 5-0-8-1.

Somerset

V. J. Marks c Gould b Jones	15
*P. M. Roebuck c Green b Jones	21
R. J. Harden not out	19
I. V. A. Richards not out	42
L-b 6, w 6, n-b 2	14

1/34 2/49   (2 wkts, 20.1 overs) 111

J. J. E. Hardy, B. C. Rose, G. V. Palmer, C. H. Dredge, J. Garner, N. S. Taylor and †T. Gard did not bat.

Bowling: Imran 5-0-23-0; le Roux 3-1-4-0; Jones 5-0-29-2; Reeve 2-0-8-0; Pigott 5-0-37-0; A. P. Wells 0.1-0-4-0.

Umpires: K. J. Lyons and D. O. Oslear.

At Worcester, June 22. SUSSEX lost to WORCESTERSHIRE by five wickets.

SUSSEX v NORTHAMPTONSHIRE

At Hastings, June 29. Northamptonshire won by 88 runs. Toss: Northamptonshire.

Northamptonshire

R. J. Bailey b C. M. Wells	14	†S. N. V. Waterton not out	13
W. Larkins c Reeve b Standing	26	N. G. B. Cook not out	0
A. J. Lamb lbw b Babington	7	L-b 6, w 9, n-b 2	17
D. J. Capel c C. M. Wells b Pigott	49		
*R. A. Harper b Reeve	43	1/23 2/30 3/74	(7 wkts, 40 overs) 188
R. J. Boyd-Moss run out	0	4/137 5/137	
D. J. Wild c and b Pigott	19	6/169 7/184	

A. Walker and N. A. Mallender did not bat.

Bowling: C. M. Wells 8-0-33-1; Pigott 8-2-27-2; Babington 8-0-39-1; Standing 8-0-35-1; Reeve 7-0-41-1; Green 1-0-7-0.

Sussex

A. M. Green b Capel	10	D. K. Standing b Harper	4
P. W. G. Parker c Harper b Cook	33	A. C. S. Pigott not out	5
A. P. Wells b Harper	17	A. M. Babington b Walker	0
C. M. Wells c and b Cook	4	L-b 5	5
*†I. J. Gould c Walker b Cook	5		
R. I. Alikhan b Wild	10	1/28 2/51 3/63	
C. P. Phillipson lbw b Harper	2	4/74 5/76 6/82	(35 overs) 100
D. A. Reeve st Waterton b Harper	5	7/88 8/94 9/97	

Bowling: Capel 7–1–21–1; Mallender 5–0–13–0; Walker 6–0–17–1; Cook 8–0–23–3; Harper 8–0–17–4; Wild 1–0–4–1.

Umpires: A. A. Jones and R. Julian.

SUSSEX v GLAMORGAN

At Hove, July 13. Sussex won by 28 runs. Toss: Sussex. Steele of Glamorgan held his 100th catch in the John Player League to dismiss A. P. Wells.

Sussex

A. M. Green c Holmes b Thomas	4	A. C. S. Pigott not out	10
P. W. G. Parker c Maynard b Ontong	12	D. K. Standing not out	8
Imran Khan lbw b Thomas	3		
C. M. Wells c Morris b Derrick	61	L-b 7, w 2, n-b 1	10
A. P. Wells c Steele b Derrick	52		
*†I. J. Gould c and b Holmes	7	1/8 2/16 3/28	(8 wkts, 40 overs) 181
C. P. Phillipson b Thomas	5	4/128 5/144 6/147	
D. A. Reeve run out	9	7/157 8/170	
A. N. Jones did not bat.			

Bowling: Thomas 8–2–19–3; Hickey 5–0–11–0; Steele 8–0–36–0; Ontong 8–1–46–1; Derrick 4–0–23–2; Holmes 7–0–39–1.

Glamorgan

J. A. Hopkins lbw b Imran	4	J. Derrick c Imran b Jones	23
H. Morris c Parker b Jones	2	J. F. Steele c Green b Jones	12
Younis Ahmed c Gould b C. M. Wells	15	D. J. Hickey not out	2
G. C. Holmes c and b C. M. Wells	11	L-b 7, w 3	10
M. P. Maynard run out	18		
*R. C. Ontong c Gould b Reeve	35	1/4 2/18 3/32	(37.4 overs) 153
J. G. Thomas c Phillipson b Pigott	20	4/35 5/77 6/109	
†T. Davies c Gould b Pigott	1	7/111 8/111 9/141	

Bowling: Imran 7–1–22–1; Jones 7.4–2–15–3; C. M. Wells 8–0–26–2; Pigott 8–0–44–2; Reeve 7–0–39–1.

Umpires: C. Cook and D. R. Shepherd.

At Leicester, July 20. SUSSEX beat LEICESTERSHIRE by 46 runs.

At Guildford, July 27. SUSSEX beat SURREY by 11 runs.

SUSSEX v ESSEX

At Eastbourne, August 3. Essex won by 39 runs in a match reduced by rain to twenty overs a side. Toss: Sussex.

Essex

*G. A. Gooch c and b Pigott	43	N. A. Foster run out	1
P. J. Prichard b Reeve	40		
A. R. Border c A. P. Wells b Jones	2	L-b 5, w 1, n-b 1	7
D. R. Pringle c Green b Pigott	11		—
K. W. R. Fletcher b Reeve	8	1/76 2/79 3/95 (7 wkts, 20 overs) 138	
B. R. Hardie not out	13	4/111 5/112	
J. P. Stephenson b Reeve	13	6/134 7/138	

†N. D. Burns, T. D. Topley and J. K. Lever did not bat.

Bowling: Imran 4–0–28–0; le Roux 2–0–16–0; Jones 4–0–22–1; C. M. Wells 3–0–26–0; Pigott 4–0–22–2; Reeve 3–0–19–3.

Sussex

P. W. G. Parker c Border b Lever	7	C. P. Phillipson not out	22
*†I. J. Gould c Pringle b Topley	5		
Imran Khan lbw b Topley	9	B 1, l-b 5, w 4	10
C. M. Wells not out	33		—
G. S. le Roux run out	6	1/14 2/18 3/28 (5 wkts, 20 overs) 99	
A. P. Wells b Foster	7	4/39 5/53	

A. M. Green, D. A. Reeve, A. C. S. Pigott and A. N. Jones did not bat.

Bowling: Lever 4–0–19–1; Topley 4–0–19–2; Gooch 4–0–22–0; Pringle 4–0–17–0; Foster 4–0–16–1.

Umpires: B. Dudleston and P. B. Wight.

At Bournemouth, August 10. SUSSEX beat HAMPSHIRE by seven wickets.

SUSSEX v KENT

At Hove, August 17. Kent won by one wicket. Toss: Sussex.

Sussex

A. P. Wells c Penn b C. S. Cowdrey	30	C. P. Phillipson not out	24
P. W. G. Parker b Penn	18		
Imran Khan lbw b C. S. Cowdrey	3	L-b 19, w 5	24
C. M. Wells b Penn	1		—
*†I. J. Gould not out	65	1/50 2/59 3/64 (5 wkts, 40 overs) 181	
G. S. le Roux run out	16	4/77 5/113	

N. J. Lenham, D. A. Reeve, A. C. S. Pigott and A. N. Jones did not bat.

Bowling: Baptiste 8–1–44–0; Ellison 8–1–40–0; C. S. Cowdrey 8–0–22–2; Penn 8–1–23–2; Underwood 8–0–33–0.

Kent

S. G. Hinks c Parker b Imran	22	†S. A. Marsh b Imran		6
S. C. Goldsmith c sub b Imran	6	C. Penn run out		0
C. J. Tavaré b Jones	8	D. L. Underwood not out		0
D. G. Aslett lbw b Reeve	31	L-b 3, w 1, n-b 1		5
*C. S. Cowdrey b Reeve	14			
G. R. Cowdrey b Reeve	13		(9 wkts, 39.2 overs)	182
E. A. E. Baptiste lbw b Imran	44	1/27 2/29 3/51		
R. M. Ellison not out	33	4/78 5/91 6/110		
		7/169 8/177 9/178		

Bowling: C. M. Wells 2–0–12–0; le Roux 8–0–39–0; Imran 8–3–31–4; Pigott 8–1–30–0; Jones 5.2–0–23–1; Reeve 8–0–44–3.

Umpires: J. Birkenshaw and D. J. Constant.

SUSSEX v MIDDLESEX

At Hove, August 24. Sussex won by 101 runs. Toss: Sussex.

Sussex

A. P. Wells c Sykes b Cowans	9	N. J. Lenham not out		7
A. M. Green st Downton b Sykes	43	D. A. Reeve not out		3
*P. W. G. Parker b Sykes	74	L-b 13, w 2		15
Imran Khan c Miller b Hughes	31			
G. S. le Roux lbw b Cowans	3	1/23 2/91 3/155	(6 wkts, 40 overs)	208
C. P. Phillipson run out		4/158 5/186 6/199		

†M. P. Speight, A. C. S. Pigott and A. N. Jones did not bat.

Bowling: Cowans 8–0–35–2; Fraser 8–1–36–0; Rose 8–1–27–0; Hughes 8–0–48–1; Sykes 8–0–49–2.

Middlesex

A. J. T. Miller b Reeve	46	S. P. Hughes b le Roux		1
K. R. Brown c Lenham b Jones	6	N. G. Cowans b Pigott		13
R. O. Butcher c Wells b Pigott	2	A. G. J. Fraser not out		2
J. D. Carr c Parker b Jones	13	L-b 3, w 5		8
C. T. Radley c Reeve b Pigott	5			
*†P. R. Downton c Parker b Jones	5	1/18 2/28 3/44	(29.2 overs)	107
G. D. Rose b Jones	0	4/57 5/68 6/68		
J. F. Sykes b le Roux	6	7/90 8/90 9/105		

Bowling: Imran 4–1–11–0; le Roux 7–2–12–2; Jones 8–0–30–4; Pigott 5.2–0–23–3; Reeve 5–0–28–1.

Umpires: N. T. Plews and A. G. T. Whitehead.

SUSSEX v YORKSHIRE

At Hove, September 7. Sussex won by seven wickets. Toss: Yorkshire.

Yorkshire

†K. Sharp run out	23	A. Sidebottom c Gould b le Roux		0
A. A. Metcalfe c Speight b le Roux	2	S. J. Dennis not out		10
M. D. Moxon c Gould b C. M. Wells	8	B 1, l-b 5, w 8		14
J. D. Love c Gould b Pigott	22			
P. E. Robinson not out	76	1/15 2/35 3/41	(7 wkts, 40 overs)	182
S. N. Hartley c Reeve b Pigott	4	4/100 5/112		
*P. Carrick c Gould b Jones	23	6/159 7/159		

C. Shaw and S. D. Fletcher did not bat.

Bowling: C. M. Wells 8–0–13–1; le Roux 8–0–33–2; Pigott 8–0–40–2; Jones 8–1–42–1; Reeve 8–0–48–0.

Sussex

A. M. Green c Sharp b Dennis	4	*†I. J. Gould not out	0
A. P. Wells run out	50	L-b 8, w 7, n-b 4	19
P. W. G. Parker not out	89		
C. M. Wells b Sidebottom	23	1/6 2/108 3/181 (3 wkts, 36.1 overs) 185	

M. P. Speight, G. S. le Roux, C. P. Phillipson, D. A. Reeve, A. C. S. Pigott and A. N. Jones did not bat.

Bowling: Sidebottom 7–0–25–1; Dennis 8–0–30–1; Shaw 8–0–29–0; Fletcher 8–0–45–0; Carrick 4.1–0–36–0; Hartley 1–0–12–0.

Umpires: H. D. Bird and J. Birkenshaw.

At Birmingham, September 14. SUSSEX beat WARWICKSHIRE by 15 runs.

WARWICKSHIRE

At Chelmsford, May 4. WARWICKSHIRE lost to ESSEX by 47 runs.

At Nottingham, May 11. WARWICKSHIRE beat NOTTINGHAMSHIRE by 48 runs.

At Leek, May 18. WARWICKSHIRE beat DERBYSHIRE by five wickets.

WARWICKSHIRE v WORCESTERSHIRE

At Birmingham, May 25. Worcestershire won by four wickets. Toss: Worcestershire. Rhodes's four stumpings in the Warwickshire innings were the most in a John Player League match.

Warwickshire

T. A. Lloyd c Rhodes b Radford	2	G. J. Parsons not out	1
D. L. Amiss st Rhodes b Illingworth	42	K. J. Kerr not out	1
A. I. Kallicharran st Rhodes b Patel	101	L-b 4, w 6, n-b 2	12
†G. W. Humpage c Radford b Weston	2		
Asif Din st Rhodes b Patel	5	1/6 2/89 3/106 (7 wkts, 40 overs) 174	
P. A. Smith c Neale b Illingworth	1	4/117 5/120	
A. J. Moles st Rhodes b Patel	7	6/172 7/173	

G. C. Small and *N. Gifford did not bat.

Bowling: Radford 8–0–32–1; Pridgeon 5–0–8–0; Inchmore 4–0–27–0; Weston 8–0–37–1; Illingworth 8–1–32–2; Patel 7–0–34–3.

Worcestershire

D. N. Patel c Smith b Parsons	8	†S. J. Rhodes c Small b Parsons	12
D. B. D'Oliveira c Humpage b Kerr	17	N. V. Radford not out	4
D. M. Smith not out	64	B 3, l-b 7, w 2	12
G. A. Hick c Small b Kerr	3		
*P. A. Neale b Moles	8	1/19 2/34 3/40 (6 wkts, 39.2 overs) 175	
M. J. Weston b Small	47	4/55 5/154 6/169	

J. D. Inchmore, R. K. Illingworth and A. P. Pridgeon did not bat.

Bowling: Small 8–1–33–1; Parsons 7–0–41–2; Moles 8–0–25–1; Kerr 8–2–22–2; Gifford 7.2–0–34–0; Lloyd 1–0–10–0.

Umpires: D. Lloyd and K. E. Palmer.

At Manchester, June 1. WARWICKSHIRE beat LANCASHIRE by 11 runs.

WARWICKSHIRE v GLAMORGAN

At Birmingham, June 8. Glamorgan won by 8 runs. Toss: Glamorgan.

Glamorgan

J. A. Hopkins b Smith	10	J. G. Thomas not out	21
H. Morris not out	97	B 1, l-b 2, w 2	10
Younis Ahmed c Small b Smith	18		—
G. C. Holmes c Lloyd b Kerr	19	1/22 2/60 3/97 (4 wkts, 40 overs)	199
*R. C. Ontong run out	24	4/169	

M. P. Maynard, †T. Davies, J. F. Steele, S. J. Base and J. Derrick did not bat.

Bowling: Small 8–1–44–0; Parsons 8–0–39–0; Smith 8–0–35–2; Kerr 8–0–39–1; Gifford 8–0–34–0.

Warwickshire

T. A. Lloyd c Ontong b Thomas	74	K. J. Kerr run out	2
D. L. Amiss run out	36	G. C. Small b Thomas	0
A. I. Kallicharran c Base b Ontong	13		
†G. W. Humpage c Ontong b Derrick	11	B 3, l-b 7, w 5	15
Asif Din b Derrick	10		—
P. A. Smith c Morris b Thomas	18	1/76 2/107 3/126 (9 wkts, 40 overs)	191
A. J. Moles not out	10	4/152 5/174 6/178	
G. J. Parsons c Steele b Derrick	2	7/188 8/191 9/191	

*N. Gifford did not bat.

Bowling: Thomas 8–0–43–3; Base 4–0–24–0; Steele 8–0–41–0; Ontong 8–1–21–1; Derrick 8–0–32–3; Holmes 4–0–20–0.

Umpires: H. D. Bird and B. Dudleston.

At Northampton, June 15. WARWICKSHIRE lost to NORTHAMPTONSHIRE by seven wickets.

WARWICKSHIRE v LEICESTERSHIRE

At Birmingham, June 22. Warwickshire won on faster scoring-rate in a match reduced by rain to 28 overs a side. Toss: Warwickshire. After a further interruption, Leicestershire were set a revised target of 144 in 21 overs.

Warwickshire

T. A. Lloyd b Agnew	12	A. J. Moles not out	2
D. L. Amiss lbw b DeFreitas	59		
A. I. Kallicharran not out	78	L-b 4, w 1, n-b 2	7
†G. W. Humpage run out	1		
Asif Din c Whitticase b DeFreitas	4	1/21 2/113 3/117 (5 wkts, 28 overs)	192
A. M. Ferreira b Taylor	29	4/127 5/185	

G. C. Small, G. J. Parsons, *N. Gifford and T. A. Munton did not bat.

Bowling: Agnew 6–0–41–1; Taylor 5–0–41–1; Willey 6–0–39–0; Benjamin 6–0–39–0; DeFreitas 5–0–28–2.

Leicestershire

L. Potter b Munton	26	†P. Whitticase b Small	2
I. P. Butcher b Small	43	J. P. Agnew b Small	0
J. J. Whitaker b Munton	12	L. B. Taylor b Small	0
*P. Willey c Lloyd b Ferreira	25	L-b 1, w 2	3
W. K. M. Benjamin run out	0		
P. D. Bowler c Moles b Ferreira	12	1/47 2/73 3/105	(21 overs) 132
P. A. J. DeFreitas not out	6	4/106 5/121 6/121	
T. J. Boon run out	3	7/128 8/132 9/132	

Bowling: Small 6–0–26–4; Parsons 5–0–24–0; Munton 5–0–27–2; Moles 3–0–37–0; Ferreira 2–0–17–2.

Umpires: D. R. Shepherd and R. A. White.

At Lord's, July 6. WARWICKSHIRE tied with MIDDLESEX.

At Portsmouth, July 20. WARWICKSHIRE lost to HAMPSHIRE by six wickets.

WARWICKSHIRE v SURREY

At Birmingham, August 3. No result.

WARWICKSHIRE v KENT

At Birmingham, August 10. No result. Toss: Warwickshire.

Kent

M. R. Benson b Gifford	17
S. G. Hinks c Humpage b Ferreira	50
C. J. Tavaré not out	5
G. R. Cowdrey not out	0
L-b 1, w 1	2

1/52 2/74   (2 wkts, 15.2 overs) 74

*C. S. Cowdrey, D. G. Aslett, E. A. E. Baptiste, R. M. Ellison, †S. A. Marsh, C. Penn and C. S. Dale did not bat.

Bowling: Parsons 3–0–16–0; Smith 2–0–11–0; Kerr 5–0–29–0; Gifford 5–0–17–1; Ferreira 0.2–0–0–1.

Warwickshire

A. J. Moles, P. A. Smith, A. I. Kallicharran, †G. W. Humpage, Asif Din, D. A. Thorne, A. M. Ferreira, G. J. Parsons, K. J. Kerr, *N. Gifford and T. A. Munton.

Umpires: B. Dudleston and R. Palmer.

WARWICKSHIRE v GLOUCESTERSHIRE

At Birmingham, August 17. Warwickshire won by 46 runs. Toss: Gloucestershire.

Warwickshire

A. J. Moles lbw b Twizell	85	A. M. Ferreira not out	8
P. A. Smith b Sainsbury	7		
A. I. Kallicharran b Payne	71	B 5, l-b 2, w 3	10
D. L. Amiss c Romaines b Bainbridge	60		
†G. W. Humpage b Twizell	3	1/13 2/149 3/227 (5 wkts, 40 overs)	284
Asif Din not out	40	4/235 5/236	

G. C. Small, T. A. Munton, K. J. Kerr and *N. Gifford did not bat.

Bowling: Sainsbury 6–0–38–1; Twizell 8–0–55–2; Bainbridge 7–0–63–1; Lloyds 8–0–49–0; Payne 7–0–46–1; Graveney 4–0–26–0.

Gloucestershire

†R. C. Russell b Gifford	43	I. R. Payne c and b Ferreira	5
C. W. J. Athey c Smith b Ferreira	64	*D. A. Graveney not out	3
J. W. Lloyds c Ferreira b Gifford	4	L-b 9, w 3	12
K. M. Curran c Moles b Small	49		
P. Bainbridge lbw b Gifford	3	1/103 2/112 3/117 (7 wkts, 40 overs)	238
P. A. Romaines c Kallicharran b Munton	33	4/129 5/183	
K. P. Tomlins not out	22	6/213 7/226	

P. H. Twizell and G. E. Sainsbury did not bat.

Bowling: Small 8–0–36–1; Smith 5–0–23–0; Munton 8–0–54–1; Kerr 3–0–20–0; Ferreira 7–0–49–2; Gifford 8–0–40–3; Asif Din 1–0–7–0.

Umpires: J. H. Hampshire and R. Julian.

WARWICKSHIRE v SOMERSET

At Birmingham, August 24. Somerset won by six wickets. Toss: Somerset.

Warwickshire

A. J. Moles lbw b Davis	15	K. J. Kerr c Richards b Marks	1
P. A. Smith lbw b Richards	6	*N. Gifford b Garner	1
A. I. Kallicharran lbw b Richards	8	T. A. Munton not out	2
D. L. Amiss b Davis	2	L-b 3, w 3, n-b 1	7
†G. W. Humpage c Felton b Taylor	13		
Asif Din c Gard b Marks	4	1/23 2/29 3/31 (30.1 overs)	88
A. M. Ferreira b Garner	28	4/45 5/51 6/55	
G. J. Parsons c Gard b Taylor	1	7/56 8/61 9/73	

Bowling: Garner 6.1–1–14–2; Richards 8–1–19–2; Davis 4–0–16–2; Marks 5–1–18–2; Taylor 7–2–18–2.

Somerset

*P. M. Roebuck lbw b Smith	1	V. J. Marks not out	31
B. C. Rose lbw b Parsons	0	L-b 3, n-b 1	4
I. V. A. Richards lbw b Parsons	1		
R. J. Harden c Humpage b Parsons	10	1/0 2/2 3/2 (4 wkts, 27.3 overs)	90
N. A. Felton not out	43	4/17	

G. V. Palmer, J. Garner, †T. Gard, M. R. Davis and N. S. Taylor did not bat.

Bowling: Parsons 6–1–11–3; Smith 2–0–6–1; Kerr 8–1–23–0; Ferreira 2–0–4–0; Gifford 5–1–21–0; Munton 3–2–10–0; Asif Din 1.3–0–12–0.

Umpires: J. Birkenshaw and R. A. White.

At Leeds, August 31. WARWICKSHIRE tied with YORKSHIRE.

WARWICKSHIRE v SUSSEX

At Birmingham, September 14. Sussex won by 15 runs. Toss: Warwickshire.

Sussex

A. M. Green c Humpage b Small	3	G. S. le Roux not out 12
A. P. Wells b Smith	11	C. P. Phillipson not out 16
*P. W. G. Parker c Ferreira b Thorne .	51	L-b 2, w 5, n-b 4 11
Imran Khan c Asif Din b Gifford	89	—
C. M. Wells lbw b Small	10	1/18 2/22 3/139 (6 wkts, 40 overs) 216
A. C. S. Pigott run out	13	4/172 5/173 6/190

†M. P. Speight, D. A. Reeve and A. N. Jones did not bat.

Bowling: Small 8–1–46–2; Smith 6–0–28–1; Ferreira 8–0–38–0; Gifford 8–1–37–1; Munton 6–0–47–0; Thorne 4–0–18–1.

Warwickshire

A. J. Moles lbw b C. M. Wells	2	G. C. Small b Pigott 5
P. A. Smith lbw b C. M. Wells	10	T. A. Munton not out 5
A. I. Kallicharran c Green b Imran ...	44	
D. L. Amiss lbw b Pigott	34	B 4, l-b 19, w 6 29
†G. W. Humpage lbw b Imran	0	—
Asif Din c Parker b Imran	25	1/11 2/24 3/95 (8 wkts, 40 overs) 201
A. M. Ferreira b Pigott	28	4/96 5/107 6/159
D. A. Thorne not out	19	7/171 8/180

*N. Gifford did not bat.

Bowling: C. M. Wells 7–0–29–2; le Roux 6–0–16–0; Reeve 6–1–20–0; Jones 5–0–19–0; Pigott 8–0–49–3; Imran 8–0–45–3.

Umpires: C. Cook and R. Julian.

WORCESTERSHIRE

WORCESTERSHIRE v KENT

At Worcester, May 11. Kent won by six wickets. Toss: Kent.

Worcestershire

T. S. Curtis c Marsh b Ellison	4	†S. J. Rhodes b Ellison 28
D. N. Patel b C. S. Cowdrey	41	N. V. Radford not out 1
G. A. Hick b Underwood	17	B 2, l-b 13, w 3 18
D. B. D'Oliveira c Dilley b C. S. Cowdrey	11	—
*P. A. Neale not out	49	1/7 2/67 3/73 (6 wkts, 40 overs) 191
M. J. Weston c Tavaré b Underwood ..	22	4/88 5/132 6/190

J. D. Inchmore, R. K. Illingworth and A. P. Pridgeon did not bat.

Bowling: Dilley 8–0–35–0; Ellison 8–0–45–2; Baptiste 8–0–30–0; C. S. Cowdrey 8–0–43–2; Underwood 8–2–23–2.

Kent

M. R. Benson c and b Radford	3	G. R. Cowdrey not out	47
S. G. Hinks c Neale b Radford	1	L-b 12, w 2	14
C. J. Tavaré c Rhodes b Pridgeon	50		
N. R. Taylor run out	28	1/4 2/5 3/66 (4 wkts, 37.1 overs)	193
*C. S. Cowdrey not out	50	4/117	

E. A. E. Baptiste, R. M. Ellison, †S. A. Marsh, G. R. Dilley and D. L. Underwood did not bat.

Bowling: Radford 7–0–42–2; Pridgeon 8–0–31–1; Weston 4–0–17–0; Inchmore 8–0–35–0; Illingworth 6.1–1–30–0; Patel 4–0–26–0.

Umpires: D. J. Constant and K. J. Lyons.

At Leeds, May 18. WORCESTERSHIRE lost to YORKSHIRE by five wickets.

At Birmingham, May 25. WORCESTERSHIRE beat WARWICKSHIRE by four wickets.

At Northampton, June 8. WORCESTERSHIRE lost to NORTHAMPTONSHIRE by 29 runs.

At Manchester, June 15. WORCESTERSHIRE lost to LANCASHIRE by 39 runs.

WORCESTERSHIRE v SUSSEX

At Worcester, June 22. Worcestershire won by five wickets. Toss: Worcestershire.

Sussex

A. M. Green c Neale b Pridgeon	8	D. A. Reeve b Inchmore	4
P. W. G. Parker c Smith b Inchmore	2	A. N. Jones not out	6
Imran Khan c Patel b Pridgeon	72	L-b 7, w 2	9
*†I. J. Gould c Rhodes b Newport	39		
C. M. Wells c D'Oliveira b Inchmore	19	1/8 2/14 3/100 (7 wkts, 40 overs)	163
A. P. Wells not out	3	4/140 5/147	
C. P. Phillipson c Neale b Pridgeon	1	6/149 7/152	

A. M. Babington and D. K. Standing did not bat.

Bowling: Pridgeon 8–1–27–3; Inchmore 8–1–23–3; Weston 8–1–23–0; Newport 8–0–42–1; Patel 8–1–41–0.

Worcestershire

T. S. Curtis c Gould b Jones	1	M. J. Weston not out	0
D. M. Smith b C. M. Wells	60		
G. A. Hick c Gould b Jones	59	L-b 7, w 3, n-b 3	13
D. N. Patel run out	3		
*P. A. Neale c Babington b Standing	16	1/4 2/83 3/90 (5 wkts, 35.1 overs)	164
D. B. D'Oliveira not out	12	4/134 5/158	

†S. J. Rhodes, A. P. Pridgeon, J. D. Inchmore and P. J. Newport did not bat.

Bowling: Imran 8–0–32–0; Jones 8–1–31–2; Reeve 8–0–33–0; C. M. Wells 4–0–22–1; Babington 3–0–23–0; Standing 4.1–1–16–1.

Umpires: R. Palmer and A. G. T. Whitehead.

WORCESTERSHIRE v HAMPSHIRE

At Worcester, June 29. Hampshire won by nine wickets. Toss: Hampshire.

Worcestershire

T. S. Curtis run out	48	N. V. Radford not out	2
D. B. D'Oliveira c R. A. Smith b Connor	11	R. K. Illingworth not out	2
G. A. Hick c R. A. Smith b Cowley	30		
D. N. Patel c and b Marshall	34	B 4, l-b 6, w 2	12
*P. A. Neale c James b Cowley	4		—
M. J. Weston b Cowley	9	1/20 2/76 3/133 (8 wkts, 40 overs) 182	
†S. J. Rhodes c Nicholas b Connor	18	4/134 5/139 6/151	
P. J. Newport c Nicholas b Connor	12	7/178 8/178	

A. P. Pridgeon did not bat.

Bowling: James 8–1–30–0; Connor 8–0–54–3; Tremlett 8–0–31–0; Cowley 8–0–33–3; Marshall 8–0–24–1.

Hampshire

V. P. Terry not out	78
D. R. Turner b Weston	22
*M. C. J. Nicholas not out	62
L-b 19, n-b 2	21

1/55   (1 wkt, 37.4 overs) 183

C. L. Smith, R. A. Smith, K. D. James, N. G. Cowley, M. D. Marshall, †R. J. Parks, T. M. Tremlett and C. A. Connor did not bat.

Bowling: Radford 8–1–26–0; Pridgeon 6.4–0–25–0; Weston 8–1–33–1; Newport 8–0–42–0; Illingworth 6–1–25–0; Patel 1–0–13–0.

Umpires: C. Cook and J. H. Hampshire.

WORCESTERSHIRE v NOTTINGHAMSHIRE

At Worcester, July 6. Nottinghamshire won by seven wickets. Toss: Nottinghamshire.

Worcestershire

T. S. Curtis b Rice	10	P. J. Newport b Rice	3
D. B. D'Oliveira c Saxelby b Hemmings	59	R. K. Illingworth not out	0
G. A. Hick c Scott b Rice	33	B 1, l-b 10, n-b 1	12
D. N. Patel lbw b K. P. Evans	29		—
*P. A. Neale b Pick	7	1/53 2/76 3/134 (7 wkts, 40 overs) 187	
M. J. Weston not out	30	4/146 5/163	
†S. J. Rhodes c and b Rice	4	6/177 7/185	

J. D. Inchmore and A. P. Pridgeon did not bat.

Bowling: Hadlee 8–2–22–0; Saxelby 8–0–38–0; Rice 8–0–33–4; Pick 8–0–34–1; Hemmings 2–0–14–1; K. P. Evans 6–0–35–1.

Nottinghamshire

B. C. Broad c Hick b Illingworth 63	R. J. Hadlee not out 34
D. W. Randall not out 67	L-b 5, w 4, n-b 4 13
P. Johnson b Illingworth 6	
*C. E. B. Rice c Neale b Illingworth .. 7	1/110 2/118 3/130 (3 wkts, 38.2 overs) 190

R. J. Evans, E. E. Hemmings, †C. W. Scott, K. P. Evans, R. A. Pick and K. Saxelby did not bat.

Bowling: Pridgeon 6.2–0–29–0; Inchmore 8–0–34–0; Weston 4–0–22–0; Patel 8–0–31–0; Newport 6–0–31–0; Illingworth 6–1–38–3.

Umpires: M. J. Kitchen and K. E. Palmer.

At Southend, July 20. WORCESTERSHIRE lost to ESSEX by 43 runs.

WORCESTERSHIRE v GLOUCESTERSHIRE

At Hereford, July 27. Worcestershire won by 3 runs. Toss: Worcestershire. D. B. D'Oliveira reached 1,000 runs to establish with B. L. D'Oliveira the first instance of a father and son scoring 1,000 runs in the John Player League.

Worcestershire

T. S. Curtis c Bainbridge b Sainsbury .. 73	M. J. Weston not out 13
D. B. D'Oliveira c Bainbridge b Burrows. 22	P. J. Newport not out 17
G. A. Hick c Russell b Bainbridge 0	L-b 8, w 5, n-b 1 14
D. N. Patel c Burrows b Sainsbury 48	
*P. A. Neale c Burrows b Twizell 29	1/60 2/60 3/141 (6 wkts, 40 overs) 233
†S. J. Rhodes c Russell b Twizell 17	4/163 5/201 6/204

R. K. Illingworth, S. M. McEwan and A. P. Pridgeon did not bat.

Bowling: Sainsbury 8–0–48–2; Burrows 8–0–38–1; Bainbridge 8–0–53–1; Twizell 8–0–47–2; Payne 8–0–39–0.

Gloucestershire

P. W. Romaines c D'Oliveira b Newport 22	P. H. Twizell b Illingworth 4
†R. C. Russell c McEwan b Pridgeon ..108	G. E. Sainsbury lbw b Pridgeon 0
*P. Bainbridge st Rhodes b Illingworth . 9	D. A. Burrows not out 1
K. M. Curran b McEwan 1	B 4, l-b 9, w 6 19
K. P. Tomlins b Newport 8	
M. W. Alleyne st Rhodes b Patel 46	1/55 2/72 3/75 (39.5 overs) 230
A. J. Wright b Pridgeon 11	4/108 5/185 6/221
I. R. Payne run out 1	7/221 8/224 9/225

Bowling: Pridgeon 8–0–23–3; Patel 8–0–62–1; Newport 8–0–52–2; McEwan 8–0–48–1; Illingworth 7.5–0–32–2.

Umpires: J. A. Jameson and B. J. Meyer.

At Weston-super-Mare, August 3. WORCESTERSHIRE lost to SOMERSET by four wickets.

At The Oval, August 10. WORCESTERSHIRE lost to SURREY by four wickets.

WORCESTERSHIRE v LEICESTERSHIRE

At Worcester, August 17. Worcestershire won by 12 runs. Toss: Leicestershire.

Worcestershire

T. S. Curtis c Willey b DeFreitas	20	R. K. Illingworth not out		9
D. M. Smith c Benjamin b Harris	27	J. D. Inchmore not out		2
G. A. Hick c Whitticase b DeFreitas	3			
D. N. Patel c Potter b Willey	31	B 4, l-b 6, w 2, n-b 3		15
*P. A. Neale lbw b DeFreitas	10			—
D. B. D'Oliveira c Bowler b Taylor	33	1/34 2/40 3/70	(8 wkts, 40 overs)	162
†S. J. Rhodes c Whitticase b DeFreitas	8	4/97 5/97 6/115		
M. J. Weston lbw b Willey	4	7/120 8/157		

S. M. McEwan did not bat.

Bowling: Benjamin 8-0-45-0; Taylor 8-1-27-1; Harris 8-2-27-1; DeFreitas 8-2-20-4; Willey 8-0-33-2.

Leicestershire

L. Potter b Inchmore	16	†P. Whitticase not out		29
*D. I. Gower c Weston b Inchmore	5	L. B. Taylor not out		14
P. Willey b Weston	10			
J. J. Whitaker c Neale b Inchmore	7	L-b 3, w 6, n-b 2		11
P. D. Bowler lbw b Hick	9			—
T. J. Boon c Neale b Weston	19	1/20 2/27 3/37	(8 wkts, 40 overs)	150
P. A. J. DeFreitas b Illingworth	20	4/41 5/67 6/91		
W. K. M. Benjamin run out	10	7/99 8/113		

G. A. R. Harris did not bat.

Bowling: McEwan 8-1-35-0; Inchmore 8-1-33-3; Weston 8-1-28-2; Hick 8-0-30-1; Illingworth 8-1-21-1.

Umpires: D. O. Oslear and R. Palmer.

WORCESTERSHIRE v GLAMORGAN

At Worcester, August 24. Worcestershire won by 63 runs. Toss: Glamorgan.

Worcestershire

T. S. Curtis b Thomas	102
†S. J. Rhodes c Morris b Steele	42
G. A. Hick not out	68
D. N. Patel not out	1
L-b 8, w 3, n-b 3	14

1/111 2/222   (2 wkts, 40 overs) 227

M. J. Weston, *P. A. Neale, D. B. D'Oliveira, P. J. Newport, R. K. Illingworth, S. M. McEwan and A. P. Pridgeon did not bat.

Bowling: Hickey 7–0–44–0; Thomas 8–0–50–1; Barwick 4–0–16–0; Ontong 8–0–32–0; Steele 8–0–44–1; Derrick 5–0–33–0.

Glamorgan

J. A. Hopkins c Neale b Weston	10	J. F. Steele not out		30
*H. Morris lbw b Weston	0	S. R. Barwick not out		29
G. C. Holmes st Rhodes b Illingworth	21			
M. P. Maynard b Illingworth	22	L-b 7, w 7		14
R. C. Ontong c Curtis b McEwan	24			
J. Derrick b Illingworth	9	1/1 2/21 3/37	(8 wkts, 40 overs)	164
J. G. Thomas c Newport b Hick	5	4/65 5/91 6/93		
†T. Davies b Illingworth	0	7/94 8/102		

D. J. Hickey did not bat.

Bowling: Weston 8–1–24–2; Pridgeon 8–0–31–0; Illingworth 8–0–25–4; McEwan 8–0–38–1; Hick 4–0–23–1; Newport 4–0–16–0.

Umpires: J. W. Holder and P. B. Wight.

At Lord's, August 31. WORCESTERSHIRE lost to MIDDLESEX by five wickets.

WORCESTERSHIRE v DERBYSHIRE

At Worcester, September 7. Derbyshire won by one wicket. Toss: Worcestershire. Barnett took his season's total of runs in the John Player League to 660, passing by 42 the previous record for Derbyshire, set by J. G. Wright in 1981.

Worcestershire

T. S. Curtis b Jean-Jacques	47	R. K. Illingworth b Holding		11
†S. J. Rhodes lbw b Finney	1	J. D. Inchmore b Warner		1
G. A. Hick c Maher b Jean-Jacques	53	S. M. McEwan not out		6
D. N. Patel b Mortensen	9	L-b 11, w 8		19
D. B. D'Oliveira c Finney b Holding	13			
*P. A. Neale b Mortensen	0	1/5 2/109 3/113	(9 wkts, 40 overs)	198
M. J. Weston c Maher b Jean-Jacques	1	4/127 5/127 6/128		
N. V. Radford not out	37	7/156 8/187 9/188		

Bowling: Finney 6–1–13–1; Mortensen 8–1–14–2; Sharma 4–0–30–0; Warner 8–0–59–1; Holding 8–0–35–2; Jean-Jacques 6–0–36–3.

Derbyshire

*K. J. Barnett c Illingworth b McEwan	78	R. Sharma run out		10
A. Hill b Illingworth	29	R. J. Finney not out		24
J. E. Morris c Rhodes b Patel	2	O. H. Mortensen not out		1
B. Roberts c Rhodes b Radford	21	B 6, l-b 12, n-b 5		23
†B. J. M. Maher b McEwan	4			
M. A. Holding b McEwan	5	1/66 2/71 3/122	(9 wkts, 40 overs)	199
A. E. Warner c Hick b McEwan	2	4/147 5/154 6/156		
M. Jean-Jacques b Illingworth	0	7/157 8/159 9/198		

Bowling: Weston 3–0–22–0; Inchmore 8–0–35–0; Radford 8–0–33–1; Illingworth 8–1–32–2; Patel 6–0–24–1; McEwan 7–0–35–4.

Umpires: C. Cook and B. J. Meyer.

YORKSHIRE

YORKSHIRE v SOMERSET

At Leeds, May 4. Yorkshire won by five wickets. Toss: Yorkshire.

Somerset

*P. M. Roebuck c Sidebottom b Carrick	51	V. J. Marks c and b Stevenson	10
J. J. E. Hardy lbw b Sidebottom	7	N. A. Felton not out	0
I. V. A. Richards c Moxon b P. J. Hartley	24	L-b 11, w 5	16
B. C. Rose c Sharp b Carrick	62		
I. T. Botham not out	45	1/10 2/61 3/153 (7 wkts, 40 overs) 217	
M. S. Turner c Carrick b P. J. Hartley	1	4/153 5/156	
J. Garner c P. J. Hartley b Carrick	1	6/157 7/202	

†T. Gard and C. H. Dredge did not bat.

Bowling: Sidebottom 8–0–28–1; Jarvis 8–1–50–0; P. J. Hartley 8–0–34–2; Stevenson 8–0–46–1; Carrick 8–1–48–3.

Yorkshire

K. Sharp b Turner	49	G. B. Stevenson not out	0
M. D. Moxon c Garner b Dredge	28		
A. A. Metcalfe c Dredge b Richards	46	L-b 13, w 4	17
J. D. Love c Turner b Dredge	44		
S. N. Hartley c Botham b Dredge	24	1/50 2/115 3/160 (5 wkts, 38.4 overs) 220	
*†D. L. Bairstow not out	12	4/206 5/210	

P. J. Hartley, P. Carrick, P. W. Jarvis and A. Sidebottom did not bat.

Bowling: Garner 7.4–2–25–0; Richards 8–0–28–1; Turner 8–0–68–1; Marks 8–0–48–0; Dredge 7–0–38–3.

Umpires: H. D. Bird and B. J. Meyer.

At The Oval, May 11. YORKSHIRE beat SURREY by six wickets.

YORKSHIRE v WORCESTERSHIRE

At Leeds, May 18. Yorkshire won by five wickets. Toss: Yorkshire.

Worcestershire

T. S. Curtis run out	11	N. V. Radford b Jarvis	0
D. B. D'Oliveira c Love b Carrick	29	J. D. Inchmore b Jarvis	3
D. M. Smith c Bairstow b Stevenson	8		
G. A. Hick b Jarvis	45	B 11, l-b 12, w 2, n-b 1	26
*P. A. Neale c Love b P. J. Hartley	6		
M. J. Weston b Carrick	4	1/25 2/44 3/74 (9 wkts, 40 overs) 163	
†S. J. Rhodes not out	30	4/104 5/119 6/131	
P. J. Newport c S. N. Hartley b Jarvis	1	7/141 8/141 9/163	

R. K. Illingworth did not bat.

Bowling: Sidebottom 8–0–40–0; Jarvis 8–4–13–4; P. J. Hartley 8–1–20–1; Stevenson 8–1–31–1; Carrick 8–0–36–2.

Yorkshire

K. Sharp b Radford	59	P. Carrick not out	4
M. D. Moxon c Rhodes b Illingworth	12		
A. A. Metcalfe b Illingworth	4	L-b 10, w 3, n-b 6	19
J. D. Love c Rhodes b Radford	36		
S. N. Hartley lbw b Weston	8	1/53 2/73 3/114 (5 wkts, 35.1 overs) 164	
G. B. Stevenson not out	22	4/132 5/156	

*†D. L. Bairstow, A. Sidebottom, P. W. Jarvis and P. J. Hartley did not bat.

Bowling: Radford 8–1–30–2; Inchmore 8–0–43–0; Weston 4.1–0–20–1; Illingworth 8–1–18–2; Newport 5–0–26–0; Hick 2–0–17–0.

Umpires: B. Leadbeater and R. A. White.

YORKSHIRE v ESSEX

At Sheffield, May 25. Yorkshire won by two wickets. Toss: Essex.

Essex

P. J. Prichard c Bairstow b Fletcher	29	N. A. Foster c Jarvis b Carrick	2
B. R. Hardie c Bairstow b Jarvis	7	J. K. Lever not out	5
A. R. Border b Sidebottom	4	D. L. Acfield run out	2
*K. W. R. Fletcher b P. J. Hartley	18	L-b 10, w 3, n-b 1	14
A. W. Lilley b Fletcher	18		
K. R. Pont b Carrick	34	1/23 2/32 3/68 (40 overs) 162	
†D. E. East c Fletcher b Sidebottom	5	4/70 5/123 6/123	
S. Turner c Bairstow b Jarvis	24	7/125 8/137 9/160	

Bowling: Sidebottom 8–0–33–2; Jarvis 8–0–38–2; P. J. Hartley 8–0–15–1; Carrick 8–0–48–2; Fletcher 8–2–18–2.

Yorkshire

K. Sharp c Fletcher b Foster	4	A. Sidebottom not out	35
M. D. Moxon lbw b Foster	43	P. W. Jarvis not out	27
J. D. Love c Turner b Acfield	30		
S. N. Hartley c Foster b Turner	2	L-b 2, w 3	5
*†D. L. Bairstow lbw b Pont	4		
P. J. Hartley c Foster b Pont	5	1/5 2/70 3/77 (8 wkts, 40 overs) 164	
P. E. Robinson b Foster	9	4/84 5/88 6/95	
P. Carrick c East b Foster	0	7/95 8/102	

S. D. Fletcher did not bat.

Bowling: Lever 8–1–25–0; Foster 8–1–38–4; Pont 8–0–27–2; Acfield 8–0–36–1; Turner 8–1–36–1.

Umpires: M. J. Kitchen and R. Julian.

YORKSHIRE v GLOUCESTERSHIRE

At Leeds, June 8. Gloucestershire won by 68 runs. Toss: Yorkshire.

Gloucestershire

A. J. Wright b Sidebottom	6	I. R. Payne b Sidebottom	0
C. W. J. Athey c Robinson b Sidebottom	74	*D. A. Graveney not out	0
P. Bainbridge b S. N. Hartley	40		
K. M. Curran c S. N. Hartley b P. J. Hartley	24	L-b 20, w 4, n-b 4	28
J. W. Lloyds lbw b P. J. Hartley	6	1/17 2/110 3/147 (6 wkts, 40 overs) 200	
K. P. Tomlins not out	22	4/158 5/190 6/193	

†R. C. Russell, C. A. Walsh and G. E. Sainsbury did not bat.

Bowling: Sidebottom 8–0–36–3; Jarvis 8–1–27–0; P. J. Hartley 8–0–40–2; S. N. Hartley 8–0–32–1; Carrick 8–0–45–0.

Yorkshire

A. A. Metcalfe st Russell b Bainbridge . 19	A. Sidebottom b Sainsbury 2		
K. Sharp c Russell b Sainsbury 2	P. J. Hartley b Walsh 1		
J. D. Love st Russell b Graveney 20	P. W. Jarvis not out 0		
G. B. Stevenson c Tomlins b Payne . . 4			
S. N. Hartley c Tomlins b Graveney . . . 11	L-b 11, w 5 16		
P. E. Robinson c Tomlins b Sainsbury . 41			
*†D. L. Bairstow c Sainsbury	1/6 2/33 3/42	(35.1 overs) 132	
b Bainbridge . 12	4/62 5/72 6/109		
P. Carrick c Curran b Walsh 4	7/125 8/130 9/132		

Bowling: Sainsbury 8–1–23–3; Walsh 5.1–1–13–2; Payne 8–0–19–1; Bainbridge 6–1–17–2; Tomlins 5–0–30–0; Graveney 3–0–19–2.

Umpires: J. A. Jameson and D. O. Oslear.

At Lord's, June 15. YORKSHIRE lost to MIDDLESEX by nine wickets.

At Luton, June 22. YORKSHIRE lost to NORTHAMPTONSHIRE by seven wickets.

YORKSHIRE v LEICESTERSHIRE

At Middlesbrough, July 6. Yorkshire won by five wickets. Toss: Leicestershire.

Leicestershire

L. Potter c Robinson b Carrick 51	W. K. M. Benjamin b Sidebottom 13		
J. C. Balderstone b Carrick 29	J. P. Agnew run out 2		
*P. Willey c Metcalfe b Carrick 7	L. B. Taylor not out 0		
T. J. Boon c Hartley b Shaw 19	L-b 11, w 5 16		
†P. Whitticase c Sharp b Shaw 7			
P. D. Bowler run out 4	1/79 2/90 3/95	(39.1 overs) 155	
P. B. Clift run out 7	4/114 5/126 6/130		
P. A. J. DeFreitas b Carrick 0	7/130 8/149 9/152		

Bowling: Sidebottom 8–0–27–1; Jarvis 7.1–0–21–0; Shaw 8–0–35–2; Fletcher 8–1–29–0; Carrick 8–1–32–4.

Yorkshire

K. Sharp c Balderstone b Benjamin . . . 1	P. Carrick not out 4		
A. A. Metcalfe lbw b Agnew 3			
S. N. Hartley c Willey b DeFreitas . . . 57	L-b 13, w 1, n-b 2 16		
P. Robinson c Potter b Agnew 68			
J. D. Love c Whitticase b Benjamin . . . 5	1/2 2/8 3/135	(5 wkts, 36.5 overs) 156	
*†D. L. Bairstow not out 2	4/149 5/152		

A. Sidebottom, P. W. Jarvis, C. Shaw and S. D. Fletcher did not bat.

Bowling: Benjamin 7–0–19–2; Agnew 8–0–23–2; DeFreitas 4.5–0–21–1; Taylor 4–0–21–0; Clift 5–0–30–0; Willey 8–1–29–0.

Umpires: J. H. Hampshire and P. B. Wight.

YORKSHIRE v NOTTINGHAMSHIRE

At Hull, July 27. Yorkshire won by 102 runs. Toss: Nottinghamshire.

Yorkshire

R. J. Blakey c Scott b Saxelby 3	P. Carrick b Pick 16	
A. A. Metcalfe lbw b Cooper 35	P. J. Hartley not out 1	
S. N. Hartley c Scott b Cooper 3	L-b 10, w 4, n-b 1 15	
P. E. Robinson c Broad b Fraser-Darling 64		
J. D. Love not out 104	1/9 2/30 3/53 (6 wkts, 40 overs) 255	
*†D. L. Bairstow run out 14	4/167 5/216 6/250	

C. Shaw, P. W. Jarvis and S. D. Fletcher did not bat.

Bowling: Cooper 8–1–16–2; Saxelby 6–0–53–1; Pick 8–0–55–1; Hemmings 4–0–26–0; Fraser-Darling 8–0–45–1; Rice 6–0–50–0.

Nottinghamshire

B. C. Broad lbw b Jarvis 4	E. E. Hemmings c Bairstow b Jarvis .. 14	
R. T. Robinson lbw b P. J. Hartley .. 0	K. Saxelby not out 6	
P. Johnson c Bairstow b Jarvis 2	K. E. Cooper b Shaw 0	
*C. E. B. Rice c Shaw b Carrick 53		
J. D. Birch b Fletcher 12	B 6, l-b 10, w 3 19	
C. D. Fraser-Darling c Jarvis b Carrick 9		
†C. W. Scott c Love b Carrick 10	1/5 2/7 3/7 4/56 5/82 (33.3 overs) 153	
R. A. Pick c P. J. Hartley b Fletcher .. 24	6/94 7/104 8/136 9/148	

Bowling: Jarvis 5–0–21–3; P. J. Hartley 8–1–33–1; Shaw 4.3–0–19–1; Fletcher 8–0–37–2; Carrick 8–1–27–3.

Umpires: J. H. Hampshire and R. Palmer.

At Manchester, August 3. LANCASHIRE v YORKSHIRE. No result.

YORKSHIRE v GLAMORGAN

At Scarborough, August 10. Yorkshire won by 19 runs. Toss: Yorkshire.

Yorkshire

S. N. Hartley c Davies b Steele 30	P. Carrick not out 39	
A. A. Metcalfe c Hopkins b Holmes ... 46	C. S. Pickles not out 16	
J. D. Love c and b Steele 10	B 2, l-b 16, w 4 22	
P. E. Robinson c Derrick b Ontong ... 4		
*†D. L. Bairstow run out 23	1/56 2/78 3/83 (6 wkts, 40 overs) 200	
D. Byas b Holmes 10	4/107 5/133 6/133	

C. Shaw, S. D. Fletcher and S. J. Dennis did not bat.

Bowling: Hickey 5–1–20–0; Barwick 5–1–10–0; Steele 8–0–28–2; Ontong 8–0–36–1; Holmes 7–0–57–2; Derrick 7–0–31–0.

Glamorgan

J. A. Hopkins c Love b Fletcher	36	J. F. Steele c Fletcher b Dennis	1
*H. Morris run out	18	S. R. Barwick not out	2
G. C. Holmes b Carrick	37	D. J. Hickey b Fletcher	0
M. P. Maynard b Shaw	24	B 4, l-b 8	12
R. C. Ontong c Dennis b Pickles	19		—
J. Derrick c Bairstow b Dennis	23	1/35 2/87 3/124	(39.4 overs) 181
†T. Davies c Carrick b Fletcher	7	4/128 5/146 6/174	
P. A. Cottey b Fletcher	2	7/176 8/178 9/181	

Bowling: Dennis 8–0–27–2; Pickles 8–0–51–1; Carrick 8–0–29–1; Shaw 8–0–30–1; Fletcher 7.4–0–32–4.

Umpires: J. W. Holder and N. T. Plews.

At Chesterfield, August 17. YORKSHIRE lost to DERBYSHIRE by ten wickets.

At Bournemouth, August 24. YORKSHIRE lost to HAMPSHIRE by seven wickets.

YORKSHIRE v WARWICKSHIRE

At Leeds, August 31. Tied. Toss: Warwickshire.

Warwickshire

A. J. Moles lbw b Dennis	3	A. M. Ferreira not out	32
P. A. Smith c Carrick b Sidebottom	17		
A. I. Kallicharran c and b Jarvis	36	B 2, l-b 20, w 1, n-b 1	24
D. L. Amiss c Love b Carrick	7		—
†G. W. Humpage not out	43	1/14 2/37 3/56	(5 wkts, 40 overs) 162
Asif Din c Bairstow b Jarvis	0	4/102 5/103	

G. C. Small, T. A. Munton, K. J. Kerr and *N. Gifford did not bat.

Bowling: Dennis 8–0–28–1; Jarvis 8–0–28–2; Sidebottom 8–0–27–1; Carrick 8–0–21–1; Fletcher 8–1–36–0.

Yorkshire

K. Sharp b Munton	5	P. W. Jarvis run out	0
A. A. Metcalfe c and b Gifford	40	S. J. Dennis not out	2
S. N. Hartley run out	5		
J. D. Love b Small	48	L-b 9, w 2, n-b 1	12
P. E. Robinson c Humpage b Ferreira	36		—
*†D. L. Bairstow b Small	7	1/15 2/27 3/54	(8 wkts, 40 overs) 162
P. Carrick run out	4	4/125 5/149 6/155	
A. Sidebottom not out	3	7/157 8/157	

S. D. Fletcher did not bat.

Bowling: Small 8–1–8–2; Smith 8–0–41–0; Munton 8–1–19–1; Ferreira 8–0–32–1; Gifford 6–1–33–1; Moles 2–0–20–0.

Umpires: H. D. Bird and J. H. Hampshire.

At Hove, September 7. YORKSHIRE lost to SUSSEX by seven wickets.

At Canterbury, September 14. KENT v YORKSHIRE. No result.

JOHN PLAYER LEAGUE RECORDS

Batting

Highest score: 176 – G. A. Gooch, Essex v Glamorgan (Southend), 1983. (282 hundreds were scored in the League.)

Most runs in a season: 814 – C. E. B. Rice (Nottinghamshire), 1977.

Most sixes in an innings: 13 – I. T. Botham, Somerset v Northamptonshire (Wellingborough School), 1986.

Most sixes by a team in an innings: 18 – Derbyshire v Worcestershire (Knypersley), 1985.

Most sixes in a season: 26 – I. V. A. Richards (Somerset), 1977.

Highest total: 310 for five – Essex v Glamorgan (Southend), 1983.

Highest total – batting second: 301 for six – Warwickshire v Essex (Colchester), 1982.

Highest match aggregate: 604 – Surrey (304) v Warwickshire (300 for nine) (The Oval), 1985.

Lowest total: 23 : – Middlesex v Yorkshire (Leeds), 1974.

Shortest completed innings: 16 overs – Northamptonshire 59 v Middlesex (Tring), 1974.

Shortest match: 2 hr 13 min (40.3 overs) – Essex v Northamptonshire (Ilford), 1971.

Biggest victories: 190 runs, Kent beat Northamptonshire (Brackley), 1973.
    There were eighteen instances of victory by ten wickets – by Derbyshire, Essex (twice), Hampshire, Leicestershire (twice), Middlesex (twice), Northamptonshire, Somerset (twice), Surrey (twice), Warwickshire, Worcestershire and Yorkshire (three times). This does not include those matches in which the side batting second was set a reduced target.

Ties: Nottinghamshire v Kent (Nottingham), 1969, in a match reduced to twenty overs.
  Gloucestershire v Hampshire (Bristol), 1972.
  Gloucestershire v Northamptonshire (Bristol), 1972.
  Surrey v Worcestershire (Byfleet), 1973.
  Middlesex v Lancashire (Lord's), 1974.
  Sussex v Leicestershire (Hove), 1974.
  Lancashire v Worcestershire (Manchester), 1975.
  Somerset v Glamorgan (Taunton), 1975.
  Warwickshire v Kent (Birmingham), 1980.
  Kent v Lancashire (Maidstone), 1981.
  Yorkshire v Nottinghamshire (Hull), 1982.
  Hampshire v Lancashire (Southampton), 1982.
  Surrey v Hampshire (The Oval), 1982.
  Worcestershire v Nottinghamshire (Hereford), 1983.
  Lancashire v Worcestershire (Manchester), 1983, in a match reduced to nineteen overs.
  Warwickshire v Worcestershire (Birmingham), 1983, Warwickshire's innings having been reduced to ten overs.
  Middlesex v Essex (Lord's), 1984.
  Essex v Leicestershire (Chelmsford), 1985.
  Northamptonshire v Lancashire (Northampton), 1985.
  Lancashire v Glamorgan (Manchester), 1985.
  Kent v Surrey (Canterbury), 1986.
  Middlesex v Warwickshire (Lord's), 1986.
  Yorkshire v Warwickshire (Leeds), 1986.

Record partnerships for each wicket

239 for 1st	G. A. Gooch and B. R. Hardie, Essex v Nottinghamshire at Nottingham	1985
273 for 2nd	G. A. Gooch and K. S. McEwan, Essex v Nottinghamshire at Nottingham	1983

215 for 3rd	W. Larkins and R. G. Williams, Northamptonshire v Worcestershire at Luton	1982
178 for 4th	J. J. Whitaker and P. Willey, Leicestershire v Glamorgan at Swansea	1984
185 for 5th	B. M. McMillan and Asif Din, Warwickshire v Essex at Chelmsford.	1986
121 for 6th	C. P. Wilkins and A. J. Borrington, Derbyshire v Warwickshire at Chesterfield	1972
101 for 7th	S. J. Windaybank and D. A. Graveney, Gloucestershire v Nottinghamshire at Nottingham	1981
95* for 8th	D. Breakwell and K. F. Jennings, Somerset v Nottinghamshire at Nottingham	1976
105 for 9th	D. G. Moir and R. W. Taylor, Derbyshire v Kent at Derby	1984
57 for 10th	D. A. Graveney and J. B. Mortimore, Gloucestershire v Lancashire at Tewkesbury	1973

Bowling

Best analyses: eight for 26, K. D. Boyce, Essex v Lancashire at Manchester, 1971; seven for 15, R. A. Hutton, Yorkshire v Worcestershire at Leeds, 1969; seven for 39, A. Hodgson, Northamptonshire v Somerset at Northampton, 1976; seven for 41, A. N. Jones, Sussex v Nottinghamshire at Nottingham, 1986; six for 6, R. W. Hooker, Middlesex v Surrey at Lord's, 1969; six for 7, M. Hendrick, Derbyshire v Nottinghamshire at Nottingham, 1972.

Four wickets in four balls: A. Ward, Derbyshire v Sussex at Derby, 1970.

Hat-tricks: A. Ward, Derbyshire v Sussex at Derby, 1970; R. Palmer, Somerset v Gloucestershire at Bristol, 1970; K. D. Boyce, Essex v Somerset at Westcliff, 1971; G. D. McKenzie, Leicestershire v Essex at Leicester, 1972; R. G. D. Willis, Warwickshire v Yorkshire at Birmingham, 1973; W. Blenkiron, Warwickshire v Derbyshire at Buxton, 1974; A. Buss, Sussex v Worcestershire at Hastings, 1974; J. M. Rice, Hampshire v Northamptonshire at Southampton, 1975; M. A. Nash, Glamorgan v Worcestershire at Worcester, 1975; A. Hodgson, Northamptonshire v Somerset at Northampton, 1976; A. E. Cordle, Glamorgan v Hampshire at Portsmouth, 1979; C. J. Tunnicliffe, Derbyshire v Worcestershire at Derby, 1979; M. D. Marshall, Hampshire v Surrey at Southampton, 1981; I. V. A. Richards, Somerset v Essex at Chelmsford, 1982; P. W. Jarvis, Yorkshire v Derbyshire at Derby, 1982; R. M. Ellison, Kent v Hampshire at Canterbury, 1983.

Most economical analysis: 8–8–0–0, B. A. Langford, Somerset v Essex at Yeovil, 1969.

Most expensive analyses: 8–0–88–1, E. E. Hemmings, Nottinghamshire v Somerset at Nottingham 1983; 7.5–0–89–3, G. Miller Derbyshire v Gloucestershire at Gloucester, 1984.

Most wickets in a season: 34 – R. J. Clapp (Somerset) 1974 and C. E. B. Rice (Nottinghamshire) 1986.

CHAMPIONS: 1969-86

1969	Lancashire	1978	Hampshire
1970	Lancashire	1979	Somerset
1971	Worcestershire	1980	Warwickshire
1972	Kent	1981	Essex
1973	Kent	1982	Sussex
1974	Leicestershire	1983	Yorkshire
1975	Hampshire	1984	Essex
1976	Kent	1985	Essex
1977	Leicestershire	1986	Hampshire

MINOR COUNTIES CHAMPIONSHIP, 1986

By MICHAEL BERRY and ROBERT BROOKE

The emergence of Cumberland and Norfolk in 1986 as the respective winners of the Championship and the limited-overs knockout brought to an end the domination of Hertfordshire, Durham and Cheshire, who since the re-organisation of Minor Counties cricket in 1983 had shared all six subsequent honours.

Cumberland, holders of the wooden spoon for a record twelve times and for so long the poor relations of the Minor Counties game, successfully built on their improvement of the previous three seasons. Their five wins in nine games took them comfortably into the Championship play-off at Worcester, where a two-wicket win over Oxfordshire saw them crowned as champions for the first time in their history. The arrival of all-rounder Bernard Reidy from Lancashire in 1983 was the main catalyst of Cumberland's improved form, and he again played a key role in 1986 with 533 runs and 27 wickets. David Lloyd, the former Lancashire and England opener, and Chris Stockdale backed him with valuable batting contributions while David Halliwell, a volatile fast bowler, set a county record by taking 44 wickets, beating the 39 by David Parsons in 1981.

For **Staffordshire**, the story was a familiar one: runners-up in the Eastern Division for the third successive season. Two new batsmen, David Banks (413 runs) and Jon Addison (290), from Worcestershire and Leicestershire respectively, plus the continued development of Jon Waterhouse, strengthened their batting, and the addition of Joey Benjamin, a fast bowler, to the attack helped promote a run that brought 34 points from their last five games.

Cambridgeshire also benefited from the acquisition of two players from the first-class game. Deprived of Derick Parry, the former West Indian Test all-rounder, by the new ruling that banned non England-qualified players, they found ample compensation in the performances of Michael Garnham, a wicket-keeper-batsman from Leicestershire, and Chris Lethbridge, a former Warwickshire seam bowler. Garnham made 566 runs and Lethbridge took 40 wickets. Nigel Gadsby sustained his consistent good form with 534 runs and Martin Stephenson, an off-spinner, enjoyed a rewarding season, his 29 wickets including the summer's only hat-trick – against Cumberland. Derek Wing, a 43-year-old seamer, also bowled well, and late in the season Cambridgeshire gave Paddy Phelan, the former Essex off-spinner, his début at the age of 48.

Frank Collyer, in his final season as captain of **Hertfordshire**, found their failure to field their main strike bowlers at the same time a considerable handicap. The highlight was the successful run in the knockout competition to the final, in which they were beaten by Norfolk, while in the Championship they had a thrilling win over Cumberland. For the future, there was promise in the batting of Martin Wright, who also shone with some brilliant work in the field. **Durham's** captain, Neil Riddell (537 runs) and John Lister (558) both scored freely, as did Steve Atkinson once his ICC Trophy commitments with Holland were finished. But Durham's bowling lacked strength. Steve Malone, a seam bowler who had played for Hampshire, failed to come up to expectations and John Johnston was often without support in a campaign in which Durham were unlucky to have two matches seriously curtailed by the weather. The presence of the former Yorkshire and England player, Chris Old (390 runs and 24 wickets), was a fillip for **Northumberland**, although their results showed no significant improvement. Kevin Corby maintained his impressive form as wicket-keeper, but the batting struggled as players were often unavailable.

Suffolk, winners of the Eastern Division in 1985, lost their second match to Cumberland, at Carlisle, by an innings and never looked likely to be serious contenders. Indeed, they had to concentrate their efforts to become the last of the Division's qualifiers for the 1987 NatWest Bank Trophy. Mike McEvoy, Gordon Morgan and Simon Clements all hit centuries and Russell Green, a fast bowler, collected 27 wickets in only six appearances.

Bedfordshire, Lincolnshire and Norfolk occupied the bottom three places in the East, Norfolk's plight being particularly surprising in view of their one-day triumph. **Bedfordshire**, having lost David Steele to retirement, could never quite put together a match-winning formula from the likes of Mike Morgan, Andy Pearson, Les McFarlane and, when available, Alan Fordham. However, they did have one day to savour, dismissing Hertfordshire for 61 for a memorable 81-run victory over their local rivals.

At **Lincolnshire**, their powerful batting, which included the talents of Neil Priestley (679 runs), Paul Todd, whose 572 runs included an innings of 180 against Suffolk, the third highest in the county's history, and Mark Fell (503), was never matched by similar bowling feats. David Marshall, with 30 wickets, was a lone spearhead. Problems with availability and the loss of Parvez Mir hit **Norfolk's** hopes, and their record might have been worse than five defeats from nine Championship games had it not been for Stephen Plumb. In one rich spell in June he scored three successive hundreds – 102 and 116 not out in the Championship against Bedfordshire, followed by 164 against Lincolnshire in Norfolk's record one-day total of 336 for five – and his aggregate for both competitions was 1,097.

In the Western Division, **Oxfordshire's** victory was closer run than Cumberland's in the Eastern, and owed much to the runs of Mike Nurton (694), Paul Fowler and Phil Garner, plus a bowling attack blessed with venom and variety. Roger Busby, their opening bowler, claimed the best return of the summer, eight for 41 against Berkshire, and finished with 36 wickets, his main support coming from Simon Porter and Ian Curtis, two spinners.

Dorset and Wiltshire provided Oxfordshire with the sternest of challenges. **Dorset**, frustrated by the weather in their final match at Taunton, were led from the front by Andrew Kennedy, their captain, with 624 runs, while Richard Merriman, a newcomer, also scored freely. The bowling was shouldered admirably by Chris Stone, who took 37 wickets, and Ian Sanders performed well. **Wiltshire's** batting was responsible for their remarkable rise from the foot of the Championship ladder. David Mercer (632 runs), Bob Lanchbury (553) and Mark Seaman (500) were at the forefront of a strong line-up which overshadowed the bowling successes of David Simpkins and John Spencer.

Somerset II won three matches in what emerged as their penultimate season of Minor Counties cricket, following their decision to withdraw from the Championship after 1987. They are the last of the first-class counties to maintain an involvement in the competition and from 1988 will be replaced in the Western Division by a Wales Minor Counties XI. **Cheshire**, the 1985 Minor Counties' champions, began well but then suffered from the weather. Ian Cockbain's elegant strokeplay produced 598 runs and Barry Wood, Stephen Crawley and Steve Yates all chipped in with useful support. However, their bowlers took fewer wickets at a higher cost. Arthur Sutton, their 47-year-old captain, marked his farewell season, after 28 years with the county, by taking 26 wickets.

The loss of Mike Milton and Richard Hayward left **Buckinghamshire** thankful for the profitable form of Paul Atkins, Andrew Harwood, Stephen Burrow and Stephen Edwards. Atkins, a nineteen-year-old, topped the Minor Counties' batting averages with 488 runs at 61.00 while Edwards finished with 36 wickets. **Devon**, for whom the ageless Doug Yeabsley took his 700th Championship wicket, enjoyed a depth of batting which included Nick Gaywood, Martin Olive, Kevin Rice and the Folland brothers, Nick and Neil.

Berkshire's failure to qualify for the 1987 NatWest Bank Trophy was certainly not the fault of Graham Roope. The former Surrey and England batsman hit 620 runs, his best performance for the county, and also took 22 wickets at 14.36 to top the Minor Counties' bowling averages. Included in that aggregate was a return of six for 21 against Shropshire, his best-ever bowling figures. Peter Lewington again demonstrated his value with 40 wickets, and Martin Lickley made 535 runs.

Shropshire, with a new captain in Stuart Mason and fresh direction from behind the scenes, failed to win a Championship game but were involved in some close finishes. John Foster, who in 1987 becomes their fourth captain in as many years, scored 683 runs and received plenty of backing from Steve Johnson (557 runs) and Mark Davies. Joe Smith topped the bowling with 31 wickets. **Cornwall**, elder statesmen Eric Willcock (567 runs) and Malcolm Dunstan apart, had few noteworthy performers in a disappointing campaign which brought just eight points from six defeats in nine Championship games, their worst record since they lost eight out of ten games in 1978.

MINOR COUNTIES UNDER-25 TO KENYA

A Minor Counties Under-25 team undertook an eleven-match tour of Kenya in February and March, 1986, winning eight matches and losing two, with one no result. The leading performers were Ian Tansley of Cheshire (later to join Derbyshire), who scored 326 runs at an average of 40.75, and the Cheshire and Lancashire fast bowler, Tony Murphy, who took 29 wickets at 13.55 each. The touring party was captained by Hertfordshire's Frank Collyer, the only over-age player in the side, and comprised: A. J. Buzza (Cornwall), P. J. Caley (Suffolk), N. T. Gadsby (Cambridgeshire), A. J. Murphy (Cheshire), E. P. Neal (Hertfordshire), N. Priestley (Lincolnshire), K. G. Rice (Devon), M. A. Roseberry (Durham), C. F. B. P. Rudd (Devon), I. Tansley (Cheshire), D. R. Thomas (Norfolk), M. A. Watts (Wiltshire) and D. A. J. Wise (Oxfordshire).

UNITED FRIENDLY INSURANCE
MINOR COUNTIES CHAMPIONSHIP, 1986

Eastern Division	Played	Won	Lost	Won 1st Inns	Drawn Tied 1st Inns	Lost 1st Inns	No Result	Points
Cumberland^{NW}	9	5	1	3	0	0	0	59
Staffordshire^{NW}	9	3	0	2	0	4	0	40
Cambridgeshire^{NW}	9	2	1*	3	0	3	0	35
Hertfordshire^{NW}	9	2	3†	2	0	2	0	34
Northumberland^{NW}	9	2	1	3	0	2	1	33
Durham^{NW}	9	1	1*	5	0	0	2	32
Suffolk^{NW}	9	2	3‡	2	0	2	0	30
Bedfordshire	9	1	1*	2	1	4	0	25
Lincolnshire	9	0	2*	1	0	4	2	14
Norfolk	9	0	5*	1	0	1	2	9

Western Division	Played	Won	Lost	Won 1st Inns	Drawn Tied 1st Inns	Lost 1st Inns	No Result	Points
Oxfordshire^{NW}	9	4	1*	1	0	2	1	50
Dorset^{NW}	9	3	1*	3	0	1	1	45
Wiltshire^{NW}	9	3	1	3	0	2	0	41
Somerset II	9	3	0	1	0	4	1	39
Cheshire^{NW}	9	2	2*	3	0	2	0	34
Buckinghamshire^{NW}	9	2	1	3	0	3	0	32
Devon^{NW}	9	1	2‡	3	1	2	0	25
Berkshire	9	1	1	2	1	3	1	23
Shropshire	9	0	4§	3	0	2	0	19
Cornwall	9	0	6*	1	0	2	0	8

* *Denotes first-innings points in one match lost outright.*
† *Denotes first-innings points in two matches lost outright.*
‡ *Denotes tie on first innings in one match lost outright.*
§ *Denotes first-innings points in two matches lost outright and a tie on first innings in one match lost outright.*
^{NW} *Denotes qualified for NatWest Bank Trophy in 1987.*
Win = 10 pts, first-innings win = 3 pts, first-innings tie = 2 pts, first-innings loss = 1 pt, No result = 2 pts.

CHAMPIONSHIP PLAY-OFF

CUMBERLAND v OXFORDSHIRE

At Worcester, September 13, 14. Cumberland won by two wickets. Toss: Cumberland. A tense finish brought victory for Cumberland off the penultimate ball after the first three deliveries of the final over had produced a dropped catch and two wickets. Hodgson, whose composure belied his nineteen years, compiled a match-winning 57, one of his three boundaries being a straight 6 off Curtis. Oxfordshire's total of 166 never looked enough, even when Busby and Arnold were restricting Cumberland to 33 runs from the opening twenty overs.

Oxfordshire

G. C. Ford b Scothern	4	R. N. Busby c Hodgson b Halliwell	...	17
M. D. Nurton c and b Woods	36	K. A. Arnold b Reidy		2
P. A. Fowler b Scothern	3	I. J. Curtis not out		0
*P. J. Garner c Clarke b Woods	36			
C. J. Clements b Halliwell	28	L-b 10, w 2		12
†A. Crossley b Halliwell	1			
G. R. Hobbins run out	27	1/15 2/19 3/75 4/87 5/89 (54.3 overs) 166		
S. R. Porter b Reidy	0	6/139 7/142 8/154 9/162		

Bowling: Halliwell 10.3-3-27-3; Scothern 11-4-32-2; Sharp 11-3-34-0; Reidy 11-1-34-2; Woods 11-1-29-2.

Cumberland

M. D. Woods c Fowler b Porter	14	†S. M. Dutton not out	6
C. J. Stockdale lbw b Busby	11	D. Halliwell not out	0
G. D. Hodgson lbw b Hobbins	57		
B. W. Reidy c Hobbins b Porter	23	B 1, l-b 10, w 2, n-b 2	15
G. J. Clarke c Ford b Garner	12		
*J. R. Moyes b Garner	17	1/18 2/38 3/94 (8 wkts, 54.5 overs) 169	
S. Sharp b Garner	9	4/118 5/143 6/157	
R. I. Cooper run out	5	7/163 8/163	

M. G. Scothern did not bat.

Bowling: Busby 11-6-10-1; Arnold 8-1-31-0; Hobbins 8-2-19-1; Porter 11-0-41-2; Curtis 11-2-34-0; Garner 5.5-1-23-3.

Umpires: D. B. Harrison and C. Smith.

KNOCKOUT FINAL

HERTFORDSHIRE v NORFOLK

At St Albans, July 20. Norfolk won by 30 runs. Toss: Hertfordshire. Norfolk, beaten by Hertfordshire in the 1984 final, were given a flying start after being put in on a pitch of greenish hue, Huggins and Plumb putting up 60 in thirteen overs. Huggins made a solid 53 and Thomas hit out for 46 off 59 balls. In reply, Hertfordshire made steady progress to 165 for three in the 42nd over, but then Plumb and Bunting each took two wickets in an over to initiate a collapse which saw the last seven wickets fall for 28 runs.

Norfolk 223 for eight (55 overs) (R. D. Huggins 53, D. R. Thomas 46); Hertfordshire 193 (50.4 overs) (D. G. Ottley 41, E. P. Neal 49).

*In the averages that follow, * against a score signifies not out, * against a name signifies the captain and † signifies a wicket-keeper.*

BEDFORDSHIRE

Secretary – A. J. PEARCE, 15 Dene Way, Upper Caldecote, Biggleswade SG18 9DL

Matches 9: Won – Hertfordshire. Lost – Durham. Won on first innings – Cambridgeshire, Lincolnshire. Tied on first innings – Norfolk. Lost on first innings – Cumberland, Northumberland, Staffordshire, Suffolk.

Batting Averages

	M	I	NO	R	HI	100s	Avge
A. Fordham	4	7	0	302	113	1	43.14
M. Morgan	9	17	2	503	83	0	33.53
A. S. Pearson	7	13	1	402	93	0	33.50
*K. V. Jones	7	12	2	315	68*	0	31.50
J. R. Wake	7	11	3	221	70	0	27.62
T. C. Thomas	8	15	4	252	46*	0	22.90
K. Gentle	7	13	0	263	60	0	20.23
†N. S. Randall	7	11	1	102	35	0	10.20
S. J. Lines	5	9	1	63	23	0	7.87
S. J. Renshaw	7	10	1	56	25*	0	6.22

Played in seven matches: S. E. Blott 0, 4*, 15*, 0; L. L. McFarlane 0*, 3*, 10*, 6*, 0*, 8, 0. Played in four matches: P. D. B. Hoare 7, 10, 5, 6, 2. Played in three matches: C. J. Proudman 5*, 13. Played in two matches: P. G. M. August 0; R. D. O. Earl 8, 9*, 17*; C. A. Musson 26, 10, 42, 15; M. G. Stedman 2, 5, 5, 54. Played in one match: B. L. Marvin 1, 39; A. Patel 10, 0*.

Bowling Averages

	O	M	R	W	BB	Avge
L. L. McFarlane	170.5	27	631	23	4-39	27.43
S. J. Renshaw	115.5	27	421	14	3-52	30.07
K. V. Jones	145	36	419	12	3-39	34.91
J. R. Wake	175.5	36	595	13	3-45	45.76
S. E. Blott	185.2	63	480	10	4-31	48.00

Also bowled: R. D. O. Earl 22–7–53–3; A. Fordham 3–0–23–0; P. D. B. Hoare 31–10–104–8; B. L. Marvin 5–2–7–1; M. Morgan 35–9–89–5; A. S. Pearson 16–5–70–2; C. J. Proudman 40.5–7–129–3.

BERKSHIRE

Secretary – C. F. V. MARTIN, Paradise Cottage, Paradise Road, Henley-on-Thames, Oxon RG9 1UB

Matches 9: Won – Cornwall. Lost – Dorset. Won on first innings – Buckinghamshire, Cheshire. Tied on first innings – Devon. Lost on first innings – Shropshire, Somerset II, Wiltshire. No result – Oxfordshire.

Batting Averages

	M	I	NO	R	HI	100s	Avge
T. M. H. James	6	6	3	169	52*	0	56.33
G. R. J. Roope	9	16	4	620	78	0	51.66
G. E. Loveday	7	13	1	430	85*	0	35.83
M. G. Lickley	9	17	1	535	102	1	33.43
M. L. Simmons	5	9	3	183	62*	0	30.50
D. B. Gorman	8	15	3	276	64	0	23.00
J. A. Claughton	4	6	1	79	27	0	15.80
*J. F. Harvey	9	12	2	148	25*	0	14.80
J. H. Jones	6	7	0	83	33	0	11.85
†M. E. Stevens	9	10	1	61	17	0	6.77
L. P. Sluman	6	6	1	31	17	0	6.20

Played in nine matches: P. J. Lewington 0*, 3, 0*, 0*, 2*. Played in three matches: S. C. Kingston 6*, 13*; K. S. Murray 9, 32*, 38, 2, 0. Played in two matches: J. C. R. Allen 1*. Played in one match: R. G. Anderson 22, 22*; P. M. New 0, 2*; J. A. Woollhead 24; K. J. Shine did not bat.

Bowling Averages

	O	M	R	W	BB	Avge
G. R. J. Roope	123	32	316	22	6-21	14.36
S. C. Kingston	69	15	172	11	4-28	15.63
P. J. Lewington	319.5	111	721	40	5-43	18.02
L. P. Sluman	128	25	361	15	5-63	24.06
T. M. H. James	84	23	291	11	3-19	26.45
J. H. Jones	140	27	417	12	3-31	34.75

Also bowled: J. C. R. Allen 24–4–88–0; R. G. Anderson 10–1–36–0; M. G. Lickley 43.3–11–139–2; P. M. New 32–9–77–5; K. J. Shine 24–9–44–0.

BUCKINGHAMSHIRE

Secretary – S. J. TOMLIN, Orchard Leigh Cottage, Bigfrith Lane, Cookham Dean SL6 9PH

Matches 9: Won – Cornwall, Devon. Lost – Cheshire. Won on first innings – Oxfordshire, Shropshire, Somerset II. Lost on first innings – Berkshire, Dorset, Wiltshire.

Batting Averages

	M	I	NO	R	HI	100s	Avge
P. D. Atkins	6	11	3	488	160*	1	61.00
S. Burrow	9	13	4	480	84*	0	53.33
*D. E. Smith	5	7	3	195	68*	0	48.75
A. R. Harwood	5	9	2	310	127*	0	44.28
S. J. Edwards	7	11	3	238	60	0	29.75
T. P. Russell	4	7	1	131	39	0	21.83
N. G. Hames	6	11	0	234	76	0	21.27
†P. A. Cooper	4	8	2	119	28	0	19.83
T. Butler	4	7	1	80	28*	0	13.33
P. D. M. Ashton	3	6	0	63	21	0	10.50
B. S. Percy	5	6	1	45	27*	0	9.00

Played in eight matches: C. D. Booden 16, 0, 1, 0. Played in six matches: A. W. Lyon 8, 4, 0. Played in five matches: †D. J. Goldsmith 11*, 6*. Played in four matches: J. K. S. Edwards 12, 33, 39*, 5; S. G. Lynch 16, 8*, 13, 7, 53. Played in three matches: K. J. Graham 24, 1, 4; R. W. M. Palmer 0, 0, 0*; T. J. A. Scriven 0, 2*. Played in two matches: W. E. Hubbick 22, 17, 27, 20*. Played in one match: G. R. Black 1; K. Roberts 1, 13; R. W. M. Tredwell did not bat.

Bowling Averages

	O	M	R	W	BB	Avge
A. W. Lyon	124	34	290	16	4-59	18.12
S. J. Edwards	225	47	669	36	8-60	18.58
C. D. Booden	214.1	45	654	25	7-19	26.16
S. Burrow	187.5	29	724	19	4-66	38.10

Also bowled: G. R. Black 15.4–3–45–4; P. A. Cooper 1–0–7–0; S. G. Lynch 54–4–248–2; R. W. M. Palmer 38–6–154–3; B. S. Percy 14.5–2–54–1; T. J. A. Scriven 11–1–50–2; R. W. M. Tredwell 16–5–40–0.

CAMBRIDGESHIRE

Secretary – P. W. GOODEN, The Redlands, Oakington Road, Cottenham, Cambridge CB4 4TW

Matches 9: Won – Norfolk, Suffolk. Lost – Cumberland. Won on first innings – Lincolnshire, Northumberland, Staffordshire. Lost on first innings – Bedfordshire, Durham, Hertfordshire.

Batting Averages

	M	I	NO	R	HI	100s	Avge
M. G. Stephenson	8	10	7	156	34*	0	52.00
†M. A. Garnham	9	17	2	566	93	0	37.73
N. T. Gadsby	9	17	1	534	147	1	33.37
J. D. R. Benson	9	17	3	368	59	0	26.28
D. C. Collard	9	9	5	98	29*	0	24.50
C. Lethbridge	9	14	1	315	87	0	24.23
I. S. Lawrence	6	11	3	166	27	0	20.75
*G. V. Miller........	9	15	0	236	76	0	15.73
G. D. Chapman	6	7	1	88	54	0	14.66
D. R. Vincent	3	6	0	34	19	0	5.66

Played in seven matches: D. C. Wing 0, 0, 2*. Played in four matches: C. W. A. Thorne 1, 7, 52*, 3, 14. Played in three matches: N. J. Adams 32, 0, 9. Played in two matches: D. C. Holliday 25*, 100*, 11; P. J. Phelan 22*, 0. Played in one match: A. D. Cuthill 20*; A. R. Davis 1, 3; G. W. Presland 8; M. Brown did not bat.

Bowling Averages

	O	M	R	W	BB	Avge
M. G. Stephenson	206.3	74	459	29	5-37	15.82
D. C. Wing	180.4	49	484	25	4-26	19.36
C. Lethbridge	285.2	49	813	40	5-43	20.32
D. C. Collard	180.4	41	563	20	3-23	28.15

Also bowled: N. J. Adams 31.3–5–95–4; J. D. R. Benson 65–14–214–5; M. Brown 18–7–35–2; G. D. Chapman 57–16–182–1; P. J. Phelan 41–3–166–2; G. W. Presland 10–1–32–1.

CHESHIRE

Secretary – J. B. Pickup, 2 Castle Street, Northwich CW8 1AB

Matches 9: Won – Buckinghamshire, Cornwall. Lost – Devon, Oxfordshire. Won on first innings – Dorset, Somerset II, Wiltshire. Lost on first innings – Berkshire, Shropshire.

Batting Averages

	M	I	NO	R	HI	100s	Avge
I. Cockbain	9	16	2	598	87	0	42.71
S. C. Yates	5	10	2	307	103*	1	38.37
S. T. Crawley	8	12	1	414	134	1	37.63
J. J. Hitchmough	9	11	3	266	96*	0	33.25
B. Wood	9	16	0	496	114	1	31.00
K. Teasdale	9	11	3	171	51*	0	21.37
*J. A. Sutton	9	9	3	114	63	0	19.00
P. H. De Prez	7	6	2	61	33	0	15.25
N. T. O'Brien	9	15	3	178	59*	0	14.83
J. S. Hitchmough	6	11	2	112	32*	0	12.44

Played in eight matches: †S. Cummings 18*, 47*, 0, 16. Played in four matches: J. F. M. O'Brien 13, 7*, 5*. Played in two matches: P. J. Dunkley 6; R. J. Owen 0*. Played in one match: G. L. Bullock 12*; P. N. Hughes 3*; A. J. Murphy 3.

Bowling Averages

	O	M	R	W	BB	Avge
B. Wood	175	60	381	22	4-27	17.31
J. F. M. O'Brien	83	28	226	12	3-35	18.83
J. A. Sutton	227	69	543	26	5-55	20.88
P. H. De Prez	129	31	352	16	4-42	22.00
N. T. O'Brien	158	41	487	21	7-56	23.19
J. S. Hitchmough	105.3	27	321	10	4-31	32.10

Also bowled: S. T. Crawley 74–16–230–5; J. J. Hitchmough 2–0–9–0; A. J. Murphy 37–5–120–3; R. J. Owen 19–6–59–1; K. Teasdale 16–2–55–1.

CORNWALL

Secretary – T. D. MENEER, c/o L. P. Dawe, 22 Berkeley Vale, Falmouth

Matches 9: Lost – Berkshire, Buckinghamshire, Cheshire, Dorset, Oxfordshire, Wiltshire. Won on first innings – Somerset II. Lost on first innings – Devon, Shropshire.

Batting Averages

	M	I	NO	R	HI	100s	Avge
M. S. T. Dunstan	7	13	2	474	118*	1	43.09
*E. G. Willcock	9	18	1	567	112	1	33.35
T. M. Thomas	7	13	2	293	85	0	26.63
P. J. Stephen	4	8	1	181	89	0	25.85
D. A. Toseland	7	9	3	148	55*	0	24.66
R. G. Furse	9	12	4	145	26*	0	18.12
J. M. Cradick	3	6	0	108	49	0	18.00
†D. J. Rowe	4	6	2	54	21*	0	13.50
T. J. Angove	4	7	0	91	49	0	13.00
G. G. Watts	4	7	0	78	32	0	11.14
A. E. Snowdon	7	13	1	125	37	0	10.41
S. Hooper	8	16	0	164	34	0	10.25
†S. P. Eva	5	7	4	20	8*	0	6.66

Played in three matches: C. C. Lovell 18, 0, 7, 5. Played in two matches: A. J. Buzza 1, 0, 0*; P. Hurley 0, 0, 7, 7; R. M. James 0, 0; C. S. Kitt 6, 45, 6; A. Machin 2, 15, 14*, 11; R. J. Perry 3*, 1, 1; M. W. Pooley 2, 6, 9, 0; R. T. Walton 1, 0, 1, 28. Played in one match: P. A. Coombe 13*, 13; S. A. Hunt 31, 6.

Bowling Averages

	O	M	R	W	BB	Avge
D. A. Toseland	183	35	638	18	5-55	35.44
R. G. Furse	189.3	31	747	20	4-71	37.35
A. E. Snowdon	117.3	14	470	12	5-34	39.16

Also bowled: A. J. Buzza 23–4–79–1; P. A. Coombe 4–2–9–0; J. M. Cradick 6–1–28–0; M. S. T. Dunstan 4.5–0–32–0; S. Hooper 0.2–0–10–0; S. A. Hunt 18–3–87–1; P. Hurley 22–4–91–0; R. M. James 28.5–7–110–1; C. S. Kitt 15–2–70–0; C. C. Lovell 41–8–133–1; A. Machin 13–2–44–1; R. J. Perry 34–11–94–2; M. W. Pooley 19–6–43–2; P. J. Stephen 2–0–17–0; T. M. Thomas 1–0–7–1; G. G. Watts 61.2–14–225–8; E. G. Willcock 4–0–17–1.

CUMBERLAND

Secretary – M. BEATY, 9 Abbey Drive, Natland, Kendal, Cumbria LA9 7QN

Matches 9: Won – Cambridgeshire, Durham, Lincolnshire, Northumberland, Suffolk. Lost – Hertfordshire. Won on first innings – Bedfordshire, Norfolk, Staffordshire.

Batting Averages

	M	I	NO	R	HI	100s	Avge
B. W. Reidy	9	14	1	533	107	1	41.00
D. Lloyd	6	9	0	326	109	1	36.22
C. J. Stockdale	9	14	0	430	102	1	30.71
S. Sharp	7	12	4	230	45	0	28.75
*J. R. Moyes	9	12	1	223	62*	0	20.27
M. D. Woods	9	13	0	249	67	0	19.15
D. Halliwell	9	11	5	110	49*	0	18.33
G. D. Hodgson	7	10	0	177	52	0	17.70
G. J. Clarke	4	6	2	67	32*	0	16.75
R. I. Cooper	5	6	1	61	23	0	12.20
†W. N. Boustead	7	6	2	10	5	0	2.50

Played in five matches: M. G. Sothern 33, 13*, 0*. Played in four matches: †S. M. Dutton 4, 4, 6*; E. K. Sample 0, 0, 5*, 1*, 4*. Played in three matches: S. D. Philbrook 41, 15, 2*, 0. Played in one match: N. Bartlett 4*; R. M. Ratcliffe 17.

Bowling Averages

	O	M	R	W	BB	Avge
D. Halliwell	284.3	76	826	44	7-41	18.77
M. D. Woods	141.4	43	353	18	6-61	19.61
B. W. Reidy	211.1	59	578	27	4-29	21.40
M. G. Sothern	142.1	32	414	13	3-41	31.84

Also bowled: G. J. Clarke 3.2–0–27–0; S. M. Dutton 2–0–7–0; D. Lloyd 125.5–37–314–9; R. M. Ratcliffe 25–10–39–2; E. K. Sample 41.3–9–150–5; C. J. Stockdale 3–0–12–0.

DEVON

Secretary – Rev. K. J. Warren, The Rectory, Lapford, Crediton EX17 6PX

Matches 9: Won – Cheshire. Lost – Buckinghamshire, Somerset II. Won on first innings – Cornwall, Shropshire, Wiltshire. Tied on first innings – Berkshire. Lost on first innings – Dorset, Oxfordshire.

Batting Averages

	M	I	NO	R	HI	100s	Avge
N. R. Gaywood	9	15	3	473	77	0	39.41
N. A. Folland	6	10	1	327	78	0	36.33
M. Olive	9	15	1	497	118*	1	35.50
K. G. Rice	9	15	1	375	119*	1	26.78
N. G. Folland	8	12	1	267	78	0	24.27
A. W. Allin	6	8	5	68	19*	0	22.66
K. Donohue	7	8	1	104	22	0	14.85
*J. H. Edwards	9	12	2	132	34	0	13.20
J. K. Tierney	9	12	1	106	30	0	9.63
†C. Pritchard	7	6	1	12	6	0	2.40

Played in eight matches: D. I. Yeabsley 4*, 6, 9*, 7*, 8. Played in three matches: P. G. Considine 1, 7*. Played in two matches: C. A. Melhuish 0, 18, 9, 4; C. F. B. P. Rudd 3, 30, 6; R. C. Turpin 5*, 16*. Played in one match: D. Beckett 0*; P. A. Brown 0, 15*; R. F. Harriott 9*.

Bowling Averages

	O	M	R	W	BB	Avge
D. I. Yeabsley	263.3	78	677	26	4-59	26.03
A. W. Allin	178	40	639	13	2-57	49.15
J. K. Tierney	158.5	18	680	13	4-78	52.30

Also bowled: D. Beckett 13–0–45–1; P. A. Brown 35–7–114–4; P. G. Considine 47–10–156–6; K. Donohue 115–17–466–6; N. A. Folland 5–0–32–0; N. G. Folland 2–0–14–0; N. R. Gaywood 8–0–38–0; M. Olive 3.3–0–17–0; K. G. Rice 4–0–17–0; C. F. B. P. Rudd 20–4–54–1.

DORSET

Secretary – D. J. W. BRIDGE, Long Acre, Tinney's Lane,
Sherborne DT9 3DY

Matches 9: Won – Berkshire, Cornwall, Shropshire. Lost – Wiltshire. Won on first innings – Buckinghamshire, Devon, Oxfordshire. Lost on first innings – Cheshire. No result – Somerset II.

Batting Averages

	M	I	NO	R	HI	100s	Avge
*A. Kennedy	8	14	2	624	100	1	52.00
C. Stone	9	13	9	192	30	0	48.00
R. V. Lewis	6	11	1	303	72	0	30.30
R. P. Merriman	9	17	2	434	84	0	28.93
S. J. Halliday	4	7	1	164	66*	0	27.33
G. S. Calway	8	14	0	350	75	0	25.00
S. J. Turrill	8	13	2	231	46	0	21.00
S. Sawney	4	7	0	133	39	0	19.00

Played in seven matches: †D. A. Ridley 1, 5*, 29*, 6*; I. D. S. Stuart 14*, 7*, 8*, 0, 5*, 30*. Played in six matches: I. E. W. Sanders 0, 1*. Played in four matches: A. R. Wingfield Digby 8, 20*, 3*, 2. Played in three matches: R. B. Hewitt did not bat. Played in two matches: S. W. D. Rintoul 0, 1*, 17*, 9; P. L. Garlick and †A. R. Richardson did not bat. Played in one match: A. M. Marsh 0; A. B. O'Sullivan did not bat.

Bowling Averages

	O	M	R	W	BB	Avge
I. E. W. Sanders	145.3	29	411	24	6-36	17.12
C. Stone	259.4	70	722	37	6-59	19.51
I. D. S. Stuart	146.2	28	515	18	4-78	28.61
A. Kennedy	110.3	29	346	10	3-35	34.60

Also bowled: P. L. Garlick 22–0–93–1; R. B. Hewitt 54.3–8–222–7; A. M. Marsh 8–2–22–0; A. B. O'Sullivan 8–1–35–0; S. Sawney 24.3–2–111–0; S. J. Turrill 41.4–5–192–5; A. R. Wingfield Digby 93–22–337–5.

DURHAM

Secretary – J. ILEY, Roselea, Springwell Avenue,
Durham DH1 4LY

Matches 9: Won – Bedfordshire. Lost – Cumberland. Won on first innings – Cambridgeshire, Hertfordshire, Norfolk, Staffordshire, Suffolk. No result – Lincolnshire, Northumberland.

Batting Averages

	M	I	NO	R	HI	100s	Avge
*N. A. Riddell	8	14	5	537	101	1	59.66
S. R. Atkinson	4	8	1	329	61	0	47.00
J. W. Lister	8	15	0	558	132	2	37.20
W. Johnson	4	7	0	242	87	0	34.57
S. Greensword	8	14	2	316	72	0	26.33
A. S. Patel	8	14	6	208	50*	0	26.00
G. Hurst	8	13	5	169	56	0	21.15

Played in seven matches: I. E. Conn 3*, 22*, 14; J. Johnston 0*. Played in six matches: P. J. Kippax 0*, 68, 28, 17. Played in five matches: †R. A. D. Mercer 2, 9, 0, 0*. Played in three matches: †A. R. Fothergill 2, 33; S. J. Malone 12. Played in two matches: G. Forster 10; G. Johnson 10, 4; D. A. Burrows did not bat. Played in one match: D. C. Jackson 23*; P. Beaney and B. R. Lander did not bat.

Bowling Averages

	O	M	R	W	BB	Avge
J. Johnston	174.2	40	446	23	4-40	19.39
I. E. Conn	127.4	19	451	19	3-11	23.73
S. J. Malone	56	7	240	10	4-34	24.00
P. J. Kippax	95	24	283	11	2-22	25.72
S. Greensword	101	27	316	12	4-42	26.33

Also bowled: P. Beaney 11-1-55-1; D. A. Burrows 47-3-224-6; G. Forster 15-8-34-1; G. Johnson 54-12-178-8; B. R. Lander 9-3-24-0; J. W. Lister 3-1-6-0; A. S. Patel 61-16-227-2; N. A. Riddell 1-0-1-0.

HERTFORDSHIRE

Secretary – D. DREDGE, 38 Santers Lane, Potters Bar EN6 2BX

Matches 9: Won – Cumberland, Norfolk. Lost – Bedfordshire, Northumberland, Suffolk. Won on first innings – Cambridgeshire, Staffordshire. Lost on first innings – Durham, Lincolnshire.

Batting Averages

	M	I	NO	R	HI	100s	Avge
A. R. Garofall	6	6	3	178	61*	0	59.33
D. G. Ottley	6	12	1	486	108	1	44.18
M. C. G. Wright	5	10	4	190	45	0	31.66
S. A. Dean	8	16	2	439	129*	1	31.35
E. P. Neal	9	17	3	331	90*	0	23.64
W. M. Osman	8	15	1	316	67	0	22.57
*F. E. Collyer	6	10	4	129	76*	0	21.50
P. A. Driver	5	8	2	112	31*	0	18.66
†M. W. C. Olley	9	11	4	123	34*	0	17.57
T. S. Smith	8	8	2	100	29*	0	16.66

Played in seven matches: W. G. Merry 18, 6*, 0, 13. Played in five matches: A. P. Wright 1, 0. Played in four matches: D. Surridge 5. Played in three matches: R. L. Johns 4*, 4, 13*. Played in two matches: J. M. Fisher 0*; N. Gilbert 1, 13, 18*; R. J. Hailey 0*; N. P. G. Wright 27, 10, 91*, 43. Played in one match: D. G. Price 2, 1; M. D. Saxby did not bat.

Bowling Averages

	O	M	R	W	BB	Avge
W. G. Merry	190	50	515	28	6-17	18.39
T. S. Smith	218.1	69	545	28	6-13	19.46
E. P. Neal	139.2	36	385	14	3-28	27.50
D. Surridge	87.2	23	283	10	5-46	28.30

Also bowled: F. E. Collyer 0.1–0–0–0; J. M. Fisher 30–1–101–4; A. R. Garofall 76–18–213–8; R. J. Hailey 74–26–158–5; R. L. Johns 51–18–122–3; D. G. Ottley 5–0–22–1; M. D. Saxby 22–3–75–2; A. P. Wright 75.3–11–286–8.

LINCOLNSHIRE

Secretary – D. H. Wright, 18 Spencer Road, Ketton, Stamford

Matches 9: Lost – Cumberland, Staffordshire. Won on first innings – Hertfordshire. Lost on first innings – Bedfordshire, Cambridgeshire, Northumberland, Suffolk. No result – Durham, Norfolk.

Batting Averages

	M	I	NO	R	HI	100s	Avge
†N. Priestley	8	14	2	679	144	2	56.58
P. A. Todd	9	16	0	572	180	1	35.75
M. A. Fell	9	16	1	503	99	0	33.53
P. R. Butler	8	14	6	268	51*	0	33.50
P. D. Johnson	3	6	1	165	60	0	33.00
T. J. Hopper	7	11	4	124	55*	0	17.71
G. Robinson	9	16	0	270	63	0	16.87
*H. Pougher	8	8	2	98	41*	0	16.33

Played in nine matches: D. Marshall 0*, 4*, 2*, 17*, 9, 4*. Played in eight matches: G. P. Gosling 0, 1*. Played in four matches: J. P. Quincey 0, 2*, 2. Played in three matches: S. Braithwaite 24, 9, 1; C. Wicks 34, 0, 12, 19, 34. Played in two matches: D. J. Allen 4; S. A. Bradford 13*, 3, 0. Played in one match: R. L. Burton 0; R. A. Dales 33; N. P. Dobbs 13*, 0*; T. F. Nicholls 9; L. A. Ward 1*, 5*; C. Beckett and P. Wood did not bat.

Bowling Averages

	O	M	R	W	BB	Avge
D. Marshall	259.1	53	853	30	5–78	28.43
T. J. Hopper	156.4	31	522	17	4–66	30.70
G. P. Gosling	120	15	469	14	4–60	33.50

Also bowled: D. J. Allen 47–14–131–4; C. Beckett 7–1–40–0; S. A. Bradford 33.3–3–127–2; S. Braithwaite 47–6–153–4; R. L. Burton 12–5–31–1; P. R. Butler 46–3–225–2; R. A. Dales 17–2–89–1; M. A. Fell 11–1–53–0; T. F. Nicholls 27–8–83–4; H. Pougher 4–0–40–0; J. P. Quincey 69–8–247–1; G. Robinson 8–0–45–1; P. A. Todd 17–2–61–0; L. A. Ward 3–0–17–0; P. Wood 24–3–108–3.

NORFOLK

Secretary – D. K. WILD, Charnwood, Hall Farm Place, New Road, Bawburgh, Norwich NR9 3LW

Matches 9: Lost – Cambridgeshire, Hertfordshire, Northumberland, Staffordshire, Suffolk. Tied on first innings – Bedfordshire. Lost on first innings – Cumberland, Durham. No result – Lincolnshire.

Batting Averages

	M	I	NO	R	HI	100s	Avge
S. G. Plumb	9	17	1	796	116*	2	49.75
J. Whitehead	6	11	2	253	37	0	28.11
P. J. Ringwood	4	8	2	162	50	0	27.00
J. R. Carter	5	10	0	258	120	1	25.80
D. R. Thomas	7	9	2	157	66*	0	22.42

	M	I	NO	R	HI	100s	Avge
*F. L. Q. Handley	7	12	0	262	87	0	21.83
S. B. Dixon	6	11	0	147	62	0	13.36
R. D. Huggins	8	14	0	178	63	0	12.71
R. A. Bunting	7	9	2	73	33	0	10.42
S. N. Waymouth	7	10	5	43	17*	0	8.60
E. R. Hodson	7	13	1	84	27*	0	7.00
†J. H. Riley	7	1	1	6	6	0	1.00

Played in five matches: P. K. Whittaker 6*, 4, 4, 2, 0*. Played in two matches: R. L. Bradford 4, 7, 22, 9; N. D. Cook 0*, 51, 3; D. E. Mattocks 12*, 0, 9; Nasir Zaidi 2, 0, 1*; G. M. Roff 35, 2; J. S. Tate 0, 10*. Played in one match: K. P. Cooper 5, 6; P. W. Thomas 1*, 0.

Bowling Averages

	O	M	R	W	BB	Avge
R. A. Bunting	154	31	453	29	6-35	15.62
P. K. Whittaker	91.4	12	360	16	4-49	22.50
S. N. Waymouth	122	26	370	15	4-93	24.66
D. R. Thomas	106.5	19	337	11	2-27	30.63
S. G. Plumb	212.3	54	588	17	4-60	34.58

Also bowled: K. P. Cooper 6-0-33-1; S. B. Dixon 2.2-0-8-1; E. R. Hodson 13-1-65-1; Nasir Zaidi 18.3-2-110-1; G. M. Roff 30-6-115-6; J. S. Tate 36-10-118-5; P. W. Thomas 13-0-39-2.

NORTHUMBERLAND

Secretary – G. H. THOMPSON, Northumberland County Cricket Ground, Osborne Avenue, Jesmond, Newcastle upon Tyne NE2 1JS

Matches 9: Won – Hertfordshire, Norfolk. Lost – Cumberland. Won on first innings – Bedfordshire, Lincolnshire, Suffolk. Lost on first innings – Cambridgeshire, Staffordshire. No result – Durham.

Batting Averages

	M	I	NO	R	HI	100s	Avge
C. M. Old	8	12	3	390	86*	0	43.33
P. G. Cormack	6	9	2	217	79*	0	31.00
G. D. Halliday	5	10	0	293	75	0	29.30
G. R. Morris	8	15	3	334	58	0	27.83
K. Pearson	6	12	2	268	74*	0	26.80
R. Dreyer	6	12	1	289	102	1	26.27
P. N. S. Dutton	5	10	0	212	64	0	21.20
J. R. Purvis	4	7	3	61	17*	0	15.25
†K. Corby	8	9	1	101	31	0	12.62
C. J. Harker	6	7	4	34	19*	0	11.33
*M. E. Younger	8	12	1	103	49*	0	9.36
P. C. Graham	7	8	3	39	10*	0	7.80

Played in four matches: S. P. Scott 2*, 0*, 0*, 0*. Played in two matches: P. G. Ingham 36, 1, 15, 33; B. C. Keenleyside 2, 12; S. G. Lishman 19, 36*, 12. Played in one match: M. F. Richardson 2, 0.

Bowling Averages

	O	M	R	W	BB	Avge
C. M. Old	223	67	521	24	4-27	21.70
S. P. Scott	65.5	18	246	10	3-61	24.60
P. C. Graham	172	55	443	18	5-31	24.61
C. J. Harker	154	32	488	18	4-48	27.11
M. E. Younger	136.4	29	465	17	6-55	27.35

Also bowled: R. Dreyer 1–1–0–0; P. N. S. Dutton 0.5–0–6–0; G. D. Halliday 41–7–133–3; P. G. Ingham 0.4–0–12–0; B. C. Keenleyside 29–3–139–0; S. G. Lishman 7–0–62–0; G. R. Morris 2–0–24–1; K. Pearson 2–1–14–0; J. R. Purvis 5–1–26–0.

OXFORDSHIRE

Secretary – J. E. O. Smith, 2 The Green, Horton-cum-Studley OX9 1AE

Matches 9: Won – Cheshire, Cornwall, Shropshire, Wiltshire. Lost – Somerset II. Won on first innings – Devon. Lost on first innings – Buckinghamshire, Dorset. No result – Berkshire.

Batting Averages

	M	I	NO	R	HI	100s	Avge
M. D. Nurton	7	15	3	694	104*	2	57.83
P. A. Fowler	6	10	2	312	76	0	39.00
*P. J. Garner ......;.	9	15	3	353	81*	0	29.41
C. J. Clements	5	7	1	148	54	0	24.66
G. C. Ford	8	13	0	249	68	0	19.15
T. A. Lester	8	11	1	181	45	0	18.10
K. A. Arnold	9	8	2	105	35*	0	17.50
S. R. Porter	9	10	1	102	29*	0	11.33
R. N. Busby	9	6	0	62	20	0	10.33
I. J. Curtis	8	6	3	14	10*	0	4.66

Played in five matches: †S. Partington 14*, 0*, 27, 4. Played in four matches: †A. Crossley 29, 23, 9, 0, 4. Played in three matches: B. J. Collis 0, 46*, 3, 15*. Played in two matches: G. R. Hobbins 1, 17; G. P. Savin 0, 0*, 0*. Played in one match: R. A. Evans 35; P. M. Jobson 4, 47*; C. W. Taylor did not bat.

Bowling Averages

	O	M	R	W	BB	Avge
R. N. Busby	220.4	54	588	36	8-41	16.33
S. R. Porter	131.2	28	431	22	5-51	19.59
I. J. Curtis	198.1	59	589	26	5-103	22.65
K. A. Arnold	180.1	46	462	16	6-45	28.87

Also bowled: B. J. Collis 3–0–20–0; R. A. Evans 18.5–5–72–1; P. J. Garner 27.5–7–63–3; G. R. Hobbins 22–10–31–7; G. P. Savin 17–0–68–1; C. W. Taylor 7–1–29–0.

SHROPSHIRE

Secretary – N. H. BIRCH, 8 Port Hill Close, Copthorne, Shrewsbury

Matches 9: Lost – Dorset, Oxfordshire, Somerset II, Wiltshire. Won on first innings – Berkshire, Cheshire, Cornwall. Lost on first innings – Buckinghamshire, Devon.

Batting Averages

	M	I	NO	R	HI	100s	Avge
J. B. R. Jones	3	6	3	172	47*	0	57.33
J. Foster	9	18	1	683	137	1	40.17
M. R. Davies	7	14	2	464	96*	0	38.66
K. Humphreys	3	6	0	212	73	0	35.33
J. S. Johnson	9	17	0	557	118	1	32.76
S. C. Gale	6	12	2	313	84	0	31.30
J. A. Smith	9	13	4	166	33	0	18.44
P. L. Ranells	5	8	2	108	30	0	18.00
†D. J. Ashley	9	13	4	134	33	0	14.88
B. J. Perry	9	11	2	121	34	0	13.44
*S. J. Mason	7	11	2	105	21*	0	11.66
G. Edmunds	9	8	4	45	24	0	11.25

Played in seven matches: J. S. Roberts 3*, 0, 1*, 2, 0*, 7*. Played in three matches: J. P. Dawson 16, 4, 4, 1*. Played in two matches: A. G. Shelley did not bat. Played in one match: M. I. Chaudry 18, 0; A. R. Williams 0.

Bowling Averages

	O	M	R	W	BB	Avge
J. A. Smith	216.2	47	665	31	5-56	21.45
B. J. Perry	158.4	25	655	27	5-32	24.25
G. Edmunds	260.1	74	770	26	4-73	29.61
J. P. Dawson	81	9	323	10	5-89	32.30

Also bowled: M. R. Davies 1–0–6–0; P. L. Ranells 62–12–211–5; J. S. Roberts 151.5–36–477–7; A. G. Shelley 26–4–116–2; A. R. Williams 24–4–72–2.

SOMERSET SECOND ELEVEN

Secretary – A. S. BROWN, County Cricket Ground, Taunton TA1 1JT

Matches 9: Won – Devon, Oxfordshire, Shropshire. Won on first innings – Berkshire. Lost on first innings – Buckinghamshire, Cheshire, Cornwall, Wiltshire. No result – Dorset.

Batting Averages

	M	I	NO	R	HI	100s	Avge
N. R. Williams	6	11	2	415	109*	0	46.11
J. G. Wyatt	6	12	1	483	86	0	43.90
R. J. Bartlett	7	13	2	458	82*	0	41.63
G. V. Palmer	8	14	3	345	39*	0	31.36
R. G. Twose	4	7	0	216	73	0	30.85
M. D. Harman	9	9	6	70	29	0	23.33
†R. J. Blitz	8	12	3	200	65	0	22.22
P. A. C. Bail	4	6	0	123	62	0	20.50
S. C. Booth	7	11	3	132	79	0	16.50
A. P. Jones	6	9	3	90	27*	0	15.00

Played in seven matches: D. J. Foster 0*, 1*, 9, 0*, 2, 0*. Played in five matches: R. V. J. Coombs 3*. Played in four matches: M. S. Turner 1, 6, 32, 27, 35. Played in three matches: J. C. M. Atkinson 64, 40*, 5, 11, 9; *P. J. Robinson 19. Played in two matches: A. R. Phillips 22. Played in one match: D. Beal 3*, 0; M. R. Davis 3; N. A. Felton 36; J. J. E. Hardy 41; D. W. Joseph 1*; J. M. Kerslake 2; N. R. Pringle 24; B. C. Rose 31, 86; N. S. Taylor 10; N. J. Waters 15, 16.

Bowling Averages

	O	M	R	W	BB	Avge
M. S. Turner	95	18	259	17	4-28	15.23
G. V. Palmer	157	30	446	20	6-57	22.30
D. J. Foster	125.2	19	382	15	4-9	25.46
M. D. Harman	222	40	693	22	4-76	31.50
A. P. Jones	92.1	15	333	10	4-31	33.30

Also bowled: J. C. M. Atkinson 27–5–61–0; D. Beal 14–2–50–0; S. C. Booth 22–2–100–1; R. V. J. Coombs 71.5–10–290–6; M. R. Davis 14–4–17–2; D. W. Joseph 36.5–12–90–3; A. R. Phillips 12–2–49–5; P. J. Robinson 2–1–4–0; N. S. Taylor 5–1–8–0; R. G. Twose 11–0–46–2; N. R. Williams 2–1–7–1; J. G. Wyatt 3–0–12–1.

STAFFORDSHIRE

Secretary – L. W. HANCOCK, 4 Kingsland Avenue, Oakhill, Stoke-on-Trent ST4 5LA

Matches 9: Won – Lincolnshire, Norfolk, Suffolk. Won on first innings – Bedfordshire, Northumberland. Lost on first innings – Cambridgeshire, Cumberland, Durham, Hertfordshire.

Batting Averages

	M	I	NO	R	HI	100s	Avge
J. P. Addison	5	10	3	290	78*	0	41.42
D. A. Banks	6	12	2	413	116	1	41.30
J. A. Waterhouse	6	11	4	231	73*	0	33.00
*N. J. Archer	9	13	3	272	75	0	27.20
P. A. Marshall	9	17	1	388	88*	0	24.25
G. S. Warner	4	8	0	177	41	0	22.12
S. J. Dean	9	18	3	295	88	0	19.66
†A. Griffiths	9	11	1	192	60	0	19.20
D. Cartledge	7	12	1	193	50*	0	17.54
D. C. Blank	9	9	2	108	52*	0	15.42
R. W. Flower	6	6	3	36	11	0	12.00

Played in seven matches: K. R. Maguire 0*, 0. Played in six matches: J. E. Benjamin 5*, 4*, 38*, 25, 25*, 1. Played in three matches: A. J. Webster 1. Played in two matches: M. E. W. Brooker 2*, 3*. Played in one match: R. I. James 0*; A. J. Mellor did not bat.

Bowling Averages

	O	M	R	W	BB	Avge
J. E. Benjamin .....:	140.3	20	439	26	4-55	16.88
A. J. Webster	91.4	24	240	12	3-23	20.00
R. W. Flower	160	55	426	21	4-22	20.28
K. R. Maguire	141ᶦ	15	520	19	3-22	27.36
D. C. Blank	230	40	717	26	5-39	27.57

Also bowled: J. P. Addison 6–0–32–0; D. A. Banks 1–0–10–0; M. E. W. Brooker 49–5–138–4; D. Cartledge 48–14–160–7; R. I. James 10–2–28–0; P. A. Marshall 1–0–13–0; A. J. Mellor 32.4–7–88–3.

SUFFOLK

Secretary – R. S. BARKER, 301 Henley Road, Ipswich IP1 6TB

Matches 9: Won – Hertfordshire, Norfolk. Lost – Cambridgeshire, Cumberland, Staffordshire. Won on first innings – Bedfordshire, Lincolnshire. Lost on first innings – Durham, Northumberland.

Batting Averages

	M	I	NO	R	HI	100s	Avge
M. S. A. McEvoy	8	15	0	490	127	1	32.66
P. J. Hayes	9	15	7	255	65*	0	31.87
P. J. Caley	8	15	1	426	79	0	30.42
G. Morgan	7	13	1	362	100	1	30.16
S. M. Clements	9	17	1	479	124	1	29.93
J. W. Edrich	6	11	0	213	37	0	19.36
†A. D. Brown	7	9	3	111	39*	0	18.50
R. Herbert	6	10	2	135	53*	0	16.87
H. J. W. Wright	3	6	1	73	26	0	14.60
P. D. Barker	6	12	0	126	28	0	10.50
M. D. Bailey	6	6	0	38	22	0	6.33
R. A. Pybus	6	6	3	9	4*	0	3.00

Played in six matches: R. C. Green 2, 0*, 0, 3*. Played in three matches: K. G. Brooks 1, 76, 0, 11, 12. Played in two matches: †N. J. Crame 20, 1*, 6, 0; C. C. Graham 4, 1, 9*, 7*; †C. Rutterford 27*, 1, 1, 0*. Played in one match: R. J. Bond 0, 6*; S. J. Halliday 74; N. Shahid 0, 0; K. J. Winder did not bat.

Bowling Averages

	O	M	R	W	BB	Avge
R. C. Green	160.4	38	397	27	6-63	14.70
P. J. Caley	62	14	217	13	5-15	16.69
M. D. Bailey	122	31	288	16	5-25	18.00
P. J. Hayes	135.3	36	348	13	3-47	26.76
R. Herbert	88.5	10	357	11	4-72	32.45
R. A. Pybus	107.2	14	448	12	3-60	37.33

Also bowled: P. D. Barker 25-9-63-4; K. G. Brooks 5-1-23-1; S. M. Clements 0.1-0-2-0; J. W. Edrich 1-0-16-1; C. C. Graham 31-5-90-2; C. Rutterford 40-10-106-5; K. J. Winder 24-3-45-3; H. J. W. Wright 38-8-121-4.

WILTSHIRE

Secretary – C. R. SHEPPARD, 45 Ipswich Street,
Swindon, Wiltshire SN2 1DB

Matches 9: Won – Cornwall, Dorset, Shropshire. Lost – Oxfordshire. Won on first innings – Berkshire, Buckinghamshire, Somerset II. Lost on first innings – Cheshire, Devon.

Batting Averages

	M	I	NO	R	HI	100s	Avge
J. J. Newman	4	7	3	204	55	0	51.00
R. J. Lanchbury	8	16	4	553	105*	1	46.08
D. J. M. Mercer	9	18	2	632	121	1	39.50
M. C. Seaman	8	16	0	500	76	0	31.25
*R. C. Cooper	9	15	2	352	70	0	27.07
B. H. White	8	16	1	394	64	0	26.26
C. R. Trembath	6	11	4	170	61	0	24.28
†J. J. Cullip	9	9	4	120	51*	0	24.00
M. A. Watts	5	6	3	62	28*	0	20.66
D. P. Simpkins	9	12	2	149	37	0	14.90

Played in seven matches: R. J. Merryweather 0, 1, 1*. Played in four matches: P. Meehan 14*, 9*, 32*; A. J. Spencer 2. Played in three matches: N. Prosser 1, 13*. Played in two matches: J. C. Barrett 4*, 1. Played in one match: K. St J. D. Emery 8; P. Jones 0*; D. R. Pike 12; R. Savage 16, 5.

Bowling Averages

	O	M	R	W	BB	Avge
A. J. Spencer	102	24	287	17	7-45	16.88
D. P. Simpkins	227.3	41	776	29	5-83	26.75
R. J. Merryweather . . .	95.3	19	328	12	3-34	27.33
M. A. Watts	114.4	17	420	14	5-51	30.00

Also bowled: J. C. Barrett 47.2–8–185–4; R. C. Cooper 30–4–129–4; K. St J. D. Emery 19–4–74–1; P. Jones 19–2–97–0; P. Meehan 47–7–154–5; J. J. Newman 3–1–9–0; D. R. Pike 12–2–25–0; N. Prosser 54–9–151–6; C. R. Trembath 117–20–395–8; B. H. White 5–0–31–0.

TOP TEN MINOR COUNTIES CHAMPIONSHIP AVERAGES, 1986

BATTING

(Qualification: 8 innings)

	M	I	NO	R	HI	100s	Avge
P. D. Atkins (*Buckinghamshire*) . . .	6	11	3	488	160*	1	61.00
N. A. Riddell (*Durham*)	8	14	5	537	101	1	59.66
M. D. Nurton (*Oxfordshire*)	7	15	3	694	104*	2	57.83
N. Priestley (*Lincolnshire*)	8	14	2	679	144	2	56.58
S. Burrow (*Buckinghamshire*)	9	13	4	480	84*	0	53.33
A. Kennedy (*Dorset*)	8	14	2	624	100	1	52.00
M. G. Stephenson (*Cambridgeshire*)	8	10	7	156	34*	0	52.00
G. R. J. Roope (*Berkshire*)	9	16	4	620	78	0	51.66
S. G. Plumb (*Norfolk*)	9	17	1	796	116*	2	49.75
C. Stone (*Dorset*)	9	13	9	192	30	0	48.00

BOWLING

(Qualification: 20 wickets)

	O	M	R	W	BB	Avge
G. R. J. Roope (*Berkshire*)	123	32	316	22	6-21	14.36
R. C. Green (*Suffolk*)	160.4	38	397	27	6-63	14.70
R. A. Bunting (*Norfolk*)	154	31	453	29	6-35	15.62
M. G. Stephenson (*Cambridgeshire*)	206.3	74	459	29	5-37	15.82
R. N. Busby (*Oxfordshire*)	220.4	54	588	36	8-41	16.33
J. E. Benjamin (*Staffordshire*)	140.3	20	439	26	4-55	16.88
I. E. W. Sanders (*Dorset*)	145.3	29	411	24	6-36	17.12
B. Wood (*Cheshire*)	175	60	381	22	4-27	17.31
P. J. Lewington (*Berkshire*)	319.5	111	721	40	5-43	18.02
W. G. Merry (*Hertfordshire*)	190	50	515	28	6-17	18.39

THE MINOR COUNTIES CHAMPIONS

1885	Norfolk	1925	Buckinghamshire	1960	Lancashire II
	Durham	1926	Durham	1961	Somerset II
	Worcestershire	1927	Staffordshire	1962	Warwickshire II
1896	Worcestershire	1928	Berkshire	1963	Cambridgeshire
1897	Worcestershire	1929	Oxfordshire	1964	Lancashire II
1898	Worcestershire	1930	Durham	1965	Somerset II
1899	Northamptonshire	1931	Leicestershire II	1966	Lincolnshire
	Buckinghamshire	1932	Buckinghamshire	1967	Cheshire
1900	Glamorgan	1933	Undecided	1968	Yorkshire II
	Durham	1934	Lancashire II	1969	Buckinghamshire
	Northamptonshire	1935	Middlesex II	1970	Bedfordshire
1901	Durham	1936	Hertfordshire	1971	Yorkshire II
1902	Wiltshire	1937	Lancashire II	1972	Bedfordshire
1903	Northamptonshire	1938	Buckinghamshire	1973	Shropshire
1904	Northamptonshire	1939	Surrey II	1974	Oxfordshire
1905	Norfolk	1946	Suffolk	1975	Hertfordshire
1906	Staffordshire	1947	Yorkshire	1976	Durham
1907	Lancashire II	1948	Lancashire II	1977	Suffolk
1908	Staffordshire	1949	Lancashire II	1978	Devon
1909	Wiltshire	1950	Surrey II	1979	Suffolk
1910	Norfolk	1951	Kent II	1980	Durham
1911	Staffordshire	1952	Buckinghamshire	1981	Durham
1912	In abeyance	1953	Berkshire	1982	Oxfordshire
1913	Norfolk	1954	Surrey II	1983	Hertfordshire
1920	Staffordshire	1955	Surrey II	1984	Durham
1921	Staffordshire	1956	Kent II	1985	Cheshire
1922	Buckinghamshire	1957	Yorkshire II	1986	Cumberland
1923	Buckinghamshire	1958	Yorkshire II		
1924	Berkshire	1959	Warwickshire II		

AN UNUSUAL DOUBLE

Phil Watson, of the NCI club in Cambridge, played for their first and second teams last year – on the same afternoon. The two teams were playing on adjoining pitches on Parker's Piece, Cambridge, which enabled Watson to open the batting for NCI's first team in a Senior League game against Cherry Hinton, and then, when he was out for 5 after fifteen overs, to field for the second team, who were one man short, in their Junior League match against Sotham. He later opened the batting for the second team and scored 46 in 25 overs before returning to field for the first team. Cambridgeshire Cricket Association said later that there appeared to be nothing in their rules to forbid such an occurrence but that this would be rectified. Not that NCI benefited from their itinerant cricketer. Both teams lost.

SECOND ELEVEN CHAMPIONSHIP, 1986

Despite the demands made on resources by first-team injuries, **Derbyshire** rose six places with three comprehensive victories. Five batsmen scored eight centuries between them, Bernard Maher's 179 not out against Worcestershire and 152 against Nottinghamshire helping him to win back his place in the first team. Chris Rudd's off-breaks brought him 43 wickets, and there was contrasting spin from the slow left-armer, Lindsay Wood, who had moved to Derby from Kent. The discovery of the year was the young Farnworth-born wicket-keeper, Karl Krikken, who never missed a chance and secured seventeen dismissals in five matches.

Essex enjoyed their best season for some years, finishing third. Ian Redpath was the most prolific in a consistent batting line-up, seven others averaging more than 30, although there were only four centuries in all. Michael Field-Buss with off-breaks, the Cambridge Blue, Andrew Golding (slow left-arm), and Ian Pont (fast-medium) were responsible for most of the bowling, each collecting more than 30 wickets, and Glenn Trimble, on an Esso Scholarship from Queensland, returned six for 84 against Surrey at The Oval. As well as filling second place in the batting averages, Neil Burns had another good season behind the stumps, his 32 dismissals including ten stumpings.

In a poor season in which they subsided to the bottom of the table, **Glamorgan** none the less recorded some useful individual performances. The outstanding batsman was Anthony Cottey, who hit three hundreds in his 954 runs, while Stephen James, from Swansea University, passed 500 runs despite playing for only half the season. Philip North, slow left-arm, took the most wickets, although Steven Watkin headed the averages. Stephen Barwick achieved the most impressive return, taking eight for 31 against Nottinghamshire at Caythorpe.

For **Gloucestershire**, still struggling near the foot of the table, Grant Bradburn took 41 wickets, including eleven for 161 against Glamorgan at Cardiff and ten for 107 against the same side at Lydney. The best innings return, though, was Henry Twizell's eight for 38 against Worcestershire at Old Hill. Five centuries were struck for the side. Ian Payne scored 107 and 140 not out in the match against Essex at Chelmsford, in which Andrew Chidgey also made 104.

Hampshire were another side to suffer from an extensive list of injuries affecting the club as a whole. A lack of penetrative bowling, especially on the final day, at times meant the difference between a draw or a win, but the team was admirably served by the Dutch seam bowler, Paul Bakker, and seventeen-year-old Kevin Shine showed real potential as a bowler, despite being restricted by a back injury for much of the season. Tony Middleton and Richard Scott both batted consistently well, and six batsmen made hundreds.

For **Kent**, bowled out by Lancashire for 24 in their first match, matters could only improve as their young players gained confidence. Trevor Ward had an excellent first season, and his 921 runs included 122 against Sussex at Maidstone. The more experienced Steven Goldsmith was also successful, and there was good support from Vince Wells, Mathew Fleming and all-rounder David Sabine. Of the bowlers, Alan Igglesden took advantage of every opportunity, earning himself a place in the first team, while Richard Davis, slow left-arm, looked to have the potential to be an asset to the county side and was given a Britannic Assurance Championship match late in the season. Chris Penn, if he was not playing for the first team, made a sound contribution, including a return of six for 75 against Surrey at Canterbury. Danny Kelleher was a useful all-rounder, especially in the second half of the season, and Paul Farbrace made a great advance in his first season as wicket-keeper.

In a memorable season, **Lancashire** won nine of their first eleven matches and remained unbeaten to become clear winners of the Championship for only the second time. Their success owed much to their all-round strength and to the leadership of David Hughes and Alan Ormrod, whose promotion to take responsibility for the first team in 1987 reflected not only their influence but the positive approach which they conveyed. David Varey fell just 17 short of 1,000 runs, with three hundreds, six others being scored for the side. Notable bowling performances included Ian Folley's eight for 44 and a match return of ten for 103 against Yorkshire at Crosby, as well as seven for 66 against Leicestershire at Manchester. Hughes, whose 46 wickets were the most for any county in the Championship in 1986, collected seven for 44 and a match haul of twelve for 99 against Nottinghamshire at Newark, while in the dismissal of Kent for 24 in their second innings at Folkestone Tony Murphy took six for 9 and Søren Henriksen four for 14.

For **Leicestershire**, who moved up five places to sixth, Chris Balderstone was the leading batsman, compiling scores of 159 against Northamptonshire at Lutterworth and 104 against Middlesex at Market Harborough, where George Ferris took six for 32. Other noteworthy returns were Paul Robinson's six for 88 against Warwickshire at Knowle & Dorridge and Ian Hopper's six for 49 against Derbyshire at Derby.

Middlesex, with the calls of the first team resulting in all but one of the staff appearing for them at some time, did well to finish fourth. "Paddy" Kasliwal from Bombay enjoyed a remarkable début in the match against Surrey at Enfield, following his six for 23 (his match figures were ten for 80) with 132 not out. He put on a record unbroken partnership of 273 for the sixth wicket with Ian Hutchinson (131 not out), also in his first season. But the most promising newcomer was Mark Ramprakash, who played with a command belying his sixteen years and represented England Young Cricketers, as did Alastair Fraser, who bowled with much pace in his first season. The slow left-arm spinner, Philip Tufnell, improved particularly towards the end of the season to finish with 45 wickets, including nine for 78 against Hampshire at Southampton, while Colin Metson, the captain, remained an excellent wicket-keeper.

The attacking cricket played by **Northamptonshire's** more settled but still inexperienced side produced many exciting matches, five being decided in the last over, and under the positive leadership of Bob Carter, they moved up four places. Richard Williams scored the most runs and took the most wickets, and there were encouraging performances from Mark Gouldstone and Alan Fordham with the bat and Mark Robinson with the ball.

Nottinghamshire, losing to the first team many of the side that won the Championship in 1985, called on 30 players in 1986 and dropped to eleventh place. The leading batsmen were Mick Newell, Duncan Martindale, and Russell and Kevin Evans, while the leading wicket-takers were Mike Bore, David Millns and Andy Afford, whose 42 wickets included eight for 107 against Northamptonshire at Newark and six for 39 against Leicestershire at Leicester.

Somerset leapt seven places to finish higher than for many years, despite five disappointingly heavy defeats that came when the side was short of batsmen owing to first-team calls. Ricky Bartlett, who made a hundred on his first-class début at Oxford, excelled in his first full season, his 160 against Worcestershire being an innings of high quality. Mark Harman, an off-spinner, was the pick of the bowlers, keeping good control of line and length, while Harvey Trump and Alan Phillips of Millfield School bowled well late in the season to raise hopes for the future.

Outstanding for **Surrey** was David Ward, one of only two players from all counties to pass 1,000 runs. He scored two centuries, as did Nick Falkner, who hit a remarkable 193 against Sussex at Hove. Left-arm spin, as purveyed by Chris Waller and Keith Medlycott, provided 64 wickets, but with few regular players throughout the season, the side slipped from second to tenth position.

With few contracted players and a long injury list, **Sussex** called on a total of 42 cricketers in their search for young talent, and they dropped eleven places. Andrew Bredin was the only bowler to take five wickets in an innings, but there was some good batting, the highest innings being 163 against Essex at Chelmsford by Keith Bradshaw, an Esso scholar from Tasmania. Other hundreds came from David Standing, who hit 157 against Middlesex, Neil Lenham, who contributed a delightful 141 against Warwickshire at Eastbourne, and Alan Wells, who reached three figures on each of his two appearances – 117 against Essex at Eastbourne, and 107 in the victory over Middlesex at Horsham.

Despite losing their last match of the season to Yorkshire by an innings and 4 runs, **Warwickshire** finished second, thanks mainly to their strong batting. Andy Moles, who headed the averages, scored four of the side's ten centuries. Tony Merrick, an Antiguan fast bowler, who was signed by the club as an overseas player for 1987, looked an outstanding prospect. The off-spinner, Adrian Pierson, bowled well in support, as did Stephen Monkhouse. Stephen Wall took the most wickets but at 32 runs apiece they were expensive.

Worcestershire, in the higher reaches of the table for much of the season, ran out of steam towards the end and had to settle for eighth place. The batting, unusually for the club in recent seasons, lacked depth and consistency, being carried by Lawrence Smith, Jonathon Wright and Stuart Lampitt. The latter, who also took the most wickets, excelled in the match against Gloucestershire at Old Hill, returning twelve for 167 and scoring 80. A match return of ten for 82 and an innings of 83 against Warwickshire at Nuneaton reflected Richard Illingworth's undoubted class, whereas Ricardo Ellcock's 24 wickets do not reveal how many he might have taken had a good number of chances been held. Shane Thomson, a sixteen-year-old from New Zealand, looked a useful cricketer, and Steve McEwan showed he is ready for the first-class game.

Outstanding for **Yorkshire**, who leapt seven places to fifth, was Richard Blakey, their Young England opening batsman. His 1,168 runs were the most in the Championship in 1986 and included four hundreds, his 273 not out against Northamptonshire being a Yorkshire record. Another highlight was the total of 486 for six declared against Glamorgan at Bradford, where Phil Robinson, Neil Hartley and Ashley Metcalfe all reached three figures.

SECOND ELEVEN CHAMPIONSHIP, 1986

	Played	Won	Lost	Drawn	Bonus Points Batting	Bonus Points Bowling	Total Points	Average
1 – Lancashire (5)	18	9	0	9	40	47	227†	12.61
2 – Warwickshire (7)	16	6	5	5	31	47	174	10.87
3 – Essex (6)	13	4	3	6	35	37	136	10.46
4 – Middlesex (3)	15	5	3	7	36	39	155	10.33
5 – Yorkshire (12)	16	5	1	10	43	38	157†	9.81
6 – Leicestershire (11)	14	4	3	7	26	40	130	9.28
7 – Somerset (14)	10	3	5	2	16	23	87	8.70
8 – Worcestershire (10) . . .	12	3	5	4	19	36	103	8.58
9 – Derbyshire (15)	14	3	3	8	26	38	112	8.00
10 – Surrey (2)	16	2	2	12	43	48	123	7.68
11 – Nottinghamshire (1) . .	15	3	4	8	27	37	112	7.46
12 – Northamptonshire (16)	14	2	4	8	33	37	102	7.28
13 – Kent (8)	15	2	3	10	27	49	108	7.20
14 – Hampshire (13)	13	1	3	9	31	39	86	6.61
15 – Sussex (4)	12	1	5	6	23	37	76	6.33
16 – Gloucestershire (17) . .	13	1	3	9	25	36	77	5.92
17 – Glamorgan (9)	16	1	3	12	28	32	72†	4.50

1985 positions in brackets.

† *Includes 12 points for a win in a one-innings match.*

Note: The averages used to determine the positions in the Championship are shown to two, uncorrected decimal places.

*In the averages that follow, * against a score signifies not out, * against a name signifies the captain and † signifies a wicket-keeper.*

DERBYSHIRE SECOND ELEVEN

Matches 14: Won – Gloucestershire, Leicestershire, Worcestershire. Lost – Lancashire, Nottinghamshire, Worcestershire. Drawn – Gloucestershire, Lancashire, Leicestershire, Northamptonshire (twice), Nottinghamshire, Yorkshire (twice).

Batting Averages

	I	NO	R	HI	Avge
A. M. Brown	22	6	832	100	52.00
†B. J. M. Maher	13	1	615	179*	51.25
K. N. Foyle	17	4	613	120	47.15
I. S. Anderson	9	0	357	115	39.66
R. Sharma	9	1	309	100	38.62
C. F. B. P. Rudd	17	5	364	74	30.33
P. G. Newman	9	0	231	89	25.66
H. V. Patel	9	2	171	68*	24.42
I. J. Tansley	20	4	306	97	19.12
D. Hallack	6	0	66	30	11.00
J. P. Taylor	10	3	64	17	9.14
A. G. Pierrepont	6	1	45	15*	9.00
†K. M. Krikken	6	1	43	19	8.60
L. J. Wood	8	4	33	14	8.25
D. E. Malcolm	7	1	37	12	6.16

Also batted: P. D. Atkins 71, 20; J. D. Benson 69; C. E. M. Bolton 0; R. J. Finney 31, 12, 32, 14; †A. M. Fraine 8; C. S. Gott 26*; M. Jean-Jacques 5, 0; S. J. Kimber 0*; †C. Marples 10, 63; G. J. Money 10, 12; A. Montgomery 6, 1; M. A. F. Nulty 14, 31; S. O. Taylor 9*; M. Wakefield 3*; J. N. Whitehouse 0. Did not bat: S. J. L. Merricks and P. E. Russell.

Bowling Averages

	O	M	R	W	Avge
R. J. Finney	29.5	10	64	5	12.80
C. F. B. P. Rudd	370	127	803	43	18.67
L. J. Wood	267.1	111	487	21	23.19
M. Jean-Jacques	60	12	168	6	28.00
R. Sharma	156.2	44	367	13	28.23
A. G. Pierrepont	93	22	260	9	28.88
P. G. Newman	91	20	262	9	29.11
D. Hallack	193	46	554	18	30.77
J. P. Taylor	244.4	36	776	23	33.73
D. E. Malcolm	218	62	541	16	33.81

Also bowled: K. N. Foyle 33.5–5–4–148–0; C. S. Gott 10–1–50–0; S. J. Kimber 34–9–125–2; S. J. L. Merricks 13–3–58–1; A. Montgomery 16–2–53–1; P. E. Russell 5–2–7–0; S. O. Taylor 4–0–11–0; M. Wakefield 53–20–117–4; J. N. Whitehouse 21–5–97–2

ESSEX SECOND ELEVEN

Matches 13: Won – Gloucestershire, Hampshire, Kent (twice). Lost – Middlesex, Surrey, Northamptonshire. Drawn – Middlesex, Northamptonshire, Nottinghamshire, Surrey, Sussex (twice).

Batting Averages

	M	I	NO	R	HI	Avge
C. Gladwin	6	11	2	401	65	44.55
†N. D. Burns	11	19	3	582	101*	36.37
C. Grinyer	6	8	2	217	72*	36.16
G. S. Trimble	8	16	1	529	120	35.26
I. Redpath	13	25	2	802	125*	34.86
R. N. Pook	3	6	0	189	52	31.50
M. G. Field-Buss	13	23	5	558	92	31.00
A. W. Lilley	3	6	0	183	64	30.50
*R. E. East	13	11	6	135	30	27.00
N. Hussain	12	22	2	519	107	25.95
I. L. Pont	9	12	1	210	58*	19.09

	M	I	NO	R	HI	Avge
B. Debenham	7	13	1	222	93	18.50
A. Mackay	11	12	2	163	42	16.30
A. K. Golding	8	10	2	125	42*	15.62
J. P. Stephenson	2	4	0	61	24	15.25
B. Sharpe	4	7	0	69	34	9.85

Played in three matches: J. H. Childs 4*, 3, 10*; T. D. Topley 1, 1*, 29, 6*. Played in one match: T. Barry, 0*, 0*; P. Bushnell 0, 2; L. S. P. Fishpool 0, 3*; N. V. Knight 4, 0; K. R. Pont 53; G. Roff 4, 0*; A. Seymour 30*, 8; P. Toogood 17.

Bowling Averages

	O	M	R	W	Avge
J. H. Childs	118	54	184	11	16.72
G. S. Trimble	110	13	384	17	22.58
T. D. Topley	102	27	262	11	23.81
I. L. Pont	309.1	57	913	34	26.85
M. G. Field-Buss	403.1	91	1,092	38	28.73
A. K. Golding	281.5	52	949	33	28.75
A. Mackay	241	37	827	18	45.94
C. Grinyer	141.5	23	411	6	68.50

Also bowled: T. Barry 24–5–69–1; P. Bushnell 16–1–77–5; R. E. East 13–4–34–0; L. S. P. Fishpool 34.5–8–116–3; C. Gladwin 36–10–93–2; N. Hussain 13.4–0–83–1; A. W. Lilley 8–3–16–0; K. R. Pont 11–2–41–0; R. N. Pook 22–6–71–0; I. Redpath 8–0–52–0; G. Roff 26–7–66–1; J. P. Stephenson 7–1–31–0; P. Toogood 43–7–111–2.

GLAMORGAN SECOND ELEVEN

Matches 16: Won – Somerset. Lost – Lancashire, Somerset, Yorkshire. Drawn – Gloucestershire (twice), Kent, Leicestershire, Nottinghamshire (twice), Surrey, Warwickshire (twice), Worcestershire (twice), Yorkshire.

Batting Averages

	M	I	NO	R	HI	Avge
S. P. James	9	14	4	559	125*	55.90
P. A. Cottey	16	26	4	954	122	43.36
A. L. Jones	8	12	0	454	85	37.83
D. B. Pauline	7	12	2	375	110	37.50
M. P. Maynard	5	7	0	248	166	35.42
J. A. Hopkins	3	4	0	124	89	31.00
S. W. Maddock	14	18	3	439	80*	29.26
*A. Jones	12	11	2	223	67	24.77
M. J. Cann	9	14	4	230	48	23.00
A. Dale	3	4	0	69	40	17.25
S. R. Barwick	9	7	4	51	16*	17.00
I. Smith	11	16	0	246	40	15.37
P. D. North	11	15	3	168	47	14.00
†M. L. Roberts	15	18	4	181	28	12.92
S. J. Moorcroft	4	3	1	16	11	8.00
A. Williams	5	6	0	43	22	7.16
S. L. Watkin	7	7	1	36	12	6.00
D. J. Hickey	4	4	2	11	8*	5.50

Played in five matches: H. G. Rogers 2*, 0*. Played in three matches: S. J. Base (57 runs). Played in two matches: I. J. F. Hutchinson 14, 7; R. N. Pook 39, 0. Played in one match: †M. Davies 1; J. Derrick 19*; G. T. Headley 0; K. D. Moye 2*, 0*; I. L. Rees 5; Younis Ahmed 39; †S. Meredith did not bat.

Bowling Averages

	O	M	R	W	Avge
S. L. Watkin	232	53	690	28	24.64
H. G. Rogers	57	11	202	7	28.85
P. D. North	334.2	116	930	32	29.06
S. R. Barwick	319.3	85	831	28	29.67
D. J. Hickey	140.3	28	400	13	30.76
I. Smith	277.3	64	741	23	32.21
S. J. Moorcroft	80.5	20	233	7	33.28
M. J. Cann	143.3	31	547	12	45.58

Also bowled: S. J. Base 28–8–64–0; P. A. Cottey 1–1–0–0; M. Davies 15–0–77–3; J. Derrick 11–5–33–0; S. W. Maddock 41.2–8–160–3; M. P. Maynard 37–3–101–2; K. D. Moye 25–2–119–2; D. B. Pauline 50–6–117–0; R. N. Pook 23–6–79–2.

GLOUCESTERSHIRE SECOND ELEVEN

Matches 13: Won – Worcestershire. Lost – Derbyshire, Essex, Warwickshire. Drawn – Derbyshire, Glamorgan (twice), Hampshire (twice), Somerset (twice), Warwickshire, Worcestershire.

Batting Averages

	M	I	NO	R	HI	Avge
I. R. Payne	6	10	2	490	140*	61.25
A. J. Wright	5	10	1	548	144	60.88
K. P. Tomlins	2	4	1	150	57	50.00
A. D. A. Chidgey	3	5	0	189	104	37.80
*J. N. Shepherd	9	8	1	260	94	37.14
J. P. Addison	9	16	0	489	163	30.56
G. E. Bradburn	11	19	5	408	67*	29.14
†A. J. Brassington	11	14	4	268	53	26.80
P. E. Hill	5	9	1	170	47	21.25
S. S. Alleyne	7	12	0	230	43	19.16
R. G. P. Ellis	5	9	0	140	37	15.55
G. E. Sainsbury	9	13	3	146	44	14.60
M. W. Alleyne	3	4	0	56	18	14.00
D. A. Burrows	11	11	3	110	41	13.75
D. J. Taylor	10	15	4	148	28*	13.45
P. H. Twizell	7	10	2	70	32	8.75
J. A. Smith	2	4	0	29	18	7.25

Played in three matches: R. T. Evans (106 runs), M. Frost (20). Played in two matches: N. M. Pritchard (29), P. M. Vincent (47). Played in one match: W. M. I. Bailey (4), J. E. Bramble (29), R. A. Bunting (13), G. H. Gilman (12), L. Gordon (0), S. Hamilton (9), A. J. Harwood (66), P. I. King (6), P. Langlais (17), C. H. H. Pegg (12), N. Pitts (8), T. W. Richings (48), P. W. Romaines (86), M. C. Seaman (19), O. C. K. Smith (37).

Bowling Averages

	O	M	R	W	Avge
G. H. Gilman	65	13	158	12	13.16
P. H. Twizell	178	56	393	27	14.55
G. E. Bradburn	296.4	97	711	41	17.34
I. R. Payne	101	27	299	14	21.35
J. N. Shepherd	128.3	35	272	10	27.20
J. P. Addison	41	4	136	4	34.00
D. J. Taylor	213.4	46	620	15	41.33
G. E. Sainsbury	206.1	61	448	10	44.80
D. A. Burrows	204.3	32	693	15	46.20
M. Frost	67	11	243	4	60.75

Also bowled: M. W. Alleyne 5–1–14–0; S. S. Alleyne 36–8–106–1; R. A. Bunting 16–1–70–0; A. D. A. Chidgey 0.1–0–4–0; L. Gordon 7–1–14–0; P. E. Hill 35–7–98–1; P. I. King 29.4–3–120–0; P. Langlais 28–9–49–1; N. Pitts 8–2–33–0; M. C. Seaman 1–0–10–0; J. A. Smith 24–2–71–2; O. C. K. Smith 13.5–3–48–1; P. M. Vincent 9–1–48–2; A. J. Wright 5–1–12–0.

HAMPSHIRE SECOND ELEVEN

Matches 13: Won – Somerset. Lost – Essex, Middlesex, Somerset. Drawn – Gloucestershire (twice), Kent (twice), Middlesex, Surrey (twice), Sussex (twice).

Batting Averages

	M	I	NO	R	HI	Avge
R. R. Savage	2	4	1	199	124*	66.33
D. R. Turner	3	4	0	193	145	48.25
S. J. Ball	3	4	2	94	46*	47.00
R. J. Scott	13	25	3	971	140	44.13
T. C. Middleton	10	19	3	678	129	42.37
M. E. O'Connor	12	19	2	553	100*	32.52
K. D. James	6	10	2	259	104*	32.37
S. J. W. Andrew	9	8	4	102	47	25.50
†A. N. Aymes	12	17	6	262	46*	23.81
*†C. F. E. Goldie	12	17	3	321	84	22.92
J. R. Ayling	10	18	5	247	33*	19.00
P. R. C. Came	3	6	0	108	38	18.00
R. J. Maru	4	5	0	60	53	12.00
M. S. D. Roberts	4	4	2	18	10*	9.00
P. J. Bakker	8	7	1	53	21	8.83
K. J. Shine	7	4	2	16	12	8.00
I. J. Chivers	11	13	1	89	41	7.41
P. Smith	4	6	1	9	4	1.80

Also batted: C. A. Connor 1*, 0*; N. G. Cowley 37, 13; R. M. F. Cox 38*, 2; N. Hutchings 22, 1; R. P. Lefebvre 45, 15; M. R. Newton 0, 0; R. A. Smith 56, 35.

Bowling Averages

	O	M	R	W	Avge
K. J. Shine	109	31	307	19	16.15
P. J. Bakker	229.5	65	606	32	18.93
R. P. Lefebvre	30	9	82	4	20.50
M. R. Newton	105.4	31	271	11	24.63
R. J. Maru	153.2	75	307	11	27.90
K. D. James	130	28	393	13	30.23
I. J. Chivers	361.4	98	931	30	31.03
P. Smith	109	25	331	10	33.10
R. J. Scott	111.1	21	369	11	33.54
S. J. W. Andrew	271.5	58	736	21	35.04
M. S. D. Roberts	90	22	237	5	47.40

Also bowled: J. R. Ayling 16–4–47–1; S. J. Ball 61–25–155–3; C. A. Connor 52–7–161–3; N. G. Cowley 27–5–77–1; C. F. E. Goldie 10.5–3–31–1; T. C. Middleton 23–4–61–2; M. E. O'Connor 1–0–6–0; D. R. Turner 3–1–6–0.

KENT SECOND ELEVEN

Matches 15: Won – Sussex (twice). Lost – Essex (twice), Lancashire. Drawn – Glamorgan, Hampshire (twice), Lancashire, Middlesex (twice), Surrey (twice), Yorkshire (twice).

Batting Averages

	I	NO	R	HI	Avge
T. R. Ward	23	3	921	122	46.05
G. R. Cowdrey	6	1	222	91	44.40
S. C. Goldsmith	22	2	633	130*	31.65
V. Wells	14	2	326	86	27.16
D. G. Aslett	11	1	264	88	26.40
M. Fleming	8	0	211	67	26.37
D. Sabine	13	1	305	95	25.41
C. S. Dale	15	6	212	50*	23.55
R. Pepper	4	0	94	40	23.50
E. A. E. Baptiste	8	0	172	60	21.50
†P. Farbrace	21	7	239	61*	17.07
J. Longley	4	0	67	38	16.75
D. J. M. Kelleher	19	1	284	59	15.77
M. Ealham	13	3	148	29	14.80
M. Dobson	4	0	48	16	12.00
S. Sharma	6	0	58	19	9.66
C. Penn	8	0	73	32	9.12
R. P. Davis	13	5	62	14*	7.75
A. P. Igglesden	7	4	9	7*	3.00

Also batted: T. M. Alderman 12, 3, 0*, 0*; C. S. Cowdrey 18, 66; J. Day 7, 14; S. G. Hinks 44, 226; K. B. S. Jarvis 0, 4, 1; N. Long 5; C. Wells 31*.

Bowling Averages

	O	M	R	W	Avge
T. M. Alderman	91.2	31	192	12	16.00
C. Penn	209.5	46	536	29	18.48
K. B. S. Jarvis	126.5	37	258	13	19.84
E. A. E. Baptiste	143.3	34	405	18	22.50
R. P. Davis	297	119	733	29	25.27
A. P. Igglesden	212.3	45	570	22	25.90
C. S. Dale	249.4	74	605	22	27.50
D. J. M. Kelleher	247	55	711	25	28.44
D. Sabine	63	6	226	5	45.20

Also bowled: D. G. Aslett 7–2–14–0; C. S. Cowdrey 2–0–13–0; G. R. Cowdrey 16–0–92–0; A. Duncan 6–0–41–0; M. Fleming 26.3–6–61–3; S. C. Goldsmith 20–4–63–0; S. G. Hinks 10–1–52–0; N. Long 21–7–73–3; C. Wells 8–0–21–0; V. Wells 11–0–69–2.

LANCASHIRE SECOND ELEVEN

Matches 18: Won – Derbyshire, Glamorgan, Kent, Nottinghamshire (twice), Somerset, Warwickshire (twice), Yorkshire. Drawn – Derbyshire, Kent, Leicestershire (twice), Northamptonshire (twice), Surrey (twice), Yorkshire.

Batting Averages

	M	I	NO	R	HI	Avge
S. J. O'Shaughnessy	7	11	4	428	113*	61.14
A. J. Murphy	13	5	4	55	24	55.00
D. W. Varey	15	25	6	983	156*	51.73
N. J. Speak	6	9	2	296	80*	42.28
*D. P. Hughes	16	23	5	746	119*	41.44
†J. Stanworth	14	10	6	136	27	34.00
K. A. Hayes	15	24	3	711	104	33.85
M. R. Chadwick	13	23	2	706	117	33.61

	M	I	NO	R	HI	Avge
I. D. Austin	16	23	5	545	93	30.27
G. D. Hodgson	4	6	2	119	64	29.75
S. Henriksen	12	12	4	236	59	29.50
D. J. Makinson	6	6	3	84	49*	28.00
A. N. Hayhurst	9	17	4	357	142	27.46
*J. A. Ormrod	10	7	2	87	25	17.40
I. Folley	7	8	2	93	31	15.50
†W. K. Hegg	6	3	0	43	19	14.33
I. C. Davidson	16	8	2	33	12*	5.50

Also batted: N. Bradshaw 26; F. J. Daly 5*; R. Ellwood 4; G. D. Mendis 29, 4; C. A. Smith 53; A. Travis 28; T. Wallwork 5; M. Watkinson 81. M. Frost and A. Smith-Butler did not bat.

Bowling Averages

	O	M	R	W	Avge
I. Folley	269.1	111	473	32	14.78
D. P. Hughes	333.5	113	710	46	15.43
A. N. Hayhurst	96.5	21	250	14	17.85
M. Watkinson	48	11	154	8	19.25
S. J. O'Shaughnessy	108.5	17	303	14	21.64
A. J. Murphy	343.5	71	1,053	42	25.07
S. Henriksen	271.3	59	767	29	26.44
I. D. Austin	89	21	212	8	26.50
I. C. Davidson	374	66	1,245	38	32.76
D. J. Makinson	125.2	21	378	9	42.00

Also bowled: M. R. Chadwick 1-1-0-0; F. J. Daly 32-7-95-0; R. Ellwood 7-1-34-0; M. Frost 55-12-200-3; K. A. Hayes 1-0-24-0; A. Smith-Butler 10-1-36-0; N. J. Speak 1-0-12-0; J. Stanworth 1-0-6-0; D. W. Varey 1-0-8-0.

LEICESTERSHIRE SECOND ELEVEN

Matches 14: Won – Northamptonshire, Nottinghamshire, Warwickshire, Worcestershire. Lost – Derbyshire, Northamptonshire, Nottinghamshire. Drawn – Derbyshire, Glamorgan, Lancashire (twice), Middlesex, Surrey, Worcestershire.

Batting Averages

	M	I	NO	R	HI	Avge
*J. C. Balderstone	8	14	0	660	159	47.14
I. P. Butcher	6	12	3	377	72	41.88
P. D. Bowler	10	16	1	526	76	35.06
P. Robinson	3	6	2	111	28	27.75
M. Blackett	10	17	2	394	77	26.26
I. Hopper	8	14	5	229	47	25.44
M. Whitmore	3	5	0	105	47	21.00
M. de Silva	6	9	0	185	61	20.55
R. A. Cobb	3	4	0	77	37	19.25
D. J. Billington	10	19	1	336	59	18.66
L. Tennant	9	13	3	148	57*	14.80
C. Pringle	3	6	0	88	40	14.66
G. A. R. Harris	7	6	2	39	20*	9.75
†P. Gill	8	11	2	87	19	9.66
L. B. Taylor	4	7	1	51	14	8.50
K. Higgs	4	6	3	25	18*	8.33
G. J. F. Ferris	5	8	2	35	14	5.83
M. Briers	7	9	3	26	8	4.33

Also batted: J. P. Agnew 3; J. Benson 25, 15; T. J. Boon 16, 33; N. E. Briers 11, 70, 13; J. Clark 20, 1; S. Crawley 14, 10; P. Downing 2, 11*, 3, 0*; R. Edmunds 0, 1, 0*, 15*; M. Gidley 0, 8; P. Greenwood 8, 9*; N. Masood 28, 18; R. V. Patel 5, 11; I. R. Payne 23; L. Potter 2*; R. Qureshi 18, 14*; O. P. J. Stephenson 0; C. Wilson 1, 3.

Bowling Averages

	O	M	R	W	Avge
L. Potter	42	19	54	10	5.40
C. Pringle	14	3	37	5	7.40
J. P. Agnew	21.2	4	57	6	9.50
N. E. Briers	27	6	73	7	10.42
R. Edmunds	27.3	8	59	5	11.80
L. Taylor	135.1	41	305	21	14.52
M. Gidley	30.5	6	91	5	18.20
I. Hopper	176.4	58	442	23	19.21
G. J. F. Ferris	128.4	33	308	16	19.25
G. A. R. Harris	202	59	513	21	24.42
M. de Silva	171.2	53	396	14	28.28
M. Briers	155	28	497	15	33.13
L. Tennant	181.4	42	548	16	34.25

Also bowled: J. C. Balderstone 55.1–14–143–3; P. D. Bowler 87–20–279–3; I. P. Butcher 4–2–17–0; S. Crawley 11–0–54–0; J. E. Fisher 6–0–22–0; K. Higgs 21.2–2–71–0; P. Higgs 17–2–50–2; P. B. G. Johnson 3–1–5–0; I. R. Payne 20–4–81–1; O. P. J. Stephenson 0.2–0–5–0.

MIDDLESEX SECOND ELEVEN

Matches 15: Won – Essex, Hampshire, Northamptonshire, Surrey, Sussex. Lost – Sussex, Warwickshire (twice). Drawn – Essex, Hampshire, Kent (twice), Leicestershire, Northamptonshire, Surrey.

Batting Averages

	M	I	NO	R	HI	Avge
P. Kasliwal	2	3	1	151	132*	75.50
A. J. T. Miller	2	4	1	205	75	68.33
I. J. F. Hutchinson	6	11	2	419	131	46.55
G. K. Brown	14	25	5	790	103	39.50
N. R. C. MacLaurin	15	26	2	860	156	35.83
K. R. Brown	11	21	2	655	125	34.47
M. R. Ramprakash	5	10	0	285	61	28.50
M. A. Roseberry	13	24	0	618	99	25.75
J. D. Carr	3	5	0	123	59	24.60
A. R. Harwood	11	20	0	489	79	24.45
G. D. Rose	12	19	2	401	72	23.58
N. F. Williams	2	4	0	78	46	19.50
J. F. Sykes	13	21	2	308	78	16.21
*†C. P. Metson	15	21	5	196	39*	12.25
A. G. J. Fraser	13	19	8	82	12	7.45
R. S. Rutnagur	3	3	0	18	6	6.00
P. C. R. Tufnell	13	13	4	43	12	4.77

Played in two matches: M. A. Cottom did not bat. Played in one match: A. A. Barnett 0*; N. G. Cowans 6*, 2*; S. P. Hughes 5; R. M. Layton 0; C. C. Lewis 34*, 3; I. M. Osbourne 14, 15; R. N. Pook 0; S. D. Weale 7*; D. W. R. Wiles 0; R. G. Woolston 0*.

Bowling Averages

	O	M	R	W	Avge
P. Kasliwal	62.1	14	178	16	11.12
M. A. Cottam	36	14	82	6	13.66
P. C. R. Tufnell	455.5	155	955	45	21.22
A. G. J. Fraser	317.2	70	904	35	25.82
G. D. Rose	316.3	50	978	31	31.54
J. F. Sykes	337.4	88	857	27	31.74

Also bowled: A. A. Barnett 9–4–25–0; G. K. Brown 71–8–235–2; K. R. Brown 3–2–2–1; J. D. Carr 49–21–72–2; N. G. Cowans 27–7–57–3; S. P. Hughes 5–0–13–1; R. M. Layton 11–2–49–1; C. C. Lewis 29–8–95–3; N. R. C. MacLaurin 15–3–52–2; I. M. Osbourne 2–1–10–0; R. N. Pook 8–1–21–1; M. R. Ramprakash 3–0–25–0; M. A. Roseberry 4.4–0–10–0; R. S. Rutnagur 5–0–22–0; S. D. Weale 8–0–42–0; D. W. R. Wiles 15–3–48–0; N. F. Williams 42–6–120–3; R. G. Woolston 36.5–11–107–3.

NORTHAMPTONSHIRE SECOND ELEVEN

Matches 14: Won – Essex, Leicestershire. Lost – Leicestershire, Middlesex, Nottinghamshire, Yorkshire. Drawn – Derbyshire (twice), Essex, Lancashire (twice), Middlesex, Nottinghamshire, Yorkshire.

Batting Averages

	M	I	NO	R	HI	Avge
*R. M. Carter	11	13	6	345	75*	49.28
R. G. Williams	12	22	3	874	115	46.00
A. Fordham	6	11	0	497	159	45.18
P. D. Atkins	7	12	2	433	117*	43.30
A. Penberthy	5	10	3	289	76	41.28
M. R. Gouldstone	12	21	0	746	128	35.52
A. C. Storie	12	23	3	589	111	29.45
†D. Ripley	9	17	2	376	84*	25.06
T. Scriven	13	19	6*	284	56	21.84
G. Smith	12	10	2	107	60	13.37
A. Walker	4	5	2	33	17	11.00
B. J. Griffiths	8	6	3	29	15*	9.66
M. Baker	6	6	0	36	17	6.00
M. Robinson	12	8	5	18	11*	6.00

Also batted: R. J. Boyd-Moss 13, 17; M. Bradley 0, 8; S. Brown 1, 2, 0, 39*; M. Frost 21; S. Inwood 17, 11; W. Larkins 19, 14, 4; N. A. Mallender 4; I. Reynolds 2*; N. Stanley 12; R. Tredwell 19*, 0; †S. N. V. Waterton 32, 87, 21*; W. Watson 46; D. J. Wild 36*, 27*. †A. Faine did not bat.

Bowling Averages

	O	M	R	W	Avge
S. Brown	66.1	8	242	14	17.28
R. G. Williams	378.5	99	890	37	24.05
A. Walker	115.4	31	281	11	25.54
M. Robinson	237	25	912	27	33.77
B. J. Griffiths	217	46	682	19	35.89
T. Scriven	345.5	91	947	25	37.88
G. Smith	230.5	36	828	21	39.42

Also bowled: P. D. Atkins 5–1–23–2; M. Baker 49–14–117–3; R. J. Boyd-Moss 6–1–19–0; R. M. Carter 12–4–21–1; A. Fordham 14–3–62–1; M. Frost 25.4–4–82–1; M. R. Gouldstone 20–1–116–1; S. Inwood 1–0–1–0; N. A. Mallender 31–10–53–1; A. Penberthy 9–2–32–0.

NOTTINGHAMSHIRE SECOND ELEVEN

Matches 15: Won – Derbyshire, Leicestershire, Northamptonshire. Lost – Lancashire (twice), Leicestershire, Yorkshire. Drawn – Derbyshire, Essex, Glamorgan (twice), Northamptonshire, Sussex, Warwickshire, Yorkshire.

Batting Averages

	M	I	NO	R	HI	Avge
D. W. Randall	2	4	0	340	177	85.00
†M. Newell	8	13	0	634	128	48.76
K. P. Evans	8	13	2	404	100*	36.72
D. J. R. Martindale	13	22	1	739	151	35.19
†C. W. Scott	9	14	1	401	68	30.84
R. J. Evans	14	24	3	590	111	28.09
*M. K. Bore	14	19	7	289	56*	24.08
B. T. Spragg	12	21	2	430	95*	22.63
G. D. Harding	6	10	1	157	51	17.44
C. D. Fraser-Darling	11	18	0	296	62	16.44
J. W. S. Porter	2	4	0	65	22	16.25
P. Pollard	8	15	0	225	42	15.00
M. E. Root	2	4	0	59	22	14.75
J. Dunn	2	4	0	44	23	11.00
K. Saxelby	4	6	1	50	29	10.00
D. J. Millns	14	17	8	87	21*	9.66
J. A. Afford	11	13	5	72	26	9.00
J. C. Bacon	3	5	0	45	21	9.00
P. M. Such	9	12	3	61	13	6.77

Played in two matches: F. J. Cooke 0*; †G. R. Sanders 2, 1, 0, 0. Played in one match: P. J. Baker 5, 0; J. D. Birch 17; M. Bradley 40, 38; D. A. Donaldson 36*, 6; N. Fenwick 1; N. R. Gaywood 59, 10; J. C. M. Lewis 6*, 2*; A. Naylor 22, 0; A. Perry 16, 0.

Bowling Averages

	O	M	R	W	Avge
K. Saxelby	87	26	182	12	15.16
M. K. Bore	295.5	117	586	30	19.53
J. A. Afford	380.2	128	882	42	21.00
K. P. Evans	152.1	30	459	16	28.68
C. D. Fraser-Darling	232	57	628	19	33.05
P. M. Such	268.1	87	602	17	35.41
D. J. Millns	299.3	51	1,005	26	38.65
G. D. Harding	64.3	15	168	4	42.00
J. C. Bacon	68	19	218	5	43.60

Also bowled: P. J. Baker 11–2–36–0; J. Dunn 11–1–45–0; R. J. Evans 25–3–119–0; N. Fenwick 14–6–36–0; J. C. M. Lewis 28–2–76–1; D. J. R. Martindale 14–0–90–0; M. Newell 6–0–23–0; P. Pollard 9–0–67–0; D. W. Randall 1–0–1–0; B. T. Spragg 3–0–19–0.

SOMERSET SECOND ELEVEN

Matches 10: Won – Glamorgan, Hampshire, Worcestershire. Lost – Glamorgan, Hampshire, Lancashire, Warwickshire, Worcestershire. Drawn – Gloucestershire (twice).

Batting Averages

	M	I	NO	R	HI	Avge
R. J. Bartlett	7	12	2	406	160	40.60
J. Szeliger	2	3	0	115	62	38.33
P. A. C. Bail	3	5	0	180	54	36.00
J. G. Wyatt	5	10	1	289	58	32.11
*R. J. Blitz	7	10	3	215	67	30.71
M. S. Turner	7	11	1	276	74*	27.60
G. V. Palmer	7	12	1	282	51	25.63
N. R. Williams	4	8	1	160	60	22.85
N. J. Waters	3	5	0	96	47	19.20
†A. Smales	2	3	0	55	28	18.33
M. R. Davis	5	6	0	83	53	13.83
M. D. Harman	8	9	3	82	21*	13.66
N. C. Pringle	2	4	0	53	26	13.25
S. C. Booth	6	11	1	110	35	11.00
J. C. M. Atkinson	3	4	0	42	16	10.50
A. P. Jones	3	4	0	38	10	9.50
A. R. Phillips	2	3	0	24	20	8.00
D. J. Foster	10	12	2	74	24	7.40
R. V. J. Coombs	5	7	2	24	13	4.80

Played in three matches: *P. J. Robinson 2, 4*. Played in one match: R. R. Baigent 4, 18; S. Baruah 31; I. T. Botham 41; M. D. Crowe 114, 14*; J. Fry 44*, 68; R. J. Harden 5; J. J. E. Hardy 111*; D. W. Joseph 1; J. M. Kerslake 0; C. A. Kirk 14, 0; N. S. Taylor 10, 21; H. R. J. Trump 8, 0; †R. J. Turner 2*, 0*; B. Jackson and R. G. Twose did not bat.

Bowling Averages

	O	M	R	W	Avge
P. J. Robinson	23.3	6	67	5	13.40
M. S. Turner	89	15	255	14	18.21
M. D. Harman	219.2	55	565	20	28.25
M. R. Davis	113.3	25	278	9	30.88
D. J. Foster	156	23	468	12	39.00
G. V. Palmer	148	31	454	9	50.44

Also bowled: P. A. C. Bail 1–0–5–0; S. C. Booth 68–23–128–3; I. T. Botham 15–2–47–2; B. Jackson 30–3–95–3; A. P. Jones 8–1–32–2; D. W. Joseph 33.3–13–64–3; A. R. Phillips 18–1–67–0; N. S. Taylor 18–4–53–3; H. R. J. Trump 39–8–128–1; N. C. Waters 1–0–5–0; N. R. Williams 27–4–98–1.

SURREY SECOND ELEVEN

Matches 16: Won – Essex, Sussex. Lost – Middlesex, Yorkshire. Drawn – Essex, Glamorgan, Hampshire (twice), Kent (twice), Lancashire (twice), Leicestershire, Middlesex, Sussex, Yorkshire.

Batting Averages

	M	I	NO	R	HI	Avge
A. Needham	7	9	1	401	96*	50.13
D. M. Ward	14	24	3	1,042	127*	49.62
C. K. Bullen	12	19	4	680	159	45.33
D. Bicknell	7	14	3	465	107*	42.27
J. D. Robinson	8	13	2	417	60	37.91
N. J. Falkner	9	15	0	567	193	37.80
D. J. Thomas	6	9	1	288	97	36.00
B. McNamara	4	8	1	249	54	35.57
W. Seabrook	2	4	1	96	53	32.00
Zahid Sadiq	15	26	0	770	142	29.62

	M	I	NO	R	HI	Avge
M. A. Feltham	6	10	2	192	81	24.00
P. D. Atkins	8	14	1	295	75	22.69
K. T. Medlycott	8	13	3	224	76*	22.40
†G. E. Brown	13	12	6	102	44*	17.00
G. Winterborne	2	4	1	50	33	16.66
R. J. Doughty	5	10	0	165	77	16.50
A. H. Gray	7	9	3	87	34*	14.50
M. P. Bicknell	5	7	2	56	23	11.20
*C. E. Waller	15	13	4	87	31*	9.67
K. D. Masters	5	3	0	8	5	2.67
J. Clifford	4	4	4	10	6*	—

Played in two matches: M. Richards 1, 1, 0*, 0. Played in one match: M. Barker 0; G. Boxall 0; J. Bramble 2*, 0; A. R. Butcher 66, 11; G. S. Clinton 7, 2; A. Goldsmith 5, 0; M. Jacobs 11*, 3; †M. Lane 24*, 1; S. Lerrigo 18, 8; M. Roberts 1, 0.

Bowling Averages

	O	M	R	W	Avge
D. J. Thomas	107.1	23	280	14	20.00
A. H. Gray	185	49	490	22	22.27
C. E. Waller	319.2	116	680	30	22.66
M. P. Bicknell	124.3	31	330	14	23.57
K. T. Medlycott	314.3	97	817	34	24.02
B. McNamara	98.4	8	303	12	25.25
A. Needham	170	58	325	12	27.08
M. A. Feltham	175	29	493	18	27.38
J. Clifford	99.3	16	344	12	28.66
C. K. Bullen	183	49	482	14	34.42
K. D. Masters	119.3	16	353	10	35.30
R. J. Doughty	141.2	30	544	12	45.33

Also bowled: P. D. Atkins 5–1–17–0; M. Barker 19–5–44–1; S. Bastian 22.5–7–65–1; G. Boxall 13–2–50–2; J. Bramble 7–1–39–0; N. J. Falkner 9–2–18–2; S. Lerrigo 23–5–71–1; N. Peters 20–6–58–2; M. Richards 22–2–92–1; M. Roberts 13–2–38–0; J. D. Robinson 11.4–1–61–0; G. Russell 36–4–126–0; D. M. Ward 8–1–41–0; G. Winterborne 36–11–82–2; Zahid Sadiq 1–0–1–0.

SUSSEX SECOND ELEVEN

Matches 12: Won – Middlesex. Lost – Kent (twice), Middlesex, Surrey, Warwickshire. Drawn – Essex (twice), Hampshire (twice), Nottinghamshire, Surrey.

Batting Averages

	I	NO	R	HI	Avge
A. P. Wells	6	0	405	117*	67.50
N. J. Lenham	6	1	225	141*	45.00
K. Bradshaw	11	0	449	163	40.81
D. K. Standing	10	0	378	157	37.80
J. Prentis	6	0	207	90	34.50
R. I. Alikhan	6	1	168	83	33.60
S. D. Myles	14	1	416	87	32.00
A. J. Pugh	14	2	326	75*	27.16
†A. Brown	3	1	53	40*	26.50
C. P. Phillipson	11	2	215	56*	23.88
*S. J. Storey	6	1	98	27*	19.60
R. G. Watson	17	0	316	44	18.58
I. P. Wadey	17	2	273	80	18.20
I. Broome	10	2	132	48	16.50

	I	NO	R	HI	Avge
C. S. Mays	7	1	96	35*	16.00
A. M. Bredin	16	3	168	27*	12.92
A. M. Babington	10	3	61	24	8.71
J. Roycroft	3	0	25	15	8.33
A. M. G. Scott	8	5	21	8*	7.00
M. Jadunath	4	0	26	8	6.50
P. Moores	3	0	19	16	6.33
I. Smith	5	2	18	8	6.00
A. Boxall	3	0	17	17	5.66
G. Garton	4	1	11	4*	3.66

Also batted: H. Abrahams 5, 4; T. Anscombe 0, 0*; J. R. T. Barclay 8, 7; M. Blackman 4*, 0; †D. Clift 2*, 1*; S. Ducat 9, 7; K. Greenfield 5, 1; R. Hanley 38, 32; †A. Harlow 25, 0; T. J. Head 9, 0*; A. N. Jones 7; D. Manuel 14, 6; D. A. Reeve 11, 1; J. Rogers 2, 1; †J. Smith 13*, 1; N. Smith 11, 8; I. C. Waring 24, 1; C. M. Wells 4, 2.

Bowling Averages

	O	M	R	W	Avge
C. M. Wells	34	9	65	6	10.83
N. Smith	27.1	0	95	7	13.57
M. Blackman	53	18	118	5	23.60
K. Bradshaw	62	8	237	10	23.70
A. M. Bredin	287.4	82	884	37	23.89
A. M. G. Scott	104	17	348	11	31.63
I. Broome	212.4	40	607	18	33.72
I. Smith	69	8	271	7	38.71
S. D. Myles	48	6	202	5	40.40
C. S. Mays	166.5	39	526	9	58.44
A. M. Babington	132.3	23	508	7	72.57

Also bowled: T. Anscombe 6–0–43–1; J. R. T. Barclay 30–5–102–3; G. Garton 40–1–193–1; M. Jadunath 9–0–55–2; A. N. Jones 25–7–82–2; N. J. Lenham 23–2–118–2; C. P. Phillipson 31–8–90–2; D. A. Reeve 35–7–101–3; J. Rogers 5–1–12–1; J. Roycroft 12–2–30–0; D. K. Standing 53.1–13–134–2; S. J. Storey 15–3–42–1.

WARWICKSHIRE SECOND ELEVEN

Matches 16: Won – Gloucestershire, Middlesex (twice), Somerset, Sussex, Worcestershire. Lost – Lancashire (twice), Leicestershire, Worcestershire, Yorkshire. Drawn – Glamorgan (twice), Gloucestershire, Nottinghamshire, Yorkshire.

Batting Averages

	M	I	NO	R	HI	Avge
A. J. Moles	9	16	5	811	136	73.72
A. M. Ferreira	5	6	2	213	109*	53.25
B. M. McMillan	4	8	0	370	150	46.25
K. J. Kerr	4	7	2	223	70*	44.60
Asif Din	2	4	0	178	102	44.50
N. M. K. Smith	5	7	2	208	64*	41.60
D. A. Thorne	5	9	2	267	86	38.14
I. G. Steer	2	3	1	73	32	36.50
W. J. P. Matthews	14	23	2	726	94	34.57
R. I. H. B. Dyer	12	22	2	682	157	34.10
G. J. Lord	10	18	3	487	110*	32.46
†G. A. Tedstone	13	20	4	461	85	28.81
G. J. Parsons	2	3	1	54	33*	27.00
S. Wall	10	11	3	157	29	19.62

	M	I	NO	R	HI		Avge
A. R. K. Pierson	8	7	2	90	25*		18.00
J. A. Waterhouse	2	4	0	71	31		17.75
D. C. Percival	3	5	2	48	36		16.00
W. Morton	5	8	2	68	26*		11.33
G. Charlesworth	5	8	1	74	15		10.57
T. A. Merrick	4	4	0	31	12		7.75
*R. N. Abberley	3	5	0	33	19		6.60
P. W. Threlfall	6	4	1	18	7		6.00
S. Monkhouse	10	7	2	30	13		6.00
D. S. Hoffman	11	9	2	22	19		3.14

Played in three matches: S. R. Bevins 15, 0; K. St J. D. Emery 5*, 6. Played in two matches: M. Bell 1*, 7*, 0*; P. Clark 3, 0; I. W. E. Stokes 28, 16; R. S. Weir 28* 0. Played in one match: J. Benson 13, 12*; M. Davies 39, 3; D. P. Dismore 0, 0; S. Green 0, 5; E. Milburn 12, 5*; T. A. Munton 1*; S. D. Myles 66, 17; J. Ratcliffe 38, 12.

Bowling Averages

	O	M	R	W	Avge
T. A. Merrick	112.3	22	248	21	11.80
G. J. Parsons	54.2	17	86	7	12.28
A. M. Ferreira	39.4	9	105	7	15.00
G. Charlesworth	33	5	91	5	18.20
B. M. McMillan	32.5	11	76	4	19.00
G. J. Lord	113	28	271	13	20.84
A. R. K. Pierson	177.5	46	498	22	22.63
A. J. Moles	154.2	42	366	16	22.87
W. Morton	92.2	28	234	9	26.00
S. Monkhouse	283.5	70	686	26	26.38
N. M. K. Smith	97.4	19	295	11	26.81
S. Wall	298	65	916	28	32.71
P. W. Threlfall	80	15	241	7	34.42
D. A. Thorne	67	17	146	4	36.50
K. St J. D. Emery	41	6	165	4	41.25
D. S. Hoffman	170.1	28	635	12	52.91

Also bowled: Asif Din 1-0-2-0; M. Bell 37-7-141-1; D. P. Dismore 15.1-1-72-0; R. I. H. B. Dyer 7-2-13-1; K. J. Kerr 38-14-67-0; W. J. P. Matthews 8.5-4-17-3; E. Milburn 4-0-18-0; T. A. Munton 27-9-73-1; S. D. Myles 7-1-25-1; I. G. Steer 3-1-7-0; R. S. Weir 37.4-5-107-3.

WORCESTERSHIRE SECOND ELEVEN

Matches 12: Won – Derbyshire, Somerset, Warwickshire. Lost – Derbyshire, Gloucestershire, Leicestershire, Somerset, Warwickshire. Drawn – Glamorgan (twice), Gloucestershire, Leicestershire.

Batting Averages

	I	NO	R	HI	Avge
L. K. Smith	19	2	806	131	47.41
R. K. Illingworth	4	0	138	83	34.50
J. P. Wright	20	0	689	111	34.45
S. R. Lampitt	16	3	414	80	31.84
I. McLaren	4	0	84	41	21.00
R. M. Ellcock	10	3	138	52	19.71
S. A. Thomson	15	4	212	36*	19.27
S. M. McEwan	11	3	149	42*	18.62
D. A. Leatherdale	9	0	156	38	17.33
P. Bent	4	0	69	30	17.25

	I	NO	R	HI	Avge
R. D. Stemp	11	2	141	30*	15.66
D. J. Hacker	10	1	139	50	15.44
A. Fraine	5	0	75	52	15.00
T. J. Hopper	4	0	53	28	13.25
J. E. M. Nicholson	5	0	47	33	9.40
S. Bramhall	6	3	22	11	7.33

Also batted: B. J. Barrett 0*, 0, 5; B. A. W. Bellamy 4, 0*; R. Bracewell 9, 0; R. L. Harvey 7, 10; J. D. Inchmore 7, 0*; S. Lloyd 14, 13; R. S. M. Morris 4*, 0; K. D. Moye 8, 9; M. F. Mulhern 1; H. V. Patel 3, 5, 10; J. R. Pickles 16; A. P. Pridgeon 11; A. C. Teskey 8; M. J. Weston 26, 139; N. White 6, 9; J. G. A. Williams 27, 19; D. Wilson 1, 3, 4; M. C. Yardley 18, 1, 8; E. Moore, C. M. Tolley and R. G. Woolstone did not bat.

Bowling Averages

	O	M	R	W	Avge
R. K. Illingworth	138.4	63	207	22	9.40
J. D. Inchmore	27	5	71	4	17.75
S. A. Thomson	163.2	31	444	19	23.36
R. M. Ellcock	196.5	35	565	24	23.54
S. R. Lampitt	262.2	79	703	28	25.10
S. M. McEwan	182.5	38	517	13	39.76
R. D. Stemp	166	46	492	9	54.66

Also bowled: B. J. Barrett 61–11–166–3; B. A. W. Bellamy 22–3–80–0; R. L. Harvey 22.3–3–104–0; T. J. Hopper 11–3–35–2; D. A. Leatherdale 9–3–28–1; E. Moore 10–0–36–0; K. D. Moye 17–2–86–1; J. R. Pickles 6–1–26–0; A. P. Pridgeon 22–9–36–1; C. M. Tolley 16–6–39–1; M. J. Weston 7–1–14–1; J. G. A. Williams 9–0–52–0; R. G. Woolstone 10.3–3–35–1; J. P. Wright 17–6–40–3.

YORKSHIRE SECOND ELEVEN

Matches 16: Won – Glamorgan, Northamptonshire, Nottinghamshire, Surrey, Warwickshire. Lost – Lancashire. Drawn – Derbyshire (twice), Glamorgan, Kent (twice), Lancashire, Northamptonshire, Nottinghamshire, Surrey, Warwickshire.

Batting Averages

	M	I	NO	R	HI	Avge
J. D. Love	3	4	1	305	145*	101.66
†R. J. Blakey	12	20	6	1,168	273*	83.42
G. Boycott	4	5	1	256	121	64.00
P. E. Robinson	11	17	3	785	151*	56.07
I. G. Swallow	11	14	2	551	114	45.91
G. B. Stevenson	8	11	2	284	63	31.55
C. S. Pickles	12	14	2	356	53	29.66
C. Shaw	6	8	4	104	29	26.00
N. G. Nicholson	10	15	2	336	67	25.84
D. Byas	12	17	1	357	65	22.31
P. N. Hepworth	7	11	0	245	41	22.27
S. A. Kellett	7	10	0	212	59	21.20
†D. N. Pike	4	6	2	78	46*	19.50
P. A. Booth	15	11	4	131	44	18.71
*S. Oldham	15	7	2	47	33	9.40

Played in eight matches: P. J. Berry 0, 24*, 0, 0. Played in seven matches: S. J. Dennis 19, 29*. Played in four matches: S. D. Fletcher 6*, 9*. Played in two matches: A. Bethel 20, 23; G. Hampshire 0; P. J. Hartley 12, 28*; S. N. Hartley 113, 101*, 23*; †A. Storr 16, 12. Played in one match: D. L. Bairstow 2; P. Carrick 18*; A. Court 3; J. Glendenen 0; A. A. Metcalfe 106; I. M. Priestley 0, 16; A. Sidebottom 0, 74*; K. Sharp 53, 13; C. Carden and P. W. Jarvis did not bat.

Bowling Averages

	O	M	R	W	Avge
S. N. Hartley	16	4	26	4	6.50
P. Carrick	35.1	16	69	8	8.62
G. Hampshire	28	8	75	4	18.75
S. Oldham	152.2	40	360	18	20.00
G. B. Stevenson	166	35	564	28	20.14
P. J. Berry	174.2	58	467	18	25.94
S. J. Dennis	148.4	34	406	15	27.06
C. S. Pickles	237	54	731	25	29.24
C. Shaw	151.3	50	384	13	29.53
P. A. Booth	460.5	153	1,149	34	33.79
I. G. Swallow	240.3	58	624	15	41.60
S. D. Fletcher	74	14	244	5	48.80
P. J. Hartley	69	12	228	4	57.00

Also bowled: R. J. Blakey 5–1–7–0; D. Byas 6–1–30–1; C. Carden 20–5–65–3; S. A. Kellett 3–0–25–0; J. D. Love 20–3–61–1; I. M. Priestley 7–1–16–1; P. E. Robinson 13–0–85–0; A. Sidebottom 4–1–16–1.

SECOND ELEVEN CHAMPIONS

1959	Gloucestershire	1969	Kent	1979	Warwickshire
1960	Northamptonshire	1970	Kent	1980	Glamorgan
1961	Kent	1971	Hampshire	1981	Hampshire
1962	Worcestershire	1972	Nottinghamshire	1982	Worcestershire
1963	Worcestershire	1973	Essex	1983	Leicestershire
1964	Lancashire	1974	Middlesex	1984	Yorkshire
1965	Glamorgan	1975	Surrey	1985	Nottinghamshire
1966	Surrey	1976	Kent	1986	Lancashire
1967	Hampshire	1977	Yorkshire		
1968	Surrey	1978	Sussex		

WARWICK UNDER-25 COMPETITION, 1986

Group A: Yorkshire qualified from Group A, winning five of their six matches and scoring more than 200 runs on all but one occasion. Their only defeat was by Derbyshire, who passed Yorkshire's 250 for three in 39 overs (P. N. Hepworth 99 not out, P. E. Robinson 51) for the loss of nine wickets in the 38th over. Lancashire, runners-up for the second year in succession, lost twice, both times to Yorkshire, while Derbyshire won three and lost three. Nottinghamshire, Group A winners in 1985, had a disastrous season and did not win a match.

Group B: This group was again well contested, with Essex and Middlesex finishing with an equal number of points but Middlesex going through to the semi-finals by virtue of one more win. It was, in the circumstances, unfortunate for Essex that both of their matches against Leicestershire were abandoned because of rain. In the matches involving the joint leaders, honours were evenly shared: Essex won the first meeting by 70 runs and Middlesex won the decisive last match of the group by 177 runs, despite T. D. Topley's hat-trick for Essex. Northamptonshire won three and lost three, but Leicestershire were without a win in the four matches they were able to play.

Group C: Kent and Surrey were again the most consistent teams, each winning four of their six matches but Surrey qualifying by virtue of their better strike-rate. Batsmen dominated both matches between these teams, Surrey scoring 243 for six in the first and 245 for four in the second, but only in the latter were Kent equal to the task, passing Surrey's score for the loss of six wickets. Hampshire won three and lost three matches, while Sussex's only win was against Surrey at Arundel.

Group D: Warwickshire continued their recent dominance of this group by winning all six of the matches they could play. Only Glamorgan, the group runners-up, were able to put any pressure on them. Gloucestershire and Somerset lost more matches than they won, and Worcestershire's middle position reflected an equal number of wins and losses.

Semi-final: *Middlesex v Yorkshire at Uxbridge, August 17.* Yorkshire won a tense, exciting contest by 2 runs. Batting first, they scored 172 for nine (D. Byas 58) and Middlesex's 170 for nine was just not enough to take them into the final.

Semi-final: *Warwickshire v Surrey at Leamington Spa, August 17.* Surrey won by 118 runs. Batting first, they amassed a total of 241 for six with B. McNamara, 77, and Zahid Sadiq, 59, the main contributors. Warwickshire's batsmen were unable to handle the spin of K. T. Medlycott (five for 24) and were 123 for nine at the end of their 39 overs.

FINAL

SURREY v YORKSHIRE

At Birmingham, August 31. Surrey won by six wickets. Put in to bat, Yorkshire lost Hepworth and Atkinson for 3 runs, but the left-handed Byas, with a fine 88 from 83 balls, saw the score to 163 and they managed 181. Surrey's openers began their reply confidently, and after Falkner had fallen to an excellent catch at square leg by Hepworth, Robinson continued to his century and ensured victory for Surrey, his unbeaten 109 containing a 6 and seventeen 4s.

Yorkshire

D. Byas c Brown b Feltham 88	†A. Storr lbw b Masters 11
P. N. Hepworth lbw b Feltham 0	C. Shaw c Falkner b Masters 11
S. Atkinson c Brown b Richards 0	P. A. Booth run out 1
N. G. Nicholson run out 22	C. Carden not out 0
*I. G. Swallow c Winterborne	B 1, l-b 8, w 3 12
b Medlycott . 32	
C. S. Pickles run out 2	1/1 2/3 3/50 4/125 5/136 (39.4 overs) 181
M. Sample lbw b Feltham 2	6/150 7/163 8/168 9/181

Bowling: Feltham 8–1–27–3; Richards 4–0–15–1; Masters 6.4–0–38–2; Bullen 8–1–25–0; Medlycott 8–0–33–1; Kendrick 5–0–34–0.

Surrey

N. J. Falkner c Hepworth b Swallow ..	28	K. T. Medlycott not out	0
J. D. Robinson not out	109	B 1, l-b 11, w 1, n-b 2	15
Zahid Sadiq b Carden	0		
*C. K. Bullen c Booth b Pickles	9	1/76 2/77 3/108 (4 wkts, 38.2 overs)	185
M. A. Feltham b Shaw	24	4/181	

G. Winterborne, †G. E. Brown, M. Richards, K. D. Masters and N. M. Kendrick did not bat.

Bowling: Shaw 7–1–21–1; Pickles 7.2–0–35–1; Booth 8–0–51–0; Swallow 8–0–25–1; Carden 8–0–41–1.

Umpires: J. H. Harris and M. J. Kitchen.

BAIN DAWES TROPHY, 1986

A new competition, organised by the TCCB, restricted to players "qualified for England" and limited to two capped players, the Bain Dawes Trophy was played in three zonal groups. The teams in each group met each other once, with the winners of each zone then playing a round-robin tournament to decide the two finalists. In 1987, the format has been extended to home and away zonal fixtures. Matches are of 55 overs per side.

North Zone: Northamptonshire gained maximum points from their five matches, on all but one occasion (when they took eight wickets) bowling out the opposition. Yorkshire, with four wins, and Derbyshire, with one win and two no-results, were second and third, followed by Nottinghamshire, Lancashire and Leicestershire, all with one win.

South-West Zone: Worcestershire also took maximum points and were followed closely by Somerset, three wins, and Gloucestershire, two wins. Glamorgan and Warwickshire made up the entry.

South-East Zone: Essex, with four wins, emerged top of a very competitive group, Kent and Surrey finishing one point behind them with three wins and a no-result each. Hampshire and Middlesex had a win apiece; Sussex went without.

Round-robin: Northamptonshire beat Worcestershire by 25 runs. Essex beat Worcestershire by 47 runs. Northamptonshire v Essex – abandoned.

FINAL

ESSEX v NORTHAMPTONSHIRE

At Chelmsford, September 8. Northamptonshire won by 14 runs. Fordham provided a solid foundation for Northamptonshire after they had chosen to bat on a lovely autumn day, and Wild and Williams capitalised to see their side set a challenging target. Williams's 95 not out came from 83 balls and included two 6s and eleven 4s. Essex began cautiously against some hostile bowling from Walker and Smith, and after the loss of Gladwin and Redpath, Lilley and Hussain brought some respectability with an 85-run partnership. Although Hussain went on to an unbeaten hundred, Essex were never able to keep up with the asking-rate of 4.5 runs an over.

Man of the Match: G. Smith.

Northamptonshire

A. C. Storie c Burns b Pook 27	T. Scriven not out 17
M. R. Gouldstone c Burns b Pont 11	
A. Fordham c East b Field-Buss 41	L-b 4, w 4, n-b 4 12
R. G. Williams not out 95	
D. J. Wild c Field-Buss b Golding 29	1/17 2/50 3/97 (5 wkts, 55 overs) 248
†D. Ripley run out 16	4/168 5/195

*R. M. Carter, G. Smith, A. Walker and M. Baker did not bat.

Bowling: Pont 11–1–41–1; Topley 11–3–29–0; Gladwin 9–0–39–0; Pook 6–0–29–1; Field-Buss 10–0–61–1; Golding 8–1–45–1.

Essex

C. Gladwin b Walker 9	A. K. Golding c Ripley b Smith 3
I. Redpath run out 7	T. D. Topley not out 2
A. W. Lilley c sub b Scriven 46	
N. Hussain not out 100	B 6, l-b 17, w 13, n-b 3 39
†N. D. Burns hit wkt b Scriven 1	
M. G. Field-Buss c Ripley b Baker 1	1/11 2/29 3/114 (8 wkts, 55 overs) 234
R. N. Pook c Wild b Smith 25	4/120 5/134 6/186
I. L. Pont b Walker 1	7/214 8/227

*R. E. East did not bat.

Bowling: Walker 11–0–35–2; Smith 11–3–31–2; Wild 11–1–37–0; Baker 11–0–59–1; Scriven 11–0–49–2.

Umpires: J. H. Hampshire and A. G. T. Whitehead.

CRICKET IN DENMARK, 1986

To those familiar with the relative strengths of the minor cricketing countries, Denmark's third place in the 1986 ICC Trophy came as no surprise. Their only defeats were by the two finalists – Zimbabwe and the reinforced Holland side. However, the absence of the leading players during the month-long tournament did have some influence on the domestic season, during which Frem and Hjørring became the third and fourth Danish clubs to celebrate their centenaries. The senior national championship and the national knockout cup were won by Svanholm, with the 1985 champions, Esbjerg, runner-up in both. One point separated the leaders in the championship. Ringsted and Aarhus earned promotion from the second division for 1987 at the expense of Køge and Nykøbing Mors, who were demoted from the first.

The women's national side, after only a decade of women's cricket in Denmark, performed respectably in Dublin against an English WCA side, Ireland and Holland. At home, AB as expected won the national title for the fifth successive year. Within the youth ranks, the junior, boys (under 16) and lilleputs (under 13) championships were respectively won by Svanholm, Esbjerg and Nørrebro. The last, in particular, marked a breakthrough, being from one of the three recently formed Pakistani clubs in Copenhagen, where a new generation is showing itself. – *Peter S. Hargreaves.*

UAU CHAMPIONSHIP, 1986

The short University season was dominated by Durham, who showed throughout a single-mindedness that had been missing for several years. In their north-eastern group, they overcame Newcastle by nine wickets and Hull by ten wickets: in the challenge rounds, Bradford were beaten by 189 runs, York by 194 runs and Sheffield by eight wickets. In the semi-finals Exeter fared no better, and Reading in the final managed to take just three wickets before Durham carried off the McKechnie Trophy. For their captain, John Stephenson, soon to make his mark for Essex against the New Zealanders, Durham's season was a personal triumph, their success owing much to his determined and skilled leadership.

After several false starts because of the unseasonal weather, the Universities completed their preliminary qualifying fixtures – 45 matches in twelve groups – and by early June the last eight in the competition had emerged. One half of the draw contained the three main contenders in Exeter, Loughborough and Durham, as well as Sheffield, while the other half had East Anglia, Liverpool, Manchester and Reading.

First Round: Cardiff beat Exeter by 120 runs: Exeter 162; Cardiff 42. Bristol lost to Loughborough (fewer wickets lost rule): Bristol 171 (R. Reed 72; I. Crossley four for 34); Loughborough 171 for nine. Leeds beat Hull by seven wickets: Hull 76; Leeds 78 for three. Durham beat Bradford by 189 runs: Durham 247 for seven (A. Fordham 96, J. P. Stephenson 50; N. Fairweather four for 54); Bradford 58 (J. N. Whitehouse seven for 25). Aberystwyth lost to Salford by six wickets: Aberystwyth 131 (M. Mahmood four for 31); Salford 132 for four (D. Whiting 54 not out). Manchester beat Keele by three wickets: Keele 66 (P. Garlick four for 17); Manchester 70 for seven (S. Sanderson six for 23). Reading beat Sussex by seven wickets: Sussex 85 (J. A. Bareham six for 19); Reading 87 for three. Kent lost to East Anglia by four wickets: Kent 112 (G. Hammersley four for 29); East Anglia 116 for six (C. Lane four for 57). *Byes:* Bangor, Brunel, Imperial College, Liverpool, Sheffield, Swansea, Warwick, York.

Second Round: Exeter beat Warwick by 10 runs: Exeter 158 for eight (A. Dunning 54; J. Gorton four for 60, G. Topp four for 41); Warwick 148 for seven (R. Turpin 73 not out; R. Belmont four for 44). Loughborough beat Swansea by two wickets: Swansea 232 for five (S. P. James 91); Loughborough 235 for eight (M. Cann four for 63). Leeds lost to Sheffield by 52 runs: Sheffield 197 (C. Hutchings 72; T. Cooper five for 38, M. Healy four for 73); Leeds 145 (C. Hutchings five for 38). Durham beat York by 194 runs: Durham 255 for six (A. Fordham 151); York 61 (J. N. Whitehouse eight for 27). Salford lost to Liverpool by three wickets: Salford 56 (N. Slater six for 19, T. Senior four for 17); Liverpool 57 for seven (M. Williams four for 13). Manchester beat Bangor by 42 runs: Manchester 180 for nine (B. Lemmon 59); Bangor 138. Reading beat Brunel by six wickets: Brunel 148; Reading 150 for four. East Anglia beat Imperial College by three wickets: Imperial College 168 for nine (N. Folland 60, R. Kelly 51); East Anglia 172 for seven.

Quarter-finals: Exeter beat Loughborough by 3 runs: Exeter 186 (T. Barry four for 66); Loughborough 183 for nine (R. Belmont four for 67). Sheffield lost to Durham by eight wickets: Sheffield 146 (J. N. Whitehouse seven for 61); Durham 147 for two (A. Fordham 72, J. P. Stephenson 55 not out). Liverpool lost to Manchester by 26 runs: Manchester 140 (N. Slater five for 24); Liverpool 114 for nine (P. Garlick four for 50). Reading beat East Anglia by four wickets: East Anglia 222 for nine (G. Hammersley 66 not out; J. A. Bareham five for 24); Reading 223 for six (R. Poole 80).

Semi-finals: These were played on June 17 at Durham and Chester-le-Street. At the Racecourse Ground, Durham, Reading beat Manchester by ten wickets after Manchester, having arrived late after choosing to travel up on the morning of the match, were tumbled out for 118 in the 50th over. Reading's pacemen, Paddy Osborn (four for 28) and John Bareham (four for 40), exploited both the humid conditions and their opponents' limp batting. Andy Parker, 74 not out, and Ian Osborne, 37 not out, were untroubled as Reading eased to a well-deserved win in the 43rd over.

At Chester-le-Street, Exeter, put in, could not come to terms with Durham's seam attack. Andy Forman claimed three early wickets and Exeter were 105 for six off 38 overs at lunch. Only Willie Dean had shown the application required, and he went on to an admirable 79 before falling to the last ball of the innings. Exeter's 187 may have seemed just enough, given the quality of their bowling, even though they were without their left-arm spinner, Rob Coombs, who had been called up by Somerset. But Durham's reply was formidable. Initially, Alan Fordham led the way, hitting four huge 6s over the pavilion, then Stephenson, who had struggled to find his best form earlier in the season, took over. He achieved his hundred as Durham reached 190 without loss in the 43rd over, their ten-wicket victory putting them in the final for the third year running.

FINAL

DURHAM v READING

At Durham, June 18. Durham won by seven wickets. Toss: Durham. A veil of drizzle drifted across the Racecourse Ground, making play impossible before lunch, and when it did commence at 2.44 p.m., it had been limited to 40 overs a side. Reading made a disastrous start, losing three wickets in the first two overs. Poole was run out first ball by O'Gorman, fielding in the gully. Oscroft and Stephenson effected a partial recovery, but it was left to Reading's captain, Phillips, to make sure Durham would be set some semblance of a target. Whitehouse once again was the spearhead for Durham and took his UAU wickets for the season to 39, a club record. As Durham began their reply, Fordham suffered his only failure of the season, and there was a misfortune when Stephenson, attempting to hook, was struck in the face and had to retire. However, in the gathering gloom, Charlesworth batted with poise and good sense to carry Durham to their eighth UAU Championship.

Reading

A. S. Parker b Whitehouse	0	P. C. M. Osborn b Whitehouse	6
I. G. Osborne c Charlesworth b Forman	0	†N. J. Kohler run out	2
R. Poole run out	0	A. C. G. Lucudi c Hiles b Forman	3
C. P. Oscroft c Hiles b Whitehouse	18	H. R. Williams b Forman	0
R. E. F. Stephenson c Hiles b Whitehouse	17	B 1, l-b 4, w 1	6
*C. C. H. Phillips not out	39	1/0 2/0 3/0 4/35 5/46 (35.4 overs) 97	
J. A. Bareham c Burton b Whitehouse	6	6/58 7/70 8/82 9/97	

Bowling: Whitehouse 18–3–64–5; Forman 17.4–6–28–3.

Durham

A. Fordham c Kohler b Williams	6	†D. M. Hiles not out	6
*J. P. Stephenson retired hurt	27		
R. C. W. Mason lbw b Osborn	6	L-b 2, w 6, n-b 2	10
T. J. G. O'Gorman b Bareham	13		
G. M. Charlesworth not out	31	1/8 2/44 3/69 (3 wkts, 34.2 overs) 99	

R. J. P. Burton, G. D. Harding, J. N. Whitehouse, A. Forman and N. C. W. Fenton did not bat.

Bowling: Osborn 17.2–4–61–1; Williams 8–2–16–1; Bareham 8–1–19–1; Lucudi 1–0–1–0.

THE LANCASHIRE LEAGUES, 1986

By CHRIS ASPIN

From time to time there arrives in one of the Northern leagues a virtually unknown professional who proves to be a cricketing genius. Last season, Werneth in the Central Lancashire League enjoyed the exhilaration of just such a discovery – Carl Hooper, a twenty year old from Guyana who will one day play for West Indies and, in all forms of cricket, score a lot of runs. Hooper missed the last two games of the season, but he still beat the record aggregate of 1,694 runs accumulated 35 years earlier by Sir Frank Worrell when he was professional for Radcliffe. At the start of his final weekend, Hooper needed 282 for the record. Against Royton he made 127 not out; the following day at Norden he struck an unbeaten 175, which gave him a total of 1,715 runs and an average of 77.95. In all, he hit eight hundreds, including an unbeaten 187 at Heywood where, on the large ground, he hit nine 6s and nineteen 4s as his side scored a record 311 for three. Werneth's gate receipts quadrupled and the club quickly re-engaged their young star for 1987.

Astonishing though Hooper's batting was, it was insufficient to take his club above sixth place in the table. The double honours of league and cup went to Littleborough, thanks largely to their professional, Ezra Moseley, who took by far the most wickets (132 at 9.12) and to David Schofield, who with 1,021 runs (40.84) and 86 wickets (9.94) won the League's batting and bowling prizes. In the Lees Wood Cup final, Littleborough, 207 for seven, beat Walsden, 206 for two, by three wickets.

It was certainly a vintage year for batsmen, with 36 centuries scored, twelve by Werneth players alone. In the return match against Heywood, the Werneth openers, Tim Orrell (125 not out) and Don Errock (80 not out), shared an unbroken partnership of 213 to give the club a ten-wicket victory. Gary Toshach, an Australian playing for Walsden, was the League's leading amateur after Schofield, scoring 1,014 runs at 48.29. Among the bowlers, Schofield's nearest rival was Mike Williamson, of Stockport, who took 65 at 15.17.

For the first time since 1938, the Lancashire League championship was decided by a play-off, Nelson, 171 for seven, beating Todmorden, 156 for eight, by 15 runs at Burnley. Todmorden also lost to Accrington in the final of the *Evening Telegraph* Cup, which was played at Accrington and drew a record "gate" of £1,740. Todmorden made 121 and Accrington 125 for seven with two balls to spare. For David Lloyd, the former Lancashire and England player, the match was especially satisfying. He had been refused permission to play as professional for Accrington, the club he grew up with, because of county umpiring commitments, but he turned out several times for them as an amateur. Having taken three for 33, he was 22 not out when the winning hit was made in the final.

The two top clubs owed much to their young professionals. For Nelson, Eric Simons, from South Africa, scored 767 runs (38.35) and took 72 wickets (16.40), and the South Australian, Darryl Scott, scored 995 runs (52.36) and took 73 wickets (16.28) for Todmorden. Only Mudassar Nazar, in the last of his six seasons with Burnley, topped 1,000 runs. Amateur batsmen to do well were Craig Smith (East Lancashire) with 853 at 37.08, Peter Wood

(Rawtenstall) with 768 at 33.39, and Ian Bell (Ramsbottom) with 733 at 31.86. Brian Knowles (Haslingden) joined the small band of players who have made 10,000 runs in their league careers.

The Australian, John Maguire, headed the bowling averages with 103 wickets at 12.11 for Church. He accounted for Bacup with a nine for 19 return and took six for 8 to help dismiss Haslingden for 25. The leading amateurs were Trevor Jones (Burnley), with 53 wickets at 17.47; Jack Houldsworth (Church), 52 at 16.34; Pat Calderbank (Nelson), 51 at 16.58; and Keith Roscoe (Rawtenstall), 51 at 21.64. Alan Barnes of Haslingden took four wickets in four balls at Bacup.

MATTHEW BROWN LANCASHIRE LEAGUE

	P	W	L	D	Pts	Professional	Runs	Avge	Wkts	Avge
Nelson	26	17	7	2*	81	E. O. Simons	767	38.35	72	16.40
Todmorden	26	17	8	1	81	D. B. Scott	995	52.36	73	16.28
Rishton	26	17	8	1	76	W. W. Davis	368	18.40	103	13.58
Burnley	26	16	9	1	70	Mudassar Nazar	1,050	55.26	57	17.15
Accrington	26	14	12	0	64	R. Tucker	679	30.86	37	21.08
Haslingden	26	12	12	2	57	H. L. Alleyne	414	24.35	66	19.19
Lowerhouse	26	12	14	0	56	A. I. C. Dodemaide	570	24.78	94	13.75
Ramsbottom	26	11	14	1	52	C. R. Norris	769	45.23	18	33.44
Enfield	26	12	14	0	51	R. J. Ratnayake	187	12.47	51	22.23
Church	26	10	16	0	50	J. N. Maguire	111	5.84	103	12.11
Colne	26	10	15	1	48	Rizwan-uz-Zaman	564	29.68	45	13.06
East Lancashire	26	10	15	1	47	S. T. Jefferies	525	30.88	60	20.06
Rawtenstall	26	9	16	1	43	T. A. Merrick	504	28.00	72	20.81
Bacup	26	8	15	3*	42	A. L. F. de Mel	670	30.45	56	19.82

* Includes 2 points for a tie.

Note: One point awarded for bowling out the opposition.

Nelson beat Todmorden in the play-off for the League championship.

TSB CENTRAL LANCASHIRE LEAGUE

	P	W	L	D	Pts	Professional	Runs	Avge	Wkts	Avge
Littleborough	30	22	6	2	100	E. A. Moseley	612	23.54	132	9.12
Royton	30	17	9	4*	78	V. A. Holder	535	23.26	107	11.81
Walsden	30	19	9	2	75	Mohsin Khan	1,202	52.26	42	22.55
Oldham	30	16	12	2	74	L. A. Lambert	255	11.09	108	14.05
Radcliffe	30	18	9	3*	72	D. Fitton	1,495	53.39	74	16.61
Werneth	30	17	9	4*	68	C. L. Hooper	1,715	77.95	41	24.20
Heywood	30	16	11	3	67	S. C. Wundke	1,471	61.29	94	19.55
Crompton	30	13	16	1	62	Shahid Aziz	309	15.45	100	14.11
Rochdale	30	14	13	3	57	R. C. Haynes	927	34.33	97	17.51
Middleton	30	10	15	5*	52	K. Boden	556	22.24	49	19.24
Castleton Moor	30	11	18	1	50	R. Malumba	334	12.85	60	25.75
Norden	30	12	14	4	50	Anwar Khan	807	36.68	72	19.75
Stockport	30	9	18	3*	45	N. Hunter	672	24.00	51	20.69
Ashton	30	8	19	3	43	Madan Lal	570	47.50	47	16.40
Milnrow	30	8	17	5*	40	S. Dublin	888	32.89	95	18.22
Hyde	30	6	21	3	31	R. Berry	1,044	38.67	49	19.35

* Includes 2 points for a tie.

Note: Five points awarded for an outright win; three for a limited win.

IRISH CRICKET IN 1986

By DEREK SCOTT

Ireland's national team began its 1986 campaign earlier than ever before, with a party of fifteen players visiting Zimbabwe in January. Wonderfully arranged by John Hick, father of the Worcestershire player, it was Ireland's fifth tour since 1879, the previous four having been to the United States and Canada. Eight matches were played, and of the six for which Irish caps were awarded, two were won, three lost and one was drawn.

Of the regular players, only Simon Corlett was not available, and with only two of the team over 30, the tour should bring its reward in years to come. D. G. Dennison, M. A. Masood, M. F. Cohen and J. A. Prior were the most successful batsmen, while the captain, M. Halliday, H. Milling and T. J. T. Patterson were the leading bowlers. Two young players, D. A. Vincent and R. S. Haire, received their first caps.

The two two-day matches in the Bulawayo area were each won by ten wickets, Halliday taking eleven for 106 and A. McBrine seven for 115 in the first, while in the low-scoring second match, Patterson's six for 27 in Matabeleland's first innings was the decisive factor. In Harare, a Schools XI was beaten in a good match before the team moved on to play two matches against Mashonaland. At Norton, when Cohen scored two fifties, rain ensured that the two-day fixture was drawn: at Wedza, in a 60-overs match, came the first defeat. Mashonaland made 338 (I. P. Butchart 84) but Ireland collapsed from 87 for two to 123 all out.

Finally, the team returned to Harare, where they encountered four days of Graeme Hick and two defeats. In the one-day match against The Stragglers, Ireland congratulated themselves on scoring 226 for eight in 50 overs, the centre-piece of which was 103 by Dennison, the first-ever century by an Irish wicket-keeper. But Hick replied with 155 not out in 116 minutes, hitting nine 6s and thirteen 4s, and The Stragglers won by eight wickets in the 34th over. Chanceless, it was the nineteen-year-old Hick's 50th century.

In the following three-day match, against the Zimbabwe CU's President's XI, containing seven international players, Hick batted for 394 minutes, hit two 6s and 34 4s, and finished with 309, the highest score against Ireland ever and the most runs scored by one player in Zimbabwe. When 14, he gave square leg an easy chance – it was to become the most expensive miss in the annals of Irish cricket – and such is cricket that it was the same miscreant fielder who caught him brilliantly on the boundary a remove of time later. Ireland, put in, had made 211, and faced with an innings defeat following Zimbabwe's 517 for nine declared, they managed to take the game into the final session before losing by an innings and 67 runs. Masood, back to form, scored 53 and 81, while Dennison made 84 in the first innings before falling victim to an attack of sunstroke which forced his retirement from the match.

In the summer, Ireland played five limited-overs matches against Yorkshire (two), Leicestershire (in the NatWest Bank Trophy) and the touring Indian team (two), as well as three-day fixtures against Wales at Coleraine, a new venue, MCC at Castle Avenue, Dublin, and Scotland at Glasgow.

Rain caused the first match against the Indians to be abandoned after eighteen overs, but next day a marvellous match ensued at Downpatrick. The

visitors were restricted to 210 for seven in 55 overs, and when Masood and
S. J. S. Warke had 75 up in the 22nd over, an Irish win was looming.
Instead, the middle order lost its way, and with 5.3 overs remaining, and five
wickets in hand, Ireland required 50. J. D. Garth, given his first cap the
previous day, got the target down to 16 from the last over, but he was
caught on the boundary for 41 off the first ball and Ireland lost by 9 runs.

Another splendid finish, this time against Wales, resulted in Ireland's only
victory of the season. Set a target of 241 in 135 minutes, the Irish achieved it
with an over to spare. In doing so, they compiled the highest total by Ireland
to win in a fourth innings. Warke scored a fine hundred and there were some
hefty blows by A. McBrine to hasten the victory.

Prior to their visit to Dublin in mid-July, MCC informed the Irish Cricket
Union of a change to their team, owing to a withdrawal because of injury.
Their replacement would be Mark Waugh, twin brother of the Australian
Test player, who was on MCC's groundstaff. Waugh scored an unbeaten 239
in 270 minutes (five 6s, 27 4s) out of 399 for seven declared and 101 not out
(91 minutes, three 6s, a 5 and nine 4s) out of 205 for two declared. Ireland
struggled to save the follow-on, despite 85 from Dennison and 68 from
Warke, but Halliday saved the day with his first half-century for Ireland. The
fourth-innings target was 279 and the match ended with Ireland 231 for eight.
In all, 1,161 runs were scored for 26 wickets, the aggregate being the highest
in a home match.

At Titwood, Glasgow, in August, the annual match against Scotland
resembled that of 1984 at the same venue, except that in 1986 the positions
were reversed and Ireland, made to follow on, had to fight hard to draw.
Their middle order collapsed in both innings, but G. D. Harrison's 68 and
Corlett's 44 not out in the second innings saved them.

New caps during the season were J. D. Garth, E. Jones and James
McBrine, twin brother of A. ("Junior"). Both McBrines played against
Scotland, the first instance of twins representing Ireland at senior level. Also
during the year, Warke, Prior and Masood reached 1,000 runs for Ireland,
with Masood's 29 innings being the fewest required for that milestone.

An under-23 party had an enjoyable five days as guests of the Scottish
Cricket Union. They lost to the East District, beat the North, were unable to
play the West because of rain and beat Scotland Under-23 in a two-day
match. Two full internationals, Garth and Rea, made centuries on the tour,
the former a brilliant 129 against Scotland. A. McBrine had match figures of
eleven for 66 as the Irish won by seven wickets.

In Ireland, the Interprovincial Cup was won by North-West, who won four
matches by bowling out the opposition each time and had their last game
ruined by rain. R. Moan, their captain, scored a century and averaged 47.60,
A. McBrine averaged 46.33, and James McBrine took sixteen wickets at 7.81.
The equivalent tournament for under-nineteens was won by North-West for
the sixth time (once shared) in sixteen years, while the under-fifteen Inter-
provincials' three-day festival was won by the Northern Cricket Union for
the first time since they won the inaugural tournament in 1976.

Irish Schools were caught on a turning wicket at Colwyn Bay and easily
beaten in two days by Wales. Against England at Chesterfield, set 191 to win
in 104 minutes, they held on to draw, scoring 117 for five.

The national clubs competition, the Schweppes Cup, was at the fifth
attempt wrested from Northern CU hands, with Phoenix, the best Leinster
club of the past fifteen years, winning the only trophy to have eluded them by

beating Donemana (North-West) in the final. To compensate, Donemana retained their North-West League title, although they lost their Cup to Coleraine, who beat Strabane in the final.

In Dublin, Phoenix were the champion runners-up – to YMCA in the Belvedere Bond League, to Clontarf in the Wiggins Teape League, and to YMCA in the Sportsgear Cup. YMCA thus achieved a league/cup double for the first time. In Munster, Waterford won the 1985 Cup in early 1986, only to have it taken from them by Limerick later in the season. Waterford were the League winners, deposing Limerick. Waringstown came back strongly after a first-innings deficit to beat North of Ireland CC in the Northern CU Cup final, which lasted eight days. However, the League had to be shared for the first time in fifteen years, with North of Ireland and Downpatrick holding the trophy for six months each.

SCOTTISH CRICKET IN 1986

By WATSON BLAIR

Scotland put behind them the frustrations of their rain-ruined preparations to win their first-ever match in the Benson and Hedges Cup, the highlight of the representative squad's most successful season for many years. Rain had made a nonsense of the two practices arranged by the Scottish Cricket Union in mid-April, and it also brought about the cancellation of the practice matches away to Essex and Derbyshire. Yet the Scots, going into their opening zonal tie relying very much on past experience and indoor nets, very nearly beat Worcestershire and the following weekend defeated Lancashire at Perth to record their first victory in the competition at the 25th attempt.

At Glasgow, the Scots needing Worcestershire, needing 110 to win, 57 for seven overnight, only for a fielding error and a surprise bowling change to let the county off the hook. Lancashire, needing to beat a total of 156 for nine, were not so fortunate: also nine wickets down, they were 3 runs short with 153 after 55 overs. Away from home, however, Scotland found sterner opposition in Nottinghamshire and Yorkshire, although there was some consolation when their opening batsman, Ian Philip, a Scottish-born Australian, won the Gold Award for his 73 runs at Trent Bridge. With Richard Swan having been man of the match for his captaincy and batting against Lancashire, this was Scotland's second Gold Award of the season. In the first round of the NatWest Bank Trophy, Kent travelled to Edinburgh, where their bowlers proved much too experienced in the requirements of limited-overs cricket, and the inability of Scotland's batsmen to force the pace told against them.

The international programme continued in July with the visit to the Nunholm ground, as part of Dumfries' octocentenary celebrations, of the Indian touring team. The Scots made three changes from the side beaten by Kent, and although losing the first by three wickets and the second by 52 runs, they put up a creditable performance in the two one-day games.

More than a month elapsed before the traditional first-class fixture against Ireland at Titwood, Glasgow. Ireland, having been asked to follow on, were still 5 runs in arrears with only three second-innings wickets in hand at the close of the third day, and with time lost during the match to rain and bad light, Scotland had every reason to feel they would otherwise have beaten their old rivals. Philip, in Scotland's innings of 396 for seven declared, had the distinction of scoring 145 in his first first-class match.

The senior squad's season ended with two matches in London later in August. At Ealing, a strong Club Cricket Conference XI was defeated by 29 runs: Scotland XI 188 for seven in 55 overs, Conference XI 159 in 51.5 overs. But at Lord's, against an MCC side captained by R. D. V. Knight, rain and bad light severely affected both days. Omar Henry and Bruce Russell hit half-centuries in Scotland's first-innings 246 for six declared, and when MCC declared at 20 for one on the second and last morning, Scotland hastened to a second declaration at 121 for six after 32 overs. The return of the rain, however, prevented MCC from taking up the challenge in earnest, and they were 180 for three at the finish.

The programme was equally busy at other levels, with Scotland B playing the UAU champions, Durham University, and Leicestershire Second XI. In the drawn game at Durham, Scotland B made 250 for seven (60 overs) and 172 for eight declared, to which Durham replied with 185 for nine (60 overs) and 228 for six. In the first of two 55-overs games at Grace Road, Leicester, a brilliant unbeaten 118 by Henry enabled a young Scottish side to win by four wickets (Leicestershire II 230 for six, Scotland B 231 for six), but the county turned the tables the next day by dismissing the Scots for 100 and passing that for the loss of three wickets. The SCU hope to extend the B programme in 1987.

For the first time, an international match was played between Scotland and Ireland at under-23 level, the Irish finishing a four-match tour by defeating their Scottish counterparts by seven wickets at Cambusdoon. Replying to Ireland's 223 for seven declared, Scotland were bowled out for 120. Forced to follow on, they fared better, scoring 179, but this was not enough to stop the Irish from winning with ten balls of the match remaining. At under-nineteen and under-sixteen, Scottish Young Cricketers played the English and Welsh Schools, while the under-seventeens and under-fifteens, playing as SCU or Districts XIs, met Somerset CA sides in the same age groups.

Although the domestic competitions were upset by the vagaries of the weather, they nevertheless produced much good cricket. The 21st final of the Scottish Cricket Cup, sponsored by Knight Frank Rutley, was won for the first time by Aberdeenshire, who beat the holders, Clydesdale, at Hamilton Crescent. Batting first, Aberdeenshire were struggling at 43 for eight, and even a final total of 111 for nine looked insufficient. However, some outstanding bowling by Dallas Moir (11–7–8–3) and Andy Bee (9.4–3–19–3) not only checked Clydesdale's scoring rate but captured vital wickets, so that when the last wicket fell, the Glasgow club were still 5 runs short with two balls remaining. Winning the Cup, in addition to their local Beneagles Scottish Counties Championship and the Famous Grouse Team of the Year award, provided the Aberdeen club with a handsome hat-trick of triumphs. The W. M. Mann (Investments) Ltd Small Clubs Cup, in only its second season, attracted a lot of interest and culminated in Ellon Gordon beating Marchmont in the final at Cupar.

Freuchie, the previous season's heroes, again qualified as Scotland's team in the Norsk Hydro Village Championship, but after knocking out Spofforth, they had to return to North Yorkshire the next week and Carlton ended their defence of the title they won at Lord's in 1985. Indeed, Yorkshire proved the stumbling-block to all of Scotland's aspirations over the border. Grange, the

East League second division club, who won the Scottish section of the William Younger Cup, were eliminated by Guisborough, and the West District were beaten by Yorkshire CA in the NCA County Championship. They had qualified as Scotland's representative by winning the Inter-District competition, and with their under-23, under-nineteen and under-sixteen teams also winning their age groups, the West made a clean sweep of the Inter-District titles.

Cricket's expansion in Scotland continued with the return of the game to Kirkcudbright, in South-West Scotland, which last boasted a club more than twenty years ago. And as if by way of additional proof, the Girvan club, disbanded in 1939, rose from the ashes as the Carrick club arranged a varied and successful programme during the summer. Nor does the game go into hibernation when the last stumps have been drawn. The Cricket Society of Scotland has monthly meetings in Edinburgh and Glasgow, and at the many sports centres in Scotland, cricket nets, six-a-sides and similar activities keep interest alive throughout the winter months. Last year, Kelso won the national "sixes", which were organised by the SCU.

The SCU now has numerous committees and sub-committees, encompassing all aspects of the game and its administration, and while it may be some time before all the activity behind the scenes reaches fruition, the Union's untiring efforts to obtain sponsorship have proved a boon from national to club level. One problem, however, that of rates, continues to tax the game's administrators, as it does the officials of many of Scotland's sporting bodies. On average, Scottish cricket clubs have a rates burden six times greater than similar clubs in England, and the SCU has pressed, and will continue to press, both local and central government for a much-needed review of the situation.

SRI LANKAN YOUNG CRICKETERS IN ENGLAND, 1986

By JOHN MINSHULL-FOGG

The Sri Lankan Young Cricketers arrived in England in mid-July for a fourteen-match tour which included three four-day "Tests" and two one-day "internationals", which were sponsored by Agatha Christie Limited. Apart from the one-day games against England Young Cricketers, at Chelmsford and Lord's, which the visitors won to become the first holders of the Agatha Christie Trophy, the tour was considerably affected by rain. Such chilly, unfamiliar conditions hampered the natural strokemakers and also meant that some of the lesser players did not obtain much match practice.

In Asanka Gurusinha, the captain, Roshan Jurangpathy and Sanjeewa Weerasinghe, the tourists had three players with experience of Test cricket in 1985-86, and Hashan Tillekeratne, the vice-captain, represented Sri Lanka against the England B touring side. These four plus Chandika Hathurusinghe, an all-rounder, Marlon Mallawaratchi and Denham Madena, the opening pair of fastish medium-pace bowlers, were the mainstays of a side which, because of the conditions, found difficulty in settling into a well-knit group. The pitches encountered were hardly suited to Weerasinghe's leg-spin, but he, Gurusinha, Tillekeratne and Jurangpathy took the eye as being adaptable to English conditions and are likely to return in future years with the senior side.

Michael Roseberry, the leading batsman in English Schools cricket for the two previous years, captained England Young Cricketers, but going in at number four did not suit him. After the one-day "internationals", Roseberry promoted himself in the order and a much-improved England won the final "Test" with something to spare. Richard Blakey of Yorkshire and Somerset's Ricky Bartlett added to their growing reputations. Following his injury early in the Headingley match, Martin Bicknell of Surrey missed three matches – although he did play for his county in their NatWest Bank Cup semi-final – and never played to his full potential. Alastair Fraser, the younger of the two Middlesex brothers, carried the brunt of the opening attack, and Graham Harding of Nottinghamshire bowled his off-spin tidily.

The find of the season, however, was sixteen-year-old Mark Ramprakash, still at Gayton High School in Harrow and very much fancied by Middlesex. He came into the Young England side after the loss of the one-day matches, and as England ended the series on a winning note, so did Ramprakash. His 6 on to the roof of the Century Restaurant stand at Trent Bridge was a stroke of power and promise for the future.

From their tour, the young Sri Lankans learned much that will help their all-round cricket, but their inexperience showed when key players were dismissed early on. What must also be said is that these young players, from both countries, deserved better public support – and publicity – than they received. The exceptions were the one-day games. At Chelmsford, the day was beautiful and the Essex crowd enjoyed a fine match. At Lord's, the groundstaff worked miracles for play to start on time following an overnight storm, and a goodly crowd, among whom was Matthew Prichard, grandson of Dame Agatha Christie, saw the President of MCC present the trophy to Gurusinha.

The tour party was: Mr Abu Fuard (*manager*), E. R. Fernando (*assistant manager*), A. P. Gurusinha (*captain*), H. P. Tillekeratne (*vice-captain*), S. Akarawita, S. Asoka, M. I. Balalle, U. C. Hathurusinghe, C. S. Jayakody, B. R. Jurangpathy, D. R. Madena, J. A. M. Mallawaratchi, R. C. A. Paulpillai, A. A. D. S. Perera, K. G. Pryantha, C. R. Soza, C. D. U. S. Weerasinghe.

RESULTS

Matches 14: Won 3, Lost 1, Drawn 8, Abandoned 2.

Note: None of the matches played was first-class.

v MCC Young Cricketers: at Barclays Bank, Ealing, July 22. Drawn. Sri Lankan Young Cricketers 193 for four dec. (A. P. Gurusinha 82); MCC Young Cricketers 162 for seven (A. Waugh 88).

v Headmasters' Conference XI: at Christ Church College ground, Oxford, July 23, 24, 25. Drawn. Sri Lankan Young Cricketers 290 (A. A. D. S. Perera 100, H. P. Tillekeratne 70, A. P. Gurusinha 62; N. H. Peters four for 31) and 74 for two (H. P. Tillekeratne 57 not out); Headmasters' Conference XI 136 (J. I. Longley 50; J. A. M. Mallawaratchi four for 27) and 330 for eight dec. (M. A. Crawley 77, N. A. Stanley 75, M. P. Speight 43).

v English Schools CA: At Manchester, July 27, 28, 29. Drawn. English Schools CA 302 for nine dec. (S. P. Titchard 95, M. A. Crawley 86; D. R. Madena four for 40); Sri Lankan Young Cricketers 44 for one. *No play on the second afternoon and third day.*

v Northern Young Cricketers: at Milnrow, July 31. Abandoned.

ENGLAND YOUNG CRICKETERS v SRI LANKA YOUNG CRICKETERS

First "Test" Match

At Leeds, August 2, 3, 4, 5. Drawn. England had much the better of a rain-affected match, although once Perera and Paulpillai had averted the follow-on, any result other than a draw seemed unlikely. Sri Lanka put England in to bat, whereupon Blakey, on his county ground, showed his promise with a half-century, following it in the second innings with an unbeaten hundred. In each innings he and Bartlett shared three-figure partnerships for the second wicket: 100 in the first and 187 in the second. Sri Lanka had six left-handed batsmen, which posed some problems for the England attack, already weakened when Bicknell, at the time the leading England-qualified bowler in the first-class averages, strained his side. England's second-innings declaration set a target of 280 in 285 minutes but Sri Lanka were content to settle for a draw.

England Young Cricketers

R. J. Blakey c Jurangpathy b Weerasinghe	55	– not out	101
T. R. Ward lbw b Mallawaratchi	12	– c Jurangpathy b Mallawaratchi	4
R. J. Bartlett run out	58	– lbw b Madena	79
*M. A. Roseberry b Jurangpathy	34	– lbw b Madena	0
M. W. Alleyne run out	66	– run out	2
I. Smith c Soza b Weerasinghe	10	– b Madena	1
†D. Ripley b Tillekeratne	4		
A. G. J. Fraser lbw b Madena	8		
G. D. Harding not out	10		
M. P. Bicknell c Perera b Jurangpathy	12		
N. M. Kendrick b Jurangpathy	0		
B 5, l-b 7, w 1, n-b 8	21	B 4, l-b 7	11

1/26 2/126 3/146 4/191 5/208   290   1/6 2/193 3/193   (5 wkts dec.) 198
6/243 7/266 8/266 9/286   4/196 5/198

Bowling: *First Innings*—Madena 25–7–54–1; Mallawaratchi 25–8–59–1; Hathurusinghe 9–2–21–0; Gurusinha 7–1–14–0; Perera 3–0–11–0; Tillekeratne 13–1–40–1; Weerasinghe 28–16–37–2; Jurangpathy 16.4–0–42–3. *Second Innings*—Madena 20.5–4–59–3; Mallawaratchi 17–5–65–1; Weerasinghe 11–2–33–0; Gurusinha 2–0–11–0; Jurangpathy 8–1–19–0.

Sri Lanka Young Cricketers

C. R. Soza b Smith	23	– lbw b Fraser	54
U. C. Hathurusinghe c and b Fraser	0	– b Kendrick	15
*A. P. Gurusinha c Bartlett b Harding	24	– b Fraser	9
H. P. Tillekeratne lbw b Smith	9	– hit wkt b Harding	1
B. R. Jurangpathy b Harding	1	– b Fraser	8
R. C. A. Paulpillai b Kendrick	39	– not out	10
A. A. D. S. Perera b Fraser	52	– not out	54
†M. I. Balalle b Smith	16		
C. D. U. S. Weerasinghe c Ward b Harding	10		
D. R. Madena c Ward b Fraser	11		
J. A. M. Mallawaratchi not out	1		
B 6, l-b 9, w 8	23	L-b 5, w 2	7

1/2 2/44 3/64 4/71 5/71   209   1/44 2/77 3/82   (5 wkts) 158
6/151 7/182 8/194 9/205   4/82 5/92

Bowling: *First Innings*—Bicknell 4–1–10–0; Fraser 24–6–64–3; Smith 20–5–54–3; Harding 24–9–44–3; Kendrick 20–12–22–1. *Second Innings*—Fraser 16–3–39–3; Smith 11–2–46–0; Kendrick 20–8–24–1; Harding 26–13–36–1; Roseberry 2–0–8–0; Alleyne 1–1–0–0.

Umpires: C. Cook and B. J. Meyer.

v Yorkshire CA Under 19: at York, August 7. Drawn. Yorkshire CA Under 19 192 for six dec. (G. Strange 81 not out, I. Priestley 59); Sri Lankan Young Cricketers 158 for four (A. A. D. S. Perera 56).

v England Young Cricketers (First Agatha Christie Trophy match): at Chelmsford, August 9. Sri Lanka Young Cricketers won by 139 runs. Sri Lanka Young Cricketers 254 for eight (55 overs) (A. P. Gurusinha 84, B. R. Jurangpathy 54); England Young Cricketers 115 (36.5 overs) (M. W. Alleyne 40, M. A. Roseberry 32; U. C. Hathurusinghe three for 30).

v England Young Cricketers (Second Agatha Christie Trophy match): at Lord's, August 11. Sri Lanka Young Cricketers won by four wickets. England Young Cricketers 158 (54.3 overs) (M. A. Roseberry 39, L. Tennant 30; D. R. Madena three for 16); Sri Lanka Young Cricketers 162 for six (48.5 overs) (U. C. Hathurusinghe 38, A. P. Gurusinha 36).

v Welsh Youth XI: at Abergavenny, August 13, 14. Drawn. Sri Lankan Young Cricketers 54 for one. *Rain stopped play.*

ENGLAND YOUNG CRICKETERS v SRI LANKA YOUNG CRICKETERS

Second "Test" Match

At Bristol, August 16, 17, 18, 19. Drawn. Again asked to bat first, England progressed evenly on the opening day to 281 for eight and extended their innings to 333 on Sunday. On a good run-making pitch, Sri Lanka lost their first wicket for 3 runs and then produced two hundreds. With Gurusinha 130 and Soza 108, they were happily placed at 257 for one at the close. Rain washed out all but eight overs of the third day, and with a draw all that was left to play for, the Sri Lankans took batting practice in considerable style on the final day. First the captain (21 4s) and Soza (sixteen 4s) increased their second-wicket stand to 289, made in 6 hours, 40 minutes, and then Tillekeratne, also a left-hander, put together an elegant, unbeaten 121 which included a 6 and fifteen 4s. When the match ended, England had employed ten bowlers, including their wicket-keeper, with only Bartlett denied all-rounder status.

England Young Cricketers

R. J. Blakey c Balalle b Hathurusinghe .	43	G. D. Harding c Soza b Mallawaratchi .	9
*M. A. Roseberry c Tillekeratne		L. Tennant run out	11
b Mallawaratchi .	23	A. G. J. Fraser c Perera b Weerasinghe	48
R. J. Bartlett c Balalle b Mallawaratchi	4	N. M. Kendrick not out	1
M. W. Alleyne b Madena	26	B 7, l-b 5, w 3, n-b 2	17
M. R. Ramprakash c Balalle b Madena	33		
I. Smith b Madena	43	1/41 2/57 3/83 4/115 5/147	333
†D. Ripley c Tillekeratne b Weerasinghe	75	6/218 7/267 8/277 9/318	

Bowling: Madena 34–5–118–3; Mallawaratchi 28–5–69–3; Hathurusinghe 18–4–61–1; Gurusinha 9–0–35–0; Weerasinghe 22–6–38–2.

Sri Lanka Young Cricketers

C. R. Soza b Smith	123	†M. I. Balalle c and b Ripley	2
U. C. Hathurusinghe c Ripley b Fraser	0	C. D. U. S. Weerasinghe not out	8
*A. P. Gurusinha b Smith	161	B 16, l-b 9, w 5, n-b 15	45
B. R. Jurangpathy c Blakey b Smith . .	34		
H. P. Tillekeratne not out	121	1/3 2/292 3/319 (7 wkts) 576	
R. C. A. Paulpillai lbw b Fraser	56	4/358 5/508	
A. A. D. S. Perera hit wkt b Tennant .	26	6/551 7/561	

D. R. Madena and J. A. M. Mallawaratchi did not bat.

Bowling: Fraser 45–9–139–2; Smith 39–8–115–3; Tennant 32–9–93–1; Harding 37–16–55–0; Kendrick 28–8–78–0; Alleyne 7–3–8–0; Blakey 6–0–20–0; Ramprakash 2–0–6–0; Roseberry 8–0–33–0; Ripley 3–2–4–1.

Umpires: J. H. Harris and A. G. T. Whitehead.

v **National Association of Young Cricketers:** at Queens' College ground, Cambridge, August 22, 23, 24. Drawn. Sri Lankan Young Cricketers 296 (B. R. Jurangpathy 63, C. D. U. S. Weerasinghe 65; M. Smith four for 67) and 119 for four; National Association of Young Cricketers 391 (G. Lloyd 121, M. A. Atherton 54).

v **Club Cricket Conference Under 25:** at Winchmore Hill, August 26. Abandoned.

v **Combined Services:** at RAF Uxbridge, August 28. Sri Lankan Young Cricketers won by six wickets. Combined Services 136 (B. R. Jurangpathy four for 38); Sri Lankan Young Cricketers 139 for four (A. P. Gurusinha 56).

ENGLAND YOUNG CRICKETERS v SRI LANKA YOUNG CRICKETERS

Third "Test" Match

At Nottingham, August 30, 31, September 1, 2. England Young Cricketers won by six wickets. Outplayed on the first two days, England showed resilience and team spirit to win this match and so take the series 1-0. Put in, Sri Lanka answered Roseberry's challenge with a first innings of 406, the main feature of which was the fifth-wicket partnership of 178 from 73 overs by Tillekeratne and Paulpillai. It was the former's second hundred of the series, and he batted with a runner after injuring his leg when 28. By the close of the second day England were in some trouble at 134 for five, having earlier been 14 for three. Alleyne and Ramprakash had steadied the innings in forthright style and on the third day Smith, 23 overnight, took England safely beyond the follow-on, his 97 including a 6 and fifteen 4s from 135 balls. Fraser, having batted well, then set England on the way to victory with three for 31 in Sri Lanka's 81 for four at the close. Next morning Berry, a slow left-arm spinner from

Yorkshire, new to the side, took three wickets to give him match figures of 47.1–25–76–6, and
with the tourists all out for 140, England had four and a half hours in which to score 257.
Roseberry and Bartlett put on 126 in 36 overs, and as England chased the runs Sri Lanka's use
of defensive fields was wrongly judged. In a regrettable incident, umpire Birkenshaw had to
reprimand Gurusinha, captain of the touring side and a Test player, for openly disputing a
disallowed appeal for leg before wicket.

Sri Lanka Young Cricketers

C. R. Soza c Harding b Berry	51 – b Fraser	9
U. C. Hathurusinghe b Bicknell	14 – b Fraser	5
*A. P. Gurusinha c and b Berry	10 – c Ripley b Fraser	18
H. P. Tillekeratne c Roseberry b Harding	125 – lbw b Bicknell	42
B. R. Jurangpathy c Blakey b Harding	46 – c Blakey b Smith	10
R. C. A. Paulpillai lbw b Fraser	81 – lbw b Fraser	12
C. S. Jayakody b Berry	6 – lbw b Berry	12
C. D. U. S. Weerasinghe b Bicknell	44 – c Harding b Berry	18
†M. I. Balalle run out	0 – b Bicknell	0
D. R. Madena c Ripley b Fraser	0 – st Ripley b Berry	6
J. A. M. Mallawaratchi not out	5 – not out	1
B 5, l-b 7, w 5, n-b 7	24 L-b 2, w 2, n-b 3	7

1/45 2/69 3/86 4/167 5/345   406   1/10 2/21 3/41 4/62 5/100   140
6/353 7/380 8/382 9/390   6/100 7/125 8/126 9/137

Bowling: *First Innings*—Bicknell 25.5–4–99–2; Fraser 37–9–101–2; Smith 19–4–62–0; Berry
37–20–55–3; Harding 25–9–63–2; Alleyne 5–1–14–0. *Second Innings*—Bicknell 19–3–56–2;
Fraser 14–2–52–4; Smith 3–1–5–1; Berry 10.1–5–21–3; Harding 3–2–4–0.

England Young Cricketers

R. J. Blakey c Balalle b Mallawaratchi	5 – b Mallawaratchi	6
*M. A. Roseberry c Soza b Mallawaratchi	6 – lbw b Gurusinha	72
R. J. Bartlett c Jurangpathy b Madena	3 – c Balalle b Weerasinghe	81
M. W. Alleyne c Jurangpathy b Madena	44 – not out	43
M. R. Ramprakash b Weerasinghe	46 – st Balalle b Weerasinghe	18
I. Smith b Weerasinghe	97 – not out	26
†D. Ripley lbw b Madena	25	
A. G. J. Fraser c Mallawaratchi b Madena	41	
G. D. Harding c Tillekeratne b Weerasinghe	0	
P. J. Berry run out	6	
M. P. Bicknell not out	2	
L-b 8, w 3, n-b 4	15 B 1, l-b 8, n-b 3	12

1/11 2/14 3/14 4/93 5/131   290   1/23 2/149 3/177   (4 wkts) 258
6/202 7/268 8/268 9/286   4/215

Bowling: *First Innings*—Madena 25.2–5–74–4; Mallawaratchi 19–3–53–2; Weerasinghe
24–4–90–3; Gurusinha 5–1–18–0; Hathurusinghe 4–0–10–0; Jurangpathy 7–0–25–0; Jayakody
2–0–12–0. *Second Innings*—Madena 15–1–50–0; Mallawaratchi 13–2–47–1; Hathurusinghe
4–0–19–0; Weerasinghe 24–1–81–2; Gurusinha 14–0–47–1; Tillekeratne 0.3–0–5–0.

Umpires: J. Birkenshaw and N. T. Plews.

SCHOOLS CRICKET IN 1986

Despite the absence through injury of the captain, M. A. Atherton, and the restricted availability of J. C. M. Atkinson, N. A. Kendrick and M. W. Alleyne owing to the calls of counties and England Young Cricketers, the English Schools side in 1986 had a core of experienced players to blend with the young players coming into the team. The batsmen scored at a good rate and in fine style, with M. R. Ramprakash and S. P. Titchard outstanding, Ramprakash going on to play for England Young Cricketers. Good support came from M. A. Crawley, N. A. Stanley, D. Leatherdale and P. A. Gover, the last named leading the side well in the absence of Atherton and setting a fine example in the field. It was a pleasure to see fielding of such a high standard, and R. J. Turner, the wicket-keeper, gave good support. The strike bowlers, P. J. Martin, I. J. Houseman and the more experienced M. J. Smith, were hampered by unresponsive pitches but bowled an attacking line and gave little away. Two promising spinners, H. R. J. Trump (off-spin) and M. A. Newton (slow left-arm), did most of the work.

Only one of the English Schools international matches, that against Scotland, was unaffected by the weather. The worst hit was the first, against Sri Lankan Young Cricketers at Manchester where English Schools, put in, were rescued from a shaky start by a third-wicket partnership of 154 between Titchard (95) and Crawley (86). Gover declared at 302 for nine, but rain brought the match to an end after seven balls on the second day with Sri Lankan Young Cricketers 45 for nine. When the match against Irish Schools at Chesterfield also ended in a draw, English Schools were in the stronger position. Despite losing the toss, as they did in all four of their international matches, they made 249 for five declared, Titchard scoring 114, and then bowled out Ireland for 164 with Trump and Newton taking four wickets each. A second declaration at 105 for two set a target of 191 in 104 minutes, of which Ireland had made 117 for five when time ran out.

Against Welsh Schools at Pontarddulais, English Schools compiled 237 for nine (Ramprakash 85) before dismissing the Welsh for 183, seven wickets falling to Trump for 58 off 23 overs. Titchard and Ramprakash had put on 95 for the first wicket when the rain again intervened. At Dartford, Scottish Young Cricketers were restricted to 166 for six in their 60 overs, whereupon the prolific opening partnership of Titchard (53) and Ramprakash (117) contributed 132 of English Schools' 256 for seven. Scotland, struggling against good tight bowling, were then dismissed for 144, Martin's pace bringing him five for 30 and Turner claiming five victims behind the stumps. The 55 runs needed for victory were scored without loss.

The second MCC Schools Oxford Festival followed the same format as the first. On the first two days, HMC Southern Schools played The Rest, while ESCA North played ESCA South, the players being rearranged into four different teams for further trial matches on the third day. A final trial – MCC Schools East against MCC Schools West – on the fourth day ended with the selection of the team to play for MCC Schools at Lord's. Finally, HMC Schools played a three-day match against Sri Lankan Young Cricketers.

HMC SOUTHERN SCHOOLS v THE REST

At Magdalen College School, Oxford, July 19, 20. Drawn. Toss: HMC Southern Schools. On a firm but slow pitch, with a fast outfield, Longley and Stanley began HMC Southern Schools' innings with a stylish century partnership which was echoed by Crawley and Foster for The

Rest. Fishpool's off-spin, well backed up, restrained the later batsmen, and to keep the game open Foster declared at The Rest's overnight score, 54 behind. Griggs dominated the Southern Schools second innings, emerging from a slow start to play some fine strokes, and Stanley was able to set a target of 258 in what became 71 overs. Some excellent catching, especially by Speight, prevented anyone playing the big innings needed for The Rest to win, and when Fishpool and Stanley looked as if they would bowl the Southern Schools to victory, The Rest's last-wicket pair played out the last four overs.

HMC Southern Schools

J. I. Longley (*Tonbridge*) c Storer b Yates	53		
*N. A. Stanley (*Bedford Modern*) c Crawley b Yates	84		
J. R. Wood (*Leighton Park*) c and b Foster	14	– (2) c Pegg b Lewis	15
†M. P. Speight (*Hurstpierpoint*) c Pegg b Smith	24	– (5) run out	13
F. J. Westlake (*Eastbourne*) b Yates	11	– (4) b Yates	22
D. H. J. Griggs (*Felsted*) not out	5	– (3) not out	105
L. S. P. Fishpool (*Bishop's Stortford*) (did not bat)		– (1) c and b Storer	33
Extras	31	Extras	15

1/124 2/160 3/184 4/203 5/222   (5 wkts dec.) 222   1/37 2/73 3/143   (4 wkts dec.) 203
                                                  4/203

J. E. Crooker (*Bedford*), N. H. Peters (*Sherborne*), H. N. Bhatia (*Rugby*) and D. W. R. Wiles (*Merchant Taylors', Northwood*) did not bat.

Bowling: *First Innings*—Smith 18-5-44-1; Nuttall 8-2-25-0; Lewis 6-1-23-0; Yates 20-2-85-3; Foster 4-0-23-1. *Second Innings*—Smith 8-2-24-0; Lewis 15-1-49-1; Nuttall 7-1-17-0; Storer 7-3-32-1; Williams 7-2-21-0; Foster 4-0-20-0; Yates 7-1-29-1.

The Rest

*S. G. Foster (*Barnard Castle*) b Peters	64	– (9) c Bhatia b Fishpool	10
M. A. Crawley (*Manchester GS*) b Fishpool	48	– (8) c Speight b Crooker	29
J. G. A. Williams (*Kelvinside*) b Peters	0	– (2) c Speight b Peters	8
R. S. M. Morris (*Stowe*) c Speight b Wiles	5	– (1) b Fishpool	37
J. Holmes (*Ellesmere*) c Stanley b Wiles	17	– (4) c Speight b Crooker	30
D. B. Storer (*Worksop*) not out	3	– (3) c Wood b Fishpool	34
G. Yates (*Manchester GS*) not out	21	– c Longley b Stanley	12
†C. H. H. Pegg (*Radley*) (did not bat)		– (6) c Fishpool b Stanley	0
J. C. M. Lewis (*Gresham's*) (did not bat)		– (5) c Speight b Stanley	39
J. D. Nuttall (*Pocklington*) (did not bat)		– not out	4
A. M. Smith (*Queen Elizabeth GS, Wakefield*) (did not bat)		– not out	8
Extras	10	Extras	15

1/112 2/113 3/120 4/142 5/144   (5 wkts dec.) 168   1/10 2/77 3/82 4/135   (9 wkts) 226
                                                5/135 6/151 7/200
                                                8/209 9/213

Bowling: *First Innings*—Peters 11-1-45-2; Crooker 11-2-28-0; Wiles 9-2-34-2; Fishpool 13-7-26-1; Bhatia 5-0-28-0. *Second Innings*—Peters 5-2-9-1; Wiles 14-2-31-0; Crooker 16-2-61-2; Bhatia 15-2-41-0; Fishpool 15-3-52-3; Stanley 6-2-17-3.

ESCA NORTH v ESCA SOUTH

At Keble College, Oxford, July 19, 20. Drawn. Toss: ESCA North. Spin bowlers controlled the match on a helpful pitch, Trump and Newton, the English Schools pair, sharing the wickets in the North's first innings. Only Titchard mastered the conditions and the attack to score 87. Ramprakash led the South's reply, setting them on the way to a 24-run lead from their 60 overs. Batting again, the North overcame an injury to Titchard and the continued threat of Kendrick's slow left-arm spin to set a target of 198 in two and a half hours. Rather than achieving it, the South looked likely losers at 90 for six, but Ramprakash and Turner held on to secure a draw.

ESCA North

†M. J. Bailey (*St Joseph's/Staffs.*) b Trump	22	– c Gover b Kendrick 9
S. P. Titchard (*Priestley/Cheshire*) c and b Trump	87	– (6) c Kidd b Kendrick 12
D. A. Leatherdale (*Pudsey/Yorks.*) b Trump	28	– b Kendrick 32
*T. M. Orrell (*Stand Coll./Lancs.*) c Ramprakash b Newton	5	– (2) st Turner b Kendrick 34
A. A. D. Gillgrass (*Bradford GS/Yorks.*) c Newton b Trump	4	– (4) c Gover b Kendrick 33
C. Tolley (*KES Stourbridge/Worcs.*) not out	13	– (5) c Gover b Kendrick 33
E. Milburn (*King Edward/Warwicks.*) b Newton	6	– c Trump b Kendrick 39
P. J. Martin (*Danum/Yorks.*) not out	6	– c and b Trump 10
G. J. Coates (*Fenton VIth Form Coll./Staffs*) (did not bat)	–	(10) st Turner b Kendrick 6
J. Boiling (*Rutlish/Surrey*) (did not bat)	–	(9) not out 2
Extras	9	Extras 11

1/58 2/125 3/150 4/150   (6 wkts dec.) 180   1/43 2/44 3/108   (9 wkts dec.) 221
5/154 6/166   4/113 5/135 6/175
                                         7/213 8/213 9/221

I. J. Houseman (*Harrogate GS/Yorks.*) did not bat.

Bowling: *First Innings*—Phillips 7–3–18–0; Pritchard 9–2–30–0; Trump 23–6–61–4; Kendrick 9–4–19–0; Newton 12–2–43–2. *Second Innings*—Phillips 6–1–24–0; Pritchard 9–3–17–0; Kendrick 35–9–83–8; Trump 17–3–53–1; Newton 15–1–33–0.

ESCA South

M. R. Newton (*Peter Symonds/Hants*) c Bailey b Coates	16	– c Gillgrass b Milburn 34
M. R. Ramprakash (*Gayton HS/Middx*) c Titchard b Tolley	87	– (7) not out 38
O. C. Smith (*Cotham GS/Avon*) b Milburn	21	– (2) c Boiling b Martin 5
I. Kidd (*John Kelly/Middx*) not out	41	– (3) c Boiling b Martin 0
P. N. Gover (*Eastleigh/Hants*) c Houseman b Martin	17	– b Coates 19
*R. G. Twose (*King's Taunton/Som.*) run out	0	– (4) c Coates b Martin 4
†R. J. Turner (*Millfield/Som.*) not out	6	– (8) not out 9
H. R. J. Trump (*Millfield/Som.*) (did not bat) ...	–	(6) c Martin b Boiling 3
Extras	16	Extras 27

1/59 2/121 3/143 4/181 5/184   (5 wkts dec.) 204   1/29 2/30 3/37 4/63   (6 wkts) 139
                                                5/70 6/90

N. Kendrick (*Wilsons/Surrey*), J. R. Pritchard (*Reading/Berks.*) and A. R. Phillips (*Millfield/Som.*) did not bat.

Bowling: *First Innings*—Houseman 13–3–46–0; Martin 10–5–21–1; Boiling 8–1–37–0; Coates 9–3–28–1; Tolley 13–2–38–1; Milburn 7–2–16–1. *Second Innings*—Houseman 6–0–19–0; Martin 11–2–36–3; Boiling 14–10–18–1; Milburn 4–0–16–1; Coates 5–0–36–1.

At Oxford, July 21. N. A. Stanley's XI won by 33 runs. N. A. Stanley's XI 205 for nine dec. (N. A. Stanley 95, J. R. Wood 51; H. R. J. Trump five for 51); T. M. Orrell's XI 172 (F. J. Westlake 60).

At Oxford, July 21. Drawn. S. G. Foster's XI 189 for eight dec. (P. A. Gover 48, D. B. Storer 40; A. R. Phillips four for 35); R. G. Twose's XI 189 for six (M. Newton 59).

At Oxford, July 22. Drawn. MCC Schools West 213 for six dec. (M. A. Crawley 114); MCC Schools East 199 for six (N. A. Stanley 89).

At Christ Church College, Oxford, July 23, 24, 25. HMC Schools drew with Sri Lankan Young Cricketers (See Sri Lankan Young Cricketers' tour section).

Details of the match between MCC Schools and the National Association of Young Cricketers may be found in Other Matches at Lord's, 1986.

Reports from the Schools

Once the weather improved, batsmen prospered in 1986, eight players from the schools reviewed here passing 1,000 runs: J. I. Longley of Tonbridge (1,141), M. P. Speight of Hurstpierpoint (1,130), M. A. Crawley of Manchester GS (1,123), N. A. Stanley of Bedford Modern (1,116), D. P. Spiller of Royal GS, Worcester (1,073), A. D. Brown of Caterham (1,061), P. I. Prichard of Shrewsbury (1,051) and R. S. M. Morris of Stowe (1,001). Crawley averaged 112.30, as well as taking 31 wickets, while Brown, Stanley and Speight all averaged more than 80. Four bowlers took 60 wickets: T. P. B. Balderson of Pocklington (64), C. M. Graham of Victoria College, Jersey (62), J. S. Waters of Royal GS, Worcester (61) and J. D. Nuttall of Pocklington (60, at an average of 8.78). Graham also scored 715 runs, and of the nine other bowlers who took 50 wickets, M. A. Atherton of Manchester GS scored 627 runs. Seven hat-tricks were reported: by J. S. Clarke and J. Holt of Hipperholme, A. D. Ferrier of Eastbourne, J. S. W. Hawkins of King's, Chester, J. S. Pritchard of Reading, A. Sharma of Forest, and J. J. Zagni of Ipswich. The outstanding return was J. Boiling's ten for 30 for Rutlish against Wallington HS.

The absence of an effective strike bowler prevented a young **Abingdon** side from converting winning positions to victories, although their positive attitude brought six wins, including excellent performances v St Edward's Oxford and Reading. The batting was led by the captain and opener, J. C. P. Haynes, while of the five main bowlers P. Lunn, with leg-breaks, posed the most problems. The outstanding performance for **Aldenham** was G. E. Peel's nine for 76 in the win over King William's College, Isle of Man. UCS, Oratory, Denstone and Liverpool College were also defeated. Much promise was shown by K. Jahangir, who played for HMC Schools Colts. **Alleyn's**, though failing to play to their potential, beat St John's Leatherhead, Emanuel and Wilson's. T. Wareham was a sensible, unselfish captain, J. Bridgeman played some fine attacking innings, and O. Lucking dismissed many good batsmen with his deceptive slow-medium 'floaters'. **Allhallows'** young and inexperienced side took comfort from some favourable draws and the loss of only one schools fixture. The captain, S. B. Claro, was well supported by J. M. Stamford with the bat and J. E. T. Clark with the ball. After losing six consecutive matches early in the season, **Ampleforth** were forced to introduce three new players, whereupon they won six of their last eight matches, beating Worksop, St Peter's York, Denstone, Oundle, Uppingham and Blundell's. The batting, apart from R. E. O'Kelly, and the opening bowling were generally poor. However, two contrasting left-arm spinners, B. R. Simonds-Gooding and D. H. Churton, who joined the XI in the second half of the season, were above average, as was W. J. Bianchi, who came in for the final matches as third seamer and headed the averages.

Ardingly, with three fast bowlers and stroke-playing batsmen, lost four of their first five matches in wet May, but when the wickets hardened they enjoyed six successive victories, Christ's Hospital, Worth and Wellingborough all being bowled out cheaply. A. M. E. Gould (left arm) and P. E. Jackson bowled with some aggression in the right conditions, and there was good support from Clark, a neat wicket-keeper, and C. M. Thorne, who took fourteen catches in close positions as well as heading the batting. Impressive for **Arnold** was fourteen-year-old S. M. Aga (slow left-arm), whose 47 wickets included returns of seven for 50 v King William's College, Isle of Man, seven for 69 v King Edward VII, Lytham, and four for 7 v Stockport GS. With only the captain, S. Davies, finding form with the bat, the side's strength lay in the bowling. There was also an outstanding prospect at **Ashville College**, who beat Bootham, Batley GS, Bradford GS, Giggleswick and Leeds GS. M. W. Yates, an opening bowler, took 45 wickets, including six for 31 v Bradford GS and four for 6 v Woodhouse Grove. Three centuries were scored for the school, two by H. M. Rogers and one by the captain, J. E. Hill.

Unbeaten until July, when some good adult sides exposed the brittleness of their batting, **Bancroft's** attributed their success to all-round effort and the positive captaincy of V. D. Masani. R. W. Hubbard's 404 runs and 42 wickets included 109 v St Albans School and eight for 44 v Essex Schools Under-19. G. J. Norgate, a wicket-keeper-batsman, set the tone for an excellent fielding side in which A. M. O'Neill took some outstanding catches, as well as winning the match v Enfield GS with his leg-breaks, returning seven for 51. **Bangor GS** enjoyed another productive season, even if the senior batsmen did not do as well as expected. Centuries were scored by G. C. Yeates, S. R. N. McClatchey and C. M. McCall, the captain, the last two also taking most wickets. Despite some inconsistency, **Barnard Castle** recorded eleven victories including those v Durham School, Queen Elizabeth GS Wakefield, Solihull School, King Edward VII Lytham and UCS London. The captain, S. G. Foster, led by example with 558 runs and 42 wickets, and played for HMC Schools against Sri Lankan Young Cricketers. **Bedford School's** young and inexperienced side went through the season unbeaten, although to have as many as fifteen draws proved frustrating. J. E. Crooker impressed with bat and ball, as exemplified by his 91 and seven for 42 v Cambridge Crusaders.

For **Bedford Modern**, who achieved a record ten wins and were undefeated by English schools, N. A. Stanley was again outstanding: his aggregate of 1,116 runs was a school record, as were his average of 85.84 and his five centuries. He captained HMC Schools v Sri Lankan Young Cricketers, and played for MCC Schools, English Schools, Northamptonshire Under-25 and their Second XI. A. J. Trott's unbeaten 150 v RGS Colchester was also a school record. An effective attack comprised A. D. McCartney, M. W. White (both fast), Stanley (fast-medium) and P. A. Owen (slow left-arm), while T. C. Taylor, with 30 dismissals, kept wicket immaculately. **Berkhamsted**, beaten only by Bishop's Stortford, were pleasantly surprised by their season, enjoying wins over Brentwood, Magdalen College School, St Albans, St Lawrence, Kimbolton and Framlingham. The bowling was led by the captain, S. Hunt (slow left-arm), and M. Player (medium). S. Fox was the most successful batsman. The leading player for **Birkenhead** was the all-rounder, P. I. Rennie, given good support in the attack by the captain, E. N. Kitchen, who took his 100th wicket for the school.

A well-balanced **Bishop's Stortford** side had an excellent season following a successful winter tour to Sri Lanka, their strong batting built on the openers, L. S. P. Fishpool and T. A. G. Lucas, who compiled a school record of 162 for the first wicket v Framlingham. In his four seasons in the XI, Fishpool, whose aggregate of 644 was the highest for the school since D. F. Cock in 1933, scored a school record of 2,171 runs, took 147 wickets with his off-spinners and held 30 catches. He played for Essex Second XI and for HMC Schools. Spin was the chief strength of a varied attack, with P. Bashford's wicket-keeping again setting the standard for a first-class fielding side. Although scoring prolifically, a young **Bloxham** side, for whom N. E. Baig was the outstanding cricketer, were limited by their inability to bowl out opposing sides. **Blundell's**, whose only schools wins came at the expense of Plymouth College and Taunton, were also hampered by the lack of a penetrative bowler, although P. G. Wilson (medium) showed promise. Fine centuries came from S. S. Patidar and the captain, A. R. Giles.

With no wins, but two close draws and a tie v the Authentics, **Bradfield College** relied heavily for runs on their captain, R. M. F. Cox. J. D. Pearce, a fifteen-year-old left-arm spinner, headed the bowling averages, while W. M. Porter (fast) took the most wickets. After a frustrating start, **Bradford GS** finished the season with victories over Woodhouse Grove, Bolton and Hymers. Fielding well, they played enterprising cricket, and it was rewarding to see less experienced players rise to the occasion when some senior players failed to reproduce their form. D. R. Chadwick had a promising first season as opener and P. R. Miles batted forcefully in the middle order, as well as bowling his off-spin intelligently in a contrasting partnership with I. J. McClay (left-arm spin). **Brentwood** won only two games, suffering from inexplicable batting collapses. They were encouraged, though, by the performance of P. Welton, a right-handed batsman of class and a useful medium-pace bowler. An inexperienced **Bromsgrove** side achieved good wins over Bloxham and King's, Worcester.

For **Canford**, the captain and left-hand bat, C. H. Forward, scored consistently, and the young W. E. Johnson showed promise, but although T. C. LeGallais and R. J. Stearn bowled well at medium pace, the attack generally lacked variety. A tour to Kenya was planned for January. In an enjoyable season which brought nine wins for **Caterham**, the power of A. D. Brown and P. J. Sidall, combined with the correct technique of J. A. Cox-Colyer and S. R. A. Miles, proved too much for most opposing bowlers. Brown was outstanding, his 1,061 runs including 105 in 39 balls v Alleyn's, 127 in 69 balls v Rutlish, 109 in 95 balls v Trinity and 189 in 113 balls v RGS Guildford. Hundreds in successive innings came from Miles v Sutton Valence and Reigate GS. **Charterhouse's** wins over Wellington College, Bradfield and Malvern were offset by heavy defeats at the hands of Tonbridge, Harrow, Eton and Rugby. In a more successful season, with only one game lost, **Cheltenham College** recorded notable victories v MCC and Haileybury, the latter thanks to a second-wicket partnership of 138 between the captain, W. J. Davies, and C. M. Harris.

Bowling out the opposition in eight of fourteen matches, **Chigwell** beat Brentwood, Enfield GS, St Edmunds Ware and John Lyon, losing only twice to schools. D. Clark was the leading bowler, well supported by M. G. Chalkley (both right-arm medium). Clark and the wicket-keeper, T. A. Coleman, shared a second-wicket stand of 125 v John Lyon. **Christ College, Brecon**, were unbeaten, but only three of their thirteen matches were won, dropped catches more than once letting the opposition escape into a draw. Opening batsmen N. S. Johnson and the captain, S. J. Harrett, provided a sound foundation to the batting, including a record 182 v Bronwydd CC (Harrett 108), but otherwise both batting and bowling lacked real power. Despite only two wins, **Christ's Hospital** were encouraged by the quality of cricket played by, and the progress of, their young side, eight of whom return in 1987. The only three-figure innings was R. T. Macro's 106 v Eastbourne. At **Clifton College**, also with a young but well-balanced side, their first six batsmen scored reliably while the bowling was a healthy combination of speed and spin. R. J. W. Holdsworth took seven Millfield wickets for 75, and there were notable wins v Winchester and Eastbourne.

Unbeaten in one of their most successful seasons, **Colfe's** defeated Eltham College, Chislehurst & Sidcup, Alleyn's, Latymer Upper, Hampton, Judd, Sevenoaks, Borden GS and Harvey GS, the latter in the final of the Kent Under-19 Cup, which they won for the first time. The school also won the Kent Under-15 Cup. The captain, C. A. Spencer, was outstanding with 900 runs, including two centuries, others coming from R. J. Harmer and a fifteen-year-old all-rounder, P. R. Whiteland, who bore the brunt of the bowling with the 6ft 10in tall J. E. M. Streeter. **Colston's**, with victories over Bristol GS, Bristol Cathedral School, Hutton GS and Marling, owed much to the high scoring of their captain, J. N. Stutt, who in his four years in the XI scored 3,028 runs with ten centuries. As the highlight of a successful season with fourteen wins, **Coventry School – Bablake** won the final of the Warwickshire Cup from King Edward's, Birmingham, the only school to have beaten them earlier in the season. They also reached the last eight of the Barclays Bank Under-17 competition. Positive batting, especially when chasing runs, brought **Cranbrook** their best results since 1968. At the end of a season of fluctuating fortunes for **Cranleigh**, R. Radbourne finally fulfilled his potential with centuries on consecutive days at the Rossall Festival v Merchant Taylors' Northwood, St Peter's York and Rossall. S. J. Watkinson (medium) headed the bowling with 53 wickets, particularly proving his hostility and stamina in the second half of the season.

Dauntsey's attributed their record of ten drawn matches in twelve to their inability to bowl sides out. The most hostile bowler was C. R. B. Page (left-arm fast-medium), while J. W. S. Porter scored the most runs, with hundreds in consecutive matches v King Edward's Bath and Wycliffe College. In a season of rebuilding, one highlight for **Dean Close** was an innings of 127 v Bloxham by P. J. Kirby, the captain and left-hand opening bat. M. H. Paget-Wilkes (medium) and T. A. Edginton (slow left-arm) had their days with both bat and ball, and as eight players were expected to return, prospects for 1987 are good. The young **Dover College** side exceeded expectations, thanks mainly to the captaincy and example of J. T. Wilson, who in addition to his playing ability inspired team loyalty and fostered a high quality of fielding. **Downside**, with average results, were hampered by their unreliable batting, but the bowling was accurate and usually penetrative, particularly that of C. E. Crossland (medium) and E. O. Thesiger (fast-medium), who was a thoughtful and decisive captain. The failure of a good batting side to achieve a target when batting second left **Dulwich College** with mixed results. G. N. Fisher was a reliable opener, the captain, I. C. Tredgett (slow left-arm), was easily the best bowler and the fielding was always keen, with M. C. Lea a fine exponent behind the stumps. A tour of Australia was planned for December, a foretaste of which came in the matches v St Peter's Adelaide and Caulfield GS, who produced the fastest bowling the XI had faced all season.

There were some outstanding performances for **Eastbourne College**. F. J. Westlake, the captain and wicket-keeper, scored a school record of 913 runs and played for Surrey Under-19; A. M. Thorpe-Beeston scored 108 in 95 minutes before lunch v St John's, Leatherhead, hitting eleven 6s, breaking two windows, smashing three slates on the school roof and losing two balls; and A. D. Ferrier (fast-medium) took a hat-trick v Collyers School. A memorable win for **The Edinburgh Academy** was the defeat of the previously unbeaten Barnard Castle. However, a lack of depth in the batting and dropped catches were a handicap later in the season, and their main strength was the spin combination of G. A. Muirhead (left-arm) and I. D. Lamond (off-breaks), who took 98 wickets between them. Undefeated for the first time in many years, **Elizabeth College, Guernsey**, were ably captained by M. J. Bacon. Highlights were returns of six for 29 by F. N. Stratford in the exciting win over Victoria College, Jersey, and six for 10 by A. B. Howe v Marlow CC, plus Bacon's 102 v King Edward VI, Southampton.

Ellesmere College, beaten only once by a school, achieved good wins over Birkenhead, Merchant Taylors' Crosby, Wrekin and Liverpool. J. Holmes again dominated the batting, support coming in the first half of the season from A. R. L. Stubbs and in the second half from J. J. Birchall, who also took the most wickets. Holmes (113 not out) and Stubbs (102 not out) put on 232 for the second wicket v Rydal. Overcoming early injuries to three prominent players, **Eltham College** won ten matches and lost only one. Their batting had depth, with three batsmen scoring hundreds, one of them being the captain and all-rounder, R. J. Hart, who scored the most runs and took the most wickets. An inexperienced **Enfield GS** team coped well with a strong fixture list, although the absence of a spinner left the attack unbalanced. Fourteen-year-old D. Bowen, with more than 500 runs, was an outstanding prospect.

Notable individual performances enhanced the season of a young **Epsom College** XI. P. Vickars (fast-medium) returned six for 13 in the 118-run victory over KCS Wimbledon and J. Gardner scored 103 as Free Foresters were defeated by one wicket. Other wins were against Christ's Hospital and Cranleigh. **Eton**, who lost only to St Edward's Oxford and St Peter's, Adelaide, defeated Marlborough, Charterhouse (bowled out for 46), Wellington College (bowled out for 73) and Hyderabad Under-19, as well as dismissing Harrow for 37 at Lord's before rain intervened. Although the opening partnership of R. D. O. MacLeay, a left-hander, and J. A. Teeger became increasingly effective, the main strength lay in the bowling, off-spinner J. D. Norman's 30 wickets including seven for 12 v Wellington and three for 1 v Harrow. The captain, F. O. S. MacDonald, dominated the cricket at **Exeter School**, scoring more than twice as many runs as the next batsman, including 137 not out v Blundell's and 103 v Wallsway. Although their bowling lacked penetration, they beat Wellington and inflicted on Truro School their sole defeat. The emergence of D. W. Ahl as an all-rounder promised well for 1987.

For **Felsted**, who defeated Oundle, The Leys, Aldenham, Brentwood and Winchester, the Knight brothers, A. V. and N. V., put on 192 for the first wicket v Bedford, both making centuries – a school record. A. V. Knight also hit 158 not out (five 6s, 24 4s) v Oundle, sharing in a second-wicket partnership of 227 with the captain, D. H. J. Griggs. In addition to scoring the most runs, Griggs formed an outstanding pace trio with B. J. S. Cooper, who took 52 wickets, and R. P. Haywood. **Fettes College**, heavily dependent on the all-round skills of M. A. M. Adam, had to contend with frequent batting collapses which left the lower order often grateful to salvage a draw. A. Sharma of **Forest** thrice took five wickets and scored fifty in the same match, his five for 26 in the defeat of Brentwood including a hat-trick. He shared 72 wickets with R. J. Davis, who took eight for 17 in the eight-wicket win over Enfield GS and six for 39 v Ilford CHS, who lost by nine wickets. There were two hundreds – a maiden 120 not out by P. J. Butler in the victory over MCC, and 100 not out v City of London from fourteen-year-old A. C. Richards, the leading run-scorer.

Although enjoying wins against Durham and Stonyhurst, **Giggleswick** were disappointed with their results. They had a dependable batsman in S. N. Youdale, and S. J. Pighills, an off-spinner, took a match-winning seven for 25 v Hipperholme GS. **Glenalmond**, inspired by their captain and Scotland Under-19 opening bowler, L. M. Porter, overcame an inauspicious start to collect two good wins and several favourable draws. E. L. Calder, another all-rounder, scored a powerful maiden century v Sedbergh, and a Colt, I. M. S. Wilson, looked especially promising. **Gresham's** owed their success to the all-round excellence of C. J. M. Lewis and the batting of fifteen-year-old H. Spence, who in his first season scored the most runs. With an accurate attack making opposing batsmen work hard for their runs, emphatic victories were recorded v Ipswich, Culford, The Leys and MCC.

Strongly placed in several drawn games, an inexperienced **Haileybury** side failed to secure a win owing to the lack of an incisive bowler and their inability to score runs quickly. J. M. Meacock's 101 not out v Dulwich and the all-round promise of B. J. B. Hall (fast-medium), who took all six Sherborne wickets to fall, were noteworthy. **Hampton** attributed their success in a season of transition to an excellent team spirit engendered by the able captaincy of S. J. Kale. The leading batsman was R. M. Holloway, whose unbeaten 111 won the game v RGS High Wycombe, and although the attack at times lacked penetration, J. C. Reeve (medium-fast) took six for 11 on his début to bring victory over John Lyon. P. Laver (off-spin) took the most wickets, while A. J. B. Sales proved a reliable wicket-keeper in his first season. **Harrow**, unbeaten by schools, defeated Wellington College, Malvern, Charterhouse and Haileybury. Their three century-makers were A. W. Sexton, M. D. S. Raper and J. J. Pethers, the latter scoring 100 not out and taking four wickets against Malvern. Highlights for **Hereford Cathedral School**, also undefeated, came in the fixture against local rivals, Belmont Abbey, in which N. R. Denny compiled his first century for the school and off-spinner A. Macdonald took six for 28. A young **Highgate** side would have benefited from a batsman who could take on the bowling. However, victory over UCS Hampstead was encouraging, as was the potential of the off-spinning all-rounder, D. N. Amato.

Inconsistent batting let **Hipperholme** down early on, but their real strength was in the bowling. Two hat-tricks were recorded, both by fast-medium bowlers: J. Holt v Read, Selby, and the captain, J. W. Clarke, in his six for 44 v Batley GS. Clarke also took six for 30 in the victory v Fulneck, while in a limited season Baldwin (fast) returned seven for 34 to bring about the defeat of Woodhouse Grove. **Hurstpierpoint** followed a tour of India at Christmas by establishing a school record of nine wins, including the final of the Langdale Trophy in which the captain, M. P. Speight, scored 162 not out v Eastbourne. Speight, who kept wicket for Sussex in the County Championship, was outstanding, his 1,130 runs extending by 353 his own record aggregate set in 1984. A young **Ipswich School** side began well with a nine-wicket win over Culford, the captain, J. J. Zagni (slow left-arm), performing the hat-trick in his six for 24. Openers R. Heap and A. M. Paul put on 151 v Framlingham, and the promising N. J. Gregory featured in several key partnerships. The school reached the semi-finals of the Barclays Under-17 Cup.

King Edward's, Birmingham, boasted strong early batting with the first three – N. Martin, P. N. J. Inglis and A. P. Hitchins – all topping 500 runs. However, with an attack which could neither contain sides, nor bowl them out, being asked to bat first was not an advantage and too many drawn games resulted. Similar problems faced **King Edward VI College, Stourbridge**, who fielded keenly and possessed attacking batsmen capable of chasing most totals. They were beaten only once in schools matches and had in C. M. Tolley an imaginative captain who represented England Schools. After an uncertain start, **King Edward VI, Southampton**, played some sound cricket, although they relied too heavily for their runs on the captain, P. A. Arnold, and M. A. Noyce. The bowling, with the 6ft 8in tall A. J. Donaldson particularly impressive, was hostile on helpful wickets. Pre-eminent in a successful season for **King Edward VII, Lytham**, was the captain, D. K. Chrispin, a forthright opening bat and off-spinner who topped both averages and scored 100 not out in twenty overs v Kirkham GS. I. C. Ball had figures of five for 16 in the win over William Hulme's GS.

King's, Taunton, ended the season by winning five of their last six games, Queen's Taunton, Allhallows, Monmouth and Blundell's numbered among their final tally of seven victories. The captain, R. G. Twose, played for Somerset Second XI, and his 44 wickets for the school included four or more on seven occasions. The best return was G. K. Barber's seven for 39 v Downside. **King's College School, Wimbledon**, with many newcomers to the side, improved steadily to finish with four wins and three losses in schools matches. R. M. Wight, a right-hand opening bat and off-spinner, made an outstanding all-round contribution, and the captain, A. D. Mallinson, scored a fine hundred v St Paul's. **King's, Bruton**, with an experienced team, were somewhat disappointed to beat only Kingswood and the XL Club, although they had the better of four draws. C. Cowell was the leading all-rounder, while the economical slow left-armer, N. Randall, headed the bowling. Unbeaten by schools, **King's, Canterbury**, built their successful season around three players; the captain, No. 3 bat and medium-fast bowler, M. B. Ryeland; opening batsman and opening bowler, J. P. Taylor; and the other opening batsman, P. P. Lacamp. A high proportion of draws could be put down partly to the weather and partly to defensive declarations by captains aware of the XI's batting strength.

Nine wins by **King's, Chester**, in their most successful season for some time included those v Duke of York's, Dover – off the last ball – Wolverhampton GS and William Hulme's GS, against whom N. J. Brown, a left-hand wicket-keeper-batsman, hit 109 not out. C. G. Oswald (opening bat and off-spinner) made a telling all-round contribution, while J. S. W. Hawkins, the leading wicket-taker, had a hat-trick in his eight for 56 v Liverpool College. The batting of R. Stott was the main feature of a sound season for the young XI of **King's, Macclesfield**, who beat King's Chester, Rossall and Abbot Beyne but lost their last three matches, at the Ipswich Festival. In contrast, **King's, Rochester**, lost three of their first four matches before positive cricket won the next seven in succession. They batted in depth, and had a marvellous opening attack in the captain, M. P. Mernagh, and I. J. Nightingale who took almost 100 wickets. There was a high standard of catching and the wicket-keeping of D. C. Walsh was quite outstanding. Schools wins were at the expense of Sutton Valence, St Edmund's, Bethany, St Lawrence, Dover College, Wellingborough and Maidstone GS. In an average but enjoyable season, **King's, Worcester**, found that their bowling was let down by brittle batting at vital times. J. A. Cooper, the captain, scored consistently, putting on 197 for the second wicket with T. A. Preston v Durham, while thirteen-year-old R. G. Tomlinson batted well when brought into the side. S. J. Jevons (fast medium) topped both averages and fielded athletically.

A limited attack held back **King William's College, Isle of Man**, only the captain, S. W. Ellis (medium-fast or off-spin), looking likely to make a breakthrough. When batting first the team did well, passing 200 on five occasions, and there were maiden hundreds from three batsmen – Ellis, 102 v Manchester GS, R. F. M. Cook, 107 v Merchant Taylors', Crosby, and Radford, 128 v the Old Boys. The loss of several promising players left **Kingston GS** short of experience, especially among the batsmen, who were unable to capitalise on winning positions established by the bowlers. Four took more than twenty wickets, with noteworthy returns coming from S. Kumar, the captain – six for 52 v St George's, Weybridge – and the opener, R. J. Williams – six Emanuel wickets for 50.

Kingswood reported their best results for 25 years with wins over Beechen Cliff, Colston's, King Edward's Bath, the XL Club and the Old Boys. The batting, much improved, was headed by the fifteen-year-old opener, R. W. Lewis, who scored more than twice as many runs as the next batsman, including 107 not out v Colston's. He also topped the bowling averages. The captain, T. Gleghorn, returned six for 27 v Wallington GS with his off-breaks and M. A. J. Earp, one of the strike bowlers, took six for 38 v King Edward's Bath, including two off the last two balls to win the match.

Ably captained by S. B. Higgo, their wicket-keeper, **Lancing College** won nine matches, schools defeated being Seaford, Cranleigh, Epsom, St Peter's, Christ's Hospital, Charterhouse and Victoria College. A strong seam attack was spearheaded by the pace of S. F. Cloke, with W. A. Gooda's gentle off-spin providing the only variety. A. J. Cunningham scored the most runs, but all the batsmen made a contribution and the averages were headed by S. N. S. Message, who joined the side midway through the season to open the innings. **Leeds GS**, with twelve drawn games and just one win, could none the less be encouraged by the performance of J. R. Goldthorp, who played for Yorkshire Under-19 and captained their successful Under-16 side. **Leighton Park's** twelve wins numbered those over Douai (by ten wickets), King James Henley (by nine wickets), Oratory, Bearwood (by 105 runs) and Reading Bluecoat. Hampshire have shown interest in J. R. Wood, a left-handed opening bat and right-arm medium-fast bowler, who, though available only for weekday matches because of club commitments, hit 926 runs at 132.28, including an unbeaten double-century (eighteen 6s) in the Barclays Bank Under-17 Cup. P. J. Newell Price (fast-medium) took six for 25 v Douai and was well supported by J. D. Thomas (medium-fast) and N. L. Stevens (slow left-arm) throughout the season.

Highlights in a frustrating season for **The Leys** were a 117-run victory over The Perse and the successful leg-spin bowling of N. R. Lankester. **Llandovery College** also reported a mediocre season, although in mitigation the young side played ten of their games against adult opposition. The most enjoyable fixture was the drawn game v Denmark Under-19. For **Lord Williams's**, who lost only to MCC, the captain R. J. Carr scored the most runs and took the most wickets with his fast bowling, while R. J. Gregory was an excellent wicket-keeper. For **Lord Wandsworth College**, undefeated by schools but with only one win, there were innings of 116 not out by S. H. Blows v Shiplake and 112 not out by the captain, D. R. W. Wood, v Farnborough Sixth Form College. Also unbeaten, but with eleven draws, **Loretto** would have welcomed more than three wins. The left-handed opener, T. R. McCreath, led the way with the bat, A. T. G. Craig (leg-spin) always bowled well, and M. C. Eglinton developed from a medium-pacer into a promising off-spinner.

The young XI of **Magdalen College School** had a mixed season, often compiling high scores only to find themselves unable to dismiss the opposition. Paradoxically, no batsman passed 500 runs, although J. C. K. Lewis, S. N. Webb (slow left-arm) and A. L. C. Winchester each captured more than twenty wickets. A young and enthusiastic **Malvern** side were ably captained by M. C. A. Pougatch, a reliable wicket-keeper who claimed 28 dismissals. The batting tended to be fragile, with J. R. Wileman, at sixteen their leading batsman, too often losing his wicket instead of going on to the big scores his talents suggested. The bowling, though steady and economical, lacked penetration. Unbeaten and with fifteen emphatic wins, **Manchester GS** had not just one but three exceptional players. M. A. Atherton topped 600 runs and took 50 wickets with his leg-spin, including six for 27 v Lytham and six for 44 v Arnold. He opened the innings with M. A. Crawley, whose 1,123 runs at an average of 112.30 passed Atherton's two-year-old record and included a run of 476 in five innings without being dismissed. Although exams and injury restricted the appearances of G. Yates, he managed 34 wickets with his off-spin and 636 runs, his best being a brilliant 207 v Duchess HS, Alnwick, at the Durham Festival – another school record – and six for 16 v RGS, Lancaster. A virtually all-spin attack also featured R. Steele (off-spin) and P. D. E. Richards (slow left-arm), who took seven Duchess HS, Alnwick, wickets for 50. Atherton, Crawley and Yates were all selected for MCC Schools, although Yates did not play in the match v NAYC. Atherton also played for NCA Young Cricketers v Combined Services and but for a broken thumb would have captained English Schools, for whom Crawley played.

Marlborough suffered their worst season for many years, the nadir coming with their dismissal for 33 by Wellington College. However, the side was young and made great progress during the season, with two Colts, G. W. Barker and A. J. Robinson, both topping 500 runs. In a period of transition, **Merchant Taylors', Crosby**, struggled early on, often being dismissed for low scores, but they finished on a high note with wins over Northern Nomads, the XL club, William Hulme's GS and King's, Macclesfield. Fifteen-year-old wicket-keeper and opening bat, R. W. Glynne-Jones, took nineteen catches and made seven stumpings as well as scoring the most runs, including 115 v Royal Military School, Dover, and S. Bell (fast-medium) returned eight for 49 v Old Crosbeians. All-round effort brought **Merchant Taylors', Northwood**, greater success than anticipated, wins in schools matches coming at the expense of St Albans, Highgate, St Paul's and St Peter's, York. They were shrewdly captained by D. W. R. Wiles, who passed 100 wickets for the XI and played for Middlesex Second XI.

The highlight for **Merchiston Castle** in an unbeaten season was their exciting finish v The Edinburgh Academy. Having followed on, Merchiston Castle could set a target of only 26, but thanks to a return of six for 13 by B. D. Cameron (left-arm medium), their opponents were dismissed for just 24. Also unbeaten and winning eight of their twelve matches, **Millfield's** strongest side ever contained a balanced attack and a potent batting force, eight players averaging more than 20. J. C. M. Atkinson, H. R. J. Trump, A. R. Phillips and the wicket-keeper, R. J. Turner, all played for English Schools, Atkinson captaining the side against Sri Lankan Young Cricketers and, with Trump and Turner, playing for HMC Schools. Atkinson appeared for Somerset in the County Championship, while Trump and Phillips played for their Second XI. The school won the Barclays Bank Under-17 competition for the third consecutive year, and the Lord's Taverners Under-15 competition. The competent batsmen of **Milton Abbey School** were frustrated by the wet weather early on, and when the pitches hardened the bowling suffered from the lack of a penetrating bowler, depending too much on the off-spin of G. Cameron-Clarke and B. A. Murray's skills behind the stumps.

Capably led by N. J. E. Foster, whose off-spin accounted for eight Culford batsmen, **Norwich School** recorded seven victories. R. J. Wilson (medium) was the leading bowler, with an eight-wicket return v St Joseph's, but the left-arm spin of all-rounder J. R. Marsh was significant. School records were set at **Oakham** by D. M. Robjohns, whose four centuries were the most in a season and whose 902 runs at 60.13 surpassed the 825 scored in 1913 by S. H. G. Humphrey. **Oundle's** inexperience resulted in poor results. Their brittle batting often collapsed after the weakness of their bowling left them facing large totals.

The batsmen of **The Perse** frequently made an enterprising bid for victory, but a general inability to bowl sides out often left them facing difficult targets. N. M. Law topped both averages, he and the captain, T. A. G. Miller, scoring by far the most runs. I. R. Styan bore the brunt of the attack, while the slow bowlers, P. J. A. Alexander and P. A. Bailey, proved their worth once the pitches hardened. Undefeated by schools in their best season ever, **Pocklington** won twelve of their last thirteen matches to take their total of victories to sixteen. They attributed this success to their opening bowlers – the captain J. D. Nuttall (left arm), 60 wickets at 8.78, and T. P. B. Balderson, 64 at 11.68 – who were ably backed by the third seamer, J. R. C. Brown (38 at 10.18). Batting second in all but one game, the young **Prior Park College** side featured in many high-scoring draws and only once managed to reach their target.

But for dropped catches, **Queen Elizabeth GS, Wakefield,** may have shown more wins and fewer draws, although they did finish the season in style, winning all three of their fixtures on a tour of Holland. The captain, A. M. Smith, played for English Schools. After a shaky start, owing to the absence through injury of key players, **Queen's College, Taunton,** realised their potential by winning the last six successive schools matches. D. N. A. Essien was the outstanding player. **Radley,** under the inspiring leadership of J. C. Smellie, were unbeaten by schools, defeating St Edward's Oxford, Abingdon, Stowe, Bradfield, Winchester and Marlborough. Three players stood out. C. H. H. Pegg, who played for Gloucestershire Second XI, was among the best schoolboy wicket-keepers with nineteen catches and nine stumpings, as well as a century v Wellington College; R. D. Stormonth-Darling, whose leg-cutters were particularly effective on damp wickets, took 40 wickets for the second season; and fourteen-year-old M. J. Lowrey, the Lord's Taverners' Under-15 Cricketer of the Year, had a remarkable first season, taking 32 wickets with his off-breaks and scoring a maiden century v Stowe.

Another school to enjoy its best season for many years was **Ratcliffe College,** for whom the captain, J. Farnell, hit 103 not out v Ruthin. P. Mestecky's medium-fast bowling brought him 58 wickets, including five in an innings six times and a return of nine for 26 v Trent College. **Reading's** young team relied heavily on the captaincy and batting of their left-handed opener, J. E. Grimsdale, and the fast bowling of J. S. Pritchard. Grimsdale scored 104 v Lord Wandsworth College, and Pritchard's 44 wickets included seven for 41 in RGS Colchester's 94 and figures of 7–2–8–9 in Oratory's 31. Six of the nine were bowled and he ended the innings with a hat-trick.

In a season of rebuilding, **Reed's** depended on their experienced players, notably J. D. F. Paris, who finished the season with five consecutive scores over 50, including two successive centuries, and T. T. Oliver, a slow left-arm spinner. First victories were gained over Trinity Croydon and another young **Reigate GS** side who, while disappointed with their results, had four good wins in July, two of them on a tour of Jersey. The captain, A. S. Clayton, led from the front with more than 500 runs, and others prominent were the opening bowler, M. T. Holman, and C. S. Bates, a fine young wicket-keeper. Noteworthy for **Repton** were a memorable tied game v Wesley College, Melbourne, and good wins v Shrewsbury and Malvern, both achieved by comfortable margins and when batting first. Sound teamwork was a feature under the decisive captaincy of G. M. Cook.

The highlight of a season of fluctuating fortunes for **Rossall's** young side was their end-of-term festival in which six teams played fifteen matches in five days. The wicket-keeper, C. D. Foster, was a sound opening batsman, well supported by the captain, P. Cartwright, and P. A. Clayton, who made a major contribution with his medium-pace bowling and batting at No. 4. Some fine cricket, especially in the field, brought ten wins for **Royal GS, Guildford,** including those at the expense of Kingston GS, Judd, Portsmouth, Wallington, Reed's, King's Worcester, Royal GS High Wycombe and KCS Wimbledon, who were dismissed for 88, seven wickets falling to P. Challinor (medium) for 18 runs. However, three consecutive defeats rather upset the record. **Royal GS, Newcastle,** enjoyed convincing wins and suffered equally convincing defeats. A highlight was a first victory over MCC. A. Atkinson, the 1987 captain, and S. Johnson performed well throughout the season.

Royal GS, Worcester, recorded wins over eight schools, the most emphatic being v Repton, when J. S. Waters produced a remarkable display of leg-spin – described by the opposition as "devastating" – to take nine for 20. Waters took 61 wickets altogether, with sound support from G. T. Burrow (slow left-arm) and D. W. Headley (fast-medium). Equally outstanding was the opening batsman, D. P. Spiller, whose 1,073 runs passed the previous school record by more than 100. He hit three hundreds, including an aggressive 139 v Royal GS, High Wycombe, and passed 50 on six other occasions. With a strong batting side consistently capable of large scores, **Rugby** beat Warwick, Oundle and Charterhouse, all by more than 100 runs, and lost only to Clifton. Fifteen-year-old B. C. A. Ellison (fast-medium) collected 51 wickets in his first season, and although conceding more than 1,000 runs, the leg-spinner H. N. Bhatia took 40 wickets and filled a vital stock role. **Rydal** were unbeaten for the first time since 1931, although more than half their fixtures were affected by the weather. Their all-rounders, M. Sherington and C. Robinson – an able captain – as well as the wicket-keeper-batsman, E. Jones, made significant contributions.

Mediocre batting, which gave the **St Albans** bowlers nothing to defend, resulted in their losing the first five matches, although an improvement came with better weather and the ability to introduce talented Colts. Apart from the wicket-keeping of D. Hopkins, most of the talent lay in the Under-15 side. A. Dalwood averaged 179 as the St Albans Colts won their County Cup competition. Pre-eminent for **St Dunstan's** was M. A. Slade, who, in addition to taking the most wickets, hit two hundreds and six fifties in the best batting figures for the school since the war. However, inability to bowl sides out prevented the side from winning at least five of their drawn matches. **St Edmund's, Canterbury,** suffered from a similar problem, their three wins being achieved when batting second. As the averages reflect, there was depth in the batting, but the only bowler with more than twenty wickets was P. J. Bryant, a leg-spinner, whose 35 included seven for 74 against Queen's, Taunton. **St Edward's, Oxford,** won four successive matches in May, largely through the fast in-swing bowling of C. G. Sharp, who took nine for 42 when Eton were dismissed for 76. The batting relied too heavily on the first three in the order – A. J. W. Brown, whose 105 not out brought the ten-wicket victory over Bradfield, J. D. Ball and G. J. Young.

Unbeaten by schools for the fourth consecutive season, **St George's, Weybridge,** had in J. Creber a polished batsman and improving leg-break bowler. He scored the most runs and took the most wickets. **St John's, Leatherhead,** beat Epsom, KCS Wimbledon, Whitgift and Royal GS, Guildford, and the Under-17s reached the South final of the Barclays Bank Cup for the second successive year. Two hundreds were hit – 106 by S. J. Walster, an opening bat and medium-pace bowler, v the Grasshoppers and 100 not out by A. C. Martin, the captain, v Whitgift. A highlight for **St Lawrence College** was the sixth-wicket partnership of 198 v Kimbolton between G. Hewitt-Coleman (109) and E. Anish (93). The absence of M. Carrington from all but four matches, owing to a broken arm, deprived the team of his aggressive batting and medium-fast bowling, but with nine of the side expected to return in 1987, prospects are good. Much promise was also shown by the **St Peter's, York,** XI, seven of whom were under sixteen. Inexperience told when they were chasing a total, and injuries to both opening bowlers, one for the whole season, severely restricted the attack. Nevertheless, M. D. Donoghue (fast-medium) and J. Brewster (off-spin) took 68 wickets between them, and the fourteen-year-old opening bat, R. Hutchinson, impressed with almost 600 runs.

Sedbergh, whose only defeat in schools matches was by one wicket at the hands of Pocklington, beat Ampleforth, Lancaster and William Hulme's GS. G. J. Porritt, with two centuries, was the leading batsman, the only other three-figure innings coming from A. J. D. Wheatley. Although the absence of an effective spin bowler was disappointing, M. W. Mewburn (left-arm fast) bowled consistently well and was generally supported by fine fielding. **Sevenoaks'** wins were v Judd and Ardingly. A. B. Hood, their main strike bowler, returned six for 22 against the latter, but when injury kept him out of the side there was an abundance of drawn games. In many of these, the XI's solid batting gave them the advantage. S. A. Ford (left-arm fast) showed promise with the ball, as well as achieving a batting average of 108 by being dismissed only once in eight innings. A strong **Sherborne** side were unbeaten and might have finished with more than seven victories, five opposing teams being eight or nine wickets down at the close. Totals of more than 200 were made regularly, with the major contributions coming from S. W. D. Rintoul and A. Kardouni, whose unbeaten 124 v Radley was a highlight. P. M. S. Slade's medium-pace bowling brought him almost twice as many wickets as the next bowler, N. H. Peters, who was fast but not as destroying as expected.

Shrewsbury's successful season featured eleven victories under the able captaincy of C. M. Bullock. D. J. Burrows headed the averages, scoring hundreds v Free Foresters, Cheltenham and Uppingham, but J. R. Prichard was the outstanding batsman, his school record of 1,051 runs including centuries v Manchester GS, MCC, Shrewsbury Saracens and Shropshire Under-19.

Sadly, a combination of bad weather and the teacher's industrial dispute severely curtailed the season for **Simon Langton GS**, who hope for more opportunities in 1987. **Solihull** enjoyed a better season than of late under the excellent captaincy of S. J. Townsley, who scored by far the most runs. R. E. Hatcliffe scored the only century, v Bromsgrove, in his first senior innings. A balanced attack featured the spin of A. A. Jowsey (slow left-arm) and P. St J. Heath (leg-breaks and googlies), the pace of M. J. Sawle and the swing and seam of P. S. Goodson. Highlights were the 1-run defeat of Royal GS, Worcester, and a semi-final appearance in the Birmingham Under-19 Cup. Despite failing to manage a win, **Stockport GS** enjoyed their cricket, their team spirit being a credit to the captaincy of P. H. Duff. M. K. Duckworth, a left-hander, and N. J. Vernon, who scored the XI's two centuries, dominated the batting, although Vernon's form fell away when he was promoted to open with Duckworth. As spearhead of the attack, R. A. Pailin (left-arm fast) was consistent.

Because of the weather, **Stonyhurst** completed only one of their first seven matches – which they lost to Giggleswick despite J. Barnes's return of seven for 13. Excellent fielding and tight bowling characterised their cricket, bringing wins over Rossall and the XL Club. The superb batting and positive captaincy of R. S. M. Morris were the basis of **Stowe's** successful season. With four hundreds, he became the first Stoic to top 1,000 runs – more than twice as many as the next batsman, his opening partner, I. O. Bendell, who hit one century. Dean Close, Mill Hill, Bradfield, Royal GS Colchester and Wellington were schools beaten, with only defeats being by Radley and Wesley College, Melbourne, both in close encounters. A. J. E. Hazzard (right-arm in-swing) was the most successful bowler, taking five wickets in a match three times and returning four for 9 v Merchant Taylors', Northwood. The ground fielding was keen and the catching safe. A young **Strathallan** XI had a disappointing season, depending unduly on the batting of the captain, G. S. R. Robertson, who played for Scotland Under-19, and the successful off-spin of K. D. Smith. In a season of rebuilding which saw 29 players represent **Sutton Valence**, D. G. Plommer twice reached three figures and was well supported by J. D. Crouch, a forcing right-hand bat. In a steady attack, D. Patel emerged as an economical leg-spinner.

Taunton School beat MCC for the third year in succession and recorded wins against seven schools, the only defeats being at the hands of Blundell's and Millfield. They attributed their success to strong batting, headed by M. Van Der Walt, a varied attack and good catching. **Tiffin** were unbeaten until the end of June, when St George's, Weybridge, inflicted their only defeat by a school. Highlights were victory over a strong Caterham XI, and a tied match v Watford GS. N. P. Warren opened the batting consistently, and was the steadiest of the opening bowlers. The lion's share of the bowling was borne by the captain, M. R. Coote (slow left-arm), whose 47 wickets took his tally over four years to 172 at 13.55 apiece. **Tonbridge**, who lost only to Pembroke School, Adelaide, beat Charterhouse, Winchester, Free Foresters, St Peter's Adelaide, Old Tonbridgians, Tonbridge CC and Kent Schools. Weakness in the bowling was offset by the remarkable batting of J. I. Longley, who, with four hundreds, became the first Tonbridgian since M. C. Cowdrey in 1950 to score 1,000 runs. His 1,141 runs broke the school record aggregate established in 1910. Longley represented HMC Schools against Sri Lankan Young Cricketers.

The relatively inexperienced **Trinity** XI, well led by G. M. Vigor, recorded good wins over King's Rochester, St Benedict's, City of London and Reigate GS. K. P. Morley's 852 runs included two hundreds, while the predominently seam attack was spearheaded by P. A. Gardner, still a Colt, T. W. Harlow and D. J. Trafford. Unbeaten until their last match, but drawing nine, **Truro School** owed much to the sound captaincy and batting of P. G. Phillips and the swing bowling of S. R. Peters (medium-fast), who took 38 wickets. The batting of **University College School** was often in difficulties, too much depending on A. D. Diamond and P. A. Teleki. The bowling, too, had its weaknesses, but R. H. H. Thompson (left-arm fast) bowled with spirit, and there were notable performances from D. O. Benaim (medium), who took seven for 26 v John Lyon, and A. S. Lal (fast-medium), six for 32 v Westfield College.

Uppingham, rebuilding, tended to be let down by their batting, although C. M. Frost played some fine innings and D. B. J. Cooke, C. R. Saunders and M. C. Renison of the younger players looked useful. Cooke, with his off-spin, was the mainstay of the bowling, support coming from the promising Colt, P. J. E. Spencer (left-arm medium). **Victoria College, Jersey**, enjoyed a ten-match tour of England in July, highlights of which were exciting last-over finishes at Hurstpierpoint and Eastbourne. The captain, C. M. Graham, confirmed his status as one of the school's best-ever all-rounders, his 715 runs and 62 wickets taking his total for the XI to 2,482 runs and 191 wickets. Spinners A. D. Brown and D. V. Carnegie ended their school careers with 122 and 102 wickets respectively.

Warwick School, unbeaten for three years, lost three times in 1986. The main problem lay in the bowling, but it was of concern that the batting depended so much on three players: A. J. Moffatt, the captain, who scored 116 v MCC and v Solihull; J. D. Stanton, who hit 111 v King Edward's, Birmingham; and T. R. Luckman, 102 v Bloxham. Without defeat until the last week of the season, **Watford GS** played positive cricket under the captaincy of their excellent wicket-keeper, I. Thomas. All-rounders M. J. H. Hanson and A. A. Chaudry were the leading players, but there were few large scores from a strong batting line-up, and the predominantly seam attack suffered from unreliable close catching. The out-cricket, however, was keen. For **Wellingborough**, with schools wins over Aylesbury GS, Alleyn's and Maidstone GS, the captain, P. S. H. Wilson, and fifteen-year-old M. I. Ingram topped 600 runs. T. K. Marriott, another fifteen-year-old, headed the bowling with 42 wickets. Fourteen-year-old J. M. Attfield showed great promise and with eight players expected to return in 1987, prospects are good.

Wellington College, another young side, played positive, attacking cricket as was seen when they successfully chased large totals to defeat Repton and Winchester. Marlborough were bowled out for 33 in their only other win. A return of six for 43 v Repton contributed towards the 42 wickets of J. R. H. Fennick (fast medium) in his first season, W. R. D. Waghorn, a left-hander, batted in attractive fashion, and P. A. Huxtable hit a maiden century v Free Foresters. Although promising more, **Wellington School, Somerset**, achieved just one victory. M. Colman's early-season seam bowling and, later, his batting, including an innings of 101 not out v Wells Cathedral School, provided some compensation. **Whitgift's** inability to bowl out the opposition offset the advantage of having a competent batting side. G. J. Thompson scored a century v Reigate GS, while the captain, N. J. Taylor's post-war school record of 808 runs included hundreds v Christ's Hospital and Domini. S. J. Hill showed promise as an off-spinner.

If disappointing in terms of results, **William Hulme's GS's** season could be deemed a success in the development both of individuals and of the team. D. M. J. Timm and G. J. O'Driscoll became good high-order batsmen, and the side was rarely short of runs. However, the inexperience showed in the bowling as they attempted to convert the advantage gained by the batsmen into wins. **Winchester**, although relatively weak, did win five matches, and there was merit in the batting of R. J. Waddington and the off-spin bowling of T. S. Maclure – hitherto a wicket-keeper – which brought him 41 wickets. Topping the averages for **Woodbridge School** was the slow left-arm bowler and No. 5 batsman, J. R. Harper. A. A. Donnison (opening bat and fast-medium bowler) scored the most runs and took the most wickets. Despite managing only one win – v Silcoates – **Woodhouse Grove** profited from their experiences and were especially encouraged by the sound technique and application of their young opening batsman, J. L. Gomersall. C. A. Miller's left-arm spin showed control and variety.

Worksop College shrugged off the loss of their first three matches to finish with more wins than losses. Well-timed declarations by R. J. Darwin, an outstanding captain, brought six thrilling finishes. The top half of the batting was sound, with D. B. Storer hitting a century v Wrekin and batting consistently, and while the attack lacked the depth of the previous year, B. D. Hackett was a useful opening bowler. His six for 26 set up the victory over Hurstpierpoint. The young **Wrekin** side, all but two of whom are expected to return in 1987, recorded only one win. The batting, somewhat unreliable, depended mainly on the captain, C. A. Fenton, who, if less successful than in 1985, still played some valuable innings. S. R. Jackson (left-arm fast-medium) and J. R. Ford (fast) developed into a good opening pair but the spinners, J. B. Rimmer (off-spin) and R. W. Barker (left-arm), took fewer wickets than expected. **Wycliffe College** ended their season in style after a poor start, winning four of their last seven matches. S. J. Reed was an outstanding captain and high-scoring opening batsman, but his bowlers lacked the accuracy he must have wanted from them. Winners of the Leicestershire County Cup for the first time, **Wyggeston and Queen Elizabeth I College** attributed their success to the consistent batting of the captain, R. M. Lee, the all-round ability of S. C. Brammar, and the penetrative fast bowling of J. L. Green and D. Bennett, both of whom played for Leicestershire Under-19.

THE SCHOOLS

(Qualification: Batting 100 runs; Bowling: 10 wickets)

* On name indicates captain.   * On figures indicates not out.

Note: The line for batting reads Innings–Not Outs–Runs–Highest Innings–Average; that for bowling reads Overs–Maidens–Runs–Wickets–Average.

ABINGDON SCHOOL

Played 19: Won 6, Lost 4, Drawn 9. Abandoned 2

Master i/c: A. Mitra

Batting—*J. C. P. Haynes 19–4–953–117–63.53; P. Lunn 18–1–426–85–25.05; N. Franklin 11–2–191–55–21.22; G. Nicholson 17–3–288–64–20.57; G. Scott 19–0–385–58–20.26; S. Green 14–1–113–23–8.69.

Bowling—S. Green 102–19–276–19–14.52; G. Nicholson 70–14–253–15–16.86; P. Williams 76–22–203–12–16.91; P. Lunn 202–50–571–26–21.96; J. Kowszun 180–55–487–21–23.19.

ALDENHAM SCHOOL

Played 15: Won 9, Lost 1, Drawn 5. Abandoned 4

Master i/c: P. K. Smith

Batting—S. C. Munyard 13–5–401–80–50.12; *D. A. Stenning 14–2–339–83–28.25; N. J. Bayley 11–2–248–65–27.55; K. Jahangir 12–0–323–74–26.91; M. S. Davies 14–1–321–66–24.69; M. H. Moledina 13–1–281–80–23.41; G. E. Peel 10–1–127–41–14.11.

Bowling—D. A. Stenning 176–61–448–33–13.57; G. E. Peel 143.5–24–458–33–13.87; R. E. Sugarman 165.9–51–399–24–16.62; J. P. Patel 100.3–20–323–12–26.91.

ALLEYN'S SCHOOL

Played 18: Won 5, Lost 6, Drawn 7

Master i/c: J. F. C. Nash

Batting—J. Bridgeman 15–3–490–81*–40.83; B. Bennett 16–3–423–90–32.53; A. Stevens 16–2–337–84*–24.07; O. Lucking 15–3–191–80–15.91; C. O'Gorman 12–2–153–48–15.30; M. Chandler 11–2–128–56–14.22; E. Bowen 13–2–141–50*–12.81.

Bowling—O. Lucking 141–28–520–37–14.05; B. Bennett 190.1–43–501–30–16.70; G. Edwards 201–57–540–27–20.00; *T. Wareham 112–16–392–17–23.05.

ALLHALLOWS SCHOOL

Played 12: Won 0, Lost 3, Drawn 9. Abandoned 2

Master i/c: P. L. Petherbridge

Batting—*S. B. Claro 11–3–200–56*–25.00; J. M. Stamford 7–1–150–86–25.00; S. C. Wheeler 10–1–153–52–17.00.

Bowling—C. D. Cuff 42–5–128–10–12.80; J. E. T. Clark 165.4–26–623–26–23.96; S. B. Claro 137.3–28–453–11–41.18.

AMPLEFORTH COLLEGE

Played 17: Won 8, Lost 7, Drawn 2. Abandoned 1

Masters i/c: J. G. Willcox and Rev. J. F. Stephens, OSB

Batting—*R. E. O'Kelly 18–2–470–105–29.37; D. S. Bennet 8–0–193–71–24.12; B. Beardmore-Gray 8–0–184–51–23.00; J. R. Elliot 17–0–283–47–16.64; P. D. Hartigan 15–2–208–46*–16.00; R. D. Booth 16–7–139–20*–15.44; M. P. Swainston 10–0–152–38–15.20; M. X. Butler 17–3–188–50*–13.42; J. G. Cummings 10–1–113–34*–12.55; B. R. Simonds-Gooding 18–2–197–35*–12.31.

Bowling—W. J. Bianchi 96.4–27–265–25–10.60; D. H. Churton 142.4–57–339–23–14.73; B. R. Simonds-Gooding 222.4–75–605–35–17.28; M. X. Butler 145–31–444–20–22.20.

ARDINGLY COLLEGE

Played 14: Won 7, Lost 6, Drawn 1. Abandoned 3

Master i/c: T. J. Brooker

Batting—C. M. Thorne 13–2–425–112*–38.63; A. M. E. Gould 11–4–190–51*–27.14; M. N. S. Dembrey 14–1–323–61*–24.84; J. J. Anderson 13–1–295–67–24.58; A. J. Butterworth 6–1–109–42*–21.80; T. W. Butterworth 12–2–195–59*–19.50; *R. A. R. Smith 9–1–149–46–18.62; C. B. Voller 7–0–108–40–15.42.

Bowling—A. M. E. Gould 162.2–33–513–32–16.03; P. E. Jackson 163.4–26–578–28–20.64; T. J. Card 59.4–4–289–14–20.64; G. Fagarazzi 84–12–307–14–21.92; J. J. Anderson 84.4–10–312–14–22.28.

ARNOLD SCHOOL

Played 15: Won 10, Lost 3, Drawn 2. Abandoned 3

Master i/c: S. Burnage

Batting—*S. Davies 12–2–406–83*–40.60; A. Lyon 15–4–285–74*–25.90; R. O. Halsall 14–3–231–79*–21.00; A. Jones 12–1–229–58–20.81; J. Muir 15–0–265–54–17.66; P. Knapman 13–2–169–59*–15.36; A. Eastwood 9–2–106–26*–15.14.

Bowling—S. M. Aga 160.4–38–459–47–9.76; J. McFarlane 182.1–49–372–27–13.77; R. O. Halsall 103.3–21–282–20–14.10; A. MacGregor 132–44–294–19–15.47.

ASHVILLE COLLEGE

Played 15: Won 6, Lost 6, Drawn 3. Abandoned 4

Master i/c: J. M. Bromley　　　　　　　　Cricket professional: P. J. Kippax

Batting—S. G. Peacock 13–4–367–65*–40.77; H. M. Rogers 13–1–353–107–29.41; *J. E. Hill 14–1–321–107–24.69; M. J. Smart 14–1–234–70–18.00; S. C. Hitchen 13–1–109–35*–9.08.

Bowling—M. W. Yates 170–52–372–45–8.26; M. J. Smart 142–36–398–35–11.37; J. A. Gunning 84–14–325–17–19.11; B. J. Drummond 87–13–315–16–19.68.

BANCROFT'S SCHOOL

Played 16: Won 6, Lost 4, Drawn 6. Abandoned 1

Master i/c: J. G. Bromfield

Batting—R. W. Hubbard 17–2–404–109–26.93; G. J. Norgate 17–3–377–83*–26.92; A. C. Knight 15–1–234–58–16.71; M. J. Goff 14–4–133–29*–13.30; *V. D. Masani 14–0–172–39–12.28; S. A. Youd 15–0–156–24–10.40.

Bowling—A. M. O'Neill 154.3–35–326–30–10.86; R. W. Hubbard 196.1–51–502–42–11.95; A. Azad 56–10–158–10–15.80; N. S. Patel 190.1–53–550–30–18.33; M. J. Goff 174.1–34–587–20–29.35.

BANGOR GRAMMAR SCHOOL
Played 19: Won 8, Lost 5, Drawn 6

Master i/c: C. C. J. Harte

Batting—S. R. N. McClatchey 18–4–367–106*–26.21; G. C. Yeates 19–2–407–110*–23.94; S. L. Mann 8–3–114–29–22.80; *C. M. McCall 17–0–365–108–21.47; S. C. McKenna 17–3–280–58*–20.00; N. S. Taylor 10–4–108–41–18.00; S. C. McGookin 18–0–283–45–15.72.

Bowling—M. W. McCord 20.2–8–38–12–3.16; S. R. N. McClatchey 201.3–63–442–33–13.39; C. M. McCall 142.3–21–428–29–14.75; N. M. Young 45–4–187–10–18.70; S. E. Skelly 139–29–391–20–19.55; N. S. Taylor 93–15–311–12–25.91.

BARNARD CASTLE SCHOOL
Played 21: Won 11, Lost 4, Drawn 6. Abandoned 3

Master i/c: C. P. Johnson

Batting—G. D. Turnbull 6–3–126–45–42.00; *S. G. Foster 17–2–558–131–37.20; M. E. Jobling 20–2–512–108*–28.44; R. D. Whittaker 18–3–418–95*–27.86; R. L. Pettit 19–3–394–63–24.62; R. J. Lawrence 16–1–277–66–18.46; N. J. Foster 15–0–271–67–18.06; T. Underwood 14–1–138–33–10.61.

Bowling—S. G. Foster 143.4–48–372–42–8.85; R. J. Irving 247–69–632–45–14.04; M. C. Fairey 127–20–473–30–15.76; N. J. Foster 235–44–842–42–20.04.

BEDFORD SCHOOL
Played 18: Won 3, Lost 0, Drawn 15. Abandoned 5

Master i/c: D. W. Jarrett   Cricket professional: R. G. Caple

Batting—J. E. Crooker 18–3–558–91–37.20; *A. P. N. Walton 18–9–293–56*–32.55; S. A. S. Cuthbert 15–2–399–55–30.69; J. Teubaner 17–2–431–68*–28.73; D. W. Young 12–7–115–24*–23.00; A. B. Cartmell 18–0–333–50–18.50; J. J. Doubleday 18–1–256–43*–15.05.

Bowling—J. E. Crooker 271.4–77–674–49–13.75; B. C. Banks 258–62–624–36–17.33; A. R. Murphy 100.2–22–258–13–19.84; C. E. Parrish 131.3–30–343–13–26.38.

BEDFORD MODERN SCHOOL
Played 17: Won 10, Lost 2, Drawn 5. Abandoned 4

Master i/c: N. J. Chinneck

Batting—*N. A. Stanley 17–4–1,116–143–85.84; A. J. Trott 15–2–414–150*–31.84; A. D. McCartney 7–1–168–44–28.00; D. C. Garratt 15–4–297–51–27.00; T. J. F. Hill 16–2–347–66–24.78; J. D. Cavanagh 12–6–137–44–22.83; R. G. Taylor 9–2–147–42–21.00.

Bowling—A. J. Trott 63.5–16–162–10–16.20; A. D. McCartney 206–35–594–36–16.50; M. W. White 150–30–404–24–16.83; N. A. Stanley 177.1–45–424–25–16.96; P. A. Owen 245.3–55–666–36–18.50.

BERKHAMSTED SCHOOL

Played 13: Won 6, Lost 1, Drawn 6. Abandoned 2

Master i/c: F. J. Davis   Cricket professional: M. Herring

Batting—S. Fox 13–1–344–88–28.66; R. Barrington 13–0–299–45–23.00; *S. Hunt 13–0–228–79–17.53; N. Allen 11–3–118–27–14.75; C. Collett 8–0–114–52–14.25; G. Barrington 12–3–120–21–13.33.

Bowling—S. Hunt 171.4–56–363–29–12.51; M. Player 164–46–435–25–17.40; P. Lane 84.3–19–243–11–22.09.

BIRKENHEAD SCHOOL

Played 15: Won 5, Lost 3, Drawn 7. Abandoned 1

Master i/c: M. H. Bowyer

Batting—M. J. Wilkie 14–3–363–101*–33.00; P. I. Rennie 15–4–350–98–31.81; A. Deakin 12–1–280–63–25.45; P. D. S. Humphreys 14–2–260–65–21.66; H. T. Roberts 13–4–183–35*–20.33.

Bowling—*E. N. Kitchen 171.3–43–427–25–17.08; P. I. Rennie 163.3–37–465–26–17.88; G. McGowan 84–10–269–14–19.21; S. N. Davies 102.2–13–324–15–21.60.

BISHOP'S STORTFORD COLLEGE

Played 14: Won 8, Lost 1, Drawn 5. Abandoned 5

Master i/c: D. A. Hopper   Cricket professional: E. G. Witherden

Batting—L. S. P. Fishpool 14–4–644–101*–64.40; T. A. G. Lucas 14–1–484–139–37.23; H. A. M. Marcelline 13–4–317–65*–35.22; P. D. K. Brooker 8–2–147–46–24.50; S. R. Hartnell 9–3–138–58*–23.00.

Bowling—P. E. B. Armitage 115–30–293–21–13.95; W. N. Wayman 113.1–25–322–21–15.33; S. R. Hartnell 163.1–42–382–22–17.36; L. S. P. Fishpool 259.1–81–557–32–17.40; C. C. Wright 130.2–25–371–11–33.72.

BLOXHAM SCHOOL

Played 16: Won 5, Lost 3, Drawn 8. Abandoned 1

Master i/c: I. K. George

Batting—N. E. Baig 16–4–562–88–46.83; J. F. Brown 16–2–464–77–33.14; M. J. Eden 17–1–441–62–27.56; N. A. Bertram 16–2–358–77*–25.57; D. A. S. Currall 10–1–220–86*–24.44; *M. W. Nash 15–0–202–48–13.46.

Bowling—N. E. Baig 224.5–38–701–41–17.09; C. R. Wollerton 155–33–504–24–21.00; E. M. Hockey 119–31–366–13–28.15; S. M. Blayney 92–10–372–12–31.00.

BLUNDELL'S SCHOOL

Played 16: Won 3, Lost 7, Drawn 6. Abandoned 2

Master i/c: E. R. Crowe   Cricket professional: E. Steele

Batting—S. S. Patidar 16–2–433–112*–30.92; *A. R. Giles 16–2–400–105–28.57; Y. A. Siddiqui 13–5–138–31*–17.25; R. K. Giles 15–1–234–78–16.71; N. C. R. Cooke-Priest 11–0–172–55–15.63; J. P. N. J. Bowers 12–0–182–40–15.16; K. J. Farrelly 13–3–147–40–14.70; A. C. B. Newark 10–0–134–50–13.40; I. C. Fudge 12–2–132–46–13.20.

Bowling—R. K. Giles 91.2–16–393–18–21.83; R. Norris 75.4–19–232–10–23.20; J. N. Munro 91.1–16–261–11–23.72; P. G. Wilson 143.4–40–402–16–25.12; S. S. Patidar 157.1–30–528–19–27.78.

BRADFIELD COLLEGE

Played 14: Won 0, Lost 6, Drawn 7, Tied 1

Master i/c: F. R. Dethridge   Cricket professional: J. F. Harvey

Batting—*R. M. F. Cox 13–0–589–96–45.30; S. W. Gammell 13–2–283–61–25.72; D. R. H. Spencer 14–0–342–73–24.42; A. C. Brown 7–0–119–34–17.00; J. J. Bates 12–3–106–24–11.77; R. W. F. Perry 12–0–132–38–11.00; N. J. Manthorp 12–1–107–48–9.72.

Bowling—J. D. Pearce 148–30–428–22–19.45; W. M. Porter 177–27–548–24–22.83; E. G. DuM. Browning 158–41–384–15–25.60; R. C. Pollock 127–25–402–14–28.71.

BRADFORD GRAMMAR SCHOOL

Played 19: Won 5, Lost 3, Drawn 11. Abandoned 4

Master i/c: A. G. Smith

Batting—R. M. Nichols 16–1–468–115–31.20; D. R. Chadwick 14–2–289–58*–24.08; *A. A. D. Gillgrass 14–1–306–79*–23.53; P. R. Miles 15–4–221–50*–20.09; R. A. Leach 15–1–257–74–18.35; P. A. Wallace 15–0–273–43–18.20; A. G. Webster 12–2–112–32–11.20.

Bowling—A. G. Webster 65.3–19–213–16–13.31; I. J. McClay 119–46–286–20–14.30; P. A. Wallace ,73.2–19–212–14–15.14; P. R. Miles 154.2–38–466–28–16.64; R. A. F. Kitchen 192.3–38–577–29–19.89; T. R. Emmott 105.2–23–322–10–32.20.

BRENTWOOD SCHOOL

Played 15: Won 2, Lost 10, Drawn 3

Master i/c: P. J. Whitcombe   Cricket professional: K. C. Preston

Batting—P. Welton 15–1–375–74*–26.78; J. G. Northwood 15–0–268–67–17.86; C. P. Davis 14–0–200–44–14.28; A. P. Connelly 15–0–197–39–13.13; S. A. Andrews 13–2–128–24*–11.63.

Bowling—S. C. Sheffield 75–13–208–10–20.80; P. I. Walker 188.4–62–512–24–21.33; Q. Ashby 85.3–18–273–10–27.30; P. Welton 187.3–39–434–15–28.93.

BRIGHTON COLLEGE

Played 18: Won 10, Lost 2, Drawn 6

Master i/c: J. Spencer   Cricket professional: J. D. Morley

Batting—R. L. Chettleburgh 18–0–602–117–33.44; *D. J. Panto 18–2–501–88*–31.31; J. G. Forster 18–1–413–67–24.29; C. P. Sweet 17–0–410–59–24.11; N. J. Hay 18–4–271–43–19.35; J. J. Burroughs 16–6–149–49–14.90.

Bowling—C. Long 202–69–470–32–14.68; D. J. Panto 312–71–1,012–50–20.24; C. P. Sweet 128.5–33–413–16–25.81; R. S. M. Wade 90.5–20–297–10–29.70.

BROMSGROVE SCHOOL

Played 14: Won 3, Lost 2, Drawn 9. Abandoned 5

Master i/c: D. Langlands

Batting—A. H. Ross 14–1–361–64–27.76; *C. E. Thomas 10–4–164–42–27.33; I. F. Barwick 14–2–257–73*–21.41; D. S. Bridge 12–2–183–62–18.30; D. Preston 13–4–157–34*–17.44; P. C. Duffy 13–0–158–37–12.15.

Bowling—D. S. Bridge 171–42–499–33–15.12; A. H. Ross 164.5–42–498–29–17.17; P. C. Duffy 68–7–243–13–18.69.

BRYANSTON SCHOOL

Played 15: Won 4, Lost 4, Drawn 7. Abandoned 2

Master i/c: M. C. Wagstaffe

Batting—*G. W. Ecclestone 15–3–518–101*–43.16; P. R. de Glanville 15–2–392–67–30.15; S. C. Ecclestone 14–0–264–47–18.85; M. K. Greenwood 13–0–210–47–16.15; H. P. Cazalet 10–2–113–38–14.12; J. G. Lengyel de Bagota 15–2–150–36–11.53; S. D. Moore 11–2–103–40–11.44.

Bowling—H. P. Cazalet 115.4–36–252–26–9.69; J. M. H. Beale 206.1–58–481–35–13.74; G. W. Ecclestone 129.2–35–346–19–18.21; J. G. Lengyel de Bagota 62.3–10–214–11–19.45; S. C. Ecclestone 88.3–17–255–13–19.61; N. D. Goodenough-Bayly 158.2–44–477–13–36.69.

CANFORD SCHOOL

Played 14: Won 5, Lost 2, Drawn 7. Abandoned 1

Master i/c: H. A. Jarvis   Cricket professional: D. Shackleton

Batting—C. H. Forward 14–3–403–77*–36.63; W. E. Johnson 12–2–349–70*–34.90; S. R. Knight 14–3–279–80*–25.36; J. H. G. Layard 11–5–120–24*–20.00; G. G. Yates 8–0–153–45–19.12.

Bowling—T. C. LeGallais 138.2–28–445–23–19.34; R. J. Stearn 165–43–478–22–21.72.

CATERHAM SCHOOL

Played 17: Won 9, Lost 4, Drawn 4

Master i/c: A. G. Simon   Cricket professional: J. Wilson

Batting—A. D. Brown 16–4–1,061–189–88.41; *S. R. A. Miles 13–3–411–100*–41.10; J. A. Cox-Colyer 17–3–528–83–37.71; P. J. Siddall 17–2–495–71*–33.00; K. J. Banks 11–2–224–62–24.88; N. D. Thomas 10–0–121–26–12.10.

Bowling—S. R. A. Miles 54–15–181–13–13.92; A. D. Brown 206.4–62–549–36–15.25; N. D. Thomas 224.4–63–575–37–15.54; J. A. Cox-Colyer 179.1–39–576–32–18.00; D. J. Paisey 78–23–199–10–19.90.

CHARTERHOUSE

Played 17: Won 5, Lost 10, Drawn 2

Master i/c: M. F. D. Lloyd   Cricket professional: R. V. Lewis

Batting—A. D. S. Hornett 4–0–136–54–34.00; A. T. Grundy 8–0–226–95–28.25; *B. T. A. Holdsworth 14–1–344–63–26.46; N. A. Stevens 13–0–294–69–22.61; S. C. Mellstrom 19–1–396–65–22.00; T. I. Beaumont 15–0–282–39–18.80; C. D. Jenkins 19–4–221–34–14.73; J. H. Gough 14–1–191–55–14.69; A. E. Ivermee 18–0–236–44–13.11.

Bowling—T. I. Beaumont 68–12–195–10–19.50; S. J. Townend 67–8–263–13–20.23; S. C. Mellstrom 146.2–19–507–24–21.12; W. D. Blacklidge 282.2–64–790–32–24.68; G. M. Bignell 104.2–15–362–14–25.85; A. E. Ivermee 148–22–542–15–36.13.

CHELTENHAM COLLEGE

Played 15: Won 5, Lost 1, Drawn 9. Abandoned 4

Master i/c: J. P. Watson   Cricket professional: M. W. Stovold

Batting—J. R. Baxter 7–5–104–37*–52.00; C. M. Harris 15–3–490–77*–40.83; O. G. Davies 11–4–224–51*–32.00; A. C. Pedrette 15–3–356–63–29.66; *W. J. Davies 15–3–347–70–28.91; R. N. Woolveridge 10–1–245–46–27.22; A. D. L. Thomas 14–1–201–63–15.46.

Bowling—D. J. Hampshire 177.5–40–441–33–13.36; R. T. Davies 97–28–310–18–17.22; O. G. Davies 125–28–390–16–24.37; W. J. Davies 100–10–411–16–25.68; C. M. Harris 157–34–551–17–32.41.

CHIGWELL SCHOOL

Played 14: Won 8, Lost 3, Drawn 3. Abandoned 2

Master i/c: D. N. Morrison

Batting—A. J. Lee 13–1–441–85–36.75; T. A. Coleman 14–4–275–65*–27.50; D. Clark 12–3–193–51*–21.44; *R. D. Mullett 9–0–134–40–14.88.

Bowling—D. Clark 153.5–30–375–36–10.41; M. G. Chalkley 151.4–30–341–24–14.20; A. J. Lee 76.1–13–245–13–18.84; M. Carpenter 84.5–9–209–10–20.90.

CHRIST COLLEGE, BRECON

Played 13: Won 3, Lost 0, Drawn 10. Abandoned 6

Master i/c: C. W. Kleiser

Batting—*S. J. Harrett 13–1–460–108–38.33; N. S. Johnson 13–2–303–69–27.54; D. O. Lloyd-Jones 12–2–270–61–27.00; M. J. Lawson 12–2–254–47*–25.40; M. J. Pearn 9–2–121–61*–17.28.

Bowling—K. L. Miller 148.5–39–410–24–17.08; J. D. Shinton 169–44–449–22–22.40; D. O. Lloyd-Jones 132–32–423–17–24.88.

CHRIST'S HOSPITAL

Played 13: Won 2, Lost 6, Drawn 5

Master i/c: R. H. Sutcliffe

Batting—*N. R. Godfrey 13–1–386–77–32.16; R. T. Aylwin 14–1–238–51*–18.30; R. T. Macro 13–0–212–106–16.30; J. P. Williams 12–1–177–56*–16.09.

Bowling—N. R. Godfrey 40–5–147–13–11.30; C. J. Thornham 75–5–326–21–15.52; M. G. Fooks 154–25–513–28–18.32; A. H. G. Sharp 115–19–386–19–20.31; P. T. V. Jenkins 128–22–427–12–35.58.

CITY OF LONDON SCHOOL

Played 12: Won 5, Lost 3, Drawn 4

Master i/c: L. M. Smith

Batting—D. M. Kutner 10–2–293–89–36.62; *W. A. Saunders 10–0–276–74–27.60; M. F. Prange 10–0–237–86–23.70; W. A. M. Solomon 12–2–237–55–23.70; N. Kapur 10–0–157–53–15.70.

Bowling—N. Kapur 131–31–398–29–13.72; D. M. Kutner 116–24–303–21–14.42.

CLIFTON COLLEGE

Played 16: Won 6, Lost 1, Drawn 9. Abandoned 3

Master i/c: D. C. Henderson   Cricket professional: F. J. Andrew

Batting—W. M. I. Bailey 16–1–505–84–33.66; W. M. Lawry 17–2–470–76*–31.33; R. J. R. Clark 6–1–144–49–28.80; *A. J. A. Cole 17–2–424–63*–28.26; R. Newman 16–1–324–87–21.60; M. J. Munro 17–0–248–51–14.58.

Bowling—R. J. W. Holdsworth 178.4–41–472–29–16.27; M. D. Parish 50–10–164–10–16.40; S. J. Midgley 141.4–27–416–25–16.64; M. J. Munro 100.5–29–299–16–18.68; I. K. R. Niven 215.2–51–561–29–19.34; D. A. Watts 101–37–291–10–29.10.

COLFE'S SCHOOL

Played 18: Won 10, Lost 0, Drawn 8

Master i/c: P. Hollingam   Cricket professional: A. Reid-Smith

Batting—*C. A. Spencer 19–4–900–120*–60.00; P. R. Whiteland 18–6–618–113*–51.50; D. E. Neil-Dwyer 12–3–382–79–42.44; M. J. Pires 12–7–120–30*–24.00; R. J. A. Harmer 16–2–296–101–21.14.

Bowling—J. E. M. Streeter 259–71–636–37–17.18; P. R. Whiteland 208–36–747–38–19.65; S. Johnson 129–24–413–22–18.77; M. J. Pires 144–24–522–16–32.62.

COLSTON'S SCHOOL

Played 17: Won 6, Lost 4, Drawn 7. Abandoned 1

Master i/c: M. P. B. Tayler   Cricket professional: R. A. Sinfield

Batting—*J. N. Stutt 16–4–702–120*–58.50; J. M. Ward 14–4–530–100*–53.00; C. E. J. Tenbroeke 12–4–240–51–30.00; J. Louch 12–1–305–83–27.72; I. Coles 12–1–237–68–21.54.

Bowling—R. L. Rees Jones 50–15–136–10–13.60; J. M. Ward 135–23–446–29–15.37; I. Coles 181.5–29–514–29–17.72; J. Louch 137–30–452–20–22.60; D. R. Rees Jones 133.5–19–441–14–31.50.

COVENTRY SCHOOL – BABLAKE

Played 25: Won 14, Lost 4, Drawn 7

Master i/c: B. J. Sutton

Batting—D. J. Barr 22–9–569–80*–43.76; *A. M. J. Kearns 13–5–297–55*–37.12; S. Wain 23–1–719–111–32.68; M. R. Edwards 12–3–289–82*–32.11; D. Ormerod 11–6–149–50*–29.80; D. Hopkins 17–4–291–69–22.38; R. J. Long 12–3–134–34*–14.88; K. L. Ashby 12–1–160–23–14.54.

Bowling—Azar Khan 59–8–238–16–14.87; A. M. J. Kearns 97–18–308–17–18.11; D. J. Barr 232.4–41–635–30–21.16; D. Hopkins 202.3–39–637–30–21.23; M. Enever 87–12–266–12–22.16; J. Walker 82.4–10–313–14–22.35.

COVENTRY SCHOOL – KING HENRY VIII

Played 15: Won 3, Lost 5, Drawn 7. Abandoned 3

Master i/c: G. P. C. Courtois

Batting—A. Dow 15–1–314–69–22.42; *P. Bond 11–0–193–34–17.54; P. Cunnington 14–4–160–35*–16.00; R. Harris 13–1–180–41–15.00; N. Ansari 11–1–131–46–13.10; P. Freeman 11–1–117–38–11.70; J. French 12–1–115–25*–10.45.

Bowling—N. Ansari 119.4–22–386–24–16.08; J. Plevin 172.4–57–414–22–18.81.

CRANBROOK SCHOOL

Played 9: Won 6, Lost 2, Drawn 1. Abandoned 4

Masters i/c: J. A. Genton and J. Furminger

Batting—G. Lister 9–3–366–78*–61.00; S. Westerman 9–0–258–98–28.66; *T. Allen 7–0–198–89–28.28; S. Rayfield 9–1–164–63–20.50.

Bowling—J. Boughton 60–9–207–12–17.25; T. Allen 120.4–28–341–18–18.94; M. Hall 142.4–39–389–20–19.45.

CRANLEIGH SCHOOL

Played 16: Won 6, Lost 3, Drawn 7. Abandoned 1

Master i/c: C. J. Lush

Batting—R. Radbourne 13–0–548–138–42.15; *E. Hellings 15–4–293–63*–26.63; R. G. Gutteridge 17–1–366–75–22.87; N. C. Radbourne 12–1–233–55–21.18; J. G. Mark 9–2–147–61*–21.00; S. J. Watkinson 17–2–252–44*–16.80; W. J. Cardwell 17–0–266–52*–15.64; P. F. Whyte 9–0–105–42–11.66.

Bowling—S. J. Watkinson 249–65–685–53–12.92; N. C. Radbourne 159–40–416–28–14.85; R. G. Gutteridge 140–26–453–30–15.10; I. Z. Khan 78–18–236–10–23.60; J. Boatswain 71–10–280–10–28.00.

CULFORD SCHOOL

Played 14: Won 2, Lost 6, Drawn 6

Master i/c: A. H. Morgan

Batting—S. Robson 10–1–279–96–31.00; A. Willman 14–2–335–67–27.91; E. Bastow 14–0–332–92–23.71; C. Fitzsimons 9–2–112–30*–16.00; M. Peskett 9–0–101–41–11.22.

Bowling—P. Marston 71–7–230–16–14.37; P. Melvin 76–0–400–17–23.52; S. Robson 93–4–313–11–28.45; C. Fitzsimons 89–9–313–11–28.45.

DAUNTSEY'S SCHOOL

Played 12: Won 1, Lost 1, Drawn 10. Abandoned 5

Master i/c: M. Johnson   Cricket professional: L. Robinson

Batting—J. W. S. Porter 11–2–554–119*–61.55; *A. Brooks 11–4–267–65*–38.14; J. S. Brazier 8–2–141–47–23.50.

Bowling—C. R. B. Page 134–38–342–19–18.00; A. Brooks 112.2–27–352–14–25.14; J. W. S. Porter 78–5–356–12–29.66.

DEAN CLOSE SCHOOL

Played 12: Won 1, Lost 5, Drawn 6. Abandoned 1

Master i/c: C. M. Kenyon					Cricket professional: D. Walker

Batting—M. H. Paget-Wilkes 13–2–326–80*–29.63; *P. J. Kirby 12–1–316–127–28.72; T. A. Edginton 13–2–253–50*–23.00; S. K. S. Chua 10–1–156–67–17.33; E. C. M. B. Kikonyogo 9–0–144–59–16.00; S. M. Cornish 10–0–131–41–13.10; T. J. Harmer 10–1–104–22–11.55.

Bowling—T. D. Postlethwaite 35.4–11–117–10–11.70; T. A. Edginton 186–46–498–29–17.17; M. H. Paget-Wilkes 109.1–21–330–14–23.57.

DOUAI SCHOOL

Played 10: Won 1, Lost 5, Drawn 4

Master i/c: J. Shaw

Batting—M. Brown 9–0–167–46–18.55; K. Blackwell 9–1–150–34*–18.75; J. Urquhart 8–0–104–49–13.00; R. Lumb 9–1–117–36*–13.00.

Bowling—J. Joyce 70–9–266–14–19.00; T. Graham 113–24–402–18–22.33; M. Parker 123–12–412–13–31.69.

DOVER COLLEGE

Played 16: Won 3, Lost 4, Drawn 9

Master i/c: D. C. Butler

Batting—J. D. Rouse 9–3–186–71*–31.00; S. P. Howkins 14–0–340–49–24.28; *J. T. Wilson 13–1–282–55–23.50; K. G. Keats 9–1–172–62*–21.50; S. M. Bradbrook 14–3–194–48–17.63; D. J. Winwood 8–1–109–27–15.57; S. Sukumganjana 14–3–151–34–13.72.

Bowling—J. T. Wilson 253–31–908–47–19.31; K. H. K. Algaith 63–7–208–10–20.80; J. K. P. Boorman 85–12–400–18–22.22.

DOWNSIDE SCHOOL

Played 12: Won 4, Lost 4, Drawn 4. Abandoned 4

Master i/c: D. Baty

Batting—P. J. A. Baldwin 11–1–297–57–29.70; N. B. Morgan 12–0–253–39–21.08; A. M. Thesiger 10–1–178–55*–19.77; C. E. Crossland 9–2–136–47–19.42; P. D. Hunt 8–1–105–76–15.00; *E. O. Thesiger 12–2–145–40–14.50; D. P. Morris 11–1–135–28–13.50.

Bowling—C. E. Crossland 126.4–31–326–23–14.17; E. O. Thesiger 172–35–494–29–17.03; P. J. A. Baldwin 88–18–268–13–20.61; B. J. Toomey 100–15–384–15–25.60.

DULWICH COLLEGE

Played 18: Won 5, Lost 4, Drawn 9. Abandoned 1

Master i/c: N. D. Cousins					Cricket professionals: W. A. Smith and A. R. Ranson

Batting—G. N. Fisher 14–3–370–65–33.63; T. D. J. Ufton 15–2–293–68*–22.53; C. A. Papadopoulos 13–6–129–48–18.42; M. C. Lea 13–1–164–49*–13.66; C. M. Coltart 15–2–171–41–13.15; P. M. King 15–1–183–41–13.07; C. B. Branson 16–2–177–41–12.64.

Bowling—*I. C. Tredgett 241.2–58–653–36–18.13; C. A. Papadopoulos 120.4–17–353–16–22.06; T. D. J. Ufton 140–31–404–18–22.44; R. F. Hollis 187.1–39–538–21–25.61; R. E. Morley 89–14–290–10–29.00.

DURHAM SCHOOL

Played 15: Won 4, Lost 6, Drawn 5. Abandoned 1

Master i/c: N. J. Willings   Cricket professional: M. Hirsch

Batting—A. Roseberry 16–0–624–98–39.00; S. H. Whitfield 15–0–347–100–23.13; N. Whitfield 15–1–298–57–21.28; *J. S. Salway 16–0–301–47–18.81; S. Monk 10–1–142–44*–15.77; A. G. Clayton 16–1–154–43–10.26.

Bowling—A. G. Clayton 257.5–66–817–49–16.67; A. Roseberry 187.4–57–514–26–19.76; S. H. Whitfield 195.3–36–682–28–24.35; N. Whitfield 93.1–16–366–14–26.14.

EASTBOURNE COLLEGE

Played 20: Won 8, Lost 5, Drawn 7

Master i/c: N. L. Wheeler   Cricket professional: A. E. James

Batting—*F. J. Westlake 20–2–913–112*–50.72; R. M. Day 20–2–625–111*–34.72; T. C. Nicholson 15–3–359–57–29.91; A. M. Thorpe-Beeston 16–0–438–108–27.37; J. D. Nicholson 10–5–100–19–20.00; R. C. A. Clarke 18–5–242–68*–18.61; P. J. T. Wright 15–4–184–32*–16.72; A. D. Ferrier 13–5–119–50*–14.87; M. A. Chapple 13–0–119–35–9.15.

Bowling—M. A. Chapple 220–50–647–36–17.97; A. D. Ferrier 117–25–399–21–19.00; R. M. Day 206–51–588–29–20.27; L. M. Valmas 191.1–35–556–25–22.24; R. C. A. Clarke 79–24–270–11–24.54; A. J. M. Crane 93–16–312–12–26.00.

THE EDINBURGH ACADEMY

Played 19: Won 7, Lost 3, Drawn 8, Tied 1

Master i/c: A. R. Dyer

Batting—T. H. Duff 18–2–513–79*–32.06; *D. I. Sutherland 20–3–403–81*–23.70; R. N. Barber 20–2–363–72*–20.16; M. T. Innes 19–0–318–64–16.73; A. J. Swarbrick 20–0–271–54–13.55; C. W. Innes 16–4–108–25*–9.00.

Bowling—M. B. Holmes 206.2–63–420–33–12.72; G. A. Muirhead 310.5–93–728–52–14.00; C. W. Innes 68–17–171–12–14.25; I. D. Lamond 266.3–86–683–46–14.84.

ELIZABETH COLLEGE, GUERNSEY

Played 18: Won 9, Lost 0, Drawn 9. Abandoned 1

Master i/c: M. E. Kinder

Batting—F. N. Stratford 12–2–290–82–29.00; *M. J. Bacon 13–1–345–102–28.75; J. Walker 12–5–159–58*–22.71; P. J. Woods 14–1–260–51–20.00; O. Marshall 10–2–156–51*–19.50; T. N. Hemery 8–0–112–44–14.00.

Bowling—P. Watts 94.3–18–213–23–9.26; A. B. Howe 98.5–23–268–22–12.18; F. N. Stratford 144.3–44–345–21–16.42; S. Sharman 111.4–27–314–19–16.52.

ELLESMERE COLLEGE

Played 16: Won 5, Lost 4, Drawn 7. Abandoned 4

Master i/c: R. K. Sethi

Batting—J. Holmes 15–3–595–113*–49.58; J. J. Birchall 13–4–375–74–41.66; A. R. L. Stubbs 15–4–364–102*–33.09; D. Marvell 8–1–164–40–23.42; *N. Owen 13–1–173–39–14.41.

Bowling—S. J. W. Taylor 84–30–171–19–9.00; J. J. Birchall 172.2–52–435–24–18.12; A. R. L. Stubbs 159.3–43–445–23–19.34; C. M. Reed 154.2–42–421–17–24.76.

ELTHAM COLLEGE

Played 19: Won 10, Lost 1, Drawn 8

Masters i/c: B. M. Withecombe and P. C. McCartney

Batting—L. A. O'Leary 13–7–387–50*–64.50; T. J. Prifti 8–4–240–104*–60.00; R. J. Churchill 15–4–451–71–41.00; C. Carpenter 7–3–123–82–30.75; J. S. Chase 6–1–153–43*–30.60; *R. J. Hart 19–2–520–101–30.58; M. J. B. Brown 17–1–413–104*–25.81; J. J. Guthrie 17–0–414–71–24.35; J. Peek 13–4–194–47–21.55; R. A. Morgan 9–3–123–49*–20.50.

Bowling—L. A. O'Leary 35–5–152–10–15.20; R. J. Hart 234–87–551–33–16.69; R. J. Churchill 170–43–516–23–22.43; N. A. O'Leary 122–27–390–16–24.37.

ENFIELD GRAMMAR SCHOOL

Played 19: Won 4, Lost 8, Drawn 7. Abandoned 3

Master i/c: J. J. Conroy

Batting—D. Bowen 18–0–516–92–28.66; M. Taylor 19–1–503–89–27.94; *S. Chandler 19–4–332–58*–22.13; M. King 11–1–190–43–19.00; N. Browne 16–4–172–41*–14.33; P. Nicholls 11–1–131–38–13.10; P. Beadle 17–0–210–50–12.35.

Bowling—M. Davies 165.5–41–411–24–17.12; J. Marshall 166.4–25–534–29–18.41; G. Rees 75.5–20–224–12–18.66; P. Nicholls 58.3–10–216–10–21.60; M. Arnold 174–28–568–26–21.84.

EPSOM COLLEGE

Played 14: Won 4, Lost 7, Drawn 3

Master i/c: M. D. Hobbs

Batting—P. J. Williams 15–0–355–64–23.66; J. Gardner 15–0–352–103–23.46; *N. Beale 13–2–204–47*–18.54; J. Jessop 13–0–240–53–18.46; J. Appleton 13–5–144–44*–18.00; A. Woods 14–0–228–58–16.28; P. Vickars 10–2–119–34–14.87; A. Nightingale 12–3–120–37–13.33; J. Saunders-Griffiths 13–0–165–43–12.69.

Bowling—P. Vickars 104–15–332–25–13.28; N. Beale 121–27–420–25–16.80; M. de Jongh 76–13–259–11–23.54; P. J. Williams 151.2–24–571–20–28.55.

ETON COLLEGE

Played 15: Won 4, Lost 2, Drawn 8, Tied 1. Abandoned 1

Master i/c: J. A. Claughton   Cricket professional: J. M. Rice

Batting—R. D. O. MacLeay 14–4–461–102*–46.10; J. A. Teeger 14–1–554–91–42.61; *A. D. A. Zagoritis 12–1–214–66–19.45; L. G. Fernandes 10–2–129–38*–16.12; W. A. C. Pym 10–2–129–69–16.12; J. B. A. Jenkins 9–0–121–42–13.44.

Bowling—J. D. Norman 146.2–57–266–30–8.86; C. York 166.4–47–391–38–10.28; H. D. Pettifer 120–34–260–19–13.68; W. A. C. Pym 131.1–36–350–24–14.58.

EXETER SCHOOL

Played 12: Won 3, Lost 4, Drawn 5. Abandoned 5

Master i/c: D. Beckett

Batting—*F. O. S. MacDonald 11–1–566–137*–56.60; M. P. Turner 8–1–191–47*–27.28; D. M. Richards 12–3–208–41–23.11; N. J. Taverner 9–0–178–35–19.77; J. D. Middleton 10–0–130–46–13.00.

Bowling—M. C. Jaquiss 89.3–32–175–19–9.21; D. W. Ahl 62–14–177–11–16.09; D. M. Richards 107.4–35–296–17–17.41; M. P. Turner 57–7–227–10–22.70.

FELSTED SCHOOL
Played 16: Won 5, Lost 3, Drawn 8. Abandoned 3

Master i/c: M. Surridge   Cricket professional: G. O. Barker

Batting—A. V. Knight 18–5–684–158*–52.61; *D. H. J. Griggs 19–2–745–97–43.82; N. V. Knight 19–1–653–100*–36.27; J. D. Collard 10–1–293–63–32.55; B. J. S. Cooper 10–5–135–37–27.00; R. P. Haywood 14–3–280–65–25.45; C. Banatvala 14–2–201–37–16.75; J. E. Bathgate 15–3–166–52–13.83.

Bowling—B. J. S. Cooper 252–49–834–52–16.03; D. H. J. Griggs 241–50–730–35–20.85; S. P. Pearce-Higgins 144–36–511–20–24.55; R. P. Haywood 232–59–715–28–25.53.

FETTES COLLEGE
Played 14: Won 1, Lost 4, Drawn 9. Abandoned 3

Master i/c: M. C. G. Peel

Batting—M. A. M. Adam 13–3–482–80–48.20; C. D. G. Hodgson 8–2–112–32–18.66; R. W. R. Hannah 12–0–166–37–13.83; J. L. MacLean 13–1–143–41–11.91; J. F. Scott 10–1–106–23*–11.77; T. K. Usher 12–0–139–32–11.58.

Bowling—M. A. M. Adam 165–50–390–20–19.50; J. F. Horton 47–10–197–10–19.70; J. Elworthy 120–25–345–17–20.29; N. Cameron 124–30–352–16–22.00.

FOREST SCHOOL
Played 19: Won 6, Lost 4, Drawn 8, Tied 1. Abandoned 2

Master i/c: K. A. Parsley   Cricket professional: H. Faragher

Batting—A. C. Richards 18–5–493–100*–37.92; R. J. Butler 15–3–395–120*–32.91; A. Sharma 16–2–341–78–24.35; P. Butler 13–1–278–91–23.16; O. G. Hansard 14–2–241–50*–20.08; *P. Patel 16–0–238–63–14.87; S. J. Hales 13–5–100–20–12.50; F. G. Cooke 13–0–105–26–8.07.

Bowling—P. Butler 51–15–159–11–14.45; A. Sharma 193.5–28–671–39–17.20; R. J. Davis 252.2–79–588–33–17.81; A. C. Richards 116–18–474–18–26.33; P. J. Clark 147.4–25–478–13–36.76.

FRAMLINGHAM COLLEGE
Played 12: Won 4, Lost 3, Drawn 5

Master i/c: S. M. Bloomfield   Cricket professional: C. Rutterford

Batting—*R. D. O. Earl 10–4–321–117*–53.50; S. C. Newbery 12–4–398–93*–49.75; M. J. Pegg 12–2–417–119–41.70; J. S. Hancock 8–2–127–28*–21.16; N. C. Gowing 9–2–144–54*–20.57.

Bowling—B. N. Foden 68–8–193–11–17.54; M. C. Kimber 94–22–263–14–18.78; R. D. O. Earl 246–76–585–28–20.89; N. J. Williams 134–30–370–13–28.46.

GIGGLESWICK SCHOOL

Played 13: Won 3, Lost 6, Drawn 4. Abandoned 3

Master i/c: J. Mayall   Cricket professional: J. Maguire

Batting—S. N. Youdale 12–0–227–51–18.91; M. P. Kaye 12–1–185–79*–16.81; C. C. Haward 12–1–140–30–12.72; C. B. Day 11–0–124–29–11.27.

Bowling—*J. M. Flint 89–21–266–21–12.66; S. J. Pighills 118–43–330–26–12.69; C. C. Haward 127–28–321–23–13.95; G. N. Topalian 90–12–277–11–25.18.

THE GLASGOW ACADEMY

Played 10: Won 3, Lost 4, Drawn 3

Master i/c: R. M. I. Williams   Cricket professional: P. A. Cooper

Batting—*G. B. A. Dyer 8–2–311–65–51.83; G. B. Robertson 6–1–110–42–22.00; A. J. R. MacDonald 8–1–121–60–17.28; G. G. H. Gemmell 7–0–109–50–15.57.

Bowling—D. M. T. Reid 33–8–59–10–5.90; M. E. Gayfer 44–7–122–11–11.09; G. B. A. Dyer 54–9–157–12–13.08; D. Mowat 55–8–178–10–17.80.

GLENALMOND

Played 12: Won 2, Lost 2, Drawn 8. Abandoned 4

Master i/c: A. James   Cricket professional: W. J. Dennis

Batting—I. M. S. Wilson 7–3–189–64*–47.25; E. L. Calder 11–1–280–107–28.00; *L. M. Porter 12–1–289–89–26.27; J. P. Brown 13–0–275–79–21.15; A. R. Linklater 13–2–210–43–19.09; A. B. P. Sanderson 13–3–183–50–18.30; J. A. Higgins 13–0–147–43–11.30.

Bowling—E. L. Calder 92–22–266–21–12.66; L. M. Porter 127.5–22–366–26–14.07; I. M. S. Wilson 73–17–193–13–14.84; M. W. J. Crow 63.3–9–231–11–21.00.

GRESHAM'S SCHOOL

Played 17: Won 8, Lost 4, Drawn 5. Abandoned 2

Master i/c: A. M. Ponder   Cricket professional: K. Taylor

Batting—J. C. M. Lewis 13–5–418–76*–52.25; H. Spence 15–0–535–130–35.66; A. Wheeler 12–4–256–51*–32.00; S. Mussellwhite 10–0–209–81–20.90; R. Dean 12–2–191–46–19.10; J. Allen 14–2–229–62–19.08; A. Clarke 9–2–116–53*–16.57.

Bowling—T. Berwick 104.5–26–287–21–13.66; J. C. M. Lewis 226.2–58–544–38–14.31; G. Roper 145.1–42–311–21–14.80; R. Jackson 111.3–34–309–18–17.16.

HABERDASHERS' ASKE'S SCHOOL, ELSTREE

Played 18: Won 4, Lost 3, Drawn 11. Abandoned 3

Master i/c: D. I. Yeabsley

Batting—A. V. Spencer 12–1–382–90–34.72; D. W. Preest 17–1–405–60–25.31; A. J. Evans 12–1–222–43*–20.18; J. D. Wellard 13–2–217–99*–19.72; M. R. Griffiths 14–4–112–26–11.20; S. G. Lloyd 14–0–145–41–10.35; *M. Badale 11–0–111–22–10.09.

Bowling—D. R. C. Gunasekera 94.2–28–247–17–14.52; D. W. Preest 156.4–42–417–23–18.13; R. P. Boseley 100–30–284–14–20.28; M. R. Griffiths 162.4–32–622–28–22.21; J. D. Wellard 149.3–32–447–17–26.29.

HAILEYBURY

Played 16: Won 0, Lost 4, Drawn 12. Abandoned 3

Master i/c: M. S. Seymour   Cricket professional: P. M. Ellis

Batting—A. P. Churchill 11–0–358–90–32.54; J. M. Meacock 17–1–465–101*–29.06; *S. J. Clarke 17–2–360–50*–24.00; B. J. B. Hall 14–1–266–52*–20.46; J. P. B. Hall 16–1–260–39–17.33; N. St J. Atkins 13–4–146–38–16.22; A. D. Braid 13–0–193–45–14.84; R. C. Green 14–7–100–15–14.28.

Bowling—S. J. Clarke 83–22–226–13–17.38; J. M. Meacock 62–11–179–10–17.90; B. J. B. Hall 240–56–690–29–23.79; N. St J. Atkins 134–44–369–14–26.35; R. C. Green 188–39–523–17–30.76; C. R. Bass 155–30–475–13–36.53.

HAMPTON SCHOOL

Played 14: Won 5, Lost 2, Drawn 7. Abandoned 2

Master i/c: G. R. Cocksworth

Batting—R. M. Holloway 16–2–665–111*–47.50; S. J. Eggleton 15–5–367–70*–36.70; *S. J. Kale 12–3–220–42–24.44; D. W. Rixon 12–2–216–54–21.60; V. A. Sheorey 15–2–267–74*–20.53; A. N. Westaway 15–1–214–42–15.28; P. Laver 12–2–125–31–12.50.

Bowling—J. C. Reeve 181.5–42–368–25–14.72; J. J. Sanders 145.5–50–350–23–15.21; J. J. Forth 136–50–293–15–19.53; P. Laver 206.2–61–541–27–20.03; S. J. Kale 161–49–372–14–26.57.

HARROW SCHOOL

Played 12: Won 4, Lost 2, Drawn 6. Abandoned 3

Master i/c: W. Snowden   Cricket professional: P. Davis

Batting—A. W. Sexton 10–4–302–101*–50.33; M. D. S. Raper 13–2–376–109–34.18; J. J. Pethers 12–1–308–100*–28.00; D. C. Manasseh 12–3–197–65–21.88; B. W. M. Burgess 10–3–145–51–20.71; *R. A. Pyman 12–1–219–58*–19.90; D. I. H. Greenall 12–0–209–64–17.41.

Bowling—R. A. Pyman 56–14–174–13–13.38; J. J. Pethers 141.5–29–447–33–13.54; M. D. S. Raper 151.2–29–379–21–18.04; D. C. Manasseh 116–25–367–18–20.38.

HEREFORD CATHEDRAL SCHOOL

Played 12: Won 5, Lost 0, Drawn 7

Master i/c: A. H. Connop

Batting—N. R. Denny 12–3–421–100*–46.77; R. Binnersley 10–3–245–40–35.00; G. Powell 12–0–358–60–29.83; *R. C. Wood 11–3–203–70*–25.37; A. S. Mills 12–1–185–48–16.81.

Bowling—A. Macdonald 91–7–397–24–16.54; C. J. Thomas 75.5–17–192–11–17.45; A. Herbert 111–32–305–16–19.06.

HIGHGATE SCHOOL

Played 12: Won 1, Lost 8, Drawn 3. Abandoned 4

Master i/c: R. W. Halstead   Cricket professional: R. E. Jones

Batting—D. N. Amato 12–1–226–54–20.54; T. de R. Sheppard 9–0–174–50–19.33; *M. G. Griffiths 11–1–164–42–16.40; R. J. M. Moxon 12–1–164–41–14.90; F. E. J. Wawn 12–2–116–25–11.60.

Bowling—J. A. Stoecker 86.4–25–215–12–17.91; M. G. Griffiths 103–26–273–15–18.20; S. McGranaghan 112.4–22–260–14–18.57; D. N. Amato 178.2–47–435–19–22.89.

HIPPERHOLME GRAMMAR SCHOOL

Played 12: Won 4, Lost 5, Drawn 3. Abandoned 1

Master i/c: R. Griffiths

Batting—I. D. Crabtree 10–3–255–66*–36.42; P. A. Ramsden 10–2–226–52*–28.25; S. Brooke 12–0–170–32–14.16; *J. W. Clarke 10–0–121–50–12.10.

Bowling—A. J. Walker 41.4–3–138–16–8.62; J. W. Clarke 125.4–37–276–25–11.04; C. D. Senior 43.5–9–142–12–11.83; G. Broadbent 39–4–141–10–14.10; J. Holt 75.4–14–313–13–24.07.

HURSTPIERPOINT COLLEGE

Played 19: Won 9, Lost 2, Drawn 8. Abandoned 4

Master i/c: M. E. Allbrook   Cricket professional: D. J. Semmence

Batting—*M. P. Speight 17–3–1,130–170–80.71; A. G. Dexter 14–6–231–50–28.87; C. J. Davey 19–2–428–68*–25.17; A. J. Reid 18–2–355–71–22.18; M. J. Hastwell 17–1–341–43–21.31; M. D. Rose 16–5–186–32*–16.90; M. S. Drake 11–2–131–45*–14.55.

Bowling—A. G. Dexter 191–39–543–30–18.10; M. S. Drake 179.5–39–540–29–18.62; M. J. Hastwell 106.4–21–303–16–18.93; S. C. Twine 194–40–622–31–20.06; C. D. J. Humphries 114.4–15–424–18–23.55; M. J. Lowndes 72.4–9–323–10–32.30.

IPSWICH SCHOOL

Played 13: Won 3, Lost 8, Drawn 2. Abandoned 1

Master i/c: P. Rees   Cricket professional: K. Winder

Batting—*J. J. Zagni 12–2–400–80–40.00; A. M. Paul 13–2–341–94*–31.00; R. Heap 13–2–331–86–30.09; R. J. Beales 9–2–179–79*–25.57; N. J. Gregory 11–2–226–72–25.11.

Bowling—J. J. Zagni 143–51–369–22–16.77; B. J. Gibbons 152–38–382–19–20.10; N. Horne 144–31–373–18–20.72.

KIMBOLTON SCHOOL

Played 15: Won 2, Lost 6, Drawn 7

Master i/c: T. J. Williams

Batting—S. Moffat 14–1–417–67–32.07; *R. M. Godden 15–0–409–59–27.26; I. A. Goldberg 15–0–364–55–24.26; A. W. Ramply 15–2–260–38–20.00; D. M. Baragwanath 9–1–120–38–15.00; A. D. Moffat 15–0–147–26–9.80.

Bowling—R. D. Ward 166.4–34–497–21–23.66; J. P. Hurley 134–21–394–16–24.62; A. W. Ramply 174.5–46–575–23–25.00; S. Moffat 146.3–26–505–15–33.66.

KING EDWARD'S SCHOOL, BIRMINGHAM

Played 18: Won 3, Lost 4, Drawn 11. Abandoned 4

Master i/c: D. H. Benson   Cricket professional: P. J. Knowles

Batting—N. Martin 15–0–720–154–48.00; P. N. J. Inglis 16–2–640–101*–45.71; A. P. Hitchins 18–0–550–62–30.55; C. Plant 17–3–302–60–21.57; *M. J. Hills 17–3–211–32–15.07; J. E. Pritchard 10–2–138–53–17.25; P. H. Henrick 10–1–123–41–13.66; P. Ashton 13–3–103–34–10.30.

Bowling—C. Plant 248.4–71–638–30–21.26; W. T. M. Pike 171–45–520–23–22.60; J. E. Pritchard 83.4–20–280–12–23.33; I. A. McNeish 80.1–25–260–11–23.63.

KING EDWARD VI COLLEGE, STOURBRIDGE

Played 16: Won 5, Lost 4, Drawn 7. Abandoned 2

Master i/c: M. L. Ryan

Batting—*C. M. Tolley 13–4–646–118*–71.77; A. W. Harris 14–4–352–51*–35.20; S. Mees 13–4–243–58–27.00; M. Jones 8–2–162–85*–27.00; R. J. George 13–0–289–60–22.23.

Bowling—T. R. Hall 58.3–20–111–12–9.25; C. M. Tolley 118.3–30–298–21–14.19; B. Darby 94.4–29–281–16–17.56; J. I. Hill 100–30–319–17–18.76; A. K. Fradgley 105–23–292–10–29.20.

KING EDWARD VI SCHOOL, SOUTHAMPTON

Played 20: Won 5, Lost 3, Drawn 12. Abandoned 5

Master i/c: R. J. Putt

Batting—*P. A. Arnold 19–6–543–56*–41.76; M. A. Noyce 17–2–479–110*–31.93; P. D. Chrispin 9–3–144–35*–24.00; J. A. Shepherd 8–1–144–55–20.57; S. A. Fisher 19–4–249–67*–16.60; P. A. W. Holden 15–1–223–33–15.92; J. E. Shepherd 15–4–154–48–14.00; A. S. Boyle 10–1–123–37–13.66.

Bowling—A. J. Donaldson 157.7–42–454–35–12.97; P. D. Chrispin 110–23–341–19–17.94; B. D. Godber 90–24–236–13–18.15; J. E. Shepherd 172.2–37–502–22–22.81; J. J. McGill 80–15–323–11–29.36.

KING EDWARD VII SCHOOL, LYTHAM

Played 20: Won 9, Lost 3, Drawn 8

Master i/c: S. T. Godfrey

Batting—*D. K. Chrispin 20–2–620–100*–34.44; M. C. Cope 18–2–516–81–32.25; A. D. Cooper 14–1–416–72–32.00; J. A. Greenslade 17–3–232–64–16.57; J. C. Friedenthal 13–3–151–36–15.10; M. P. Mullarkey 17–3–197–41*–14.07; E. J. McKnight 12–1–122–23–12.20.

Bowling—D. K. Chrispin 134.2–36–362–35–10.34; S. J. Stammers 176.3–49–409–34–12.02; I. C. Ball 196.1–66–406–26–15.61; P. M. Robbins 86.5–30–225–13–17.30; J. N. Derbyshire 51–7–207–11–18.81; M. P. Mullarkey 115–19–398–20–19.90.

KING'S COLLEGE, TAUNTON

Played 14: Won 7, Lost 1, Drawn 6. Abandoned 1

Master i/c: P. A. Dossett   Cricket professional: R. E. Marshall

Batting—S. D. Painter 13–8–345–67*–69.00; A. J. Berry 13–4–333–85–37.00; M. B. Taylor 7–1–146–77–24.33; *R. G. Twose 13–0–247–72–19.00; N. Dyer 13–0–182–51–14.00; N. Coulson 12–2–101–32–10.10.

Bowling—R. G. Twose 285.1–91–629–44–14.29; G. K. Barber 200.1–52–464–29–16.00; N. Keyte 77–23–179–10–17.90; D. J. Battishill 98–25–295–14–21.07.

KING'S COLLEGE SCHOOL, WIMBLEDON

Played 14: Won 4, Lost 5, Drawn 5. Abandoned 2

Master i/c: A. G. P. Lang   Cricket professional: R. A. Dare

Batting—R. M. Wight 13–3–466–94–46.60; *A. D. Mallinson 13–1–289–101–24.08; R. M. Hussey 13–0–311–99–23.92; N. R. H. Cartwright 9–1–138–47–17.25; J. H. Cantor 9–2–116–27*–16.57; K. P. Robert 13–1–185–40–15.41; E. J. Heaver 13–0–174–45–13.38.

Bowling—R. M. Wight 193.4–45–657–38–17.28; J. Q. Cooper 109.2–25–364–19–19.15; T. A. Preston 78–8–339–16–21.18; M. S. Raynsford 112–19–426–11–38.72.

KING'S SCHOOL, BRUTON

Played 12: Won 2, Lost 4, Drawn 6. Abandoned 4

Master i/c: D. C. Elstone

Batting—C. Cowell 12–2–326–82*–32.60; W. Campbell-Stanway 9–3–136–40–22.66; R. Browne 12–1–242–54–22.00; P. Lee 12–1–228–45–20.72; A. Gent 8–2–110–42–18.33; M. Walton 12–0–141–36–11.75.

Bowling—N. Randall 108–34–261–25–10.44; C. Cowell 122–28–344–18–19.11; M. Walton 113–25–324–14–23.14; *S. Griffin 93.4–23–270–11–24.54.

THE KING'S SCHOOL, CANTERBURY

Played 14: Won 5, Lost 1, Drawn 8

Master i/c: A. W. Dyer   Cricket professional: D. V. P. Wright

Batting—*M. B. Ryeland 15–4–389–76–35.36; P. P. Lacamp 15–2–451–81–34.69; J. P. Taylor 13–0–324–77–24.92; I. D. S. Linney 12–0–152–33–12.66; D. M. Ives 13–0–162–30–12.46; D. G. Stocks 12–1–114–27–10.36.

Bowling—J. P. Taylor 200.1–88–378–34–11.11; M. B. Ryeland 222.5–58–575–38–15.13; M. Durham 116.1–19–378–17–22.23; A. J. H. Brown 91.5–14–319–14–22.78.

THE KING'S SCHOOL, CHESTER

Played 20: Won 9, Lost 3, Drawn 8. Abandoned 3

Master i/c: K. H. Mellor

Batting—N. J. Brown 13–4–418–109*–46.44; C. A. Lewis 20–2–471–90–26.16; G. W. Jones 8–2–132–40–22.00; *A. J. Martin 18–1–369–100–21.70; C. G. Oswald 19–2–363–61–21.35; T. R. Blackmore 19–5–242–31*–17.28; A. R. H. Mais 15–5–150–63–15.00; J. S. W. Hawkins 13–2–116–24–10.54.

Bowling—C. G. Oswald 114.2–43–252–27–9.33; J. S. W. Hawkins 175–46–370–33–11.21; R. J. Willis 85.5–22–212–18–11.77; O. C. A. Read 63–13–164–13–12.61; G. S. Powell 153.5–29–423–29–14.58; D. B. Claringdon 174.5–40–509–18–28.27.

THE KING'S SCHOOL, MACCLESFIELD

Played 22: Won 4, Lost 6, Drawn 12. Abandoned 2

Master i/c: D. M. Harbord

Batting—R. Stott 20–1–626–92–32.94; J. Burdekin 21–3–430–46–23.88; S. White 13–5–162–51–20.25; S. Swindells 20–1–380–59–20.00; C. Fitches 19–2–321–61–18.88; A. Palin 16–0–232–55–14.50; A. Bates 17–1–169–48–10.56; R. Wright 15–4–113–36*–10.27; E. Fitzgerald 18–4–128–35–9.14.

Bowling—R. Stott 44-4-197-12-16.41; S. White 200-46-596-26-22.92; J. Burdekin 196-47-584-25-23.36; A. Palin 146-23-495-20-24.75; C. Fitches 276-64-863-34-25.38; P. Hammond 131-15-509-13-39.15.

KING'S SCHOOL, ROCHESTER

Played 15: Won 9, Lost 4, Drawn 2. Abandoned 2

Master i/c: J. S. Irvine

Batting—S. I. Andrews 15-2-451-126*-34.69; *M. P. Mernagh 11-1-321-73-32.10; R. N. Eastburn 12-1-345-100*-31.36; M. R. Eastburn 11-4-146-27*-20.85; D. C. Walsh 11-0-220-44-20.00; R. J. Bailey 10-3-122-50*-17.42; S. J. Chambers 12-1-160-33-14.54.

Bowling—M. P. Mernagh 227.2-65-514-51-10.07; I. J. Nightingale 230.3-80-534-47-11.36.

KING'S SCHOOL, WORCESTER

Played 18: Won 4, Lost 4, Drawn 10

Master i/c: D. P. Iddon

Batting—S. J. Jevons 13-2-345-72-31.36; T. A. Preston 17-1-468-87-29.25; *J. A. Cooper 17-3-324-99-23.14; C. P. Burnham 10-3-151-66*-21.57; R. G. Tomlinson 6-1-104-46-20.80; D. L. Evans 15-1-272-55*-19.42; J. R. I. Mills 16-0-242-64-15.12; C. M. Rogers 12-1-150-51-13.63.

Bowling—S. J. Jevons 121.3-27-349-24-14.54; R. L. Brown 161.1-29-547-27-20.25; A. P. Blackmore 154-34-485-21-23.09; C. P. Burnham 119.2-26-368-14-26.28; J. R. I. Mills 111.5-26-394-14-28.14.

KING WILLIAM'S COLLEGE, ISLE OF MAN

Played 15: Won 2, Lost 9, Drawn 4

Master i/c: T. M. Manning   Cricket professional: D. Mark

Batting—J. C. Radford 15-1-492-128-35.14; *S. W. Ellis 16-1-474-102-31.60; R. F. M. Cook 9-0-249-107-27.66; M. F. Batey 11-1-227-64-22.70; P. W. Townsend 16-1-285-86-19.00; A. P. Woodward 16-0-204-52-12.75.

Bowling—S. W. Ellis 293-50-944-49-19.26; J. C. Radford 185.1-35-656-21-31.23.

KINGSTON GRAMMAR SCHOOL

Played 19: Won 1, Lost 13, Drawn 5

Master i/c: R. J. Sturgeon

Batting—*S. Kumar 19-1-463-68*-25.72; D. J. Railton 19-0-405-61-21.31; N. J. Stafford 18-3-282-37*-18.80; S. J. Dixon 16-9-110-18*-15.71; R. J. Williams 18-2-217-36-13.56; C. M. J. Hancock 19-0-255-66-13.42; D. C. Newhouse 17-1-153-42-9.56; R. A. Iley 18-0-164-27-9.11.

Bowling—N. J. Stafford 152.3-18-534-26-20.53; S. J. Dixon 158.1-32-479-23-20.82; R. J. Williams 151-24-509-24-21.20; S. Kumar 217.1-25-736-28-26.28; J. Weston 102.2-16-456-13-35.07.

KINGSWOOD SCHOOL

Played 13: Won 5, Lost 4, Drawn 4. Abandoned 2

Master i/c: R. J. Lewis

Batting—R. W. Lewis 12-2-524-107*-52.40; R. A. P. Kent 11-2-264-92*-29.33; R. D. Udy 11-1-211-57-21.10; C. N. J. Law 10-1-130-47-14.44.

Bowling—R. W. Lewis 107–26–325–21–15.47; M. A. J. Earp 119.4–22–359–21–17.09; T. Gleghorn 103.4–14–380–21–18.09; R. D. Udy 77–8–300–13–23.07.

LANCING COLLEGE

Played 17: Won 9, Lost 4, Drawn 4. Abandoned 2

Master i/c: E. A. Evans-Jones   Cricket professional: R. G. Davies

Batting—S. N. S. Message 7–0–235–75–33.57; A. J. Cunningham 16–2–445–92–31.78; *S. B. Higgo 14–3–280–58–25.45; J. B. Higgo 16–1–305–68–20.33; G. J. Atkins 12–2–176–45–17.60; D. A. Beater 13–1–190–47–15.83; T. E. J. Selmon 10–0–134–35–13.40; T. P. Mackenzie 12–4–101–35*–12.62; P. M. Rimmer 12–2–126–31*–12.60; W. A. Gooda 14–2–145–36–12.08.

Bowling—T. P. Mackenzie 130.1–37–354–30–11.80; S. F. Cloke 203.2–33–524–44–11.90; T. W. Poerscourt-Egerton 146–41–368–25–14.72; A. J. Cunningham 137.4–26–421–21–20.04; W. A. Gooda 101–37–271–13–20.84.

LEEDS GRAMMAR SCHOOL

Played 18: Won 1, Lost 5, Drawn 12

Master i/c: I. R. Briars

Batting—J. R. Goldthorp 17–3–634–118–45.28; G. O. J. Hill 16–3–420–81*–32.30; G. R. Tyler 18–0–334–65–18.55; J. F. Harrison 16–0–288–73–18.00; C. M. Siddle 15–0–243–60–16.20; D. Hyde 17–2–242–60*–16.13; A. J. McFarlane 10–0–151–38–15.10; D. M. Payne 16–4–140–53–11.66.

Bowling—J. Shaw 23–2–130–12–10.83; C. M. Siddle 164–43–513–34–15.08; A. J. Metcalfe 116–22–404–18–22.44; G. R. Tyler 182–34–726–28–25.92; I. D. Johnson 89–11–438–12–36.50.

LEIGHTON PARK SCHOOL

Played 21: Won 12, Lost 5, Drawn 4. Abandoned 1

Master i/c: R. C. Boyd   Cricket professional: M. Lickley

Batting—J. R. Wood 12–5–926–202*–132.28; J. C. Berridge 6–2–225–100*–56.25; S. K. Bhundia 11–1–241–42–24.10; J. D. Thomas 13–1–221–51–18.41; R. S. E. Sykes 10–2–146–61*–18.25; F. W. Brazel 11–1–169–77–16.90; *J. S. Shingles 11–1–167–43–16.70; A. D. S. Park 12–1–153–36–13.90; M. Harris 17–2–178–33–11.86; P. J. Newell Price 15–2–150–47–11.53.

Bowling—J. R. Wood 101–20–252–21–12.00; P. J. Newell Price 188–45–523–41–12.75; J. D. Thomas 130–26–429–30–14.30; J. S. Shingles 48–10–169–11–15.36; N. L. Stevens 120–15–451–27–16.70.

THE LEYS SCHOOL

Played 18: Won 3, Lost 10, Drawn 5. Abandoned 3

Master i/c: P. R. Chamberlain   Cricket professional: D. Gibson

Batting—*S. P. Barker 16–0–303–79–18.93; N. R. Lankester 16–0–297–51–18.56; R. E. Symes 16–0–296–71–18.50; C. W. Barker 7–0–122–42–17.42; P. R. Searle 10–0–173–71*–17.30; D. O. Solomon 15–0–199–42–13.26; S. M. Baker 14–2–157–26–13.08; M. D. R. Fairey 16–0–194–47–12.12; A. D. Terry 15–1–101–24–7.21.

Bowling—P. R. Searle 43–10–130–10–13.00; N. R. Lankester 151.5–34–507–35–14.48; S. P. Barker 218–44–634–29–21.86; S. C. Hawtrey-Woore 82.1–21–290–13–22.30; A. D. Terry 226.2–45–487–20–24.35.

LLANDOVERY COLLEGE

Played 14: Won 3, Lost 7, Drawn 4

Master i/c: T. G. Marks

Batting—K. J. Whiskerd 13–1–331–87*–27.58; N. G. Phillips 14–0–152–35–10.85; D. J. R. Evans 14–0–147–43–10.50; I. C. Hughes 12–0–117–36–9.75; S. Smith-Wrench 13–0–124–34–9.53; R. A. R. Evans 14–0–106–51*–7.57.

Bowling—R. S. Williams 103.4–36–226–15–15.06; *G. H. M. Forster 66–11–193–11–17.54; R. A. R. Evans 89–20–242–12–20.16; D. J. R. Evans 87.5–10–402–16–25.12.

LORD WANDSWORTH COLLEGE

Played 8: Won 1, Lost 2, Drawn 5. Abandoned 4

Master i/c: A. G. Whibley

Batting—*D. R. W. Wood 8–1–312–112*–44.57; C. R. W. Gould 7–0–212–78–30.28; S. H. Blows 8–1–191–116*–27.28; P. S. Roades 7–1–109–44–18.16.

Bowling—S. P. Lawrence 68–10–241–10–24.10.

LORD WILLIAMS'S SCHOOL

Played 11: Won 4, Lost 1, Drawn 6. Abandoned 3

Masters i/c: A. M. Brannan and G. M. D. Howat

Batting—R. J. Carr 9–1–398–93*–49.75; D. J. Brooks 8–1–230–45*–32.85; S. M. Alexander 7–0–137–34–19.57; R. J. Gregory 7–0–132–36–18.85; T. Fairn 8–2–102–33–17.00.

Bowling—R. J. Carr 187.2–37–521–29–17.96; S. M. Alexander 93.5–14–332–11–30.18.

LORETTO SCHOOL

Played 14: Won 3, Lost 0, Drawn 11. Abandoned 1

Master i/c: R. G. Selley

Batting—R. C. Fraser 10–0–281–71–28.10; T. R. McCreath 14–0–333–97–23.78; M. R. Hinton 12–2–231–91–23.10; A. G. Shepherd-Cross 14–0–302–64–21.57; A. T. G. Craig 13–4–186–41–20.66.

Bowling—A. T. G. Craig 162–31–360–28–12.85; M. C. Eglinton 233–64–600–39–15.38; J. A. N. Macaulay 169–43–440–22–20.00.

MAGDALEN COLLEGE SCHOOL

Played 17: Won 4, Lost 4, Drawn 9. Abandoned 4

Master i/c: N. A. Rollings

Batting—A. D. Redman 14–4–344–60*–34.40; J. C. K. Lewis 15–6–286–53*–31.77; *M. E. Mackinlay 15–0–420–79–28.00; T. J. Stockwin 16–1–367–60–24.46; J. M. Hutton 15–2–234–92–18.00; J. A. Turner 12–2–176–39–17.60.

Bowling—S. N. Webb 88.2–7–353–24–14.70; J. C. K. Lewis 150.4–34–444–26–17.07; T. E. J. Waters 105–21–293–17–17.23; M. E. Mackinlay 63–11–204–10–20.40; R. J. Suckling 77.1–11–277–13–21.30; A. L. C. Winchester 154.5–25–543–24–22.62.

MALVERN COLLEGE

Played 19: Won 4, Lost 6, Drawn 9. Abandoned 4

Master i/c: A. J. Murtagh   Cricket professional: R. W. Tolchard

Batting—J. R. Wileman 18–3–606–81–40.40; J. R. Rawes 18–1–415–78–24.41; I. K. Timberlake 14–2–266–63–22.16; A. M. Searle 16–2–301–46–21.50; *M. C. A. Pougatch 17–4–273–30–21.00; N. W. G. Gough 7–0–128–32–18.28; G. N. Lunt 16–2–238–49*–17.00; E. G. Maughan 16–2–185–41–13.21.

Bowling—P. M. Montague-Fuller 126.3–29–326–20–16.30; H. C. Douglas-Pennant 248.2–48–575–28–20.53; I. P. G. Elliott 111.2–16–449–20–22.45; M. J. Barrett-Greene 204.1–62–521–23–22.65; A. M. Searle 59.1–15–229–10–22.90; G. N. Lunt 183.5–34–625–24–26.04.

MANCHESTER GRAMMAR SCHOOL

Played 21: Won 15, Lost 0, Drawn 6. Abandoned 1

Master i/c: D. Moss

Batting—M. A. Crawley 18–8–1,123–110*–112.30; G. Yates 13–5–636–207–79.50; *M. A. Atherton 15–2–627–99–48.23; P. M. Crawley 12–1–254–57–23.09; A. B. Gaskarth 12–5–109–30*–15.57; N. W. Davenport 12–2–153–53–15.30.

Bowling—P. D. E. Richards 134.1–55–274–30–9.13; M. A. Atherton 307.4–99–622–50–12.44; G. Yates 249.3–92–466–34–13.70; M. A. Crawley 269.5–75–605–31–19.51.

MARLBOROUGH COLLEGE

Played 15: Won 2, Lost 5, Drawn 8. Abandoned 2

Master i/c: P. J. Lough   Cricket professional: R. R. Savage

Batting—A. J. Robinson 17–1–562–104–35.12; G. W. Barker 17–1–546–107*–34.12; S. C. G. Thomson 7–2–148–39–29.60; *A. J. Fane 15–0–400–87–26.66; J. S. Kerr 17–2–384–65–25.60; M. R. Sidley 15–4–203–43–18.45; A. B. Robb 12–2–111–32–11.10.

Bowling—A. B. Robb 187–44–632–26–24.30; S. F. C. Pole 190.4–33–696–28–24.85; S. Moorhead 149.5–16–691–18–38.38.

MERCHANT TAYLORS' SCHOOL, CROSBY

Played 18: Won 4, Lost 9, Drawn 5. Abandoned 3

Master i/c: Rev. D. A. Smith   Cricket professional: G. E. Trim

Batting—R. W. Glynne-Jones 16–0–414–115–25.87; M. W. Appleton 17–1–350–100–21.87; *N. A. Hanley 15–2–249–54*–19.15; N. M. Dixon 16–0–271–79–16.93; P. M. Snell 14–3–184–47–16.72; A. J. Dawson 15–4–146–57*–13.27; M. Watkinson 14–1–139–48–10.69.

Bowling—S. Bell 34–10–114–10–11.40; N. A. Hanley 117.5–19–426–20–21.30; A. J. Dawson 82–13–317–14–22.64; M. Watkinson 167.4–30–553–19–29.10.

MERCHANT TAYLORS' SCHOOL, NORTHWOOD

Played 19: Won 6, Lost 2, Drawn 11. Abandoned 5

Master i/c: W. M. B. Ritchie

Batting—A. J. Teskey 18–1–561–72–33.00; A. P. Solomons 17–5–318–60*–26.50; A. Coker 19–0–501–75–26.36; N. J. Boxall 17–3–366–51*–26.14; J. L. Hampel 18–3–369–64–24.60; D. Cornelius 14–2–262–54*–21.83; P. K. Alsop 9–3–116–38*–19.33; D. Bowden 10–1–146–36–16.22; *D. W. R. Wiles 13–3–100–38*–10.00.

Bowling—D. W. R. Wiles 309–71–808–48–16.83; D. Bowden 63–16–222–13–17.07; J. L. Hampel 244–67–621–34–18.26; A. P. Thompson 234.5–54–623–34–18.32.

MERCHISTON CASTLE SCHOOL

Played 12: Won 4, Lost 0, Drawn 8. Abandoned 1

Masters i/c: M. C. L. Gill and S. J. Dight

Batting—M. E. R. Paton 14–1–379–83–29.15; *L. M. Mair 13–2–266–52–24.18; A. J. K. Wilson 11–0–241–41–21.90; N. R. Ballantyne 14–1–223–66–17.15; P. Walton 12–1–110–44*–10.00.

Bowling—S. J. K. Laird 84.5–22–199–18–11.05; B. D. Cameron 202.2–55–441–33–13.36; N. R. Ballantyne 94.2–23–255–19–13.42; I. W. Hunter 145–30–390–22–17.72; C. F. Lyon 149–45–346–17–20.35.

MILLFIELD SCHOOL

Played 12: Won 8, Lost 0, Drawn 4. Abandoned 4

Master i/c: F. N. Fenner   Cricket professional: G. Wilson

Batting—*J. C. M. Atkinson 8–2–374–135–62.33; I. J. H. Smith 9–2–255–103*–36.42; R. W. Hill 9–1–278–60–34.75; H. R. J. Trump 12–2–285–88–28.50; P. J. Stephenson 8–0–202–74–25.25; P. A. Baverstock 8–1–173–72–24.71; A. R. Phillips 7–2–113–51–22.60; J. H. A. Biggs 7–0–151–66–21.57; R. J. Turner 13–2–168–67–15.27.

Bowling—J. M. Box 39–11–106–12–8.83; D. J. Knight 67.4–21–163–13–12.53; J. C. M. Atkinson 88–24–191–15–12.73; H. R. J. Trump 182–61–424–27–15.70; P. J. Stephenson 128–34–322–14–23.00; A. R. Phillips 111.3–31–279–12–23.25.

MILTON ABBEY SCHOOL

Played 10: Won 2, Lost 2, Drawn 6. Abandoned 3

Master i/c: S. T. Smail

Batting—R. J. Jessurun 6–3–112–39*–37.33; J. M. A. Boscawen 10–0–241–56–24.10; B. A. Murray 10–1–203–54–22.55; E. S. H. Spicer 10–1–160–64*–17.77; R. C. Hunnisett 10–0–103–47–10.30.

Bowling—G. Cameron-Clarke 116.3–19–366–24–15.25; R. F. Jessurun 93.5–16–298–18–16.55.

NORWICH SCHOOL

Played 16: Won 7, Lost 1, Drawn 8. Abandoned 3

Master i/c: P. J. Henderson

Batting—J. G. Crane 15–3–415–81–34.58; J. R. Marsh 15–4–315–69–28.63; S. O'Callaghan 11–1–263–64–26.30; *N. J. E. Foster 14–2–286–59–23.83.

Bowling—R. J. Wilson 132–27–396–28–14.14; J. R. Marsh 146.4–31–409–24–17.04; D. P. Heath 97–25–306–17–18.00; P. D. Lee 108–23–351–19–18.47; N. J. E. Foster 135.1–31–434–23–18.86.

NOTTINGHAM HIGH SCHOOL

Played 19: Won 6, Lost 1, Drawn 12. Abandoned 1

Master i/c: D. A. Slack   Cricket professional: H. Latchman

Batting—M. Saxelby 17–2–864–138*–57.60; N. A. Hunt 16–6–510–98–51.00; P. R. D. Briggs 20–3–638–133*–37.52; J. W. A. Morris 8–5–101–39–33.66; T. J. Deas 15–3–350–58*–29.16; R. I. Atkinson 14–1–327–66–25.15; R. J. Crampton 12–3–161–25*–17.88; R. L. C. Jones 12–2–169–52–16.90; *A. J. Floyd 14–1–189–67–14.53.

Bowling—J. G. Hampson 40–10–115–12–9.58; M. Saxelby 184.1–54–403–27–14.92; T. J. Deas 311.3–93–828–50–16.56; R. L. C. Jones 86.5–15–295–14–21.07; J. W. A. Morris 167.2–25–560–24–23.33; A. J. Belfield 109.1–15–416–14–29.71.

OAKHAM SCHOOL

Played 18: Won 3, Lost 1, Drawn 14

Master i/c: J. Wills

Batting—D. M. Robjohns 18–3–902–121–60.13; D. J. K. Webb 16–1–525–109*–35.00; B. James 6–0–159–61–26.50; A. S. England 18–2–355–54–22.18; F. Cooke 12–2–209–56–20.90; C. N. Wood 13–3–140–25*–14.00; P. J. R. Neild 13–2–29–100–9.09.

Bowling—S. V. Aldis 213.3–38–642–39–16.46; P. J. R. Neild 212.3–55–605–27–22.40; A. S. England 118.2–25–347–10–34.70.

OUNDLE SCHOOL

Played 17: Won 2, Lost 8, Drawn 7. Abandoned 4

Master i/c: M. J. Goatly   Cricket professional: A. Watkins

Batting—*C. D. Squire 17–3–535–79–38.21; T. I. Macmillan 16–0–591–156–36.93; A. R. Turner 12–1–299–69–27.18; P. D. Eakins 12–1–245–37–22.27; C. A. Barraclough 8–0–147–62–18.37; J. A. S. Shervington 11–2–145–65–16.11.

Bowling—R. H. J. Jenkins 207–39–665–36–18.47; R. B. Waters 92–14–287–14–20.50; A. J. Douglas 118–20–405–14–28.92; J. A. S. Shervington 73–7–301–10–30.10; A. G. Macmillan 85–6–431–11–39.18; E. Riddington 139–17–536–13–41.23.

THE PERSE SCHOOL

Played 19: Won 2, Lost 6, Drawn 11. Abandoned 3

Master i/c: A. W. Billinghurst   Cricket professional: D. C. Collard

Batting—N. M. Law 18–0–535–93–29.72; *T. A. G. Miller 17–0–445–88–26.17; D. R. S. Woodhouse 7–1–132–44–22.00; J. P. Toner 15–1–296–53–21.14; J. G. S. Agar 7–0–135–44–19.28; T. J. H. Moynihan 14–1–200–79–15.38; P. J. A. Alexander 15–1–205–44–14.64; I. R. Styan 16–0–230–47–14.37.

Bowling—N. M. Law 124–28–434–19–22.84; I. R. Styan 229–62–654–27–24.22; P. A. Bailey 97.3–18–339–12–28.25; T. D. F. Charlton 137–13–480–12–40.00; P. J. A. Alexander 173.1–26–659–16–41.18; M. A. Melford 178.2–41–530–11–48.18.

PLYMOUTH COLLEGE
Played 16: Won 6, Lost 4, Drawn 6. Abandoned 1

Master i/c: T. J. Stevens

Batting—*S. A. Stevenson 11–1–391–77–39.10; S. Summers 12–2–291–79–29.10; A. D. Kerr 9–3–129–44–21.50; G. W. Waldock 11–0–233–69–21.18; C. D. Colgate 11–1–210–39–21.00; S. A. Lucas 11–3–116–26*–14.50.

Bowling—J. Potts 95–19–245–24–10.20; B. S. Fox 59–8–151–14–10.78; C. D. L. Vinson 71–26–177–14–12.64; S. A. Lucas 122–35–288–22–13.09; R. N. Furneaux 92–19–302–22–13.72.

POCKLINGTON SCHOOL
Played 23: Won 16, Lost 2, Drawn 5

Master i/c: D. Nuttall

Batting—S. A. Clarke 16–3–444–76–34.15; M. J. Baker 23–2–629–73*–29.95; T. P. B. Balderson 21–3–480–67*–26.66; J. E. Haynes 22–1–444–84–21.14; *J. D. Nuttall 15–6–182–43*–20.22; J. R. L. Brown 11–3–120–31–15.00; A. T. Pettinger 17–2–219–49*–14.60; P. M. Lee 17–2–170–58–11.33; P. J. Kemp 13–1–136–27–11.33; U. R. D. Alexander 13–4–102–26*–11.33.

Bowling—J. D. Nuttall 261–88–527–60–8.78; J. R. L. Brown 181–61–387–38–10.18; T. P. B. Balderson 305–86–748–64–11.68.

PRIOR PARK COLLEGE
Played 12: Won 1, Lost 3, Drawn 8. Abandoned 5

Master i/c: J. J. Gidney   Cricket professional: P. B. Fisher

Batting—M. I. Woodhouse 10–3–231–76*–33.00; B. D. Moorhouse 12–1–349–91–31.72; J. I. Reid 10–2–244–69–30.50; I. P. Fox 8–1–192–60–27.42; J. L. Powell 7–2–135–50*–27.00; A. D. Hadley 8–0–179–38–22.37.

Bowling—J. L. Powell 103–24–368–23–16.00; B. D. Moorhouse 70–12–265–13–20.38.

QUEEN ELIZABETH GRAMMAR SCHOOL, WAKEFIELD
Played 12: Won 4, Lost 2, Drawn 6. Abandoned 4

Master i/c: T. Barker   Cricket professional: V. Harihiran

Batting—S. K. Das 10–3–259–64–37.00; *A. M. Smith 9–2–248–88*–35.42; J. Wild 8–4–124–38*–31.00; S. Barnsley 11–0–208–67–18.90; C. J. Robinson 10–3–100–34–14.28; M. Whitmore 10–1–119–41*–13.22.

Bowling—P. R. Worth 81.5–22–224–18–12.44; A. Wilson 70–15–192–14–13.71; J. M. Booth 69.4–14–191–13–14.69; A. M. Smith 93–22–213–11–19.36; J. Wild 94–21–280–12–23.33.

QUEEN'S COLLEGE, TAUNTON
Played 15: Won 6, Lost 2, Drawn 6, Tied 1

Master i/c: J. W. Davies

Batting—J. J. Wilson 12–3–371–62–41.22; D. N. A. Essien 13–0–429–95–33.00; *A. Tanner 15–1–337–109*–24.07; M. R. Scholfield 12–0–270–65–22.50; C. A. E. Essien 13–5–158–58*–19.75; D. Abell 14–2–229–62–19.08.

Bowling—D. N. A. Essien 198.5–57–424–37–11.45; C. A. E. Essien 172.1–38–465–36–12.91; D. Knight 109–46–205–12–17.08; A. Tanner 104–35–278–14–19.85.

RADLEY COLLEGE

Played 15: Won 8, Lost 1, Drawn 6

Master i/c: G. de W. Waller   Cricket professionals: A. G. Robinson and A. R. Wagner

Batting—C. H. H. Pegg 15–6–447–101–49.66; M. J. Lowrey 11–4–321–102*–45.85; J. G. K. Pearce-Smith 13–1–293–59–24.41; J. S. Myers 14–2–222–57*–18.50; J. O. D. Evans 8–2–108–41–18.00; *J. C. Smellie 11–1–164–54–16.40.

Bowling—R. D. Stormonth-Darling 269–99–531–40–13.27; J. S. Myers 57–14–187–14–13.35; M. J. Lowrey 200–67–433–32–13.53; H. W. Astor 176–50–491–21–23.38.

RATCLIFFE COLLEGE

Played 17: Won 4, Lost 2, Drawn 11. Abandoned 1

Master i/c: C. W. Swan

Batting—*J. Farnell 17–3–510–103*–36.42; R. D. Roopnarinesingh 11–4–200–67*–28.57; R. J. J. d'Mello 17–2–377–60–25.13; P. F. Copp 17–1–296–92–18.50.

Bowling—P. A. Mestecky 259–72–692–58–11.93; J. Farnell 90–11–333–26–12.80; A. W. Baxter 86–20–258–17–15.17; R. J. J. d'Mello 67–13–228–12–19.00.

READING SCHOOL

Played 15: Won 5, Lost 4, Drawn 6. Abandoned 2

Master i/c: R. G. Owen   Cricket professional: A. Dindar

Batting—T. J. C. Dance 2–1–157–98*–157.00; J. N. S. Hampton 11–1–325–55–32.50; *J. E. Grimsdale 15–1–402–104–28.71; O. D. Beckett 15–0–397–86–26.46; J. S. Pritchard 13–1–230–56–19.16; R. M. Hawkins 12–2–140–27–14.00; P. R. Auty 14–0–190–64–13.57.

Bowling—J. S. Pritchard 220–48–598–44–13.59; J. N. S. Hampton 59–6–300–11–27.27; D. J. Whitwell 136–21–540–17–31.76.

REED'S SCHOOL

Played 16: Won 6, Lost 3, Drawn 7. Abandoned 1

Master i/c: G. R. Martin

Batting—J. D. F. Paris 16–6–751–119*–75.10; C. A. Potts 13–4–434–84–48.22; T. T. Oliver 7–4–104–30–34.66; L. E. Jones 16–2–438–73–31.28; *S. H. K. Maddock 15–2–228–45–17.53; M. R. Viner 11–2–142–44*–15.77; S. Shiells 14–0–142–32–10.14.

Bowling—T. T. Oliver 241.2–54–772–39–19.79; R. Taylor 69.1–17–215–10–21.50; R. Pakenham 205–47–751–29–25.89; A. J. Masters 144.4–37–479–18–26.61.

REIGATE GRAMMAR SCHOOL

Played 18: Won 4, Lost 5, Drawn 9. Abandoned 3

Master i/c: D. C. R. Jones   Cricket professional: H. Newton

Batting—*A. S. Clayton 18–0–545–79–30.27; P. J. Brookes 11–4–181–78–25.85; S. J. Virley 19–1–387–74*–21.50; J. S. Burrow 18–0–372–46–20.66; T. Humphries 19–0–356–67–18.73; C. S. Bates 18–3–272–39*–18.13; D. M. Gregory 12–1–189–78–17.18.

Bowling—R. J. Sullivan 94–17–328–20–16.40; P. J. Brookes 139.2–30–431–21–20.52; M. T. Holman 258.3–51–809–38–21.28; A. S. Clayton 111.3–12–451–19–23.73; D. N. Abbott 105.2–15–402–16–25.12.

REPTON SCHOOL

Played 19: Won 3, Lost 5, Drawn 11. Abandoned 3

Master i/c: M. Stones   Cricket professional: M. K. Kettle

Batting—C. E. Wall 17–3–650–98–46.42; *G. M. Cook 17–2–554–111*–36.93; A. J. Needler 7–2–101–51–20.20; M. W. Gresley 14–1–259–73–19.92; S. C. Hall 14–4–185–51–18.50; J. H. Sookias 17–0–301–60–17.70; R. W. A. Pyne 10–3–122–47*–17.42; M. J. Priestley 14–0–239–54–17.07; D. J. Anderson 14–2–171–38–14.25.

Bowling—R. W. A. Pyne 242–60–753–47–16.02; P. J. A. Heathcote 62–12–198–12–16.50; D. J. Anderson 230–52–671–37–18.13; C. E. Wall 168–32–542–26–20.84; G. M. Cook 86–16–264–10–26.40.

ROSSALL SCHOOL

Played 17: Won 3, Lost 8, Drawn 6. Abandoned 1

Master i/c: R. J. Clapp

Batting—C. D. Foster 17–0–366–71–21.52; P. L. Smith 10–1–179–64–19.88; P. A. Clayton 17–2–293–72–19.53; *P. Cartwright 17–0–316–86–18.58; A. G. Smith 11–2–133–28–14.77; D. M. Indo 16–4–166–43–13.83; B. M. Evans 10–1–113–29–12.55; J. G. Brown 14–2–137–36–11.41.

Bowling—M. Beech 85–26–193–12–16.08; A. G. Smith 132–33–339–17–19.94; P. A. Clayton 218–47–664–32–20.75; W. E. Hayes 77–16–283–10–28.30.

THE ROYAL GRAMMAR SCHOOL, GUILDFORD

Played 19: Won 10, Lost 4, Drawn 5. Abandoned 1

Master i/c: S. B. R. Shore

Batting—*M. C. Cain 18–4–503–82–35.92; T. Smith 19–1–492–84–27.33; S. Forber 16–1–368–57–24.53; N. Canning 19–0–359–66–18.89; P. Challinor 15–1–248–72–17.71; J. Hoyle 11–4–108–37–15.42; C. Richards 13–2–161–45–14.63; N. Moore 16–1–133–25–8.86.

Bowling—T. Jeveons 131.2–30–401–26–15.42; P. Challinor 62–11–266–17–15.64; N. Canning 120–13–457–27–16.92; C. Richards 156.1–25–513–24–21.37; J. Hoyle 147.1–18–481–19–25.31.

THE ROYAL GRAMMAR SCHOOL, NEWCASTLE

Played 15: Won 5, Lost 4, Drawn 6

Master i/c: D. W. Smith

Batting—A. Atkinson 13–3–336–57–33.60; C. Hall 14–3–285–65–25.90; S. Johnson 13–2–266–73*–24.18; *P. Hollis 14–1–188–43–14.46; T. Meears-White 15–1–163–38–11.64.

Bowling—N. Brown 53–11–139–13–10.69; A. Atkinson 165.1–40–452–36–12.55; P. Hollis 65–20–132–10–13.20; S. Johnson 170–54–385–25–15.40; S. Curtis 74.3–11–248–13–19.07.

THE ROYAL GRAMMAR SCHOOL, WORCESTER

Played 25: Won 10, Lost 5, Drawn 10. Abandoned 1

Master i/c: C. N. Boyns   Cricket professional: M. J. Horton

Batting—D. P. Spiller 24–0–1,073–139–44.70; G. T. Burrow 25–2–685–62–29.78; *D. P. Norris 24–2–611–96–27.77; D. W. Headley 23–8–381–60*–25.40; L. M. Haddigan 13–3–239–42–23.90; M. J. Ridlinton 24–1–510–80–22.17; S. P. Chapman 12–2–141–29–14.10; M. J. Walker 17–2–210–40–14.00; S. D. Bradley 18–5–152–36*–11.69.

Bowling—J. S. Waters 361–82–987–61–16.18; D. P. Spiller 80–22–227–14–16.21; D. W. Headley 277–67–706–32–22.06; G. T. Burrow 173–36–510–22–23.18; S. P. Chapman 95–18–323–11–29.36; M. J. Walker 126–29–415–10–41.50.

RUGBY SCHOOL

Played 14: Won 4, Lost 1, Drawn 9. Abandoned 1

Master i/c: P. J. Rosser   Cricket professional: W. J. Stewart

Batting—C. W. Semmens 16–1–506–92*–33.73; A. J. Holmes 16–0–480–96–30.00; M. Rowlands 8–3–141–46–28.20; Y. J. Khan 16–0–446–83–27.87; H. N. Bhatia 14–7–170–53*–24.28; *T. H. A. Arulampalam 16–1–318–71–21.20; S. T. Carfoot 8–1–123–67*–17.57; R. R. Montgomerie 10–1–153–53–17.00; R. A. Sutton 12–1–160–59–14.54; A. G. H. Lamberty 15–2–171–32–13.15.

Bowling—B. C. A. Ellison 237.3–56–694–51–13.60; A. G. H. Lamberty 88.3–19–308–12–25.66; H. N. Bhatia 318.2–83–1,058–40–26.45; M. Rowlands 91.4–24–284–10–28.40.

RYDAL SCHOOL

Played 12: Won 4, Lost 0, Drawn 7, Tied 1

Master i/c: M. H. Stevenson   Cricket professional: R. W. C. Pitman

Batting—*C. F. Robinson 11–0–294–77–26.72; M. Morrison 12–3–210–61–23.33; M. Sherrington 12–2–187–85–18.70; S. Dale-Jones 12–4–125–41–15.62.

Bowling—S. Woodhead 104–26–297–28–10.60; C. F. Robinson 75–24–189–14–13.50; A. Higson 79–20–178–10–17.80; M. Sherrington 156–36–416–21–19.80.

ST ALBANS SCHOOL

Played 10: Won 2, Lost 6, Drawn 2

Master i/c: N. Woodsmith   Cricket professional: G. Cooper

Batting—D. Rourke 7–0–128–78–18.28; T. Preest 9–0–138–44–15.33; S. Thomas 7–0–107–45–15.28; A. Grimberg 10–0–103–39–10.30.

Bowling—J. Smart 113–39–286–18–15.88; A. Pepper 143–32–413–19–21.73.

ST DUNSTAN'S COLLEGE

Played 14: Won 4, Lost 2, Drawn 8. Abandoned 3

Master i/c: C. Matten

Batting—M. A. Slade 15–5–785–131*–78.50; M. J. Dowse 14–0–425–86–30.35; S. Tyler 13–1–300–62*–25.00; G. R. S. Scovell 10–1–221–52–24.55; J. Platford 9–1–126–61–15.75; R. E. Moyse 14–1–182–33*–14.00; E. L. Moseley 10–0–132–42–13.20.

Bowling—R. E. Moyse 55–13–177–11–16.09; M. A. Slade 170–49–530–31–17.09; J. Dall 65–13–222–12–18.50; G. R. S. Scovell 147–19–626–24–26.08.

ST EDMUND'S SCHOOL, CANTERBURY

Played 16: Won 3, Lost 7, Drawn 6

Master i/c: H. W. Scott   Cricket professional: D. V. P. Wright

Batting—N. C. Kennett 14–1–346–65–26.61; P. J. Bryant 11–3–193–50*–24.12; A. J. C. Eagar 15–1–283–78–20.21; M. R. Lunn 12–1–201–74*–18.27; N. A. Bryant 14–0–219–48–15.64; M. N. Pelham 12–1–143–29–13.00; D. M. Fenton 12–3–108–38–12.00; *D. H. Hopkins 14–1–153–56–11.76; M. J. E. Horton 14–0–156–39–11.14.

Bowling—P. J. Bryant 169–20–664–35–18.97; M. R. Lunn 91–19–337–16–21.06; D. M. Fenton 110.3–19–405–19–21.31; D. Blench 93–21–333–13–25.61.

ST EDWARD'S SCHOOL, OXFORD

Played 14: Won 4, Lost 4, Drawn 6

Master i/c: E. C. Danziger   Cricket professional: B. R. Edrich

Batting—A. J. W. Brown 14–2–454–105*–37.83; J. D. Ball 14–3–340–85–30.90; G. J. Young 12–1–330–76–30.00; M. R. Jepp 11–2–161–43–17.88.

Bowling—C. G. Sharp 198–57–422–31–13.61; J. P. Young 106–23–368–23–16.00; J. R. Kelly 188–38–497–14–35.50.

ST GEORGE'S, WEYBRIDGE

Played 15: Won 4, Lost 2, Drawn 9. Abandoned 3

Master i/c: B. O'Gorman

Batting—J. Creber 14–2–522–111–43.50; S. Cook 11–2–329–101*–36.55; *G. Parmenter 10–6–124–42–31.00; P. Dobson 7–1–139–58–23.16; J. Ruffell 10–1–158–65*–17.55; S. Cherriman 11–2–136–63*–15.11; G. Peters 12–1–159–64–14.45; S. Henderson 10–1–117–28–13.00; M. Todd 11–2–116–33–12.88; O. Holder 12–2–100–29–10.00.

Bowling—G. Parmenter 167.1–40–464–32–14.50; J. Creber 166.2–24–693–34–20.38; A. Regan 97–26–304–14–21.71; H. J. Harper 97–21–308–13–23.69.

ST JOHN'S SCHOOL, LEATHERHEAD

Played 16: Won 4, Lost 4, Drawn 8

Master i/c: A. B. Gale   Cricket professional: E. Shepperd

Batting—S. J. Walster 16–0–639–106–39.93; *A. C. Martin 16–3–426–100*–32.76; S. E. Penfold 16–1–470–81–31.33; D. A. Gordon 13–5–176–45*–22.00; A. C. Hibbert 14–1–185–50*–14.23; O. S. D. Brown 13–2–150–39–13.63; I. B. George 16–1–169–46–11.26; A. T. Georgiou 12–1–105–29*–9.54.

Bowling—A. C. Martin 88.1–17–333–23–14.47; S. J. Walster 174.2–26–503–25–20.12; T. P. Fairclough 82–9–343–16–21.43; J. H. Smart 98–24–285–13–21.92; D. S. McDaniel 86–14–341–13–26.23; S. E. Penfold 101.3–12–471–17–27.70.

ST LAWRENCE COLLEGE

Played 19: Won 4, Lost 5, Drawn 10

Master i/c: N. O. S. Jones   Cricket professional: L. A. C. D'Arcy

Batting—G. Hewitt-Coleman 9–1–274–109–34.25; *A. O. Uzor 19–1–516–93*–28.66; P. N. Unachukwu 16–4–318–77–26.50; R. S. Chhabra 17–3–320–63*–22.85; G. G. Philpott 10–2–177–55*–22.12; E. Anish 17–2–307–93–20.46; N. Abbasi 16–2–184–35–13.14; L. M. Willsmer 13–2–102–28–9.27.

Bowling—G. G. Philpott 108.5–19–336–26–12.92; L. M. Willsmer 76.1–13–236–16–14.75; G. Hewitt-Coleman 111–26–336–19–17.68; J. R. H. Miller 117–21–511–22–23.22; A. O. Uzor 182.2–29–682–18–37.88.

ST PAUL'S SCHOOL

Played 17: Won 5, Lost 1, Drawn 11. Abandoned 1

Master i/c: G. Hughes   Cricket professional: E. W. Whitfield

Batting—*J. P. Partridge 17–1–580–141*–36.25; H. C. G. B. Brooks 17–4–457–107*–35.15; R. Frost 17–1–412–79–25.75; J. M. York 16–1–294–58–19.60; P. L. Graham 17–2–261–38–17.40; D. M. Redstone 14–5–152–32–16.88; R. J. Smith 11–4–117–40*–16.71; S. W. Filmer 14–0–136–33–9.71.

Bowling—J. E. G. Pearson 63.3–25–143–10–14.30; H. C. G. B. Brooks 171.4–42–439–26–16.88; T. A. Kiggell 73–23–204–10–20.40; D. M. Redstone 61.5–9–218–10–21.80; R. J. Smith 146.5–30–498–21–23.71; R. Frost 164.1–50–433–18–24.05.

ST PETER'S SCHOOL, YORK

Played 19: Won 4, Lost 3, Drawn 12

Master i/c: D. Kirby   Cricket professional: K. Mohan

Batting—N. G. Wilkinson 18–3–533–87–35.53; R. Hutchinson 19–1–585–96–32.50; P. J. E. Brierley 18–1–431–68–25.35; N. D. Muirhead 19–2–357–101*–21.00; M. Reid 13–3–189–45–18.90; J. Brewster 18–3–255–38–17.00; D. M. D. White 19–0–307–55–16.15; *S. Forman 13–2–102–39*–9.27.

Bowling—M. D. Donoghue 250.2–41–730–32–22.81; J. Brewster 253.2–64–835–36–23.19; S. Forman 123.4–26–445–17–26.17; N. G. Wilkinson 117–31–377–14–26.92; P. R. H. Gair 100–15–417–12–34.75.

SEDBERGH SCHOOL

Played 13: Won 5, Lost 3, Drawn 5. Abandoned 4

Master i/c: M. J. Morris

Batting—G. J. Porritt 14–3–537–101*–48.81; A. J. D. Wheatley 9–2–252–117*–36.00; *J. I. Foggitt 14–3–342–70–31.09; M. W. Mewburn 11–5–126–32–21.00; J. R. C. Dakin 12–0–223–63–18.58; N. M. Poulsen 13–0–216–42–16.61.

Bowling—H. J. A. Daniels 82–13–234–17–13.76; M. W. Mewburn 164–30–412–26–15.84; A. M. Skinner 70–18–186–11–16.90; J. I. Foggitt 130.5–39–335–19–17.63; J. R. C. Dakin 70.3–18–209–10–20.90.

SEVENOAKS SCHOOL

Played 14: Won 2, Lost 2, Drawn 10. Abandoned 3

Master i/c: I. J. B. Walker

Batting—S. A. Ford 8–7–108–24*–108.00; *C. J. Crang 14–1–325–84–25.00; S. C. West 14–1–281–51–21.61; P. Hodder-Williams 13–0–274–55–21.07; A. Griffiths 9–3–113–30*–18.83; N. C. Baker 12–0–214–55–17.83; J. D. Fry 12–1–166–47–15.09; A. R. Abayanayaka 12–2–110–36–11.00.

Bowling—A. B. Hood 127.4–42–294–23–12.78; A. Griffiths 121.1–24–407–22–18.50; S. A. Ford 112–24–320–16–20.00.

SHERBORNE SCHOOL

Played 16: Won 7, Lost 0, Drawn 9. Abandoned 1

Master i/c: M. J. Cleaver   Cricket professional: C. Stone

Batting—S. W. D. Rintoul 14–3–553–87–50.27; *A. Kardouni 15–3–440–124*–36.66; T. R. Ashworth 11–2–320–100*–35.55; N. H. Peters 14–2–401–74–33.41; A. C. James 8–4–119–31*–29.75; F. C. E. Millar 7–2–139–60*–27.80; D. J. Stober 11–3–178–43–22.25; R. D. Youngman 11–0–200–63–18.18.

Bowling—P. M. S. Slade 199.3–63–476–45–10.57; N. H. Peters 136.5–49–313–24–13.04; A. C. James 62–22–161–12–13.41; A-R. Vassigh 89–24–240–16–15.00; F. C. E. Millar 115.3–18–378–20–18.90; A. P. Houldsworth 121.5–30–298–15–19.86.

SHREWSBURY SCHOOL

Played 22: Won 11, Lost 3, Drawn 8. Abandoned 1

Master i/c: C. M. B. Williams   Cricket professional: P. H. Bromley

Batting—D. J. Burrows 20–7–859–118*–66.07; J. R. Prichard 23–2–1,051–138–50.04; N. J. Miller 15–1–453–81–32.35; *C. M. Bullock 24–4–592–82–29.60; M. J. Lascelles 16–7–255–64*–28.33; J. R. T. Griffiths 15–3–257–44–21.41; G. M. Hutchinson 16–4–199–71*–16.58; J. M. Jones 12–1–106–56–9.63.

Bowling—D. J. Burrows 205.5–48–567–36–15.75; R. G. Atkin 172.4–27–575–30–19.16; J. R. T. Griffiths 48.5–9–199–10–19.90; R. N. Batkin 205.4–33–647–29–22.31; M. J. Lascelles 246.5–54–869–34–25.55.

SOLIHULL SCHOOL

Played 21: Won 5, Lost 5, Drawn 11

Master i/c: M. R. Brough   Cricket professional: W. Hogg

Batting—*S. J. Townsley 20–3–706–97–41.52; M. A. C. Fitzpatrick 16–2–427–77–30.50; R. E. Hatcliffe 9–3–165–100*–27.50; A. J. P. Morton 19–1–403–52*–22.38; R. Lucas 21–5–327–55*–20.43; M. J. Sawle 11–5–122–25–20.33; P. S. Goodson 13–1–237–70*–19.75; M. Crockart 12–4–100–27–12.50.

Bowling—P. S. Goodson 208–24–706–31–22.77; M. J. Sawle 183.3–28–689–25–27.56; A. A. Jowsey 198–18–794–24–33.08; P. St J. Heath 72–4–365–10–36.50.

STOCKPORT GRAMMAR SCHOOL
Played 13: Won 0, Lost 4, Drawn 9. Abandoned 2

Master i/c: C. Dunkerley

Batting—M. K. Duckworth 13–1–390–96–32.50; N. J. Vernon 13–2–351–100*–31.90;
H. Grayson 6–0–121–34–20.16; I. R. Millner 6–0–101–31–16.83; M. J. Blood
12–2–154–47–15.40; *P. H. Duff 13–1–157–36–13.08.

Bowling—M. K. Duckworth 44–5–151–10–15.10; R. A. Pailin 143.4–13–515–25–25.75; M. J.
Seed 102.5–21–318–12–26.50.

STONYHURST COLLEGE
Played 9: Won 2, Lost 2, Drawn 5. Abandoned 3

Master i/c: J. M. Fairburn

Batting—A. Desforges 6–1–102–40–20.40; J. Smith 8–2–107–42*–17.83; R. Barton
9–0–118–40–13.11.

Bowling—J. Barnes 91–29–166–21–7.90; M. Barton 67–9–205–13–15.76; *R. Fee
113–36–279–14–19.92.

STOWE SCHOOL
Played 18: Won 7, Lost 2, Drawn 9. Abandoned 2

Master i/c: G. A. Cottrell   Cricket professional: M. J. Harris

Batting—*R. S. M. Morris 18–4–1,001–115*–71.50; I. O. Bendell 17–2–411–109*–27.40;
J. M. J. Phillips 16–4–328–78*–27.33; J. C. Mahbubani 15–3–181–41–15.08; R. B.
Pumfrey 12–2–142–30*–14.20.

Bowling—A. J. E. Hazzard 247–73–562–43–13.06; R. B. Pumfrey 104–19–318–21–15.14;
H. R. Thomas 141.2–26–377–22–17.13; R. S. M. Morris 160–42–415–19–21.84; R. B. K.
Giles 149.4–30–403–11–36.63.

STRATHALLAN SCHOOL
Played 17: Won 3, Lost 6, Drawn 8. Abandoned 3

Master i/c: R. J. W. Proctor

Batting—*G. S. R. Robertson 15–1–628–88–44.85; R. E. M. Reah 14–0–296–72–21.14;
A. G. A. Bullard 15–0–262–45–17.46; R. Moffat 11–1–113–50–11.30; D. F. Lennox
15–3–134–30–11.16; K. D. Smith 16–4–120–36–10.00.

Bowling—K. D. Smith 255.1–49–773–46–16.80; M. Bargon 63.2–12–180–10–18.00; C. N. C.
Henderson 192.2–34–617–29–21.27; G. S. R. Robertson 162.5–29–538–19–28.31.

SUTTON VALENCE SCHOOL
Played 16: Won 2, Lost 6, Drawn 8. Abandoned 1

Master i/c: D. Pickard

Batting—D. G. Plommer 16–4–322–128*–26.83; A. Rogers 9–4–115–35–23.00; A. Pound
12–0–210–74–17.50; J. D. Crouch 16–0–279–72–17.43; R. J. Harrison 12–0–194–66–16.16;
A. G. Hewson 16–0–218–50–13.62.

Bowling—A. Pound 155–28–351–23–15.26; D. Patel 120–21–393–18–21.83; *R. J. Ashton
134–32–428–17–25.17; J. D. Crouch 180–20–691–22–31.40.

TAUNTON SCHOOL

Played 14: Won 8, Lost 2, Drawn 4. Abandoned 4

Master i/c: R. P. Smith   Cricket professional: A. Kennedy

Batting—M. Van Der Walt 14–1–603–123–46.38; A. Habib 14–5–331–66*–37.77; *C. B. Walker 14–1–399–119–30.69; R. J. L. Craddock 14–1–390–56*–30.00; V. J. Pike 7–1–142–44–23.66; M. N. P. Adam 9–3–140–47*–23.33; N. M. Raw 11–1–107–27–10.70.

Bowling—J. D. Seward 118.1–35–310–26–11.92; V. J. Pike 140.2–40–297–19–15.63; A. F. M. Dowdney 92–27–185–11–16.81; C. B. Walker 113.5–33–305–16–19.06; M. N. P. Adam 76.3–16–313–15–20.86; M. B. Goodman 103–28–244–11–22.18.

TIFFIN SCHOOL

Played 16: Won 5, Lost 4, Drawn 6, Tied 1. Abandoned 2

Master i/c: M. J. Williams

Batting—N. P. Warren 16–0–416–66–26.00; A. D. Young 11–3–194–36–24.25; N. D. Cecil 15–3–248–44*–20.66; S. J. Crowter 12–3–149–74–16.55; S. P. Randall 13–0–213–63–16.38; G. J. Affleck 14–0–209–45–14.92; P. K. Somers 11–0–159–34–14.45; S. C. Watson 10–0–132–37–13.20; *M. R. Coote 16–4–158–24–13.16.

Bowling—M. R. Coote 213.1–65–527–47–11.21; J. E. Gale 62.5–15–177–13–13.61; N. P. Warren 163–36–453–25–18.12; S. C. Watson 131.4–27–429–22–19.50; S. P. Randall 67–11–209–10–20.90.

TONBRIDGE SCHOOL

Played 19: Won 7, Lost 1, Drawn 11

Master i/c: D. R. Walsh   Cricket professional: H. J. Mutton

Batting—J. I. Longley 18–1–1,141–156*–67.11; K. B. Saro-Wiwa 18–4–469–59*–33.50; J. A. G. Waters 12–2–260–78–26.00; *J. S. Lazell 18–1–427–103*–25.11; R. T. W. Heale 9–1–149–34*–18.62; R. D. Gill 12–0–223–41–18.58; J. J. Mantovani 15–4–201–49–18.27; P. D. Mantovani 11–2–161–50–17.88; J. Owen-Browne 15–6–158–34*–17.55.

Bowling—J. P. Nolan 106–37–273–20–13.65; N. A. Langley 139–32–444–27–16.44; W. J. Chaloner 279–83–705–31–22.74; J. Owen-Browne 203–71–528–22–24.00.

TRINITY SCHOOL, CROYDON

Played 24: Won 10, Lost 4, Drawn 10. Abandoned 4

Masters i/c: B. Widger and A. Gist

Batting—K. P. Morley 23–3–852–120*–42.60; *G. M. Vigor 21–0–665–91–31.66; P. A. Gardner 15–6–265–55–29.44; M. R. D. Hollands 21–2–414–120–21.78; H. R. Stanford 11–3–169–31–21.12; P. J. Mander 22–0–440–78–20.00; D. J. Trafford 23–1–409–59–18.59; D. M. P. Turner 12–0–112–30–9.33; N. A. Zain 17–0–152–35–8.94.

Bowling—D. M. P. Turner 78.2–16–220–20–11.00; J. W. Harlow 161.5–25–478–34–14.05; P. A. Gardner 237.1–49–627–43–14.58; D. J. Trafford 180.5–36–572–35–16.34; G. M. Vigor 109–21–337–19–17.73; A. J. Budge 99–15–356–12–29.66.

TRURO SCHOOL

Played 12: Won 2, Lost 1, Drawn 9. Abandoned 2

Master i/c: A. J. D. Aldwinckle

Batting—*P. G. Phillips 11–0–309–78–28.09; R. A. Miller 11–1–190–49*–19.00; D. C. Barrington 11–0–206–54–18.72; J. A. Johnston 10–0–130–35–13.00.

Bowling—S. R. Peters 152–35–339–38–8.92; P. G. Phillips 49.2–2–199–13–15.30; S. N. Chakraborty 72.3–9–229–12–19.08.

UNIVERSITY COLLEGE SCHOOL

Played 14: Won 2, Lost 9, Drawn 3. Abandoned 2

Master i/c: T. Roberts   Cricket professional: W. G. Jones

Batting—A. D. Diamond 12–0–342–69–28.50; P. A. Teleki 13–0–308–66–23.69; K. A. G. Watling 13–0–197–53–15.15; *G. Sanders 14–2–162–63*–13.50; A. G. B. Bloch 11–1–128–43–12.80; D. O. Benaim 12–3–106–27*–11.77.

Bowling—D. O. Benaim 102.5–25–320–21–15.23; A. S. Lal 131.5–26–450–21–21.42; R. H. H. Thompson 124–21–366–15–24.40; G. Sanders 157.2–26–614–15–40.93.

UPPINGHAM SCHOOL

Played 12: Won 2, Lost 4, Drawn 6. Abandoned 2

Master i/c: P. L. Bodily   Cricket professional: M. R. Hallam

Batting—M. C. Renison 12–3–272–52*–30.22; A. S. Waters 8–2–173–54*–28.83; C. M. Frost 12–0–304–68–25.33; D. B. J. Cooke 13–0–327–88–25.15; S. R. Green 10–2–116–24–14.50; C. R. Saunders 13–1–170–32–14.16; P. H. Marsh 8–0–109–33–13.62.

Bowling—D. B. J. Cooke 174.1–41–488–29–16.82; P. J. E. Spencer 166.2–39–420–21–20.00; C. R. Saunders 111.1–23–346–12–28.83; B. O. H. Robson 75–9–434–11–39.45.

VICTORIA COLLEGE, JERSEY

Played 24: Won 10, Lost 6, Drawn 8. Abandoned 1

Master i/c: D. A. R. Ferguson   Cricket professional: R. A. Pearce

Batting—*C. M. Graham 23–3–715–106*–35.75; P. J. Le Cornu 26–2–800–102*–33.33; A. J. Wright 22–0–629–85–28.59; I. G. Le Couteur 21–4–326–75–19.17; I. Furness 18–4–234–74*–16.71; A. J. Clarke 18–6–193–63*–16.08; A. D. Brown 19–5–208–33*–14.85; D. J. Pearce 11–3–112–60*–14.00; J. W. Kellett 24–1–286–51–12.43.

Bowling—C. M. Graham 301.3–87–683–62–11.01; A. J. Wright 230.1–64–556–43–12.93; A. D. Brown 214–45–633–34–18.61; P. J. Le Cornu 106.5–21–318–16–19.87; D. V. Carnegie 187.3–37–617–31–19.90; S. G. Ritzema 77–19–202–10–20.20.

WARWICK SCHOOL

Played 14: Won 2, Lost 3, Drawn 9. Abandoned 2

Master i/c: I. B. Moffatt   Cricket professional: N. Horner

Batting—*A. J. Moffatt 14–1–611–116–47.00; J. D. Stanton 13–0–384–111–29.53; T. R. Luckman 13–0–282–102–21.69; M. A. Cooke 9–2–113–28–16.14; J. C. Seccombe 11–2–100–30–11.11; C. G. Stanton 13–0–143–42–11.00.

Bowling—D. A. Wilson 155.4–43–529–23–23.00; J. N. Beachus 143.3–23–507–18–28.16; J. D. Stanton 95–25–312–11–28.36.

WATFORD GRAMMAR SCHOOL

Played 11: Won 5, Lost 2, Drawn 4. Abandoned 5

Master i/c: D. Green

Batting—C. E. Mann 4–1–114–82*–38.00; M. J. H. Hanson 11–3–270–72–33.75; A. A. Chaudry 10–0–329–80–32.90; R. M. Nicholls 10–1–252–51–28.00; G. D. Gregory 11–1–119–47–11.90.

Bowling—C. E. Ahye 75–19–195–16–12.18; A. A. Chaudry 152.3–33–416–31–13.41; M. J. H. Hanson 155.5–31–497–26–19.11.

WELLINGBOROUGH SCHOOL

Played 19: Won 5, Lost 5, Drawn 9

Master i/c: C. J. Ford   Cricket professional: J. C. J. Dye

Batting—M. I. Ingram 18–2–624–110*–39.00; *P. S. H. Wilson 19–2–653–80*–38.41; J. C. Whitehead 12–6–145–56*–24.16; J. M. Attfield 15–5–223–61*–22.30; A. D. Woodward 13–6–154–27–22.00; T. K. Marriott 17–0–373–60–21.94; S. P. H. Gane 16–1–215–33–14.33; J. J. Attfield 17–1–184–40–11.50.

Bowling—T. K. Marriott 245.3–50–766–42–18.23; R. J. Cousins 214.3–52–514–23–22.34; J. J. Attfield 124.4–23–454–18–25.22; S. P. H. Gane 197.5–33–726–28–25.92.

WELLINGTON COLLEGE

Played 16: Won 3, Lost 7, Drawn 6. Abandoned 1

Masters i/c: D. J. Mordaunt and K. M. Hopkins   Cricket professional: P. J. Lewington

Batting—W. R. D. Waghorn 16–1–484–69*–32.26; *J. S. Hodgson 17–3–374–65–26.71; M. C. K. Hodgson 5–1–101–36–25.25; P. A. Huxtable 16–0–343–113–21.43; J. M. Benkert 9–0–182–57–20.22; W. Kemp 9–0–174–50–19.33; J. S. White 17–2–248–49–16.53.

Bowling—R. C. H. Bruce 108–26–274–17–16.11; J. R. H. Fenwick 251.9–68–701–42–16.69; P. A. Huxtable 128–33–324–14–23.14; J. S. Hodgson 202.2–48–613–22–27.86; B. P. Alexander 134–29–506–18–28.11.

WELLINGTON SCHOOL, SOMERSET

Played 9: Won 1, Lost 2, Drawn 6. Abandoned 3

Master i/c: P. M. Pearce

Batting—M. Colman 8–2–294–101*–49.00; J. Austin 8–4–129–53–32.25; J. Clist 9–0–221–53–24.55; J. Govier 9–1–162–67–20.25; J. Vallance 9–2–136–61–19.42; *M. Salter 9–0–148–50–16.44.

Bowling—M. Colman 120.5–74–305–24–12.70; S. Kitto 74.5–32–203–13–15.61.

WESTMINSTER SCHOOL

Played 13: Won 2, Lost 0, Drawn 11. Abandoned 1

Master i/c: J. A. Cogan   Cricket professional: R. Gilson

Batting—*J. D. Kershen 13–2–526–125*–47.81; J. R. D. Hyam 11–2–339–71*–37.66; D. J. Cogan 11–1–284–94*–28.40; J. G. R. Griffiths 11–0–285–74–25.90; A. T. Coles 11–1–166–59*–16.60.

Bowling—B. C. Baird 101–17–308–17–18.11; J. G. R. Griffiths 97–10–328–18–18.22; B. M. I. Hyam 122–17–360–18–20.00.

WHITGIFT SCHOOL

Played 19: Won 6, Lost 3, Drawn 10. Abandoned 3

Master i/c: P. C. Fladgate   Cricket professional: A. Long

Batting—*N. J. Taylor 18–3–808–104–53.86; G. J. Thompson 17–3–534–100*–38.14; T. P. Bureau 18–1–398–83*–23.41; I. L. H. Scarisbrick 18–1–381–76–22.41; R. Slatford 14–7–111–26*–15.85; C. Nott 11–2–129–44–14.33; P. J. Wallis 11–1–134–28*–13.40.

Bowling—J. A. M. Bulloch 83–27–191–19–10.05; R. Slatford 207.1–31–600–25–24.00; H. Gallagher 196.4–35–625–25–25.00; S. J. Hill 212.5–35–627–24–26.12.

WILLIAM HULME'S GRAMMAR SCHOOL

Played 19: Won 4, Lost 9, Drawn 6. Abandoned 1

Master i/c: I. J. Shaw

Batting—A. G. Cleary 15–3–536–90–44.66; D. M. J. Timm 18–1–581–114–34.17; C. W. Timm 20–3–472–75*–27.76; G. J. O'Driscoll 19–1–449–55–24.94; S. P. Hinds 11–6–105–27*–21.00; *K. G. Rushton 11–0–188–48–17.09; M. J. Braddock 13–4–123–63–13.66.

Bowling—K. G. Rushton 107–20–416–17–24.47; D. M. J. Timm 157.2–14–631–21–30.04; A. P. Cleary 148.3–34–515–17–30.29.

WINCHESTER COLLEGE

Played 19: Won 5, Lost 6, Drawn 8. Abandoned 1

Master i/c: J. F. X. Miller   Cricket professional: V. Broderick

Batting—R. J. Waddington 16–2–484–84–34.57; B. C. Winzer 17–4–338–48–26.00; J. G. B. Warren 16–0–292–67–18.25; M. A. T. Hall 7–0–117–40–16.71; *B. D. Thornycroft 16–3–204–42–15.69; M. I. Riaz 13–0–170–59–13.07; A. P. S. Casstles 15–4–105–45–9.54.

Bowling—J. E. Byng 93.2–19–312–20–15.60; T. S. Maclure 244.4–49–691–41–16.85; B. D. Thornycroft 97.3–6–280–12–23.33; M. W. Smith 112–23–312–12–26.00; C. G. Tiley 134–35–391–13–30.07; B. C. Winzer 197–30–664–15–44.26.

WOODBRIDGE SCHOOL

Played 14: Won 6, Lost 2, Drawn 6

Cricket professional: J. A. Pugh

Batting—J. R. Harper 13–4–282–53*–31.33; A. A. Donnison 13–1–301–45–25.08; J. S. Daniel 11–2–211–71*–23.44; S. Waddington 14–1–260–51–20.00; *M. G. Harvey 12–0–213–36–17.75.

Bowling—J. R. Harper 97–26–269–20–13.45; A. A. Donnison 119–25–339–25–13.56; J. W. Griffiths 101–22–259–19–13.63; R. M. Hallam 70.2–10–224–16–14.00; N. Henchie 125–24–357–22–16.22.

WOODHOUSE GROVE SCHOOL

Played 12: Won 1, Lost 4, Drawn 7. Abandoned 4

Master i/c: E. R. Howard   Cricket professional: D. Stranger

Batting—J. L. Gomersall 11–2–240–63*–26.66; N. C. Harps 10–0–157–33–15.70; N. T. Fox 11–1–146–29–14.60; *M. E. Fox 11–2–118–29–13.11.

Bowling—C. A. Miller 81–19–245–14–17.50; N. Hague 97–18–283–13–21.76; M. E. Fox 77–8–290–13–22.30.

WORKSOP COLLEGE

Played 16: Won 5, Lost 4, Drawn 7

Master i/c: N. S. Broadbent   Cricket professional: A. Kettleborough

Batting—D. B. Storer 15–4–703–100*–63.90; M. J. W. Hallam 16–2–374–68–26.71; *R. J. Darwin 16–2–369–100–26.35; N. E. Green 15–3–263–69–21.91; C. P. Green 14–1–159–28–12.23.

Bowling—B. D. Hackett 192.5–45–504–35–14.40; B. St J. B. Bowser 71–13–186–12–15.50; P. K. R. Patel 144–27–475–23–20.65; C. P. Green 129.5–19–443–19–23.31; D. B. Storer 136–29–440–16–27.50.

WREKIN COLLEGE

Played 15: Won 1, Lost 6, Drawn 8

Master i/c: T. J. Murphy   Cricket professional: T. J. Harrison

Batting—*C. A. Fenton 15–2–423–80–32.53; S. R. Jackson 13–3–207–63*–20.70; R. W. Barker 15–0–219–52–14.60; D. H. A. Horton 15–3–173–51*–14.41; J. B. Rimmer 14–1–180–39–13.84; A. T. Eley 11–0–129–41–11.72.

Bowling—S. R. Jackson 155–34–392–26–15.07; C. A. Fenton 116–24–276–15–18.40; A. D. McDonald 102–17–318–15–21.20; J. R. Ford 88–15–299–11–27.18; J. B. Rimmer 124–20–415–12–34.58.

WYCLIFFE COLLEGE

Played 15: Won 4, Lost 3, Drawn 8. Abandoned 3

Master i/c: M. Eagers   Cricket professional: K. Biddulph

Batting—*S. J. Reed 15–2–612–91*–47.07; P. R. Pitman 11–2–262–54*–29.11; M. F. Brown 14–4–270–45–27.00; N. A. Hitchings 8–3–115–40*–23.00; J. D. Trigg 10–0–189–43–18.90; S. G. Cady 13–1–203–45–16.91; J. A. H. Tovey 14–0–159–29–11.35.

Bowling—S. E. King 52.4–13–185–12–15.41; R. N. Giles 148.3–31–358–18–19.88; M. F. Brown 118.4–23–509–21–24.23; N. A. Hitchings 115.4–26–344–10–34.40.

WYGGESTON & QUEEN ELIZABETH I COLLEGE

Played 10: Won 5, Lost 2, Drawn 3. Abandoned 3

Master i/c: G. G. Wells

Batting—*R. M. Lee 7–1–181–65–30.16; S. C. Brammar 9–2–206–39–29.42; K. T. Roberts 7–1–113–45*–18.83.

Bowling—J. L. Green 66.5–17–145–15–9.66; D. J. Herrington 47–11–134–10–13.40.

OVERSEAS CRICKET, 1985-86

Note: Throughout this section, matches not first-class are denoted by the use of a dagger.

ENGLAND IN THE WEST INDIES, 1985-86

By JOHN THICKNESSE

It would be less than fair to David Gower and the team he captained in the West Indies to label the tour simply a disaster. Their record, true enough, was all of that – another "blackwash" in the Test series and only two wins, compared to ten defeats, in fourteen matches. Much went wrong, too, that with firmer captaincy and management might not have.

But there were many mitigating circumstances, of which the brilliance of the opposition, captained by Viv Richards, and the poor quality of too many of the pitches were the most decisive. In cold fact, England never had a hope. That they could and should have done better, few who saw them would dispute. Their lack of commitment was reflected in their attitude to practice, a department in which West Indies showed them up as amateurs. However, any chance England had of competing in the series – slender at the best of times on the record of West Indies since the middle 1970s – vanished to all practical purposes when the batsmen reached the first Test in Jamaica without having met, in four matches, one pitch on which to find their confidence. On top of that, they had been deprived by injury of Mike Gatting, who had been in better form than anyone. Gatting, the vice-captain, had his nose broken by Malcolm Marshall in the first one-day international, misjudging the ball to hook, and the consequences were long-lasting both in playing terms and psychologically.

Three days after Gatting's injury, England were in the thick of the Test series on a dangerous Kingston pitch, and within two more had been beaten by ten wickets after being demolished twice in 88 overs and two balls. Almost overnight another star fast bowler, Patrick Patterson, had risen in the firmament. Raw at that stage, but very quick, he took seven wickets on his début and left more mental scars and bruises than Marshall on a fast, uneven pitch. Well grassed for about four yards either side of centre, and bare in the areas forward of the popping-creases, the playing surface could not have underlined with greater emphasis the disparity between the two teams' bowling strength if its preparation had been left to West Indies' four-pronged pace attack itself.

England might conceivably have recovered from that unnerving experience had Gatting been on hand to pump some ginger into them. But while he was at home for three weeks, having attention to his nose, the side was like a ship without a rudder. It was a great credit to Gower that he pulled his batting together to average 37 in the Tests, having scored only 27 runs in five innings before the series started. But his inability to lift a beaten team's morale, with Graham Gooch as the temporary vice-captain, was as apparent as in 1984. Gower is among the most graceful figures in the game, a lovely natural strokeplayer who is well liked by his fellow-players, not least because of his unselfishness. But instead of the strong leader England needed in those crucial weeks, they had a dilettante. Regrettably, it was not only that he had no faith in practice – a weakness exacerbated by Ian Botham's presence – but sometimes he seemed even to lack interest. In the opening fixture, for example, against Windward Islands in St Vincent, he not only decided not to play, but on the second day went sailing. There was scant encouragement in that for Greg Thomas and David Smith, the two "first tourists".

To lose 0-2, or 1-3, would have been a good result for England, given the known gulf between the teams. For the margin to have been as close as that, however, certain key players, notably among the batsmen, had to play to top ability. In the event, Gower was the only one to average more than 30 in the Tests, while of the bowlers only John Emburey enhanced his reputation. His success should be measured not by his Test average (32.00) but rather by the fact that he dismissed Richie Richardson, the West Indies number three, in six successive innings. By the final Test, he had him in his grip.

Though it undoubtedly reflected upon the inconsistency of England's faster bowlers that Emburey, with fourteen, should be the leading wicket-taker, he bowled his off-spin beautifully. A word for Thomas in that context, though. A poor fourth Test cost him his place in Antigua in the final Test, and he showed that he needed to work hard on his line. But he bowled with a bit of pace and no lack of heart. Picked on debatable credentials – a succession of injuries and only 34 wickets in the Championship for Glamorgan in 1985 – he vindicated the selectors' judgement. He has it in him to be England's spearhead.

Another pleasant surprise was how little the anti-apartheid protests infringed themselves on matters. There were many threats before the tour of strong reaction to the presence of four players – Gooch, Emburey, Peter Willey and Les Taylor – who had toured South Africa under the banner of the South African Breweries XI in 1982. Noisy demonstrations were staged outside Queen's Park Oval in Port-of-Spain during England's first fortnight there, but at no stage did they become physical, and they had largely fizzled out by the time the team returned to Trinidad at the end of March. England were under police escort in every island; but there is nothing new in that on modern tours to "third world" countries.

The demonstrations, and a number of hostile editorials in the local press, were nevertheless a factor in the team's decline through the effect they had on Gooch. As captain of that side in South Africa, he was invariably the main target of the protesters' opprobrium. Ironically, his superb 129 not out – England's only hundred – in the one-day international at Port-of-Spain did more than anything to take the wind out of the protesters' sails. Unfortunately he took no steps to prevent his edginess being apparent to the team, and feelings were mixed when he was persuaded by Gower to stay on for the final Test, rather than make a protest of his own, following a derogatory article by Lester Bird, the Deputy Prime Minister of Antigua, by flying home from Trinidad. Donald Carr, the secretary of the Test and County Cricket Board, made a special journey to discuss that issue with Gooch; but it was Gower, by appealing to his loyalty, who talked him out of a move that might well have damaged his career.

Botham had a dreadful tour in every imaginable way. England may not have fared any better in results had he not been picked, but they could only have pulled together better. His aversion to net practice set a bad example, and only once, when he was under threat of being dropped, did he produce a good performance with the ball. Allegations in a British Sunday newspaper concerning his behaviour during the fortnight in Barbados added to the problems of Tony Brown, the manager. It was a hard tour for him, complicated by the fact that Bob Willis, his assistant, who was in charge of practice, lacked the imagination or initiative to make the best of poor facilities.

The worst error of the selection panel – choosing only two opening batsmen in Gooch and Tim Robinson – was camouflaged to a certain extent by the arrival of Wilf Slack as batting reinforcement after the first of Gatting's injuries. (Rejoining the tour in mid-March, Gatting immediately suffered a broken thumb in the match against Barbados.) But the folly of tackling a West Indies tour on the assumption that both openers would hit form, while avoiding injury themselves, was shown clearly enough by Robinson's exposure to the fast bowlers. In 21 innings he was bowled nine times and had a single-figure average in the Tests.

Phil Edmonds, the other spinner, took only three expensive wickets in the first three Tests. Nevertheless, as one of the most determined members of the party, he made a gallant attempt to show the senior batsmen that even a tailender could sometimes frustrate the opposition by ignoring short-pitched balls and by taking every opportunity to play forward in defence. His omission from the last two Tests was due more to the repeated batting breakdowns higher in the order than to the shortage of his wickets. For following a visit by P. B. H. May, the chairman of selectors, to Barbados, where the tourists lost three times, England's priority was to "stop the rot". The resultant inclusion of an extra batsman left no room for Edmonds: to the cost not only of balance in attack but also of a standard of fielding that on more than one occasion embarrassingly reflected the lack of proper preparation.

Smith, preferred to Slack at Port-of-Spain in the fourth Test, justified his selection by top-scoring in each innings, a feat which, had he followed it with a good match at St John's, must have enhanced his prospects in England in 1986. However, he withdrew on the morning of the final Test with a recurrence of his back trouble. Willey and Richard Ellison, after starting strongly in the first Test with, respectively, a sterling 71 and an analysis of five for 78 in 33 overs, also met later disappointment. Willey's second-highest Test score was 26, and he was struggling to keep his place when, on an unaccompanied evening run in Trinidad, he badly jarred an old knee injury and flew home before the final week. It was a sorry reward for the training schedule he had imposed upon himself to retain peak fitness at the age of 36. Ellison, unlucky in the second Test, missed the third through illness and was neglected for the fourth in conditions suited to his method.

Allan Lamb was another to fall back after encouraging beginnings, while Neil Foster never did himself full justice and Taylor and Bruce French were given little opportunity. Taylor despite a steady effort in the first one-day international. For French, the tour was a disheartening repetition of his Indian experience in 1984-85, the selectors seeming scarcely to look beyond Paul Downton as wicket-keeper in the major games, even though his batting was no longer a factor in his favour. He passed 20 once in nineteen innings, and his performance with the gloves was uneven.

It must be reiterated, though, that through their fast bowlers West Indies were always certain winners in the conditions that prevailed. It was fitting that Richards should crown their superiority with his devastating 56-ball hundred in the final Test, the fastest ever in Test cricket in terms of balls received. But there are ways and ways of losing. Once England fell love-two behind, they seemed to lose their appetite to fight. There were certain notable exceptions, but for the last month of the tour too many of the team, sub-consciously or otherwise, gave the appearance of scoring off the days before they could return to England. At nearly £900 a week per head, they owed the Test selectors, and the British public, a good deal more than that.

ENGLAND TOUR RESULTS

Test matches – Played 5: Lost 5.
First-class matches – Played 10: Won 1, Lost 7, Drawn 2.
Win – Jamaica.
Losses – Windward Islands, West Indies (5), Barbados.
Draws – Leeward Islands, Trinidad & Tobago.
Non first-class matches – Played 4: Won 1, Lost 3. *Win* – West Indies. *Losses* – West Indies (3).

TEST MATCH AVERAGES

WEST INDIES – BATTING

	T	I	NO	R	HI	100s	Avge
D. L. Haynes	5	9	3	469	131	1	78.16
I. V. A. Richards	5	6	1	331	110*	1	66.20
R. B. Richardson	5	9	2	387	160	2	55.28
R. A. Harper	2	3	1	100	60	0	50.00
M. D. Marshall	5	5	1	153	76	0	38.25
C. G. Greenidge	5	6	0	217	58	0	36.16
H. A. Gomes	5	6	0	191	56	0	31.83
M. A. Holding	4	4	0	124	73	0	31.00
C. A. Best	3	4	1	78	35	0	26.00
P. J. L. Dujon	4	4	0	85	54	0	21.25
J. Garner	5	5	1	52	24	0	13.00
B. P. Patterson	5	5	3	12	9	0	6.00

Played in one Test: T. R. O. Payne 5; C. A. Walsh 3.

* *Signifies not out.*

BOWLING

	O	M	R	W	BB	Avge
J. Garner	156.1	30	436	27	4-43	16.14
M. D. Marshall	169.3	36	482	27	4-38	17.85
C. A. Walsh	33	6	103	5	4-74	20.60
B. P. Patterson	118.1	19	426	19	4-30	22.42
M. A. Holding	102.4	16	385	16	3-47	24.06

Also bowled: H. A. Gomes 1–1–0–0; R. A. Harper 38–15–55–4; I. V. A. Richards 20–7–29–0; R. B. Richardson 1–0–5–0.

ENGLAND – BATTING

	T	I	NO	R	HI	100s	Avge
D. I. Gower	5	10	0	370	90	0	37.00
G. A. Gooch	5	10	0	276	53	0	27.60
A. J. Lamb	5	10	0	224	62	0	22.40
D. M. Smith	2	4	0	80	47	0	20.00
P. Willey	4	8	0	136	71	0	17.00
I. T. Botham	5	10	0	168	38	0	16.80
W. M. Slack	2	4	0	62	52	0	15.50
R. M. Ellison	3	6	0	82	36	0	13.66
J. G. Thomas	4	8	4	45	31*	0	11.25
J. E. Emburey	4	8	2	64	35*	0	10.66
P. R. Downton ...	5	10	0	91	26	0	10.11
R. T. Robinson ...	4	8	0	72	43	0	9.00
P. H. Edmonds ...	3	6	2	36	13	0	9.00
N. A. Foster	3	6	1	24	14	0	4.80

Played in one Test: M. W. Gatting 15, 1.

* *Signifies not out.*

BOWLING

	O	M	R	W	BB	Avge
J. E. Emburey	153	34	448	14	5-78	32.00
N. A. Foster	83.5	8	285	7	3-76	40.71
R. M. Ellison	82.3	19	294	7	5-78	42.00
J. G. Thomas	86	13	364	8	4-70	45.50
I. T. Botham	134.5	16	535	11	5-71	48.63

Also bowled: P. H. Edmonds 92.3–16–260–3; G. A. Gooch 7–3–27–1; A. J. Lamb 0.0–0–1–0; P. Willey 4–0–15–1.

Note: A. J. Lamb's only delivery in the first Test was a no-ball.

ENGLAND AVERAGES – FIRST-CLASS MATCHES

	M	I	NO	R	HI	100s	Avge
M. W. Gatting	5	9	0	317	80	0	35.22
A. J. Lamb	8	16	1	438	78	0	29.20
D. I. Gower	8	16	0	447	90	0	27.93
G. A. Gooch	9	18	0	443	53	0	24.61
I. T. Botham	8	16	0	379	70	0	23.68
D. M. Smith	5	10	1	195	47	0	21.66
R. T. Robinson	9	18	0	359	76	0	19.94
W. M. Slack	4	8	1	134	52	0	19.14
P. Willey	7	14	0	259	71	0	18.50
R. M. Ellison	6	11	0	183	45	0	16.63
J. E. Emburey	7	12	2	165	38	0	16.50
P. H. Edmonds	7	12	4	118	20	0	14.75
P. R. Downton	8	16	3	134	26	0	10.30
J. G. Thomas	6	12	6	57	31*	0	9.50
N. A. Foster	7	12	2	60	14	0	6.00
L. B. Taylor	4	6	3	14	9	0	4.66
B. N. French	2	3	0	9	9	0	3.00

* *Signifies not out.*

BOWLING

	O	M	R	W	BB	Avge
L. B. Taylor	93.3	17	259	13	3-27	19.92
P. Willey..........	81.4	17	162	8	2-38	20.25
N. A. Foster	180.3	33	583	23	6-54	25.34
R. M. Ellison	162.3	32	513	18	5-78	28.50
J. E. Emburey	239.2	56	648	21	5-78	30.85
P. H. Edmonds	233.4	43	590	18	4-38	32.77
J. G. Thomas	135	19	547	14	4-70	39.07
I. T. Botham	180.5	26	671	15	5-71	44.73

Also bowled: M. W. Gatting 3-0-15-1; G. A. Gooch 17-6-56-1; A. J. Lamb 0.0-0-1-0.

FIELDING

P. R. Downton 16 (11 ct [1 as sub], 5 st), G. A. Gooch 10, I. T. Botham 6, B. N. French 6 (5 ct, 1 st), J. E. Emburey 5 (1 as sub), A. J. Lamb 5, J. G. Thomas 5, M. W. Gatting 4, D. I. Gower 4, R. T. Robinson 4, W. N. Slack 4 (1 as sub), P. Willey 3, P. H. Edmonds 2, N. A. Foster 2, L. B. Taylor 2, R. M. Ellison 1, D. M. Smith 1.

WINDWARD ISLANDS v ENGLAND XI

At Arnos Vale, St Vincent, February 1, 2, 3, 4. Windward Islands won by seven wickets. Having won what should have been a decisive toss, and through the spin of Edmonds earned a small first-innings lead, England then suffered a second batting collapse which left them unable to stop the Windwards from completing their first victory over a touring team. On an awkward turning pitch, uneven in pace and bounce, and on an outfield over which the firmest hits pulled up short of the boundary, each run had to be earnt, the overall scoring-rate being 1.8 an over. Hinds, bowling off-spin over the wicket to a two-seven field, turned the game on the third afternoon, when England lost seven wickets for 33 after Smith had been bowled by a full toss. Gatting's 77 (173 minutes, 200 balls) was more than double the next best score on either side, while England's second-innings 94 was their lowest score on a Test-match tour of the West Indies.

England XI

G. A. Gooch b Etienne	27	– c and b Collymore	10
R. T. Robinson b Collymore	9	– lbw b Collymore	7
D. M. Smith b Collymore	0	– b Hinds	18
*M. W. Gatting c Charles b Hinds	77	– (5) b Etienne	14
A. J. Lamb b Hinds	5	– (4) lbw b Hinds	6
P. Willey c Mahon b Marshall	16	– b Hinds	2
†P. R. Downton c Cadette b Collymore	16	– c and b Etienne	2
P. H. Edmonds c Cadette b Collymore	14	– not out	18
N. A. Foster lbw b Collymore	4	– c Lewis b Hinds	1
J. G. Thomas b Thomas	5	– c sub b Etienne	5
L. B. Taylor not out	4	– lbw b Hinds	0
B 1, l-b 1, n-b 7	9	B 4, l-b 2, w 1, n-b 4	11

1/27 2/29 3/56 4/63 5/121   186   1/21 2/23 3/42 4/61 5/63   94
6/145 7/169 8/176 9/178   6/65 7/67 8/73 9/79

Bowling: *First Innings*—Collymore 23-4-34-5; Thomas 13.5-3-26-1; Hinds 22-3-61-2; Etienne 19-4-37-1; Marshall 24-8-26-1. *Second Innings*—Collymore 12-6-17-2; Thomas 9-2-13-0; Hinds 22.5-8-21-5; Etienne 20-3-37-3.

Windward Islands

*L. D. John lbw b Foster	15	– c Thomas b Willey	22
†I. Cadette st Downton b Edmonds	17		
L. A. Lewis c Downton b Edmonds	3	– (2) c Lamb b Edmonds	30
J. D. Charles c Gatting b Thomas	30	– (3) lbw b Willey	24
L. C. Sebastien c Robinson b Willey	26	– not out	11
S. L. Mahon lbw b Thomas	0	– (4) not out	12
R. A. Marshall c Lamb b Willey	1		
D. J. Collymore not out	31		
S. J. Hinds c Taylor b Edmonds	1		
J. T. Etienne st Downton b Edmonds	4		
W. L. Thomas c and b Thomas	9		
B 2, l-b 4, n-b 25	31	B 6, n-b 8	14

1/28 2/39 3/58 4/105 5/108   168   1/30 2/86 3/94   (3 wkts) 113
6/114 7/131 8/138 9/143

Bowling: *First Innings*—Thomas 16–4–54–3; Foster 7–3–11–1; Edmonds 25–5–38–4; Taylor 7–1–17–0; Willey 26–8–42–2. *Second Innings*—Thomas 6–0–15–0; Foster 2–1–4–0; Edmonds 22–2–48–1; Willey 24.4–6–38–2; Taylor 1–0–2–0.

Umpires: L. H. Barker and G. T. Browne.

LEEWARD ISLANDS v ENGLAND XI

At St John's, Antigua, February 7, 8, 9, 10. Drawn. A poor all-round display by England enabled the Leewards to avoid defeat, despite being below full strength and losing an important toss. Richards (resting) and Baptiste and Merrick (injured) were absent, while Ferris was off the field in England's second innings. Otto, the acting-captain, was the only batsman to come to terms with a pitch of changing moods. When it was damp and seaming in the first innings he scored 55; when it was slow and bounceless in the second he stayed in for five hours for a determined 92. England, left 70 minutes plus twenty overs to score 116, compounded an uneven performance in the field by batting feebly. Never up with the required rate, they were obliged to settle for a draw as Richardson returned five for 40 – his first wickets in a first-class game.

Leeward Islands

A. L. Kelly c Thomas b Ellison	12	– lbw b Botham	16
L. L. Lawrence c Emburey b Ellison	6	– lbw b Thomas	35
R. B. Richardson c Gatting b Thomas	19	– c and b Thomas	27
E. E. Lewis c Thomas b Foster	6	– b Emburey	36
*R. M. Otto c Gooch b Foster	55	– lbw b Botham	92
K. L. T. Arthurton c Botham b Ellison	11	– b Foster	13
†McC. V. Simon lbw b Emburey	16	– lbw b Foster	0
N. C. Guishard b Gatting	54	– lbw b Foster	17
W. K. M. Benjamin b Emburey	30	– b Foster	5
J. D. Thompson c Gooch b Emburey	3	– lbw b Ellison	1
G. J. F. Ferris not out	2	– not out	11
B 4, l-b 8, n-b 10	22	B 9, l-b 7, w 1, n-b 18	35

1/13 2/41 3/42 4/70 5/105   236   1/19 2/73 3/97 4/163 5/194   288
6/140 7/140 8/229 9/232   6/194 7/242 8/253 9/261

Bowling: *First Innings*—Botham 14–4–51–0; Ellison 13–1–37–3; Thomas 10–1–37–1; Foster 13–6–33–2; Emburey 16.2–3–51–3; Gatting 3–0–15–1. *Second Innings*—Botham 9.1–2–28–2; Ellison 16–2–49–1; Emburey 26–6–64–1; Thomas 17–1–77–2; Foster 20–3–54–4.

England XI

G. A. Gooch c Otto b Thompson	53	– c Simon b Benjamin	0
R. T. Robinson c Benjamin b Guishard	68	– b Richardson	32
*D. I. Gower c Guishard b Thompson	5	– b Richardson	9
M. W. Gatting c Richardson b Ferris	71	– b Richardson	8
A. J. Lamb c Simon b Guishard	64	– c Simon b Benjamin	1
I. T. Botham b Ferris	40	– b Benjamin	4
†P. R. Downton b Ferris	4	– not out	10
J. E. Emburey c Simon b Ferris	38	– lbw b Richardson	6
R. M. Ellison c Simon b Guishard	21	– lbw b Richardson	1
J. G. Thomas not out	1	– not out	1
N. A. Foster lbw b Benjamin	14		
B 11, l-b 10, n-b 9	30	B 8, l-b 9, w 1, n-b 4	22

1/118 2/134 3/160 4/271 5/307   409   1/1 2/20 3/42 4/46   (8 wkts) 94
6/328 7/331 8/390 9/390   5/59 6/75 7/81 8/89

Bowling: *First Innings*—Ferris 31–5–91–4; Benjamin 30.1–11–60–1; Guishard 48–7–124–3; Thompson 38–6–93–2; Otto 5–1–16–0; Richardson 3–0–4–0. *Second Innings*—Benjamin 17–2–37–3; Richardson 17–2–40–5.

Umpires: A. E. Weekes and P. C. White.

JAMAICA v ENGLAND XI

At Kingston, February 13, 14, 15, 16. England XI won by 158 runs. Holding's decision to put England in misfired after a promising beginning. On a pitch of patchy grass, England were 56 for three; but Gatting and Lamb added 147 and the eventual 371 gave them the initiative for the remainder of the match. Jamaica, who were without Patterson at the request of the West Indies selectors, were further weakened when Holding pulled a hamstring. A third-wicket stand between Neita and Dujon enabled them to avoid the follow-on, but resistance crumbled on the final afternoon when, on a worn pitch, Ellison and Edmonds were too good for some young and inexperienced batsmen. Walsh, with a devastating assault on Gower in the second innings, made sure of becoming Holding's replacement in West Indies' squad for the one-day international.

England XI

G. A. Gooch c Dujon b Walsh	36	– b Walsh	6
R. T. Robinson c Daley b Holding	9	– b Daley	19
*D. I. Gower c F. A. Cunningham b Holding	2	– c Adams b Walsh	11
M. W. Gatting c Adams b Walsh	80	– b Neita	15
A. J. Lamb c Neita b Adams	78	– not out	60
I. T. Botham c Walsh b Adams	32	– c Dujon b Neita	38
†P. R. Downton c Neita b Walsh	4	– not out	7
J. E. Emburey b Daley	25		
R. M. Ellison c F. A. Cunningham b Daley	32		
P. H. Edmonds not out	15		
L. B. Taylor c Dixon b Daley	0		
B 24, l-b 7, n-b 27	58	B 14, l-b 3, w 1, n-b 3	21

1/22 2/30 3/56 4/203 5/258   371   1/19 2/37 3/47   (5 wkts dec.) 177
6/262 7/280 8/323 9/371   4/99 5/147

Bowling: *First Innings*—Walsh 33–9–84–3; Holding 13.3–1–44–2; Daley 34.2–6–119–3; Dixon 6–0–28–0; Adams 14–2–50–2; Davidson 5–0–15–0. *Second Innings*—Walsh 12–3–32–2; Daley 16–1–37–1; Dixon 13–1–44–0; Adams 8–4–13–0; Neita 11–2–29–2; Davidson 3–1–5–0.

Jamaica

F. A. Cunningham c Downton b Taylor	14 – lbw b Taylor		7
G. Powell lbw b Taylor	36 – c Downton b Ellison		19
M. C. Neita c Emburey b Taylor	66 – b Taylor		40
†P. J. L. Dujon c Downton b Ellison	39 – c Taylor b Edmonds		31
C. A. Davidson run out	30 – c Emburey b Edmonds		40
L. Cunningham lbw b Ellison	0 – c Robinson b Ellison		9
J. C. Adams c and b Botham	13 – c Gower b Edmonds		3
D. C. Dixon st Downton b Emburey	1 – b Edmonds		6
A. G. Daley b Botham	14 – b Emburey		1
C. A. Walsh not out	0 – not out		0
*M. A. Holding absent injured	– absent injured		
B 2, l-b 3, n-b 4	9	B 5, l-b 2, n-b 5	12

1/32 2/72 3/146 4/180 5/184   222   1/28 2/95 3/104 4/112 5/146   168
6/203 7/205 8/219 9/222   6/154 7/165 8/168 9/168

Bowling: *First Innings*—Botham 13.2–3–31–2; Taylor 18–2–70–3; Ellison 15–2–45–2; Edmonds 16–4–40–0; Emburey 19–6–31–1. *Second Innings*—Botham 6–1–13–0; Taylor 13–3–28–2; Ellison 17–4–36–2; Emburey 8–2–16–1; Gooch 7–3–24–0; Edmonds 19–4–44–4.

Umpires: L. U. Bell and J. R. Gayle.

†WEST INDIES v ENGLAND

First One-day International

At Kingston, Jamaica, February 18. West Indies won by six wickets. A bad injury to Gatting, whose nose was broken when he missed an attempted hook off Marshall from a ball which cannoned off his face into the stumps, did far more damage to England than West Indies' easy victory. They won with thirteen balls to spare in a match reduced by eight overs by their own slow over-rate, four fast bowlers and off-spinner Harper managing only 46 overs in the allowed 200 minutes. After England had been sent in, Patterson made immediate inroads by dismissing Robinson and Gower with his fourth and eighth balls in international cricket. Marshall prevented a full recovery by bowling Gatting and Gooch, and though Lamb and Willey added 62 off sixteen overs, England could not put West Indies under pressure. But for careless strokes by Gomes and Richardson with 4 runs needed, the margin would have been eight wickets.

Man of the Match: M. D. Marshall.

England

G. A. Gooch b Marshall	36	N. A. Foster not out	5
R. T. Robinson b Patterson	0	J. G. Thomas not out	0
*D. I. Gower c Richards b Patterson	0		
M. W. Gatting b Marshall	10	B 8, l-b 2, w 4, n-b 11	25
A. J. Lamb c Greenidge b Marshall	30		
P. Willey c Richardson b Marshall	26	1/2 2/10 3/47 (8 wkts, 46 overs) 145	
†P. R. Downton lbw b Garner	8	4/63 5/125 6/125	
J. E. Emburey b Garner	5	7/137 8/143	

L. B. Taylor did not bat.

Bowling: Garner 10–0–18–2; Patterson 7–0–17–2; Walsh 9–0–42–0; Marshall 10–1–23–4; Harper 10–0–35–0.

West Indies

C. G. Greenidge c Downton b Thomas	45	R. A. Harper not out	1
D. L. Haynes c Downton b Foster	35	B 4, l-b 2, n-b 5	11
R. B. Richardson lbw b Gooch	32		
H. A. Gomes st Downton b Willey	19	1/84 2/89 3/142 (4 wkts, 43.5 overs) 146	
†P. J. L. Dujon not out	3	4/142	

*I. V. A. Richards, M. D. Marshall, J. Garner, B. P. Patterson and C. A. Walsh did not bat.

Bowling: Taylor 7-2-17-0; Thomas 8-1-35-1; Foster 10-1-44-1; Emburey 10-3-19-0; Willey 6.5-0-25-1; Gooch 2-2-0-1.

Umpires: D. M. Archer and A. J. Gaynor.

WEST INDIES v ENGLAND

First Test Match

At Kingston, Jamaica, February 21, 22, 23. West Indies won by ten wickets. Only while Gooch and Robinson batted without undue difficulty in the first hour of the match did England promise to give West Indies a harder fight than in 1984. Of the five West Indian victories in that series in England, two were achieved on the fourth day: at Sabina Park, after two England collapses, they had almost an hour to spare on the third when Haynes and Richardson completed the formality of scoring the 5 runs needed in West Indies' second innings. Once again the cause of England's defeat was their inability to play exceptional fast bowling, much of it short-pitched. Their problems were accentuated by a fast, uneven surface and the presence in the West Indies ranks of Patterson, a 24-year-old Jamaican who, after failing to make much impact in a handful of games for Lancashire in 1985, forced his way into the West Indies team by his performances in the Shell Shield. Described before the Test as the fastest bowler in the Caribbean after Marshall, Patterson left no doubt in the England batsmen's minds that the order should have been reversed. A heavyweight of 6ft 2in, with a sprinting run and powerful delivery, in England's second innings he bowled at a pace comparable to that of Jeff Thomson of Australia in his prime. Deprived of the new ball by the prior claims of Marshall and Garner, he none the less took seven for 74 in his first Test and won the match award.

England went into the game weakened by Gatting's injury in the one-day international. (He returned home for further treatment after two days' play.) Lamb was the only other batsman in true form following four games on sub-standard pitches, and the England batsmen were further incommoded by an inadequate sightscreen at the Southern end, which was too low to frame the hands of bowlers more than six feet tall. The Jamaica Cricket Association had been unable to grant England's request to have it raised, lodged after their problems facing Walsh and Holding in the Jamaica match, because to do so would have obscured the view of an estimated 200 spectators to whom tickets had been sold. All Patterson's wickets were taken from that end.

After Gower won the toss, Gooch and Robinson reached 32 before the latter was caught at slip in the thirteenth over off a break-back that clipped the bat as he tried to withdraw it. Little could they have suspected it, but England had used up one-seventh of their batting time in both innings put together. The collapse rapidly took shape. Gower, having started against Patterson with a top-edged 6 over the four slips, was soon lbw to Holding, playing round a full-length ball, and Smith, in his first Test, was caught at the wicket from a ball he could have left.

Gooch defended skilfully, repeatedly killing chest-high balls to keep them from Haynes at short leg. But ten minutes after lunch he was unable to control a steeply rising ball from Marshall and was caught in the gully. From then on only Lamb produced the necessary resolution, fortitude and patience to cope with the surfeit of short bowling. He lost Botham, Willey and Downton, the first two to mis-played attacking strokes, before Garner bowled him with a shooter that struck off stump no more than six inches above the base. The same fate befell Robinson in the second innings.

When West Indies batted, Thomas, England's other new cap, opened with one of the most fiery overs of the match. Haynes edged his first ball head high between first and second slip, and was dropped by Willey in the gully from a square-cut off the second. The sixth, fast and lifting, just missed bat and head. Willey's proved a costly miss. With Greenidge punishing Thomas and Botham, the first wicket put on 79 in eighteen overs before Greenidge retired hurt with a cut forehead after mis-hooking Botham, and when West Indies reached 85 for no wicket (in two hours) by the close, the outlook for England was depressing.

On the second day, however, England gained the initiative through the accuracy of Ellison and Edmonds, aided by the cautious batting of a team determined to consolidate and by Richards's decision not to bat at number five. Gomes made sure the task was carried out, batting self-denyingly for 220 minutes, and Best made a good impression, opening his Test account with a hook for 6, third ball, off Botham and sharing a stand of 68 with Gomes.

Tactical considerations notwithstanding, it was a fine effort by England to take seven for 183 off 75 overs in the day.

By dismissing Marshall and Greenidge, who returned at 247 for seven, Ellison next morning completed five or more wickets in an innings in his third successive Test; the product of persevering accuracy. But Dujon's handsome 54 extended West Indies' lead to 148, which, with the pitch playing as it had been, looked enough to give them victory. In practice England, apart from Willey, batted acquiescently after Robinson and Gooch had been dismissed for 0.

England

G. A. Gooch c Garner b Marshall	51	– b Marshall	0
R. T. Robinson c Greenidge b Patterson	6	– b Garner	0
*D. I. Gower lbw b Holding	16	– c Best b Patterson	9
D. M. Smith c Dujon b Patterson	1	– (7) c Gomes b Marshall	0
A. J. Lamb b Garner	49	– c sub (R. A. Harper) b Patterson	13
I. T. Botham c Patterson b Marshall	15	– b Marshall	29
P. Willey c Dujon b Holding	0	– (4) b Garner	71
†P. R. Downton c Dujon b Patterson	2	– c Haynes b Holding	3
R. M. Ellison c Haynes b Patterson	9	– b Garner	11
P. H. Edmonds not out	5	– lbw b Patterson	7
J. G. Thomas b Garner	0	– not out	1
N-b 5	5	B 5, n-b 3	8

1/32 2/53 3/54 4/83 5/120   159   1/1 2/3 3/19 4/40 5/95   152
6/127 7/138 8/142 9/158   6/103 7/106 8/140 9/146

Bowling: *First Innings*—Marshall 11–1–30–2; Garner 14.3–0–58–2; Patterson 11–4–30–4; Holding 7–0–36–2; Richards 1–1–0–0; Richardson 1–0–5–0. *Second Innings*—Marshall 11–4–29–3; Garner 9–2–22–3; Holding 12–1–52–1; Patterson 10.5–0–44–3.

West Indies

C. G. Greenidge lbw b Ellison	58		
D. L. Haynes c Downton b Thomas	32	– (1) not out	4
J. Garner c Edmonds b Botham	24		
R. B. Richardson lbw b Botham	7	– (2) not out	0
H. A. Gomes lbw b Ellison	56		
C. A. Best lbw b Willey	35		
*I. V. A. Richards lbw b Ellison	23		
†P. J. L. Dujon c Gooch b Thomas	54		
M. D. Marshall c sub (J. E. Emburey) b Ellison	6		
M. A. Holding lbw b Ellison	3		
B. P. Patterson not out	0		
B 2, l-b 4, n-b 3	9	N-b 1	1

1/95 2/112 3/115 4/183 5/222   307   (no wkt) 5
6/241 7/247 8/299 9/303

In the first innings, C. G. Greenidge, when 47, retired hurt at 79 and resumed at 247.

Bowling: *First Innings*—Botham 19–4–67–2; Thomas 28.5–6–82–2; Ellison 33–12–78–5; Edmonds 21–6–53–0; Willey 4–0–15–1; Gooch 2–1–6–0. *Second Innings*—Thomas 1–0–4–0; Lamb 0.0–0–1–0.

Umpires: D. M. Archer and J. R. Gayle.

TRINIDAD & TOBAGO v ENGLAND XI

At Port-of-Spain, February 28, March 1, 2. Drawn. England were in danger of wasting Robinson's solid 76, made in 191 minutes, when a mid-innings collapse reduced them to 156 for six after Nanan had put them in to bat. But on a green pitch without much pace, Trinidad lacked support for Gray, and by adding 50 for the seventh wicket Willey and Emburey made sure that the final total was respectable. England, selecting their side before leaving Jamaica in expectation of conditions favouring the spinners, were also ill-equipped. However, Foster and Taylor earned a lead of 120 with five and a half hours remaining on the final day. Largely through lack of concentration England were 41 for four before Smith and Slack, in his first match after being summoned from the England B tour in Sri Lanka, added 60 in 63 minutes. Despite disposing of the Trinidad openers cheaply, England never looked like winning in the three hours following the declaration.

England XI

G. A. Gooch c Mohammed b Gray	23	– lbw b Gray	12
R. T. Robinson lbw b Gray	76	– c Mohammed b Gilman	6
W. N. Slack c Bodoe b Nanan	0	– (6) not out	37
*D. I. Gower b Nanan	43	– c Simmons b Gilman	7
†B. N. French b Gray	0		
D. M. Smith c Rajah b Gray	7	– (3) not out	23
P. Willey st Williams b Mahabir	27	– (5) c Williams b Gray	10
J. E. Emburey b Mahabir	32		
P. H. Edmonds c and b Gray	12		
N. A. Foster c Bodoe b Nanan	1		
L. B. Taylor not out	1		
B 5, w 1, n-b 1	7	L-b 3, w 3	6

1/50 2/55 3/145 4/145 5/145   229   1/21 2/21 3/30   (4 wkts dec.) 101
6/156 7/206 8/215 9/218   4/41

Bowling: *First Innings*—Gray 24.3–9–50–5; Gilman 8–1–35–0; Simmons 6–2–18–0; Nanan 28–9–54–3; Mahabir 21–6–48–2; Bodoe 5–0–19–0. *Second Innings*—Gray 11–2–39–2; Gilman 12–1–44–2; Nanan 4–0–12–0; Mahabir 2–1–3–0.

Trinidad & Tobago

P. V. Simmons b Emburey	24	– c Gooch b Foster	6
M. Richardson lbw b Foster	0	– c Gooch b Taylor	1
N. Gomez c French b Taylor	2	– c Slack b Edmonds	39
A. Rajah c Willey b Taylor	12	– not out	55
D. I. Mohammed lbw b Foster	6	– c Foster b Willey	5
M. Bodoe lbw b Foster	9		
†D. Williams b Foster	17	– (6) not out	0
*R. Nanan c French b Foster	26		
A. H. Gray c Smith b Foster	2		
G. Mahabir c Emburey b Taylor	2		
G. Gilman not out	0		
B 1, l-b 5, w 2, n-b 1	9	B 1, l-b 6, w 1, n-b 2	10

1/2 2/9 3/42 4/46 5/50   109   1/10 2/10 3/90 4/112   (4 wkts) 116
6/61 7/84 8/88 9/96

Bowling: *First Innings*—Taylor 14–5–27–3; Foster 16.4–5–54–6; Gooch 3–0–5–0; Emburey 8–4–15–1; Edmonds 1–0–2–0. *Second Innings*—Foster 7–3–16–1; Taylor 9–1–31–1; Emburey 9–1–23–0; Edmonds 9–1–29–1; Willey 5–1–10–1.

Umpires: Mohammed Hosein and S. Mohammed.

†WEST INDIES v ENGLAND

Second One-day International

At Port-of-Spain, Trinidad, March 4. England won by five wickets. A leg-bye off the final ball brought England victory in a match reduced by rain to 37 overs a side. Described by many as the best one-day international played in the West Indies, it was made for the crowd of 16,000 by two great innings: 82 off 39 balls by Richards (four 6s, six 4s), and 129 not out by Gooch (126 balls, one 6, seventeen 4s) which, though hit at a slower pace, was comparable in the controlled power of Gooch's strokeplay. That it earned him the match award in competition with Richards's spectacular innings was proof of its quality. It was further enhanced by the facts that Gooch was on the field throughout the match; was under continuous pressure to maintain an asking-rate of 6.2 an over; and gave no semblance of a chance. Slack, who shared a second-wicket stand of 89 in seventeen overs, was the only other England batsman to score more than 20 as the target contracted to 100 off twelve overs, 59 off six, 27 off three, and nine off the last, which was bowled by Patterson following some heavy punishment of Garner. In West Indies' innings, Richards was in the form that makes him impossible to bowl to. The length of the ball, and especially its line, were immaterial as he scored his runs out of 117 in nine overs, overtaking Richardson who had a start of 38. The biggest of his 6s was a straight drive off Botham out of the ground, a hit of more than 100 yards.

Man of the Match: G. A. Gooch.

West Indies

D. L. Haynes b Foster	53	R. A. Harper not out		0
C. A. Best run out	10	L-b 4, n-b 1		5
R. B. Richardson not out	79			—
*I. V. A. Richards c Foster b Botham	82	1/37 2/106 3/223	(3 wkts, 37 overs)	229

H. A. Gomes, †T. R. O. Payne, M. D. Marshall, J. Garner, C. A. Walsh and B. P. Patterson did not bat.

Bowling: Botham 8-1-59-1; Foster 10-1-42-1; Ellison 8-0-57-0; Emburey 8-2-48-0; Willey 3-0-19-0.

England

G. A. Gooch not out	129	D. M. Smith not out		10
I. T. Botham c Richards b Garner	8			
W. N. Slack c Payne b Walsh	34	B 1, l-b 7, n-b 6		14
A. J. Lamb b Garner	16			—
*D. I. Gower run out	9	1/9 2/98 3/143	(5 wkts, 37 overs)	230
P. Willey c Richards b Garner	10	4/170 5/183		

†P. R. Downton, R. M. Ellison, J. E. Emburey and N. A. Foster did not bat.

Bowling: Garner 9-1-62-3; Patterson 6-0-30-0; Walsh 9-0-49-1; Marshall 10-1-59-0; Harper 3-0-22-0.

Umpires: C. E. Cumberbatch and S. Mohammed.

WEST INDIES v ENGLAND

Second Test Match

At Port-of-Spain, Trinidad, March 7, 8, 9, 11, 12. West Indies won by seven wickets. Up to the start of England's second innings, the second Test developed along similar lines to the first, except that at Queen's Park Oval Richards won the toss and put England in to bat. Both sides made two changes, Walsh and Payne replacing the injured Holding and Dujon for West Indies, and Slack and Emburey coming in for Robinson, who was unwell, and Smith for England. Payne and Slack won their first Test caps.

The pitch had nothing like the pace of Kingston, but none the less England were bowled out for 176 in 44.4 overs, of which 106 came from Gower and Lamb for the fourth wicket. After Gooch (fourth ball) and Slack had fallen to Marshall in his first three overs, Gower and Lamb scored their runs at a rate of 7 an over, punishing Patterson and Walsh heavily. Patterson, lacking rhythm and over-stepping regularly, was a shadow of the bowler who had begun so auspiciously in Kingston. In the latter stages of the partnership, however, England encountered, in the shape of a shower, the first of the ill luck that was to dog them on three of the first four days. Considered at first too light to stop play, it freshened a slow pitch enough for Garner to have Gower lbw with a ball, delivered over the wicket, which cut back from about off stump. Shortly there was a twenty-minute interruption: but the important breakthrough had been made. When play resumed, the remaining six wickets crashed in 90 minutes. Gower, hooking and pulling with rediscovered certainty, and Lamb both hit eleven 4s; but no other batsman reached double figures.

An ill-conceived spell by Botham, who gave away 39 in five overs with the new ball in the hope of inducing Greenidge or Haynes to hook a catch to one of two long-legs, enabled West Indies to reach 67 for one in 70 minutes by the close. But though Haynes and Richardson were to strengthen West Indies' advantage with a stand of 150, England, in the person of Ellison, were again notably unlucky. In a 90-minute spell, his out-swing beat the bat eight times, Haynes in one over playing and missing at three successive balls. Nevertheless, with Richardson producing many splendid off-side strokes, the score rose steadily; rapidly when Botham, replacing Ellison, gave away 26 in four erratic overs. Richardson, hammering Thomas on the leg side, reached a fluent hundred in 34 overs.

Only at 198 did Gower belatedly pair Edmonds with Emburey – and almost instantly West Indies lost their impetus. When Richardson (175 minutes, one 6, nineteen 4s) was caught at the wicket off a mistimed sweep, he became the first of seven batsmen to fall to the spinners in a combined spell of 45 uninterrupted overs. Haynes was brought to a standstill, and only Richards, whose 34 came off twenty balls with two 6s and four 4s, briefly jeopardised the England strategy. However, when England took the new ball soon after Garner's dismissal, Marshall found support from Walsh and Patterson as he took his score to 62 not out in two hours and West Indies to a lead of 223.

England, starting their second innings 50 minutes before lunch on the third day, could not have made a worse start. Slack, tardily sent back by Gooch, was run out without scoring. Walsh broke a second-wicket stand of 79 when Gower missed one of the increasing number of shooters, and 40 minutes later he ended Gooch's three-hour innings with a late in-swinger as the batsman played no stroke. At 168 for three at the close, England's slim chance of escape rested on Willey, Lamb and Botham following the rest day. But within an hour all three were out, Payne redeeming an untidy match behind the stumps with a diving catch in front of slip to extend Botham's unsuccessful run. Shooters were by then a common occurrence, and England were in danger of defeat by an innings when Emburey, glancing Walsh to backward short-leg, was eighth out at 214.

However, Richards's decision to take a new ball brought an unexpected development. Being harder than the old one, its bounce was higher and more consistent, and the threat of the shooter disappeared. Garner dismissed Edmonds, but for two hours the last pair, Ellison and Thomas, defied the four fast bowlers with ease. Relying more on the forward stroke than their seniors, they doggedly added 72 and were looking good for more when Ellison was adjudged lbw.

West Indies, needing 93, made through Greenidge a strong effort to score them in the 90 minutes to close of play. In the event, with England pairing the spinners after six overs and Greenidge caught at extra-cover, they were 17 short. Victory was a formality when the fifth day dawned bright and clear; but by dismissing Richardson and Gomes, Emburey confirmed what a hard task West Indies might have faced had their target been 200.

The game was played against a background of demonstrations from a small group of anti-apartheid protesters, but there was no trouble inside the ground and, without being large, the gates were satisfactory. Marshall, who completed 200 wickets in his 42nd Test when he dismissed Downton, won the match award.

England

G. A. Gooch c Best b Marshall	43	2 – lbw b Walsh	47
W. N. Slack c Payne b Marshall	2	2 – run out	0
*D. I. Gower lbw b Garner	66	b Walsh	47
P. Willey c Payne b Patterson	5	b Marshall	26
A. J. Lamb c Marshall b Garner	62	lbw b Walsh	40
I. T. Botham c Richardson b Marshall	2	c Payne b Marshall	1
J. E. Emburey c Payne b Garner	0	c Best b Walsh	14
†P. R. Downton c Marshall b Walsh	8	lbw b Marshall	5
R. M. Ellison lbw b Marshall	4	lbw b Marshall	36
P. H. Edmonds not out	3	c Payne b Garner	13
J. G. Thomas b Patterson	4	not out	31
L-b 4, n-b 14	18	B 20, l-b 11, w 1, n-b 27	59

1/2 2/11 3/30 4/136 5/147   176   1/2 2/82 3/109 4/190 5/192   315
6/148 7/153 8/163 9/165   6/197 7/214 8/214 9/243

Bowling: *First Innings*—Marshall 15-3-38-4; Garner 15-4-45-3; Patterson 8.4-0-60-2; Walsh 6-2-29-1. *Second Innings*—Garner 21-5-44-1; Marshall 32.2-9-94-4; Richards 7-4-7-0; Walsh 27-4-74-4; Patterson 16-0-65-0; Gomes 1-1-0-0.

West Indies

C. G. Greenidge c Lamb b Thomas	37	– c Lamb b Edmonds	45
D. L. Haynes st Downton b Emburey	67	– not out	39
R. B. Richardson c Downton b Emburey	102	– c Gooch b Emburey	9
H. A. Gomes st Downton b Emburey	30	– b Emburey	0
C. A. Best b Edmonds	22	– not out	0
*I. V. A. Richards c Botham b Edmonds	34		
†T. R. O. Payne c Gower b Emburey	5		
M. D. Marshall not out	62		
J. Garner c Gooch b Emburey	12		
C. A. Walsh c Edmonds b Thomas	3		
B. P. Patterson c Gooch b Botham	9		
L-b 11, w 1, n-b 4	16	L-b 2	2

1/59 2/209 3/242 4/257 5/298   399   1/72 2/89 3/91   (3 wkts) 95
6/303 7/327 8/342 9/364

Bowling: *First Innings*—Botham 9.4-0-68-1; Thomas 20-4-86-2; Ellison 18-3-58-0; Edmonds 30-5-98-2; Emburey 27-5-78-5. *Second Innings*—Thomas 5-1-21-0; Ellison 3-1-12-0; Edmonds 12.3-3-24-1; Emburey 10-1-36-2.

Umpires: D. M. Archer and C. E. Cumberbatch.

BARBADOS v ENGLAND XI

At Bridgetown, March 14, 15, 16, 17. Barbados won by three wickets. Gatting, rejoining the team after convalescing at home, had the misfortune to break his thumb within twenty hours of his return; one of several factors that contributed to Barbados's third post-war victory over MCC or England. It was achieved without Greenidge, Haynes and Marshall, and its source was ineffectual batting in England's first innings when, after winning the toss, they were bowled out for 171. Gatting's dismissal was the turning-point. Having shown no after-effects of his facial injury in scoring 36 in 85 minutes, he had no counter to a ball of medium pace from Greene which lifted steeply to his bottom hand, whence it looped to second slip. England lost their seven remaining wickets between lunch and tea. Though handicapped by other injuries, the tourists fought back under Willey's acting-captaincy to leave Barbados 267 to win. Shooters were by then a regular occurrence, but the good technique of two policemen, Johnson and Reifer, saw the Shell Shield champions home in the fourth of the final twenty overs. Botham, who damaged his left ankle, bowled only 3.3 overs, but favoured by much good luck he hit his first fifty on two tours, his 70 in three hours being the highest score on either side.

England XI

R. T. Robinson st Payne b Reifer	40	– c Best b Greene	21
W. N. Slack c Payne b Greene	12	– b Reid	23
D. M. Smith c Payne b Greene	24	– lbw b Garner	43
*M. W. Gatting c Best b Greene	36	– absent injured	
P. Willey b Garner	8	– (4) b Reid	60
I. T. Botham b Estwick	27	– (5) lbw b Estwick	70
R. M. Ellison c Payne b Greene	2	– (6) c Reid b Greene	45
†B. N. French c Payne b Estwick	0	– (7) b Estwick	9
P. H. Edmonds c Payne b Estwick	3	– (8) b Reid	20
N. A. Foster not out	6	– (9) c and b Best	10
L. B. Taylor c Inniss b Greene	9	– (10) not out	0
L-b 1, w 2, n-b 1	4	L-b 7, n-b 4	11

1/51 2/63 3/115 4/115 5/151   171   1/35 2/67 3/103 4/193 5/240   312
6/151 7/151 8/155 9/157   6/256 7/282 8/312 9/312

Bowling: *First Innings*—Garner 9-4-21-1; Estwick 18-7-38-3; Greene 20-1-72-5; Reifer 8-0-18-1; Reid 5-1-17-0; Broomes 1-0-4-0. *Second Innings*—Garner 16-3-31-1; Estwick 22-1-58-2; Greene 27-4-74-2; Reid 38-8-70-3; Broomes 15-1-44-0; Best 5.3-0-20-1; Reifer 2-1-8-0.

Barbados

A. S. Gilkes c Willey b Taylor	52	– c French b Foster 32
M. Inniss run out	28	– lbw b Taylor 6
C. A. Best c and b Ellison	2	– b Edmonds 42
†T. R. O. Payne b Taylor	1	– c French b Foster 7
N. A. Johnson st French b Edmonds	40	– b Willey 56
L. N. Reifer c sub b Edmonds	35	– not out 59
V. S. Greene c Willey b Ellison	5	– (8) c Foster b Edmonds 6
W. E. Reid c Slack b Ellison	25	– (7) c Robinson b Willey ... 14
*J. Garner c French b Edmonds	4	– not out 23
N. da C. Broomes not out	11	
R. O. Estwick b Taylor	1	
L-b 9, n-b 4	13	B 7, l-b 8, n-b 8 23

1/70 2/76 3/80 4/97 5/154   217   1/22 2/61 3/71 4/129   (7 wkts) 268
6/167 7/185 8/192 9/216   5/170 6/208 7/222

Bowling: *First Innings*—Botham 3.3–0–13–0; Foster 15–3–57–0; Edmonds 21.3–6–45–3; Ellison 15–3–36–3; Taylor 19.3–4–46–3; Willey 4–1–11–0. *Second Innings*—Foster 16–1–69–2; Ellison 4–1–16–0; Taylor 12–1–38–1; Edmonds 27.4–5–84–2; Willey 18–1–46–2.

Umpires: N. D. B. Harrison and S. E. Parris.

†WEST INDIES v ENGLAND

Third One-day International

At Bridgetown, Barbados, March 19. West Indies won by 135 runs. After Gower had won the toss, Botham and in particular Foster put in accurate, lively spells to help restrict West Indies to 249 in 46 overs on a very fast outfield. England's batsmen, however, were brushed aside in 39 overs by bowling of much higher pace. Fatalism set in when Gooch was given out, caught at the wicket, in the fifth over, and much of the subsequent batting lacked commitment. England's best chance of holding West Indies to a manageable total had disappeared when Richards, mistiming an angled stroke off Foster, was missed at slip at 5. His 62 (56 balls, two 6s, seven 4s) was ended by a superbly judged overhead catch by Foster on the long-off boundary at the end of an over by Emburey which had already cost 20.

Man of the Match: I. V. A. Richards.

West Indies

C. G. Greenidge c Downton b Foster ..	31	M. D. Marshall c and b Botham 9
D. L. Haynes b Foster	28	M. A. Holding not out 0
R. B. Richardson b Botham	62	B 4, w 2, n-b 1 7
*I. V. A. Richards c Foster b Emburey	62	
†P. J. L. Dujon c Lamb b Foster	23	1/61 2/64 3/181 (7 wkts, 46 overs) 249
R. A. Harper not out	24	4/195 5/225
J. Garner b Emburey	3	6/239 7/248

H. A. Gomes and B. P. Patterson did not bat.

Bowling: Botham 9–2–39–2; Thomas 7–1–50–0; Foster 9–0–39–3; Willey 6–0–21–0; Gooch 6–1–41–0; Emburey 9–0–55–2.

England

G. A. Gooch c Dujon b Garner	6	J. E. Emburey c Dujon b Patterson 15
R. T. Robinson c Richardson b Marshall	23	N. A. Foster not out 9
W. N. Slack c Dujon b Holding	9	J. G. Thomas c Richards b Patterson .. 0
*D. I. Gower lbw b Marshall	0	L-b 3, w 3, n-b 5 11
A. J. Lamb c Marshall b Holding	18	
I. T. Botham c Garner b Marshall	14	1/18 2/42 3/42 (39 overs) 114
P. Willey c Greenidge b Harper	9	4/46 5/69 6/81
†P. R. Downton b Harper	0	7/82 8/85 9/113

Bowling: Garner 6–2–6–1; Patterson 9–1–38–2; Marshall 6–2–14–3; Holding 10–1–29–2; Harper 8–1–24–2.

Umpires: D. M. Archer and L. H. Barker.

WEST INDIES v ENGLAND

Third Test Match

At Bridgetown, Barbados, March 21, 22, 23, 25. West Indies won by an innings and 30 runs. A disastrous third day, on which fifteen wickets were lost for 211, condemned England to their eighth successive defeat by West Indies. Only once before had England suffered a losing run of equal length, against Australia in the first two series after the First World War. This Bridgetown Test, which enabled West Indies to retain the Wisden Trophy, did particular damage to Gower's team in that it was watched by an estimated 4,000 British spectators, among them the chairman of selectors. It did nothing to lessen Mr May's disappointment that after two days England were seemingly as well placed as any side since Pakistan six Kensington Oval Tests earlier (1976-77) to prevent West Indies winning, only to lose before lunch on the fourth. Before returning home, May called for greater resolve, questioning the team's attitude. Out of loyalty to Willis, his assistant, who was responsible for practice, Brown, the manager, refuted that, but May's sentiments were widely shared.

Dujon and Holding returned for West Indies, while for England, Robinson replaced Slack and Foster came in for Ellison, who was unwell. Gower, winning what looked an essential toss, followed the normal practice for the ground by putting his opponents in to bat, but the move misfired. If there was life in the pitch, Botham and Thomas were unable to extract it, and though Foster dismissed Greenidge in the eighth over (his own first), West Indies were 115 for one at lunch off 25. Richardson made a brilliant start, hitting nine 4s in reaching 50 off 44 deliveries, straight-driving, cutting and hooking with confidence and power. Twenty minutes before lunch, however, forcing Thomas off the back foot to extra cover, he was dropped by Gooch at 55. That miss, in conjunction with a life for Haynes at 51 (Edmonds at square leg from a hook off Botham) consigned England to a wait of 260 minutes for a second wicket. Haynes, doggedly adhesive, had helped Richardson add 194 when, in the first over of another Foster spell, he was caught by the only slip.

After their erratic start, England bowled and fielded well to limit West Indies to 269 for two, Richardson 150 not out, off 81 overs in the day. Much of the credit went to Emburey who, by pitching the ball on off and middle stumps to a three-six leg-side field, made the Antiguan labour 270 minutes for the last hundred of his runs. At 92 he survived a concerted appeal for a catch off his gloves by Downton, diving forward past the batsman's legs.

Emburey won his due reward after 25 minutes on the second morning when Richardson misjudged the ball to sweep and was lbw after batting for 347 minutes in his second hundred in successive Tests. Thus began England's best day of the series to that date. Though Richards, caressing Emburey for two driven 6s, played masterfully to reach 50 in 80 minutes, the innings fell apart directly the new ball was taken after 108 overs, following a long spell in harness by the spinners. Thirteen minutes before lunch, in Thomas's first over, Gomes chipped low to Gower at square leg and West Indies were 361 for four: 90 minutes into the afternoon they were all out for 418. Thomas, striking the vital blow when he had Richards caught by Downton off a late out-swinger first ball after lunch, took four for 14 in 6.1 overs, yorking Holding and having Garner caught at second slip to polish off the innings.

Robinson, in two minds whether to hook or take evasive action, was caught off his gloves in the last over before tea. But Gooch and Gower, playing with great skill, negotiated a lengthy passage of dull light to take England to 110 for one by close of play. On the third day, however, their splendid effort came to nothing. Bowling of high class destroyed the first innings; much poor batting accounted for six wickets in the second. It was clear England were up against it when the twelfth ball of the day, bowled to Gooch by Garner, missed off stump a few inches off the ground. There was swing and movement off the ground as well. The collapse started when Gower edged a ball that did little more than hold its line to give Dujon the second of five catches in the innings. But Gooch (who went 37 minutes before adding to his overnight 46) and Lamb received near unplayable balls, while Willey was the victim of a poor decision. Botham batted soundly for an hour, but then his concentration went, he skied a hook five minutes before lunch, and the tail was swept aside.

With the sky clearing, conditions were easier when England followed on 229 behind. But once Patterson bowled Gooch and Robinson in one of the fastest spells of the match, determination was in short supply. England's capitulation reached an ignominious level when Gower chased a wide half-volley and Botham swished 21 in four overs before getting out a minute from the close. After a rainy rest day, play was twice interrupted when the game resumed. But despite a fighting stand of 50 between Downton and Emburey, West Indies completed their victory ten minutes before lunch. Richardson won the match award.

West Indies

C. G. Greenidge c Botham b Foster	... 21	M. A. Holding b Thomas	23
D. L. Haynes c Botham b Foster	84	M. D. Marshall run out	4
R. B. Richardson lbw b Emburey	160	J. Garner c Gooch b Thomas	0
H. A. Gomes c Gower b Thomas	33	B. P. Patterson not out	0
*I. V. A. Richards c Downton b Thomas	51	B 2, l-b 9, w 3, n-b 2	16
C. A. Best lbw b Foster	21		
†P. J. L. Dujon c sub (W. N. Slack)		1/34 2/228 3/286 4/361 5/362	418
b Botham	5	6/367 7/406 8/413 9/418	

Bowling: Botham 24-3-80-1; Thomas 16.1-2-70-4; Foster 19-0-76-3; Edmonds 29-2-85-0; Emburey 38-7-96-1.

England

G. A. Gooch c Dujon b Garner	53	– b Patterson	11
R. T. Robinson c Dujon b Marshall	3	– b Patterson	43
*D. I. Gower c Dujon b Marshall	66	– c Marshall b Garner	23
P. Willey c Dujon b Marshall	5	– lbw b Garner	17
A. J. Lamb c Richardson b Marshall	5	– c and b Holding	6
I. T. Botham c Dujon b Patterson	14	– (7) c Dujon b Garner	21
†P. R. Downton lbw b Holding	11	– (8) c Dujon b Holding	26
J. E. Emburey c Best b Patterson	0	– (9) not out	35
P. H. Edmonds c Richardson b Patterson	4	– (6) lbw b Garner	4
N. A. Foster lbw b Holding	0	– c Richardson b Holding	0
J. G. Thomas not out	4	– b Patterson	0
B 4, l-b 8, w 2, n-b 10	24	L-b 1, n-b 12	13

1/6 2/126 3/134 4/141 5/151	189	1/48 2/71 3/94 4/108 5/108	199
6/168 7/172 8/181 9/185		6/132 7/138 8/185 9/188	

Bowling: *First Innings*—Marshall 14-1-42-4; Garner 14-4-35-1; Patterson 15-5-54-3; Holding 13-4-37-2; Richards 3-0-9-0. *Second Innings*—Marshall 13-1-47-0; Garner 17-2-69-4; Patterson 8.4-2-28-3; Holding 10-1-47-3; Richards 4-1-7-0.

Umpires: D. M. Archer and L. H. Barker.

†WEST INDIES v ENGLAND

Fourth One-day International

At Port-of-Spain, Trinidad, March 31. West Indies won by eight wickets. England put up a performance which exposed to a crowd of 21,000 what depths of incompetence they had reached. That P. B. H. May's criticisms had fallen on deaf ears as far as the captain was concerned had become clear in Barbados on the previous Friday when, after two days off following the Test defeat, the first practice was made optional – and Gower himself was one of the six who failed to attend. In the circumstances it was apposite that when Gower, in surrender, came on to bowl with West Indies needing eight to win, Haynes and Richards scored 9 off his only two deliveries; a single by Haynes being turned into a 5 by a throw over Downton's head with no-one backing up, then Richards completing his 50 with a cover drive next ball. England's batting, fielding and – apart from Emburey and Edmonds – their bowling proclaimed the lack of practice and resolve on a slow pitch which, had they been in the right frame of mind, would have given them an even chance of levelling the series.

Man of the Match: J. Garner.

England

G. A. Gooch c Richards b Marshall ...	10	J. E. Emburey not out	2
R. T. Robinson b Marshall	55	P. H. Edmonds b Garner	0
*D. I. Gower b Walsh	20		
A. J. Lamb c Dujon b Walsh	16	B 1, l-b 4, w 2, n-b 3	10
I. T. Botham c Harper b Garner	29		
P. Willey c Greenidge b Marshall	6	1/15 2/49 3/88 (9 wkts, 47 overs) 165	
†P. R. Downton c Greenidge b Marshall	12	4/126 5/138 6/154	
R. M. Ellison b Garner	5	7/161 8/165 9/165	

N. A. Foster did not bat.

Bowling: Marshall 9-0-37-4; Garner 9-1-22-3; Holding 9-1-32-0; Walsh 10-0-25-2; Harper 10-0-44-0.

West Indies

C. G. Greenidge b Foster 0
D. L. Haynes not out 77
R. B. Richardson c Gooch b Emburey 31
*I. V. A. Richards not out 50
    L-b 7, w 1 8

1/0 2/75   (2 wkts, 38.2 overs) 166

H. A. Gomes, †P. J. L. Dujon, R. A. Harper, M. D. Marshall, M. A. Holding, J. Garner and C. A. Walsh did not bat.

Bowling: Foster 6-1-27-1; Ellison 7-0-30-0; Botham 5-0-24-0; Edmonds 10-1-38-0; Emburey 10-2-31-1; Gower 0.2-0-9-0.

Umpires: C. E. Cumberbatch and S. Mohammed.

WEST INDIES v ENGLAND

Fourth Test Match

At Port-of-Spain, Trinidad, April 3, 4, 5. West Indies won by ten wickets. Botham's first worthwhile contributions of the series and two encouraging innings by Smith were England's only consolations from another overwhelming defeat. As at Kingston (first Test) and Bridgetown (third), the pitch gave West Indies enough advantage for their fast bowlers to win the upper hand against batsmen in peak form, so it followed that against a disillusioned England team a rapid wicket-taking rate was not far short of a formality. In the event it took West Indies fewer overs (103.4) to demolish England twice than it did to bowl them out in the second innings of the previous Test at Queen's Park Oval. When the second innings of this match was tidied up in 38 overs, Haynes and Richardson scored the 39 needed to win off 35 deliveries, West Indies' ninth successive victory over England coming 70 minutes before the end of the third day – about fifteen minutes earlier than in Kingston, where the margin was the same.

The pitch, a hotch-potch of thick grass and bare brown patches, was described as the greenest ever seen in Port-of-Spain. It was two-paced, uneven in bounce throughout, and after two days criss-crossed by cracks. On the third morning when, under the supervision of the umpires, groundstaff shaved off an eighth of an inch of grass, the resultant clippings weighed about two pounds. England's cricket lacked distinction, and not only with the bat, as Thomas's analysis makes clear. But what remained of their fighting spirit had undoubtedly been diminished by the seemingly calculated nature of the pitch's preparation.

Smith's relative success – he was top scorer in each innings – was significant. Having been omitted from the second and third Tests, he was the only batsman whose confidence was more or less intact. By England's modest standards of the series, he was beginning to impose himself when he was caught behind square-leg off a well-hit hook in the first innings, and deceived by Holding's movement to be lbw without offering a stroke in the second. He took Edmonds's place in the side beaten at Bridgetown, while for West Indies Harper, the off-spinner, came in for Best, though in the event he did not bowl a ball.

Having won the toss, West Indies were in the ascendant from the fourth over when Garner, bowling at his quickest, had Robinson caught at third slip. At 31 for three, all to Garner, it required little imagination to see England collapsing for a hundred. But with Smith coping skilfully with the variations in bounce, especially with balls that rose chest high, and Lamb surviving an easy chance to Harper at third slip at 11, the fourth wicket put on 92. Then Botham, after a shaky start, sustained his concentration for 165 minutes before swinging wildly across Holding to be last out for 38, his highest Test score in the West Indies. There was still time for West Indies to have two overs batting before the close.

Thomas's inability to control either line or length damaged England's slim chance of remaining in contention. Greenidge and Haynes shared eight 4s in his opening four-over spell, and he was hardly less expensive later. However, Gomes, well caught by Downton low to his left, and Richards, with whom he shared a partnership of 102, the highest of the match, were the only batsmen to master the problems for any length of time. Richards, who passed 6,000 runs in Tests at the start of his innings, played superbly, responding to England's tactics of bowling clear of his off stump with a variety of exquisite off-side strokes to beat the six-man field. He looked sure to make his first Test hundred on the ground since 1975-76 when, half an hour before the close, Botham had him lbw with a breakback that kept low. When Botham next morning polished off the tail, he completed only his third five-wicket bag in eighteen Tests against West Indies, raising his tally overall to 352.

Once Gooch, hooking, top-edged the third ball of the innings straight up in the air, England never looked like overcoming their deficit of 112. Robinson, bat crooked and far away from body, was bowled off the inside edge for his fifth single-figure score in six innings in the series; Gower was adjudged lbw when he turned his back on a short ball, bowled over the wicket, which kept low; Lamb was beaten by a great delivery from Patterson which pitched on middle stump and struck the top of off. Hard enough to play in conditions favouring the bat, as in 1984 in England, the quality of West Indies' pace quartet made for something less than gripping contests on pitches such as this.

The Man of the Match award was won by Richards.

England

G. A. Gooch c Richards b Garner	14	– c Dujon b Marshall	0
R. T. Robinson c Marshall b Garner	0	– b Garner	5
*D. I. Gower c Dujon b Garner	10	– lbw b Patterson	22
D. M. Smith c Greenidge b Patterson	47	– lbw b Holding	32
A. J. Lamb b Holding	36	– b Patterson	11
I. T. Botham b Holding	38	– c Gomes b Marshall	25
P. Willey c Richardson b Garner	10	– lbw b Marshall	2
†P. R. Downton c Garner b Marshall	7	– not out	11
J. E. Emburey c Haynes b Marshall	8	– b Holding	0
N. A. Foster c Richards b Holding	0	– b Marshall	14
J. G. Thomas not out	5	– b Garner	0
L-b 3, w 1, n-b 21	25	B 5, l-b 7, n-b 16	28

1/8 2/29 3/31 4/123 5/124   **200**   1/0 2/30 3/30 4/75 5/105   **150**
6/151 7/168 8/181 9/190   6/109 7/115 8/126 9/150

Bowling: *First Innings*—Marshall 23-4-71-2; Garner 18-3-43-4; Patterson 10-2-31-1; Holding 14.3-3-52-3. *Second Innings*—Marshall 10-2-42-3; Garner 9-3-15-3; Holding 10-1-45-2; Patterson 9-1-36-2.

West Indies

C. G. Greenidge lbw b Emburey	42		
D. L. Haynes c Botham b Foster	25	– (1) not out	17
R. B. Richardson b Emburey	32	– (2) not out	22
H. A. Gomes c Downton b Foster	48		
*I. V. A. Richards lbw b Botham	87		
†P. J. L. Dujon c Downton b Botham	5		
M. D. Marshall b Emburey	5		
R. A. Harper lbw b Botham	21		
M. A. Holding b Botham	25		
J. Garner not out	5		
B. P. Patterson c Downton b Botham	3		
L-b 10, w 3, n-b 1	14		

1/58 2/74 3/111 4/213 5/244   312   (no wkt) 39
6/249 7/249 8/300 9/306

Bowling: *First Innings*—Botham 24.1–3–71–5; Thomas 15–0–101–0; Foster 24–3–68–2; Emburey 27–10–62–3. *Second Innings*—Botham 3–0–24–0; Foster 2.5–0–15–0.

Umpires: C. E. Cumberbatch and S. Mohammed.

WEST INDIES v ENGLAND

Fifth Test Match

At St John's, Antigua, April 11, 12, 13, 15, 16. West Indies won by 240 runs. Richards's 110 not out in West Indies' second innings, the fastest Test hundred ever in terms of balls received (56 to reach three figures, 58 in all), made the final Test historic on two counts. The other was West Indies' achievement in emulating Australia, previously the only country to win all five home Tests on more than one occasion. Their previous five-love victory was over India in 1961-62, matching Australia's feats against England (1920-21) and South Africa (1931-32), the series in which Sir Donald Bradman made 806 runs in four completed innings. In addition, West Indies also won all five Tests of the 1984 series in England.

Richards's display, making him the obvious candidate for the match award, would have been staggering at any level of cricket. What made it unforgettable for the 5,000 or so lucky enough to see it was that he scored it without blemish at a time when England's sole aim was to make run-scoring as difficult as possible to delay a declaration. Botham and Emburey never had fewer than six men on the boundary and sometimes nine, yet whatever length or line they bowled, Richards had a stroke for it. His control and touch were as much features of the innings as the tremendous power of his driving. As can be calculated from the following table, he was within range of his hundred six balls before completing it (with a leg-side 4 off Botham), while from the time he reached 83 off 46 balls there had been no doubt, assuming he stayed in, that he would trim several deliveries off J. M. Gregory's previous record of 67 for Australia against South Africa at Johannesburg in 1921-22. The full innings went:

··36126141 (24 off 10)	··211·412·1 (36 off 20)	112·2111·· (45 off 30)	
·1·1624441 (68 off 40)	12··664612 (96 off 50)	··21·461 (110 off 58)	

Plundered in 83 minutes out of 146 while he was at the wicket, it had to be, by any yardstick, among the most wonderful innings ever played.

Though it was not until the sixth of the final twenty overs that Downton's dismissal enabled West Indies to complete their second successive "blackwash" over Gower's side, England's defeat was in one way their worst of the series. With the exception of the second Test, the pitch was the only one that did not overtly help West Indian-style fast bowling; and by winning the toss Gower gave his bowlers their best chance of exploiting any moisture beneath the surface following heavy rain the weekend before the match.

In the event, there were only two junctures when England were remotely in contention – 40 minutes before lunch on the second day when Haynes, having deservedly completed his first hundred of the series, was caught at mid-on to make West Indies 291 for six; and when Gooch and Slack opened the third innings with a partnership of 127, England's highest of the rubber.

Both positions flattered to deceive. With Gower misguidedly over-bowling Botham in the hope he would collect the extra two wickets he needed to overtake Lillee's world record of dismissals, West Indies added 183 at almost 5 an over for their last four wickets (Marshall, Harper and Holding shared eight 6s). And within ten overs of Gooch's dismissal, England were 159 for four and in danger of being forced to follow on. Having taken two of the four wickets that fell on the first day – Richards was caught off a mis-hook at deep fine-leg – Botham emerged from the match with two for 225. The nearest he came to drawing level with Lillee (355) was when, with Marshall 12, Slack, diving to his left, missed a well-hit pick-up at square leg.

The game was not without its controversial moments, all of them, regrettably, centring on Richards in the field. But the first day, which was declared a public holiday and drew a full house of 10,000, established a carnival atmosphere which made the fifth Test the most enjoyable of the series. It was played in perfect weather: scorching hot but always with a sea-breeze.

Four weeks to the day after having his right thumb broken, Gatting was fit to play, while Slack and Ellison replaced Willey, who had returned to England, and Thomas. Smith's enforced withdrawal with back trouble within hours of the start gave Robinson another chance, this time at number three. Overnight there had been doubts about Gower's fitness following a blow on the right wrist, received while batting against Marshall in the previous Test, but Smith's indisposition settled the matter. West Indies were unchanged.

Haynes capped a consistent series with 131 (440 minutes, fifteen 4s) and 70; Gooch put together a pair of hard-earned 51s; Slack produced an innings of the type which should have seen him included in the original sixteen; Gower, with his captaincy possibly at stake, batted more than seven hours in the match. For once, too, there was an important contribution from a West Indian spinner, Harper striking at vital moments four times; and Emburey continued his mastery of Richardson by dismissing him for the fifth and sixth times in seven completed innings. Less encouragingly, West Indies bowled 40 no-balls which were not scored from: the most in any Test innings.

Notwithstanding his haughty treatment of the umpires in his stubborn pursuit of a ball to the liking of his bowlers, Richards, however, stood alone. For West Indian spectators, the only thing the series had lacked until the last Test was the sight of the greatest player in the world in full majestic flow. If anyone forgets that extraordinary *tour de force*, it can truthfully be said that he did not deserve to see it in the first place.

The Man of the Series award was presented to Marshall, who spearheaded West Indies' attack throughout the rubber, taking 27 wickets.

West Indies

C. G. Greenidge b Botham	14		
D. L. Haynes c Gatting b Ellison	131	– (1) run out	70
R. B. Richardson c Slack b Emburey	24	– (2) c Robinson b Emburey	31
H. A. Gomes b Emburey	24		
*I. V. A. Richards c Gooch b Botham	26	– (3) not out	110
†P. J. L. Dujon b Foster	21		
M. D. Marshall c Gatting b Gooch	76		
R. A. Harper c Lamb b Foster	60	– (4) not out	19
M. A. Holding c Gower b Ellison	73		
J. Garner run out	11		
B. P. Patterson not out	0		
B 2, l-b 11, w 1	14	B 4, l-b 9, w 1, n-b 2	16
	474		**246**

1/23 2/63 3/137 4/178 5/232   474   1/100 2/161   (2 wkts dec.) 246
6/291 7/351 8/401 9/450

Bowling: *First Innings*—Botham 40-6-147-2; Foster 28-5-86-2; Ellison 24.3-3-114-2; Emburey 37-11-93-2; Gooch 5-2-21-1. *Second Innings*—Botham 15-0-78-0; Foster 10-0-40-0; Emburey 14-0-83-1; Ellison 4-0-32-0.

England

G. A. Gooch lbw b Holding	51	– lbw b Holding	51
W. N. Slack c Greenidge b Patterson	52	– b Garner	8
R. T. Robinson b Marshall	12	– run out	3
*D. I. Gower c Dujon b Marshall	90	– (5) c Dujon b Harper	21
A. J. Lamb c and b Harper	1	– (6) b Marshall	1
M. W. Gatting c Dujon b Garner	15	– (7) b Holding	1
I. T. Botham c Harper b Garner	10	– (8) b Harper	13
†P. R. Downton c Holding b Garner	5	– (9) lbw b Marshall	13
R. M. Ellison c Dujon b Marshall	6	– (4) lbw b Garner	16
J. E. Emburey not out	7	– c Richardson b Harper	0
N. A. Foster c Holding b Garner	10	– not out	0
B 5, l-b 6, n-b 40	51	B 10, l-b 10, w 2, n-b 21	43

1/127 2/132 3/157 4/159 5/205		310
6/213 7/237 8/289 9/290		

1/14 2/29 3/84 4/101 5/112		170
6/124 7/147 8/166 9/168		

Bowling: First Innings—Marshall 24–5–64–3; Garner 21.4–2–67–4; Patterson 14–2–49–1; Holding 20–3–71–1; Harper 26–7–45–1; Richards 2–0–3–0. *Second Innings*—Marshall 16.1–6–25–2; Garner 17–5–38–2; Patterson 15–3–29–0; Holding 16–3–45–2; Harper 12–8–10–3; Richards 3–1–3–0.

Umpires: L. H. Barker and C. E. Cumberbatch.

FUTURE TOURS

1987	Pakistanis to England World Cup in India and Pakistan	1989-90	Sri Lankans and Pakistanis to Australia Indians to Pakistan
1987-88	England to Pakistan and New Zealand England to Australia† New Zealanders to Australia Sri Lankans to Australia	1990	England to West Indies Indians to New Zealand and Sri Lanka New Zealanders and Indians to England New Zealanders to Pakistan
1988	Australians to West Indies West Indians to England Sri Lankans to England Australians to Pakistan New Zealanders to India	1990-91	England to Australia West Indians to Sri Lanka and India Sri Lankans to Pakistan
1988-89	England to Sri Lanka and India West Indians and Pakistanis to Australia Pakistanis to New Zealand	1991	New Zealanders to Australia* Pakistanis to India* Sri Lankans to New Zealand* Australians to West Indies* West Indians to England
1989	Indians to West Indies Pakistanis to Sri Lanka* Australians to England		

* Signifies unconfirmed. † *For Australian Bicentenary only.*

ENGLAND B IN SRI LANKA, 1985-86

By MIKE SELVEY

The idea of an England B tour was conceived because it was considered by some that the transition from county to Test match cricket was, in many instances, too great. It was thought that an attempt to bridge the gap, by selecting a secondary squad to play matches against international-class opposition, would be a positive step towards the development of future Test players. There would also be a bonus for the selectors in that they could assess the performances of certain players at a level above county cricket without having to select them for full Test matches. Such a tour, therefore, could have an eliminating aspect to it.

The original schedule was for an eleven-week tour encompassing three countries – a warm-up, good-will visit to Bangladesh, a series of first-class and one-day matches in Sri Lanka, and finally matches in Zimbabwe. However, the unacceptability to the governments of Bangladesh and Zimbabwe of some players with South African connections – Bill Athey, Kim Barnett, Martyn Moxon, Chris Smith and Mark Nicholas, the captain – led to the cancellation by the TCCB of these two legs. The rearranged schedule produced a seven-week tour of Sri Lanka instead.

The selectors decided to adhere to the second-team principle rather than choose only promising youngsters – a blend of youth and experience is a healthy one – but although the batting looked sound on paper, the bowling decidedly lacked balance. To select a battery of seam bowlers and only one spin bowler for a tour of hot, mostly humid countries with slow, turning wickets was folly, as the subsequent performances illustrated. At the same time, the selectors are to be congratulated on their choice of wicket-keeper, Steven Rhodes of Worcestershire. Not only was his 'keeping of the highest class, and his enthusiasm boundless, but his batting showed technique, tenacity and a flair which could make him a cornerstone of future England sides. It was unfortunate that he blotted his copybook with an outburst on the final day of the tour.

The results were disappointing. The one-day series was lost twice, first by two to one and then, after it was extended, by three to two. (The constant changes to the itinerary provided an unnecessary difficulty for the manager, Mr Peter Lush, and his team.) In addition, the seven first-class games, five of which were unofficial "Tests" over four days, were all drawn. When the opportunity did present itself, most notably in the second "Test" at the Colombo Cricket Club ground, where an uncharacteristically fast, bouncy pitch was suited to the England seamers, the tourists were unable to take advantage of it. In the third "Test", on an atrocious pitch at the Asgiriya Stadium in Kandy, the home side were 6 for five in their second innings, but recovered. It was in this match that the England B team, contrary to instructions from the TCCB in London, played their assistant manager, Norman Gifford.

Individually there were few outstanding successes, and these came mostly from the batting ranks. Wilf Slack and Smith scored heavily and consistently, both demonstrating the concentration and single-mindedness needed to bat for long periods in uncomfortable conditions. The highest score of the tour, a career-best 184, came from Athey in the last match, but in general he lacked consistency. Of the rest, Nicholas played superbly in Kandy, but was otherwise somewhat erratic, Derek Randall, until near the end, paid the penalty for inadequate preparation, and Moxon could benefit from becoming less stiff in his method. Barnett's opportunities were curtailed by the debilitating virus which forced him to retire during the second "Test" and necessitated his early return home.

None of the bowlers enhanced his reputation, although the conditions were mostly against the seamers. Jonathan Agnew and Derek Pringle were steady, while David Lawrence impressed not with his figures but with the physical effort he put into his bowling and his willingness to learn. Tim Tremlett was unable to find the movement he had obtained in England, and Norman Cowans, notwithstanding his returning the best figures of the tour (six for 50) in the last match, was a disappointment. However, the tour was regarded as something of a rehabilitation for Nick Cook, who responded well to the challenge of being the only spinner, bowling intelligently in the one-day games and producing what would, with support, have been a match-winning performance in the first "Test". However, he was unable to take full advantage of the Kandy wicket in the third "Test" and thereafter he was less effective.

Perhaps the most pleasant surprise of the visit (a former name of the island was Serendip) was the quality of the young Sri Lankan cricketers, particularly the batsmen. Of the six hundreds scored against the tourists, three were by teenagers – Asanka Gurusinha, Roshan Mahanama and Hashan Tillekeratne. The standard of the Sri Lankan fielding was exceptionally high, unlike that of England, who disappointed at times, and given that their bowling develops at the same rate as the other aspects of their game, Sri Lanka could be a major cricket country in the coming years.

The future of such "B" tours is uncertain. They are expensive operations, but to be effective they do need to parallel a major tour as far as possible. This means selecting a full, balanced squad, a deficiency highlighted in Sri Lanka by Barnett's illness and the need for a second spin bowler. In addition, the "Tests" should have been played over five days rather than four. Had this been the case, England might well have emerged on top. There is, too, the problem, political as well as logistical, of which countries to play at this level. Nevertheless, if as a result there is the early emergence of one or two players who might otherwise have taken longer to develop, and their entry to the full Test arena is less difficult than it might have been, then the exercise will have been justified.

ENGLAND B TOUR RESULTS

First-class matches – Played 7: Drawn 7.
Draws – Sri Lanka Colts, Sri Lanka Board President's XI, Sri Lanka (5).
Non first-class matches – Played 5: Won 2, Lost 3. *Wins* – Sri Lanka (2). *Losses* – Sri Lanka (3).

ENGLAND B AVERAGES – FIRST-CLASS MATCHES

BATTING

	M	I	NO	R	HI	100s	Avge
C. L. Smith	6	9	1	419	116	1	52.37
S. J. Rhodes	7	10	4	292	77*	0	48.66
C. W. J. Athey	7	11	1	451	184	1	45.10
W. N. Slack	6	10	0	431	96	0	43.10
D. W. Randall	5	8	1	212	92	0	30.28
K. J. Barnett	4	6	2	112	51*	0	28.00
M. C. J. Nicholas	6	8	1	172	49	0	24.57
M. D. Moxon	4	5	0	110	52	0	22.00
D. R. Pringle	5	8	3	105	38*	0	21.00
D. V. Lawrence	5	5	1	63	27	0	15.75
N. G. B. Cook	7	7	2	68	39	0	13.60
T. M. Tremlett	5	5	1	27	21	0	6.75
J. P. Agnew	6	4	0	10	9	0	2.50

Played in three matches: N. G. Cowans 2*, 0*. Played in one match: N. Gifford 4*.

Signifies not out.

BOWLING

	O	M	R	W	BB	Avge
N. Gifford	53	14	128	7	4-81	18.28
D. R. Pringle	129.5	37	273	12	4-23	22.75
J. P. Agnew	185.3	36	458	17	3-57	26.94
N. G. B. Cook	340.5	121	739	24	6-69	30.79
N. G. Cowans	83	22	229	7	6-50	32.71
D. V. Lawrence	145	22	525	7	3-50	75.00

Also bowled: C. W. J. Athey 12–2–51–2; K. J. Barnett 11–2–52–2; M. D. Moxon 5–1–15–0; M. C. J. Nicholas 18–5–45–1; D. W. Randall 0.4–0–7–1; W. N. Slack 8–1–15–0; C. L. Smith 23.5–6–72–1; T. M. Tremlett 123–35–302–3.

FIELDING

C. W. J. Athey 13, S. J. Rhodes 12 (9 ct, 3 st), M. D. Moxon 5, M. C. J. Nicholas 5, D. W. Randall 5, N. G. B. Cook 4, N. Gifford 3, T. M. Tremlett 3, D. R. Pringle 2, K. J. Barnett 1, D. V. Lawrence 1, C. L. Smith 1.

SRI LANKA COLTS v ENGLAND B

At P. Saravanamuttu Stadium, Colombo, January 12, 13, 14. Drawn. The opening match of the tour was a disappointment for England B, but taking into account the length of time since the end of the English season and the lack of practice afforded in Sri Lanka owing to bad weather, their shortcomings were understandable. The Colts' innings, after Nicholas had put them in, was dominated by an unbeaten century from Ranatunga, a Test player, who looked a class above every other batsman in the match. England B's bowlers, except for Lawrence, who struggled for rhythm and was twice warned for running on the pitch, performed steadily without being penetrative, but their batting was inept and only Rhodes's application avoided the follow-on. Although a result was never likely, the Colts caused some embarrassment, and even more worryingly, Nicholas sustained a groin strain in attempting a quick single.

Sri Lanka Colts

D. M. Vonhagt b Cook	20	– c Rhodes b Agnew	18
D. Ranatunga b Cook	44	– c Athey b Tremlett	35
S. L. Anthonisz b Cook	0	– not out	33
*A. Ranatunga not out	120		
B. R. Jurangpathy c Barnett b Pringle	2		
H. P. Tillekeratne lbw b Lawrence	12	– (4) not out	11
N. A. C. P. Rodrigo b Agnew	9		
†A. G. D. Wickremasinghe lbw b Pringle	2		
S. D. Anurasiri b Pringle	0		
C. P. Ramanayake b Agnew	5		
K. N. Amalean c Nicholas b Agnew	1		
B 10, l-b 5, n-b 17	32	B 1, l-b 2, n-b 2	5

1/39 2/40 3/140 4/143 5/182   247   1/21 2/83   (2 wkts dec.) 102
6/220 7/236 8/236 9/245

Bowling: *First Innings*—Agnew 22.1-3-57-3; Lawrence 13-2-65-1; Pringle 24-7-41-3; Cook 25-10-55-3; Tremlett 13-6-14-0. *Second Innings*—Agnew 9-1-17-1; Lawrence 8-2-27-0; Cook 8.2-3-35-0; Tremlett 8-1-20-1.

England B

K. J. Barnett lbw b Amalean	7	– b Rodrigo	15
W. N. Slack c Rodrigo b Anurasiri	32	– b Anurasiri	7
C. W. J. Athey c Vonhagt b Amalean	4	– not out	53
*M. C. J. Nicholas lbw b Ramanayake	25	– retired hurt	1
D. W. Randall lbw b Ramanayake	0	– st Wickremasinghe b Jurangpathy	1
D. R. Pringle b Anurasiri	1	– not out	16
†S. J. Rhodes not out	21		
T. M. Tremlett lbw b Anurasiri	0		
N. G. B. Cook b Amalean	4		
D. V. Lawrence st Wickremasinghe b Anurasiri	11		
J. P. Agnew c Vonhagt b Anurasiri	0		
L-b 5, w 2	7	L-b 2, n-b 1	3

1/16 2/20 3/62 4/62 5/63   112   1/11 2/42 3/59   (3 wkts) 96
6/76 7/76 8/93 9/112

Bowling: *First Innings*—Amalean 19-5-51-3; Ramanayake 12-6-16-2; Anurasiri 23.4-8-38-5; Jurangpathy 3-2-2-0. *Second Innings*—Amalean 5-0-26-0; Ramanayake 8-4-6-0; Anurasiri 10-2-32-1; Rodrigo 4-2-4-1; Jurangpathy 6-3-20-1; Tillekeratne 1-0-6-0.

Umpires: B. C. Cooray and S. Ponnadurai.

SRI LANKA BOARD PRESIDENT'S XI v ENGLAND B

At P. Saravanamuttu Stadium, Colombo, January 16, 17, 18. Drawn. Winning the toss and batting on a docile pitch, the President's XI lost only two wickets on the opening day when Barnett, captain in place of the injured Nicholas, resorted to eight bowlers. The England B reply, which went well into the afternoon of the last day, was ponderous in the searing heat. Only Athey played fluently, but Smith's century, in his first innings of the tour, was a testament to his patience and application for six hours and nineteen minutes.

Sri Lanka Board President's XI

*S. Wettimuny run out	57			
†A. M. de Silva c Randall b Barnett	24	– (1) not out	37	
S. Warnakulasuriya c Cook b Cowans	93			
A. P. Gurusinha c Moxon b Lawrence	82			
R. S. Mahanama not out	13	– (3) not out	15	
M. A. R. Samarasekera c Athey b Cook	47			
S. M. S. Kaluperuma (did not bat)		– (2) c Moxon b Barnett	50	
B 1, l-b 6, w 3, n-b 5	15	B 2, l-b 2	4	

1/79 2/93 3/270 4/272 5/331   (5 wkts dec.) 331   1/89   (1 wkt) 106

T. L. Fernando, E. A. R. de Silva, K. G. Perera and A. K. Kuruppuarachchi did not bat.

Bowling: *First Innings*—Lawrence 20–1–79–1; Cowans 19–7–50–1; Cook 35.5–14–76–1; Tremlett 23–6–62–0; Barnett 4–0–17–1; Athey 1–0–12–0; Smith 2–0–13–0; Slack 7–0–15–0. *Second Innings*—Lawrence 5–1–18–0; Cowans 5–2–9–0; Tremlett 5–0–26–0; Cook 7–3–16–0; Smith 8–4–13–0; Barnett 4–1–20–1.

England B

M. D. Moxon c Perera b E. A. R. de Silva	44	T. M. Tremlett b E. A. R. de Silva	0
W. N. Slack c Gurusinha		N. G. B. Cook c Kaluperuma	
b Kuruppuarachchi	10	b E. A. R. de Silva	0
C. L. Smith c A. M. de Silva		D. V. Lawrence b E. A. R. de Silva	27
b Kuruppuarachchi	116	N. G. Cowans not out	2
D. W. Randall c A. M. de Silva			
b E. A. R. de Silva	13	B 4, l-b 3, w 2, n-b 2	11
*K. J. Barnett b Fernando	11		
C. W. J. Athey c Wettimuny b Perera	41	1/15 2/79 3/108	288
†S. J. Rhodes c Mahanama		4/153 5/226 6/258 7/259	
b Kuruppuarachchi	13	8/259 9/265	

Bowling: Fernando 13–5–45–1; Kuruppuarachchi 19–8–37–3; Perera 17–2–45–1; E. A. R. de Silva 50.5–20–85–5; Samarasekera 21–8–43–0; Kaluperuma 11–2–26–0.

Umpires: F. R. S. de Mel and K. T. Ponnambalam.

SRI LANKA v ENGLAND B

First Unofficial "Test"

At Sinhalese Sports Club, Colombo, January 20, 21, 22, 23. Drawn. Nicholas's decision to bat first looked questionable when three wickets fell for 50, but a stand of 125 between Slack, who went on to make a defiant 96, and Smith regained the initiative. With the wicket already taking spin, and the young Warnaweera, bowling off-spin at medium pace – albeit with a dubious action – posing a special problem, it needed determined batting by the lower order, in particular an inventive career-best 77 not out from Rhodes, for England B to reach a secure total of 363 midway through the second day. By the close they had established a hold on the game, Cook having removed the first four batsmen at a personal cost of 27 runs. However, Gurusinha, a promising nineteen-year-old left-hander, stroked an elegant hundred in just over five hours, with twelve boundaries, and although the new ball finished off the innings, Sri Lanka avoided the follow-on. Cook's six for 69, achieved with the help of fine catching by Athey, was his first five-wicket haul since he took eleven wickets for England against Pakistan in Karachi in 1984. With runs needed quickly if England were to force a win, the loss of an hour to rain at the end of the third day was bound to be a crucial influence. Rhodes again batted impressively for his second half-century of the match, and Nicholas eventually set a challenging target of 240 in a minimum of 53 overs. Cook again bowled well to have Sri Lanka in difficulty, but he lacked adequate spin support and sensible batting from Gurusinha and Ratnayeke saw Sri Lanka to safety.

England B

M. D. Moxon b Ratnayeke	8	– b Amalean	4
W. N. Slack c Vonhagt b Anurasiri	96	– c de Alwis b A. Ranatunga	21
*M. C. J. Nicholas lbw b Ratnayeke	11		
C. W. J. Athey b Warnaweera	5	– (5) run out	6
C. L. Smith lbw b Warnaweera	62	– (4) b Warnaweera	2
K. J. Barnett b Samarasekera	12	– not out	16
D. R. Pringle c de Alwis b Ratnayeke	27	– not out	9
†S. J. Rhodes not out	77	– (3) c A. Ranatunga b Warnaweera	57
T. M. Tremlett c Gurusinha b Warnaweera	21		
N. G. B. Cook c de Alwis b D. Ranatunga	39		
J. P. Agnew c and b D. Ranatunga	0		
B 1, l-b 3, n-b 1	5	L-b 5, w 1	6

1/15 2/39 3/50 4/175 5/197	363	1/12 2/47 3/56　　(5 wkts dec.)	121
6/197 7/243 8/277 9/363		4/78 5/104	

Bowling: First Innings—Ratnayeke 22–2–56–3; Amalean 17–4–55–0; Warnaweera 39–10–97–3; Anurasiri 34–12–67–1; Guneratne 14–2–53–0; Samarasekera 5–2–20–1; D. Ranatunga 2.4–0–11–2. *Second Innings*—Ratnayeke 6–2–11–0; Amalean 7–1–22–1; Warnaweera 14.3–3–49–2; A. Ranatunga 8–1–22–1; Anurasiri 5–1–12–0.

Sri Lanka

D. M. Vonhagt c Athey b Cook	22	– c Tremlett b Cook	11
D. Ranatunga c Moxon b Cook	30	– b Cook	26
M. A. R. Samarasekera c Tremlett b Cook	32	– (4) c Athey b Cook	5
*A. Ranatunga lbw b Cook	0	– (3) c Athey b Cook	0
A. P. Gurusinha c Rhodes b Agnew	111	– not out	21
S. D. Anurasiri c Athey b Cook	8		
†R. G. de Alwis c Cook b Tremlett	11		
J. R. Ratnayeke c Athey b Agnew	14	– (6) not out	42
R. P. W. Guneratne c Moxon b Agnew	2		
K. N. Amalean not out	3		
K. P. J. Warnaweera c Athey b Cook	1		
B 2, l-b 5, n-b 4	11	B 4, l-b 1, n-b 1	6

1/49 2/58 3/64 4/121 5/165	245	1/31 2/31 3/41 4/53　　(4 wkts)	111
6/193 7/236 8/239 9/240			

Bowling: First Innings—Agnew 27–6–77–3; Pringle 16–4–40–0; Tremlett 22–7–45–1; Cook 44.4–20–69–6; Smith 2–0–7–0. *Second Innings*—Agnew 7–2–17–0; Pringle 8–2–27–0; Cook 17–7–28–4; Tremlett 11–5–15–0; Barnett 3–1–15–0; Smith 1–0–4–0; Athey 1–1–0–0.

Umpires: K. T. Francis and P. W. Vidanagamage.

SRI LANKA v ENGLAND B

Second Unofficial "Test"

At Colombo Cricket Club, Colombo, January 26, 27, 28, 29. Drawn. Choosing to bowl first on a hard, well-grassed pitch which should have been suited to their pace attack, England B, on the first day in particular, were unable to take advantage of it, and with poor catching a contributory factor they let slip an opportunity to establish a lead in the series. The ball bounced and deviated alarmingly at times, beating the bat frequently and on several occasions clearing the wicket-keeper, yet only two wickets fell all day, both to Pringle, as Sri Lanka put on 231. Wettimuny, missed by Moxon at third slip off the fourth ball of the innings, was 116 not out at the close, his first century since his epic 190 at Lord's in 1984. Next day Agnew, the best of the English seamers, ended the Sri Lankan captain's marathon of almost seven and three-quarter hours, but with Sri Lanka batting well into the second afternoon before declaring, the match was effectively beyond England B's reach.

Although there was still movement for the seam bowlers, as well as some turn, the Sri Lankan attack was equally ineffective and all the English batsmen made useful runs. Barnett and Rhodes saw the third day out with England B 300 for six, and on the fourth morning the Derbyshire captain completed a lengthy half-century (204 minutes), all the while batting in a sweater despite the 100-degree temperature and sapping humidity. It was to be his last innings of the tour. When Sri Lanka batted a second time, England B fielded three substitutes and Rhodes made a marvellous leg-side stumping off the bowling of Nicholas.

Sri Lanka

*S. Wettimuny b Agnew		138		
†A. M. de Silva c Rhodes b Pringle		12	– (1) st Rhodes b Nicholas	39
S. Warnakulasuriya c Rhodes b Pringle		22	– (4) not out	27
A. Ranatunga c Smith b Pringle		52		
R. S. Mahanama c Moxon b Agnew		58	– not out	32
S. M. S. Kaluperuma b Cook		70	– (2) c Rhodes b Agnew	0
H. P. Tillekeratne c and b Athey		17	– (3) c Nicholas b Cook	17
A. L. F. de Mel b Athey		11		
E. A. R. de Silva not out		6		
K. G. Perera not out		0		
B 12, l-b 16, w 7, n-b 7		42	B 4, l-b 6, w 1, n-b 1	12

1/47 2/135 3/232 4/279 5/358   (8 wkts dec.) 428   1/1 2/61 3/61   (3 wkts) 127
6/402 7/408 8/427

A. K. Kuruppuarachchi did not bat.

Bowling: *First Innings*—Agnew 32–12–59–2; Lawrence 28–3–114–0; Pringle 35–12–72–3; Nicholas 7–1–28–0; Cook 48–13–110–1; Athey 5–0–17–2. *Second Innings*—Agnew 4–0–18–1; Lawrence 11–3–33–0; Nicholas 11–4–17–1; Slack 1–1–0–0; Cook 5–2–7–1; Moxon 5–1–15–0; Athey 5–1–22–0; Smith 3–1–5–0.

England B

M. D. Moxon lbw b Perera	52		N. G. B. Cook not out	14
W. N. Slack c Tillekeratne			D. V. Lawrence b Perera	0
b E. A. R. de Silva	50		J. P. Agnew c sub (D. Bulankulame)	
C. L. Smith lbw b de Mel	76		b E. A. R. de Silva	9
C. W. J. Athey b Kaluperuma	41			
*M. C. J. Nicholas b Kuruppuarachchi	38		B 9, l-b 9, n-b 1	19
K. J. Barnett retired ill	51			
D. R. Pringle lbw b Perera	5		1/107 2/127 3/207	365
†S. J. Rhodes c sub (A. P. Gurusinha)			4/256 5/282 6/293 7/335	
b Perera	10		8/350 9/365	

Bowling: de Mel 27–7–89–1; Kuruppuarachchi 22–3–77–1; Ranatunga 3–1–10–0; E. A. R. de Silva 46–18–69–2; Perera 38–13–67–4; Kaluperuma 12–3–28–1; Warnakulasuriya 2–0–7–0.

Umpires: H. C. Felsinger and D. C. C. Perera.

SRI LANKA v ENGLAND B

First One-day "International"

At Moratuwa, February 1. Sri Lanka won by four wickets. From the moment Sri Lanka won the toss, England B were outplayed in every department of the game. All the batsmen struggled with their timing against accurate bowling and outstanding fielding, and only a third-wicket partnership of 77 between Randall and Nicholas lent substance to the total. Sri Lanka, by contrast, were untroubled. Kuruppu, who began by driving a straight 4 and pulling a 6 in Cowans's first over, hit 80 from 73 balls, including two 6s and six 4s.

England B

M. D. Moxon c A. M. de Silva		†S. J. Rhodes c Ranasinghe	
b Ramanayake .	12	b Ramanayake .	6
C. L. Smith c Mahanama		T. M. Tremlett not out	17
b Ramanayake .	7	N. G. B. Cook c Ranasinghe	
D. W. Randall b Ranasinghe	34	b Ramanayake .	18
*M. C. J. Nicholas c de Mel		N. G. Cowans not out	2
b E. A. R. de Silva .	38	B 4, l-b 8, w 5	17
C. W. J. Athey c A. M. de Silva			
b Ranasinghe .	6	1/26 2/27 3/104 (8 wkts, 45 overs) 162	
D. R. Pringle c A. M. de Silva		4/104 5/112 6/118	
b E. A. R. de Silva .	5	7/127 8/157	

J. P. Agnew did not bat.

Bowling: de Mel 9–0–41–0; Ramanayake 9–1–36–4; Rodrigo 9–1–24–0; Ranasinghe 9–2–28–2; E. A. R. de Silva 9–2–21–2.

Sri Lanka

D. S. B. P. Kuruppu b Cook	80	*A. L. F. de Mel lbw b Agnew	12
†A. M. de Silva lbw b Pringle	5	H. P. Tillekeratne not out	1
S. Warnakulasuriya b Cook	21	L-b 7	7
S. M. S. Kaluperuma c Rhodes b Tremlett	11		
R. S. Mahanama not out	24	1/32 2/87 3/118 (6 wkts, 41.3 overs) 163	
S. K. Ranasinghe c Cowans b Tremlett	2	4/126 5/145 6/161	

N. A. C. P. Rodrigo, E. A. R. de Silva and C. P. Ramanayake did not bat.

Bowling: Agnew 8–2–18–1; Cowans 5–0–26–0; Pringle 8.3–2–29–1; Tremlett 8–0–45–2; Nicholas 3–0–18–0; Cook 9–2–20–2.

Umpires: F. R. S. de Mel and H. C. Felsinger.

SRI LANKA v ENGLAND B

Second One-day "International"

At Ketterama Stadium, Colombo, February 2. Sri Lanka won by four wickets. This was the inaugural match in the new 40,000-seat stadium which was constructed in just six months at the instigation of Sri Lanka's Prime Minister. England B again lost the toss, and even allowing for consistent bowling and brilliant fielding, their total was below expectations. Sri Lanka began cautiously, and Cook again bowled well, but Vonhagt played the anchor role and there were mature, astute innings from Gurusinha and Samarasekera. Ratnayake won the match with a 6 over long-on off Tremlett.

England B

M. D. Moxon c and b Perera	29	N. G. B. Cook c Ranatunga	
C. W. J. Athey c Gurusinha		b Samarasekera .	0
b Ranatunga .	70	N. G. Cowans b Samarasekera	0
D. W. Randall run out	4	J. P. Agnew not out	2
*M. C. J. Nicholas c Mahanama b Perera	1	B 1, l-b 3, n-b 2	6
C. L. Smith lbw b Ratnayake	28		
D. R. Pringle c and b Rajadurai	5	1/59 2/65 3/82 (9 wkts, 45 overs) 178	
†S. J. Rhodes c Mahanama b Ratnayake	15	4/120 5/132 6/155	
T. M. Tremlett not out	18	7/164 8/165 9/170	

Bowling: Ratnayake 9–1–34–2; Amalean 9–2–24–0; Ranatunga 9–0–35–1; Samarasekera 4–0–22–2; Perera 9–1–34–2; Rajadurai 5–0–25–1.

Sri Lanka

D. M. Vonhagt c Cook b Pringle 38	R. S. Mahanama not out 39
†L. K. de Alwis c Pringle b Cowans ... 9	R. J. Ratnayake not out 18
P. A. de Silva c Tremlett b Pringle 11	
*A. Ranatunga st Rhodes b Cook 13	L-b 4, w 1, n-b 2 7
A. P. Gurusinha c Moxon b Cook 21	
M. A. R. Samarasekera c Tremlett	1/14 2/25 3/54 (6 wkts, 41.2 overs) 182
b Pringle . 26	4/81 5/97 6/153

K. N. Amalean, B. Rajadurai and K. G. Perera did not bat.

Bowling: Agnew 8–0–52–0; Cowans 8–0–30–1; Pringle 9–1–35–3; Tremlett 7.2–0–39–0; Cook 9–0–22–2.

Umpires: H. C. Felsinger and K. T. Francis.

SRI LANKA v ENGLAND B

Third One-day "International"

At Kandy, February 4. England B won by 4 runs. The tourists made up for their inadequate performances in the first two one-day games by winning a close match with polished, professional cricket. The result was in doubt until the last over, from which Sri Lanka needed 10 runs to win with their last pair at the crease. Pringle ensured they did not score them. Put in, England B recovered through Smith and Nicholas, the captain showing his best form of the tour. An exhilarating partnership of 60 in seven overs between Rhodes and Pringle followed. Sri Lanka's reply began with Lawrence bowling a ten-ball over, but in his fourth over he found his rhythm to take two wickets. Cook again bowled well, with off-spin support from Tremlett and Smith.

England B

M. D. Moxon c Gurusinha	D. R. Pringle c A. Ranatunga
b Ratnayeke . 7	b Ratnayeke . 24
W. N. Slack run out 11	T. M. Tremlett not out 7
C. W. J. Athey b Ratnayeke 6	N. G. B. Cook run out 1
*M. C. J. Nicholas c Silva	D. V. Lawrence not out 8
b Samarasekera . 50	L-b 6, w 4, n-b 3 13
C. L. Smith c Tillekeratne	
b Wijesuriya . 28	1/24 2/25 3/32 (9 wkts, 45 overs) 194
D. W. Randall c Silva b Ramanayake . 5	4/99 5/116 6/117 7/177
†S. J. Rhodes c Tillekeratne b John ... 34	8/178 9/180

Bowling: Ratnayeke 9–1–41–3; John 9–3–42–1; Ramanayake 9–1–34–1; A. Ranatunga 3–0–16–0; Samarasekera 6–0–30–1; Wijesuriya 9–0–25–1.

Sri Lanka

†S. A. R. Silva c Moxon b Smith 53	V. B. John lbw b Cook 2
D. Ranatunga c Rhodes b Lawrence ... 5	C. P. Ramanayake run out 5
P. A. de Silva c Cook b Lawrence 0	R. G. C. E. Wijesuriya run out 12
A. P. Gurusinha run out 15	
*A. Ranatunga c Cook b Tremlett 22	B 1, l-b 7, w 4, n-b 5 17
M. A. R. Samarasekera c Tremlett	
b Pringle . 29	1/24 2/24 3/54 (45 overs) 190
H. P. Tillekeratne not out 22	4/96 5/139 6/139
J. R. Ratnayeke st Rhodes b Cook 8	7/158 8/160 9/173

Bowling: Tremlett 9–0–22–1; Lawrence 6–0–30–2; Nicholas 9–0–42–0; Pringle 9–1–30–1; Cook 9–0–43–2; Smith 3–1–15–1.

Umpires: D. P. Buultjens and B. C. Cooray.

SRI LANKA v ENGLAND B

Third Unofficial "Test"

At Kandy, February 6, 7, 8, 9. Drawn. With the pitch at the Asgiriya Stadium being devoid of grass and held together before the match only by heavy watering, which delayed the start, there was little point in England B playing an extra seam bowler, as was their original intention. Instead, they included Gifford, their 45-year-old assistant manager, as a second spinner in spite of previous instructions from Lord's that he should play only if there was a shortage of players.

The toss was important, and Sri Lanka won it and batted. Nicholas introduced spin after only eight overs, but although Cook and Gifford took two wickets each on the first day, good batting by de Silva and Gurusinha ensured Sri Lanka of a sound start. They were 235 for five at the close, and a final total of 271 was too many for the pitch. Neither England spinner should have been happy with his performance. England B, on the other hand, were made to struggle against the fast off-spin of Warnaweera and the leg-spin of Weerasinghe, another teenager. Only Nicholas, who played a fine technical innings, showed any confidence. With a first-innings lead of 111, Sri Lanka appeared to be comfortably placed, but in a sensational start to their second innings, the English attack reduced them to 6 for five before a century partnership in even time between Mahanama and Ranasinghe restored the initiative. Dias's declaration left England B to score 292 in slightly more than seven hours. That they survived all the last day for a draw was due to the obdurate batting of first Slack and Athey and later Rhodes and Pringle, who had added an unbeaten 71 when bad light stopped play with eight overs remaining.

The standard of umpiring in this match left much to be desired. At the same time, the umpires were not helped by the unnecessary pressure put on them by certain Sri Lankan fieldsmen.

Sri Lanka

D. Ranatunga b Gifford	19	– c Rhodes b Pringle	1
†S. A. R. Silva c Randall b Gifford	30	– c Gifford b Agnew	0
P. A. de Silva lbw b Cook	81	– c Rhodes b Agnew	0
A. P. Gurusinha c Randall b Agnew	67	– c and b Gifford	1
*R. L. Dias c Athey b Gifford	20	– (6) c and b Gifford	0
R. S. Mahanama c Athey b Cook	5	– (5) c Nicholas b Gifford	47
S. K. Ranasinghe run out	7	– run out	68
J. R. Ratnayeke lbw b Gifford	0	– c Tremlett b Cook	31
C. D. U. S. Weerasinghe st Rhodes b Cook	0	– (10) not out	4
V. B. John run out	25	– (9) b Cook	22
K. P. J. Warnaweera not out	0	– not out	3
B 6, l-b 9, n-b 2	17	L-b 1, n-b 2	3

1/42 2/72 3/180 4/222 5/235   271   1/1 2/1 3/2 4/6   (9 wkts dec.) 180
6/235 7/235 8/236 9/261   5/6 6/106 7/133
                                        8/165 9/173

Bowling: *First Innings*—Agnew 14–2–43–1; Pringle 11–2–25–0; Cook 39–15–95–3; Gifford 36–11–81–4; Tremlett 8–3–12–0. *Second Innings*—Agnew 9.2–1–22–2; Pringle 7–3–15–1; Gifford 17–3–47–3; Cook 17–0–72–2; Tremlett 6–1–23–0.

England B

W. N. Slack b Weerasinghe	30	– b de Silva	67
C. W. J. Athey c de Silva b Weerasinghe	16	– c Weerasinghe b Warnaweera	38
C. L. Smith c de Silva b Weerasinghe	20	– c Silva b Warnaweera	18
*M. C. J. Nicholas b Warnaweera	46	– c Gurusinha b Warnaweera	1
D. W. Randall c Ranatunga b Warnaweera	25	– lbw b Warnaweera	0
†S. J. Rhodes lbw b Warnaweera	2	– not out	40
D. R. Pringle st Silva b Weerasinghe	8	– not out	38
T. M. Tremlett lbw b Warnaweera	0		
N. G. B. Cook c Ranatunga b Warnaweera	0		
N. Gifford not out	4		
J. P. Agnew c Silva b Weerasinghe	1		
L-b 3, w 4, n-b 1	8	B 4, l-b 7, w 4, n-b 4	19

1/46 2/69 3/76 4/109 5/121   160   1/60 2/105 3/113   (5 wkts) 221
6/139 7/144 8/144 9/155   4/113 5/150

Bowling: *First Innings*—Ratnayeke 9-1-28-0; John 3-1-7-0; Warnaweera 35-16-72-5; Weerasinghe 30.3-12-49-5; de Silva 2-1-1-0. *Second Innings*—Ratnayeke 5-0-28-0; John 5-1-24-0; Ranasinghe 6.1-1-20-0; Warnaweera 37-16-53-4; Weerasinghe 28-10-69-0; de Silva 16-8-16-1.

Umpires: D. P. Buultjens and F. R. S. de Mel.

SRI LANKA v ENGLAND B

Fourth One-day "International"

At P. Saravanamuttu Stadium, Colombo, February 11. Sri Lanka won by 8 runs. The first of the two additional one-day matches was dominated by the nineteen-year-old Mahanama. Coming in with Sri Lanka 10 for three, he produced a breathtaking display of strokeplay, allied to cheeky running between the wickets. His unbeaten 111, the first century by a Sri Lankan in such a match on home soil, came from 121 balls with nine 4s and a huge 6. England B needed 21 from the last over, and when Smith hit 2, 6, 2, followed by a no-ball off the fourth delivery, there was still a chance. It ended with the run-out of Smith.

Sri Lanka

†D. S. B. P. Kuruppu c Rhodes b Tremlett	1	T. L. Fernando c Cowans b Nicholas	17
S. Warnakulasuriya c Rhodes b Lawrence	7	C. P. Ramanayake c Rhodes b Nicholas	1
*R. S. Madugalle c and b Tremlett	2		
A. P. Gurusinha c Pringle b Cowans	13	L-b 2, w 2	4
R. S. Mahanama not out	111		
M. A. R. Samarasekera c Rhodes b Cowans	3	1/4 2/10 3/10 (8 wkts, 44 overs) 185
S. K. Ranasinghe c Nicholas b Pringle	26	4/54 5/61 6/137
		7/172 8/185

K. N. Amalean and K. G. Perera did not bat.

Bowling: Tremlett 9-1-29-2; Lawrence 7-0-25-1; Pringle 9-2-46-1; Cowans 9-1-39-2; Cook 2-0-10-0; Nicholas 8-0-34-2.

England B

M. D. Moxon lbw b Amalean	13	D. V. Lawrence c sub b Ranasinghe	0
W. N. Slack c Kuruppu b Ramanayake	11	N. G. B. Cook not out	0
C. W. J. Athey lbw b Amalean	0	N. G. Cowans not out	0
*M. C. J. Nicholas b Perera	18	B 2, l-b 10, w 3	15
C. L. Smith run out	67		
†S. J. Rhodes c Kuruppu b Ranasinghe	13	1/23 2/23 3/30 (9 wkts, 44 overs) 177
D. R. Pringle lbw b Ranasinghe	12	4/59 5/90 6/108 7/164
T. M. Tremlett b Ranasinghe	28	8/164 9/177

Bowling: Ramanayake 6-1-14-1; Amalean 8-1-38-2; Fernando 7-2-22-0; Perera 9-1-20-1; Ranasinghe 9-1-43-4; Samarasekera 5-0-28-0.

Umpires: P. W. Vidanagamage and B. W. Wimalaratne.

SRI LANKA v ENGLAND B

Fifth One-day "International"

At Nondescripts Cricket Club, Colombo, February 13. England B won by seven wickets. Slack's fighting innings of 122 not out (four 6s, seven 4s), his first century in limited-overs cricket, together with his partnership of 146 with Smith, took England to the highest total of the series with ten balls to spare. For Sri Lanka, Samarasekera struck straight and cleanly to include three 6s and six 4s in his 68.

Sri Lanka

D. S. B. P. Kuruppu c Slack b Agnew .	0	S. K. Ranasinghe not out	38
S. Warnakulasuriya c Rhodes b Agnew .	8		
*R. S. Madugalle run out	19	B 1, l-b 1, n-b 4	6
R. S. Mahanama lbw b Cowans	6		
M. A. R. Samarasekera c sub b Tremlett	68	1/0 2/14 3/27 (5 wkts, 45 overs) 204	
H. P. Tillekeratne not out	59	4/50 5/130	

J. R. Ratnayeke, †A. M. de Silva, K. N. Amalean and S. D. Anurasiri did not bat.

Bowling: Agnew 9-1-44-2; Tremlett 9-0-41-1; Cowans 9-0-34-1; Cook 9-1-22-0; Nicholas 9-0-61-0.

England B

M. D. Moxon st de Silva b Anurasiri . .	6	C. L. Smith not out	60
W. N. Slack not out	122		
C. W. J. Athey c Tillekeratne		B 1, l-b 5, n-b 8	14
b Samarasekera .	3		
*M. C. J. Nicholas run out	2	1/29 2/49 3/61 (3 wkts, 43.2 overs) 207	

D. W. Randall, †S. J. Rhodes, T. M. Tremlett, N. G. B. Cook, J. P. Agnew and N. G. Cowans did not bat.

Bowling: Ratnayeke 8-0-27-0; Amalean 9-0-33-0; Anurasiri 9-1-30-1; Samarasekera 8-0-41-1; Warnakulasuriya 3-0-15-0; Ranasinghe 6.2-0-55-0.

Umpires: M. D. D. N. Gooneratne and P. W. Vidanagamage.

SRI LANKA v ENGLAND B

Fourth Unofficial "Test"

At Colombo Cricket Club, Colombo, February 16, 17, 18, 19. Drawn. Sri Lanka included only two Test players – Madugalle and Ratnayake – while England B's selection of Randall was something of a gamble in view of his recent form. However, Nicholas had detected a new determination in Randall, and as the Colombo Club pitch, in the second "Test", had behaved in a similar fashion to some at Trent Bridge, he reasoned that the selection could be justified. Events proved him right as England B, put in on a dampish pitch, made 240 for three on the first day. Slack followed up his brilliant one-day century with a competent 85 and Randall worked hard for his 92, the pair adding 164 for the second wicket, the highest stand of the tour, in three and a half hours. After Nicholas's declaration Lawrence dismissed Warnakulasuriya in the second over, but by now the pitch was ideal for batting and Samarasekera and Madugalle took Sri Lanka to 161. Samarasekera, who drove and cut powerfully, reached his hundred just before the close. He was out to Tremlett on the third morning, having hit one 6 and sixteen 4s, and before another run was added Madugalle was struck in the face by a rising ball from Agnew which deflected from, and broke, his right thumb. Assisted by a number of dropped catches, Sri Lanka batted throughout the day with Mahanama playing soundly and Fernando hitting three 6s and six 4s in a bright maiden first-class fifty. When Sri Lanka declared at their overnight score, England used the final day for batting practice until bad light stopped play in mid-afternoon.

England B

W. N. Slack run out	85	– c sub (C. Mahesh) b Perera	33
C. W. J. Athey c Wickremasinghe b Kuruppuarachchi	26	– c Tillekeratne b Samarasekera	37
D. W. Randall c Wickremasinghe b Ratnayake	92	– not out	60
*M. C. J. Nicholas lbw b Fernando	49		
N. G. B. Cook c Wickremasinghe b Kuruppuarachchi	10		
C. L. Smith c Warnakulasuriya b Kuruppuarachchi	51	– (4) c and b Perera	4
†S. J. Rhodes c Wickremasinghe b Kuruppuarachchi	26	– (5) not out	22
T. M. Tremlett not out	6		
D. V. Lawrence b Perera	2		
N. G. Cowans not out	0		
B 4, l-b 11, n-b 7	22	B 5, l-b 5, n-b 1	11

1/42 2/206 3/233 4/273   (8 wkts dec.) 369   1/73 2/81 3/99   (3 wkts) 167
5/281 6/354 7/359 8/364

J. P. Agnew did not bat.

Bowling: First Innings—Ratnayake 20–1–60–1; Kuruppuarachchi 30–6–85–4; Fernando 28–6–69–1; Samarasekera 8–0–31–0; Perera 33–11–73–1; Tillekeratne 3–0–8–0; Ranasinghe 9–1–28–0. *Second Innings*—Kuruppuarachchi 10.4–2–25–0; Fernando 8–0–23–0; Perera 24–4–61–2; Samarasekera 13–3–24–1; Tillekeratne 6–3–24–0.

Sri Lanka

S. Warnakulasuriya c Randall b Lawrence	4	†A. G. D. Wickremasinghe not out	29
M. A. R. Samarasekera b Tremlett	110	T. L. Fernando st Rhodes b Smith	56
*R. S. Madugalle retired hurt	57	K. G. Perera not out	0
R. S. Mahanama b Lawrence	67	B 7, l-b 11, w 3, n-b 6	27
H. P. Tillekeratne c Cook b Agnew	37	1/8 2/182 3/276 (6 wkts dec.) 390	
S. K. Ranasinghe c Rhodes b Agnew	3	4/298 5/304 6/390	

R. J. Ratnayake and A. K. Kuruppuarachchi did not bat.

Bowling: Agnew 24–4–58–2; Lawrence 20–1–73–2; Tremlett 27–6–85–1; Cowans 24–5–75–0; Cook 28–12–68–0; Smith 3.5–0–13–1.

Umpires: A. C. Felsinger and K. T. Ponnambalam.

SRI LANKA v ENGLAND B

Fifth Unofficial "Test"

At Galle, February 22, 23, 24, 25. Drawn. England were denied the chance of victory by an extraordinary display of skill, courage and composure by Tillekeratne, a seventeen-year-old schoolboy, who batted in untroubled fashion for an hour on the third evening and throughout the final day to finish with an unbeaten 105, his maiden first-class hundred (265 balls, eleven 4s). Nor was the quality of his innings detracted from by an incident, born of English frustration, which happened when Sri Lanka were nine wickets down and Tillekeratne was 90. (At that point England, needing approximately 7 runs an over from seventeen overs, could still win the match and thus the series.) Tillekeratne touched a delivery from Lawrence to the diving Rhodes, who claimed the catch. The batsman, however, remained in his ground, intimating that the ball had not carried, and he was adjudged not out, whereupon he was subjected to harsh words from Lawrence, and then to a furious outburst from the wicket-keeper. Both players subsequently received an "official reprimand" from the England B management.

Sri Lanka chose to bat first on an unevenly grassed pitch and struggled on the first day against the pace of Cowans and the accuracy of Pringle. The England B innings was founded on a marathon effort from Athey, who batted for twenty minutes short of eight hours for his 184 (fifteen 4s). There was another competent innings from Smith, who appeared down the order and batted with a runner because of illness. By the end of the third day Sri Lanka had reduced the deficit of 104 by 96 for the loss of three wickets; but by then Tillekeratne was already well entrenched.

Sri Lanka

D. M. Vonhagt b Cowans	0	– c Pringle b Agnew	0
D. Ranatunga lbw b Cowans	25	– b Cook	15
*S. Warnakulasuriya c Nicholas b Pringle	23	– lbw b Agnew	50
M. A. R. Samarasekera c Rhodes b Pringle	6	– c Pringle b Cook	8
H. P. Tillekeratne c Athey b Cowans	5	– not out	105
D. C. Wickremasinghe lbw b Cowans	87	– lbw b Lawrence	3
†A. M. de Silva c Athey b Pringle	34	– lbw b Lawrence	26
T. L. Fernando c Lawrence b Cowans	32	– c Nicholas b Lawrence	9
S. D. Anurasiri lbw b Cowans	0	– c Randall b Pringle	1
R. S. Abeysekera not out	1	– b Cook	23
C. P. Ramanayake c Cook b Pringle	0	– b Randall	25
B 11, n-b 7	18	B 4, l-b 2, n-b 1	7

1/2 2/51 3/52 4/62 5/157   231   1/0 2/42 3/64 4/98 5/116   272
6/175 7/208 8/224 9/231   6/173 7/187 8/199 9/229

In the first innings, D. Ranatunga, when 16, retired at 41 and resumed at 157.

Bowling: *First Innings*—Agnew 18-2-44-0; Cowans 20-5-50-6; Lawrence 17-0-66-0; Pringle 16.5-4-23-4; Cook 23-6-37-0. *Second Innings*—Agnew 19-3-46-2; Cowans 15-3-45-0; Cook 43-16-71-3; Lawrence 23-9-50-3; Pringle 12-3-30-1; Smith 4-1-17-0; Randall 0.4-0-7-1.

England B

M. D. Moxon c sub (K. G. Perera) b Fernando	2
C. W. J. Athey c Warnakulasuriya b Ramanayake	184
D. W. Randall c Samarasekera b Anurasiri	21
*M. C. J. Nicholas lbw b Abeysekera	1
†S. J. Rhodes c sub (K. G. Perera) b Ramanayake	24

N. G. B. Cook retired ill	1
C. L. Smith not out	70
D. R. Pringle c Anurasiri b Ramanayake	1
D. V. Lawrence not out	23
B 4, l-b 1, n-b 3	8

1/5 2/48 3/59   (6 wkts dec.) 335
4/151 5/267 6/285

N. G. Cowans and J. P. Agnew did not bat.

Bowling: Ramanayake 35-9-91-3; Fernando 16-1-47-1; Anurasiri 50-10-128-1; Abeysekera 27-6-64-1.

Umpires: H. C. Felsinger and M. D. D. N. Gooneratne.

THE INDIANS IN SRI LANKA, 1985-86

By R. MOHAN

Lacking any kind of match practice for months after the 1984-85 home season had ended, and with a team hastily assembled in August, the Indians were under-prepared for their visit to Sri Lanka. They were also at a further disadvantage in conditions which the Sri Lankan seam attack was accustomed to exploiting. The home team had trained assiduously for months, and for this reason alone the fledgling Test nation deserved the historic and emotive maiden win it scored in the three-match series.

India's bowling was even more limited than usual, but what let the team down was the batting. This never attained the levels it had in the two limited-overs successes earlier in the year – first in Melbourne and then in Sharjah. The political background against which this series was organised, with the Indian government viewing it as a diplomatic initiative, was never likely to inspire confidence in cricketers touring the island in troubled times.

With only two three-day matches and a one-day international before the first Test, the Indians were hardly in a position to find their form before the three Tests were played off the reel. Indeed, with a bit of luck the Sri Lankans might well have won the first Test, rain robbing them of a session of play on the final day. However, the chance that had slipped away was encashed in the second Test in which the Sri Lankans outbowled and outbatted the Indians. In the final hour, Rumesh Ratnayake dived to take a return catch from a defiant Kapil Dev to end the Indian innings and signal a fine triumph. Sri Lanka had seized the chance which India had given them by losing four first-innings wickets cheaply on the fourth morning, the home batsmen sparkling as they set up a target which the Indians could not be expected to attain. Only some unconvincing umpiring, about which the Indians unfortunately stated their misgivings in very clear terms, detracted from the merits of a splendid victory.

Finding their feet somewhat late on tour, the Indians seized the initiative only in the final Test, but here too the Sri Lankan captain, Duleep Mendis, and his deputy, Roy Dias, were too good for the Indian attack. They increased their rescue stand to 216 on the final day and took their team close to snatching victory from the jaws of defeat. When they were out, both having hit hundreds, the late-order batsmen played out time to force a draw and keep intact the hard-earned lead in the series.

Sri Lanka introduced some promising youngsters in the warm-up matches. Asanka Gurusinha, a teenage left-handed batsman, was the best of them. But the advent of Saliya Ahangama, a resourceful medium-pacer who capably exploited the mildly seaming conditions, helped the Test effort. Asantha de Mel, his fitness and form under a cloud, did well to strike form in the Tests and so dispelled doubts about his place in the team.

With Sunil Gavaskar opting to bat in the middle order, India were never given a solid start in the series. Krish Srikkanth made runs consistently for the first time in a revived Test career, but of the senior middle-order batsmen, Dilip Vengsarkar waged a near-lone battle for India. His unbeaten 98 was instrumental in India's staving off defeat in the first Test, and it was indicative of the difference between the two sides that there were five Test centuries by Sri Lankans against the one by an Indian (Mohinder Amarnath).

The young Indian leg-spinner, Laxman Sivaramakrishnan, injured a finger on his bowling hand early on tour and never played the expected role of strike spinner. The slow left-armer, Maninder Singh, who took his place in two Tests, shone in patches and returned his best Test figures of four for 31 in the first innings of the third Test. However, he flattered to deceive when his team needed a better striking-rate in the fourth innings on a pitch increasingly helpful to spin.

Sri Lanka's victory in the series was a triumph for the seniors in the team such as Mendis, Dias, Ranjan Madugalle and de Mel. They had been fixtures in the Sri Lankan team since the country's Test baptism in February 1982, and they played leading parts in the Test win at the Tamil Union ground in Colombo. Ratnayake, with a slinging action, bowled consistently well throughout the series, the Indian batsmen never learning to judge his change of pace correctly, while Amal Silva, the wicket-keeper, set a new record for a three-Test series with 22 dismissals, including nine in the first Test.

The one-day series was shared 1-1 with the decisive third match being declared a no result because of interference from the weather and bad light.

INDIAN TOUR RESULTS

Test matches – Played 3: Lost 1, Drawn 2.
First-class matches – Played 5: Lost 1, Drawn 4.
Loss – Sri Lanka.
Draws – Sri Lanka Colts, Sri Lanka Board President's XI, Sri Lanka (2).
Non first-class matches – Played 3: Won 1, Lost 1. No result 1. *Win* – Sri Lanka. *Loss* – Sri Lanka. *No result* – Sri Lanka.

TEST MATCH AVERAGES

SRI LANKA – BATTING

	T	I	NO	R	HI	100s	Avge
L. R. D. Mendis	3	6	1	310	124	1	62.00
R. L. Dias	3	6	1	273	106	1	54.60
R. S. Madugalle	3	5	1	177	103	1	44.25
A. Ranatunga	3	5	0	185	111	1	37.00
P. A. de Silva	3	6	1	168	75	0	33.60
S. A. R. Silva	3	6	1	151	111	1	30.20
S. Wettimuny	3	5	0	103	34	0	20.60
A. L. F. de Mel	3	4	1	26	16	0	8.66
F. S. Ahangama	3	3	1	11	11	0	5.50
R. J. Ratnayake	3	3	1	9	7	0	4.50

Played in one Test: E. A. R. de Silva 1*; B. R. Jurangpathy 1, 0; C. D. U. S. Weerasinghe 3.

*Signifies not out.

BOWLING

	O	M	R	W	BB	Avge
F. S. Ahangama	133.3	32	348	18	5-52	19.33
R. J. Ratnayake	162.5	35	459	20	6-85	22.95
A. L. F. de Mel	150.3	30	438	12	5-64	36.50

Also bowled: E. A. R. de Silva 27–11–38–0; B. R. Jurangpathy 4–0–24–0; R. S. Madugalle 1–0–10–0; A. Ranatunga 49–20–102–2; C. D. U. S. Weerasinghe 19–8–36–0.

INDIA – BATTING

	T	I	NO	R	HI	100s	Avge
M. Amarnath	2	4	1	216	116*	1	72.00
S. M. Gavaskar	3	6	1	186	52	0	37.20
D. B. Vengsarkar	3	6	1	177	98*	0	35.40
K. Srikkanth	3	6	0	187	64	0	31.16
L. S. Rajput	2	4	0	105	61	0	26.25
R. J. Shastri	3	6	0	157	81	0	26.16
Kapil Dev	3	6	0	128	78	0	21.33
Chetan Sharma	3	5	2	57	38	0	19.00
M. Azharuddin	3	6	0	112	43	0	18.66
S. Viswanath	3	5	0	31	20	0	6.20

Played in two Tests: Maninder Singh 0, 3, 0*. Played in one Test: R. M. H. Binny 19; Gopal Sharma 10*, 1; L. Sivaramakrishnan 18, 21.

Signifies not out.

BOWLING

	O	M	R	W	BB	Avge
Chetan Sharma	109	12	383	14	5-118	27.35
Kapil Dev	129.4	30	372	11	3-74	33.81
Maninder Singh	86.3	27	212	6	4-31	35.33
R. J. Shastri	122.3	31	270	6	3-74	45.00

Also bowled: M. Amarnath 15-2-31-1; R. M. H. Binny 12-0-49-2; Gopal Sharma 15-6-35-0; L. Sivaramakrishnan 38-5-117-0.

INDIAN AVERAGES – FIRST-CLASS MATCHES

BATTING

	M	I	NO	R	HI	100s	Avge
M. Amarnath	2	4	1	216	116*	1	72.00
D. B. Vengsarkar	4	7	1	310	133	1	51.66
S. M. Gavaskar	5	9	2	243	52	0	34.71
M. Azharuddin	5	9	1	265	66	0	33.12
Kapil Dev	4	7	0	186	78	0	26.57
K. Srikkanth	5	9	0	233	64	0	25.88
L. S. Rajput	4	7	0	174	61	0	24.85
R. J. Shastri	4	7	0	168	81	0	24.00
L. Sivaramakrishnan ..	3	4	0	61	21	0	15.25
Chetan Sharma	5	7	2	72	38	0	14.40
S. Viswanath	5	7	0	92	38	0	13.14
Gopal Sharma	3	4	2	25	12	0	12.50

Played in three matches: Maninder Singh 0*, 0, 3, 0*. Played in two matches: R. S. Ghai 1, 1. Played in one match: R. M. H. Binny 19.

Signifies not out.

BOWLING

	O	M	R	W	BB	Avge
Chetan Sharma	140	15	483	17	5-118	28.41
Kapil Dev	147.5	34	411	13	3-74	31.61
Maninder Singh	134.3	39	329	8	4-31	41.12
R. J. Shastri	153.3	45	317	7	3-74	45.28

Also bowled: M. Amarnath 15–2–31–1; M. Azharuddin 4–0–24–0; R. M. H. Binny 12–0–49–2; S. M. Gavaskar 6–2–19–0; R. S. Ghai 34–7–101–1; L. S. Rajput 5–1–19–0; Gopal Sharma 76–20–161–4; L. Sivaramakrishnan 89–15–238–4; K. Srikkanth 4–0–30–0; D. B. Vengsarkar 7–0–31–1.

FIELDING

S. Viswanath 16 (15 ct, 1 st), M. Azharuddin 5, L. Sivaramakrishnan 5 (1 as sub), S. M. Gavaskar 4, D. B. Vengsarkar 4, Maninder Singh 3, L. S. Rajput 3, Chetan Sharma 2, Kapil Dev 2, R. M. H. Binny 1, Gopal Sharma 1, R. J. Shastri 1, K. Srikkanth 1.

SRI LANKA COLTS XI v INDIANS

At Nondescripts Cricket Club, Colombo, August 21, 22, 23. Drawn. Feeling their way at the start of the tour, the Indians were kept in the field for an inordinately long time while the opener, Warnakulasuriya, compiled his maiden first-class hundred and an unbeaten 174 containing two 6s and fifteen 4s. The Colts captain, Ranatunga, batted aggressively for his half-century. When the Indians batted, only Vengsarkar applied himself seriously to what had essentially become batting practice, and he scored a century before the match petered out. Weerasinghe, a teenage leg-spinner, enhanced his reputation with five wickets.

Sri Lanka Colts

†S. A. R. Silva c Sivaramakrishnan b Chetan	46	– c Vengsarkar b Chetan 12
S. Warnakulasuriya not out	174	
R. S. Mahanama st Viswanath b Gopal	11	– (2) c Viswanath b Chetan 10
*A. Ranatunga c Gavaskar b Shastri	51	– c Chetan b Gopal 15
A. P. Gurusinha c Gopal b Ghai	15	
H. P. Tillekeratne c Viswanath b Sivaramakrishnan	11	– (3) not out 8
B. R. Jurangpathy c Sivaramakrishnan b Vengsarkar	61	– (5) not out 0
C. D. U. S. Weerasinghe not out	1	
B 5, l-b 4, w 5, n-b 1	15	B 1, l-b 1, n-b 6 8

1/77 2/98 3/184   (6 wkts dec.) 385   1/21 2/31 3/53   (3 wkts) 53
4/227 5/254 6/376

K. G. Perera, F. S. Ahangama and A. K. Kuruppuarachchi did not bat.

Bowling: *First Innings*—Chetan 15–2–40–1; Ghai 15–4–44–1; Sivaramakrishnan 27–4–64–1; Shastri 31–14–47–1; Gopal 29–8–58–1; Gavaskar 6–2–19–0; Srikkanth 4–0–30–0; Azharuddin 4–0–24–0; Vengsarkar 7–0–31–1; Rajput 5–1–19–0. *Second Innings*—Chetan 6–0–17–2; Ghai 6–0–21–0; Sivaramakrishnan 4–1–11–0; Gopal 3–2–2–1.

Indians

K. Srikkanth b Ahangama	16	Chetan Sharma c Perera b Weerasinghe	1
L. S. Rajput c Gurusinha b Ahangama	24	L. Sivaramakrishnan b Jurangpathy	1
M. Azharuddin c Tillekeratne		R. S. Ghai c Gurusinha b Jurangpathy	1
b Weerasinghe	28	Gopal Sharma not out	2
D. B. Vengsarkar b Ahangama	133		
S. M. Gavaskar c Ranatunga		B 3, l-b 1, w 2, n-b 8	14
b Weerasinghe	27		
*R. J. Shastri c Perera b Weerasinghe	11	1/26 2/71 3/75 4/157 5/177	296
†S. Viswanath lbw b Weerasinghe	38	6/251 7/253 8/262 9/266	

Bowling: Ahangama 25.2–5–88–3; Kuruppuarachchi 13–2–32–0; Weerasinghe 41–8–114–5; Perera 12–4–29–0; Jurangpathy 12–1–20–2; Ranatunga 1–0–9–0.

Umpires: A. C. Felsinger and L. Saverimuttu.

†SRI LANKA v INDIA

First One-day International

At Sinhalese Sports Club, Colombo, August 25. India won by two wickets. Four big innings marked the first-ever one-day international between Sri Lanka and India in Sri Lanka, the most decisive being Vengsarkar's 89 off 66 balls. This enabled India to keep pace with an asking-rate which had climbed above 6 an over, and victory was achieved in the final over. Shastri had anchored the Indian reply with a steady 67. The Sri Lankan innings, which had been drifting against a well-directed seam attack, was revived splendidly in a 110-run stand between Dias and Ranatunga.

Man of the Match: R. L. Dias.

Sri Lanka

†S. A. R. Silva c Chetan b Shastri	36	P. A. de Silva b Chetan	4
J. R. Ratnayeke c Shastri b Amarnath	13	A. L. F. de Mel not out	2
R. S. Madugalle c and b Gopal	3	L-b 10	10
R. L. Dias b Chetan	80		
A. Ranatunga b Chetan	64	1/34 2/40 3/82 (6 wkts, 45 overs) 241	
*L. R. D. Mendis not out	29	4/192 5/227 6/231	

R. J. Ratnayake, R. G. C. E. Wijesuriya and V. B. John did not bat.

Bowling: Kapil Dev 9–1–47–0; Chetan 9–2–50–3; Gopal 9–0–21–1; Amarnath 8–0–40–1; Shastri 5–0–35–1; Sivaramakrishnan 5–0–38–0.

India

R. J. Shastri c Ratnayeke b Ranatunga	67	Chetan Sharma run out	8
K. Srikkanth c de Mel b Wijesuriya	29	†S. Viswanath not out	7
M. Azharuddin b Wijesuriya	7	L. Sivaramakrishnan not out	1
D. B. Vengsarkar c Ratnayeke		L-b 6, w 1, n-b 1	8
b Ratnayake	89		
*Kapil Dev c Silva b Ratnayeke	24	1/61 2/81 3/135 (8 wkts, 44.3 overs) 242	
S. M. Gavaskar run out	0	4/185 5/196 6/200	
M. Amarnath c Silva b Ratnayeke	2	7/221 8/234	

Gopal Sharma did not bat.

Bowling: de Mel 8.3–1–54–0; John 9–0–32–0; Ratnayake 9–0–35–2; Wijesuriya 8–0–56–2; Ratnayeke 6–0–32–1; Ranatunga 4–0–27–1.

Umpires: H. C. Felsinger and P. W. Vidanagamage.

SRI LANKA BOARD PRESIDENT'S XI v INDIANS

At Moratuwa, August 26, 27, 28. Drawn. A hundred by Gurusinha, a young left-hander of elegant, assured strokeplay, was the feature of a colourless match in this suburb of Colombo. The tourists, frustrated by the difficulties of adjusting to new conditions after a long break from Test and domestic cricket, had some consolation in Azharuddin's two half-centuries, while Ahangama, an industrious seam bowler, impressed his national selectors with a long spell in the Indians' first innings.

Indians

L. S. Rajput c Senanayake b Wijesuriya	28	– c Wettimuny b Samarasekera ... 17
K. Srikkanth c de Alwis b Ahangama	7	– c de Alwis b Ramanayake 23
M. Azharuddin b Kaluperuma	66	– not out 59
S. M. Gavaskar b Wijesuriya	12	– not out 18
†S. Viswanath c and b Kaluperuma	23	
*Kapil Dev b Ahangama	58	
L. Sivaramakrishnan b Ramanayake	21	
Chetan Sharma c sub b Ramanayake	14	
Gopal Sharma run out	12	
R. S. Ghai c de Alwis b Samarasekera	1	
Maninder Singh not out	0	
B 2, l-b 4, n-b 1	7	L-b 4, w 2 6

1/17 2/59 3/95 4/129 5/154   249   1/44 2/44   (2 wkts) 123
6/209 7/231 8/246 9/248

Bowling: *First Innings*—Ahangama 18–2–51–2; Ramanayake 11–4–20–2; Samarasekera 23.1–4–57–1; Wijesuriya 29–7–66–2; Kaluperuma 15–1–49–2. *Second Innings*—Ahangama 4–0–20–0; Samarasekera 11–2–37–1; Wijesuriya 9–1–25–0; Ramanayake 5–0–12–1; Kaluperuma 4–1–15–0; de Silva 2–0–10–0; Madugalle 1–1–0–0.

Sri Lanka Board President's XI

S. Wettimuny c Viswanath b Gopal ... 83	M. A. R. Samarasekera c Chetan
C. P. Senanayake c Azharuddin	b Maninder . 9
b Kapil Dev . 15	R. G. C. E. Wijesuriya c and b Maninder 21
S. M. S. Kaluperuma	F. S. Ahangama c Rajput b Gopal 2
c and b Sivaramakrishnan . 37	C. P. Ramanayake not out 9
*R. S. Madugalle c Viswanath	
b Sivaramakrishnan . 30	B 4, l-b 10, n-b 3 17
P. A. de Silva c Rajput	
b Sivaramakrishnan . 0	1/25 2/94 3/171 (9 wkts dec.) 361
A. P. Gurusinha not out 100	4/171 5/173 6/229
†R. G. de Alwis c and b Kapil Dev ... 38	7/242 8/318 9/325

Bowling: Kapil Dev 18.1–4–39–2; Chetan 10–1–43–0; Maninder 48–12–117–2; Ghai 13–3–36–0; Sivaramakrishnan 20–5–46–3; Gopal 29–4–66–2.

Umpires: F. R. S. de Mel and K. T. Ponnambalam.

SRI LANKA v INDIA

First Test Match

At Sinhalese Sports Club, Colombo, August 30, 31, September 1, 3, 4. Drawn. Sri Lanka came within an ace of scoring their maiden win in Test cricket, only resolute batting by Vengsarkar and interference from typically tropical weather denying them their opportunity. In a match of fluctuating fortunes, the home team took all the honours and at one point, as 17 were taken off Kapil Dev's first over, threatened to meet the target of 123 runs in eleven overs.

A painstaking half-century by Gavaskar, batting in the middle order, helped India consume time in their first innings as de Mel led the Sri Lankan seam attack with a haul of five wickets. There was a memorable début for Ahangama when he had Azharuddin caught behind off his fourth ball in Test cricket, the catch being the first of Silva's six in the innings. The Sri Lankans were in early trouble against Chetan Sharma before Madugalle and Ranatunga, with their maiden Test hundreds, got the better of an Indian attack whose penetration was nullified as the days became brighter. Madugalle batted for 403 minutes, Ranatunga for over five and a half hours.

There was little hint of the trouble to come for India when they began their second essay on the fourth morning. However, Ratnayake, who had sent back Rajput and Gavaskar in the space of four balls in the evening, struck in quick succession to capture three wickets in fifteen balls on the final day after rain had accounted for one vital session and dented the home side's ambitions. Only Vengsarkar's unbeaten 98 in six and three-quarter hours ensured that India went ahead by more than 100 runs in the last twenty overs.

Sri Lanka changed their batting order in an attempt to meet their target, and Aravinda de Silva sounded the challenge by hooking Kapil Dev for 6 the moment the second innings began. India had as many as seven men on the boundary as the first four overs produced 38 runs, but in trying to keep up the frenetic pace, Sri Lanka lost three wickets in eight balls and had settled for a draw when bad light brought an early finish.

India

L. S. Rajput c Silva b Ahangama	32	– c Silva b Ratnayake	61
K. Srikkanth b Ratnayake	2	– c Silva b Ratnayake	9
M. Azharuddin c Silva b Ahangama	3	– lbw b Ahangama	16
D. B. Vengsarkar c Silva b de Mel	6	– not out	98
S. M. Gavaskar run out	51	– c de Mel b Ratnayake	0
R. J. Shastri c Silva b de Mel	9	– lbw b Ratnayake	40
*Kapil Dev c Silva b de Mel	36	– c sub (S. D. Anurasiri)	
		b Ratnayake	6
†S. Viswanath c E. A. R. de Silva b de Mel	20	– c Silva b Ratnayake	0
Chetan Sharma c Silva b de Mel	38	– run out	4
Gopal Sharma not out	10	– lbw b Ahangama	1
Maninder Singh lbw b Ratnayake	0	– b Ahangama	3
L-b 5, w 1, n-b 5	11	B 4, 1-b 3, n-b 6	13

1/19 2/30 3/47 4/49 5/65   218   1/23 2/54 3/130 4/130 5/188   251
6/101 7/143 8/202 9/218   6/206 7/206 8/220 9/229

Bowling: *First Innings*—de Mel 28–8–64–5; Ratnayake 24.2–7–64–2; Ahangama 23–3–60–2; E. A. R. de Silva 12–5–18–0; Ranatunga 10–8–7–0. *Second Innings*—de Mel 30–3–84–0; Ratnayake 41–10–85–6; Ahangama 27.3–10–49–3; E. A. R. de Silva 15–6–20–0; Ranatunga 6–2–6–0.

Sri Lanka

S. Wettimuny c Viswanath b Chetan	13		
†S. A. R. Silva c Azharuddin b Chetan	7	– (6) not out	1
R. S. Madugalle c and b Maninder	103	– (5) not out	5
R. L. Dias c Azharuddin b Chetan	4	– (3) c Srikkanth b Kapil Dev	0
*L. R. D. Mendis c Gavaskar b Maninder	51	– (2) c Kapil Dev b Chetan	18
A. Ranatunga b Shastri	111	– (4) run out	15
P. A. de Silva c Azharuddin b Shastri	33	– (1) c Maninder b Kapil Dev	21
A. L. F. de Mel c Viswanath b Kapil Dev	16		
R. J. Ratnayake lbw b Kapil Dev	2		
E. A. R. de Silva not out	1		
F. S. Ahangama c Viswanath b Kapil Dev	0		
L-b 5, n-b 1	6	L-b 1	1

1/18 2/29 3/33 4/118 5/262   347   1/38 2/39 3/44 4/58   (4 wkts) 61
6/317 7/342 8/346 9/346

Bowling: *First Innings*—Kapil Dev 30.4–8–74–3; Chetan 25–3–81–3; Shastri 34–9–70–2; Maninder 40–12–82–2; Gopal 15–6–35–0. *Second Innings*—Kapil Dev 4–0–36–2; Chetan 4–0–24–1.

Umpires: H. C. Felsinger and K. T. Francis.

SRI LANKA v INDIA

Second Test Match

At P. Saravanamuttu Stadium, Colombo, September 6, 7, 8, 10, 11. Sri Lanka won by 149 runs. Sri Lanka's epochal Test win, in only their fourteenth Test match, came despite their own slow batting at the start, but their well-directed seam attack, bowling on and outside off stump, put them well in the hunt by establishing a convincing first-innings lead. India's woeful catching on the first day enabled Silva and Madugalle to build a steady foundation of 168 by the close, and Dias's polished 95 increased the advantage on the second day. Although the last six wickets fell for 17, the Sri Lankan bowlers maintained it by capturing three Indian wickets for 6 runs by the end of the day's play.

Despite half-centuries from Srikkanth, Gavaskar and Amarnath on the third day, India frittered away their margin of safety by losing four quick wickets for 34 runs on the fourth morning. This left Sri Lanka, 141 runs ahead, time to set up a declaration on the fourth afternoon, and Dias and Aravinda de Silva obliged with quick-fire knocks that left their bowlers a whole day to bring about the country's first Test win.

Notwithstanding two dubious decisions on the final morning, India, set a target of 348 in 333 minutes plus twenty overs, could have batted out for a draw. However, Ratnayake swung the match for Sri Lanka by running through the middle order. A defiant 78 by Kapil Dev produced moments of anxiety before Ratnayake dived to take a smart return catch to dismiss the Indian captain and seal the victory which led to a nationwide celebration and a public holiday the following day. Silva's century and nine dismissals in the match were an unprecedented feat by a wicket-keeper in a Test match.

Sri Lanka

S. Wettimuny run out	19	– c Rajput b Chetan	32
†S. A. R. Silva c Viswanath b Shastri	111	– c Vengsarkar b Kapil Dev	11
R. S. Madugalle lbw b Chetan	54		
R. L. Dias c Viswanath b Chetan	95	– not out	60
*L. R. D. Mendis c Shastri b Amarnath	51	– not out	13
A. Ranatunga lbw b Chetan	21		
P. A. de Silva c Azharuddin b Chetan	2	– (3) b Shastri	75
A. L. F. de Mel lbw b Shastri	0		
R. J. Ratnayake c Sivaramakrishnan b Shastri	7		
C. D. U. S. Weerasinghe b Chetan	3		
F. S. Ahangama not out	0		
L-b 3, w 4, n-b 15	22	B 4, l-b 6, n-b 5	15

1/74 2/169 3/229 4/328 5/368   385   1/46 2/48 3/180   (3 wkts dec.) 206
6/372 7/375 8/375 9/379

Bowling: *First Innings*—Kapil Dev 32–10–69–0; Chetan 33–3–118–5; Shastri 45.3–11–74–3; Sivaramakrishnan 31–4–90–0; Amarnath 15–2–31–1. *Second Innings*—Kapil Dev 20–4–73–1; Chetan 13–1–55–1; Shastri 13–4–41–1; Sivaramakrishnan 7–1–27–0.

India

L. S. Rajput c Silva b de Mel	0	– lbw b de Mel	12
K. Srikkanth c Mendis b Ahangama	64	– lbw b Ratnayake	25
M. Azharuddin c Silva b Ratnayake	0	– c Silva b de Mel	25
D. B. Vengsarkar c Ranatunga b Ratnayake	1	– c Silva b Ratnayake	0
L. Sivaramakrishnan c Wettimuny b Ratnayake	18	– (9) c Silva b de Mel	21
S. M. Gavaskar st Silva b Ranatunga	52	– (5) c Silva b Ratnayake	19
M. Amarnath c Ahangama b de Mel	60	– (6) c de Silva b Ratnayake	10
R. J. Shastri c Silva b Ahangama	17	– (7) c Silva b Ahangama	4
*Kapil Dev c Ratnayake b Ahangama	6	– (8) c and b Ratnayake	78
†S. Viswanath c Wettimuny b Ratnayake	7	– lbw b Ahangama	0
Chetan Sharma not out	4	– not out	0
B 4, l-b 6, w 1, n-b 4	15	L-b 2, n-b 2	4

1/0 2/1 3/3 4/79 5/88   244   1/39 2/39 3/41 4/84 5/84   198
6/178 7/218 8/229 9/238   6/98 7/98 8/168 9/169

Bowling: *First Innings*—de Mel 31–8–63–2; Ratnayake 25.1–5–76–4; Ahangama 18–3–59–3; Weerasinghe 16–7–28–0; Ranatunga 5–1–8–1. *Second Innings*—de Mel 22–4–64–3; Ratnayake 23.2–6–49–5; Ahangama 14–3–56–2; Weerasinghe 3–1–8–0; Ranatunga 4–0–19–0.

Umpires: S. Ponnadurai and P. W. Vidanagamage.

SRI LANKA v INDIA

Third Test Match

At Kandy, September 14, 15, 16, 18, 19. Drawn. A magnificent rearguard action by Sri Lanka's two most accomplished batsmen, Mendis and Dias, kept India at bay, and by forcing the draw Sri Lanka sealed their first-ever series win. There had been a qualitative improvement in India's batting which, however, was not so apparent in their first innings; and on a good batting pitch, the Indians had bowled more purposefully than they had in the rest of the series.

With a forceful contribution from Srikkanth, India held the upper hand at the close of the third day (149 for one) and were in a strong position to set themselves a deadline for the declaration. Amarnath anchored the middle order with his ninth Test century and Azharuddin, after a disappointing series, ran into late form to enable India to give their bowlers a full eight hours in which to bowl out the opposition. They made a good start as Sri Lanka lost three wickets cheaply in the last session of the penultimate day, Kapil Dev becoming India's leading wicket-taker (267) when Silva was caught behind. However, Sri Lanka's captain and vice-captain swung the game away from India with their amazing counter-attack, and by lunch on the final day there was even a chance that Sri Lanka might score an improbable victory. The 216-run stand was broken just before the tea interval by a run-out and the seamers returned in the hope of running through the late middle order. Dias (seventeen 4s) batted for 312 minutes; Mendis (two 6s, eleven 4s) for 318 minutes.

Time, however, was no longer on India's side, and in the mandatory overs' period de Silva and de Mel held on with a degree of skill and luck. The umpires called off play for bad light twenty minutes before the scheduled close and Sri Lanka were left the winners of the series.

India

R. J. Shastri c Madugalle b de Mel	6	– c Silva b Ahangama	81
K. Srikkanth b Ahangama	40	– lbw b Ahangama	47
M. Amarnath lbw b Ahangama	30	– not out	116
D. B. Vengsarkar run out	62	– lbw b Ahangama	10
M. Azharuddin c Silva b Ahangama	25	– (6) b Ratnayake	43
S. M. Gavaskar c Silva b Ratnayake	49	– (7) not out	15
*Kapil Dev lbw b Ahangama	0	– (5) b Ranatunga	2
R. M. H. Binny c de Mel b Ahangama	19		
Chetan Sharma c Wettimuny b de Mel	11		
†S. Viswanath c Silva b Ratnayake	4		
Maninder Singh not out	0		
L-b 1, w 1, n-b 1	3	L-b 5, w 4, n-b 2	11

1/10 2/66 3/111 4/161 5/180   249   1/74 2/178 3/206   (5 wkts dec.) 325
6/180 7/212 8/241 9/242   4/211 5/289

In the first innings, Chetan Sharma, when 4, retired hurt at 237 and resumed at 242.

Bowling: *First Innings*—de Mel 26.3–5–97–2; Ratnayake 26–5–88–2; Ahangama 24–7–52–5; Ranatunga 8–5–11–0. *Second Innings*—de Mel 13–2–66–0; Ratnayake 23–2–97–1; Ahangama 27–6–72–3; Ranatunga 16–4–51–1; Jurangpathy 4–0–24–0; Madugalle 1–0–10–0.

Sri Lanka

S. Wettimuny c Viswanath b Kapil Dev	34	– c Vengsarkar b Chetan	5
†S. A. R. Silva lbw b Binny	19	– c Viswanath b Kapil Dev	2
R. S. Madugalle c and b Binny	5	– c Viswanath b Kapil Dev	10
R. L. Dias c Viswanath b Chetan	8	– run out	106
*L. R. D. Mendis c sub (L. Sivaramakrishnan) b Maninder	53	– c Gavaskar b Chetan	124
A. Ranatunga c Vengsarkar b Maninder	38	– b Chetan	0
F. S. Ahangama c Gavaskar b Maninder	11		
P. A. de Silva run out	8	– (7) not out	29
B. R. Jurangpathy c Viswanath b Kapil Dev	1	– (8) lbw b Kapil Dev	0
A. L. F. de Mel c Viswanath b Maninder	1	– (9) not out	9
R. J. Ratnayake not out	0		
L-b 4, n-b 16	20	B 8, l-b 4, w 4, n-b 6	22

1/36 2/44 3/68 4/80 5/153   198   1/5 2/8 3/34 4/250   (7 wkts) 307
6/173 7/196 8/197 9/198   5/250 6/266 7/267

Bowling: *First Innings*—Kapil Dev 19–4–46–2; Binny 12–0–49–2; Chetan 14–1–40–1; Shastri 6–2–28–0; Maninder 12.3–4–31–4. *Second Innings*—Kapil Dev 24–4–74–3; Chetan 20–4–65–3; Maninder 34–11–99–0; Shastri 24–5–57–0.

Umpires: D. P. Buultjens and M. D. D. N. Gooneratne.

†SRI LANKA v INDIA

Second One-day International

At P. Saravanamuttu Stadium, Colombo, September 21. Sri Lanka won by 14 runs. In a match badly affected by rain and shortened to 28 overs a side, Madugalle's rare aggression guided Sri Lanka to a challenging total. Vengsarkar sustained the Indian reply, but the Sri Lankan fielders backed up their seam bowlers so well that India dropped behind the required run-rate.

Man of the Match: R. S. Madugalle.

Sri Lanka

†S. A. R. Silva b Kapil Dev	11	J. R. Ratnayeke not out	26
P. A. de Silva c Kapil Dev b Shastri	24		
R. L. Dias b Gopal	27	L-b 4, w 1, n-b 1	6
*L. R. D. Mendis run out	20		
A. Ranatunga b Binny	7	1/21 2/54 3/86 (5 wkts, 28 overs) 171	
R. S. Madugalle not out	50	4/86 5/98	

A. L. F. de Mel, R. J. Ratnayake, R. G. C. E. Wijesuriya and V. B. John did not bat.

Bowling: Kapil Dev 5–0–26–1; Chetan 6–0–49–0; Shastri 6–0–22–1; Binny 5–0–42–1; Gopal 6–1–28–1.

India

R. J. Shastri st Silva b Wijesuriya	25	*Kapil Dev not out	6
K. Srikkanth b John	10	L-b 2, w 2	4
M. Azharuddin c Mendis b John	26		
D. B. Vengsarkar run out	50	1/12 2/60 3/75 (4 wkts, 28 overs) 157	
S. M. Gavaskar not out	36	4/143	

M. Amarnath, R. M. H. Binny, Chetan Sharma, †S. Viswanath and Gopal Sharma did not bat.

Bowling: de Mel 3–0–20–0; John 6–0–26–2; Ratnayake 6–0–33–0; Ratnayeke 6–0–34–0; Wijesuriya 5–0–31–1; Ranatunga 2–0–11–0.

Umpires: B. C. Cooray and K. T. Francis.

†SRI LANKA v INDIA

Third One-day International

At P. Saravanamuttu Stadium, Colombo, September 22. No result. When bad light prevented any further play – it was felt in some quarters that the offer to go off was made prematurely – Sri Lanka were perilously placed at 32 for four in reply to India's 194 in 40 overs. Vengsarkar, with his third half-century of the series, had pushed up his side's run-rate after India had started shakily. With the light deteriorating, the Sri Lankans set out to chase 72 in fifteen overs (the minimum overs required for a result) and lost wickets quickly.

Man of the Match: D. B. Vengsarkar.

India

R. J. Shastri lbw b Ratnayeke	45	S. M. Gavaskar not out	39
K. Srikkanth b de Mel	8	R. M. H. Binny not out	8
M. Azharuddin run out	13	B 3, l-b 5, w 1	9
D. B. Vengsarkar b Ratnayake	55		—
M. Amarnath c Silva b Ratnayake	5	1/25 2/55 3/84 (6 wkts, 40 overs)	194
*Kapil Dev c Wijesuriya b Ranatunga	12	4/102 5/135 6/173	

Chetan Sharma, †S. Viswanath and Gopal Sharma did not bat.

Bowling: de Mel 8–0–39–1; John 8–2–22–0; Ratnayake 7–0–41–2; Ranatunga 6–0–23–1; Ratnayeke 7–0–38–1; Wijesuriya 4–0–23–0.

Sri Lanka

†S. A. R. Silva b Kapil Dev	1	A. Ranatunga not out	0
P. A. de Silva c Vengsarkar b Chetan	2	L-b 1, w 1	2
R. L. Dias c Kapil Dev b Chetan	12		—
*L. R. D. Mendis not out	14	1/4 2/4 3/26 (4 wkts, 9.2 overs)	32
R. S. Madugalle c Viswanath b Kapil Dev	1	4/32	

J. R. Ratnayeke, A. L. F. de Mel, R. J. Ratnayake, R. G. C. E. Wijesuriya and V. B. John did not bat.

Bowling: Kapil Dev 5–0–20–2; Chetan 4.2–0–11–2.

Umpires: D. C. C. Perera and K. T. Ponnambalam.

THE SRI LANKANS IN PAKISTAN, 1985-86

By QAMAR AHMED

The Sri Lankans arrived in Pakistan in October bubbling with confidence after their first-ever victory in a Test series – against India at home the previous month – but their tour, Sri Lanka's second to Pakistan, proved to be a disappointment for them. They lost the three-match Test series 2-0 and were outplayed in the four one-day internationals.

Their failure was due mainly to the inability of their experienced batsmen – Sidath Wettimuny, Roy Dias, Ranjan Madugalle and the captain, Duleep Mendis – to strike form. Only Aravinda de Silva, who celebrated his twentieth birthday and scored his maiden Test hundred at Faisalabad, displayed his skills and realised his promise. He went on to make another hundred in the final Test at Karachi, in difficult circumstances, against fine bowling by Imran Khan, Abdul Qadir and Tauseef Ahmed.

The Sri Lankan bowling, except for Ravi Ratnayeke and Asantha de Mel, was equally unimpressive. Ratnayeke took ten wickets in the series, eight of them for 83 in Pakistan's first innings in the second Test, the best return by any Sri Lankan bowler. That match, the first played at Sialkot, was won for Pakistan by the excellent bowling of Imran Khan, who had match figures of nine for 95. Imran was playing in a Test series for the first time after an absence of two years because of injury. At Karachi, de Mel's six for 109, his best figures in Test cricket, gave Sri Lanka a chance to win the third Test and so square the series. But it was Pakistan's off-spinner, Tauseef Ahmed, who had the final say in a bowlers' match by taking five for 54 in Sri Lanka's second innings to win it for the home side. In defence of both Sri Lanka's batsmen and bowlers, there was little time for them to adjust to Pakistani conditions before the one-day internationals and Test matches began. Their itinerary provided only one warm-up match, and that was abandoned because of rain.

The first Test at Faisalabad was destined to be a dull, dreary affair once the decision to play the match on a newly laid pitch was overturned by the Pakistan chairman of selectors, Hanif Mohammad. Despite strong protests by the local cricket association and other administrators, Test cricket was again played on a lifeless pitch which produced a feast of runs and few wickets.

The series saw the retirement of Pakistan's most prolific batsman, Zaheer Abbas, who announced his decision during the second Test in Sialkot, the city of his birth. His farewell Test was to have been the match at Karachi but he withdrew from the team. He did make himself available for the Sharjah Cup one-day tournament in November but was not selected. In his 78 Tests, Zaheer scored 5,062 runs, including twelve hundreds, at an average of 44.79. Another resignation was Javed Miandad's from the captaincy of Pakistan. Imran Khan took over for the one-day series against the visiting West Indians.

SRI LANKAN TOUR RESULTS

Test matches – Played 3: Lost 2, Drawn 1.
First-class matches – Played 3: Lost 2, Drawn 1. Abandoned 1.
Losses – Pakistan (2).
Draw – Pakistan.
Abandoned – BCCP President's XI.
Non first-class matches – Played 4: Lost 4. Losses – Pakistan (4).

TEST MATCH AVERAGES

PAKISTAN – BATTING

	T	I	NO	R	HI	100s	Avge
Javed Miandad	3	3	1	306	203*	1	153.00
Mudassar Nazar	3	5	2	253	78	0	84.33
Qasim Omar	3	4	0	218	206	1	54.50
Mohsin Khan	2	4	1	143	50	0	47.66
Imran Khan	3	2	0	69	63	0	34.50
Salim Yousuf	2	3	1	63	27	0	31.50
Abdul Qadir	3	2	0	29	19	0	14.50
Salim Malik	3	2	0	26	22	0	13.00
Wasim Akram	3	2	1	9	5*	0	9.00

Played in two Tests: Zaheer Abbas 4. Played in one Test: Ashraf Ali did not bat; Jalal-ud-Din did not bat; Mohsin Kamal 4*; Ramiz Raja 52; Shoaib Mohammad 33; Tauseef Ahmed 1.

Signifies not out.

BOWLING

	O	M	R	W	BB	Avge
Imran Khan	120.4	37	271	17	5-40	15.94
Tauseef Ahmed	45.2	18	104	6	5-54	17.33
Abdul Qadir	102.2	26	279	9	5-44	31.00
Wasim Akram	103.5	31	251	8	2-17	31.37

Also bowled: Jalal-ud-Din 39–12–89–1; Mohsin Kamal 29–5–88–4; Mudassar Nazar 34.2–5–69–4; Shoaib Mohammad 2–1–4–0

SRI LANKA – BATTING

	T	I	NO	R	HI	100s	Avge
P. A. de Silva	3	5	0	250	122	2	50.00
A. Ranatunga	3	5	1	169	79	0	42.25
R. J. Ratnayake	3	5	1	102	56	0	25.50
S. Wettimuny	3	5	0	124	52	0	24.80
J. R. Ratnayeke	3	5	1	90	36	0	22.50
S. A. R. Silva	2	3	0	64	35	0	21.33
R. L. Dias	3	5	0	87	48	0	17.40
R. S. Madugalle	3	5	0	75	65	0	15.00
L. R. D. Mendis	3	5	0	55	20	0	11.00
A. L. F. de Mel......	3	5	0	39	18	0	7.80
R. G. C. E. Wijesuriya	3	5	2	19	8	0	6.33

Played in one Test: A. P. Gurusinha 17, 12.

BOWLING

	O	M	R	W	BB	Avge
J. R. Ratnayeke	81.5	14	297	10	8-83	29.70
R. J. Ratnayake	75	8	275	6	2-48	45.83
A. L. F. de Mel	77	8	349	7	6-109	49.85

Also bowled: P. A. de Silva 5–0–22–0; R. S. Madugalle 7–1–18–0; A. Ranatunga 22–1–93–0; R. G. C. E. Wijesuriya 73.4–21–189–1.

BCCP PRESIDENT'S XI v SRI LANKANS

At Rawalpindi, October 9, 10, 11. Abandoned owing to rain and the wet conditions at the Pindi Club ground. A limited-overs exhibition match was played on the scheduled third day, the Sri Lankans winning by seven wickets.

BCCP President's XI 101 (34 overs); Sri Lankans 104 for three (31.4 overs) (R. S. Madugalle 45 not out).

†PAKISTAN v SRI LANKA

First One-day International

At Peshawar, October 13. Pakistan won by eight wickets. Mendis and de Mel, coming together at 69 for six, looked as if they might lift Sri Lanka, who were put in to bat, to a respectable total. However, Mendis was bowled by Qadir for 23, and later de Mel, who hit Qadir for 16 in one over, was run out. Mudassar Nazar and Shoaib Mohammad put on 113 runs for the first wicket to set Pakistan on the way to a comfortable victory.

Man of the Match: Mudassar Nazar.

Sri Lanka

†S. A. R. Silva b Tahir 25	R. J. Ratnayake b Tahir 19
P. A. de Silva c Ashraf b Imran 0	R. G. C. E. Wijesuriya lbw b Imran ... 0
R. S. Madugalle b Zakir 0	V. B. John not out 3
R. L. Dias b Mudassar 5	B 4, l-b 3, w 9, n-b 7 23
*L. R. D. Mendis b Qadir 23	
A. Ranatunga lbw b Qadir 11	1/2 2/11 3/35 (39.2 overs) 145
J. R. Ratnayeke b Mudassar 0	4/50 5/66 6/69
A. L. F. de Mel run out 36	7/90 8/126 9/133

Bowling: Imran 8–0–22–2; Zakir 8–2–21–1; Mudassar 8–0–32–2; Tahir 7.2–0–29–2; Qadir 8–0–34–2.

Pakistan

Mudassar Nazar lbw b de Mel 40
Shoaib Mohammad not out 72
Ramiz Raja b Wijesuriya 7
*Javed Miandad not out 8
    B 4, l-b 3, w 7, n-b 6 20

1/113 2/138   (2 wkts, 32.5 overs) 147

Zaheer Abbas, Salim Malik, Imran Khan, †Ashraf Ali, Tahir Naqqash, Abdul Qadir and Zakir Khan did not bat.

Bowling: de Mel 8–2–27–1; John 5–0–28–0; Ratnayake 5–1–22–0; Wijesuriya 6–1–18–1; Ratnayeke 4.5–0–33–0; Ranatunga 4–0–12–0.

Umpires: Javed Akhtar and Khizar Hayat.

PAKISTAN v SRI LANKA

First Test Match

At Faisalabad, October 16, 17, 18, 20, 21. Drawn. The newly laid pitch at the Iqbal Stadium was rejected on the morning of the match by Hanif Mohammad, the chairman of Pakistan's selectors, on the grounds that it was dangerous. What followed was a high-scoring game in which only thirteen wickets fell while 1,034 runs were scored. Sri Lanka, after winning the toss, batted into the third day to compile their highest score in Test cricket, 479, de Silva batting for eight and a half hours and hitting three 6s and seventeen 4s. Not out 93 at the close of play on his twentieth birthday, de Silva moved to his maiden Test hundred the following morning with a 6 off Imran. In reply Pakistan were 555 for three when the match was called off soon after tea on the fifth day, Qasim Omar and Javed Miandad having completed their second and third double-centuries respectively. Their partnership of 397 for the third wicket was the eighth highest in Test cricket and the second highest for the third wicket.

Sri Lanka

S. Wettimuny lbw b Qadir	52	A. L. F. de Mel c Ashraf b Wasim	17	
†S. A. R. Silva c Shoaib b Imran	17	R. J. Ratnayake lbw b Qadir	56	
R. S. Madugalle b Mudassar	5	R. G. C. E. Wijesuriya not out	7	
R. L. Dias c Ashraf b Jalal-ud-Din	48			
*L. R. D. Mendis lbw b Imran	15	B 4, l-b 11, w 2, n-b 10	27	
A. Ranatunga c Shoaib b Qadir	79			
P. A. de Silva c Ashraf b Imran	122	1/23 2/40 3/125 4/129 5/165	479	
J. R. Ratnayeke run out	34	6/286 7/352 8/391 9/443		

Bowling: Imran 49–15–112–3; Wasim 42.3–12–98–1; Jalal-ud-Din 39–12–89–1; Mudassar 13.3–3–29–1; Qadir 54.3–17–132–3; Shoaib 2–1–4–0.

Pakistan

Mudassar Nazar lbw b Ratnayake	78
Shoaib Mohammad c Silva b Ratnayake	33
Qasim Omar b Ratnayeke	206
*Javed Miandad not out	203
B 6, l-b 17, w 1, n-b 11	35

1/86 2/158 3/555   (3 wkts) 555

Zaheer Abbas, Salim Malik, Imran Khan, †Ashraf Ali, Abdul Qadir, Wasim Akram and Jalal-ud-Din did not bat.

Bowling: de Mel 27–3–106–0; Ratnayake 32–4–93–2; Ratnayeke 29.5–3–117–1; Wijesuriya 44–13–102–0; Ranatunga 18–1–74–0; Madugalle 7–1–18–0; de Silva 5–0–22–0.

Umpires: Khizar Hayat and Mahboob Shah.

†PAKISTAN v SRI LANKA

Second One-day International

At Gujranwala, October 23. Pakistan won by 15 runs. Mendis put Pakistan in on a lively wicket and was rewarded with three wickets falling for 68 runs. However, Zaheer entered to build the innings, first with Ramiz and then, when Ramiz was out in the 22nd over, with Salim Malik for the next eighteen overs. Helped by de Silva's fine 86, the Sri Lankans appeared well set to reach their target, but accurate bowling by Mudassar and Tahir, plus three run-outs at crucial stages, arrested their advance.

Man of the Match: P. A. de Silva.

Pakistan

Mudassar Nazar c Silva b Ratnayake . .	11	Imran Khan not out 1
Shoaib Mohammad c Madugalle b de Mel	4	
Ramiz Raja b Wijesuriya	45	L-b 7, w 11, n-b 2 20
*Javed Miandad c Silva b Ratnayake . .	10	
Zaheer Abbas c de Silva b Ratnayake .	61	1/6 2/49 3/68　　(5 wkts, 40 overs) 224
Salim Malik not out	72	4/106 5/222

†Salim Yousuf, Tahir Naqqash, Abdul Qadir and Zakir Khan did not bat.

Bowling: de Mel 6–0–41–1; John 8–1–17–0; Ratnayake 8–0–51–3; Ratnayeke 6–0–44–0; Wijesuriya 8–0–40–1; Ranatunga 4–0–24–0.

Sri Lanka

†S. A. R. Silva c Yousuf b Qadir	19	R. J. Ratnayake run out 9
P. A. de Silva run out	86	J. R. Ratnayeke not out 0
R. S. Madugalle c Miandad b Qadir . . .	7	L-b 10, w 4, n-b 3 17
R. L. Dias c Tahir b Imran	43	
*L. R. D. Mendis run out	4	1/53 2/65 3/161　　(7 wkts, 40 overs) 209
A. Ranatunga not out	17	4/163 5/169
A. L. F. de Mel b Tahir	7	6/195 7/209

R. G. C. E. Wijesuriya and V. B. John did not bat.

Bowling: Imran 8–0–47–1; Zakir 3–0–23–0; Qadir 8–0–25–2; Mudassar 8–0–39–0; Shoaib 6–0–30–0; Tahir 7–0–35–1.

Umpires: Mian Aslam and Shakoor Rana.

†PAKISTAN v SRI LANKA

Third One-day International

At Lahore, October 25. Pakistan won by five wickets. A crowd of some 40,000 saw Miandad win the toss and put Sri Lanka in to bat. Madugalle, whose partnership of 93 with Ranatunga steadied the innings, hit four 6s and three 4s in his highest score in a one-day international. With Miandad in delightful form, Pakistan kept in touch with the asking-rate of 6 an over and won with nine balls to spare.

Man of the Match: Javed Miandad.

Sri Lanka

†S. A. R. Silva lbw b Tahir	19	R. J. Ratnayake c Zaheer
P. A. de Silva lbw b Imran	0	b Mohsin Kamal . 26
R. S. Madugalle c Imran b Mudassar .	73	R. G. C. E. Wijesuriya not out 6
A. Ranatunga b Tahir	39	B 4, l-b 15, w 8 27
R. L. Dias c Malik b Mudassar	9	
*L. R. D. Mendis not out	27	1/2 2/42 3/135　　(7 wkts, 38 overs) 228
A. L. F. de Mel c Yousuf b Tahir	2	4/151 5/165 6/174 7/211

V. B. John and F. S. Ahangama did not bat.

Bowling: Imran 7–1–33–1; Mohsin Kamal 6–1–18–1; Qadir 8–0–26–0; Tahir 8–0–59–3; Mudassar 6–0–41–2; Malik 2–0–22–0; Shoaib 1–0–10–0.

Pakistan

Mudassar Nazar run out	16	Imran Khan not out 2
Shoaib Mohammad lbw b de Mel	14	
Ramiz Raja c de Mel b Ratnayake	56	B 1, l-b 5, w 6, n-b 6 18
*Javed Miandad not out	91	
Zaheer Abbas b Ranatunga	21	1/27 2/53 3/130　　(5 wkts, 36.3 overs) 231
Salim Malik c de Mel b Ratnayake	13	4/188 5/206

†Salim Yousuf, Tahir Naqqash, Abdul Qadir and Mohsin Kamal did not bat.

Bowling: de Mel 7–0–38–1; John 8–0–45–0; Ratnayake 6.3–0–50–2; Ahangama 3–0–23–0; Wijesuriya 8–0–46–0; Ranatunga 4–0–23–1.

Umpires: Amanullah Khan and Shakoor Rana.

PAKISTAN v SRI LANKA

Second Test Match

At Sialkot, October 27, 28, 29, 31. Pakistan won by eight wickets. Jinnah Park became the 59th Test match venue and Pakistan's eleventh. Sri Lanka, put in, were bowled out on the first day for 157, Imran taking four for 55 on a pitch which helped the seam bowlers throughout. Except for their openers, Mudassar and Mohsin Khan, and their captain, Pakistan's batsmen were no more secure on the second day as Ratnayeke claimed eight wickets for 83, the best bowling by a Sri Lankan in a Test match and eclipsing Ratnayake's six wickets against India the previous month. Play was held up three times as the Sri Lankan fielders protested over the turning down of an appeal for a catch at the wicket against Miandad off Ratnayake. On the third day Pakistan dismissed the touring side for 200, Imran's five wickets giving him match figures of nine for 95, and went into the rest day with 1 run in the book. The remaining 98 required for victory were scored without difficulty on the fourth morning to give Pakistan victory with more than a day and a half to spare.

Sri Lanka

S. Wettimuny c Yousuf b Imran	45	– lbw b Imran	0
†S. A. R. Silva c Omar b Mudassar	12	– c Wasim b Mudassar	35
R. S. Madugalle c Yousuf b Mohsin Kamal	0	– c Miandad b Mohsin Kamal	65
R. L. Dias c Omar b Mohsin Kamal	21	– lbw b Mudassar	7
*L. R. D. Mendis c Mudassar b Mohsin Kamal	20	– c Yousuf b Wasim	3
A. Ranatunga not out	25	– c Malik b Imran	28
P. A. de Silva hit wkt b Imran	2	– c Yousuf b Wasim	8
J. R. Ratnayeke c Yousuf b Imran	0	– not out	17
A. L. F. de Mel lbw b Wasim	1	– b Imran	0
R. J. Ratnayake b Imran	1	– c sub (Ramiz Raja) b Imran	2
R. G. C. E. Wijesuriya lbw b Wasim	8	– lbw b Imran	0
B 6, l-b 2, w 3, n-b 11	22	B 9, l-b 10, n-b 16	35

1/41 2/41 3/81 4/99 5/101   157   1/0 2/98 3/111 4/121 5/147   200
6/101 7/110 8/130 9/131   6/163 7/188 8/188 9/200

In the first innings, R. L. Dias, when 5, retired hurt at 49 and resumed at 170.

Bowling: *First Innings*—Imran 19–3–55–4; Wasim 14.2–4–38–2; Mohsin Kamal 17–3–50–3; Mudassar 6–1–6–1. *Second Innings*—Imran 18.3–5–40–5; Mohsin Kamal 12–2–38–1; Wasim 19–4–74–2; Qadir 1.1–0–1–0; Mudassar 11.5–1–28–2.

Pakistan

Mudassar Nazar c Silva b Ratnayake	78	– not out	24
Mohsin Khan lbw b Ratnayeke	50	– run out	44
Qasim Omar c Wijesuriya b Ratnayeke	1	– c Ranatunga b de Mel	3
*Javed Miandad lbw b Ratnayeke	40		
Zaheer Abbas b Ratnayeke	4		
Salim Malik lbw b Ratnayeke	22		
Imran Khan c sub (A. P. Gurusinha) b Ratnayeke	6		
†Salim Yousuf lbw b Ratneyeke	23	– (4) not out	13
Abdul Qadir c Silva b Ratnayeke	10		
Wasim Akram c Silva b Ratnayeke	4		
Mohsin Kamal not out	4		
B 5, l-b 3, w 1, n-b 8	17	B 4, l-b 4, n-b 8	16

1/88 2/93 3/181 4/185 5/209   259   1/76 2/82   (2 wkts) 100
6/216 7/216 8/245 9/252

Bowling: *First Innings*—de Mel 15–3–63–0; Ratnayake 18–2–77–2; Ratnayeke 23.2–5–83–8; Ranatunga 3–0–18–0; Wijesuriya 4–1–10–0. *Second Innings*—Ratnayake 6–0–24–0; de Mel 10–1–43–1; Ratnayeke 7.4–1–25–0.

Umpires: Javed Akhtar and Mian Aslam.

†PAKISTAN v SRI LANKA

Fourth One-day International

At Hyderabad, November 3. Pakistan won by 89 runs. Sri Lanka put Pakistan in to bat, but after an early breakthrough they were frustrated first by Ramiz Raja and then by Miandad as the Pakistanis maintained a scoring rate of 5 runs an over. Madugalle, who was fielding at third man, was injured when he was hit by a stone thrown from the stands. However, he recovered in time to bat and was one of five Sri Lankan wickets to fall for 80 in 21 overs. Mendis played a captain's innings but was fighting a lone battle.

Pakistan

Mudassar Nazar c and b Wijesuriya ...	29	Abdul Qadir not out	20
Mohsin Khan lbw b John	6	Tahir Naqqash not out	7
Ramiz Raja lbw b Ratnayeke	45		
*Javed Miandad c sub		B 4, l-b 7	11
(S. Warnakulasuriya) b Ratnayeke .	56		
Zaheer Abbas c Gurusinha b Ratnayeke	26	1/12 2/81 3/91 (7 wkts, 39 overs)	216
Salim Malik c Mendis b Wijesuriya ...	16	4/127 5/163	
†Salim Yousuf b Ratnayake	0	6/168 7/195	

Tauseef Ahmed and Mohsin Kamal did not bat.

Bowling: de Mel 8–1–42–0; John 8–1–34–1; Ratnayake 8–0–45–1; Wijesuriya 5–0–25–2; Ratnayeke 6–0–34–3; Ranatunga 4–0–25–0.

Sri Lanka

P. A. de Silva c Mohsin Khan		R. J. Ratnayake c Mohsin Kamal	
b Mohsin Kamal .	19	b Zaheer .	2
J. R. Ratnayeke c Yousuf		R. G. C. E. Wijesuriya not out	12
b Mohsin Kamal .	8	V. B. John c Malik b Qadir	7
R. S. Madugalle c Tahir b Mudassar ..	9		
R. L. Dias b Mudassar	13		
*L. R. D. Mendis st Yousuf b Qadir ...	46	L-b 7, w 1, n-b 2	10
A. Ranatunga c Tahir b Tauseef	1		
†A. P. Gurusinha run out	0	1/20 2/34 3/41 (37.2 overs)	127
A. L. F. de Mel c sub		4/69 5/80 6/83	
(Shoaib Mohammad) b Zaheer .	0	7/87 8/91 9/112	

Bowling: Mohsin Kamal 4–0–26–2; Tahir 3–0–12–0; Mudassar 8–0–23–2; Tauseef 8–2–20–1; Qadir 7.2–2–13–2; Zaheer 7–0–26–2.

Umpires: Feroze Butt and Shakeel Khan.

PAKISTAN v SRI LANKA

Third Test Match

At Karachi, November 7, 8, 9, 11. Pakistan won by ten wickets. Sri Lanka, who elected to bat, were bowled out twice on a pitch which took spin from the first day. In the first innings it was the leg-spinner, Abdul Qadir, who did the damage; in the second, the off-spinner, Tauseef Ahmed, took five wickets in a Test for the first time. In between, de Mel, moving the ball skilfully off the seam, dismissed the top six batsmen in the Pakistan order to return his best figures for Sri Lanka. It was not an easy match for batsmen. However, Miandad, Ramiz, who replaced Zaheer, and Imran each played crucial, responsible innings on the second day as Pakistan, 68 for four at lunch, improved to 294 for nine at the close. Only de Silva, with his second hundred of the series (265 minutes, sixteen 4s) could match their dedication. Of Sri Lanka's 216 for eight at the end of the third day, he had scored 103 not out. In contrast to the difficulties of the first three days, Mudassar and Mohsin hit off the runs required for victory in almost even time. In Sri Lanka's second innings Imran took over the captaincy, Javed Miandad having fractured his right thumb, and when Imran was unfit on the fourth day, Mudassar led the side.

Sri Lanka

S. Wettimuny b Wasim	17	– c Yousuf b Imran	10
J. R. Ratnayeke b Qadir	36	– c Yousuf b Imran	3
R. S. Madugalle lbw b Wasim	0	– (8) b Tauseef	5
R. L. Dias c Yousuf b Imran	7	– c Malik b Qadir	4
*L. R. D. Mendis c Miandad b Qadir	15	– (7) b Imran	2
A. Ranatunga c Miandad b Tauseef	12	– (5) c Yousuf b Wasim	25
P. A. de Silva c and b Qadir	13	– (3) c Yousuf b Tauseef	105
†A. P. Gurusinha lbw b Imran	17	– (6) c Yousuf b Tauseef	12
A. L. F. de Mel st Yousuf b Qadir	3	– b Tauseef	18
R. J. Ratnayake not out	21	– c Omar b Tauseef	22
R. G. C. E. Wijesuriya lbw b Qadir	2	– not out	2
B 5, l-b 10, w 1, n-b 3	19	B 5, l-b 11, n-b 6	22

1/27 2/28 3/60 4/89 5/90   162   1/14 2/15 3/57 4/104 5/132   230
6/106 7/122 8/125 9/151   6/139 7/157 8/191 9/221

Bowling: *First Innings*—Imran 20–9–36–2; Wasim 14–7–17–2; Tauseef 22–10–50–1; Qadir 20.5–5–44–5. *Second Innings*—Imran 14.1–5–28–3; Wasim 14–4–24–1; Qadir 25.5–4–102–1; Mudassar 3–0–6–0; Tauseef 23.2–8–54–5.

Pakistan

Mudassar Nazar c Gurusinha b de Mel	16	– not out	57
Mohsin Khan c Gurusinha b de Mel	13	– not out	36
Qasim Omar c Ranatunga b de Mel	8		
*Javed Miandad lbw b de Mel	63		
Salim Malik b de Mel	4		
Ramiz Raja c and b de Mel	52		
Imran Khan c Ratnayake b Ratnayeke	63		
†Salim Yousuf lbw b Ratnayake	27		
Abdul Qadir c Wettimuny b Wijesuriya	19		
Tauseef Ahmed b Ratnayake	1		
Wasim Akram not out	5		
B 13, l-b 8, w 2, n-b 1	24	B 1, l-b 3, n-b 1	5

1/27 2/43 3/60 4/68 5/153   295   (no wkt) 98
6/228 7/259 8/288 9/290

Bowling: *First Innings*—de Mel 22–1–109–6; Ratnayake 15–2–48–2; Ratnayeke 15–4–48–1; Wijesuriya 22–5–68–1; Ranatunga 1–0–1–0. *Second Innings*—de Mel 3–0–28–0; Ratnayake 4–0–33–0; Ratnayeke 6–1–24–0; Wijesuriya 3.4–2–9–0.

Umpires: Khizar Hayat and Mahboob Shah.

THE NEW ZEALANDERS IN AUSTRALIA, 1985-86

By D. J. CAMERON

Perhaps because New Zealand cricket had existed in the shade of Australia for so many decades – one Test was played in 1946, and regular Test exchanges did not start until 1973-74 – Australian cricket loomed over New Zealand. So it was with a sense of wonderment, and delight, that New Zealanders, in November and December 1985, greeted the success of Jeremy Coney's team as they took, by two Tests to one, their first-ever series against Australia. With a little more luck it might have been 3-0, for between New Zealand's innings victory in the first Test at the Gabba and the six-wicket win at Perth, New Zealand narrowly missed victory in the nip and tuck struggle at Sydney. It was, in fact, only New Zealand's third series victory outside New Zealand. Pakistan 1969-70 and Sri Lanka 1983-84 provided the earlier instances.

Were New Zealand so good, or Australia so bad? It was a little bit of both. For a decade or so, New Zealand bowlers had toiled on Australian pitches which favoured truly fast bowlers and proficient, shot-making batsmen. New Zealand never had quite enough of either. Yet in late 1985 New Zealand were presented with pitches which, at the vital times, favoured the skilled medium-fast bowler who could hit the seam rather than the man who might hit the helmet. These same pitches, with not enough bounce to delight the cutters and the hookers, were allies to the batsman who played sensibly and straight. In other words New Zealand, and especially Richard Hadlee, the sharpest and finest-tempered of New Zealand's bowling swords, found pitches very much of the New Zealand mould, except for that strip of spinning mischief at Sydney.

From the moment Hadlee laid waste the Australian first innings of the first Test, nine wickets for 52, a display which justified the use of that overworked adjective "great", he and the New Zealanders had the Australians in their grip. Hadlee, who caught the tenth wicket in that first innings, took six more in the second. In the second Test, on a drudge of a pitch, he still acquired seven wickets. At Perth, on a bony, slowish pitch, he took another eleven, taking his total for the series to 33; few as a result of bouncers, many through the artistry of a medium-fast bowler on pitches which gave him such a vast canvas.

With Ewen Chatfield's probing support, and with the summoning of the off-spinner, John Bracewell, for the second and third Tests, the New Zealand bowlers seldom gave the slow-footed, prodding Australian batsmen any respite. This did not happen by accident. G. M. Turner, the former New Zealand and Worcestershire batsman, was appointed cricket manager for the side, and from his friends in England he learnt the strong and weak points of those Australians who toured there earlier in the year.

Apart from their record-breaking first innings in Brisbane, the New Zealanders never found pitches of sufficient pace or trustworthiness to produce big scores. But throughout the series their batting, like their bowling and fielding, was tightly organised and disciplined. Apart from some weak batting on the spinner's pitch at Sydney, the New Zealanders worked solidly at their batting. They took their time and they played straight so that, with Turner's work in the background and Coney's cheery leadership, their whole team effort was tidily integrated.

Martin Crowe almost stole Hadlee's considerable thunder at the Gabba with the classicism of his 188 which, with John Reid's fluent if less spectacular 108, produced the match-winning stand of 224 for the third wicket. Like too many others he faltered at Sydney, but at Perth he hit 71 and 42 not out, all the time playing within his considerable powers. In the Tests, John Wright had four scores of 35 or more, while his equally diligent opening partner, Bruce Edgar, hit three half-centuries.

The Australians, still recovering from their 1-3 series defeat in England, had lost some of their playing sub-structure to the unofficial tour of South Africa. On the other hand, the Australian players were newly armed with expansive contracts from the Australian Cricket Board and encouraged by the official urging that they were the best cricketers in the country. Allan Border, by deed and word, tried mightily to rebuild the defences of Australian cricket, but in many cases he was using bricks of sand. Too many of his batsmen, and even Border himself, produced a technique which made them vulnerable to a bowler of Hadlee's class. Too often his faster bowlers, on pitches of no real pace, tried to blast and bounce the New Zealand batsmen out – and seemed dismayed when the pitch and the batsmen did not oblige.

In January the New Zealanders, with Stuart Gillespie and Bruce Blair in place of Lance Cairns, who had retired, and Trevor Franklin, returned to Australia for the Benson and Hedges World Series Cup contest with Australia and India. This time they found less success. For one thing, they had lost the drill that Geoff Howarth used to bring to their one-day play. They had adequate bowling, and potentially good batting, but perhaps only two or three times did the two marry. They found the Australian bowling more geared to the seaming and sometimes indifferent one-day pitches, while the Indians, perhaps below their best one-day form, were still full of uncomfortable surprises.

The New Zealanders complained publicly about pitches which placed too much emphasis, in one-day matches, on winning the toss, and they were often less than impressed with some of the umpiring. But in reality they played below their own form and hopes, whereas Australia had improved, at least in one-day tactics, and the Indians just pipped New Zealand for a place in the finals.

NEW ZEALAND TOUR RESULTS

Test matches – Played 3: Won 2, Lost 1.
First-class matches – Played 6: Won 2, Lost 1, Drawn 3.
Wins – Australia (2).
Loss – Australia.
Draws – South Australia, Queensland, New South Wales.
Non first-class matches – Played 13: Won 3, Lost 6. Drawn 3, No result 1. *Wins* – India (2), Australia. *Losses* – India (3), Australia (3). *Draws* – Queensland Combined XI, Queensland Country XI, Prime Minister's XI. *No result* – Australia.

TEST MATCH AVERAGES

AUSTRALIA – BATTING

	T	I	NO	R	HI	100s	Avge
A. R. Border	3	6	1	279	152*	1	55.80
G. R. J. Matthews . . .	3	6	0	247	115	1	41.16
G. M. Ritchie	3	6	0	180	89	0	30.00
W. B. Phillips	3	6	0	177	63	0	29.50
D. C. Boon	3	6	0	175	81	0	29.16
D. W. Hookes	2	4	1	59	38*	0	19.66
C. J. McDermott	2	4	0	61	36	0	15.25
G. F. Lawson	2	4	0	47	21	0	11.75
D. R. Gilbert	3	5	2	25	12*	0	8.33
R. B. Kerr	2	4	0	31	17	0	7.75
R. G. Holland	3	5	1	4	4	0	1.00

Played in one Test: R. J. Bright 1; A. M. J. Hilditch 0, 12; S. P. O'Donnell 20*, 2*; K. C. Wessels 70, 3.

Signifies not out.

BOWLING

	O	M	R	W	BB	Avge
R. J. Bright	51.5	15	126	5	3-39	25.20
R. G. Holland	158	51	370	13	6-106	28.46
D. R. Gilbert	122.3	31	288	8	3-48	36.00
G. R. J. Matthews . . .	92	25	216	6	3-110	36.00
G. F. Lawson	104.5	27	210	5	4-79	42.00

Also bowled: A. R. Border 0.1-0-0-0; D. W. Hookes 1-0-2-0; C. J. McDermott 77-13-212-3; S. P. O'Donnell 11-6-17-0; K. C. Wessels 1-0-7-0.

NEW ZEALAND – BATTING

	T	I	NO	R	HI	100s	Avge
M. D. Crowe	3	5	1	309	188	1	77.25
B. A. Edgar	3	5	0	209	74	0	41.80
J. G. Wright	3	5	0	182	46	0	36.40
J. F. Reid	3	5	0	169	108	1	33.80
R. J. Hadlee	3	4	0	111	54	0	27.75
V. R. Brown	2	3	1	51	36*	0	25.50
J. J. Crowe	3	5	1	73	35	0	18.25
I. D. S. Smith	3	4	1	54	28	0	18.00
J. V. Coney	3	5	0	72	22	0	14.40

Played in two Tests: J. G. Bracewell 83*, 2*, 28*; E. J. Chatfield 3. Played in one Test: S. L. Boock 37, 3; B. L. Cairns 0; M. C. Snedden did not bat.

Signifies not out.

BOWLING

	O	M	R	W	BB	Avge
R. J. Hadlee	169.3	42	401	33	9-52	12.15
E. J. Chatfield	96	30	184	7	3-33	26.28
J. G. Bracewell	89.5	27	195	7	3-91	27.85

Also bowled: S. L. Boock 51.5-18-102-3; V. R. Brown 57-13-176-1; B. L. Cairns 40-7-109-0; J. V. Coney 49-23-79-3; M. D. Crowe 21-5-55-0; M. C. Snedden 30-4-111-1.

NEW ZEALAND AVERAGES – FIRST-CLASS MATCHES

BATTING

	M	I	NO	R	HI	100s	Avge
M. D. Crowe	4	7	2	562	242*	2	112.40
B. A. Edgar	6	10	0	389	122	1	38.90
J. J. Crowe	6	11	4	252	79*	0	36.00
J. V. Coney	6	11	2	303	89	0	33.66
J. G. Wright	6	11	0	331	46	0	30.09
J. F. Reid	5	9	0	241	108	1	26.77
R. J. Hadlee	5	6	0	151	54	0	25.16
V. R. Brown	5	8	3	121	36*	0	24.20
I. D. S. Smith	5	7	3	93	28	0	23.25
S. L. Boock	4	3	0	40	37	0	13.33
B. L. Cairns	4	3	0	29	25	0	9.66
E. J. Chatfield	3	2	0	3	3	0	1.50

Played in three matches: M. C. Snedden 26. Played in two matches: J. G. Bracewell 83*, 2*, 28*. Played in one match: T. J. Franklin 13; E. B. McSweeney 26*.

Signifies not out.

BOWLING

	O	M	R	W	BB	Avge
R. J. Hadlee	241.3	64	537	37	9-52	14.51
J. G. Bracewell	89.5	27	195	7	3-91	27.85
E. J. Chatfield	139	44	252	8	3-33	31.50
S. L. Boock	202.5	49	560	17	4-83	32.94
V. R. Brown	189	29	624	14	4-75	44.57
M. C. Snedden	107	12	364	6	4-88	60.66
B. L. Cairns	145.5	31	389	6	2-46	64.83

Also bowled: J. V. Coney 66-26-132-3; M. D. Crowe 21-5-55-0.

FIELDING

J. V. Coney 10, I. D. S. Smith 10 (8 ct, 2 st), J. J. Crowe 8, V. R. Brown 6, M. D. Crowe 4, J. F. Reid 4, J. G. Wright 4, J. G. Bracewell 3, B. L. Cairns 3, E. J. Chatfield 3, B. A. Edgar 3, R. J. Hadlee, T. J. Franklin 2 (1 as sub), E. B. McSweeney 2 (1 ct, 1 st), S. L. Boock 1.

†At Townsville, October 18, 19, 20. Drawn. Queensland Combined XI 202 (N. Jelich 48, I. Stenhouse 42; V. R. Brown four for 85) and 68 for two; New Zealanders 345 for seven dec. (T. J. Franklin 98, B. A. Edgar 115, J. J. Crowe 48).

†At Carrara, October 22, 23. Drawn. New Zealanders 247 for five dec. (T. J. Franklin 47, J. F. Reid 79, M. D. Crowe 97 not out); Queensland Country XI 160 for seven (R. Williams 54, W. London 41).

SOUTH AUSTRALIA v NEW ZEALANDERS

At Adelaide, October 26, 27, 28, 29. Drawn. Sunshine and a serene pitch made this match a batting exercise, even if there was a slightly undignified scramble for a draw by the New Zealanders on the last afternoon. South Australia's declaration had left them to score 265 at about 5 runs an over and, seeking match practice, the New Zealanders had shuffled their batting order. They were 171 for seven with twelve overs remaining, but Coney and McSweeney made sure of the draw. In the first innings, Martin Crowe hit one 6 and 41 4s in his career-best innings of 242 not out.

South Australia

A. M. J. Hilditch lbw b Hadlee	7	– c McSweeney b Hadlee	1
G. A. Bishop c Hadlee b Cairns	11	– st McSweeney b Boock	202
R. J. Zadow c Boock b Hadlee	26	– lbw b Cairns	0
*D. W. Hookes c Coney b Brown	106	– lbw b Boock	14
P. R. Sleep c Coney b Brown	12	– not out	133
D. F. G. O'Connor c and b Brown	11	– not out	12
†W. B. Phillips c J. J. Crowe b Boock	44		
T. B. A. May not out	42		
A. K. Zesers c Coney b Snedden	9		
G. C. Small b Cairns	0		
B 1, l-b 2, w 1, n-b 6	10	L-b 2, w 1, n-b 8	11

1/15 2/40 3/61 4/112   (9 wkts dec.) 278   1/15 2/17 3/47   (4 wkts dec.) 373
5/159 6/190 7/234   4/344
8/273 9/278

I. R. Carmichael did not bat.

Bowling: *First Innings*—Hadlee 19–6–38–2; Snedden 16–1–69–1; Cairns 15.5–4–46–2; Boock 20–5–51–1; Brown 29–5–71–3. *Second Innings*—Hadlee 12–3–30–1; Cairns 26–8–44–1; Boock 33–5–104–2; Brown 28–3–97–0; Snedden 19–1–68–0; Coney 6–1–28–0.

New Zealanders

J. G. Wright c Hilditch b Small	8	– (2) c Bishop b May	41
B. A. Edgar c Phillips b Small	1	– (1) c Zesers b May	16
M. D. Crowe not out	242	– (7) c Bishop b Hookes	11
*J. V. Coney run out	89	– (8) not out	17
J. J. Crowe not out	42	– lbw b May	38
B. L. Cairns (did not bat)		– c O'Connor b Sleep	25
V. R. Brown (did not bat)		– (3) c Hookes b May	10
R. J. Hadlee (did not bat)		– (4) c Hookes b Sleep	19
†E. B. McSweeney (did not bat)		– not out	26
L-b 2, n-b 3	5	B 3, l-b 3	6

1/9 2/15 3/260   (3 wkts dec.) 387   1/59 2/62 3/78 4/108   (7 wkts) 209
                                                    5/146 6/155 7/171

M. C. Snedden and S. L. Boock did not bat.

Bowling: *First Innings*—Small 19–5–49–2; Carmichael 24–7–79–0; Zesers 25–8–69–0; May 31–10–96–0; Sleep 9–2–40–0; O'Connor 2–0–30–0; Hookes 9–4–22–0. *Second Innings*—Small 6–2–13–0; Carmichael 7–2–15–0; Zesers 7–3–16–0; May 23–6–67–4; Sleep 13–2–49–2; Hookes 5–0–43–1.

Umpires: A. R. Crafter and B. E. Martin.

QUEENSLAND v NEW ZEALANDERS

At Brisbane, November 1, 2, 3, 4. Drawn. Coney gave Queensland first use of what became an easy-paced pitch and centuries by Courtice and Border took them through to lunch on the second day for a total of 407. After a hesitant start, with Wright and Reid going to Trimble in one over at 34, Edgar steadied the innings with a solid 122 (329 minutes), and a lively 79 by Crowe allowed the New Zealanders to declare. Queensland scored their 232 for six declared in smart fashion, with Phillips's 77 coming from 80 balls with three 6s and five 4s, but the New Zealanders, needing 309 to win from 65 overs, again sought batting practice rather than victory.

Queensland

R. B. Kerr c Coney b Snedden	20	– (2) lbw b Hadlee	39
K. C. Wessels b Snedden	25	– (1) lbw b Boock	42
B. A. Courtice c Edgar b Boock	112	– (8) not out	21
*A. R. Border c Wright b Cairns	102		
G. M. Ritchie lbw b Snedden	7	– (3) c Wright b Brown	18
G. S. Trimble c Reid b Snedden	49	– (5) c sub b Boock	26
A. B. Henschell c Coney b Boock	24	– (4) c Smith b Boock	0
†R. B. Phillips c Crowe b Brown	30	– (6) not out	77
C. J. McDermott c Reid b Boock	4	– (7) b Boock	1
H. Frei c Coney b Brown	7		
J. R. Thomson not out	11		
L-b 4, n-b 12	16	B 3, l-b 1, n-b 4	8

1/45 2/56 3/218 4/234 5/320   407   1/69 2/92 3/96   (6 wkts dec.) 232
6/334 7/366 8/378 9/389   4/120 5/156 6/159

Bowling: *First Innings*—Hadlee 26–7–53–0; Cairns 36–9–94–1; Snedden 30–5–88–4; Coney 3–1–10–0; Boock 19–4–75–3; Brown 18.5–0–83–2. *Second Innings*—Hadlee 15–6–15–1; Cairns 8–0–34–0; Snedden 12–1–28–0; Boock 29–5–83–4; Brown 10–1–68–1.

New Zealanders

J. G. Wright c McDermott b Trimble	18	– (2) lbw b Frei	13
B. A. Edgar c Phillips b Wessels	122		
J. F. Reid c Border b Trimble	0	– (1) c Courtice b Trimble	20
*J. V. Coney c Frei b McDermott	44	– (7) not out	46
J. J. Crowe not out	79	– (8) not out	0
V. R. Brown not out	33	– (3) c Henschell b Frei	0
†I. D. S. Smith (did not bat)		– (4) c Courtice b McDermott	14
R. J. Hadlee (did not bat)		– (5) c Wessels b Trimble	21
M. C. Snedden (did not bat)		– (6) c Wessels b Henschell	26
L-b 4, w 1, n-b 30	35	L-b 3, n-b 9	12

1/34 2/34 3/157 4/248   (4 wkts dec.) 331   1/25 2/30 3/47 4/78   (6 wkts) 152
                                    5/81 6/152

B. L. Cairns and S. L. Boock did not bat.

Bowling: *First Innings*—McDermott 21–2–54–1; Frei 28–7–72–0; Thomson 20–2–74–0; Trimble 18–4–48–2; Henschell 11–0–65–0; Wessels 2–1–14–1. *Second Innings*—McDermott 9–0–36–1; Frei 6–2–14–2; Trimble 15–3–30–2; Henschell 18–4–55–1; Courtice 3–0–11–0; Ritchie 1–0–3–0.

Umpires: M. W. Johnson and C. D. Timmins.

AUSTRALIA v NEW ZEALAND

First Test Match

At Brisbane, November 8, 9, 10, 11, 12. New Zealand won by an innings and 41 runs. When Coney sent Australia in to bat on a pitch which seemed to have some moisture in it, and with cloudy, humid weather aiding the faster bowlers, there was no early indication of the drama that this Test would provide. Wessels, 38 not out, led Australia to lunch at 72 for two, and he had 69 not out, and Australia 146 for four, when bad light cut short the first day. Hadlee's fifteen overs had brought him four wickets for 35, and early on the second, humid morning he dismissed Wessels for 70 (186 balls). He then demolished the Australian innings with one of the outstanding pieces of contemporary Test match bowling, having taken all eight by the time Australia were 175 for eight. He missed the chance of all ten wickets by taking a well-judged catch in the deep from Lawson to give Brown his first wicket in Test cricket, whereupon Brown returned the favour by catching Holland and Australia were all out for 179, with Hadlee returning figures of 23.4-4-52-9. Only J. C. Laker (twice in 1956 at Manchester) and G. A. Lohmann (in 1895-96 in Johannesburg) had recorded better analyses in Test cricket.

The Australians had no bowler to match Hadlee's control and movement off the pitch, which had lost much of its spite, and staunch batting by Reid (71 not out) and Martin Crowe (58 not out) took New Zealand to 209 for two at stumps. On the third day they tightened New Zealand's grip on the match, reaching their centuries within five minutes of each other, Crowe from 197 balls with sixteen 4s, Reid 234 balls, fifteen 4s. It took a great diving catch by Border to remove Reid when the stand was worth 224, a New Zealand Test match record for the third wicket. Crowe, however, surged on, accompanied by free hitting from Coney and Jeff Crowe, hitting 26 4s in all before edging a delivery from Matthews into his stumps after 328 balls. Next Hadlee arrived to torment the Australians again – 50 from 41 balls with three 6s and four 4s – and New Zealand were 553 for seven at stumps, their highest score in Tests. Coney declared on the fourth morning with a lead of 374.

In a little more than two hours Hadlee, Chatfield and Snedden had Australia 67 for five, but Border found a stout ally in Matthews, who hit his first Test hundred from 171 balls and then saw Border to his fifteenth from 196 balls. However, when Hadlee took the second new ball fourteen minutes from stumps and Matthews caught for 115, Border, 106 not out, was Australia's last hope as they went into the final day at 266 for six. He stood alone as Hadlee took three of the last four wickets to finish with match figures of 52.3-13-123-15, the best match return by a New Zealand bowler. Border's undefeated 152, off 303 balls in just over seven and a half hours, included two 6s and twenty 4s.

The attendance for the five days was 16,044. Hadlee was named as Man of the Match in what had been New Zealand's most overwhelming Test victory away from home.

Australia

K. C. Wessels lbw b Hadlee	70	– (2) c Brown b Chatfield	3
A. M. J. Hilditch c Chatfield b Hadlee	0	– (1) c Chatfield b Hadlee	12
D. C. Boon c Coney b Hadlee	31	– c Smith b Chatfield	1
*A. R. Border c Edgar b Hadlee	1	– not out	152
G. M. Ritchie c M. D. Crowe b Hadlee	8	– c Coney b Snedden	20
†W. B. Phillips b Hadlee	34	– b Hadlee	2
G. R. J. Matthews b Hadlee	2	– c Coney b Hadlee	115
G. F. Lawson c Hadlee b Brown	8	– (9) c Brown b Chatfield	7
C. J. McDermott c Coney b Hadlee	9	– (8) c and b Hadlee	5
D. R. Gilbert not out	0	– c Chatfield b Hadlee	10
R. G. Holland c Brown b Hadlee	0	– b Hadlee	0
B 9, l-b 5, n-b 2	16	L-b 3, n-b 3	6

1/1 2/70 3/72 4/82 5/148   179   1/14 2/16 3/16 4/47 5/67   333
6/150 7/159 8/175 9/179   6/264 7/272 8/291 9/333

Bowling: *First Innings*—Hadlee 23.4-4-52-9; Chatfield 18-6-29-0; Snedden 11-1-45-0; M. D. Crowe 5-0-14-0; Brown 12-5-17-1; Coney 7-5-8-0. *Second Innings*—Hadlee 28.5-9-71-6; Chatfield 32-9-75-3; Snedden 19-3-66-1; M. D. Crowe 9-2-19-0; Brown 25-5-96-0; Coney 3-1-3-0.

New Zealand

B. A. Edgar c Phillips b Gilbert	17	R. J. Hadlee c Phillips b McDermott	54
J. G. Wright lbw b Matthews	46	†I. D. S. Smith not out	2
J. F. Reid c Border b Gilbert	108		
M. D. Crowe b Matthews	188	B 2, l-b 11, n-b 32	45
*J. V. Coney c Phillips b Lawson	22		
J. J. Crowe c Holland b Matthews	35	1/36 2/85 3/309 4/362 (7 wkts dec.) 553
V. R. Brown not out	36	5/427 6/471 7/549	

M. C. Snedden and E. J. Chatfield did not bat.

Bowling: Lawson 36.5-8-96-1; McDermott 31-3-119-1; Gilbert 39-9-102-2; Matthews 31-5-110-3; Holland 22-3-106-0; Border 0.1-0-0-0; Wessels 1-0-7-0.

Umpires: A. R. Crafter and R. A. French.

NEW SOUTH WALES v NEW ZEALANDERS

At Sydney, November 15, 16, 17, 18. Drawn. Presented with a bare, brown pitch, New Zealand rested Hadlee, Martin Crowe and Snedden. New South Wales batted first on winning the toss, but two breaks for rain held them to 148 for three at the close of the first day. Matthews followed his Brisbane Test century with 111, and the New Zealanders did well to hold the state to 300. Their batting, however, fared badly against Holland's leg-spin, but Wellham, the home captain, spared them the embarrassment of having to follow on. More rain, a declaration at 128 for six, and rain again allowed the tourists to meander through to a draw.

New South Wales

M. A. Taylor c Reid b Boock	29	– c and b Brown	5
M. E. Waugh c Brown b Boock	17	– run out	0
*D. M. Wellham run out	86	– (6) b Brown	0
P. S. Clifford c Cairns b Brown	6	– (5) c Cairns b Chatfield	40
G. R. J. Matthews c and b Cairns	111	– (7) not out	32
S. R. Waugh c Crowe b Brown	21	– (3) c Wright b Boock	6
†G. C. Dyer b Cairns	1	– (4) c Edgar b Brown	41
M. J. Bennett c Crowe b Brown	17	– not out	1
P. A. Blizzard c Crowe b Boock	4		
D. R. Gilbert c Franklin b Brown	0		
R. G. Holland not out	0		
B 2, l-b 5, n-b 1	8	B 2, n-b 1	3

1/44 2/57 3/68 4/248 5/258   300   1/0 2/11 3/13   (6 wkts dec.) 128
6/268 7/284 8/300 9/300   4/81 5/81 6/117

Bowling: *First Innings*—Cairns 17-1-59-2; Chatfield 27-9-39-0; Boock 39-10-105-3; Coney 8-1-15-0; Brown 26.1-5-75-4. *Second Innings*—Chatfield 16-5-29-1; Cairns 3-2-3-0; Boock 11-2-40-1; Brown 20-2-54-3.

New Zealanders

T. J. Franklin b Gilbert	13		
B. A. Edgar b Blizzard	0	– c S. R. Waugh b Bennett	41
J. F. Reid b Holland	18	– c Dyer b Bennett	34
*J. G. Wright lbw b Holland	31	– (1) c Gilbert b Bennett	38
J. V. Coney b Holland	25	– c Gilbert b Bennett	10
J. J. Crowe b Holland	3	– (4) c and b Holland	17
S. L. Boock c Clifford b Holland	0		
V. R. Brown c Dyer b Holland	6	– (6) not out	21
†I. D. S. Smith not out	18	– (7) not out	7
B. L. Cairns b Holland	4		
E. J. Chatfield c Gilbert b Holland	0		
B 1, n-b 1	2	B 6, l-b 1	7

1/0 2/20 3/54 4/58 5/62   120   1/73 2/104 3/131   (5 wkts) 175
6/81 7/93 8/104 9/112   4/141 5/161

Bowling: *First Innings*—Gilbert 14–11–12–1; Blizzard 6–2–17–1; Matthews 5–1–21–0; Bennett 22–7–36–0; Holland 25–10–33–8. *Second Innings*—Gilbert 7–1–19–0; Blizzard 4–1–12–0; Holland 31–7–77–1; Matthews 8–6–4–0; Bennett 23–9–56–4.

Umpires: R. A. Emerson and A. G. Marshall.

AUSTRALIA v NEW ZEALAND

Second Test Match

At Sydney, November 22, 23, 24, 25, 26. Australia won by four wickets. Contrary to all expectations Border sent New Zealand in to bat on a grassless, drab pitch after leaving out his fastest bowler, McDermott, and bringing in a left-arm spinner, Bright. Border's decision appeared to be going against him when Wright and Edgar put on 60 by lunch, but in the next four hours he was proved right as his spin bowlers, Bright and Holland, swept through the New Zealand innings. Only Bracewell, hastily summoned from New Zealand to bowl his off-spinners, and Boock, with a Test highest score of 35, remained, and yet these two, the former strong and confident of stroke, the latter all obdurate defence, took New Zealand to 217 for nine by the close and next day increased their last-wicket partnership to 124, the highest for the series between the two countries. Hadlee had time to take the first Australian wicket before lunch.

The seam and spin combination of Hadlee and Bracewell quickly reduced Australia to 71 for five and Matthews should have been stumped at 79 for five. Instead this irrepressible left-hander and the stolid Ritchie took Australia into the third day at 175 for five. Ritchie was dropped by Boock in Hadlee's first over, but Hadlee dismissed Matthews at 186 and Ritchie at 224 (after 281 minutes), and New Zealand gained a lead of 66 runs. When, by late on the third day, Wright and Edgar had fashioned a 100-run stand for the first wicket, New Zealand had the match in their grasp – and promptly dropped it. From 119 for three overnight, they were all out soon after lunch on the fourth day for 193.

Bad light and then rain after tea suited neither team, but the rain cleared for Australia to start the last day at 36 for one. It returned to halt play for 68 minutes, and when the match resumed Australia needed 199 from 61 overs with nine wickets in hand. Boon and Phillips added 105 for the second wicket, and at tea Australia were 141 for two, requiring 119 from a minimum of 32 overs. From the last twenty overs 90 runs were needed and the light was fading badly – as was New Zealand's catching. Boon, after a fine innings of 81 in 267 minutes, was out at 192, but Matthews was dropped off Hadlee when 2. It was a costly miss, for he and his fellow left-hander, Hookes, struck out boldly, against the old ball and the new, hitting 64 off nine and a half overs. Hookes was dropped with the victory 2 runs away, and Australia levelled the series with 23 balls to spare.

Bracewell was made Man of the Match, for which the attendance was 37,540.

New Zealand

J. G. Wright c O'Donnell b Bright	38	– c and b Matthews ... 43
B. A. Edgar c Border b Holland	50	– c and b Holland ... 52
J. F. Reid c Kerr b Holland	7	– b Matthews ... 19
M. D. Crowe run out	8	– b Holland ... 0
*J. V. Coney c Border b Holland	8	– b Holland ... 7
J. J. Crowe b Holland	13	– c and b Holland ... 6
V. R. Brown lbw b Holland	0	– b Bright ... 15
†I. D. S. Smith c Hookes b Bright	28	– c and b Bright ... 12
R. J. Hadlee lbw b Holland	5	– lbw b Gilbert ... 26
J. G. Bracewell not out	83	– not out ... 2
S. L. Boock lbw b Gilbert	37	– c Boon b Bright ... 3
B 6, l-b 8, n-b 2	16	B 1, l-b 4, n-b 3 ... 8

1/79 2/92 3/109 4/112 5/128   293   1/100 2/106 3/107 4/119 5/131   193
6/128 7/161 8/166 9/169   6/137 7/162 8/163 9/190

Bowling: *First Innings*—Gilbert 20.3–6–41–1; O'Donnell 6–2–13–0; Bright 34–12–87–2; Matthews 17–3–32–0; Holland 47–19–106–6. *Second Innings*—Gilbert 9–2–22–1; O'Donnell 5–4–4–0; Holland 41–16–68–4; Matthews 30–11–55–2; Bright 17.5–3–39–3.

Australia

†W. B. Phillips b Bracewell	31	– c Bracewell b Boock	63
R. B. Kerr lbw b Hadlee	7	– c Wright b Bracewell	7
D. C. Boon lbw b Hadlee	0	– c Reid b Bracewell	81
*A. R. Border b Bracewell	20	– st Smith b Bracewell	11
G. M. Ritchie c J. J. Crowe b Hadlee	89	– c M. D. Crowe b Hadlee	13
D. W. Hookes run out	0	– not out	38
G. R. J. Matthews c Smith b Hadlee	50	– lbw b Hadlee	32
S. P. O'Donnell not out	20	– not out	2
R. J. Bright lbw b Boock	1		
D. R. Gilbert c Smith b Hadlee	0		
R. G. Holland st Smith b Boock	0		
B 5, l-b 2, n-b 2	9	B 3, l-b 9, n-b 1	13

1/19 2/22 3/48 4/71 5/71   227   1/27 2/132 3/144 4/163   (6 wkts) 260
6/186 7/224 8/225 9/226   5/192 6/258

Bowling: First Innings—Hadlee 24-2-65-5; M. D. Crowe 5-2-15-0; Bracewell 25-9-51-2; Boock 29.5-14-53-2; Brown 13-3-35-0; Coney 1-0-1-0. *Second Innings*—Hadlee 27.1-10-58-2; M. D. Crowe 2-1-7-0; Bracewell 30-7-91-3; Boock 22-4-49-1; Brown 7-0-28-0; Coney 9-1-15-0.

Umpires: M. W. Johnson and B. E. Martin.

AUSTRALIA v NEW ZEALAND

Third Test Match

At Perth, November 30, December 1, 2, 3, 4. New Zealand won by six wickets. With the Test series level, and faced by a new, uncertain pitch on the renovated WACA ground, both teams approached the final Test tentatively. New Zealand brought in Cairns, for what was to be his last Test, while Australia rebuilt their new-ball attack around Lawson and McDermott. As a sideline, the relaid outfield promised to present more problems than the pitch, for it was soft and spongy and unlikely to contribute to fast scoring.

Coney put Australia in, but this time Chatfield, not Hadlee, did the early damage. However, he strained a groin muscle, and after lunch (74 for two) it was Hadlee and Coney who reduced Australia to 140 for seven by tea. Some big hitting by McDermott helped them to 203, with Hadlee again taking five wickets.

Martin Crowe, with Edgar as his ally, fought through the second day, lifting New Zealand to 184 for two at stumps, but when he followed Edgar, out early on the third day, the rest of the New Zealand batting had to scramble for runs against steadfast bowling from Lawson and Holland.

Australia, beginning their second innings 96 in arrears, were 38 for two at the end of the third day, but a hard-fought rearguard action by Border, Boon and Ritchie carried them to 207 for five. In what may well have been the final turning-point of the match Bracewell bowled Hookes with a shooter, and Hadlee had Matthews lbw before Australia finished the fourth day at 239 for seven. When, next morning, Hadlee dismissed Lawson and Gilbert in nine balls, and Bracewell trapped McDermott, the last seven Australian batsmen had gone for 64 and New Zealand needed 164 to win – from about half that number of overs – on a wearing, cracking pitch.

Edgar and Wright provided a solid start (Wright was completely undone by an impossible skidder at 77) and Martin Crowe and Reid took the score to 121, even though Reid was uncomfortable and uncertain for much of the time. Coney drew New Zealand closer; and, finally accompanied by his brother, Crowe marched on resolutely to the win with ten overs to spare.

Hadlee, with eleven wickets in the match, 33 in the series and 299 in 60 Tests, was the Man of the Match, the attendance being 46,800.

Australia

†W. B. Phillips c Smith b Chatfield	37	– c Smith b Chatfield	10
R. B. Kerr c Smith b Chatfield	17	– b Hadlee	0
D. C. Boon c Bracewell b Hadlee	12	– b Hadlee	50
*A. R. Border c Smith b Hadlee	12	– b Hadlee	83
G. M. Ritchie lbw b Coney	6	– c M. D. Crowe b Coney	44
D. W. Hookes c Bracewell b Coney	14	– b Bracewell	7
G. R. J. Matthews b Hadlee	34	– lbw b Hadlee	14
G. F. Lawson c J. J. Crowe b Hadlee	11	– c J. J. Crowe b Hadlee	21
C. J. McDermott b Chatfield	36	– lbw b Bracewell	11
D. R. Gilbert not out	12	– b Hadlee	3
R. G. Holland c M. D. Crowe b Hadlee	4	– not out	0
L-b 6, n-b 2	8	B 2, l-b 5, n-b 9	16

1/38 2/63 3/78 4/85 5/85   203   1/3 2/28 3/109 4/195 5/207   259
6/114 7/131 8/159 9/190   6/214 7/234 8/251 9/255

Bowling: *First Innings*—Hadlee 26.5-6-65-5; Cairns 14-1-50-0; Chatfield 16-6-33-3; Coney 21-11-43-2; Bracewell 6-3-6-0. *Second Innings*—Hadlee 39-11-90-6; Cairns 26-6-59-0; Chatfield 30-9-47-1; Bracewell 28.5-8-47-2; Coney 8-5-9-1.

New Zealand

J. G. Wright c Phillips b Lawson	20	– (2) b Gilbert	35
B. A. Edgar c Hookes b McDermott	74	– (1) c Border b Matthews	16
J. F. Reid b Gilbert	7	– c Phillips b Gilbert	28
M. D. Crowe lbw b McDermott	71	– not out	42
*J. V. Coney c Phillips b Lawson	19	– b Gilbert	16
J. J. Crowe lbw b Holland	17	– not out	2
R. J. Hadlee c Hookes b Holland	26		
†I. D. S. Smith c Matthews b Lawson	12		
J. G. Bracewell not out	28		
B. L. Cairns c Ritchie b Holland	0		
E. J. Chatfield c Phillips b Lawson	3		
B 1, l-b 7, n-b 14	22	B 7, l-b 7, n-b 11	25

1/43 2/55 3/184 4/191 5/215   299   1/47 2/77 3/121 4/149   (4 wkts) 164
6/253 7/256 8/273 9/276

Bowling: *First Innings*—Lawson 47-12-79-4; McDermott 33-9-66-2; Gilbert 31-9-75-1; Holland 40-12-63-3; Matthews 5-3-6-0; Hookes 1-0-2-0. *Second Innings*—Lawson 21-7-35-0; Gilbert 23-5-48-3; McDermott 13-1-27-0; Matthews 9-3-13-1; Holland 8-1-27-0.

Umpires: R. C. Isherwood and P. J. McConnell.

†At Canberra, January 22. Drawn. Prime Minister's XI 48 for no wkt (12.5 overs) v New Zealanders.

New Zealand's matches v Australia and India in the Benson and Hedges World Series Cup may be found in that section.

THE INDIANS IN AUSTRALIA, 1985-86

By DICKY RUTNAGUR

The fifth Indian team to visit Australia for a Test series surpassed its predecessors only in that it finished the tour (excluding the World Series Cup matches) unbeaten. But its merit is more exactly reflected by the fact that, for the first time in three tours, India failed to win a Test match – and that at a time when Australia were reckoned to be at their weakest ever.

It was to the disadvantage of the Indians that the tour was very short, and this handicap was the more severely felt because rain interfered with every first-class match save the first, against South Australia, which the tourists won. Little practice was gained from the second against Victoria, the only other fixture before the first Test, the weather taking its toll on every day. The one remaining state game, against Tasmania, between the first and second Tests, was abandoned without a ball being bowled. That scope for practice was so limited was an encumbrance which the Indians brought on themselves by asking for an abbreviated itinerary, preferring to play earlier in a one-day competition in Sharjah.

Just prior to this series, India had lost a rubber to Sri Lanka while Australia were beaten by New Zealand. In some eyes, therefore, the series was seen as a contest for international cricket's wooden spoon. And often the quality of both teams' play merited such a tag, Australia particularly plumbing low depths.

India's main batsmen scored abundantly. Sunil Gavaskar was the most prolific, registering two centuries and averaging 117.33 in the Tests. However, except for Krish Srikkanth and, once, Mohammad Azharuddin, the others did not fit their rate of scoring to the side's needs. In the last Test the first three batsmen all hit hundreds, but so slow were Gavaskar and Mohinder Amarnath over their record second-wicket stand that Kapil Dev had to promote himself to make up lost time.

Kapil Dev took eight wickets in the first innings of the opening Test. But otherwise the Indians' bowling strength was centred on their two finger-spinners, Ravi Shastri and Shivlal Yadav, and one of the reasons for India's inability to convert their superiority into wins was the loss of form of their young leg-spinner, Laxman Sivaramakrishnan. Inadequate as it was, India's bowling was made to appear even less effective by sub-standard fielding. In contrast, Australia's fielding on the ground was neater and more athletic. But they too dropped catches in plenty, and the tone of their out-cricket was lowered by the limitations of Wayne Phillips as wicket-keeper.

Indeed, Australia revealed many weaknesses. The middle-order batting, after Allan Border, was never dependable. However, David Boon, promoted to open, filled the position with distinction, scoring two hundreds. Border was only a short way behind him in the final aggregates. Greg Matthews, resilient and more mature, proved another batting success with two match-saving innings, including a century. Inaccurate at the start of the series, the Australians bowled with improving tidiness and discipline. But their attack lacked a cutting edge. The only bowler to yield an impressive return was the newcomer, Bruce Reid, left-arm fast-medium, who bowled an excellent line and, using his height (6ft 8in), extracted a menacing degree of bounce.

With the pitch docile, rain intervening often, and catches going down, the first Test was drawn. The loss of all play after tea on the final day denied India almost certain victory in the second Test, after which Kapil Dev, India's captain, claimed that they were deprived also by poor umpiring. Such setbacks notwithstanding, India could have clinched the match had they batted more positively, and had Kapil Dev not erred tactically during the last-wicket stand between Border and Gilbert in the second innings. His reluctance to attack Border gave Australia breathing space in terms of time and runs. The scorecard would suggest that the third Test, too, was within India's reach, and indeed they did have a chance on the last day. They would have been better placed to seize it if, again, they had kept an eye on the clock while batting on the second day.

INDIAN TOUR RESULTS

Test matches – Played 3: Drawn 3.
First-class matches – Played 5: Won 1, Drawn 4. Abandoned 1.
Win – South Australia.
Draws – Victoria, Australia (3).
Abandoned – Tasmania.
Non first-class matches – Played 14: Won 7, Lost 7. Abandoned 1. *Wins* – Victoria Country XI, New Zealand (3), Australia (2), Australian Country XI. *Losses* – Australia (5), New Zealand (2). *Abandoned* – Australian Capital Territory XI.

TEST MATCH AVERAGES

AUSTRALIA – BATTING

	T	I	NO	R	HI	100s	Avge
G. M. Ritchie	2	3	1	159	128	1	79.50
D. C. Boon	3	6	1	323	131	2	64.60
A. R. Border	3	5	0	298	163	1	59.60
G. R. J. Matthews .	3	5	1	191	100*	1	47.75
G. R. Marsh	3	6	1	176	92	0	35.20
D. W. Hookes	2	3	0	76	42	0	25.33
R. J. Bright	3	5	2	56	28	0	18.66
W. B. Phillips	3	5	0	67	22	0	13.40
D. R. Gilbert	2	3	1	15	10*	0	7.50
S. R. Waugh	2	4	0	26	13	0	6.50
B. A. Reid	3	4	0	20	13	0	5.00
C. J. McDermott	2	3	0	3	2	0	1.00

Played in one Test: R. G. Holland 1*; M. G. Hughes 0.

* Signifies not out.

BOWLING

	O	M	R	W	BB	Avge
B. A. Reid	133.2	42	325	11	4-100	29.54
D. R. Gilbert	63	4	225	4	2-81	56.25

Also bowled: R. J. Bright 123–34–282–1; R. G. Holland 21–6–113–1; D. W. Hookes 2–0–4–1; M. G. Hughes 38–6–123–1; C. J. McDermott 69–20–200–3; G. R. J. Matthews 77–11–236–2; S. R. Waugh 18–5–69–2.

INDIA – BATTING

	T	I	NO	R	HI	100s	Avge
S. M. Gavaskar	3	4	1	352	172	2	117.33
M. Amarnath	3	4	1	223	138	1	74.33
K. Srikkanth	3	4	0	291	116	1	72.75
D. B. Vengsarkar	3	4	2	120	75	0	60.00
M. Azharuddin	3	3	1	113	59*	0	56.50
N. S. Yadav	3	2	1	47	41	0	47.00
R. J. Shastri	3	2	0	91	49	0	45.50
Kapil Dev	3	3	0	135	55	0	45.00
S. M. H. Kirmani	3	2	0	42	35	0	21.00
R. M. H. Binny	2	2	0	38	38	0	19.00

Played in two Tests: Chetan Sharma 54; L. Sivaramakrishnan 15.

Signifies not out.

BOWLING

	O	M	R	W	BB	Avge
N. S. Yadav	191.1	75	334	15	5-99	22.26
Kapil Dev	118	31	276	12	8-106	23.00
R. J. Shastri	205	71	386	14	4-87	27.57

Also bowled: M. Amarnath 6-0-18-0; R. M. H. Binny 27-7-67-1; Chetan Sharma 37-5-128-0; L. Sivaramakrishnan 57-5-210-3.

INDIAN AVERAGES – FIRST-CLASS MATCHES

BATTING

	M	I	NO	R	HI	100s	Avge
S. M. Gavaskar	4	5	1	360	172	2	90.00
Chetan Sharma	3	3	1	148	67	0	74.00
M. Amarnath	5	7	2	297	138	1	59.40
M. Azharuddin	5	6	1	245	77	0	49.00
K. Srikkanth	5	7	0	342	116	1	48.85
Kapil Dev	4	5	0	223	88	0	44.60
D. B. Vengsarkar	5	7	2	187	75	0	37.40
N. S. Yadav	5	4	2	67	41	0	33.50
R. J. Shastri	4	3	0	92	49	0	30.66
R. M. H. Binny	3	3	0	82	44	0	27.33
S. M. H. Kirmani	4	4	0	69	35	0	17.25
L. Sivaramakrishnan	4	2	0	19	15	0	9.50

Played in one match: R. S. Ghai 0*; R. R. Kulkarni did not bat; A. Malhotra 67, 12; K. S. More 35*.

Signifies not out.

BOWLING

	O	M	R	W	BB	Avge
Kapil Dev	153	42	356	18	8-106	19.77
N. S. Yadav	245.1	85	478	19	5-99	25.15
R. J. Shastri	258	85	495	14	4-87	35.35
L. Sivaramakrishnan	120.4	12	427	11	3-75	38.81
Chetan Sharma	72	9	257	5	4-55	51.40

Also bowled: M. Amarnath 16–4–37–0; R. M. H. Binny 39–14–91–2; R. S. Ghai 13–3–40–1; R. R. Kulkarni 11–1–27–0.

FIELDING

S. M. H. Kirmani 10 (8 ct, 2 st), L. Sivaramakrishnan 8, Kapil Dev 6, Chetan Sharma 6, K. Srikkanth 5, M. Azharuddin 4, S. M. Gavaskar 3, K. S. More 2 (1 ct, 1 st), D. B. Vengsarkar 2, M. Amarnath 1, R. S. Ghai 1, A. Malhotra 1, R. J. Shastri 1, N. S. Yadav 1.

†At Canberra, November 27. Australian Capital Territory XI v Indians. Abandoned without a ball being bowled because of rain.

SOUTH AUSTRALIA v INDIANS

At Adelaide, November 29, 30, December 1, 2. Indians won by four wickets. Eighteen wickets fell cheaply on a green pitch providing much movement before the batsmen came into their own. Kapil Dev and Chetan Sharma routed South Australia, who opted to bat first, before tea and the Indians, in trouble against the left-arm fast-medium of Parkinson, were 129 for eight before being rallied by an exciting partnership of 84 between Malhotra and Chetan Sharma. The pitch had eased by the time the Indian innings ended and South Australia made good the deficit with only one wicket lost. Darling, in lean form hitherto, dropped down the order and rediscovered his touch with one of his side's two hundreds. The Indians' fitness problems tempted Hilditch to leave them all of the last day to get 326, which they reached with twelve overs to spare.

South Australia

*A. M. J. Hilditch lbw b Kapil Dev	17	– c Chetan b Kapil Dev 0
G. A. Bishop c Kirmani b Chetan	14	– c Kapil Dev b Sivaramakrishnan 93
W. M. Darling c Sivaramakrishnan b Kapil Dev	0	– (6) not out 107
D. F. G. O'Connor lbw b Kapil Dev	20	– c Malhotra b Sivaramakrishnan 58
P. R. Sleep c Kirmani b Kapil Dev	22	– c Kirmani b Chetan 19
R. J. Zadow c Kirmani b Chetan	11	– (3) c Chetan b Yadav 120
†D. J. Kelly c Chetan b Sivaramakrishnan	16	– c Chetan b Sivaramakrishnan ... 2
T. B. A. May b Chetan	2	– lbw b Kapil Dev 0
A. K. Zesers c Kirmani b Sivaramakrishnan	9	– run out 25
S. D. H. Parkinson lbw b Chetan	0	– not out 4
P. W. Gladigau not out	12	
B 2, l-b 8, w 1, n-b 1	12	L-b 2, n-b 5 7

1/26 2/26 3/38 4/78 5/82   135   1/0 2/149 3/268   (8 wkts dec.) 435
6/101 7/109 8/118 9/121   4/290 5/296 6/307
                            7/325 8/423

Bowling: *First Innings*—Kapil Dev 15–8–24–4; Chetan 17–2–55–4; Amarnath 6–2–6–0; Yadav 5–2–6–0; Shastri 9–3–16–0; Sivaramakrishnan 8.3–1–18–2. *Second Innings*—Kapil Dev 20–3–56–2; Chetan 18–2–74–1; Shastri 44–11–93–0; Amarnath 4–2–13–0; Sivaramakrishnan 27–2–124–3; Yadav 25–4–73–1.

Indians

R. J. Shastri c sub b Parkinson	1		
K. Srikkanth lbw b Parkinson	4	– (1) b Zesers	42
M. Amarnath c Kelly b Parkinson	4	– (8) not out	24
D. B. Vengsarkar c Kelly b Gladigau	24	– lbw b May	43
M. Azharuddin c Bishop b Sleep	25	– c Kelly b May	77
A. Malhotra c Kelly b Gladigau	67	– (3) lbw b Zesers	12
†S. M. H. Kirmani b Parkinson	20	– (2) c O'Connor b Parkinson	7
*Kapil Dev c Kelly b Parkinson	0	– (6) run out	88
L. Sivaramakrishnan c Kelly b Zesers	4		
Chetan Sharma c Bishop b Parkinson	67	– (7) not out	27
N. S. Yadav not out	16		
B 3, l-b 7, w 1, n-b 2	13	B 4, l-b 4, w 1	9

1/2 2/12 3/13 4/63 5/72   245   1/47 2/55 3/84   (6 wkts) 329
6/99 7/99 8/129 9/213   4/131 5/266 6/281

Bowling: *First Innings*—Gladigau 20–3–56–2; Parkinson 21.2–3–56–6; Zesers 27–6–65–1; Sleep 15–4–42–1; May 4–0–16–0. *Second Innings*—Gladigau 5.4–0–24–0; Parkinson 17–1–84–1; Zesers 27.2–5–80–2; Sleep 21–2–63–0; May 18–2–70–2.

Umpires: M. P. O'Brien and M. G. O'Connell.

†At Warrnambool, December 4. Indians won by six wickets. Victoria Country XI 116 (38 overs); Indians 175 for six (50 overs) (D. B. Vengsarkar 66 not out). The Indians passed the Victoria Country XI's score for four wickets and batted on.

VICTORIA v INDIANS

At Melbourne, December 6, 7, 8, 9. Drawn. Rain interfered with every day and in all took away 674 minutes of playing time from a match dominated by the bowlers. Victoria's innings, propped up by Jones, who was striving to regain his place in the Test side, lasted until the third morning. Yadav bowled accurately and thoughtfully, but Sivaramakrishnan's figures flattered him. The little leg-spinner was erratic, and his form, so close to the first Test, must have disconcerted the Indians. The tourists made a disastrous start against Hughes, a pace bowler with a bushy moustache and an exceptionally long run, and Hickey, who claimed Gavaskar for his first first-class wicket. India were 15 for three at lunch on the third day but were then steadied by Amarnath, their captain for the match.

Victoria

M. B. Quinn c More b Ghai	31	M. G. Hughes run out	23
D. F. Whatmore c Azharuddin b Binny	19	D. J. Hickey c Gavaskar	
D. M. Jones c and b Sivaramakrishnan	83	b Sivaramakrishnan	0
P. W. Young c Azharuddin b Yadav	29	S. P. Davis not out	0
J. D. Siddons run out	12	B 1, l-b 1, w 1, n-b 2	5
G. R. Parker st More b Sivaramakrishnan	2		
*R. J. Bright c Ghai b Yadav	10	1/24 2/73 3/142 4/161 5/175	233
†M. G. D. Dimattina lbw b Yadav	19	6/190 7/192 8/233 9/233	

Bowling: Binny 12–7–24–1; Kulkarni 11–1–27–0; Sivaramakrishnan 28.1–4–75–3; Ghai 13–3–40–1; Yadav 24–4–65–3.

Indians

S. M. Gavaskar c Jones b Hickey	.....	8	N. S. Yadav lbw b Hughes	 4
K. Srikkanth c Siddons b Hughes	.....	5	R. S. Ghai not out	 0
*M. Amarnath b Davis	....	46		
D. B. Vengsarkar c Dimattina b Hughes		0	B 4, l-b 3, n-b 3	 10
M. Azharuddin c Parker b Bright	.....	30		—
R. M. H. Binny b Parker	....	44	1/13 2/13 3/13 4/76	(7 wkts) 182
†K. S. More not out	....	35	5/103 6/153 7/176	

L. Sivaramakrishnan and R. R. Kulkarni did not bat.

Bowling: Hughes 26–12–42–3; Hickey 18–4–52–1; Davis 18–5–24–1; Bright 15–6–17–1; Siddons 7–1–25–0; Parker 7–3–15–1.

Umpires: D. W. Holt and L. J. King.

AUSTRALIA v INDIA

First Test Match

At Adelaide, December 13, 14, 15, 16, 17. Drawn. Adverse weather, which cost 300 minutes' play during the last three days, was only one of the factors leading to the draw. The pitch, although grassy, catered mainly to the batsmen, and the bowling on both sides was moderate. Moreover, both sides adopted a cautious approach: Australia had just lost a series to New Zealand for the first time, and India were under-prepared and consequently less than confident.

Australia included three new caps in Marsh, a top-order batsman, and pace bowlers Hughes and Reid, the latter a last-minute replacement for Gilbert, who was injured. The Indians played three seamers and two finger-spinners. Notwithstanding the pitch's greenness and an overcast sky, Australia elected to bat first and lost two early wickets. However, despite losing Border at 124, they ended the first day comfortably placed at 248 for four, India having relinquished the initiative by dropping chances. Boon and Ritchie, who staged a fourth-wicket partnership of 117, were missed off Shastri at 83 and 26 respectively. Boon, out to the second new ball, batted 336 minutes and 255 balls for his 123 (his first Test century), and Ritchie, 55 not out overnight, batted doggedly until 37 minutes before tea on the second day, his 128 occupying six and a half hours.

If India had to wait almost until lunch for their first success on the second day, it was because Kapil Dev overlooked Hookes's well-known weakness against spin. His dismissal, immediately he was confronted by Yadav, was followed by a useful stand between Ritchie and Matthews, but once it was broken, Australia's remaining four wickets fell for only 6 runs. Kapil Dev, who took five wickets in 21 balls, had final figures of eight for 106, the best by an Indian overseas.

India now could hope only for a draw, yet with Srikkanth in full flow, and the Australian bowling wayward, they raced to 95 in only 25 overs. When they resumed on the third day, Gavaskar, who had survived a chance at the wicket, off McDermott, could not continue his undefeated innings of 39, a blow on the forearm having left him temporarily incapacitated. Amarnath, too, could not bat in his accustomed position because of an allergy. However, Chetan Sharma, the night-watchman, denied Australia any advantage, and Gavaskar resumed his innings at the fall of the fifth wicket to remain unbeaten with 166 (551 minutes, 416 balls) after putting on 94 with Yadav, an Indian record for the last wicket against Australia. India's 520 was their highest total against Australia.

Kapil Dev was the Man of Match, the attendance for the five days being 29,833.

Australia

†W. B. Phillips c Yadav b Kapil Dev	11		
D. C. Boon c Vengsarkar b Kapil Dev	123	– (1) not out	11
G. R. Marsh c Chetan b Binny	5	– (2) not out	2
*A. R. Border b Kapil Dev	49		
G. M. Ritchie c Kirmani b Kapil Dev	128		
D. W. Hookes b Yadav	34		
G. R. J. Matthews lbw b Kapil Dev	18		
R. J. Bright not out	5		
C. J. McDermott lbw b Kapil Dev	0		
B. A. Reid c Gavaskar b Kapil Dev	2		
M. G. Hughes c Vengsarkar b Kapil Dev	0		
L-b 4, n-b 2	6	L-b 3, n-b 1	4

1/19 2/33 3/124 4/241 5/318   381   (no wkt) 17
6/374 7/375 8/375 9/381

Bowling: *First Innings*—Kapil Dev 38-6-106-8; Binny 24-7-56-1; Chetan 19-3-70-0; Yadav 27-6-66-1; Shastri 38-11-70-0; Amarnath 3-0-9-0. *Second Innings*—Kapil Dev 3-1-3-0; Chetan 2-0-9-0; Yadav 2-1-2-0; Shastri 1-1-0-0.

India

S. M. Gavaskar not out	166	R. M. H. Binny c Phillips b McDermott	38
K. Srikkanth c Ritchie b McDermott	51	†S. M. H. Kirmani c Boon b Reid	7
Chetan Sharma c Phillips b Reid	54	N. S. Yadav c Hughes b Hookes	41
D. B. Vengsarkar c Phillips b Hughes	7		
M. Azharuddin c Phillips b Reid	17	B 2, l-b 7, w 1, n-b 12	22
M. Amarnath c Marsh b McDermott	37		
R. J. Shastri b Reid	42	1/95 2/131 3/171 4/187 5/247	520
*Kapil Dev lbw b Bright	38	6/273 7/333 8/409 9/426	

S. M. Gavaskar, when 39, retired hurt at 97 and resumed at 247.

Bowling: McDermott 48-14-131-3; Hughes 38-6-123-1; Reid 53-22-113-4; Bright 44-15-80-1; Matthews 17-2-60-0; Hookes 2-0-4-1.

Umpires: A. R. Crafter and S. G. Randell.

TASMANIA v INDIANS

At Hobart, December 20, 21, 22, 23. Abandoned without a ball being bowled because of rain.

AUSTRALIA v INDIA

Second Test Match

At Melbourne, December 26, 27, 28, 29, 30. Drawn. Australia, who except for Matthews and Border batted poorly, were saved by the weather and by the Indians' lacking a sense of urgency. India, who had almost all of the post-lunch play on the last day in which to score 126 to win, were 59 for two at tea when the weather intervened.

The pitch was well grassed, but not green, and yet the ball turned from the first day. By the third, Australia lodged a protest about its quality, even though India were in the process of compiling a big score. Anticipating a turning pitch, India had included Sivaramakrishnan, despite his lack of form, while Gilbert had returned for Hughes in the Australian side. Waugh, a batsman and medium-pace bowler, won his Test cap because Ritchie had fractured toes.

India won the toss and bowled, a tactic inconsistent with their selection of an extra spinner. It succeeded, however. Damp underneath, the pitch helped the spinners and Australia were 127 for six before tea. A seventh-wicket partnership between Matthews and Bright enabled them to

reach 210 for eight by the close, all the wickets having fallen to spin, and Matthews, 54
overnight, continued his defiance next morning. Taking 50 off the last 70 balls, he deservedly
reached his century, which included a 6 and ten 4s. Of the 46 he and Gilbert put on for the last
wicket, Matthews scored 41.

India were twice interrupted by bad light, losing 65 minutes, but this was compensated for by
a rollicking 86, off 89 balls, from Srikkanth. At the close India were 187 for three from 56 overs,
and they conceded no ground on the third morning until just before lunch. In the afternoon,
however, the innings lost momentum until Kapil Dev came in at 291 for five, half an hour before
tea, and struck 55 from 50 balls. When 46, he became only the third all-rounder, after G. S.
Sobers and I. T. Botham, to score 3,000 runs and take 200 wickets in Tests. India finished the
day 431 for nine.

Australia, 183 behind, went in again with almost two days left, and that they were not beaten
on the fourth day was due to Border's skill in playing spin and his fortitude. Having batted for
228 minutes, he was unbeaten at the close with 98 in a total of 228 for eight. In the last over
before the close, Reid, seemingly caught at slip, off Yadav, was adjudged not out, and although
he did not remain for long next morning, the decision gave Kapil Dev added ammunition with
which to attack the umpiring. Gilbert dug in again, staying for 115 minutes while Border, whom
the Indians were reluctant to attack, added 64. The Australian captain was last out for a heroic
163, from 358 balls, containing sixteen 4s. The weather forecast for the final day was
unfavourable, yet the Indians seemed to have ignored it, judging by their tactics against
Australia's last pair and by their approach afterwards to getting the required runs.

Border was the Man of the Match. The attendance was 81,715.

Australia

†W. B. Phillips b Yadav	7	– (7) c Srikkanth b Yadav	13
D. C. Boon lbw b Shastri	14	– c and b Kapil Dev	19
G. R. Marsh c Sivaramakrishnan b Yadav	30	– (1) c Sivaramakrishnan b Shastri	19
*A. R. Border c and b Sivaramakrishnan	11	– (3) st Kirmani b Yadav	163
D. W. Hookes b Shastri	42	– (4) c Srikkanth b Shastri	0
S. R. Waugh c Kapil Dev b Sivaramakrishnan	13	– (5) b Shastri	5
G. R. J. Matthews not out	100	– (6) c Azharuddin b Sivaramakrishnan	16
R. J. Bright b Shastri	28	– lbw b Kapil Dev	20
C. J. McDermott c Kapil Dev b Shastri	1	– c and b Shastri	2
B. A. Reid c Srikkanth b Kapil Dev	1	– c Sivaramakrishnan b Yadav	13
D. R. Gilbert c Kirmani b Yadav	4	– not out	10
B 5, l-b 6	11	B 11, l-b 16, n-b 1	28

1/22 2/26 3/41 4/90 5/109   262   1/32 2/54 3/54 4/84 5/126   308
6/127 7/193 8/195 9/216   6/161 7/202 8/205 9/231

Bowling: *First Innings*—Kapil Dev 23–6–38–1; Binny 3–0–11–0; Shastri 37–13–87–4; Yadav
27.5–10–64–3; Sivaramakrishnan 13–2–51–2. *Second Innings*—Kapil Dev 22–7–53–2;
Amarnath 3–0–9–0; Shastri 47–13–92–4; Yadav 38.5–15–84–3; Sivaramakrishnan 13–1–43–1.

India

S. M. Gavaskar b Gilbert	6	– b Reid	8
K. Srikkanth lbw b Gilbert	86	– c Bright b Reid	38
M. Amarnath c Phillips b Reid	45	– not out	3
D. B. Vengsarkar c and b Matthews	75	– not out	1
M. Azharuddin b Matthews	37		
R. J. Shastri c Phillips b Waugh	49		
*Kapil Dev c Hookes b Reid	55		
R. M. H. Binny c Matthews b Reid	0		
†S. M. H. Kirmani c Phillips b Waugh	35		
L. Sivaramakrishnan c Phillips b Reid	15		
N. S. Yadav not out	6		
B 4, l-b 15, n-b 17	36	B 4, l-b 1, n-b 4	9

1/15 2/116 3/172 4/246 5/291   445   1/39 2/57   (2 wkts) 59
6/370 7/372 8/420 9/425

Bowling: *First Innings*—McDermott 15–5–52–0; Gilbert 22–1–81–2; Reid 38.2–11–100–4; Bright 31–8–76–0; Matthews 31–7–81–2; Waugh 11–5–36–2. *Second Innings*—McDermott 6–1–17–0; Gilbert 4–0–9–0; Reid 8–1–23–2; Bright 7–4–5–0.

Umpires: R. A. French and R. C. Isherwood.

AUSTRALIA v INDIA

Third Test Match

At Sydney, January 2, 3, 4, 5, 6. Drawn. Inept batting on the last day took Australia close to defeat in a match which, at the end of the fourth day, looked destined to peter out. Only eight wickets fell on the first four days and then a dozen, all Australian, crashed on the fifth.

For the first time in the series, Australia included the leg-spinner, Holland, a match-winner in the previous two Test matches played in Sydney. This time, however, the pitch was much firmer than on those occasions, and also very slow, and India registered their first total of 600 on foreign soil. No Indian had previously made a Test hundred in Sydney: this time the first three batsmen, Gavaskar, Srikkanth and Amarnath, passed the landmark. Gavaskar and Srikkanth, who, batting for much of the time with a runner, reached his hundred off only 97 balls, put on 191, and at the end of the first day India were 334 for one, Gavaskar 132 not out. Srikkanth, later named as Man of the Match, was dropped at first slip when only 2 while Gavaskar had two escapes, at 3 and 27.

Despite India's strong position, Gavaskar and Amarnath batted with extreme caution as they took their stand to the highest for any Indian wicket against Australia. They added only 64 before lunch, prompting Kapil Dev to promote himself in the order to hasten the scoring. There was a brilliant onslaught also from Azharuddin before the declaration, half an hour before the close.

Australia's reply began with a partnership of 217 between Boon (131 off 311 balls) and Marsh. Australia's highest opening partnership against India, it was also their highest for the first wicket against any country at the SCG. Although three wickets fell in the space of 44 runs on the fourth day, Australia, 347 for four with Border 64 not out, looked safe when bad light stopped play 68 minutes early. (A heavy storm had reduced the third day [Australia 169 without loss] by 105 minutes.) Just 54 runs were required to save the follow-on, but on the final morning Border holed out to long-on. His concentration may have wavered because his wife, at the time, was in labour in a Brisbane hospital. By the time the new Border had arrived, Australia were following on. Matthews, who had helped Border check the collapse on the fourth day, was also out to an injudicious stroke, and the last five wickets fell for just 9 runs.

A little over four hours remained when Australia followed on and the crisis appeared to be over when the opening stand occupied 72 minutes. However, Border's decision to bat lower down the order produced further problems, and when he was out with seven overs remaining, Australia were in danger of defeat. Ritchie, batting for 166 minutes, and Bright saw them through. India's spinners, Shastri and Yadav, took all but one of the wickets that fell in the day.

The attendance for the match was 67,528.

India

S. M. Gavaskar b Holland	172	M. Azharuddin not out	59
K. Srikkanth b Reid	116	B 5, l-b 9, n-b 22	36
M. Amarnath c Bright b Gilbert	138		—
*Kapil Dev b Gilbert	42	1/191 2/415 (4 wkts dec.)	600
D. B. Vengsarkar not out	37	3/485 4/510	

R. J. Shastri, †S. M. H. Kirmani, Chetan Sharma, L. Sivaramakrishnan and N. S. Yadav did not bat.

Bowling: Gilbert 37–3–135–2; Reid 34–8–89–1; Bright 41–7–121–0; Holland 21–6–113–1; Matthews 29–2–95–0; Waugh 7–0–33–0.

Australia

D. C. Boon b Kapil Dev	131	– (2) run out	25
G. R. Marsh c Gavaskar b Shastri	92	– (1) lbw b Yadav	28
*A. R. Border c Chetan b Shastri	71	– (7) c Sivaramakrishnan b Yadav	4
G. M. Ritchie c Kapil Dev b Yadav	14	– (3) not out	17
†W. B. Phillips c Srikkanth b Shastri	14	– c Srikkanth b Shastri	22
G. R. J. Matthews c Amarnath b Yadav	40	– c Kapil Dev b Yadav	17
S. R. Waugh c Sivaramakrishnan b Yadav	8	– (4) lbw b Shastri	0
R. J. Bright c Kirmani b Shastri	3	– not out	0
D. R. Gilbert c Azharuddin b Yadav	1		
B. A. Reid st Kirmani b Yadav	4		
R. G. Holland not out	1		
L-b 14, n-b 3	17	B 3, l-b 2, n-b 1	6

1/217 2/258 3/277 4/302 5/369   396   1/57 2/57 3/60 4/87   (6 wkts) 119
6/387 7/388 8/390 9/395   5/111 6/115

Bowling: First Innings—Kapil Dev 25-8-65-1; Shastri 57-21-101-4; Yadav 62.3-21-99-5; Sivaramakrishnan 22-2-79-0; Chetan 13-2-38-0. *Second Innings*—Kapil Dev 7-3-11-0; Yadav 33-22-19-3; Chetan 3-0-11-0; Shastri 25-12-36-2; Sivaramakrishnan 9-0-37-0.

Umpires: P. J. McConnell and S. G. Randell.

†At Adelaide, January 28. Indians won by five wickets. Australian Country XI 181 for six (50 overs) (J. R. Hogg 59, S. J. Scuderi 55); Indians 182 for five.

India's matches v Australia and New Zealand in the Benson and Hedges World Series Cup may be found in that section.

THE WEST INDIANS IN PAKISTAN, 1985-86

By QAMAR AHMED

No sooner had Pakistan's home series against Sri Lanka finished than West Indies, after a stopover in Sharjah for games against India and Pakistan, arrived in Pakistan to play five one-day internationals. In nineteen previous one-day matches between the two countries, Pakistan had won only three – and all of those in Australia. This time, led by Imran Khan and putting up a brave fight against some hostile bowling by Malcolm Marshall, Michael Holding, Tony Gray and Courtney Walsh, they won two and kept the series alive until the last match, which West Indies won by eight wickets to clinch the rubber. The main attraction of the series was the batting of Vivian Richards who, captaining West Indies for the first time on tour, hit half-centuries in the first three matches and scored 260 runs in the five matches with an average of 86.66.

†PAKISTAN v WEST INDIES

First One-day International

At Gujranwala, November 27. West Indies won by eight wickets. Toss: West Indies. Richard's 80 not out was made from 39 deliveries.
Man of the Match: I. V. A. Richards.

Pakistan

Mudassar Nazar c Walsh b Holding . . .	77	†Salim Yousuf not out 0
Mohsin Khan c Dujon b Walsh	17	
Ramiz Raja b Harper	17	B 3, l-b 13, w 8, n-b 5 29
Javed Miandad lbw b Harper	22	
*Imran Khan c Harper b Holding	45	1/29 2/74 3/113 (5 wkts, 40 overs) 218
Salim Malik not out	11	4/169 5/218

Wasim Akram, Abdul Qadir, Mohsin Kamal and Tauseef Ahmed did not bat.

Bowling: Marshall 8-0-47-0; Garner 6-1-24-0; Walsh 8-0-39-1; Holding 8-1-39-2; Harper 8-2-37-2; Richards 2-0-16-0.

West Indies

D. L. Haynes c sub (Shoaib Mohammad) b Wasim . 39	*I. V. A. Richards not out 80
R. B. Richardson lbw b Mohsin Kamal 5	B 1, l-b 8, w 13 22
A. L. Logie not out 78	1/8 2/105 (2 wkts, 35.3 overs) 224

†P. J. L. Dujon, M. D. Marshall, R. A. Harper, M. A. Holding, J. Garner, A. H. Gray and C. A. Walsh did not bat.

Bowling: Wasim 6-1-31-1; Mohsin Kamal 5.3-1-34-1; Qadir 6-1-39-0; Mudassar 5-0-31-0; Tauseef 5-1-46-0; Imran 8-0-34-0.

Umpires: Athar Zaidi and Khizar Hayat.

†PAKISTAN v WEST INDIES

Second One-day International

At Lahore, November 29. Pakistan won by six wickets. Toss: Pakistan. Abdul Qadir avenged the rough treatment he received in the first match by taking four wickets as the West Indian batting collapsed. A capacity crowd of 25,000 saw Pakistan's first home win against West Indies in a one-day international.

Man of the Match: Abdul Qadir.

West Indies

D. L. Haynes b Zakir	26	M. A. Holding st Yousuf b Qadir	0
R. B. Richardson c Ramiz b Wasim	22	A. H. Gray not out	7
A. L. Logie b Zakir	9	C. A. Walsh c Wasim b Qadir	7
*I. V. A. Richards b Mudassar	53	B 3, l-b 7, w 4, n-b 2	16
H. A. Gomes b Qadir	23		
†P. J. L. Dujon b Qadir	4	1/45 2/61 3/70	(36.2 overs) 173
R. A. Harper c Malik b Mudassar	5	4/129 5/143 6/151	
M. D. Marshall b Wasim	1	7/156 8/156 9/164	

Bowling: Imran 5–1–25–0; Wasim 5–0–24–2; Zakir 8–0–31–2; Mohsin Kamal 8–0–40–0; Qadir 5.2–0–17–4; Mudassar 5–0–26–2.

Pakistan

Mudassar Nazar c Walsh b Gray	15	Salim Malik not out	26
Mohsin Khan lbw b Gray	43	B 1, l-b 8, w 2, n-b 5	16
Ramiz Raja c and b Holding	12		
Javed Miandad b Harper	41	1/23 2/47 3/124	(4 wkts, 38.3 overs) 175
*Imran Khan not out	22	4/126	

†Salim Yousuf, Abdul Qadir, Wasim Akram, Mohsin Kamal and Zakir Khan did not bat.

Bowling: Marshall 7.3–0–38–0; Gray 8–0–36–2; Walsh 8–0–32–0; Holding 7–1–33–1; Harper 8–0–27–1.

Umpires: Amanullah Khan and Shakoor Rana.

†PAKISTAN v WEST INDIES

Third One-day International

At Peshawar, December 2. West Indies won by 40 runs. Toss: West Indies. Richards was again the difference between the two teams, hitting four 6s and five 4s and taking a heavy toll of the bowling of Imran, Qadir and Mudassar as he scored 66 off 39 balls.

Man of the Match: I. V. A. Richards.

West Indies

D. L. Haynes c Mohsin Kamal b Imran	60	†P. J. L. Dujon not out	9
R. B. Richardson st Yousuf b Tauseef	27	R. A. Harper not out	0
H. A. Gomes run out	15	B 4, l-b 13, w 3, n-b 4	24
*I. V. A. Richards c Mohsin Khan b Imran	66	1/70 2/100 3/169	(5 wkts, 40 overs) 201
A. L. Logie lbw b Imran	0	4/170 5/192	

M. D. Marshall, M. A. Holding, J. Garner and C. A. Walsh did not bat.

Bowling: Imran 7–0–39–3; Wasim 6–0–24–0; Tauseef 8–1–24–1; Mohsin Kamal 8–0–31–0; Qadir 6–1–42–0; Mudassar 5–0–24–0.

Pakistan

Mudassar Nazar c and b Holding	19	Wasim Akram b Holding	9
Mohsin Khan c Harper b Marshall	6	Mohsin Kamal b Marshall	5
Ramiz Raja run out	38	Tauseef Ahmed not out	3
Javed Miandad c Gomes b Holding	2	B 3, l-b 9, w 3, n-b 4	19
*Imran Khan b Harper	8		
Salim Malik b Walsh	7	1/15 2/37 3/47 (39.3 overs)	161
Abdul Qadir b Marshall	37	4/65 5/80 6/106	
†Salim Yousuf b Holding	8	7/138 8/142 9/149	

Bowling: Marshall 8–1–36–3; Garner 8–1–22–0; Walsh 8–0–36–1; Holding 7.3–0–17–4; Harper 8–1–38–1.

Umpires: Ikram Rabbani and Mian Aslam.

†PAKISTAN v WEST INDIES

Fourth One-day International

At Rawalpindi, December 4. Pakistan won by five wickets. Toss: Pakistan. Controlled spin bowling by Tauseef and Qadir helped restrict West Indies to 199. Had Richardson not been dropped when 13 by Zulqarnain, the wicket-keeper, who was making his first appearance for Pakistan, the target might even have been smaller. For the first time in the series, Pakistan's openers put on 50 for the first wicket.

Man of the Match: Shoaib Mohammad.

West Indies

D. L. Haynes run out	23	M. D. Marshall c Zulqarnain b Wasim	20
R. B. Richardson not out	92	M. A. Holding c Imran b Wasim	2
A. L. Logie c sub (Tahir Naqqash)		J. Garner not out	1
b Tauseef	0	B 4, l-b 10, w 1, n-b 2	17
*I. V. A. Richards c Zulqarnain b Shoaib	21		
H. A. Gomes run out	1	1/57 2/57 3/99 (8 wkts, 40 overs)	199
†P. J. L. Dujon run out	12	4/100 5/124 6/136	
R. A. Harper lbw b Qadir	10	7/166 8/198	

C. A. Walsh did not bat.

Bowling: Imran 6–0–33–0; Wasim 6–0–41–2; Tauseef 6–2–12–1; Mohsin Kamal 6–0–44–0; Shoaib 8–0–30–1; Qadir 8–2–25–1.

Pakistan

Shoaib Mohammad c Walsh b Garner	53	Abdul Qadir not out	0
Qasim Omar lbw b Walsh	27		
Javed Miandad not out	67	B 9, l-b 15, n-b 7	31
Salim Malik c Haynes b Harper	14		
*Imran Khan run out	8	1/57 2/141 3/171 (5 wkts, 39.1 overs)	203
Ramiz Raja c and b Richards	3	4/184 5/195	

Wasim Akram, Mohsin Kamal, Tauseef Ahmed and †Zulqarnain did not bat.

Bowling: Marshall 8–2–27–0; Garner 8–1–33–1; Walsh 8–0–43–1; Harper 8–0–41–1; Richards 2–0–6–1; Holding 5.1–0–29–0.

Umpires: Shakoor Rana and Tariq Atta.

†PAKISTAN v WEST INDIES

Fifth One-day International

At Karachi, December 6. West Indies won by eight wickets. Toss: West Indies. Expectations of a thrilling match to decide the series were dashed as Pakistan's batsmen struggled against the pace and accuracy of Marshall and Holding. Intermittent crowd disturbances – hundreds invaded the field of play when Pakistan were 87 for four and a stand was set alight – reduced Pakistan's innings to 38 overs.

Man of the Match: M. D. Marshall.

Pakistan

Mohsin Khan c Richardson b Marshall	54	Wasim Akram b Holding		0
Shoaib Mohammad c Richardson b Gray	1	†Zulqarnain not out		4
Ramiz Raja c Dujon b Marshall	0	L-b 4, w 4, n-b 1		9
Salim Malik run out	7			—
*Imran Khan run out	19	1/2 2/3 3/14	(7 wkts, 38 overs)	127
Javed Miandad b Holding	28	4/45 5/116		
Abdul Qadir not out	5	6/117 7/119		

Mohsin Kamal and Tauseef Ahmed did not bat.

Bowling: Marshall 8–1–25–2; Gray 6–4–14–1; Walsh 8–0–20–0; Holding 8–0–35–2; Harper 6–0–20–0; Richards 2–0–9–0.

West Indies

D. L. Haynes c Mohsin Khan		*I. V. A. Richards not out		40
b Mohsin Kamal	39	B 1, l-b 5, w 7, n-b 3		16
R. B. Richardson lbw b Wasim	13			—
H. A. Gomes not out	20	1/26 2/77	(2 wkts, 34.1 overs)	128

A. L. Logie, †P. J. L. Dujon, R. A. Harper, M. D. Marshall, M. A. Holding, C. A. Walsh and A. H. Gray did not bat.

Bowling: Wasim 8–0–25–1; Mohsin Kamal 6–1–47–1; Qadir 8–2–19–0; Imran 8–2–19–0; Tauseef 3.1–0–12–0.

Umpires: Mahboob Shah and Shakeel Khan.

THE AUSTRALIANS IN NEW ZEALAND, 1985-86

By R. T. BRITTENDEN

New Zealand maintained their recent record against visiting teams when they won the three-match series against Australia by one Test to nil. In the previous seven years, they had met each of the other Test-playing countries at home and enjoyed series victories over all of them, whereas the 1981-82 series against Australia had been drawn. With a 2-1 Test success over their neighbours earlier in the summer, New Zealand could look upon the season as a late flowering, and a full one, of their somewhat elderly team.

After an even but rain-ruined contest at Wellington, the Australians gained a 25-run lead in the Test at Christchurch. But after rain had accounted for most of the fourth day, the Australians suffered another of the batting collapses which had marked their cricket of late before Allan Border, their captain, saved them with his second century of the match. At Auckland, in a fascinating final Test, Australia went from 193 for one to 314 all out, yet when New Zealand yielded a lead of 56, with the pitch taking increasing spin, the match and the series appeared to be Australia's. However, John Bracewell's off-breaks wrecked the Australian second innings – their 103 was by 59 the lowest score they have made against New Zealand – and their spin bowlers failed to take similar advantage of the pitch. New Zealand won by eight wickets.

Border had with him a team which was the best available – bearing in mind the unavailability of those players who toured South Africa – and one which, it was hoped, would mend Australia's ailing fortunes. On the evidence presented, it still had some way to go, though after forthright talking by Border it did manage to redeem some self-respect by squaring the four-match one-day series which concluded the tour. Border showed clearly that he was a class above the others, while David Boon, a predominantly front-foot player, and Geoff Marsh, correct and careful, looked capable of being Australia's opening pair in the years ahead. Greg Ritchie played two of the series' most assertive innings, but Greg Matthews could point only to his 130 in the first Test. The free-scoring Wayne Phillips had a disappointing tour, but twenty-year-old Stephen Waugh already looked an accomplished all-round player.

The bowling was very ordinary. Craig McDermott, so successful in England in 1985, was ineffective. Both he and Bruce Reid, the left-arm fast bowler, delivered an unnecessary number of no-balls. Matthews, the principal spinner, was accurate, but the slow bowling could almost certainly have profited from the presence of Bob Holland, the New South Wales leg-spinner.

Jeremy Coney, with successive scores of 101 not out, 98 and 93 carried the New Zealand batting almost single-handed, although there was a gallant century from Martin Crowe at Christchurch. The bowlers, Bracewell, in the last two Tests, Richard Hadlee – as ever – and Ewen Chatfield, all distinguished themselves.

AUSTRALIAN TOUR RESULTS

Test matches – Played 3: Lost 1, Drawn 2.
First-class matches – Played 5: Won 1, Lost 1, Drawn 3.
Win – Northern Districts.
Loss – New Zealand.

Draws – New Zealand (2), Central Districts.
Non first-class matches – Played 6: Won 4, Lost 2. *Wins* – Auckland, Nelson, New Zealand (2).
    Losses – New Zealand (2).

TEST MATCH AVERAGES

NEW ZEALAND – BATTING

	T	I	NO	R	HI	100s	Avge
J. V. Coney	3	3	1	292	101*	1	146.00
M. D. Crowe	3	4	1	179	137	1	59.66
R. J. Hadlee	3	3	1	105	72*	0	52.50
J. G. Wright	2	4	1	129	59	0	43.00
K. R. Rutherford	3	4	1	115	65	0	38.33
J. F. Reid	3	4	1	50	32	0	16.66
B. A. Edgar	3	5	0	80	38	0	16.00
I. D. S. Smith	3	2	0	25	22	0	12.50
J. G. Bracewell	2	2	0	24	20	0	12.00

Played in three Tests: E. J. Chatfield 2*, 1*. Played in two Tests: G. B. Troup 10. Played in one Test: T. J. Franklin 0; S. R. Gillespie 28; G. K. Robertson 12.

* Signifies not out.

BOWLING

	O	M	R	W	BB	Avge
J. G. Bracewell	125.3	48	229	15	6-32	15.26
R. J. Hadlee	157.5	36	387	16	7-116	24.18
E. J. Chatfield	136	48	254	8	3-19	31.75

Also bowled: J. V. Coney 35–8–103–3; M. D. Crowe 5–3–8–0; S. R. Gillespie 27–2–79–1; J. F. Reid 1–1–0–0; G. K. Robertson 24–6–91–1; G. B. Troup 77–10–240–3.

AUSTRALIA – BATTING

	T	I	NO	R	HI	100s	Avge
A. R. Border	3	5	1	290	140	2	72.50
D. C. Boon	3	5	1	176	70	0	44.00
G. R. Marsh	3	5	0	204	118	1	40.80
G. M. Ritchie	3	5	0	164	92	0	32.80
G. R. J. Matthews ...	3	5	0	148	130	1	29.60
W. B. Phillips	3	5	0	135	62	0	27.00
S. R. Waugh	3	5	0	87	74	0	17.40
R. J. Bright	2	4	1	47	21*	0	15.66
T. J. Zoehrer	3	5	0	71	30	0	14.20
B. A. Reid	3	4	3	9	8	0	9.00
C. J. McDermott	2	3	0	17	9	0	5.66

Played in one Test: S. P. Davis 0; D. R. Gilbert 15.

* Signifies not out.

BOWLING

	O	M	R	W	BB	Avge
S. R. Waugh	36	9	83	5	4-56	16.60
G. R. J. Matthews ...	111	47	236	8	4-61	29.50
B. A. Reid	101.1	18	294	9	4-90	32.66
C. J. McDermott	56.3	10	156	3	2-47	52.00

Also bowled: A. R. Border 4-3-1-0; R. J. Bright 63-22-138-2; S. P. Davis 25-4-70-0; D. R. Gilbert 33-8-115-2.

AUSTRALIAN AVERAGES – FIRST-CLASS MATCHES

BATTING

	M	I	NO	R	HI	100s	Avge
A. R. Border	4	6	1	367	140	2	73.40
D. C. Boon	4	7	1	302	109	1	50.33
G. R. Marsh	5	8	1	349	118	2	49.85
G. M. Ritchie	5	8	1	292	92	0	41.71
G. R. J. Matthews ...	5	8	1	223	130	1	31.85
W. B. Phillips	5	9	0	251	62	0	27.88
B. A. Reid	5	6	4	54	28*	0	27.00
T. J. Zoehrer	5	8	0	172	71	0	21.50
S. R. Waugh	5	8	0	124	74	0	15.50
R. J. Bright	4	7	1	82	21*	0	13.66
C. J. McDermott	3	5	0	40	19	0	8.00
D. R. Gilbert	2	2	0	15	15	0	7.50
S. P. Davis	3	3	2	3	2*	0	3.00

Signifies not out.

BOWLING

	O	M	R	W	BB	Avge
S. R. Waugh	53	12	151	7	4-56	21.57
B. A. Reid	132.4	24	372	13	4-25	28.61
G. R. J. Matthews ...	153	52	388	12	4-61	32.33
R. J. Bright	115.2	33	305	9	5-42	33.88
C. J. McDermott	79.3	15	240	6	3-61	40.00

Also bowled: A. R. Border 4-3-1-0; S. P. Davis 71-13-214-3; D. R. Gilbert 51-11-184-3; W. B. Phillips 2-0-6-0.

FIELDING

T. J. Zoehrer 9 (7 ct, 2 st), G. R. J. Matthews 5, S. R. Waugh 4, A. R. Border 3, G. R. Marsh 3, R. J. Bright 2 (1 as sub), D. C. Boon 2, W. B. Phillips 2, S. P. Davis 1, C. J. McDermott 1, B. A. Reid 1, G. M. Ritchie 1.

†At Auckland, February 15. Australians won by six wickets. Auckland 250 for seven (50 overs) T. J. Franklin 79, J. J. Crowe 66); Australians 252 for four (47.4 overs) (D. C. Boon 57, G. R. Marsh 78, G. M. Ritchie 66 not out).

NORTHERN DISTRICTS v AUSTRALIANS

At Hamilton, February 16, 17, 18. Australians won by four wickets. Only 142 minutes' play was possible on the first day when Northern Districts, who elected to bat, put on 83 for one. Howarth, the former New Zealand captain, declared next day, and the Australians replied in kind with 153 for one from 35 overs. Bright's slow left-arm spin destroyed the Northern Districts second innings and the Australians scored the winning runs by four o'clock on the third day of what was to be a very brief build-up to the Tests.

Northern Districts

L. M. Crocker b Gilbert	30	– (2) b Bright	23
R. E. W. Mawhinney not out	26	– (1) b Reid	0
D. J. White c Zoehrer b Davis	53	– c Waugh b Reid	8
B. R. Blair not out	51	– c Waugh b Bright	46
*G. P. Howarth (did not bat)		– st Zoehrer b Bright	6
C. M. Kuggeleijn (did not bat)		– c Davis b Bright	5
†B. A. Young (did not bat)		– lbw b Davis	31
M. J. Child (did not bat)		– c Matthews b Bright	0
S. J. Scott (did not bat)		– b Reid	17
K. Treiber (did not bat)		– b Reid	8
S. M. Carrington (did not bat)		– not out	1
L-b 3, n-b 4	7	B 8, l-b 8, n-b 6	22

1/56 2/110   (2 wkts dec.) 167   1/0 2/23 3/64 4/84 5/95   167
                                                    6/101 7/101 8/145 9/162

In the first innings, R. E. W. Mawhinney retired hurt at 13 and resumed at 110.

Bowling: *First Innings*—Reid 10–2–22–0; Davis 13–3–38–1; Gilbert 10–1–39–1; Bright 11.2–6–23–0; Matthews 11–1–42–0. *Second Innings*—Reid 12.3–2–25–4; Davis 11–3–23–1; Bright 18–3–42–5; Gilbert 8–2–30–0; Waugh 4–2–11–0; Phillips 1–0–4–0; Matthews 7–2–16–0.

Australians

G. R. Marsh not out	44		
W. B. Phillips c and b Scott	44	– (1) c Crocker b Carrington	12
G. R. J. Matthews not out	57		
†T. J. Zoehrer (did not bat)		– (2) c Child b Treiber	30
S. R. Waugh (did not bat)		– (3) c Young b Treiber	3
*A. R. Border (did not bat)		– (4) st Young b Treiber	77
R. J. Bright (did not bat)		– (5) c and b Child	2
B. A. Reid (did not bat)		– (6) not out	28
D. R. Gilbert (did not bat)		– (7) c and b Treiber	0
G. M. Ritchie (did not bat)		– (8) not out	27
B 4, l-b 4	8	B 1, n-b 2	3

1/76   (1 wkt dec.) 153   1/17 2/22 3/92 4/110   (6 wkts) 182
                                                  5/136 6/136

S. P. Davis did not bat.

Bowling: *First Innings*—Carrington 6–1–18–0; Treiber 5–2–7–0; Scott 11–3–45–1; Kuggeleijn 7–1–41–0; Child 5–2–25–0; Blair 1–0–9–0. *Second Innings*—Carrington 9–2–25–1; Treiber 23–5–92–4; Scott 4–0–24–0; Kuggeleijn 3–0–14–0; Child 11–1–23–1; Mawhinney 1–1–0–0; Crocker 0.4–0–3–0.

Umpires: B. L. Aldridge and R. L. McHarg.

NEW ZEALAND v AUSTRALIA

First Test Match

At Wellington, February 21, 22, 23, 24, 25. Drawn. The Australians started the series competently as Boon and Marsh continued their form of the final Test against India. Then they had partnerships of 217 and 57. This time they put on 104, showing scant regard for some wayward bowling. Ritchie and Matthews, each 55 not out, made it Australia's day by adding 119 runs for them to be 285 for four at the close.

Coney's decision to field, on winning the toss, must have come from force of habit. This was the nineteenth Test between the two countries; fourteen times the captain winning the toss had elected to bat second. New Zealand, winning the toss, had batted first only in 1946, and that may have caused Coney some misgivings. New Zealand on that occasion were out for 42 and 54.

Ritchie batted superbly, Matthews was all industry. They continued on the second day to score 213, an Australian fifth-wicket record against New Zealand, and at lunch Australia were firmly in command at 363 for four. At 97 Matthews offered a straightforward catch to Crowe off Hadlee, and he went on to make his hundred in 254 minutes and bat in all for 306 minutes. But the rest of the batting fell apart, the last five wickets adding only 56 runs. Hadlee, whose 61st Test appearance equalled the New Zealand record of B. E. Congdon, took his Test aggregate to 302 wickets.

After the loss of Franklin, the left-handers, Edgar and Reid, batted purposefully. Gillespie, playing in his first Test, came in as night-watchman with almost six overs to go and was to bat during three sessions of the game; in time for 114 minutes for almost an hour was lost on the third morning through appeals against the light. With New Zealand in danger of a large deficit, Coney batted with typical composure, while Rutherford, who had a Test aggregate of 12 runs in seven innings, a legacy of the West Indies tour, hit eleven 4s in his resolute sixth-wicket partnership of 109. Hadlee matched his captain in confidence, and when rain brought play to a halt at 12.18 p.m. on the fourth day, he and Coney had scored 100 in 110 minutes and added 132 for the seventh wicket, another New Zealand record against Australia. Coney reached his hundred, in 286 minutes from 191 balls, as the rain began to fall, and the match was not resumed.

Australia

D. C. Boon c Smith b Troup	70	C. J. McDermott b Hadlee	2
G. R. Marsh c Coney b Chatfield	43	B. A. Reid not out	0
W. B. Phillips b Gillespie	32	S. P. Davis c and b Hadlee	0
*A. R. Border lbw b Hadlee	13		
G. M. Ritchie b Troup	92	B 2, l-b 9, w 4, n-b 9	24
G. R. J. Matthews c Rutherford b Coney	130		
S. R. Waugh c Smith b Coney	11	1/104 2/143 3/166	435
†T. J. Zoehrer c sub (J. G. Bracewell)		4/166 5/379 6/414	
b Coney	18	7/418 8/435 9/435	

Bowling: Hadlee 37.1–5–116–3; Chatfield 36–10–96–1; Troup 28–6–86–2; Gillespie 27–2–79–1; Coney 18–7–47–3.

New Zealand

T. J. Franklin c Border b McDermott	0	*J. V. Coney not out	101
B. A. Edgar c Matthews b Matthews	38	R. J. Hadlee not out	72
J. F. Reid c Phillips b Reid	32		
S. R. Gillespie c Border b Reid	28	B 2, l-b 6, w 1, n-b 15	24
M. D. Crowe b Matthews	19		
K. R. Rutherford c sub (R. J. Bright)		1/0 2/57 3/94 4/115	(6 wkts) 379
b Reid	65	5/138 6/247	

†I. D. S. Smith, G. B. Troup and E. J. Chatfield did not bat.

Bowling: McDermott 25.3–5–80–1; Davis 25–4–70–0; Reid 31–6–104–3; Matthews 37–10–107–2; Border 4–3–1–0; Waugh 4–1–9–0.

Umpires: F. R. Goodall and S. J. Woodward.

NEW ZEALAND v AUSTRALIA

Second Test Match

At Christchurch, February 28, March 1, 2, 3, 4. Drawn. Although Hadlee produced another outstanding effort, the match belonged to Border. He propped up a calamitous decline in Australia's fortunes with his 140 in the first innings, and when his side was in danger of defeat on the last day, he hit an unbeaten 114, so joining G. S. Chappell, S. M. Gavaskar, G. A. Headley and C. L. Walcott in scoring two hundreds in a Test match twice.

Coney put Australia in on a pitch which had a distinctly green look about it, but they were only one down, for 58, at lunch. In the 40 minutes after, however, Hadlee took three wickets in his six-over spell, Chatfield claimed one, and Australia were 74 for five. Border found in Waugh an able lieutenant. He scored his first Test fifty stylishly, and at the close Australia were 224 for five, Border 84 not out, having just passed 6,000 runs in Tests. Next morning, a period of indecision with runs coming off inadvertent edges, the Australian captain was dropped in the slips off Hadlee before reaching his seventeenth Test hundred.

New Zealand lost ground rapidly, being 48 for three at the close of the second day and then 48 for four. Coney led a remarkable recovery, and Crowe, eight 4s in his 50, displayed a mastery which matched his performance at Brisbane before, mistiming a hook from Reid, he was struck on the jaw and had to be assisted from the field to receive ten stitches. Returning after Coney and Smith had added a half-century he immediately counter-attacked, 29 runs coming from three overs. He went to his century from 156 balls (eighteen 4s) and kept attacking until he was caught in the deep, last out within seconds of the close of play, for 137, which included 21 4s. It was a display which drew comparisons with Sutcliffe's epic innings for New Zealand at Johannesburg in 1953-54.

Only 48 minutes' play was possible on the fourth day (Australia 49 for two) but on the last day Australia, with six wickets gone, led by only 155. However, Border, the Man of the Match, went phlegmatically on, moving up the Australian Test aggregates behind G. S. Chappell and Sir Donald Bradman and ending New Zealand's prospects of victory.

Australia

G. R. Marsh b Hadlee	28	– (2) lbw b Bracewell ... 15
D. C. Boon c Coney b Hadlee	26	– (1) c Coney b Troup ... 6
W. B. Phillips c Smith b Chatfield	1	– b Hadlee ... 25
*A. R. Border b Chatfield	140	– not out ... 114
G. M. Ritchie lbw b Hadlee	4	– c Smith b Bracewell ... 11
G. R. J. Matthews c Smith b Hadlee	6	– c sub (J. J. Crowe) b Hadlee ... 3
S. R. Waugh lbw b Hadlee	74	– c Smith b Bracewell ... 1
†T. J. Zoehrer c Coney b Hadlee	30	– c Rutherford b Bracewell ... 13
R. J. Bright c Smith b Bracewell	21	– not out ... 21
D. R. Gilbert b Hadlee	15	
B. A. Reid not out	1	
B 1, l-b 9, n-b 8	18	L-b 6, w 1, n-b 3 ... 10

1/57 2/58 3/58 4/64 5/74   364   1/15 2/32 3/76   (7 wkts dec.) 219
6/251 7/319 8/334 9/358   4/120 5/129
                                  6/130 7/166

Bowling: *First Innings*—Hadlee 44.4–8–116–7; Troup 34–4–104–0; Chatfield 36–13–56–2; Coney 9–0–28–0; Bracewell 27–9–46–1; Crowe 2–1–4–0. *Second Innings*—Hadlee 25–4–47–2; Troup 15–0–50–1; Chatfield 17–6–29–0; Bracewell 33–12–77–4; Reid 1–1–0–0; Coney 3–1–10–0.

New Zealand

B. A. Edgar lbw b Reid	8	– c and b Matthews	9
J. G. Wright c Zoehrer b Gilbert	10	– not out	4
J. F. Reid c Zoehrer b Waugh	2	– not out	0
M. D. Crowe c Waugh b Reid	137		
K. R. Rutherford lbw b Gilbert	0		
*J. V. Coney c Reid b Waugh	98		
R. J. Hadlee c Zoehrer b Reid	0		
†I. D. S. Smith b Waugh	22		
J. G. Bracewell c Marsh b Reid	20		
G. B. Troup lbw b Waugh	10		
E. J. Chatfield not out	2		
B 6, l-b 8, n-b 16	30	N-b 3	3

1/17 2/29 3/29 4/48 5/124	339	1/13	(1 wkt) 16
6/190 7/263 8/311 9/331			

In the first innings, M. D. Crowe, when 51, retired hurt at 117 and resumed at 190.

Bowling: *First Innings*—Reid 34.3–8–90–4; Gilbert 26–4–106–2; Waugh 23–6–56–4; Bright 18–6–51–0; Matthews 6–1–22–0. *Second Innings*—Gilbert 7–4–9–0; Reid 4–0–7–0; Matthews 3–3–0–1.

Umpires: B. L. Aldridge and F. R. Goodall.

†At Nelson, March 6. Australians won by 82 runs. Australians 276 for seven (50 overs) (G. M. Ritchie 46, G. R. J. Matthews 66, R. J. Bright 48 not out); Nelson 194 for nine (50 overs) (G. N. Edwards 55).

CENTRAL DISTRICTS v AUSTRALIANS

At New Plymouth, March 8, 9, 10. Drawn. An easy-paced pitch, and Pukekura Park's short boundaries, produced an entertaining match. A chanceless century by Boon and an impressive 71 in 85 minutes (three 6s, nine 4s) by Zoehrer enabled the Australians to score at a rate of almost 5 an over. Central Districts, 27 for three at the end of the first day, had Crowe, their captain, to thank for their first-innings lead. He hit two 6s and fifteen 4s in his 97, and Duff matched him in his power of stroke. By the close the Australians were 131 for two, 417 runs being scored in the day. On the third day, however, the task of scoring 302 in approximately three hours was beyond the home team.

Australians

D. C. Boon c C. J. Smith b Stirling	109	– (2) run out	17
G. R. Marsh b Stirling	0	– (1) c Blain b Stirling	101
W. B. Phillips lbw b G. K. Robertson	12	– c Crowe b Visser	48
G. M. Ritchie c Blain b Stirling	21	– c Glover b Duff	80
G. R. J. Matthews c I. D. S. Smith b Visser	13	– c and b Duff	5
S. R. Waugh c Blain b G. K. Robertson	34	– c sub b Stirling	0
†T. J. Zoehrer b Duff	71	– c and b Stirling	0
*R. J. Bright lbw b G. K. Robertson	17	– c and b Duff	16
C. J. McDermott lbw b G. K. Robertson	19	– b Briasco	4
S. P. Davis not out	2	– (11) not out	1
B. A. Reid absent ill		– (10) c Glover b Duff	17
B 2, l-b 3, w 2, n-b 4	11	B 9, l-b 2, w 1, n-b 4	16

1/2 2/24 3/76 4/95 5/163	309	1/19 2/114 3/214 4/229 5/232	305
6/222 7/283 8/288 9/309		6/242 7/282 8/287 9/287	

Bowling: *First Innings*—G. K. Robertson 20.5–2–70–4; Stirling 14–1–91–3; Visser 14–0–69–1; Duff 21–5–68–1; Crowe 1–0–6–0. *Second Innings*—G. K. Robertson 16–2–66–0; Stirling 13–2–56–3; Duff 34.3–12–87–4; Visser 11–3–66–1; Briasco 3–1–19–1.

Central Districts

P. S. Briasco c Marsh b McDermott	1	– run out	29
C. J. Smith lbw b McDermott	13	– c Zoehrer b Davis	38
S. P. Robertson c Matthews b McDermott	2		
*M. D. Crowe c McDermott b Bright	97	– (3) c Marsh b Matthews	42
†T. E. Blain c Bright b Matthews	30	– (4) c and b Matthews	16
S. W. Duff b Waugh	71	– (7) not out	2
R. Glover c and b Matthews	28		
I. D. S. Smith not out	23		
D. A. Stirling c Zoehrer b Waugh	6	– (5) c Ritchie b Bright	10
G. K. Robertson not out	33	– (6) not out	1
B 1, l-b 3, n-b 5	9	B 4, l-b 1, w 1, n-b 5	11

1/7 2/18 3/22 4/125 5/153   (8 wkts dec.) 313   1/63 2/80 3/126   (5 wkts) 149
6/249 7/253 8/269   4/141 5/146

P. J. Visser did not bat.

Bowling: *First Innings*—McDermott 18–4–61–3; Davis 15–2–53–0; Matthews 21–2–82–2; Waugh 13–1–57–2; Bright 13–1–56–1. *Second Innings*—Reid 9–2–31–0; McDermott 5–1–23–0; Bright 10–1–46–1; Davis 7–1–30–1; Matthews 3–0–12–2; Phillips 1–0–2–0.

Umpires: D. A. Kinsella and K. Thomson.

NEW ZEALAND v AUSTRALIA

Third Test Match

At Auckland, March 13, 14, 15, 16, 17. New Zealand won by eight wickets. Border elected to bat, and despite a green tinge to the pitch Hadlee and Robertson, appearing in his first Test, were played comfortably. Boon was caught off one of the few to lift, but Marsh and Phillips batted for most of the day, their stand of 168 being a record for Australia's second wicket against New Zealand. Marsh's century, which took him 258 minutes, was almost inevitable, so competently did he play. At 227 for four overnight Australia were comfortably placed, and with Ritchie and Zoehrer in command the next morning, a score in excess of 400 seemed in prospect. However, Bracewell, with flighted off-breaks and ready turn, changed the course of the game as the last six Australian wickets fell for 36.

Matthews struck back with three wickets for Australia before the close (75 for three) and the success of the two off-spinners on the second day did not augur well for the side batting fourth. New Zealand lost five wickets for 107 before Coney, striking the ball confidently, and Hadlee added 63, and then Coney, in perhaps his finest Test innings, assisted by Robertson, took New Zealand to 258, a deficit of 56. Australia were 32 for two at the close, with Boon 13 not out, and he was to stay there, not out at the finish, the tenth Australian to carry his bat through a Test innings. There was little sign of fight from the others as Bracewell, whose match figures of ten for 106 made him not only the Man of the Match but the first New Zealand spin bowler to capture ten wickets in a Test match, achieved a vast amount of turn.

New Zealand required 160 to win and it seemed a difficult task, but Matthews bowled too flat to make the most of the wicket. Wright produced one of his best Test match innings and Rutherford played pluckily. At 62 Rutherford was given out, but Zoehrer signalled that the catch had not been properly made, Border chivalrously waved him back, and New Zealand finished the day 85 for one. On the fifth day Wright completed his second half-century of the match and Crowe's succession of boundaries eased New Zealand to victory.

Australia

D. C. Boon c Coney b Hadlee	16	– (2) not out	58
G. R. Marsh c Coney b Hadlee	118	– (1) lbw b Hadlee	0
W. B. Phillips c Smith b Bracewell	62	– c Bracewell b Chatfield	15
*A. R. Border c Smith b Chatfield	17	– (5) b Bracewell	6
†T. J. Zoehrer c Coney b Robertson	9	– (4) lbw b Chatfield	1
G. M. Ritchie c Smith b Chatfield	16	– lbw b Chatfield	1
G. R. J. Matthews b Bracewell	5	– st Smith b Bracewell	4
S. R. Waugh c Reid b Bracewell	1	– b Bracewell	0
R. J. Bright c Smith b Hadlee	5	– b Bracewell	0
C. J. McDermott lbw b Bracewell	9	– b Bracewell	6
B. A. Reid not out	0	– c Hadlee b Bracewell	8
B 2, l-b 11, n-b 3	16	L-b 4	4

1/25 2/193 3/225 4/225 5/278   314   1/0 2/28 3/35 4/59 5/62   103
6/293 7/294 8/301 9/309   6/71 7/71 8/71 9/85

Bowling: *First Innings*—Hadlee 31-12-60-3; Robertson 24-6-91-1; Chatfield 29-10-54-2; Crowe 3-2-4-0; Bracewell 43.3-19-74-4; Coney 5-0-18-0. *Second Innings*—Hadlee 20-7-48-1; Chatfield 18-9-19-3; Bracewell 22-8-32-6.

New Zealand

J. G. Wright c Zoehrer b McDermott	56	– c Boon b Matthews	59
B. A. Edgar lbw b Matthews	24	– b Reid	1
K. R. Rutherford b Matthews	0	– not out	50
M. D. Crowe lbw b Matthews	0	– not out	23
J. F. Reid c Phillips b Bright	16		
*J. V. Coney c Border b McDermott	93		
R. J. Hadlee b Reid	33		
†I. D. S. Smith b Waugh	3		
J. G. Bracewell c Boon b Bright	4		
G. K. Robertson st Zoehrer b Matthews	12		
E. J. Chatfield not out	1		
B 7, l-b 8, n-b 1	16	B 18, l-b 4, n-b 5	27

1/73 2/73 3/73 4/103 5/107   258   1/6 2/106   (2 wkts) 160
6/170 7/184 8/203 9/250

Bowling: *First Innings*—McDermott 17-2-47-2; Reid 19-2-63-1; Matthews 34-15-61-4; Bright 22-4-58-2; Waugh 5-1-14-1. *Second Innings*—McDermott 14-3-29-0; Reid 12.4-2-30-1; Matthews 31-18-46-1; Bright 23-12-29-0; Waugh 4-1-4-0.

Umpires: R. L. McHarg and S. J. Woodward.

†NEW ZEALAND v AUSTRALIA

First One-day International

At Dunedin, March 19. New Zealand won by 29 runs. On a pitch which favoured seam bowling, and on a slow outfield, New Zealand did well to score 186. Davis was so demanding that he set a trans-Tasman record, bowling his ten overs for just 12 runs, but after a lull between the 22nd over and the 43rd there was sufficient aggression. Blain, in his first match for New Zealand, scored 24 off eighteen balls. Hadlee conceded only 15 runs from his nine overs, with four wickets, and Marsh needed 96 balls for his 35.

Man of the Match: M. D. Crowe and R. J. Hadlee (shared).   *Attendance*: 12,600.

New Zealand

K. R. Rutherford b Gilbert	23	R. J. Hadlee not out	21
B. A. Edgar c Phillips b Gilbert	35	†T. E. Blain not out	24
M. D. Crowe b Reid	47	L-b 10, w 2, n-b 1	13
*J. V. Coney c Marsh b Waugh	5		
J. G. Wright run out	6	1/65 2/72 3/80 (6 wkts, 50 overs) 186	
B. R. Blair c Waugh b McDermott	12	4/87 5/117 6/146	

J. G. Bracewell, S. R. Gillespie and E. J. Chatfield did not bat.

Bowling: McDermott 10-0-40-1; Davis 10-2-12-0; Reid 10-1-53-1; Gilbert 10-2-35-2; Waugh 10-0-36-1.

Australia

D. C. Boon c Rutherford b Chatfield	13	D. R. Gilbert b Crowe	2
G. R. Marsh b Hadlee	35	B. A. Reid c Crowe b Hadlee	2
†W. B. Phillips c Blain b Gillespie	23	S. P. Davis not out	0
*A. R. Border c Blain b Crowe	3	L-b 12, w 3	15
G. M. Ritchie c and b Bracewell	9		
G. R. J. Matthews c Wright b Bracewell	26	1/13 2/52 3/55 (47 overs) 157	
S. R. Waugh c Crowe b Hadlee	29	4/82 5/122 6/124	
C. J. McDermott lbw b Hadlee	0	7/126 8/142 9/157	

Bowling: Hadlee 9-5-15-4; Chatfield 8-2-19-1; Gillespie 10-2-39-1; Crowe 10-4-23-2; Bracewell 7-0-30-2; Coney 3-0-19-0.

Umpires: B. L. Aldridge and G. C. Morris.

†NEW ZEALAND v AUSTRALIA

Second One-day International

At Christchurch, March 22. New Zealand won by 53 runs. On a much faster wicket and outfield, New Zealand were given a flying start by Edgar and Rutherford, whose opening partnership of 125 took 111 minutes. Coney scored the fastest of the three half-centuries – off 50 balls. Only Boon, who hit nine 4s in his 47, looked capable of a substantial reply, and McDermott brought the later part of the innings to life by hitting 37 from 29 balls.
Man of the Match: J. V. Coney. *Attendance:* 20,500.

New Zealand

K. R. Rutherford c Waugh b Reid	64	†T. E. Blain not out	0
B. A. Edgar b Reid	74	J. G. Bracewell not out	2
M. D. Crowe c Ritchie b Waugh	12	L-b 8, w 2, n-b 2	12
*J. V. Coney run out	64		
J. G. Wright c Matthews b McDermott	6	1/125 2/150 3/170 (7 wkts, 49 overs) 258	
R. J. Hadlee c Ritchie b Davis	11	4/191 5/212	
B. R. Blair c McDermott b Davis	13	6/246 7/256	

S. R. Gillespie and E. J. Chatfield did not bat.

Bowling: McDermott 10-1-50-1; Davis 10-1-51-2; Reid 10-0-44-2; Gilbert 5-0-29-0; Matthews 5-0-29-0; Waugh 9-0-47-1.

Australia

G. R. Marsh run out	9	D. R. Gilbert run out	5
D. C. Boon c and b Gillespie	47	B. A. Reid c Crowe b Chatfield	3
*A. R. Border c Blair b Crowe	27	S. P. Davis not out	1
G. M. Ritchie c Crowe b Hadlee	31	L-b 8, w 2	10
G. R. J. Matthews c Wright b Bracewell	13		
†W. B. Phillips run out	12	1/27 2/67 3/99 (45.4 overs) 205	
S. R. Waugh b Hadlee	10	4/132 5/137 6/150	
C. J. McDermott b Chatfield	37	7/160 8/189 9/204	

Bowling: Hadlee 10–2–36–2; Chatfield 8.4–3–38–2; Gillespie 8–0–51–1; Crowe 7–0–27–1; Bracewell 10–2–37–1; Coney 2–0–8–0.

Umpires: F. R. Goodall and R. L. McHarg.

†NEW ZEALAND v AUSTRALIA

Third One-day International

At Wellington, March 26. Australia won by three wickets with three balls to spare. An exhilarating partnership of 86 by Phillips and Waugh for the sixth wicket carried them there, although the run of play had suggested another Australian defeat. When Rutherford and Martin Crowe put on 50 in 29 minutes a big score was in prospect, but thereafter New Zealand's tempo dropped abruptly. When Australia batted, Marsh went 29 balls without scoring, and at 142 for five after 39 overs their cause looked hopeless. However, Phillips repeatedly cleared the covers and a requirement of 88 off eleven overs was reduced by 80 in 62 deliveries. Hadlee began the last over with Australia 1 run in arrears. Phillips went first ball, Waugh to the second, but McDermott played the third to the point boundary to give Australia a dramatic win.

Man of the Match: W. B. Phillips and S. R. Waugh (shared).   *Attendance:* 14,500.

New Zealand

K. R. Rutherford c Davis b Matthews	79	J. G. Bracewell c Marsh b Davis		0
B. A. Edgar st Phillips b Matthews	29	S. R. Gillespie not out		0
M. D. Crowe b McDermott	28			
*J. V. Coney run out	24	B 7, l-b 8, n-b 1		16
J. J. Crowe b Waugh	16			
B. R. Blair run out	19	1/86 2/145 3/146	(9 wkts, 50 overs)	229
R. J. Hadlee run out	7	4/184 5/190 6/205		
†T. E. Blain c Phillips b Davis	11	7/224 8/228 9/229		

E. J. Chatfield did not bat.

Bowling: McDermott 10–1–41–1; Davis 10–1–37–2; Reid 7–0–32–0; Waugh 7–0–31–1; Matthews 10–0–42–2; Bright 6–0–31–0.

Australia

D. C. Boon b Chatfield	1	R. J. Bright not out		0
G. R. Marsh c Coney b M. D. Crowe	53	C. J. McDermott not out		4
*A. R. Border c Blain b M. D. Crowe	21	B 2, l-b 10, w 1, n-b 6		19
G. M. Ritchie run out	1			
S. R. Waugh run out	71	1/12 2/54 3/56	(7 wkts, 49.3 overs)	232
G. R. J. Matthews b Gillespie	9	4/108 5/142		
†W. B. Phillips lbw b Hadlee	53	6/228 7/228		

B. A. Reid and S. P. Davis did not bat.

Bowling: Hadlee 9.3–3–26–1; Chatfield 10–3–48–1; Gillespie 10–0–45–1; M. D. Crowe 8–1–44–2; Bracewell 10–0–46–0; Coney 2–0–11–0.

Umpires: B. L. Aldridge and G. C. Morris.

†NEW ZEALAND v AUSTRALIA

Fourth One-day International

At Auckland, March 29. Australia won by 44 runs to level the series 2-2. After the start was delayed by rain, resulting in a 45-over match, Australia struggled until Ritchie and Matthews came together for the fifth wicket and added 100 from 90 deliveries. Ritchie was dropped off a straightforward return catch by Gray when 6. New Zealand's middle order failed, and a brave effort from Hadlee came too late to arrest the decline.

Man of the Match: G. R. J. Matthews.   *Attendance:* 34,000.

Australia

G. R. Marsh run out	19	C. J. McDermott not out	12
D. C. Boon b Bracewell	40	B. A. Reid b Hadlee	1
*A. R. Border run out	21	S. P. Davis run out	0
G. M. Ritchie b Gray	53	B 1, l-b 12, n-b 1	14
S. R. Waugh run out	1		
G. R. J. Matthews b Chatfield	54	1/25 2/86 3/87 (44.5 overs)	231
†W. B. Phillips c Blain b Chatfield	10	4/96 5/196 6/209	
R. J. Bright b Hadlee	6	7/209 8/229 9/231	

Bowling: Hadlee 8.5–0–35–2; Chatfield 9–0–37–2; Gillespie 8–1–55–0; Crowe 2–0–15–0; Bracewell 9–0–31–1; Gray 8–0–45–1.

New Zealand

K. R. Rutherford run out	12	J. G. Bracewell c Matthews b Waugh	20
B. A. Edgar c Boon b Reid	22	S. R. Gillespie not out	18
M. D. Crowe c Border b Matthews	14	E. J. Chatfield not out	7
*J. V. Coney run out	11	B 1, l-b 16, n-b 1	18
B. R. Blair c Boon b Matthews	11		
†T. E. Blain c and b Matthews	7	1/32 2/53 3/59 (9 wkts, 45 overs)	187
R. J. Hadlee c Matthews b Davis	40	4/77 5/78 6/100	
E. J. Gray c Phillips b Reid	7	7/112 8/149 9/161	

Bowling: McDermott 9–1–23–0; Davis 8–2–28–1; Reid 9–1–30–2; Matthews 9–1–33–3; Waugh 9–1–45–1; Boon 1–0–11–0.

Umpires: R. L. McHarg and S. J. Woodward.

THE PAKISTANIS IN SRI LANKA, 1985-86

By GERRY VAIDYASEKERA

A strong Pakistani team, with a popular and tactful manager in Salim Asghar Mian, toured Sri Lanka from February to April, the longest stay of any visiting side. The reason for their extended stay was their participation in the 1985-86 Asia Cup tournament and the concurrent Triangular Tournament in which New Zealand played the host country and Pakistan. Pakistan lost to Sri Lanka in the final of the Asia Cup but won the Triangular Tournament from New Zealand. Of the seven one-day internationals they played in Sri Lanka, Pakistan won five and lost only one. The Test series against Sri Lanka was squared 1-1.

During the second Test match, which Sri Lanka won by eight wickets, the Pakistan team were said to be considering returning home in protest at the standard of umpiring and the behaviour of the spectators. In the end, good sense prevailed. However, the umpires originally assigned to stand in the third Test of the series were changed before that match. A feature of the two one-day tournaments was the use of neutral umpires.

Sri Lanka missed not having a steady opening partnership when batting and a fast opening bowler when in the field. Their batting depended to a great extent on the two talented left-handers, Arjuna Ranatunga and Asanka Gurusinha, while the attack comprised seam bowlers and the left-arm spinner, Don Anurasiri, a new cap. In the high standard of their fielding, though, the Sri Lankans outshone Pakistan, some of whose displays drew criticism from their captain, Imran Khan.

Imran was the leading wicket-taker in the Test matches, and Wasim Akram, left-arm fast-medium, also served his side well. Tauseef Ahmed, the off-spinner, bowled Pakistan to victory on a pitch taking turn in the first Test. Pakistan's experienced batting line-up rarely played to its full potential on pitches which, overall, favoured the seam bowlers. Ramiz Raja was the most consistent, and there were instances of reputations being maintained in innings from Javed Miandad, Mohsin Khan and Salim Malik. Zulqarnain, the latest in Pakistan's efforts to find a regular successor to Wasim Bari, kept wicket well. Manzoor Elahi joined the touring party for the Asia Cup matches.

PAKISTANI TOUR RESULTS

Test matches – Played 3: Won 1, Lost 1, Drawn 1.
First-class matches – Played 5: Won 1, Lost 1, Drawn 3.
Win – Sri Lanka.
Loss – Sri Lanka.
Draws – Sri Lanka Colts, Sri Lanka Board President's XI, Sri Lanka.
Non first-class matches – Played 7: Won 5, Lost 1. No result 1. Abandoned 1. *Wins* – Sri Lanka (3), Bangladesh, New Zealand. *Loss* – Sri Lanka. *No result* – Sri Lanka. *Abandoned* – Sri Lanka.

TEST MATCH AVERAGES

SRI LANKA – BATTING

	T	I	NO	R	HI	100s	Avge
A. P. Gurusinha	2	4	2	187	116*	1	93.50
A. Ranatunga	3	5	1	316	135*	1	79.00
P. A. de Silva	3	6	1	95	37	0	19.00
L. R. D. Mendis	3	4	0	73	58	0	18.25
A. L. F. de Mel	3	4	1	48	23	0	16.00
R. S. Mahanama	2	4	0	63	41	0	15.75
R. G. de Alwis	2	2	0	28	18	0	14.00
J. R. Ratnayeke	3	4	0	56	38	0	14.00
S. Wettimuny	3	6	0	66	37	0	11.00
S. D. Anurasiri	2	2	0	12	8	0	6.00

Played in one Test: K.N. Amalean 2; E. A. R. de Silva 10*, 4*; R. L. Dias 11, 26; R. J. Ratnayake 4, 4; A. K. Kuruppuarachchi 0*; S. A. R. Silva 3; K. P. J. Warnaweera 3, 0.

Signifies not out.

BOWLING

	O	M	R	W	BB	Avge
A. K. Kuruppuarachchi	25.2	3	85	7	5-44	12.14
J. R. Ratnayeke	74.4	16	208	11	5-37	18.90
A. L. F. de Mel	76.2	15	259	10	3-39	25.90

Also bowled: K. N. Amalean 18.2–1–59–3; S. D. Anurasiri 19–12–21–0; E. A. R. de Silva 17–7–37–1; A. Ranatunga 27.3–11–68–2; R. J. Ratnayake 23–2–57–3; K. P. J. Warnaweera 7.3–2–26–1.

PAKISTAN – BATTING

	T	I	NO	R	HI	100s	Avge
Ramiz Raja	3	4	0	178	122	1	44.50
Salim Malik	3	4	0	155	54	0	38.75
Mudassar Nazar	3	4	0	93	81	0	23.25
Qasim Omar	3	4	0	85	52	0	21.25
Javed Miandad	3	4	0	63	36	0	15.75
Abdul Qadir	2	2	0	31	20	0	15.50
Mohsin Khan	3	4	0	50	35	0	12.50
Imran Khan	3	4	0	48	33	0	12.00
Tauseef Ahmed	2	3	1	24	23*	0	12.00
Wasim Akram	3	4	0	30	19	0	7.50
Zulqarnain	3	4	0	24	13	0	6.00

Played in one Test: Mohsin Kamal 1*, 13*; Zakir Khan 0*.

Signifies not out.

BOWLING

	O	M	R	W	BB	Avge
Tauseef Ahmed	39	13	117	9	6-45	13.00
Imran Khan	116	27	270	15	4-69	18.00
Wasim Akram ..:....	97.3	35	204	8	4-55	25.50
Abdul Qadir	65.3	12	174	5	3-29	34.80

Also bowled: Mohsin Kamal 15-0-52-2; Mudassar Nazar 31-6-84-1; Salim Malik 2-1-2-0; Zakir Khan 45-10-150-3.

PAKISTANI AVERAGES – FIRST-CLASS MATCHES

BATTING

	M	I	NO	R	HI	100s	Avge
Ramiz Raja	5	7	2	323	122	1	64.60
Salim Malik	5	6	0	278	106	1	46.33
Mohsin Khan	4	6	1	163	101*	1	32.60
Qasim Omar	5	7	0	165	62	0	23.57
Javed Miandad	4	6	0	119	43	0	19.83
Mudassar Nazar	4	6	0	114	81	0	19.00
Tauseef Ahmed	3	4	2	38	23*	0	19.00
Imran Khan	4	5	0	86	38	0	17.20
Abdul Qadir	2	2	0	31	20	0	15.50
Wasim Akram	5	5	0	34	19	0	6.80
Zulqarnain	5	5	1	24	13	0	6.00

Played in three matches: Mohsin Kamal 1*, 13*; Zakir Khan 0*, 3, 0*. Played in one match: Salim Yousuf 1; Shoaib Mohammad 8; Rizwan-uz-Zaman 18.

Signifies not out.

BOWLING

	O	M	R	W	BB	Avge
Tauseef Ahmed	62	20	151	10	6-45	15.10
Imran Khan	135	34	301	17	4-69	17.70
Wasim Akram	143.3	56	291	12	4-55	24.25
Abdul Qadir	65.3	12	174	5	3-29	34.80
Zakir Khan	94	24	275	7	3-80	39.28

Also bowled: Mohsin Kamal 51-4-215-3; Mudassar Nazar 43-8-135-1; Qasim Omar 1-0-5-0; Rizwan-uz-Zaman 7-2-5-0; Salim Malik 3-1-3-0; Zulqarnain 1-0-3-0.

FIELDING

Zulqarnain 11 (9 ct, 2 st), Imran Khan 6, Mohsin Khan 4, Ramiz Raja 4, Salim Malik 3, Javed Miandad 3, Mudassar Nazar 2, Mohsin Kamal 1, Qasim Omar 1, Salim Yousuf 1, Shoaib Mohammad 1 (as sub), Wasim Akram 1.

SRI LANKA COLTS v PAKISTANIS

At Kurunegala, February 19, 20, 21. Drawn. There was a good attendance on all three days for the first visit, after more than 30 years, of a touring team to the picturesque Welagadera Stadium. Put in to bat on a damp wicket, the Pakistanis used the match to accustom themselves to the conditions against a side containing six spin bowlers. Mohsin Khan faced 143 balls for his second-innings hundred, adding 101 for the third wicket in 103 minutes with Miandad and an unbroken 96 in 80 minutes with Ramiz. The Colts' captain, Vonhagt, played elegantly for his 88, hitting ten 4s in a stay of 247 minutes.

Pakistanis

Mudassar Nazar c and b de Silva	21	– c de Alwis b de Silva	0
Mohsin Khan c Vonhagt b Herath	12	– not out	101
Qasim Omar c de Alwis b de Silva	18	– b de Silva	0
Javed Miandad c de Alwis b de Silva	13	– c and b C. D. U. S. Weerasinghe	43
Ramiz Raja not out	37	– not out	50
Salim Malik c de Alwis b C. D. U. S. Weerasinghe	17		
*Imran Khan c de Alwis b C. D. U. S. Weerasinghe	38		
Zakir Khan not out	0		
B 2, l-b 5	7	B 4, l-b 2, n-b 1	7

1/26 2/42 3/66   (6 wkts dec.) 163   1/4 2/4 3/105   (3 wkts) 201
4/105 5/105 6/163

†Zulqarnain, Wasim Akram and Mohsin Kamal did not bat.

Bowling: *First Innings*—de Silva 17–4–51–3; Herath 20–7–50–1; Vonhagt 4–0–12–0; C. D. U. S. Weerasinghe 11–2–32–2; Jayawardena 3–0–11–0. *Second Innings*—de Silva 11–2–37–2; Herath 11–1–41–0; C. D. U. S. Weerasinghe 15–1–58–1; Jayawardena 5–0–23–0; Jurangpathy 3–0–19–0; H. P. O. Weerasinghe 6–1–17–0.

Sri Lanka Colts

*D. M. Vonhagt c Mohsin Khan b Zakir	88	H. P. O. Weerasinghe not out	38
†L. K. de Alwis c Mohsin Kamal b Imran	15	O. Herath c and b Imran	10
D. Bulankulame c Imran b Wasim	53	R. S. Jayawardena not out	6
D. C. Wickremasinghe lbw b Zakir	40	B 2, l-b 3, w 4, n-b 21	30
B. R. Jurangpathy c Mohsin Khan b Mohsin Kamal	13		
R. Paulpillai c and b Wasim	14	1/29 2/172 3/176 4/241 (7 wkts dec.) 307

5/241 6/253 7/269

C. D. U. S. Weerasinghe and S. de Silva did not bat.

Bowling: Imran 19–7–31–2; Wasim 24–9–62–2; Zakir 23–5–64–2; Mohsin Kamal 20–2–94–1; Mudassar 12–2–51–0.

Umpires: D. P. Buultjens and P. W. Vidanagamage.

SRI LANKA v PAKISTAN

First Test Match

At Kandy, February 23, 24, 25, 27. Pakistan won by an innings and 20 runs. Mendis's decision to bat first was not supported by his batsmen, who struggled to reach 100 against Imran's pace and movement off the seam and the spin of Tauseef and Qadir on a treacherous pitch, which earlier in the month, when England B played Sri Lanka, had assisted the spin bowlers from the first session. Sri Lanka suffered further setbacks from injuries to Silva and Warnaweera, an off-spin bowler playing in his first Test. In Silva's absence, P. A. de Silva kept wicket. Pakistan also found batting difficult on the first day, losing four wickets for 58, but on the second day

Mudassar and Salim Malik increased their fifth-wicket stand to 102 (192 minutes). Mudassar batted in all for 364 minutes, facing 239 balls, and was later named as Man of the Match. A lively 39 in half an hour for the last wicket between Tauseef and Wasim saw Pakistan establish a lead of 121, which Sri Lanka reduced by 7 without loss before the close. Next day they lost two wickets in the twelve overs permitted by the weather, and after the rest day they gave little resistance as Tauseef returned his best figures in Test cricket. The match was over soon after lunch, even though some 30 minutes had been lost when the umpires, followed by the Sri Lankan batsmen, Dias and Ranatunga, returned to the pavilion in protest at the abuse delivered by the fieldsmen when an appeal for a catch, from Ranatunga to forward short leg, was turned down. Play resumed after Imran apologised to the umpires.

Sri Lanka

S. Wettimuny lbw b Imran	0	– c Ramiz b Wasim	8
†S. A. R. Silva c Zulqarnain b Wasim	3	– absent injured	
P. A. de Silva c Zulqarnain b Imran	11	– b Tauseef	5
R. L. Dias b Tauseef	11	– b Tauseef	26
*L. R. D. Mendis c Mudassar b Imran	6	– c Mudassar b Tauseef	4
A. Ranatunga b Tauseef	18	– st Zulqarnain b Tauseef	33
J. R. Ratnayeke b Qadir	4	– (2) b Imran	7
A. L. F. de Mel b Tauseef	23	– (7) b Tauseef	0
R. J. Ratnayake c Malik b Qadir	4	– (8) st Zulqarnain b Tauseef	4
E. A. R. de Silva not out	10	– (9) not out	4
K. P. J. Warnaweera c Imran b Qadir	3	– (10) b Imran	0
L-b 7, w 2, n-b 7	16	L-b 3, w 6, n-b 1	10

1/0 2/14 3/25 4/37 5/44   109   1/14 2/19 3/31 4/43 5/74   101
6/59 7/69 8/78 9/100   6/74 7/80 8/100 9/101

Bowling: *First Innings*—Imran 9–0–20–3; Wasim 8–3–21–1; Tauseef 13–4–32–3; Qadir 12.4–3–29–3. *Second Innings*—Imran 16–5–29–2; Wasim 5–3–5–1; Qadir 7–1–19–0; Tauseef 15–7–45–6.

Pakistan

Mudassar Nazar c Mendis b Ratnayake	81	Abdul Qadir b Ratnayake ... 11
Mohsin Khan lbw b de Mel	1	†Zulqarnain b de Mel ... 5
Qasim Omar lbw b Ratnayake	11	Tauseef Ahmed not out ... 23
Javed Miandad lbw b E. A. R. de Silva	4	Wasim Akram run out ... 19
Ramiz Raja lbw b Warnaweera	3	B 4, w 7 ... 11
Salim Malik c P. A. de Silva b de Mel	54	
*Imran Khan c sub (R. S. Mahanama)		1/1 2/28 3/49 4/52 5/154 6/167 230
b Ranatunga	7	7/173 8/181 9/191

Bowling: de Mel 17.2–5–50–3; Ratnayeke 10–1–26–0; Ratnayake 23–2–57–3; Warnaweera 7.3–2–26–1; E. A. R. de Silva 17–7–37–1; Ranatunga 15.3–6–30–1.

Umpires: A. C. Felsinger and S. Ponnadurai.

†SRI LANKA v PAKISTAN

First One-day International

At Kandy, March 2. Pakistan won by eight wickets in a match reduced by rain from 45 to 25 overs per side. Pakistan put Sri Lanka in to bat and restricted them to 124 by means of tight bowling and a slow over-rate. Ranasinghe's 41, on his first appearance for his country, came off 49 balls, but it needed 16 from Wasim's last over to set a challenging target. However, with Mohsin scoring 59 off 57 balls (one 6, seven 4s) and Mudassar 41 off 50 balls, Pakistan always had overs and wickets in hand.

Man of the Match: Mohsin Khan.

Sri Lanka

†A. M. de Silva b Zakir	8	R. S. Mahanama not out	15
S. K. Ranasinghe c Qadir b Tauseef	41	A. L. F. de Mel not out	16
P. A. de Silva b Imran	21	L-b 3, n-b 1	4
A. Ranatunga c Ramiz b Qadir	2		
*L. R. D. Mendis c Wasim b Qadir	5	1/30 2/68 3/71 (6 wkts, 23 overs) 124	
R. L. Dias c Miandad b Qadir	12	4/78 5/83 6/101	

R. J. Ratnayake, S. D. Anurasiri and K. G. Perera did not bat.

Bowling: Imran 4-0-15-1; Wasim 4-0-34-0; Zakir 5-0-22-1; Tauseef 5-0-27-1; Qadir 5-0-23-3.

Pakistan

Mudassar Nazar c A. M. de Silva b Ranasinghe	41	Ramiz Raja not out	0
Mohsin Khan c A. M. de Silva b Ratnayake	59	L-b 6, n-b 1	7
Javed Miandad not out	18	1/66 2/124 (2 wkts, 21.3 overs) 125	

Salim Malik, *Imran Khan, Abdul Qadir, Tauseef Ahmed, †Zulqarnain, Wasim Akram and Zakir Khan did not bat.

Bowling: de Mel 4.3-1-25-0; Ratnayake 4-0-17-1; Ranasinghe 5-0-31-1; Ranatunga 2-0-12-0; Anurasiri 4-0-19-0; Perera 2-0-15-0.

Umpires: K. T. Francis and S. Ponnadurai.

SRI LANKA BOARD PRESIDENT'S XI v PAKISTANIS

At Galle, March 4, 5, 6. Drawn. With the tourists resting five of their senior players, Salim Malik, who captained the Pakistan Under-23 team to Sri Lanka in 1985, led the side and, on winning the toss, chose to bat. Play did not begin until half an hour after lunch as a result of the wet outfield, and tight bowling and good fielding restricted the Pakistanis to 115 for two off 58 overs. Malik's hundred on the second day took 191 minutes and contained three 6s and nine 4s; Ramiz batted for 173 minutes for his 58 and Qasim Omar 245 minutes for his 62. When the home side batted, Abeysekera hit an entertaining 41 not out off 62 balls and put on 77 in 85 minutes for the sixth wicket with D. C. Wickremasinghe.

Pakistanis

Rizwan-uz-Zaman c and b Ramanayake	18	Wasim Akram c Bulankulame b Amalean	4
Shoaib Mohammad c Amalean b Abeysekera	8	Zakir Khan c Bulankulame b Amalean	3
Qasim Omar c Warnakulasuriya b Anurasiri	62	Tauseef Ahmed not out	14
Ramiz Raja c Mahanama b Anurasiri	58	Zulqarnain not out	0
*Salim Malik c sub b Abeysekera	106	B 1, l-b 4, w 1, n-b 5	11
†Salim Yousuf c and b Anurasiri	1	1/27 2/29 3/123 4/167 (8 wkts dec.) 285	
Mohsin Kamal did not bat.		5/170 6/193 7/223 8/282	

Bowling: Ramanayake 17-2-50-1; Amalean 18-5-52-2; Abeysekera 46-10-106-2; Anurasiri 37-11-72-3; Bulankulame 1-1-0-0.

Sri Lanka Board President's XI

D. Bulankulame b Tauseef	10	†A. G. D. Wickremasinghe b Wasim	0
*S. Warnakulasuriya c Yousuf b Zakir	48	R. S. Abeysekera not out	41
D. Ranatunga c Malik b Zakir	16	B 6, w 1, n-b 4	11
R. S. Mahanama c Zulqarnain b Wasim	33		
H. P. Tillekeratne retired hurt	10	1/47 2/72 3/85 (5 wkts) 209	
D. C. Wickremasinghe not out	40	4/122 5/132	

K. N. Amalean, S. D. Anurasiri and C. P. Ramanayake did not bat.

Bowling: Wasim 22–12–25–2; Zakir 26–9–61–2; Tauseef 23–7–34–1; Rizwan 7–2–5–0; Mohsin Kamal 16–2–69–0; Malik 1–0–1–0; Omar 1–0–5–0; Zulqarnain 1–0–3–0.

Umpires: M. D. D. N. Gooneratne and K. T. Ponnambalam.

†SRI LANKA v PAKISTAN

Second One-day International

At Moratuwa, March 8. No result. Sri Lanka won the toss and put Pakistan in to bat. Rain prevented the Sri Lankans from commencing their innings.

Pakistan

Mudassar Nazar c Kuruppu b Ramanayake .	29	Wasim Akram c Ranasinghe b Anurasiri 7
Mohsin Khan c Mahanama b de Mel . .	16	Tauseef Ahmed not out 0
Ramiz Raja c Kuruppu b Ramanayake .	6	Zakir Khan not out 5
Javed Miandad c Kuruppu b Ranasinghe	30	L-b 8, w 1, n-b 1 10
Salim Malik c Mahanama b Ramanayake	1	1/34 2/55 3/72 (8 wkts, 38 overs) 125
*Imran Khan c de Silva b Amalean . . .	20	4/76 5/108 6/112
Abdul Qadir run out	1	7/120 8/120

†Zulqarnain did not bat.

Bowling: de Mel 8–1–25–1; Amalean 7–1–15–1; Ramanayake 6–0–25–3; Ranasinghe 9–0–30–1; Anurasiri 8–2–22–1.

Sri Lanka

†D. S. B. P. Kuruppu, S. K. Ranasinghe, P. A. de Silva, R. L. Dias, *L. R. D. Mendis, A. Ranatunga, R. S. Mahanama, A. L. F. de Mel, C. P. Ramanayake, S. D. Anurasiri and K. N. Amalean.

Umpires: H. C. Felsinger and K. T. Ponnambalam.

†SRI LANKA v PAKISTAN

Third One-day International

At Ketterama Stadium, Colombo, March 9. Abandoned.

†SRI LANKA v PAKISTAN

Fourth One-day International

At Sinhalese Sports Club, Colombo, March 11. Pakistan won by eight wickets. Put in to bat, Sri Lanka were saved by Ranatunga, whose 74 not out, off 89 balls, included a 6 off Qadir and four 4s. Rain interrupted Pakistan's reply in the fourteenth over (45 for no wicket), and when play resumed 90 minutes later in bright sunshine they required a further 57 runs off 10.1 overs, their target having been amended to 102 off 24 overs. This they achieved with an over to spare.

Man of the Match: A. Ranatunga.

Sri Lanka

†D. S. B. P. Kuruppu c Zulqarnain			A. L. F. de Mel b Wasim	13
		b Zakir .	4	C. P. Ramanayake b Wasim	0

†D. S. B. P. Kuruppu c Zulqarnain b Zakir . 4
S. K. Ranasinghe c Imran b Wasim ... 14
R. L. Dias c Miandad b Wasim 1
*L. R. D. Mendis c Zulqarnain b Zakir 0
R. S. Mahanama c Zulqarnain b Qadir . 22
A. Ranatunga not out 74
P. A. de Silva c Malik b Qadir 11

A. L. F. de Mel b Wasim 13
C. P. Ramanayake b Wasim 0
S. D. Anurasiri not out 4
    B 1, l-b 4, w 8, n-b 4 17
                       —

1/13 2/23 3/24   (8 wkts, 38 overs) 160
4/25 5/86 6/122
7/149 8/149

K. N. Amalean did not bat.

Bowling: Imran 8–2–22–0; Wasim 9–1–28–4; Zakir 9–0–42–2; Tauseef 2–0–10–0; Qadir 9–0–47–2; Mudassar 1–0–6–0.

Pakistan

Mudassar Nazar c Kuruppu
           b Ranasinghe . 35
Mohsin Khan b Amalean 30
Javed Miandad not out 22

Ramiz Raja not out 13
    L-b 2, n-b 1 3
                   —
1/65 2/71   (2 wkts, 23 overs) 103

Salim Malik, *Imran Khan, Abdul Qadir, Tauseef Ahmed, Wasim Akram, Zakir Khan and †Zulqarnain did not bat.

Bowling: de Mel 8–1–22–0; Amalean 7–1–31–1; Ramanayake 3–0–20–0; Ranasinghe 5–0–28–1.

Umpires: H. C. Felsinger and P. W. Vidanagamage.

SRI LANKA v PAKISTAN

Second Test Match

At Colombo Cricket Club, Colombo, March 14, 15, 16, 18. Sri Lanka won by eight wickets. Kuruppuarachchi, a left-arm medium-fast bowler and one of three new caps, gave Sri Lanka the start they needed when he dismissed Mudassar with his third ball in Test cricket; and de Mel backed up Mendis's decision to insert Pakistan on a green pitch with two wickets to make the touring side 12 for three. By the end of the day Pakistan were all out for 132, the lowest Test score against Sri Lanka, the last five wickets having fallen for 8 runs in 30 balls. Sri Lanka were 21 without loss and batted throughout the second day to the security of 248 for six. Ranatunga, 69 not out overnight, went on to reach 1,000 Test runs the next morning, and his innings of 305 minutes (175 balls) was the foundation of Sri Lanka's lead of 141 with more than two and a half days remaining.

Pakistan again lost wickets quickly at the start, and although Omar for a time threatened to swing the game away from Sri Lanka with a half-century in 50 balls (eight 4s), Pakistan went into the rest day only 13 runs ahead with one wicket in hand. With the weather holding, Sri Lanka achieved their second victory in Test cricket before lunch on the fourth day.

Two controversial incidents, in addition to disputed decisions, marred the third day. The replacement of a damaged ball after sixteen overs of Pakistan's second innings produced an objection from the batsmen when an umpire began rubbing the new ball on the ground to effect "a similar amount of wear". They reported the matter to the Pakistan manager, who came on to the field of play with a 1985 *Wisden* to show the relevant Law to the umpires. Later Miandad, angered by the lbw decision which dismissed him and riled by the jeering of the crowd, mounted the stairs of the pavilion in search of a spectator who had thrown a stone at him.

Pakistan

Mudassar Nazar c de Alwis b Kuruppuarachchi	3	– lbw b Kuruppuarachchi	1
Mohsin Khan lbw b Kuruppuarachchi	35	– c de Silva b de Mel	2
Qasim Omar lbw b de Mel	3	– c de Alwis b Ratnayeke	52
Javed Miandad c de Alwis b de Mel	0	– (5) lbw b Ratnayeke	36
Ramiz Raja lbw b de Mel	32	– (4) c de Alwis b Ratnayeke	21
Salim Malik c Mahanama b Kuruppuarachchi	42	– c Wettimuny b Ratnayeke	30
*Imran Khan c Mendis b Ratnayeke	8	– c de Silva b de Mel	0
Tauseef Ahmed b Ratnayeke	0	– (9) lbw b Ratnayeke	1
Wasim Akram c de Mel b Kuruppuarachchi	0	– (8) c Ranatunga b de Mel	0
†Zulqarnain c de Silva b Kuruppuarachchi	1	– lbw b Kuruppuarachchi	5
Mohsin Kamal not out	1	– not out	13
L-b 4, w 2, n-b 1	7	B 1, l-b 6, n-b 4	11

1/3 2/12 3/12 4/72 5/78	132	1/6 2/6 3/72 4/93 5/131	172
6/124 7/124 8/130 9/131		6/136 7/136 8/145 9/154	

Bowling: *First Innings*—de Mel 16–6–39–3; Kuruppuarachchi 14.5–2–44–5; Ratnayeke 17.4–8–29–2; Ranatunga 1–0–12–0; Anurasiri 2–1–4–0. *Second Innings*—de Mel 16–1–79–3; Kuruppuarachchi 10.3–1–41–2; Ratnayeke 17–3–37–5; Anurasiri 2–0–8–0.

Sri Lanka

S. Wettimuny c Zulqarnain b Mudassar	37	– c Malik b Imran	7
R. S. Mahanama run out	10	– c Zulqarnain b Imran	8
A. P. Gurusinha c Imran b Wasim	23	– not out	9
P. A. de Silva c sub (Shoaib Mohammad) b Mohsin Kamal	37	– not out	1
A. Ranatunga c Omar b Wasim	77		
*L. R. D. Mendis c Mohsin Khan b Imran	5		
J. R. Ratnayeke c Imran b Wasim	38		
†R. G. de Alwis c Miandad b Mohsin Kamal	10		
A. L. F. de Mel c Zulqarnain b Imran	11		
S. D. Anurasiri c Ramiz b Wasim	4		
A. K. Kuruppuarachchi not out	0		
B 7, l-b 3, w 4, n-b 7	21	B 2, l-b 2, w 1, n-b 2	7

1/40 2/69 3/82 4/130 5/147	273	1/19 2/31	(2 wkts) 32
6/227 7/248 8/265 9/272			

Bowling: *First Innings*—Imran 27–5–78–2; Wasim 27.3–9–55–4; Mohsin Kamal 15–0–52–2; Mudassar 14–2–36–1; Tauseef 11–2–40–0; Malik 1–0–2–0. *Second Innings*—Imran 7–2–18–2; Wasim 6–1–10–0.

Umpires: K. T. Francis and D. C. C. Perera.

SRI LANKA v PAKISTAN

Third Test Match

At P. Saravanamuttu Stadium, Colombo, March 22, 23, 24, 26, 27. Drawn. Sri Lanka fought bravely to keep the series level, the nineteen-year-old Gurusinha, in only his third Test, and the 21-year-old Ranatunga batting throughout the fifth day, which began with Sri Lanka 83 for three. Gurusinha batted for 495 minutes (307 balls) and hit fourteen 4s; Ranatunga for 341 minutes (208 balls) with four 6s and fourteen 4s. However, Pakistan missed five catches and two stumpings on the final day, Ranatunga escaping six times. Sri Lanka were also helped by the rain, which washed out all but two hours, twenty minutes of the fourth day.

Winning the toss and batting, Sri Lanka made cautious progress to 191 for four on the first day. Including the last one-day international, Ranatunga's fifty was his third in successive innings against Pakistan, while Mendis's signalled a welcome return to form. Pakistan were again in early trouble, but Ramiz Raja led the recovery to 180 for five by the close of the second day. On the third he advanced to his first Test hundred, and when lbw to the persevering Ratnayeke had batted for 388 minutes (242 balls) and hit seventeen 4s. Pakistan's lead of 37 grew in significance when Sri Lanka lost both opening batsmen at 18 and finished the day 24 for two. But first the rain and then Sri Lanka's two young left-handers were to have the final say.

Sri Lanka

S. Wettimuny c Ramiz b Wasim	0	– c Ramiz b Wasim		14
R. S. Mahanama c Zulqarnain b Qadir	41	– b Imran		4
A. P. Gurusinha c Zulqarnain b Imran	39	– not out		116
A. Ranatunga c Imran b Zakir	53	– (5) not out		135
P. A. de Silva c Mohsin b Zakir	16	– (4) c Miandad b Imran		25
*L. R. D. Mendis c Zulqarnain b Imran	58			
J. R. Ratnayeke c Miandad b Zakir	7			
†R. G. de Alwis b Imran	18			
A. L. F. de Mel not out	14			
S. D. Anurasiri b Imran	8			
K. N. Amalean lbw b Qadir	2			
B 7, l-b 9, w 6, n-b 3	25	B 19, l-b 7, w 1, n-b 2		29

1/12 2/79 3/109 4/149 5/202   281   1/18 2/18 3/83   (3 wkts) 323
6/218 7/251 8/260 9/272

Bowling: *First Innings*—Imran 32–11–69–4; Wasim 22–8–41–1; Zakir 24–6–80–3; Mudassar 7–2–19–0; Qadir 23.5–3–56–2. *Second Innings*—Wasim 29–11–72–1; Imran 25–4–56–2; Zakir 21–4–70–0; Qadir 22–5–70–0; Mudassar 10–2–29–0; Malik 1–1–0–0.

Pakistan

Mudassar Nazar c de Alwis b de Mel	8	Abdul Qadir b Amalean		20
Mohsin Khan lbw b Amalean	12	†Zulqarnain c de Alwis b Ratnayeke		13
Qasim Omar c de Alwis b Ratnayeke	19	Wasim Akram run out		11
Javed Miandad lbw b Amalean	23	Zakir Khan not out		0
Ramiz Raja lbw b Ratnayeke	122	B 10, l-b 7, w 1, n-b 10		28
Salim Malik c sub (S. M. S. Kaluperuma) b Ratnayeke	29			
*Imran Khan c de Alwis b Ranatunga	33			

1/24 2/32 3/49 4/87 5/158   318
6/234 7/278 8/305 9/318

Bowling: de Mel 27–3–91–1; Amalean 18.2–1–59–3; Ratnayeke 30–4–116–4; Anurasiri 15–11–9–0; Ranatunga 11–5–26–1.

Umpires: D. P. Buultjens and H. C. Felsinger.

Pakistan's matches v Bangladesh, New Zealand and Sri Lanka in the Asia Cup and Triangular Tournament may be found in the section on the Asia Cup, 1985-86.

BENSON AND HEDGES WORLD SERIES CUP, 1985-86

†AUSTRALIA v NEW ZEALAND

At Melbourne, January 9 (day/night). No result. Rain, soon after New Zealand, who were put in, began to bat, prevented much play in the afternoon and reduced the match to 31 overs a side, which Australia's slow over-rate further cut to 29 overs. Crowe struck a memorable 71 from 58 balls, and a total of 161 for seven favoured a New Zealand win. However, the rain returned and did not allow Australia even fifteen overs in which to achieve a target of 84.

Attendance: 39,000.

New Zealand

J. G. Wright run out	5	B. R. Blair not out	7
B. A. Edgar b Davis	17	†E. B. McSweeney not out	2
M. D. Crowe b Gilbert	71	L-b 5, w 3, n-b 2	10
J. F. Reid c Phillips b Davis	7		
*J. V. Coney c Phillips b Waugh	24	1/10 2/30 3/50 (7 wkts, 29 overs)	161
R. J. Hadlee b Gilbert	5	4/127 5/137	
J. G. Bracewell c Waugh b McDermott	13	6/146 7/152	

S. L. Boock and E. J. Chatfield did not bat.

Bowling: McDermott 6-1-20-1; Davis 6-1-30-2; Reid 6-0-36-0; Matthews 4-0-24-0; Gilbert 5-0-33-2; Waugh 2-0-13-1.

Australia

†W. B. Phillips, D. C. Boon, *A. R. Border, G. M. Ritchie, D. W. Hookes, S. R. Waugh, G. R. J. Matthews, C. J. McDermott, B. A. Reid, D. R. Gilbert and S. P. Davis.

Umpires: A. R. Crafter and R. C. Isherwood.

†INDIA v NEW ZEALAND

At Brisbane, January 11. India won by five wickets. The ball swung for a time in the morning, but afterwards conditions were ideal for batting. New Zealand, again sent in, started boldly, Crowe (76 from 83 balls) and Edgar (75 from 118 balls) adding 130 in 26 overs. India, whose requirement was larger than their highest score ever achieved batting second, were given a flying start by Gavaskar with 27 (one 6, four 4s) from seventeen balls. Srikkanth hit seven 4s in his 50, Amarnath had a 6 and eight 4s in his 61 before being fourth out at 162, and finally Kapil Dev and Shastri, with an unbroken, 87-run stand, won the match with two overs to spare.

Man of the Match: Kapil Dev.   *Attendance:* 10,209.

New Zealand

B. A. Edgar b Kapil Dev	75	S. R. Gillespie b Chetan	7
J. G. Wright c Kirmani b Binny	2	S. L. Boock run out	0
M. D. Crowe c and b Amarnath	76	E. J. Chatfield not out	1
J. F. Reid b Shastri	11	L-b 15, w 1, n-b 3	19
R. J. Hadlee c Amarnath b Yadav	22		
*J. V. Coney b Azharuddin b Yadav	11	1/12 2/142 3/171 (9 wkts, 50 overs)	259
B. R. Blair not out	29	4/196 5/209 6/223	
†E. B. McSweeney b Chetan	6	7/238 8/254 9/256	

Bowling: Kapil Dev 10-0-28-1; Binny 6-1-29-1; Chetan 7-0-43-2; Amarnath 10-1-40-1; Yadav 8-0-51-2; Shastri 9-0-53-1.

India

K. Srikkanth run out	50	R. J. Shastri not out	36
S. M. Gavaskar b Chatfield	27		
M. Amarnath b Boock	61	L-b 8, w 4, n-b 1	13
M. Azharuddin run out	13		
D. B. Vengsarkar c Coney b Gillespie	9	1/40 2/137 3/154 (5 wkts, 48 overs) 263	
*Kapil Dev not out	54	4/162 5/176	

R. M. H. Binny, Chetan Sharma, †S. M. H. Kirmani and N. S. Yadav did not bat.

Bowling: Chatfield 9-2-51-1; Hadlee 10-3-42-0; Blair 3-0-27-0; Gillespie 9-1-39-1; Coney 6-0-36-0; Boock 10-0-55-1; Crowe 1-0-5-0.

Umpires: M. W. Johnson and B. E. Martin.

†AUSTRALIA v INDIA

At Brisbane, January 12. Australia won by four wickets. Runs were hard to come by on the same pitch on which India and New Zealand had aggregated 522 runs in 98 overs on the previous day. India, put in, were restrained after a disastrous start – the result of their openers' excesses – by accurate bowling from Australia's seam attack. They were only 113 for eight with sixteen overs left, but Chetan Sharma and Kirmani kept them in the match. Australia made heavy weather of their task. A series of poor strokes reduced them from 20 without loss to 48 for five in 64 balls before Matthews and Waugh put the innings on an even keel.

Man of the Match: G. R. J. Matthews.   *Attendance*: 21,145.

India

S. M. Gavaskar b Davis	5	†S. M. H. Kirmani c Matthews	
K. Srikkanth c Matthews b McDermott	6	b McDermott	27
M. Amarnath c Phillips b Gilbert	13	N. S. Yadav not out	0
D. B. Vengsarkar run out	19		
M. Azharuddin b Waugh	35	L-b 6, w 2, n-b 2	10
*Kapil Dev run out	16		
R. J. Shastri b Reid	0	1/5 2/13 3/29 (43 overs) 161	
R. M. H. Binny lbw b Waugh	8	4/69 5/100 6/100	
Chetan Sharma run out	22	7/102 8/113 9/160	

Bowling: McDermott 9-1-32-2; Davis 7-2-11-1; Gilbert 9-1-42-1; Waugh 10-0-46-2; Reid 8-1-24-1.

Australia

†W. B. Phillips c Amarnath b Binny	8	G. R. J. Matthews not out	46
D. C. Boon c Gavaskar b Binny	14	C. J. McDermott not out	24
*A. R. Border c Kirmani b Chetan	16	L-b 9, w 1	10
D. W. Hookes c Azharuddin b Binny	5		
G. M. Ritchie c and b Chetan	1	1/20 2/27 3/45 (6 wkts, 45.2 overs) 164	
S. R. Waugh b Yadav	40	4/45 5/48 6/127	

D. R. Gilbert, B. A. Reid and S. P. Davis did not bat.

Bowling: Kapil Dev 9.2-1-31-0; Binny 10-2-38-3; Chetan 6-0-28-2; Shastri 10-1-23-0; Amarnath 3-0-11-0; Yadav 7-1-24-1.

Umpires: R. A. French and S. G. Randell.

†AUSTRALIA v NEW ZEALAND

At Sydney, January 14 (day/night). Australia won by four wickets. Sent in on a seaming pitch, far too lively for a one-day match, New Zealand were 25 for two after fifteen overs and 53 for four at the halfway point as the batsmen had to try to survive, rather than attack. Coney (58 from 86 balls) and Hadlee (21 from 24) provided the main resistance in a seventh-wicket stand.

New Zealand fought back to have Australia 87 for four in the 29th over, only to drop Ritchie in the 30th when he was 25. He battled on to 68 with victory within touching distance, and Australia won with almost five overs to spare.

Man of the Match: D. R. Gilbert.   *Attendance:* 36,170.

New Zealand

B. A. Edgar c Ritchie b Davis	0	†E. B. McSweeney b Gilbert		3
J. G. Wright st Phillips b Matthews	22	S. R. Gillespie c Matthews b Davis		1
M. D. Crowe c Phillips b Gilbert	9	E. J. Chatfield not out		4
J. F. Reid c Phillips b Waugh	9	L-b 2, w 3, n-b 3		8
J. J. Crowe c Marsh b Reid	12			
*J. V. Coney c Boon b Gilbert	58	1/1 2/19 3/42	(49.2 overs)	152
J. G. Bracewell c and b Gilbert	5	4/44 5/68 6/84		
R. J. Hadlee c Phillips b Gilbert	21	7/140 8/144 9/147		

Bowling: McDermott 9–3–21–0; Davis 8.2–3–17–2; Gilbert 10–0–46–5; Matthews 10–1–17–1; Waugh 3–0–12–1; Reid 9–0–37–1.

Australia

D. C. Boon lbw b Gillespie	21	G. R. J. Matthews c M. D. Crowe		
G. R. Marsh c McSweeney b Chatfield	13		b Chatfield	1
*A. R. Border st McSweeney		C. J. McDermott not out		1
	b Bracewell	16	L-b 5, w 4, n-b 2	11
G. M. Ritchie c McSweeney b Hadlee	68			
†W. B. Phillips c Coney b Hadlee	3	1/34 2/41 3/72	(6 wkts, 45.1 overs)	153
S. R. Waugh not out	19	4/87 5/151 6/152		

B. A. Reid, D. R. Gilbert and S. P. Davis did not bat.

Bowling: Hadlee 10–0–42–2; Chatfield 10–3–21–2; Gillespie 7.1–0–30–1; Bracewell 10–2–29–1; Coney 5–0–15–0; M. D. Crowe 3–1–11–0.

Umpires: B. E. Martin and S. G. Randell.

†AUSTRALIA v INDIA

At Melbourne, January 16 (day/night). India won by eight wickets. India, tempted by the long boundaries at the MCG, included Sivaramakrishnan, their leg-spinner, and with rain forecast they gained an advantage by winning the toss and batting second. Australia, under extra pressure because of the need to accelerate early for fear of rain, were 50 for five before Waugh rallied them with 73 from 104 balls. Two interruptions for rain reduced each side's innings by five overs. A moving ball and the accuracy of the Australian seamers made run-getting difficult, but after Srikkanth was run out, Gavaskar and Amarnath batted with considerable expertise.

Man of the Match: S. R. Waugh.   *Attendance:* 52,612.

Australia

G. R. Marsh b Kapil Dev	5	D. R. Gilbert c Sivaramakrishnan		
D. C. Boon run out	23		b Chetan	7
G. R. J. Matthews run out	11	B. A. Reid c Srikkanth b Binny		4
*A. R. Border b Binny	0	S. P. Davis run out		6
G. M. Ritchie c More b Shastri	3	L-b 8, w 1, n-b 1		10
S. R. Waugh not out	73			
†W. B. Phillips b Sivaramakrishnan	7	1/18 2/31 3/31	(44.2 overs)	161
C. J. McDermott c Azharuddin		4/40 5/50 6/80		
	b Chetan	12	7/100 8/128 9/141	

Bowling: Kapil Dev 8.2–2–25–1; Binny 9–1–39–2; Shastri 9–1–23–1; Chetan 9–0–29–2; Sivaramakrishnan 9–1–37–1.

India

K. Srikkanth run out	22
S. M. Gavaskar c Phillips b Reid	59
M. Amarnath not out	58
M. Azharuddin not out	11
L-b 5, w 2, n-b 5	12

1/37 2/126   (2 wkts, 40.2 overs) 162

A. Malhotra, *Kapil Dev, R. M. H. Binny, R. J. Shastri, †K. S. More, Chetan Sharma and
L. Sivaramakrishnan did not bat.

Bowling: McDermott 8.2-1-29-0; Davis 9-3-16-0; Reid 9-0-39-1; Gilbert 7-0-41-0;
Waugh 3-0-16-0; Matthews 4-0-16-0.

Umpires: M. W. Johnson and S. G. Randell.

†INDIA v NEW ZEALAND

At Perth, January 18. New Zealand won by three wickets. Exasperated with his ill-luck, Coney
entrusted the toss to Hadlee, whose success was important only in that it gave New Zealand
knowledge of their target – the smallest they had ever had to pursue in a one-day international.
From start to finish the conditions favoured the bowlers, with the ball seaming and bouncing
eccentrically on a green, newly laid pitch. Snedden justified his late inclusion ahead of the off-
spinner, Bracewell, with three for 23. At 76 for two after 25 overs New Zealand were winning
comfortably, but the finish became keenly disputed when Kapil Dev returned for his second
spell and, bowling with a packed slip cordon, took a wicket in each of his first three overs.
Man of the Match: M. D. Crowe.   *Attendance:* 11,199.

India

K. Srikkanth run out	0	R. M. H. Binny c Wright b Snedden		1
S. M. Gavaskar c M. D. Crowe		†K. S. More c Snedden b Chatfield		2
b Gillespie	9	L. Sivaramakrishnan not out		2
M. Amarnath c M. D. Crowe b Snedden	30			
M. Azharuddin b M. D. Crowe	11	L-b 6, w 6, n-b 2		14
A. Malhotra c Wright b Hadlee	15			
R. J. Shastri c McSweeney b Chatfield	23	1/0 2/23 3/58	(44.2 overs)	113
*Kapil Dev c J. J. Crowe b Hadlee	0	4/60 5/93 6/93		
Chetan Sharma c McSweeney b Snedden	6	7/104 8/106 9/108		

Bowling: Chatfield 9.2-4-9-2; Hadlee 8-1-16-2; Gillespie 10-2-20-1; Snedden 8-2-23-3;
M. D. Crowe 4-0-20-1; Coney 5-0-19-0.

New Zealand

B. A. Edgar c Gavaskar b Binny	13	†E. B. McSweeney c Kapil Dev b Chetan		5
J. G. Wright c Kapil Dev b Chetan	13	M. C. Snedden not out		0
M. D. Crowe c Azharuddin b Kapil Dev	33	L-b 3, w 2, n-b 8		13
J. F. Reid c Gavaskar b Kapil Dev	14			
J. J. Crowe c Gavaskar b Kapil Dev	0	1/28 2/31 3/77	(7 wkts, 40.1 overs)	115
*J. V. Coney not out	19	4/83 5/86		
R. J. Hadlee b Chetan	5	6/95 7/111		

S. R. Gillespie and E. J. Chatfield did not bat.

Bowling: Kapil Dev 10-4-26-3; Binny 8.1-0-25-1; Chetan 8-0-26-3; Amarnath 2-0-8-0;
Shastri 10-2-17-0; Sivaramakrishnan 2-0-10-0.

Umpires: R. C. Isherwood and P. J. McConnell.

†AUSTRALIA v NEW ZEALAND

At Perth, January 19. Australia won by four wickets. The same pitch that was used for the low-scoring match the previous day again gave the seam bowlers exaggerated help, but this time New Zealand lost the toss and batted before a capacity crowd. Batting was always difficult against the fast, well-directed Australian bowling, although Jeff Crowe was helped by an extraordinary mixture of full tosses and long-hops from Trimble. Marsh and Border took Australia to 61 from 22 overs, and though there was a flutter of interest when Border (58 from 104 balls) was fifth out, Phillips (two 6s and three 4s) put Australia ahead with 29 balls to spare.

Man of the Match: A. R. Border.   *Attendance:* 24,640.

New Zealand

B. A. Edgar c Border b Waugh	10	R. J. Hadlee not out	15
J. G. Wright b Davis	9	†E. B. McSweeney not out	0
M. D. Crowe c Boon b Waugh	1	B 2, l-b 10, w 2, n-b 3	17
J. F. Reid b Reid	11		
J. J. Crowe run out	63	1/12 2/13 3/32 (6 wkts, 50 overs) 159	
*J. V. Coney c Marsh b Matthews	33	4/36 5/118 6/156	

M. C. Snedden, S. R. Gillespie and E. J. Chatfield did not bat.

Bowling: McDermott 10–1–20–0; Davis 10–3–13–1; Waugh 10–3–28–2; Reid 10–1–36–1; Trimble 4–0–32–0; Matthews 6–0–18–1.

Australia

D. C. Boon c Coney b Hadlee	6	†W. B. Phillips not out	28
G. R. Marsh c McSweeney b M. D. Crowe	20	G. S. Trimble not out	0
*A. R. Border run out	58		
G. M. Ritchie c Reid b Coney	5	L-b 10, w 3, n-b 1	14
S. R. Waugh c J. J. Crowe b Chatfield	23		
G. R. J. Matthews c M. D. Crowe b Hadlee	7	1/9 2/61 3/78 (6 wkts, 45.1 overs) 161	
		4/117 5/131 6/144	

C. J. McDermott, B. A. Reid and S. P. Davis did not bat.

Bowling: Chatfield 10–0–39–1; Hadlee 9.1–1–35–2; Gillespie 8–2–23–0; Snedden 6–0–20–0; M. D. Crowe 8–1–16–1; Coney 4–1–18–1.

Umpires: R. A. French and S. G. Randell.

†AUSTRALIA v INDIA

At Sydney, January 21 (day/night). Australia won by 100 runs. This match ended the consistent pattern of the series in that the outcome of the toss did not decide the winner. Put in, Australia thrived on a mild pitch. Marsh, scoring the first century of the competition off 145 balls, and Boon put on 152 in 31 overs and three balls, and then Border set about the weary attack. Once the volatile Srikkanth was out for 20, India were never in the hunt. Gavaskar remained unbeaten with 92, his highest one-day score for India, but he did his team no service in that, by going so slowly, he reduced their scoring-rate for the competition, a factor which would have been vital had two countries finished level on points and wins.

Man of the Match: G. R. Marsh.   *Attendance:* 31,241.

Australia

G. R. Marsh c Azharuddin b Chetan	125	C. J. McDermott run out	2
D. C. Boon c Amarnath b Shastri	83	G. R. J. Matthews not out	1
*A. R. Border c Srikkanth b Chetan	52	L-b 9, w 2, n-b 4	15
†W. B. Phillips c Kapil Dev b Chetan	7		
G. M. Ritchie run out	1	1/152 2/273 3/282 (6 wkts, 50 overs) 292	
S. R. Waugh not out	6	4/283 5/283 6/286	

D. R. Gilbert, B. A. Reid and S. P. Davis did not bat.

Bowling: Kapil Dev 10–0–68–0; Binny 7–0–48–0; Chetan 9–0–61–3; Amarnath 10–0–36–0; Shastri 10–0–42–1; Sivaramakrishnan 4–0–28–0.

India

K. Srikkanth c Border b Davis	20	M. Azharuddin not out	17
S. M. Gavaskar not out	92	L-b 8, w 2, n-b 4	14
M. Amarnath c Matthews b Gilbert	16		
A. Malhotra c Matthews b Gilbert	5	1/31 2/74 3/93 (4 wkts, 50 overs)	192
*Kapil Dev c McDermott b Matthews	28	4/158	

R. J. Shastri, Chetan Sharma, R. M. H. Binny, †K. S. More and L. Sivaramakrishnan did not bat.

Bowling: McDermott 9–0–27–0; Davis 7–0–30–1; Reid 10–0–28–0; Gilbert 10–0–36–2; Matthews 10–0–49–1; Waugh 3–0–10–0; Marsh 1–0–4–0.

Umpires: M. W. Johnson and P. J. McConnell.

†INDIA v NEW ZEALAND

At Melbourne, January 23 (day/night). New Zealand won by five wickets. The match produced the closest finish of the series, the winning run coming off the penultimate ball. India, put in, were in low spirits after two consecutive defeats and also because of the absence of Gavaskar, troubled by an injured back. They were slow to find momentum but Amarnath and Vengsarkar shored up the innings and a late sally by Binny and Chetan Sharma (16 off Hadlee's last over) was invaluable. Indeed, the Indian score might have sufficed had their bowling been tighter. Starting well, New Zealand sailed a smooth course until Martin Crowe (93 balls) was fourth out at 185, with 44 balls remaining, whereupon the batsmen laboured a little. However, Coney, coolheaded, saw them home.

Man of the Match: M. D. Crowe. *Attendance*: 13,864.

India

R. J. Shastri lbw b Hadlee	6	R. M. H. Binny b Chatfield	11
K. Srikkanth c and b Chatfield	9	†K. S. More not out	1
M. Amarnath c and b Bracewell	74		
D. B. Vengsarkar b Bracewell	43	B 2, l-b 3, w 3	8
M. Azharuddin run out	12		
*Kapil Dev c Bracewell b Chatfield	47	1/15 2/16 3/98 (8 wkts, 50 overs)	238
A. Malhotra c Wright b Chatfield	7	4/115 5/182 6/205	
Chetan Sharma not out	20	7/205 8/220	

N. S. Yadav did not bat.

Bowling: Chatfield 10–2–28–4; Hadlee 10–1–52–1; M. D. Crowe 5–0–13–0; Boock 8–0–51–0; Coney 7–0–36–0; Bracewell 10–0–53–2.

New Zealand

J. G. Wright st More b Amarnath	39	R. J. Hadlee not out	1
B. A. Edgar c Vengsarkar b Shastri	30		
M. D. Crowe c Shastri b Kapil Dev	67	B 1, l-b 7, w 2	10
J. F. Reid run out	35		
J. J. Crowe b Kapil Dev	30	1/49 2/112 3/176 (5 wkts, 49.5 overs)	239
*J. V. Coney not out	27	4/185 5/235	

†E. B. McSweeney, S. L. Boock, J. G. Bracewell and E. J. Chatfield did not bat.

Bowling: Kapil Dev 10–1–36–2; Binny 5.5–1–31–0; Chetan 10–0–57–0; Amarnath 5–0–26–1; Shastri 10–0–30–1; Yadav 9–0–51–0.

Umpires: B. E. Martin and P. J. McConnell.

†INDIA v NEW ZEALAND

At Adelaide, January 25. India won by five wickets, thus ending a run of three defeats. The result reflected a marked improvement in their bowling and fielding, although Hadlee was dropped at mid-wicket when 9 with New Zealand 75 for six and went on to make a rousing 71 with two 6s and five 4s before he was out in the last over. India, again without Gavaskar, could not come to terms easily with the green, lively pitch and were 26 for three after fifteen overs. They were no more comfortably placed when Vengsarkar was fourth out for a handsome 32, but the initiative was wrested by a partnership of 73 between Azharuddin, who hit eight boundaries and was gloriously dominant against the off-spin of Bracewell, and Malhotra. Once again the team winning the toss won the match.

Man of the Match: M. Azharuddin.   *Attendance:* 8,782.

New Zealand

J. G. Wright c More b Binny	7	†E. B. McSweeney b Chetan	5
B. A. Edgar c Vengsarkar b Binny	2	S. R. Gillespie b Kapil Dev	4
M. D. Crowe c More b Shastri	28	E. J. Chatfield not out	4
J. F. Reid c Vengsarkar b Kulkarni	9	L-b 4, w 5, n-b 2	11
J. J. Crowe c Malhotra b Kulkarni	7		
*J. V. Coney c and b Shastri	4	1/12 2/13 3/37	(49.2 overs) 172
R. J. Hadlee b Kapil Dev	71	4/57 5/58 6/65	
J. G. Bracewell c Kapil Dev b Amarnath	20	7/119 8/130 9/144	

Bowling: Kapil Dev 9.2-3-24-2; Binny 7-1-13-2; Chetan 10-0-46-1; Kulkarni 9-1-28-2; Shastri 10-1-36-2; Amarnath 4-0-21-1.

India

R. J. Shastri lbw b Hadlee	2	A. Malhotra c Reid b Gillespie	33
K. Srikkanth c Coney b Gillespie	16	*Kapil Dev not out	6
M. Amarnath c McSweeney b Gillespie	5	B 1, l-b 4, w 6	11
D. B. Vengsarkar c M. D. Crowe b Gillespie	32		
M. Azharuddin not out	69	1/2 2/25 3/26	(5 wkts, 46 overs) 174
		4/85 5/158	

Chetan Sharma, R. M. H. Binny, R. R. Kulkarni and †K. S. More did not bat.

Bowling: Hadlee 10-3-28-1; Chatfield 10-5-13-0; Gillespie 10-3-30-4; M. D. Crowe 4-0-25-0; Coney 5-0-29-0; Bracewell 7-0-44-0.

Umpires: A. R. Crafter and R. A. French.

†AUSTRALIA v INDIA

At Adelaide, January 26. Australia won by 36 runs. On the evidence of the video camera, India had some reason to feel aggrieved when Waugh, whose dashing 81 so heavily tipped the scales, was not adjudged run out when 7. On the other hand the Indians had only themselves to blame when they let him off 4 runs later. Waugh, pulling and driving with great authority, hit two 6s and four 4s. India, who elected to bat second, were 75 for four in reply in the twentieth over but began to challenge as Gavaskar and Shastri added 97 from seventeen overs. Kapil Dev and Chetan Sharma put India ahead of the clock, but their dismissal to consecutive balls from Reid snuffed out Indian hopes. As a result of this victory Australia qualified for the finals.

Man of the Match: B. A. Reid.   *Attendance:* 28,236.

Australia

D. C. Boon c Kulkarni b Ghai	27	D. R. Gilbert run out	1
G. R. Marsh c Vengsarkar b Chetan	25	B. A. Reid not out	1
*A. R. Border c Kapil Dev b Shastri	9		
G. M. Ritchie run out	28	L-b 12, w 7, n-b 3	22
S. R. Waugh c Kapil Dev b Chetan	81		
G. R. J. Matthews c More b Chetan	44	1/50 2/60 3/79 (8 wkts, 50 overs)	262
†W. B. Phillips not out	23	4/134 5/226 6/250	
C. J. McDermott b Kapil Dev	1	7/255 8/257	

S. P. Davis did not bat.

Bowling: Kapil Dev 10-2-50-1; Kulkarni 10-1-53-0; Ghai 10-1-54-1; Shastri 10-1-33-1; Chetan 10-0-60-3.

India

K. Srikkanth lbw b McDermott	10	R. R. Kulkarni not out	5
S. M. Gavaskar c Phillips b Reid	77	R. S. Ghai run out	1
M. Amarnath c Phillips b McDermott	0	†K. S. More run out	0
D. B. Vengsarkar c Border b Reid	17	B 6, l-b 7, w 3, n-b 5	21
M. Azharuddin c Border b Reid	2		
R. J. Shastri c Border b McDermott	55	1/26 2/26 3/60 (45.3 overs)	226
*Kapil Dev c Phillips b Reid	25	4/75 5/172 6/182	
Chetan Sharma c McDermott b Reid	13	7/218 8/218 9/220	

Bowling: McDermott 8-1-20-3; Davis 7.3-0-38-0; Gilbert 10-1-50-0; Reid 10-0-53-5; Waugh 5-0-26-0; Matthews 5-0-26-0.

Umpires: R. C. Isherwood and P. J. McConnell.

†AUSTRALIA v NEW ZEALAND

At Adelaide, January 27. New Zealand won by 206 runs. The New Zealand experiment of opening with Bracewell failed in the first over, but Edgar, Martin Crowe and Wright moved the innings along briskly. With the next four batsmen hitting out freely New Zealand reached an imposing but not impossible score to justify Coney's decision to bat. However, the Australian batting, facing Hadlee in his dominant Test match mood, and Chatfield at his most economical, collapsed dramatically. Coney caught brilliantly, and in 26.3 overs Australia were all out for 70, equalling their lowest score in one-day matches. It was New Zealand's biggest win and Australia's biggest defeat in terms of runs in one-day internationals.

Man of the Match: R. J. Hadlee. *Attendance:* 25,742.

New Zealand

J. G. Bracewell c Border b McDermott	0	B. R. Blair b Davis	21
B. A. Edgar c Border b Reid	61	†E. B. McSweeney not out	4
M. D. Crowe c Border b Reid	26	L-b 9, w 5, n-b 1	15
J. G. Wright c Gilbert b McDermott	61		
R. J. Hadlee c McDermott b Davis	24	1/0 2/37 3/157 (7 wkts, 50 overs)	276
*J. V. Coney c Phillips b Reid	40	4/160 5/224	
J. J. Crowe not out	24	6/226 7/272	

S. R. Gillespie and E. J. Chatfield did not bat.

Bowling: McDermott 10-1-70-2; Davis 10-0-46-2; Reid 10-1-41-3; Matthews 10-0-49-0; Gilbert 10-0-61-0.

Australia

G. R. Marsh c Coney b Hadlee	0		D. R. Gilbert c and b Bracewell	8
D. C. Boon c McSweeney b Hadlee	10		B. A. Reid lbw b Blair	1
S. R. Waugh c Coney b Chatfield	3		S. P. Davis not out	0
G. S. Trimble c Coney b Hadlee	4		L-b 3, w 1, n-b 4	8
G. R. J. Matthews lbw b Gillespie	4			
*A. R. Border c Gillespie b Chatfield	9		1/0 2/10 3/15 (26.3 overs)	70
†W. B. Phillips c Chatfield b Bracewell	22		4/20 5/31 6/47	
C. J. McDermott c Wright b Gillespie	1		7/55 8/68 9/70	

Bowling: Hadlee 5–1–14–3; Chatfield 7–2–9–2; Gillespie 5–0–21–2; M. D. Crowe 4–0–13–0; Bracewell 3.3–1–3–2; Blair 2–0–7–1.

Umpires: A. R. Crafter and B. E. Martin.

†AUSTRALIA v NEW ZEALAND

At Sydney, January 29 (day/night). Australia won by 99 runs. Australia elected to bat first and after a strong start were 123 for one at 30 overs. Thereafter the batting lost some momentum, although Jones hit 53 from 58 balls. New Zealand persisted, and failed again, with Bracewell as an opener, and they never recovered from the dismissal of Martin Crowe in the fifth over. Wright existed for 65 balls, but Hadlee apart (30 from 37 balls), the New Zealand batsmen could not attack quickly enough against accurate Australian bowling. Reid swept away the tail with only the second hat-trick in one-day international matches.
Man of the Match: D. C. Boon. *Attendance:* 26,283.

Australia

D. C. Boon b Gillespie	64		C. J. McDermott not out	6
G. R. Marsh b Bracewell	37		D. R. Gilbert not out	6
*A. R. Border run out	29		B 1, l-b 8, n-b 5	14
D. M. Jones lbw b Hadlee	53			
S. R. Waugh run out	17		1/98 2/124 3/147 (7 wkts, 50 overs)	239
G. R. J. Matthews c Wright b Chatfield	10		4/185 5/217	
†W. B. Phillips b Hadlee	3		6/224 7/225	

B. A. Reid and S. P. Davis did not bat.

Bowling: Hadlee 10–1–36–2; Chatfield 10–1–48–1; Gillespie 10–0–48–1; Bracewell 10–1–43–1; M. D. Crowe 1–0–11–0; Coney 9–0–44–0.

New Zealand

J. G. Bracewell b McDermott	0		†E. B. McSweeney c Border b Reid	1
B. A. Edgar c Phillips b Davis	18		S. R. Gillespie b Reid	0
M. D. Crowe b McDermott	9		E. J. Chatfield b Davis	0
J. G. Wright c Waugh b Matthews	24		L-b 7, w 2, n-b 2	11
*J. V. Coney b Gilbert	25			
J. J. Crowe b Davis	19		1/0 2/14 3/39 (42.4 overs)	140
R. J. Hadlee not out	30		4/77 5/91 6/122	
B. R. Blair c Marsh b Reid	3		7/133 8/137 9/137	

Bowling: McDermott 7–1–28–2; Davis 9.4–2–25–3; Reid 9–2–29–3; Matthews 10–0–27–1; Gilbert 7–0–24–1.

Umpires: R. A. French and R. C. Isherwood.

†AUSTRALIA v INDIA

At Melbourne, January 31 (day/night). India won by six wickets. Fine bowling by Kapil Dev, who took two of his four wickets in his last over, prevented Australia, who won the toss, from putting together a formidable total after Marsh and Boon had begun with 146 from 32 overs and three balls. The out-of-form Srikkanth enjoyed some luck in making a brisk 27, but Australia's tight attack so controlled India's run-rate that they did not reach 100 until the 29th over. Two overs later, however, Gavaskar and Vengsarkar (88 balls) launched the offensive and Kapil Dev made certain of an Indian victory with 23 from nineteen balls.

Man of the Match: D. B. Vengsarkar.   *Attendance:* 57,169.

Australia

G. R. Marsh c Gavaskar b Shastri	....	74	C. J. McDermott lbw b Kapil Dev	....	0
D. C. Boon c Kapil Dev b Shastri	....	76	D. R. Gilbert not out	....	7
*A. R. Border c Malhotra b Kapil Dev		18	L-b 3, w 1		4
D. M. Jones b Kapil Dev	....	33			
†W. B. Phillips run out	....	8	1/146 2/161 3/194	(7 wkts, 50 overs)	235
S. R. Waugh b Kapil Dev	....	3	4/212 5/212		
D. M. Wellham not out	....	12	6/224 7/224		

B. A. Reid and S. P. Davis did not bat.

Bowling: Kapil Dev 9–0–30–4; Binny 6–1–24–0; Chetan 7–0–29–0; Sivaramakrishnan 8–0–52–0; Shastri 10–0–43–2; Azharuddin 10–0–54–0.

India

S. M. Gavaskar b Gilbert	....	72	Chetan Sharma not out	....	6
K. Srikkanth c Jones b Davis	....	27	L-b 14, w 3, n-b 2	....	19
A. Malhotra c Davis b Gilbert	....	14			
D. B. Vengsarkar not out	....	77	1/46 2/79 3/181	(4 wkts, 48.5 overs)	238
*Kapil Dev c Wellham b Davis	....	23	4/230		

M. Azharuddin, R. M. H. Binny, R. J. Shastri, L. Sivaramakrishnan and †K. S. More did not bat.

Bowling: McDermott 9.5–0–55–0; Davis 10–2–40–2; Reid 9–0–34–0; Gilbert 10–0–43–2; Waugh 6–0–34–0; Border 4–0–18–0.

Umpires: A. R. Crafter and M. W. Johnson.

†NEW ZEALAND v INDIA

At Launceston, February 2. India won when New Zealand fell 22 runs short of a revised target of 190 off 45 overs. Both sides needed to win this match to join Australia in the finals, and all the early advantage was with New Zealand, who put India in to bat on a lively pitch. Yet the New Zealanders chose to produce their most indifferent performance of the series. Jeff Crowe dropped Chetan Sharma when the score was 130 for seven, whereupon he and Binny cracked 53 in 34 minutes. New Zealand again could not score quickly enough but received the bonus, after a break for rain, of having their target reduced to 190 with 100 needed from fifteen overs and seven wickets in hand. However, Kapil Dev came back when New Zealand needed 59 from seven overs, with five wickets intact, and destroyed their chances by taking three wickets in six balls.

Man of the Match: Chetan Sharma.   *Attendance:* 9,786.

India

K. Srikkanth lbw b Snedden	....	22	R. M. H. Binny lbw b Hadlee	....	24
S. M. Gavaskar c McSweeney b Hadlee		1	R. R. Kulkarni c Gillespie b Chatfield	..	9
M. Amarnath c McSweeney b Gillespie		24	†K. S. More not out	....	1
A. Malhotra c Snedden b Gillespie	....	39			
M. Azharuddin c McSweeney			L-b 7, w 7, n-b 2	....	16
b M. D. Crowe	.	3			
R. J. Shastri b Snedden	....	23	1/1 2/52 3/56	(9 wkts, 48 overs)	202
*Kapil Dev lbw b Gillespie	....	2	4/64 5/119 6/127		
Chetan Sharma not out	....	38	7/127 8/180 9/199		

Bowling: Hadlee 10–5–17–2; Chatfield 9–0–43–1; Gillespie 9–0–54–3; Snedden 10–0–46–2; M. D. Crowe 10–2–35–1.

New Zealand

J. J. Crowe c Kulkarni b Binny 3	M. C. Snedden c Binny b Kapil Dev . . 1
B. A. Edgar c More b Shastri 26	S. R. Gillespie not out 15
M. D. Crowe c and b Binny 10	E. J. Chatfield not out 0
J. F. Reid b Kulkarni 37	L-b 8, w 7 15
*J. V. Coney c Shastri b Kapil Dev . . 37	
R. J. Hadlee c Azharuddin b Chetan . . 5	1/7 2/27 3/48 (9 wkts, 45 overs) 168
B. R. Blair c Srikkanth b Binny 19	4/102 5/113 6/135
†E. B. McSweeney b Kapil Dev 0	7/135 8/147 9/163

Bowling: Kapil Dev 9-1-26-3; Binny 9-1-26-3; Chetan 9-1-35-1; Shastri 9-0-33-1; Kulkarni 9-0-40-1.

Umpires: A. R. Crafter and S. G. Randell.

QUALIFYING TABLE

	P	W	L	NR	Pts
Australia	10	6	3	1	13
India	10	5	5	0	10
New Zealand	10	3	6	1	7

†AUSTRALIA v INDIA

First Final Match

At Sydney, February 5 (day/night). Australia won by 11 runs. Excellent bowling, especially by Davis and Matthews, was Australia's greatest asset in a close rain-affected contest. The course of the match was also influenced by Gavaskar's dropping a slip chance in the first over. This not only reprieved Boon; it also damaged Gavaskar's finger, so preventing him from opening the Indian innings. Australia, put in, were 69 without loss when the ground was struck by a storm and it was a wonder that play restarted. Wickets fell rapidly, but Jones made an invaluable 30 not out. When India batted, Davis not only took two early wickets but also restricted the scoring, and the Indian rally, when it came, was cut short by Matthews.

Attendance: 26,559.

Australia

D. C. Boon c Malhotra b Shastri 50	C. J. McDermott run out 0
G. R. Marsh c Chetan b Azharuddin . . 36	B. A. Reid not out 4
D. M. Wellham b Amarnath 6	
*A. R. Border c Azharuddin b Shastri . . 12	B 1, l-b 6, w 2, n-b 4 13
D. M. Jones not out 30	
S. R. Waugh b Azharuddin 1	1/69 2/86 3/110 (8 wkts, 44 overs) 170
G. R. J. Matthews run out 7	4/118 5/122 6/135
†T. J. Zoehrer b Kapil Dev 11	7/164 8/164

S. P. Davis did not bat.

Bowling: Kapil Dev 9-2-21-1; Binny 7-0-30-0; Chetan 5-0-34-0; Amarnath 5-0-21-1; Shastri 9-0-31-2; Azharuddin 9-0-26-2.

India

R. J. Shastri c Zoehrer b Davis 8	Chetan Sharma not out 19
K. Srikkanth b Davis 0	R. M. H. Binny b Border 16
M. Amarnath c Marsh b Matthews 13	†K. S. More b Davis 2
D. B. Vengsarkar c Jones b Waugh 45	B 2, l-b 6, w 2, n-b 1 11
M. Azharuddin b Matthews 1	
S. M. Gavaskar c Jones b Border 32	1/4 2/11 3/40 (43.4 overs) 159
*Kapil Dev b Matthews 0	4/52 5/82 6/82
A. Malhotra c and b Border 12	7/112 8/126 9/149

Bowling: McDermott 5-0-26-0; Davis 7.4-3-10-3; Reid 9-2-34-0; Matthews 9-0-27-3; Waugh 8-1-31-1; Border 5-0-23-3.

Umpires: R. A. French and M. W. Johnson.

†AUSTRALIA v INDIA

Second Final Match

At Melbourne, February 9 (day/night). Australia won by seven wickets and so won the finals 2-0. The margin of victory was a true index of Australia's superiority in all departments. The pitch was damp and of poor quality but, considering that it provided ample turn, India with their two spin bowlers should have thrived. Put in, the Indians were bowled out for 187, four of their last six batsmen being run out and Amarnath being dismissed "handled the ball" (the first instance in a one-day international) after pushing away a turning ball from Matthews that spun back towards his wicket. Matthews accounted more directly for Srikkanth, with a spectacular return catch, and Vengsarkar, two of the three batsmen to contribute significantly. With Border scoring a commanding 65, Australia comfortably drove home the advantage of a sound start.

Man of the Finals: G. R. J. Matthews			*Attendance:* 72,192.

India

S. M. Gavaskar c Border b Davis	11	R. M. H. Binny c and b Reid	4
K. Srikkanth c and b Matthews	37	†K. S. More run out	1
M. Amarnath handled the ball	15	N. S. Yadav not out	1
D. B. Vengsarkar b Matthews	41	L-b 7, w 4, n-b 2	13
*Kapil Dev c Zoehrer b Reid	1		
M. Azharuddin run out	14		**(50 overs) 187**
R. J. Shastri run out	49		
Chetan Sharma run out	0		

1/34 2/66 3/70
4/71 5/108 6/151
7/151 8/163 9/168

Bowling: McDermott 10-0-35-0; Davis 10-1-23-1; Reid 10-0-37-2; Waugh 3-0-15-0; Matthews 10-1-37-2; Border 7-0-33-0.

Australia

G. R. Marsh lbw b Kapil Dev	9	D. M. Jones not out	19
D. C. Boon run out	44		
D. M. Wellham c Azharuddin		B 1, l-b 2, w 5	8
b Kapil Dev	43		
*A. R. Border not out	65	1/31 2/77 3/144	**(3 wkts, 47.2 overs) 188**

S. R. Waugh, G. R. J. Matthews, †T.J. Zoehrer, C. J. McDermott, B. A. Reid and S. P. Davis did not bat.

Bowling: Kapil Dev 9-1-26-2; Binny 2-0-13-0; Chetan 8.2-0-42-0; Azharuddin 8-0-37-0; Yadav 10-0-27-0; Shastri 10-1-40-0.

Umpires: A. R. Crafter and P. J. McConnell.

SHARJAH CHALLENGE CUP, 1985-86

West Indies, who were on their way to play a series of limited-overs internationals in Pakistan, met India and Pakistan in a $100,000 (approx. £75,000) round-robin tournament in Sharjah. They beat both countries to win the new Challenge Cup.

PAKISTAN v WEST INDIES

At Sharjah, November 15. West Indies won by seven wickets. Toss: Pakistan.

Pakistan

Mudassar Nazar c Logie b Holding ...	18	*Imran Khan not out	25
Mohsin Khan not out	86	B 1, l-b 6, w 4, n-b 3	14
Qasim Omar c Richards b Gray	2		—
Ramiz Raja c and b Garner..........	35	1/50 2/58 (4 wkts, 45 overs)	196
Javed Miandad b Marshall	16	3/142 4/161	

Salim Malik, †Salim Yousuf, Wasim Akram, Abdul Qadir and Tauseef Ahmed did not bat.

Bowling: Garner 9-1-59-1; Gray 8-1-32-1; Holding 5-0-17-1; Marshall 8-1-30-1; Harper 9-2-26-0; Richards 6-0-25-0.

West Indies

D. L. Haynes b Wasim	0	A. L. Logie not out	6
R. B. Richardson not out	99	L-b 8, n-b 3	11
H. A. Gomes c Yousuf b Mudassar ...	32		—
*I. V. A. Richards c Yousuf b Imran ..	51	1/0 2/72 3/177 (3 wkts, 44.1 overs)	199

†P. J. L. Dujon, M. D. Marshall, R. A. Harper, J. Garner, M. A. Holding and A. H. Gray did not bat.

Bowling: Wasim 8.1-1-40-1; Imran 9-0-41-1; Mudassar 9-0-32-1; Tauseef 9-1-38-0; Qadir 9-0-40-0.

Umpires: H. D. Bird and D. R. Shepherd.

INDIA v PAKISTAN

At Sharjah, November 17. Pakistan won by 48 runs. Toss: India.

Pakistan

Mudassar Nazar c Vengsarkar		Salim Malik not out	12
b Sivaramakrishnan .	67		
Mohsin Khan run out	2	L-b 8, w 1, n-b 1	10
Ramiz Raja c Gavaskar b Binny	66		—
Javed Miandad not out	37	1/18 2/118 (4 wkts, 45 overs)	203
*Imran Khan run out	9	3/169 4/185	

†Salim Yousuf, Mohsin Kamal, Wasim Akram, Abdul Qadir and Tauseef Ahmed did not bat.

Bowling: Kapil Dev 7-1-26-0; Binny 9-1-36-1; Chetan 7-1-40-0; Shastri 9-1-26-0; Sivaramakrishnan 9-0-40-1; Amarnath 4-0-27-0.

India

S. M. Gavaskar st Yousuf b Tauseef	63	Chetan Sharma b Mudassar	1
K. Srikkanth c Yousuf b Mohsin Kamal	4	†S. M. H. Kirmani not out	5
M. Azharuddin lbw b Wasim	3	L. Sivaramakrishnan run out	1
D. B. Vengsarkar c Malik b Tauseef	27		
R. J. Shastri run out	12	B 2, l-b 9, w 4, n-b 2	17
*Kapil Dev lbw b Tauseef	0		
M. Amarnath b Mudassar	11	1/9 2/28 3/84 (40.4 overs) 155	
R. M. H. Binny c Tauseef		4/115 5/118 6/129	
b Mohsin Kamal	11	7/135 8/139 9/151	

Bowling: Wasim 7.4–2–15–1; Mohsin Kamal 7–0–27–2; Mudassar 9–0–43–2; Imran 1.1–0–3–0; Qadir 6.5–0–26–0; Tauseef 9–2–30–3.

Umpires: H. D. Bird and D. R. Shepherd.

INDIA v WEST INDIES

At Sharjah, November 22. West Indies won by eight wickets. Toss: India.

India

*S. M. Gavaskar not out	76	Kapil Dev not out	28
K. Srikkanth b Garner	6		
M. Amarnath c Richards b Garner	0	L-b 17, w 4, n-b 8	29
D. B. Vengsarkar c Garner b Holding	6		
M. Azharuddin run out	35	1/10 2/11 3/25 4/125 (4 wkts, 45 overs) 180	

R. J. Shastri, R. M. H. Binny, †S. M. H. Kirmani, R. S. Ghai and L. Sivaramakrishnan did not bat.

Bowling: Marshall 9–2–35–0; Garner 9–4–11–2; Walsh 9–1–37–0; Holding 9–3–28–1; Harper 9–0–52–0.

West Indies

D. L. Haynes not out	72
R. B. Richardson b Ghai	72
H. A. Gomes b Kapil Dev	10
*I. V. A. Richards not out	24
L-b 8	8

1/114 2/147   (2 wkts, 41.3 overs) 186

A. L. Logie, †P. J. L. Dujon, M. D. Marshall, R. A. Harper, J. Garner, M. A. Holding and C. A. Walsh did not bat.

Bowling: Kapil Dev 8–1–29–1; Binny 7–0–36–0; Ghai 8.3–0–54–1; Shastri 9–1–27–0; Sivaramakrishnan 9–0–32–0.

Umpires: H. D. Bird and D. R. Shepherd.

ASIA CUP, 1985-86

By GERRY VAIDYASEKERA

The Second Asia Cup tournament, for the John Player Gold Leaf Trophy, was contested in Sri Lanka by the host country, Pakistan and Bangladesh. India, the 1983-84 champions, withdrew from the tournament and their place was taken by New Zealand, who did not participate in the Asia Cup itself but played in a concurrent Triangular Tournament, also sponsored by John Player, against Pakistan and Sri Lanka. Bangladesh won a place in the tournament as winners of the South-East Asian Cricket Conference Tournament which had been played in Dacca in February 1984.

For the first time in a country which was a full member of the ICC, neutral umpires stood in the matches. H. D. Bird and D. R. Shepherd of England, Mahboob Shah of Pakistan, and two local umpires, H. C. Felsinger and P. W. Vidanagamage, made up the five-man panel.

†SRI LANKA v PAKISTAN

At P. Saravanamuttu Stadium, Colombo, March 30. Pakistan won by 81 runs. Toss: Sri Lanka. This was Pakistan's eleventh victory in fifteen one-day internationals against Sri Lanka, who had won only two. Pakistan took control of the match as Mohsin and Ramiz added 69 off fourteen overs for the second wicket.
Man of the Match: Mohsin Khan.

Pakistan

Mudassar Nazar c de Silva b de Mel ..	15	Wasim Akram c sub b Ratnayeke 24
Mohsin Khan c and b Anurasiri	39	†Zulqarnain not out 11
Ramiz Raja c Kuruppu b Ratnayeke ..	26	Zakir Khan b Ratnayeke 1
Javed Miandad c Dias b Anurasiri	9	
Qasim Omar st Kuruppu b Ranatunga .	16	B 5, l-b 7, w 2, n-b 1 15
Manzoor Elahi c Kuruppu b Ranatunga	6	
*Imran Khan c de Silva b de Mel	21	1/18 2/87 3/87 4/108 (45 overs) 197
Abdul Qadir c Anurasiri b Amalean	14	5/118 6/119 7/141 8/179 9/187

Bowling: de Mel 9-1-40-2; Amalean 7-1-30-1; Ratnayeke 9-1-32-3; Samarasekera 2-0-19-0; Anurasiri 9-1-27-2; Ranatunga 9-0-37-2.

Sri Lanka

†D. S. B. P. Kuruppu c and b Qadir ..	34	A. L. F. de Mel c Zulqarnain b Manzoor 0
M. A. R. Samarasekera c Imran b Zakir	5	S. D. Anurasiri c Imran b Qadir 5
A. P. Gurusinha c Zulqarnain b Zakir .	8	K. N. Amalean c Imran b Qadir 9
R. L. Dias c Miandad b Zakir	0	
A. Ranatunga c Zulqarnain b Manzoor .	7	B 4, l-b 3, w 7 14
*L. R. D. Mendis c Zulqarnain b Imran	0	
P. A. de Silva c Miandad b Manzoor ..	12	1/24 2/32 3/32 4/52 (33.5 overs) 116
J. R. Ratnayeke not out	22	5/53 6/67 7/83 8/94 9/105

Bowling: Wasim 6-1-17-0; Zakir 6-0-34-3; Manzoor 9-1-22-3; Imran 5-0-12-1; Qadir 7.5-1-24-3.

Umpires: H. D. Bird and D. R. Shepherd.

†BANGLADESH v PAKISTAN

At Moratuwa, March 31. Pakistan won by seven wickets. Toss: Pakistan. This was Bangladesh's first one-day match against a full member of the ICC.
Man of the Match: Wasim Akram.

Bangladesh

Raquibul Hassan c Zulqarnain b Zakir	5	Jahangir Badsha b Wasim	0
Nurul Abedin c Zulqarnain b Imran	0	†Hafizur Rahman b Imran	8
*Ashraf Hossain b Wasim	0	Ghulam Nowsher not out	1
Minhazul Abedin c Manzoor b Wasim	6	Samiur Rahman st Zulqarnain b Qadir	0
Shaheedur Rahman c and b Qadir	37	L-b 4, w 4, n-b 1	9
Rafiqul Alam c Ramiz b Wasim	14		
Farooque Chowdhury c Zulqarnain		1/3 2/4 3/15 4/27 5/68	(35.3 overs) 94
b Qadir	14	6/70 7/79 8/93 9/93	

Bowling: Imran 7-3-11-2; Wasim 9-2-19-4; Zakir 7-1-27-1; Manzoor 5-1-18-0; Qadir 7.3-1-15-3.

Pakistan

Mudassar Nazar not out	47	Qasim Omar not out	3
Mohsin Khan lbw b Jahangir	28	L-b 4, w 1	5
Ramiz Raja lbw b Jahangir	0		
Javed Miandad c Hafizur b Ashraf	15	1/44 2/53 3/85	(3 wkts, 32.1 overs) 98

Manzoor Elahi, *Imran Khan, Abdul Qadir, Wasim Akram, †Zulqarnain and Zakir Khan did not bat.

Bowling: Ghulam 7-1-32-0; Samiur 7-1-15-0; Chowdhury 6-0-13-0; Jahangir 9-1-23-2; Ashraf 3-0-7-1; Raquibul 0.1-0-4-0.

Umpires: H. C. Felsinger and P. W. Vidanagamage.

†SRI LANKA v BANGLADESH

At Kandy, April 2. Sri Lanka won by seven wickets. Toss: Sri Lanka. Bangladesh scored only 49 in the first twenty overs. For Sri Lanka Gurusinha (89 balls) and Ranatunga put on the last 68 runs off 11.3 overs.
Man of the Match: A. P. Gurusinha.

Bangladesh

Raquibul Hassan lbw b Ranatunga	12	Jahangir Badsha run out	1
Nurul Abedin c Mahanama b Ratnayeke	13	Samiur Rahman c Dias b Amalean	4
*Ashraf Hossain c Kuruppu b Ranatunga	10	Ghulam Nowsher not out	3
Minhazul Abedin run out	40	B 1, l-b 4, w 3, n-b 2	10
Shaheedur Rahman c Mendis			
b Ratnayeke	25	1/26 2/29 3/49	(8 wkts, 45 overs) 131
Rafiqul Alam b Amalean	10	4/92 5/119 6/119	
Farooque Chowdhury not out	3	7/120 8/126	

†Hafizur Rahman did not bat.

Bowling: de Mel 9-1-30-0; Amalean 9-2-15-2; Ratnayeke 9-1-41-2; Ranatunga 9-1-17-2; Anurasiri 9-2-23-0.

Sri Lanka

†D. S. B. P. Kuruppu c Samiur b Ghulam	3	A. Ranatunga not out	41
R. S. Mahanama c Hafizur b Chowdhury	25	B 3, l-b 7, w 9	19
A. P. Gurusinha not out	44		
R. L. Dias c Raquibul b Ashraf	0	1/8 2/63 3/64 (3 wkts, 31.3 overs)	132

*L. R. D. Mendis, P. A. de Silva, J. R. Ratnayeke, A. L. F. de Mel, S. D. Anurasiri and K. N. Amalean did not bat.

Bowling: Ghulam 9–0–45–1; Samiur 3–0–15–0; Jahangir 6–0–18–0; Chowdhury 8.3–2–22–1; Ashraf 5–0–22–1.

Umpires: Mahboob Shah and D. R. Shepherd.

---

†SRI LANKA v NEW ZEALAND

At Ketterama Stadium, Colombo, April 5. New Zealand won by six wickets. Toss: New Zealand. In their first match of the Triangular Tournament, the New Zealand seam bowlers kept Sri Lanka's strokemakers in check throughout. Rutherford hit 34 off 45 balls and put on 62 for the first wicket with Wright in 15.1 overs.

Man of the Match: M. C. Snedden.

Sri Lanka

†D. S. B. P. Kuruppu c McSweeney		J. R. Ratnayeke not out	22
b Snedden .	23	C. P. Ramanayake run out	0
R. S. Mahanama lbw b Snedden	12	S. D. Anurasiri run out	0
A. P. Gurusinha c J. J. Crowe b Watson	14	B 8, l-b 5, n-b 2	15
A. Ranatunga c McSweeney b Snedden .	23		
*L. R. D. Mendis c Gray b Bracewell	24	1/39 2/40 3/79 (9 wkts, 43 overs)	137
P. A. de Silva c J. J. Crowe b Watson .	4	4/88 5/96 6/96	
S. K. Ranasinghe c Gray b Watson ...	0	7/130 8/136 9/137	

K. N. Amalean did not bat.

Bowling: Robertson 8–2–26–0; Watson 9–2–15–3; Gray 9–0–15–0; Snedden 9–1–26–3; Bracewell 8–0–42–1.

New Zealand

K. R. Rutherford c Mahanama		J. G. Bracewell not out	16
b Ratnayeke .	34		
*J. G. Wright c and b Ranatunga	24	B 4, l-b 8, w 3, n-b 1	16
M. D. Crowe c Mahanama b Ranatunga	4		
J. J. Crowe run out	21	1/62 2/71 3/72 (4 wkts, 36.2 overs)	140
T. E. Blain not out	25	4/110	

†E. B. McSweeney, G. K. Robertson, W. Watson, E. J. Gray and M. C. Snedden did not bat.

Bowling: Amalean 7–0–29–0; Ramanayake 3–0–20–0; Ratnayeke 7–1–24–1; Anurasiri 9–1–19–0; Ranatunga 6–0–17–2; Ranasinghe 2–0–7–0; de Silva 2.2–0–12–0.

Umpires: H. D. Bird and Mahboob Shah.

---

†SRI LANKA v PAKISTAN

Asia Cup Final

At Sinhalese Sports Club, Colombo, April 6. Sri Lanka won by five wickets to win the John Player Gold Leaf Trophy. Toss: Sri Lanka. In response to the requests of the large crowd, the President of Sri Lanka, Mr J. R. Jayawardene, declared a public holiday to commemorate the victory. Pakistan were 72 for five after 26 overs, but Miandad gave the innings substance with a chanceless 67 (four 4s) off 100 balls. The last nine overs yielded 91 runs. With Imran off the field because of a leg injury, Sri Lanka made a steady start. The loss of three wickets set them back before de Silva and Ranatunga added 97 off 16.1 overs. Ranatunga's 57 came off 65 balls, de Silva's 52 off 66 balls. The match was considered to be part of the Triangular Tournament.

Man of the Match: Javed Miandad.　　　　*Man of the Series:* A. Ranatunga.

Pakistan

Mudassar Nazar b de Mel	2	Wasim Akram c Gurusinha b Amalean.	6
Mohsin Khan run out	7	†Zulqarnain not out	1
Ramiz Raja c Mahanama b Amalean	2		
Javed Miandad c Ratnayeke b Amalean	67	L-b 4, w 8, n-b 2	14
*Imran Khan lbw b Ratnayeke	2		
Salim Malik c and b Anurasiri	23	1/7 2/10 3/24　　(9 wkts, 45 overs)	191
Manzoor Elahi b Amalean	37	4/32 5/72 6/137	
Abdul Qadir c de Mel b Ratnayeke	30	7/179 8/185 9/191	

Zakir Khan did not bat.

Bowling: de Mel 9-2-21-1; Amalean 9-1-46-4; Ratnayeke 8-0-50-2; Ranatunga 9-1-27-0; Anurasiri 9-0-24-1; de Silva 1-0-19-0.

Sri Lanka

†D. S. B. P. Kuruppu c Malik b Qadir	30	R. L. Dias not out	0
R. S. Mahanama c Qadir b Manzoor	21		
A. P. Gurusinha c Zulqarnain b Qadir	4	B 1, l-b 6, w 2	9
P. A. de Silva c sub b Mudassar	52		
A. Ranatunga c Mohsin b Qadir	57	1/40 2/59 3/64　　(5 wkts, 42.2 overs)	195
*L. R. D. Mendis not out	22	4/161 5/191	

J. R. Ratnayeke, A. L. F. de Mel, S. D. Anurasiri and K. N. Amalean did not bat.

Bowling: Wasim 7.2-2-22-0; Zakir 6-0-36-0; Manzoor 9-0-30-1; Qadir 9-0-32-3; Malik 3-0-19-0; Mudassar 8-0-49-1.

Umpires: H. D. Bird and D. R. Shepherd.

†NEW ZEALAND v PAKISTAN

At Sinhalese Sports Club, Colombo, April 7. Pakistan won by four wickets. Toss: Pakistan. As Sri Lanka, Pakistan and New Zealand each won a match, Pakistan were adjudged champions of the Triangular Tournament by virtue of their faster run-rate.

Man of the Match: M. D. Crowe.　　　　*Man of the Tournament:* Javed Miandad.

New Zealand

K. R. Rutherford c Tauseef b Wasim	9	†T. E. Blain b Mohsin Kamal	0
*J. G. Wright st Zulqarnain b Tauseef	42	E. J. Gray b Wasim	1
M. D. Crowe c Manzoor b Mohsin Kamal	75	M. C. Snedden not out	2
J. J. Crowe run out	42	B 1, l-b 14, w 6	21
B. R. Blair c Zulqarnain b Mohsin Kamal	0		
G. K. Robertson c Zulqarnain b Mohsin Kamal	7	1/16 2/102 3/181　　(8 wkts, 42 overs)	214
		4/182 5/194 6/202	
J. G. Bracewell not out	15	7/202 8/211	

E. J. Chatfield did not bat.

Bowling: Wasim 9-2-19-2; Mohsin Kamal 8-0-47-4; Manzoor 9-0-33-0; Qadir 9-1-51-0; Tauseef 6-0-38-1; Mudassar 1-0-11-0.

Pakistan

Mudassar Nazar run out	20	Abdul Qadir not out	11
Mohsin Khan c Snedden b Chatfield	16	Wasim Akram not out	8
Ramiz Raja c Blair b Gray	25	L-b 10	10
*Javed Miandad b Snedden	68		
Salim Malik run out	32	1/31 2/42 3/110 (6 wkts, 40.4 overs) 217	
Manzoor Elahi c M. D. Crowe b Snedden	27	4/162 5/173 6/206	

†Zulqarnain, Tauseef Ahmed and Mohsin Kamal did not bat.

Bowling: Chatfield 9–4–18–1; Robertson 7–0–39–0; Snedden 7.4–0–56–2; M. D. Crowe 3–0–21–0; Bracewell 9–0–41–0; Gray 5–0–32–1.

Umpires: H. C. Felsinger and P. W. Vidanagamage.

THE CRICKETER CUP WINNERS, 1967-1986

Sponsored by The Cricketer

1967   REPTON PILGRIMS   beat Radley Rangers by 96 runs.

Final Sponsored by Champagne Mercier

1968	OLD MALVERNIANS	beat Harrow Wanderers by five wickets.
1969	OLD BRIGHTONIANS	beat Stowe Templars by 156 runs.
1970	OLD WYKEHAMISTS	beat Old Tonbridgians by 94 runs.

Final Sponsored by Moët & Chandon

1971	OLD TONBRIDGIANS	beat Charterhouse Friars on faster scoring-rate.
1972	OLD TONBRIDGIANS	beat Old Malvernians by 114 runs.
1973	RUGBY METEORS	beat Old Tonbridgians by five wickets.
1974	OLD WYKEHAMISTS	beat Old Alleynians on faster scoring-rate.
1975	OLD MALVERNIANS	beat Harrow Wanderers by 97 runs.
1976	OLD TONBRIDGIANS	beat Old Blundellians by 170 runs.
1977	SHREWSBURY SARACENS	beat Oundle Rovers by nine wickets.
1978	CHARTERHOUSE FRIARS	beat Oundle Rovers by nine wickets.
1979	OLD TONBRIDGIANS	beat Uppingham Rovers by 5 runs.
1980	MARLBOROUGH BLUES	beat Old Wellingtonians by 31 runs.
1981	CHARTERHOUSE FRIARS	beat Old Wykehamists by nine wickets.
1982	OLD WYKEHAMISTS	beat Old Malvernians on faster scoring-rate.
1983	REPTON PILGRIMS	beat Haileybury Hermits by seven wickets.
1984	OLD TONBRIDGIANS	beat Old Malvernians by seven wickets.
1985	OUNDLE ROVERS	beat Repton Pilgrims by three wickets.
1986	OLD MALVERNIANS	beat Downside Wanderers by six wickets.

From 1967 to 1983 the final was played at Burton Court, Chelsea. Since then, it has been played at Vincent Square, Westminster.

AUSTRAL-ASIA CUP, 1985-86

By QAMAR AHMED

The first Austral-Asia Cup tournament, played in Sharjah in April as part of the Cricketers' Benefit Fund Series, was won by Pakistan off the last ball of the final against India. With 4 runs needed to win, Javed Miandad struck Chetan Sharma's final delivery for his third 6.

India, put in to bat, were given an excellent start by Gavaskar, Srikkanth and Vengsarkar, who put on 200 for the loss of only one wicket. However, they slumped from 216 for two to 245 for seven when Imran Khan and Wasim Akram returned to the attack. Pakistan's requirement of just under 5 an over drifted to 9 with ten overs remaining, but Miandad and Abdul Qadir picked up the rate in their fifth-wicket stand of 71 and Miandad kept the impetus going with exciting running between the wickets. His 110, as he faced the final ball from Chetan Sharma, contained only two 6s and two 4s, but with India's field set to prevent a third 4, he won the match in the most dramatic manner. It was Pakistan's first major success in a limited-overs tournament and they won $40,000 in prizemoney.

Five countries participated in the tournament: Australia, New Zealand and Sri Lanka, in addition to India and Pakistan. Sri Lanka, as winners of the Asia Cup, qualified automatically for the semi-finals, where they were joined by the winners of the first-round matches, India and Pakistan, plus New Zealand, who went through as the first-round loser with the lesser margin of defeat. Following a practice established in previous competitions in Sharjah, neutral umpires were employed, D. M. Archer and A. Gaynor, from West Indies, standing in all five matches.

The beneficiaries of the tournament were Vijay Hazare, Javed Miandad, Dilip Vengsarkar and Wazir Mohammad.

†INDIA v NEW ZEALAND

At Sharjah, April 10. India won by three wickets. Toss: India. Rain delayed the start of the match by one hour.
Man of the Match: E. J. Chatfield.

New Zealand

K. R. Rutherford b Maninder	12	G. K. Robertson b Azad	0
M. C. Snedden c Patil b Maninder	26	†E. B. McSweeney not out	18
M. D. Crowe lbw b Madan Lal	1		
*J. J. Crowe not out	36	L-b 12	12
T. E. Blain c Patil b Maninder	0		
B. R. Blair run out	0	1/37 2/42 3/48 (8 wkts, 44 overs) 132
J. G. Bracewell b Shastri	25	4/48 5/48 6/81
E. J. Gray b Shastri	2	7/95 8/96

E. J. Chatfield did not bat.

Bowling: Kapil Dev 6–3–7–0; Binny 5–0–12–0; Madan Lal 7–1–12–1; Maninder 9–0–23–3; Shastri 9–0–25–2; Azad 8–0–41–1.

India

S. M. Gavaskar c McSweeney b Chatfield	0	†C. S. Pandit not out 33
K. Srikkanth c Blair b Chatfield	11	Madan Lal not out 8
M. Azharuddin c and b Chatfield	6	L-b 5 5
S. M. Patil b M. D. Crowe	7	
R. J. Shastri st McSweeney b Gray	25	1/0 2/8 3/19 (7 wkts, 41.4 overs) 134
K. Azad b Bracewell	30	4/25 5/81
*Kapil Dev c Blain b Snedden	9	6/81 7/116

R. M. H. Binny and Maninder Singh did not bat.

Bowling: Chatfield 9–5–14–3; Robertson 4–0–13–0; M. D. Crowe 5–1–16–1; Snedden 7–1–24–1; Bracewell 9–1–34–1; Gray 7.4–1–28–1.

Umpires: D. M. Archer and A. Gaynor.

†AUSTRALIA v PAKISTAN

At Sharjah, April 11. Pakistan won by eight wickets. Toss: Australia.
Man of the Match: Mudassar Nazar.

Australia

D. C. Boon c Mohsin Khan b Tauseef	44	C. J. McDermott run out 1
G. R. Marsh c Mudassar b Qadir	26	†T. J. Zoehrer run out 5
D. M. Jones lbw b Tauseef	8	L-b 10, w 1, n-b 1 12
G. M. Ritchie not out	60	
S. R. Waugh c Zulqarnain b Wasim ...	26	1/63 2/79 3/90 (7 wkts, 50 overs) 202
G. R. J. Matthews c Miandad		4/140 5/195
b Mohsin Kamal .	20	6/197 7/202

*R. J. Bright, B. A. Reid and S. P. Davis did not bat.

Bowling: Wasim 10–0–38–1; Mohsin Kamal 10–0–51–1; Manzoor 10–0–58–0; Tauseef 10–1–19–2; Qadir 10–0–26–1.

Pakistan

Mudassar Nazar b Reid 95
Mohsin Khan lbw b Bright 46
Ramiz Raja not out 56
Manzoor Elahi not out 2
    L-b 5, w 2 7

1/80 2/195   (2 wkts, 49.1 overs) 206

*Javed Miandad, Salim Malik, Abdul Qadir, Wasim Akram, Tauseef Ahmed, †Zulqarnain and Mohsin Kamal did not bat.

Bowling: McDermott 10–2–29–0; Davis 8–2–28–0; Reid 9.1–0–51–1; Waugh 6–1–25–0; Bright 10–1–28–1; Matthews 6–0–40–0.

Umpires: D. M. Archer and A. Gaynor.

SEMI-FINALS

†INDIA v SRI LANKA

At Sharjah, April 13. India won by three wickets. Toss: India.
Man of the Match: S. M. Gavaskar.

Sri Lanka

R. S. Mahanama c Patil b Chetan	 9	R. J. Ratnayake c Azad b Chetan	 1
P. A. de Silva c Maninder b Chetan	... 5	J. R. Ratnayeke run out	 3
A. P. Gurusinghe b Azad	 68	S. D. Anurasiri not out	 2
R. L. Dias b Maninder	 9		
*L. R. D. Mendis c Azharuddin		B 1, l-b 12, n-b 1	 14
b Madan Lal . 32			
A. Ranatunga run out	 28	1/8 2/20 3/58	(9 wkts, 50 overs) 205
†R. G. de Alwis run out	 19	4/129 5/135 6/165	
A. L. F. de Mel not out	 15	7/188 8/195 9/201	

Bowling: Kapil Dev 10–1–39–0; Chetan 9–1–35–3; Madan Lal 8–0–40–1; Maninder 10–2–19–1; Shastri 8–0–40–0; Azad 5–0–19–1.

India

S. M. Gavaskar c de Silva b de Mel	... 71	†C. S. Pandit run out	 2
K. Srikkanth st de Alwis b Anurasiri	.. 59	Madan Lal not out	 1
M. Azharuddin b de Mel	 30	B 1, l-b 6, n-b 1	 8
S. M. Patil b de Mel	 10		
K. Azad c Gurusinghe b Anurasiri	 1	1/93 2/165 3/170	(7 wkts, 49.1 overs) 206
*Kapil Dev c Dias b Anurasiri	 3	4/171 5/175	
R. J. Shastri not out	 21	6/191 7/194	

Chetan Sharma and Maninder Singh did not bat.

Bowling: de Mel 10–0–40–3; Ratnayake 9.1–0–36–0; Anurasiri 10–0–40–3; Ratnayeke 10–0–38–0; de Silva 3–0–9–0; Ranatunga 7–0–36–0.

Umpires: D. M. Archer and A. Gaynor.

†NEW ZEALAND v PAKISTAN

At Sharjah, April 15. Pakistan won by ten wickets. Toss: Pakistan.
Man of the Match: Abdul Qadir.

New Zealand

K. R. Rutherford c Miandad b Imran .	2	E. J. Chatfield c sub (Qasim Omar)	
M. C. Snedden b Wasim	 0	b Manzoor . 2	
M. D. Crowe c Qadir b Wasim	 9	W. Watson not out	 1
*J. J. Crowe c Zulqarnain b Wasim	... 1		
E. J. Gray b Manzoor	 17	B 1, l-b 5, w 8, n-b 2	 16
B. R. Blair b Qadir	 9		
J. G. Bracewell b Qadir	 0	1/4 2/15 3/18	(35.5 overs) 64
T. E. Blain b Qadir	 0	4/32 5/32 6/32	
†E. B. McSweeney c Wasim b Qadir	... 7	7/32 8/48 9/55	

Bowling: Imran 7–2–11–1; Wasim 7–3–10–3; Qadir 10–4–9–4; Tauseef 10–2–20–0; Manzoor 1.5–0–8–2.

Pakistan

Mudassar Nazar not out 32
Mohsin Khan not out 34

(no wkt, 22.4 overs) 66

Ramiz Raja, Javed Miandad, Salim Malik, *Imran Khan, Manzoor Elahi, Abdul Qadir, Wasim Akram, Tauseef Ahmed and †Zulqarnain did not bat.

Bowling: Chatfield 3–2–3–0; Watson 7–0–15–0; Gray 8.4–3–22–0; Bracewell 4–0–26–0.

Umpires: D. M. Archer and A. Gaynor.

FINAL

†INDIA v PAKISTAN

At Sharjah, April 18. Pakistan won by one wicket. Toss: Pakistan.
Man of the Match: Javed Miandad.　　　*Man of the Tournament:* S. M. Gavaskar.

India

K. Srikkanth c Wasim b Qadir 75	†C. S. Pandit not out 0		
S. M. Gavaskar b Imran 92			
D. B. Vengsarkar b Wasim 50	L-b 6, w 2, n-b 1 9		
K. Azad b Wasim 0			
*Kapil Dev b Imran 8	1/117 2/216 3/216　(7 wkts, 50 overs) 245		
Chetan Sharma run out 10	4/229 5/242		
R. J. Shastri b Wasim 1	6/245 7/245		

M. Azharuddin, Madan Lal and Maninder Singh did not bat.

Bowling: Imran 10–2–40–2; Wasim 10–1–42–3; Manzoor 5–0–33–0; Mudassar 5–0–32–0; Qadir 10–2–49–1; Tauseef 10–1–43–0.

Pakistan

Mudassar Nazar lbw b Chetan 5	Wasim Akram run out 3
Mohsin Khan b Madan Lal 36	†Zulqarnain b Chetan 0
Ramiz Raja b Maninder 10	Tauseef Ahmed not out 1
Javed Miandad not out 116	
Salim Malik run out 21	L-b 11 11
Abdul Qadir c sub (R. Lamba)	
b Kapil Dev . 34	1/9 2/39 3/61　　(9 wkts, 50 overs) 248
*Imran Khan b Madan Lal 7	4/110 5/181 6/209
Manzoor Elahi c Shastri b Chetan 4	7/215 8/235 9/241

Bowling: Kapil Dev 10–1–45–1; Chetan 9–0–51–3; Madan Lal 10–0–53–2; Maninder 10–0–36–1; Shastri 9–0–38–0; Azharuddin 2–0–14–0.

Umpires: D. M. Archer and A. Gaynor.

CRICKET IN AUSTRALIA, 1985-86

By JOHN MACKINNON

New South Wales won the Sheffield Shield for the second consecutive year, doing so in a manner similar to their success in 1984-85. As then it was their tail-end batsmen who thwarted Queensland in the final, though this time, instead of scoring the winning runs, they batted through the last nine overs to draw a match which the Queenslanders had to win if they were to take the Shield for the first time. New South Wales retained the trophy by virtue of finishing at the top of the table and had every reason to be satisfied with their performance. Only three players had appeared in the previous year's final, the others having dispersed variously to New Zealand, South Africa and Pakistan; or, in the case of Peter Clifford, been omitted.

As the composition of the New South Wales team would suggest, the Sheffield Shield competition of 1985-86 could be described as a contest of the reserves. States were affected not only by the demands of Test matches and one-day internationals, both at home and in New Zealand, but also by the defections to South Africa. South Australia and Western Australia each called upon twenty players for the ten-match programme, and no team used fewer than eighteen. It was especially unfortunate that both the Sheffield Shield final and the McDonald's Cup final were contested in the absence of players required by their country. The Australian Cricket Board recognised this, and it was hoped that in 1986-87 the state teams would see more of their international representatives.

In 1984-85, the Board lengthened the playing time of a Sheffield Shield day to six and a half hours. However, this had no significant effect on the number of outright results obtained and for the season under review the playing time was reduced back to six hours a day. In addition, the points gained for an outright win were reduced from twelve to eight; though in the event there were neither more nor fewer outright wins than there had been the previous season.

In Mark Taylor and Steve Small, New South Wales had two capable opening batsmen. Taylor, a solidly built left-hander, went close to 1,000 first-class runs in his first year. The middle-order batting, however, gave cause for concern, especially when Greg Matthews and Stephen Waugh were required by Australia. Neither Dirk Wellham nor Peter Clifford found his touch consistently, and it was as well for New South Wales that Greg Dyer's batting complemented his wicket-keeping skills. Mark O'Neill came into the side midway through the campaign and hit three consecutive hundreds, though a month separated the second and third of them. Of the bowlers, Murray Bennett and Bob Holland were effective when the SCG pitch favoured spin, and Mike Whitney made a timely return to form when Geoff Lawson was out with a back injury.

Queensland again looked back on their season as one of missed opportunities, especially so as it was the last for both Jeff Thomson and Kepler Wessels. Queensland's bowling resources were thin and Thomson will not be easily replaced. He was by some way their leading wicket-taker, although in his quest for speed he bowled 205 no-balls. Glen Trimble bowled effectively at medium pace, Harry Frei was versatile, but the selection of 44-year-old Malcolm Francke was not a progressive move. Having decided not to play in

Test cricket, Wessels played in all the Shield matches and his batting generally compensated for the frequent absences of Allan Border. He was well supported by Trimble and Andrew Courtice, but Robbie Kerr promised more than he achieved. Ray Phillips kept wicket to the highest standard and was again the country's leading wicket-keeper with 42 dismissals.

Victoria had the most settled side in the competition. Paul Hibbert and Dav Whatmore had very good seasons, Michael Quinn and Jamie Siddons were the best of the younger players, but Dean Jones, after a lean start, was inconsistent and had a relatively disappointing season. Of the bowlers, Simon Davis and Merv Hughes were a strong opening pair, and when Davis was called up for Australia, Dennis Hickey bowled fast and looked a good prospect. With the MCG wicket conducive to spin, Ray Bright bowled steadily to win back his Test place.

The Western Australians were unhappy about their relaid pitch at the WACA ground, and only at the end of the season did it win the batsmen's confidence. Graeme Wood, out of Test match contention, had a prolific year, hitting three hundreds after moving to number four in the order. Geoff Marsh batted well at number three for Western Australia and became Australia's opener, and Mike Veletta realised his potential with two hundreds and six fifties. The faster bowlers did especially well. Bruce Reid was drafted into the Test side for the series against the Indians and at 6ft 8in became Australia's tallest player; another tall left-armer, Chris Matthews, produced some effective spells; and Ken MacLeay was among the country's leading wicket-takers. Tim Zoehrer, a fine wicket-keeper, was rewarded with selection for Australia in the World Series Cup finals and later won his first cap in New Zealand.

South Australia had another disappointing year. Having failed to lure Joel Garner from Barbados, they recruited Gladstone Small of Warwickshire. He bowled at a lively pace but, apart from the steady seam bowling of Andrew Zesers, lacked support. The batting, too, was inconsistent. David Hookes earned a temporary recall to the Test team with some boisterous innings, Glen Bishop won a reputation as a second-innings specialist, and Peter Sleep returned after a year's absence to give some sound performances. Andrew Hilditch, however, faded badly and was omitted from the side in mid-season. Jamie Pyke came in for the last match and looked to be an all-rounder of promise. It was hoped that John Inverarity's appointment as coach would bring more stability.

Tasmania again had a poor season. David Boon's absence from all but three matches was a serious loss. Much was expected of the West Indian fast bowler, Winston Davis, but Roger Brown was the only other bowler of substance and often carried the attack single-handed.

The 1985-86 season was always going to be a struggle and so it proved. The loss of fifteen players to South Africa affected both the Test team and the state teams, and while playing standards were open to criticism, so too were some of the pitches. In Perth, the new WACA pitch was nowhere near ready for first-class cricket; in Sydney, the pitch continued to favour spin bowlers, at least until the New Year; and the MCG was equally helpful to spin on the first day because of excessive watering in its preparation. However, the Adelaide Oval produced a splendid pitch and was a credit to the curator, Les Burdett.

The umpires did not have an easy time. The incidence of players being reported for various misdemeanours, mainly dissent, was on the increase, and unhappily it was often the senior players who were involved. The players' tribunal has become a thing of the past, but a more responsible attitude by some captains would be a help.

If the performance of the Test team reflected the state of the domestic competition, then the Sheffield Shield can only get better. Australia have some fine young players on the threshold of international cricket, yet on the evidence of the 1985-86 season the gap in the standard between state and Test cricket has grown wider. Players such as Kerr, Trimble and Hookes have great state records, but have failed when playing for Australia. In all, the national selectors chose 24 players for eighteen representative matches. Access to the coveted green cap has become, perhaps, too readily available. The players need a better grounding for cricket at the highest level and the Sheffield Shield must involve the top players more if it is to fulfil that required role.

FIRST-CLASS AVERAGES, 1985-86

BATTING

(Qualification: 500 runs)

	M	I	NO	R	HI	100s	Avge
M. D. O'Neill (*NSW*)	6	9	2	588	178*	3	84.00
A. R. Border (*Qld*)	11	19	2	1,247	194	6	73.35
G. M. Wood (*WA*)	10	15	3	741	133	3	61.75
P. A. Hibbert (*Vic*)	10	16	3	694	148	3	53.38
G. R. J. Matthews (*NSW*)	11	19	2	890	184	4	52.35
G. R. Marsh (*WA*)	8	14	3	563	176	2	51.18
D. C. Boon (*Tas*)	9	17	1	818	196	3	51.12
M. A. Taylor (*NSW*)	12	20	1	937	118	2	49.31
K. C. Wessels (*Qld*)	13	22	1	1,030	167	3	49.04
G. A. Bishop (*SA*)	11	21	1	965	224*	3	48.25
D. W. Hookes (*SA*)	12	22	1	1,001	243	3	47.66
M. R. J. Veletta (*WA*)	10	16	1	715	130	2	47.66
P. R. Sleep (*SA*)	12	22	4	793	139	3	44.05
G. M. Ritchie (*Qld*)	11	20	3	738	128	1	43.41
S. M. Small (*NSW*)	9	14	0	605	123	2	43.21
D. J. Buckingham (*Tas*) ...	10	18	1	687	121	1	40.41
D. F. Whatmore (*Vic*)	11	18	1	676	127	2	39.76
G. S. Trimble (*Qld*)	11	19	3	606	112	1	37.87
D. M. Jones (*Vic*)	11	17	1	603	113	1	37.68
B. A. Courtice (*Qld*)	12	20	3	614	112	2	36.11
J. D. Siddons (*Vic*)	11	16	0	540	107	1	33.75
G. C. Dyer (*NSW*)	12	17	2	503	88*	0	33.53
R. B. Kerr (*Qld*)	12	20	1	609	102	1	32.05
M. B. Quinn (*Vic*)	11	18	0	535	103	1	29.72
D. M. Wellham (*NSW*) ...	12	19	0	562	86	0	29.57
R. J. Zadow (*SA*)	11	20	1	540	144	2	28.42

*Signifies not out.

BOWLING

(Qualification: 20 wickets)

	O	M	R	W	BB	Avge
M. R. Whitney (*NSW*)	195.3	43	483	22	6-75	21.95
S. P. Davis (*Vic*)	243.1	74	550	25	6-19	22.00
C. D. Matthews (*WA*)	283.2	62	757	31	5-23	24.42
G. F. Lawson (*NSW*)	248.5	64	513	21	4-79	24.43
K. H. MacLeay (*WA*)	378.4	99	913	35	6-93	26.09
G. S. Trimble (*Qld*)	263.2	59	759	29	5-50	26.17
M. J. Bennett (*NSW*)	446.1	144	877	32	4-38	27.41
D. R. Gilbert (*NSW*)	290.3	62	794	28	4-16	28.36
B. A. Reid (*WA*)	367.1	99	875	30	6-54	29.17
M. G. Hughes (*Vic*)	390	77	1,125	37	5-53	30.41
G. C. Small (*SA*)	415.4	74	1,244	39	7-42	31.90
G. R. J. Matthews (*NSW*)	274.4	82	639	20	5-22	31.95
R. G. Holland (*NSW*)	661.4	214	1,555	48	8-33	32.40
A. K. Zesers (*SA*)	563.3	169	1,309	40	6-73	32.73
J. R. Thomson (*Qld*)	372.3	42	1,385	42	6-72	32.98
R. L. Brown (*Tas*)	384.2	61	1,365	41	7-80	33.29
S. D. H. Parkinson (*SA*)...	261.3	52	913	27	6-56	33.81
W. W. Davis (*Tas*)	287.5	65	768	22	7-128	34.91
R. J. Bright (*Vic*)	499.5	170	1,024	27	6-74	37.93
H. Frei (*Qld*)	449.4	103	1,216	32	4-71	38.00
C. J. McDermott (*Qld*)	309.4	64	867	22	4-116	39.41

SHEFFIELD SHIELD, 1985-86

	Played	Won	Drawn	Lost	1st Inns Pts	Pts
New South Wales	10	4	5	1	24	56
Queensland	10	4	6	0	20*	54
Victoria	10	2	7	1	32	48
Western Australia	10	2	7	1	24*	42
South Australia	10	2	4	4	12	28
Tasmania	10	0	3	7	4	4

Outright win = 8 pts; lead on first innings = 4 pts.

* *First-innings points shared in one match.*

SOUTH AUSTRALIA v WESTERN AUSTRALIA

At Adelaide, October 17, 18, 19, 20. Drawn. Western Australia 4 pts. Western Australia, set a target of 276 at 5½ runs an over to gain outright points, soon gave up the chase and the match ended with the captains, Hookes and Wood, accusing each other of negative tactics. After winning the toss, South Australia struggled on a damp pitch, but Sleep, back after a season out of the state side, held the innings together with a fine century. Small worked up a lively pace when Western Australia batted, forcing Veletta to retire hurt with a bruised hand, and only Zoehrer's late defiance brought them first-innings points. Zadow scored his first first-class hundred in South Australia's second innings, and as the wicket dried out the batsmen on both sides took the opportunity of practice.

South Australia

A. M. J. Hilditch c Zoehrer b MacLeay	1	– c Bush b Clough 7
G. A. Bishop c Marsh b Clough	4	– c and b Bush 108
R. J. Zadow b MacLeay	8	– c sub b Bush 144
*D. W. Hookes c Reid b Clough	40	– c Bush b Reid 82
P. R. Sleep c Reid b Bush	105	– not out 11
D. F. G. O'Connor c Zoehrer b MacLeay	5	
†W. B. Phillips c Zoehrer b MacLeay	26	– (6) not out 1
T. B. A. May c Andrews b Reid	3	
A. K. Zesers not out	31	
G. C. Small c Andrews b Clough	16	
I. R. Carmichael c Marsh b Reid	1	
L-b 11, w 2, n-b 2	15	N-b 4 4

1/1 2/11 3/23 4/77 5/92   255   1/31 2/186 3/345   (4 wkts dec.) 357
6/147 7/169 8/206 9/254   4/345

Bowling: *First Innings*—Reid 31.4–8–71–2; MacLeay 30–8–83–4; Clough 25–4–71–3; Bush 12–4–19–1; Andrews 2–2–0–0. *Second Innings*—Reid 24.4–5–90–1; MacLeay 17–3–68–0; Clough 22–6–75–1; Bush 28–3–104–2; Andrews 5–1–20–0.

Western Australia

*G. M. Wood c Hilditch b Small	10	– (2) not out 53
M. R. J. Veletta c Phillips b Small	87	
G. R. Marsh c Zadow b Small	11	– not out 50
M. W. McPhee c Zadow b Zesers	18	– (1) c Phillips b Small 4
G. J. Ireland lbw b Small	50	
W. S. Andrews lbw b Zesers	29	
K. H. MacLeay c Phillips b Carmichael	3	
†T. J. Zoehrer not out	94	
G. E. W. Bush c Hilditch b Small	3	
B. A. Reid c Hookes b May	16	
P. M. Clough c Hookes b Sleep	1	
B 3, l-b 2, w 1, n-b 9	15	B 4, l-b 3, w 1, n-b 2 10

1/19 2/33 3/56 4/159 5/178   337   1/5   (1 wkt) 117
6/204 7/257 8/275 9/320

M. R. J. Veletta retired hurt at 134 and resumed at 204.

Bowling: *First Innings*—Small 29–7–89–5; Carmichael 25–7–68–1; Zesers 26–4–71–2; May 20–2–61–1; Sleep 14.2–1–43–1. *Second Innings*—Small 6–0–30–1; Carmichael 10–2–25–0; Zesers 6–1–12–0; May 9–2–14–0; Sleep 12–4–29–0.

Umpires: M. G. O'Connell and G. W. Pellen.

QUEENSLAND v VICTORIA

At Brisbane, October 18, 19, 20, 21. Drawn. Queensland 4 pts. With Victoria's first innings taking up almost two days, and the over-rate not helped by McDermott and Thomson's profligate bowling of no-balls, the cricket was pedestrian until Border's seven-hour 194, only 6 short of his career-best score, put some life into the game. Ritchie and Trimble also batted enterprisingly for two and a quarter hours, and finally McDermott and Frei, both reaching their highest Shield scores, put on 96 in better than even time against the tired attack. The same pair then undermined Victoria's second innings, and only some defiant batting by Hibbert and Dimattina foiled Queensland's late bid for victory.

Victoria

M. B. Quinn b Thomson	46	– (2) lbw b Thomson	19
D. F. Whatmore c Phillips b Frei	109	– (1) lbw b Frei	7
D. M. Jones c Courtice b Thomson	16	– c Courtice b McDermott	6
P. A. Hibbert c Phillips b Thomson	65	– (6) not out	31
J. D. Siddons lbw b McDermott	33	– c Phillips b McDermott	17
†M. G. D. Dimattina c Trimble b McDermott	46	– (8) not out	15
P. W. Young b Henschell	11	– (4) b McDermott	20
A. I. C. Dodemaide c Ritchie b McDermott	32	– (7) c Phillips b Frei	6
*R. J. Bright b Frei	38		
M. G. Hughes c Wessels b McDermott	1		
S. P. Davis not out	0		
L-b 1, w 1, n-b 32	34	B 12, l-b 1, n-b 3	16

1/148 2/174 3/197 4/272 5/317   431   1/12 2/19 3/64   (6 wkts) 137
6/339 7/367 8/429 9/431   4/64 5/89 6/104

Bowling: *First Innings*—McDermott 37-8-116-4; Frei 38.1-9-91-2; Thomson 30-2-137-3; Henschell 37-8-57-1; Border 4-2-11-0; Wessels 8-1-18-0. *Second Innings*—McDermott 15-4-41-3; Frei 10-3-31-2; Thomson 13-3-28-1; Henschell 14-5-24-0.

Queensland

R. B. Kerr c Whatmore b Dodemaide	0	C. J. McDermott c Dodemaide b Hughes	72
B. A. Courtice c Whatmore b Hughes	4	H. Frei run out	43
K. C. Wessels c Dimattina b Davis	32	J. R. Thomson not out	2
*A. R. Border b Dodemaide	194		
G. M. Ritchie st Dimattina b Bright	86	L-b 3, w 1, n-b 4	8
G. S. Trimble c Dimattina b Dodemaide	90		
A. B. Henschell b Dodemaide	7		539
†R. B. Phillips c Bright b Hughes	1		

1/4 2/4 3/49 4/216 5/384
6/400 7/419 8/425 9/521

Bowling: Dodemaide 34.2-7-151-4; Hughes 34-4-116-3; Davis 25-4-106-1; Bright 26-3-127-1; Young 1-0-11-0; Siddons 4-0-25-0; Hibbert 1-1-0-0.

Umpires: M. W. Johnson and M. J. King.

TASMANIA v NEW SOUTH WALES

At Hobart, October 25, 26, 27, 28. Drawn. New South Wales 4 pts. Boon gave New South Wales first use of a damp pitch, but three early wickets to his seam bowlers merely opened the way for Clifford and Matthews. Clifford survived a number of blows to his body from Davis, but capitalised on some erratic leg-spin bowling by Saunders. Matthews, dropped at 23 by Saunders, made his highest score, as did Steve Waugh, whose first Shield hundred was a lively innings. Boon, batting for nearly nine hours and playing strongly on the on-side, particularly on the drive, provided the backbone of Tasmania's solid reply. As the conditions became easier, so a draw became the most likely result.

New South Wales

M. A. Taylor c Hill b Davis	12	– (2) not out	56
M. E. Waugh c Saunders b Davis	13	– (1) c Buckingham b Hill	28
*D. M. Wellham b Brown	14		
P. S. Clifford c Soule b Brown	98		
G. R. J. Matthews c Buckingham b Ray	184		
S. R. Waugh b Davis	107		
†G. C. Dyer c Ray b Brown	35		
G. F. Lawson c Bradshaw b Brown	23		
M. J. Bennett not out	20	– (3) not out	20
D. R. Gilbert c Woolley b Saunders	22		
R. G. Holland c Goodman b Ray	10		
B 4, l-b 7, n-b 12	23	B 1, w 2, n-b 4	7

1/25 2/36 3/60 4/194 5/368   561   1/67   (1 wkt) 111
6/483 7/486 8/514 9/544

Bowling: *First Innings*—Davis 38–8–129–3; Hill 32–9–94–0; Brown 35–2–166–4; Ray 35.5–6–102–2; Saunders 10–1–59–1. *Second Innings*—Davis 12–6–9–0; Hill 12–1–44–1; Brown 6–1–17–0; Ray 5–3–3–0; Saunders 12–0–37–0.

Tasmania

M. Ray c Bennett b Gilbert 7	R. L. Brown b Lawson 27
G. W. Goodman lbw b Gilbert 14	W. W. Davis lbw b Lawson 9
*D. C. Boon c S. R. Waugh b Gilbert .196	M. A. Hill not out 1
K. Bradshaw b Gilbert 26	
R. D. Woolley c M. E. Waugh b Holland 16	L-b 8, w 3, n-b 15 26
D. J. Buckingham c Clifford b Matthews 41	
S. L. Saunders b Holland 51	1/10 2/41 3/121 4/140 5/226 429
†R. E. Soule b Lawson 15	6/373 7/375 8/416 9/419

Bowling: Lawson 37–11–85–3; Gilbert 32–5–108–4; Bennett 29–10–48–0; Holland 41–11–119–2; Matthews 24–11–39–1; S. R. Waugh 5–0–22–0.

Umpires: W. Elliott and S. G. Randell.

NEW SOUTH WALES v VICTORIA

At Newcastle, November 1, 2, 3, 4. New South Wales won by 90 runs. New South Wales 8 pts, Victoria 4 pts. Victoria controlled the game for three days, but requiring 169 for victory they collapsed against the off-spin bowling of Matthews, who returned his best figures, and the leg-spin of Holland. Bright put New South Wales in, whereupon the 21-year-old opener, Taylor, batted for four hours. Hughes bowled fast and well on the green pitch to take five wickets in an innings for the first time. The solid batting of Whatmore and the fluent strokes of Siddons ensured that Victoria would gain a useful first-innings lead, but when New South Wales batted again, Clifford held the Victorian pace attack at bay until, looking for his hundred, he missed a long hop from O'Donnell and was out for 98 for the second match in succession. Lawson and Bennett helped increase Victoria's target, which looked less achievable when Lawson and Gilbert made an early breakthrough. Matthews and Holland were too good for the later batsmen.

New South Wales

M. A. Taylor c Whatmore b Hughes 77	– c Whatmore b O'Donnell 7
M. E. Waugh c Dimattina b Hughes 0	– b Hughes 4
*D. M. Wellham c Dimattina b Hughes 15	– lbw b O'Donnell 22
P. S. Clifford c Siddons b Dodemaide 29	– lbw b O'Donnell 98
G. R. J. Matthews b Davis 35	– run out 28
S. R. Waugh lbw b O'Donnell 15	– c Whatmore b Dodemaide 11
†G. C. Dyer c Dodemaide b Hughes 14	– lbw b O'Donnell 2
G. F. Lawson c Whatmore b O'Donnell 23	– b Davis 30
M. J. Bennett c O'Donnell b Hughes 1	– not out 26
D. R. Gilbert not out 16	– c O'Donnell b Davis 0
R. G. Holland run out 0	– c Davis b O'Donnell 6
B 1, l-b 4, w 1, n-b 1 7	L-b 3, w 1, n-b 6 10

1/2 2/24 3/72 4/154 5/166   232   1/11 2/15 3/62 4/132 5/147   244
6/182 7/192 8/202 9/223   6/177 7/192 8/225 9/225

Bowling: *First Innings*—Hughes 24–4–74–5; Dodemaide 12–5–21–1; Davis 12–0–48–1; Bright 13–5–31–0; O'Donnell 15.5–3–53–2. *Second Innings*—Hughes 25–4–90–1; Dodemaide 11–4–36–1; Davis 14–5–32–2; Bright 11–4–17–0; O'Donnell 24.2–5–66–5.

Victoria

M. B. Quinn c Dyer b Gilbert	5	– b Gilbert	1
D. F. Whatmore c Taylor b Bennett	72	– c Dyer b Lawson	0
D. M. Jones b S. R. Waugh	19	– c Dyer b Lawson	9
P. A. Hibbert b Gilbert	14	– c Dyer b Matthews	21
S. P. O'Donnell b Gilbert	10	– b Matthews	4
J. D. Siddons c Taylor b Lawson	76	– c Wellham b Holland	5
A. I. C. Dodemaide c M. E. Waugh b Lawson	0	– b Holland	11
*R. J. Bright b Gilbert	39	– b Matthews	16
†M. G. D. Dimattina c Bennett b Lawson	48	– b Matthews	7
M. G. Hughes c Dyer b Lawson	8	– b Matthews	0
S. P. Davis not out	3	– not out	0
L-b 6, n-b 8	14	L-b 3, n-b 1	4

1/8 2/50 3/91 4/116 5/153   308   1/1 2/1 3/17 4/37 5/42   78
6/154 7/228 8/278 9/299   6/42 7/71 8/71 9/71

Bowling: *First Innings*—Lawson 32.4–4–82–4; Gilbert 26–4–84–4; S. R. Waugh 14–5–25–1; Holland 15–2–51–0; Bennett 18–5–40–1; M. E. Waugh 1–1–0–0; Matthews 8–2–20–0. *Second Innings*—Lawson 8–3–7–2; Gilbert 6–2–12–1; S. R. Waugh 5–0–17–0; Holland 15–9–17–2; Matthews 15.5–9–22–5.

Umpires: R. A. Emerson and R. A. French.

WESTERN AUSTRALIA v TASMANIA

At Perth, November 1, 2, 3, 4. Western Australia won by an innings and 7 runs. Western Australia 12 pts. Tasmania struggled on the newly laid pitch at the WACA ground after Boon had won the toss. Boon himself was dropped twice in an innings of four and a half hours. Western Australia also found batting difficult, being further hampered by the lush outfield, which kept boundaries to a minimum, but Veletta batted determinedly for six hours to ensure that his side gained a big first-innings lead. Tasmania's second innings was a virtual procession as the tall left-arm fast bowler, Reid, produced a number of unplayable deliveries.

Tasmania

G. W. Goodman c Zoehrer b MacLeay	0	– (2) c MacLeay b Clough	9
M. Ray run out	0	– (1) b Reid	27
*D. C. Boon st Zoehrer b Andrews	64	– lbw b Reid	0
K. Bradshaw st Zoehrer b Bush	7	– b Andrews	8
R. D. Woolley c Zoehrer b MacLeay	5	– (6) b Reid	40
D. J. Buckingham c Zoehrer b MacLeay	0	– (5) c Zoehrer b Reid	45
S. L. Saunders run out	11	– c Zoehrer b Reid	8
†R. E. Soule c McPhee b Bush	2	– run out	9
R. L. Brown b Andrews	1	– b Reid	0
W. W. Davis c MacLeay b Bush	8	– c Andrews b MacLeay	6
M. A. Hill not out	0	– not out	0
L-b 2, w 2	4	B 11, l-b 2, w 1, n-b 3	17

1/1 2/5 3/39 4/52 5/52   102   1/19 2/20 3/45 4/63 5/128   169
6/88 7/93 8/94 9/98   6/143 7/161 8/161 9/167

Bowling: *First Innings*—Reid 21–12–15–0; MacLeay 16–8–22–3; Clough 9–3–15–0; Bush 27.4–7–31–3; Andrews 12–1–17–2. *Second Innings*—Reid 32–8–54–6; MacLeay 14.3–3–31–1; Clough 12–2–22–1; Bush 23–7–31–0; Andrews 14–6–18–1.

Western Australia

*G. M. Wood c Soule b Davis	10	G. E. W. Bush c Soule b Hill	1
M. R. J. Veletta c Ray b Davis	85	B. A. Reid b Brown	1
G. R. Marsh lbw b Ray	46	P. M. Clough not out	0
M. W. McPhee c Buckingham b Hill	23		
G. J. Ireland b Ray	6	B 3, l-b 8, w 1, n-b 13	25
W. S. Andrews b Ray	20		
K. H. MacLeay b Brown	23	1/25 2/116 3/154 4/166 5/212	278
†T. J. Zoehrer b Brown	38	6/212 7/270 8/276 9/278	

Bowling: Davis 36–11–64–2; Hill 25–9–54–2; Ray 33–10–80–3; Brown 22.4–5–49–3; Saunders 7–2–16–0; Bradshaw 3–1–4–0.

Umpires: R. J. Evans and P. J. McConnell.

VICTORIA v TASMANIA

At Melbourne, November 8, 9, 10, 11. Drawn. Victoria 4 pts. Rain washed out the first day's play at the St Kilda ground. With the exception of Bradshaw and Woolley, the Tasmanian batsmen struggled against Victoria's seam bowlers, Hughes and Davis, on a pitch that gave them some help, and a final total of 328 was praiseworthy in the circumstances. Victoria also experienced difficulties early on, but Bright and Dimattina, who hit his first Shield fifty, saw that they collected the first-innings points.

Tasmania

G. W. Goodman lbw b Davis	38	W. W. Davis c McCarthy b Hughes	0
*M. Ray b Bright	25	R. L. Brown c Dodemaide b Davis	31
R. S. Hyatt c McCarthy b Davis	3	M. A. Hill c Siddons b Hughes	0
K. Bradshaw c Dimattina b Hughes	87		
R. D. Woolley c Dimattina b Hughes	70	L-b 6, w 1, n-b 5	12
†R. E. Soule c Hibbert b Davis	4		
D. J. Buckingham c Whatmore b Davis	17	1/49 2/52 3/77 4/215 5/225	328
S. L. Saunders not out	41	6/255 7/255 8/259 9/320	

Bowling: Hughes 29.5–6–81–4; McCarthy 24–3–59–0; Bright 31–14–61–1; Dodemaide 21–5–48–0; Davis 35–11–73–5.

Victoria

D. F. Whatmore c Saunders b Hill	6	*R. J. Bright not out	61
M. B. Quinn c Ray b Brown	38	†M. G. D. Dimattina not out	54
D. M. Jones c Davis b Hill	8	B 2, l-b 6, w 2, n-b 12	22
P. A. Hibbert b Ray	62		
J. D. Siddons c Woolley b Brown	74	1/9 2/22 3/100	(6 wkts) 332
A. I. C. Dodemaide c Saunders b Brown	7	4/175 5/205 6/230	

R. C. A. M. McCarthy, M. G. Hughes and S. P. Davis did not bat.

Bowling: Davis 43–14–101–0; Hill 30–3–88–2; Brown 37–10–105–3; Ray 18–9–26–1; Saunders 1–0–4–0.

Umpires: D. W. Holt and R. C. Isherwood.

SOUTH AUSTRALIA v QUEENSLAND

At Adelaide, November 15, 16, 17, 18. Queensland won by five wickets. Queensland 12 pts. Enterprising captaincy brought about two declarations, though Hookes's initiative in setting Queensland to score 285 in 81 overs was upset by a splendid partnership of 210 in just over three hours between Border and Wessels. South Australia lost the match in their first innings. All the batsmen made a start on an excellent pitch but none went on to play the major innings which the situation demanded. In Queensland's reply Kerr played stylishly for three hours, and there was some big hitting by Border at the end, but the South Australian bowling after Small and Zesers looked thin.

South Australia

Batsman	First Innings		Second Innings	
A. M. J. Hilditch c Kerr b Trimble	46	–	c Courtice b Henschell	59
G. A. Bishop c Frei b Thomson	19	–	c Henschell b Thomson	44
W. M. Darling c Wessels b Thomson	16	–	b Thomson	4
*D. W. Hookes c Kerr b Frei	47	–	c Trimble b Frei	102
†W. B. Phillips c Phillips b McDermott	46	–	c Ritchie b Thomson	23
P. R. Sleep c Kerr b Trimble	9	–	lbw b McDermott	21
R. J. Zadow c McDermott b Thomson	52	–	not out	7
T. B. A. May c Border b Thomson	17	–	(9) not out	6
A. K. Zesers c Kerr b Thomson	2			
G. C. Small c Henschell b Thomson	7	–	(8) lbw b McDermott	0
I. R. Carmichael not out	8			
B 1, l-b 1, w 1, n-b 18	21		B 2, l-b 7, n-b 13	22

1/45 2/72 3/107 4/157 5/181   290   1/102 2/109 3/120   (7 wkts dec.) 288
6/214 7/262 8/273 9/279   4/214 5/256 6/274
                                         7/274

Bowling: *First Innings*—McDermott 29-3-71-1; Frei 17-5-42-1; Thomson 24.1-4-72-6; Henschell 16-4-40-0; Trimble 13-1-63-2. *Second Innings*—McDermott 15-5-35-2; Frei 23-4-92-1; Thomson 10-0-50-3; Henschell 27-5-89-1; Trimble 3-0-13-0.

Queensland

Batsman	First Innings		Second Innings	
B. A. Courtice b Zesers	36	–	(2) c Hilditch b May	4
R. B. Kerr c Hookes b Zesers	80	–	(1) c Hilditch b Small	4
K. C. Wessels c Phillips b Small	1	–	c Phillips b Zesers	107
G. M. Ritchie c Phillips b Small	16	–	(5) not out	24
G. S. Trimble b Zesers	24	–	(6) c Bishop b May	3
*A. R. Border not out	88	–	(4) c Hookes b Zesers	119
A. B. Henschell not out	40	–	not out	17
L-b 7, n-b 2	9		L-b 6, n-b 1	7

1/115 2/122 3/124 4/165   (5 wkts dec.) 294   1/4 2/30 3/240 4/243   (5 wkts) 285
5/175   5/250

†R. B. Phillips, C. J. McDermott, H. Frei and J. R. Thomson did not bat.

Bowling: *First Innings*—Small 32-7-77-2; Carmichael 14-5-46-0; Zesers 31-10-67-3; May 17-4-48-0; Sleep 8-0-49-0. *Second Innings*—Small 10-0-32-1; Carmichael 21-2-75-0; Zesers 16-1-56-2; May 25.5-3-86-2; Hookes 7-0-30-0.

Umpires: B. E. Martin and R. B. Woods.

WESTERN AUSTRALIA v VICTORIA

At Perth, November 15, 16, 17, 18. Drawn. Victoria 4 pts. Once again the pitch and slow outfield had a large bearing on the course of the match. After Wood had put Victoria in, his pace attack made short work of their innings, with the left-armer, Matthews, in his second Shield game, especially effective in the overcast conditions. However, Davis was even more devastating when Western Australia batted, taking the last five wickets for 16 and returning career-best figures of six for 19. Victoria's second innings was a more determined affair. Quinn, dropped twice, batted for five and a half hours, and Jones, after an early escape, returned to form over a similar length of time, his hundred including three 6s. Bright's declaration left Western Australia to score 320 off 117 overs, but this was not practicable in the conditions. Wood and Marsh were both dropped off Hughes on the last morning, but thereafter they resisted stoutly, the match ending early when Marsh reached his century after seven hours.

Victoria

M. B. Quinn c Zoehrer b MacLeay	3	c Andrews b MacLeay	62
D. F. Whatmore c Andrews b Reid	29	c Ireland b MacLeay	22
P. A. Hibbert c Ireland b Matthews	9	run out	19
D. M. Jones b Reid	0	c Matthews b Reid	113
S. P. O'Donnell b Matthews	6	c Zoehrer b Matthews	22
J. D. Siddons b Matthews	7	c Veletta b Reid	7
A. I. C. Dodemaide c Zoehrer b MacLeay	27	not out	33
*R. J. Bright b Matthews	6	b Matthews	3
†M. G. D. Dimattina c Veletta b Matthews	2	not out	2
M. G. Hughes not out	9		
S. P. Davis c Veletta b Reid	3		
B 1, l-b 3, n-b 6	10	L-b 6, w 1, n-b 12	19

1/3 2/29 3/38 4/51 5/58   111   1/33 2/73 3/182   (7 wkts dec.) 302
6/64 7/70 8/76 9/99   4/232 5/247 6/271
                                      7/288

Bowling: *First Innings*—Reid 19.1–4–41–3; MacLeay 18–5–43–2; Matthews 21–8–23–5. *Second Innings*—Reid 40–7–113–2; MacLeay 27–11–35–2; Matthews 31–4–84–2; Bush 19–5–40–0; Andrews 12–3–24–0.

Western Australia

*G. M. Wood c Dimattina b O'Donnell	14	c Dimattina b O'Donnell	82
M. R. J. Veletta c Dimattina b Hughes	0	c Dimattina b Hughes	7
G. R. Marsh c Dodemaide b Hughes	2	not out	100
M. W. McPhee lbw b O'Donnell	0	not out	4
G. J. Ireland lbw b Davis	19		
W. S. Andrews lbw b Davis	12		
G. E. W. Bush c Siddons b Davis	5		
†T. J. Zoehrer c Whatmore b Davis	15		
K. H. MacLeay c Hibbert b Davis	10		
C. D. Matthews lbw b Davis	6		
B. A. Reid not out	3		
L-b 6, n-b 2	8	B 6, l-b 5, n-b 8	19

1/7 2/11 3/14 4/25 5/47   94   1/8 2/189   (2 wkts) 212
6/54 7/69 8/84 9/87

Bowling: *First Innings*—Hughes 17–4–36–2; O'Donnell 20–7–33–2; Davis 15.4–4–19–6. *Second Innings*—Hughes 25–4–78–1; O'Donnell 24–6–29–1; Davis 18–3–29–0; Bright 22–10–22–0; Dodemaide 11–1–28–0; Hibbert 6–0–10–0; Siddons 2–0–5–0.

Umpires: P. J. McConnell and D. G. Weser.

TASMANIA v SOUTH AUSTRALIA

At Launceston, November 22, 23, 24, 25. South Australia won by nine wickets. South Australia 12 pts. With both sides bereft of points in the competition, South Australia made the most of batting first and went on to gain maximum points as the wicket deteriorated. Sleep held South Australia's early batting together and then Kelly and Parkinson saw them to a big total, Parkinson hitting his first-ever fifty before producing his best form with the ball at left-arm fast-medium. Following on, Tasmania's batsmen fought harder and Hyatt made his highest score. No-one, however, could master the medium-pace bowling of the eighteen-year-old Zesers, and South Australia just beat the weather as they hit the few runs needed for victory.

South Australia

*A. M. J. Hilditch c Bradshaw b Davis	29	– not out	7
G. A. Bishop run out	37	– b Davis	0
W. M. Darling c Hyatt b Brown	18	– not out	8
D. F. G. O'Connor lbw b Brown	31		
P. R. Sleep c Soule b Hyatt	99		
R. J. Zadow c Soule b Hill	21		
†D. J. Kelly c and b Brown	79		
T. B. A. May c Hyatt b Brown	10		
A. K. Zesers c Soule b Davis	22		
S. D. H. Parkinson c Davis b Ray	10		
P. W. Gladigau not out	10		
B 1, l-b 8, w 3, n-b 12	24	L-b 2, w 1, n-b 2	5

1/63 2/74 3/91 4/150 5/204   **442**   1/7   (1 wkt) **20**
6/287 7/304 8/331 9/387

Bowling: First Innings—Davis 43–12–126–2; Brown 39–10–159–4; Hill 20–5–52–1; Ray 17.3–3–36–1; Hyatt 15–6–34–1; Saunders 4–0–26–0. *Second Innings*—Davis 2–0–3–1; Hill 2–0–11–0; Woolley 0.4–0–4–0.

Tasmania

*M. Ray c Parkinson b May	49	– (2) c Kelly b May	47
G. W. Goodman b Parkinson	4	– (1) c Parkinson b Zesers	10
R. S. Hyatt lbw b May	12	– c Hilditch b Zesers	80
R. D. Woolley lbw b Parkinson	22	– b May	10
D. J. Buckingham b Parkinson	0	– (6) lbw b Parkinson	22
†R. E. Soule not out	35	– (8) not out	31
K. Bradshaw b Parkinson	4	– (5) lbw b Sleep	37
S. L. Saunders c Zadow b Sleep	13	– (7) c May b Zesers	14
W. W. Davis b Zesers	0	– lbw b Zesers	1
R. L. Brown b Zesers	1	– c May b Sleep	10
M. A. Hill c Bishop b Sleep	4	– c and b Sleep	10
B 2, l-b 5, n-b 4	11	B 16, l-b 7, n-b 4	27

1/7 2/41 3/89 4/89 5/103   **159**   1/21 2/83 3/107 4/171 5/209   **299**
6/114 7/143 8/144 9/146   6/230 7/244 8/254 9/271

Bowling: First Innings—Gladigau 13–2–35–0; Parkinson 24–9–41–4; May 26–10–42–2; Zesers 26–17–28–2; Sleep 6.4–3–6–2. *Second Innings*—Gladigau 20–6–40–0; Parkinson 15–5–42–1; May 24–6–58–2; Zesers 45–17–65–4; Sleep 32–10–71–3.

Umpires: I. W. Batt and S. G. Randell.

QUEENSLAND v WESTERN AUSTRALIA

At Brisbane, November 29, 30, December 1, 2. Drawn. Queensland 2 pts, Western Australia 2 pts. Thomson took his 300th wicket for Queensland when he had Wood caught at cover, but Veletta and Marsh occupied the next five hours in a splendid partnership of 254. MacLeay saw to it that Western Australia controlled the game, first with a forceful innings of 60 and then by dismissing Barsby and Wessels with consecutive balls in his second over. Queensland's recovery was helped by six catches going down, including one off Henschell who, reprieved when he was 2, batted well for 261 minutes. Rain prevented play on the last day and the first-innings points were shared.

Western Australia

*G. M. Wood c Henschell b Thomson	13	C. D. Matthews b Frei	24
M. R. J. Veletta b Frei	130	B. A. Reid not out	23
G. R. Marsh b Frei	138	G. E. W. Bush c Maranta b Brown	4
M. W. McPhee c Barsby b Thomson	10		
G. J. Ireland c Maranta b Henschell	39	L-b 4, w 1, n-b 16	21
W. S. Andrews c and b Trimble	41		
†T. J. Zoehrer b Henschell	24	1/28 2/282 3/308 4/308 5/389	527
K. H. MacLeay b Brown	60	6/395 7/427 8/485 9/509	

Bowling: Frei 34–10–91–3; Twible 26–5–70–0; Thomson 23–3–103–2; Maranta 18–3–69–0; Henschell 33–8–97–2; Trimble 21–7–59–1; Brown 10.1–0–34–2.

Queensland

B. A. Courtice c Veletta b Matthews	48	†R. B. Phillips not out	24
T. J. Barsby c Bush b MacLeay	0		
*K. C. Wessels c Wood b MacLeay	0	L-b 3, n-b 12	15
G. S. Trimble c Zoehrer b Reid	41		
A. B. Henschell not out	85	1/0 2/0 3/67	(5 wkts) 225
A. N. Brown c Reid b MacLeay	12	4/131 5/176	

M. G. Maranta, P. W. Twible, H. Frei and J. R. Thomson did not bat.

Bowling: Reid 26–8–59–1; MacLeay 20–5–44–3; Matthews 24–7–58–1; Bush 22–7–57–0; Andrews 4–2–4–0.

Umpires: M. W. Johnson and C. D. Timmins.

TASMANIA v QUEENSLAND

At Devonport, December 6, 7, 8, 9. Queensland won by seven wickets. Queensland 12 pts. Tasmania were struggling from the first day, when they collapsed to Queensland's veteran opening bowlers, Thomson and Frei, and then lost their two opening bowlers, Davis and Hill, with leg injuries. Bradshaw, an occasional bowler, helped Brown rein in Queensland in mid-innings, and had Boon not dropped Phillips before he had scored, Queensland's lead might have been restricted. Ritchie batted soundly for three and a half hours and was joined by Phillips in a stand of 130 for the sixth wicket. Tasmania's second innings, enlivened by Bradshaw and Buckingham's 113 in two hours, was helped by Thomson's contribution of 28 no-balls to go with the 19 he bowled in the first innings. Queensland took only an hour to hit off the winning runs as rain and fog threatened.

Tasmania

M. Ray b Frei	1	– (2) c Kerr b Frei	49
R. S. Hyatt c Frei b Thomson	0	– (3) c Trimble b Frei	27
*D. C. Boon c Phillips b Thomson	44	– (1) c Phillips b Trimble	16
K. Bradshaw c Border b Thomson	1	– c Ritchie b Trimble	49
R. D. Woolley c Wessels b Frei	14	– c Phillips b Thomson	0
D. J. Buckingham c Frei b Thomson	21	– c Henschell b Trimble	60
S. L. Saunders c Phillips b Thomson	0	– c Phillips b Thomson	13
†R. E. Soule c Twible b Trimble	15	– c Ritchie b Frei	53
R. L. Brown run out	5	– run out	9
W. W. Davis c Kerr b Trimble	21	– c Thomson b Frei	8
M. A. Hill not out	4	– not out	3
L-b 2, n-b 28	30	L-b 9, n-b 39	48
1/4 2/10 3/14 4/43 5/97	156	1/41 2/122 3/123 4/124 5/237	335
6/98 7/101 8/107 9/134		6/239 7/289 8/301 9/315	

Bowling: *First Innings*—Thomson 17–2–76–5; Frei 9–2–24–2; Twible 5–1–16–0; Trimble 12.2–4–38–2. *Second Innings*—Thomson 32–3–122–2; Frei 27.1–8–71–4; Twible 13–4–27–0; Trimble 19–3–61–3; Henschell 14–2–32–0; Border 3–0–13–0.

Queensland

R. B. Kerr b Brown	27				
B. A. Courtice c Brown b Hyatt	77				
K. C. Wessels b Bradshaw	69	– not out	20
G. M. Ritchie c Soule b Brown	89	– (2) c Soule b Bradshaw	49
G. S. Trimble c Ray b Bradshaw	2	– (4) c Hyatt b Buckingham	1
A. B. Henschell b Brown	3	– (5) not out	1
†R. B. Phillips c sub b Hyatt	56			
*A. R. Border c Boon b Brown	8	– (1) b Bradshaw	11
P. W. Twible not out	18			
H. Frei c Ray b Hyatt	14			
J. R. Thomson not out	17			
B 2, l-b 9, n-b 16	27	L-b 3	3

1/69 2/194 3/194 4/197 (9 wkts dec.) 407   1/21 2/80 3/83 (3 wkts) 85
5/200 6/330 7/344
8/363 9/382

Bowling: *First Innings*—Davis 14.2–4–31–0; Hill 4–1–12–0; Brown 47.4–16–124–4; Bradshaw 27–5–85–2; Ray 13–3–31–0; Saunders 4–1–30–0; Hyatt 17–7–54–3; Woolley 9–0–29–0. *Second Innings*—Brown 6–0–31–0; Bradshaw 7–1–40–2; Buckingham 2–0–9–1; Boon 0.4–0–2–0.

Umpires: W. Elliott and S. G. Randell.

NEW SOUTH WALES v WESTERN AUSTRALIA

At Sydney, December 7, 8, 9, 10. New South Wales won by 151 runs. New South Wales 12 pts. Wood took the unusual step, at the SCG, of sending New South Wales in to bat and paid the penalty when Western Australia collapsed on the fourth day as the Sydney pitch played to form. However, when Bower joined Taylor on the first day, New South Wales were in trouble at 56 for four. Their stand of 104 in two and a quarter hours effected a recovery which Bennett, Lawson and Holland consolidated. Western Australia's batsmen were confounded by the New South Wales spin attack in their first innings, and late on the third day, after daring hitting by Wellham and Matthews had made a declaration possible, were chasing a victory target of 257. The seemingly generous equation indicated what Wellham thought of the wicket, and the only threats to New South Wales were Veletta and some big storm-clouds.

New South Wales

S. M. Small c Zoehrer b MacLeay	4	– lbw b Reid	4
M. A. Taylor c and b Mulder	65	– c Andrews b MacLeay	10
*D. M. Wellham c Zoehrer b Reid	11	– b Andrews	55
P. S. Clifford c Ireland b Bush	16	– c Andrews b Bush	22
G. R. J. Matthews c Veletta b Bush	0	– c Zoehrer b Reid	49
R. J. Bower run out	63	– not out	3
†G. C. Dyer lbw b MacLeay	22	– not out	3
M. J. Bennett not out	55		
G. F. Lawson lbw b MacLeay	24		
D. R. Gilbert b MacLeay	0		
R. G. Holland c Wood b Reid	16		
L-b 4, n-b 6	10	B 4, n-b 7	11

1/12 2/36 3/56 4/56 5/160 286   1/19 2/21 3/75 (5 wkts dec.) 157
6/175 7/213 8/256 9/256   4/151 5/151

Bowling: *First Innings*—Reid 26.2–3–74–2; MacLeay 23–5–58–4; Mulder 26–7–49–1; Bush 38–9–92–2; Andrews 8–5–9–0. *Second Innings*—Reid 13–1–33–2; MacLeay 7–0–30–1; Mulder 7–0–38–0; Bush 10–2–47–1; Andrews 3–1–5–1.

Western Australia

*G. M. Wood c Small b Bennett	51	– c Dyer b Matthews 12
M. R. J. Veletta lbw b Gilbert	5	– b Holland 55
G. R. Marsh b Matthews	35	– st Dyer b Holland 5
M. W. McPhee c Bower b Bennett	0	– c Taylor b Gilbert 3
G. J. Ireland c Gilbert b Bennett	9	– c Dyer b Gilbert 5
W. S. Andrews st Dyer b Bennett	30	– lbw b Gilbert 0
†T. J. Zoehrer st Dyer b Holland	5	– c Dyer b Gilbert 1
K. H. MacLeay lbw b Gilbert	14	– c Dyer b Lawson 2
B. A. Reid not out	11	– c and b Lawson 9
B. Mulder b Matthews	4	– not out 3
G. E. W. Bush c Bennett b Matthews	4	– b Lawson 4
B 5, l-b 8, w 3, n-b 3	19	B 7, l-b 3 10

1/48 2/95 3/101 4/101 5/132   187   1/29 2/49 3/62 4/84 5/84   105
6/143 7/145 8/173 9/183   6/88 7/90 8/98 9/105

Bowling: *First Innings*—Lawson 12-2-31-0; Gilbert 10-1-30-2; Holland 34-16-52-1; Bennett 33-12-47-4; Matthews 6.5-3-14-3. *Second Innings*—Lawson 7.2-1-11-3; Gilbert 10-3-16-4; Holland 19-5-34-2; Bennett 15-6-19-0; Matthews 13-7-15-1.

Umpires: R. A. Emerson and A. G. Marshall.

NEW SOUTH WALES v SOUTH AUSTRALIA

At Sydney, December 13, 14, 15, 16. New South Wales won by an innings and 115 runs. New South Wales 12 pts. Darling batted brilliantly, scoring his 97 in two and a half hours, as South Australia capitulated to the New South Wales spin bowlers on the first day. The New South Wales batsmen showed greater application. Taylor, in his first Shield season, scored his first century. It took him six hours, but he opened the way for a dashing display by Waugh, who followed his hundred by immediately bowling Bishop, catching Sleep and running out Darling. South Australia's second innings followed a predictable course and Lawson took the opportunity to bowl himself back into form after being dropped from the Test team.

South Australia

*A. M. J. Hilditch c Waugh b Bennett	12	– lbw b Lawson 0
G. A. Bishop c and b Holland	18	– b Waugh 0
R. J. Zadow lbw b Holland	2	– b Holland 46
D. F. G. O'Connor lbw b Holland	0	– lbw b Lawson 4
P. R. Sleep b Holland	6	– c Waugh b Bennett 19
W. M. Darling c Holland b Bennett	97	– run out 3
†D. J. Kelly c Small b O'Neill	3	– b Lawson 27
T. B. A. May c Bower b O'Neill	3	– (9) b Holland 0
C. L. Harms c O'Neill b Bennett	25	– (8) not out 29
A. K. Zesers not out	3	– c O'Neill b Bennett 0
G. C. Small st Dyer b Bennett	0	– c O'Neill b Bennett 9
L-b 6	6	B 4, l-b 6, n-b 1 11

1/30 2/32 3/32 4/39 5/42   175   1/0 2/0 3/4 4/49 5/55   148
6/57 7/85 8/166 9/173   6/108 7/109 8/111 9/126

In the second innings R. J. Zadow retired hurt and resumed at 108.

Bowling: *First Innings*—Lawson 6-1-18-0; Waugh 5-1-12-0; Holland 33-17-46-4; Bennett 23.5-12-38-4; O'Neill 17-2-55-2. *Second Innings*—Lawson 15-6-20-3; Waugh 5-2-15-1; Holland 26-8-39-2; Bennett 25.5-13-32-3; O'Neill 9-3-32-0.

New South Wales

S. M. Small c Sleep b Small	66	M. J. Bennett b Zesers	15
M. A. Taylor c O'Connor b May	118	M. D. O'Neill not out	38
*D. M. Wellham st Kelly b Sleep	41	B 5, l-b 14, w 1, n-b 3	23
W. J. S. Seabrook b May	8		
S. R. Waugh not out	119	1/143 2/224 3/240 (6 wkts dec.) 438	
R. J. Bower run out	10	4/240 5/266 6/315	

†G. C. Dyer, G. F. Lawson and R. G. Holland did not bat.

Bowling: Small 37–7–90–1; May 41–11–86–2; Zesers 23–5–64–1; Harms 27.3–8–69–0; Sleep 41–9–110–1.

Umpires: R. A. Emerson and A. G. Marshall.

VICTORIA v QUEENSLAND

At Melbourne, December 13, 14, 15, 16. Drawn. Victoria 4 pts. When Victoria's captain, Jones, opted to extend his innings until late on the third day, Wessels responded in kind and Queensland's second innings occupied almost seven hours. Queensland's fortunes fell away dramatically after they reached 177 for two on the first day with Courtice and Trimble in full flow. Davis, well supported by his slip fielders and Dimattina, dismissed the middle order with a spell of three for 0 in three overs and finished with six for 53, fine bowling on the slow MCG wicket. Victoria's two stalwarts, Whatmore and Hibbert, put on 106 for the third wicket in two hours. Whatmore, the dominant partner, deserved a century, and after his dismissal for 90, Hibbert, dropped by Trimble when 2, added a further 184 in four hours with the 21-year-old Siddons, who hit his first Shield hundred.

Queensland

T. J. Barsby c Dimattina b Davis	31	– (2) c Dimattina b Dodemaide	9
B. A. Courtice c Dimattina b Davis	60	– (1) not out	111
*K. C. Wessels c Dodemaide b Hickey	15	– c Dimattina b Dodemaide	24
G. S. Trimble c Whatmore b Jones	75	– not out	41
A. B. Henschell c Whatmore b Davis	5		
N. Jelich c Dimattina b Dodemaide	30		
†R. B. Phillips c Dimattina b Davis	0		
M. G. Maranta c Jones b Davis	4		
P. W. Twible c Dimattina b Davis	39		
H. Frei b Hibbert b Dodemaide	9		
J. R. Thomson not out	13		
L-b 5, n-b 2	7	B 7, l-b 3, n-b 2	12
1/38 2/59 3/177 4/185 5/191	288	1/13 2/58 (2 wkts) 197	
6/191 7/203 8/248 9/266			

Bowling: *First Innings*—Hickey 8–3–17–1; Dodemaide 34–7–101–2; Davis 34.5–14–53–6; Emerson 16–3–68–0; Hibbert 5–2–14–0; Jones 10–2–30–1. *Second Innings*—Dodemaide 28–10–48–2; Davis 32–19–46–0; Emerson 17–4–40–0; Hibbert 9–3–12–0; Jones 9–2–19–0; Siddons 4–1–11–0; Young 6–2–11–0.

Victoria

M. B. Quinn c Phillips b Frei	12	†M. G. D. Dimattina not out	23
D. F. Whatmore c Wessels b Thomson	90	S. P. Davis run out	2
*D. M. Jones c Trimble b Thomson	9		
P. A. Hibbert c Phillips b Twible	137	B 5, l-b 12, n-b 6	23
P. W. Young c and b Trimble	8		
J. D. Siddons c Wessels b Twible	107	1/31 2/46 3/152 (9 wkts dec.) 456	
A. I. C. Dodemaide run out	31	4/177 5/361 6/393	
D. A. Emerson b Trimble	14	7/416 8/452 9/456	

D. J. Hickey did not bat.

Bowling: Thomson 22–2–78–2; Frei 30–5–80–1; Maranta 25–2–78–0; Twible 35.2–5–82–2; Henschell 4–0–16–0; Trimble 27–2–99–2; Jelich 1–0–6–0.

Umpires: R. C. Isherwood and L. J. King.

QUEENSLAND v SOUTH AUSTRALIA

At Brisbane, December 20, 21, 22, 23. Queensland won by 110 runs. Queensland 12 pts. Queensland established a sound position on the first day through the forceful batting of Wessels and Border and made it impregnable on the second morning as Trimble displayed his powerful strokes. He was on course for his first Shield hundred when Border declared. The Queensland bowlers met little resistance from the South Australian batsmen until Darling and Small added 51 in 33 minutes for the last wicket, so avoiding the follow-on. Queensland, with a rearranged order, were in considerable embarrassment at 59 for five, but when Border declared on the fourth morning McDermott and Thomson bowled fast and accurately to set up the win.

Queensland

R. B. Kerr hit wkt b Parkinson	19	– (2) b Parkinson	6
B. A. Courtice b Parkinson	0	– (1) b Zesers	11
K. C. Wessels c Phillips b Sleep	85	– c Hilditch b Small	3
*A. R. Border c Phillips b Zesers	118	– (7) c Hookes b Zesers	30
G. M. Ritchie c Phillips b Small	24	– (4) b Small	63
G. S. Trimble not out	87	– b Zesers	10
A. B. Henschell c Hookes b Small	12	– (8) not out	21
†R. B. Phillips c Phillips b Small	23	– (5) c sub b Parkinson	3
C. J. McDermott c Parkinson b Small	6	– lbw b Small	2
H. Frei not out	4	– not out	6
B 5, l-b 4, w 2, n-b 2	13	B 4, l-b 2, w 1	7

1/3 2/38 3/181 4/230 5/257	(8 wkts dec.) 391	1/13 2/16 3/39 (8 wkts dec.) 162
6/313 7/360 8/372		4/48 5/59 6/107
		7/147 8/151

J. R. Thomson did not bat.

Bowling: *First Innings*—Small 31–4–109–4; Parkinson 21–3–85–2; Zesers 21–8–64–1; May 8–0–26–0; Sleep 11–2–49–1; Hookes 14–2–49–0. *Second Innings*—Small 16–2–55–3; Parkinson 13–2–41–2; Zesers 21–5–43–3; Hookes 9–2–17–0.

South Australia

A. M. J. Hilditch c Ritchie b Thomson	12	– lbw b Frei	3
G. A. Bishop b Trimble	14	– c Wessels b McDermott	9
R. J. Zadow b Henschell	40	– c Wessels b McDermott	1
*D. W. Hookes c Phillips b Trimble	7	– c Wessels b Trimble	72
†W. B. Phillips c Border b Henschell	33	– c Phillips b Thomson	14
P. R. Sleep lbw b Frei	18	– not out	49
W. M. Darling not out	60	– c Kerr b Thomson	6
A. K. Zesers c Phillips b Thomson	5	– b Thomson	0
S. D. H. Parkinson c Border b Trimble	4	– (10) c Wessels b Trimble	3
T. B. A. May b McDermott	5	– (11) c Wessels b Thomson	10
G. C. Small c Trimble b McDermott	33	– (9) c Frei b Henschell	12
B 1, l-b 7, w 1, n-b 11	20	B 5, l-b 3, n-b 5	13

1/26 2/34 3/44 4/116 5/118	251	1/11 2/13 3/15 4/49 5/112 192
6/156 7/170 8/193 9/200		6/118 7/123 8/152 9/164

Bowling: *First Innings*—McDermott 18.4–4–47–2; Frei 15–2–58–1; Thomson 19–3–61–2; Trimble 19–9–41–3; Henschell 22–14–36–2. *Second Innings*—McDermott 19–5–55–2; Frei 6–2–14–1; Thomson 13.2–2–29–4; Trimble 13–2–47–2; Henschell 9–2–39–1.

Umpires: M. W. Johnson and C. D. Timmins.

VICTORIA v NEW SOUTH WALES

At Melbourne, December 20, 21, 22, 23. Drawn. Victoria 4 pts. Rain on the final day brought to an end a game in which it took Victoria until after lunch on the third day to achieve a lead on the first innings. Apart from Lawson, who made his highest first-class score, the New South Wales batsmen were tied down by Bright, and the Victorians were equally ineffective until Hibbert and Bright put on 185 for the seventh wicket, a record in matches against New South Wales. Hibbert batted for seven hours, Bright for four hours, and neither gave a chance. When New South Wales batted a second time, Small, aged 30, hit his first Shield century. Jones, Victoria's vice-captain, received a suspended fine for abusing the umpires after being caught by Small, and the spirit of the game was further tarnished by the unnecessary appealing of the Victorian players during Small's second innings.

New South Wales

S. M. Small c Hibbert b Bright	25	– b Dodemaide	123
M. A. Taylor c Young b Davis	46	– c Whatmore b Hughes	40
*D. M. Wellham c Jones b Bright	5	– c Davis b Bright	63
R. J. Bower c Whatmore b Bright	18	– not out	40
G. R. J. Matthews c Dimattina b Bright	13		
S. R. Waugh c Siddons b Bright	32	– (5) not out	41
†G. C. Dyer b Bright	7		
M. J. Bennett c Dimattina b Hughes	1		
G. F. Lawson c Quinn b Davis	63		
P. A. Blizzard not out	18		
R. G. Holland c Dodemaide b Davis	2		
B 2, l-b 5, w 4	11	B 4, l-b 6, n-b 2	12

1/45 2/65 3/95 4/106 5/129   241   1/103 2/226 3/234   (3 wkts) 319
6/139 7/140 8/168 9/234

Bowling: *First Innings*—Hughes 16-3-50-1; Davis 24.4-7-64-3; Dodemaide 15-3-45-0; Bright 36-12-74-6; Jones 2-1-1-0. *Second Innings*—Hughes 16-1-70-1; Davis 14-2-56-0; Dodemaide 27-5-76-1; Bright 26-6-56-1; Jones 9-1-33-0; Hibbert 2-0-9-0; Quinn 2-0-5-0; Whatmore 1-0-4-0.

Victoria

M. B. Quinn lbw b Lawson	3	†M. G. D. Dimattina not out	2
D. F. Whatmore b Blizzard	6	M. G. Hughes c Taylor b Bennett	4
P. W. Young b Matthews	9		
P. A. Hibbert c Blizzard b Bennett	148	B 2, l-b 8, n-b 4	14
D. M. Jones c Small b Matthews	12		
J. D. Siddons run out	1	1/10 2/12 3/38 (9 wkts dec.) 273
A. I. C. Dodemaide c Taylor b Bennett	5	4/57 5/66 6/79
*R. J. Bright c Matthews b Bennett	69	7/264 8/268 9/273

S. P. Davis did not bat.

Bowling: Lawson 26-9-49-1; Blizzard 15-3-30-1; Matthews 25-7-52-2; Waugh 16-5-30-0; Bennett 26.4-6-71-4; Holland 11-3-31-0.

Umpires: M. G. Gandy and D. E. Holden.

SOUTH AUSTRALIA v TASMANIA

At Adelaide, January 10, 11, 12, 13. South Australia won by 55 runs. South Australia 8 pts, Tasmania 4 pts. Tasmania, chasing 316 in 86 overs, were going well at 244 for four, but then six wickets fell for 16 as their tailenders again showed little aptitude with the bat. South Australia won off the second ball of the last over. Harris hit a hundred on his first-class début, and in Tasmania's first innings Buckingham scored a determined maiden Shield hundred, but the best performance of the match came from Bishop, who took advantage of some moderate bowling, hitting 28 4s and scoring his runs in four and three-quarter hours.

South Australia

G. A. Bishop c Hyatt b Cooley	45	– not out	224
A. S. Watson c Soule b Brown	30	– c Soule b Brown	22
*R. J. Zadow lbw b Cooley	25	– c Buckingham b Brown	8
P. R. Sleep c Soule b Brown	3	– c Buckingham b Hyatt	13
W. M. Darling c Woolley b Brown	7	– c Bennett b Brown	4
S. C. Wundke c Bradshaw b Ray	42	– c Cooley b Hyatt	39
†D. J. Kelly c Dell b Brown	85	– c Hyatt b Brown	14
C. L. Harms not out	43	– not out	5
G. C. Small c Ray b Brown	12		
A. K. Zesers b Brown	0		
S. D. H. Parkinson lbw b Brown	0		
B 2, l-b 6, w 2, n-b 11	21	B 9, l-b 1, n-b 6	16

1/56 2/100 3/107 4/113 5/118   313   1/49 2/64 3/114   (6 wkts dec.) 345
6/223 7/286 8/309 9/313   4/129 5/210 6/320

Bowling: *First Innings*—Brown 29.3–5–80–7; Cooley 24–5–87–2; Dell 6–1–40–0; Ray 17–5–44–1; Hyatt 13–1–44–0; Bradshaw 9–5–10–0. *Second Innings*—Brown 21–2–103–4; Cooley 12–0–83–0; Dell 1–0–15–0; Ray 6–2–33–0; Hyatt 28–5–77–2; Bradshaw 6–0–24–0.

Tasmania

*M. Ray b Parkinson	52	– c Kelly b Zesers	10
E. J. Harris c Sleep b Parkinson	11	– b Harms	118
R. J. Bennett c Watson b Zesers	23	– run out	15
K. Bradshaw c Bishop b Parkinson	11	– (6) b Small	62
R. D. Woolley b Harms	94	– c Bishop b Sleep	16
D. J. Buckingham c Small b Zesers	121	– (4) b Zesers	15
R. S. Hyatt b Small	5	– c Bishop b Harms	14
†R. E. Soule b Harms	3	– b Harms	0
C. R. Dell c Parkinson b Harms	4	– c Wundke b Sleep	0
R. L. Brown not out	0	– not out	1
T. J. Cooley b Zesers	0	– c Parkinson b Harms	0
B 6, l-b 11, w 2	19	B 5, l-b 2, w 1, n-b 1	9

1/36 2/75 3/100 4/113 5/289   343   1/27 2/82 3/112 4/145 5/244   260
6/294 7/321 8/341 9/343   6/244 7/246 8/259 9/259

Bowling: *First Innings*—Small 29–8–76–1; Parkinson 24–4–86–3; Zesers 28.1–9–77–3; Harms 22–5–49–3; Sleep 10–3–26–0; Wundke 4–1–12–0. *Second Innings*—Small 18–2–65–1; Parkinson 4–2–12–0; Zesers 14–4–40–2; Harms 28.2–10–60–4; Sleep 21–6–76–2.

Umpires: M. P. Brien and R. B. Woods.

WESTERN AUSTRALIA v NEW SOUTH WALES

At Perth, January 10, 11, 12, 13. Western Australia won by an innings and 46 runs. Western Australia 12 pts. This was the first outright defeat for New South Wales in more than two years. After Wood won the toss, his bowlers dismissed New South Wales on a green pitch for their lowest score against Western Australia. Matthews captured the last five wickets in ten balls soon after lunch. Blizzard, with three early wickets, threatened to achieve similar success when Western Australia batted, but he lacked support and Wood and Andrews added 216 in four and a quarter hours. Wood batted for six hours without giving a chance, while Andrews, who had not passed 50 before, hit his maiden first-class hundred. New South Wales batted throughout the third day, but only just into the fourth. Dyer concentrated well for four hours. MacLeay's out-swing troubled all the batsmen and he would have had even better figures with greater support from his fieldsmen.

New South Wales

S. M. Small lbw b MacLeay	3	– lbw b MacLeay	48
M. A. Taylor run out	12	– c Ireland b MacLeay	23
*D. M. Wellham c Veletta b MacLeay	28	– c Zoehrer b MacLeay	14
P. S. Clifford b MacLeay	0	– c Gonnella b MacLeay	35
R. J. Bower c Gonnella b Capes	4	– (7) c Wood b MacLeay	43
M. D. O'Neill lbw b Matthews	24	– (5) c Zoehrer b Matthews	39
†G. C. Dyer lbw b Matthews	7	– (6) c Andrews b Breman	68
M. J. Bennett not out	2	– c Gonnella b Breman	12
P. A. Blizzard lbw b Matthews	0	– c Ireland b MacLeay	12
R. G. Holland b Matthews	1	– b Matthews	2
M. R. Whitney b Matthews	0	– not out	0
N-b 2	2	B 1, l-b 10, w 1, n-b 13	25

1/3 2/37 3/43 4/43 5/47   83   1/70 2/82 3/101 4/143 5/223   321
6/76 7/81 8/81 9/83   6/249 7/297 8/319 9/321

Bowling: *First Innings*—Matthews 8.5-0-40-5; MacLeay 14-5-25-3; Capes 10-6-14-1; Breman 4-1-4-0. *Second Innings*—Matthews 35-7-93-2; MacLeay 38.1-10-93-6; Capes 12-0-53-0; Breman 21-9-47-2; Moody 9-2-24-0.

Western Australia

G. J. Ireland c Small b Blizzard	1	T. G. Breman not out	22
M. R. J. Veletta c Small b Blizzard	16	K. H. MacLeay not out	41
P. Gonnella c Dyer b Blizzard	10		
*G. M. Wood b Bower b Bennett	133	B 10, l-b 3, w 2, n-b 15	30
T. M. Moody c sub b Bower	19		
W. S. Andrews c Whitney b Bennett	139	1/7 2/21 3/53 4/91 (7 wkts dec.) 450
†T. J. Zoehrer c Blizzard b Bennett	39	5/307 6/384 7/391	

C. D. Matthews and P. A. Capes did not bat.

Bowling: Whitney 22-3-84-0; Blizzard 31-7-72-3; Holland 30-8-107-0; Bower 10-2-55-1; Bennett 32-8-85-3; O'Neill 12-2-34-0.

Umpires: R. J. Evans and W. M. Powell.

SOUTH AUSTRALIA v NEW SOUTH WALES

At Adelaide, January 16, 17, 18, 19. Drawn. South Australia 4 pts. A match featuring some spectacular individual efforts was spoiled by unsavoury incidents on the last day. As a result of one, Bower, the New South Wales batsman, was given a suspended fine of $A250 for dissent against umpire Pellen when given out, caught behind; and in another, South Australia's fast bowler, Small, was warned for intimidatory bowling after delivering two short-pitched deliveries at O'Neill from well over the popping crease. Small had bowled superbly in New South Wales's first innings on a pitch offering only a little help, and Taylor, who opened the innings, had done well to bat for four and a half hours. On the second day Hookes made full use of the short boundaries square of the wicket to score his first-ever double-hundred, his five-and-a-quarter-hour innings featuring ten 6s and 26 4s. His sixth-wicket partnership of 195 with Kelly was a record for matches between the two states. O'Neill's second-innings 178 not out, only his second first-class hundred, matched Hookes's for exciting strokeplay. Batting for four and three-quarter hours, he hit five 6s and 23 4s.

New South Wales

S. M. Small c Bishop b Small	3	– b Small	54
M. A. Taylor b Zesers	92	– b Parkinson	100
*D. M. Wellham c Zadow b Small	0	– b Sleep	41
P. S. Clifford c Kelly b Zesers	29	– lbw b Sleep	17
R. J. Bower b Small	4	– c Kelly b Parkinson	30
M. D. O'Neill c Watson b Small	24	– not out	178
†G. C. Dyer c Sleep b Small	26	– c Kelly b Harms	88
M. J. Bennett c Kelly b Small	12	– not out	14
P. A. Blizzard not out	12		
R. G. Holland c and b Hookes	7		
M. R. Whitney b Small	4		
B 1, l-b 9, w 2, n-b 4	16	B 2, l-b 3, w 4, n-b 4	13

1/12 2/12 3/81 4/90 5/145   239   1/127 2/187 3/213   (6 wkts) 535
6/183 7/203 8/204 9/230   4/224 5/271 6/471

Bowling: *First Innings*—Small 22.4–4–42–7; Parkinson 17–4–48–0; Zesers 21–4–51–2; Harms 26–5–85–0; Hookes 2–0–3–1. *Second Innings*—Small 31–5–113–1; Parkinson 24–2–105–2; Zesers 41–13–78–0; Harms 27–2–103–1; Hookes 5–0–22–0; Sleep 33–7–109–2.

South Australia

G. A. Bishop c Wellham b Holland	29	G. C. Small c Dyer b Whitney	14
A. S. Watson lbw b Blizzard	3	A. K. Zesers not out	27
R. J. Zadow c Dyer b Blizzard	0	S. D. H. Parkinson c Holland b Bennett	36
*D. W. Hookes c Dyer b Blizzard	243		
P. R. Sleep run out	4	B 1, l-b 2, n-b 4	7
W. M. Darling c O'Neill b Whitney	7		
†D. J. Kelly c Bower b Holland	42	1/8 2/8 3/74 4/90 5/127	435
C. L. Harms c Wellham b Blizzard	23	6/322 7/346 8/365 9/373	

Bowling: Whitney 33–7–110–2; Blizzard 32–4–118–4; Holland 33–11–91–2; Bennett 16.4–2–75–1; O'Neill 9–2–22–0; Bower 1–0–16–0.

Umpires: B. E. Martin and G. W. Pellen.

VICTORIA v WESTERN AUSTRALIA

At Melbourne, January 18, 19, 20, 21. Drawn. Victoria 4 pts. Western Australia went into the last day with ten wickets in hand and needing a further 277 for outright points. That they fell short of their target was due as much to some tentative batting as to some skilful bowling, especially by Bright. Throughout the match batsmen on both sides had difficulties as the spinners achieved considerable turn and Western Australia fought back well after trailing by 133 on the first innings.

Victoria

D. F. Whatmore c Gonnella b Mulder	21	– c Zoehrer b Matthews	5
M. B. Quinn c Gonnella b Mulder	53	– c Veletta b MacLeay	14
D. M. Jones c Moody b Mulder	37	– c Wood b MacLeay	72
P. A. Hibbert c Andrews b Mulder	10	– c Breman b Mulder	18
P. W. Young c Zoehrer b Breman	10	– c Zoehrer b MacLeay	37
J. D. Siddons c Mulder b Andrews	45	– b Matthews	17
A. I. C. Dodemaide not out	63	– not out	5
*R. J. Bright c Zoehrer b Matthews	26	– (9) b Matthews	0
†M. G. D. Dimattina run out	5	– (8) lbw b Matthews	2
C. R. Miller b Mulder	0	– c Wood b Mulder	9
M. G. Hughes b Mulder	9	– run out	0
B 7, l-b 5, n-b 4	16	B 1, l-b 3, n-b 3	7

1/47 2/116 3/121 4/131 5/148   295   1/14 2/26 3/54 4/145 5/167   186
6/201 7/262 8/283 9/283   6/168 7/170 8/176 9/186

Bowling: *First Innings*—Matthews 23-7-49-1; MacLeay 18-6-38-0; Breman 12-2-39-1; Mulder 39-10-125-6; Andrews 15-3-32-1. *Second Innings*—Matthews 23.5-5-54-4; MacLeay 22-5-50-3; Breman 6-0-28-0; Mulder 15-5-35-2; Andrews 6-0-15-0.

Western Australia

T. M. Moody c Whatmore b Bright	29	– c Dimattina b Hughes 14
M. R. J. Veletta c Hibbert b Dodemaide	26	– lbw b Bright 55
P. Gonnella b Bright	0	– lbw b Dodemaide 49
*G. M. Wood b Bright	0	– not out 67
R. B. Gartrell b Hughes	46	– (6) lbw b Miller 7
W. S. Andrews b Bright	11	– (7) b Bright 22
†T. J. Zoehrer c Dimattina b Dodemaide	4	– (5) st Dimattina b Bright 13
T. G. Breman c Miller b Bright	20	– not out 13
K. H. MacLeay not out	10	
C. D. Matthews c Quinn b Miller	11	
B. Mulder b Miller	0	
N-b 5	5	B 3, l-b 6, n-b 6 15

1/55 2/55 3/55 4/61 5/80   162   1/43 2/121 3/147   (6 wkts) 255
6/97 7/135 8/141 9/162   4/171 5/185 6/234

Bowling: *First Innings*—Hughes 14-4-39-1; Dodemaide 21-7-52-2; Miller 8-1-19-2; Bright 30-12-44-5; Jones 2-0-8-0. *Second Innings*—Hughes 23-5-69-1; Dodemaide 22-4-58-1; Miller 21-5-48-1; Bright 48-20-62-3; Jones 2-1-5-0; Siddons 1-0-4-0.

Umpires: R. Guy and L. J. King.

QUEENSLAND v NEW SOUTH WALES

At Brisbane, January 24, 25, 26, 27. Drawn. New South Wales 4 pts. Wellham's decision to put Queensland in went awry. Had O'Neill caught Kerr at second slip, Waugh, the only bowler to make any impression, might have undermined the Queensland innings; instead Kerr batted for three and a half hours and Smart for seven and a half hours as he compiled his first Shield hundred. That New South Wales, beginning their innings late on the second day, achieved first-innings points was due to the enterprising batting of Wellham and O'Neill, who hit his second successive hundred and batted in all for four and a half hours. On the final day Holland made his first fifty in first-class cricket. Wellham and Dyer were reported by umpire Johnson for dissent, but the Australian Cricket Board's commissioner, R. R. Lindwall, considered the incident "not serious enough to warrant a decision against the players".

Queensland

B. A. Courtice c Taylor b Waugh	10	– (2) c Waugh b Bennett 23
R. B. Kerr c Taylor b Waugh	84	– (1) not out 50
*K. C. Wessels c Dyer b Waugh	20	– b O'Neill 13
C. B. Smart c Dyer b Whitney	133	– run out 5
T. J. Barsby c Wellham b Blizzard	30	– not out 6
A. B. Henschell c Dyer b Waugh	14	
†R. B. Phillips c Dyer b Whitney	1	
H. Frei b Whitney	19	
J. R. Thomson b Blizzard	14	
F. M. Francke c Dyer b Whitney	22	
D. Tazelaar not out	14	
B 6, l-b 15, n-b 7	28	B 1, l-b 4, n-b 3 8

1/27 2/61 3/143 4/197 5/227   389   1/64 2/83 3/91   (3 wkts) 105
6/228 7/282 8/312 9/366

Bowling: *First Innings*—Whitney 30.3-5-73-4; Blizzard 24-7-49-2; Waugh 33-5-130-4; Bennett 27-12-50-0; Holland 26-8-62-0; O'Neill 4-2-4-0. *Second Innings*—Whitney 6-2-7-0; Blizzard 8-0-24-0; Waugh 8-1-18-0; Bennett 22-9-24-1; Holland 10-3-17-0; O'Neill 10-7-10-1.

New South Wales

S. M. Small b Francke	46	P. A. Blizzard c Barsby b Francke	24
M. A. Taylor c Henschell b Thomson	41	R. G. Holland b Henschell	53
*D. M. Wellham c Courtice b Tazelaar	72	M. R. Whitney not out	10
P. S. Clifford c sub b Tazelaar	6		
M. D. O'Neill run out	147	L-b 6, w 1, n-b 26	33
M. E. Waugh c Phillips b Henschell	12		—
†G. C. Dyer lbw b Tazelaar	23	1/103 2/124 3/155 4/238 5/272	487
M. J. Bennett lbw b Thomson	20	6/328 7/370 8/419 9/431	

Bowling: Thomson 25–1–116–2; Frei 33–7–110–0; Tazelaar 24–2–84–3; Francke 45–7–132–2; Henschell 12.2–6–36–2; Wessels 5–4–3–0.

Umpires: M. W. Johnson and M. J. King.

TASMANIA v WESTERN AUSTRALIA

At Hobart, January 24, 25, 26, 27. Drawn. Western Australia 4 pts. Three declarations failed to bring about a result as the batsmen on both sides enjoyed the ideal batting conditions. All the Western Australian top-order batsmen made runs against the weak Tasmanian bowling, with Moody unfortunate not to reach a maiden hundred. Gonnella refused a run and at the same time stranded his partner. Tasmania were in dire straits at 88 for four but Bradshaw, partnered first by Buckingham, then by Woolley, led the recovery during an innings of six hours. Woolley batted more forcefully and Tasmania avoided the follow-on early on the fourth morning. Western Australia sought quick runs, but Wood's declaration evoked a passive response from the home team.

Western Australia

T. M. Moody run out	94	– b Cooley	59
M. R. J. Veletta c Soule b Bradshaw	53	– run out	9
P. Gonnella c Bradshaw b Brown	134	– c Bennett b Cooley	36
*G. M. Wood lbw b Tame	102		
R. B. Gartrell b Tame	104	– (6) not out	1
W. S. Andrews not out	31	– (4) c Soule b Cooley	11
†T. J. Zoehrer b Brown	0		
T. G. Breman c Soule b Brown	11	– (5) c Woolley b Harris	6
B 2, l-b 10, w 1, n-b 11	24	L-b 2, n-b 5	7

1/133 2/164 3/393 4/411   (7 wkts dec.) 553   1/16 2/98 3/117   (5 wkts dec.) 129
5/540 6/541 7/553   4/124 5/129

K. H. MacLeay, C. D. Matthews and B. Mulder did not bat.

Bowling: *First Innings*—Brown 37.2–2–152–3; Cooley 19–1–78–0; Tame 35–4–127–2; Ray 21–3–69–0; Hyatt 21–5–77–0; Bradshaw 9–0–38–1. *Second Innings*—Brown 7–0–24–0; Cooley 4–0–33–3; Tame 8–0–67–0; Harris 0.3–0–3–1.

Tasmania

*M. Ray b Matthews	0	– (2) c Gartrell b Matthews	13
E. J. Harris c Zoehrer b Matthews	31	– (1) c Veletta b Mulder	21
R. J. Bennett run out	2	– lbw b Breman	21
K. Bradshaw b Mulder	112	– st Zoehrer b Mulder	22
†R. E. Soule c MacLeay b Matthews	1		
D. J. Buckingham st Zoehrer b Andrews	57	– (5) not out	52
R. D. Woolley not out	124	– not out	22
R. S. Hyatt c Mulder b Matthews	7		
M. P. Tame c Gonnella b Breman	32	– (6) b Breman	3
R. L. Brown not out	17		
B 8, l-b 2, n-b 14	24	B 10, l-b 3, n-b 4	17

1/8 2/13 3/84 4/88   (8 wkts dec.) 407   1/21 2/47 3/61   (5 wkts) 171
5/183 6/257 7/277 8/357   4/111 5/118

T. J. Cooley did not bat.

Bowling: *First Innings*—Matthews 36.2–5–116–4; MacLeay 31–6–83–0; Breman 28–10–45–1; Mulder 47–13–129–1; Andrews 10–2–24–1. *Second Innings*—Matthews 11–0–34–1; MacLeay 6–0–24–0; Breman 18–4–43–2; Mulder 23–5–55–2; Veletta 1–0–1–0; Moody 1–0–1–0.

Umpires: P. Howard and S. G. Randell.

VICTORIA v SOUTH AUSTRALIA

At Melbourne, January 25, 26, 27, 28. Drawn. Victoria 4 pts. This was Bright's 100th game for Victoria, and his performances with the bat, the ball and as captain fitted the occasion. However, his second-innings declaration, which set South Australia to make 356 on the fourth day, drew a disappointing response. For Victoria, Whatmore hit his highest score in four and a half hours, but few of the Victorians came to terms with the accurate medium-pace bowling of Zesers. South Australia's first innings was notable for Watson's splendid 97 and for Hughes being warned and subsequently banned from bowling for running on the pitch.

Victoria

D. F. Whatmore c Harms b Parkinson	127 – b Parkinson	50
M. B. Quinn c Kelly b Zesers	33 – c Kelly b Small	54
D. M. Jones c Watson b Zesers	1 – run out	91
P. A. Hibbert c and b Harms	32 – (6) not out	5
J. D. Siddons b Sleep	2 – (4) c Sleep b Small	36
A. I. C. Dodemaide c Hookes b Zesers	48 – (5) b Zesers	9
†M. G. D. Dimattina c Zadow b Zesers	4	
*R. J. Bright not out	67	
P. W. Jackson c Watson b Zesers	0	
M. G. Hughes c sub b Zesers	19	
C. R. Miller b Sleep	0	
B 4, l-b 7, n-b 1	12	B 5, l-b 9, w 1, n-b 1 16

1/86 2/100 3/158 4/171 5/218   345   1/107 2/125 3/209 (5 wkts dec.) 261
6/232 7/262 8/262 9/344   4/232 5/261

Bowling: *First Innings*—Small 22–4–54–0; Parkinson 14–2–64–1; Harms 20–2–62–1; Zesers 38–13–73–6; Hookes 4–0–14–0; Sleep 14.2–2–67–2. *Second Innings*—Small 18–0–85–2; Parkinson 13.1–2–48–1; Zesers 23–6–75–1; Sleep 14–1–39–0.

South Australia

A. M. J. Hilditch c Whatmore b Bright	15 – not out	84
A. S. Watson b Bright	97 – c sub b Miller	59
R. J. Zadow b Miller	2 – run out	8
*D. W. Hookes run out	23 – run out	9
P. R. Sleep c Dimattina b Hughes	52 – not out	10
W. M. Darling c Dimattina b Hughes	13	
†D. J. Kelly c Dimattina b Bright	4	
C. L. Harms b Jackson	20	
G. C. Small c sub b Jackson	12	
A. K. Zesers b Miller	0	
S. D. H. Parkinson not out	2	
B 2, l-b 1, n-b 8	11	B 8, l-b 8, n-b 3 19

1/52 2/63 3/110 4/175 5/205   251   1/118 2/148 3/166 (3 wkts) 189
6/212 7/219 8/242 9/249

Bowling: *First Innings*—Hughes 12.1–2–34–2; Dodemaide 12–3–29–0; Bright 42–18–73–3; Miller 16–3–61–2; Jackson 29.5–9–51–2. *Second Innings*—Hughes 10–1–29–0; Dodemaide 12–3–33–0; Bright 25–12–32–0; Miller 19–8–39–1; Jackson 19–8–36–0; Dimattina 1–0–4–0.

Umpires: R. C. Bailhache and D. E. Holden.

QUEENSLAND v TASMANIA

At Brisbane, January 31, February 1, 2, 3. Queensland won by six wickets. Queensland 12 pts.
The home team were in early trouble against Davis and Brown until Wessels and Phillips put on
180 in three and a quarter hours. Wessels enjoyed a certain amount of good fortune against
Davis, being dropped twice by Bennett in the slips and being "dismissed" twice off no-balls.
Tazelaar and Thomson took their toll of the thwarted bowlers with a last-wicket stand of 56 in
27 minutes. With Thomson suffering from a sore neck when Tasmania batted, Trimble opened
the attack with Frei and achieved his best-ever figures. When Tasmania followed on,
Thomson rejoined the attack and, though he was to bowl 26 no-balls, helped to start another
collapse. Bennett batted throughout the third day, putting on 123 in two and three-quarter
hours with Buckingham, but after his dismissal on the fourth morning, the result was never
in doubt.

Queensland

R. B. Kerr c Bennett b Davis	12	– (2) c and b Brown	9
B. A. Courtice c Soule b Brown	3	– (1) c Harris b Davis	0
*K. C. Wessels c Soule b Davis	167	– c Soule b Davis	45
G. M. Ritchie c Woolley b Davis	0	– not out	23
C. B. Smart b Davis	7	– c Bradshaw b Davis	7
G. S. Trimble c Soule b Davis	9	– not out	12
†R. B. Phillips c Bradshaw b Brown	71		
H. Frei c Harris b Brown	4		
F. M. Francke b Davis	2		
D. Tazelaar not out	29		
J. R. Thomson b Davis	24		
L-b 6, n-b 31	37	B 5, l-b 3, n-b 5	13

1/21 2/22 3/26 4/70 5/89   365   1/0 2/55 3/61 4/77   (4 wkts) 109
6/79 7/287 8/308 9/309

Bowling: *First Innings*—Brown 30–3–124–3; Davis 37.3–5–128–7; Tame 19–5–46–0;
Bradshaw 11–1–36–0; Ray 13–4–25–0. *Second Innings*—Brown 7–2–34–1; Davis 8–0–41–3;
Tame 1–0–3–0; Bradshaw 1–0–12–0; Soule 1.4–0–11–0.

Tasmania

*M. Ray b Frei	0	– (2) c Phillips b Trimble	1
E. J. Harris b Trimble	2	– (1) b Thomson	5
R. J. Bennett c Phillips b Trimble	31	– c Kerr b Thomson	110
K. Bradshaw c Tazelaar b Trimble	7	– c Phillips b Tazelaar	10
R. D. Woolley c Phillips b Tazelaar	10	– c Kerr b Tazelaar	4
D. J. Buckingham c Tazelaar b Trimble	43	– c Wessels b Trimble	62
R. S. Hyatt c Smart b Tazelaar	7	– not out	33
†R. E. Soule not out	51	– b Thomson	0
M. P. Tame b Trimble	7	– c Phillips b Frei	4
R. J. Brown c Phillips b Francke	12	– c Phillips b Frei	1
W. W. Davis c sub b Francke	10	– c Phillips b Frei	0
B 2, n-b 12	14	B 6, l-b 10, w 4, n-b 28	48

1/1 2/7 3/34 4/63 5/73   194   1/4 2/10 3/63 4/73   278
6/131 7/131 8/145 9/182   5/196 6/264 7/265
8/275 9/278

Bowling: *First Innings*—Frei 17–2–38–1; Trimble 22–5–50–5; Tazelaar 16–1–73–2; Francke
13–3–31–2. *Second Innings*—Thomson 26–2–109–3; Trimble 21–4–32–2; Frei 15.3–6–24–3;
Tazelaar 22–5–55–2; Francke 18–4–36–0; Wessels 7–4–6–0.

Umpires: M. J. King and C. D. Timmins.

NEW SOUTH WALES v TASMANIA

At Sydney, February 21, 22, 23. New South Wales won by an innings and 47 runs. New South Wales 12 pts. In taking only three days to beat Tasmania, New South Wales secured a place in the Shield final. The Sydney wicket was once again at the centre of a controversy, the faster bowlers finding a ridge at one end which led to a confrontation between Davis, the West Indian bowler, and Whitney, who was struck twice by him while batting. The umpires' report led to Whitney being fined $A250 and to a reprimand for Davis. The New South Wales opening batsman, Small, played a courageous innings to set up his team's lead, and when Tasmania batted again the combination of pace and spin from Whitney, Holland and Bennett was too much for them.

Tasmania

*M. Ray c Dyer b Waugh	8	– (2) c P. L. Taylor b Whitney	9
E. J. Harris c P. L. Taylor b Whitney	57	– (1) b Holland	37
R. J. Bennett c Dyer b Waugh	24	– c Waugh b Whitney	0
K. Bradshaw c Dyer b Whitney	0	– c M. A. Taylor b Whitney	3
R. D. Woolley c Holland b Bennett	11	– c Waugh b Holland	15
D. J. Buckingham c Bennett b Whitney	36	– c P. L. Taylor b Holland	10
R. S. Hyatt c Small b P. L. Taylor	9	– c Small b Bennett	0
B. A. Cruse c Bennett b P. L. Taylor	16	– lbw b Bennett	0
†R. E. Soule c M. A. Taylor b Bennett	13	– not out	9
R. L. Brown not out	27	– b Holland	10
W. W. Davis st Dyer b Bennett	1	– c Dyer b Holland	7
L-b 2, w 2, n-b 4	8	B 6, l-b 1	7
	210		107

1/22 2/89 3/90 4/105 5/105
6/129 7/154 8/180 9/194

1/21 2/21 3/31 4/70 5/71
6/72 7/72 8/86 9/99

Bowling: *First Innings*—Whitney 18–4–40–3; Waugh 15–5–31–2; Holland 23–6–42–0; P. L. Taylor 20–4–42–2; Bennett 24.1–7–53–3. *Second Innings*—Whitney 8–3–12–3; Waugh 7–3–15–0; Holland 12.4–6–25–5; P. L. Taylor 8–1–24–0; Bennett 19–9–23–2; Bower 1–0–1–0.

New South Wales

S. M. Small c Soule b Ray	118	M. J. Bennett not out	57
M. A. Taylor c Soule b Ray	44	R. G. Holland b Davis	15
*D. M. Wellham c Bennett b Ray	4	M. R. Whitney c Woolley b Brown	19
P. S. Clifford c Soule b Davis	0		
R. J. Bower c Soule b Davis	7	B 3, l-b 4, n-b 14	21
M. E. Waugh c Buckingham b Ray	1		
†G. C. Dyer c Soule b Ray	59	1/96 2/104 3/109 4/145 5/150	364
P. L. Taylor c Cruse b Davis	19	6/215 7/267 8/275 9/308	

Bowling: Davis 41–2–105–4; Brown 22.4–2–79–1; Hyatt 19–2–54–0; Bradshaw 1–0–4–0; Cruse 13–2–36–0; Ray 35–12–79–5.

Umpires: R. A. Emerson and R. A. French.

SOUTH AUSTRALIA v VICTORIA

At Adelaide, February 21, 22, 23, 24. Victoria won by eight wickets. Victoria 8 pts, South Australia 4 pts. Victoria, 68 for five on the second afternoon and looking set to follow on, fought back to win with time and wickets to spare. First Dodemaide batted splendidly to rescue them, and then Hickey bowled with speed and aggression in South Australia's second innings, six of his seven wickets coming from catches by the wicket-keeper, Dimattina. Finally, Victoria's opening batsmen made light work of their task. Whatmore, having batted an hour for 2 runs in the first innings, now spent two hours making 84, and Quinn batted enterprisingly for four hours in making his first century.

South Australia

A. M. J. Hilditch c Dimattina b Hickey	16	c Dimattina b Hickey	12
A. S. Watson run out	44	c Dimattina b Hickey	15
R. J. Zadow c Dimattina b Dodemaide	0	lbw b Dodemaide	19
*D. W. Hookes b Hickey	62	c Dimattina b Hickey	11
G. A. Bishop c Hickey b Dodemaide	0	c Siddons b Hickey	8
P. R. Sleep c Siddons b Hickey	16	c Dimattina b Hickey	33
†D. J. Kelly c Dimattina b Hughes	82	c Dimattina b Hickey	12
N. R. Plummer c Hibbert b Jackson	49	c Whatmore b Hughes	42
A. K. Zesers not out	12	c Jones b Parker	32
G. C. Small not out	6	c Dimattina b Hickey	22
S. D. H. Parkinson (did not bat)	–	not out	0
L-b 15, n-b 1	16	B 1, l-b 2, w 1, n-b 1	5

1/38 2/45 3/112 4/123   (8 wkts dec.) 303   1/24 2/31 3/43 4/51 5/93   211
5/127 6/151 7/259 8/288   6/114 7/115 8/172 9/207

Bowling: *First Innings*—Hickey 27-4-93-3; Hughes 19-3-54-1; Dodemaide 24-8-68-2; Jackson 19-4-48-1; Jones 5-0-17-0; Parker 2-0-8-0. *Second Innings*—Hickey 28.5-10-81-7; Hughes 28-7-64-1; Dodemaide 27-15-37-1; Jackson 12-5-19-0; Parker 4-0-7-1.

Victoria

D. F. Whatmore b Parkinson	2	c Small b Hookes	84
M. B. Quinn b Parkinson	29	run out	103
*D. M. Jones lbw b Parkinson	0	not out	57
P. A. Hibbert lbw b Parkinson	0	not out	0
J. D. Siddons c Hookes b Plummer	44		
G. R. Parker b Small	15		
A. I. C. Dodemaide c and b Zesers	80		
†M. G. D. Dimattina c Hookes b Zesers	10		
P. W. Jackson lbw b Small	2		
M. G. Hughes b Zesers	47		
D. J. Hickey not out	8		
B 3, l-b 6, w 2, n-b 2	13	B 11, l-b 12, n-b 1	24

1/36 2/39 3/39 4/39 5/68   250   1/139 2/261   (2 wkts) 268
6/122 7/140 8/145 9/233

Bowling: *First Innings*—Small 24-3-87-2; Parkinson 20-7-50-3; Zesers 34-13-46-4; Plummer 17-3-48-1; Hookes 1-0-10-0. *Second Innings*—Small 15-1-54-0; Parkinson 7-1-33-0; Zesers 22-7-44-0; Plummer 14.2-0-53-0; Hookes 4-0-20-1; Sleep 9-2-33-0; Zadow 1-0-6-0; Watson 1-0-2-0.

Umpires: B. E. Martin and R. B. Woods.

WESTERN AUSTRALIA v QUEENSLAND

At Perth, February 21, 22, 23, 24. Drawn. Western Australia 4 pts. With rain preventing any play on the first day, interest centred on the struggle for first-innings points. Wood was in excellent form for Western Australia in an innings of three hours, being especially severe on the faster bowlers. Queensland were 99 for five, and although Henschell and Barsby pulled them round with 145 in two hours, their last pair still needed 27 to obtain the points. They just failed when Thomson was caught behind, swinging at the medium-pace bowler, Breman.

Western Australia

T. M. Moody c Henschell b Thomson	39	– c Phillips b Thomson	0
M. R. J. Veletta c Smart b Thomson	0	– not out	78
P. Gonnella c Barsby b Trimble	27	– lbw b Tazelaar	61
*G. M. Wood c Tazelaar b Wessels	121		
R. B. Gartrell run out	24	– (4) not out	36
W. S. Andrews b Henschell	43		
†M. J. Cox c Phillips b Henschell	2		
T. G. Breman c Phillips b Frei	22		
K. H. MacLeay not out	21		
G. D. Porter c Phillips b Frei	0		
C. D. Matthews c Phillips b Frei	0		
L-b 2, w 2, n-b 19	23	L-b 3, w 3, n-b 14	20

1/3 2/41 3/110 4/185 5/268   **322**   1/2 2/133   (2 wkts) **195**
6/272 7/276 8/322 9/322

Bowling: *First Innings*—Thomson 12–0–83–2; Frei 25.5–2–84–3; Trimble 9–1–43–1; Tazelaar 8–0–40–0; Henschell 15–4–41–2; Wessels 10–2–29–1. *Second Innings*—Thomson 6–0–23–1; Frei 16–1–47–0; Trimble 7–2–16–0; Tazelaar 22–4–61–1; Henschell 5–4–1–0; Wessels 15–3–44–0.

Queensland

R. B. Kerr c Veletta b MacLeay	28		H. Frei c Veletta b Breman	13
B. A. Courtice c MacLeay b Breman	9		D. Tazelaar not out	10
*K. C. Wessels c Cox b MacLeay	1		J. R. Thomson c Cox b Breman	10
C. B. Smart lbw b Breman	32			
G. S. Trimble b Matthews	4		L-b 10, w 1, n-b 19	30
T. J. Barsby c Andrews b Breman	67			
A. B. Henschell b Matthews	110		1/29 2/34 3/48 4/57 5/99	319
†R. B. Phillips lbw b Breman	5		6/244 7/256 8/296 9/296	

Bowling: Matthews 25–8–75–2; MacLeay 31–7–90–2; Breman 21–2–76–6; Porter 17–5–38–0; Andrews 6–0–30–0.

Umpires: R. J. Evans and T. A. Prue.

NEW SOUTH WALES v QUEENSLAND

At Sydney, February 28, March 1, 2, 3. Drawn. New South Wales 4 pts. Queensland's failure to take even first-innings points left New South Wales on top of the Shield table – and thus with home advantage in the final. Yet on the first evening Queensland were 218 for one with Kerr and Wessels in total command. Then Holland took three wickets in fourteen balls and Queensland were struggling. New South Wales were given a splendid foundation by Mark Taylor with an innings of six and a quarter hours. O'Neill, whose powerful strokeplay produced twelve boundaries on the slow outfield, hit his third consecutive hundred for the state but was dropped three times in four and a half hours at the wicket.

Queensland

B. A. Courtice c Dyer b Holland	20	– (2) not out	35
R. B. Kerr c and b Holland	102		
*K. C. Wessels b Holland	93		
†R. B. Phillips lbw b Waugh	11	– (5) not out	7
C. B. Smart c Dyer b Holland	0	– (1) b Whitney	4
G. S. Trimble c P. L. Taylor b Whitney	19	– (3) c M. A. Taylor b Waugh	0
T. J. Barsby not out	56		
A. B. Henschell c P. L. Taylor b Waugh	15	– (4) c M. A. Taylor b Whitney	43
H. Frei c Waugh b Whitney	1		
J. R. Thomson b Holland	14		
F. M. Francke c Dyer b Waugh	1		
L-b 3, n-b 4	7	L-b 2, n-b 5	7

1/51 2/218 3/219 4/221 5/242   **339**   1/7 2/8 3/85   (3 wkts) **96**
6/257 7/278 8/279 9/326

Bowling: *First Innings*—Waugh 18.4–4–49–3; Whitney 23–5–63–2; Holland 43–15–92–5; Bennett 37–6–77–0; P. L. Taylor 11–5–27–0; O'Neill 7–3–15–0; Bower 6–1–13–0. *Second Innings*—Waugh 10–4–13–1; Whitney 11–3–15–2; Holland 11–3–20–0; Bennett 7–5–2–0; P. L. Taylor 8–0–22–0; O'Neill 7–1–22–0.

New South Wales

S. M. Small c Phillips b Frei	22	M. J. Bennett c Frei b Francke	14
M. A. Taylor c Phillips b Thomson	89	R. G. Holland st Phillips b Francke	19
*D. M. Wellham c Phillips b Trimble	4	M. R. Whitney not out	0
R. J. Bower c Barsby b Trimble	57		
M. D. O'Neill b Wessels	117	B 3, l-b 11, n-b 15	29
M. E. Waugh c Phillips b Wessels	27		
†G. C. Dyer c Phillips b Frei	19	1/35 2/48 3/147 4/239 5/338	440
P. L. Taylor c Smart b Henschell	43	6/343 7/371 8/403 9/440	

Bowling: Thomson 32–5–92–1; Frei 36–11–75–2; Trimble 40–12–95–2; Francke 32.3–8–86–2; Henschell 20–3–53–1; Wessels 12–4–25–2.

Umpires: R. A. French and A. G. Marshall.

TASMANIA v VICTORIA

At Devonport, February 28, March 1, 2. Victoria won by nine wickets. Victoria 12 pts. Tasmania, their batsmen overwhelmed by the hostile bowling of Hughes, Hickey and O'Donnell, suffered their seventh defeat of the season. Victoria, on the other hand, were never troubled by the depleted Tasmanian attack and Hibbert hit his third hundred of the season. Following an injury to Dimattina, Jones kept wicket for Victoria.

Tasmania

R. J. Bennett b Dodemaide	22	– (2) c O'Donnell b Hughes	1
E. J. Harris c Dodemaide b O'Donnell	49	– (1) b Hickey	17
*M. Ray b Hughes	44	– c Siddons b Hughes	0
K. Bradshaw c Dodemaide b O'Donnell	0	– (5) b Hickey	0
D. J. Buckingham c Whatmore b O'Donnell	49	– (4) c Whatmore b Hickey	36
R. D. Woolley c Siddons b Hughes	0	– c Jones b Hickey	17
R. S. Hyatt b Hughes	38	– retired hurt	1
†R. E. Soule c Jackson b O'Donnell	25	– c sub b Hickey	27
R. L. Brown c Jones b Hughes	3	– c Siddons b Hughes	5
T. J. Cooley c Jones b Hughes	0	– c Hibbert b Hughes	0
W. W. Davis not out	0	– not out	11
B 3, l-b 7, n-b 1	11		
1/33 2/111 3/119 4/127 5/130	241	1/1 2/1 3/50 4/54 5/71	115
6/193 7/225 8/239 9/239		6/72 7/93 8/93 9/115	

Bowling: *First Innings*—Hughes 23–6–53–5; Hickey 20–1–68–0; Dodemaide 23–5–48–1; O'Donnell 24.3–7–52–4; Jackson 4–1–10–0. *Second Innings*—Hughes 10–1–23–4; Hickey 13.3–1–52–5; Dodemaide 2–0–9–0; O'Donnell 8–3–31–0.

Victoria

D. F. Whatmore c Woolley b Brown	4	– (2) not out	23
M. B. Quinn b Brown	24	– (1) c sub b Cooley	5
*D. M. Jones c Davis b Ray	70		
P. A. Hibbert c Woolley b Brown	124		
J. D. Siddons c Buckingham b Bradshaw	57		
S. P. O'Donnell c Soule b Brown	25		
A. I. C. Dodemaide not out	4		
P. W. Jackson (did not bat)		– (3) not out	0
L-b 6, w 2, n-b 10	18	N-b 3	3
1/13 2/83 3/135	(6 wkts dec.) 326	1/27	(1 wkt) 31
4/249 5/315 6/326			

M. G. Hughes, D. J. Hickey and †M. G. D. Dimattina did not bat.

Bowling: *First Innings*—Davis 13–3–31–0; Brown 31.4–1–102–4; Cooley 10–0–69–0; Bradshaw 6–0–32–1; Ray 16–2–57–1; Hyatt 9–1–29–0. *Second Innings*—Brown 5–0–16–0; Cooley 4.5–0–15–1.

Umpires: J. Hinds and S. G. Randell.

WESTERN AUSTRALIA v SOUTH AUSTRALIA

At Perth, February 28, March 1, 2, 3. Drawn. Western Australia 4 pts. Wood's decision to put South Australia in was foiled by the best pitch in Perth of the season. Sleep, having survived a difficult chance to MacLeay before he had scored, batted stubbornly for seven and a half hours, and Pyke played encouragingly in his first match, hitting two 6s and eight 4s. After an unsteady start, Western Australia took control through a partnership of 167 in 201 minutes between Veletta and Gartrell. When they both fell to Pyke's medium pace, the left-handed Andrews hit out aggressively to obtain first-innings points for Western Australia on the final morning. South Australia's declaration after 50 overs set Western Australia a target of 181 in 31 overs, and although Gonnella and Wood took them to 54 in the tenth over, the steadiness of Small and Pyke curtailed the run-chase. As wickets fell regularly, Wood was content to hold out for a draw.

South Australia

A. M. J. Hilditch lbw b MacLeay	1	– c Andrews b Matthews 28
A. S. Watson b Mulder	39	– run out 26
P. R. Sleep c Cox b Breman	139	– b Matthews 0
*D. W. Hookes c Cox b Matthews	20	– (8) st sub b Andrews 28
G. A. Bishop c Cox b Moody	36	– st sub b Andrews 50
S. C. Wundke c Cox b Breman	35	– (4) c Mulder b Moody 28
†D. J. Kelly c Matthews b Mulder	39	– (6) b Breman 5
J. K. Pyke c Breman b Matthews	77	– (7) not out 8
A. K. Zesers b Breman	5	– c Matthews b Breman 0
G. C. Small st Cox b Mulder	0	– not out 1
S. D. H. Parkinson not out	7	
B 4, l-b 14, w 2, n-b 14	34	B 1, l-b 3, w 1, n-b 2 7

1/1 2/103 3/135 4/197 5/294   432   1/30 2/30 3/78   (8 wkts dec.) 181
6/306 7/388 8/399 9/408   4/95 5/121 6/145
                                           7/177 8/180

Bowling: *First Innings*—Matthews 36.2–5–112–2; MacLeay 39–9–72–1; Breman 29–9–74–3; Mulder 47–21–112–3; Moody 19.5–5–44–1. *Second Innings*—Matthews 8–2–19–2; MacLeay 7–3–24–0; Breman 8–1–26–2; Mulder 10–2–47–0; Moody 9–3–27–1; Andrews 8–3–33–2; Wood 0.1–0–1–0.

Western Australia

T. M. Moody b Zesers	46	– c Hookes b Small 2
M. R. J. Veletta c Watson b Pyke	107	– (9) c Hookes b Small 2
P. Gonnella c Zesers b Small	0	– (2) c Kelly b Pyke 37
*G. M. Wood c Zesers b Small	9	– (3) not out 64
R. B. Gartrell c and b Pyke	92	– (4) c Kelly b Small 3
W. S. Andrews not out	82	– (5) c Hookes b Pyke 11
†M. J. Cox c Zesers b Parkinson	31	– (8) c Bishop b Pyke 3
T. G. Breman not out	45	– (6) b Small 0
K. H. MacLeay (did not bat)		– (7) c Wundke b Pyke 2
C. D. Matthews (did not bat)		– not out 1
B 5, l-b 13, w 1, n-b 2	21	B 1, l-b 2 3

1/71 2/80 3/93 4/260   (6 wkts dec.) 433   1/10 2/54 3/57   (8 wkts) 128
5/268 6/348   4/92 5/92 6/95
                                              7/98 8/125

B. Mulder did not bat.

Bowling: *First Innings*—Small 34–10–77–2; Parkinson 25–5–96–1; Pyke 24–6–84–2; Zesers 39–10–112–1; Hookes 1–0–4–0; Sleep 4–0–42–0. *Second Innings*—Small 16–2–47–4; Parkinson 2–0–22–0; Pyke 9–3–27–4; Zesers 2–0–13–0; Hookes 1–0–16–0; Sleep 1–1–0–0.

Umpires: R. J. Evans and P. J. McConnell.

SHEFFIELD SHIELD FINAL

NEW SOUTH WALES v QUEENSLAND

At Sydney, March 14, 15, 16, 17, 18. Drawn. Queensland needed to win the match in order to lift the Sheffield Shield from New South Wales, and for the second successive year they were foiled by the New South Wales tailenders. Bennett and Holland batted through the last nine overs to save their side from defeat. Queensland's first innings, although formidable, took them nearly two days to compile, Wessels, their captain, batting dourly and setting an example which was followed by Kerr and Trimble. Trimble hit his first hundred, while for the holders, Whitney bowled spiritedly to achieve his best return. New South Wales dropped seven catches. Dyer's batting made up for some poor wicket-keeping and his enterprising partnership with Waugh enabled New South Wales to save the follow-on. Queensland showed more urgency in the second innings but were tied down by some good spin bowling from Bennett and Taylor. Thomson, making his farewell appearance in first-class cricket, was given a standing ovation by a crowd of 3,300 on the last day. In all, 16,900 attended the final.

Queensland

B. A. Courtice c Dyer b Bower	8	– (2) st Dyer b Bennett	22
R. B. Kerr c M. A. Taylor b Whitney	64	– (1) st Dyer b Bennett	34
*K. C. Wessels c Dyer b Whitney	166	– c Small b P. L. Taylor	29
C. B. Smart c M. A. Taylor b Whitney	0	– (5) b P. L. Taylor	2
T. J. Barsby c Dyer b Whitney	0	– (7) c M. A. Taylor b P. L. Taylor	10
G. S. Trimble b Waugh	112	– (4) run out	0
A. B. Henschell not out	44	– (6) not out	20
†R. B. Phillips c M. A. Taylor b P. L. Taylor	5	– c Bower b P. L. Taylor	6
H. Frei c Small b Whitney	1	– not out	1
J. R. Thomson c Dyer b Whitney	0		
D. Tazelaar not out	3		
B 6, l-b 8, w 1, n-b 18	33	L-b 2, w 3, n-b 4	9

1/34 2/141 3/148 4/148 5/327 (9 wkts dec.) 436 1/62 2/71 3/71 (7 wkts dec.) 133
6/412 7/425 8/426 9/427   4/85 5/106 6/122
                                               7/131

Bowling: *First Innings*—Whitney 34–7–65–6; Waugh 27–4–71–1; Bower 7–1–28–1; Holland 39–7–92–0; Bennett 27–5–65–0; P. L. Taylor 25–3–78–1; O'Neill 6–1–23–0. *Second Innings*—Whitney 10–4–14–0; Waugh 5–0–25–0; Holland 5–0–25–0; Bennett 13–0–36–2; P. L. Taylor 13–1–31–4.

New South Wales

S. M. Small c Courtice b Frei	39	– c Kerr b Wessels	50
M. A. Taylor c Phillips b Tazelaar	41	– c Phillips b Frei	30
M. J. Bennett c Phillips b Tazelaar	11	– (9) not out	2
*D. M. Wellham lbw b Henschell	7	– (3) run out	80
R. J. Bower c Tazelaar b Frei	3	– (4) c Phillips b Tazelaar	0
M. D. O'Neill b Henschell	20	– (5) c Phillips b Henschell	1
M. E. Waugh c Phillips b Thomson	41	– (6) c Smart b Wessels	24
†G. C. Dyer not out	88	– (7) run out	0
P. L. Taylor c Smart b Thomson	0	– (8) lbw b Tazelaar	42
R. G. Holland lbw b Thomson	5	– not out	0
M. R. Whitney c Smart b Tazelaar	0		
B 4, l-b 4, w 1, n-b 30	39	B 3, l-b 3, w 2, n-b 9	17

1/53 2/95 3/112 4/116 5/124   294   1/64 2/97 3/115 4/116 (8 wkts) 258
6/149 7/248 8/251 9/264   5/182 6/184 7/254 8/254

Bowling: *First Innings*—Thomson 29–3–91–3; Frei 37–7–87–2; Tazelaar 22–4–48–3; Henschell 19–2–48–2; Trimble 2–0–12–0. *Second Innings*—Thomson 19–5–41–0; Frei 26–8–71–1; Tazelaar 20–6–57–2; Henschell 29–13–45–1; Trimble 2–0–12–0; Wessels 16–5–26–2.

Umpires: R. A. French and M. W. Johnson.

SHEFFIELD SHIELD WINNERS

1892-93	Victoria	1938-39	South Australia
1893-94	South Australia	1939-40	New South Wales
1894-95	Victoria	1940-46	No competition
1895-96	New South Wales	1946-47	Victoria
1896-97	New South Wales	1947-48	Western Australia
1897-98	Victoria	1948-49	New South Wales
1898-99	Victoria	1949-50	New South Wales
1899-1900	New South Wales	1950-51	Victoria
1900-01	Victoria	1951-52	New South Wales
1901-02	New South Wales	1952-53	South Australia
1902-03	New South Wales	1953-54	New South Wales
1903-04	New South Wales	1954-55	New South Wales
1904-05	New South Wales	1955-56	New South Wales
1905-06	New South Wales	1956-57	New South Wales
1906-07	New South Wales	1957-58	New South Wales
1907-08	Victoria	1958-59	New South Wales
1908-09	New South Wales	1959-60	New South Wales
1909-10	South Australia	1960-61	New South Wales
1910-11	New South Wales	1961-62	New South Wales
1911-12	New South Wales	1962-63	Victoria
1912-13	South Australia	1963-64	South Australia
1913-14	New South Wales	1964-65	New South Wales
1914-15	Victoria	1965-66	New South Wales
1915-19	No competition	1966-67	Victoria
1919-20	New South Wales	1967-68	Western Australia
1920-21	New South Wales	1968-69	South Australia
1921-22	Victoria	1969-70	Victoria
1922-23	New South Wales	1970-71	South Australia
1923-24	Victoria	1971-72	Western Australia
1924-25	Victoria	1972-73	Western Australia
1925-26	New South Wales	1973-74	Victoria
1926-27	South Australia	1974-75	Western Australia
1927-28	Victoria	1975-76	South Australia
1928-29	New South Wales	1976-77	Western Australia
1929-30	Victoria	1977-78	Western Australia
1930-31	Victoria	1978-79	Victoria
1931-32	New South Wales	1979-80	Victoria
1932-33	New South Wales	1980-81	Western Australia
1933-34	Victoria	1981-82	South Australia
1934-35	Victoria	1982-83	New South Wales
1935-36	South Australia	1983-84	Western Australia
1936-37	Victoria	1984-85	New South Wales
1937-38	New South Wales	1985-86	New South Wales

New South Wales have won the Shield 39 times, Victoria 24, South Australia 12, Western Australia 9, Queensland 0, Tasmania 0.

†McDONALD'S CUP, 1985-86

At Adelaide, October 13. Western Australia won by two wickets. South Australia 199 for eight (50 overs) (D. F. G. O'Connor 61, S. C. Wundke 45; B. A. Reid four for 40); Western Australia 200 for eight (49.1 overs) (G. R. Marsh 92 not out; S. C. Wundke four for 36).

At Brisbane, October 13. Drawn. Queensland 235 for eight (50 overs) (R. B. Kerr 50, K. C. Wessels 47, G. M. Ritchie 74 not out; M. A. Hill five for 29); Tasmania 45 for no wkt (11 overs).

At Melbourne, November 28. Victoria won by 8 runs. Victoria 209 for eight (50 overs) (D. F. Whatmore 51, P. W. Young 83); Tasmania 201 for seven (50 overs) (K. Bradshaw 43, D. J. Buckingham 43 not out).

At Sydney, December 5. New South Wales won by 1 run. New South Wales 235 for five (50 overs) (D. M. Wellham 62, P. S. Clifford 52, R. J. Bower 45 not out); Western Australia 234 for seven (50 overs) (G. M. Wood 59, G. R. Marsh 73).

At Melbourne, December 11. Queensland won by seven wickets. Victoria 170 (49.4 overs) (P. W. Young 43); Queensland 133 for three (35 overs) (T. J. Barsby 52, B. A. Courtice 52).

At Sydney, December 18. New South Wales won by four wickets. South Australia 203 for eight (50 overs) (W. M. Darling 41, W. B. Phillips 66 not out); New South Wales 204 for six (47.5 overs) (M. A. Taylor 59, S. R. Waugh 47).

Semi-Finals

At Sydney, February 15. Victoria won by four wickets. New South Wales 191 for nine (50 overs) (P. S. Clifford 73); Victoria 194 for six (48.1 overs) (P. W. Young 97 not out, D. M. Jones 48).

At Brisbane, February 16. Queensland won by seven wickets. Queensland 212 (48.4 overs) (R. B. Kerr 74, T. J. Barsby 55 not out); Western Australia 214 for three (44 overs) (M. R. J. Veletta 105 not out).

FINAL

†WESTERN AUSTRALIA v VICTORIA

At Melbourne, March 10. Western Australia won by 19 runs. Toss: Victoria. The match was replayed after rain had interrupted the scheduled final.
Attendance: 3,065

Western Australia

T. M. Moody c Dodemaide b Hickey ..	14	K. H. MacLeay not out	11
M. R. J. Veletta c Jones b Hickey	0	G. D. Porter run out	0
P. Gonnella c Siddons b Hickey	8	C. D. Matthews run out	1
*G. M. Wood c Ephraims b Hickey ...	0	L-b 6, w 5, n-b 2	13
R. B. Gartrell c Whatmore b Hickey ..	1		
W. S. Andrews c Siddons b Hughes ...	71	1/2 2/18 3/18	(38 overs) 167
†M. J. Cox b Jones	38	4/19 5/37 6/117	
T. G. Breman run out	10	7/140 8/164 9/165	

Bowling: Hickey 8–2–26–5; Dodemaide 7–3–17–0; Hughes 7–1–24–1; Parker 4–0–30–0; O'Donnell 8–0–41–0; Jones 4–0–23–1.

Victoria

M. C. Ephraims c MacLeay b Matthews	21	
D. F. Whatmore c Wood b Porter	34	
*D. M. Jones c Veletta b Breman	0	
P. W. Young run out	17	
J. D. Siddons b Porter	22	
S. P. O'Donnell c Wood b Moody	2	
A. I. C. Dodemaide c Gartrell b MacLeay	25	
G. R. Parker c Cox b Porter	0	

†M. G. D. Dimattina c and b Moody .. 3
M. G. Hughes not out 9
D. J. Hickey run out 2
B 2, l-b 7, w 3, n-b 1 13

1/34 2/38 3/78   (36.5 overs) 148
4/82 5/106 6/108
7/108 8/111 9/143

Bowling: Matthews 8–2–16–1; MacLeay 5.5–0–30–1; Breman 7–1–30–1; Porter 8–0–28–3; Moody 8–1–35–2.

Umpires: R. C. Bailhache and R. C. Isherwood.

KNOCKOUT COMPETITION WINNERS

Australasian Knockout: 1969-70 New Zealand; 1970-71 Western Australia; 1971-72 Victoria; 1972-73 New Zealand.

Gillette Cup: 1973-74 Western Australia; 1974-75 New Zealand; 1975-76 Queensland; 1976-77 Western Australia; 1977-78 Western Australia; 1978-79 Tasmania.

McDonald's Cup: 1979-80 Victoria; 1980-81 Queensland; 1981-82 Queensland; 1982-83 Western Australia; 1983-84 South Australia; 1984-85 New South Wales; 1985-86 Western Australia.

THE ASHES

"In affectionate remembrance of English cricket which died at The Oval, 29th August, 1882. Deeply lamented by a large circle of sorrowing friends and acquaintances, R.I.P. N.B. The body will be cremated and the Ashes taken to Australia."

Australia's first victory on English soil over the full strength of England, on August 29, 1882, inspired a young London journalist, Reginald Shirley Brooks, to write this mock "obituary". It appeared in the *Sporting Times*.

Before England's defeat at The Oval, by 7 runs, arrangements had already been made for the Hon. Ivo Bligh, afterwards Lord Darnley, to lead a team to Australia. Three weeks later they set out, now with the popular objective of recovering the Ashes. In the event, Australia won the first Test by nine wickets, but with England winning the next two it became generally accepted that they brought back the Ashes.

It was long accepted that the real Ashes – a small urn believed to contain the ashes of a bail used in the third match – were presented to Bligh by a group of Melbourne women. At the time of the 1982 centenary of The Oval Test match, however, evidence was produced which suggested that these ashes were the remains of a ball and that they were given to the England captain by Sir William Clarke, the presentation taking place before the Test matches in Australia in 1883. The certain origin of the Ashes, therefore, is the subject of some dispute.

After Lord Darnley's death in 1927, the urn was given to MCC by Lord Darnley's Australian-born widow, Florence. It can be seen in the cricket museum at Lord's, together with a red and gold velvet bag, made specially for it, and the scorecard of the 1882 match.

CRICKET IN SOUTH AFRICA, 1985-86

By PETER SICHEL

The first of two visits by an Australian team, together with a condensed domestic programme, assured cricket followers in South Africa of an abundance of good cricket. Certainly the Australians, after a slow start in acclimatising to new conditions, provided much-needed international stimulus to South African players unable to play official Test cricket. The two teams were well balanced, with South Africa winning the third of the "Test" matches after two draws. The "Tests" were well supported, particularly at Cape Town, and the one-day games were always played before packed grounds.

Fast bowling dictated the series, 89 of the 95 wickets taken falling to the seamers. For the visitors, Carl Rackemann excelled with 28 wickets, and had Alderman and Hogg not been dogged by injuries, the result might have been different. Rackemann never stopped trying, even in the most adverse conditions, and no South African batsman could truthfully say that he had mastered his seam and swing bowling. Of the batsmen, John Dyson, Steve Smith and Mike Taylor stood out, leaving South Africans wondering why they had failed to gain regular places in the Australian Test team. Kim Hughes led the side with commendable astuteness, and also produced glimpses of his batting class, but neither he nor the vice-captain, Graham Yallop, scored as many runs as anticipated.

The South Africans, unused to competition of this nature, did falter on occasions. The exceptions were Clive Rice, Henry Fotheringham, the evergreen Graeme Pollock and Kevin McKenzie. Called up from a south-coast beach to replace the injured Ken McEwan, McKenzie played several innings of maturity and sound strokeplay and topped the "Test" batting averages with 220 runs at 73.33. Pollock hit a hundred at Durban, and although not the player of ten years earlier, he was always dominant at the wicket. Garth le Roux and Hugh Page bore the brunt of the attack, and le Roux and Clive Rice both took hat-tricks in the third "Test" at Johannesburg. Alan Kourie did not live up to his reputation in domestic cricket, and perhaps the quick-footed Hughes had something to do with his length being uncharacteristically off target.

In the domestic competitions, Western Province enjoyed a most successful season, winning not only the Currie Cup but also the Benson and Hedges Trophy, the Southern Cross Shield and the Firestone Challenge Trophy; and they were the beaten finalists in the Nissan Shield, which was won by Transvaal. Having obtained the services as manager and coach of Robin Jackman, formerly of Surrey, Western Province played their best cricket for some time. McEwan and le Roux both produced consistently outstanding performances, McEwan topping the Currie Cup averages at a shade over 71, and le Roux taking 39 wickets, the most in the competition. They were well supported by their colleagues in a fine team effort.

Transvaal did not enjoy their best season. Page and Neal Radford bowled well, but Sylvester Clarke was sorely missed for much of the summer. However, the season did mark the emergence of Brian McMillan as a cricketer of rare ability. Sadly, Kourie, for the first time in many summers, failed to make an impact with the ball. But his batting was as solid as before, and he remained a difficult batsman to dislodge, his eye and courage being his hallmark.

Northern Transvaal, having lost Mandy Yachad to Transvaal and gained Roy Pienaar from Western Province, were always there or thereabouts, and they were always difficult to beat in Pretoria. Pienaar's batting was a delight; as a strokeplayer he had few peers in the country. Natal again disappointed, in spite of Collis King's enjoying his best season in South Africa. The Kent fast bowler, Graham Dilley, also had a fine season, capturing 30 wickets in the Currie Cup, and Rob Bentley again impressed. Their captain, Darryl Bestall, missed several matches through injury. Eastern Province won only one match, but with young players of the calibre of Philip Amm, Mark Rushmere and Tim Shaw they can only improve their position. The news that Kepler Wessels would be assisting them in 1986-87 could have been the spur that was needed in the Eastern Cape.

Most interest was shown in the emergence of Border and Orange Free State in the premier competition, and in spite of winning only one match between them, they justified their promotion. For Border, Lorrie Wilmot made a welcome return to first-class cricket and Faoud Bacchus, having his best season in South Africa, did much to ensure a good start to their innings. Their problems lay in their attack. The Free State, soundly led by Chris Broad of Nottinghamshire, enhanced their reputation, with fine performances from Corrie van Zyl, a lively fast-medium bowler, and Joubert Strydom, son of Steve Strydom, the international rugby referee and himself a fine cricketer.

Boland, captained by Stephen Jones, won the Castle Bowl for the second time in three years. However, many observers feel that the time has come to introduce one single competition, the thinking being that players can only improve with sterner competition provided by the stronger provinces.

FIRST-CLASS AVERAGES, 1985-86

BATTING

(Qualification: 8 innings, 400 runs, average 30.00)

	M	I	NO	R	HI	100s	Avge
C. R. Norris (*Transvaal B*)	6	11	4	477	126*	3	68.14
K. S. McEwan (*W. Province*)	7	11	2	510	142	2	56.66
B. M. McMillan (*Transvaal/Transvaal B*)	5	9	1	419	129	1	52.37
M. W. Rushmere (*E. Province*)	8	15	4	570	128	1	51.81
R. G. Pollock (*Transvaal*)	9	15	2	671	113	2	51.61
R. M. Bentley (*Natal*)	6	9	1	410	134*	1	51.25
H. R. Fotheringham (*Transvaal*)	11	20	2	841	114*	3	46.72
A. L. Wilmot (*Border*)	7	12	2	448	108*	1	44.80
S. J. Cook (*Transvaal*)	11	20	1	840	124	2	44.21
K. A. McKenzie (*Transvaal*)	9	14	2	511	110	1	42.58
M. S. Venter (*Transvaal/Transvaal B*)	7	12	1	459	225*	1	41.72
S. F. A. F. Bacchus (*Border*)	7	12	0	494	134	1	41.16
L. P. Vorster (*Transvaal B*)	6	11	1	404	95	0	40.40
A. G. Elgar (*W. Province/W. Province B*)	7	11	0	438	81	0	39.81
P. G. Amm (*E. Province*)	6	11	0	431	82	0	39.18
A. M. Ferreira (*N. Transvaal*)	8	14	1	499	105	1	38.38
R. F. Pienaar (*N. Transvaal*)	7	14	0	534	90	0	38.14
B. C. Broad (*OFS*)	7	12	1	416	101*	1	37.81
S. A. Jones (*Boland*)	8	14	0	518	132	1	37.00
P. N. Kirsten (*W. Province*)	10	17	1	516	83	0	32.25
S. Nackerdien (*Boland*)	8	16	2	444	122	1	31.71

*Signifies not out.

BOWLING

(Qualification: 25 wickets, average 25.00)

	O	M	R	W	BB	Avge
B. A. Matthews (*W. Province/W. Province B*)	303.4	77	625	42	5-32	14.88
G. R. Dilley (*Natal*)	206.4	57	486	30	7-63	16.20
E. O. Simons (*W. Province*)	190	40	474	28	5-52	16.92
H. A. Page (*Transvaal*)	280.1	62	751	42	5-31	17.88
N. V. Radford (*Transvaal*)	213.5	37	627	35	5-52	17.91
G. S. le Roux (*W. Province*)	334.3	66	884	49	5-54	18.04
P. Anker (*Boland*)	308.2	105	562	31	5-34	18.12
O. Henry (*Boland*)	344	116	757	38	7-82	19.92
C. J. P. G. van Zyl (*OFS*)	277	67	624	31	5-54	20.12
S. T. Jefferies (*W. Province*)	293.4	72	810	35	5-30	23.14
C. D. Mitchley (*N. Transvaal*)	238.5	43	695	30	5-26	23.16
J. C. van Duyker (*N. Transvaal B*)	231.4	44	643	26	4-29	24.73

Note: Runs debited to these bowlers do not include wides and no-balls.

CURRIE CUP, 1985-86

	Played	Won	Lost	Drawn	Bonus Points Batting	Bonus Points Bowling	Total Pts
Western Province	6	4	0	2	26	25	91
Transvaal	6	2	0	4	20	27	67
Northern Transvaal	6	1	1	4	20	27	57
Natal	6	1	1	4	19	23	52
Eastern Province	6	1	2	3	10	19	39
Border	6	1	2	3	12	14	36
Orange Free State	6	0	4	2	14	22	36

Semi-final: Transvaal beat Northern Transvaal by 277 runs.
Final: Western Province drew with Transvaal and won the trophy.

EASTERN PROVINCE v BORDER

At Port Elizabeth, October 25, 26, 27. Drawn. Eastern Province 3 pts, Border 3 pts.

Border

S. F. A. F. Bacchus b Armitage	40	– c Rushmere b Watson	7
N. P. Minnaar lbw b van Vuuren	29	– b Watson	29
†V. G. Cresswell b Shaw	4	– b van Vuuren	15
E. N. Trotman b van Vuuren	6	– c Michau b Armitage	26
I. L. Howell run out	36	– c Watson b Birrell	28
A. L. Wilmot lbw b van Vuuren	38	– lbw b Shaw	34
G. L. Hayes c Richardson b Watson	29	– not out	20
*R. B. C. Ranger c Birrell b Armitage	0	– not out	4
G. C. G. Fraser not out	4		
G. M. Gower lbw b van Vuuren	0		
J. A. Carse c Birrell b Watson	2		
B 6, l-b 7, w 2	15	L-b 5, w 1	6

1/51 2/58 3/67 4/104 5/142　　　　　203　　1/12 2/52 3/55 4/94　　(6 wkts) 169
6/170 7/187 8/199 9/200　　　　　　　　　　5/132 6/146

Bowling: *First Innings*—Watson 17–4–36–2; Capel 18–9–25–0; van Vuuren 16–8–28–4; Shaw 25–5–63–1; Armitage 14–4–34–2; Birrell 1–0–2–0. *Second Innings*—Watson 15–2–49–2; Capel 9–1–19–0; van Vuuren 15–8–22–1; Shaw 21–13–19–1; Armitage 15–7–23–1; Birrell 9–3–31–1.

Eastern Province

P. G. Amm c and b Howell	60	R. L. S. Armitage not out 71
A. V. Birrell c Bacchus b Carse	7	T. G. Shaw not out 43
T. B. Reid lbw b Howell	21	B 11, l-b 7, w 2 20
*†D. J. Richardson c Cresswell b Ranger	19	
M. W. Rushmere st Cresswell b Bacchus	36	1/30 2/69 3/114 (7 wkts dec.) 311
M. Michau st Cresswell b Ranger	26	4/114 5/148
D. J. Capel st Cresswell b Howell	8	6/167 7/194

M. K. van Vuuren and W. K. Watson did not bat.

Bowling: Carse 16–3–38–1; Trotman 13–4–33–0; Gower 5–1–5–0; Fraser 4–0–15–0; Ranger 38–8–68–2; Howell 52–18–99–3; Hayes 3–1–9–0; Bacchus 13–3–24–1.

Umpires: D. H. Bezuidenhout and H. R. Martin.

Wides not debited to bowlers' analyses.

ORANGE FREE STATE v WESTERN PROVINCE

At Bloemfontein, October 25, 26, 28. Western Province won by an innings and 24 runs. Western Province 21 pts, Orange Free State 4 pts.

Western Province

A. G. Elgar c van Heerden b Holder ..	25	E. O. Simons c East b van Zyl 5
L. Seeff c Strydom b Player	51	†R. J. Ryall not out 8
P. N. Kirsten lbw b van Heerden	25	
K. S. McEwan c East b van Zyl	142	B 9, l-b 12, w 1, n-b 7 29
D. J. Cullinan c East b Player	43	
*A. P. Kuiper b Beukes	23	1/45 2/99 3/113 (8 wkts dec.) 402
G. S. le Roux c van Zyl b Beukes	0	4/237 5/321 6/323
S. T. Jefferies not out	51	7/326 8/358

M. B. Minnaar did not bat.

Bowling: van Zyl 18–4–45–2; Player 23–3–93–2; Beukes 28–8–77–2; Holder 15–1–59–1; van Heerden 18–1–99–1.

Orange Free State

*B. C. Broad c and b Jefferies	4	– c McEwan b Kirsten	25
R. A. le Roux c McEwan b le Roux	0	– b le Roux	41
D. P. le Roux c Elgar b Jefferies	10	– c Kuiper b Kirsten	0
J. J. Strydom c Ryall b Jefferies	53	– (8) not out	39
†R. J. East lbw b Minnaar	29	– c McEwan b le Roux	15
C. J. van Heerden b le Roux	9	– b le Roux	5
J. M. Truter c Simons b Jefferies	5	– (4) c Minnaar b Kirsten	16
A. P. Beukes c and b Simons	17	– (7) b Minnaar	18
V. A. Holder b Minnaar	28	– b Kirsten	0
C. J. P. G. van Zyl c Kuiper b Simons	11	– c and b Kirsten	9
B. T. Player not out	7	– lbw b Kirsten	0
B 2, l-b 10, w 10, n-b 1	23	L-b 12, w 1, n-b 1	14

1/9 2/19 3/22 4/42 5/88 196 1/56 2/56 3/90 4/102 5/111 182
6/129 7/135 8/176 9/178   6/112 7/167 8/168 9/180

Bowling: *First Innings*—le Roux 17–5–38–2; Jefferies 18–9–38–4; Simons 14.2–4–47–2; Minnaar 12–3–46–2; Seeff 1–0–4–0. *Second Innings*—le Roux 16–5–27–3; Jefferies 12–4–23–0; Simons 8–2–9–0; Minnaar 29–11–61–1; Kirsten 21.3–7–48–6.

Umpires: P. M. de Klerk and A. J. Norton.

Wides and no-balls not debited to bowlers' analyses.

NATAL v NORTHERN TRANSVAAL

At Durban, October 26, 27, 28. Drawn. Natal 4 pts, Northern Transvaal 8 pts.

Natal

B. J. Whitfield c Geringer b Ontong	51	– c du Preez b Clare	25
M. B. Logan lbw b Grobler	6	– c Day b Clare	60
R. M. Bentley b Mitchley	85	– c Day b Ontong	35
*D. Bestall b Ontong	0	– c Barnard b Clare	8
N. P. Daniels c Barnard b Ontong	7	– b Barnard	5
†T. R. Madsen lbw b Mitchley	18	– c Barnard b Ontong	21
G. S. Cowley c and b Mitchley	8	– c Day b Clare	75
R. K. McGlashan c sub b Ontong	7	– c Verdoorn b Ontong	31
G. R. Dilley c Day b Ontong	0	– c Barnard b Ontong	8
I. L. Pont c Day b Mitchley	11	– c Geringer b Weideman	5
E. J. Hodkinson not out	0	– not out	2
B 2, l-b 3, w 1, n-b 4	10	B 6, l-b 8, n-b 3	17

1/14 2/105 3/107 4/122 5/175   203   1/75 2/92 3/100 4/114 5/161   292
6/180 7/185 8/188 9/203   6/182 7/257 8/274 9/279

Bowling: *First Innings*—Grobler 14–6–37–1; Weideman 6–0–21–0; Mitchley 19.1–3–57–4; Clare 12–1–30–0; Geringer 3–0–15–0; Ontong 20–9–33–5. *Second Innings*—Weideman 9–3–20–1; Mitchley 9–0–41–0; Clare 28–8–70–4; Ontong 50.3–20–106–4; Barnard 22–10–35–1; du Preez 1–0–3–0.

Northern Transvaal

V. F. du Preez c Madsen b Dilley	22	– c Bestall b Pont	1
R. C. Ontong lbw b Pont	5	– (7) not out	15
*L. J. Barnard run out	40	– run out	56
†N. T. Day c Bestall b Bentley	88	– (6) not out	12
A. M. Ferreira c Daniels b Hodkinson	40	– b McGlashan	4
A. Geringer c Bentley b McGlashan	45	– (4) st Madsen b McGlashan	10
K. D. Verdoorn c Bentley b McGlashan	9	– (2) c McGlashan b Bentley	30
I. F. N. Weideman c Logan b Hodkinson	14		
C. D. Mitchley c Madsen b Dilley	8		
G. Grobler not out	7		
M. D. Clare c Madsen b Dilley	0		
B 2, l-b 8, w 1, n-b 6	17	B 1, l-b 6, n-b 2	9

1/28 2/30 3/87 4/152 5/252   295   1/1 2/67 3/93   (5 wkts) 137
6/254 7/266 8/277 9/294   4/107 5/108

Bowling: *First Innings*—Dilley 16.3–4–42–3; Pont 10–2–47–1; Hodkinson 17–4–34–2; McGlashan 35–10–104–2; Cowley 14–5–27–0; Daniels 1–0–6–0; Bentley 11–4–18–1. *Second Innings*—Dilley 8–3–18–0; Pont 5–1–15–1; Hodkinson 2–1–6–0; McGlashan 9–1–44–2; Daniels 3–1–6–0; Bentley 10–3–39–1.

Umpires: L. J. Rautenbach and D. D. Schoof.

Wides and no-balls not debited to bowlers' analyses.

NORTHERN TRANSVAAL v BORDER

At Pretoria, November 8, 9, 11. Border won by two wickets. Border 16 pts, Northern Transvaal 9 pts.

Northern Transvaal

V. F. du Preez lbw b Howell	51	– c Ball b Trotman 5
R. F. Pienaar c Trotman b Ballantyne	6	– c Trotman b Bacchus 30
*L. J. Barnard c Ball b Bacchus	19	– b Ballantyne 93
†N. T. Day b Ballantyne	117	– c Ball b Bacchus 17
R. C. Ontong lbw b Hayes	41	
A. Geringer c Ball b Howell	36	– (5) c Bacchus b Trotman 34
A. M. Ferreira run out	44	– (6) not out 22
K. D. Verdoorn not out	7	
C. D. Mitchley not out	0	
B 4, l-b 2, w 13, n-b 3	22	B 2, l-b 10, w 2, n-b 4 ... 18

1/39 2/86 3/90 4/190   (7 wkts dec.) 343   1/6 2/82 3/116   (5 wkts dec.) 219
5/252 6/335 7/342   4/185 5/219

G. Grobler and M. D. Clare did not bat.

Bowling: *First Innings*—Carse 10–0–43–0; Trotman 18–2–59–0; Ballantyne 12–0–47–2; Howell 28–8–71–2; Bacchus 17–4–43–1; Hayes 13–5–31–1; Fraser 4–1–18–0; Ranger 2–0–9–0. *Second Innings*—Carse 2.4–0–15–0; Trotman 14–0–70–2; Ballantyne 9.5–1–31–1; Howell 6–3–23–0; Bacchus 6.2–1–18–2; Hayes 2–0–14–0; Ranger 6–0–30–0.

Border

S. F. A. F. Bacchus lbw b Clare	70	– c Barnard b Mitchley 43
N. P. Minnaar b Grobler	19	– c Day b Mitchley 1
G. C. G. Fraser c du Preez b Mitchley	14	– run out 20
E. N. Trotman c Day b Mitchley	15	– lbw b Ferreira 40
I. L. Howell c Day b Mitchley	0	– c Barnard b Ferreira 26
A. L. Wilmot c Day b Mitchley	78	– not out 48
G. L. Hayes c Barnard b Clare	8	– c Day b Ontong 92
*R. B. C. Ranger c Barnard b Mitchley	6	– c Day b Clare 0
M. R. Ballantyne c du Preez b Grobler	23	– c Barnard b Ontong 30
†T. R. Ball c Ferreira b Ontong	6	– not out 4
J. A. Carse not out	0	
B 4, l-b 7, n-b 3	14	L-b 7, n-b 2 9

1/54 2/90 3/116 4/116 5/123   253   1/16 2/53 3/77 4/125   (8 wkts) 313
6/151 7/178 8/224 9/253   5/140 6/148 7/220 8/290

In the second innings A. L. Wilmot retired hurt at 142 and resumed at 220.

Bowling: *First Innings*—Clare 22–6–60–2; Grobler 14–3–78–2; Ontong 14–1–35–1; Mitchley 13.1–4–26–5; Ferreira 7–1–17–0; Pienaar 3–0–23–0. *Second Innings*—Clare 25–3–80–1; Grobler 10–2–43–0; Ontong 16–4–62–2; Mitchley 24.3–5–73–2; Ferreira 13–2–46–2.

Umpires: S. G. Moore and F. E. Wood.

Wides and no-balls not debited to bowlers' analyses.

TRANSVAAL v ORANGE FREE STATE

At Johannesburg, November 8, 9, 11. Transvaal won by an innings and 88 runs. Transvaal 19 pts, Orange Free State 2 pts.

Transvaal

S. J. Cook c East b Donald 5	†R. V. Jennings c D. P. le Roux
H. R. Fotheringham c East	b van Zyl . 5
b van Heerden .110	N. V. Radford not out 14
M. Yachad c East b Holder 39	B 8, l-b 8, w 3, n-b 6 25
R. G. Pollock c Holder b Beukes 50	
*C. E. B. Rice b Beukes 23	1/13 2/78 3/194 (7 wkts dec.) 358
K. A. McKenzie lbw b van Zyl 40	4/229 5/263
A. J. Kourie not out 47	6/298 7/325

H. A. Page and S. T. Clarke did not bat.

Bowling: van Zyl 32–9–72–2; Donald 24–5–55–1; Player 12–0–42–0; Holder 18–2–58–1; van Heerden 14–2–51–1; Beukes 22–5–55–2.

Orange Free State

*B. C. Broad c Rice b Page 17	– c Pollock b Clarke 1
R. A. le Roux b Radford 2	– lbw b Radford 35
D. P. le Roux c Jennings b Page 41	– c sub b Clarke 8
C. J. van Heerden c and b Kourie 44	– c Radford b Page 8
J. M. Truter c Pollock b Kourie 17	– c Jennings b Page 12
†R. J. East c Jennings b Radford 1	– c Yachad b Clarke 10
A. P. Beukes b Kourie 1	– lbw b Page 0
V. A. Holder c Rice b Page 6	– lbw b Page 0
C. J. P. G. van Zyl b Kourie 0	– c McKenzie b Radford 27
B. T. Player not out 2	– lbw b Radford 14
A. A. Donald b Page 5	– not out 2
L-b 5, w 2, n-b 5 12	L-b 3, n-b 2 5

1/4 2/54 3/92 4/118 5/126	148	1/6 2/30 3/49 4/60 5/74	122
6/130 7/134 8/134 9/142		6/77 7/77 8/78 9/111	

Bowling: *First Innings*—Clarke 11–3–34–0; Radford 14–2–38–2; Page 12–2–28–4; Kourie 24–12–36–4. *Second Innings*—Clarke 17–6–23–3; Radford 9.1–2–17–3; Page 17–3–48–4; Kourie 10–2–29–0.

Umpires: G. D. Baker and O. R. Schoof.

Wides and no-balls not debited to bowlers' analyses.

NATAL v ORANGE FREE STATE

At Durban, November 15, 16, 17. Drawn. Natal 10 pts, Orange Free State 8 pts.

Natal

B. J. Whitfield c East b van Heerden 24	– b van Zyl 2
M. B. Logan c East b van Zyl 2	– lbw b Beukes 28
R. M. Bentley lbw b van Zyl 17	– c van Heerden b van Zyl 10
*D. Bestall c van Heerden b Player 11	– (11) c East b van Zyl 2
†M. J. Pearse run out 3	– (4) b Donald 0
C. L. King c Strydom b Player 154	– (5) c East b Donald 25
N. P. Daniels b Donald 37	– b van Zyl 48
G. S. Cowley c East b van Heerden 39	– c Strydom b Player 0
R. K. McGlashan c Broad b Beukes 20	– (6) lbw b van Zyl 13
G. R. Dilley st East b Beukes 1	– (9) c Green b Beukes 17
T. J. Packer not out 6	– (10) not out 16
B 2, l-b 4, w 2, n-b 16 24	L-b 8, n-b 4 12

1/13 2/47 3/60 4/67 5/86	338	1/3 2/22 3/23 4/55 5/76	173
6/163 7/242 8/324 9/331		6/101 7/102 8/152 9/160	

Bowling: *First Innings*—van Zyl 23–3–58–2; Donald 15–3–58–1; van Heerden 17–1–69–2; Player 10–2–40–2; Beukes 17.3–3–70–2; R. A. le Roux 2–0–19–0. *Second Innings*—van Zyl 25–7–54–5; Donald 15–3–54–2; van Heerden 1–1–0–0; Player 7–0–24–1; Beukes 25–13–29–2.

Orange Free State

A. M. Green lbw b Cowley	32	– c sub b Dilley	0
R. A. le Roux c King b Dilley	13	– b King	7
D. P. le Roux lbw b Packer	1	– c Pearse b King	10
J. J. Strydom run out	56	– lbw b Packer	9
*B. C. Broad not out	101	– b King	7
C. J. van Heerden b McGlashan	1	– not out	15
†R. J. East b McGlashan	59	– b Bentley	46
A. P. Beukes not out	23	– not out	13
B 2, l-b 13, w 1, n-b 6	22	B 5, l-b 6, w 1, n-b 1	13

1/14 2/81 3/104 4/130 (6 wkts dec.) 308   1/0 2/19 3/26 4/42 (6 wkts) 120
5/142 6/229   5/44 6/105

C. J. P. G. van Zyl, B. T. Player and A. A. Donald did not bat.

Bowling: *First Innings*—Dilley 20–3–58–1; Packer 23–3–60–1; McGlashan 17–7–59–2; Cowley 15.4–2–56–1; Daniels 23–12–50–0; Bentley 2–1–3–0. *Second Innings*—Dilley 13–5–14–1; Packer 8–1–14–1; Cowley 7–2–8–0; Daniels 4–2–17–0; Bentley 10–7–27–1; King 15–6–27–3.

Umpires: B. Glass and D. A. Sansom.

Wides and no-balls not debited to bowlers' analyses.

NORTHERN TRANSVAAL v WESTERN PROVINCE

At Pretoria, November 15, 16, 18. Drawn. Northern Transvaal 8 pts, Western Province 7 pts.

Northern Transvaal

V. F. du Preez c Ryall b le Roux	43	– lbw b le Roux	6
R. F. Pienaar c Ryall b Jefferies	40	– b Simons	79
*L. J. Barnard lbw b Kuiper	22	– b le Roux	13
†N. T. Day c Ryall b Simons	10	– b Minnaar	6
K. D. Verdoorn c le Roux b Simons	4	– c Elgar b Simons	30
A. Geringer c le Roux b Simons	8	– not out	67
R. C. Ontong c Ryall b Kuiper	0	– not out	25
A. M. Ferreira b Jefferies	105		
C. D. Mitchley b Simons	36		
P. S. de Villiers c Minnaar b Simons	3		
M. D. Clare not out	4		
B 5, l-b 15, n-b 4	24	B 1, l-b 12, w 1, n-b 2	16

1/79 2/89 3/121 4/121 5/130   299   1/18 2/59 3/75 (5 wkts dec.) 242
6/133 7/133 8/256 9/284   4/125 5/178

Bowling: *First Innings*—le Roux 22–2–72–1; Jefferies 21.2–4–74–2; Simons 26–7–52–5; Minnaar 11–1–27–0; Kuiper 12–3–32–2; Kirsten 7–2–18–0. *Second Innings*—le Roux 15–4–37–2; Jefferies 23–4–57–0; Simons 21–3–46–2; Minnaar 24–9–46–1; Kirsten 6–0–40–0.

Western Province

A. G. Elgar b Ontong	66 – b Mitchley	5
L. Seeff c Day b Mitchley	4 – not out	44
P. N. Kirsten c Day b de Villiers	41 – not out	38
K. S. McEwan b Mitchley	36
D. J. Cullinan c Verdoorn b Ontong	4
*A. P. Kuiper c Clare b Mitchley	22

```
G. S. le Roux c Geringer b Pienaar .......... 30
S. T. Jefferies b Pienaar ................... 18
E. O. Simons c Day b Clare ................. 28
†R. J. Ryall lbw b Clare ................... 4
M. B. Minnaar not out ..................... 1
       B 5, l-b 5, w 1, n-b 7 ............. 18          B 8, l-b 2, n-b 2 ........ 12
```

1/21 2/109 3/122 4/138 5/175   272   1/13   (1 wkt) 99
6/188 7/225 8/252 9/268

Bowling: *First Innings*—Clare 12.4–1–63–2; Mitchley 19–6–41–3; Ferreira 6–1–22–0; de Villiers 5–0–20–1; Ontong 30–7–75–2; Barnard 2–0–2–0; Pienaar 14–5–31–2. *Second Innings*—Clare 7–3–15–0; Mitchley 8–1–29–1; de Villiers 1–1–0–0; Ontong 12–2–33–0; Pienaar 5–2–10–0.

Umpires: J. W. Peacock and O. R. Schoof.

Wides and no-balls not debited to bowlers' analyses.

EASTERN PROVINCE v TRANSVAAL

At Port Elizabeth, November 22, 23, 24. Drawn. Eastern Province 7 pts, Transvaal 9 pts.

Transvaal
```
S. J. Cook c Richardson b Watson ........... 17 – b Watson ................... 5
H. R. Fotheringham c Capel b Armitage ...... 56 – not out ...................114
M. Yachad c and b Shaw .................... 90 – c Capel b Armitage ......... 27
R. G. Pollock c Reid b Shaw ................ 1 – not out ................... 52
*C. E. B. Rice b van Vuuren ................ 73
K. A. McKenzie c Michau b van Vuuren ..... 18
†R. V. Jennings not out .................... 20
N. V. Radford c Armitage b van Vuuren ...... 0
H. A. Page c Rushmere b Shaw ............. 15
S. T. Clarke b Shaw ....................... 2
K. J. Kerr not out ........................ 0
       L-b 5, n-b 1 ....................... 6          B 1, l-b 8 ............. 9
```

1/24 2/126 3/216 4/258   (9 wkts dec.) 298   1/12 2/80   (2 wkts dec.) 207
5/267 6/267 7/292
8/296 9/298

Bowling: *First Innings*—Watson 24–5–64–1; van Vuuren 25–8–46–3; Capel 10–1–38–0; Shaw 34–5–98–4; Armitage 14–1–46–1. *Second Innings*—Watson 17–4–30–1; van Vuuren 4–1–6–0; Capel 13–2–51–0; Shaw 20–2–66–0; Armitage 12–1–45–1.

Eastern Province
```
P. G. Amm b Kerr .......................... 55 – c Yachad b Kerr ........... 65
I. K. Daniell c Rice b Radford ............. 18 – b Clarke ................... 1
T. B. Reid run out ......................... 32 – c Kerr b Page ............. 41
*†D. J. Richardson lbw b Radford .......... 21 – c Jennings b Page ......... 0
M. Michau b Kerr .......................... 42 – not out ................... 50
R. L. S. Armitage c Page b Kerr ........... 14 – c sub b Kerr .............. 15
D. J. Capel c Cook b Page ................. 14 – c Rice b Page ............. 7
M. W. Rushmere c Pollock b Kerr .......... 40 – not out ................... 15
T. G. Shaw not out ........................ 24
W. K. Watson b Radford .................... 4
M. K. van Vuuren c Rice b Page ............ 2
       L-b 6, n-b 5 ....................... 11          L-b 11, w 1, n-b 5 ...... 17
```

1/24 2/84 3/126 4/142 5/157   277   1/16 2/90 3/90 4/131   (6 wkts) 211
6/187 7/214 8/267 9/274   5/162 6/182

Bowling: *First Innings*—Clarke 17–3–53–0; Radford 18–1–70–3; Kerr 37–9–101–4; Page 14–1–42–2. *Second Innings*—Clarke 12–0–50–1; Radford 12–0–35–0; Kerr 17–1–67–2; Page 13–0–42–3.

Umpires: B. J. Meyer and G. Rossiter.

Wides and no-balls not debited to bowlers' analyses.

NATAL v WESTERN PROVINCE

At Durban, November 23, 24, 25. Western Province won by 107 runs. Western Province 20 pts, Natal 7 pts.

Western Province

P. H. Rayner c Madsen b Dilley	4	– c King b Hodkinson	6
L. Seeff c Madsen b Dilley	15	– c Cooper b Hodkinson	9
P. N. Kirsten c Cowley b Dilley	6	– c Madsen b Hodkinson	52
K. S. McEwan c Daniels b Bentley	101	– not out	82
D. J. Cullinan c Madsen b Dilley	46	– c Pearse b Cooper	24
*A. P. Kuiper c Dilley b Cooper	36	– not out	55
G. S. le Roux not out	57		
S. T. Jefferies b Bentley	12		
E. O. Simons not out	15		
L-b 4, w 8, n-b 10	22	L-b 2, n-b 5	7

1/4 2/19 3/30 4/113   (7 wkts dec.) 314   1/14 2/21 3/82   (4 wkts dec.) 235
5/194 6/244 7/272   4/118

†R. J. Ryall and M. B. Minnaar did not bat.

Bowling: *First Innings*—Dilley 21–3–73–4; Hodkinson 15–2–50–0; Cooper 16–1–41–1; King 9–1–43–0; Cowley 13–4–23–0; Daniels 6–0–23–0; Bentley 11–1–39–2. *Second Innings*—Dilley 11–1–30–0; Hodkinson 13–3–31–3; Cooper 6–0–27–1; Cowley 10–1–28–0; Daniels 15–4–48–0; Bentley 17–3–64–0.

Natal

B. J. Whitfield lbw b le Roux	3	– lbw b le Roux	0
M. B. Logan c le Roux b Kuiper	39	– lbw b le Roux	33
*R. M. Bentley c Kirsten b Minnaar	45	– c Seeff b le Roux	5
C. L. King c McEwan b Minnaar	69	– b Jefferies	2
†T. R. Madsen lbw b le Roux	4	– c Simons b Minnaar	24
M. J. Pearse c Ryall b Simons	9	– lbw b Simons	17
N. P. Daniels c Jefferies b Minnaar	19	– c Minnaar b le Roux	9
G. S. Cowley not out	40	– b Simons	35
G. R. Dilley b Jefferies	0	– lbw b le Roux	19
E. J. Hodkinson b le Roux	1	– lbw b Kuiper	4
K. R. Cooper b le Roux	9	– not out	0
L-b 13, w 1, n-b 8	22	B 15, l-b 7, w 2, n-b 10	34

1/5 2/82 3/115 4/134 5/152   260   1/0 2/23 3/33 4/69 5/79   182
6/197 7/208 8/210 9/234   6/96 7/144 8/148 9/179

Bowling: *First Innings*—le Roux 20–5–45–4; Jefferies 20–2–80–1; Simons 14–1–43–1; Minnaar 23–7–65–3; Kuiper 3–0–5–1. *Second Innings*—le Roux 19–3–54–5; Jefferies 16–3–47–1; Simons 9–1–28–2; Minnaar 12–5–19–1; Kuiper 2–2–0–1; Kirsten 1–1–0–0.

Umpires: P. M. de Klerk and J. P. Smit.

Wides and no-balls not debited to bowlers' analyses.

WESTERN PROVINCE v EASTERN PROVINCE

At Cape Town, November 29, 30. Western Province won by an innings and 19 runs. Western Province 19 pts, Eastern Province 5 pts.

Western Province

P. H. Rayner c Bauermeister b Capel	28	†R. J. Ryall c Rushmere b Watson		18
A. G. Elgar c Capel b Watson	30	D. Norman not out		15
L. Seeff c Capel b Armitage	40	M. B. Minnaar c Armitage b Watson		8
P. N. Kirsten c Bauermeister b Watson	51			
K. S. McEwan b Watson	8	B 1, l-b 14, w 6, n-b 12		33
*A. P. Kuiper c Richardson b Capel	33			—
G. S. le Roux c Rushmere b Watson	0	1/63 2/65 3/155 4/170 5/185		266
S. T. Jefferies c Richardson b Armitage	2	6/189 7/200 8/234 9/252		

Bowling: Watson 22.5–9–47–6; Bauermeister 9–0–34–0; Capel 13–6–28–2; Rayment 14–3–48–0; Armitage 28–8–76–2.

Eastern Province

A. van N. Snyman b Jefferies	4	– c Ryall b le Roux		2
*†D. J. Richardson lbw b Jefferies	0	– c and b Jefferies		19
T. B. Reid b le Roux	0	– c Minnaar b Norman		18
M. Michau b le Roux	1	– c Ryall b Kuiper		21
R. L. S. Armitage b le Roux	24	– c Ryall b Jefferies		18
M. W. Rushmere c Rayner b Jefferies	15	– b le Roux		17
D. J. Capel c Seeff b Norman	11	– c Ryall b le Roux		4
A. V. Birrell lbw b Kuiper	12	– not out		9
K. G. Bauermeister c Seeff b Jefferies	5	– c Ryall b Norman		18
P. A. Rayment lbw b Jefferies	0	– b Norman		19
W. K. Watson not out	9	– b Minnaar		1
B 2, l-b 3, w 1, n-b 4	10	B 1, l-b 4, w 1, n-b 4		10

1/0 2/6 3/6 4/17 5/46	91	1/2 2/27 3/65 4/66 5/98	156
6/59 7/61 8/66 9/74		6/102 7/104 8/126 9/154	

Bowling: *First Innings*—le Roux 12–4–17–3; Jefferies 17–9–30–5; Norman 7–1–22–1; Minnaar 3–1–8–0; Kuiper 1.4–0–4–1. *Second Innings*—le Roux 14–3–41–3; Jefferies 16–7–37–2; Norman 11–3–17–3; Minnaar 13.1–1–28–1; Kuiper 6–1–19–1; Kirsten 1–0–4–0.

Umpires: W. Richard and D. A. Sansom.

Wides and no-balls not debited to bowlers' analyses.

BORDER v NATAL

At East London, November 29, 30, December 1. Drawn. Border 3 pts, Natal 7 pts.

Border

S. F. A. F. Bacchus c McGlashan b Cowley	16	– c Pearse b Cowley		38
N. P. Minnaar c Daniels b Hodkinson	7	– c Hodkinson b McGlashan		48
†V. G. Cresswell b Hodkinson	2	– lbw b McGlashan		50
E. N. Trotman lbw b Hodkinson	0	– run out		8
I. L. Howell c Daniels b Lister-James	18	– b McGlashan		17
A. L. Wilmot lbw b Cowley	24	– c Hodkinson b McGlashan		5
G. L. Hayes b Dilley	2	– lbw b Dilley		0

G. L. Long b Dilley	0	– c Scott b Dilley	21
*R. B. C. Ranger c Pearse b Hodkinson	6	– lbw b Dilley	12
M. R. Ballantyne b Dilley	0	– not out	11
T. Hardiman not out	0	– not out	0
L-b 3, n-b 3	6	B 1, l-b 8, w 2, n-b 4	15

1/10 2/18 3/18 4/30 5/48   81   1/67 2/100 3/121 4/168 (9 wkts) 225
6/55 7/65 8/77 9/77   5/179 6/179 7/179
                                    8/212 9/225

Bowling: *First Innings*—Dilley 16-6-24-3; Hodkinson 13.2-6-26-4; Cowley 8-5-6-2; Bentley 3-1-8-0; Lister-James 5-1-11-1; McGlashan 2-2-0-0. *Second Innings*—Dilley 20-5-61-3; Hodkinson 4-0-9-0; Cowley 9-0-36-1; Bentley 8-5-9-0; Lister-James 4-1-15-0; McGlashan 28-8-72-4; King 2-0-8-0.

Natal

B. J. Whitfield lbw b Trotman	3	C. M. Lister-James c Hayes b Ballantyne	30
†M. J. Pearse c Cresswell b Hardiman	2	G. R. Dilley not out	9
*R. M. Bentley not out	134	B 7, l-b 2, w 2, n-b 1	12
C. L. King lbw b Long	40		
D. A. Scott c Cresswell b Howell	4	1/5 2/9 3/78 (7 wkts dec.) 287	
N. P. Daniels b Howell	53	4/97 5/199	
G. S. Cowley run out	0	6/199 7/264	

R. K. McGlashan and E. J. Hodkinson did not bat.

Bowling: Hardiman 20-3-52-1; Trotman 24-11-52-1; Ballantyne 15-3-58-1; Howell 27-7-54-2; Long 16-5-58-1; Bacchus 1-0-1-0.

Umpires: H. R. Martin and S. G. Moore.

Wides and no-balls not debited to bowlers' analyses.

TRANSVAAL v NORTHERN TRANSVAAL

At Johannesburg, November 29, 30, December 1. Drawn. Transvaal 6 pts, Northern Transvaal 7 pts.

Northern Transvaal

V. F. du Preez c Jennings b Radford	2	– c Pollock b Kourie	49
R. F. Pienaar b Rice	34	– c Cook b Hooper	17
*L. J. Barnard lbw b Rice	24	– lbw b Rice	32
†N. T. Day c Jennings b Rice	6	– c Kourie b Clarke	15
K. D. Verdoorn c Rice b Clarke	74	– c Jennings b Rice	1
A. Geringer b Radford	9	– not out	6
R. C. Ontong c Jennings b Kourie	16	– not out	3
A. M. Ferreira c Fotheringham b Radford	39		
C. D. Mitchley b Radford	1		
P. S. de Villiers not out	2		
M. D. Clare lbw b Radford	0		
L-b 8, w 3, n-b 4	15	L-b 2, w 1, n-b 2	5

1/7 2/65 3/66 4/75 5/96   222   1/32 2/96 3/106   (5 wkts) 128
6/150 7/212 8/219 9/222   4/107 5/124

Bowling: *First Innings*—Clarke 23-6-55-1; Radford 20.5-4-52-5; Hooper 12-1-32-0; Rice 16-5-27-3; Kourie 16-6-41-1. *Second Innings*—Clarke 11-2-24-1; Radford 4-0-18-0; Hooper 6-2-25-1; Rice 13-6-24-2; Kourie 14-4-32-1.

Transvaal

S. J. Cook c Barnard b Clare 37	†R. V. Jennings b Ferreira 1
H. R. Fotheringham c Barnard	N. V. Radford b Clare 8
b Mitchley . 16	S. T. Clarke lbw b Clare 29
M. S. Venter c Day b Mitchley 14	J. J. Hooper not out 3
R. G. Pollock c Ferreira b Clare 78	B 1, l-b 16, n-b 16 33
*C. E. B. Rice c Day b Clare 0	
K. A. McKenzie c Pienaar b Ferreira . 23	1/59 2/78 3/95 4/95 5/134 243
A. J. Kourie c Barnard b de Villiers ... 1	6/153 7/154 8/189 9/220

Bowling: Clare 18.5–0–70–5; Mitchley 23–4–65–2; Ferreira 19–4–51–2; de Villiers 10–1–24–1.

Umpires: C. M. P. Coetzee and B. J. Meyer.

Wides and no-balls not debited to bowlers' analyses.

BORDER v TRANSVAAL

At East London, December 13, 14, 15. Transvaal won by eight wickets. Transvaal 21 points, Border 2 pts.

Border

S. F. A. F. Bacchus c Jennings b Page	0	– c Jennings b Kerr	95
N. P. Minnaar c Kourie b Page	10	– c Cook b Kourie	13
†V. G. Cresswell lbw b Kourie	30	– c Jennings b Radford	4
E. N. Trotman c Pollock b Kourie	29	– c and b Kerr	63
*I. L. Howell c Page b Kerr	13	– c Kerr b Kourie	9
A. L. Wilmot c Pollock b Page	26	– c Yachad b Kerr	65
G. L. Hayes c Jennings b Page	4	– not out	65
G. L. Long c Cook b Page	5	– c Kerr b Kourie	14
M. R. Ballantyne c Rice b Kourie	4	– b Radford	30
G. M. Gower c Kerr b Kourie	2	– lbw b Rice	1
T. Hardiman not out	0	– lbw b Radford	0
B 1, l-b 3, n-b 3	7	B 5, l-b 5	10

1/0 2/25 3/72 4/77 5/97	130	1/36 2/43 3/145 4/164 5/219 369
6/114 7/122 8/128 9/130		6/264 7/288 8/363 9/364

Bowling: *First Innings*—Page 12–3–31–5; Radford 7–1–26–0; Kourie 23.4–8–51–4; Kerr 11–4–15–1. *Second Innings*—Page 11–1–39–0; Radford 13–2–35–3; Kourie 49–7–147–3; Kerr 38–7–123–3; Rice 4–2–15–1.

Transvaal

S. J. Cook b Howell	41	– not out	46
H. R. Fotheringham c Hardiman b Howell	27	– c Ballantyne b Hayes	36
M. Yachad b Howell	18	– run out	0
R. G. Pollock c Howell b Ballantyne	113		
*C. E. B. Rice c Minnaar b Bacchus	80		
K. A. McKenzie b Long	39		
A. J. Kourie not out	54		
†R. V. Jennings not out	13		
N. V. Radford (did not bat)		– (4) not out	12
B 1, l-b 13, w 3, n-b 1	18	B 3, l-b 2, w 1	6

1/55 2/77 3/104 4/290	(6 wkts dec.) 403	1/75 2/75 (2 wkts) 100
5/292 6/369		

H. A. Page and K. J. Kerr did not bat.

Bowling: *First Innings*—Hardiman 10–0–42–0; Gower 19–3–58–0; Howell 27–9–77–3; Trotman 17–1–66–0; Long 9–0–36–1; Bacchus 10–1–27–1; Ballantyne 12–1–58–1; Hayes 5–0–21–0. *Second Innings*—Hardiman 3–0–17–0; Gower 3–0–11–0; Howell 10–5–14–0; Trotman 6–1–21–0; Ballantyne 6–2–7–0; Hayes 7.4–2–24–1.

Umpires: P. M. de Klerk and J. P. Smit.

Wides and no-balls not debited to bowlers' analyses.

TRANSVAAL v NATAL

At Johannesburg, December 19, 20, 21. Drawn. Transvaal 5 pts, Natal 7 pts.

Transvaal

S. J. Cook lbw b Cowley	36	– c Madsen b Cowley	82
H. R. Fotheringham c Madsen b Dilley	3	– c Daniels b Hodkinson	7
M. Yachad c Madsen b King	10	– c Madsen b Dilley	12
R. G. Pollock b Dilley	26	– b Lister-James	13
*C. E. B. Rice lbw b Cowley	0	– not out	27
K. A. McKenzie c Bestall b Dilley	31	– not out	38
A. J. Kourie lbw b Dilley	13		
†R. V. Jennings not out	50		
N. V. Radford c Daniels b Dilley	0		
H. A. Page c Bestall b Dilley	12		
R. W. Hanley c Bestall b Dilley	2		
L-b 6, w 1, n-b 6	13	L-b 8, w 4, n-b 4	16

1/5 2/28 3/72 4/73 5/83   196   1/30 2/86 3/105 4/135   (4 wkts) 195
6/103 7/149 8/149 9/178

Bowling: *First Innings*—Dilley 24.5–8–63–7; Hodkinson 24–2–72–0; King 3–1–5–1; Cowley 17–1–43–2. *Second Innings*—Dilley 9–2–21–1; Hodkinson 20–6–30–1; King 12–4–41–0; Cowley 10–1–35–1; Lister-James 15–2–42–1; Logan 1–1–0–0; Bentley 1–0–10–0.

Natal

B. J. Whitfield c Pollock b Hanley	32	C. M. Lister-James c Jennings b Radford	42
M. B. Logan c Kourie b Radford	6	G. R. Dilley not out	8
R. M. Bentley b Hanley	3		
C. L. King c Jennings b Page	7	L-b 10, w 1, n-b 5	16
*D. Bestall not out	69		
†T. R. Madsen lbw b Page	0	1/14 2/38 3/51 (8 wkts dec.)	200
N. P. Daniels c Radford b Page	0	4/53 5/53 6/55	
G. S. Cowley c Jennings b Radford	17	7/91 8/180	

E. J. Hodkinson did not bat.

Bowling: Page 25–7–57–3; Radford 22–4–52–3; Hanley 21–7–33–2; Rice 7–1–19–0; Kourie 9.4–3–23–0.

Umpires: G. Rossiter and D. D. Schoof.

Wides and no-balls not debited to bowlers' analyses.

NORTHERN TRANSVAAL v EASTERN PROVINCE

At Pretoria, December 19, 20, 21. Drawn. Northern Transvaal 6 pts, Eastern Province 9 pts.

Eastern Province

P. G. Amm c du Preez b Mitchley	45	– c Ferreira b Ontong	82
A. V. Birrell c Barnard b Mitchley	0	– c Barnard b Clare	12
*†D. J. Richardson c de Villiers b Clare	42	– c Barnard b de Villiers	20
M. Michau lbw b Mitchley	34	– c Ontong b Pienaar	12

R. L. S. Armitage lbw b Ontong	56	– c de Villiers b Barnard	26
M. W. Rushmere c Day b Mitchley	44	– not out	34
D. G. Emslie c Geringer b Mitchley	15	– (8) c Verdoorn b Ontong	7
T. G. Shaw not out	35	– (9) not out	21
P. A. Rayment c Barnard b Clare	3		
M. K. van Vuuren c Barnard b Clare	2	– (7) c du Preez b Barnard	6
W. K. Watson b Clare	18		
B 5, l-b 15, n-b 5	25	L-b 4, w 4, n-b 2	10

1/4 2/94 3/107 4/174 5/203   319   1/23 2/54 3/81   (7 wkts dec.) 230
6/249 7/268 8/273 9/281   4/142 5/161 6/177 7/197

Bowling: *First Innings*—Clare 27.5–3–112–4; Mitchley 30–7–73–5; Ferreira 11–0–28–0; de Villiers 2–0–20–0; Ontong 22–7–44–1; Pienaar 8–2–17–0. *Second Innings*—Clare 12–1–41–1; Mitchley 3–0–12–0; de Villiers 10–0–24–1; Ontong 18–2–60–2; Pienaar 8–2–28–1; Barnard 11–0–55–2.

Northern Transvaal

V. F. du Preez c Emslie b van Vuuren	11	– run out	36
R. F. Pienaar c Michau b Rayment	43	– lbw b van Vuuren	6
*L. J. Barnard c Shaw b van Vuuren	0	– b Shaw	54
†N. T. Day lbw b van Vuuren	0	– c and b van Vuuren	62
K. D. Verdoorn c Richardson b Shaw	22	– run out	32
A. Geringer lbw b Rayment	3	– c van Vuuren b Watson	26
R. C. Ontong c Amm b Shaw	31	– (8) not out	10
A. M. Ferreira c Michau b Armitage	95	– c Emslie b Shaw	25
C. D. Mitchley c Watson b Shaw	0	– run out	1
P. S. de Villiers not out	23	– not out	4
M. D. Clare c Richardson b Armitage	4		
L-b 5, w 2, n-b 2	9	L-b 1, n-b 3	4

1/19 2/19 3/37 4/73 5/81   241   1/12 2/92 3/119 4/187   (8 wkts) 260
6/82 7/195 8/199 9/223   5/196 6/243 7/246 8/256

Bowling: *First Innings*—Watson 15–2–56–0; van Vuuren 16–4–45–3; Rayment 11–1–42–2; Shaw 26–12–54–3; Armitage 8.3–2–35–2. *Second Innings*—Watson 12–2–51–1; van Vuuren 13–1–51–2; Rayment 3–0–20–0; Shaw 23–4–76–2; Armitage 12–1–58–0; Birrell 2–2–0–0.

Umpires: K. E. Liebenberg and S. G. Moore.

Wides and no-balls not debited to bowlers' analyses.

WESTERN PROVINCE v BORDER

At Cape Town, January 10, 11. Western Province won by an innings and 21 runs. Western Province 20 pts, Border 2 pts.

Western Province

P. H. Rayner c Cresswell b Trotman	34	S. T. Jefferies not out	15
A. G. Elgar c Howell b Trotman	81		
P. N. Kirsten c Cresswell b Howell	83	B 7, l-b 9, w 2, n-b 2	20
D. J. Cullinan b Trotman	30		
*A. P. Kuiper c Cresswell b Howell	3	1/47 2/200 3/203 (7 wkts dec.) 388
S. D. Bruce c and b Bacchus	36	4/215 5/242
G. S. le Roux b Trotman	86	6/323 7/388

†R. J. Ryall, E. O. Simons and M. B. Minnaar did not bat.

Bowling: Hardiman 5–1–25–0; Trotman 32–4–94–4; Ballantyne 14–0–66–0; Long 6–0–27–0; Howell 37–2–130–2; Bacchus 7–1–26–1.

Border

†V. G. Cresswell c Cullinan b le Roux	12	– lbw b Simons	51
N. P. Minnaar c Simons b le Roux	33	– c Ryall b Minnaar	28
G. C. G. Fraser c Rayner b le Roux	1	– c Ryall b Minnaar	39
M. R. Ballantyne c le Roux b Jefferies	7	– (10) b le Roux	15
S. F. A. F. Bacchus c le Roux b Jefferies	17	– (4) run out	9
E. N. Trotman c Ryall b Jefferies	0	– (5) c Ryall b Jefferies	28
A. L. Wilmot c Ryall b Simons	4	– (6) lbw b Minnaar	8
G. L. Hayes run out	21	– (7) c Ryall b Jefferies	6
G. L. Long lbw b Simons	0	– (9) lbw b Minnaar	13
*I. L. Howell run out	2	– (8) not out	34
T. Hardiman c Ryall b le Roux	12	– b le Roux	6
L-b 3, w 1, n-b 2	6	B 2, l-b 10, w 1, n-b 2	15

1/17 2/39 3/53 4/75 5/75   115   1/42 2/117 3/128 4/167 5/167   252
6/75 7/87 8/87 9/96   6/180 7/182 8/197 9/246

Bowling: *First Innings*—le Roux 12.4–3–42–4; Jefferies 13–2–39–3; Simons 9–3–22–2; Minnaar 8–4–6–0. *Second Innings*—le Roux 14.4–1–54–2; Jefferies 19–1–58–2; Simons 10–1–35–1; Minnaar 21–3–61–4; Kirsten 6–2–17–0; Kuiper 4–0–12–0.

Umpires: D. H. Bezuidenhout and D. H. Scheepers.

Wides and no-balls not debited to bowlers' analyses.

ORANGE FREE STATE v EASTERN PROVINCE

At Bloemfontein, January 10, 11, 13. Eastern Province won by one wicket. Eastern Province 15 pts, Orange Free State 7 pts.

Orange Free State

D. P. le Roux c Shaw b Birrell	92	– c Richardson b Shaw	36
A. M. Green c and b Shaw	27	– c Michau b Shaw	17
C. J. van Heerden c Michau b Watson	30	– c and b Shaw	24
J. J. Strydom c Amm b van Vuuren	0	– c Richardson b Shaw	11
*B. C. Broad c Birrell b Armitage	18	– c Emslie b Armitage	17
A. P. Beukes b Birrell	7	– (7) c Richardson b Rayment	40
†R. J. East c Birrell b Shaw	11	– (6) st Richardson b Shaw	27
P. Grobler c Richardson b Shaw	2	– c Richardson b Shaw	3
C. J. P. G. van Zyl not out	14	– c Rayment b Shaw	9
B. T. Player b Watson	0	– not out	0
A. A. Donald run out	1	– c Richardson b Rayment	0
B 2, l-b 4, w 2, n-b 2	10	B 1, l-b 6, w 1, n-b 6	14

1/56 2/134 3/150 4/174 5/174   212   1/23 2/78 3/87 4/114 5/128   198
6/191 7/193 8/197 9/200   6/163 7/183 8/198 9/198

Bowling: *First Innings*—Watson 21–8–32–2; van Vuuren 13–3–30–1; Shaw 36–8–73–3; Rayment 4–1–20–0; Armitage 9–2–28–1; Birrell 9–1–19–2. *Second Innings*—Watson 1–0–1–0; van Vuuren 9–2–20–0; Shaw 36–13–79–7; Rayment 13.5–4–27–2; Armitage 16–4–44–1; Birrell 3–1–13–0.

Eastern Province

P. G. Amm b Donald	27	– b Donald	12
A. V. Birrell lbw b van Zyl	8	– c Beukes b van Zyl	59
*†D. J. Richardson b Player	4	– lbw b Beukes	50
M. Michau b Donald	2	– (5) lbw b Beukes	3
R. L. S. Armitage c East b Donald	0	– (6) c and b van Heerden	10
M. W. Rushmere b van Zyl	78	– (4) c East b van Zyl	40

D. G. Emslie b Grobler .... 12 – c Beukes b van Heerden 0
T. G. Shaw c East b Donald .... 6 – c and b Beukes 8
P. A. Rayment c and b van Zyl .... 2 – (11) not out 13
W. K. Watson not out .... 22 – not out 4
M. K. van Vuuren c East b Donald .... 20 – (9) run out 5
    B 2, l-b 10, n-b 1 13   B 4, l-b 10, n-b 2 16

1/35 2/46 3/46 4/46 5/53   194   1/20 2/114 3/138 4/151   (9 wkts) 220
6/94 7/116 8/148 9/153   5/184 6/188 7/188
                                      8/199 9/203

Bowling: *First Innings*—van Zyl 23–12–36–3; Donald 20–6–46–5; Grobler 8–1–21–1; Player 16–3–46–1; Beukes 8–0–20–0; van Heerden 5–0–12–0. *Second Innings*—van Zyl 23–4–72–2; Donald 11–0–46–1; Player 4–0–27–0; Beukes 20–6–51–3; van Heerden 3–1–8–2.

Umpires: D. D. Schoof and T. Wood.

Wides and no-balls not debited to bowlers' analyses.

BORDER v ORANGE FREE STATE

At East London, January 31, February 1, 3. Drawn. Border 10 pts, Orange Free State 5 pts.

Border

S. F. A. F. Bacchus c and b Beukes ...134 | G. L. Hayes not out 11
N. P. Minnaar c East b van Heerden .. 12 |
G. L. Long c van Heerden b Donald .. 73 | B 6, l-b 8, w 7, n-b 7 28
†V. G. Cresswell b le Roux b Player .. 39 |
E. N. Trotman b Player .... 74 | 1/46 2/138 3/222   (5 wkts dec.) 479
A. L. Wilmot not out .... 108 | 4/301 5/419

*I. L. Howell, G. M. Gower, I. Foulkes and M. R. Ballantyne did not bat.

Bowling: Donald 17–3–62–1; Pringle 16–1–59–0; van Heerden 10–1–61–1; Player 25–3–105–2; Beukes 26–3–94–1; Broad 13–1–70–0.

Orange Free State

D. P. le Roux b Trotman .... 7 | M. Pringle c Bacchus b Foulkes 26
A. M. Green c Howell b Trotman ..... 12 | B. T. Player not out 7
D. van der Merwe c Long b Trotman .. 10 |
†R. J. East c Howell b Foulkes .... 76 | B 3, l-b 9, w 2, n-b 4 18
*B. C. Broad c Cresswell b Foulkes ... 65 |
J. J. Strydom not out ....100 | 1/23 2/34 3/35 4/155   (8 wkts) 363
C. J. van Heerden c Howell b Foulkes . 10 | 5/199 6/219
A. P. Beukes c and b Hayes .... 32 | 7/263 8/341

A. A. Donald did not bat.

Bowling: Gower 3.2–0–12–0; Trotman 18–2–46–3; Howell 35–12–81–0; Long 9–2–18–0; Bacchus 3–0–14–0; Ballantyne 7–2–21–0; Hayes 21–2–54–1; Foulkes 40–7–99–4.

Umpires: D. H. Bezuidenhout and A. A. Matthews.

Wides and no-balls not debited to bowlers' analyses.

EASTERN PROVINCE v NATAL

At Port Elizabeth, February 7, 8, 9. Natal won by an innings and 13 runs. Natal 17 pts.

Eastern Province

I. K. Daniell c Logan b King	41	– lbw b McGlashan	7
A. V. Birrell lbw b Dilley	9	– c McGlashan b Dilley	0
*†D. J. Richardson b McGlashan	19	– (5) b Bentley	5
M. Michau c Whitfield b McGlashan	31	– (3) b Bentley	38
M. W. Rushmere c McGlashan b Dammann	0	– (4) c Bestall b Bentley	128
R. L. S. Armitage b McGlashan	5	– (6) lbw b Dilley	8
D. J. Capel b McGlashan	12	– c and b Hodkinson	10
T. G. Shaw c and b McGlashan	4	– c Cowley b Dilley	22
W. K. Watson c Logan b Dilley	36	– c Whitfield b Dilley	0
M. K. van Vuuren c Madsen b Dilley	1	– st Madsen b Bentley	29
P. A. Rayment not out	8	– not out	1
L-b 1	1	B 7, l-b 8, n-b 11	26

1/45 2/55 3/76 4/105 5/112   167   1/3 2/8 3/118 4/163 5/174   274
6/120 7/141 8/154 9/167   6/187 7/223 8/226 9/269

Bowling: First Innings—Dilley 23.2–7–50–3; Hodkinson 11–4–36–0; King 7–2–14–1; Dammann 7–1–13–1; McGlashan 24–7–53–5. *Second Innings*—Dilley 24–10–32–4; Hodkinson 12–5–19–1; Dammann 10–2–27–0; McGlashan 46–14–129–1; Cowley 3–1–2–0; Bentley 33.2–16–37–4; Bestall 4–2–2–0.

Natal

B. J. Whitfield c Daniell b Shaw	140	†T. R. Madsen b Watson	1
M. B. Logan run out	72	G. R. Dilley b Watson	6
R. M. Bentley st Richardson b Armitage	76	B 3, l-b 10, w 1, n-b 1	15
C. L. King c Daniell b Watson	77		
*D. Bestall not out	65	1/144 2/291 3/313 (7 wkts dec.) 454
G. S. Cowley c Michau b Shaw	2	4/424 5/437 6/440 7/454

H. F. Dammann, R. K. McGlashan and E. J. Hodkinson did not bat.

Bowling: Watson 18.4–3–68–3; van Vuuren 24–6–62–0; Rayment 11–2–38–0; Shaw 49–7–142–2; Armitage 30–3–88–1; Birrell 9–0–33–0; Capel 1–0–8–0.

Umpires: J. W. Peacock and O. R. Schoof.

Wides and no-balls not debited to bowlers' analyses.

ORANGE FREE STATE v NORTHERN TRANSVAAL

At Bloemfontein, February 7, 8, 10. Northern Transvaal won by 6 runs. Northern Transvaal 19 pts, Orange Free State 10 pts.

Northern Transvaal

V. F. du Preez c East b Donald	15	– c East b Donald	6
R. F. Pienaar c East b Green	90	– lbw b van Zyl	24
*L. J. Barnard c East b Green	17	– b Donald	26
†N. T. Day b Beukes	62	– c Broad b Green	21
K. D. Verdoorn b van Zyl	2	– c Broad b Donald	1
A. Geringer c East b Player	13	– c East b Donald	6
A. M. Ferreira b Beukes	27	– (8) b van Zyl	36
R. C. Ontong c Donald b Beukes	26	– (7) c Horwitz b Green	33
W. F. Morris c van Heerden b Green	0	– b van Zyl	8
C. D. Mitchley c van Zyl b Green	0	– b Donald	19
M. D. Clare not out	1	– not out	0
B 5, l-b 8, n-b 6	19	B 6, l-b 9, w 8, n-b 3	26

1/60 2/131 3/132 4/147 5/179   272   1/8 2/56 3/75 4/85 5/85   206
6/243 7/253 8/266 9/270   6/103 7/163 8/176 9/200

Bowling: *First Innings*—van Zyl 16–5–42–1; Donald 12–1–26–1; Player 13–2–53–1; Beukes 15–2–32–3; van Heerden 5–1–20–0; Green 18.3–4–59–4; Broad 5–1–21–0. *Second Innings*—van Zyl 24–7–41–3; Donald 17.2–3–43–5; Beukes 24–5–56–0; Green 20–9–40–2.

Orange Free State

O. M. Horwitz lbw b Clare	14	– c Geringer b Morris	39
A. M. Green b Barnard	104	– lbw b Mitchley	8
C. J. van Heerden st Day b Morris	31	– (8) c Barnard b Morris	17
J. J. Strydom c Day b Ferreira	17	– lbw b Ontong	15
*B. C. Broad c sub b Ontong	56	– c Ferreira b Ontong	17
†R. J. East c Day b Clare	7	– c Day b Morris	9
D. van der Merwe lbw b Morris	19	– (3) lbw b Morris	6
A. P. Beukes lbw b Barnard	26	– (7) c Day b Morris	10
C. J. P. G. van Zyl st Day b Morris	1	– c Barnard b Ontong	5
B. T. Player c du Preez b Morris	11	– not out	2
A. A. Donald not out	17	– c Ferreira b Morris	0
B 4, l-b 13, n-b 4	21	B 14, l-b 3, n-b 3	20

1/26 2/96 3/150 4/218 5/234   324   1/24 2/33 3/67 4/85 5/96   148
6/243 7/289 8/294 9/295   6/110 7/132 8/140 9/148

Bowling: *First Innings*—Clare 9–0–30–2; Mitchley 12–1–37–0; Ferreira 12–2–40–1; Ontong 20–2–92–1; Barnard 16–4–28–2; Morris 26.4–6–76–4. *Second Innings*—Mitchley 9–1–29–1; Ferreira 4–1–12–0; Ontong 13–5–21–3; Morris 17–1–66–6.

Umpires: K. E. Liebenberg and B. J. Meyer.

Wides and no-balls not debited to bowlers' analyses.

WESTERN PROVINCE v TRANSVAAL

At Cape Town, February 8, 9, 10. Drawn. Western Province 4 pts, Transvaal 7 pts.

Transvaal

*S. J. Cook b le Roux	124	– c Minnaar b Simons	3
M. Yachad c Ryall b Kuiper	12	– run out	23
M. S. Venter b Kuiper	0	– b Minnaar	49
H. R. Fotheringham c Seeff b Minnaar	42	– c Simons b Minnaar	44
B. Roberts b Kirsten	9	– not out	43
B. M. McMillan c Ryall b le Roux	85	– not out	15
A. J. Kourie c Kuiper b le Roux	2		
†R. V. Jennings c Rayner b le Roux	19		
H. A. Page lbw b Kirsten	51		
N. V. Radford lbw b Simons	0		
S. T. Clarke not out	0		
L-b 11, n-b 9	20	L-b 6, w 2, n-b 3	11

1/37 2/37 3/117 4/130 5/243   364   1/9 2/40 3/111   (4 wkts dec.) 188
6/257 7/285 8/355 9/360   4/147

Bowling: *First Innings*—le Roux 22.4–4–52–4; Simons 13–3–27–1; Kuiper 27–3–96–2; Minnaar 42–12–103–1; Kirsten 28–6–66–2. *Second Innings*—le Roux 11–3–19–0; Simons 15–2–52–1; Kuiper 5–1–7–0; Minnaar 27–8–49–2; Kirsten 18–7–50–0.

Western Province

P. H. Rayner c McMillan b Clarke	0	– c Roberts b Radford	0
A. G. Elgar c Jennings b Page	29	– c Jennings b Page	48
L. Seeff lbw b Radford	7	– b Kourie	24
P. N. Kirsten b Radford	13	– c Radford b Page	19
K. S. McEwan run out	56	– not out	47
D. J. Cullinan c Jennings b Page	49	– not out	6
*A. P. Kuiper c Yachad b Kourie	33		

G. S. le Roux c Venter b Page 13
E. O. Simons b Kourie 7
†R. J. Ryall c Clarke b Kourie 4
M. B. Minnaar not out 3
    B 1, l-b 5, n-b 3 9   B 3, l-b 5, n-b 1 9

1/0 2/19 3/49 4/57 5/145   223   1/9 2/75 3/79 4/120   (4 wkts) 153
6/191 7/202 8/216 9/216

Bowling: *First Innings*—Clarke 17-5-36-1; Radford 16-3-58-2; Page 15-3-39-3; McMillan 4-1-13-0; Kourie 28-6-68-3. *Second Innings*—Clarke 13-3-30-0; Radford 9-3-25-1; Page 13-5-39-2; McMillan 2-1-3-0; Kourie 22-6-40-1; Fotheringham 2-0-7-0.

Umpires: L. J. Rautenbach and D. A. Sansom.

Wides and no-balls not debited to bowlers' analyses.

SEMI-FINAL

TRANSVAAL v NORTHERN TRANSVAAL

At Johannesburg, February 14, 15, 16, 17. Transvaal won by 277 runs.

Transvaal

*S. J. Cook c Morris b Ferreira .... 27 – c Day b Ferreira 51
M. Yachad c Ferreira b Weideman .... 6 – b Weideman 5
M. S. Venter c Day b Ontong .... 63 – c Morris b Weideman 0
H. R. Fotheringham c Mitchley b Weideman . 28 – lbw b Morris 64
K. A. McKenzie c Geringer b Pienaar ..... 11 – c Barnard b Morris 84
B. M. McMillan c Day b Ontong .... 80 – c Ferreira b Morris 53
A. J. Kourie c Day b Mitchley .... 37 – lbw b Mitchley 25
†R. V. Jennings run out .... 15 – not out 23
H. A. Page c and b Ontong .... 0 – b Weideman 0
N. V. Radford not out .... 21 – b Weideman 0
S. T. Clarke c Mitchley b Weideman ...... 11 – not out 2
    B 4, l-b 6, n-b 10 20   B 4, l-b 2, w 2, n-b 5 13

1/8 2/54 3/110 4/129 5/152   319   1/20 2/20 3/83   (9 wkts dec.) 320
6/222 7/225 8/260 9/293   4/147 5/240 6/282
                                            7/304 8/307 9/307

Bowling: *First Innings*—Mitchley 13-2-46-1; Weideman 21-3-62-3; Ferreira 17-5-61-1; Pienaar 25-7-59-1; Ontong 19-4-57-3; Morris 5-2-14-0. *Second Innings*—Mitchley 24-4-54-1; Weideman 19.5-6-60-4; Ferreira 15-6-48-1; Pienaar 6-0-24-0; Ontong 17-3-54-0; Morris 20-3-67-3.

Northern Transvaal

V. F. du Preez c Venter b Radford .... 1 – b Clarke 11
R. F. Pienaar c Fotheringham b Kourie ...... 74 – c Jennings b Radford 0
*L. J. Barnard c Cook b Clarke .... 18 – lbw b Radford 1
†N. T. Day b Clarke .... 0 – c Fotheringham b Radford 16
K. D. Verdoorn c McMillan b Radford ...... 31 – c Cook b Clarke 55
R. C. Ontong c Yachad b Radford .... 0 – c Yachad b Kourie 50
A. Geringer c McKenzie b Page .... 19 – c Jennings b Clarke 2
A. M. Ferreira c Jennings b Kourie .... 5 – b Clarke 0
I. F. N. Weideman not out .... 32 – lbw b Clarke 0
W. F. Morris c Kourie b Radford .... 19 – b Clarke 4
C. D. Mitchley c Jennings b Radford ...... 10 – not out 0
    B 3, l-b 4, w 2 9   L-b 3, w 1, n-b 1 5

1/7 2/22 3/82 4/82 5/129   218   1/4 2/8 3/25 4/29 5/126   144
6/143 7/148 8/154 9/201   6/130 7/130 8/130 9/144

Bowling: *First Innings*—Clarke 24–5–60–2; Radford 19.5–7–57–5; Page 21–7–47–1; McMillan 11–4–22–0; Kourie 14–4–23–2. *Second Innings*—Clarke 11–3–19–6; Radford 10–2–33–3; Page 7–0–22–0; McMillan 6–0–34–0; Kourie 8.1–0–31–1.

Umpires: D. H. Bezuidenhout and D. D. Schoof.

Wides and no-balls not debited to bowlers' analyses.

FINAL

WESTERN PROVINCE v TRANSVAAL

At Cape Town, March 7, 8, 9, 10. Drawn. Western Province won the Currie Cup by virtue of heading the league table.

Western Province

A. G. Elgar c Jennings b Radford	65	– b Radford	5
L. Seeff c Fotheringham b Clarke	44	– c Kourie b Page	9
P. N. Kirsten c Jennings b Radford	66	– c Jennings b Radford	1
K. S. McEwan c Jennings b Page	28	– b Clarke	1
D. J. Cullinan b Page	56	– c Jennings b Page	12
*A. P. Kuiper c McKenzie b Radford	48	– not out	20
G. J. Turner not out	26	– c Jennings b Page	1
G. S. le Roux not out	6	– c McKenzie b Kourie	3
S. T. Jefferies (did not bat)		– c McKenzie b Clarke	1
†R. J. Ryall (did not bat)		– not out	17
B 4, l-b 15, w 5, n-b 5	29	B 4, l-b 3, n-b 3	10

1/123 2/123 3/192 4/233   (6 wkts dec.) 368   1/5 2/7 3/8 4/26   (8 wkts) 80
5/298 6/356   5/29 6/31 7/48 8/49

B. A. Matthews did not bat.

Bowling: *First Innings*—Clarke 24–7–74–1; Radford 25–2–96–3; Kourie 21–6–56–0; Page 18–3–74–2; McMillan 12–3–39–0. *Second Innings*—Clarke 13–7–16–2; Radford 14–4–15–2; Kourie 11–5–21–1; Page 11–6–18–3.

Transvaal

S. J. Cook c Ryall b Matthews	23	– c Ryall b Jefferies	102
H. R. Fotheringham c Seeff b Kuiper	59	– lbw b le Roux	0
B. M. McMillan c Kuiper b Jefferies	4	– c Ryall b le Roux	34
R. G. Pollock c Matthews b le Roux	32	– c Ryall b Matthews	26
*C. E. B. Rice b Matthews	1	– c Ryall b Matthews	0
K. A. McKenzie c Ryall b Jefferies	7	– c Seeff b Matthews	0
A. J. Kourie lbw b le Roux	46	– c Seeff b le Roux	82
†R. V. Jennings lbw b Jefferies	1	– c Kuiper b Jefferies	6
H. A. Page c Ryall b Jefferies	16	– c Cullinan b Jefferies	7
N. V. Radford b Jefferies	10	– (11) not out	13
S. T. Clarke not out	0	– (10) b Jefferies	15
L-b 6, w 3, n-b 4	13	B 3, l-b 3, w 4, n-b 3	13

1/41 2/54 3/117 4/122 5/126   212   1/1 2/82 3/142 4/142 5/142   298
6/144 7/155 8/194 9/212   6/222 7/236 8/252 9/270

Bowling: *First Innings*—le Roux 19–3–72–2; Jefferies 19.2–5–50–5; Kuiper 12–1–30–1; Matthews 22–8–47–2. *Second Innings*—le Roux 24–3–67–3; Jefferies 33–4–90–4; Kuiper 7–1–20–0; Matthews 26–6–66–3; Kirsten 17–2–42–0.

Umpires: D. H. Bezuidenhout and O. R. Schoof.

Wides and no-balls not debited to bowlers' analyses.

CURRIE CUP WINNERS

1889-90	Transvaal	1952-53	Western Province
1890-91	Griqualand West	1954-55	Natal
1892-93	Western Province	1955-56	Western Province
1893-94	Western Province	1958-59	Transvaal
1894-95	Transvaal	1959-60	Natal
1896-97	Western Province	1960-61	Natal
1897-98	Western Province	1962-63	Natal
1902-03	Transvaal	1963-64	Natal
1903-04	Transvaal	1965-66	Natal/Transvaal (Tied)
1904-05	Transvaal	1966-67	Natal
1906-07	Transvaal	1967-68	Natal
1908-09	Western Province	1968-69	Transvaal
1910-11	Natal	1969-70	Transvaal/W. Province (Tied)
1912-13	Natal	1970-71	Transvaal
1920-21	Western Province	1971-72	Transvaal
1921-22	Transvaal/Natal/W. Prov. (Tied)	1972-73	Transvaal
1923-24	Transvaal	1973-74	Natal
1925-26	Transvaal	1974-75	Western Province
1926-27	Transvaal	1975-76	Natal
1929-30	Transvaal	1976-77	Natal
1931-32	Western Province	1977-78	Western Province
1933-34	Natal	1978-79	Transvaal
1934-35	Transvaal	1979-80	Transvaal
1936-37	Natal	1980-81	Natal
1937-38	Natal/Transvaal (Tied)	1981-82	Western Province
1946-47	Natal	1982-83	Transvaal
1947-48	Natal	1983-84	Transvaal
1950-51	Transvaal	1984-85	Transvaal
1951-52	Natal	1985-86	Western Province

SAB CASTLE BOWL, 1985-86

	Played	Won	Lost	Drawn	Tied	Bonus Points Batting	Bowling	Total Pts
Boland	6	4	1	0	1	13	30	88
Western Province B	6	4	1	1	0	9	25	74
Eastern Province B	6	2	1	1	2	10	23	63
Natal B	6	2	2	1	1	14	24	63
Griqualand West	6	1	3	2	0	12	28	50
Transvaal B	6	0	1	5	0	20	20	40
Northern Transvaal B ...	6	0	4	2	0	12	26	38

At Kimberley, October 25, 26, 27. Griqualand West won by an innings and 1 run. Griqualand West 360 for nine dec. (D. J. Callaghan 43, A. D. Methven 62, C. W. Symcox 100 not out; K. G. Bauermeister four for 92); Eastern Province B 173 (K. G. Bauermeister 55, P. A. Rayment 41) and 186 (D. G. Emslie 69; B. E. van der Vyver five for 56). *Griqualand West 21 pts, Eastern Province B 4 pts.*

At Pretoria, October 25, 26, 28. Natal B won by 139 runs. Natal B 348 (A. C. Hudson 62, M. J. Pearse 74, J. R. Sheard 40, C. M. Lister-James 88 not out; E. du P. Klopper four for 108) and 165 for eight dec. (A. C. Hudson 71, P. S. de Villiers five for 33); Northern Transvaal B 246 (C. P. L. de Lange 104, L. J. E. Coetzee 41) and 128 (J. A. O'Donoghue five for 39). *Natal B 19 pts, Northern Transvaal B 6 pts.*

At Stellenbosch, November 15, 16, 18. Boland won by 147 runs. Boland 343 for nine dec. (C. Spilhaus 45, S. Nackerdien 81, O. Henry 117) and 159 for six dec. (M. C. Smit 49, S. A. Jones 45); Natal B 204 (D. A. Scott 94, P. Anker five for 48; O. Henry five for 95) and 151 (P. Anker five for 34). *Boland 19 pts, Natal B 5 pts.*

At Constantia, Cape Town, November 21, 22, 23. Western Province B won by three wickets. Natal B 253 (A. C. Hudson 44, K. D. Dawson 53) and 151 (C. M. Lister-James 54 not out; D. Norman six for 56); Western Province B 201 for eight dec. (A. G. Elgar 43, G. J. Turner 69 not out; M. R. Hobson five for 56) and 207 for seven (A. G. Elgar 41, S. D. Bruce 44). *Western Province B 14 pts, Natal B 5 pts.*

At Johannesburg, November 22, 23, 24. Drawn. Eastern Province B 223 (D. J. Ferrant 43, M. B. Billson 53; G. N. MacNab four for 29) and 311 for seven (M. J. P. Ford 96, D. G. Emslie 82, D. J. Ferrant 40, K. G. Bauermeister 61 not out); Transvaal B 460 for five dec. (B. Roberts 53, M. S. Venter 225 not out, B. M. McMillan 129). *Transvaal B 9 pts, Eastern Province B 3 pts.*

At Pietersburg, November 29, 30, December 2. Drawn. Northern Transvaal B 372 for six dec. (W. Kirsh 43, C. P. L. de Lange 44, L. J. E. Coetzee 75 not out, P. L. Symcox 107) and 106 (W. H. van Wyk seven for 55); Transvaal B 344 for eight dec. (L. H. Vorster 50, C. R. Norris 101, R. W. Adair 63) and 120 for five (G. L. Ackermann four for 51). *Northern Transvaal B 7 pts, Transvaal B 7 pts.*

At Uitenhage, November 28, 29, 30. Eastern Province B won by four wickets. Western Province B 241 (I. M. Wingreen 103, D. B. Rundle 49) and 163 for seven dec. (B. de K. Robey four for 73); Eastern Province B 148 (I. K. Daniell 43; B. A. Matthews four for 50, B. P. Martin four for 40) and 259 for six (D. G. Emslie 111 not out, P. A. Tullis 64 not out). *Eastern Province B 15 pts, Western Province B 8 pts.*

At Durban, November 29, 30, December 1. Natal B won by five wickets. Griqualand West 128 (A. D. Hall five for 22) and 210 (P. J. R. Steyn 63; J. A. O'Donoghue five for 51); Natal B 191 (G. W. Symmonds four for 50) and 150 for five (M. D. Mellor 41, A. C. Hudson 70). *Natal B 16 pts, Griqualand West 5 pts.*

At Plumstead, Cape Town, December 12, 13, 14. Western Province B won by 41 runs. Western Province B 137 (S. van Rooyen four for 50) and 174 (T. N. Lazard 43; O. Henry five for 67); Boland 148 (S. A. Jones 65) and 122 (W. M. van der Merwe five for 35). *Western Province B 15 pts, Boland 5 pts.*

At Johannesburg, December 13, 14, 15. Drawn. Transvaal B 276 (B. Roberts 43, L. H. Vorster 51, G. E. McMillan 56, B. McBride 58; P. McLaren five for 68) and 184 for four dec. (B. Roberts 79, L. W. Griessel 42, M. S. Venter 41); Griqualand West 182 (P. C. Botha four for 28) and 173 for nine (P. R. J. Steyn 54). *Transvaal B 9 pts, Griqualand West 3 pts.*

At Union Ground, Port Elizabeth, December 19, 20, 21. Eastern Province B won by six wickets. Northern Transvaal B 279 (M. J. R. Rindel 115) and 201 (A. Da Costa 47, M. J. R. Rindel 47; K. G. Bauermeister four for 45); Eastern Province B 201 (A. van N. Snyman 41, I. K. Daniell 48, D. J. Callaghan 44; J. C. van Duyker four for 58) and 283 for four (A. van N. Snyman 92, I. K. Daniell 113). *Eastern Province B 17 pts, Northern Transvaal B 9 pts.*

At Stellenbosch, December 26, 27, 28. Boland won by eight wickets. Boland 407 for eight dec. (G. Vermeulen 58, S. Nackerdien 122, N. M. Lambrechts 84, S. A. Jones 85) and 37 for two; Transvaal B 133 (O. Henry five for 46) and 307 (B. Roberts 65, L. P. Vorster 52, B. McBride 66 not out). *Boland 17 pts, Transvaal B 2 pts.*

At Kimberley, January 10, 11, 12. Western Province B won by 3 runs. Western Province B 252 for nine dec. (G. J. Turner 58, D. Norman 56) and 177 (T. N. Lazard 40; G. W. Symmonds four for 57); Griqualand West 251 (P. J. R. Steyn 53, L. Potter 41, L. M. Phillips 47, G. J. Parsons 52; B. A. Matthews four for 47) and 175 (L. Potter 57, L. M. Phillips 43; B. A. Matthews four for 32). *Western Province B 17 pts; Griqualand West 8 pts.*

At Albany Sports Club Ground, Port Elizabeth, January 10, 11, 13. Tied. Eastern Province B 189 (D. J. Capel 54, P. A. Tullis 43; O. Henry four for 46) and 278 (I. K. Daniell 116, D. J. Capel 60; I. W. Callen four for 71); Boland 211 (S. Nackerdien 40, S. A. Jones 53) and 256 (C. Spilhaus 82, S. Nackerdien 60; A. L. Hobson four for 39). *Boland 12 pts, Eastern Province B 11 pts.*

At Pretoria, January 23, 24, 25. Boland won by 8 runs. Boland 180 (A. Watts 57) and 224 (S. Nackerdien 42; P. S. de Villiers four for 48); Northern Transvaal B 147 (A. Da Costa 43; I. W. Callen five for 59) and 249 (P. L. Symcox 64, G. L. Ackermann 43; O. Henry seven for 82). *Boland 16 pts, Northern Transvaal B 5 pts.*

At Constantia, Cape Town, February 1, 2, 3. Western Province B won by 119 runs. Western Province B 186 and 138 (T. N. Lazard 40; J. C. van Duyker four for 31); Northern Transvaal B 136 (M. W. Pfaff 48) and 69 (J. During five for 20). *Western Province B 16 pts, Northern Transvaal B 5 pts.*

At Johannesburg, February 7, 8, 9. Drawn. Transvaal B 248 (G. E. McMillan 59, K. J. Kerr 74; B. A. Matthews five for 32) and 193 for three dec. (C. R. Norris 101 not out, K. J. Rule 61 not out); Western Province B 126 for seven dec. (G. J. Turner 42 not out) and 3 for one. *Transvaal B 6 pts, Western Province B 4 pts.*

At Pietermaritzburg, February 7, 8, 9. Tied. Natal B 367 (A. C. Hudson 58, M. J. Pearse 48, J. A. O'Donoghue 53, C. Lowe 64; A. L. Hobson seven for 114) and 204 for five dec. (M. D. Mellor 45, M. J. Pearse 43); Eastern Province B 279 (J. W. Furstenburg 122, A. L. Hobson 41; J. A. O'Donoghue five for 102) and 292 (T. B. Reid 87, D. G. Emslie 69). *Natal B 13 pts, Eastern Province B 13 pts.*

At Kimberley, February 13, 14, 15. Drawn. Griqualand West 282 (F. W. Swarbrook 104 not out, A. D. Methven 40, G. J. Parsons 50; G. L. Ackermann five for 48) and 206 for seven dec. (L. Potter 70, A. D. Methven 44; J. C. van Duyker four for 71); Northern Transvaal B 190 (P. L. Symcox 51, C. P. L. de Lange 49) and 154 for six (P. L. Symcox 52). *Northern Transvaal B 8 pts, Griqualand West 6 pts.*

At Pietermaritzburg, March 1, 2, 3. Drawn. Transvaal B 321 for six dec. (M. Yachad 45, L. P. Vorster 70, C. R. Norris 126 not out) and 215 for six dec. (M. Yachad 71, L. P. Vorster 95); Natal B 254 (M. D. Mellor 51, M. J. Pearse 90) and 132 for five (D. A. Scott 49 not out). *Transvaal B 7 pts, Natal B 5 pts.*

At Stellenbosch, March 6, 7, 8. Boland won by nine wickets. Boland 262 (O. Henry 50, S. A. Jones 58; L. Potter four for 52) and 45 for one. Griqualand West 116 and 190. *Boland 19 pts, Griqualand West 5 pts.*

OTHER FIRST-CLASS MATCH

At Stellenbosch, October 3, 4, 5. Boland won by two wickets. SA Defence Force 177 (O. Henry four for 44) and 148 (A. Watts four for 54); Boland 160 and 166 for eight (L. P. Jacobs 52, M. C. Smit 52; C. J. van Heerden four for 45).

†NISSAN SHIELD, 1985-86

At Stellenbosch, October 12. Natal won by 39 runs. Natal 200 for seven (R. M. Bentley 104); Boland 161.

At East London, October 12. Western Province won by 58 runs. Western Province 222 for nine (P. H. Rayner 86, P. N. Kirsten 72; G. M. Gower four for 24); Border 164 for nine (M. B. Minnaar five for 23).

At Durban, October 19. Natal won by four wickets. Eastern Province 220 for six (P. G. Amm 72, D. J. Richardson 56); Natal 221 for six (B. J. Whitfield 48, M. B. Logan 63, C. L. King 69).

At Bloemfontein, October 19. Northern Transvaal won by four wickets. Orange Free State 211 for six (D. P. le Roux 41); Northern Transvaal 214 for six (L. J. Barnard 50, N. T. Day 78 not out).

At Kimberley, October 19. Transvaal won by 74 runs. Transvaal 247 for eight (H. R. Fotheringham 50, M. Yachad 74; G. P. van Rensburg four for 64); Griqualand West 173 for seven (A. D. Methven 61 not out).

At Port Elizabeth, October 23. Natal won by 123 runs. Natal 216 for seven (B. J. Whitfield 44, M. B. Logan 88); Eastern Province 93 (R. K. McGlashan four for 19).

SEMI-FINALS

First leg: At Durban, November 3. Natal won by 9 runs. Natal 240 for seven (M. B. Logan 87, R. M. Bentley 42, C. L. King 50); Western Province 231 (P. N. Kirsten 52, A. P. Kuiper 50; G. R. Dilley four for 47, T. J. Packer five for 32).

First leg: At Pretoria, November 3. Transvaal won by eight wickets. Northern Transvaal 167 (R. C. Ontong 40 not out); Transvaal 168 for two (S. J. Cook 66 not out, R. G. Pollock 59 not out).

Second leg: At Johannesburg, December 7. Transvaal won by eight wickets. Northern Transvaal 227 (R. F. Pienaar 102); Transvaal 229 for two (S. J. Cook 82, K. A. McKenzie 76 not out).

Second leg: At Cape Town, December 7. Western Province won by four wickets. Natal 235 for six (R. M. Bentley 65, D. Bestall 57 not out; E. O. Simons five for 45); Western Province 236 for six (A. G. Elgar 84, K. S. McEwan 76).

Third leg: At Durban, January 14. Western Province won by six wickets. Natal 204 for eight (R. M. Bentley 73); Western Province 207 for four (A. G. Elgar 45, D. J. Cullinan 57 not out).

FINAL

TRANSVAAL v WESTERN PROVINCE

At Johannesburg, February 22. Transvaal won by seven wickets.

Western Province

P. H. Rayner b Clarke	0	G. S. le Roux run out		28
A. G. Elgar c Jennings b McMillan	6			
P. N. Kirsten b Kourie	44	B 1, l-b 10, w 10, n-b 2		23
K. S. McEwan run out	66			
D. J. Cullinan lbw b Kourie	16	1/0 2/30 3/90 4/125	(6 wkts)	230
*A. P. Kuiper not out	47	5/172 6/230		

E. O. Simons, J. During, †R. J. Ryall and B. A. Matthews did not bat.

Bowling: Clarke 11-1-34-1; Radford 11-2-44-0; Page 11-1-39-0; McMillan 11-0-50-1; Kourie 11-2-40-2.

Transvaal

S. J. Cook b le Roux	39	*C. E. B. Rice not out		59
H. R. Fotheringham c le Roux b Simons	71	L-b 4, w 8, n-b 1		13
B. M. McMillan not out	39			
R. G. Pollock c Elgar b Kirsten	13	1/109 2/118 3/140	(3 wkts)	234

K. A. McKenzie, A. J. Kourie, †R. V. Jennings, H. A. Page, N. V. Radford and S. T. Clarke did not bat.

Bowling: Matthews 11-3-25-0; Simons 7-1-34-0; During 8-0-40-0; le Roux 11-0-41-1; Kirsten 11-0-49-1; Kuiper 6-1-32-0.

Umpires: D. H. Bezuidenhout and D. A. Sansom.

Wides and no-balls not debited to bowlers' analyses.

AUSTRALIAN TEAM IN SOUTH AFRICA, 1985-86

ORANGE FREE STATE v AUSTRALIAN XI

At Bloemfontein, November 22, 23, 25. Drawn. Toss: Australian XI.

Australian XI

J. Dyson c Player b van Heerden	141	– (2) c van Heerden b Beukes 52
S. B. Smith c van Heerden b Donald	47	
G. N. Yallop c R. A. le Roux b van Heerden	35	– c D. P. le Roux b Beukes 62
*K. J. Hughes lbw b van Zyl	17	– c R. A. le Roux b Beukes 3
M. D. Haysman run out	14	– (1) c Broad b van Heerden 7
M. D. Taylor lbw b van Zyl	42	– (5) not out 102
T. V. Hohns b Donald	14	– (6) c East b van Heerden 46
†S. J. Rixon not out	17	– (7) not out 21
R. J. McCurdy c van Heerden b van Zyl	1	
B 2, l-b 5, n-b 10	17	B 1, l-b 5, n-b 2 8

1/69 2/146 3/171 4/206   (8 wkts dec.) 345   1/31 2/108 3/128   (5 wkts dec.) 301
5/305 6/317 7/344 8/345   4/133 5/220

C. G. Rackemann and T. M. Alderman did not bat.

Bowling: *First Innings*—van Zyl 26.4–5–55–3; Donald 20–3–70–2; Player 12–0–56–0; Beukes 15–1–52–0; van Heerden 24–5–78–2; Broad 7–1–27–0. *Second Innings*—van Zyl 8–5–17–0; Donald 13–1–30–0; Player 11–0–43–0; Beukes 23.4–1–106–3; van Heerden 16–2–56–2; Green 6–0–43–0.

Orange Free State

R. A. le Roux c Hohns b McCurdy	5	– (2) c Rixon b Alderman 10
A. M. Green c Taylor b Rackemann	29	– (1) not out 46
D. P. le Roux c Rixon b McCurdy	32	– not out 18
J. J. Strydom c Rixon b Rackemann	0	
*B. C. Broad c Rixon b Rackemann	88	
C. J. van Heerden c Dyson b Hohns	46	
†R. J. East c Dyson b McCurdy	27	
A. P. Beukes c Alderman b Hohns	51	
C. J. P. G. van Zyl c Taylor b McCurdy	17	
B. T. Player c Yallop b Hohns	11	
A. A. Donald not out	4	
B 2, l-b 1, w 1, n-b 5	9	L-b 1, n-b 1 2

1/18 2/34 3/34 4/103 5/188   319   1/32   (1 wkt) 76
6/216 7/258 8/292 9/307

Bowling: *First Innings*—McCurdy 24–2–91–4; Alderman 13–3–40–0; Rackemann 19–3–71–3; Hohns 28.5–5–114–3. *Second Innings*—McCurdy 6–1–16–0; Alderman 11–2–43–1; Rackemann 4–0–16–0; Haysman 2–2–0–0.

Umpires: G. R. Brown and D. H. Scheepers.

†At Pretoria, November 27. Northern Transvaal won by 7 runs. Northern Transvaal 211 for nine (50 overs) (A. Geringer 50, A. M. Ferreira 61); Australian XI 204 (49.2 overs) (K. J. Hughes 72).

PRESIDENT'S XI v AUSTRALIAN XI

At Pretoria, November 29, 30, December 2. Australian XI won by five wickets. Toss: President's XI.

President's XI

P. G. Amm c Rixon b Hogg	22	– c Taylor b Maguire	20
M. D. Logan b Alderman	16	– c Taylor b Alderman	19
*M. Yachad b Alderman	1	– c Rixon b Maguire	3
D. J. Cullinan c Dyson b Maguire	14	– b Alderman	0
S. Nackerdien c Alderman b Maguire	10	– c Hughes b Maguire	12
†T. R. Madsen b Maguire	54	– (10) b Maguire	0
O. Henry c Rixon b Hogg	0	– (6) c Hughes b Maguire	19
E. O. Simons lbw b Hogg	0	– (7) b Hogg	18
H. A. Page lbw b Rackemann	12	– (8) not out	16
C. J. P. G. van Zyl not out	12	– (9) c Rixon b Hogg	2
A. A. Donald b Alderman	4	– run out	12
L-b 3, n-b 2	5	L-b 3, n-b 2	5
	150		**126**

1/34 2/39 3/42 4/60 5/81   1/33 2/41 3/43 4/56 5/58
6/86 7/88 8/125 9/135   6/96 7/96 8/103 9/104

Bowling: First Innings—Hogg 13–2–45–3; Alderman 10.5–2–24–3; Rackemann 10–1–37–1; Maguire 15–4–41–3. *Second Innings*—Hogg 10–0–28–2; Alderman 14–3–37–2; Maguire 14.2–1–58–5.

Australian XI

J. Dyson c Madsen b van Zyl	0	– (2) c Nackerdien b Page	28
S. B. Smith c Madsen b Page	6	– (1) c Nackerdien b Simons	17
†G. Shipperd c Nackerdien b van Zyl	37	– lbw b Simons	0
*K. J. Hughes c Yachad b Donald	73	– c sub b Page	16
M. D. Taylor lbw b Simons	1	– not out	19
M. D. Haysman lbw b Simons	4	– c Nackerdien b Simons	4
S. J. Rixon c van Zyl b Donald	5	– not out	5
J. N. Maguire c Simons b van Zyl	20		
C. G. Rackemann c Cullinan b Page	11		
R. M. Hogg not out	9		
T. M. Alderman c and b Simons	0		
L-b 7, n-b 13	20	L-b 1, n-b 1	2
	186	(5 wkts)	**91**

1/0 2/10 3/113 4/118 5/125   1/31 2/31 3/56
6/137 7/146 8/162 9/185   4/64 5/79

Bowling: First Innings—van Zyl 18–3–33–3; Page 26–4–73–2; Simons 12.4–1–37–3; Donald 11–0–24–2; Henry 10–5–12–0. *Second Innings*—van Zyl 9–0–24–0; Page 11.1–4–26–2; Simons 8–0–40–3.

Umpires: D. H. Bezuidenhout and O. R. Schoof.

†At Johannesburg, December 4. Transvaal won by 58 runs. Transvaal 269 for three (50 overs) (S. J. Cook 60, H. R. Fotheringham 72, M. Yachad 40, R. G. Pollock 59 not out); Australian XI 211 for six (50 overs) (S. B. Smith 93, M. D. Haysman 42).

BORDER v AUSTRALIAN XI

At East London, December 6, 7, 8. Drawn. Toss: Australian XI.

Border

S. F. A. F. Bacchus c Rixon b Rackemann	25	G. L. Long not out	25
N. P. Minnaar c Dyson b Rackemann	21	M. R. Ballantyne c Yallop b Maguire	8
G. C. G. Fraser lbw b Rackemann	2	T. Hardiman st Rixon b Hogan	0
†V. G. Cresswell hit wkt b Rackemann	14		
E. N. Trotman b Maguire	48	L-b 2, n-b 6	8
A. L. Wilmot b Maguire	10		
*I. L. Howell c Haysman b Maguire	5	1/46 2/48 3/51 4/73 5/103	**168**
G. L. Hayes c Hogan b Maguire	2	6/117 7/133 8/142 9/165	

Bowling: Rackemann 11–0–52–4; Maguire 18–3–66–5; Faulkner 14–3–42–0; Hogan 2.2–0–6–1.

Australian XI

†S. J. Rixon c Cresswell b Hardiman .. 0	S. P. Smith c Cresswell b Trotman 29
J. Dyson c Fraser b Howell 62	T. G. Hogan c Trotman b Hardiman .. 2
M. D. Haysman c Minnaar b Long 39	J. N. Maguire not out 0
*G. N. Yallop c Cresswell b Long 6	L-b 8, n-b 4 12
M. D. Taylor b Trotman 54	
T. V. Hohns lbw b Bacchus 23	1/0 2/100 3/112 4/112 (8 wkts) 236
P. I. Faulkner not out 9	5/183 6/196 7/231 8/234

C. G. Rackemann did not bat.

Bowling: Hardiman 14–1–50–2; Ballantyne 16–2–48–0; Trotman 20–3–33–2; Long 17–4–40–2; Howell 21–6–32–1; Bacchus 7–1–15–1; Fraser 3–0–10–0.

Umpires: D. A. Sansom and D. D. Schoof.

†At Port Elizabeth, December 11. Australian XI won by 5 runs. Australian XI 222 for seven (50 overs) (J. Dyson 78, G. N. Yallop 50); Eastern Province 217 for nine (50 overs) (D. J. Richardson 61).

EASTERN PROVINCE v AUSTRALIAN XI

At Port Elizabeth, December 13, 14, 15. Eastern Province won by two wickets. Toss: Australian XI.

Australian XI

S. B. Smith c Richardson b Rayment 40	– c Rayment b van Vuuren 13
J. Dyson c Richardson b van Vuuren 5	– not out 71
G. Shipperd b Rayment 6	– not out 14
*K. J. Hughes st Richardson b Shaw 72	
G. N. Yallop b van Vuuren 7	
M. D. Haysman not out 125	
†S. J. Rixon c and b Shaw 28	
T. G. Hogan b Shaw 63	
C. G. Rackemann b Shaw 0	
R. J. McCurdy c Amm b Birrell 17	
L-b 5, w 3, n-b 11 19	L-b 1, w 2 3

1/14 2/50 3/73 4/94 5/188	(9 wkts dec.) 382	1/42	(1 wkt dec.) 101
6/238 7/354 8/354 9/382			

R. M. Hogg did not bat.

Bowling: *First Innings*—Watson 18–1–56–0; van Vuuren 24–3–84–2; Shaw 39–6–116–4; Rayment 20–3–54–2; Armitage 19–1–65–0; Birrell 0.4–0–2–1. *Second Innings*—Watson 5–0–14–0; van Vuuren 8–1–25–1; Shaw 9–3–25–0; Rayment 4–0–16–0; Birrell 9–1–20–0.

Eastern Province

P. G. Amm c Rixon b Rackemann 10	– run out 34
A. V. Birrell st Rixon b Hogan 8	– c and b Hogan 38
*†D. J. Richardson c Hughes b Hogan 7	– c Hogan b Hogg 64
M. Michau c and b Hogan 53	– lbw b Hogg 26
R. L. S. Armitage not out 98	– c sub b Hogg 9
M. W. Rushmere lbw b Hogan 7	– not out 46

```
D. G. Emslie b Hogan ...................... 19 – (9) run out .................. 1
T. G. Shaw c Rixon b Hogan ............... 17 – (7) c and b Rackemann ....... 3
P. A. Rayment c Rixon b Hogan ........... 0 – (10) not out ................. 11
W. K. Watson c and b Hogan .............. 2 – (8) c Smith b Hogg ........... 9
M. K. van Vuuren run out ................. 0
        B 5, l-b 5, n-b 4 ................. 14        B 2, l-b 6, w 1 ........... 9
```
```
1/14 2/24 3/28 4/134 5/146       235   1/71 2/72 3/121 4/135    (8 wkts) 250
6/183 7/219 8/221 9/233                5/187 6/198 7/215 8/219
```

Bowling: *First Innings*—Hogg 11–1–42–0; Rackemann 25.4–7–59–1; Hogan 40–12–86–8; McCurdy 4–0–17–0; Haysman 5–1–21–0. *Second Innings*—Hogg 23–3–71–4; Rackemann 9.4–0–64–1; Hogan 22–0–107–1.

Umpires: C. M. P. Coetzee and L. J. Rautenbach.

BOLAND v AUSTRALIAN XI

At Stellenbosch, December 17, 18, 19. Drawn. Toss: Boland.

Boland

```
J. B. Munnik c Hughes b Alderman .......... 10 – run out ................... 0
C. Spilhaus c Smith b Maguire ............. 1 – lbw b Maguire ............. 1
S. Nackerdien c Shipperd b Alderman ....... 14 – c Haysman b Maguire ........ 8
†L. J. Kets b Faulkner .................... 4 – b Faulkner ................ 24
O. Henry c Haysman b Hohns ................ 50 – c Haysman b Hogan .......... 23
N. M. Lambrechts b Hohns .................. 13 – not out ................... 52
*S. A. Jones c Maguire b Faulkner ..........132 – c and b Hogan ............. 26
M. C. Smit c Alderman b Hohns ............. 8 – not out ................... 12
A. Watts b Hogan .......................... 16
S. van Rooyen c Alderman b Hogan .......... 0
P. Anker not out .......................... 10
        L-b 7, w 4, n-b 2 ................. 13        B 7, l-b 6 ............. 13
```
```
1/7 2/26 3/31 4/31 5/66          271   1/5 2/9 3/21 4/55      (6 wkts) 159
6/129 7/139 8/208 9/208                5/80 6/116
```

Bowling: *First Innings*—Maguire 26–2–99–1; Alderman 12–3–13–2; Faulkner 9.4–2–19–2; Hohns 25–8–69–3; Hogan 22–7–64–2. *Second Innings*—Maguire 14–5–20–2; Alderman 9–1–22–0; Faulkner 8–1–28–1; Hohns 18–5–42–0; Hogan 22–9–34–2; Haysman 1–1–0–0; Yallop 1–1–0–0.

Australian XI

```
S. B. Smith c Watts b Anker .........112   T. G. Hogan c sub b van Rooyen ..... 4
†G. Shipperd c Smit b Watts ......... 16   J. N. Maguire not out ............. 2
*K. J. Hughes c Watts b Anker .......116   T. M. Alderman not out ............ 1
G. N. Yallop c Spilhaus b Anker ..... 26        B 4, l-b 9, n-b 2 ........... 15
M. D. Taylor run out ................ 1
M. D. Haysman st Kets b Henry ....... 41   1/42 2/251 3/254       (9 wkts dec.) 456
T. V. Hohns c Henry b Anker ......... 90   4/265 5/309 6/353
P. I. Faulkner c Spilhaus b van Rooyen 32  7/426 8/442 9/453
```

Bowling: van Rooyen 33–11–79–2; Anker 45–5–126–4; Henry 35–7–128–1; Jones 10–2–30–0; Watts 16–1–55–1; Smit 16–5–25–0.

Umpires: H. R. Martin and W. Richard.

†At Cape Town, December 21. Australian XI won by 48 runs. Australian XI 260 for four (50 overs) (J. Dyson 126 not out, K. J. Hughes 61); Western Province 212 for nine (50 overs) (P. N. Kirsten 96, D. J. Cullinan 41; R. M. Hogg four for 36).

†At Durban, December 23. Australian XI won by 28 runs. Australian XI 234 for six (50 overs) (S. B. Smith 61, G. N. Yallop 63); Natal 206 (49.3 overs) (A. C. Hudson 43, T. R. Madsen 40; J. N. Maguire four for 39).

SOUTH AFRICA v AUSTRALIAN XI

At Durban, December 26, 27, 28, 29. Drawn. Toss: South Africa.

South Africa

S. J. Cook lbw b Hogg	52	– c Haysman b Hogg	2
H. R. Fotheringham c Rixon b Hogg	70	– (6) not out	100
P. N. Kirsten c Rixon b Hogg	2	– (2) c Rixon b Hogg	5
R. G. Pollock c Hughes b Rackemann	108	– b Rackemann	6
K. S. McEwan c Rixon b Rackemann	4	– (3) c Haysman b Rackemann	5
*C. E. B. Rice c Dyson b Hogg	11	– (5) c Hogan b Rackemann	9
A. J. Kourie c Haysman b Hogg	1	– run out	44
G. S. le Roux c Rixon b Rackemann	9	– c Haysman b Hogan	28
†R. V. Jennings c Rixon b Rackemann	46		
S. T. Jefferies not out	43		
H. A. Page c Hogan b Rackemann	10		
B 11, l-b 17, w 5, n-b 4	37	B 3, n-b 1	4

1/124 2/130 3/133 4/148 5/184   393   1/2 2/7 3/16 4/23   (7 wkts dec.) 203
6/186 7/237 8/327 9/359   5/30 6/130 7/203

Bowling: *First Innings*—Hogg 32-13-88-5; Rackemann 42.1-6-115-5; Hogan 16-4-62-0; Maguire 24-2-79-0; Hohns 5-2-21-0. *Second Innings*—Hogg 13-6-26-2; Rackemann 15-4-28-3; Hogan 14.4-1-77-1; Maguire 9-1-22-0; Hohns 8-1-38-0; Haysman 4-1-9-0.

Australian XI

J. Dyson c Jennings b Jefferies	29	– (2) c Cook b Page	4
G. Shipperd b Kourie	59	– (1) lbw b le Roux	6
M. D. Haysman lbw b Jefferies	0	– not out	3
*K. J. Hughes c Pollock b Page	38	– not out	17
M. D. Taylor c Jennings b Jefferies	109		
T. V. Hohns c Kourie b Rice	10		
†S. J. Rixon c Rice b Jefferies	20		
T. G. Hogan c Rice b Kirsten	53		
J. N. Maguire c Kirsten b Page	10		
C. G. Rackemann c Jennings b le Roux	8		
R. M. Hogg not out	12		
L-b 5, w 3, n-b 3	11	L-b 1, n-b 1	2

1/51 2/51 3/115 4/160 5/185   359   1/4 2/12   (2 wkts) 32
6/236 7/315 8/331 9/343

Bowling: *First Innings*—le Roux 24-1-77-1; Jefferies 34-10-100-4; Page 25.3-6-84-2; Rice 8-1-21-1; Kourie 27-6-72-1; Kirsten 1-1-0-1. *Second Innings*—le Roux 6-2-24-1; Page 5-2-7-1.

Umpires: D. H. Bezuidenhout and O. R. Schoof.

SOUTH AFRICA v AUSTRALIAN XI

At Cape Town, January 1, 2, 3, 4. Drawn. Toss: South Africa.

South Africa

S. J. Cook lbw b McCurdy	91	– c Rixon b Rackemann	70
H. R. Fotheringham c Rixon b Rackemann	10	– b Rackemann	31
P. N. Kirsten b Rackemann	72	– c Haysman b Rackemann	20
R. G. Pollock b Hogg	79	– c Dyson b McCurdy	3
*C. E. B. Rice c Haysman b McCurdy	21	– not out	27
K. A. McKenzie lbw b Hogg	20	– (7) not out	18
A. J. Kourie c Rixon b Rackemann	8		
G. S. le Roux c Dyson b McCurdy	45	– (6) c Haysman b Rackemann	15
†R. V. Jennings c Dyson b McCurdy	9		
S. T. Jefferies c Hughes b Rackemann	22		
H. A. Page not out	33		
B 5, l-b 8, n-b 7	20	L-b 15, n-b 3	18

1/37 2/169 3/204 4/287 5/287   430   1/86 2/121 3/128   (5 wkts dec.) 202
6/308 7/352 8/367 9/384   4/156 5/176

Bowling: *First Innings*—Hogg 29–6–85–2; Rackemann 37.2–3–118–4; McCurdy 30–1–133–4; Hogan 30–6–81–0. *Second Innings*—Hogg 14–2–43–0; Rackemann 26–1–106–4; McCurdy 12–2–38–1.

Australian XI

J. Dyson c Jennings b Kirsten	95	– (2) c Jennings b Page	33
G. Shipperd b Jefferies	17	– (1) lbw b le Roux	8
M. D. Haysman b Jefferies	4	– lbw b Rice	33
*K. J. Hughes b Kirsten	53	– not out	97
R. M. Hogg c Jennings b Page	0		
M. D. Taylor c and b Kirsten	22	– (5) c McKenzie b Kourie	17
G. N. Yallop b le Roux	51	– (6) not out	24
†S. J. Rixon b le Roux	11		
T. G. Hogan lbw b le Roux	28		
R. J. McCurdy not out	4		
C. G. Rackemann b le Roux	2		
L-b 10, n-b 7	17	L-b 10, w 1, n-b 1	12

1/25 2/30 3/135 4/142 5/171   304   1/31 2/54 3/106 4/185   (4 wkts) 224
6/230 7/255 8/260 9/302

Bowling: *First Innings*—le Roux 20.3–3–56–4; Jefferies 19–3–59–2; Page 16–3–39–1; Kourie 16–3–58–0; Rice 10–3–21–0; Kirsten 17–3–61–3. *Second Innings*—le Roux 13–3–23–1; Jefferies 13–4–32–0; Page 11–2–41–1; Kourie 23–7–54–1; Rice 13–3–30–1; Kirsten 17–4–34–0.

Umpires: D. A. Sansom and D. D. Schoof.

SOUTH AFRICAN UNIVERSITIES v AUSTRALIAN XI

At Port Elizabeth, January 6, 7, 8. Drawn. Toss: Australian XI.

South African Universities

P. H. Rayner c Shipperd b Alderman	30	– c Haysman b Faulkner	25
P. G. Amm b Faulkner	13	– c Shipperd b Alderman	30
*R. F. Pienaar c Taylor b Faulkner	9	– (4) st Shipperd b Hohns	82
D. J. Cullinan lbw b Alderman	5	– (5) b Alderman	10
M. W. Rushmere c Yallop b Hohns	25	– (6) not out	45
J. J. Strydom b Faulkner	0	– (7) not out	23
T. G. Shaw c Hogan b Hohns	66		

†B. McBride c Hogan b Maguire .... 42 – (3) c Shipperd b Maguire 9
P. A. Rayment c Shipperd b Maguire 0
M. R. Hobson not out 5
    B 1, l-b 9, w 2, n-b 12 24   L-b 4, n-b 9 13

1/32 2/50 3/70 4/78 5/81   (9 wkts dec.) 219   1/38 2/54 3/84   (5 wkts dec.) 237
6/126 7/187 8/197 9/219   4/120 5/192

B. A. Matthews did not bat.

   Bowling: *First Innings*—Maguire 20.1–4–42–2; Alderman 19–5–32–2; Faulkner 17–4–45–3; Hogan 14–3–38–0; Hohns 19–3–52–2. *Second Innings*—Maguire 16–4–43–1; Alderman 17–7–36–2; Faulkner 14–2–41–1; Hohns 10–0–59–1; Haysman 10–0–54–0.

Australian XI

J. Dyson c Rayner b Rayment .... 29 – (2) c Pienaar b Rayment 1
†G. Shipperd c McBride b Matthews .... 14 – (7) c McBride b Matthews 48
M. D. Haysman c Pienaar b Matthews .... 40 – c Shaw b Matthews 12
G. N. Yallop c Cullinan b Hobson .... 15 – (8) c Cullinan b Matthews 20
M. D. Taylor c McBride b Matthews .... 43 – (4) c Shaw b Rayment 70
T. V. Hohns c Shaw b Rayment .... 2 – c McBride b Pienaar 6
*K. J. Hughes c McBride b Matthews .... 1 – (1) c Rayner b Rayment 22
P. I. Faulkner not out .... 31 – (5) c McBride b Shaw 6
J. N. Maguire b Pienaar .... 10 – (10) not out 2
T. M. Alderman b Pienaar .... 19 – (11) not out 0
T. G. Hogan absent ill .... – (9) b Rayment 12
    L-b 11, w 1, n-b 4 16   B 1, l-b 2, w 1 4

1/35 2/55 3/79 4/141 5/144   220   1/10 2/36 3/38 4/51   (9 wkts) 203
6/145 7/162 8/189 9/220   5/70 6/151 7/185
                                   8/201 9/203

   Bowling: *First Innings*—Matthews 26–8–47–4; Hobson 13–2–43–1; Rayment 18–2–69–2; Pienaar 10–2–27–2; Shaw 9–5–23–0. *Second Innings*—Matthews 16–3–49–3; Hobson 2–0–9–0; Rayment 17–3–63–4; Pienaar 9–0–44–1; Shaw 9–3–35–1.

                Umpires: J. W. Peacock and L. J. Rautenbach.

NORTHERN TRANSVAAL v AUSTRALIAN XI

At Pretoria, January 10, 11, 13. Australian XI won by 25 runs. Toss: Australian XI.

Australian XI

G. Shipperd c Day b Clare .... 46 – (2) lbw b Mitchley 79
P. I. Faulkner c and b Mitchley .... 7 – (1) c Day b Pienaar 109
M. D. Taylor c Verdoorn b Ferreira .... 66 – not out 101
*K. J. Hughes c du Preez b Mitchley .... 33 – not out 27
†S. J. Rixon c Geringer b Mitchley 14
T. V. Hohns b Mitchley 15
T. G. Hogan c Mitchley b Clare 7
J. N. Maguire c Ferreira b Grobler 8
R. J. McCurdy b Grobler 14
R. M. Hogg b Ontong 13
T. M. Alderman not out 0
    L-b 2, w 1, n-b 3 6   B 1, l-b 3, n-b 6 10

1/10 2/116 3/141 4/163 5/174   229   1/161 2/248   (2 wkts dec.) 326
6/185 7/192 8/207 9/229

   Bowling: *First Innings*—Clare 14–5–44–2; Mitchley 18–4–60–4; Grobler 8–1–44–2; Pienaar 6–0–14–0; Ferreira 11–2–30–1; Ontong 9.2–1–35–1. *Second Innings*—Clare 13–3–34–0; Mitchley 14–1–57–1; Grobler 10–0–71–0; Pienaar 8–0–30–1; Ferreira 12–0–52–0; Ontong 14–2–66–0; Geringer 2–0–12–0.

Northern Transvaal

V. F. du Preez c Hughes b McCurdy	0	– lbw b Hogg	0
R. F. Pienaar b McCurdy	8	– c and b Alderman	4
*L. J. Barnard c Rixon b Alderman	4	– c Hogan b Faulkner	37
†N. T. Day c Rixon b McCurdy	5	– lbw b Hogan	34
K. D. Verdoorn c Shipperd b Alderman	44	– lbw b Alderman	58
A. Geringer b McCurdy	0	– c Rixon b Faulkner	30
R. C. Ontong b Alderman	3	– run out	85
A. M. Ferreira c Shipperd b McCurdy	25	– b Maguire	32
C. D. Mitchley c Shipperd b Hogg	58	– b Alderman	1
G. Grobler b Faulkner	23	– c Taylor b Maguire	24
M. D. Clare not out	0	– not out	0
L-b 16, n-b 4	20	B 16, l-b 7, w 8, n-b 4	35

1/0 2/7 3/18 4/19 5/19   190   1/0 2/8 3/87 4/132 5/160   340
6/28 7/83 8/132 9/186   6/214 7/271 8/282 9/338

Bowling: *First Innings*—McCurdy 16–1–85–5; Alderman 14–6–38–3; Hogg 6–1–26–1; Maguire 3–0–14–0; Faulkner 3–0–11–1. *Second Innings*—McCurdy 4–0–11–0; Alderman 17–6–44–3; Hogg 17–2–75–1; Maguire 23–5–85–2; Hogan 22–7–63–1; Faulkner 9.2–1–39–2.

Umpires: P. M. de Klerk and J. P. Smit.

SOUTH AFRICA v AUSTRALIAN XI

At Johannesburg, January 16, 17, 18, 20, 21. South Africa won by 188 runs. Toss: Australian XI.

South Africa

S. J. Cook b Hogg	5	– lbw b Alderman	21
H. R. Fotheringham lbw b Alderman	19	– c Rixon b Rackemann	5
P. N. Kirsten c Rixon b Rackemann	12	– b Faulkner	10
R. G. Pollock c Rixon b Rackemann	19	– not out	65
*C. E. B. Rice c Faulkner b Rackemann	9	– c Rixon b Rackemann	50
K. A. McKenzie c Rixon b Rackemann	72	– c Alderman b Rackemann	110
A. J. Kourie c Rixon b Rackemann	14	– lbw b Alderman	0
G. S. le Roux c Alderman b Rackemann	23	– c Rixon b Rackemann	18
†R. V. Jennings c Rixon b Rackemann	0	– run out	0
H. A. Page not out	14	– lbw b Alderman	2
C. J. P. G. van Zyl c Rixon b Rackemann	13	– c Rixon b Alderman	2
B 2, l-b 8, n-b 1	11	L-b 17, w 2, n-b 3	22

1/12 2/31 3/51 4/69 5/86   211   1/25 2/31 3/80 4/204 5/207   305
6/155 7/166 8/166 9/191   6/242 7/242 8/258 9/274

In the second innings R. G. Pollock, when 51, retired hurt at 94, and resumed at 274.

Bowling: *First Innings*—Hogg 4–3–3–1; Alderman 28–6–68–1; Rackemann 26.4–3–84–8; Faulkner 13–4–46–0. *Second Innings*—Alderman 37–6–116–4; Rackemann 30.1–6–107–4; Faulkner 19–0–65–1.

Australian XI

S. B. Smith c Pollock b van Zyl	116	– c Jennings b van Zyl	14
J. Dyson c Rice b Page	9	– not out	18
G. Shipperd b le Roux	44	– b le Roux	3
*K. J. Hughes lbw b van Zyl	0	– c Jennings b le Roux	0
M. D. Taylor c Jennings b Page	21	– lbw b le Roux	0
G. N. Yallop c Jennings b van Zyl	20	– b Rice	6

P. I. Faulkner c McKenzie b Rice .... 25 – c Fotheringham b Rice 7
†S. J. Rixon lbw b van Zyl .... 3 – b Page 2
C. G. Rackemann lbw b Rice .... 8 – b Rice 2
T. M. Alderman not out .... 3 – c Jennings b Page 1
R. M. Hogg b Rice .... 0 – c Jennings b Page 0
    L-b 13, w 1, n-b 4 18   B 2, l-b 5, n-b 1 8

1/45 2/159 3/159 4/192 5/214   267 1/24 2/29 3/29 4/29 5/36   61
6/230 7/237 8/263 9/267   6/48 7/53 8/60 9/61

Bowling: *First Innings*—le Roux 25–6–68–1; van Zyl 27–4–83–4; Page 26–8–37–2; Rice 24–8–43–3; Kourie 4–0–23–0. *Second Innings*—le Roux 7–2–11–3; van Zyl 8–3–16–1; Page 7.4–0–19–3; Rice 6–2–8–3.

Umpires: D. D. Schoof and O. R. Schoof.

†At Johannesburg, January 24. Australian XI won by 46 runs. Australian XI 197 for five (50 overs) (J. Dyson 57, S. B. Smith 56); South Africa 151 (41.5 overs).

†At Durban, January 26. Australian XI won by four wickets. South Africa 221 for six (50 overs) (H. R. Fotheringham 71, C. E. B. Rice 91); Australian XI 224 for six (49.3 overs) (S. B. Smith 70, J. Dyson 41).

†At Port Elizabeth, January 28. South Africa won by 72 runs. South Africa 223 for nine (50 overs) (S. J. Cook 45, K. A. McKenzie 62, C. E. B. Rice 78 not out); Australian XI 151 (40.1 overs) (M. D. Taylor 43; G. S. le Roux five for 13).

†At Cape Town, January 30. South Africa won by 24 runs. South Africa 234 for nine (50 overs); Australian XI 210 (48.2 overs) (K. J. Hughes 60; C. E. B. Rice four for 45).

†At Johannesburg, February 1. South Africa won by five wickets. Australian XI 185 for seven (49 overs) (G. N. Yallop 42); South Africa 189 for five (39.4 overs) (H. R. Fotheringham 43).

†At Kimberley, February 3. Griqualand West won by six wickets. Australian XI 219 for nine (50 overs) (M. D. Taylor 50); Griqualand West 221 for four (47.4 overs) (F. W. Swarbrook 65, L. Potter 120).

†At Pretoria, February 5. South Africa won by six wickets. Australian XI 272 for six (50 overs) (J. Dyson 115, K. J. Hughes 46, M. D. Taylor 49); South Africa 273 for four (48.2 overs) (S. J. Cook 76, C. E. B. Rice 95 not out, K. A. McKenzie 57 not out).

CRICKET IN THE WEST INDIES, 1985-86

By TONY COZIER

After two consecutive seasons during which the leading West Indian players were on tour in Australia, leaving the Shell Shield considerably devalued, the West Indies' domestic competition was restored to full strength in 1985-86 after its sponsors had expressed their concern about its decline. The Board of Control ensured the presence of the leading players in 1986 by stipulating that Test selection would be conditional on their participation in at least two Shield matches. As a result, some players were obliged to forego tempting offers from Australian club and state teams, and in the event Windward Islands' fast bowler, Winston Davis, overlooked for the West Indies team which toured Sharjah and Pakistan in November and December, was the only Test cricketer to accept an overseas contract, opting to play for Tasmania. Because of the Board's ruling, the standard of cricket in the Shell Shield improved – and with the Test series against England to follow, public interest increased.

The established players were dominant; none more so that the Barbadians. After a disappointing season in 1984-85, when they relinquished their hold on the championship to finish one from bottom, Barbados reclaimed their traditional position as holders of the Shield: their twelfth title in the twenty years of the competition. Joel Garner was appointed captain for the first time and committed himself totally to the job, bowling more overs than any other fast bowler in the Shell Shield and setting a Barbados record of 28 wickets, at an average of 13.50, in their five matches. Principal support came from his fellow Test bowler, Malcolm Marshall (23 wickets in four matches), and Carlisle Best, his predecessor as captain, who led the Shield scoring for the second successive season, being the only batsman to score more than 500 runs. West Indies' opening batsmen, Gordon Greenidge and Desmond Haynes, also scored more than 300 runs for Barbados.

Barbados regained the Shield before the start of their final match, having beaten the 1985 champions, Trinidad & Tobago, Windward Islands and, in what was the decisive match, Jamaica. But amidst the celebrations there was concern that there was little to show from the non-Test players, the selectors having found it necessary to use as many as nineteen players in the five matches. However, a satisfactory season was rounded off when Barbados defeated the touring England team by three wickets.

Bowlers of all types prevailed on pitches which, on the whole, were inconsistent in bounce and brought adverse comment from several captains, as they did later from the England management. By way of illustration, there were only two totals in excess of 400 compared with nine under 150 in the Shield. Nowhere was batting more hazardous than at Sabina Park, where Jamaica's formidable fast-bowling quartet of Courtney Walsh, Patrick Patterson, Michael Holding, the captain, and Aaron Daley dismissed Guyana for the lowest total ever in the Shell Shield – 41 – and Leeward Islands, including Vivian Richards and Richie Richardson, for 77.

Jamaica, on the strength of their fast bowling, won their two matches at Sabina Park but then lost all three away from home when their fragile batting was exposed. Trinidad & Tobago, with a victory over Windward Islands in the final match, moved up to finish second, while Leeward Islands, with potentially powerful batting led by Richards and Richardson, took third place despite their opening match, against Windward Islands, having been abandoned because of a sodden outfield.

Apart from the three leading Barbadians, only two other batsmen scored 300 runs in the Shield – and both were from Guyana, where batting conditions were excellent. Mark Harper, elder brother of the West Indies Test all-rounder and new Guyana captain, Roger, was brought into the team for the last three games and at last came good after ten seasons in first-class cricket. He took centuries off Barbados and Leeward Islands for 398 runs from five innings and an average of 132.66. The left-handed Timur Mohamed's 332 runs came mainly from the competition's highest innings, an unbeaten 200 against Windward Islands.

Just as familiar batsmen were prominent, so too among the bowlers. The Trinidadian captain and off-spinner, Ranjie Nanan, in his fourteenth Shield season, passed Andy Roberts as the highest wicket-taker in the Shell Shield (185 to 180), taking 30 wickets at 14.73 runs each. The two Guyanese off-spinners, Clyde Butts with 28 and Roger Harper with 22, also put forward a case for spin bowlers. Walsh was the leading fast bowler, bowling consistently well throughout the competition for his 29 wickets, but Patterson caught the public attention in his first full season with his speed and menacing aggression. He had seven for 24 on the opening day of the Shell Shield against Leeward Islands and, if he never quite reproduced those figures, he was always a threat for both Jamaica and West Indies.

The absence of any outstanding player from among the reserves was not confined to Barbados alone and performances highlighted the obvious gap between Test and Shield level. Winston Benjamin, the 21-year-old Leeward Islands fast bowler, was as impressive as anyone in his début season, claiming twenty wickets with a high, easy action and good control.

The limited-overs Geddes Grant-Harrison Line Trophy final was a repeat of that of 1984 when Jamaica and Leeward Islands were the teams and the venue was Antigua. The outcome was the same as well, Jamaica winning comfortably by six wickets. Of the two other annual domestic first-class fixtures, the Texaco Trophy in Trinidad was cancelled by the authorities as it clashed with the team's preparations for the Shell Shield, while in the Guystac Trophy in Guyana, Demerara county, needing 35 to win, found themselves 28 for six before they scraped to victory against Berbice.

Two Northern Telecom youth tournaments were staged during the season, the first in Guyana, the second in Trinidad & Tobago. The former was dominated by the Young West Indies all-rounder, Carl Hooper, who led Guyana to the championship with 404 runs (average 80.80) and 33 wickets (average 11.15) in the five matches. The latter produced a thrilling climax with the title depending on the last ball of the tournament. But Barbados, unable to dislodge Leeward Islands' last pair, had to be content with a draw, and Trinidad & Tobago consequently won the championship.

FIRST-CLASS AVERAGES, 1985-86

BATTING

(Qualification: 250 runs, average 35)

	M	I	NO	R	HI	100s	Avge
M. A. Harper (*Guyana*)	4	7	2	434	149*	2	86.80
D. L. Haynes (*Barbados*)	10	18	3	914	131	3	60.93
R. M. Otto (*Leeward I*)	5	8	1	396	165	1	56.57
I. V. A. Richards (*Leeward I*) ...	9	11	1	518	132	2	51.80
C. A. Best (*Barbados*)	9	15	1	640	179	2	45.71
L. L. Lawrence (*Leeward I*)	4	6	0	269	113	2	44.83
C. G. Greenidge (*Barbados*)	9	14	1	578	90	0	44.46
T. Mohamed (*Guyana*)	5	9	1	332	200*	1	41.50
R. A. Harper (*Guyana*)	8	14	3	433	72	0	39.36
R. B. Richardson (*Leeward I*) ...	10	17	2	575	160	2	38.33
A. Rajah (*T & T*)	5	9	1	297	69	0	37.12
A. F. D. Jackman (*Guyana*)	6	11	0	391	120	1	35.54

Signifies not out.

BOWLING

(Qualification: 20 wickets)

	O	M	R	W	BB	Avge
J. Garner (*Barbados*)	322.1	68	866	57	6-28	15.19
R. Nanan (*T & T*)	253.3	56	508	33	5-52	15.39
M. D. Marshall (*Barbados*)	304.3	58	854	50	6-85	17.08
C. A. Walsh (*Jamaica*)	216	37	680	39	8-92	17.43
C. G. Butts (*Guyana*)	274	72	593	34	6-57	17.44
R. A. Harper (*Guyana*)	247.5	64	553	30	4-29	18.43
B. P. Patterson (*Jamaica*)	246.5	44	813	41	7-24	19.82
A. H. Gray (*T & T*)	158.3	26	478	24	5-50	19.91
W. K. M. Benjamin (*Leeward I*)	158	37	400	20	5-47	20.00
M. A. Holding (*Jamaica*)	193.1	34	680	33	4-38	20.60
S. J. Hinds (*Windward I*)	166.5	30	467	22	6-19	21.22
J. T. Etienne (*Windward I*)	181.2	35	445	18	6-35	24.72
G. Mahabir (*T & T*)	171	33	499	20	4-31	24.95

Note: Matches taken into account are Shell Shield, Guystac Trophy and those against the England touring team in the West Indies.

SHELL SHIELD, 1985-86

	Played	Won	Lost	Drawn	1st-inns lead in drawn match	Abandoned	Pts
Barbados	5	3	0	2	2	0	64
Trinidad & Tobago ..	5	3	2	0	0	0	48
Leeward Islands	4	1	1	2	1	1	32
Jamaica	5	2	3	0	0	0	32
Windward Islands ...	4	1	3	0	1	1	25*
Guyana	5	1	2	2	0	0	24

1st-innings lead in one match lost outright.

Win = 16 pts; draw or abandoned game = 4 pts; 1st-innings lead in match lost outright = 5 pts; 1st-innings lead in drawn match = 4 pts.

JAMAICA v GUYANA

At Kingston, January, 9, 10, 11. Jamaica won by three wickets. Toss: Jamaica. Jamaica 16 pts.

Guyana

A. A. Lyght c Holding b Patterson	0	– c Holding b Walsh	9
C. B. Lambert b Patterson	0	– c Dujon b Walsh	24
T. Mohamed c Holding b Walsh	1	– (4) c Patterson b Walsh	57
A. F. D. Jackman c Powell b Patterson	1	– (3) c Lewis b Holding	11
R. Seeram b Patterson	0	– (6) c Powell b Walsh	7
D. I. Kallicharran c Heron b Patterson	0	– (8) b Walsh	5
*R. A. Harper c Holding b Patterson	18	– (7) c Heron b Walsh	65
†M. R. Pydanna c Dujon b Walsh	0	– (9) b Daley b Walsh	1
C. G. Butts b Walsh	6	– (10) c Holding b Walsh	0
R. F. Joseph c and b Patterson	4	– (5) c Dujon b Holding	3
L. A. Lambert not out	0	– not out	5
B 4, n-b 7	11	B 7, l-b 1, n-b 7	15

1/2 2/4 3/4 4/4 5/6 6/9   41   1/24 2/46 3/60 4/85 5/112   202
7/11 8/31 9/41   6/131 7/142 8/152 9/152

Bowling: *First Innings*—Walsh 8-1-13-3; Patterson 7.1-2-24-7. *Second Innings*—Walsh 19.3-2-92-8; Patterson 15-3-63-0; Holding 8-2-20-2; Daley 5-0-19-0.

Jamaica

W. W. Lewis b Harper	23	– c L. A. Lambert b Harper	7
F. A. Cunningham c Kallicharran b L. A. Lambert	8	– lbw b Kallicharran	20
G. Powell c L. A. Lambert b Harper	7	– c Kallicharran b Harper	13
M. C. Neita c Kallicharran b Butts	2	– (5) c C. B. Lambert b Harper	5
G. A. Heron c Harper b Butts	12	– (7) c C. B. Lambert b Butts	11
†P. J. L. Dujon c C. B. Lambert b Harper	13	– st Pydanna b Kallicharran	0
C. A. Davidson not out	12	– (8) not out	22
A. G. Daley b Harper	0	– (9) not out	18
*M. A. Holding c Jackman b Kallicharran	34	– (4) c Butts b Harper	5
C. A. Walsh c Pydanna b Kallicharran	1		
B. P. Patterson c Jackman b Kallicharran	0		
B 1, n-b 13	14	B 5, l-b 8, n-b 5	18

1/34 2/52 3/54 4/54 5/79   126   1/21 2/50 3/59 4/67   (7 wkts) 119
6/79 7/82 8/125 9/126   5/67 6/69 7/92

Bowling: *First Innings*—Joseph 7-1-25-0; L. A. Lambert 7-1-26-1; Harper 15-3-37-4; Butts 10-3-25-2; Kallicharran 4.5-1-12-3. *Second Innings*—Joseph 3-0-11-0; L. A. Lambert 3-1-7-0; Harper 21-6-29-4; Butts 12-2-23-1; Kallicharran 14.2-1-36-2.

Umpires: L. H. Barker and A. J. Gaynor.

BARBADOS v TRINIDAD & TOBAGO

At Bridgetown, January 10, 11, 12. Barbados won by an innings and 13 runs. Toss: Trinidad & Tobago. Barbados 16 pts.

Barbados

D. L. Haynes c D. Williams b Gray ...	4	G. N. Linton c Moosai b Nanan	23
C. A. Best run out	179	*J. Garner run out	5
T. A. Hunte c Simmons b Nanan ...	25	E. L. Reifer not out	51
R. I. C. Holder c and b Nanan	0	W. T. Greenidge b Gray	10
T. R. O. Payne c Nanan b Antoine ..	17	B 3, l-b 2, w 1, n-b 3	9
†M. C. Worrell c Gabriel b Nanan ...	14		—
M. D. Marshall c K. C. Williams		1/4 2/73 3/73 4/119 5/150	350
b Nanan .	13	6/172 7/233 8/246 9/295	

Bowling: Gray 20.5-1-75-2; K. C. Williams 8-1-24-0; Antoine 17-1-95-1; Mahabir 15-1-69-0; Nanan 28-3-82-5.

Trinidad & Tobago

R. S. Gabriel c Marshall b Greenidge	19	– c Greenidge b Marshall	9
P. V. Simmons b Garner	12	– b Garner	35
A. L. Logie run out	20	– c Worrell b Garner	32
H. A. Gomes c Best b Marshall	15	– c Worrell b Garner	11
P. Moosai c Worrell b Garner	26	– c Best b Linton	20
*R. Nanan lbw b Marshall	6	– (7) c sub b Greenidge	10
K. C. Williams lbw b Marshall	39	– (6) c Best b Linton	16
†D. Williams hit wkt b Garner	0	– st Worrell b Linton	10
A. H. Gray c Hunte b Garner	4	– lbw b Marshall	1
G. S. Antoine not out	6	– not out	3
G. Mahabir b Garner	0	– c Worrell b Greenidge	5
B 7, l-b 7, w 3, n-b 13	30	B 4, l-b 3, w 1	8

1/22 2/39 3/73 4/89 5/104	177	1/80 2/85 3/110 4/124 5/134	160
6/132 7/132 8/151 9/172		6/148 7/152 8/152 9/160	

Bowling: *First Innings*—Garner 15.1-1-55-5; Greenidge 6-0-29-1; Marshall 16-1-48-3; Linton 4-1-12-0; Reifer 4-0-19-0. *Second Innings*—Marshall 11-3-27-2; Greenidge 8.3-3-25-2; Reifer 8-0-31-0; Linton 10-2-39-3; Best 4-0-9-0; Garner 10-4-22-3.

Umpires: D. M. Archer and J. R. Gayle.

WINDWARD ISLANDS v LEEWARD ISLANDS

At Castries, January 10, 11, 12, 13. Abandoned without a ball bowled because of the soaked outfield. Windward Islands 4 pts, Leeward Islands 4 pts.

JAMAICA v LEEWARD ISLANDS

At Kingston, January 16, 17, 18. Jamaica won by ten wickets. Toss: Leeward Islands. Jamaica 16 pts.

Jamaica

W. W. Lewis b Benjamin	13	– not out	6
F. A. Cunningham c Williams b Baptiste	17	– not out	0
G. Powell run out	22		
M. C. Neita b Guishard	33		
G. A. Heron b Benjamin	12		
†P. J. L. Dujon b Benjamin	75		
C. A. Davidson lbw b Benjamin	1		

```
A. G. Daley c Otto b Benjamin . . . . . . . . . . . .    2
*M. A. Holding b Merrick . . . . . . . . . . . . . . . .   21
C. A. Walsh c Richards b Merrick . . . . . . . . . .    0
B. P. Patterson not out . . . . . . . . . . . . . . . . .    2
    B 8, l-b 4, w 3, n-b 17 . . . . . . . . . . . . .   32        B 4 . . . . . . . . . . . . . . . . . .    4

1/17 2/46 3/91 4/109 5/166          230          (no wkt) 10
6/177 7/179 8/203 9/203
```

Bowling: *First Innings*—Merrick 16-1-64-2; Benjamin 16.4-5-47-5; Baptiste 13-4-24-1; Ferris 8-1-17-0; Guishard 20-7-42-1; Richards 13-2-24-0. *Second Innings*—Benjamin 0.5-0-6-0.

Leeward Islands

```
A. L. Kelly retired hurt . . . . . . . . . . . . . . . . . . . .   8 – (11) c Dujon b Patterson . . . . . . .    2
R. B. Richardson b Patterson . . . . . . . . . . . . . . .   5 – (1) c Neita b Patterson . . . . . . . .    1
E. E. Lewis lbw b Walsh . . . . . . . . . . . . . . . . . . .   3 – (2) c Powell b Holding . . . . . . . .   30
R. M. Otto c Neita b Patterson . . . . . . . . . . . . . .   0 – (6) c Daley b Walsh . . . . . . . . . .   22
*I. V. A. Richards c Powell b Walsh . . . . . . . . . .   2 – (3) c Walsh b Patterson . . . . . . . .    5
†S. I. Williams c Dujon b Patterson . . . . . . . . . .   0 – (4) c Lewis b Holding . . . . . . . . .   16
E. A. E. Baptiste c and b Walsh . . . . . . . . . . . . .  13 – (5) c Heron b Daley . . . . . . . . . .   58
N. C. Guishard c Dujon b Walsh . . . . . . . . . . . . .   2 – (7) b Holding . . . . . . . . . . . . . . .    0
T. A. Merrick c Neita b Holding . . . . . . . . . . . .   1 – (8) c Walsh b Patterson . . . . . . . .    6
W. K. M. Benjamin b Daley . . . . . . . . . . . . . . .  14 – (9) b Holding . . . . . . . . . . . . . . .    0
G. J. F. Ferris not out . . . . . . . . . . . . . . . . . . .  21 – (10) not out . . . . . . . . . . . . . . .    8
    B 2, l-b 3, n-b 3 . . . . . . . . . . . . . . . . .    8        B 4, l-b 3, n-b 7 . . . . . .   14

1/14 2/19 3/21 4/21 5/21            77    1/1 2/14 3/53 4/65 5/138        162
6/31 7/37 8/39 9/77                      6/145 7/150 8/150 9/156
```

Bowling: *First Innings*—Walsh 12-1-23-4; Patterson 9-4-18-3; Holding 5-0-21-1; Daley 2.2-0-10-1. *Second Innings*—Walsh 8-1-42-1; Patterson 9.3-2-37-4; Holding 8-0-52-4; Daley 4-0-24-1.

Umpires: D. M. Archer and L. U. Bell.

BARBADOS v WINDWARD ISLANDS

At Bridgetown, January 17, 18, 19, 20. Barbados won by 118 runs. Toss: Windward Islands. Barbados 16 pts.

Barbados

```
C. G. Greenidge c Maurice b Murphy . . . . . . . .   6 – c Hinds b Etienne . . . . . . . . . . .   59
D. L. Haynes run out . . . . . . . . . . . . . . . . . . . .  81 – c Lewis b Etienne . . . . . . . . . . .  112
C. A. Best b Etienne . . . . . . . . . . . . . . . . . . . .  33 – st Cadette b Hinds . . . . . . . . . .   54
T. A. Hunte b Etienne . . . . . . . . . . . . . . . . . . .  12 – c Murphy b Etienne . . . . . . . . .   15
†T. R. O. Payne c Hinds b Etienne . . . . . . . . . .   7 – not out . . . . . . . . . . . . . . . . . . .   22
R. I. C. Holder lbw b Etienne . . . . . . . . . . . . . .   0 – (7) not out . . . . . . . . . . . . . . . .    5
M. D. Marshall c Murphy b Etienne . . . . . . . . .   2
G. N. Linton handled the ball . . . . . . . . . . . . . .   1
*J. Garner c Murphy b Etienne . . . . . . . . . . . . .  17 – (6) c Mahon b Hinds . . . . . . . . . .   56
N. da C. Broomes b Collymore . . . . . . . . . . . . .   0
W. T. Greenidge not out . . . . . . . . . . . . . . . . .   5
    B 3, l-b 4, n-b 4 . . . . . . . . . . . . . . . . .   11        B 8, l-b 3, w 2, n-b 2 . . . .   15

1/23 2/77 3/105 4/121 5/121        175    1/143 2/190 3/239   (5 wkts dec.) 338
6/135 7/153 8/157 9/157                   4/249 5/331
```

Bowling: *First Innings*—Collymore 15-7-36-1; Murphy 8-0-48-1; Hinds 10-0-49-0; Etienne 16.2-8-35-6. *Second Innings*—Collymore 20-4-59-0; Murphy 8-0-54-0; Etienne 38-6-114-3; Hinds 29-4-97-2; Charles 3-1-3-0.

Windward Islands

L. C. Sebastien c Broomes b Marshall	6	– (5) lbw b Garner 69
*L. D. John c Haynes b Garner	4	– (1) b Marshall 10
L. A. Lewis c C. G. Greenidge b Marshall	6	– lbw b Marshall 24
F. X. Maurice run out	13	– b Marshall 3
J. D. Charles lbw b Marshall	11	– (6) run out 82
S. L. Mahon c Marshall b Garner	4	– (7) c Payne b Marshall 14
†I. Cadette b Marshall	5	– (2) c Holder b Marshall 43
D. J. Collymore not out	14	– c Broomes b Marshall 8
J. T. Etienne c C. G. Greenidge b Linton	7	– b W. T. Greenidge 8
S. J. Hinds b W. T. Greenidge	0	– c Garner b W. T. Greenidge ... 6
S. A. E. Murphy st Payne b Linton	3	– not out 3
B 6, l-b 4, n-b 11	21	B 5, l-b 8, w 3, n-b 15 ... 31

1/12 2/19 3/21 4/45 5/45   94   1/42 2/81 3/88 4/91 5/225   301
6/54 7/81 8/81 9/81   6/277 7/282 8/284 9/293

In the second innings S. L. Mahon, when 13, retired hurt at 271, and resumed at 277.

Bowling: *First Innings*—Marshall 13–5–39–4; Garner 10–3–24–2; Broomes 2–1–6–0; Linton 4.4–2–7–2; W. T. Greenidge 5–3–8–1. *Second Innings*—Marshall 28–5–85–6; Garner 19–4–82–1; W. T. Greenidge 14.1–3–58–2; Broomes 11–3–17–0; Linton 17–1–46–0.

Umpires: L. H. Barker and A. E. Weekes.

TRINIDAD & TOBAGO v GUYANA

At Pointe-á-Pierre, January 17, 18, 19, 20. Trinidad & Tobago won by 264 runs. Toss: Trinidad & Tobago. Trinidad & Tobago 16 pts.

Trinidad & Tobago

R. S. Gabriel c Mohamed b Butts	45	– c Pydanna b Solomon 10
P. V. Simmons c Harper b Solomon	0	– c Harper b L. A. Lambert 3
A. L. Logie c Harper b Butts	38	– (4) lbw b Solomon 16
H. A. Gomes c C. B. Lambert b Butts	2	– (3) not out 168
A. Rajah lbw b Kallicharran	1	– b Butts 57
P. Moosai c Mohamed b Kallicharran	5	– c Seeram b Solomon 36
K. C. Williams c Mohamed b Kallicharran	18	– lbw b Harper 29
*R. Nanan c C. B. Lambert b Butts	1	– b Harper 1
†D. Williams b L. A. Lambert	37	– b Butts 13
A. H. Gray b Butts	2	– c Solomon b Harper 15
G. Mahabir not out	17	– c Lyght b Harper 0
B 4, l-b 3, n-b 7	14	B 8, l-b 8, w 2, n-b 5 23

1/1 2/58 3/68 4/73 5/79   180   1/8 2/18 3/44 4/173 5/251   371
6/117 7/123 8/123 9/130   6/314 7/318 8/343 9/370

Bowling: *First Innings*—L. A. Lambert 9.3–0–49–1; Solomon 6–0–13–1; Butts 20–6–43–5; Kallicharran 16–0–68–3. *Second Innings*—L. A. Lambert 15–4–43–1; Solomon 20–4–82–3; Butts 43–9–102–2; Harper 26.5–3–63–4; Kallicharran 18–1–62–0; C. B. Lambert 1–0–3–0.

Guyana

A. A. Lyght c D. Williams b Gray	19	– (2) lbw b K. C. Williams 19
C. B. Lambert c Gray b Mahabir	33	– (1) c sub b Gray 3
T. Mohamed c Simmons b Gray	0	– (4) b K. C. Williams 4
K. G. Edwards c Simmons b Nanan	3	– (5) lbw b Gray 16
*R. A. Harper lbw b Nanan	7	– (6) lbw b Mahabir 8
A. F. D. Jackman run out	25	– (3) lbw b Nanan 16

D. I. Kallicharran run out .... 0 – (8) c Gabriel b K. C. Williams . 15
†M. R. Pydanna lbw b Nanan .... 9 – (9) c Nanan b Mahabir 5
C. G. Butts c and b Mahabir .... 22 – (7) st D. Williams b Mahabir ... 33
L. A. Lambert b Mahabir .... 10 – c Gomes b Mahabir 2
C. V. Solomon not out .... 13 – not out 1
    L-b 6, n-b 2 8   B 10, l-b 3, n-b 3 16

1/36 2/36 3/57 4/62 5/70   149   1/6 2/45 3/45 4/50 5/73   138
6/78 7/100 8/113 9/128   6/73 7/107 8/127 9/137

Bowling: *First Innings*—Gray 17–3–46–2; K. C. Williams 2–0–6–0; Nanan 26–8–51–3; Mahabir 13.1–3–40–3. *Second Innings*—Gray 12–1–40–2; K. C. Williams 19–3–48–3; Nanan 10–7–6–1; Mahabir 7–1–31–4.

Umpires: J. R. Gayle and S. Mohammed.

LEEWARD ISLANDS v BARBADOS

At Nevis, January 24, 25, 26, 27. Drawn. Toss: Barbados. Leeward Islands 4 pts, Barbados 8 pts.

Barbados

C. G. Greenidge lbw b Ferris .... 90 – c Arthurton b Ferris 70
D. L. Haynes b Guishard ....118 – c and b Willett 14
C. A. Best c Lawrence b Willett .... 9 – run out 47
T. A. Hunte b Willett .... 1 – b Guishard 39
†T. R. O. Payne lbw b Ferris .... 62 – retired hurt 18
S. R. Greaves run out .... 21 – (7) lbw b Guishard 2
G. N. Linton lbw b Benjamin .... 0 – (8) lbw b Benjamin 0
*J. Garner b Benjamin .... 10 – (6) run out 22
R. O. Estwick lbw b Ferris .... 0 – not out 0
N. da C. Broomes not out 0
W. T. Greenidge lbw b Benjamin 0
     B 9, l-b 11, w 3, n-b 2 25   B 8, l-b 14, n-b 2 24

1/166 2/203 3/208 4/265 5/318   336   1/38 2/129 3/149   (7 wkts dec.) 236
6/328 7/328 8/336 9/336   4/229 5/233 6/236 7/236

Bowling: *First Innings*—Benjamin 24.5–6–59–3; Ferris 24–3–64–3; Willett 49–20–91–2; Guishard 36–10–78–1; Richards 10–3–24–0. *Second Innings*—Benjamin 17–2–40–1; Ferris 12–5–30–1; Richards 30–6–60–0; Willett 17–5–48–1; Guishard 17.3–4–36–2.

Leeward Islands

R. B. Richardson b W. T. Greenidge .... 10 – c Garner b Broomes 21
L. L. Lawrence c Payne b Estwick .... 10 – c sub b Broomes 113
E. E. Lewis c Hunte b W. T. Greenidge ...... 12 – not out 108
R. M. Otto lbw b Garner .... 50 – not out 2
*I. V. A. Richards b Garner 16
K. L. T. Arthurton lbw b Garner 9
†S. I. Williams c W. T. Greenidge b Garner ... 45
N. C. Guishard b Garner 1
W. K. M. Benjamin c C. G. Greenidge b Linton 21
E. T. Willett b Garner 0
G. J. F. Ferris not out 8
     L-b 6, n-b 1 7   B 3, l-b 6, n-b 3 12

1/17 2/32 3/34 4/58 5/81   189   1/43 2/246   (2 wkts) 256
6/155 7/157 8/159 9/159

Bowling: *First Innings*—Garner 14–4–28–6; W. T. Greenidge 12–3–48–2; Estwick 8–1–33–1; Linton 12.5–3–49–1; Greaves 5–0–25–0. *Second Innings*—Garner 16–2–40–0; W. T. Greenidge 13–2–55–0; Broomes 32–6–74–2; Estwick 20–7–34–0; Linton 7–0–40–0; Best 3–1–4–0.

Umpires: S. Mohammed and P. C. White.

TRINIDAD & TOBAGO v JAMAICA

At Port-of-Spain, January 24, 25, 26, 27. Trinidad & Tobago won by ten wickets. Toss: Jamaica. Trinidad & Tobago 16 pts.

Jamaica

W. W. Lewis c D. Williams b K. C. Williams	5	– lbw b K. C. Williams	1
O. W. Peters c Rampersad b Gray	5	– lbw b Gray	5
G. Powell c Logie b K. C. Williams	16	– c Rajah b Nanan	27
M. C. Neita c Gabriel b Gray	6	– st D. Williams b Mahabir	38
†P. J. L. Dujon c Logie b K. C. Williams	9	– c Gabriel b Mahabir	22
C. A. Davidson not out	67	– b Mahabir	19
M. A. Tucker c and b Mahabir	16	– b Nanan	29
*M. A. Holding c Gabriel b Nanan	31	– c D. Williams b Nanan	3
A. G. Daley b Nanan	21	– c Mahabir b Nanan	6
C. A. Walsh c Mahabir b Nanan	4	– not out	3
B. P. Patterson c Rampersad b Nanan	0	– b Nanan	0
B 4, l-b 3, n-b 4	11	B 8, l-b 4	12

1/11 2/11 3/20 4/39 5/48   191   1/1 2/13 3/68 4/78 5/110   165
6/77 7/126 8/185 9/191   6/115 7/126 8/144 9/163

Bowling: *First Innings*—Gray 16–2–53–2; K. C. Williams 10–1–40–3; Mahabir 15–0–50–1; Nanan 16.4–3–34–4; Gomes 3–1–7–0. *Second Innings*—Gray 14–3–33–1; K. C. Williams 6–2–13–1; Nanan 28.5–9–52–5; Mahabir 32–7–55–3.

Trinidad & Tobago

R. S. Gabriel c Dujon b Walsh	41	– not out	33
C. Rampersad c Daley b Walsh	23		
H. A. Gomes c Powell b Patterson	0		
A. L. Logie lbw b Patterson	79		
A. Rajah b Tucker	49		
P. Moosai c Holding b Tucker	25	– (2) not out	12
K. C. Williams c Daley b Holding	30		
†D. Williams lbw b Patterson	26		
*R. Nanan c Holding b Daley	17		
A. H. Gray not out	0		
G. Mahabir c Davidson b Daley	0		
L-b 6, n-b 14	20	N-b 2	2

1/35 2/36 3/135 4/157 5/204   310   (no wkt) 47
6/251 7/285 8/310 9/310

Bowling: *First Innings*—Walsh 22–4–70–2; Patterson 29–4–82–3; Tucker 20–4–64–2; Holding 21–6–55–1; Daley 14–3–33–2. *Second Innings*—Patterson 4–0–15–0; Holding 3–1–15–0; Tucker 2–1–15–0; Daley 1–0–2–0.

Umpires: M. N. Baksh and C. E. Cumberbatch.

GUYANA v WINDWARD ISLANDS

At Berbice, January 24, 25, 26, 27. Guyana won by an innings and 16 runs. Toss: Guyana. Guyana 16 pts.

Guyana

A. A. Lyght c Etienne b Hinds 20	D. I. Kallicharran run out 3		
C. B. Lambert run out 61	C. G. Butts not out 17		
A. F. D. Jackman c Cadette b Etienne 83	L-b 5, w 1 6		
T. Mohamed not out 200			
M. A. Harper c Lewis b Hinds 37	1/100 2/186 3/243 (7 wkts dec.) 502		
†K. G. Edwards b Hinds 3	4/252 5/300		
*R. A. Harper c Lewis b Collymore ... 72	6/460 7/465		

L. A. Lambert and C. V. Solomon did not bat.

A. A. Lyght retired hurt at 19 and resumed at 252.

Bowling: Collymore 22–1–75–1; Murphy 21–2–100–0; Kentish 24–3–78–0; Etienne 34–4–118–1; Hinds 34–3–121–3; Charles 2–0–5–0.

Windward Islands

*L. D. John c Butts b R. A. Harper 70	– c Kallicharran b L. A. Lambert	11
†I. Cadette c and b Kallicharran 25	– b Solomon	15
L. A. Lewis lbw b R. A. Harper 22	– c Edwards b Solomon	0
F. X. Maurice c R. A. Harper b Butts 0	– c C. B. Lambert b Solomon	20
L. C. Sebastien c R. A. Harper b Butts 15	– b Butts	29
J. D. Charles c Kallicharran b Butts 1	– c L. A. Lambert b Butts	114
D. J. Collymore c Kallicharran b Butts 7	– c M. A. Harper b Kallicharran .	36
T. Z. Kentish c Lyght b R. A. Harper 13	– lbw b R. A. Harper	1
J. T. Etienne not out 18	– c R. A. Harper b Kallicharran ..	1
S. J. Hinds b Butts 0	– c R. A. Harper b Butts	42
S. A. E. Murphy b Butts 1	– not out	7
B 1, l-b 1, w 1, n-b 8 11	B 7, l-b 2, w 3, n-b 15 ...	27

1/63 2/109 3/116 4/140 5/141   183   1/21 2/25 3/48 4/76 5/102   303
6/149 7/150 8/174 9/177   6/212 7/224 8/225 9/281

Bowling: *First Innings*—L. A. Lambert 4–0–21–0; Solomon 4–0–18–0; Butts 33.3–11–57–6; Kallicharran 14–2–43–1; R. A. Harper 20–5–42–3. *Second Innings*—L. A. Lambert 5–0–35–1; Solomon 17–1–79–3; Kallicharran 27–0–84–2; Butts 17.1–4–48–3; R. A. Harper 17–2–48–1.

Umpires: D. M. Archer and C. Duncan.

BARBADOS v JAMAICA

At Bridgetown, January 31, February 1, 2, 3. Barbados won by 73 runs. Toss: Jamaica. Barbados 16 pts.

Barbados

C. G. Greenidge c Cunningham b Holding 23	– c Walsh b Daley	30
D. L. Haynes c Patterson b Holding 30	– c Heron b Patterson	65
C. A. Best c Dujon b Patterson 78	– c Powell b Holding	0
†T. R. O. Payne c Dujon b Daley 38	– b Holding	22
T. A. Hunte c Dujon b Daley 0	– lbw b Holding	0

S. R. Greaves c Davidson b Walsh	7	– lbw b Daley	0
M. D. Marshall c Davidson b Holding	11	– b Patterson	17
W. E. Reid c Dujon b Walsh	0	– (9) c Dujon b Walsh	3
†J. Garner c Davidson b Holding	1	– (8) c Dujon b Daley	11
R. O. Estwick c Davidson b Daley	8	– lbw b Daley	6
W. T. Greenidge not out	3	– not out	0
L-b 8, n-b 17	25	B 9, l-b 3, n-b 6	18

1/58 2/66 3/148 4/148 5/164   224   1/66 2/73 3/99 4/103 5/104   172
6/183 7/186 8/194 9/220   6/147 7/153 8/165 9/168

Bowling: *First Innings*—Walsh 23–3–74–2; Patterson 15–3–45–1; Holding 12–2–38–4; Daley 19–3–59–3. *Second Innings*—Patterson 17–4–37–2; Walsh 12–4–38–1; Daley 22–10–46–4; Holding 15–4–39–3.

Jamaica

O. W. Peters c Payne b Marshall	6	– lbw b Garner	5
F. A. Cunningham c Payne b W. T. Greenidge	24	– lbw b Garner	34
G. Powell c Haynes b Garner	0	– c C. G. Greenidge b Garner	9
M. C. Neita c C. G. Greenidge b Marshall	2	– run out	12
†P. J. L. Dujon c Haynes b Estwick	69	– not out	58
G. A. Heron c Payne b Marshall	1	– (8) lbw b Garner	4
C. A. Davidson b Marshall	0	– (6) lbw b Marshall	20
*M. A. Holding c and b Garner	5	– (7) b Marshall	0
A. G. Daley b Garner	8	– c Payne b Marshall	3
C. A. Walsh b Marshall b Reid	19	– b Garner	4
B. P. Patterson not out	1	– b Garner	2
L-b 1, n-b 6	7	B 17, l-b 4, n-b 9	30

1/12 2/12 3/19 4/60 5/63   142   1/16 2/37 3/58 4/104 5/153   181
6/63 7/78 8/99 9/125   6/153 7/161 8/169 9/179

Bowling: *First Innings*—Marshall 16–2–35–4; Garner 16–1–47–3; Estwick 9–2–44–1; W. T. Greenidge 5–1–14–1; Reid 4.2–3–1–1. *Second Innings*—Marshall 24–4–73–3; Garner 23.5–6–42–6; Reid 16–2–30–0; Estwick 7–2–13–0; Greaves 1–0–2–0.

Umpires: M. N. Baksh and S. E. Parris.

LEEWARD ISLANDS v TRINIDAD & TOBAGO

At Basseterre, January 31, February 1, 2, 3. Leeward Islands won by an innings and 1 run. Toss: Trinidad & Tobago. Leeward Islands 16 pts.

Leeward Islands

A. L. Kelly lbw b K. C. Williams	24	T. A. Merrick lbw b Mahabir 0
L. L. Lawrence c Simmons b Gray	19	W. K. M. Benjamin not out 10
R. B. Richardson b Nanan	50	
E. E. Lewis b Mahabir	28	B 1, l-b 9, w 2, n-b 4 16
R. M. Otto b Mahabir	165	
*I. V. A. Richards b Nanan	132	1/35 2/51 3/109 (8 wkts dec.) 503
†McC. V. Simon c Simmons b Nanan	8	4/141 5/378 6/405
N. C. Guishard not out	51	7/464 8/464

G. J. F. Ferris did not bat.

Bowling: Gray 12–1–53–1; K. C. Williams 15–0–93–1; Nanan 51–9–136–3; Simmons 10–0–61–0; Mahabir 42.5–9–138–3; Gomes 3–0–12–0.

Trinidad & Tobago

R. S. Gabriel lbw b Merrick	2	– c Benjamin b Guishard	13
P. V. Simmons b Guishard	52	– c and b Guishard	65
H. A. Gomes lbw b Ferris	23	– (5) c Lawrence b Guishard	6
A. L. Logie b Benjamin	5	– c Guishard b Richards	14
A. Rajah lbw b Merrick	69	– (6) c Simon b Richards	30
P. Moosai c and b Richards	25	– (3) lbw b Guishard	12
K. C. Williams lbw b Richards	0	– st Simon b Guishard	8
†D. Williams lbw b Richards	42	– c Lawrence b Richards	3
*R. Nanan c Richards b Merrick	0	– not out	29
A. H. Gray not out	54	– lbw b Richards	4
G. Mahabir c Kelly b Guishard	6	– c Kelly b Benjamin	8
B 5, l-b 3, w 1, n-b 15	24	L-b 4, w 2, n-b 2	8

1/4 2/53 3/68 4/114 5/171   302   1/33 2/72 3/89 4/100 5/137   200
6/173 7/210 8/211 9/283   6/151 7/159 8/160 9/179

Bowling: *First Innings*—Benjamin 22–5–72–1; Merrick 12–0–67–3; Ferris 12–1–40–1; Guishard 38.5–11–74–2; Richards 25–8–40–3. *Second Innings*—Merrick 4–1–16–0; Ferris 4–0–17–0; Guishard 38–15–84–5; Richards 37–7–80–4; Benjamin 1–1–0–1.

Umpires: M. A. Hippolyte and A. E. Weekes.

WINDWARD ISLANDS v JAMAICA

At St Vincent, February 6, 7, 8, 9. Windward Islands won by eight wickets. Toss: Windward Islands. Windward Islands 16 pts.

Jamaica

F. A. Cunningham b Thomas	15	– hit wkt b Hinds	24
W. W. Lewis c Charles b Collymore	14	– b Thomas	0
G. Powell c Marshall b Hinds	20	– (6) run out	40
M. C. Neita run out	10	– (3) lbw b Thomas	17
†P. J. L. Dujon c Cadette b Hinds	2	– c John b Hinds	4
C. A. Davidson c Sebastien b Etienne	5	– (4) c Collymore b Hinds	10
M. A. Tucker c and b Hinds	14	– c Charles b Collymore	9
*M. A. Holding c Thomas b Hinds	3	– c sub b Thomas	12
A. G. Daley c Marshall b Hinds	2	– b Etienne	47
C. A. Walsh c Thomas b Hinds	6	– c Marshall b Hinds	14
B. P. Patterson not out	0	– not out	3
L-b 6, n-b 1	7	B 9, l-b 6, n-b 5	20

1/24 2/40 3/63 4/63 5/66   98   1/3 2/33 3/58 4/65 5/66   200
6/72 7/87 8/89 9/97   6/92 7/109 8/160 9/178

Bowling: *First Innings*—Collymore 9–0–22–1; Thomas 9–0–27–1; Etienne 12–3–24–1; Hinds 12–2–19–6. *Second Innings*—Collymore 9–0–27–1; Thomas 23–3–61–3; Etienne 19–3–40–1; Marshall 8–0–17–0; Hinds 23–9–40–4.

Windward Islands

*L. D. John b Patterson	18	– not out	44
L. A. Lewis c Dujon b Walsh	32		
J. D. Charles c Davidson b Walsh	2	– lbw b Walsh	0
S. L. Mahon c Cunningham b Daley	24	– not out	7
L. C. Sebastien c Dujon b Walsh	52		
R. A. Marshall c Daley b Walsh	9		

†I. Cadette b Patterson	18	– (2) c Cunningham b Tucker	41
D. J. Collymore b Walsh	21		
S. J. Hinds c Daley b Walsh	0		
W. L. Thomas not out	6		
J. T. Etienne b Walsh	0		
B 12, l-b 1, n-b 9	22	N-b 3	3

1/53 2/55 3/98 4/119 5/156   204   1/66 2/77   (2 wkts) 95
6/190 7/195 8/195 9/204

In the first innings L. A. Lewis retired at 29 and resumed at 195.

Bowling: *First Innings*—Walsh 23.3-3-75-7; Patterson 18-4-48-2; Holding 5-2-11-0; Daley 12-2-23-1; Tucker 9-3-34-0. *Second Innings*—Walsh 10-0-34-1; Patterson 5-0-18-0; Daley 3-0-18-0; Tucker 7-1-25-1.

Umpires: G. T. Browne and S. Mohammed.

GUYANA v BARBADOS

At Essequebo, February 6, 7, 8, 9. Drawn. Toss: Guyana. Guyana 4 pts, Barbados 8 pts.

Guyana

C. B. Lambert c Greenidge b Reid	47	– c Reifer b Reid	57
R. Seeram lbw b Garner	0	– (6) c Best b Reid	6
†S. Bamfield b Greene	15	– (2) c Marshall b Greene	21
T. Mohamed run out	33	– c Garner b Linton	6
M. A. Harper not out	149	– not out	64
A. F. D. Jackman run out	18	– (3) st Payne b Linton	14
*R. A. Harper st Payne b Reid	20	– lbw b Greene	23
D. I. Kallicharran b Marshall	5	– not out	32
C. G. Butts c Best b Greene	16		
L. A. Lambert c Reifer b Linton	15		
C. V. Solomon lbw b Garner	1		
L-b 7, n-b 6	13	B 6, l-b 2, n-b 7	15

1/4 2/31 3/92 4/104 5/151   332   1/41 2/82 3/98 (6 wkts dec.) 238
6/201 7/223 8/270 9/313   4/108 5/118 6/161

Bowling: *First Innings*—Marshall 14-2-39-1; Garner 8-0-32-2; Linton 16-2-51-1; Greene 21-4-75-2; Best 12-1-42-0; Reid 22-2-86-2. *Second Innings*—Marshall 5-0-7-0; Garner 9-6-6-0; Greene 21-2-80-2; Linton 37-6-94-2; Reid 22-7-43-2.

Barbados

C. G. Greenidge c c C. B. Lambert b R. A. Harper	66	– retired hurt	17
D. L. Haynes b R. A. Harper	12	– c M. A. Harper b Kallicharran	9
C. A. Best c Bamfield b Solomon	111	– lbw b Kallicharran	7
†T. R. O. Payne c Kallicharran b Solomon	62	– c R. A. Harper b Butts	9
N. A. Johnson b Solomon	6		
L. N. Reifer b Butts	9	– (5) b Kallicharran	0
M. D. Marshall c sub b Butts	1	– not out	7
V. S. Greene b R. A. Harper	17		
G. N. Linton c Bamfield b Solomon	1		
*J. Garner b Butts	44		
W. E. Reid not out	13	– (6) not out	4
B 6, l-b 7, n-b 10	23	B 4, l-b 4, n-b 1	9

1/50 2/97 3/238 4/245 5/279   365   1/31 2/40 3/40 4/48 (4 wkts) 62
6/287 7/287 8/288 9/328

In the second innings C. G. Greenidge retired hurt at 31.

Bowling: *First Innings*—L. A. Lambert 3–0–14–0; Solomon 24–6–78–4; Butts 47.4–11–102–3; R. A. Harper 42–13–104–3; Kallicharran 17–5–43–0; M. A. Harper 4–1–11–0. *Second Innings*—Solomon 4–1–9–0; M. A. Harper 2–1–2–0; R. A. Harper 5–1–11–0; Butts 13–5–17–1; Kallicharran 10–4–15–3.

Umpires: C. E. Cumberbatch and D. J. Narine.

GUYANA v LEEWARD ISLANDS

At Bourda, February 12, 13, 14, 15. Drawn. Toss: Guyana. Guyana 4 pts, Leeward Islands 8 pts.

Guyana

C. B. Lambert c Simon b Benjamin	0	– c Otto b Guishard	48
A. F. Sattaur c Richards b Proctor	17	– c Simons b Benjamin	0
A. F. D. Jackman c Williams b Guishard	67	– c Guishard b Benjamin	35
T. Mohamed b Benjamin	0	– c Williams b Ambrose	31
M. A. Harper c Simon b Ambrose	42	– c Williams b Ambrose	106
†S. Bamfield c Richardson b Guishard	13	– b Proctor	83
*R. A. Harper lbw b Benjamin	32	– not out	17
D. I. Kallicharran run out	29	– c Otto b Proctor	14
C. G. Butts lbw b Guishard	1	– c Lewis b Proctor	0
M. O. Grenville c Simon b Ambrose	7	– (11) not out	6
C. V. Solomon not out	1	– (10) c Otto b Proctor	1
L-b 4, n-b 5	9	L-b 4, n-b 7	11

1/0 2/25 3/27 4/109 5/133   218   1/1 2/81 3/91 4/140   (9 wkts) 352
6/146 7/193 8/198 9/212   5/306 6/315 7/343
                                             8/344 9/346

Bowling: *First Innings*—Benjamin 16–3–39–3; Ambrose 17–1–61–2; Proctor 12–1–39–1; Richardson 5–0–19–0; Guishard 27–7–55–3; Richards 1–0–1–0. *Second Innings*—Benjamin 13–2–40–2; Ambrose 21–4–79–2; Proctor 13–1–46–4; Guishard 37–7–119–1; Richards 5–2–7–0; Otto 20–2–46–0; Lewis 3–0–11–0.

Leeward Islands

R. B. Richardson c Bamfield b R. A. Harper	55	N. C. Guishard b Butts	8
L. L. Lawrence c Bamfield b Butts	86	W. K. M. Benjamin c R. A. Harper b Butts	16
E. E. Lewis c M. A. Harper b Butts	12	E. J. Proctor c Grenville b Kallicharran	2
R. M. Otto c Lambert b R. A. Harper	10	E. L. C. Ambrose not out	0
*I. V. A. Richards c Solomon b R. A. Harper	32	B 4, l-b 5, n-b 2	11
S. I. Williams c Bamfield b Kallicharran	42		
†McC. V. Simon c Sattaur b Butts	31		305

1/138 2/150 3/167 4/183 5/210 6/263 7/287 8/297 9/305

Bowling: Solomon 9–1–38–0; Grenville 2–0–19–0; R. A. Harper 33–7–75–3; Butts 39–12–98–5; Kallicharran 28.3–7–66–2.

Umpires: D. M. Archer and R. W. Haynes.

WINDWARD ISLANDS v TRINIDAD & TOBAGO

At Roseau, February 13, 14, 15, 16. Trinidad & Tobago won by four wickets. Toss: Windward Islands. Trinidad & Tobago 16 pts, Windward Islands 5 pts.

Windward Islands

*L. D. John b Gray	33	– c Gray b Mahabir	44
†I. Cadette lbw b Gray	84	– c Simmons b Gray	5
L. A. Lewis lbw b Nanan	10	– c and b Gray	2
J. D. Charles lbw b Nanan	0	– (5) c and b Nanan	1
L. C. Sebastien b Nanan	2	– (4) b Nanan	22
S. L. Mahon b Gray	25	– lbw b Mahabir	6
R. A. Marshall lbw b Gray	0	– st Williams b Mahabir	2
D. J. Collymore c Gomes b Nanan	3	– b Mahabir	17
S. J. Hinds not out	8	– (10) c Gabriel b Nanan	3
W. L. Thomas lbw b Gray	5	– (9) c Gabriel b Nanan	5
J. T. Etienne b Nanan	3	– not out	8
B 7, l-b 12, w 1, n-b 14	34	B 8, l-b 4, n-b 6	18

1/58 2/92 3/92 4/102 5/153	**207**	1/11 2/19 3/86 4/90 5/92	**133**
6/161 7/178 8/184 9/196		6/100 7/122 8/122 9/133	

Bowling: First Innings—Gray 23–4–72–5; St Hilaire 3–0–27–0; Nanan 29.3–6–60–5; Mahabir 11–4–23–0; Gomes 1–0–6–0. *Second Innings*—Gray 8–0–17–2; St Hilaire 4–0–24–0; Simmons 6–0–17–0; Nanan 13.3–3–21–4; Mahabir 12–1–42–4.

Trinidad & Tobago

R. S. Gabriel b Thomas	0	– not out	20
P. V. Simmons c Lewis b Etienne	36	– c Hinds b Collymore	0
H. A. Gomes c Hinds b Thomas	6	– b Collymore	12
A. L. Logie b Thomas	2	– c Etienne b Thomas	0
A. Rajah b Collymore	12	– lbw b Collymore	12
D. I. Mohammed c Charles b Etienne	46	– lbw b Thomas	49
†D. Williams b Thomas	2	– c Mahon b Thomas	50
*R. Nanan run out	61	– not out	8
A. H. Gray b Marshall	4		
D. V. St Hilaire c Charles b Marshall	2		
G. Mahabir not out	1		
B 3, l-b 2, n-b 5	10	B 1, n-b 7	8

1/1 2/15 3/17 4/37 5/61	**182**	1/3 2/6 3/19 4/57	(6 wkts) **159**
6/64 7/173 8/174 9/181		5/131 6/132	

In the second innings R. S. Gabriel retired hurt at 3 and resumed at 131.

Bowling: First Innings—Collymore 12–6–22–1; Thomas 24–3–63–4; Hinds 11–1–46–0; Etienne 17–2–26–2; Marshall 12.5–4–20–2. *Second Innings*—Collymore 15.5–2–59–3; Thomas 15–0–53–3; Etienne 6–2–14–0; Hinds 3–0–13–0; Marshall 8–0–19–0.

Umpires: J. A. Simon and P. C. White.

SHELL SHIELD WINNERS

1965-66	Barbados	1976-77	Barbados
1966-67	Barbados	1977-78	Barbados
1968-69	Jamaica	1978-79	Barbados
1969-70	Trinidad	1979-80	Barbados
1970-71	Trinidad	1980-81	Combined Islands
1971-72	Barbados	1981-82	Barbados
1972-73	Guyana	1982-83	Guyana
1973-74	Barbados	1983-84	Barbados
1974-75	Guyana	1984-85	Trinidad & Tobago
1975-76 {	Trinidad / Barbados	1985-86	Barbados

OTHER FIRST-CLASS MATCH

GUYSTAC TROPHY, 1985-86

BERBICE v DEMERARA

At Bourda, November 1, 2, 3, 4. Demerara won by four wickets. Toss: Demerara.

Berbice

C. B. Lambert c and b Grenville	3	– c Lyght b Charles	15
A. F. Sattaur c Bamfield b Charles	16	– run out	48
K. G. Edwards c M. A. Harper b Butts	99	– c S. Seeram b Butts	39
D. Persaud c Bamfield b Grenville	15	– b Butts	6
D. I. Kallicharran c R. Seeram b R. A. Harper	38	– c Butts b R. A. Harper	46
L. Bhansingh c Charles b R. A. Harper	3	– lbw b Matthews	10
*†M. R. Pydanna c R. A. Harper b Butts	3	– lbw b R. A. Harper	5
J. Angus c Bamfield b Butts	18	– run out	7
L. A. Lambert lbw b Matthews	13	– lbw b Butts	0
R. F. Joseph c R. Seeram b Matthews	2	– c Charles b Matthews	0
C. V. Solomon not out	0	– not out	0
B 2, l-b 9, w 2, n-b 7	20	B 12, l-b 4, w 3, n-b 5	24

1/5 2/29 3/57 4/160 5/164   230   1/17 2/98 3/109 4/137 5/181   200
6/173 7/207 8/224 9/230   6/184 7/195 8/196 9/200

Bowling: *First Innings*—Grenville 10-0-68-2; Charles 8-0-39-1; Butts 20.4-2-48-3; Matthews 9-1-29-2; R. A. Harper 18-6-35-2. *Second Innings*—Grenville 7-1-26-0; Charles 9-1-40-1; M. A. Harper 4-2-9-0; Matthews 8.4-0-26-2; Butts 18-7-30-3; R. A. Harper 12-3-53-2.

Demerara

A. A. Lyght lbw b L. A. Lambert	33	– lbw b Joseph	3
†S. Bamfield b L. A. Lambert	27	– c Bhansingh b Solomon	3
R. Seeram b Angus	2	– run out	6
A. F. D. Jackman st Pydanna b Kallicharran	120	– c and b Joseph	1
M. A. Harper run out	35	– c Edwards b Joseph	1
S. Seeram c Angus b L. A. Lambert	12	– b Solomon	0
*R. A. Harper lbw b Joseph	61	– not out	10
G. E. Charles c Edwards b L. A. Lambert	37	– not out	0
C. G. Butts not out	12		
S. Matthews run out	21		
M. O. Grenville c Pydanna b Joseph	4		
B 4, l-b 7, w 3, n-b 18	32	B 1, l-b 6, n-b 5	12

1/52 2/72 3/97 4/168 5/197   396   1/10 2/16 3/22 4/26   (6 wkts) 36
6/285 7/342 8/362 9/391   5/26 6/28

Bowling: *First Innings*—L. A. Lambert 23-3-117-4; Joseph 11.4-0-58-2; Solomon 16-0-71-0; Kallicharran 18-0-72-1; Angus 26-10-50-1; Bhansingh 3-0-17-0. *Second Innings*—Solomon 5-1-6-2; Joseph 5-0-23-3.

†GEDDES GRANT-HARRISON LINE TROPHY, 1985-86

Zone A

At Kingston, January 7. Jamaica won by six wickets. Guyana 137 for eight (45 overs) (A. G. Daley four for 26); Jamaica 138 for four (39.2 overs) (W. W. Lewis 56).

At Tobago, January 15. Trinidad & Tobago won by seven wickets. Guyana 106 for eight (36 overs); Trinidad & Tobago 108 for three (25.1 overs) (P. V. Simmons 62).

At Port-of-Spain, January 22. Jamaica won by 49 runs. Jamaica 180 for nine (49 overs) (O. W. Peters 74 not out); Trinidad & Tobago 131 (38.4 overs) (P. V. Simmons 59).

Zone B

At Castries, January 8. Leeward Islands won by five wickets. Windward Islands 108 for three (28 overs); Leeward Islands 111 for five (25.4 overs).

At Bridgetown, January 15. Barbados won by 146 runs after Windward Islands' target was reduced to 252 off 41 overs. Barbados 276 for three (45 overs) (D. L. Haynes 44, C. A. Best 45, T. A. Hunte 75, T. R. O. Payne 100 not out); Windward Islands 105 for seven (41 overs).

At Basseterre, January 22. Leeward Islands won by three wickets. Barbados 213 for eight (50 overs) (C. A. Best 40); Leeward Islands 216 for seven (45.4 overs) (S. I. Williams 45 not out).

FINAL

LEEWARD ISLANDS v JAMAICA

At St John's, March 1. Jamaica won by six wickets. Toss Jamaica.
Man of the Match: M. C. Neita.

Leeward Islands

R. B. Richardson b Walsh	0	N. C. Guishard run out		23
L. L. Lawrence c Cunningham		W. K. M. Benjamin not out		21
b Patterson	4	G. J. F. Ferris not out		1
E. E. Lewis run out	28	B 7, l-b 2, w 2, n-b 15		26
R. M. Otto c Cunningham b Patterson	0			
*I. V. A. Richards c Daley b Walsh	60	1/0 2/15 3/17	(8 wkts, 39 overs)	169
S. I. Williams c Adams b Barrett	0	4/86 5/93 6/116		
†McC. V. Simon c Adams b Daley	6	7/117 8/157		

E. L. C. Ambrose did not bat.

Bowling: Walsh 10-1-39-2; Patterson 9-1-32-2; Daley 10-1-40-1; Barrett 9-0-38-1; Neita 1-0-11-0.

Jamaica

F. A. Cunningham c Otto b Ferris	12	A. G. Daley not out		20
G. Powell run out	33	B 4, l-b 6, w 1, n-b 6		17
M. C. Neita c Simon b Richardson	67			
A. B. Williams c Simon b Ambrose	0	1/15 2/75 3/75	(4 wkts, 34.3 overs)	173
C. A. Davidson not out	24	4/138		

*†P. J. L. Dujon, J. C. Adams, H. Barrett, C. A. Walsh and B. P. Patterson did not bat.

Bowling: Ferris 5-1-9-1; Benjamin 6-0-32-0; Richards 5-1-25-0; Ambrose 10-1-32-1; Guishard 6-0-40-0; Richardson 2.3-0-25-1.

Umpires: C. Mack and A. E. Weekes.

CRICKET IN NEW ZEALAND, 1985-86

By C. R. BUTTERY

At the start of the season Otago looked the team least likely to win the Shell Trophy. With basically the same players who won only one match the previous season, their prospects were not promising, yet under the inspiring leadership of Warren Lees, the cautious approach of past seasons disappeared. Attacking fields were set whenever possible and a positive attitude prevailed at all times. Nowhere was this more apparent than in the game against Central Districts at Oamaru at the end of January. Set to score 342 to win in 182 minutes plus twenty overs, the Otago batsmen achieved their victory for the loss of six wickets, Richard Hoskin leading the way with 111 off 133 balls.

Otago won four matches outright and their only upset was defeat by Northern Districts when the batting failed in both innings. There were, however, some anxious moments in their final match against Canterbury. A first-innings lead would bring sufficient points for Otago to remain top of the table, but the task of overhauling Canterbury's 401 looked immense. Once again, however, Otago's positive attitude was evident. Solid contributions by all the recognised batsmen, including a well-compiled 134 from Stuart McCullum, saw them pass Canterbury's total with only five wickets down and the Shell Trophy was theirs. The opening batsmen, Ken Rutherford and McCullum, each had a satisfactory series, Rutherford scoring three hundreds, including a hundred in each innings against Northern Districts, and playing with success in the Test matches against Australia later in the season. Despite a disastrous series in the West Indies earlier in 1985, he looked New Zealand's best batting prospect since Martin Crowe. The veteran pace bowler, John Cushen, was Otago's most successful bowler, finishing with 31 wickets.

Auckland, the runners-up, suffered from the loss of key players to the national team, Jeff Crowe, John Reid, John Bracewell, Martin Snedden and Stuart Gillespie all being unavailable for much of the season. Nevertheless they did win four games and perhaps only lack of consistency in the batting stopped them from winning the trophy. Trevor Franklin passed 50 six times and Peter Webb was dismissed below double figures only once, but the other batsmen had moderate success. Although Mark Greatbatch virtually won the match against Central Districts with not out scores of 119 and 88, his next highest innings was 24. Gary Troup bowled well to take 30 wickets but Willie Watson failed to repeat his successes of the previous season. In Bracewell's absence, Dipak Patel's all-round ability proved invaluable. The Worcestershire professional scored 469 runs, including a fine 174 against Canterbury, and took 29 wickets.

Wellington, the holders, were affected by adverse weather conditions which ruined their chances of at least one outright victory. Like Auckland they were without several leading players – Jeremy Coney, Ewen Chatfield, Bruce Edgar and Ervin McSweeney – and in the circumstances third place could be considered satisfactory. They were the only side to avoid an outright defeat. Lancashire's Paul Allott made a major contribution to the side with 30 wickets, but the outstanding player was undoubtedly Evan Gray. He scored more runs and took more wickets than any other Wellington player, and it was indicative of the strength of New Zealand cricket that he was unable to command a regular Test place. His 34 wickets included a return of eight for 37 and match figures of fourteen for 151 against Canterbury at Hutt Recreation Ground.

Although Northern Districts won three matches they never looked like being in contention for the trophy. Their most successful batsman was David White, whose 578 runs included an innings of 209 against Central Districts. Chris Kuggeleijn and Lindsay Crocker also made useful contributions but the batting in general was not strong. The unavailability of Lance Cairns, Cliff Dickeson and Brendon Bracewell left a big gap in the bowling, and some large scores were compiled against the side. Northern Districts did, however, have the satisfaction of outright victories over the two leading sides, Auckland and Otago.

Central Districts had an unhappy season, winning only one match. Once again their bowling lacked penetration and their problems were compounded by the failure of the leading batsmen to score as heavily as in 1984-85. John Smith was their most consistent batsman with two hundreds and three other scores over 50, while Ron Hart hit 207 against Wellington but made only another 172 runs from ten innings. Gary Robertson was the leading bowler with 32 wickets, and with scores of 50 not out, 66 not out and 99 not out he also headed Central Districts' batting averages. Perhaps the brightest feature was the emergence of Tony Blain as a potential international wicket-keeper-batsman in the same mould as his team-mate, Ian Smith.

Without Richard Hadlee and John Wright to strengthen the side, Canterbury failed to achieve an outright victory and led on the first innings only twice. David Boyle batted confidently in his three matches, but generally the batting could not be relied on. Nor was there any depth in the bowling. Much was expected of Sean Tracy, a fast bowler who had previously played for Auckland, but although he took Canterbury to the brink of victory against Central Districts by taking five of the six second-innings wickets to fall, he was unable to find the same form in other matches.

The one-day Shell Cup competition was played between December 27 and January 4 at the peak of the Christmas holiday period. This, together with New Zealand's Test players all being available, attracted large crowds. Canterbury's four wins in five games won them the cup but it could just as easily have gone to Auckland or Wellington. At the start of the final round, these three sides had three wins each: but while Canterbury beat Otago, the Wellington v Auckland game was drawn because of rain. Reid was the outstanding batsman of the series with scores of 46, 99 not out, 118 and 49 for Auckland, but what the crowds enjoyed most was the big hitting of Cairns. The towering 6s in his innings of 52 in fewer than six overs for Northern Districts against Auckland, and of 60 in 48 balls against Wellington will long be remembered by those fortunate enough to see Cairns at his swashbuckling best in what was his farewell season.

FIRST-CLASS AVERAGES, 1985-86

BATTING

(Qualification: 5 completed innings, average 35)

	I	*NO*	*R*	*HI*	*Avge*
M. D. Crowe (*Central Districts*)	6	1	318	137	63.60
P. N. Webb (*Auckland*)	13	5	441	115	55.12
D. J. Boyle (*Canterbury*)	6	1	267	149	53.40
K. R. Rutherford (*Otago*)	17	2	753	126	50.20
E. J. Gray (*Wellington*)	13	2	545	128*	49.54
S. J. McCullum (*Otago*)	13	1	585	134	48.75
G. K. Robertson (*Central Districts*)	11	4	303	99*	43.28
T. D. Ritchie (*Wellington*)	13	3	420	60	42.00
R. N. Hoskin (*Otago*)	12	2	401	111	40.10
C. J. Smith (*Central Districts*)	17	0	674	103	39.64
M. J. Greatbatch (*Auckland*)	12	4	316	119*	39.50
T. J. Franklin (*Auckland*)	16	1	592	176	39.46
D. J. White (*Northern Districts*)	17	2	578	209	38.53
R. T. Hart (*Central Districts*)	11	1	379	207	37.90
D. J. Walker (*Otago*)	11	2	341	106	37.88
R. H. Vance (*Wellington*)	13	0	488	114	37.53
P. J. Kelly (*Auckland*)	9	1	292	93	36.50
D. N. Patel (*Auckland*)	14	1	469	174	36.07
A. H. Jones (*Wellington*)	11	3	286	99	35.75
C. M. Kuggeleijn (*Northern Districts*) ...	14	2	424	74	35.33

* *Signifies not out.*

BOWLING

(Qualification: 20 wickets)

	O	*M*	*R*	*W*	*Avge*
P. J. W. Allott (*Wellington*)	230.4	80	460	30	15.33
J. G. Bracewell (*Auckland*)	178.3	64	358	22	16.27
E. J. Gray (*Wellington*)	330.2	119	748	34	22.00
J. A. J. Cushen (*Otago*)	350.1	133	711	31	22.93
G. B. Troup (*Auckland*)	286.5	81	695	30	23.16
V. R. Brown (*Canterbury*)	211.1	70	487	20	24.35
N. A. Mallender (*Otago*)	227.1	48	597	24	24.87
D. N. Patel (*Auckland*)	355.1	105	756	29	26.06
S. W. Duff (*Central Districts*)	218.2	56	604	21	28.76
S. J. Scott (*Northern Districts*)	271.1	67	721	24	30.04
G. K. Robertson (*Central Districts*)	269.4	41	967	32	30.21
S. M. Carrington (*Northern Districts*) ...	259.5	43	792	25	31.68
J. K. Lindsay (*Otago*)	187.3	45	647	20	32.35
D. A. Stirling (*Central Districts*)	217	31	863	26	33.19
P. J. Visser (*Central Districts*)	298.3	72	903	26	34.73

SHELL TROPHY, 1985-86

	Played	Won	Lost	Drawn	1st Inns Pts	Pts
Otago...............	8	4	1	3	22*	70
Auckland............	8	4	2	2	20	68
Wellington	8	3	0	5	20†	56
Northern Districts	8	3	3	2	12	47‡
Central Districts.......	8	1	4	3	14*	24‡
Canterbury	8	0	5	3	8	8

Outright win = 12 pts; lead on first innings = 4 pts.

* *First-innings points shared in one match.*   † *First-innings points shared in two matches.*

‡ *Central Districts were penalised 2 points and Northern Districts 1 point for failing to achieve an average rate of seventeen overs per hour during the season.*

CANTERBURY v AUCKLAND

At Lancaster Park, Christchurch, January 6, 7, 8. Auckland won by an innings and 34 runs. Auckland 16 pts. Toss: Auckland.

Auckland

T. J. Franklin run out................176		*P. N. Webb not out	1
P. A. Horne c Latham b Thiele 32			
M. J. Greatbatch c MacDonald b Brown 7		B 1, l-b 3, w 1, n-b 1	6
D. N. Patel b Thiele 174			
D. G. Scott not out 50		1/52 2/65 3/343 (5 wkts dec.)	454
A. J. Hunt lbw b Thiele 8		4/426 5/449	

†P. J. Kelly, G. B. Troup, B. J. Barrett and W. Watson did not bat.

Bowling: Thiele 32.3–7–103–3; Tracy 17–1–86–0; Latham 3–1–13–0; Brown 25–1–76–1; Stead 12–1–43–0; MacDonald 21–4–74–0; Hartshorn 21–8–55–0.

Canterbury

A. Nathu c Kelly b Troup	8	– c Greatbatch b Watson	5
P. G. Kennedy c Franklin b Barrett	22	– b Barrett	14
P. E. McEwan c Kelly b Patel	22	– c Hunt b Patel	34
*V. R. Brown c Webb b Patel	11	– c Kelly b Patel	30
R. T. Latham c Franklin b Hunt	64	– c Horne b Patel	9
D. W. Stead c Franklin b Patel	46	– not out	31
D. J. Hartshorn lbw b Barrett	38	– b Hunt	15
†A. W. Hart c Greatbatch b Patel	0	– b Watson	12
G. K. MacDonald c Kelly b Hunt	9	– c Kelly b Watson	0
C. H. Thiele b Barrett	4	– c Horne b Patel	17
S. R. Tracy not out	1	– c Horne b Barrett	7
B 2, l-b 4, n-b 4	10	B 3, n-b 8	11

1/20 2/37 3/62 4/71 5/171	235	1/15 2/37 3/83 4/97 5/97	185
6/187 7/187 8/206 9/228		6/127 7/153 8/153 9/178	

Bowling: *First Innings*—Troup 10–2–29–1; Watson 7–2–16–0; Patel 31–8–76–4; Barrett 12–1–54–3; Hunt 21–7–54–2. *Second Innings*—Troup 10–2–26–0; Watson 16–2–44–3; Patel 34–11–62–4; Barrett 11.3–2–43–2; Hunt 3–0–7–1.

Umpires: B. L. Aldridge and F. R. Goodall.

CENTRAL DISTRICTS v OTAGO

At Palmerston North, January 6, 7, 8. Otago won by 259 runs. Otago 16 pts. Toss: Central Districts.

Otago

K. R. Rutherford c Stirling b Robertson	126	– b Murphy	67
S. J. McCullum lbw b Robertson	0	– b Stirling	9
R. N. Hoskin c Guthardt b Visser	13	– c Guthardt b Stirling	75
K. J. Burns b Robertson	14	– c Visser b Murphy	0
D. J. Walker c I. D. S. Smith b Briasco	5	– c Guthardt b Stirling	30
T. J. Wilson b Murphy	3	– (9) run out	15
B. J. McKechnie lbw b Murphy	0	– (6) b Stirling	1
*†W. K. Lees c I. D. S. Smith b Visser	22	– (7) lbw b Stirling	6
J. K. Lindsay not out	17	– (8) lbw b Visser	21
N. A. Mallender b Visser	0	– not out	23
J. A. J. Cushen b Robertson	0	– not out	6
L-b 7, n-b 9	16	L-b 3, n-b 7	10

1/4 2/37 3/97 4/136 5/141   216   1/37 2/97 3/97   (9 wkts dec.) 263
6/141 7/194 8/198 9/211   4/159 5/161 6/173
                                       7/201 8/224 9/245

Bowling: *First Innings*—Robertson 15.2-1-67-4; Murphy 20-8-42-2; Visser 20-5-47-3; Stirling 6-0-28-0; Duff 7-1-14-0; Briasco 4-2-11-1. *Second Innings*—Robertson 19-4-68-0; Murphy 12-4-31-2; Visser 23-6-67-1; Stirling 21-2-82-5; Briasco 2-0-12-0; Hayward 1-1-0-0.

Central Districts

R. T. Hart lbw b Mallender	0	– (2) c Lees b Cushen	5
C. J. Smith c Lees b Mallender	39	– (1) lbw b Mallender	2
P. S. Briasco c Cushen b Mallender	14	– b McKechnie	7
*R. E. Hayward c McCullum b Cushen	8	– c Lees b McKechnie	23
I. D. S. Smith c Hoskin b Cushen	1	– c Hoskin b Cushen	19
†D. J. Guthardt c Rutherford b Cushen	16	– c Rutherford b Lindsay	10
D. A. Stirling c Rutherford b Cushen	12	– c McKechnie b Lindsay	33
G. K. Robertson c Wilson b McKechnie	5	– c Lees b McKechnie	0
S. W. Duff lbw b Cushen	1	– not out	15
A. J. Murphy c Mallender b Cushen	0	– c and b Lindsay	0
P. J. Visser not out	0	– lbw b McKechnie	0
L-b 1, n-b 3	4	L-b 2, w 1, n-b 3	6

1/0 2/14 3/61 4/63 5/76   100   1/2 2/11 3/25 4/47 5/66   120
6/83 7/90 8/91 9/95   6/84 7/92 8/110 9/114

Bowling: *First Innings*—Mallender 14-2-36-3; Cushen 26-12-34-6; McKechnie 15-10-19-1; Wilson 4-2-6-0; Lindsay 2-1-4-0. *Second Innings*—Mallender 11-5-14-1; Cushen 15-4-28-2; McKechnie 18.2-6-38-4; Lindsay 14-5-38-3.

Umpires: D. A. Kinsella and J. G. Reardon.

NORTHERN DISTRICTS v WELLINGTON

At Gisborne, January 6, 7, 8. Wellington won by four wickets. Wellington 16 pts. Toss: Wellington.

Northern Districts

L. M. Crocker c Milne b Allott	18	– c Larsen b Beyeler	29
R. E. W. Mawhinney b Maguiness	19	– c Milne b Allott	30
D. J. White c Milne b Beyeler	43	– c Vance b Gray	67
*G. P. Howarth c Gray b Beyeler	16	– b Jones	18
B. G. Cooper lbw b Allott	6	– (8) c Milne b Allott	10
C. M. Kuggeleijn c Larsen b Maguiness	58	– (5) b Allott	3
†B. A. Young c Ormiston b Maguiness	17	– (6) lbw b Allott	0
G. E. Bradburn c Larsen b Gray	4	– (7) c and b Maguiness	17
S. J. Scott c and b Allott	11	– b Beyeler	18
S. M. Carrington not out	1	– b Allott	10
K. B. Hancock c Milne b Maguiness	0	– not out	0
B 1, l-b 3, w 2	6	L-b 3, w 1, n-b 2	6

1/29 2/70 3/85 4/91 5/121   199   1/43 2/68 3/107 4/139 5/139   208
6/155 7/163 8/196 9/198   6/166 7/175 8/190 9/200

Bowling: *First Innings*—Beyeler 22–6–48–2; Allott 24–10–46–3; Gray 26–11–69–1; Maguiness 22.2–11–32–4. *Second Innings*—Beyeler 22–6–45–2; Allott 18.3–7–56–5; Gray 32–17–60–1; Maguiness 14–3–25–1; Jones 10–4–19–1.

Wellington

J. G. Boyle c Kuggeleijn b Hancock	9	– (2) run out	14
R. W. Ormiston c and b Bradburn	21	– (1) c Kuggeleijn b Hancock	7
*R. H. Vance c Young b Carrington	48	– c Young b Carrington	8
†J. D. Milne b Howarth b Bradburn	12		
E. J. Gray b Hancock	11	– (6) c Young b Hancock	26
A. H. Jones c Young b Hancock	8	– (5) not out	23
T. D. Ritchie c Young b Carrington	60	– (4) lbw b Scott	0
G. R. Larsen c White b Scott	92	– (7) b Hancock	0
P. J. W. Allott c Hancock b Scott	13	– (8) not out	2
S. J. Maguiness c Mawhinney b Carrington	18		
F. Beyeler not out	8		
B 2, l-b 13, w 3	18	B 4, l-b 3, w 3	10

1/21 2/47 3/91 4/95 5/111   318   1/8 2/25 3/31 4/35   (6 wkts) 90
6/114 7/251 8/268 9/302   5/82 6/86

Bowling: *First Innings*—Carrington 23–4–63–3; Hancock 24–2–107–3; Scott 28.5–9–68–2; Bradburn 28–13–43–2; White 4–0–18–0; Kuggeleijn 2–1–4–0. *Second Innings*—Carrington 7–0–23–1; Hancock 7–1–37–3; Scott 4–2–6–1; Bradburn 2–0–12–0; Kuggeleijn 1.1–0–5–0.

Umpires: T. A. McCall and K. Thomson.

CANTERBURY v NORTHERN DISTRICTS

At Christchurch, January 10, 11, 12. Drawn. Canterbury 4 pts. Toss: Canterbury.

Northern Districts

L. M. Crocker c Hartshorn b Tracy	105	– not out	38
R. E. W. Mawhinney c Hart b McNally	1	– lbw b Thiele	20
D. J. White b McNally	11		
*G. P. Howarth c Hartshorn b McNally	0		
B. G. Cooper c Thiele b Hartshorn	83		

C. M. Kuggeleijn c Hart b Tracy 73
†B. A. Young c Nathu b Tracy 4
G. E. Bradburn c Hart b Hartshorn 19
S. J. Scott c Hart b McNally 6
S. M. Carrington c sub b Tracy 53
K. B. Hancock not out 10
        L-b 16, w 1, n-b 1 18

1/14 2/44 3/44 4/169 5/230   383   1/58   (1 wkt) 58
6/234 7/273 8/306 9/329

Bowling: *First Innings*—Thiele 20-3-87-0; McNally 29-8-97-4; Tracy 15.5-1-70-4; Latham 7-1-40-0; Hartshorn 22-3-70-2; Brown 1-0-3-0. *Second Innings*—Thiele 3.4-1-10-1; McNally 3-1-13-0; Tracy 5-0-15-0; Stead 6-3-20-0.

Canterbury

A. Nathu c Young b Hancock 9	S. R. McNally run out 13
P. G. Kennedy c Kuggeleijn b Bradburn 10	C. H. Thiele not out 9
P. E. McEwan c Hancock b Bradburn .118	
*V. R. Brown b Bradburn 134	B 1, l-b 12, w 4, n-b 2 19
R. T. Latham not out 66	
D. W. Stead c Young b Scott 8	1/13 2/48 3/238 (8 wkts dec.) 387
D. J. Hartshorn c Young b Scott 0	4/307 5/326 6/334
†A. W. Hart run out 1	7/335 8/371

S. R. Tracy did not bat.

Bowling: Carrington 24-3-102-0; Hancock 21-3-99-1; Bradburn 23-7-80-3; Scott 29-6-78-2; Kuggeleijn 4-1-15-0.

Umpires: B. L. Aldridge and F. R. Goodall.

OTAGO v AUCKLAND

At Dunedin, January 10, 11, 12. Drawn. Otago 4 pts. Toss: Otago.

Auckland

T. J. Franklin lbw b Mallender .... 16 – c Burns b Cushen 5
P. A. Horne c Mallender b Cushen 4
D. G. Scott lbw b Cushen ... 52 – (2) c Lees b Mallender 4
D. N. Patel c Walker b Mallender .... 10 – not out 11
M. J. Greatbatch c Rutherford b Cushen .... 24 – (3) not out 19
A. J. Hunt c Lindsay b Cushen 18
*P. N. Webb c Lees b Mallender 49
†P. J. Kelly c Lindsay b Mallender 12
G. B. Troup c Walker b Wilson 12
W. Watson run out 0
B. J. Barrett not out 0
     B 1, l-b 4, n-b 3 8   L-b 1 1

1/9 2/61 3/85 4/87 5/120   205 1/9 2/9   (2 wkts) 40
6/137 7/164 8/186 9/197

Bowling: *First Innings*—Mallender 25.5-6-68-4; Cushen 29-13-51-4; McKechnie 11-3-21-0; Wilson 13-2-50-1; Walker 6-2-10-0. *Second Innings*—Mallender 7-2-20-1; Cushen 7-2-17-1; McKechnie 1-0-2-0.

Otago

K. R. Rutherford c Kelly b Troup	....	10	T. J. Wilson not out	....	26
S. J. McCullum b Troup	....	33	N. A. Mallender c Kelly b Troup	.....	16
R. N. Hoskin lbw b Troup	....	46	J. A. J. Cushen c Webb b Barrett	.....	12
K. J. Burns b Barrett	....	47			
D. J. Walker c Kelly b Troup	....	6	B 5, l-b 13, n-b 2	....	20
J. K. Lindsay c Franklin b Barrett	....	10			
*†W. K. Lees b Patel	....	13	1/18 2/50 3/131 4/154 5/157		243
B. J. McKechnie b Barrett	....	4	6/178 7/180 8/193 9/216		

Bowling: Troup 23–9–43–5; Barrett 15.5–3–51–4; Patel 29–7–74–1; Watson 12–3–36–0; Scott 9–2–21–0.

Umpires: D. E. C. McKechnie and G. C. Morris.

WELLINGTON v CENTRAL DISTRICTS

At Wellington, January 10, 11, 12. Drawn. Wellington 2 pts, Central Districts 2 pts. Toss: Wellington.

Central Districts

R. T. Hart c Ritchie b Maguiness	.....	207	D. A. Stirling not out	....	3
C. J. Smith c Ormiston b Gray	....	101			
P. S. Briasco b Beyeler	....	42	B 8, l-b 23, w 1	....	32
*R. E. Hayward lbw b Maguiness	.....	35			
†D. J. Guthardt run out	....	13	1/250 2/374 3/378	(6 wkts dec.)	433
I. D. S. Smith lbw b Larsen	....	0	4/417 5/417 6/433		

G. W. Walton, G. K. Robertson, A. J. Murphy and P. J. Visser did not bat.

Bowling: Beyeler 33–7–88–1; Allott 8–1–16–0; Maguiness 52.3–14–127–2; Larsen 30–8–86–1; Gray 32–11–62–1; Jones 6–0–23–0.

Wellington

J. G. Boyle c Guthardt b Murphy	.....	70	T. D. Ritchie not out	....	58
R. W. Ormiston lbw b Visser	....	7			
*R. H. Vance run out	....	66	B 10, l-b 6, n-b 4	....	20
E. J. Gray c sub b Visser	....	5			
A. H. Jones not out	....	54	1/16 2/155 3/159 4/184	(4 wkts)	280

†J. D. Milne, G. R. Larsen, P. J. W. Allott, S. J. Maguiness and F. Beyeler did not bat.

Bowling: Robertson 12–1–55–0; Visser 20–4–60–2; Stirling 15–2–56–0; Murphy 11–2–33–1; Walton 24–8–48–0; Briasco 3–1–12–0.

Umpires: D. A. Greenfield and M. M. Spring.

AUCKLAND v CENTRAL DISTRICTS

At Auckland, January 14, 15, 16. Auckland won by four wickets. Auckland 16 pts. Toss: Auckland.

Central Districts

C. J. Smith lbw b Morrison	....	41	– (2) c sub b Hunt	....	70
R. T. Hart c Troup b Morrison	....	56	– (1) run out	....	15
P. S. Briasco run out	....	39	– b Hunt	....	18
†T. E. Blain c Kelly b Morrison	....	6	– c Webb b Patel	....	1
*R. E. Hayward lbw b Barrett	....	49	– c and b Webb	....	9
D. J. Guthardt c Greatbatch b Patel	....	17	– c Kelly b Webb	....	2

D. A. Stirling b Troup .... 36 – hit wkt b Patel 35
G. K. Robertson c Kelly b Troup .... 3 – not out 50
G. W. Walton c Greatbatch b Troup .... 7 – b Patel 11
A. J. Murphy not out .... 0 – b Troup 1
P. J. Visser not out .... 0 – not out 0
    L-b 5, n-b 18 23   B 6, l-b 8, n-b 2 16

1/112 2/115 3/129 4/182   (9 wkts dec.) 277   1/56 2/99 3/100   (9 wkts dec.) 228
5/224 6/258 7/267   4/120 5/122 6/122
8/276 9/277   7/168 8/210 9/227

Bowling: *First Innings*—Troup 22–7–41–3; Barrett 20–6–38–1; Morrison 20-2–68–3; Watson 16–4–52–0; Patel 27–9–54–1; Hunt 10–4–19–0. *Second Innings*—Troup 9-3–20–1; Barrett 5–0–24–0; Morrison 13–4–24–0; Watson 6–2–15–0; Patel 16.1–5–52–3; Hunt 13–2–45–2; Webb 8–1–34–2.

Auckland

T. J. Franklin c Briasco b Stirling .... 0 – c Blain b Visser 9
D. G. Scott b Stirling .... 79 – lbw b Murphy 26
M. J. Greatbatch not out ....119 – not out 88
D. N. Patel c Blain b Robertson .... 29 – b Walton 7
*P. N. Webb not out .... 42 – run out 22
A. J. Hunt (did not bat) .... – run out 25
†P. J. Kelly (did not bat) .... – run out 15
G. B. Troup (did not bat) .... – not out 20
    L-b 2, w 2, n-b 5 9   B 2, l-b 10, w 1, n-b 3 16

1/0 2/160 3/209   (3 wkts dec.) 278   1/17 2/48 3/75   (6 wkts) 228
                                             4/107 5/152 6/180

W. Watson, D. K. Morrison and B. J. Barrett did not bat.

Bowling: *First Innings*—Stirling 20–7–55–2; Visser 20.4–4–55–0; Robertson 15–3–34–1; Murphy 16–3–58–0; Walton 19–7–65–0; Briasco 3–0–9–0. *Second Innings*—Stirling 11–0–50–0; Visser 3–0–11–1; Robertson 8.5–1–48–0; Murphy 6–0–26–1; Walton 14–1–57–1; Briasco 5–0–24–0.

Umpires: D. B. Cowie and T. A. McCall.

OTAGO v NORTHERN DISTRICTS

At Alexandra, January 14, 15, 16. Otago won by ten wickets. Otago 16 pts. Toss: Otago.

Northern Districts

L. M. Crocker lbw b Mallender .... 7 – (7) c Wilson b Lindsay 21
R. E. W. Mawhinney lbw b Mallender .... 37 – (1) c Lees b Wilson 48
D. J. White c Lindsay b Wilson .... 9 – lbw b McKechnie 1
G. W. McKenzie c Lees b Cushen .... 21 – c Lindsay b Walker 30
B. G. Cooper c Lees b McKechnie .... 49 – lbw b Lindsay 6
*C. M. Kuggeleijn c McKechnie b Lindsay .... 74 – st Lees b Walker 3
†B. A. Young c Walker b Wilson .... 0 – (2) b Cushen 16
G. E. Bradburn c Lees b Mallender .... 16 – b Walker 0
S. J. Scott lbw b Wilson .... 20 – c Lees b McKechnie 32
S. M. Carrington c Lees b Lindsay .... 0 – c Burns b Lindsay 10
K. B. Hancock not out .... 0 – not out 0
    B 4, l-b 11, n-b 9 24   L-b 8 8

1/11 2/30 3/83 4/93 5/159   257   1/66 2/67 3/74 4/81 5/88   175
6/172 7/220 8/255 9/255   6/119 7/119 8/149 9/173

Bowling: *First Innings*—Mallender 20–3–59–3; McKechnie 23–11–27–1; Cushen 27–13–46–1; Wilson 21.1–6–43–3; Lindsay 22–7–67–2. *Second Innings*—Mallender 7–2–16–0; McKechnie 10–3–18–2; Cushen 17–8–24–1; Wilson 6–2–12–1; Lindsay 18–5–55–3; Walker 9–2–42–3.

Otago

J. K. Lindsay c Young b Carrington 10	
K. R. Rutherford c Mawhinney b Kuggeleijn . .105 – (1) not out 104	
S. J. McCullum c McKenzie b Kuggeleijn ..... 42 – (2) not out 66	
R. N. Hoskin not out 55	
K. J. Burns lbw b Carrington 24	
D. J. Walker not out 12	
B 2, l-b 5, w 5, n-b 1 13	B 1, l-b 3 4

1/21 2/164 3/174 4/236   (4 wkts dec.) 261   (no wkt) 174

*†W. K. Lees, B. J. McKechnie, T. J. Wilson, J. A. J. Cushen and N. A. Mallender did not bat.

Bowling: *First Innings*—Carrington 13–4–28–2; Hancock 7–1–31–0; Scott 29.4–8–61–0; Bradburn 21–4–62–0; White 4–0–10–0; Kuggeleijn 29–8–62–2. *Second Innings*—Carrington 8–0–34–0; Scott 6–2–14–0; Bradburn 10–0–40–0; White 4–0–29–0; Kuggeleijn 5–0–14–0; Cooper 5.5–0–34–0; Mawhinney 1–0–5–0.

Umpires: D. E. C. McKechnie and N. F. Tapper.

WELLINGTON v CANTERBURY

At Lower Hutt, January 14, 15, 16. Wellington won by 70 runs. Wellington 12 pts, Canterbury 4 pts. Toss: Wellington.

Wellington

R. W. Ormiston c Hart b Thiele .... 31 – (2) c Hart b Brown 33	
J. G. Boyle c Hartshorn b Tracy .... 3 – (1) lbw b Thiele 56	
*R. H. Vance lbw b McNally ....114 – c Kennedy b Brown 47	
E. J. Gray c Hart b Thiele .... 44 – lbw b McNally 5	
A. H. Jones c Hartshorn b Thiele .... 10 – c Hartshorn b Brown 33	
T. D. Ritchie b Brown .... 41 – c Hart b McNally 2	
G. R. Larsen lbw b McNally .... 2 – c Hartshorn b Brown 0	
†J. D. Milne b McNally .... 0 – lbw b Brown 2	
S. J. Maguiness not out .... 19 – b McNally 3	
F. Beyeler b McNally .... 6 – lbw b Brown 30	
W. M. Aberhart c Hart b Thiele .... 4 – not out 0	
L-b 2, n-b 2 4	B 6, l-b 3, w 1, n-b 1 11

1/6 2/60 3/138 4/174 5/229   278   1/62 2/106 3/121 4/179 5/185   222
6/237 7/249 8/249 9/261   6/185 7/185 8/190 9/190

Bowling: *First Innings*—Tracy 14–0–51–1; McNally 18–4–39–4; Thiele 26.5–7–74–4; Brown 23–8–63–1; McEwan 13–3–49–0. *Second Innings*—Tracy 3–0–20–0; McNally 29–13–65–3; Thiele 15–2–49–1; Brown 23–9–53–6; McEwan 4–1–5–0; Hartshorn 3–1–9–0; Stead 1–0–12–0.

Canterbury

A. Nathu c Ormiston b Larsen .... 38 – (2) c and b Gray 44	
P. G. Kennedy lbw b Gray .... 15 – (5) st Milne b Gray 9	
†A. W. Hart c Milne b Gray .... 44 – (8) c Beyeler b Gray 1	
P. E. McEwan c Boyle b Gray .... 30 – (1) b Larsen 12	
*V. R. Brown c Ormiston b Gray .... 10 – (3) b Gray 1	
R. T. Latham c Vance b Larsen .... 25 – (4) c Beyeler b Gray 18	
D. W. Stead c Milne b Jones .... 52 – (6) c Boyle b Gray 22	

D. J. Hartshorn c and b Gray	32	– (7) b Larsen	2
S. R. McNally b Gray	16	– c Jones b Gray	0
C. H. Thiele not out	10	– not out	8
S. R. Tracy b Jones	4	– c Ormiston b Gray	0
B 5, l-b 12, n-b 4	21	B 10, l-b 6	16

1/33 2/98 3/136 4/142 5/146   297   1/35 2/36 3/62 4/88 5/107   133
6/202 7/256 8/281 9/286   6/120 7/125 8/125 9/125

Bowling: *First Innings*—Beyeler 10–4–30–0; Aberhart 14–3–42–0; Maguiness 14–6–22–0; Gray 50–19–114–6; Larsen 27–11–46–2; Jones 12.1–3–26–2. *Second Innings*—Beyeler 3–0–8–0; Aberhart 2–0–10–0; Maguiness 2–0–5–0; Gray 26.1–12–37–8; Larsen 14–2–34–2; Jones 10–5–23–0.

Umpires: M. M. Spring and K. Thomson.

AUCKLAND v WELLINGTON

At Auckland, January 18, 19, 20. Drawn. Wellington 4 pts. Toss: Wellington.

Auckland

T. J. Franklin c and b Gray	60	– not out	18
P. A. Horne c Milne b Molony	19	– not out	17
M. J. Greatbatch c Ormiston b Aberhart	4		
D. N. Patel b Molony	89		
A. J. Hunt lbw b Gray	20		
*P. N. Webb c Gray b Allott	63		
†P. J. Kelly c Boyle b Larsen	20		
G. B. Troup c Vance b Allott	7		
D. K. Morrison retired hurt	0		
M. J. Bradley c Milne b Larsen	6		
W. Watson not out	4		
B 4, l-b 7, w 2	13	B 4, l-b 2, n-b 1	7

1/47 2/67 3/142 4/202   (9 wkts dec.) 305   (no wkt) 42
5/202 6/243 7/256 8/291 9/305

Bowling: *First Innings*—Allott 36.1–17–57–2; Aberhart 19–6–50–1; Molony 26–6–75–2; Larsen 28–7–47–2; Gray 28–6–65–2. *Second Innings*—Allott 4–1–4–0; Aberhart 4–0–17–0; Ritchie 2–1–2–0; Vance 2–0–13–0.

Wellington

R. W. Ormiston c Hunt b Troup	6	D. M. Molony b Watson	5
J. G. Boyle c Franklin b Bradley	32	†J. D. Milne c Franklin b Watson	36
*R. H. Vance c Patel b Bradley	5	W. M. Aberhart c Greatbatch b Patel	24
E. J. Gray not out	67		
A. H. Jones lbw b Watson	99	B 1, l-b 12, w 2, n-b 11	26
T. D. Ritchie lbw b Bradley	31		
G. R. Larsen c Kelly b Morrison	48	1/22 2/34 3/66 4/126 5/251 383
P. J. W. Allott c Hunt b Morrison	4	6/269 7/274 8/284 9/347

Bowling: Troup 29–4–61–1; Watson 26–2–78–3; Bradley 25–5–55–3; Morrison 32–7–89–2; Patel 27–9–72–1; Hunt 5–1–15–0.

Umpires: N. W. Stoupe and S. J. Woodward.

CANTERBURY v OTAGO

At Christchurch, January 18, 19, 20. Otago won by eight wickets. Otago 16 pts. Toss: Canterbury.

Canterbury

A. Nathu lbw b Wilson	29	– c Burns b Cushen	10
P. G. Kennedy c Burns b Mallender	2	– c Lees b Mallender	5
P. E. McEwan run out	27	– run out	63
*V. R. Brown c Lees b Mallender	10	– b Cushen	6
R. T. Latham b Wilson	26	– c Rutherford b Lindsay	40
D. W. Stead b Cushen	14	– (7) b Lindsay	11
D. J. Hartshorn not out	47	– (8) lbw b Cushen	32
†A. W. Hart b Mallender	1	– (6) b Lindsay	9
S. R. McNally c Burns b Wilson	17	– c Walker b Cushen	29
G. K. MacDonald c McKechnie b Mallender	14	– not out	2
S. R. Tracy run out	1	– b Cushen	6
B 2, l-b 8, w 1, n-b 6	17	B 4, l-b 4, n-b 7	15

1/8 2/63 3/66 4/77 5/116   205   1/8 2/23 3/57 4/124 5/132   228
6/120 7/132 8/162 9/202   6/146 7/158 8/206 9/222

Bowling: *First Innings*—Mallender 21–3–68–4; Cushen 20–10–43–1; McKechnie 18–7–40–0; Wilson 13–1–42–3; Lindsay 4.3–2–2–0. *Second Innings*—Mallender 14–2–45–1; Cushen 23.3–7–54–5; McKechnie 10–3–26–0; Wilson 4–0–28–0; Lindsay 18–4–67–3.

Otago

K. R. Rutherford lbw b McNally	11	– c sub b MacDonald	35
S. J. McCullum c Hart b Hartshorn	40	– b Brown	21
R. N. Hoskin c MacDonald b McEwan	24	– not out	6
K. J. Burns run out	93	– not out	8
N. A. Mallender st Hart b McEwan	0		
D. J. Walker c Stead b McNally	106		
J. K. Lindsay lbw b Brown	13		
*†W. K. Lees lbw b Brown	11		
B. J. McKechnie lbw b McNally	9		
T. J. Wilson c Hart b Brown	31		
J. A. J. Cushen not out	3		
B 9, l-b 9, n-b 1	19	B 2, l-b 2	4

1/13 2/66 3/84 4/89 5/236   360   1/46 2/60   (2 wkts) 74
6/259 7/273 8/296 9/327

Bowling: *First Innings*—Tracy 16–1–69–0; McNally 21–3–83–3; McEwan 18–3–70–2; Hartshorn 12–3–41–1; Brown 21.2–7–41–3; MacDonald 15–2–38–0. *Second Innings*—Tracy 5–1–33–0; McNally 2–2–0–0; Brown 10.1–6–16–1; MacDonald 8–4–21–1.

Umpires: B. L. Aldridge and N. F. Tapper.

NORTHERN DISTRICTS v CENTRAL DISTRICTS

At Hamilton, January 18, 19, 20. Northern Districts won by nine wickets. Northern Districts 16 pts. Toss: Central Districts.

Central Districts

C. J. Smith c Mawhinney b Child	25	– (2) c Kuggeleijn b Scott	103
R. T. Hart c Kuggeleijn b Child	5	– (1) b Child	3
P. S. Briasco c Young b Carrington	15	– c sub b Child	2
†T. E. Blain c Young b Carrington	6	– run out	70
*R. E. Hayward b Carrington	1	– c Kuggeleijn b Carrington	25
R. L. Glover b Bradburn b Carrington	8	– c sub b Carrington	0
D. A. Stirling run out	7	– b Child	26

G. K. Robertson c Carrington b Bradburn ..... 35 – not out 66
S. W. Duff c and b Bradburn .... 45 – c Young b Child 2
G. W. Walton not out .... 0 – c Crocker b Bradburn 10
P. J. Visser c Scott b Bradburn .... 0 – b Carrington 0
      B 1 1   B 4, l-b 4, w 2, n-b 1 11

1/19 2/46 3/46 4/49 5/61   148   1/14 2/18 3/134 4/196 5/200   318
6/68 7/68 8/138 9/148   6/222 7/252 8/261 9/305

Bowling: *First Innings*—Carrington 14-2-38-4; Scott 13-4-15-0; Child 21-5-56-2; Bradburn 16.4-3-38-3. *Second Innings*—Carrington 30.5-6-118-3; Scott 19-7-35-1; Child 28-7-69-4; Bradburn 23-5-57-1; Kuggeleijn 7-3-17-0; McKenzie 2-0-10-0; White 1-0-4-0.

Northern Districts

L. M. Crocker c Hayward b Visser .... 16 – not out 11
R. E. W. Mawhinney c Walton b Visser ..... 75 – b Duff 10
D. J. White st Blain b Duff .... .209 – not out 12
G. W. McKenzie b Duff 49
B. G. Cooper b Duff 29
*C. M. Kuggeleijn not out 27
M. J. Child c and b Duff 5
†B. A. Young not out 2
      B 3, l-b 12, w 1, n-b 3 19   B 1, w 2 3

1/19 2/218 3/360 4/381   (6 wkts dec.) 431   1/16   (1 wkt) 36
5/412 6/424

G. E. Bradburn, S. J. Scott and S. M. Carrington did not bat.

Bowling: *First Innings*—Stirling 12-2-49-0; Visser 28-8-83-2; Robertson 14-2-51-0; Briasco 11-6-19-0; Walton 35-8-96-0; Duff 44-9-111-4; Hayward 6-4-7-0. *Second Innings*—Stirling 0.4-0-6-0; Visser 7-1-18-0; Duff 6-0-11-1.

Umpires: D. B. Cowie and T. A. McCall.

CENTRAL DISTRICTS v CANTERBURY

At Levin, January 25, 26, 27. Drawn. Central Districts 4 pts. Toss: Canterbury.

Central Districts

R. T. Hart st Hart b Stead .... 48 – b Tracy 26
C. J. Smith lbw b Thiele .... 2 – c Stead b Tracy 1
P. S. Briasco c McEwan b Thiele .... 3 – (7) not out 8
T. E. Blain c Hart b Tracy .... 33 – (3) c Stead b Tracy 5
S. P. Robertson c Thiele b Tracy .... 2 – (8) not out 3
*R. E. Hayward not out .... 69 – (4) b Tracy 0
†I. D. S. Smith c McNally b Brown .... 81 – (5) c Kennedy b Thiele 4
D. A. Stirling not out .... 29 – (6) c Hart b Tracy 0
      B 5, l-b 10 15   B 4 4

1/6 2/16 3/88 4/93   (6 wkts dec.) 282   1/11 2/17 3/17 4/28   (6 wkts) 51
5/101 6/231   5/32 6/45

G. K. Robertson, S. W. Duff and P. J. Visser did not bat.

Bowling: *First Innings*—Thiele 19-3-67-2; McNally 22-5-86-0; Tracy 14-5-24-2; Stead 18-5-54-1; Brown 7.4-0-36-1. *Second Innings*—Thiele 7-0-22-1; Tracy 11-4-19-5; Stead 3-1-6-0.

Canterbury

P. G. Kennedy b Visser	10	– (6) lbw b Stirling 20
A. Nathu c I. D. S. Smith b Visser	26	– c Visser b G. K. Robertson 153
*V. R. Brown c S. P. Robertson b G. K. Robertson	17	– lbw b Visser 5
D. J. Hartshorn c S. P. Robertson b G. K. Robertson	6	– (8) c Briasco b Stirling 32
R. T. Latham b Visser	0	– (4) c G. K. Robertson b Visser . 16
D. W. Stead lbw b G. K. Robertson	6	– (7) c C. J. Smith b Stirling 42
†A. W. Hart c I. D. S. Smith b Visser	0	– (9) not out 10
S. R. McNally c G. K. Robertson b Visser	0	– (10) b G. K. Robertson 6
P. E. McEwan c Duff b G. K. Robertson	0	– (5) lbw b G. K. Robertson 4
C. H. Thiele not out	0	– (1) b Stirling 6
S. R. Tracy c Hayward b Visser	0	– c I. D. S. Smith b G. K. Robertson . 0
L-b 2, n-b 1	3	B 2, l-b 4, n-b 17 23

1/18 2/56 3/62 4/62 5/62   68   1/19 2/28 3/45 4/55 5/90   317
6/66 7/68 8/68 9/68   6/209 7/292 8/307 9/316

Bowling: *First Innings*—Stirling 7-2-22-0; Visser 11.4-5-29-6; G. K. Robertson 5-1-15-4. *Second Innings*—Visser 31-6-89-2; G. K. Robertson 21-1-76-4; Stirling 25-5-75-4; Duff 24-6-64-0; Briasco 2-0-7-0; Hayward 2-2-0-0.

Umpires: D. A. Kinsella and J. Nilsson.

NORTHERN DISTRICTS v AUCKLAND

At Tauranga, January 25, 26, 27. Northern Districts won by four wickets. Northern Districts 12 pts, Auckland 4 pts. Toss: Northern Districts.

Auckland

P. A. Horne c White b Scott	3	– c Mawhinney b Bradburn 25
D. G. Scott c Young b Scott	7	– c Child b Scott 9
T. J. Franklin c Kuggeleijn b Bradburn	64	– lbw b Child 26
D. N. Patel st Young b Bradburn	34	– c Crocker b Bradburn 23
M. J. Greatbatch c Bradburn b Carrington	20	– c Crocker b Child 0
*P. N. Webb run out	16	– (7) not out 10
R. B. Reid not out	23	– (6) b Bradburn 0
†P. J. Kelly c Cooper b Bradburn	0	– c McKenzie b Carrington 1
G. B. Troup c Scott b Bradburn	1	– b Carrington 12
D. K. Morrison not out	0	– run out 0
M. J. Bradley (did not bat)	–	– c White b Bradburn 0
B 2, l-b 1, n-b 2	5	L-b 3, n-b 1 4

1/11 2/14 3/71 4/126   (8 wkts dec.) 173   1/21 2/42 3/67 4/69 5/70   120
5/148 6/164 7/165 8/166   6/95 7/96 8/108 9/109

Bowling: *First Innings*—Carrington 11-0-23-1; Scott 14-6-40-2; Child 15-5-42-0; Kuggeleijn 12-4-12-0; Bradburn 22-6-53-4. *Second Innings*—Carrington 15-7-29-2; Scott 5-0-18-1; Child 9-2-30-2; Bradburn 18.1-4-40-4.

Northern Districts

L. M. Crocker b Bradley	23	– c Greatbatch b Bradley 20
R. E. W. Mawhinney b Troup	9	– b Patel 5
D. J. White c Scott b Troup	7	– c Webb b Patel 9
G. W. McKenzie c Kelly b Bradley	7	– c Scott b Bradley 20
B. G. Cooper c Bradley b Patel	15	– hit wkt b Troup 10

*C. M. Kuggeleijn c Kelly b Troup .... 26 – not out 35
M. J. Child c Kelly b Troup .... 22 – b Morrison 21
†B. A. Young c Kelly b Bradley .... 3 – not out 14
G. E. Bradburn not out 6
S. J. Scott b Patel 28
S. M. Carrington c Horne b Troup 0
    L-b 3, n-b 4 7   B 1, l-b 4, n-b 4 9

1/19 2/27 3/46 4/58 5/64   153   1/12 2/24 3/49 4/70   (6 wkts) 143
6/114 7/115 8/121 9/150   5/76 6/119

    Bowling: *First Innings*—Troup 18.1–6–43–5; Patel 15–1–46–2; Morrison 3–0–19–0; Bradley 11–1–37–3; Scott 3–1–5–0. *Second Innings*—Troup 13–6–18–1; Patel 29–6–53–2; Morrison 8.5–2–28–1; Bradley 18–4–39–2.

           Umpires: D. B. Cowie and K. Thomson.

WELLINGTON v OTAGO

At Wellington, January 25, 26, 27. Drawn. Wellington 2 pts, Otago 2 pts. Toss: Wellington.

Otago

K. R. Rutherford lbw b Allott 0   K. B. Ibadulla c Milne b Gray 5
S. J. McCullum b Gray 94   N. A. Mallender not out 52
R. N. Hoskin b Allott 5   J. A. J. Cushen not out 9
K. J. Burns c Milne b Allott 10   B 5, l-b 4 9
D. J. Walker b Allott 89
J. K. Lindsay b Allott 34   1/2 2/24 3/46   (9 wkts dec.) 320
*†W. K. Lees c Jones b Molony 9   4/172 5/235 6/248
B. J. McKechnie run out 5   7/250 8/258 9/266

    Bowling: Allott 37–9–79–5; Molony 14.2–0–39–1; Gray 32–7–95–2; Griffiths 19–3–57–0; Larsen 8–0–29–0; Jones 5–1–12–0.

Wellington

J. G. Boyle c Lees b Cushen 12   G. R. Larsen not out 0
R. W. Ormiston lbw b Mallender 5
*R. H. Vance c Burns b Lindsay 59   B 1, l-b 4, n-b 2 7
E. J. Gray not out 128
A. H. Jones c McKechnie b Ibadulla .. 26   1/15 2/19 3/103   (5 wkts) 268
T. D. Ritchie c McCullum b Lindsay .. 31   4/163 5/238

P. J. W. Allott, D. M. Molony, †J. D. Milne and A. A. Griffiths did not bat.

    Bowling: Mallender 6–1–16–1; Cushen 27–9–40–1; McKechnie 7–3–15–0; Lindsay 32–6–128–2; Ibadulla 24–5–64–1.

        Umpires: R. L. McHarg and S. J. Woodward.

AUCKLAND v CANTERBURY

At Auckland, January 29, 30, 31. Auckland won by 195 runs. Auckland 16 pts. Toss: Auckland.

Auckland

P. A. Horne lbw b Thiele	1	– b Stead	62
D. G. Scott c sub b Thiele	27	– c Latham b Brown	37
T. J. Franklin lbw b Tracy	51	– c Brown b Stead	0
D. N. Patel c MacDonald b Brown	2	– c Latham b Brown	10
M. J. Greatbatch c Nathu b Brown	12	– not out	15
*P. N. Webb b Brown	84	– not out	10
†P. J. Kelly c McEwan b Brown	84		
G. B. Troup not out	8		
D. K. Morrison not out	5		
B 10, l-b 8	18	B 10, l-b 2	12

1/1 2/69 3/80 4/88   (7 wkts dec.) 292   1/107 2/107 3/109   (4 wkts dec.) 146
5/114 6/274 7/280   4/117

M. J. Bradley and W. Watson did not bat.

Bowling: *First Innings*—Tracy 16–3–64–1; Thiele 22–7–49–2; McNally 13–6–27–0; Brown 30–12–46–4; Stead 9–2–30–0; MacDonald 8–1–29–0; McEwan 8–3–29–0. *Second Innings*—Tracy 4–1–15–0; Brown 24–7–59–2; Stead 17–9–35–2; MacDonald 9–2–25–0.

Canterbury

D. J. Boyle b Patel	0	– lbw b Patel	36
A. Nathu c Franklin b Morrison	14	– c Franklin b Troup	8
P. E. McEwan c Kelly b Patel	13	– c Greatbatch b Troup	4
*V. R. Brown b Bradley	17	– c Greatbatch b Watson	4
R. T. Latham c Troup b Watson	5	– c Greatbatch b Patel	13
D. W. Stead not out	24	– b Patel	37
†A. W. Hart b Bradley	1	– (8) not out	12
S. R. McNally b Patel	16	– (7) c Webb b Patel	1
G. K. MacDonald c Webb b Patel	0	– b Patel	0
C. H. Thiele b Troup	0	– c Scott b Troup	3
S. R. Tracy c Kelly b Troup	1	– c Scott b Troup	7
B 10, l-b 5, n-b 3	18	L-b 5, w 1, n-b 3	9

1/0 2/26 3/31 4/43 5/65   109   1/19 2/23 3/37 4/58 5/101   134
6/69 7/104 8/104 9/107   6/108 7/115 8/115 9/120

Bowling: *First Innings*—Patel 31–11–47–4; Troup 11.2–7–11–2; Bradley 7–3–15–2; Morrison 4–1–5–1; Watson 8–0–16–1. *Second Innings*—Troup 17.2–6–41–4; Patel 31–13–41–5; Bradley 9–2–24–0; Morrison 6–2–9–0; Watson 4–1–14–1.

Umpires: D. A. Kinsella and N. W. Stoupe.

OTAGO v CENTRAL DISTRICTS

At Oamaru, January 29, 30, 31. Otago won by four wickets. Otago 12 pts, Central Districts 4 pts. Toss: Otago.

Central Districts

R. T. Hart retired hurt	0	– (10) run out	14
C. J. Smith c Cushen b Lindsay	22	– (1) c Smith b Cushen	1
P. S. Briasco c McCullum b Lindsay	109	– (2) lbw b Mallender	12
T. E. Blain b Lindsay	63	– (3) c Lees b McKechnie	31
*R. E. Hayward c McCullum b Cushen	10	– (4) c Walker b Lindsay	43
†I. D. S. Smith c Lees b Cushen	84	– (7) c Hoskin b Cushen	8
D. A. Stirling not out	52	– (8) c Rutherford b Lindsay	0

S. W. Duff (did not bat)		– (5) c Lees b McKechnie	51
G. W. Walton (did not bat)		– (6) c Rutherford b Lindsay	36
G. K. Robertson (did not bat)		– (9) not out	99
P. J. Visser (did not bat)		– lbw b McKechnie	0
L-b 3, n-b 1	4	L-b 4, n-b 1	5

1/61 2/197 3/204 4/219   (5 wkts dec.) 344   1/1 2/26 3/68 4/113 5/174   300
5/344   6/174 7/185 8/185 9/300

Bowling: *First Innings*—Mallender 22-7-37-0; Cushen 31.4-9-90-2; McKechnie 19-5-53-0; Wilson 6-0-21-0; Lindsay 31-6-115-3; Walker 6-0-25-0. *Second Innings*—Mallender 20-2-67-1; Cushen 38-14-100-2; McKechnie 17.5-4-42-3; Lindsay 24-6-87-3.

Otago

K. R. Rutherford c Hayward b Visser	42	– c Briasco b Duff	70
S. J. McCullum b Stirling	77	– c C. J. Smith b Duff	38
R. N. Hoskin c Briasco b Walton	24	– c Duff b Visser	111
K. J. Burns st I. D. S. Smith b Duff	43	– lbw b Duff	16
D. J. Walker c Visser b Duff	6	– st I. D. S. Smith b Duff	3
J. K. Lindsay c Blain b Duff	29	– (7) not out	65
*†W. K. Lees c I. D. S. Smith b Visser	1	– (8) not out	12
B. J. McKechnie c Hayward b Duff	35		
N. A. Mallender c Visser b Duff	20		
T. J. Wilson c sub b Duff	9	– (6) c Hart b Walton	22
J. A. J. Cushen not out	1		
B 4, l-b 4, n-b 8	16	B 3, l-b 2	5

1/89 2/136 3/166 4/193 5/214   303   1/108 2/113 3/145   (6 wkts) 342
6/221 7/265 8/282 9/302   4/149 5/176 6/323

Bowling: *First Innings*—Stirling 10-1-62-1; Visser 19-5-56-2; Duff 14.5-7-36-6; Robertson 12-1-60-0; Walton 17-0-81-1. *Second Innings*—Stirling 2-0-15-0; Visser 16.1-2-77-1; Duff 24-2-119-4; Robertson 9-0-55-0; Walton 18-1-71-1.

Umpires: F. R. Goodall and G. C. Morris.

WELLINGTON v NORTHERN DISTRICTS

At Wellington, January 29, 30, 31. Drawn. Northern Districts 4 pts. Toss: Wellington.

Northern Districts

L. M. Crocker b Allott	3	– c Ritchie b Allott	37
R. E. W. Mawhinney b Larsen	110	– c Vance b Cederwall	3
D. J. White c Milne b Cederwall	15	– c Milne b Allott	47
B. G. Cooper lbw b Allott	6	– c Milne b Allott	31
*G. P. Howarth b Allott	5	– run out	79
C. M. Kuggeleijn lbw b Allott	47	– c Vance b Allott	2
M. J. Child b Molony	1	– b Gray	37
†B. A. Young c Milne b Cederwall	8	– not out	1
S. J. Scott lbw b Allott	0	– c Jones b Larsen	6
S. M. Carrington b Cederwall	0		
K. Treiber not out	0		
B 2, l-b 5, w 1, n-b 9	17	B 7, l-b 12, n-b 6	25

1/9 2/61 3/74 4/88 5/188   212   1/10 2/94 3/111   (8 wkts dec.) 268
6/193 7/208 8/208 9/209   4/158 5/164 6/233
                                        7/261 8/268

Bowling: *First Innings*—Allott 26-9-40-5; Cederwall 20.3-1-58-3; Larsen 21-9-43-1; Molony 17-4-40-1; Jones 2-1-6-0; Gray 7-2-18-0. *Second Innings*—Allott 32-10-59-4; Cederwall 8-0-52-1; Larsen 36-12-65-1; Molony 6-0-41-0; Gray 10-2-32-1.

Wellington

R. W. Ormiston run out	52	– (2) lbw b Carrington	0
J. G. Boyle b Carrington	19	– (1) c Howarth b Carrington	4
*R. H. Vance c Young b Carrington	7	– st Young b Scott	84
E. J. Gray c Howarth b Carrington	0	– run out	71
A. H. Jones lbw b Treiber	10	– c and b Scott	5
T. D. Ritchie not out	37	– not out	41
G. R. Larsen lbw b Treiber	1	– (8) not out	20
G. N. Cederwall c Young b Child	3	– (7) c Young b Scott	0
P. J. W. Allott c Cooper b Child	8		
†J. D. Milne lbw b Child	13		
D. M. Molony lbw b Child	12		
B 6, l-b 6, w 3, n-b 5	20	B 9, l-b 15, n-b 1	25

1/53 2/72 3/82 4/94 5/101   182   1/1 2/10 3/165 4/171   (6 wkts) 250
6/107 7/112 8/130 9/148   5/192 6/192

Bowling: *First Innings*—Carrington 20–1–59–3; Treiber 14–2–42–2; Scott 16–0–43–0; Child 10.3–0–26–4. *Second Innings*—Carrington 20–2–78–2; Treiber 15–3–46–2; Scott 15–5–33–3; Child 12–3–34–0; Kuggeleijn 9–2–35–0.

Umpires: B. L. Aldridge and M. M. Spring.

CANTERBURY v WELLINGTON

At Christchurch, February 2, 3, 4. Wellington won by 69 runs. Wellington 16 pts. Toss: Wellington.

Wellington

R. W. Ormiston b Roberts	24	– (2) c Latham b Roberts	8
J. G. Boyle c Nathu b Roberts	1	– (1) c Stead b Thiele	26
*R. H. Vance c Brown b Thiele	14	– c Hart b McNally	16
E. J. Gray c Thiele b McNally	2	– b Brown	53
A. H. Jones c Boyle b Thiele	17	– (11) not out	1
T. D. Ritchie c Hart b Roberts	30	– (5) c Nathu b Roberts	27
G. R. Larsen lbw b Thiele	9	– (6) c Hart b Stead	40
P. J. W. Allott not out	66	– b Thiele	42
†J. D. Milne c Kennedy b McNally	6	– (7) c and b Nathu	23
S. J. Maguiness c Nathu b Roberts	54	– (9) b Stead	1
D. M. Molony b Roberts	4	– (10) not out	14
L-b 11, w 1, n-b 3	15	L-b 9, w 2	11

1/2 2/33 3/38 4/59 5/99   242   1/18 2/50 3/88   (9 wkts dec.) 262
6/105 7/115 8/132 9/228   4/136 5/136 6/202
                                    7/212 8/214 9/251

Bowling: *First Innings*—Thiele 20–4–59–3; Roberts 16.3–1–77–5; McNally 14–2–57–2; Stead 7–3–19–0; Brown 3–0–19–0. *Second Innings*—Thiele 19–4–42–2; Roberts 18–3–67–2; McNally 17–4–42–1; Stead 16–6–37–2; Brown 11–5–21–1; McEwan 4–1–16–0; Nathu 10–2–28–1.

Canterbury

D. J. Boyle c Milne b Molony	9	– (2) c and b Gray	68
A. Nathu c Milne b Gray	42	– (1) c Ormiston b Maguiness	8
P. E. McEwan b Maguiness	17	– c Gray b Larsen	4
*V. R. Brown run out	12	– (6) c Milne b Maguiness	11
R. T. Latham c Maguiness b Molony	13	– c and b Molony	47
D. W. Stead c Milne b Molony	2	– (7) c and b Maguiness	18

P. G. Kennedy c Ormiston b Gray .... 19 – (4) c Ritchie b Vance 81
†A. W. Hart b Gray .... 0 – (9) b Gray 15
S. R. McNally c Milne b Maguiness ...... 0 – (8) c Maguiness b Molony 22
C. H. Thiele not out .... 12 – c Larsen b Molony 0
S. J. R. Roberts b Larsen .... 0 – not out 1
L-b 3, w 1, n-b 3 7   B 13, l-b 10, w 1, n-b 3 .. 27

1/9 2/37 3/69 4/85 5/87   133   1/25 2/32 3/175 4/177 5/204   302
6/106 7/106 8/106 9/132   6/242 7/266 8/294 9/294

Bowling: *First Innings*—Allott 3–0–11–0; Molony 18–2–62–3; Larsen 11.2–1–28–1; Maguiness 21–10–29–2; Gray 5–5–0–3. *Second Innings*—Molony 20–3–69–3; Larsen 24.3–5–59–1; Maguiness 34–9–70–3; Gray 30.3–11–60–2; Vance 7–4–11–1; Ormiston 3–0–10–0.

Umpires: R. L. McHarg and N. F. Tapper.

CENTRAL DISTRICTS v AUCKLAND

At New Plymouth, February 2, 3, 4. Central Districts won by six wickets. Central Districts 16 pts. Toss: Auckland.

Auckland

T. J. Franklin b G. K. Robertson .... 69 – b G. K. Robertson 8
D. G. Scott c Visser b G. K. Robertson ...... 13 – c I. D. S. Smith b Visser 3
M. J. Greatbatch c S. P. Robertson
  b G. K. Robertson . 2 – b G. K. Robertson 6
D. N. Patel c Duff b Stirling .... 22 – c I. D. S. Smith
  b G. K. Robertson . 10
R. B. Reid c Hayward b G. K. Robertson .... 22 – lbw b G. K. Robertson 25
*P. N. Webb b Duff .... 24 – c S. P. Robertson b Martin 115
A. J. Hunt b Visser .... 23 – (8) not out 79
†P. J. Kelly c Stirling b Martin .... 33 – (9) not out 34
G. B. Troup c G. K. Robertson b Martin 8
D. K. Morrison b G. K. Robertson .... 5 – (7) c Briasco b Stirling 17
W. Watson not out 0
L-b 5, w 1, n-b 1 7   L-b 12, n-b 1 13

1/23 2/30 3/75 4/128 5/140   228   1/10 2/12 3/24   (7 wkts dec.) 310
6/177 7/180 8/213 9/226   4/35 5/100
                                             6/143 7/251

Bowling: *First Innings*—G. K. Robertson 15.4–3–47–5; Visser 22–7–51–1; Stirling 13–2–49–1; Martin 11–2–37–2; Duff 12–3–39–1. *Second Innings*—G. K. Robertson 25–7–68–4; Visser 20–9–44–1; Stirling 12.2–1–52–1; Martin 21–6–81–1; Duff 23–6–48–0; Briasco 1–0–4–0; Hayward 2–1–1–0.

Central Districts

P. S. Briasco c Troup b Scott .... 91 – c Webb b Morrison 79
C. J. Smith c Kelly b Scott .... 89 – c Hunt b Scott 80
S. P. Robertson c Kelly b Franklin 16
T. E. Blain not out .... 35 – (3) not out 77
S. W. Duff not out .... 14 – (4) run out 17
*R. E. Hayward (did not bat) .... – (5) lbw b Troup 0
†I. D. S. Smith (did not bat) .... – (6) not out 23
B 1, l-b 4, n-b 4 9   B 5, l-b 3, n-b 1 9

1/172 2/195 3/230   (3 wkts dec.) 254   1/148 2/190 3/226   (4 wkts) 285
                                               4/226

G. K. Robertson, K. W. Martin, D. A. Stirling and P. J. Visser did not bat.

Bowling: *First Innings*—Troup 11–6–17–0; Morrison 10–5–19–0; Watson 5–0–20–0; Patel 40–15–69–0; Scott 20–7–44–2; Hunt 14–2–50–0; Franklin 6–1–21–1; Reid 3–0–9–0. *Second Innings*—Troup 11–2–46–1; Morrison 8–0–35–1; Watson 12–0–62–0; Patel 15–1–58–0; Scott 16–0–61–1; Hunt 3–0–13–0; Greatbatch 0.3–0–2–0.

Umpires: J. G. Reardon and S. J. Woodward.

NORTHERN DISTRICTS v OTAGO

At Hamilton, February 2, 3, 4. Northern Districts won by eight wickets. Northern Districts 16 pts. Toss: Northern Districts.

Otago

K. R. Rutherford c Crocker b Scott	12	– lbw b Carrington	12
S. J. McCullum c McKenzie b Carrington	2	– c Crocker b Child	29
R. N. Hoskin c Mawhinney b Treiber	19	– lbw b Scott	0
K. J. Burns c Young b Treiber	7	– lbw b Child	6
D. J. Walker c McKenzie b Treiber	2	– c Kuggeleijn b Scott	6
J. K. Lindsay c Young b Treiber	10	– c White b Treiber	21
*†W. K. Lees c Young b Treiber	2	– not out	62
B. J. McKechnie c McKenzie b Treiber	24	– c Crocker b Treiber	7
T. J. Wilson run out	1	– run out	0
N. A. Mallender c Kuggeleijn b Treiber	19	– c Young b Scott	19
J. A. J. Cushen not out	0	– lbw b Scott	0
L-b 2, n-b 2	4	B 1, l-b 4, w 2, n-b 5	12

1/5 2/28 3/36 4/40 5/54   102   1/27 2/43 3/45 4/53 5/55   180
6/56 7/64 8/68 9/101   6/119 7/137 8/137 9/167

Bowling: *First Innings*—Carrington 14–5–21–1; Treiber 20.1–7–42–7; Scott 16–1–37–1. *Second Innings*—Carrington 15–3–49–1; Treiber 16–5–38–2; Scott 13.4–3–42–4; Child 15–5–34–2; Kuggeleijn 2–0–12–0.

Northern Districts

L. M. Crocker run out	0	– c Walker b Lindsay	67
R. E. W. Mawhinney b Cushen	7	– lbw b Cushen	45
D. J. White c Rutherford b Mallender	4	– not out	41
G. W. McKenzie lbw b Mallender	17	– not out	25
*G. P. Howarth c Lindsay b McKechnie	4		
C. M. Kuggeleijn c Lindsay b McKechnie	26		
M. J. Child lbw b Cushen	0		
†B. A. Young not out	30		
S. J. Scott c Hoskin b McKechnie	10		
S. M. Carrington c Lees b Mallender	0		
K. Treiber c Lees b Mallender	0		
L-b 1, n-b 4	5	B 4	4

1/1 2/13 3/13 4/22 5/51   103   1/108 2/112   (2 wkts) 182
6/52 7/79 8/103 9/103

Bowling: *First Innings*—Mallender 16.2–2–31–4; Cushen 25–13–38–2; McKechnie 17–6–33–3. *Second Innings*—Mallender 11–2–22–0; McKechnie 5–0–16–0; Cushen 20–7–47–1; Wilson 5–2–15–0; Lindsay 17–3–53–1; Rutherford 7.2–2–25–0.

Umpires: T. A. McCall and N. W. Stoupe.

AUCKLAND v NORTHERN DISTRICTS

At Auckland, February 6, 7, 8. Auckland won by 138 runs. Auckland 16 pts. Toss: Northern Districts.

Auckland

T. J. Franklin b Child	10	– c Kuggeleijn b Scott	80
P. A. Horne c White b Carrington	0	– b Scott	116
J. F. Reid run out	26	– run out	26
D. N. Patel c Blair b Scott	11	– c Blair b Kuggeleijn	37
A. J. Hunt b Scott	0	– (6) not out	13
*P. N. Webb b Scott	5	– (8) not out	0
J. G. Bracewell c Mawhinney b Kuggeleijn	54	– (5) run out	0
M. C. Snedden c Mawhinney b Scott	20		
†P. J. Kelly c Treiber b Child	93		
S. R. Gillespie c White b Child	1	– (7) lbw b Kuggeleijn	3
G. B. Troup not out	29		
B 4, l-b 5	9	L-b 7, n-b 1	8

1/1 2/24 3/35 4/37 5/51   258   1/197 2/218 3/242   (6 wkts dec.) 283
6/88 7/124 8/146 9/155   4/246 5/275 6/279

Bowling: *First Innings*—Carrington 21–3–54–1; Treiber 15–4–50–0; Scott 25–8–77–4; Child 16.3–5–49–3; Kuggeleijn 7–4–19–1. *Second Innings*—Carrington 9–3–30–0; Treiber 1–0–5–0; Scott 22–3–85–2; Child 18–2–50–0; Kuggeleijn 25–3–70–2; Blair 8–1–36–0.

Northern Districts

L. M. Crocker lbw b Patel	39	– b Snedden	12
R. E. W. Mawhinney c Gillespie b Bracewell	22	– lbw b Gillespie	2
D. J. White c and b Bracewell	20	– c Webb b Bracewell	22
B. R. Blair lbw b Patel	9	– b Bracewell	3
*G. P. Howarth run out	25	– c Webb b Gillespie	15
C. M. Kuggeleijn c Franklin b Troup	44	– c Kelly b Gillespie	1
M. J. Child c Bracewell b Gillespie	4	– (8) not out	66
†B. A. Young not out	21	– (7) b Snedden	23
S. J. Scott c Webb b Troup	10	– b Snedden	10
S. M. Carrington st Kelly b Bracewell	1	– (11) b Bracewell	15
K. Treiber c Franklin b Bracewell	8	– (10) b Troup	21
B 1, l-b 3, n-b 2	6	B 5, l-b 8, n-b 1	14

1/50 2/75 3/93 4/95 5/150   199   1/7 2/38 3/42 4/45 5/52   204
6/159 7/179 8/192 9/199   6/63 7/110 8/122 9/159

Bowling: *First Innings*—Troup 13–4–41–2; Gillespie 13–3–33–1; Snedden 15–3–40–0; Bracewell 27–9–43–4; Patel 17–4–38–2. *Second Innings*—Troup 12–6–18–1; Gillespie 15–7–15–3; Snedden 19–2–47–3; Bracewell 26–7–86–3; Patel 13–5–14–0); Hunt 2–0–11–0.

Umpires: D. B. Cowie and J. G. Reardon.

CENTRAL DISTRICTS v WELLINGTON

At Napier, February 6, 7, 8. Drawn. Wellington 4 pts. Toss: Central Districts.

Wellington

J. G. Boyle run out	5	– (2) lbw b G. K. Robertson	1
R. A. Verry c I. D. S. Smith b Stirling	16	– (1) c Duff b Visser	16
*R. H. Vance c S. P. Robertson b Visser	4	– c I. D. S. Smith	
		b G. K. Robertson	16
E. J. Gray b Martin	24	– c Visser b Stirling	109
R. W. Ormiston c I. D. S. Smith b Stirling	34	– c I. D. S. Smith b Stirling	29
T. D. Ritchie c Briasco b G. K. Robertson	13	– run out	49
†E. B. McSweeney c Martin b Stirling	32	– not out	20

G. R. Larsen not out	16	– not out	1
P. J. W. Allott b Stirling	0		
S. J. Maguiness c Stirling b G. K. Robertson	27		
E. J. Chatfield c I. D. S. Smith b G. K. Robertson	0		
L-b 5, n-b 3	8	L-b 7, n-b 1	8

1/5 2/12 3/55 4/55 5/92   179   1/7 2/35 3/35   (6 wkts dec.) 249
6/125 7/140 8/140 9/179   4/91 5/219 6/234

Bowling: *First Innings*—G. K. Robertson 18-4-39-3; Visser 15-2-35-1; Stirling 17-2-46-4; Martin 13-3-52-1; Duff 4-3-2-0. *Second Innings*—Robertson 19-2-57-2; Visser 17-5-46-1; Stirling 18-2-69-2; Martin 20-4-65-0; Duff 4-2-5-0.

Central Districts

P. S. Briasco lbw b Allott	6	– c Verry b Gray	60
C. J. Smith b Chatfield	29	– c McSweeney b Maguiness	18
S. P. Robertson b Gray	35	– c McSweeney b Allott	11
T. E. Blain c McSweeney b Allott	8	– c McSweeney b Allott	18
S. W. Duff c Gray b Maguiness	11	–(9) not out	7
*R. E. Hayward c Allott b Gray	12	–(5) c Maguiness b Gray	58
†I. D. S. Smith c Allott b Gray	10	–(6) c McSweeney b Gray	20
D. A. Stirling not out	21	–(7) c Maguiness b Allott	37
G. K. Robertson b Gray	0	–(8) run out	0
K. W. Martin c Ritchie b Allott	14		
P. J. Visser c McSweeney b Chatfield	1		
L-b 5, n-b 1	6	L-b 4	4

1/14 2/46 3/56 4/80 5/99   153   1/61 2/83 3/103 4/116   (8 wkts) 233
6/109 7/115 8/115 9/152   5/151 6/206 7/207 8/233

Bowling: *First Innings*—Allott 27-12-46-3; Chatfield 35.5-18-36-2; Maguiness 17-6-29-1; Larsen 1-1-0-0; Gray 23-11-37-4. *Second Innings*—Allott 15-4-46-3; Chatfield 16-5-33-0; Maguiness 11-5-32-1; Gray 28.4-5-99-3; Verry 5-1-14-0; Vance 2-0-5-0.

Umpires: D. A. Kinsella and J. Nilsson.

OTAGO v CANTERBURY

At Dunedin, February 6, 7, 8. Drawn. Otago 4 pts. Toss: Otago.

Canterbury

D. J. Boyle c Lees b Cushen	149	–(2) not out	5
A. Nathu run out	0	–(1) not out	23
P. E. McEwan lbw b Boock	70		
P. G. Kennedy lbw b Cushen	53		
R. T. Latham c Hoskin b McKechnie	81		
*V. R. Brown c Lees b McKechnie	1		
D. W. Stead lbw b McKechnie	0		
S. R. McNally c Lees b Mallender	3		
†A. W. Hart not out	17		
A. J. Hintz not out	1		
B 2, l-b 14, n-b 10	26		

1/0 2/115 3/255 4/332   (8 wkts dec.) 401   (no wkt) 28
5/333 6/340 7/345 8/398

S. J. R. Roberts did not bat.

Bowling: *First Innings*—Mallender 32-9-98-1; Cushen 37-11-85-2; McKechnie 43-14-108-3; Boock 36-13-57-1; Lindsay 3-0-20-0; Rutherford 6-2-17-0. *Second Innings*—Cushen 7-1-14-0; Lindsay 2-0-11-0; Hoskin 4-2-3-0.

Otago

K. R. Rutherford c Latham b Roberts . 44	*†W. K. Lees not out 13
S. J. McCullum c Brown b Hintz 134	
R. N. Hoskin c Kennedy b Stead 23	B 9, l-b 10, w 3, n-b 3 25
K. J. Burns c Kennedy b McEwan 29	
D. J. Walker not out 76	1/98 2/151 3/223 (5 wkts dec.) 403
J. K. Lindsay lbw b Hintz 59	4/251 5/367

B. J. McKechnie, N. A. Mallender, S. L. Boock and J. A. J. Cushen did not bat.

Bowling: Roberts 22–5–60–1; McNally 27–6–83–0; Hintz 21–3–75–2; Brown 32–15–54–0; Stead 28–3–92–1; McEwan 10–6–10–1; Nathu 6–1–9–0; Hart 1–0–1–0.

Umpires: D. E. C. McKechnie and G. C. Morris.

OVERS BOWLED AND RUNS SCORED IN THE BRITANNIC ASSURANCE CHAMPIONSHIP, 1986

	Over-rate per hour			Run-rate per 100 balls		
	1st half	*2nd half*	*Total*	*1st half*	*2nd half*	*Total*
Derbyshire (11)	18.87	18.61	18.76	49.49	52.23	50.49
Essex (1)	18.62	18.70	18.67	47.81	55.11	51.94
Glamorgan (17)	18.54	18.69	18.61	44.22	43.91	44.06
Gloucestershire (2)	18.22*	17.47‡	17.86	52.14	52.80	52.49
Hampshire (6)	18.61	18.99	18.78	50.46	53.99	52.21
Kent (8)	18.68	18.22*	18.45	43.59	51.84	47.05
Lancashire (15)	17.11‡	17.81†	17.46	48.51	45.21	46.93
Leicestershire (7)	17.59†	18.15*	17.87	48.91	50.65	49.75
Middlesex (12)	17.66†	18.30*	17.96	49.23	51.47	50.48
Northamptonshire (9)	18.62	19.00	18.81	56.69	55.45	56.10
Nottinghamshire (4)	18.74	18.97	18.85	53.77	56.02	54.82
Somerset (16)	18.54	18.74	18.63	57.78	58.42	58.10
Surrey (3)	18.51	18.53	18.52	53.04	63.71	58.19
Sussex (14)	18.55	18.63	18.60	48.48	56.59	52.70
Warwickshire (12)	18.89	18.86	18.87	51.43	50.12	50.84
Worcestershire (5)	18.54	18.75	18.64	52.85	62.34	57.26
Yorkshire (10)	18.50	18.90	18.64	53.09	56.43	54.30
1986 average rate			18.49			52.22
1985 average rate			18.43			52.61
1984 average rate			16.88			51.82
1983 average rate			18.96			50.68
1982 average rate			19.06			51.38
1981 average rate			18.62			50.86
1980 average rate			18.95			50.47
1979 average rate			19.36			48.37
1978 average rate			19.45			47.53

1986 Championship positions are shown in brackets.

   * £2,000 fine.   † £3,000 fine.   ‡ £4,000 fine.

Note: In 1984, no financial penalty was incurred for failure to achieve a required over-rate, and the figures for that year do not make any allowance for the fall of wickets, which the figures for earlier years do.

CRICKET IN INDIA, 1985-86

By P. N. SUNDARESAN

With no touring team visiting India in the season under review, the domestic competitions became the focal point. The selectors were able to concentrate on the Irani Trophy match and the Duleep Trophy competition which began the season before choosing their team to Australia, while later in the season the Ranji Trophy championship provided an opportunity for last-minute claims to a place in the team to tour England. In the first two competitions, Ravi Shastri was the triumphant captain on both occasions as Bombay won the Irani Trophy and West Zone claimed the Duleep Trophy by beating South Zone in the final. The three matches in the latter competition produced eight hundreds, with Lalchand Rajput taking the palm for his 221 for West Zone against North Zone. In this same match, Shastri took eight wickets for 145 in North Zone's only innings.

Three more member associations of the Indian Cricket Board were admitted to the Ranji Trophy championship: Goa in the South Zone, Himachal Pradesh in the North, and Tripura in the East. This raised the number of participants to 27, but in effect their entry only weakened the championship as all three were of inadequate strength. Indeed, one consequence of the admission of Himachal Pradesh was that Jammu and Kashmir were able to register their first innings victory in something like three decades. Furthermore, only Goa, being contiguous to Bombay, and so having the opportunity to draft talent from that state, can be expected to improve in the coming years.

The success story of the season was provided by Andhra. They have often been in the habit of causing upsets in the South Zone, but this time they exceeded all previous achievements by winning the zone league and entering the knockout stage for the first time. Such success should have gladdened the soul of C. K. Nayudu, India's first Test captain, who led Andhra in their first Ranji Trophy match against Mysore in 1953-54. In the quarter-finals, Andhra lost to Rajasthan on a rain-affected pitch at Jaipur after their decision to bat first had misfired.

Delhi, losing finalists in the previous two seasons, won the Ranji Trophy at the third attempt with a convincing victory over Haryana. Haryana had reached the final with a 150-run win over Bombay, champions of the past two seasons. This semi-final was a splendid match, with Kapil Dev and Shastri back from the tour of Australia to captain Haryana and Bombay respectively. Shastri was looking for a hat-trick of trophies, but his decision to insert Haryana rebounded on him when they made 423, Ravinder Chadda scoring an unbeaten 159. Kapil Dev's opening spells in both innings carried the main thrust for Haryana when Bombay batted, and Sarkar Talwar, with his contrasting off-spin bowling, provided him with fine support, taking six wickets in Bombay's first innings and three in the second.

In the final, however, the placid turf at the Feroz Sha Kotla gave little support to Kapil Dev's men as Mohinder Amarnath struck an immaculate 194 and there were also hundreds from Manoj Prabhakar (115), Kirti Azad (107) and Ajay Sharma (110) as Delhi gained a first-innings lead of 350. With the young left-arm spinner, Maninder Singh, then running into his best form, taking eight for 54 in Haryana's second innings, Delhi emerged worthy champions. Delhi's earlier matches were highlighted by a forceful 231 against Maharashtra by their young opening batsman, Raman Lamba – the highest individual score of the season and a record for Delhi – which, coupled with 110 in the semi-final against Rajasthan, helped him win a place in the Indian team to England.

However, it was another Delhi batsman, Kirti Azad, who headed the first-class averages, 834 of his 858 runs coming in Ranji Trophy matches. With a double-century against Himachal Pradesh and three other hundreds, two of them in the knockout rounds, he led the Ranji Trophy averages with 92.66. Talwar was the season's leading wicket-taker with 46, but Maninder Singh's 39 wickets represent a better performance in that 24 were taken in the Ranji Trophy knockout to Talwar's fifteen.

The bowling feat of the season was Pradeep Sunderam's ten wickets in an innings for 78 for Rajasthan against Vidarbha in a Central Zone Ranji Trophy match. Having thus emulated Premansu Chatterjee of Bengal, who took ten for 20 against Assam in 1956-57, Sunderam, a medium-fast bowler, took six second-innings wickets to surpass Chatterjee's Indian record of fifteen for 109 against Madhya Pradesh in 1955-56, his match figures being sixteen for 154. Another notable bowling feat was performed by R. P. Singh and K. K. Sharma, of Uttar Pradesh, who shared all twenty wickets in a Central Zone match against Rajasthan.

FIRST-CLASS AVERAGES, 1985-86

BATTING

(Qualification: 500 runs)

	I	NO	R	HI	100s	Avge
K. Azad (*Delhi*)	11	1	858	215	4	85.80
M. D. Gunjal (*Maharashtra*)	8	0	677	176	3	84.62
M. Prabhakar (*Delhi*)	10	3	502	119	3	71.71
C. S. Pandit (*Bombay*)	11	3	570	130*	2	71.25
R. Lamba (*Delhi*)	11	1	691	231	3	69.10
K. Bhaskar Pillai (*Delhi*)	13	5	544	140	3	68.00
K. V. S. D. Kamaraju (*Andhra*)	11	1	552	110*	2	55.20
D. Meher Baba (*Andhra*)	11	0	557	134	1	50.63
A. Malhotra (*Haryana*)	12	1	549	116	1	49.90
L. S. Rajput (*Bombay*)	16	2	670	221	1	47.85
R. Chadda (*Haryana*)	13	0	581	159	2	44.69

Signifies not out.

BOWLING

(Qualification: 25 wickets)

	O	M	R	W	Avge
Azim Khan (*Maharashtra*)	193.4	48	454	26	17.46
Maninder Singh (*Delhi*)	325.5	102	691	3?	17.71
P. Sunderam (*Rajasthan*)	137	25	486	??	
Avinash Kumar (*Bihar*)	214.1	48	578		
S. Talwar (*Haryana*)	417.2	57	1,147		
K. D. Mokashi (*Bombay*)	336	63	987		

Note: Matches taken into account are Ranji Trophy, Duleep Trophy and Ir

RANJI TROPHY, 1985-86

*In the following scores, (M) indicates that the match was played on coir matting, (T) that it was played on turf, and * by the name of the team indicates that they won the toss.*

Central Zone

At Indore (T), November 17, 18, 19. Drawn. Uttar Pradesh* 453 for five dec. (S. Chaturvedi 122, Yusuf Ali Khan 139, R. Sapru 60, K. B. Kala 51 not out) and 151 for three (S. S. Khandkar 53, S. Chaturvedi 46); Madhya Pradesh 464 for nine dec. (Sanjeeva Rao 79, A. Laghate 48, M. Hassan 50, M. Sahni 58, D. Nilosey 40; Mazhar Ali four for 120). *Uttar Pradesh 9 pts, Madhya Pradesh 5 pts.*

At Jodhpur (M), November 17, 18, 19. Rajasthan won by 9 runs. Rajasthan* 218 (B. Thakre five for 44) and 115 (S. Takle four for 50, V. Gawate four for 30); Vidarbha 140 (P. Sahasrabudhe 45; P. Sunderam ten for 78) and 184 (V. Gawate 50 not out; P. Sunderam six for 76). *Rajasthan 27 pts, Vidharba 11 pts.*

At Jaipur (T), November 23, 24, 25. Rajasthan won by ten wickets. Railways* 203 (R. Jadhav 59) and 115 (S. Mudkavi four for 42, S. Vyas six for 43); Rajasthan 298 for nine dec. (P. Shastri 59, A. Mudkavi 50 not out) and 21 for no wkt. *Rajasthan 26 pts, Railways 5 pts.*

At Nagpur (T), November 23, 24, 25. Drawn. Vidarbha 302 for eight dec. (P. Hingnikar 51, V. Telang 48, V. Gawate 61, S. Takle 66; N. Hirwani four for 90) and 292 (P. P. Pandit 53, S. Phadkar 127; D. Nilosey four for 93); Madhya Pradesh* 214 (S. Lahore 53; V. Gawate four for 80, S. Takle four for 45) and 330 for eight (Sanjeeva Rao 72, M. Sahni 123; U. Gani five for 115). *Vidarbha 13 pts, Madhya Pradesh 10 pts.*

At Gwalior (T), December 14, 15, 16. Drawn. Madhya Pradesh* 158 (C. P. Singh 54; H. Joshi four for 38) and 241 (M. Hassan 68, Bhupinder Singh 43; I. Rajkumar four for 62, H. Joshi four for 83); Railways 283 (P. Karkera 59, R. Jadhav 41, P. Banerjee 57; N. Hirwani seven for 64) and 66 for four. *Railways 8 pts, Madhya Pradesh 6 pts.*

At Meerut (T), December 14, 15, 16. Drawn. Vidarbha 135 (R. P. Singh four for 33) and 49 for two; Uttar Pradesh* 38 for no wkt dec. and 30 for no wkt. *Uttar Pradesh 5 pts.*

At Agra (T), December 20, 21, 22. Uttar Pradesh won by nine wickets. Railways 202 (P. Karkera 55, P. Vedraj 47; Gopal Sharma six for 64) and 194 (N. Churi 45; R. S. Hans six for 66, Gopal Sharma four for 69); Uttar Pradesh 192* (K. B. Kala 49, A. G. Mathur 48; H. Joshi five for 54) and 205 for one (S. S. Khandkar 121 not out, S. Chaturvedi 63). *Uttar Pradesh 26 pts, Railways 6 pts.*

At Bhinmal (T), December 20, 21, 22. Madhya Pradesh won by four wickets. Rajasthan* 100 (S. Mudkavi 44; S. Jain four for 17, N. Hirwani five for 35) and 168 (S. Mudkavi 45, S. Vyas 41; N. Hirwani six for 98); Madhya Pradesh 202 (C. P. Singh 68) and 67 for six. *Madhya Pradesh 24 pts, Rajasthan 7 pts.*

At Yavatmal (M), December 27, 28, 29. Drawn. Railways 154 for eight dec. (G. Tank 46; B. Thakre four for 41) and 422 for nine (A. Burrows 193, K. Fernandes 42, P. Banerjee 46; H. Wasu four for 92); Vidarbha* 460 (P. Hingnikar 100, R. Pankule 76, S. Hedaoo 95, P. Sahasrabudhe 46). *Vidarbha 8 pts, Railways 7 pts.*

At Allahabad (T), December 27, 28, 29. Uttar Pradesh won by 147 runs. Uttar Pradesh 219 for eight dec. (S. Chaturvedi 40, S. Anand 58, Gopal Sharma 46; P. Sunderam six for 94) and 258 for two dec. (S. S. Khandkar 131 not out, S. Chaturvedi 42, Yusuf Ali Khan 61); Rajasthan* 169 (S. Vyas 43; K. K. Sharma seven for 43) and 161 (A. Asava 47 not out; R. P. Singh six for 75, K. K. Sharma four for 50). *Uttar Pradesh 30 pts, Rajasthan 7 pts.*

Uttar Pradesh 70 pts, Rajasthan 67 pts, Madhya Pradesh 45 pts, Vidarbha 32 pts, Railways ?6 pts. Uttar Pradesh and Rajasthan qualified for the knockout stage.

East Zone

At Calcutta (T), December 28, 29, 30. Bengal won by an innings and 221 runs. Bengal* 408 for six dec. (P. Roy 177, Arun Lal 113; A. Deb Burman four for 124); Tripura 101 (G. Shome, jun. four for 46) and 86. *Bengal 32 pts, Tripura 1 pt.*

At Balasore (T), December 28, 29, 30. Orissa won by an innings and 35 runs. Orissa 419 for four dec. (K. Dubey 51, A. Jayaprakash 142 not out, A. Bharadwaj 71, S. Mitra 103 not out); Assam* 203 (R. Bora 44, P. Bora 43 not out) and 181 (R. Bora 85; S. Mitra five for 16). *Orissa 30 pts, Assam 6 pts.*

At Talcher (T), January 4, 5, 6. Orissa won by an innings and 19 runs. Orissa* 365 for six dec. (K. Dubey 54, S. Das 124, A. Jayaprakash 66, D. Mahanty 64); Tripura 182 (S. Paul 100; H. Praharaj four for 28) and 164 (R. K. Sen 44 not out; S. Mitra five for 60, D. Mahanty four for 35). *Orissa 31 pts, Tripura 3 pts.*

At Ranchi (T), January 4, 5, 6. Bihar won by an innings and 84 runs. Assam* 141 (S. Dutta 65; A. Kumar four for 31, M. R. Bhalla four for 32) and 228 (S. Dutta 68, R. Bora 59; A. Kumar five for 47); Bihar 453 for five dec. (R. Deora 145, H. Gidwani 60, Baldev Singh 195; H. Barua four for 114). *Bihar 29 pts, Assam 3 pts.*

At Calcutta (T), January 9, 10, 11. Bengal won by four wickets. Assam 402 (S. Dutta 71, Amal Das 73, R. Bora 107, S. Uzir 54 not out) and 121; Bengal* 274 for eight (Arun Lal 50, R. Dani 69 not out) and 284 for six (Arun Lal 91, S. Mukherjee 42). *Bengal 28 pts, Assam 9 pts.*

At Ranchi (T), January 9, 10, 11. Bihar won by an innings and 140 runs. Bihar* 320 (R. Deora 75, H. Gidwani 62, S. S. Karim 57; A. Das six for 76); Tripura 92 (V. Venkatram five for 17) and 88 (V. Venkatram four for 38). *Bihar 32 pts, Tripura 4 pts.*

At Rourkela (T), January 15, 16, 17. Drawn. Bengal 152 for two dec. (Arun Lal 63 not out) and 13 for no wkt; Orissa* 250 for six dec. (K. Dubey 56, S. Das 47, A. Bhardwaj 45). *Orissa 3 pts, Bengal 3 pts.*

At Nowgong (T), January 15, 16, 17. Assam won by six wickets. Tripura* 79 (N. Konwar four for 18, H. Barua four for 29) and 155 (T. Dey Roy 57; N. Konwar four for 68); Assam 196 (S. Dutta 40, G. Hazarika 50; S. Das Gupta five for 51) and 39 for four. *Assam 23 pts, Tripura 6 pts.*

At Ranchi (T), January 23, 24, 25. Drawn. Bihar* 532 for five dec. (R. Deora 104, A. Dayal 174, H. Gidwani 57, B. D. Gossein 111) and 155 (P. Nandy five for 24); Bengal 393 for eight dec. (M. Das 55, A. Mitra 91, P. Nandy 105, A. Bhattacharjee 71 not out) and 155 for seven (P. Roy 46). *Bihar 12 pts, Bengal 10 pts.*

At Baripada (T), January 29, 30, 31. Bihar won by ten wickets. Bihar* 451 (R. Deora 70, A. Dayal 54, H. Gidwani 69, B. D. Gossein 45, S. Roy 56, S. S. Karim 59) and 11 for no wkt; Orissa 245 (K. Dubey 45, D. Mahanty 70; A. Kumar four for 62) and 213 (A. Kumar seven for 83). *Bihar 28 pts, Orissa 8 pts.*

Bihar 101 pts, Bengal 73 pts, Orissa 72 pts, Assam 41 pts, Tripura 14 pts. Bihar and Bengal qualified for the knockout stage.

North Zone

At Srinagar (T), September 15, 16, 17. Delhi won by an innings and 111 runs. Jammu and Kashmir 83 (M. Prabhakar four for 42) and 212 (S. Chowdhary 40, Zahoor Bhat 77); Delhi* (406 for five dec. (S. C. Khanna 155, K. Bhaskar Pillai 101 not out, A. Sharma 41). *Delhi 30 pts, Jammu and Kashmir 4 pts.*

At Srinagar (T), September 20, 21, 22. Punjab won by eight wickets. Jammu and Kash (A. Aijaz 121; Harjinder Singh six for 72) and 91 (Umesh Kumar four for 5); Punjab* ? dec. (N. S. Sidhu 65, Kulwant Singh 51, D. Chopra 81 not out, M. I. Singh 54) and / *Punjab 27 pts, Jammu and Kashmir 6 pts.*

At Srinagar (T), September 30, October 1, 2. Jammu and Kashmir won by an innings and 66 runs. Himachal Pradesh* 112 (Idris four for 31) and 197 (R. Dutt 46; N. Khanday five for 64); Jammu and Kashmir 375 (A. Aijaz 100, R. Pandit 87, S. Chowdhary 54, K. Drabhu 62). *Jammu and Kashmir 30 pts, Himachal Pradesh 3 pts.*

At Srinagar (T), October 4, 5, 6. Drawn. Haryana 243 (R. Dogra 57, Salim Ahmed 42; D. Pandit four for 44) and 198 for six (A. Malhotra 42, R. Chadda 71); Jammu and Kashmir* 138 (S. Chowdhary 40; Chetan Sharma four for 46, S. Talwar four for 56). *Haryana 10 pts, Jammu and Kashmir 7 pts.*

At Srinagar (T), October 8, 9, 10. Drawn. Services 264 (B. Ghosh 72, A. Jha 74; R. Pandit four for 34); Jammu and Kashmir* 45 for three. *Jammu and Kashmir 4 pts, Services 4 pts.*

At Jalandhar (T), November 2, 3, 4. Drawn. Punjab* 356 (Balkar Singh 82, N. S. Sidhu 85, K. P. Amarjeet 53) and 16 for no wkt; Delhi 322 for four dec. (M. Prabhakar 104, R. Lamba 80, K. Azad 75 not out). *Delhi 4 pts, Punjab 3 pts.*

At Chandigarh (T), November 2, 3, 4. Haryana won by an innings and 61 runs. Haryana* 307 (Satya Dev 49, S. Talwar 79; R. K. Verma four for 92); Services 104 (S. Talwar seven for 44) and 142 (K. Srikant 40; S. Talwar four for 60). *Haryana 28 pts, Services 4 pts.*

At Jalandhar (T), November 7, 8, 9. Punjab won by an innings and 154 runs. Himachal Pradesh* 89 (D. Chopra five for 43) and 182 (Inderjit Singh 42; D. Chopra four for 53, M. I. Singh six for 61); Punjab 425 for five dec. (Y. Dutta 59, K. P. Amarjeet 86, D. Chopra 51, Yashpal Sharma 129 not out, Kulwant Singh 46 not out). *Punjab 32 pts, Himachal Pradesh 3 pts.*

At Delhi (T), November 7, 8, 9. Delhi won by ten wickets. Haryana 225 (R. Jolly 100; M. Prabhakar four for 56) and 202 (Ashwani Kumar 42); Delhi* 400 for five dec. (R. Lamba 110, S. C. Khanna 55, K. Azad 82, K. Bhaskar Pillai 81 not out) and 31 for no wkt. *Delhi 26 pts, Haryana 5 pts.*

At Delhi (T), November 12, 13, 14. Services won by an innings and 27 runs. Himachal Pradesh* 265 (Inderjit Singh 74, V. Sen 76) and 195 (Inderjit Singh 62, V. Sen 62; V. Gohil five for 54); Services 487 for nine dec. (K. Srikant 157, Ratan Das 111, Roshan 69). *Services 31 pts, Himachal Pradesh 7 pts.*

At Faridabad (T), November 12, 13, 14. Haryana won by nine wickets. Punjab* 172 (Yashpal Sharma 70; Kapil Dev four for 44, Chetan Sharma four for 65) and 165; Haryana 250 (R. Chadda 63, R. Jolly 41, Chetan Sharma 46 not out) and 88 for one. *Haryana 25 pts, Punjab 6 pts.*

At Rohtak (T), November 17, 18, 19. Haryana won by an innings and 138 runs. Himachal Pradesh* 144 (S. Talwar six for 40, Sharanjit Singh four for 61) and 171 (Darshan Singh 50; S. Talwar four for 65, Sharanjit Singh six for 79); Haryana 453 for six dec. (D. Sharma 49, R. Chadda 156, R. Jolly 82, Satya Dev 48 not out). *Haryana 30 pts, Himachal Pradesh 2 pts.*

At Delhi (T), November 25, 26, 27. Delhi won by an innings and 165 runs. Himachal Pradesh 164 (Inderjit Singh 43, Harish Kumar 66; Madan Lal four for 49) and 112 (S. Valson six for 40); Delhi* 441 for five dec. (K. Azad 215, K. Bhaskar Pillai 140). *Delhi 32 pts, Himachal Pradesh 2 pts.*

At Patiala (T), November 30, December 1, 2. Drawn. Punjab* 287 (R. Kalsi 87, Balkar Singh 75; B. Ghosh six for 56) and 192 for four dec. (K. P. Amarjeet 54 not out, Y. Dutta 67); Services 181 (Ratan Das 43) and 126 for three (Ratan Das 57 not out). *Services 8 pts, Punjab 7 pts.*

At Delhi (T), December 10, 11, 12. Drawn. Delhi* 350 for four dec. (S. C. Khanna 54, Gursharan Singh 114 not out, K. Azad 114) and 87 for four; Services 107. *Delhi 8 pts, Services 3 pts.*

Delhi 100 pts, Haryana 98 pts, Punjab 75 pts, Jammu and Kashmir 51 pts, Services 50 pts, Himachal Pradesh 17 pts. Delhi and Haryana qualified for the knockout stage.

South Zone

At Vasco (M), November 30, December 1, 2. Kerala won by six wickets. Goa* 188 (S. Pednekar 40; Ajay Varma four for 60) and 153 (N. Raote 72; S. Santosh five for 43); Kerala 196 and 148 for four (K. Jayaraman 54 not out). *Kerala 26 pts, Goa 9 pts.*

At Badravathi (M), December 7, 8, 9. Karnataka won by six wickets. Goa* 322 (N. Phadte 156; A. R. Bhat four for 90) and 136 (M. Desai 57, A. R. Bhat four for 46, H. Surendra four for 19); Karnataka 335 for six dec. (M. R. Srinivasaprasad 106, R. D. Khanvilkar 88, G. R. Viswanath 69; S. Pednekar four for 69) and 124 for four (M. R. Srinivasaprasad 51). *Karnataka 25 pts, Goa 7 pts.*

At Madras (T), December 14, 15, 16. Tamil Nadu won by an innings and 98 runs. Tamil Nadu* 260 for seven dec. (V. Sivaramakrishnan 50, A. Jabbar 46, M. Gautham 56; T. S. Mahadevan four for 102); Kerala 80 (S. Vasudevan six for 27) and 82 (M. Gautham four for 16, S. Vasudevan four for 36). *Tamil Nadu 31 pts, Kerala 3 pts.*

At Bellary (M), December 21, 22, 23. Drawn. Kerala* 316 (S. Santosh 79, K. Jayaraman 59, S. Ramesh 59; Teshwant four for 56) and 330 (T. Mathew 111, S. Santosh 49, S. Rajesh 65, S. Ramesh 64; P. K. Rathod four for 84); Karnataka 251 (R. Khanvilkar 64, G. R. Viswanath 50; Ajay Varma five for 82) and 177 for three (S. Viswanath 59, M. R. Srinivasaprasad 51). *Karnataka 10 pts, Kerala 9 pts.*

At Vizianagaram (T), December 21, 22, 23. Drawn. Andhra 593 for nine dec. (M. F. Rehman 141, K. V. S. D. Kamaraju 83, D. Meher Baba 61, K. B. Ramamurthy 100 not out, J. K. Ghiya 110; S. Vasudevan four for 137) and 176 for seven (D. Meher Baba 61; M. Gautham four for 47); Tamil Nadu* 321 for four dec. (V. Sivaramakrishnan 86, P. C. Prakash 125 not out, A. Jabbar 51 not out). *Andhra 9 pts, Tamil Nadu 9 pts.*

At Dharwar (T), December 28, 29, 30. Drawn. Tamil Nadu* 218 (P. C. Prakash 107 not out; J. Abhiram four for 42) and 292 (V. Sivaramakrishnan 42, Robin Singh 62, S. Vasudevan 45; H. Surendra five for 111); Karnataka 279 (M. R. Srinivasaprasad 64, B. P. Patel 41; S. Vasudevan six for 57) and 24 for two. *Karnataka 10 pts, Tamil Nadu 8 pts.*

At Sirpur (M), December 28, 29, 30. Drawn. Andhra* 283 (L. K. Adiseshu 88, J. K. Ghiya 59; M. V. Narasimha Rao six for 112) and 461 for nine dec. (M. F. Rehman 81, G. A. Pratapkumar 42, V. Chamudeswarnath 63, D. Meher Baba 71, K. B. Ramamurthy 51 retired; Harimohan four for 106); Hyderabad 300 for five dec. (A. Azeem 93, V. Mohanraj 71, M. V. Narasimha Rao 78 not out) and 64 for three. *Andhra 8 pts, Hyderabad 8 pts.*

At Cuddapah (M), January 4, 5, 6. Andhra won by an innings and 79 runs. Goa* 150 (S. Mahadevan 79, J. K. Ghiya four for 43) and 121 (J. K. Ghiya five for 49); Andhra 350 (L. K. Adiseshu 63, K. V. S. D. Kamaraju 47, D. Meher Baba 134 not out; S. Mahadevan four for 82). *Andhra 32 pts, Goa 5 pts.*

At Tellicherry (M), January 4, 5, 6. Hyderabad won by an innings and 91 runs. Kerala 178 (K. Jayaraman 46; M. V. Narasimha Rao five for 44) and 115 (R. Yadav seven for 58); Hyderabad* 384 (A. Azeem 56, V. Mohanraj 80, K. A. Qayyum 49, Etheshamuddin 58, R. Yadav 47; T. S. Mahadevan eight for 108). *Hyderabad 32 pts, Kerala 6 pts.*

At Madras (T), January 11, 12, 13. Drawn. Tamil Nadu 226 for seven dec. (V. Sivaramakrishnan 84, R. Madhavan 79) v Hyderabad*. *Tamil Nadu 2 pts, Hyderabad 3 pts.*

At Visakhapatnam (T), January 11, 12, 13. Drawn. Andhra* 334 (K. V. S. D. Kamaraju 55, K. B. Ramamurthy 54, G. A. Pratapkumar 79 not out; Jeswant four for 64) and 162 for six dec. (K. B. Ramamurthy 50 not out; Jeswant four for 60); Karnataka 214 (M. R. Srinivasaprasad 41, G. R. Viswanath 44, C. F. Saldana 41. *Andhra 8 pts, Karnataka 7 pts.*

At Hyderabad (T), January 17, 18, 19. Drawn. Karnataka 449 for eight dec. (G. Saldana 91, R. Khanvilkar 55, G. R. Viswanath 160 not out, Jeswant 60) and 224 for nine (S. Viswanath 41, R. Khanvilkar 70, G. R. Viswanath 54 not out; Kanwaljit Singh five for 39); Hyderabad* 309 for seven dec. (V. Mohanraj 54, V. Jaisimha 80 not out, Etheshamuddin 59). *Karnataka 9 pts, Hyderabad 8 pts.*

At Madras (T), January 18, 19, 20. Tamil Nadu won by an innings and 110 runs. Tamil Nadu 328 (P. C. Prakash 49, V. Sivaramakrishnan 110; T. S. Mahadevan five for 98); Goa* 108 (S. Pednekar 44; R. Mishra four for 11, S. Vasudevan four for 35) and 110 (N. Phadte 46; R. Venkatesh five for 16). *Tamil Nadu 32 pts, Goa 4 pts.*

At Tellicherry (M), January 18, 19, 20. Andhra won by 137 runs. Andhra 250 (K. V. S. D. Kamaraju 68, G. A. Pratapkumar 42) and 263 for eight dec. ((K. V. S. D. Kamaraju 108, M. S. Kumar 57 not out, D. Meher Baba 47); Kerala* 215 (K. Jayaraman 73; J. K. Ghiya seven for 74) and 161 (S. Ramesh 40 not out; M. F. Rehman four for 11). *Andhra 29 pts, Kerala 8 pts.*

At Margao (T), January 25, 26, 27. Hyderabad won by an innings and 87 runs. Goa* 194 (H. Mohan four for 56) and 220 (S. Kangralkar 69, C. Ashok 50 not out; R. Yadav four for 68); Hyderabad 501 for five dec. (A. Azeem 136, V. Mohanraj 113, Arun Paul 72, K. A. Qayyum 65 not out, V. Jaisimha 63). *Hyderabad 30 pts, Goa 3 pts.*

Andhra 86 pts, Tamil Nadu 82 pts, Hyderabad 81 pts, Karnataka 61 pts, Kerala 52 pts, Goa 28 pts. Andhra and Tamil Nadu qualified for the knockout stage.

West Zone

At Pune (T), November 23, 24, 25. Drawn. Baroda 292 (A. D. Gaekwad 69, R. Parikh 62, G. Tilakraj 66) and 179 for nine dec. (A. D. Gaekwad 49; Azim Khan five for 17); Maharashtra* 325 (R. Poonawala 61, M. D. Gunjal 89; D. V. Pardeshi four for 82) and 35 for no wkt. *Maharashtra 10 pts, Baroda 7 pts.*

At Surat (M), November 23, 24, 25. Bombay won by nine wickets. Gujarat 290 (S. Talati 41, P. Desai 70, S. Amarnath 89) and 82 (S. M. Patil six for 20); Bombay* 301 for four dec. (L. S. Rajput 54, S. S. Hattangadi 141 not out, S. M. Patil 59) and 72 for one. *Bombay 28 pts, Gujarat 4 pts.*

At Baroda, December 21, 22, 23. Drawn. Gujarat* 305 (S. Talati 82, A. Saheba 51, S. Amarnath 50) and 214 for nine dec. (S. Talati 81, A. Saheba 43; T. Arothe six for 57); Baroda 234 (A. D. Gaekwad 71, M. Narula 45, T. Arothe 44; M. Patel four for 75, H. Patel four for 71) and 142 for four (G. Tilakraj 59 not out). *Gujarat 13 pts, Baroda 8 pts.*

At Bombay (T), December 21, 22, 23. Drawn. Saurashtra* 308 for four dec. (K. Chauhan 52, B. Jadeja 76, A. Pandya 110 not out) and 316 for four dec. (K. Chauhan 143, S. Keshwala 80 not out); Bombay 322 for three dec. (S. S. Hattangadi 76, J. Sanghani 80, C. S. Pandit 65 not out, S. M. Patil 60 not out) and 102 for five. *Saurashtra 10 pts, Bombay 7 pts.*

At Baroda (T), December 28, 29, 30. Drawn. Bombay* 340 (L. S. Rajput 52, J. Sanghani 67, S. M. Patil 111, S. V. Manjrekar 40 not out) and 182 for two dec. (S. V. Manjrekar 112 not out); Baroda 321 (R. Parikh 47, G. Tilakraj 53, M. Narula 73, D. V. Pardeshi 42) and 106 for five. *Bombay 12 pts, Baroda 5 pts.*

At Pune (T), December 28, 29, 30. Maharashtra won by seven wickets. Saurashtra* 213 (A. Patel 46) and 233 (R. Badiyani 60, S. Keshwala 47, N. Oza 56; Azim Khan four for 34); Maharashtra 403 for four dec. (R. Poonawala 111, V. Khedkar 110, S. Kalyani 95, M. D. Gunjal 64) and 44 for three. *Maharashtra 25 pts, Saurashtra 5 pts.*

At Bombay (T), January 4, 5, 6. Drawn. Maharashtra* 289 (M. D. Gunjal 125, Azim Khan 64; P. Kasliwal five for 91) and 381 for seven dec. (M. D. Gunjal 54, S. Jadhav 93, Azim Khan 40 not out, P. P. Pradhan 45); Bombay 300 for four dec. (S. M. Patil 66, C. S. Pandit 130 not out) and 95 for no wkt. *Bombay 9 pts, Maharashtra 8 pts.*

At Rajkot (T), January 4, 5, 6. Drawn. Saurashtra* 288 (B. Jadeja 65, N. Oza 42, A. Patel 43) and 242 for five dec. (R. Badiyani 108 not out, S. Keshwala 50); Gujarat 274 (A. Saheba 52, B. Mistry 52, P. Desai 44; B. Radia five for 61) and 137 for three. *Saurashtra 12 pts, Gujarat 10 pts.*

At Bulsar (T), January 18, 19, 20. Maharashtra won by nine wickets. Gujarat* 225 (A. Saheba 86, P. Desai 60 not out; Azim Khan five for 54) and 194 (B. K. Patel 53; Azim Khan four for 48); Maharashtra 357 for six dec. (R. Poonawala 48, V. Khedkar 127, S. Kalyani 86, M. D. Gunjal 54) and 60 for one. *Maharashtra 26 pts, Gujarat 5 pts.*

At Gandhidham (M), January 18, 19, 20. Drawn. Saurashtra 308 for five dec. (R. Badiyani 40, A. Pandya 138, S. Keshwala 51; D. V. Pardeshi four for 66) and 204 for one (B. Jadeja 78 not out, B. Pujara 103 not out); Baroda* 483 for six dec. (R. Parikh 123, A. D. Gaekwad 108, S. S. Hazare 65, M. Narula 100 not out). *Saurashtra 7 pts, Baroda 5 pts.*

Maharashtra 69 pts, Bombay 56 pts, Saurashtra 34 pts, Gujarat 32 pts, Baroda 25 pts. Maharashtra and Bombay qualified for the knockout stage.

KNOCKOUT STAGE

MAHARASHTRA v BENGAL

At Pune (T), February 7, 8, 9, 10. Drawn. Maharashtra were declared winners by virtue of their first-innings lead. Toss: Maharashtra.

Maharashtra

R. Poonawala b Bhattacharjee	84		
V. Khedkar c Das b Shome, sen.	3	– c Das b Arun Lal	68
S. Kalyani c Chatterjee b Shome, jun.	9	– st Das b Arun Lal	24
*M. D. Gunjal c Das b Shome, jun.	176		
B. Joglekar c Banerjee b Nandy	177		
†P. R. Pradhan c Das b Chatterjee	17	– c Roy b Arun Lal	50
S. Jadhav lbw b Mukherjee	42	– not out	62
Azim Khan c Shome, jun. b Nandy	32	– not out	23
S. C. Gudge not out	5	– lbw b Arun Lal	39
V. V. Oak lbw b Nandy	1		
S. V. Ranjane lbw b Chatterjee	1		
B 4, l-b 6, w 11, n-b 5	26	B 4, l-b 3, w 4, n-b 1	12
	573	(4 wkts)	278
Penalty for 3 overs short	12		

1/38 2/76 3/107 4/391 5/420   585   1/112 2/141 3/170 4/221
6/512 7/565 8/565 9/572

Bowling: *First Innings*—G. Shome, sen. 22-3-99-1; G. Shome, jun. 27-7-89-2; Chatterjee 28.3-3-103-2; Bhattacharjee 23-3-86-1; Nandy 23-1-87-3; Mukherjee 25-1-81-1; Banerjee 2-0-15-0; Arun Lal 1-0-3-0. *Second Innings*—G. Shome, sen. 9-2-31-0; G. Shome, jun. 5-1-23-0; Banerjee 1-0-14-0; Chatterjee 5-1-28-0; Mukherjee 6-1-16-0; Arun Lal 27-6-79-4; Roy 13-1-47-0; Mitra 9-0-33-0.

Bengal

P. Roy c Pradhan b Oak	37	A. Bhattacharjee c sub b Gudge	7
†M. Das c Ranjane b Jadhav	28	S. Mukherjee not out	18
*Arun Lal b Jadhav	58	G. Shome, sen. c and b Azim	37
U. Chatterjee c sub b Oak	0		
A. Mitra b Gudge	106	L-b 4, w 1, n-b 21	26
U. Banerjee c Kalyani b Azim	32		
Pronab Nandy b Ranjane	0		373
G. Shome, jun. c Joglekar b Ranjane	24		

1/74 2/76 3/76 4/168 5/261
6/268 7/301 8/318 9/318

Bowling: Oak 27-5-100-2; Ranjane 25-6-61-2; Azim 29-8-60-2; Jadhav 23-5-41-2; Gudge 31-4-94-2; Gunjal 1-0-13-0.

Umpires: R. Mehra and V. K. Ramaswamy.

UTTAR PRADESH v TAMIL NADU

At Kanpur (T), February 7, 8, 9, 10. Drawn. Tamil Nadu won on the toss of a coin after rain prevented Uttar Pradesh from completing their first innings. Toss: Tamil Nadu.

Tamil Nadu

B. Arun c Chaturvedi b Singh	22	S. Vasudevan run out	65
W. V. Raman lbw b Gopal	58	S. Venkatesh not out	38
V. Sivaramakrishnan b Hans	43	*†B. Reddy c Sekhar b Gopal	45
R. Madhavan c Chaturvedi b Gopal	0		
P. C. Prakash c K. K. Sharma b Hans	70	B 13, l-b 6, w 2, n-b 23	44
A. Jabbar c Sapru b Gopal	29		—
Robin Singh lbw b Singh	19	1/44 2/110 3/110 4/114 5/203	508
R. Mishra c Kala b K. K. Sharma	75	6/261 7/265 8/375 9/433	

Bowling: Singh 17–1–89–2; K. K. Sharma 20–0–114–1; Gopal 60.3–12–125–4; Kala 2–1–2–0; Hans 43–14–90–2; Mazhar 23–3–69–0.

Uttar Pradesh

S. S. Khandkar c Sivaramakrishnan b Arun	2
†S. Chaturvedi not out	74
Yusuf Ali Khan not out	56
B 4, n-b 13	17
1/5 (1 wkt)	149

R. P. Singh, K. K. Sharma, Gopal Sharma, K. B. Kala, *R. S. Hans, Mazhar Ali, R. Sapru and S. Anand did not bat.

Bowling: Arun 14–2–64–1; Mishra 9–3–12–0; Vasudevan 10–2–26–0; Robin 7–0–41–0; Venkatesh 4–2–2–0.

Umpires: S. Chaturvedi and C. K. Sathe.

QUARTER-FINALS

TAMIL NADU v BOMBAY

At Madras (T), February 14, 15, 16, 17. Drawn. Bombay were declared winners by virtue of their first-innings lead. Toss: Tamil Nadu.

Tamil Nadu

K. Srikkanth b Patil	38		
W. V. Raman c Hattangadi b Sawant	34	– c Manjrekar b Kasliwal	17
V. Sivaramakrishnan b Patil	6	– not out	4
P. C. Prakash c and b Patil	9	– c Sanghani b Sawant	79
A. Jabbar run out	43		
R. Mishra c sub b Sawant	12	– c Manjrekar b Thakkar	6
Robin Singh not out	36	– not out	73
R. Venkatesh b Thakkar	12	– c Pandit b Mokashi	13
B. Arun c Thakkar b Kasliwal	34	– c Manjrekar b Thakkar	8
L. Sivaramakrishnan run out	6		
*†B. Reddy c sub b Patil	0		
L-b 1, w 1, n-b 1	3	B 1, l-b 4, n-b 7	12

1/54 2/62 3/85 4/98 5/122   233   1/25 2/54 3/161 4/168   (5 wkts) 212
6/149 7/163 8/225 9/233   5/207

Bowling: *First Innings*—Kasliwal 13–5–31–1; Patil 30.2–11–54–4; Mokashi 31–6–95–0; Sawant 16–3–26–2; Thakkar 13–7–7–1; Rajput 5–1–19–0. *Second Innings*—Kasliwal 8–1–36–1; Patil 5–1–10–0; Mokashi 16–3–56–1; Sawant 16–3–36–1; Thakkar 19–6–58–2; Hattangadi 3–0–11–0.

Bombay

L. S. Rajput b L. Sivaramakrishnan	... 95	A. Sawant c Mishra b Venkatesh	 20
S. S. Hattangadi c and		P. Kasliwal c Jabbar b Raman	 17
b L. Sivaramakrishnan .	31	R. Thakkar run out	 29
J. Sanghani c sub b Jabbar	 46	K. D. Mokashi not out	 7
S. V. Manjrekar c Robin b Jabbar	 44	B 2, l-b 4, n-b 4	 10
*S. M. Patil c Robin b Jabbar	 1		
†C. S. Pandit c sub b Venkatesh	 27	1/75 2/168 3/182 4/190 5/243	300
G. A. Parkar lbw b Jabbar	 53	6/265 7/290 8/327 9/358	

Bowling: Arun 6.5–1–19–0; Robin 5–0–10–0; Venkatesh 46–2–140–2; Raman 24–7–39–1; L. Sivaramakrishnan 38–5–98–2; Jabbar 42–13–63–4; Srikkanth 2–0–4–0; Mishra 1–0–1–0.

Umpires: J. D. Ghosh and J. D. Roy.

MAHARASHTRA v DELHI

At Pune (T), February 14, 15, 16, 17. Drawn. Delhi were declared winners by virtue of their first-innings lead. Toss: Delhi.

Delhi

R. Lamba c Poonawala b Gudge	231	– c Oak b Azim	 62
†S. C. Khanna c Pradhan b Gudge	 93	– lbw b Ranjane	 10
Gursharan Singh run out	 6	– c Pradhan b Oak	 4
K. Azad c Jadhav b Gudge	 0	– c Jadhav b Gudge	 37
K. Bhaskar Pillai c Kalyani b Ranjane	 35	– not out	 20
M. Prabhakar c Gudge b Jadhav	119		
*Madan Lal c Kalyani b Jadhav	 46	– not out	 26
A. Sharma c Kalyani b Gudge	 23		
R. C. Shukla not out	 18		
Maninder Singh run out	 9		
S. Valson c Kalyani b Azim	 2		
B 4, l-b 6, w 5, n-b 7	 22	B 1	 1
1/191 2/223 3/225 4/323 5/407	604	1/12 2/25 3/102 (4 wkts dec.)	160
6/500 7/548 8/573 9/594		4/113	

Bowling: *First Innings*—Oak 18–2–82–0; Ranjane 23–3–68–1; Poonawala 2–0–22–0; Azim 44.4–5–108–1; Jadhav 38–4–96–2; Gudge 60–6–214–4; Kalyani 1–0–4–0. *Second Innings*—Oak 7–2–27–1; Ranjane 8–1–25–1; Poonawala 5–1–18–0; Azim 12–3–24–1; Gudge 14–2–45–1; Kalyani 5–0–11–0; Khedkar 3–0–9–0.

Maharashtra

R. Poonawala c Sharma b Madan Lal	 13	– b Maninder	 32
V. Khedkar b Maninder	 95		
†P. R. Pradhan lbw b Shukla	 23	– not out	 1
S. Kalyani c Khanna b Azad	 71		
*M. D. Gunjal lbw b Azad	104		
B. Joglekar c Madan Lal b Azad	 2		
S. Jadhav b Maninder	 1	– not out	 10
V. V. Oak c Khanna b Shukla	 6		
Azim Khan c Gursharan b Maninder	 6		
S. C. Gudge not out	 17	– lbw b Maninder	 17
S. V. Ranjane b Azad	 4	– lbw b Maninder	 0
B 1, l-b 4, n-b 5	 10	B 4	 4
1/18 2/95 3/176 4/261 5/272	352	1/50 2/59 3/59 (3 wkts)	64
6/280 7/303 8/326 9/348			

Bowling: *First Innings*—Madan Lal 7–0–37–1; Prabhakar 5–0–20–0; Valson 5–0–27–0; Maninder 48–9–112–3; Shukla 31–6–91–2; Azad 16.4–2–42–4; Sharma 4–0–18–0. *Second Innings*—Madan Lal 1–1–0–0; Maninder 3–1–7–3; Gursharan 3–0–24–0; Khanna 4–0–29–0.

Umpires: N. N. Patwardhan and K. V. Ramani.

BIHAR v HARYANA

At Jamshedpur (T), February 14, 15, 16, 17. Drawn. Haryana were declared winners by virtue of their first-innings lead. Toss: Haryana.

Haryana

Ashwani Kumar lbw b Venkatram	31	– c and b Venkatram	26
Deepak Sharma c Das b Venkatram	45	– c sub b Venkatram	93
R. Dogra c Gidwani b Kuldip	11	– b Venkatram	7
A. Malhotra b Kuldip	2	– b Venkatram	48
*R. Chadda c Roy b Randhir	17	– c sub b Venkatram	5
Aman Kumar run out	43	– c Gossein b Kumar	3
R. Jolly st Deora b Venkatram	41	– c Kumar b Randhir	50
†Salim Ahmed c Kuldip b Venkatram	19	– b Dayal	18
Satya Dev c Kuldip b Venkatram	0	– c Deora b Randhir	45
Chetan Sharma not out	31	– not out	72
S. Talwar c Dayal b Kuldip	27	– c Kumar b Dayal	2
L-b 2, n-b 1	3	B 6, l-b 9, w 1	16

1/50 2/71 3/83 4/103 5/119   270   1/63 2/71 3/161 4/183 5/187   385
6/189 7/189 8/212 9/217   6/199 7/276 8/317 9/369

Bowling: *First Innings*—Randhir 17–6–51–1; Kuldip 20.1–3–68–3; Gidwani 5–0–13–0; Kumar 22–5–37–0; Venkatram 31–5–99–5. *Second Innings*—Randhir 16–1–45–2; Kuldip 10–1–35–0; Gidwani 11–0–48–0; Kumar 29–8–76–1; Venkatram 31–8–83–5; Dayal 6.3–1–29–2; Roy 9–2–25–0; Das 2–0–10–0; Deora 2–0–19–0.

Bihar

A. Dayal run out	47	Avinash Kumar c Ashwani Kumar	
R. Deora lbw b Chetan	1	b Deepak	30
H. Gidwani c Jolly b Talwar	38	Randhir Singh not out	18
B. D. Gossein lbw b Chetan	2	Kuldip Singh run out	0
S. Roy lbw b Talwar	33	B 3, l-b 1, n-b 9	13
†S. S. Karim lbw b Deepak	1		
U. Das lbw b Chetan	53	1/8 2/73 3/77 4/108 5/141	268
*V. Venkatram lbw b Chetan	32	6/142 7/217 8/220 9/266	

Bowling: Chetan 31–6–83–4; Jolly 9–2–34–0; Deepak 39–16–48–2; Talwar 45–5–99–2.

Umpires: M. I. Mohammad Ghouse and V. Vikramraju.

RAJASTHAN v ANDHRA

At Jaipur (T), February 14, 15, 16, 17. Drawn. Rajasthan were declared winners by virtue of their first-innings lead. Toss: Andhra.

Andhra

L. K. Adiseshu c P. Shastri b Parminder	1	– b Rathore	0
V. S. Prasad c and b S. Shastri	16	– c Dalbir b S. Mudkavi	35
M. Rehman c P. Shastri b Parminder	5	– b Rathore	0
K. V. S. D. Kamaraju c Jain b Parminder	0	– not out	110
M. S. Kumar lbw b Vyas	41		

D. Meher Baba run out	76	– c Parminder b Vyas	60
*K. B. Ramamurthy c Asava b Vyas	5		
J. K. Ghiya c Jain b S. Mudkavi	8	– not out	7
M. Pratapkumar b S. Shastri	10		
†Krishnamohan lbw b S. Shastri	13		
K. Ravishankar not out	5		
L-b 4, w 1	5	B 4, l-b 6, w 2, n-b 3	15

1/1 2/15 3/15 4/66 5/66   185   1/1 2/1 3/123 4/220   (4 wkts) 227
6/95 7/106 8/128 9/161

Bowling: *First Innings*—Rathore 8-2-21-0; Parminder 11-4-26-3; S. Shastri 22-6-55-3; S. Mudkavi 18.4-5-37-1; Vyas 18-6-42-2. *Second Innings*—Rathore 10-1-23-2; Parminder 12-1-53-0; A. Mudkavi 5-0-20-0; Vyas 8-0-31-1; P. Shastri 5-2-9-0; S. Shastri 13-4-29-0; S. Mudkavi 17-2-52-1.

Rajasthan

Dalbir Singh run out	109	*S. Vyas c Meher Baba b Kumar	31
Parminder Singh c Kumar b Ghiya	58	†D. Jain c and b Meher Baba	35
P. Shastri c Krishnamohan b Kumar	69	R. Rathore not out	12
S. Mudkavi c Pratapkumar b Ghiya	52		
A. Asawa lbw b Ramamurthy	9	L-b 1, w 1, n-b 1	3
S. Jain c Pratapkumar b Ghiya	13		
A. Mudkavi c Krishnamohan b Ghiya	13	1/88 2/229 3/241 4/269 5/308	431
S. Shastri c Krishnamohan b Prasad	27	6/317 7/353 8/355 9/398	

Bowling: Ghiya 60-16-123-4; Ramamurthy 14-4-35-1; Ravishankar 22-3-84-0; Meher Baba 11.5-1-23-1; Rahman 4-1-10-0; Prasad 30-11-54-1; Kamaraju 7-0-30-0; Kumar 12-1-49-2; Pratapkumar 8-1-22-0.

Umpires: S. R. Bose and S. Phukan.

SEMI-FINALS

BOMBAY v HARYANA

At Bombay (T), March 15, 16, 17, 18. Haryana won by 150 runs. Toss: Bombay.

Haryana

Ashwani Kumar b Kulkarni	3	– c Parkar b Shastri	24
Deepak Sharma c Hattangadi b Mokashi	48	– lbw b Shastri	5
Aman Kumar b Mokashi	40	– lbw b Mokashi	19
A. Malhotra c Parkar b Mokashi	49	– c Pandit b Mokashi	63
R. Chadda not out	159	– c Vengsarkar b Shastri	28
*Kapil Dev c Sippy b Mokashi	39	– c Parkar b Mokashi	24
R. Jolly c Sawant b Mokashi	15	– c and b Sawant	36
Chetan Sharma c Sippy b Sandhu	19	– c Pandit b Sandhu	18
†Salim Ahmed c Vengsarkar b Sandhu	13	– c Vengsarkar b Shastri	12
S. Talwar c Parkar b Mokashi	20	– not out	9
Sharanjit Singh run out	2	– st Pandit b Shastri	2
B 2, l-b 7, w 2, n-b 5	16	B 8, l-b 1, w 1, n-b 2	12

1/3 2/62 3/147 4/150 5/227   423   1/14 2/41 3/69 4/129 5/154   252
6/261 7/294 8/352 9/401   6/199 7/221 8/239 9/243

Bowling: *First Innings*—Sandhu 19-1-85-2; Kulkarni 22-3-93-1; Shastri 33-5-80-0; Mokashi 34.4-4-140-6; Sawant 7-1-16-0. *Second Innings*—Sandhu 11-1-38-1; Sippy 2-0-5-0; Kulkarni 1-0-2-0; Shastri 35.5-11-65-5; Mokashi 29-4-96-3; Rajput 3-0-12-0; Sawant 5-0-25-1.

Bombay

L. S. Rajput b Kapil Dev	3	– c Kapil Dev b Chetan	2
S. S. Hattangadi lbw b Kapil Dev	9	– c Chadda b Kapil Dev	28
A. Sippy c Sharanjit b Talwar	61	– lbw b Kapil Dev	3
D. B. Vengsarkar c Sharanjit b Kapil Dev	0	– lbw b Kapil Dev	14
G. A. Parkar c Salim b Kapil Dev	51	– b Talwar	39
*R. J. Shastri c Chetan b Talwar	65	– c Kapil Dev b Talwar	3
†C. S. Pandit c Salim b Talwar	57	– not out	99
B. S. Sandhu c Salim b Talwar	17	– c Kapil Dev b Deepak	6
R. R. Kulkarni c Deepak b Talwar	22	– c Chadda b Talwar	29
A. Sawant not out	1	– c Chadda b Sharanjit	1
K. D. Mokashi c Sharanjit b Talwar	0	– c sub b Deepak	0
B 2, l-b 2, n-b 6	10	L-b 1, n-b 4	5

1/9 2/22 3/22 4/127 5/137   296   1/11 2/18 3/39 4/59 5/116   229
6/236 7/260 8/279 9/296   6/120 7/130 8/184 9/196

Bowling: *First Innings*—Kapil Dev 15–4–47–4; Chetan 12–1–41–0; Talwar 29.3–1–103–6; Sharanjit 15–0–58–0; Deepak 13–1–43–0. *Second Innings*—Chetan 9–0–31–1; Kapil Dev 14–1–33–3; Talwar 21–2–94–3; Jolly 1–0–1–0; Deepak 7.3–0–23–2; Sharanjit 9–0–46–1.

Umpires: N. C. Sen and R. S. Rathore.

RAJASTHAN v DELHI

At Kota (T), March 15, 16, 17. Delhi won by 204 runs. Toss: Delhi.

Delhi

R. Lamba c A. Mudkavi b S. Shastri	12	– b S. Shastri	110
S. C. Khanna st Jain b S. Shastri	5	– c A. Mudkavi b P. Shastri	22
A. Sharma b S. Shastri	4	– b S. Shastri	9
K. Azad run out	47	– c A. Mudkavi b S. Shastri	118
M. Amarnath b Ratan	39	– c A. Mudkavi b S. Mudkavi	5
*Madan Lal c Vyas b Ratan	36	– c A. Mudkavi b S. Shastri	56
K. Bhaskar Pillai c and b Ratan	25	– st Jain b S. Shastri	7
M. Prabhakar st Jain b Ratan	14	– b Vyas	14
R. C. Shukla c A. Mudkavi b Ratan	4	– b S. Shastri	1
Maninder Singh c S. Mudkavi b Vyas	0	– not out	0
†Shashikant not out	0	– c Asawa b S. Shastri	1
B 2, l-b 4	6	B 14, l-b 1	15

1/16 2/17 3/30 4/108 5/110   192   1/107 2/132 3/177 4/194 5/314   358
6/153 7/175 8/179 9/180   6/326 7/351 8/353 9/357

Bowling: *First Innings*—Sunderam 4–1–11–0; Parminder 2–0–6–0; S. Shastri 18–4–46–3; Ratan 23.2–7–72–5; S. Mudkavi 2–0–17–0; Vyas 10–2–34–1. *Second Innings*—Parminder 9–1–17–0; S. Shastri 40.2–13–94–7; S. Mudkavi 23–4–72–1; Ratan 27–4–115–0; Vyas 8–0–22–1; P. Shastri 7–1–18–1; S. Mudkavi 1–0–5–0.

Rajasthan

Dalbir Singh c Sharma b Madan Lal	0	– c and b Azad	34
Parminder Singh st Shashikant b Maninder	7	– b Prabhakar	3
P. Shastri run out	1	– c Shashikant b Madan Lal	14
S. Mudkavi c Lamba b Azad	88	– b Maninder	23
A. Asawa c Shashikant b Azad	12	– b Azad	4
A. Mudkavi c Shukla b Maninder	5	– c Bhaskar Pillai b Maninder	38

S. Shastri c Prabhakar b Azad . . . . 7 – c Lamba b Maninder 52
*S. Vyas c Bhaskar Pillai b Maninder . . . . 0 – c Shashikant b Maninder 0
†D. Jain not out . . . . 37 – lbw b Azad 0
Ratan Singh c Prabhakar b Azad . . . . 3 – c Sharma b Azad 0
P. Sunderam run out . . . . 2 – not out 1
       B 4, l-b 3 7   B 4, w 2, n-b 2 8

1/0 2/5 3/14 4/43 5/58   169   1/13 2/20 3/65 4/76 5/94   177
6/94 7/94 8/130 9/149   6/148 7/148 8/155 9/155

Bowling: *First Innings*—Madan Lal 4-1-10-1; Prabhakar 1-1-0-0; Maninder 30-8-77-3; Azad 23.5-3-59-4; Sharma 3-1-7-0; Shukla 4-0-9-0. *Second Innings*—Prabhakar 5-0-13-1; Madan Lal 8-0-33-1; Maninder 26.1-10-57-4; Shukla 9-1-18-0; Azad 18-1-52-4.

Umpires: M. Y. Gupte and R. R. Kadam.

FINAL

DELHI v HARYANA

At Delhi (T), March 28, 29, 30, 31, April 1. Delhi won by an innings and 141 runs. Toss: Haryana.

Haryana

Ashwani Kumar c Shashikant b Azad . . . . 74 – c Shashikant b Maninder 12
Deepak Sharma c Lamba b Madan Lal . . . . 26 – b Maninder 36
Aman Kumar c Prabhakar b Maninder . . . . 32 – c Madan Lal b Prabhakar 7
A. Malhotra c Bhaskar Pillai b Azad . . . . 34 – b Maninder 98
R. Chadda c Sharma b Maninder . . . . 17 – st Shashikant b Maninder 2
R. Jolly c Shukla b Maninder . . . . 9 – lbw b Maninder 16
*Kapil Dev c Prabhakar b Azad . . . . 2 – b Maninder 25
†Salim Ahmed run out . . . . 55 – lbw b Maninder 1
Chetan Sharma c Shashikant b Prabhakar . . . . . 18 – c Azad b Maninder 0
S. Talwar b Prabhakar . . . . 0 – not out 0
Sharanjit Singh not out . . . . 4 – absent injured
       L-b 5, n-b 12 17   B 4, l-b 2, n-b 6 12

1/68 2/123 3/150 4/180 5/203   288   1/28 2/40 3/46 4/52 5/106   209
6/205 7/207 8/268 9/268   6/140 7/204 8/204 9/209

Bowling: *First Innings*—Madan Lal 14-1-55-1; Prabhakar 14.5-1-54-2; Maninder 41-15-66-3; Azad 32-9-90-3; Shukla 6-1-15-0; Sharma 2-1-3-0. *Second Innings*—Madan Lal 7-1-13-0; Prabhakar 10-2-25-1; Maninder 33.1-17-54-8; Azad 22-2-83-0; Shukla 6-0-20-0; Sharma 1-0-8-0.

Delhi

R. Lamba c Sharanjit b Chetan 25   R. C. Shukla lbw b Talwar 15
S. C. Khanna lbw b Chetan 5   Maninder Singh not out 14
M. Prabhakar run out 115   †Shashikant b Deepak 7
K. Azad c Aman Kumar b Talwar 107
M. Amarnath c Deepak b Talwar 194   B 5, l-b 7, w 5, n-b 13 30
K. Bhaskar Pillai c Salim b Kapil Dev . . 2
*Madan Lal b Talwar 14   1/9 2/47 3/230 4/299 5/311   638
A. Sharma c Deepak b Jolly 110   6/363 7/565 8/604 9/629

Bowling: Chetan 25-3-101-2; Kapil Dev 38-8-148-1; Talwar 58-4-194-4; Sharanjit 20.3-6-58-0; Deepak 31.2-3-90-1; Jolly 9-1-23-1; Malhotra 4-0-12-0.

Umpires: S. Banerjee and V. K. Ramaswamy.

RANJI TROPHY WINNERS

1934-35	Bombay	1960-61	Bombay
1935-36	Bombay	1961-62	Bombay
1936-37	Nawanagar	1962-63	Bombay
1937-38	Hyderabad	1963-64	Bombay
1938-39	Bengal	1964-65	Bombay
1939-40	Maharashtra	1965-66	Bombay
1940-41	Maharashtra	1966-67	Bombay
1941-42	Bombay	1967-68	Bombay
1942-43	Baroda	1968-69	Bombay
1943-44	Western India	1969-70	Bombay
1944-45	Bombay	1970-71	Bombay
1945-46	Holkar	1971-72	Bombay
1946-47	Baroda	1972-73	Bombay
1947-48	Holkar	1973-74	Karnataka
1948-49	Bombay	1974-75	Bombay
1949-50	Baroda	1975-76	Bombay
1950-51	Holkar	1976-77	Bombay
1951-52	Bombay	1977-78	Karnataka
1952-53	Holkar	1978-79	Delhi
1953-54	Bombay	1979-80	Delhi
1954-55	Madras	1980-81	Bombay
1955-56	Bombay	1981-82	Delhi
1956-57	Bombay	1982-83	Karnataka
1957-58	Baroda	1983-84	Bombay
1958-59	Bombay	1984-85	Bombay
1959-60	Bombay	1985-86	Delhi

IRANI TROPHY, 1985-86

At Nagpur (T), October 24, 25, 26, 27, 28. Drawn. Bombay were declared winners by virtue of their first-innings lead. Bombay* 472 (L. S. Rajput 50, R. J. Shastri 112, C. S. Pandit 123, R. R. Kulkarni 97; R. S. Ghai six for 130) and 400 (S. S. Hattangadi 85, D. B. Vengsarkar 83, S. M. Patil 78, R. J. Shastri 68); Rest of India 312 (M. Azharuddin 100 not out, A. Malhotra 52, Kapil Dev 70; R. J. Shastri four for 68) and 342 for seven (P. Shastri 44, M. Prabhakar 74, M. Azharuddin 49, K. Bhaskar Pillai 103 not out; K. D. Mokashi four for 101).

DULEEP TROPHY, 1985-86

At Vijayawada (T), October 5, 6, 7, 8. Abandoned. East Zone beat Central Zone on the toss of a coin, rain having prevented any play.

At Trivandrum (T), October 11, 12, 13, 14. Drawn. West Zone were declared winners by virtue of their first-innings lead. West Zone* 575 for seven dec. (L. S. Rajput 221, S. M. Gavaskar 72, D. B. Vengsarkar 110, R. J. Shastri 55, B. Mistry 58; Maninder Singh five for 145) and 52 for one; North Zone 519 (S. C. Khanna 52, N. S. Sidhu 47, M. Amarnath 136, A. Malhotra 116, Kapil Dev 45, Yashpal Sharma 76; R. J. Shastri eight for 145).

At Secunderabad (T), October 11, 12, 13, 14. Drawn. South Zone were declared winners by virtue of their first-innings lead. South Zone 293 for seven dec. (K. Srikkanth 49, K. A. Qayyum 60, S. M. H. Kirmani 61 not out); East Zone* 229 (H. Praharaj 43).

FINAL

SOUTH ZONE v WEST ZONE

At Bangalore (T), October 17, 18, 19, 20. West Zone won by nine wickets. Toss: South Zone.

South Zone

*K. Srikkanth c Patil b Sandhu	4	– c Rajput b Patel	120
C. S. Sureshkumar lbw b Patel	13	– b Kulkarni	8
M. Azharuddin c Gavaskar b Patel	6	– b Kulkarni	1
R. Madhavan b Shastri	3	– c Sandhu b Shastri	19
R. M. H. Binny run out	115	– lbw b Patel	15
R. D. Khanvilkar c More b Kulkarni	98	– run out	1
†S. M. H. Kirmani c and b Kulkarni	6	– lbw b Patel	22
L. Sivaramakrishnan lbw b Shastri	10	– run out	2
B. Arun c and b Patel	29	– b Patel	4
A. R. Bhat c Mistry b Patel	0	– c Gavaskar b Shastri	13
N. S. Yadav not out	7	– not out	19
B 3, l-b 3, n-b 8	14	B 1, l-b 6, n-b 5	12

1/4 2/29 3/36 4/36 5/242   305   1/40 2/43 3/79 4/116 5/118   236
6/259 7/259 8/281 9/305   6/177 7/184 8/198 9/205

Bowling: First Innings—Sandhu 12–2–45–1; Kulkarni 19–1–73–2; Shastri 38–16–66–2; Patel 33.5–8–86–4; Mistry 5–1–9–0; Gaekwad 3–0–9–0; Patil 4–0–11–0. *Second Innings*—Sandhu 7–1–27–0; Kulkarni 10–1–19–2; Shastri 25.2–5–75–2; Patel 36–3–95–4; Mistry 8–2–13–0.

West Zone

A. D. Gaekwad c Kirmani b Binny	6		
L. S. Rajput c Khanvilkar b Madhavan	25	– not out	31
S. M. Gavaskar lbw b Yadav	119	– c Sivaramakrishnan b Yadav	44
D. B. Vengsarkar c Azharuddin b Yadav	147		
S. M. Patil b Arun	65		
*R. J. Shastri not out	55		
B. Mistry c Khanvilkar b Yadav	7		
†K. S. More c Arun b Yadav	6	– not out	9
B. S. Sandhu c Arun b Bhat	6		
A. Patel c sub b Yadav	0		
R. R. Kulkarni lbw b Yadav	0		
B 4, l-b 7, n-b 6	17	B 4, n-b 1	5

1/15 2/84 3/226 4/352 5/398   453   1/78   (1 wkt) 89
6/414 7/429 8/444 9/445

Bowling: First Innings—Binny 10–3–15–1; Arun 20–2–78–1; Bhat 43–13–90–1; Khanvilkar 9–2–23–0; Sivaramakrishnan 24–3–92–0; Yadav 51–10–109–6; Madhavan 15–3–33–1; Srikkanth 1–0–2–0. *Second Innings*—Arun 3–1–9–0; Bhat 4–1–11–0; Sivaramakrishnan 3–0–26–0; Yadav 9–3–18–1; Madhavan 4–1–15–0; Azharuddin 1–0–2–0; Sureshkumar 1–0–4–0.

Umpires: P. G. Pandit and R. S. Rathore.

CRICKET IN PAKISTAN, 1985-86

By QAMAR AHMED and ABID ALI KAZI

A first-class season which occupied seven months saw a record 102 matches played in Pakistan in 1985-86. That figure could have been as high as 111 had not seven matches in the Quaid-e-Azam Trophy, one in the Patron's Trophy and one against the visiting Sri Lankan team been abandoned because of rain or cancelled for various reasons. The Sri Lankans toured Pakistan in October and November, playing three Test matches and four one-day internationals. Pakistan won both series: 2-0 and 4-0 respectively. In staging the second Test, Sialkot, the Punjab town famous for the manufacture of sports goods, became the 59th Test match venue. Sri Lanka's visit was followed by that of West Indies, who won by three matches to two over an evenly contested one-day series.

The opening first-class tournament of the season, the BCCP Patron's Trophy, was won by Karachi Whites for the third season in succession since its restoration in 1983-84 to first-class status. They took the trophy by virtue of their 20-run lead on the first innings over Lahore City Whites in a final which lost its first two days to rain. The tournament was contested by seventeen city and zonal teams divided into four groups. Rizwan-uz-Zaman, of Karachi Blues, scored the most runs (670 in four matches, including two hundreds), and there were double-hundreds from Masood Anwar of Rawalpindi and Ali Zia of Lahore City Whites. The leading wicket-taker was Iqbal Sikandar, of Karachi Whites, whose 29 wickets were taken at 9.48 apiece.

Under its revised format, only Karachi and Lahore, the breeding grounds of the Test players, and the top five departmental teams from the 1984-85 competition gained direct entry to the Quaid-e-Azam Trophy, the national championship. The other departmental teams were relegated to a non first-class qualifying tournament, from which the Agriculture Development Bank of Pakistan (ADBP) emerged to fill the sixth departmental place in the Quaid-e-Azam. Making up the complement of twelve sides were four zonal teams: Zone A comprising players from Hyderabad, Sukkur and Quetta; Zone B from Bahawalpur, Multan and Lahore; Zone C from Gujranwala, Sargodha and Faisalabad; and Zone D from Rawalpindi, Peshawar, Dera Ismail Khan and Hazara. The intention was to provide participation for players from all parts of the country, but in practice the new format was not a success because the zonal teams performed poorly.

The new arrangement did, however, benefit Karachi, who took advantage of the failure of teams like PIA, MCB and National Bank to qualify by acquiring players from them to enhance their own squad. The result was that, after a lapse of fifteen years, Karachi won the Quaid-e-Azam Trophy for the tenth time. With a spin-bowling trio of Ijaz Faqih, Iqbal Qasim and Iqbal Sikandar, and consistent batting from Rizwan, Moin-ul-Atiq, Asif Mujtaba and Zafar Ahmed, they won seven of their eleven matches without undue difficulty. The runners-up, Railways, also had a successful spin-bowling combination in Mohammad Nazir and Nadeem Ghauri.

The PACO Cup, which is contested by the top four teams from the Quaid-e-Azam, plus the winners of the Patron's Trophy, was won by the hosts, captained by Shahid Mahboob. With Karachi the winners of both earlier competitions, PACO had qualified as the fifth-placed team in the Quaid-e-Azam but were deserving champions, winning three of their four matches. The Wills Cup, Pakistan's leading one-day competition, was regained by PIA, who beat United Bank by 3 runs. It was their fourth victory in the five tournaments played since 1981.

The season was a good one for bowlers, with no fewer than thirteen taking 50 or more wickets. Karachi's Ijaz Faqih was the leading wicket-taker with 107 at an average of 16.06, which bettered Abdul Qadir's record for a season of 103, set in 1982-83. Sajjad Akbar of Lahore was the next highest with 96. There were three hat-tricks, all in the Quaid-e-Azam: two by Aamer Wasim, Sialkot and Zone C's left-arm spinner, against Lahore and Railways, and one by the Quetta and Zone A medium-pace bowler, Habib Baloch, against HBFC. Aamer Wasim's hat-trick dismissals against Lahore were all lbw, only the sixth such occurrence in first-class cricket. Nine batsmen passed 1,000 runs in the season, Ijaz Ahmed of Gujranwala and PACO leading the way with 1,476 at an average of 46.12, while Rizwan-uz-Zaman headed the averages with 1,198 runs at 92.15, including five centuries in eight matches. Anil Dalpat of Karachi was the leading wicket-keeper with 67 dismissals (39ct, 28st), closely followed by Ashraf Ali, of Lahore City and United Bank, with 62 (53ct, 9st).

The averages and scores which follow were submitted by Abid Ali Kazi.

FIRST-CLASS AVERAGES, 1985-86

BATTING

(Qualification: 600 runs, average 40)

	M	I	NO	R	HI	100s	Avge
Rizwan-uz-Zaman (*Karachi*)	8	15	2	1,198	175	5	92.15
Moin-ul-Atiq (*Karachi*)	12	17	5	972	203*	4	81.00
Nasir Valika (*United Bank*)	12	21	8	865	100*	1	66.53
Asif Mujtaba (*Karachi*)	16	22	6	869	131*	1	54.31
Arshad Pervez (*Sargodha/Habib Bank*)	14	24	3	1,113	119	3	53.00
Shahid Saeed (*Railways*)	14	27	2	1,210	136	3	48.40
Zafar Ahmed (*Karachi*)	15	23	5	864	117*	3	48.00
Ijaz Ahmed (*Gujranwala/PACO*)	18	33	1	1,476	182	5	46.12
Ali Zia (*Lahore City/United Bank*)	17	26	2	1,091	229*	3	45.45
Masood Anwar (*Rawalpindi/ADBP*)	14	22	2	903	202*	2	45.15
Saadat Ali (*Lahore City/United Bank*)	17	29	1	1,210	140	2	43.21
Shahid Anwar (*Lahore City/Lahore*)	18	33	3	1,279	163*	3	42.63
Tariq Javed (*Rawalpindi/Zone D*)	11	19	2	718	154*	2	42.23
Shakir Javed (*Faisalabad/Zone C*)	9	18	2	673	164	2	42.06
Aamer Malik (*Lahore City/ADBP/Lahore*)	14	24	1	938	122	4	40.78
Mansoor Rana (*Lahore City/ADBP/Lahore*)	19	31	3	1,124	140	2	40.14
Umar Rasheed (*PACO*)	14	25	4	841	112	1	40.04

* *Signifies not out.*

BOWLING

(Qualification: 50 wickets)

	O	M	R	W	BB	Avge
Mohammad Nazir (*Railways*)	783.2	274	1,269	88	6-41	14.42
Iqbal Sikandar (*Karachi*)	342.5	70	1,038	65	6-29	15.96
Ijaz Faqih (*Karachi*)	743	160	1,719	107	6-20	16.06
Iqbal Qasim (*Karachi*)	453.3	117	1,024	62	7-39	16.51
Sajjad Akbar (*Lahore City/Lahore*)	687.1	168	1,626	96	7-40	16.93
Mohammad Riaz (*Lahore City/Zone D*)	402	89	1,049	61	8-66	17.19
Saleem Jaffer (*Karachi/United Bank*)	452	85	1,539	80	6-20	19.23
Nadeem Ghauri (*Railways*)	727.5	198	1,678	87	7-38	19.28
Akram Raza (*Lahore City/Lahore*)	494.2	112	1,179	58	7-82	20.32
Ghaffar Kazmi (*Lahore City/ADBP*)	512.5	79	1,490	65	7-55	22.92
Mohammad Altaf (*Bahawalpur/Zone B*)	397.1	62	1,217	53	6-63	22.96
Masood Anwar (*PACO*)	535.4	122	1,328	55	6-55	24.14
Shahid Mahboob (*Quetta/PACO*)	592.2	66	2,088	72	7-63	29.00

Note: Matches taken into account are the BCCP Patron's Trophy, Quaid-e-Azam Trophy, PACO Cup and three Test matches against the Sri Lankan touring team in Pakistan.

BCCP PATRON'S TROPHY, 1985-86

Note: First innings closed at 75 overs.

Group A

At Hyderabad, November 8, 9, 10. The ground being unavailable, the match between Sukkur and Quetta was postponed. When it was not played at a later date, the points were shared. *Sukkur 5 pts, Quetta 5 pts.*

At National Stadium, Karachi, November 14, 15. Karachi Whites won by an innings and 126 runs. Sukkur 117 (Jalal-ud-Din five for 32) and 79 (Iqbal Sikandar six for 29, Ijaz Faqih four for 14); Karachi Whites 322 for five (Moin-ul-Atiq 177 not out, Asif Mujtaba 50). *Karachi Whites 18 pts, Sukkur 3 pts.*

At National Stadium, Karachi, November 19, 20. Karachi Whites won by an innings and 50 runs. Quetta 115 (Iqbal Qasim four for 15) and 124 (Shahid Mahboob 76; Iqbal Sikandar six for 36); Karachi Whites 289 for four (Asif Mujtaba 131 not out, Ijaz Faqih 112). *Karachi Whites 18 pts, Quetta 2 pts.*

At Hyderabad, November 19, 20, 21. Hyderabad won by 103 runs. Hyderabad 282 (Nadeem Jamal 149, Rasheed Ghanchi 52; Mohammad Younus five for 87) and 172 (Ghulam Ali 46; Javed Ali four for 59); Sukkur 209 for eight (Israr Ahmed 108) and 142 (Arif Amin 44; Anwar Iqbal six for 43). *Hyderabad 18 pts, Sukkur 6 pts.*

At National Stadium, Karachi, November 24, 25, 26. Drawn. Quetta 326 for six (Rashid Raza 56, Imran Khan 66, Raees Ahmed 102 not out) and 218 for five dec. (Tehsin Ahmed 102 not out); Hyderabad 185 (Ghulam Ali 64; Raees Ahmed five for 54) and 264 for seven (Nadeem Jamal 120, Afzal Chaudhri 46). *Quetta 10 pts, Hyderabad 4 pts.*

At Hyderabad, December 3, 4. Karachi Whites won by an innings and 70 runs. Hyderabad 128 and 100 (Iqbal Sikandar six for 35); Karachi Whites 298 for six (Moin-ul-Atiq 41, Asif Mujtaba 77, Ijaz Faqih 89). *Karachi Whites 18 pts, Hyderabad 3 pts.*

Karachi Whites 54 pts, Hyderabad 25 pts, Quetta 17 pts, Sukkur 14 pts. Karachi Whites qualified for the semi-finals.

Group B

At Bahawalpur, November 8, 9, 10. Karachi Blues won by 133 runs. Karachi Blues 207 (Rizwan-uz-Zaman 46, Nasir Shah 46; Mohammad Altaf five for 61) and 243 for eight dec. (Rizwan-uz-Zaman 80, Nasir Shah 54; Mohammad Altaf four for 52); Bahawalpur 158 (Rizwan-uz-Zaman five for 16) and 159 (Jahangir Alvi 41; Rizwan-uz-Zaman five for 27). *Karachi Blues 16 pts, Bahawalpur 5 pts.*

At Multan, November 8, 9, 10. Lahore City Blues won by eight wickets. Multan 229 (Rizwan Sattar 62, Manzoor Elahi 43; Sajjad Akbar five for 71, Ghaffar Kazmi four for 47) and 161 (Sajid Waheed 46; Sajjad Akbar four for 26, Ghaffar Kazmi four for 63); Lahore City Blues 282 for nine (Tanvir Ahmed 109, Nadeem Younus 45; Shahid Butt four for 68) and 111 for two (Tanvir Ahmed 50). *Lahore City Blues 18 pts, Multan 7 pts.*

At Bahawalpur, November 13, 14, 15. Lahore City Blues won by nine wickets. Bahawalpur 118 (Mohammad Altaf 41) and 185 (Abdur Rahim 61, Rashid Shera 63; Sajjad Akbar four for 42); Lahore City Blues 238 (Saadat Ali 56; Mohammad Altaf six for 63) and 66 for one. *Lahore City Blues 17 pts, Bahawalpur 4 pts.*

At Montgomery Biscuit Factory Ground, Sahiwal, November 13, 14, 15. Karachi Blues won by 165 runs. Karachi Blues 223 (Nadeem Moosa 71, Rashid Khan 67 not out; Manzoor Elahi four for 52) and 299 for eight dec. (Rizwan-uz-Zaman 81, Shaukat Mirza 41; Zulfiqar Ali four for 85); Multan 164 (Javed Ilyas 52; Azeem Hafeez four for 63) and 193 (Zahoor Elahi 50, Manzoor Elahi 41; Azeem Hafeez five for 90). *Karachi Blues 16 pts, Multan 5 pts.*

At Bahawalpur, November 18, 19, 20. Drawn. Multan 139 (Mohammad Zahid five for 27) and 389 for seven dec. (Zahoor Elahi 71, Manzoor Elahi 129, Rizwan Sattar 109; Mohammad Zahid five for 131); Bahawalpur 226 (Qasim Shera 89) and 225 for six (Jahangir Alvi 50, Qasim Shera 88). *Bahawalpur 9 pts, Multan 4 pts.*

At Gaddafi Stadium, Lahore, November 18, 19, 20. Drawn. Karachi Blues 291 for three (Rizwan-uz-Zaman 113 not out, Zahid Ahmed 125 not out) and 295 for four (Rizwan-uz-Zaman 175, Nasir Shah 65 not out); Lahore City Blues 242 (Ashraf Ali 65, Shafiq Ahmed 72, Mohammad Riaz 49; Rashid Khan five for 59). *Karachi Blues 10 pts, Lahore City Blues 5 pts.*

Karachi Blues 42 pts, Lahore City Blues 40 pts, Bahawalpur 18 pts, Multan 16 pts. Karachi Blues qualified for the semi-finals.

Group C

At Gujranwala, October 29, 30. Faisalabad won by an innings and 94 runs. Gujranwala 76 (Tanvir Shaukat six for 47) and 84; Faisalabad 254 for nine (Mohammad Ashraf 83, Wasim Hyder 42 not out; Tahir Mahmood five for 62). *Faisalabad 18 pts, Gujranwala 4 pts.*

At LCCA Ground, Lahore, October 29, 30, 31. Drawn. Lahore City Whites 260 for six (Mohammad Ishaq 119, Shahid Anwar 41) and 195 for two (Shahid Anwar 56, Mansoor Rana 71 not out); Sargodha 212 (Arshad Pervez 107 not out; Ghayyur Qureshi five for 41). *Lahore City Whites 10 pts, Sargodha 5 pts.*

At Sargodha, November 3, 5, 6. Sargodha won by six wickets. Lahore Division 176 (Aziz-ur-Rehman seven for 67) and 170 (Sarfraz Azeem 43, Altaf Shah 55); Sargodha 133 (Shahid Tanvir six for 44) and 214 for four (Tasnim Abidi 40, Arshad Pervez 61 not out). *Sargodha 14 pts, Lahore Division 5 pts.*

At LCCA Ground, Lahore, November 3, 5, 6. Lahore City Whites won by nine wickets. Gujranwala 225 (Ijaz Ahmed 52, Tahir Mahmood 49, Farhat Masood 59) and 215 (Tahir Mahmood 81; Ghayyur Qureshi six for 44) and 123 for one (Shahid Anwar 54 not out). *Lahore City Whites 18 pts, Gujranwala 7 pts.*

At Faisalabad, November 9, 10, 11. Faisalabad won by 89 runs. Faisalabad 137 (Shakir Javed 43; Shahid Tanvir four for 34) and 349 for nine dec. (Shakir Javed 164, Anwar Awais 75); Lahore Division 228 for eight (Maqsood Raza 58, Shahid Tanvir 68; Humayun Farkhan five for 90) and 169 (Sarfraz Azeem 77 not out). *Faisalabad 14 pts, Lahore Division 7 pts.*

At Sargodha, November 9, 10, 11. Drawn. Gujranwala 120 (Aziz-ur-Rehman four for 30) and 378 for eight dec. (Ijaz Ahmed 131, Farhat Masood 80, Nadeem Ahsan 50 not out); Sargodha 127 (Arshad Pervez 50; Farhat Masood five for 43) and 145 for four (Talat Imtiaz 49 not out, Azhar Sultan 61). *Sargodha 6 pts, Gujranwala 4 pts.*

At Sialkot, November 14, 15. Gujranwala won by an innings and 41 runs. Lahore Division 136 (Farhat Masood six for 37) and 108 (Farhat Masood four for 19); Gujranwala 285 for eight (Sajjad Bashir 123, Mohammad Ayub 43, Nadeem Ahsan 47; Saif-ur-Rehman five for 78). *Gujranwala 18 pts, Lahore Division 4 pts.*

At LCCA Ground, Lahore, November 14, 15, 16. Drawn. Faisalabad 203 (Mohammad Ashraf 51; Ali Zia eight for 60) and 267 for six (Anwar Awais 57, Shakir Javed 55); Lahore City Whites 383 for four (Shahid Anwar 76, Ali Zia 229 not out, Naved Anjum 43). *Lahore City Whites 10 pts, Faisalabad 4 pts.*

At LCCA Ground, Lahore, November 19, 20. Lahore City Whites won by an innings and 64 runs. Lahore City Whites 375 for five dec. (Shahid Anwar 46, Mansoor Rana 140, Ali Zia 45, Naved Anjum 101 not out); Lahore Division 131 (Maqsood Raza 57; Naeem Taj seven for 42) and 180 (Shahid Tanvir 100; Tahir Shah five for 33). *Lahore City Whites 18 pts, Lahore Division 3 pts.*

At Sargodha, November 19, 20, 21. Faisalabad won by five wickets. Sargodha 161 (Tanvir Afzal four for 49) and 221 (Mohammad Nawaz 47, Arshad Pervez 56; Tanvir Afzal five for 92); Faisalabad 280 for nine (Mohammad Ashraf 49, Anwar Awais 61, Shakir Javed 79, Mushtaq Sohail 42) and 106 for five (Aziz-ur-Rehman four for 26). *Faisalabad 18 pts, Sargodha 5 pts.*

Lahore City Whites 56 pts, Faisalabad 54 pts, Gujranwala 33 pts, Sargodha 30 pts, Lahore Division 19 pts. Lahore City Whites qualified for the semi-finals.

Group D

At Pindi Club Ground, Rawalpindi, October 29, 30. Rawalpindi won by an innings and 175 runs. Rawalpindi 354 for two (Masood Anwar 202 not out, Raja Afaq 116 not out); Hazara 114 and 65 (Sabih Azhar six for 29). *Rawalpindi 18 pts, Hazara 1 pt.*

At Shahi Bagh Stadium, Peshawar, October 29, 30. Peshawar won by an innings and 114 runs. Dera Ismail Khan 87 and 84 (Farrukh Zaman four for 15); Peshawar 285 for two (Aamir Mirza 82, Ibrar-ul-Haq 138). *Peshawar 18 pts, Dera Ismail Khan 1 pt.*

At Pindi Club Ground, Rawalpindi, November 3, 5. Rawalpindi won by an innings and 46 runs. Dera Ismail Khan 131 (Sajid Hussain seven for 65) and 107 (Sabih Azhar four for 30, Sajid Hussain four for 22); Rawalpindi 284 for three (Masood Anwar 78, Azmat Jalil 62, Tariq Javed 80, Raja Afaq 49 not out). *Rawalpindi 18 pts, Dera Ismail Khan 2 pts.*

At Shahi Bagh Stadium, Peshawar, November 3, 5. Peshawar won by an innings and 78 runs. Peshawar 302 for four (Aamir Mirza 72, Abdur Rahim 55, Ibrar-ul-Haq 112 not out); Hazara 103 (Khawar Nadeem 53; Mohammad Saleem four for 37, Khurshid Akhtar four for 16) and 121 (Farrukh Zaman six for 32). *Peshawar 18 pts, Hazara 2 pts.*

At Wah Cantt, November 9, 10, 11. Drawn. Dera Ismail Khan 214 (Sardar Badshah 65); Hazara 221 for eight (Rizwan Bokhari 70, Wajid Elahi 46). *Hazara 8 pts, Dera Ismail Khan 6 pts.*

At Shahi Bagh Stadium, Peshawar, November 9, 10, 11. Drawn. Peshawar 135 (Aamir Mirza 55; Raja Afaq four for 33) and 131 (Pervez Chaughtai 43); Rawalpindi 112 (Nasir Javed 44; Khurshid Akhtar four for 38). *Peshawar 6 pts, Rawalpindi 4 pts.*

Peshawar 42 pts, Rawalpindi 40 pts, Hazara 11 pts, Dera Ismail Khan 9 pts. Peshawar qualified for the semi-finals.

Semi-finals

At LCCA Ground, Lahore, November 23, 24, 25, 26. Lahore City Whites won by 266 runs. Lahore City Whites 454 for eight (Tahir Shah 90, Mansoor Rana 98, Wasim Raja 129; Zahid Ahmed five for 94) and 239 (Ali Zia 87); Karachi Blues 263 for nine (Rizwan-uz-Zaman 93, Shaukat Mirza 75; Akram Raza five for 90) and 164 (Rizwan-uz-Zaman 72; Tahir Shah four for 26).

At National Stadium, Karachi, December 9, 10, 11. Karachi Whites won by ten wickets. Peshawar 171 (Aamer Mirza 41; Ijaz Faqih five for 55) and 202 (Farrukh Zaman 54); Karachi Whites 315 for three (Moin-ul-Atiq 66, Sajid Ali 82, Mansoor Akhtar 101 not out, Sajid Riaz 48 not out) and 59 for no wkt.

Final

At Gaddafi Stadium, Lahore, December 15, 16, 17, 18, 19. Drawn. Karachi Whites declared winners by virtue of their first-innings lead. Karachi Whites 182 (Mansoor Akhtar 59; Ali Zia four for 37) and 68 for two; Lahore City Whites 162 (Aamer Sohail 49; Iqbal Qasim four for 26).

QUAID-E-AZAM TROPHY, 1985-86

	Matches	Won	Lost	Drawn	Abandoned	Pts
Karachi	11	7	1	3	0	154
Railways	11	6	0	4	1	147
Lahore	11	5	1	3	2	131
United Bank	11	5	3	3	0	127
PACO	11	4	3	3	1	115
ADBP	11	4	3	4	0	112
HBFC	11	3	0	6	2	110
Zone D	11	3	4	2	2	105
Habib Bank	11	2	3	5	1	93
Zone B	11	3	7	0	1	91
Zone C	11	1	7	1	2	84
Zone A	11	0	11	0	0	34

Note: First innings closed at 85 overs.

At National Stadium, Karachi, January 8, 9, 10. Karachi won by an innings and 5 runs. Zone A 127 (Ijaz Faqih four for 24) and 242 (Nadeem Jamal 46, Raj Hans 71; Hasan Askari four for 46, Ijaz Faqih five for 67); Karachi 374 for one (Basit Ali 41, Moin-ul-Atiq 203 not out, Zafar Ahmed 113 not out). *Karachi 18 pts, Zone A 1 pt.*

At Bahawalpur, January 8, 9, 10. Zone B won by five wickets. Habib Bank 317 (Arshad Pervez 119, Extras 42; Bilal Rana five for 100, Mohammad Altaf five for 85) and 108 (Shakeel Shah six for 51, Bilal Rana four for 30); Zone B 201 (Rizwan Sattar 66; Abdur Raqeeb five for 69) and 226 for five (Farooq Shera 95). *Zone B 16 pts, Habib Bank 8 pts.*

At Pindi Club Ground, Rawalpindi, January 8, 9, 10. Railways won by 236 runs. Railways 258 for eight (Shahid Saeed 41, Abdul Sami 65, Hammad Butt 47; Sajid Hussain five for 72) and 235 (Talat Mirza 44, Mohammad Nazir 41; Sajid Hussain five for 94); Zone D 170 (Mohammad Arif, sen. 55 not out; Nadeem Ghauri four for 93, Mohammad Nazir six for 41) and 87 (Nadeem Ghauri five for 28, Mohammad Nazir five for 32). *Railways 18 pts, Zone D 5 pts.*

At Hyderabad, January 8, 9, 10, 11. Drawn. HBFC 227 for nine (Ijaz Ahmed 54; Mian Fayyaz five for 70) and 266 for nine dec. (Tariq Alam 50, Raees Ahmed 67; Mian Fayyaz four for 69); PACO 247 (Raees Ahmed four for 99) and 195 for five (Ijaz Ahmed 113 not out). *PACO 9 pts, HBFC 7 pts.*

At LCCA Ground, Lahore, January 8, 9, 10, 11. Lahore won by 208 runs. Lahore 305 for seven (Wasim Ali 63, Sajjad Akbar 81, Akram Raza 53, Haafiz Shahid 47 not out) and 243 (Shahid Anwar 100, Sajjad Akbar 45; Aamer Wasim four for 48, including an all-lbw hat-trick); Zone C 229 (Mohammad Nawaz 41, Saadat Gul 65; Haroon Rashid five for 78) and 111 (Mohammad Ashraf 43). *Lahore 18 pts, Zone C 7 pts.*

At Hyderabad, January 13, 14, 15. PACO won by an innings and 46 runs. Zone A 194 (Ghulam Ali 44; Shahid Mahboob five for 79, Mian Fayyaz four for 50) and 138 (Mian Fayyaz six for 37); PACO 378 for nine (Siddiq Patni 50, Ijaz Ahmed 182, Tahir Mahmood 42 not out). *PACO 18 pts, Zone A 5 pts.*

At Sialkot, January 13, 14, 15. United Bank won by an innings and 56 runs. Zone C 103 (Saleem Jaffer six for 18, Tauseef Ahmed four for 18) and 127 (Saleem Jaffer six for 50); United Bank 286 (Saadat Ali 84, Ali Zia 41, Naved Anjum 63; Tanvir Afzal five for 38). *United Bank 18 pts, Zone C 4 pts.*

At National Stadium, Karachi, January 13, 14, 15, 16. Drawn. Karachi 252 for six (Basit Ali 101, Ijaz Faqih 59) and 292 for five dec. (Rizwan-uz-Zaman 149); HBFC 214 for nine (Sagheer Abbas 116 not out; Ijaz Faqih five for 72) and 137 for eight (Iqbal Sikandar five for 70). *Karachi 10 pts, HBFC 5 pts.*

At LCCA Ground, Lahore, January 13, 14, 15, 16. Lahore won by seven wickets. ADBP 329 for eight (Tanvir Ahmed 84, Atif Rauf 71, Ghaffar Kazmi 65) and 192 (Manzoor Elahi 50; Afzaal Butt four for 39); Lahore 267 (Shahid Anwar 56, Aamer Sohail 49, Ameer Akbar 60, Zulqarnain 44; Raja Afaq four for 64, Ghaffar Kazmi five for 92) and 255 for three (Shahid Anwar 89, Aamer Sohail 45, Ramiz Raja 59). *Lahore 18 pts, ADBP 8 pts.*

At Bahawalpur, January 18, 19, 20. HBFC won by four wickets. Zone B 216 (Farooq Shera 63; Kazim Mehdi five for 46) and 161 (Zahoor Elahi 58, Farooq Shera 43; Kazim Mehdi five for 49); HBFC 225 (Tahir Rasheed 55, Ijaz Ahmed 42, Rafat Alam 53; Bilal Rana five for 79) and 155 for six. *HBFC 17 pts, Zone B 6 pts.*

At National Stadium, Karachi, January 18, 19, 20, 21. Drawn. Habib Bank 166 (Sultan Rana 53; Shahid Mahboob seven for 84) and 492 (Agha Zahid 147, Arshad Pervez 53, Tehsin Javed 48, Salim Malik 67, Anwar Miandad 66; Mian Fayyaz four for 145); PACO 377 for six (Ijaz Ahmed 102, Umar Rasheed 112, Moin Mumtaz 58 not out) and 79 for two (Ijaz Ahmed 54). *PACO 10 pts, Habib Bank 4 pts.*

At Faisalabad, January 18, 19, 20, 21. Drawn. Railways 302 for nine (Shahid Saeed 129 not out, Hammad Butt 47, Musleh-ud-Din 81; Wasim Hyder four for 45) and 323 (Hammad Butt 43, Shahid Saeed 45, Mohammad Nazir 46, Shahid Pervez 88; Aamer Wasim six for 121, including a hat-trick); Zone C 269 (Mohammad Ashraf 42, Shakir Javed 60, Wasim Hyder 61; Nadeem Ghauri four for 104) and 208 for nine (Mohammad Ashraf 57, Mohammad Nawaz 65; Mohammad Nazir five for 58). *Railways 10 pts, Zone C 8 pts.*

At LCCA Ground, Lahore, January 18, 19, 20, 21. United Bank won by 194 runs. United Bank 188 (Shafiq Ahmed 46; Afzaal Butt four for 68) and 379 for nine dec. (Saadat Ali 106, Shafiq Ahmed 109, Naved Anjum 51, Ashraf Ali 57 not out); Lahore 226 for six (Akram Raza 76, Ameer Akbar 47) and 147 (Ameer Akbar 45). *United Bank 14 pts, Lahore 7 pts.*

At Pindi Club Ground, Rawalpindi, January 18, 19, 20, 21. Drawn. ADBP 177 (Ghaffar Kazmi 58, Maqsood Kundi 74 not out; Sajid Hussain four for 51) and 390 for nine dec. (Aamer Malik 113, Mansoor Rana 50, Atif Rauf 50; Nasir Javed five for 73); Zone D 233 (Mohammad Riaz 70; Ghaffar Kazmi five for 99, Raja Afaq five for 80) and 276 for nine (Tariq Javed 50, Mohammad Riaz 78, Shahid Javed 45; Khatib Rizwan five for 104). *Zone D 9 pts, ADBP 5 pts.*

At National Stadium, Karachi, January 23, 24, 25. Karachi won by seven wickets. PACO 111 (Ijaz Ahmed 44; Ijaz Faqih six for 20) and 260 (Khalid Alvi 64, Ijaz Ahmed 42, Umar Rasheed 72; Iqbal Qasim four for 85, Ijaz Faqih four for 73); Karachi 297 for two (Rizwan-uz-Zaman 140, Moin-ul-Atiq 111 not out) and 79 for three. *Karachi 18 pts, PACO 1 pt.*

At Hyderabad, January 23, 24, 25. Habib Bank won by an innings and 89 runs. Zone A 92 (Abdur Raqeeb six for 23) and 128 (Raj Hans 56; Abdur Raqeeb five for 49, Anwar Miandad four for 22); Habib Bank 309 for four (Agha Zahid 60, Arshad Pervez 90, Anwar Miandad 62). *Habib Bank 18 pts, Zone A 2 pts.*

At Faisalabad, January 23, 24, 25, 26. ADBP won by eight wickets. Zone C 320 for five (Bilal Ahmed 47, Mansoor Khan 109 not out, Shakir Javed 55) and 141 (Zakir Khan four for 60, Khatib Rizwan four for 21); ADBP 331 for eight (Masood Anwar 40, Mansoor Rana 50, Ghaffar Kazmi 67) and 132 for two (Masood Anwar 72, Mansoor Rana 43 not out). *ADBP 17 pts, Zone C 8 pts.*

At Pindi Club Ground, Rawalpindi, January 23, 24, 25, 26. Abandoned without a ball bowled owing to rain. *Zone D 9 pts, Lahore 9 pts.*

At National Stadium, Karachi, January 28, 29. Karachi won by an innings and 67 runs. Zone B 117 (Iqbal Qasim seven for 39) and 102 (Ijaz Faqih five for 53, Iqbal Sikandar five for 20); Karachi 286 for three (Rizwan-uz-Zaman 154 not out, Basit Ali 70, Zafar Ahmed 51 not out). *Karachi 18 pts, Zone B 2 pts.*

At Bahawalpur, January 28, 29. HBFC won by an innings and 113 runs. Zone A 80 (Kazim Mehdi six for 13) and 65 (Rafat Alam five for 25); HBFC 258 (Saleem Taj 43, Mohammad Javed 49, Tahir Rasheed 81 not out; Habib Baloch five for 74, including a hat-trick). *HBFC 18 pts, Zone A 4 pts.*

At Gaddafi Stadium, Lahore, January 28, 29, 30, 31. Drawn. ADBP 227 (Aamer Malik 45, Mansoor Rana 82, Manzoor Elahi 65; Sikander Bakht five for 49) and 357 for seven dec. (Tanvir Ahmed 50, Mansoor Rana 72, Atif Rauf 102 not out); United Bank 260 (Saadat Ali 82, Ashraf Ali 52) and 60 for one. *United Bank 10 pts, ADBP 7 pts.*

At LCCA Ground, Lahore, January 28, 29, 30, 31. Drawn. Railways 267 for nine (Shahid Saeed 49, Babar Altaf 51, Mohammad Nazir 49) and 218 (Talat Mirza 93); Lahore 180 for nine (Sajjad Akbar 41; Mohammad Nazir five for 65) and 267 for nine (Shahid Anwar 51, Aamer Sohail 45, Akram Raza 60; Mohammad Nazir six for 96). *Railways 10 pts, Lahore 5 pts.*

At Shahi Bagh Stadium, Peshawar, January 28, 29, 30, 31. Zone D won by 213 runs. Zone D 215 (Tariq Javed 85, Aamir Mirza 44; R. Ghulam Abbas seven for 42) and 302 (Aamir Mirza 82, Mohammad Saleem 44, Shahid Javed 51; Aamer Wasim five for 118, Tanvir Afzal four for 88); Zone C 183 (Wasim Hyder 40; Mohammad Riaz five for 58) and 121 (Mohammad Riaz six for 56). *Zone D 16 pts, Zone C 5 pts.*

At Bahawalpur, February 2, 3. Zone B won by nine wickets. Zone A 111 (Qasim Shera six for 50, Mohammad Altaf four for 32) and 140 (Nadeem Jamal 43; Qasim Shera six for 54); Zone B 193 (Shahid Tanvir 48, Qasim Shera 41, Bilal Rana 41) and 62 for one. *Zone B 15 pts, Zone A 4 pts.*

At National Stadium, Karachi, February 2, 3, 4, 5. Drawn. Karachi 92 (Salim Malik five for 19) and 429 (Rizwan-uz-Zaman 66, Asif Mujtaba 99, Zafar Ahmed 117 not out, Anil Dalpat 61, Extras 46; Abdul Qadir four for 178); Habib Bank 203 (Zaheer Ahmed 42; Ijaz Faqih four for 81) and 286 for eight (Arshad Pervez 59, Salim Malik 71, Abdul Qadir 46 not out; Ijaz Faqih six for 106). *Habib Bank 8 pts, Karachi 4 pts.*

At Faisalabad, February 2, 3, 4, 5. Railways won by 242 runs. Railways 301 for seven (Talat Mirza 50, Shahid Saeed 95, Abid Sarwar 64; Khatib Rizwan four for 83) and 218 (Abid Sarwar 54; Ghaffar Kazmi four for 52); ADBP 155 (Aamer Malik 76; Mohammad Nazir four for 17) and 122 (Mohammad Nazir four for 22). *Railways 18 pts, ADBP 5 pts.*

At Pindi Club Ground, Rawalpindi, February 2, 3, 4, 5. United Bank won by four wickets. Zone D 206 (Tariq Javed 43, Mohammad Riaz 67, Shahid Javed 41; Saleem Jaffer five for 52) and 160 (Tariq Javed 40, Mohammad Arif, sen. 40; Tauseef Ahmed six for 59); United Bank 199 (Nasir Valika 77 not out; Mohammad Riaz eight for 66) and 169 for six (Saadat Ali 80). *United Bank 15 pts, Zone D 6 pts.*

At Bahawalpur, February 7, 8, 9, 10. PACO won by two wickets. Zone B 332 for five (Zahoor Elahi 74, Farooq Shera 123 not out) and 142 (Shahid Mahboob seven for 63); PACO 321 for nine (Khalid Alvi 40, Siddiq Patni 57, Ijaz Ahmed 48, Umar Rasheed 77) and 157 for eight (Tahir Mahmood 61 not out; Shakeel Shah five for 64). *PACO 17 pts, Zone B 8 pts.*

At Faisalabad, February 7, 8, 9, 10. Drawn. Railways 228 (Hammad Butt 69, Shahid Pervez 57; Sikander Bakht five for 41) and 157 for four (Abdul Sami 48, Talat Mirza 48); United Bank 237 (Saadat Ali 72, Nasir Valika 51; Nadeem Ghauri five for 85). *United Bank 9 pts, Railways 7 pts.*

At LCCA Ground, Lahore, February 7, 8, 9, 10. Drawn. HBFC 266 for five (Munir-ul-Haq 134 not out) and 153 for one (Noor-ul-Qamar 70, Saleem Taj 56 not out); Habib Bank 282 for six (Tehsin Javed 46, Anwar Miandad 67, Sultan Rana 54, Azhar Khan 77 not out). *Habib Bank 9 pts, HBFC 7 pts.*

At Bahawalpur, February 13, 14, 15. United Bank won by an innings and 276 runs. United Bank 360 for five (Saadat Ali 60, Shafiq Ahmed 124, Nasir Valika 100 not out; Habib Baloch four for 141); Zone A 49 (Saleem Jaffer six for 20) and 35 (Shahid Aziz five for 6). *United Bank 18 pts, Zone A 3 pts.*

At National Stadium, Karachi, February 13, 14, 15, 16. Drawn. Railways 240 (Abdul Sami 68; Iqbal Sikandar four for 39) and 317 (Shahid Saeed 61, Abid Sarwar 142; Ijaz Faqih six for 79); Karachi 282 for six (Moin-ul-Atiq 54, Zafar Ahmed 52, Asif Mujtaba 49, Zafar Ali 54, Ijaz Faqih 53 not out) and 123 for five. *Karachi 10 pts, Railways 6 pts.*

At Sialkot, February 13, 14, 15, 16. Abandoned without a ball bowled owing to rain. *Zone C 9 pts, HBFC 9 pts.*

At LCCA Ground, Lahore, February 13, 14, 15, 16. Abandoned without a ball bowled owing to rain. *Lahore 9 pts, Habib Bank 9 pts.*

At Pindi Club Ground, Rawalpindi, February 13, 14, 15, 16. Abandoned without a ball bowled owing to rain. *Zone D 9 pts, PACO 9 pts.*

At Hyderabad, February 19, 20. Railways won by an innings and 202 runs. Railways 374 for nine (Abid Sarwar 122, Hammad Butt 56, Mohammad Nazir 41, Shahid Pervez 59 not out); Zone A 91 (Nadeem Ghauri five for 42, Mohammad Nazir four for 24) and 81 (Nadeem Ghauri seven for 38). *Railways 18 pts, Zone A 4 pts.*

At National Stadium, Karachi, February 19, 20, 21. Karachi won by an innings and 14 runs. ADBP 200 (Masood Anwar 82; Iqbal Qasim four for 78, Iqbal Sikandar four for 54) and 180 (Mansoor Rana 47; Ijaz Faqih five for 59); Karachi 394 for two (Moin-ul-Atiq 161, Sajid Ali 157 not out). *Karachi 18 pts, ADBP 3 pts.*

At Bahawalpur, February 19, 20, 21, 22. United Bank won by 227 runs. United Bank 283 (Ali Zia 133, Naved Anjum 42; Mohammad Altaf four for 50) and 269 for eight dec. (Shafiq Ahmed 76, Ashraf Ali 53 not out; Qasim Shera five for 90); Zone B 158 (Qasim Shera 58; Sikander Bakht four for 43) and 167 (Abdur Rahim 42; Shahid Aziz six for 44). *United Bank 18 pts, Zone B 5 pts.*

At LCCA Ground, Lahore, February 19, 20, 21, 22. Drawn. Lahore 301 for four (Shahid Anwar 163 not out, Wasim Ali 50 not out) and 72 for one; PACO 279 for seven (Ijaz Ahmed 46, Moin Mumtaz 51, Tahir Mahmood 48; Akram Raza seven for 82). *Lahore 10 pts, PACO 6 pts.*

At Pindi Club Ground, Rawalpindi, February 19, 20, 21, 22. Drawn. Zone D 161 (Ali Ahmed four for 68, Raees Ahmed four for 31) and 254 for seven dec. (Mujahid Hameed 89, Shahid Javed 59 not out); HBFC 147 (Tahir Rasheed 41, Tariq Alam 43; Mohammad Riaz six for 64) and 99 for five. *Zone D 7 pts, HBFC 4 pts.*

At Faisalabad, February 19, 20, 21, 22. Habib Bank won by seven wickets. Zone C 197 (Anwar Awais 53) and 180 (Saadat Gul 47 not out; Waheed Niazi five for 73); Habib Bank 267 for nine (Arshad Pervez 96; Wasim Hyder four for 83, Naeem Khan four for 45) and 111 for three. *Habib Bank 18 pts, Zone C 5 pts.*

At Hyderabad, February 25, 26, 27. ADBP won by ten wickets. Zone A 116 (Ghaffar Kazmi seven for 55) and 234 (Iqbal Malik 53, Sajid Ali 43); ADBP 345 for three (Aamer Malik 105, Masood Anwar 166, Mansoor Rana 60 not out) and 9 for no wkt. *ADBP 18 pts, Zone A 2 pts.*

At Bahawalpur, February 25, 26, 27. Railways won by nine wickets. Zone B 139 (Shahid Tanvir 71; Mohammad Nazir four for 46) and 232 (Bilal Rana 117; Sibtain Hyder six for 38); Railways 319 (Abdul Sami 100, Shahid Saeed 70, Extras 47; Mohammad Altaf four for 87) and 53 for one. *Railways 18 pts, Zone B 4 pts.*

At Pindi Club Ground, Rawalpindi, February 25, 26, 27. Zone D won by eight wickets. Habib Bank 166 (Mohammad Riaz seven for 74) and 160 (Arshad Pervez 60 not out; Mohammad Riaz eight for 70); Zone D 277 for four (Tariq Javed 154 not out) and 50 for two. *Zone D 18 pts, Habib Bank 3 pts.*

At National Stadium, Karachi, February 25, 26, 27, 28. Karachi won by six wickets. United Bank 241 for nine (Shafiq Ahmed 72, Naved Anjum 47, Shahid Butt 40 not out; Ijaz Faqih five for 93) and 293 (Shafiq Ahmed 45, Ali Zia 59, Ashraf Ali 62 not out; Rashid Khan four for 54); Karachi 268 for nine (Sajid Khan 46, Asif Mujtaba 69 not out; Ali Zia four for 62) and 269 for four (Sajid Khan 73, Asif Mujtaba 51, Ijaz Faqih 79 not out). *Karachi 18 pts, United Bank 7 pts.*

At Faisalabad, February 25, 26, 27, 28. PACO won by two wickets. Zone C 268 for six (Bilal Ahmed 40, Shakir Javed 105 not out, Saadat Gul 50 not out) and 305 (Mohammad Ashraf 108, Wasim Hyder 54 not out; Mohammad Anwar five for 73); PACO 289 for nine (Moin Mumtaz 50, Yahya Toor 59; Aamer Wasim four for 94) and 286 for eight (Siddiq Patni 62, Moin Mumtaz 71, Tahir Mahmood 52). *PACO 17 pts, Zone C 8 pts.*

At LCCA Ground, Lahore, February 25, 26, 27, 28. Drawn. HBFC 253 (Saleem Taj 52, Ijaz Ahmed 42, Shaukat Mirza 45; Sajjad Akbar six for 67) and 341 (Munir-ul-Haq 64, Shaukat Mirza 43, Tahir Rasheed 75, Tariq Alam 107; Akram Raza four for 81); Lahore 251 for nine (Ameer Akbar 72; Kazim Mehdi five for 82) and 228 for one (Shahid Anwar 101 not out, Aamer Sohail 86). *HBFC 10 pts, Lahore 8 pts.*

At National Stadium, Karachi, March 3, 4, 5. Karachi won by an innings and 25 runs. Zone C 163 (Sajid Bashir 52; Ijaz Faqih four for 41) and 183 (Mansoor Khan 42, Sajid Bashir 69; Ijaz Faqih four for 59, Iqbal Qasim five for 48); Karachi 371 for four (Sajid Ali 113, Zafar Ahmed 104 not out, Asif Mujtaba 44, Ijaz Faqih 45 not out). *Karachi 18 pts, Zone C 3 pts.*

At Sargodha, March 3, 4, 5. Railways won by 192 runs. Railways 303 (Talat Mirza 51, Babar Altaf 80, Ajmal Hussain 60; Abdur Raqeeb four for 69) and 193 (Abdur Raqeeb five for 80); Habib Bank 169 (Nadeem Ghauri four for 75, Mohammad Nazir five for 51) and 135 (Arshad Pervez 57; Nadeem Ghauri five for 72, Mohammad Nazir five for 34). *Railways 18 pts, Habib Bank 5 pts.*

At LCCA Ground, Lahore, March 3, 4, 5. Lahore won by an innings and 102 runs. Zone A 147 (Sajjad Akbar four for 29, Asim Butt four for 21) and 184 (Mansoor Khan 71; Afzaal Butt four for 73); Lahore 433 (Shahid Anwar 74, Aamer Sohail 101, Tahir Shah 44, Mohammad Jamil 101, Sajjad Akbar 68; Afzal Chaudhri five for 118). *Lahore 18 pts, Zone A 4 pts.*

At Bahawalpur, March 3, 4, 5, 6. Zone B won by 16 runs. Zone B 82 (Mohammad Riaz six for 32) and 446 (Abdur Rahim 132, Farooq Shera 135, Bilal Rana 73; Mohammad Riaz four for 165); Zone D 252 for eight (Tariq Javed 111 not out) and 260 (Mohammad Arif, jun. 50, Shahid Javed 54). *Zone B 14 pts, Zone D 8 pts.*

At Faisalabad, March 3, 4, 5, 6. PACO won by three wickets. United Bank 316 for six (Saadat Ali 140, Ali Zia 44, Nasir Valika 76 not out) and 194 (Nasir Valika 66, Ashraf Ali 72 not out; Shahid Mahboob four for 46); PACO 277 for seven (Umar Rasheed 51, Yahya Toor 61 not out, Nadeem Ahsan 55 not out; Shahid Butt four for 91) and 237 for seven (Umar Rasheed 92, Moin Mumtaz 45; Shahid Butt four for 63). *PACO 17 pts, United Bank 8 pts.*

At Gaddafi Stadium, Lahore, March 3, 4, 5, 6. Drawn. HBFC 272 for six (Tahir Rasheed 102 not out, Tariq Alam 100) and 226 (Shaukat Mirza 74, Tariq Alam 42 not out; Ghaffar Kazmi four for 57); ADBP 237 (Manzoor Elahi 63; Ali Ahmed seven for 70) and 162 for six (Aamer Malik 68 not out; Ali Ahmed four for 78). *HBFC 10 pts, ADBP 6 pts.*

At Gymkhana Ground, Karachi, March 8, 9, 10. Karachi won by six wickets. Zone D 110 (Ijaz Faqih six for 49) and 243 (Shahid Javed 65, Mujahid Hameed 64; Iqbal Qasim six for 73); Karachi 262 (Zafar Ahmed 62, Sajid Riaz 46 not out; Shakeel Ahmed four for 43) and 94 for four (Asif Mujtaba 41 not out). *Karachi 18 pts, Zone D 4 pts.*

At Gaddafi Stadium, Lahore, March 9, 10, 11. HBFC won by 30 runs. HBFC 100 (Ehteshamud-Din four for 56, Sikander Bakht five for 40) and 208 (Mohammad Javed 88; Ehtesham-ud-Din four for 68); United Bank 72 (Mohinder Kumar five for 36) and 206 (Shahid Butt 44 not out; Ali Ahmed seven for 80). *HBFC 14 pts, United Bank 4 pts.*

At Faisalabad, March 9, 10, 11, 12. Railways won by 165 runs. Railways 194 (Shahid Saeed 52) and 313 for nine dec. (Shahid Saeed 136); PACO 214 for seven (Yahya Toor 61; Nadeem Ghauri five for 103) and 128 (Tahir Mahmood 53; Nadeem Ghauri seven for 69). *Railways 15 pts, PACO 6 pts.*

At Sialkot, March 9, 10, 11, 12. Zone C won by an innings and 25 runs. Zone A 156 (Shahid Nazir four for 31) and 261 (Hameed-ul-Haq 81, Raj Hans 52; Tariq Mahmood eight for 69); Zone C 442 for eight (Khawar Malik 59, Abdul Waheed 100, Sajid Bashir 109, Wasim Hyder 56). *Zone C 18 pts, Zone A 5 pts.*

At LCCA Ground, Lahore, March 9, 10, 11, 12. Lahore won by 47 runs. Lahore 165 (Asim Butt 44) and 309 (Tahir Shah 55, Akram Raza 59, Sajjad Akbar 53 not out); Zone B 292 for nine (Abdur Rahim 86, Farooq Shera 100 not out; Sajjad Akbar four for 80) and 135 (Bilal Rana 51 not out; Tahir Shah five for 47). *Lahore 15 pts, Zone B 8 pts.*

At Bahawalpur, March 15, 16, 17, 18. ADBP won by six wickets. PACO 189 (Moin Mumtaz 50) and 180 (Tahir Mahmood 58; Raja Afaq four for 40); ADBP 155 (Mian Fayyaz five for 42) and 216 for four (Tanvir Ahmed 66, Ghaffar Kazmi 96 not out). *ADBP 15 pts, PACO 5 pts.*

At Sargodha, March 15, 16, 17, 18. Abandoned without a ball bowled owing to rain. *Railways 9 pts, HBFC 9 pts.*

At Shahi Bagh Stadium, Peshawar, March 15, 16, 17, 18. Zone D awarded a walkover against Zone A who failed to arrive. *Zone D 14 pts.*

At Gaddafi Stadium, Lahore, March 17, 18, 19, 20. Drawn. United Bank 117 (Liaqat Ali seven for 42) and 383 (Mansoor Akhtar 65, Saadat Ali 51, Shafiq Ahmed 41, Nasir Valika 75 not out, Ashraf Ali 40, Extras 51; Agha Zahid four for 65); Habib Bank 108 (Sikander Bakht six for 54) and 86 for three. *United Bank 6 pts, Habib Bank 4 pts.*

At LCCA Ground, Lahore, March 17, 18, 19, 20. Lahore won by 82 runs. Lahore 134 and 155 (Ijaz Faqih four for 44, Asif Mujtaba four for 39); Karachi 110 (Akram Raza six for 29) and 97 (Sajjad Akbar seven for 40). *Lahore 14 pts, Karachi 4 pts.*

At Bahawalpur, March 21, 22, 23. ADBP won by an innings and 5 runs. Zone B 116 (Ghaffar Kazmi four for 11) and 206 (Tariq Ismail 41; Ghaffar Kazmi six for 75); ADBP 327 (Manzoor Elahi 115; Qasim Shera five for 105). *ADBP 18 pts, Zone B 4 pts.*

At Sialkot, March 27, 28, 29, 30. The ground being unavailable, the match between Zone C and Zone B was postponed. When it was not played at a later date, the points were shared. *Zone C 9 pts, Zone B 9 pts.*

At National Stadium, Karachi, March 27, 28, 29, 30. Drawn. Habib Bank 249 for nine (Arshad Pervez 101; Raja Afaq five for 88) and 315 for eight (Anwar Miandad 88, Zaheer Ahmed 55; Raja Afaq five for 125); ADBP 252 for nine (Masood Anwar 51, Atif Rauf 55). *ADBP 10 pts, Habib Bank 7 pts.*

QUAID-E-AZAM TROPHY WINNERS

1953-54	Bahawalpur	1972-73	Railways
1954-55	Karachi	1973-74	Railways
1956-57	Punjab	1974-75	Punjab A
1957-58	Bahawalpur	1975-76	National Bank
1958-59	Karachi	1976-77	United Bank
1959-60	Karachi	1977-78	Habib Bank
1961-62	Karachi Blues	1978-79	National Bank
1962-63	Karachi A	1979-80	PIA
1963-64	Karachi Blues	1980-81	United Bank
1964-65	Karachi Blues	1981-82	National Bank
1966-67	Karachi	1982-83	United Bank
1968-69	Lahore	1983-84	National Bank
1969-70	PIA	1984-85	United Bank
1970-71	Karachi Blues	1985-86	Karachi

PACO CUP, 1985-86

	Played	Won	Lost	Drawn	Points
PACO	4	3	0	1	59
Lahore	4	2	0	2	50
United Bank	4	2	2	0	50
Railways	4	0	3	1	22
Karachi	4	0	2	2	20

Lahore took second position by virtue of their superior overall run-rate.

Note: First innings closed at 85 overs.

At Gaddafi Stadium, Lahore, March 22, 23, 24. United Bank won by an innings and 4 runs. Railways 132 (Hammad Butt 41; Saleem Jaffer six for 64) and 148 (Saleem Jaffer five for 69); United Bank 284 (Nasir Valika 47, Ashraf Ali 63; Sibtain Hyder four for 107). *United Bank 18 pts, Railways 4 pts.*

At LCCA Ground, Lahore, March 22, 23, 24, 25. Drawn. Karachi 193 (Sajid Khan 93; Sajjad Akbar seven for 50) and 309 (Sajid Ali 86, Basit Ali 98, Zafar Ali 51); Lahore 287 for eight (Shahid Anwar 40, Mohammad Jamil 96, Wasim Ali 60; Ijaz Faqih six for 105) and 144 for five. *Lahore 10 pts, Karachi 5 pts.*

At LCCA Ground, Lahore, March 27, 28, 29. Lahore won by 7 runs. Lahore 187 (Shahid Anwar 60, Akram Raza 45; Nadeem Ghauri five for 92, Mohammad Nazir five for 47) and 141 (Ameer Akbar 46; Nadeem Ghauri four for 54, Mohammad Nazir six for 62); Railways 169 (Sajjad Akbar six for 53) and 152 (Hammad Butt 66 not out; Akram Raza four for 38). *Lahore 15 pts, Railways 5 pts.*

At Gaddafi Stadium, Lahore, March 27, 28, 29, 30. United Bank won by 66 runs. United Bank 285 (Mansoor Akhtar 80, Naved Anjum 59, Waheed Mirza 42; Jalal-ud-Din five for 80; Barkatullah four for 59) and 276 (Shafiq Ahmed 42, Nasir Valika 60 not out); Karachi 216 (Asif Mujtaba 79, Zafar Ahmed 50; Naved Anjum four for 42) and 279 (Basit Ali 81, Zafar Ahmed 49, Anil Dalpat 56; Saleem Jaffer four for 61). *United Bank 18 pts, Karachi 6 pts.*

At Gaddafi Stadium, Lahore, April 1, 2, 3. PACO won by eight wickets. PACO 299 (Ijaz Ahmed 117, Umar Rasheed 43, Tahir Mahmood 57; Nadeem Moosa four for 34) and 92 for two (Ijaz Ahmed 40); Karachi 148 (Zafar Ahmed 43; Shahid Mahboob seven for 74) and 239 (Sajid Ali 42, Zafar Ahmed 48; Masood Anwar six for 55). *PACO 18 pts, Karachi 4 pts.*

At LCCA Ground, Lahore, April 1, 2, 3, 4. Lahore won by four wickets. United Bank 241 (Mansoor Akhtar 44, Naved Anjum 43; Akram Raza four for 67, Sajjad Akbar five for 76) and 363 for eight dec. (Saadat Ali 85, Shafiq Ahmed 43, Ali Zia 89, Nasir Valika 57 not out; Akram Raza five for 104); Lahore 250 for six (Tahir Shah 86, Aamer Malik 74) and 355 for six (Ameer Akbar 82, Aamer Malik 101, Mansoor Rana 46). *Lahore 18 pts, United Bank 6 pts.*

At Gaddafi Stadium, Lahore, April 6, 7, 8, 9. Drawn. Railways 230 (Talat Mirza 44, Shahid Saeed 81; Haseeb-ul-Hasan five for 75) and 274 (Shahid Saeed 109, Abdul Sami 45; Raza Khan five for 76); Karachi 155 and 196 for nine (Haseeb-ul-Hasan 46; Sibtain Hyder four for 52). *Railways 9 pts, Karachi 5 pts.*

At LCCA Ground, Lahore, April 6, 7, 8, 9. PACO won by three wickets. United Bank 274 for six (Mansoor Akhtar 78, Saadat Ali 69, Nasir Valika 46 not out; Masood Anwar six for 97) and 270 (Saadat Ali 48, Shafiq Ahmed 72, Ali Zia 51; Masood Anwar four for 73); PACO 283 (Umar Rasheed 82, Moin Mumtaz 52; Shahid Aziz five for 112) and 262 for seven (Ijaz Ahmed 93, Tahir Mahmood 57, Shahid Mahboob 49; Shahid Aziz six for 101). *PACO 17 pts, United Bank 8 pts.*

At Gaddafi Stadium, Lahore, April 11, 12, 13, 14. PACO won by seven wickets. Railways 139 (Shahid Mahboob four for 72, Masood Anwar four for 19) and 255 (Shahid Saeed 90, Hammad Butt 46); PACO 282 for eight (Ijaz Ahmed 45, Shahid Mahboob 100 not out); Mohammad Nazir four for 102) and 114 for three (Khalid Alvi 46). *PACO 18 pts, Railways 4 pts.*

At Gaddafi Stadium, Lahore, April 16, 17, 18, 19. Drawn. Lahore 221 for nine (Aamer Malik 41, Sajjad Akbar 40; Shahid Mahboob six for 104) and 323 for five dec. (Shahid Anwar 44, Aamer Malik 122, Mansoor Rana 116; Masood Anwar four for 112); PACO 218 for six dec. (Siddiq Patni 42, Ijaz Ahmed 53, Umar Rasheed 61 not out, Moin Mumtaz 43; Sajjad Akbar four for 75) and 17 for one. *Lahore 7 pts, PACO 6 pts.*

†WILLS CUP, 1985-86

Semi-finals

At National Stadium, Karachi, September 20. United Bank won by five wickets. Lahore 175 for six (45 overs) (Ghaffar Kazmi 52); United Bank 179 for five (43.3 overs) (Mudassar Nazar 44, Ali Zia 51 not out).

At Pindi Club Ground, Rawalpindi, September 20. PIA won by eight wickets. Habib Bank 120 (34.2 overs) (Azeem Hafeez four for 22); PIA 123 for two (32.4 overs) (Rizwan-uz-Zaman 40, Asif Mohammad 44 not out).

Final

At Gaddafi Stadium, Lahore, September 27. PIA won by 3 runs. PIA 257 for three (45 overs) (Shoaib Mohammad 111 not out, Zaheer Abbas 65, Asif Mujtaba 55 not out); United Bank 254 for nine (45 overs) (Saadat Ali 83, Shafiq Ahmed 46).

CRICKET IN SRI LANKA, 1985-86

By GERRY VAIDYASEKERA

This was a memorable season for Sri Lanka. It began with their historic win over India in September, their first Test match victory, which also resulted in their first series success. Later in the season, four countries visited the island, all at about the same time. The extended tour by England B, which led to the discovery of such promising players as Asanka Gurusinha, Roshan Mahanama, Kausik Amalean and Kosala Kuruppuarachchi, overlapped the arrival of the Pakistanis, who played three Tests and three one-day internationals before taking part in the Asia Cup and Triangular invitation tournaments. Bangladesh played in the Asia Cup, while New Zealand, on their way to Sharjah for the Austral-Asia Cup, completed the trio for the Triangular Tournament.

The domestic season started with the inter-district competition for the J.R. Jayawardene Challenge Trophy. The preliminary rounds were played over three days, with the semi-finals and final being of four days' duration for the first time. In one semi-final, Roger Wijesuriya, a slow left-arm spin bowler, performed the hat-trick. In a repeat of the previous year's final, Gampaha beat Matara-Hambantota Districts to win the trophy for the second year in succession. Other personal feats of distinction occurred in a three-day national trial game when Kapila Jayasooriya (67 not out of 182) and Ashley de Silva (108 not out of 218) carried their bats in the first innings of their respective XIs.

Sinhalese Sports Club, captained by Sidath Wettimuny, and Nondescripts, led by Ranjan Madugalle, were joint-winners of the Lakspray Trophy, the premier cricket competition. Arjuna Ranatunga won the award for the best batsman, Ravi Ratnayeke for the best bowler, and Saman Kumara for the best wicket-keeper. Sinha Sports Club, of Ambalangoda, playing in the tournament for the first time, won the Pure Beverages Trophy, and Sinhalese Sports Club, captained by Ranatunga, took the Bristol Trophy. Colombo South Schools were the All-Island Schools under-seventeen zonal champions.

Off the field of play, though not away from it, there were several notable events. In February, Ketterama Stadium, situated in Colombo and one of the most modern cricket grounds in Asia, was opened by the Prime Minister, Mr R. Premadasa, in the presence of the visiting England cricketers. In the limited-overs match with which the stadium was inaugurated, Sri Lanka defeated England B by four wickets. In another official ceremony, Sri Lanka's president, Mr J. R. Jayawardene, opened the new headquarters of the Board of Control, built at a cost of Rs7.5 million. And the future of cricket in Sri Lanka received a further boost when the government approved the establishment of a Cricketers' Benevolent Fund for the welfare of players. Finally, Mrs Owen Herath created history when she was elected president of the Puttalam District Cricket Association, the first woman to hold such office in a district association.

CRICKET IN ZIMBABWE, 1985-86

By ALWYN PICHANICK

Although the unfortunate cancellation of the tour by the England B team removed from the fixture list one of the season's main attractions, Zimbabwe nevertheless were hosts to two first-class touring teams in 1985-86 as part of their build-up to the 1986 ICC Trophy. Both were from Australia.

The first visitors, in September and October, were the Young Australians, a powerful combination which included four players with Test match experience and three who were to become Test cricketers during the course of the season. Over the three weeks they were in Zimbabwe, the Young Australians played two first-class and five one-day matches against Zimbabwe, plus one-day games against Zimbabwe Districts and Zimbabwe B. The first three-day match was drawn, but the touring team won the second as a result of fine fast bowling by Dave Gilbert. In the one-day encounters, however, Zimbabwe stretched their unbeaten record to eighteen by winning the series 5-0, and improved it to nineteen when they beat New South Wales in March.

New South Wales, the Sheffield Shield winners, were making a hastily organised tour which replaced the England B tour, and they followed an itinerary almost identical to that of the Young Australians. They, too, drew the first and won the second first-class game, but they also won the limited-overs series by three matches to two, so ending Zimbabwe's unbeaten run in one-day cricket. The Zimbabwe selectors used the one-day and three-day matches against New South Wales to provide as much cricket as possible for the candidates for the Zimbabwe team to visit England for the ICC Trophy, and to some extent this affected the strength of the teams which opposed the visitors.

During the season Graeme Hick, who scored two first-class hundreds against the Young Australians, and Kevin Curran demonstrated how much they had benefited from playing county cricket in England. Both were unavailable for Zimbabwe in the ICC competition, but happily, Zimbabwe revealed their depth of playing strength by retaining the Associate Members' Trophy, and for the second time in succession gained entry to the World Cup.

David Houghton captained the team outstandingly, and despite his additional responsibilities he batted and kept wicket well. Andy Pycroft, the former captain, continued to bat with distinction, and Grant Paterson, Andrew Waller and Gary Wallace all made substantial contributions. On the visit to England, Robin Brown shouldered great responsibility and proved that he remained an excellent opening batsman.

The attack was built around John Traicos and Peter Rawson, and the progress of the young fast bowler, Eddo Brandes, was especially pleasing. Ian Butchart and Ali Shah, the all-rounders, made an important contribution, with Butchart in particular playing some exciting innings at critical times in the one-day games against the Young Australians and New South Wales. His bowling in the ICC Trophy final at Lord's was vital to the team's success. There were also a number of young players on the fringe of national selection making good progress, and two of them, Chris Cox, a left-arm spinner, and David Brain, a left-arm medium-pacer, were included in the squad chosen to defend the ICC Trophy.

ZIMBABWE v YOUNG AUSTRALIANS

At Harare, September 20, 21, 23. Drawn. Toss: Zimbabwe.

Young Australians

B. A. Courtice c Butchart b Rawson	2	– (2) lbw b Rawson	29
*R. B. Kerr c Butchart b Curran	6	– (1) lbw b Curran	26
D. M. Jones c and b Butchart	20	– b Traicos	70
P. S. Clifford c Houghton b Rawson	9	– b Traicos	29
G. A. Bishop c Houghton b Rawson	32	– b Curran	15
S. L. Saunders b Butchart	19	– lbw b Rawson	29
A. I. C. Dodemaide c Hick b Rawson	41	– not out	36
†M. G. Dimattina lbw b Traicos	5	– lbw b Rawson	14
B. A. Reid c Houghton b Rawson	14	– b Traicos	0
D. R. Gilbert c Hick b Curran	14	– c Shah b Curran	4
R. L. Brown not out	4	– not out	0
L-b 5, w 2, n-b 2	9	B 9, l-b 7, w 2, n-b 2	20

1/4 2/18 3/36 4/41 5/78   175   1/43 2/72 3/136 4/173   (9 wkts) 272
6/98 7/112 8/137 9/164   5/175 6/210 7/241
                                                    8/242 9/248

Bowling: *First Innings*—Rawson 27.5–11–56–5; Curran 19–6–58–2; Butchart 15–3–45–2; Traicos 9–3–11–1. *Second Innings*—Rawson 33–9–65–3; Curran 23–7–61–3; Butchart 8–2–29–0; Traicos 36–12–78–3; Shah 8–4–19–0; Hick 5–3–4–0.

Zimbabwe

R. D. Brown c and b Brown	22
G. A. Paterson b Gilbert	8
A. H. Shah c Gilbert b Brown	3
*A. J. Pycroft c Saunders b Gilbert	37
G. A. Hick lbw b Brown	127
†D. L. Houghton c Kerr b Reid	35
A. C. Waller lbw b Reid	0
K. M. Curran not out	49
I. P. Butchart c Dodemaide b Reid	38
P. W. E. Rawson c Kerr b Reid	1
A. J. Traicos c Dimattina b Dodemaide	7
B 6, l-b 4, w 2, n-b 6	18

1/13 2/16 3/69 4/115 5/208   345
6/210 7/253 8/322 9/328

Bowling: Gilbert 30–3–97–2; Brown 22.2–4–90–3; Reid 26–5–91–4; Dodemaide 22.5–6–53–1; Saunders 2.4–1–4–0.

Umpires: D. B. Arnott and I. D. Robinson.

†At Harare, September 22. Zimbabwe won by three wickets. Young Australians 234 for seven (50 overs) (R. B. Kerr 63, D. M. Jones 62); Zimbabwe 238 for seven (47.4 overs) (G. A. Paterson 73).

†At Bulawayo, September 28. Zimbabwe won by one wicket. Young Australians 220 for eight (50 overs) (D. M. Jones 55, G. A. Bishop 43, S. R. Waugh 42; I. P. Butchart five for 56); Zimbabwe 221 for nine (49.5 overs) (P. W. E. Rawson 45 not out; A. I. C. Dodemaide four for 28).

†At Bulawayo, September 29. Zimbabwe won by eight wickets. Young Australians 113 (43.5 overs); Zimbabwe 114 for two (29.1 overs) (G. A. Paterson 65 not out).

ZIMBABWE v YOUNG AUSTRALIANS

At Harare, October 1, 2, 3. Young Australians won by 65 runs. Toss: Zimbabwe.

Young Australians

*R. B. Kerr b Curran	3	– (2) c and b Butchart	68
B. A. Courtice c Rawson b Traicos	29	– (1) c Houghton b Butchart	59
M. R. J. Veletta c Houghton b Curran	4		
D. M. Jones c Pycroft b Butchart	59	– (3) not out	43
G. A. Bishop c Shah b Butchart	10	– (4) not out	41
S. R. Waugh c Houghton b Curran	30		
S. L. Saunders c Paterson b Rawson	53		
A. I. C. Dodemaide run out	0		
†M. G. Dimattina not out	64		
L-b 4, n-b 3	7	L-b 3, n-b 3	6

1/7 2/22 3/84 4/103   (8 wkts dec.) 259   1/119 2/140   (2 wkts dec.) 217
5/109 6/147 7/147 8/259

B. A. Reid and D. R. Gilbert did not bat.

Bowling: *First Innings*—Rawson 21.5-5-57-1; Curran 24-6-69-3; Traicos 28-9-62-1; Butchart 12-1-43-2; Hick 9-1-24-0. *Second Innings*—Rawson 8-1-23-0; Curran 15-1-57-0; Traicos 17-1-71-0; Butchart 13-1-63-2.

Zimbabwe

R. D. Brown c Veletta b Gilbert	13	– c Dimattina b Gilbert	0
G. A. Paterson c Courtice b Gilbert	0	– c Dimattina b Gilbert	12
A. J. Traicos c Kerr b Dodemaide	6	– (11) c Saunders b Waugh	0
G. A. Hick c Bishop b Gilbert	7	– (3) c Veletta b Gilbert	154
*A. J. Pycroft lbw b Gilbert	18	– (4) b Reid	1
†D. L. Houghton b Gilbert	2	– (5) c Jones b Gilbert	37
K. M. Curran b Gilbert	3	– c Dimattina b Gilbert	17
A. H. Shah c Veletta b Gilbert	0	– c Veletta b Reid	22
I. P. Butchart c Dimattina b Dodemaide	32	– b Gilbert	1
A. C. Waller run out	27	– (6) b Waugh	9
P. W. E. Rawson not out	6	– (10) not out	20
B 1, l-b 7, n-b 4	12	L-b 6, n-b 6	12

1/1 2/19 3/35 4/35 5/37   126   1/0 2/33 3/37 4/135 5/178   285
6/55 7/55 8/60 9/108   6/235 7/240 8/247 9/284

Bowling: *First Innings*—Gilbert 18-7-43-7; Reid 7-4-20-0; Dodemaide 12-3-27-2; Waugh 6.5-0-28-0. *Second Innings*—Gilbert 20-4-75-6; Reid 25-3-66-2; Dodemaide 19-3-63-0; Saunders 2-0-18-0; Waugh 14-2-57-2.

Umpires: D. B. Arnott and K. Kanjee.

†At Harare, October 5. Zimbabwe won by 108 runs. Zimbabwe 217 for nine (50 overs) (G. A. Paterson 46, D. L. Houghton 40); Young Australians 109 (40.2 overs) (A. I. C. Dodemaide 45).

†At Harare, October 6. Zimbabwe won by 23 runs. Zimbabwe 208 for nine (50 overs) (A. J. Pycroft 68, A. C. Waller 44); Young Australians 185 for eight (50 overs) (M. G. Dimattina 59 not out, R. L. Brown 40 not out; K. M. Curran four for 38).

†At Harare, March 22. Zimbabwe won by four wickets. New South Wales 232 for seven (50 overs) (P. S. Clifford 55); Zimbabwe 234 for six (49 overs) (D. L. Houghton 68, A. C. Waller 57 not out).

†At Harare, March 23. New South Wales won by two wickets. Zimbabwe 220 (49.4 overs) (A. J. Pycroft 52, P. W. E. Rawson 53; M. E. Waugh four for 52); New South Wales 224 for eight (49.2 overs) (M. A. Taylor 50, T. Bayliss 57).

ZIMBABWE v NEW SOUTH WALES

At Harare, March 28, 29, 31. Drawn. Toss: Zimbabwe.

Zimbabwe

R. D. Brown c Clifford b P. L. Taylor	33	– c O'Neill b Whitney	5
A. H. Shah c Dyer b Waugh	0	– b Whitney	10
G. A. Hick c Dyer b Done	40	– c Waugh b Whitney	4
A. J. Pycroft c Holland b P. L. Taylor	90	– c Whitney b P. L. Taylor	61
*†D. L. Houghton c M. A. Taylor b Holland	19	– c Clifford b P. L. Taylor	66
A. C. Waller b Holland	30	– c Small b P. L. Taylor	0
G. C. Wallace c P. L. Taylor b Holland	22	– not out	6
P. W. E. Rawson not out	48	– c Waugh b Whitney	9
I. P. Butchart b Holland	1	– c Holland b P. L. Taylor	18
E. A. Brandes b Done	7		
A. J. Traicos b Whitney	0		
B 2, l-b 4, w 2, n-b 9	17	B 4, l-b 3, n-b 3	10

1/4 2/65 3/100 4/174 5/198   307   1/16 2/20 3/27   (8 wkts dec.) 189
6/229 7/254 8/268 9/290   4/136 5/151 6/154
                                                   7/165 8/189

Bowling: *First Innings*—Whitney 20.5–6–40–1; Waugh 14–4–40–1; Holland 28–8–95–4; Done 18–2–74–2; P. L. Taylor 19–6–52–2. *Second Innings*—Whitney 13–2–37–3; Waugh 12–4–29–0; Holland 12–2–38–0; P. L. Taylor 13–4–39–5; Done 2–0–21–0; O'Neill 5–0–18–0.

New South Wales

S. M. Small c Butchart b Rawson	12	– c Houghton b Rawson	25
M. A. Taylor c Hick b Rawson	23	– c Rawson b Brandes	3
P. S. Clifford c Pycroft b Rawson	18	– c Houghton b Traicos	44
R. J. Bower c Traicos b Rawson	4	– lbw b Rawson	11
M. D. O'Neill c Hick b Butchart	19	– c Houghton b Butchart	15
M. E. Waugh c Houghton b Brandes	23	– not out	51
*†G. C. Dyer c Hick b Rawson	85	– not out	8
P. L. Taylor c and b Brandes	12		
R. P. Done not out	10		
L-b 6, n-b 2	8	B 5, l-b 3, n-b 1	9

1/16 2/49 3/58 4/83 5/83   (8 wkts dec.) 214   1/8 2/42 3/56   (5 wkts) 166
6/116 7/144 8/214   4/87 5/136

R. G. Holland and M. R. Whitney did not bat.

Bowling: *First Innings*—Rawson 22.5–1–92–5; Brandes 14–3–58–2; Butchart 9–3–23–1; Traicos 9–2–21–0; Shah 4–1–14–0. *Second Innings*—Rawson 10–3–23–2; Brandes 7–1–36–1; Traicos 18–4–40–1; Hick 4–1–15–0; Butchart 7–0–27–1; Shah 6–2–13–0; Brown 1–0–4–0.

Umpires: R. Jackson and K. Kanjee.

†At Harare, March 30. Zimbabwe won by two wickets. New South Wales 224 for nine (50 overs) (M. A. Taylor 73); Zimbabwe 226 for eight (49.4 overs) (G. A. Paterson 44, G. A. Hick 77, A. C. Waller 52).

†At Bulawayo, April 2. New South Wales won by 61 runs. New South Wales 186 (49.5 overs) (M. E. Waugh 61); Zimbabwe 125 (35.5 overs) (R. P. Done five for 21).

ZIMBABWE v NEW SOUTH WALES

At Harare, April 4, 5, 7. New South Wales won by 70 runs. Toss: Zimbabwe.

New South Wales

S. M. Small c Meman b Jarvis	9	– c Waller b Brandes	12
M. A. Taylor c Houghton b Rawson	2	– c Brown b Brandes	18
T. Bayliss b Rawson	5	– c Butchart b Jarvis	46
R. J. Bower c Houghton b Butchart	31	– b Brandes	0
M. D. O'Neill c Pycroft b Butchart	132	– not out	55
M. E. Waugh b Butchart	83	– not out	19
*†G. C. Dyer not out	30		
P. L. Taylor not out	12		
L-b 4, w 1, n-b 5	10	B 1, l-b 3, n-b 1	5

1/13 2/17 3/23 4/103 (6 wkts dec.) 314 1/24 2/35 3/35 (4 wkts dec.) 155
5/271 6/271 4/107

R. P. Done, R. G. Holland and M. R. Whitney did not bat.

Bowling: *First Innings*—Rawson 18.3-4-76-2; Jarvis 15-2-44-1; Brandes 14-2-43-0; Cox 14-1-51-0; Butchart 15-2-53-3; Meman 11-0-43-0. *Second Innings*—Brandes 8-1-38-3; Rawson 9-1-41-0; Jarvis 12-2-31-1; Cox 4-0-22-0; Butchart 6-0-19-0.

Zimbabwe

R. D. Brown lbw b Holland	22	– st Dyer b Holland	18
*†D. L. Houghton b Whitney	14	– b P. L. Taylor	55
A. C. Waller b Waugh	5	– (5) c Done b Holland	12
A. J. Pycroft not out	58	– c M. A. Taylor b P. L. Taylor	9
G. C. Wallace c Waugh b Done	12	– (6) st Dyer b O'Neill	70
P. W. E. Rawson c Small b Done	2	– (7) st Dyer b Holland	26
I. P. Butchart c Dyer b Done	14	– (8) lbw b O'Neill	8
B. Meman lbw b P. L. Taylor	36	– (3) lbw b Holland	6
E. A. Brandes c Dyer b Done	11	– c and b P. L. Taylor	0
M. P. Jarvis b Whitney	3	– c Whitney b P. L. Taylor	1
C. Cox c Waugh b P. L. Taylor	0	– not out	0
L-b 4, n-b 3	7	B 4, l-b 5, w 1	10

1/21 2/28 3/53 4/55 5/72 184 1/48 2/72 3/91 4/94 5/106 215
6/78 7/97 8/157 9/173 6/170 7/190 8/190 9/215

In the first innings A. J. Pycroft, when 6, retired hurt at 35 and resumed at 97.

Bowling: *First Innings*—Whitney 15-3-41-2; Waugh 12-5-25-1; Done 15-2-54-4; Holland 10-4-37-1; P. L. Taylor 9.5-2-23-2. *Second Innings*—Whitney 8-4-9-0; Waugh 5-1-16-0; Done 9-2-33-0; Holland 29-10-71-4; P. L. Taylor 18.2-4-58-4; O'Neill 11-4-19-2.

Umpires: K. Kanjee and I. D. Robinson.

†At Harare, April 6. New South Wales won by four wickets. Zimbabwe 224 for nine (50 overs) (P. W. E. Rawson 48); New South Wales 226 for six (48.3 overs) (M. E. Waugh 54, P. S. Clifford 67 not out, G. C. Dyer 42).

CRICKET IN CANADA, 1986

By KENNETH R. BULLOCK

The 1986 season was expected to be a milestone in the history of Canadian cricket. The national senior team were to visit England to participate in the third ICC Trophy tournament, and preparations in the previous two seasons had gone according to plan, culminating in victories over Bermuda and the USA in Bermuda in May 1985. Strong performances against MCC and the USA had also raised hopes to a high level of expectation. Consequently, it was a shock when Canada lost their first two ICC Trophy matches to the USA and Holland. Victories over Papua New Guinea, Hong Kong, Gibraltar and Israel kept them in contention, but a defeat by Bermuda sealed their fate. The last match, against Fiji, was won.

There is little doubt that the Canadian side did not perform to their potential. Bowan Singh, the all-rounder, who had contributed so much to the defeats of Bermuda and the USA in 1985, experienced a poor tour, and three new players added to the side were also a disappointment. Furthermore, Holland proved to be a much improved side and the USA and Bermuda played to their full potential. Now the Canadian selectors must analyse the results and begin to build anew for 1990.

From August 2-8, the fourteenth National Senior tournament was held in Winnipeg, Manitoba, all matches being played at Assinniboine Park. The weather was kind and all matches were completed. Ontario, fielding a young side with limited experience in competition at National level, surprised everyone by taking the Ed Bracht Trophy once again. They played hard and well, winning five consecutive matches before losing their final one to Manitoba. Quebec were runners-up by virtue of defeating British Columbia and Manitoba; British Columbia were third, Manitoba fourth, Alberta fifth, Nova Scotia sixth and Saskatchewan last. At the junior level, two national under-eighteen training camps were held in Toronto and Vancouver, with 24 boys from Ontario, Quebec and Nova Scotia attending the eastern camp and 31 the camp in Vancouver. The junior selectors were present to assess the candidates for the team to visit Ireland in 1987 for the seventh International Youth Festival.

The Board of Directors of the Canada Cricket Association held its semi-annual meeting in Toronto in April and its Annual General Meeting in Edmonton, Alberta, in December. Jack Kyle was re-elected President for his ninth term. Also during the year the groundwork was laid for the formation of a Canadian Association of Cricket Umpires. There are more than 500 certificated umpires in Canada, and it is hoped they will take the opportunity to participate in this new association.

In 1987, Canada is the host for the biennial match between Canada and the USA, which will be played at Winnipeg, Manitoba.

WOMEN'S CRICKET, 1986

By NETTA RHEINBERG

The Women's Cricket Association celebrated its Diamond Jubilee Year (1926-1986) with a festival match on June 8 which commemorated the first recorded women's cricket match in 1745. Then, at Gosden Common in Surrey, the "maids of Hambleton" beat the "maids of Bramley" by eight notches. The festival match was played on the same site, by courtesy of the Bramley Cricket Club, and as far as possible in the same atmosphere. Sheep cropped the pitch, a notcher scored, and the game was accompanied by gambling and drinking. Funds raised were shared between the WCA and the British Sports Association for the Disabled.

On August 9, an official but informal dinner was held at Colwall, the picturesque village in the shadow of the Malvern Hills, where the first idea of the Association was mooted. It is known to all today as the "cradle" of women's cricket. Unfortunately, the match arranged for the next day, between present and past internationals, was ruined by rain, but the weekend of reunion and nostalgia was most successful.

The year had started inauspiciously with some controversy following the WCA's ban from international cricket on members of a privately raised team which had visited South Africa during the winter. This resulted in the resignation of Mrs Rachael Heyhoe Flint from her job as the Association's PRO although she did not, as reported by the media, sever her relations with the WCA.

There was also anxiety over the financing of the forthcoming tour by India, their first ever to England, but in February sponsorship worth £30,000 was offered by the Uni-Vite Nutrition Company.

INDIAN WOMEN IN ENGLAND, 1986

The Indians, clearly well coached, possessed good batting technique and steady but not aggressive bowling. Their concentration was admirable and their fielding fair, if sometimes unathletic. However, they seemed to lack experience of tactics in a four-day game, laying undue stress on not being beaten and on breaking records rather than taking the slightest risk in trying to win. This attitude of caution was most noticeable, especially in the Tests, in their slow batting, which let them down in the limited-overs internationals. They lost all three, while the three Test matches were drawn. Nevertheless, it has to be remembered that the Indian Women's Cricket Association is a young one, and few, if any, countries have made such strides in ability in such a comparatively short time.

At Leicester, June 22. *First one-day international.* England won by five wickets. India 190 for six (48 overs) (S. Aggarwal 72); England 191 for five (46.2 overs) (J. Court 67, J. Brittin 44).

ENGLAND v INDIA

First Test Match

At Collingham, Yorkshire, June 26, 27, 29, 30. Drawn. India, having won the toss, were 203 for seven at the end of the first day, with Kulkarni, captain in the absence of the injured Edulji, 61 not out. Next day she registered her maiden Test century, her 118 including thirteen 4s, taking 351 minutes and contributing towards two world record partnerships: 106 for the eighth wicket with Desai and 90 for the ninth with Singhal. With Brittin unable to bat, having broken a finger while fielding, England began shakily but recovered to 55 for two by the close. On the third day Potter and Cooke took their partnership to 107, but when the last six batsmen mustered only 21 between them, England trailed by 125. However, they had India 75 for six at the close and all out at lunch on the final day, leaving England with five hours to score 254 to win. Anchored by Cooke's first Test hundred (269 minutes), they finished just 24 runs short but were not helped by India's tactics. In the penultimate hour only seven overs were bowled, an attitude which led to an official protest by England and gave rise to friction between the two sides.

India

G. Banerji c Stother b McConway	38	– c Stinson b Starling	8
S. Aggarwal c McConway b Starling	6	– b Smith	0
S. Shah c Hodges b Starling	21	– c McConway b Starling	12
*S. Kulkarni b Court	118	– st Stinson b McConway	11
S. Rangaswamy c Stinson b Potter	16	– b McConway	0
S. Gupta b Potter	7	– not out	33
R. Punekar lbw b Potter	0	– c May b Stother	2
†V. Kulpana c Stinson b McConway	0	– b Starling	34
M. Desai b Starling	54	– c Hodges b Smith	2
M. Singhal c Smith b Starling	44	– c sub b Potter	0
A. Ghosh not out	8	– c Smith b Potter	13
B 5, l-b 4, n-b 2	11	B 6, l-b 5, w 1, n-b 1	13

1/10 2/61 3/84 4/105 5/113   323   1/3 2/9 3/22 4/30 5/65   128
6/113 7/114 8/220 9/310   6/65 7/93 8/113 9/114

Bowling: First Innings—Starling 30–12–61–4; Potter 30–4–52–3; McConway 35–14–56–2; Court 3–0–14–1; Stother 21–5–65–0; Smith 16–6–53–0; May 3–0–13–0. *Second Innings*—Starling 21–6–36–3; Smith 17–8–30–2; McConway 8–4–11–2; Potter 5.3–0–17–2; Stother 17–6–23–1; May 1–1–0–0.

England

*C. Hodges b Rangaswamy	7	– st Kulpana b Kulkarni	68
L. Cooke c Singhal b Rangaswamy	72	– run out	117
J. Court c Shah b Gupta	0	– b Gupta	20
S. Potter not out	86	– c Kulkarni b Rangaswamy	6
J. May c Shah b Gupta	1	– not out	4
H. Stother run out	4	– c Shah b Rangaswamy	4
†A. Stinson c Singhal b Gupta	7	– not out	1
G. Smith b Rangaswamy	0		
G. McConway st Kulpana b Kulkarni	9		
A. Starling b Rangaswamy	0		
B 4, l-b 1, n-b 7	12	L-b 7, n-b 2	9

1/28 2/34 3/141 4/147   (9 wkts dec.) 198   1/149 2/186 3/209   (5 wkts) 229
5/159 6/181 7/182   4/221 5/223
8/197 9/198

J. Brittin did not bat.

Bowling: *First Innings*—Rangaswamy 29.3–11–42–4; Gupta 29–8–57–3; Kulkarni 19–4–52–1; Ghosh 14–5–27–0; Shah 6–3–8–0; Desai 3–0–7–0. *Second Innings*—Rangaswamy 18–1–72–2; Gupta 18–2–66–1; Kulkarni 17–2–58–1; Shah 8–2–26–0.

Umpires: J. Bragger and J. West.

ENGLAND v INDIA

Second Test Match

At Blackpool, July 3, 4, 6, 7. Drawn. A threatened boycott of the match by the Indians, as a consequence of the WCA's protest at their time wasting in the first Test, was averted after discussions involving both sides. On a slow pitch with a fast outfield, India batted for all but 75 minutes of the first two days, their innings dominated by Aggarwal, who reached her hundred in five hours and batted in all for 6 hours, 27 minutes. Banerji, Kulkarni and Venugopal arrived at 50 in 169, 240 and 161 minutes respectively. England spent the third day avoiding the follow-on, but hopes that they might be set a target after declaring at their overnight score evaporated as the Indians occupied the crease for another four hours on the last day.

India

G. Banerji c McConway b May	60	– c and b Potter 75
S. Aggarwal b Starling	132	– b Smith 7
S. Shah c Hodges b Starling	27	– not out 62
S. Kulkarni b Potter	78	– not out 18
S. Gupta c and b McConway	7	
S. Rangaswamy b Metcalf	1	
R. Venugopal c Hodges b Smith	55	
R. Punekar run out	47	
†M. Singhal not out	1	
A. Ghosh c Starling b McConway	2	
B 8, l-b 2, w 3, n-b 3	16	B 3, l-b 3, w 1, n-b 7 14

1/109 2/187 3/270 4/294   (9 wkts dec.) 426   1/30 2/138   (2 wkts dec.) 176
5/295 6/343 7/417
8/424 9/426

*D. Edulji did not bat.

Bowling: *First Innings*—Starling 31–9–69–2; McConway 34.2–15–38–2; Smith 23–5–64–1; Metcalf 22–3–78–1; May 32–6–75–1; Potter 28–3–81–1; Hodges 5–2–11–0. *Second Innings*—Smith 13–1–43–1; Potter 8–3–18–1; Starling 8–1–17–0; McConway 17–5–35–0; Metcalf 5–0–23–0; May 7–2–13–0; Court 11–3–21–0; Hodges 1–1–0–0.

England

*C. Hodges c and b Kulkarni	51	– c Rangaswamy b Edulji 25
L. Cooke c Kulkarni b Edulji	64	– b Gupta 11
J. Powell not out	115	– not out 11
J. Court b Rangaswamy	43	– not out 4
S. Potter c Singhal b Edulji	49	
J. May b Edulji	1	
G. Metcalf c Banerji b Kulkarni	5	
G. McConway not out	3	
B 7, l-b 4, n-b 8	19	B 1, n-b 2 3

1/105 2/131 3/215 4/322   (6 wkts dec.) 350   1/31 2/41   (2 wkts) 54
5/334 6/347

G. Smith, A. Starling and †J. Lee did not bat.

Bowling: *First Innings*—Edulji 44–17–92–3; Kulkarni 33–4–97–2; Rangaswamy 14–5–30–1; Ghosh 18–4–48–0; Gupta 12–2–32–0; Venugopal 6–0–25–0; Banerji 2–1–3–0; Shah 3–0–12–0. *Second Innings*—Gupta 11–3–27–1; Edulji 6–4–5–1; Rangaswamy 9–6–10–0; Kulkarni 5–2–11–0.

Umpires: V. Reichwald and V. Williams.

ENGLAND v INDIA

Third Test Match

At Worcester, July 12, 13, 14, 15. Drawn. Any prospect of a result was denied by Aggarwal's marathon innings of 9 hours, 23 minutes, at the end of which she passed by 1 run the world record of Betty Snowball which had stood since 1935. The following delivery Aggarwal skied to the wicket-keeper to end India's innings. England had opened the way by declaring at their first day's total, their position having been established by centuries from Brittin, in 184 minutes, and Hodges, in 246. Their 207 in 199 minutes was a record for the second wicket in a Test match in England. On the second day, as India made patient progress to 232 for six, McConway, the England spin bowler, took four wickets for 14 in 23 overs, and on the final day Potter scored a maiden Test hundred as the match, and the series, moved inexorably to a draw.

England

J. Brittin c Aggarwal b Edulji	125	– c Singhal b Gupta		0
L. Cooke c Shah b Sridar	10	– c Rangaswamy b Gupta		16
*C. Hodges not out	121	– c Shah b Ghosh		46
J. Court b Edulji	15	– b Gupta		42
S. Potter b Edulji	13	– c and b Kulkarni		102
J. Powell b Edulji	12	– c Kalpana b Edulji		30
†A. Stinson b Sridar	6	– run out		3
G. McConway st Kalpana b Kulkarni	14	– not out		0
J. May not out	1			
B 7, l-b 2, w 2, n-b 4	15	B 4, l-b 3, w 2, n-b 5		14

1/20 2/227 3/253 4/281   (7 wkts dec.) 332   1/0 2/34 3/100   (7 wkts dec.) 253
5/299 6/306 7/330   4/164 5/238 6/247 7/253

G. Smith and A. Starling did not bat.

Bowling: *First Innings*—Edulji 42–8–94–4; Sridar 13–3–46–2; Kulkarni 27–0–99–1; Rangaswamy 8–0–31–0; Gupta 6–0–24–0; Shah 5–1–13–0; Banerji 4–0–16–0. *Second Innings*—Gupta 22–9–50–3; Edulji 27–13–30–1; Kulkarni 20–3–46–1; Ghosh 14–5–26–1; Shah 13–7–17–0; Sridar 12–3–42–0; Rangaswamy 7–3–10–0; Banerji 6–0–25–0.

India

G. Banerji run out	22	– c May b Starling		19
S. Aggarwal c Stinson b Smith	190	– not out		24
S. Shah c Hodges b McConway	21	– not out		4
S. Kulkarni c Court b McConway	35			
S. Gupta b McConway	0			
†V. Kalpana lbw b McConway	5			
S. Rangaswamy c McConway b Smith	16			
M. Singhal c Hodges b McConway	35			
*D. Edulji c Powell b McConway	0			
A. Ghosh c Stinson b McConway	1			
S. Sridar not out	20			
B 9, l-b 5, w 6, n-b 9	29	B 2, l-b 1, w 1, n-b 3		7

1/42 2/107 3/161 4/161 5/177   374   1/25   (1 wkt) 54
6/228 7/298 8/298 9/316

Bowling: *First Innings*—McConway 42–27–34–7; Smith 22.4–2–68–2; Starling 34–3–99–0; Potter 23–8–50–0; Hodges 18–6–28–0; May 17–3–42–0; Court 7–2–23–0; Brittin 5–1–16–0. *Second Innings*—Starling 7–4–17–1; Smith 7–2–28–0; McConway 5–3–6–0.

Umpires: J. Burns and A. Garton.

At Osterley, July 26. *Second one-day international.* England won by six wickets. India 65 (33.2 overs) (G. McConway three for 12, S. Potter three for 11); England 68 for four (34 overs) (A. Ghosh four for 17).

At Banstead, July 27. *Third one-day international.* England won by 41 runs. England 140 for nine (36 overs); India 99 (36.3 overs) (G. McConway three for 21).

CAREER FIGURES OF PLAYERS RETIRING OR NOT RETAINED

BATTING

	M	I	NO	R	HI	100s	Avge	1,000r in season
J. R. T. Barclay	274	434	44	9,677	119	9	24.81	4
G. D. Barlow	251	404	59	12,387	177	26	35.90	7
G. Boycott	609	1,014	162	48,426	261*	151	56.83	23 + 3
R. G. P. Ellis	40	73	3	2,020	105*	2	28.85	0
B. J. Griffiths	177	138	51	290	16	0	3.33	0
A. Hill	258	447	47	12,356	172*	18	30.89	5
J. D. Inchmore	218	246	53	3,137	113	1	16.25	0
G. Monkhouse	75	86	33	1,158	100*	1	21.84	0
C. P. Phillipson	168	226	61	3,052	87	0	18.49	0
P. I. Pocock	554	585	156	4,867	75*	0	11.34	0
K. R. Pont	198	305	44	6,558	125*	7	25.12	0
J. F. Steele	379	605	85	15,054	195	21	28.95	6
S. Turner	261	513	101	9,411	121	4	22.84	0
Younis Ahmed	450	746	114	25,388	221*	44	40.17	13

BOWLING AND FIELDING

	R	W	BB	Avge	5 W/i	10 W/m	Ct
J. R. T. Barclay	9,936	324	6-61	30.66	9	1	216
G. D. Barlow	68	3	1-6	22.66	0	0	136
G. Boycott	1,459	45	4-14	32.42	0	0	264
R. G. P. Ellis	271	5	2-40	54.20	0	0	21
B. J. Griffiths	12,899	444	8-50	29.05	13	0	36
A. Hill	365	9	3-5	40.55	0	0	97
J. D. Inchmore	14,777	510	8-58	28.97	18	1	72
G. Monkhouse	4,682	173	7-51	27.06	2	0	35
C. P. Phillipson	5,213	153	6-56	34.07	4	0	136
P. I. Pocock	42,648	1,607	9-57	26.53	60	7	185
K. R. Pont	3,189	96	5-17	33.21	2	0	92
J. F. Steele	15,793	584	7-29	27.04	16	0	413
S. Turner	21,351	821	6-26	26.00	27	1	217
Younis Ahmed	1,899	41	4-10	46.31	0	0	239

BIRTHS AND DEATHS OF CRICKETERS

The qualifications are as follows:

1. All players who have appeared in a Test match.

2. Players who have appeared in 50 or more first-class matches during their careers and, if dead, were still living ten years ago.

3. Players who appeared in fifteen or more first-class matches in the 1986 English season.

4. English county captains, county caps and captains of Oxford and Cambridge Universities who, if dead, were still living ten years ago.

5. Oxford and Cambridge Blues of the last ten years. Earlier Blues may be found in previous *Wisdens*.

6. All players chosen as *Wisden* Cricketers of the Year, including the Public Schoolboys chosen for the 1918 and 1919 Almanacks. Cricketers of the Year are identified by the italic notation *CY* and year of appearance.

7. Players or personalities not otherwise qualified who are thought to be of sufficient interest to merit inclusion.

Key to abbreviations and symbols

CUCC – Cambridge University, OUCC – Oxford University.

Australian states: NSW – New South Wales, Qld – Queensland, S. Aust. – South Australia, Tas. – Tasmania, Vic. – Victoria, W. Aust. – Western Australia.

Indian teams: Guj. – Gujarat, H'bad – Hyderabad, Ind. Rlwys – Indian Railways, Ind. Serv. – Indian Services, J/K – Jammu and Kashmir, Karn. – Karnataka (Mysore to 1972-73), M. Pradesh – Madhya Pradesh (Central India [C. Ind.] to 1939-40, Holkar to 1954-55, Madhya Bharat to 1956-57), M'tra – Maharashtra, Naw. – Nawanagar, Raja. – Rajasthan, S'tra – Saurashtra (West India [W. Ind.] to 1945-46, Kathiawar to 1949-50), S. Punjab – Southern Punjab (Patiala to 1958-59, Punjab since 1968-69), TC – Travancore-Colchin (Kerala since 1956-57), TN – Tamil Nadu (Madras to 1959-60), U. Pradesh – Uttar Pradesh (United Provinces [U. Prov.] to 1948-49), Vidarbha (CP & Berar to 1949-50, Madhya Pradesh to 1956-57).

New Zealand provinces: Auck. – Auckland, Cant. – Canterbury, C. Dist. – Central Districts, N. Dist. – Northern Districts, Wgtn – Wellington.

Pakistani teams: B'pur – Bahawalpur, HBL – Habib Bank Ltd, HBFC – House Building Finance Corporation, IDBP – Industrial Development Bank of Pakistan, Kar. – Karachi, MCB – Muslim Commercial Bank, NBP – National Bank of Pakistan, NWFP – North-West Frontier Province, PIA – Pakistan International Airlines, Pak. Us – Pakistan Universities, Pak. Rlwys – Pakistan Railways, PWD – Public Works Department, R'pindi – Rawalpindi, UBL – United Bank Ltd.

South African provinces: E. Prov. – Eastern Province, Griq. W. – Griqualand West, N. Tvl – Northern Transvaal, NE Tvl – North-Eastern Transvaal, OFS – Orange Free State, Rhod. – Rhodesia, Tvl – Transvaal, W. Prov. – Western Province.

West Indies islands: B'dos – Barbados, BG – British Guiana (Guyana since 1966), Jam. – Jamaica, T/T – Trinidad and Tobago, Comb. Is. – Combined Islands.

* *Denotes Test player.* ** *Denotes appeared for two countries. There is a list of Test players country by country from page 85.*
† *Denotes also played for team under its previous name.*

Aamer Hameed (Pak. Us, Lahore, Punjab & OUCC) b Oct. 18, 1954

Abberley, R. N. (Warwicks.) b April 22, 1944

*A'Beckett, E. L. (Vic.) b Aug. 11, 1907

*Abdul Kadir (Kar. & NBP) b May 5, 1944

*Abdul Qadir (HBL, Lahore & Punjab) b Sept. 15, 1955

*Abel, R. (Surrey; *CY 1890*) b Nov. 30, 1857, d Dec. 10, 1936

Abell, Sir G. E. B. (OUCC, Worcs. & N. Ind.) b June 22, 1904

Aberdare, 3rd Lord (*see* Bruce, Hon. C. N.)

*Abid Ali, S. (H'bad) b Sept. 9, 1941

Abrahams, J. (Lancs.) b July 21, 1952

*Absolom, C. A. (CUCC & Kent) b June 7, 1846, d July 30, 1889

Acfield D. L. (CUCC & Essex) b July 24, 1947

*Achong, E. (T/T) b Feb. 16, 1904, d Aug. 29, 1986

Ackerman, H. M. (Border, NE Tvl, Northants, Natal & W. Prov.) b April 28, 1947

A'Court, D. G. (Glos.) b July 27, 1937

Adam, Sir Ronald, 2nd Bt (Pres. MCC 1946-47) b Oct. 30, 1885, d Dec. 26, 1982

Adams, P. W. (Cheltenham & Sussex; *CY 1919*) b 1900, d Feb. 28, 1962

*Adcock, N. A. T. (Tvl & Natal; *CY 1961*) b March 8, 1931

*Adhikari, H. R. (Guj., Baroda & Ind. Serv.) b July 31, 1919

*Afaq Hussain (Kar., Pak. Us, PIA & PWD) b Dec. 31, 1939

Afford, J. A. (Notts.) b May 12, 1964

*Aftab Baloch (PWD, Kar., Sind, NBP & PIA) b April 1, 1953

*Aftab Gul (Punjab U., Pak. Us & Lahore) b March 31, 1946

*Agha Saadat Ali (Pak. Us, Punjab, B'pur & Lahore) b June 21, 1929

*Agha Zahid (Pak. Us, Punjab, Lahore & HBL) b Jan. 7, 1953

*Agnew, J. P. (Leics.) b April 4, 1960

*Ahangama, F. S. (SL) b Sept. 14, 1959

Ahluwalia, M. S. (CUCC) b Dec. 27, 1965

Ainsworth, Lt-Cdr M. L. Y. (Worcs.) b May 13, 1922, d Aug. 28, 1978

Aird, R. (CUCC & Hants; Sec. MCC 1953-62, Pres. MCC 1968-69) b May 4, 1902, d Aug. 16, 1986

Aitchison, Rev. J. K. (Scotland) b May 26, 1920

Alabaster, G. D. (Cant., N. Dist. & Otago) b Dec. 10, 1933

*Alabaster, J. C. (Otago) b July 11, 1930

Alcock, C. W. (Sec. Surrey CCC 1872-1907, Editor *Cricket* 1882-1907) b Dec. 2, 1842, d Feb. 26, 1907

Alderman, A. E. (Derbys.) b Oct. 30, 1907

*Alderman, T. M. (W. Aust. & Kent; *CY 1982*) b June 12, 1956

Aldridge, K. J. (Worcs & Tas.) b March 13, 1935

Alexander of Tunis, 1st Lord (Pres. MCC 1955-56) b Dec. 10, 1891, d June 16, 1969

*Alexander, F. C. M. (CUCC & Jam.) b Nov. 2, 1928

*Alexander, G. (Vic.) b April 22, 1851, d Nov. 6, 1930

*Alexander, H. H. (Vic.) b June 9, 1905

Alikhan, R. I. (Sussex) b Dec. 28, 1962

*Alim-ud-Din (Rajputna, Guj., Sind, B'pur, Kar. & PWD) b Dec. 15, 1930

*Allan, D. W. (B'dos) b Nov. 5, 1937

*Allan, F. E. (Vic.) b Dec. 2, 1849, d Feb. 9, 1917

Allan, J. M. (OUCC, Kent, Warwicks. & Scotland) b April 2, 1932

*Allan, P. J. (Qld) b Dec. 31, 1935

Allbrook, M. E. (CUCC, Kent & Notts.) b Nov. 15, 1954

*Allcott, C. F. W. (Auck.) b Oct. 7, 1896, d Nov. 21, 1973

Allen, A. W. (CUCC & Northants) b Dec. 22, 1912

Allen, B. O. (CUCC & Glos.) b Oct. 13, 1911, d May 1, 1981

*Allen, D. A. (Glos.) b Oct. 29, 1935

*Allen, Sir G. O. (CUCC & Middx; Pres. MCC 1963-64; *special portrait 1987*) b July 31, 1902

Allen, J. C. (Leewards) b Aug. 18, 1951

Allen, M. H. J. (Northants & Derbys.) b Jan. 7, 1933

*Allen, R. C. (NSW) b July 2, 1858, d May 2, 1952

Alletson, E. B. (Notts.) b March 6, 1884, d July 5, 1963

Alley, W. E. (NSW & Som.; *CY 1962*) b Feb. 3, 1919

Alleyne, H. L. (B'dos & Worcs.) b Feb. 28, 1957

*Allom, M. J. C. (CUCC & Surrey; Pres. MCC 1969-70) b March 23, 1906

*Allott, P. J. W. (Lancs. & Wgtn) b Sept. 14, 1956

Altham, H. S. (OUCC, Surrey & Hants; Pres. MCC 1959-60) b Nov. 30, 1888, d March 11, 1965

*Amalean, K. N. (SL) b April 7, 1965

*Amarnath, Lala (N. Ind., S. Punjab, Guj., Patiala, U. Pradesh & Ind. Rlwys) b Sept. 11, 1911

*Amarnath, M. (Punjab & Delhi; *CY 1984*) b Sept. 24, 1950

*Amarnath, S. (Punjab & Delhi) b Dec. 30, 1948

*Amar Singh, L. (Patiala, W. Ind. & Naw.) b Dec. 4, 1910, d May 20, 1940

*Amerasinghe, A. M. J. G. (SL) b Feb. 2, 1954

*Ames, L. E. G. (Kent; *CY 1929*) b Dec. 3, 1905

**Amir Elahi (Baroda, N. Ind., S. Punjab & B'pur) b Sept. 1, 1908, d Dec. 28, 1980

*Amiss, D. L. (Warwicks.; *CY 1975*) b April 7, 1943

Anderson, I. S. (Derbys. & Boland) b April 24, 1960

*Anderson, J. H. (W. Prov.) b April 26, 1874, d March 11, 1926

*Anderson, R. W. (Cant., N. Dist., Otago & C. Dist.) b Oct. 2, 1948

*Anderson, W. McD. (Otago, C. Dist. & Cant.) b Oct. 8, 1919, d Dec. 21, 1979

Andrew, C. R. (CUCC) b Feb. 18, 1963

*Andrew, K. V. (Northants) b Dec. 15, 1929

*Andrews, B. (Cant., C. Dist. & Otago) b April 4, 1945

*Andrews, T. J. E. (NSW) b Aug. 26, 1890, d Jan. 28, 1970

Andrews, W. H. R. (Som.) b April 14, 1908

Angell, F. L. (Som.) b June 29, 1922

*Anil Dalpat (Kar. & PIA) b Sept. 20, 1963

*Anurasiri, S. D. (SL) b Feb. 25, 1966

*Anwar Hussain (N. Ind., Bombay, Sind & Kar.) b July 16, 1920

*Anwar Khan (Kar., Sind & NBP) b Dec. 24, 1955

*Appleyard, R. (Yorks.; *CY 1952*) b June 27, 1924

*Apte, A. L. (Ind. Us, Bombay & Raja.) b Oct. 24, 1934

*Apte, M. L. (Bombay & Bengal) b Oct. 5, 1932

*Archer, A. G. (Worcs.) b Dec. 6, 1871, d July 15, 1935

*Archer, K. A. (Qld) b Jan. 17, 1928

*Archer, R. G. (Qld) b Oct. 25, 1933

*Arif Butt (Lahore & Pak. Rlwys) b May 17, 1944

Arlott, John, (Writer & Broadcaster) b Feb. 25, 1914

*Armitage, R. L. S. (E. Prov. & N. Tvl) b July 9, 1955

*Armitage, T. (Yorks.) b April 25, 1848, d Sept. 21, 1922

Armstrong, N. F. (Leics.) b Dec. 22, 1892

Armstrong, T. R. (Derbys.) b Oct. 13, 1909

*Armstrong, W. W. (Vic.; *CY 1903*) b May 22, 1879, d July 13, 1947

*Arnold, E. G. (Worcs.) b Nov. 7, 1876, d Oct. 25, 1942

*Arnold, G. G. (Surrey & Sussex; *CY 1972*) b Sept. 3, 1944

*Arnold, J. (Hants) b Nov. 30, 1907, d April 4, 1984

Arnold, P. (Cant. & Northants) b Oct. 16, 1926

*Arun Lal, J. (Delhi & Bengal) b Aug. 1, 1955

*Asgarali, N. (T/T) b Dec. 28, 1920

Ashdown, W. H. (Kent) b Dec. 27, 1898, d Sept. 15, 1979

*Ashley, W. H. (W. Prov.) b Feb. 10, 1862, d July 14, 1930

*Ashraf Ali (Lahore, Income Tax, Pak Us, Pak Rlwys & UBL) b April 22, 1958

Ashton, C. T. (CUCC & Essex) b Feb. 19, 1901, d Oct. 31, 1942

Ashton, G. (CUCC & Worcs.) b Sept. 27, 1896, d Feb. 6, 1981

Ashton, Sir H. (CUCC & Essex; *CY 1922*; Pres. MCC 1960-61) b Feb. 13, 1898, d June 17,1979

Asif Din, M. (Warwicks.) b Sept. 21, 1960

*Asif Iqbal (H'bad, Kar., Kent, PIA & NBP; *CY 1968*) b June 6, 1943

*Asif Masood (Lahore, Punjab U. & PIA) b Jan. 23, 1946

Aslett, D. G. (Kent) b Feb. 12, 1958

*Astill, W. E. (Leics.; *CY 1933*) b March 1, 1888, d Feb. 10, 1948

*Athey, C. W. J. (Yorks. & Glos.) b Sept. 27, 1957

Atkinson, C. R. M. (Som.) b July 23, 1931

*Atkinson, D. St E. (B'dos & T/T) b Aug. 9, 1926

*Atkinson, E. St E. (B'dos) b Nov. 6, 1927

Atkinson, G. (Som. & Lancs.) b March 29, 1938

Atkinson, T. (Notts.) b Sept. 27, 1930

Attenborough, G. R. (S. Aust.) b Jan. 17, 1951

*Attewell, W. (Notts.; *CY 1892*) b June 12, 1861, d June 11, 1927

Austin, Sir H. B. G. (B'dos) b July 15, 1877, d July 27, 1943

*Austin, R. A. (Jam.) b Sept. 5, 1954

Avery, A. V. (Essex) b Dec. 19, 1914

Aworth, C. J. (CUCC & Surrey) b Feb. 19, 1953

Aylward, J. (Hants & All-England) b 1741, d Dec. 27, 1827

*Azad, K. (Delhi) b Jan. 2, 1959

*Azeem Hafeez (Kar. & Allied Bank) b July 29, 1963

*Azhar Khan (Lahore, Punjab, Pak. Us., PIA & HBL) b Sept. 7, 1955

*Azharuddin, M. (H'bad) b Feb. 8, 1963

*Azmat Rana (B'pur, PIA, Punjab, Lahore & MCB) b Nov. 3, 1951

*Bacchus, S. F. A. F. (Guyana, W. Prov. & Border) b Jan. 31, 1954

*Bacher, Dr A. (Tvl) b May 24, 1942

*Badcock, C. L. (Tas. & S. Aust.) b April 10, 1914, d Dec. 13, 1982

*Badcock, F. T. (Wgtn & Otago) b Aug. 9, 1895, d Sept. 19, 1982

*Baichan, L. (Guyana) b May 12, 1946

*Baig, A. A. (H'bad, OUCC & Som.) b March 19, 1939

Bail, P. A. C. (Som. & CUCC) b June 23, 1965

Bailey, Sir D. T. L. (Glos.) b Aug. 5, 1918

Bailey, J. (Hants) b April 6, 1908

Bailey, J. A. (Essex & OUCC; Sec. MCC 1974-   ) b June 22, 1930

Bailey, R. J. (Northants) b Oct. 28, 1963

*Bailey, T. E. (Essex & CUCC; *CY 1950*) b Dec. 3, 1923

Bainbridge, P. (Glos.; *CY 1986*) b April 16, 1958

*Bairstow, D. L. (Yorks. & Griq. W.) b Sept. 1, 1951

Baker, C. S. (Warwicks.) b Jan. 5, 1883, d Dec. 16, 1976

Baker, R. P. (Surrey) b April 9, 1954

*Bakewell, A. H. (Northants; *CY 1934*) b Nov. 2, 1908, d Jan. 23, 1983

*Balaskas, X. C. (Griq. W., Border, N. Prov., Tvl & NE Tvl) b Oct. 15, 1910

*Balderstone, J. C. (Yorks. & Leics.) b Nov. 16, 1940

Baldry, D. O. (Middx & Hants) b Dec. 26, 1931

Baldwin, H. G. (Surrey; Umpire) b March 16, 1893, d March 7, 1969

*Banerjee, S. A. (Bengal & Bihar) b Nov. 1, 1919

*Banerjee, S. N. (Bengal, Naw., Bihar & M. Pradesh) b Oct. 3, 1911, d Oct. 14, 1980

*Bannerman, A. C. (NSW) b March 21, 1854, d Sept. 19, 1924

*Bannerman, Charles (NSW) b July 23, 1851, d Aug. 20, 1930

Bannister, J. D. (Warwicks.) b Aug. 23, 1930

*Baptiste, E. A. E. (Kent & Leewards) b March 12, 1960

*Baqa Jilani, M. (N. Ind.) b July 20, 1911, d July 2, 1941

Barber, A. T. (OUCC & Yorks.) b June 17, 1905, d March 10, 1985

*Barber, R. T. (Wgtn & C. Dist.) b June 23, 1925

*Barber, R. W. (Lancs., CUCC & Warwicks; *CY 1967*) b Sept. 26, 1935

*Barber, W. (Yorks.) b April 18, 1901, d Sept. 10, 1968

Barclay, J. R. T. (Sussex & OFS) b Jan. 22, 1954

*Bardsley, W. (NSW; *CY 1910*) b Dec. 7, 1882, d Jan. 20, 1954

Baring, A. E. G. (Hants) b Jan. 21, 1910, d Aug. 29, 1986

Barker, G. (Essex) b July 6, 1931

Barling, T. H. (Surrey) b Sept. 1, 1906

Barlow, A. (Lancs.) b Aug. 31, 1915, d May 9, 1983

Barlow, E. A. (OUCC & Lancs.) b Feb. 24, 1912, d June 27, 1980

*Barlow, E. J. (Tvl, E. Prov., W. Prov., Derbys. & Boland) b Aug. 12, 1940

*Barlow, G. D. (Middx) b March 26, 1950

*Barlow, R. G. (Lancs.) b May 28, 1851, d July 31, 1919

Barnard, H. M. (Hants) b July 18, 1933

Barnard, L. J. (Tvl & N. Tvl) b Jan. 5, 1956

Barnes, A. R. (Sec. Aust. Cricket Board 1960-81) b Sept. 12, 1916

*Barnes, S. F. (Warwicks. & Lancs.; *CY 1910*) b April 19, 1873, d Dec. 26, 1967

*Barnes, S. G. (NSW) b June 5, 1916, d Dec. 16, 1973

*Barnes, W. (Notts.; *CY 1890*) b May 27, 1852, d March 24, 1899

*Barnett, B. A. (Vic.) b March 23, 1908, d June 29, 1979

*Barnett, C. J. (Glos.; *CY 1937*) b July 3, 1910

Barnett, K. J. (Derbys. & Boland) b July 17, 1960

Barnwell, C. J. P. (Som.) b June 23, 1914

Baroda, Maharaja of (Manager, Ind. in Eng., 1959) b April 2, 1930

*Barratt, F. (Notts.) b April 12, 1894, d Jan. 29, 1947

Barratt, R. J. (Leics.) b May 3, 1942

*Barrett, A. G. (Jam.) b April 5, 1942

Barrett, B. J. (Auck., C. Dist. & Worcs.) b Nov. 16, 1966

*Barrett, J. E. (Vic.) b Oct. 15, 1866, d Feb. 9, 1916

Barrick, D. W. (Northants) b April 28, 1926

*Barrington, K. F. (Surrey; *CY 1960*) b Nov. 24, 1930, d March 14, 1981

Barrington, W. E. J. (CUCC) b Jan. 4, 1960

Barron, W. (Lancs. & Northants) b Oct. 26, 1917

Barrow, A. (Natal) b Jan. 23, 1955

*Barrow, I. (Jam.) b Jan. 6, 1911, d April 2, 1979

Bartholomew, P. C. S. (T/T) b Oct. 9, 1939

*Bartlett, E. L. (B'dos) b March 18, 1906, d Dec. 21, 1976

*Bartlett, G. A. (C. Dist. & Cant.) b Feb. 3, 1941

Bartlett, H. T. (CUCC, Surrey & Sussex; *CY 1939*) b Oct. 7, 1914

Bartley, T. J. (Umpire) b March 19, 1908, d April 2, 1964

Barton, M. R. (OUCC & Surrey) b Oct. 14, 1914

*Barton, P. T. (Wgtn) b Oct. 9, 1935

*Barton, V. A. (Kent & Hants) b Oct. 6, 1867, d March 23, 1906

Barwick, S. R. (Glam.) b Sept. 6, 1960

Bates, D. L. (Sussex) b May 10, 1933

*Bates, W. (Yorks.) b Nov. 19, 1855, d Jan. 8, 1900

Bath, B. F. (Tvl) b Jan. 16, 1947

*Baumgartner, H. V. (OFS & Tvl) b Nov. 17, 1883, d April 8, 1938

Baxter, A. D. (Devon, Lancs., Middx & Scotland) b Jan. 20, 1910, d Jan. 28, 1986

*Bean, G. (Notts & Sussex) b March 7, 1864, d March 16, 1923

Bear, M. J. (Essex & Cant.) b Feb. 23, 1934
*Beard, D. D. (C. Dist. & N. Dist.) b Jan. 14, 1920, d July 15, 1982
*Beard, G. R. (NSW) b Aug. 19, 1950
Beauclerk, Lord Frederick (Middx, Surrey & MCC) b May 8, 1773, d April 22, 1850
Beaufort, 10th Duke of (Pres. MCC 1952-53) b April 4, 1900, d Feb. 5, 1984
Beaumont, D. J. (CUCC) b Sept. 1, 1944
*Beaumont, R. (Tvl) b Feb. 4, 1884, d May 25, 1958
*Beck, J. E. F. (Wgtn) b Aug. 1, 1934
Becker, G. C. (W. Aust.) b March 13, 1936
Bedford, P. I. (Middx) b Feb. 11, 1930, d Sept. 18, 1966
*Bedi, B. S. (N. Punjab, Delhi & Northants) b Sept. 25, 1946
*Bedser, A. V. (Surrey; *CY 1947*) b July 4, 1918
Bedser, E. A. (Surrey) b July 4, 1918
Beet, G. (Derbys.; Umpire) b April 24, 1886, d Dec. 13, 1946
*Begbie, D. W. (Tvl) b Dec. 12, 1914
Beldham, W. (Hambledon & Surrey) b Feb. 5, 1766, d Feb. 20, 1862
*Bell, A. J. (W. Prov. & Rhod.) b April 15, 1906, d Aug. 2, 1985
Bell, R. V. (Middx & Sussex) b Jan. 7, 1931
*Bell, W. (Cant.) b Sept. 5, 1931
Bellamy, B. W. (Northants) b April 22, 1891, d Dec. 20, 1985
Benaud, J. (NSW) b May 11, 1944
*Benaud, R. (NSW; *CY 1962*) b Oct. 6, 1930
Benjamin, W. K. M. (Leewards & Leics.) b Dec. 31, 1964
Bennett, B. W. P. (CUCC) b Feb. 6, 1955
Bennett, C. T. (CUCC, Surrey & Middx) b Aug. 10, 1902, d Feb. 3, 1978
Bennett, D. (Middx) b Dec. 18, 1933
Bennett, G. M. (Som.) b Dec. 17, 1909, d July 26, 1982
*Bennett, M. J. (NSW) b Oct. 16, 1956
Bennett, N. H. (Surrey) b Sept. 23, 1912
Bennett, R. (Lancs.) b June 16, 1940
*Benson, M. R. (Kent) b July 6, 1958
Bensted, E. C. (Qld) b Feb. 11, 1901, d Jan. 21, 1980
Bentley, R. M. (Rhod., Zimb. & Natal) b Nov. 3, 1958
Bernard, J. R. (CUCC & Glos.) b Dec. 7, 1938
Berry, L. G. (Leics.) b April 28, 1906, d Feb. 5, 1985
*Berry, R. (Lancs., Worcs. & Derbys.) b Jan. 29, 1926
Bessant, J. G. (Glos.) b Nov. 11, 1892, d Jan. 18, 1982
*Best, C. A. (B'dos) b May 14, 1959
Bestall, D. (N. Tvl, Natal & E. Prov.) b May 28, 1952
*Betancourt, N. (T/T) b June 4, 1887, d Oct. 12, 1947

Beukes, A. P. (Griq. W. & OFS) b May 24, 1953
Bezuidenhout, S. J. (E. Prov.) b July 11, 1946
Bhalekar, R. B. (M'tra) b Feb. 17, 1952
*Bhandari, P. (Delhi & Bengal) b Nov. 27, 1935
*Bhat, R. (Karn.) b April 16, 1958
Bick, D. A. (Middx) b Feb. 22, 1936
Bickmore, A. F. (OUCC & Kent) b May 19, 1899, d March 18, 1979
Biddulph, K. D. (Som.) b May 29, 1932
Biggs, A. L. (E. Prov.) b April 26, 1946
*Bilby, G. P. (Wgtn) b May 7, 1941
*Binks, J. G. (Yorks.; *CY 1969*) b Oct. 5, 1935
*Binny, R. M. H. (Karn.) b July 19, 1955
*Binns, A. P. (Jam.) b July 24, 1929
Birch, J. D. (Notts.) b June 18, 1955
*Bird, H. D. (Yorks. & Leics.; Umpire) b April 19, 1933
*Bird, M. C. (Lancs. & Surrey) b March 25, 1888, d Dec. 9, 1933
Bird, R. E. (Worcs.) b April 4, 1915, d Feb. 20, 1985
*Birkenshaw, J. (Yorks., Leics. & Worcs.) b Nov. 13, 1940
*Birkett, L. S. (B'dos, BG & T/T) b April 14, 1904
Birrell, H. B. (E. Prov., Rhod. & OUCC) b Dec. 1, 1927
*Bisset, Sir Murray (W. Prov.) b April 14, 1876, d Oct. 24, 1931
*Bissett, G. F. (Griq. W., W. Prov. & Tvl) b Nov. 5, 1905, d Nov. 14, 1965
Bissex, M. (Glos.) b Sept. 28, 1944
*Blackham, J. McC. (Vic.; *CY 1891*) b May 11, 1854, d Dec. 28, 1932
*Blackie, D. D. (Vic.) b April 5, 1882, d April 18, 1955
Blackledge, J. F. (Lancs.) b April 15, 1928
*Blain, T. E. (C. Dist.) b Feb. 17, 1962
Blair, B. R. (Otago) b Dec. 27, 1957
*Blair, R. W. (Wgtn & C. Dist.) b June 23, 1932
Blair, W. L. (Otago) b May 11, 1948
Blake, D. E. (Hants) b April 27, 1925
Blake, Rev. P. D. S. (OUCC & Sussex) b May 23, 1927
*Blanckenberg, J. M. (W. Prov. & Natal) b Dec. 31, 1893, 'presumed dead'
*Bland, K. C. (Rhod., E. Prov. & OFS; *CY 1966*) b April 5, 1938
Blenkiron, W. (Warwicks.) b July 21, 1942
Bligh, Hon. Ivo (*see* 8th Earl of Darnley)
Block, S. A. (CUCC & Surrey) b July 15, 1908, d Oct. 7, 1979
Blofeld, H. C. (CUCC) b Sept. 23, 1939
Blundell, Sir E. D. (CUCC & NZ) b May 29, 1907, d Sept. 24, 1984
*Blunt, R. C. (Cant. & Otago; *CY 1928*) b Nov. 3, 1900, d June 22, 1966
*Blythe, C. (Kent; *CY 1904*) b May 30, 1879, d Nov. 8, 1917

*Board, J. H. (Glos.) b Feb. 23, 1867, d April 16, 1924
*Bock, E. G. (Griq. W., Tvl & W. Prov.) b Sept. 17, 1908, d Sept. 5, 1961
Boddington, R. A. (Lancs.) b June 30, 1892, d Aug. 5, 1977
Bodkin, P. E. (CUCC) b Sept. 15, 1924
*Bolton, B. A. (Cant. & Wgtn) b May 31, 1935
*Bolus, J. B. (Yorks., Notts. & Derbys.) b Jan. 31, 1934
*Bond, G. E. (W. Prov.) b April 5, 1909, d Aug. 27, 1965
Bond, J. D. (Lancs. & Notts.; *CY 1971*) b May 6, 1932
*Bonnor, G. J. (Vic. & NSW) b Feb. 25, 1855, d June 27, 1912
*Boock, S. L. (Otago & Cant.) b Sept. 20, 1951
Boon, D. C. (Tas.) b Dec. 29, 1960
Boon, T. J. (Leics.) b Nov. 1, 1961
*Booth, B. C. (NSW) b Oct. 19, 1933
Booth, B. J. (Lancs. & Leics.) b Dec. 3, 1935
Booth, F. S. (Lancs.) b Feb. 12, 1907, d Jan. 21, 1980
*Booth, M. W. (Yorks.; *CY 1914*) b Dec. 10, 1886, d July 1, 1916
Booth, P. (Leics.) b Nov. 2, 1952
Booth, R. (Yorks. & Worcs.) b Oct. 1, 1926
*Borde, C. G. (Baroda & M'tra) b July 21, 1934
*Border, A. R. (NSW, Glos, Qld & Essex; *CY 1982*) b July 27, 1955
Bore, M. K. (Yorks. & Notts.) b June 2, 1947
Borrington, A. J. (Derbys.) b Dec. 8, 1948
*Bosanquet, B. J. T. (OUCC & Middx; *CY 1905*) b Oct. 13, 1877, d Oct. 12, 1936
Boshier, B. S. (Leics.) b March 6, 1932
*Botham, I. T. (Som.; *CY 1978*) b Nov. 24, 1955
*Botten, J. T. (NE Tvl & N. Tvl) b June 21, 1938
Boucher, J. C. (Ireland) b Dec. 22, 1910
Bourne, W. A. (B'dos & Warwicks.) b Nov. 15, 1952
*Bowden, M. P. (Surrey & Tvl) b Nov. 1, 1865, d Feb. 19, 1892
Bowditch, M. H. (W. Prov.) b Aug. 30, 1945
*Bowes, W. E. (Yorks.; *CY 1932*) b July 25, 1908
*Bowley, E. H. (Sussex & Auck.; *CY 1930*) b June 6, 1890, d July 9, 1974
Bowley, F. L. (Worcs.) b Nov. 9, 1873, d May 31, 1943
Bowman, R. (OUCC & Lancs.) b Jan. 26, 1934
Box, T. (Sussex) b Feb. 7, 1808, d July 12, 1876
*Boyce, K. D. (B'dos & Essex; *CY 1974*) b Oct. 11, 1943
*Boycott, G. (Yorks. & N. Tvl; *CY 1965*) b Oct. 21, 1940

Boyd-Moss, R. J. (CUCC & Northants) b Dec. 16, 1959
Boyes, G. S. (Hants) b March 31, 1899, d Feb. 11, 1973
*Boyle, H. F. (Vic.) b Dec. 10, 1847, d Nov. 21, 1907
*Bracewell, B. P. (C. Dist., Otago & N. Dist.) b Sept. 14, 1959
Bracewell, J. G. (Otago & Auck.) b April 15, 1958
*Bradburn, W. P. (N. Dist.) b Nov. 24, 1938
*Bradley, W. M. (Kent) b Jan. 2, 1875, d June 19, 1944
*Bradman, Sir D. G. (NSW & S. Aust.; *CY 1931*) b Aug. 27, 1908
Bradshaw, J. C. (Leics.) b Jan. 25, 1902, d Nov. 8, 1984
Brain, B. M. (Worcs. & Glos.) b Sept. 13, 1940
*Brann, W. H. (E. Prov.) b April 4, 1899, d Sept. 22, 1953
Brassington, A. J. (Glos.) b Aug. 9, 1954
Bratchford, J. D. (Qld) b Feb. 2, 1929
*Braund, L. C. (Surrey & Som.; *CY 1902*) b Oct. 18, 1875, d Dec. 22, 1955
Bray, C. (Essex) b April 6, 1898
Brayshaw, I. J. (W. Aust.) b Jan. 14, 1942
Brazier, A. F. (Surrey & Kent) b Dec. 7, 1924
Breakwell, D. (Northants & Som.) b July 2, 1948
*Brearley, J. M. (CUCC & Middx; *CY 1977*) b April 28, 1942
*Brearley, W. (Lancs.; *CY 1909*) b March 11, 1876, d Jan. 30, 1937
Breddy, M. N. (CUCC) b Sept. 23, 1961
*Brennan, D. V. (Yorks.) b Feb. 10, 1920, d Jan. 9, 1985
Brettell, D. N. (OUCC) b March 10, 1956
Brickett, D. J. (E. Prov.) b Dec. 9, 1950
Bridge, W. B. (Warwicks.) b May 29, 1938
Bridger, Rev. J. R. (Hants) b April 8, 1920, d July 14, 1986
Brierley, T. L. (Glam. & Lancs.) b June 15, 1910
Briers, N. E. (Leics.) b Jan. 15, 1955
*Briggs, John (Lancs.; *CY 1889*) b Oct. 3, 1862, d Jan. 11, 1902
*Bright, R. J. (Vic.) b July 13, 1954
*Briscoe, A. W. (Tvl) b Feb. 6, 1911, d April 22, 1941
Bristowe, W. R. (OUCC) b Nov. 17, 1963
*Broad, B. C. (Glos. & Notts.) b Sept. 29, 1957
Broadbent, R. G. (Worcs.) b June 21, 1924
Brocklehurst, B. G. (Som.) b Feb. 18, 1922
*Brockwell, W. (Kimberley & Surrey; *CY 1895*) b Jan. 21, 1865, d July 1, 1935
Broderick, V. (Northants) b Aug. 17, 1920
Brodhurst, A. H. (CUCC & Glos.) b July 21, 1916
*Bromfield, H. D. (W. Prov.) b June 26, 1932

*Bromley, E. H. (W. Aust. & Vic.) b Sept. 2, 1912, d Feb. 1, 1967
*Bromley-Davenport, H. R. (CUCC, Bombay Eur. & Middx) b Aug. 18, 1870, d May 23, 1954
Brookes, D. (Northants; *CY 1957*) b Oct. 29, 1915
Brookes, W. H. (Editor of *Wisden* 1936-39) b Dec. 5, 1894, d May 28, 1955
Brooks, R. A. (OUCC & Som.) b June 14, 1943
*Brown, A. (Kent) b Oct. 17, 1935
Brown, A. D. (CUCC) b May 18, 1962
Brown, A. S. (Glos.) b June 24, 1936
*Brown, D. J. (Warwicks.) b Jan. 30, 1942
Brown, D. W. J. (Glos.) b Feb. 26, 1942
Brown, E. (Warwicks.) b Nov. 27, 1911
*Brown, F. R. (CUCC, Surrey & Northants; *CY 1933*; Pres. MCC 1971-72) b Dec. 16, 1910
*Brown, G. (Hants) b Oct. 6, 1887, d Dec. 3, 1964
Brown, J. (Scotland) b Sept. 24, 1931
*Brown, J. T. (Yorks.; *CY 1895*) b Aug. 20, 1869, d Nov. 4, 1904
*Brown, L. S. (Tvl, NE Tvl & Rhod.) b Nov. 24, 1910, d Sept. 1, 1983
Brown, R. D. (Zimb.) b March 11, 1951
Brown, S. M. (Middx) b Dec. 8, 1917
*Brown, V. R. (Cant.) b Nov. 3, 1959
*Brown, W. A. (NSW & Qld; *CY 1939*) b July 31, 1912
Brown, W. C. (Northants) b Nov. 13, 1900, d Jan. 20, 1986
*Browne, C. R. (B'dos & BG) b Oct. 8, 1890, d Jan. 12, 1964
Browne, D. W. (CUCC) b April 4, 1964
Bruce, Hon. C. N. (3rd Lord Aberdare) (OUCC & Middx) b Aug. 2, 1885, d Oct. 4, 1957
Bruce, S. D. (W. Prov. & OFS) b Jan. 11, 1954
Bruce, W. (Vic.) b May 22, 1864, d Aug. 3, 1925
Bruyns, A. (W. Prov. & Natal) b Sept. 19, 1946
Bryan, G. J. (Kent) b Dec. 29, 1902
Bryan, J. L. (CUCC & Kent; *CY 1922*) b May 26, 1896, d April 23, 1985
Bryan, R. T. (Kent) b July 30, 1898, d July 27, 1970
*Buckenham, C. P. (Essex) b Jan. 16, 1876, d Feb. 23, 1937
Buckingham, J. (Warwicks.) b Jan. 21, 1903
Budd, E. H. (Middx & All-England) b Feb. 23, 1785, d March 29, 1875
Budd, W. L. (Hants) b Oct. 25, 1913, d Aug. 23, 1986
Buggins, B. L. (W. Aust.) b Jan. 29, 1935
Bull, C. L. (Cant.) b Aug. 19, 1946
Bull, D. F. E. (Qld) b Aug. 13, 1935

Bull, F. G. (Essex; *CY 1898*) b April 2, 1875, d Sept. 16, 1910
Buller, J. S. (Yorks. & Worcs.) b Aug. 23, 1909, d Aug. 7, 1970
Burden, M. D. (Hants) b Oct. 4, 1930
*Burge, P. J. (Qld; *CY 1965*) b May 17, 1932
*Burger, C. G. de V. (Natal) b July 12, 1935
Burgess, G. I. (Som.) b May 5, 1943
*Burgess, M. G. (Auck.) b July 17, 1944
Burke, C. (Auck.) b March 22, 1914
*Burke, J. W. (NSW; *CY 1957*) b June 12, 1930, d Feb. 2, 1979
*Burke, S. F. (NE Tvl & OFS) b March 11, 1934
*Burki, Javed (Pak. Us, OUCC, Punjab, Lahore, Kar., R'pindi & NWFP) b May 8, 1938
*Burn, E. J. K. (K. E.) (Tas.) b Sept. 17, 1862, d July 20, 1956
Burnet, J. R. (Yorks.) b Oct. 11, 1918
Burnley, I. D. (CUCC) b March 11, 1963
Burnup, C. J. (CUCC & Kent; *CY 1903*) b Nov. 21, 1875, d April 5, 1960
Burrough, H. D. (Som.) b Feb. 6, 1909
Burrow, B. W. (Griq. W.) b Feb. 8, 1940
Burton, D. C. F. (CUCC & Yorks.) b Sept. 13, 1887, d Sept. 24, 1971
*Burton, F. J. (Vic. & NSW) b 1866, d Aug. 25, 1929
Burtt, J. W. (C. Dist.) b June 11, 1944
*Burtt, T. B. (Cant.) b Jan. 22, 1915
Bury, T. E. O. (OUCC) b May 14, 1958
Buse, H. T. F. (Som.) b Aug. 5, 1910
Bushby, M. H. (CUCC) b July 29, 1931
Buss, A. (Sussex) b Sept. 1, 1939
Buss, M. A. (Sussex & OFS) b Jan. 24, 1944
Buswell, J. E. (Northants) b July 3, 1909
*Butcher, A. R. (Surrey) b Jan. 7, 1954
*Butcher, B. F. (Guyana; *CY 1970*) b Sept. 3, 1933
Butcher, I. P. (Leics.) b July 1, 1962
*Butcher, R. O. (Middx, B'dos & Tas.) b Oct. 14, 1953
*Butler, H. J. (Notts.) b March 12, 1913
Butler, L. C. (Wgtn) b Sept. 2, 1934
*Butler, L. S. (T/T) b Feb. 9, 1929
*Butt, H. R. (Sussex) b Dec. 27, 1865, d Dec. 21, 1928
*Butts, C. G. (Guyana) b July 8, 1957
Butterfield, L. A. (Cant.) b Aug. 29, 1913
Buxton, I. R. (Derbys.) b April 17, 1938
*Buys, I. D. (W. Prov.) b Feb. 3, 1895, dead
Bynoe, M. R. (B'dos) b Feb. 23, 1941

Caccia, Lord (Pres. MCC 1973-74) b Dec. 21, 1905
Caesar, Julius (Surrey & All-England) b March 25, 1830, d March 6, 1878
Caffyn, W. (Surrey & NSW) b Feb. 2, 1828, d Aug. 28, 1919
Caine, C. Stewart (Editor of *Wisden* 1926-33) b Oct. 28, 1861, d April 15, 1933

*Cairns, B. L. (C. Dist., Otago & N. Dist.) b Oct. 10, 1949

Calder, H. L. (Cranleigh; *CY 1918*) b 1900

*Callaway, S. T. (NSW & Cant.) b Feb. 6, 1868, d Nov. 25, 1923

*Callen, I. W. (Vic. & Boland) b May 2, 1955

*Calthorpe, Hon. F. S. Gough- (CUCC, Sussex & Warwicks.) b May 27, 1892, d Nov. 19, 1935

*Camacho, G. S. (Guyana) b Oct. 15, 1945

*Cameron, F. J. (Jam.) b June 22, 1923

*Cameron, F. J. (Otago) b June 1, 1932

*Cameron, H. B. (Tvl, E. Prov. & W. Prov.; *CY 1936*) b July 5, 1905, d Nov. 2, 1935

*Cameron, J. H. (CUCC, Jam. & Som.) b April 8, 1914

Campbell, K. O. (Otago) b March 20, 1943

*Campbell, T. (Tvl) b Feb. 9, 1882, d Oct. 5, 1924

Cannings, V. H. D. (Warwicks. & Hants) b April 3, 1919

Capel, D. J. (Northants & E. Prov.) b Feb. 6, 1963

Caple, R. G. (Middx & Hants) b Dec. 8, 1939

Cardus, Sir Neville (Cricket Writer) b April 3, 1888, d Feb. 27, 1975

*Carew, G. McD. (B'dos) b June 4, 1910, d Dec. 9, 1974

*Carew, M. C. (T/T) b Sept. 15, 1937

*Carkeek, W. (Vic.) b Oct. 17, 1878, d Feb. 20, 1937

*Carlson, P. H. (Qld) b Aug. 8, 1951

*Carlstein, P. R. (OFS, Tvl, Natal & Rhod.) b Oct. 28, 1938

Carmody, D. K. (NSW & W. Aust.) b Feb. 16, 1919, d Oct. 21, 1977

Carpenter, D. (Glos.) b Sept. 12, 1935

Carpenter, R. (Cambs. & Utd England XI) b Nov. 18, 1830, d July 13, 1901

*Carr, A. W. (Notts.; *CY 1923*) b May 21, 1893, d Feb. 7, 1963

*Carr, D. B. (OUCC & Derbys.; *CY 1960*; Sec. TCCB 1974-86) b Dec. 28, 1926

*Carr, D. W. (Kent; *CY 1910*) b March 17, 1872, d March 23, 1950

Carr, J. D. (OUCC & Middx) b June 15, 1963

Carrick, P. (Yorks. & E. Prov.) b July 16, 1952

Carrigan, A. H. (Qld) b Aug. 26, 1917

Carrington, E. (Derbys.) b March 25, 1914

*Carter, C. P. (Natal & Tvl) b April 23, 1881, d Nov. 8, 1952

*Carter, H. (NSW) b Halifax, Yorks. March 15, 1878, d June 8, 1948

Carter, R. G. (Warwicks.) b April 14, 1933

Carter, R. G. M. (Worcs.) b July 11, 1937

Carter, R. M. (Northants & Cant.) b May 25, 1960

Cartwright, H. (Derbys.) b May 12, 1951

*Cartwright, T. W. (Warwicks., Som. & Glam.) b July 22, 1935

Carty, R. A. (Hants) b July 28, 1922

Cass, G. R. (Essex, Worcs. & Tas.) b April 23, 1940

Castell, A. T. (Hants) b Aug. 6, 1943

Castle, F. (Som.) b April 9, 1909

Catt, A. W. (Kent & W. Prov.) b Oct. 2, 1933

*Catterall, R. H. (Tvl, Rhod., Natal & OFS; *CY 1925*) b July 10, 1900, d Jan. 2, 1961

Causby, J. P. (S. Aust.) b Oct. 27, 1942

*Cave, H. B. (Wgtn & C. Dist.) b Oct. 10, 1922

Cederwall, B. W. (Wgtn) b Feb. 24, 1952

Chadwick, D. (W. Aust.) b March 29, 1941

Chalk, F. G. H. (OUCC & Kent) b Sept. 7, 1910, d Feb. 20, 1943

*Challenor, G. (B'dos) b June 28, 1888, d July 30, 1947

*Chandrasekhar, B. S. (†Karn.; *CY 1972*) b May 17, 1945

*Chang, H. S. (Jam.) b July 22, 1952

*Chapman, A. P. F. (Uppingham, OUCC & Kent; *CY 1919*) b Sept. 3, 1900, d Sept. 16, 1961

*Chapman, H. W. (Natal) b June 30, 1890, d Dec. 1, 1941

Chapman, T. A. (Leics. & Rhod.) b May 14, 1919, d Feb. 19, 1979

*Chappell, G. S. (S. Aust., Som. & Qld; *CY 1973*) b Aug. 7, 1948

*Chappell, I. M. (S. Aust. & Lancs.; *CY 1976*) b Sept. 26, 1943

*Chappell, T. M. (S. Aust., W. Aust. & NSW) b Oct. 21, 1952

*Chapple, M. E. (Cant. & C. Dist.) b July 25, 1930, d July 31, 1985

*Charlton, P. C. (NSW) b April 9, 1867, d Sept. 30, 1954

*Charlwood, H. R. J. (Sussex) b Dec. 19, 1846, d June 6, 1888

Chatfield, E. J. (Wgtn) b July 3, 1950

Chatterton, W. (Derbys.) b Dec. 27, 1861, d March 19, 1913

*Chauhan, C. P. S. (M'tra & Delhi) b July 21, 1947

Cheatle, R. G. L. (Sussex & Surrey) b July 31, 1953

*Cheetham, J. E. (W. Prov.) b May 26, 1920, d Aug. 21, 1980

Chester, F. (Worcs.; Umpire) b Jan. 20, 1895, d April 8, 1957

Chesterton, G. H. (OUCC & Worcs.) b July 15, 1922

*Chevalier, G. A. (W. Prov.) b March 9, 1937

Childs, J. H. (Glos. & Essex; *CY 1987*) b Aug. 15, 1951

Childs-Clarke, A. W. (Middx & Northants) b May 13, 1905, d Feb. 19, 1980

*Chipperfield, A. G. (NSW) b Nov. 17, 1905

Chisholm, R. H. E. (Scotland) b May 22, 1927

*Chowdhury, N. R. (Bihar & Bengal) b May 23, 1923, d Dec. 14, 1979
*Christiani, C. M. (BG) b Oct. 28, 1913, d April 4, 1938
*Christiani, R. J. (BG) b July 19, 1920
*Christopherson, S. (Kent; Pres. MCC 1939-45) b Nov. 11, 1861, d April 6, 1949
*Christy, J. A. J. (Tvl & Qld) b Dec. 12, 1904, d Feb. 1, 1971
*Chubb, G. W. A. (Border & Tvl) b April 12, 1911, d Aug. 28, 1982
Clark, D. G. (Kent; Pres. MCC 1977-78) b Jan. 27, 1919
Clark, E. A. (Middx) b April 15, 1937
*Clark, E. W. (Northants) b Aug. 9, 1902, d April 28, 1982
Clark, L. S. (Essex) b March 6, 1914
Clark, T. H. (Surrey) b Oct. 4, 1924, d June 15, 1981
*Clark, W. M. (W. Aust.) b Sept. 19, 1953
Clarke, Dr C. B. (B'dos, Northants & Essex) b April 7, 1918
Clarke, R. W. (Northants) b April 22, 1924, d Aug. 3, 1981
*Clarke, S. T. (B'dos, Surrey & Tvl) b Dec. 11, 1954
Clarke, William (Notts.; founded All-England XI & Trent Bridge ground) b Dec. 24, 1798, d Aug. 25, 1856
Clarkson, A. (Yorks. & Som.) b Sept. 5, 1939
Claughton, J. A. (OUCC & Warwicks.) b Sept. 17, 1956
*Clay, J. C. (Glam.) b March 18, 1898, d Aug. 12, 1973
Clay, J. D. (Notts.) b Oct. 15, 1924
Clayton, G. (Lancs. & Som.) b Feb. 3, 1938
Clements, S. M. (OUCC) b April 19, 1956
*Cleverley, D. C. (Auck.) b Dec. 23, 1909
Clift, Patrick B. (Rhod., Leics. & Natal) b July 14, 1953
Clift, Philip B. (Glam.) b Sept. 3, 1918
Clinton, G. S. (Kent, Surrey & Zimb.-Rhod.) b May 5, 1953
*Close, D. B. (Yorks. & Som.; *CY* 1964) b Feb. 24, 1931
Cobb, R. A. (Leics.) b May 18, 1961
Cobden, F. C. (CUCC) b Oct. 14, 1849, d Dec. 7, 1932
Cobham, 10th Visct (Hon. C. J. Lyttelton) (Worcs.; Pres. MCC 1954) b Aug. 8, 1909, d March 20, 1977
*Cochrane, J. A. K. (Tvl & Griq. W.) b July 15, 1909
*Coen, S. K. (OFS, W. Prov., Tvl & Border) b Oct. 14, 1902, d Jan. 28, 1967
*Colah, S. M. H. (Bombay, W. Ind. & Naw.) b Sept. 22, 1902, d Sept. 11, 1950
Colchin, Robert ("Long Robin") (Kent & All-England) b Nov. 1713, d April 1750
*Coldwell, L. J. (Worcs.) b Jan. 10, 1933
Coleman, C. A. R. (Leics.) b July 7, 1906, d June 14, 1978

*Colley, D. J. (NSW) b March 15, 1947
Collin, T. (Warwicks.) b April 7, 1911
*Collinge, R. O. (C. Dist., Wgtn & N. Dist.) b April 2, 1946
*Collins, H. L. (NSW) b Jan. 21, 1889, d May 28, 1959
Collins, R. (Lancs.) b March 10, 1934
*Colquhoun, I. A. (C. Dist.) b June 8, 1924
*Commaille, J. M. M. (W. Prov., Natal, OFS & Griq. W.) b Feb. 21, 1883, d July 27, 1956
*Compton, D. C. S. (Middx & Holkar; *CY* 1939) b May 23, 1918
Compton, L. H. (Middx) b Sept. 12, 1912, d Dec. 27, 1984
*Coney, J. V. (Wgtn; *CY* 1984) b June 21, 1952
*Congdon, B. E. (C. Dist., Wgtn, Otago & Cant.; *CY* 1974) b Feb. 11, 1938
*Coningham, A. (NSW & Qld) b July 14, 1863, d June 13, 1939
*Connolly, A. N. (Vic. & Middx) b June 29, 1939
Connor, C. A. (Hants) b March 24, 1961
Constable, B. (Surrey) b Feb. 19, 1921
Constant, D. J. (Kent & Leics.; Umpire) b Nov. 9, 1941
*Constantine, Lord L. N. (T/T & B'dos; *CY* 1940) b Sept. 21, 1902, d July 1, 1971
Constantine, L. S. (T/T) b May 25, 1874, d Jan. 5, 1942
*Contractor, N. J. (Guj. & Ind. Rlwys) b March 7, 1934
*Conyngham, D. P. (Natal, Tvl & W. Prov.) b May 10, 1897
*Cook, C. (Glos.) b Aug. 23, 1921
*Cook, F. J. (E. Prov.) b 1870, dead
*Cook, G. (Northants & E. Prov.) b Oct. 9, 1951
Cook, G. G. (Qld) b June 29, 1910, d Sept. 12, 1982
*Cook, N. G. B. (Leics. & Northants) b June 17, 1956
Cook, S. J. (Tvl) b July 31, 1953
Cook, T. E. (Sussex) b Feb. 5, 1901, d Jan. 15, 1950
*Cooper, A. H. C. (Tvl) b Sept 2, 1893, d July 18, 1963
*Cooper, B. B. (Middx, Kent & Vic.) b March 15, 1844, d Aug. 7, 1914
Cooper, F. S. Ashley- (Cricket Historian) b March 17, 1877, d Jan. 31, 1932
Cooper, G. C. (Sussex) b Sept. 2, 1936
Cooper, H. P. (Yorks. & N. Tvl) b April 17, 1949
Cooper, K. E. (Notts.) b Dec. 27, 1957
Cooper, K. R. (Natal) b April 1, 1954
Cooper, N. H. C. (Glos. & CUCC) b Oct. 14, 1953
*Cooper, W. H. (Vic.) b Sept. 11, 1849, d April 5, 1939
*Cope, G. A. (Yorks.) b Feb. 23, 1947

Cope, J. E. B. (OUCC) b May 5, 1966

*Copson, W. H. (Derbys.; *CY 1937*) b April 27, 1908, d Sept. 14, 1971

Cordle, A. E. (Glam.) b Sept. 21, 1940

*Corling, G. E. (NSW) b July 13, 1941

Cornford, J. H. (Sussex) b Dec. 9, 1911, d June 17, 1985

*Cornford, W. L. (Sussex) b Dec. 25, 1900, d Feb. 6, 1964

Cornwallis, Capt. Hon. W. S. (2nd Lord Cornwallis) (Kent) b March 14, 1892, d Jan. 4, 1982

Corrall, P. (Leics.) b July 16, 1906

Corran, A. J. (OUCC & Notts.) b Nov. 25, 1936

Cosh, N. J. (CUCC & Surrey) b Aug. 6, 1946

*Cosier, G. J. (Vic., S. Aust. & Qld) b April 25,1953

*Cottam, J. T. (NSW) b Sept. 5, 1867, d Jan. 30, 1897

*Cottam, R. M. H. (Hants & Northants) b Oct. 16, 1944

*Cotter, A. (NSW) b Dec. 3, 1884, d Oct. 31, 1917

Cotterell, T. A. (CUCC) b May 12, 1963

Cotton, J. (Notts. & Leics.) b Nov. 7, 1940

Cottrell, G. A. (CUCC) b March 23, 1945

Cottrell, P. R. (CUCC) b May 22, 1957

Coulson, S. S. (Leics.) b Oct. 17, 1898, d Oct. 3, 1981

*Coulthard, G. (Vic.) b Aug. 1, 1856, d Oct. 22, 1883

*Coventry, Hon. C. J. (Worcs.) b Feb. 26, 1867, d June 2, 1929

Coverdale, S. P. (CUCC & Yorks.) b Nov. 20, 1954

Cowan, M. J. (Yorks.) b June 10, 1933

Cowan, R. S. (OUCC & Sussex) b March 30, 1960

*Cowans, N. G. (Middx) b April 17, 1961

*Cowdrey, C. S. (Kent) b Oct. 20, 1957

Cowdrey, G. R. (Kent) b June 27, 1964

*Cowdrey, M. C. (OUCC & Kent; *CY 1956*; Pres. MCC 1986-87) b Dec. 24, 1932

*Cowie, J. (Auck.) b March 30, 1912

Cowley, G. S. (E. Prov. & Natal) b March 1, 1953

Cowley, N. G. (Hants) b March 1, 1953

*Cowper, R. M. (Vic. & W. Aust.) b Oct. 5, 1940

Cox, A. L. (Northants) b July 22, 1907

Cox, G., jun. (Sussex) b Aug. 23, 1911, d March 30, 1985

Cox, G. R. (Sussex) b Nov. 29, 1873, d March 24, 1949

*Cox, J. L. (Natal) b June 28, 1886, d July 4, 1971

*Coxon, A. (Yorks.) b Jan. 18, 1916

Crabtree, H. P. (Essex) b April 30, 1906, d May 28, 1982

Craig, E. J. (CUCC & Lancs.) b March 26, 1942

*Craig, I. D. (NSW) b June 12, 1935

Cranfield, L. M. (Glos.) b Aug. 29, 1909

Cranmer, P. (Warwicks.) b Sept. 10, 1914

*Cranston, J. (Glos.) b Jan. 9, 1859, d Dec. 10, 1904

*Cranston, K. (Lancs.) b Oct. 20, 1917

*Crapp, J. F. (Glos.) b Oct. 14, 1912, d Feb. 15, 1981

*Crawford, J. N. (Surrey, S. Aust., Wgtn & Otago; *CY 1907*) b Dec. 1, 1886, d May 2, 1963

Crawford, N. C. (CUCC) b Nov. 26, 1958

Crawford, P. (NSW) b Aug. 3, 1933

Crawley, A. M. (OUCC & Kent; Pres. MCC 1972-73) b April 10, 1908

Crawley, L. G. (CUCC, Worcs. & Essex) b July 26, 1903, d July 9, 1981

Cray, S. J. (Essex) b May 29, 1921

Cresswell, G. F. (Wgtn & C. Dist.) b March 22, 1915, d Jan. 10, 1966

*Cripps, G. (W. Prov.) b Oct. 19, 1865, d July 27, 1943

*Crisp, R. J. (Rhod., W. Prov. & Worcs.) b May 28, 1911

*Croft, C. E. H. (Guyana & Lancs.) b March 15, 1953

*Cromb, I. B. (Cant.) b June 25, 1905, d March 6, 1984

Crookes, N. S. (Natal) b Nov. 15, 1935

Cross, G. F. (Leics.) b Nov. 15, 1943

*Crowe, J. J. (S. Aust. & Auck.) b Sept. 14, 1958

*Crowe, M. D. (Auck., C. Dist. & Som.; *CY 1985*) b Sept. 22, 1962

Crump, B. S. (Northants) b April 25, 1938

Crush, E. (Kent) b April 25, 1917

Cuffy, T. (T/T) b Nov. 9, 1949

Cullinan, M. R. (SA Us & OUCC) b April 3, 1957

Cumbes, J. (Lancs., Surrey, Worcs. & Warwicks.) b May 4, 1944

*Cunis, R. S. (Auck. & N. Dist.) b Jan. 5, 1941

Cunningham, K. G. (S. Aust.) b July 26, 1939

*Curnow, S. H. (Tvl) b Dec. 16, 1907, d July 28, 1986

Curran, K. M. (Glos. & Zimb.) b Sept. 7, 1959

Curtis, I. J. (OUCC & Surrey) b May 13, 1959

Curtis, T. S. (Worcs. & CUCC) b Jan. 15, 1960

Cuthbertson, G. B. (Middx, Sussex & Northants) b March 28, 1901

Cutmore, J. A. (Essex) b Dec. 28, 1898, d Nov. 30, 1985

*Cuttell, W. R. (Lancs.; *CY 1898*) b Sept. 13, 1864, d Dec. 9, 1929

*Da Costa, O. C. (Jam.) b Sept. 11, 1907, d Oct. 1, 1936

Dacre, C. C. (Auck. & Glos.) b May 15, 1899, d Nov. 2, 1975

Daer, A. G. (Essex) b Nov. 22, 1906, d July 16, 1980

Daft, Richard (Notts. & All-England) b Nov. 2, 1835, d July 18, 1900

Dakin, G. F. (E. Prov.) b Aug. 13, 1935

Dalmeny, Lord (6th Earl of Rosebery) (Middx & Surrey) b Jan. 8, 1882, d May 30, 1974

*Dalton, E. L. (Natal) b Dec. 2, 1906, d June 3, 1981

*Dani, H. T. (M'tra & Ind. Serv.) b May 24, 1933

*Daniel, W. W. (B'dos, Middx & W. Aust.) b Jan. 16, 1956

Dansie, N. (S. Aust.) b July 2, 1928

*D'Arcy, J. W. (Cant., Wgtn & Otago) b April 23, 1936

Dare, R. (Hants) b Nov. 26, 1921

*Darling, J. (S. Aust.; *CY 1900*) b Nov. 21, 1870, d Jan. 2, 1946

*Darling, L. S. (Vic.) b Aug. 14, 1909

Darling, W. M. (S. Aust.) b May 1, 1957

*Darnley, 8th Earl of (Hon. Ivo Bligh) (CUCC & Kent; Pres. MCC 1900) b March 13, 1859, d April 10, 1927

Davey, J. (Glos.) b Sept. 4, 1944

*Davidson, A. K. (NSW; *CY 1962*) b June 14, 1929

Davidson, J. E. (CUCC) b Oct. 23, 1964

Davies, A. G. (CUCC) b May 5, 1962

Davies, Dai (Glam.) b Aug. 26, 1896, d July 16, 1976

Davies, Emrys (Glam.) b June 27, 1904, d Nov. 10, 1975

*Davies, E. Q. (E. Prov., Tvl & NE Tvl) b Aug. 26, 1909, d Nov. 11, 1976

Davies, R. (NSW) b July 22, 1946

Davies, H. D. (Glam.) b July 23, 1932

Davies, H. G. (Glam.) b April 23, 1913

Davies, J. G. W. (CUCC & Kent; Pres. MCC 1985-86) b Sept. 10, 1911

Davies, T. (Glam.) b Oct. 25, 1960

*Davis, B. A. (T/T & Glam.) b May 2, 1940

*Davis, C. A. (T/T) b Jan. 1, 1944

Davis, E. (Northants) b March 8, 1922

*Davis, I. C. (NSW & Qld) b June 25, 1953

Davis, M. R. (Som.) b Feb. 26, 1962

Davis, P. C. (Northants) b May 24, 1915

Davis, R. C. (Glam.) b Jan. 1, 1946

*Davis, S. P. (Vic.) b Nov. 8, 1959

*Davis, W. W. (Windwards & Glam.) b Sept. 18, 1958

Davison, B. F. (Rhod., Leics, Tas. & Glos.) b Dec. 21, 1946

Davison, I. (Notts.) b Oct. 4, 1937

Dawkes, G. O. (Leics. & Derbys.) b July 19, 1920

*Dawson, E. W. (CUCC & Leics.) b Feb. 13, 1904, d June 4, 1979

*Dawson, O. C. (Natal & Border) b Sept. 1, 1919

Dawson, T. A. J. (OUCC) b Jan. 29, 1963

Day, A. P. (Kent; *CY 1910*) b April 10, 1885, d Jan. 22, 1969

Day, N. T. (Tvl & N. Tvl) b Dec. 31, 1953

*de Alwis, R. G. (SL) b Feb. 15, 1959

*Dean, H. (Lancs.) b Aug. 13, 1884, d March 12, 1957

Deane, H. G. (Natal & Tvl) b July 21, 1895, d Oct. 21, 1939

*De Caires, F. I. (BG) b May 12, 1909, d Feb. 2, 1959

*De Courcy, J. H. (NSW) b April 18, 1927

Deed, J. A. (Kent) b Sept. 12, 1901, d Oct. 19, 1980

DeFreitas, P. A. J. (Leics.) b Feb. 18, 1966

Delisle, G. P. S. (Middx & OUCC) b Dec. 25, 1934

*Dell, A. R. (Qld) b Aug. 6, 1947

*de Mel, A. L. F. (SL) b May 9, 1959

*Dempster, C. S. (Wgtn, Leics., Scotland & Warwicks.; *CY 1932*) b Nov. 15, 1903, d Feb. 14, 1974

*Dempster, E. W. (Wgtn) b Jan. 25, 1925

*Denness, M. H. (Scotland, Kent & Essex; *CY 1975*) b Dec. 1, 1940

Dennett, E. G. (Glos.) b April 27, 1880, d Sept. 14, 1937

Denning, P. W. (Som.) b Dec. 16, 1949

Dennis, F. (Yorks.) b June 11, 1907

Dennis, S. J. (Yorks. & OFS) b Oct. 18, 1960

*Denton, D. (Yorks.; *CY 1906*) b July 4, 1874, d Feb. 16, 1950

Denton, W. H. (Northants) b Nov. 2, 1890, d April 23, 1979

Deodhar, D. B. (M'tra; oldest living Ranji Trophy player) b Jan. 14, 1892

*Depeiza, C. C. (B'dos) b Oct. 10, 1927

Derrick, J. (Glam.) b Jan. 15, 1963

*Desai, R. B. (Bombay) b June 20, 1939

De Saram, F. C. (OUCC & Ceylon) b Sept. 5, 1912, d April 11, 1983

*de Silva, D. S. (SL) b June 11, 1942

*de Silva, E. A. R. (SL) b March 28, 1956

*de Silva, G. R. A. (SL) b Dec. 12, 1952

*de Silva, P. A. (SL) b Oct. 17, 1965

de Smidt, R. (W. Prov.) b Nov. 24, 1883, d Aug. 3, 1986

De Vaal, P. D. (Tvl) b Dec. 3, 1945

Devereux, L. N. (Middx, Worcs. & Glam.) b Oct. 20, 1931

Dewdney, C. T. (Jam.) b Oct. 23, 1933

Dewes, A. R. (CUCC) b June 2, 1957

*Dewes, J. G. (CUCC & Middx) b Oct. 11, 1926

Dews, G. (Worcs.) b June 5, 1921

*Dexter, E. R. (CUCC & Sussex; *CY 1961*) b May 15, 1935

*Dias, R. L. (SL) b Oct. 18, 1952

Dibbs, A. H. A. (Pres. MCC 1983-84) b Dec. 9, 1918, d Nov. 28, 1985

*Dick, A. E. (Otago & Wgtn) b Oct. 10, 1936

Dickeson, C. W. (N. Dist.) b March 26, 1955

*Dickinson, G. R. (Otago) b March 11, 1903, d March 17, 1978

*Dilley, G. R. (Kent & Natal) b May 18, 1959

Diment, R. A. (Glos. & Leics.) b Feb. 9, 1927

*Dipper, A. E. (Glos.) b Nov. 9, 1885, d Nov. 7, 1945

Divecha, R. V. (Bombay, OUCC, Northants, Vidarbha & S'tra) b Oct. 18, 1927

Diver, A. J. D. (Cambs., Middx, Notts. & All-England) b June 6, 1824, d March 25, 1876

Dixon, A. L. (Kent) b Nov. 27, 1933

*Dixon, C. D. (Tvl) b Feb. 12, 1891, d Sept. 9, 1969

Dodds, T. C. (Essex) b May 29, 1919

Doggart, G. H. G. (CUCC, Durham & Middx) b June 2, 1897, d June 7, 1963

*Doggart, G. H. G. (CUCC & Sussex; Pres. MCC 1981-82) b July 18, 1925

Doggart, S. J. G. (CUCC) b Feb. 8, 1961

Doherty, M. J. D. (Griq. W.) b March 14, 1947

*D'Oliveira, B. L. (Worcs.; *CY 1967*) b Oct. 4, 1931

D'Oliveira, D. B. (Worcs.) b Oct. 19, 1960

*Dollery, H. E. (Warwicks. & Wgtn; *CY 1952*) b Oct. 14, 1914

Dollery, K. R. (Qld, Auck., Tas. & Warwicks.) b Dec. 9, 1924

*Dolphin, A. (Yorks.) b Dec. 24, 1885, d Oct. 23, 1942

*Donnan, H. (NSW) b Nov. 12, 1864, d Aug. 13, 1956

*Donnelly, M. P. (Wgtn, Cant., Middx, Warwicks. & OUCC; *CY 1948*) b Oct. 17, 1917

*Dooland, B. (S. Aust. & Notts.; *CY 1955*) b Nov. 1, 1923, d Sept. 8, 1980

Dorrinton, W. (Kent & All-England) b April 29, 1809, d Nov. 8, 1848

Dorset, 3rd Duke of (Kent) b March 24, 1745, d July 19, 1799

*Doshi, D. R. (Bengal, Notts. & Warwicks.) b Dec. 22, 1947

Doughty, R. J. (Glos. & Surrey) b Nov. 17, 1960

*Douglas, J. W. H. T. (Essex; *CY 1915*) b Sept. 3, 1882, d Dec. 19, 1930

Dowding, A. L. (OUCC) b April 4, 1929

Dowe, U. G. (Jam.) b March 29, 1949

Dower, R. R. (E. Prov.) b June 4, 1876, d Sept. 15, 1964

Dowling, D. F. (Border, NE Tvl & Natal) b July 25, 1914

*Dowling, G. T. (Cant.) b March 4, 1937

Downton, P. R. (Kent & Middx) b April 4, 1957

Draper, E. J. (E. Prov. & Griq. W.) b Sept. 27, 1934

*Draper, R. G. (E. Prov. & Griq. W.) b Dec. 24, 1926

Dredge, C. H. (Som.) b Aug. 4, 1954

*Druce, N. F. (CUCC & Surrey; *CY 1898*) b Jan. 1, 1875, d Oct. 27, 1954

Drybrough, C. D. (OUCC & Middx) b Aug. 31, 1938

*D'Souza, A. (Kar., Peshawar & PIA) b Jan. 1, 1938

*Ducat, A. (Surrey; *CY 1920*) b Feb. 16, 1886, d July 23, 1942

*Duckworth, C. A. R. (Natal & Rhod.) b March 22, 1933

*Duckworth, G. (Lancs.; *CY 1929*) b May 9, 1901, d Jan. 5, 1966

Dudleston, B. (Leics., Glos. & Rhod.) b July 16, 1945

*Duff, R. A. (NSW) b Aug. 17, 1878, d Dec. 13, 1911

*Dujon, P. J. (Jam.) b May 28, 1956

*Duleepsinhji, K. S. (CUCC & Sussex; *CY 1930*) b June 13, 1905, d Dec. 5, 1959

*Dumbrill, R. (Natal & Tvl) b Nov. 19, 1938

*Duminy, J. P. (OUCC, W. Prov. & Tvl) b Dec. 16, 1897, d Jan. 31, 1980

*Duncan, J. R. F. (Qld & Vic.) b March 25, 1944

*Dunell, O. R. (E. Prov.) b July 15, 1856, d Oct. 21, 1929

Dunning, B. (N. Dist.) b March 20, 1940

*Dunning, J. A. (Otago & OUCC) b Feb. 6, 1903, d June 24, 1971

*Du Preez, J. H. (Rhod. & Zimb.) b Nov. 14, 1942

Du Preez, V. F. (N. Tvl) b Sept. 6, 1958

*Durani, S. A. (S'tra, Guj. & Raja.) b Dec. 11, 1934

Durose, A. J. (Northants) b Oct. 10, 1944

*Durston, F. J. (Middx) b July 11, 1893, d April 8, 1965

*Du Toit, J. F. (SA) b April 5, 1868, d July 10, 1909

Dye, J. C. J. (Kent, Northants & E. Prov.) b July 24, 1942

Dyer, D. D. (Natal & Tvl) b Dec. 3, 1946

*Dyer, D. V. (Natal) b May 2, 1914

Dyer, R. I. H. B. (Warwicks.) b Dec. 22, 1958

*Dymock, G. (Qld) b July 21, 1946

*Dyson, A. H. (Glam.) b July 10, 1905, d June 7, 1978

Dyson, J. (Lancs.) b July 8, 1934

*Dyson, John (NSW) b June 11, 1954

*Eady, C. J. (Tas.) b Oct. 29, 1870, d Dec. 20, 1945

Eagar, E. D. R. (OUCC, Glos. & Hants) b Dec. 8, 1917, d Sept. 13, 1977

Eagar, M. A. (OUCC & Glos.) b March 20, 1934

Eaglestone, J. T. (Middx & Glam.) b July 24, 1923

Ealham, A. G. E. (Kent) b Aug. 30, 1944

East, D. E. (Essex) b July 27, 1959

East, R. E. (Essex) b June 20, 1947

East, R. J. (OFS) b March 31, 1953

Eastman, G. F. (Essex) b April 7, 1903

Eastman, L. C. (Essex & Otago) b June 3, 1897, d April 17, 1941

*Eastwood, K. H. (Vic.) b Nov. 23, 1935

*Ebeling, H. I. (Vic.) b Jan. 1, 1905, d Jan. 12, 1980

Eckersley, P. T. (Lancs.) b July 2, 1904, d Aug. 13, 1940

Edbrooke, R. M. (OUCC) b Dec. 30, 1960

Eddy, V. A. (Leewards) b Feb. 14, 1955

*Edgar, B. A. (Wgtn) b Nov. 23, 1956

Edinburgh, HRH Duke of (Pres. MCC 1948-49, 1974-75) b June 10, 1921

Edmeades, B. E. A. (Essex) b Sept. 17, 1941

*Edmonds, P. H. (CUCC, Middx & E. Prov.) b March 8, 1951

Edmonds, R. B. (Warwicks.) b March 2, 1941

Edrich, B. R. (Kent & Glam.) b Aug. 18, 1922

Edrich, E. H. (Lancs.) b March 27, 1914

Edrich, G. A. (Lancs.) b July 13, 1918

*Edrich, J. H. (Surrey; *CY 1966*) b June 21, 1937

*Edrich, W. J. (Middx; *CY 1940*) b March 26, 1916, d April 23, 1986

*Edwards, G. N. (C. Dist.) b May 27, 1955

*Edwards, J. D. (Vic.) b June 12, 1862, d July 31, 1911

Edwards, M. J. (CUCC & Surrey) b March 1, 1940

*Edwards, R. (W. Aust. & Vic.) b Dec. 1, 1942

*Edwards, R. M. (B'dos) b June 3, 1940

Edwards, T. D. W. (CUCC) b Dec. 6, 1958

*Edwards, W. J. (W. Aust.) b Dec. 23, 1949

Eele, P. J. (Som.) b Jan. 27, 1935

Eggar, J. D. (OUCC, Hants & Derbys.) b Dec. 1, 1916, d May 3, 1983

*Ehtesham-ud-Din (Lahore, Punjab, PIA, NBP & UBL) b Sept. 4, 1950

*Elgie, M. K. (Natal) b March 6, 1933

Elliott, C. S. (Derbys.) b April 24, 1912

*Elliott, H. (Derbys.) b Nov. 2, 1891, d Feb. 2, 1976

Elliott, Harold (Lancs.; Umpire) b June 15, 1904, d April 15, 1969

Ellis, G. P. (Glam.) b May 24, 1950

Ellis, J. L. (Vic.) b May 9, 1890, d July 26, 1974

Ellis, R. G. P. (OUCC & Middx) b Oct. 20 1960

Ellison, C. C. (CUCC) b Feb. 11, 1962

*Ellison, R. M. (Kent; *CY 1986*) b Sept. 21, 1959

Elms, R. B. (Kent & Hants) b April 5, 1949

*Emburey, J. E. (Middx & W. Prov.; *CY 1984*) b Aug. 20, 1952

*Emery, R. W. G. (Auck. & Cant.) b March 28, 1915, d Dec. 18, 1982

*Emery, S. H. (NSW) b Oct. 16, 1885, d Jan. 7, 1967

*Emmett, G. M. (Glos.) b Dec. 2, 1912, d Dec. 18, 1976

*Emmett, T. (Yorks.) b Sept. 3, 1841, d June 30, 1904

*Endean, W. R. (Tvl) b May 31, 1924

*Engineer, F. M. (Bombay & Lancs.) b Feb. 25, 1938

Enthoven, H. J. (CUCC & Middx) b June 4, 1903, d June 29, 1975

*Evans, A. J. (OUCC, Hants & Kent) b May 1, 1889, d Sept. 18, 1960

Evans, D. G. L. (Glam.; Umpire) b July 27, 1933

*Evans, E. (NSW) b March 6, 1849, d July 2, 1921

Evans, G. (OUCC, Glam. & Leics.) b Aug. 13, 1915

Evans, J. B. (Glam.) b Nov. 9, 1936

*Evans, T. G. (Kent; *CY 1951*) b Aug. 18, 1920

Every, T. (Glam.) b Dec. 19, 1909

Eyre, T. J. P. (Derbys.) b Oct. 17, 1939

Ezekowitz, R. A. B. (OUCC) b Jan. 19, 1954

Faber, M. J. J. (OUCC & Sussex) b Aug. 15, 1950

Fagg, A. E. (Kent) b June 18, 1915, d Sept. 13, 1977

Fairbairn, A. (Middx) b Jan. 25, 1923

Fairbrother, N. H. (Lancs.) b Sept. 9, 1963

*Fairfax, A. G. (NSW) b June 16, 1906, d May 17, 1955

Fairservice, C. (Kent & Middx) b Aug. 21, 1909

Fairservice, W. J. (Kent) b May 16, 1881, d June 26, 1971

Falcon, M. (CUCC) b July 21, 1888, d Feb. 27, 1976

Fallows, J. A. (Lancs.) b July 25, 1907, d Jan. 20, 1974

*Fane, F. L. (OUCC & Essex) b April 27, 1875, d Nov. 27, 1960

Fantham, W. E. (Warwicks.) b May 14, 1918

*Farnes, K. (CUCC & Essex; *CY 1939*) b July 8, 1911, d Oct. 20, 1941

*Farooq Hamid (Lahore & PIA) b March 3, 1945

*Farrer, W. S. (Border) b Dec. 8, 1936

*Farrimond, W. (Lancs.) b May 23, 1903, d Nov. 14, 1979

*Farrukh Zaman (Peshawar, NWFP, Punjab & MCB) b April 2, 1956

*Faulkner, G. A. (Tvl) b Dec. 17, 1881, d Sept. 10, 1930

*Favell, L. E. (S. Aust.) b Oct. 6, 1929

*Fazal Mahmood (N. Ind., Punjab & Lahore; *CY 1955*) b Feb. 18, 1927

Fearnley, C. D. (Worcs.) b April 12, 1940

Featherstone, N. G. (Tvl, N. Tvl, Middx & Glam.) b Aug. 20, 1949

'Felix', N. (Wanostrocht) (Kent, Surrey & All-England) b Oct. 4, 1804, d Sept. 3, 1876

Fell, D. J. (CUCC) b Oct. 27, 1964

*Fellows-Smith, J. P. (OUCC, Tvl & Northants) b Feb. 3, 1932

Felton, N. A. (Som.) b Oct. 24, 1960

*Fender, P. G. H. (Sussex & Surrey; *CY 1915*) b Aug. 22, 1892, d June 15, 1985

Fenner, D. (Border) b March 27, 1929

*Ferguson, W. (T/T) b Dec. 14, 1917, d Feb. 23, 1961

Fernandes, M. P. (BG) b Aug. 12, 1897, d May 8, 1981

*Fernando, E. R. N. S. (SL) b Dec. 19, 1955

Ferrandi, J. H. (W. Prov.) b April 3, 1930

Ferreira, A. M. (N. Tvl & Warwicks.) b April 13, 1955

**Ferris, J. J. (NSW, Glos. & S. Aust.; *CY 1889*) b May 21, 1867, d Nov. 21, 1900

*Fichardt, C. G. (OFS) b March 20, 1870, d May 30, 1923

Fiddling, K. (Yorks. & Northants) b Oct. 13, 1917

*Fielder, A. (Kent; *CY 1907*) b July 19, 1877, d Aug. 30, 1949

Findlay, T. M. (Comb. Is. & Windwards) b Oct. 19, 1943

Findlay, W. (OUCC & Lancs.; Sec. Surrey CCC, Sec. MCC 1926-36) b June 22, 1880, d June 19, 1953

*Fingleton, J. H. (NSW) b April 28, 1908, d Nov. 22, 1981

*Finlason, C. E. (Tvl & Griq. W.) b Feb. 19, 1860, d July 31, 1917

Finney, R. J. (Derbys.) b Aug. 2, 1960

Firth, J. (Yorks. & Leics.) b June 27, 1918, d Sept. 6, 1981

Firth, Rev. Canon J. D'E. E. (Winchester, OUCC & Notts.; *CY 1918*) b Jan. 21, 1900, d Sept. 21, 1957

Fisher, B. (Qld) b Jan. 20, 1934, d April 6, 1980

*Fisher, F. E. (Wgtn & C. Dist.) b July 28, 1924

Fisher, P. B. (OUCC, Middx & Worcs.) b Dec. 19, 1954

*Fishlock, L. B. (Surrey; *CY 1947*) b Jan. 2, 1907, d June 26, 1986

Flanagan, J. P. D. (Tvl) b Sept. 20, 1947

*Flavell, J. A. (Worcs.; *CY 1965*) b May 15, 1929

*Fleetwood-Smith, L. O'B. (Vic.) b March 30, 1910, d March 16, 1971

Fletcher, D. A. G. (Rhod. & Zimb.) b Sept. 27, 1948

Fletcher, D. G. W. (Surrey) b July 6, 1924

*Fletcher, K. W. R. (Essex; *CY 1974*) b May 20, 1944

Fletcher, S. D. (Yorks.) b June 8, 1964

*Floquet, C. E. (Tvl) b Nov. 3, 1884, d Nov. 22, 1963

*Flowers, W. (Notts.) b Dec. 7, 1856, d Nov. 1, 1926

Foat, J. C. (Glos.) b Nov. 21, 1952

*Foley, H. (Wgtn) b Jan. 28, 1906, d Oct. 16, 1948

Folley, I. (Lancs.) b Jan. 9, 1963

Foord, C. W. (Yorks.) b June 11, 1924

Forbes, C. (Notts.) b Aug. 9, 1936

Ford, D. A. (NSW) b Dec. 12, 1930

*Ford, F. G. J. (CUCC & Middx) b Dec. 14, 1866, d Feb. 7, 1940

Ford, N. M. (OUCC, Derbys. & Middx) b Nov. 18, 1906

Ford, R. G. (Glos.) b March 3, 1907, d Oct. 1981

Foreman, D. J. (W. Prov. & Sussex) b Feb. 1, 1933

Fosh, M. K. (CUCC & Essex) b Sept. 26, 1957

Foster, D. G. (Warwicks.) b March 19, 1907, d Oct. 13, 1980

*Foster, F. R. (Warwicks.; *CY 1912*) b Jan. 31, 1889, d May 3, 1958

Foster, G. N. (OUCC, Worcs. & Kent) b Oct. 16, 1884, d Aug. 11, 1971

Foster, H. K. (OUCC & Worcs.; *CY 1911*) b Oct. 30, 1873, d June 23, 1950

Foster, M. K. (Worcs.) b Jan. 1, 1889, d Dec. 3, 1940

*Foster, M. L. C. (Jam.) b May 9, 1943

*Foster, N. A. (Essex) b May 6, 1962

Foster, P. G. (Kent) b Oct. 9, 1916

*Foster, R. E. (OUCC & Worcs.; *CY 1901*) b April 16, 1878, d May 13, 1914

*Fothergill, A. J. (Som.) b Aug. 26, 1854, d Aug. 1, 1932

Fotheringham, H. R. (Natal & Tvl) b April 4, 1953

Foulkes, I. (Border & OFS) b Feb. 22, 1955

Fowler, A. J. B. (Middx) b April 1, 1891, d May 7, 1977

*Fowler, G. (Lancs.) b April 20, 1957

Fowler, W. P. (Derbys., N. Dist. & Auck.) b March 13, 1959

*Francis, B. C. (NSW & Essex) b Feb. 18, 1948

Francis, D. A. (Glam.) b Nov. 29, 1953

*Francis, G. N. (B'dos) b Dec. 7, 1897, d Jan. 12, 1942

*Francis, H. H. (Glos. & W. Prov.) b May 26, 1868, d Jan. 7, 1936

Francke, F. M. (SL & Qld) b March 29, 1941

*Francois, C. M. (Griq. W.) b June 20, 1897, d May 26, 1944

*Frank, C. N. (Tvl) b Jan. 27, 1891, d Dec. 26, 1961

*Frank, W. H. B. (SA) b Nov. 23, 1872, d Feb. 16, 1945
 Franklin, H. W. F. (OUCC, Surrey & Essex) b June 30, 1901, d May 25, 1985
*Franklin, T. J. (Auck.) b March 18, 1962
 Franks, J. G. (OUCC) b Sept. 23, 1962
*Frederick, M. C. (B'dos, Derbys. & Jam.) b May 6, 1927
*Fredericks, R. C. (†Guyana & Glam.; *CY 1974*) b Nov. 11, 1942
*Freeman, A. P. (Kent; *CY 1923*) b May 17, 1888, d Jan. 28, 1965
*Freeman, D. L. (Wgtn) b Sept. 8, 1914
*Freeman, E. W. (S. Aust.) b July 13, 1944
*Freer, F. W. (Vic.) b Dec. 4, 1915
*French, B. N. (Notts.) b Aug. 13, 1959
 Frost, G. (Notts.) b Jan. 15, 1947
 Fry, C. A. (OUCC, Hants & Northants) b Jan. 14, 1940
*Fry, C. B. (OUCC, Sussex & Hants; *CY 1895*) b April 25, 1872, d Sept. 7, 1956
*Fuller, E. R. H. (W. Prov.) b Aug. 2, 1931
*Fuller, R. L. (Jam.) b Jan. 30, 1913
*Fullerton, G. M. (Tvl) b Dec. 8, 1922
 Fulton, R. W. (Cant.) b Aug. 5, 1951
 Funston, G. K. (NE Tvl & Griq. W.) b Nov. 21, 1948
*Funston, K. J. (NE Tvl, OFS & Tvl) b Dec. 3, 1925
*Furlonge, H. A. (T/T) b June 19, 1934

 Gabriel, R. S. (T/T) b June 5, 1952
*Gadkari, C. V. (M'tra & Ind. Serv.) b Feb. 3, 1928
*Gaekwad, A. D. (Baroda) b Sept. 23, 1952
*Gaekwad, D. K. (Baroda) b Oct. 27, 1928
*Gaekwad, H. G. (†M. Pradesh) b Aug. 29, 1923
 Gale, R. A. (Middx) b Dec. 10, 1933
*Gallichan, N. (Wgtn) b June 3, 1906, d March 25, 1969
*Gamsy, D. (Natal) b Feb. 17, 1940
*Gandotra, A. (Delhi & Bengal) b Nov. 24, 1948
*Gannon, J. B. (W. Aust.) b Feb. 8, 1947
*Ganteaume, A. G. (T/T) b Jan. 22, 1921
 Gard, T. (Som.) b June 2, 1957
 Gardiner, H. A. B. (Rhod.) b Jan. 3, 1944
 Gardiner, S. J. C. (CUCC) b March 19, 1947
 Gardner, F. C. (Warwicks.) b June 4, 1922, d Jan. 13, 1979
 Gardner, L. R. (Leics.) b Feb. 23, 1934
 Garland-Wells, H. M. (OUCC & Surrey) b Nov. 14, 1907
 Garlick, P. L. (CUCC) b Aug. 2, 1964
 Garlick, R. G. (Lancs. & Northants) b April 11, 1917
*Garner, J. (B'dos, Som. & S. Aust.; *CY 1980*) b Dec. 16, 1952
 Garnham, M. A. (Glos. & Leics.) b Aug. 20, 1960

*Garrett, T. W. (NSW) b July 26, 1858, d Aug. 6, 1943
*Gaskin, B. M. (BG) b March 21, 1908, d May 2, 1979
*Gatting, M. W. (Middx; *CY 1984*) b June 6, 1957
*Gaunt, R. A. (W. Aust. & Vic.) b Feb. 26, 1934
*Gavaskar, S. M. (Bombay & Som.; *CY 1980*) b July 10, 1949
*Gay, L. H. (CUCC, Hants & Som.) b March 24, 1871, d Nov. 1, 1949
 Geary, A. C. T. (Surrey) b Sept. 11, 1900
*Geary, G. (Leics.; *CY 1927*) b July 9, 1893, d March 6, 1981
*Gedye, S. G. (Auck.) b May 2, 1929
*Gehrs, D. R. A. (S. Aust.) b Nov. 29, 1880, d June 25, 1953
*Ghavri, K. D. (S'tra & Bombay) b Feb. 28, 1951
*Ghorpade, J. M. (Baroda) b Oct. 2, 1930, d March 29, 1978
*Ghulam Abbas (Kar., NBP & PIA) b May 1, 1947
*Ghulam Ahmed (H'bad) b July 4, 1922
*Gibb, P. A. (OUCC, Scotland, Yorks. & Essex) b July 11, 1913, d Dec. 7, 1977
 Gibbons, H. H. (Worcs.) b Oct. 10, 1904, d Feb. 16, 1973
*Gibbs, G. L. (BG) b Dec. 27, 1925, d Feb. 21, 1979
*Gibbs, L. R. (†Guyana, S. Aust. & Warwicks.; *CY 1972*) b Sept. 29, 1934
 Gibbs, P. J. K. (OUCC & Derbys.) b Aug. 17, 1944
 Gibson, C. H. (Eton, CUCC & Sussex; *CY 1918*) b Aug. 23, 1900, d Dec. 31, 1976
 Gibson, D. (Surrey) b May 1, 1936
 Gibson, J. G. (N. Dist. & Auck.) b Nov. 12, 1948
*Giffen, G. (S. Aust.; *CY 1894*) b March 27, 1859, d Nov. 29, 1927
*Giffen, W. F. (S. Aust.) b Sept. 20, 1861, d June 29, 1949
*Gifford, N. (Worcs. & Warwicks.; *CY 1975*) b March 30, 1940
*Gilbert, D. R. (NSW) b Dec. 19, 1960
*Gilchrist, R. (Jam. & H'bad) b June 28, 1934
 Giles, R. J. (Notts.) b Oct. 17, 1919
 Gill, A. (Notts.) b Aug. 4, 1940
 Gill, L. L. (Tas. & Qld; oldest surviving Sheffield Shield player) b Nov. 19, 1891
 Gilhouley, K. (Yorks. & Notts.) b Aug. 8, 1934
 Gillespie, S. R. (Auck.) b March 2, 1957
 Gilliat, R. M. C. (OUCC & Hants) b May 20, 1944
*Gilligan, A. E. R. (CUCC, Surrey & Sussex; *CY 1924*; Pres. MCC 1967-68) b Dec. 23, 1894, d Sept. 5, 1976

*Gilligan, A. H. H. (Sussex) b June 29, 1896, d May 5, 1978

Gilligan, F. W. (OUCC & Essex) b Sept. 20, 1893, d May 4, 1960

*Gilmour, G. J. (NSW) b June 26, 1951

*Gimblett, H. (Som.; *CY 1953*) b Oct. 19, 1914, d March 30, 1978

Gladstone, G. (*see* Marais, G. G.)

Gladwin, Chris (Essex) b May 10, 1962

*Gladwin, Cliff (Derbys.) b April 3, 1916

*Gleeson, J. W. (NSW & E. Prov.) b March 14, 1938

*Gleeson, R. A. (E. Prov.) b Dec. 6, 1873, d Sept. 27, 1919

*Glover, G. K. (Kimberley & Griq. W.) b May 13, 1870, d Nov. 15, 1938

Glover, T. R. (OUCC) b Nov. 26, 1951

Goddard, G. F. (Scotland) b May 19, 1938

*Goddard, J. D. C. (B'dos) b April 21, 1919

*Goddard, T. L. (Natal & NE Tvl) b Aug. 1, 1931

*Goddard, T. W. (Glos.; *CY 1938*) b Oct. 1, 1900, d May 22, 1966

Goel, R. (Patiala & Haryana) b Sept. 29, 1942

Goldie, C. F. E. (CUCC & Hants) b Nov. 20, 1960

Golding, A. K. (Essex & CUCC) b Oct. 5, 1963

Goldstein, F. S. (OUCC, Northants, Tvl & W. Prov.) b Oct. 14, 1944

*Gomes, H. A. (T/T & Middx; *CY 1985*) b July 13, 1953

Gomes, S. A. (T/T) b Oct. 18, 1950

*Gomez, G. E. (T/T) b Oct. 10, 1919

*Gooch, G. A. (Essex & W. Prov.; *CY 1980*) b July 23, 1953

Goodway, C. C. (Warwicks.) b July 10, 1909

Goodwin, K. (Lancs.) b June 25, 1938

Goodwin, T. J. (Leics.) b Jan. 22, 1929

*Goonatillake, H. M. (SL) b Aug. 16, 1952

Goonesena, G. (Ceylon, Notts., CUCC & NSW) b Feb. 16, 1931

*Gopalan, M. J. (Madras) b June 6, 1909

*Gopinath, C. D. (Madras) b March 1, 1930

*Gordon, N. (Tvl) b Aug. 6, 1911

Gore, A. C. (Eton & Army; *CY 1919*) b May 14, 1900

Gorman, S. R. (CUCC) b April 28, 1965

Gothard, E. J. (Derbys.) b Oct. 1, 1904, d Jan. 17, 1979

Gould, I. J. (Middx, Auck. & Sussex) b Aug. 19, 1957

*Gover, A. R. (Surrey; *CY 1937*) b Feb. 29, 1908

*Gower, D. I. (Leics.; *CY 1979*) b April 1, 1957

Gowrie, 1st Lord (Pres. MCC 1948-49) b July 6, 1872, d May 2, 1955

Grace, Dr Alfred b May 17, 1840, d May 24, 1916

Grace, Dr Alfred H. (Glos.) b March 10, 1866, d Sept. 16, 1929

Grace, C. B. (Clifton) b March 1882, d June 6, 1938

*Grace, Dr E. M. (Glos.) b Nov. 28, 1841, d May 20, 1911

Grace, Dr Edgar M. (MCC) (son of E. M. Grace) b Oct. 6, 1886, d Nov. 24, 1974

*Grace, G. F. (Glos.) b Dec. 13, 1850, d Sept. 22, 1880

Grace, Dr Henry (Glos.) b Jan. 31, 1833, d Nov. 15, 1895

Grace, Dr H. M. (father of W. G., E. M. and G. F.) b Feb. 21, 1808, d Dec. 23, 1871

Grace, Mrs H. M. (mother of W. G., E. M. and G. F.) b July 18, 1812, d July 25, 1884

*Grace, Dr W. G. (Glos.; *CY 1896*) b July 18, 1848, d Oct. 23, 1915

Grace, W. G., jun. (CUCC & Glos.) b July 6, 1874, d March 2, 1905

*Graham, H. (Vic. & Otago) b Nov. 29, 1870, d Feb. 7, 1911

Graham, J. N. (Kent) b May 8, 1943

*Graham, R. (W. Prov.) b Sept. 16, 1877, d April 21, 1946

*Grant, G. C. (CUCC, T/T & Rhod.) b May 9, 1907, d Oct. 26, 1978

*Grant, R. S. (CUCC & T/T) b Dec. 15, 1909, d Oct. 18, 1977

Graveney, D. A. (Glos.) b Jan. 21, 1953

Graveney, J. K. (Glos.) b Dec. 16, 1924

*Graveney, T. W. (Glos., Worcs. & Qld; *CY 1953*) b June 16, 1927

Graves, P. J. (Sussex & OFS) b May 19, 1946

Gray, A. H. (T/T & Surrey) b May 23, 1963

*Gray, E. J. (Wgtn) b Nov. 18, 1954

Gray, J. R. (Hants) b May 19, 1926

Gray, L. H. (Middx) b Dec. 16, 1915, d Jan. 3, 1983

Greasley, D. G. (Northants) b Jan. 20, 1926

Green, A. M. (Sussex & OFS) b May 28, 1960

Green, D. J. (Derbys. & CUCC) b Dec. 18, 1935

Green, D. M. (OUCC, Lancs. & Glos.; *CY 1969*) b Nov. 10, 1939

Green, Brig. M. A. (Glos. & Essex) b Oct. 3, 1891, d Dec. 28, 1971

*Greenough, T. (Lancs.) b Nov. 9, 1931

*Greenidge, A. E. (B'dos) b Aug. 20, 1956

*Greenidge, C. G. (Hants & B'dos; *CY 1977*) b May 1, 1951

*Greenidge, G. A. (B'dos & Sussex) b May 26, 1948

Greensmith, W. T. (Essex) b Aug. 16, 1930

*Greenwood, A. (Yorks.) b Aug. 20, 1847, d Feb. 12, 1889

Greenwood, H. W. (Sussex & Northants) b Sept. 4, 1909, d March 24, 1979

Greenwood, P. (Lancs.) b Sept. 1i, 1924

Greetham, C. (Som.) b Aug. 28, 1936

*Gregory, David W. (NSW; first Australian captain) b April 15, 1845, d Aug. 4, 1919

*Gregory, E. J. (NSW) b May 29, 1839, d April 22, 1899

*Gregory, J. M. (NSW; *CY 1922*) b Aug. 14, 1895, d Aug. 7, 1973

*Gregory, R. G. (Vic.) b Feb. 26, 1916, d June 10, 1942

*Gregory, S. E. (NSW; *CY 1897*) b April 14, 1870, d August 1, 1929

*Greig, A. W. (Border, E. Prov. & Sussex; *CY 1975*) b Oct. 6, 1946

*Greig, I. A. (CUCC, Border & Sussex) b Dec. 8, 1955

*Grell, M. G. (T/T) b Dec. 18, 1899, d Jan. 11, 1976

*Grieve, B. A. F. (Eng.) b May 28, 1864, d Nov. 19, 1917

Grieves, K. J. (NSW & Lancs.) b Aug. 27, 1925

*Grieveson, R. E. (Tvl) b Aug. 24, 1909

*Griffin, G. M. (Natal & Rhod.) b June 12, 1939

*Griffith, C. C. (B'dos; *CY 1964*) b Dec. 14, 1938

Griffith, G. ("Ben") (Surrey & Utd England XI) b Dec. 20, 1833, d May 3, 1879

*Griffith, H. C. (B'dos) b Dec. 1, 1893, d March 18, 1980

Griffith, K. (Worcs.) b Jan. 17, 1950

Griffith, M. G. (CUCC & Sussex) b Nov. 25, 1943

*Griffith, S. C. (CUCC, Surrey & Sussex; Sec. MCC 1962-74; Pres. MCC 1979-80) b June 16, 1914

Griffiths, B. J. (Northants) b June 13, 1949

Griffiths, Sir W. H. (CUCC & Glam.) b Sept. 26, 1923

Grimes, A. D. H. (CUCC) b Jan. 8, 1965

Grimmett, C. V. (Wgtn, Vic. & S. Aust.; *CY 1931*) b Dec. 25, 1891, d May 2, 1980

Grimshaw, N. (Northants) b May 5, 1911

Gripper, R. A. (Rhod.) b July 7, 1938

*Groube, T. U. (Vic.) b Sept. 2, 1857, d Aug. 5, 1927

*Grout, A. T. W. (Qld) b March 30, 1927, d Nov. 9, 1968

Grove, C. W. (Warwicks. & Worcs.) b Dec. 16, 1912, d Feb. 15, 1982

Grover, J. N. (OUCC) b Oct. 15, 1915

Groves, B. S. (Border & Natal) b March 1, 1947

Groves, M. G. M. (OUCC, Som. & W. Prov.) b Jan. 14, 1943

Grundy, J. (Notts. & Utd England XI) b March 5, 1824, d Nov. 24, 1873

*Guard, G. M. (Bombay & Guj.) b Dec. 12, 1925, d March 13, 1978

*Guest, C. E. J. (Vic. & W. Aust.) b Oct. 7, 1937

*Guha, S. (Bengal) b Jan. 31, 1946

**Guillen, S. C. (T/T & Cant.) b Sept. 24, 1924

Guise, J. L. (OUCC & Middx) b Nov. 25, 1903

*Gunasekera, Y. (SL) b Nov. 8, 1957

**Gul Mahomed (N. Ind., Baroda, H'bad, Punjab & Lahore) b Oct. 15, 1921

*Guneratne, R. P. W. (SL) b Jan. 26, 1962

*Gunn, G. (Notts.; *CY 1914*) b June 13, 1879, d June 28, 1958

Gunn, G. V. (Notts.) b June 21, 1905, d Oct. 14, 1957

*Gunn, J. (Notts.; *CY 1904*) b July 19, 1876, d Aug. 21, 1963

Gunn, T. (Sussex) b Sept. 27, 1935

*Gunn, William (Notts.; *CY 1890*) b Dec. 4, 1858, d Jan. 29, 1921

*Gupte, B. P. (Bombay, Bengal & Ind. Rlwys) b Aug. 30, 1934

*Gupte, S. P. (Bombay, Bengal, Raja. & T/T) b Dec. 11, 1929

*Gurusinha, A. P. (SL) b Sept. 16, 1966

Gurr, D. R. (OUCC & Som.) b March 27, 1956

*Guy, J. W. (C. Dist., Wgtn, Northants, Cant., Otago & N. Dist.) b Aug. 29, 1934

Hacker, P. J. (Notts., Derbys. & OFS) b July 16, 1952

Hadlee, B. G. (Cant.) b Dec. 14, 1941

*Hadlee, D. R. (Cant.) b Jan. 6, 1948

*Hadlee, R. J. (Cant., Notts. & Tas.; *CY 1982*) b July 3, 1951

*Hadlee, W. A. (Cant. & Otago) b June 4, 1915

Hafeez, A. (*see* Kardar)

Hagan, D. A. (OUCC) b June 25, 1966

*Haig, N. E. (Middx) b Dec. 12, 1887, d Oct. 27, 1966

*Haigh, S. (Yorks.; *CY 1901*) b March 19, 1871, d Feb. 27, 1921

Halfyard, D. J. (Kent & Notts.) b April 3, 1931

*Hall, A. E. (Tvl & Lancs.) b Jan. 23, 1896, d Jan. 1, 1964

*Hall, G. G. (NE Tvl & E. Prov.) b May 24, 1938

Hall, I. W. (Derbys.) b Dec. 27, 1939

Hall, Louis (Yorks.; *CY 1890*) b Nov. 1, 1852, d Nov. 19, 1915

Hall, T. A. (Derbys. & Som.) b Aug. 19, 1930, d April 21, 1984

*Hall, W. W. (B'dos, T/T & Qld) b Sept. 12, 1937

Hallam, A. W. (Lancs. & Notts.; *CY 1908*) b Nov. 12, 1869, d July 24, 1940

Hallam, M. R. (Leics.) b Sept. 10, 1931

Halliday, S. J. (OUCC) b July 13, 1960

*Halliwell, E. A. (Tvl & Middx; *CY 1905*) b Sept. 7, 1864, d Oct. 2, 1919

*Hallows, C. (Lancs.; *CY 1928*) b April 4, 1895, d Nov. 10, 1972

Hallows, J. (Lancs.; *CY 1905*) b Nov. 14, 1873, d May 20, 1910

*Halse, C. G. (Natal) b Feb. 28, 1935

*Hamence, R. A. (S. Aust.) b Nov. 25, 1915

Hamer, A. (Yorks. & Derbys.) b Dec. 8, 1916

Hammond, H. E. (Sussex) b Nov. 7, 1907, d June 16, 1985

*Hammond, J. R. (S. Aust.) b April 19, 1950

*Hammond, W. R. (Glos.; *CY 1928*) b June 19, 1903, d July 1, 1965

*Hampshire, J. H. (Yorks., Derbys. & Tas.) b Feb. 10, 1941

*Hands, P. A. M. (W. Prov.) b March 18, 1890, d April 27, 1951

*Hands, R. H. M. (W. Prov.) b July 26, 1888, d April 20, 1918

*Hanif Mohammad (B'pur, Kar. & PIA; *CY 1968*) b Dec. 21, 1934

*Hanley, M. A. (Border & W. Prov.) b Nov. 10, 1918

Hanley, R. W. (E. Prov., OFS, Tvl & Northants) b Jan. 29, 1952

*Hanumant Singh (M. Pradesh & Raja.) b March 29, 1939

Harden, R. J. (Som.) b Aug. 16, 1965

Hardie, B. R. (Scotland & Essex) b Jan. 14, 1950

*Hardikar, M. S. (Bombay) b Feb. 8, 1936

*Hardinge, H. T. W. (Kent; *CY 1915*) b Feb. 25, 1886, d May 8, 1965

*Hardstaff, J. (Notts.) b Nov. 9, 1882, d April 2, 1947

*Hardstaff, J., jun. (Notts. & Auck.; *CY 1938*) b July 3, 1911

Hardy, J. J. E. (Hants & Som.) b Oct. 10, 1960

Harfield, L. (Hants) b Aug. 16, 1905, d Nov. 19, 1985

*Harford, N. S. (C. Dist. & Auck.) b Aug. 30, 1930, d March 30, 1981

*Harford, R. I. (Auck.) b May 30, 1936

Harman, R. (Surrey) b Dec. 28, 1941

*Haroon Rashid (Kar., Sind, NBP, PIA & UBL) b March 25, 1953

*Harper, R. A. (Guyana & Northants) b March 17, 1963

*Harris, 4th Lord (OUCC & Kent; Pres. MCC 1895) b Feb. 3, 1851, d March 24, 1932

Harris, David (Hants & All-England) b 1755, d May 19, 1803

Harris, M. J. (Middx, Notts., E. Prov. & Wgtn) b May 25, 1944

*Harris, P. G. Z. (Cant.) b July 18, 1927

*Harris, R. M. (Auck.) b July 27, 1933

*Harris, T. A. (Griq. W. & Tvl) b Aug. 27, 1916

Harrison, L. (Hants) b June 8, 1922

*Harry, J. (Vic.) b Aug. 1, 1857, d Oct. 27, 1919

Hart, G. E. (Middx) b Jan. 13, 1902

*Hartigan, G. P. D. (Border) b Dec. 30, 1884, d Jan. 7, 1955

*Hartigan, R. J. (NSW & Qld) b Dec. 12, 1879, d June 7, 1958

*Hartkopf, A. E. V. (Vic.) b Dec. 28, 1889, d May 20, 1968

Hartley, A. (Lancs.; *CY 1911*) b April 11, 1879, d Oct. 1918

*Hartley, J. C. (OUCC & Sussex) b Nov. 15, 1874, d March 8, 1963

Hartley, P. J. (Warwicks. & Yorks.) b April 18, 1960

Hartley, S. N. (Yorks. & OFS) b March 18, 1956

Harty, I. D. (Border) b May 7, 1941

Harvey, J. F. (Derbys.) b Sept. 27, 1939

*Harvey, M. R. (Vic.) b April 29, 1918

Harvey, P. F. (Notts.) b Jan. 15, 1923

*Harvey, R. L. (Natal) b Sept. 14, 1911

*Harvey, R. N. (Vic. & NSW; *CY 1954*) b Oct. 8, 1928

Harvey-Walker, A. J. (Derbys.) b July 21, 1944

*Haseeb Ahsan (Peshawar, Pak. Us, Kar. & PIA) b July 15, 1939

Hassan, B. (Notts.) b March 24, 1944

*Hassett, A. L. (Vic.; *CY 1949*) b Aug. 28, 1913

*Hastings, B. F. (Wgtn, C. Dist. & Cant.) b March 23, 1940

*Hathorn, C. M. H. (Tvl) b April 7, 1878, d May 17, 1920

*Hawke, 7th Lord (CUCC & Yorks.; *CY 1909*; Pres. MCC 1914-18) b Aug. 16, 1860, d Oct. 10, 1938

*Hawke, N. J. N. (W. Aust., S. Aust. & Tas.) b June 27, 1939

Hawker, Sir Cyril (Essex; Pres. MCC 1970-71) b July 21, 1900

Hawkins, D. G. (Glos.) b May 18, 1935

*Hayes, E. G. (Surrey & Leics.; *CY 1907*) b Nov. 6, 1876, d Dec. 2, 1953

*Hayes, F. C. (Lancs.) b Dec. 6, 1946

*Hayes, J. A. (Auck. & Cant.) b Jan. 11, 1927

Hayes, K. A. (OUCC & Lancs.) b Sept. 26, 1962

Hayes, P. J. (CUCC) b May 20, 1954

Haygarth, A. (Sussex; Historian) b Aug. 4, 1825, d May 1, 1903

*Haynes, D. L. (B'dos) b Feb. 15, 1956

Haynes, R. W. (Glos.) b Aug. 27, 1913, d Oct. 16, 1976

Hayward, T. (Cambs. & All-England) b March 21, 1835, d July 21, 1876

*Hayward, T. W. (Surrey; *CY 1895*) b March 29, 1871, d July 19, 1939

Haywood, P. R. (Leics.) b March 30, 1947

*Hazare, V. S. (M'tra, C. Ind. & Baroda) b March 11, 1915

Hazell, H. L. (Som.) b Sept. 30, 1909

Hazlerigg, Lord, formerly Hon. A. G. (CUCC & Leics.) b Feb. 24, 1910

*Hazlitt, G. R. (Vic. & NSW) b Sept. 4, 1888, d Oct. 30, 1915
*Headley, G. A. (Jam.; *CY 1934*) b May 30, 1909, d Nov. 30, 1983
*Headley, R. G. A. (Worcs. & Jam.) b June 29, 1939
Hearn, P. (Kent) b Nov. 18, 1925
*Hearne, Alec (Kent; *CY 1894*) b July 22, 1863, d May 16, 1952
**Hearne, Frank (Kent & W. Prov.) b Nov. 23, 1858, d July 14, 1949
*Hearne, G. A. L. (W. Prov.) b March 27, 1888, d Nov. 13, 1978
*Hearne, George G. (Kent) b July 7, 1856, d Feb. 13, 1932
*Hearne, J. T. (Middx; *CY 1892*) b May 3, 1867, d April 17, 1944
*Hearne, J. W. (Middx; *CY 1912*) b Feb. 11, 1891, d Sept. 13, 1965
Hearne, Thos. (Middx) b Sept. 4, 1826, d May 13, 1900
Hearne, Thos., jun. (Lord's Ground Superintendent) b Dec. 29, 1849, d Jan. 29, 1910
Heath, G. E. M. (Hants) b Feb. 20, 1913
Heath, M. (Hants) b March 9, 1934
Hedges, B. (Glam.) b Nov. 10, 1927
Hedges, L. P. (Tonbridge, OUCC, Kent & Glos.; *CY 1919*) b July 13, 1900, d Jan. 12, 1933
*Heine, P. S. (NE Tvl, OFS & Tvl) b June 28, 1928
Hemmings, E. E. (Warwicks. & Notts.) b Feb. 20, 1949
Hemsley, E. J. O. (Worcs.) b Sept. 1, 1943
*Henderson, M. (Wgtn) b Aug. 2, 1895, d June 17, 1970
Henderson, R. (Surrey; *CY 1890*) b March 30, 1865, d Jan. 29, 1931
Henderson, S. P. (CUCC, Worcs. & Glam.) b Sept. 24, 1958
*Hendren, E. H. (Middx; *CY 1920*) b Feb. 5, 1889, d Oct. 4, 1962
*Hendrick, M. (Derbys. & Notts.; *CY 1978*) b Oct. 22, 1948
Hendriks, J. L. (Jam.) b Dec. 21, 1933
*Hendry, H. L. (NSW & Vic.) b May 24, 1895
Henry, O. (W. Prov., Boland & Scotland) b Jan. 23, 1952
Henwood, P. P. (OFS & Natal) b May 22, 1946
Herman, O. W. (Hants) b Sept. 18, 1907
Herman, R. S. (Middx, Border, Griq. W. & Hants) b Nov. 30, 1946
Heron, J. G. (Zimb.) b Nov. 8, 1948
*Heseltine, C. (Hants) b Nov. 26, 1869, d June 13, 1944
Heseltine, P. J. (OUCC) b June 21, 1960
Hever, N. G. (Middx & Glam.) b Dec. 17, 1924
Hewetson, E. P. (OUCC & Warwicks.) b May 27, 1902, d Dec. 26, 1977

Hewett, H. T. (OUCC & Som.; *CY 1893*) b May 25, 1864, d March 4, 1921
Hewitt, S. G. P. (CUCC) b April 6, 1963
*Hibbert, P. A. (Vic.) b July 23, 1952
Hick, G. A. (Worcs. & Zimb.; *CY 1987*) b May 23, 1966
Higgins, H. L. (Worcs.) b Feb. 24, 1894, d Sept. 15, 1979
*Higgs, J. D. (Vic.) b July 11, 1950
*Higgs, K. (Lancs. & Leics.; *CY 1968*) b Jan. 14, 1937
Hignell, A. J. (CUCC & Glos.) b Sept. 4, 1955
*Hilditch, A. M. J. (NSW) b May 20, 1956
Hill, Alan (Derbys. & OFS) b June 29, 1950
*Hill, Allen (Yorks.) b Nov. 14, 1843, d Aug. 29, 1910
*Hill, A. J. L. (CUCC & Hants) b July 26, 1871, d Sept. 6, 1950
*Hill, C. (S. Aust.; *CY 1900*) b March 18, 1877, d Sept. 5, 1945
Hill, E. (Som.) b July 9, 1923
Hill, G. (Hants) b April 15, 1913
*Hill, J. C. (Vic.) b June 25, 1923, d Aug. 11, 1974
Hill, L. W. (Glam.) b April 14, 1942
Hill, M. (Notts., Derbys & Som.) b Sept. 14, 1935
Hill, N. W. (Notts.) b Aug. 22, 1935
Hill, W. A. (Warwicks.) b April 27, 1910
Hills, J. J. (Glam.; Umpire) b Oct. 14, 1897, d Oct. 1969
Hills, R. W. (Kent) b Jan. 8, 1951
Hill-Wood, C. K. (OUCC & Derbys.) b June 5, 1907
Hill-Wood, Sir W. W. (CUCC & Derbys.) b Sept. 8, 1901, d Oct. 10, 1980
Hilton, C. (Lancs. & Essex) b Sept. 26, 1937
Hilton, J. (Lancs. & Som.) b Dec. 29, 1930
*Hilton, M. J. (Lancs.; *CY 1957*) b Aug. 2, 1928
*Hime, C. F. W. (Natal) b Oct. 24, 1869, d Dec. 6, 1940
*Hindlekar, D. D. (Bombay) b Jan. 1, 1909, d March 30, 1949
Hinks, S. G. (Kent) b Oct. 12, 1960
*Hirst, G. H. (Yorks.; *CY 1901*) b Sept. 7, 1871, d May 10, 1954
*Hitch, J. W. (Surrey; *CY 1914*) b May 7, 1886, d July 7, 1965
Hitchcock, R. E. (Cant. & Warwicks.) b Nov. 28, 1929
*Hoad, E. L. G. (B'dos) b Jan. 29, 1896, d March 5, 1986
*Hoare, D. E. (W. Aust.) b Oct. 19, 1934
*Hobbs, Sir J. B. (Surrey; *CY 1909, special portrait 1926*) b Dec. 16, 1882, d Dec. 21, 1963
*Hobbs, R. N. S. (Essex & Glam.) b May 8, 1942
Hobson, D. L. (E. Prov. & W. Prov.) b Sept. 3, 1951

*Hodges, J. H. (Vic.) b July 31, 1856, d Jan. 17, 1933

Hodgkinson, G. F. (Derbys.) b Feb. 19, 1914

Hodgson, A. (Northants) b Oct. 27, 1951

Hodgson, K. I. (CUCC) b Feb. 24, 1960

Hoffman, D. S. (Warwicks.) b Jan. 13, 1966

Hofmeyr, M. B. (OUCC & NE Tvl) b Dec. 9, 1925

*Hogan, T. G. (Vic.) b Sept. 23, 1956

*Hogg, R. M. (S. Aust.) b March 5, 1951

Hogg, W. (Lancs. & Warwicks.) b July 12, 1955

Hohns, T. V. (Qld) b Jan. 23, 1954

Holder, V. A. (B'dos, Worcs. & OFS) b Oct. 8, 1945

*Holding, M. A. (Jam., Lancs., Derbys. & Tas.; *CY 1977*) b Feb. 16, 1954

*Hole, G. B. (NSW & S. Aust.) b Jan. 6, 1931

*Holford, D. A. J. (B'dos & T/T) b April 16, 1940

*Holland, R. G. (NSW) b Oct. 19, 1946

Holliday, D. C. (CUCC) b Dec. 20, 1958

*Hollies, W. E. (Warwicks.; *CY 1955*) b June 5, 1912, d April 16, 1981

Hollingdale, R. A. (Sussex) b March 6, 1906

Holmes, Gp Capt. A. J. (Sussex) b June 30, 1899, d May 21, 1950

*Holmes, E. R. T. (OUCC & Surrey; *CY 1936*) b Aug. 21, 1905, d Aug. 16, 1960

Holmes, G. C. (Glam.) b Sept. 16, 1958

*Holmes, P. (Yorks.; *CY 1920*) b Nov. 25, 1886, d Sept. 3, 1971

Holt, A. G. (Hants) b April 8, 1911

*Holt, J. K., jun. (Jam.) b Aug. 12, 1923

Home of the Hirsel, Lord (Middx; Pres. MCC 1966-67) b July 2, 1903

Hone, Sir B. W. (S. Aust. & OUCC) b July 1, 1907, d May 28, 1978

*Hone, L. (MCC) b Jan. 30, 1853, d Dec. 31, 1896

Hooker, J. E. H. (NSW) b March 6, 1898, d Feb. 12, 1982

Hooker, R. W. (Middx) b Feb. 22, 1935

*Hookes, D. W. (S. Aust.) b May 3, 1955

*Hopkins, A. J. Y. (NSW) b May 4, 1874, d April 25, 1931

Hopkins, J. A. (Glam.) b June 16, 1953

Hopkins, V. (Glos.) b Jan. 21, 1911, d Aug. 6, 1984

*Hopwood, J. L. (Lancs.) b Oct. 30, 1903, d June 15, 1985

*Horan, T. P. (Vic.) b March 8, 1854, d April 16, 1916

*Hordern, H. V. (NSW & Philadelphians) b Feb. 10, 1883, d June 17, 1938

*Hornby, A. N. (Lancs.) b Feb. 10, 1847, d Dec. 17, 1925

Horner, N. F. (Yorks. & Warwicks.) b May 10, 1926

Hornibrook, P. M. (Qld) b July 27, 1899, d Aug. 25, 1976

Horsfall, R. (Essex & Glam.) b June 26, 1920, d Aug. 25, 1981

Horton, H. (Worcs. & Hants) b April 18, 1923

Horton, J. (Worcs.) b Aug. 12, 1916

*Horton, M. J. (Worcs. & N. Dist.) b April 21, 1934

Hossell, J. J. (Warwicks.) b May 25, 1914

*Hough, K. W. (Auck.) b Oct. 24, 1928

*Howard, A. B. (B'dos) b Aug. 27, 1946

Howard, A. H. (Glam.) b Dec. 11, 1910

Howard, B. J. (Lancs.) b May 21, 1926

Howard, K. (Lancs.) b June 29, 1941

*Howard, N. D. (Lancs.) b May 18, 1925, d May 31, 1979

Howard, Major R. (Lancs.; MCC Team Manager) b April 17, 1890, d Sept. 10, 1967

Howarth, G. P. (Auck., Surrey & N. Dist.) b March 29, 1951

*Howarth, H. J. (Auck.) b Dec. 25, 1943

Howat, M. G. (CUCC) b March 2, 1958

*Howell, H. (Warwicks.) b Nov. 29, 1890, d July 9, 1932

*Howell, W. P. (NSW) b Dec. 29, 1869, d July 14, 1940

Howland, C. B. (CUCC, Sussex & Kent) b Feb. 6, 1936

*Howorth, R. (Worcs.) b April 26, 1909, d April 2, 1980

Hughes, D. P. (Lancs. & Tas.) b May 13, 1947

*Hughes, K. J. (W. Aust.; *CY 1981*) b Jan. 26, 1954

*Hughes, M. G. (S. Aust. & Essex) b Nov. 23, 1961

Hughes, S. P. (Middx & N. Tvl) b Dec. 20, 1959

Huish, F. H. (Kent) b Nov. 15, 1869, d March 16, 1957

Hulme, J. H. A. (Middx) b Aug. 26, 1904

Human, J. H. (CUCC & Middx) b Jan. 13, 1912

Humpage, G. W. (Warwicks. & OFS; *CY 1985*) b April 24, 1954

Humphries, D. J. (Leics. & Worcs.) b Aug. 6, 1953

*Humphries, J. (Derbys.) b May 19, 1876, d May 8, 1946

Hunt, A. V. (Scotland & Bermuda) b Oct. 1, 1910

*Hunt, W. A. (NSW) b Aug. 26, 1908, d Dec. 31, 1983

*Hunte, C. C. (B'dos; *CY 1964*) b May 9, 1932

*Hunte, E. A. C. (T/T) b Oct. 3, 1905, d June 26, 1967

Hunter, David (Yorks.) b Feb. 23, 1860, d Jan. 11, 1927

*Hunter, Joseph (Yorks.) b Aug. 3, 1855, d Jan. 4, 1891

Hurd, A. (CUCC & Essex) b Sept. 7, 1937

*Hurst, A. G. (Vic.) b July 15, 1950

Hurst, R. J. (Middx) b Dec. 29, 1933
*Hurwood, A. (Qld) b June 17, 1902, d Sept. 26, 1982
*Hussain, M. Dilawar (C. Ind. & U. Prov.) b March 19, 1907, d Aug. 26, 1967
*Hutchings, K. L. (Kent; *CY 1907*) b Dec. 7, 1882, d Sept. 3, 1916
Hutchinson, J. M. (Derbys.) b Nov. 29, 1896
*Hutchinson, P. (SA) b Jan. 26, 1862, d Sept. 30, 1925
*Hutton, Sir Leonard (Yorks.; *CY 1938*) b June 23, 1916
*Hutton, R. A. (CUCC, Yorks. & Tvl) b Sept. 6, 1942
Huxford, P. N. (OUCC) b Feb. 17, 1960
Huxter, R. J. A. (CUCC) b Oct. 29, 1959
*Hylton, L. G. (Jam.) b March 29, 1905, d May 17, 1955

*Ibadulla, K. (Punjab, Warwicks., Tas. & Otago) b Dec. 20, 1935
*Ibrahim, K. C. (Bombay) b Jan. 26, 1919
*Iddon, J. (Lancs.) b Jan. 8, 1902, d April 17, 1946
*Ijaz Butt (Pak. Us, Punjab, Lahore, R'pindi & Multan) b March 10, 1938
*Ijaz Faqih (Kar., Sind, PWD & MCB) b March 24, 1956
*Ikin, J. T. (Lancs.) b March 7, 1918, d Sept. 15, 1984
*Illingworth, R. (Yorks. & Leics.; *CY 1960*) b June 8, 1932
Illingworth, R. K. (Worcs.) b Aug. 23, 1963
*Imran Khan (Lahore, Worcs., OUCC, PIA & Sussex; *CY 1983*) b Nov. 25, 1952
*Imtiaz Ahmed (N. Ind., Comb. Us, NWFP, Pak. Serv., Peshawar & PAF) b Jan. 5, 1928
*Imtiaz Ali (T/T) b July 28, 1954
Inchmore, J. D. (Worcs. & N. Tvl) b Feb. 22, 1949
*Indrajitsinhji, K. S. (S'tra & Delhi) b June 15, 1937
Ingle, R. A. (Som.) b Nov. 5, 1903
Ingleby-Mackenzie, A. C. D. (Hants) b Sept. 15, 1933
Inman C. C. (Ceylon & Leics.) b Jan. 29, 1936
Innes, G. A. S. (W. Prov. & Tvl) b Nov. 16, 1931, d July 19, 1982
*Inshan Ali (T/T) b Sept. 25, 1949
*Insole, D. J. (CUCC & Essex; *CY 1956*) b April 18, 1926
*Intikhab Alam (Kar., PIA, Surrey, PWD, Sind & Punjab) b Dec. 28, 1941
*Inverarity, R. J. (W. Aust. & S. Aust.) b Jan. 31, 1944
*Iqbal Qasim (Kar., Sind & NBP) b Aug. 6, 1953
*Irani, J. K. (Sind) b Aug. 18, 1923, d Feb. 25, 1982

*Iredale, F. A. (NSW) b June 19, 1867, d April 15, 1926
Iremonger, J. (Notts.; *CY 1903*) b March 5, 1876, d March 25, 1956
*Ironmonger, H. (Qld & Vic.) b April 7, 1882, d June 1, 1971
*Ironside, D. E. J. (Tvl) b May 2, 1925
*Irvine, B. L. (W. Prov., Natal, Essex & Tvl) b March 9, 1944
*Israr Ali (S. Punjab, B'pur & Multan) b May 1, 1927
*Iverson, J. B. (Vic.) b July 27, 1915, d Oct. 24, 1973

*Jackman, R. D. (Surrey, W. Prov. & Rhod.; *CY 1981*) b Aug. 13, 1945
*Jackson, A. A. (NSW) b Sept. 5, 1909, d Feb. 16, 1933
Jackson, A. B. (Derbys.) b Aug. 21, 1933
Jackson, Sir A. H. M. (Derbys.) b Nov. 9, 1899, d Oct. 11, 1983
*Jackson, Rt Hon. Sir F. S. (CUCC & Yorks.; *CY 1894*; Pres. MCC 1921) b Nov. 21, 1870, d March 9, 1947
Jackson, G. R. (Derbys.) b June 23, 1896, d Feb. 21, 1966
*Jackson, H. L. (Derbys.; *CY 1959*) b April 5, 1921
Jackson, John (Notts. & All-England) b May 21, 1833, d Nov. 4, 1901
Jackson, P. F. (Worcs.) b May 11, 1911
Jacques, T. A. (Yorks.) b Feb. 19, 1905
*Jahangir Khan (N. Ind. & CUCC) b Feb. 1, 1910
*Jai, L. P. (Bombay) b April 1, 1902, d Jan. 29, 1968
*Jaisimha, M. L. (H'bad) b March 3, 1939
Jakeman, F. (Yorks. & Northants) b Jan. 10, 1920, d May 18, 1986
*Jalal-ud-Din (PWD, Kar., IDBP & Allied Bank) b June 12, 1959
James, A. E. (Sussex) b Aug. 7, 1924
*James, K. C. (Wgtn & Northants) b March 12, 1904, d Aug. 21, 1976
James, R. M. (CUCC & Wgtn) b Oct. 2, 1934
*Jameson, J. A. (Warwicks.) b June 30, 1941
*Jamshedji, R. J. D. (Bombay) b Nov. 18, 1892, d April 5, 1976
*Jardine, D. R. (OUCC & Surrey; *CY 1928*) b Oct. 23, 1900, d June 18, 1958
Jardine, M. R. (OUCC & Middx) b June 8, 1869, d Jan. 16, 1947
*Jarman, B. N. (S. Aust.) b Feb. 17, 1936
Jarrett, D. W. (OUCC & CUCC) b April 19, 1952
*Jarvis, A. H. (S. Aust.) b Oct. 19, 1860, d Nov. 15, 1933
Jarvis, K. B. S. (Kent) b April 23, 1953
Jarvis, P. W. (Yorks.) b June 29, 1965
*Jarvis, T. W. (Auck. & Cant.) b July 29, 1944

*Javed Akhtar (R'pindi & Pak. Serv.) b Nov. 21, 1940
*Javed Miandad (Kar., Sind, Sussex, HBL, Glam. & H'bad; *CY 1982*) b June 12, 1957
*Jayantilal, K. (H'bad) b Jan. 13, 1948
*Jayasekera, R. S. A. (SL) b Dec. 7, 1957
Jayasinghe, S. (Ceylon & Leics.) b Jan. 19, 1931
Jefferies, S. T. (W. Prov., Derbys. & Lancs.) b Dec. 8, 1959
Jefferson, R. I. (CUCC & Surrey) b Aug. 15, 1941
*Jeganathan, S. (SL) b July 11, 1951
*Jenkins, R. O. (Worcs.; *CY 1950*) b Nov. 24, 1918
Jenkins, V. G. J. (OUCC & Glam.) b Nov. 2, 1911
*Jenner, T. J. (W. Aust. & S. Aust.) b Sept. 8, 1944
Jennings, C. B. (S. Aust.) b June 5, 1884, d June 20, 1950
Jennings, K. F. (Som.) b Oct. 5, 1953
Jennings, R. V. (Tvl) b Aug. 9, 1954
Jepson, A. (Notts.) b July 12, 1915
*Jessop, G. L. (CUCC & Glos.; *CY 1898*) b May 19, 1874, d May 11, 1955
Jesty, T. E. (Hants., Border, Griq. W., Cant. & Surrey; *CY 1983*) b June 2, 1948
Jewell, Major M. F. S. (Sussex & Worcs.) b Sept. 15, 1885, d May 28, 1978
*John, V. B. (SL) b May 27, 1960
Johnson, C. (Yorks.) b Sept. 5, 1947
*Johnson, C. L. (Tvl) b 1871, d May 31, 1908
Johnson, G. W. (Kent & Tvl) b Nov. 8, 1946
*Johnson, H. H. H. (Jam.) b July 17, 1910
Johnson, H. L. (Derbys.) b Nov. 8, 1927
*Johnson, I. W. (Vic.) b Dec. 8, 1918
Johnson, L. A. (Northants) b Aug. 12, 1936
*Johnson, L. J. (Qld) b March 18, 1919, d April 20, 1977
Johnson, P. (Notts.) b April 24, 1965
Johnson, P. D. (CUCC & Notts.) b Nov. 12, 1949
*Johnson, T. F. (T/T) b Jan. 10, 1917, d April 5, 1985
Johnston, B. A. (Broadcaster) b June 24, 1912
*Johnston, W. A. (Vic.; *CY 1949*) b Feb. 26, 1922
Jones, A. (Glam., W. Aust., N. Tvl & Natal; *CY 1978*) b Nov. 4, 1938
Jones, A. A. (Sussex, Som., Middx, Glam., N. Tvl & OFS) b Dec. 9, 1947
Jones, A. L. (Glam.) b June 1, 1957
*Jones, A. O. (Notts. & CUCC; *CY 1900*) b Aug. 16, 1872, d Dec. 21, 1914
Jones, B. J. R. (Worcs.) b Nov. 2, 1955
*Jones, C. M. (C. E. L.) (BG) b Nov. 3, 1902, d Dec. 10, 1959
*Jones, D. M. (Vic.) b March 24, 1961
*Jones, Ernest (S. Aust. & W. Aust.) b Sept. 30, 1869, d Nov. 23, 1943

Jones, E. C. (Glam.) b Dec. 14, 1912
Jones, E. W. (Glam.) b June 25, 1942
*Jones, I. J. (Glam.) b Dec. 10, 1941
Jones, K. V. (Middx) b March 28, 1942
*Jones, P. E. (T/T) b June 6, 1917
Jones, P. H. (Kent) b June 19, 1935
Jones, S. A. (W. Prov. & Boland) b April 14, 1955
*Jones, S. P. (NSW, Qld & Auck.) b Aug. 1, 1861, d July 14, 1951
Jones, W. E. (Glam.) b Oct. 31, 1916
Jordaan, A. H. (N. Tvl) b Aug. 22, 1947
Jordan, A. B. (C. Dist.) b Sept. 5, 1949
Jordan, J. M. (Lancs.) b Feb. 7, 1932
Jorden, A. M. (CUCC & Essex) b Jan. 28, 1947
Jordon, R. C. (Vic.) b Feb. 17, 1937
*Joshi, P. G. (M'tra) b Oct. 27, 1926
Joshi, U. C. (S'tra, Ind. Rlwys, Guj. & Sussex) b Dec. 23, 1944
*Joslin, L. R. (Vic.) b Dec. 13, 1947
Jowett, D. C. P. R. (OUCC) b June 24, 1931
Judd, A. K. (CUCC & Hants) b Jan. 1, 1904
Judge, P. F. (Middx, Glam. & Bengal) b May 23, 1916
Julian, R. (Leics.) b Aug. 23, 1936
*Julien, B. D. (T/T & Kent) b March 13, 1950
*Jumadeen, R. R. (T/T) b April 12, 1948
*Jupp, H. (Surrey) b Nov. 19, 1841, d April 8, 1889
*Jupp, V. W. C. (Sussex & Northants; *CY 1928*) b March 27, 1891, d July 9, 1960
*Jurangpathy, B. R. (SL) b June 25, 1967

*Kallicharran, A. I. (Guyana, Warwicks., Qld, Tvl & OFS; *CY 1983*) b March 21, 1949
*Kaluperuma, L. W. (SL) b May 25, 1949
*Kaluperuma, S. M. S. (SL) b Oct. 22, 1961
*Kanhai, R. B. (†Guyana, T/T, W. Aust., Warwicks. & Tas.; *CY 1964*) b Dec. 26, 1935
*Kanitkar, H. S. (M'tra) b Dec. 8, 1942
*Kapil Dev (Haryana, Northants & Worcs.; *CY 1983*) b Jan. 6, 1959
Kaplan, C. J. (OFS) b Jan. 26, 1909
**Kardar, A. H. (formerly Abdul Hafeez) (N. Ind., OUCC, Warwicks. & Pak. Serv.) b Jan. 17, 1925
Katz, G. A. (Natal) b Feb. 9, 1947
Kayum, D. A. (OUCC) b Oct. 13, 1955
*Keeton, W. W. (Notts.; *CY 1940*) b April 30, 1905, d Oct. 10, 1980
Keighley, W. G. (OUCC & Yorks.) b Jan. 10, 1925
*Keith, H. J. (Natal) b Oct. 25, 1927
Kelleher, H. R. A. (Surrey & Northants) b March 3, 1929
*Kelleway, C. (NSW) b April 25, 1886, d Nov. 16, 1944
Kelly, J. (Notts.) b Sept. 15, 1930

*Kelly, J. J. (NSW; *CY 1903*) b May 10, 1867, d Aug. 14, 1938

Kelly, J. M. (Lancs. & Derbys.) b March 19, 1922, d Nov. 13, 1979

*Kelly, T. J. D. (Vic.) b May 3, 1844, d July 20, 1893

*Kempis, G. A. (Natal) b Aug. 4, 1865, d May 19, 1890

*Kendall, T. (Vic. & Tas.) b Aug. 24, 1851, d Aug. 17, 1924

Kennedy, A. (Lancs.) b Nov. 4, 1949

*Kennedy, A. S. (Hants; *CY 1933*) b Jan. 24, 1891, d Nov. 15, 1959

*Kenny, R. B. (Bombay & Bengal) b Sept. 29, 1930, d Nov. 21, 1985

*Kent, M. F. (Qld) b Nov. 23, 1953

*Kentish, E. S. M. (Jam. & OUCC) b Nov. 21, 1916

*Kenyon, D. (Worcs.; *CY 1963*) b May 15, 1924

*Kerr, R. B. (Qld) b June 16, 1961

*Kerr, J. L. (Cant.) b Dec. 28, 1910

Kerr, K. J. (Tvl & Warwicks.) b Sept. 11, 1961

Kerslake, R. C. (CUCC & Som.) b Dec. 26, 1942

Kettle, M. K. (Northants) b March 18, 1944

*Khalid Hassan (Punjab & Lahore) b July 14, 1937

*Khalid Wazir (Pak.) b April 27, 1936

*Khan Mohammad (N. Ind., Pak. Us, Som., B'pur, Sind, Kar. & Lahore) b Jan. 1, 1928

Kidd, E. L. (CUCC & Middx) b Oct. 18, 1889, d July 2, 1984

Kilborn, M. J. (OUCC) b Sept. 20, 1962

*Killick, Rev. E. T. (CUCC & Middx) b May 9, 1907, d May 18, 1953

Kilner, Norman (Yorks. & Warwicks.) b July 21, 1895, d April 28, 1979

*Kilner, Roy (Yorks.; *CY 1924*) b Oct. 17, 1890, d April 5, 1928

Kimpton, R. C. M. (OUCC & Worcs.) b Sept. 21, 1916

*King, C. L. (B'dos, Glam., Worcs. & Natal) b June 11, 1951

*King, F. McD. (B'dos) b Dec. 14, 1926

King, I. M. (Warwicks. & Essex) b Nov. 10, 1931

King, J. B. (Philadelphia) b Oct. 19, 1873, d Oct. 17, 1965

*King, J. H. (Leics.) b April 16, 1871, d Nov. 18, 1946

*King, L. A. (Jam. & Bengal) b Feb. 27, 1939

Kingsley, Sir P.G.T. (OUCC) b May 26, 1908

*Kinneir, S. P. (Warwicks.; *CY 1912*) b May 13, 1871, d Oct. 16, 1928

*Kippax, A. F. (NSW) b May 25, 1897, d Sept. 4, 1972

Kirby, D. (CUCC & Leics.) b Jan. 18, 1939

*Kirmani, S. M. H. (†Karn.) b Dec. 29, 1949

Kirsten, P. N. (W. Prov., Sussex & Derbys.) b May 14, 1955

Kirton, K. N. (Border & E. Prov.) b Feb. 24, 1928

*Kischenchand, G. (W. Ind., Guj. & Baroda) b April 14, 1925

Kitchen, M. J. (Som.) b Aug. 1, 1940

*Kline, L. F. (Vic.) b Sept. 29, 1934

*Knight, A. E. (Leics.; *CY 1904*) b Oct. 8, 1872, d April 25, 1946

*Knight, B. R. (Essex & Leics.) b Feb. 18, 1938

*Knight, D. J. (OUCC & Surrey; *CY 1915*) b May 12, 1894, d Jan. 5, 1960

Knight, J. M. (OUCC) b March 16, 1958

Knight, R. D. V. (CUCC, Surrey, Glos. & Sussex) b Sept. 6, 1946

Knight, W. H. (Editor of *Wisden* 1870-79) b Nov. 29, 1812, d Aug. 16, 1879

*Knott, A. P. E. (Kent & Tas.; *CY 1970*) b April 9, 1946

Knott, C. H. (OUCC & Kent; oldest living Blue) b March 20, 1901

Knott, C. J. (Hants) b Nov. 26, 1914

Knowles, J. (Notts.) b March 25, 1910

Knox, G. K. (Lancs.) b April 22, 1917

*Knox, N. A. (Surrey; *CY 1907*) b Oct. 10, 1884, d March 3, 1935

Kortright, C. J. (Essex) b Jan. 9, 1871, d Dec. 12, 1952

*Kotze, J. J. (Tvl & W. Prov.) b Aug. 7, 1879, d July 7, 1931

Kourie, A. J. (Tvl) b July 30, 1951

*Kripal Singh, A. G. (Madras & H'bad) b Aug. 6, 1933

*Krishnamurthy, P. (H'bad) b July 12, 1947

Kuiper, A. P. (W. Prov.) b Aug. 24, 1959

*Kulkarni, U. N. (Bombay) b March 7, 1942

*Kumar, V. V. (†TN) b June 22, 1935

*Kunderan, B. K. (Ind. Rlwys & Mysore) b Oct. 2, 1939

*Kuruppuarachchi, A. K. (SL) b Nov. 1, 1964

*Kuys, F. (W. Prov.) b March 21, 1870, d Sept. 12, 1953

Lacey, Sir F. E. (CUCC & Hants; Sec MCC 1898-1926) b Oct. 19, 1859, d May 26, 1946

*Laird, B. M. (W. Aust.) b Nov. 21, 1950

*Laker, J. C. (Surrey, Auck. & Essex; *CY 1952*) b Feb. 9, 1922, d April 23, 1986

*Lall Singh (S. Punjab) b Dec. 12, 1909, d Nov. 19, 1985

*Lamb, A. J. (W. Prov. & Northants; *CY 1981*) b June 20, 1954

Lamb, T. M. (OUCC, Middx & Northants) b March 24, 1953

Lamba, R. (Delhi) b Jan. 2, 1958

Lambert, G. E. (Glos. & Som.) b May 11, 1919

Lambert, R. H. (Ireland) b July 18, 1874, d March 24, 1956

Lambert, Wm (Surrey) b 1779, d April 19, 1851

Lampard, A. W. (Vic. & AIF) b July 3, 1885, d Jan. 11, 1984

*Lance, H. R. (NE Tvl & Tvl) b June 6, 1940

Langdale, G. R. (Derbys. & Som.) b March 11, 1916

Langford, B. A. (Som.) b Dec. 17, 1935

*Langley, G. R. (S. Aust.; *CY 1957*) b Sept. 14, 1919

*Langridge, James (Sussex; *CY 1932*) b July 10, 1906, d Sept. 10, 1966

Langridge, J. G. (John) (Sussex; *CY 1950*) b Feb. 10, 1910

Langridge, R. J. (Sussex) b April 13, 1939

*Langton, A. B. C. (Tvl) b March 2, 1912, d Nov. 27, 1942

*Larkins, W. (Northants & E. Prov.) b Nov. 22, 1953

*Larter, J. D. F. (Northants) b April 24, 1940

*Larwood, H. (Notts.; *CY 1927*) b Nov. 14, 1904

Lashley, P. D. (B'dos) b Feb. 11, 1937

Latchman, A. H. (Middx & Notts.) b July 26, 1943

*Laughlin, T. J. (Vic.) b Jan. 30, 1951

*Laver, F. (Vic.) b Dec. 7, 1869, d Sept. 24, 1919

Lawrence, D. V. (Glos.) b Jan. 28, 1964

*Lawrence, G. B. (Rhod. & Natal) b March 31, 1932

Lawrence, J. (Som.) b March 29, 1914

Lawrence, M. P. (OUCC) b May 6, 1962

*Lawry, W. M. (Vic.; *CY 1962*) b Feb. 11, 1937

*Lawson, G. F. (NSW & Lancs.) b Dec. 7, 1957

Leadbeater, B. (Yorks.) b Aug. 14, 1943

*Leadbeater, E. (Yorks. & Warwicks.) b Aug. 15, 1927

Leary, S. E. (Kent) b April 30, 1933

Lea, A. E. (CUCC) b Sept. 29, 1962

Lee, C. (Yorks. & Derbys.) b March 17, 1924

Lee, F. S. (Middx & Som.) b July 24, 1905, d March 30, 1982

Lee, G. M. (Notts. & Derbys.) b June 7, 1887, d Feb. 29, 1976

*Lee, H. W. (Middx) b Oct. 26, 1890, d April 21, 1981

Lee, I. S. (Vic.) b March 24, 1914

Lee, J. W. (Middx & Som.) b Feb. 1, 1904, d June 20, 1944

Lee, P. G. (Northants & Lancs.; *CY 1976*) b Aug. 27, 1945

*Lee, P. K. (S. Aust.) b Sept. 15, 1904, d Aug. 9, 1980

*Lees, W. K. (Otago) b March 19, 1952

*Lees, W. S. (Surrey; *CY 1906*) b Dec. 25, 1875, d Sept. 10, 1924

Leese, Sir Oliver, Bt (Pres. MCC 1965-66) b Oct. 27, 1894, d Jan. 20, 1978

*Legall, R. A. (B'dos & T/T) b Dec. 1, 1925

Legard, E. (Warwicks.) b Aug. 23, 1935

*Leggat, I. B. (C. Dist.) b June 7, 1930

*Leggat, J. G. (Cant.) b May 27, 1926, d March 8, 1973

*Legge, G. B. (OUCC & Kent) b Jan. 26, 1903, d Nov. 21, 1940

Lenham, L. J. (Sussex) b May 24, 1936

Lenham, N. J. (Sussex) b Dec. 17, 1965

*le Roux, F. L. (Tvl & E. Prov.) b Feb. 5, 1882, d Sept. 22, 1963

le Roux, G. S. (W. Prov. & Sussex) b Sept. 4, 1955

le Roux, R. A. (OFS) b May 27, 1950

*Leslie, C. F. H. (OUCC & Middx) b Dec. 8, 1861, d Feb. 12, 1921

Lester, E. (Yorks.) b Feb. 18, 1923

Lester, G. (Leics.) b Dec. 27, 1915

Lester, Dr J. A. (Philadelphia) b Aug. 1, 1871, d Sept. 3, 1969

L'Estrange, M. G. (OUCC) b Oct. 12, 1952

Lethbridge, C. (Warwicks.) b June 23, 1961

*Lever, J. K. (Essex & Natal; *CY 1979*) b Feb. 24, 1949

*Lever, P. (Lancs. & Tas.) b Sept. 17, 1940

*Leveson Gower, Sir H. D. G. (OUCC & Surrey) b May 8, 1873, d Feb. 1, 1954

*Levett, W. H. V. (Kent) b Jan. 25, 1908

Lewington, P. J. (Warwicks.) b Jan. 30, 1950

*Lewis, A. R. (CUCC & Glam.) b July 6, 1938

Lewis, C. (Kent) b July 27, 1908

Lewis, D. J. (OUCC & Rhod.) b July 27, 1927

*Lewis, D. M. (Jam.) b Feb. 21, 1946

Lewis, E. B. (Warwicks.) b Jan. 5, 1918, d Oct. 19, 1983

Lewis, E. J. (Glam. & Sussex) b Jan. 31, 1942

*Lewis, P. T. (W. Prov.) b Oct. 2, 1884, d Jan. 30, 1976

Lewis, R. V. (Hants) b Aug. 6, 1947

*Leyland, M. (Yorks.; *CY 1929*) b July 20, 1900, d Jan. 1, 1967

*Liaqat Ali (Kar., Sind, HBL & PIA) b May 21, 1955

Liddicutt, A. E. (Vic.) b Oct. 17, 1891, d April 8, 1983

Lightfoot, A. (Northants) b Jan. 8, 1936

Lill, J. C. (S. Aust.) b Dec. 7, 1933

*Lillee, D. K. (W. Aust.; *CY 1973*) b July 18, 1949

*Lilley, A. A. (Warwicks.; *CY 1897*) b Nov. 28, 1866, d Nov. 17, 1929

Lilley, A. W. (Essex) b May 8, 1959

Lilley, B. (Notts.) b Feb. 11, 1895, d Aug. 4, 1950

Lillywhite, Fred (Sussex; Editor of *Lillywhite's Guide to Cricketers*) b July 23, 1829, d Sept. 15, 1866

Lillywhite, F. W. ("William") (Sussex) b June 13, 1792, d Aug. 21, 1854

*Lillywhite, James, jun. (Sussex) b Feb. 23, 1842, d Oct. 25, 1929

*Lindsay, D. T. (NE Tvl, N. Tvl & Tvl) b Sept 4, 1939

*Lindsay, J. D. (Tvl & NE Tvl) b Sept. 8, 1909

*Lindsay, N. V. (Tvl & OFS) b July 30, 1886, d Feb. 2, 1976

*Lindwall, R. R. (NSW & Qld; *CY 1949*) b Oct. 3, 1921

*Ling, W. V. S. (Griq. W. & E. Prov.) b Oct. 3, 1891, d Sept. 26, 1960

*Lissette, A. F. (Auck. & N. Dist.) b Nov. 6, 1919, d Jan. 24, 1973

Lister, J. (Yorks. & Worcs.) b May 14, 1930

Lister, W. H. L. (Lancs.) b Oct. 7, 1911

Littlewood, D. J. (CUCC) b Oct. 28, 1955

Livingston, L. (NSW & Northants) b May 3, 1920

Livingstone, D. A. (Hants) b Sept. 21, 1933

Livsey, W. H. (Hants) b Sept. 23, 1893, d Sept. 12, 1978

*Llewellyn, C. B. (Natal & Hants; *CY 1911*) b Sept. 26, 1876, d June 7, 1964

Llewellyn, M. J. (Glam.) b Nov. 27, 1953

Lloyd, B. J. (Glam.) b Sept. 6, 1953

*Lloyd, C. H. (†Guyana & Lancs.; *CY 1971*) b Aug. 31, 1944

*Lloyd, D. (Lancs.) b March 18, 1947

*Lloyd, T. A. (Warwicks. & OFS) b Nov. 5, 1956

Lloyds, J. W. (Som., OFS & Glos.) b Nov. 17, 1954

*Loader, P. J. (Surrey and W. Aust.; *CY 1958*) b Oct. 25, 1929

Lobb, B. (Warwicks. & Som.) b Jan. 11, 1931

*Lock, G. A. R. (Surrey, Leics. & W. Aust.; *CY 1954*) b July 5, 1929

Lock, H. C. (Surrey) b May 8, 1903, d May 18, 1978

Lockwood, Ephraim (Yorks.) b April 4, 1845, d Dec. 19, 1921

*Lockwood, W. H. (Notts. & Surrey; *CY 1899*) b March 25, 1868, d April 26, 1932

Lockyer, T. (Surrey & All-England) b Nov. 1, 1826, d Dec. 22, 1869

*Logan, J. D. (SA) b June 24, 1880, d Jan. 3, 1960

*Logie, A. L. (T/T) b Sept. 28, 1960

*Lohmann, G. A. (Surrey, W. Prov. & Tvl; *CY 1889*) b June 2, 1865, d Dec. 1, 1901

Lomax, J. G. (Lancs. & Som.) b May 5, 1925

Long, A. (Surrey & Sussex) b Dec. 18, 1940

Longfield, T. C. (CUCC & Kent) b May 12, 1906, d Dec. 21, 1981

Lord, Thomas (Middx; founder of Lord's) b Nov. 23, 1755, d Jan. 13, 1832

*Love, H. S. B. (NSW & Vic.) b Aug. 10, 1895, d July 22, 1969

Love, J. D. (Yorks.) b April 22, 1955

Lowndes, W. G. L. F. (OUCC & Hants) b Jan. 24, 1898, d May 23, 1982

*Lowry, T. C. (Wgtn, CUCC & Som.) b Feb. 17, 1898, d July 20, 1976

*Lowson, F. A. (Yorks.) b July 1, 1925, d Sept. 8, 1984

*Loxton, S. J. E. (Vic.) b March 29, 1921

*Lucas, A. P. (CUCC, Surrey, Middx & Essex) b Feb. 20, 1857, d Oct. 12, 1923

Luckes, W. T. (Som.) b Jan. 1, 1901, d Oct. 27, 1982

*Luckhurst, B. W. (Kent; *CY 1971*) b Feb. 5, 1939

Luddington, R. S. (OUCC) b April 8, 1960

Lumb, R. G. (Yorks.) b Feb. 27, 1950

*Lundie, E. B. (E. Prov., W. Prov. & Tvl) b March 15, 1888, d Sept. 12, 1917

Lynch, M. A. (Surrey & Guyana) b May 21, 1958

*Lyon, B. H. (OUCC & Glos.; *CY 1931*) b Jan. 19, 1902, d June 22, 1970

Lyon, J. (Lancs.) b May 17, 1951

Lyon, M. D. (CUCC & Som.) b April 22, 1898, d Feb. 17, 1964

*Lyons, J. J. (S. Aust.) b May 21, 1863, d July 21, 1927

Lyons, K. J. (Glam.) b Dec. 18, 1946

*Lyttelton, Rt Hon. Alfred (CUCC & Middx; Pres. MCC 1898) b Feb. 7, 1857, d July 5, 1913

Lyttelton, Rev. Hon. C. F. (CUCC & Worcs.) b Jan. 26, 1887, d Oct. 3, 1931

Lyttelton, Hon. C. J. (*see* 10th Visct Cobham)

Lyttelton, Hon. R. H. (Eton) b Jan. 18, 1854, d Nov. 7, 1939

*McAlister, P. A. (Vic.) b July 14, 1869, d May 10, 1938

*Macartney, C. G. (NSW & Otago; *CY 1922*) b June 27, 1886, d Sept. 9, 1958

*Macaulay, G. G. (Yorks.; *CY 1924*) b Dec. 7, 1897, d Dec. 14, 1940

*Macaulay, M. J. (Tvl, W. Prov., OFS, NE Tvl & E. Prov.) b April 19, 1939

*MacBryan, J. C. W. (CUCC & Som.; *CY 1925*) b July 22, 1892, d July 15, 1983

*McCabe, S. J. (NSW; *CY 1935*) b July 16, 1910, d Aug. 25, 1968

McCanlis, M. A. (OUCC, Surrey & Glos.) b June 17, 1906

*McCarthy, C. N. (Natal & CUCC) b March 24, 1929

McConnon, J. E. (Glam.) b June 21, 1922

*McCool, C. L. (NSW, Qld & Som.) b Dec. 9, 1915, d April 5, 1986

McCorkell, N. T. (Hants) b March 23, 1912

*McCormick, E. L. (Vic.) b May 16, 1906

*McCosker, R. B. (NSW; *CY 1976*) b Dec. 11, 1946

McCullum, S. J. (Otago) b Dec. 6, 1956

*McDermott, C. J. (Qld; *CY 1986*) b April 14, 1965

*McDonald, C. C. (Vic.) b Nov. 17, 1928

*McDonald, E. A. (Tas., Vic. & Lancs.; *CY 1922*) b Jan. 6, 1891, d July 22, 1937

*McDonnell, P. S. (Vic., NSW & Qld) b Nov. 13, 1858, d Sept. 24, 1896

McEvoy, M. S. A. (Essex & Worcs.) b Jan. 25, 1956

McEwan, K. S. (E. Prov., W. Prov., Essex & W. Aust; *CY 1978*) b July 16, 1952

*McEwan, P. E. (Cant.) b Dec. 19, 1953

McFarlane, L. L. (Northants, Lancs. & Glam.) b Aug. 19, 1952

*McGahey, C. P. (Essex; *CY 1902*) b Feb. 12, 1871, d Jan. 10, 1935

*MacGibbon, A. R. (Cant.) b Aug. 28, 1924

*McGirr, H. M. (Wgtn) b Nov. 5, 1891, d April 14, 1964

*McGlew, D. J. (Natal; *CY 1956*) b March 11, 1929

*MacGregor, G. (CUCC & Middx; *CY 1891*) b Aug. 31, 1869, d Aug. 20, 1919

*McGregor, S. N. (Otago) b Dec. 18, 1931

McHugh, F. P. (Yorks. & Glos.) b Nov. 15, 1925

*McIlwraith, J. (Vic.) b Sept. 7, 1857, d July 5, 1938

Macindoe, D. H. (OUCC) b Sept. 1, 1917, d March 3, 1986

*McIntyre, A. J. (Surrey; *CY 1958*) b May 14, 1918

McIntyre, J. M. (Auck. & Cant.) b July 4, 1944

*Mackay, K. D. (Qld) b Oct. 24, 1925, d June 13, 1982

McKay-Coghill, D. (Tvl) b Nov. 4, 1941

*McKenzie, G. D. (W. Aust. & Leics.; *CY 1965*) b June 24, 1941

McKenzie, K. A. (NE Tvl & Tvl) b July 16, 1948

*McKibbin, T. R. (NSW) b Dec. 10, 1870, d Dec. 15, 1939

*McKinnon, A. H. (E. Prov. & Tvl) b Aug. 20, 1932, d Dec. 2, 1983

*MacKinnon, F. A. (CUCC & Kent) b April 9, 1848, d Feb. 27, 1947

McLachlan, I. M. (CUCC & S. Aust.) b Oct. 2, 1936

*MacLaren, A. C. (Lancs.; *CY 1895*) b Dec. 1, 1871, d Nov. 17, 1944

*McLaren, J. W. (Qld) b Dec. 24, 1887, d Nov. 17, 1921

MacLarnon, P. G. (OUCC) b Sept. 24, 1963

McLaughlin, J. J. (Qld) b Feb. 18, 1930

*Maclean, J. A. (Qld) b April 27, 1946

Maclean, J. F. (Worcs. & Glos.) b March 1, 1901, d March 9, 1986

*McLean, R. A. (Natal; *CY 1961*) b July 9, 1930

*McLeod, C. E. (Vic.) b Oct. 24, 1869, d Nov. 26, 1918

*McLeod, E. G. (Auck. & Wgtn) b Oct. 14, 1900

*McLeod, R. W. (Vic.) b Jan. 19, 1868, d June 15, 1907

McMahon, J. W. (Surrey & Som.) b Dec. 28, 1919

*McMahon, T. G. (Wgtn) b Nov. 8, 1929

*McMaster, J. E. P. (Eng.) b March 16, 1861, d June 7, 1929

McMillan, G. E. (Tvl & N. Tvl) b Nov. 18, 1953

*McMillan, Q. (Tvl) b June 23, 1904, d July 3, 1948

*McMorris, E. D. A. (Jam.) b April 4, 1935

McNally, J. P. (Griq. W.) b Nov. 27, 1907

*McRae, D. A. N. (Cant.) b Dec. 25, 1912

*McShane, P. G. (Vic.) b 1857, d Dec. 11, 1903

McSweeney, E. B. (C. Dist. & Wgtn) b March 8, 1957

McVicker, N. M. (Warwicks. & Leics.) b Nov. 4, 1940

*McWatt, C. A. (BG) b Feb. 1, 1922

*Madan Lal (Punjab & Delhi) b March 20, 1951

*Maddocks, L. V. (Vic. & Tas.) b May 24, 1926

*Madray, I. S. (BG) b July 2, 1934

Madson, M. B. (Natal) b Sept. 29, 1949

*Madugalle, R. S. (SL) b April 22, 1959

*Maguire, J. N. (Qld) b Sept. 15, 1956

*Mahanama, R. S. (SL) b May 31, 1966

Maher, B. J. M. (Derbys.) b Feb. 11, 1958

*Mahmood Hussain (Pak. Us, Punjab, Kar., E. Pak. & NTB) b April 2, 1932

*Mailey, A. A. (NSW) b Jan. 3, 1886, d Dec. 31, 1967

*Majid Khan (Lahore, Pak. Us, CUCC, Glam., PIA, Qld & Punjab; *CY 1970*) b Sept. 28, 1946

*Maka, E. S. (Bombay) b March 5, 1922

*Makepeace, H. (Lancs.) b Aug. 22, 1881, d Dec. 19, 1952

Makinson, D. J. (Lancs.) b Jan. 12, 1961

*Malhotra, A. (Haryana) b Jan. 26, 1957

Mallender, N. A. (Northants & Otago) b Aug. 13, 1961

*Mallett, A. A. (S. Aust.) b July 13, 1945

Mallett, A. W. H. (OUCC & Kent) b Aug. 29, 1924

Mallett, N. V. H. (OUCC) b Oct. 30, 1956

*Malone, M. F. (W. Aust. & Lancs.) b Oct. 9, 1950

Malone, S. J. (Essex, Hants & Glam.) b Oct. 19, 1953

*Maninder Singh (Delhi) b June 13, 1963

*Manjrekar, V. L. (Bombay, Bengal, Andhra, U. Pradesh, Raja. & M'tra) b Sept. 26, 1931, d Oct. 18, 1983

*Mankad, A. V. (Bombay) b Oct. 12, 1946

*Mankad, V. (M. H.) (W. Ind., Naw., M'tra, Guj., Bengal, Bombay & Raja.; *CY 1947*) b April 12, 1917, d Aug. 21, 1978

*Mann, A. L. (W. Aust.) b Nov. 8, 1945
*Mann, F. G. (CUCC & Middx; Pres. MCC 1984-85) b Sept. 6, 1917
*Mann, F. T. (CUCC & Middx) b March 3, 1888, d Oct. 6, 1964
Mann, J. P. (Middx) b June 13, 1919
*Mann, N. B. F. (Natal & E. Prov.) b Dec. 28, 1920, d July 31, 1952
Manning, J. S. (S. Aust. & Northants) b June 11, 1924
Mansell, P. N. F. (Rhod.) b March 16, 1920
*Mansoor Akhtar (Kar., UBL & Sind) b Dec. 25, 1956
*Mantri, M. K. (Bombay & M'tra) b Sept. 1, 1921
Manzoor Elahi (Multan & Pak. Rlwys) b April 15, 1963
*Maqsood Ahmed (S. Punjab, R'pindi & Kar.) b March 26, 1925
*Marais, G. G. ("G. Gladstone") (Jam.) b Jan. 14, 1901, d May 19, 1978
Marie, G. V. (OUCC) b Feb. 17, 1945
*Markham, L. A. (Natal) b Sept. 12, 1924
*Marks, V. J. (OUCC & Som.) b June 25, 1955
Marlar, R. G. (CUCC & Sussex) b Jan. 2, 1931
Marner, P. T. (Lancs. & Leics.) b March 31, 1936
Marples, C. (Derbys.) b Aug. 3, 1964
*Marr, A. P. (NSW) b March 28, 1862, d March 15, 1940
*Marriott, C. S. (CUCC, Lancs. & Kent) b Sept. 14, 1895, d Oct. 13, 1966
Marsden, R. (OUCC) b April 2, 1959
Marsden, Tom (Eng.) b 1805, d Feb. 27, 1843
Marsh, F. E. (Derbys.) b July 7, 1920
*Marsh, G. R. (W. Aust.) b Dec. 31, 1958
*Marsh, R. W. (W. Aust.; *CY 1982*) b Nov. 11, 1947
Marsh, S. A. (Kent) b Jan. 27, 1961
Marshall, Alan (Qld & Surrey; *CY 1909*) b June 12, 1883, d July 23, 1915
Marshall, J. M. A. (Warwicks.) b Oct. 26, 1916
*Marshall, M. D. (B'dos & Hants; *CY 1983*) b April 18, 1958
*Marshall, N. E. (B'dos & T/T) b Feb. 27, 1924
*Marshall, R. E. (B'dos & Hants; *CY 1959*) b April 25, 1930
Martin, E. J. (Notts.) b Aug. 17, 1925
*Martin, F. (Kent; *CY 1892*) b Oct. 12, 1861, d Dec. 13, 1921
*Martin, F. R. (Jam.) b Oct. 12, 1893, d Nov. 23, 1967
Martin, J. D. (OUCC & Som.) b Dec. 23, 1941
*Martin, J. W. (NSW & S. Aust.) b July 28, 1931
*Martin, J. W. (Kent) b Feb. 16, 1917

Martin, S. H. (Worcs., Natal & Rhod.) b Jan. 11, 1909
*Martindale, E. A. (B'dos) b Nov. 25, 1909, d March 17, 1972
Maru, R. J. (Middx & Hants) b Oct. 28, 1962
*Marx, W. F. E. (Tvl) b July 4, 1895, d June 2, 1974
*Mason, J. R. (Kent; *CY 1898*) b March 26, 1874, d Oct. 15, 1958
*Massie, H. H. (NSW) b April 11, 1854, d Oct. 12, 1938
*Massie, R. A. L. (W. Aust.; *CY 1973*) b April 14, 1947
*Matheson, A. M. (Auck.) b Feb. 27, 1906, d Dec. 31, 1985
*Mathias, Wallis (Sind, Kar. & NBP) b Feb. 4, 1935
*Matthews, A. D. G. (Northants & Glam.) b May 3, 1904, d July 29, 1977
Matthews, C. S. (Notts.) b Oct. 17, 1929
*Matthews, G. R. J. (NSW) b Dec. 15, 1959
*Matthews, T. J. (Vic.) b April 3, 1884, d Oct. 14, 1943
*Mattis, E. H. (Jam.) b April 11, 1957
Maudsley, R. H. (OUCC & Warwicks.) b April 8, 1918, d Sept. 29, 1981
*May, P. B. H. (CUCC & Surrey; *CY 1952*; Pres. MCC 1980-81) b Dec. 31, 1929
Mayer, J. H. (Warwicks.) b March 2, 1902, d Sept. 6, 1981
Mayes, R. (Kent) b Oct. 7, 1921
Maynard, C. (Warwicks. & Lancs.) b April 8, 1958
Maynard, M. P. (Glam.) b March 21, 1966
*Mayne, E. R. (S. Aust. & Vic.) b July 2, 1882, d Oct. 26, 1961
*Mayne, L. C. (W. Aust.) b Jan. 23, 1942
*Mead, C. P. (Hants; *CY 1912*) b March 9, 1887, d March 26, 1958
*Mead, W. (Essex; *CY 1904*) b March 25, 1868, d March 18, 1954
Meads, E. A. (Notts.) b Aug. 17, 1916
*Meale, T. (Wgtn) b Nov. 11, 1928
*Meckiff, I. (Vic.) b Jan. 6, 1935
Mee, A. A. G. (OUCC) b May 29, 1963
*Meher-Homji, K. R. (W. Ind. & Bombay) b Aug. 9, 1911, d Feb. 10, 1982
*Mehra, V. L. (E. Punjab, Ind. Rlwys & Delhi) b March 12, 1938
*Meintjes, D. J. (Tvl) b June 9, 1890, d July 17, 1979
*Melle, M. G. (Tvl & W. Prov.) b June 3, 1930
Melluish, M. E. L. (CUCC & Middx) b June 13, 1932
*Melville, A. (OUCC, Sussex, Natal & Tvl; *CY 1948*) b May 19, 1910, d April 18, 1983
Mence, M. D. (Warwicks. & Glos.) b April 13, 1944
Mendis, G. D. (Sussex & Lancs.) b April 20, 1955
*Mendis, L. R. D. (SL) b Aug. 25, 1952

*Mendonca, I. L. (BG) b July 13, 1934

Mercer, J. (Sussex, Glam. & Northants; *CY 1927*) b April 22, 1895

*Merchant, V. M. (Bombay; *CY 1937*) b Oct. 12, 1911

*Merritt, W. E. (Cant. & Northants) b Aug. 18, 1908, d June 9, 1977

*Merry, C. A. (T/T) b Jan. 20, 1911, d April 19, 1964

Metcalfe, A. A. (Yorks.) b Dec. 25, 1963

*Meuleman, K. D. (Vic. & W. Aust.) b Sept. 5, 1923

Meuli, E. M. (C. Dist.) b Feb. 20, 1926

Meyer, B. J. (Glos.) b Aug. 21, 1932

Meyer, R. J. O. (CUCC, Som. & W. Ind.) b March 15, 1905

Mian Mohammad Saaed (N. Ind. Patiala & S. Punjab; Pak.'s first captain) b Aug. 31, 1910, d Aug. 23, 1979

*Middleton, J. (W. Prov.) b Sept. 30, 1865, d Dec. 23, 1913

Middleton, T. C. (Hants.) b Feb. 1, 1964

**Midwinter, W. E. (Vic. & Glos.) b June 19, 1851, d Dec. 3, 1890

*Milburn, B. D. (Otago) b Nov. 24, 1943

*Milburn, C. (Northants & W. Aust.; *CY 1967*) b Oct. 23, 1941

*Milkha Singh, A. G. (Madras) b Dec. 31, 1941

Miller, A. J. T. (OUCC & Middx) b May 30, 1963

*Miller, A. M. (Eng.) b Oct. 19, 1869, d June 26, 1959

*Miller, G. (Derbys. & Natal) b Sept 8, 1952

*Miller, K. R. (Vic., NSW & Notts.; *CY 1954*) b Nov. 28, 1919

*Miller, L. S. M. (C. Dist. & Wgtn) b March 31, 1923

Miller, R. (Warwicks.) b Jan. 6, 1941

*Miller, R. C. (Jam.) b Dec. 24, 1924

*Milligan, F. W. (Yorks.) b March 19, 1870, d March 31, 1900

*Millman, G. (Notts.) b Oct. 2, 1934

Mills, C. H. (Surrey, Kimberley & W. Prov.) b Nov. 26, 1867, d July 26, 1948

Mills, G. H. (Otago) b Aug. 1, 1916

Mills, J. E. (Auck.) b Sept. 3, 1905, d Dec. 11, 1972

Mills, J. M. (CUCC & Warwicks.) b July 27, 1921

Mills, J. P. C. (CUCC & Northants) b Dec. 6, 1958

Milner, J. (Essex) b Aug. 22, 1937

*Milton, C. A. (Glos.; *CY 1959*) b March 10, 1928

*Milton, W. H. (W. Prov.) b Dec. 3, 1854, d March 6, 1930

*Minnett, R. B. (NSW) b June 13, 1888, d Oct. 21, 1955

"Minshull", John (scorer of first recorded century) b *circa* 1741, d Oct. 1793

*Miran Bux, (Pak. Serv., Punjab & R'pindi) b April 20, 1907

*Misson, F. M. (NSW) b Nov. 19, 1938

*Mitchell, A. (Yorks.) b Sept. 13, 1902, d Dec. 25, 1976

*Mitchell, B. (Tvl; *CY 1936*) b Jan. 8, 1909

Mitchell, C. G. (Som.) b Jan. 27, 1929

**Mitchell, F. (CUCC, Yorks. & Tvl; *CY 1902*) b Aug. 13, 1872, d Oct. 11, 1935

*Mitchell, T. B. (Derbys.) b Sept. 4, 1902

*Mitchell-Innes, N. S. (OUCC & Som.) b Sept. 7, 1914

Mobey, G. S. (Surrey) b March 5, 1904

*Modi, R. S. (Bombay) b Nov. 11, 1924

*Mohammad Aslam (N. Ind. & Pak. Rlwys) b Jan. 5, 1920

*Mohammad Farooq (Kar.) b April 8, 1938

*Mohammad Ilyas (Lahore & PIA) b March 19, 1946

*Mohammad Munaf (Sind, E. Pak., Kar. & PIA) b Nov. 2, 1935

*Mohammad Nazir (Pak. Rlwys) b March 8, 1946

*Mohsin Kamal (Lahore & Allied Bank) b June 16, 1963

*Mohsin Khan (Pak. Rlwys, Kar., Sind., Pak. Us & HBL) b March 15, 1955

*Moir, A. McK. (Otago) b July 17, 1919

Moir, D. G. (Derbys. & Scotland) b April 13, 1957

*Mold, A. W. (Lancs.; *CY 1892*) b May 27, 1863, d April 29, 1921

*Moloney, D. A. R. (Wgtn, Otago & Cant.) b Aug. 11, 1910, d July 15, 1942

Monckton of Brenchley, 1st Lord (Pres. MCC 1956-57) b Jan. 17, 1891, d Jan. 9, 1965

Monkhouse, G. (Surrey) b April 26, 1954

*Moodie, G. H. (Jam.) b Nov. 25, 1915

*Moon, L. J. (CUCC & Middx) b Feb. 9, 1878, d Nov. 23, 1916

*Mooney, F. L. H. (Wgtn) b May 26, 1921

Moore, D. N. (OUCC & Glos.) b Sept. 26, 1910

Moore, H. I. (Notts.) b Feb. 28, 1941

Moore, R. H. (Hants) b Nov. 14, 1913

*More, K. S. (Baroda) b Sept. 4, 1962

Morgan, D. C. (Derbys.) b Feb. 26, 1929

Morgan, J. T. (CUCC & Glam.) b May 7, 1907, d Dec. 18, 1976

Morgan, M. (Notts.) b May 21, 1936

*Morgan, R. W. (Auck.) b Feb. 12, 1941

*Morkel, D. P. B. (W. Prov.) b Jan. 25, 1906, d Oct. 6, 1980

*Morley, F. (Notts.) b Dec. 16, 1850, d Sept. 28, 1884

Morley, J. D. (Sussex) b Oct. 20, 1950

*Moroney, J. (NSW) b July 24, 1917

Morrill, N. D. (OUCC) b Dec. 9, 1957

*Morris, A. R. (NSW; *CY 1949*) b Jan. 19, 1922

Morris, H. (Glam.) b Oct. 5, 1963

Morris, H. M. (CUCC & Essex) b April 16, 1898, d Nov. 18, 1984

Morris, J. E. (Derbys.) b April 1, 1964

Morris, R. E. T. (W. Prov.) b Jan. 28, 1947

*Morris, S. (Vic.) b June 22, 1855, d Sept. 20, 1931

Morrisby, R. O. G. (Tas.) b Jan. 12, 1915

*Morrison, B. D. (Wgtn) b Dec. 17, 1933

*Morrison, J. F. M. (C. Dist. & Wgtn) b Aug. 27, 1947

Mortensen, O. H. (Denmark & Derbys.) b Jan. 29, 1958

*Mortimore, J. B. (Glos.) b May 14, 1933

Mortlock, W. (Surrey & Utd Eng. XI) b July 18, 1832, d Jan. 23, 1884

Moseley, E. A. (B'dos, Glam. & E. Prov.) b Jan. 5, 1958

Moseley, H. R. (B'dos & Som.) b May 28, 1948

*Moses, H. (NSW) b Feb. 13, 1858, d Dec. 7, 1938

*Moss, A. E. (Middx) b Nov. 14, 1930

*Moss, J. K. (Vic.) b June 29, 1947

*Motz, R. C. (Cant.; *CY 1966*) b Jan. 12, 1940

Moulding, R. P. (OUCC & Middx) b Jan. 3, 1958

*Moule, W. H. (Vic.) b Jan. 31, 1858, d Aug. 24, 1939

*Moxon, M. D. (Yorks. & Griq. W.) b May 4, 1960

Moylan, A. C. D. (CUCC) b June 26, 1955

Mubarak, A. M. (CUCC) b July 4, 1951

*Mudassar Nazar (Lahore, Punjab, Pak. Us, HBL, PIA & UBL) b April 6, 1956

*Muddiah, V. M. (Mysore & Ind. Serv.) b June 8, 1929

*Mufasir-ul-Haq (Kar., Dacca, PWD, E. Pak. & NBP) b Aug. 16, 1944, d July 27, 1983

Muncer, B. L. (Middx & Glam.) b Oct. 23, 1913, d Jan. 18, 1982

Munden, V. S. (Leics.) b Jan. 2, 1928

*Munir Malik (Punjab, R'pindi, Pak. Serv. & Kar.) b July 10, 1934

Munton, T. A. (Warwicks.) b July 30, 1965

**Murdoch, W. L. (NSW & Sussex) b Oct. 18, 1854, d Feb. 18, 1911

*Murray, A. R. A. (E. Prov.) b April 30, 1922

*Murray, B. A. G. (Wgtn) b Sept. 18, 1940

*Murray, D. A. (B'dos) b Sept. 29, 1950

*Murray, D. L. (T/T, CUCC, Notts. & Warwicks.) b May 20, 1943

*Murray, J. T. (Middx; *CY 1967*) b April 1, 1935

Murray-Willis, P. E. (Worcs. & Northants) b July 14, 1910

Murrell, H. R. (Kent & Middx) b Nov. 19, 1879, d Aug. 15, 1952

Murrills, T. J. (CUCC) b Dec. 22, 1953

*Musgrove, H. (Vic.) b Nov. 27, 1860, d Nov. 2, 1931

*Mushtaq Ali, S. (C. Ind., Guj., †M. Pradesh & U. Pradesh) b Dec. 17, 1914

*Mushtaq Mohammad (Kar., Northants & PIA; *CY 1963*) b Nov. 22, 1943

Muzzell, R. K. (W. Prov., Tvl and E. Prov.) b Dec. 23, 1945

Mynn, Alfred (Kent & All-Eng.) b Jan. 19, 1807, d Oct. 31, 1861

*Nadkarni, R. G. (M'tra & Bombay) b April 4, 1932

*Nagel, L. E. (Vic.) b March 6, 1905, d Nov. 23, 1971

*Naik, S. S. (Bombay) b Feb. 21, 1945

*Nanan, R. (T/T) b May 29, 1953

*Naoomal Jaoomal, M. (N. Ind. & Sind) b April 17, 1904, d July 18, 1980

*Narasimha Rao, M. V. (H'bad) b Aug. 11, 1954

Nash, J. E. (S. Aust.) b April 16, 1950

*Nash, L. J. (Tas. & Vic.) b May 2, 1910, d July 24, 1986

Nash, M. A. (Glam.) b May 9, 1945

*Nasim-ul-Ghani (Kar., Pak. Us, Dacca, E. Pak., PWD & NBP) b May 14, 1941

*Naushad Ali (Kar., E. Pak., R'pindi, Peshawar, NWFP, Punjab & Pak. Serv.) b Oct. 1, 1943

*Navle, J. G. (Rajputna, C. Ind., Holkar & Gwalior) b Dec. 7, 1902, d Sept. 7, 1979

*Nayak, S. V. (Bombay) b Oct. 20, 1954

*Nayudu, Col. C. K. (C. Ind., Andhra, U. Pradesh & Holkar; *CY 1933*) b Oct. 31, 1895, d Nov. 14, 1967

*Nayudu, C. S. (C. Ind., Holkar, Baroda, Bengal, Andhra & U. Pradesh) b April 18, 1914

*Nazar Mohammad (N. Ind. & Punjab) b Aug. 5, 1921

*Nazir Ali, S. (S. Punjab & Sussex) b June 8, 1906, d Feb. 18, 1975

Neale, P. A. (Worcs.) b June 5, 1954

*Neblett, J. M. (B'dos & BG) b Nov. 13, 1901, d March 28, 1959

Needham, A. (Surrey) b March 23, 1957

Neilson, D. R. (Tvl) b Dec. 17, 1948

*Nel, J. D. (W. Prov.) b July 10, 1928

Nelson, G. W. (Border) b Nov. 14, 1941

Nevell, W. T. (Middx, Surrey & Northants) b June 13, 1916

*Newberry, C. (Tvl) b 1889, d Aug. 1, 1916

Newdick, G. A. (Wgtn) b Jan. 11, 1949

Newell, M. (Notts.) b Feb. 25, 1965

*Newham, W. (Sussex) b Dec 12, 1860, d June 26, 1944

Newland, Richard (Sussex) b *circa* 1718, d May 29, 1791

Newman, G. C. (OUCC & Middx) b April 26, 1904, d Oct. 13, 1982

*Newman, J. (Wgtn & Cant.) b July 3, 1902

Newman, J. A. (Hants & Cant.) b Nov. 12, 1884, d Dec. 21, 1973

Newman, P. G. (Derbys.) b Jan. 10, 1959

Newport, P. J. (Worcs.) b Oct. 11, 1962

*Newsom, E. S. (Tvl & Rhod.) b Dec. 2, 1910

Newstead, J. T. (Yorks.; *CY 1909*) b Sept. 8, 1877, d March 25, 1952

*Niaz Ahmed (Dacca, PWD, E. Pak. & Pak. Rlwys) b Nov. 11, 1945

Nicholas, M. C. J. (Hants) b Sept. 29, 1957

Nicholls, D. (Kent) b Dec. 8, 1943

Nicholls, R. B. (Glos.) b Dec. 4, 1933

*Nichols, M. S. (Essex; *CY 1934*) b Oct. 6, 1900, d Jan. 26, 1961

Nicholson, A. G. (Yorks.) b June 25, 1938, d Nov. 4, 1985

*Nicholson, F. (OFS) b Sept. 17, 1909, d July 30, 1982

*Nicolson, J. F. W. (Natal & OUCC) b July 19, 1899, d Dec. 13, 1935

*Nissar, Mahomed (Patiala, S. Punjab & U. Pradesh) b Aug. 1, 1910, d March 11, 1963

*Nitschke, H. C. (S. Aust.) b April 14, 1905, d Sept. 29, 1982

*Noble, M. A. (NSW; *CY 1900*) b Jan. 28, 1873, d June 21, 1940

*Noblet, G. (S. Aust.) b Sept. 14, 1916

*Noreiga, J. M. (T/T) b April 15, 1936

Norfolk, 16th Duke of (Pres. MCC 1957-58) b May 30, 1908, d Jan. 31, 1975

Norman, M. E. J. C. (Northants & Leics.) b Jan. 19, 1933

*Norton, N. O. (W. Prov. & Border) b May 11, 1881, d June 27, 1968

*Nothling, O. E. (NSW & Qld) b Aug. 1, 1900, d Sept. 26, 1965

*Nourse, A. D. ("Dudley") (Natal; *CY 1948*) b Nov. 12, 1910, d Aug. 14, 1981

*Nourse, A. W. ("Dave") (Natal, Tvl & W. Prov.) b Jan. 26, 1878, d July 8, 1948

Nugent, 1st Lord (Pres. MCC 1962-63) b Aug. 11, 1895, d April 27, 1973

*Nunes, R. K. (Jam.) b June 7, 1894, d July 22, 1958

*Nupen, E. P. (Tvl) b Jan. 1, 1902, d Jan. 29, 1977

*Nurse, S. M. (B'dos; *CY 1967*) b Nov. 10, 1933

Nutter, A. E. (Lancs. & Northants) b June 28, 1913

*Nyalchand, S. (W. Ind., Kathiawar, Guj. & S'tra) b Sept. 14, 1919

Nye, J. K. (Sussex) b May 23, 1914

Nyren, John (Hants) b Dec. 15, 1764, d June 28, 1837

Nyren, Richard (Hants & Sussex) b 1734, d April 25, 1797

Oakes, C. (Sussex) b Aug. 10, 1912

Oakes, J. (Sussex) b March 3, 1916

*Oakman, A. S. M. (Sussex) b April 20, 1930

Oates, T. W. (Notts.) b Aug. 9, 1875, d June 18, 1949

Oates, W. F. (Yorks. & Derbys.) b June 11, 1929

O'Brien, F. P. (Cant. & Northants) b Feb. 11, 1911

*O'Brien, L. P. (Vic.) b July 2, 1907

*O'Brien, Sir T. C. (OUCC & Middx) b Nov. 5, 1861, d Dec. 9, 1948

*Ochse, A. E. (Tvl) b March 11, 1870, d April 11, 1918

*Ochse, A. L. (E. Prov.) b Oct. 11, 1899, d May 6, 1949

*O'Connor, J. (Essex) b Nov. 6, 1897, d Feb. 22, 1977

*O'Connor, J. D. A. (NSW & S. Aust.) b Sept. 9, 1875, d Aug. 23, 1941

Odendaal, A. (CUCC & Boland) b May 4, 1954

*O'Donnell, S. P. (Vic.) b June 26, 1963

*Ogilvie, A. D. (Qld) b June 3, 1951

*O'Keeffe, K. J. (NSW & Som.) b Nov. 25, 1949

*Old, C. M. (Yorks., Warwicks. & N. Tvl; *CY 1979*) b Dec. 22, 1948

*Oldfield, N. (Lancs & Northants) b May 5, 1911

*Oldfield, W. A. (NSW; *CY 1927*) b Sept. 9, 1894, d Aug. 10, 1976

Oldham, S. (Yorks. & Derbys.) b July 26, 1948

Oldroyd, E. (Yorks.) b Oct. 1, 1888, d Dec. 27, 1964

*O'Linn, S. (Kent, W. Prov. & Tvl) b May 5, 1927

Oliver, P. R. (Warwicks.) b May 9, 1956

*O'Neill, N. C. (NSW; *CY 1962*) b Feb. 19, 1937

Ontong, R. C. (Border, Tvl, N. Tvl & Glam.) b Sept. 9, 1955

Ord, J. S. (Warwicks.) b July 12, 1912

Orders, J. O. D. (OUCC) b Aug. 12, 1957

*O'Reilly, W. J. (NSW; *CY 1935*) b Dec. 20, 1905

O'Riordan, A. J. (Ireland) b July 20, 1940

Ormiston, R. W. (C. Dist. & Wgtn) b Oct. 19, 1955

Ormrod, J. A. (Worcs. & Lancs.) b Dec. 22, 1942

O'Shaughnessy, S. J. (Lancs.) b Sept. 9, 1961

Oslear, D. O. (Umpire) b March 3, 1929

*O'Sullivan, D. R. (C. Dist. & Hants) b Nov. 16, 1944

Outschoorn, L. (Worcs.) b Sept. 26, 1918

*Overton, G. W. F. (Otago) b June 8, 1919

*Owen-Smith, H. G. O. (W. Prov., OUCC & Middx; *CY 1930*) b Feb. 18, 1909

Owen-Thomas, D. R. (CUCC & Surrey) b Sept. 20, 1948

*Oxenham, R. K. (Qld) b July 28, 1891, d Aug. 16, 1939

Packe, M. St J. (Leics.) b Aug. 21, 1916, d Dec. 20, 1978

*Padmore, A. L. (B'dos) b Dec. 17, 1946
Page, J. C. T. (Kent) b May 20, 1930
Page, M. H. (Derbys.) b June 17, 1941
*Page, M. L. (Cant.) b May 8, 1902
*Pai, A. M. (Bombay) b April 28, 1945
*Paine, G. A. E. (Middx & Warwicks.; *CY 1935*) b June 11, 1908, d March 30, 1978
*Pairaudeau, B. H. (BG & N. Dist.) b April 14, 1931
*Palairet, L. C. H. (OUCC & Som.; *CY 1893*) b May 27, 1870, d March 27, 1933
Palairet, R. C. N. (OUCC & Som.; Joint-Manager MCC in Australia 1932-33) b June 25, 1871, d Feb. 11, 1955
Palia, P. E. (Madras, U. Prov., Bombay, Mysore & Bengal) b Sept. 5, 1910, d Sept. 9, 1981
*Palm, A. W. (W. Prov.) b June 8, 1901, d Aug. 17, 1966
*Palmer, C. H. (Worcs. & Leics.; Pres. MCC 1978-79) b May 15, 1919
*Palmer, G. E. (Vic. & Tas.) b Feb. 22, 1860, d Aug. 22, 1910
*Palmer, K. E. (Som.) b April 22, 1937
Palmer, R. (Som.) b July 12, 1942
Palmer, R. W. M. (CUCC) b June 4, 1960
*Pandit, C. S. (Bombay) b Sept. 30, 1961
Pardon, Charles Frederick (Editor of *Wisden* 1887-90) b March 28, 1850, d April 18, 1890
Pardon, Sydney H. (Editor of *Wisden* 1891-1925) b Sept. 23, 1855, d Nov. 20, 1925
*Parfitt, P. H. (Middx; *CY 1963*) b Dec. 8, 1936
Paris, C. G. A. (Hants; Pres. MCC 1975-76) b Aug. 20, 1911
Parish, R. J. (Aust. Administrator) b May 7, 1916
*Park, R. L. (Vic.) b July 30, 1892, d Jan. 23, 1947
*Parkar, G. A. (Bombay) b Oct. 24, 1955
*Parkar, R. D. (Bombay) b Oct. 31, 1946
Parkar, Z. (Bombay) b Nov. 22, 1957
*Parker, C. W. L. (Glos.; *CY 1923*) b Oct. 14, 1882, d July 11, 1959
Parker, E. F. (Rhod. & Griq. W.) b April 26, 1939
*Parker, G. M. (SA) b May 27, 1899, d May 1, 1969
Parker, G. W. (CUCC & Glos.) b Feb. 11, 1912
Parker, J. F. (Surrey) b April 23, 1913, d Jan. 27, 1983
*Parker, J. M. (N. Dist. & Worcs.) b Feb. 21, 1951
Parker, J. P. (Hants) b Nov. 29, 1902, d Aug. 9, 1984
*Parker, N. M. (Otago & Cant.) b Aug. 28, 1948
*Parker, P. W. G. (CUCC, Sussex & Natal) b Jan. 15, 1956

*Parkhouse, W. G. A. (Glam.) b Oct. 12, 1925
*Parkin, C. H. (Yorks. & Lancs.; *CY 1924*) b Feb. 18, 1886, d June 15, 1943
*Parkin, D. C. (E. Prov., Tvl & Griq. W.) b Feb. 18, 1870, d March 20, 1936
Parks, H. W. (Sussex) b July 18, 1906, d May 7, 1984
*Parks, J. H. (Sussex & Cant.; *CY 1938*) b May 12, 1903, d Nov. 21, 1980
*Parks, J. M. (Sussex & Som.; *CY 1968*) b Oct. 21, 1931
Parks, R. J. (Hants) b June 15, 1959
Parr, F. D. (Lancs.) b June 1, 1928
Parr, George (Notts. & All-England) b May 22, 1826, d June 23, 1891
*Parry, D. R. (Comb. Is. & Leewards) b Dec. 22, 1954
*Parsana, D. D. (S'tra, Ind. Rlwys & Guj.) b Dec. 2, 1947
Parsons, A. B. D. (CUCC & Surrey) b Sept. 20, 1933
Parsons, A. E. W. (Auck. & Sussex) b Jan. 9, 1949
Parsons, G. J. (Leics., Warwicks., Boland & Griq. W.) b Oct. 17, 1959
Parsons, Canon J. H. (Warwicks.) b May 30, 1890, d Feb. 2, 1981
*Partridge, J. T. (Rhod.) b Dec. 9, 1932
Partridge, N. E. (Malvern, CUCC & Warwicks.; *CY 1919*) b Aug. 10, 1900, d March 10, 1982
Partridge, R. J. (Northants) b Feb. 11, 1912
*Pascoe, L. S. (NSW) b Feb. 13, 1950
*Passailaigue, C. C. (Jam.) b Aug. 1902, d Jan. 7, 1972
*Patankar, C. T. (Bombay) b Nov. 24, 1930
**Pataudi, Iftikhar Ali, Nawab of (OUCC, Worcs., Patiala, N. Ind. & S. Punjab; *CY 1932*) b March 16, 1910, d Jan. 5, 1952
*Pataudi, Mansur Ali, Nawab of (Sussex, OUCC, Delhi & H'bad; *CY 1968*) b Jan. 5, 1941
*Patel, B. P. (Karn.) b Nov. 24, 1952
Patel, D. N. (Worcs. & Auck.) b Oct. 25, 1958
*Patel, J. M. (Guj.) b Nov. 26, 1924
Paterson, R. F. T. (Essex) b Sept. 8, 1916, d May 29, 1980
Pathmanathan, G. (OUCC, CUCC & SL) b Jan. 23, 1954
*Patiala, Maharaja of (N. Ind., Patiala & S. Punjab) b Jan. 17, 1913, d June 17, 1974
*Patil, S. M. (Bombay) b Aug. 18, 1956
*Patil, S. R. (M'tra) b Oct. 10, 1933
*Patterson, B. P. (Jam., Tas. & Lancs.) b Sept. 15, 1961
Pauline, D. B. (Surrey & Glam.) b Dec. 15, 1960
Paulsen, R. G. (Qld & W. Aust.) b Oct. 18, 1947

Pawson, A. G. (OUCC & Worcs.) b May 30, 1888, d Feb. 25, 1986

Pawson, H. A. (OUCC & Kent) b Aug. 22, 1921

Payn, L. W. (Natal) b May 6, 1915

*Payne, T. R. O. (B'dos) b Feb. 13, 1957

*Paynter, E. (Lancs.; *CY 1938*) b Nov. 5, 1901, d Feb. 5, 1979

Payton, D. H. (C. Dist.) b Feb. 19, 1945

Payton, W. R. D. (Notts.) b Feb. 13, 1882, d May 2, 1943

Pearce, G. (Sussex) b Oct. 27, 1908, d June 16, 1986

Pearce, J. P. (OUCC) b April 18, 1957

Pearce, T. A. (Kent) b Dec. 18, 1910, d Aug. 11, 1982

Pearce, T. N. (Essex) b Nov. 3, 1905

*Pearse, C. O. C. (Natal) b Oct. 10, 1884, d May 7, 1953

Pearse, D. K. (Natal) b May 1, 1958

Pearson, D. B. (Worcs.) b March 29, 1937

*Peate, E. (Yorks.) b March 2, 1856, d March 11, 1900

Peck, I. G. (CUCC & Northants) b Oct. 18, 1957

*Peebles, I. A. R. (OUCC, Middx & Scotland; *CY 1931*) b Jan. 20, 1908, d Feb. 28, 1980

*Peel, R. (Yorks.; *CY 1889*) b Feb. 12, 1857, d Aug. 12, 1941

*Pegler, S. J. (Tvl) b July 28, 1888, d Sept. 10, 1972

*Pellew, C. E. (S. Aust.) b Sept. 21, 1893, d May 9, 1981

*Penn, F. (Kent) b March 7, 1851, d Dec. 26, 1916

Pepper, C. G. (NSW and Aust. Serv.; Umpire) b Sept. 15, 1918

Perkins, C. G. (Northants) b June 4, 1911

*Perks, R. T. D. (Worcs.) b Oct. 4, 1911, d Nov. 22, 1977

Perrin, P. A. (Essex; *CY 1905*) b May 26, 1876, d Nov. 20, 1945

Perryman, S. P. (Warwicks. & Worcs.) b Oct. 22, 1955

*Pervez Sajjad (Lahore, PIA & Kar.) b Aug. 30, 1942

Petchey, M. D. (OUCC) b Dec. 16, 1958

*Petherick, P. J. (Otago & Wgtn) b Sept. 25, 1942

*Petrie, E. C. (Auck. & N. Dist.) b May 22, 1927

Pfuhl, G. P. (W. Prov.) b Aug. 27, 1947

*Phadkar, D. G. (M'tra, Bombay, Bengal & Ind. Rlwys) b Dec. 10, 1925, d March 17, 1985

Phebey, A. H. (Kent) b Oct. 1, 1924

Phelan, P. J. (Essex) b Feb. 9, 1938

*Philipson, H. (OUCC & Middx) b June 8, 1866, d Dec. 4, 1935

*Phillip, N. (Comb. Is., Windwards & Essex) b June 12, 1948

Phillipps, J. H. (NZ Manager) b Jan. 1, 1898, d June 8, 1977

Phillips, R. B. (NSW & Qld) b May 23, 1954

*Phillips, W. B. (S. Aust.) b March 1, 1958

Phillipson, C. P. (Sussex) b Feb. 10, 1952

Phillipson, W. E. (Lancs.) b Dec. 3, 1910

*Philpott, P. I. (NSW) b Nov. 21, 1934

Piachaud, J. D. (OUCC, Hants & Ceylon) b March 1, 1937

Pick, R. A. (Notts.) b Nov. 19, 1963

Pickles, L. (Som.) b Sept. 17, 1932

Pienaar, R. F. (Tvl, W. Prov. & N. Tvl) b July 17, 1961

*Pierre, L. R. (T/T) b June 5, 1921

*Pigott, A. C. S. (Sussex & Wgtn) b June 4, 1958

Pilch, Fuller (Norfolk & Kent) b March 17, 1804, d May 1, 1870

Pilling, H. (Lancs.) b Feb. 23, 1943

*Pilling, R. (Lancs.; *CY 1891*) b July 5, 1855, d March 28, 1891

Pinch, C. J. (NSW & S. Aust.) b June 23, 1921

Pithey, A. J. (Rhod. & W. Prov.) b July 17, 1933

*Pithey, D. B. (Rhod., OUCC, Northants, W. Prov., Natal & Tvl) b Oct. 10, 1936

Pitman, R. W. C. (Hants) b Feb. 21, 1933

*Place, W. (Lancs.) b Dec 7, 1914

Platt, R. K. (Yorks. & Northants) b Dec. 21, 1932

*Playle, W. R. (Auck. & W. Aust.) b Dec. 1, 1938

Pleass, J. E. (Glam.) b May 21, 1923

*Plimsoll, J. B. (W. Prov. & Natal) b Oct. 27, 1917

Pocock, N. E. J. (Hants) b Dec. 15, 1951

*Pocock, P. I. (Surrey & N. Tvl) b Sept. 24, 1946

*Pollard, R. (Lancs.) b June 19, 1912, d Dec. 16, 1985

*Pollard, V. (C. Dist. & Cant.) b Burnley Sept. 7, 1945

Pollock, A. J. (CUCC) b April 19, 1962

*Pollock, P. M. (E. Prov.; *CY 1966*) b June 30, 1941

*Pollock, R. G. (E. Prov. & Tvl; *CY 1966*) b Feb. 27, 1944

*Ponsford, W. H. (Vic.; *CY 1935*) b Oct. 19, 1900

Pont, K. R. (Essex) b Jan. 16, 1953

*Poole, C. J. (Notts.) b March 13, 1921

Pooley, E. (Surrey & first England tour) b Feb. 13, 1838, d July 18, 1907

*Poore, M. B. (Cant.) b June 1, 1930

*Poore, Brig-Gen. R. M. (Hants & SA; *CY 1900*) b March 20, 1866, d July 14, 1938

Pope, A. V. (Derbys.) b Aug. 15, 1909

*Pope, G. H. (Derbys.) b Jan. 27, 1911

*Pope, R. J. (NSW) b Feb. 18, 1864, d July 27, 1952

Popplewell, N. F. M. (CUCC & Som.) b Aug. 8, 1957

Portal of Hungerford, 1st Lord (Pres. MCC 1958-59) b May 21, 1893, d April 22, 1971

Porter, A. (Glam.) b March 25, 1914

Pothecary, E. A. (Hants) b March 1, 1906

*Pothecary, J. E. (W. Prov.) b Dec. 6, 1933

Potter, G. (Sussex) b Oct. 26, 1931

Potter, J. (Vic.) b April 13, 1938

Potter, L. (Kent, Griq. W. & Leics.) b Nov. 7, 1962

*Pougher, A. D. (Leics.) b April 19, 1865, d May 20, 1926

Pountain, F. R. (Sussex) b April 23, 1941

Powell, A. G. (CUCC & Essex) b Aug. 17, 1912, d June 7, 1982

*Powell, A. W. (Griq. W.) b July 18, 1873, d Sept. 11, 1948

*Prabhakar, M. (Delhi) b April 15, 1963

Prasanna, E. A. S. (†Karn.) b May 22, 1940

Pratt, R. C. E. (Surrey) b May 5, 1928, d June 7, 1977

Pratt, R. L. (Leics.) b Nov. 15, 1938

Prentice, F. T. (Leics.) b April 22, 1912, d July 10, 1978

Pressdee, J. S. (Glam. & NE Tvl) b June 19, 1933

Preston, Hubert (Editor of *Wisden* 1944-51) b Dec. 16, 1868, d Aug. 6, 1960

Preston, K. C. (Essex) b Aug. 22, 1925

Preston, Norman (Editor of *Wisden* 1951-80) b March 18, 1903, d March 6, 1980

Pretlove, J. F. (CUCC & Kent) b Nov. 23, 1932

Price, D. G. (CUCC) b Feb. 7, 1965

Price, E. J. (Lancs. & Essex) b Oct. 27, 1918

*Price, J. S. E. (Middx) b July 22, 1937

Price, M. R. (Glam.) b April 20, 1960

*Price, W. F. (Middx) b April 25, 1902, d Jan. 13, 1969

Prichard, P. J. (Essex) b Jan. 7, 1965

*Prideaux, R. M. (CUCC, Kent, Northants, Sussex & OFS) b July 13, 1939

Pridgeon, A. P. (Worcs.) b Feb. 22, 1954

*Prince, C. F. H. (W. Prov., Border & E. Prov.) b Sept. 11, 1874, d March 5, 1948

*Pringle, D. R. (CUCC & Essex) b Sept. 18, 1958

Pritchard, T. L. (Wgtn, Warwicks. & Kent) b March 10, 1917

*Procter, M. J. (Glos., Natal, W. Prov. & Rhod.; *CY 1970*) b Sept. 15, 1946

Prodger, J. M. (Kent) b Sept. 1, 1935

*Promnitz, H. L. E. (Border, Griq. W. & OFS) b Feb. 23, 1904, d Sept. 7, 1983

Prouton, R. O. (Hants) b March 1, 1926

Puckett, C. W. (W. Aust.) b Feb. 21, 1911

Pugh, C. T. M. (Glos.) b March 13, 1937

Pullan, D. A. (Notts.) b May 1, 1944

*Pullar, G. (Lancs. & Glos.; *CY 1960*) b Aug. 1, 1935

Pullinger, G. R. (Essex) b March 14, 1920, d Aug. 4, 1982

*Puna, N. (N. Dist.) b Oct. 28, 1929

*Punjabi, P. H. (Sind & Guj.) b Sept. 20, 1921

Pycroft, A. J. (Zimb.) b June 6, 1956

Pydanna, M. (Guyana) b Jan. 27, 1950

*Qasim Omar (Kar. & MCB) b Feb. 9, 1957

Quaife, B. W. (Warwicks. & Worcs.) b Nov. 24, 1899, d Nov. 28, 1984

*Quaife, William (W. G.) (Warwicks. & Griq. W.; *CY 1902*) b March 17, 1872, d Oct. 13, 1951

Quick, I. W. (Vic.) b Nov. 5, 1933

Quinlan, J. D. (OUCC) b April 18, 1965

*Quinn, N. A. (Griq. W. & Tvl) b Feb. 21, 1908, d Aug. 5, 1934

*Rabone, G. O. (Wgtn & Auck.) b Nov. 6, 1921

*Rackemann, C. G. (Qld) b June 3, 1960

*Radford, N. V. (Lancs., Tvl & Worcs.; *CY 1986*) b June 7, 1957

*Radley, C. T. (Middx; *CY 1979*) b May 13, 1944

*Rae, A. F. (Jam.) b Sept. 30, 1922

*Rai Singh, K. (S. Punjab & Ind. Serv.) b Feb. 24, 1922

Rait Kerr, Col. R. S. (Sec. MCC 1936-52) b April 13, 1891, d April 2, 1961

*Rajindernath, V. (N. Ind., U. Prov., S. Punjab, Bihar & E. Punjab) b Jan. 7, 1928

*Rajinder Pal (Delhi, S. Punjab & Punjab) b Nov. 18, 1937

Rajput, L. S. (Bombay) b Dec. 18, 1961

Ralph, L. H. R. (Essex) b May 22, 1920

*Ramadhin, S. (T/T & Lancs.; *CY 1951*) b May 1, 1929

*Ramaswami, C. (Madras) b June 18, 1896

*Ramchand, G. S. (Sind, Bombay & Raja.) b July 26, 1927

*Ramiz Raja (Lahore & Allied Bank) b July 14, 1962

*Ramji, L. (W. Ind.) b 1900, d Dec. 20, 1948

Ramsamooj, D. (T/T & Northants) b July 5, 1932

*Ranasinghe, A. N. (SL) b Oct. 13, 1956

*Ranatunga, A. (SL) b Dec. 1, 1963

*Randall, D. W. (Notts.; *CY 1980*) b Feb. 24, 1951

Randhir Singh (Orissa & Bihar) b Aug. 16, 1957

*Rangachari, C. R. (Madras) b April 14, 1916

*Rangnekar, K. M. (M'tra, Bombay & †M. Pradesh) b June 27, 1917, d Oct. 11, 1984

*Ranjane, V. B. (M'tra & Ind. Rlwys) b July 22, 1937

*Ranjitsinhji, K. S., afterwards H. H. the Jam Saheb of Nawanagar (CUCC & Sussex; *CY 1897*) b Sept. 10, 1872, d April 2, 1933

*Ransford, V. S. (Vic.; *CY 1910*) b March 20, 1885, d March 19, 1958

Ransom, V. J. (Hants & Surrey) b March 17, 1918

*Rashid Khan (PWD, Kar. & PIA) b Dec. 15, 1959

Ratcliffe, R. M. (Lancs.) b Nov. 29, 1951

Ratnayake, R. J. (SL) b Jan. 2, 1964

*Ratnayeke, J. R. (SL) b May 2, 1960

Rawlinson, H. T. (OUCC) b Jan. 21, 1963

Rayment, A. W. H. (Hants) b May 29, 1928

Raymer, V. N. (Qld) b May 4, 1918

Read, H. D. (Surrey & Essex) b Jan. 28, 1910

*Read, J. M. (Surrey; *CY 1890*) b Feb. 9, 1859, d Feb. 17, 1929

*Read, W. W. (Surrey; *CY 1893*) b Nov. 23, 1855, d Jan. 6, 1907

Reddick, T. B. (Middx, Notts. & W. Prov.) b Feb. 17, 1912, d June 1, 1982

*Reddy, B. (TN) b Nov. 12, 1954

Redman, J. (Som.) b March 1, 1926, d Sept. 19, 1981

*Redmond, R. E. (Wgtn & Auck.) b Dec. 29, 1944

*Redpath, I. R. (Vic.) b May 11, 1941

Reed, B. L. (Hants) b Sept. 9, 1937

*Reedman, J. C. (S. Aust.) b Oct. 9, 1865, d March 25, 1924

Rees, A. (Glam.) b Feb. 17, 1938

Reeve, D. A. (Sussex) b April 2, 1963

Reeves, W. (Essex; Umpire) b Jan. 22, 1875, d March 22, 1944

*Rege, M. R. (M'tra) b March 18, 1924

*Rehman, S. F. (Punjab, Pak. Us & Lahore) b June 11, 1935

*Reid, B. A. (W. Aust.) b March 14, 1963

*Reid, J. F. (Auck.) b March 3, 1956

*Reid, J. R. (Wgtn & Otago; *CY 1959*) b June 3, 1928

Reid, K. P. (E. Prov. & Northants) b July 24, 1951

*Reid, N. (W. Prov.) b Dec 26, 1890, d June 10, 1947

Reidy, B. W. (Lancs.) b Sept. 18, 1953

*Relf, A. E. (Sussex & Auck.; *CY 1914*) b June 26, 1874, d March 26, 1937

*Renneburg, D. A. (NSW) b Sept. 23, 1942

Revill, A. C. (Derbys. & Leics.) b March 27, 1923

Reynolds, B. L. (Northants) b June 10, 1932

Reynolds, G. R. (Qld) b Aug. 24, 1936

Rhodes, A. E. G. (Derbys.) b Oct. 10, 1916, d Oct. 18, 1983

*Rhodes, H. J. (Derbys.) b July 22, 1936

Rhodes, S. D. (Notts.) b March 24, 1910

Rhodes, S. J. (Yorks. & Worcs.) b June 17, 1964

*Rhodes, W. (Yorks.; *CY 1899*) b Oct. 29, 1877, d July 8, 1973

Rice, C. E. B. (Tvl & Notts.; *CY 1981*) b July 23, 1949

Rice, J. M. (Hants) b Oct. 23, 1949

*Richards, A. R. (W. Prov.) b 1868, d Jan. 9, 1904

*Richards, B. A. (Natal, Glos., Hants & S. Aust.; *CY 1969*) b July 21, 1945

Richards, C. J. (Surrey & OFS) b Aug. 10, 1958

Richards, G. (Glam.) b Nov. 29, 1951

*Richards, I. V. A. (Comb. Is., Leewards, Som. & Qld; *CY 1977*) b March 7, 1952

*Richards, W. H. M. (SA) b Aug. 1862, d Jan. 4, 1903

*Richardson, A. J. (S. Aust.) b July 24, 1888, d Dec. 23, 1973

Richardson, A. W. (Derbys.) b March 4, 1907, d July 29, 1983

Richardson, D. J. (E. Prov. & N. Tvl) b Sept. 16, 1959

*Richardson, D. W. (Worcs.) b Nov. 3, 1934

Richardson, G. W. (Derbys.) b April 26, 1938

*Richardson, P. E. (Worcs. & Kent; *CY 1957*) b July 4, 1931

*Richardson, R. B. (Leewards) b Jan. 12, 1962

*Richardson, T. (Surrey & Som.; *CY 1897*) b Aug. 11, 1870, d July 2, 1912

*Richardson, V. Y. (S. Aust.) b Sept. 7, 1894, d Oct. 29, 1969

*Richmond, T. L. (Notts.) b June 23, 1890, d Dec. 29, 1957

Rickards, K. R. (Jam. & Essex) b Aug. 23, 1923

Riddington, A. (Leics.) b Dec. 22, 1911

Ridge, S. P. (OUCC) b Nov. 23, 1961

*Ridgway, F. (Kent) b Aug. 10, 1923

Ridings, P. L. (S. Aust.) b Oct. 2, 1917

*Rigg, K. E. (Vic.) b May 21, 1906

Riley, H. (Leics.) b Oct. 3, 1902

*Ring, D. T. (Vic.) b Oct. 14, 1918

Rist, F. H. (Essex) b March 30, 1914

Ritchie, G. G. (Tvl) b Sept. 16, 1933

*Ritchie, G. M. (Qld) b Jan. 23, 1960

*Rixon, S. J. (NSW) b Feb. 25, 1954

*Rizwan-uz-Zaman (Kar. & PIA) b Sept. 4, 1962

*Roach, C. A. (T/T) b March 13, 1904

*Roberts, A. D. G. (N. Dist.) b May 6, 1947

*Roberts, A. M. E. (Comb. Is., Leewards, Hants, NSW & Leics.; *CY 1975*) b Jan. 29, 1951

*Roberts, A. T. (Windwards) b Sept. 18, 1937

*Roberts, A. W. (Cant. & Otago) b Aug. 20, 1909, d May 13, 1978

Roberts, B. (Tvl & Derbys.) b May 30, 1962

Roberts, Pascal (T/T) b Dec 15, 1937

Roberts, W. B. (Lancs. & Victory Tests) b Sept. 27, 1914, d Aug. 24, 1951

*Robertson, G. K. (C. Dist.) b July 15, 1960

*Robertson, J. B. (W. Prov.) b June 5, 1906, d July 5, 1985

*Robertson, J. D. (Middx; *CY 1948*) b Feb. 22, 1917

Robertson, S. D. (Rhod.) b May 1, 1947

*Robertson, W. R. (Vic.) b Oct. 6, 1861, d June 24, 1938

Robertson-Glasgow, R. C. (OUCC & Som.) b July 15, 1901, d March 4, 1965

Robins, D. H. (Warwicks.) b June 26, 1914

Robins, R. V. C. (Middx) b March 13, 1935

*Robins, R. W. V. (CUCC & Middx; *CY 1930*) b June 3, 1906, d Dec. 12, 1968

Robinson, A. L. (Yorks.) b Aug. 17, 1946

Robinson, Emmott (Yorks.) b Nov. 16, 1883, d Nov. 17, 1969

Robinson, Ellis P. (Yorks. & Som.) b Aug. 10, 1911

Robinson, H. B. (OUCC & Canada) b March 3, 1919

Robinson, M. (Glam., Warwicks., H'bad & Madras) b July 16, 1921

Robinson, P. E. (Yorks.) b Aug. 3, 1963

Robinson, P. J. (Worcs. & Som.) b Feb. 9, 1943

Robinson, Ray (Writer) b July 8, 1908, d July 6, 1982

*Robinson, R. D. (Vic.) b June 8, 1946

*Robinson, R. H. (NSW, S. Aust. & Otago) b March 26, 1914, d Aug. 10, 1965

*Robinson, R. T. (Notts.; *CY 1986*) b Nov. 21, 1958

Robson, E. (Som.) b May 1, 1870, d May 23, 1924

Rochford, P. (Glos.) b Aug. 27, 1928

*Rodriguez, W. V. (T/T) b June 25, 1934

Roe, B. (Som.) b Jan. 27, 1939

Roebuck, P. G. P. (CUCC & Glos.) b Oct. 13, 1963

Roebuck, P. M. (CUCC & Som.) b March 6, 1956

Rogers, J. J. (OUCC) b Aug. 20, 1958

Rogers, N. H. (Hants) b March 9, 1918

Rogers, R. E. (Qld) b Aug. 24, 1916

Romaines, P. W. (Northants, Glos. & Griq. W.) b Dec. 25, 1955

*Roope, G. R. J. (Surrey & Griq. W.) b July 12, 1946

*Root, C. F. (Derbys. & Worcs.) b April 16, 1890, d Jan. 20, 1954

*Rorke, G. F. (NSW) b June 27, 1938

*Rose, B. C. (Som.; *CY 1980*) b June 4, 1950

Rosebery, 6th Earl of (*see* Dalmeny, Lord)

*Rose-Innes, A. (Kimberley & Tvl) b Feb. 16, 1868, d Nov. 22, 1946

Rosendorff, N. (OFS) b Jan. 22, 1945

Ross, C. J. (Wgtn & OUCC) b June 24, 1954

Rotherham, G. A. (Rugby, CUCC, Warwicks. & Wgtn; *CY 1918*) b May 28, 1899, d Jan. 31, 1985

Rouse, S. J. (Warwicks.) b Jan. 20, 1949

Routledge, R. (Middx) b July 7, 1920

*Routledge, T. W. (W. Prov. & Tvl) b April 18, 1867, d May 9, 1927

*Rowan, A. M. B. (Tvl) b Feb. 7, 1921

*Rowan, E. A. B. (Tvl; *CY 1952*) b July 20, 1909

*Rowe, C. G. (Wgtn & C. Dist.) b June 30, 1915

Rowe, C. J. C. (Kent & Glam.) b May 5, 1953

Rowe, E. J. (Notts.) b July 21, 1920

*Rowe, G. A. (W. Prov.) b June 15, 1874, d Jan. 8, 1950

*Rowe, L. G. (Jam. & Derbys.) b Jan. 8, 1949

*Roy, A. (Bengal) b June 5, 1945

*Roy, Pankaj (Bengal) b May 31, 1928

*Roy, Pranab (Bengal) b Feb. 10, 1957

*Royle, Rev. V. P. F. A. (OUCC & Lancs.) b Jan. 29, 1854, d May 21, 1929

*Rumsey, F. E. (Worcs., Som. & Derbys.) b Dec. 4, 1935

*Russell, A. C. [C. A. G.] (Essex; *CY 1923*) b Oct. 7, 1887, d March 23, 1961

Russell, P. E. (Derbys.) b May 9, 1944

Russell, R. C. (Glos.) b Aug. 15, 1963

Russell, S. E. (Middx & Glos.) b Oct. 4, 1937

*Russell, W. E. (Middx) b July 3, 1936

Russom, N. (CUCC & Som.) b Dec. 3, 1958

Rutherford, I. A. (Worcs. & Otago) b June 30, 1957

*Rutherford, J. W. (W. Aust.) b Sept. 25, 1929

*Rutherford, K. R. (Otago) b Oct. 26, 1965

Rutnagur, R. S. (OUCC) b Aug. 9, 1964

Ryan, M. (Yorks.) b June 23, 1933

Ryan, M. L. (Cant.) b June 7, 1943

*Ryder, J. (Vic.) b Aug. 8, 1889, d April 3, 1977

Rydon, R. A. (OUCC) b Nov. 27, 1964

*Sadiq Mohammad (Kar., PIA, Tas., Essex, Glos. & UBP) b May 3, 1945

Sadler, W. C. H. (Surrey) b Sept. 24, 1896, d Feb. 12, 1981

*Saeed Ahmed (Punjab, Pak. Us, Lahore, PIA, Kar., PWD & Sind) b Oct. 1, 1937

*Saggers, R. A. (NSW) b May 15, 1917

Sainsbury, G. E. (Essex & Glos.) b Jan. 17, 1958

Sainsbury, P. J. (Hants; *CY 1974*) b June 13, 1934

*St Hill, E. L. (T/T) b March 9, 1904, d May 21, 1957

*St Hill, W. H. (T/T) b July 6, 1893, d 1957

*Salah-ud-Din (Kar., PIA & Pak. Us) b Feb. 14, 1947

Sale, R., jun. (OUCC, Warwicks. & Derbys.) b Oct. 4, 1919

*Saleem Altaf (Lahore & PIA) b April 19, 1944

*Salim Malik (Lahore & HBL) b April 16, 1963

*Salim Yousuf (Sind, Kar., IDBP & Allied Bank) b Dec. 7, 1959

Salvi, N. M. (OUCC) b May 21, 1965

Sampson, H. (Yorks. & All-England) b March 13, 1813, d March 29, 1885

*Samuelson, S. V. (Natal) b Nov. 21, 1883, d Nov. 18, 1958

Sanderson, J. F. W. (OUCC) b Sept. 10, 1954

*Sandham, A. (Surrey; *CY 1923*) b July 6, 1890, d April 20, 1982

*Sandhu, B. S. (Bombay) b March 1, 1956

*Sardesai, D. N. (Bombay) b Aug. 8, 1940

*Sarfraz Nawaz (Lahore, Punjab, Northants, Pak. Rlwys & UBL) b Dec. 1, 1948

*Sarwate, C. T. (CP & B, M'tra, Bombay & †M. Pradesh) b June 22, 1920

*Saunders, J. V. (Vic. & Wgtn) b Feb. 3, 1876, d Dec. 21, 1927

Saunders, S. L. (Tas.) b June 27, 1960

Savage, J. S. (Leics. & Lancs.) b March 3, 1929

Savage, R. Le Q. (OUCC & Warwicks.) b Dec. 10, 1955

Savill, L. A. (Essex) b June 30, 1935

Saville, G. J. (Essex) b Feb. 5, 1944

Saxelby, K. (Notts.) b Feb. 23, 1959

*Saxena, R. C. (Delhi & Bihar) b Sept. 20, 1944

Sayer, D. M. (OUCC & Kent) b Sept. 19, 1936

*Scarlett, R. O. (Jam.) b Aug. 15, 1934

Schmidt, E. (E. Prov. & OFS) b Sept. 21, 1950

Schofield, R. M. (C. Dist.) b Nov. 6, 1939

Scholes, W. J. (Vic.) b Feb. 5, 1950

Schonegevel, D. J. (OFS & Griq. W.) b Oct. 9, 1934

*Schultz, S. S. (CUCC & Lancs.) b Aug. 29, 1857, d Dec. 18, 1937

*Schwarz, R. O. (Middx & Natal; *CY 1908*) b May 4, 1875, d Nov. 18, 1918

Scott, A. M. G. (CUCC) b March 31, 1966

*Scott, A. P. H. (Jam.) b July 29, 1934

Scott, Christopher J. (Lancs.) b Sept. 16, 1959

Scott, Colin J. (Glos.) b May 1, 1919

*Scott, H. J. H. (Vic.) b Dec. 26, 1858, d Sept. 23, 1910

Scott, M. E. (Northants) b May 8, 1936

*Scott, O. C. (Jam.) b Aug. 25, 1893, d June 16, 1961

*Scott, R. H. (Cant.) b March 6, 1917

Scott, S. W. (Middx; *CY 1893*) b March 24, 1854, d Dec. 8, 1933

*Scott, V. J. (Auck.) b July 31, 1916, d Aug. 2, 1980

*Scotton, W. H. (Notts.) b Jan. 15, 1856, d July 9, 1893

Seabrook, F. J. (CUCC & Glos.) b Jan. 9, 1899, d Aug. 7, 1979

*Sealey, B. J. (T/T) b Aug. 12, 1899, d Sept. 12, 1963

*Sealy, J. E. D. (B'dos & T/T) b Sept. 11, 1912, d Jan. 3, 1982

Seamer, J. W. (Som. & OUCC) b June 23, 1913

Sebastian, L. C. (Windwards) b Oct. 31, 1955

*Seccull, A. W. (Kimberley, W. Prov. & Tvl) b Sept. 14, 1868, d July 20, 1945

Seeff, L. J. (W. Prov.) b May 1, 1959

*Sekar, T. A. P. (TN) b March 28, 1955

*Selby, J. (Notts.) b July 1, 1849, d March 11, 1894

Sellers, A. B. (Yorks.; *CY 1940*) b March 5, 1907, d Feb. 20, 1981

*Sellers, R. H. D. (S. Aust.) b Aug. 20, 1940

*Selvey, M. W. W. (CUCC, Surrey, Middx, Glam. & OFS) b April 25, 1948

*Sen, P. (Bengal) b May 31, 1926, d Jan. 27, 1970

*Sen Gupta, A. K. (Ind. Serv.) b Aug. 3, 1939

*Serjeant, C. S. (W. Aust.) b Nov. 1, 1951

Seymour, James (Kent) b Oct. 25, 1879, d Sept. 30, 1930

*Seymour, M. A. (W. Prov.) b June 5, 1936

*Shackleton, D. (Hants.; *CY 1959*) b Aug. 12, 1924

*Shafiq Ahmed (Lahore, Punjab, NBP & UBL) b March 28, 1949

*Shafqat Rana (Lahore & PIA) b Aug. 10, 1943

Shahid Israr (Kar. & Sind) b March 1, 1950

*Shahid Mahmoud (Kar., Pak. Us & PWD) b March 17, 1939

*Shalders, W. A. (Griq. W. & Tvl) b Feb. 12, 1880, d March 18, 1917

*Sharma, Chetan (Haryana) b Jan. 3, 1966

*Sharma, Gopal (U. Pradesh) b Aug. 3, 1960

*Sharma, P. (Raja.) b Jan. 5, 1948

Sharma, R. (Derbys.) b June 27, 1962

Sharp, G. (Northants) b March 12, 1950

Sharp, H. P. (Middx) b Oct. 6, 1917

*Sharp, J. (Lancs.) b Feb. 15, 1878, d Jan. 28, 1938

Sharp, K. (Yorks. & Griq. W.) b April 6, 1959

*Sharpe, D. (Punjab, Pak. Rlwys, Lahore & S. Aust.) b Aug. 3, 1937

*Sharpe, J. W. (Surrey & Notts.; *CY 1892*) b Dec. 9, 1866, d June 19, 1936

*Sharpe, P. J. (Yorks. & Derbys.; *CY 1963*) b Dec. 27, 1936

*Shastri, R. J. (Bombay) b May 27, 1962

*Shaw, Alfred (Notts. & Sussex) b Aug. 29, 1842, d Jan. 16, 1907

Shaw, C. (Yorks.) b Feb. 17, 1964

Shaw, J. H. (Vic.) b Oct. 18, 1932

*Sheahan, A. P. (Vic.) b Sept. 30, 1946

Sheffield, J. R. (Essex & Wgtn) b Nov. 19, 1906

*Shepherd, B. K. (W. Aust.) b April 23, 1937

*Shepherd, D. J. (Glam.; *CY 1970*) b Aug. 12, 1927

Shepherd, D. R. (Glos.) b Dec. 27, 1940

*Shepherd, J. N. (B'dos, Kent, Rhod. & Glos.; *CY 1979*) b Nov. 9, 1943

Shepherd, T. F. (Surrey) b Dec. 5, 1889, d Feb. 13, 1957

*Sheppard, Rt Rev. D. S. (Bishop of Liverpool) (CUCC & Sussex; *CY 1953*) b March 6, 1929

*Shepstone, G. H. (Tvl) b April 8, 1876, d July 3, 1940

*Sherwell, P. W. (Tvl) b Aug. 17, 1880, d April 17, 1948

*Sherwin, M. (Notts.; *CY 1891*) b Feb. 26, 1851, d July 3, 1910

*Shillingford, G. C. (Comb. Is. & Windwards) b Sept. 25, 1944

*Shillingford, I. T. (Comb. Is. & Windwards) b April 18, 1944

*Shinde, S. G. (Baroda, M'tra & Bombay) b Aug. 18, 1923, d June 22, 1955

Shipman, A. W. (Leics.) b March 7, 1901, d Dec. 12, 1979

Shipperd, G. (W. Aust.) b Nov. 11, 1956

Shirreff, A. C. (CUCC, Hants, Kent & Som.) b Feb. 12, 1919

*Shivnarine, S. (Guyana) b May 13, 1952

*Shoaib Mohammad (Kar. & PIA) b Jan. 8, 1962

*Shodhan, R. H. (Guj. & Baroda) b Oct. 18, 1928

Short, A. M. (Natal) b Sept. 27, 1947

*Shrewsbury, Arthur (Notts.; *CY 1890*) b April 11, 1856, d May 19, 1903

*Shrimpton, M. J. F. (C. Dist. & N. Dist.) b June 23, 1940

*Shuja-ud-Din, Col. (N. Ind., Pak. Us, Pak. Serv., B'pur & R'pindi) b April 10, 1930

*Shukla, R. C. (Bihar & Delhi) b Feb. 4, 1948

*Shuter, J. (Kent & Surrey) b Feb. 9, 1855, d July 5, 1920

*Shuttleworth, K. (Lancs. & Leics.) b Nov. 13, 1944

*Sidebottom, A. (Yorks. & OFS) b April 1, 1954

*Sidhu, N. S. (Punjab) b Oct. 20, 1963

*Siedle, I. J. (Natal) b Jan. 11, 1903, d Aug. 24, 1982

*Sievers, M. W. (Vic.) b April 13, 1912, d May 10, 1968

*Sikander Bakht (PWD, PIA, Sind, Kar. & UBL) b Aug. 25, 1957

Silk, D. R. W. (CUCC & Som.) b Oct. 8, 1931

*Silva, S. A. R. (SL) b Dec. 12, 1960

Sime, W. A. (Notts.) b Feb. 8, 1909, d May 5, 1982

Simmons, J. (Lancs. & Tas.; *CY 1985*) b March 28, 1941

*Simpson, R. B. (NSW & W. Aust.; *CY 1965*) b Feb. 3, 1936

*Simpson, R. T. (Notts. & Sind; *CY 1950*) b Feb. 27, 1920

*Simpson-Hayward, G. H. (Worcs.) b June 7, 1875, d Oct. 2, 1936

Sims, Sir Arthur (Cant.) b July 22, 1877, d April 27, 1969

*Sims, J. M. (Middx) b May 13, 1903, d April 27, 1973

*Sinclair, B. W. (Wgtn) b Oct. 23, 1936

*Sinclair, I. McK. (Cant.) b June 1, 1933

*Sinclair, J. H. (Tvl) b Oct. 16, 1876, d Feb. 23, 1913

*Sincock, D. J. (S. Aust.) b Feb. 1, 1942

*Sinfield, R. A. (Glos.) b Dec. 24, 1900

Singh, Charan K. (T/T) b 1938

Singh, Swaranjit (CUCC, Warwicks., E. Punjab & Bengal) b July 18, 1931

Singleton, A. P. (OUCC, Worcs. & Rhod.) b Aug. 5, 1914

*Sivaramakrishnan, L. (TN) b Dec. 31, 1965

Siviter, K. (OUCC) b Dec. 10, 1953

Skeet, C. H. L. (OUCC & Middx) b Aug. 17, 1895, d April 20, 1978

Skelding, Alec (Leics.) b Sept. 5, 1886, d April 17, 1960

Skinner, A. F. (Derbys. & Northants) b April 22, 1913, d Feb. 28, 1982

Skinner, D. A. (Derbys.) b March 22, 1920

Skinner, L. E. (Surrey & Guyana) b Sept. 7, 1950

*Slack, W. N. (Middx & Windwards) b Dec. 12, 1954

Slade, D. N. F. (Worcs.) b Aug. 24, 1940

Slade, W. D. (Glam.) b Sept. 27, 1941

*Slater, K. N. (W. Aust.) b March 12, 1935

Sleep, P. R. (S. Aust.) b May 4, 1957

*Slight, J. (Vic.) b Oct. 20, 1855, d Dec. 9, 1930

Slocombe, P. A. (Som.) b Sept. 6, 1954

*Smailes, T. F. (Yorks.) b March 27, 1910, d Dec. 1, 1970

Smales, K. (Yorks. & Notts.) b Sept. 15, 1927

*Small, G. C. (Warwicks.) b Oct. 18, 1961

Small, John, sen. (Hants & All-England) b April 19, 1737, d Dec. 31, 1826

*Small, J. A. (T/T) b Nov. 3, 1892, d April 26, 1958

*Small, M. A. (B'dos) b Feb. 12, 1964

Smart, J. A. (Warwicks.) b April 12, 1891, d Oct. 3, 1979

Smedley, M. J. (Notts.) b Oct. 28, 1941

*Smith, A. C. (OUCC & Warwicks.; Chief Exec. TCCB 1987–   ) b Oct. 25, 1936

Smith, A. J. S. (Natal) b Feb. 8, 1951

*Smith, Sir C. Aubrey (CUCC, Sussex & Tvl) b July 21, 1863, d Dec. 20, 1948

*Smith, C. I. J. (Middx; *CY 1935*) b Aug. 25, 1906, d Feb. 9, 1979

*Smith, C. J. E. (Tvl) b Dec. 25, 1872, d March 27, 1947

*Smith, C. L. (Natal, Glam. & Hants; *CY 1984*) b Oct. 15, 1958

Smith, C. S. (CUCC & Lancs.) b Oct. 1, 1932

*Smith, C. W. (B'dos) b July 29, 1933

*Smith, Denis (Derbys.; *CY 1936*) b Jan. 24, 1907, d Sept. 12, 1979

*Smith, D. B. M. (Vic.) b Sept. 14, 1884, d July 29, 1963

Smith, D. H. K. (Derbys. & OFS) b June 29, 1940

*Smith, D. M. (Surrey & Worcs.) b Jan. 9, 1956

*Smith, D. R. (Glos.) b Oct. 5, 1934

*Smith, D. V. (Sussex) b June 14, 1923

Smith, Edwin (Derbys.) b Jan. 2, 1934

*Smith, E. J. (Warwicks.) b Feb. 6, 1886, d Aug. 31, 1979

*Smith, F. B. (Cant.) b March 13, 1922

*Smith, F. W. (Tvl) No details of birth or death known

Smith, G. (Kent) b Nov. 30, 1925

Smith, G. J. (Essex) b April 2, 1935

*Smith, Harry (Glos.) b May 21, 1890, d Nov. 12, 1937

*Smith, H. D. (Otago & Cant.) b Jan. 8, 1913, d Jan. 25, 1986

*Smith, I. D. S. (C. Dist.) b Feb. 28, 1957

Smith, K. D. (Warwicks.) b July 9, 1956

Smith, L. D. (Otago) b Dec. 23, 1914, d Nov. 1, 1978

Smith, M. J. (Middx) b Jan. 4, 1942

*Smith, M. J. K. (OUCC, Leics. & Warwicks.; *CY 1960*) b June 30, 1933

Smith, N. (Yorks. & Essex) b April 1, 1949

*Smith, O. G. (Jam.; *CY 1958*) b May 5, 1933, d Sept. 9, 1959

Smith, P. A. (Warwicks.) b April 5, 1964

Smith, Ray (Essex) b Aug. 10, 1914

Smith, Roy (Som.) b April 14, 1930

Smith, R. A. (Natal & Hants) b Sept. 13, 1963

Smith, R. C. (Leics.) b Aug. 3, 1935

*Smith, S. B. (NSW) b Oct. 18, 1961

Smith, S. G. (T/T, Northants & Auck.; *CY 1915*) b Jan. 15, 1881, d Oct. 25, 1963

*Smith, T. P. B. (Essex; *CY 1947*) b Oct. 30, 1908, d Aug. 4, 1967

*Smith, V. I. (Natal) b Feb. 23, 1925

Smith, W. A. (Surrey) b Sept. 15, 1937

Smith, W. C. (Surrey; *CY 1911*) b Oct. 4, 1877, d July 16, 1946

*Smithson, G. A. (Yorks. & Leics.) b Nov. 1, 1926, d Sept. 6, 1970

*Snedden, C. A. (Auck.) b Jan. 7, 1918

*Snedden, M. C. (Auck.) b Nov. 23, 1958

Snellgrove, K. L. (Lancs.) b Nov. 12, 1941

*Snooke, S. D. (W. Prov. & Tvl) b Nov. 11, 1878, d April 4, 1959

*Snooke, S. J. (Border, W. Prov. & Tvl) b Feb. 1, 1881, d Aug. 14, 1966

*Snow, J. A. (Sussex; *CY 1973*) b Oct. 13, 1941

Snowden, A. W. (Northants) b Aug. 15, 1913, d May 7, 1981

Snowden, W. (CUCC) b Sept. 27, 1952

*Sobers, Sir G. S. (B'dos, S. Aust. & Notts.; *CY 1964*) b July 28, 1936

*Sohoni, S. W. (M'tra, Baroda & Bombay) b March 5, 1918

Solanky, J. W. (E. Africa & Glam.) b June 30, 1942

Solkar, E. D. (Bombay & Sussex) b March 18, 1948

*Solomon, J. S. (BG) b Aug. 26, 1930

*Solomon, W. R. T. (Tvl & E. Prov.) b April 23, 1872, d July 12, 1964

*Sood, M. M. (Delhi) b July 6, 1939

Southern, J. W. (Hants) b Sept. 2, 1952

*Southerton, James (Surrey, Hants & Sussex) b Nov. 16, 1827, d June 16, 1880

Southerton, S. J. (Editor of *Wisden* 1934-35) b July 7, 1874, d March 12, 1935

*Sparling, J. T. (Auck.) b July 24, 1938

Spencer, C. T. (Leics.) b Aug. 18, 1931

Spencer, J. (CUCC & Sussex) b Oct. 6, 1949

Spencer, T. W. (Kent) b March 22, 1914

Sperry, J. (Leics.) b March 19, 1910

*Spofforth, F. R. (NSW & Vic.) b Sept. 9, 1853, d June 4, 1926

*Spooner, R. H. (Lancs.; *CY 1905*) b Oct. 21, 1880, d Oct. 2, 1961

*Spooner, R. T. (Warwicks.) b Dec. 30, 1919

Springall, J. D. (Notts.) b Sept. 19, 1932

*Srikkanth, K. (TN) b Dec. 21, 1959

*Srinivasan, T. E. (TN) b Oct. 26, 1950

*Stackpole, K. R. (Vic.; *CY 1973*) b July 10, 1940

Standen, J. A. (Worcs.) b May 30, 1935

Standing, D. K. (Sussex) b Oct. 21, 1963

*Stanyforth, Lt-Col. R. T. (Yorks.) b May 30, 1892, d Feb. 20, 1964

*Staples, S. J. (Notts.; *CY 1929*) b Sept. 18, 1892, d June 4, 1950

Starkie, S. (Northants) b April 4, 1926

*Statham, J. B. (Lancs.; *CY 1955*) b June 16, 1930

*Stayers, S. C. (†Guyana & Bombay) b June 9, 1937

Stead, B. (Yorks., Essex, Notts. & N. Tvl) b June 21, 1939, d April 15, 1980

Stead, D. W. (Cant.) b May 26, 1947

*Steel, A. G. (CUCC & Lancs.; Pres. MCC 1902) b Sept. 24, 1858, d June 15, 1914

*Steele, D. S. (Northants & Derbys.; *CY 1976*) b Sept. 29, 1941

Steele, J. F. (Leics., Natal & Glam.) b July 23, 1946

Stephens, E. J. (Glos.) b March 23, 1910

Stephenson, G. R. (Derbys. & Hants) b Nov. 19, 1942

*Stephenson, H. H. (Surrey & All-England) b May 3, 1832, d Dec. 17, 1896

Stephenson, H. W. (Som.) b July 18, 1920

Stephenson, Lt-Col. J. W. A. (Essex & Worcs.) b Aug. 1, 1907, d May 20, 1982

Stevens, Edward ("Lumpy") (Hants) b *circa* 1735, d Sept. 7, 1819

*Stevens, G. B. (S. Aust.) b Feb. 29, 1932

*Stevens, G. T. S. (UCS, OUCC & Middx; *CY 1918*) b Jan. 7, 1901, d Sept. 19, 1970

*Stevenson, G. B. (Yorks.) b Dec. 16, 1955

Stevenson, K. (Derbys. & Hants) b Oct. 6, 1950

Stevenson, M. H. (CUCC & Derbys.) b June 13, 1927

Stewart, A. J. (Surrey) b April 8, 1963

*Stewart, M. J. (Surrey; *CY 1958*) b Sept. 16, 1932

*Stewart, R. B. (SA) b Sept. 3, 1856, d Sept. 12, 1913

Stewart, R. W. (Glos. & Middx) b Feb. 28, 1945

Stewart, W. J. (Warwicks. & Northants) b Aug. 31, 1934

*Stirling, D. A. (C. Dist.) b Oct. 5, 1961

Stocks, F. W. (Notts.) b Nov. 6, 1917

*Stoddart, A. E. (Middx; *CY 1893*) b March 11, 1863, d April 4, 1915

*Stollmeyer, J. B. (T/T) b April 11, 1921

*Stollmeyer, V. H. (T/T) b Jan. 24, 1916

*Storer, W. (Derbys.; *CY 1899*) b Jan. 25, 1867, d Feb. 28, 1912

Storey, S. J. (Surrey & Sussex) b Jan. 6, 1941

Stott, L. W. (Auck.) b Dec. 8, 1946

Stott, W. B. (Yorks.) b July 18, 1934

Stovold, A. W. (Glos. & OFS) b March 19, 1953

*Street, G. B. (Sussex) b Dec. 6, 1889, d April 24, 1924

*Stricker, L. A. (Tvl) b May 26, 1884, d Feb. 5, 1960

Stringer, P. M. (Yorks. & Leics.) b Feb. 23, 1943

*Strudwick, H. (Surrey; *CY 1912*) b Jan. 28, 1880, d Feb. 13, 1970

Strydom, W. T. (OFS) b March 21, 1942

*Studd, C. T. (CUCC & Middx) b Dec. 2, 1860, d July 16, 1931

*Studd, G. B. (CUCC & Middx) b Oct. 20, 1859, d Feb. 13, 1945

Studd, Sir Peter M. (CUCC) b Sept. 15, 1916

Sturt, M. O. C. (Middx) b Sept. 12, 1940

*Subba Row, R. (CUCC, Surrey & Northants; *CY 1961*) b Jan. 29, 1932

*Subramanya, V. (Mysore) b July 16, 1936

Such, P. M. (Notts.) b June 12, 1964

Sudhakar Rao, R. (Karn.) b Aug. 8, 1952

Sueter, T. (Hants & Surrey) b *circa* 1749, d Feb. 17, 1827

*Sugg, F. H. (Yorks., Derbys. & Lancs.; *CY 1890*) b Jan. 11, 1862, d May 29, 1933

Sullivan, J. (Lancs.) b Feb. 5, 1945

Sully, H. (Som. & Northants) b Nov. 1, 1939

*Sunderram, G. R. (Bombay & Raja.) b March 29, 1930

Sunnucks, P. R. (Kent) b June 22, 1916

*Surendranath, R. (Ind. Serv.) b Jan. 4, 1937

Surridge, D. (CUCC & Glos.) b Jan. 6, 1956

Surridge, W. S. (Surrey; *CY 1953*) b Sept. 3, 1917

*Surti, R. F. (Guj., Raja. & Qld) b May 25, 1936

*Susskind, M. J. (CUCC, Middx & Tvl) b June 8, 1891, d July 9, 1957

*Sutcliffe, B. (Auck., Otago & N. Dist.; *CY 1950*) b Nov. 17, 1923

*Sutcliffe, H. (Yorks.; *CY 1920*) b Nov. 24, 1894, d Jan. 22, 1978

Sutcliffe, S. P. (OUCC & Warwicks.) b May 22, 1960

Sutcliffe, W. H. H. (Yorks.) b Oct. 10, 1926

Suttle, K. G. (Sussex) b Aug. 25, 1928

Sutton, R. E. (Auck.) b May 30, 1940

*Swamy, V. N. (Ind. Serv.) b May 23, 1924, d May 1, 1983

Swanton, E. W. (Middx; Writer) b Feb. 11, 1907

Swarbrook, F. W. (Derbys., Griq. W. & OFS) b Dec. 17, 1950

Swart, P. D. (Rhod., W. Prov., Glam. & Boland) b April 27, 1946

*Swetman, R. (Surrey, Notts & Glos.) b Oct. 25, 1933

Sydenham, D. A. D. (Surrey) b April 6, 1934

Symington, S. J. (Leics.) b Sept. 16, 1926

*Taber, H. B. (NSW) b April 29, 1940

*Taberer, H. M. (OUCC & Natal) b Oct. 7, 1870, d June 5, 1932

*Tahir Naqqash (Servis Ind., MCB, Punjab & Lahore) b June 28, 1959

Tait, A. (Northants & Glos.) b Dec. 27, 1953

*Talat Ali (Lahore, PIA & UBL) b May 29, 1950

Talbot, R. O. (Cant. & Otago) b Nov. 26, 1903, d Jan. 5, 1983

*Tallon, D. (Qld; *CY 1949*) b Feb. 17, 1916, d Sept. 7, 1984

Tamhane, N. S. (Bombay) b Aug. 4, 1931

*Tancred, A. B. (Kimberley, Griq. W. & Tvl) b Aug. 20, 1865, d Nov. 23, 1911

*Tancred, L. J. (Tvl) b Oct. 7, 1876, d July 28, 1934

*Tancred, V. M. (Tvl) b 1875, d June 3, 1904

Tang Choon, R. P. (T/T) b 1914, d Sept. 5, 1985

*Tapscott, G. L. (Griq. W.) b Nov. 7, 1889, d Dec. 13, 1940

*Tapscott, L. E. (Griq. W.) b March 18, 1894, d July 7, 1934

*Tarapore, K. K. (Bombay) b Dec. 17, 1910, d June 15, 1986

Tarbox, C. V. (Worcs.) b July 2, 1891, d June 15, 1978

*Tarrant, F. A. (Vic., Middx & Patiala; *CY 1908*) b Dec. 11, 1880, d Jan. 29, 1951

Tarrant, George F. (Cambs. & All-England) b Dec. 7, 1838, d July 2, 1870

*Taslim Arif (Kar., Sind & NBP) b May 1, 1954

*Tate, F. W. (Sussex) b July 24, 1867, d Feb. 24, 1943

*Tate, M. W. (Sussex; *CY 1924*) b May 30, 1895, d May 18, 1956

*Tattersall, R. (Lancs.) b Aug. 17, 1922

*Tauseef Ahmed (PWD & UBL) b May 10, 1958

*Tavaré, C. J. (OUCC & Kent) b Oct. 27, 1954

Tayfield, A. (Natal, Tvl & NE Tvl) b June 21, 1931

*Tayfield, H. J. (Natal, Rhod. & Tvl; *CY 1956*) b Jan. 30, 1929

*Taylor, A. I. (Tvl) b July 25, 1925

Taylor, B. (Essex; *CY 1972*) b June 19, 1932

*Taylor, B. R. (Cant. & Wgtn) b July 12, 1943

*Taylor, Daniel (Natal) b Jan. 9, 1887, d Jan. 24, 1957

*Taylor, D. D. (Auck. & Warwicks.) b March 2, 1923, d Dec. 5, 1980

Taylor, D. J. S. (Surrey, Som. & Griq. W.) b Nov. 12, 1942

Taylor, G. R. (Hants) b Nov. 25, 1909, d Oct. 31, 1986

*Taylor, H. W. (Natal, Tvl & W. Prov.; *CY 1925*) b May 5, 1889, d Feb. 8, 1973

*Taylor, J. M. (NSW) b Oct. 10, 1895, d May 12, 1971

*Taylor, J. O. (T/T) b Jan. 3, 1932

*Taylor, K. (Yorks. & Auck.) b Aug. 21, 1935

Taylor, K. A. (Warwicks.) b Sept. 29, 1916

*Taylor, L. B. (Leics. & Natal) b Oct. 25, 1953

Taylor, M. L. (Lancs.) b July 16, 1904, d March 14, 1978

Taylor, M. N. S. (Notts. & Hants) b Nov. 12, 1942

Taylor, N. R. (Kent) b July 21, 1959

Taylor, N. S. (Yorks., Surrey & Som.) b June 2, 1963

Taylor, R. M. (Essex) b Nov. 30, 1909, d Jan. 1984

*Taylor, R. W. (Derbys.; *CY 1977*) b July 17, 1941

Taylor, T. J. (OUCC & Lancs.) b March 28, 1961

Taylor, T. L. (CUCC & Yorks.; *CY 1901*) b May 25, 1878, d March 16, 1960

Taylor, W. (Notts.) b Jan. 24, 1947

Tennekoon, A. P. B. (SL) b Oct. 29, 1946

*Tennyson, 3rd Lord (Hon. L. H.) (Hants; *CY 1914*) b Nov. 7, 1889, d June 6, 1951

*Terry, V. P. (Hants) b Jan. 14, 1959

*Theunissen, N. H. (W. Prov.) b May 4, 1867, d Nov. 9, 1929

Thomas, D. J. (Surrey & N. Tvl) b June 30, 1959

*Thomas, G. (NSW) b March 21, 1938

*Thomas, J. G. (Glam. & Border) b Aug. 12, 1960

Thompson, A. W. (Middx) b April 17, 1916

*Thompson, G. J. (Northants; *CY 1906*) b Oct. 27, 1877, d March 3, 1943

Thompson, J. R. (CUCC & Warwicks.) b May 10, 1918

*Thompson, Nathaniel (NSW) b April 21, 1838, d Sept. 2, 1896

Thompson, P. M. (OFS & W. Prov.) b April 25, 1948

Thompson, R. G. (Warwicks.) b Sept. 26, 1932

*Thoms, G. R. (Vic.) b March 22, 1927

*Thomson, A. L. (Vic.) b Dec. 2, 1945

*Thomson, J. R. (NSW, Qld & Middx) b Aug. 16, 1950

*Thomson, K. (Cant.) b Feb. 26, 1941

*Thomson, N. I. (Sussex) b Jan. 23, 1929

Thorne, D. A. (Warwicks & OUCC) b Dec. 12, 1964

Thornton, C. I. (CUCC, Kent & Middx) b March 20, 1850, d Dec. 10, 1929

*Thornton, P. G. (Yorks., Middx & SA) b Dec. 24, 1867, d Jan. 31, 1939

*Thurlow, H. M. (Qld) b Jan. 10, 1902, d Dec. 3, 1975

Tilly, H. W. (Middx) b May 25, 1932

Timms, B. S. V. (Hants & Warwicks.) b Dec. 17, 1940

Timms, J. E. (Northants) b Nov. 3, 1906, d May 18, 1980

Timms, W. W. (Northants) b Sept. 28, 1902, d Sept. 30, 1986

Tindall, M. (CUCC & Middx) b March 31, 1914

Tindall, R. A. E. (Surrey) b Sept. 23, 1935

*Tindill, E. W. T. (Wgtn) b Dec. 18, 1910

*Titmus, F. J. (Middx, Surrey & OFS; *CY 1963*) b Nov. 24, 1932

Todd, L. J. (Kent) b June 19, 1907, d Aug. 20, 1967

Todd, P. A. (Notts.) b March 12, 1953

*Tolchard, R. W. (Leics.) b June 15, 1946

Tomlins, K. P. (Middx & Glos.) b Oct. 23, 1957

*Tomlinson, D. S. (Rhod. & Border) b Sept. 4, 1910

Tompkin, M. (Leics.) b Feb. 17, 1919, d Sept. 27, 1956

Toogood, G. J. (OUCC) b Nov. 19, 1961

*Toohey, P. M. (NSW) b April 20, 1954

Tooley, C. D. M. (OUCC) b April 19, 1964

Tordoff, G. G. (CUCC & Som.) b Dec. 6, 1929

*Toshack, E. R. H. (NSW) b Dec. 15, 1914

Townsend, A. (Warwicks.) b Aug. 26, 1921

Townsend, A. F. (Derbys.) b March 29, 1912

*Townsend, C. L. (Glos.; *CY 1899*) b Nov. 7, 1876, d Oct. 17, 1958

*Townsend, D. C. H. (OUCC) b April 20, 1912

*Townsend, L. F. (Derbys. & Auck.; *CY 1934*) b June 8, 1903

Toynbee, M. H. (C. Dist.) b Nov. 29, 1956

*Traicos, A. J. (Rhod. & Zimb.) b May 17, 1947

*Travers, J. P. F. (S. Aust.) b Jan. 10, 1871, d Sept. 15, 1942

*Tremlett, M. F. (Som. & C. Dist.) b July 5, 1923, d July 30, 1984

Tremlett, T. M. (Hants) b July 26, 1956

*Tribe, G. E. (Vic. & Northants; *CY 1955*) b Oct. 4, 1920

*Trim, J. (BG) b Jan. 24, 1915, d Nov. 12, 1960

Trimble, S. C. (Qld) b Aug. 16, 1934

*Trimborn, P. H. J. (Natal) b May 18, 1940

**Trott, A. E. (Vic., Middx & Hawkes Bay; *CY 1899*) b Feb. 6, 1873, d July 30, 1914

*Trott, G. H. S. (Vic.; *CY 1894*) b Aug. 5, 1866, d Nov. 10, 1917

*Troup, G. B. (Auck.) b Oct. 3, 1952

*Trueman, F. S. (Yorks.; *CY 1953*) b Feb. 6, 1931

*Trumble, H. (Vic.; *CY 1897*) b May 12, 1867, d Aug. 14, 1938

*Trumble, J. W. (Vic.) b Sept. 16, 1863, d Aug. 17, 1944

*Trumper, V. T. (NSW; *CY 1903*) b Nov. 2, 1877, d June 28, 1915

*Truscott, P. B. (Wgtn) b Aug. 14, 1941

*Tuckett, L. (OFS) b Feb. 6, 1919

*Tuckett, L. R. (Natal & OFS) b April 19, 1885, d April 8, 1963

*Tufnell, N. C. (CUCC & Surrey) b June 13, 1887, d Aug. 3, 1951

Tuke, Sir Anthony (Pres. MCC 1982-83) b Aug. 22, 1920

Tunnicliffe, C. J. (Derbys.) b Aug. 11, 1951

Tunnicliffe, H. T. (Notts.) b March 4, 1950

Tunnicliffe, J. (Yorks.; *CY 1901*) b Aug. 26, 1866, d July 11, 1948

*Turnbull, M. J. (CUCC & Glam.; *CY 1931*) b March 16, 1906, d Aug. 5, 1944

Turner, A. (NSW) b July 23, 1950

*Turner, C. T. B. (NSW; *CY 1889*) b Nov. 16, 1862, d Jan. 1, 1944

Turner, D. R. (Hants & W. Prov.) b Feb. 5, 1949

Turner, F. M. (Leics.) b Aug. 8, 1934

*Turner, G. M. (Otago, N. Dist. & Worcs.; *CY 1971*) b May 26, 1947

Turner, S. (Essex & Natal) b July 18, 1943

*Twentyman-Jones, P. S. (W. Prov.) b Sept. 13, 1876, d March 8, 1954

Twining, R. H. (OUCC & Middx; Pres. MCC 1964-65) b Nov. 3, 1889, d Jan. 3, 1979

*Tyldesley, E. (Lancs.; *CY 1920*) b Feb. 5, 1889, d May 5, 1962

*Tyldesley, J. T. (Lancs.; *CY 1902*) b Nov. 22, 1873, d Nov. 27, 1930

*Tyldesley, R. K. (Lancs.; *CY 1925*) b March 11, 1897, d Sept. 17, 1943

*Tylecote, E. F. S. (OUCC & Kent) b June 23, 1849, d March 15, 1938

*Tyler, E. J. (Som.) b Oct. 13, 1864, d Jan. 21, 1917

*Tyson, F. H. (Northants; *CY 1956*) b June 6, 1930

Ufton, D. G. (Kent) b May 31, 1928

*Ulyett, G. (Yorks.) b Oct. 21, 1851, d June 18, 1898

*Umrigar, P. R. (Bombay & Guj.) b March 28, 1926

*Underwood, D. L. (Kent; *CY 1969*) b June 8, 1945

Unwin, F. St G. (Essex) b April 23, 1911

*Valentine, A. L. (Jam.; *CY 1951*) b April 29, 1930

*Valentine, B. H. (CUCC & Kent) b Jan. 17, 1908, d Feb. 2, 1983

*Valentine, V. A. (Jam.) b April 4, 1908, d July 6, 1972

Vance, R. H. (Wgtn) b March 31, 1955

*van der Bijl, P. G. (W. Prov. & OUCC) b Oct. 21, 1907, d Feb. 16, 1973

*van der Bijl, V. A. P. (Natal, Middx & Tvl; *CY 1981*) b March 19, 1948

Van der Gucht, P. I. (Glos. & Bengal) b Nov. 2, 1911

*Van der Merwe, E. A. (Tvl) b Nov. 9, 1904, d Feb. 28, 1971

*Van der Merwe, P. L. (W. Prov. & E. Prov.) b March 14, 1937

van Geloven, J. (Yorks. & Leics.) b Jan. 4, 1934

*Van Ryneveld, C. B. (W. Prov. & OUCC) b March 19, 1928

van Vuuren, M. K. (E. Prov.) b Aug. 20, 1958

Varachia, R. (First Pres. SA Cricket Union) b Oct. 12, 1915, d Dec. 11, 1981

Varey, D. W. (CUCC & Lancs.) b Oct. 15, 1961

Varey, J. G. (OUCC) b Oct. 15, 1961

*Varnals, G. D. (E. Prov., Tvl & Natal) b July 24, 1935

Vaulkhard, P. (Notts. & Derbys.) b Sept. 15, 1911

*Vengsarkar, D. B. (Bombay; *CY 1987*) b April 6, 1956

*Veivers, T. R. (Qld) b April 6, 1937

*Venkataraghavan, S. (†TN & Derbys.) b April 21, 1946

Verdoorn, K. D. (N. Tvl) b July 24, 1955

*Verity, H. (Yorks.; *CY 1932*) b May 18, 1905, d July 31, 1943

*Vernon, G. F. (Middx) b June 20, 1856, d Aug. 10, 1902

Vernon, M. T. (W. Aust.) b Feb. 9, 1937

Vigar, F. H. (Essex) b July 7, 1917

*Viljoen, K. G. (Griq. W., OFS & Tvl) b May 14, 1910, d Jan. 21, 1974

*Vincent, C. L. (Tvl) b Feb. 16, 1902, d Aug. 24, 1968

*Vine, J. (Sussex; *CY 1906*) b May 15, 1875, d April 25, 1946

*Vintcent, C. H. (Tvl & Griq. W.) b Sept. 2, 1866, d Sept. 28, 1943

Virgin, R. T. (Som., Northants & W. Prov.; *CY 1971*) b Aug. 26, 1939

*Viswanath, G. R. (†Karn.) b Feb. 12, 1949

*Viswanath, S. (Karn.) b Nov. 29, 1962

*Vivian, G. E. (Auck.) b Feb. 28, 1946

*Vivian, H. G. (Auck.) b Nov. 4, 1912, d Aug. 12, 1983

*Voce, W. (Notts.; *CY 1933*) b Aug. 8, 1909, d June 6, 1984

*Vogler, A. E. E. (Middx, Natal, Tvl & E. Prov.; *CY 1908*) b Nov. 28, 1876, d Aug. 9, 1946

*Vizianagram, Maharaj Kumar Sir Vijaya of (U. Prov.) b Dec. 28, 1905, d Dec. 2, 1965

*Waddington, A. (Yorks.) b Feb. 4, 1893, d Oct. 28, 1959

Waddington, J. E. (Griq. W.) b Dec. 30, 1918, d Nov. 24, 1985

*Wade, H. F. (Natal) b Sept. 14, 1905, d Nov. 22, 1980

Wade, T. H. (Essex) b Nov. 24, 1910

*Wade, W. W. (Natal) b June 18, 1914

*Wadekar, A. L. (Bombay) b April 1, 1941

Wadsworth, K. J. (C. Dist. & Cant.) b Nov. 30, 1946, d Aug. 19, 1976

*Wainwright, E. (Yorks.; *CY 1894*) b April 8, 1865, d Oct. 28, 1919

*Waite, J. H. B. (E. Prov. & Tvl) b Jan. 19, 1930

*Waite, M. G. (S. Aust.) b Jan. 7, 1911, d Dec. 16, 1985

*Walcott, C. L. (B'dos & BG; *CY 1958*) b Jan. 17, 1926

*Walcott, L. A. (B'dos) b Jan. 18, 1894, d Feb. 28, 1984

Walden, F. I. (Northants; Umpire) b March 1, 1888, d May 3, 1949

Walford, M. M. (OUCC & Som.) b Nov. 27, 1915

Walker, A. (Northants) b July 7, 1962

Walker, A. K. (NSW & Notts.) b Oct. 4, 1925

Walker, C. (Yorks. & Hants) b June 27, 1920

Walker, C. W. (S. Aust.) b Feb. 19, 1909, d Dec. 21, 1942

Walker, I. D. (Middx) b Jan. 8, 1844, d July 6, 1898

*Walker, M. H. N. (Vic.) b Sept. 12, 1948

*Walker, P. M. (Glam., Tvl & W. Prov.) b Feb. 17, 1936

Walker, W. (Notts.; oldest living County Champ. player) b Nov. 24, 1892

*Wall, T. W. (S. Aust.) b May 13, 1904, d March 25, 1981

*Wallace, W. M. (Auck.) b Dec. 19, 1916

Waller, C. E. (Surrey & Sussex) b Oct. 3, 1948

*Walsh, C. A. (Jam. & Glos.; *CY 1987*) b Oct. 30, 1962

Walsh, J. E. (NSW & Leics.) b Dec. 4, 1912, d May 20, 1980

*Walter, K. A. (Tvl) b Nov. 5, 1939

*Walters, C. F. (Glam. & Worcs.; *CY 1934*) b Aug. 28, 1905

*Walters, F. H. (Vic. & NSW) b Feb. 9, 1860, d June 1, 1922

Walters, J. (Derbys.) b Aug. 7, 1949

*Walters, K. D. (NSW) b Dec. 21, 1945

Walton, A. C. (OUCC & Middx) b Sept. 26, 1933

*Waqar Hassan (Pak. Us, Punjab, Pak. Serv. & Kar.) b Sept. 12, 1932

*Ward, Alan (Derbys., Leics. & Border) b Aug. 10, 1947

*Ward, Albert (Yorks. & Lancs.; *CY 1890*) b Nov. 21, 1865, d Jan. 6, 1939

Ward, B. (Essex) b Feb. 28, 1944

Ward, D. (Glam.) b Aug. 30, 1934

*Ward, F. A. (S. Aust.) b Feb. 23, 1909, d March 25, 1974

*Ward, J. T. (Cant.) b March 11, 1937

*Ward, T. A. (Tvl) b Aug. 2, 1887, d Feb. 16, 1936

Ward, William (MCC & Hants) b July 24, 1787, d June 30, 1849

*Wardle, J. H. (Yorks.; *CY 1954*) b Jan. 8, 1923, d July 23, 1985

*Warnapura, B. (SL) b March 1, 1953

*Warnaweera, K. P. J. (SL) b Nov. 23, 1960

Warne, F. B. (Worcs., Vic. & Tvl) b Oct. 3, 1906

Warner, A. E. (Worcs. & Derbys.) b May 12, 1959

*Warner, Sir Pelham (OUCC & Middx; *CY 1904, special portrait 1921*) b Oct. 2, 1873, d Jan. 30, 1963

*Warr, J. J. (CUCC & Middx) b July 16, 1927

*Warren, A. R. (Derbys.) b April 2, 1875, d Sept. 3, 1951

*Washbrook, C. (Lancs.; *CY 1947*) b Dec. 6, 1914

*Wasim Akram (Lahore & PACO) b Sept. 7, 1966

*Wasim Bari (Kar., PIA & Sind) b March 23, 1948

*Wasim Raja (Lahore, Sargodha, Pak. Us, PIA, Punjab & NBP) b July 3, 1952

Wass, T. G. (Notts.; *CY 1908*) b Dec. 26, 1873, d Oct. 27, 1953

Wassell, A. (Hants) b April 15, 1940

*Watkins, A. J. (Glam.) b April 21, 1922

*Watkins, J. C. (Natal) b April 10, 1923

*Watkins, J. R. (NSW) b April 16, 1943

Watkinson, M. (Lancs.) b Aug. 1, 1961

*Watson, C. (Jam. & Delhi) b July 1, 1938
Watson, F. B. (Lancs.) b Sept. 17, 1898, d Feb. 1, 1976
*Watson, G. D. (Vic., W. Aust. & NSW) b March 8, 1945
Watson, G. G. (NSW, W. Aust. & Worcs.) b Jan. 29, 1955
*Watson, W. (Yorks. & Leics.; *CY 1954*) b March 7, 1920
*Watson, W. (Auck.) b Aug. 31, 1965
*Watson, W. J. (NSW) b Jan. 31, 1931
Watson, W. K. (Border, N. Tvl, E. Prov. & Notts.) b May 21, 1955
*Watt, L. (Otago) b Sept. 17, 1924
Watts, E. A. (Surrey) b Aug. 1, 1911, d May 2, 1982
Watts, H. E. (CUCC & Som.) b March 4, 1922
Watts, P. D. (Northants & Notts.) b March 31, 1938
Watts, P. J. (Northants) b June 16, 1940
*Waugh, S. R. (NSW) b June 2, 1965
*Wazir Ali, S. (C. Ind., S. Punjab & Patiala) b Sept. 15, 1903, d June 17, 1950
*Wazir Mohammad (B'pur & Kar.) b Dec. 22, 1929
*Webb, M. G. (Otago & Cant.) b June 22, 1947
*Webb, P. N. (Auck.) b July 14, 1957
Webb, R. T. (Sussex) b July 11, 1922
Webb, S. G. (Manager Australians in England 1961) b Jan. 31, 1900, d Aug. 5, 1976
*Webbe, A. J. (OUCC & Middx) b Jan. 16, 1855, d Feb. 19, 1941
Webster, J. (CUCC & Northants) b Oct. 28, 1917
Webster, Dr R. V. (Warwicks. & Otago) b June 10, 1939
Webster, W. H. (CUCC & Middx; Pres. MCC 1976-77) b Feb. 22, 1910, d June 19, 1986
*Weekes, E. D. (B'dos; *CY 1951*) b Feb. 26, 1925
*Weekes, K. H. (Jam.) b Jan. 24, 1912
Weeks, R. T. (Warwicks.) b April 30, 1930
*Weerasinghe, C. D. U. S. (SL) b March 1, 1968
*Weir, G. L. (Auck.) b June 2, 1908
*Wellard, A. W. (Som.; *CY 1936*) b April 8, 1902, d Dec. 31, 1980
*Wellham, D. M. (NSW) b March 13, 1959
Wellings, E. M. (OUCC & Surrey) b April 6, 1909
Wells, A. P. (Sussex) b Oct. 2, 1961
Wells, B. D. (Glos. & Notts.) b July 27, 1930
Wells, C. M. (Sussex, Border & W. Prov.) b March 3, 1960
Wenman, E. G. (Kent & England) b Aug. 18, 1803, d Dec. 31, 1879
Wensley, A. F. (Sussex) b May 23, 1898, d June 17, 1970

*Wesley, C. (Natal) b Sept. 5, 1937
*Wessels, K. C. (OFS, W. Prov., N. Tvl, Sussex & Qld) b Sept. 14, 1957
West, G. H. (Editor of *Wisden* 1880-86) b 1851, d Oct. 6, 1896
*Westcott, R. J. (W. Prov.) b Sept. 19, 1927
Weston, M. J. (Worcs.) b April 8, 1959
*Wettimuny, M. D. (SL) b June 11, 1951
*Wettimuny, S. (SL; *CY 1985*) b Aug. 12, 1956
*Wharton, A. (Lancs. & Leics.) b April 30, 1923
*Whatmore, D. F. (Vic.) b March 16, 1954
Wheatley, K. J. (Hants) b Jan. 20, 1946
Wheatley, O. S. (CUCC, Warwicks. & Glam.; *CY 1969*) b May 28, 1935
Whitaker, Haddon (Editor of *Wisden* 1940-43) b Aug. 30, 1908, d Jan. 5, 1982
Whitaker, J. J. (Leics.; *CY 1987*) b May 5, 1962
Whitcombe, P. A. (OUCC & Middx) b April 23, 1923
White, A. F. T. (CUCC, Warwicks. & Worcs.) b Sept. 5, 1915
*White, D. W. (Hants & Glam.) b Dec. 14, 1935
White, E. C. S. (NSW) b July 14, 1913
*White, G. C. (Tvl) b Feb. 5, 1882, d Oct. 17, 1918
*White, J. C. (Som.; *CY 1929*) b Feb. 19, 1891, d May 2, 1961
White, Hon. L. R. (5th Lord Annaly) (Middx & Victory Test) b March 15, 1927
White, R. A. (Middx & Notts.) b Oct. 6, 1936
White, R. C. (CUCC, Glos. & Tvl) b Jan. 29, 1941
*White, W. A. (B'dos) b Nov. 20, 1938
Whitehead, J. P. (Yorks. & Worcs.) b Sept. 3, 1925
Whitehouse, J. (Warwicks.) b April 8, 1949
*Whitelaw, P. E. (Auck.) b Feb. 10, 1910
Whitfield, B. J. (Natal) b March 14, 1959
Whitfield, E. W. (Surrey & Northants) b May 31, 1911
Whiting, N. H. (Worcs.) b Oct. 2, 1920
Whitington, R. S. (S. Aust. & Victory Tests; Writer) b June 30, 1912, d March 13, 1984
*Whitney, M. R. (NSW & Glos.) b Feb. 24, 1959
Whittaker, G. J. (Surrey) b May 29, 1916
Whitticase, P. (Leics.) b March 15, 1965
Whittingham, N. B. (Notts.) b Oct. 22, 1940
*Whitty, W. J. (S. Aust.) b Aug. 15, 1886, d Jan. 30, 1974
*Whysall, W. W. (Notts.; *CY 1925*) b Oct. 31, 1887, d Nov. 11, 1930
*Wiener, J. M. (Vic.) b May 1, 1955
*Wight, C. V. (BG) b July 28, 1902, d Oct. 4, 1969

*Wight, G. L. (BG) b May 28, 1929

Wight, P. B. (BG, Som., & Cant.) b June 25, 1930

*Wijesuriya, R. G. C. E. (SL) b Feb. 18, 1960

Wilcox, D. R. (CUCC & Essex) b June 4, 1910, d Feb. 6, 1953

Wild, D. J. (Northants) b Nov. 28, 1962

*Wiles, C. A. (B'dos & T/T) b Aug. 11, 1892, d Nov. 4, 1957

Wilkins, A. H. (Glam., Glos. & N. Tvl) b Aug. 22, 1953

Wilkins, C. P. (Derbys., Border, E. Prov. & Natal) b July 31, 1944

*Wilkinson, L. L. (Lancs.) b Nov. 5, 1916

Wilkinson, P. A. (Notts.) b Aug. 23, 1951

Wilkinson, Col. W. A. C. (OUCC) b Dec. 6, 1892, d Sept. 19, 1983

Willatt, G. L. (CUCC, Notts. & Derbys.) b May 7, 1918

*Willett, E. T. (Comb. Is. & Leewards) b May 1, 1953

Willett, M. D. (Surrey) b April 21, 1933

*Willey, P. (Northants, E. Prov. & Leics.) b Dec. 6, 1949

Williams, A. B. (Jam.) b Nov. 21, 1949

Williams, C. B. (B'dos) b March 8, 1926

Williams, Lord C. C. P. (OUCC & Essex) b Feb. 9, 1933

Williams, D. L. (Glam.) b Nov. 20, 1946

*Williams, E. A. V. (B'dos) b April 10, 1914

Williams, N. F. (Middx, Windwards & Tas.) b July 2, 1962

Williams, R. G. (Northants) b Aug. 10, 1957

*Williams, R. J. (Natal) b April 12, 1912, d May 14, 1984

Williamson, J. G. (Northants) b April 4, 1936

*Willis, R. G. D. (Surrey, Warwicks. & N. Tvl; *CY 1978*) b May 30, 1949

*Willoughby, J. T. (SA) b Nov. 7, 1874, d *circa* 1955

Willsher, E. (Kent & All-England) b Nov. 22, 1828, d Oct. 7, 1885

Wilmot, A. L. (E. Prov.) b June 1, 1943

Wilmot, K. (Warwicks.) b April 3, 1911

Wilson, A. (Lancs.) b April 24, 1921

Wilson, A. E. (Middx & Glos.) b May 18, 1910

*Wilson, Rev. C. E. M. (CUCC & Yorks.) b May 15, 1875, d Feb. 8, 1944

*Wilson, D. (Yorks. & MCC) b Aug. 7, 1937

Wilson, E. F. (Surrey) b June 24, 1907, d March 3, 1981

*Wilson, E. R. (CUCC & Yorks.) b March 25, 1879 d July 21, 1957

Wilson, J. V. (Yorks.; *CY 1961*) b Jan. 17, 1921

*Wilson, J. W. (Vic. & S. Aust.) b Aug. 20, 1921, d Oct. 13, 1985

Wilson, P. H. L. (Surrey, Som. & N. Tvl) b Aug. 17, 1958

Wilson, R. C. (Kent) b Feb. 18, 1928

Wiltshire, J. R. (Auck. & C. Dist.) b Jan. 20, 1952

*Wimble, C. S. (Tvl) b Jan. 9, 1864, d Jan. 28, 1930

Windows, A. R. (Glos. & CUCC) b Sept. 25, 1942

Winfield, H. M. (Notts.) b June 13, 1933

Wingfield Digby, Rev. A. R. (OUCC) b July 25, 1950

Winn, C. E. (OUCC & Sussex) b Nov. 13, 1926

Winslow, P. L. (Sussex, Tvl & Rhod.) b May 21, 1929

Wisden, John (Sussex; founder John Wisden and Co. and *Wisden's Cricketers' Almanack*) b Sept. 5, 1826, d April 5, 1884

*Wishart, K. L. (BG) b Nov. 28, 1908, d Oct. 18, 1972

Wolton, A. V. G. (Warwicks.) b June 12, 1919

*Wood, A. (Yorks.; *CY 1939*) b Aug. 25, 1898, d April 1, 1973

*Wood, B. (Yorks., Lancs., Derbys. & E. Prov.) b Dec. 26, 1942

Wood, C. J. B. (Leics.) b Nov. 21, 1875, d June 5, 1960

Wood, D. J. (Sussex) b May 19, 1914

*Wood, G. E. C. (CUCC & Kent) b Aug. 22, 1893, d March 18, 1971

*Wood, G. M. (W. Aust.) b Nov. 6, 1956

*Wood, H. (Kent & Surrey; *CY 1891*) b Dec. 14, 1854, d April 30, 1919

*Wood, R. (Lancs. & Vic.) b March 7, 1860, d Jan. 6, 1915

*Woodcock, A. J. (S. Aust.) b Feb. 27, 1948

Woodcock, John C. (Editor of *Wisden* 1980-86) b Aug. 7, 1926

*Woodfull, W. M. (Vic.; *CY 1927*) b Aug. 22, 1897, d Aug. 11, 1965

Woodhead, F. G. (Notts.) b Oct. 30, 1912

Woodhouse, G. E. S. (Som.) b Feb. 15, 1924

**Woods, S. M. J. (CUCC & Som.; *CY 1889*) b April 14, 1867, d April 30, 1931

Wookey, S. M. (CUCC & OUCC) b Sept. 2, 1954

Wooler, C. R. D. (Leics. & Rhod.) b June 30, 1930

Wooller, W. (CUCC & Glam.) b Nov. 20, 1912

Woolley, C. N. (Glos. & Northants) b May 5, 1886, d Nov. 3, 1962

*Woolley, F. E. (Kent; *CY 1911*) b May 27, 1887, d Oct. 18, 1978

*Woolley, R. D. (Tas.) b Sept. 16, 1954

*Woolmer, R. A. (Kent, Natal & W. Prov.; *CY 1976*) b May 14, 1948

*Worrall, J. (Vic.) b May 12, 1863, d Nov. 17, 1937

*Worrell, Sir F. M. M. (B'dos & Jam.; *CY 1951*) b Aug. 1, 1924, d March 13, 1967

Worsley, D. R. (OUCC & Lancs.) b July 18, 1941

Worsley, Sir W. A. 4th Bt (Yorks.; Pres. MCC 1961-62) b April 5, 1890, d Dec. 4, 1973

*Worthington, T. S. (Derbys.; *CY 1937*) b Aug. 21, 1905, d Aug. 31, 1973

Wright, A. (Warwicks.) b Aug. 25, 1941

Wright, A. J. (Glos.) b July 27, 1962

*Wright, C. W. (CUCC & Notts.) b May 27, 1863, d Jan. 10, 1936

*Wright, D. V. P. (Kent; *CY 1940*) b Aug. 21, 1914

*Wright, J. G. (N. Dist. & Derbys.) b July 5, 1954

*Wright, K. J. (W. Aust. & S. Aust.) b Dec. 27, 1953

Wright, L. G. (Derbys.; *CY 1906*) b June 15, 1862, d Jan. 11, 1953

Wright, M. J. E. (N. Dist.) b Jan. 17, 1950

Wyatt, J. G. (Som.) b June 19, 1963

*Wyatt, R. E. S. (Warwicks. & Worcs.; *CY 1930*) b May 2, 1901

*Wynne, O. E. (Tvl & W. Prov.) b June 1, 1919, d July 13, 1975

*Wynyard, E. G. (Hants) b April 1, 1861, d Oct. 30, 1936

Yachad, M. (N. Tvl & Tvl) b Nov. 17, 1960

*Yadav, N. S. (H'bad) b Jan. 26, 1957

*Yajurvindra Singh (M'tra & S'tra) b Aug. 1, 1952

*Yallop, G. N. (Vic.) b Oct. 7, 1952

*Yardley, B. (W. Aust.) b Sept. 7, 1947

*Yardley, N. W. D. (CUCC & Yorks.; *CY 1948*) b March 19, 1915

Yardley, T. J. (Worcs. & Northants) b Oct. 27, 1946

Yarnold, H. (Worcs.) b July 6, 1917, d Aug. 13, 1974

*Yashpal Sharma (Punjab) b Aug. 11, 1954

Yawar Saeed (Som. & Punjab) b Jan. 22, 1935

*Yograj Singh (Haryana & Punjab) b March 25, 1958

Young, D. M. (Worcs. & Glos.) b April 15, 1924

*Young, H. I. (Essex) b Feb. 5, 1876, d Dec. 12, 1964

*Young, J. A. (Middx) b Oct. 14, 1912

*Young, R. A. (CUCC & Sussex) b Sept. 16, 1885, d July 1, 1968

*Younis Ahmed (Lahore, Kar., Surrey, PIA, S. Aust., Worcs. & Glam.) b Oct. 20, 1947

*Yuile, B. W. (C. Dist.) b Oct. 29, 1941

*Zaheer Abbas (Kar., Glos., PWD, Dawood Indust., Sind & PIA; *CY 1972*) b July 24, 1947

*Zakir Khan (Sind) b April 3, 1963

*Zoehrer, T. J. (W. Aust.) b Sept. 25, 1961

*Zulch, J. W. (Tvl) b Jan. 2, 1886, d May 19, 1924

*Zulfiqar Ahmed (B'pur & PIA) b Nov. 22, 1926

*Zulqarnain (Pak. Rlwys) b May 25, 1962

ADDRESSES OF REPRESENTATIVE BODIES

INTERNATIONAL CRICKET CONFERENCE: J. A. Bailey, Lord's Ground, London NW8 8QN.

ENGLAND: Cricket Council, A. C. Smith, Lord's Ground, London NW8 8QN.

AUSTRALIA: Australian Cricket Board, D. L. Richards, 70 Jolimont Street, Jolimont, Victoria 3002.

WEST INDIES: West Indies Cricket Board of Control, G. S. Camacho, 8B Caledonia Avenue, Kingston 5, Jamaica.

INDIA: Board of Control for Cricket in India, R. S. Mahendra, Vijay Nagar Colony, Bhiwani 125 021.

NEW ZEALAND: New Zealand Cricket Council, G. T. Dowling, PO Box 958, Christchurch.

PAKISTAN: Board of Control for Cricket in Pakistan, Lt-Col. Rafi Nasim, Gaddafi Stadium, Lahore.

SRI LANKA: Board of Control for Cricket in Sri Lanka, Nuski Mohamed, 302 Galle Road, Colombo 7.

SOUTH AFRICA: South African Cricket Union, Dennis Carlstein, PO Box 55009, Northlands 2116, Transvaal.
South African Cricket Board, A. I. Mangera, PO Box 54059, Vrededorp 2141, Transvaal.

ARGENTINA: Argentine Cricket Association, R. H. Gooding, c/o The English Club, 25 de Mayo 586, 1002 Buenos Aires.

BANGLADESH: Bangladesh Cricket Control Board, Syed Ashraful Huq, The Stadium, Dacca.

BERMUDA: Bermuda Cricket Board of Control, C. W. Butterfield, PO Box 992, Hamilton.

CANADA: Canadian Cricket Association, K. R. Bullock, PO Box 1364, Brockville, Ontario, K6V 5Y6.

DENMARK: Danish Cricket Association, Lars Kruse, Vedelsgade 12, 13, DK-4180 Soroe.

EAST AFRICA: East and Central African Cricket Conference, S. Patel, PO Box 71712, Ndola, Zambia.

FIJI: Fiji Cricket Association, P. I. Knight, PO Box 300, Suva.

GIBRALTAR: Gibraltar Cricket Association, T. J. Finlayson, 21 Sandpits House, Withams Road.

HONG KONG: Hong Kong Cricket Association, S. K. Sipahimalani, Centre for Media Resources, University of Hong Kong, Knowles Bldg, Pokfulam Road.

ISRAEL: Israel Cricket Association, G. Kandeli, 35/7 Minz Street, Petach Tiqua.

KENYA: Kenya Cricket Association, P. S. Gill, PO Box 46480, Nairobi.

MALAYSIA: Malaysian Cricket Association, K. Sivanesan, c/o Perbadanan Kemajuan, Negeri Selangor, Persiaran Barat, P. Jaya, Selangor.

NETHERLANDS: Royal Netherlands Cricket Association, Hon. Secretary, Willem de Nevijgerlaan 96A, 2582 ET's – Gravenhage.

PAPUA NEW GUINEA: Papua New Guinea Cricket Board of Control, N. R. Agonia, PO Box 812, Port Moresby.

SINGAPORE: Singapore Cricket Association, R. Sivasubramaniam, 5000-D Marine Parade Road 22-16, Laguna Park, Singapore 1544.

USA: United States of America Cricket Association, Naseeruddin Khan, 2361 Hickory Road, Plymouth Meeting, Pennsylvania 19462.

WEST AFRICA: West Africa Cricket Conference, The Hon. Major General M. S. Tarawalle, c/o HQN RSLMF, Freetown, Sierre Leone.

ZIMBABWE: Zimbabwe Cricket Union, A. L. A. Pichanick, PO Box 452, Harare.

BRITISH UNIVERSITIES SPORTS FEDERATION: 28 Woburn Square, London WC1.

CLUB CRICKET CONFERENCE: D. J. Annetts, 353 West Barnes Lane, New Malden, Surrey, KT3 6JF.

ENGLAND SCHOOLS' CRICKET ASSOCIATION: C. J. Cooper, 68 Hatherley Road, Winchester, Hampshire SO22 6RR.

IRISH CRICKET UNION: D. Scott, 45 Foxrock Park, Foxrock, Dublin 18, Ireland.

MINOR COUNTIES CRICKET ASSOCIATION: D. J. M. Armstrong, Thorpe Cottage, Mill Common, Ridlington, North Walsham, NR28 9TY.

NATIONAL CRICKET ASSOCIATION: B. J. Aspital, Lord's Ground, London NW8 8QN.

SCARBOROUGH CRICKET FESTIVAL: Lt Cdr H. C. Wood, MBE, North Marine Road, Scarborough, North Yorkshire, YO12 7TJ.

SCOTTISH CRICKET UNION: R. W. Barclay, Admin. Office, 18 Ainslie Place, Edinburgh, EH3 6AU.

COMBINED SERVICES: Colonel R. M. Brennan, c/o ASCB, Clayton Barracks, Aldershot, Hampshire.

THE SPORTS COUNCIL: John Wheatley, Director-General, 16 Upper Woburn Place, London WC1 0QP.

ASSOCIATION OF CRICKET UMPIRES: L. J. Cheeseman, 16 Ruden Way, Epsom Downs, Surrey, KT17 3LN.

WOMEN'S CRICKET ASSOCIATION: 16 Upper Woburn Place, London WC1 0QP.

The addresses of MCC, the First-Class Counties, and Minor Counties are given at the head of each separate section.

OBITUARIES

ACHONG, ELLIS EDGAR ("PUSS"), died in Port-of-Spain, Trinidad, on August 29, 1986, aged 82. A left-arm spin bowler, he was the first cricketer of Chinese extraction to play Test cricket, appearing for West Indies in six matches against England and taking eight wickets at 47.25. Chosen to tour England in 1933, he played in all three Tests but with limited success, and in all first-class matches that season took 71 wickets. Essentially an orthodox slow left-armer, at Manchester he had Robins stumped by a ball which, bowled with a wrist-spinner's action, turned into the right-hander from the off and gave rise to the use in England of the word "chinaman" to describe such a delivery. After 1935 he played in the Lancashire leagues until 1951, and having returned to live in Trinidad he stood as an umpire in the 1953-54 Port-of-Spain Test between West Indies and England. In all first-class matches he took 110 wickets at 30.23, his best figures being seven for 73 for Trinidad against British Guiana in 1932-33.

AIRD, RONALD, MC, died at his home at Yapton on August 16, 1986, aged 84. Until he was over 80 he had been a very fit man, playing golf regularly and constant in his attendance at race meetings, but in the last two or three years his health had failed, his activities had been sadly restricted, and it was clear to his friends that one who had always been so full of life had now ceased to enjoy it.

Good cricketer though he was, Ronny Aird will always be chiefly remembered for his work at Lord's, which covered first to last 60 years. Appointed Assistant Secretary in 1926 when W. Findlay was promoted to Secretary, he continued to serve under Col. Rait Kerr and himself succeeded as Secretary in 1952. He retired in 1962, but was President in 1968-69 and a Trustee from 1971 to 1983, when he became a Life Vice-President, remaining active on the committee almost to the end. I can remember Lord Cornwallis, who as an ex-President and a Trustee was in a position to know, saying of him as far back as 1950, when he was still only Assistant Secretary, "No-one realises how much that man has done for Lord's".

It was never Aird's way to seek the limelight. His name seldom appeared in the press. He was not responsible for any startling reforms or innovations. But as one of the papers said after his death, "Lord's was never a happier place than during his secretaryship". There was an aura of happiness and it was a joy just to be there, whatever the occasion: all the staff in the pavilion, the tennis-court or elsewhere greeted one as an old friend. This atmosphere was typical of Aird himself and his greatness lay rather in what he was than in what he did. One could not imagine him ever being involved in rows or unpleasantness. He was completely imperturbable. Whatever happened, he remained his own smiling, courteous self. Not that he could not be firm enough when occasion demanded it. This was well shown in his chairmanship, which evoked widespread admiration, of the highly contentious special meeting in 1968 on relations with South Africa.

S. C. Griffith, who was Assistant Secretary under him before succeeding him as Secretary, writes: "He was the best man to work for that a man ever had; a wonderful person and a very true friend. He was a kind man and a tremendous lover of his fellow human-beings. I was very proud to work for him."

No less notable on a smaller scale was his work for I Zingari, of which he was an officer for more than 50 years, being successively Secretary and Treasurer. He played an important part in raising the club from the low esteem in which it was held in the 1920s and making it again one to which people are proud to belong and for which they enjoy playing. No-one has better deserved the honour bestowed on him a few years ago when he was appointed a Freeman of the club. In his later days, his wisdom and experience were of the greatest value, too, to the Friends of Arundel Castle Cricket in their formative years.

He got his colours at Eton in 1919, when he made 60, top score, against Winchester and was also the team's wicket-keeper. In 1920 he was replaced behind the wicket by M. Ll. Hill, who afterwards kept for Somerset, but he made 49 against Winchester and 44 not out at Lord's and was described as "perhaps the soundest batsman on the side". In 1921, when he headed the averages, he played a memorable innings of 112 not out, which enabled Eton to win after J. L. Guise had scored 278 for Winchester.

Like many another good strokeplayer, he took some time to acclimatise himself to first-class cricket. Though he had had a trial for Hampshire in 1921, he was never in the running for a Blue at Cambridge in 1922 and did little later in the season for his county. In 1923 his average for Cambridge was only 15 and he probably owed his Blue to an innings of 64 against Yorkshire, who had Robinson, Waddington, Macaulay and Rhodes to bowl for them. The next highest score was 30. Playing again regularly for Hampshire after term, he was disappointing. However, next year, being down from Cambridge, he was able for the only time in his life to play a full season's county cricket and scored 1,072 runs with an average of 24.36, including hundreds against Sussex, when he and Mead added 266 for the third wicket, and Somerset. After this his place in the side was secure when he was available, but from 1926 on his first-class cricket was limited to two or three matches on his annual holiday and to an occasional appearance for MCC at Lord's. In 1926 he made 113 against Kent and in 1929 obtained the highest score of his career, 159 against Leicestershire in a total of 272. Altogether for Hampshire between 1921 and 1938 he scored 3,603 runs with an average of 22.24. Later he was for many years the county's President. He continued to play club cricket after the war when his commitments allowed. One's picture of him is the typical graceful Etonian bat with lovely wrists and the racket-player's off-side strokes, but in fact he could score all round the wicket and played well off his legs. For many years, too, he was one of the best covers in England.

A natural games player, he was in two Eton rackets pairs which reached the final at Queen's and in 1922 was second string to R. H. Hill at Cambridge: they won the doubles but Aird lost his single. In 1923 he was first string and won both his matches. Later he concentrated on tennis and became especially formidable at Lord's, where he won the Silver Racket six times between 1933 and 1949. In the challenge for the Gold Racket he was defeated twice by Lord Aberdare and four times by W. D. Macpherson, both amateur champions. At Cambridge he was virtually promised a soccer Blue if he would learn to head the ball, but he found that this, especially when the ball was wet, gave him such headaches that he did not think it worth it. In later life he was a National Hunt Steward.

He was a man of wide and varied talents and interests, so varied that few of his friends can have been aware of them all, just as few knew the details of his war record. They knew of course that he had been a major in the Royal Tank Regiment, that he had won the Military Cross in the desert and been wounded. They did not know that he had been in almost a record number of tanks that were totally destroyed and that twice he had been the only survivor; that he had been wounded twice, once severely, and that on both these occasions his one thought had been to get back to active service as soon as possible. Few of his friends can have known the full story, but none will be surprised when he hears it.

ALSTON, HALLAM NEWTON EGERTON, who died on October 19, 1985, aged 77, appeared only in first-class cricket, for Somerset against Surrey in 1933, but he had something to remember it by. His one wicket was that of Hobbs. Apart from that, his analysis of seven overs for 6 runs against the powerful Surrey batting of those days on The Oval wicket shows that he must have bowled with commendable steadiness. Educated at Cheltenham, where he was in the XI, he was for many years a formidable all-rounder in club cricket; an attacking batsman, a fast-medium opening bowler and a good slip or gully. One feat deserves to be recorded. For the Somerset Stragglers against the United Services at Mount Wise in 1935, he and his partner put up 240 for the first wicket in the first innings and 209 unbeaten in the second, each making a century both times, and Alston finished the match by taking six for 18.

AWDRY, AMBROSE LEONARD, who died on October 10, 1986, aged 72, was one of the famous Wiltshire cricketing family. A steady medium-paced bowler, who flighted the ball well, he headed the Winchester averages in 1932 and later for a few seasons did valuable work for the county as an all-rounder.

BARING, AMYAS EVELYN GILES, died in hospital on August 29, 1986, aged 76. Going up to Cambridge from Gresham's, Holt, he did little at Fenner's in his first two summers, though in the second he did have one trial for the University, and later that summer, 1930, he played regularly for Hampshire. His 32 wickets for them cost him 40.78 runs each, but he had innumerable slip catches dropped off him and he attracted attention both by his pace and by his spirit. When, therefore, he started 1931 with ten for 57 in the Seniors' match, he might have expected a good trial: it was never of course likely that he would displace Farnes, but he might have made a formidable opening partner for him. Instead, he was quickly discarded, and while Cambridge were playing Oxford at Lord's, he was playing for Hampshire against Essex at Colchester, where, on a fast, crumbling wicket, he took nine for 26 in the first innings. Nor was this a flash in the pan. For the county that season he took 74 wickets at 22.16. He hoped to play regularly the following season, but a bad car accident later in 1931, in which he dislocated both knees, stopped any question of cricket. It was a tribute to his courage and perseverance that he was able to play a match or two in 1933, bowling at a much reduced pace, and even more that in 1934 he was bowling apparently as fast as ever. Unfortunately, he was seldom available, but against Middlesex at Lord's he took nine wickets and against the Australians at Southampton had Woodfull, Brown and Bradman out for 6, finishing with five for 121. After this he was unable to make more than an occasional appearance until 1939, when he took 34 wickets at 22.52, including ten for 110 against Kent at Canterbury. He did not play for Hampshire after the war. With a high action, he was genuinely fast and a great trier. He did not swing the ball much but could make it run away and could at times make it lift awkwardly. His cricket began and ended with his bowling. In all first-class matches he took 197 wickets at 28.46.

BAXTER, ARTHUR DOUGLAS ("SANDY"), who died in hospital at Edenbridge on January 28, 1986, aged 76, might have taken a high place among the bowlers of the day had he ever been able to play regularly. In a first-class career extending from 1929 to 1939, he played only 42 matches, but in these he took 189 wickets at 21.74. His one spell of continuous cricket was for E. R. T. Holmes's MCC team in Australia and New Zealand in 1935-36. Apart from this, he made three appearances for Lancashire and two for Middlesex, played for the Gentlemen in 1934, and otherwise for such sides as MCC, Free Foresters, H. D. G. Leveson Gower's XI and for his native Scotland. Yet in 1935, for instance, for Leveson Gower's XI against Oxford University at Reigate, he took thirteen for 72 and later in the season, again for Leveson Gower, eleven for 125 against Wyatt's MCC side to the West Indies at Scarborough. He bowled normally fast in-swingers, but is said to have dismissed one Queensland batsman with a ball which, starting "outside the off-stump, dipped in very late, pitched on the middle-and-leg, then whipped away and took the top of the middle-and-off". On this trip, in the first-class matches he took 31 wickets at 27.87, and in all matches 58 at 17.93. He was a bowler pure and simple, and the generally accepted view was that, had he not overlapped with C. S. Marriott, he would have been the worst bat and field of his time in first-class cricket. None the less everyone loved to have him on a side. He was so cheerful and friendly, enjoyed his cricket so much, and helped others to enjoy theirs. He had been in the XI at Loretto and originally played for Devon.

BELLAMY, BENJAMIN WALTER (BEN), who died in hospital on December 20, 1985, aged 94, had been the oldest surviving County Championship player. Joining the Northamptonshire staff in 1912, he had to wait until Walter Buswell retired at the end of 1921 to become their regular wicket-keeper, though he had played a few times in 1920 and 1921. His first match was against Surrey, when P. G. H. Fender hit his record century in 35 minutes and 1,475 runs were scored for the loss of 27 wickets. A competent and reliable 'keeper, he held his place until the end of 1935, when he gave way to the New Zealander, K. C. James. In his early matches he had gone in last, but by perseverance and determination he soon worked his way up the order and as early as 1922 made the highest score of his career, a chanceless 168 against Worcestershire at Worcester. His best season as a batsman was 1928 when he scored 1,116 runs with an average of 22.77, including 118 against Surrey at Northampton and 65 and 100 against Gloucestershire at Bristol, where he and Claude Woolley in the second innings put on 203 for the second wicket. His fourth and last hundred was 110 not out against Glamorgan in 1934. Two years after his retirement, he was recalled in a crisis for a couple of matches as a batsman and in the first, against Derbyshire, made 83 in the second innings, the next highest score being 29. Tall and rather clumsily built, though in his young days he had played inside-forward for Northampton Town, he had no grace of style to recommend him nor any great variety of stroke, but his concentration and determination not to get out made him invaluable to a side which, for most of his career, was one of the weakest in batting ever to play in the Championship. Altogether he scored 9,247 runs with an average of 16.54, besides catching 529 batsmen and stumping 125. From 1936 to 1957 he was coach at Bedford School. His old captain, W. C. Brown, wrote of him only a week or two before his own death: "A dedicated professional cricketer, his impeccable conduct on and off the field was a tribute to the game and earned him the respect of all who knew him."

BRADSHAW, WALTER HULATT, died on July 13, 1986, aged 77. Going up to Oxford from Malvern, he got his Blue in his second summer, 1930, as an opening bowler and retained his place the following year. Many University bowlers have been far from first-class, but few have given more convincing proof. In his two years his 22 wickets cost 38.46 runs each, his one reputable analysis being four for 15 against Leveson Gower's XI at Eastbourne – although, not seriously regarded as a batsman, he did make 81 in 50 minutes against Gloucestershire. It was therefore a surprise, when meeting him a few years later, back from a teaching appointment in India, to find that he had developed into a formidable bowler while playing in the Ranji Trophy there. Tall and strong, he bowled fast-medium with a high action off a short run, could bring the ball back sharply from the off and also make it lift sharply. At this time he must surely, given the opportunity, have taken wickets in first-class cricket in England. He was for many years a master of Stowe, where he ran the cricket. He also gained a soccer Blue.

BRIDGER, REV. JOHN RICHARD, died in a motor accident at Burley on July 14, 1986 aged 66. A son of E. J. Bridger, who in a long career took more than 1,500 wickets for Dulwich CC, he was in the Rugby XI from 1935 to 1938, when he was captain and had a remarkable match against Marlborough. He made 153 in three hours, held four catches in the first innings and took five for 54 in the

second with his leg-breaks. Leaving Rugby at Easter 1939, he went up to
Cambridge in October and, being as a theological student exempt from military
service, played in four war-time matches against Oxford, besides representing the
University at rugger, hockey, lawn tennis and squash. No Blues were awarded in
those years and the average standard of the University side was little above that of
a good college side before the war, but no-one could doubt that Bridger would
have got a Blue at any time. He gave further evidence of this in some of the war-
time matches at Lord's. When Championship cricket was resumed in 1946, he had
the advantage over his contemporaries that he had been able to keep in practice
and to gain valuable experience with good players. His batting was based on an
eminently sound method and he was a brilliant field, and it was no surprise when,
in his first match for Hampshire, he made 50 against Sussex and followed it in the
next with 39 and 142 against Middlesex. In his second innings, lasting 4 hours, 40
minutes, he added 179 for the second wicket with G. Hill. Unfortunately, being
now a schoolmaster, he was available only in the holidays and, though he
continued to play until 1954, he managed for the county only 38 matches in all, in
which he scored 1,725 runs with an average of 27.82, including two centuries. He
occasionally captained the side.

BROADHEAD, WILFRED BEDFORD, who died at his home in Wath,
Yorkshire, after a long illness, on April 2, 1986, aged 82, was for many years
prominent in Yorkshire league cricket and played frequently for the Yorkshire
Colts and for the Second XI. On his one appearance for the county, against Kent
at Tonbridge in 1929, he went in first with Holmes in a side weakened by the
absence of Sutcliffe and Leyland. He made only 3 and 2, but had the satisfaction
of catching Woolley.

BROWN, WILLIAM CECIL, who died in hospital in Hove on January 20,
1986, aged 85, did great and unselfish service for Northamptonshire between the
wars in the dimmest period of their history, when they were seldom far from the
bottom of the table and once went three seasons without winning a match. At
Charterhouse he had been nowhere near the XI and at Jesus, Cambridge, was no
more than a college player, but by 1925 he had by keenness and application
become good enough to fill the occasional vacancy in the county side. By 1928 he
had secured a regular place, and in that year he scored 877 runs with an average of
21.92, having made the only century of his career, 103 not out against Glamorgan
at Northampton. Often handicapped by ill-health or injury, he never did as well
again, but he frequently played useful innings, defending or attacking as the
occasion demanded. For instance, in 1931 at Trent Bridge, coming in at 18 for
five, he helped Bakewell to add 106 in 80 minutes against an attack which
included Larwood, Voce and Staples. Brown continued to play until 1937,
captaining the side from 1932 to 1935 and scoring in all 2,601 runs with an average
of 14.06. From 1938 to 1942 he acted as Northamptonshire's Honorary Secretary.
He had an encyclopaedic knowledge of the county and of everyone in it during his
lifetime who had attained any prominence in the games-playing or sporting world,
and this constantly proved a great help to *Wisden's* obituaries. Indeed, on the day
he went into hospital he wrote a note in his usual firm and immaculate hand to tell
us of the death of Ben Bellamy.

BUDD, WILLIAM LLOYD, who died in hospital on August 23, 1986, aged 72,
will be better remembered as, from 1969 to 1982, a first-class umpire who stood in
four Tests than for his performances as a player. He was tried for Hampshire
between 1934 and 1938 as a steady fast-medium in-swing bowler and a hard-
hitting tail-end bat, but only in 1935 and 1937 did he appear at all frequently, and

in both years his wickets were expensive. He did play two notable innings: 67 not out against Glamorgan at Bournemouth in 1935, when he and A. L. Hosie added 125 for the last wicket, and 77 not out against Surrey at The Oval in 1937. He reappeared in a few matches in 1946. Apart from war service with the county police, his whole life was given to cricket, playing, coaching or umpiring, and he was a man universally loved and esteemed. For Hampshire he scored in all 941 runs with an average of 11.47 and took 64 wickets at 39.15.

BULLOCK, PERCY GEORGE, died at Wythall on December 1, 1986, aged 93. A right-handed bat, he played in three games as a professional for Worcestershire in 1921 with little success. At the time of his death he was the oldest surviving Worcestershire cricketer.

CAMM, JOHN SUTCLIFFE, died at Berkeley on September 18, 1985, aged 60. A left-hand bat and a slow left-arm bowler, he played for Gloucestershire Second XI in 1949 and 1950.

CATLOW, CHARLES STANLEY, died at Northampton on March 7, 1986, aged 78. A batsman of great natural gifts with a beautiful style, he was captain of Haileybury in 1926, but his first-class cricket was limited to two matches for Northamptonshire in 1929 in which he met with no success.

COLDHAM, JOHN MAURICE, who died in hospital at Woking after a long period of ill-health on July 25, 1986, aged 85, was three years in the Repton XI and captain in the last, 1919. His record was not outstanding at school, but in 1918 when he was seventeen, playing at Scarborough in a match sufficiently important for the full scores to be given in *Wisden*, he made 11 and 24 not out against a Yorkshire side which had Rhodes and Hirst to bowl for them. It was not till 1923, Coldham having first gone out to India, that he went up to Oxford, and in August 1924, playing for Norfolk against Staffordshire, he made 48 [run out] against the bowling of Barnes. The side's total was 115 and his captain, Michael Falcon, with 19 was the only other batsman to score double figures. This secured Coldham his county cap and also a place in what was originally a Norfolk side to play the South Africans but finished up as a Minor Counties one. The South Africans had that great bowler, S. J. Pegler, but Coldham made 40 and 20 and had much to do with his side's victory in a close match. After this it is not surprising that for many years his place in the strong Norfolk side was never in doubt when he was available: what is surprising, and shows the strength of University batting in those days, is that he had in three years only one trial for Oxford. Tall and strong, he was a good, upstanding batsman, a fine slip and, if required, a competent wicket-keeper. He was for many years a master at Sedbergh, where he ran the cricket for 21 seasons.

COPLEY, SYDNEY HERBERT, who died in hospital in the Isle of Man on April 1, 1986, aged 80, will be remembered for one feat. On the last day of the first Test at Trent Bridge in 1930, England, who had one substitute in the field already, required another and Copley, then on the Nottinghamshire staff, was sent out. Australia, requiring 429 to win, were 229 for three with McCabe and Bradman well set and 195 minutes to go. At this point McCabe on-drove Tate, and Copley, covering a lot of ground, threw himself forward and, as he fell, held the catch in both hands near his ankles. But for this Australia would probably have saved the match and might even have won it. A right-hand bat and slow left-arm bowler, Copley was on the Nottinghamshire staff from 1924 to 1930 but appeared only once for the county, against Oxford University in 1930. From 1933 to 1938 he was professional at Cupar, and from 1939 to his retirement in 1975 coach and head groundsman at King William's College, Isle of Man.

CURNOW, SYDNEY HARRY (SYD), who died in Perth, Australia, on July 28, 1986, aged 78, played in seven Test matches for South Africa, opening the batting in all but one of his fourteen innings and scoring 168 runs. Such a record, however, does not indicate his true ability, and in all first-class matches he scored 3,409 runs with an average of 42.08. Going into the Transvaal side in 1928-29 for the trial series for the team to England, he failed to score in his first innings but made 92 in the second, showing a sound defensive technique and making a special impression in the field with his quick gathering and fast, sure returns. In 1929-30 he followed an innings of 99 against Natal with 108 against Griqualand West and 162 against Orange Free State, putting on 204 for the first wicket with A. Langebrink against the Free State. When Chapman's team visited South Africa the following season, he was chosen for the first Test at the Old Wanderers ground in Johannesburg, where South Africa won by 28 runs – a victory which eventually provided them with their first series win over England since 1909-10. With scores of 13 and 8 he failed to retain his place for Newlands but was recalled for the last two Tests. His other four Tests were played in Australia in 1931-32, and he made his highest score of 47 in the third Test at Melbourne. When the teams returned there for the final Test, his 16 in the second innings was the only South African score in double figures as their first innings of 36 was followed by 45 on a vicious "sticky" wicket. The match, which produced only 234 runs, was completed in 5 hours, 53 minutes. The next season, in the South African Tournament in Cape Town, his talent was in full bloom as he scored 641 runs with an average of 91.57 and hit three centuries: 192 not out against Western Province, 105 against Natal and 224 for the North against the South, the highest of his nine hundreds. He continued to represent Transvaal until 1945-46 and at the beginning of the 1970s he went to live in Western Australia.

CUSH, FRANK, OBE, who died in Australia in November 1985, aged 92, was Chairman of the Australian Board of Control from 1955 to 1959. He was an Honorary Life Member of MCC.

DAER, ARTHUR GEORGE, who died at Torquay on July 16, 1980, aged 73, but whose death was not recorded in *Wisden*, was an amateur who played for Essex from 1925 to 1935, and from 1929 to 1934 was a frequent member of the side. A fast-medium opening bowler who relied more on movement off the seam than on swerve, he could, in the words of one of his contemporaries, "have some of the old pros in a muddle at times". When in 1930 he took 51 wickets at 30.86, besides playing some useful innings and having a batting average of 20.42, it was hoped that he would develop into a valuable all-rounder but he never fulfilled his promise. At times he was effective: in 1933 he took nine for 93 against Gloucestershire at Cheltenham and nine for 95 against Sussex at Horsham. However, as his figures show, he was not sufficiently consistent. In all matches for Essex he took 195 wickets at 31.70 and scored 1,469 runs with an average of 14.83. His highest score was 59 against Worcestershire at Leyton in 1932. A "character", who helped to enliven any side on which he played, later he kept a pub in Romford and built a cricket school in the back yard.

DAER, HARRY BRUCE, brother of the above, died at Plymouth on December 19, 1980, aged 62. An opening bowler, he had some trials for Essex as a professional in 1938 and 1939 but did not meet with any success.

DEEPAL, HARSHA, who died in Sri Lanka in 1986, aged 24, as the result of a motor accident, was a stylish left-handed bat and right-arm medium-pace bowler who toured Pakistan in 1983-84 with the Sri Lankan Under-23 team. He had in 1980-81 represented his country against India in an Under-20 series and played for Sri Lanka Colts against the touring Zimbabweans that same season.

de SMIDT, RUPERT, who died in Cape Town, South Africa, on August 3, 1986, aged 103, was believed to be the oldest first-class cricketer. A fast bowler, he played four times for Western Province between 1911 and 1913, taking sixteen wickets at 18.00 apiece.

DUNN, PERCY JOHN HAMPDEN, who died on June 5, 1986, aged 78, as the result of an accident, was one of the best bowlers in London club cricket in the 1930s. A tall medium-pace right-armer, he played for Beckenham, Butterflies and the Band of Brothers and on several occasions represented the Club Cricket Conference. He had been in the Westminster XI in 1925, when he headed their bowling averages.

DURNELL, THOMAS WILFRED, who died on April 10, 1986, aged 84, was a fast-medium bowler with a high action who might have made a big difference to Warwickshire between the wars had he been more frequently available. As it was, after a match or two in 1921 he did not appear again until 1927 when, on his first appearance, he created quite a sensation by taking three for 60 and seven for 29 against Northamptonshire at Edgbaston and came out top not only of the Warwickshire averages but of the first-class bowling averages with fourteen wickets at 12.78. A few matches in the next three seasons showed that this was no fluke, but after that he was seen no more. In fourteen first-class matches he had taken 42 wickets with an average of 28.33. Most of his cricket was played for Smethwick in the Birmingham League.

EARL, KENNETH JOHN, died in hospital on October 13, 1986, aged 60. As a right-arm fast-medium bowler for Northumberland from 1948 to 1965, he took 270 wickets and in 1950 played two first-class matches for the Minor Counties against MCC and the West Indians. In the first of these, at Lord's, he took five for 75 in the second innings.

EDRICH, WILLIAM JOHN (BILL), DFC, who died at Chesham as the result of an accident on April 23, 1986, aged 70, was a cricketer who would have been the answer to prayer in the troubled England sides of today and especially in the West Indies in 1985-86. Endlessly cheerful, always optimistic and physically courageous, he was a splendid hitter of short-pitched fast bowling and took the blows he received as a part of the game. When he made 16 in an hour and three-quarters on a hideous wicket at Brisbane in the first innings of the first Test in 1946-47, an innings which *Wisden's* correspondent described as "one of the most skilful batting displays I have ever seen", it was reckoned that he was hit ten times by Lindwall, Miller and Toshack. So far from being demoralised by this experience, he scored in the series 462 runs with an average of 46.20, and that for a side which lost three Tests, two of them by an innings, and drew the other two. Moreover, his cricket did not end with his batting. Though he stood only 5ft 6in tall, and had a low, slinging action, he could off a run of eleven strides bowl genuinely fast for a few overs. Admittedly it was a terrible proof of the weakness of English bowling after the war that at this period he often had to open in Test matches. It is barely credible that in 1950, when his 22 wickets in the season cost him just under 50 runs each, he opened in both of West Indies' innings at Lord's. In fairness it must be added that Walcott, who made 168 not out in the second innings, was missed off him in the slips at 9. Still, in a reasonably strong side he was a valuable change as a fifth or sixth bowler, always apt to upset a good batsman by his unexpected speed. Like many natural athletes, he originally made a reputation as a tireless outfield, but he was soon found to be too valuable in the slips to spend much time elsewhere. One way and another he was always in the game, always trying his hardest.

He came of a Norfolk farming family, which sometimes produced its own XI. Three of his brothers played with some success in first-class cricket and his cousin, John, had later a distinguished Test match career. Bill Edrich first appeared for Norfolk in 1932 at the age of sixteen, and by 1936 had scored 1,886 runs for them in the Minor Counties Championship alone, not to mention an innings of 111 against the 1935 South African side. By then he had begun to qualify for Middlesex, and in 1936 he made three hundreds in first-class cricket for MCC and came second in the first-class averages with an average of 55. So it was no surprise when next year, in his first full season of first-class cricket, he scored 2,154 runs with an average of 44.87, heading the batting, and was picked for Lord Tennyson's side in India. In 1938 he started by making 1,000 runs before the end of May, a target he achieved only with the help of an unexpectedly generous action by Bradman who, captaining the Australians against Middlesex on May 31, made an otherwise meaningless declaration to give him a chance of getting the last 20 runs. After this feat his place in the England side was secure; so secure that he kept it right through the series even though failure followed failure and six innings produced only 67 runs. In the following winter, as a member of the side to South Africa, his ill luck pursued him, five innings bringing 21 runs. At last, in the second innings of the timeless fifth Test, when England were set 696 to win, he saved the side by batting 7 hours, 40 minutes for 219. Timeless or not, the match was abandoned when the score stood at 654 for five: the rain came down, everyone had had enough, and the Englishmen left to catch their boat.

The sequel to this innings is perhaps the strangest part of the story. There can surely be no parallel for a batsman failing in eight consecutive Tests and yet keeping his place, but one would at any rate expect that, when he had at last justified the selectors' confidence, he would have retained it. Instead, in 1939, though his average for the season was 49.68, he did not play in a Test against the West Indians, and in 1946, when Test cricket was resumed after seven years' interval, he had only one match against India and did not bat in that. Moreover he was only a late choice for the 1946-47 tour of Australia. Let anyone justify these inconsistencies who can.

During the war Edrich had joined the RAF and had a distinguished career, winning the DFC as a bomber pilot. Up to the war he had played as a professional; after it he became an amateur. Furthermore, until 1938 he had normally opened the innings. When he played his great innings in South Africa, he had been moved down the order, and in 1939 Brown and Robertson established themselves in the Middlesex side as a great opening pair. Thenceforward Edrich's normal place was first wicket. It was in Australia in 1946-47 that he showed himself indisputably a Test player. His batting in the first Test has been mentioned. In the second he scored 71 and 119 and made a gallant attempt to stave off an innings defeat. He followed this with 89 in the third Test and 60 in the fifth.

In England in 1947 came his *annus mirabilis*. Scoring in all 3,539 runs with an average of 80.43 he beat Hayward's 41-year-old aggregate of 3,518: however, Compton beat it by even more. What is not sufficiently appreciated is that, but for a strained arm, which stopped him bowling after the beginning of August, he might well have equalled J. H. Parks's astonishing record of 3,000 runs and 100 wickets: Edrich had already taken 67 wickets. In 1946 he had taken 73 at 19.28. In the Tests in 1947 against South Africa he made 552 runs with an average of 110.40. At Manchester he made 191, adding 228 with Compton for the third wicket in 196 minutes. At Lord's in the previous Test, also for the third wicket, they had added 370. Edrich made 189.

In 1948, in the disastrous series against Australia, his sole notable contribution was 111 in the fourth Test at Leeds, but next year against New Zealand he averaged 54 with only one century. In 1950 he contributed a typically gallant 71 in the second innings of the first Test at Manchester, but at Lord's in the second he failed abjectly in each innings. His scores were 8 and 8: it would have been better for his reputation if he had taken two first balls. Each time he stayed long enough to make it clear that he was completely out of his depth with Ramadhin and Valentine. Nothing worse for the morale of the younger members of the side can be imagined. Inevitably he was dropped for the two remaining Tests, but for Middlesex he scored much as usual and it was a great surprise when he was omitted from the team for Australia at the end of the season. The Australians themselves were astonished, and when the side proved to be incontestably the worst batting one England had ever sent out, and all the new choices were failures, there were those who thought that his courage and experience might have turned the scale in a series which was closer than the results indicated. No reasons were given at the time for his omission, but in fact an ill-advised late-night party during the first Test against West Indies, followed by his calamitous showing in the second, had convinced the selectors, and not least the captain elect, that the team would be better without him. By a generous gesture Edrich himself was at the station to see the team off and to wish them well.

Although few could have foreseen it at the time, this was the beginning of the end for Edrich. Never again was he to be the force in Tests that he had been. Recalled as Hutton's opening partner for the last three Tests against Australia in 1953, he made 64 at Leeds and was 55 not out when the Ashes were regained at The Oval after a period of eighteen years. But he did not do much in his one Test against Pakistan in 1954, and although at the end of that summer he was picked for Australia, only a fighting 88 in the second innings of the first Test showed what he could once do. That was the end of his career for England. For Middlesex he still made runs, if not on the scale of his great years. In 1951 and 1952 he shared the captaincy with Compton: this, like most such diarchies, was not a success. From 1953, he was sole captain, a position in which he certainly could not be blamed for lack of enterprise. At last in 1957, though he got his 1,000 runs, for the fifteenth time, his average dropped to 22.92 and he felt it was time to resign. Next year he played in about half the matches with only moderate results, and at the end of the season he accepted the captaincy of Norfolk, for whom he continued to score runs and to take wickets with slow off-breaks until 1972.

When his first-class career ended he was 42, an age at which many great batsmen have still been batting with almost undiminished powers. However, Edrich had always relied rather on his natural gifts, his wonderful eye, his physical strength and courage than on a studiously sound technique. Granted that he was always well behind the ball when playing a fast bowler, he had a markedly right-handed grip and his best strokes were the cut, the hook and the pulled drive. His bat did not have that pendulum-like swing up and down the line which is the foundation of real soundness. Still, he had done enough for fame and had given much pleasure to many thousands of spectators.

In first-class cricket he had scored 36,965 runs, with an average of 42.39 and made 86 centuries, nine of them double-centuries: he took 479 wickets at 33.31 and held 526 catches. His highest score was 267 not out for Middlesex against Northamptonshire at Northampton in 1947. For Middlesex his figures were 25,738 runs with an average of 43.40 and 328 wickets at 30.41, and in Tests he made 2,440 runs with an average of 40, including six hundreds: he also took 41 wickets at 41.29 and held 39 catches.

ELLIOTT, GEORGE O. J., who died early in 1986, aged 68, was secretary of Leicestershire from 1945 to 1949. He had previously been founder, secretary and captain of the West of England XI which raised much money for war charities in 1944 and 1945.

FISHLOCK, LAURENCE BARNARD, died peacefully in hospital after an operation on June 26, 1986, aged 79. For years he was one of the mainstays of the Surrey side; the first left-hand batsman of any prominence they had had since the early 1870s. Season after season he topped their averages, usually with more than 2,000 runs and an average of about 50. He was largely a county player: a little older than most, he was 28 when he got his cap. Four years later came the war, and when first-class cricket was resumed he was 39, an age when men are retiring from Test cricket rather than starting it. So in all he played in only four Tests: two in 1936 against India, another, also against India, in 1946, and one in Australia in 1946-47. In these he did little. He had also gone on the 1936-37 tour of Australia and on that, though in the opinion of most people he was lucky to be preferred to Paynter, he was equally unlucky to miss six crucial weeks through a broken bone in his right hand. No touring side has suffered so much from injuries as that one and, had he remained fit, Fishlock must, whether in form or not, have had ample opportunity of proving himself. By a cruel stroke of fortune, he again broke a finger on his second tour.

Joining the Surrey staff in 1930, he played against Oxford at The Oval in 1931 and made 41 not out in the second innings, but it was 1934 before he had a real trial, making 598 runs with an average of 31.47. Next year, playing regularly, he made more than 1,000 runs and hit three hundreds, but this hardly prepared people for his advance in 1936. Scoring 2,129 runs with an average of 53.22, he represented the Players at Lord's, took part in two Test trials and in two Tests, and made 100 in each innings for Surrey against Sussex at The Oval. In 1937, after his unlucky winter in Australia, he had almost the only poor spell of his life. In May and June he could get no runs, but then D. J. Knight, whose return to the side after a gap of many years had been only a qualified success, dropped out, Fishlock was moved up to open, a position he continued to occupy to within a year or two of his retirement, and runs immediately began to flow. They included two hundreds in one match against Yorkshire at The Oval, a feat which no one had performed since Knight in 1919. In 1938 he made a century in a Test trial, but with Leyland and Paynter in form and English batting crushingly strong, he had no chance in the Tests.

Trained as an engineer, he spent the war mostly in London making aircraft parts for the RAF and so was able to play some cricket, which meant in 1946 he could take up more or less where he left off, making 2,241 runs with an average of 50.47 and being one of the Five Cricketers of the Year in the 1947 *Wisden*. He continued to score as heavily as ever and in 1948 played the highest innings of his career, 253 against Leicestershire at Leicester. In 1952 he still got his 1,000 runs and played some valuable innings which helped Surrey to win the Championship that launched them on their astonishing sequence of seven consecutive Championships, but he wisely decided to retire while the going was good. Later he coached at St Dunstan's, Catford.

Playing with a sedulously straight bat, he was primarily a front-of-the-wicket player, driving equally well straight or through the covers but also forcing hard off his back foot. Like most left-handers, he was strong to square leg as well. He was a splendid field, especially in the deep, as one might expect for in his young days he had been an amateur soccer international and, later turning professional, had played for a succession of clubs. In all first-class cricket, he scored 25,376 runs with an average of 39.34 and made 56 centuries.

FLOWER, ARTHUR WILLIAM, who died at Eastbourne on June 6, 1986, aged 66, was Secretary of Middlesex County Cricket Club from 1964 to 1980.

FLYNN, ARNOLD EDWARD, who died at Modbury, South Australia, on September 28, 1986, aged 70, was a polished batsman in Lindsay Hassett's Australian Forces team which played in the Middle East in 1941 and 1942 against English, South African and New Zealand Forces teams. In his later years he was the inspiration behind the Adelaide University Cricket Club.

FLYNN, BRIAN, died on August 3, 1986, aged 57, following a yachting accident off Darwin, Australia. A leg-spin bowler who appeared to possess immense potential, he played for Queensland from 1952-53 till 1955-56, having been unable to gain a place for his native New South Wales because of the presence of Benaud. Although he had some spectacular successes, notably seven for 127 (including the last five for 33) and four for 91 against South Australia in 1952-53, and eight for 148 against New South Wales, that season's Sheffield Shield winners, in 1953-54, his 48 first-class wickets were taken at an average of 38.70.

GOLDIE, ERIC, who died on July 8, 1986, played regularly for Devon from 1928 to 1932. He was a good attacking opening bat and a fine field.'

GRIMSHAW, RON, who died in hospital in Oxford on June 26, 1986, aged 64, was the cricket correspondent for the *Oxford Mail*. He had been reporting the University's cricket and rugger since 1951.

HADINGHAM, ANTHONY WALLACE GWYNNE, died suddenly in South Africa on July 14, 1986, aged 73. Four years in the St Paul's XI, he made 55 in the Freshmen's match at Cambridge in 1932 and was drafted straight into the University side. After innings of 69 against Essex and 80 against the Indians, when he and A. T. Ratcliffe added 144 in 125 minutes, he was given his Blue but did little at Lord's. Next year, though he started with 34 against Cambridge, going in first, which paved the way for a remarkable Cambridge win, he lost his place. In 1932 he made one appearance for Surrey but did not bat in a match ruined by rain. Short and slightly built, he was primarily an off-side player, a good driver and cutter. Until he emigrated to South Africa in 1946, he was one of the mainstays of Wimbledon cricket.

HARFIELD, LEWIS, died in Winchester Hospital on November 19, 1985, aged 80. Born at Cheriton, near Winchester, he joined the Hampshire staff in 1925 and, after a few trials for the county in 1926 and 1927, played frequently in 1928, when he scored 578 runs with an average of 16.05. In 1929 he made his place secure and received his cap, his record of 1,216 runs with an average of 26.43 and a highest score of 89 against Sussex at Hove representing admirably consistent batting. Against Kent at Folkestone he made 83 and 69, but more significant, in view of the quality of the opposition, was 86 against Yorkshire at Bournemouth, when he and Mead added 183 in three and three-quarter hours for the third wicket. A determined player with a sound defence, he had strokes on both sides of the wicket and was an especially good hooker. Probably his right position was as an opener, though he often went in lower. An operation kept him out of the side throughout the whole of 1930, and when he resumed his place in 1931 he made 84 in his first innings, but thereafter his batting fell off markedly and his average dropped to 19.12. It was clear that he could no longer stand the strain of first-class cricket. In May 1932 the county received such a discouraging medical report of him that they had no choice but to terminate his agreement. In his brief career he made in all 2,460 runs for them with an average of 20.00.

HARRIS, LESLIE JOHN, who died on October 28, 1985, aged 70, played three matches for Glamorgan in 1947 as a medium-pace bowler and after moving to Kent did wonderful work for the Primary Club, through which cricketers who are out first ball raise money for the blind.

HIGHTON, EDWARD FREDERICK WILLIAM, died on October 9, 1985, aged 61. In 1951, when Statham was playing in a Test, he opened the Lancashire bowling at Colchester and took one for 49. This was his only match for the county, but in the previous season, while a member of the Second XI, he had represented the Minor Counties against MCC at Lord's and taken six wickets. He was a fast-medium right-arm bowler.

HIGSON, PETER, who died in Hove on April 19, 1986, aged 81, was in the Cheltenham XI as a batsman and later captained Lancashire Second XI, making an occasional appearance in the county side. He was a son of T. A. Higson, who played for Lancashire and Derbyshire and had been an England selector.

HILL, ANTHONY EWART LEDGER, who died in Winchester on October 25, 1986, aged 85, was a son of that splendid Hampshire batsman, A. J. L. Hill. In his three years in the Marlborough XI, he showed considerable promise and in 1919, his last season, not only made 50 against Rugby but also, though only a change bowler, took in the two innings eight for 99 and turned into a victory a match which seemed a certain draw. However, in eighteen matches for Hampshire between 1920 and 1930 he never did himself justice and his highest score was 24. All who played with him will remember him as a beautiful field. It was typical of a charming and modest man that the only story the writer ever heard him tell of his county career was how he missed Fender (who went on to make 184) on the boundary at The Oval when he had made 22 and a kindly spectator suggested that he would be more use on the top of the gasometer. Typically, too, he did not bother to add what *Wisden* says: that the sun was in his eyes at the time. A search of *Wisden* fails to confirm the story, often repeated, that he and his father once played for the county in the same match.

HOAD, EDWARD LISLE GOLDSWORTHY (TEDDY), who died in Bridgetown, Barbados, on March 5, 1986, aged 90, was West Indies' first captain in a Test match in the West Indies and, at the time of his death, their oldest Test cricketer. A tall, correct right-handed bat, he was slow in running into form when he came to England in 1928 but went on to head the West Indians' averages with 765 runs at 36.42 and in all matches passed 1,000 runs. An unbeaten innings of 149 against Worcestershire gained him a place in the side for the second Test at Old Trafford, but after scores of 13 and 4 he did not play at The Oval. At the end of the tour, he scored 145 in a 12-a-side game against J. Cahn's team at the Loughborough Road ground in Nottingham, followed by 124 against a strong Leveson Gower's XI at Scarborough, going in at the fall of the first wicket and, batting with skill and judgement, being last out. But his dropping of Haig probably allowed Leveson Gower's XI to avoid the follow-on and they recovered to win the match. When F. S. G. Calthorpe's team visited the West Indies in 1929-30, he made 147 for Barbados against them, putting up 261 with Tarilton, and he then captained West Indies in the drawn first Test match at Bridgetown. Opening the innings, he scored 24 and 0 and did not play in the other Tests, the captaincy in those times being the preserve of the home island. He did, nevertheless, appear twice more for West Indies, scoring 6 and 36 at Lord's and 1 and 14 at Old Trafford in 1933, when he scored 1,083 runs with an average of 27.76 on the tour.

Against Sussex at Hove, he made 149 not out and with H. C. Griffith put on 138 for the tenth wicket, which more than 50 years on remained a West Indian record. In all first-class cricket between 1921-22 and 1937-38 he scored 3,502 runs, including eight centuries, with an average of 38.48 and took 53 wickets at 36.28 with his leg-spin bowling.

HODGSON, DAVID GLYNN McPHERSON, died in Cape Town, South Africa, on December 15, 1985, aged 46. A middle-order batsman for Western Province in the 1960s and early 1970s, he was Secretary of its Cricket Union at the time of his death.

HORROCKS, WILLIAM JOHN, who died at Melbourne on November 15, 1985, aged 80, was a batsman of great possibilities which, in this country at any rate, he failed to fulfil. With a strong defence, he had strokes all round the wicket and a particularly beautiful square cut. He was, moreover, a splendid field. Born at Warrington, which then was in Lancashire, he went out to Australia at the age of seven and came into prominence by scoring 75 not out for Western Australia, followed by 31 and 76 for an Australian XI, against Percy Chapman's MCC side at Perth and 51 and 39 next season against Harold Gilligan's side. Returning to England in 1931, he played his first match for Lancashire against the New Zealanders at Liverpool and made 72, helping Hallows in an opening stand of 184 in two hours and a half. A fortnight later, going in against Nottinghamshire at Old Trafford with the score 53 for three, he batted for more than four hours to make 100 not out in a total of 249, and at the end of the season he was second in the county's averages with 343 runs and an average of 34.30. However, in 1932, after a few early failures, he was relegated to the second XI, but neither in that year nor the next could he get any runs for them, and in 1933 he severed his connection with Lancashire and returned to Australia. That he had not, in fact, lost his batting was shown by a fine innings of 140 for Combined Western Australia against G. O. Allen's side in 1936-37, when he and C. L. Badcock put on 306 for the second wicket. In all first-class cricket between 1926-27 and 1936-37 he scored 1,255 runs, including three centuries, with an average of 33.02.

HORTON, WILLIAM HERBERT FRANCIS KENNETH, who died on October 31, 1986, aged 80, was in the Stonyhurst XI as a batsman and in 1927 had two trials for Middlesex without success. Later he played some first-class cricket in India.

INCLEDON-WEBBER, LT.-COL. GODFREY STURDY, who died on April 28, 1986, aged 81, was in the Eton XI in 1922, when he made 80 against Winchester, and 1923. A good natural all-round cricketer, he lacked the concentration to make full use of his gifts.

IRANI, JAMSHED KHUDADAAD ("JEMI"), died in Karachi, Pakistan, on February 25, 1982, aged 60. He kept wicket for India in their inaugural Test match against Australia, at Brisbane in 1947-48, and also in the second at Sydney, scoring 3 runs and making three dismissals (2 ct, 1 st). At the age of fourteen he had played for Sind in the Ranji Trophy.

JACKSON, PETER FREDERICK, died on October 23, 1986, aged 53. Head of the batting averages at Merchant Taylors', Northwood, in 1950, he later played occasionally for Buckinghamshire, but will be better remembered as for many years the leading spirit in Amersham cricket and their chief run-getter.

JAKEMAN, FREDERICK, died in Huddersfield on May 18, 1986, aged 66. Born at Holmfirth, he was a left-handed batsman who Yorkshire hoped might train on into Leyland's successor. However, in a number of trials in 1946 and 1947 he failed to come up to expectations and in 1949 he appeared in the Northamptonshire side, scoring 969 runs with an average of 31.06 and making hundreds against Derbyshire and Sussex. Next year he was slightly less successful, but in 1951 he jumped right to the front with 1,989 runs and an average of 56.82. Fourth in the first-class averages, he made six hundreds, including 258 not out against Essex at Northampton in five hours and twenty minutes, which beat by 1 run the record score for the county which had been shared by Bakewell and Brookes. He had a wonderful spell in July when four consecutive innings produced 558 runs for once out. In 1952 he missed a third of the matches through injury and was disappointing, his average falling to 29, and in 1953 he completely lost both his form and his place in the side. In 1954 he started with a fine century against Sussex, but he could not keep it up and his last match for the county was against Surrey early in August. After some years in league cricket he was a first-class umpire from 1961 to 1972. Short and strongly built, he was quick on his feet and a fine driver and puller. He should have had a longer career than he did, but he lacked concentration and did not keep himself as fit as he might have. He had a safe pair of hands in the deep, but was apt to damage his arm in throwing. In his first-class career he scored 5,952 runs with an average of 32 and made eleven hundreds. His son later had a brief trial for Northamptonshire.

KENNY, RAMNATH BHAURA, died on November 21, 1985, aged 55. A sound right-handed bat, with quick footwork and stylish strokeplay, and an off-break bowler of almost medium pace, he played in five Tests for India: at Calcutta against West Indies in 1958-59 and four times against Benaud's Australian side in 1959-60, scoring in all 245 runs with an average of 27.22 and a highest innings of 62. Playing for Bombay from 1950-51 to 1960-61, and then for Bengal until 1963-64, he scored in all first-class cricket 3,079 runs with an average of 50.47 and took fifteen wickets at 31.20. Among his eleven hundreds, three in 1956-57 came in successive innings with the third, 218 against Madras, remaining his highest score. A qualified coach, he helped in the development of the young Sunil Gavaskar, and it was while playing and coaching professionally in the north of England that he played for Cumberland.

KIRSTEN, NOEL, who died in South Africa on September 30, 1986, aged 59, held a national wicket-keeping record which, although equalled, had not been bettered. For Border against Rhodesia at East London in 1959-60, he took six catches and made one stumping to record seven dismissals in an innings: he had nine in the match. He played eighteen matches for Border between 1946-47 and 1960-61, scoring 163 runs, taking 27 catches and making five stumpings. His son, Peter, played for Western Province and Derbyshire as well as representing South Africa.

LAKER, JAMES CHARLES (JIM), who died at Putney on April 23, 1986, aged 64, will always be remembered for his bowling in the Test match at Old Trafford in 1956, when he took nineteen Australian wickets for 90, nine for 37 in the first innings and ten for 53 in the second. No other bowler has taken more than seventeen wickets in a first-class match, let alone in a Test match. The feat is unique and, rash though it may seem to say, may well remain so. Ten wickets in an innings, more than any other achievement in cricket, must contain a large element of luck: however well a man bowls, the odds must always be that his partner will pick up a wicket. In this case these odds were heavier than usual because Lock at the other end was, on such a wicket, as great a spinner as Laker and bowled superbly. What turned the scale was that Laker was bowling off-breaks whereas Lock relied on the left-armer's natural leg-break, and the Australians at that period were wholly inexperienced in playing off-breaks, especially on a wicket which, heavily marled and almost devoid of grass, might have been designed for an off-spinner.

Since the days of Howell and Trumble at the turn of the century, Australian wickets had become so unresponsive to finger-spin that the off-break had virtually disappeared and sides relied on pace and wrist-spin – Gregory and McDonald, Lindwall, Miller and Johnston or again Hordern, Mailey, Grimmett and O'Reilly. Against these two types of bowler the essential is to get into line, so that the bat can swing straight down the path of the ball. But the batsman who follows this principle against vicious off-spin soon finds himself reduced to an ugly jab right across the line, and the result is always likely to be an lbw or a catch to one of the close-fielders. Moreover, so accurate was Laker that these fielders could stand very close indeed. In any case this was the weakest Australian batting side for more than 60 years, with the possible exception of 1912 when four of their essential batsmen refused to come. In particular, they lacked a great attacking genius like Trumper, Macartney or Bradman who would refuse to be dictated to and who might have disrupted the entire plan. Indeed, the Australians had had a foretaste earlier in the season of what might happen when, for Surrey at The Oval, Laker had taken ten for 88 in the first innings, the only instance of a bowler performing the feat twice in one season. Altogether that summer he played seven times against the Australians and took 63 wickets for 10 runs each.

Born at Frizinghall, near Bradford, Laker was brought up in Yorkshire and in his schooldays was a batsman and a fast bowler. It was B. B. Wilson who, in indoor nets early in the war, suggested that he should change to off-spin and, while serving in the Middle East and having the chance of playing Army cricket with a number of distinguished players, he turned the advice to good account. Before being demobilised he was billeted at Catford and joined the cricket club, whose president then was Andrew Kempton, who for years did so much for young Surrey cricketers. Kempton recommended him to The Oval and, after playing twice for Surrey in 1946 against the Combined Services, he was taken on the county staff, the Surrey authorities having first made sure that Yorkshire were not interested. He soon made his place secure in the Surrey side in 1947 and headed their bowling averages. At the end of the season he was picked for the largely experimental MCC side which G. O. Allen was taking to the West Indies and was one of the few successes among the untried players. In the first innings of the first Test he took seven for 103 (six of them on the second morning for 25) and, though handicapped later by strained stomach muscles, he came out top of the averages.

However, in England in 1948 he suffered a severe setback. The Australian side that year was, at a modest computation, one of the strongest batting sides in the history of cricket, and nothing in Laker's limited experience had prepared him for such an ordeal. On his second appearance against them, for MCC at Lord's, he was hit for nine 6s on the second morning. None the less he was chosen for the first Test and created a sensation by being easily the top scorer in the first innings with 63 made in 90 minutes: the total was 165 and he and Bedser added 89 for the ninth wicket. He also took three early wickets, Morris, Barnes and Miller, but after that he was ineffective, as he was too in the second Test. Dropped for the third Test, he was recalled for the fourth, in which Australia, set to get 404 in 344 minutes, got them within a quarter of an hour of time. The pitch was taking spin, the ball was lifting – a few years later, Laker would have been in his element. Unfortunately he failed to keep a length: moreover, although there was a spot just where a slow left-armer or leg-spinner could have used it, it was no help to him.

Altogether that season his fourteen wickets against the Australians cost him 59.35 runs each, and it was probably this, and especially the treatment he received at Lord's, which led the selectors to feel that, however successful he might be in county cricket, he was not really a Test match bowler.

Yet in the coming years, in the immensely strong Surrey sides which won the Championship season after season, he and Lock proved themselves one of the greatest combinations on a turning wicket in cricket history, comparable with Peel and Briggs for England, Blythe and Woolley for Kent or Parker and Goddard for Gloucestershire. Laker may well have thought that, when he took eight for 2 for England against the Rest at Bradford in 1950, his place in the England side was secure, but in the next six years he was often left out in England and went on only one tour abroad, to the West Indies, where it has to be admitted that he was terribly expensive. However, he did have his successes in England. It was, for instance, undoubtedly he who won the final Test against South Africa in 1951 with four for 64 and six for 55, and after taking more than 100 wickets for Surrey alone that season he was included among the Five Cricketers of the Year in the 1952 *Wisden*.

After 1956 the attitude of the selectors naturally changed. In 1957 Laker played in four Tests against West Indies, missing one through illness, and again in 1958 in four of the five against New Zealand. In 1956-57 he was one of the MCC side in South Africa, where he met with fair success, and at last in 1958-59 was picked for a tour of Australia, where he topped the bowling averages both in the Tests and in all first-class matches. But he was by now feeling the strain and opted out of the New Zealand part of the tour which followed. In England in 1959 he was not the bowler he had been: his 78 wickets cost 24.61 runs each and he was much handicapped by an arthritic finger. At the end of the season he retired from the Surrey side, having taken for them, over thirteen years, 1,395 wickets at 17.37 in 309 matches: eleven times he had more than 100 wickets in a season. However, in 1962 he was persuaded by his friend, Trevor Bailey, to turn out for Essex, and for three years he appeared for them in 30 matches as an amateur. He was still capable of discomfiting the best players.

In 1960 he had published a book, *Over to Me*, which gave so much offence to the authorities at Lord's and The Oval that they withdrew his honorary membership of MCC and Surrey, although these were restored some years later, and at the time of his death he was Chairman of Surrey's cricket committee. Meanwhile he had found himself a new career as a television cricket commentator: he had, of course, a deep knowledge of his subject, he was admirably clear and, though outspoken, never unfair.

In all first-class matches he took 1,944 wickets at 18.41 and scored 7,304 runs with an average of 16.60, including two centuries, both for Surrey. In 46 Test matches, he took 193 wickets at 21.24. He was also a good close-fielder.

LALL SINGH, who died in Kuala Lumpur on November 19, 1985, aged 76, appeared for India against England in the inaugural Test match between the two countries. Of Indian origin, he was born in Malaya, as it was then, and was the only Malayan to play for India. A century for the Federated Malay States led to his travelling to Calcutta, sponsored by a Kuala Lumpur businessman, for the trials for the side to visit England in 1932, and scores of 99 and 48 won him inclusion. In the only Test match of the tour, at Lord's, his scores were 15 and 29, and in the second innings he put on 74 in 40 minutes with Amar Singh for the eighth wicket. In England's first innings he had run out Woolley from mid-on, and it was for his brilliant fielding, as much as his entertaining batting, that he left an impression. "It would be idle to pretend", said *Wisden*, "that he had a particularly strong defence." In all matches on the tour he made 520 runs, with a highest score of 52. He played in India for Southern Punjab and Hindus for four more seasons but never again for India. In all first-class cricket he scored 1,123 runs with an average of 24.95 and one hundred.

LAUGHLIN, ERROL THOMAS, died in Kingwilliamstown, South Africa, on April 22, 1986, aged 38, following a motor accident. An attacking batsman and off-spin bowler, he made his début for Rhodesia in 1969-70 but from 1976-77 represented Border. Playing for Leicestershire Second XI in 1972 he scored 522 runs with an average of 32.50 and took fourteen wickets at 22.21. In first-class cricket, he made 946 runs, average 18.54, with a highest score of 101 for Border against Transvaal B in 1981-82, and took 29 wickets, average 30.48. He was, at the time of his death, manager of Border.

LAWTON, RANDALL, died in July 1986 at the age of 84. Born in Yorkshire, he was a good fast bowler and a useful tail-end hitter who was a regular member of the Staffordshire side in the 1930s.

LINDSAY, THE HON. PATRICK, who died on January 9, 1986, aged 57, was a fast-medium opening bowler in the Eton sides of 1946 and 1947. In 1946, when he bowled particularly well at Lord's, he began the first innings with a spell of six overs for 1 run and one wicket.

LOWE, RICHARD GEOFFREY HARVEY, died on July 5, 1986, aged 82. Captain of Westminster in 1923, he was probably the best all-rounder in the Public Schools, but was prevented by a bad back from playing any cricket in the first summer at Cambridge. He duly got his Blue in 1925, doing particularly well as a bowler, but his batting was disappointing until, sent in at Bath to open, he made 83 (his highest score in first-class cricket) and helped E. W. Dawson to put up 154. An attempt after this to convert him into a regular opener in 1926 failed: indeed so unsuccessful was he both as a batsman and a bowler that his place was in jeopardy and he saved it only by an admirable innings of 80 against Surrey at The Oval. Lucky it was for Cambridge that he did so. At Lord's he took five for 22 in the first innings, which he finished with a hat-trick, clean-bowling the last two men with yorkers, and followed this with three for 34 in the second. Thanks to him, Cambridge won a splendid match by 34 runs, and later that month he played two matches for Kent. In 1927 he was disappointing but retained his place. A left-handed bat, he bowled fast-medium right with a high arm, coming quick off the pitch and sometimes bringing it back. He could also swing the ball a bit both ways, but at Cambridge he was used as a stock bowler rather than as an opener. He played soccer for four years for the University, was captain, and also played in an amateur international against Scotland in 1924. For many years headmaster of a prep school in Sussex, he lived in Kent in his retirement and gave valuable assistance with Band of Brothers cricket in August. In all first-class cricket he made 697 runs with an average of 18.83 and took 70 wickets at 26.24.

McCOOL, COLIN LESLIE, died in hospital in New South Wales on April 5, 1986, aged 70. He was an outstanding all-round cricketer in Australia in the post-war years and, from 1956 to 1960, for Somerset. Short in stature but of strong build, he was a right-handed batsman most adept square of the wicket, either with wristy cuts or vigorous hooks, and there were few better players of spin bowling on a difficult pitch. His own spin bowling, a clever mixture of leg-breaks and googlies, had lost something in accuracy by the time he played for Somerset, and English wickets did not always give him the bounce which encourages his type abroad, but in his expansively flighted deliveries and the mystery of the turn came a manifestation of an art that was to disappear from English grounds. He was also a fine slip fielder.

Although he played seven times for his home state of New South Wales before war service with the RAAF, it was with Queensland that he caught the attention of the Australian selectors in 1945-46 with six for 36 against New South Wales, seven for 106 and 172 as he "scattered the field by carefree batting" at Adelaide, and four for 102 and seven for 74 against the Australian Services. His 172 against South Australia remained the highest score of his career. Taken to New Zealand for the first-ever Test between the two countries, he scored 7 and, put on to bowl at the end, produced figures of 0.2–0–0–1 as Australia won by an innings and 103 runs. In 1946-47, after taking sixteen wickets against Hammond's MCC side before the first Test, he was especially successful in the series. At Brisbane, on the second evening, he attacked the subdued England bowling to reach 92 not out, but resuming after the rest day he added only 3 more runs before playing back to Wright and being lbw. At Sydney he took eight wickets, including five for 109, and at Melbourne, hooking and driving with absolute confidence, he scored an unbeaten 104 after going in with Yardley on a hat-trick and Australia 188 for five. Five for 44 in the second innings of the final Test, again at Sydney, saw him finish the series with eighteen wickets at 27.27, Australia's leading wicket-taker with Lindwall, and he scored 272 runs with an average of 54.40. He did little in his three Tests against India the next season, and his thirteen wickets in the Sheffield Shield cost 48.61 each, but he went to England with Bradman's team in 1948. However, with a new ball available after 55 overs and a formidable attack waiting to use it, there was no place for McCool in the Test side. He was, moreover, handicapped by a worn spinning finger, a legacy of his triumphs in 1946-47, which blistered and continually bled, and while he ended with 57 wickets at 17.82, he did not reach his best until late in the tour. In South Africa in 1949-50 he again took 50 wickets, as well as scoring 438 runs, and he played in all five Tests, his five for 41 at Cape Town being his best return in a Test match. But in 1950-51, although he was the leading wicket-taker in the Shield that season, he did not get a Test against England; nor against West Indies the following season. By choosing to play as a professional for East Lancashire in the leagues, he precluded the possibility of selection for the Australians to England in 1953 and at 37 his Test career was over. He had scored, in his fourteen appearances, 459 runs with an average of 35.50, taken 36 wickets at 26.61 and held fourteen catches.

McCool was 40 when he began his career with Somerset and his talents and his influence were apparent from the start. He failed by 34 runs to reach 2,000 runs and after four seasons at the foot of the table, Somerset finished fifteenth in the Championship. Against Johnson's Australians at Taunton, he scored 90 and then 116 in 95 minutes, one of his three hundreds that year. Next season, with another Australian, Bill Alley, also on the staff, Somerset climbed to eighth, and in 1958 they won twelve games and were third: their best season ever. His 1,590 runs that year included his highest score for the county, 169 against Worcestershire at Stourbridge, and the best bowling of his career, eight for 74 on a sporting pitch at Trent Bridge. He was given a testimonial in 1959, when he scored 1,769 runs and took 64 wickets, and after 1960 he retired and returned to Australia. In his five seasons in English cricket he had scored 8,225 runs with an average of 33.70 and taken 232 wickets at 28.17: only in 1960, when he scored 1,222 runs, had his aggregate dropped below 1,500. In all first-class matches, 251, he scored 12,420 runs with eighteen centuries and an average of 32.85, took 602 wickets at 27.47 and held 262 catches. He also made two stumpings.

MacFARLANE, ROBERT, who died on February 13, 1986, aged 77, played for Scotland against Ireland in 1939 and with innings of 48 and 22 made a useful contribution to a substantial victory.

MACINDOE, DAVID HENRY, Vice-Provost of Eton, died suddenly of a heart attack on March 3, 1986, aged 68. Going up to Oxford after two years in the Eton XI, he took nine for 59 in the Freshmen's match in 1937 and, getting immediately into the 'Varsity side, finished up with 42 wickets at 23.52. Against Cambridge he took in the match six for 92 and such an impression did he create that he was picked for the Gentlemen at Lord's, the first freshman straight from school to be picked purely as a bowler since S. M. J. Woods in 1888. In 1938 he was again picked for the Gentlemen, this time against the Australians, but in neither of these two matches did he meet with much success. In 1938 he was terribly overbowled for Oxford and his figures suffered accordingly. Altogether he played in four University matches, of which Oxford won three and the fourth was drawn, and in 1946 he captained the side. Indeed, it was fortunate that he was available, for his personality and experience were invaluable in restarting Oxford cricket on the right lines. Taking what was in those days a longish run for a bowler of his pace, he bowled fast-medium in-swingers with a high action. As a bat he had no great pretensions, but in 1939 he scored 43 not out and 51 against the Minor Counties. His own county cricket was played for Buckinghamshire and his first-class career ended when he came down in 1946. However, his interest in the game continued unabated to the end and he had still much to contribute to it. Returning as a master to Eton, he ran the cricket there from 1949 to 1960 and also collaborated with his predecessor, C. H. Taylor, in an admirable little instructional book, *Cricket Dialogue*. For some years he ran the Oxford Harlequins tour in August and he served on the committee both of IZ and of the Butterflies.

MacLEAN, COL. JOHN FRANCIS, died on March 9, 1986, aged 85. One of the many good cricketers who never got into the XI at Eton, he never when up at Cambridge had a trial at Fenner's either; but, keeping wicket for Worcestershire throughout the summer of 1922, he created such an impression that he was picked as first-string wicket-keeper for the MCC side which A. C. MacLaren was taking to New Zealand and Australia that winter. Of this side he was the last survivor. He fully justified his selection, keeping for the most part quite beautifully and playing many useful innings. On the whole tour he made 458 runs with an average of 21.80. In the first representative match against New Zealand he made 84 and helped his captain add 157 for the eighth wicket. In the third he and T. C. Lowry added 106 in an hour for the sixth wicket, his share being 53. In 1923 he again kept admirably for Worcestershire throughout the season and also played a sensational innings against Nottinghamshire at Worksop. The side's total was 239, of which he made 121 in an hour and a half off the bowling of Barratt, Sam Staples and Richmond. Unfortunately, after this year he could not find time for much first-class cricket. He played his last match for Worcestershire in 1924 and after that his only county cricket was six matches for Gloucestershire between 1930 and 1932. In his career he scored 2,112 runs with an average of 21.55, caught 57 batsmen and stumped 43. A brilliant wicket-keeper, he lacked perhaps the consistency of the top-class professionals, but this was a fault which experience could well have cured. As a batsman, he was a tremendously hard hitter.

MATHESON, ALEXANDER MALCOLM, who died in Auckland, New Zealand, on December 31, 1985, aged 79, played for New Zealand in the fourth Test at Auckland in 1929-30 and was a member of their side to England in 1931, playing his only other Test at Manchester, where play did not start until the last afternoon. That New Zealand side were fairly strong in batting, but their bowling was hopelessly weak and Matheson, though his 44 wickets cost 23.81 runs each, came third in the averages and narrowly missed being second. His best performance was in his first match, when he took four good Hampshire wickets for 49 and bowled the almost unbowlable Mead; but in a miserably wet and cold summer, and handicapped at times by a strained leg muscle, he did not live up to this promise. By the time the New Zealanders reached Canterbury in August he was reduced to the indignity, for a fast-medium bowler, of having seven men on the boundary for Woolley, who promptly cut him for 4 between slip and wicket-keeper. Playing for Auckland from 1926-27 to 1939-40 and for Wellington from 1944-45 to 1946-47, he took altogether in first-class cricket 194 wickets at 28.52 and scored 1,844 runs with an average of 23.64. His highest score, and his only century, was 112 for Auckland against Canterbury in 1937-38. On the tour of England, when his usual place was last, he made 72 against Scotland at Glasgow. He had also been a first-class rugger player and in 1946 refereed the international between New Zealand and Australia at Auckland.

MORRIS, HAROLD MARSH, died at Brighton on November 18, 1984, aged 86. A member of the Repton XI in 1915 and 1916, he had a good record as a batsman in both seasons and was captain in the second. At Cambridge in 1919 he scored consistently in the trials, but on his one appearance for the University, against the AIF side, was unlucky enough to make a pair. However, playing for Essex in the vacation, he made 60 against Middlesex in his second match and kept his place until the end of the season. Indeed, he remained a regular member of the side until 1926 and, if his average seldom exceeded 20, it never fell much below it. He played many useful innings and one outstanding one of 111 in three hours against Middlesex at Lord's in 1923, which saved Essex from an apparently certain defeat. But his main asset to the county was his superb fielding, whether at cover or in the country, which was all the more noticeable in a side which had more than its share of stately, not to say static, veterans. Ironically in 1927, when he could no longer play regularly, he surpassed all he had done before by scoring 143 against Somerset at Taunton and following it a week or two later with 166 against Hampshire at Southampton, he and Russell adding 233 for the fourth wicket in 140 minutes. By now it had become clear that the county needed a new captain. A severe illness had virtually ended J. W. H. T. Douglas's great career as a bowler and had also affected his fielding, while the avoidance of any risk when batting had almost become an obsession. Still, had the committee found what he regarded as a suitable successor, he would no doubt have served loyally under him as long as he was wanted. Instead, at the end of 1927, they appointed Morris and Douglas never played for the county again. Not only did he doubt Morris's qualifications as a captain, but he did not regard him as a good enough player and reckoned that he was not sufficiently dedicated to do the job properly. As it turned out, Morris was less difficult than Douglas had been in his later years, and in some ways things went better. However, he was too often absent and in 1932 appeared twice only: this was the end of his first-class career. In all matches for Essex he scored 6,941 runs with an average of 19.77 and made three centuries. A good stylist, who drove and cut well, he looked at his best capable of more than he in fact accomplished. In 1927 he went with Lord Tennyson's side to Jamaica.

NASH, LAURENCE JOHN, died in hospital in Heidelberg, Victoria, on July 24, 1986, aged 76. He played in two Test matches for Australia, both at Melbourne: the fifth Test of 1931-32, in which South Africa were dismissed for 36 and 45 on a "sticky", and the fifth against England in 1936-37 which Australia won to retain the Ashes. A right-arm fast bowler, not tall but powerfully built, he made the ball rise awkwardly and got his first Test after taking seven for 50 for Tasmania against the South Africans, his best-ever figures. He took four for 18 and one for 4 but did not play for Australia again until he was a surprise inclusion for the decisive match against G. O. Allen's team, the series being level at two Tests apiece after Australia had been 2-0 down. He had upset the Englishmen with his lifting deliveries when taking two for 21 and two for 16 for Victoria against MCC, and in the Test he bowled fast and well, taking four for 70 as England failed to avoid the follow-on and one for 34. In 22 matches, seventeen of them for Tasmania, he scored 953 runs, with an average of 28.02 and one hundred, and took 69 wickets at 28.33. He was famous as an Australian Rules footballer.

PARTHSARATHY, R. T., who died on February 4, 1986, aged 65, played for Madras in the Ranji Trophy championship in 1947-48 as a right-handed bat and medium-pace bowler and in later life was prominent as a commentator on cricket for All-India radio.

PAWSON, ALBERT GUY, CMG, who died in Lamerton, Devon, on February 25, 1986, aged 97, had been for some years not only the oldest surviving cricket Blue but the oldest first-class cricketer of any standing. Three years in the Winchester XI and captain in the last two, he went up to Oxford in 1907. Their wicket-keeper that year had been D. R. Brandt and he in 1908 kept throughout the term, Pawson merely getting a chance against the Gentlemen of England, when he made 41 not out, which remained his highest score in first-class cricket. However, Worcestershire arriving without a wicket-keeper for the last match in The Parks, Pawson, though he had no qualification for them, filled the vacancy, and so well did he keep, stumping three men in quick succession off the intricate lobs of G. H. Simpson-Hayward, that his place was never in question for the rest of his time in residence. He kept four years at Lord's, and such was the impression he created on his first appearance in 1908 that, had not Gentlemen v Players for once preceded the University Match, he must have been picked for the Gentlemen. He captained Oxford in 1910. Meanwhile, in 1909, Lord Hawke, anxious to find a successor for himself as captain and also for David Hunter as wicket-keeper, invited Pawson, who was born in Yorkshire, at Bramley, to play four matches for them. He duly accepted, but on the Authentics' northern tour he injured a finger so badly that he had to withdraw. In any case he was by no means certain that he would have been prepared to give up for cricket a career in the Sudanese service. He rose high in the Sudan, becoming Governor of the Blue Nile, and for years he played hardly any cricket. On retiring in 1934, he took the game up again and from then till the war played much club cricket, largely, as he was living in Kent, for the Band of Brothers, and it was still easy to see what a fine 'keeper he must have been in his young days. He continued to play village cricket until he was 70. His elder brother had been a member of the Oxford side of 1903 and he had two sons in the Winchester XI, the younger of whom, H. A., captained Oxford, played for the Gentlemen and for Kent, and like his father had to refuse the captaincy of the county side.

PEARCE, GEORGE SMART, died at Horsham, where he had lived all his life, on June 16, 1986, aged 77. Between 1928 and 1933 he had a number of trials for Sussex without accomplishing much, but in late August 1933, at the suggestion of W. L. Knowles, the county Secretary, he was picked to fill a last-minute vacancy against Yorkshire at Hove. Sussex won by an innings and Pearce played his full part. Going in tenth he made 40 and, after taking the valuable wicket of Holmes in the first innings, he took five for 34 in the second. He played in the two remaining fixtures and scored 32 against the Indians and 80 against Essex at Leyton. In 1934, therefore, he received a good trial but did only moderately,

scoring 455 runs with an average of 19.78 and taking 49 wickets at 25.86. At times
he bowled well but he was inconsistent. A poor season in 1935 was redeemed only
by an innings of 76 off Kent at Hastings, which included three 6s and eight 4s,
followed by a stubborn but valuable 54 at Old Trafford in the next match. In 1936
he played twice only, both times against Cambridge, and in the second match
made 47. This was his last appearance for the county. An attacking batsman and a
right-arm fast-medium bowler, he was a player of distinct possibilities, but the
Sussex batting was so strong that he seldom rose above the tail, while for bowling
of his pace they already had Tate, Cornford and Hammond. He probably
reckoned that a well-established butcher's in his home town offered a more secure
future than the changes and chances of a cricket professional's life. For Sussex, he
scored in all 1,295 runs with an average of 18.76 and took 89 wickets at 29.07.

RAPHAEL, GEOFFREY LEWIS, died in hospital in London on June 12,
1986, aged 76. A medium-pace away-swinger, who could also turn the ball both
ways and had a beautiful action, he seemed likely, when he got his colours at
Harrow at the age of sixteen, to become a first-class bowler. Unfortunately he
never fulfilled his promise, though by his last year at Harrow, 1928, he had made
himself into a useful opening bat. Later that summer he played one match for
Middlesex.

RIGHTON, EDWARD GRANTHAM, who died on May 2, 1986, aged 73,
made four appearances for Worcestershire as a batsman between 1934 and 1936
without much success. His father had played four times for the county before the
Great War.

ROBERTSON, JOHN BENJAMIN, died in South Africa on July 5, 1985,
aged 79. He played in three Test matches for South Africa against Australia in
1935-36 as a spin bowler, taking six wickets at 53.50. He gained selection on the
strength of taking eight for 96 for Western Province against the touring side, but
this was on a pitch taking spin. In the same match, which the Australians won
by an innings, Fleetwood-Smith took twelve wickets for 103. In all first-class
matches, Robertson took 65 wickets at 24.20.

ROSE, ALFRED, who died in hospital at Worksop on June 21, 1985, aged 91,
made one appearance for Derbyshire as a bat in 1924 and failed to score. He was
asked to play again later in the summer but replied that he was too old for that
class of cricket.

RUDDLE, MARCUS POOLE, died in Dublin in March 1986, aged 81. A
right-hand batsman and right-arm medium-pace bowler, he made one
unsuccessful appearance for Ireland in 1937, but was a consistent performer over
the years for the Pembroke, Phoenix and Clontarf clubs. In recent years he
organised the Esso All-Ireland Under-19 competition.

RUSHWORTH, ALFRED WILLIAM, died in Hobart, Tasmania, on
December 30, 1985, aged 87. A dependable right-handed bat, he made his first-
class début in 1922-23 in the match in which Victoria took 1,059 runs off
Tasmania and he went on to play another 23 matches for the island state, scoring
783 runs with an average of 18.64 and holding 30 catches, many of them in the
slips.slips. Captain of Tasmania twelve times, he later became a state selector.

SENANAYAKE, ROBERT PARAKRAMA, died in Colombo, Sri Lanka, on
April 26, 1986, aged 72. He was President of the Ceylon Cricket Association and
Board of Control for Cricket in Sri Lanka for more than twenty years, and it was

during his term of office that his country became an Associate Member of the ICC and the steps were taken towards full membership, which was attained in 1981. A stylish opening batsman, after a successful schoolboy career as captain of St Thomas's College he went up to Cambridge and played in the trials there in 1933 and 1934. He later opened for Ceylon against G. O. Allen's MCC side when they stopped at Colombo on their way to Australia. His father and brother were respectively the first and second Prime Ministers of Sri Lanka.

SMITH, HORACE DENNIS, who died in Christchurch, New Zealand, on January 25, 1986, aged 73, was one of the ten bowlers who have taken a wicket with their first ball in Test cricket. Moreover it was his only wicket in his only Test match. A right-arm medium-fast bowler, in the first Test at Christchurch against Jardine's side in March 1933 the twenty-year-old Smith bowled Paynter with the first ball of the second over, the ball swinging late between bat and pad to hit the left-handers middle and leg stumps. With Sutcliffe having been caught behind off the first ball of the match, from Badcock, England were 4 for two. Had Hammond been caught at slip in the first over, England might have been three wickets down: instead Hammond went on to 227 and England scored 560 for eight. In his twenty overs, Smith conceded 113 runs, and for the second Test he was named twelfth man. He played six times for Otago and four for Canterbury, and in his eleven matches took seventeen wickets at 33.52 and scored 404 runs with an average of 22.44.

SPRINKS, HENRY ROBERT JAMES, who died at Bramshaw, near Lyndhurst, on May 23, 1986, aged 80, was an amateur who played in 21 matches for Hampshire as a fast bowler between 1925 and 1929. Though at times he suggested possibilities, his 29 wickets cost 46.13 runs each and his most notable performance was to add 99 in three-quarters of an hour with Livesey for the last wicket against Kent at Dover in 1928. His share was 40.

STUART, ROBERT LIVINGSTONE, died on June 6, 1986, aged 77. Captain of Highgate in 1927, he returned to Argentina, where he was born, and was a member of the South American side in England in 1932. On this tour he made 608 runs with an average of 33.70, his outstanding performance being an innings of 137 against the Army, when for three hours, twenty minutes he displayed a full range of beautifully executed strokes all round the wicket.

TARAPORE, KEKI KHURSEDJI, died in hospital in Bombay on June 15, 1986, aged 76, after being knocked down by a moped. As a slow left-arm bowler and right-handed bat in the lower order, he played without success in one Test match for India in 1948-49 against West Indies at Delhi. His nineteen overs cost 72 runs: he himself scored 2. This was his last season of a career which began in 1937-38, and in all first-class matches he took 148 wickets at 28.77 and scored 441 runs with an average of 11.30. His best bowling was eight for 91 for Bombay against Nawanagar. Later in life he was Secretary of the Board of Control for Cricket in India and manager of the Indian team to England, in 1967, to Australia, in 1967-68, and to the West Indies, in 1970-71.

TAYLOR, GEORGE RAMMELL, who died suddenly on October 31, 1986, aged 76, captained Hampshire in 1939. He had been a useful bat in the XI at Lancing but would never have claimed to be more than a club player and before taking on the captaincy had made only one appearance for the county, in 1935. A local solicitor, in 1939 he averaged 9.79 and his highest score was 41 against Lancashire. He maintained to the end of his life a keen interest in the county cricket club.

TAYLOR, HOWARD, who died on December 30, 1985, aged 77, was captain of Mill Hill in 1926 and, as a formidable all-rounder, was one of the XV who represented the Public Schools against the Australians that year at Lord's. For many years he was a valuable member of the Blackheath side, and in 1937 he played three matches for Kent without conspicuous success. He could hardly have been subjected to a more searching test on his first appearance, which was against Yorkshire at Tonbridge, and, if he was unlucky enough to get a pair, he had the considerable consolation of bowling Sutcliffe. Right-arm medium to slow-medium, he was a stock bowler rather than an opener. By profession he was a stockbroker.

TIMMS, WILFRID WALTER, who died at Godalming on September 30, 1986, aged 84, was such a modest, self-effacing, unpretentious man that in later years many who knew him as a distinguished teacher of French and Spanish never realised that he had been a well-known cricketer. He made his reputation by a performance which is still unique. In 1921, when captain of Northampton Grammar School, he was given leave by the school to play for the county against Kent in May and then against Essex in June. In this second match, Essex made a vast score and Northamptonshire followed on 381 behind, with only a draw to play for and little hope of that. But Timms, who had made 23 in the first innings, helped Haywood, their star batsman, to add 212 and then added 123 with George Thompson. Northamptonshire finished 64 on with five wickets in hand: Timms, who had batted for five and three-quarter hours for 154 not out, was carried off the field in triumph on the shoulders of his schoolfellows. Two men, I. D. Walker and S. H. Day, had made centuries for their counties the year before leaving school, but no schoolboy before or since has played an innings of that size or length in a county match. Later that season, Timms played for Northamptonshire throughout the summer holidays, on occasion captaining the side, and scored 533 runs with an average of 28.05.

It was therefore a great disappointment that in four years at Cambridge he failed to get a Blue. In his first three years he had only three innings for the University altogether. In his last year he averaged 17.10 for them and made 78 not out against Leicestershire, but that was as far as he got. Perhaps, in view of what he had already accomplished, he deserved a better trial, but Cambridge batting at that period was strong and he never shone in the field, where a weak throwing arm was a grave handicap. Meanwhile he continued to play for his county in the vacations, but did little in 1922 or 1923. It was not until 1925 that, with 837 runs and an average of 29.89, he showed his true form. Slightly built, he had in 1921 scored largely behind the wicket by cuts and deflections. Now he had the strength to drive and made full use of this when, in 1926, he made 128 against Warwickshire in his first match and 112 against Leicestershire in the next, heading the averages in county matches with 33.29. He was, in fact, the soundest batsman they had and continued to play for them in the holidays until 1932. Altogether he made 3,855 runs for them, including four centuries, and averaged 22.81.

After some years as a master at Oundle, he moved in 1930 to Charterhouse, where he ran the cricket from 1932 to 1946. Charterhouse had always been a famous soccer school: the cricket had been neglected. J. T. Morgan, captain of Cambridge in 1930, once said that in his time in the school, cricket had been regarded merely as a means of keeping the footballers fit in the summer. There had never been a "Master in Charge of Cricket" in the ordinary sense of the phrase. Indeed, only twice had there been a first-class cricketer on the staff: F. G. Inge in 1865 and C. B. Fry in 1896 and 1897, an episode of which both he and his biographers have understandably thought it best to say as little as possible. The school had, of course, produced good players and sometimes good XIs, but they owed little to the system or the coaching. Within a few years of Timms taking over, however, it had become one of the best cricket schools in England.

The extent of his achievement is to be measured not by the two great batsmen who were in the school under him, John Lomas, now sadly forgotten by all save his contemporaries, and Peter May, though both these acknowledged their debt to him, but by the inexhaustible supply of supporting players who ensured a series of good XIs. Timms himself would have been the first to acknowledge his debt to the professionals who helped him, Bob Relf from 1932 to 1937, Willis Walker to tide over a gap in 1938, and George Geary from 1939 on, but he would have been too modest to say that Geary was entirely his own selection. At that time there were several famous professionals in the market, some with even more distinguished records. Timms was adamant throughout that he wanted primarily a bowler, not a bat, and that the bowler he wanted was Geary. Generations of Carthusians will attest the wisdom of his choice. They will also attest that in any list of the great Public School coaches, Timms should hold an honoured place.

Peter May writes: He was of great assistance to me in developing the basics of my batting. He was always patient and encouraging: we valued his advice because he had been successful himself in county cricket. He was a very fine player of the cut.

WADDINGTON, JACK E., died in South Africa on November 24, 1985, aged 66. A right-arm slow bowler who relied more on accuracy of line and length than spin, he was South Africa's youngest first-class cricketer when, aged 15 years 320 days, he made his début for Griqualand West against Eastern Province in 1934-35, and when he retired 25 years later he was the leading wicket-taker in the Currie Cup with 317 at an average of 21.75. His 53 wickets in 1952-53 made him one of only three bowlers to take 50 wickets in a Currie Cup season.

WAGENER, JACK GORDON, died at Eastbourne on June 18, 1986, aged 81. A left-hand bat with plenty of strokes and an inclination to attack, and a right-arm fast-medium in-swinger, he had a fine record in the Bradfield XI and at Cambridge might well have been in the running for a Blue in years when there was less talent. As it was, going in number ten for the University against Yorkshire in 1927, he made 40 and put on 77 for the ninth wicket with J. T. Morgan, and a week or two later, again batting at ten, he scored 37 not out for Sussex against the University. However, this was as far as he got, though he afterwards did play a few more matches for Sussex. Becoming a schoolmaster, he was for many years in charge of cricket at Rossall. He had one curious experience in club cricket. Playing for Eastbourne against the Cryptics he was out for 98, two separate short runs having been called against him after he had passed 90.

WAITE, MERVYN GEORGE, died in Adelaide, Australia, on December 16, 1985, aged 74. A hard-hitting batsman and medium-pace bowler, who also bowled off-breaks, he played two Test matches for Australia on the 1938 tour of England, at Leeds and The Oval, and opened the bowling. At The Oval, where England made 903 for seven declared, his analysis was 72–16–150–1, the wicket being that of Compton, bowled for 1 after coming in when the score was 547 for four. As only 8 runs had been added since Paynter was lbw to O'Reilly without scoring, the Australians might have viewed this as a breakthrough but for the presence of Hutton at the other end. On the tour, Waite did well enough as an all-rounder "without making himself indispensable" to score 684 runs with an average of 25.33 and take 56 wickets at 25.96. At Bramall Lane, on a pitch affected by rain, he took seven for 101 in Yorkshire's first innings with a mixture of swing and off-spin: as well as securing him a place in the Leeds Test, these were his best bowling figures. He did not take a wicket at Headingley, but his partnership of 37, of which he scored 3, for the seventh wicket with Bradman saw Australia edge ahead on the first innings and helped Bradman move towards his third century in successive Test innings on the ground. Australia won this match to retain the Ashes. In 1939-40, as South Australia compiled 821 for seven declared against Queensland, he scored 137, the only hundred of his career, and added 281 with C. L. Badcock in a record fifth-wicket partnership for the state. It was also against Queensland, after the war, that he made his last appearance, finishing with memorable figures of four for 11 as Queensland scored 101 to win by five wickets. In all first-class cricket, from 1930-31 till 1945-46, he scored 3,888 runs with an average of 27.77, took 192 wickets at 31.61 and held 66 catches. His innings of 239 for West Torrens against Port Elizabeth in 1935-36 was still a record for the Adelaide District competition at the time of his death.

WATKINS, WILLIAM RICHARD, died on October 15, 1986, aged 82. As a right-handed bat in the middle order and right-arm slow bowler who could turn the ball both ways, he played 27 times for Middlesex as a professional between 1930 and 1937. His highest score for them was 83 against Surrey at Lord's in 1933, when he helped Hendren add 174 and, though he could not save the match, turned what looked like a walkover into an honourable defeat. For MCC against Kent at Folkestone in 1936, he batted for two and three-quarter hours without mistake to score his only hundred, 115, and with Bill Edrich put on 198 for the fourth wicket. His best bowling was also for MCC, against Cambridge at Lord's in 1939 when he occasioned some surprise by taking five for 31 in 9.4 overs in the first innings. In all first-class cricket he scored 867 runs with an average of 18.84 and took eighteen wickets at 20.88. He later became coach of MCC's groundstaff.

WEBSTER, WILLIAM HUGH ("TAGGE"), died after a long illness on June 19, 1986, aged 76. Going up to Cambridge from Highgate, where he had been a successful all-rounder, he was not seriously in the running for a Blue in his first two years and in 1932, given a good trial, did little and seemed to have lost his chance. However, playing for the Foresters against the University in the last match of term he was, for almost the first time in his life, sent in first, and in innings of 29 and 42 he showed such powers of concentration and defence that he was taken on tour as an opener and, confirming the good impression he had created, played in that capacity at Lord's. Doubtless his superb fielding (he was an amateur soccer international) had something to do with the choice. Between 1930 and 1947 he played 45 matches for Middlesex. Altogether in first-class cricket he scored 1,870 runs with an average of 19.89, including one century, 111 for Middlesex against Gloucestershire at Bristol in 1936, and some rather mild left-arm medium-pace bowling brought him 21 wickets at 22.76. In later life he served on the MCC committee and was President of the club in 1977. He was President of Middlesex in 1980.

WEIGHTMAN, WESLEY, who died on July 29, 1986, aged 78, played for Durham for some years in the 1930s. A good bat, he was the county's Honorary Treasurer from 1970 to 1981 and President from 1982 to 1986.

WILCOX, ALFRED GEORGE SIDNEY, who died on July 30, 1986, aged 66, played for Gloucestershire as an amateur in 1939 and as a professional from 1946 to 1949. A left-handed bat, who sometimes opened, he made many runs for the Second XI, but could never quite secure a regular place in the county side. Altogether he scored 835 runs with an average of 15.75. His highest score was 73 against Hampshire at Bournemouth in 1948.

WILLIAMSON, CHARLES RICHARD, who died in Bradford on February 4, 1986, aged 85, was one of the best-known cricket writers in England. Known to everyone as "Dick", he reported on cricket and soccer for almost 65 years and was acquainted with every Yorkshire player for more than 50 years. He possessed a keen mind for statistical detail and thus was accepted as the final arbiter in many press-box arguments. After working for the Bradford *Telegraph and Argus* and the *Yorkshire Sports*, he became the agency man on Yorkshire's home grounds and for almost twenty years never missed a game.

WILSON, MAJOR CYRIL JOHN, who died suddenly on May 7, 1986, aged 86, was in the Eton XI in 1916, when he headed the batting averages, and in 1917, when he made 80 against Harrow, but he will be better remembered for his services to Greenjacket cricket. Apart from all the runs he made for them, he was for years their secretary.

WRIGHTSON, ROGER WILFRID, died at Whitehaven on September 13, 1986, aged 46. Born at Elsecar in Yorkshire, he played for Essex, where his father was a schoolmaster and where he had been brought up, in twelve matches as a left-handed batsman between 1965 and 1967. His highest score was 84 against Warwickshire at Clacton in 1965, when he batted for more than four hours and was top scorer in a total of 163. Later he played for Cumberland.

I ZINGARI RESULTS, 1986

Matches – 25: Won 10, Lost 5, Drawn 9, Abandoned 1.

May 3	Charterhouse School	Won by five wickets
May 10	Honourable Artillery Company	Lost by 33 runs
May 11	Sandhurst Wanderers	Won by 12 runs
May 18	Staff College, Camberley	Lost by five wickets
May 24	Eton Ramblers	Drawn
June 7	Hurlingham CC	Drawn
June 8	Lord Porchester's XI	Drawn
June 14	Eton College	Drawn
June 17	Winchester College	Drawn
June 21	Guards CC	Won by 108 runs
June 22	London New Zealand CC	Won by five wickets
June 28	Harrow School	Won by seven wickets
June 29	Lavinia, Duchess of Norfolk's XI	Drawn
July 5	Earl of Bessborough's XI	Drawn
July 6	Hagley CC	Drawn
July 12	Green Jackets Club	Won by one wicket
July 13	Rickling Green CC	Lost by two wickets
July 19	Bradfield Waifs	Lost by eight wickets
July 27	Royal Armoured Corps	Won by 113 runs
August 2	Band of Brothers	Won by nine wickets
August 3	R. Leigh-Pemberton's XI	Abandoned
August 9, 10	South Wales Hunts XI	Drawn
August 30	Hampshire Hogs	Lost by six wickets
August 31	J. H. Pawle's XI	Won by three wickets
September 7	Captain R. H. Hawkin's XI	Won by 128 runs

PAKISTAN v WEST INDIES, 1986-87

On the fourth day of the first Test, West Indies unexpectedly collapsed to the pace of Imran Khan and the spin of Abdul Qadir to suffer only their second defeat in 37 Tests since 1981-82, the other being by Australia in Sydney in 1984-85. However, they won the second Test comprehensively by an innings in three days to level the series, and the third Test was drawn.

First Test: At Faisalabad, October 24, 26, 27, 28, 29. Pakistan won by 186 runs. Pakistan 159 (Imran Khan 61; A. H. Gray four for 39) and 328 (Mohsin Khan 40, Qasim Omar 48, Salim Yousuf 61, Wasim Akram 66); West Indies 248 (D. L. Haynes 40, R. B. Richardson 54; Wasim Akram six for 91) and 53 (Imran Khan four for 30, Abdul Qadir six for 16).

Second Test: At Lahore, November 7, 8, 9. West Indies won by an innings and 10 runs. Pakistan 131 (Javed Miandad 46; M. D. Marshall five for 33) and 77 (C. A. Walsh four for 21); West Indies 218 (C. G. Greenidge 75, I. V. A. Richards 44; Imran Khan five for 59, Abdul Qadir four for 96).

Third Test: At Karachi, November 20, 21, 22, 24, 25. Drawn. West Indies 240 (R. B. Richardson 44, I. V. A. Richards 70; Abdul Qadir four for 107) and 211 (D. L. Haynes 88 not out; Imran Khan six for 46); Pakistan 239 (Ramiz Raja 62, Javed Miandad 76; C. G. Butts four for 73) and 125 for seven.

West Indies won the one-day international series 4-1, Pakistan preventing a clean sweep by winning the last match.

Full details of the West Indians' tour of Pakistan will appear in the 1988 edition of Wisden.

INDIA v AUSTRALIA, 1986-87

India and Australia featured in the second-ever tied Test when, with the scores level in the first Test at Madras, G. R. J. Matthews trapped Maninder Singh lbw with the fifth ball of the final over. The other Test to have been tied, also with just one ball remaining, was between Australia and West Indies at Brisbane in 1960-61. The second Test was ruined by rain, which restricted play to six and a half hours, and the third was also drawn, after both sides had compiled large first-innings totals. On the fourth day no wicket fell, for only the tenth time in Tests.

First Test: At Madras, September 18, 19, 20, 21, 22. Tied. Australia 574 for seven dec. (D. C. Boon 122, D. M. Jones 210, A. R. Border 106, G. R. J. Matthews 44; N. S. Yadav four for 142) and 170 for five dec. (D. C. Boon 49); India 397 (K. Srikkanth 53, M. Azharuddin 50, R. J. Shastri 62, Kapil Dev 119; G. R. J. Matthews five for 103) and 347 (S. M. Gavaskar 90, M. Amarnath 51, M. Azharuddin 42, R. J. Shastri 48 not out; G. R. J. Matthews five for 146, R. J. Bright four for 94).

Second Test: At Delhi, September 26, 27, 28, 29, 30. Drawn. Australia 207 for three dec. (D. C. Boon 67, T. J. Zoehrer 52 not out); India 107 for three.

Third Test: At Bombay, October 15, 16, 17, 18, 19. Drawn. Australia 345 (G. R. Marsh 101, D. C. Boon 47, A. R. Border 46; N. S. Yadav four for 84) and 216 for two (D. C. Boon 40, D. M. Jones 73 not out, A. R. Border 66 not out); India 517 for five dec. (S. M. Gavaskar 103, D. B. Vengsarkar 164 not out, R. J. Shastri 121 not out; G. R. J. Matthews four for 158).

India won the one-day international series 3-2. Rain prevented a result being achieved in the third of the six matches.

Full details of the Australians' tour of India will appear in the 1988 edition of Wisden.

INTERNATIONAL CRICKET CONFERENCE

On June 15, 1909, representatives of cricket in England, Australia and South Africa met at Lord's and founded the Imperial Cricket Conference. Membership was confined to the governing bodies of cricket in countries within the British Commonwealth where Test cricket was played. India, New Zealand and West Indies were elected as members on May 31, 1926, Pakistan on July 21, 1953, and Sri Lanka on July 21, 1981. South Africa ceased to be a member of the ICC on leaving the British Commonwealth in May, 1961.

On July 15, 1965, the Conference was renamed the International Cricket Conference and new rules were adopted to permit the election of countries from outside the British Commonwealth.

CONSTITUTION

Chairman: The President of MCC for the time being or his nominee.
Secretary: The Secretary of MCC.
Foundation members: United Kingdom and Australia.
Full members: India, New Zealand, West Indies, Pakistan and Sri Lanka.
Associate members*: Argentina (1974), Bangladesh (1977), Bermuda (1966), Canada (1968), Denmark (1966), East Africa (1966), Fiji (1965), Gibraltar (1969), Hong Kong (1969), Israel (1974), Kenya (1981), Malaysia (1967), Netherlands (1966), Papua New Guinea (1973), Singapore (1974), USA (1965), West Africa (1976) and Zimbabwe (1981).
Affiliate members*: Italy (1984), Switzerland (1985).
* *Year of election shown in parentheses.*

MEMBERSHIP

The following governing bodies for cricket shall be eligible for election.

Foundation Members: The governing bodies for cricket in the United Kingdom and Australia are known as Foundation Members, and while being Full Members of the Conference such governing bodies have certain additional rights as set out in the rules of the Conference.

Full Members: The governing body for cricket recognised by the Conference of a country, or countries associated for cricket purposes, of which the representative teams are accepted as qualified to play official Test matches.

Associate Members: The governing body for cricket recognised by the Conference of a country, or countries associated for cricket purposes, not qualifying as Full Members but where cricket is firmly established and organised.

Chairman: J. Buzaglo (*Gibraltar*). *Deputy Chairman:* K. R. Bullock (*Canada*). *Hon. Treasurer:* G. Davis (Israel).

TEST MATCHES

1. Duration of Test Matches

Within a maximum of 30 hours' playing time, the duration of Test matches shall be a matter for negotiation and agreement between the two countries in any particular series of Test matches.

When agreeing the Playing Conditions prior to the commencement of a Test series, the participating countries may:

    (a) Extend the playing hours of the last Test beyond the limit of 30 hours, in a series in which, at the conclusion of the penultimate match, one side does not hold a lead of more than one match.

    (b) Allow an extension of play by one hour on any of the first four days of a Test match, in the event of play being suspended for one hour or more on that day, owing to weather interference.

(c) Play on the rest day, conditions and circumstances permitting, should a full day's play be lost on either the second or third scheduled days of play.

(d) Make up time lost in excess of five minutes in each day's play owing to circumstances outside the game, other than acts of God.

Note. The umpires shall determine when such time shall be made up. This could, if conditions and circumstances permit, include the following day.

2. Qualification Rules

A cricketer is qualified to play in a Test match or one-day international either by birth or residence.

(a) Qualification by birth. A cricketer, unless debarred by the Conference, is always eligible to play for the country of his birth.

(b) Qualification by residence. A cricketer, unless debarred by the Conference, shall be eligible to play for any country in which he is residing and has been residing during the four immediately preceding years, provided that he has not played for the country of his birth during that period.

Note. Notwithstanding anything hereinbefore contained, any player who has once played in a Test match or one-day international for any country shall not afterwards be eligible to play in a Test match or one-day international against that country, without the consent of its governing body.

FIRST-CLASS MATCHES

1. Definitions

(a) A match of three or more days' duration between two sides of eleven players officially adjudged first-class shall be regarded as a first-class fixture.

(b) In the following Rules the term "governing body" is restricted to Foundation Members, Full Members and Associate Members of the conference.

2. Rules

(a) Foundation and Full Members of the ICC shall decide the status of matches of three or more days' duration played in their countries.

(b) In matches of three or more days' duration played in countries which are not Foundation Members or Full Members of the ICC:

   (i) If the visiting team comes from a country which is a Foundation or Full Member of the ICC, that country shall decide the status of matches.

   (ii) If the visiting team does not come from a country which is a Foundation or Full Member of the ICC, or is a Commonwealth team composed of players from different countries, the ICC shall decide the status of matches.

Notes

(a) Governing bodies agree that the interest of first-class cricket will be served by ensuring that first-class status is *not* accorded to any match in which one or other of the teams taking part cannot on a strict interpretation of the definition be adjudged first-class.

(b) In case of any disputes arising from these Rules, the Secretary of the ICC shall refer the matter for decision to the Conference, failing unanimous agreement by postal communication being reached.

3. First-class Status

The following matches shall be regarded as first-class, subject to the provisions of Definitions (a) being completely complied with:

(a) In the British Isles and Eire
The following matches of three or more days' duration shall automatically be considered first-class:

 (i) County Championship matches.
 (ii) Official representative tourist matches from Full Member countries unless specifically excluded.
 (iii) MCC v any first-class county.
 (iv) Oxford v Cambridge and either University against first-class counties.
 (v) Scotland v Ireland.

(b) In Australia
 (i) Sheffield Shield matches.
 (ii) Matches played by teams representing states of the Commonwealth of Australia between each other or against opponents adjudged first-class.

(c) In India
 (i) Ranji Trophy matches.
 (ii) Duleep Trophy matches.
 (iii) Irani Trophy matches.
 (iv) Matches played by teams representing state or regional associations affiliated to the Board of Control between each other or against opponents adjudged first-class.
 (v) All three-day matches played against representative visiting sides.

(d) In New Zealand
 (i) Shell Trophy matches.
 (ii) Matches played by teams representing major associations of the North and South Islands against opponents adjudged first-class.

(e) In Pakistan
 (i) Matches played by teams representing divisional associations affiliated to the Board of Control, between each other or against teams adjudged first-class.
 (ii) Matches between the divisional associations and the Universities past and present XI.
 (iii) Quaid-e-Azam Trophy matches.
 (iv) BCCP Trophy Tournament matches.
 (v) Pentangular Trophy Tournament matches.

(f) In Sri Lanka
 (i) Matches of three days or more against touring sides adjudged first-class.
    At the time of going to press details of domestic competitions with first-class status were not available.

(g) In West Indies
 (i) Matches played by teams representing Barbados, Guyana, Jamaica, Trinidad, the Windward Islands and the Leeward Islands, either for the Shell Shield or against other opponents adjudged first-class.
 (ii) The final of the inter-county tournament in Guyana between Berbice, Demerara and Essequibo.
 (iii) The Beaumont Cup match in Trinidad & Tobago.

(h) In all Foundation and Full Member countries represented on the Conference
 (i) Test matches and matches against teams adjudged first-class played by official touring teams.
 (ii) Official Test Trial matches.
 (iii) Special matches between teams adjudged first-class by the governing body or bodies concerned.

QUALIFICATION AND REGISTRATION

Regulations Governing the Qualification and Registration of Cricketers in Test and Competitive County Cricket

1. QUALIFICATIONS FOR ENGLAND

Subject to the overriding discretion of the Test and County Cricket Board, acting with the consent of the International Cricket Conference, the qualifications for playing for England shall be:

(a) That the cricketer was born in the British Isles; or

(b) That the cricketer's father or mother was born in the British Isles and that he himself is residing and has been resident therein during the preceding four consecutive years; or

(c) That the cricketer is residing and has been resident in the British Isles during the preceding ten consecutive years; or

(d) That the cricketer is residing and has been resident in the British Isles during the preceding four consecutive years and since the day before his fourteenth birthday.

All these qualifications apply only if the cricketer has not played for any other country in a Test match or (if the Board so decides) any other international match during the specified period of residence or in the case of (a) during the previous four years.

In the case of (b), if the cricketer has played first-class cricket in his country of origin before commencing his period of residence in the British Isles, the four-year period shall be increased to such number of years (not exceeding ten) as equals four years plus one year for each season of first-class cricket he played in his country of origin. In the case of (b) and (c), if, following the commencement of his period of residence in the British Isles, the cricketer plays first-class cricket in his country of origin (other than as an overseas cricketer in circumstances approved by the Board), then if previously qualified for England under (b) or (c) he shall cease to be so qualified. If he was in the course of acquiring residential qualification, his period of residence in the British Isles shall be treated as terminated, and a new period of residence will be required.

It is also required that the player shall have made a declaration in writing to the Board that it is his desire and intention to play for England and in (b), (c) and (d) that he shall be a British or Irish citizen.

2. QUALIFICATIONS FOR REGISTRATION FOR COMPETITIVE COUNTY CRICKET

(a) A cricketer qualified for England shall only be qualified for registration for:

    (i) The county of his birth.

    (ii) The county in which he is residing and has been resident for the previous twelve consecutive months.

    (iii) The county for which his father regularly played.

(b) In addition, a cricketer qualified for England shall be qualified for registration for a county if:

    (i) He has none of the above qualifications for any county and is not registered for one; or

    (ii) Although qualified for and/or registered by one or more counties, the county or counties concerned have confirmed in writing that they do not wish to register him or retain his registration.

This paragraph (b), however, will not permit registration of a player who has been under contract to a county for the previous season and has failed to accept the offer of a new contract for the new season. It does not prevent his application for a Special Registration.

3. REGISTRATION

Normally new registrations take place during the close season, but in exceptional circumstances a county may apply to register a player in the course of a season.

No cricketer may be registered for more than one county at any one time or, subject to the overriding discretion of the Board, for more than one county during any one season. However, this shall not prevent a player qualified to play for England, and already registered for a minor county, from being registered for a first-class county with the consent of the minor county concerned, who will not lose his registration.

Except with the Board's approval no county may have registered for it more than 35 cricketers at any one time.

4. SPECIAL REGISTRATION

The qualification for county cricket may be wholly or partially waived by the Board and a cricketer qualified to play for England may be "specially registered" should the Board conclude that it would be in the best interest of competitive county cricket as a whole. For this purpose the Board shall have regard to the interests of the cricketer concerned and any other material considerations affecting the county concerned including, if applicable, the cricketer's age and the other Special Registrations of the county in previous years.

No application for Special Registration will be entertained in respect of a cricketer who has a contract of employment with another county in the absence of that county's consent, except during the period between January 1 and the start of the new season, if the cricketer's contract is due to expire in that period.

5. CRICKETERS NOT QUALIFIED TO PLAY FOR ENGLAND

No county shall be entitled to play more than one unqualified cricketer in any competitive match, except where two unqualified cricketers were registered for the county on November 28, 1978 or if *bona fide* negotiations had been begun before that date and were completed before the 1979 season.

The player must have remained registered without a break and had a contract of employment with the county since the start of the 1979 season, except in any season during which he was a member of an official touring team to the British Isles.

Although there is no restriction on the number of unqualified cricketers who may be registered by a county, it is the Board's policy that in normal circumstances *not more than two unqualified cricketers should be registered by any one county.*

If a registered overseas player is invited to play for his country for the whole or part of a tour of the British Isles, his county must release him and, except with the prior consent of the Board, may not play him during that tour.

Note: A citizen of a country within the European Economic Community, although he is not qualified to play for England, is not regarded as an unqualified cricketer for the purposes of registration, provided he satisfies the requirements as set out in Regulation 1 (except that for "British Isles" read "EEC").

6. NEGOTIATIONS BETWEEN COUNTIES AND CRICKETERS

No county may approach or be involved in discussions with any unregistered cricketer who is not qualified for that county with a view to offering him a trial or registering him:

    (i) During the currency of a season without having given not less than fourteen days' previous notice in writing; or

    (ii) During the close season without having given notice in writing

to any county for which he is qualified for registration by virtue of birth or residence before making any such approach or engaging in any such discussions.

No county may approach or be involved in discussions with any cricketer under the age of sixteen on April 15 in the current year, unless the cricketer is qualified for registration by that county or is not qualified for registration by any other first-class county.

7. RESIDENCE

A player does not interrupt his qualifying period of residence by undertaking government service or occasional winter work for business reasons outside the county in which his residence is situated.

The qualifying period cannot run while the cricketer has a contract with or is registered by another county.

MAIN RULES AND PLAYING CONDITIONS
OF LIMITED-OVERS COMPETITIONS

The following rules, playing conditions and variations of the Laws of Cricket are common to all three county competitions – the Benson and Hedges Cup (55 overs a side), the NatWest Bank Trophy (60 overs) and the Refuge Assurance League (40 overs):

Status of Matches

Matches shall not be considered first-class.

Declarations

No declarations may be made at any time.

Restriction on Placement of Fieldsmen

At the instant of delivery a minimum of four fieldsmen (plus the bowler and wicket-keeper) must be within an area bounded by two semi-circles centred on each middle stump (each with a radius of 30 yards) and joined by a parallel line on each side of the pitch. In the event of an infringement, the square-leg umpire shall call "No-ball". The fielding circle should be marked by painted white "dots" at five-yard intervals.

Fieldsman Leaving the Field

In addition to Law 2.8, a player who suffers an injury caused by an external blow (e.g. not a pulled muscle) and has to leave the field for medical attention may bowl immediately on his return.

Mode of Delivery

No bowler may deliver the ball under-arm.

Limitation of Overs by Any One Bowler

No bowler may deliver more than one fifth of the allocated overs, except that where the total of overs is not divisible by five, an additional over shall be allowed to the minimum number of bowlers necessary to make up the balance.

Wide-ball – Judging a Wide

Umpires are instructed to apply a very strict and consistent interpretation in regard to the Law in order to prevent negative bowling wide of the wicket or over the batsman's head.

The following criteria should be adopted as a guide to umpires:

1. If the ball passes either side of the wicket sufficiently wide to make it virtually impossible for the striker to play a "normal cricket stroke" both from where he is standing and from where he should normally be standing at the crease, the umpire shall call and signal "Wide".

2. If the ball passes over head-height of the striker standing upright at the crease, the umpire shall call and signal "Wide".

Note: The above provisions do not apply if the striker makes contact with the ball.

The Bowling of Fast, Short-pitched Balls

A bowler shall be limited to one fast, short-pitched ball per over. If he bowls a second, the umpire shall call and signal "No ball". If the bowler is no-balled a second time in the innings for the same offence, the bowler shall be warned, and after a further offence he shall be taken off and not allowed to bowl again in the innings.

RULES COMMON TO THE BENSON AND HEDGES CUP AND THE NATWEST BANK TROPHY

The Result

1. *A Tie.*

In the event of a tie, the following shall apply:

    (i) The side taking the greater number of wickets shall be the winner.

    (ii) If both sides are all out, the side with the higher overall scoring-rate shall be the winner.

    (iii) If the result cannot be decided by either of the first two methods, the winner shall be the side with the higher rate after 30 overs or, if still equal, after twenty or, if still equal, after ten.

2. *Unfinished Match*

If a match remains unfinished after the allocated number of days, the winner shall be the side which has scored the faster in runs per over throughout the innings, provided that at least twenty overs have been bowled at the side batting second. If the scoring-rate is the same, the side losing fewer wickets in the first twenty overs of each innings shall be the winner.

If, however, at any time on the last day the umpires are satisfied that there is insufficient time remaining to achieve a definite result or, where applicable, for the side batting second to complete its maximum number of overs, they shall order a new match to be started, allowing an equal number of overs per side (minimum ten overs per side) bearing in mind the time remaining for play until scheduled close of play. In this event, team selection for the new match will be restricted to the eleven players and twelfth man originally chosen, unless authorised otherwise in advance by the Secretary of the Board. If, however, the team batting second has received twenty overs or more when the umpires decide that there is insufficient time remaining to achieve a definite result, the match shall not be resumed nor shall a new match be started.

In the event of no result being obtained within this rule, the captains should agree, if circumstances (outdoors or indoors) permit, to a bowling contest to achieve a result, five cricketers from each team to bowl overarm, two deliveries each, at three stumps at a distance of 22 yards. The team scoring the greater number of hits shall be the winner. If the scores are equal, the same cricketers will bowl one ball each alternately to achieve a result on a "sudden death" basis. If circumstances make this form of contest impossible, the match shall be decided by the toss of a coin, except in a Benson and Hedges zonal match which shall be declared to have "No Result".

3. *Over-rates*

All teams are expected to complete the bowling of their overs within an allotted playing time. In the event of their failing to do so, the full quota of overs will be completed but the fielding team will be fined £100 per over which it has failed to bowl in the allotted time. If the innings is limited in advance, the calculations will be revised accordingly.

RULES AND PLAYING CONDITIONS APPLYING ONLY TO THE BENSON AND HEDGES CUP

Duration of Play

The matches, of 55 overs per side, will be completed in one day, if possible, but two days will be allocated for zonal league matches and three days for knockout matches in case of weather interference. Matches started on Saturday but not completed may only be continued on Sunday with the approval of the Board.

Normal hours will be 11 a.m. to 7.00 p.m. The umpires may order extra time if they consider a finish can be obtained on any day.

Over-rates

The allotted playing-time for completing 55 overs is 3 hours, 25 minutes.

Intervals

Lunch 1.15-1.55. The tea interval in an uninterrupted match will be taken at 4.30 or after 35 overs of the innings of the side batting second, whichever is the later. In a match which has had a delayed start or which is unlikely to be finished in a day, the tea interval will be at 4.30.

Qualification of Players

The University qualification will take precedence in respect of those players who are also qualified for county clubs and no cricketer may play for more than one team in the same year's competition.

Scoring System

In the zonal league matches the winning team scores two points. In a "no result" match each side scores one point.

    If two or more teams in any zone finish with an equal number of points, their position in the table shall be based on the faster rate of taking wickets in all zonal league matches. This is calculated by total balls bowled, divided by wickets taken.

RULES AND PLAYING CONDITIONS APPLYING ONLY TO THE NATWEST BANK TROPHY

Duration and hours of play

The matches, of 60 overs per side, will be completed in one day, if possible, but three days will be allocated in case of weather interference.

    Cup Final only: If the match starts not less than half an hour late, owing to weather or the state of the ground, and not more than one and a half hours late, each innings shall be limited to 50 overs. If, however, the start is delayed for more than one and a half hours, the 60-over limit shall apply.

    Normal hours will be 10.30 a.m. to 7.10 p.m. The umpires may order extra time if, in their opinion, a finish can be obtained on any day.

    The captains of the teams in the final shall be warned that heavy shadows may move across the pitch towards the end of the day and that no appeal against the light will be considered in such circumstances.

Over-rates

The allotted playing-time for completing 60 overs is 3 hours, 45 minutes.

RULES AND PLAYING CONDITIONS APPLYING ONLY TO THE REFUGE ASSURANCE LEAGUE

Hours of play

Normal hours of play shall be 2.00-7.00 p.m. (1.30-6.30 for televised matches) with a tea interval of twenty minutes at the end of the over in progress at 4.20 p.m. (3.50 for televised matches), or between innings, whichever is the earlier. The duration and time of the tea interval can be varied in the case of an interrupted match. Close of play shall normally be at 7.00 p.m. (6.30 for televised matches) but play may continue after that time if, in the opinion of the umpires, the overs remaining can be completed by 7.10 p.m. (6.40 p.m.)

Length of Innings

  (i) In an uninterrupted match:

    (a) Each side shall bat for 40 overs unless all out earlier.

    (b) If the side fielding first fails to bowl 40 overs by 4.20 p.m. (3.50 for televised matches), the over shall be completed and the side batting second shall receive the same number of overs as their opponents.

    (c) If the team batting first is all out within two minutes of the scheduled time for the tea interval, the innings of the side batting second shall be limited to the same number of overs as their opponents have received, the over in which the last wicket falls to count as a complete over.

(ii) In matches where the start is delayed or play is suspended so:

    (a) The object shall be to rearrange the number of overs so that both teams may receive the same number of overs (minimum ten each). The calculation of the overs to be bowled shall be based on an average rate of one over per 3½ minutes or part thereof in the time remaining before 7.00 p.m. (6.30 p.m. for televised matches).

    (b) If the start is delayed by not more than an hour and the match is thereby reduced to no fewer than 31 overs a side, the time of the close of the first innings shall be fixed allowing 3½ minutes for each over. If the team fielding first fails to bowl the revised number of overs by the agreed time, the principles set out in (i) b and c shall apply.

    (c) Where play is suspended after the match has started on the basis of each team batting for more than twenty overs, the number of overs should be rearranged so that both teams may bat for the same number of overs (minimum of 20 each); the calculation as above.

    (d) If, owing to a suspension of play during or immediately prior to the start of the innings of the team batting second, it is not possible for that team to have the opportunity of batting for the same number of overs (minimum 20 overs) as their opponents, they will bat for a number of overs to be calculated as above. The team batting second shall not bat for a greater number of overs than their opponents unless the latter have been all out in fewer than the agreed number of overs.

    (e) If there is insufficient time to provide for a match as above (20 overs minimum), that match shall be void and, conditions permitting, a new match of ten overs each side shall be played provided play begins no later than 5.40 p.m. (5.10 for televised matches). If there is any suspension of play during the ten-overs match, it will be abandoned as a "No result".

Over-rates

In uninterrupted matches or matches of not less than 31 overs per team, which are not subsequently interrupted, the team fielding first will be fined £100 for each over below the full quota bowled by the scheduled time for the tea interval and the team fielding second for each over below the full quota bowled by the scheduled time for the close of play. In matches of less than 31 overs, or in the event of interruptions after the start of play, teams will be expected to achieve a rate of eighteen overs per hour but no automatic fine will be imposed.

The Result

    (i) Where both sides have had the opportunity to bat for the same number of overs and the scores are level, the result is a tie, no account being taken of the number of wickets which have fallen.

    (ii) If, owing to suspension of play, the number of overs in the innings of the side batting second has to be revised, their target score, which they must exceed to win the match, shall be calculated by multiplying the revised number of overs by the average runs per over scored by the side batting first. If the target score involves a fraction, the final scores cannot be equal and the result cannot be a tie.

    (iii) If a match is abandoned before the side batting second has received its allotted number of overs, the result shall be decided on the average run-rate throughout both innings, provided the team batting second has received not less than twenty overs.

    (iv) If a result cannot be achieved as above, the match shall be declared "No result".

    (v) If the team batting first has been all out without using its full quota of overs, the calculation of the run-rate shall be based on the full quota of overs to which it was entitled.

Scoring of points

    (i) The team winning a match to score four points.

    (ii) In a "tie" each team to score two points.

    (iii) In a "No Result" match each team to score two points.

    (iv) If two or more teams finish with an equal number of points for any of the first four places, their final positions will be decided by:

        (a) The most wins or, if still equal

        (b) The most away wins or, if still equal

        (c) The higher run-rate throughout the season.

MEETINGS IN 1986

TCCB SPRING MEETING

At its Spring Meeting, held at Lord's on March 6, the TCCB considered the findings of the enquiry into the standards of English cricket, which was chaired by C. H. Palmer, rejected a return to uncovered pitches and proposed an amendment to the Law relating to dangerous bowling. The proposal, to be presented to the ICC meeting in July, aimed at removing from the umpires the responsibility of deciding whether bouncers were aimed at intimidating batsmen, and suggested that Law 42.8 should start: "The bowling of short-pitched balls is unfair if, in the opinion of the umpire at the bowler's end, they are either frequent or by their length, line or height are likely to inflict physical injury on the striker standing upright at the crease. The relative skill of the striker shall be taken into consideration . . . ." The ICC would also be given a report of the circumstances under which Bangladesh and Zimbabwe refused to accept the England B team during the previous winter, and the ICC would be asked to consider the position of both countries in the light of ICC's agreement that countries should not interfere with the selection of visiting sides.

The meeting rejected by nine votes to six, with four abstentions, a return to uncovered pitches as recommended by the Palmer Report. It was decided to defer other proposals made by the Report until later in the year. It was also decided that, when the weather prevented a result in the NatWest Bank Trophy and knockout stages of the Benson and Hedges Cup, where possible the game should be decided by a bowling competition involving five players from either side bowling two balls each at a set of stumps. Should such a contest be impossible, the match would be decided by the toss of a coin. F. J. Titmus, who played 53 times for England, was appointed an England selector, to join P. B. H. May (chairman), P. J. Sharpe and A. C. Smith, following the retirement of A. V. Bedser, who had been a selector since 1962. An application by A. I. Kallicharran to be regarded as "English qualified" was rejected: having appeared in a Test for West Indies in 1980, he would have to wait until 1990.

TCCB EXECUTIVE COMMITTEE

A special meeting of the Executive Committee of the TCCB was convened at Lord's on May 19, following the admission by I. T. Botham in *The Mail on Sunday* the previous day that he had been a casual user of the drug marijuana, or cannabis, since the age of eighteen. As a result of this meeting, Botham was omitted from the England squad, announced the previous day, to play against India in the two Texaco Trophy internationals and it was decided that he would not be selected again until investigations into his drug-taking had been completed.

TCCB DISCIPLINE COMMITTEE

At a meeting of the Discipline Committee of the TCCB at Lord's on May 29, which lasted for almost seven hours, I. T. Botham faced charges of bringing the game into disrepute since becoming an England cricketer by: a) using cannabis; b) admitting to using cannabis; c) denying in the past that he had used cannabis; d) making public pronouncements without the clearance of his county. Finding Botham guilty on charges b, c, and d, the committee suspended him from all first-class cricket until and including July 31. The committee also requested a meeting with the chairman of the TCCB's Overseas Tours Committee, D. J. Insole, and the chairman of selectors, P. B. H. May, to discuss discipline on England tours. The Discipline Committee comprised P. Bromage (chairman), Dr A. Burnett, S. Cama, A. Cawdry, W. Craven, E. Crush, D. A. Graveney, J. K. Graveney and A. E. Moss.

CRICKET COUNCIL APPEALS COMMITTEE

The Appeals Committee of the Cricket Council met at Lord's on June 12 to consider an appeal from I. T. Botham against the suspension imposed by the TCCB Discipline Committee. Botham's claim that the suspension was unfair was argued by Mr Robert Alexander, QC. After a hearing of approximately five and a half hours, the committee, chaired by Mr Desmond Perrett, QC, upheld the suspension.

INTERNATIONAL CRICKET CONFERENCE

At the Annual Meeting of the International Cricket Conference, held at Lord's on July 9, 10, a decision was taken to reduce the matches of the 1987 World Cup from 60 to 50 overs a side in the hope that they might be completed in one day, even though two days would be set aside for each game. India and Pakistan, the member countries staging the World Cup, were asked to ensure that they were aware of any political problems. The Conference drew to the attention of members its earlier statement that outside interference in the selection of national teams would not be tolerated. However, no action was taken against Bangladesh and Zimbabwe following the refusal of these countries to accept the England B team because it contained cricketers who had played in South Africa, the Conference accepting their explanation that the restriction was imposed by their governments. No decision was reached on the matters of short-pitched bowling and over-rates in Test cricket. The TCCB's proposal (see TCCB Spring Meeting) was not thought likely to provide a satisfactory answer in the long term, while an Australian proposal to ban the bouncer altogether was considered to be too drastic as it would penalise the bowler who uses it as a legitimate method of attack and also as it would make the game too uniform. Instead, it was agreed that the ICC would send a letter to all governing bodies, to be forwarded to all first-class umpires, stressing that they would have the strongest backing for a strict interpretation of Law 42.8. Australia's suggestion that floodlights be used to complete a day's play in a Test match interrupted by bad light was also left unresolved.

TCCB SUMMER MEETING

At its Summer Meeting, held at Lord's on August 1, the TCCB discussed the management of England teams in the light of the manager's report of the previous winter's tour to the West Indies. While agreeing that there were deficiencies in the planning and execution of the tour, the Board accepted the report, the contents of which would not be made public. So that future tours would be better organised, the Board drew up Terms of Reference for the position of assistant manager, giving emphasis to players' fitness, practice facilities and day-to-day discipline. The assistant manager would be a selector on tour. The Board also agreed to review the role of the assistant manager at its Spring Meeting in 1987 with a view to the appointment continuing, possibly with a change of title, during the English season. It was felt that it was not right for cricket in England that one man should have full control of the England team. P. M. Lush was appointed manager, M. J. Stewart assistant manager, and M. W. Gatting captain of the England team to Australia in 1986-87.

The Board heard that a resolution might be put to the 1987 meeting of ICC, defining sporting contacts with South Africa more precisely and stipulating that players who, after a certain date, continued to have sporting links with South Africa would not be eligible to play Test cricket.

TCCB WINTER MEETING

At its Winter Meeting, held at Lord's on December 11, the TCCB discussed the restructuring of county cricket for the 1988 season and beyond. The Board agreed that, for the first time, four-day matches would be played in the County Championship, the counties voting by fifteen to two for a programme of six four-day and sixteen three-day matches in preference to one of eight four-day and sixteen three-day games, as recommended by the Palmer Report, or to retaining the present system. The new-style Championship would be tried for at least three seasons and it was expected that the four-day games would be played at the beginning and at the end of the season, so as not to clash with the one-day competitions. No decision was taken as to how bonus points, if any, would be awarded. The meeting decided also that there would be no quarter-finals in the league cup competition, the winners of the four zones becoming the semi-finalists [Benson and Hedges' existing sponsorship expires in 1987]; and it was confirmed that at the end of the season there would be a knockout competition involving the top four teams in the Refuge Assurance Sunday League, the semi-finals to be played in mid-week and the final, for the Refuge Assurance Cup, on a Sunday at a Test match ground. From the 1987 season, cricketers from all universities, and not just Oxford and Cambridge, would be eligible for the Combined Universities team in the Benson and Hedges Cup.

It was agreed that the TCCB would propose to the Annual Meeting of the ICC in 1987 that bouncers should be restricted to one per over, with a bowler receiving only one warning, and that from 1989 bowlers' run-ups should be limited to 30 yards.

THE CRICKETERS' ASSOCIATION

The Cricketers' Association was formed in 1968, to work with the Test and County Cricket Board for the overall good of first-class cricket and its players. Membership is not compulsory, though the large majority of registered first-class cricketers are members. Players' views are communicated to the TCCB through representation on the Registration, Cricket and Discipline sub-committees.

Officers, 1986-87

President: J. Arlott.

Chairman: G. Cook (Northamptonshire).

Treasurer: D. A. Graveney (Gloucestershire).

Secretary: J. D. Bannister,
1a Pargeter Street, Walsall,
Staffordshire W5 8RP
(Telephone: 0922-27164/27669).

In 1986, the Executive committee concentrated on improving insurance cover for the Association's 355 members. It was decided to provide, free of charge to members, cover against a player being forced to retire from first-class cricket prematurely because of injury or illness. Sums varying from £2,500 to £10,000 were insured, with the higher amounts available to the younger players.

Minimum wage scales were negotiated for the 1987 season, with the new basic figure for a capped player rising to £8,000. More players than not will receive in excess of this figure, which in all cases will be supplemented by sponsors' prizemonies and awards. Additionally, $5\frac{1}{2}\%$ of each player's salary – after he has been on a county staff for two years – is paid by his club into a Group Retirement scheme, jointly administered by representative trustees from the Association and the TCCB.

Of great concern to the Association is the threatened proposal to come before the ICC in July this year. This would make ineligible for Test cricket any player who coaches or plays cricket as an individual in South Africa. The Reg Hayter award for the Cricketers' Cricketer of the Year, voted for by county cricketers who had one vote for a player of their own club and a second for a player from another club, was won in 1986 by C. A. Walsh.

CRICKET BOOKS, 1986

By JOHN ARLOTT

This has been a quite outstanding year for cricket writing in general and for anthologies in particular. Indeed, it is not possible to record a finer year's output. A total of 71 titles has been submitted, and it is difficult to escape the conclusion that the entire standard of writing on the game has risen in the 26 years of this notice. That comment applies to virtually every department of cricket-book writing from appreciation to the hardest of statistics.

Barclays World of Cricket (Collins Willow; £25) is the third edition of this heavyweight work, revised to coincide with the bicentenary of MCC. E. W. Swanton continues as General Editor with George Plumptre as Editor and John Woodcock as Consultant Editor; and once again these three have combined to produce an encyclopaedia at once authoritative and written with a distinction unusual in a reference book. They are joined in this instance by Robert Brooke as statistician. There has been some judicious concentration since the last – 1980 – version; nevertheless there is an increase of 64 pages and of another 50 illustrations. The result is a handsome and generous survey, coverage and history of the game. It will be difficult for anyone to match, leave alone excel, this highly expert study with its wide range of authoritative writers.

Starting with Grace: A Pictorial Celebration of Cricket 1864-1986 (Stanley Paul; £14.95), by Bob Willis and Patrick Murphy, has been compiled with the collaboration of the BBC Hulton Picture Library, the major source of cricket pictures. It is indeed a pictorial celebration; it does not attempt to be a history – that will come from another source – but it is immensely revealing and absorbing. It is not concerned merely with photographs of cricketers in action nor with portraits of them, for again and again the photographs capture character. The starting date of 1864 saw the legalisation of round-arm bowling and, equally historically significant, the first-class début of W. G. Grace. The text is both perceptive and revealing, both technically sound and witty. The triumph, however, lies in the pictures. Technically they also are often interesting, but they are above all human and absorbing. Whether you want Denis Compton happily dancing with Anna Neagle, or the same man with Ted Dexter and Gary Sobers almost desperately watching a horse race on television, or a colourful picture of Sri Lanka's inaugural Test match with England, these illustrations are intriguing, entertaining and completely delightful.

In *Cricket* (Allison & Busby; £14.95), C. L. R. James has met the long-standing demand for more of his cricket-writing. His first book, *Beyond a Boundary*, was accepted as the new, modern, classic of the game. This is a gathering of 85 of his essays and letters since then. Some may be disappointed that this is not the major, unified work its predecessor was. It has, though, the same clarity, humanity, perception, technical appreciation and personal-isation. It is, too, important that the letters, though personally addressed, do round off, in his instinctively logical fashion, the arguments of his other writings. Above all, though, it has that lucidity which illuminated the first book. "Cricketers already mature when Bradman appeared might want to play like Bradman. They couldn't. They hadn't the outlook. They hadn't the temper. They had inhibitions Bradman never knew." No-one else has written on cricket with such a combination of simplicity of style and yet profundity of thought as Mr James exhibits. He has a superb sense of historic perspective and cricket should be grateful to him. If this book is not all it might have been, it is almost certainly better than any other contemporary cricket writer could have produced: a contemplative pleasure to read.

England v Australia: Test Match Records 1877-1985 (Collins Willow; £6.95), edited by David Frith, is a paper-bound, 256-page book of scores and records. It should be noted, though, that Mr Frith takes the term "Test Match" quite literally as meaning international matches played between England and Australia. With a foot in both camps and having already written a substantial pictorial history of those games, he was adequately fitted for this task, which is almost purely analytical. That is to say, he does not give full scores but provides detailed figures of all other relevant facts about those games. It bears the look of a standard work.

Cricket's Unforgettable Cliff-hangers (Jaico Books, 121 Mahatma Gandhi Road, Bombay-400 038; Rs15.00), by J. K. Colabawalla, is a 160-page paperback. The author describes himself as an avid cricket fan; he has followed the game for more than seventeen years, has passed the written examination of the Bombay Cricket Association, and has presented sports programmes for All-India Radio. His subjects are six closely contested cricket matches; with some lesser-known statistics, and wit in cricket.

Gents & Players (Robson Books; £8.95), by Frank Keating, includes cricket among its subjects but is, as usual, concerned with the whole field of sport, sports writing and sports thinking. Mr Keating, despite his heavy journalistic commitment, retains enthusiasm for the subject and freshness in his writing. He deals with both play and players: football – rugby and soccer – tennis, golf, grouse shooting, or the race-track, the great modern figures in sport and some from yesterday. He is readable and relishable on the highest level of sports writing.

In *A Season for All Men* (The Book Guild Ltd, Lewes, Sussex; £8.50), E. Valentine Joyce picks five great cricket seasons to study, enjoy and analyse. They are 1902, 1928, 1938, 1947 and 1955. They are all, in their different ways, quite epic English summers; nostalgic either through reading or actual watching; for no-one, surely, remembers such a range of seasons. Of the many tempting samples, one is irresistible. In Cheltenham Week of 1928 Wally Hammond had, even for such a great all-rounder, an amazing period. Gloucestershire beat both Surrey and Worcestershire and Mr Joyce observes that "Hammond the all-rounder came splendidly into his own; after such a week, who would have denied his right to the mantle of England's newest champion? 362 runs, 16 wickets and 13 catches – not a bad return for a five-day week. Short of taking the gloves for a spell, it is difficult to see what more he could have done. If it was not quite Hammond's season, this surely was his week." The book closes with 37 utterly nostalgic photo reproductions of cigarette cards of England and Australian cricketers of the 1930s.

The Boundary Book Second Innings (Pelham Books; £14.95), compiled and edited by Leslie Frewin, which indexes 147 printed items, contains nine cartoons and is decorated by some quite distinguished line drawings, is a most splendid collection. A fold-over announces "every copy sold helps to buy a Lord's Taverners New Horizons minibus for disabled children". The contributions by famous cricketers and writers past and present make this a superb gift book, and as such its price is reasonable, for it is doubtful if a better collection could be made.

Quick Singles: Memories of Summer Days & Cricket Heroes (Dent; £8.95), edited by Christopher Martin-Jenkins and Mike Seabrook ("past contributor to *The Cricketer* and erstwhile player of unfulfilled promise"), is a book of cricket delights: 33 essays and memories by cricket enthusiasts who are neither professional cricket writers nor, with the single exception of Peter Gibbs, practising cricket technicians. Its list of contributors alone proves convincing: Bob Hawke, Prime Minister of Australia; Paul Jennings, Lord Home of the Hirsel, Roy Hattersley, Barry Norman, Lawrence Durrell, Tim Rice, William Deedes, Brian Redhead, Brian Boothroyd, John Fowles. It is a most formidable batting order. Neither does it disappoint.

The Character of Cricket (Pavilion/Michael Joseph; £12.95), by Tim Heald, is a novel, cricketing joy. The idea of a cricket book not concerned with actual play sounded potentially pedestrian. This is, though, in Mr Heald's own words, "The entire experience of visiting each ground with an eye for the detail that the busy match reporter takes for granted: the Fuller Pilch memorial; the loos at the Vauxhall End; P. G. Wodehouse's tie; the British Telecom tent . . . conversations with the kind of people who give the game its backbone." There are strange stories, unexpected people, quotations from a Betjeman poem and another by John Clare. Perhaps the most striking quality about the book is provided by the illustrations of Paul Cox; totally novel, human and evocative. The people are right, the places are right. These pictures have been drawn by a man who knows his cricket and his cricketers and they do the author proud.

After Stumps Were Drawn (Collins; £8.95), selected by Jack Pollard, with a foreword by Sir Donald Bradman, is described simply as "The best of Ray Robinson's cricket writing". It is a collection of work by a man who was painstaking, prolific and much respected. Ray Robinson was a profound note-taker who, by his precision and care for facts, built up some of the finest and most complete cricket writing ever produced. He was studious, generous, and he cared deeply for cricket, which he served both modestly and superbly. This is a book which should be on every cricket reader's shelves.

Beyond the Far Pavilions (Pavilion/Michael Joseph; £10.95), by Leo Cooper and Allen Synge, is a most impressive collection of cricketing minutiae. It covers the globe from a Hertfordshire prep school to the Arizona Desert by way of Finland and Corfu. It is surprising, diverting and, simultaneously, scholarly. The compilers have been conscientious, with a taste for cricket, a nose for the unusual and a sense of humour which never debases their subject.

Wet Wickets and Dusty Balls: A Diary of a Cricketing Year (Hamish Hamilton; £9.95), by Ian Miller, is a domestic comedy, full of domesticity and finding comedy in Netherpopham and Mugsborough with unerring precision. At the end Patel helps Elizabeth to choose her birthday present to the author. "It was a polyplastic Duncan Fearnley, the right length too."

A Guide to First-Class Cricket Matches Played in India (Association of Cricket Statisticians, Haughton Mill, Retford, Nottinghamshire) is yet another title in the encyclopaedic output of the Association. Its 208 closely printed octavo pages cover "All cricket matches played on the Indian Sub-Continent, except for matches in Ceylon/Sri Lanka and, since July 1947, in Pakistan and Bangladesh".

A Maidan View (Allen & Unwin; £11.95), by Mihir Bose, is sub-titled "The Magic of Indian Cricket". The author, though, has not been prepared, like some, to fall back on the word "Magic" to explain all. Indeed, he is at pains to make the great attempt at the impossible – to place cricket in Indian

culture from its haphazard introduction by the British, through its adoption by the Indian princes and on to the present day. He makes it clear that cricket is not, in fact, the most popular sport in India; but he is concerned to place it and its heroes in that society and to define the Maidan – the cricketing oval of the urban environment. This is the boldest attempt yet to describe Indian cricket as viewed from the outside – but from the immediate outside, not from a distance. It should be read by everybody concerned with the social setting of cricket wherever it is played.

The literature and history of Indian cricket grow steadily. Therefore the centenary of the first Parsee cricketers' tour of England – in 1886 – has been marked with two books. Vasant Raiji is the author of *India's Hambledon Men* (Tyeby Press, Thakkar Estate, 20 Chapsi Bhimji Road, Mazgaon, Bombay-400 010; Rs50 or £5), which has a foreword by Dom Moraes. A painstaking history, it also traces the doings of subsequent Parsee teams; of G. F. Vernon's, Lord Hawke's and Oxford University Authentics' tours in India between 1889 and 1903; Presidency matches 1892-1906 and some historic scorecards involving Parsees, especially in their matches with the Europeans in India. The 156 pages have been most thoroughly and carefully collected and arranged.

Parsee Cricket Centenary – 1886-1986 (from the author, 3 Dallas Place, St Ives, NSW 2075, Australia; £1), by Kersi Meher-Homji, has been issued in a limited edition of 130 copies. Kersi Meher-Homji is himself a practising cricketer, now living in Australia, who states: "The booklet is neither a 'Who's Who' nor a history of Parsee cricket. It is just an interesting collection." He goes on: "This booklet attempts to pay tribute to the never-say-die Parsee cricketers from Dr Dhunjishah Patel, the captain of the pioneering team of 1886 to England, P. D. Kanga, Dr Mehelashah Pavri and K. M. Mistry, to the more recent heroes; Polly Umrigar, Rusi Modi, Nari Contractor, Rusi Surti, Farokh Engineer." It is an interesting sidelight with a quite unexpected Australian angle.

India is the setting, also, for another of the year's fiction contributions, the novel, *Slow Turn* (Michael Joseph; £9.95), by Mike Marqusee. The author is a freelance writer and a keen amateur cricketer who lives in North London. This is his first novel. It is a thriller about "a makeshift team of has-beens from English county cricket" who tour India. They arrive in Madras to find that one of the tour umpires has been murdered. From that point the thriller develops against the background of Indian life, politics and cricket.

Derbyshire Bowlers (J. H. Hall & Sons Ltd, Siddals Road, Derby, DE1 2PZ; £2.50), by John Shawcroft, is the latest title in the "Derbyshire Heritage Series". It is a 56-page octavo on an epic cricketing subject. Quoting Wilf Taylor, who was associated with the county club, eventually as secretary, for more than 70 years, "It was always a fight but invariably our bowlers saw us through". The story runs from the Mycroft era through those mighty bowlers of pace to Paul Newman and Martin Jean-Jacques.

The History of Kent County Cricket, Appendix "I" 1964-1984 (Kent County Cricket Club; £6) keeps up to date the most voluminous of county cricket histories which began with Lord Harris's first publication of 1907 (which included appendices A to D). This is the fifth of the supplements which maintain that stately progress.

Yorkshire Cricketers 1863-1985 (The Association of Cricket Statisticians, Haughton Mill, Retford, Nottinghamshire; £2.25) is a 47-page quarto in the now established format of this scholarly and exhaustive series. It is sufficient to say that it takes its place rightfully and ought to satisfy Yorkshiremen.

The History of Lascelles Hall Cricket Club: a Famous Nursery of Yorkshire Cricket 1825-1968 (Lascelles Hall CC; no price given) is a 34-page octavo giving a potted history of a most historic club reverberant with epic names from Joe Ambler to John Thewlis. It might have run to many more pages without tiring the enthusiasts or even the poets of pages 16 and 21; but leaving the last word to Ephraim Lockwood on his first sight of Niagara Falls, "If this is Niagara, then give me Lascelles Hall".

Rawtenstall Cricket Club 1886-1986 (from Brian Manning, 205 Haslingden Old Road, Rawtenstall; £2.50) is a 48-page quarto, generously illustrated; a centenary brochure for yet another of those sturdy Lancashire clubs which have played such a part in the county's history. There is no more impressive dip into its history than that which reveals S. F. Barnes as its professional from 1931 to 1933; even the considerable names that follow cannot dim that eminence. It is a happily readable record.

Grass Roots (South Shields CC; no price given), by Clive Crickmer, is a history of South Shields Cricket Club 1850-1984; and has a foreword by Colin Milburn. It is a remarkably generous, well-illustrated and produced 358-page octavo which makes it unusually large in the field of club histories. Both the author and the illustrator ensure, too, that it is not without humour, and it is warm with the fellowship of the game in that part of the north-east.

A History of Cricket at Reading School (Reading School; no price given) celebrates the school's quincentenary and the 60th anniversary of the Old Redingensians CC. It is a most pleasantly made 80-page octavo with all the statistics and an essay on "My Schooldays" by the school's most eminent cricketer, H. E. ("Tom") Dollery.

Queensland versus Victoria: A Statistical Survey (available in England from Appleby's Books, 5 St John's Street, Keswick, Cumbria; £5.25: or from Roger Page, 55 Tarcoola Drive, Yallambie, Victoria, Australia \$A10.50), by John King, is the fifth of his statistical histories of series of first-class matches between Australian states. A 44-page quarto, it is, as usual, cyclostyled, workmanlike, and thorough.

L.B.W. – Laughter Before Wicket (Allen & Unwin; £10.95) is edited by Peter Haining, who describes it as "100 years of humorous cricket short stories". It is important to notice that they are in general humorous but do not attempt to be funny. Once more not all the authors are experts in the field of cricket. For instance, J. M. Barrie, Anthony Trollope, Sir Arthur Conan Doyle and E. W. Hornung all made their reputations away from the game; though there are several who did not. Just a few of the stories are well worn; others are not. For instance, Ian Hay, Stephen Leacock and Leslie Thomas are not generally known as cricket humorists. Without, however, making over-fine distinctions about humour and cricket, this is 315 pages of satisfying read for the cricketer and it is decorated with some delightfully amusing drawings by an artist who deserves more credit than he is granted.

Seasons Past (Stanley Paul; £16.95), edited by Christopher Martin-Jenkins, is a collection of diaries from *The Cricketer*, covering nineteen seasons from 1967 to 1985 by five of their contributors, including Alan Gibson, Tony Lewis, Mike Brearley and Peter Roebuck. Photographic illustrations – a few in colour – provide pleasant decoration but the text is likely to prove more satisfying to most readers.

Summer of Suspense (Partridge Press; £10.95) is yet another of Patrick Eagar's books of cricket photographs. It is a book possible only from a photographer who watches so closely that he misses no worthwhile moment in a match. He enjoys it; he keeps the camera trained on the action; and he catches it in the key moment. With some of the photographs in this book he won the Benson and Hedges Sport Photographer's Portfolio Award for 1986. The text is again by Alan Ross: lively, informative and a perfect complement to the photographs. Mr Eagar has virtually created a fresh significance and standard of cricket photography: it is both alive and a pleasure. His publisher and printer have lived up to the challenge.

Cricket Rebels (QB Books, Horwitz Grahame Books Ltd, 506 Miller Street, Cammeray, Sydney, NSW 2062, Australia; $A5.95), by Chris Harte and Warwick Hadfield, is an account of the "rebel" tour of South Africa in 1985-86 by Australian cricketers under Kim Hughes. A 174-page paperback quarto, it is quite unlike any other cricket tour book ever written. Among its sixteen pages of photographs and photo-reproductions is one of Kim Hughes's hand-written statement of·resignation from the Australian Test captaincy. There are careful biographical sketches of the players involved, but such chapter headings as "Gleneagles and legal eagles", "Rebels in revolt", "A Barrage of writs" and "Legal tangles", as well as appendices of a letter to Mr Hawke and an ACB player contract, emphasise the unusual content, form and theme of a book which deserves a place in the files of cricket's history as something less than a happy record.

Reflections (Weston Creek CC, 14 Hyndes Crescent, Holder, ACT 2611, Australia; no price given) is a 48-page octavo on the Weston Creek (Australia) tour of England in August 1985. The account gives full scores and provides a story of enjoyment, humour and good comradeship.

India's Tour of Australia 1985-86 (Al-Faisel Publications, 1433 Qasimjan Street, Delhi-110 006;˙5/-), by S. Pervez Qaiser, is a souvenir-type 32-page publication with portraits and potted biographies of the players and skeleton records of previous tours.

In *Wickets, Catches and the Odd Run* (Collins Willow; £9.95), Trevor Bailey shows not only his technical observation and understanding of cricket but his sense of humour and his relish for its better anecdotes. Among the aspects of his success were his knowledge and appreciation of his opponents as well as his colleagues. Here he goes back to his accomplished schooldays at Dulwich and his service in the Royal Marines, and then follows to his first-class cricket and on down to today, when he is a respected commentator and correspondent. He is both a relisher and relishable so far as cricket is concerned. The theme of his book is appreciation carried through to enjoyment.

Ian Botham is the central figure of two books. The first, *High Wide and Handsome* (Collins Willow; £10.95), is subtitled "The story of a very special year" and is by Frank Keating. It is concerned with the season of 1985 which, he says, "Even by his own glittering standards was a dazzling one for Ian Botham". If this is largely an admiring account, for his subject moves the author to much enthusiasm, it is also perceptive and the superlatives are given intelligent endorsement in quotations of men whose opinions must be respected. It is, too, as one would expect from Mr Keating, an exhilarating read which will give pleasure to readers in years to come who have never known either the subject or the author. *It Sort of Clicks* (Collins Willow; £9.95) is credited to "Ian Botham talking to Peter Roebuck". It is an

understanding portrait, drawn in the days before late 1986 while the two were still teammates sharing a mutual respect. It blends Botham's opinions with Roebuck's against the background of Somerset county cricket in modern times. The combination is sometimes perfect; on other occasions at odds. It is revealing on the subject of their opponents and their colleagues, and it analyses many attitudes, including that between Botham and the press. At one point Roebuck writes, "A few years ago Ian Botham was fat, a fact he was able to hide from himself until he saw some photos". At another point, though, he says: "No, for all Botham's flaws, he stands alone as an all-rounder, to the supreme irritation of those of solemn attitude." The whole is made the more intriguing by subsequent developments in the relationship between the two.

Greg Chappell (Collins; £9.95) is the authorised biography, by an Australian feature writer, of that country's outstanding batsman in recent years. The subject's towering statistical records are duly presented in an appendix. The story, however, transcends figures; and it has humanity, perception and true understanding, especially of the changing background against which he played. There is, too, some extremely revealing and hitherto unpublished material concerning his relationship with Sir Donald Bradman from their correspondence.

Good Enough? (Pelham Books; £10.95), by Chris Cowdrey and Jonathan Smith, has as its text Chris Cowdrey's remark, "I don't mind if I am not as good as my father as long as I am good enough". By no means every cricketer, certainly not every cricketer embarking on an autobiographical study, even if it disavows autobiography – and with a collaborator – could write as freely, easily and in so dignified a fashion of his performance on the field where his father was so outstanding. The younger Cowdrey has much to contribute to the game, our understanding of it, and the pleasure of those who play with him and those who watch him. This is a fundamentally happy book.

A Right Ambition (Collins Willow; £8.95), by David Gower – "with Derek Hodgson " – is a thoughtful, technical and generous book. Even when he is discussing the making of strokes, their flaws and virtues, Gower is always thinking below the surface. He is especially illuminating about his opponents. "Batting against Lillee has been one of the most enjoyable experiences of my career, even when he had won the day." He is illuminating, too, about Mike Brearley. "He certainly appeared to have a phenomenal memory for opposing players. He brought his intelligence to bear in an almost academic fashion in his deliberations on the cricket field, and at that stage of my career I was quite happy to accept without too much question all that happened under his control."

McGilvray: The Game is Not the Same . . . (David & Charles; £9.95), "As told to Norman Tasker", is the cricketing life of Alan McGilvray, as a player from 1933-34 with New South Wales, as the state captain in the period of Bradman, O'Reilly, Oldfield, Kippax and McCabe, and from 1935 as a broadcaster who continued through many years, much respected in his own country and Britain. A thoughtful man with a sharp eye for the nuances of cricket, and a dry sense of humour, the man whom Brian Johnston addressed as "McGillers" has written a book of considerable wisdom. Few men have had the privilege to be so close to the game on the highest level for half a century, and if it is, for many, nostalgic, it also contains informed opinions that will be of value to the cricket researchers of years to come.

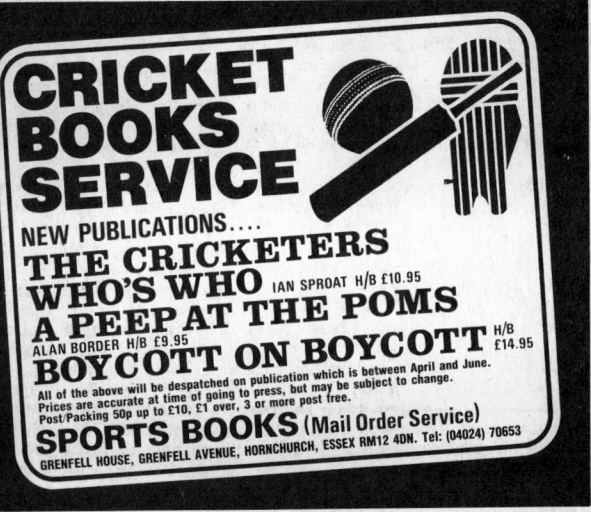

'Tiger' O'Reilly: 60 Years in Cricket (Collins; £9.95) is the autobiography of that very considerable performer for New South Wales and Australia, and subsequently, for many years, a cricket reporter and critic. Bill O'Reilly says simply enough, "From the day I made my first appearance for North Sydney I seem to have stirred up plenty of interest with my unusual type of medium-paced leg-spinner-cum-wrong'un". In that, however, he underestimates himself; for he was, over nearly twenty years, one of the most unrelentingly attacking spin bowlers the game has known. Surprisingly enough, he played in only 27 Tests; but in them, over a period of good batting pitches, he took 144 wickets at 22.59. He was a schoolmaster who wrote two books on cricket tours; knew the game inside out and commented on it with utter fairness. If he was – and indeed he was – a most ferocious bowler in his attitude towards batsmen, he proved with the years a man of kindness and an observer of justice.

Trumper: The Definitive Biography (Hodder and Stoughton; £12.95), by Peter Sharpham, is a result of much research backed by convincing statistics; its text ends, evocatively, with Hugh Trumble's comment, "Trumper stands alone as the best batsman of all time". That statement may not be accepted without question outside Australia but Trumper, who died at the age of 37, was unquestionably a charismatic figure and remains a legend in the social as well as the sporting history of Australia. Mr Sharpham follows Jack Fingleton as a biographer of Trumper. He has worked patiently on his subject and has also succeeded in discovering some interesting photographs for reproduction.

Hedley Verity: Portrait of a Cricketer (Kingswood Press; £12), by Alan Hill, is somewhat surprisingly the first full-length biography of that great Yorkshire left-arm bowler who met his death in Sicily during the last war. In less than ten years of first-class cricket, he took 1,956 wickets, including 144 in Test matches, at 14.90. The fact that he achieved those figures on good wickets and against opposition which included Don Bradman gives some indication of his quality. His accuracy was immaculate but while he is often described as a slow left-arm bowler, he was not of the slow "flighty" type but tended to push the ball through rather in the manner of Underwood. He was difficult to attack and utterly persistent in all circumstances. He was a thoughtful and a likeable person and Mr Hill has done him honest Yorkshire justice.

J. B. Hobbs, His Record Innings-by-Innings (Association of Cricket Statisticians; no price given) is by Derek Lodge, with an introduction by Ronald Mason, and "a note on Sandham". It is a 44-page statistical analysis of the career of "The Master", recorded with scholarly care and precision. It shows in cool figures just how great were his achievements.

The 1986 Cricketers' Who's Who (Queen Anne Press; £8.95), compiled and edited by Iain Sproat, with Ralph Dellor as Associate Editor, is a now familiar annual publication. Arranged in alphabetical rather than county order, it is well illustrated and contains all the facts – and in many cases more – than could reasonably be asked by the average follower of the game.

Frank Tyson – The Cricket Coaching Manual (Pelham Books; £8.95) is a well-made, and both substantially and valuably illustrated, book of technical instruction. Even when he was the fastest bowler in the world, Frank Tyson studied his cricket intently and here is the product of that study. The illustrations from time to time reveal the fact that the original publication was in Australia, but Mr Tyson's thought is international as far as cricket is

concerned. There is a foreword by his old friend, colleague and fellow-Lancastrian, Keith Andrew, who is the director of coaching of the National Cricket Association in England. He found the book, as will all informed readers, "All Tyson – erudite, thorough and, like his bowling, something special to make you sit up and take notice".

The Asda Cricket Challenge (Dennis Fairey and Associates, Chiltern House, 184 High Street, Berkhamsted, Hertfordshire HP4 3AP; £2) is a handsomely produced and illustrated 88-page quarto souvenir of the Asda matches at the Scarborough Festival of 1986. There is much colour illustration – the cover, an aerial view of the ground, is most impressive – and it has fifteen varied and interesting feature articles on the Festival and its history.

1986 International Golden Oldies Cricket Festival (Air New Zealand; £1) is a souvenir programme with feature articles on those Brighton matches played last year. Local and cricketing information is attractively laid out.

A Cricket Diary 1987 (Long-Handle Press, 18 Ashley Avenue, Lower Weston, Bath BA1 3DS; £3.95 post free) is compiled once more by John Dixon, formerly the Gloucestershire medium-pace bowler. It has useful notes for the cricketers, some nostalgic anniversary dates, and some diverting and well-chosen illustrations.

Playfair Cricket Annual 1986 (Queen Anne Press; £1.75) is the 39th edition and the first not to be edited by Gordon Ross, on whose death the office passed to Bill Frindall. He has maintained the original format in a carefully made 256-page pocket-size reference book, which must be of value, and already his hand is to be seen in a few thoughtful changes.

ACS Cricket Year Book 1986 (Newnes Books; £3.50) is compiled by Peter Wynne-Thomas, Philip Bailey and John Stockwell for the Association of Cricket Statisticians. A 224-page octavo, it is exhaustive in its recording of the figures of current players of all nations, a characteristic example of ACS thoroughness.

The County Yearbooks which follow in general carry scores of county matches of the preceding season, Second XI information and feature articles.

The Essex County Cricket Club 1986 Handbook (Essex CCC, County Ground, Chelmsford CM2 0PG; £3, plus 46p postage) celebrates with a "Double Trophy Edition". It includes contributions by Tony Lewis, Ray Illingworth, Trevor Bailey, Doug Insole, Ralph Dellor, Stanley Wilmot, David Lemmon, Keith Fletcher, Graham Gooch, Bernard Webber and Francis Ponder. It runs to 232 pages – a celebration indeed.

Hampshire Handbook 1986 (Hampshire CCC, County Ground, Southampton SO9 2TY; £2.50) is edited by Tony Mitchener, taking over from Peter Marshall, who has had to retire for business reasons after eight years in that office. This issue also marks the retirement of Geoffrey Ford as club chairman and A. K. James as secretary, whose services are recognised in a tribute by Cecil Paris, the club's president. There are also features by John Hughes, Patrick Symes, Victor Isaacs, John Southern (on Hampshire Colts), Colin Savage, Frank Bailey and Chris Kirkland, as well as notes on the playing staff and poetic tributes, two by Imogen Grosberg and one by Kenneth East.

Kent County Cricket Club Annual 1986 (Kent CCC, St Lawrence Ground, Canterbury; £2) contains a feature article on Alan Knott by Leslie Ames and features by Derek Carlaw on the story of Kent county matches – obviously

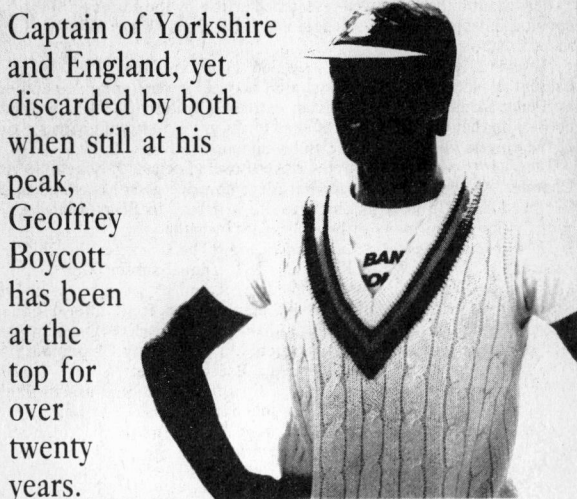

the first of a projected series – Don Beney and Gerald Dineley; plus sections of records by John F. Griffiths and Howard Milton.

Middlesex County Cricket Club Review 1985-86 (Middlesex CCC, Lord's Ground, London NW8 8QN; £4, post free). There are feature articles by Mike Gatting, Charles Oliver, David Green, Paul Downton and Terence Prittie.

Irish Cricket Union Yearbook 1986 (Irish Cricket Union, 22 St Catherine's Court, Newgrove Avenue, Sandymount, Dublin 4; £1) is edited by Francis Xavier Carty. It contains full details and averages of all matches played by Ireland in the relevant twelve months, including the tour to Zimbabwe and, of course, a provincial round-up and statistics from 1855 to 1986.

West Indies Cricket Annual 1986 (produced for Benson and Hedges [Overseas] Ltd by Caribbean Communications, 116 Queens Road, Hersham, Walton-on-Thames, Surrey KT12 5LL; no price given) is once more edited by Tony Cozier. It is a most attractively produced 88-page quarto, generously illustrated, with some pictures in colour. The Five Cricketers of the Year are Carlisle Best, Joel Garner, Desmond Haynes, Malcolm Marshall and Patrick Patterson; and there is a well-researched article by the editor on West Indian opening batsmen, a most valuable island-by-island Who's Who, and all the relevant statistics.

Weston Creek Cricket Year 1985-86 (Weston Creek CC, 14 Hyndes Cresent, Holder, ACT 2611, Australia; no price given), compiled and edited by Percy Samara-Wickrama, is an extremely informative 100-page octavo booklet on that club, its progress at all levels in 1985-86, with career statistics of the players and a list of the club's honours.

The Twelfth Man (Wombwell Cricket Lovers Society, J. Sokell, Secretary, Chamfer, 42 Woodstock Road, Barnsley; no price given) is edited by John Featherstone. It makes its chief feature a tribute to Brian Johnston, with contributions from many of his colleagues over the years.

The Cricketer Quarterly Facts and Figures (The Cricketer, Beech Hanger, Ashurst, Tunbridge Wells, Kent TN3 9ST, annual subscription UK £5.90; £1.30 a copy) moved into its thirteenth year and its second year under the editorship of Bill Frindall, with his emphasis on fresh information of a factual kind, as in such items as "Botham's Greatest Hits" and a thoughtful feature on the increase of drawn matches in the County Championship.

Cricketer International (The Cricketer, Beech Hanger, Ashurst, Tunbridge Wells, Kent TN3 9ST; £1 monthly), edited by Christopher Martin-Jenkins, passed into its 67th volume since its foundation in 1921. Among its regular contributors, apart from the editor, were Robert Brooke, E. W. Swanton, Alan Lee, Christopher Bazalgette and Andrew Longmore.

Wisden Cricket Monthly (Editorial, 6 Beech Lane, Guildown, Guildford, Surrey GU2 5ES; 95p or £12.35 for twelve issues annually), edited by David Frith, has regular contributions by E. M. Wellings, Doug Ibbotson, David Foot, Tony Lewis, Neil Hallam, Bob Willis and David Gower, as well as the editor. It maintains an informed interest in cricketana.

Cricketer (Newspress Pty, 603-611 Little Lonsdale Street, Melbourne, Victoria 3001, Australia; monthly October to April, $A2.75) continues under the editorship of Ken Piesse. It carries many feature articles by such contributors as Richard Cashman, Craig Regan, Jack Pollard and Ashley Mallett. It incorporates Burroughs Australian Cricket Guide.

The New Zealand Cricket Player (RPL Sporting Publications, 3rd Floor, Communications House, 12 Heather Street, Parnell, Auckland, New

Zealand; nine times a year, $NZ2.25) is edited by Don Cameron and among its contributors are Brent Edwards, Gary Dixon and Bob Monteith. It diligently follows New Zealand cricket and the performances of New Zealand sides overseas.

Australian Cricket Journal (Details of subscription from GPO Box 696, Adelaide, South Australia 5001, Australia), edited by Chris Harte, is a quarterly which in September 1986 entered its second year. It has an unusual and entirely healthy – indeed, stimulating – literary and historic bias; and publishes much original and valuable research.

Two titles published in 1986 involved John Arlott, and like the three that follow later have been included in the number of titles submitted. *Arlott in Conversation with Mike Brearley* (Hodder & Stoughton; £9.95) provides on the page the three Channel 4 television programmes. The subject matter is wide-ranging, for there has always been more to John Arlott than cricket, and Mike Brearley was just the man to draw him on, coaxing insights and reminiscences rather as he coaxed wickets from Botham: it was not so much a matter of asking but knowing when to ask.

In *John Arlott's 100 Greatest Batsmen* (Queen Anne Press; £14.95), the list has been compiled with much heart-searching, and essentially it is a personal list, even if he has had to omit some personal favourites. The hundred are presented in alphabetical order, from Abel to Zaheer, with each essay accompanied by an illustration – some are in colour – and statistics. The essence, though, is the writer's feeling for his fellow-man and his ability to paint with words: as of his Hampshire favourite, Philip Mead. "An unforgettable figure, his style was not graceful: for years at number four for Hampshire, he came out at a slightly pin-toed toddle; he had drooping shoulders, deep chest, wide hips and powerful bowed legs; and his deeply lined face was always solemn."

It is David Foot's portraits of cricketers, created similarly with a few words, which makes *Sunshine, Sixes and Cider:* A History of Somerset Cricket (David & Charles; £12.95) more than simply the story of a county cricket club, albeit one which throughout its colourful history has been a byword for eccentricity and unpredictability. The print was scarcely dry before Somerset added another, yet-to-be-written chapter by its decisions of last year. But here is Mr Foot on Bill Alley in 1961. "The crease was his God-given territory. He occupied it with the mannerisms of a lusty, lovable black-sheep squire. There were none of the divisive trappings of the elevated landowner .... He wasn't quite top-drawer – that was what everyone found so engaging." One hopes there would still be a place for him at Taunton.

David Foot has also written the biographical notes for *The Lord's Taverners Cricket Clinic* (David & Charles; £9.95), in which twenty leading cricketers have provided advice and comment on all aspects of the game: for example, Peter May on driving, Bill O'Reilly on leg-spin, Mike Brearley on captaincy and Richie Benaud on the psychological approach. Those last two could just as easily have been transposed. It is well presented, with photographs by Ken Kelly and line illustrations by Rodger Towers, and reflects the concern of the Lord's Taverners to encourage and assist young people to play cricket.

These notices began with a heavyweight work: it is fitting that they should end with one. *Men in White* (Moa Publications, PO Box 26092, Auckland 3, New Zealand; or from Southern Booksellers, 84 Bohemia Road, St Leonards-on-Sea, Sussex TN37 6JL; £25), by Don Neely, Richard King and Francis Payne, is "The History of New Zealand International Cricket 1894-1985". As such, it includes, in its 656 pages, Test matches and one-day internationals as well as matches played by New Zealand sides on tour and at home: each match has a report and scorecard; and the reader learns of more than cricket alone. For example, in Paris, after the 1949 tour of England, where the players were treated to a night at the *Folies Bergère*, some of them "were financially embarrassed when the city banks closed in the wake of a devaluation of the British pound". It is generously and handsomely illustrated, nostalgically so at times, and enlivened by cartoons and caricatures and colour. The foreword by Walter Hadlee is a fine essay. Neely, a New Zealand selector, and the mainspring of this book, apologises in his preface to his children for missing five years of their lives. He has, instead, filled them with a volume of which his family and New Zealand cricket can be justifiably proud.

CRICKET ASSOCIATIONS AND SOCIETIES

AUCKLAND CRICKET SOCIETY: *Secretary* Tom Lindsay, PO Box 56059, Auckland, New Zealand.

AUSTRALIAN CRICKET SOCIETY: *Secretary* Christopher Harte, GPO Box 696, Adelaide, 5001, South Australia.

ADELAIDE BRANCH: *Secretary* Gerald Fishpool, 49 Johnstone Street.

BRISBANE BRANCH: *Secretary* Robert Spence, GPO Box 1498, Brisbane 4001, Queensland.

CANBERRA BRANCH: *Secretary* Julian Oakley, GPO Box 50, Canberra, 2600, ACT.

MELBOURNE BRANCH: *Secretary* Colin Barnes, 4 Hornby Street, Beaumaris, 3193, Victoria.

PERTH BRANCH: *Secretary* Kevin Collins, 11 Brindley Street, Belmont, 4104, Western Australia.

SYDNEY BRANCH: *Secretary* Ronald Cardwell, 92 Victoria Road, West Pennant Hills, 2120, New South Wales.

BLACKLEY CRICKET SOCIETY: *Secretary* D. N. Butterfield, 7 Bayswater Terrace, Halifax, West Yorkshire, HX3 0NB.

CHESTERFIELD CRICKET SOCIETY: *Secretary* B. Holling, 24 Woodland Way, Old Tupton, Chesterfield, Derbyshire.

COUNCIL OF CRICKET SOCIETIES, THE: *Secretary* J. Featherstone, 205 Hyde Park Road, Leeds, Yorkshire LS6 1AH.

CRICKET SOCIETY, THE: *Secretary* E. C. R. Rice, 50 Westbrook, Saltdean, West Sussex BN2 8FZ.

CRICKET SOCIETY, THE (Midland Branch): *Secretary* Dr A. A. Walker, "Sarnia", Hernes Nest, Bewdley, DY12 2ET.

CRICKET STATISTICIANS, ASSOCIATION OF: *Secretary* P. Wynne-Thomas, The Bungalow, Haughton Mill, Retford, Nottinghamshire.

EAST RIDING CRICKET SOCIETY: *Secretary* R. P. Thompson, 151 Park Avenue, Hull HU5 3EX.

ESSEX CRICKET SOCIETY: *Secretary* M. K. Smith, 12 Woodcote Road, Leigh-on-Sea, Essex SS9 3NP.

FYLDE CRICKET SOCIETY: *Secretary* S. Kennedy, 36 Torquay Avenue, Marton, Blackpool, Lancashire.

HAMPSHIRE CRICKET SOCIETY: *Secretary* F. Bailey, 7 Lightfoot Grove, Basingstoke, Hampshire.

HEAVY WOOLLEN CRICKET SOCIETY: *Secretary* G. S. Cooper, 27 Milford Grove, Gomersal, Cleckheaton, West Yorkshire.

INDIA, THE CRICKET SOCIETY OF: *Secretary* Sandeep Singh Nakai, House No. 122, Sector 8-A, Chandigarh, India.

LANCASHIRE AND CHESHIRE CRICKET SOCIETY: *Secretary* H. W. Pardoe, Crantock, 117a Barlow Moor Road, Didsbury, Manchester, M20 8TS.

LINCOLNSHIRE CRICKET LOVERS' SOCIETY: *Secretary* C. Kennedy, 26 Eastwood Avenue, Grimsby, South Humberside, DN34 5BE.

MERSEYSIDE CRICKET SOCIETY: *Secretary* W. T. Robins, 11 Yew Tree Road, Hunts Cross, Liverpool, L25 9QN.

NATAL CRICKET SOCIETY: *Secretary* Haydn Bradfield, PO Box 3046, Durban 4000, South Africa.

NORTHERN CRICKET SOCIETY: *Secretary* R. S. Marsh, 113 Crossgates Lane, Leeds, Yorkshire LS15 7PJ.

NOTTINGHAM CRICKET LOVERS' SOCIETY: *Secretary* G. Blagdurn, 2 Inham Circus, Chilwell, Beeston, Nottinghamshire, NG9 4FN.

PAKISTAN ASSOCIATION OF CRICKET STATISTICIANS: *Secretary* Abid Ali Kazi, 5-A, 11/1 Sunset Lane, Phase 11, Defence Housing Society, Karachi, Pakistan.

ROTHERHAM CRICKET SOCIETY: *Secretary* J. A. R. Atkin, 15 Gallow Tree Road, Rotherham, South Yorkshire S65 3FE.

SCOTLAND, CRICKET SOCIETY OF: *Secretary* A. J. Robertson, 5 Riverside Road, Eaglesham, Glasgow, G76 0DQ.

SOMERSET WYVERNS: *Secretary* M. J. W. Richards, "Wyvern", 3 Ash Road, Tring, Hertfordshire.

SOPHIANS, THE: *Secretary* A. K. Hignell, 79 Coed Glas Road, Llanishen, Cardiff.

SOUTH AFRICAN CRICKET SOCIETY: *Secretary* Ronald Ryninks, PO Box 78040, Sandton, Transvaal, 2146, South Africa.

STOURBRIDGE AND DISTRICT CRICKET SOCIETY: *Secretary* R. Barber, 6 Carlton Avenue, Pedmore, Stourbridge, DY9 9ED.

SUSSEX CRICKET SOCIETY: *Secretary* A. A. Dumbrell, 6 Southdown Avenue, Brighton, East Sussex, BN1 6EG.

UPPINGHAM SCHOOL CRICKET SOCIETY: *Secretary* Dr E. J. R. Boston, The Common Room, Uppingham School, Rutland.

WEST LANCASHIRE CRICKET SOCIETY: *Secretary* J. N. Renshaw, 206 Fylde Road, Southport, Merseyside PR9 9YB.

WOMBWELL CRICKET LOVERS' SOCIETY: *Secretary* J. Sokell, 42 Woodstock Road, Barnsley, South Yorkshire, S75 1DX.

ZIMBABWE, CRICKET SOCIETY OF: *Secretary* L. G. Morgenrood, 10 Elsworth Avenue, Belgravia, Harare, Zimbabwe.

1284

FIXTURES, 1987

Indicates Sunday play. † Not first-class.

Saturday, April 18
Cambridge — Cambridge U. v Essex

Wednesday, April 22
Lord's — MCC v Essex
Oxford — Oxford U. v Kent
Cambridge — Cambridge U. v Lancs.

Saturday, April 25
Chesterfield* — Derbys. v Sussex
Bristol* — Glos. v Essex
Southampton* — Hants v Northants
Lord's* — Middx v Yorks.
Nottingham* — Notts. v Surrey
Taunton — Somerset v Lancs.
Birmingham* — Warwicks. v Glam.
Worcester* — Worcs. v Kent
Cambridge — Cambridge U. v Leics.

Wednesday, April 29
Chelmsford — Essex v Warwicks.
Canterbury — Kent v Glam.
Manchester — Lancs. v Middx
The Oval — Surrey v Derbys.
Hove — Sussex v Glos.
Oxford — Oxford U. v Hants
Cambridge — Cambridge U. v Northants

Thursday, April 30
Arundel — †Lavinia, Duchess of Norfolk's XI v Pakistanis (1 day)

Saturday, May 2
The Oval* — Surrey v Pakistanis

†Benson and Hedges Cup (1 day)
Derby — Derbys. v Northants
Swansea — Glam. v Sussex
Bristol — Glos. v Notts.
Canterbury — Kent v Minor Counties
Taunton — Somerset v Essex
Birmingham — Warwicks. v Yorks.
Worcester — Worcs. v Lancs.
Oxford — Combined Universities v Hants

Wednesday, May 6
Canterbury — Kent v Pakistanis
Swansea — Glam. v Lancs.

Leicester — Leics. v Essex
Lord's — Middx v Northants
Taunton — Somerset v Surrey
Worcester — Worcs. v Sussex
Leeds — Yorks. v Hants
Cambridge — Cambridge U. v Derbys.

Saturday, May 9
Chelmsford* — Essex v Pakistanis

†Benson and Hedges Cup (1 day)
Bristol — Glos. v Leics.
Southampton — Hants v Middx
Nottingham — Notts. v Derbys.
Taunton — Somerset v Combined Universities
The Oval — Surrey v Kent
Hove — Sussex v Minor Counties
Leeds — Yorks. v Lancs.
Perth (North Inch)‡ — Scotland v Warwicks.

‡ *To continue on Sunday if necessary.*

Tuesday, May 12
Derby — †Derbys. v Pakistanis (1 day)

†Benson and Hedges Cup (1 day)
Chelmsford — Essex v Middx
Southampton — Hants v Somerset
Canterbury — Kent v Sussex
Southport — Lancs. v Scotland
Leicester — Leics. v Notts.
Northampton — Northants v Glos.
The Oval — Surrey v Glam.
Leeds — Yorks. v Worcs.

Thursday, May 14
Taunton — †Somerset v Pakistanis (1 day)

†Benson and Hedges Cup (1 day)
Chelmsford — Essex v Hants
Manchester — Lancs. v Warwicks.
Leicester — Leics. v Derbys.
Lord's — Middx v Combined Universities
Nottingham — Notts. v Northants
Hove — Sussex v Surrey
Worcester — Worcs. v Scotland
Oxford (Christ Church) — Minor Counties v Glam.

Saturday, May 16

| Hove* | Sussex v Pakistanis |

†Benson and Hedges Cup (1 day)

Derby	Derbys. v Glos.
Cardiff	Glam. v Kent
Lord's	Middx v Somerset
Northampton	Northants v Leics.
Birmingham	Warwicks. v Worcs.
Oxford (Christ Church)	Minor Counties v Surrey
Cambridge	Combined Universities v Essex
Glasgow (Hamilton Crescent)‡	Scotland v Yorks.

‡ *To continue on Sunday if necessary.*

Wednesday, May 20

Chelmsford	Essex v Glam.
Bournemouth	Hants. v Notts.
Dartford	Kent v Sussex
Leicester	Leics. v Lancs.
Birmingham	Warwicks. v Surrey
Worcester	Worcs. v Derbys.
Leeds	Yorks. v Somerset
Oxford	Oxford U. v Glos.
Cambridge	Cambridge U. v Middx

Thursday, May 21

| The Oval | †ENGLAND v PAKISTAN (1st 1-day Texaco Trophy) |
| Lord's | †MCC v MCC Young Cricketers (1 day) |

Saturday, May 23

Nottingham	†ENGLAND v PAKISTAN (2nd 1-day Texaco Trophy)
Derby	Derbys. v Warwicks.
Cardiff	Glam. v Yorks.
Manchester	Lancs. v Worcs.
Northampton	Northants v Leics.
Taunton	Somerset v Glos.
The Oval	Surrey v Essex
Hove	Sussex v Middx
Oxford	Oxford U. v Notts.

Monday, May 25

| Birmingham | †ENGLAND v PAKISTAN (3rd 1-day Texaco Trophy) |

Wednesday, May 27

| Leeds or Dublin (Rathmines) | Yorks. (3 days) or †Ireland (2 days) v Pakistanis |

†Benson and Hedges Cup – Quarter-Finals
(1 day)

Saturday, May 30

Lord's*	Middx v Pakistanis
Chesterfield	Derbys. v Glam.
Southampton	Hants. v Glos.
Leicester	Leics. v Somerset
Northampton	Northants v Kent
Worcester	Worcs. v Essex
Middlesbrough	Yorks. v Notts.
Oxford	Oxford U. v Warwicks.

Wednesday, June 3

Swansea	Glam. v Hants
Bristol	Glos. v Lancs.
Tunbridge Wells	Kent v Surrey
Lord's	Middx v Essex
Taunton	Somerset v Notts.
Birmingham	Warwicks. v Leics.
Sheffield	Yorks. v Worcs.

Thursday, June 4

| Manchester | ENGLAND v PAKISTAN (1st Cornhill Test, 5 days) |

Saturday, June 6

Swansea*	Glam. v Somerset
Tunbridge Wells	Kent v Essex
Leicester	Leics. v Worcs.
Lord's	Middx v Glos.
Northampton	Northants v Surrey
Nottingham	Notts. v Lancs.
Horsham	Sussex v Hants
Harrogate	Yorks. v Derbys.

Wednesday, June 10

†Benson and Hedges Cup – Semi-Finals
(1 day)

| Harrogate | †Tilcon Trophy (3 days) |

Thursday, June 11

| Glasgow (Titwood) | †Scotland v Pakistanis (1 day) |

Saturday, June 13

Bletchley (Manor Fields)*	Northants v Pakistanis
Ilford	Essex v Kent
Cardiff	Glam. v Warwicks.
Manchester	Lancs. v Notts.
Bath	Somerset v Middx
The Oval	Surrey v Hants
Worcester	Worcs. v Leics.

Monday, June 15

| Downpatrick | †Ireland v Glos. (1 day) |

Tuesday, June 16

| Downpatrick | †Ireland v Glos. (1 day) |

Wednesday, June 17

Derby	Derbys. v Lancs.
Ilford	Essex v Northants
Basingstoke	Hants v Yorks.
Bath	Somerset v Kent
Hove	Sussex v Glam.
Birmingham	Warwicks. v Notts.
Worcester	Worcs. v Glos.
Cambridge	Cambridge U. v Surrey

Thursday, June 18

| Lord's | ENGLAND v PAKISTAN (2nd Cornhill Test, 5 days) |

Saturday, June 20

Southampton	Hants v Middx
Liverpool	Lancs. v Kent
Leicester	Leics. v Sussex
Luton	Northants v Warwicks.
Nottingham	Notts. v Worcs.
Leeds	Yorks. v Essex
Oxford	Oxford U. v Glam.

Wednesday, June 24

| Oxford | Oxford & Cam. U. v Pakistanis |

†NatWest Bank Trophy – First Round
(1 day)

High Wycombe	Bucks. v Somerset
Wisbech	Cambs. v Derbys.
Darlington	Durham v Middx
Cardiff	Glam. v Cheshire
Southampton	Hants v Dorset
Manchester	Lancs. v Glos.
Leicester	Leics. v Oxon.
Northampton	Northants v Ireland
Jesmond	Northumb. v Essex
Nottingham	Notts. v Suffolk
Edinburgh (Myreside)	Scotland v Kent
Burton upon Trent	Staffs. v Warwicks.
The Oval	Surrey v Herts.
Hove	Sussex v Cumb.
Trowbridge	Wilts. v Yorks.
Worcester	Worcs. v Devon

Saturday, June 27

Leicester*	Leics. v Pakistanis
Chelmsford	Essex v Somerset
Gloucester	Glos. v Worcs.
Canterbury	Kent v Notts.
Manchester	Lancs. v Derbys.
Lord's	Middx v Glam.
Northampton	Northants v Yorks.
Guildford	Surrey v Sussex
Birmingham	Warwicks. v Hants

Wednesday, July 1

Swansea	Glam. v Northants
Gloucester	Glos. v Hants
Canterbury	Kent v Yorks.
Manchester	Lancs. v Essex
Leicester	Leics. v Derbys.
The Oval	Surrey v Middx
Birmingham	Warwicks. v Somerset
Kidderminster	Worcs. v Notts.
Lord's	Oxford U. v Cambridge U.

Thursday, July 2

| Leeds | ENGLAND v PAKISTAN (3rd Cornhill Test, 5 days) |

Saturday, July 4

Heanor*	Derbys. v Hants
Swansea*	Glam. v Glos.
Northampton	Northants v Lancs.
Nottingham	Notts. v Yorks.
The Oval	Surrey v Leics.
Hove	Sussex v Kent
Worcester	Worcs. v Warwicks.
Lord's	†Eton v Harrow (1 day)

Wednesday, July 8

†NatWest Bank Trophy – Second Round
(1 day)

Leicester or Oxford (Morris Motors)	Leics. or Oxon. v Hants or Dorset
Glasgow (Titwood) or Canterbury	Scotland or Kent v Cambs. or Derbys.
Hove or Netherfield, Kendal	Sussex or Cumb. v Lancs. or Glos.
Trowbridge or Leeds	Wilts or Yorks. v Glam. or Cheshire
Sunderland or Uxbridge	Durham or Middx v Notts. or Suffolk
Northampton or Dublin	Northants or Ireland v Surrey or Herts.
Stone or Birmingham	Staffs. or Warwicks. v Bucks. or Somerset
Jesmond or Chelmsford	Northumb. or Essex v Worcs. or Devon

Thursday, July 9

| Burton upon Trent | †Minor Counties v Pakistanis (2 days) |

Saturday, July 11

Lord's	†BENSON AND HEDGES CUP FINAL (1 day)
Nottingham, Manchester or Birmingham	Notts., Lancs. or Warwicks. v Pakistanis
Dublin (Malahide)*	†Ireland v Northants (2 days)

Wednesday, July 15

Cardiff	Glam. v Pakistanis
Derby	Derbys. v Kent
Southend	Essex v Hants
Bristol	Glos. v Middx
Nottingham	Notts. v Leics.
Taunton	Somerset v Worcs.
The Oval	Surrey v Yorks.
Nuneaton	Warwicks. v Sussex

Thursday, July 16

| Lord's | England v Australia (WCA Silver Jubilee 1-day International) |

Saturday, July 18

Worcester*	Worcs. v Pakistanis
Southend	Essex v Derbys.
Cardiff	Glam. v Surrey
Bristol	Glos. v Northants
Bournemouth*	Hants v Warwicks.
Lord's	Middx v Notts.
Taunton	Somerset v Leics.
Hastings	Sussex v Yorks.
Coleraine*	Ireland v Scotland (3 days)

Wednesday, July 22

Derby	Derbys. v Notts.
Portsmouth	Hants v Sussex
Folkestone	Kent v Glos.
Southport	Lancs. v Warwicks.
Leicester	Leics. v Middx
Northampton	Northants v Somerset
The Oval	Surrey v Worcs.
Leeds	Yorks. v Glam.
Lord's	†MCC v MCC Schools (1 day)

Thursday, July 23

| Birmingham | ENGLAND v PAKISTAN (4th Cornhill Test, 5 days) |

| Lord's | †MCC Schools v National Association of Young Cricketers (1 day) |

Friday, July 24

| Lord's | †NCA Young Cricketers v Combined Services |

Saturday, July 25

Bristol	Glos. v Derbys.
Portsmouth	Hants v Essex
Manchester	Lancs. v Notts.
Leicester	Leics. v Yorks.
Lord's	Middx v Kent
Northampton	Northants v Sussex
Worcester	Worcs. v Somerset

Wednesday, July 29

†NatWest Bank Trophy – Quarter-Finals (1 day)

Thursday, July 30

| Jesmond | †England XI v Rest of the World XI (1 day) |

Friday, July 31

| Jesmond | †England XI v Rest of the World XI (1 day) |

Saturday, August 1

Southampton*	Hants v Pakistanis
Cheltenham	Glos. v Leics.
Canterbury	Kent v Derbys.
Lord's	Middx v Surrey
Weston-super-Mare	Somerset v Glam.
Eastbourne	Sussex v Notts.
Birmingham	Warwicks. v Northants
Leeds	Yorks. v Lancs.
Worcester	England v Australia (Women's Test, 4 days)

Wednesday, August 5

Chesterfield	Derbys. v Yorks.
Abergavenny	Glam. v Leics.
Cheltenham	Glos. v Surrey
Canterbury	Kent v Middx
Manchester	Lancs. v Northants
Worksop	Notts. v Warwicks.
Weston-super-Mare	Somerset v Hants
Eastbourne	Sussex v Essex
Lord's	†MCC v Ireland (2 days)

Thursday, August 6

The Oval	ENGLAND v PAKISTAN (5th Cornhill Test, 5 days)

Saturday, August 8

Chesterfield	Derbys. v Surrey
Cheltenham	Glos. v Kent
Southampton	Hants v Lancs.
Hinckley	Leics. v Warwicks.
Lord's	Middx v Worcs.
Northampton	Northants v Essex
Nottingham	Notts. v Somerset
Sheffield	Yorks. v Sussex

Sunday, August 9

Arundel	†Lavinia, Duchess of Norfolk's XI v Rest of the World XI (1 day)
Welshpool	†Wales v Ireland (3 days)

Wednesday, August 12

†NatWest Bank Trophy – Semi-Finals (1 day)

Nottingham, Manchester or Birmingham	Notts., Lancs. or Warwicks. v Rest of the World XI
Aberdeen (Mannofield)	†Scotland v MCC (3 days)

Saturday, August 15

Bristol*	Glos. v Rest of the World XI
Derby	Derbys. v Leics.
Chelmsford	Essex v Middx
Nottingham	Notts. v Northants
Taunton	Somerset v Yorks.
The Oval	Surrey v Kent
Hove	Sussex v Warwicks.
Worcester	Worcs. v Glam.

Sunday, August 16

†Warwick Under-25 Semi-Finals (1 day) (or Sunday, August 23)

Wednesday, August 19

Chelmsford	Essex v Notts.
Cardiff	Glam. v Middx
Bournemouth	Hants v Kent
Lytham	Lancs. v Sussex
Northampton	Northants v Worcs.
The Oval	Surrey v Somerset
Birmingham	Warwicks. v Glos.
Scarborough	Yorks. v Leics.

Thursday, August 20

Lord's	MCC v REST OF THE WORLD XI (MCC Bicentenary Match, 5 days)

Saturday, August 22

Derby	Derbys. v Essex
Neath	Glam. v Notts.
Bournemouth	Hants v Somerset
Wellingborough School	Northants v Middx
Nottingham	Notts. v Glos.
Hove	Sussex v Surrey
Birmingham	Warwicks. v Lancs.

Sunday, August 23

†Warwick Under-25 Semi-Finals (1 day) (if not played on Sunday, August 16)

Wednesday, August 26

Maidstone	Kent v Lancs.
Leicester	Leics. v Notts.
Uxbridge	Middx v Warwicks.
Northampton	Northants v Derbys.
The Oval	Surrey v Glam.
Hove	Sussex v Somerset
Worcester	Worcs. v Hants
Leeds	Yorks. v Glos.

Friday, August 28

Lord's	†National Club Cricket Championship Final (1 day)

Saturday, August 29

Colchester	Essex v Surrey
Maidstone	Kent v Hants
Manchester	Lancs. v Glos.
Leicester	Leics. v Northants
Uxbridge	Middx v Sussex
Nottingham	Notts. v Derbys.
Birmingham	Warwicks. v Worcs.
Hove	England v Australia (Women's Test, 4 days)

Sunday, August 30

Birmingham	†Warwick Under-25 Final (1 day)
Llanelli	Glam. v Somerset (1 day, Buckleys Brewery Trophy)

Monday, August 31

Lord's	†Norsk Hydro Village Cricket Championship Final (1 day)

Wednesday, September 2	
Colchester	Essex v Worcs.
Cardiff	Glam. v Derbys.
Bristol	Glos. v Somerset
Southampton	Hants v Leics.
Nottingham	Notts. v Sussex
The Oval	Surrey v Northants
Birmingham	Warwicks. v Kent
Scarborough	Yorks. v MCC

Saturday, September 5	
Lord's	†NATWEST BANK TROPHY FINAL (1 day)

Sunday, September 6	
Scarborough	†Lancs. v Derbys. (1 day), Asda Cricket Challenge

Monday, September 7	
†Bain Dawes Trophy Final (1 day)	

Scarborough	†Yorks. v Hants (1 day), Asda Cricket Challenge

Tuesday, September 8	
Scarborough	†Asda Cricket Challenge Final (1 day)

Wednesday, September 9	
Manchester	Lancs. v Surrey
Leicester	Leics. v Glos.
Lord's	Middx v Hants
Nottingham	Notts. v Glam.
Taunton	Somerset v Derbys.
Hove	Sussex v Northants
Scarborough	Yorks. v Warwicks.

Saturday, September 12	
Derby	Derbys. v Middx
Chelmsford	Essex v Lancs.
Bristol	Glos. v Glam.
Canterbury	Kent v Leics.
Worcester	Worcs. v Northants

PAKISTANI TOUR, 1987

APRIL		
30 Arundel		†v Lavinia, Duchess of Norfolk's XI (1 day)
MAY		
2 The Oval*		v Surrey
6 Canterbury		v Kent
9 Chelmsford*		v Essex
12 Derby		†v Derbys. (1 day)
14 Taunton		†v Somerset (1 day)
16 Hove*		v Sussex
21 The Oval		†v ENGLAND (1st 1-day Texaco Trophy)
23 Nottingham		†v ENGLAND (2nd 1-day Texaco Trophy)
25 Birmingham		†v ENGLAND (3rd 1-day Texaco Trophy)
27 Leeds or Dublin (Rathmines)		v Yorks. (3 days) or †Ireland (2 days)
30 Lord's*		v Middx
JUNE		
4 Manchester		v ENGLAND (1st Cornhill Test, 5 days)
11 Glasgow (Titwood)		†v Scotland (1 day)

13 Bletchley (Manor Fields)*	v Northants
18 Lord's	v ENGLAND (2nd Cornhill Test, 5 days)
24 Oxford	v Oxford & Cambridge Universities
27 Leicester*	v Leics.

JULY	
2 Leeds	v ENGLAND (3rd Cornhill Test, 5 days)
9 Burton upon Trent	†v Minor Counties (2 days)
11 Nottingham, Manchester or Birmingham	v Notts., Lancs. or Warwicks.
15 Cardiff	v Glam.
18 Worcester*	v Worcs.
23 Birmingham	v ENGLAND (4th Cornhill Test, 5 days)

AUGUST	
1 Southampton*	v Hants
6 The Oval	v ENGLAND (5th Cornhill Test, 5 days)

†REFUGE ASSURANCE LEAGUE, 1987

MAY

3–Derbys. v Northants (Derby); Glam. v Sussex (Cardiff); Leics. v Hants (Leicester); Notts. v Kent (Nottingham); Somerset v Essex (Taunton); Warwicks. v Yorks. (Birmingham); Worcs. v Lancs. (Worcester).

10–Hants v Surrey (Southampton); Kent v Worcs. (Canterbury); Lancs. v Glam. (Manchester); Sussex v Derbys. (Hove); Yorks. v Northants (Leeds).

17–Essex v Leics. (Chelmsford); Glam. v Kent (Swansea); Glos. v Warwicks. (Bristol); Middx v Somerset (Lord's); Northants v Hants (Northampton); Surrey v Lancs. (The Oval).

24–Derbys. v Worcs. (Derby); Glam. v Yorks. (Cardiff); Kent v Middx (Canterbury); Lancs. v Hants (Manchester); Somerset v Glos. (Taunton); Surrey v Essex (The Oval).

31–Hants v Glos. (Southampton); Lancs. v Somerset (Manchester); Northants v Sussex (Northampton); Notts. v Leics. (Nottingham); Warwicks. v Derbys. (Birmingham); Worcs. v Essex (Worcester); Yorks. v Kent (Middlesbrough).

JUNE

7–Leics. v Worcs. (Leicester); Middx v Glos. (Lord's); Northants v Notts. (Northampton); Surrey v Warwicks. (The Oval); Sussex v Hants (Horsham); Yorks. v Derbys. (Sheffield).

14–Essex v Kent (Ilford); Glam. v Notts. (Ebbw Vale); Glos. v Sussex (Swindon); Hants v Derbys. (Southampton); Leics. v Surrey (Leicester); Somerset v Warwicks. (Bath); Worcs. v Middx (Worcester).

21–Derbys. v Glos. (Ilkeston); Hants v Middx (Basingstoke); Lancs. v Kent (Manchester); Northants v Glam. (Luton); Notts. v Worcs. (Nottingham); Somerset v Sussex (Bath); Warwicks. v Essex (Birmingham); Yorks. v Surrey (Leeds).

28–Glos. v Worcs. (Gloucester); Kent v Somerset (Canterbury); Lancs. v Derbys. (Manchester); Middx v Glam. (Lord's); Surrey v Northants (Guildford); Sussex v Notts. (Hove); Warwicks. v Hants (Birmingham).

JULY

5–Essex v Sussex (Chelmsford); Middx v Leics. (Lord's); Northants v Lancs. (Tring); Notts. v Yorks. (Nottingham); Worcs. v Warwicks. (Worcester).

12–Derbys. v Glam. (Cheadle); Essex v Glos. (Chelmsford); Hants v Worcs. (Southampton); Lancs. v Leics. (Manchester); Surrey v Somerset (The Oval); Warwicks. v Notts. (Birmingham); Yorks. v Middx (Scarborough).

19–Essex v Derbys. (Southend); Glam. v Surrey (Cardiff); Glos. v Yorks. (Bristol); Kent v Northants (Canterbury); Notts. v Middx (Nottingham); Somerset v Leics. (Taunton); Sussex v Lancs. (Hastings).

26–Glam. v Warwicks. (Swansea); Hants v Essex (Portsmouth); Lancs. v Notts. (Manchester); Leics. v Yorks. (Leicester); Middx v Derbys. (Lord's); Northants v Glos. (Finedon); Worcs. v Somerset (Worcester).

AUGUST

2–Glos. v Leics. (Cheltenham); Kent v Derbys. (Canterbury); Middx v Surrey (Lord's); Somerset v Glam. (Weston-super-Mare); Sussex v Worcs. (Eastbourne); Warwicks. v Northants (Birmingham); Yorks. v Lancs. (Scarborough).

9–Derbys. v Surrey (Chesterfield); Glos. v Kent (Cheltenham); Hants v Glam. (Bournemouth); Leics. v Warwicks. (Leicester); Middx v Lancs. (Lord's); Northants v Essex (Northampton); Notts. v Somerset (Nottingham); Yorks. v Sussex (Hull).

16-Derbys. v Leics. (Derby); Essex v Middx (Chelmsford); Glam. v Worcs. (Swansea); Notts. v Hants (Nottingham); Somerset v Yorks. (Taunton); Surrey v Kent (The Oval); Sussex v Warwicks. (Hove).

23-Glam. v Essex (Neath); Glos. v Notts. (Moreton-in-Marsh); Hants v Somerset (Bournemouth); Leics. v Kent (Leicester); Northants v Middx (Wellingborough School); Sussex v Surrey (Hove); Warwicks. v Lancs. (Birmingham); Worcs. v Yorks. (Worcester).

30-Derbys. v Notts. (Derby); Essex v Yorks. (Colchester); Kent v Hants (Maidstone); Lancs. v Glos. (Manchester); Leics. v Northants (Leicester); Middx v Sussex (Lord's); Worcs. v Surrey (Hereford).

SEPTEMBER

6-Kent v Sussex (Canterbury); Leics. v Glam. (Leicester); Notts. v Essex (Nottingham); Somerset v Northants (Taunton); Surrey v Glos. (The Oval); Warwicks. v Middx (Birmingham); Yorks. v Hants (Leeds).

13-Derbys. v Somerset (Derby); Essex v Lancs. (Chelmsford); Glos. v Glam. (Bristol); Kent v Warwicks. (Canterbury); Surrey v Notts. (The Oval); Sussex v Leics. (Hove); Worcs. v Northants (Worcester).

†MINOR COUNTIES' CHAMPIONSHIP, 1987

All matches are of two days' duration.

MAY

24-Lincs. v Herts. (Sleaford); Northumb. v Beds. (Jesmond).

26-Cumb. v Beds. (Carlisle); Durham v Herts. (Hartlepool).

27-Suffolk v Cambs. (Framlingham College).

31-Salop. v Somerset II (Shrewsbury).

JUNE

2-Cheshire v Somerset II (Warrington).

7-Cumb. v Cambs. (Barrow); Lincs. v Durham (Bourne).

8-Cheshire v Cornwall (Toft).

9-Northumb. v Cambs. (Jesmond).

10-Herts. v Staffs. (Watford Town CC); Salop. v Cornwall (Shifnal).

17-Cambs. v Norfolk (Wisbech).

18-Somerset II v Bucks. (Taunton).

21-Beds. v Staffs. (Henlow); Northumb. v Lincs. (Jesmond).

30-Staffs. v Lincs. (Knypersley).

JULY

5-Bucks. v Salop. (Slough); Cornwall v Devon (Falmouth); Herts. v Beds. (Hitchin); Lincs. v Norfolk (Burghley Park); Northumb. v Cumb. (Jesmond); Oxon. v Cheshire (Christ Church College).

6-Staffs. v Durham (Brewood).

7-Herts. v Cambs. (Hertford CC); Wilts. v Cheshire (Devizes).

12-Oxon. v Berks. (Morris Motors).

14-Suffolk v Herts. (Bury St Edmunds).

15-Devon v Dorset (Sidmouth); Staffs. v Cambs. (Leek).

19-Cheshire v Dorset (Boughton Hall, Chester); Cornwall v Berks. (Truro); Durham v Northumb. (Chester-le-Street); Lincs. v Suffolk (Grimsby Town); Oxon. v Bucks. (Aston Rowant).

20-Wilts. v Somerset II (Trowbridge).

21-Devon v Berks. (Torquay); Salop. v Dorset (Wellington).

26-Berks. v Wilts. (Falkland CC, Newbury); Oxon. v Salop (Banbury XX).

27-Norfolk v Beds. (Lakenham); Suffolk v Cumb. (Ipswich School).

28-Cornwall v Bucks. (Wadebridge); Staffs. v Northumb. (Stone); Wilts. v Salop. (Chippenham).

29-Cambs. v Beds. (Fenner's, Cambridge); Norfolk v Cumb. (Lakenham).

30-Berks. v Dorset (Finchampstead); Devon v Bucks. (Exmouth).

31-Norfolk v Suffolk (Lakenham).

AUGUST

2-Salop. v Cheshire (St George's, Telford).

3-Norfolk v Staffs. (Lakenham); Somerset II v Devon (Taunton).

5 – Cambs. v Lincs. (Fenner's, Cambridge);
Dorset v Somerset II (Sherborne School);
Norfolk v Herts. (Lakenham); Suffolk v
Staffs. (Mildenhall); Wilts. v Oxon.
(Marlborough College).

9 – Beds. v Lincs. (Goldington Bury,
Bedford); Berks. v Salop. (Kidmore
End); Cheshire v Beds. (High
Wycombe); Cumb. v Durham (Millom);
Suffolk v Northumb. (Ransome &
Reavell, Ipswich).

10 – Cornwall v Oxon. (Falmouth); Wilts. v
Dorset (Swindon).

11 – Berks. v Cheshire (Bracknell); Herts. v
Northumb. (St Albans).

12 – Devon v Oxon. (Bovey Tracey); Durham
v Suffolk (Stockton-on-Tees).

13 – Dorset v Bucks. (Dorchester); Somerset
II v Berks. (Bristol Imperial).

16 – Beds. v Durham (Wardown Park,
Luton); Bucks. v Wilts. (Marlow); Dorset

v Oxon. (Weymouth); Lincs. v Cumb.
(Lincoln Lindum).

18 – Beds. v Suffolk (Southill Park); Cambs. v
Durham (March); Cheshire v Devon
(Bowdon); Dorset v Cornwall
(Dorchester); Herts. v Cumb. (Potters
Bar); Somerset II v Oxon. (Glastonbury
CC).

20 – Salop. v Devon (Bridgnorth); Somerset II
v Cornwall (Taunton).

23 – Cornwall v Wilts. (St Austell);
Northumb. v Norfolk (Jesmond); Cumb.
v Staffs. (Netherfield, Kendal).

25 – Devon v Wilts. (Newton Abbot);
Durham v Norfolk (Sunderland).

30 – Bucks. v Berks. (Amersham).

SEPTEMBER

10 – Final Play-off (1 day) (Worcester).

The composition of the Eastern and Western
Divisions may be found on page 801.

†MINOR COUNTIES KNOCKOUT COMPETITION, 1987

All matches are of one day's duration.

Qualifying Round

May 31 Berks. v Oxon. (Hurst, near
Reading); Herts. v Beds. (West
Herts. CC, Watford); Lincs. v
Durham (Appleby Frodingham).

First Round

June 14 Berks. or Oxon. v Staffs. (Reading
School or Christ Church College);
Bucks. v Salop. (Beaconsfield);
Cambs. v Herts. or Beds. (Trinity
Old, Cambridge); Cheshire v Cumb.
(Oxton); Cornwall v Wilts. (Truro);

Devon v Dorset (Instow); Lincs. or
Durham v Northumb. (Market
Rasen or Durham City); Suffolk v
Norfolk (To be arranged).

Quarter-finals to be played on June 28.

Semi-finals to be played on July 12.

Final to be played on July 26.

†SECOND ELEVEN CHAMPIONSHIP, 1987

All matches are of three days' duration.

APRIL

29—Glam. v Somerset (Cardiff); Glos. v Warwicks. (Bristol); Yorks. v Northants (Leeds).

MAY

6—Derbys. v Northants (Derby); Glam. v Leics. (Cardiff); Lancs. v Kent (Manchester); Notts. v Yorks. (Steetley, Shireoaks); Somerset v Glos. (Weston-super-Mare); Surrey v Hants (The Oval).

13—Leics. v Derbys. (Lutterworth); Middx v Kent (Uxbridge); Northants v Worcs. (Wolverton, Milton Keynes); Notts. v Essex (Boots Ground, Nottingham); Glos. v Somerset (Bristol); Sussex v Surrey (Horsham); Warwicks v Lancs. (Griff & Coton, Nuneaton); Yorks. v Glam. (Elland).

20—Derbys. v Notts. (Chesterfield); Glos. v Glam. (Bristol); Hants v Middx (Southampton); Lancs. v Northants (Ramsbottom CC); Leics. v Surrey (Uppingham School); Somerset v Kent (Taunton); Worcs. v Warwicks. (Old Hill CC).

27—Hants v Glos. (Bournemouth); Kent v Glam. (Folkestone); Lancs. v Notts. (Northern CC, Crosby); Leics. v Northants (Market Harborough); Surrey v Middx (Guildford); Yorks. v Warwicks. (York).

JUNE

3—Derbys. v Yorks. (Shipley); Glam. v Lancs. (Abergavenny); Kent v Surrey (Canterbury); Leics. v Warwicks. (Leicester); Northants v Essex (Northampton); Sussex v Middx (Hove).

10—Derbys. v Leics. (Chesterfield); Glam. v Glos. (Ammanford); Hants v Kent (Bournemouth); Lancs. v Yorks. (Preston CC); Middx v Northants (Ealing CC); Somerset v Worcs. (Westlands, Yeovil); Sussex v Essex (Eastbourne); Warwicks. v Notts. (Coventry and North Warwickshire CC).

17—Glos. v Hants (Bristol); Kent v Middx (Canterbury); Lancs. v Derbys. (Manchester); Notts. v Northants (Collingham & District CC, Newark); Surrey v Leics. (The Oval); Warwicks. v Worcs. (Leamington Town CC).

24—Essex v Kent (Ilford); Glos. v Derbys. (Lydney); Hants v Somerset (Bournemouth); Middx v Warwicks. (Harefield); Northants v Lancs. (Old Northamptonians CC); Notts. v Glam. (Central Avenue, Worksop); Worcs. v Leics. (Worcester); Yorks. v Surrey (Scarborough).

JULY

1—Derbys. v Lancs. (Derby); Essex v Surrey (Chelmsford); Kent v Hants (Dover or Canterbury); Middx v Leics. (Lensbury Club, Teddington); Northants v Yorks. (Northampton); Notts. v Sussex (Nottingham); Somerset v Warwicks. (Taunton).

8—Glam. v Surrey (Swansea); Glos. v Worcs. (Bristol); Kent v Sussex (Maidstone); Leics. v Notts. (Hinckley); Northants v Derbys. (Overstone Park CC); Somerset v Lancs. (Taunton); Warwicks. v Yorks. (Old Edwardians CC).

15—Leics. v Lancs. (Leicester); Middx v Essex (Enfield CC); Northants v Notts. (Wellingborough School); Sussex v Hants (Hove); Warwicks. v Glam. (Olton CC); Worcs. v Somerset (Worcester); Yorks. v Derbys. (Bawtry Road, Sheffield).

22—Essex v Hants (Leigh-on-Sea); Middx v Surrey (South Hampstead CC); Northants v Leics. (Woughton or Milton Keynes); Notts. v Lancs. (Worthington Simpson); Somerset v Glam. (Taunton); Worcs. v Glos. (Worcester); Yorks. v Kent (Todmorden).

29—Glam. v Yorks. (Pontarddulais); Kent v Essex (Blackheath); Lancs. v Leics. (Middleton CC); Northants v Middx (Bedford Modern School); Somerset v Hants (Taunton); Surrey v Sussex (Banstead); Warwicks. v Glos. (Walmley CC); Worcs. v Derbys. (Royal GS, Worcester).

AUGUST

5 – Derbys. v Glos. (Ilkeston); Essex v Northants (Chelmsford); Leics. v Glam. (Leicester); Middx v Hants (Harrow CC); Surrey v Lancs. (Purley CC); Warwicks. v Sussex (Birmingham); Yorks. v Notts. (Marske-by-Sea).

9 – Essex v Notts. (Chelmsford).

12 – Glam. v Worcs. (Swansea); Notts. v Leics. (Worthington Simpson); Surrey v Kent (Guildford); Warwicks. v Middx (Studley CC); Yorks. v Lancs. (Harrogate).

19 – Glos. v Essex (Bristol); Hants v Sussex (Southampton); Kent v Lancs. (Canterbury); Notts. v Derbys. (Worksop College); Surrey v Yorks. (Guildford); Warwicks. v Leics. (Moseley CC); Worcs. v Glam. (Worcester).

26 – Derbys. v Worcs. (Bass, Burton upon Trent); Essex v Middx (Romford); Glam. v Warwicks. (Swansea); Lancs. v Surrey (Manchester); Somerset v Hants (Taunton); Sussex v Kent (Hastings).

SEPTEMBER

2 – Glam. v Notts. (Usk); Kent v Yorks. (Canterbury); Lancs. v Warwicks. (Manchester); Leics. v Worcs. (Hinckley); Middx v Sussex (Watford Town CC); Surrey v Essex (Banstead).

9 – Essex v Sussex (Southend); Hants v Surrey (Southampton).

†WARWICK UNDER-25 COMPETITION, 1987

All matches are of one day's duration.

MAY

4 – Leics. v Middx. (Leicester).

11 – Glam. v Somerset (Gorseinon).

18 – Lancs. v Yorks. (Manchester); Leics. v Northants (Leicester).

19 – Warwicks. v Worcs. (Birmingham).

25 – Glam. v Worcs. (Usk); Hants v Kent (Southampton).

26 – Sussex v Surrey (Arundel); Worcs. v Somerset (Worcester).

JUNE

1 – Derbys. v Yorks. (Heanor); Sussex v Hants (Arundel).

2 – Northants v Essex (Finedon); Surrey v Hants (The Oval).

9 – Middx v Northants (Harrow CC).

15 – Lancs. v Derbys. (East Lancs. CC, Blackburn); Somerset v Warwicks. (Taunton).

16 – Leics. v Essex (Leicester).

22 – Glos. v Warwicks. (Bristol); Kent v Sussex (Tonbridge School).

23 – Essex v Middx (Wanstead CC); Warwicks. v Glam. (Birmingham).

29 – Yorks. v Notts. (Doncaster).

30 – Somerset v Glos. (Taunton).

JULY

6 – Glos. v Glam. (Bristol); Notts. v Derbys. (Farnsfield).

13 – Worcs. v Glos. (Worcester).

14 – Surrey v Kent (The Oval).

20 – Notts. v Lancs. (Collingham and District CC).

AUGUST

16 – Semi-Finals.

23 – Semi-Finals (if not played on August 16).

30 – FINAL (Birmingham).

†BAIN DAWES TROPHY, 1987

All matches are of 55 overs per side.

APRIL

28–Yorks. v Northants (Leeds).

MAY

4–Glos. v Somerset (Bristol).

5–Glos. v Worcs. (Bristol); Notts. v Yorks. (Steetley, Shireoaks).

11–Kent v Surrey (Gore Court, Sittingbourne); Sussex v Hants (Arundel); Worcs. v Warwicks. (Worcester); Yorks. v Leics. (Elland).

12–Glam. v Somerset (Swansea); Leics. v Derbys. (Lutterworth).

18–Somerset v Glam. (Taunton); Surrey v Sussex (Banstead).

19–Derbys. v Notts. (Chesterfield); Glos. v Glam. (Bristol); Hants v Middx (Southampton); Lancs. v Northants (Manchester).

25–Yorks. v Notts. (Hull).

26–Lancs. v Notts. (Softon, Liverpool); Northants v Leics. (Uppingham School).

JUNE

1–Essex v Kent (Chelmsford); Notts. v Leics. (Nottingham); Surrey v Middx (The Oval); Warwicks. v Glos. (Birmingham).

2–Derbys. v Yorks. (Heanor); Glam. v Glos. (Pontarddulais); Sussex v Kent (Hastings); Warwicks. v Worcs. (Birmingham).

8–Hants v Sussex (Southampton); Warwicks v Somerset (Birmingham); Worcs. v Glos. (Worcester).

9–Derbys. v Leics. (Heanor); Glam. v Warwicks. (Croesyceiliog); Hants v Kent (Bournemouth); Lancs. v Yorks. (Haslingden); Sussex v Essex (Eastbourne).

15–Glam. v Worcs. (Ynysygerwn); Kent v Sussex (Canterbury); Leics. v Northants (Leicester); Surrey v Essex (Oxted CC).

16–Lancs. v Derbys. (Manchester); Middx v Surrey (Lensbury Club, Teddington);

Notts. v Northants (Worksop College); Somerset v Warwicks. (Taunton).

22–Essex v Middx (Wanstead CC); Notts. v Derbys. (Boots Ground, Nottingham); Worcs. v Somerset (Worcester).

23–Northants v Lancs. (Baker Perkins Ground, Peterborough); Sussex v Surrey (Horsham).

29–Derbys. v Northants (Ilkeston CC); Middx v Sussex (Ealing CC); Somerset v Glos. (Taunton); Surrey v Kent (The Oval); Worcs. v Glam. (Worcester).

30–Derbys. v Lancs. (Derby); Essex v Surrey (Access Ground, Southend); Kent v Hants (Dover or Canterbury); Leics. v Yorks (Leicester).

JULY

6–Hants v Surrey (Southampton); Kent v Essex (Canterbury); Somerset v Worcs. (Taunton).

7–Glos. v Warwicks. (Bristol); Leics. v Notts. (Hinckley); Middx v Hants (Harefield).

13–Hants v Essex (Southampton); Middx v Kent (Potters Bar); Yorks. v Lancs. (Elland).

14–Leics. v Lancs. (Leicester); Middx v Essex (Enfield CC); Northants v Notts. (Northampton); Surrey v Kent (The Oval); Warwicks. v Glam. (Moseley CC); Yorks. v Derbys. (Bawtry Road, Sheffield).

20–Northants v Derbys. (Northampton); Surrey v Hants (The Oval); Sussex v Middx (Hove).

21–Essex v Hants (Chalkwell Park, Westcliff); Northants v Yorks. (Bedford Modern School); Notts. v Lancs. (Nottingham).

27–Kent v Middx (Canterbury).

28–Essex v Sussex (Chelmsford); Lancs. v Leics. (Heywood CC).

SEPTEMBER

7–FINAL.

ERRATA IN WISDEN, 1973

Page 577   Worcestershire were 202 all out v Somerset, not 202 for nine dec. R. M. Carter
            was *run* out 0.

WISDEN, 1983

Page 293   C. W. J. Athey scored 114* for Yorkshire v Surrey at The Oval, not 140*.

WISDEN, 1985

Page 793   F. E. Collyer of Hertfordshire scored an unbeaten 68, not 65.
Page 800   In Cheshire's averages, K. Tedsdale should read K. Teasdale.

WISDEN, 1986

Page 134   Zaheer Abbas had played 89 not out innings to September 1985, not 39. This
             correction applies also to the figures on page 136.
Page 138   At the end of "Fast Scoring", G. Fowler and S. J. O'Shaughnessy's partnership
             was in 1983, not 1984.
Page 256   A. Needham hit 124 before lunch on the first day, not the second.
Page 271   D. L. Underwood took ten for 136 for Kent v Essex at Dartford, not ten for 36.
Page 277   R. B. Phillips's 20 dismissals should read: 18 ct, 2 st; 5 ct, 2 st as sub.
Pages 300-1 In the last line on page 300, it incorrectly states that M. W. Gatting was 96
             when A. J. Lamb was run out. Gatting was in fact 96 when I. T. Botham was
             dismissed.
Page 303   Fifth Test match, 5th paragraph. I. T. Botham hit his first and third balls for 6
             and his fourth for 4, not as stated.
Page 413   In the match report of Hampshire v Sussex, it states incorrectly that G. D.
             Mendis had "received only four balls in the preceding five overs". He did, in
             fact, receive fifteen balls in the last five overs of the innings and scored 15 runs
             off them.
Page 899   N. F. M. Popplewell's highest innings was 172 (Somerset v Essex, Southend,
             1985), not 143.
Page 1216   Laurie, Lt-Col. Laurence Ernest, should read Liddell, Lt-Col. Laurence Ernest
             (Laurie).

WISDEN, 1987

Page 140   C. G. Greenidge's not out innings should read 64, not 84, and his average
            should be 45.76.
Page 192   The most Test match appearances for Pakistan are 81 by Wasim Bari, not 78 by
            Zaheer Abbas. Wasim Bari played 24 Tests v England, 19 v Australia, 9 v West
            Indies, 11 v New Zealand and 18 v India.

Advice has been received concerning the incorrect recording in *Wisden* of the umpire, T. G.
Wilson. Corrections are as follows: *Wisden* 1977 – page 627, T. G. (not T. C.) Wilson; page
671, T. G. Wilson. *Wisden* 1979 – page 649, T. G. (not R. T.) Wilson. *Wisden* 1980 – page 611,
T. G. Wilson (not H. Horton). *Wisden* 1984 – page 656, T. G. (not G. C.) Wilson.